WHO'S WHO
IN
ECONOMICS

A Biographical Dictionary
of Major Economists
1700–1986

Also by Mark Blaug

Introduction to the Economics of Education, Penguin Books, 1970
The Methodology of Economics, Cambridge University Press, 1980
Great Economists Since Keynes, Wheatsheaf Books, 1984
Economic Theory in Retrospect, Cambridge University Press, 4th edition, 1985
Economic History and the History of Economics, Wheatsheaf Books, 1986
Great Economists Before Keynes, Wheatsheaf Books, 1986

Edited works

Who's Who in Economics: A Biographical Dictionary 1700–1981
   (with Paul Sturges), Wheatsheaf Books, 1983

WHO'S WHO IN ECONOMICS

A Biographical Dictionary of Major Economists 1700–1986

Second Edition

edited by

MARK BLAUG
*University of London Institute of Education
and University of Buckingham*

The MIT Press
Cambridge, Massachusetts

MIT Press editions, 1983 and 1986

First edition published in Great Britain in 1983,
second edition in 1986, by Wheatsheaf Books Ltd

Library of Congress Cataloging in Publication Data

Who's who in economics.
  Includes index.
  1. Economists—Biography.   I. Blaug, Mark.
  HB76.W47   1986   330'.092'2 [B]   86–2837
  ISBN 0–262–02256–7

Printed and bound in Great Britain

Contents

Preface

The title of this book begs two questions: What is an 'economist'? and What is a *major* economist'? There is no perfect answer to either question but a stab at an answer is necessary if we are to justify our choice of names to include and exclude from this dictionary.

There are many economists in the world. There are few economists in the world. Both of these statements are perfectly true: it all depends on how we define an 'economist'. In America, the 1960 Census of Population classified 22,424 individuals as instructors or practitioners in the area of 'economics'; however, the 1964 National Register of Scientific and Technical Personnel counted only 12,143 American scientists and technicians as claiming professional competence in some branch of 'economics'. Other definitions of an economist are possible, such as having one's highest degree in economics, being a member of at least one professional association of economists, having work experience primarily in the field of economics, being currently employed in a job with the title 'economist', and identifying oneself as an 'economist'. Depending on which criterion is chosen, we can obtain 5000 or 17,000 economists in the United States in 1964 (Tolles and Melichar, 1968) and what is true of America is just as true of the rest of the world.

I have chosen to define an economist as one who publishes more or less regularly in one of the hundreds of learned journals of economics. This is unfair to the many dedicated teachers of economics who publish little if anything, to business and government economists whose writings are never published, and to economists working for international agencies whose writings frequently remain anonymous. My choice of the publication criterion, however, was dictated by the prior choice of a criterion of eminence in economics. The dictionary definition of 'eminence' is 'one who stands high as compared with others, especially in his own calling'. But who is to judge high standing as compared with others? Presumably, none other than the peer group, which is to say that eminent or major economists are those who receive prizes and honorary degrees, are nominated and elected to offices in professional associations of economists, and are frequently cited in the writings of other economists. In fact, we may virtually reduce the concept of eminence to frequency of citations, because the number of times particular economists are footnoted in journal articles over a period of years has been shown to be highly correlated with the award of Nobel prizes, with election to offices in leading professional associations, and with differences in salaries earned (Quandt, 1976; Bordo and Landlau, 1979; Grubel, 1979; Hamermesh, Johnson, and Weisbrod, 1982).

There are good reasons why scholars cite the works of other scholars. Nothing is as fundamental to science as the notion that scientific knowledge is public and freely available to all: there is no such thing as an inalienable property right in new ideas. The practice of citing authorities is therefore an attempt to provide incentives to intellectual pioneers by giving public recognition to their priority claims. For that reason all scientific communities develop informal mechanisms for penalising individuals who, in effect, infringe the property rights of others by failing to acknowledge their influences and sources of inspiration. Nevertheless, this informal mechanism operates imperfectly, and citation practices are frequently abused: witness the typical doctoral dissertation with endless citations of the works of the candidate's supervisors, the common habit of advertising one's own works by self-citations however irrelevant to the theme in question, the tendency of members of a particular school of thought to cite each other, and the widespread inclination to cite 'stars' in the profession to show that the author is knowledgeable. Moreover, there is the opposite tendency to refer to really famous scholars by name without citing their works, lest a citation be construed as an insult to the intelligence of one's audience (Garfield, 1979).[1]

However, despite these qualifications in equating scholarly 'eminence' with the frequency of citation counts, it is difficult to conceive of any other single indicator that is equally revealing of peer recognition of scientific achievement. I have therefore selected all the living economists in this dictionary on the grounds that they are frequently cited by their colleagues.

In the first edition of this dictionary, my co-editor and I diluted this criterion by adding a sprinkling of names of economists whose works are rarely cited but whose outstanding achievements in advising policy-makers in business and governments are widely acknowledged. Needless to say, these purely subjective additions opened the door to endless objections that so-and-so should have been included. For the top hundred or so economists in the world, it hardly matters which criterion of 'eminence' one adopts because they would appear under almost all the criteria one could devise. It is only when we extend the list of major economists to several hundreds that we encounter difficulties in choosing a purely objective criterion that truly reflects majority opinion in economics rather than the invidious judgements of one or two individuals who happen to be editing a biographical dictionary. Recognising the inherent limitations of my judgement, I might instead have assembled a committee of experts to adjudicate the selection process but a trial run with a mini-committee suggested that the opinions of such a committee would be no less objectionable than my own judgement. I have therefore chosen in this second edition to adhere rigidly to the objective method of citation frequencies. No doubt, this favours academic economists over business and government economists. But until someone devises an operational measure of 'eminence' in economics that does not rest on publications, I would rather be damned for parochial exactitude than for encyclopedic arbitrariness.

The data source for citation frequencies is the Social Sciences Citation Index (SSCI), published tri-annually since 1966 by the Institute of Scientific Information in Philadelphia, Pennsylvania, and available on computer (SOCIAL–SCISEARCH on DIALOG database). SSCI indexes citations from more than 5000 social science periodicals of 45 countries, including 200 economic journals as well as some non-journal economic books, such as proceedings, symposia, and monographic series, treating each chapter or monograph as though it were an article appearing in a journal. SSCI does not distinguish among social scientists by fields of specialisation, but the type of journal in which the citations appear allows one to distinguish between economists and other social scientists.

SSCI has no rival on its own grounds. Its list of journals is amazingly comprehensive and includes virtually all the 220 journals indexed in the 22 volumes of the *Index of Economic Articles 1886–1980* (AEA, 1985), and all but 92 of the even

---

[1] Even a statement about citation practices may require a citation.

larger set of 300 economic journals indexed in the current *Journal of Economic Literature*; on the other hand, it includes 25 journals not indexed in SSCI under the headings 'Economics; Business, Finance; Industrial Relations & Labor; Operations Research and Management Science; Planning and Development' (ISI, 1982); it is worth noting that the list includes 88 journals published in languages other than English. To sum up: I define an 'economist' as someone who publishes articles in this list of over 200 economic journals indexed in SSCI.

I confined the citation count to the twelve-year period 1972–83 and counted about 1200 economists in the order of frequency with which they were cited over the period as a whole. The rank order of citation frequencies reveals a number of discontinuities, one of which occurred around the number 1000, at which point the frequency count converges on two to three citations per year. I have therefore selected the number 1000 as the cut-off point between major and minor economists, a decision which is nevertheless arbitrary as the line might instead have been drawn at 800 or 1200. In other words, I struck a compromise between too few and too many names, bearing in mind the practical uses of a dictionary of this kind.

It proved impossible to let the computer do all the work. SSCI includes self-citations and to have eliminated all of this would have required an extremely expensive program. In addition, SSCI credits all jointly authored articles to the first name to appear in the credit list of the article, the result of which is to undercount all those economists who habitually publish jointly and whose last name begins with a letter near the end of the alphabet. To have eliminated this shortcoming by means of appropriate computer programming likewise proved to be expensive. Finally, there is the even more serious difficulty that SSCI mindlessly lists different authors as they are cited by whatever name and whatever set of initials accompanying the name in the original publication. Thus, to give just one example at random, the economist Ezra J. Mishan appears in several guises as Mishan E., Mishan E. J., Mishan J. E., Mishan E. H., Mishan E. I., Mishan E. Z., and Mishan E. K. In this particular case, these are all versions of one and the same economist, so that the program of citation frequencies might simply have asked the computer to add them together. But this trick will not work for Bhagwati, J., Bhagwati J. N., Bhagwati J. D., Bhagwati M., and Bhagwati N., because Bhagwati J. is also the name of a sociologist. This last problem simply cannot be eliminated by any feasible exercise in programming. In consequence it proved necessary to check every name by hand in order to catch cases of joint authorship and to avoid counting non-economists of the same name. I can only hope that the resulting introduction of human error over a sample as large as 1000 has been kept to a minimum.

The total number of 1000 living economists seems to be something like the top 6 per cent of all living, cited economists, at least if an 'economist' is defined as someone who published more or less regularly in an economic journal: vol. 21 of the AEA *Index of Economic Articles* lists about 10,000 economists as having published at least one article in the year 1979; if we go back to 1960 to count all the additional names of economists who published in the 1960s and 1970s, one adds about 7000 names; assuming all those 7000 were still living in 1979, the total stock of living, publishing economists is 17,000, of whom 1000 is almost 6 per cent. In short, by publishing this biographical dictionary, the editor appears to have made 16 times as many enemies as friends!

The roughly 1000 entries of living economists comprise the following elements:

1 full name,
2 year and place of birth,
3 title of current post, with name and location of current employer,
4 previous posts,
5 degrees received (in economics unless otherwise stated),
6 offices held, prizes won and honours received,
7 editorial duties, if any,
8 principal fields of interest (see Appendix 1),
9 chief publications (limited to ten books and ten articles),
10 statement of principal contributions to economics (in 300 words or less).

The authors of the entries for living economists are the economists themselves: each was asked to supply the relevant information, including a statement of their principal contributions to economics as they — and not I — conceive them (where no information under any of the ten headings was supplied, the heading in question was deleted). I obtained an 88 per cent response rate to my mailing but I may have failed to locate some of the economists from whom no reply was received (see Appendix 4). Special problems were encountered in obtaining information about recently deceased economists: contact with friends and colleagues of the deceased was usually successful but in one or two cases no information was obtainable from any of the standard sources, thus vindicating my belief that there is a need for a dictionary of this kind. The entries for the almost 400 dead economists (marked with an asterisk) were written by myself on the basis of standard sources; I selected the 400 names by a critical comparison of the dead economists listed in the indexes of leading histories of economic thought.[1]

I sincerely hope that this volume will fill an empty niche in the scanty reference shelf of fellow economists and students of economics. I wish to express my thanks to Gottfried Bombach, Roger Cardinal, Jean-Claude Eicher, Herbert Grubel, the late Fritz Machlup, Christian Morrisson, Dennis O'Brien, Pedro Schwartz and the late Sidney Weintraub for valuable advice on my selection procedures at an early stage of preparation for this volume; to N. Georgescu-Roegen, Rolf Henricksson, Bruce Larsons, Claude Menard, Ingrid Metzger-Buddenberg, Mona McKay, Mary Rowlatt, Evert Schoorl, George J. Stigler, and Rita Tullberg for providing valuable information on some recently deceased economists; to Max Alter, assisted by Lakis Kaonides and Jose-Miguel Albala, for preparing the rank order of citation frequencies from SSCI; and to R. Bolick of MIT Press and Edward Elgar of Wheatsheaf Books for helping me to make the second edition of this dictionary a better and more informative volume than the first edition. Particular thanks go to Paul Sturges, the co-editor of the first edition of this book, who was forced by personal circumstances to withdraw from this edition almost as soon as we had started.

---

[1] The ratio 5:2 of living to dead economists is, if anything, too favourable to dead economists. In economics, as in other branches of human knowledge, over 90 per cent of all the economists that have ever lived are alive now. On the other hand, the standard of 'eminence' rises as one goes backward in time, which explains the disproportionate number of entries for nineteenth- and early twentieth-century economists.

References

AEA (1985), *Index of Economic Articles 1886–1980*, Homewood, Ill., Richard D. Irwin, vols 1–22.

Bordo, M. D. and Landau, D. (1979), 'The pattern of citations in economic theory 1945–68: an exploration towards a quantitative history of thought', *HOPE*, 2, Summer, pp. 241–53.

Garfield, E. (1979), *Citation Indexing: Its Theory and Application in Science, Technology, and Humanities*, New York, Wiley.

Grubel, H. G. (1979), 'Citation counts for leading economists', *Econ. Notes* (Monte Dei Paschi de Siena Journal), 2, pp. 134–45.

Hamermesh, D. S., Johnson, G. E., and Weisbrod, B. A. (1982), 'Scholarship Citations and Salaries: Economic Rewards in Economics', *SEJ*, 49, 2, October, pp. 472–81.

ISI Institute of Scientific Information (1982), 'Source Journals Arranged Alphabetically Within Subject Categories', *Source Publications for Social Sciences Citation Index*, Philadelphia, Penn., ISI.

Quandt, R. E. (1976), 'Some quantitative aspects of the economics journal literature', *JPE*, 84, 4, August, pp. 741–55.

Tolles, A. N. and Melichar, E. (1968), 'Who are the economists?', *Studies of the Structure of Economists' Salaries and Income, AER*, 58, 5, pt. 2, December, pp. 123–53.

Mark Blaug
London, September 1985

List of Economic Journals Included in SSCI (ISI, 1982)

Economics

Acta Deconomica
African Economic History
Agricultural Economics Research
Akron Business and Economic Review
American Economic Review
American Journal of Agricultural
  Economics
American Journal of Economics and
  Sociology
Annales de Sciences Economiques
  Appliquées
Annals of Public and Co-operative
  Economy
Applied Economics
Australian Economic History Review
Australian Economic Papers
Australian Journal of Agricultural
  Economics
Bell Journal of Economics
Betriebswirtschaftliche Forschung und
  Praxis
British Tax Review
Brookings Papers on Economic
  Activity
Bulletin for International Fiscal
  Documentation
Cahiers Economiques de Bruxelles
Cambridge Journal of Economics
Canadian Journal of Economics
Chinese Economic Studies
Contributions to Political Economy
Desarrollo Economico
Developing Economies
Eastern European Economics
Econometrica
Economic and Social Review
Economic Bulletin for Europe
Economic Development and Cultural
  Change
Economic Geography
Economic History Review
Economic Inquiry
Economic Journal
Economic Record
Economica

Economics Letters
Economie Appliquée
Economist
Ekonomicko-Matematicky Obzor
Ekonomicky Casopis
Ekonomiska Samfundets Tidskrift
Energy Economics
European Economic Review
Explorations in Economic History
Food Policy
Forum-American Bar Association
Giornale degli Economisti e Annali di
  Economia
History of Political Economy
Hitotsubashi Journal of Economics
Insurance Mathematics & Economics
Inter-American Economic Affairs
International Economic Review
International Journal of Social
  Economics
International Monetary Fund Staff
  Papers
Jahrbücher für Nationalökonomie und
  Statistik
Japanese Economic Studies
Journal of Accounting & Economics
Journal of Agricultural Economics
Journal of Banking & Finance
Journal of Comparative Economics
Journal of Developing Areas
Journal of Development Economics
Journal of Econometrics
Journal of Economic Behaviour &
  Organization
Journal of Economic Dynamics &
  Control
Journal of Economic Education
Journal of Economic History
Journal of Economic Issues
Journal of Economic Literature
Journal of Economic Psychology
Journal of Economic Studies
Journal of Economic Theory
Journal of Economics and Business
Journal of Environmental Economics
  and Management

Journal of Financial and Quantitative
  Analysis
Journal of Financial Economics
Journal of Industrial Economics
Journal of International Economics
Journal of Law & Economics
Journal of Macroeconomics
Journal of Mathematical Economics
Journal of Monetary Economics
Journal of Political Economy
Journal of Post-Keynesian Economics
Journal of Public Economics
Journal of Taxation
Journal of Transport Economics and
  Policy
Journal of Urban Economics
Kyklos
Malayan Economic Review
Manchester School of Economic and
  Social Studies
Matekon
National Tax Journal
National Westminster Bank Quarterly
  Review
Nationalokonomisk Tidsskrift
Nebraska Journal of Economics and
  Business
New Zealand Economic Papers
Osterreichische Osthefte
Oxford Bulletin of Economics and
  Statistics
Oxford Economic Papers New Series
Politicka Economie
Problemas del Desarrollo
Problems of Communism
Problems of Economics
Public Choice
Public Finance
Quarterly Journal of Economics
Quarterly Review of Economics and
  Business
Review of Black Political Economy
Review of Business and Economic
  Research
Review of Economic Conditions in
  Italy
Review of Economic Studies
Review of Economics and Statistics
Review of Radical Political Economics
Review of Social Economy
Revista Brasileira de Economia
Revue d'Etudes Comparatives
  est-ouest
Revue Economique
Rivista di Economia Agraria
Rivista Internazionali di Scienze
  Economiche e Commerciali

Scandinavian Journal of Economics
Scottish Journal of Political Economy
Socio-Economic Planning Sciences
South African Journal of Economics
Southern Economic Journal
Soviet Studies
Three Banks Review
Tijdschrift voor Economische en
  Sociale Geografie
Trimestre Economico
Weltwirtschaftliches Archiv
World Development
World Economy
Zeitschrift für Nationalökonomie

Business, Finance

Abacus
Accounting Organizations and Society
Accounting Review
Banking Law Journal
Barclays Review
Bulletin for International Fiscal
  Documentation
Finance and Trade Review
Financial Management
Institutional Investor
International Monetary Fund Staff
  Papers
Journal of Accountancy
Journal of Accounting Research
Journal of Corporate Taxation
Journal of Finance
Journal of Futures Markets
Journal of Money Credit and Banking
Journal of Real Estate Taxation
Journal of Risk and Insurance
Journal of Taxation
Lloyds Bank Review
Managerial Finance
National Tax Journal
Public Finance Quarterly
Review of Business and Economic
  Research
Taxes

Industrial Relations & Labour

Arbitration Journal
British Journal of Industrial Relations
Business Lawyer
Compensation Review
Economic and Industrial Democracy
Employee Relations Law Journal
Industrial & Labor Relations Review

Industrial Relations
International Labour Review
Journal of Collective Negotiations in
  the Public Sector
Journal of Human Resources
Journal of Labor Research
Labor History
Labor Law Journal
Monthly Labor Review
Public Personnel Management
Relations Industrielle/Industrial
  Relations
Work and Occupations

*Operations Research & Management
Science*

Behavioral Science
European Journal of Operational
  Research
Interfaces
Journal of Systems Management
Management Science
Omega-International Journal of
  Management Science
Operations Research
Organization Studies

Planning & Development

Development and Change
Development — Seeds of Change —
  Village through Global Order
Ekistics
Futures
Futuribles
Growth and Change
Habitat International
IDS Bulletin — Institute of
  Development Studies
Journal of Forecasting
Journal of Regional Science
Journal of Rural Development
Journal of the American Planning
  Association
Local Government Studies
Long Range Planning
Policy Sciences
Research Policy
Revue Canadienne d'Etudes du
  Developpement — Canadian
  Journal of Development Studies
Social Policy & Administration
Socio-Economic Planning Sciences
Soviet Studies
Technological Forecasting and Social
  Change
Third World Planning Review
Transportation

Abbreviations

J.	—	Journal
Jr.	—	Junior
Labs.	—	Laboratories
LDS	—	Less Developed Countries
Lect.	—	Lecturer
Math.	—	Mathematical, Mathematician
Maths.	—	Mathematics
MP	—	Member of Parliament
Nat.	—	National
Obit.	—	Obituary
OR	—	Operations Research
Philo.	—	Philosophy
Pol.	—	Policy
Polit.	—	Political
Pop.	—	Population
Pres.	—	President
Prof.	—	Professor
Pt.	—	Part
Q.	—	Quarterly
Quant.	—	Quantitative
Repr.	—	Reprinted
Res.	—	Research
Rev.	—	Review
Soc.	—	Society
Sr.	—	Senior
Stat.	—	Statistical, Statistician
Stats.	—	Statistics
Stud.	—	Studies
Suppl.	—	Supplement
Temp.	—	Temporary
Transl.	—	Translation
Univ.	—	University
Vis.	—	Visiting
Vol.	—	Volume

Associations, Institutions, Publishers

AAA	—	*American Accounting Association*
AAAS	—	*American Academy of Arts and Sciences*
AAEA	—	*American Agricultural Economics Association*
AAUP	—	*American Association of University Professors*
ACLS	—	*American Council of Learned Societies*
AEA	—	*American Economic Association*
AEI	—	*American Enterprise Institute*
AFA	—	*American Finance Association*
AHA	—	*American History Association*
ANU	—	*American National University*
ASA	—	*American Statistical Association*
AT & T	—	*American Telephones & Telegraph*
A & U	—	*Allen & Unwin, London, UK*
AUTE	—	*Association of University Teachers of Economics, UK*
BA	—	*British Academy*
BAAS	—	*British Association for the Advancement of Science*
BIT	—	*Bureau International du Travail or ILO*
CBE	—	*Commander of the British Empire*

CEA	—	Canadian Economic Association
CEPREMAP	—	Centre d'Etudes Prespectives d'Économie Mathematique Appliquée a la Planification, France
CNRS	—	Centre National de la Recherche Scientifique, Paris, France
CORE	—	Centre for Operations Research and Econometrics, Belguim
CREDOC	—	Centre de Recherche pour l'Étude et l'Observation des Condition de Vie, France
CUP	—	Cambridge University Press, Cambridge, UK
EEA	—	Eastern Economic Association, USA
EEC	—	European Economic Community
EHA	—	Economic History Association, USA
EHS	—	Economic History Society, UK
Em Soc	—	Econometric Society
FAO	—	Food and Agricultural Organisation, UN
HMSO	—	Her Majesty's Stationery Office, UK
IARIW	—	International Association for Research in Income and Wealth
IBRD	—	International Bank for Reconstruction and Development
IEA	—	International Economic Association
IIPF	—	International Institute of Public Finance
ILO	—	International Labour Office
IMF	—	International Monetary Fund
INEA	—	Institute of Economic Affairs, UK
INSEE	—	Institut National de la Statistique et des Études Économiques, France
IRRA	—	Industrial Relations Research Association, USA
ISER	—	Institute of Social and Economic Research, University of York, UK
JHUP	—	Johns Hopkins University Press
LASA	—	Latin America Studies Association
LSE	—	London School of Economics and Political Science, London, UK
MEA	—	Midwest Economics Association, USA
MIT	—	Massachusetts Institute of Technology, Cambridge, Mass., USA
NAS	—	National Academy of Sciences, USA
NBER	—	National Bureau of Economic Research, New York, NY, USA
N-H	—	North–Holland Publishing Co., Amersterdam, The Netherlands
NIESR	—	National Institute of Economic and Social Research, London, UK
NSF	—	National Science Foundation, USA
NTA	—	National Tax Association, USA
NYU	—	New York University, NYC, New York, USA
OBE	—	Order of the British Empire
OECD	—	Organisation for Economic Co-operation and Development
OEEC	—	Organisation of European Economic Co-operation
OPEC	—	Organisation of Petroleum Export Countries
ORSA	—	Operations Research Society of America
OUP	—	Oxford University Press, Oxford, UK
PAA	—	Population Association of America

RES	—	Royal Economic Society, UK
RSA	—	Regional Science Association, USA
RSS	—	Royal Statistical Society, UK
SEA	—	Southern Economic Association, USA
SIAM	—	Society for Industrial and Applied Mathematics
SSRC	—	Social Science Research Council, UK or USA
TIAA	—	Teachers Insurance and Annuity Association, USA
UCLA	—	University of California, Los Angeles, Calif., USA
UN	—	United Nations
UNCTAD	—	UN Conference on Trade and Development
UNESCO	—	UN Educational Scientific and Cultural Organisation
UNDP	—	UN Development Programme
UNECA	—	UN Economic Commission for Africa
UNECAFE	—	UN Economic Commission for Asia and the Far East
UNECE	—	UN Economic Commission for Europe
UNECLA	—	UN Economic Commission for Latin America
UNICEF	—	UN International Children's Educational Fund
Univ. Camb.	—	University of Cambridge, Cambridge, UK
WEA	—	Western Economic Association, USA
WHO	—	World Health Organisation, UN
WRSA	—	Western Regional Science Association, USA

Journals

ACES Bull.	—	*Association for Comparative Economic Studies Bulletin*
AEP	—	*Australian Economic Papers*
AER	—	*American Economic Review*
AJAE	—	*American Journal of Agricultural Economics*
Bell JE	—	*Bell Journal of Economics*
BER	—	*Bulletin of Economic Research*
BJIR	—	*British Journal of Industrial Relations*
BNLQR	—	*Banca Nazionale del Lavoro Quarterly Review*
BOIS	—	*Bulletin of the Oxford University Institute of Economics and Statistics*
Camb JE	—	*Cambridge Journal of Economics*
CJE	—	*Canadian Journal of Economics*
CSSH	—	*Comparative Studies in Society and History*
DE	—	*De Economist*
Ec	—	*Economica*
Econ App	—	*Economie Appliquée*
Econ Int	—	*Economia Internazionale*
Econom	—	*The Economist*
EDCC	—	*Economic Development and Cultural Change*
EHR	—	*Economic History Review*
EI	—	*Economic Inquiry*
EJ	—	*Economic Journal*
Ekon Tids	—	*Ekonomisk Tidskrift*
Em	—	*Econometrica*
ER	—	*Economic Record*
ESQ	—	*Economic Studies Quarterly*
ESS	—	*Encyclopaedia of the Social Sciences*, E. R. A. Seligman and A. J. Johnson (eds) (Macmillan, 1930–5, 15 vols)
Europ ER	—	*European Economic Review*
For Aff	—	*Foreign Affairs*
HOPE	—	*History of Political Economy*

IESS	—	*International Encyclopedia of the Social Sciences*, D. L. Sills (ed.) (Macmillan and Free Press, 1968, 18 vols)
ILO Bull Lab Stat	—	*ILO Bulletin of Labour Statistics*
ILRR	—	*Industrial Labor Relations Review*
Int ER	—	*International Economic Review*
Int Lab Rev	—	*International Labour Review*
JASA	—	*Journal of the American Statistical Association*
J Bank Fin	—	*Journal of Banking and Finance*
J Bank Res	—	*Journal of Bank Research*
J Bus	—	*Journal of Business*
J Comp E	—	*Journal of Comparative Economics*
JDE	—	*Journal of Development Economics*
J Dev Stud	—	*Journal of Development Studies*
J Ec Behav	—	*Journal of Economic Behaviour and Organization*
J Ec Dyn	—	*Journal of Economic Dynamics and Control*
JEEM	—	*Journal of Environmental Economics and Management*
JEH	—	*Journal of Economic History*
JEI	—	*Journal of Economic Issues*
JEL	—	*Journal of Economic Literature* ·
J Em	—	*Journal of Econometrics*
JET	—	*Journal of Economic Theory*
J Eur EH	—	*Journal of European Economic History*
JFE	—	*Journal of Farm Economics*
J Fin	—	*Journal of Finance*
J Fin Econ	—	*Journal of Financial Economics*
JHE	—	*Journal of Health Economics*
JHR	—	*Journal of Human Resources*
JI Bus Stud	—	*Journal of International Business Studies*
J Ind E	—	*Journal of Industrial Economics*
J Int E	—	*Journal of International Economics*
J Lab E	—	*Journal of Labor Economics*
J Law E	—	*Journal of Law and Economics*
J Math E	—	*Journal of Mathematical Economics*
JMCB	—	*Journal of Money, Credit and Banking*
J Mon E	–	*Journal of Monetary Economics*
JMS	—	*Journal of Management Studies*
JNS	—	*Jahrbücher für Nationalökonomie und Statistik*
JPE	—	*Journal of Political Economy*
J Post Keyn E	—	*Journal of Post-Keynesian Economics*
J Pub E	—	*Journal of Public Economics*
J Reg S	—	*Journal of Regional Science*
JRSS	—	*Journal of the Royal Statistical Society*
JSP	—	*Journal of Social Policy*
JSW	—	*Jahrbüch für Sozialwissenschaften*
J Transp EP	—	*Journal of Transport Economics and Policy*
JUE	—	*Journal of Urban Economics*
Kyk	—	*Kyklos*
LBR	—	*Lloyds Bank Review*
MBR	—	*Midland Bank Review*
MLR	—	*Monthly Labor Review*
MS	—	*Manchester School of Economic and Social Studies*
OBES	—	*Oxford Bulletin of Economics and Statistics*
OEP	—	*Oxford Economic Papers*
PDR	—	*Pakistan Development Review*
PF	—	*Public Finance*

Pol Meth	—	*Political Methodology*
QJE	—	*Quarterly Journal of Economics*
QREB	—	*Quarterly Review of Economics and Business*
RE	—	*Revue Économique*
REP	—	*Revue d'Économie Politique*
REStat	—	*Review of Economics and Statistics*
REStud	—	*Review of Economic Studies*
RISE	—	*Revista Internazionale di Scienze Economiche e Commerciali*
Riv Intern	—	*Revista Internazionale*
RIW	—	*Review of Income and Wealth*
RSE	—	*Review of Social Economy*
SAJE	—	*South African Journal of Economics*
Scand JE	—	*Scandinavian Journal of Economics*
SEJ	—	*Southern Economic Journal*
SJPE	—	*Scottish Journal of Political Economy*
Swed JE	—	*Swedish Journal of Economics*
Urb Stud	—	*Urban Studies*
WA	—	*Weltwirtschaftliches Archiv*
WD	—	*World Development*
WEJ	—	*Western Economic Journal*
YBESR	—	*Yorkshire Bulletin of Economic and Social Research*
YEE	—	*Yale Economic Essays*
ZGS	—	*Zeitschrift für die gesamte Staatswissenschaft*
ZN	—	*Zeitschrift für Nationalökonomie*

Geographic – American States

AL	—	Alabama
AR	—	Arkansas
AZ	—	Arizona
CA	—	California
CO	—	Colorado
CT	—	Connecticut
DC	—	District of Columbia
FL	—	Florida
GA	—	Georgia
HI	—	Hawaii
IA	—	Iowa
ID	—	Idaho
IL	—	Illinois
IN	—	Indiana
KS	—	Kansas
KY	—	Kentucky
LA	—	Louisiana
MA	—	Massachusetts
MD	—	Maryland
ME	—	Maine
MI	—	Michigan
MO	—	Missouri
MS	—	Mississippi
MT	—	Montana
NB	—	Nebraska
NDak	—	North Dakota
NH	—	New Hampshire
NJ	—	New Jersey
NY	—	New York

NC	—	North Carolina
NM	—	New Mexico
NV	—	Nevada
OH	—	Ohio
OK	—	Oklahoma
OR	—	Oregon
PA	—	Pennsylvania
RI	—	Rhode Island
SC	—	South Carolina
SD	—	South Dakota
TN	—	Tennessee
TX	—	Texas
UT	—	Utah
VA	—	Virginia
VI	—	Virgin Islands
VT	—	Vermont
WA	—	Washington
WI	—	Wisconsin
WV	—	West Virginia
WY	—	Wyoming

A

AARON, Henry Jacob

Born 1936, Chicago, IL, USA.
Current Post Sr. Fellow, Brookings Inst., Prof. Econ., Univ. Maryland, MD, USA, 1979–.
Past Posts Instr. Econ., Harvard Univ., 1963–6; Sr. Staff Econ., US President's Council Econ. Advisers, 1966–7; Assoc. Prof., Prof. Econ., Univ. Maryland, 1967–74, 1974–7; Chairman, Panel Housing Allowance Experiments, US Dept. Housing and Urban Devlp., 1975–7; Vis. Prof. Econ., Harvard Univ., 1974; Sr. Fellow, Brookings Inst., 1968–77; Ass. Secretary Planning and Educ., US Dept. Health, Educ. and Welfare, 1977–9; Chairman, US Advisory Council Social Security, 1978–9.
Degrees BA (Polit. Science and Econ.) UCLA, 1958; MA (Russian Regional Stud.), PhD Harvard Univ., 1960, 1963.
Offices and Honours Disting. Policy Fellow, Grad. School Public Pol., Univ. Cal. Berkeley, 1981; Member, Exec. Committee, AEA, 1978–81; Member, Comm. Behavioral Social Sciences and Educ., Nat. Res. Council, 1983–; Member, Board Dirs., Abt Assoc., 1978–; Trustee, MAA, 1983–.
Editorial Duties Ed. Boards, *JHE*, *Knowledge*, *Public Fin. Q.*
Principal Fields of Interest 931 Urban Economics; 913 Economics of Health.
Publications Books: 1. *Urban Finance and Economic Development: A Case Study of Mexico City* (with O. Oldman, R. Bied, S. Kass), (Harvard Univ. Press, 1967); 2. *Social Security: Perspectives for Reform* (with J. Pechman, M. Taussig), (Brookings Inst., 1968); 3. *Shelter and Subsidies: Who Benefits from Federal Housing Policies?* (Brookings Inst., 1972); 4. *The New View of Property Taxation* (Brookings Inst., 1975); 5. *Politics and the Professors: the Great Society in Transition* (Brookings Inst., 1978); 6. *How Taxes Affect Economic Behavior*, co-ed. (with J. Pechman), (Brookings Inst., 1981); 7. *The Value-Added Tax: Lessons from Europe*, ed. (Brookings Inst., 1981); 8. *VAT Experience of Some European Countries* (Kluwer, 1982); 9. *Economic Effects of Social Security* (Brookings Inst., 1982); 10. *The Peculiar Problem of Taxing Life Insurance Companies* (Brookings Inst., 1983)
Articles: 1. 'Efficiency and equity in the optimal supply of a public good' (with M. C. McGuire), *REStat*, 51(1), Feb. 1969; 2. 'Public goods and income distribution' (with M. C. McGuire), *Em*, 38(6), Nov. 1970; 3. 'Income taxes and housing', *AER*, 60(5), Dec. 1970; 4. 'Inefficiency of transfers in kind: the case of housing assistance' (with G. von Furstenberg), *WEJ*, 9(2), June 1971; 5. 'Tax reform and the composition of investment' (with F. S. Russek Jr. and N. M. Singer), *Nat. Tax J.*, 25(1), March 1972; 6. 'Tax changes and the composition of fixed investment: an aggregate simulation' (with F. S. Russek Jr. and N. M. Singer), *REStat*, 54(4), Nov. 1972; 7. 'New views on property tax incidence', *AER*, 64(2), May 1974; 8. 'Inflation and the income tax', *AER*, 66(2), May 1976; 9. 'The use of income maintenance experiment findings in public policy 1977–1978' (with J. Todd), in *Proceedings of Industrial Relations Res. Assoc. Series 1978*, Aug. 1978; 10. 'Rationing hospital care: lessons from Britain' (with W. Schwartz), *New England J. Medicine*, 5. 1984.
Principal Contributions In all of my work, I have tried to apply economic theory and methods to questions of public policy to produce analyses of immediate use in formulating policy. This course has necessitated some attention to institutional details and to political constraints. Most of my work has concerned taxation and transfer programmes, in cash or in kind, including housing policy, social security, income-tested cash assistance. One study examined the way social science research was used in the USA in formulating the programme of the Great Society. Recent work has included a study of budget limits on the provision of hospital care, of the taxation of life insurance companies, of tax-reform options in the USA and the economic effects of social security.

ABEL, Andrew B.

Born 1952, Washington, DC, USA.
Current Post John L. Loeb Assoc. Prof. Econ., Harvard Univ., Cambridge, USA, 1983–.
Past Posts Ass. Prof., Univ. Chicago, 1978–80; Ass. Prof., Harvard Univ., 1980–3.
Degrees BA Princeton Univ., 1974; PhD MIT, 1978.
Editorial Duties Ed. Board, *QJE*, 1983–.
Principal Fields of Interest 023 Macroeconomic Theory; 311 Domestic Monetary and Financial Theory and Policy.
Publications *Books:* 1. *Investment and the Value of Capital* (Garland Publishing, 1979); 2. *The Collected Papers of Franco Modigliani*, 3 Vols, ed. (MIT Press, 1980).
Articles: 1. 'Empirical investment equations: an integrative framework', in *On the State of Macroeconomics. Carnegie Rochester Conf. Series Public Pol.*, 12, Spring, 1980; 2. 'Taxes, inflation and the durability of capital', *JPE*, 89(3), June 1981; 3. 'An intertemporal model of saving and investment' (with O. Blanchard), *Em*, 51(3), May 1983; 4. 'A dynamic model of investment and capacity utilization', *QJE*, 96(3), Aug. 1981; 5. 'Dynamic effects of permanent and temporary tax policies in a q model of investment,' *JMon E*, 9(3), May 1982; 6. 'Optimal investment under uncertainty', *AER*, 73(1), March 1983; 7. 'An integrated view of tests of rationality, market efficiency and the short-run neutrality of monetary policy' (with F. Mishkin), *JMon E*, 11(1), Jan. 1983; 8. 'Market structure and the durability of goods', *REStud*, 50(4), Oct. 1983; 9. 'Tax neutrality in the presence of adjustment costs', *QJE*, 98(4), Nov. 1983; 10. 'Energy price uncertainty and optimal factor intensity: a mean variance analysis', *Em*, 51(6), Nov. 1983.
Principal Contributions Theoretical and empirical research on the determinants of investment. Use of adjustment costs to provide theoretical underpinnings of the q theory of investment in both deterministic and stochastic environments. Application of adjustment cost/q theoretic models to analyse effects of various tax policies. Analysis of aggregate implications of individual lifetime uncertainty.

ABRAMOVITZ, Moses

Born 1912, New York City, NY, USA.
Current Post Managing Ed., *JEL*, 1981–; Coe Prof. Amer. Econ. Hist. Emeritus, Stanford Univ., 1977–.
Past Posts Instr. Econ., Tutor Division Hist. Govt. and Econ., Harvard Univ., 1936–8; Res. Assoc., NBER, 1938–42; Lect. Econ., Columbia Univ., 1940–2, 1946–8; Principal Econ., US War Production Board, 1942; Principal Econ., US Office Strategic Services, 1943; Private, US Army, 1943–5; Dir. Business Cycle Stud., NBER, 1946–8; Prof. Econ. and Cas. Prof. Amer. Econ. Hist., Stanford Univ., 1948–77; Vis. Prof., Univ. Penn., 1955–6; Econ. Adviser, Secretary Gen., OECD, 1962–3.
Degrees BA Harvard Univ., 1932; PhD Columbia Univ., 1939.
Offices and Honours Sheldon Fellow, Harvard Univ., 1932–3; Columbia Univ. Fellow, 1934–5; US SSRC Fellow, 1935–6; Seligman Prize, Columbia Univ., 1939; Dir., NBER, 1956–; Fellow, AAAS, 1960, Inst. Advanced Study Behavioral Sciences, Stanford, CA, 1961–2; Vis. Fellow, All Souls Coll., Oxford, 1968; Disting. Fellow, ASA, AEA; Exec. Comm., Vice-Pres., Pres., AEA, 1965–7, 1969, 1979–80.
Editorial Duties Ed. Board, Managing Ed. *JEL*, 1975–7, 1981–.
Principal Fields of Interest 110 Economic Growth; 131 Economic Structures; 042 N. American Economic History.
Publications *Books:* 1. *Price Theory for a Changing Economy* (Columbia Univ. Press, 1939); 2. *Inventories and Business Cycles* (NBER, 1950); 3. *Capital Formation and Economic Growth*, ed. (Princeton Univ. Press, 1955); 4. *The Growth of Public Employment in Great Britain* (with V. Eliasberg), (Princeton Univ. Press, 1957).
Articles: 1. 'Resource and output

trends in the United States since 1870', *AER*, 46(2), May 1956; 2. 'The nature and significance of Kuznets cycles', *EDCC*, 9 April 1966, repr. in *Readings in Business Cycles*, eds. R. A. Gordon and L. R. Klein (Richard D. Irwin, 1965); 3. 'Evidence of long swings in aggregate construction since the Civil War', *NBER, Occasional Paper 90* (Columbia Univ. Press, 1964); 4. 'The passing of the Kuznets Cycle', *Ec*, N.S. 35, Nov. 1968; 5. 'Manpower, capital and technology', in *Human Resources and Economic Welfare, Essays in Honor of Eli Ginzberg*, ed. I. Berg (Columbia Univ. Press, 1972); 6. 'Reinterpreting economic growth: parables and realities' (with P. A. David), *AER*, 43(2), May 1973; 7. 'In pursuit of full employment', in *Jobs for Americans*, ed. E. Ginzberg (Prentice-Hall, 1976); 8. 'Rapid growth potential and its realization: the experience of capitalist economies in the postwar period', in *Economic Growth and Resources*, ed. E. Malinvaud (Macmillan, 1979); 9. 'The retreat from economic advance', in *Progress and its Discontents*, eds. G. A. Almond, M. Chodorow and R. H. Pearce (Univ. California Press, 1982); 10. 'Welfare quandaries and productivity concerns', *AER*, 71(1), March, 1981.

Principal Contributions My earliest work was in price theory. I considered market behaviour and prices when firms operated in a changing environment rather than in stationary conditions. I studied inventories as one method of adapting to change. This led me to the National Bureau and to work on inventories and business cycles. Using Kuznets' new GNP estimates, I showed the close cyclical conformity between inventory accumulation and output and helped establish the importance of inventory accumulation in accounting for output fluctuations, especially for output change in the early portions of cyclical expansions and recessions. This work also revealed the disparate behaviour of different kinds of commodity stocks — purchased materials, goods in process and manufacturers' stocks of goods ready for sale. Beginning in the 1950s, I studied the economic growth of the industrialised countries from several angles. I worked on the 'long swings' in growth and helped to show that they were not just supply-side phenomena but rather a complicated interaction between the intensities of resource-use on the one side and the growth of population, labour force and capital stock on the other. An early paper, using Kendrick's data, helped reveal the importance of the Residual in accounting for long-term growth and pointed to changes in scale, education, and the allocation of labour as factors underlying the large Residual. Later work, with Paul David, uncovered the relatively large role of capital accumulation in nineteenth-century growth in the USA. We attribute this to an interaction between the capital-using technological progress of the time and capital accumulation. Study of the postwar growth of industrialised countries helped to show the strong inverse relation between countries' initial levels of productivity and their subsequent pace of progress.

ACKLEY, Hugh Gardner

Born 1915, Indianapolis, IN, USA.
Current Post Prof. Emeritus, Univ. Michigan, Ann Arbor, MI, USA, 1984–.
Past Posts Instr., Ohio State Univ., 1939–40, Univ. Michigan, 1940–1; Cons., Nat. Resources Plan Board, 1940–1; Econ., US Office Price Admin., 1941–3, 1944–6; US Office of Strategic Service, 1943–4; Ass. Prof., Assoc. Prof., Prof., Henry Carter Adams Disting. Prof. Polit. Econ., Univ. Michigan, 1946–7, 1947–52, 1952–69, 1969–83; Cons., US Econ. Stabilization Agency, 1950–1; Econ. Adviser, Ass. Dir., US Office Price Stabilization, 1951–2; Member, Chairman US President's Council Econ. Advisers, 1962–8, 1964–8; US Ambassador Italy, 1968–9; Member, Nat. Advisory Council Social Security, 1978–80; Columnist, *Dun's Review, Dun's Business Month*, 1971–; Fulbright Res. Scholar, Italy, 1956–7; Ford Foundation Faculty Res. Fellow, Italy, 1961–2; Member, Sr. Adviser, Assoc. Staff, Brookings Inst., 1976–8, 1979–; Trustee, Joint Council Econ. Educ., 1971–77: Dir., NBER, 1971–80;

Vis. Comm., Dept. Econ., MIT, 1971–7.

Degrees BA Western Michigan Univ., 1936., Hon LLD, MA, PhD Univ. Michigan, 1964, 1937, 1940; Hon LLD Kalamazoo Coll., 1967.

Offices and Honours Chairman, Comm. Res. Publications, Comm. Honors and Awards, Vice-Pres., Advisory Comm. US Bureau Census, Pres., Disting. Fellow, AEA, 1960–1, 1959–61, 1962, 1974–6, 1982, 1983; Fellow, AAAS, 1968–; Cavaliere del Gran Croce, Republica d'Italia, 1969; Disting. Alumnus Award, Western Mich. Univ., 1970; Member, Amer. Philo. Soc., 1972; Disting. Faculty Achievement Award, Univ. Mich., 1977; Dir., US SSRC, 1959–61; Res. Scholar, Rockefeller Foundation Center, Bellagio, 1977.

Editorial Duties Ed. Board, *AER*, 1953–6.

Principal Fields of Interest 023 Macroeconomic Theory.

Publications *Books:* 1. *Macroeconomic Theory* (Macmillan, 1961, Maruzen, 1964; transls., Japanese, Iwanami Shoten, 1964, 1969; Spanish, Union Tipografica, 1965; Portuguese, Enio Matheus Guazzelli, 1969; Italian, Einaudi, 1971; Indonesian, Yayasan Penebut Univ., 1973); 2. *Un Modello Econometrico dello Sviluppo Italiano nel Dopoguerra* (Guiffre, 1963; transl., Japanese, 1964); 3. *Annual Report of the Council Economic Advisers*, in *Economic Report of the President* (with others), (US Govt. Printing Office, 1965, 1966, 1967, 1968); 4. *Policies for the Promotion of Economic Growth* (US Dept. Labor, 1966); 5. *Stemming World Inflation* (Atlantic Inst., 1971; transl., French); 6. *Macroeconomics: Theory and Policy* (Macmillan, 1978).

Articles: 1. 'Spatial competition in a discontinuous market', *QJE*, 56, Feb. 1942; 2. 'Relative price changes and aggregate consumer demand' (with D. B. Suits), *AER*, 40(5), Dec. 1950; 3. 'The multiplier time period: money, inventories, and flexibility', *AER*, 41(3), June 1951; 4. 'The wealth-saving relationship', *JPE*, 59, April 1951; 5. 'The Keynesian analysis of Italian economic problems', *BNQLR*, 10, Sept. 1957; 6. 'Administered prices and

the inflationary process', *AER*, 49(2), May 1959; 7. 'The future of wage and price controls', *Atlantic Econ. Rev.*, 22, 1972; 8. 'An incomes policy for the 1970's', *REStat*, 54(3), Aug. 1972; 9. 'Italy in the 1970s: down the drain to Bangladesh?', *Challenge*, 22, 1979; 10. 'Commodities and capital: prices and quantities', AER, 73(2), May 1983.

Principal Contributions: I was attracted into economics by the macroeconomic phenomenon of Depression; yet my graduate studies concentrated on microeconomics. These led quickly into government consulting and then to the wartime staffs of the Office of Price Administration and the Office of Strategic Services. Later, I helped to manage the Korean War controls. My first and perhaps best book — a study of Korean controls — is available only in microfilm. But apparently it gets intensive use whenever a possible defence emergency causes officials to ask their economists about controls.

Returning to teaching in 1952, I readily accepted reassignment to macroeconomics. My lectures evolved into an extraordinarily successful textbook, translated into many languages, and apparently somewhere still in use. Understanding inflation always seemed to me to require integration into macroeconomics of a somewhat institutional view of wage and price determination. This view found expression in 1959 Congressional testimony that I consider among my best work. It was broadly consistent with concurrent and later work by Schultze, Okun, and others, and provided my rationale for incomes policies.

Services as Member and later Chairman of the Council of Economic Advisers also involved teaching macroeconomics: persuading Presidents Kennedy and Johnson and Congress to cut taxes to create jobs. As the stimulus succeeded, and as Vietnam then produced overemployment, the effort to 'jawbone' wage and price restraint became more necessary but more difficult. President Johnson accepted our advice to ask for higher taxes but enactment was too long delayed. Appointment as Ambassador to Italy after the CEA service reflected a longstanding interest in the Italian economy, expressed in an earlier series of articles and a monograph. Later I analysed Japanese macro-policies.

ADAMS, F. Gerard

Born 1929, USA.
Current Post Prof. Econ. and Fin., Univ. Penn., Philadelphia, PA, USA, 1970–.
Past Posts Inst., Univ. Michigan, 1952–6; Econ., Cal. Texas Oil Corp., 1956–9; Econ., Cie Française des Petroles, 1959–61; Ass. Prof., Assoc. Prof., Univ. Penn., 1961–5, 1965–70; Cons. Forecasting, OECD, Paris, Catholic Univ., Louvain, 1973; Vis. Prof., Univ. Kobe, Japan, 1976; Sr. Staff, US President's Council Econ. Advisers, Washington, DC, 1968–9; Vis. Lect., Univ. Singapore, 1981; Vis. Scholar, Confindustria, Rome, 1984.
Degrees BA, MA, PhD Univ. Michigan, 1949, 1951, 1956.
Editorial Duties Assoc. Ed., *J. Pol. Modeling, Bus. Econ., Forecasting, J. Data Use.*
Principal Fields of Interest 130 Economic Fluctuations; 212 Econometric Models; 723 Energy.
Publications *Books:* 1. *An Econometric Analysis of International Trade* (with H. Eguchi and F. J. M. Meyer zu Schlochtern), (OECD, 1969); 2. *Econometric Models of World Agricultural Commodity Markets* (with J. R. Behrman), (Ballinger, 1976); 3. *Stabilizing World Commodity Markets*, co-ed. (with S. A. Klein), (D. C. Heath, 1978); 4. *Econometric Modeling of World Commodity Policy*, co-ed. (with J. R. Behrman), (D. C. Heath, 1978); 5. *Modeling the Multi-regional Economic System*, (ed. with N. J. Glickman), (D. C. Heath, 1980); 6. *Commodity Exports and Economic Development* (with J. R. Behrman), (D. C. Heath, 1982); 7. *Global Econometrics: Essays in Honor of L. R. Klein*, co-ed. (with B. Hickman), (MIT Press, 1983); 8. *Industrial Policies for Growth and Competitiveness*, co-ed. (with L. R. Klein), (D. C. Heath, 1983); 9. *Industrial Policies for Growth and Competitiveness II*,

Empirical Studies, co-ed. (with L. R. Klein), (D. C. Heath, 1984).
Articles: 1. 'The size of individual incomes; socioeconomic variables and chance variation', *REStat*, 40, Nov. 1958; 2. 'Consumer attitudes, buying plans and purchases of durable goods', *REStat*, 46, Nov. 1964; 3. 'Prediction with consumer attitudes: the time series–cross section paradox', *REStat*, 47, Nov. 1965; 4. 'The time path of undeveloped land prices during urbanization', *REStat*, 48, May 1966; 5. 'Aggregate economic policy and the presidential transition 1968–9', *Public Pol.*, Winter 1969; 6. 'An economic linear programming model of the US petroleum refining industry' (with J. M. Griffin), *JASA*, 67, Sept. 1972; 7. 'From econometric models of the nation to models of industries and firms', *Wharton Q.*, 1973; 8. 'On the specification and simulation of a regional econometric model: a model of Mississippi' (with C. Brooking and N. J. Glickman), *REStat*, 57, Aug. 1975; 9. 'The law of the sea treaty and regulation of module exploitation', *J. Pol. Modeling*, 2, Jan. 1980; 10. 'Can Latin America carry its international debt? ' (with E. Sanchez and M. Adams), *J. Pol. Modeling*, 5, Dec. 1983.
Principal Contributions My work in applied econometrics has gradually developed from a focus on individual macro-level behavioural equations to a concern with the linkages between econometric model systems and their application. I have been greatly concerned with stretching the limits of macro-modelling in the direction of models of industries and commodity markets. This calls for a broad scope, not only with respect to the structural form and estimation of relationships — i.e. use of engineering data and models and use of sectoral accounting systems — but also with respect to spelling out the structure of the critical linkages between various models. Thus recent work has involved links between the national economy and sector commodity models, linking commodities into the world model system, global models between producer and consumer (also debtor and creditor) countries, and most recently a concern with the impact

of industrial policies within countries and on their international linkages. This leads naturally to a concern with the study of the restructuring of the world economy.

ADAMS, Walter

Born 1922, Vienna, Austria.
Current Post Disting. Univ. Prof. Econ., Michigan State Univ., E. Lansing, MI., USA, 1970–.
Past Posts Instr., Yale Univ., 1945–7; Ass. Prof., Assoc. Prof., Prof., Pres., Michigan State Univ., 1947–70, 1969–70; Vis. Prof., Univ. Grenoble, 1966, Salzburg Seminar, 1959, 1960, Falkenstein Seminar, 1971, 1972, Univ. Paris, 1982, Wake Forest Univ., 1983; Econ. Cons. US Congressional Commission, 1950, 1952, 1959; Member, US Attorney General Nat. Comm. Study Antitrust Laws, 1953–5; Member, US Advisory Comm. Internat. Educ. and Cultural Affairs, 1961–9.
Degrees BA Brooklyn Coll, 1942; MA, PhD Yale Univ., 1946, 1947; Hon. LLD Central Mich. Univ., 1973, Michigan State Univ., 1979.
Offices and Honours Pres., AAUP, 1972–4, Midwest Econ. Assoc., 1979–80, Assoc. Social Econ., 1980–1.
Editorial Duties Ed. Boards, *QREB*, 1981–, *Women's Pol. Stud. Yearbook*, 1976–, *Econ. Perspectives*, 1979–.
Principal Fields of Interest 600 Industrial Organisation; 400 International Economy.
Publications *Books:* 1. *Readings in Economics* (Macmillan, 1948); 2. *The Structure of American Industry* (Macmillan, 1950, 1982); 3. *Monopoly in America* (Macmillan, 1955); 4. *From Mainstreet to the Left Bank* (Michigan State Univ. Press, 1959); 5. *Is the World our Campus?* (Michigan State Univ. Press, 1960); 6. *The Brain Drain*, ed. (Macmillan, 1968).
Articles: 1. 'The aluminium case', *AER*, 41(5), Dec. 1951; 2. 'Competition, monopoly and countervailing Power', *QJE*, 67, Nov. 1953; 3. 'Atomic energy', *Columbia Law Rev.*, Feb. 1955; 4. 'The role of competition in the regulated industries', *AER*, 48(2), May 1958; 5. 'Steel imports and vertical oligopoly power', *AER*, 54(4), Sept. 1964; 6. 'Big steel, invention and innovation' (with J. B. Dirlam), *QJE*, 80, May 1966; 7. 'The military–industrial complex and the new industrial state', *AER*, 58(2), May 1968; 8. 'The military-industrial complex: a market structure analysis', *AER*, 62(2), May 1972; 9. 'Tacit vertical collusion and the labor industrial complex', *Nebraska Law Rev.*, Fall 1983; 10. 'Countervailing or coalescing power?', *J Post Keyn E*, 6(2), Winter 1983.
Principal Contributions Throughout my professional career I have been concerned with the impact of concentrated economic power on democratic societies. In studying economic organisation, I have raised the central questions: 'Who makes what decisions, at what cost, on whose behalf, for whose benefit and with what consequences? To whom are decision makers accountable and what mechanisms are available to correct their mistakes?' One focus of my studies has been the analysis of individual industries exhibiting high levels of concentration, viz. steel, automobiles, petroleum, etc., in order to understand the relation between structure, conduct and performance, and (hopefully) to make recommendations for public policy based on this analysis. In these studies, I have applied not only the traditional tools of microeconomic theory, but also an historical and comparative approach.

For many years, I have been concerned with the proper role of the State in microeconomic organisation. I was among the first American economists (1955) to advocate deregulation of the trucking and airline industries, arguing that the US regulatory scheme in those industries was not an instrument for protecting consumers from exploitation but for protecting vested interests from competition. Similarly, and for the same reasons, I have fought against the growing move of protectionism in the United States and especially protection of such oligopolies as steel and automobiles. Here, too, I found that the role of the State was being perverted from servant of the public to a mask for monopolistic privilege. Lately, I have also explored some macroeconomic consequnces of concentrated economic power following the notion of 'entitlements inflation' (*Anspruchsinflation*) observed by G. Haberler as a problem not only in the United States but in other Western democracies. In some circumstances — where vested interests can subvert government stabilisation efforts — it is demonstrable that a good micro-policy is the most effective macroeconomic public policy.

Finally, a word about methodology. There is a danger, I think, that the current fascination with technique — the penchant to demonstrate virtuosity in the use of high-powered mathematical tools — is diverting economists from the study of substantive issues. Some of our colleagues seem oblivious of the fact that algebra and geometry are a complement to, not a substitute for, thought. No wonder that intelligent laymen satirise our profession for having embraced a kind of rigour which resembles rigor mortis. It is time for the pendulum of fashion to swing back toward a more eclectic methodology in our discipline.

ADELMAN, Irma

Born 1930, Rumania.
Current Post Prof. Agric. and Resource Econ., Prof. Econ., Univ. Cal. Berkeley, CA, USA, 1979–.
Past Posts Instr., Lect., Univ. Cal. Berkeley, 1956–7, 1957–8; Vis. Ass. Prof., Mills Coll., Oakland, CA, 1958–9; Acting Ass. Prof., Ass. Prof., Stanford Univ., 1960–1, 1961–2; Assoc. Prof., Johns Hopkins Univ., 1962–6; Prof. Econ., Northwestern Univ., Evanston, IL. 1966–72; Fellow, Center Advanced Study Behavioral Sciences, Stanford, 1970–1; Sr. Econ., Devlp. Res. Center, IBRD, 1971–2; Prof. Econ., Univ. Maryland, Coll. Park, 1972–9; Cleveringa Chair, Leiden Univ., Fellow, Netherlands Inst. Advanced Study, 1977–8.
Degrees BS(Bus. Admin.), MA, PhD Univ. Cal. Berkeley, 1950, 1951, 1955.
Offices and Honours Vice-Pres., AEA, 1979–80; Fellow, Exec. Comm., AAAS; Fellow, Em. Soc.; Phi Beta Kappa; Order Bronze Tower, Govt. S. Korea.
Editorial Duties Ed. Boards, *JEL*, 1969–75, *AER*, 1976–8, *J. Pol. Modeling*, 1979–, *J. Comp. E*, 1980–; Assoc. Ed., *JDE*, 1974–.
Principal Fields of Interest 040 Economic History; 110 Economic Growth; Development; Planning Theory and Policy; 210 Econometrics, Statistical and Mathematical Methods and Models.
Publications *Books:* 1. *Theories of Economic Growth and Development* (Stanford Univ. Press, 1964; transl. Spanish, Fondo de Cultura Econ., 1964); 2. *The Theory and Design of Economic Development*, co-ed. (with E. Thorbecke), (JHUP, 1966); 3. *Society, Politics and Economic Development: A Quantitative Approach* (with C. T. Morris), (JHUP, 1967); 4. *Practical Approaches to Development Planning: Korea's Second Five-Year Plan* (JHUP, 1969); 5. *Economic Growth and Social Equity in Developing Countries* (with C. T. Morris), (Stanford Univ. Press, 1973); 6. *Income Distribution Policy in Developing Countries: A Case Study of Korea* (with S. Robinson), (Stanford Univ. Press, 1977).

Articles: 1. 'A stochastic analysis of the size distribution of firms', *JASA*, 53(284), Dec. 1958; 2. 'The dynamic properties of the Klein-Goldberger model' (with F. L. Adelman), *Em*, 27(4), Oct. 1959, repr. in *Reading in Business Cycles*, eds. R. A. Gordon and L. R. Klein (Richard D. Irwin, 1964), and *Readings in Econometrics*, eds. A. Zellner (Little, Brown, 1968); 3. 'On an index of quality change' (with Z. Grilliches), *JASA*, 56(295), Sept. 1961; 4. 'A factor analysis of the interrelationship between social and political variables and per capita GNP' (with C. T. Morris), *QJE*, 79(4), Nov. 1965; 5. 'The measurement of institutional characteristics of nations: methodological considerations'(with C. T. Morris), *JDE*, 8(3), April 1972; 6. 'Development economics — a reassessment of goals', *AER*, 65(2), May 1975; 7. 'Policies for equitable growth' (with C. T. Morris and S. Robinson), *WD*, 4(7), 1976; 8. 'Redistribution before growth: a strategy for developing countries' (Martinus Nijhof, 1978); 9. 'An inquiry into the course of poverty in the nineteenth and early twentieth centuries' (with C. T. Morris), in *Economic Growth and Resources: Trends and Factors*, ed. R. L. Matthews (Macmillan, 1979); 10. 'Some thoughts on the restructuring of north–south interactions', *J. Pol. Modeling*, 2(2), May 1980.

Principal Contributions I was first attracted to economics by a desire to contribute to the solution of the problems of worldwide poverty. Thus, my basic interest was in the study of economic development even before economic development was recognised as a modern academic subdiscipline. Several basic strands have run through all my work since the very beginning. An interest in long- and short-term economic dynamics; an interest in the quantification of qualitative phenomena; an interest in interactions among economic, social and political forces; an interest in the analysis of institutional change; an interest in stochastic elements; and, last but not least, an interest in policies to remedy widespread and persistent poverty and inequality. In each of these areas, my work combines empirical analysis (including data development) with a broad range of statistical and operations research techniques. I have used both inductive and deductive methodologies; conventional, quantised, and qualitative data; and descriptive, normative, and optimising approaches.

Much of my work deals with economic planning; with a quantitative delineation of long-term economic, institutional, and political change; and with income distribution and basic needs. Together with Professor Cynthia Taft Morris, I pioneered the use of multivariate techniques to quantify interactions among economic, social and political forces in economic development. Together with Professor Sherman Robinson, I pioneered the development of the technique of computable general equilibrium models for economic planning and policy analysis and in its application to developing countries. My work contributed to the reorientation of the focus of development policy toward income distribution and basic needs in the early 1970s. My current interests are in land reform, agricultural-development-led industrialisation, the modelling of institutional change, quantitative economic history, planning under uncertainty, and trends in income distribution and poverty.

ADELMAN, Morris Albert

Born 1917, New York City, NY, USA.
Current Post Prof. Econ., MIT, Cambridge, MA., USA, 1960–.
Past Posts Econ., US War Production Board, 1941–2; Econ., Fed. Reserve Board, 1946; Ass. Prof., Assoc. Prof., MIT, 1948–60.
Degrees BSS City Coll. NY, 1938; PhD Harvard Univ., 1948.
Offices and Honours Wells Prize, Harvard Univ., 1948; US SSRC Fellow, 1947–8; Ford Faculty Fellow, 1962–3; Award Contributions Mineral Econ., Amer. Inst. Mining, Metallurgical and Petroleum Engineers, 1979; Pres., Award for Contribs. Energy Econ., Internat. Assoc., 1980–1, 1983.
Editorial Duties Ed. Board, *Ind. Energy Econ.*
Principal Fields of Interest 723 Energy.
Publications Books: 1. *A&P Cost-Price: Behavior and Public Policy* (Harvard Univ. Press, 1959); 2. *The Supply and Price of Natural Gas* (Blackwell, 1962); 3. *Alaskan Oil: Price and Supply* (with P. Bradley, *et al.*), (Praeger, 1971); 4. *The World Petroleum Market* (JHUP, 1972); 5. *Resources in an Uncertain Future* (with J. Houghton, *et al.*), (Ballinger, 1983).
Articles: 1. 'Is the oil shortage real: oil companies as tax collectors', *Foreign Policy*, 9, Winter 1972–3; 2. 'The world oil cartel: scarcity, economics, and politics', *QREB*, 16(2), Summer 1976; 3. 'Constraints on the world oil monopoly price', *Resources and Energy*, 1(1), Sept. 1978; 4. 'Alternative methods of supply forecasting' (with others), in *Advances in the Economics of Energy and Resources*, 2

(JAI Press, 1979); 5. 'Energy–income coefficients: their use and abuse', *Energy Econ.*, 2(1), Jan. 1980; 6. 'Worldwide production costs for oil and gas' (with others), in *Advances in the Economics of Energy and Resources*, 3 (JAI Press, 1980); 7. 'Coping with supply insecurity', *Energy J.*, 3(2), April 1982; 8. 'OPEC as a cartel', in *OPEC Behavior and World Oil Prices*, eds. J. M. Griffin and D. A. Teece (A&U, 1982).

Principal Contributions Early work was on antitrust policy, and on some case studies, particularly in retailing. Over the last twenty-odd years, my published research has been devoted mostly to oil and natural gas as studies in competition and monopoly with account taken of the peculiarities of supply and cost, and the role of governments as market participants. Winston Churchill called World War II 'the unnecessary war' because its victims could have prevented it. In 1972, I argued that the then-small oil price increases promised more harm to come and were preventable and unnecessary because they resulted from monopoly, not scarcity.

AFTALION, Albert*

Dates and Birthplace 1874–1956, Bulgaria.

Posts Held Prof., Univ. Lille, 1904–20, Univ. Paris, 1920–40.

Publications *Books:* 1. *L'oeuvre économique de Simonde de Sismondi* (1899); 2. *Essai d'une théorie des crises générales et périodiques* (1909); 3. *Les crises périodiques de surproduction*, 2 vols (1913); 4. *Les fondements du socialisme: étude critique* (1923); 5. *La valeur de la monnaie dans l'économie contemporaine*, 2 vols (1927, 1948), 6. *L'or et la monnaie, leur valeur: les mouvements de l'or* (1938).

Career One of the professors appointed to chairs in economics in the law faculties of the universities of France after 1878 who questioned the free trade *laissez-faire* orthodoxy of the 'Paris group' and gradually introduced more scientific content into French economics. He is best known for his 'real' theory of business cycles, including the statement in 1909 of the 'acceleration principle' of derived demand (restated and named by J. M. Clark in 1917). Much of his later work dealt with the nature of the French inflation 1919–24 and the causes of international gold movements between the two world wars.

Secondary Literature F. Perroux *et al.*, *L'oeuvre scientifique d'Albert Aftalion* (Domat-Montchrestien, 1945); D. Villey, 'Aftalion, Albert', *IESS*, vol. 1.

AHMAD, Syed

Born 1930, Bishunpur, Muzaffarpur, Bihar, India.

Current Post Prof. Econ., McMaster Univ., Hamilton, Ont., Canada, 1972– .

Past Posts Lect., Muslim Univ., Aligarh, India, 1956–7; Lect., Sr. Lect., Prof., Univ. Khartoum, Sudan, 1957–70; Prof. Econ. Theory, Univ. Kent, Canterbury, UK, 1970–2

Degrees BA, MA, LLB Muslim Univ., Aligarh, 1950, 1952, 1952; MSc, DSc London Univ., 1956, 1978.

Offices and Honours Silver Jubilee Medal Disting. Services, Univ. Khartoum, 1980.

Editorial Duties Ed. Boards, *E. African J. Econ., Pakistan J. Applied Econ.*

Principal Fields of Interest 621 Technological Change; 311 Domestic Monetary and Financial Theory and Policy; 022 Microeconomic Theory.

Publications *Articles:* 1. 'The international relation of demand and the preference system of the firm', *OEP*, 10(1), Feb. 1958; 2. 'On the international supply of capital goods', *Indian Econ. Rev.*, 5(1), Feb. 1960; 3. 'Harrod on Domar's theory of growth', *EJ*, 71, June 1961; 4. 'Saving wealth relation and the measure of the real value of assets', *JPE*, 70(3), June 1962; 5. 'On the theory of induced invention', *EJ*, 76, June 1966; 6. 'Is money net wealth?', *OEP*, 22(3), Nov. 1970; 7. 'The 'paradox of bliss' and money as net wealth', *JMCB*, 7(3), Aug. 1975; 8. 'Transactions demand for money and the quantity theory', *QJE*, 91(2), May 1977; 9. 'Induced adjustment and the role of agriculture in economic development: a case study of Syria and Egypt' (with A. Kubursi), in *Technology Transfer and Change in the Arab World* (Pergamon, 1978); 10. 'Metzler and the classical theory of interest: comment', *AER*, 54(5), Dec. 1981.

Principal Contributions Developed the concept of the 'innovation possibility curve' (IPC), which provides an analytical basis for Hicks's intuition of 'price-induced' technological change, and for identifying losses due to inappropriate technologies. Stressed the importance of using an appropriate marginal approach to evaluate 'wealth' in the form of money and other nominal assets, and explored the implications of the choice of the unit of measurement for such evaluation. The central theme of most of the contributions in these and other fields is the role and measurement of capital in its various aspects: variable and fixed capital; the economic longevity of capital equipment; technical change as a means of changing the efficiency of capital and other co-operating factors; and the appropriate approaches to measuring capital and wealth. Recent work includes empirical research on capital and technological change in the development of a number of Middle-Eastern countries, and a nearly-completed book on capital theory.

AIGNER, Dennis John

Born 1937, Los Angeles, CA, USA.
Current Post Prof. Econ., Univ. Southern Cal., Los Angeles, CA, USA, 1976–.
Past Posts Stat., US Forest Service, Berkeley, CA., 1960–2; Ass. Prof. Econ., Assoc. Prof., Dir., Computer Lab., Coll. Bus. Admin., Univ. Illinois, 1962–6, 1964–6, 1966–7; Assoc. Prof. Econ., Dir. Data and Computation Center Social Sciences, Chairman, Social Systems Res. Inst., Univ. Wisconsin, Madison, 1967–70, 1967–73, 1971–6; Vis. Prof. Econ., Univ. Hawaii, 1970; Vis., CORE, Univ. Catholique de Louvain, Belgium, 1970–1; Vis. Prof., Univ. Wisconsin, 1982; Vis. Lect, ASA Program Stats., 1980–3; Cons., Rand Corp., Santa Monica, CA, 1976.
Degrees BS (Agric. Econ.), MA (Stat.), PhD (Agric. Econ.) Univ. Cal. Berkeley, 1959, 1962, 1963.
Offices and Honours Fulbright Scholar, Belgium, 1970–1; Fellow, Em Soc., 1972; H. I. Romnes Faculty Fellow, Univ. Wisconsin, 1976; Fulbright Scholar, Israel, 1983.
Editorial Duties Co-Ed., *JEm*, 1972; Assoc. Ed., *Rev. Public Data Use*, 1980–.
Principal Fields of Interest 211 Econometrics.
Publications Books: *Principles of Statistical Decision-Making* (Macmillan, 1968); 2. *Basic Econometrics* (Prentice-Hall, 1971); 3. *Latent Variables in Socioeconomic Models*, co-ed. (with A. S. Goldberger), (N-H, 1977); 4. *Modelling and Forecasting Time-of-Day and Seasonal Electricity Demands*, *Annals of Applied Econometrics, 1979, 1*, co-ed. (with A. Lawrence), (N-H, 1979); 5. *Experimental Design in Econometrics*, *Annals of Applied Econometrics 1979, 2*, co-ed. (with C. Morris), (N-H 1979); 6. *Modelling and Analysis of Electricity Demand by Time-of-Day*, ed. (Electric Power Res. Inst., 1979); 7. *Electricity Demand and Consumption by Time-of-Use: A Survey* (with D. Poirier), (Electric Power Res. Inst., 1979); 8. *Specification and Estimation of Frontier Production, Profit and Cost Functions, Annals of Applied Econometrics, 1980, 2*, co-ed (with P. Schmidt), (N-H 1980); 9. *Welfare Econometrics of Peak-Load Pricing for Electricity, Annals of Applied Econometrics, 1984, 3*, ed. (N-H 1984).

Articles: 1. 'On estimating the industry production function' (with S. Chu), *AER*, 58(4), Sept. 1968; 2. 'Estimation of Pareto's law from grouped observations' (with A. S. Goldberger), *JASA*, 65, June 1970; 3. 'Estimation and prediction from aggregate data when aggregates are measured more accurately than their components' (with S. M. Goldfeld), *Em*, 42, Jan. 1974; 4. 'An appropriate econometric framework for estimating a labor supply function from the SEO file', *IntER*, 15(1), Feb. 1974; 5. 'On the explanatory power of dummy variable regression' (with A. S. Goldberger and G. Kalton), *IntER* 16(3), June 1975; 6. 'Identification and estimation of dynamic shock-error models' (with A. Maravall), in *Latent Variables in Socioeconomic Models*, eds. D. J. Aigner and A. S. Goldberger (N-H 1977); 7. 'Statistical theories of discrimination in labor markets' (with G. Cain), *ILRR*, 30(1), Jan. 1977; 8. 'Formulation and estimation of stochastic frontier production functions' (with C. A. K. Lovell and P. Schmidt), *J Em*, 6, July 1977; 9. 'Correcting for truncation bias in the analysis of experiments in time-of-day pricing of electricity' (with J. A. Hausman), *Bell JE*, 11, Spring 1980, repr. *Evaluation Studies Review Annual, Vol. 5*, eds. E. Stromsdorfer and G. Farkas (Sage Publications, 1980); 10. 'Time-of-day electricity consumption response to temperature and the ownership of air conditioning appliances' (with L. Lillard), *J. Bus. and Econ. Stat.*, 2, Jan. 1984.

Principal Contributions I began my research endeavours with an interest in the errors-in-variables 'problem' in econometrics. This has remained a theme throughout my work, which now spans twenty years. Of course our attitude about this 'problem' has since evolved into an appreciation of its possibilities for an enhanced model specification and ultimate solution. The errors-in-variables problem also serves as an interface with the quantitative branches of other social sciences, notably psychology and sociology.

The other major theme of my work has evolved from the estimation of frontier production, cost and profit functions. Standard microeconomic theory talks about a production function that derives from technical efficiency in the utilisation of inputs, yet most empirical work estimates an average production function. This line of research has since resulted in a means to evaluate the technical and economic efficiency of individual firms in an industry and related issues. Most recently I have been involved in the design,

conduct and analysis of large-scale social experiments for the purpose of measuring customer response to time-differentiated prices for electricity in the US.

AKERLOF, George Arthur

Born 1940, New Haven, CT, USA.
Current Post Prof., Univ. Cal. Berkeley, 1977–.
Past Posts Ass. Prof., Assoc. Prof., Univ. Cal. Berkeley, 1960–70, 1970–1; Sr. Econ., US President's Council Econ. Advisers, 1973–4; Vis. Res. Econ., Board Governors, Fed. Reserve Board, 1977–8; Prof., LSE, 1978–80; Vis. Prof., Indian Stat. Inst., Planning Unit, New Delhi, 1967–8.
Degrees BA Yale Univ., 1962; PhD MIT, 1966.
Editorial Duties Ed. Boards, *AER*, *QJE*, *J Ec Behav*.
Principal Fields of Interest 022 Microeconomic Theory; 023 Macroeconomic Theory; 026 Economics of Uncertainty and Information.
Publications *Books:* 1. *An Economic Theorist's Book of Tales* (CUP, 1984).
Articles: 1. 'Relative wages and the rate of inflation', *QJE*, 83(3), Aug. 1969; 2. 'The market for "lemons": quality uncertainty and the market mechanism', *QJE*, 84(3), Aug. 1970; 3. 'The economics of caste and of the rat race and other woeful tales', *QJE*, 90(4), Nov. 1976; 4. 'The economics of "tagging" as applied to the optimal income tax, welfare programs and manpower planning', *AER*, 68(1), March 1978; 5. 'Irving Fisher on his head: the consequences of constant target-threshold monitoring of bank accounts', *QJE*, 92(2), May 1978; 6. 'Jobs as dam sites', *REStud*, 48(1), Jan. 1981; 7. 'Labor contracts as partial gift exchange', *QJE*, 97(4), Nov. 1982; 8. 'The economic consequences of cognitive dissonance' (with W. Dickens), *AER*, 72(3), June 1982; 9. 'Can small deviations from rationality make significant differences to economic equilibria?' (with J. Yellen), *AER*, 75(4), Sept. 1985; 10. 'A new rational model of the business cycle with wage and price inertia' (with J. Yellen), *QJE*, forthcoming 1986.

ÅKERMAN, Gustaf*

Dates and Birthplace 1888–1959 Vienna, Austro-Hungary.
Posts Held Civil servant, Swedish Foreign Affairs Dept., 1915–18; Ass. Prof., Univ. Lund, 1923; Prof., Univ. Goteborg, 1931–53.
Degrees Jur. kandidat, Univ. Uppsala, 1913; Dr Univ. Lund, 1923.
Publications *Books:* 1. *Real Kapital und Kapitalzins*, 2 vols (1923–4); 2. *Om den Industriella Rationaliseringen* (1931); 3. *Mjölleregleringen* (1937); 4. *Engelsk Arbetslöshet och Arbetslöshetspolitik* (1947).
Career Elder brother of Johann Henrik, an economist and historian in his own right, whose 1923–4 book on capital theory led Wicksell to reformulate his own theory of fixed capital formation. Like Böhm-Bawerk, Åkerman was inspired by his reading of John Rae. He partially reformulated his ideas in a 1931 book, and also worked on industrial rationalisation, price regulations, economic fluctuations and employment questions.
Secondary Literature K. Wicksell, *Lectures on Political Economy,* vol. 1, App. 2 (Macmillan, 1934).

ÅKERMAN, Johan Henrik

Dates and Birthplace 1891–1961, Stockholm, Sweden.
Posts Held Ass. Prof., Prof., Prof. Emeritus, Univ. Lund, 1932–43, 1943–60, 1960–1.
Degrees Fil. Lic., Dr Univ. Lund, 1927, 1929.
Publications *Books:* 1. *Economic Progress and Economic Crises* (1932); 2. *Das Problem der sozialökonomischen Synthese* (1938); 3. *Structures et cycles économiques,* 2 vols (1955–7); 4. *Theory of industrialism* (1960).
Articles: 1. 'Economic plans and causal analysis', *Ekonomisk Tidskrift,* 1942, repr. in *Internat. Econ. Papers,* 4, eds. A. T. Peacock, *et al.* (Macmillan, 1954).
Career Swedish economist who devoted his life to the development of a theoretical framework for the explanation of historical change. His approach did not find favour in the English-speaking world, since it relegated economic analysis to a minor role in the study of economic structures and denied its ability to explain the origins of and change in such structures.
Secondary Literature H. Hegeland, ed., *Money, Growth and Methodology and Other Essays in Economics in Honour of Johan Akerman* (Gleerup Lund, 1961).

ALBACH, Horst

Born 1931, Essen, W. Germany.
Current Post Prof. Management, Inst. für Gesellschafts- und Wirtschaftswissenschaften der Univ. Bonn, W. Germany, 1961–.
Past Posts Ass. Prof., Cologne Univ., 1956–8, Darmstadt Inst. Technology, 1959; Assoc. Prof., Graz Univ., 1960, Kiel Univ., 1960–1.
Degrees Diplom-Kaufmann, Diplom-Volkswirt, PhD, Habilitation Cologne Univ., 1956, 1957, 1958, 1960; Hon. Dr Stockholm School Econ., 1973, Helsinki School Econ., 1976.
Offices and Honours Council Econ. Experts, Fed. Republic of Germany, 1978–83; Board Econ. Advisers, Fed. Ministry Econ.; Dir., Inst. Res. on Small and Medium-Sized Firms; Chairman, Board of Scientific Advisers, Wissenschaftszentrum Berlin; Board Scientific Advisers, Inst. für Höhere Studien, Wien; Pres., German Internat. Management Assoc., German Operations Res. Soc.; Vice Chairman, Board Experts, Fed. Govt. on Vocational Training 1970–4; Vice-Pres., Scientific Comm., National Science Council, 1974–7, German Econ. Assoc.; Universitätsseminar der Wirtschaft, German Management Training Centre.
Editorial Duties Exec. Ed., *Zeitschrift für Betriebswirtschaft;* Co-ed., *USW Schriften für Führungskräfte, Beiträge zur betriebswirtschaftlichen Forschung, Bonner betriebswirtschaftliche Schriften, J. Bus. Strategy.*
Principal Fields of Interest 010 General Economics; 110 Economic Growth, Development, and Planning

Theory and Policy; 200 Quantitative Economic Methods and Data.

Publications *Books:* 1. *Wirtschaftlichkeitsrechnung bei unsicheren Erwartungen* (Westdeutscher Verlag, 1959); 2. *Investition und Liquidität*, (Gabler Verlag, 1962; transl., Japanese, Diamond Publishing, 1964); 3. *Die degressive Abschreibung* (Gabler Verlag, 1967); 4. *Beiträge zur Unternehmensplanung* (Gabler Verlag, 1969, 1971; transl., Japanese, Chikura Shobo, 1983); 5. *Steuersystem und unternehmerische Investionspolitik* (Gabler Verlag, 1970); 6. *Kosten und Finanzierung der beruflichen Bildung* (with F. Edding, Th. Dams, H. Gerfin, J. Münch), (Bertelsmann Verlag, 1975); 7. *Als-Ob-Konzept und zeitlicher Vergleichsmarkt* (J. C. B. Mohr, Paul Siebeck, 1976); 8. *Mitarbeiterführung* (with T. Gabelin), (Gabler Verlag, 1977); 9. *Finanzkraft und Marktbeherrschung* (J. C. B. Mohr, Paul Siebeck, 1981); 10. *Zur Versorgung der Deutschen Wirtschaft mit Risikokapital* (Inst. Mittelstandsforschung, 1983). *Articles:* 1. 'Zur Theorie des wachsenden Unternehmens', in *Theorien des Einzelwirtschaftlichen und des gesamwirtschaftlichen Wachstums*, ed., W. Krelle (J. C. B. Mohr, 1965); 2. 'Innerbetrieblich Lenkpreise als Instrument dezentraler Unternehmensführung Schmalenbachs', *Zeitschrift für betreibswirtschaftliche Forschung*, 26, 3/4, March–April, 1974; 3. 'Kritische Wachstumsschwellen in der Unternehmenssentwicklung', *Zeitschrift für Betriebswirtschaft*, 46(10), Oct. 1976; 4. 'Capital Budgeting and Risk Management', in *Quantitative Wirtschaftsforschung*, ed. E. Helmstädter (J. C. B. Mohr, 1977); 5. 'Strategische Unternehmensplanung bei erhöhter Unsicherheit', *Zeitschrift für Betriebswirtschaft*, 48(8), Aug. 1978; 6. 'The capital structure of the firm: empirical investigations in the financing behavior of German industrial firms' (with B. Geisen), *Liiketaloudellinen Aikakauskirja*, 28(2), 1979; 7. 'Average and best practice production functions in German industry', *J Ind E*, 29, Sept. 1980; 8. 'Zur Prognose der Rentabilitatsentwicklung deutscher Industrie-aktien-gesellschaften', *Zeitschrift für Betriebswirtschaft*, 51(10), Oct. 1981; 9. 'Innovationen für Wirtschaftswachstum und internationale Wettbewerbsfähigkeit', in *Technische Innovationen und Wirtschaftskraft* (Rheinisch-Westfälische Akademie der Wissenschaften, 1983); 10. 'The rate of return in German manufacturing industry: measurement and policy implications', in *Measuring Profitability and Capital Costs: An International Study*, ed. D. Holland (J. C. B. Mohr, 1984).

ALCHIAN, Armen A.

Born 1914, Fresno, CA, USA.

Current Post Prof. Econ., UCLA, 1964–.

Past Posts Econ., Rand Corp., 1947–64.

Degrees BA, PhD Stanford Univ., 1936, 1944.

Offices and Honours Member, Mont Pelerin Soc.; Pres., WEA, 1974; Member, AAAS, 1978.

Principal Fields of Interest 022 Microeconomic Theory; 511 Organisation and Decision Theory.

Publications *Books:* 1. *University Economics* (with W. R. Allen), (Wadsworth, 1964, 1972); 2. *Exchange and Production* (Wadsworth, 1964, 1983); 3. *Economic Forces at Work* (Liberty, 1978). *Articles:* 1. 'Uncertainty, evolution and economic theory', *JPE*, 58, June 1950; 2. 'Costs and outputs', in *The Allocation of Economic Resources*, eds. M. Abramovitz, et al. (Stanford Univ. Press, 1959); 3. 'The meaning and validity of the inflation-induced lag of wages' (with R. A. Kessel), *AER*, 50(1), March 1960; 4. 'Information costs, pricing and resource unemployment', *WEJ*, 7(2), June 1969; 5. 'Production, information, cost and economic organization', *AER*, 62(5), Dec. 1972; 6. 'Vertical integration, appropriable rents and the competitive contracting process' (with B. Klein and R. G. Crawford), *J Law E*, 21(2), Oct. 1978; 7. 'Specificity, specialization and coalitions', *ZGS*, 140(1), March 1984.

Principal Contributions Analysis of effects of inflation on common stock prices; effects of property rights systems; organisation theory.

ALDCROFT, Derek Howard

Born 1936, Abergele, North Wales, UK.
Current Post Prof. Econ. Hist., Leicester Univ., England, 1976–.
Past Posts Teaching Ass., Lect., Glasgow Univ., 1960–2, 1964–7; Ass. Lect., Sr. Lect., Reader, Leicester Univ., 1962–3, 1967–70, 1970–3; Prof. Econ. Hist., Sydney Univ., Australia 1973–6.
Degrees BA, PhD Manchester Univ., 1958, 1962.
Offices and Honours Houblon-Norman Award 1968, 1972; Overseas Vis. Fellow, Australia, 1979; Council, EHS, 1983–.
Editorial Duties Chairman, Ed. Board, *J Transport Hist.*, 1971–8; Ed. Board, *Bus. Hist. Rev.*, 1971–3; Advisory Panel, *Econ. Rev.*, 1983–.
Principal Fields of Interest 110 Economic Growth; 044 European Economic History.
Publications *Books:* 1. *British Railways in Transition* (Macmillan, 1968); 2. *British Transport* (with H. J. Dyos), (Leicester Univ. Press, 1969); 3. *The Inter-War Economy: Britain 1919–1939* (Batsford, 1970); 4. *The British Economy 1870–1939* (with H. W. Richardson), (Macmillan, 1970); 5. *British Transport since 1914* (David and Charles, 1975); 6. *From Versailles to Wall Street: The International Economy 1919–1929* (Allen Lane Penguin, 1977); 7. *The East Midlands Economy* (Pointon York, 1979); 8. *The European Economy 1914–1980* (Croom Helm, 1980); 9. *The British Economy Between the Wars* (Philip Allen, 1983); 10. *Full Employment — The Elusive Goal* (Wheatsheaf Books, 1984).
Articles: 1. 'Economic progress in Britain in the 1920s', *SJPE*, 13, Nov. 1966; 2. 'Economic growth in Britain in the interwar years: a reassessment', *EHR*, 20, Aug. 1967; 3. 'The development of the managed economy before 1939', *J Contemporary Hist.*, 1969; 4. 'The impact of British monetary policy, 1919–1939', *Internat. Rev. Banking Hist.*, 3, 1970; 5. 'Innovation on the railways: the lag in diesel and electric traction', *J. Transp. EP*, 1, 1969; 6. 'A new chapter in transport history: the twentieth-century revolution', *J Transp. Hist.*, 3, 1976; 7. 'The economy, management and foreign competition, 1870–1914', in *Industry, Education and the Economy in the Nineteenth Century*, eds. G. Roderick and M. Stephens (Falmer Press, 1981); 8. 'Britain's economic decline 1870–1980', in *The British Malaise: Industrial Performance, Education and Training in Britain Today*, eds. G. Roderick and M. Stephens (Falmer Press, 1982); 9. 'Urban transport problems in historical perspective', in *Business, Banking and Urban History: Essays in Honour of S. G. Checkland*, eds. D. H. Aldcroft and A. Slaven (John Donald, 1982); 10. 'Relearning the lessons of the past', *Econ. Rev.*, 1, 1983.
Principal Contributions My research interests have been centred on modern economic issues and much of my work crosses the boundary disciplines between economics and economic history. I have for many years written on two major themes: growth and structural change in advanced economies, and transport problems of the twentieth century. I have made some important contributions to the reinterpretation of Britain's interwar growth performance and more recently I shifted attention to the post-1950 period. Since I believe that there are often lessons to be learned from the study of the past, I have always attempted to relate my historical work to contemporary problems. This is demonstrated clearly in my latest work *Full Employment — The Elusive Goal*, which examines the constraints to generating full employment in the 1930s and 1980s. This work also shifts my focus of interest towards macro-policy issues of the twentieth century and the controversies between rival schools of thought. Increasingly, as I work in this area, I incline to the view that viable growth and employment cannot be determined by government policy in the long run unless a stable financial framework is maintained.

ALEXANDER, Sidney Stuart

Born 1916, Forest City, PA, USA.
Current Post Prof. Econ. Management, MIT, 1956–.
Past Posts Econ., IMF, 1948–52; Adviser, Columbia Broadcasting System, 1952–6.
Degrees BS, MS, PhD Harvard Univ., 1936, 1938, 1946.
Principal Fields of Interest 121 Economic Studies of Less Industrialised Countries; 431 Balance of Payments; 723 Energy.
Publications *Books:* 1. (principal contributor) *The Outlook for Key Commodities. The Outlook for Energy Sources,* in *Resources for Freedom: Report to the President by the President's Materials Policy Commission,* 2, 3 (US Govt Printing Office, 1952).
Articles: 1. 'Effects of a devaluation on the trade balance', *IMF Staff Papers,* 2, April 1952; 2. 'Economics and business planning', in *Economics and the Policy Maker,* eds. S. S. Alexander, *et al.* (Brookings Inst., 1959); 3. 'The impersonality of normative judgements', in *Essays in Honor of Sir Roy Harrod,* eds. W. A. Eltis, *et al.* (OUP, 1970); 4. 'Social evaluation through notional choice', *QJE,* 88(4), Nov. 1974.
Principal Contributions Theory of effects of a devaluation on the trade balance; foundations of normative judgements in social policy; economics and politics of the Middle East; economics of energy and mineral supply.

ALIBER, Robert Z.

Born 1930, Keene, NH, USA.
Current Post Prof. Internat. Econ. and Fin., Grad. School Bus., Univ. Chicago, Chicago, IL., USA, 1980–.
Past Posts Ass. Instr., Yale Univ., 1958–9; Staff Econ., Comm. Econ. Devlp., Washington, DC, 1961–4; Sr. Econ. Adviser, Agency Internat. Devlp., US Dept. State, Washington, DC, 1964–5; Instr., Johns Hopkins School Advanced Internat. Stud., Washington, DC, 1964–5; Assoc. Prof. Internat. Econ. and Fin., Grad. School Bus., Univ. Chicago, 1965–80; Vis. Prof., Salzburg Seminar Amer. Stud., Salzburg; Vis. Scholar, Fed. Reserve Bank San Franciso; National Westminster Prof. Internat. Fin., London Grad. School Bus. Stud., 1978; Vis. Prof., Amos Tuck School Bus. Admin., Dartmouth Coll., Hanover, NH, 1983; Vis. Prof., Williams Coll., Williamstown, MA, 1983.
Degrees BA Williams Coll., 1952; BA, MA Univ. Camb., 1954, 1957; PhD Yale Univ., 1962.
Offices and Honours Secretary, Assoc. Public Policy Analysis and Management, 1978–81.
Editorial Duties Ed. Board, *J Internat. Bus Stud.*
Principal Fields of Interest 310 Domestic Monetary and Financial Theory and Institutions; 430 Balance of Payments; International Finance; 440 International Investment and Foreign Aid.
Publications *Books:* 1. *The Management of the Dollar in International Finance* (Princeton Univ. Press, 1964); 2. *Guidelines, Informal Controls and the Market Place,* co-ed. (with G. P. Schultz), (Univ. Chicago Press, 1966); 3. *The International Money Game* (Basic, Macmillan, 1973, 1983; transls., Japanese, Sangyo Nohristsu Daigaku, Spanish, Biblioteca de Ciencias Economicas, Portuguese, Zahar Editores); 4. *National Monetary Policies and the International Financial System* (Univ. Chicago Press, 1974, 1982); 5. *The Political Economy of Monetary Reform,* ed. (Macmillan, 1977); 6. *Exchange Risk and Corporate International Finance* (with T. Mayer and J. S. Duesenberry), (Macmillan, 1978, Halsted, 1979); 7. *Stabilizing World Financial Arrangements* (Trade Policy Res. Centre, 1979); 8. *Your Money and Your Life* (Basic, 1982); 9. *Money, Banking and the Economy* (W. W. Norton, 1981, 1984).
Articles: 1. 'The costs and benefits of the US role as a reserve currency country', *QJE,* 78, Aug. 1964; 2. 'The theory of the international corporation: a theory of direct foreign investment', in *The International Corporation,* ed. C. P. Kindleberger (MIT Press, 1970); 3. 'Uncertainty, currency areas, and the exchange rate system',

Ec, N.S. 39, Nov. 1972; 4. 'Floating exchange rates: the twenties and the seventies', in *Flexible Exchange Rates and the Balance of Payments* (N-H., 1980); 5. 'The integration of offshore and domestic markets for national currencies', *J Mon E*, 6(3), Summer 1980.

Principal Contributions The microfoundations of international finance, including the pricing of exchange risk and of political risk as well as the other factors which segment national financial markets. I have explored the consequences of segmentation of these markets for international corporate financial management and national financial management, and also given attention to the evolution of international financial arrangements and the expansion of the domain of national currency areas.

ALLAIS, Maurice Felix Charles

Born 1911, Paris, France.

Current Post Prof. d'Econ., Dir., Centre d'Analyse Economique, Ecole Nationale Supérieure des Paris, 1944–.

Past Posts Service des Mines de Nantes et Conrole des Chemins de Fer, 1937–43; Armée des Alpes, 1939–40; Dir., Bureau de Documentation et de Statistique Miniére, 1943–8; Dir. de Recherche, CNRS, 1946–80; Prof. d'Econ. Thèorique, Institut de Statistique de l'Univ. de Paris, 1947–68; Membre, Comité National, CNRS, 1947–80; Commission de l'Energie du Conseil Economique et Social, 1960–1; Pres., Comité d'Experts pour l'Etude des Options de la Politique Tarifaire dans les Transport, EEC, 1963–4; Prof. d'Econ., Inst. de Hautes Etudes Internat. de Genève, 1967–70; Disting. Vis. Scholar, Center Thomas Jefferson, Univ. Virginia, 1958–9.

Degrees Ancien élève, Ecole Polytechnique, Paris, 1933, Ecole Nationale Supérieure des Mines de Paris, 1936; Ingenieur-Dr Univ. Paris, 1949; Dr Hon. Univ. Groningen, Netherlands, 1964.

Offices and Honours Prix Laplace, Prix Rivot, l'Académie des Sciences de l'Ecole Polytechnique, 1933; Prix Charles Dupin, Académie des Sciences

Morales et Politiques, 1943; Lanchester Prize, Johns Hopkins Univ.; OR Soc. Amer. for outstanding paper on OR, 1957, 1958; Prix Joseph Dutens, Académie des Sciences Morales et Polit., 1959; Prix Galabert, Societé Française d'Astronautique, 1959; Laureate, Gravity Res. Foundation, USA, 1959; Grand Prix, Communauté Atlantique de l'Assoc. Française, 1960; Grand Prix André Arnoux, Assoc. pour la Liberté Econ. et le Progrès Social, 1968; Medaille d'or, Societé d'Encouragement pour l'Industrie Nationale, 1970, CNRS, 1978; Prix Robert Blanche, Prix Zerilli Marimo, Academie des Sciences Morales et Polit., 1983, 1984; Fellow, Soc. Internat. d'Em, 1949–; Membre, Inst. Internat. de Statistique, 1951; Fellow, OR Soc. Amer., 1958; Hon. Member, AEA, 1976; Officier, Ordre des Palmes Académiques, 1949; Ordre de la Légion d'Honneur, 1977; Chevalier, Ordre de l'Econ. Nat., 1977.

Editorial Duties Ed. Boards, *REP*, 1952–, *Em*, 1959–69; Council, *Em Soc*, 1960–5.

Principal Fields of Interest 000 General Economics; Theory; History; Systems; 100 Economic Growth; Development; Planning; Fluctuations; 300 Domestic Monetary and Fiscal Theory and Institutions.

Publications *Books:* 1. *A la Récherche d'une Discipline Economique — Première Partie: L'Economie Pure* (Ateliers Industrie, 1943, Imprimerie Nationale, 1952); 2. *Abondance ou Misère* (Libraire de Medicis, 1946); 3. *Economie et Interêt* (Imprimerie Nationale, 1947); 4. *Les Fondements Comptables de la Macroéconomique* (Presses Univ. de France, 1954); 5. *L'Europe Unie, Route de la Prosperité* (Calmann-Levy, 1959); 6. *Le Tiers-Monde au Carrefour, Centralisation Autoritaire ou Planisme Concurrentiel* (Editions des Cahiers Africains, 1961; transl., Italian, *Il Terzo Mondo al Bivio*, Editore, 1962); 7. *La Liberalisation des Rélations Economiques Internationales — Accords Commerciaux et Integration Economique* (Gauthier-Villars, 1970; transl., English (abridged) as *Customs Unions and Trade Agreements, Encyclopedia Britannica*, 1974,

5); 8. *L'Inflation Française et la Crois-sance — Mythologies et Realité* (Editions ALEPS, 1974); 9. *L'Impôt sur le Capital et la Réforme Monétaire* (Hermann, 1976); 10. *La Theorie Generale des Surplus* (Inst. de Sciences Maths. et Econ. Appliquées, 1981).

Articles: 1. 'Method of appraising economic prospects of mining exploration over large territories — Algerian Sahara case study', *MS*, July 1957; 2. 'The influence of the capital output ratio on real national income', *Em*, 30(4), Oct. 1962, repr. in *Readings in Welfare Economics*, eds. K. J. Arrow and T. Scitovsky (Richard D. Irwin, 1969); 3. 'The role of capital in economic development', in *The Role of Econometric Analysis in the Formulation of Development Plans* (Pontifical Academy of Sciences, 1963); 4. 'Réformulation de la théorie quantitative de la monnaie', *Bull. Sedeis*, Sept. 1965, transl. English (abridged) as 'A Restatement of the quantity theory of money', *AER*, 56(5), Dec. 1966; 5. 'Growth and inflation', *JMCB*, 1(3), Aug. 1969; 6. 'Theories of general economic equilibrium and maximum efficiency', in *Equilibrium and Disequilibrium in Economic Theory*, ed. G. Schwödiauer (Reidel, 1977; transl., Spanish, *El Trimestre Economico*, Julio–Sept. 1972; 7. 'The psychological rate of interest', *JMCB*, 6(3), Aug. 1974; 8. 'The foundations of a positive theory of choice involving risk and a criticism of the postulates and axioms of the American school', in *Expected Utility Hypothesis and the Allais' Paradox; Contemporary Discussions on Rational Decisions under Uncertainty with Allais' Rejoinder*, eds. M. Allais and E. E. Hagen (Reidel, 1979); 9. 'The so-called Allais' paradox and rational decisions under uncertainty', *ibid*; 10. 'Frequence, probabilité et Hazard', *J. de la Soc. de Statistique*, 2, 3, 1983; transl., English (abridged) as 'Frequency, probability and chance', in *Foundations of Utility and Risk Theory with Applications*, eds. J. Stigum and R. Wenstop (Reidel, 1983).

Principal Contributions Reformulation of general economic equilibrium maximum efficiency and economic calculus theories without any hypothesis of convexity. New concepts: distributable surplus and economic loss for the whole economy; first presentation and analysis of the utility possibility curve. Critical analysis of currently accepted theories. Capital and interest theory reformulation: new concepts; primary income; characteristic functions; maximum capitalistic efficiency. Invariant general model of production as a function of interest rate verified by empirical data. First demonstration of the 'golden rule of capital accumulation'. Risk theory: critical analysis of neo-Bernoullian theories of expected utility — 'Allais' Paradox'. Cardinal utility empirical determination; representation by an invariant function. Generalisation of expected utility theory by consideration of cardinal utility moments and probability of ruin. Generalisation of general economic equilibrium and maximum efficiency theories. Application to mining research. Monetary dynamics: hereditary and relativistic unitary formulation of demand for money and of interest rate, which leads to extraordinary empirical verifications over time and space. Monetary dynamic fundamental equation. Generating of limit cycles. Synthesis of capital and monetary dynamic theories. New concepts: psychological rate of interest, rate of forgetfulness, psychological time, invariant functions of desired cash balances and psychological rate of interest. Time series: Schuster test generalisation for autocorrelated time series. Test of a quasi-periodic structure. Critical analysis of probability and randomness concepts. Theorem (T); chance simulation by sum of periodic functions. Numerous contributions: to critical analysis of French economic policy, 1945–83; to pure and applied theory of international trade, especially of EEC; to basic industries: energy, transportation, and mining research; to fiscal and monetary policy.

ALLEN, Bruce Templeton

Born 1938, Oak Park, IL, USA.
Current Post Prof. Econ., Michigan

State Univ., East Lansing, MI, USA, 1977–.

Past Posts Ass. Prof., Assoc. Prof. Econ., Michigan State Univ., 1965–71, 1971–7.

Degrees BA De Pauw Univ., 1960; MBA Univ. Chicago, 1961; PhD Cornell Univ., 1965.

Principal Fields of Interest 612 Public Policy towards Monopoly and Competition; 512 Managerial Economics; 611 Market Structure: Industrial Orientation and Corporate Strategy.

Publications *Books:* 1. *The Market for Electrical Generating Equipment* (with A. Melnik), (Michigan State Univ., Inst. Public Utilities, 1973); 2. *Study Guide to Microeconomics*, ed. M. Beadley (Scott Fulesman, 1985).

Articles: 1. 'Market concentration and wage increases', *ILRR*, 21, April 1968; 2. 'Concentration and economic progress: note', *AER*, 59(4), Sept. 1969; 3. 'Vertical integration and market foreclosure: the case of cement and concrete', *J Law E*, 14(1), April 1971; 4. 'Industrial reciprocity: a statistical analysis', *J Law E*, 18(5), Oct. 1975; 5. 'Average concentration in manufacturing, 1947–1972', *JEI*, 10(3), Sept. 1976; 6. 'Tacit collusion and market sharing: the case of steam turbine generators', *Industrial Organization Rev.*, 4, 1976; 7. 'On not being "stuck in cement"', *Industrial Organization Rev.*, 6, 1978; 8. 'Cross-media ownership, regulatory scrutiny, and pricing behaviour' (with M. O. Wirth), *J. Econ. Bus.*, 33, Fall 1980; 9. 'Structure and stability in gasoline markets', *JEI*, 15(1), March 1981; 10. 'Concentration, scale economies, and the size distribution of plants', *QREB*, 23, Winter 1983.

Principal Contributions Some years ago, a department committee evaluating me for promotion characterised my work approximately as follows: 'Allen is the author of a small number of articles, primarily econometric tests of existing hypotheses in industrial organization.' This remains a description of my interests and the research that has followed them. My work has followed several of the last twenty years' themes in industrial organisation: relations between market structure and such performance characteristics as wage and productivity behaviour; determinants, changes, and description of market structures; mergers and acquisitions of all types, and their antitrust treatment; a variety of topics in market behaviour, including tacit collusion, market foreclosure, reciprocity, and nonprice competition, as well as their antitrust treatment; and industry-level research requiring and yielding an acquaintance with such industries as cement, petroleum products, turbine generators and nuclear power reactors.

When I left graduate school in 1965, I had the strong opinion that market structure was the prime determinant of the behaviour of an industry's firms, and that this in turn largely determined how a market performed. Accordingly, a focus on structure and its apparent consequences marked most of my early work. However, this interest has shifted over the years to a greater concern with the behaviour and interaction of sellers. Similar market structures can support a richer variety of behavioural forms than I had suspected. It is in this area that I find most of the analytical puzzles, particularly when seller conduct appears to be irreconcilable with any sort of profit maximisation. Since my major teaching consists of MBA-level managerial economics instead of industrial organisation, this research interest dovetails helpfully with my work in the classroom.

ALLEN, Roy G. D.*

Dates and Birthplace 1906–83, Stoke-on-Trent, Staffordshire, England.

Posts Held Prof. Stats., LSE, 1944–73; Cons., UK Royal Commission Civil Liability, 1947–8.

Degrees BA, MA Univ. Camb., 1927, 1932; DSc Univ. London, 1944; Hon. DSc(Social Science) Univ. Southampton, 1970.

Offices and Honours Fellow, BA, 1952; CBE, 1954; Knighted, 1966; Hon. Fellow, Sidney Sussex Coll. Camb., 1971; Member, Official UK Commission Retail Prices Index Advisory Comm., Civil Aviation Authority, Inquiry Decimal Currency, Impact Rates Comm., and others.

Publications *Books:* 1. *Mathematical Analysis for Economists* (Macmillan, 1938); 2. *Statistics for Economists* (Hutchinson, 1949); 3. *Macroeconomic Theory* (Macmillan, 1967); 4. *Index Numbers in Theory and Practice* (Macmillan, 1975); 5. *Introduction to National Accounts Statistics* (Macmillan, 1980).

Articles: 1. 'The nature of indifference curves', *REStud*, 1, Feb. 1934; 2. 'A reconsideration of the theory of value' (with J. R. Hicks), *Ec*, N.S. 1–2, Feb., May 1934; 3. 'The supply of engineering labour under boom conditions' (with B. Thomas), *EJ*, 49, June 1939; 4. 'Index numbers of retail prices 1938–51', *Applied Stats.*, 1, June 1952; 5. 'On official statistics and official statisticians', *JRSS*, 133, pt. 4, 1970.

Career Although he worked on a variety of practical problems, such as national accounting statistics, the design and calculation of retail price indexes, and the analysis of family budgets based on family expenditure surveys, he is best known for his pioneer work with Hicks on indifference curves. His *Mathematical Analysis for Economists* (1938) in particular was so many years ahead of its time that it can still be studied with profit today.

ALLINGHAM, Michael

Born 1943, London, England.
Current Post Prof. Econ. Theory, Univ. Kent, Canterbury, England, 1977–.
Past Posts Univ. Edinburgh, 1967–9; Univ. Essex, 1969–71; Northwestern Univ., 1971–2; Univ. Penn., 1972–3; Univ. Bristol, 1973–4; LSE, 1974–7.
Degrees MA, PhD Univ. Edinburgh, 1966, 1969.
Principal Fields of Interest 010 General Economics.
Publications *Books:* 1. *Equilibrium and Disequilibrium* (Ballinger, 1973); 2. *General Equilibrium* (Macmillan, 1975); 3. *Resource Allocation and Economic Policy*, co-ed. (Macmillan, 1976); 4. *Value* (Macmillan, 1983).
Articles: 1. '*Tatônnement* stability: an econometric approach', *Em*, 40(1),

Jan. 1972; 2. 'On progression and leisure', *AER*, 62(3), June 1972; 3. 'Qualitative economics and comparative status' (with M. Morishima), in *Theory of Demand: Real and Monetary*, ed. M. Morishima, *et al.* (OUP, 1973); 4. 'Equilibrium and stability', *Em*, 42(4), June 1974; 5. 'Second best and decentralization' (with G. C. Archibald), *JET*, 10(2), Apr. 1975; 6. 'Towards an ability tax', *J Pub E*, 4(4), Nov. 1975; 7. 'Future price oscillations', *Em*, 43(3), May 1976; 8. 'Stability of monopoly', *Em*, 44(3), May 1976; 9. 'Progressive taxation', *J Pub E*, 8(3), Jan. 1979.

Principal Contributions 'Pure economics is, in essence, the theory of the determination of prices under a hypothetical regime of free competition' (Léon Walras). My work has explored this theory.

ALONSO, William

Born 1933, Buenos Aires, Argentina.
Current Post R. Saltonstall Prof. Pop. Policy, Center Pop. Stud., Harvard Univ., 1976–.
Past Posts Instr. City Planning, Univ. Penn., 1959–60; Ass. Prof., Assoc. Prof. Regional Planning, Harvard Univ., 1959–67; Dir. and Prof. Regional and Urban Planning, Bandung Inst. Technology, Indonesia, UN Expert, 1960–1; Vis. Prof., Univ. Central de Venezuela, 1962; Acting Dir., Centre Urban Stud., Harvard Univ., 1963–5; Vis. Lect., Yale Univ., 1966; Prof. Regional Planning, Univ. Cal. Berkeley, 1966–7; Vis. Prof. Econ., Stanford Univ., 1975; Dir., Centre Pop Stud., Harvard Univ., 1976–8.
Degrees BA (Architectural Science), MCP Harvard Univ., 1954, 1956; PhD (Regional Science) Univ. Penn., 1960.
Offices and Honours National Scholar, 1950–6; Guggenheim Foundation Fellow, 1973–4; Pres., Regional Science Assoc., 1979–80; Fellow, AAAS, 1983–.
Principal Fields of Interest 840 Demographic Economics; 930 Urban Economics; 940 Regional Economics.
Publications *Books:* 1. *Location and Land Use* (Harvard Univ. Press, 1964);

2. *Regional Development and Planning*, co-ed. (with J. R. P. Friedmann), (MIT Press, 1964); 3. *Regional Policy*, co-ed. (With J. R. P. Friedmann), (MIT Press, 1975); 4. *Population Interactions among Rich and Poor Countries*, ed. (forthcoming, 1986); 5. *The Politics of Numbers: Essays on the Political Economy of National Statistics*, co-ed. (with P. Starr), (Basic Books, forthcoming, 1986).

Articles: 1. 'The historic and the structural theories of urban form: their implications for urban renewal', *Land Econ*, 40, May 1964; 2. 'A reformulation of classical location theory and its relation to the theory of rent', *Papers Regional Science Assoc*, 19, 1967; 3. 'Predicting best with imperfect data', *J Amer. Inst. Planners*, 34(4), July 1968; 4. 'Urban and regional imbalances in economic development', *EDCC*, 17, July 1969; 5. 'What are new towns for?', *Urban Stud.*, Feb. 1970; 6. 'The economics of urban size', *Papers Regional Science Assoc.*, 26, 1971; 7. 'Problems, purposes and implicit policies for a national strategy of urbanization', in US Commission on Population Growth and the American Future, V, *Population Distribution and Policy*, ed. S. M. Mazie (US Govt. Printing Office, 1972); 8. 'Urban zero population growth', *Daedalus*, Fall 1973; 9. 'A theory of movements', in *Human Settlement Systems*, ed. N. Hansen (Ballinger, 1979); 10. 'Five bell shapes in development', *Regional Science Papers*, 45, 1980.

Principal Contributions An interest in the spatial order of societies has characterised much of my work. My *Location and Land Use*, a rewarmed doctoral dissertation, used microeconomics to build a model of land markets and urban form and was written in what then passed for mathematical economics. The book was well received, stayed in print for twenty years and became a standard footnote in some areas of urban economics. But just how different economics was a generation ago is illustrated by a delay of several years in the book's publication: Harvard University Press understandably hesitated to publish because it received quite negative comments from many referees, eminent land economists who as institutionalists were offended by what seemed to them a bloodless and mechanical approach.

Since then the bulk of my work, both as an academic and a policy adviser, has been on urban and regional development and policy, both in poor and in rich countries. Such issues are in part economic, to be sure, but to deal with them one must consider institutions, politics, historical and social factors, and I have tried to do this without worrying about disciplinary boundaries. Imperfect knowledge is intrinsic to these messy issues, and this has made me curious about conceptualisation, categorisation and measurement in their social context. This aspect of my work is illustrated by an early article (see No. 3 above) and by a forthcoming book (*The Politics of Numbers*).

While these concerns have led me away from the stern standards of microeconomic fundamentalism, I retain a love for the crystalline beauty of formal models. Indeed, in spite of my limited mathematics (recently characterised as 'Mickey Mouse' by a student), I am working with pleased excitement on a generalising statement about the form underlying 'from–to' accounting, or transition models, as used in several disciplines. I have only published one paper (see No. 9 above) on this, but I have learned a great deal since then and in the coming years hope to provide an intellectual scheme that unifies gravity models, input-output tables, log-linear contingency tables and other such. The value of this work, if any, is not to recommend any particular model in this vast family, but to clarify the commonalities and differences of their structure. This may help in certain cases in the choice, design, calibration and use of models of this type.

AMEMIYA, Takeshi

Born 1935, Tokyo, Japan.
Current Post Prof. Econ., Stanford Univ., Stanford, CA, USA, 1974–.
Past Posts Ass. Prof., Stanford Univ., 1964–6; Lect., Hitotsubashi Univ.,

Tokyo, 1966–8; Assoc. Prof., Stanford Univ., 1968–74; Sr. Fellow, NBER Computer Res. Center, Cambridge, MA, 1975; Vis. Scholar, LSE, 1976; Vis. Prof., Kyoto Univ., 1981.

Degrees BA Internat. Christian Univ., Tokyo, 1958; MA Amer. Univ., 1961; PhD Johns Hopkins Univ., 1964.

Offices and Honours Ford Foundation Doctoral Dissertation Fellow, Johns Hopkins Univ., 1963–4; Guggenheim Foundation Fellow, 1975–6; Japan Soc. Promotion of Science Fellow, 1981; Fellow, Council, Em Soc; Fellow, ASA.

Editorial Duties Assoc. Ed., *Em*, 1970–5, *JASA*, 1970–3; Co-ed., *Em*, 1981–2, *J Em*, 1982–.

Principal Fields of Interest 211 Econometric and Statistical Methods and Models.

Publication Books: 1. *Studies in Econometrics, Time Series, and Multivariate Statistics*, co-ed. (with S. Karlin and L. A. Goodman), (Academic Press, 1983); 2. *Censored or Truncated Regression Models* (N-H., 1984); 3. *Advanced Econometrics* (Harvard Univ. Press, 1985).

Articles: 1. 'A comparative study of alternative estimators in a distributed-lag model' (with W. A. Fuller), *Em*, 35, July–Oct. 1967; 2. 'Generalized least squares with an estimated autocovariance matrix', *Em*, 41, July 1973; 3. 'Regression analysis when the dependent variable is truncated normal', *Em*, 41, Nov. 1973; 4. 'Multivariate regression and simultaneous equation models when the dependent variables are truncated normal', *Em*, 42, Nov. 1974; 5. 'The nonlinear two stage least squares estimator', *J Em*, 2, July 1974; 6. 'The maximum likelihood, the minimum chi-square, and the nonlinear weighted least squares estimator in the general qualitative response model', *JASA*, 71, June 1976; 7. 'The maximum likelihood and the nonlinear three-stage least squares estimator in the general nonlinear simultaneous equation model', *Em*, 45, May 1977; 8. 'The n^2–order mean squared errors of the maximum likelihood and the minimum logit chi-squared estimator', *Annals Stats.*, 8, May 1980; 9. 'Qualitative response models: a survey', *JEL*, 19(4), Dec. 1981; 10. 'The two-stage least absolute deviations estimators', *Em*, 50, May 1982.

Principal Contributions All my work is concerned with theory of estimation and prediction in econometric models, especially large sample theory. Early work was mainly concerned with time series and simultaneous equations models. Research in the last ten years has concentrated on the analysis of various nonlinear econometric models, such as qualitative response models, censored or truncated regression models, and nonlinear simultaneous equations models. The first two types of models are the ones most frequently used by econometricians in recent years. Among my more important contributions in recent years are a simple consistent estimator in censored or truncated regression models, the nonlinear two state least squares estimator, and the two stage least absolute deviations estimator.

AMOROSO, Luigi*

Dates and Birthplace 1886–1965, Naples, Italy.

Posts Held Prof. Polit. Econ., Univ. Rome; Former Exec., Banco di Napoli and Instituto Nazionale Assicurazioni; Dir., Banco Nazionale del Lavoro.

Degrees Dr (Maths.), Univ. Rome.

Offices and Honours Fellow, Em Soc; Cavaliere Italian Republic.

Publications Books: 1. *Lezioni di Economia Matematica* (1921); 2. *Principii di Economica Corporativa* (1938); 3. *Meccanica Economica* (1942); 4. *Economica di Mercato* (1949).

Articles: 1. 'The static supply curve', *Giornale degli Economisti*, 1930, repr. in *Internat. Econ. Papers*, 4, eds. A. T. Peacock, *et al.* (Macmillan, 1954); 2. 'Vilfredo Pareto', *Em*, 6, Jan. 1938.

Career A follower of Pareto, who was inspired by the desire to simplify the structure of economic theory. His proof in a 1928 *Annali di Economia* article of the 'existence' of Walrasian general equilibrium when utility functions are interdependent and not just 'additive' is one of his major achievements. During the Fascist period he was able, unlike some colleagues, to continue working in Italy. His *Principii*, written during this period, has discussions of money and equilibrium quite free from political implications and, in the third part, an economic theory of Fascism stated in analytical terms, which remains within the mainstream of economic science.

ANDERSON, James*

Dates and Birthplace 1739–1808, Hermiston, Scotland.
Degree LLD Univ. Aberdeen, 1780.
Publications *Books:* 1. *Observations on the Means of Exciting a Spirit of National Industry* (1777); 2. *An Enquiry into the Nature of the Corn Laws* (1777); 3. *Recreations in Agriculture, Natural History, Arts and Miscellaneous Literature*, 6 vols (1799–1802).
Career Gentleman farmer and prolific writer on agriculture and corn law questions, chiefly in his periodical *The Bee*, and his series of *Recreations*. His discovery of the 'Ricardian' theory of rent arose from his agricultural studies. It is first stated in the *Observations*, where he concluded that the rent of land is a premium paid for the privilege of cultivating soils that are more fertile than others and that its payment equalises the profits of farmers tilling land of different qualities. The same idea is formulated more precisely in the *Enquiry*.
Secondary Literature E. Cannan, *A History of the Theories of Production and Distribution in English Political Economy* (Staples Press, 1898).

ANDO, Albert K.

Born 1929, Tokyo, Japan.
Current Post Prof. Econ. Fin., Univ. Penn., USA, 1976–.
Past Post Assoc. Prof. Econ., MIT.
Degrees BS Seattle Univ., 1951; MA St Louis Univ., 1953; MS, PhD (Math. Econ.) Carnegie Inst. Technology (now Carnegie-Mellon Univ.), 1956, 1959.
Offices and Honours Ford Foundation Faculty Res. Fellow, 1966–7; Fellow, Em Soc.; Chairman, Sub-

comm. Monetary Res., US SSRC, 1967–; Guggenheim Foundation Fellow, 1970–1.
Editorial Duties Assoc. Ed, *JASA*, 1966–9, *J Em*, 1972–6; Ed. Board, *AEA*, 1973–4.
Principal Fields of Interest 023 Macroeconomic Theory.
Publications *Books:*1. *Essays on Social Science Models* (with H. A. Simon and F. M. Fisher), (MIT Press, 1963); 2. *Studies in Stabilization Policies* (with E. C. Brown, *et al.*), (Brookings Inst. 1968); 3. *International Aspects of Stabilization Policies*, ed. (Fed. Reserve Bank Boston, 1975).
Articles: 1. 'The relative stability of monetary velocity and the investment multiplier' (with F. Modigliani), *AER*, 55(4), Sept. 1965; 2. 'Some aspects of stabilization policies, the monetarist controversy, and the MPS model', *Int ER*, 15(3), Oct. 1974; 3. 'Some reflections on describing structure of financial sectors', in *The Brookings Model: Perspective and Recent Developments*, eds. L. R. Klein and G. Fromm (N-H, 1975); 4. 'Some stabilization problems of 1971–5, with an application of optimal control algorithms', in *Frontiers of Quantitative Economics*, ed. M. Intriligator (N-H, 1977); 5. 'On a theoretical and empirical basis of macroeconometric models', in *Proceedings of the Conference on Methodology of Large-scale Econometric Models*, ed. J. Kmenta (N–H, 1981).
Principal Contributions Theoretical and empirical investigation of consumer behaviour. Theory of aggregation and partitions in dynamic systems. Macroeconomic models, with emphasis on interactions between growth and cyclical fluctuations. Monetary and financial aspects of the US economy.

ANDREWS, Philip Walter Sawford*

Dates and Birthplace 1914–71, Southampton, England.
Posts Held Ass. Lect. Econ., Univ. Coll., Southampton, 1935–6; Worker Educ. Assoc. (Southern District), 1936–7; Res. Staff, Social Stud. Res. Group, Oxford, 1937–41; Lect. Econ.,

New Coll., Oxford, 1941–8; Chief Stats., Social Reconstruction Survey, Fellow, Nuffield Coll. Oxford, 1941–6, 1946–67; Special Univ. Lect. Econ., Univ. Oxford, 1951–67; Prof. Econ., Univ. Lancaster, 1967–71.

Degrees BSc Univ. London External, 1934; MA Univ. Oxford, 1944.

Offices and honours Open Foundation Scholar, Univ. Coll., Southampton, 1931–4; British Assoc. Exhibitioner, 1934; First Bley Stein Memorial Lect., UCLA, 1963.

Editorial Duties General Ed., *J Ind E*, 1952–71; Ed. Board, *OEP*, 1948–52.

Publications *Books:* 1. *Manufacturing Business* (Macmillan, 1949); 2. *Oxford Studies in the Price Mechanism*, co-ed. (with T. Wilson), (OUP, 1951); 3. *Capital Development in Steel: A study of the United Steel Companies Ltd* (with E. Brunner), (Blackwell, 1941); 4. *The Life of Lord Nuffield* (with E. Brunner), (Blackwell, 1951); 5. *Fair Trade* (with F. A. Friday), (Macmillan, 1960); 6. *On Competition in Economic Theory* (Macmillan, 1964); 7. *The Eagle Ironworks, Oxford* (with E. Brunner), (Mills & Boon, 1965); 8. *Industrial Uses of Economic Theory* (UCLA, 1963); 9. *Studies in Pricing* (with E. Brunner), (Macmillan, 1975). **Articles:** 1. 'Post war public companies', *EJ*, 47, Sept. 1937; 2. 'Summary of replies to questions on the effects of the rate of interest' (with J. E. Meade), *OEP*, 1, Oct. 1938; 3. 'A reconsideration of the theory of the individual business', *OEP*, N.S. 1(1), Jan. 1949; 4. 'Some aspects of competition in the real trade', *OEP* N.S. 2(2), June 1950; 5. 'Productivity and the businessman' (with E. Brunner), *OEP*, N.S. 2(2), Nov. 1950; 6. 'Industrial economics as a specialist subject', *J Ind E*, 1(1), Nov. 1952; 7. 'Limités economiques à la dimension et à la croissance des enterprises individuelles', *RE*, Jan. 1956; 8. 'Business profits and the quiet life' (with E. Brunner), *J Ind E*, 11, Nov. 1962; 9. 'The recent controversy over resale price maintenance' (with F. A. Friday), *JRSS*, 125, pt. 4, 1962; 10. 'Economic theory and management studies', in *Bedrijseconomische Vertennigen* (Elsevier, 1965).

Career Andrews presented in *Manufacturing Business* a 'normal cost' price theory (to be contrasted with 'full cost') which emphasised the importance of the industrial environment within which firms operate. In later work, collaborating with Elisabeth Brunner, he extended his analysis to incorporate theories of investment, retail trade and collusion, emphasising the importance of competitive forces within our oligopolistic world. Acceptance of his work was hindered by the fundamental nature of his challenge to the traditional equilibrium framework of microeconomics and by the way in which he used industrial investigations in his published work. Though valuable applied studies, they led many to assume mistakenly that his objectives were descriptive, rather than the creation of a new positive theory of industrial economics.

ANGELL, James Waterhouse

Born 1898, Chicago, IL, USA.

Current Post Retired, 1966–.

Past Posts Lect., Prof., Columbia Univ., 1924–66.

Degrees BA, MA, PhD Harvard Univ., 1918, 1921, 1924.

Offices and Honours Vice-Pres., AEA, 1940; US Minister, Allied Commission Reparations, Germany, 1945–6.

Principal Fields of Interest 311 Monetary Theory and Policy.

Publications *Books:* 1. *The Theory of International Prices — History, Criticism and Restatement* (Harvard Univ. Press, 1926); 2. *The Recovery of Germany* (Prentice-Hall, 1929); 3. *Financial Policy of the United States* (Prentice-Hall, 1933); 4. *The Behaviour of Money* (Prentice-Hall, 1936); 5. *Investment and Business Cycles* (Prentice-Hall, 1941).

Career (editor's entry) Monetary economist who also wrote on international prices and business cycles. The *Theory of International Prices* was a history of ideas relating to exchange rates, which was eclipsed by Jacob Viner's later researches. *The Behavior of Money* summarises much of Angell's empirical work on money, which again suffered neglect as a result of being published in the same year as Keynes's *General Theory*.

Secondary Literature J-K. Lee and D. C. Wellington, 'Angell and the stable money rule', *JPE*, 92(5), Oct. 1984.

ANTONELLI, Etienne*

Dates and Birthplace 1879–1971, Valencia, Spain.

Posts Held Prof., Conservatoire National des Arts et Métiers, Paris, 1932; Prof. Law, Univ. Montpellier, 1934–52.

Degree Dr Law, Univ. Paris.

Offices and Honours Deputy, Haute-Savoie, 1924–32; Member, Conseil de la Fondation des Sciences Politiques, Paris; Commander, Légion d'Honneur; Croix de guerre (1914–18); Chevalier des Palmes Académiques.

Publications *Books:* 1. *Principes d'économie pure* (1914); 2. *Traité d'économie politique* (1927); 3. *L'économie pure du capitalisme* (1939); 4. *Manuel d'économie politique*, 2 vols (1945–6); 5. *Etudes d'économie humaniste, 2 vols (1957–8); 6. Structures des économies présentes (1962).*

Career A follower, life-long friend and literary executor of Walras, he gave a course of lectures with a Walrasian structure at the Collège Libre des Sciences Sociales as early as 1912. This later appeared as *Principes . . .* in 1914. His earliest work had been on the state protection of viticulture and later work ranged widely, including specific studies of the social security system.

AOKI, Masanao

Born 1931, Hiroshima, Japan.

Current Post Prof. System Science, UCLA, USA, 1976–; Econ., Inst. Social Econ. Res., Osaka Univ., Osaka, Japan, 1981–.

Past Posts Ass. Prof., UCLA, 1960–4, 1965–8; Vis. Assoc. Prof., Univ. Cal. Berkeley, 1964–5; Vis. Prof., Univ. Camb., 1971–2; Prof., Univ. Illinois, 1974–5; Vis. Prof., Stanford Univ., 1975, 1976, Woodrow Wilson School, Princeton Univ., 1980.

Degrees BS, MS (Physics) Univ. Tokyo, 1953, 1955; PhD (Eng.) UCLA, 1960; DSc (Control Theory) Tokyo Inst. Technology, 1966.

Offices and Honours Fulbright Fellow, 1956–8; Vis. Fellow, Clare Hall Camb., 1971–2; US SSRC Training Fellow, 1975–6; Fellow, Inst. Electrical Eng. Control System Soc., 1976, Em Soc., 1978; Pres., Soc. Econ. Dynamics and Control, 1981–2.

Editorial Duties Assoc. Ed., *IEEE Trans. Auto. Control*, 1970–1, 1975–6, *Info. Science*, 1969–83, *J Ec Dyn.*, 1978–83; Ed., *J Ec Dyn*, 1983, *Int. ER*, 1984; Ed.-at-large, *Applied Maths.* (Marcel Dekker, 1969–81); Ed. Board, *Internat. Series Econ. Modeling* (Kluwer-Nijhoff, 1983–).

Principal Fields of Interest 130 Economic Fluctuations; Forecasting; Stabilisation; and Inflation; 210 Quantitative Economic Methods; 430 Balance of Payments; International Finance.

Publications *Books:*1. *Optimization of Stochastic Systems: In Discrete-Time Systems* (Academic Press, 1967, transl., Russian, 1971); 2. *Introduction to Optimization Techniques* (Macmillan 1971; transl., Russian, 1977); 3. *Optimal Control and Dynamic Analysis of Economic Systems* (N-H, 1976); 4. *Dynamic Analysis of Open Economics* (Academic Press, 1981); 5. *Macroeconomic Time Series: System Theoretic Perspectives* (Springer-Verlag, 1983); 6. *Time Series Analysis and Japanese Economy* (in Japanese) (Oriental Economist, 1984).

Articles: 1. 'Successive approximations in solving some control system optimization problems', *J Math. Analysis and Applications*, 5(3), Dec. 1962; 2. 'On performance losses in some adaptive control systems: 1', *Basic Eng. Trans. ASME*, 87(1), Jan. 1965; 3. 'Control of large scale dynamic systems by aggregation', *Inst. Electrical Eng. Trans. Auto Control*, 13(3), June 1968; 4. 'On decentralized linear stochastic control problems with quadratic cost', *Inst. Electrical Eng. Trans. Auto Control*, 18(3), June 1973; 5. 'Noninteracting control of macroeconomic variables', *J Em*, 2, 1974; 6. 'Local controllability of a decentralized economic system', *REStud*, 41, Jan. 1974;

7. 'Output decisions by a firm: an example of dual control problem with information externality', in *Adaptive Economics*, eds. T. Groves and R. Day (Academic Press, 1975); 8. 'Interaction among economic agents under imperfect information: an example', in *New Trends in Dynamic Systems Theory and Economics*, eds. M. Aoki and A. Marzollo (Academic Press, 1979); 9. 'Perturbation and robustness analysis of a closed macroeconomic model', *J Ec Dyn*, 1, Feb. 1979; 10. 'A dynamic model of trade adjustment and the Marshall–Lerner condition', *WA*, 119(2), 1983.

Principal Contributions Early work concentrated on adapting the statistical decision-theoretic approach to deal with control problems of discrete-time dynamic systems with imprecisely known characteristics, or operating in imprecisely known environments. My monograph, *Optimization of Stochastic Systems*, provides a framework for treating these systems as parameter of large-scale dynamic systems or systems composed of several interdependent subsystems with central or independent decision agents, so-called decentralised dynamic systems. From these systems, my interests eventually settled on dynamic problems associated with open economy macroeconomics and problems of policy effectiveness studies in systems of interdependent economies. I have attempted to conduct comparative dynamic analysis in open economy macroeconomics and to introduce to the economic profession some techniques and concepts from system theory that I found useful. My 1976 book provides a set of tools and concepts to conduct comparative dynamic analysis of economic models. My 1981 book mostly analyses adjustment processes in two and three country models of the world under floating exchange rate regimes. My 1983 lecture notes set out a procedure that has been developed in system theory for systematic construction of state space or Markovian models from vector-valued time series data.

ARCHIBALD, George Christopher

Born 1926, Glasgow, Scotland.
Current Post Prof. Econ., Univ. British Columbia, Canada.
Past Posts Lect., LSE, 1950–64; Reader Econ., Prof. Econ., Univ. Essex, England, 1964–7, 1967–71.
Degrees BSc, MA Univ. Camb., 1950, 1951.
Offices and Honours Fellow, Em Soc., 1976, Royal Soc. Canada, 1979.
Principal Fields of Interest 010 General Economics.
Publications *Books:* 1. *An Introduction to a Mathematical Treatment of Economics* (with R. G. Lipsey), (Weidenfeld & Nicolson, 1967, 1977, Harper & Row; transl., Portuguese, Biblioteca de Ciencias Sociais, 1970); 2. *The Theory of the Firm*, ed. (Penguin, 1971, 1974).
Articles: 1. 'Monetary and value theory: a critique of Lange and Patinkin' (with R. G. Lipsey), *REStud*, 26, Oct. 1958, repr. in *Monetary Theory*, ed. R. S. Thorn (Random House, 1963), and *Readings in Monetary Theory*, ed. R. W. Clower (Penguin Books, 1976); 2. 'Chamberlain versus Chicago', *REStud*, 29, Oct. 1961, repr. in *The Theory of the Firm*, ed. G. C. Archibald (Penguin, 1971), and *Readings in Industrial Organization*, ed. C. K. Rowley (Macmillan, 1976); 3. 'The qualitative content of maximizing models', *JPE*, 73, Feb. 1965, repr. in *Readings in Industrial Organization, op. cit.*, and *The Theory of Demand: Real and Monetary*, ed. M. Morishima (OUP, 1973); 4. 'Excess demand for labour, unemployment and the Phillips curve: a theoretical and empirical study' (with R. Kemmiss and J. W. Perkins), in *Inflation and Labour Markets*, ed. D. Laidler and D. Purdy (Manchester Univ. Press, 1974); 5. 'Non-paternalism and the basic theorems of welfare economics' (with D. Donaldson), *CJE*, 9(3), Aug. 1976.

ARMSTRONG, Wallace Edwin*

Dates and Birthplace 1896–1980, England.
Posts Held Ass. Anthropologist,

Papuan Govt., 1921–2; Lect., Social Anthrop., Lect. Econ., Univ. Camb., 1921–2, 1926–39; Lect., Sr. Lect., Reader, Prof. Econ., Univ. of Southampton, 1939–49, 1949–53, 1958–61.
Degrees BA Univ. Camb., 1918.
Offices and Honours Anthony Wilkin Studentship for Ethnological Res. New Guinea, 1919–22.
Publications *Books:* 1. *Rossel Island* (1928); 2. *Saving and Investment* (1936).
Articles: 1. 'The determinateness of the utility function', *EJ*, 49, Sept. 1939; 2. 'Uncertainty and the utility function', *EJ*, 58, March 1948; 3. 'Utility and the theory of welfare', *OEP*, N.S. 3, Oct. 1951.
Career Developed an hetorodox theory of consumer behaviour, which sought to reinstate cardinal measurement of utility and interpersonal comparisons of utility.
Secondary Literature See T. Majumdar, *The Measurement of Utility* (Macmillan, 1958) Ch. 9.

ARNDT, Heinz Wolfgang

Born 1915, Breslau, Germany.
Current Post Emeritus Prof., Vis. Fellow, Devlp. Stud. Centre, ANU, Canberra, Australia, 1980–.
Past Posts Res. Ass., Royal Inst. Internat. Affairs, London, 1941–3; Ass. Lect., Manchester Univ. 1943–6; Sr. Lect., Sydney Univ., 1946–50; Prof. Econ., ANU, 1950–80; Vis. Prof., Univ. S. Carolina, 1953–4; Indian Stat. Inst., Calcutta, 1958–9; UNEC, Geneva, 1960–1; Dep. Dir., Country Stud. Div., OECD, 1972; Cons., UNCTAD, 1966, Asian Devlp. Bank, 1982, UNIDO, 1983, 1984.
Degrees BA, MA, B.Litt. Oxford Univ, 1936, 1938, 1940.
Offices and Honours Hon. Secretary, Australia SSRC, 1958–9; Pres., Australian and New Zealand Econ. Soc., 1957–9; Member, Governing Council, UN Asian Devlp. Inst., Bangkok, 1969–75; Country Vice Pres., Soc. Internat. Devlp., 1968–78; Fellow, Australian Academy Social Sciences.
Editorial Duties Ed. Board, *ER*,

1955–75; *Internat. Devlp. Rev.*, 1970–8; Ed., *Bull. Indonesian Econ. Stud.*, 1965–82.
Principal Fields of Interest 310 Domestic Monetary Theory and Institutions; 112 Economic Development Theory; 121 Economic Studies of LDCs.
Publications *Books:* 1. *The Economic Lessons of the Nineteen-Thirties* (OUP, 1944, 1963; trans., Italian 1949, Japanese 1978); 2. *The Australian Trading Banks* (Cheshire 1957, with C. P. Harris, Melbourne Univ. Press, 1965, with D. W. Stammer, 1973, with W. J. Blackert, 1977); 3. *The Australian Economy: A Volume of Readings* (with W. M. Corden), (Cheshire 1963, 1972); 4. *Taxation in Australia: Agenda for Reform* (with R. I. Downing, and others), (Melbourne Univ. Press, 1964); 5. *A Small Rich Industrial Country: Studies in Australian Development, Trade and Aid* (Cheshire, 1968); 6. *The Australian Economy: A Second Volume of Readings* (with A. H. Boxer), (Cheshire, 1972); 7. *Australia and Asia: Economic Essays* (ANU Press, 1972); 8. *The Rise and Fall of Economic Growth: A Study in Contemporary Thought* (Longman Cheshire 1978, Univ. Chicago Press, 1984); 9. *The Indonesian Economy: Collected Papers* (Chopmen Publications, 1983).
Articles: 1. 'The concept of liquidity in international monetary theory', *REStud*, 15(1), 1947; 2. 'A suggestion for simplifying the theory of international capital movements', *Econ. Int.*, 7, Aug. 1954; 3. 'External economies in economic growth', *ER*, 31, Nov. 1955; 4. 'Banking in hyperinflation', *Bull. Indonesian Econ. Stud.*, 1966; 5. 'The modus operandi of protection', *ER*, 55, June 1979; 6. 'Economic development: a semantic history', *EDCC*, 29(3), April 1981; 7. 'The "trickle down" myth', *EDCC*, 31(5), Oct. 1983; 8. 'Political economy', *ER*, 60, Nov. 1984.
Principal Contributions After writing *The Economic Lessons of the Nineteen-Thirties* during World War II, guided by Paul Rosenstein-Rodan, I taught macroeconomics and wrote about some issues in international

monetary theory and policy. In Australia, I concentrated for some years on studies of the Australian banking system and capital market. Increasing interest in economic development problems, reinforced by a spell in India, led to almost twenty years of specialisation on development issues in SE Asia, especially Indonesia. But some work, both theoretical and applied, went on side by side on domestic and international macroeconomics. In recent years, a major interest has been the history of thought about the ends of economic policy, changing emphasis on economic growth in DCs, and changing meanings of 'development' for and in LDCs.

ARROW, Kenneth Joseph

Born 1921, New York City, NY, USA.
Current Post Joan Kenney Prof. Econ., Prof. OR., Stanford Univ., Stanford, USA, 1979–.
Past Posts Prof. Econ., Stats, and OR, Stanford Univ., 1953–68; Prof. Econ., Harvard Univ., 1968–74; James Bryant Conant Univ. Prof., Harvard Univ., 1974–9.
Degrees BSc (Social Science) City Coll. NY, 1940; MA, PhD Columbia Univ., 1941, 1951; LLD Univ. Chicago, 1967, City Univ., NY, 1972, Hebrew Univ., Jerusalem, 1975; Hon. degrees, Univs., Harvard, 1968, Vienna, 1974, Columbia, 1973, Yale, 1974, René Descartes, 1975, Helsinki, 1976.
Offices and Honours Member, NAS, Amer. Philo. Soc.; Fellow, AAAS; Foreign Hon. Member, Finnish Academy Sciences; Corresponding Member, BA; Pres., Em Soc, 1956; John Bates Clark Medal, AEA, 1957; Pres., Inst. Management Sciences, 1963; Nobel Prize in Econ., 1972; Pres., AEA, 1973; Pres., WEA, 1980–1; Pres., IEA, 1983–6; Pres., Internat. Soc. Inventory Res., 1983–; Order of the Rising Sun (2nd Class), Japan.
Principal Fields of Interest 025 Social Choice; 021 General Equilibrium Theory; 513 Business and Public Administration.
Publications *Books:* 1. *Social Choice and Individual Values* (Wiley, 1951, Yale Univ. Press, 1963); 2. *Studies in the Mathematical Theory of Inventory and Production* (with S. Karlin and H. Scarf), (Stanford Univ. Press, 1958); 3. *Public Investment, the Rate of Return, and Optimal Fiscal Policy* (with M. Kurz), (JHUP, 1970); 4. *Essays in the Theory of Risk-bearing* (N–H, 1971); 5. *The Limits of Organisation* (Norton, 1971); 6. *General Competitive Analysis* (with M. F. Hahn), (N–H, 1971); 7. *Studies in Resource Allocation Processes* (with L. Hurwicz), (CUP, 1977); 8. *Collected Papers*, 6 vols. (Harvard Univ. Press, Blackwell, 1983–5).
Principal Contributions Study of collective choice based on individual preferences and logical difficulties in aggregation. Properties of general equilibrium systems in economics: existence, stability and optimality. General equilibrium economics of uncertainty, including concept of contingent markets, measures of risk-aversion and their implications for demand for risky commodities, effect of differential information on economic behaviour, with its implications for medical economics and for social institutions more generally. Estimation of production functions, especially CES (constant elasticity of substitution) functions, and measurement of real value added. Optimal social investment policy; and optimal inventory policy.
Secondary Literature C. C. von Weizsäcker, 'Kenneth Arrow's contributions to economics', *Scand JE*, 74(4), Dec. 1972, repr. in *Contemporary Economists in Perspective*, 1, eds. H. W. Spiegel and W. J. Samuels (JAI Press, 1984).

ARTHUR, W. Brian

Born 1945, Belfast, N. Ireland.
Current Post Dean and Virginia Morrison Prof. Pop. Stud., Prof. Econ., Stanford Univ., Food Res. Inst., Stanford, CA, USA, 1983–.
Past Posts Ass. Prof. Econ., Univ. Cal. Berkeley, 1973–4; Assoc., Pop. Council, NY, 1974–7; Vis. Scholar,

Office Pop. Res., Princeton Univ., 1976–7; Res. Scholar, System and Decision Sciences, Internat. Inst. Applied Systems Analysis, Laxenberg, Austria, 1977–82; Vis. Prof., Food Res. Inst., Stanford Univ., 1982–3.

Degrees BSc (Electrical Eng.) Queen's Univ. Belfast, N. Ireland, 1966; MA (OR) Univ. Lancaster, England, 1967; MA (Maths.) Univ. Michigan, 1969; MA, PhD (OR) Univ. Cal. Berkeley, 1973, 1973.

Offices and Honours Univ. Belfast Foundation Prize, 1966; Univ. Cal. Fellow, 1969–70.

Editorial Duties Assoc. Ed., *Theoretical Pop. Biology*.

Principal Fields of Interest 840 Demographic Economics; 020 General Economic Theory; 110 Economic Growth; Development; and Planning Theory and Policy.

Publications *Books:* 1. *Mathematical Modelling at IIASA*, co-ed. (with R. Levien and A. Wierzbicki), (Internat. Inst. Applied Systems Analysis, 1982).

Articles: 1. 'Large-scale simulation models in population and development: what use to planners?' (with G. McNicoll), *Pop. and Devlp. Rev.*, 1, Dec. 1975; 2. 'Optimal time paths with age-dependence: a theory of population policy' (with G. McNicoll), *REStud*, 44(1), Feb. 1977; 3. 'Samuelson, population and intergenerational transfers' (with G. McNicoll), *Int ER*, 19, Feb. 1978; 4. 'Stochastic control of linear, discrete-time, distributed lag models', *Internat. J. Control*, 28, Oct. 1978; 5. 'An analytical survey of population and development in Bangladesh' (with G. McNicoll), *Pop. and Devlp. Rev.*, 4, March 1978; 6. 'Age and earnings in the labor market: implications of the 1980s labor bulge', in *Human Resources, Employment and Development*, eds. P. Streeten and H. Maier (Macmillan, 1983); 7. 'The economics of risks to life', *AER*, 71(1), March 1981; 8. 'Why a population converges to stability', *Amer. Math. Monthly*, 88, Oct. 1981; 9. 'The analysis of linkages in demographic theory', *Demography*, 21, Feb. 1984; 10. 'A generalized urn problem and its applications' (in Russian), (with Y. Ermoliev and Y. Kaniovski),

Kibernetika, 19, Feb. 1983; transl., English, *Cybernetics*, 19, Sept. 1983.

Principal Contributions Early work in optimal control of dynamic systems with an age dimension led to a lasting interest in population and its interactions with the economy. Introduced functional calculus to demography, thereby settling several major open problems in population analysis; provided simple but rigorous proofs of the two central theorems of population dynamics. Clarified effect of population growth in overlapping generations models and the effect of population age-structural changes on the economy. First rigorous analysis of the value of altering mortality risks. Detailed study of Bangladesh's economic development and population interactions (with G. NcNicoll). Recent research on the theory of economic allocation under increasing returns (decreasing supply costs) introduces probability theory to resolve the indeterminacy issues. Resulting theorems (with Soviet co-authors) generalise deterministic, fixed-point dynamical stability results to stochastic case.

ARTIS, Michael John

Born 1938, Croydon, Surrey, England.

Current Post Prof. Econ., Manchester Univ., UK, 1976–.

Past Posts Ass. Res. Officer, Oxford Univ. Inst. Econ. and Stats., 1959–63; Lect., Sr. Lect., Adelaide and Flinders Univs., S. Australia, 1964–7; Sr. Res. Officer, Review Ed., NIESR, London, UK, 1967–72; Prof. Appl. Econ., Swansea Univ. Coll., 1972–5.

Degrees BA Univ. Oxford, 1959.

Offices and Honours Res. Fellow, Centre Econ. Policy Res., London, UK, 1984–.

Editorial Duties Ass. Ed., Ed., *Nat. Inst. Econ. Rev.*, 1967–72; Managing Ed., *MS*, 1975–.

Principal Fields of Interest 130 Economic Fluctuations; Forecasting; Stabilisation and Inflation; 311 Domestic Monetary and Financial Theory and Policy; 431 Balance of Payments;

Mechanisms of Adjustment; Exchange Rates.

Publications *Books:* 1. *Foundations of British Monetary Policy* (Blackwell, 1964); 2. *Essays in Economic Analysis*, co-ed. (with A. R. Nobay), (CUP, 1975); 3. *Studies in Modern Economic Analysis*, co-ed (with A. R. Nobay), (Blackwell, 1977); 4. *Contemporary Economic Analysis*, co-ed. (with A. R. Nobay), (Croom Helm, 1978); 5. *Essays in Fiscal and Monetary Policy*, co-ed. (with A. R. Nobay), (OUP, 1981); 6. *Monetary Control in the United Kingdom* (with M. K. Lewis), (Philip Allan, 1981); 7. *Demand Management, Supply Constraints and Inflation*, co-ed. (with A. R. Nobay), (Manchester Univ. Press, 1982).

Articles: 1. 'Liquidity and the attack on the quantity theory', *BOIS*, 23(4), Nov. 1961; 2. 'Two aspects of the monetary debate' (with A. R. Nobay), *Nat. Inst. Econ. Rev.*, 49, Aug. 1969; 3. 'Fiscal policy in post-war Australia' (with R. H. Wallace), in *Readings in Australian Fiscal and Monetary Policy*, ed. N. Runcie (London Univ. Press, 1971); 4. 'Fiscal policy for stabilization', in *The Economic Record on the Labour Government*, ed. W. Beckerman (Duckworth, 1972); 5. 'The demand for money in the UK' (with M. K. Lewis), *MS*, 44(2), June 1976; 6. 'Inflation, real wages and the terms of trade' (with M. H. Miller), in *Inflation, Development and Integration*, ed. J. K. Bowers (Leeds Univ. Press, 1979); 7. 'Income policies: some rationales', in *Incomes Policies, Inflation and Relative Pay*, eds. J. L. Fallick and R. F. Elliott (A&U, 1981); 8. 'Monetary targets and exchange rate: a case for conditional targets' (with D. A. Currie), *OEP*, 33, Suppl., July 1981, repr. in *The Money Supply and the Exchange Rate*, eds. W. A. Eltis and A. J. N. Sinclair (OUP, 1981); 9. 'Using the treasury model to measure the impact of fiscal policy' (with C. J. Green), in *Demand Management, Supply Constraints and Inflation*, eds. M. J. Artis, C. J. Green, D. G. Leslie and G. Smith (Manchester Univ. Press, 1982); 10. 'Why do forecasts differ?', *Bank of England Academic Panel Paper*, 1982.

Principal Contributions My central interest has always been, as it still is, in macroeconomic policy. This is a big field, implying parallel interests in macroeconomic theory, forecasting and modelling, policy design, the measurement of policy effects and the institutional setting of policy formation. Over a period of time, the balance of my interests in these areas has tended to shift from the less formal towards the more technical aspects of the subject matter, though not with any clear intention that the former were undeserving of further pursuit. In fact, it is a current intention of mine to attempt to redress the balance somewhat by revisiting some of the themes raised in my first monograph on *The Foundations of British Monetary Policy*, where the historical and institutional setting of monetary policy formation was given pride of place.

ASHENFELTER, Orley Clark

Born 1942, San Francisco, CA, USA.

Current Post Prof. Econ., Dir., Industrial Relations Section, Princeton Univ., Princeton, NJ, USA, 1972–.

Past Posts Dir., Office Evaluation, US Dept. Labor, 1972–3; Lect., Ass. Prof., Assoc. Prof. Econ., Princeton Univ., 1968–72; Benjamin Meeker Vis. Prof., Univ. Bristol, 1981.

Degrees BA Claremont Men's Coll., CA, 1964; PhD Princeton Univ., 1970.

Offices and Honours Project on Women, Urban Inst. 1975–; Guggenheim Foundation Fellow, 1976–7; Fellow, Ragnar Frisch Prize, Em Soc 1977, 1983; Advisory Panel AEA, Panel of Stats., Nat. Commission Employment and Unemployment Stats., 1977–81; Vis. Scholar, Fed. Reserve Bank Philadelphia, 1979–80; Macro Advisory Panel, Nat. Commission Employment Policy, 1980–1; Advisory Board, Inst. Labor and Management Relations, Rutgers Univ., 1979–; Exec. Comm., Conference Res. in Income and Wealth, NBER, 1982.

Editorial Duties Ed. Boards *JUE*, 1974, *J. Labor Res.*, 1980–; *PDR*, 1981–, *J Labor Econ.*, 1983–; Managing Ed., *AER*, 1985–.

Principal Fields of Interest 211 Econometric and Statistical Methods and Models; 821 Theory of Labour Markets and Leisure; 833 Labour Management Relations.

Publications *Books:* 1. *Discrimination in Labor Markets* (with A. Rees), (Princeton Univ. Press, 1973); 2. *Labor and the National Economy* (with W. G. Bowen), (W. W. Norton, 1975); 3. *Evaluating the Labor Market Effects of Social Programs* (with J. Blum), (Industrial Relations Section, Princeton Univ., 1976); 4. *Equal Rights and Industrial Relations* (with L. Hausman, B. Rustin, R. Schubert and D. Slaiman), (Industrial Relations Res. Assoc., 1977); 5. *Essays in Labor Market Analysis (In memory of Yochanan Peter Comay)*, co-ed. (with W. Oates), (Halsted Press, 1978).

Articles: 1. 'Wage movements and the labour market equilibrium hypothesis' (with J. Altayi) *Ec*, N.S. 47, Aug. 1980; 2. 'Anticipated unemployment, temporary layoffs, and compensating wage differentials' (with J. Abowd), in *Studies in Labor Markets*, ed. S. Rosen (Univ. Chicago Press, 1981); 3. 'Economic implications of an aging population', in *Aging: A Challenge to Science and Society*, II, *Medicine and Social Science* (OUP, 1981); 4. 'Employment statistics: the interaction of economics and policy' (with G. Solon), *AER*, 72(2), May 1982; 5. 'Time-series representation of economic variables and alternative models of the labor market' (with D. Card), *REStud*, 49(5), Special Issue 1982; 6. 'The withering away of a full employment goal,' *Canadian Public Policy*, March 1983; 7. 'Determining participation in income-tested social programs', *JASA*, 78, Sept. 1983; 8. 'The pitfalls in judging arbitrator impartiality by win–loss tallies under final offer arbitration' (with D. Bloom), *Labor Law J.*, Aug. 1983, repr. in *Proceedings of the 1983 Spring Meeting*, ed. B. Dennis (Industrial Relations Res. Assoc., 1983); 10. 'Models of arbitrator behavior: theory and evidence' (with D. Bloom), *AER*, 74(1), March 1984.

Principal Contributions Most of my research is designed to set out methods for, and the results of, empirical tests of economic models of aspects of the labour market. Some of the tests have even been successful!

ASHLEY, William James*

Dates and Birthplace 1860–1927, London, England.

Posts Held Prof. Polit. Econ., Constitutional Hist., Univ. Toronto, 1888–92; Prof. Econ. Hist., Harvard Univ., 1892–1901; Prof. Commerce, Univ. Birmingham, 1901–25.

Degrees BA Univ. Oxford, 1881.

Offices and Honours Vice-Pres., RES; Pres., Econ. Section, BA, 1907, 1924; Knighted, 1917.

Publications *Books:* 1. *The Tariff Problem* (1903, 1920); 2. *The Christian Outlook, Being the Sermons of an Economist* (1925); 3. *The Bread of our Forefathers: an Inquiry into Economic History* (1928); 4. *An Introduction to English Economic History and Theory*, 2 vols (1888–93, 1931–6); 5. *The Economic Organisation of England: an Outline History* (1914, 1949).

Career Economic historian with direct ties to the German Historical School. At Oxford as a student and private tutor, he fell under the influence of Arnold Toynbee. He held that the principles of orthodox economics were not universally true and that modifications or fresh theories were needed for different societies and different times. Thus is the context of his own times, he favoured State action to assist trade unions and factory legislation, whilst supporting Joseph Chamberlains imperial preference policies. In *Economic Organisation ...*, he wrote in favour of a corporativist system in which industry and labour both take on a corporative character and are regulated by the State in the interests of the whole community.

Secondary Literature A. Ashley, *William James Ashley: A Life* (King, 1932); B. Semmel, 'Ashley, William James', *IESS*, 1.

ASIMAKOPULOS, Athanasios (Tom)

Born 1930, Montreal, Quebec, Canada.
Current Post Prof. Econ., McGill Univ., Montreal, Quebec, Canada, 1966–.
Past Posts Vis. Lect., McGill Univ., 1956–7; Ass. Prof., Royal Military Coll. Canada, Kingston, Ont.; Ass. Prof., Assoc. Prof., McGill Univ., 1959–63, 1963–6; Vis. Prof., Monash Univ., 1973–4.
Degrees BA (Econ. & Polit. Science) McGill Univ., 1951; MA, PhD Univ. Camb., 1953, 1959.
Offices and Honours C. D. Howe Memorial Foundation Fellow, 1965–6; Canada Council Leave Fellow, 1972–3; Canada Social Sciences and Humanities Res. Council Fellow, 1979–80; Member, Exec. Council, CEA, 1967–9; Fellow, Royal Soc. Canada, 1976–.
Editorial Duties Managing Ed., *CJE*, 1968–72; Ed. Boards, *J Post Keyn E*, 1977–; Ed. Adviser, *Greek Econ. Rev.*, 1979–.
Principal Fields of Interest 022 Microeconomic Theory; 023 Macroeconomic Theory; 915 Social Security.
Publications *Books:* 1. *The Reliability of Selected Price Indexes as Measures of Price Trends* (Queen's Printer, 1964); 2. *An Introduction to Economic Theory: Microeconomics* (OUP, 1978; transls., Italian, Il Mulino, 1982; Spanish, Edicions Vicens–Vives, 1984); 3. *The Nature of Public Pension Plans: Intergenerational Equity, Funding and Saving* (Econ. Council Canada, 1980).
Articles: 1. 'The definition of neutral inventions', *EJ*, 73, Dec. 1963, repr. in *Il Problema des progresso technologico nell' analisi economica*, ed. B. Jossa (Franco Angeli Editore, 1968); 2. 'A synoptic view of some simple models of growth' (with J. C. Weldon), *CJE*, 31(1), Feb. 1965; 3. 'The biological interest rate and the social utility function', *AER*, 57(1), March 1967; 4. 'On the theory of government pension plans' (with J. C. Weldon), *CJE*, 1(4), Nov. 1968; 5. 'A Robinsonian growth model in one-sector notation', *AEP*, 8, June 1969; 6. 'Keynes, Patinkin, his-

torical time, and equilibrium analysis', *CJE*, 6(3), May 1973; 7. 'The short-period incidence of taxation;' (with J. B. Burbidge), *EJ*, 84, June 1974; 8. 'A Kaleckian theory of income distribution', *CJE*, 8(3), Aug. 1975; 9. 'Keynes' theory of effective demand revisited', *AEP*, 21, June 1982; 10. 'Kalecki and Keynes on finance, investment and saving', *CJE*, 7, Sept–Dec. 1983.
Principal Contributions My writings reflect a continuing interest in economic theory, what it is, how it has developed, and how it is used. Many of my publications arise from attempts to explain particular aspects of economic theory to my students and dissatisfaction with what is available for them to study. My approach to the teaching of microeconomics is very much affected by my study of macroeconomics where the analytical techniques and habits of mind of microeconomics are often applied uncritically. The study of Robinson's theory of growth led to a careful reading of Kalecki, and their work has influenced my treatment of Keynes's theory. The nature of public pensions, with specific attention to their evolution and prospects in Canada, has become my main area of immediate policy interest. The theoretical approach taken (with J. C. Weldon) reflects the lessons drawn from history (and Keynes) and explicitly recognises the inability of current governments to determine the precise content of the future pensions of their constituents, and the usefulness of a properly-specified social welfare function for the discussion of the provisions of a public pension plan.

ATKINSON, Anthony Barnes

Born 1944, Caerleon, Monmouth, Wales.
Current Post Prof. Econ., LSE, London, 1980–.
Past Posts Fellow, St John's Coll. Camb., 1967–71; Prof. Econ., Univ. Essex, 1971–6; Vis. Prof., MIT, 1973; Prof. Polit. Econ., Univ. Coll. London, 1976–9; UK Royal Commission Distribution Income and Wealth, 1978–9.

Degrees BA, MA Univ. Camb., 1966, 1969.

Offices and Honours Fellow, Exec. Comm., Em Soc., 1974, 1982–; Chairman, Econ. Comm., UK–SSRC, 1978–80; Pres., UK Assoc. Polytechnic Teachers Econ., 1982–.

Editorial Duties Ed., *J Pub E*, 1971–; Assoc. Ed., *JET*, 1971–9; Ed. Board, *REStud*, 1968–74.

Principal Fields of Interest 320 Fiscal Theory and Policy; 910 Welfare, Health and Education; 020 General Economic Theory.

Publications *Books:* 1. *Poverty in Britain and the Reform of Social Security* (CUP 1969); 2. *Unequal Shares* (Allen Lane Penguin, 1972); 3. *Economics of Inequality* (OUP, 1975, 1983); 4. *Distribution of Personal Wealth in Britain* (with A. J. Harrison), (CUP, 1978); 5. *Lectures on Public Economics* (with J. E. Stiglitz), (McGraw-Hill, 1980); 6. *Social Justice and Public Policy* (Wheatsheaf Books, MIT Press, 1982); 7. *Parents and Children* (with A. K. Maynard and C. C. Trinder) (Heinemann, 1983).

Articles: 1. 'On the measurement of inequality', *JET* 2(3), Sept. 1970; 2. 'The structure of indirect taxation and economic efficiency' (with J. E. Stiglitz), *J Pub E*, 2(1), Feb. 1972; 3. 'Mortality multipliers and the estate duty method' (with A. J. Harrison), *OBES*, 37(1), Feb. 1975; 4. 'On the switch from direct to indirect taxation' (with N. H. Stern and J. Gomulka), *J Pub E*, 14(2), Oct. 1980; 5. 'On the reliability of income data in the family expenditure survey 1970–77' (with J. Micklewright), *JRSS*, Series A, 146(1), 1983.

Principal Contributions Measurement of wide inequality and the relationship between social values and statistical measures. Explanation of income inequality with particular reference to intergenerational transmission of advantage and disadvantage. Role of social security and income maintenance. Modern public economics and the development of criteria for the design of taxation and public expenditure policy in a world of complexity, multiple objectives and second-best constraints.

ATTWOOD, Thomas*

Dates and Birthplace 1783–1856, Birmingham, W. Midlands, England.

Post Held Banker.

Publications *Books:* 1. *The Remedy: or, Thoughts on the Present Distress* (1816); 2. *A Letter to Nicholas Vansitart, on the Creation of Money and on its Action upon National Prosperity* (1817); 3. *Observations on Currency, Population, and Pauperism* (1818); 4. *Letter to the Earl of Liverpool* (1819); 5. *The Scotch Banker* (1828).

Career He and his brother Matthias (1779–1851), also a banker and able economist, first emerged as spokesmen for the distressed industrial areas of the West Midlands in the post-Napoleonic war period. He favoured a well-managed paper currency as a means of avoiding the deflation he associated with the gold standard then in force. His case was considered wildly unorthodox and his speech-making and pamphleteering activities in the Birmingham Union, though they mobilised local political sentiment, ultimately led to his arguments being ignored. Despite repeated mention in J. S. Mill's *Principles*, the name of Thomas Attwood practically disappeared from economics until modern times when Hawtrey and Viner drew attention to him once again.

Secondary Literature F. W. Fetter, ed. *Selected Economic Writings of Thomas Attwood* (LSE, 1964).

AUERNHEIMER, Leonardo

Born 1936, Alta Gracia, Cordoba, Argentina.

Current Post Assoc. Prof. Econ., Texas A&M Univ., Coll. Station, Texas, USA, Sr. Investigator, Centro de Estudios Macroecon. de Argentina (CEMA), Buenos Aires, Argentina, 1977–.

Past Posts Cons., Ford Foundation, 1965–6; Teach. Ass., Univ. Buenos Aires, 1966–85; Vis. Prof., Univ. Vicosa, Brasil, 1972–3; Ass. Prof., Texas A&M Univ., 1973–77; Con., Vis. Prof., Centro de Estudios Monetarios Latinoamericanos, Mexico City,

1975, CEMA, 1980–1; Vis. Scholar, Univ. Göttingen, W. Germany, 1983.

Degrees Licenciado, Univ. Buenos Aires, 1965; MA, PhD Univ. Chicago, 1970, 1973.

Principal Fields of Interest 023 Macroeonomic Theory; 311 Domestic Monetary and Financial Theory and Policy; 431 Balance of Payments; Mechanisms of Adjustment; Exchange Rates.

Publications *Books:* 1. *The Essentials of Money and Banking* (with R. B. Ekelund, Jr.), (Wiley, 1982).

Articles: 1. 'The honest government guide to the revenues from the creation of money', *JPE*, 82, May–June 1974; 2. 'The effects of inflationary finance on stability', *SEJ*, 42, Jan. 1976; 3. 'Rentals, prices, stocks and flows', *SEJ*, 42, July 1976; 4. 'Market organization and the durability of durable goods' (with T. R. Saving), *Em*, 45, Jan–March 1975; 5. 'Adaptive-regressive expectations and the price level', *J Mon E*, 5, Jan. 1979; 6. 'The price change equation in simple models of monetary adjustment', *SEJ*, 49, Oct. 1982; 7. 'Deficit, government expenditures and the inflation tax: two models of passive money', *Cuadernos de Econ.*, April 1983; 8. 'The revenue maximising inflation rate, and the treatment of the transition', *JMCB*, 15, Aug. 1983.

Principal Contributions Early work reflected an interest in the theory and implications of the revenues from the creation of fiat money. In particular, the 1974 *JPE* piece showed the correct and general specification of those revenues taking account of transitional but, as it turns out, essential elements. In addition, this early paper is considered as the first reference in the monetary literature of instances where 'time inconsistency' could arise. Later work, in part inspired by the stabilisation experiments of the Southern Cone countries during the late 1970s, is related to expectations, the 'fiscal' constraint, and the connection between debt and money printing financing of government expenditures under both monetary and exchange rate rules. In addition to my interest in macro and monetary theory, I have made incur-

sions in the theory of capital and depreciation; in particular the work with T. R. Saving shows the robustness of durability with respect to alternative forms of market organisation.

AUMANN, Robert John

Born 1930, Frankfurt-am-Main, W. Germany.

Current Post Prof. Maths., Hebrew Univ., Jerusalem, Israel; Teacher Stats., Tel-Aviv Univ., Tel Aviv, Israel, 1981–.

Past Posts Res. Ass., Res. Assoc., Princeton Univ., Em Res. Program, 1954–6, 1960–2; Vis. Prof. Stats., Yale Univ., 1964–5; Ford Vis. Res. Prof. Econ., Univ. Cal. Berkeley, 1971; Vis. Prof., CORE, Univ. Catholique de Louvain, 1972, 1978, 1984, Stanford Univ., 1975–6, 1980–1; Fellow, Inst. Advanced Stud., Hebrew Univ., 1979–80; Visitor, Bell Labs., 1956, US Nat. Bureau Standards, 1957–8, Rand Corp., Santa Monica, 1963, 1968, Univ. Cal. Berkeley, 1964, Stanford Univ., 1971–84.

Degrees BS City Coll., NY, 1950; SM, PhD (Maths.) MIT, 1952, 1955.

Offices and Honours Fellow, Em Soc., 1966; AAAS, 1974; Harvey Prize, Technion, Israel, 1983.

Editorial Duties Ed. Board, *Internat. J. Game Theory*, 1971, *SIAM J. Applied Maths.*, 1976–80; Advisory Board, *J Math E*, 1974–, *Maths. of Op R.*, 1979–; Assoc. Ed., *JET*, 1974–9. *Em*, 1975–8; Area Ed., *Game Theory, Maths. of OR.*, 1975–9.

Principal Fields of Interest 026 Economics of Uncertainty and Information; 021 General Equilibrium Theory; 213 Mathematical Methods and Models.

Publications *Books:* 1. *Values of Non-Atomic Games* (with L. S. Shapley), (Princeton Univ. Press, 1974; transl., Russian, Mir, 1977).

Articles: 1. 'Acceptable points in general cooperative n-person games', in *Contributions to the Theory of Games*, vol. 4 (Princeton Univ. Press, 1959); 2. 'Utility theory without the completeness axiom', *Em*, 30(4), July 1962, 32(1), Jan.–April 1964; 3. 'Markets with a continuum of traders', *Em*,

32(1), Jan.–April 1964; 4. 'The bargaining set for cooperative games' (with M. Maschler), in *Advances in Game Theory* (Princeton Univ. Press, 1964); 5. 'Integrals of set-valued functions', *J Math. Analysis & Applications*, 12, 1965; 6. 'Existence of competitive equilibria in markets with a continuum of traders', *Em*, 34(1), Jan. 1966; 7. 'Subjectivity and correlation in randomized strategies', *J Math. E*, 1, 1974; 8. 'Values of markets with a continuum of traders, *Em*, 43(4), July 1975; 9. 'Agreeing to disagree', *Annals Stats.*, 4, 1976; 10. 'An axiomatization of the non-transferable utility value', *Em*, 53, 1985.

Principal Contributions The main focus of my work has long been multiperson interactive decision theory — more commonly called Game Theory — and its economic and politico-economic applications. Related work has been in one person decision theory (utilities, subjective probabilities), in general equilibrium theory, and in the development of relevant mathematical tools. Some areas of specific contributions (with considerable overlap) have been: (1) non-atomic continua as models for large numbers of individually insignificant agents, in particular as an expression of 'perfect competition'; (2) repeated games as models for co-operation and bargaining in environments where information may be either complete or incomplete; this theory enables 'rational analysis of phenomena such as co-operation, altruism, revenge, threats (self-destructive or otherwise), partial or complete concealment of information, signalling and trusting or mistrusting signals, the relationship between using information and revealing it, and so on; (3) development of the Shapley value as a tool for economic analysis, and specifically the non-transferable utility Shapley value; applications have been to general equilibrium, fixed prices, voting, taxation, and public goods; (4) the Bargaining Set for co-operative games (which subsequently led to the development of the Kernel, Nucleus and related concepts); and (5) models of differential information, specifically the notions of common knowledge and correlated equilibrium and their applications.

AUPETIT, Albert*

Dates and Birthplace 1876–1943, Sancerre, Cher, France.

Posts Held Teacher, l'Ecole Pratique des Hautes Etudes, Paris, 1910–14; Secretary–Gen., Banque de France, 1920–6; Prof., l'Ecole des Sciences Polit., Paris, 1921; Businessman, 1926–43.

Offices and Honours Commander, Légion d'Honneur; Member, Inst. de France, 1936.

Publications *Books:* 1. *Essai sur la théorie générale de la monnaie* (1901); 2. *Les grands marchés financiers: France* (1912).

Articles: 1. 'L'oeuvre économique de Cournot', *Revue de métaphysique et de morale,* 13, 1905.

Career One of Walras' few immediate followers, his *Essai* ... is a brilliant and neglected product of his early years. It was both a significant step in the development of the theory of money and an early reformulation of Walrasian equilibrium theory.

Secondary Literature G. Pirou, 'Nécrologie: Albert Aupetit', *REP*, 55(3–4), 1945.

AUSPITZ, Rudolf*

Dates and Birthplace 1837–1906, Austro-Hungary.

Posts Held Businessman, dealing in sugar, and member of Parliament.

Publications *Books:* 1. *Untersuchungen über die Theorie des Preises* (with R. Lieben), (1889).

Career Joint author with Richard Lieben (1842–1919) of one of the outstanding early works in mathematical economics. The chief theoretical concern of their *Untersuchungen* ... was partial equilibrium, which they discussed intensively in diagrammatic form, utilising total and marginal curves. In common with Jevons, they incorporated the idea of disutility of labour and they utilised the concept of consumer surplus. Their discussion of monopoly is similar to that of Pareto, who along with Edgeworth and Irving Fisher was deeply influenced by their book.

Secondary Literature J. A. Schumpeter, 'Rudolf Auspitz', *ESS*, vol. 2; G. Tintner, 'Auspitz, Rudolf, and Lieben, Richard', *IESS*, vol. 1.

AYRES, Clarence Edwin*

Dates and Birthplace 1891–1972, Lowell, MA, USA.

Posts Held Taught philosophy at Univs. Chicago, Amherst and Reed, 1917–30; Prof. Econ., Univ. Texas, 1930–68.

Degrees BA Brown Univ., 1912, 1914; PhD Univ. Chicago, 1917.

Publications *Books:* 1. *The Problem of Economic Order* (1938); 2. *The Theory of Economic Progress* (1944, 1978); 3. *The Divine Right of Capital* (1946); 4. *The Industrial Economy* (1952); 5. *Toward a Reasonable Society* (1961).

Career The leading representative of the institutional school in the years after World War II. He developed a theoretical system for institutionalism in which 'technological behaviour' is set alongside 'ceremonial behaviour' as determinants of economic progress. This method enabled him to assess the importance of institutions as agents for economic change. His policy prescriptions included a form of negative income tax. Although his influence inside the economics profession has proved limited, outside it his work has been well received.

Secondary Literature W. Breit, 'Ayres, Clarence E.', *IESS*, 18; *Science and Ceremony: The Institutional Economics of C. E. Ayres*, eds. W. Breit and W. P. Culbertson Jr. (Univ. Texas Press, 1976).

AZARIADIS, Costas

Born 1943, Athens, Greece.

Current Post Prof. Econ., Univ. Penn., Philadelphia, PA, USA, 1981–.

Past Posts Ass. Prof., Brown Univ., 1973–7; Assoc. Prof., Univ. Penn.,

1977–81; Vis. Fellow, Inst. Advanced Study, Hebrew Univ., 1977; Vis. Assoc. Prof., Princeton Univ., 1980; Vis. Prof., Ecole des Hautes Etudes Sciences Sociales, Paris, 1983.

Degrees Dipl(Eng.) National Technical Univ., Athens., 1969; MSIA, PhD Carnegie-Mellon Univ., 1971, 1975.

Editorial Duties Guest Ed., *QJE*, 1983.

Principal Fields of Interest 023 Macroeconomic Theory.

Publications *Articles:* 1. 'Implicit contracts and underemployment equilibria', *JPE*, 83(6), Dec. 1975; 2. 'Implicit contracts and related topics: a survey', in *The Economics of the Labour Market* (HMSO, 1981); 3. 'A re-examination of natural rate theory', *AER*, 71(5), Dec. 1981; 4. 'Self-fulfilling prophecies', *JET*, 25(3), Dec. 1981; 5. 'Employment with asymmetric information', *QJE*, 98(3), Suppl. 1983; 6. 'Predetermined prices and the allocation of social risks' (with R. Cooper), *QJE*, 100(2), May, 1985; 7. 'Sunspots and cycles' (with R. Gusnerie), forthcoming, 1986.

Principal Contributions A combination of slow progress and lack of imagination has kept me working on the same substantive topics over the last decade; unemployment is one of them, the effect of beliefs on equilibrium is the other. I became involved early on with the theory of implicit contracts which I saw as an attempt to say something interesting about sluggish prices and quantity rationing. Advances, especially recent ones, in the incentives literature have made it possible for many of us to analyse involuntary underemployment in a rigorous way. Still, we have no satisfactory explanation of wage rigidity, no logically coherent theory of rationing, and no general equilibrium paradigm that places these labour-market phenomena in proper macroeconomic perspective. Much work remains to be done here.

Beliefs are something I always like to know more about. How are they formed? How do they interact with equilibrium? What are 'optimism' and 'pessimism'? Temporary equilibrium says that beliefs *drive* equilibrium. The rational expectations literature requires beliefs to be *validated* by equilibrium. Which one is right? The answer is both. The 'sunspots' literature, to which I contributed in the early 1980s, is an example of rational expectations equilibria which are completely driven by arbitrarily formed beliefs. The trouble with such equilibria is, of course, that there are too many of them. It is of some interest to know which, if any, are reachable from given prior beliefs, and how the economy behaves while beliefs and equilibrium converge. If there is method in this madness, it must have something to do with a larger effort to build up the logical foundations of macroeconomics. I see my own work, past and future, as part of that larger effort.

B

BABBAGE, Charles*

Dates and Birthplace 1792–1871, Teignmouth, Devon, England.
Post Held Lucasian Chair Maths, Univ. Camb., 1828–39.
Degrees BA, MA Univ. Camb., 1814, 1817.
Offices and Honours Co-founder Stat. Soc., Astronomical Soc., and BAAS; Fellow, Royal Soc., 1816.
Publications *Books:* 1. *On the Economy of Machinery and Manufactures* (1832, 1841); 2. *Passages from the Life of a Philosopher* (1864).
Career Mathematician and, through his work on the 'difference engine' and the 'analytical engine', a pioneer of computer technology. The mechanical problems encountered in his own workshop during the government-financed work on his 'difference engine' led him to a general interest in manufacturing problems. *Economy of machinery . . .* was the result of an investigative tour of British and European factories. It is his interest in the use of accurate mathematical and statistical work in various fields, including economics, which justifies his reputation as a forerunner of operations research.
Secondary Literature P. and E.

Morrison, 'Babbage, Charles', *IESS*, 1.

BABEAU, André Yves Georges

Born 1934, Boulogne s/Seine, France.
Current Post Prof. Econ., Univ. Paris-Dauphine, Paris, France, 1982–.
Past Posts Chargé de course, Maître Conference, Univ. Lille, 1962–4, 1964–7; Prof., Univ. Paris-Nanterre, 1968–81; Dir., CREDOC, Paris, 1978–84.
Degrees Dr Sciences Econ., Agrège Science Econ., Diplôme de l'Inst, d'Etudes Polit., Paris, 1959, 1964.
Offices and Honours Member, Comité Nat., CNRS, 1968–75; Conseil Nat. de la Stat., 1973–8; Chairman, Comité d'Action spécifique 'Analyse quantitative de l'économie française', 1981.
Editorial Duties Ed. Boards, *RE* 1964, *Consommation-Revue de Socio-Econ.* 1978–, *RIW*, 1980–.
Principal Fields of Interest 911 General Welfare Programme; 920 Consumer Economics.
Publications *Books:* 1. *Les conseils ouvriers en Pologne* (Edns Armand-Colin, 1959; transl., Spanish, 1963); 2. *Problèmes techniques de planification* (with P. H. Derycke), (Edns Jirey, 1967); 3. *Le profit* (Presses Univ. de France, 1969, 1984; transl., Spanish, 1972); 4. *Analyse quantitative des décisions de l'entreprise. La décision de production* (with M. Desplas), (Edns Bordas, 1973); 5. *Partage des surplus et inflation* (with A. Masson and D. Strauss-Kahn), (Edns Cujas, 1975); 6. *Calcul économique appliqué: problèmes resolus de micro-économie* (Edns Dunod, 1975, 1982); 7. *La richesse du Français, epargne, plus-value, heritage* (with D. Strauss-Kahn), (Presses Univ. de France, 1977).
Articles: 1. 'La détention des valeurs mobilières par les particuliers', *RE*, 15, July 1964; 2. 'Le patrimoine des salaries et inactifs de 1949 a 1967' (with A. Masson and D. Strauss-Kahn), *RE*, 25(4), July 1974; 3. 'Economies of scale in households' cash balances: a series of empirical tests', *Europ ER*, 5(2), Aug. 1974; 4. 'La situation des ménages dans

l'inflation, 1965–74', *REP*, 5, 1976; 5. 'The application of the constant price method for evaluating the transfers related to inflation: the case of French households', *RIW*, 24(4), Dec. 1978; 6. 'Le coût de la sécurité du consommateur', *Consommation*, 25(4), Oct.–Dec. 1978; 7. 'L'évolution du rapport patrimoine/revenu au cours du cycle de vie: une comparaison France–Canada', *Consommation-Revue de Socio-Econ.*, April 1982; 8. 'Le rapport macroéconomique du patrimoine au revenu des ménages', *RE*, 1, 1983; 9. 'Finances publiques et politiques sociales: explication de leurs evolutions et développement dans les économies de marché' (IIPF, 1983); 10. 'The macroeconomic wealth-income ratio of household', *RIW*, 29(4), Dec. 1983.

Principal Contributions My first field of interest was macroeconomic planning and simultaneously the microeconomic production function (with some estimations of the elasticity of substitution between factors). Then I began to scrutinise household saving behaviour and wealth accumulation. My interest in saving concerned macroeconomic saving as well as disaggregated savings (housing investment, stocks and shares, and so on). As far as wealth accumulation is concerned, my main interest was in measuring the influence of inflation on the value of different assets. I also tried to test the stability hypothesis of the wealth-income ratio. More recently, I have studied consumption behaviour, being primarily interested in the composition of household consumption. Very lately, I tried to determine the influence of family size in the estimation of life standard distributions.

BACH, George Leland

Born 1915, Victor, IA, USA.
Current Post Frank E. Buck Prof. Emeritus, Econ. Public Policy, Stanford Univ., Stanford, CA, USA, 1981–.
Past Posts Dean, Grad. School Industrial Admin., Maurice Falk Prof. Econ. Social Science, Carnegie-Mellon Univ., 1949–63, 1963–6; Prof., Stanford Univ., 1966–81.

Degrees BA, Hon LLD Grinnell Coll., 1936, 1956; PhD Univ. Chicago, 1940; Hon. LLD Carnegie-Mellon Univ., 1967.
Offices and Honours Fellow, AAAS; Trustee, Vice Chairman, Joint Council Econ. Education; Study Dir., Hoover Commission, 1949–50; Ford Foundation Faculty Fellow, 1960–1; Chairman, Nat. Task Force Econ. Educ., 1960–3; Chairman, Board Dirs., Pittsburgh Branch, Fed. Reserve System, 1960–6; Chairman, AEA Comm. Econ. Educ., 1962–76; Dow-Jones Award Disting. Service Bus. Educ., 1975; AEA Joint Council Econ. Educ. Award, 1977; Walter Gores Award Excellence in Teaching, 1978.
Principal Fields of Interest 012 Teaching of Economics.
Publications *Books:* 1. *Economics: An Introduction to Analysis and Policy* (Prentice-Hall, 1948, 1980); 2. *Federal Reserve Policy-Making* (Alfred A. Knopf, 1950); 3. *Inflation: A Study in Economics, Ethics and Politics* (Brown Univ. Press, 1958); 4. *Making Monetary and Fiscal Policy* (Brookings Inst., 1971); 5. *The New Inflation* (Brown Univ. Press, 1973).
Articles: 1. 'Monetary-fiscal policy reconsidered', *JPE*, 57, Oct. 1949; 2. 'The redistributional effects of inflation' (with A. Ando), *REStat*, 39, Feb. 1957; 3. 'The differential effects of tight money' (with C. J. Huizenga), *AER*, 51(1), March 1961; 4. 'Economic education: aspirations and achievements' (with P. Saunders), *AER*, 55(3), June 1965; 5. 'Inflation and the redistribution of wealth' (with J. Stephenson), *REStat*, 56(1), Feb. 1974.
Principal Contributions Early analysis of Federal Reserve policy-making; early empirical analysis of differential impact of inflation on different income groups, stressing combined interaction of economic, political and social forces;

effects of 'tight money' policy; earliest attempt to measure the effectiveness of different approaches to teaching economics, with new tests of economic understanding; new approaches to teaching elementary economics at colleges and pre-college levels.

BAER, Werner

Born 1931, Offenbach, W. Germany.
Current Post Prof. Econ., Univ. Illinois Urbana-Champaign, Urbana, IL, USA, 1974–.
Past Posts Instr., Harvard Univ., 1958–61; Ass. Prof., Yale Univ., 1961–5; Assoc. Prof., Prof., Vanderbilt Univ., 1965–9, 1969–74; Vis. Prof., Univ. Sao Paulo, Brazil, 1966–8, Vargas Foundation, Rio de Janeiro, 1966–8; Vis. Scholar, Brazilian Planning Ministry, 1975, Brazilian Census Bureau, 1978.
Degrees BA Queens Coll., 1953; MA, PhD Harvard Univ., 1955, 1958.
Offices and Honours Rhodes Fellow, Univ. Oxford, 1975; Gold Medal Award, Federal Univ. Pernambuco, Brazil, 1981; Brazil's Order Southern Cross, 1982.
Editorial Duties Ed. Board, *WD*, *Cambridge Latin Amer. Stud.* (CUP, 1977–82), *Luso-Brasilian Rev.*, *Revista Paraguaya de Estudios Sociologicos*, *Revista Latinoamericana de Historia Economica y Social*.
Principal Fields of Interest 440 International Investment and Foreign Aid; 121 Economic Studies of Developing Countries; 134 Inflation and Deflation.
Publications *Books:* 1. *The Puerto Rican Economy* (Univ. Puerto Rico Press, 1962); 2. *Inflation and Growth in Latin America*, co-ed. (with I. Kerstenetzky), (Richard D. Irwin, 1964); 3. *Industrialization and Economic Development in Brazil* (Richard D. Irwin, 1965); 4. *The Development of the Brazilian Steel Industry* (Vanderbilt Univ. Press, 1969); 5. *O Setor Privado Nacional* (with A. V. Villela), (IPEA, 1980); 6. *Dimensoes do Desenvolvimento Brasileiro*, co-ed. (with P. Geiger and P. Haddad), (Editora Campus, 1978); 7. *Export Diversification and the New Protectionism*, co-ed. (with M. Gillis) (Univ. Illinois Press, 1981); 8. *The Brazilian Economy: Growth and Development* (Praeger, 1983).
Articles: 1. 'Multiple exchange rates and multiple policy objectives' (with M. E. A. Herve), *Ec*, N.S. 29, May 1962; 2. 'Profit illusion and policy mak-

ing in an inflationary economy' (with M. Simonsen), *OEP*, 17, July 1963; 3. 'Employment and industrialization in developing countries' (with M. E. A. Herve), *QJE*, 80, Feb. 1966; 4. 'Import substitution in Latin America', *Latin American Res. Rev.*, Spring 1972; 5. 'The changing role of the state in the Brazilian economy' (with I. Kerstenetzky and A. Villela), *WD*, 1(7) Nov. 1973; 6. 'Indexing in Brazil' (with P. Beckerman), *WD*, 2(8), Dec. 1974; 7. 'Technology, employment and development', *WD*, 4(2), Feb. 1976; 8. 'Changes in the Inter-American economic system' (with D. Coes), in *The Future of the Inter-American System*, ed. T. J. Farer (Praeger, 1979); 9. 'Toward a service oriented growth strategy' (with L. Samuelson), *WD*, 3(6), June 1981; 10. 'State enterprise and the distribution of income: Brazil and Peru' (with A. Figueroa) in *Authoritarian Capitalism*, eds. T. C. Bruneau and P. Faucher (Westview Press, 1981).
Principal Contributions My major interest has been and still is the process of import-substitution industrialisation in Latin America. In my earlier work I concentrated on analysing import substitution policies, their justification based on the Prebisch-type of critique of traditional trade theory, their success in stimulating growth and their negative side-effects — penalising agriculture, increasing the concentration of income, worsening regional disequilibria, and contributing to inflationary pressures. In more recent years I have concentrated on studying the nature of post-import substitution economies — the role of state enterprises and banks; the changing role of multinationals and domestic private firms; the successes and failures of indexing as a measure to cope with inflation; the use of tax and credit incentives to remedy resource misallocation resulting from import substitution; and the role of the service sector in the development process. The latter studies have convinced me that economists have to adapt their theories to the behaviour pattern of institutions and individuals in newly industrialised countries.

BAGEHOT, Walter*

Dates and Birthplace 1826–77, Langport, Somerset, England.
Posts Held Banker; Ed., *The Economist*, 1861–77.
Degrees BA, MA Univ. London, 1846, 1848.
Publications *Books:* 1. *Collected Works of Walter Bagehot*, ed. N. St John-Stevas, vols. 9–11 (1966–78).
Career Chiefly known for his analysis of government in *The English Constitution* (1865–7). In his contributions to *The Economist* and in *Lombard Street* (1873), however, he developed a theory of central banking which highlighted the role of the Bank of England in maintaining confidence in the banking system. A posthumous volume of *Economic Studies* (1880) was all that existed of a projected treatise on political economy. His aim was to move away from the more abstract side of economics and to place emphasis on the importance of cultural and sociological factors in economic analysis.
Secondary Literature N. St John-Stevas, *Walter Bagehot: a Study of His Life and Thought* (The Economist, Indiana Univ. Press, 1959); H. S. Gordon, 'Bagehot, Walter. Economic contributions', *IESS*, 1.

BAILEY, Elizabeth Ellery

Born 1938, New York City, NY, USA.
Current Post Dean, Grad. School Industrial Admin., Carnegie-Mellon Univ., Pittsburgh, PA, USA, 1983–.
Past Posts Sr. Technical Aide, Assoc. Member Technical Staff, Bell Labs., 1960–73; Adjunct Ass. Prof., Adjunct Assoc. Prof. Econ, NYU., 1973–7; Supervisor, Econ. Analysis Group, Res. Head, Econ. Res. Dept., Bell Labs., 1973–7; Commissioner, Vice-Chairman, Acting Chairman, US Civil Aeronautics Board, 1977–83, 1981–3, 1981.
Degrees BA Radcliffe Coll., 1960; MS (Computer Science), Stevens Inst. Technology, 1966; PhD Princeton Univ., 1972.
Offices and Honours Board Trustees, Princeton Univ., 1978–82; Exec. Comm., Head, Comm. Status Women, AEA, 1981–3, 1980–2; Board, Standard Oil Ohio, 1984–, Presbyterian Hospital, 1984–, Pennsylvania Power & Light, 1983–; Advisory Board, Center Econ. Policy Res., Stanford Univ., 1983–5, Inst. Res. Poverty, Univ. Wisconsin-Madison, 1983–4, AEI Center Study Govt. Regulation, 1980–.
Editorial Duties Ed. Board, *AER*, 1977–9, *J. Ind. E*, 1977, *Info. Econ. and Policy*, 1982–4, Series on Regulation of Econ. Activity (MIT Press, 1982–5), *Encyclopaedia of Economics* (McGraw-Hill), 1982–5.
Principal Fields of Interest 610 Industrial Organisation and Public Policy; 020 General Economic Theory.
Publications *Books:* 1. *Economic Theory of Regulatory Constraint* (D. C. Heath, 1973); 2. *Selected Economics Papers of William J. Baumol*, ed. (NYU Press, 1976); 3. *Deregulating the Airlines* (with D. R. Graham and D. P. Kaplan), (MIT Press, 1984).
Articles: 1. 'Resource allocation and the regulated firm' (with J. C. Malone), *Bell JE*, 1(1), Spring 1970; 2. 'Peak load pricing under regulatory contraint', *JPE*, 18, July–Aug. 1972; 3. 'Reversals in peak and offpeak prices' (with L. J. White), *Bell JE*, 5, Spring 1974, repr. in *Regulation in Future Perspective: The Little Engine that Might*, ed. W. G. Shepherd and T. G. Cies (Ballinger, 1974); 4. 'Innovation and Regulation', *J Pub E*, 3(3), Aug. 1974; 5. 'Weak invisible hand theorems on pricing and entry in a multi-product nautral monopoly' (with W. J. Baumol and R. D. Willig), *AER*, 67(3), June 1977; 6. 'Optimal price policy following product-specific technical change', *J Ind E*, 28, Dec. 1979; 7. 'The Contestability of airline markets during the transition to deregulation' (with J. C. Panzar), *Law and Contemporary Problems*, 44(1), Winter 1981, repr. in *Reprints for Antitrust Law and Econ.*, 14(1); 8. 'Income distributional concerns in regulatatory policy making' (with R. D. Willig), in *Studies in Public Regulation*, ed. G. Fromm (MIT Press, 1981); 9. 'Contestability and the design of regulatory and antitrust policy',

AER, 71(2), May 1981; 10. 'Market
structure and multiproduct industries'
(with A. F. Friedlaender), *JEL*, 20(3),
Sept. 1982.

Principal Contributions I began my
economics career at Bell Laboratories
as one of the founding members of an
Economics Research department. Our
work broadened industrial organisation
by developing models of regulated
monopolies, of optimal pricing under
regulatory constraints, and finally
multiproduct enterprises. I was given
the opportunity to go to Washington, to
participate in the deregulation of the
airline industry. This post gave me a
unique opportunity to put economic
theory into practice. A remarkable confluence of new theoretical tools aided
immensely in providing a framework
for practical action. I have recently
assumed the post of Dean of a major
business school and hope to continue
here to use the theoretical and scientific
base of economics to address major
problems of our times.

BAILEY, Martin J.

Born Taft, CA, USA.
Current Post Econ. Adviser, Under-
Secretary Econ. Affairs, US State
Dept., 1983–.
Past Posts Vis. Res. Prof. Econ.,
Univ. Catolica de Chile, Santiago,
1956–7; Staff Econ., US Cabinet
Comm. Price Stability for Econ.
Growth, 1959; Ass. Prof., Assoc.
Prof., Prof. Econ., Univ. Chicago,
1955–9, 1959–64, 1964–5; Econ., Act-
ing Assoc. Dir., Econ. Polit. Stud.
Div., US Inst. Defense Analyses,
1963–4, 1964–7; Vis. Fellow, Grad.
School Industrial Admin., Carnegie-
Mellon Univ., 1973–4; Prof. Econ.,
Univ. Maryland, 1974–.
Degrees BA UCLA, 1951; MA, PhD
Johns Hopkins Univ., 1953, 1956.
Offices and Honours Phi Beta
Kappa, 1951; Beta Gamma Sigma,
1971; Ford Foundation Faculty Res.
Fellow, 1960–1.
Editorial Duties Advisory Board,
JMCB.
Principal Fields of Interest 320 Fiscal
Theory and Policy; 130 Economic Fluc-

tuations, Forecasting and Inflation; 020
Theory of Social Choice.
Publications *Books:* 1. *National In-
come and the Price Level* (McGraw-
Hill, 1962, 1971); 2. *The Taxation of
Income from Capital*, co-ed. (with A.
C. Harberger), (Brookings Inst.,
1968); 3. *Reducing Risks to Life:
Measurement of the Benefits* (AEI,
1980).
Articles: 1. 'Edgeworth's taxation
paradox, and the nature of demand
functions', *Em*, 22(1), Jan. 1954; 2.
'The interpretation and application of
the compensation principle', *EJ*, 64,
March 1954; 3. 'The Marshallian
demand curve', *JPE*, 62(3), June 1954;
4. 'The welfare cost of inflationary
finance', *JPE*, 64(2), April 1956; 5.
'Saving and the rate of interest', *JPE*,
65(4), Aug. 1956, 68(1), Feb. 1959; 6.
'Possibility of rational social choice in
an economy', *JPE*, 87(1), Feb. 1979; 7.
'The marginal utility of income does
not increase' (with M. Olson and P.
Wonnacott), *AER*, 70(3), June 1980; 8.
'Positive time preference' (with M.
Olson), *JPE*, 89(1), Feb. 1981; 9.
'Risks, costs and benefits of fluoro-
carbon regulation', *AER*, 72(2), May
1982; 10. 'Optimal market choice in the
presence of pollution externalities'
(with R. A. Collinge), *JEEM*, 10(3),
Sept. 1983.
Principal Contributions Overall my
work has ranged over several fields,
including economic theory (micro and
macro), public finance and social
choice. My early work was divided
about equally between macro-theory
and public finance. In macro-theory,
my papers on inflationary finance and
on the saving function were followed by
a graduate textbook and treatise,
National Income and the Price Level.
Its innovations, still of some topical
relevance, included the development
of a Fisherian approach to inflation
within the IS-LM framework, and the
development of what would now be
called a rational expectations approach
to multipliers and the fiscal impact. In
public finance, I published papers on
benefit-cost analysis, tax analysis, and
the theory of social choice; these interests, and their specialised applications, continue to the present.

From time to time, I have published papers on various aspects of income taxation, covering both incidence and incentive effects. My work on benefit-cost analysis started with the rate-of-return issue in capital budgeting, and has since ranged into particular fields of application such as defence, health and safety. Starting in the early 1960s, I became interested in government service, first in the Defense Department, later at the Treasury Department (in tax policy), and currently at the State Department. This service alternated with my regular academic career. My defence work led me away from the fundamentals of project evaluation to questions of incentive structure in government, a field closely related to my recent work on externalities and optimal local government.

BAILEY, Samuel*

Dates and Birthplace 1791–1870, Sheffield, S. Yorkshire, England.
Post Held Businessman.
Publications Books: 1. *A Critical Dissertation on the Nature, Measures and Causes of Value* (1825, 1931); 2. *Letter to a Political Economist* (1826).
Career Launched the first really effective analytical attack on Ricardo's system with *A Critical Dissertation . . .* , but the book received only a small part of the recognition it deserved. His ideas were too novel, and from his comparative isolation in Sheffield he was not equipped to push home his attack. He is particularly trenchant on Ricardo's labour theory of value, the defects in the concept of real value and Ricardo's theory of profits. Works which take a similar line include *Observations on Certain Verbal Disputes on Political Economy* (anon.) (1821), which has often been incorrectly attributed to Bailey himself.
Secondary Literature R. M. Rauner, *Samuel Bailey and the Classical Theory of Value* (G. Bell & Sons, 1961).

BAILY, Martin Neil

Born 1945, Exeter, Devon, England.
Current Post Sr. Fellow, Econ. Stud. Program, Brookings Inst., Washington, DC, USA, 1979–.
Past Posts Lect., Univ. Nairobi, Kenya, 1972; Ass. Prof., MIT, 1972–3; Ass. Prof., Assoc. Prof., Yale Univ., 1973–9; Vis. Prof., Univ. de Los Andes, Colombia, 1975; Res. Ass., NBER, 1978–.
Degrees BA, MA Univ. Camb. 1966, 1970; MA Simon Fraser Univ., Canada, 1968; PhD MIT, 1972.
Offices and Honours Bachelor Scholar, Coll. Prize, Christ's Coll. Cambridge; Ford Foundation Fellow, 1968–70; Canada Council Fellow, 1970–2; Sr. Adviser, Brookings Panel Econ. Activity, 1976–.
Principal Fields of Interest 110 Economic Growth; 130 Economic Fluctuations; 820 Labour Markets, Public Policy.
Publications Books: 1. *The Battle Against Unemployment and Inflation*, co-ed. (W. W. Norton, 1982); 2. *Workers, Jobs and Inflation*, ed. (Brookings Inst., 1982).
Articles: 1. 'Research and development costs and returns', *JPE*, 80(1), Jan.–Feb. 1972; 2. 'Wages and employment under uncertain demand', *REStud*, 41(1), Jan. 1974; 3. 'Dynamic monopsony and structural change', *AER*, 65(3), June 1975; 4. 'Contract theory and the moderation of inflation by recession and controls', *Brookings Papers Econ. Activity*, 7(3), Dec. 1976; 5. 'On the theory of layoffs and unemployment', *Em*, 45(5), July 1977; 6. 'The macroeconomic impact of selective public employment and wage subsidies' (with J. Tobin), *Brookings Papers Econ. Activity*, 8(2), Sept. 1977; 7. 'Stabilization policy and private economic behavior', *Brookings Papers Econ. Activity*, 9(1), Jan. 1978; 8. 'Some aspects of optimal unemployment insurance', *JPE*, 10(3), Dec. 1978; 9. 'Productivity and the services of capital and labor', *Brookings Papers Econ. Activity*, 12(1), April 1981; 10. 'The productivity growth slowdown by industry', *Brookings Papers Econ. Activity*, 13(2), Sept. 1982.

Principal Contributions In early research both the depletion of innovation possibilities and federal regulation were found to have slowed new drug development. Dissertation research then developed the theory of implicit labour contracts, showing that a risk-neutral firm will stabilise the wage and vary employment in response to product demand fluctuations when workers maintain a long-term relation with the firm. Subsequent work examined the choice between layoffs and hours variations and demonstrated that the unemployment insurance programme could encourage layoffs. A third paper showed that workers with seniority would choose a stable rather than a flexible wage, and layoffs rather than hours reductions, thereby shifting the costs of recession to junior workers.

Joint research with Tobin developed and tested a framework for analysing the impact of public policies on the natural rate of unemployment. The papers showed the conditions under which such policies will be successful or not and how changes in relative wages can defeat the intent of policy measures. My interests then turned to an alternative to the equilibrium business cycle model: an economy prone to endogenous fluctuations can become more stable as it anticipates the benefits of stabilisation policy. Theoretical and empirical analysis supported this idea.

A 1980 study of the slowdown in aggregate productivity growth argued that the flow of capital services may have declined as a result of structural changes such as the rise in energy costs, economic regulation, and the expansion of foreign trade. Evidence for the hypothesis was found in the decline in the market value of capital, and, in a later paper, in the fact that the slowdown has been most severe in the capital-intensive industries. Current research is examining in detail the pattern of industrial innovation in the 1970s to see if it has slowed relative to earlier periods, or changed its direction.

BAIN, Joe S.

Born 1912, Spokeane, WA, USA.
Current Post Emeritus Prof., Univ. Cal. Berkeley, USA, 1975–.
Past Posts Res. Assoc., Public Admin., Harvard Univ., 1951–2; Ford Res. Prof., Prof. Econ., Univ. Cal. Berkeley, 1963–4, 1939–75.
Degrees BA UCLA, 1935; MA, PhD Harvard Univ., 1939, 1940.
Offices and Honours Phi Beta Kappa, 1934; Vis. Lect., Univ. Washington, Seattle, 1966, Boston Coll., Mass., 1967; Vice-Pres., Disting. Fellow, AEA, 1968, 1982.
Editorial Duties Ed. Board, *AER*, 1951–4.
Principal Fields of Interest 610 Industrial Organisation.
Publications *Books:* 1. *Economics of the Pacific Coast Petroleum Industry* (Univ. Cal. Press, 1944–7); 2. *Pricing, Distribution and Employment: Economics of an Enterprise System* (Henry Holt, 1948, 1953); 3. *Barriers to New Competition: Their Character and Consequences in Manufacturing Industries* (Harvard Univ. Press, 1956); 4. *Industrial Organization* (Wiley, 1959, 1968); 5. *Northern California's Water Industry: the Comparative Efficiency of Public Enterprise in Developing a Scarce Natural Resource* (with R. E. Caves and J. Margolis), (Johns Hopkins Univ. Press, 1966); 6. *Essays on Price Theory and Industrial Organization* (Little, Brown & Co., 1972).
Principal Contributions Writing and teaching in the areas of price theory and industrial organisation, in which the latter augments and incorporates price theory, in so far as that explains and predicts market structure, conduct and performance – and their interrelationship. Most novel contribution has involved identifying and quantifying 'barriers to entry' as an important dimensions of market structures, finding their sources, spinning a theory of the effects of these barriers on efficiency and pricing in monopolised and oligopoly industries, measuring such barriers and testing for their predicted effects.
Secondary Literature *Essays on Industrial Organization in Honor of Joe*

S. Bain, eds. R. T. Masson and P. D. Qualls (Ballinger, 1976).

BALASSA, Bela

Born 1928, Budapest, Hungary.
Current Post Prof. Polit. Écon., Johns Hopkins Univ., 1967–.
Past Posts Cons., World Bank, Washington, DC, 1961–; Ass. Prof., Assoc. Prof., Yale Univ., 1959–67; Vis. Ass. Prof., Univ. Cal. Berkeley, 1961–2; Vis. Assoc. Prof., Columbia Univ., 1963–4; Prof. Associé, Univ. de Paris IX (Dauphine), 1971–2; Prof. Invité, Inst. d'Études Polit., Paris, 1983–4; Prof. Invité, Univ. de Paris 1 (Pantheon, Sorbonne), 1984.
Degrees Diplomkaufmann Hungary Academy Foreign Trade, 1948; Dr. juris rerumque Politicarum Univ. Budapest, 1951; MA, PhD Yale Univ., 1958, 1959.
Offices and Honours Pres., Assoc. Comparative Econ., 1970–1; Pres., Assoc. Comparative Econ. Stud., 1979–80; Laureate, Inst. de France, 1980; Bernhard Harms Prize Internat. Econ., 1984.
Editorial Duties Ed. Boards, *AER*, 1973–5, *PDR*, 1975–; Assoc. Ed., *J Int E*, *REStat*.
Principal Fields of Interest 110 Economic Growth; Development; and Planning Theory and Practice; 410 International Trade Theory; 420 Trade Relations; Commercial Policy; International Economic Integration.
Publications *Books:* 1. *The Hungarian Experience in Economic Planning* (Yale Univ. Press, 1959); 2. *The Theory of Economic Integration* (R. D. Irwin, 1961, 1973; Greenwood Press, 1982; transls. Japanese, Dayiyamondo, 1963, Spanish, UTEMA, 1964, Portuguese, M. Texeira, 1964, Czech, Makladatelstue Svobota, 1966); 3. *Trade Prospects for Developing Countries* (R. D. Irwin, 1964; transls. Spanish, Fondo de Cultura Econ., 1967, Portuguese, Victor Publicaciones, 1969); 4. *Trade Liberalization Among Industrial Countries: Objectives and Alternatives* (McGraw-Hill, 1967); 5. *The Structure of Protection in Developing Countries* (with others), (JHUP, 1971; transl.

Spanish, CEMLA, 1972); 6. *European Economic Integration* (with others), (N-H., 1975); 7. *Policy Reform in Developing Countries* (Pergamon, 1977; transls. Chinese, 1978, Spanish, CEMLA, 1979); 8. *The Newly Industrializing Countries in the World Economy* (Pergamon, 1981; transls. French, Economico, 1985, Spanish, CEMLA, 1984); 9. *Development Strategies in Semi-Industrial Economies* (with others), (JHUP, 1982); 10. *Change and Challenge in the World Economy* (Macmillan, 1985).
Articles: 1. 'Success criteria for economic systems', *YEE*, 1(1), 1960, repr. in *Comparative Economic Systems Models and Cases*, ed. M. Bornstein (Richard D. Irwin, 1965, 1969), and *Ekonomiska System*, ed. A. Lindbeck (AB Raben & Sjorgen, 1971); 2. 'An empirical demonstration of classical comparative costs theory', *REStat*, 45(3), Aug. 1963, repr. in *Echange International et Croissance*, ed. J. Lassudrie-Duchene (Ec., 1972); 3. 'The purchasing power parity doctrine: a reappraisal', *JPE*, 72(6), Dec. 1964, repr. in *International Finance*, ed. R. W. Cooper (Penguin, 1969), and *Intercambio y desarrollo*, ed. R. French-Davis (Fondo de Cultura Economica, 1981); 4. 'Tariff protection in industrial countries: an evaluation', *JPE*, 72(6), Dec. 1965, repr. in *Readings in International Economics*, eds. R. E. Caves and H. G. Johnson (Richard D. Irwin, 1978); 5. 'Tariff reductions and trade in manufacturers among the industrial countries', *AER*, 56(3), June 1966; 6. 'Trade creation and trade diversion in the European common market', *EJ*, 77, March 1967, repr. in *International Economic Integration*, ed. P. Robson (Penguin, 1971), and in *Integracion economica*, eds. S. Andic and S. Teitel (Fondo de Cultura Economica, 1977); 7. 'Growth strategies in semi-industrial countries', *QJE*, 84(1), Feb. 1970, repr. in *Bobbs-Merrill Reprints in Economics*, 23 (Bobbs-Merrill, 1972), and in *Revista Espanola de Economica*, Jan–April, 1971; 8. 'The changing pattern of comparative advantage in manufactured goods', *REStat*, 61(2), May 1979; 9. 'The process of industrial development and alternative development

strategies',in *Essays in International Finance*, 141, Dec. 1980, repr. in *International Economic Policies and their Theoretical Foundations*, ed. J. M. Letiche (Academic Press, 1982); 10. 'The economic consequences of social policies in the industrial countries', *Bernhard-Harms Memorial Lecture*, 11, 1984.

Principal Contributions Early work concerned the history of economic thought, in particular Karl Marx and J. S. Mill. Introduced concept of success criteria for economic systems, including static efficiency, dynamic efficiency, rate of economic growth, consumer satisfaction, and income distribution; subsequently suggested methods for measuring dynamic efficiency. Study on Hungarian planning was followed by work on economic reforms in Hungary and China and comparative investigations of developed, developing, and socialist economies. Book on the theory of economic integration remains standard reference; it was followed by work on trade liberalisation and on the practical experience of integration schemes. Introduced new methods to analyse trade creation and trade diversion and investigated the dynamic effects of integration.

Contributions to international economics included the development of new concepts, such as the effective rate of protection (simultaneously with H. G. Johnson and W. M. Corden), intra-industry vs. inter-industry specialisation, 'revealed' comparative advantage, and horizontal vs. vertical specialisation, as well as methods of analysis for the practical application of these concepts. Further developed the purchasing power parity doctrine and introduced the 'stages' approach to comparative advantage. Work on developing countries centred on policy choices. I was an early proponent of outward-oriented policies, and introduced new methods of analysis for the study of external shocks and policy responses to these shocks. The application of theoretical principles to practical situations led to advising in a large number of developing countries over the last two decades. Among developed countries, concentrated on the French economy and examined the economic consequence of social policies in Western Europe.

BALDWIN, Robert Edward

Born 1924, Niagara Falls, NY, USA.
Current Post Hilldale Prof. Econ., Univ. Wisconsin-Madison, Madison, WI, USA, 1982–.
Past Posts Instr., Univ. Buffalo, 1945–6; Instr., Ass. Prof., Harvard Univ., 1950–2, 1952–7; Assoc. Prof., Prof., Univ. Cal., Berkeley, 1957–62, 1962–4; Chief Econ., Office US Trade Representative, 1963–4; Prof., F. W. Taussig Res. Prof., Univ. Wisconsin, 1964–82, 1974; Res. Prof., Brookings Inst., 1967–8; Cons., US Dept. Labor, 1974–5, World Bank, 1978–9; Res. Assoc., NBER, 1982–.
Degrees BA Univ. Buffalo, 1945; PhD Harvard Univ., 1950.
Offices and Honours Ford Foundation Foreign Area Training Fellow, 1960–1; Ford Foundation Faculty Res. Fellow, 1969–70.
Editorial Duties Former Ed. Board, *AER*; Assoc. Ed., *J Int E, REStat, World Economy, PDR*.
Principal Fields of Interest 410 International Trade Theory;420 Trade Relations: Commercial Policy; International Integration; 120 Economic Development Studies.
Publications *Books:* 1. *Economic Development, Theory, History, Policy* (with G. M. Meier), (Wiley, 1957; transls., Spanish, Polish, Arabic, Vietnamese, Indonesian); 2. *Economic Development and Growth* (Wiley, 1966, 1972); 3. *Economic Development and Export Growth: A Study of Northern Rhodesia, 1920–1960* (Univ. Cal. Press, 1966); 4. *Nontariff Distortions of International Trade* (Brookings Inst., 1970; transl., Swedish); 5. *Disease and Economic Development: The Economic Impact of Parasitic Disease in St Lucia* (with B. Weisbrod, *et. al*), (Univ. Wisconsin Press, 1973); 6. *International Trade and Finance: Readings*, co-ed. (with J.D. Richardson), (Little Brown, 1974, 1981); 7. *Foreign Trade Regimes and Economic Development: The Philippines* (Univ. Chicago Press,

1975); 8. *Recent Issues and Initiatives in US Trade Policy*, ed. (NBER, 1984); 9. *The Structure and Evolution of Recent US Trade Policy*, co-ed. (with A. S. Krueger), (Univ. Chicago Press, 1984); 10. *The Political Economy of U.S. Import Policy* (MIT Press, 1986). *Articles:* 1. 'Equilibrium in international trade: a diagrammatic analysis', *QJE*, 62, Nov. 1948; 2. 'The new welfare economics and gains in international trade', *QJE*, 66, Feb. 1952, repr. in *Readings in International Trade*, eds. H.S. Ellis and L.A. Meltzler (Blakiston, 1968); 3. 'A comparison of welfare criteria', *REStud*, 21(2), 1954; 4.'The effects of tariffs on international and domestic prices', *QJE*, 74, Feb. 1960; 5. 'Export technology and development from a subsistence level', *EJ*, 73, March 1963; 6. 'The case against infant industry protection', *JPE*, 77(3), May–June 1969; 7. 'Determinants of the commodity structure of trade', *AER*, 61(1), March 1971; 8. 'Welfare effects on the United States of a significant multilateral tariff reduction', *J Int E*, 10(3), Aug. 1980; 9. 'The political economy of protectionism', in *Import Competition and Response*, ed. J. Bhagwati (Univ. Chicago Press, 1982); 10. 'The inefficiency of trade policy', *Essays in Internat. Fin.*, 150, Princeton Univ., 1982.

Principal Contributions Have divided research efforts between international trade and economic development. In trade theory developed the so-called 'Baldwin-envelope' to indicate the general equilibrium conditions under various trade policies and to compare the welfare implications of these different policies. Tested the Leontief Paradox with later US data and demonstrated the need for modifying the two-factor Heckscher-Ohlin model by taking account of human capital and differences in technology. In development, established the first undergraduate course at Harvard in this field and wrote with G. M. Meier one of the early texts on development. In study of Zambia demonstrated the significance of the form of export activities in shaping a country's development pattern. Later analysed trade and exchange rate policies in the Philippines.

After serving as first chief economist in Office of US Trade Representative became interested in trade policy, and wrote a book indicating the importance of nontariff trade distortion and the need to improve international trading rules governing their use. Also developed import model for quantifying the trade and employment effects of multilateral trade negotiations that reduce trade barriers. Recently have focussed on the political economy of trade policy, especially the manner in which US trade policy is implemented.

BALL, Robert James

Born 1933, Saffron Walden, Essex, England.

Current Post Prof. Econ., London Bus. School, London, UK, Chairman, Legal and General Group, London, UK, 1965–.

Past Posts Lect., Sr. Lect. Econ., Univ. Manchester, 1960–3, 1963–5; Principal, London Bus. School, London, 1972–84.

Degrees MA Univ. Oxford, 1957; PhD Univ. Penn., 1973.

Offices and Honours Fellow, Em Soc, RES; Companion, British Inst. Management; Knighted, 1984.

Editorial Duties Ed. Board, *Omega*.

Principal Fields of Interest 130 Economic Fluctuations: Forecasting Stabilisation and Inflation; 212 Construction and Use of Econometric Models; 311 Domestic Monetary and Financial Theory and Policy.

Publications *Books: 1. An Econometric Model of the United Kingdom* (with L. R. Klein, *et. al*), (Blackwell, 1961); 2. *Inflation and the Theory of Money* (A&U, 1964); 3. *Inflation*, co-ed. (with P. Doyle), (Penguin, 1969); 4. *The International Linkage of National Economic Models* (N-H, 1973); 5. *Money and Employment* (Macmillan, 1982). *Articles:* 1. 'Some econometrics of the determination of absolute prices and wages' (with L. R. Klein), *EJ*, 69, Sept. 1959; 2. 'The relationship between aggregate consumption and wealth' (with P. Drake), *Int ER*, 5, Jan. 1964; 3. 'Short term employment functions in British manufacturing industry' (with E. B. A. St Cyr), *REStud*, 33, July 1966; 4. 'An economic approach to short-run analysis of the UK economy, 1955–66' (with T. Burns), *OR Q.*, 19, Autumn 1968; 5. 'The inflationary mechanism in the United Kingdom economy' (with T. Burns), *AER*, 66(4), Sept. 1976, repr. in *The Managed Economy*, ed. C. Feinstein (OUP, 1983); 6. 'The role of exchange-rate changes in balance of payments adjustment: the United Kingdom case' (with T. Burns and J. Laury), *EJ*, 87, March 1977; 7. 'Stabilisation policy in Britain 1964–81' (with T. Burns), in *Demand Management*, ed. M. Posner (Heinemann Educational Books, 1978); 8. 'Long run portfolio equilibrium and balance of payments adjustments in econometric models' (with T. Burns), in *Modelling the International Transmission Mechanism* (N-H, 1979); 9. 'The London Business School model of the UK economy: an exercise in international monetarism' (with T. Burns and P. J. Warburton), in *Economic Modelling*, ed., P. Ormerod (Heinemann, 1980).

Principal Contributions Development and practical usage of econometric forecasting and policy methods relating to the UK economy. Continuous interest in matters relating to inflation, and general macroeconomic policy. Ancillary contributions have been made to the determination of specific economic variables such as wage rates (1959), consumption (1963 and 1964), interest rates (1965), employment (1966), inventories and investment (1963 and 1964), exports (1966) and prices (1972).

BALOGH, Thomas*

Dates and Birthplace 1905–85, Budapest, Hungary.

Posts Held Res. Ass., Banque de France, Reichsbank, 1930–4; Lect., Univ. Coll. London, 1934–40; Fellow, Balliol Coll. Oxford, 1945–73; Reader Econ., Univ. Oxford, 1960–73; UK Minister of Energy, 1974–5; Deputy Chairman, British Nat. Oil Corp., 1976–9; Hon. Res. Fellow, University Coll. London, 1979–85.

Degrees Dr Rer. pol., Hon. Dr Econ. Budapest Univ., 1927, 1977; MA Univ. Oxford, 1945.

Offices and Honours Rockefeller Foundation Fellow, 1928–30; Deputy Chief, UN Refugee Admin. Mission Hungary, 1946–7; Econ. Adviser, Indian Planning Commission, 1955, 1960, Govt. Malta, 1955–7, Govt. Jamaica, 1956, FAO, 1957–9, UNECA, 1960; UK Cabinet, 1964–7.

Publications *Books:* 1. *Studies in Financial Organisation* (CUP, 1946); 2. *Unequal Partners* (Blackwell, 1963); 3. *Economics of Poverty* (Weidenfeld & Nicholson, 1966); 4. *Labour and Inflation* (Fabian Soc., 1970); 5. *Fact and Fancy in International Economic Relations* (Pergamon, 1971); 6. *The Irrelevance of Conventional Economics* (Weidenfeld & Nicholson, 1982). *Articles:* 1. 'The apotheosis of the dilettante', in *The Establishment*, ed. H. Thomas (Bond, 1959).

Career Early postwar advocate of foreign exchange controls and an incomes policy in the face of what he predicted would be a chronic 'dollar shortage' for the foreseeable future. As an influential adviser to Wilson's UK Labour Government in the 1960s, he failed to convince Wilson to devalue. In the 1970s he played a key role in recasting UK policy on North Sea oil. His *Irrelevance of Conventional Economics* underlined his lifelong dislike of neoclassical economics.

BARAN, Paul Alexander*

Dates and Birthplace 1910–64, Ukraine, Russia.

Posts Held Res. Assoc., Inst. Social Res., Frankfurt, Germany, 1931–3; Econ., US Office Strategic Service, Washington, DC, 1940–7; Prof. Econ., Stanford Univ., 1948–64.

Degrees PhD Univ. Berlin, 1932; MA Harvard Univ., 1941.

Publications *Books:* 1. *The Political Economy of Growth* (1957); 2. *Monopoly Capital* (with P. M. Sweezy), (1966); 3. *The Longer View: Essays Toward a Critique of Political Economy* (1969).

Career Generally considered the intellectual founder of the 'dependency' school which holds that economic development in the advanced capitalist countries is functionally related to underdevelopment in the Third World. One of the foremost Marxist theorists in the West of the monopoly stage of capitalist development.

Secondary Literature *Paul A. Baran 1910–1964: A Collective Portrait*, eds. P. M. Sweezy and L. Huberman (Monthly Review Press, 1965).

BARDHAN, Pranab Kumar

Born 1939, Calcutta, India.
Current Post Prof. Econ., Univ. Cal. Berkeley, CA, USA, 1977–.
Past Posts Lect. Econ., Calcutta Univ., Ass. Prof., 1961–2; Prof. Econ., MIT, 1966–9; Prof., Indian Stat. Inst., New Delhi, 1969–73; Prof., Delhi School Econ., 1973–6.
Degrees BA Presidency Coll., Calcutta 1958; MA Calcutta Univ., 1960; PhD Univ. Camb., 1966.
Offices and Honours Stevenson Prize, Univ. Camb., 1964; Indian Universities Grants Commission Nat. Lect., 1975; Guggenheim Foundation Fellow, 1981–2; US SSRC Fellow, 1982–3.
Editorial Duties Ed. Board, *AER, Indian Econ. Rev.*; Co-ed., *Sankhya*; Assoc. Ed., *Int ER*.
Principal Fields of Interest 410 International Trade Theory; 130 Economic Growth: Development and Planning; 710 Agriculture.
Publications *Books:* 1. *Economic Growth, Development and Foreign Trade: A Study in Pure Theory* (Wiley, 1970); 2. *Poverty and Income Distribution in India*, co-ed. (with T. N. Srinivasan), (Stat Publishing Soc., 1974); 3. *Agrarian Relations in West Bengal* (with A. Rudra), (Somaiya, 1983); 4. *Land, Labour and Rural Poverty: Essays in Development Economics* (Columbia Univ. Press, 1984); 5. *The Political Economy of Development in India* (Blackwell, 1984).
Articles: 1. 'Equilibrium growth in the international economy', *QJE*, 79(3), Aug. 1965; 2. 'International trade theory in a vintage capital model', *Em*, 34, Oct. 1966; 3. 'Equilibrium growth with economic obsolescence of machines', *QJE*, 83(2), May 1969; 4. 'On optimum subsidy to a learning industry: an aspect of the theory of infant industry protection', *Int ER*, 12(1), Feb. 1971; 5. 'Optimum growth and allocation of foreign exchange', *Em*, 39(6), Nov. 1971; 6. 'On life and death questions', *Econ. and Polit. Weekly*, Aug. 1974; 7. 'Wages and unemployment in a poor agrarian economy', *JPE*, 87(3), June 1979; 8. 'Interlocking factor markets and agrarian development', *OEP*, 32(1), March 1980; 9. 'Imports, domestic production and transnational vertical integration', *JPE*, 90(4), 1982; 10. 'Labour tying in a poor agrarian economy', *QJE*, 97(3), Aug. 1983.
Principal Contributions My early work mostly involved formal models of economic growth and international trade. Since then my interests have branched out into the area of economic development, particularly agrarian institutions, implicit contracts in land, labour and credit transactions, and the interrelationship between the State and social and economic structures.

BARLOW, Robin

Born 1934, Blackburn, Lancashire, England.
Current Post Prof. Econ., Dir., Center Res. Econ. Devlp., Univ. Michigan, USA, 1978–.
Past Posts Ass. Prof., Assoc. Prof., Univ. Michigan, 1961–78; Vis. Prof., Univ. Clermont-Ferrand, France, 1981–2, 1984.
Degrees BA Univ. Oxford, 1954; MBA, PhD Univ. Michigan, 1958, 1961.
Offices and Honours Ford Foundation Foreign Area Training Fellow, 1959–61.
Principal Fields of Interest 121 Economic Studies of Less Industrialised Countries; 841 Demographic Economics; 913 Economics of Wealth.
Publications *Books:* 1. *Economic Behavior of the Affluent* (with H. E. Brazer and J. N. Morgan), (Brookings Inst., 1966); 2. *The Economic Effects of*

Malaria Eradication (Bureau Public Health Econ., Univ. Michigan, 1969); 3. *A Resource Allocation Model for Child Survival* (with H. N. Barnum, L. Fajardo and A. Pradilla), (Oelgeschlager, Gunn and Hain, 1980); 4. *Case Studies in the Demographic Impact of Asian Development Projects*, ed. (Center Res. Econ. Devlp., Univ. Michigan, 1982).

Articles: 1. 'Efficiency aspects of local school finance', *JPE*, 78(5), Sept–Oct. 1970; 2. 'Policy analysis with a disaggregated economic-demographic model' (with G. W. Davies), *JPE*, 3(1), Feb. 1974; 3. 'Applications of a health planning model in Morocco', *Internat. J Health Services*, 6, 1976; 4. 'A test of alternative methods of making GNP comparisons', *EJ*, 87, Sept. 1977; 5. 'Health and economic development: a theoretic and empirical review', in *Research in Human Capital and Development* (JAI Press, 1979); 6. 'Economic growth in the Middle East, 1950–72', *Internat. J Middle Eastern Stud.*, 14, 1982.

Principal Contributions Health economics and public finance. Estimated the economic effects of malaria control in Sri Lanka by using a large-scale model to simulate the growth of per capita income with and without control. Measured the cost-effectiveness of selected health interventions in Morocco and Colombia. In the Colombian study, undertaken with H. N. Barnum, linear programming techniques were used in discovering the optimal set of interventions against infant mortality. Used a median-voter model to estimate whether the property tax in Michigan led to an excessive or inadequate level of school expenditures. Collaborated in a survey of the working and investing behaviour of high-income Americans. Studied problems of comparing the national incomes of different countries, with particular reference to the Middle East.

BARNETT, Andy Hubbard

Born 1945, Westminster, SC, USA.
Current Post Assoc. Prof. Econ.,

Auburn Univ., Auburn, AL, USA, 1982–.

Past Posts Instr. Clemson Univ., 1970–2; Instr., Assoc. Prof., Univ. S. Carolina, 1975–82.

Degrees BA Presbyterian Coll., 1968; MA Clemson Univ., 1970; PhD Univ. Virginia, 1978.

Principal Fields of Interest 024 Welfare Theory; 320 Public Finance; 720 Natural Resources.

Publications *Books:* 1. *The US Textile Mill Products Industry: Strategies for the 1980s and Beyond* (with B. Toyne, *et al.*), (Univ. S. Carolina Press, 1983); 2. *The Global Textile Industry* (with B. Toyne, *et al.*), (A&U, 1984).

Articles: 1. 'Allocating environmental resources' (with B. Yandle, Jr.), *PF*, 28(1), 1973; 2. 'Old answers to "new" problems: Henry George, property rights and environmental quality' (with B. Yandle, Jr.), *Amer. J Econ. and Sociology*, 33, Oct. 1974; 3. 'The Pigouvian tax rule under monopoly', *AER*, 70(5), Dec. 1980; 4. 'An extension of the Dolbear triangle' (with J. Bradley, Jr.), *SEJ*, 47(1), Jan. 1981; 5. 'A scheme for soliciting accurate evaluations of public goods', *Public Fin. Q.*, 9, Apr. 1981; 6. 'The impact of unions and productivity: a skeptical view' (with J. T. Addison), *BJIR*, 20(2), July 1982; 7. 'Taxation and pollution control: an illustration', *Rev. Regional Stud.*, June, 1984.

Principal Contributions Initial efforts in economics were concerned with natural resources, including the evolution of property rights, optimal control of environmental externalities and public policy. More recent works deal with the theory of externalities and public goods, with brief diversions into labour and industrial organisation. Current interests are in social decision mechanisms and market failures.

BARON, David P.

Born 1940, Kankakee, IL, USA.
Current Post Prof. Bus., Econ. and the Environment, Grad. School Bus., Stanford Univ., Stanford, CA, USA, 1981–.

Past Posts Prof., Grad. School Management, Northwestern Univ., Evanston, IL, 1968–81; Vis. Prof., Univ. D'Aux-Marseille, France, 1973–4, Katholieke Univ. Leuven, Belgium, 1977–8.

Degrees BS Univ. Michigan, 1962; MBA Harvard Univ., 1964; DBA Indiana Univ., 1968.

Editorial Duties Ed. Board, *AER*, 1975–8; Assoc. Ed., *Decision Science*, 1978–83.

Principal Fields of Interest 020 General Economic Theory; 610 Industrial Organisation and Public Policy.

Publications Books: 1. *The Export–Import Bank: An Economic Analysis* (Academic Press, 1983).

Articles: 1. 'Flexible exchange rates, forward markets, and the level of trade', *AER*, 66(1), March 1976; 2. 'A model of regulation under uncertainty and a test of regulatory bias' (with R. A. Taggart), *Bell JE*, 8, Spring 1977; 3. 'On the relationship between complete and incomplete financial market models', *Int ER*, 20, Feb. 1979; 4. 'Models of the firm and international trade under uncertainty' (with R. Forsythe), *AER*, 69(4), Sept. 1979; 5. 'The investment banking contract for new issues under asymmetric information: deregulation and the incentive problem' (with B. Holstrom), *J Fin*, 35, Dec. 1980; 6. 'On the design of regulatory price adjustment mechanisms' (with R. DeBondt), *JET*, 24, Feb. 1981; 7. 'Price regulation, quality, and asymmetric information', *AER*, 71(1), March 1981; 8. 'Regulating a monopolist with unknown costs' (with R. B. Myerson), *Em*, 50, July 1982; 9. 'Regulation and information in a continuing relationship' (with D. Besanko), *Information Econ. and Pol.*, 1984; 10. 'Regulation, asymmetric information, and auditing' (with D. Besanko), *Rand JE*, 15, Dec. 1984.

Principal Contributions Contributed to the theory of information economics, choice under uncertainty, and industrial organisation. Applied research has focussed on regulation, export financing, corporate finance, and investment banking. Current interests are regulation, industrial organisation, public policy, and political economy.

BARONE, Enrico*

Dates and Birthplace 1859–1924, Italy.

Post Held Army Officer; Prof., War Coll., Turin; Prof., Istituto di Scienze Econ., Rome, 1907.

Publications *Books:* 1. *Le Opere Economiche*, 3 vols (1894–1924, 1936–7).

Articles: 1. 'The ministry of production in the collectivist state', 1908, in *Collectivist Economic Planning*, ed. F. A. Hayek (1935); 2. 'Related costs in the economics of transport', *Giornale degli Economisti*, 1921, repr. in *Internat. Econ. Papers*, 5, eds. A. T. Peacock *et al.* (Macmillan, 1955).

Career One of the outstanding early mathematical economists, whose chief contribution was made whilst serving as an army officer. Introduced to economics by Pantaleoni, his major achievements were in international trade theory, the theory of the firm, welfare economics and general equilibrium theory. In international trade theory, he used the concept of consumer surplus to demonstrate that protective tariffs tend to reduce economic welfare. His work on the theory of the firm, largely unpublished and now lost, used marginal productivity analysis as the basis of the firm's supply functions for output and demand functions for inputs. He then used this to refine the Walrasian analysis of general equilibrium. His demonstration that a ministry of production in a collectivist economy could plan production rationally is perhaps his best known contribution.

Secondary Literature R. E. Kuenne, 'Barone, Enrico', *IESS*, 2.

BARRO, Robert J.

Born 1944, New York City, NY, USA.

Current Post Disting. Prof. Arts, Sciences and Econ., Univ. Rochester, USA, 1984–.

Past Posts Ass. Prof. Econ., Brown Univ., 1968–72; Assoc. Prof., Prof. Econ., Univ. Chicago, 1973–5, 1982–4; Prof. Econ., Univ. Rochester, 1975–82; Vis. Fellow, Hoover Inst., Stanford Univ., 1977–8; Res. Assoc., NBER, 1978–.

Degrees BS (Physics) Cal. Inst. Technology, 1965; PhD Harvard Univ., 1969.

Offices and Honours Fellow, Em Soc, 1980–.

Editorial Duties Ed., *JPE*, 1973–5, 1982–4; NSF Rev. Panel Econ., 1976–8; Assoc. Ed., *J Mon E*, 1976–80, 1984, *Em*, 1978–81.

Principal Fields of Interest 023 Macroeconomic Theory.

Publications *Books:* 1. *Money, Employment and Inflation* (with H. Grossman), (CUP, 1976); 2. *The Impact of Social Security on Private Savings* (AEI, 1978); 3. *Money, Expectations, and Business Cycles* (Academic Press, 1981); 4. *Macroeconomics* (Wiley, 1984).

Articles: 1. 'A general disequilibrium model of income and employment' (with H. Grossman), *AER*, 61(1), March 1971; 2. 'Are government bonds net wealth?', *JPE*, 82(6), Nov.–Dec. 1974; 3. 'Rational expectations and the role of monetary policy', *J Mon E*, 2(1), Jan. 1976; 4. 'Unanticipated money growth and unemployment in the United States', *AER*, 67(3), March 1977; 5. 'On the determination of the public debt', *JPE*, 87(5), pt. 1, Oct. 1979; 6. 'A positive theory of monetary policy in a natural rate model' (with D. Gordon), *JPE*, 91(4), Aug. 1983.

Principal Contributions Development of the 'new classical macroeconomics'. Stressed the implications of incomplete information and rational expectations for understanding the business-cycle role of money and for evaluating monetary policy. Empirical work has sought to test the 'natural rate' hypothesis, with stress on the distinction between anticipated and unanticipated movements in monetary aggregates. Recent research involves the application of analogous approaches to the fiscal area, including analyses of public debt, government expenditures and tax rates. Conditions for the neutrality of deficits (the 'Ricardian theorem') have been studied, as has the relation of optimal taxation over time to a positive theory of debt creation. Earlier research concerned developments of the disequilibrium (Keynesian) approach to macro-analysis.

BARTEN, Anton Peter

Born 1930, Amsterdam, The Netherlands.

Current Post Prof. Econ., Catholic Univ. Louvain, Leuven, Belgium, 1971–.

Past Posts Staff, Centraal Planbureau, The Hague, Netherlands, 1955–60; Res. Assoc. Em, Netherlands School Econ., Rotterdam, Netherlands, 1960–6; Acting Assoc. Prof. Econ., Univ. Cal. Berkeley, 1962–3; Res. Assoc., Social Systems Res. Inst., Univ. Wisconsin, Madison, 1963; Res. Prof. Econ. and Social Sciences, Catholic Univ. Louvain, Belgium, 1966–71; Staff, Dir., CORE, Univs. Louvain, Brussels, 1966–9, 1971–4; Vis. Prof. Em, Grad. School Bus., Univ. Chicago, 1969–70, Univ. Penn., Philadelphia, PA, 1984.

Degrees Dr. Univ. Amsterdam, 1957; Dr. Netherlands School Econ., Rotterdam, 1966.

Offices and Honours Kluwer Award Social Sciences, 1968; Fellow, Em Soc. 1969–; Fellow, Assoc. Scientifique Européenne d'Economie Appliquée, 1969–; Officer Order Crown Belgium, 1975.

Editorial Duties Assoc. Ed., *Em*, 1969–72; Ed. Board, *Europ. ER* 1969–.

Principal Fields of Interest 022 Microeconomics Theory; 210 Econometric, Statistical, and Mathematical Methods and Models; 920 Consumer Economics.

Publications *Books:* 1. *Theorie en Empirie van een Volledig Stelsel van Vraagvergelijkingen* (Pasmans, 1966); 2. *Technisch-economisch Model van de Energieproductie* (with Y. Smeers, and others), (Programmatie van het Wetenschapsbeleid, 1978); 3. *Methodological Aspects of Macroeconomic Model Construction* (Cabay, 1981); 4. *Energy, The Evaluation of the Communities' Geothermal Energy, Production and Utilization of Hydrogen, and Systems Analysis: Development of Models R & D Subprogrammes* (with A. D. Brown, and others), (Directorate General Res. Science and Educ., Commission OEEC, 1981).

Articles: 1. 'Consumer demand functions under conditions of almost additive preferences', *Em*, 32, Jan.–April 1964; 2. 'Family composition, prices and expenditure patterns' in *Econometric Analysis for National Economic Planning* (Butterworths, 1964); 3. 'Evidence on the Slutsky conditions for demand equations', *REStat*, 49, Feb. 1967; 4. 'Estimating demand equations', *Em*, 36, April 1968; 5. 'Maximum likelihood estimation of a complete system of demand equations', *Europ ER*, 1(1), Jan. 1969; 6. 'An import allocation model for the Common Market', *Cahiers économiques de Bruxelles*, 50, 1971; 7. 'The negativity condition in consumer demand' (with E. Geyskens), *Europ ER*, 6(3), July 1975; 8. 'COMET, a medium-term macroeconomic model for the European Economic Community' (with G. d'Alcantara and G. J. Carrin), *Europ ER*, 7(1), Jan. 1976; 9. 'The systems of consumer demand functions approach: a review', *Em*, 45(1), Jan. 1977, repr. in *Frontiers of Quantitative Economics* ed. M. D. Intriligator (N-H, 1977); 10. 'Consumer theory' (with V. Bohm), in *Handbook of Mathematical Economics, II*, ed. M. D. Intriligator (N-H, 1982).

Principal Contributions One line of research consists in the development of the Hicks–Allen approach to consumer theory into the direction of a tool of empirical analysis. This has involved further elaboration of the theory (e.g. the Fundamental Matrix Equation of Demand Theory), collection of data (Netherlands 1921–62), functional form specification (with H. Theil, the Rotterdam system) and statistical methodology of allocation systems (invariance for identity of residual class, negative definite matrix estimation). As a by-product, the way in which family composition may affect consumption patterns was elaborated.

Another line of research goes back to the beginning of my professional career as a member of the team for the construction of a macroeconometric model for The Netherlands to be used by the Central Planning Bureau. Since the late 1960s, macroeconometric model construction has been undertaken for and under contract with the European Commission. This project consists of an interlinked set of identically specified national sub-models for EEC member-countries. In the course of its existence, this COMET model has developed into a worldwide model with emphasis on the EEC.

BARTOLI, Henri

Born 1918, Lyon, France.
Current Post Prof. Econ., Univ. Paris I Panthéon Sorbonne, Paris, 1971–.
Past Posts Ass. Faculté de Droit de Lyon, 1941–3; Thiers Fellow, Ass. Facilité de Droit, Paris, 1943–4; Inst. de Science Econ. Appliquée, 1944–5; Prof. Faculté de Droit et des Sciences Econ., Grenoble, 1945–59; Prof. Faculté de Droit et des Sciences Econ., Paris, 1959–71; Cons., Missions, Angleterre, 1945, Pologne, 1955, 1962, Chine Populaire, 1958, URSS, 1958, Algérie, 1962, 1964, 1970, 1983, Maroc, 1963, 1979, Portugal, 1975, Canada, 1979, Cameroun, 1979, Tunisie, 1981, Bénin et Togo, 1982, Italie, 1962, 1981, 1982, Grèce, 1982, 1983.
Degrees Baccalauréat, Licence Droit Doctorat en Droit Univ. Lyon, 1937, 1940, 1943; Agrégation de l'Enseignement Supérieur, 1945.
Offices and Honours Cabinet, Ministre de l'Economie, Governement Provisoire de France, Août–Nov., 1944; Econ. Comm., CNRS, 1965–74; Boards Dir., ISMEA, CREDOC, CRESST; Advisory Comm., Vie sociale dans l'enterprise, French Ministry Industrie et Recherche; Member, Conseil Nat. de l'Enseignement Supérieur, 1970–5; Officier de la Légion d'Honneur; L'Ordre Nat. du Mérite; La Médaille de la Résistance.
Editorial Duties Ed. Boards, *Esprit*, 1945, 1976, *Econ. App.*, 1950–, *Cahiers de l'Inst. de Science Econ App* (*Economies et Sociétés*), 1950–, *RISE*, 1962.
Principal Fields of Interest 031 History of Economic Thought; 053 Comparative Economic Systems; 800 Manpower, Labour, Population.
Publications *Books:* 1. *Essai d'étude théorique de l'autofinancement de la nation* (Vinay 1943); 2. *Le financement de la reprise* (Domat-Montchrestien 1945); 3. *La doctrine économique et social de Karl Marx* (Seuil, 1950); 4. *Science économique et travail* (Dallox, 1957; trad., Italien, Scienza Economica

e Lavoro, 1967); 5. *Economie et création collective* (Economica, 1977).

Articles: 1. 'La méthod marxiste', in *Actes du Congrès des economistes de langue française* (Domat-Montchrestien, 1950); 2. 'Théories marxistes', in *Fluctuations cycliques* (Domat-Montchrestien, 1954); 3. 'Note sur le déterminisme et l'indeterminisme en économique', *Cahiers de l'Inst. de Science Écon App.*, Dec. 1958; 4. 'La rationalité des décisions de politique économique et la crise du pouvoir dans les nations capitalistes industrielles', *Econ App*, Jan.–Feb., 1962; 5. 'Mathematisation du temps économique et adequation du cadre theorique au cadre réel', *RISE*, 9, 1962; 6. 'Analyse et signification des migrations de main d'oeuvre', *Cahiers de l'Inst. de Science Econ App*, Sept. 1966; 7. 'Emploi et industrialisation', *Econ App*, Dec. 1968; 8. 'La stratégie des besoins essentiels face aux situations d'extrême pauvreté', *Economies et Sociétés*, Jan. 1980; 9. 'Pertinence et actualité du concept de plein emploi', in *Population travail, chômage* (Economica, 1982); 10. 'Le problème des régions dans la pensée économique', *Annali di Economia e Giornale Degli Economisti*, 9–10, 1983.

Principal Contributions My early works concentrated on the financing of the French economy during and after the war, as well as on problems of the history of economic thought (Physiocratic theory of value). In the following period, many of my works were concerned with Marx's economic thought and Marxist method. My book *La doctrine économique et sociale de Karl Marx* was the result of that research. In the 1950s, my interests turned to labour economics and to comparative systems. This led to the preparation of my advanced text, *Science économique et travail*, and the creation in 1967 of the 'Séminaire d'économie du travail', of which I assumed the direction. The principal research themes of the seminar are: employment, wages, manpower programmes, working conditions, human labour costs, industrial relations, poverty (see Nos. 7, 8, 9 above).

In my view, labour is the fundamental economic category from which all economics may be elaborated. The interpretation of economics in my book arises from the idea of work as the source of social/production relations. As far as the contents of the formal principles of economic reasoning are concerned, priority is given to assuring the basic necessities of life (basic needs) at the lowest human cost to labour, and the book proposes a new conception of economic systems as a combination of sub-systems (economic, legal, social, cultural, technological, etc.) which are partially autonomous and are governed by the characteristics of various periods in time. More recently, I have also studied some aspects of cultural economics, which has led to the creation, under my direction, of a research group on the economy of the theatre, music, and painting, in the framework of the Seminar on Labour Economics. Italian speaking, I am the writer of the periodic Italian thought chronicle in *RE* and am writing a book about the history of Italian economic thought.

BARTON, John*

Dates and Birthplace 1789–1852, London, England.

Post Held Private income.

Publications *Books:* 1. *Economic Writings*, 2 vols, ed. G. Sotiroff (1962).

Career His fame arose from one incident: Ricardo's reading of Barton's *Observations* . . . caused him to change his mind on the question of whether the introduction of machines could ever harm the working class. The third (1821) edition of Ricardo's *Principles* includes a new chapter on machinery, incorporating Barton's pessimistic analysis of the effects of machinery. Although Barton published several other pamphlets, his analysis never reached the same level of originality and his views were largely ignored. His attempts to influence opinion through his political correspondence with the Duke of Richmond and his membership of the Statistical Society were similarly ineffective.

Secondary Literature G. Sotiroff, 'Barton, John', *IESS*, 2.

BARZEL, Yoram

Born 1931, Jerusalem.
Current Post Prof. Econ., Univ. Washington, USA, 1970–.
Past Posts Ass. Prof., Assoc. Prof. Econ., Univ. Washington, 1961–6, 1966–70; Res. Fellow, Falk Foundation, Jerusalem, Israel, 1963–4; Vis. Res. Fellow, Univ. Coll., London, 1970–1; Vis. Scholar, Hoover Inst., Stanford Univ., 1974–5, 1981–2; Vis. Prof. Econ., Washington Univ., St Louis, MO, 1984.
Degrees BA, MA Hebrew Univ., 1953, 1956; PhD Univ. Chicago, 1961.
Offices and Honours Univ. Fellow, Hebrew Univ., 1954–5; Univ. Fellow, Univ. Chicago, 1957–8; Ford Foundation Fellow, 1960–1; Ford Faculty Fellow, 1970–1.
Principal Fields of Interest 022 Microeconomic Theory; 611 Market Structure.
Publications *Books:* 1. *The Political Economy of the Oil Import Quota* (with C. D. Hall), (Hoover Inst. Press, Stanford Univ., 1977).
Articles: 1. 'The production function and technical change in steam-power industry', *JPE*, 72, April 1964; 2. 'The optimal timing of innovations', *REStat*, 50, Aug. 1968; 3. 'Excess capacity in monopolistic competition', *JPE*, 78(5), Sept.–Oct. 1970; 4. 'Investment, scale and growth', *JPE*, 79(1), March–April 1971; repr. in *Benefit Cost Analysis* (Aldine–Atherton, 1972); 5. 'Assets, subsistence, and the supply curve of labor' (with R. J. McDonald), *AER*, 63(4), Sept. 1973; 6. 'A theory of rationing by waiting', *J Law E*, 17(1), April 1974; 7. 'An alternative approach to the analysis of taxation', *JPE*, 84(6), Dec. 1976; 8. 'An economic analysis of slavery', *J Law E*, 20(1), April 1977; 9. 'Some fallacies in the interpretation of information costs', *J Law E*, 20(2), Oct. 1977; 10. 'Measurement costs and the organization of markets', *J Law E*, 25(1), April 1982.
Principal Contributions In the first phase of my research I concentrated on the microeconomics of technical change. My studies of the electric power industry showed that the increase in output per unit of input was largely accounted for by increases in the scale of operations. Questions of innovations induced by scale, and of 'premature' innovative activity in the competition to capture the returns were explored next. Subsequent work looked at methods of public choice related to public goods. The next stage in my work, greatly influenced by Steven N. S. Cheung, is concerned with the costs of transacting and the specifications of property rights. The central idea is that because of costs such as measuring, metering and policing the terms of exchange, rights to the gains from trade in any transaction are not fully delineated. Transactors may attempt to capture these gains, using resources in the process. However, both individually, and in their aggregate behaviour, transactors will erect institutions and impose constraints on themselves to reduce the loss from competing the gains away. My main endeavour is to explain the existence of private and government constraints such as the 'pig in a poke', tie-in sales, and the prohibition of price discrimination. The work also attempts to provide a rationale for institutions such as voting in the economic sphere, the existence of consumer-owned production facilities and the prevalence of non-profit organisations. These explanations attempt to be operational: refutable implications are derived from transaction costs considerations; many are capable of being tested by using readily available, 'conventional' data.

BASEVI, Giorgio

Born 1938, Genoa, Italy.
Current Post Prof. Internat. Econ., Univ. Bologna, Bologna, Italy, 1976–.
Past Posts Econ., EEC, Brussels, 1965–6; Assoc. Prof., Univ. Catholique de Louvain, Belgium, 1966–71; Assoc. Prof., Univ. Bologna, 1971–6; Vis. Prof., Johns Hopkins Univ., Bologna Center, 1967–84, Univ. Libre de Bruxelles, 1973–5, Univ. Catholique de Louvain, 1974–7, Katholike Univ. Leuven, 1974–6, Univ. de Montreal, 1982.
Degrees Laurea Econ. Univ. Genoa, 1961; MA, PhD Univ. Chicago, 1962, 1965.

Editorial Duties Ed. Board, *Empirical Econ.*

Principal Fields of Interest 310 domestic Monetary and Financial Theory; 410 International Trade Theory; 430 Balance of Payments; International Finance.

Publications *Books:* 1. *Teoria pura del Commercio Internazionale* (Angeli, 1967); 2. *La Billancia dei Pagamenti*, ed. (Mulino, 1971); 3. *La Bilancia dei Pagamenti Italiana* (with A. Soci), (Mulino, 1978); 4. *West Germany: A European and Global Power*, co-ed. (with W. L. Kohl), (D. C. Heath, 1980); 5. *Macroeconomic Prospects and Policies for the European Community* (with R. Dornbusch, O. Blanchard, W. Buiter and R. Layard), (Centre Europ. Policy Stud., 1983).

Articles: 1. 'Vault cash and the shift in the desired level of free reserves', *JPE*, 71(4), Aug. 1963; 2. 'The United States tariff structure: estimates of effective rates of protection of US industries and industrial labour', *REStat*, 48(2), May 1966; 3. 'The restrictive effect of the US tariff and its welfare value', *AER*, 58(4), Sept. 1968; 4. 'Domestic demand and ability to export', *JPE*, 78(2), March–April 1970; 5. 'Aggregation problems in the measurement of effective protection', in *Effective Tariff Protection*, eds. H. G. Grubel and H. G. Johnson (Grad. Inst. Internat. Stud., 1971); 6. 'Commodity trade equations in project Link', in *The International Linkage of National Economic Models*, ed. P. J. Ball (N-H, 1973); 7. 'Balances of payments and exchange markets. A cost correspondence', *Europ ER*, 4, Dec. 1973; 8. 'The 1974 increase in oil price: optimum tariff on transfer problem?' (with A. Steinherr), *WA*, 112(2), 1976; 9. 'Vicious and virtuous circles. A theoretical analysis and a policy proposal for managing exchange rates' (with P. de Grauwe), *Europ ER*, 10, 1977; 10. 'Monetary authorities' reaction functions in a model of exchange-rate determination for the European monetary system' (with M. Calzolari), in *Exchange Rates in Multicountry Econometric Models*, eds. P. de Grauwe and T. Peeters (Macmillan, 1983).

Principal Contributions My first few years of research were mainly in the field of pure trade theory, particularly with reference to protectionism. I soon felt, however, that the Heckscher-Ohlin-Samuelson paradigm was subject to rapidly decreasing returns to research efforts, or at least to mine. I then moved my interests to the theory and policy of balance of payments and exchange rate determination. In between, however, particularly during the early 1970s, I was heavily involved in building a large econometric model for Italy within Project LINK directed by Lawrence Klein at the University of Pennsylvania. At present my interests go beyond both the real and monetary theory of international economics. I am currently working on the stability characteristics of economies burdened by large public and foreign debt. While my best-known publications probably remain the first ones connected with the theory of effective protection, I feel that the problems I am dealing with at present are more interesting and may lead me to some positive contribution.

BASMANN, Robert Leon

Born 1926, Davenport, IA, USA.

Current Post Sr. Res. Fellow, Univ. Texas, Austin, TX, Prof. Econ., Texas A & M Univ., College Station, TX, USA, 1976–.

Past Posts Vis. Ass. Prof., Northwestern Univ., 1956–7; Econ., Res. Specialist, General Electric Co., 1957–61; Assoc. Prof. Econ., Univ. Chicago, 1961–3; Vis. Prof. Econ., Univ. Minnesota, 1963; Prof. Econ., Purdue Univ., 1963–9; J. Fishsmith Prof. Econ., Brigham Young Univ., 1974; Adjunct Prof., Univ. New Mexico, 1976.

Degrees BS(Science), MS, PhD Iowa State Univ., 1950, 1953, 1955.

Offices and Honours Fulbright Scholar, Univ. Oslo, Norway, 1955–6; Fellow, Em Soc., 1966; *WEJ* Best Article Award, 1973.

Editorial Duties Co-Ed., *Advances in Em* (JAI Press).

Principal Fields of Interest 211 Econometric and Statistical Models; 610 Industrial Organisation and Policy; 020 General Economic Theory.

Publications *Articles:* 1. 'A theory of

demand with variable consumer preferences', *Em*, 24, Jan. 1956, repr. in *The Evolution of Modern Demand Theory*, eds. R. Ekelund, W. P. Gramm and E. Furuboth (D. C. Heath, 1971); 2. 'A generalised classical method of linear estimation of coefficients in a structural equation', *Em*, 25, Jan. 1957, repr. in *Selected Readings in Econometrics from Econometrica*, eds. J. W. Hooper and M. Nerlove (MIT Press, 1970); 3. 'On finite sample distributions of generalized classical linear identifiability test statistics', *JASA*, 56, Dec. 1960, repr. in *Readings in Econometric Theory*, eds. J. M. Dowling and F. R. Glahe (Colorado Univ. Press, 1970); 4. 'Remarks concerning the application of exact finite sample distribution function of GCL estimators in econometric statistical inference', *JASA*, 58, Dec. 1963; 5. 'The role of the economic historian in predictive testing of proffered "economic laws"', *Explorations Entrepreneurial Hist.*, 2(3), 1965, repr. in *The New Economic History*, ed. R. Andreano (Wiley & Sons, 1970); 6. 'The Brookings quarterly econometric model: science or number mysticism? Argument and evidence in the Brookings–SSRC philosophy of econometrics', in *Problems and Issues in Current Econometric Practice*, ed. K. Brunner (Ohio State Univ. Press, 1972), repr. in *Erkenntnisprobleme der Oekonometrie*, ed. L. Czayka (Verlag Anton Hain, 1978); 7. 'Exact finite sample distributions for some econometric estimators and test statistics', in *Frontiers of Quantitative Economics*, 2, eds. M. D. Intriligator and D. A. Kendrick (N-H, 1974); 8. 'Modern logic and the suppositious weakness of the empirical foundations of economic science', *Schweizerische Zeitschrift für Volkswirtschaft und Stat*, 2, 1975. 9. 'Budget constraint prices as preference-changing parameters of generalized Fechner-Thurstone direct utility functions' (with D. J. Molina and D. J. Slottje), *AER*, 73(3), June 1983; 10. 'Note on aggregation of Fechner-Thurstone direct utility functions' (with D. J. Molina and D. J. Slottje), *Econ. Letters*, 14, 1984.

Principal Contributions Early graduate study interest was in the statistical estimation of cost and revenue functions for multiproduct firms in monopolistic competition caused by the susceptibility of commodities to product differentiation. Early work centred on the framework of relations among shifts of average revenue functions due to variations of the parameters of direct utility functions caused by systematic and stochastic changes in the consumers' environments and in particular the confounding effect of those parameter changes on statistical estimates of cross-elasticities of demand for monopolistic competitors' products. This effort evolved into pioneering econometric estimation and testing methods for simultaneous economic equation systems and the development of exact distribution theory for econometric statistical estimators and test statistics for dynamical as well as nondynamical models. Current work in econometric methodology concentrates on the development of a practicable standard of policy model validation adapted to rules of evidence and concepts used in the 'finding of fact' in hearings held by regulatory commissions, in the judicial review of commission remedies, and in civil litigation. Present work on econometric methods is an investigation of some nonparametric cost-of-living indexes and their practical application where tastes have changed between the base period and the current period.

BASTABLE, Charles Francis*

Dates and Birthplace 1855–1945, Charleville, Cork, Ireland.
Posts Held Prof. Polit. Econ. and Jurisprudence, Trinity Coll., Dublin, 1882–1932, Queens Coll., Galway, 1883–1903.
Degrees MA, LLD Trinity Coll.
Offices and Honours Pres., Section F, BAAS, 1894; Fellow, BA.
Publications *Books:* 1. *The Theory of International Trade* (1887); 2. *Public Finance* (1892).

Career Best known for his work on international trade, restating in a more complete form the classical 'Ricardian' theory of trade. He was largely a follower of J. S. Mill, though not uncritically so, as when in a famous 1889 *QJE* article he exposed flaws in Mill's views on international payments. His *Public Finance* is generally descriptive, but does include some theoretical discussion of taxation.

Secondary Literature J. Viner, *Studies in the Theory of International Trade* (Harper & Bros., 1937).

BASTIAT, Frederic*

Dates and Birthplace 1801–50, Bayonne, France.
Offices and Honours Leading founder of *Associations pour la liberté des échanges*; Secretary, Paris Assoc.; Member, Constituent Assembly, 1848, subsequently Legislative Assembly.
Publications *Books:* 1. *Economic Harmonies* (1849), ed. G. B. de Huszar (1964); 2. *Economic Sophisms* (1846), ed. A. Goddard (1964).
Career Inspired by the successes of the British Anti-Corn Law League, he became a lifetime campaigner for free trade. His brilliant first article in this vein in the *Journal des Economistes* (1844) was succeeded by his popular series of *Sophismes économiques* (1845). These included the famous 'Petition of the candlemakers', a satirical attack on protectionism using the analogy of candlemakers who petition for the suppression of unfair competition from sunlight. He also directed controversial writings at Proudhon and the socialist writers. His *Harmonies économiques*, of which a first volume appeared before his death, was an attempt at a systematic exposition of his economic ideas. His analysis is considerably inferior to his satirical powers, and his theory of value, rejecting the Ricardian emphasis on costs and sacrifices for a system based on the exchange of services, is perhaps the most interesting contribution.
Secondary Literature H. Durand, 'Bastiat, Frederic', *IESS*, 2; G. C. Roche III, *Frederic Bastiat: A Man Alone* (Arlington House, 1971).

BATOR, Francis M.

Born 1925, Budapest, Hungary.
Current Post Prof. Polit. Econ., Harvard Univ., USA, 1968–.

Past Posts Sr. Econ. Adviser, Agency Internat. Devlp., US Dept. State, 1963–4; Sr. Staff, Nat. Security Council, White House, 1964–5; Dep. Special Ass., US President for Nat. Security Affairs, White House, 1965–7.
Degrees BS, PhD MIT, 1949, 1956; Hon. MA Harvard Univ., 1967.
Offices and Honours Member, Inst. Strategic Stud., Council Foreign Relations; Fellow, AAAS; Guggenheim Foundation Fellow, 1959; Cons., Rand Corp., 1960–3, 1970–; US Member, UN Consultative Group on Econ. Projections, 1962; Special Cons., US Secretary Treasury, 1967–9; Member, US President's Advisory Comm. Internat. Monetary Arrangements, 1967–9; Cons., US Under-Secretary of State for Polit. Affairs, 1967–9; Disting. Service Award, US Treasury Dept., 1968; US Member, UN Expert Group Internat. Monetary Arrangements, 1969–; Member, Foreign Affairs Task Force; Chairman, N. Atlantic Study Group, Democratic Advisory Council Elected Officials, 1970–6.
Principal Fields of Interest 023 Microeconomic Theory; 723 Energy.
Publications *Books:* 1. *The Question of Government Spending: Public Needs and Private Wants* (Harper & Bros., 1960, Collier Books, 1962; transl., Spanish, 1964); 2. *Energy, the Next Twenty Years*, co-ed. (Ballinger, 1979).
Articles: 1. 'On capital productivity, input allocation and growth', *QJE*, 71, Feb. 1957; 2. 'The simple analytics of welfare maximization', *AER*, 47(1), March 1957, repr. in *Readings in Microeconomics*, ed. D. R. Kamerschen (Wiley, 1969), and *Readings in Microeconomics*, eds. W. Breit and H. M. Hochman (Holt, 1971), and *Price Theory*, ed. H. Townsend (Penguin, 1971), and Bobbs-Merrill Repr. Series in Econ. (Bobbs-Merrill, 1974); 3. 'The anatomy of market failure', *QJE*, 72, Aug. 1958, repr. in Breit and Hochman, *op. cit.*, and *The New Public Finance*, eds. O. A. Davis and G. Tullock (Allyn & Bacon, 1970), and Bobbs-Merrill Repr. Series in Econ. (Bobbs-Merrill, 1974); 4. 'Budgetary reform: notes on principles and strategy', *REStat*, 45, May 1963, repr. in *Macroeconomic Readings,* ed. R. Lindauer (Free Press,

1968), and *Readings in Money, National Income and Stabilization Policy*, eds. H. Smith and R. Teigen (Richard D. Irwin, 1970); 5. 'The political economics of international money', *Foreign Affairs*, Oct. 1968, repr. in *Economics and Society: Readings and Problems*, eds. S. Silver and N. Ginsberg (Appleton, Century-Crofts, 1982).

Principal Contributions Early work dealt with welfare economics, externality theory, market failure, and the role of government; also with fiscal and monetary policy. While in government, worked on trade, aid, balance of payments, and international monetary reform (the Special Drawing Rights), as well as on non-economic defence and foreign policy issues. Recently: macroeconomics and the US macroeconomy, with special attention to energy and inflation.

BAUER, Otto*

Dates and Birthplace 1881–1938, Vienna, Austro-Hungary.
Degrees Dr Law, Univ. Vienna, 1906.
Publications *Books:* 1. *Die Nationalitätenfrage und die Sozialdemokratie* (1907, 1924); 2. *Nationalkampf oder Klassenkampf?* (1911); 3. *Zwischen zwei Weltkriegen* (1936).
Articles: 'Die Akkumulation des Kapitals', *Die Neue Zeit,* 31,(1), 1912–3.
Career Leading Marxist who challenged Kautsky on the question of agrarian policy. His work for the Austrian Social Democratic Party prevented him doing full justice to his analytical abilities. In addition to his work on agrarian policy, his earlier contribution on capital accumulation is also of outstanding quality. In the Marxist literature, however, he is best remembered for his analysis of the question of nationality.
Secondary Literature J. Braunthal ed., *Eine Auswahl aus seinem Lebenswerk mit einem Lebensbild Otto Bauers* (1961).

BAUER, Peter Thomas

Born Hungary.
Current Post Prof. Emeritus, LSE, 1984–.
Recent Posts Smuts Reader, Univ. Camb., 1956–60; Fellow, Gonville and Caius Coll. Camb., 1946–60, 1968–84; Prof. Econ., LSE, 1960–84.
Degree MA Univ. Camb.
Offices and Honours Fellow, BA, 1975–; Created life peer, 1983.
Principal Fields of Interest 121 Economic Studies of Less Industrialised Countries.
Publications *Books:* 1. *The Rubber Industry* (Harvard Univ. Press, 1948); 2. *West African Trade* (CUP, 1954, Routledge & Kegan Paul, 1963); 3. *Markets, Market Control and Marketing Reform* (with B. S. Yamey), (Weidenfeld & Nicolson, 1968); 4. *Dissent on Development* (Weidenfeld & Nicolson, 1972, Harvard Univ. Press, 1972, 1976); 5. *Equality, the Third World and Economic Delusion* (Weidenfeld & Nicolson, Harvard Univ. Press, 1981); 6. *Reality and Rhetoric: Studies in the Economics of Development* (Weidenfeld & Nicolson, Harvard Univ. Press, 1984).
Articles: 'The working of rubber regulations', *EJ,* 56, Sept. 1946; 2. 'Economic progress and occupational distribution' (with B. S. Yamey), *EJ,* 56, Dec. 1951; 3. 'Reduction in the fluctuations of incomes of primary producers' (with F. W. Paish), *EJ,* 62, Dec. 1952; 4. 'Economic history as theory', *Ec,* N.S, 38, May 1971; 5. 'East–West/North–South' (with B. S. Yamey), *Commentary,* 70(3), Sept. 1980.
Principal Contributions Critique of received opinion on various issues, including economic progress and occupational distribution, the vicious circle of poverty, the widening gap of income differences within and between countries; analysis of conceptual and practical problems of price and income stabilisation; discussion of the operation of marketing boards and commodity agreements in LDCs; role of cash crops in economic advance of LDCs; and systematic critique of the operation of foreign aid.

BAUMOL, William Jack

Born 1922, New York City, NY, USA.
Current Post Prof. Econ., Princeton Univ., Princeton, NJ, and NYU, NY, 1971–.
Past Posts Jr. Econ., US Dept. Agric., 1942–3, 1946; Ass. Lect., LSE, 1947–9; Prof. Econ., Princeton Univ., 1954–71.
Degrees BSS Coll. City NY, 1942; PhD Univ. London, 1949; Hon. LLD Rider Coll., 1965; Hon. Dr. Stockholm School Econ., 1971; Hon. Dr. Humane Letters, Knox Coll., 1973; Hon. Dr. Univ. Basel, 1973.
Offices and Honours Pres., Atlantic Econ. Soc., AEA, EEA, Assoc. Environmental Resource Economists; Vice-Pres., AAUP; Guggenheim Foundation Fellow, 1957–8; Ford Faculty Fellow, 1965–6; Hon. Fellow, LSE, 1970; AAAS, 1971; John R. Commons Award, Omicron Delta Epsilon, 1975; Townsend Harris Medal, Alumni Assoc. City Coll. NY, 1975; Amer. Philo. Soc., 1977; Disting. Fellow, AEA, 1982; Disting. Member, Econ. Assoc. Puerto Rico, 1984; Fellow, Em Soc.
Principal Fields of Interest 022 Microeconomic Theory; 024 Welfare Theory; 610 Industrial Organisation and Public Policy.
Publications *Books:* 1. *Economic Dynamics* (Macmillan, 1951, 1970; transls., Spanish, 1964, 1971, Japanese, 1961, 1973, Greek, 1974); 2. *Welfare Economics and the Theory of the State* (Longmans Green, 1952, Harvard Univ. Press, 1965); 3. *Business Behavior, Value and Growth* (Macmillan, 1959, Harcourt, Brace & World, 1966; transls., Japanese, 1963, 1969, Italian, 1972); 4. *Economic Theory & Operations Analysis* (Prentice-Hall, 1961, 1976; transls., Russian, 1962, 1965, French, 1963, Hindi, 1963, Spanish, 1964, Japanese, 1965, Italian, 1968, Hungarian, 1968); 5. *Performing Arts: The Economic Dilemma* (with W. G. Bowen), (Twentieth Century Fund, 1966); 6. *The Theory of Environmental Policy* (with W. E. Oates), (Prentice-Hall, 1975); 7. *Economics, Environmental Policy and the Quality of Life* (with W. E. Oates and S. A. B. Blackman), (Prentice-Hall, 1979); 8. *Eco-*

nomics: Principles and Policy (with A. Blinder), (Harcourt Brace Jovanovich, 1979, 1984); 9. *Contestable Markets and the Theory of Industry Structure* (with R. D. Willig and J. S. Panzar), (Harcourt Brace Jovanovich, 1982); 10. *Superfairness: Applications and Theory* (MIT Press, 1986).
Articles: 1. 'The transactions demand for cash: an inventory theoretic approach', *QJE*, 66, Nov. 1952; 2. 'Macroeconomics of unbalanced growth: the anatomy of urban crisis', *AER*, 57(3), June 1967; 3. 'Optimal departures from marginal cost pricing' (with D. Bradford), *AER*, 60(3), June 1970; 4. 'Quasi-optimality: the price we must pay for a price system', *JPE*, 87(3), June 1970; 5. 'Subsidies to new energy sources: do they add to energy stocks?' (with E. Wolff), *JPE*, 89(5), Oct. 1981; 6. 'Contestable markets: an uprising in the theory of industry structure', *AER*, 72(1), March 1982; 7. 'Applied fairness theory and rationing policy', *AER*, 72(4), Sept. 1982; 8. 'Marx and the iron law of wages', *AER*, 73(2), May 1983; 9. 'On the career of a microeconomist', *BNLQR*, 147, Dec. 1983.
Principal Contributions Most of my work has related to welfare economics and its applications. My first book showed how the theory of externalities could be extended to provide the foundations of a theory of the State. Since then I and W. E. Oates have applied welfare theory to environmental issues showing, for example, how a subsidy to firms which reduce emissions could decrease each firm's pollution output and yet increase the pollution generated by the industry. More recently J. Panzar and R. Willig and I worked on the theory of contestable markets which showed circumstances sufficient to elicit socially desirable behaviour from industries with a small number of incumbent firms. The analysis also provided for the special case of perfect ease of entry and exit which may be the first comprehensive theory of the determination of industry structure in particular for cases involving multiproduct firms. I also have produced a model of unbalanced growth showing how cer-

tain types of service such as education, medicine and the arts have been condemned by lagging productivity to rising relative costs and to absorption of an ever growing share of the economy's resources if the quantities demanded keep up with the rest of the economy.

BECCARIA, Cesare Bonesana, Marquis of*

Dates and Birthplace 1738–94, Milan, Italy.

Posts Held Prof. Polit. Econ., Milan, 1768–70; Official, Austrian administration of Milan, 1770–94.

Publications Books: 1. *An Essay on Crimes and Punishments* (1764, 1963); 2. *Elementi di Economia Pubblica* (1804).

Articles: 1. 'An attempt at an analysis of smuggling', *Il Caffe*, 1764; repr. in *Precursors of Mathematical Economics: an Anthology*, eds. W. J. Baumol and S. M. Goldfeld (LSE, 1968).

Career His early text on criminal law was an enormous international success and influenced the penal policies of many countries. His starting point was the utilitarian principle of the greatest happiness of the greatest number, according to which the test of the seriousness of a crime, and hence the nature of the punishment, is always social injury and not private intention. His brief tenure of the Milan chair produced a set of lectures, published posthumously, which touched on all the main current fields of economic analysis, and which contain a surprising number of hints of theoretical developments to come.

Secondary Literature C. Phillipson, *Three Criminal Law Reformers: Beccaria, Bentham, Romilly* (Dent, 1923); M. P. Mack, 'Beccaria', *IESS*, 2; P. Groenewegen, 'Turgot, Beccaria and Smith', in *Alto Polo, Italian Economics, Past and Present*, ed. P. Groenewegen and J. Halevi (Univ. of Sydney, 1983).

BECKER, Gary Stanley

Born 1930, Pottstown, PA, USA.

Current Post Prof. Econ. and Sociology, Univ. Chicago, 1970–.

Past Posts Ass. Prof. Econ., Univ. Chicago, 1954–7; Ass. Prof., Assoc. Prof., Prof. Econ., Arthur Lehman Prof. Econ., Columbia Univ., 1957–60, 1960–8, 1968–9; Ford Foundation Vis. Prof. Econ., Univ. Chicago, 1969–70.

Degrees BA Princeton Univ., 1951; MA, PhD Univ. Chicago, 1953, 1955; Hon. Degrees, Hebrew Univ., Jerusalem, 1985, Knox Coll., Galesburg, IL, 1985.

Offices and Honours NAS; AAAS; ASA; Em Soc; Exec. Board, Mont Pelerin Soc.; Founding Member, Vice-Pres. Nat. Academy Education, 1965–7; W. S. Woytinsky Award, Univ. Michigan, 1965; John Bates Clark Medal, Vice-Pres., AEA, 1967, 1974; Professional Achievement Award, Univ. Chicago Alumni Assoc., 1968.

Principal Fields of Interest 850 Human Capital.

Publications Books: 1. *The Economics of Discrimination* (Univ. Chicago Press, 1957, 1971); 2. *Human Capital* (Columbia Univ. Press, 1964, 1975); 3. *Economic Theory* (Alfred A. Knopf, 1971); 4. *The Economic Approach to Human Behavior* (Univ. Chicago Press, 1976); 5. *A Treatise on the Family* (Harvard Univ. Press, 1981).

Principal Contributions The first to provide a neoclassical analysis of discrimination in labour markets. Among the first to develop the implications of human capital theory. After analysing the allocation of time of economic agents, generalised the argument into the so-called 'new economics of the family', providing a standard explanation of such phenomena as marriage, divorce, the decision to have children, the decision to educate children, etc.

Secondary Literature J. R. Shackleton, 'Gary S. Becker: the economist as empire-builder', in *Twelve Contemporary Economists*, eds. J. R. Shackleton and G. Locksley (Macmillan, 1981).

BECKERMAN, Wilfred

Born 1925, Croydon, Surrey, England.
Current Post Fellow, Balliol Coll., Univ. Reader Econ., Univ. Oxford, 1977–.
Past Posts Lect., Univ. Nottingham, 1950–2; Econ. Adviser, Head Div., OEEC, Paris, 1952–61; Dir. Res. Project, NIESR, 1962–4; Fellow, Balliol Coll. Oxford, 1964–9; Econ. Adviser, Pres. UK Board of Trade, 1967–9; Prof. Polit. Econ., Univ. London, 1969–75; Elie Halévy Vis. Prof., Inst. Nat. d' Etudes Politiques, Paris, 1977–8; Vis. Fellow, Woodrow Wilson Center, Washington, DC, 1982; Cons., OECD, ILO, World Bank; Vis. Prof., Univ. Dijon, 1983.
Degrees BA, MA, PhD Univ. Camb., 1948, 1951, 1951.
Offices and Honours Member, UK Royal Commission Environmental Pollution, 1970–3; Pres., Section F, BAAS, 1978; Governor, Council, Exec. Comm., NIESR, 1972–; Res. Scholar, Rockefeller Center, Bellagio, Italy, 1980.
Editorial Duties Ed. Board, *JEEM, J. Public Pol.*
Principal Fields of Interest 221 National Income Accounting; 824 Labour Market Studies: Wages, Employment; 914 Economics of Poverty.
Publications *Books:* 1. *The British Economy in 1975* (with others), (CUP, 1965); 2. *International Real Income Comparisons* (OECD, 1966); 3. *Introduction to National Income Analysis* (Weidenfeld & Nicolson, 1968, 1980; transls., Spanish, 1970, 1971, Portuguese, 1979); 4. *The Labour Government's Economic Record, 1964–70*, ed. and contrib. (Duckworth, 1972); 5. *In Defence of Economic Growth* (CUP, 1974, as *Two Cheers for the Affluent Society*, St Martin's Press, 1975; transls., Swedish, 1975, Dutch, 1976, Japanese, 1976); 6. *Leisure, Equality and Welfare* (OECD, 1978); 7. *Slow Growth in Britain: Causes and Cure,* ed. and contrib. (OUP, 1979); 8. *Poverty and the Impact of Income Maintenance Programmes* (ILO, 1979); 9. *Poverty and Social Security in Britain since 1961* (with S. Clark), (OUP, 1982).

Articles: 1. 'Price changes and the stability of the balance of trade', *Ec*, N. S. 19, Nov. 1952; 2. 'Interdependence of consumer preferences in the theory of income distribution' (with S. F. James), *EJ*, 63, March 1953; 3. 'The economist as a modern missionary', *EJ*, 66, March 1956; 4. 'The world trade matrix multiplier and the stability of world trade', *Em*, 24, July 1956; 5. 'Projecting Europe's growth', *EJ*, 72, Dec. 1962; 6. 'International comparisons of income levels: a suggested new measure' (with R. Bacon), *EJ*, 76, Sept. 1966; 7. 'The international distribution of incomes' (with R. Bacon), in *Unfashionable Economics: Essays in Honour of Lord Balogh*, ed. P. Streeten (Weidenfeld and Nicolson, 1970); 8. 'Economists, scientists and environmental catastrophe', *OEP*, 24(3), Nov. 1972; 9. 'The impact of income maintenance payments on poverty in Britain', *EJ*, 89, June 1979, repr. in *Wealth, Income and Inequality*, ed. A. B. Atkinson (OUP, 1980); 10. 'Human resources: are they worth preserving?', in *Human Resources, Employment and Development,* eds. P. Streeten and G. Maier (Macmillan, 1983).

Principal Contributions During ten years at OEEC and OECD (1952–61) I had varied policy interests. Then in the 1960s I concentrated on analysis of growth determinants (including advocacy of an export-led growth model), as well as methods of international real income comparisons. As a result of membership of a Royal Commission (1970–3) I became involved in environmental economics, which led to my playing a prominent part in the then major controversy over the desirability and costs of economic growth. Moved in the mid-1970s to the relative obscurity and peace of detailed work on poverty and the impact of social security programmes in various countries. But by 1978 it was clear that the major cause of increased poverty in the modern world was the return to large-scale unemployment and stagnation, and also that the most interesting work going on was in macroeconomics, so in an attempt chiefly to understand it I drifted back into mainstream macroeconomics.

I still occasionally dip a finger in the

real income comparison pie, or the poverty pie, but I am currently chiefly interested in the mechanism by which induced sharp changes in flexible prices of primary products feed back on to the industrialised countries' economies inflation rates. Overall my contributions have been mainly of a quantitative nature in the areas indicated above, but my main contribution was, I suppose, the less exclusively measurement-oriented battle that I fought in *In Defence of Economic Growth* in the early 1970s, just when we entered a period in which there was no more growth to defend.

BECKMANN, Martin Joseph

Born 1924, Ratingen, W. Germany.
Current Post Prof. Econ., Brown Univ., Providence, RI, USA, 1961–; Prof. Applied Maths., Technical Univ. Munich, W. Germany, 1969–.
Past Posts Res. Assoc., Cowles Commission Res. Econ., Ass. Prof. Yale Univ., 1951–5, 1955–9; Vis. Prof., Univ. Heidelberg, 1959; Assoc. Prof., Brown Univ., 1959–61; Prof. Emeritus, OR and Econ., Univ. Bonn, W. Germany, 1962–9; Tinbergen Chair, Erasmus Univ., Rotterdam, Netherlands, 1982.
Degrees Vordiplom Univ. Gottingen, 1947; Diplom., Dr. Rer. Pol. Univ. Freiburg, 1949, 1950; Hon. Dr. Rer Pol Univ. Karlsruhe, 1971; Hon. Dr. Phil. h.c. Univ. UMEA, Sweden, 1981.
Offices and Honours Postdoctoral Fellow Polit. Econ., Univ. Chicago, 1950–1; Fellow, Center Advanced Study Behavioral Sciences, Stanford, CA, 1955–6; Fellow, Em Soc; Member, Internat. Inst. Stats.; Pres., Western Regional Science Assoc., 1976–7; Pres., Regional Science Assoc. 1979–80.
Editorial Duties Managing Ed. (with W. Krelle), *Lecture Notes in Economic and Mathematical Systems* (Springer-Verlag); Assoc. Ed., *Transportation Science*.
Principal Fields of Interest 213 Mathematical Methods and Models; 511 Organisation and Decision Theory; 940 Regional Economics.
Publications *Books:* 1. *Studies in the Economics of Transtation* (with C. B.

McGuire and C. B. Winston), (Yale Univ. Press, 1956); 2. *Lineare Planungsrechnung — Linear Programming* (Fachverlag für Wirtschaftstheorie und Okonometrie, 1959); 3. *Location Theory* (Random House, 1968; transl. Japanese, 1970); 4. *Dynamic Programming of Economic Decisions* (Springer-Verlag, 1968); 5. *Mathematik für Okonomen*, I (with H. P. Kunzi), (Springer-Verlag, 1967, 1971) 6. *Mathematik für Okonomen*, II (with H. P. Kunzi), (Springer-Verlag, 1970); 7. *Rank in Organizations* (Springer-Verlag, 1978); 8. *Tinbergen Lectures in Organization Theory* (Springer-Verlag, 1983).

Articles; 1. 'A continuous model of transportation', *Em*, 20(4), Oct. 1952; 2. 'Assignment problems and the location of economic activities' (with T. C. Koopmans), *Em*, 25(1), Jan. 1957; repr. in The Bobbs-Merrill Reprint Series Econ., 177 (Bobbs-Merrill, 1958); 3. 'City hierarchies and the distribution of city size', *EDCC*, 6(3), April 1958; repr. in The Bobbs-Merrill Reprint Series Social Sciences, 338 (Bobbs-Merrill, 1959); 4. 'Some aspects of returns to scale in business administrations', *QJE*, 74, Aug. 1960; 5. 'A Wicksellian model of growth', *RISE*, 12, March 1966; 6. 'Neutral inventions and production functions' (with R. Sato), *REStud*, 35(1), Jan. 1968; 7. 'Simultaneous price and quantity adjustment in a single market' (with H. E. Ryder, Jr.), *Em*, 37(3), July 1969; 8. 'A note on cost estimation and the optimal bidding strategy', *Operations Res.*, 22(3), May–June, 1974; 9. 'Spatial price policies revisited', *Bell JE*, 7(2), Autumn, 1976; 10. 'Management production functions and the theory of the firm', *JET*, 14(1), Feb. 1977.

Principal Contributions Early work was focussed on competitive spatial market equilibrium and on the efficient utilisation of transportation facilities, developing appropriate linear and non-linear programming models under the influence of T. C. Koopmans. My interests then shifted to sequential decision-making as exemplified by inventory and production control, and to the economic insights found in dynamic programming. Through Jacob Marschak I was motivated to study the economics of organisations, particularly the economic functions of supervision and rank. I have tackled the returns to scale in management problem through the use of production functions. I have maintained an interest in the economics of transportation and have introduced utility methods into the modelling of traveller behaviour. More recently I have returned to location theory as the foundation of Regional Science an Urban Economics. Perhaps my best known contribution has been a simple model explaining the quantitative relationships in a central place hierarchy and the distribution of city sizes.

BEESLEY, Michael E

Born 1924, Birmingham, W. Midlands, England.
Current Post Prof. Econ., London Grad. Bus. School, 1965–.
Past Posts Chief Econ. Adviser UK Ministry Transport, 1965–8, Cons. Chief Econ. Adviser, UK Dept Environment, 1968–9; Dir., Small Bus. Unit, Dir., Inst. Public Sector Management, London Grad. Bus. School, 1973, 1977.
Degrees BCom., PhD Univ. Birmingham, 1945, 1955.
Editorial Duties Managing Ed., *J Transp EP*; Ed. Board, *Appl. Econ.*
Offices and Honours Member, UK Dept Transport, Standing Advisory Comm. Trunk Road Assessment; Dir., Transmark Ltd.
Principal Fields of Interest 933 Urban Transportation Economics.
Publications *Books:*1. *Urban Transport: Studies in Economic Policy* (Butterworths, 1973); 2. *Corporate Social Responsibility — A Re-assessment* (with T. C. Evans), (Croom Helm, 1978); 3. *Liberalisation of the Use of British Telecommunications Network* (HMSO, 1981).
Articles: 1. 'The birth and death of industrial establishments', *J Ind E*, 4(1), Oct. 1955; 2. 'Estimating the social benefit of constructing an underground railway in London' (with C. D. Foster), *JRSS*, 126, pt. 1, 1963, repr. in AEA *Readings in Welfare Economics*, eds. K. J. Arrow and T. Scitovsky (Richard D. Irwin, A&U, 1969); 3. 'Urban form, car ownership and public policy', *Urb Stud*, 1(2), Nov. 1964; 4. 'The value of time spent in travelling: some new evidence', *Ec*, N.S. 32, May 1965; 5. 'Competition and supply in London taxis', *J Transp EP*, 13(1), Jan. 1979.
Principal Contributions Development of cost-benefit analysis, as applied particularly to transport projects. The analysis of regulation and the relation between management requirements and the application of economic analysis.

BEHRMAN, Jere Richard

Born 1940, Indianapolis, IN, USA.
Current Post William P. Kenan Jr. Prof. Econ., Assoc. Dir., Joseph H. Lauder Inst. Management and Internat. Stud., Co-Dir., Center Analysis of Developing Economies, Univ. Penn., Philadelphia, PA, USA., 1983–.
Past Posts Ass. Prof., Assoc. Prof., Univ. Penn., 1965–8, 1969–71; Cons., World Bank, 1966–9, 1972–3, 1977–8, 1980–4; Res. Assoc. Cons., MIT–Ford Foundation Project, Office Nat. Econ. Planning, Santiago, Chile, 1968–71; Vis. Seminar Co-ordinator, Univ. Catolica, Santiago, Chile, 1969; Res. Assoc., NBER, 1969–79; Res. Investigator-Cons., Wharton Em Forecasting Assoc. Inc., Philadelphia, PA, 1970–1, 1977–81; Prof. Univ. Penn., 1971–83; Vis. Lect., Princeton Univ., 1973; Res. Investigator-Cons., Brookings–SIECA Project, Guatemala, 1973–6; Res. Investigator-Cons., UN Devlp. Programme Project, Panama, 1975–6; Cons., Harvard Inst. Internat. Devlp., Central Bank Nicaragua, Managua, Nicaragua, 1975–6; Cons., INCAE, Nicaragua, 1976–7; Res. Investigator-Cons., SIECA, Guatemala, 1976–8; Co-Investigator, Ford-Rockefeller-US Agency Internat. Devlp. Project, Nicaragua, 1977–81; Res. Assoc., Center Latin Amer. Devlp. Stud., Boston Univ., 1978–9; Academic Vis., Econ., ICERD, LSE, London, 1979–81; Cons., Nat. Council Applied Econ. Res., India, 1980; Vis. Scientist, ICRISAT, India, 1980–4; USIS Tours India, Pakistan, Sri Lanka, Bangladesh, Nepal, 1980, 1981; Cons., Ministry Fin. and Devlp. Planning, Botswana, 1982.

Degrees BA (Physics) Williams Coll., MA, USA, 1962; PhD MIT, 1966.

Offices and Honours Phi Beta Kappa, 1961; AAEA Award Merit, Outstanding Res. Agric. Econ. Hon. Fellow, Univ. Wisconsin–Madison, 1976–7; Ford Foundation Fellow, 1971–2; Guggenheim Foundation Fellow, 1979–80; Fellow, Em Soc., 1980–; Compton Fellow, 1980–1.

Editorial Duties Ed. Board, Book Review Ed., *JDE*, 1976, 1982–.

Principal Fields of Interest 121 Economic Studies of Less Industrialised Countries; 800 Manpower; Labour; Population; 400 International Economics.

Publications *Books:* 1. *Supply Response in Underdeveloped Agriculture: A Case Study of Four Major Annual Crops in Thailand 1937–63* (N-H, 1968); 2. *Econometric Models of World Agricultural Commodity Markets: Coffee, Cocoa, Tea, Wool, Cotton, Sugar, Wheat, Rice* (with F. G. Adams), (Ballinger, 1976); 3. *Foreign Trade Regimes and Economic Development: Chile* (Columbia Univ. Press, 1976); 4. *International Commodity Agreements: An Evaluation of the UNCTAD Integrated Commodity Programme* (Overseas Devlp. Council, 1977); 5. *Macroeconomic Policy in a Developing Country: The Chilean Experience* (N-H, 1977); 6. *Econometric Modelling of World Commodity Policy,* co-ed. (with F. G. Adams), (D. C. Heath, 1982); 7. *Development, the International Economic Order and International Commodity Agreements* (Addison-Wesley, 1978); 8. *Short-Term Macroeconomic Policy in Latin America,* co-ed. (with J. A. Hanson), (Ballinger, 1979); 9. *Socioeconomic Success: A Study of the Effects of Genetic Endowments, Family Environment and Schooling* (with Z. Hrubec, P. Taubman, and T. J. Wales), (N-H, 1980); 10. *Commodity Exports and Economic Development: The Commodity Problem and Policy in Developing Countries* (with F. G. Adams), (D. C. Heath, 1982).

Articles: 1. 'Sectoral elasticities of substitution between capital and labor in a developing economy: time series analysis in the case of postwar Chile', *Em*, 40(2), March 1972; transl. Spanish, *Cuadernos de Economia*, 9(26), April 1972; 2. 'Short-run flexibility in a developing economy', *JPE* 80(2), March–April 1972; 3. 'Sectoral investment determination in a developing economy', *AER*, 62(5), Dec. 1972; 4. 'Country and sectoral variations in manufacturing elasticities of substitution between capital and labor', in *Trade and Employment in Developing Countries, 2: Factor Supply and Substitution*, ed. A. Krueger (Univ. Chicago Press, 1982); 5. 'Parental preferences and provision for progeny' (with R. A. Pollak and P. Taubman), *JPE*, 90(1), Feb. 1982; 6. 'The impact of minimum wages on the distribution of earnings for major race-sex groups: a dynamic analysis' (with P. Taubman and R. Sickles), *AER*, 73(4), Sept. 1983; 7. 'The quality of schooling: quantity alone is misleading' (with N. Birdsall), *AER*, 73(5), Dec. 1983; 8. 'Does geographical aggregation cause overestimates of the return to schooling?' (with N. Birdsall), *OBES*, 46(1), Feb. 1984; 9. 'Micro determinants of female migration in a developing country: labor market, demographic marriage market, and economic marriage market incentives' (with B. L. Wolfe,), in *Research in Population Economics*, eds. T. P. Schultz and K. I. Wolpin (JAI Press, 1984). 10. 'The socioeconomic impact of schooling in a developing country' (with B. L. Wolfe), *REStat*, 66(2), May 1984.

Principal Contributions Primary research interests in applied research related to numerous dimensions of economic development. Secondary research interests pertain to human capital, household behaviour, intergenerational mobility and inequality in US. Early work in mid-1960s focussed upon market responsiveness in developing agriculture, with evidence presented of considerable responsiveness in contrast to widespread myth of non-economic peasants. Next major area of study concerned fiscal, macro and foreign sector policy within overall empirical models of Latin American economies, which pointed to some flexibility, but still limited range of policy options. Also wrote 1976 volume on Chile in Bhagwati–Krueger NBER project on trade liberalisation in developing countries, which suggested some substantial costs to inward orientation. Continued work on international primary commodity markets started in mid-1960s, with widely-cited 1977 quantitative evaluation of UNCTAD/Integrated Commodity Programme that questioned many previous positive and negative claims about the programme. Followed by major study integrating econometric models of international primary markets and developing economies that implied very little negative impact of market instabilities on developing economies.

Extensive study of family background using US adult twin males in late 1970s suggested that standard estimates of returns to schooling were biassed upwards substantially and that genetic variance was quite important in the variance of socioeconomic success. At the same time and continuing into 1980s, a series of studies on women in Latin America suggested, *inter alia*, that the role of schooling had been misunderstood in the past due to the failure to control for family background and that integration of marriage with labour market changes insights regarding investment and migration. Also in early 1980s development of new intra-household models, the estimation of which suggested a parental inequality aversion so strong that parents do not follow a pure investment strategy, that parents favour girls in the US though not in India, that parental age is critical, and that US intergenerational mobility is great. Also several studies of returns to schooling suggest that they are overstated in standard estimates by failure to control for school quality and by geographical aggregation bias.

BELL, Carolyn Shaw

Born 1920, Framingham, MA, USA.
Current Post Katharine Coman Prof. Econ., Wellesley Coll., Wellesley, MA, USA, 1963–.
Past Posts Econ., US Office Price Admin., Washington, DC, 1941–5; Ass. Prof. Econ., Wellesley Coll., 1951–63.
Degrees BA Mount Holyoke Coll., 1941; PhD London Univ., 1949; Hon.

Doc. Humane Letters Babson Coll., 1983.
Offices and Honours Exec. Comm., AEA, 1975–7; Exec. Board, EEA, 1983–.
Editorial Duties Ed. Board, *Challenge*, 1972–., *JEL*, 1983–., *J Evolutionary Econ.*, 1983–., *J Econ. Educ.*, 1983–.
Principal Fields of Interest 850 Human Capital; 910 Welfare, Health and Education; 010 General Economics.
Publications *Books:* 1. *The Economics of Consumption* (with W. W. Cochrane), (McGraw Hill, 1956); 2. *Consumer Choice in the American Economy* (Random House, 1957); 3. *The Economics of the Ghetto* (Bobbs-Merrill, 1971); 4. *Coping in a Troubled Society: An Environmental Approach to Mental Health* (with others), (D. C. Heath, 1974).

Articles: 1. 'Economics sex and gender', *Social Science Q.*, 55(3), Dec. 1974; 2. 'The economics of might have been', *MLR*, 97(11), Nov. 1974; 3. 'Should every job support a family?', *Public Interest*, Summer 1975; 4. 'The economics of work and the labor force', in *Working Woman*, eds. B. Yates and N. Harkess (Mayfield, 1977); 5. 'Economic data, policy-making and the law', *Boston Coll. Law Rev.*, 21(5), June 1982; 6. 'Minimum wages and personal income', in *The Economics of Legal Minimum Wages*, ed. J. Rottenberg (AEI, 1981); 7. 'Demand, supply and labor market analysis', *JEI*, 15(2), June 1981; 8. 'Human capital formation and the decision makers', *JEI*, 18(2), June 1984.
Principal Contributions Looking at familiar data from a different perspective has prompted much of my analysis of income. I am convinced that the basic unit of microanalysis, whether household or family, cannot be successful for explanations of both income and expenditure (or saving). Hence I have looked at the relation between individual earnings or income and family or household income in much of my work. It has also led me to give special attention to family members as individuals, especially women and children. My other strong concern has to do with the quality of our basic economic data and

how to use them properly. Finally, I believe in writing economics to be read outside the profession: I believe in writing for daily newspapers, speaking on TV, and so on. Economists should not be so unintelligible to the general public.

BENASSY, Jean-Pascal, E.

Born 1948, Paris, France.
Current Post Dir. de Recherche, CNRS, Paris, Res. Assoc., CEPREMAP, Paris, Dir., Laboratoire d'Econ. Polit., Ecole Normale Supérieure, Paris, France, 1979–.
Past Posts Visit. Prof., Univ. Cal. Berkeley, 1977–8.
Degrees Ecole Normale Supérieure, Section Sciences, DEA (Maths. and Stats.) Univ. Paris VI, 1967, 1970; Inst. d'Etudes Polit., Section Econ. et Fin., 1970; PhD Univ. Cal. Berkeley, 1973; Doctorat Univ. de Paris I, 1980.
Offices and Honours Fellow, Em. Soc.
Editorial Duties Assoc. Ed., *J Ec Behav*.
Principal Fields of Interest 020 General Economic Theory; 130 Economic Fluctuations; 430 Balance of Payments.
Publications *Books:* 1. *The Economics of Market Disequilibrium* (Academic Press, 1982); 2. *Macro-économie et théorie du déséquilibre* (Dunod, 1984); 3. *Macroeconomics: An Introduction to the Non-Walrasian Approach* (Academic Press, 1986).
Articles: 1. 'Neo-Keynesian Disequilibrium Theory in a Monetary Economy', *REStud*, 42(4), Oct. 1975; 2. 'Disequilibrium exchange in barter and monetary economies', *EI*, 13(2), June 1975; 3. 'Théorie néo-Keynésienne du déséquilibre dans une économie monétaire', *Cahiers du Séminaire d'Econométrie*, 17, 1976; 4. 'The disequilibrium approach to monopolistic price setting and general monopolistic equilibrium', *REStud*, 43(1), Feb. 1976; 5. 'A Neo-Keynesian model of price and quantity determination in disequilibrium', in *Equilibrium and Disequilibrium in Economic Theory*, ed. G. Schwödiauer (D. Reidel, 1977); 6. 'On quantity signals and the foundations of effective demand theory', *Scand JE*, 79(2), 1977; 7. 'Cost and Demand In-

flation Revisited: A Neo-Keynesian Approach', *Econ App*, 31(1–2), 1978; 8. 'The three regimes of the IS-LM model: a non-Walrasian analysis', *Europ ER*, 23(1), Sept. 1983; 9. 'A non-Walrasian model of the business cycle', *J Ec Behav*, 5(1), March 1984; 10. 'Tariffs and Pareto optimality in international trade: the case of unemployment', *Europ ER*, 26(3), Dec. 1984.
Principal Contributions I have devoted most of my research to the microeconomic foundations of macroeconomics in situations where all markets do not clear, with emphasis on both the microeconomic theory of non-Walrasian equilibria and their macroeconomic applications. My early work developed the microeconomic aspects of the theory: functioning of non-clearing markets, the formation of quantity signals, a general theory of rational demand and supply behaviour under quantity rationing, price setting by decentralised agents outside Walrasian equilibrium, and the effects of expectations — notably quantity expectations — on current outcomes. Though the above concepts can also be used to study dynamics, a main contribution has been the development of several concepts of non-Walrasian equilibrium, with varying degrees of price rigidity. These include, notably, a fix-price equilibrium, and an equilibrium with endogenous price-making where decentralised agents set prices in a framework of imperfect competition. In all these concepts, general schemes for formulating price and quantity expectations are explicitly incorporated.

In later work, I applied the above concepts to a number of traditional macroeconomic topics such as unemployment, inflation, IS-LM, international trade and tariffs, business cycles and a few others, emphasising in particular the policy implications of the theory. My current research deals with macroeconomic implications of various price and expectations schemes, as well as with further development of the microeconomic foundations of price and expectations formation out of Walrasian equilibrium.

BENHAM, Frederick Charles Courtnay*

Dates 1902–62.
Posts Held Econ. Adviser, Comptroller for Devlp. and Welfare in W. Indies, 1942–5; Prof. Commerce, Univ. London, 1945–7; Econ. Adviser, Commissioner-General for UK in SE Asia, 1947–55; Sir Henry Price Res. Prof. Internat. Affairs, Royal Inst. of Internat. Affairs, 1955–62.
Offices and Honours CBE, 1945.
Publications 1. *British Monetary Policy* (1932); 2. *Economics* (1938, 8th ed., ed. F. W. Paish, 1967); 3. *The National Income of British Guiana* (1942); 4. *The Colombo Plan and Other Essays* (1956); 5. *A Short Introduction to the Economy of Latin America* (with H. A. Holley), (1960); 6. *Economic Aid to Underdeveloped Countries* (1961).

Career Author of the most widely used prewar textbook in elementary economics in Britain and expert on development economics, working particularly on national income accounting in the West Indies and South-East Asia.

BENHAM, Lee Kenneth

Born 1940, Searcy, AR, USA.
Current Post Prof. Econ., Washington Univ., St Louis, MO, USA, 1974–.
Past Posts Instr., Ass. Prof., School Bus., Univ. Chicago, 1967–74.
Degrees BA Knox Coll., Galesburg, IL, 1962; PhD Stanford Univ., 1970.
Principal Fields of Interest 610 Industrial Organisation and Public Policy; 913 Economics of Health.
Publications *Books:* 1. *Readings in Labor Market Analysis*, co-ed. (Holt, Rinehard, Winston, 1971).
Articles: 1. 'The labor market for registered nurses: a three equation model', *REStat*, 53(3), Aug. 1971; 2. 'The effect of advertising on the price of eyeglasses', *J Law E*, 15(2), Oct. 1972; 3. 'Benefits of women's education within marriage', *JPE*, pt. 2, 82(2), Mar–April 1974, repr. in *Economics of the Family: Marriage Children and Human Capital*, ed. T. W. Schultz (Univ. Chicago Press, 1974); 4. 'Health, hours, and wages' (with M. Grossman), in *The Economics of Health and Medical Care*, ed. M. Perlman (Macmillan, 1974); 5. 'Regulating through the professions: a perspective on information control' (with A. Benham), *J Law E*, 18(2), Oct. 1975; 6. 'The impact of incremental medical services on health status, 1963–1970' (with A. Benham), in *Equity in Health Services*, ed. R. Andersen, *et al.* (Ballinger, 1975); 7. 'Guilds and the form of competition in the health care sector', in *Competition in the Health Care Sector*, ed. W. Greenberg (Aspen Systems Corp., 1978); 8. 'The informers' tale' (with A. Benham), in *Regulating the Professions: A Public Policy Symposium*, eds. R. Blair and S. Rubin (D. C. Heath, 1980); 9. 'Employment, earnings, and psychiatric diagnosis' (with A. Benham), in *Economic Aspects of Health*, ed. V. Fuchs (Univ. Chicago Press, 1982).

Principal Contributions My early work examined labour markets and the economics of health. Investigation of the impact of information and advertising on market organisation and prices evolved out of my interests in the regulation of professional labour markets. Licensed professionals have generally restricted advertising by their members. I first studied the consequences of advertising bans in No. 2 above. A companion paper (No. 5, with Alexandra Benham) provided additional evidence that such bans are associated with significantly higher prices and an altered industry structure. The political economy of self-regulating occupations has been the subject of several further studies. Currently, my interest in the role of information continues, and I am also examining the impact of political climate on the costs of contracting and the organisation of firms.

BEN-PORATH, Yoram

Born 1937, Ramat Gan, Israel.
Current Post Prof. Econ., Hebrew Univ. Jerusalem, 1977–; Dir., Maurice Falk Inst. Econ. Res. Israel, Jerusalem, 1979–.
Past Posts Ass. Prof. Econ., Univ. Chicago, 1967; Lect., Sr. Lect., Assoc. Prof. Econ., Hebrew Univ., 1967–70,

1970–2, 1973–7; Cons., Rand Corp., CA, 1968–; Vis. Lect. Econ., Harvard Univ., 1971–2; Vis. Prof. Econ., UCLA, 1976–7; Fellow, Inst. Advanced Stud., Hebrew Univ., Jerusalem, 1977–8.

Degrees BA, MA Hebrew Univ. Jerusalem, 1961, 1963; PhD Harvard Univ., 1967.

Offices and Honours Israel Tax Reform Commission, 1975; Fellow, Em Soc, 1977–; Internat. Comm. Pop. and Income Distribution, 1980–2; Member, Standing Comm., Hebrew Univ., 1977–81.

Editorial Duties Assoc. Ed., *REStat*, 1972–.

Principal Fields of Interest 111 Economic Growth Theory; 320 Public Finance; 800 Manpower, Labour, Population.

Publications *Books:* 1. *The Arab Labor Force in Israel* (The Maurice Falk Inst. Econ. Res. Israel, 1966); 2. *Family Aspects of Income Distribution*, ed. (Suppl., *Pop. and Devlp. Review*, 8, 1982).

Articles: 1. 'The production of human capital and the life-cycle of earnings', *JPE*, 75(4), pt. 1, Aug. 1967; 2. 'Fertility in Israel: an economist's interpretation — differentials and trends, 1950–76', in *Economic Development and Population Growth in the Middle East*, eds. C. A. Cooper and S. S. Alexander (American Elsevier, 1972); 3. 'Labor force participation rates and the supply of labor', *JPE*, 81(3), May–June 1973; 4. 'Short-term fluctuations in fertility and economic activity in Israel', *Demography*, May 1973; 5. 'Economic analysis of fertility in Israel: point and counterpoint', *JPE*, 81(2), pt. 2, March–April 1973; 6. 'First generation effects on second generation fertility', *Demography*, Aug. 1975; 7. 'Fertility response to child mortality, micro-data from Israel', *JPE*, 84(2), pt. 2, Aug. 1976; 8. 'Do sex differences really matter?' (with F. Welch), *QJE*, 90(2), May 1980; 9. 'The political economy of a tax reform: Israel 1975' (with M. Bruno), *JPE*, 7(3), June 1977; 10. 'The F-connection: families, friends and firms and the organization of exchange', *Pop. and Devlp Rev.*, 6(1), March 1980.

Principal Contributions Mostly worked in the economics of human resources — human capital, labour supply and economics of the family. Papers reflect a dialogue between empirical work and theory — mostly extensions of microeconomic analysis to non-market activities. The theoretical model of human capital accumulation which generates the concave life-cycle of earnings was preceded by empirical work on this topic. Interest in population generated by Kuznet's work led to a series of empirical and micro-theoretical studies of fertility. This work on the family led to questions on the role of families in the institutional set-up of the economy and the importance of identity of transactions in a world of imperfect information. Interest in another border area, political economy, is reflected in an early paper which identified a political business cycle in Israel, analysis of the tax reform and recent work on the response of the public sector to demographic pressures.

BENSTON, George J.

Born 1932, New York City, NY, USA.

Current Post Prof. Accounting, Econ. and Fin., Grad. School Management, Univ. Rochester, Rochester, NY, USA, 1976–.

Past Posts Instr., Ass. Prof. Accounting, Georgia State Coll., Atlanta, GA, 1956–8; Ass. Prof. Accounting, Grad. School Bus., Univ. Chicago, 1962–6; Vis. Ass. Prof. Fin., Univ. Cal. Berkeley, 1963; Assoc. Prof. Accounting and Fin., Coll. Bus. Admin., Univ. Rochester, 1966–9; Disting. Vis. Faculty, Amer. Accounting Assoc. Doctoral Consorti, 1972, 1978; Vis. Prof., London Grad. School Bus. Stud., LSE, 1971, Hebrew Univ., Jerusalem, 1973, 1979, 1981; Lect., Law and Conservation Center, Emory Univ., Atlanta, GA, 1979–.

Degrees BA (Liberal Arts and Accounting), Queens Coll., NYC, 1952; MBA (Accounting and Taxation), NYU, 1953; Chartered Public Accountant Univ. N. Carolina, 1955; PhD Univ. Chicago, 1963.

Offices and Honours Woodrow Wilson Fellow, 1958–9; US Steel Foundation Fellow, 1958–9, 1959–60; Fed. Reserve

Bank Chicago Res. Fellow, 1960–1; Ford Foundation Dissertation Fellow, 1961–2; Beta Gamma Sigma; Phi Beta Kappa; Beta Gama Sigma Disting. Scholar, 1975.

Editorial Duties Assoc. Ed., *J Fin, JMCB, J Bank Res., Account. J, J Fin. Res., J. Account. & Public Policy, J. Account. and Econ., Account Rev., Wall Street Rev. Books.*

Principal Fields of Interest 310 Domestic Monetary and Financial Theory and Institutions; 540 Accounting; 610 Industrial Organisation and Public Policy.

Publications *Books:* 1. *Corporate Financial Disclosure in the UK and the USA* (D. C. Heath, Inst. Chartered Accountants in England and Wales, 1976); 2. *Contemporary Cost Accounting and Control* (Dickenson, 1970, CBI Publishing, 1977); 3. *Federal Reserve Membership: Consequences, Costs, Benefits and Alternatives* (Assoc. Reserve City Bankers Chicago, 1978); 4. *An Empirical Study of Mortgage Redlining* (with D. Horsky and H. M. Weingartner), (Salomon Bros. Center, NYU, 1978); 5. *Conglomerate Mergers: Causes, Consequences and Remedies* (AEI, 1980); 6. *Investors' Use of Published Financial Accounting Data: A Review of the Evidence from Research* (Univ. Glasgow Press, 1981); 7. *Financial Services: The Changing Institutions and Government Policy* (Prentice-Hall, 1983).

Articles: 1. 'Published corporate accounting data and stock prices', *J. Account Res., Empirical Res. in Account.: Selected Studies,* 1967; 2. 'Required disclosure and the stock markets: an evaluation of the securities exchange act of 1934', *AER,* 63(1), March 1973; 3. 'A transactions cost approach to the theory of financial intermediation' (with C. W. Smith Jr.), *J Fin,* 31(2), May 1976; 4. 'The impact of maturity regulation on high interest rate lenders and borrowers', *J Fin E Con,* 4(1), Jan. 1977; 5. 'Rate ceiling implications of the cost structure of consumer finance companies', *J Fin,* 32(4), Sept. 1977; 6. 'The market for public accounting services: demand, supply and regulation', *Accounting J.,* 2, 1979–80; 7. 'Accounting numbers and economic values',

Antitrust Bull., 27, Spring 1982; 8. 'The economics of gender discrimination in employee fringe benefits: Manhart revisited', *Univ Chicago Law Rev.,* 49, Spring 1982; 9. 'Scale economies in banking: a restructuring and reassessment' (with C. A. Hanweck and B. B. Humphrey), *JMCB,* 14(4), pt. 1, Nov. 1982; 10. 'Federal regulation of banking: analysis and policy recommendations', *J Bank Res.,* 13(4), Winter 1982.

Principal Contributions Having been a practicing CPA and then a banker before getting a PhD in economics, I teach and do research in several fields. Banking (or, rather, financial services) is the principal focus of my work. This area provides the researcher with interesting problems in regulation, market structure, production functions, and the effects of changing economic and technological conditions. Excellent data are available for empirical estimations and tests of hypotheses. In this regard, I have conducted research on economies of scale and operating costs in commercial banks, thrift insititutions, and consumer finance companies. With respect to regulation, I have conducted studies on bank examination and supervision, banking structure, the payments system, mortgage redlining, and deposit insurance. Accounting is another area in which I have continued to work.

In adition to analyses of costs, I have been concerned with issues of disclosure and the Securities and Exchange Commission. I conducted the first empirical study of the relationship between accounting data and stock prices. I also initiated a study on the effects and effectiveness of SEC accounting disclosure requirements. Additional work in accounting includes analyses of accounting standards and social responsibility in accounting. Most of this work has relied strongly on economic analysis. Some economic subjects on which I have written include the use of accounting data for antitrust and economic analysis, sex discrimination in employment, and standing to sue in price fixing cases.

BENTHAM, Jeremy*

Dates and Birthplace 1748–1832, London, England.
Post Held Private income.
Degrees BA, MA Univ. Oxford, 1763, 1766.
Offices Called to the bar, 1817.
Publications *Books:* 1. *A Fragment on Government* (1776, 1951); 2. *An Introduction to the Principles of Morals and Legislation* (1780, 1823, 1948); 3. *Rationale of Judicial Evidence*, 5 vols, ed. J. S. Mill (1827); 4. *The Works of Jeremy Bentham*, 11 vols., ed. J. Bowring (1838–43, 1962); 5. *Jeremy Bentham's Economic Writings*, 3 vols, ed. W. Stark (1952); 6. *The Collected Works of Jeremy Bentham*, 36 vols. ed. J. Burns (1968 — in progress).
Career Bentham is remembered both as a pioneer of social science and as a tireless advocate of administrative, legal and parliamentary reform. He found in the principle of utility, and in particular in his notorious 'felicific calculus', an exact standard by which questions of reform could be settled. The reforms he pressed for were directed towards his four ends of good government: subsistence, abundance, security and equality. He interpreted the economics of Adam Smith in the light of the search for abundance and advocated a state which provided guaranteed employment, minimum wages and a variety of social benefits. Much of his influence on ideas and legislation was through a small but enthusiastic circle of pupils and disciples, amongst whom were many economists, including Ricardo, and James and John Stuart Mill. Only a small portion of his vast literary output was published in his own lifetime, and a complete edition of his works projected in 36 volumes is still in preparation. Even his strictly economic writings, a small part of the whole, contain many remarkable contributions that have only come to be properly appreciated in recent times.
Secondary Literature M. P. Mack, 'Bentham, Jeremy', *IESS*, 2.

BERG, Elliot Joseph

Born 1927, New York City, NY, USA
Current Post Pres., Elliot Berg Assoc., Alexandria, VI, USA, 1982–.
Past Posts Field Organiser, NY Branch, United World Federalists, 1950–1; Admin. Staff, Foreign Policy Assoc., NYC, 1951–2; Res. Fellow, African Res. and Stud. Program, Boston Univ., 1954–5; Teaching Fellow, Ass. Prof. Econ., Harvard Univ., 1959–64; Project Dir., Harvard Advisory Group, Liberia, 1964–6; Prof. Econ., Dir. Center Econ. Devlp., Univ. Michigan, 1966–83; Cons., World Bank, 1980–1, Govt. Expenditure Analysis Division, IMF, 1981–2; Adjunct Prof., Georgetown Univ., 1983–4, Univ. Clermont-Ferrand, France, 1979–.
Degrees BA NYU, 1949; MA Columbia Univ., 1955; PhD Harvard Univ., 1960.
Offices and Honours Phi Beta Kappa; French Govt. Fellow, 1952–4; Jacob Wertheim Fellow, Harvard Univ., 1955–7; Ford Foundation Foreign Area Training Fellow, 1957–9; Ford Foundation Faculty Res. Fellow, 1959–70; Grand Commander Order of the Star of Africa, Govt. of Liberia, 1966.
Principal Fields of Interest 113 Economic Planning; 121 Economic Studies Less Industrialised Countries; 443 International Aid.
Publications *Books:* 1. *A New American Policy for Africa* (Africa League, 1960); 2. *The Recent Economic Evolution of the Sahel* (Univ. Michigan Press, 1975); 3. *Marketing Price Policy and Storage of Foodgrains in the Sahel. A Survey* (Univ. Michigan Press, 1977); 4. *Accelerated Development in Sub-Saharan Africa* (World Bank, 1981); 5. *Changing the Public-Private Mix: A Survey of Some Recent Experiences in LDCs* (IMF, 1983); 6. *Absorptive Capacity in the Sahel* (OECD, 1983).
Articles: 1. 'The economic basis of political choice in French West Africa', *Amer. Polit. Science Rev.*, June 1960; 2. 'Backward sloping labor supply functions in dual economies — the Africa case', *QJE*, 75, Aug. 1961, 76, Nov. 1962; 3. 'Trade unions' (with J. Butler), in *Political Parties and National Integration in Tropical Africa* (Univ. Cal.

Press, 1964); 4. Socialism and economic development in tropical Africa', *QJE*, 78, Nov. 1964; 5. 'The economics of migrant labor in West Africa', in *Urbanization and Migration in West Africa* (Univ. Cal. Press, 1965); 6. 'Major issues in wage policy in Africa', in *Industrial Relations and Economic Development* (Macmillan, 1966); 7. 'Wage structure in less-developed countries', in *Wage Policy Issues in Economic Development* (CRED, 1968); 9. 'Esquisse d'un modèle bureaucratique du choix des projets', *Annales Econ.*, 14, 1980; 10. 'The World Bank strategy', in *Africa in Economic Crisis* (Macmillan, 1984).

Principal Contributions I became an economist because I was interested in world poverty — why countries grow or don't grow. I started working on African problems mainly because my first preference, China, was not at that time open to outside study. Two perceptions emerged early in my career; these I tried to explain to my students, and are now reflected in my analytic work and consulting. The first is that policy is a lot more important than most economists have ever allowed. This was especially evident in the field of development, which was from its infancy dominated by mechanistic models of the growth process. The second perception is that organisational irrationality explains more of what happens in the world than any set of analytic propositions based on assumptions of 'rational' behaviour. Neither of these perceptions is particularly congenial to academic economics, which explains my decision to leave the academy (at least full-time) and concentrate on consulting. My main contributions in this work have been to offer candid assessments of policies and programmes, and, especially in recent years, to find ways that individual initiative and market forces can be harnessed more effectively in developing countries.

BERGLAS, Eitan

Born 1934, Tel Aviv, Israel.
Current Post Prof. Econ., Dir., Sapir Res. Inst., Tel Aviv Univ., 1981.
Past Posts Econ. Adviser, Israeli Govt., 1964–7; Sr. Lect. Econ., Assoc. Prof., Tel Aviv Univ., 1966–71, 1971–75; Vis. Xerox Prof., Univ. Rochester, NY, 1974–6; Vice-Rector, Tel Aviv Univ., 1977–8; Dir. Budget, Israeli Govt., 1978–9.

Degrees BA Hebrew Univ., Jerusalem, 1960; MA, PhD Univ. Chicago, 1962, 1963.

Offices and Honours Member, Israeli Comm. Fin. Higher Educ., 1970–2; Israeli Tax Reform Commission, 1971–3; Israeli Commission Wages Public Sector, 1977–9; Pres., Israeli Econ. Assoc., 1984.

Principal Fields of Interest 320 Fiscal Theory & Policy; Public Finance; 480 International Economics; 930 Urban Economics.

Publications *Articles:* 1. 'Real exchange rate and devaluation' (with A. Razin), *J Int E*, 3(2), May 1973; 2. 'Devaluation, monetary policy and border tax adjustments', *CJE*, 7(1), Feb. 1974; 3. 'Distribution of tastes and skills and the provision of local public goods', *J Pub E*, 6(4), Nov. 1976; 4. 'On the theory of clubs', *AER*, 66(2), May 1976; 5. 'Pollution control and intercommunity trade', *Bell JE*, 8(1), Spring 1977; 6. 'The export of technology' (with R. W. Jones) in *Optimal Policies, Control Theory and Technology Exports*, eds. K. Brunner and A. Metzler (Wiley, 1977), repr. in *International Trade: Essays in Theory*, ed. R. W. Jones (N-H, 1979); 7. 'Preferential trading theory: the n–commodity case', *JPE*, 87(2), April 1979; 8. 'Clubs, local public goods and transportation models: a synthesis' (with D. Pines), *J Pub E*, 15(2), April 1981; 9. 'Harmonization of commodity taxes: destination, origin and restricted origin principles', *J Pub E*, 16(5), Dec. 1981; 10. 'User charges, local public services and taxation of land rents', *PF*, 37(2), 1982.

Principal Contributions My early work was related to problems of balance of payments theory. In these works I have used the monetary approach to the balance of payments though I have tended to emphasise the effect of fiscal policy on the balance of payments. Later I have moved to problems of a system of communities. This research is an extension of the theory of clubs to questions related to provision of public services in an urban context when cities are regarded as groupings of people that collectively provide and consume some public services and at the same time co-operate in the production process. In my work I have emphasised the effect of social mobility on the distribution of production. I have characterised the equilibrium allocation of local public goods, and tax structures and studied the conditions under which costless mobility results in an efficient allocation. In another line of research I have contributed to the development of the theory of preferential trading by extending the analysis to the case of many goods. This analysis shows that some important results of the two-good custom union theory do not extend to the case where the number of goods exceeds two. This extended model has been used to analyse problems of fiscal harmonisation.

BERGMANN, Barbara Rose

Born 1927, New York City, NY, USA.

Current Post Prof. Econ., Univ. Maryland, MD, USA, 1971–.

Past Posts Econ., US Bureau Labor Stats, NY Regional Office, 1949–53; Teaching Fellow Econ., Instr. Econ., Harvard Univ., 1954–8, 1958–61; Sr. Res. Assoc., Harvard Econ. Res. Project, 1960–1; Econ., NY Metropolitan Region Study, 1957–61; Sr. Staff Econ., US President's Council Econ. Advisers, 1961–2; Assoc. Prof. Econ., Brandeis Univ., 1962–4; Sr. Staff, Brookings Inst., 1963–5; Sr. Econ. Adviser, Agency Internat. Devlp., US Dept. State, 1966–7; Assoc. Prof. Econ., Univ. Maryland, 1965–71.

Degrees BA (Maths., Econ.) Cornell Univ., 1948; MA PhD Harvard Univ., 1959.

Offices and Honours Phi Beta Kappa; Pres., EEA, 1974; Vice-Pres., AEA, 1976; Member, Advisory Board Women's Law Project, Center Law and Social Policy, 1974–80; Board Dirs., Public Interest Econ. Center, 1975–6, US Congressional Budget Office, Panel Econ. Advisers, 1977–,

AEA Advisory Comm., US Census Bureau, 1977–82, Price Advisory Comm., US Council Wage and Price Stability, 1979–80; Council, AAUP, 1980–3; Chair, Comm. Status of Women in Econ. Profession, AEA, 1982–; Columnist, *NY Times*, 1981–2.

Editorial Duties Ed. Boards, *AER*, 1970–3, *Challenge, Signs, Women and Politics*.

Principal Fields of Interest 211 Econometric and Statistical Models and Methods; 800 Manpower; Labour; Population.

Publications Books: 1. *Projection of a Metropolis* (with B. Chinitz and E. Hoover), (Harvard Univ. Press, 1961); 2. *Structural Unemployment in the United States* (with D. Kaun), (US Dept. Commerce, 1967).

Articles: 1. 'Alternative measures of structural unemployment', in *Employment Policy and the Labor Market*, ed. A. M. Ross (Univ. Cal. Press, 1965); 2. 'Investment in the human resources of Negroes', in *Federal Programs for the Development of Human Resources*, Joint Econ. Comm., US Congress (US Govt. Printing Office, 1968), repr. in *Race and Poverty, The Economics of Discrimination*, ed. J. F. Kain (Prentice Hall, 1969); 3. 'The effect on white incomes of discrimination in employment', *JPE*, 79(2), March–April 1971; 4. 'The occupational standing of negroes by areas and industries' (with J. R. Lyle), *JHR*, 6(4), Fall 1971; 5. 'Assessing the impact of alternative economic outcomes on social objectives', in *Input Output Techniques*, eds. A. Brody and A. P. Carter (N-H, 1973); 6. 'Can racial discrimination be ended under capitalism?', in *Issues in Political Economy: Orthodox and Radical Approaches*, ed. J. Weaver (Allyn and Bacon, 1972), repr. in *Economics: Mainstream Readings and Radical Critiques*, ed. D. Mermelstein (Random House, 1973); 7. 'The 1973 report of the president's council of economic advisors: the economic role of women' (with I. Adelman), *AER*, 63(4), Sept. 1973; 8. 'Combining microsimulation and regression: a "prepared" regression of poverty incidence on unemployment and growth', *Em*, 41(5), Sept. 1973; 9. 'Unemployment rate targets and anti-inflation policy as more women enter the workforce' (with C. Vickery and K. Swartz), *AER*, 68(2), May 1978; 10. 'Discrimination and unemployment', in *Unemployment in Western Countries*, eds. E. Malinvaud and J–P. Fitoussi (Macmillan, 1980).

Principal Contributions My principal interests lie in the fields of sex roles in economic life, in the use of computer simulation of economic systems as an alternative to economic theory as currently practised, and in the reform of the methods of data collection. What unifies these interests is a dissatisfaction with economic study as currently practised.

My work on sex roles has been designed to elucidate the caste-like character of assignments to economic role by sex, and to chart out a more just and humane future. Another focus of my work in the sex-role field has been the causes, form and effect of discrimination in the labour market. My work in computer simulation has produced a group of smaller models of dynamic processes: labour force entry of wives, labour turnover as a generator of unemployment durations, inventory accumulation as a mode of avoidance of customer loss, changes in product characteristics in a monopolistically competitive industry (the latter two are still in draft). I have also engaged in building a large model which deals with macroeconomic phenomena (GNP, production, employment, inflation), but which is built up from computer code which describes the activity of individual business firms and individual consumer-workers.

In my presidential address to the Eastern Economic Association, I criticised current practice, in which economists have contact with the real world of economic actors in only two ways: by throwing into our computers the third-hand data we get in the form of government statistics, and through introspection while sitting in our chairs. I believe the lack of first-hand data-gathering work to be at the root of much of what is nonproductive in our professional practice. I have recently started to perform research myself in which direct contact with economic actors is a feature.

BERGSON, Abram

Born 1914, Baltimore, MD, USA.
Current Post George F. Baker Prof. Econ., Harvard Univ., Cambridge, MA, USA, 1971–.
Past Posts Ass. Prof. Econ., Univ. Texas, 1940–2; Chief Econ. Subdivision, US Office Strategic Services, 1942–5; Member, American Reparations Delegation, Moscow, 1945; Ass. Prof., Assoc. Prof., Prof. Econ., Columbia Univ., 1946–56; Prof. Econ., Harvard Univ., 1956–70; Cons., RAND Corp., Santa Monica, CA, 1948–; Board Dirs., US SSRC, 1962–8; Member, Chairman, Social Science Advisory Board, US Arms Control and Disarmament Agency, 1966–73, 1971–3; Chairman, Advisory Committee Nat. Income Estimates, World Bank, 1983.
Degrees BA Johns Hopkins Univ., 1933; MA PhD Harvard Univ., 1935, 1940; Hon. LLD, Univ. Windsor, Canada, 1979.
Offices and Honours Phi Beta Kappa, 1933; Sheldon Travelling Fellow, Harvard Univ., 1937, 1939–40; Ford Faculty Res. Fellow, 1962; Fellow, Center Behavioral Science, Stanford, 1963–4; AAAS, Amer. Phil. Soc.; NAS; Award, Disting. Contrib., Amer. Assoc. Advancement Slavic Stud., 1975; Disting. Fellow, AEA, 1970; Council, IEA, 1974–77; Pres., Comparative Econ. Assoc., 1981.
Editorial Duties Ed. Boards, *Slavic and E. Europ. Rev.*, *JEL*, *J Comp E*, *Social Choice and Welfare*; Hon. ed., *Soviet Economy*.
Principal Fields of Interest 024 Welfare Theory; 027 Economics of Centrally Planned Economies; 052 Socialist and Communist Economic Systems.
Publications *Books:* 1. *The Structure of Soviet Wages: A Study in Socialist Economics* (Harvard Univ. Press, 1944; transl., Japanese, 1950); 2. *Soviet Economic Growth: Conditions and Perspectives*, ed. and contrib. (Row Peterson, 1953; transl., Japanese 1955); 3. *Real National Income of Soviet Russia*, (Harvard Univ. Press, 1961; transl., Japanese, 1965); 4. *Economic Trends in the Soviet Union*, ed. and contrib. (Harvard Univ. Press, 1963); 5. *The Economics of Soviet Planning* (Yale

Univ. Press, 1964); 6. *Essays in Normative Economics* (Harvard Univ. Press, 1966); 7. *Planning and Productivity under Soviet Socialism* (Columbia Univ. Press, 1968); 8. *Productivity and the Social System — The USSR and the West* (Harvard Univ. Press, 1978); transl., Spanish, 1981); 9. *Welfare, Planning and Employment: Selected Essays in Economic Theory* (MIT Press, 1982); 10. *The Soviet Economy: Towards the Year 2000*, co-ed. (with H. Levine) (A&U, 1983).

Articles: 1. 'Note on consumers' surplus', *JEL*, 13(1), March 1975; 2. 'Notes on the production function in Soviet post-war industrial growth', *J Comp E*, 3(2), June 1979; 3. 'Are the Russians oversaving?', in *Festgabe für Ota Sik*, eds. U. Gartner and J. Kosta (Duncker and Humboldt, 1979); 4. 'The geometry of COMECON trade', *Europ ER*, 14(3), Dec. 1980; 5. 'Paul A. Samuelson: the Harvard days', in *Samuelson and Neoclassical Economics*, ed. G. Feiwel (Kluwer–Nijhoff, 1981); 6. 'Soviet consumption in Western perspective', *Econ. Notes* (Monte dei Paschi di Siena), 2, 1982; 7. 'Entrepreneurship under labor participation: the Yugoslav case', in *Entrepreneurship*, ed. J. Ronen (D. C. Heath, 1982); 8. 'Pareto on social welfare', *JEL*, 21(1), March 1983; 9. 'On the measurement of real Soviet defense expenditures', in *Marxism, Central Planning and the Soviet Economy*, ed. P. Desai (MIT Press, 1983).

Principal Contributions *Welfare Economics:* An early (1936, repr. 1966, 1982) article analysed the implications, for the individual's indifference map and utility function, of the conditions that Ragnar Frisch imposed in order to measure utility. A utility function of the sort since referred to as CES emerged, and some of its properties were delineated. Another essay, also early (1938, repr. 1966, 1982) introduced the concept of a social welfare function into welfare economics, and used it in order to make explicit the value premises underlying different formulations. More recently (1973, 1979 and 1980, all repr. 1982), a series of essays sought to clarify consumers' and producers' surplus in a general equilibrium context, and presented on that basis an alternative to the widely-held view of the unimportance of monopoly welfare losses.

Socialist planning theory and public enterprise pricing: Two essays (1948, repr. 1966, 1982; 1967, repr. 1982) surveying theoretic literature on socialist planning, among other things, considered at an early stage the possibility that incentives of enterprise managers could result in inefficient actions. Two subsequent (1972, repr. 1982; 1978, repr. 1982) essays deal with public enterprise: one re-examining the question of the second-best optimum price for a public enterprise and the other exploring how to reward public enterprise management in order to induce it to take an appropriate attitude towards risk.

Comparative systems: An early (1944) monograph represents an effort to clarify the principles of relative wage determination in the USSR. Another volume (1961) brought to a conclusion over a decade of research by myself and others attempting systematically to compile measures of Soviet real national income that conform to Western national income methodology. More recently, a short volume (1968) and a number of essays (repr. 1978) seek to clarify the 'static' and 'dynamic' efficiency of the Soviet and East European economies. The Soviet planning process is also examined from the standpoint of efficiency in my *Economics of Soviet Planning* (1964).

BERGSTROM, Theodore Carl

Born 1940, Cambridge, MA, USA.
Current Post Prof. Econ., Univ. Michigan, Ann Arbor, MI, USA, 1975–.
Past Posts Ass. Prof., Assoc. Prof., Prof. Econ., Washington Univ., St Louis, MO, 1966–75.
Degrees BA (Maths.) Carleton College., 1962; PhD Stanford Univ., 1968.
Principal Fields of Interest 021 General Equilibrium Theory; 022 Microeconomic Theory; 321 Fiscal Theory and Policy.
Publications *Articles:* 1. 'A "Scandinavian consensus" solution for efficient income distribution among non-

malevolent consumers', *JET*, 2, Dec. 1970; 2. 'On the existence and optimality of competitive equilibrium for a slave economy', *REStud*, 38, Jan. 1971; 3. 'Private demands for public goods' (with R. Goodman), *AER*, 63(3), June 1973; 4. 'The core when strategies are restricted by law', *REStud*, 42(2), April 1975; 5. 'How to dispose of free disposability — at no cost', *J Math E*, 3, 1976; 6. 'When is a man's life worth more than his human capital?', in *The Value of Life and Safety*, ed. M. Jones-Lee (N-H, 1982); 7. 'On capturing oil rents with a national excise tax', *AER*, 72(1), March 1982; 8. 'Microeconomic estimates of demand for local public goods' (with D. Rubinfeld and P. Shapiro), *Em*, 50(5), Sept. 1982; 9. 'Independence of allocative efficiency from distribution in the theory of public goods' (with R. Cornes), *Em*, 51(6), Nov. 1983; 10. 'Counting Groves-Ledyard equilibria via degree theory' (with C. Simon), *J Math E*, 11(4), Oct. 1983.

Principal Contributions Much of my work consists of applications of the techniques of modern mathematical economics to problems of social interaction. Examples include work on benevolent consumers, competitive equilibrium with slavery, law and the core when there are externalities, the valuation of human life, the theory of health insurance, voting theory, and the theory of marriage and the family. I have also done work on the foundations of the theory of general equilibrium, welfare economics, and public finance. This research includes contributions to the technical literature on the existence of competitive equilibrium (for example, dispensing with the assumptions of free disposal and monotonicity), the existence of Lindahl equilibrium and its properties, and the determination of necessary and sufficient conditions for the Pareto optimal supply of public goods to be independent of income distribution. A third area of interest is empirical estimates of demand for local public goods. I developed (with R. Goodman) a theory and method for estimating individual demand functions for public goods from cross-sectional data on the expenditures of munici-palities and on the economic and demographic characteristics of their populations. More recently, D. Rubinfeld, P. Shapiro, and I have developed a method for estimating demand functions for public goods from individual survey data.

BERKELEY, George*

Dates and Birthplace 1685–1753, Kilkenny, Ireland.

Post Held Bishop of Cloyne, Ireland, 1734–52.

Degrees BA, MA Trinity Coll., Dublin, 1704, 1707.

Publications *Books:* 1. *An Essay Towards Preventing the Ruine of Great Britain* (1721, 1953); 2. *The Querist* (1735–7, 1953); 3. *A Word to the Wise* (1749, 1953); 4. *The Works of George Berkeley*, 9 vols., eds. A. A. Luce and T. E. Jessop (1948–57).

Career Best known as a philosopher and critic of Hobbes and Locke, his work on economic questions is largely contained in *The Querist* in which the problems of Ireland are discussed as a series of some 900 questions. The originality of his method is its application of moral and theological concepts to the question of economic development. He argued that Irish development needed positive government intervention and the creation of an appropriate moral and social environment through the efforts of the Church. His work in economics, as distinct from his philosophical writings, seems to have had little impact on later thinkers.

Secondary Literature I. D. S. Ward, 'Berkeley, George', *IESS*, 2.

BERNDT, Ernst Rudolph

Born 1946, Crespo, Entre Rios, Argentina.

Current Post Prof. Applied Econ., Sloan School Management, MIT; Res. Assoc., NBER, Cambridge, MA, USA, 1980–.

Past Posts Res. Econ., Exec. Office US President, Washington DC, 1971–2; Ass. Prof. Econ., Univ. British

Columbia, Vancouver, Canada, 1976–80; Vis. Scholar, MIT, 1977–8.

Degrees BA Valparaiso Univ., Valparaiso, IN, 1968; MS, PhD Univ. Wisconsin, 1971, 1972.

Offices and Honours Canada Council Sabbatical Leave Fellow, 1977–8; Member, US, NAS Comm. Nuclear and Alternative Energy Systems, 1976–80.

Editorial Duties Assoc. Book Review Ed., *JASA*, 1977–81; Ed. Board, *Resources and Energy*, 1979–, *Energy J*, 1979–; Assoc. Ed., *J Bus. Admin.*, 1982–; *J Em*, 1983–.

Principal Fields of Interest 211 Econometric and Statistical Methods and Models; 620 Economics of Technological Change: 720 Natural Resources.

Publications *Books:* 1. *Modeling and Measuring Natural Resource Substitution*, co-ed. (with B. Field), (Wiley, 1981).

Articles: 1. 'The internal structure of functional relationships: separability, substitution and aggregation', *REStud*, 40(3), July 1973; 2. 'The translog function and the substitution of equipment, structures and labor in US manufacturing' (with L. R. Christensen), *J Em*, 1(1), 1973; 3. 'Estimation and inference in nonlinear structural models' (with B. H. Hall, R. E. Hall and J. A. Hausman), *Annals Econ. and Social Measurement*, Oct. 1974; 4. 'Estimation and hypothesis testing in singular equation systems with autoregressive disturbances', *Em*, 43(5–6), July–Aug., 1975; 5. 'Technology, prices and the derived demand for energy', *REStat*, 57(3), Aug. 1975; 6. 'Conflict among criteria for testing hypotheses in the multivariate linear regression model' (with N. E. Savin), *Em*, 45(5), July 1977; 7. 'Engineering and econometric interpretation of energy-capital complementarity' (with D. O. Wood), *AER*, 69(3), June 1979; 8. 'Energy price increases and the productivity slowdown in United States manufacturing', in *The Decline in Productivity Growth* (Fed. Reserve Bank Boston, 1980); 9. 'Capacity utilization measures: underlying economic theory and an alternative approach' (with C. J. Morrison), *AER*, 71(2), May 1981; 10. 'Short run labor productivity in a dynamic model' (with C. J. Morrison), *J Em*, 16, Dec. 1981.

Principal Contributions I think of myself as an applied econometrician with a special interest in microeconomic topics. My early research involved empirical implementation of translog production and cost functions. Subsequent theoretical research focussed on relationships among the concepts of functional separability, substitution elasticities, and consistent aggregation. This mix of economic theory and empirical implementations then led me to examine alternative criteria for testing hypothesis in multiple equation systems, and also extended to a consideration of problems in consistently specifying vector autoregressive processes in singular equation systems. In the last decade much of my empirical research has involved modelling the special relationship between energy and capital, and examining implications of the OPEC energy price increases on investment, capacity output and productivity. The initial framework employed a static optimisation framework but by the late 1970s I was involved in estimation of dynamic factor demand models. Currently my research is a mix of analyses of energy-productivity interactions, the integration of hedonic price analyses with the theory of cost and production, the measurement of consumers' evaluations of technical design innovations in the Swedish and US automobile markets, and an evaluation of productivity performance in the 200 US electric power industries.

BERNHOLZ, Peter

Born 1929, Bad Salzuflen, Westphalia, W. Germany.

Current Post Prof., Dir., Inst. Sozialwissenschaften, Univ. Basel, Switzerland, 1971–.

Pasts Posts Dozent, Univ. Frankfurt, 1964–6; Prof., Technische Univ. Berlin, 1966–71; Vis. Prof., MIT, 1969, Virginia Polytechnic Inst., 1974, 1978, Stanford Univ., 1981; Dean, Philosophisch–Historische Fakultät, Univ. Basel, 1982–3.

Degrees Diplom-Volkswirt, Dr. Rer.

Pol. Univ. Marburg, 1953, 1955; Habilitation Univ. Frankfurt, 1862.

Offices and Honours Rockefeller Fellow, Harvard Univ., Stanford Univ., 1963–4; Member, Verein für Sozialpolitik; Member, Pres. Europ. Section, Public Choice Soc., 1974–80, 1980–; Member, Mont Pelerin Soc.; Member, Scientific Advisory Board, W. German Econ. Ministry, 1974–.

Editorial Duties Ed. Board, *J. Public Choice*.

Principal Fields of Interest 311 Monetary Theory and Policy; 430 International Monetary Economics; 025 Public Choice and Social Choice.

Publications *Books:* 1. *Mehrergiebigkeit ängerer Produktionswege und reine Kapitaltheorie* (Marburg Dissertation, 1955); 2. *Aussenpolitik und internationale Wirtschaftsbeziehungen* (Klostermann, 1966); 3. *Grundlagen der politischen Ökonomie* 3 vols. (Siebeck, 1972–9); 4. *Währungskrisen und Währungsordnung* (Hoffman & Campe, 1974); 5. *Flexible Exchange Rates in Historical Perspective* (Princeton Stud. Internat. Fin., 49, 1982); 6. *The International Game of Power* (Mouton, 1984).

Articles: 1. 'Economic policies in a democracy', *Kyk*, 19(1), 1966; 2. 'Erwerbkosten, Laufzeit und Charakter zimstrangender Forderungen als Bestimmungsgründe der Geldnachfrage der Haushalte', *ZGS*, 123(1), Jan. 1967; 3. 'Log-rolling, Arrow-paradox and cyclical majorities', *Public Choice*, 15, Summer 1973; 4. 'On the reasons of the influence of interest groups on political decision-making', *Zeitschrift für Wirtschafts und Sozialwissenschaften*, 33(1), 1974; 5. 'A general two-period neo-Austrian model of capital' (with M. Faber and W. Reiss), *JET*, 17(1), March 1978; 6. 'Steady state and superiority of roundaboutness' (with M. Faber), *ZGS*, 134(4), Dec. 1978; 7. 'A general social dilemma: profitable exchange and intransitive group preferences', *ZN*, 40(2), 1980; 8. 'Expanding welfare state, democracy and free market economy: are they compatible?', *ZGS*, 138(3), Sept. 1982; 9. 'Externalities as a necessary condition for cyclical social preferences', *QJE*, 47(4), Nov. 1982; 10. 'Inflation and monetary constitu-

tions in historical perspective', *Kyk*, 36(3), 1983.

Principal Contributions Early interest in intertemporal problems encouraged work on Austrian-capital and on monetary theory. Austrian capital theory was reformulated (later together with M. Faber, W. Reiss and G. Stephan) and the explanations of Böhm-Bawerk and Schumpeter for positive interest integrated. It was proved that the fact of a higher interest than growth rate in neoclassical balanced growth models is caused by superior roundabout production processes.

In public choice theory, imperfect information of voters, economic growth and interest groups were shown to bring about the support of stagnating industries by democratic governments. Moreover, it was demonstrated that vote-trading benefitting majorities implies the presence of cyclical social preferences with separable individual preferences. The ensuing discussion suggested a similar but more general theorem for all non-oligarchic societies. Additionally, Sen's 'Dilemma of a Paretian Liberal' holds true under the same broad conditions. This institutional interpretation of Arrow's theorem was recently followed by the proof that, for any profile of individual preferences and non-oligarchic setting, there exists an assignment of rights to different subsets of society to decide among different pairs of outcomes removing cyclical social preferences and Sen's dilemma.

Interest in international monetary problems led to an analysis of many countries and periods, demonstrating that systematic deviations of flexible exchange rates from purchasing power parity depend on the direction and durability of relative inflation rates; purchasing power is re-established only after up to twelve years. This research suggested the study of earlier economists who had already formulated some of the theorems.

BERNOULLI, Daniel*

Dates and Birthplace 1700–82, Switzerland.

Posts Held Prof. Maths, St Petersburg, 1725–33; Prof. Medicine and Botany, Basle, 1733–50; Prof. Physics, Basle, 1750.

Degree Graduate in medicine.

Offices and Honours 10 prizes, French Academy of Sciences.

Publications 1. *Specimen Theoriae Novae de Mensura Sortis* (1738), repr. as 'Exposition of a new theory on the measurement of risk', *Em*, 22, 1954, and in *Precursors in Mathematical Economics: An Anthology*, ed. W. J. Baumol and S. M. Goldfield (1968).

Career Member of the second generation of the remarkable Swiss family which produced nine mathematicians of the highest ability in three generations. His chief interests were in theoretical physics, mechanics and probability. The *Specimen* ... arises from his discussion of the so-called 'Petersburg paradox', according to which the actuarial value of a 'fair' gamble is infinite, which contradicts the observation that gamblers will nevertheless refuse fair wagers involving large sums. Bernoulli resolved the paradox by asserting that gamblers are evaluated in terms of the actuarial value of the utilities of a gamble; by assuming diminishing marginal utility of income, he showed that the expected utility of a 'fair' gamble is negative.

Secondary Literature P. A. Samuelson, 'St Petersburg paradoxes: defanged, dissected and historically described', *JEL*, 18(1), March 1977.

BERNSTEIN, Eduard*

Dates and Birthplace 1850–1932, Berlin, Germany.

Post Held Bank employee; political exile in Switzerland and England, 1878–1901.

Publications *Books*: 1. *Evolutionary Socialism: A Criticism and Affirmation* (1899, 1909, 1961); 2. *Wie ist wissenschaftlicher Socialismus möglich?* (1901).

Career Leading Marxist socialist, personal friend of Friedrich Engels, and an important theoretician of the German Social Democratic Party (SPD) in the closing decade of the nineteenth century. His observation of the discrepancies between socialist doctrine and the economic development of Western Europe led him to break with orthodox Marxism. In *Evolutionary Socialism* ... , he used statistical data to show how capitalism was differentiating rather than polarising classes, and then moved from this exposure of specific Marxist predictions to an attack on the theory of the economic determinism of the historical process. His 'revisionism' was condemned by the SPD in 1903, but its recent postwar policy has incorporated many of his ideas.

Secondary Literature P. Gay, *The Dilemma of Democratic Socialism: Eduard Bernstein's Challenge to Marx* (Columbia Univ. Press, 1952, Collier Books, 1962); C. Gneuss, 'Bernstein, Eduard', *IESS*, 2.

BERRY, Robert Albert

Born 1937, St Marys, Ontario, Canada.

Current Post Prof. Econ., Univ. Toronto, Toronto, Ont., Canada, 1974–.

Past Posts Res. Staff Econ., Ass. Prof., Ass. Dir., Econ. Growth Center, Assoc. Prof., Yale Univ., 1962–5, 1965–7, 1966–8, 1970–2, 1967–72; Econ. Adviser, Ford Foundation, Bogota, Columbia, 1968–9; Adviser, Head Planning Dept., Columbia, 1970–1; Assoc. Prof., Univ. Western Ontario, 1972–4; Member, ILO World Employment Mission, Philippines, 1973; Econ., World Bank, 1974–5; Member, Musgrave Tax Mission, Bolivia, 1976; Cons. World Bank Missions, Pakistan, Colombia, 1980.

Degrees BA Univ. Western Ontario, 1959; PhD Princeton Univ., 1963.

Editorial Duties Ed. Board, *Sociedad y Desarrolo*, 1979–; *North-South Canadian J. Latin Amer. Stud.*, 1975–, *Canadian J. Devlp. Stud.*, 1979–.

Principal Fields of Interest 121 Economic Development Studies of Less Industrialised Countries; 824 Labour Market Studies: Wages and Employment; 717 Land Reform and Land Use.

Publications *Books*: 1. *Income Distribution in Colombia* (with M. Urritia),

(Yale Univ. Press, 1976); 2. *Agrarian Structure and Productivity in Developing Countries* (with W. Cline), (JHUP, 1979); 3. *Economic Policy and Income Distribution in Colombia*, co-ed. (with R. Soligo), (Westview Press, 1980); 4. *Politics of Compromise: Coalition Government in Colombia* (with R. Hellman and M. Solaun), (Transactions Press, 1980); 5. *Essays on Industrialization in Colombia*, ed. (Arizona State Univ. Press, 1983).

Articles: 1. 'Some welfare aspects of international migration' (with R. Soligo), *JPE*, 77(5), Sept.–Oct. 1969; 2. 'Land distribution, income distribution and the productive efficiency of Colombian Agriculture', *Food Res. Inst. Stud.*, 12(3), 1973; 3. 'Open unemployment as a social problem in Urban Colombia: myth and reality', *EDCC* 23(2), Jan. 1975; 4. 'Emigration of highly educated manpower: a problem for Colombian education policy' (with M. T. Mendez), in *The Brain Drain and Taxation: Theory and Empirical Analysis*, ed. J. Bhagwati (N-H, 1976); 5. 'Import substitution and beyond: Colombia' (with F. Thoumi), *WD*, 5(1–2), Jan.–Feb. 1977; 6. 'Labour market performance in developing countries: a survey' (with R. Sabot), *WD*, 6(1–2) Nov.–Dec. 1978; 7. 'A positive interpretation of the expansion of urban services in Latin America, with some Colombian evidence', *J. Devlp. Stud.*, 14(2), Jan. 1978; 8. 'Trade policies and income distribution in developing countries: some necessary complications and some preliminary soundings in Colombia' (with C. F. Diaz-Alejandro), in *Economic Policy and Income Distribution in Colombia*, eds. A. Berry and R. Soligo (Westview Press, 1980); 9. 'Land reform and the adequacy of world food production', in *International Dimensions of Land Reform*, ed. J. D. Montgomery (Westview Press, 1984); 10. 'Changes in the world distribution of income between 1950 and 1977' (with F. Bourguignon and C. Morrisson), *EJ*, forthcoming, 1986.

Principal Contributions My work to date has focussed mainly on agriculture, labour markets, and income distribution in developing countries, with special attention to Columbia. One major thread has been the effects of agrarian structure, and especially the size distribution of farms, on agricultural output and on the distribution of income generated by agriculture. The potential productivity advantages of small farms are demonstrated and interpreted in this work. More recently I have been studying small-scale industry with a view to assessing the extent of parallelism between the two sectors in this regard. Work on labour markets (especially Columbia's) has been mainly in the context of an attempt to assess the sources of income and welfare inequality in developing countries, and its relation to public policy. Studies of open urban unemployment in Columbia led me to question the centrality of this phenomenon in the interpretation of the economic setting of poorer families in the less developed countries. Intensive data work on income distribution trends in Columbia and the Philippines reflects concern that such causal analyses have little chance of paying off unless data problems are given high priority.

BERTRAND, Joseph Louis Francois*

Dates and Birthplace 1822–1900, Paris, France.

Posts Held Teacher Maths., Collège St Louis, 1841–8, Lycée Henri IV, 1852–6; Prof. Maths., L'Ecole Polytechnique, 1856–95, Collège de France, 1862–1900.

Degrees BA 1838, Dr. Science 1839.

Offices Member, Académie des Sciences, 1856.

Editorial Duties Ed. *Journal des savants*, 1865–1900.

Publications *Articles:* 1. 'Review of Walras, *Théorie mathématique de la richesse sociale*, and Cournot, *Recherches sur les principes mathématiques de la théorie de richesses*', *Journal des Savants*, Sept. 1883.

Career An eminent mathematician who in a review of Cournot and Walras launched an attack on current mathematical economics. His remarks were chiefly directed against Cournot whose argument he can be said to have grasped only imperfectly. Though he treated Walras more kindly, the latter struggled with Bertrand's objections to the concept of 'tâtonnement' for the rest of his career. Bertrand's article was treated as an authoritative refutation of the mathematical approach by opponents of mathematical economics.

Secondary Literature G. H. Bryan, 'Joseph Bertrand', *Nature*, 61, 1899–1900.

BETTELHEIM, Charles Oscar

Born 1913, Paris, France.
Current Post Dr. d'Etudes, l'Ecole des Hautes Etudes en Sciences Sociales, Paris, 1948–.
Past Posts Chargé de cours, Faculté de Sciences Econ., Caen, 1939–40; Dir., Centre de Recherches Sociales et des Relations Internat. du Ministere du Travail, Paris, 1944–8; Réprésentant, Conférence Internat. du Commerce, 1947; Prof., l'Ecole Nat. d'Admin., Paris, 1948–52; Prof., l'Institut d'Etudes du Devlp. Econ. et Social, 1958–64.
Degrees Licence Lettres, Diplome d'Etudes Superieures de Philo., Diplome d'Etudes Superieures de Droit Privé, Diplome d'Etudes Superieures d'Econ. Polit., Dr d'Etat en Droit Univ. de Paris, 1934, 1936, 1936, 1937, 1939.
Offices and Honours Lauréat, l'Académie Française, 1963.
Editorial Duties Ed., *Problèmes de Planification*, 1960–72, *Collection Economie et Socialisme* (F. Maspero, 1964–79).
Principal Fields of Interest 052 Socialist and Communist Economic Systems; 121 Economic Studies of Less Industrialised Countries.
Publications *Books:* 1. *La planification sovietique* (M. Rivière, 1939, 1946); 2. *L'économie allemande sous le nazisme* (M. Rivière, 1945, F. Maspero, 1971); 3. *L'économie sovietique*, ed. (Sirey, 1950); 4. *L'Inde independante* (A. Colin, 1962, F. Maspero, 1971); 5. *Planification et croissance accelerée* (F. Maspero, 1964, 1970); 6. *La transition vers l'économie socialiste* (F. Maspero, 1968, 1977); 7. *Calbul économique et*

formes de propriété (F. Maspero, 1970); 8. *Revolution culturelle et organisation industrielle en Chine* (F. Maspero, 1973); 9. *Questions sur la Chine après la mort de Mao-Tse-toung* (F. Maspero, 1978); 10. *Class Struggles in the USSR: First Period, 1917–1923, Second Period, 1923–1930, Third and Fourth Periods, 1930–1941* (Monthly Review Press, Harvester Press, 1976, 1978, 1983, 1984).

Articles: 1. 'Cuba en 1965: résultats et perspectives', *Economie et Politique*, 132, July 1965; 2. 'Le problème des prix dans les pays socialistes d'Europe', *La Pensée*, 133, 134, June-Aug. 1967; 3. 'The transition between socialism and capitalism', *Monthly Rev.*, March 1969; 4. 'Chine et URSS: deux modèles d'industrialisation', *Les Temps Modernes*, Aug.–Sept. 1970; 5. 'En Chine, naissance d'une nouvèlle morale proletarienne', *Le Monde Diplomatique*, 212, Nov. 1971; 6. 'State property and socialism', *Economy and Society*, II, 1973; 7. 'Le stalinisme en tant qu'idéologie du capitalisme d'état' (with B. Chavance), *Les Temps Modernes*, May 1979; 8. 'La dissidence et la crise de la formation sociale sovietique', in *Dissenso e democrazia eni paesi dell'Est* (Vallecchi, 1979); 9. 'Economic politics and political economy in China', in *Post-industrial Society*, ed. B. Gustafson (Croom Helm, 1979); 10. 'La NEP, les années trente et l'industrialization', in *L'industrialisation de l'URSS dans les années 1930* (Editions de l'Ecole des Hautes Etudes en Sciences Sociales, 1982).

Principal Contributions I began my work as an economist with a descriptive study of Soviet planning, in the course of which I discovered the principal theoretical problems of a planned economy (1939). I continued these studies in a book on the Nazi economy (1945). I then became interested in the problems of employment and unemployment in connection with my post at the French Ministry of Labour (1944–50). More recently, I have worked on the planning problems of Third World countries, in particular India (1953–6), Guinea and Mali (1959–62) and, finally, Cuba (1962–7).

My work is in the Marxist tradition

but, in the course of my studies, I have found myself forced to transform certain traditional Marxist concepts, such as the concept of productive forces as a determinant of historical change. From 1974 to 1983 I wrote on the economic, social and political history of the USSR with the object of characterising the dynamics of change in the Soviet economy since the Revolution; these caused me to revise some of my earlier views on Soviet planning. Parallel to my work on the Soviet economy, I also studied the economic history of communist China, which belies many of the official declarations of what transpired there. I hope eventually to bring all these studies together in a reconsideration of the communist experience with centrally-planned economies.

BEVERIDGE, William Henry*

Dates and Birthplace 1879–1963, Bengal, India.

Posts Held Fellow, Univ. Coll. Oxford, 1902–9; Civil Servant, 1908–19; Director, LSE, 1919–37; Master, Univ. Coll. Oxford, 1937–44.

Degrees Classics, Bachelor of Civil Law Univ. Oxford, 1902, 1904.

Offices and Honours Knighted, 1919; created peer, 1945.

Publications Books: 1. *Unemployment: A Problem of Industry* (1909); 2. *Prices and Wages in England from the Twelfth to the Nineteenth Century* (1939); 3. Interdepartmental committee on social insurance and allied services, *Social Insurance and Allied Services*, Cmnd. 6352 (The Beveridge Report) (1942); 4. *Full Employment in a Free Society* (1944); 5. *Voluntary Action: A Report on Methods of Social Advance (1948).*

Career His early economic work on unemployment, his work as a civil servant, his directorship of the London School of Economics (1932–7), and his scholarly work on the history of wages and prices, are all dwarfed by the wartime investigations on social insurance which resulted in the Beveridge Report of 1942. This document was the blueprint for the Labour government's social legislation after 1945. Beveridge's

work was the culmination of efforts begun by Beatrice Webb, with Beveridge's assistance, in the Minority Report of the Royal Commission on the Poor Laws of 1909.

Secondary Literature M. Cole, 'Beveridge, William Henry', *IESS*, 2.

BEWLEY, Truman Fassett

Born 1941, Bridgeport, CT, USA.

Current Post Alfred Cowles Prof. Econ., Yale Univ., New Haven, CT, USA, 1983–.

Past Posts Ass. Prof., Assoc. Prof. Econ., Harvard Univ., 1972–5, 1975–8; Prof. Econ., Northwestern Univ., 1978–83.

Degrees BA (Hist.) Cornell Univ., 1963; PhD, PhD (Maths.), Univ. Cal. Berkeley, 1970, 1971.

Offices and Honours Fellow, Em Soc., 1978; Guggenheim Foundation Fellow, 1982–3.

Editorial Duties Assoc. Ed., *J Math. E*; Advisory Ed., *Econ. Letters*.

Principal Fields of Interest 021 General Equilibrium Theory; 023 Macroeconomic Theory.

Publications Articles: 1. 'Existence of equilibria in economies with infinitely many commodities', *JET*, 4(3), Dec. 1972; 2. 'Edgeworth's conjecture' (with E. Kohlberg), *Em*, 41(3), May 1973; 3. 'The asymptotic theory of stochastic games', *Mathematics of Operations Res.*, 1(3), Aug. 1976; 4. 'The permanent income hypothesis: a theoretical interpretation', *JET*, 15(2), Dec. 1977; 5. 'A critique of Tiebout's theory of local public expenditures', *Em*, 49(3), May; 1981; 6. 'An integration of equilibrium theory and turnpike theory', *J Math E*, 10(2–3), Sept. 1982; 7. 'A difficulty with the optimum quantity of money', *Em*, 51(5), Sept. 1983.

Principal Contributions My first two papers were concerned with problems in mathematical economics. These were the existence of equilibrium in an economy with infinitely many commodities and the convergence of an economy to the set of equilibria as the number of traders is allowed to go to infinity. After this, I worked with Kohlberg on the theory of stochastic games. Our main result was that such games have an asymptotic value when future payoffs are not discounted. Most of my papers since my work with Kohlberg have been concerned with inter-temporal general equilibrium theory. My intention is to apply the methods of general equilibrium theory to macro-economic questions.

BHAGWATI, Jagdish N.

Born 1934, Bombay, India.
Current Post Arthur Lehman Prof. Econ., Columbia Univ., New York City, USA.
Past Posts Prof. Econ., MIT, 1968–78; Ford Internat. Prof. Econ., MIT, 1978–80.
Degrees BCom. Univ. Bombay, 1954; BA, MA Univ. Camb., 1956, 1962; PhD MIT, 1967.
Offices and Honours Frank Graham Memorial Lecture, Princeton Univ., 1967; Lal Bahadur Shastri Lectures, 1973; V. K. Ramaswami Memorial Lecture, 1979; Fellow, Em Soc., 1973; Mahalanobis Memorial Medal, Indian Em Soc., 1974.
Editorial Duties Ed. Boards, *WD*, *JDE*, *AER*, 1968–71, Founding Ed., *J Int E*, 1971–.
Principal Fields of Interest 410 International Trade Theory.
Publications *Books:* 1. *Trade, Tariffs and Growth* (Weidenfeld & Nicolson, MIT Press, 1969); 2. *Planning for Industrialisation: India* (with P. Desai), (MIT Press, 1970, 1979); 3. *Illegal Transactions and International Trade: Theory and Measurement* (N-H, 1974, 1975); 4.*The Brain Drain and Taxation: Theory and Empirical Analysis* (N-H, 1976); 5. *Foreign Trade Regimes and Economic Development: The Anatomy of Exchange Control and its Consequences* (Ballinger, 1978); 6. *Lectures on International Trade* (with T. N. Srinivasan), (MIT Press, 1983).
Articles: 1. 'Domestic distortions, tariffs and the theory of optimum subsidy' (with V. K. Ramaswami), *JPE*, 71, Feb. 1963; 2. 'Distortions and immiserizing growth: a generalization', *REStud*, 35, Oct. 1968; 3. 'The generalized theory of distortions and welfare',

in *Trade, Balance of Payments and Growth: Essays in Honor of C. P. Kindleberger*, eds J. Bhagwati, *et al.* (N-H, 1971); 4. 'Education in a "job ladder" model and the fairness-in-hiring rule' (with T. N. Srinivasan), *J Pub E*, 7(1), Feb. 1977; 5. 'Shadow prices for project selection in the presence of distortions: effective rates of protection and domestic resource costs' (with T. N. Srinivasan), *JPE*, 86(1), Feb. 1978.
Principal Contributions Theoretical writings in international trade, education, migration and public finance. In international economics, principal theoretical contributions include the theory of immiserising growth, and the theory of policy intervention in the presence of distortions. Developed the theory of education based on the job-ladder model and fairness-in-hiring rule. Raised and analysed the theoretical public-finance problem of appropriate tax jurisdiction in the presence of international mobility of people. Developed the general theory of directly-unproductive, profit-seeking activities to analyse the welfare effects of lobbying, tax-evading and other such activities. Important policy work relates to efficient trade regimes for development.

BICKERDIKE, Charles Frederick*

Dates and Birthplace 1876–1961, England.
Posts Held Lect., Univ. Manchester, 1911–12; Civil Servant, UK Board Trade, UK Ministry Labour, 1912–41.
Degrees BA, MA Univ. Oxford, 1899, 1910.
Honours OBE, 1937.
Publications *Articles:* 1. 'The theory of incipient taxes', *EJ*, 16, Dec. 1906; 2. 'Relation of the general supply curve to a "particular expenses" curve', *EJ*, 17, Dec. 1907; 3. 'Monopoly and differential prices', *EJ*, 21, March 1911; 4. 'A non-monetary cause of fluctuations in employment', *EJ*, 24, Sept. 1914; 5. 'The instability of foreign exchange', *EJ*, 30, March 1920; 6. 'Saving and the monetary system', *EJ*, 35, Sept. 1925.
Career His chief work was done during the free trade controversies at the

turn of the century. He was a protégé of Edgeworth, who said of him that he was the only person since Mill who had found something original and worthwhile to say on the protectionist side of the case. He also worked with Edgeworth on mathematical treatments of economic questions. His last article foreshadows Harrod-Domar type growth problems.

Secondary Literature V. Tarascio, 'Bickerdike's monetary growth theory', *HOPE*, 12(3), Summer 1980.

BIENAYMÉ, Alain Marie André Paul

Born 1934, Toulon, France.
Current Post Prof. Econ., Paris IX Dauphine Univ., France; Member, Conseil Econ. et Social, 1974–.
Past Posts Prof. Econ., Dijon Univ., 1964–8; Econ. Adviser to Pres. Fauré, Ministry Agric. Educ. Social Affairs, Assemblée Nat., 1966–78; Member, Governing Board, Internat. Inst. Educ. Planning, Paris, 1969–76; Rapporteur, French Economic Plans.
Degrees Dr., Agregé, Grad. Private Law Paris 1956, 1957, 1964.
Offices and Honours Chairman, Comm. General Econ. Problems and Business Cycles, Conseil Econ. et Social; Trustee, Internat. Council Educ. Devlp., NY; Fellow, Inst. Ajijic Sobre Educ. Internat., Guadalajara, Mexico; Silver Medal, CNRS, Paris, 1977.
Editorial Duties Ed. Board, *RE*, *Revue Française de gestion*; *Revue de l'inst. de previsions econ. et financières pour le developpement des entreprises (IPECODE)*.
Principal Fields of Interest 510 Administration; 600 Industrial Organisation; Technological Change; Industry Studies; 912 Economics of Education.
Publications *Books: Croissance et monnaie en plein emploi* (Cujas, 1964); 2. *Politique de l'innovation et repartition des revenus* (Cujas, 1966); 3. *L'entreprise et le pouvoir economique*, ed. (Dunod, 1969); 4. *Croissance des entreprises*, 2 vols. (Bordas, 1971–3); 5. *Higher Education Systems: France* (with F. E. Bourricaud and S. Quiers),

(Internat. Council Educ. Devlp., 1978); 6. *Strategies de l'entreprise competitive* (Masson, 1980); 7. *Entreprise, marché, etat* (Presse Univ. de France, 1982).

Articles: 1. 'Le rôle du plan dans la restructuration de l'appareil de production', *REP*, Aug. 1974; 2. 'Theories de l'organisation industrielle: les cas français et belge', *Cahiers de l'ISMEA, Economies et Sociétés*, Série H.S., 18, 1975; 3. 'L'application de la théorie des organisations a l'université,' *RE*, 27(2), March 1976; 4. 'L'offre competitive', *Economie et Statistique, INSEE*, Dec. 1976; 5. 'Le principe des transferts croissants', REP, 3, 1977; 6. 'Incomes policy in France', *LBR*, 128, April 1978, repr. *RE*, 30(1), Jan. 1979; 7. L'entreprise sans ombres', in *Entreprise et organisation — Mélanges en l'honneur de Mme J. Aubert-Krier (Economica*, 1978); 8. 'Resource allocation and planning in formal education', in *The Future of Formal Education*, ed. T. Husén (Almqvist & Wiksell Internat., 1980); 9. 'Le degré d'autonomie d'une politique nationale pour l'industrie', *Chroniques d'actualités de la SEDEIS*, 15, Jan. 1983; 10. 'Educational research and policy — how do they relate?', in *The Case of France: Higher Education*, eds. T. Husèn and M. Kogan (Pergamon, 1983).

Principal Contributions Research has been conducted in three main fields: 1. I first explored the consequences of new sets of axioms relative to the main economic regulations in our mixed economies. Instead of pure market economies regulated under the assumption of 'complete competition', I attempted to derive the main consequences of a full-employment economy on real growth and money supply determination by private demand (1964). More recently (1982), a second set of axioms focusses on the competition between markets and organisations in resource allocation processes, its consequence on stagflation, investment decision and business strategies.

2. Next, I focussed on industrial economics, giving evidence of intersectoral transfers of productivity gains (1966, 1977), the growth of business firms (1971, 1973), and the competitive

constraints facing middle-sized countries (1970, 1983).

3. A third field concerns enquiries and contributions in the international comparative analysis of education systems, using public policy analysis, organisational and economic theory (1976, 1983).

BIERWAG, Gerald O.

Born 1936, Rupert, ID, USA.
Current Post Prof. Econ. and Fin., Coll. Bus. and Public Admin., Univ. Arizona, Tucson, AZ, 1982–.
Past Posts Ass. Prof., Assoc. Prof., Prof. Econ., Univ. Oregon, 1962–5, 1966–8, 1968–82; Vis. Prof. Econ., Warwick Univ., 1968–9; Vis. Prof. Fin., Univ. Arizona, 1981–2.
Degrees BA Univ. Idaho, 1958; PhD Northwestern Univ., 1962.
Offices and Honours Pres., Western Fin. Assoc., 1985; Exec. Comm., Western Econ. Assoc., 1977–8, Western Fin. Ass., 1981–3; Winner Graham-Dodd Scroll, Awarded Financial Analysts Federation, 1983.
Editorial Duties Ed. Board, *AER*, 1981–4, *J. Fin. Res.*, 1981–; Assoc. Ed., *J. Fin. and Quant. Analysis*, 1977–, *EI*, 1977–80.
Principal Fields of Interest 521 Business Finance; 211 Econometric and Statistical Methods.
Publications *Books:* 1. *Innovations in Bond Portfolio Management; Duration Analysis and Immunization*, co-ed. (JAI Press, 1983).
Articles: 1. 'Aggregate Koyck functions' (with M Grove), *Em*, 34, Oct. 1966; 2. 'A model of the term structure of interest rates' (with M. Grove), *REStat*, 44, Feb. 1967; 3. 'Slutsky equations for assets' (with M. Grove), *JPE*, 76, Jan.–Feb. 1968; 4. 'Optimal TIC bids on serial bond issues', *Management Science*, 22(11), July 1976; 5. 'Immunization, duration and the term structure of interest rates', *J Fin. Quant. Analysis*, 12, Dec. 1977; 6. 'Measures of duration', *EI*, 16(4), Oct. 1978; 7. 'An immunization strategy is a mini-max strategy' (with C. Khang), *J Fin.*, 34(3), May 1979; 8. 'The primary market for municipal bonds: bidding rules

and the cost of borrowing', in *Contemporary Studies in Economic and Financial Analysis* (JAI Press, 1981); 9. 'Duration: its development and use in bond portfolio management' (with G. Kaufman and A. Toevs), *Financial Analysts J.*, July–Aug., 1983.
Principal Contributions Chronologically, principal contributions and interests developed as follows:

The application of linear programming techniques to determine optimal land reform schemes, and a demonstration of their second-best properties that arise because optimal farm sizes cannot change quickly in response to changes in product prices (1962–4); innovations in production techniques, balanced growth of LDCs, and the international terms of trade; this research explores the implications of Hicksian production innovations for LDC growth and investment policies and the terms of trade (1962–4); optimal portfolio selections and the term structure of interest rates. Studies of diversification and equilibrium term structures under the expectations hypothesis; this research explored the econometric applications of new distributed lag techniques to term structure movements (1964–71); optimal micro-economic decision-making under uncertainty under the expected utility hypothesis (1971–4); optimal bidding constraints on competitive municipal bond issues; this research led to practical procedures for minimising interest costs; the developed techniques are in common use today (1974–8); immunisation of portfolios of fixed income securities so as to avoid risks inherent in volatile interest rates; procedures in common use by pension funds and other investing institutions in the US; this research has led to measurements of risk undertaken in non-immunised portfolios; methods were devised for the empirical estimation of equilibrium models of bond pricing (1976–80); applications of immunisation procedures to management techniques of depository institutions and the measurement of pertinent interest-rate risk; some of this research may be relevant to the eventual imposition of risk sensitive deposit insurance premiums (1980–4).

BINSWANGER, Hans

Born 1943, Kreuzlingen, Switzerland.
Current Post Chief, Agric. Res.
Unit, World Bank, Washington, DC,
USA, 1980–.
Past Posts Principal Econ., Internat.
Crops Res. Inst. Semi-Arid Tropics,
Hyderabad, India, 1975–80; Res.
Assoc., Univ. Minnesota, 1973–4;
Assoc., Agric. Devlp. Council, NY,
1974–80.
Degrees Certificat (Polit. Sciences)
Univ. Paris, 1964; MSc (Agric. Sciences)
Eidgenossische Technische Hoch-
schule, Zurich, Switzerland, 1969; PhD
N. Carolina State Univ., 1973.
Offices and Honours Fellow, Swiss
Board of Schools, 1969; Award for
Excellence in Publication, Amer.
Assoc. Agric. Econ.
Editorial Duties Assoc. Ed., *AJAE*,
1983–4.
Principal Fields of Interest 620
Economics of Technological Change;
710 Agriculture; 110 Economic Growth
and Development.
Publications *Books:* 1. *The Econ-
omics of Tractors in South Asia: An
Analytical Review* (Agric. Devlp.
Council, 1978); 2. *Induced Innovation:
Technology, Institutions & Develop-
ment* (with V. Ruttan and others),
(JHUP, 1978); 3. *Rural Household
Studies in Asia*, co-ed. (with R. Even-
son, C. Florenzo, B. White), (Singa-
pore Univ. Press, 1980); 4. *Thailand,
Rural Growth and Employment* (with
others), (World Bank, 1983); 5. *Rural
Labor Markets in Asia: Contractual
Arrangements, Employment and
Wages*, co-ed. (with M. Rosenzweig),
(Yale Univ. Press, 1984).
Articles: 1. 'A cost function approach
to the measurement of elasticities of
factor demand and elasticities of substi-
tution;', *AJAE*, 56(2), May 1974; 2.
'The measurement of technical change
biases with many factors of production',
AER, 64(5), Dec. 1974; 3. 'The role of
sectoral technical change in develop-
ment: Japan, 1880–1965' (with M.
Yamaguchi), *AJAE*, 57(2), May 1975;
4. 'Equity and efficiency issues in *ex
ante* allocation of research resources',
Indian J. Agric. Econ., 32(3), July-
Sept. 1977; 5. 'Attitudes toward risk,

experimental measurement of rural
India', *AJAE*, 62(3), Aug. 1980; 6.
'Attitudes toward risk, theoretical implications of an experiment in rural
India', *EJ*, 91, Dec. 1981; 7. 'Income
distribution in agriculture: a unified
approach' (with J. B. Quizon), *AJAE*,
65(3), Aug. 1983; 8. 'Risk aversion and
credit constraints in farmers' decision
making, a reinterpretation' (with D. A.
Sillers), *J Dev Stud*, 20(1), Oct. 1983; 9.
'Production relations in agriculture'
(with M. Rosenzweig), Discussion
Paper 5, Agric. Res. Unit, World
Bank, 1983; 10. 'Flexible consumer
demand functions and linear estimations: reply' (with G. Swamy), *AJAE*,
67(1), Feb. 1985.
Principal Contributions The theory
of induced innovation maintains that
the rate and direction of technical
change are influenced by output and
factor prices. By measuring biasses in
a many-factor framework, I demonstrated its empirical relevance for US
agriculture; I also provided better
micro-economic foundations. Work in
India concentrated on the role of risk in
agricultural development. An experimental study demonstrated that almost
all rural people are risk averse, but not
even the poorest of the poor act according to simple or lexicographic safety-
based rules. These results have been
confirmed in three other countries.
However, the experimental behaviour
is also inconsistent with the standard
subjective expected utility theory.
Such inconsistencies are common in
experiments with small payoffs. In the
Indian experiment, the payoffs were
large in relation to the incomes of the
respondents.

In a review of theories of rural labour
markets and contractual arrangements,
Mark Rosenzweig and I found that
models of rural wage determination
make assumptions inconsistent with
basic assumptions in most rural contractual choice models. We therefore
attempted to build a theory of agricultural production relations (factor markets, output markets, contractual
arrangements and farm size), based on
consistent behavioural and material
determinants. Risk, information costs,
moral hazard and incentives problem

are fully incorporated. So are specific technological features of agriculture such as its spatial dispersion and the physical attributes of factors of production. In such a system, capital and insurance markets are poorly developed, which constrains other factor markets and contractual arrangements. I have also worked on agricultural mechanisation, research resource allocation and other technical agricultural topics. Jaime Quizon and I have developed a unified approach to modelling income distribution in agriculture. This approach is now being implemented in an econometrically estimated general equilibrium model of India's agricultural sector.

BISH, Robert Lee

Born 1942, Seattle, WA, USA.
Current Post Prof. Econ. and Public Admin., Univ. Victoria, British Columbia, Canada, 1981–.
Past Posts Ass. Prof. Econ. and Public Affairs, Univ. Washington, 1968–72; Assoc. Prof. Econ. and Urban Stud., Univ. Southern Cal., 1972–5; Assoc. Prof. Urban Stud., Univ. Maryland, 1976–81.
Degrees BA Univ. Southern Cal., 1964; MA, PhD Indiana Univ., 1966, 1968.
Offices and Honours Phi Beta Kappa; Omicron Delta Epsilon.
Editorial Duties Ed. Board, *Urban Affairs*.
Principal Fields of Interest 025 Social Choice; 931 Urban Economic and Public Policy; 324 State and Local Govt. Finance.
Publications *Books:* 1. *The Public Economy of Metropolitan Areas* (Rand-McNally, 1971); 2. *Understanding Urban Government: Metropolitan Reform Reconsidered* (with V. Ostrom), (AEI, 1973); 3. *Financing Government* (with H. Groves), (Holt, Rinehart, Winston, 1973); 4. *Urban Economics and Policy Analysis* (with H. Nourse), (McGraw-Hill, 1975); 5. *Coastal Resource Use: Decisions on Puget Sound* (with R. Warren and others), (Univ. Washington Press, 1975); 6.

Governing Puget Sound (Univ. Washington Press, 1981).
Articles: 1. 'Public housing: the magnitude and distribution of direct benefits and effects on housing consumption', *J Reg S*, 9(3), 1969; 2. 'A neglected issue in public goods theory: the monopsony problem' (with P. O'Donoghue), *JPE*, 78, Nov.–Dec. 1970; 3. 'Scale and monopoly problems in urban government services' (with R. Warren), *Urban Affairs Q.*, 8, Sept. 1972; 4. 'Allocating coastal resources: trade off and rationing processes' (with L. Craine and others), in *The Water's Edge*, ed. B. Ketchun (MIT, 1972); 5. 'Urban health, education and welfare program in a federal system', in *Services to People*, ed. S. Mushkin (Georgetown Univ. Press, 1974); 6. 'The assumption of knowledge in policy analysis', *Pol. Stud. J.*, 3, Spring 1975; 7. 'Fiscal equalization through court decisions: policy making without evidence', *Sage Urban Affairs Annual Rev.*, 10, 1976; 8. 'Environmental resource management: public or private', in *Managing the Commons* ed. G. Hardin (Freeman Press, 1977); 9. 'Intergovernmental relations in the United States: concepts and implications from a public choice perspective', in *Interorganizational Policy Making: Limits to Coordination and Central Control* eds. K. Hanf and F. W. Scharpf (Sage, 1978); 10. 'Local government diversity and federal grant programs: design and modification of the coastal energy impact program', in *Making Ocean Policy*, ed. F. Hoole, and others (Westview Press, 1981).
Principal Contributions Work has focussed on the integration of microeconomic theory with classical political theory on constitutions and federalism for the analysis of outcomes to be predicted from alternative institutional arrangements. Theory development and application has emphasised the structure of governments in urban areas, law and property rights systems for coastal resource decision-making, and the operation of federal systems. Current work involves comparisons between the parliamentary-federal system in Canada and the congressional-federal system in the United States.

BISHOP, Robert Lyle

Born 1916, St Louis, MO, USA.
Current Post Prof. Econ., MIT, Cambridge, USA, 1963–.
Degrees BA, MA, PhD Harvard Univ., 1937, 1942, 1949.
Principal Fields of Interest 022 Microeconomic Theory.
Publications *Articles:* 1. 'Elasticities, cross-elasticities, and market relationships', *AER*, 42(5), Dec. 1952; 2. 'Duopoly: collusion or warfare?', *AER*, 50(5), Dec. 1960; 3. 'Game-theoretic analyses of bargaining', *QJE*, 77, Nov. 1963; 4. 'The effects of specific and valorem taxes', *QJE*, 82, May 1968; 5. 'Monopoly', *IESS*, 10, 1968.
Principal Contributions Demand theory and consumer's surplus; monopolistic competition — market classification and welfare aspects; bargaining theory as applied to both bilateral monopoly and oligopoly; miscellaneous problems of micro-equilibrium involving taxes, vertical relationships, factor demand and monopsony; critiques of Smith, Ricardo and Marx.

BLACK, Duncan

Born 1908, Motherwell, Lanarkshire, Scotland.
Current Post Emeritus Prof. Econ., Univ. Coll. N. Wales, Bangor, UK, 1968–.
Past Posts Ass. Lect. Econ., Univ. Dundee, Scotland, 1932–4; Ass. Lect., Lect., Prof. Econ., Univ. Coll. N. Wales, 1934–40, 1940–5, 1952–68; Lect. Econ., Queen's Univ., Belfast, N. Ireland, 1945–6; Lect. Social Econ., Glasgow Univ., 1946–52.
Degrees MA (Maths. and Physics), MA (Econ. and Polit. Philo.), PhD Glasgow Univ., 1929, 1932, 1937.
Offices and Honours Res. Fellow Law and Econ., Law School, Univ. Chicago, 1968–9; NSF Fellow, Virginia Polytechnic Inst., 1970–1; Hon. Foreign Fellow, AAAS; Fellow, Em Soc; Benjamin Lippincott Prize, Amer. Polit. Science Assoc., 1983.
Principal Fields of Interest 025 Social Choice.
Publications *Books:* 1. *The Incidence of Income Taxes* (Macmillan, 1939); 2. *Committee Decisions with Complementary Valuation* (with R. A. Newing), (William Hodge, 1951); 3. *The Theory of Committee and Elections* (CUP, 1958; partly transl., Italian, in *Economia del Benessere e Democrazia*, eds. F. Forte and G. F. Mosetto (Franco Angeli Editore, 1972).
Principal Contributions The Festschrift volume, *Towards a Science of Politics*, ed. G. Tullock (Public Choice Center, Virginia Polytechnic Inst. and State Univ., 1981) provides a biographical sketch by R. H. Coase and also gives a discussion of my work by B. Grufman.

BLACK, Fischer

Born 1938, Washington, DC, USA.
Current Post Prof. Fin., MIT, Mass., 1975–.
Past Posts Prof. Fin., Univ. Chicago, 1971–5.
Degrees BA Harvard Coll., 1959; PhD Harvard Univ., 1964.
Principal Fields of Interest 521 Business Finance.
Publications *Articles:* 1. 'Banking and interest rates in a world without money: the effects of uncontrolled banking', *J Bank Res*, 1, Autumn 1970; 2. 'The pricing of options and corporate liabilities' (with M. Scholes), *JPE*, 81, May–June 1973; 3. 'The effects of dividend yield and dividend policy on common stock prices and returns' (with M. Scholes), *J Fin Econ*, 1(1), May 1974; 4. 'Global monetarism in a world of national currencies', *Columbia J. World Bus.*, 13, Spring 1978; 5. 'The magic in earnings: economic earnings versus accounting earnings', *Fin. Analysis J.*, 36, Nov.–Dec. 1980.
Principal Contributions Application of general equilibrium theory to realistic models of the pricing of options; expected returns on stocks; business cycles; monetary policy; and international trade and investment.

BLACK, John Donald*

Dates and Birthplace 1883–1960, Jefferson County, WI, USA.

Posts Held Teacher, High School, Rice Lake, WI, 1905–7; Instr. Rhetoric, Michigan Coll. Mines, 1911–5; Instr. Econ., Univ. Wisconsin, 1917–8; Prof., Agric. Econ., Univ. Minnesota, 1927; Prof. Econ., Harvard Univ., 1927–56; Chief Econ., Federal Forum Board, 1931–2, US Dept. Agric., 1949–53, Tennessee Valley Authority, 1940–60; Cons., US Forestry Service, 1950, FAO, UN ECLA, 1956–7; Vis. Prof., Michigan Univ., 1958; Cons., Amer. Univ. Beirut, 1958.

Degrees BA, MA, PhD Univ. Wisconsin, 1909, 1910, 1918.

Offices and Honours Certificate Extraordinary Achievement, Nat. Planning Assoc., 1951; Pres., Americ. Farm Econ. Assoc., 1932, AEA, 1955; Phi Beta Kappa; Alpha Zeta; Alpha Gamma Rho.

Publications *Books:* 1. *Introduction to Production Economics* (1926); 2. *Agricultural Reform in the United States* (1929); 3. *Production Organization* (1929); 4. *The Dairy Industry and the AAA* (1938); 5. *Parity, Parity, Parity* (1942); 6. *Food Enough* (1943); 7. *A Food and Nutrition Program for the Nation* (1944); 8. *Federal-State-Local Relations in Agriculture* (1949); 9. *The Rural Economy of New England* (1952); 10. *Economics for Agriculture* (1952).

Career Doyen of American agricultural economists and the most prolific and influential writer on American agriculture in the interwar and early postwar period.

BLACK, Robert Denis Collison

Born 1922, Dublin, Ireland.

Current Post Prof. Emeritus, Queen's Univ. Belfast, Belfast, N. Ireland, 1985–.

Past Posts Deputy, Polit. Econ., Trinity Coll., Dublin, 1943–5; Ass. Lect., Lect., Sr. Lect., Reader, Prof. Econ., Queen's Univ., Belfast, 1945–6, 1946–58, 1958–61, 1961–2, 1962–85; Vis. Prof., Yale Univ., 1964–5.

Degrees BA, BCom, PhD, Trinity Coll., Dublin, 1941, 1943, 1945.

Offices and Honours Rockefeller Fellow, 1950–1; Council, RES, 1963–81; Council, Econ. and Social Res.

Inst., Dublin, 1963–; Chairman, Comm. Social Science Res., Ireland, 1973–80; Ford Foundation Study Award, 1974; Fellow, BA, 1974–; Member, Royal Irish Academy, 1974; Res. Fellow, Japan Soc. Promotion Science, 1980; Hon. Fellow, Trinity Coll., Dublin, 1982–; Pres., Stat. and Social Inquiry Soc., Ireland, 1983–; Pres., Sect. F, BAAS, 1985.

Editorial Duties Ed. Boards, *HOPE*, 1969–, *Hist. Econ. Thought Soc. Newsletter*, 1968–; *Econ. and Social Rev.*, 1969.

Principal Fields of Interest 031 History of Economic Thought.

Publications *Books:* 1. *Centenary History of the Statistical and Social Inquiry Society of Ireland* (Eason & Son, 1947); 2. *Economic Thought and the Irish Question, 1817–1870* (CUP, 1960); 3. *A Catalogue of Pamphlets on Economic Subjects, published between 1750 and 1900 and now housed in Irish Libraries* (Queen's Univ., A. M. Kelley, 1969); 4. *Economic Writings of Mountifort Longfield*, ed. (A. M. Kelley, 1971); 5. *The Theory of Political Economy by W. S. Jevons*, ed. (Penguin, 1971); 6. *Readings in the Development of Economic Analysis, 1776–1848*, ed. (David & Charles, Barnes & Noble, 1971, 1973); 7. *Papers and Correspondence of William Stanley Jevons*, 7 vols., ed. (Macmillan, 1972–81); 8. *The Marginal Revolution in Economics*, co-ed. (with A. W. Coats and C. D. Goodwin), (Duke Univ. Press, 1973).

Articles: 1. 'Trinity College, Dublin, and the theory of value, 1832–1863', *Ec*, N.S. 12, Aug. 1945; 2. 'The classical economists and the Irish problem', *OEP*, 5(1), March 1953; 3. 'Jevons and Cairnes', *Ec*, N.S. 27, Aug. 1960; 4. 'Parson Malthus, the general and the captain', *EJ*, 77, March 1967; 5. 'Economic policy in Ireland and India in the time of J. S. Mill', *EHR*, Second Series, 21(2), Aug. 1968; 6. 'History of economic thought', in *Information Sources in Economics*, ed. J. Fletcher (Butterworths, 1971, 1984); 7. 'Smith's contribution in historical perspective', in *The Market and the State*, eds. A. S. Skinner and T. Wilson (OUP, 1976; transl., Japanese, Keizai Seminar, 1977); 8.

'Ralph George Hawtrey, 1879–1975', *Proceedings BA*, 63, 1977; 9. 'William Stanley Jevons', in *Pioneers of Modern Economics*, eds. D. P. O'Brien and J. R. Presley (Macmillan, 1981); 10. 'The present position and prospects of political economy', in *Methodological Controversy in Economics, Historical Essays in honour of T. W. Hutchison*, ed. A. W. Coats (JAI Press, 1983).

Principal Contributions These have largely developed from two lasting interests in (i) the relation between economic theories and policies and (ii) the relation between the lives of economists and their doctrines. Early studies dealt with the theories (mainly of value and distribution) developed by Irish economists during the classical period. Subsequently nineteenth-century Ireland provided the basis for a full-scale historical case study of theory-policy relations. Many problems encountered during its preparation in tracing necessary manuscript and pamphlet sources stimulated work devoted to improving the bibliographical resources for the history of ideas and to preserving and making accessible the unpublished papers of leading economists. A major effort in this latter direction was the tracing and editing of the papers and correspondence of W. S. Jevons for the Royal Economic Society.

BLACK, Stanley Warren

Born 1939, Charlotte, NC, USA.
Current Post Georges Lurcy Prof. Econ., Univ. N. Carolina, Chapel Hill, NC, USA, 1983–.
Past Posts Ass. Prof. Econ., Princeton Univ., 1966–71; Assoc. Prof., Prof. Econ., Vanderbilt Univ., 1972–6, 1977–83; Res. Fellow, Inst. Internat. Econ. Studies, Stockholm, Sweden, 1975–6; Special Ass. Undersecretary Econ. Affairs, US Dept. State, 1977–8; Vis. Prof. Econ., Yale Univ., 1980–1.
Degrees BA Univ. N. Carolina, 1961; MA, PhD Yale Univ., 1963, 1965.
Offices and Honours Vice-Pres., SEA, 1982–3.
Editorial Duties Ed. Board, *SEJ*, 1980–3.
Principal Fields of Interest 310 Domestic Monetary and Financial Theory; 430 Balance of Payments; International Finance.

Publications *Books:* 1. *Floating Exchange Rates and National Economic Policy* (Yale Univ. Press, 1977); 2. *Politics versus Markets: International Differences in Macroeconomic Policies* (AEI, 1982).

Articles: 1. 'Theory and policy analysis of short-term movements in the balance of payments', *YEE*, 8(1), 1968; 2. 'International money markets and flexible exchange rates', *Princeton Stud. Internat. Fin.*, 32, 1973; 3. 'Rational response to shocks in a dynamic model of capital asset pricing', *AER*, 66(5), Dec. 1976; 4. 'Exchange rate policies for less developed countries in a world of floating rates', *Princeton Essays Internat. Fin.*, 119, 1976; 5. 'The effects of alternative monetary control procedures on exchange rates and output', *JMCB*, 14(4), Nov. 1982; 6. 'The use of monetary policy for internal and external balance in ten industrial countries', in *Exchange Rates and International Macroeconomics*, ed. J. Frenkel (Univ. Chicago Press, 1983); 7. 'The effect of alternative intervention policies on the variability of exchange rates in a stochastic exchange rate model: the "Harrod" effect', in *Exchange Rate Management Under Uncertainty*, ed. J. Bhandari (MIT Press, 1984).

Principal Contributions Extended theory of spot and forward exchange rates and developed modern theory of asset market determination of exchange rates; introduced rational expectations concept into foreign exchange theory; including empirical applications. Developed criteria for exchange-rate policies of developing countries. Estimated reaction functions for monetary policy in multi-country study; cross-country comparisons showed effects of economic structure and political choices on inflation and unemployment. Developed a political choice theory for this problem. Recent work aimed at understanding empirical exchange-rate relationships, including reasons for time-varying coefficients. Analyzed 'Harrod' effect, showing how behaviour of risk-averse speculators will vary with government policy in exchange market in a stochastic, rational expectations model.

BLACKORBY, Charles

Born 1938, N Dak., USA.
Current Post Prof., Univ. British Columbia, Vancouver, Canada.
Degrees BA Harvard Univ., 1960; PhD Johns Hopkins Univ., 1965.
Principal Fields of Interest 022 Microeconomic Theory.
Publications *Books:* 1. *Duality, Separability, and Functional Structure: Theory and Economic Applications* (with D. Primont and R. Russell), (Elsevier, N-H, 1978).
Articles: 1. 'Degrees of cardinality and aggregate partial ordering', *Em*, 43(5–6), Sept.–Nov. 1975; 2. 'On testing separability restrictions with flexible functional forms' (with D. Primont and R. Russell), *J Em*, 5(2), March 1977; 3. 'Utility versus equity: some plausible quasi-orderings' (with D. Donaldson), *J Pub E*, 7(3), July 1977; 4. 'Expenditure functions, local duality, and second order approximations' (with W. E. Diewert), *Em*, 47(3), May 1979; 5. 'Ethical indices for the measurement of poverty' (with D. Donaldson), *Em*, 49(4), May 1980.

BLANC, Jean Joseph Louis*

Dates and Birthplace 1811–82, Madrid, Spain.
Posts Held Journalist, Ed., Professional writer, Exiled in England, 1848–70.
Offices and Honours Member, Provisional Govt. of France, 1848; Member, National Assembly, Chamber of Deputies, 1870–82.
Publications *Books:* 1. *L'organisation du travail* (1839).
Career His reputation as a leading socialist writer was made by his articles in *La revu du progrès social*, which were collected as *L'organisation*. The 1848 Revolution enabled him to become president of a *Commission du gouvernement pour les travailleurs* in which he spoke in favour of extreme socialist programmes. He advocated the takeover of bankrupted factories and shops by the State in which profits would be divided according to the needs of the workers; he later proposed equal shares for all members of these producer co-operatives. His writings have been attacked as impractical and imprecise, but his philanthropic character is recognised even by his critics; in fact the major role he assigned to the State in his schemes made them more practical than those of Owen and St-Simon.
Secondary Literature L. A. Loubere, *Louis Blanc* (Northwestern Univ. Press, 1961).

BLANQUI, Jerome Adolphe*

Dates and Birthplace 1798–1854, France.
Posts Held Head, Ecole de Commerce, Paris, 1830–54; Prof. Polit. Econ., Conservatoire des Arts et Métiers, Paris, 1833–54
Offices and Honours Member of Chamber of Deputies representing Gironde; Member, Académie des Sciences Morales et Polit., 1838.
Publications *Books:* 1. *Résumé de l'histoire du commerce et de l'industrie* (1826); 2. *Précis élémentaire d'économie politique* (1826); 3. *History of Political Economy in Europe* (1837, 1968).
Career Brother of Louis Auguste Blanqui the revolutionist, with whom he is sometimes confused. He was an inspiring lecturer and diligent researcher whose studies involved him in extensive travel throughout Europe. His chief concern was with labour economics, but his work on the history of economics enjoyed international acclaim and remained useful for many years, particularly for its treatment of ancient and medieval economic thought. He was Say's successor at the Conservatoire des Arts et Métiers.

BLAU, Julian H.

Born 1917, New York City, NY, USA.
Current Post Prof. Maths., Antioch Coll., Yellow Springs, OH, 1952–.

Past Posts Instr. Maths., MIT, 1948–9; Ass. Prof. Maths., Penn. State Coll., 1949–52; Res. Mathematician, Mental Health Res. Inst., Univ. Michigan, 1963; Co-dir., SSRC Res. Training Inst., Stanford Univ., 1964.

Degrees BS (Maths.) City Coll., NY, 1938; MA (Maths.) NYU, 1939; PhD (Maths.) Univ. N. Carolina, 1948.

Offices and Honours Blumenthal Fellow, NYU, 1938–40; Teaching Fellow, Univ. N. Carolina, 1940–2; Vis. Lect., Math. Assoc. Amer., 1964–5; NSF Faculty Fellow, 1966–7.

Editorial Duties Ed. Board, *Social Choice and Welfare.*

Principal Fields of Interest 024 Welfare Theory; 025 Social Choice.

Publications *Articles:* 1. 'The space of measures on a given set', *Fundamental Mathematics*, 1951; 2. 'The existence of social welfare functions', *Em*, 25(2), April 1957, repr. in *Selected Readings in Economic Theory from Econometrics*, ed. K. J. Arrow (MIT Press, 1971); 3. 'Transformation of probabilities', *Proceedings Amer. Math. Soc.*, 12, Aug. 1961; 4. 'Arrow's theorem with weak independence', *Ec.* N.S. 38, Nov. 1971; 5. 'A direct proof of Arrow's theorem', *Em*, 40(1), Jan. 1972; 6. 'Liberal values and independence', *REStud*, 42(3), July 1975; 7. 'Neutrality, monotonicity, and the right of veto: a comment', *Em*, 44(3), May 1976; 8. 'Social decision functions and the veto' (with R. Deb), *Em*, 45(4), May 1977; 9. 'Semiorders and collective choice', *JET*, 21(1), Aug. 1979.

Principal Contributions I was attracted to economics by Arrow's book *Social Choice and Individual Values*, with its interplay of social theory and logic. I corrected the hypothesis of Arrow's General Possibility Theorem; using a potentially powerful technique invented by Arrow in his proof of the case of exactly three alternatives, and ideas of my own, I extended the validity of the theorem to any larger set of alternatives. Later, originally for pedagogical reasons, I replaced my ponderous barnacled proof by a clearer, more direct argument. I was especially interested in Arrow's condition of independence of irrelevant alternatives, which gives the subject its form, and

weakened it so that in general only a small minority of sets were assumed independent; this minority sufficed for Arrow's Theorem. Used this idea also in weakening Sen's liberalism and attempted to resolve the Liberal Paradox for the case of two people. I studied enlarging the range of the social preference and, for semiorder and many weaker variants, proved that Arrow's conclusion extends to these cases. For acyclic social preferences, I proved (with Deb) the existence of a vetoer if there are enough alternatives, and also the existence of a group veto in a partition of society. My interest in social choice led me to consider proportional representation and variants mandated by actual constitutions. I characterised these axiomatically in terms of coalitional invariance and included the case of an infinite number of 'political positions'.

BLAUG, Mark

Born 1927, Den Haag, The Netherlands.

Current Post Prof. Emeritus, Univ. London Inst. Educ., London, England, Cons. Prof. Econ., Dir., Employment Res. Centre, Univ. Buckingham, Buckingham, England, 1984–.

Past Posts Ass. Lect., Queen's Coll., NY, 1951–2; Stat., US Dept. Labor, NY, 1952–3; Ass. Prof., Yale Univ., 1954–62; Vis. Reader, Univ. Manchester, 1960–1; Sr. Lect., Reader, Prof., Econ. of Educ. Univ. London Inst. Educ., 1963–5, 1965–9, 1969–84; Prof., Univ. Chicago, 1965–6; Parttime Lect., LSE, 1963–78; Cons., Ford Foundation, Bangkok, Thailand, 1969–70; Member ILO World Employment Programme Missions, Ethiopia, 1972, Philippines, 1973, Sudan, 1975, Lesotho, 1978; Member, World Bank Missions, India, 1970, China, 1983; Vis. Prof., European Univ. Inst., Florence, Italy, 1981–2; Fellow, Inst. Advanced Study, Humanities and Social Sciences, The Netherlands, 1983–4.

Degrees BA Queen's Coll., NY, 1950; MA, PhD Columbia Univ., 1952, 1955.

Offices and Honours Guggenheim Foundation Fellow, 1958–9; Res. Fellow, US SSRC, 1962–3; Vice-Chairman, Econ. Comm., UK SSRC, 1972–6; Member, Econ. Comm., UK Comm. Nat. Academic Awards, 1973–5, Educ. Comm., CNRS, Frace, 1973–5; Advisory Comm., Internat. Inst. Applied Systems Analysis, Laxenberg, Austria, 1971–82; Res. Scholar, Rockefeller Foundation Center, Bellagio, Italy, 1974; Pres., UK Assoc. Polytechnic Teachers Econ., 1978–81.

Editorial Duties Ed. Board, *HOPE*, 1969, *Higher Educ*, 1972–, *J. Cultural Econ.*, 1980–, *Econ. Educ. Rev.* 1980, *Internat. J. Educ. Dev.*, 1981–, *Econ. and Philo.*, 1984.

Principal Fields of Interest 036 Economic Methodology; 031 History of Economic Thought; 912 Economics of Education.

Publications *Books:* 1. *Ricardian Economics. A Historical Study* (Yale Univ. Press, 1958, Greenwood Press, 1974; transl. Japanese, Bokutakusha, 1980); 2. *Economic Theory in Retrospect* (Richard D. Irwin, 1962, Cambridge Univ. Press, 1985; transls., Italian, Editore Boringhieri, 1970, German, Nymphenburger Verlagshandlung, 1971, Portuguese, Teizeira & Ca., 1976, Japanese, Keizai Shimpo Sha, 1981, French, Economica, 1981, Spanish, Fondo de Cultura Economica, 1983); 3. *The Causes of Graduate Unemployment in India* (with R. Layard and M. Woodhall), (Allen Lane/Penguin, 1969); 4. *An Introduction to the Economics of Education*(Allen Lane/Penguin, 1970, Penguin, 1972; transl., Portuguese, Editore Globo, 1975); 5. *Education and the Employment Problem in the Developing Countries* (ILO, 1973; transls. French, ILO, 1974, Spanish, ILO, 1974); 6. *The Practice of Manpower Forecasting. A Collection of Case Studies* (with B. Ahamad), (Elsevier, 1973); 7. *The Cambridge Revolution: Success or Failure? A Critical Analysis of Cambridge Theories of Value and Distribution* (INEA, 1974, 1975; transls. Japanese, Keizai Shimpo Sha, 1977, Italian, Liguori Editore, 1978); 8. *The Economics of the Arts*, ed. (Martin Robertson, Praeger, 1976); 9. *The Methodology of Economics, or How Do Economists Explain* (CUP, 1980; transls., French, Editions Librairie Economica, 1983, Spanish, Alianza Editorial, 1984); 10. *Great Economists since Keynes* (Wheatsheaf Books, 1984).

Articles: 1. 'The classical economists and the factory acts — a reexamination', *QJE*, 72, May 1958, repr. in *The Classical Economists and Economic Policy*, ed. A. W. Coats (Methuen, 1971); 2. 'The productivity of capital in the Lancashire cotton industry during the nineteenth century', *EHR*, 2(13), April 1961, repr. in *Business History. Selected Readings*, ed. K. A. Tucker (Frank Cass., 1977); 3. 'A survey of the theory of process innovations', *Ec*, N.S. 30, Feb. 1963, repr. in *Progresso Technico e Sviluppo Economico*, ed. B. Jossa (Franco Angeli Editore, 1966), and *Penguin Modern Economics: Economics of Technical Change,* ed. N. Rosenberg (Penguin, 1971); 4. 'The myth of the old poor law and the making of the new', *JEH*, 23, June 1963, repr. in *Essays in Social History*, eds. M. W. Flinn and T. C. Smout (Clarendon Press, 1974); 5. 'An economic analysis of personal earnings in Thailand', *EDCC*, 23(1), Oct. 1974; 6. 'Kuhn versus Lakatos, or paradigms versus research programmes in the history of economics', *HOPE*, 7(4), Winter 1975, repr. in *Method and Appraisal in Economics*, ed. S. J. Latsis (CUP, 1976), and *Paradigms and Revolutions*, ed. G. Gutting (Univ. Notre Dame Press, 1980; transl., Spanish, *Revista Espanola de Economia*, VI, Enero-Abril, 1976; 7. 'The empirical status of human capital theory: a slightly jaundiced survey', *JEL*, 14(3), Sept. 1976, repr. in *Public Economics and Human Resources*, ed. V. Halberstadt and A. J. Culver (Editions Cujas, 1977); 8. 'Why are Covent Garden seat prices so high?', *J. Cultural Econ.*, 2(1), June 1978, repr. Royal Opera House (Covent Garden, 1978); 9. 'A methodological appraisal of radical economics', in *Methodological Controversy in Economics: Historical Essays in Honor of T. W. Hutchison*, ed. A. W. Coats (JAI Press, 1983); 10. 'Where are we now in the economics of education?', Univ. London Inst. Educ.,

1983, repr. *Econ. Educ. Rev.*, 4(1), 1985.

Principal Contributions Early work was concentrated on British economic history, including a revisionist interpretation of the Old Poor Laws and the history of economic thought, particularly the classical era dominated by Ricardo. My advanced text, *Economic Theory in Retrospect*, however, covers the entire period from Adam Smith to Milton Friedman. It was an attempt to write a purely analytical history of economics as a story of steady, cumulative progress. In the 1960s, my interests shifted to the economics of education and for some years I worked in the tradition of human capital theory. For many years I was alone in attacking the manpower forecasting approach to educational planning, which was then very much in vogue. Subsequently, I moved away from human capital theory towards other ways of thinking about the economic value of education. Alternative methods of financing education (vouchers, loans, full-cost fees) have long been a principal focus of interest. Much of my work in the economics of education in the 1970s has taken the form of international missions to Third World countries. Have also studied public subsidies to the performing arts in Britain. More recently, have returned to a lifelong concern with the methodology of economics and the appraisal of competing research programmes in economics.

BLINDER, Alan Stuart

Born 1945, New York City, NY, USA.

Current Post Gordon S. Rentschler Memorial Prof. Econ., Princeton Univ., Princeton, NJ, USA, 1982–.

Past Posts Instr. Fin., Rider Coll., Trenton, NJ, 1968–9; Instr. Econ., Boston State Coll., Boston, MA, 1969; Ass. Prof., Assoc. Prof., Prof. Econ., Princeton Univ., 1971–6, 1976–9, 1979–82.

Degrees BA Princeton Univ., 1967; MSc LSE, 1968; PhD MIT, 1971.

Offices and Honours W. S. Woytinsky Award, 1981; Bicentennial Preceptor, Princeton Univ., 1975–8.

Editorial Duties Ed. Board, *JEL*, 1981–, *J Mon.E*, 1981–; Assoc. Ed., *J Pub E*, 1982–.

Principal Fields of Interest 130 Economic Fluctuations, Forecasting Stabilisation; and Inflation.

Publications *Books:* 1. *Toward an Economic Theory of Income Distribution* (MIT Press, 1974, 1977); 2. *General Equilibrium Systems: Essays in Memory of Rafael Lusky,* co-ed. (with P. Friedman), (Academic Press, 1977); 3. *Economics: Principles and Policy* (with W. J. Baumol), (Harcourt Brace Jovanovich, 1979, 1982); 4. *Economic Policy and the Great Stagflation* (Academic Press, 1979; transl., Japanese, 1982).

Articles: 1. 'Does fiscal policy matter?' (with R. M. Solow), *J Pub E* 2(4), Nov. 1973; 2. 'Distribution effects and the aggregate consumption function', *JPE*, 83(3), June 1975; 3. 'Human capital and labor supply: a synthesis' (with Y. Weiss), *JPE*, 84(3), June 1976; 4. 'Reconsidering the work disincentive effects of social security' (with R. Gordon and D. Wise), *Nat. Tax J.*, 33(4), Dec. 1980; 5. 'Market wages, reservation wages, and retirement decisions' (with R. H. Gordon), *J Pub E*, 14(2), Oct. 1980; 6. 'Temporary income taxes and consumer spending', *JPE*, 80(1), Feb. 1981; 7. 'Inventories, rational expectations, and the business cycle' (with S. Fischer), *J Mon E*, 8(3), Nov. 1981; 8. 'Retail inventory behavior and business fluctuations', *Brookings Papers Econ. Activity*, 2, 1981; 9. 'Inventories and sticky prices: more on the microfoundations of macroeconomics', *AER*, 72(3), June 1982; 10. 'Money, credit constraints, and economic activity' (with J. E. Stiglitz), *AER*, 73(2), May 1983.

Principal Contributions Inventories, income distribution, fiscal policy and social security and pensions.

BLISS, Christopher John Emile

Born 1940, London, England.
Current Post Nuffield Reader Inter-

nat. Econ., Fellow, Nuffield Coll. Oxford, 1977–.

Past Posts Fellow, Christ's Coll. Camb., 1965–71; Univ. Lect., Univ. Camb., 1965–71, 1966–71; Prof. Econ., Univ. Essex, 1971–7.

Degrees BA, PhD Univ. Camb., 1962, 1966.

Offices and Honours Fellow, Em Soc, 1978; Dir., General Funds Investment Trust, 1980–.

Editorial Duties Managing Ed., Ass. Ed., *REStud*, 1967–71.

Principal Fields of Interest 021 General Equilibrium Theory.

Publications *Books:* 1. *Capital Theory and the Distribution of Income* (N-H, 1975); 2. *Palanpur: the Economy of an Indian Village* (with N. H. Stern), (OUP, 1982).

Articles: 1. 'On putty-clay', *REStud*, 35, April 1968; 2. 'Heterogeneous capital the production function and the theory of distribution: comment', *REStud*, 37(3), July 1970; 3. 'Prices, markets and planning', *EJ*, 82, March 1972; 4. 'Heterogeneous capital and the Heckscher–Ohlin–Samuelson theory of trade: discussion', in *Essays in Modern Economics*, eds. M. Parkin and A. R. Nobay (Longman, 1973); 5. 'The reappraisal of Keynes' economics: an appraisal', in *Current Economic Problems*, eds. M. Parkin and A. R. Nobay (CUP, 1975); 6. 'Capital theory in the short-run', in *Modern Capital Theory*, eds. M. Brown, K. Sato and P. Zarembka (N-H, 1976); 7. 'Productivity, wages and nutrition: part 1: the theory, part 11: some observations', *JDE*, 5(4), Dec. 1978; 8. 'Temporary equilibrium with rationed borrowing and consistent plans', in *Advances in Economic Theory*, ed. M. Baranzini (N-H, 1982); 9. 'Two views of macroeconomics', *OEP*, 35(1), March 1983; 10. 'Dragon-slaying and ballroom dancing' (with B. Nalebuff), *JPE*, forthcoming, 1986.

Principal Contributions My chief and continuing fascination since I was introduced to economics as an undergraduate has been economic theory. I have explored this in many directions, including some which are quite abstract. The temptation to pursue an idea as far as it will go, or to strip something down to its very barest essentials, is one which I have been neither able nor inclined to resist. Among my published works are one or two pieces whose greatest merit may well be their beauty. Despite this, my fascination with the abstract has always had to compete with an unquenchable interest in the world of experience and reality. I have always felt the force of what Emmanuel Lasker (speaking of chess) called 'the merciless facts', and I cannot help but feel contempt for those who run away from them. This is reflected in my approach to economics and in my general philosophy, including my political philosophy. Being interested in things has been to some extent a vice for me. By drawing me into various studies and hobbies it has ensured that the single-minded devotion to specialised scholarship which I admire in others has not been my way. Similarly, within economics I have spread myself too widely to make myself the master of any one area. I am always embarrassed to be asked what area I work in. The enquiry deserves a short answer but I am seldom working in one area alone. Today my chief interest is macroeconomic theory. I am appalled by the gap between what we observe and what theory can explain, and I would like to make that gap smaller.

BLOCK, Michael Kent

Born 1942, New York City, NY, USA.

Current Post Assoc. Prof. Public Policy and Econ., Coll. Bus. and Public Admin., Univ. Arizona, Tucson, AZ, 1976–.

Past Posts Res. Econ., Bank America, 1964–5; Econ. Planning Assoc., San Francisco, 1965; Ass. Prof. Econ., Univ. Santa Clara, Santa Clara, CA, 1969–72; Ass. Prof., Assoc. Prof., OR and Admin. Science, Naval Postgrad. School, Monterey, CA, 1972–4, 1974–5; Res. Fellow, Hoover Inst., Stanford Univ., Stanford, CA, 1975–6.

Degrees BA, MA, PhD Stanford Univ., 1964, 1969, 1972.

Offices and Honours Phi Beta Kappa.

Editorial Duties Ed. Board, *Law and Human Behavior*.

Principal Fields of Interest 916 Economics of Crime; 612 Public Policy Toward Monopoly and Competition; 613 Public Utilities and Costs of Government Regulation.

Publications *Books:* 1. *Student Workbook: Bach's Economics* (with H. G. Demmert), (Prentice-Hall, 1974, 1980); 2. *Sherman Act Indictments: 1955–1980* (with J. M. Claudbault), (Federal Legal Publications, 1982).

Articles: 1. 'The allocation of effort under uncertainty: The case of risk averse behavior' (with J. M. Heineke), *JPE*, 81(2), pt. 2, April–May 1973; 2. 'Crime and punishment reconsidered' (with R. C. Lind), *J. Legal Stud.*, Jan. 1975; 3. 'A labor theoretic approach to criminal choice' (with J. M. Heinecke), *AER*, 65(3), June 1975; 4. 'A choice theoretic approach to crimes punishable by imprisonment' (with R. C. Lind), *J. Legal Stud.* June 1975; 5. 'The cost of antitrust deterrence: why not hang a price fixer now and then?' (with J. G. Sidak), *Georgetown Law J.*, June 1980; 6. 'The level of theft, the size of the public sector, and the distribution of income: some interesting empirical findings', in *White Collar and Economic Crime*, eds. P. M. Wickman and T. Dailey (D. C. Heath, 1982); 7. 'Some simple analytics of international deterrence' (with R. C. Lind), *Amer. Polit. Science Rev.*, Sept. 1981; 8. 'The deterrent effect of antitrust enforcement' (with F. C. Nold and J. G. Sidak), *JPE*, 89(3), June 1981; 9. 'The effectiveness of recent US government criminal antitrust enforcement efforts in the construction industry' (with J. S. Feinstein and F. C. Nold), in *Internationale Forschungserebwisse auf dem gemeit der Wirtschaftskrimiwalität*, ed. K. Liebl (Centaurus, 1984); 10. 'Asymmetric information and collusive behavior in auction markets' (with J. S. Feinstein and F. C. Nold), *AER*, 75(3), June 1984.

Principal Contributions Throughout my career I have been interested in the application of economic analysis to legal issues. My early research efforts were centred around the individual choice problem, specifically the criminal's or potential criminal's choice of how much, if any, effort to devote to stealing and how much effort to devote to working. The application of the traditional choice theoretic model to this rather unusual problem led to contributions in two areas. First, the direct results of this application, including the finding that the deterrence results derived by Gary Becker and refined by Issac Ehrlich held only under quite special circumstances. While this result is cited quite frequently and is a technically correct point that needed to be made, I've come to regard it as an appropriate activity only for a newly minted PhD. Second, and I think somewhat more important than the direct implications of this application, were my 'spin off' results. In order to derive general deterrence results, it was necessary to solve the labour supply problem under uncertainty. I think the results here, especially the implication that income uncertainty may actually increase the labour supply, are more durable and certainly of more general interest than the deterrence results.

Over time my focus has shifted and I have become much more concerned with empirical verification of theory. My recent work is concerned with the decision to fix prices. In a sense this has brought me closer to the mainstream in economics. Moreover, I think in this area it is the empirical testing of the deterrent effort, i.e., estimating the effect of antitrust enforcement on prices, that has been my contribution. At this stage of my career, I am somewhat more interested in solving the problem of 'how do we test it' than in signing derivatives.

BLOMQUIST, Glenn C.

Born 1945, Paterson, NJ, USA.

Current Post Assoc. Prof. Econ. and Public Admin., Univ. Kentucky, Lexington, KY, USA, 1981–.

Past Posts Ass. Prof., Illinois State Univ., Normal, IL, 1976–80; Ass. Prof., Univ. Kentucky, Lexington, KY, 1980–1; Vis. Scholar, Univ. Chicago, 1984.

Degrees BA Ohio Wesleyan Univ., Delaware, OH, 1967; MA Ohio State

Univ., Columbia, OH, 1969; PhD
Univ. Chicago, 1977.

Editorial Duties Advisory Board,
Growth and Change, 1982.

Principal Fields of Interest 931 Urban Economics; 720 Natural Resources;
921 Consumer Economics.

Publications *Books:* 1. *Environmental Policy: Elements of Environmental Analysis* (with G. S. Tolley and P. E. Graves), (Ballinger, 1981); 2. *Environmental Policy: Water Quality*, co-ed. (with G. S. Tolley), (Ballinger, 1983); 3. *The Regulation of Motor Vehicle and Traffic Safety (AEI, 1984)*.
Articles: 1. 'The effect of electric utility power plant location on area property value', *Land Econ.*, 50, Feb. 1974; 2. 'Value of life saving: implications of consumption activity', *JPE*, 87(4), June 1979; 3. 'Passive restraints: an economist's view' (with S. Peltzman), in *The Scientific Basis of Health and Safety Regulation* (Brookings Inst., 1981); 4. 'The value of life: an empirical perspective', *EI*, 19(1), Jan. 1981; 5. 'Hedonic prices, demands for urban housing amenities and benefit estimates' (with L. Worley), *JUE*, 9(2), March 1981; 6. 'Specifying the demand for urban housing characteristics: the exogeneity issue' (with L. Worley), in *Economics of Urban Amenities* (Academic Press, 1982); 7. 'Estimating the value of life and safety: recent developments', in *The Value of Life and Safety* (N-H, 1982); 8. 'Measurement of the benefits of water quality improvements', in *Environmental Policy: Water Quality*, eds. G. C. Blomquist and G. S. Tolley (Ballinger, 1983); 9. 'Toward improved water quality policy' (with G. S. Tolley), in *Environmental Policy: Water Quality, op.cit.*; 10. 'The 55 m.p.h. speed limit and gasoline consumption', *Resources and Energy*, 6, forthcoming, 1986.

Principal Contributions In general my work deals with the theory and measurement of the benefits of public policy concerning health, safety and environment. There are three related areas of research. The first area focusses on valuing reductions in risk to life and limb. The emphasis is on preference-based measures of values of life-saving rather than some variant of earnings. The second area attempts to develop

further the implicit market approach. Housing markets are analysed to estimate the values of urban and environmental amenities. The third area consists of positive and prescriptive work on environmental and traffic safety regulation.

I am interested in the economic rationale for and contribution of economic analysis to social regulation. In *Environmental Policy: Elements of Environmental Policy*, Tolley and I offer a benefit-cost based, multidisciplinary framework for the design and evaluation of environmental policy. I have also given specific attention to valuing improvements in water quality and the implementation of water quality policy. In *The Regulation of Motor Vehicle and Traffic Safety*, I turn to a comprehensive review and economic critique of two decades of traffic safety regulation in the US. In other works I have analysed seat belt usage in automobiles, mandatory passive restraints, and the national speed limit. I am continuing to work on benefit estimation. Currently I am investigating the performance of markets in which there are risks to health and safety and limits to rationality. Also I am working on developing approaches to benefit estimation as alternatives to those based on implicit markets.

BLOOMFIELD, Arthur Irving

Born 1914, Montreal, Quebec, Canada.

Current Post Prof. Econ., Univ. Penn., Philadelphia, PA, USA, 1978–.

Past Posts Econ., Sr. Econ., Fed. Reserve Bank NY, 1941–52, 1953–8; Cons., US Foreign Econ. Admin., 1944–5, US Intermat. Coop. Admin. 1949–50; Financial Adviser, UN Civil Assistance Command, UN Korean Reconstruction Agency, Pusan, Korea, 1951–2; Member, Foreign Aid Team Indochina, US Mutual Security Admin. 1953; Sr. Econ., US Commission Foreign Econ. Policy, 1953; Cons., US Foreign Operations Admin. Indochina, 1954, US Internat. Coop. Admin. Seoul, Korea, 1956, 1960; Vis. Prof., Johns Hopkins Univ. 1961, Princeton Univ.

1963; Cons., Ford Foundation, Malaysia, 1964; Vis. Prof., City Univ. NY, 1965; Cons., US Agency Internat. Devlp. Kinshasa, Democratic Republic of Congo, 1966, 1967, 1968; Bureau of Intelligence and Res., US Dept. State, 1969–78; Vis. Prof., Univ. Melbourne, 1972; Cons., Central Bank Malaysia, Kuala Lumpur, 1983.

Degrees BA, MA McGill Univ., Montreal, Canada, 1935, 1936; PhD Univ. Chicago, 1942.

Offices and Honours US SSRC Pre-Doctoral Fellow, 1939–40; Guggenheim Foundation Fellow, 1956; Rockefeller Foundation Fellow, 1957–8; Ford Foundation Faculty Res. Fellow, 1962–3.

Editorial Duties Ed. Board, *J Post Keyn E*, 1978.

Principal Fields of Interest 430 Balance of Payments; International Finance; 031 History of Economic Thought; 311 Domestic Monetary and Financial Theory and Policy.

Publications *Books:* 1. *Capital Imports and the American Balance of Payments 1934–39* (Univ. Chicago Press, 1950, Augustus M. Kelley, 1966; transl. Japanese, Shinhyoron, 1974); 2. *Banking Reform in South Korea* (with J. P. Jensen) (Fed. Reserve Bank NY, 1951); 3. *Speculative and Flight Movements of Capital in Postwar International Finance* (Princeton Univ. Press, 1954); 4. *Monetary Policy under the International Gold Standard, 1880–1914* (Fed. Reserve Bank NY, 1959; transl. Spanish, CEMLA, 1970); 5. *Short-term Capital Movements under the Pre-1914 Gold Standard* (Princeton Univ. Press, 1963); 6. *Patterns of Fluctuation in International Investment before 1914* (Princeton Univ. Press, 1968).

Articles: 1. 'Foreign-trade doctrines of the physiocrats', *AER*, 28(5), Dec. 1938, repr. in *Essays in Economic Thought.*, eds. J. J. Spengler and W. R. Allen (Rand McNally, 1960); 2. 'The mechanism of adjustment of the American balance of payments: 1919–29', *QJE*, 57(2), May 1943; 3. 'Foreign exchange rate theory and policy', in *The New Economics*, ed. S. E. Harris (A. A. Knopf, 1947); 4. 'Monetary policy in underdeveloped countries', in *Public Policy*, Yearbook Grad. School Public Admin. Harvard Univ., VII, ed. C. J. Friedrich and S. E. Harris (Vermont Printing, 1957); 5. 'Rules of the game of international adjustment?', in *Essays in Money and Banking in Honour of R. S. Sayers*, eds. C. R. Whittlesey and J. S. G. Wilson (OUP, 1968); 6. 'Recent trends in international economies', *Annals Amer. Academy Polit. and Social Science*, 386, Nov. 1969, repr. in *Dimensions of Macroeconomics*, ed. S. Mittra (Random House, 1971); 7. 'Managing the managed float' (with W. J. Ethier), *Princeton Essays in International Finance*, 112, Oct. 1975; 8. 'Adam Smith and the theory of international trade', in *Essays on Adam Smith*, eds. A. S. Skinner and T. Wilson (OUP, 1975); 9. 'Impact of growth and technology on trade in nineteenth century British thought', *HOPE*, 11(4), Fall 1978; 10. 'British thought on the influence of foreign trade and investment on growth, 1800–1880', *HOPE*, 13(1), Spring 1981.

Principal Contributions My main interest during my professional career has been in problems of international finance, especially those relating to capital movements and exchange rates; and much of my research and writing, both at the Federal Reserve and at the University of Pennsylvania, has been in this broad area. In the late 1950s and in the 1960s my interests shifted from current problems to international financial history, and I wrote a number of monographs, I believe among the first of their kind, on the pre-1914 gold standard and its functioning. More recently a considerable part of my research and writing has turned to the history of economic thought, especially nineteenth-century theories of trade and growth. Over the past thirty-five years as a whole I have also been on a large number of short-term assignments, many for the US Government, in the Far East, Africa and the Caribbean, where I advised on the establishment of central banks and/or monetary policy. A number of published studies has emerged from these assignments.

BLUESTONE, Barry Alan

Born 1944, New York City, NY, USA.

Current Post Prof. Econ., Dir., Social Welfare Res. Inst., Boston Coll., Chestnut Hill, MA, USA, 1982–.

Past Posts Res. Fellow, Inst. Labor and Industrial Relations, Univ. Mich., 1968–71; Ass. Prof., Assoc. Prof., Boston Coll., 1971–6, 1977–81.

Degrees BA, MA, PhD Univ. Michigan, 1966, 1967, 1970.

Offices and Honours Osterweil Prize Econ., 1966; Woodrow Wilson Fellow, 1966–7; John Eliot Parker Award Labor Econ., 1971; Aspen Inst. Fellow, 1983; C. Wright Mills Award (Honorable Mention), 1983.

Editorial Duties Ed. Board, *Review Radical Polit. Econ.*, 1978–80

Principal Fields of Interest 820 Labour Markets; Public Policy; 914 Economics of Poverty; 940 Regional Economics.

Publications *Books:* 1. *Low Wages and the Working Poor* (with M. Murphy and M. Stevenson), (Univ. Michigan Press, 1973); 2. *Aircraft Industry Dynamics: An Analysis of Competition, Capital and Labor* (with P. Jordan and M. Sullivan), (Auburn House, 1981); 3. *The Retail Revolution* (with P. Hanna, S. Kuhn and L. Moore), (Auburn House, 1981); 4. *Corporate Flight: The Causes and Consequences of Economic Dislocation* (with L. Baker and B. Harrison), (Progressive Alliance Books, 1981); 5. *The Deindustrialization of America* (with B. Harrison), (Basic Books, 1982).

Articles: 1. 'Low wage industries and the working poor', *Poverty and Human Resources*, 3, April 1968; 2. 'The tripartite economy: labor markets and the working poor', *Poverty and Human Resources*, 5, July 1970; 3. 'Ecology and class conflict' (with R. England), *Rev. Radical Polit. Econ.*, 3, Fall 1971; 4. 'The incidence and regulation of plant closings' (with B. Harrison), *Pol. Stud. J.*, Dec. 1981; 5. 'Industrial policy priorities in the trade jungle' (with S. O'Cleirecain), *World Pol. J.*, 1, 1984; 6. 'Why corporations close profitable plants,' *Working Papers*, 7, May 1980; 7. 'Storm clouds on the horizon: labor market crisis and industrial policy', *Econ. Educ. Project*, May 1984; 8. 'Is deindustrialization a myth? Capital mobility vs. absorptive capacity in the US economy', *The Annals*, Fall 1984.

Principal Contributions My early work focussed on low wage employment and dual labour market theory. Research on wage determination led me to conclude that, for the majority of the US labour force, factors other than human capital dominated the wage determination process. In particular, unionisation and racial and gender discrimination were key factors for all groups of workers except highly skilled professionals. Following up on a number of hypotheses raised by this early work, I turned my attention to pursuing a number of industry studies, in particular aircraft and retail trade. Research into these industries suggested the links between capital investment, capital mobility, labour market strategies and regional development. Along with research carried out by my colleague B. Harrison, these industry studies led me to investigate the problem of plant closings and worker dislocation in the United States. This, in turn, generated the basis for our joint work on deindustrialisation. Changes in corporate behaviour in the postwar period toward enterprise location and labour-management relations is the central theme of this work. Most recently, Harrison and I have been investigating changes in the structure of the US labour market and how these changes may affect the distribution of income and family living standards.

BOADWAY, Robin William

Born 1943, Regina, Saskatchewan, Canada.

Current Post Prof. Econ., Queen's Univ., Kingston, Ont., Canada, 1980–.

Past Posts Lect., Royal Military Coll., Kingston, Ont., 1969–72; Lect., Ass. Prof., Assoc. Prof., Queen's Univ., 1972–3, 1973–6, 1976–80.

Degrees B.Eng., Royal Military Coll., 1964; BA, B.Phil. Univ. Oxford, 1966, 1967; PhD Queen's Univ., 1973.

Offices and Honours Rhodes Scholar,

1964–7; Univ. Chicago Post-Doctoral Fellow, 1976–7; US SSRC Leave Fellow, 1980–1; Harry Johnson Memorial Prize, CEA, 1978.

Principal Fields of Interest 320 Fiscal Theory and Policy; Public Finance; 024 Welfare Theory; 915 Social Security.

Publications *Books:* 1. *Canadian Banking and Monetary Policy*, co-ed. (with J. P. Cairns and H. H. Binhammer), (McGraw-Hill, 1972); 2. *The Impact of the Mining Industries on the Canadian Economy* (with J. Treddenick), (Centre Resource Stud., Queen's Univ., 1977); 3. *Public Sector Economics* (Little-Brown, 1979; with D. Wildasin, 1984); 4. *Canadian Tax Policy* (with H. Kitchen), (Canadian Tax Foundation, 1980); 5. *Intergovernmental Transfers in Canada* (Canadian Tax Foundation, 1980); 6. *Equalization in a Federal State: An Economic Analysis* (with F. R. Flatters), (Econ. Council Canada, 1982); 7. *Welfare Economics* (Blackwell, 1984).

Articles: 1. 'The welfare foundations of cost-benefit analysis', *EJ*, 84, Dec. 1974; 2. 'Cost-benefit rules in general equilibrium', *REStud*, 42, July 1975; 3. 'Integrating equity and efficiency in applied welfare economics', *QJE*, 90, Nov. 1976; 4. 'Public investment decision rules in a neo-classical growing economy', *Int ER*, 19, June 1978; 5. 'A general equilibrium computation of the effects of the Canadian tariff structure' (with J. M. Treddenick), *CJE*, 11, Aug. 1978; 6. 'A characterization of piecemeal second best policy' (with R. G. Harris), *J Pub E*, 8, Oct. 1977; 7. 'Depreciation and interest deductions and the effect of the corporation income tax on investment' (with N. Bruce), *J Pub E*, 11, Feb. 1979; 8. 'Long-run tax incidence: a comparative dynamic approach', *REStud*, 46, July 1979; 9. 'Unemployment insurance and redistributive taxation' (with A. J. Oswald), *J Pub E*, 20, March 1983; 10 'On the neutrality of flow-of-funds corporate taxation' (with N. Bruce and J. Mintz), *Ec*, N.S. 50, Feb. 1983.

Principal Contributions Most of my work has been in three principal areas — welfare economics, fiscal federalism and corporate taxation. My early work in welfare economics was intended to show that the evaluation of welfare change from policy changes could not in general ignore either equity or distortions elsewhere. This was followed by some work on incorporating equity and distortions into policy rules. A synthesis of my views on welfare economics may be found in my book *Welfare Economics*.

In fiscal federalism, I have studied the inequities and inefficiencies arising out of decentralised federal systems of government and the appropriate system of federal grants to correct for these. A good part of my work on corporate taxation has been joint with Neil Bruce and Jack Mintz. Much of it has centred on the effect of the corporate tax on the investment and financial decision of the firm, including investment not only in depreciable capital but also in inventories. This analysis led to a consideration of the design of the ideal corporate tax system and its relation with the personal tax system. The work culminated in an empirical study estimating the effective tax rates in Canada for various types of capital and for various years.

I have also done some work in other areas — investigating the use of the unemployment insurance scheme as an instrument for equity, analysing the role of regional subsidiaries in a model with regional unemployment differentials, and some general equilibrium computational work on the Canadian economy. My current research concerns estimating the impact of capital taxation on savings.

BODKIN, Ronald George

Born 1936, Philadelphia, PA, USA.
Current Post Prof. Econ., Univ. Ottawa, Ottawa, Ont., Canada, 1975–.
Past Posts Instr., Lect., Univ. Penn., 1957–60, 1961–2; Lect., Ass. Prof., Res. Staff, Vis. Res. Assoc., Cowles Foundation, Yale Univ., 1962–5, 1971–2; Vis. Lect., Univ. Colorado, 1964; Assoc. Prof., Prof., Univ. W. Ontario, 1965–75; Dir., CANDIDE Project, Econ. Council Canada, 1972–4; Prof. Invité d'économétrie, Univ. Genève, 1984.

Degrees BA Swarthmore Coll., Swarthmore, PA, USA, 1957; MA, PhD, Univ. Penn., 1959, 1962.

Offices and Honours Canada Council Leave Fellow, 1971–2; Pres., EEA, 1982–3.

Editorial Duties Ed. Board, *CJE*, 1968–70, *Int ER* 1969, *Eastern Econ. J.*, 1973–6, and *J. Post Keyn. E.*, 1978.

Principal Fields of Interest 212 Construction, Analysis and Use of Econometric Models; 023 Macroeconomic Theory; 031 History of Economic Thought.

Publications *Books:* 1. *The Wage-Price-Productivity Nexus* (Univ. Pennsylvania Press, 1966); 2. *Price Stability and High Employment: The Options for Canadian Economic Policy* (with E. P. Bond, G. L. Reuber, and T. R. Robinson), (Queen's Printer, 1967); 3. *The Tracking Properties of CANDIDE Model I. Over the Sample Period 1955–68* (with K. S. R. Murthy and Tom Siedule), (Info. Canada, 1975); 4. *CANDIDE Model 1.1*, co-ed. (with S. M. Tanny), (Info. Canada, 1975).

Articles: 1. 'Windfall income and consumption', *AER*, 43(4), Sept. 1959, repr. in *Consumption and Saving*, II, eds. W. Friend and R. Jones (Univ. Pennsylvania Press, 1960); 2. 'Income, the price level and generalized multipliers in Keynesian economics' (with R. J. Ball), *Metroeconomica* 15(2–3), Aug.–Dec. 1963, repr. in *Inflation: Selected Readings*, eds. J. Ball and P. Doyle (Penguin, 1969); 3. 'Empirical aspects of the trade-offs among three goals: high level employment, price stability and economic growth' (with L. R. Klein and M. Abe), in Commission on Money and Credit, *Inflation, Growth and Employment* (Prentice-Hall, 1964); 4. 'Nonlinear estimation of aggregate production functions' (with L. R. Klein), *REStat*, 49(1), Feb. 1967; 5. 'Real wages and cyclical variations in employment: a reconsideration', *CJE*, 2(3), Aug. 1969; 6. 'Additively consistent relationships for personal savings and the categories of consumption expenditures, U.S.A. 1949–1963', *Eastern Econ. J.*, 1(1), Jan. 1974; 7. 'Keynesian econometric concepts: consumption functions, investment functions, and "the" multiplier', in *Modern Economic Thought*, ed. S. Weintraub, (Univ. Pennsylvania Press, 1977); 8. '*Ex ante* Forecasting with several econometric models of the Canadian economy' (with V. Cano-Lamy, and others), *J Post Keyn. E*, 1(3), Spring 1979; 9. 'The challenge of inflation and unemployment in Canada during the 1980s: would a tax-based incomes policy help?', *Canadian Public Policy — Analyse de Politiques*, 7 Suppl. April 1981; 10. 'Conjectural Nobel prizes in economics: 1770 to 1890' (with E. G. West), *Eastern Econ. J.*, 9(3), July–Sept. 1983.

Principal Contributions Under the guidance of Irwin Friend, my research interests began with a study of the consumption function in general and the permanent income hypothesis in particular. Lawrence R. Klein came to the University of Pennsylvania in 1958 and interested me in a variety of problems in theoretical and applied econometrics. During the 1960s I was strongly interested in wage-price macroeconomics, as I was still confident at that time that a stable trade-off curve existed (into the indefinite future) between the goals of full employment and price stability. I still retain an interest in wage-price theory and policy, such as tax-based incomes policy. From 1972–4 I headed a project team concerned with a major Canadian econometric model, CANDIDE, and this sparked my current interest in writing a history of macroeconometric modelling, which I am doing with Kanta Marwah of Carleton Univ. and Prof. Lawrence R. Klein. This current project ties in with a maverick interest that I have had for some time in the history of economic thought.

BOHM, Peter Jan Gunnar

Born 1935, Stockholm, Sweden.

Current Post Prof. Econ., Univ., Stockholm, 1970–.

Degrees PhD, Docent Stockholm School Econ., Univ. Stockholm, 1964, 1970, 1971.

Offices and Honours Judge, Market Court, Sweden, 1971–.

Editorial Duties Ed., *Swed JE*, 1968–72; Assoc. Ed., *J Pub E*, 1983–.

Principal Fields of Interest 022 Microeconomic Theory; 024 Welfare Theory; 320 Fiscal Theory and Policy; Public Finance.

Publications *Books:* 1. *External Economies in Production* (Almqvist & Wiksell, 1964, 1967); 2. *Resource Allocation and the Credit Market* (Almqvist & Wiksell, 1967); 3. *Pricing of Copper in International Trade — A Case Study of the Price Stabilization Problem* (Nordts, 1968); 4. *Social Efficiency — A Concise Introduction to Welfare Theory* (Macmillan, Halsted Press, 1973, 1975); 5. *Deposit-refund Systems: Theory and Applications to Environmental, Conservation, and Consumer Policy* (JHUP, 1981).

Articles: 1. 'On the theory of second best', *REStud*, 34(3), July 1967; 2. 'An approach to the problem of estimating demand for public goods', *Swed JE*, 73(1), March 1971; 3. 'Pollution: taxation or purification?', *Kyk*, 25(3), 1972; 4. 'Estimating demand for public goods: an experiment', *Europ ER*, 3(1), April 1972; 5. 'Estimating willingness to pay: why and how?', *Scand JE*, 81(2), April 1979.

Principal Contributions Contributions to externality theory and to the analysis of environmental policy. Public goods: theory, methods for revealing preferences and experimental applications. Comprehensive analysis of deposit-refund systems: theory and applications. Concise introductory textbook on welfare theory. Contributions to second-best theory. Analysis of price stabilisation schemes. Allocative efficiency of different ways of organising the credit market. Cost-benefit analysis of industrial projects and policy proposals in Sweden. Economic theory of transportation policy.

BÖHM-BAWERK, Eugen von*

Dates and Birthplace 1851–1914, Austro-Hungary.

Posts Held Prof. Econ., Univ. Innsbruck, 1881–9; Civil servant, Austrian Ministry of Fin., 1889–1904; Minister of Fin., 1895, 1897, 1900; Prof. Econ., Univ. Vienna, 1904–14.

Degrees Graduate in Law, Univ. Vienna.

Publications *Books:* 1. *Capital and Interest*, 3 vols, eds. G. D. Huncke and H. F. Sennholz (1884–1912, 1959); 2. *Gesammelte Schriften*, 10 vols, ed. F. X. Weiss (1924–6); 3. *Shorter Classics of Eugene von Böhm-Bawerk* (1881–1914, 1962).

Career One of the greatest figures of the Austrian school, who expanded and reworked Menger's marginal utility theory. His theory of interest, based on the 'three reasons' for interest, was his major personal contribution. Other significant influences were Thünen and Rae, whose ideas on roundabout production he developed as an element of his capital theory. This aroused furious controversy with fellow economists, into which he entered enthusiastically, writing almost as much in defence of the theory as in its original formulation. Even today there is less than total agreement as to the meaning and significance of his theory of capital and interest. Böhm-Bawerk's considerable polemical skills were further demonstrated by *The Close of the Marxian System* (1896), which remains one of the most powerful attacks on Marxist economics ever written. In his government service he participated in the introduction of a gold currency. His resignation as Minister of Finance came when military expenditure threatened to unbalance the budget.

Secondary Literature J. Schumpeter, 'Eugen von Böhm-Bawerk', in *Ten Great Economists from Marx to Keynes* (OUP, 1951); E, Kauder, 'Böhm-Bawerk, Eugen von', *IESS*, 2; R. E. Kuenne, *Eugene von Böhm-Bawerk* (Columbia Univ. Press, 1971).

BOISGUILBERT, Pierre Le Pesant, Sieur de*

Dates and Birthplace 1646–1714, Normandy, France.

Posts Held Landowner and member, Noblesse de la robe.

Publications *Books:* 1. *Le détail de la France* (1695); 2. *Factum de la France* (1706).

Career Though much concerned

with workaday economic facts and policy, he soon developed deeper theoretical interests. From his country home in Normandy he developed the idea, which was to take on central importance for the physiocrats, that agriculture was the most essential sector of the economy and should be given preference over the demands of manufacturing. To this end he advocated high prices for agricultural products, leading to a rural population with a greater capacity to consume goods and a swifter circulation of money. His policy propositions were probably easy to disregard because of his exaggerated claims for them, but he can be seen with hindsight as a major contributor to the development of macroeconomic theory in the early eighteenth century.

Secondary Literature H. Van Dyke Roberts, *Boisguilbert* (Columbia Univ. Press, 1935); J. J. Spengler, *et al.*, *Pierre de Boisguilbert et la naissance de l'économie politique*, 2 vols (Presses Univ. de France, 1966).

BOITEUX, Marcel Paul

Born 1922, Niort, France.
Current Post Chairman, Electricité de France, 1978–.
Past Posts Econ., CNRS, Paris, 1945–9; Prof. Econ., Ecole Supérieure d'Electricité, 1957–62, Ecole Nationale des Ponts et Chaussées, Paris, 1963–7; Member, Chairman, Consulting Comm. Scientific and Technical Res. France, 1965–8, 1966–7; General Manager, Electricité de France, 1967–8.
Degrees Agrégé (Maths.) Ecole Normale Supérieure, 1945; Diplôme, Inst. d'Etudes Politiques, 1947; Hon. Dr. Yale Univ., 1982.
Offices and Honours Pres., Em Soc., 1959, French OR Soc., 1960; Internat. Federation OR Soc., 1965–6; Chairman, Européen Centre Public Entreprises, 1983–.
Principal Fields of Interest 227 Prices; 024 Welfare Theory.
Publications *Articles:* 1. 'La tarification des demandes en pointe', *Revue Générale d'Electricité*, 1949; 2. 'Sur la gestion des monopoles publics restreints

à l'équilibre budgétaire', *Em*, 24(1), Jan. 1956; 3. 'L'amortissement peut-il jouer un rôle dans le calcul économique?', *Revue de Recherche Opérationnelle*, 1(5), 1957; 4. 'Marginal cost pricing of electricity', in *Marginal Cost Pricing in Practice*, ed. J. R. Nelson (Prentice-Hall, 1964); 5. 'Note sur le taux d'actualisation', *REP*, 79, 1969.
Principal Contributions Marginal cost pricing. Second-best theory. Welfare economic.

BOLAND, Lawrence Arthur

Born 1939, Peoria, IL, USA.
Current Post Prof. Econ., Simon Fraser Univ., Burnaby, British Columbia, Canada, 1978–.
Past Posts Ass. Prof., Univ. Wisconsin-Milwaukee, 1965–6; Ass. Prof., Assoc. Prof., Simon Fraser Univ., 1966–70, 1970–8; Vis. Ass. Prof., Boston Univ., 1968.
Degrees BS Bradley Univ, Peoria, IL, 1962; MS, PhD Univ. Illinois, Urbana, IL, 1963, 1966.
Offices and Honours NDEA Fellow, 1962–5.
Editorial Duties Ed. Board. *Philo. Social Science*, 1975–, *CJE*, 1979–82.
Principal Fields of Interest 036 Economic Methodology; 022 Microeconomic Theory; 011 General Economics.
Publications *Books:* 1. *The Foundations of Economic Method* (A & U, 1982); 2. *Methodology for a New Microeconomics* (A & U, forthcoming, 1986). *Articles:* 1. 'Conventionalism and economic theory', *Philo. Science*, 37(2), June 1970; 2. 'An institutional theory of economic technology and change', *Philo. Social Science*, 1(3), Sept. 1971; 3. 'The law of demand, weak axiom of revealed preference and price-consumption curves', *AEP*, 14(1), June 1975; 4. 'Uninformative economic models', *Atlantic Econ. J.*, 3(2), Nov. 1975; 5. 'Testability in economic science', *SAJE*, 45(1), March 1977; 6. 'Time in economics vs. economics in time: the "Hayek Problem"', *CJE*, 11(2), May 1978, repr. in *Schriftenreihe für interdisziplinare Okonomie* (forthcoming, 1986); 7. 'A critique of Friedman's critics', *JEL*, 17(2), June

1979, repr. in *How Economists Explain: A Reader in Methodology*, eds. W. L. Marr and B. Raj (Univ. Press America, 1983), and *Hacienda Publica Espanola* (Inst. de Estudios Fiscales, 1985); 8. 'On the role of knowledge in economic theory' (with G. Newman), *AEP*, 18(1), June 1979; 9. 'Knowledge and the role of institutions in economic theory', *JEI*, 8(4), 1979; 10. 'On the futility of criticizing the neoclassical maximization hypothesis', *AER*, 71(5), Dec. 1981.

Principal Contributions After switching from engineering studies to economics late in my undergraduate degree, and after completing PhD studies exclusively devoted to mathematical economics, I decided that most mathematical models of economic theories were inherently empty since they never dealt with the actual process of decision-making that we are supposedly explaining. Very early it was clear to me that any realistic explanation of an individual's behaviour must include assumptions concerning how the individual processes information such as that concerning his or her own utility or preferences as well as that concerning existing prices. This led immediately to the study of methodology and epistemology.

Unfortunately, when I decided to study methodology it was not highly regarded by the profession. Until the late 1970s, editors of major economics journals were reluctant to publish anything concerning methodology. In the 1960s the low regard was quite understandable since little of the methodology literature seemed to have any direct effect on economic theory. My purpose has always been to show that methodology can matter. All that is required is the recognition that every decision maker must have a methodology. In one sense, it may be easily claimed that, of course, everyone has a methodology. But on closer examination, that claim usually presumes that everyone has the same methodology (namely, inductive learning). Such an examination eventually led to my 1982 book, *The Foundations of Economic Method*, which criticises the role of presumed induction in economic theory and shows that this presumption has

generated impossible avant-garde theoretical problems. More recently, in my *Methodology for a New Microeconomics*, I examine the methodological problems of recent attempts to focus microeconomics on the study of disequilibrium systems — again, I try to show how methodology matters.

BONAR, James*

Dates and Birthplace 1852–1941, Perth, Scotland.
Post Held Civil Servant, 1881–1919.
Degrees BA Univ. Oxford, 1877; LLD Univ. Glasgow, 1886; Hon. DLitt. Univ. Camb., 1935.
Offices and Honours Founder, Vice-Pres., RES; Vice-Pres., RSS; Pres., Section F, BAAS, 1898; Fellow, BA, 1930.
Publications *Books:* 1. *Malthus and His Work* (1885, 1924); 2. *Philosophy and Political Economy* (1893, 1922); 3. *Elements of Political Economy* (1903).
Career An historian of economics, concentrating on the work of Smith, Malthus and Ricardo. He also introduced the work of the Austrian economists to a largely unaware English-speaking public. His *Philosophy and Political Economy* was much appreciated in continental Europe. He contributed extensively to Palgrave's *Dictionary of Political Economy* and published many articles in the *Economic Journal*.
Secondary Literature G. F. Shirras, 'Obituary: James Bonar', *EJ*, 51, April 1941.

BORCH, Karl Henrik

Born 1919, Sarpsborg, Norway.
Current Post Prof. Insurance, Norwegian School Bus., Bergen, Norway, 1963–.
Past Posts Ass. Actuary, Samvirke Insurance, Oslo, Norway, 1945–7; Scientific Officer, UNESCO, Cairo, Teheran, Delhi, 1947–51; Res. Fellow, Cowles Commission, Univ. Chicago, 1952; Regional Repres., UNICEF, Brazzaville, 1952–3; Head, Productivity Measurement Service, OEEC,

Paris, 1954–9; Res. Fellow, Norwegian School Bus., 1959–62; Res. Assoc., Princeton Univ., 1962–3; Vis. Prof, UCLA, 1964–5, 1981, Nuffield Coll. Oxford, 1967, Ohio State Univ., 1968–9, Bonn Univ, 1972–3, Swedish School Econ., 1975, Univ. Ottawa, 1976.
Degrees MA (Actuarial Science), PhD (Maths.) Univ. Oslo, 1947, 1963.
Offices and Honours Fellow, Em Soc, 1963; Member, Internat. Stat. Inst., 1968, Norwegian Academy of Science, 1981; Prize, Accademia dei Lincei, Rome, 1975.
Editorial Duties Ed., *Productivity Measurement Rev.*, 1955–9; Ed. Board, *Productivity Measurement Rev.* 1959–66, *Theory and Decision*, 1970–, *Internat. J. Game Theory*, 1971–81, *Fin. Rev.* 1976–, *J. Bank Fin* 1977–, *Econ. Letters*, 1978–.
Principal Fields of Interest 021 General Equilibrium Theory; 213 Mathematical Methods and Models.
Publications *Books:* 1. *The Economics of Uncertainty* (Princeton Univ. Press, 1968; transls., German, Oldenbourg, 1969, Japanese, Nihon Seisan Hombu, 1973, Spanish, Editorial Tecnos, 1976); 2. *Risk and Uncertainty* co-ed. (with J. Mossin), (Macmillan, 1968); 3. *The Mathematical Theory of Insurance*(D. C. Heath, 1974).
Articles: 1. 'The safety loading of reinsurance premiums', *Skandinavisk Aktuarietidskrift*, 1960; 2. 'Equilibrium in a reinsurance market', *Em*, 30, July 1962; 3. 'The theory of risk', *JRSS*, Ser. B, 1967; 4. 'The place of uncertainty in the theories of the Austrian school', in *Carl Menger and the Austrian School of Economics,* eds. J. R. Hicks and W. Weber (OUP, 1973); 5. 'Capital markets and the supervision of insurance', *J. Risk and Insurance*, 41, 1976; 6. 'The monster in Loch Ness', *J. Risk and Insurance*, 43(3), Sept. 1976; 7. 'Optimal life insurance', *Geneva Papers on Risk and Insurance*, 6, Oct. 1977; 8. 'The price of moral hazard', *Scandinavian Actuarial J.*, 1980; 9. 'The three markets for private insurance', *Geneva Papers on Risk and Insurance*, 20, July 1981; 10. 'Optimal strategies in a game of economic survival', *Naval Research Logistics Q.*, 29, 1982.
Principal Contributions My actuarial training led to mathematical statistics, and then to game theory, which gave me an idea of what economics was all about. When in 1959 I got a research post which game me almost complete freedom, as long as my work was relevant to insurance, I naturally set out to develop an economic theory of insurance. As most universities' courses in insurance attract few students, I have had to teach many other subjects. My book, *The Economics of Uncertainty*, is really a set of lecture notes written when no students registered for a course on the economics of insurance.

BORCHERDING, Thomas Earl

Born 1939, Cincinnati, OH, USA.
Current Post Prof. Econ., Claremont Grad. School, Claremont, CA, USA, 1984–.
Past Posts Ass. Prof., Univ. Washington, Seattle, 1966–71; Assoc. Prof. Econ., Res. Assoc., Center Study of Public Choice, Virginia Polytechnic Inst. and State Univ., 1971–3; Nat. Fellow, Hoover Inst., Stanford Univ., 1974–5; Prof. Law and Econ., Univ. Toronto, 1978–9; Vis. Sr. Scholar, Hoover Inst., Stanford Univ., 1979–80; Assoc. Prof., Prof. Econ., Simon Fraser Univ., Canada, 1971–84.
Degrees BA Univ. Cincinnati, 1961; PhD Duke Univ., 1966.
Offices and Honours Phi Beta Kappa, 1961; US Nat. Defense Educ. Act Fellow, 1961–4; Ford Foundation Dissertation Fellow, 1964–5; Relm Foundation Fellow, 1965–6, 1969; Omicron Delta Epsilon, 1973; Earhart Fellow, 1973, 1974 and 1980; Canadian SSRC Sabbatical Fellow, 1979–80.
Editorial Duties Ed. Boards, *CJE*, 1975–8, *Pakistan J. Econ.*, 1980–1, *Cato J.*, 1984–; Co-ed., *EI*, 1980.
Principal Fields of Interest 022 Microeconomic Theory; 025 Social Choice; Bureaucratic Performance; 320 Public Finance.
Publications *Books:* 1. *Budgets and Bureaucrats: The Source of Government Growth*, ed. (Duke Univ. Press, 1977); 2. *The Egg Marketing Board: A Case Study of Monopoly and Its Social Costs* (Fraser Inst., 1983).

Articles: 1. 'The firm, the industry and the demand for inputs' (with L. Bassett), *CJE*, 3(1), Feb. 1970; 2. 'Externalities and output taxes' (with L. Bassett), *SEJ*, 36(2), April 1970; 3. 'A neglected cost of a voluntary military', *AER*, 61(1), March 1971; 4. 'The demand for the services of non-federal governments' (with R. Deacon), *AER*, 62(5), Dec. 1972; 5. 'The economics of school integration: public choice with tie-ins', *Public Choice*, 31, Fall 1977; 6. 'Why do all the good apples go East?: Alchian and Allen's substitution theorem revisited' (with E. Silberberg), *JPE*, 86(1), Feb. 1978; 7. 'Competition, exclusion and the optimal supply of public goods', *J Law E*, 21, April 1978; 8. 'Expropriation of private property and the basis for compensation' (with J. Knetsch), *Univ. Toronto Law J.*, 29, Summer 1979; 9. 'Comparing the efficiency of private and public production: a survey of the evidence from five federal countries' (with W. Pommerehne and F. Schneider), *ZN*, Suppl., 2, 1982; 10. 'Toward a positive theory of public sector supply arrangements', in *Public Enterprise in Canada: The Calculus of Instrument Choice*, ed. J. R. S. Pritchard (Butterworths, 1983).

Principal Contributions In the main, my research has ranged over several issues of public choice economics. Beginning with my dissertation and more recently, this work has asked by how much, in what areas, and why does the democratic State grow? To aid this enquiry, a median-voter model of public sector demand was formulated in a choice-theoretic, empirically verifiable framework (1972) and extended to non-competitive bureaucratic circumstances (1977). Whether these collectively provided goods and services are highly consumption indivisible ('public goods') or are rent-seeking redistributions has also been a positive theme explored in the context of government budgets (1972, 1977), market regulation (1981) and public enterprise (1982, 1983). The issue of why State action takes various supply forms — contracting out, public bureaucracy or regulation — is a more recent interest (1982, 1983). As a side issue the question of why compensation to supplying agents is generally paid under the first two institutions, but not the last, was also pursued (1979).

Currently, my efforts are shifting to the question of the efficacy of policy analysis in worlds of rationally formed political expectations, reflecting the discussion of the value of openly available analyses of marketable assets. The parallels are not close because of the great differences in transactions costs between representative politics and highly transferable, monitorable private assets. Given this understanding, the possibilities and limitations of fiscal and monetary manipulations by incumbents, the so-called 'political business cycle', is now being considered. I continue to work on the possibilities and limitations of complex-contracting and co-ordination of n-person public goods demands through private market mechanisms, a task begun with my 1978 paper on the subject.

BORDO, Michael David

Born 1942, Montreal, Quebec, Canada.

Current Post Prof. Econ., Coll. Bus. Admin., Univ. S. Carolina, Columbia. SC, USA, 1981–; Research Assoc., NBER, 1982–.

Past Posts Ass. Prof., Carleton Univ., Ottawa, 1969–76; Res. Assoc., NBER, 1970; Academic Vis., LSE 1973, Haifa Univ., Israel, 1975; Vis. Ass. Prof., UCLA, 1976; Assoc. Prof., Carleton Univ., 1976–81; Vis. Assoc. Prof., Lund Univ, Sweden, 1977, UCLA, 1980; Vis. Scholar, Fed. Reserve Bank St Louis, 1981; Res. Staff, Exec. Dir., US Congressional Gold Commission, 1981–2.

Degrees BA McGill Univ., 1963; MSc LSE, 1965; PhD Univ. Chicago, 1972.

Offices and Honours Canada Council Doctoral Fellow, 1967–9.

Editorial Duties Ed. Board, *Explor. Econ. Hist.*, 1984.

Principal Fields of Interest 310 Domestic Monetary and Financial Theory and Policy; 041 Economic History;

General; 432 International Monetary Arrangements.

Publications *Books:* 1. *A Retrospective on the Classical Gold Standard, 1821–1931,* co-ed. (with A. J. Schwartz), (Univ. Chicago Press, 1984).

Articles: 1. 'John E. Cairnes on the effects of the Australian gold discoveries 1851–73: an early application of the methodology of positive economics', *HOPE,* 7(3), Fall 1975; 2. 'The income effects of the sources of new money: a comparison of the United States and the United Kingdom: 1870–1913', *Explor. Econ. Hist.,* 14(1), Jan. 1977; 3. 'Issues in monetary economics and their impact on research in economic history' (with A. J. Schwartz), in *Recent Developments in the Study of Business and Economic History: Essays in Memory of Herman E. Kroos,* ed. R Gallman (Johnson Assoc., 1977); 4. 'The effects of monetary change on relative commodity prices and the role of long term contracts', *JPE,* 88(6), Dec. 1980; 5. 'The long run behavior of income velocity of circulation: a cross country comparison of five advanced countries 1870–1975' (with L. Jonung), *EI,* 19(1), Jan. 1981; 6. 'Money and prices in the nineteenth century: was Thomas Tooke right?' (with A. J. Schwartz), *Explor. Econ. Hist.,* 18(2), May 1981; 7. 'Currency substitution and the demand for money: some evidence for Canada' (with E. U. Choudhri), *JMCB,* 14(1), Feb. 1982; 8. 'Some aspects of the monetary economics of Richard Cantillon', *J Mon E,* 11(4), Aug. 1983; 9. 'The classical gold standard: some lessons for today', *Fed. Reserve Bank St Louis Econ. Rev.,* 63(6), May 1981; 10. 'The gold standard: the traditional approach', in *A Retrospective on the Classical Gold Standard 1821–1931,* eds. M. D. Bordo and A. J. Schwartz (Univ. Chicago Press, 1984).

Principal Contributions A dominant theme of much of my research over the past fifteen years has been the extension of the modern quantity theory of money to economic history. My early work, stemming from my dissertation at the University of Chicago, was to ascertain whether the first-round effects of monetary change had a significant impact on nominal income. My interest in first-round effects has since led me to study the seminal works on the subject by Richard Cantillon in the eighteenth century and John Cairnes in the nineteenth, and to examine recent evidence for the US, for the pattern of response of relative prices to monetary change predicted by the theories of these early writers.

Since 1976, I have collaborated with Anna J. Schwartz of the NBER on a number of papers in monetary history. Our work includes a survey article in 1977 and two articles comparing, for the late nineteenth-century US and UK, the modern quantity theory of inflation to that of the cost-push view.

I have also been engaged in a project with Lars Jonung of Lund University examining the evidence for the past century for a number of countries on the determinants of the long-run behaviour of the income velocity of money, following the approach of Knut Wicksell. Recently I have been interested in the historical aspects of international monetary arrangements. This interest has led to a number of papers on the operation of the classical gold standard, a survey of the traditional approach to the classical gold standard, and the organisation with Anna J. Schwartz of an NBER-sponsored conference on the classical gold standard.

BORTKIEWICZ, Ladislaus Von*

Dates and Birthplace 1868–1931, St Petersburg, Russia.

Posts Held Lect., Univs. Strasburg, St Petersburg; Prof., Univ. Berlin, 1901–33

Degrees Grad., Univ. St Petersburg; PhD Univ. Göttingen, 1893.

Offices and Honours Member, Internat. Stat. Inst., Swedish Academy of Sciences.

Publications *Articles:* 1. 'On the correction of Marx's fundamental theoretical construction in the third volume of *Capital*' (1896); repr. in E von Böhm-Bawerk, *Karl Marx and the Close of his System,* ed. P. M. Sweezy (1949); 2. 'Value and price in the Marxian system' (1907); repr. in *Internat. Econ. Papers,* 2, (1952).

Career A mathematical statistican and mathematical economist. Perhaps his outstanding economic work was an analysis of the so-called 'Transformation problem' in Marxist economics, which attempted to fill the gaps in Marx's own arguments; it went largely unnoticed in Marxist circles until P. M. Sweezy rediscovered it in his *Theory of Capitalist Development* (1942). He also wrote notably on the concept of price index numbers. Vigorous controversy with Böhm-Bawerk on the role of time preference in the theory of interest and with Alfred Weber on the geometrical respresentation of the location of industries was typical of his many contributions to economics, most of which appeared in articles and reviews.

Secondary Literature J. A. Schumpeter, 'Ladislaus van Bortkiewicz: 1868–1931', in *Ten Great Economists from Marx to Keynes* (OUP, 1951); E. J. Gumbel, 'Bortkiewicz, Ladislaus von', *IESS*, 2.

BORTS, George Herbert

Born 1927, New York City, NY, USA.

Current Post Prof. Econ., Brown Univ., Providence, RI, USA, 1960–.

Past Posts Instr. Stats., Illinois Inst. Technology, 1948–9; Res. Fellow, Cowles Commission, Univ. Chicago, 1949–50; Ass. Prof., Assoc. Prof. Econ., Brown Univ., 1950–4, 1955–9; Res. Assoc., NBER, 1954–5.

Degrees BA Columbia Univ., 1947; MA, PhD Univ. Chicago, 1949, 1953, Hon. MA Brown Univ., 1957.

Offices and Honours Res. Fellow, US SSRC, 1948–9; Ford Foundation Faculty Res. Fellow, LSE, 1960–1; Guggenheim Foundation Fellow, 1975–6.

Editorial Duties Managing Ed., *AER*, 1969–80

Principal Fields of Interest 430 Balance of Payments; International Finance; 615 Economics of Transportation; 940 Regional Economics.

Publications *Books:* 1.*Economic Growth in a Free Market* (with J. L. Stein), (Columbia Univ. Press, 1964).

Articles: 1. 'Increasing returns in the railway industry', *JPE,* 62, Aug. 1954;

2. 'The estimation of rail cost functions', *EM,* 28, Jan. 1960; 3. 'Regional cycles of manufacturing in the United States, 1914–1953', *Occasional Paper 73* (NBER, 1960); 4. 'Exploring the uneconomic region of the production function' (with E. J. Mishan), *REStud,* 29(4), 1962–3; 5. 'The equalization of returns and regional economic growth', *AER,* 50(3), June 1960; 6. 'Professor Meade on economic growth', *Ec*, N.S. 29, Feb. 1962; 7. 'The estimation of produced income by state and region', in *The Behavior of Income Shares* (Princeton Univ. Press, 1964); 8. 'A theory of long–run international capital movements', *JPE,* 73, Aug. 1964; 9. 'Capital movements and economic growth in developed countries' (with K. J. Kopecky), in *International Mobility and Movement of Capital,* eds. F. Machlup, W. S. Salant and L. Tarshis (St Martin's Press, 1972); 10. 'The monetary approach to the balance of payments with an empirical application to the case of Panama' (with J. A. Hanson), in *Short-Term Macroeconomic Policy in Latin America,* eds. J. Behrman and J. A. Hanson (Columbia Univ. Press, 1979).

Principal Contributions My major interests have been transporation economics, international and regional economics. Other work that I have done in regulation and price theory has emerged from problems suggested by these areas. The motivation is curiosity about the effects of government policies on economic events in one's own and neighbouring regions and countries, as well as a desire to understand conditions of optimality and the policies to achieve them. I am deeply interested in economic theory as a vehicle for understanding the world; as well as a framework for prescribing optimality. While philosophically convinced of the superiority of solutions relying on free markets, I have come to realise that deeper problems consist of finding what can most effectively be freed from the control of government and other noncompetitive forms of organisation, and perfecting the capacity of individuals and institutions to make use of the market.

BOS, Dieter Josef

Born 1940, Prague, Czechoslovakia.
Current Post Dir., Inst. Econ., Univ. Bonn, Bonn, W. Germany, 1979–.

Past Posts Ass., Univ. Vienna, 1965–71; Prof. Econ., Univ. Graz, Austria, 1971–5; Prof. Econ., Univ. Vienna, Austria, 1975–9; Vis. Prof., Harvard Univ., 1981; Board Dirs., Sonderforschungsbereich 21 on Economic Modelling, Bonn, W. Germany; Vis. Prof., LSE 1975–.

Degrees Dr. Juris, Dr. Rer. Pol. Univ. Vienna, Austria, 1963, 1968.

Offices and Honours Dr. Theodor Korner Prize, Vienna, 1967; Dr. Leopold Kunschak Prize, Vienna, 1971; Directory, Austrian Econ. Assoc., 1975.

Editorial Duties Managing Ed., *ZN*, 1973; Ed. Board, *Empirica*, 1974–.

Principal Fields of Interest 614 Public Enterprises; 321 Fiscal Theory and Policy; 025 Social Choice; Bureaucratic Performance.

Publications *Books:* 1. *Offentliche Auftrage in Österreich* (Jupiter-Verlag, 1968); 2. *Wirtschaftsgeschehen und Staatsgewalt* (Herder-Verlag, 1970); 3. *Eine ökonomische Theorie des Finanzausgleichs* (Springer-Verlag, 1971); 4. *Simulationsanalysen zur Österreichischen Pensionsdynamik* (with R. Holzmann), (Verlag Österreichischen Akademie Wissenschaften, 1976); 5. *Steuerfunktionen in Prognose — und Entscheidungsmodellen* (with B. Genser), (Verlag Österreichischen Akademie Wissenschaften, 1977); 6. *Economic Theory of Public Enterprise* (Springer-Verlag, 1981); 7. *Public Production*, co-ed. (with R. A. Musgrave and J. Wiseman), (Springer-Verlag, 1982); 8. *Beitrage zue neueren Steuertheorie*, co-ed. (with M. Rose and C. Seidl), (Springer-Verlag, 1984); 9. *Entrepreneurship*, co-ed. (with A. Bergson and J. Meyer), (Springer-Verlag, 1984); 10. *Public Enterprise Economics* (N-H, 1985).

Articles: 1. 'Offentliche personalausgaben', in *Handbuch der Finanzwissenschaft*, 1, eds. F. Neumark, H. Haller and N. Andel (Mohr-Verlag, 1977); 2. 'Cost of living indices and public pricing', *Ec*, N.S. 45, Feb. 1978; 3. 'Distributional effects of maximi-

sation of passenger miles', *J Transp EP*, 12, Sept. 1978; 4. 'Zur theorie des finanzausgleichs', in *Schriften des Vereins fur Sozialpolitik, Probleme des Finanzausgleichs*, I, ed. W. Dreibig (Duncker & Humblot, 1978); 5. 'A voting paradox of fiscal federalism', *J Pub E*, 11, June 1979; 6. 'Offentliche unternehmungen', in *Handbuch der Finanzwissenschaft*, 2, eds. F. Neumark, H. Haller and N. Andel (Mohr-Verlag, 1980); 7. 'The democratic decision on fees versus taxes', *Kyk*, 33(1), Feb. 1980; 8. 'On the quality of publicly supplied goods' (with B. Genser and R Holzmann), *Ec*, N.S. 49, Aug. 1982; 9. 'Crisis of the tax state', *Public Choice*, 38, Dec. 1982; 10. 'Cost-axiomatic regulatory pricing' (with G. Tillmann), *J Pub E*, 22, Nov. 1983.

Principal Contributions I began as an institutional economist, accentuating the connections between law and economics. My ever increasing desire for general results, however, changed me gradually into a mathematical economist. But I always remained interested in those fields of economic theory where government regulations prevail and consumers or entrepreneurs react upon these regulations. In dealing with such regulatory activities, I find the normative approaches (Pareto optimality, fairness, maximisation of social welfare functions) as interesting as the positive approaches (actual behaviour of bureaucrats, voters, public enterprises management, etc.). The confrontation between normative and positive economics characterises much of my work, most clearly to be seen in my advanced textbook on *Public Enterprise Economics* (1985). This book summarises my own previous theoretical work on public sector pricing, extends it and fits it into the general framework of public pricing theory. The theoretical derivations are empirically tested on data for London Transport.

Other recent research deals with the economics of taxation, in search of adequate theoretical foundations of income tax progressivity. As I am one of too few mathematical public economists in the German-speaking countries, I am engaged in encouraging young economists to research in this field. Last, but not least, I devote much time to the editing of 'my' journal, *ZN,* which I have switched into an English-written journal with a high theoretical level in the last ten years.

BOS, Hendricus Cornelis

Born 1926, Den Haag, The Netherlands.
Current Post Prof. Devlp. Planning and Econ. of Centrally Planned Systems, Erasmus Univ., Rotterdam, Netherlands, 1965–.
Past Posts Sr. Lect., Res. Fellow, Dir., Netherlands Econ. Inst., 1953–65, 1951–68, 1960–78; Vis. Res. Fellow, Cowles Foundation, Yale Univ. 1961.
Degrees Doctoranous, Doctoraat Netherlands School Econ., 1953, 1964.
Editorial Duties Ed. Board, *J. Pol. Modeling.*
Principal Fields of Interest 050 Economic Systems; 100 Economic Growth; 400 International Economics.
Publications *Books:* 1. *A Discussion on Methods of Monetary Analysis and Norms for Monetary Policy* (Rotterdam Univ. Press, 1956, 1965); 2. *Mathematical Models of Growth* (with J. Tinbergen), (McGraw-Hill, 1962; transls., French, Spanish, Russian); 3. *Econometrics of Education Planning* (with J. Tinbergen), (OECD, 1965); 4. *Spatial Dispersion of Economic Activity* (Rotterdam Univ. Press, 1965; transls., Italian, Russian); 5. *Private Foreign Investment in Developing Countries* (with M. Snaders and C. Secchi), (Reidel, 1974).
Principal Contributions I have started research on such diverse subjects as income distribution in the USSR, methodological aspects of monetary analysis, and estimating national income of the Netherlands in the nineteenth century. Since the mid 1950s, I have concentrated my activities on problems of developing countries, in particular the national and international planning aspects: macro planning models, education planning, economic co-operation among developing countries, and appraisal of foreign direct investment. More recently, my interest has shifted to international trade, financial and monetary aspects

of the North-South relations; also, since 1965 I have kept an interest in East-European economics.

BOSKIN, Michael Jay

Born 1945, New York City, NY, USA.
Current Post Prof. Econ., Stanford Univ., Stanford, CA, USA; Res. Assoc., NBER, Cambridge, MA, USA, 1978–.
Past Posts Instr., Univ. Cal. Berkeley, 1969–70; Vis. Prof., Harvard Univ., 1977–8.
Degrees BA, MA, PhD Univ. Cal. Berkeley, 1967, 1968, 1971.
Offices and Honours Phi Beta Kappa; Chancellor's Award Outstanding Undergrad., Univ. Cal., 1967; Woodrow Wilson Fellow; Ford Foundation Fellow; Nat. Tax Assoc. Award Outstanding Doctoral Dissertation, 1971; Mellon Foundation Faculty Res. Fellow, 1973; Member, Exec. Comm., WEA, 1980–.
Principal Fields of Interest 212 Construction, Analysis and Use of Econometic Models; 320 Fiscal Policy and Theory; Public Finance; 915 Social Security.
Publications *Books:* 1.*The Crisis in Social Security,* ed. (Inst. Contemporary Stud., 1977); 2. *Federal Tax Reform,* ed. (Inst. Contemporary Stud., 1978); 3. *Economics and Human Welfare; Essays in Honor of Tibor Scitovsky,* ed. (Academic Press, 1979); 4. *The Economics of Taxation,* co-ed. (with H. Aaron), (Brookings Inst., 1980); 5. *The Economy in the 1980s: A Program for Stability and Growth,* ed. (Inst. Contemporary Stud., 1980); 6. *The Federal Budget; Economics and Politics,* co-ed. (with A. Wildavsky), (Inst. Contemporary Stud., 1982); 7. *Social Security Solutions* (Twentieth Century Fund, 1985); 8. *The Real Federal Budget* (Harvard Univ. Press, 1985).
Articles: 1. 'Some lessons from the new public finance' (with J. Stiglitz), *AER,* 67(1), March 1977; 2. 'Effects of the charitable deduction on contributions by low income and middle income households; evidence from the national survey of philanthropy' (with M. S. Feldstein), *REStat,* 59(3), Aug. 1977;

3. 'Taxation, saving and the rate of interest', *JPE*, pt. 2, 86(2), April 1978; 4. 'Optimal redistributive taxation when individual welfare depends upon relative income' (with E. Sheshinski), *QJE*, 92(4), Nov. 1978; 5. 'Interrelationships among the choice of tax base, tax rates and the unit and time period of account in the design of an optimal tax system', in *Economics of Taxation,* eds. H. Aaron and M. J. Boskin (Brookings Inst., 1980); 6. 'Some issues in supply-side economics', in *Supply Shocks, Incentives and National Wealth,* eds. K. Brunner and A. H. Meltzer (McGraw-Hill, 1981); 7. 'Federal government deficits: myths and realities', *AER,* 72(2), May 1982; 8. 'Optimal tax treatment of the family: married couples' (with E. Sheshinski), *J Pub E,* 20(3), Apr. 1983; 9. 'Modelling alternative solutions to the long-run social security funding problem' (with M. Avrin and K. Cone), in *Behavioral Simulations of Tax Policy,* ed. M. Feldstein (Harvard Univ. Press, 1983); 10. 'The effect of social security on retirement in the early 1970s' (with M. Hurd), *QJE,* forthcoming, 1985.

Principal Contributions My research has focussed on analytical and empirical studies of the supply of factors for production and the implication of these results for public policy. My early work studied the implications of differential labour supply responses of primary and secondary earners in the family and their implications for tax policy. More recently, I have analysed retirement decisions and their interaction with social security. Also, I have focussed my attention on the determinants of saving behaviour in the United States, with special emphasis on the potential effects of fiscal policy. Drawing out these implications for factor supply has been the source of a series of articles on various topics in optimal taxation, or it might be termed sensible supply-side economics. My recent econometric work has attempted to combine disaggregated information on households with national income accounts data to build an econometric/demographic model for explaining postwar trends in wealth, saving, and their determinants in the US. My explorations in optimal tax theory and its application to various policy problems has led me to reexamine the conceptual and accounting foundations of federal government budgeting in the US. Among my current work is an attempt to improve concepts and measurements within the federal budget in order to enable proper cost-benefit analysis to be carried out. I am also investigating the tail-end of the life-cycle, long-run financial problems in social insurance programmes, and alternative methods of comparing economic well-being at different points in the life-cycle. Throughout my work I have attempted to combine economic analysis and careful econometric studies with substantive policy issues.

BOULDING, Kenneth Ewart

Born 1910, Liverpool, England.
Current Post Dir. Program Res. Polit. and Econ. Change, Inst. Behavioral Sciences, Univ. Colorado, Boulder, CO, USA, 1981–; Disting. Prof. Emeritus, Univ. Colorado, 1980–.
Past Posts Prof. Econ., Univ. Michigan, 1949–67; Co-dir., Res. Dir., Dir., Center Res. Conflict Resolution, Univ. Michigan, 1961–4, 1964–5, 1965–6; Dir., Program Res. General Social Econ. Dynamics, Inst. Behavioral Sciences, Prof. Econ., Disting. Prof. Econ., Univ. Colorado, 1967–81, 1976–7, 1977–80.
Degrees BA (Polit., Phil., Econ.), MA Univ. Oxford, 1931, 1939.
Offices and Honours John Bates Clark Medal, Pres., AEA, 1949, 1968; Amer. Council Learned Socs. Prize Disting. Scholarship Humanities, 1962; Frank E. Seidman Disting. Award Polit. Econ., 1976; Pres., AAAS 1979; Member, Sr. Member, Inst. Medicine, NAS, 1975–; Corresp. Fellow, BA, 1982; Pres., Section F, BAAS, 1982–3.
Principal Fields of Interest 020 General Economic Theory.
Publications *Books:* 1.*Economic Analysis* (Harper, 1941, 1966); 2. *The Reconstruction of Economics* (Wiley, 1950); 3. *The Image* (Univ. Michigan Press, 1956); 4. *Conflict and Defense* (Harper, 1962); 5. *Ecodynamics* (Sage, 1978); 6. *Collected Papers,* 1, 2, ed.

F. R. Glahe (Colorado Assoc. Univ. Press, 1971), 3, 4, 5, ed. L. Singell (1973, 1974, 1975); 7. *Beasts, Ballads, and Bouldingisms: A Collection of Writings by Kenneth Boulding,* ed, R. P. Beilock (Transaction Books, 1980); 8. *Evolutionary Economics* (Sage 1981); 9. *A Preface to Grants Economics: The Economy of Love and Fear*(Praeger, 1981).

Principal Contributions Synthesised neoclassical and Keynesian economic theory into a coherent whole in *Economic Analysis*, especially fourth edition (1966). Urged economics down a new path in *The Reconstruction of Economics* (1949) with emphasis on stocks rather than flows and macro-theory of functional distribution. In work on *Evolutionary Economics,* have urged an integration of economic with biological concepts of ecological equilibrium and dynamics and genetic production. Exchange is only one of three major organisers of social life, the others being the threat system and the integrative system; in work on *Grants Economics* I have argued that one-way transfers should be integrated into the body of economic theory. Elsewhere I have taken the view that economic policy cannot be judged by economic criteria alone and that a larger normative theory of evaluative judgement is possible.

Secondary Literature C. E. Kerman, *Creative Tension: The Life and Thought of Kenneth Boulding* (Basic Books, 1974); G. Harcourt, 'A man for all systems: talking with Kenneth Boulding', *J Post Keyn. E,* 6(1), 1983.

BOWEN, Howard Rothmann

Born 1908, Spokane, WA, USA.
Current Post Pres. Emeritus; Prof. Econ. and Educ., Claremont Grad. School, 1969–.
Past Posts Instr., Ass. Prof., Assoc. Prof. Econ., Univ. Iowa, 1935–42; Econ., US Dept. Commerce, 1942–4; Chief Econ., US Joint Congressional Comm. Internal Revenue Taxation, 1944–5; Econ., Irvine Trust Co., 1945–7; Prof. Econ., Univ. Illinois, 1947–52; Williams Coll., 1952–5; Pres., Grunnell

Coll., Univ. Iowa, 1955–64, 1964–9; Chancellor, Claremont Grad. School, 1970–5; Dir., Bankers Life Co., 1965–81.
Degrees BA Washington State Univ., 1929; MA, PhD Univ. Iowa, 1933, 1935; Hon. Doctorates, 20 Univs.
Offices and Honours Member, US Tax Mission Japan, 1949; Chairman, Govt. Comm. Econ. and Social Trends Iowa, 1958; Member, Fed. Advisory Comm. Intergovt. Relations, 1961–4; Chairman, Nat. Comm. Technology, Automation and Econ. Progress, 1964–6; Pres., Amer. Assoc. Higher Educ., 1975–; Pres., WEA, 1977; Pres., Nat. Academy Educ. Assoc. Study Higher Educ., 1980; Phi Kappa Phi; Phi Beta Kappa.
Principal Fields of Interest 912 Economics of Education.
Publications *Books:* 1. *Toward Social Economy* (Rhinehart, 1948, Southern Illinois Press, 1977); 2. *Who Benefits from Higher Education and Who Should Pay?* (with P. Servelle), (Amer. Assoc. for Higher Educ., 1972); 3. *Financing Higher Education* (Assoc. Amer. Colleges, 1974); 4. *Freedom and Control in a Democratic Society* (Amer. Council of Life Insurance, 1976); 5. *Investment in Learning* (Jossey-Bass, 1977); 6. *The Cost of Higher Education* (Jossey-Bass, 1980); 7. *The State of the Nation and the Agenda for Higher Education* (Carnegie Commission on Higher Educ., 1981).

BOWLES, Samuel

Born 1939, New Haven, CT, USA.
Current Post Prof. Econ., Univ. Massachusetts, Amherst, MA, USA.
Past Posts Assoc. Prof. Econ., Harvard Univ., 1971–4.
Degrees BA Yale Univ., 1960; PhD Harvard Univ., 1965.
Offices and Honours Member, Union Radical Polit. Econ., 1969–; Member, Steering Comm. Center Popular Econ., 1978–; Guggenhiem Foundation Fellow, 1978–9.
Editorial Duties Ed. Board, *Rev. Radical Polit. Econ.,* 1974–6.
Principal Fields of Interest 850 Human

Capital; 022 Microeconomic Theory; 051 Capitalist Economic Systems.

Publications *Books:* 1. *Planning Educational Systems for Economic Growth* (Harvard Univ. Press, 1969); 2. *Notes and Problems in Microeconomic Theory* (with D. Kendrick and P. Dixon), (Markham, 1970, N-H, 1980); 3. *Schooling in Capitalist America* (with H. Gintis), (Basic Books, 1976; transls., German, Spanish, Japanese, and Italian); 4. *Beyond the Waste Land: A Democratic Alternative to Economic Decline* (with D. M. Gordon and T. E. Weisskopf), (Doubleday, 1983); 5. *Understanding Capitalism: Competition, Command and Change in the US Economy* (with R. C. Edwards), (Harper and Row, 1984).

Articles: 1. 'The efficient allocation of resources in education', *QJE,* 81, May 1967; 2. 'Schooling and inequality from generation to generation', *JPE,* 80(3), pt. 2, May–June 1972; 3. 'The "inheritance of IQ" and the intergenerational reproduction of economic inequality' (with V. Nelson), *REStat,* 56(1), Feb. 1974; 4. 'Heterogeneous labor and the Marxian theory of value: a critique and reformulation' (with H. Gintis), *Camb JE,* 1(2), 1977; 5. 'Structure and practice in the labor theory of value', *Rev. Radical Polit. Econ.,* 13(1), March 1981; 6. 'The production process and a competitive economy: Walrasian, Marxian and neo-Hobbesian models', *AER,* 75(1), March 1985.

Principal Contributions Textbook in advanced microeconomic theory, and principal writings in the economics of human resources (particularly education) and in Marxist economic theory. In both areas focussed on the processes whereby systems of power and privilege are perpetuated over time and may be modified or overcome. In recent years, turned to the interface of political and economic theory.

BOWLEY, Arthur Lyon*

Dates and Birthplace 1869–1957, Bristol, Avon, England.
Posts Held Part-time Reader Stats., 1895–1919; Lect., Maths. and Econ.,

Univ. Extension Coll., Reading, 1900–19; Prof. Stats., LSE, 1919–36.
Degree BA (Maths.) Univ. Camb., 1891.
Offices and Honours Various offices in BAAS, RSS, and Internat. Stat. Inst., Ed., *London and Camb. Econ. Service,* 1925–45; Knighted, 1950.
Publications *Books:* 1. *A Short Account of England's Foreign Trade in the Nineteenth Century* (1893, 1922); 2. *Wages and Income in the United Kingdom since 1860* (1900, 1937); 3. *Livelihood and Poverty* (with A. R. Bennett-Hurst), (1915); 4. *The Mathematical Groundwork of Economics* (1924); 5. *Has Poverty Diminished?* (with M. H. Hogg), (1925); 6. *Family Expenditure: A Study of its Variables* (with R. G. D. Allen), (1935); 7. *Studies in the National Income,* ed. (1942).

Career Began his career as a mathematician but turned to economics because of its relevance to problems of social reform. His early work on wages and prices made extensive use of historical and statistical data and he remained an applied statistician rather than an economist or economic historian. Nevertheless, his advocacy over many years of the use of statistics and mathematics in economics, though unspectacular, influenced generations of economists. He was a constant critic of government statistics and the inadequate sampling techniques used. His various outstanding publications on wages were an important contribution to questions of the distribution of national income.

Secondary Literature R. G. D. Allen, 'Bowley, Arthur Lyon', *IESS,* 2; A. Darnell, 'A. L. Bowley', in *Pioneers of Modern Economics in Britain,* eds. D. P. O'Brien and J. R. Presley (Macmillan, 1981).

BOWMAN, Mary Jean

Born 1908, New York City, NY, USA.
Current Post Emeritus Prof. Econ. and Educ., Univ. Chicago, 1974–.
Past Posts City Supervisor, US Bureau Labor Stats., 1934; Instr., Ass. Prof., Iowa State Univ., 1935–43; Dir., NW

Central Region Consumer Purchases Survey, US Dept. Agric., 1935–6; Vis. Prof., Univ. Minnesota, 1941; Sr. Econ., US Bureau Labor Stats., 1944–6; Vis. Prof., Univ. Cal. Berkeley, 1948–9; Contract Res., Resources for the Future, 1957–9; Res. Assoc. Prof., Prof. Econ. and Educ., Univ. Chicago, 1958–74; Disting. Vis. Prof., Zagreb, Yugoslavia, 1973, Uppsala Univ., Sweden, 1974, LSE, 1975; Cons., Brazil, 1976, World Bank, 1978–.

Degrees BA Vassar Coll., 1930; MA Radcliffe Coll., 1932; PhD Harvard Univ., 1938.

Offices and Honours Phi Beta Kappa; Virginia Swinburne Brownell Prize Econ., Vassar Coll., 1930; Res. Fellow, Radcliffe Coll., 1932–3; Fulbright Res. Fellow, Sweden, 1956–7; Exec. Comm., AEA 1969–71; Board Trustees, TIAA, 1972–6; Guggenheim Foundation Fellow, 1974; Member, UK-US Exchange Program Econ. of Educ., Ford Foundation, 1976–82; Disting. Service Medal, Teachers Coll., Columbia Univ., 1982.

Editorial Duties Ed., *JPE*, 1959–60; *Internat. J. Social Econ.*, 1978–; Ed. Board, *Econ. Educ. Rev.* 1980–.

Principal Fields of interest 022 Microeconomic Theory; 912 Economics of Education; 111 Economic Development.

Publications *Books:* 1. *Economic Analysis and Public Policy* (with G. L. Bach), (Prentice-Hall, 1943, 1949); 2. *Expectations, Uncertainty and Business Behavior*, ed. (SSRC, 1958); 3. *Resources and People in East Kentucky: Problems and Prospects of a Lagging Economy* (with W. W. Haynes), (JHUP, 1963); 4. *Education and Economic Development*, co-ed. (with C. A. Anderson), (Aldine, 1965); 5. *Readings in the Economics of Education*, ed. (UNESCO, 1968); 6. *Where Colleges Are and Who Attends* (with C. A. Anderson and V. Tinto), (McGraw-Hill, 1972); 7. *Elites and Change in the Kentucky Mountains* (with D. Plunkett), (Univ. Press Kentucky, 1973); 8. *Learning and Earning* (with A. Sohlman and B-C. Ysander), (Swedish Nat. Board Univs. and Colls., 1978); 9. *Educational Choice and Labor Markets in Japan* (Univ. Chicago Press, 1981); 10. *Collective Choice in Education*, ed. (Kluwer Nijhoff, 1982).

Articles: 1. 'A graphical analysis of personal income distribution in the United States', *AER*, 35(4), Sept. 1945, repr. in *Readings in the Theory of Income Distribution*, eds. W. J. Fellner and F. Machlup (Blakiston, 1946); 2. 'The land grant colleges and universities in human resource development', *JEH*, 20(4), Dec. 1962; 3. 'Educational shortage and excess', *CJE*, 29(4), Nov. 1963; 4. 'Schultz, Denison and the contribution of eds. to national income growth', *JPE*, 57(5), Oct. 1964; 5. 'The costing of human resource development', in *The Economics of Education*, eds. E. A. G. Robinson and J. Vaizey (Macmillan, 1966); 6. 'Schooling, experience and gains and losses in human capital through migration' (with R. G. Myers), *JASA*, 62(3), Sept. 1967, repr. in *Human Capital Formation and Manpower Development*, ed. R. A. Wykstra (The Free Press, 1971), and *Investment in Human Capital*, ed. B. F. Kiker (South Carolina Univ. Press, 1971); 7. 'Expectations, uncertainty and investments in human beings', in *Uncertainty and Expectations in Economics*, eds. C. F. Carter and J. L. Ford (Blackwell, 1972); 8. 'Human capital and economic modernization in historical perspective' (with C. A. Anderson), in *Schooling and Society*, ed. L. Stone (JHUP, 1976); 9. 'Out-of-school formation of human resources', in *Economic Dimensions of Education*, ed. D. M. Windham (Nat. Academy of Educ., 1979); 10. 'Choice in the spending of time', in *The Social Sciences, their Nature and Uses*, ed. W. H. Kruskal (Univ. Chicago Press, 1982).

Principal Contributions My first contribution (1943) was the development of a text aimed at teachers of introductory economics and at students in intermediate theory in which the focus was directly on fundamental questions in resource allocation and income distribution. (I invited G. L. Bach to collaborate as the specialist on macroeconomics.) Among subsequent offshoots was an analysis of the concepts and measures of income inequality and their implications (1945).

Expectations and decision-making

under uncertainty has been a focus of my concerns in three contexts. First was the attempt to bring order out of seeming chaos in contributions to the analysis of *Expectations, Uncertainty and Business Behavior* (1958). Later on I adapted Schackle's model in a theoretical treatment of human investment decisions (1972). This and other adaptations from enterprise research were joined in a book on *Educational Choice and Labor Markets in Japan* (1981).

For two decades I have stressed the importance of out-of-school learning. Involved are such questions as life-cycle development and cohort versus age patterns, including the processes of skill transfers within and across countries over time. A two-pronged attack on the spread of schooling in LDCs combines elements of the 'new home economics' that better specify the options faced by individuals and families with an analysis that takes into account the nature of the 'information fields' in which they anticipate. Years ago I applied this dual approach in a study of migration in the Ivory Coast, students have carried it on, and I am doing so currently in a study of Mexican education.

With colleagues from Chile and France I have recently completed a comparative study of the political economy of public support of higher education in three countries.

BOYER, Russell Stewart

Born 1944, New York City, NY, USA.

Current Post Prof. Econ., Univ. Western Ontario, Canada, 1982–.

Past Posts Econ., Fed. Reserve System, 1969, 1972, 1973; Ass. Prof., Assoc. Prof., Univ. Western Ontario, 1970–82; Res. Fellow, LSE, 1974–5; Vis. Assoc. Prof., Carnegie-Mellon Univ., 1979–80.

Degrees BA (Physics) Columbia Univ., 1964; MA (Physics) Univ. Wisconsin, 1965; PhD Univ. Chicago, 1971.

Offices and Honours NY State Regents Fellow, 1960–4; Nat. Science Foundation Fellow, 1964–5; Univ.

Chicago Fellow, 1967–9; NSF Res. Fellow, 1970; Sabbatical Leave Fellow, Canada Social Sciences and Humanities Research Council, 1979–80.

Editorial Duties Ed. Board, *J. Internat. Money and Fin.*

Principal Fields of Interest 310 Domestic Monetary and Financial Theory and Institutions; 430 Balance of Payments, International Finance.

Publications *Articles:* 1. 'Commodity markets and bond markets in a small, fixed-exchange-rate economy', *CJE*, 8(1), Feb. 1975; 2. 'Devaluation and portfolio balance', *AER*, 67(2), March 1977; 3. 'Commercial policy under alternative exchange rate regimes', *CJE*, 10(2), May 1977; 4. 'Financial policies in an open economy', *Ec*, 45(1), Feb. 1978; 5. 'Currency mobility and balance of payments adjustment', in *A Monetary Approach to International Adjustment*, eds. B. H. Putnam and D. S. Wilford (Praeger, 1978); 6. 'Optimal foreign exchange market intervention', *JPE*, 86(6), Dec. 1978; 7. 'The dynamic adjustment path for perfectly foreseen changes in monetary policy' (with R. J. Hodrick), *J Mon E*, 9(2), March 1982.

Principal Contributions My research interests have always been focussed on characteristics of assets and their implications for macroeconomic behaviour. At the University of Chicago it was strongly influenced by Professor Mundell and fellow graduate students in the International Economic Workshop (Rudiger Dornbusch, Jacob Frenkel, Michael Mussa, and Douglas Purvis). Early success in thinking in this area occurred in the more relaxed atmosphere of the Federal Reserve System. During the summers of 1969 and 1972, I was a Research Fellow there, where there were active discussions with Lance Girton, Dale Henderson and Don Roper. During the earlier summer, I initiated the idea that the formation of one-bank holding companies could be based on eliminating the inefficiency caused by the failure to pay interest on demand deposits. While this research was not published, the ideal of this motivation is now widely recognised in financial circles. In the summer of 1972, I initiated the idea of currency substitution and the indeterminancy of exchange rates that occurs in the case of perfect substitution. This idea presaged the asset approach to exchange rates which has developed subsequently. While at the London School of Economics, I formalised work on imperfect capital mobility models and began thinking about re-valuation effects on foreign-currency-denominated assets. That these effects could cause potential instability for debtor countries is now widely recognised. Back at Western with David Laidler and Michael Parkin as new senior colleagues, I became interested in the open economy implications of the Poole problem. Working with junior colleagues recently, I have incorporated rational expectations into models, and applied them to Canadian data. The basic thrust of this recent work is to make the link between the empirical regularities which exchange rates exhibit and the models which can generate such behaviour.

BRADFORD, David F.

Born 1939, Cambridge, MA, USA.
Current Post Prof. Econ. and Public Affairs, Princeton Univ., 1975–.
Past Posts Res. Ass., Fed. Reserve Bank Boston, 1961; Res. Econ., Operations Evaluation Group, Center Naval Analyses, Washington, DC, 1962; Ass. Secretary Defense, 1964; Cons., Military Manpower Policy Study, US Office Ass. Secretary Defense, 1964–5; Acting Instr. Econ., Res. Assoc., Stanford Univ., 1965–6; Ass. Prof. Econ., Assoc. Dean, Dir. Grad. Program, Woodrow Wilson School Public and Internat. Affairs, Assoc. Prof. Econ. and Public Affairs, Princeton Univ., 1966–7, 1974–5, 1978–80, 1971–5; Deputy Ass. Secretary Tax Policy, US Treasury Dept., 1975–6.
Degrees BA Amherst Coll., 1960, Stanford Univ., 1961; MS (Applied Maths.) Harvard Univ., 1962; PhD Stanford Univ., 1966.
Offices and Honours Nat. Merit Scholar, 1956–60; Assoc. Conferee, Merrill Center Econ., 1959; Phi Beta Kappa, 1960; Woodrow Wilson Fellow, 1960–1; Workshop Fellow, Stanford Univ., 1962–3; Ford Foundation Dissertation Fellow, 1963–4; US Treasury Dept. Exceptional Service Award, 1976; Fulbright Fellow, Louvain, Belgium, 1977; Advisory Comm., Tax Policy Studies Program, AEA, 1978–; Fellow, Em Soc, Nat. Tax Assoc.
Editorial Duties Ed. Boards, *AER*, 1977–9, *Econ. Letters*, 1978–.
Principal Fields of Interest 022 Microeconomic Theory.
Publications *Books:* 1. *Deferment Policy in Selective Service* (Princeton Univ. Industrial Relations Section, 1969).

Articles: 1. 'The enlistment decision under draft uncertainty', *QJE*, 86, Nov. 1968; 2. 'Optimal departures from marginal cost pricing' (with W. J. Baumol), *AER*, 60(3), June 1970; repr. in Japanese, in *Expressways and Automobiles*, 14(4), 14(5), 1971; 3. 'Constraints on public action and rules for social decision', *AER*, 60(4), Sept. 1970; 4. 'Towards a predictive theory of intergovernmental grants' (with W. E. Oates), *AER*, 64(2), May 1971; repr. in Spanish, in *Financiacion de las Autonomias*, ed. A. Giminez (H. Blume Ediciones, 1979); 5. 'Detrimental externalities and non-convexity of the production set' (with W. J. Baumol), *Ec*, N.S. 39, May 1972; 6. 'Constraints on government investment opportunities and the choice of discount rate', *AER*, 65(5), Dec. 1975; repr. in *Public Expenditure and Policy Analysis*, eds. R. H. Haveman and J. Margolis (Houghton Mifflin, 1983); 7. 'A formal model of external effects and corrective taxes', App. to *The Theory of Environmental Policy*, eds. W. J. Baumol and W. E. Oates (Prentice-Hall, 1975); 8. 'The optimal taxation of commodities and income' (with H. S. Rosen), *AER*, 66(2), May 1976; 9. 'The value of information for crop forecasting with Bayesian speculators: theory and empirical results' (with H. H. Kelejian), *Bell JE*, 9, Spring 1978; 10. 'The possibilities for an expenditure tax', *Nat Tax J*, 35(3), Sept. 1982.

BRAEUTIGAM, Ronald Ray

Born 1947 Tulsa, OK, USA.
Current Post Prof. Econ., Northwestern Univ., Evanston, IL, USA, 1983–.
Past Posts Staff Econ., US Office Telecommunications, Exec. Office US President, Washington, DC, 1972–3; Lect., Stanford Univ., 1974–5; Ass. Prof., Assoc. Prof. Econ., Northwestern Univ., 1975–80, 1980–3; Vis. Prof. Econ., Cal. Inst. Technology, 1978–9; Sr. Res. Fellow, Internat. Inst. Management, Wissenschaftszentrum, Berlin, 1981.
Degrees BSc (Petroleum Eng.) Univ. Tulsa, 1969; MSc, PhD (Eng.–Econ.) Stanford Univ., 1971, 1975.
Editorial Duties Ed. Board, *Series on Regulation* (MIT Press, 1979–); Assoc. Ed. *J Ind E*, 1983–; Rev. Panel, *NSF Program Regulatory Policy* Res., 1984–.
Principal Fields of Interest 610 Industrial Organisation and Public Policy; 613 Public Utilities; 630 Industry Studies.
Publications *Books:* 1. *The Regulation Game: Strategic Use of Administrative Process* (with B. M. Owen), (Ballinger, 1978).
Articles: 1. 'Optimal pricing with intermodal competition', *AER*, 69(1), March 1979; 2. 'An analysis of fully distributed cost pricing in regulated industries', *Bell JE*, 11(1), Spring, 1980; 3. 'The workback method and the value of helium', *Public Policy*, 29, Winter 1981; 4. 'The deregulation of natural gas', in *Case Studies in Regulation: Revolution and Reform*, eds. L. Weiss and M. Klass (Little-Brown, 1981); 5. 'The estimation of a hybrid cost function for a railroad firm', *REStat*, 64(3), Aug. 1982; 6. 'Demand uncertainty and the regulated firm' (with J. Quirk), *Int ER*, Feb. 1984; 7. 'Socially optimal pricing with rivalry and economies of scale', *Rand J. Econ.*, 15(1), Spring 1984; 8. 'The regulation of surface freight transport' (with R. Noll), *REStat*, 66(1), Feb. 1984.
Principal Contributions Early work was addressed to the need for reform in several areas of the regulated sector of the US economy. The principal contributions of this work were to show how decisions regarding industry structure and pricing should be co-ordinated. Several of the articles are designed to show the economic theory behind this idea, and in some cases the methodology has been applied. *The Regulation Game* shows how firms can circumvent the intent of regulation, and is in part written as a 'How To' manual based on observed or strongly possible strategies that firms may employ in the face of regulatory restraint. Other articles in part reflect a rather extensive effort to investigate the empirical properties of the cost characteristics of regulated firms in the railroad industry, and demonstrate how standard econometric methodology can be combined with information about engineering process functions to yield a better understanding of the nature of underlying technology. In recent years the research has also focussed on law and economics to an increasing extent. The major thread of the research remains the effects of regulation on the allocation of economic resources, and on alternative schemes for improving economic efficiency with better pricing schemes and entry policies, particularly in telecommunications, transportation, and energy.

BRAINARD, William Crittenden

Born 1935, Jersey City, NJ, USA.
Current Post Prof. Econ., Yale Univ., 1969–.
Past Posts Res. Staff, Dir., Cowles Foundation, Yale Univ., 1961, 1976–81; Ass. Prof., Assoc. Prof. Econ., Yale Univ., 1962–4, 1966–9; Res. Assoc., Brookings Inst., Washington, DC, 1965–6; Vis. Prof., Univ. Cal. San Diego, 1970–1, Univ. Essex, England, 1975–6.
Degrees BA (Physics) Oberlin Coll., 1957; MA, PhD Yale Univ., 1959, 1963.
Offices and Honours Fellow, Em Soc.
Editorial Duties Co-ed., *Brookings Papers Econ. Activity.*
Principal Fields of Interest 311 Domestic Monetary and Financial Theory.
Publications *Articles:* 1. 'Financial intermediaries and the effectiveness of monetary controls' (with J. Tobin), *AER*, 53(2), May 1963; 2. 'Financial intermediaries and a theory of monetary

control', *Yale Econ. Essays*, 4(2), 1964; 3. 'Some simple propositions concerning cost-push inflation' (with M. C. Lovell), *AER*, 56(4), Sept. 1966; 4. 'Uncertainty and the effectiveness of policy', *AER*, 57(2), May 1967, repr. in *Targets and Indicators of Monetary Policy*, ed. K. Brunner (Chandler, 1969); 5. 'A simulation policy game for teaching macroeconomics' (with F. Trenery Dolbear Jr. and R. Attiyeh), *AER*, 58(2), May 1968; 6. 'Pitfalls in financial model building' (with J. Tobin), *AER*, 58(2), May 1968; 7. 'Social risk and financial markets' (with F. T. Dolbear Jr.), *AER*, 61(2), May 1971; 8. 'Empirical monetary macro-economics: what have we learned in the last 25 years?' (with R. Cooper), *AER*, 65(2), May 1975; 9. 'Asset markets and the cost of capital' (with J. Tobin), in *Economic Progress, Private Values and Public Policy, Essays in Honor of William Fellner* (N-H, 1977); 10. 'A model of US financial and nonfinancial economic behavior' (with D. K. Backus, G. Smith and J. Tobin), *JMCB*, 12(2), May 1980.

BRAY, John Francis*

Dates and Birthplace 1809–97, Washington, DC, USA.

Posts Held Printer, photographer, farmer.

Publications *Books:* 1. *Labour's Wrongs and Labour's Remedy* (1839, 1931); 2. *A Voyage from Utopia,* ed. M. F. Lloyd-Prichard (1957).

Career During a lengthy period of residence in England 1822–42 he wrote his chief work, *Labour's Wrongs*, which owed much to his own experience of working conditions in the printing industry. His argument is in the Ricardian socialist tradition, claiming that the employer takes the whole product of a worker's labour and returns only a fraction to him as wages. He argued in favour of communal property organised through the medium of corporations, owned and founded by the workers, and issuing money representing labour-time.

Secondary Literature H. J. Carr, 'John Francis Bray', *Ec*, N.S. 7, Nov. 1940.

BRECHER, Richard A.

Born 1946, Boston, MA, USA.

Current Post Prof. Econ., Carleton Univ., Ottawa, Ont., Canada, 1981–.

Past Posts Ass. Prof. Econ., Res. Staff, Econ. Growth Center, Yale Univ., 1971–7; Academic Vis., LSE, 1974–5; Vis., Nuffield Coll. Oxford, 1974–5; Assoc. Prof. Econ., Carleton Univ., 1977–81; Vis. Scholar, Columbia Univ., 1981–2.

Degrees BA (Econ. and Anthrop.) McGill Univ., 1967; MA, PhD Harvard Univ., 1970, 1971.

Offices and Honours Res. Fellow, Canada Council, 1974–5; Leave Fellow, Canada Social Sciences and Humanities Res. Council, 1981–2.

Editorial Duties Assoc. Ed., Co-ed., Ed., *J Int E*, 1981–2, 1982, 1983–.

Principal Fields of Interest 410 International Trade Theory; 422 Commercial Policy; 441 International Investment and Capital Markets.

Publications *Articles:* 1. 'Minimum wage rates and the pure theory of international trade', *QJE*, 88(1), Feb. 1974; 2. 'Tariffs, foreign capital and immiserizing growth' (with C. F. Diaz Alejandro), *J Int E*, 7(4), Nov. 1977, repr. in *Internat. Trade: Selected Readings*, ed. J. N. Bhagwati (MIT Press, 1981); 3. 'Money, employment, and trade-balance adjustment with rigid wages', *OEP*, 30(1), March 1978; 4. 'Foreign ownership and the theory of trade and welfare' (with J. N. Bhagwati), *JPE*, 89(3), June 1981; 5. 'Immiserizing investment from abroad: the Singer-Prebisch thesis reconsidered' (with E. U. Choudhri), *QJE*, 97(1), Feb. 1982; 6. 'The Leontief paradox, continued' (with E. U. Choudhri), *JPE*, 90,(4), Aug. 1982; 7. 'Optimal policy in the presence of licensed technology from abroad', 90(5), Oct. 1982; 8. 'Immiserizing transfers from abroad' (with J. N. Bhagwati), *J Int E*, 13(3–4), Nov. 1982; 9. 'The generalized theory of transfers and welfare: bilateral transfers in a multilateral world' (with J. N. Bhagwati and T. Hatta), *AER*, 73(4), Sept. 1983; 10. 'New products and the factor content of international trade' (with E. U. Choudhri), *JPE*, 92(5), Oct. 1984.

Principal Contributions Early work

focussed on the theory of international trade with unemployment in the presence of real-wage rigidity. Attention then shifted to foreign ownership and its implications for commercial policy. Subsequent writings dealt with the factor content of international trade in commodities. Recent work emphasises the theory of transfers and welfare.

BRECHLING, Frank Paul Richard

Born 1931, Wismar, Germany.
Current Post Prof., Univ. Maryland, Coll. Park, MD, USA, 1979–.
Past Posts Ass. Prof., Assoc. Prof., Northwestern Univ., 1966–79.
Degrees BA Trinity Coll., Dublin, 1955.
Principal Fields of Interest 023 Macroeconomic Theory.
Publications *Books:* 1. *The Theory of Interest Rates*, co-ed. (with F. H. Hahn), (Macmillan, 1965); 2. *Investment and Employment Decisions* (Manchester Univ. Press, 1975).
Articles: 1. 'A note on bond-holding and the liquidity preference theory of interest', *REStud*, 24, June 1957; 2. 'Trade credit and monetary policy' (with R. G. Lipsey), *EJ*, 73, Dec. 1963; 3. 'The relationship between output and employment in British manufacturing industries', *REStud*, 32, July, Oct. 1965; 4. 'Wage inflation and the structure of regional unemployment', *JMCB*, pt. II, 5(1), Feb. 1973; 5. 'The incentive effects of the US unemployment insurance tax', in *Research in Labor Economics*, ed. R. G. Ehrenberg (JAI Press, 1977).
Principal Contributions Empirical investigation of employment and investment decisions. Analysis of the unemployment insurance system.

BREMS, Hans J.

Born 1915, Viborg, Denmark.
Current Post Prof. Econ., Univ. Illinois, Urbana Champaign, IL, USA, 1954–.
Past Posts Ass. Prof., Univ. Copenhagen, 1943–51; Lect., Univ. Cal. Berkeley, 1951–4; Vis. Prof., Univs. Cal. Berkeley, 1959, Kiel, 1961, 1972, Göttingen, 1964, Hamburg, 1967, Uppsala, 1968, 1982, Lund, 1970, 1975, Göteborg, 1972, Copenhagen, 1975, 1982, Stockholm, 1980, Basel, 1982, and Zurich, 1983.
Degrees PhD Univ. Copenhagen, 1950; Hon. Dr, Svenska Handelshogskolan, Helsinki, 1970.
Offices and Honours Member, Royal Danish Academy Sciences and Letters, 1979–.
Editorial Duties Ed. Board, *HOPE*, 1985–.
Principal Fields of Interest 020 General Economic Theory; 031 History of Thought; 111 Economic Growth Theory and Models.
Publications *Books:* 1. *Product Equilibrium under Monopolistic Competition* (Harvard Univ. Press, 1951); 2. *Output, Employment, Capital and Growth* (Harper, 1959, Greenwood Press, 1973); 3. *Quantitative Economic Theory* (Wiley, 1968); 4. *Labor, Capital, and Growth* (D. C. Heath, 1973); 5. *Inflation, Interest and Growth* (D. C. Heath, 1980; transl. German, *Dynamische Makrotheorie — Inflation, Zins und Wachstum* (J. C. B. Mohr, P. Siebeck, 1980); 6. *Fiscal Theory — Government, Inflation, and Growth* (D. C. Heath, 1983).
Articles: 1. 'Input-output coefficients as measures of product quality', *AER*, 47(1), March 1957; 2. 'Devaluation, a marriage of the elasticity and the absorption approaches,' *EJ*, 67, March 1957; 3. 'A growth model of international direct investment', *AER*, 60(3), June 1970; 4. 'Ricardo's long-run equilibrium', *HOPE*, 2(2), Fall 1970; 5. 'Alternative theories of pricing, distribution, saving and investment', *AER*, 69(1), March 1979; 6. 'Richard Cantillon: resources and population', *Econ App.*, 36(2–3), 1983.
Principal Contributions Early work attempted to measure product quality by input-output coefficients (1957), to optimise it, and to determine a product-quality equilibrium under duopoly (1951, 1968). J. Friedman, *Oligopoly Theory* (CUP, 1983) calls this work 'a major effort that did not take hold'. Later work moved to international economics and attempted to marry the

elasticity and the absorption approaches to devaluation (1957) and to see international direct investment as part of a two-country neoclassical growth model with a flexible exchange rate (1970). Three books (1973, 1980, and 1983) set out modern growth theory and attempted to apply it to monetary and fiscal theory by adding to it bonds, government, inflation, interest rates, money, shares, and taxation. Occasionally I have worked in the history of economic thought. For example, my 1970 Ricardo model incorporated fixed capital ('machinery') and is still, I believe, the only mathematical Ricardo model to do so. A forthcoming volume, *Pioneers of Economic Theory*, will examine the theories of a score of major pioneers as models set out in algebra or calculus and solved to check consistency and properties claimed.

BRENTANO, Lujo*

Dates and Birthplace 1844–1931, Frankfurt-am-Main, Germany.
Posts Held Prussian Stat. Office, 1867–71; Prof., Univs., Berlin, 1871–2, Breslau, 1872–82, Strasbourg, 1882–8, Vienna, 1888–9, Leipzig, 1889–91 and Munich, 1891–1931.
Degrees Dr Law Univ. Heidelberg, 1866; Dr Econ., Univ. Göttingen, 1867.
Offices and Honours Founder member, Verein für Sozialpolitik.
Publications *Books:* 1. *On the History and Development of Guilds, and the Origins of Trade Unions* (1870); 2. *Hours and Wages in Relation to Production* (1876, 1894); 3. *The Relation of Labour to the Law of Today* (1877, 1898); 4. *Die Deutschen Getreidezölle* (1911); 5. *Eine Geschichte der wirtschaftlichen Entwicklung Englands*, 4 vols (1927–9); 6. *Mein Leben im Kampf um die soziale Entwicklung Deutschlands* (1931).
Career Economic historian whose works are notable for clarity of exposition. He was also an inspiring teacher in his various university posts. His interest in economics began after the completion of his law studies and his work under Ernst Engel in the Prussian Statistical Office turned his interest towards trade unions. He was an advocate of unions as a means of improving the living standards of the worker. Economic liberalism and an attachment to English institutions were other consistent features of his work.
Secondary Literature J. J. Sheehan, *The Career of Lujo Brentano* (Chicago Univ. Press, 1966); H. Kisch, 'Brentano, Lujo', *IESS*, 2.

BRESCIANI-TURRONI, Constantino*

Dates and Birthplace 1882–1963, Verona, Italy.
Posts Held Prof. Stats and Econ., various Italian Univs. and Univ. Cairo; Pres., Banco di Roma, 1945; Exec. Dir., IBRD, 1947–53; Italian Minister Foreign Trade, 1953.
Degrees Grad., Univ. Verona.
Publications *Books:* 1. *The Economics of Inflation* (1931, 1937); 2. *Le Previsioni Economiche* (1932); 3. *Economic Policy for the Thinking Man* (1942, 1950); 4. *Il Programma Economico-Sociale del Liberalismo* (1946); 5. *Saggi di Economia* (1961).
Career The last great representative of the Italian classical school, he nevertheless moved beyond the conventional classical methodology in his studies of monetary theory and policy. His work for the Reparations Commission in Germany after World War I resulted in his great work on inflation and confirmed his opinion that monetary methods were necessary to control inflation. He was a major architect of Italy's post-World War II reconstruction and his later publications concentrated on policy advice.
Secondary Literature F. M. Tamagna, 'Bresciani-Turroni, Constantino', *IESS*, 2.

BRETON, Albert

Born 1929, Montmarte, Saskatchewan, Canada.
Current Post Prof. Econ., Univ. Toronto, Ont., Canada, 1970–.
Past Posts Ass. Prof., Univ. de

Montreal, 1957–65; Dir. Res., Social Res. Group, Montreal, 1956–65; Vis. Assoc. Prof., Carleton Univ., Ottawa, 1964–5; Sr. Lect., Reader, LSE, 1966–9; Invited Prof., Univ. Catholique Louvain, Belgium, 1968; Vis. Prof., Harvard Univ., 1969–70.

Degrees BA Coll. de S. Boniface, 1951; PhD Columbia Univ., 1965.

Offices and Honours Gust Instr., MIT, 1959–60; Post-Doctoral Fellow, Univ. Chicago, 1965–6; Killam Sr. Res. Scholar, 1972, 1974, 1977–8; Fellow, Royal Soc. Canada, 1976–; Vice-Chairman, Fed. Cultural Policy Rev. Comm., 1979–82; Commissioner, Canadian Royal Comm. Union and Devlp. Prospects Canada, 1982–.

Editorial Duties Ed. Board, *PF, Finances Publiques*, 1975–.

Principal Fields of Interest 320 Fiscal Theory and Policy: Public Finance; 025 Social Choice; Bureaucratic Performance; 023 Macroeconomic Theory.

Publications *Books:* 1. *Discriminatory Government Policies in Federal Countries* (Private Planning Assoc. Canada, 1967); 2. *The Economic Theory of Representative Government* (Aldine, 1974); 3. *The Economic Constitution of Federal States* (with A. Scott), (Univ. Toronto Press, 1978); 4. *The Design of Federations* (with A. Scott), (Inst. Res. Public Policy, 1980); 5. *Why Disunity? An Analysis of Linguistic and Regional Cleavages in Canada* (with R. Breton), (Inst. Res. Public Policy, 1980); 6. *The Logic of Bureaucratic Conduct* (with R. Wintrobe), (CUP, 1982); 7. *Marriage, Population and the Labour Force Participation of Women* (Econ. Council Canada, 1984).

Articles: 1. 'The economics of nationalism', *JPE*, 72, Aug. 1964; 2. 'A theory of government grants', *CJE*, 31, May 1965; 3. 'A theory of the demand for public goods', *CJE*, 32, Nov. 1966; 4. 'An economic theory of social movements' (with R. Breton), *AER*, 59(2), May 1969; 5. 'Public goods and the stability of federalism', *Kyk*, 23, Nov. 1970; 6. 'The economics of bilingualism' (with P. Miezkowski), in *The Political Economy of Fiscal Federalism*, ed. W. E. Oates (D. C. Heath, 1977); 7. 'A theory of "moral" suasion' (with R. Wintrobe), *CJE*, 12, May 1978; 8.

'Nationalism and language policies', *CJE*, 12, Nov. 1978; 9. 'Federalism versus centralism in regional growth', in *Public Finance and Economic Growth*, eds. D. Biehl, K. W. Roskamp and W. F. Stolper (Wayne State Univ. Press, 1983); 10. 'Some economics of liberty and regression: efficient regulation in markets for ideas' (with R. Wintrobe), in *Government, Democracy and Social Choice: Essays in Honour of Duncan Black*, ed. P. M. Jackson (Wheatsheaf Books, 1984).

Principal Contributions My earlier work on nationalism produced a new theory of that phenomenon and the first model of what was later to be rediscovered as 'the' theory of rent-seeking. It also generated a conviction that a deeper understanding of public economics would require that more attention be given to the supply side of the government sector. My book on *Representative Government* stressed such an approach. My later work with Ronald Wintrobe developed a new theory of bureaucracy that was the first to stress that these organisations are not mainly authority structures, but networks of exchange relationships based on trust; and that bureaucracies are not, in general, monopolies, but systems of competing bureaus.

From the very beginning, my interest in governmental supply had led me to the study of federalism. After developing a theory of federalism based on the properties of public goods, I was, with Anthony Scott, among the first to suggest a theory of federalism based on organisational or transaction costs. In the 1970s, with Peter Wieszkowski, I provided the first economic theory of bilingualism as a prolegomena to an understanding of the supply of language policies by governments in Canada and virtually everywhere in the world.

BRITO, Dagobert Llanos

Born 1941, Guanajuato, Mexico.

Current Post George A. Peterkin Prof. Polit. Econ., Rice Univ., TX, USA, 1984–.

Past Posts Instr., Rice Univ., 1969–70; Ass. Prof., Univ. Wisconsin–Madison, 1970–3; Assoc. Prof. Econ. and Polit. Science, Ohio State Univ., 1972–5; Vis. Prof., MIT, 1974; Prof. Econ. and Polit. Science, Ohio State Univ., 1976–9; Vis. Prof., Rice Univ., 1978–9; Prof. and Dir., Murphy Inst. Polit. Econ., Tulane Univ., 1979–81, 1981–4.

Degrees BA, MA, PhD Rice Univ., 1967, 1970, 1970.

Offices and Honours Rice Fellow, 1967–9.

Principal Fields of Interest 020 General Economic Theory; 024 Public Finance.

Publications *Books:* 1. *Strategies for Managing Nuclear Proliferation — Economic and Political Issues*, co-ed. (with M. D. Intriligator and A. Wick), (D. C. Heath, 1983).

Articles: 1. 'A dynamic model of an armaments race', *Int ER*, 13(2), June 1972; 2. 'Heterogeneous labor inputs and nineteenth century Anglo-American managerial behavior' (with J. G. Williamson), *Explor. Econ. Hist.*, 10(3), Spring 1973; 3. 'Estimation, prediction and economic control', *Int ER*, 14(3), Oct. 1973; 4. 'Becker's theory of the allocation of time and the St Petersburg paradox', *JET*, 10(1), Feb. 1975; 5. 'Some properties of the optimal income tax' (with W. H. Oakland), *Int ER*, 8(2), June 1977; 6. 'A new approach to the Nash bargaining problem' (with A. M. Buoncristiani and M. D. Intriligator), *Em*, 45(5), July 1977; 7. 'On the monopolistic provision of excludable public goods' (with W. H. Oakland), *AER*, 70(4), Sept. 1980; 8. 'Nuclear proliferation and the probability of nuclear war' (with M. D. Intriligator), *Public Choice*, 36, 1981; 9. 'Strategic arms limitation treaties and innovations in weapon technology' (with M. D. Intriligator), *Public Choice*, 36, 1981; 10. 'Can arms races lead to war?' (with M. D. Intriligator), *J. Conflict Resolution*, 1985.

Principal Contributions Arms races and the causes of war have been problems which have received relatively little attention from economists in recent years. This neglect is in a way surprising since many of the essential features of these phenomena — allocation of resources, externalities, the production of public goods, organisational be-

haviour, etc. — are subjects that have been of central concern to the economics profession. An important component of my research effort for the past fourteen years has been applying developments in economic theory to the problem of the arms race and the outbreak of war. The goal of this research — which has been joint with M. D. Intriligator since 1972 — is to develop a formal theory of arms accumulation and war outbreak which is based on the postulates of rationality and maximizing behaviour on the part of the agents involved. It is not our belief that all aspects of arms races and war can be explained by rational behaviour; however, we do believe that rational behaviour does explain major components of these phenomena, and, in particular, we believe that it is these components which can be addressed by policy. Our work on this problem has led to over twenty published papers in various journals and edited volumes. My other interest in economics is pure theory. In that field I have worked on the St Petersburg Paradox and on the taxation of capital in the context of models of heterogeneous agents with self selection.

BRITTAN, Samuel

Born N.e.

Current Post Econ. Writer, Ass. Ed., *Financial Times*, London, 1966–, 1978–.

Recent Posts Econ. Ed., *Observer*, 1961–4; Adviser, UK Dept. Econ. Affairs, 1965.

Degrees BA Univ. Camb.

Offices and Honours Sr. Wincott Award, Financial Journalists, 1971; Res. Fellow, Vis. Fellow, Nuffield Coll. Oxford, 1973–4, 1973.

Principal Fields of Interest 050 Economic Systems.

Publications *Books:* 1. *The Price of Economic Freedom: A Guide to Flexible Rates* (Macmillan, 1970); 2. *Is There an Economic Consensus?* (Macmillan, 1973); 3. *Capitalism and the Permissive Society* (Macmillan, 1973); 4. *The Delusion of Incomes Policy* (with P. Lilley), (Temple Smith, 1977); 5. *The Economic Consequences of Democracy*

(Temple Smith, 1977); 6. *How to End the 'Monetarist' Controversy* (INEA, 1981); 7. *The Role and Limits of Government* (Temple Smith, 1983).

Articles: 1. 'How British is the British sickness?', *J Law E*, 21(2), Oct. 1978; 2. 'A people's stake in North sea oil', *LBR*, 130, April 1978; 3. 'Inflation and democracy', in *The Political Economy of Inflation*, eds. J. Hirsch and J. E. Goldthorpe (Martin Robertson, 1978); 4. 'The European monetary system: a compromise that could be worse than either extreme', in *The World Economy* (Trade Pol. Res. Centre, 1979); 5. 'Hayek, the new right, and the crisis of social democracy', *Encounter*, Jan. 1980; 6. 'The Wenceslas myth', *Encounter*, May 1981; 7. 'Two cheers for utilitarianism' *OEP*, 35(3), Nov, 1983; 8. 'The politics and economics of privatisation', *Polit. Q.*, 54(2), April–June, 1984.

Principal Contributions Pioneering work on interaction between economic doctrine and political influences in British economic policy; critical analysis of the 'left-right' spectrum in relation to economic and other policy. Reinterpretation of free-market doctrines in relation to alternative value systems; systemic weaknesses of democratic political economies; empirical examination of degree of consensus among economists; role of money GDP as ultimate target for financial policy; and property rights in national resources with special reference to State-owned corporations and North Sea oil.

BROCK, William Allen

Born 1941, Philadelphia, PA, USA.
Current Post F. P. Ramsey Prof. Econ., Univ. Wisconsin-Madison, WI, 1975–.
Past Posts Ass. Prof. Econ. and Maths., Vis. Assoc. Prof., Univ. Rochester, Rochester, NY, 1969–71, 1973; Assoc. Prof. Econ., Univ. Chicago, 1972–5; Assoc. Prof., Prof. Econ., Cornell Univ., 1974–7.
Degrees BA (Maths.) Univ. Missouri, 1965; PhD (Maths.) Univ. Cal. Berkeley, 1969.
Offices and Honours Bernard Fried-

man Memorial Prize, Univ. Cal. Berkeley, 1968; Fellow, Em Soc., 1974; Sherman Fairchild Disting. Scholar, Cal. Inst. Technology, 1978; Romnes Faculty Fellow, Univ. Wisconsin-Madison, 1981.
Editorial Duties Assoc. Ed., *JET, IER*, 1972–; Advisory Ed., *Advanced Textbook in Economics Series* (N-H, 1983).
Principal Fields of Interest 111 Economic Growth Theory; 206 Microeconomic Theory; 611 Industrial Organisation Theory.
Publications *Books:* 1. *The Impact of Federal Regulations and Taxes on Business Formation, Dissolution and Growth* (with D. S. Evans), (Holmes and Meiers, 1985); 2. *Stability Analysis in Economic Theory* (with A. G. Malliaris), (N-H, 1985).

Articles: 1. 'On existence of weakly maximal programs in a multisector economy', *REStud*, 37(2), April 1970; 2. 'Optimal economic growth and uncertainty: the discounted case' (with L. J. Mirman), *JET*, 4(3), June 1972; 3. 'Money and growth: the case of long run perfect foresight', *Int ER*, 15(3), Oct. 1974; 4. 'Some results of global asymptotic stability of difference equations' (with J. A. Scheinkman), *JET*, 10(2), April 1975; 5. 'Economics of special interest politics: case of the tariff' (with S. P. Magee), *AER*, 68(2), May 1978; 6. 'Global asymptotic stability results for multi-sector models of optimal growth under uncertainty when future utilities are discounted' (with M. Majumdar), *JET*, 18(2), Aug. 1978; 7. 'Global asymptotic stability of optimal control: a survey of recent results', in *Frontiers of Quantitative Economics*, 3, ed. M. Intriligator (N-H, 1978); 8. 'Asset prices in a production economy', in *Economics of Information and Uncertainty*, ed. J. J. McCall (N-H, 1982); 9. 'The analysis of macroeconomic policies in perfect foresight equilibrium', *Int ER*, 22(1), Feb. 1981; 10. 'Pricing, predation and entry barriers in regulated industries', in *Breaking Up Bell: Essays on Industrial Organization and Regulation*, ed. D. S. Evans (N-H, 1983).
Principal Contributions Became fascinated with economic science while writing econometric software in the

early 1960s. Contributed to the existence theory of optima and stability theory of multisector optimal growth models in the cases of certainty and uncertainty. Showed how, by suitable interpretation, these normative models can be turned into positive models of business cycles and asset price fluctuations. This led to later work by others that showed it is harder to reject these models with aggregate time series data than was suspected. Was the first to formally examine in rational expectations models the logical possibility of hyperinflationary price-level bubbles and speculative bubbles where the asset's price diverges from its market fundamental in markets for assets including fiat money. Discovered that bootstrap equilibria and bubbles could exist even in contexts where fiat money was intrinsically useful. This work led to development by others of the first econometric tests for bubbles. Developed an asset pricing model that showed how real discount rates on future asset earnings increase as perceptions of future consumption deteriorate and why asset returns covary. This work has led to work by others that clarified (resolved?) the controversy over whether asset prices fluctuate too much to be consistent with market efficiency.

Developed an alternative notion of sustainability against entry of natural monopoly that is appropriate for technologies requiring large sunk costs. It is much easier than the impression given by the received sustainability literature for a true natural monopoly to drive out entrants in such situations. Showed that, contrary to received thoughts, the relative strength of incentives for a regulated dominant firm over an unregulated dominant firm to indulge in predatory cross subsidisation depends upon the dominant firm's expectations concerning the time profile in regulatory tightness that it faces.

BRONFENBRENNER, Martin

Born 1914, Pittsburg, PA, USA.
Current Post Prof. Internat. Econ., School Internat. Politics, Econ. and Bus., Aoyama Gakuin Univ., Tokyo, Japan, 1984–.

Past Posts Instr., Ass. Prof. Econ. and Stats., Central YMCA Coll., Chicago, 1938–40; Ass. Econ. Analyst, Assoc. Econ. Analyst, US Treasury, Washington, 1940–1; State Fed. Reserve Bank, Chicago, 1941–3; Japanese Language Student Officer, US Navy, 1943–6; Fin. Econ., Fed. Reserve Bank, Chicago, 1946–7; Assoc. Prof., Prof. Econ., Univ. Wisconsin, 1947–57; Tax Econ., Tokyo, 1949–50; Cons. Econ., UNECAFE, Bangkok, 1953; Prof. Econ., Michigan State Univ., 1957–8, Univ. Minnesota, 1958–62, Carnegie-Mellon Univ., 1962–71; Prof. Japanese Hist., Duke Univ., 1971–84; Vis. Fellow, Center Advanced Study Behavioral Sciences, Stanford, Salzburg Seminar Amer. Stud., Inst. Devlp. Stud., Univ. Sussex, Center East Asian Stud., Kyoto Nankai Univ., Tianjin, China.

Degrees BA Washington Univ., St Louis, 1934; PhD Univ. Chicago, 1939; Certificate (Japanese Language) Univ. Colorado, 1944.

Offices and Honours Pres., SEA, 1978–9, Hist. Econ. Soc., 1981–2, Atlantic Econ. Assoc., 1982–3; Vice Pres., AEA, 1984.

Editorial Duties Ed. Board, *AER*, *JEL, HOPE, EDCC, SEJ*.

Principal Field of Interests 020 General Economic Theory; 120 Country Studies (Japan); 053 Comparative Economic Systems.

Publications Books: 1. *Is the Business Cycle Obsolete?*, ed. (Wiley, 1969); 2. *Academic Encounter* (Free Press, 1969); 3. *Income Distribution Theory* (Aldine, 1971); 4. *Tomioka Stories* (Exposition, 1976); 5. *Macroeconomic Alternatives* (A.H.M., 1979); 6. *Economics* (with W. Gardner and W. Sichel), (Macmillan, 1983).

Articles: 1. 'Cross-section studies in the Cobb-Douglas Function' (with P. H. Douglas), *JPE*, 47, Dec. 1939; 2. 'Production functions, Cobb-Douglas, Intraform', *Em*, 12, Jan. 1944; 3. 'The appeal of confiscation in economic development',*EDCC*, 3, April 1955, repr. in *The Economics of Underdevelopment*, eds. A. N. Agarwala and S. P. Singh (OUP, 1958); 4. 'A reformulation of naive profit theory', *SEJ*, 26, April

1960; 5. 'Liquidity functions in the American economy' (with T. Mayer), *Em*, 28, Oct. 1960; 6. 'Survey of inflation theory' (with F. D. Holzman), *AER,* 53(4), Sept. 1962; 7. 'Elements of stagflation theory', *ZN*, 36(1–2), July 1976; 8. 'Marginal-efficiency theory of Japanese growth', in *Economic Growth and Resources*, 5, ed. S. Tsam (Macmillan, 1978); 9. 'The market economist in the directed economy', SEJ, 46(4), April 1980; 10. 'Notes on Reagonomics', in *Technology, Organization and Market Structure* eds. R. Sato and M. J. Beckmann (Springer-Verlag, 1983).

Principal Contributions My principal apology for the shallowness of my footprints on the sands of time, professionally speaking, is that I never intended to become a professional economist. Rather I am a perpetual student flitting between fields, sufficiently pessimistic about the real world to accept Academia as the best available refuge therefrom, but regretting my failure to get started in economic journalism. I maintain that there is no such thing as a pure economist. Economics is adulterated on one side by the keeping up of facts, statutes and court decisions, and on the other side by applied mathematicians and computerologists 'all dressed up with no place to go'. I spent the first half of my forty academic years as a 'what does it all mean?' theorist among the fact-mongers and the second half as a historian among computer-jockeys simulating 'obfuscation functions'.

My work in comparative economic systems and on doctrinal history can be summarised in the proposition that, both before and after choosing among the various policy and methodology religions available for True Believers, from Marxism to astrology, one should learn something about the others, sympathetically interpreted. My work in distribution theory may be summed up in the proposition that the distribution of income and wealth is an important factor in judging an economic system on welfare grounds, but that such emotive terms as 'maldistribution', 'exploitation', and 'poverty' are all subjective and mean whatever one wants them to mean, neither more nor less. My work in economic development, and to some extent in international economics generally, fits into a pattern also. The developing countries of the 'North' have hampered the development of the semi-developed countries of the 'South' primarily by denying poor countries access to rich-country markets. I don't think either Meiji or postwar Japan could have 'made it' under contemporary protectionism. The way to remedy this is to dismantle the barriers, at whatever cost to our rich-country labour and farm aristocracies.

BROWN, Arthur Joseph

Born 1914, Great Warford, Cheshire, England.
Current Post Emeritus Prof., Univ. Leeds, UK, 1979–.
Past Posts Fellow, All Souls Coll. Oxford, 1937–46; Head, Econ. Section, UK Foreign Office Res. Dept., 1943–5; Member, Econ. Section, UK Cabinet Office, 1945–7; Prof. Econ., Univ. Leeds, 1947–9; Vis. Prof., Columbia Univ., 1950, ANU, 1963; Member, E. African Econ. and Fiscal Commission, 1960, UK Secretary State's Advisory Group on Central Africa, 1962, UN Expert Group, Econ. and Social Consequences Disarmament, 1961–2; Head, Regional Econ. Res. Project, NIESR, 1966–72; UK Hunt Comm. Intermediate Areas, 1967–9; EEC Group Role of Public Fin. in Eur. Integration, 1975–7; UK Univ. Grants Comm., 1969–78; Pro-Vice-Chancellor, Univ. Leeds, 1975–7.
Degrees BA, DPhil Univ. Oxford, 1936, 1939; Hon. DLitt Univ. Bradford, 1975, Univ. Sheffield, 1979, Univ. Kent, 1979; Hon. LLD Univ. Aberdeen, 1978.
Offices and Honours Jr. Webb Medley Prize, Sr. Webb Medley Prize, Univ. Oxford, 1935, 1936; Pres., Section F, BAAS, 1958; Fellow, BA 1972; CBE, 1974; Pres., RES, 1976–8.
Editorial Duties Ed. Board, *YBESR,* 1948–79.
Principal Fields of Interest 134 Inflation and Deflation; 311 Domestic Monetary and Financial Theory and Policy; 423 Economic Integration.
Publications *Books:* 1. *Industrialisation and Trade* (Royal Inst. Internat.

Affairs, 1943); 2. *Applied Economics: Aspects of the World Economy in War and Peace* (A&U, Rinehart, 1947); 3. *The Great Inflation 1939–51* (OUP, 1955, Garland, 1983); 4. *Introduction to the World Economy* (A&U, Rinehart, 1959; transls., Portuguese, Zahar, 1960, Spanish, Taurus, 1960, Dutch, Aula, 1963, Hindi, 1963, Japanese, Diamond, 1965, Greek, Papaysis, 1968); 5. *The Framework of Regional Economics in the United Kingdom* (CUP, 1972); 6. *Regional Economic Problems* (with E. M. Burrows), (A&U, Rinehart, 1977).

Articles: 1. 'The liquidity preference schedules of the London clearing banks', *OEP*, 1(1), Oct. 1938; 2. 'Interest, prices and the demand schedule for idle money', *OEP*, 1(2), May 1939, repr. in *Oxford Studies in the Price Mechanism*, eds. T. Wilson and P. S. W. Andrews (OUP, 1951); 3. 'The fundamental elasticities in international trade', in *ibid.*; 4. 'Inflation and the British economy', *EJ*, 68, Sept. 1958; 5. 'Economic separatism versus a common market', *YBESR*, 18(1–2), May–Nov. 1961; 6. 'Britain and the world economy, 1870–1914', *YBESR*, 17(1), May 1965; 7. 'UV analysis', in *The Concept and Measurement of Involuntary Unemployment*, ed. G. D. N. Worswick (A&U, 1976); 8. 'Inflation and the British sickness', *EJ*, 89, March 1979; 9. 'Inflation in the world economy', *Proceedings of the BA*, 66, 1980.

Principal Contributions Have tried to be guided by Keynes's precept that economists should aspire to be useful people, like dentists. First research (1936–9) was on liquidity preference, including estimation of banks' asset-demand functions and the demand function for idle money. In wartime, turned to comparison of economic war efforts and to foreign trade elasticities and other topics related to postwar reconstruction. A combination of these interests led to work on wartime and postwar inflations, including elucidation of the price-wage spiral, and an adumbration of the Phillips curve and the probable need for incomes policies (1947–55). After a period spent mostly on a textbook with an international comparative emphasis, invitations to serve on various advisory bodies led to work on customs unions between developing countries, with special reference to demand effects and economies of scale, and on economic consequences of disarmament. The former led to regional economics and, through a government initiative, direction of a study of that aspect of the UK economy, the keynote of which was the relation between frictions of factor-movement and unemployment (1966–72). Several of these lines of interest were combined in work on possible development of the EEC (MacDougall Group, 1975–77). More recently, pure curiosity has led back to an attempt to make sense of the last thirty years' experience of inflation by an international comparative study to see how well or badly my insights of 1955 survive.

BROWN, Harry Gunnison*

Dates and Birthplace 1880–1975, Troy, NY, USA.

Posts Held Prof., Yale Univ., 1909–15; Prof., Univ. Missouri, 1915–50.

Degrees BA Williams Coll., 1904; PhD Yale Univ., 1909.

Offices and Honours Founder, member, Ed. Council, *Amer. J. Econ. and Sociology*.

Publications *Books:* 1. *Transportation Rates and their Regulation* (1916); 2. *Principles of Commerce* (1916); 3. *Economics of Taxation*; 4. *The Economic Basis of Tax Reform* (1932); 5. *Basic Principles of Economics* (1942).

Career Academic follower of Henry George who continued to advocate land value taxation throughout a long career. His work on business administration introduced economic principles as a basis for the subject. In retirement, he acted as a consultant to local authorities modernising their tax structures.

Secondary Literature W. Lissner, 'In memoriam: H. G. Brown', *Amer. J Econ. and Sociology*, 34, 1975.

BROWN, Murray

Born 1929, Alden, NY, USA.
Current Post Goodyear Prof. Econ.,

State Univ. NY, Buffalo, NY, USA, 1972–.

Past Posts Res. Ass., NBER, 1955–6; Lect., City Coll. NY, 1955–6; Ass. Prof. Econ., Wharton School, Univ. Penn., 1956–62; Res. Assoc., US Commission Money and Credit, 1960; Vis. Scholar, Econometric Inst., Netherlands School Econ., 1962; Cons., Office Bus. Econ., US Dept. Commerce, 1962–4, Organization Amer. States, 1965, US Dept. Justice, 1965; Prof. Econometrics, George Washington Univ., 1964–7; Res. Assoc., Center Econ. Stud. and Plans, Rome, Italy, 1966–; Prof., State Univ. NY, Buffalo, 1967–72; Vis. Prof., Univ. Perugia, 1974–5, Univ. Rome, 1981.

Degrees BA Univ. Buffalo, 1952; PhD New School Social Res., NY, 1956.

Offices and Honours Vis. Scholar, Einaudi Foundation, Italy; Hiram J. Halle Fellow, 1955–6; Special Award Effective Teaching, Univ. Penn., 1960; Ford Faculty Fellow, 1961–2; Guggenheim Foundation Fellow, 1965–6; Advisory Comm. Econ., NY Academy Sciences; Fulbright Fellow, 1981.

Principal Fields of Interest 023 Macroeconomic Theory; 026 Economics of Uncertainty and Information; Game Theory and Bargaining Theory; 021 Technological Change; Innovation; Research and Development.

Publications *Books:* 1.*On the Theory and Measurement of Technological Change* (CUP, 1966); 2. *The Theory and Empirical Analysis of Production,* ed. (NBER, 1967); 3. *Essays in Modern Capital Theory,* co-ed. (with K. Sato and P. Zarembka), (N-H, 1976); 4. *A Regional-National Econometric Model of Italy,* co-ed. (Pion, 1978).

Articles: 1. 'The structure of stochastic difference equation models', *Em,* 27(1), Jan. 1959; 2. 'Overinvestment during prosperity', *EJ,* 71, Sept. 1961; 3. 'A measure of technological change and returns to scale' (with J. Popkin), *REStat,* 44(4), Nov. 1962; 4. 'Technological change and the distribution of income' (with J. S. deCani), *IER,* 4(3), Sept. 1963; 5. 'A measure of the relative exploitation of capital and labor', *REStat,* 48(2), May 1966; 6. 'Toward an econometric accommodation of the capital-intensity perversity phenomemon',

Em, 41(5), Sept. 1973; 7. 'Substitution-composition effects, capital intensity uniqueness and growth', *EJ,* 79, June 1969; 8. 'The S-branch utility tree: a generalization of the linear expenditure system' (with D. Heien), *Em.* 40(4), July 1972; 9. 'The measurement of capital aggregates — a post switching problem', in *The Measurement of Capital,* ed. D. Usher (NBER, 1980); 10. 'Marriage and household decision making: a bargaining analysis' (with M. Manser), *IER,* 21(1), Feb. 1980.

Principal Contributions In seeking to measure and decompose the technological change residual of the aggregate growth rate, I found a method in the early 1960s to measure the length of technological epochs. This was then used to quantify Hicksian nonneutral as distinct from neutral technological change. A byproduct of that work was the discovery of a new production function form (along with John D. Cani), the CES, which was employed extensively to measure factors affecting the distribution of income, capital-labour exploitation and technological change in the US and elsewhere.

At about the same time, the reswitching phenomenon surfaced, providing a fundamental critique of aggregate neoclassical production economics; addressing that problem, I showed in a 1969 *EJ* article that a stringent condition for the validity of aggregate production specifications is that there be a high degree of capital-labour substitution. This led to further investigations of the aggregation conditions, under which well-behaved production functions can be specified and tested (surveyed in the 1980 NBER volume on capital measurement). An interest in household demand theory resulted in a new specificaton for a complete system of demand equations in a 1972 *Em* article but, more fundamentally, the question of what exactly constitutes a household was addressed. Rather than specify an aggregate-type household utility function, co-operative game theory was used and a general household utility decision-making framework evolved. This considerably enlarged the set of refutable hypotheses in the area of family economics.

BROWNING, Edgar K.

Born Front Royal, VA, USA.
Current Post Prof. Econ., Texas
A & M Univ., Coll. Station, TX, USA,
1984–.
Past Posts Ass. Prof., Assoc. Prof.,
Prof., Univ. Virginia, 1969–74, 1974–7,
1977–84; Vis. Scholar, UCLA, 1978.
Degrees BA Univ. Virginia, 1965;
PhD Princeton Univ., 1971.
Offices and Honours Sequicentennial
Assoc. Center Advanced Stud., Univ.
Virginia, 1974–5, 1982; Adjunct Scholar,
AEI, 1977–; Vice-Pres., SEA, 1983–4.
Editorial Duties Ed. Board, *SEJ*,
1980–2, *Public Fin. Q.*, 1981–.
Principal Fields of Interest 320 Fiscal
Theory and Policy; Public Finance; 022
Microeconomic Theory; 910 Welfare,
Health and Education.
Publications *Books:* 1. *Redistribution
and the Welfare System* (AEI, 1975); 2.
Public Finance and the Price System
(with J. M. Browning), (Macmillan,
1979, 1983); 3. *The Distribution of
the Tax Burden* (with W. R. Johnson),
(AEI, 1979); 4. *Microeconomic Theory
and Applications*, (with J. M. Browning), (Little, Brown, 1983).
Articles: 1. 'Alternative programs for
income redistribution: the NIT and
NWT', *AER* 63(1), March 1973, repr.
in *Benefit-Cost and Policy Analysis:
1973*, ed. R. Haveman (Aldine, 1974); 2.
'The diagrammatic analysis of multiple
consumption externalities', *AER*,
64(4), Sept. 1974; 3. 'Why the social
insurance budget is too large in a democracy', *EI*,13, Sept. 1975; 4. 'The
marginal cost of public funds', *JPE*,
84(2), April 1976; 5. 'The marginal welfare cost of income redistribution',
SEJ, 44, July 1978; 6. 'How much more
equality can we afford?', *Public Interest*,
43, Spring 1976, repr. in *Economics: A
Reader*, ed. K. Elzinga (Basic Books,
1978) and *Current Issues in the American
Economy*, ed. R. Puth (Wiley, 1978); 7.
'The burden of taxation', *JPE*, 86(4),
Aug. 1978, repr. in *Income Inequality:
Trends and International Comparisons*,
ed. J. Moroney (D. C. Heath, 1980); 8.
'A theory of paternalistic in-kind transfers', *EI*,19, Oct. 1981; 9. 'The distributional and efficiency effects of increasing the minimum wage: a simula-

tion' (with W. Johnson), *AER*, 73(1),
March 1983; 10. 'The trade-off between equality and efficiency' (with W.
Johnson), *JPE*, 92(4), April 1984.
Principal Contributions Much of my
work has been motivated by the recognition that the distributional aspects of
public policies are extremely important
in determining what policies the political process actually implements, and by
the relative lack of attention given to
the analysis and evaluation of redistributional policies in the economics literature. Early work focussed on welfare
programmes, welfare reform and the
measurement of economic inequality.
More recently, I have emphasised the
relevance of efficiency costs for the
evaluation of tax and expenditure programmes, including programmes intended to reduce economic inequality.
My work continues to concentrate on
the microeconomic effects of public
policies, especially tax and expenditure
policies.

BRUNNER, Karl

Born 1916, Zurich, Switzerland.
Current Post Fred H. Gowen Prof.
Econ., Univ. Rochester, Prof. Econ.,
Univ. Berne, 1971–.
Past Posts Res. Assoc., Swiss Nat.
Bank, 1943–5; Lect., Handelshoch-
schule, St Gäleen, 1946–9; Res. Assoc.,
Swiss Inst. Internat. Econ., 1945–8;
Adviser, Swiss Watch Chamber Com-
merce, 1948–9; Cons., EEC, 1948–9;
Ass. Prof., Assoc. Prof., Prof., UCLA,
1951–7, 1957–62 , 1962–6; Vis. Prof.,
Univ. Wisconsin, 1965, Michigan State
Univ., 1965–6, Northwestern Univ.,
1966; Everett Reese Prof., Ohio State
Univ., 1966–71.
Degrees Dr Univ. Zurich, 1943;
Hon. Dr Catholic Univ. Louvain, 1966,
Univ. St Gallen, 1982.
Offices and Honours Rockefeller
Fellow, 1949–51; Vice-Pres., Pres.,
WEA, 1972, 1973.
Editorial Duties Ed., *JMCB*, 1969–
74, *J Mon E*, 1974–84.
Principal Fields of Interest 311 Dom-
estic Monetary and Finance Theory
and Policy; 321 Fiscal Theory and Policy.
Publications *Books:* 1. *Problems*

and Issues in Current Econometric Practice, ed. (Ohio State Univ., 1972); 2. *Konstanz Seminar on Monetary Theory and Monetary Policy,* ed. (Duncker & Humbolt, 1972); 3. *The First World and the Third World,* ed. (Univ. Rochester Policy Center, 1978); 4. *Economics and Social Institutions,* ed. (Martinus Nijhoff, 1979); 5. *The Great Depression Revisited,* ed. (Kluwer Nijhoff, 1981).

Articles: 1. 'Survey of selected issues in monetary theory', *Schweizerische Zeitschrift für Volkswirtschaft und Statistik,* 1, 1971; 2. 'Inflation, money and the role of fiscal arrangements: an analytic framework for the inflation problem', in *The New Inflation and Monetary Policy,* ed. M. Monti (Macmillan, 1976); 3. 'Milton Friedman in our time', in *Economics and Social Institutions* ed. K. Brunner (Martinus Nijhoff, 1979); 4. 'Stagflation, persistent unemployment and the permanence of economic shocks' (with A. Cukierman and A. H. Meltzer), *J Mon E,* 6(4), Sept. 1980; 5. 'Epilogue: understanding the great depression', in *The Great Depression Revisited,* ed. K. Brunner (Kluwer Nijhoff, 1981); 6. 'A fascination with economics', *BNLQR,* 135, Dec. 1980; 7. 'The control of monetary aggregates', in *Controlling Monetary Aggregates,* 3 (Fed. Reserve Bank Boston, 1981); 7. 'Money and economic activity, inventories and business cycles' (with A. Cukierman and A. H. Meltzer), *J Mon E,* 11(3), May 1983; 8. 'Monetary policy and monetary order', *Aussenwirtschaft,* 39(3), Sept. 1984.

Principal Contributions Three strands of ideas have attracted my attention over the past thirty years. Monetary theory had already stirred my interest in Switzerland. An increasing interest concerning the nature of our cognitive endeavours directed my attention to philosophy of science. These two strands occupied most of my time during the 1950s and 1960s, and influenced each other. My research in the field of money supply analysis reveals this aspect most clearly. This was motivated by a realisation that the literature offered at best some fragments of a theory explaining the behaviour of the money stock. This

work eventually ignited a growing interest in the nature and role of monetary policy-making and the role of institutional arrangements. The questions pursued were also extended to address the nature of the interaction between the real sector and the monetary sector. This extension was motivated by a basic dissatisfaction with the dominant paradigm expressed by the standard IS/LM framework, which under one possible interpretation seems false, and under the alternative interpretation seems to suffer from a very limited range of application.

The last strand of my interests gradually emerged in the early 1970s, which I began to appreciate the importance of an analysis directed to understanding of political institutions. This appreciation was initially fostered by an interest in the central bank behaviour and the drift into a pattern of policy with an inflationary bias. This perspective led to exploration of the nature of substantive issues underlying apparently 'ideological' conflicts. Work in the range of the political economy of alternative institutional orders and the analysis of alternative explanations of the business cycle will occupy my future agenda.

BRUNO, Michael

Born 1932, Hamburg, W. Germany.
Current Post Prof. Econ., Hebrew Univ., Jerusalem, 1970–.
Past Posts Sr. Econ., Joint Dir. Res., Bank of Israel, 1957–61, 1961–4; Lect., Sr. Lect., Assoc Prof., Hebrew Univ., 1963–4, 1965, 1966–7; Vis. Prof., MIT, 1965–6, 1970–1, 1981, Harvard Univ., 1970–1, 1976–7; Dir. Res., Falk Inst. Econ. Res., Israel, 1972–5; Sr. Econ. Policy Adviser, Israeli Minister Fin., 1975–6; Vis. Res. Prof., Inst. Internat. Econ Stud., Stockholm, 1978; Res. Assoc., NBER, Cambridge, Mass., 1979–.
Degrees BA, MA Univ Camb., 1956, 1960; PhD Stanford Univ., 1962.
Offices and Honours Fellow, Member Council, Vice-Pres., Em Soc, 1967, 1967–8, 1984; Member, Israel AAAS, 1975; Foreign Hon. Member, AAAS, 1982; Rothschild Prize Social Science,

1974; Pres., Israel Econ. Assoc., 1977–9.

Principal Fields of Interest 023 Macroeconomic Theory; 110 Economic Growth, Development; 400 International Economics.

Publications *Books:* 1. *Interdependence, Resource Use and Structural Change in Israel* (Bank of Israel, 1962); 2. *Economics of Worldwide Stagflation* (with J. Sachs), (Harvard Univ. Press, 1984).

Articles: 1. 'Development alternatives in an open economy: the case of Israel' (with H. B. Chenery), *EJ*, 72, March 1962; 2. 'The nature and significance of the reswitching of techniques' (with E. Burmeister and E. Sheshinski), *QJE*, 80(4), Nov. 1966; 3. 'Optimal patterns of trade and development', *REStat.*, 49, Nov. 1967; 4. 'Estimation of factor contribution to growth under structural disequilibrium', *Int ER*, Feb. 1968; 5. 'Fundamental duality relations in the pure theory of capital and growth', *REStud.*, 36, May 1969; 6. 'Domestic resource costs and effective protection: clarification and synthesis', *JPE*, Jan/Feb. 1972; 7. 'Market distortions and gradual reform', *REStud.*, 39(3), July 1972; 8. 'The two-sector open economy and the real exchange rate', *AER*, 66(4), Sept. 1976; 9. 'Price and output adjustment; micro foundations and aggregation', *J Mon E,* 5(2), April 1979; 10. 'Import prices and stagflation in the industrial countries: a cross-section analysis', *EJ* 90, Sept. 1980.

Principal Contributions Early work has concentrated on trade and development issues, structural change and formulation of development policy in open economies. In this context I have applied input-output analysis and linear and dynamic programming methods to the analysis of factor use and shadow pricing, especially of foreign exchange, for investment allocation criteria in an open industrialising economy. During this period (1957–65) I also contributed to the estimation of production functions, especially under disequilibrium in factor markets. A visit to MIT in 1965–6 shifted my interests partly into capital and growth theory where I worked on the reswitching problem, optimal growth theory with discrete technologies, and duality. The next policy-induced research area in the 1970s has been concerned with public economics, in particular the design of income maintenance schemes and tax reform under inflation. Since the mid-1970s, I have shifted my interests back to trade and macroeconomics of open economies, first working on the dynamics of wage and price adjustment and subsequently on the theoretical and empirical analysis of stagflation in industrial countries. This has entailed a systematic formulation of the impact of supply shocks in individual economies and on international capital flows as well as an attempt to account for the poor output, productivity and inflation performance of the industrial world in the last decade.

BUCHANAN, David*

Dates and Birthplace 1779–1848, Montrose, Scotland.

Posts Held Journalist and Ed., *Weekly Register,* 1808–9, *Caledonian Mercury,* 1810–27, *Edinburgh Courant,* 1826–48.

Publications *Books:* 1. *Adam Smith's Wealth of Nations*, 3 vols (1814); 2. *Inquiry into the Taxation and Commercial Policy of Great Britain* (1844).

Career His edition of Smith was an important pre-Ricardian commentary, which criticised various aspects of Smith's work, including the theory of rent, in an able fashion. He developed an argument in favour of progressive taxation in the supplement to the edition. His later *Inquiry . . .* contains a spirited critique of current taxation practices and an attack on the Ricardian theory of rent. He was also a contributor to the *Edinburgh Review* and *Encyclopaedia Britannica,* 7th edn.

BUCHANAN, James M.

Born 1919, Murfreesboro, TN, USA.

Current Post Univ. Disting. Prof., General Dir., Center Stud. Public Choice, Virginia Polytechnic Inst., Blacksburg, VA, USA, 1969–.

Recent Posts McIntire Prof. Econ.,

Dir., Thomas Jefferson Center Polit. Econ., Univ. Virginia, 1956–68; Prof. Econ., UCLA, 1968–9.

Degrees BS Univ. Middle Tennessee, 1940; MA Univ. Tennessee, 1941; PhD Univ. Chicago, 1948.

Offices and Honours Co-founder (with G. Tullock), Public Choice Soc., 1962; Pres., SEA, 1963; Exec. Comm., 1967–9, Vice-Pres., AEA, 1972; Law Econ. Prize, Univ. Miami Law Econ. Center, 1977; Exec. Comm., Mont Pelerin Soc., 1980–1; Vice-Pres., WEA, 1982.

Principal Fields of Interest 024 Welfare Theory.

Publications *Books:* 1. *Calculus of Consent* (with G. Tullock), (Univ. Michigan Press, 1962); 2. *Cost and Choice* (Markham Publishing, 1969, Univ. Chicago Press, 1979); 3. *The Limits of Liberty* (Univ. Chicago Press, 1975); 4. *Freedom in Constitutional Contract* (Texas A & M Univ. Press, 1978); 5. *The Power to Tax* (with G. Brennan), (CUP, 1980).

Articles: 1. 'Individual choice in voting and the market', *JPE*, 62, Aug. 1954; 2. 'Externality' (with W. C. Stubblebine), *Ec*, N.S. 29, Nov. 1962; 3. 'A contractarian paradigm for applying economic theory', *AER*, 65(2), May 1975; 4. 'Markets, states, and the extent of morals', *AER*, 68(2), May 1978; 5. The homogenization of heterogeneous inputs' (with R. D. Tollison), *AER*, 71(1), March 1981.

Principal Contributions Integration of the analysis of political decision-making (public choice) into the corpus of economic theory, which is the source for what is now called 'public sector economics'. Extension and application of economic analysis to constitutional choices among social-political rules and institutions. Critique of Keynesian macroeconomic policy based on analysis of political decision structure. Clarification of theory of opportunity cost. Critique of post-Keynesian theory of public debt.

Secondary Literature G. Locksley, 'Individuals, contracts and constitutions: the political economy of James M. Buchanan', in *Twelve Contemporary Economists*, eds. V. R. Shackleton and G. Locksley (Macmillan, 1981); D. G.

Mueller, 'On Buchanan', *Contemporary Economists in Perspective,* eds. H. W. Spiegel and W. J. Samuels, 2 (JAI Press, 1984).

BUDD, Edward C.

Born 1920, Summit, NJ, USA.

Current Post Prof. Econ., Penn. State Univ., Univ. Park, PA, USA, 1961–.

Past Posts Price Econ., US Office Price Admin., Fresno, San Francisco, CA, 1944–6; Ass. Prof. Econ., Univ. Illinois, 1949–51; Instr. Econ., Univ. Oregon, 1951–2; Instr., Ass. Prof., Yale Univ., 1952–61; Cons., Bureau Econ. Analysis, US Dept. Commerce, 1966–70.

Degrees BA (Econ. and Hist.), PhD Univ. Cal. Berkeley, 1942, 1954.

Offices and Honours Phi Beta Kappa, 1942; Exec. Comm., Conference Res. Income and Wealth, NBER, 1970–2; Public Service Union Liberal Arts Alumni Award, Distinction Social Sciences, 1983.

Editorial Duties Ed. Board, *RIW*, 1977–83.

Principal Fields of Interest 010 General Economics; 200 Quantitative Economic Methods and Data; 900 Welfare Programmes, etc.

Publications *Books:* 1.*Inequality and Poverty,* ed. (W. W. Norton, 1967); 2. *Size Distribution of Family Personal Income: Methodology and Estimates for 1964* (with D. Radner and J. Hinrichs), (Bureau Econ. Analysis, US Dept. Commerce, 1973).

Articles: 1. 'Factor demand with a variable quantity of cooperating factors', *AER*, 41(3), Sept. 1951; 2. 'The product side: some theoretical aspects' (with E. Hagen), in *A Critique of the US Product and Income Accounts* (Princeton Univ. Press, 1958); 3. 'US factor shares, 1850–1910', in *Trends in the American Economy in the 19th Century* (Princeton Univ. Press, 1960); 4. 'The state of income distribution theory', in *Income Distribution Analysis* (Univ. N. Carolina, 1966); 5. 'Postwar changes in the size distribution of income in the US', *AER*, 60(2), May 1970; 6. 'The impact of inflation on the distribution of income and wealth' (with D. F. Seiders), *AER*, 61(2), May 1971; 7.'The creation of a microdata file for estimating the size distribution of income', *RIW*, 17(4), Dec. 1971; 8. 'The BEA and CPS size distributions: some comparisons for 1964' (with D. B. Radner), in *The Personal Distribution of Income and Wealth* (Columbia Univ. Press, 1975); 9. 'Macroeconomic fluctuations and the size distribution of income and earnings in the US' (with T. C. Whiteman), in *Income Distribution and Economic Inequality* (Halsted Press, Wiley, 1978); 10. 'An accounting framework for transfer payments and its implications for the size distribution of income' (with D. B. Radner and T. C. Whiteman), in *Social Accounting for Transfers* (Chicago Univ. Press, 1984).

Principal Contributions Historical studies of the US income distribution between labour and property income and among persons and households. Contributed to the conceptual framework of national income accounting. Primarily concerned with the development of microdata systems for estimating the personal distribution of income by size of income and socioeconomic characteristics of recipients and integrating these into the framework provided by the national income accounts. Originated methods for estimating the distribution of family personal income, using microdata files from household field surveys, income tax returns, audit studies, and other government administrative records, and carried out the estimation process for 1964 and 1972. With D. B. Radner, was the first to develop methods for statistically matching microdata files, using field surveys and tax return data. Have also been concerned with estimating the effect of macroeconomic fluctuations, as well as other variables, on income distribution. With D. F. Seiders, developed a new method, using microdata files, for estimating the distributional effects of inflation and unemployment on the size distribution of income and wealth.

BUITER, Willem Hendrik

Born 1949, Den Haag, The Netherlands.

Current Post Cassell Prof. Econ., LSE, 1982–.

Past Posts Ass. Prof. Econ. and Internat. Affairs, Princeton Univ., 1975–6, 1977–9; Lect. Econ., LSE, 1976–7; Cons., Fin. Stud. Division, Res. Dept., IMF, 1979; Vis. Scholar, Fiscal Affairs Dept., IMF, 1982; Prof. Econ., Bristol Univ., 1980–2.

Degrees BA Univ. Camb., 1971; PhD Yale Univ., 1975.

Offices and Honours Res. Assoc., NBER, 1979–; Specialist Adviser, UK House of Commons Select Comm. Treasury and Civil Service, 1980–; Member, Brookings Panel Econ. Activity, 1981, 1983; Adviser, Commission EEC, 1982–; Programme Dir. Internat. Macroeconomics, UK Centre Econ. Policy Res., 1983–.

Editorial Duties Assoc. Ed., *World Politics*, 1978, *EJ*, 1980–, *J Ec Dyn*, 1980–; Ed. Board, *REStud*, 1980–.

Principal Fields of Interest 130 Economic Fluctuations; Forecasting; Stablisations; and Inflation; 300 Domestic Monetary and Fiscal Theory and Institutions; 430 Balance of Payments; International Finance.

Publications *Books:* 1. *Temporary and Long-Run Equilibrium* (Garland, 1979).

Articles: 1. 'Long-run effects of fiscal and monetary policy on aggregate demand' (with J Tobin), in *Monetarism*, ed. J Stein (N-H, 1976); 2. 'Crowding out and the effectiveness of fiscal policy', *J Pub E*, 7, June 1977; 3.'Walras' law and all that', *Int ER*, 21, Feb. 1980; 4. 'The macroeconomics of Dr. Pangloss: a critical survey of the new classical macroeconomics', *EJ*, 90, March 1980; 5. 'Time preference and international lending and borrowing in an overlapping generations model', *JPE*, 89, Aug. 1981; 6. 'Monetary policy and international competitiveness' (with M. H. Miller), *OEP*, 33, Suppl., July 1981; 7. 'The superiority of contingent rules over fixed rules in models with rational expectations', *EJ*, 91, Sept. 1981; 8. 'Real effects of anticipated and unanticipated money: some problems of estimation and hypothesis testing', *J Mon E*, 11, March 1983; 9. 'Changing the rules: economic consequences of the Thatcher regime' (with M. H. Miller), *Brookings Papers Econ. Activity*, 21, 1983; 10. 'Saddle-point problems in continuous time rational expectations models', *Em*, 52, May 1984.

Principal Contributions The common thread in most of my work concerns monetary and fiscal policy evaluation and design. Increasingly, an open economy or multi-country framework approach has been adopted. One set of papers aimed to save the rational expectations revolution from the new classical macroeconomics. A continuing concern is the development of dynamic models with tolerable microfoundations, that have sufficient plausible market imperfections (especially in financial markets) for a non-trivial potential role for monetary, fiscal and financial policy to emerge. Given policy 'effectiveness', the search for credible or time-consistent policies is the next item on the agenda. As part of this research programme, I am trying to integrate the allocative and stabilisation aspects of budgetary and monetary policy. I have cautious hopes for the applicability of simple nonco-operative dynamic game theory to the problem of decentralised policy design in open, interdependent economies.

BUKHARIN, Nikolai Ivanovich*

Dates and Birthplace 1888–1938, Moscow, Russia.

Posts Held Ed., *Pravda, Novy Mir Izvestia*; Member, Russian Politburo, Comintern.

Publications *Books:* 1. *The Economic Theory of the Leisure Class* (1914, 1927, 1968); 2. *Imperialism and the World Economy* (1915, 1972); 3. *The Economy of the Transformation Period* (1920, 1971); 4. *ABC of Communism* (with E. Preobrazhensky), (1921, 1969); 5. *The Theory of Historical Materialism* (1921).

Career One of the chief theorists of the Russian Revolution and the Soviet State, he became a revolutionary whilst studying economics. He was an exile with Lenin in the years 1911–17 when he wrote a number of theoretical works, including an analysis of imperialism, on which Lenin drew repeatedly. For a while, in the 1920s, he was an ally of Stalin who nevertheless had him expelled from his positions of influence in 1929. He argued for a policy of industrialisation at the expense of the peasantry but drew back from Stalin's adoption of an extreme version of his argument. He was indicted in the third round of the Moscow Trials and was executed in 1938.

Secondary Literature P. Knirsch, *Die ökonomischen Anschauungen Nikolaj I. Bucharins* (Ost-Europa Inst., 1959); S. F. Cohen, *Bukharin and the Bolshevik Revolution* (Alfred A. Knopf, 1973).

BULLOCK, Charles Jesse*

Dates and Birthplace 1869–1941, Boston, MA, USA.

Posts Held Instr. Econ., Cornell Univ., 1895–9; Prof., Williams Coll., 1899–1903; Prof. Econ., Harvard Univ., 1903–35.

Degrees BA Univ. Boston, 1889; PhD Univ. Wisconsin, 1895.

Offices Fellow, AAAS.

Publications *Books:* 1. *The Finances of the United States 1775–89* (1895); 2. *Introduction to the Study of Economics* (1897); 3. *Essays on the Monetary History of the USA* (1900); 4. *Economic Essays* (1936); 5. *Politics, Finance and Consequences* (1939).

Articles: 1. 'The variation of productive forces', *QJE*, 16, Aug. 1902.

Career His *QJE* paper of 1902, positing a general law of variation of productive forces, is an important contribution to the theory of substitution, then a neglected field despite Marshall's work on it. He presided over the Harvard Univ. Comm. on Econ. Res., which owes its fame to the development of the 'three curve barometer' as an indicator of turning points in the business cycle.

BURMEISTER, Edwin

Born 1939, Chicago, IL, USA.
Current Post Commonwealth Prof.

Econ., Univ. Virginia, Charlottesville, VA, USA, 1979–.

Past Posts Ass. Prof., Assoc. Prof., Prof. Econ., Wharton School, Univ. Penn., 1965–8, 1968–71, 1972–6; Vis. Prof., Duke Univ., 1971–2, 1981–2, Res. School Social Sciences, ANU, 1974–5, Univ. Chicago, 1980; Prof. Econ., Member Center Advanced Stud., Univ. Virginia, 1976–9.

Degrees BA, MA Cornell Univ., 1961, 1962; PhD MIT, 1965.

Offices and Honours Hon. Woodrow Wilson Fellow, 1961–2; Fellow, Em Soc.; Guggenheim Foundation Fellow, 1974.

Editorial Duties Acting Ed., Assoc. Ed., *Int ER*, 1970–1, 1971–6; Ed. Board, *JEL*, 1979–; Internal Ed. Board, Irving Fisher and Frank Taussig Awards, 1975–.

Principal Fields of Interest 020 General Economic Theory; 200 Quantitative Economic Methods and Data; 520 Business Finance and Investment.

Publications *Books:* 1. *Mathematical Theories of Economic Growth* (with A. Dobell), (Macmillan 1970; transls., Spanish, Bosch Casa Editorial, 1973, Italian, Etas Libri, 1975, Japanese, Keiso Shobo, 1976); 2. *Economic Model Performance: Comparative Simulation Studies of the U.S. Economy*, co-ed. (with L. R. Klein), (Univ. Pennsylvania Press, 1976); 3. *Capital Theory and Dynamics* (CUP, 1980; transls., French, Spanish, 1985).

Articles: 1. 'The nature and implications of the reswitching of techniques' (with M. Bruno and E. Sheshinski), *QJE*, 80, Nov. 1966, repr. in *Readings in Mathematical Economics, 2*, ed. P. Newman (JHUP, 1968); 2. 'The factor-price frontier, duality and joint production' (with K. Kuga), *REStud*, 37(1) Jan. 1970; 3. 'Money, public debt, inflation and real interest' (with E. S. Phelps), *JMCB*, 3(2), May 1971; 4. 'The "saddlepoint property" and the structure of dynamic heterogeneous capital good models' (with C. Caton, A. Dobell and S. A. Ross), *Em*, 41(1), Jan. 1973; 5. 'Maximin paths of heterogeneous capital accumulation and the instability of paradoxical steady states' (with P. J. Hammond), *Em*, 45(4), May 1977; 6. 'Professor Pasinetti's

"unobtrusive postulate," regular economies, and the existence of a well-behaved aggregate production function', *REP*, 89(5), Sept.–Oct. 1979; 7. 'On some conceptual issues in rational expectations modelling', *JMCB*, 12(4), pt. 2, Nov. 1980; 8. 'On the uniqueness of dynamically efficient steady states', *Int ER*, 22(1), Feb. 1981; 9. 'Kalman filtering estimation of unobserved rational expectations with an application to the German hyperinflation' (with K. D. Wall), *J Em*, 20(3), Nov. 1982; 10. 'Sraffa, labor theories of value and the economics of wage rate determination', *JPE*, 92(3), June 1984.

Principal Contributions Capital theory and economic growth were subjects that dominated my research for the first decade of my career. Although these areas remain of interest to me, more recently I have been investigating problems associated with macroeconomic models; in particular, the dynamic properties of rationally formed expectations have been the subject of several papers. These efforts also have induced me to do econometric work in which Kalman filtering techniques are employed to obtain estimates of unobserved variables.

The theme which unites my work is dynamics. Current research is focussed on financial economics and its interface with the dynamic properties of the financial sectors in macroeconomic models. This work involves both theoretical and empirical studies.

BURNS, Arthur F.

Born 1904, Stanislau, Austro-Hungary.

Current Post US Ambassador, Federal Republic of Germany, 1981–.

Past Posts Ass. Stats, Gilder Fellow, Columbia Univ., 1926–7; Instr., Ass. Prof., Assoc. Prof., Prof. Econ., Rutgers Univ., 1927–30, 1930–1933, 1933–43, 1943–58; Res. Assoc., Res. Staff, Dir. Res. Pres., Chairman, NBER, 1930–1, 1933–69; Chief Stat., 1945–53, 1957–67; 1967–8; US Railway Emergency Board, 1942; Chairman, US President's Advisory Board Econ. Growth and Stability, 1953–6; Chairman, US President's Council Econ. Advisers, 1953–6; Chairman, Cabinet Comm., Small Bus., 1956; Member, US Advisory Council Social Security Fin., 1957–8; Vis. Prof., J. B. Clark Prof. Econ., Columbia Univ., 1942–4, 1959–69; Member, NY Temp. State Commission Econ. Expansion, 1959–60; Member, US President's Advisory Comm. Labor-Management Policy, 1961–6; Member, NY Governor's Comm. Min. Wage, 1964; Vis. Prof. Econ., Stanford Univ., 1968; Counsellor, US President, 1969–70; Chairman, Board Governors, Fed. Reserve System, 1970–8; Alternate Governor, IMF, 1973–8; Disting. Scholar, AEI; Disting. Prof. Lect., Georgetown Univ., 1978–81.

Degrees BA, MA, PhD Columbia Univ., 1925, 1925, 1934; Hon. LLD From 37 American Univs. and Colls., and from 6 foreign Univs.

Offices and Honours Phi Beta Kappa; Pres., Disting. Fellow, AEA, 1959; Fellow, ASA; Pres., Academy Polit. Science, 1962–8; Dir., Nation Wide Securities Co., 1957–68, Dividend Shares Inc., 1958–68, Calvin Bullock Company, 1957–68, 1978–81; Disting. Public Service Award, US Tax Foundation, 1969; Korean Govt., Mugunghwha Decoration, 1970; Disting. Service Award, Investment Educ., 1970; Award Excellence, Columbia Univ., 1974; Jefferson Award, Amer. Inst. Public Service, 1976; Alexander Hamilton Award, US Treasury, 1976; Commander, French Legion of Honour, 1977; Japanese Order Rising Sun, First Class, 1978; German Grand Cross Order of Merit, 1978; Frank E. Seidman Disting. Award Polit. Econ., 1978; Francis Boyer Award, AEI Public Pol. Res., 1978; Charles Waldo Haskins Award, NYU, 1983.

Principal Fields of Interest 131 Economic Fluctuations.

Publications *Books:* 1. *Principal Trends in the United States since 1870* (Princeton Univ. Press, 1934); 2. *Measuring Business Cycles*(with W. C. Mitchell), (NBER, 1946); 3. *Economic Research and the Keynesian Thinking of our Times* (NBER, 1946); 4. *Frontiers of Economic Knowledge* (Princeton Univ. Press, 1954); 5. *Prosperity with-*

out Inflation (Columbia Univ. Press, 1957); 6. *The Management of Prosperity* (Columbia Univ. Press., 1966); 7. *Full Employment, Guideposts and Economic Stability* (with P. A. Samuelson), (Wiley, 1967); 8. *The Defense Sector and the American Economy* (with J. K. Javits and C. J. Hitch), (Wiley, 1968); 9. *The Business Cycle in a Changing World* (Columbia Univ. Press, 1969); 10. *Reflections of an Economic Policy Maker* (AEI, 1978).

Principal Contributions Studies of the process of economic growth, causes of business cycle fluctuations, methods of economic forecasting, and policies for managing national prosperity.

Secondary Literature G. H. Moore, 'Burns, Arthur F.', *IESS,* 18.

BURNS, Arthur Robert*

Dates and Birthplace 1895–1981, London, England.

Posts Held Prof. Econ., Columbia Univ., NYC, 1933–62; Sr. Adviser, US Foreign Econ. Admin., 1940–5.

Degrees BSc, PhD LSE, 1926, 1928.

Publications *Books:* 1. *Money and Monetary Policy in Early Times* (1927); 2. *The Decline of Competition* (1936); 3. *Comparative Economic Organisation (1955).*

Career *The Decline of Competition* was a major influence in the USA in disseminating the theories of Chamberlin and Robinson in undergraduate teaching. After World War II, he turned increasingly to the subject of economic development, once again from the vantage point of institutionalism.

BURSTEIN, Meyer Louis

Born 1926, Neenah, WI, USA.

Current Post Prof. Econ., York Univ., Downsview, Ont., Canada, 1981–.

Past Posts Assoc. Prof. Econ., Northwestern Univ., 1955–64; Prof., Univ. Western Ontario, Canada, 1964–5; Vis. Prof. Math. Econ., Birmingham Univ., England, 1965–6; Cons., US Dept. Defense, 1966–7; Esmée Fairbain Prof. Econ. Fin. and Investment, Warwick Univ., England, 1967–9;

Cons. for Cambodia, US Dept. State, 1974–5; Prof. Econ., Univ. College Buckingham, England, 1974–7; Vis. Prof. Econ., State Univ. NY, Buffalo, Univ. Cal. Santa Barbara, 1978–9, Univ. Miami, 1980–1, Univ. Cal. Davis, 1983, Univ. Virginia, Charlottesville, 1983.

Degrees BPhil, JD, MA, PhD Univ. Chicago, 1947, 1950, 1955, 1957.

Offices and Honours Life Member, Univ. Chicago Law Review Assoc.

Principal Fields of Interest 023 Macroeconomic Theory; 310 Domestic Monetary Theory; 610 Industrial Organisation and Public Policy.

Publications *Books:* 1. *Money* (Schenkman, 1963); 2. *The Cost of Trucking; Econometric Analysis* (with others), (Northwestern Univ. Press, 1964); 3. *Economic Theory: Equilibrium and Change* (Wiley, 1968); 4. *Resource Allocation and Economic Policy,* co-ed. (with M. G. Allingham), (Macmillan, 1976); 5. *New Directions in Economic Policy* (Macmillan, 1978); 6. *Modern Monetary Theory* (Macmillan, 1985).

Articles: 1.'Demand for household refrigeration in the United States', in *Studies in the Demand for Durable Goods,* ed. A. C. Harberger (Univ. Chicago Press, 1959); 2. 'The economics of tie-in sales', *REStat* 42(10), Feb. 1960; 3. 'A theory of full line forcing', *Northwestern Univ. Law Rev.* 56(1), March–April 1960; 4. 'On the invariance of demand for cash and other assets' (with R. W. Clower), *REStud.,* 28(1), Oct. 1960; 5. 'Measurement of quality changes in durable goods', *MS,* 29, Sept. 1961; 6. 'Colonial currency & contemporary monetary theory: a review article', *Explor. Entrepreneurial Hist.,* N.S. 3(3), 1966; 7. 'Some more Keynesian economics', *EI,* 13(1), March 1975; 8. 'Stock-flow analysis', in *Encyclopedia of Economics,* ed. D Greenwald (McGraw-Hill, 1982); 9. 'Diffusion of knowledge based products', *EI,* 22(4), Oct 1984.

Principal Contributions I should select the following four contributions. Influenced by A. Harberger and G. Chow, I was concerned to obtain correct models of stock-flow goods that could be estimated. This led to contri-butions to measurement of quality change in durable goods and, after meeting R. Clower in 1957, to stock/flow formalisations that have helped explain short- and long-run effects of money supply changes and effects of changes in the cost of production of money. Owing directly to lectures by M. Friedman (in turn influenced by A. Director), I became interested in tied sales. I took the analysis beyond simple price discrimination (metering devices, for example) into the field of general excise taxation, owing much to Hotelling.

I have contributed to understanding of time in economic theory — owing much to J. Robinson. In 1963 I showed that the dynamics of models of *tatônnement* are not robust for deep, properly 'macro' theory; and in 1968 that the stationary state of Marshall and Pigou is rooted in physical science. As far back as 1963, I tried to show that disequilibrium in macroeconomics cannot usefully be worked up from Walrasian models. Rather, disequilibrium can have two proper connotations. One is 'weak': agents (in general, price quoters) may be disappointed or surprised by their results (an idea obviously related to Clower's dual constraint). The other is 'strong': agents may not be able collectively to solve the welfare-optimisation problem conjugate to their collective decisions on prices and outputs. In neither case is disequilibrium properly characterised by the excess demand or supply derived from reaction to the auctioneer's quotations. If this point ever gets properly understood widely in the profession, I may be able to claim a part of the credit.

BUTT, Issac*

Dates and Birthplace 1813–79, Donegal, Ireland.

Posts Held Lawyer; Whately Prof. Econ., Trinity Coll., Dublin, 1836–41.

Degrees BA, LLB, MA, LLD Trinity Coll., Dublin, 1835, 1836, 1840, 1840.

Offices and Honours MP, 1852–65, 1871–9; Leader, Home Rule Party, 1871–9.

Publications *Books:* 1. *A Practical Treatise on the New Law of Compensa-*

tion to Tenants in Ireland (1871); 2. *Home Government for Ireland* (1874).

Career Politican who, as leader of the Home Rule movement, formulated the programme later adopted by the Irish Nationalist Party. Whilst holding the Whately Chair in Dublin, he contributed to the Irish tradition on value theory initiated by Longfield. His programme for Ireland included major land reforms.

Secondary Literature R. D. C. Black, 'Trinity College, Dublin, and the Theory of Value, 1823–63', *Ec*, N.S. 12, Aug. 1945.

BUTZ, William F.

Born 1943, Lafayette, IN, USA.
Current Post Assoc. Dir. Demographic Fields, US Bureau Census, 1982–.
Past Posts Econ., Sr. Econ., Deputy Dir. Labor and Pop. Stud. Program, Rand Corp., 1970–8, 1978–82; Vis. Lect. Econ., UCLA, 1976–82.
Degrees BA Indiana Univ., 1965.
Offices and Honours Danforth Grad. Fellow.
Principal Fields of Interest 112 Economic Development Model and Theories; 841 Demographic Economics; 851 Human Capital.
Publications *Articles:* 1. 'Measurement of health and nutrition effects of large-scale nutrition intervention projects' (with J. P. Habicht), in *Estimating the Impact of Nutrition and Health Programs*, ed. R. Klein (Plenum Press, 1979); 2. 'The emergency of countercyclical US fertility' (with M. P. Ward), *AER*, 69(3), June 1979; 3. 'Completed fertility and its timing' (with M. P. Ward), *JPE*, 88(5), Oct. 1980; 4. 'The role of breastfeeding in economic development: a theoretical exposition', in *Research in Human Capital and Development*, 2, ed. I. Siradgeldin (JAI Press, 1981); 5. 'Household composition and interhousehold exchange in Malaysia' (with J. E. Stan), *Pop. and Devlp. Rev.*, Aug. 1982; 6. 'Assessing socioeconomic correlates of birthweight in peninsular Malaysia: ethnic differences and changes over time' (with J. DaVanzo and J. P. Habicht),

Social Science and Medicine, 1983; 7. 'Environmental factors in the relationship between breastfeeding and infant mortality: the role of water and sanitation in Malaysia' (with J. P. Habicht and J. DaVanzo), *Amer. J. Epidemiology*, July 1984; 8. 'The contraceptive role of breastfeeding' (with J. P. Habicht and L. Meyers, J. DaVanzo), *Pop. Stud.*, Summer 1985.

Principal Contributions My interest in economic research began with the interactions between microeconomics of the family, on the one hand, and nutrition, health, and fertility, on the other hand. At that time (early 1970s), no appropriate microdata existed, so I initiated and designed two large surveys in Guatemala and Malaysia to fill this gap. Much of my career has been spent in collaborating with demographers, epidemologists and other economists – – analysing their data and publishing the results. These interests spilled over into analyses of US fertility. In teaching economic development courses, I have concentrated on the microeconomics of development. Accepting a job in charge of the demographic data and research at the US Census Bureau was a major career shift — toward broader subject matters and toward administration.

BYRON, Raymond Peter

Born 1941, Sydney, New S. Wales, Australia.
Current Post Reader Econometrics, ANU, Canberra, Australia, 1979–.
Past Posts Temp. Lect., Univ. Western Australia, 1965, Univ. Adelaide, 1966; Res. Officer, NIESR, London, 1968–9; Res. Fellow, Fellow, ANU, 1969–72; Vis. Prof., CORE, Louvain, Belgium, 1972–3; Reader Econometrics, ANU, 1972–5; Res. Officer, Devlp. Res. Center, World Bank, USA, 1976–8; Vis. Prof., Univ. Florida, 1984.
Degrees BEc Univ. Western Australia, 1964; MSc, PhD LSE, 1965, 1969.
Offices and Honours Bowley Prize, LSE, 1969; Member, Em Soc.
Editorial Duties Ed. Boards, *Em, Numerical Analysis, Devlp. Econ.*
Principal Fields of Interest 211 Econometric Methods.

Publications *Articles:* 1. 'A simple method for estimating systems of separable demand equations', *REStud.*, 37(2), April 1970; 2. 'The restricted Aitken estimation of sets of demand relations', *Em*, 38(6), Nov. 1970; 3. 'Testing structural specification by using the unrestricted reduced form', *Em*, 42(5), Sept. 1974; 4. 'Testing for misspecification in econometric systems using full information', *Int ER*, 13(3), Oct. 1972; 5. 'Efficient estimation and inference in large econometric systems', *Em*, 45(6), Sept. 1977; 6. 'The estimation of large social account matrices', *JRSS*, 142(4), 1979; 7. 'Linearised estimation of nonlinear single equation functions', *Int ER*, 24(1), Feb. 1983; 8. 'A note on the estimation of symmetric systems', *Em*, 50(6), Nov. 1982.

Principal Contributions My early efforts related to testing the validity of economic hypotheses — confronting the hypothesis with the data. Applications were in demand analysis (symmetry of income-compensated substitution effects, separability of utility functions) and to the specification of macroeconometric models. During this period (1966–9) my work probably represented one of the earliest formal applications of Wald tests in econometrics. Subsequently I became interested in computational and numerical problems relating to econometrics with applications to systems of equations, large macro models, social accounting matrices, and large symmetric systems. More recently I have written on nonlinear estimation procedures and the tendency of asymptotic test statistics to over-reject infinite sample situations. My current interests relate to developing countries and to applying econometrics in data-poor situations.

C

CAGAN, Phillip D.

Born 1927, Seattle, WA, USA.
Current Post Prof. Econ., Columbia Univ., New York City, USA, 1966–.
Past Posts Res. Ass. Sr. Res. NBER Staff, 1953–4, 1965; Ass. Prof., Univ. Chicago, 1955–8; Assoc. Prof., Prof.,

Brown Univ., 1959–61, 1962–4; Vis. Assoc. Prof., Carnegie-Mellon Univ., 1962.
Degrees BA UCLA, 1948; MA, PhD Univ. Chicago, 1951, 1954.
Offices and Honours Ford Faculty Fellow, 1963; Fellow, Em Soc, 1975–.
Editorial Duties Ed. Board, *AER*, 1971–3; Advisory Board, *JMCB*, 1975–; Assoc. Ed., *REStat.*, 1972–.
Principal Fields of Interest 311 Domestic Monetary and Financial Theory and Policy; 131 Economic Fluctuations; 134 Inflation.
Publications *Books:* 1. *Determinants and Effects of Changes in the Money Stock 1875–1960* (NBER, 1965); 2. *The Channels of Monetary Effects on Interest Rates* (NBER, 1972); 3. *The Hydra-Headed Monster: The Problem of Inflation in the United States* (AEI, 1974); 4. *The Financial Effects of Inflation* (with R. Lipsey), (Ballinger, 1978); 5. *Persistent Inflation* (Columbia Univ. Press, 1979); 6. *The Consumer Price Index — Issues and Alternatives* (with G. Moore), (AEI, 1981).

Articles: 1. 'The monetary dynamics of hyperinflations', in *Studies in the Quantity Theory of Money*, ed. M. Friedman (Univ. Chicago Press, 1956); 2. 'Why do we use money in open market operations?', *JPE*, 66, Feb. 1958; 3. 'The demand for currency relative to total money supply', *JPE*, 66, Aug. 1958; 4. 'Measuring quality changes and the purchasing power of money: an exploratory study of automobiles', *Nat. Banking Rev.*, 3 Dec. 1965, repr. in *Price Indexes and Quality Change*, ed. Z. Griliches (Harvard Univ. Press, 1971); 5. 'Changes in the cyclical behavior of interest rates', *REStat.*, 48, Aug. 1966; 6. 'The lag in monetary policy as implied by the time pattern of monetary effects on interest rates' (with A. Gandolfi), *AER*, 59(2), May, 1969; 7. 'Has the growth of money substitutes hindered monetary policy?' (with A. J. Schwartz), *JMCB*, 7(2), May 1975; 8. 'Changes in the recession behavior of wholesale prices in the 1920s and post-world war II', *Explor. Econ. Res.*, 2, Winter 1975; 9. 'Financial innovations and the erosion of monetary controls', in *Contemporary Economic Problems*, ed. W. Fellner

(AEI, 1979); 10. 'The choice among monetary aggregates as targets and guides for monetary policy', *JMCB*, 14(4), Nov. 1982.

Principal Contributions After my early study of hyperinflations, the study of the US money supply occupied me for many years. While still associated with the NBER, I also did related studies of interest rates and saving behaviour. But my research interests have mainly involved issues in current monetary policy and the nature of inflation and problems of combating it. A major problem is the slow adjustment of prices, and several of my studies focussed on price behaviour. I expect to continue writing about the problem of combating inflation and in particular examining further how to conduct an anti-inflationary monetary policy under financial innovations, and how to fashion monetary controls in the payments regime of the future.

CAIN, Glen G.

Born 1933, Chicago, IL, USA.
Current Post Prof., Univ. Wisconsin-Madison, USA, 1963–.
Degrees BA Lake Forest Coll., 1955; MA Univ. Cal. Berkeley, 1956; PhD Univ. Chicago, 1960.
Offices and Honours Member, Nat. Commission Employment Unemployment Stats., 1977–9.
Editorial Duties Ed., *JHR*, 1973–5.
Principal Fields of Interest 820 Labour Markets; 851 Human Capital.
Publications *Books: 1. Married Women in the Labor Force* (Univ. Chicago Press, 1966); 2. *Income Maintenance and Labor Supply: Econometric Studies* (with H. Watts), (Markham Press, 1973).
Articles: 1. 'Problems in making policy inferences from the Coleman report' (with H. Watts), *Amer. Sociological Rev.*, April 1970; 2. 'Estimation of a model of labor supply, fertility, and wages of married women' (with M. Dooley), *JPE*, 84(4), pt. 2, Aug. 1976; 3. 'The challenge of segmented labor market theories to orthodox theory: a survey', *JEL*, 14(4), Dec. 1976; 4. 'Issues in the analysis of selection bias' (with

B. Barnow and A. Goldberger), in *Evaluation Studies Review Annual*, 5, eds. E. Stromsdorfer and G. Farkas (Sage Publications, 1980); 5. 'Welfare economics of policies toward women', *J Labor E*, 2, pt. 2, Oct. 1984; 6. 'The effect of unions on wages in hospitals', in *Research in Labor Economics*, ed. R. Ehrenberg (JAI Press, 1981).

CAIRNCROSS, Alexander Kirkland

Born 1911, Lesmahagow, Strathclyde, Scotland.
Current Post Retired, Fellow, St Anthony's Coll. Oxford, 1978–.
Past Posts Lect., Polit. Econ., Univ. Glasgow, 1935–9; Lect., Agric. Econ., West of Scotland Agric Coll., Glasgow, 1935–9; Econ. Ass., UK War Cabinet Office, 1940–1; Admin. Officer, UK Board of Trade, 1941; Ass. Dir., Deputy Dir., Dir., UK Ministry Aircraft Production, 1941–5; Econ. Advisory Panel, Berlin, 1945–6; Staff, *The Economist*, 1946; Econ. Advisor, UK Board of Trade, 1946–9; Dir., Econ. Division, OEEC, 1950; Prof. Appl. Econ., Univ. Glasgow, 1951–61; Dir., Econ. Devlp. Inst., IBRD, Washington, 1955–6; Econ. Adviser, UK Govt., 1961–4; Head, UK Govt. Econ. Service, 1964–9; Master, St Peter's Coll. Oxford, 1969–78; Vis. Prof., Brookings Inst., Washington, 1972; Leverhulme Vis. Prof., Bangalore, Delhi, Bombay, 1980–1.
Degrees MA Univ. Glasgow, 1933; PhD Univ. Camb., 1936; Hon. Dr, eight universities; Hon. Fellow, LSE, St Peter's Coll. Oxford.
Offices and Honours Fellow, BA, 1961; Pres., RES, 1968–70; Pres., Scottish Econ. Soc., 1969–71; Pres., BAAS, 1970–1; Foreign Hon. Member, AAAS, 1973; Council Management, NIESR; Leverhulme Emeritus Fellow, 1983–; Chancellor, Univ. Glasgow, 1972–.
Editorial Duties Ed., *SJPE*, 1954–61, *Social and Econ. Stud.* (Univ. Glasgow), 1953–61.
Principal Fields of Interest 012 Teaching of Economics; 113 Economic Planning; 134 Inflation and Deflation.
Publications *Books: 1. Introduction to Economics* (Butterworths, 1944,

1982); 2. *Home and Foreign Investment, 1870–1913* (CUP, 1953, Kelley, 1967); 3. *Factors in Economic Development* (A&U, 1962; transl., Spanish, 1964); 4. *Economic Development and the Atlantic Provinces* (Atlantic Provinces Res. Board, 1961); 5. *Monetary Policy in a Mixed Economy* (Almqvist Wiksell, 1960); 6. *Essays in Economic Management* (A&U, 1971); 7. *Control of Long-term International Capital Movements* (Brookings Inst., 1973); 8. *Inflation, Growth and International Finance* (with B. Eichengreen), (A&U, 1975); 9. *Sterling in Decline* (Blackwell, 1983); 10. *Years of Recovery 1945–51* (Methuen, 1984).

Articles: 1. 'Academics and policy-makers', in *Changing Perceptions of Economic Policy*, ed. F. Cairncross (Methuen, 1981); 2. 'The relationship between monetary and fiscal policy', in *Proceedings of the British Academy* (OUP, 1981); 3. 'The post-war years 1945-77', in *The Economic History of Britain since 1700*, 2, eds. B. Houd and D. McCloskey (CUP, 1981); 4. 'Reflections on innovation', in *Inflation, Development and Integration*, ed. J. K. Bowers (Leeds Univ. Press, 1979); 5. 'The limitations of shadow rates', in *Employment, Income Distribution and Development Strategy*, ed. A. K. Cairncross and M. Puri (Macmillan, 1976); 6. 'Economic growth and stagnation in the United Kingdom before the first world war', in *The Theory and Experience of Economic Development*, eds. M. Gersovitz, *et al.* (A&U, 1982); 7. 'The market and the state', in *The Market and the State*, eds. T. Wilson and A. S. Skinner (OUP, 1976); 8. 'What is de-industrialisation?', in *De-industrialisation*, ed. F. Blackaby (Heinemann, 1979).

Principal Contributions My pre-war interests from 1931 onwards were mainly in international economics; beginning with an undergraduate thesis on the transfer problem, followed by a doctoral dissertation on the interaction of home and foreign investment along Keynesian lines and leading on to studies of labour integration, capital movements and building cycles that were interrupted by the war. All of these studies (parts of which were eventually published in 1953) mix theory with an examination of the historical record, paying due regard to the uncertainties of the statistical data. In an effort to make economic theory and its practical implications more intelligible to the layman (and to myself), I wrote an elementary textbook which was virtually completed at the outbreak of war in 1939. Wartime experience sharpened my interest in problems of economic management and policy and in the genesis and impact of technical change. It seemed to me then that current treatment of economic growth (itself a neglected subject) overlooked the importance of managerial factors, gave far too much prominence to capital accumulation and tended to treat technical change, mistakenly, as exogenous.

Since 1939 I have spent only nine years as a university teacher. In the middle of administrative and advisory duties, my contributions to economics have been limited to essays and addresses, reports, prefaces, reviews and editorial comment. In the 1950s I took an interest in regional and industrial problems, then in economic development, and finally in monetary theory. In the 1960s and 1970s I wrote on a wide variety of subjects in applied economics, mainly from the angle of planning and economic management and revisited briefly, after forty years, the subject of international capital movements. After my retirement in 1978, I returned to the economic history of the recent past, with occasional forays into analysis of current policy.

CAIRNES, John Elliott*

Dates and Birthplace 1823–75, C. Louth, Ireland.

Posts Held Whately Prof. Econ., Univ. Dublin, 1856–61; Prof. Polit. Econ. and Jurisprudence, Univ. Galway, 1859–70; Prof. Polit. Econ., Univ. Coll. London, 1866–72.

Degrees BA Trinity Coll., Dublin, 1848; MA Univ. Dublin, 1854.

Publications *Books:* 1. *The Character and Logical Method of Political Economy* (1857, 1965); 2. *The Slave Power* (1862); 3. *Essays in Political Economy,*

Theoretical and Applied (1873, 1965);
4. *Some Leading Principles of Political Economy Newly Expounded* (1874, 1965).

Career Often referred to as 'the last of the classical economists', he was the author of what was the definitive statement of the methodology of the classical school in *The Character and Logical Method. . . .* He showed his ability to apply this method to particular cases in a number of studies, the most influential of which was *The Slave Power*. This analysis of the social consequences of an economy based on slavery did much to influence British opinion in favour of the Unionists in the American Civil War. His *Leading Principles . . .* was an attempt to restore the strength of the classical structure damaged by his mentor's (J. S. Mill's) abandonment of the wages fund doctrine in 1869. It attempted, among other things, to generalise the concept of non-competing groups to both domestic and international trade.

Secondary Literature R. D. C. Black, 'Cairnes, John Elliott', *IESS*, 2.

CAMERON, Rondo Emmett

Born 1925, Linden, TX, USA.
Current Post William Rand Kenan, Jr. Prof., Emory Univ., Atlanta, GA, USA, 1970–.
Past Posts Instr. Econ., Yale Univ., 1951–2; Ass. Prof., Assoc. Prof. Econ. and Hist., Univ. Wisconsin-Madison, 1952–6, 1957–61, 1961–9; Vis. Prof. Econ., Univ. Chicago, 1956–7; Fulbright Vis. Prof., Univ. Glasgow, 1962–3; Special Field Representative, Rockefeller Foundation Latin America, Santiago, Chile, 1965–7.
Degrees BA, MA Yale Univ., 1948, 1949; PhD Univ. Chicago, 1952.
Offices and Honours Fulbright Scholar, France, 1950–1; Guggenheim Foundation Fellow, 1954–5, 1970–1; Fellow, Center Advanced Study Behavioral Sciences, Stanford, CA, 1958–9; Tawney Lect., EHS, 1963; Vice-Pres., Pres., EHA, 1970–1, 1974–5; Fellow, Woodrow Wilson Center for Scholars, Washington, DC, 1974–5;

Member, Exec. Comm., Internat. EHA, 1974–86.
Editorial Duties Amer. Rev. Corresp., *EHR*, 1961–5; Rev. Ed., Ed., *JEH*, 1968–9, 1975–81; Ed. Board, *Social Science Hist. Revue Internat. d'Histoire de la Banque, Zeitschrift für Unternehmensgeschichte.*
Principal Fields of Interest 044 European Economic History; 122 Economic Studies of More Industrialised Countries; 123 Comparative Economic Studies.
Publications *Books:* 1. *France and the Economic Development of Europe, 1800–1914* (Princeton Univ. Press, 1961, Octagon Books, 1975; transls., French, Spanish, 1971); 2. *The European World: A History* (with J. Blum and T. G. Barnes), (Little, Brown, 1966, 1971), and as *The Emergence of the European World* and *The European World Since 1815: Triumph and Transition* (Little, Brown, 1970); 3. *Banking in the Early Stages of Industrialization* (with O. Crisp, H. T. Patrick, and R. Tilly), (OUP, 1967; transls., Japanese, Nikon Hyoronska, 1973, Spanish, Editorial Tecnos, 1974, Italian, Societa editrice il Mulino, 1975); 4. *Civilizations, Western and World* (with R. S. Lopez, T. G. Barnes and J. Blum), 2 vols (Little, Brown, 1975); 5. *Europe in Review*, co-ed. (with G. L. Hosse, H. G. Hill and M. B. Petrovich), (Rand, McNally, 1964); 6. *Essays in French Economic History*, ed. (Richard D. Irwin, 1970); 7. *Civilization Since Waterloo*, ed. (F. E. Peacock, 1971); 8. *Banking and Economic Development: Some Lessons of History*, ed. (OUP, 1972).
Articles: 1. 'The credit mobilier and the economic development of Europe', *JPE*, 61, Dec. 1953; 2. 'Le développement économique de l'Europe au XIXe siècle: le rôle de la France', *Annales Economies, Sociétés, Civilisations*, April–June 1957; transl., Arabic, UNESCO, 1957; 3. 'Economic growth and stagnation in France, 1815–1914', *J. Modern Hist*, 30, March 1958, repr. in *The Experience of Economic Growth: Case Studies in Economic History*, ed. B. E. Supple (Alfred A. Knopf, 1959), and *The Economic Development of Western Europe*, 4, eds. W.

C. Scoville and J. C. Laforce (D. C. Heath, 1970), and Bobbs-Merrill *Reprints in European History* (Bobbs-Merrill, 1971), and *Europe and the Industrial Revolution* ed. S. Lieberman (Schenkmann 1972); 4. 'Imperialism and technology', in *Technology in Western Civilizations*, eds. M. Kranzberg and C. W. Pursell, Jr. (OUP, 1967); 5. 'Some lessons of history for developing nations', *AER*, 57(2), May 1967; transls. Spanish, *Cuadernos de economia*, April 1967, Portuguese, *Ensaios Sobre Cafe e Desenvolvento Economico* (Inst. Brasileiro do Cafe, 1973); 6. 'The international diffusion of technology and economic development in the modern economic epoch', in *Sixth International Congress of Economic History, 5 themes* (Internat. EHA, 1974; transl., Portuguese *A Moderna Historia Economica*, eds. C. M. Pelaez and M. Buescu (Inst. Brasileiro do Cafe, 1976)); 7. 'Economic history pure and applied', *JEH*, 36, March 1976; 8. 'Les origens historiques due sous-développement économique contemporaine', *Mondes en Développement*, 19, 1977; 9. 'Technology, institutions and long-term economic change', in *Economics in the Long View*, 1, *Models and Methodology*, eds. C. P. Kindleberger and G. di Tella (Macmillan, 1982); 10. 'French economic growth: a radical revision' (with C. E. Freedeman), *Social Science Hist.*, 7, Winter 1983.

Principal Contributions Application of economic principles to the elucidation and understanding of concrete historical events and, conversely, the application of historical knowledge to the improvement and understanding of economic principles.

CAMPBELL, Colin Dearborn

Born 1917, Cooperstown, NY, USA.
Current Post Loren M. Berry Prof. Econ., Dartmouth Coll., Hanover, NH, USA, 1966–.
Past Posts Econ., Board of Governors, Fed. Reserve System, Washington, DC, 1954–6; Ass. Prof., Assoc. Prof., Dartmouth Coll., 1956–66; Econ., Brookings Tax Advisory Group, Republic Korea, 1960; Dir., Dartmouth Nat.

Bank, Hanover, NH, 1961–; Dir., Thomas Jefferson Center Foundation, Charlottesville, VA, 1972–; Dir., Student Loan Marketing Assoc., Washington, DC, 1973–5; Adjunct Scholar, AEI, 1974–.
Degrees BA Harvard Univ., 1938; MA Univ. Iowa, 1941; PhD Univ. Chicago, 1950.
Principal Fields of Interest 310 Domestic Monetary and Financial Theory and Institutions; 324 State and Local Government Finance; 915 Social Security.
Publications *Books:* 1. *An Introduction to Money and Banking* (with R. G. Campbell), (Dryden Press, 1972, 1984); 2. *A Comparative Study of the Fiscal Systems of New Hampshire and Vermont, 1940–1974* (with R. G. Campbell), (Wheelabrator Foundation, 1976); 3. *Income Redistribution*, ed. (AEI, 1977); 4. *Financing Social Security*, ed. (AEI, 1979); 5. *Social Security's Financial Crises* (Internat. Inst. Econ. Res., 1983); 6. *Controlling the Cost of Social Security*, ed. (D. C. Heath, 1984).

Articles: 1. 'Are property tax rates increasing?', *JPE*, 59(5), Oct. 1951; 2. 'Hyperinflation in China, 1937–49' (with G. C. Tullock), *JPE*, 62(3), June 1954; 3. 'Soviet price reductions for consumer goods, 1948–54' (with R. G. Campbell), *AER*, 45(4), Sept. 1955; 4. 'Some little-understood aspects of Korea's monetary and fiscal systems' (with G. C. Tullock), *AER*, 47(3), June 1957; 5. 'Social insurance in the United States: a program in search of an explanation', *J Law E*, 12(2), Oct. 1969; 6. 'The velocity of money and the rate of inflation: recent experiences in South Korea and Brazil', in *Varieties of Monetary Experience*, ed. D. Meiselman (Univ. Chicago Press, 1970); 7. 'Conflicting views on the effect of old-age and survivors insurance on retirement' (with R. G. Campbell), *EI*, 14(3), Sept. 1976.

Principal Contributions I teach undergraduate courses on money and banking and the principles of economics and have co-authored with my wife a textbook on money and banking, now in its fifth edition. My PhD dissertation was on property taxation, and in recent years I have returned to that topic. I am interested in why governments of states vary in efficiency, and believe that greater reliance on property taxation may have the desirable effect of increasing efficiency. A second topic of my research has been inflation. This involves examining how people attempt to adjust to inflation and the effect of inflation on the velocity of money. A third area of my research and writing is social security: primarily the difficulties encountered in indexing old-age and survivors' benefits for inflation, the unexpected financial problems that now plague the system, the surprising cuts that US Congress has made in some types of benefits, and the redistributional effects of social security.

CAMPBELL, Robert

Born 1921, San Mateo, CA, USA.
Current Post Prof. Econ., Univ. Oregon, 1952–.
Degrees BA, PhD, Univ. Cal. Berkeley, 1947, 1953; BS US Merchant Marine Academy, 1960.
Offices and Honours AAAS.
Principal Fields of Interest 031 History of Economic Thought.
Publications *Books:* 1. *People and Markets* (Benjamin/Cummings, 1978).
Articles: 1. *Libraries of the Pacific Northwest*, contrib. (Univ. Washington Press, 1960); 2. *The Social Sciences View School Administration*, contrib. (Prentice-Hall, 1965); 3. 'The demand for higher education in the US, 1919–1964' (with B. N. Siegel), *AER*, 57(3), June 1967; 4. 'Economics and health in the history of ideas', *Annales Cisalpines d'Histoire Sociale*', serie I, 1975; 5. 'The Keynesian revolution 1920–70', in *Fontana Economic History of Europe: The Twentieth Century – 1*, 5, ed. C. Cipolla (Fontana, 1979).

CANARD, Nicolas Francois*

Dates and Birthplace 1750–1833, France.
Posts Held Prof. Maths., Coll. de Moulins, France.
Publications *Books:* 1. *Principes d'économie politique* (1801); 2. *Mém-oires sur les causes qui produisent la stagnation et le décroissement du commerce en France* (1826).
Career Canard's *Principes . . .* , whilst otherwise unremarkable, had the distinction of being recognised by the French Academy, which failed to notice Cournot and Walras. The book is sometimes claimed to be an early example of mathematical economics, but its use of mathematics is in fact confined to some algebraic formulas.

CANES, Michael Edwin

Born 1941, Jerusalem, Israel.
Current Post Vice Pres., American Petroleum Inst., Washington DC.
Past Posts Econ. US Center Naval Analyses, Arlington, VA, 1969–72; Ass. Prof., Grad. School Management, Univ. Rochester, 1972–4; Sr. Econ. Dep. Dir., Dir. Policy Analysis Dept., Amer. Petroleum Inst., Washington DC, 1974–8, 1978–82.
Degrees BS (Maths.), Univ. Chicago, 1963; MBA Grad. School Bus., Univ. Chicago, 1965; MSc LSE, 1966; PhD UCLA, 1970.
Offices and Honours Exec. Board, Washington, DC, Chapter, Internat. Assoc. Energy Econ.
Principal Fields of Interest 720 Natural Resources; 610 Industrial Organization and Public Policy; 630 Industry Studies.
Publications *Articles:* 1. 'Discounting and the evaluation of public investments: comment', *Appl. Econ.*, 5(3), Sept. 1973; 2. 'The public interest in restricting the quality of team play', in *Government and the Sport Business* (Brookings Inst., 1974); 3. 'The simple economics of incentive contracting: note', *AER*, 86(3), June 1976; 4. 'The market for pro football betting', in *Gambling and Society*, ed. W. R. Eadington (Charles C. Thomas, 1976); 5. 'Stock prices and the publication of second-hand information' (with P. Lloyd-Davies), *J. Bus.*, 51(1), Jan. 1978; 6. 'The divestiture of horizontally diversified petroleum companies', *Oil & Gas Tax Q.*, 27(2), Dec. 1978; 7. 'Pipelines and public policy' (with D. A. Norman), in *Oil Pipelines and Public*

Policy, ed. E. J. Mitchell (AE Inst., 1979); 8. 'Rational United States energy policies', *Middle East Review*, 16(4), Summer 1984; 9. 'Long-term contracts and market forces in the natural gas market' (with D. A. Norman), *J. Energy and Dev.*, 10(1), Autumn 1984.

Principal Contributions My principal contributions have taken the form of utilisation of economic analysis to inform private and public policy-makers of the consequences of actions taken in the energy area. This has involved utilisation of two distinct skills; application of theory and statistical methods to energy-related problems, and translation of results into language and policy choices familiar to decision makers. Most of this work has involved US oil and gas markets. Issues there have included price controls, taxation, the vertical and horizontal diversification of energy companies, contract terms between sellers and buyers of raw energy, and the rate of leasing of publicly owned lands. My contributions have encompassed theoretical explanations of vertical and horizontal diversification of energy companies, empirical tests of alternative explanations of such diversification, theoretical explanation of various terms in producer-pipeline natural gas contracts, and explanation and testing of alternative theories of oil pipeline sizing decisions. Generally speaking, the results of my analyses have implied the relaxation of socially imposed constraints on energy markets, or a refraining from initial imposition. While a very large number of factors bear on social decisions in energy, those implications are consistent with the general thrust of US energy policy over the past decade or so.

CANNAN, Edwin*

Dates and Birthplace 1861–1935, Madeira, Spain.

Posts Held Lect., Prof. Econ., LSE, 1895–1926.

Degrees BA, MA Univ. Oxford, 1884, 1887; Hon. LLD Univ. Glasgow; Hon. LittD Univ. Manchester.

Offices Pres., Econ. Section, BAAS, 1902, 1931; Pres., RES, 1932–4.

Publications *Books:* 1. *Elementary Political Economy* (1888); 2. *A History of the Theories of Production and Distribution in English Political Economy From 1776 to 1848* (1898, 1917, 1953); 3. *The Economic Outlook* (1912); 4. *Wealth* (1914); 5. *Money* (1918); 6. *Review of Economic Theory* (1929, 1953); 7. *An Economist's Protest* (1927); 8. *Modern Currency and the Regulation of its Value* (1931).

Career His edition of Smith's *Wealth of Nations* (1904) is perhaps his chief monument because of the outstanding quality of the introduction and explanatory notes. However, his work as a teacher at LSE, where he inspired several generations of students, is another source of his reputation. His teaching was not particularly modern in terms of tools and techniques, but it was based on a deep knowledge of the great writers in the subject which also informs many of his books, including his one undisputed masterpiece, *A History of the Theories of Production and Distribution*. The outspoken and commonsensical style of his various works make them still readable and useful.

Secondary Literature A. L. Bowley, 'Obituary: Edwin Cannan', *EJ*, 45, June 1935.

CANTILLON, Richard*

Dates and Birthplace 1680(?)–1734, Ireland(?)

Posts Held Banker.

Publications *Books:* 1. *Essay on the Nature of Commerce* (1755, 1959).

Career Little definite is known about Cantillon except that he was Irish and turned briefly from a successful banking career, mainly in France, to write one of the most outstanding works in the history of the subject – the *Essay*. ... This was circulated in manuscript for many years after his death and was extremely influential, at least throughout the eighteenth century. However, it was necessary for Jevons to rediscover it in 1881 after a prolonged neglect. His ideas on population, determination of prices, wages and interest, the role of the entrepreneur, banking, and the influence of money supply on the economy are increasingly quoted and appreciated.

Secondary Literature J. J. Spengler, 'Cantillon, Richard', *IESS*, 2; A. E. Murphy, 'Richard Cantillon — An Irish Banker in Paris', in *Economists and the Irish Economy*, ed. A. E. Murphy (Irish Academic Press, 1984).

CARAVALE, Giovanni Alfredo

Born 1935, Rome, Italy.
Current Post Prof. Polit. Econ., Univ. Rome La Sapienza, 1979–.
Past Posts Lect. Econ. Fiscal Policy, Univ. Pescara, 1964–5; Lect., Prof., Polit. Econ., Univ. Peruvia, 1968–72, 1972–9.
Degrees Dottorato Univ. Rome, 1957; Libera Docenza Universitaria, 1963; Prof. Straordinario Econ. Politica, 1972; Prof. Ordinario Econ. Politica, 1975.
Offices and Honours Member, Soc. Italiana degli Economisti.
Editorial Duties Ed., *Seminari de Economia, Collana dell'Istituto di Economia* (Univ. Perugia).
Principal Fields of Interest 010 General Economics, Theory, History, Systems; 100 Economic Growth, Development, Planning, Fluctuations; 600 Industrial Organisation, Technological Change, Industry Studies.
Publications *Books:* 1. *Il Creditor al Consumo* (Utet, 1960); 2. *Cicli Economici e Trend* (Giuffre, 1961); 3. *Fluttuazioni e Sviluppo nella Dinamica di Squilibrio* (Iscona, 1967); 4. *Un Modello Ricardiano di Sviluppo Economico* (with D. Tosato), (Boringhieri, 1974; transl. as *Ricardo and the Theory of Value, Distribution and Growth* (Routledge & Kegan Paul, 1980); 5. *The Crisis in Economic Theories*, ed. (Franco Angeli, 1983); 6. *The Legacy of Ricardo*, ed. (Blackwell, 1984).
Articles: 1. 'Oligopolio differenziato e processo di sviluppo', *Econ Internat.*, 18, 1965; 2. 'Aspetti economici dell'evoluzione tecnologica', *Annali della Faculta di Econ. e Commercio di Perugia*, 1977; 3. 'Politica dei redditi', *Enciclopedia Italiana*, 4, Appendice (1977); 4. 'Saggio di profitto e merce

tipo nella teoria di Ricardo' (with D. Tosato), *Rivista Politica Econ.*, 1, 1978; 5. 'L'economia Italiana nel commercio internazionale', *Annali della Faculta di Econ e Commercio di Perugia*, 1978; 6. 'Note sulla teoria Ricardiana del valore, della distribuzione e dello sviluppo', *Giornale degli Economisti e Annali di Economia*, 3–4, 1982.
Principal Contributions The analysis of the economic effects of consumer credit especially with reference to the cyclical behaviour of the economy. Hence the interest in the connection between fluctuations and long-term growth, and the formulation of a comprehensive scheme for a joint interpretation of these two types of phenomenon. In this context, the analytical definition (1967) of a dynamic 'wages function' (relation between rate of increase in wages and unemployment) in terms later repeated in the literature, and the study of the role played by oligopolistic market structures with product differentiation. The rigorous definition of a unifying interpretative schema for Ricardo's problems of value, distribution and growth in which the central problem of Ricardo's investigation — the determination of the rate of profit and its relation to the accumulation process in the presence of diminishing returns — finds a satisfactory and general solution. Building on these results, the clarification of the relationship between Ricardo's theory of value and P. Sraffa's theory of prices and distribution. The indication of the reasons for the present crisis in the ultimate foundations of both mainstream and unorthodox theories — viewed as a necessary step in any attempt at 'reconstruction' of economics as a science.

CARDOZO, Jacob Newton*

Dates and Birthplace 1786–1873, GA, USA.
Posts Held Journalist and newspapers ed.
Publications *Books:* 1. *Notes on Political Economy* (1826).
Career A critic of both Malthus and Ricardo, chiefly on the grounds that their theories did not fit American circumstances. In his view, the Ricardian

theory of distribution did not sufficiently take into account the potential for expansion of manufacturing, and the Malthusian tendency of population growth to outstrip the food supply was merely a product of the imperfect social conditions of the Old World. He was a strong supporter of free trade.

Secondary Literature M. M. Leiman, *Jacob N. Cardozo* (Columbia Univ. Press, 1966).

CAREY, Henry Charles*

Dates and Birthplace 1793–1879, Philadelphia, PA, USA.
Posts Held Publisher and other business interests.
Publications *Books:* 1. *Essay on the Rate of Wages* (1835, 1960); 2. *Principles of Political Economy*, 3 vols. (1837–1940, 1960); 3. *The Past, the Present and the Future* (1848); 4. *The Slave Trade* (1853, 1862); 5. *Principles of Social Science*, 3 vols (1858–60, 1963).
Career A businessman-economist with a distinctly American view of the subject; his prolific writings concentrated on the harmony of economic interests. This involved a break with Malthus' and Ricardo's ideas on free trade, population, rent and wages. Increasingly he became a committed protectionist, arguing in *The Slave Trade* that protection would end slavery in the South by stimulating industry and fostering economic links with the North. His works made extensive use of historical and statistical data, the latter frequently presented in graphic terms. His long-term influence on economics has been slight despite the wide currency of his writings in his own time.
Secondary Literature A. D. H. Kaplan, *Henry Charles Carey: A Study in American Economic Thought* (JHUP, 1931); H. W. Spiegel, 'Carey, Henry C.', *IESS*, 2.

CARGILL, Thomas F.

Born 1942, Oakland, CA, USA.
Current Post Prof. Econ., Univ. Nevada, Reno, NV, USA, 1978–.

Past Posts Lect., Univ. Cal. Davis, 1968–9; Vis. Lect., Cal State Univ., Sacramento, 1969; Ass. Prof., Purdue Univ., IN, 1969–73; Assoc. Prof., Univ. Nevada, 1973–8; Vis. Scholar, Comptroller Currency, Washington, DC, 1980; Vis. Prof., Univ. Cal Davis, 1982, 1983; Vis. Scholar, Hoover Inst., Stanford Univ., 1983; Bank of Japan, Toyko, Japan, 1984.
Degrees AA City Coll., San Francisco, 1962; BS Univ. San Francisco, 1964; MA, PhD Univ. Cal. Davis, 1965, 1968.
Offices and Honours Ford Foundation Doctoral Dissertation Fellow, 1967; Outstanding Res. Award. Univ. Nevada, 1977.
Principal Fields of Interest 311 Domestic Monetary and Financial Theory and Institutions; 132 Economic Forecasting and Econometric Models.
Publications *Books:* 1. *Money, the Financial System, and Monetary Policy* (Prentice-Hall 1979, 1983); 2. *Financial Deregulation and Monetary Control* (with G. G. Garcia), (Hoover Inst. Press, 1982; transl., Japanese, Toyo Keizai Shimposha, 1983); 3. *A Supplement on the Garn-St Germain Depository Institutions Act of 1982: Progress Toward Deregulation* (with G. G. Garcia), (Prentice-Hall, 1983).
Articles: 1. 'An empirical investigation of the wage-lag hypothesis', *AER*, 59(5), Dec. 1969; 2. 'A spectral approach to estimating the distributed lag relationship between long and short term interest rates' (with R. A. Meyer), *Int ER*, 13, June 1972; 3. 'Early applications of spectral methods to economic time series', *HOPE*, 6(1), Spring 1974; 4. 'The term structure of interest rates: a test of the expectations hypothesis', *J Fin*, 30, June 1975; 5. 'Anticipated price changes and nominal interest rates in the 1950s', *REStat.*, 58, Aug. 1976; 6. 'Clark Warburton and the development of monetarism since the great depression', *HOPE*, 11(3), Fall 1979; 7. 'The term structure of inflationary expectations and market efficiency' (with R. A. Meyer), *J Fin*, 35, March 1980; 8. 'A tribute to Clark Warburton, 1896–1979', *JMCB*, 13, Feb. 1981; 9. 'Revealed preferences in macroeconomic policy decision' (with

R. A. Meyer), *J Macroecon.*, 3, Spring 1981; 10. 'Dynamic portfolio behavior of commercial banks: an integrated analysis' (with R. A. Meyer), *QREB*, 22, Spring 1982.

Principal Contributions My interest has focussed on two major areas: monetary/financial economics and applied econometrics. In addition, I have been interested in the historical development of economics. Early work applied a variety of econometric methods to the wage-price relationship, interest rates, commodity markets, long-swings, and monetary impacts on the economy. Interest then shifted to methodological issues regarding time and frequency domain distributed lag estimators and alternative ways of incorporating time-varying behaviour into econometric models. In the late 1970s, interest focussed more specifically on financial markets and institutions, portfolio optimisation, and methods to analyse regulatory impacts on commercial banks. As a result of my experience at the Comptroller of the Currency at the time the Depository Institutions Deregulation and Monetary Control Act was enacted, major effort has been devoted to the study of financial reform both from a domestic and international perspective.

Overall, my interest has focussed on policy issues and the need to apply well-designed quantitative methods for their analysis. At the same time, institutional and historical perspectives have been important. This is reflected by my work on the history of spectral methods, Warburton's role in the development of monetarism, the historical development of financial reform, and the financial reform process in the 1980s.

CARLSON, John Allyn

Born 1933, Boston, MA, USA.
Current Post Prof. Econ., Purdue Univ., W Lafayette, IN, USA, 1973–.
Past Posts Vis. Ass. Prof., Cornell Univ., 1961–2; Guest Scholar, Brookings Inst., 1967–8; Res. Fellow Econ. Stats., Univ. Manchester, 1971–2; Hon. Res. Fellow, Univ. Coll. London, 1980.

Degrees BS (Maths.) Denison Univ., 1955; PhD Johns Hopkins Univ., 1961.
Offices and Honours Phi Beta Kappa, 1955.
Principal Fields of Interest 020 General Economic Theory; 130 Economic Fluctuations, Forecasting, Stabilisation and Inflation; 200 Quantitative Economic Methods and Data.
Publications *Books:* 1. *Macroeconomic Adjustments* (Holt, Rinehart and Winston, 1970).

Articles: 1. 'Forecasting errors and business cycles', *AER*, 57(3), June, 1967; 2. 'An invariably stable cobweb model', *REStud.*, 35, July 1968; 3. 'The production lag', *AER*, 63(1), March 1973; 4. 'Aggregate inventory behavior: a critical study of a class of models' (with W. Wehrs), in *Trade, Stability and Macroeconomics: Essays in Honor of Lloyd Metzler*, eds. G. Horwich and P. A. Samuelson (Academic Press, 1974); 5. 'Inflation expectations' (with M. Parkin), *Ec*, 42, May 1975, repr. in *Inflation in the United Kingdom*, eds. M. Parkin and M. T. Sumner (Manchester Univ. Press, 1978); 6. 'Are price expectations normally distributed?', *JASA*, 70, Dec. 1975; 7. 'A study of price forecasts', *Annals Econ. Social Measurement*, 6, Winter 1977; 8. 'Expected inflation and interest rates', *EI*, 17, Oct. 1979; 9. 'Money demand responsiveness to the rate of return on money: a methodological critique' (with J. Frew), *JPE*, 88(3), June 1980; 10. 'Discrete equilibrium price dispersion' (with R. P. McAfee), *JPE*, 91(3), June 1983.
Principal Contributions An early interest in economic adjustment processes began with experiments in which patterns of expectations played critical roles in changes in market prices and aggregate output (Nos. 1, 2 above). As inflation became a widespread phenomenon, series of inflation expectations were developed from survey data, with careful attention to information available to those surveyed and with concern about the plausibility of assumptions utilised in creating the expectations series (Nos. 5, 6, 7). Relationships between inflation expectations and interest rates have also been studied (No. 8). The dispersion

exhibited by different people's price expectations led to studies of the dispersion of actual prices and then to formulations of models of price dispersion, with emphasis on testable implications (No. 10). Continuing interests in what may or may not be inferred from available information show up in a number of ways. Lags attributable to production time have been estimated for different industries from accounting data (No. 3). Seemingly paradoxical parameter estimates in inventory investment models have been examined critically (No. 4). And a methodological piece warns of inappropriate inferences when constructed data may automatically support the hypothesis under investigation (No. 9).

CARNOY, Martin

Born 1938, Warsaw, Poland.
Current Post Prof. Educ. and Econ., Stanford Univ., Stanford, CA, USA, 1979–.
Past Posts Econ., Brookings Inst., Washington DC, 1964–8; Ass. Prof., Assoc. Prof., Stanford Univ., 1969–79; Vis. Scholar, Internat. Inst. Educ. Planning, Paris, France, 1978–9.
Degrees BS Cal. Inst. Technology, Pasadena, CA, 1960; MA, PhD Univ. Chicago, 1961, 1964.
Offices and Honours Ford Foundation Fellow, 1961–2.
Principal Fields of Interest 912 Economics of Education.
Publications *Books:* 1. *Industrialization in a Latin American Common Market* (Brookings Inst., 1972; transl., Spanish, Instituto Turcato di Tella, 1975); 2. *Cost-Benefit Analysis in Education: A Case Study of Kenya* (with H. Thias), (JHUP, 1972); 3. *Schooling in a Corporate Society*, ed. (David McKay, 1972, 1975); 4. *Education as Cultural Imperialism* (David McKay, 1974; transls., Spanish, Siglo Veintiuno Editores, 1977, Italian, Feltrinelli Editore, 1980); 5. *Education and Employment: A Critical Appraisal* (Internat. Inst. Educ. Planning, 1977); 6. *Can Educational Policy Equalize Income Distribution in Latin America?* (with J. Lobo *et al.*), (ILO, 1979);

7. *Economic Democracy* (with D. Shearer), (M. E. Sharpe, 1980); 8. *Cuba: Cambio Economico y Reforma Educativa, 1955–78* (with J. Werthein), (Editorial Nueva Imagen, 1980); 9. *A New Social Contract* (with D. Shearer and R. Rumberger), (Harper and Row, 1983); 10. *The State and Political Theory* (Princeton Univ. Press, 1984).
Articles: 1. 'Rates of return to schooling in Latin America', *JHR*, 2(3), Summer 1967; transl., Spanish, *Cuadernos de Economica*, 4(13), 1967; 2. 'Earnings and schooling in Mexico', *EDCC*, 15(4), July 1967; 3. 'A welfare analysis of Latin American integration: six industry studies', *JPE*, 78(4), pt. 1, July-Aug. 1970, repr. Brookings Inst., 1971; 4. 'Explaining differentials in earnings among large Brazilian cities' (with M. Katz), *Urb Stud*, 8(1), Feb. 1971; 5. 'The economic costs and returns to educational television', *EDCC*, 23(2), Jan. 1975; 6. 'The return to schooling in the United States' (with D. Marenbach), *JHR*, 10(3), Summer 1975; 7. 'Evaluation of educational media: some issues' (with H. Levin), *Instructional Science*, 4, 1975; 8. 'Education and economic development: the first generation', *EDCC*, 25, Suppl., 1977; 9. 'Segmentation in the US labor market: its effects on the mobility and earnings of whites and blacks' (with R. Rumberger), *Camb J Econ.*, 4, June 1980; 10 'Education industrial democracy and the state', *J. Econ. and Industrial Democracy*, 2(2), May 1981.
Principal Contributions Throughout my career, economics of education has been an important interest. My doctoral thesis on the returns to education in Mexico made the first estimates of earnings functions and estimates of rates of return to education corrected for parents' socioeconomic background. In the mid-1960s, I left research on education to write several books on the Latin American trade and industrialisation, and — as part of that research — to organise joint studies with economists from around the hemisphere. A study in Kenya for the World Bank returned me to my primary interest, but my Kenya results made me question the human capital approach. The product of this questioning was *Educa-*

tion as *Cultural Imperialism*, which attempted to show that educaton did not spread as a 'civilizing force' or even because the returns from schooling were high; rather, education was a useful way for economically and politically dominant groups to incorporate young people into an inequitable international division of labour. In the last decade I have altered my position somewhat. My studies on the American economy and theories of the State have convinced me that the public sector is not only crucial for economists to understand, but that its structure and operation are the expression both of dominant groups and social movements for change. Thus, the expansion and nature of public education is a complex process, the result of pressures for greater social equity and conflicting pressures for social reproduction. I have developed this view in my forthcoming book, *Schooling and Work in the Democratic State.*

CARR, Jack Leslie

Born 1944, Toronto, Ont., Canada.
Current Post Prof., Univ Toronto, Toronto, Ont., Canada, 1978–.
Past Posts Ass. Prof., Assoc. Prof., Univ. Toronto, 1968–73, 1973–8; Vis. Assoc. Prof., UCLA, 1975–6.
Degrees BCom Univ. Toronto, 1965; MA, PhD, Univ. Chicago, 1968, 1971.
Offices and Honours Hon. Woodrow Wilson Fellow, 1965; Lily Hon. Fellow, 1965–8; Canada Council Leave Fellow, 1975; Leave Fellow, Canada Social Sciences and Humanities Res. Council, 1982.
Principal Fields of Interest 023 Macroeconomic Theory; 134 Inflation and Deflation; 311 Domestic Monetary and Financial Theory and Policy.
Publications *Books:* 1. *Cents and Nonsense: The Economics of Canadian Policy Issues* (with F. Mathewson and J. McManus), (Holt, Rinehart and Winston, 1972); 2. *Essays in Monetary Aspects of Inflation* (with K. Nold and S. Winder), (Info. Canada, 1973); 3. *The Macroeconomic Effects of an Arctic Gas Pipeline on the Canadian Economy*

(with G. V. Jump and J. A. Sawyer), (Inst. Policy Analysis, Univ. Toronto, 1974); 4. *The Structure of a National Financial Facility for the Canadian Credit Union Systems: Studies for Decision Making: Study No. 2* (Nat. Assoc. Canadian Credit Unions, 1976); 5. *Wage and Price Controls: Panacea for Inflation or Prescription for Disaster* (Fraser Inst., 1976); 6. *The Money Supply and Monetary Policy* (Inst. Policy Analysis, Univ. Toronto, 1978); 7. *Liability Rules and Insurance Markets* (with P. J. Halpern), (Consumer and Corp. Affairs Canada, 1981); 8. *Tax-Based Income Policies: A Cure for Inflation* (with W. Scarth and R. Schuettlinger), (Fraser Inst. 1982).
Articles: 1. 'Money supply, interest rates and the yield curve' (with L. B. Smith), *JMCB*, 4(3), Aug. 1972; 2. 'A suggestion for the treatment of serial correlation: a case in point', *CJE*, 5(2), May 1972; 3. 'Correcting the yield curve: a re-interpretation of the duration problem' (with P. J. Halpern and J. S. McCallum), *J Fin*, 29(4), Sept. 1974; 4. 'A suggestion for a new monetary indicator' (with L. B. Smith), *J Mon E*, 1(3), July 1975; 5. 'The operation of the Canadian economy under fixed and flexible exchange rates: simulation results from the TRACE model' (with G. V. Jump and J. A. Sawyer), *CJE*, 9(1), Feb. 1976; 6. 'Tax effects, price expectations and the nominal rate of interest' (with L. B. Smith and J. E. Pesando), *EI*, 14(2), June 1976; 7. 'The zero coupon yield curve: a response to the comments', *J Fin*, 33(4), Sept. 1978; 8. 'The role of money supply shocks in the short-run demand for money' (with M. R. Darby), *J Mon E*, 8(2), Sept. 1981; 9. 'Ricardo and the non-neutrality of money in a world with taxes' (with J. Ahiakpor), *HOPE*, 14(2), Summer 1982; 10. 'The economics of symbols, clan names and religion' (with J. Landa), *J. Legal Stud.*, June 1983.
Principal Contributions My earlier work was concentrated entirely in the area of monetary economics. I was one of the early researchers to distinguish formally between anticipated and unanticipated money supply growth. I investigated the effects of anticipated and

unanticipated money on economic activity, interest rates and inflation rates. Towards the middle of the 1970s my research interests broadened significantly. I developed an interest in history of thought (in particular, history of monetary thought), in law and economics (I did work on liability rules), in the economics of religion and the economics of language.

In a sense I view all these other interests as developing naturally from my interest in monetary economics. Money is a method of reducing the costs of making exchange. Language can be viewed as performing a similar role and much of law and economics can be viewed as the search for an efficient set of laws which best facilitate exchange. From the beginning of my professional career I have always had an interest in policy. This has stemmed from my belief that economics must eventually be of use in formulating governmental policy. My very first book, *Cents and Nonsense,* examined how formal economic analysis could be used to analyse a wide variety of policy problems facing Canada. This interest in policy has been maintained to the present.

CARTER, Anne Pitts

Born 1925, New York City, NY, USA.

Current Post Dean Faculty, Fred C. Hecht Prof. Econ., Brandeis Univ., Waltham, MA, USA, 1976–.

Past Posts Instr., Brooklyn Coll., NYC, 1947–9; Ass. Prof., Smith Coll., Northampton, MA, 1951–3; Ass. Prof., Dir. Res., Harvard Econ. Res. Project, Harvard Univ., 1966–8, 1968–72; Vis. Prof., Prof. Econ., Brandeis Univ., 1971–2, 1972–6.

Degrees BA Queen's Coll., NYC, 1945; PhD Harvard-Radcliffe, 1949; Hon. DSc Lowell Univ., MA, 1975.

Offices and Honours Fellow, Em Soc; Sponsor, Federation Amer. Scientists; Dir., Resources for the Future, 1976–; Cons., Data Resources Inc., 1977–; Member, US Dept. Commerce Technical Advisory Board, 1977–80.

Editorial Duties Ed. Boards, *QJE,*

1970–, *REStat,* 1970–, *Eastern Econ. J.,* 1978–81, *JEL,* 1977–80.

Principal Fields of Interest 222 Input-Output Analysis; 620 Economics of Technological Change; 112 Economic Development Models and Theories.

Publications *Books:* 1. *Structural Change in the American Economy* (Harvard Univ. Press, 1970; transl., Russian, Statistika, 1974); 2. *The Future of the World Economy* (with W. Leontief and P. P. Petri), (OUP, 1976); 3. *Contributions to Input-Output Analysis,* co-ed. (with A. Brody), (N-H, 1970); 4. *Applications of Input-Output Analysis,* co-ed. (with A. Brody), (N-H, 1970); 5. *Input-Output Technique,* co-ed. (with A. Brody), (N-H, 1972); 6. *Energy and the Environment, A Structural Analysis,* ed. (Univ. Press New England, 1976).

Articles: 1. 'Capital coefficients as economic parameters: the problem of instability', in *Problems of Capital Formation* (Princeton Univ. Press, 1957); 2. 'Investment, capacity utilization and changes in input structure in the tin can industry', *REStat,* 42, Aug. 1960; 3. 'Incremental flow coefficients for a dynamic input-output model with changing technology', in *Structural Interdependence and Economic Development,* ed. T. Barna (Macmillan, 1963); 4. 'The economics of technological change', *Scientific Amer.,* April 1966; 5. 'Changes in the structure of the American economy, 1947 to 1958 and 1962', *REStat,* 49(3), May 1967; 6. 'A linear programming system analyzing embodied technological change', in *Contributions to Input-Output Analysis,* eds. A. P. Carter and A. Brody (N-H, 1970); 7. 'Applications of input-output analysis to energy problems', *Science,* 19, April 1974; 8. 'Energy environment and economic growth', *Bell JE,* 5(2), Autumn 1974; transl., Hungarian, *Szigma,* July 1974; 9. 'Factors affecting the long term prospects of developing regions' (with P. Petri), *J. Pol. Modeling,* 1, Sept. 1979; 10. 'International effects of energy conservation', *Scand JE,* 83(2), June 1981.

Principal Contributions My early work consisted of quantitative studies of the diffusion of new techniques in specific narrowly defined sectors such as cotton textiles, metal containers, nuts, bolts and screws. These studies aimed to show how investment paced changes in the industry average production function, given the parameters of a 'best practice' technique, as derived from the technical literature of the sector. Later I broadened this enquiry to the description and explanation of changes in input-output coefficients over time. To do this it was necessary to prepare comparable sets of coefficients for successive periods and to assemble auxiliary data on prices, investment and labour productivity. This work, performed at the Harvard Economic Research Project, helped lay the basis for the time series of comparable tables and related data now published as a regular part of the US National Accounts.

In the late 1960s and early 1970s I extended this work to the areas of environmental pollution and economy-wide energy analysis and explored the effects of changing input-output structures on income distribution using partially closed models. During the mid-1970s I worked with Petri and Leontief to construct the UN World Model: an attempt to analyse the global economy in terms of 15 regional disaggregated models linked by trade and other global equations. This model was used to simulate a number of broad policy options and to study particular problems of energy, trade and economic development. For the past several years I have been absorbed in administrative responsibilities rather than research. My current interest lies in exploring how society controls the pace and direction of technical change.

CARVER, Thomas Nixon*

Dates and Birthplace 1865–1961, Kirkville, IA, USA.

Posts Held Prof. Econ. and Sociology, Oberlin Coll., 1894–1900; Prof. Econ., Harvard Univ., 1900–32; Vis. Prof., Univ. Southern Cal., 1932–40.

Degrees BA Univ. Southern Cal., 1891; PhD Cornell Univ., 1894.

Offices and Honours Pres., AEA, 1916.

Publications *Books:* 1. *The Distribution of Wealth* (1904, 1918); 2. *Principles of Rural Economics* (1911, 1932); 3. *The Present Economic Revolution in the United States* (1925); 4. *The Essential Factors in Social Evolution* (1935).

Career A social philosopher of a down-to-earth kind, befitting his early years as a farmer. Free enterprise capitalism was equated in his economic theory with moral virtue as well as national prosperity. His chief work was on the distribution of income and wealth, but he also did pioneering work in the economics of agriculture. A vigorous controversialist, he continued to present his views in articles and through teaching to the end of his life.

Secondary Literature O. H. Taylor, 'Carver, Thomas Nixon', *IESS*, 2.

CASAROSA, Carlo

Born 1942, Calcinaia, Pisa, Italy.

Current Post Prof. Straordinario Econ., Univ. Pisa, 1981–.

Past Posts Ass. Ordinario, Scuola Superiore, Pisa, 1969–80; Prof. Incaricato Econ., Univ. Pisa, 1972–80, Univ. Florence, 1973–5.

Editorial Duties Ed. Board, *Quaderni di storia dell'Economia Politica*, 1983; *Economia Politica*, 1984.

Principal Fields of Interest 023 Macroeconomic Theory; 031 History of Economic Thought; 321 Fiscal Theory and Policy.

Publications *Articles:* 1. 'Modelli di crescita, il problema dell'occupazione e la finanza pubblica', *Studi Economici*, 24, 1969; 2. 'Macroeconomia', App. 4 in A. Pesenti, *Manuale di Economia Politica* (Editori Riuniti, 1970); 3. 'Il problema dell'esistenza dell'equilibrio temporaneo nei modelli monetari', *Rivista di Politica Econ.*, 53, Oct. 1973; 4. 'La teoria ricardiana della distribuzione e dello sviluppo economico', *Rivista di Politica Econ.*, 64, Aug.–Sept. 1974; 5. 'A new formulation of the Ricardian system', *OEP*, 30(1), March 1978; 6. 'Commenti a un recente studio di Modigliani e Padoa-Schioppa', *Moneta e Credito*, 121(1), March 1978; 7. 'Un contributo all'analisi dei fondamenti microeconomici della teoria

Keynesiana della domanda effettiva', *Rivista di Politica Econ.*, 68, Nov. 1978; 8. 'The microfoundations of Keynes's aggregate supply and expected demand analysis', *EJ*, 91, March 1981; 9. 'Debt, interest and inflation: appearance and reality', *Rivista di Politica Econ., Selected Papers*, 1982; 10. 'The new view of the Ricardian theory of distribution and economic growth', in *Advances in Economic Theory*, ed. M. Baranzini (Blackwell, 1983).

Principal Contributions Challenged the established view of the Ricardian theory of distribution and presented an alternative reconstruction of this theory, centred on the notion of dynamic equilibrium. Subsequently related my work to the parallel work of Hicks and Hollander and formulated what is now known as the 'New View' of the Ricardian theory. Explored the micro-foundations of Keynes's aggregate supply and expected demand analysis and showed that such analysis is an extension of the Marshallian theory of the competitive firm to the system as a whole: Keynes's macroeconomic propositions do not depend on the type of entrepreneurial behaviour which is assumed. In the area of fiscal policy showed that Keynesian solutions to short-run 'Keynesian' problems might cause classical problems in the medium run, and that the substitution of social contributions with either direct or indirect taxation would improve the trade-off between employment and inflation in a fully indexed economy. Dealt with the problem of inflation accounting, with special attention to interest payments and warned against the use of nominal instead of real magnitudes.

CASS, David

Born 1937, Honolulu, HI, USA.

Current Post Prof. Econ., Co-Dir., Center Analytic Res. Econ. and Social Sciences, Univ. Penn., Philadelphia, PA, USA, 1974–.

Past Posts Ass. Prof., Assoc. Prof., Res. Staff, Cowles Foundation, Yale Univ., 1964–70; Prof., Carnegie-Mellon Univ., 1970–4; Vis. Prof., Hebrew Univ., 1976, Univ. Paris, 1981, 1984, Univ. Geneva, 1984.

Degrees BA Univ. Oregon, 1958; PhD Stanford Univ., 1965.

Offices and Honours Phi Beta Kappa; Guggenheim Foundation Fellow, 1970–1; Fellow, Em. Soc., 1971; Mary Elizabeth Morgan Prize Excellence in Econ., Univ. Chicago, 1976; Sherman Fairchild Disting. Scholar, Cal. Inst. Technology, 1978–9.

Editorial Duties Amer. Ed., *REStud*, 1968–72; Assoc. Ed., *JET*, 1968–82, *J Fin Econ*, 1973–8.

Principal Fields of Interest 021 General Equilibrium Theory; 026 Economics of Uncertainty and Information; 111 Economic Growth Theory and Models.

Publications *Books:* 1. *Selected Readings from Econometrica*, co-ed. (with L. W. McKenzie), (N-H, 1974); 2. *The Hamilton Approach to Economic Dynamics*, co-ed. (with K. Shell), (Academic Press, 1976).

Articles: 1. 'Optimum growth in an aggregate model of capital accumulation', *REStud*, 32(3), July 1965; 2. 'A re-examination of the pure consumption loans model' (with M. E. Yaari), *JPE*, 74(4), Aug. 1966; 3. 'Individual saving, aggregate capital accumulation and efficient growth' (with M. E. Yaari), in *Essays in the Theory of Optimal Economic Growth*, ed. K. Shell (MIT Press, 1967); 4. 'The structure of investor preferences and asset returns, and separability in portfolio allocation' (with J. E. Stiglitz), *JET*, 2(2), June 1970; 5. 'On capital over-accumulation in the aggregative, neoclassical model of economic growth: a complete characterization', *JET*, 4(2), April 1972; 6. 'On the Wicksellian point-input, point-output model of capital accumulation: a modern view (or, neoclassicism slightly vindicated)', *JPE*, 81(1), Jan.–Feb. 1973; 7. 'Duality: a symmetric approach from the economist's vantage point', *JET*, 7(3), March 1974; 8. 'The structure and stability of competitive dynamical systems' (with K. Shell), *JET*, 12(1), Feb. 1976; 9. 'The role of money in supporting the Pareto optimality of competitive equilibria in consumption-loan type models' (with M. Okuno and I. Zilcha), *JET*, 20(1), Feb. 1979, repr. in *Models of Monetary Economics*, eds. J. H. Kareken and N. Wallace (Fed. Reserve Bank Minneapolis, 1980); 10. 'Do sunspots matter?' (with K. Shell), *JPE*, 91(2), April 1983.

Principal Contributions My main original interest was in the pure theory of capital, especially in characterising efficient and optimal growth. I have also had continuing interests in individual behaviour under uncertainty, and in the modern development of Walrasian general equilibrium theory (especially in its intertemporal aspects). Most recently I have been combining all three interests in studies (several joint with my long-time colleague from graduate school, Karl Shell) focussing on the role of 'sunspots' (i.e. self-fulfilling beliefs about what 'really causes' prices) in decentralised market economies.

CASSEL, Karl Gustav*

Dates and Birthplace 1866–1945, Stockholm, Sweden.
Posts Held Prof., Stockholm Univ.
Degrees Dr (Maths.) Uppsala Univ., 1895.
Publications *Books:* 1. *Socialpolitik* (1902, 1923); 2. *The Nature and Necessity of Interest* (1903); 3. *The Theory of Social Economy* (1918, 1932); 4. *The World's Monetary Problems* (1921).
Articles: 1. 'Keynes' *General Theory*', *Int Lab Rev*, 36, June 1937; 2. 'The principles of railway rates for passengers', *Archiv für Eisenbahnwesen*, 1900, repr. in *Internat. Econ. Papers*, 6, eds. A. T. Peacock, *et al.* (Macmillan, 1956).
Career Studied economics in Germany and gained his chief fame from *The Theory of Social Economy*, which was widely sold and translated. This textbook was based on his earlier published papers and presents a simplified version of Walrasian general equilibrium theory. Whilst rejecting utility theory and even marginalism, he still gave his work a thoroughly neoclassical emphasis. He was an important figure in the discussion of German repara-

tions after World War I, wrote extensively on fiscal and monetary problems, and examined the problems of unemployment. He stood out against Keynesian remedies for the depression and rejected the *General Theory* in a very critical review.
Secondary Literature K. Wicksell, *Lectures on Political Economy*, vol. 1, App. 1 (Macmillan, 1934); K. G. Landgren, 'Cassel, Karl Gustav', *IESS, 2*.

CASSON, Mark Christopher

Born 1945, Warrington, Cheshire, England.
Current Post Prof. Econ., Univ. Reading, Berkshire, England, 1981–.
Past Posts Lect., Reader Econ., Univ. Reading, 1969–77, 1977–81.
Degrees BA Univ. Bristol, 1966.
Principal Fields of Interest 026 Economic Uncertainty and Information; 131 Economic Fluctuations; 442 International Business.
Publications *Books:* 1. *Introduction to Mathematical Economics* (with P. J. Buckley), (Nelson, 1973); 2. *The Future of the Multinational Enterprise* (with P. J. Buckley), (Macmillan, 1976); 3. *Alternatives to the Multinational Enterprise* (Macmillan, 1979); 4. *Youth Unemployment* (Macmillan, 1979); 5. *Unemployment: A Disequilibrium Approach* (Martin Robertson, 1981); 6. *The Entrepreneur: An Economic Theory* (Martin Robertson, 1982); 7. *The Economics of Unemployment: An Historical Perspective* (Martin Robertson, MIT Press, 1983); 8. *The Growth of International Business*, ed. (A&U, 1983); 9. *The Theory of the Multinational Enterprise: Selected Papers* (with P. J. Buckley), (Macmillan, 1984).
Articles: 1. 'Linear regression with error in the deflating variable', *Em*, 41(3), Sept. 1973; 2. 'Generalised errors in variables regression', *REStud*, 41(2), June 1973; 3. 'A theory of international operations', in *European Research in International Business*, eds. M. Ghertman and J. Leontiades (N-H, 1978); 4. 'New theories of aggregate unemployment', in *Economics of*

Unemployment in Britain, ed. J. Cready (Butterworths, 1981).

Principal Contributions 'How markets really work' has for several years been my major research interest. It began with a fairly narrow interest in 'market failure' but has developed into a broader study of the impact of legal, social, cultural and political influences on market behaviour. The study of market failure has led me to range over topics as diverse as unemployment (viewed as a consequence of labour market failure) and the multinational enterprise (viewed as an institutional response to failures in markets for technology and semi-processed materials). My most ambitious work is on entrepreneurship. I regard the entrepreneur as someone who specialises in taking judgemental decisions about what kind of trade should take place; he organises markets and appropriates some of the gains from trade by skilful bargaining; by organising markets he helps others to economise on their transaction costs. I now believe that the crucial determinants of transaction costs are social rather than economic. Transaction costs, it could be said, are much lower when trade takes place within a social group than when it takes place between social groups. Work in progress is focussed upon the dynamics of the formation of social groups, and upon the role of entrepreneurs in promoting the division of labour within them. The analysis will be applied to classical issues such as the comparitive growth of nations. It will also be applied to more specific subjects such as the comparative performance of multinational firms and to international differentials in rates of unemployment. I prefer limited success in tackling really big issues to complete success in tackling much smaller ones.

CAVES, Richard Earl

Born 1931, Akron, OH, USA.
Current Post Prof. Econ., Harvard Univ., MA., USA, 1962–.
Past Posts Ass. Prof., Assoc. Prof. Econ., Univ. Cal. Berkeley, 1957–60, 1960–2.

Degrees BA Oberlin Coll., 1953; MA, PhD Harvard Univ., 1956, 1958.
Offices and Honours Wells Prize, Harvard Univ., 1957–8; Henderson Prize, 1962.
Principal Fields of Interest 400 International Economics.
Publications *Books:* 1. *Trade and Economic Structure* (Harvard Univ. Press, 1960); 2. *Air Transport and its Regulators* (Harvard Univ. Press, 1962); 3. *Capital Transfers and Economic Policy: Canada, 1951, 1962* (with G. L. Reuber), (Harvard Univ. Press, 1971); 4. *Industrial Organization in Japan* (with M. Uekusa), (Brookings Inst., 1976); 5. *Competition in the Open Economy* (with M. E. Porter and A. M. Spence), (Harvard Univ. Press, 1980); 6. *Multinational Enterprise and Economic Analysis* (CUP, 1982).
Articles: 1. 'International corporations: the industrial economics of foreign investment', *Ec*, N.S. 38, Feb. 1971; 2. 'Causes of direct investment: foreign firms' shares in Canadian and United Kingdom manufacturing industries', *REStat*, 56(3), Aug. 1974; 3. 'From entry barriers to mobility barriers' (with M. E. Porter), *QJE*, 91(2), May 1977; 4. 'Monopolistic export industries, trade taxes, and optimal competition policy' (with A. A. Augquier), *EJ*, 89, Sept. 1979; 5. 'Industrial organization, corporate strategy and structure', *JEL*, 18(1), March 1980; 6. 'The decline of dominant firms, 1905–1929' (with M. Fortunato and P. Ghemawat), *QJE*, 99(3), Aug. 1984.
Principal Contributions Intersection between the fields of international trade and industrial organisation, including the effect of international trade on the structure and performance of national markets and on industrial policy, the structure and behaviour of multinational enterprises, export-led growth of national industries and economies, and transnational comparisons of industrial organisation. Other research areas include the effects of regulation on industrial structure and behaviour, the consequences of resource commitments that create barriers to entry and exit, and the effect of market structure on the internal organisation and thus the behaviour of firms.

CHADWICK, Edwin*

Dates and Birthplace 1800–90, Longsight, Lancashire, England.

Posts Held Secretary to Jeremy Bentham, 1830–4; Sub-ed., *Examiner*, 1831–3; Ass. Commissioner, Royal Commissioners UK Poor Law Enquiry, 1832–3, 1833–4; Secretary, UK Poor Law Commission, 1934–7; Metropolitan Commissioner Sewers, 1848–9.

Degrees Lawyer, 1830.

Offices and Honours Member, l'Inst. Français, 1862; Central Comm., BA, 1873; Pres., Assoc. Sanitary Inspectors, 1883; Knighted, 1889.

Publications *Books:* 1. *Report on the Sanitary Condition of the Labouring Population of Great Britain* (1842), ed. M. W. Flinn (1965); 2. *Report on the Metropolitan Water Supply* (1850); 3. *The Health of Nations: Review of the Works of Edwin Chadwick*, 2 vols., ed. B. W. Richardson (1887).

Career One of the great social reformers of the Victorian age who implemented many of Bentham's practical suggestions for reforming the Poor Laws, the police, the prison system, and, above all, the public health system of Britain. He has recently been hailed as an important forerunner of the so-called 'Chicago theory of regulation'.

Secondary Literature S. E. Fine, *The Life and Times of Sir Edwin Chadwick* (Methuen, 1952); R. B. Ekelund, Jr. and R. F. Hebert, *A History of Economic Theory and Method* (McGraw-Hill, 1983), chap. 9.

CHALMERS, Thomas*

Dates and Birthplace 1780–1847, Fife, Scotland.

Posts Held Clergyman, Church of Scotland; Prof. Moral Philosophy and Polit. Econ., Univ. St Andrews, 1823–8; Prof. Theology, Univ. Edinburgh, 1828–43; Prof. Divinity, New Coll. (Free Church), Edinburgh, 1843.

Degrees DD Univ. Glasgow, 1816; DCL Univ. Oxford, 1835.

Offices and Honours Fellow, Vic-Pres., Royal Soc. Edinburgh.

Publications *Books:* 1. *Enquiry into the Extent and Stability of National Resources* (1808); 2. *Political Economy* (1832).

Career Successful evangelical preacher and church leader whose interest in pauperism and other economic problems began with his parish work. His successful organisation of a system of poor relief in his parish helped to make him a confirmed opponent of the Poor Laws. His *Political Economy* was not a systematic theory, but an attempt to show how moral improvement could stem from the adoption of particular economic policies. His enthusiasm for the theory of population and the theory of general gluts made him more Malthusian than Malthus. His remedy for over-population was self-restraint, enjoined by Christian education. His gift for describing economic phenomena in telling phrases, of which 'the margin of cultivation' is perhaps the best known, was much greater than the orginality of his analysis.

CHAMBERLAIN, Neil Wolverton

Born 1915, Charlotte, N C, USA.

Current Post Armand G. Erpf Prof. Emeritus, Columbia Univ., 1981–.

Past Posts Dir. Program Econ. Devlp., Ford Foundation, 1957–60; Dept. Econ., Yale Univ., 1960–7; Grad. School Bus., Columbia Univ., 1967–80.

Degrees BA, MA Western Reserve Univ., 1937, 1939; PhD Ohio State Univ., 1942.

Offices and Honours Brookings Res. Fellow, 1940; Ford Foundation Res. Fellow, 1957; Trustee, Salzburg Seminar Amer. Stud., 1957–79; Pres., IRRA, 1967.

Editorial Duties Ed. Board, *AER*, 1959–62.

Principal Fields of Interest 113 Economic Planning Theory; 820 Labour Markets.

Publications *Books:* 1. *Collective Bargaining* (McGraw-Hill, 1951, 1965); 2. *A General Theory of Economic Process* (Harper, 1955); 3. *The Firm: Microeconomic Planning and Action* (McGraw-Hill, 1962); 4. *Private and Public Planning* (McGraw-Hill, 1965); 5. *Forces of Change in Western Europe*

(McGraw-Hill, 1980); 6. *Social Strategy and Corporate Structure* (Macmillan, 1982).

Articles: 1. 'The nature and scope of collective bargaining', *QJE*, 58, May 1944; 2. 'The organized business in America', *JPE*, 52, June 1944; 3. 'Collective bargaining and the concept of contract', *Columbia Law Rev.*, 48, Sept. 1948; 4. 'The union challenge to management control', *ILRR*, 16, Jan. 1963; 5. 'Some second thoughts on the concept of human capital', in *Proceedings of the Twentieth Annual Winter Meeting: the Development and Use of Manpower* (IRRA, 1967).

Principal Contributions The development and elaboration of certain concepts permitting the blending of institutional and social analysis with economic theory. These include aspects of collective bargaining and bargaining power; economic counterpoint (the necessary simultaneous tendencies towards equilibrium and disequilibrium, within both firm and economy); the interplay between technical-economic and political-organisation co-ordination within the firm and economy; ingredients of economic planning, and the nature and role of social values in economic systems.

CHAMBERLIN, Edward Hastings*

Dates and Birthplace 1899–1967, La Conner, WA, USA.

Posts Held Prof. Econ., Harvard Univ., 1927–67.

Degrees BA Univ. Iowa; MA Univ. Michigan, 1922; PhD Harvard Univ., 1927.

Offices and Honours Ed., *QJE*, 1948–58; Disting. Fellow, AEA, 1965.

Publications *Books:* 1. *The Theory of Monopolistic Competition* (1933, 1937, 1938, 1942, 1946); 2. *Towards a More General Theory of Value* (1957).

Career The *Theory of Monopolistic Competition* and Joan Robinson's *Economics of Imperfect Competition* were independent contributions to the theory of limited competition published in the same year. Chamberlin's book was based on his 1927 thesis, and his later work was essentially

concerned with elaborating and buttressing his theory. The book turned attention from the analysis of an industry to the examination of the role of the firm. He saw markets as involving the whole range of variables from pure competition to monopoly with competition and monopoly blended in between the two extremes.

Secondary Literature R. E. Kuenne, ed., *Monopolistic Competition Theory: Studies in Impact* (Wiley & Sons, 1967); J. W. Markham, 'Chamberlin, Edward H.', *IESS*, 18; R. Robinson, *Edward H. Chamberlin* (Columbia Univ. Press, 1971).

CHAMPERNOWNE, David Gawen

Born 1912, Oxford, England.

Current Post Prof. Fellow Emeritus, Trinity Coll. Camb., 1979–.

Past Posts Prof. Stats., Univ. Oxford, 1949–50; Reader Econ., Prof. Econ. Stats., Emeritus Prof., Univ. Camb., 1959–69, 1969–78, 1976–9.

Degrees MA Univ. Camb., 1938; MA Univ. Oxford, 1945.

Offices and Honours Fellow, BA.

Editorial Duties Co-ed., *EJ*, 1971–5.

Principal Fields of Interest 020 General Economic Theory.

Publications *Books:* 1. *Uncertainty and Estimation in Economics* (Oliver & Boyd, Holden Day, 1969); 2. *Distribution of Income between Persons* (CUP, 1973).

Articles: 1. 'Unemployment, basic and monetary: the classical analysis and the Keynesian', *REStud*, 3, June 1936; 2. 'The uneven distribution of unemployment in the United Kingdom, 1929–36, Pt 1–2', *REStud*, 5, Feb. 1938, 6, Feb. 1939; 3. 'A note on J. V. Neumann's article on "A model of economic equilibrium"', *REStud*, 13(1), 1945; 4. 'A model of income distribution', *EJ* 63, June 1953; 5. 'The production function and the theory of capital: a comment', *REStud*, 21(2), 1954; 6. 'Expectations and the links between the economic future and the present', in *Keynes' General Theory, Reports of Three Decades*, ed. R. Lekachman (Macmillan, 1964); 7. 'A comparison of measures of income distribution', *EJ*,

84, Dec. 1974; 8. 'Income distribution and egalitarian policy: the outlook in 1980', in *Inkomensverdeling en Openbare Financien,* eds. P. J. Eijgelshoven and L. J. van Gemerden (Het Spectrum, 1981).

Principal Contributions Explanation of economic inequality of various types. The unequal experience during the 1930s of different regions and of different types of industry in the UK. Models of personal distribution of income and wealth, using stochastic variables to represent miscellaneous influences. Estimation from time-series and other economic statistics. Bayesian methods. Effects of ignorance and disagreement about the economic future on the working of market mechanisms.

CHAPMAN, Sydney John*

Dates and Birthplace 1871–1951, Wells, Norfolk, England.
Posts Held Lect., Univ. Coll., Cardiff, 1899–1901; Prof., Univ. Manchester, 1901–17; Secretary, UK Board Trade, 1918–27; Chief Econ. Adviser, UK Govt., 1927–32.
Degrees BA Univ. London, 1891.
Offices and Honours Pres., Section F, BAAS, 1909; Vice-Pres., RSS, 1916; Member and Chairman of many UK Govt. and League of Nations Comms.; Knighted, 1920.
Publications *Books:* 1. *The Lancashire Cotton Industry* (1904); 2. *Work and Wages,* 3 vols (1904–14); 3. *The Cotton Industry and Trade* (1905); 4. *Outlines of Political Economy* (1911).
Career His early career included successful publications and the building up of a thriving commerce faculty at Manchester. Wartime government service drew him from academic life into the Civil Service. His wide knowledge of industry and his theoretical ability enabled him to handle such matters as the return to tariff protection in 1932.

CHENERY, Hollis Burnley

Born 1918, Richmond, VA, USA.
Current Post Prof. Econ., Harvard Univ., 1983–.

Past Posts Ass. Admin., US Agency Internat. Devlp., Washington DC, 1961–5; Prof. Econ., Member Center Internat. Affairs, Harvard Univ., 1965–70; Econ. Adviser to Pres., World Bank, 1970–2; Vice-Pres., Devlp. Pol., World Bank, Washington, DC, 1972–82.
Degrees BS (Maths.) Univ. Arizona, 1939; BS (Eng.) Univ. Oklahoma, 1941; MA Univ. Virginia, 1947; PhD Harvard Univ., 1950; Hon. PhD Netherlands School Econ., 1968.
Offices and Honours Fellow, Council, Em Soc; Fellow, AAAS; Guggenheim Memorial Foundation Fellow, 1960–1.
Principal Fields of Interest 112 Economic Development Models; 411 International Trade Theory.
Publications *Books:* 1. *Interindustry Economics* (with P. Clark), (Wiley, 1959); 2. *Studies in Development Planning* (Harvard Univ. Press, 1971); 3. *Redistribution with Growth: An Approach to Policy* (with others), (OUP, 1974); 4. *Patterns of Development, 1950–1970* (with M. Syrquin), (OUP, 1975); 5. *Structural Change and Development Policy* (OUP, 1979).
Articles: 1. 'Overcapacity and the acceleration principle', *Em,* 20, Jan. 1952; 2. 'Patterns of industrial growth' *AER,* 50(4), Sept. 1960; 3. 'Capital-labour substitution and economic efficiency' (with K. Arrow, *et al.*), *REStat* 43, Aug. 1961; 4. 'Comparative advantage and development policy', *AER,* 51(1), March 1961; 5. 'Foreign assistance and economic development' (with A. Strout), *AER,* 56(4), Sept. 1966.
Principal Contributions Comparative analysis of patterns of development and systematic changes in the structure of production; estimation of production functions (including the original CES production function). Allocation of resources in developing countries, effect of interdependence and economies of scale, planning models for different types of country. International economic development, the 'two-gap model', effects of limited foreign exchange, role of international capital flows, and international aspects of industrialisation. Distributional aspects of development policy, relations between efficiency and equity.

CHENG, Pao Lun

Born 1922, Shanghai, China.
Current Post Prof. Fin. and Econ., Simon Fraser Univ., Burnaby, British Columbia, Canada, 1982–.
Past Posts Instr., Ass. Prof., Univ. Missouri, 1949–51, 1956–7; Instr., Ass. Prof., Prof., Univ. New Mexico, 1954–6, 1956–7, 1981–2; Lect., Michigan State Univ., 1957–8; Assoc. Prof., Prof., Univ. Mass., 1958–62, 1962–74; Prof., Simon Fraser Univ., 1974–81.
Degrees BS Nat. Chiao Tung Univ., Shanghai, China, 1944; MA Univ. Missouri, 1949; PhD Univ. Wisconsin, 1956.
Offices and Honours Univ. Fellow, Univ. Wisconsin, 1951; Ford Foundation Faculty Res. Fellow, 1964–5.
Principal Fields of Interest 026 Economics of Uncertainty and Information; 213 Mathematical Methods and Models; 521 Business Finance.
Publications *Articles:* 1. 'Optimum bond portfolio selections', *Management Science,* 8(4), July 1962; 2.'Bargaining power and wage negotiation', *ILRR,* 22(1), Oct. 1968; 3. 'The common level of assessment in propery taxation', *Nat. Tax J.,* 23(1), March 1970; 4. 'Statistical control of assessment uniformity', *Management Science,* 16(10), June 1970; 5.'Portfolio returns and the random walk theory', *J Fin,* 26(1), March 1971; 6. 'Statistical biases and security rates of return' (with K. Deets), *J. Fin. Quant. Analysis,* 6(3), June 1971; 7. 'Systematic risk and the horizon problem', *J. Fin. Quant. Analysis,* 8(2), March 1973; 8. 'Default risk, scale, and the homemade leverage theorem: note', *AER,* 65(4), Sept. 1975; 9. 'An alternative test of the CAPM' (with R. Grauer), *AER,* 70(4), Sept. 1980; 10. 'Divergent rates, financial restrictions and relative prices in capital market equilibrium', *J. Fin. Quant. Analysis,* 15(2), Sept. 1980.
Principal Contributions Early interest began with the business cycles and the statistical indicators of the NBER. A shift in direction took place when financial economics and portfolio theory made their debut in the early 1960s. Along with the valuation and assessment of real properties under uncertainty, energy was directed towards the valuation of financial assets and the statistical properties of rates of return. Current interest has been in the area of testing the mean-variance valuation model and studying asset pricing and covered interest arbitrage when markets are imperfect.

CHERBULIEZ, Antoine Elisee*

Dates and Birthplace 1797–1869, Geneva, Switzerland.
Posts Held Lawyer and magistrate; Prof. Law and Polit. Econ., Univ. Geneva, 1833; Prof. Polit. Econ., Univ. Zürich, 1851.
Publications *Books:* 1. *Riche ou pauvre* (1840); 2. *Précis de la science économique* (1862).
Career Turning to the study of economics when past the age of forty, he produced one of the best textbook expositions of classical economics. Though containing no original contribution of his own, the *Précis* ... enjoyed widespread and justified success. Cherbuliez was also known as an opponent of Proudhon and the socialists.

CHETTY, V. K.

Born 1938, Puduvayal, India.
Current Post Prof. Econ., Indian Stat. Inst., New Delhi, India, 1972–.
Past Posts Lect. Stats., Annamalai Univ., 1959–62; Ass. Prof., Univ. Wisconsin, 1966–7; Assoc. Prof., Columbia Univ., 1967–71; Vis. Prof., CORE, Belgium, 1971–2, Univ. Warwick, 1981; Cowles Foundation, Yale Univ., 1982.
Degrees BSc (Stats.) Annamalai Univ., 1959; MSc, PhD Univ. Wisconsin, 1965, 1966.
Offices and Honours NBER Res. Fellow, 1969–70; US SSRC Fellow, 1971–2.
Editorial Duties Assoc. Ed., *J. Bus. and Econ. Stats., J. Quant. Econ.*
Principal Fields of Interest 021 General Equilibrium Theory; 300 Monetary Economics; 110 Planning.
Publications *Articles:* 1. 'Pooling of time series and cross-section data', *Em,* 36, April 1968, repr. in *Bobbs-Merrill*

Reprint Series Economics (Bobbs-Merrill, 1974); 2. 'Bayesian analysis of Haavelmo's models', *Em*, 36, July–Oct. 1968, repr. in *Collected Papers in Honour of L. J. Savage,* eds. A. Zellner and S. E. Fienberg (Wiley, 1980); 3. 'On measuring the nearness of the near-moneys', *AER*, 59(3), June 1969, repr. in *Monetary Economics: Readings on Current Issues,* eds. W. E. Gibson and C. G. Kaufman (Wiley, 1978); 4. 'Temporary competitive equilibrium in a monetary economy with uncertain technology and many planning periods' (with D. Dasgupta), *J Math E*, 5(1), March 1978; 5. 'Efficiency of temporary equilibria' (with D. Dasgupta), *J Math E*, 7(1), March 1980.

Principal Contributions Eary work related to econometric methods, in particular to studies of finite sample properties of estimators of simultaneous equations systems from a Bayesian viewpoint. Applications of Bayesian methods to study distributed lags with special reference to demand for financial assets. Developed simple models to study the substitutability among financial assets. In order to formulate Bayesian priors based on economic theory and to build models incorporating money, I developed an interest in economic theory. Studied existence of temporary general equilibria with many periods and uncertain technology and efficiency properties of such equilibria. Worked on non-Walrasian general equilibrium models with price rigidities and rationing. Using these models I studied problems of price and distribution control in Indian industries.

CHEUNG, Steven Ng Sheong

Born 1935, Hong Kong.
Current Post Prof. Econ., Univ. Hong Kong, Hong Kong, 1982–.
Past Posts Ass. Prof., Cal. State Coll., Long Beach, 1965–7; Ass. Prof., Univ. Chicago, 1968–9; Assoc. Prof., Prof., Univ. Washington, 1969–72, 1972–84.
Degrees BA, MA, PhD UCLA, 1961, 1962, 1967.
Offices and Honours Mont Pelerin Soc.; Trustees Cal. State Coll., Disting. Teaching Award, 1966; Post-Doctoral Fellow Polit. Econ., Univ. Chicago, 1967–8.
Editorial Duties Ed., *Asian Econ. J.*
Principal Fields of Interest 020 General Economics Theory; 000 General Economics; Theory; History; Systems.
Publications *Books:* 1. *The Theory of Share Tenancy* (Univ. Chicago Press, 1969); 2. *Contractual Arrangements and the Capturability of Returns in Innovation; Report of a Pilot Investigation* (Nat. Technical Info. Service, 1976); 3. *The Myth of Social Cost* (INEA, 1978; transls., Spanish, 1980, Chinese, 1983); 4. *Will China Go "Capitalist"?'* (INEA, 1982; transl., Chinese, 1982); 5. *A Tangerine Seller Speaks* (in Chinese), (Hong Kong Econ. J., 1984)

Articles: 1. 'Private property rights and sharecropping', *JPE*, 76, Nov.–Dec. 1968; 2. 'Transaction costs, risk aversion, and the choice of contractual arrangements', *J Law E*, 12(1), April 1969; 3. 'The structure of a contract and the theory of a non-exclusive resource', *J Law E*, 13(1), April 1970; 4. 'The enforcement of property rights in children, and the marriage contract', *EJ*, 82, June 1972; transl., Chinese, 1981; 5. 'The fable of the bees: an economic investigation', *J Law E*, 16(1), April 1973; 6. 'A theory of price control', *J Law E*, 17(1), April 1974; 7. 'Why are better seats "underpriced"?', *EI*, 15(4), Oct. 1977; 8. 'Rent control and housing reconstruction; the postwar experience of prewar premises in Hong Kong', *J Law E*, 22(1), April 1979; 9. 'Property rights in trade secrets', *EI* 19(1), Jan. 1982; 10. 'The contractual nature of the firm', *J Law E*, 26(1), April 1983.

Principal Contributions A conviction about the importance of property rights in affecting economic behaviour has led to an almost exclusive focus on various aspects of transaction costs. Research interests comprise economic explanation of pricing and contractual arrangements, including sharecropping, bee-keeping rentals, ticket pricing, rent and price controls, patent and trade-secret licensing, and the pricing and contractual structures of various industries. Recent investigations are into the relation between economic systems and transaction costs/property rights structures.

CHEVALIER, Michel*

Dates and Birthplace 1806–79, Limoges, France.
Post Held Prof., Collège de France, Paris, 1940–79.
Offices and Honours Councillor of State, 1838; Deputy, 1845; Senator; Grand Officier, Légion d'Honneur; Member, Académie des Sciences Morales et Politiques.
Publications *Books:* 1.*Cours d'économie politique*, 3 vols. (1842–50); 2. *L'organisation du travail* (1848); 3. *Questions politiques et sociales* (1852).
Career In his youth a St-Simonian (experiencing imprisonment in 1832), he was in later life a respectable professor frequently employed by the French government. The Cobden-Chevalier commercial treaty between Britain and France (1860) is the best known product of this work. His factual work is of the highest standard, much of it derived from his government service. However, his *Cours* ... , based on his lectures at the Collège, is analytically unremarkable. His later politics were anti-socialist and included determined attacks on the ideas of Louis Blanc, collected as *L'organisation* ... and *Questions* ...

CHEYSSON, Jean-Jacques Emile*

Dates and Birthplace 1836–1910, France.
Posts Held Prof. Polit. Econ., Ecole Libre des Sciences Politiques, Paris, 1882, Ecole des Mines, Paris, 1885.
Offices and Honours Member, Paris Inst. Societé de Stat. de Paris, Societé Internat. de Stat., Societé d'Econ. Sociale.
Publications *Books:* 1. *Oeuvres choisies* (1911).
Career Engineer-economist in the Ecole des Mines tradition laid down by Dupuit, whose greatest work is prob-

ably his published lecture of 1887, *Statistique geometrique*. This is a highly developed series of analytical arguments, touching on a wide range of topics. It overflows with original and striking ideas on statistical demand, revenue and cost curves, location and transporation rates, wages, profit maximisation, market supply areas, etc.
Secondary Literature C. Colson, 'Notice sur la vie et les travaux de M. Emile Cheysson', *Séances et travaux* (Academie des sciences morales et politiques, 1913); R. F. Hébert, 'The theory of input selection and supply areas in 1887: Emile Cheysson', *HOPE,* 6(1), Feb. 1974.

CHIANG, Alpha Chung-i

Born 1927, Shanghai, China.
Current Post Prof. Econ., Univ. Connecticut, Storrs, CT, USA, 1964–.
Past Posts Lect., Univ Bridgeport, CT, 1953–4; Ass. Prof., Assoc. Prof., Denison Univ., OH, 1954–64; Vis. Prof., New Asia Coll., Hong Kong, 1960–1, Cornell Univ., 1966–7.
Degrees BA St John's Univ., Shanghai, China, 1946; MA Univ. Colorado, 1948; PhD Columbia Univ., 1954.
Offices and Honours Ford Foundation Faculty Res. Fellow, 1957; Vice-Pres., Pres., Ohio Assoc. Econ. and Polit. Scientists, 1962–3, 1963–4; NSF Science Faculty Fellow, 1963–4; Board Dirs., Connecticut Product Devlp. Corp., appointed Governor State, 1972–5.
Editorial Duties Ed. Boards, *Academia Econ. Papers, Academia Sinica,* China, 1973–.
Principal Fields of Interest 023 Macroeconomic Theory; 110 Economic Development and Growth Theory; 213 Mathematical Methods and Models.
Publications *Books:* 1. *Exercises in Aggregate Economics* (Holt, Rinehart & Winston, 1964, 1969); 2. *Fundamental Methods of Mathematical Economics* (McGraw-Hill, 1967, 1984; transls., Spanish, Amorrortu Editores, 1971, Italian, Editore Boringhiere, 1978, Japanese, McGraw-Hill Kogakusha, 1979, Portuguese, Editora

McGraw-Hill Brasil, 1982, Turkish, Internat. Communication Agency, 1983, Indonesian, Penerbit Erlangga, 1983).

Articles: 1. 'The "demonstration effect" in a dual economy', *Amer. J. Econ. and Sociology,* 18(3), April 1959, repr. in Portuguese, *Revista Brasileira de Ciencias Socias,* 1(1), Nov. 1961, German, *Konsum und Nachtfrage,* eds. E. and M. Streissler (Kieppenheuer & Witsch, 1966); 2. 'Instalment credit control: a theoretical analysis', *JPE,* 67(4), Aug. 1959; 3. 'Religion, proverbs and economic mentality', *Amer. J. Econ. and Sociology,* 20(3), April 1961; 4. 'The short-run effects of instalment credit control', *CJE,* 27(3), Aug. 1961; 5. 'Maximum-speed development through austerity' (with J. C. H. Fei), in *The Theory and Design of Economic Development,* eds. I Adelman and E. Thorbecke (JHUP, 1966); 6. 'The fundamental cause of economic stagnation' (with J. C. H. Fei), in *Economic Development of Tropical Agriculture,* ed. W. W. McPherson (Univ. Florida Press, 1968); 7. 'Income distribution and the profit rate in two-class models of dynamic equilibrium', *RISE,* 19(3), March 1972; 8. 'A simple generalization of the Kaldor-Pasinetti theory of profit rate and income distribution', *Ec,* N.S. 40, Aug. 1973; 9. 'A linear model of general equilibrium' (with J. C. H. Fei), *Academia Econ. Papers,* 2(2), Sept. 1974; 10. 'Hicks-neutral and Harrod-neutral technological progress: the solution of a puzzle', *RISE,* 28(4), April 1981.

Principal Contributions Although I have published articles in several journals, I am perhaps most closely identified with the teaching of mathematics to economists via my *Fundamental Methods of Mathematical Economics.* Now in its third edition, this book grew out of the personal frustration, during my student days as well as the early years of my teaching career, with mathematics books that give overly concise and often enigmatic explanations. Years of compounding of such frustration led me to challenge myself to design a 'teachable' book and the result is *Fundamental Methods.* A sequel volume is now being planned, to cover the methods of dynamic optimisation (calculus of variations, optimal control theory) — a topic which is very much in use today, and which needs a 'teachable' text.

CHIPLIN, Brian

Born 1945, Bournemouth, Dorset, England.
Current Post Prof. Industrial Econ., Univ. Nottingham, Nottingham, England, 1984–.
Past Posts Viyella Res. Fellow, Univ. Nottingham, 1966–7; Lect., Sr. Lect. Industrial Econ., Univ. Nottingham, 1967–80, 1980–4; Vis. Prof. Econ., State Univ. NY, Buffalo, USA, 1979–80, Univ. Cal. Irvine, USA, 1982–3.
Degrees BA (Industrial Econ.) Univ. Nottingham, 1966.
Principal Fields of Interest 610 Industrial Organisation; 820 Labour Markets; 917 Economics of Minorities.
Publications *Books:* 1. *The Cotton and Allied Textile Industry* (Moodies Services, 1973); 2. *Acquisitions and Mergers: Government Policy in Europe* (Wilton House Fin. Times, 1975); 3. *Sex Discrimination in the Labour Market* (with P. J. Sloane), (Macmillan, 1976); 4. *The Economics of Advertising* (with B. Sturges), (Holt, Rinehart & Winston, 1981); 5. *Tackling Discrimination at the Workplace* (with P. J. Sloane), (CUP, 1982).
Articles: 1. 'Sexual discrimination in the labour market' (with P. J. Sloane), *BJIR,* 12, Nov. 1974, repr. in *The Economics of Women and Work,* ed. A. M. Amsden (Penguin, 1980); 2. 'Personal characteristics and sex differences in professional employment' (with P. J. Sloane), *EJ,* 86, Dec. 1976; 3. 'Non-convexity or indifference surfaces in the case of labour market discrimination', *AER,* 66(5), Dec. 1976; 4. 'An evaluation of sex discrimination: some problems and a suggested reorientation', in *Women in the Labour Market,* eds. C. S. Lloyd, *et al.* (Columbia Univ. Press, 1979); 5. 'Some economic issues of a workers' co-operative economy', in *The Political Economy of Co-operation and Participation,* ed. A. Clarke (OUP, 1980); 6. 'An alternative

approach to the measurement of sex discrimination: an illustration from university entrance', *EJ*, 90, Dec. 1980; 7. 'Competition policy and state enterprises in the UK' (with D. M. Wright), *Antitrust Bull.*, 27, Winter 1982; 8. 'Risk-bearing and self-management' (with T. W. Buck), *Kyk*, 36(2), 1983.

Principal Contributions Main research and publications have been in the area of labour economics and particularly the analysis and measurement of sex discrimination. Have become increasingly concerned with hiring/promotion decisions as they operate at the level of the individual enterprise. More recently I have become concerned with organisational efficiency under alternative institutional arrangements, e.g. State entrance and workers' co-operatives.

CHIPMAN, John S.

Born 1926, Montreal, Quebec, Canada.

Current Post Prof. Econ., Univ. Minnesota, USA, 1960–.

Past Posts Post-Doctoral Fellow Polit. Econ., Univ. Chicago, 1950–1; Ass. Prof. Econ., Harvard Univ., 1951–5; Assoc. Prof. Econ., Univ Minnesota, 1955–60; Vis. Prof. Econ., Harvard Univ., 1966–7.

Degrees BA (Econ. and Polit. Science), MA (Econ. and Polit. Science) McGill Univ., 1947, 1948; PhD Johns Hopkins Univ., 1951.

Offices and Honours Fellow, Member Council, Em Soc, 1957, 1976–7, 1981–; Fellow, Center Advanced Study Behavioral Sciences, Stanford, CA, 1972–3; Fellow, ASA, 1974; Fellow, AAAS, 1979; Guggenheim Foundation Fellow, 1980–1; James Murray Luck Award NAS, 1981.

Editorial Duties Assoc. Ed., *Em*, 1959–69; Co-ed., Ed., *JInt E*, 1971–6, 1977–; Assoc. Ed., *Canadian J. Stats.*, 1980–.

Principal Fields of Interest 411 International Trade Theory.

Publications *Books:* 1. *The Theory of Intersectoral Money Flows and Income Formation* (JHUP, 1951); 2. *Preferences, Utility and Demand* (with L.

Hurwicz, *et al.*), (Harcourt Brace Jovanovich, 1971); 3. *Flexible Exchange Rates and the Balance of Payments: Essays in Memory of Egon Sohmen*, co-ed. (with C. P. Kindleberger), (N-H, 1980).

Articles: 1. 'On least squares with insufficient observations', *JASA*, 59, 1964; 2. 'A survey of the theory of international trade: Pts 1–3', *Em*, 33–4, July, Oct. 1965, Jan. 1966; 3. 'External economies of scale and competitive equilibrium', *QJE*, 84(3), Aug. 1970; 4. 'A renewal model of economic growth: the discrete case', in *Mathematical Topics in Economic Theory and Computation*, eds. R. H. Day and S. M. Robinson (SIAM Publications, 1972); 5. 'Estimation and aggregation in econometrics: an application of the theory of generalized inverses', in *Generalized Inverses and Applications*, ed. M. Z. Nashed (Academic Press, 1976).

Principal Contributions Multsectoral extensions of Keynesian multiplier. Contributions to utility and portfolio theory. Synthesis of international trade theory. Development of the theory of international capital movements and their effects on terms of trade and exchange rates. A model of competitive equilibrium under increasing returns to scale with accompanying tax-subsidy scheme. Analysis of internal-rate-of-return criterion in the context of a renewal model of economic growth. Derivation of conditions for aggregation of preferences and (with J. C. Moore) for validity of conventional welfare measures. Introduction of minimum-bias and minimum-mean-square error estimation and the theory of best approximate aggregation, with application to econometric models of international trade.

CHISWICK, Barry Raymond

Born 1942, New York City, NY, USA.

Current Post Res. Prof. Econ., Survey Res. Laboratory, Univ. Illinois, Chicago , IL, USA, 1978–.

Past Posts Ass. Prof., Assoc. Prof., UCLA, 1966–71; Vis. Ass. Prof.,

Univ. Chicago, 1969; Assoc. Prof., Columbia Univ., 1969–71; Res. Analyst, NBER, 1970–3; Assoc. Prof., Prof., Grad. Center, Queens Coll., City Univ. NY, 1971–5; Vis. Res. Econ., Princeton Univ., 1973; Sr. Staff Econ., US President's Council Econ. Advisers, 1973–7; Sr. Fellow, Vis. Scholar, Hoover Inst., Stanford Univ., 1977–8, 1984–5; Adjunct Scholar, AEI, 1978–.

Degrees BA Brooklyn Coll., NY, 1962; MA, PhD Columbia Univ., 1964, 1967.

Offices and Honours Ford Foundation Doctoral Dissertation Fellow, 1964–5; ASA Nat. Council, 1976–7; ASA Census Advisory Comm., 1980–; Pres., Univ. NBER Conference Res. Income and Wealth, 1978–; National Comm. Vital and Health Stats., 1981–.

Editorial Duties Ed. Board, *Internat. Migration Rev.*, 1983–.

Principal Fields of Interest 022 Microeconomic Theory; 200 Quantitative Economic Methods and Data; 800 Manpower, Labour, Population.

Publications *Books:* 1. *Income Inequality: Regional Analyses within a Human Capital Framework* (Columbia Univ. Press, 1974); 2. *Statistics and Econometrics* (with S. Chiswick), (Univ. Park Press, 1975); 3. *Human Resources and Income Distribution: Issues and Policies,* co-ed. (with J. O'Neill), (Univ. Norton, 1977); 4. *The Employment of Immigrants in the United States* (AEI, 1982); 5. *The Gateway: US Immigration Issues and Policies,* ed. (AEI, 1982); 6. *The Dilemma of American Immigration: Beyond the Golden Door* (with P. Cafferty, A Greeley, T. Sullivan), (Transaction Books, 1983).

Articles: 1. 'Education and the distribution of earnings' (with G. S. Becker), *AER,* 56(2), May 1966, repr. in *Human Capital,* by G. S. Becker (Columbia Univ. Press, 1975); 2. 'Time series changes in income inequality in the United States since 1939, with projections to 1985' (with J. Mincer), *JPE,* 80(3), pt. 2, May–June 1972; 3. 'Racial discrimination in the labor market: a test of alternative hypotheses', *JPE,* 81(6), Nov.–Dec. 1973, repr. in *Patterns of Racial Discrimination, II, Em-*

ployment and Income, eds. G. von Furstenberg, *et al.* (D. C. Heath, 1974); 4. 'The demand for nursing home care: an analysis of the substitution between institutional and non-institutional care', *JHR,* 11(3), Summer 1976; 5. 'Hospital utilization: an analysis of SMAS differences in hospital admission rates, occupancy rates and bed rates', *Explor. Econ. Res.,* 3(3), Summer 1976; 6. 'The income transfer system: impact, viability and proposals for reform', in *Contemporary Economic Problems,* ed. W. Fellner (AEI, 1977); 7. 'The effect of Americanization on the earnings of foreign-born men', *JPE,* 86(5), Oct. 1978; 8. 'The economic progress of immigrants: some apparently universal pattern', in *Contemporary Economic Problems,* ed. W. Fellner (AEI, 1979), repr. in *The Gateway: US Immigration Issues and Policies,* ed. B. R. Chiswick (AEI, 1982); 9. 'The impact of immigration on the level and distribution of economic well-being', in *ibid.;* 10. 'The earnings and human capital of American Jews', *JHR,* 18(3), Summer 1983.

Principal Contributions Research has focussed on the theoretical and empirical analysis of investment in human capital, employment and earnings with special attention to the determination of optimal public policies. Research on public policy formation complemented by staff position on the President's Council of Economic Advisers and consulting for various government agencies and commissions.

Involved in the development and early application of the 'human capital earnings function', now a standard technique for analyses of earnings. Demonstrated its usefulness for estimating rates of return to schooling and for analysing income distribution.

Pioneered empirical research on income distribution (across geographic areas and over time) using a systematic model based on human capital theory. Public policy interest led to an analytical synthesis of the US income transfer system and its economic impact. This was accompanied by research on specific issues such as public educational policies, discrimination, screening, and unemployment compensation.

An interest in health economics led to the first econometric model of the supply and demand for nursing-home care and the first economic model for analysing optimal hospital size and vacancy rates.

Pioneered systematic research on the adjustment (human capital investment, earnings, employment, occupation) of immigrants, thereby opening a new field of research for economists. Model based on skill transferability and self-selection shown to be very powerful in understanding immigrant adjustment. The first to model the link between the impact of immigration and explicit and implicit immigration policies.

Current research focusses on the determinants of racial and ethnic group differences in economic outcomes. Pioneered a series of systematic studies of the 'successful' US minorities (Chinese, Japanese and Jews). Developing and testing alternative models of inter-group differences in fertility, investment in human capital, and labour market outcomes.

CHOW, Gregory

Born 1929, Macau, S. China.
Current Post Prof. Econ., Class of 1913 Prof. Polit. Econ., Dir., Econometric Res. Program, Princeton Univ., NJ, 1971–.
Past Posts Staff Member, Manager Econ. Models, IBM Res. Center Yorktown Heights, NY, 1962–70; Vis. Prof., Cornell Univ., 1964–5; Adjunct Prof., Columbia Univ., 1965–71; Academia Sinica, Lect., Taiwan Univ., 1966; Vis. Prof., Harvard Univ., 1967.
Degrees BA Cornell Univ., 1951; MA, PhD Univ. Chicago, 1952, 1955.
Offices and Honours Fellow, Em Soc, ASA, Academia Sinica; Adviser, Econ. Planning Council, Taiwan; Chairman, AEA Comm. Exchanges with People's Republic China; Pres., Soc. Econ. Dynamics Control, 1979–80.
Editorial Duties Ed. Boards, *AER*, 1970–2, *Annals Econ. Social Measurements*, 1972–8; Assoc. Ed., *REStat*, 1972–, *Int ER*, 1972–; Co-ed., *JED*, 1978–81; Chief Ed., *Econ. Science Technology Rev.* (in Chinese), 1980–4.

Principal Fields of Interest 023 Macroeconomic Theory; 212 Econometric Models.
Publications *Books:* 1. *Demand for Automobiles in the United States: A Study in Consumer Durables* (N-H, 1957), transl. Spanish, 1965; 2. *Analysis and Control of Dynamic Economic Systems* (Wiley, 1975); 3. *Econometric Analysis by Control Methods* (Wiley, 1981); 4. *Evaluating the Reliability of Macroeconomic Models* (with P. Corsi), (Wiley, 1982); 5. *Econometrics* (McGraw-Hill, 1983); 6. *The Chinese Economy* (Harper & Row, 1985).
Articles: 1. 'Tests of equality between sets of coefficients in two linear regressions', *Em*, 28, July 1960; 2. 'Multiplier, accelerator, and liquidity preference in the determination of national income in the United States', *REStat*, 44(1), Feb. 1967; 3. 'Technological change and the demand for computers', *AER*, 57(5), Dec. 1967; 4 'Effect of uncertainty on optimal control policies', *Int ER*, 14(3), Oct. 1973; 5. 'Estimation of rational expectations models', *JEc Dyn*, 2, 1980.
Principal Contributions Pioneered the study of the demand for consumer durables (including automobiles) and for computers. Conducted empirical studies in macroeconomics, including the demand for money and the modelling of the macroeconomy of the US. Contributed to econometric methods, including the 'Chow-test' of stability of regression coefficients; methods to estimate systems of simultaneous equations; an information criterion for the selection of econometric models; and the estimation of econometric models under rational expectations. Developed stochastic control methods and pioneered the study of stabilisation policies and economic planning using these methods.

CHRIST, Carl Finley

Born 1923, Chicago, IL, USA.
Current Post Abram G. Hutzler Prof. Econ., Johns Hopkins Univ., Baltimore, MD, USA, 1977–.
Past Posts Jr. Physicist, Manhattan Project, 1943–5; Instr. Physics, Prince-

ton Univ., 1945–6; Res. Assoc., Cowles Commission, Univ. Chicago, 1946–50; Ass. Prof., Assoc. Prof., Prof. Polit. Econ., Johns Hopkins Univ., 1950–3, 1953–5, 1961–6, 1969–70; Assoc. Prof., Univ. Chicago, 1955–61; Vis. Prof., Univ. Tokyo, 1959; Keynes Vis Prof., Univ. Essex, England, 1966–7; Lect., Kyoto Amer. Studies Seminar, 1977; Cons., Fed. Reserve Board, 1979.

Degrees BS (Physics), PhD Univ. Chicago, 1943, 1950.

Offices and Honours Phi Beta Kappa, 1943; Sigma XI, 1946; Fellow, ASA, 1970; Fellow, Em Soc, 1967–; US SSRC Fellow, 1948–50; Sr. Fulbright Res. Fellow, Univ. Camb., 1954–5; Council Member, RES; Fellow, Center Advanced Study Behavioral Sciences, Stanford, 1960–1; Vice-Pres., AEA, 1980.

Editorial Duties Ed. Board, *AER,* 1969–73.

Principal Fields of Interest 210 Econometric Methods; 311 Domestic Monetary; 321 Fiscal Theory.

Publications *Books:* 1. *Econometric Models and Methods* (Wiley, 1966; transls., Japanese, Kajima, 1973, Spanish, Limusa, 1974).

Articles: 1. 'A simple macroeconomic model with a government budget restraint', *JPE,* 76, Jan.–Feb. 1968; 2. 'Judging the performance of econometric models of the US economy', *Int ER,* 16, Feb. 1975, repr. in *Econometric Model Performance: Comparative Simulation Studies of the US Economy,* eds. L. R. Klein and E. Burmeister (Univ. Pennsylvania Press, 1976); 3. 'An evaluation of the economic policy proposals of the joint economic committee of the 92nd and 93rd congresses', in *Institutions, Policies, and Economic Performance,* eds. K. Brunner and A. H. Meltzer, repr. in *Carnegie-Rochester Conference Series on Public Policy,* 20 (N-H, 1976); 4. 'Some dynamic theory of macroeconomic policy effects on income and prices under the government budget restraint', *J Mon E,* 4, Jan. 1978; 5. 'On fiscal and monetary policies and the government budget restraint', *AER,* 69(4), Sept. 1979; 6. 'Changes in the financing of the federal debt and their impact on the US economy, 1948–90', in US Congress, Joint Econ. Comm., *Special Study on Economic Change, 6, Federal Finance: The Pursuit of American Goals* (US Govt. Printing Office, 1980); 7. 'The mythology of tax cuts' (with A. A. Walters), *Policy Rev.,* 16, Spring 1981; 8. 'Analysis of stability in macroeconomic models with a government budget restraint', *Revista de Econometria,* 2, April 1982; 9. 'Rules vs. discretion in monetary policy', *CATO J,* 3, Spring 1983.

Principal Contributions Early work was in econometrics. Dissertation was a test of the forecasts made by Klein's Model III (published in NBER volume, *Conference on Business Cycles,* 1951). Prepared a textbook in econometrics. Have maintained an interest in the testing of econometric models by examining their forecasting performance. Recent work has been in macroeconomics, especially the interaction of monetary and fiscal policy through the govenment budget restraint. This restraint requires that the central government's expenditure must be financed by some combination of taxing, borrowing from owners of existing money, borrowing from the central bank (i.e. printing new money), and depleting stocks of assets (gold, foreign exchange, etc). It means that a government cannot choose all the macroeconomic policy variables freely; they must satisfy the government budget restraint. Policy multipliers that take this into account differ from those that ignore it. Such considerations are relevant to open-economy macroeconomic models as well as to closed-economy models. One of the most satisfying aspects of academic economics is the excellent students I have taught at Chicago and at Johns Hopkins, many of whom are already listed in this directory, and many more of whom surely will be.

CHRISTALLER, Walter*

Dates and Birthplace 1893–1969, Bavaria, Germany.

Posts Held City planner, Minicipality Berlin, 1921–30.

Degrees Student, Univ. Heidelberg, 1913–14; PhD Univ. Erlangen, 1933.

Offices and Honours Gold Medal,

Sweden; Hon. Fellow, Assoc. Amer. Geographers.

Publications *Books:* 1. *Central Places in Southern Germany* (1933, 1966).

Articles: 1. 'How I discovered the theory of central places' (1968), in *Man, Space and Environment*, eds. P. W. English and R. C. Mayfield (1972).

Career Following in the footsteps of Thünen and Alfred Weber, Christaller developed an abstract theory of the location of cities, emphasising tertiary activities (whereas Thünen and Weber had focussed on the primary and secondary sectors), which reached the conclusion that cities tend to be located in the centre of hexagonal market areas. This theory has had a major impact on economic geography and even as Thünen has been called 'the father of location theory', Christaller has been dubbed 'the father of theoretical geography'.

Secondary Literature B. J. L. Berry and A. Pred, *Central Place Studies: A Bibliography of Theory and Applications* (Regional Science Res. Inst., 1965); B. J. L. Berry and W. L. Garrison, 'Recent developments of central place theory', in *Urban Economics. Theory, Development and Planning*, eds. W. H. Leahy, *et al.* (Free Press, 1970).

CHRISTENSEN, Laurits Ray

Born 1941, Manitowoc, WI, USA.
Current Post Prof. Econ., Univ. Wisconsin-Madison, WI, USA; Pres., Laurits R. Christensen Assoc. Inc., 1981–.
Past Posts Cons., US Treasury, 1971–2, US Bureau Labor Stats., 1972–3; Vis. Assoc. Prof., Univ. British Columbia, Canada, 1973.
Degrees BA Cornell Univ., 1964; MS (Stats.), PhD Univ. Cal. Berkeley, 1960, 1968.
Editorial Duties Ed. Board, *AER*, 1976–8.
Principal Fields of Interest 200 Quantitative Economic Methods and Data; 600 Industrial Organisation.
Publications *Articles*: 1. 'Measuring economic performance in the private sector' (with D. W. Jorgenson), in *The Measurement of Economic and Social Performance*, ed. M. Moss (NBER, 1973); 2. 'Transcendental logarithmic production frontiers' (with D. W. Jorgenson and L. J. Lau), *REStat*, 55(1), Feb. 1973; 3. 'The internal structure of functional relationships: separability substitution, and aggregation' (with E. R. Berndt), *REStud*, 40(3), July 1973; 4. 'Testing for the existence of a consistent aggregate index of labor inputs' (with E. R. Berndt), *AER*, 64(3), June 1974; 5. 'Economies of scale in US electric power generation' (with W. H. Greene), *JPE*, 84(4), Aug. 1976, repr. in *Managerial Economics: Concepts, Application, and Cases* (Dun-Donnelly, 1977); 6. 'Global properties of flexible functional forms' (with D. W. Caves), *AER*, 70(3), June 1980; 7. 'The relative efficiency of public and private firms in a competitive environment: the case of Canadian railroads' (with D. W. Caves), *JPE*, 88(5), Oct. 1980; 8. 'Economic performance in regulated and unregulated environments: a comparison of US and Canadian railroads' (with D. W. Caves and J. A. Swanson), *QJE*, 96(4), Nov. 1981; 9. 'The economic theory of index numbers and the measurement of input, output, and productivity' (with D. W. Caves and W. E. Diewert), *Em*, 50(6), Nov. 1982; 10. 'A Comparison of different methodologies in a case study of residential time-of-use electricity pricing' (with D. W. Caves and J. A. Herriges), *J Em*, 26(1–2), Sept.–Oct. 1984.

Principal Contributions My career in economic research has been greatly influenced by the work of my mentor, Dale W. Jorgenson. I spent the first several years following my PhD collaborating with Jorgenson on several projects. We developed a system of national economic accounts that emphasised consistency of interrelationships. We applied the system to the USA and later to several other countries. Jorgenson, Lawrence J. Lau and I developed the ideas for translog functional forms at Berkeley during the summer of 1969. This provided the basis for much of my subsequent empirical work.

In 1971 I began a series of collaborations with my PhD students at the

University of Wisconsin, involving more microeconomic data sets, first aggregate manufacturing data and later individual firm data for electric utilities, railroads, airlines, etc. The principal contributions to develop from this were: (1) making use of economic principles to develop better data sets than had been used for previous industry studies; and (2) modelling the structure of cost and production in more general ways than had been the norm. For example, Berndt and I were the first seriously to study substitution possibilities in situations with more than two inputs. Greene and I were the first to use a flexible functional form to study return to scale issues. Caves and I pioneered in the area of multiproduct cost functions.

A central theme of my work throughout my career has been the proper estimation of differences in productivity across time and economic entities. My most recent work has involved extensive study of consumer behaviour at the household level in response to diurnal peak-load pricing for electricity.

CICCHETTI, Charles J.

Born 1943.
Current Post Prof. Econ. Environmental Stud., Univ. Wisconsin-Madison, USA, 1979–; Vice-Pres., Nat. Econ. Res. Assoc., White Plains, NY, USA, 1984–.
Past Posts Econ., Resources for the Future, Washington DC, 1969–72; Assoc. Lect., Assoc. Prof., Univ. Wisconsin, 1972, 1974–9; Dir., Wisconsin Energy Office, 1975–6; Chairman, Commissioner, Public Service Commission, WI, 1977–9, 1977–80.
Degrees BA Colorado Coll., 1965; PhD Rutgers Univ., 1969.
Offices and Honours Special Energy Counsellor to Governor P. J. Luce, State of Wisconsin, 1975–6.
Editorial Duties Ed. Boards, *JEEM, Energy Systems and Policy, J Law E.*
Principal Fields of Interest 613 Public Utilities; 721 Natural Resources; 723 Energy.
Publications *Books:* 1. *A Primer for Environmental Preservation* (MSS

Modular Publications, 1973); 2. *Studies in Electric Utility Regulation* (with J. Jurewitz), (Ballinger, 1975); 3. *Energy System Forecasting, Planning and Pricing,* ed. (with W. Foell), (Univ. Wisconsin Monograph, 1975); 4. *The Measurement of Congestion Costs: A Case Study of the Spanish Peaks Primitive Area* (with K. Smith), (Ballinger, 1976); 5. *The Marginal Costs and Pricing of Electricity: An Applied Approach* (with W. Gillen and P. Smolensky), (Ballinger, 1977).

Articles: 1. 'Benefits or costs', in *Benefit Cost and Policy Analysis 1972,* eds. W. Niskanen, *et al.* (Aldine Press, 1972); 2. 'An economic analysis of the Trans-Alaska Pipeline', in *Benefit Cost and Policy Analysis 1973,* eds. R. Haveman, *et al.* (Aldine Press, 1974); 3. 'Some institutional and conceptual thoughts on the measurement of indirect and intangible benefits and costs', in *Benefit Cost Analysis and Water Pollution Control Policy,* eds. H. Peskin and E. Seskin (Urban Inst., 1974); 4. 'Congestion, optimal use and benefit estimation: a case study of wilderness recreation' (with V. K. Smith), in *Social Experiments and Social Program Evaluation,* eds. J. G. Albert and M. Kamrass (Ballinger, 1974); 5. 'Public utility pricing: a synthesis of marginal cost, regulatory constraints, Averch-Johnson bias, and peak load pricing' (with J. Jurewitz), in *Studies in Electric Utility Regulation,* eds. C. Cicchetti and J. Jurewitz (Ballinger, 1975).

CLAGUE, Christopher Karran

Born 1938, Washington, DC, USA.
Current Post Prof. Econ., Univ. Maryland, College Park, MD, USA, 1979–.
Past Posts Instr., Harvard Univ., 1965–7; Sr. Staff Econ., US President's Council Econ. Advisers, Washington, DC, 1967–8; Ass. Prof., Assoc. Prof., Univ. Maryland, 1968–71, 1971–9; Vis. Prof., Boston Univ., Center Latin American Devlp. Stud., 1974–5, Univ. Cal. Berkeley, 1983.
Degrees BA Swarthmore Coll., 1960, PhD Harvard Univ., 1966.

Offices and Honours Doherty Fellow, 1964–5.

Editorial Duties Ed. Board, *SEJ*, 1977–9.

Principal Fields of Interest 110 Economic Growth; 400 International Economics.

Publications *Books:* 1. *Haiti: the Politics of Squalor* (with R. Rothberg), (Houghton Mifflin, 1971); 2. *Capital Utilization: A Theoretical Empirical Analysis* (with R. Betancourt), (CUP, 1981).

Articles: 1. 'An international comparison of industrial efficiency: Peru and the United States', *REStat*, 44(4), May 1967; 2. 'Capital-labor substitution in manufacturing in underdeveloped countries', *Em*, 37(3), July 1969; 3. 'The determinants of efficiency in manufacturing industries in an underdeveloped country,' *EDCC*, 18(2), June 1970, repr. in *Workers and Managers in Latin America*, eds. S. Davis and L. W. Goodman (D. C. Heath, 1972); 4. 'Tariff preferences and separable utility', *AER*, 61(2), May 1971; 5. 'Legal strategies for dealing with heroin addiction', *AER*, 63(2), May 1973, repr. in *The Economics of Crime*, eds. R. Andreano and J. J. Siegfried (Wiley, 1980); 6. 'Information costs, corporate hierarchies, and earnings inequality', *AER*, 67(1), Feb. 1977; 7. 'The effects of marriage and fertility patterns on the transmission and distribution of wealth', *JHR*, 12(2), Spring 1977; 8. 'The theory of capital utilization in labor-managed enterprises' (with R. Betancourt), *QJE*, 91(3), Aug. 1977; 9. 'An econometric analysis of capital utilization' (with R. Betancourt), *Int ER*, 19(1), Feb. 1978.

Principal Contributions My intellectual work can be divided into four areas. (1) Economic development with special reference to Latin America, 1965–70 and 1983–present. In my dissertation I analysed at the factory level the reasons for differences in labour productivity between Peru and the US. I maintained an interest in Peru and did a study of the economic development of Haiti (1970). In the last year I have returned to the study of Latin American economic development.

(2) International trade, 1965–72, 1978–present. I did studies of the trade effects of tariff discrimination, in which I emphasised an Armington-type substitution among goods from different countries (1971). I also collaborated in a study of the relationship between the absolute purchasing-power parity and the exchange rate (1972), a topic to which I have returned in the last few years.

(3) Poverty, income distribution and social mobility, 1973–77. Stimulated by some work of Pryor on the effects of assortative mating and fertility differences by income on the concentration of material wealth, I argued first that the intergenerational transmission of wealth in the US consists primarily of human rather than financial capital and second that marriage and fertility patterns do play a role in the perpetuation of inequality. In another paper I suggested that income inequality is increased by the phenomenon of *esprit de corps* in successful corporations. I also did an economic analysis of strategies for dealing with heroin addiction.

(4) Capital utilisation, 1972–present (mostly with Roger Betancourt). Our initial interest in multiple shifts stemmed from a concern to increase modern-sector employment in developing countries. We found the duration of operations to be a largely neglected variable in production theory, with important implications for econometric estimation of production functions. Recently with Panagariya, we have been incorporating variable capital utilisation into two-sector models of international trade.

CLAPHAM, John Harold*

Dates and Birthplace 1873–1946, Salford, England.

Posts Held Fellow, King's Coll. Camb., 1898–1904; Prof. Econ., Univ. Leeds, 1902–8; UK Board Trade, 1916–18; Dean, Vice-Provost, King's Coll., 1908–46, Prof. Econ. Hist., Univ. Camb., 1928–46.

Degree BA Univ. Camb., 1895.

Offices and Honours Pres., EHS, BA; Knighted, 1943.

Publications *Books:* 1. *The Woollen*

and Worsted Industries (1907); 2. The Economic Development of France and Germany 1815–1914 (1921, 1961); 3. An Economic History of Modern Britain, 3 vols (1926–38, 1950–2); 4. The Bank of England, 2 vols (1944); 5. A Concise Economic History of Britain (1949, 1957).

Articles: 1. 'Of empty economic boxes', EJ, 32, Sept. 1922, 32, Dec. 1922.

Career Originally an historian, he turned to British economic history under the guidance of Marshall. Both as a writer of broad surveys of economic history and as a teacher he was a major influence on the development of the discipline in Britain. His technique remained that of the historian, but he was nevertheless very much aware of developments in economic theory. By providing what he felt were neutral accounts of the development of institutions and changes in economic circumstances, he provided a basis for future work on themes and problems in economic history.

Secondary Literature P. Mathias, 'Clapham, John Harold', IESS, 2.

CLARK, Colin Grant

Born 1905, London, England.
Current Post Cons. Econ. Res., Univ. Queensland, St Lucia, Australia, 1977–.
Past Posts Under-Secretary Labour and Industry, Fin. Adviser, Treasury, State of Queensland, Australia, 1938–52; Vis. Prof., Univ Chicago, 1952; Dir., Agric. Econ. Inst., Oxford Univ., 1953–69; Fellow, Monash Univ., Australia, 1969–78; Econ., Inst. Pol. Stud., London, 1976–7.
Degrees MA, Dr Letters Univ. Oxford, 1931, 1971; MA Univ. Camb., 1935; PhD Sacro Cuore Univ., Milan, 1955; PhD Tilburg Univ., The Netherlands, 1962.
Offices and Honours Fellow, Brasenose Coll., Oxford, 1961; Corresp. Fellow, BA, 1978.
Principal Fields of Interest 110 Economic Growth.
Publications Books: 1. Conditions of Economic Progress (Macmillan, 1940,

1957); 2. Growthmanship (INEA, 1961); 3. Economics of Subsistence Agriculture (with M. R. Haswell), (Macmillan, 1964); 4. Population, Growth and Land Use (Macmillan, 1967, 1977); 5. Poverty before Politics (INEA, 1977); 6. The Economics of Irrigation (with I. Carruthers), (Liverpool Univ. Press, 1981); 7. Regional and Urban Location (Queensland Univ. Press, 1982); 8. Wages and Profits in Japan (Nikon Keizai Shimbun, 1984).

Articles: 1. 'Public finance and changes in the value of money', EJ, 55, Dec. 1945.

Principal Contributions Quantitative international studies of national products. Questioning of capital investment as determining factor in growth. Study of limitations of taxation and proposals for its reduction.

Secondary Literature H. W. Arndt, 'Clark, Colin', IESS, 18.

CLARK, John Bates*

Dates and Birthplace 1847–1938, Providence, RI, USA.
Posts Held Prof., Smith Coll., 1881–93, Amherst Coll., 1893–5, Columbia Univ., 1895–1923.
Degree BA Amherst Coll., 1872.
Offices and Honours Founder, Pres., AEA, 1888; Head, Econ. and Hist. Div., Carnegie Endowment Internat. Peace, 1911–23.
Publications Books: 1. The Philosophy of Wealth (1886); 2. The Distribution of Wealth (1899, 1902); 3. Essentials of Economic Theory (1907); 4. Social Justice without Socialism (1914).

Career His earlier articles show the influence of his German academic socialist teachers and show him as a critic of capitalism. His Philosophy ... was a reworking of these articles. At Columbia his intellectual position gradually shifted towards wholehearted support for capitalism. His Distribution ... again reworked previously published materials into treatise form and contains the marginal productivity theory of distribution, which he developed in response to certain writings of Henry George. It also contained his theory of capital, in which capital goods are distinguished from social capital, with the marginal productivity of social capital, not of specific capital goods, determining the role of interest. This involved him in lively controversy with various contemporaries, particularly Böhm-Bawerk. His later *Essentials . . .* contained his attempt to move from what he considered the static analysis of his earlier work to a more dynamic model.

Secondary Literature A. H. Clark and J. M. Clark, *John Bates Clark: A Memorial* (Columbia Univ. Press, 1938); G. J. Stigler, *Production and Distribution Theories* (Macmillan, 1941); J. M. Clark, 'Clark, John Bates', *IESS*, 2.

CLARK, John Maurice*

Dates and Birthplace 1884–1963, MA, USA.

Posts Held Assoc. Prof. Econ., Amherst, MA, 1910–5; Prof., Univ. Chicago, 1915–26; Prof. Econ., Columbia Univ., 1926–57.

Degrees BA Amherst Coll., 1905; MA, PhD Columbia Univ., 1906, 1910.

Offices and Honours Pres., F. A. Walker Medal, AEA, 1922, 1952.

Publications *Books:* 1. *Standards of Reasonableness in Local Freight Discriminations* (1910); 2. *Studies in the Economics of Overhead Costs* (1923, 1962); 3. *Social Control of Business* (1926, 1939); 4. *The Costs of the World War to the American People* (1931); 5. *Strategic Factors in Business Cycles* (1934); 6. *Preface to Social Economics* (1936); 7. *Alternative to Serfdom* (1948, 1960); 8. *The Ethical Basis of Economic Freedom* (1955); 9. *Competition as a Dynamic Process* (1961).

Articles: 1. 'Toward a concept of workable competition', *AER,* 30(3), June 1940.

Career Son of John Bates Clark and his successor in the search for an understanding of the dynamic elements in economics. Despite his thorough acquaintance with the techniques of abstract analysis, he chose to express his arguments in purely verbal terms. His interests ranged widely within economics and he published on the business cycle (inventing the acceleration principle), economic costs of war, public works, the labour market and many other topics. The chief problem to which he addressed himself was the implications of competition on welfare and public policy. He considered perfect competition both theoretically and practically unattainable and sought to distinguish it from a realistic concept of 'workable competition'.

Secondary Literature J. W. Markham, 'Clark, John Maurice', *IESS,* 2; C. A. Hickman, *J. M. Clark* (Columbia Univ. Press, 1975).

CLARK, Peter K.

Born 1944, Spokane, WA, USA.

Current Post Vis. Prof. Econ. and Management, Yale Univ., USA, 1983–.

Past Posts Ass. Prof., Assoc. Prof., Univ. Minnesota; Fiscal Analyst, US Congressional Budget Office; Sr Staff Econ., US President's Council Econ. Advisers; Vis. Assoc. Prof., Stanford Univ.; Chief, Nat. Income Section, Governors Fed. Reserve Board.

Degrees BS (Physics) Cal. Inst. Technology, 1965; PhD Harvard Univ., 1970.

Offices and Honours NBER Faculty Res. Fellow, 1973–4; Hoover Nat. Fellow, 1979–80.

Principal Fields of Interest 023 Macroeconomic Theory; 132 Economic Forecasting and Econometric Models; 226 Productivity and Growth: Theory and Models.

Publications *Articles:* 1. 'A subordinated stochastic process model with finite variance for speculative prices', *Em,* 41, Jan. 1973; 2. 'Capital formation and the recent productivity showdown', *J Fin,* 33(3), June 1978; 3. 'Potential GNP in the United States, 1948–1980', *RIW,* 25(2), June 1979; 4. 'Investment in the 1970s: theory, performance and prediction', *Brookings Papers Econ. Activity,* 1, 1979, 5. 'Inflation and the productivity decline', *AER,* 72(2), May 1982.

Principal Contributions Early work focussed on the idea that economic processes might not evolve at a constant rate, and that an adjusted time scale, or operational time, could be important in understanding the statistical properties of economic series. The transformation to operational time was successful in explaining the empirical distribution of price changes and returns in financial markets. A position as Senior Staff Economist at the Council of Economic Advisers led to a shift in research interest toward macroeconomic issues, including the natural rate of unemployment, potential GNP, the determinants of business capital formation, and the sources of economic growth. In 1977, some of this work was the basis for the upward revision of the official employment rate and the downward revision of potential GNP. Recent interest has focussed on the worldwide slowdown in productivity growth and its relationship to the emergence of chronic inflation.

CLAWSON, Marion

Born 1905, Elko, NV, USA.
Current Post Sr. Fellow Emeritus, Resources for the Future, Washington DC, USA, 1970–.
Past Posts Jr. Agric. Econ., Agric. Experimental Station, Univ. Nevada; Agric. Econ., US Bureau Agric. Econ., Washington, DC; Regional Admin., Dir., US Dept. Interior, Washington, DC; Cons., Econ. Advisory Staff, Jerusalem, Israel; Dir., Land Use and Management, Dir., Land and Water Stud., Acting Pres., Vice-Pres., Cons., Resources for the Future, Washington, DC; Regents Prof., Univ. Cal. Berkeley; Walker-Ames Prof., Univ. Washington, Seattle; Vis. Prof., Duke Univ., Durham, NC.
· **Degrees** BS, MS (Agric.) Univ. Nevada, 1926, 1929; PhD Harvard Univ., 1943.
Offices and Honours Vice-Pres., Pres., Western Agric. Econ. Assoc.; Vice-Pres., AAEA; Fellow, AAAS; Pres., Forest Hist. Soc.; Disting. Service Award, American Forestry Assoc.
Editorial Duties Ed. Boards, *Landscape Planning, Environmental Professional.*
Principal Fields of Interest 721 Natural Resources; 718 Rural Economics; 041 Economic History; General.
Publications *Books:* 1. *Economics of Outdoor Recreation* (with J. L. Knetsch), (JHUP, 1966); 2. *The Agricultural Potential of the Middle East* (with H. Landsberg and L. T. Alexander), (Amer. Elsevier, 1971); 3. *Planning and Urban Growth: An Anglo-American Comparison* (with P. Hall), (JHUP, 1973); 4. *Forests for Whom and For What?* (JHUP, 1975); 5. *The Economics of US Nonindustrial Private Forests* (Resources for the Future, 1978); 6. *The Federal Lands Revisited* (Resources for the Future, 1983).
Articles: 1. 'The federal land policy and management act of 1976 in a broad historical perspective', *Arizona Law Rev.*, 21(2), 1979; 2. 'An eclectic and inclusive approach to resource policy analysis', *J Bus Admin*, 11(1), Fall 1979, 11(2), Spring 1980; 3. 'Wilderness as one of many land uses', *Idaho Law Rev.*, 16(3), Summer 1980; 4. 'Methods of measuring the demand for and value of outdoor recreation' (Resources for the Future, 1981); 5. 'Competitive land use in American forestry and agriculture', *J. Forest Hist.*, 25(4), Oct. 1981; 6. 'An economic classification of US "commerical" forests', *J Forestry*, 79(11), Nov. 1981; 7. 'The role of the agricultural economist', *J. NE Econ. Council*, 12(2), Fall 1983.
Principal Contributions My major contributions have been (1) bringing social science analysis to problems of forestry, outdoor recreation, and other uses of natural resources; (2) eclectic and comprehensive analysis of natural resource problems, to integrate ecological, economic efficiency, economic equity, and socio-cultural considerations; (3) consideration of use of land, water, and other natural resources for such varied purposes as agriculture, forestry, urban occupancy, outdoor recreation, mineral development, and transportation use, all on an equal plane of analysis.

CLAY, Henry*

Dates and Birthplace 1883–1954, Bradford, W. Yorkshire, England.

Posts Held Lect., Workers' Educ. Tutorial Classes, 1909–17; Econ., UK Ministry Labour, 1917–9; Fellow, New Coll. Oxford, 1919–21; Stanley Jevons Prof. Polit. Econ., Prof. Social Econ., Univ. Manchester, 1922–7, 1927–30; Econ. Adviser, Bank of England, 1930–44; Warden, Nuffield Coll. Oxford, 1944–9.

Degrees MA, MCom Univ. Oxford, 1904.

Offices and Honours Member, Econ. and Wage Commission, S. Africa, 1925, UK Royal Commission Unemployment Insurance, 1931; Knighted, 1946.

Publications *Books:* 1. *Economics. An Introduction for the General Reader* (1916); 2. *The Problem of Industrial Relations* (1929); 3. *The Post-War Unemployment Problem* (1929).

Career Prominent British monetary and applied economist of the interwar period, the epitome of a 'classical economist' in the sense of the term defined by Keynes. Founded NIESR in 1938.

CLINE, William Richard

Born 1941, Denver, CO, USA.

Current Post Sr. Fellow, Inst. Internat. Econ., Washington, DC, 1982–.

Past Posts Instr., Yale Univ., 1966; Lect., Ass. Prof., Princeton Univ., 1967–9, 1969–70; Ford Foundation Vis. Prof., Brazilian Planning Ministry and Univ. Sao Paulo, 1970–1; Deputy Dir. Devlp. and Trade Res., Office Ass. Secretary Internat. Affairs, US Treasury, 1971–3; Sr. Fellow, Brookings Inst., 1973–81.

Degrees BA Princeton Univ., 1963; MA, PhD Yale Univ., 1964, 1969.

Offices and Honours Woodrow Wilson Fellow, 1964; National Defense Foreign Language Fellow, 1966; Ford Foreign Area Fellow, 1965.

Editorial Duties Assoc. Ed, *JDE*.

Principal Fields of Interest 100 Economic Growth; 400 International Economics.

Publications *Books:* 1. *Economic Consequences of a Land Reform in Brazil* (N-H, 1970); 2. *Potential Effects of Income Redistribution on Economic Growth: Latin American Cases* (Praeger, 1972); 3. *International Monetary Reform and the Developing Countries* (Brookings Inst., 1976); 4. *Trade Negotiations in the Tokyo Round* (with N. Kawanabe, T. Kronsjo and T. Williams), (Brookings Inst., 1978); 5. *Economic Integration in Developing Countries*, co-ed. (with E. Delgado), (Brookings Inst., 1978); 6. *Agrarian Structure and Productivity in Developing Countries* (with R. A. Berry), (JHUP, 1979); 7. *Economic Stabilization in Developing Countries*, co-ed. (with S. Weintraub), (Brookings Inst., 1980); 8. *World Inflation and the Developing Countries* (Brookings Inst., 1980); 9. *Trade Policy in the 1930s* (Inst. Internat. Econ., 1983); 10. *International Debt: Systemic Risk and Policy Response* (Inst. Internat. Econ., 1984).

Articles: 1. 'Measurement of debt servicing capacity: an application of discriminant analysis' (with C. R. Frank, Jr.), *J Int E*, 1(3), Aug. 1971; 2. 'Cost-benefit analysis of irrigation projects in northeastern Brazil', *AJAE*, 55(4), Nov. 1973; 3. 'Interrelationships between agricultural strategy and rural income distribution', *Food Research Inst. Stud.*, 11(2), 1973; 4. 'Distribution and development: a survey of literature', *JDE*, 1(4), Feb. 1975; 5. 'Policy instruments for rural income distribution', in *Income Distribution and Growth in Less-Developed Countries*, eds. C. R. Frank, Jr. and R. Webb (Brookings Inst., 1977); 6. 'Imports and consumer prices: a survey analysis', *J. Retailing*, 55(1), Spring 1979; 7. 'Commodity prices and the world distribution of income', *J. Pol. Modelling*, 2(1), Jan. 1980; 8. 'Can the East Asian model of development be generalized?', *WD*, 10(2), Feb. 1982; 9. 'Mexico's crisis, the world's peril', *Foreign Pol.*, 49, Winter 1982–3; 10. 'Economic stabilization in developing countries: theory and stylized facts', in *IMF Conditionality*, ed. J. Williamson (Inst. Internat. Econ., 1983).

Principal Contributions The common theme of my work has been the application of theory and quantitative modelling to the examination of policy issues in international and development economics. My early work focussed on distributional issues, using production functions and land-use patterns to simulate the impact of hypothetical land reform in Brazil, and applying empirical consumption functions and input-output relationships to simulate growth effects of income redistribution, in both cases challenging conventional views of adverse effect. In the mid-1970s, my work concentrated on international economics with implications for developing countries: the effects of international floating exchange rates on developing countries, quantitative effects of trade negotiations, proposals for a new economic order, and consequences of world inflation for developing countries. The principal laboratory for my work on development has been Latin America, the subject of ongoing consulting work. In 1982–3 I returned to an early empirical interest — debt servicing capacity of developing countries — and carried out projections of balance of payments and debt for major debtor countries to determine whether the debt crisis of the early 1980s was one of temporary illiquidity or fundamental insolvency. I have found computer-based simulation, often on a data-intensive basis, to be a useful means of narrowing the range of debate. Work on issues such as international debt and trade policy has also suggested the importance of taking political as well as economic factors into account.

CLOTFELTER, Charles Thomas

Born 1947, Birmingham, AL, USA.
Current Post Vice Provost, Academic Pol. and Planning, Duke Univ., Prof. Public Pol. Stud. and Econ., Duke Univ. Durham, NC, USA, 1984–.
Past Posts Teaching Fellow, Harvard Univ., 1972–4; Tutor Econ., Harvard Coll., 1972–4; Ass. Prof. Econ., Univ. Maryland, College Park, MD, 1974–9; Fin. Econ., Office Tax Analysis, US Treasury Dept., 1978–9; Assoc. Prof. Public Pol. Stud. and Econ., Duke Univ., 1979–84; Vis. Scholar, Inst.

Res. Social Sciences, Univ. N. Carolina, Chapel Hill, 1982; Res Assoc., NBER, 1982–.
Degrees BA (Hist); Duke Univ. 1969; MA, PhD Harvard Univ. 1972, 1974.
Offices and Honours Brookings Econ. Policy Fellow, 1978–9; Vice-Pres., SEA, 1983–4.
Principal Fields of Interest 320 Fiscal Theory and Policy: Public Finance; 930 Urban Economics; 910 Welfare, Health and Education.
Publications *Articles:* 1. 'The effect of school desegregation on housing prices', *REStat*, 57, Nov. 1975; 2. 'Public spending for higher education: an empirical test of two hypotheses', *Public Fin.*, 31(2), 1976; 3. 'Public services, private substitutes, and demand for protection against crime', *AER*, 67(5), Dec. 1977; 4. 'Private security and the public safety', *JUE*, 5, July 1978; 5. 'Urban school desegregation and declines in white enrolment: a reexamination', *Urban Econ.*, 6, July 1979; 6. 'Equity, efficiency and the taxation of in-kind compensation', *Nat. Tax J.*, 32, March 1979; 7. 'Tax incentives and charitable giving: evidence from a panel of taxpayers', *Public Econ.*, 13, June 1980; 8. 'Permanent versus transitory tax effects and the realization of capital gains' (with G. E. Auten), *QJE*, 98, Nov. 1982; 9. 'Tax evasion and tax rates: an analysis of individual returns', *REStat*, 65, Aug. 1983; 10. 'Tax-induced distortions and the business-pleasure borderline: the case of travel and entertainment', *AER*, 73(5), Dec. 1983
Principal Contributions I have emphasised empirical analysis applied to public policy and private behaviour. The work on desegregation and private protection points up some of the unintended effects of public policies. The work on tax policy explores a variety of forms of behaviour that are influenced, in varying degrees, by provisions of federal tax laws.

CLOWER, Robert Wayne

Born 1926, Pullman, WA, USA.
Current Post Prof. Econ., UCLA, 1972–.
Past Posts Instr. Econ., Washington State Univ., 1948–9; Ass. Tutor, New Coll. Oxford, 1950–2; Ass. Prof., Washington State Univ., 1952–6; Vis. Prof. Econ., Univ. Punjab, Lahore, Pakistan, 1954–6; Assoc. Prof., Prof. Econ., Northwestern Univ., 1957–62, 1963–71; Dir., Econ. Survey Liberia, Monrovia, Liberia, 1961–2; Vis. Prof., Camb. Univ., 1962; John Maynard Keynes Vis. Prof. Econ., Univ. Essex, 1965–6; Vis. Prof. Econ., Makerere Coll., Kampala, Uganda, 1965, Monash Univ., Melbourne, Australia, 1972; Bank of Italy Res. Staff Seminar, Perugia, Italy, 1973; Vis. Prof., Inst. Advanced Study, Vienna, Austria, 1974.
Degrees BA, MA Washington State Univ., 1948, 1949; MLitt, DLitt Oxford Univ., 1952, 1978.
Offices and Honours Rhodes Scholar, 1949–52; Nuffield Coll. Student, 1950–2; Chairman, Oxford-London-Cambridge Joint Econ. Seminars, 1950–2; Ford Foundation Faculty Res. Fellow, 1960–1; Guggenheim Memorial Fellow, 1965–6; Amer. Cons. Ed., Penguin Books, 1966–84; Hon. Fellow, Brasenose Coll. Oxford, 1978–; Fellow, Em Soc, 1978–; Exec. Comm., AEA, 1978–80; Erskine Fellow, Canterbury Univ., New Zealand, 1982; Vice-Pres., Pres., WEA Internat., 1985–6, 1986–7.
Editorial Duties Ed. Board, AER, 1963–6; Managing Ed., EI, 1973–9, AER, 1980–5.
Principal Fields of Interest 010 General Economics; 300 Domestic Monetary Theory; Fiscal Theory and Institutions; 600 Industrial Organisation.
Publications Books: 1. Introduction to Mathematical Economics (with D. W. Bushaw), (Richard D. Irwin, 1957); 2. Intermediate Economic Analysis (with J. F. Due), (Richard D. Irwin, 1961, 1966); 3. Puerto Rico Shipping and the US Maritime Laws (with J. Harris), (Northwestern Univ., 1965); 4. Growth without Development, an Economic Survey of Liberia (with G.

Dalton, A. Walters and M. Harwitz), (Northwestern Univ. Press, 1966); 5. Monetary Theory, ed. (Penguin, 1969, transl. Italian, La Teoria Monetaria, Franco Angeli, 1972); 6. Microeconomics (with J. F. Due), (Richard D. Irwin, 1972; transl. Spanish, Biblioteca Technos de Ciencias Economicas, 1978); 7. Money and Markets: Selected Essays of R. W. Clower, ed. D. A. Walker (CUP, 1984).
Articles: 1. 'An investigation into the dynamics of investment', AER, 44(1), March 1954; 2. 'Some theory of an ignorant monopolist', EJ, 69, Dec. 1959; 3. 'The Keynesian conterrevolution: a theoretical appraisal', in The Theory of Interest Rates, eds. F. W. Hahn and F. Brechling (Macmillan, 1965), repr. in Macroeconomic Themes, ed. J. Surrey (OUP, 1976), and in La Nueva Teoria Monetaria, ed. J. Saltes (Madrid Libres, 1978), and in Modern Macroeconomics, eds. T. Korliras and R. Thorn (Harper & Row, 1979); 4. 'A reconsideration of the microfoundations of monetary theory', WEJ, Dec. 1967; 5. 'Income, wealth and the theory of consumption' (with M. B. Johnson), in Essays in Honour of Sir John Hicks (Edinburgh Univ. Press, 1968), repr. in Macroeconomic Themes, ed. J. Surrey (OUP, 1966); 6. 'The coordination of economic activities: a Keynesian perspective', AER, 65(2), May 1975; 7. 'Reflections on the Keynesian perplex', ZN, 35(1–2), July 1975; 8. 'The anatomy of monetary theory', AER, 67(2), May 1977; 9. 'The transactions theory of the demand for money: a reconsideration' (with P. W. Howitt), JPE, 88(3), June 1978; 10. 'The genesis and control of inflation', in The Stability of Contemporary Economic Systems, eds. O. Kyn and W. Schrettl (Vandenhoeck & Ruprecht, 1979).
Principal Contributions I have been concerned throughout my professional career with the study of disequilibrium adjustment processes at both the microeconomic (household and firm) and macroeconomic level. This perspective underlies my early interest in stock-flow analysis, my later work on the micro-foundation of macroeconomics and monetary theory, and my current interest in the theory of

ongoing systems of monetary exchange. Though regarded by some of my colleagues as an idiosyncratic iconoclast, I consider myself to be a thoroughly constructive critic of conventional wisdom. My principal contributions have, I think, shed fresh light on central questions of economics concerning the self-organising and self-adjustment capabilities of decentralised economic systems. One way and another, I think I have helped to add sense to a discipline that is (and probably always will be) remarkably full of nonsense.

COASE, Ronald Harry

Born 1910, Middlesex, England.
Current Post Retired. Prof. Emeritus Econ., Sr. Fellow Law Econ., Univ. Chicago Law School, 1979–.
Past Posts Prof., Univs. Buffalo, 1951–8, Viriginia, 1958–64, Chicago, 1964–79.
Degrees BCom, DSc Univ. London, 1932, 1951.
Offices and Honours Fellow, AAAS, 1978; Disting. Fellow, AEA, 1979.
Principal Fields of Interest 010 General Economics.
Publications *Books:* 1. *British Broadcasting: A Study in Monopoly* (Longmans Green, Harvard Univ. Press, 1950).
Articles: 1. 'The nature of the firm', *Ec*, N.S. 4, Nov. 1937, repr. in *Readings in Price Theory*, eds. G. J. Stigler and K. E. Boulding (Richard D Irwin, 1952); 2. 'The marginal cost controversy', *Ec*, N.S. 13, Aug. 1946; 3. 'The problem of social costs', *J Law E*, 3, Oct. 1960; 4. 'The lighthouse in economics', *J Law E*, 17(2), Oct. 1974; 5. 'Marshall on method', *J Law E*, 18(1), April 1975.
Principal Contributions See K. G. Elzinga, 'Coase, R. H.', *IESS*, 18.

COATS, A. W.

Born 1924, Southall, Middlesex, England.
Current Post Emeritus Prof. Econ. and Social Hist., Univ. Nottingham, England; Res. Prof. Econ., Duke Univ., Durham, NC, USA, 1984–.

Past Posts Lect., Prof. Econ. and Social Hist., Univ. Nottingham, 1953–62, 1964–82; Reader, Econ. and Social Hist., Univ. York, England, 1963–4; Vis. Prof., Univs. Columbia, 1962, Virginia, 1962–3, Wisconsin, 1963, 1967, Stanford, 1967, Texas, Austin, 1978, Emory, Atlanta, 1979, 1983, Western Australia, Perth, 1980.
Degrees BSc, MSc Univ. London, 1948, 1950; PhD Johns Hopkins Univ., 1953.
Offices and Honours Gladstone Memorial Prize, Univ. Coll., Exeter, 1949; Fellow, English Speaking Union, Univ. Pittsburgh, 1950–1, Gustav Bissing, Johns Hopkins Univ., 1952–3, Rockefeller Foundation, 1958–9, Netherlands Inst. Advanced Stud., 1972–3, Nat. Humanities Center, N. Carolina, 1983–4; Pres., Hist. of Econ. Soc., USA, 1984–5.
Editorial Duties Ed. Boards, *YBESR*, 1963–4, *HOPE*, 1969–, *Res. Hist. Econ. Thought and Methodology* (JAI Press, 1983); Ed., *Hist. of Econ. Thought Newsletter*, 1968–71.
Principal Fields of Interest 031 History of Economic Thought; 036 Economic Methodology; 040 Economic History.
Publications *Books:* 1. *Essays in American Economic History*, co-ed. (with R. M. Robertson), (Arnold, 1969); 2. *The Classical Economists and Economic Policy*, ed. (Methuen, 1971); 3. *The Marginal Revolution in Economics*, co-ed. (with R. D. Collison Black and C. D. Goodwin), (Duke Univ. Press, 1972); 4. *English Poor Laws 1807–1833, English Poor Laws 1834–1870, Charity 1815–1870, Scottish Poor Laws 1815–1870*, ed. (Farnborough, 1973); 5. *El Papel del Economists En La Administracion Publica*, ed. (Revista Espanola de Economia, 1979); 6. *Economists in Government: An International Comparative Study*, ed. (Duke Univ. Press, 1981); 7. *Methodological Controversy in Economics: Historical Essays in Honor of T. W. Hutchison*, ed. (JAI Press, 1983).
Articles: 1. 'Changing attitudes to labour in the mid-eighteenth century', *EHR*, N.S. 11, Aug. 1958, repr. in *Essays in Social History*, eds. M. W. Flinn and T. C. Smout (OUP, 1974); 2. 'The first two decades of the American

Economic Association', *AER,* 50(4), Sept. 1960; 3. 'Sociological aspects of British economics, 1880–1930', *JPE,* 75(5), Oct. 1967; 4. 'The origins and early development of the Royal Economic Society', *EJ,* 78, June 1968; 5. 'Political economy and the tariff reform campaign of 1903', *J Law E,* 11, April 1968; 6. 'Is there a "structure of scientific revolutions" in economics?', *Kyk,* 23(2), 1969, repr. in *How Economists Explain: A Reader in Methodology,* eds. W. Marr and B. Raj (Univ. Press Amer., 1983); 7. 'The role of scholarly journals in the history of economics: an essay', *JEL,* 9(1), March 1971; 8. 'Economics and psychology: the death and resurrection of a research program', in *Method and Appraisal in Economics,* ed. S. Latsis (CUP, 1967); 9. 'The current crisis in economics in historical perspective', *Nebraska J. Econ. and Bus.,* 16(3), Summer 1977; 10. 'The culture and the economists: American-British differences', *HOPE,* 12(4), Spring 1980.

Principal Contributions Research focussed on British and American economic thought and policy, late seventeenth century to present day, emphasising links between economic thought, economic history, the role of economic ideas in intellectual history, and the relevance of the history of economics to the training of economists. Have undertaken pioneering research in the history of learned societies in economics in Britain and USA, and on the role of professional economists in post-1945 governments and international agencies. Methodological controversy has proved to be an enduring source of insights into developments in economic theory, technique, policy, ideology, and the organisation and structure of the social science professions. Have stressed the subtle inter-relationships between 'internal' and 'external' influences on the development of economics as a science, discipline, and profession. Principal influences: T. W. Hutchison, F. Machlup, M. Polanyi, T. S. Kuhn, and I. Lakatos. Current and prospective concern with the growth of relativism and subjectivism in the post-positivist era.

COBDEN, Richard*

Dates and Birthplace 1804–65, Sussex, England.

Posts Held Businessman; MP for Stockport, West Riding and Rochdale.

Publications *Books:* 1. *Speeches on Questions of Public Policy*(1870).

Career Self-made and largely self-educated, his campaign for free trade in corn through the Anti-Corn Law League (founded 1838) made him the most famous advocate of *laissez faire* policies. His activities in parliament and public lectures helped to realise the repeal of the Corn Laws in 1846. He was an outspoken opponent of aggressive foreign policy and involvement in war, arranging the 1860 trade treaty with France and supporting the case of the North in the American Civil War. He has no claim as a contributor to the development of economic ideas but a great claim as a populariser and political user of economic concepts. The Manchester base of the League led to the use of the phrase 'Manchester School' (coined by Disraeli) for free trade liberalism in politics and economic thought.

Secondary Literature W. D. Grampp, *The Manchester School of Economics* (Stanford Univ. Press, 1960).

CODDINGTON, Alan*

Dates and Birthplace 1941–82, Doncaster, S. Yorkshire, England.

Posts Held Sir Ellis Hunter Memorial Fellow Econ., Univ. York, 1965–6; Ass. Lect. Econ., 1966–7; Lect. Econ., 1967–75; Hallsworth Fellow Polit. Econ., Univ. Manchester, 1974–5; Sr. Lect. Econ., 1975–7; Reader Econ., 1977–9; Prof. Econ., 1981–2, Queen Mary Coll., Univ. London.

Degrees BSc Univ. Leeds, 1963; DPhil Univ. York 1966.

Publications *Books:* 1. *Theories of the Bargaining Process* (1968); 2. *Keynesian Economics: The Search for First Principles* (1983).

Articles: 1. 'Positive economics', *CJE,* 5(1), Feb. 1972; 2. 'Creaking semaphore and beyond', *British J. Philo. Science,* 26, 1975; 4. 'The rationale of general equilibrium theory', *EI*, 13(4), Dec. 1975.

Career Wrote on the theory of bargaining processes, the influence of positivist ideas on methodological discussion in economics, methodological status of the theory of general competitive equilibrium, and the analytical foundations of Keynesian economics.

COEN, Robert M.

Born 1939, Columbus, OH, USA.

Current Post Prof. Econ., Northwestern Univ., Evanston, IL, USA, 1975–.

Past Posts Ass. Prof. Econ., Stanford Univ., 1965–71; Assoc. Prof. Econ., Northwestern Univ., 1971–5; Vis. Assoc. Prof. Econ., Univ Massachusetts, 1974; Vis. Lect., Inst. Advanced Stud., Vienna, 1975, 1977, 1982; Res. Scholar, Internat. Inst. Appl. Systems Analysis, Laxenburg, Austria, 1979–80.

Degrees BA Harvard Univ., 1961; MA, PhD Northwestern Univ., 1964, 1967.

Offices and Honours Member, Em Soc, NTA; Brookings Inst. Res. Fellow, 1964–5; Exec. Comm., NBER Conference Res. Income and Wealth, 1973–6.

Principal Fields of Interest 213 Econometric Models; 323 National Taxation.

Publications *Books:* 1. *An Annual Growth Model of the US Economy* (with B. G. Hickman), (N-H, 1976). *Articles:* 1. 'Effects of tax policy on investment in manufacturing', *AER*, 58(2), May 1968; 2. 'Investment behaviour, the measurement of depreciation, and tax policy', *AER*, 65(1), March 1975; 3. 'Alternative measures of capital and its rates of return in United States manufacturing', in *The Measurement of Capital*, ed. D. Usher (Univ. Chicago Press, 1980); 4. 'Investment and growth in an econometric model of the United States' (with B. G. Hickman), *AER*, 70(2), May 1980; 5. 'Tax policy, federal deficits, and US growth in the 1980s' (with B. G. Hickman), *Nat. Tax J.*, 37(1), March 1984.

Principal Contributions Empirical study of the effects of taxation on capital formation. Determination of average service lives and depreciation patterns of plant and equipment. Evaluations of tax depreciation policy. Construction of a medium-term econometric model of the US to study potential and actual growth over a 10–12 year horizon.

COHEN STUART, Arnold Jacob*

Dates and Birthplace 1855–1921, Den Haag, The Netherlands.

Posts Held Supervisor Waterworks, Java, Dutch East Indies, 1878; Lawyer in Amsterdam; Employee, Dir., Royal Dutch Petroleum Co., 1900, 1906–21.

Degrees Dr Law, Univ. Amsterdam.

Publications *Books:* 1. *Bijdrage Tot de Theorie der Progressieve Inkomstenbelasting* (1889).

Career His attention was turned whilst a student of law to the question of the distribution of the burden of taxation. He reinterpreted J. S. Mill's principle (that justice is achieved when each taxpayer incurs an equal sacrifice) to mean that the sacrifice of each taxpayer should be in the same ratio to the total satisfaction which each taxpayer derives from his income. This permits a higher rate of progression in taxes than Mill's own version of the principle, and was widely accepted in the Edwardian era.

Secondary Literature F. Y. Edgeworth, 'Obituary: Arnold Jacob Cohen Stuart', *EJ*, 31, Sept. 1921; *Classics in the Theory of Public Finance*, eds. R. A. Musgrave and A. T. Peacock (Macmillan, 1958).

COHN, Gustav*

Dates and Birthplace 1840–1919, Germany.

Posts Held Teacher, Riga Polytechnic, 1869–72; Prof., Zürich Polytechnic, 1875–84; Prof., Univ. Göttingen, 1884–1919.

Publications *Books:* 1. *Untersuchungen über die Englische Eisenbahnpolitik*, 2 vols (1874–5); 2. *Finanzlage der Schweiz* (1877); 3. *Volkswirtschaftliche Aufsätze* (1882); 4. *System der Nationalökonomie*, 3 vols (1885–98); 5. *Nationalökonomische Studien* (1886); 6. *Zur Geschichte und Politik des*

Verkehrwesens (1900); 7. *Zur Politik des Deutschen Finanz- Verkehrs- und Verwaltungswesens* (1905).

Career His chief contributions were to transport economics and public finance. His studies of English railway economics laid the foundations for future treatises on railway theory and policy. He was one of the founders of the modern discipline of public finance. He wrote particularly tellingly on equity in taxation.

Secondary Literature E. R. A. Seligman, 'Cohn, Gustav', *ESS*, 3.

COLE, George Douglas Howard*

Dates and Birthplace 1889–1959, London, England.

Posts Held Fellow, Magdalen, All Souls and Nuffield Coll. Oxford; Chichele Prof. Social and Polit. Theory, Univ. Oxford, 1944–57.

Degrees BA Univ. Oxford.

Offices and Honours Pres., Chairman, Fabian Soc., 1939–46, 1948–50, 1952–9.

Publications *Books:* 1. *The World of Labour* (1913, 1919); 2. *Self Government in Industry* (1917, 1920); 3. *Guild Socialism Restated* (1920); 4. *Life of Robert Owen* (1925, 1930); 5. *Gold Credit and Employment* (1930); 6. *What Marx Really Meant* (1934, 1937); retitled, *The Meaning of Marxism* (1950); 7. *Principles of Economic Planning* (1935); 8. *The Common People 1746–1946* (with R. Postgate), (1938, 1956); 9. *Money: Its Present and Future* (1944, 1947); 10. *History of Socialist Thought,* 5 vols (1952–60).

Career Developed a brand of socialism, known as 'guild socialism', which sought to reconcile syndicalism and State socialism. As a teacher, he inspired several generations among whom were numbered many leaders of emergent Third World countries. His actual involvement in politics was less successful than his voluminous writings. These fell into three categories: factual surveys of world politics and economics, works on economic theory, and historical work. He was also consulted as an adviser by all sections of the labour and trades union movements.

Secondary Literature R. Postgate, 'Cole, G. D. H.', *IESS*, 2; M Cole, *The Life of G. D. H. Cole* (St Martin's Press, 1971); L. P. Carpenter, *G. D. H. Cole: An Intellectual Biography* (CUP, 1973).

COLLARD, David Anthony

Born 1937, Tiverton, Devon, England.

Current Post Prof. Econ., Univ. Bath, UK, 1978.

Past Posts Ass. Lect., Lect., Univ. College, Cardiff, Wales, 1960–4; Lect., Univ. Bristol, 1964–78.

Degrees BA, MA Univ. Camb., 1960, 1962.

Editorial Duties Book Rev. Ed., *EJ*, 1983.

Principal Fields of Interest 010 General Economics.

Publications *Books:* 1. *The New Right : A Critique* (Fabian Soc., 1968); 2. *Mathematical Investigation of the Effects of Machinery* (1838) by J. E. Tozer, ed. (A. M. Kelly, 1968); 3. *Prices, Markets and Welfare* (Faber & Faber, 1972); 4. *Altruism and Economy* (Martin Robertson, 1978, 1981); 5. *Income and Distribution: Limits to Redistribution* (with M. Slater and R. Lecomber), (Colston Res. Soc., 1981).

Articles: 1. 'The production of commodities', *EJ*, 73, March 1963, repr. in *Une Nouvelle Approche en Economie Politique*, ed. J. Faccarelle and N. Lavergne (Presses Univ. de France, 1977); 2. 'Walras, Patinkin and the money *tâtonnement*', *EJ*, 76, Sept. 1966; 3. 'Immigration and discrimination: some economic aspects', in *Economic Issues in Immigration* (INEA, 1970); 4. 'Léon Walras and the Cambridge caricature', *EJ*, 83, June 1973; 5. 'Price and prejudice in the housing market', *EJ*, 83, June 1973; 6. 'Exclusion by estate agents: an analysis', *Appl. Econ.*, 3(4), Dec. 1973; 7. 'Edgeworth's propositions on altruism', *EJ*, 85, June 1975; 8. 'Social dividend and negative income tax', in *Taxation and Social Policy*, ed. C. T. Sandford (Heinemann, 1980); 9. 'A. C. Pigou', in *Pioneers of Modern Economics in Britain*, ed D. P. O'Brien and J. R. Presley (Macmillan, 1981);

10. 'Pigou on expectations and the cycle', *EJ*, 93, June 1983.

Principal Contributions Since the early 1960s I have written on many topics in economics that have attracted my attention: Sraffa, methodology, Walras, racial discrimination, immigration, Edgeworth, Pigou, philanthropy, and so on. These fit broadly into two categories: history of economic thought, and welfare economics. My most influential publication so far has been *Altruism and Economy*: in retrospect my work on race, housing and discrimination in the 1970s may be seen as the reverse side of that coin. Although I hope my work is technically competent, I have also tried to stress the political economy of economics, e.g. in my early pamphlet *The New Right: A Critique*. My interests continue to lie in enriching the assumptions we make in our analysis of human action.

COLM, Gerhard*

Dates and Birthplace 1897–1968, Hanover, W. Germany.

Posts Held Econ., Fed. Stat. Bureau, Berlin, 1921–7; Instr., Ass. Prof., Assoc. Prof., Prof. Econ., Inst. World Econ., Kiel Univ., 1927–33; Prof. Econ., New School Social Res., 1933–9; Fiscal Expert., Dept. Commerce, Washington, 1939–40; Prof. Lect., George Washington Univ., 1940–62; Principal Fiscal Analyst, US Bureau Budget, 1940–6; Econ., US President's Council Econ. Advisers, 1946–52; Chief Econ., Nat. Planning Assoc., 1952–68; Special Mission, Amer. Military Govt., Germany, 1946.

Degrees Dr Rer. Pol. Freiburg Univ., 1921; Dr Rer. Pol. h.c. Univ. Frankfurt, 1961, New School Social Res., 1964.

Offices and Honours Bernard Harms Prize, Inst. World Econ., 1964.

Publications *Books:* 1. *Economic Consequences of Recent American Tax Policy* (with F. Lehmann), (1938); 2. *Who Pays the Taxes* (with H. Tarasov), (1942); 3. *The American Economy in 1960* (with M. Young), (1952); 4. *Essays in Public Finance and Fiscal Policy* (with H. O. Nicol), (1955); 5.

The Economy of the American People (with T. Geiger), (1958, 1967).

Career Prominent interwar tax expert who pursued a long and distinguished career in public finance.

COLQUHOUN, Patrick*

Dates and Birthplace 1745–1820, Dumbarton, Scotland.

Posts Held Businessman.

Offices and Honours Lord Provost of Glasgow, 1782–3; City Magistrate, London, 1792–1818.

Publications *Books:* 1. *Treatise on the Police of the Metropolis* (1795); 2. *A New and Appropriate System of Education for the Labouring Poor* (1806); 3. *Treatise on Indigence* (1806); 4. *Treatise on the Population of the British Empire* (1814, 1815).

Career Social reformer whose works contain schemes for improved policing, savings banks, boards of education and a national poor rate. He is best known for the very carefully calculated estimate of national income contained in his 1814 work. Arguing that all wealth is produced by labour, his figures showed that the labouring population only received one-fifth of what it produced. His figures were widely quoted by socialist writers.

Secondary Literature M. Beer, 'Colquhoun, Patrick', *ESS*, 3.

COLSON, Clement-Leon*

Dates and Birthplace 1853–1939, Versailles, France.

Posts Held Lect., Ecole Polytechnique, Ecole des-Ponts-et-Chaussées, Ecole Libre des Sciences Polit., Paris, 1880–1921; Inspecteur-general des-Ponts-et-Chaussées, 1908.

Degrees Lic. en Droit, Paris, 1878.

Offices and Honours Vice-Pres., Conseil Superieour de Stat., Chairman, Econ. Stat. Section, Internat. Stat. Inst., 1923–9.

Publications *Books:* 1. *La garantie d'interêts et son application en France* (1888); 2. *Transports et tarifs* (1890); 3. *Cours d'économie politique* (1901–7); 4. *Organisme et désordre social* (1912);

5. *L'outillage économique de la France* (1921).

Career An engineer-economist who published his lectures in book form over a period of years. His economic and statistical views developed in close relationship to each other, and railway statistics naturally figured heavily in his total output. He was an important adviser to the French government after 1914 on transport, exchange, commerce and other economic matters. Among the important decisions on which he advised was the devaluation of the franc.

Secondary Literature 'Obituary: Clement-Leon Colson', *JRSS*, 102, 1939.

COLWELL, Stephen*

Dates and Birthplace 1800–71, VA, USA.

Posts Held Lawyer; Iron merchant.

Offices and Honours Member, US Revenue Commission, 1865.

Publications *Books:* 1. *The Relative Position in our Industry of Foreign Commerce, Domestic Production and Internal Trade* (1850); 2. 'Introduction' to F. List, *National System of Political Economy* (1856); 3. *The Ways and Means of Commercial Payment* (1858); 4. *The Claims of Labour* (1861); 5. *Gold, Banks and Taxation* (1864); 6. *State and National Systems of Banks* (1864).

Career American protectionist whose analysis of the credit system is probably his major achievement. He produced a series of reports for the government on taxation and other economic questions.

Secondary Literature H. C. Carey, *Memoir of Stephen Colwell* (1871).

COMANOR, William S.

Born 1937, Philadelphia, PA, USA.

Current Post Prof. Econ., Univ. Cal. Santa Barbara, CA, 1975–.

Past Posts Teaching Fellow, Instr. Econ., Ass. Prof., Harvard Univ., 1961–3, 1964–5, 1966–8; Special Econ. Ass., Ass. Attorney General US Dept. Justice, 1965–6; Assoc. Prof. Econ.,

Grad. School Bus., Stanford Univ., 1968–73; Fulbright Vis. Lect., Univ. Tokyo, 1972; Vis. Assoc. Prof. Econ., Harvard Univ., 1973–4; Prof. Econ., Univ. Western Ontario, 1974–5; Dir., Bureau Econ., Fed. Trade Commission, 1978–80.

Degrees BA Haverford Coll., Haverford, PA, 1959; PhD Harvard Univ., 1963.

Offices and Honours Phi Beta Kappa, 1959; Harvard Univ. Fellow, 1959; NSF Fellow, 1963; Fulbright Fellow, 1972.

Editorial Duties Ed. Boards, *REStat, Antitrust Bull., Reprints Antitrust Law and Econ., J Ind E, Decision and Managerial Econ., Internat. J. Advertising.*

Principal Fields of Interest 022 Microeconomics; 600 Industrial Organisation and Public Policy.

Publications *Books:* 1. *Advertising and Market Power* (with T. A. Wilson), (Harvard Univ. Press, 1974); 2. *National Health Insurance in Ontario: the Effects of a Policy of Cost Control* (AEI, 1980).

Articles: 1. 'Research and competitive product differentiation in the pharmaceutical industry in the United States', *Ec*, N.S. 31, Nov. 1964; 2. 'Research and technical change in the pharmaceutical industry', *REStat*, 47, May 1965; 3. 'Advertising market structure and performance' (with T. A. Wilson), *REStat*, 49, Nov. 1967; 4. 'Vertical territorial and customer restrictions: white motor and its aftermath', *Harvard Law Rev.*, May 1968; 5. 'The cost of planning, the FCC and cable television' (with B. M. Mitchell), *J Law E*, 15(1), April, 1972; 6. 'Racial discrimination in American industry', *Ec*, N.S. 40, Nov. 1973; 7. 'Monopoly and the distribution of wealth' (with R. H. Smiley), *QJE*, 89(2), May 1975; 8. 'The effect of advertising on competition: a survey' (with T. A. Wilson), *JEL*, 17(2), June 1979; 9. 'Conglomerate mergers: considerations for public policy', in *The Conglomerate Corporation: An Antitrust Law and Economics Symposium*, eds. R. Blair and R. Lanzillotti (Oelgeschlager, Gunn & Hain, 1981); 10. 'Strategic behaviour and antitrust analysis' (with H. E. Frech), *AER*, 74(2), May 1984.

Principal Contributions Writing and teaching in the field of industrial organisation, with primary attention paid to the determinants and effects of restrictions on competition. This has led to studies of the economy generally as well as of specific industries, and also of the roles of advertising and research expenditures for various dimensions of efficiency. Particular attention has been paid to the economics of the pharmaceutical industry, and to the effective conduct of antitrust policy.

COMMONS, John Roger*

Dates and Birthplace 1862–1945, Hollandsburg, OH, USA.
Posts Held Teacher Econ., Univs. Wesleyan, Oberlin, Indiana and Syracuse, 1890–9; Prof., Univ. Wisconsin, 1904.
Degree BA Oberlin Coll., 1888.
Offices and Honours Pres., AEA.
Publications Books: 1. The Distribution of Wealth (1893, 1968); 2. A Documentary History of American Industrial Society, 10 vols (1910–11, 1958); 3. History of Labor in the United States, 4 vols (1918–35); 4. Legal Foundations of Capitalism (1924, 1959); 5. Institutional Economics (1934, 1959); 6. Myself (1934, 1963); 7. The Economics of Collective Action, ed. K. H. Parsons (1950, 1956).
Career Both a theorist and a successful maker of economic policy. His early interest in both the German historical school and marginalism was the inspiration for The Distribution of Wealth. In his later theoretical works he developed an analysis of collective action by the State, and a wide range of other institutions, which he saw as essential to understanding economic life. This institutional theory was closely related to his remarkable successes in fact-finding and drafting legislation on a wide range of social issues for the State of Wisconsin. The State became a laboratory for progressive innovations whose success later gave Commons a similar role at the federal level. Indeed, his practical work has been remembered more favourably than his theory which reached its fullest form in Institutional Economics. He was also a major historian of American labour.

Secondary Literature J. Dorfman, 'Commons, John R.', IESS, 3; L. G. Harter, John R. Commons: His Assault on Laissez-Faire (Oregon State Univ. Press, 1962).

CONDILLAC, Etienne Bonnot De*

Dates and Birthplace 1714–80, Grenoble, France.
Posts Held Private income; Tutor, Duke of Parma, 1758–67.
Publications Books: 1. La commerce et le gouvernement considérés relativement l'un à l'autre (1776); 2. Oeuvres philosophique de Condillac, 3 vols, ed. G. Le Roy (1947–51).
Career Philosopher, educationalist and economist. His philosophical work was based on Locke and Newton, preferring reliance on observation and experience to Descartes' emphasis on fixed principles. His educational work arose from his tutorship of the young Duke of Parma for whom he prepared a systematic course of study. His economic writings were neglected in his own time. He stressed the economic interdependence of all occupations and classes, the role of national and international markets, and the significance of competition and the price system when not impaired by monopoly and other restrictions on trade. All this was expressed in the simplest terms he could achieve. He was rediscovered by the late nineteenth-century utility theorists as a forerunner.
Secondary Literature J. J. Spengler, 'Condillac, Étienne Bonnot de', IESS, 3.

CONDORCET, Marie Jean Antoine Nicolas Caritat, Marquis de*

Dates and Birthplace 1743–94, Ribemont, Picardy, France.
Posts Held Ass. Secretary, French Académie des Siences, 1769; Inspecteur des Monnaies, 1774.
Offices and Honours Member, French Legislative Assembly and Convention; Member, Académie Française, 1782.
Publications Books: 1. Essai sur l'application de l'analyse a la probabilité des décisions rendues a la pluralité des

voix (1785); 2. *Sketch for a Historical Picture of the Progress of the Human Mind* (1795, 1955); 3. *Oeuvres*, 12 vols eds. A. Condorcet, J. O'Connor and M. F. Arago (1847–9).

Career Distinguished as a writer, administrator and politician, he sought to combine mathematics and philosophy in his writings. Thus he applied the calculus of probabilities to social phenomena, including voting patterns. His social philosophy was one of progress, based on a programme of public education. His works include statistical descriptions of different societies and economic analysis, which moved somewhat beyond physiocratic theories to absorb current concepts of collective welfare. His association with the Girondins in the Convention directly led to his death in prison. His application of mathematics to social and economic questions was later taken up by Poisson and Cournot.

Secondary Literature G. G. Granger, 'Condorcet', *IESS*, 3; K. M. Baker, *Condorcet: From Natural Philosophy to Social Mathematics* (Univ. Chicago Press, 1975).

COOLEY, Thomas Ferguson

Born 1943, Rutland, PA, USA.
Current Post Prof. Econ., Univ. Cal. Santa Barbara, USA, 1980–.
Past Posts Ass. Prof. Econ., Tufts Univ., Medford, MA, 1971–6; Vis. Ass. Prof., Carnegie-Mellon Univ., 1973; Vis. Prof., Univ. Western Australia, 1974; Res. Assoc., NBER, 1973–7; Faculty Assoc., Joint Center Urban Stud., MIT and Harvard, 1976–80; Vis. Prof., Birkbeck Coll., London, 1979–80, Stockholm School Econ., 1984.
Degrees BS Reusselaer Polytechnic Inst., 1965; MA, PhD Univ. Penn., 1967, 1971.
Editorial Duties Ed. Board, *AER* 1981–.
Principal Fields of Interest 023 Macroeconomic Theory; 132 Economic Forecasting; 211 Econometric and Statistical Methods.
Publications *Books:* 1. *Water Shortage: An Analysis of the California Drought* (with R. Berk, *et al.*), (ABT Press, 1981).
Articles: 1. 'Tests of an adaptive regression model', *REStat*, 55(2), April 1973; 2. 'An adaptive regression model' (with E. C. Prescott), *Int ER*, 14(2), June 1973; 3. 'A comparison of robust and varying parameter estimates of a macroeconomic model', *Annals Econ. and Social Measurement*, 4(3), June 1975; 4. 'Estimation in the presence of stochastic parameter variation' (with E. C. Prescott), *Em*, 44(1), Jan. 1976; 5. 'Rational expectations in American agriculture 1867–1914' (with S. J. DeCanio), *REStat*, 59(1), Feb. 1977; 6. 'Identification and estimation of money demand' (with S. J. LeRoy), *AER*, 71(1), Dec. 1981; 7. 'A theory of growth controls' (with C. J. LaCivita), *JUE*, 12(3), June 1982; 8. 'Specification analysis by discriminating priors', *Em Rev.*, 1(1), 1982; 9. 'A new view of the market structure performance debate' (with J. Bothwell), *J Ind E*, 32(4), Nov. 1984; 10. 'Econometric policy evaluation: a note' (with S. J. LeRoy), *AER*, 74(3), June 1984.
Principal Contributions My initial work was on the development of methods for estimating models with time-varying parameters. I used these methods to study the implied rationality of industrial forecasting. Subsequently, I have worked on methods of sensitivity analysis for econometric models. I have written on the identifiability of money demand functions. More recently I have written on the nature of structural models and abuses of nonstructural models. Currently I am working on maximum likelihood methods of prediction.

COOPER, Richard Newell

Born 1934, Seattle, WA, USA.
Current Post Maurits C. Boas Prof. Internat. Econ., Harvard Univ., Cambridge, MA, USA.
Past Posts Ass. Lect., LSE, 1958; Sr. Staff Econ., US President's Council Econ. Advisers, 1961–3; Ass. Prof., Prof. Econ., Provost, Yale Univ., 1963–5, 1966–77, 1972–4; Dep. Ass. Secretary Internat. Monetary Affairs,

Under Secretary Econ. Affairs, US Dept. State, 1965–6; 1977–81; Cons., US Dept. Treasury, 1963–9, Agency Internat. Devlp., 1967–9, US Nat. Security Council, 1969–70, Harvard Devlp. Advisory Service, 1970–2, US Navy, 1975–.

Degrees BA Oberlin Coll., 1956; MSc LSE, 1958; PhD Harvard Univ., 1962; LLD Oberlin Coll., 1978.

Offices and Honours Phi Beta Kappa, 1955; Marshall Scholar, 1956–8; Brookings Fellow, 1960–1; Ford Foundation Faculty Fellow, 1970–1; Fellow Center Study Behavioral Sciences, Stanford, 1975–6.

Editorial Duties Ed. Boards, *J Int E,* 1970, *Foreign Pol.,* 1970–7, *QJE,* 1981–.

Principal Fields of Interest 300 Domestic Monetary and Fiscal Theory and Institutions; 400 International Economics.

Publications *Books:* 1. *The Economics of Interdependence* (McGraw-Hill, 1968, Columbia Univ. Press, 1980); 2. *International Finance,* ed. (Penguin, 1969; transl., Spanish, 1971); 3. *Sterling, European Monetary Unification, and the International Monetary System* (British-North Amer. Comm., 1972; transl., French, 1984); 4. *Towards a Renovated World Monetary System* (with M. Kaji and C. Segre), (Trilateral Commission, 1973); 5. *A Reordered World* (Ptomac Press, 1973); 6. *Economic Mobility and National Economic Policy* (Almqvist and Wiksell, 1974); 7. *Towards a Renovated International System* (with K. Kaiser and M. Kosaka), (Trilateral Commission, 1977); 8. *The International Monetary System Under Flexible Rates,* co-ed (with J. de Macedo, P. Kenen and J. von Ypersele), (Ballinger, 1982); 9. *Economic Policy in an Interdependent World* (MIT Press, 1985).

Articles: 1. 'Uncertainty and diversification in international trade' (with W. C. Brainard), in *Studies in Agricultural Economics, Trade and Development* (Food Res. Inst., 1968); 2. 'Macroeconomic policy adjustments in interdependent economies', *QJE,* 83(1), Feb. 1969; 3. 'Eurodollars, reserve dollars and asymmetries in the international monetary system', *J Int E,* 2(4), Sept. 1972, repr. in *Europe and the*

Evolution of the International Monetary System, ed. A. Swoboda (Sijthoff, 1973); 3. 'An analysis of devaluation in developing countries', in *International Trade and Money,* eds. M. Connally and A. Swoboda (A&U, 1973); 5. 'Prolegomena to the choice of an international system', *International Organisation,* Winter 1975, repr. in *World Politics and International Economics,* eds. C. F. Bergsten and L. Krause (Brookings Inst., 1975), and in Spanish, *Boletin Mensuel,* Feb. 1976; 6. 'Worldwide versus regional integration: is there an optimal size to an integrated area?', in *Economic Integration: Worldwide, Regional, Sectional,* ed. F. Machlup (Macmillan, 1976); 7. 'An economist's view of the oceans', *J. World Trade Law,* July 1975; 8. 'A new international economic order for mutual gain', *Foreign Pol.,* Spring 1977, repr. in *Towards a New Strategy for Development,* eds. H. Brookfield, *et al.* (Pergamon, 1979), and in Italian in *Gli Stati Uni e L'Ordine Mondiale,* ed. C. M. Santoro (Boringhiera, 1978); 9. 'The gold standard: historical facts and future prospects', *Brookings Papers Econ. Activity,* 1, 1982; 10. 'Economic interdependence and coordination of economic policies', in *Handbook in International Economics,* II, eds. R. Jones and P. Kenen (N-H, 1974).

Principal Contributions Most of my published work has been concerned with trade policy, the workings of the international monetary system, macroeconomic management of open economies, and the analysis of currency devaluations. It has often been motivated by experience in the US government and as a consultant for other governments or policy-oriented institutes. As a result, it has a strong empirical and even institutional flavour compared with much professional writing, taking into account some of the constraints that policy-makers face in the short run, and being concerned with the process by which the constraints may be relaxed in the longer run. It has occasionally involved excursions into economic history of the nineteenth century and earlier. A central theme of my major book, *The Economics of Interdependence* and some subsequent work has been that countries find themselves working under constraints imposed by the markets in which they trade goods, services and financial claims, and that the evolution of these markets will over time alter the opportunities and effectiveness of traditional economic policy actions and create new opportunities for different actions. In particular, relatively open economies will face a different set of constraints and opportunities from those of relatively closed ones. I have also been concerned with the gains to be derived from international co-operation in economic management, both among economically advanced countries and between them and less developed countries, including energy policies, commodity policies, and foreign aid as well as macroeconomic policies.

COPELAND, Morris A.

Born 1895, Rochester, NY, USA.
Current Post Robert Thorner Prof. Emeritus, Cornell Univ., USA, 1965–.
Recent Posts Prof., Cornell Univ. 1942–65; Univ. Missouri, 1965–8; State Univ. New York, 1969–71.
Degrees BA, DHL Amherst Coll. 1917, 1957; PhD Univ. Chicago, 1921.
Offices and Honours Fellow, ASA; Pres., AEA, 1957.
Principal Fields of Interest 224 National Wealth and Balance Sheets.
Publications *Books:* 1. *A Study of Money Flows in the United States* (NBER, 1952); 2. *Fact and Theory in Economics: The Testament of an Institutionalist, Collected Papers of Morris A. Copeland*, ed. C. Morse (Cornell Univ. Press, 1958); 3. *Trends in Government Financing* (Princeton Univ. Press, 1961); 4. *Our Free Enterprise Economy* (Macmillan, 1965, Sunshine Press, 1980); 5. *Toward Full Employment in Our Free Enterprise Economy* (Fordham Univ. Press, 1966).
Articles: 1. 'Communities of economic interest and the price system', in *Trends of Economics*, ed. R. G. Tugwell (Alfred A. Knopf, 1924); 2 'National income and its distribution', in NBER, *Recent Economic Changes*, 2, (McGraw-Hill, 1938); 3. 'On the scope and method

of economics', in *Thorstein Veblen: A Critical Appraisal*, ed. D. Dowd (Cornell Univ. Press, 1958).
Principal Contributions Development of money flows (theory, method and use) now used by almost all national banks all over the world. Other contributions include cross-disciplinary work.
Secondary Literature 1. J. Cohen, 'Copeland's money flows after twenty-five years; a survey', *JEL*, 10(1), March 1972; 2. J. Millar, 'Institutionalism from a natural science point of view; an intellectual profile of Morris A. Copeland', in *Institutional Economics* (Nijhoff, 1974).

CORDEN, Warner Max

Born 1927, Breslau, Germany.
Current Post Prof. Econ., ANU, Canberra, Australia.
Past Posts Res. Officer, Argus & Australian Ltd., 1950–1, Commonwealth Australia, 1951–5, NIESR, 1955–7; Lect., Sr. Lect., Univ. Melbourne, 1958–61; Sr. Res. Fellow, Prof. Fellow, ANU, 1962–7, Nuffield Reader Internat. Econ., Fellow, Nuffield Coll. Oxford, 1967–76; Vis. Prof., Univ. Cal. Berkeley, 1965, Monash Univ., 1969, Univ. Minnesota, 1971, La Trobe Univ., 1971, Princeton Univ., 1973, Univ. Melbourne, 1974, City Univ., London, 1978, 1979, 1980, Inst. Internat. Econ. Stud., Stockholm, 1982, European Univ. Inst., Florence, Italy, 1983.
Degrees B Com, M Com Univ. Melbourne, 1949, 1953; PhD Univ. London, 1956; MA Univ. Oxford, 1967.
Offices and Honours Pres., Econ. Soc. Australia New Zealand, 1977–80; Fellow, Academy Social Sciences Australia; Member, Group of Thirty.
Editorial Duties Ed. Board, *OEP*, 1968–76; Assoc. Ed. *J Int E*, 1971–80.
Principal Fields of Interest 400 International Economics.
Publications *Books:* 1. *Recent Developments in the Theory of International Trade* (Princeton Internat. Fin. Section, Princeton Univ., 1965); 2. *Australian Economic Policy Discussion: A Survey* (Melbourne Univ. Press, 1968); 3. *The Theory of Protection* (OUP, 1971;

transl., French, Economica, 1977); 4. *Monetary Integration* (Princeton Internat. Fin. Section, Princeton Univ., 1972); 5. *Trade Policy and Economic Welfare* (OUP, 1974; transls., Spanish, Ediciones ICE, 1978, French, Economica, 1980); 6. *Inflation, Exchange Rates and the World Economy* (OUP, 1977, 1981; transl., Italian, Editore Boringhieri, 1981).

Articles: 1. 'The calculation of the cost of protection', *ER*, 33, April, 1957; 2. 'Tariffs, subsidies and the terms of trade', *Ec*, N.S. 24, Aug. 1957; 3. 'The geometric representation of policies to attain internal and external balance', *REStud*, 28, Oct. 1960; 4. 'The structure of a tariff system and the effective protective rate', *JPE*, 74(4), June 1966, repr. in *International Trade: Selected Readings*, ed. J. Bhagwati (MIT Press, 1981); 5. 'The effects of trade on the rate of growth', in *Trade, Balance of Payments and Growth* eds. J. Bhagwati, *et al.* (N-H, 1971); 6. 'Economies of scale and customs union theory', *JPE*, 80(3), April 1972; 7. 'Taxation, real wage rigidity and employment', *EJ*, 91, June 1981; 8. 'Booming sector and deindustrialisation in a small open economy' (with J. P. Neary), *EJ*, 92, Dec. 1982.

Principal Contributions Worked on international trade theory and the application of theory to policy, favouring simple geometric and verbal exposition. Main contributions have been on growth and trade, theory of protection, monetary integration, customs union theory, internal-external balance theory, booming sector economics and, more recently, the international monetary system. Best known for developing in several articles and one book the theory of tariff structure and effective protection. Also in this area, produced the first paper on the theory of the cost of protection, developed the concept of the 'conservative social welfare function' to explain actual protection policies, and sought to systematise the theory of trade policy in *Trade Policy and Economic Welfare* and several other surveys. Contributed extensively over many years to the analysis of protection and of macroeconomic policies in Australia, thus providing the basis for several theoretical contributions.

CORRY, Bernard Alexander

Born 1930, London, England.
Current Post Prof. Econ., Queen Mary Coll., Univ. London, 1968–.
Past Posts Lect. Econ., Univ. Durham, 1956–8; Lect., Reader Econ., LSE, 1958–64, 1964–8; Vis. Prof., Univ. Cal. Berkeley, 1965–6; Sr. Econ. Adviser, UK Dept. Employment & Productivity, 1968–70.
Degrees BSc LSE, 1951; PhD Univ. London, 1958.
Offices and Honours Chairman, AUTE, 1979–84; Council, RES, 1975–80; Governor, NIESR, 1978–.
Editorial Duties Rev. Ed., *Ec*, 1962–8; Ed. Boards, *Appl. Econ.*, 1972–, *J. Econ. Stud.*, 1972–.
Principal Fields of Interest 031 History of Economic Thought; 810 Labour Economics.
Publications *Books:* 1. *Money, Saving and Investment in English Economics 1800–1850* (Macmillan, 1962); 2. *Essays in Honour of Lord Robbins*, co-ed. (with M. H. Peston), (Weidenfeld & Nicholson, 1970).

Articles: 1. 'The theory of the economic effects of government expenditure in English classical political economy', *Ec*, 25, Feb. 1958; 2. 'Malthus and Keynes — a reconsideration', *EJ*, 69, Dec. 1959; 3. 'Progress and profits', *Ec*, 28, May 1960; 4. 'Technological innovation and relative shares', *AER*, 56(2), May 1966; 5. 'The Phillips relation: a theoretical explanation' (with D. W. Laidler), *Ec*, 34, May 1967; 6. 'Activity rates and unemployment: the experience of the United Kingdom 1951–66' (with J. A. Roberts), *Appl. Econ.*, 2(3), 1970; 7. 'Lauderdale and public debt: a reconsideration', in *Essays in Honour of Lord Robbins*, eds. B. A. Corry and M. H. Peston (Weidenfeld and Nicolson, 1970); 8. 'Activity rates and unemployment: the UK experience: some further results', *Appl. Econ.*, 6(3), 1974; 9. 'Keynes' place in the history of economic thought', in *Keynes and Laissez-Faire*, ed. A. P. Thirlwall (Macmillan, 1978); 10. 'Female unemployment' (with J. Nugent), in *Women and the Labour Market*, ed. M. Evans (Tavistock, 1982).
Principal Contributions Keynes's

General Theory was undoubtedly the economics text that influenced me the most and its dominant influence remains with me — even though many of my friends now regard it as a hindrance to better economic understanding. I was drawn to economics via politics and to Keynes because of childhood memories of the 1930s and the evils that mass unemployment brings. The great personal influence on my economic studies was unquestionably Lionel Robbins, as it was for so many generations of LSE students. From him I learned a love of, and respect for, scholarship, an interest in methodology (with the important additional influence of Karl Popper), a concern for economic policy, and many other things. My main research areas have been, and remain, the history of economic thought — or rather the history of economic analysis — and labour economics. In both of these areas the macroeconomic aspects have been my prime concern.

My main contribution to the history of economic theory has been an attempt to understand classical macro-theory and to assess the 'Keynesian' element in the pre-Keynes literature, mainly in the classical period; and my current research is taking this story through the neoclassical period. In labour economics (in collaboration with J. A. Roberts and J. Nugent), I have been concerned with the female labour market and in particular the responsiveness of activity rates to unemployment. My current interest here is in the operation of the market for part-time employees. I remain firmly convinced of the importance and current relevance of Keynes's economics and still feel that, in the main, he has not been correctly interpreted especially with respect to the real wage/employment relationship. It is this relationship which is my major theoretical concern at the moment.

COSSA, Luigi*

Born 1831–96, Milan, Italy.
Posts Held Prof. Polit. Econ., Univ. Pavia, 1858–96.
Publications *Books:* 1. *Primi Elementi d'Economia Politica* (1860); 2. *Primi*

Elementi di Scienza Delle Finanze (1868); 3. *Guida Allo Studio Dell' Economia Politica* (1876); 4. *Saggia d'Economia Politica* (1878).
Current Post Known chiefly for inspiring teaching which formed a generation of Italian economists into a school. He had studied in Germany with Roscher and this encouraged him to take up work in the history of economics. His emphasis was not on any particular view of the discipline but on sound methods. The *Guida . . .* is effectively a history of economics, and for its time it was a remarkable achievement.
Secondary Literature A. Loria, 'Obituary — Luigi Cossa', *EJ*, 6, Sept. 1896.

COTTA, Alain

Born 1933, Nice, France.
Current Post Prof. Econ., Univ. Paris-Dauphine, Paris, France, 1968–; Prof. Econ., L'Ecole des Hautes Etudes, Paris, France, 1962–.
Past Posts Prof., Univ. Caen, 1960–1; Vis. Prof., LSE, 1962, Univ. Purdue, 1967–8; Dir., Centre Recherches, Univ. Paris-Dauphine, 1971–.
Degrees Diplome Ecole des Hautes Etudes, 1954; Dr, Agregé Paris, France, 1955, 1960.
Offices and Honours Member, Commission des Comptes de la Nation, 1974, Haut Comité de la Population, 1978, Trilateral Commission, 1982.
Principal Fields of Interest 010 General Economics.
Publications *Books:* 1. *Theorie gènérale du capital, de la croissance et des fluctuations* (Dunod, 1967); 2. *Les choix économiques de la grande entreprise* (Dunod, 1969); 3. *Croissance et inflation en France depuis 1962* (Presses Univ. de France, 1974); 4. *Le capitalisme* (Presses Univ. de France, 1977, 1979); 5. *Reflexions sur la grande transition* (Presses Univ. de France, 1979).
Articles: 1. 'Les effets d'une éventuelle baisse du prix du petrole', *CIRCE*, March 1983; 2. 'L'entreprise publique: realité économique ou realité politique', *Revue Commentaire*, June 1983; 3. 'Investissement industriel et croissance

de l'économie française', *RE*, June 1983; 4. 'Staying solvent by the light of the moon', *Internat. Management*, Aug. 1983; 5. 'Il faut denationaliser pour relever le défi de l'an 2000', *Magazine Hebdo*, Dec. 1983; 6. 'Le travail souterrain-un phenomène de societé', *BIT*, Feb. 1983; 7. 'L'inflation annuelle encore et toujours a 10%?', *Le Figaro*, Jan. 1984; 8. 'Die Geldpolitik in Frankreich', *Revue Allemande*, Feb. 1984; 9. 'Quel degré de verité a-t-on atteint', *Le Figaro*, May 1984; 10. 'La figure de Fraser ou la hantise d'un point', *Le Figaro*, July 1984.

Principal Contributions My first interest in economics had been the theory of capital and subsequently the theory of growth. For long I was preoccupied with analysing the main processes of decision which determine or influence the specific waves of accumulation of capital. So I went into the theory of oligopoly and big enterprises. Two new fields appeared to deserve investigation. One is the theory of power, which involves some use of knowledge of sociology or psychosociology of organisations. The other is the continuous extension of worldwide markets. I am now mainly interested in strategy of firms and states regarding the evolution of world economies.

COURBIS, Raymond

Born 1937, Algeria.
Current Post Prof. Econ., Univ. Paris-Nanterre, France, 1974–.
Past Posts Chargé de mission, French Ministry Fin., 1962–71; Assoc. Prof., Univ. Tours, France, 1972–3; Dir., GAMA (Group for Applied Macroeconomic Analysis), 1972–; Assoc. Prof., Ecole Polytechnique, 1972–83; Econ. Adviser, ENA (Nat. School Admin.), 1972–82; Scientific Adviser, INSEE, 1972–5; Vis. Prof., Univ. Birmingham, 1973, Laval Univ., Canada, 1977.
Degrees Ingénieur Civil Ecole des Mines de Paris, 1961; Diploma Stud. Econ. Programming, 1962; Diploma, Dr d'Etat Univ. Paris 1, 1969, 1971.
Offices and Honours Prize, Member Comm., French Econ. Assoc., 1971,

1978; Member, Consultative Comm. Univs., 1977–80; Member, CNRS, 1980–; Member, Jury 'Concours d'-agregation' Econ., 1978–9.
Editorial Duties Ed., *Prévision et Analyse Economique*; Ed. Boards, *Europ ER*, 1979–, *Internat. Regional Science Rev.*, 1980–, *Revue d'Economie Regionale et Urbaine*, 1981–.
Principal Fields of Interest 023 Macroeconomic Theory; 221 National Income Accounting; 941 Regional Economics.
Publications *Books:* 1. *Prevision des prix et étude sectorielle des entreprises pendant la preparation du Ve Plan* (Imprimerie Nationale, 1968); 2. *La détermination de l'équilibre général en économie concurrencée* (CNRS, 1971, 1980); 3. *Le modele FIFI* (with M. Aglietta, H. Bussery and C. Seibel), (INSEE, 1973, 1975); 4. *Competitivite et croissance en économie concurrencée* (Dunod, 1975); 5. *La méthode des comptes de surplus et ses applications macroéconomiques* (with Ph. Temple), (INSEE, 1975); 6. *Les modèles de prix* (Dunod, 1975); 7. *Modèles régionauz et modèles régionaux-nationaux*, ed. (Cujas, CNRS, 1979); 8. *Construction d'un tableau d'échanges inter-industriels et inter-régionaux de l'économie française* (with C. Pommier), (Economica and Documentation Française, 1979); 9. *Le modèle MOGLI* (with A. Fonteneau, C. Le Van and P. Voisin), (Economica, 1980); 10. *International Trade and Multi-country Models*, ed. (Economica, 1981).

Articles: 1. 'Le comportement d'-autofinancement des entreprises', *Econ App*, 21(3–4), 1968; 2. 'Développement économique et concurrence étrangère', *RE*, 20(1), Jan. 1969; 3. 'Compatabilité nationale à prix constants et à productivité constante', *RIW*, 15(1), March 1969; 4. 'The FIFI model used in the preparation of the French plan', *Econ. of Planning*, 12(1–2), 1972; 5. 'The REGINA model, a regional-national model', *Econ. of Planning*, 12(3), 1972, repr. in *Regional Science and Urban Econ.*, 9(2–3), May–Aug. 1979; 6. 'La théorie des économies concurrencées, fondement du modèle FIFI', *RE*, 24(6), Nov. 1973, 25(5), Sept. 1974; 7. 'Une réformulation dynamique de la théorie des économies concurrencées', *Econ*

App, 33(1), 1980; 8. 'Multiregional modeling and the interaction between regional and national development: a general theoretical framework', in *Modeling the Multiregional System*, eds. F. G. Adams and N. J. Glickman (D. C. Heath, 1980); 9. 'Measuring effects of French regional policy by means of a regional-national model', *Regional Science and Urban Econ.*, 12(1), Feb. 1982; 10. 'Integrated multiregional modeling in Western Europe', in *Multiregional Economic Modeling: Practice and Prospects*, eds. B. Issaev, P. Nimkamp, P. Rietveld and F. Snickars (N-H, 1982).

Principal Contributions *Macroeconomic Theory:* Introduced in French planning, in the mid-1960s, the differentiation between 'exposed', and 'sheltered' sectors and proposed the theory of 'competitive economies' ('economies concurrencées') for open economies, which emphasised supply and led to the supply-oriented policies of the French VIth and VIIth Plans. More general than the 'Scandinavian model', the 'competitive economies' theory does not only consider price and wage determination but is a complete theory of overall equilibrium and growth. In 1980, the first version was generalised in a dynamic one, that unifies demand- and supply-oriented approaches. The Keynesian approach is valuable in the short term but intertemporal adjustments are such that economy appears as supply-driven in the long term.

Regional Theory: Emphasised both the important impact of regional factors on national development and the role of supply at the regional level. Proposed to distinguish 'demand-located' industries (where regional demand determines regional production) and 'free-located' industries (where, in the medium term, regional production depends on the regional capital stock, this latter being itself determined by regional investments and the location behaviour of multiregional firms).

Modelling (for the French economy): Main builder of FIFI (a national medium-term model used for the VIth and VIIth Plans); project leader and builder of REGINA (a regional-national model used for the VIIth Plan), MOGLI (annual short-term-medium-term model), PROTEE (quarterly) and ANAIS (input-output).

National Accounting: Proposed a general framework for consistent and balanced national accounts at constant prices. Adjustments terms are introduced, and interpreted in terms both of price transfers and productivity gains. It is one of the foundations of the French method of the 'surplus accounts'.

Regional Accounting: Built a multi- and inter-regional input-output table for the French economy.

COURCELLE-SENEUIL,   Jean Gustave*

Dates and Birthplace 1813–92, Vauxains, Dordogne, France.

Posts Held Journalist, Businessman and Govt. employee; Prof. Polit. Econ., Univ. Santiago, Chile, 1852–62; retired in France, re-entering journalism and politics.

Offices and Honours Officer, Légion d'Honneur; Councillor of State, France, 1879.

Publications *Books:* 1. *Le crédit et la banque* (1840); 2. *Traité des opérations de banque* (1853); 3. *Traité des entreprises industrielles, commerciales et agricoles* (1855); 4. *Traité théoretique et pratique d'économie politique* (1858); 5. *Cours de comptabilité*, 4 vols (1867); 6. *Liberté et socialisme* (1868); 7. *Adam Smith* (1888).

Career A writer of able works of a practical and factual kind, but with no claims as a theorist. He did attempt some simple graphical presentations which are of interest and used his own distinctive terminology — plutology for theory, and ergonomy for applied economics — which gained no currency. His work in government gave him considerable opportunity for the application of his economic ideas, which remained of the liberal, free trade variety.

COURNOT, Antoine Augustin*

Dates and Birthplace 1801–76, Gray, Haute-Saône, France.

Posts Held Literary Adviser, Tutor, household of Marshall St-Cyr, 1823–33; Prof. Maths., Univ. Lyons, 1834–5; Admin. posts, Académie de Grenoble, 1835, Univ. and Académie Dijon, 1854–62.

Degrees Licentiate Sciences, Paris, 1823; DSc, 1829.

Publications *Books:* 1. *Researches into the Mathematical Principle of Wealth* (1838, 1929, 1960); 2. *Principes de la théorie des richesses* (1863); 3. *Revue sommaire des doctrines économiques* (1877).

Career Beginning as a mathematician, he applied mathematics first to economic questions and then to a general philosophy of the world. His theory of markets and prices and his 'law of demand' in *Recherches . . .* is so devised as to be empirically testable, and is hence a genuine contribution to econometrics. By retaining the element of uncertainty in his argument, he avoided the pitfall of seeming to give economics too great a precision by its expression in mathematical terms. His theory of markets was revolutionary in that it began with the consideration of monopoly and moved by successive stages through duopoly and oligopoly to perfect competition. In this, and numerous other features, his work could only be truly appreciated long after his death.

Secondary Literature H. Guitton, 'Cournot, Antoine Augustin', *IESS*, 3; R. D. Theocharis, *Early Developments in Mathematical Economics* (Macmillan, 2nd edn., 1983), chap. 9.

COWLING, Keith George

Born 1936, Scunthorpe, Lincolnshire, England.

Current Post Prof. Econ., Univ. Warwick, Coventry, England, 1969–.

Past Posts Ass. Lect., Lect., Sr. Lect., Reader, Univ. Manchester, 1961–2, 1963–5, 1965–6, 1966–9; Econ. Planning Cons., FAO, 1963–5; Vis. Fellow, Econ. Res. Inst., Dublin, 1965; Cons., UK Nat. Board Prices and Incomes, 1966–7; Cons., Working Group Member, UK Nat. Econ. Devlp. Office, 1966–8; Res. Adviser, West Midlands Econ. Planning Board, 1967–9; Vis. Prof., Washington Univ., St Louis, MO, USA, 1969–70; Co-Dir., Dir., Centre Industrial Econ. and Bus. Res., Univ. Warwick, 1970–3.

Degrees BSc Univ. London, 1957; PhD Univ. Illinois, 1967.

Offices and Honours Council, RES, 1980–; Member, Econ. Study Soc., 1971–4; Member, UK SSRC Management and Industrial Relations Comm., 1978–82; Member, Steering Comm. Europ. Assoc. Res. in Industrial Econ.

Editorial Duties Ed., *Internat. J. Industrial Organization*, 1982–; Corresp. Ed., *MS*, 1982–; Assoc. Ed., *J Ind E*, 1977–82.

Principal Fields of Interest 610 Industrial Organisation and Public Policy.

Publications *Books:* 1. *Determinants of Wage Inflation in Ireland* (Econ. Res. Inst., 1965); 2. *Resource Structure of Agriculture: An Economic Analysis* (with D. Metcalf and A. J. Rayner), (Pergamon, 1967); 3. *Market Structure and Corporate Behaviour*, ed. (Gray-Mills, 1972); 4. *Advertising and Economic Behaviour* (with J. Cable, M. Kelly and T. McGuinness), (Macmillan, 1975); 5. *Mergers and Economic Performance* (with others), (CUP, 1980); 6. *Monopoly Capitalism* (Macmillan, 1982).

Articles: 1. 'Wage inflation in the UK: a regional analysis' (with D. Metcalf), *BOIS*, 19(1), March 1967; 2. 'Price, quality and market share' (with A. J. Rayner), *JPE*, 78(5), Nov.–Dec. 1970; 3. 'Price, quality and advertising competition' (with J. Cubbin), *Ec*, 38, Nov. 1971; 4. 'Hedonic prices for UK cars' (with J. Cubbin), *EJ*, 82, Sept. 1972; 5. 'On the theoretical specification of industrial structure — performance relationship, *Europ ER*, 8, July 1976; 6. 'Price-cost margins and market structure' (with M. Waterson), *Ec*, 43, Aug. 1976; 7. 'Social costs of monopoly power' (with D. Mueller), *EJ*, 88, Dec. 1978; 8. 'Oligopoly, distribution and the rate of profit', *Europ ER*, 13, March 1981; 9. 'Wage share, concentration and unionism' (with I. Molho), *MS*, 49, June 1982; 10. 'Advertising and labor supply' (with J. Brack), *Kyk*, 36(2), 1983.

Principal Contributions My early research was on the factor markets serving agriculture, culminating in the book on *Resource Structure of Agriculture*. This work led my research interests in two directions: first into a more general interest in labour market analysis — with work on disaggregated Phillips curves, and second, into a more long-term concern with oligopolistic market structures. In pursuing the second interest, I initially focussed on the specification and estimation of demand functions facing firms operating in oligopolistic markets, with price, quality and advertising as decision variables. The central aim was to begin to understand the degree of market power possessed by the major corporations, and its determinants. A fairly major study of the impact and determinants of advertising investment, published as *Advertising and Economic Behaviour*, formed a particular extension of these interests. Some theoretical work on the links between market structure and the degree of monopoly was coupled with attempts at empirical estimation and subsequently with an analysis of the social costs of monopoly power. All this led gradually towards my central concern in recent years: the impact of the existence of monopoly power, and in many cases growing monopoly power, on the functioning of the macroeconomic system as a whole. This led to the publication of my book on *Monopoly Capitalism* and subsequently to papers on the internationalisation of production and deindustrialisation, and, going a little deeper, to a more recent one focussing on economic obstacles to democracy.

CRAGG. John Gordon

Born 1937, Toronto, Ont., Canada.

Current Post Prof. Econ., Univ. British Columbia, Vancouver, British Columbia, Canada, 1979–.

Past Posts Ass. Prof., Univ. Chicago, 1964–7; Prof., Assoc. Prof., Univ. British Columbia, 1967–9; Dir. Res.,

Canadian Prices & Incomes Commission, Ottawa, 1969–.

Degrees BA (Philo. and Econ.) McGill Univ., 1958; BA Univ. Camb., 1960; PhD Princeton Univ., 1965.

Editorial Duties Ed. Board, *Econometric Corp. Fin.*.

Principal Fields of Interest 211 Econometric and Statistical Methods.

Publications *Books:* 1. *Expectations and the Valuation of Shares* (with B. G. Malkiel), (Univ. Chicago Press, 1982); 2. *Wage Changes and Labour Flows in Canada* (Prices & Incomes Commission, Canada, 1973).

Articles: 1. 'On the relative small-sample properties of several structural equation estimators', *Em*, 35(1), 1967; 2. 'Empirical evidence on the incidence of the corporation income tax' (with A. C. Harberger and P. Mieszkowski), *JPE*, 75(6), Dec. 1967; 3. 'The consensus and accuracy of some predictions of the growth of corporate earnings' (with B. G. Malkiel), *J Fin*, 23(1), March 1968; 4. 'The issuing of corporate securities' (with N. D. Baxter), *JPE*, 78(6), Dec. 1970; 5. 'Corporate choice among long-term financing instruments' (with N. D. Baxter), *REStat*, 52(3), Aug. 1970; 6. 'The demand for automobiles' (with R. S. Uhler), *CJE*, 3, Aug. 1970; 7. 'The structure of the asset portfolios of households', *REStud*, 38(3), July 1971; 8. 'Some statistical models for limited dependent variables with application to the demand for durable goods', *Em*, 39(5), Sept. 1971; 9. 'Estimation and testing in time-series regression models with heteroscedastic disturbances', *J Em*, 20(1), Oct. 1982; 10. 'More efficient estimation in the presence of heteroscedasticity of unknown form', *Em*, 51(3), May 1983.

Principal Contributions Showed by Monte Carlo investigation of the small sample properties of simultaneous equations estimators that only weak general rankings were evident and even these depend on exact structure used. Participated in initial application of discrete choice of models and multi-nominal logic model to the issue of financial securities and selection of durable goods. Developed some models for limited dependent variables widening the scope of tobit-type models. Examined nature of security analysts' forecasts and their role in security valuation.

CRANDALL, Robert Warren

Born 1940, Akron, OH, USA.
Current Post Sr. Fellow, Brookings Inst., Washington, DC, USA, 1977–.
Past Posts Ass. Prof., Assoc. Prof, Econ., MIT, 1966–72, 1972–4; Deputy Dir., Council Wage and Price Stability, Exec. Office US President, Washington, DC, 1975–8; Adjunct Assoc. Prof. Econ., George Washington Univ., Washington, DC, 1976–7.
Degrees BA Univ. Cincinnati, 1962; MA, PhD Northwestern Univ., 1965, 1968.
Offices and Honours Johnson Res. Fellow, Brookings Inst., 1965–6.
Principal Fields of Interest 420 Trade Relations and Commercial Policy; 600 Industrial Organisation; 720 Conservation and Pollution.
Publications *Books:* 1. *The US Steel Industry in Recurrent Crisis* (Brookings Inst., 1981); 2. *The Scientific Basis of Health and Safety Regulation* (Brookings Inst., 1981); 3. *Controlling Industrial Pollution* (Brookings Inst., 1983).
Articles: 1. 'Vertical integration and the market for repair parts in the US automobile industry', *J Ind E*, 16(3), July 1968; 2. 'The economic effect of television network program ownership', *J Law E*, 14(2), Oct. 1971; 3. 'F.C.C. regulation, monopsony, and network television program costs', *Bell JE*, 3(2), Autumn 1972; 4. 'A reexamination of the prophecy of doom for cable television' (with L. Fray), *Bell JE* 5(1), Spring 1974; 5. 'The profitability of cable television', *J Bus*, 47(4), Oct. 1974; 6. 'Pollution controls and productivity growth in basic industries', in *Productivity Measurement in Regulated Industries*, eds. H. Ewing and J. Stevenson (Academic Press, 1981); 7. 'The cost of automobile safety and emissions regulation to the consumer' (with L. Lave and T. Keeler), *AER*, 72(2), May 1982; 8. 'Automobile safety regulation and offsetting behavior' (with J. Graham), *AER*, 74(2), May 1984.
Principal Contributions Examined the relationship between vertical integration and repair parts pricing as a mechanism of extracting consumer surplus in the sale of automobiles. Studied the relationship between vertical integration and monopoly power in television programming and the motion picture industry. More recently, explored the political economy of health, safety, and environmental regulation. Environmental regulation was shown to be partly a reaction by legislators from declining areas to new industrial growth in the South and West of the USA. Examined the effects of federal regulation of the automobile, discovering substantial benefits from safety regulation, but at some expense to nonoccupants' safety. Analyses of the effects of trade protection on declining steel and automobile industries, demonstrating the limited benefits of protection and the substantial welfare and redistributive costs. Predicted the current decline in the US steel industry, based upon simple notions of comparative advantage.

CROCKER, Thomas Tom

Born 1936, Bangor, ME, USA.
Current Post Prof. Econ., Univ. Wyoming, Laramie, WY, USA, 1975–.
Past Posts Timber Cruiser, Surveyor, Scaler, St Regis Paper Co., Bucksport, ME, 1952–61; Instr., Ass. Prof. Econ., Univ. Wisc.-Milwaukee, 1963–70; Assoc. Prof., Res. Assoc. Statewide Air Pollution Res. Center, Univ. Cal. Riverside, 1970–5; Res. Assoc., Boalt School Law, Univ. Cal. Berkeley, 1973; Res. Human Resources, Penn. State Univ., State Coll., PA, 1974.
Degrees BA Bowdoin Coll., 1959; PhD Univ. Missouri, Columbia.
Offices and Honours Chair, Technical Comm. Econ. Effects, Air Pollution Control Assoc., 1971–4; Member, Science Advisory Board, Co-Chair, Strategic Environ. Assessment System Rev. Panel, US Environmental Protection Agency, 1973–6; Member, Econ. Assessment Rev. Panel, Occupational Safety and Health Admin., US Dept. Labor, 1975–7; Member, Comm. on Odors, Comm. Prevention Significant Environmental Deterioration, NAS, Comm. Alkyl Benzene Derivatives,

NAS–Nat. Res. Council, 1978–9, 1979–81, 1979–80; Member, Rev. Comm. Health Econometric Res., Children's Hospital Pittsburgh, 1983–.

Editorial Duties Member, Ed. Boards, *JEEM*, 1973–; *J. Air Pollution Control Assoc.*, 1974–83.

Principal Fields of Interest 022 Microeconomic Theory; 024 Welfare Theory; 722 Conservation and Pollution.

Publications *Books:* 1. *Environmental Economics* (with A. J. Rogers), (Dryden Press, 1971; transl., Japanese, Charles E. Tuttle, 1973); 2. *Economics Perspectives on Acid Deposition Control*, ed. (Butterworths, 1984).

Articles: 1. 'The structuring of atmospheric pollution control systems', in *The Economics of Air Pollution*, ed. H. Wolozin (W. W. Norton, 1966); 2. 'Property values and air pollution' (with R. J. Anderson, Jr), *Em*, 38, Oct. 1970; 3. 'Externalities, property rights, and transactions costs: an empirical study', *J Law E*, 14, Oct. 1971; 4. 'Contractual choice', *Natural Resources J.*, 13, Oct. 1973; 5. 'Benefit-cost analysis of benefit-cost analyses', in *Cost Benefit Analysis and Water Pollution Policy*, eds. H. M. Peskin and E. P. Seskin (Urban Inst., 1975); 6. 'Property rights to geothermal resources: part II' (with S. Sato), *Ecology Law Q.*, 6, June 1977; 7. 'Transactions networks, economic growth, and income distribution', in *Comparative Public Policy: Public Goods and Public Policy*, eds. W. Loehr and T. Sandler (Sage Publications, 1978); 8. 'The advantages of contingent valuation methods for benefit-cost analysis' (with D. Brookshire), *Public Choice*, 36, 1981; 9. 'Hours of work, labor productivity and environmental conditions' (with R. L. Horst, Jr), *REStat*, 62, Aug. 1981; 10. 'Assessing the adequacy of natural science information: a Bayesian approach' (with R. M. Adams and R. W. Katz), *REStat*, 66(4), Nov. 1984.

Principal Contributions My enduring hope has been to make theoretical and empirical contributions to the development of techniques for valuing non-marketed goods, particularly environmental goods, and to gain insight into the efficiency and equity properties of alternative institutional forms for allocating natural resources. Air pollution problems have frequently served as a practical vehicle for these efforts. A major recent focus has been the assessment, generally within a Bayesian context, of the adequacy and treatment of natural science information in benefit-cost analyses. In retrospect, probably my most provocative idea was the original suggestion of tradeable effluent permit systems for pollution control. Efforts to develop teaching programmes in resource and environmental economics and to keep non-specialists and non-economists informed about what is happening in the field have complemented these research activities.

CROSLAND, Charles Anthony*

Dates and Birthplace 1918–77, Newbury, Berkshire, England.

Posts Held Fellow, Lect. Econ., Trinity Coll., Oxford, 1947–50; MP (Labour), 1950–5, 1959–77; UK Minister Econ. Affairs, 1964–5; UK Secretary State Educ. and Science, 1965–7; Pres., UK Board Trade, 1967–9; UK Secretary State Local Govt., 1967–70, Environment, 1974–6, Foreign and Commonwealth Affairs, 1976–7; Pres., Council of Ministers, EEC, 1977.

Degrees BA (Philo., Politics, Econ.) Univ. Oxford, 1939.

Offices and Honours Fellow, Trinity Coll., Oxford; Chairman, Fabian Soc., 1961–2; Council Member, Consumer Assoc., 1958–63; Exec. Comm., Town and Country Planning Assoc., 1971–2.

Publications *Books:* 1. *New Fabian Essays* (with others), (1952); 2. *Britain's Economic Problems* (1953); 3. *The Future of Socialism* (1956); 4. *The Conservative Enemy* (1962); 5. *The Politics of Education* (with L. Boyle and M. Kogan), (1971); 6. *Socialism Now and Other Essays* (1974).

Career A prominent figure in the British Labour government of the 1960s and 70s, he is best remembered for his major opus, *The Future of Socialism*. This immensely influential book defined for a whole generation a bright new vision of 'socialism', defined in the anti-Marxist sense as a society of greater equality, common ownership of the means of production being dismissed as an irrelevance; it married a Keynesian stance on fiscal policy with an emphasis on generous welfare expenditures.

CUKIERMAN, Alex

Born 1938, Paris, France.
Current Post Assoc. Prof. Econ., Tel-Aviv Univ., Tel-Aviv, Israel, 1979–.
Past Posts Lect. Econ., Sr. Lect. Econ., Tel-Aviv Univ., Tel-Aviv, Israel, 1972–6, 1976–9; Vis. Lect., Northwestern Univ., 1976; Vis. Assoc. Prof., NYU, 1977–8, Carnegie-Mellon Univ., 1978–9; Cons., EEC, 1982; Dir., Horowitz Inst. Res. Developing Countries, Tel-Aviv Univ., 1983; Vis. Prof. Econ., Carnegie-Mellon Univ., 1984–5.
Degrees BA, MA Hebrew Univ., 1963, 1967; PhD MIT, 1972.
Principal Fields of Interest 134 Inflation and Deflation; 131 Economic Fluctuations; 023 Macroeconomic Theory.
Publications *Books:* 1. *The Capital Market in Israel* (with B. Shahar and J. Bronfeld), (Weidenfeld & Nicholson, 1971; transl., Hebrew, Shoken, 1972); 2. *Inflation, Stagflation and Relative Prices Under Imperfect Information* (CUP, 1984; transl., Italian, Edizioni de Communita, 1984).
Articles: 1. 'A test of expectational processes using information from the capital markets — the Israeli case', *Int ER,* 18, Oct. 1977; 2. 'The horizontal integration of the banking firm, credit rationing and monetary policy', *REStud,* 45, Feb. 1978; 3. 'Rational expectations and the role of monetary policy: a generalization', *J Mon E,* 5, April 1979; 4. 'Differential inflationary expectations and the variability of the rate of inflation: theory and evidence' (with P. Wachtel), *AER,* 69(4), Sept. 1979; 5. 'The effects of wage indexation on macroeconomics fluctuations: a generalization', *J Mon E,* 6, April 1980; 6. 'The effects of uncertainty on investment under risk neutrality with endogenous information, *JPE,* 88, June 1980; 7. 'Stagflation persistent unemployment and the permanence of economic shocks' (with K. Brunner and L. A. Meltzer), *J Mon E,* 6, Oct. 1980; 8. 'Relative price variabil-ity, inflation and the allocative efficiency of the price system', *J Mon E,* 8, April 1982; 9. 'Money and economic activity, inventories and business cycles' (with K. Brunner and L. A. Meltzer), *J Mon E,* 11, May 1983; 10. 'Relative price variability and inflation — a survey and further results', in *Carnegie-Rochester Conference Series on Public Pol.,* 19, Autumn 1983.

Principal Contributions Investigated the interactions between relative price variability and inflation within equilibrium frameworks in which money is fundamentally neutral, with particular emphasis on the relationships among the following: the distribution of inflationary expectations across individuals, inflation variance, inflation uncertainty, relative price variability, and general nominal uncertainty. Contributed to the development of the argument that slow learning about permanent changes in productivity causes stagflation. Participated in development of macro-inventory models of the business cycle with particular emphasis on employment, interest rates and the transmission of monetary policy. Investigated the effects of wage indexation on macroeconomic stability and the real effects of nonneutral tax structures in inflationary environments. Did empirical work on the inflation-induced distortions of the national accounts.

Current work includes the formulation and characterisation of the credibility of monetary policy-makers. Earlier work focussed on the tests of inflationary expectation's formulation and expected devaluation using information from the Israeli index and foreign-exchange linked bond markets. It also included descriptive work on the Israeli capital market with particular emphasis on its various indexation characteristics as well as the development of formal models of credit rationing and a small-scale macroeconomic model of the Israeli economy. Throughout my active research years I was and still am keenly interested in the causes and consequence of inflation. However, emphasis and method used changed over the years. My early work on the subject focussed on the Phillips curve, using a disequilibrium full information framework, while more recent work is based on various equilibrium, incomplete information models and deals with a wider range of the real effects of inflation. Current research is guided by the belief that full understanding of inflation requires a theory of government behaviour.

CULBERTSON, John Mathew

Born 1921, Detroit, MI, USA.
Current Post Prof. Econ., Univ. Wisconsin-Madison, WI, USA, 1968–.
Past Posts Econ., Board Governors, Fed. Reserve System, 1950–7; Ass. Prof. Commerce, Ass. Prof. Econ. and Commerce, 1957–9, 1962–8; Vis. Assoc. Prof., Univ. Michigan, 1960; Vis. Prof. Econ., Univ. Cal. Berkeley, 1962–3, 1966–7; Dir., Fin. and Fiscal Res. Center, Social Systems Res. Inst., 1963–5, 1967–8; Cons., Feb. Reserve Bank, St Louis, 1959–60; Sub-Comm. Internat. Fin., US Congress Banking and Currency Comm., 1963; USAID Mission Bolivia, 1965, Vis. Prof., Univ. Paris I, 1983.
Degrees BA, MA, PhD Univ. Michigan, 1946, 1947, 1956.
Editorial Duties Assoc. Ed., *J Fin*, 1964–7.
Principal Fields of Interest 010 General Economics; 100 Economic Growth; Development; Planning; Fluctuations; 400 International Economics.
Publications *Books:* 1. *Full Employment or Stagnation?* (McGraw-Hill, 1964); 2. *Macroeconomic Theory and Stabilization Policy* (McGraw-Hill, 1968); 3. *Economic Development: An Ecological Approach* (Alfred A. Knopf, 1971); 4. *Money and Banking* (McGraw-Hill, 1972, 1977); 5. *Public Finance and Stabilization Policy: Essays in Honor of Richard A. Musgrave*, co-ed. (with W. Smith), (N-H, 1974).
Articles: 1. 'The term structure of interest rates', *QJE*, 71, Nov. 1957; 2. 'A positive debt management program', *REStat*, 41, May 1959; 3. 'Friedman on the lag in effect of monetary policy', *JPE*, 68, Dec. 1960; 4. 'The use of monetary policy', *SEJ*, 28, Oct. 1961; 5. 'Government financial policy in the effective market economy', in *Banking*

and Monetary Studies, ed. D. Carson (Richard D. Irwin, 1963); 6. 'The interest rate structure: towards completion of the classical system', in *The Theory of Interest Rates,* eds. F. H. Hahn and F. P. R. Brechling (Macmillan, 1965); 7. 'Stabilization policy in an evolutionary economics', in *Public Finance and Stabilization policy: Essays in Honor of Richard A. Musgrave,* eds. J. M. Culberbon and W. L. Smith (N-H, 1974); 8. 'Ecology, economics and the quality of life', in *Historical Ecology: Essays on Environment and Social Change,* ed. L. J. Bilsky (Kennikat Press, 1980); 9. 'Interest rates in a naturalistic economics', *Economies et Societés,* 14, Feb.–April 1980; 10. 'The new potentiality for realizing evolutionary-institutional economics', *JEI,* 18(2), June 1984.

Principal Contributions My work has been directed towards the development of a realist or causal economics, in contrast to *a priori,* 'theoretical' economics. This kind of work in economics was well received in the 1950s but with the rise of formalistic economics in the 1960s it became unfashionable and difficult to publish.

My doctoral dissertation developed a causal interpretation of the term structure of interest rates and criticised what now can be seen as a pioneer work in modern formalistic economics, the interpretation of the structure of interest rates on the basis of a simple pattern of hypothetical 'expectations'. The methodological points made in that work were generalised in my 1968 book. They were developed to incorporate new ideas and tools of current science and were applied to other topics of economics in later work, much of which was not published.

The recent fragmentation of formalistic economics, the rising criticism of its unrealism, the successes of the empirical, evolutionary sciences, and the challenge to logical positivism by the new realist philosophy of science now seems to be creating an intellectual climate in which realist or causal economics can receive a hearing, and perhaps will become the dominant approach in the years ahead. I plan in the next few years to publish in a series of books a coherent version of a modern realist (or causal, or institutionalist, empirical, social, historical) economics. In this work, I emphasise that the recently dominant 'theoretical economics' gains its appeal to economists from its formal rituals and its substance from eighteenth-century natural-harmony ideology. The needs of economic policy urgently call for its replacement with an economics that provides realistic causal explanations of the workings of actual economies, and that belongs to the intellectual world of modern scientific thought.

CULYER, Anthony John

Born 1942, Croydon, Surrey, England.
Current Post Prof. Econ., Univ. York, Heslington, York, England, 1979–.
Past Posts Teaching Ass., UCLA, 1964–5; Tutor, Ass. Lect., Univ. Exeter, 1965–6, 1966–9; Lect., Sr. Lect., Reader, Univ. York, 1969–72, 1972–6, 1976–9; Ass. Dir., Dep. Dir., Inst. Social Econ. Res., Univ. York, 1971–9, 1979–82; Sr. Res. Assoc., Ontario Econ. Council, Vis. Lect., Queen's Univ., Ont., Canada, 1976; Vis. Prof., Univ. Otago, New Zealand, 1979; ANU, 1979.
Degree BA Univ. Exeter, 1964.
Offices and Honours Fullbright Scholar, 1964–5; Adviser to Chief Scientist, UK Dept. Health and Social Security, 1979–; Hon. Adviser, US Office Health Econ., 1980–; Convenor, UK SSRC European Workshop Health Indicators, 1980–2; Member, Scientific Comm. UK IIPF, 1975–6, 1982–3; Member, UK North Allerton Health Authority, 1981–; Organiser, UK SSRC Health Economists' Study Group, 1971–; Member, Health Service Research Comm. EEC, 1983–.
Editorial Duties Co-Ed., *JHE*; Ed., *York-Nuffield Portfolios*; Ed. Board, *BER*, 1976–84.
Principal Fields of Interest 913 Economics of Health; 911 General Welfare Programmes; 02 Welfare Theory.
Publications *Books:* 1. *The Price of Blood* (with M. H. Cooper), (INEA,

1968); 2. *Economics of Social Policy* (Martin Robertson, 1973; transl., Japanese, 1976); 3. *Economic Policies and Social Goals,* co-ed. (with K. G. Wright), (Martin Robertson, 1974); 4. *Need and the National Health Service* (Martin Robertson, 1976); 5. *Human Resources and Public Finance,* co-ed. (with V. Halberstadt), (Cujas, 1977); 6. *Economic Aspects of Health Services* co-ed. (with K. G. Wright), (Martin Robertson, 1978); 7. *Measuring Health: Lessons for Ontario* (Univ. Toronto Press, 1978); 8. *The Political Economy of Social Policy* (Martin Robertson, 1980, 1983); 9. *Health Indicators,* ed. (Martin Robertson, 1983); 10. *Economics* (Blackwell, 1985).
Articles: 1. 'A utility-maximising view of universities', *SJPE*, 17(3), Nov. 1970; 2. 'The nature of the commodity "health care" and its efficient allocation', *OEP*, 23(2), July 1971, repr. in *Penguin Modern Economics: Health Economics,* eds. A. J. Culyer and M. H. Cooper (Penguin, 1973); 3. 'Medical care and the economics of giving', *Ec*, N.S. 38, Aug. 1971; 4. 'Social indicators: health' (with A. Williams, and others), *Social Trends,* 1(2), 1971, repr. in *Social Indicators and Social Policy,* eds. A. Schonfield and S. Shaw (Heinemann, 1972); 5. 'Blood and altruism: an economic review', in *Blood Policy: Issues and Alternatives,* ed. D. B. Johnson (AEI, 1978); 6. 'The quality of life and the limits of cost benefit analysis', in *Public Economics and the Quality of Life,* eds. L. Wingo and A. Evans (JHUP, 1977); 7. 'Need, values and health status measurement', in *Economic Aspects of Health Services,* eds. A. J. Culyer and K. G. Wright (Martin Robertson, 1978); 8. 'Externality models and health' (with H. Simpson), *ER*, 56(15), June 1980; 9. 'Economics, social policy and social administration: the interplay between topics and disciplines', *JSP*, 10(3), 1981; 10. 'Joint products and multijurisdictional spillovers' (with T. Sandler), *QJE*, 97(4), Sept. 1982.
Principal Contributions Told by noneconomic students of social policy and by fellow economists in the 1960s that resource allocation in the social services was not a proper economic

subject, I risked an economist's career devoted to the contrary view and rapidly earned the enmity of the left for No. 1 in the above lists of books and articles and that of the right for No. 4 in the book list. Having thus established my impeccable credentials for impartiality in a politically treacherous terrain, the main thrust of my work has been in trying to provide suitable conceptual material, case studies and general propaganda to enhance effectiveness, efficiency and fairness at all levels of responsibility for the finance and organisation of the welfare state, especially health services and health-related activities, both public and private. The search for a satisfactory rationale for that extraordinary institutional feature of the twentieth century, the welfare state, has been a connecting thread throughout. This main stream has had tributaries, mostly concerning other aspects of applying welfare economics to phenomena, puzzles and problems both as economists and as *real* decision makers see them.

CUNNINGHAM, William*

Dates and Birthplace 1849–1919, Edinburgh, Scotland.

Posts Held Univ. Extension Lect., 1874–8; Lect., Fellow, Univ. Camb., 1878–91; Prof. Econ., King's Coll. London, 1891–7; Lect., Harvard Univ., 1899, 1914.

Degrees BA Univ. Camb., 1872.

Offices and Honours Officer, BA, Royal Hist. Soc.; Pres., Econ. Section, BAAS, 1891, 1905.

Publications *Books:* 1. *The Growth of English Industry and Commerce,* 3 vols (1882, 1910–12); 2. *Outlines of English Industrial History* (with E. A. McArthur), (1895); 3. *Modern Civilisation in Some of its Economic Aspects* (1896); 4. *The Rise and Decline of the Free Trade Movement* (1905); 5. *The Case Against Free Trade* (1911); 6. *The Progress of Capitalism in England* (1916, 1925).

Articles: 1. 'The perversion of economic history', *EJ,* 2, Sept. 1892.

Career He established economic history as an independent discipline in British universities by outlining its subject matter, establishing its methods, and stimulating teaching and research. His advocacy of the historical method in economics caused some controversy and influenced Marshall to revise the economic history sections in his *Principles.* Cunningham initiated a revision of opinion on mercantilism and advocated protectionism as a current policy. In addition to his considerable volume of academic achievement, he was also a practising clergyman.

Secondary Literature R. M. Hartwell, 'Cunningham, William', *IESS,* 4.

CYERT, Richard Michael

Born 1921, Winona, MI, USA.

Current Post Pres., Carnegie-Mellon Univ., Pittsburg, PA, USA, 1972–.

Past Posts Officer, US Navy, 1943–6; Instr., Univ. Minnesota, 1946; Instr., City Univ., NY, 1948; Instr., Ass. Prof., Assoc. Prof., Prof. Econ. and Industrial Admin., Dean, Grad. School Industrial Admin., Carnegie-Mellon Univ., 1948–9, 1949–55, 1955–60, 1960–2, 1962–72.

Degrees BS Univ. Minnesota, 1943; PhD Columbia Univ., 1951; Hon. Dr Phil. Gothenburg Univ., Sweden, 1972; Hon. Dr Univ. Leuven, Belgium, 1973; Hon. Dr Law, Waynesburg Coll., Waynesburg, PA, 1979; Hon. Dr Science, Westminster Coll., New Wilmington, PA, 1979; Hon. Dr Law, Allegheny Coll., Meadville, PA, 1980; Hon. Dr Educ., Bethany Coll., VA, 1984.

Offices and Honours Ford Foundation Faculty Res. Fellow, 1959–60; Guggenheim Foundation Fellow, 1967–8; Medal, Hofstra Univ., 1973; Fellow, ASA, 1973; Outstanding Achievement Award, Univ. Minnesota, 1975; Fellow, Em Soc, 1977, AAAS, 1980; Pittsburg Vectors Man of Year Award, 1984; Stat. of Year Award, Pittsburg Chapter ASA, 1984.

Editorial Duties Ed. Board, *Behavioral Science.*

Principal Fields of Interest 020 General Economic Theory; 610 Industrial Organisation and Public Policy; 510 Administration.

Publications *Books:* 1. *A Behavioral Theory of the Firm* (with J. G. March), (Prentice-Hall, 1963), repr. in *Entscheidungstheorie, Texte und Analysen,* eds. E Witte and A. L. Thimm (Gabler Verlag, 1977); 2. *Theory of the Firm: Resource Allocation in a Market Economy* (with K. J. Cohen), (Prentice-Hall, 1965; transls., Italian, Etas Kompass, 1967, Spanish, Libreria 'El Alteneo' Editorial, 1973); 3. *Management of Non-Profit Organizations: With Emphasis on Universities* (D. C. Heath, 1975); 4. *The American Economy, 1960–2000: A Retrospective and Prospective Look* (Free Press, 1983).

Articles: 1. 'Oligopoly price behavior and the business cycle', *JPE,* 63, Feb. 1955; 2. 'Organizational structure and pricing behavior in an oligopolistic market' (with J. G. March), *AER,* 45(1), March 1955, repr. in *Price Policies and Practices,* eds. R. Mulvihill and M. Paranka (Wiley, 1967); 3. 'Computer models in dynamic economics' (with K. J. Cohen), *QJE,* 75(1), Feb. 1961, repr. in *Price Theory,* ed. H. Townsend (Penguin, 1971); 4. 'Behavioral rules and the theory of the firm' (with M. I. Kamien), in *Prices: Issues in Theory, Practice and Public Policy,* eds. A. Phillips and O. E. Williamson (Univ. Pennsylvania Press, 1967), repr. in *Readings in Industrial Economics,* eds. C. K. Rowley (Macmillan, 1972); 5. 'Multiperiod decision models with alternating choice as a solution to the duopoly problem', *QJE,* 84(3), Aug. 1970; 6. 'An analysis of cooperation and learning in a duopoly contest' (with M. H. DeGroot), *AER,* 63(1), March 1973.

Principal Contributions My original interests were in oligopoly theory. I was interested, in particular, in seeing what statistical regularities in behaviour could be determined by statistical techniques. My first paper tested the hypothesis that oligopolists followed price changes during the up-swing, but not during the down-swing of a business cycle. In trying to develop theoretical models of oligopoly behaviour, I got the idea that more knowledge was needed about the internal variables that affected decision-making within the firm. This idea developed because it

was clear that the market forces were not the determinate factors. This interest then led to learning more about organisation theory and doing some specific empirical studies of decision-making within oligopolistic firms. Ultimately, this work led to the writing of *A Behavioral Theory of the Firm.* This book has been classified as a citation classic because of the large number of times it has been cited. This book was written with James G. March and has had a wide impact in a number of the social sciences.

In the course of attempting to develop more complex models that could encompass some of the knowledge about behaviour that had been learned from the empirical studies, I became interested in simulation. An article by Kalman Cohen and myself in the 1961 *QJE* was, so far as I know, the first article on the possibilities of simulation for developing dynamic economic models. I became somewhat discouraged about simulation models because I believe they were describing but not explaining. In the search for new methodologies for model building, I became interested in Bayesian analysis. Together with M. DeGroot, I have over the last fifteen years been applying Bayesian analysis to economic theory. In this process, we have made a large number of contributions to oligopoly theory. This work will be forthcoming shortly in book form. We have been able to develop models with utility functions that incorporate learning about utilities on the part of the individual.

D

DALTON, Edward Hugh*

Dates and Birthplace 1887–1962, Neath, Glamorgan, Wales.
Posts Held Lect., Reader Econ., LSE, 1914, 1920–36; MP (Labour), 1924–31, 1935–62; UK Minister of Econ. Warfare, 1940–2; Pres., UK Board Trade, 1942–5; UK Chancellor Exchequer, 1945–7.
Degrees MA King's Coll. Camb., 1909; DSc LSE, 1913.

Offices and Honours Council, Royal Stat. Soc.; Created Life Peer, 1960.

Publications *Books:* 1. *Inequality of Incomes in Modern Communities* (1920, 1929); 2. *Principles of Public Finance* (1923, 1957); 3. *London Essays in Economics,* co-ed. (with T. E. Gregory), (1929); 4. *Practical Socialism for Britain* (1935); 5. *Memoirs,* 3 vols (1952–62).

Career Notable postwar British Labour Politician who wrote authoritatively on issues of taxation. His *Principles of Public Finance* was a leading textbook in the interwar period.

DALY, George

Born 1940, Painesville, OH, USA.

Current Post Dean, Coll. Bus. Admin., Univ. Iowa, Iowa City, IA, USA, 1984–.

Past Posts Ass. Prof., Assoc. Prof., Miami Univ., 1965–9, 1969–71; Ass. Prof., Univ. Texas, Austin, 1969–70; Assoc. Prof., Prof., Dean, Coll. Social Sciences, Univ. Houston, 1971–4, 1974–84, 1979–83; Exec. Secretary, Climatic Impact Assessment Program, US Dept. Transportation, 1973–4; Chief Econ., Office Energy Res. and Develp., Exec. Office US President, 1974; Ass. Dir., Inst. Defense Analyses, Washington, DC, 1977–9; Vis. Prof., Univ. Virginia, 1979.

Degrees BA Miami Univ., 1962; MA, PhD Northwestern Univ., 1965, 1967.

Principal Fields of Interest 010 General Economics; 025 Social Choice; Bureaucratic Performance.

Publications *Articles:* 1. 'Externalities, extortion and allocative efficiency' (with J. F. Giertz), *AER,* 64(5), Dec. 1974; 2. 'Transfers and Pareto optimality' (with J. F. Giertz), *J Pub E,* 5(1–2), Jan.–Feb. 1976; 3. 'On welfare programs and donor-recipient adjustments' (with J. F. Giertz), *Pub Fin. Q.,* Oct. 1976; 4. 'Reply to Bromley', *AER,* 68(5), Dec. 1978; 5. 'Estimating the value of a missing market: the economics of directory assistance' (with T. Mayor), *J Law E,* 6(3), April 1980; 6. 'Externalities, property rights and the baseball players' labor market' (with W. J. Moore), *EI,* 18(1), Jan. 1981; 7.

'Politics as a filter', *Public Choice,* Spring 1981; 8. 'Price competition and the acquisition of weapon systems', *J. Pol. Analysis and Management,* forthcoming, 1985; 9. 'The future of OPEC: price hikes versus cartel instability' (with J. Griffin and H. Steele), *Energy J.,* forthcoming, 1985; 10. 'Reason and rationality during energy crises' (with T. Mayor), *JPE,* forthcoming, 1986.

Principal Contributions My work has concentrated on issues related to public policy and the processes through which it is made.

DANIELSEN, Albert Leroy

Born 1934, Council Bluffs, IA, USA.

Current Post Prof. Econ., Univ. Georgia, Athens, GA, USA, 1980–.

Past Posts Instr., Pfeiffer Coll., 1962, 1963; Ass. Prof., Assoc. Prof., Univ. Georgia, 1963–8, 1968–80; Acting Dir., Office Internat. Market Analysis, US Dept. Energy, Washington DC, 1977–8; Special Ass., Dep. Ass., Secretary Internat. Energy Res., US Dept. Energy, 1978.

Degrees BS (Industrial Management) Clemson Univ., 1960; PhD Duke Univ., 1966.

Offices and Honours Nat. Defense Educ. Act Fellow, 1960–1, 1961–2, 1962–3; Intergovernmental Personnel Act Program Participant, US Dept. of Energy, 1976–8; US SSRC and Fullbright Res. Award, 1982–; Dir., Annual Georgia Public Utilities Conf., Atlanta, GA, 1981–; Exec. Committee, Internat. Assoc. Energy Economists, 1981–4.

Principal Fields of Interest 723 Energy; 613 Public Utilities; 611 Market Structure.

Publications *Books:* 1. *The Evolution of OPEC* (Harcourt, Brace Jovanovich, 1982); 2. *Current Issues in Public Utility Economics: Essays in Honor of James C. Bonbright* (with D. R, Kamerschen) (D. C. Heath, 1983).

Articles: 1. 'A positive theory of trade and compensation', *SEJ,* 40(4), April 1974; 2. 'A theory of exchange, philanthropy and appropriation', *Public Choice,* Winter 1976; 3. 'Cartel rivalry and the world price of oil', *SEJ,*

42(3), Jan. 1976; 4. 'Some empirical evidence on the variables associated with the ranking of economics journals' (with C. D. DeLorme), *SEJ*, 43(2), Oct. 1976; 5. 'An empirical investigation of voting on energy issues' (with P. H. Rubin), *Public Choice*, Winter, 1977; 6. 'An analysis of oil price legislation and regulation in the United States', *J. World Trade Law*, Sept. 1979; 7. 'The role of speculation in the oil price ratchet process', *Resources and Energy*, 2(1), Oct. 1979; 8. 'The theory and measurement of OPEC stability', *SEJ*, 47(1), July 1980; 9. 'World oil price increases: sources and solutions' (with E. B. Selby, Jr.), *Energy J.*, 1(4), Oct. 1980; 10. 'Oil price increases as leading indicators of new car sales' (with J. E. Hillard), *Resources and Energy*, 5(2), Oct. 1982.

Principal Contributions Work orientated toward problems of the day. Early publications in economics of education and human capital; borrowing a phrase from Abraham Lincoln, 'the world will little note nor long remember' those efforts. The gasoline 'shortages' in 1973 and the October oil embargo kindled my interest in oil markets. Convinced that the traditional theory of cartel behaviour was inadequate for analysing the world oil market, I concluded that the theory is one-sided: it is incapable of explaining how an existing cartel arises in the first place. Coined the term 'Cartel Rivalry' to describe a more dynamic theory of cartel formation, breakdown and reformation. Jury still out on this competing models designed to explain the level and stability of oil prices. Most economists are still wedded to the 'traditional' theory. I did additional work on the theory and measurement of cartel stability and concluded that the stability of a particular institution is an empirical matter that cannot be decided on theoretical grounds alone. I then questioned the theory which leads to the conclusion that inventory accumulation and drawdown serve to stabilise production and prices and arrived at the finding that inventory accumulation tends to drive prices higher during periods of 'shortage', and more or less 'permanently' raises prices

in a cartelised market. The jury is still out on this issue too.

DARBY, Michael Rucker

Born Dallas, TX, USA.
Current Post Prof. Econ., UCLA, USA, 1978–.
Past Posts Ass. Prof. Econ., Ohio State Univ., 1970–3; Vis. Ass. Prof. Econ., Assoc. Prof. Econ., UCLA, 1972–3, 1973–8; Harry Scherman Res. Fellow, NBER, NY, 1974–5; Vis. Fellow, Hoover Inst., Stanford Univ., 1977–8.
Degrees BA Dartmouth Coll., 1967; MA, PhD Univ. Chicago, 1968, 1970.
Offices and Honours Sr. Fellow, Dartmouth Coll, 1966–7; NSF Grad. Fellow, 1967–70; Woodrow Wilson Hon. Fellow, 1967–8; Lilly Honor Fellow, 1967–70; Fed. Deposit Insurance Corp. Grad. Fellow, 1969–70; Fed. Deposit Insurance Corp., Prize Best Dissertation, 1969–70.
Editorial Duties Book Review Ed., *JMCB*, 1973–4; Ed., *J. Internat. Money and Fin.*, 1981–; Ed. Board, *AER*, 1983–.
Principal Fields of Interest 300 Domestic Monetary and Fiscal Theory and Institutions; 430 Balance of Payments; International Finance; 200 Quantitative Economic Methods and Data.
Publications *Books:* 1. *Macroeconomics: The Theory of Income, Employment and the Price Level* (McGraw-Hill, 1976); 2. *Have Controls Ever Worked? The Post-War Record* (with M. Parkin), (Fraser Inst., 1976); 3. *The Effects of Social Security on Income and the Capital Stock* (*AEI*, 1979); 4. *Intermediate Economics* (McGraw-Hill, 1979; transl. Japanese, McGraw-Hill-Kogakusha, 1981); 5. *The International Transmission of Inflation* (with J. R. Lothian, A. E. Gandolfi, J. Schwartz and A. C. Stockman), (Univ. Chicago Press, 1983); 6. *Labor Force, Employment and Productivity in Historical Perspective* (UCLA Inst. Industrial Relations, 1984); 7. *Macroeconomics* (with M. T. Melvin), (Scott Foresman & Co., 1985).
Articles: 1. 'The allocation of transi-

tory income among consumers' assets', *AER*, 62(5), Dec. 1972; 2. 'Free competition and the optimal amount of fraud' (with E. Karni), *J Law E*, 16(1), April 1973; 3. 'The financial and tax effects of monetary policy on interest rates', *EI*, 13(2), June 1975; 4. 'Three-and-a-half million U.S. employees have been mislaid: or, an explanation of unemployment, 1934–41', *JPE*, 84(1), Feb. 1976; 5. 'Price and wage controls: the first two years', *Carnegie-Rochester Conf. Series on Public Pol.*, 2, April 1976; 6. 'Rational expectations under conditions of costly information', *J Fin*, 31(3), June 1976; 7. 'The consumer expenditure function', *Explor. in Econ. Res.*, 4(5), Winter–Spring 1977–8.

Principal Contributions My thesis (Article No. 1 above) developed two principal concepts: the shock-absorber money demand and investment of transitory income in consumers' durable goods. The latter idea led to my deriving Friedman's permanent income estimator from a perpetual inventory of wealth and correcting previous upward-biassed estimates of its current income weight. An integrated model of consumer expenditures — as opposed to consumption — culminated this line of research (Article No. 7 above). Although shock-absorber money demand was featured in the dynamic-adjustment model introduced in my three textbooks, only in 1976 did I begin work with Carr on its simplified specification.

Anomalies frequently reflect measurement without theory. So I showed that the post-1933 'counter-example' to the natural-rate hypothesis arose from counting WPA (Works Project Admin.) workers as unemployed (Article No. 4 above). In a series of papers, the 1971–4 price controls were shown to systematically bias both price indices and deflated variables. The post-1965 productivity slowdown proved explicable when the effects of age, sex, education and immigration on labour input are computed.

During 1977–81 I wrote the papers included in *The International Transmission of Inflation*. These specified, estimated and simulated the quarterly Mark III International Transmission Model for eight countries and demonstrated that US monetary policy was the major independent cause of the 1970s world inflation, that both goods and assets are imperfect substitutes internationally, and that nonreserve countries exercised short-run money control to a degree which ultimately destroyed the Bretton Woods System.

Beside these major themes, I developed the tax or 'Darby Effect' of inflation on interest rates (Article No. 3 above), with Karni analysed the market structures of 'credence goods' industries (No. 2 above), studied the formation of economically rational expectations (No. 6 above) and demonstrated in my social security monograph that 'bequest assets' dwarf 'life cycle' assets in the US.

D'ARGE, Ralph Clair

Born 1941, Los Angeles, CA, USA.
Current Post John S. Bugas Disting. Prof. Econ., Univ. Wyoming, Laramie, WY, 1974–.
Past Posts Ass. Prof. Econ., Univ. New Mexico, Albuquerque, NM, 1967–9; Vis. Scholar, Resources for the Future, Washington, DC, 1972; Prof. Econ., Univ. Cal. Riverside, 1972–4; Scholar, Rockefeller Center, Bellagio, Italy, 1974.
Degrees BS (Agric. Econ.) Cal. State Univ., Chico, 1963; MS (Agric. Econ.), MA, PhD Cornell Univ., 1965, 1967, 1969.
Offices and Honours Pres., Assoc. Environmental Resource Econ., 1980; Member, Environmental Stud. Board, NAS, 1976–82; Member, Environmental Advisory Comm., 1978–80; Adviser to UNCTAD, WHO, OECD, NAS, NSF.
Editorial Duties Managing Ed., *JEEM*, 1973–; Assoc. Ed., Nat. Advisory Council, *Nat. Resource J.*, 1974–81, 1981–; Ed. Board, *JEI*, 1973–6.
Principal Fields of Interest 721 Natural Resources, 020 General Economic Theory; 710 Agriculture.
Publications *Books:* 1. *Economics of the Environment: A Materials Balance Approach* (with A. V. Kneese and R. U. Ayres), (JHUP, 1970); 2. *Quantita-*

tive Water Resource Basin Planning: An Analysis of the Pecos Basin (New Mexico Water Resources Inst., 1970); 3. *Water Resources Planning and Social Goals: Conceptualization Toward a New Methodology* (with D. F. Peterson, *et al.*), (US Govt. Printing Office, 1971); 4. *Economic and Social Measures of Biologic and Climatic Change*, ed. (USDOT, 1975); 5. *Experiments in Valuing Non-Market Goods: A Case Study of Alternative Benefit Measures of Air Pollution Control in the South Coast Air Basin of Southern California* (with D. Brookshire, W. Schulze and M. Thayer), (EPA, 1979).

Articles: 1. 'Pervasive external costs and the response of society' (with A. V. Kneese), in *The Analysis and Evaluation of Public Expenditures: The PPB System*, Joint Econ. Compendium, US Congress (US Govt. Printing Office, 1969); 2. 'Essay on economic growth and environmental quality', *Swed JE*, 73(1), March 1971, repr. in *Economics of Environment: Papers from Four Nations*, eds. P. Bohm and A. V. Kneese (St Martin's Press, 1982), and *Readings in Advanced Economics*, ed. R. Fels (Richard D. Irwin, 1974); 3. 'Economic growth and the natural environment', in *Environmental Quality Analysis: Theory and Methods in the Social Sciences*, eds. A. V. Kneese and B. T. Bower (JHUP, 1972); 4. 'Economic growth and the environment' (with K. C. Kogiku), *REStud*, 40(1), Jan. 1973; 5. 'The Coase proposition, information, and long-run equilibrium' (with W. Schulze), *AER*, 63(4), Sept. 1974; 6. 'Adjustment issues of impacted communities or, are boomtowns bad?' (with C. Brookshire), *Natural Resources J.*, 20(3), July 1980; 7. 'An experiment on the economic valuation of visibility' (with R. Rowe and D. Brookshire), *JEEM*, 7(1), March 1980.

Principal Contributions At Cornell University, I became interested in water and other natural resource problems. There seemed to be a substantial void between economic models and biological-physical principles. For the next ten years, my research focussed on discovering methods of connecting economic methodology with concepts

and models from the physical and biological sciences. Early research efforts were concentrated on water resources planning models embodying benefit-cost analysis and engineering design. This led to involvement in a large-scale interdisciplinary effort to develop a more holistic planning methodology, later identified as 'Tech Com'. At the same time, I became interested in linking pure welfare models with physical principles and co-developed with Kneese and Ayres the first general equilibrium-welfare model explicitly including conservation and matter-energy. Shortly thereafter I developed the first linkage between economic growth models and concepts of pollution and conservation and introduced the 'spaceship theorem'.

A secondary but continuing interest in international trade theory led me to explore how pollution may influence patterns of international trade and also to examine the problem of trans-frontier pollution. During this period, Kneese and I thought that the field of resource economics had matured and broadened enough to sustain a scientific journal, so we founded *JEEM*. After completing studies on the stratosphere and conducting research on neutrality of environmental laws and property rights, I became interested in pricing the environment and estimating monetary values of public goods in general. This interest led to a substantial ongoing research effort on techniques to reveal preferences for nonmarket goods, including the 'contingent valuation method'. Finally, my interest continues on problems of managing the global commons which most recently involved the carbon dioxide problem.

DASGUPTA, Partha Sarathi

Born 1942, Dacca, Bangladesh.
Current Post Prof. Econ., Univ. Camb., Fellow, St John's Coll. Camb., 1984–.
Past Posts Reader Econ., Prof. Econ., LSE, 1975–8, 1978–84; Vis. Prof., Stanford Univ., 1974–5; 1983–4, Delhi School Econ., 1978.
Degrees BSc (Physics) Univ. Delhi,

1962; BA (Maths.), PhD Univ. Camb., 1965, 1968.

Offices and Honours Fellow, Em Soc, 1975.

Principal Fields of Interest 121 Economic Studies of Less Industrialised Countries; 721 Natural Resources.

Publications *Books:* 1. *Guidelines for Project Evaluation* (with S. A. Marglin and A. K. Sen), (UN, 1972); 2. *Economic Theory and Exhaustible Resources* (with G. M. Heal), (CUP, James Nisbet, 1979); 3. *The Control of Resources* (Blackwell, 1982).

Articles: 1. 'On the concept of optimum population', *REStud*, 36, July 1969; 2. 'The optimal depletion of exhaustible resources' (with G. M. Heal), *REStud*, Symposium, 1974; 3. 'Benefit cost analysis and trade policies' (with J. E. Stiglitz), *JPE*, 82(1), Jan.–Feb. 1974; 4. 'On some alternative criteria for justice between generations', *J Pub E*, 3(4), Nov. 1974; 5. 'The implementation of social choice rules' (with P. J. Hammond and E. S. Maskin), *REStud*, 46(2), April 1979; 6. 'Industrial structure and the nature of innovative activity' (with J. E. Stiglitz), *EJ*, 90, June 1980; 7. 'Uncertainty, industrial structure and the speed of R & D' (with J. E. Stiglitz), *Bell JE*, 11(1), Jan. 1980; 8. 'Utilitarianism, information and rights', in *Utilitarianism and Beyond*, eds. A. K. Sen and B. Williams (CUP, 1982); 9. 'Resource depletion, research and development and the social role of discount', in *Discounting for Time and Risk in Energy Planning*, ed. R. Lind (JHUP, 1982); 10. 'Strategic considerations in invention and innovation: the case of natural resources' (with R. Gilbert and J. E. Stiglitz), *Em*, (51(5), Sept. 1983.

Principal Contributions Economic theory with major bias towards normative issues, dealing with capital and optimal growth theory, taxation and trade, development planning, welfare and justice, natural resources, industrial structure and technical change, incentive compatibility in planning mechanisms, game theory and the economics of malnutrition.

DAVENANT, Charles*

Dates and Birthplace 1656–1714, England.

Posts Held Commissioner of Excise, 1678–89; Polit. Pamphleteer; Inspector General Exports and Imports, 1702–14; MP, 1698–1707.

Publications *Books:* 1. *A Memorial Concerning the Coyn of England* (1695), and *A Memorial Concerning Creditt* (1696), in *Two Manuscripts by Charles Davenant*, ed. A. P. Usher (1942); 2. *The Political and Commercial Works of That Celebrated Writer Charles D'Avenant*, 5 vols, ed. C. Whitworth (1771).

Career A political and economic writer of considerable literary skill and with a firm grasp of Petty's political arithmetic. The exigencies of financial survival as a pamphleteer give some of his work an apparent inconsistency which lays him open to the charge of writing solely for immediate advantage. His main original contributions were in the theories of money, international trade and finance, and public finance. These were not, however, isolated insights, for they sprang from an unusually coherent view of the relations between the elements of economic life.

Secondary Literature D. A. G. Waddell, 'Davenant, Charles', *IESS*, 4.

DAVENPORT, Herbert Joseph*

Dates and Birthplace 1861–1931, Wilmington, VT, USA.

Posts Held Teacher Econ., Univ. Chicago, 1902–8; Prof., Dean, Univ. Missouri, 1908–16; Prof., Cornell Univ., 1916–29.

Degree PhD Univ. Chicago, 1898.

Offices and Honours Pres., AEA, 1920.

Publications *Books:* 1. *Outlines of Economic Theory* (1896); 2. *Value and Distribution* (1908); 3. *Economics of Enterprise* (1913, 1943); 4. *The Economics of Alfred Marshall* (1935).

Career A pupil and admirer of Veblen, although his conviction that most economic doctrines were relative truths did not lead him to the study of institutions. He sought a theory based on prices and excluding the psychological elements of Marshall and the Austrians. He used the concept of opportunity cost and in his avoidance of utility theory pointed in the direction of the indifference curve approach. In many other respects, his writings bristle with indications of later developments in economics.

Secondary Literature H. W. Spiegel, 'Davenport, Herbert J.', *IESS*, 4.

DAVID, Paul Allan

Born 1935, New York City, NY, USA.
Current Post William Robertson Coe Prof. Amer. Econ. Hist., Stanford Univ., CA, USA, 1976–.
Past Posts Ass. Prof., Assoc. Prof., Prof. Econ., Stanford Univ., 1961–6, 1966–9, 1969–76; Vis. Fellow, All Souls Coll. Oxford, 1968–9, Vis. Prof. Econ., Harvard Univ., 1972–3; Pitt Prof. Amer. Hist. and Inst., Fellow, Churchill Coll. Camb., 1977–8; Fellow, Center Advanced Study Behavioral Sciences, Stanford Univ., 1978–9.
Degrees BA, PhD Harvard Univ., 1956, 1973.
Offices and Honours Fulbright Scholar, 1956–8; Guggenheim Foundation Fellow, 1975–6; Fellow, Internat. Em Soc; Vice-Pres., EHA, 1978–9; Fellow, AAAS.
Editorial Duties Ed. Board, *JEH*, 1969–77; Assoc. Ed., *Explor. Econ. Hist.*, 1973–, *Hist. Methods*, 1980–.
Principal Fields of Interest 042 North American Economic History; 841 Economic Demography; 621 Technology.
Publications *Books:* 1. *Nations and Households in Economic Growth: Essays in Honor of Moses Abramovitz*, co-ed. (with M. W. Reder), (Academic Press, 1974); 2. *Technical Choice, Innovation and Economic Growth: Essays on American and British Experience in the Nineteenth Century* (CUP, 1975); 3. *Reckoning with Slavery: A Critical Study in the Quantitative History of American Negro Slavery* (with H. Gutman, R. Sutch, P. Temin and G. Wright), (OUP, 1976).

Articles: 1. 'Biased efficiency growth and capital-labor substitution in the U.S., 1899–1960' (with T. van de Klundert), *AER*, 55(3). June 1965; 2. 'The mechanization of reaping in the ante-bellum Midwest', in *Industrialization in Two Systems*, ed. H. Rosovsky (Wiley, 1966); 3. 'The growth of real product in the US before 1940: a new evidence, controlled conjectures', *JEH*, 22(2), June 1967; 4. 'Learning by doing and tariff protection: a reconsideration of the case of the ante-bellum cotton textile industry', *JEH*, 23(3), Sept. 1970; 5. 'Economic growth in America: historical parables and realities' (with M. Abramovitz), *DE*, 12(3), May–June 1973; 6. 'Private savings: ultra-rationality, aggregation and "Denison's Law"' (with J. L. Scadding), *JPE*, 82(2), pt. 1, March–April 1974; 7. 'A bicentenary contribution to the history of the cost of living in America' (with P. Solar), *Res. Econ. Hist.*, 2, 1977; 8. 'Invention and accumulation in America's economic growth: a nineteenth century parable', in *International Organization, National Policies and Economic Development*, eds. K. Brunner and A. H. Meltzer (Wiley, 1977); 9. 'Rudimentary contraceptive methods and the America transition to marital fertility control, 1855–1915' (with W. C. Sunstrom), in *Long-Term Factors in America Economic Growth* (NBER, 1985).
Principal Contributions Extending and refining the uses of quantitative and theoretical methods of economics in studying economic history — particularly technological change in agriculture and industry, structural transformations connected with urbanisation and industrialisation, and the sources of long-term growth in the US — formed the main concerns of my early work. Interpreting the consequences of the institution of slavery for American economic development, and exploring, in that connection, the inherent limitations of neoclassical analysis as means of inferring micro-motives from macro-outcomes (market phenomena), also occupied my attention, along with that of some others. Three themes that had emerged in my writings by the mid-1970s have become dominant motifs of

my subsequent work in the areas of technological, demographic and institutional history: (1) the implications of non-convexities, due to scale economies and learning effects in production and consumption, which give rise to path-dependent dynamic processes and thereby necessitate an historical approach to economic analysis; (2) the importance for long-term economic change of the nature of the externalities that arise in economic-demographic interactions, and the role of social institutions in determining such interactions; and (3) the effects of the strategic behaviour of agents within social and economic institutions upon the performance and long-run viability of specific institutional arrangements.

DAVIDSON, David*

Dates and Birthplace 1854–1942, Sweden.
Posts Held Prof. Econ., Uppsala Univ., 1890.
Degree PhD (Law) Uppsala Univ., 1877.
Offices and Honours Ed., *Ekon Tids,* 1899–1939.
Publications Books: 1. *Bidrag Till Läran om de Ekonomiska Lagarna för Kapitalbildningen* (1878); 2. *Bidrag Till Jordränteteoriens Historia* (1880); 3. *Europas Centralbanker* (1886); 4. *Om Beskattningsnormen Vid Inkomstskatten* (1889).
Career One of the founders of neo-classical economics in Sweden, frequently engaged in controversies with Cassell and Wicksell. His published thesis, *Bidrag Till Läran ...* was both an analysis of capital along classical lines, and an economic theory based on the structure of wants. The book established his reputation and in later years he became an enthusiastic student of Ricardo's writings and editor of Scandinavia's leading economic journal.
Secondary Literature E. F. Heckscher, 'David Davidson', *Internat. Econ. Papers,* 2 (Macmillan, 1952); K. G. Landren, 'Davidson, David', *IESS,* 4; C. G. Uhr, *Economic Doctrines of David Davidson* (Almqvist & Wiksell, 1975).

DAVIDSON, PAUL

Born 1930, New York City, NY, USA.
Current Post Prof. Econ., Assoc. Dir., Bureau Econ. Res., Rutgers Univ., New Brunswick, NJ, USA, 1966–.
Past Posts Instr. Physiological Chemistry, Univ. Penn., 1951–2; Instr. Econ., Univ. Penn., 1955–8; Assoc. Prof., Rutgers Univ., 1958–60; Ass. Dir., Econ. Div., Continental Oil Co., 1960–1; Ass. Prof., Assoc. Prof. Econ., Univ. Penn., 1961–3, 1963–6; Vis. Lect., Univ. Bristol, England, 1964–5; Sr. Vis., Univ. Camb., 1970–1; Member, Brookings Panel, 1974; Vis. Prof., Inst. Advanced Stud., Vienna 1980, 1984; Prof. Internat. Summer School Centro di Studi Economici Avanzati, Trieste, 1980.
Degrees BS Brooklyn Coll., NY, 1950; MBA City Univ. NY, 1955; PhD Univ. Penn., 1959.
Offices and Honours Consumer Expenditures Study Fellow, Ford Foundation, 1956–7; Fulbright Hayes Fellow, 1964–5; Rutgers Faculty Res. Fellow, 1970–1; George Miller Disting. Lect., Univ. Illinois, Urbana, 1972; Lindbeck Award Res., 1976; Rutgers Faculty Res. Fellow, 1980.
Editorial Duties Ed. Board, *Energy J.,* 1980–3; Ed., *J Post Keyn E,* 1978–.
Principal Fields of Interest 023 Macroeconomic Theory; 311 Domestic Monetary and Financial Theory and Policy; 432 International Monetary Arrangements.
Publications Books: 1. *Theories of Aggregate Income Distribution* (Rutgers Univ. Press, 1960); 2. *Aggregate Supply and Demand Analysis* (with E. Smolensky), (Harper & Row, 1964; transl., Japanese, 1966); 3. *The Demand and Supply of Outdoor Recreation* (with C. J. Cicchetti and J. J. Seneca), Bureau Econ. Res., Rutgers Univ., repr. Bureau Outdoor Recreation, US Dept. Interior, 1969; 4. *Money and the Real World* (Macmillan, 1972, 1978, Halsted Press, Wiley, 1973, 1978); 5. *Milton Friedman's Monetary Theory: A Debate With His Critics* (with others), (Univ. Chicago Press, 1974; transl., Japanese, 1978); 6. *Inter-*

national Money and the Real World (Macmillan, 1982, Halsted Press, Wiley, 1982).

Articles: 1. 'Employment and income multipliers and the price level', *AER,* 52(4), Sept. 1962; 2. 'Public policy problems of the domestic crude oil industry', *AER,* 53(1), March 1963, repr. in *Economics of Natural and Environmental Resources,* ed. V. L. Smith (Gordon and Breach, 1977); 3. 'A Keynesian view of Patinkin's theory of employment', *EJ,* 77, Sept. 1967, repr. in *Disequilibrio, Inflaciton y Desempleo,* ed. Vincens-Vives (Editorales, 1978); 4. 'A Keynesian view of Friedman's theoretical framework for monetary analysis', *JPE,* 80(5), Sept.–Oct. 1972; 5. 'Money as cause and effect' (with S. Weintraub), *EJ,* 83, Dec. 1973, repr. in *Keynes, Keynesians and Monetarists,* ed. S. Weintraub (Univ. Penn. Press, 1978); 6. 'Oil: its time allocation and project independence' (with L. H. Falk and H. Lee), *Brookings Papers Econ. Activity,* 2, 1974; 7. 'Money and general equilibrium', *Econ App,* 30(4), 1977; 8. 'The United States internal revenue service: the fourteenth member of OPEC?', *J Post Keyn E,* 1(1), Winter 1979; 9. 'Post Keynesian economics: solving the crisis in economic theory', *Public Interest,* Special Issue, 1980, repr. in *The Crisis in Economic Theory,* eds. D. Bell and I. Kristol (Basic Books, 1981); 10. 'Rational expectations: a fallacious foundation for studying crucial decision-making processes', *J Post Keyn E,* 5(2), Winter, 1982–3.

Principal Contributions Early work was on income distribution and its relationship to the development of macroeconomic analytical thought from Ricardo and Marx, through the neoclassical revolution, to Keynes and eminent Post-Keynesians such as Boulding, Kaldor, J. Robinson and Weintraub. While working for an international oil company in the 1960s, I developed a second area of expertise in natural resource economics — oil and water resource use. With the collaboration of my graduate students (J. J. Seneca and C. Cicchetti), we did a landmark econometric analysis of the 'Demand and Supply of Outdoor Recreation' for over twenty specific

recreational activities. This second area of expertise led to a further comprehension of real world micro-demand and supply analysis in which government rules, regulation and tax laws have an impact. In this area I developed (with the aid of Seneca and Cicchetti) the first econometric cross-sectional analysis of the demand for communication in which various cross elasticities were estimated (see my testimony, Fed. Communications Commission, Docket No. 16258, 1968). I have developed the concepts and analysis of aggregate supply and aggregate demand, money, finance and liquidity, nonergodic analysis, the role of finance and financial markets, the use of spot and forward markets for organising production activities in an nonergodic environment. These concepts are essential for analysing inflation and unemployment phenomena. I have also developed the concepts of user costs and the importance of economics and monopoly rents to analyse the economics of natural resources.

My most recent contribution has been in highlighting why those axioms underlying mainstream neoclassical economics — e.g. (1) the growth substitution axiom, (2) the axiom of reals and (3) the ergodic world axiom — are not applicable to any economic system where contracts are made in the form of money (hence all existence proofs are jeopardised) and where the future is uncertain in a nonergodic sense. In other words, I have developed a logical model which, unlike mainstream macro-theory, is applicable to the real world in which we happen to live.

DAVIS, Otto Anderson

Born 1934, Florence, SC, USA.
Current Post Prof. Econ., Public Pol., Carnegie-Mellon Univ., Pittsburg, PA, USA, 1982–.
Past Posts Assoc. Prof. Econ., Prof. Econ., Prof. Polit. Econ., Assoc. Dean, Dean, School Urban Public Affairs, Carnegie-Mellon Univ., 1965–7, 1967–8, 1969–81, 1968–75, 1975–81.
Degrees BA (Econ. and Hist.)

Wofford Coll., 1956; MA, PhD Univ. Virginia, 1957, 1960.

Offices and Honours Pres., Public Choice Soc., 1970–2; Fellow, Center Advanced Study Behavioral Sciences, Stanford, CA, 1974–5; Fellow, Em Soc, 1978; Member, Pol. Council, Assoc. Public Pol. Analysis and Management, 1979.

Principal Fields of Interest 320 Fiscal Theory and Policy.

Publications *Articles:* 1. 'The economics of urban renewal' (with A. Whinston), *Law Contemporary Problems,* 26, Winter 1961, repr. in *Economics, Readings, Issues, and Cases,* ed. E. Mansfield (Norton, 1974); 2. 'Welfare economics and the theory of second best' (with A. Whinston), *REStud,* 32, Jan. 1965; 3. 'A theory of the budgetary process' (with M. A. H. Dempster and A. Wildavsky), *Amer. Polit. Science Rev.,* 60, Sept. 1966, repr. in *Dimensions of Macroeconomics,* ed. S. Mittra (Random House, 1971); 4. 'Social preference orderings and majority rule' (with M. H. DeGroot and M. J. Hinich), *Em,* 40(1), Jan. 1972; 5. 'A simultaneous equations model of the educational process' (with A. E. Boardman and P. R. Sanday), *J Pub E,* 7(1), Feb. 1977; 6. 'Enterprise zones; new deal, old deal, or no deal?' (with D. DiPasquale), *Cato J,* 2(2), Fall 1982; 7. 'The jitneys: a study of grassroots capitalism' (with N. J. Johnson), *J. Contemporary Stud.,* 7, Winter 1984.

Principal Contributions Both theoretical and empirical work on imperfect markets especially where externalities are important. A second area has been public choices including contributions to the theory of public choice and the study of institutions in which such choices are made. A third area has been the evaluation of public policies including contributions to benefit-cost analysis and urban problems. Finally, there have been contributions to the field of public finance both in a theoretical and empirical sense as well as at a practical level where tax and expenditure decisions are made.

DEANE, Phyllis Mary

Born 1918, Hong Kong.

Current Post Emerita Prof. Econ. Hist., Univ. Camb., UK; Hon. Fellow Newnham Coll. Camb., 1983–.

Past Posts Res. Officer, NIESR, London, 1941–5; Res. Officer, UK Colonial Office, 1947–9; Sr. Res. Officer, Dept. Applied Econ., Univ. Camb., 1950–61; Res. Cons., Univ. W. Indies, 1953; Technical Adviser, UK Ministry Overseas Devlp., 1950–65; Lect. Econ., Reader Econ. Hist., Prof. Econ. Hist., Univ. Camb., 1961–71, 1971–81, 1981–3; Co-ordinator, Ford Foundation Devlp. Programme, Univ. Buenos Aires, 1962–5; Vis. Fellow, Johns Hopkins Univ., 1956; Vis. Prof., Pittsburg Univ., 1969, Queens Univ., Canada, 1975.

Degrees MA (Econ. and Hist.) Glasgow Univ., 1940; MA Univ. Camb., 1950.

Offices and Honours Carnegie Res. Fellow, Univ. Glasgow, 1940–1; Colonial Res. Fellow, 1945–7; Pres., IARIW, 1967–9; Council, Pres., RES, 1968–80, 1980–2; Council, EHS, 1973–; Governor, NIESR, 1974–; Soc. Scholars, Johns Hopkins Univ., 1976–; Fellow, Royal Hist. Soc., 1971–; BA, 1980–; Exec. Comm., IEA, 1983–.

Editorial Duties Managing Ed., Rev. Ed., *EJ,* 1969–75; Member, *Syndics CUP,* 1975–81.

Principal Fields of Interest 041 Economic History: General; 031 History of Economic Thought; 036 Economic Methodology.

Publications *Books:* 1. *The Future of the Colonies* (with J. Huxley), (Pilot Press, 1944); 2. *Colonial Social Accounting* (CUP, 1953, Archon Books, 1973); 3. *Studies in Social and Financial Accounting; Income and Wealth Series,* 9 (Bowes & Bowes, 1961); 4. *British Economic Growth, 1688–1959* (CUP, 1962, 1967); 5. *Abstract of British Historical Statistics* (with B. R. Mitchell), (CUP, 1962); 6. *The First Industrial Revolution* (CUP, 1965, 1979; transls., Spanish, Edicions 62, 1968, Portuguese, Zahar Brazil, 1969, Japanese, Shakai Shiso Sha, 1973, Italian, Il Mulino, 1979); 7. *Evolution of Economic Ideas* (CUP, 1978; transls., Japanese, Iwanami

Shoten, 1979, Portuguese, Zahar Brazil, 1980, Italian, Laterza, 1981, Hungarian, Kozgazdasagi, 1984).

Articles: 1. 'The implications of early national income estimates for the measurement of longterm economic growth', *EDCC*, 14(1), Nov. 1955, repr. in *The Causes of the Industrial Revolution in England*, ed. R. M. Hartwell (Methuen, 1967); 2. 'Capital formation in Britain before the railway age', *EDCC*, 60(3), April 1961, repr. in *Capital Formation in the Industrial Revolution*, ed. F. Crouzet (Methuen, 1972); 3. 'New estimates of GNP for the United Kingdom, 1830–1914', *RIW*, 14(2), June 1968; 4. 'The industrial revolution in Britain', in *Fontana Economic History of Europe*, ed. C. Cipolla, 4(1) (Collins/Fontana, Harvester Press, 1973); 5. 'The role of capital in the industrial revolution', *Explor. Econ. Hist* 10(4), Summer 1973; 6. 'War and industrialisation', in *War and Economic Development*, ed. J. Winter (CUP, 1975); 7. 'The relevance of recent trends in economic history to the information needs of research workers in the field', in *The Organization and Retrieval of Economic Knowledge*, ed. M. Perlman (Macmillan, 1977); 8. 'Inflation in history', in *Perspectives on Inflation* ed. D. Heathfield (Longman, 1979); 9. 'The scope and method of economic science', *EJ*, 93, March 1983; 10. 'Introduction' to J. N. Keynes, *Scope and Method of Political Economy* (Kelley, 1984; transl., Italian, Instituto della Enclipedia Italiana, 1984).

Principal Contributions My first major research effort was an attempt to apply and adapt to selected Third World countries national accounting techniques first developed by Meade and Stone for the UK war economy; this was during the war, and based on data available in the Colonial Office. Subsequently I was able to spend nearly two years in Central Africa updating and strengthening the estimates with material collected in village surveys and from local and central government records. For most of the 1950s and 1960s I worked in the national accounting field — developing a system of regional accounts for the UK, using a national accounts framework to estimate and analyse the dimensions of long-term British economic growth 1688–1959, and going as consultant to Third World governments or research institutes. By the 1970s my researches on historical aspects of economic growth in today's advanced countries was taking precedence and I had begun to develop a related interest in the history of economic ideas; it is in these areas that most of my work is currently concentrated.

DEATON, Angus Stewart

Born 1945, Edinburgh, Scotland.
Current Post Prof. Econ. Internat. Affairs, Woodrow Wilson School, Princeton Univ., 1983–.
Past Posts Econ., Bank England, 1967–8; Res. Officer, Dept. Appl. Econ., Univ. Camb., 1969–76; Fellow, Dir. Studies Econ., Fitzwilliam Coll. Camb., 1972–6; Prof. Em, Bristol Univ., 1976–83; Vis. Prof., Princeton Univ., 1979–80; Cons., World Bank, 1980–.
Degrees BA, MA, PhD Univ. Camb., 1967, 1971, 1974.
Offices and Honours First Recipient, Em Soc Frisch Medal, 1978; Fellow, Council, Em Soc, 1979, 1981–.
Editorial Duties Ass. Ed. *REStud*, 1975–80; Assoc. Ed., Co-ed., Ed., *Em*, 1978–80, 1980–4, 1984–; Co-ed., *Em Soc Monographs Quant. Ec.*, 1980–.
Principal Fields of Interest 024 Welfare Theory; 210 Econometric, Statistical and Mathematical Methods and Models; 920 Consumer Economics.
Publications *Books:* 1. *Models and Projections of Demand in Post-War Britain* (Chapman & Hall, Halsted Press, 1972); 2. *Economics and Consumer Behaviour* (with J. Muellbauer), (CUP 1980); 3. *Essays in the Theory and Measurement of Consumer Behaviour*, ed. (CUP, 1981).
Articles: 1. 'Models of consumer behaviour: a survey' (with A. Brown), *EJ* 82(4), Dec. 1972; 2. 'The analysis of consumer demand in the United Kingdom 1900–1970', *Em*, 42(2), March 1974; 3. 'A reconsideration of the empirical implications of additive

preference', *EJ*, 84(3), June 1974; 4. 'Involuntary savings through unanticipated inflation', *AER*, 67(5), Dec. 1977; 5. 'Equity, efficiency and the structure of indirect taxation', *J Pub E*, 8(3), Dec. 1977; 6. 'Testing non-tested non-linear regression models' (with M. H. Pesaran), *Em*, 46(3), May 1978; 7. 'The distance function and consumer behaviour with applications to index numbers and optimal taxation', *REStud*, 46(3), July 1979; 8. 'Testing linear versus logarithmic regression models' (with G. B. A. Evans), *REStud*, 47(1), Jan. 1980; 9. 'An almost ideal demand system' (with J. Muellbauer), *AER*, 70(3), June 1980; 10. 'Optimal taxation and the structure of preferences', *Em*, 49(5), Sept. 1981.

Principal Contributions My work on consumer behaviour has primarily been concerned with building satisfactory econometric models, which conform to the evidence, which make theoretical sense, and which distinguish clearly the respective roles of theoretical assumption and empirical evidence. I have developed specific models of consumer choice that can reasonably be applied to the data and have worked on the choice of functional form, on the development of applicable duality theory, and on extensions of the theory to encompass demographic variables, imperfectly perceived prices, quantity rationing, and intertemporal choice under uncertainty. I have also worked on tools of statistical inference, particularly for testing 'non-tested' i.e. distinct econometric models.

In public economics I have worked towards the implementation of the theory of tax reform, optimal taxation and shadow prices and discovered serious pitfalls in the way of simple evaluation in practice. Most recently, I have been concerned with household behaviour in poor countries, with the methodology of welfare comparisons and the identification of poverty, with the pattern of demand in relation to development, and with the assessment of public policy in poor countries, particularly in relation to food distribution schemes. I regard my main contributions as empirical: showing that additive preferences do not describe reality, that simple-minded models of choice in terms of income and prices are rejected by the evidence, and that rational-expectations life-cycle models of consumption and labour supply do not describe behaviour in reality. More generally, I have attempted to forge closer links between best-practice econometric analysis and economic theory over a wide range of applied problems. I have also tried to write clearly.

DEBREU, Gerard

Born 1921, Calais, France.

Current Post Prof. Econ. and Maths., Univ. Cal. Berkeley, USA, 1962–.

Past Posts Res. Assoc., CNRS, 1946–8; Res. Assoc., Cowles Commission Res. Econ., Univ. Chicago, 1950–5; Assoc. Prof. Econ., Cowles Foundation Res. Econ., Yale Univ., 1955–61; Vis. Prof. Econ., Cowles Foundation, Yale Univ., 1961, 1976; Vis. CORE, Prof., Univ. Louvain, Belgium, 1971, 1972, Univ. Canterbury, Christchurch, New Zealand, 1973; Prof., Miller Inst. Basic Res. Science, Univ. Cal. Berkeley, 1973–4; Res. Assoc., CEPREMAP, Paris, France, 1980.

Degrees Agregé, DSc (Maths.) Univ. Paris, France, 1946, 1956; Hon. Degrees: Dr Rer. Pol. h.c. Univ. Bonn, 1977; Dr en Sciences Econ. h.c., Univ. Lausanne, 1980; DSc, h.c. Northwestern Univ., 1981; Dr h.c. Univ. Sciences Sociales de Toulouse, 1983.

Offices and Honours Rockefeller Foundation Fellow, 1948–50; Fellow, Center Advanced Study Behavioral Sciences, Stanford, 1960–1; Guggenheim Foundation Fellow, 1968–9; Erskine Fellow, 1969; Pres., *Em Soc.*, 1971; Overseas Fellow, 1972; Chevalier de la Légion d'Honneur, 1976; Sr. US Scientists Award, Alexander von Humboldt Foundation, Univ. Bonn, 1977; Member, NAS, 1977; Disting. Fellow, *AEA*, 1982; Nobel Prize in Econ., 1983; Commandeur de l'Ordre National du Mérite, 1984.

Editorial Duties Assoc. Ed., *Int ER*, 1959–69; Ed. Board, *JET*, 1972–; Advisory Board, *J Math E*, 1974–; *SIAM*

J. Appl. Maths., 1976–9; Corresp., *The Math. Intelligencer*, 1983–4.

Principal Fields of Interest 021 General Equilibrium Theory; 022 Microeconomic Theory; 024 Welfare Theory.

Publications *Books:* 1. *Theory of Value, An Axiomatic Analysis of Economic Equilibrium* (Wiley, 1959, Yale Univ. Press, 1971; transls. French, Dunod, 1966, Spanish, Bosch, 1973, German, Springer-Verlag, 1976, Japanese, Toyo Keizai Shinpo-Sha, 1977); 2. *Mathematical Economics: Twenty Papers of Gerard Debreu* (CUP, 1983).

Articles: 1. 'A social equilibrium existence theorem', *Proceedings Nat. Academy Sciences*, 38, 1952; 2. 'Existence of an equilibrium for a competitive economy' (with K. J. Arrow), *Em*, 22, July 1954; 3. 'Valuation equilibrium and Pareto optimum', *Proceedings Nat. Academy Sciences*, 40, 1954, repr. in *Readings in Welfare Economics*, eds. K. J. Arrow and T. J. Scitovsky (Richard D. Irwin, 1969), transl., German, *Mathematische Wirtschaftstheorie*, eds. M. J. Beckmann and R. Sato (Keipenheuer and Witsch, 1975); 4. 'Representation of a preference ordering by a numerical function', in *Decision Processes*, eds. R. M. Thrall, C. H. Coombs, and R. L. Davis (Wiley, 1954), repr. in *Readings in Mathematical Economics, I, Value Theory*, ed. P. Newman (JHUP, 1968), transl., German, *Mathematische Wirtschaftstheorie, op. cit.*; 5. 'Market equilibrium', *Proceedings Nat. Academy Sciences*, 42, 1956; 6. 'A limit theorem on the core of an economy' (with H. Scarf), *IER*, 4, Sept. 1963, transl., German, in *Mathematische Wirtschaftstheorie, op. cit.*; 7. 'Neighboring economic agents', *La Décision*, 171(3), May 1969; 8. 'Economies with a finite set of equilibria', *Em*, 38(3), May 1970; 9. 'Smooth preferences', *Em* 40(4), July 1972; 10. 'Excess demand functions', *J Math E*, 1, 1974.

Principal Contributions Measurement of underutilisation of resources. Characterisation of Pareto optima. Existence theorems for social equilibrium and for economic equilibrium. Theory of contingent commodities. Representation theorems for prefer-ences by means of (continuous, additively decomposed, differentiable, or at least concave) utility functions. Theorems on the convergence of the core for a sequence of large economies. Topologies on the set of preferences. Characterisation of the excess demand function of an economy.

DeCANIO, Stephen J.

Born 1942, Crow Agency, MI, USA.
Current Post Prof. Econ., Univ. Cal. Santa Barbara, CA, USA, 1981–.

Past Posts Teaching Ass., MIT, 1969–70; Instr. Econ., Simmons Coll., 1969; Ass. Prof. Econ., Tufts Univ., 1970–2; Ass. Prof., Assoc. Prof. Econ., Yale Univ., 1972–6, 1976–8; Assoc. Prof. Econ., Univ. Cal. Santa Barbara, 1978–81.

Degrees BA (Maths.) Univ. Cal. Berkeley, 1964; PhD MIT, 1972.

Principal Fields of Interest 042 North American (excluding Mexico) Economic History; 210 Econometric, Statistical and Mathematical Methods and Models; 612 Public Policy towards Monopoly and Competition.

Publications *Books:* 1. *Agriculture in the Postbellum South: The Economics of Production and Supply* (MIT Press, 1974).

Articles: 1. 'Cotton, "Overproduction" in late nineteenth-century southern agriculture', *JEH*, 33(3), Sept. 1973; 2. 'Productivity and income distribution in the post-bellum south', *JEH*, 34(2), June 1974; 3. 'Rational expectations in American agriculture, 1867–1919' (with T. F. Cooley), *REStat*, 59(1), Feb. 1977; 4. 'Inflation and the wage lag during the American Civil War' (with J. Mokyr), *Explor. Econ. Hist.*, 14(4), Oct. 1977; 5. 'Rational expectations and learning from experience', *QJE*, 93(1), Feb. 1979; 6. 'Accumulation and discrimination in the post-bellum south', *Explor. Econ. Hist.*, 16(2), April 1979; 7. 'Proposition 13 and the failure of economic politics', *Nat. Tax J.*, 32(2), June 1979; 8. 'Economic losses from forecasting error in agriculture', *JPE*, 88(2), April 1980; 9. 'Two hidden sources of productivity growth in American agriculture' (with

W. N. Parker), *Agric. Hist.*, 56(2), Oct. 1982; 10. 'Delivered pricing and multiple basing point equilibria; a re-evaluation', *QJE*, 99(2), May 1984.

Principal Contributions Most of my early work dealt with the economic history of the post-bellum American South. The main focus was development of evidence and methods suitable to determine whether discrimination, exploitation, and other market failures were primarily responsible for the economic and political situation of the freedmen. My conclusion was that market forces were a positive rather than an oppressive factor, and that the chief source of the poverty of the blacks was their lack of property. This, in turn, was a consequence of the prohibition of property ownership by slaves and the other inequities of slavery. My other work in economic history has been concerned with agricultural supply (particularly the assessment of farmers' performance in farming expectations) and the economics of wartime finance. In addition to the research in economic history, I have explored the theoretical question of whether agents' expectations converge to rational expectations equilibria. Most recently, I have compared the efficiency of different pricing systems in a context of spatial competition.

DEHEZ, Pierre Jules Eric

Born 1948, Gent, Belgium.
Current Post Ass. Prof., European Univ. Inst., Florence, Italy, 1982–.
Past Posts Res. Assoc., CORE, Univ. de Louvain, 1975–81; Vis. Prof., Univ. Mannheim, 1981; Vis. Ass. Prof., Univ. Illinois, 1981–2; Vis., Univ. de Namur, 1982.
Degrees Licence et Maitrise Univ. Louvain, 1973; PhD jointly LSE, Univ. Bonn, Univ. de Louvain, 1980.
Offices and Honours Aspirant, Fonds Nat. Belge de la Recherche Scientifique, 1975–9; Forschungsstipendiat, Deutscher Akademischer Austauschdients, 1976–7.
Principal Fields of Interest 021 General Equilibrium Theory; 022 Microeconomic Theory; 213 Mathematical Methods and Models.

Publications *Articles:* 1. 'A note on advertising policy under uncertainty and dynamic conditions' (with A. Jacquemin), *J Ind E*, 24(1), Feb. 1975; 2. 'On disequilibrium savings and public consumption' (with J. J. Gobszewicz), *ZN*, 39(1–2), Jan.–Feb. 1979; 3. 'Employment and dividend policy of the firm under risk', *REStud*, 47(3), April 1980; 4. 'Apports de la théorie de l'équilibre general temporaire en analyse macroéconomique', *Recherches Econ. de Louvain* 46(1), 1980; 5. 'State-dependent utility, the demand for insurance and the value of safety' (with J. Drèze), in *The Value of Life and Safety*, ed. M. J. Lee (N-H, 1982); 6. 'Stationary Keynesian equilibria', *Europ ER*, 19(2–3), Oct. 1982; 7. 'On supply-constrained equilibria' (with J. Drèze), *JET*, 31, 1984; 8. 'Rigidité des prix relatifs, rationements de l'offre et inflation' (with J. Drèze), *Cahiers du Seminaire d'Econometrie*, 26, 1984.

Principal Contributions The general field of interest is economic theory with mathematics used as a language. Special focus is on the relation between microeconomic theory from a non-Walrasian temporary point of view and macroeconomics. Several contributions deal with the effect of (short-run) price rigidities and liquidity constraints on economic activity and, more recently, with price linkages as a factor of stagflation. Another field of permanent interest is decision-making under uncertainty.

DEL VECCHIO, Gustavo*

Dates and Birthplace 1883–1972, Lugo, Italy.
Posts Held Prof. Polit. Econ., Univs., Trieste, 1920–6, Bologna, 1926–48, Rome, 1948; Rector, Univ. Borconi di Milano, 1934–48.
Degree Grad. Law Univ. Bologna, 1904.
Offices and Honours Italian Ministry Treasury, 1947–8; Governor, IMF, 1948–50; Member, Nat. Econ. Council, Italy, 1958.
Publications *Books:* 1. *La teoria*

dello sconte (1914); 2. *Ricerche sopra la teoria generale della moneta* (1932); 3. *Vecchie e nove teorie economiche* (1933); 4. *Progressi della teoria economica* (1934); 5. *Lezioni di economia politica*, 5 vols (1937–54); 6. *La sintesi economica e la teoria del reddito* (1950); 7. *L'introduzione alla finanza* (1954); 8. *Capitale e interesse* (1956).

Career Monetary theorist whose ideas had a base in the Walrasian theory of money. Published his views first in a series of papers beginning in 1909 and summed them up in the *Ricerche ...* and *Capitale e interesse*.

Secondary Literature L. dal Pane, 'Commemorazione di Gustavo del Vecchio', in G. Busino, *et al.*, *Studi Inediti in Memoria di Gustavo del Vecchio* (1974).

De MARCHI, Neil Barry

Born 1939, Katanning, Western Australia.

Current Post Prof. Econ., Duke Univ., Durham, NC, USA, 1986–.

Past Posts Lect., Monash Univ., Victoria, Australia, 1964–7; Ass. Prof., Assoc. Prof., Duke Univ., 1971–6, 1977–86; Vis. Reader, Univ. Western Australia, 1973; Assoc. Prof., Univ. Amsterdam, 1976–7; Adjunct-Dir., Econ. Res., Algemene Bank Nederland, Amsterdam, 1980–3.

Degrees BEc Univ. Western Australia, 1960; BPhil Univ. Oxford, 1964; PhD ANU, 1970.

Offices and Honours Rhodes Scholar, 1961–4; Nuffield Dominion Fellow, London, 1970–1; Assoc., Brookings Inst., 1973–4, 1977–9; Cons., Dutch Govt. Comm. Re-Industrialisation in Netherlands, 1982; Member, Nat. Exec., Hist. Econ. Soc., 1984–5.

Editorial Duties Co-ed., *HOPE*, 1971–; Ed., *ABN Bank Econ. Rev*, 1980–3; Ed. Board, *Econ. and Philo.*, 1984–.

Principal Fields of Interest 031 History of Economic Thought; 036 Economic Methodology; 310 Domestic Monetary and Financial Theory and Policy.

Publications *Articles:* 1. 'The empirical content and longevity of Ricardian economics', *Ec*, N.S. 37, Aug. 1970; 2. 'Mill and Cairnes and the emergence of marginalism in England', *HOPE*, 4, Fall 1972, repr. in *The Marginal Revolution*, eds. C. D. W. Goodwin, R. D. C. Black and A. W. Coats (Duke Univ. Press, 1973); 3. 'The noxious influence of authority: a correction of Jevons' charge', *J Law E*, 16, April 1973; 4. 'Malthus and Ricardo's inductivist critics: four letters to William Whewell' (with R. P. Sturges), *Ec*, N.S. 40, Nov. 1973; 5. 'The first Nixon administration: prelude to controls', in *Exhortation and Controls: The Search for a Wage-Price Policy, 1945–1971*, ed. C. D. W. Goodwin (Brookings Inst., 1975); 6. 'Anomaly and the progress of economics: the case of the Leontief paradox', in *Method and Appraisal in Economics*, ed. S. J. Latsis (CUP, 1976); 7. 'Energy policy under Nixon: mainly putting out fires', in *Energy Policy in Perspective*, ed. C. D. Goodwin (Brookings Inst., 1981); 8. 'The Ford administration: energy as a political good', in *Energy Policy in Perspective, op. cit.*; 9. 'The case for James Mill', in *Methodological Controversy in Economics: Historical Essays*, ed. A. W. Coats (JAI Press, 1983); 10. 'Methodology: A Comment on Frazer and Boland' (with A. Hirsch), *AER*, 74(4), Sept. 1984.

Principal Contributions My research and writing reflects a continuing interest in the history of economics and its methodology and in economic policy. All of it is motivated in one way or another by certain questions about the nature and uses of economic inquiry, viewed in some particular historical context. Some questions are taken from the philosophy of science and use the history of economics as test material: may we reinterpret classical economic theory in a Popperian manner?; what can we learn from Kuhn about why the marginal revolution didn't occur earlier in England?; does commitment to a well-defined research programme adequately explain economists' reluctance to give up theory in the face of untoward empirical findings?; etcetera. In large part, however, I have looked at the actual practices of economics — how they go about the business of getting warrantable beliefs out of their enquiries. This motivated my early interest in Ricardo and Mill. It should issue soon in separate studies of Keynes (his 'moments of transition') and of Friedman. Currently I am exploring the rise and role of econometrics. The third of my triad of interests is economic policy, especially domestic and international macroeconomic and financial policy, and energy policy. This interest has taken two forms: studies of US anti-inflation and energy policy in the 1970s; and hands-on involvement in macroeconomic assessment for an international commercial bank. Besides middle-brow analysis of policy options, the issues that concern me here are how macroeconomic explanations are derived; how economic analysis engages policy-makers; how economists have become committed to their own stories; and how they attempt to persuade others.

DEMSETZ, Harold

Born 1930, Chicago, IL, USA.
Current Post Prof. Econ., UCLA, 1971–.
Past Posts Instr. Ass. Prof., Univ. Michigan, 1958–60; Assoc. Prof., UCLA, 1960–3; Prof., Univ. Chicago, 1963–71; Disting. Vis. Prof., Washington Univ., St Louis, 1982–3.
Degrees BS Univ. Illinois, 1953; MBA, MA, PhD Northwestern Univ., 1954, 1959, 1959.
Offices and Honours Disting. Teaching Prize, WEA, 1981; Dir., Econ. Bus. Program, UCLA, 1983–.
Editorial Duties Ed. Board, *Supreme Court Econ. Rev.*
Principal Fields of Interest 610 Industrial Organisation; 612 Public Policy towards Monopoly and Competition; 613 Public Utilities.
Publications *Books:* 1. *Economic, Legal and Political Dimensions of Competition* (N-H, 1982).
Articles: 1. 'The nature of equilibrium in monopolistic competition', *JPE,* 67, Feb. 1959; 2. 'Towards a theory of property rights', *AER,* 57(2), May 1967; 3. 'The cost of transacting', *QJE,* 82, Feb. 1968; 4. Why regulate utilities', *J Law E,* 16, April 1968; 5. 'When does the rule of liability matter?', *J. Legal Stud.,* Jan. 1972; 6. 'Production, information costs and economic organization' (with A. A. Alchian), *AER,* 62(5), Dec. 1972; 7. 'Industrial structure, market rivalry, and public policy', *J Law E,* 16(1), April 1973, repr. in *The Impact of Large Firms on the U.S. Economy,* eds. J. F. Weston and S. I. Orstein (D. C. Heath, 1973); 8. 'The systems of belief about monopoly', in *Industrial Concentration: The New Learning,* eds. R. Goldschmid, H. M. Mann, and J. F. Weston (Little Brown, 1974); 9. 'Barrier to entry', *AER,* 72(1), March 1982; 10. 'The structure of corporate ownership and the theory of the firm', *J Law E,* 26(2), June 1983.

Principal Contributions A look back over my work reveals three continuing interests. The first is a curiosity about why certain institutional arrangements arise and survive. This is revealed in my work on property rights, the theory of the firm, and the causes of industrial concentration, and it continues in work I am now doing on the ownership structure of firms. The second interest is in resolving certain theoretical problems that at one time or another have puzzled me. Here I would place my work on monopolistic competition and natural monopoly; is excess capacity implied by monopolistic competition?; is monopoly price implied by natural monopoly? My third interest has been to bring empirical evidence to bear as much as is practical. Approximately half of my written work is substantially empirical. This includes my work on transaction cost, industrial structure, and the ownership structure of the firm. In no case is the empirical work purely descriptive, rather it is used to examine whether a fairly simple look at data supports or undermines the proposition under consideration. If I have a special talent, it is to simplify a problem to the point where 'geometric thinking' can grasp its essentials and where a few quantifiable relationships stand out. Problems requiring complex mathematical and econometric techniques seem to dull my interest. I think this is because solutions that demand such complexity are very difficult for me to interpret with great confidence. I am grateful for the ample supply of bright, young scholars predisposed to take on these problems.

DENIS, Hector*

Dates and Birthplace 1842–1913, Belgium.
Posts Held Prof., Univ. Brussels.
Offices and Honours Member, Belgian Chamber of Representatives.
Publications *Books:* 1. *L'Impôt sur le revenu* (1881); 2. *L'Impôt* (1889); 3. *La dépression économique et sociale et l'historie des prix,* 2 vols (1895); 4. *Histoire des systèmes économiques et socialistes* (1897); 5. *Discours philosophiques d'Hector Denis* (1919).
Career Idealistic socialist who sought an inductive basis for his viewpoint. Some of his work on taxation was done as a basis for legislation and showed the necessary increase in public expenditure that would follow the expansion of government activity. His work on the history of economic ideas was probably his most significant contribution.
Secondary Literature L. Bertrand, 'Denis, Hector', *ESS*, 5.

DENISON, Edward Fulton

Born 1915, Omaha, NB, USA.
Current Post Sr. Fellow Emeritus, Brookings Inst., Washington, DC, USA, 1978–.
Past Posts Econ., Ass. Dir., Office Bus. Econ., US Dept. Commerce, 1941–62; Econ., Assoc. Dir., Res. Comm. Econ. Devlp., 1956–62; Sr. Fellow, Division Econ. Stud., Brookings Inst., 1962–78; Ford Rotating Res. Prof., Univ. Cal. Berkeley, 1966–7; Assoc. Dir., Nat. Econ. Accounts, Bureau Econ. Analysis, US Dept. Commerce, Washington, 1979–82.
Degrees BA Oberlin Coll., 1936; MA, PhD Brown Univ., 1938, 1941; Grad., Nat. War Coll., 1951.
Offices and Honours Vice-Pres., Disting. Fellow, AEA; Fellow, AAS, IARIW, Nat. Econ. Club; Shiskin Award, Washington Stat. Soc.
Principal Fields of Interest 122 Economic Studies of More Industrialised Countries; 221 National Income Accounting; 226 Productivity and Growth; Theory and Data.
Publications *Books:* 1. *The Sources of Economic Growth in the United States*

and the Alternatives Before Us (Comm. for Econ. Devlp., 1962); 2. *Why Growth Rates Differ: Post-war Experience in Nine Western Countries* (Brookings Inst., 1967; transl., Russian, 1971); 3. *Accounting for United States Economic Growth, 1929–1969* (Brookings Inst., 1974); 4. *How Japan's Economy Grew so Fast* (with W. K. Chung), (Brookings Inst., 1976); 5. *Accounting for Slower Economic Growth: the United States in the 1970s* (Brookings Inst., 1979).
Articles: 1. 'National income and product statistics of the United States, 1929–46' (with M. Gilbert, *et al.*), *Survey of Current Bus.*, 27, Suppl., July 1947; 2. 'Theoretical aspects of quality change, capital consumption and net capital formation', in *Problems of Capital Formation: Concepts, Measurement, and Controlling Factors, Studies in Income and Wealth*, 19 (Princeton Univ. Press, 1957); 3. 'A note on private saving', *REStat*, 40, Aug. 1958; 4. 'The unimportance of the embodied question', *AER*, 54(1), March 1964; 5. 'Measuring the contribution of education (and the residual) to economic growth', in *The Residual Factor and Economic Growth* (OECD, 1964), repr. in *The Economics of Education*, eds. E. A. G. Robinson and J. E. Vaizey (St Martin's Press, 1966), and *Readings in the Economics of Education* (UNESCO, 1968), transls., in Italian, *L'Istruzione come investimento* (Centro Studi Investimento Sociali, 1966) and *Il Fattore Tesiddo* (Centro Studi Investimenti Sociali, 1968), in German, *Bildungsinvestitionen und Wirtschaftswachstum*, ed. K. Hüfner (Ernst Klett, 1970); 6. 'Welfare measurement and the GNP', *Survey of Current Bus.*, 51, Jan. 1971, repr. in *The Quality of Life Concept: A Potential New Tool for Decision Makers* (Environmental Protection Agency, 1973), and *Readings in Macroeconomics*, eds. W. E. Mitchell, J. H. Hand and I. Walters (McGraw-Hill, 1974); 7. 'Effects of selected changes in the institutional and human environment upon output per unit of input', *Survey of Current Bus.*, 58, Jan. 1978; 8. 'Is US growth understated because of the underground economy? Employment ratios suggest not', *RIW*, March 1982; 9. 'The interruption of

productivity growth in the United States', *EJ*, 93, Suppl., March 1983; 10. 'International transactions in measures of the nation's production', *Survey Current Bus.*, 61, May 1981.

Principal Contributions Developed growth accounting (sources-of-growth analysis) and applied it to the study of growth in ten advanced countries and to the study of differences in their levels of output. Contributed to the theory and practice of measurement of capital stock, especially with respect to quality changes. Demonstrated unreality of embodiment models. Showed stability of total private saving rate. Participated in development of concepts and estimates for the national income accounts of USA. Measured and analysed professional incomes.

DE QUINCEY, Thomas*

Dates and Birthplace 1785–1859, Manchester, England.

Posts Held Professional essayist.

Publications *Books:* 1. *The Logic of Political Economy* (1841); 2. *Collected Writings of Thomas De Quincey*, vol 9. *Political Economy and Politics*, ed. D. Masson (1897, 1970).

Career Chiefly known for the famous *Confessions of an English Opium Eater* (1821) and for his voluminous writings in the periodical literature on a wide range of subjects, including political economy. The content of his economic writing is purely Ricardian, but his expositional style was so striking that he proved to be one of Ricardo's most effective disciples. J. S. Mill quoted frequently from *The Logic ...*, and thus ensured De Quincey's economic work such lasting interest as it retains.

DESAI, Meghnad Jagdishchandra

Born 1940, Baroda, Gujarat, India.

Current Post Prof. Econ., LSE, London, UK, 1983–.

Past Posts Assoc. Specialist, Agric. Econ., Univ. Cal. Berkeley, 1963–5; Lect., Sr. Lect., Reader Econ., LSE, 1965–77, 1977–80, 1980–3.

Degrees BA, MA Univ. Bombay, 1958, 1960; PhD Univ. Penn, 1964.

Editorial Duties Ed. Board, *REStud*, 1973–83.

Principal Fields of Interest 020 General Economic Theory; 040 Economic History; 210 Econometric Models.

Publications *Books:* 1. *Marxian Economic Theory* (Gray-Mills, Blackwell, 1974); 2. *Applied Econometrics* (Philip Allan, 1976); 3. *Marxian Economics* (Blackwell, 1979); 4. *Testing Monetarism* (Frances Pinter, 1981).

Articles: 1. 'An econometric model of the world tin economy', *Em*, 34(1), Jan. 1966; 2. 'Some issues in econometric history', *EHR*, 21(1), April 1968; 3. 'A test of the hypothesis of disguised unemployment' (with D. Mazunder), *Ec*, N.S. 37, Feb. 1970; 4. 'Inflation and growth cycles in a model of the class struggle', *JET*, 6(6), Dec. 1973; 5. 'The Phillips curve: a revisionist interpretation', *Ec*, N.S. 42, Feb. 1975; 6. 'Fiscal policy simulations and stabilization policy' (with S. G. B. Henry), *REStud*, 42, July 1975; 7. 'The consolation of slavery', *EHR*, 29(5), Aug. 1976; 8. 'Bequests and inheritance in nuclear families and joint families' (with A. Shah), *Ec*, N.S. 50, May 1983.

Principal Contributions My doctoral research was in applied econometrics of commodity markets and the model of the tin economy (No. 1 above) was the largest commodity model of its kind, the first to be simulated for stabilisation policy. My applied econometric work continued in building macroeconomic models of the UK economy again with a view to exploring problems of stabilisation policy. In the early 1970s, my interests changed to a study of inflation and unemployment. I had always been interested in Marxian economics and am more Keynesian than not. This combination led to my first paper in economic theory which had to do with an extension of Godwin's model of the growth cycle. This interprets the phenomena of inflation and unemployment in a Marx type model. This work led me to a new insight into the nature of the Phillips curve. My 1975 paper (No. 5 above) is unorthodox and original in advancing an interpretation of the Phillips curve that accounts for the econometric method used by Phillips and ties it up with a causal interpretation. This is the problem of separating the short-run disequilibrium dynamics which generates the data from the underlying long-run disequilibrium. This is where economic theory and econometric method meet and this area has formed my major research interest in recent years. Moving from an understanding of the nature of Phillips' work, I concluded that the need was to endogenise unemployment as well as wages and prices but that there were few available models that did the job. Goodwin's model was one. I came across a paper by Stein that purported to test for a Keynesian as against a monetarist explanation of inflation. This led me to a study of the problem of testing the validity of alternative models from the same data act; which eventually resulted in the book, *Testing Monetarism*.

My other major interest is in Marxian economics. My 1974 book was the first major textbook in this area since Sweezy's *Theory of Capitalist Development*. It does three things not previously done in this area. It advances the notion that Marxian labour values are not directly observable and hence the value-price transformation is similar to the econometric problem of going from the reduced form (observable) to the structural (unobservable). It summarises the value-price debate and also brings out the economy-wide nature of the transformation problem. Secondly, the book revised the Marxian notion of the three circuits of capital. This is necessary in order to bring out the monetary nature of Marx's theory usually ignored in earlier discussions. Thirdly, it provides a critique of Marx's model of accumulation. I show that Marx's work kills a coherent analysis of the dynamic disequilibrium of capitalism despite assertions to the contrary.

DESTUTT DE TRACY, Antoine-Louis-Claude*

Dates and Birthplace 1754–1836, Paris, France.
Posts Held Army officer and politician.
Offices and Honours Commandant,

Légion d'Honneur; Member, L'Inst. de France, 1794; Member, Académie Française, 1808.
Publications *Books:* 1. *Traité d'économie politique* (1823).
Career Wrote a treatise on economics as part of a series of *Eléments d'idéologie* begun in 1801. As a philosopher in the eighteenth-century mould, he brought to economic ideas a logical rigour which was not matched with equal originality. His insistence that value should be measured in invariant units just as other quantities are measured in given units was taken up by Ricardo. His concept of 'ideology' was taken up and transformed by Marx and Engels.

DE TRAY, Dennis Normam

Born 1944, Napoleon, OH, USA.
Current Post Chief, Living Standards Res. Unit Devlp. Res. Dept., World Bank, Washington, DC, 1983–.
Past Posts Assoc. Econ., Econ., Sr. Econ., Rand Corp., Santa Monica, CA, 1972–6, 1978–83; Assoc., Internat. Programs Div., Population Council, Res. Res. Adviser, Pakistan Inst. Devlp. Econ., Islamabad, Pakistan, 1976–8.
Degrees BS Cornell Univ., 1966; MS Utah State Univ., 1967; MA, PhD Univ. Chicago, 1972.
Offices and Honours Rockefeller Foundation Fellow, 1967–8; Fellow, Nat. Inst. Mental Health, 1968–71.
Principal Fields of Interest 824 Labour Market Studies, Wages, Employment; 851 Human Capital; 921 Consumer Economics, Levels of Living.
Publications *Articles:* 1. 'Child quality and the demand for children', *JPE*, March–April 1973, repr. in *Economics of the Family*, ed. T. W. Schultz (Univ. Chicago Press, 1974); 2. 'The sensitivity of male labor supply estimates to choice of assumption' (with D. H. Greenberg and J. DaVauzo), *REStat*, 58(3), Aug. 1976; 3. 'Population growth and educational policies: an economic perspective', in *Population and Development*, ed. R. Ridker (Resources for the Future, 1976); 4. 'On estimating sex differences in earnings' (with D. H. Greenberg), *SEJ*, 44(2), Oct. 1977; 5. 'On the care and handling of regression specifications

in fertility research', *Pakistan Devlp. Rev.*, 16(3), Autumn 1977; 6. 'The demand for children in a "natural fertility" population', *Pakistan Devlp. Rev.*, 18(1), Spring 1979; 7. 'On the microeconomics of family behavior in developing countries', in *Rural Household Stud. in Asia*, eds. H. P. Bingswanger, *et al.* (Singapore Univ. Press, 1980); 8. 'Veteran status as a screening device', *AER*, 72(1), March 1982; 9. 'Children's work activities in Malaysia', *Pop. and Devlp. Rev.*, 9(3), Sept. 1983; 10. 'Son preference in Pakistan: an analysis of intentions versus behaviour', in *Res. in Pop. Econ.*, 5, 1984, eds. T. P. Schultz and I. Wolpin (JAI Press, 1986).

Principal Contributions Most of my professional career has focussed on trying to understand household behaviour and the effect of that behaviour on human resource and human capital issues, broadly defined. I have been especially interested in the consequences of household decision-making for the design and analysis of public policy. Until 1976 I worked almost exclusively on household behaviour in the context of US policy issues, for example, fertility, education, labour supply, and welfare reform. My work during that period is probably most closely associated with the 'quantity verses quality' theory of fertility determination.

At that time I left Rand temporarily to serve as Resident Research Adviser at the Pakistan Institute of Economic Development in Islamabad, Pakistan. Two years in that post critically altered my research interests and my thinking about the production of useful microeconomic research. I came to realise that the theoretical constructs with which I had analysed US family behaviour and the questions I had addressed were often much more pertinent to conditions and problems in developing than in developed countries. I also became concerned during that period over the fact that microeconomic research on household behaviour often had little or no perceptible effect on policy decision-making. This waste of intellectual and financial resources led me to concentrate on developing better ways of organising research and dissemination activities in order to serve nonacademic, policy-oriented research consumers more effectively. For me the solution entailed a shift in emphasis away from pure research to pre- and post-research activities — supplementing an interest in selectivity or simultaneity bias with concerns about data generation and the 'selling' of research and policy findings. My interests today have to do mainly with ways of improving the value of household-level microeconomic research as a policy decision-making tool.

DE VITI DE MARCO, Antonio*

Dates and Birthplace 1858–1943, Lecre, Italy.

Posts Held Prof. Polit. Econ. and Public Fin., Univs. Camermo, Macerata, Piava, Roma, 1887–1925.

Offices and Honours MP, 1900–21.

Editorial Duties Joint Ed., *Giornale degli economisti*, 1890–1913.

Publications *Books:* 1. *Il caratlere seouco dell'economia finanziari* (1881); 2. *Moneta e prezzi* (1885); 3. *La funzione della banca* (1898); 4. *Saggi di economia e finanza* (1899); 5. *I prima principi dell'economia finanziara* (1928); 6. *Un trentennio de lotte politicha (1894–1922)* (1930).

Career Founder of the Italian tradition of public finance as an autonomous branch of economics. Vigorous free-trader who was politically active in a number of anti-protectionist organisations.

Secondary Literature J. M. Buchanan, '*La scienza della Finanze*: the Italian tradition in fiscal theory', in *Fiscal Theory and Political Economy* (Univ. N. Carolina Press, 1960).

DEWEY, Donald Jefferson

Born 1922, Solon, VT, USA.

Current Post Prof. Econ., Columbia Univ., New York, NY, USA, 1965–.

Past Posts Instr., Indiana Univ., 1947; Ass. Prof., Assoc. Prof., Duke Univ., 1950–7, 1958–60; Assoc. Prof., Columbia Univ., 1960–5.

Degrees BA Univ. Chicago, 1943; MA Univ. Iowa, 1947.

Offices and Honours Disting. Article

Award, JPE, 1948; Postdoctoral Fellow, Polit. Econ., Univ. Chicago, 1949–50; Sr. Fulbright Fellow, Univ. London, 1956–7; Ford Faculty Fellow, 1966–7.

Principal Fields of Interest 022 Microeconomic Theory; 031 History of Economic Thought; 610 Industrial Organisation and Public Policy.

Publications *Books:* 1. *Monopoly in Economics and Law* (Rand McNally, 1959, 1964); 2. *Modern Capital Theory* (Columbia Univ. Press, 1965); 3. *The Theory of Imperfect Competition: A Radical Reconstruction* (Columbia Univ. Press, 1969); 4. *Microeconomics: The Analysis of Markets and Prices* (OUP, 1975).

Articles: 1. 'Occupational choice in a collectivist economy', *JPE*, 56(6), Dec. 1948; 2. 'Professor Schumpeter on socialism: the case of Britain', *JPE*, 58(3), June 1950; 3. 'Negro employment in southern industry', *JPE*, 60(4), Aug. 1952; 4. 'Imperfect competition no bar to efficient production', *JPE*, 66(1), Feb. 1958; 5. 'Labor turnover as an index of unemployment in the United States, 1919–58', *J Ind E*, 8(3), June 1960; 6. 'Antitrust legislation', in *International Encyclopedia of the Social Sciences*, ed. D. L. Sills (Macmillan, 1968); 7. 'Industrial concentration and the rate of profit: some neglected theory', *J Law E*, 19(2), April 1976; 8. 'Information, entry, and welfare: the case for collusion', *AER*, 69(4), Sept. 1979; 9. 'Antitrust and its alternatives: a compleat guide to the welfare trade-offs', in *Antitrust and Regulation*, ed. R. Grierson (D. C. Heath, 1985).

Principal Contributions In my life in economics I believe that I have done something to show how racial discrimination 'really' operated in American labour markets before 1965; tied up a few loose ends in mainstream capital theory; helped to rescue the treatment of monopolistic and/or imperfect competition from the wilderness into which it had been driven by the uncritical disciples of Edward Chamberlin and Joe Bain; and made a contribution to improving the quality of economic and legal thought applied to the problems of regulation and antitrust. Since first reading Frank Knight and Joseph Schumpeter I have been fascinated by the interaction between ideas and events in the formation of economic policies but as yet have reached few firm conclusions.

DHRYMES, Phoebus J.

Born 1932, Ktima, Cyprus.
Current Post Prof. Econ., Columbia Univ., NY, USA, 1974–.
Recent Posts Ass. Prof., Assoc. Prof. Econ., Univ. Penn., 1964–73;
Degrees BA Univ. Texas, Austin, 1957; PhD MIT, 1961; Hon. MA Univ. Penn., 1971.
Offices and Honours Fellow, Em Soc, 1967, ASA, 1970.
Editorial Duties Founding co-ed., *J Em*, 1973–7.
Principal Fields of Interest 211 Econometric and Statistical Methods and Models.

Publications *Books:* 1. *Econometrics: Statistical Foundations and Applications* (Harper & Row, 1970, Springer-Verlag, 1974); 2. *Distributed Lags: Problems of Estimation and Formulation* (Holden-Day, 1971, N-H, 1981); 3. *Introductory Econometrics* (Springer-Verlag, 1978); 4. *Mathematics for Econometrics* (Springer-Verlag, 1978); 5. *Domestic Consequences of an Overvalued Currency* (Centre of Planning and Econ. Res., Athens, 1978).

Articles: 1. 'On the theory of the monopolistic multiproduct firm under uncertainty', *Int ER*, 5, Sept. 1964; 2. 'Some extensions and tests of the CES class of production functions', *REStat*, 47, Nov. 1965; 3. 'Efficient estimation of distributed lags with auto-correlated errors', *Int ER*, 10(1), Feb. 1969; 4. 'Alternative asymptotic tests of significance and related aspects of 2SLS and 3SLS estimated parameters', *REStud*, 36, April, 1969; 5. 'Restricted and unrestricted reduced forms: asymptotic distribution and relative efficiency', *Em*, 41(1), Jan. 1973.

Principal Contributions In simultaneous equations theory: elucidation of the relationship between the classical methods such as least squares, and simultaneous equations methods such as two and three stage least squares. Applications of asymptotic theory to econometric problems. Solution of the problem of predictive efficiency when predicting with a simultaneous equations model. Development of the theory of estimation of distributed lags. Development of the theory of estimation of CES production functions. Derivation of the contemporary theory of the demand for labour as derived from microprinciples and applications to major sectors of the US economy.

DIAMOND, Peter Arthur

Born 1940, New York City, NY, USA.
Current Post Prof., MIT, Cambridge, MA, USA, 1970–.
Past Posts Ass. Prof., Acting Assoc. Prof., Univ. Cal. Berkeley, 1963–5, 1965–6; Overseas Fellow, Churchill Coll. Camb., 1965–6; Assoc. Prof., MIT, 1966–70; Vis. Prof., Univ. Coll., Nairobi, 1968–9, Hebrew Univ., Jerusalem, 1969; Vis. Fellow, Balliol Coll. Oxford, 1973–4; Vis. Prof., Harvard School Public Health, 1977–8; Vis. Scholar, Harvard Law School, 1982–3.
Degrees BA (Maths.) Yale Univ., 1960; PhD MIT, 1963.
Offices and Honours US SSRC Fellow, 1965; Guggenheim Foundation Fellow, 1966–7, 1982–3; Fellow, Council, Em Soc, 1968, 1981–7; Fellow AAAS, 1978; Mahalanobis Memorial Award, 1980.
Editorial Duties Assoc. Ed., *JET*, 1969–71, *J Pub E*, 1971–; Ed. Board, *AER*, 1979–81.
Principal Fields of Interest 020 General Economic Theory.
Publications *Books:* 1. *Uncertainty in Economics: Readings and Exercises*, co-ed. (with M. Rothschild), (Academic Press, 1978); 2. *A Search Equilibrium Approach to the Micro Foundations of Macroeconomics* (MIT Press, 1984).
Articles: 1. 'The evaluation of infinite utility streams', *Em*, 33(1), Jan. 1965; 2. 'National debt in a neoclassical growth model', *AER*, 55(5), Dec. 1965; 3. 'The role of a stock market in a general equilibrium model with technological uncertainty', *AER* 57(4), Sept. 1967; 4. 'Optimal taxation and public production, I, II' (with J. A.

Mirrlees), *AER*, 61(1), 61(3), March, June 1971; 5. 'A model of price adjustment', *JET*, 3(2), June 1971; 6. 'Accident law and resource allocation', *Bell JE*, 5(2), Autumn 1974; 7. 'A model of social insurance with variable retirement' (with J. A. Mirrlees), *J Pub Ed*, 10(3), Dec. 1978; 8. 'An equilibrium analysis and breach of contract 1: steady states' (with E. Maskin), *Bell JE*, 10(1), Spring 1979; 9. 'Protection, trade adjustment assistance, and income distribution', in *Import Competition and Response*, ed. J. Bhagwati (Univ. Chicago Press, 1982); 10. 'Aggregate demand management in search equilibrium', *JPE*, 90(5), Sept. 1982.
Principal Contributions Early work was on infinite horizon preferences and growth theory. Normative analyses have reconsidered the implications of the Walrasian model in the presence of overlapping generations, in the absence of some markets (especially insurance markets), and in the absence of the ability to costlessly redistribute income among individuals. Recent work has concentrated on the implications of the absence of a Walrasian auctioneer.

DIAZ-ALEJANDRO, Carlos F.*

Dates and Birthplace 1937–85, La Habana, Cuba.
Posts Held Ass. Prof., Prof. Econ., Growth Center, Yale Univ., 1961–5, 1969–83; Econ. Staff Comm. Nine, Alliance for Progress, Organization Amer. States, 1962–3; Assoc. Prof. Econ., Univ. Minnesota, 1965–9; Cons., Interamer. Comm. Alliance Progress, Pan Amer. Union, 1965–6; MIT/ODEPLAN, Santiago, Chile, Project Andean Common Market, 1967–8; Member, Commission Internat. Devlp. ('Pearson Commission'), 1968–9; Vis. Prof. Econ., Pontificia Univ. Catolica Rio de Janeiro, 1971; Vis. Scholar, Nuffield Coll. Oxford, 1975–6; Prof. Econ., Columbia Univ., New York, 1983–5.
Degrees BS (Bus.) Miama Univ., Ohio, 1957; PhD MIT, 1961.
Offices and Honours Cons., Commission US-Latin Amer. Relations ('Linowitz Commission'), 1975; Chair-

man, Joint Comm. Latin Amer. Stud., US SSRC, 1976–9; Member, Council Foreign Relations, New York, 1977–; Member, AEA Pol. Advisory Board, Econ. Inst., Boulder, CO, 1977–80; Member, Academic Panel Consultative Group Internat. Econ. Monetary Affairs, Rockefeller Foundation, 1978; Member, US Bipartisan Commission Central Amer., 1979–.

Editorial Duties Ed. Board, *WD* (UK); Co-ed., *JDE*, 1976–85.

Principal Fields of Interest 047 Latin American Economic History; 431 Balance of Payments.

Publications *Books:* 1. *Exchange Rate Devaluation in a Semi-Industrialized Country: The Experience of Argentina, 1955–6* (MIT Press, 1966; transl. Spanish, Amorrortu, 1975); 2. *Essays on the Economic History of the Argentine Republic* (Yale Univ. Press, 1970; transl., Spanish, Amorrortu, 1965); 3. *Foreign Trade Regimes and Economic Development: Columbia* (Columbia Univ. Press, 1976); 4. *Politica Economica en Centro y Periferia: Enasyos en Homenaje a Felipe Pazos*, co-ed. (with S. Teitel and V. E. Tokman), (Fondo de Cultura Econ., 1976).

Articles: 1. 'Latin American debt: I don't think we are in Kansas anymore', *Brookings Papers Econ. Activity*, 2, 1984; 2. 'The post-1971 international financial system and the less developed countries', in *A World Divided: The Less Developed Countries in the International Economy*, ed. G. K. Helleiner (CUP, 1975); 3. 'Tariffs, foreign capital and immiserizing growth' (with R. Brecher), *J Int E*, 7(4), Nov. 1977; 4. 'International markets for exhaustible resources, less developed countries, and multinational corporations', in *Research in International Business and Finance*, vol 1, *The Economic Effects of Multinational Corporations*, ed. R. G. Hawkins (JAI Press, 1979); 5. 'Latin America in the 1930s', in *Latin America in the 1930s: The Role of the Periphery in World Crisis*, ed. R. Thorp (Macmillan, 1984).

Principal Contributions Analysis of trade and payments of semi-industrialised countries. Analytical economic history of Latin America.

DICKINSON, Henry Douglas*

Dates and Birthplace 1899–1968, England.

Posts Held Res., LSE, 1922–4; Ass. Lect., Reader, Univ. Leeds, 1924–47; Sr. Lect., Prof., Univ. Bristol, 1947–64.

Degrees BA Univ. Camb., 1922.

Publications *Books:* 1. *Institutional Revenue* (1932); 2. *Economics of Socialism* (1939).

Articles: 1. 'Price formation in a socialist community', *EJ*, 43, June 1933.

Career Historian of economic thought, whose interest in both the Austrian school and Marx is revealed in *Institutional Revenue*. This developed into a theory of the socialist economy which involved an original model of 'market socialism'.

Secondary Literature M. H. Dobb, 'Obit.: H. D. Dickinson', *Hist. Econ. Thought Newsletter*, 3. 1968.

DICKS-MIREAUX, Leslie

Born 1924, England.

Current Post Assoc. Dir., PRO-NED, London, England, 1984–.

Past Posts Sr. Res. Officer, NIESR, London, 1956–62; Sr. Econ., Nat. Econ. Devlp. Office, London, 1962–6; Head, Short-Term Forecasting Div., Econ. Stats. Dept., OECD, Paris, 1966–7; Special Adviser, Bank of England, 1967–84.

Degrees BSc King's Coll., London, 1948.

Principal Fields of Interest 311 Domestic Monetary Theory and Policy.

Publications *Articles:* 1. 'The excess demand for labour: a study of conditions in Great Britain, 1946–1956' (with J. C. R. Dow), *OEP*, 10, Feb. 1956; 2. 'The determinants of wage inflation, United Kingdom, 1946–1956' (with J. C. R. Dow), *JRSS*, 122, pt. 2, 1959; 3. 'The interrelationship between cost and price changes, 1946–1959: a study of inflation in post-war Britain', *OEP*, 13, Oct. 1961; 4. 'The wages structure and some implications for incomes policy' (with J. R. Shepherd), *Nat. Inst. Econ. Review*, 22, 1962; 5. 'Cost-push or demand-pull: a study of inflation in the UK', *Woolwich Econ. Papers,* 1963; 6. 'The Radcliffe report—ten years after: a summary of empirical evidence', in *Money in Britian 1959–1969,* eds. D. R. Croome and H. G. Johnson (OUP, 1970); 7. 'British monetary experience 1973–1977', in *Geld-und Währungspolitik im Umbruch* (Fisher, 1983).

Principal Contributions The determinants of general wage and price inflation, in particular quantitative attempts to distinguish for Britain between the separate roles of cost factors and demand factors in the inflationary process.

DIEHL, Karl*

Dates and Birthplace 1864–1943, Frankfurt-am-Main, Germany.
Posts Held Prof., Univ. Rostock, 1898, Univ. Königsberg, 1899, Univ. Freiburg, 1908–43.
Publications *Books:* 1. *P. J. Proudhon, seine Lehre und sein Leben,* 3 vols (1888–96); 2. *Sozialwissenschaftliche Erläuterungen zu David Ricardos Grundgesetzen,* 2 vols (1905); 3. *Theoretische Nationalökonomie,* 4 vols (1916–33).
Career Studied in Berlin, Halle and Vienna. His tenure of the Freiburg chair further enhanced its prestige. Teaching by the seminar method, he attracted and held a large number of students. His views were largely of an institutionalist type, though he relied very much on the English classics as a starting point. *Theoretische Nationalökonomie* reveals his theoretical ability and his willingness to turn theory to the solving of practical problems. He was also a Proudhon scholar of considerable note.
Secondary Literature A. Hesse, 'Diehl, Karl', in *Handwörterbuch der Sozialwissenschaften,* 2, eds. E. V. Beckerath, *et al.* (Gustav Fischer, 1959).

DIETZEL, Carl August*

Dates and Birthplace 1829–84, Germany.
Posts Held Privatdozent, Heidelberg Univ; Prof., Marburg Univ., 1867.

Degrees Dr Heidelberg Univ., 1956.
Publications *Books:* 1. *Das System der Staatsanleihen im Zusammenhang der Volkswirtschaft Betrachtet* (1855); 2. *Diebesteuerung der Aktiengesellschaften im Verleindung mit der Gemeindebesteuerung* (1859); 3. *Die Volkswirtschaft und ihr Verhältnis zi Gesellschaft und Staat.* (1864).
Career German writer on finance who overturned the accepted idea that public credit is inherently different from private credit. His legitimisation of public credit was reflected in many subsequent German writers.
Secondary Literature F. Meisel, 'Dietzel, Karl August', *ESS,* 5.

DIETZEL, Heinrich*

Dates and Birthplace 1857–1935, Germany.
Posts Held Prof., Univ. Dorpat, 1885–90, Univ. Bonn, 1890–1935.
Publications *Books:* 1. *Karl Rodbertus* (1886–8); 2. *Theoretische Sozialökonomik* (1895).
Career A representative of classical economics in Germany opposed to the mainstream dominated by the historical school and popular Marxism. His pupils held a number of university chairs and high government posts by the time of his death. He wrote illuminatingly on the methods of economic research and a wide variety of questions, such as free trades unions, public loans and taxation. He also wrote a good deal on Rodbertus and the early socialists. Throughout his career he was an enthusiastic propagandist for free trade.
Secondary Literature P. Arndt, 'Heinrich Dietzel (obit.)', *EJ,* 45, Dec. 1935.

DIEWERT, Walter Erwin

Born 1941, Vancouver, British Columbia, Canada.
Current Post Prof. Econ., Univ. British Columbia, Vancouver, Canada, 1974–.
Past Posts Ass. Prof., Univ. Chicago, 1968–70; Vis. Prof., Harvard Univ.,

1970; Assoc. Prof., Univ. British Columbia, 1970–4; Res. Cons., Canadian Dept. Manpower and Immigration, Ottawa, 1970–3; Vis. Prof., Stanford Univ., 1972, 1973, 1977, 1978, 1980, 1981; Res. Cons. Stats., Canada, Ottawa, 1983; Vis. Prof., Univ. Amsterdam, 1983; Univ. Sydney, 1983.

Degrees BA (Maths.), MA (Maths.) Univ. British Columbia, 1963, 1965; PhD Univ. Cal. Berkeley, 1969.

Offices and Honours Univ. Cal. Best Thesis Econ. Award, 1969; Fellow, Em Soc., 1975; Royal Soc. Canada, 1982.

Editorial Duties Assoc. Ed., *J Em*, 1973–83, *AER*, 1978–81.

Principal Fields of Interest 020 General Economic Theory; 200 Quantitative Economic Methods; 410 International Trade Theory.

Publications *Books:* 1. *Price Level Measurement*, co-ed. (with C. Montmarquette), (Stats. Canada, 1983).

Articles: 1. 'An application of the Shephard duality theorem: a generalized Leontief production function', *JPE*, 79(3), May–June 1971; 2. 'Applications of duality theory', in *Frontiers of Quantitative Economics*, II, eds. M. Intriligator and D. Kendrick (N-H, 1974); 3. 'Exact and superlative index numbers', *J Em*, 4(2), June 1976; 4. 'Frank Knight's theorem in linear programming revisited' (with A. D. Woodland), *Em*, 45(2), March 1977; 5. 'Nine kinds of quasiconcavity and concavity' (with M. Avriel and I. Zang), *JET*, 25(3), Dec. 1981; 6. 'The comparative dynamics of efficient programs of capital accumulation and resource depletion' (with T. R. Lewis), in *Economic Theory of Natural Resources*, eds. W. Eichhorn, *et al.* (Physical Verlag, 1982); 7. 'A fundamental matrix equation of production theory with applications to the theory of international trade', in *Methods of Operations Research, 46*, ed. P. Stahly (Verlag Anton Hain, 1983); 8. 'The measurement of waste within the production sector of an open economy', *Scand. JE,* 85(2), 1983; 9. 'The theory of the output price index and the measurement of real output charge', in *Price Level Measurement,* eds. W. E. Diewert and C. Montmarquette (Stats. Canada,

1983); 10. 'Cost benefit analysis and project evaluation: a comparison of alternative approaches', *J Pub E,* 22(3), Dec. 1983.

Principal Contributions My early research was directed towards finding functional forms for production and utility functions that could provide second order approximations to arbitrary linearly homogeneous functions, i.e., finding 'flexible' functional forms. This work led me into duality theory, which investigates under what conditions technology sets or preferences can be represented by functions of prices. Duality theory proved to be useful not only in solving the econometric problems involved in estimating preferences or technology, but also in deriving comparative statics theorems in complex models, such as general equilibrium models with unions, governments or international trade. Since most microeconomic problems can be phrased in terms of constrained maximisation problems, some of my research has been concerned with the mathematical properties of these problems. Thus Woodland and I used the properties of inverse bordered Hessian matrices to prove comparative statics theorems in production and trade theory. My interest in the mathematics of optimisation theory also led to some research (with Avriel and Zang) characterising different types of quasiconcavity. Other measurement problems that I have worked on are: (1) the determination of an optimal or 'superlative' functional form for an index number formula; (2) nonparametric approximations or bounds for preferences and technology sets; (3) alternative concepts for measuring the deadweight loss due to distortions and the derivation of second order approximations to these theoretical loss measures; and (4) the determination of shadow prices in order to evaluate projects in a distorted economy. My recent research topics in the area of production theory include: (1) developing the comparative statics of a finite horizon intertemporal profit maximisation problem (with T. Lewis); (2) the economics of transfer pricing; and (3) modelling the effects of an innovation.

DIVISIA, François*

Dates and Birthplace 1889–1964, Tizi–Ouzou, Algeria.

Posts Held Govt. Engineer, 1919; Res. and Teaching, French Ministry Nat. Educ; Prof., L'Ecole Nationale des Ponts êt Chaussés, 1932–50.

Offices and Honours Chevalier, Légion d'Honneur; Pres., Soc. d'Econométrie, 1935; Pres., Soc. de Stat. de Paris, 1939; Foreign Member, Accademia Nazionale dei Lincei, 1951.

Publications *Books:* 1. *L'indice monétaire de la théorie de la monnaie* (1926); 2. *Economique rationelle* (1928); 3. *L'épargne et la richesse collective* (1928); 4. *Exposés d'économique*, 3 vols (1951–65); 5. *Traitement économétrique de la monnaie, l'intérêt, l'emploi* (1962).

Career Originally trained as an engineer, his part-time economic work was recognised by his appointment to a teaching post with the Ministry of National Education. His first major publication, *L'indice* . . . contained the monetary index known as the Divisia index. *Economique Rationelle* made his reputation with its concise and practical statement of his views. He was moved by what he saw as lack of precision in Keynes's *General Theory* to offer a microeconomic alternative in the form of *Traitement économétrique* . . . His work was a major contribution to the development of econometrics.

Secondary Literature R. Roy, 'Divisia, François', *IESS*, 4.

DIXIT, Avinash K.

Born 1944, Bombay, India.

Current Post Prof. Econ. and Internat. Affairs, Princeton Univ., Princeton, NJ, USA, 1980–.

Past Posts Acting Ass. Prof., Univ. Cal. Berkeley, 1968–9; Tutor Econ., Balliol Coll. Oxford, 1970–4; Prof. Econ., Univ. Warwick, Coventry, UK, 1974–80; Vis. Prof., MIT, 1977.

Degrees BSc (Maths. and Physics) Bombay Univ., 1963; BA (Maths.) Univ. Camb., 1965; PhD MIT, 1968.

Offices and Honours Ford Foundation Doctoral Fellow, 1967–8; Fellow, Council Em Soc., 1977, 1980–2.

Editorial Duties Ed. Board, Ass. Ed., *REStud,* 1970–80, 1975–8; Assoc. Ed., *JET,* 1972–5; Assoc. Ed, *Em,* 1978–83; Co-ed., *Bell JE,* 1981–3.

Principal Fields of Interest 410 International Trade Theory; 420 Trade Relations, Commercial Policy, Economic Integration; 610 Industrial Organisation and Public Policy.

Publications *Books:* 1. *Optimization in Economic Theory* (OUP, 1976; transl., Janpanese, 1982); 2. *The Theory of Equilibrium Growth* (OUP, 1976); 3. *Theory of International Trade* (with V. Norman), (CUP, 1980; transl., German, 1982).

Articles: 1. 'Marketable surplus and dual development', *JET,* 1(2), Aug. 1969; 2. 'Models of dual economies', in *Models of Economic Growth,* eds. J. A. Mirrlees and N. H. Stern (Macmillan, 1973); 3. 'The optimum factory town', *Bell JE,* 4(2), Autumn 1973; 4. 'Welfare effects of tax and price changes', *JPE,* 4(2), Feb. 1975; 5. 'Monopolistic competition and optimum product diversity' (with J. E. Stiglitz), *AER,* 67(3), June 1977; 6. 'The balance of trade in a model of temporary equilibrium with rationing', *REStud,* 45(3), Oct. 1978; 7. 'The role of investment in entry-deterrence', *EJ,* 90, March 1980; 8. 'The relationship between factor endowments and commodity trade' (with A. Woodland), *J Int E,* 13(2), Nov. 1982; 9. 'International trade policy for oligopolistic industries', *EJ,* 94, Suppl., March 1984; 10. 'Tax policy in open economies', in *Handbook of Public Economics,* eds. A. Auerbach and M. Feldstein (N-H, 1984).

Principal Contributions Have contributed to theoretical research in several areas of economics, including international trade, industrial organisation, public finance, and growth and development. The work mainly concerns characterisation of market equilibria and design of policies.

DIXON, Peter Bishop

Born 1946, Melbourne, Victoria, Australia.

Current Post Dir., Inst. App. Econ. and Social Res., Univ. Melbourne, Parkville, Victoria, Australia, 1984–.

Past Posts Teaching Ass., Harvard Univ., 1970–2; Econ., IMF, Washington DC, 1972–4; Vis. Econ., Reserve Bank Australia, Sydney, 1974–5; Res. Cons. and Assoc. Dir., Sr. Adviser, IMPACT Project, Melbourne, 1975–82, 1982–; Sr. Lect., Monash Univ., Melbourne, 1975–8; Prof. Econ., La Trobe Univ., Melbourne, 1978–84; Vis. Prof., Harvard Univ., 1982–3.

Degrees BEc Monash Univ., 1968; MA, PhD Harvard Univ., 1970, 1972.

Offices and Honours Fellow, Academy Social Sciences in Australia, 1982; Res. Medal Royal Soc. Victoria (with A. A. Powell), 1983.

Editorial Duties Ed. Board, *Australian Econ. Rev.*

Principal Fields of Interest 021 General Equilibrium Theory; 200 Quantitative Economic Methods and Data; 222 Input-Output.

Publications *Books:* 1. *The Theory of Joint Maximization* (N-H, 1975); 2. *Structural Adaptation in an Ailing Macroeconomy* (with A. A. Powell and B. R. Parmenter), (Melbourne Univ. Press, 1979); 3. *Notes and Problems in Microeconomic Theory* (with S. Bowles and D. Kendrick), (N-H, 1980; transl., Spanish, Editorial Hispano Europea, 1983); 4. *ORANI: A Multisectoral Model of the Australian Economy* (with B. R. Parmenter, J. Sutton and D. P. Vincent), (N-H, 1982).

Articles: 1. 'Insecticide requirements in an efficient agricultural sector' (with O. Dixon and J. Miranowski), *REStat,* 55(4), Nov. 1973; 2. 'Effective exchange rates and the International Monetary Fund's multilateral exchange rate model: a review', *AEP,* 15, June 1976; 3. 'Durable goods in the extended linear expenditure system' (with C. Lluch), *RÉStud,* 44(2), June 1977; 4. 'Some causes of structural maladjustment in the Australian economy' (with B. R. Parmenter and J. Sutton), *Econ. Papers,* 57, Jan. 1978; 5. 'Economies of scale, commodity disaggregation and the costs of protection', *AEP,* 17, June 1978; 6. 'Advances in input-output modeling: a review article' (with B. R. Parmenter), *J. Pol. Modeling,* 1(2), 1979; 7. 'The estimation of supply response in Australian agriculture: the CRESH/CRETH projection system' (with D. P. Vincent and A. A. Powell), *Int ER,* 21(1), Jan. 1980; 8. 'A tax-wage bargain in Australia: is a free lunch possible?' (with W. M. Corden), *ER,* 56, Sept. 1980; 9. 'Some economic implications of technical change in Australia to 1990–91: an illustrative application of the SNAPSHOT model' (with D. P. Vincent), *ER,* 56, Dec. 1980; 10. 'A measure of the incidence of the costs of structural change: the experience of birthplace groups in the Australian labour force during the seventies' (with S. M. Bonnell), *ER,* 59, Dec. 1983.

Principal Contributions My principal contributions have been in applied general equilibrium economics. Initial work in this area was with large-scale linear programming models of multi-country trade (see, for example, my *Theory of Joint Maximization*). Later I adopted a Johansen framework which allows easier incorporation of subsitiution possibilities. Together with Alan Powell, Brian Parmenter and other colleagues at the Melbourne University-based IMPACT Project, I implemented ORANI, a Johansen model of the Australian economy. The initial version of ORANI was completed in 1977. It continues to be updated and extended. With 120 sectors, 70 labour types, 6 regions and a myriad of substitution possibilities, ORANI is regarded as one of the world's most detailed applied general equilibrium models. While of the Johansen class, the model extends Johansen's original formulation by allowing for multiproduct industries and multi-industry products, by incorporating econometric estimates of numerous substitutions and transformation elasticities, by including a detailed treatment of marginal industries, by adding a regional dimension and by eliminating the linearisation errors in Johansen's computational procedure without destroying its simplicity. The model is used regularly by government agencies in Australia and by university research workers. Among the numerous applications are analyses of the effects on industries, occupations and regions of changes in tariffs, the exploitation for export of mineral resources, changes in world commodity prices, changes in the costs of employing labour, changes in the domestic pricing policy for oil and the substitution of indirect for direct taxes. In my writings, I have emphasised the need for rigorous theoretical specifications as a basis for empirical research. I have argued that it is only by close attention to theory that one can hope to create models capable of giving insight into the implications of disturbances which push the economy away from previously established historical trends.

DMITRIEV, Vladimir Karpovich*

Dates and Birthplace 1868–1913, Smolensk, Russia.
Posts Held Excise Controller, 1896–9.
Degrees Grad. Polit. Econ., Univ. Moscow, 1896.
Publications *Books:* 1. *Economic Essays* (1904, 1974).
Career The first Russian mathematical economist, his work was influnced by Ricardo and Cournot. During his lifetime and up to the Russian Revolution, his work received some favourable notice, mainly from outside Russia but also from within. Nevertheless, his writings were literally rediscovered in the 1960s when the work of Sraffa on Ricardo illuminated Dmitriev's pioneering interpretation of Ricardo. Since his ideas, though not Marxian, are compatible with Marxian ideas, it has proved possible to use his precedents to legitimise the introduction of mathematical methods into Russian economics.
Secondary Literature D. M. Nuti, 'Introduction' to V. K. Dmitriev, *Economic Essays* (CUP, 1974); R. M. Larsen, 'Dmitriev's Smithian Model', *SJPE*, 24(3), Nov. 1977.

DOBB, Maurice Herbert*

Dates and Birthplace 1900–76, England.
Posts Held Lect., Reader Econ., Univ. Camb., 1924–67.
Degrees BA Univ. Camb., 1921; PhD LSE, 1924.
Publications *Books:* 1. *Capitalist Enterprise and Social Progress* (1925); 2. *Soviet Economic Development Since 1917* (1928, 1966); 3. *Political Economy and Capitalism* (1937); 4. *Studies in the Development of Capitalism* (1946); 5. *An Essay on Economic Growth and Planning* (1960, 1969); 6. *Theories of Value and Distribution since Adam Smith* (1973).
Career Marxist economist whose greatest efforts were directed towards developing a theoretical framework for the analysis of capitalism. This led him inevitably into the examination of theories of value and the total rejection of neoclassical theory. His sympathetic examination of Soviet economic experience under Stalin was later applied to the economic development of the Third World, which became one of his main interests in later life. His work in Marxist economics made few concessions to new interpretations, but this did not prevent him from obtaining considerable influence and worldwide respect. Among his many contributions to the history of ideas was his editorship of Ricardo's *Works and Correspondence* with Piero Sraffa.
Secondary Literature J. Eatwell, 'Dobb, Maurice H.', *IESS*, 18; Maurice Dobb memorial issue, *Camb JE*, 2, March 1978.

DOERINGER, Peter Brantley

Born 1941, Boston, MA, USA.
Current Post Prof. Econ., Dir., Inst. Employment Pol., Boston Univ., Boston, MA, USA, 1974–.
Past Posts Teaching Fellow, Instr., Ass. Prof., Harvard Univ., 1963–6, 1966–7, 1967–72; Cons., Equal Employment Opportunity Commission, 1966–7; Arbitrator, Amer. Arbitration Assoc., 1968–; Mediator, Joint Labor-Management Comm. Police and Fire

MA, 1981–; Lect., LSE, 1971–2; Assoc. Prof., Harvard Univ., 1972–4; Dir., Harvard Univ. Inst. Manpower Admin., 1972–82; Cons., Secretary, US Dept. Labor, 1974–5.

Degrees BA, MA, PhD Harvard Univ., 1962, 1965, 1966.

Offices and Honours Member, Nat. Academy Arbitrators, 1978–.

Editorial Duties Ed. Board, *REStat*; Gen. Ed., Boston Stud. in Appl. Econ. (Kluwer–Nijhoff).

Principal Fields of Interest 810 Manpower Training and Allocation; Labour Force and Supply; 820 Labour Markets; Public Policy; 830 Trade Unions; Collective Bargaining; Labour-Management Relations.

Publications *Books:* 1. *Programs to Employ the Disadvantaged*, ed. (Prentice-Hall, 1969); 2. *Internal Labor Markets and Manpower Analysis* (with M. J. Piore), (D. C. Heath, 1971); 3. *Industrial Relations In International Perspective*, ed. (Macmillan 1981); 4. *Workplace Perspectives on Education and Training Policy*, ed. (Martinus-Nijhoff, 1981); 5. *Jobs and Training in the Eighties: Vocational Training and the Labor Market*, co-ed. (with B. Vermeulen), (Martinus-Nijhoff, 1981).

Articles: 1. 'Equal employment opportunity in Boston' (with M. J. Piore), *Industrial Relations*, 9, May 1970; 2. 'Is there a dual labour market in Great Britain?' (with N. F. Q. Bosanquet), *EJ*, 83, June 1973; 3. 'Dual labor markets and unemployment' (with M. J. Piore), *Public Interest*, 38, Winter, 1975; 4. 'Economic trends in New England: a perspective for higher education in New England in the 1980s' (with P. Pannell and P. Tandon), in *Business and Academia: Partners in New England's Economic Renewal*, eds. J. C. Hoy and M. H. Bernstein (Univ. Press New England, 1981); 5. 'Manpower strategies for growth and diversity in New England's high technology sector' (with P. Pannell), in *New England's Vital Resource: The Labor Force*, eds. J. C. Hoy and M. C. Bernstein (Amer. Council Educ., 1982); 6. 'Budget watching as a spectator sport', in *Proceedings of the Thirty-Fourth Annual Meeting of the Industrial Relations Res. Assoc.* (IRRA, 1981); 7. 'Unions: economic performance and economic structure', in *The Economics of Trade Unions*, ed. J. J. Rosa (Klswer-Nijhoff, 1983); 8. 'Internal labor markets and paternalism in rural areas', in *Internal Labor Markets*, ed. P. Osterman (MIT Press, 1984); 9. 'Union effects on low wage labor markets: the case of the service employees international union', in *Advances in Industrial Relations*, eds. D. Lipsky and J. M. Douglas (JAI Press, 1983).

Principal Contributions Almost all of my research has been 'institutional' in that it involves the study of workplace employment systems. The most widely-known aspect of this research has been on labour market segmentation (dual labour markets). The most significant contribution, however, has been the documentation of how economic institutions (such as internal labour markets) constrain and redirect economic behaviour. The focus upon workplace employment systems has allowed my research to branch out in various directions — education and training, discrimination, poverty and labour market disadvantage, and manpower planning. By relying more on field research than on econometric modelling, I have been able to study economic decision-making directly. This has given my research a firm grounding in economic reality. It has also been an advantage in contributing to policy discussions, an activity which I believe should be the ultimate goal of applied economics. From time to time, my research has intersected with new developments in neoclassical economics — human capital, search theory, implicit contracts and the economics of information. In recent years, however, I have become less interested in the efficiency dimension of economic institutions than in how such institutions develop legitimacy and influence income distribution. I have also become more concerned with the evolution of economic systems, as seen through historical and comparative studies, and in the institutional foundations of such evolution.

DOLBEAR, F. Trenery, Jr

Born 1935, Scranton, PA, USA.
Current Post Prof. Econ., Brandeis Univ., Waltham, MA, USA, 1974–.
Past Posts Ass. Instr., Acting Instr., Yale Univ., 1959–60, 1961–3; Ass. Prof., Carnegie Inst. Technology, 1963–6; Vis. Ass. Prof. Bus. Econ., Stanford Univ., 1966–7; Brookings Econ. Pol. Fellow, US Bureau of the Budget, 1967–8; Assoc. Prof., Brandeis Univ., 1968–74; Vis. Assoc. Prof., Univ. Essex, England, 1975–6; Academic Vis., LSE, 1983.
Degrees BA Williams Coll., 1957; MA, PhD Yale Univ., 1958, 1963.
Principal Fields of Interest 020 General Economic Theory; 012 Teaching of Economics.
Publications *Articles:* 1. 'Individual choice under uncertainty: an experimental study', *YEE*, 3(2), Fall 1963; 2. 'Asymmetry between bribes and charges' (with M. I. Kamien and N. L. Schwartz), *Water Resources Res.*, 2(1), First Qtr 1966; 3. 'Inconsistent behavior in lottery choice experiments' (with L. Lave), *Behavioral Science*, 12(1), Jan. 1967; 4. 'The possibility of oversupply of local public goods: a critical note' (with W. C. Brainard), *JPE*, 75(1), Feb. 1967; 5. 'On the theory of optimum externality', *AER*, 57(1), March 1967; 6. 'Collusion in oligopoly: an experiment on the effect of numbers and information' (with L. B. Lave, *et al.*), *QJE*, 82, May 1968; 7. 'A simulation policy game for teaching macroeconmics' (with R. Attiyeh and W. Brainard), *AER*, 58(2), May 1968; 8. 'Social risk and financial markets' (with W. Brainard), *AER*, 61(2), May 1971; 9. 'Teaching macroeconomics with a computer simulation', ERIC Document Repro. Service, 1972; 10. 'Computer simulation exercises for economic statistics' (with L. Pulley), *J Econ Educ*, 15(1), Winter 1984.
Principal Contributions Clarification of conceptual difficulties in allocation theory relating to externalities, public goods, and social risk. Also a continuing interest in experimental economics which dates from doctoral dissertation on the problem of choice under uncertainty. Recent efforts have been devoted to designing computer exercises for more effective teaching of difficult concepts in macroeconomics and in statistics.

DOMAR, Evsey David

Born 1914, Lodz, Russia (now Poland).
Current Post Ford Internat. Prof. Econ. Emeritus, MIT, Cambridge, MA, USA, 1984–.
Past Posts Econ., Board of Governors, Fed. Reserve System, 1943–6; Ass. Prof. Econ., Carnegie Inst. Technology, 1946–7; Ass. Prof. Econ., Res. Assoc., Cowles Commission, Univ. Chicago, 1947–8; Assoc. Prof., Prof. Polit. Econ., Johns Hopkins Univ., 1948–55, 1955–8; Prof. Econ., Ford Internat. Prof. Econ., MIT, 1958–72, 1972–84; Vis. Lect., Univ. Buffalo, 1949; Vis. Assoc. Prof., Russian Inst., Columbia Univ., 1951–3, 1954–5; Vis. Fulbright Prof., Oxford Univ., 1952–3, Vis. Prof., MIT, 1957, Harvard Univ., 1962, Stockholm School Econ., 1972, La Trobe Univ., Melbourne, Australia, 1974, Hebrew Univ., Jerusalem, 1979; Cons., RAND Corp., 1951–81, Ford Foundation, 1954–8, Brookings Inst., 1956–9, NSF, 1958, 1967–9, Batelle Memorial Inst., 1959–60, OECD, 1961–2, Inst. Defense Analysis, 1961–2.
Degrees BA UCLA, 1939; MA (Math. Stats.), Univ. Michigan 1941; MA, PhD Harvard Univ., 1943, 1947.
Offices and Honours Exec. Comm., Vice-Pres., Disting. Fellow, AEA, 1962–5, 1970, 1984; Fellow, AAAS, 1962–; Fellow, Center Advanced Study Behavioral Sciences, 1962–3; Recipient, John R. Commons Award, Omicron Delta Epsilon, 1965; Fellow, Em Soc, 1968–; Pres., Assoc. Comparative Econ., 1970.
Editorial Duties Ed. Boards, *AER*, 1957–9, *Amer. Econ.*, 1963–, *J Comp E*, 1976–82.
Principal Fields of Interest 023 Macroeconomic Theory; 041 Economic History; General; 053 Comparative Economic Systems.
Publications *Books:* 1. *Essays in the Theory of Economic Growth* (OUP,

1957; transls., Japanese, Polish, Slovak, Spanish, Italian and Hungarian; Greenwood Press, 1982).

Articles: 1. 'Proportional income taxation and risk-taking' (with R. A. Musgrave), *QJE*, 58(3), May 1944; 2. 'On the measurement of technological change', *EJ*, 71, Dec. 1961; 3. 'The Soviet collective farm as a producer cooperative', *AER*, 56(4), Sept. 1966; 4. 'An index-number tournament', *QJE*, 81(2), May 1967; 5. 'The causes of slavery or serfdom: a hypothesis', *JEH*, 30(1), March 1970; 6. 'On the optimal compensation of a socialist manager', *QJE*, 88(1), Feb. 1974; 7. 'On the measurement of comparative efficiency', in *Comparison of Economic Systems*, ed. A. Eckstein (Univ. Cal. Press, 1971); 8. 'On the profitability of Russian serfdom' (with M. J. Machina), *JEH*, 44(4), Dec. 1984.

Principal Contributions Began in the theory of taxation (the effects of income tax on risk-taking) and moved quickly to the theory of growth and the construction of growth models. When this field became overcrowded (it is customary in our profession to beat every new idea to death), I left it for comparative economic systems with emphasis on the economics of socialism, where I am still working. At the same time, developed an interest in the theory of slavery and serfdom. (A long paper on the profitability of Russian serfdom is ready for publication.) In connection with preparing a course on problems in economic history, developed several models, such as on the drive to the Indies, on the Black Death, etc.

DONGES, Juergen B.

Born 1940, Seville, Spain.
Current Post Vice-Pres., Inst. World Econ., Kiel, W. Germany, Hon. Prof. Polit. Econ., Univ. Kiel, 1973–.
Past Posts Res. Ass., Univ. Saarbrücken, 1966–9; Div. Chief, Inst. World Econ. Kiel, 1969–72.
Degrees Diplom-Volkswirt, Dr Rer. Pol. Univ. Saarbrücken, 1966, 1969.
Offices and Honours Advisory Board, German Fed. Ministry Econ. Co–op.,

Bonn, 1973; Scientific Council, European Inst. Public Admin., Masstricht, Netherlands, 1981–; Adviser, German Soc. Foreign Pol., Bonn, 1983–; Inst. Econ. Stud., Madrid, Spain, 1984–; Cons., various internat. organisations 1972; Madrid Center Econ. Stud. and Communications, 1978–83.
Editorial Duties Co-ed. *Die Weltwirtschaft*, 1970, 1971, 1973; Ed. Board, *Biblioteca del Pensamiento Economico Moderno*, 1979–83, *The World Economy*, 1984.
Principal Fields of Interest 400 International Economics; 120 Country Studies; 600 Industrial Organisation; Technological Change; Industry Studies.
Publications *Books:* 1. *Über das Inflationsproblem in Entwicklungsländern* (Heymanns, 1970); 2. *Brazil's Trotting Peg* (AEI, 1971, 1972); 3. *Protektion und Branchenstruktur der westdeutschen Wirtschaft* (with G. Fels, *et al.*), (J. C. B. Mohr, 1973); 4. *Industrial Development Policies for Indonesia* (with B. Stecher and F. Wolter), (J. C. B. Mohr, 1974); 5. *Übertragung von Technologien an Entwicklungslander* (with J. P. Agarwal, *et al.*), (J. C. B. Mohr, 1975); 6. *La Industrializacion en Espana* (Oikos-Tau, 1976); 7. *Aussenwirtschaftsstrategien und Industrialisierung in Entwicklungsländern* (with L. Muller-Ohlsen), (J. C. B. Mohr, 1978); 8. *Aussenwirtschafts und Entwicklungspolitik* (Springer, 1981); 9. *What is Wrong with the European Communities?* (INEA, 1981; transl., Spanish, Instituto de Economia de Mercado, 1981); 10. *The Second Enlargement of the European Community* (with K. W. Schatz, *et al.*), (J. C. B. Mohr, 1982; transl., Portuguese, Edicoes 70, 1983).
Articles: 1. 'Shaping Spain's export industry', *WD*, 1(9), Sept. 1973; transl., Spanish, *Informacion Comercial Espanola*, Sept.–Oct. 1973; 2. 'Zur theorie de effektiven protektion', *ZGS*, 131(2), April 1975; 3. 'The expansion of manufactured exports in developing countries' (with J. Riedel), *WA*, 113(1), 1977; 4. 'The Third World demand for a new international economic order', *Kyk*, 30(2), 1977; 5. 'UNCTAD's integrated programme for commodities', *Resources Policies*,

5, March 1979, repr. in *Le rôle de l'Europe dans le nouvel ordre économique international*, ed. Inst. d'Etudes Européennes (Editions de l'Université Bruxelles, 1979); 6. 'Foreign investment in Portugal' (Fundacao Calouste Gulbenkian, 1980); 7. 'Industrial policies in West Germany's not so market-oriented economy', *World Econ.*, 3(2), Sept. 1980; 8. 'Structural policy issues in production and trade', in *East-West-South: Economic Interactions between Three Worlds*, ed. C. T. Saunders (Macmillan, 1981); 9. 'Reappraisal of foreign trade strategies for industrial development', in *Reflections on a Troubled World Economy*, eds. F. Machlup, G. Fels and H. Muller-Groeling (Macmillan, 1983); 10. 'Is European integration now due to inertia or conviction?', *World Econ.*, 7(1), March 1984.

Principal Contributions Early work was concentrated on testing alternative development and trade theories, with emphasis on developing countries. Then interest shifted to the analysis of the impact of economic policies on growth, resource allocation, foreign trade and foreign investment. Contributed to empirical analysis of changes in the international division of labour. Currently engaged in research on European economic integration and on economic policy problems of West Germany. Other main work has been in analysing Spain's economic growth in comparative perspective.

DORFMAN, Robert

Born 1916, New York City, NY, USA.
Current Post David A. Wells Prof. Polit. Econ., Harvard Univ., Cambridge, MA, USA, 1972–.
Past Posts Ass. Stat., US Bureau Labor Stat., 1939–41; Stat., US Office Price Admin., 1941–3; Operations Analyst, US Air Force, S.W. Pacific Theatre, Washington, DC, 1943–6, 1948–50; Assoc. Prof. Econ., Univ. Cal. Berkeley, 1950–5; Prof. Econ., Harvard Univ., 1955–72; Cons., Agency for Internat. Devlp., Arms Control and Disarmament Agency, Brookings Inst., US President's Council Econ. Advisers, Devlp. Advisory Service, Harvard Univ., Energy Info. Agency, IBRD, Commission Pop. and the Amer. Future, RAND Corp.
Degrees BA, MA Columbia Univ., 1936, 1937; PhD Univ. Cal. Berkeley, 1950.
Offices and Honours Newton Booth Fellow, Univ. Cal. Berkeley, 1947–8; Ford Faculty Res. Fellow, 1958–9; Council, ORSA, 1959–62; Fellow, Center Advanced Study Behavioral Science, 1960–1; Member, US President's Commission to Appraise Employment and Unemployment Stats., 1962–3; Member, White House Interior Team on Waterlogging and Salinity in W. Pakistan, 1962–3; Council, Em Soc. 1962–4; Member, Division Behavioral Sciences, Nat. Res. Council, 1963–5; Pres., Inst. Management Science, 1965–6; Ford Faculty Res. Fellow, Univ. Cal. Berkeley, 1965–6; Exec. Comm., AEA, 1968–71; Guggenheim Foundation Fellow, 1970–1; Member, Nat. Academy Sciences Rev. Comm., Environmental Impact of Oil and Gas Production on the Outer Continental Shelf, 1973–4; Member, Environmental Studies Board, Comm. Environmental Decision-Making, Chairman, Comm. Prototype Analysis of Pesticides, Nat. Res. Council, 1974–7, 1975–7, 1978–9; Vice-Pres., AEA, 1982.
Editorial Duties Ed. Boards, *QJE*, 1976–; Amer. Ed., *REStud*, 1953–63.
Principal Fields of Interest 022 Microeconomic Theory; 722 Conservation and Pollution; 213 Mathematical Methods and Models.
Publications Books: 1. *Application of Linear Programming to the Theory of The Firm* (Prentice-Hall, 1951); 2. *The Economic Status of the Aged* (with P. O. Steiner), (Univ. Cal. Press, 1957); 3. *Linear Programming and Economic Analysis* (with P. A. Samuelson and R. M. Solow), (McGraw-Hill, 1958); 4. *Design of Water Resource Systems* (with A. Maass, M. Hufschmidt, and others), (Harvard Univ. Press, 1962); 5. *The Price System* (Prentice-Hall, 1964); 6. *Measuring Benefits of Government Investments*, ed. (Brookings Inst., 1965); 7. *Prices and Markets* (Prentice-

Hall, 1967, 1978); 8. *Models for Managing Regional Water Quality* (with H. D. Jacoby and H. A. Thomas, Jr.), (Harvard Univ. Press, 1972); 9. *Economics of the Environment, Selected Readings*, co-ed. (with N. S. Dorfman), (W. W. Norton, 1972, 1977).

Articles: 1. 'The detection of defective members of large populations', *Annals Math. Stats.*, 14, Dec. 1943; 2. 'Optimal advertising and optimal quality' (with P. O. Steiner), *AER*, 44(5), Dec. 1954; 3. 'A graphical exposition of Böhm-Bawerk's interest theory', *REStud*, 26, Feb. 1959; 4. 'An economic interpretation of optimal control theory', *AER*, 59(5), Dec. 1969; 5. 'The functions of the city', in *Thinking About Cities*, ed. A. H. Pascal (Dickenson, 1970); 6. 'Production, Theory of', *Encyclopedia Britannica* (Enc. Britannica, 15th edn., 1974); 7. 'Incidence of the benefits and costs of environmental programs', *AER*, 67(1), Feb. 1977; 8. 'Forty years of cost-benefit analysis', in *Econometric Contributions to Public Policy*, eds. R. Stone and W. Peterson (Macmillan, 1978); 9. 'A formula for the Gini coefficient', *REStat*, 61(1), Feb. 1979; 10. 'The meaning of internal rates of return', *J Fin*, 36(5), Dec. 1981.

Principal Contributions My shots have been scattered. My first publications were in the area of applied mathematical statistics. My doctoral dissertation was, probably, the pioneering effort in applying non-linear programming, which had not yet been invented, to the theory of the monopolistically competitive firm. It was followed, in 1958, by a full-dress interpretation of microeconomic theory in linear programming terms, written with P. A. Samuelson and R. M. Solow. At about that time, my interest in natural resource economics developed, and I began participating in the Harvard Water Program. *Design of Water Resource Systems*, written with other members of the Program, was the major result of that enterprise.

The interest in natural resource economics led in several directions. One was toward public investments in general, resulting in the symposium, *Measuring Benefits of Government Investments*, 'General Equilibrium with Public Goods' (1969), and several related papers. A second was toward development policies for less developed countries, which was pursued by active consultation in a number of less developed countries but only minor published contributions. And, finally this interest led directly into environmental economics, where it still continues, and to the collection, *Economics of the Environment*, to *Regulating Pesticides*, the report of a National Research Council committee that I chaired, and to numerous papers.

Off this main line, I am especially pleased to have written the early paper on advertising (with P. O. Steiner), the expository article on optimal control theory, and the article on internal rates of return.

DORNBUSCH, Rudiger

Born 1942, Krefeld, W. Germany.

Current Post Prof. Econ., MIT, USA, 1978–.

Past Posts Ass. Prof., Univ. Rochester, 1972–3; Assoc. Prof., Univ. Chicago, 1974–8.

Degrees Licence de sciences politiques Univ. Geneva, Switzerland, 1966; MA, PhD Univ. Chicago, 1969, 1971.

Offices and Honours Fellow, Em Soc, 1979; Fellow, AAAS, 1980.

Principal Fields of Interest 431 Balance of Payments; 023 Macroeconomic Theory.

Publications *Books:* 1. *International Economic Policy*, co-ed. (with J. Frenkel), (JHUP, 1979); 2. *Open Economy Macroeconomics* (Basic Books, 1980); 3. *Macroeconomics* (with S. Fisher), (McGraw-Hill, 1981); 4. *Economics* (with S. Fisher), (McGraw-Hill, 1985); 5. *Dollars, Debts, and Deficits* (MIT Press, 1986).

Articles: 1. 'Devaluation, money and non-traded goods', *AER*, 63(5), Dec. 1973; 2. 'Expectations and exchange rate dynamics', *JPE*, 84(6), Dec. 1976; 3. 'Comparative advantage, trade and payments in Ricardian model with a continuum of goods' (with S. Fischer and P. A. Samuelson), *AER*, 67(5), Dec. 1977.

Principal Contributions Work on exchange-rate problems and open economy macroeconomics.

DOUGHERTY, Christopher Robert Sykes

Born 1943, Leeds, W. Yorkshire, England.

Current Post Sr. Lect. Econ., LSE, London, England, 1972–.

Past Posts Cons., Econ. Educ. and Manpower, Harvard Univ. Devlp. Advisory Service, Nat. Planning Dept., Bogota, Colombia, 1967–8; Res. Fellow, King's Coll. Camb., 1968–72.

Degrees BA Univ. Camb., 1965; PhD Univ. Harvard, 1972.

Principal Fields of Interest 113 Economic Planning Theory and Policy; 810 Manpower Training and Allocation; Labour Force and Supply.

Publications *Books:* 1. *Interest and Profit* (Methuen, Columbia Univ. Press, 1980).

Articles: 1. 'Dynamic input-output, trade and development' (with M. Bruno and M. Fraenkel), in *Applications of Input-Output Analysis*, eds. A. P. Carter and A. Brody (N-H, 1969); 2. 'The optimal allocation of investment in education', in *Studies in Development Planning*, ed. H. B. Chenery (Harvard Univ Press, 1971); 3. 'Substitution and the structure of the labour force', *EJ*, 82, March 1972; 4. 'Estimates of labor aggegation functions', *JPE*, 80(6), Nov.–Dec. 1972; 5. 'On the rate of return and the rate of profit', *EJ*, 82, Dec. 1972; 6. 'Measuring the effects of the misallocation of labour' (with M. J. Selowsky), *REStat*, 55(3), Aug. 1973; 7. 'On the secular macroeconomic consequences of technical progress', *EJ*, 84, Sept. 1974; 8. 'The distribution of schooling and the distribution of earnings: raising the school leaving age in 1973' (with M. Blaug and G. C. Psacharopoulos), *MS*, 50(1), March 1982; 9. 'Manpower development planning in the United Kingdom', in *The Practice of Manpower Planning Revisited*, ed. M. Debeauvais (Internat. Inst. Educ. Planning, 1985).

Principal Contributions My interest in manpower development planning dates from the time that I was given that assignment as a junior member of the Harvard Development Advisory Service group attached to the Colombian National Planning Department. The manpower requirements approach was the dominant planning methodology but its assumptions had begun to be questioned, notably by Robinson Hollister. My early papers were directed to providing further empirical evidence of their implausibility and to developing rate-of-return analysis as an alternative approach for educational planning. The latter led to close associations with George Psacharopoulos and Marcelo Selowsky.

When I returned to Cambridge as a Research Fellow the capital theory controversy was at its height. It seemed to me at the time (and it still does) that much of the controversy was attributable to a wilful misrepresentation of the neoclassical position by some of its opponents. My paper on the rate of return was a response to the bizarre charge that the Fisherian approach to the determination of the rate of profit was logically defective. The book attempting to sort out the positions of the different camps absorbed rather too much time over the following years.

In 1980 I returned to manpower development planning after a gap of ten years. A consultancy for the ILO in that year gave me new field experience and made me realise that the problems of planning manpower development were deeper than I had previously thought. It made me aware that training needs assessment was only one function of a national planning unit, others being the promotion of administrative efficiency within the manpower development sector, monitoring labour and training markets, and the promotion of cost-effectiveness in the use of resources in a more general sense than that adopted in rate-of-return analysis. In recent consultancy work with the World Bank and the ILO I have been advocating an approach which is managerial, rather than strictly economic, and which focusses on adaptive processes rather than the blueprint approach to planning.

DOUGLAS, Paul Howard*

Dates and Birthplace 1892–1976, Salem, MA, USA.

Posts Held Teacher Econ., Univ. Illinois, 1916–7, Reed Coll., 1917–18, Univ. Washington, 1919–20; Prof., Univ. Chicago 1920–49, Amherst Coll., 1924–7, New School Social Res., NY, 1967–9.

Degrees BA Bowdoin Coll., 1913; MA, PhD Columbia Univ., 1915, 1921.

Offices and Honours US Senator, Illinois, 1948–66; Pres., AEA, 1948.

Publications *Books:* 1. *Real Wages in the United States* (1930, 1966); 2. *The Theory of Wages* (1934, 1964); 3. *Ethics in Government* (1952, 1972).

Articles: 1. 'Are there laws of production?', *AER*, 38, March 1948; 2. 'Comments on the Cobb-Douglas production function', in *The Theory and Empirical Analysis of Production*, ed. M. Brown (1967); 3. 'The Cobb-Douglas production function once again: its history, its testing, and some empirical values', *JPE*, 84(3), Oct. 1976.

Career A pioneer econometrician whose work had as its starting point the marginal productivity theory of his teacher, John Bates Clark. In cooperation with Charles W. Cobb, he was responsible for the now famous 'Cobb-Douglas' production function. His work at Chicago as a teacher enabled him to organise research projects designed to test the marginal productivity theory of distribution. *The Theory of Wages* contains his main contribution to this field. As Senator for Illinois for almost 20 years, he drafted and fought for the passage of a number of important pieces of economic legislation.

Secondary Literature G. C. Cain, 'Douglas, Paul H.', *IESS*, 18; P. A. Samuelson, 'Paul Douglas' measurement of production functions and marginal productivities', *JPE,* 87(5), pt. 1. Oct. 1979.

DOWNS, Anthony

Born 1930, Evanston, IL., USA.

Current Post Sr. Fellow, Brookings Inst., Washington, DC, USA, 1977–.

Past Posts Chairman, Real Estate Res. Corp., 1959–77.

Degrees BA(Polit. Theory and Internat. Relations) Carleton Coll., 1948–52; MA, PhD Stanford Univ., 1952, 1956.

Offices and Honours Lambda Alpha; AEA, AAAS; Nat. Academy Public Admin.

Principal Fields of Interest 931 Urban Economics; 970 Economies of Politics.

Publications *Books:* 1. *An Economic Theory of Democracy* (Harper & Row, 1957); 2. *Inside Bureaucracy* (Little Brown, 1967); 3. *Urban Problems and Prospects* (Rand McNally, 1970, 1976); 4. *Racism in America* (US Civil Rights Commission, 1970); 5. *Federal Housing Subsidies* (Health-Lexington, 1973); 6. *Opening up the Suburbs* (Yale Univ. Press, 1973); 7. *Neighborhoods and Urban Development* (Brookings Inst., 1981); 8. *Urban Decline and the Future of American Cities* (with others), (Brookings Inst., 1982); 9. *Rental Housing in the 1980s* (Brookings Inst., 1983).

Articles: 1. 'Alternative futures for the American ghetto', *Daedalus,* Fall 1968; 2. 'Up and down with ecology', *Public Interest,* Summer 1972; 3. 'The automotive population explosion', *Traffic Q.,* July 1979; 4. 'Too much capital for housing?', *Brookings Bull.,* Summer, 1980; 5. 'Inflation and mortgage interest rates', *Real Estate Rev.,* Winter 1981.

Principal Contributions Application of economic analysis to political theory concerning democratic political parties and bureaucratic organisations, including analysis of impacts of uncertainty and ignorance. Analysis of racial segregation in US cities, its causes and effects. Analysis of dynamics of urban development as related to neighbourhood change and falling population in large US cities. Analysis of real-estate capital flows.

DRÈZE, Jacques H.J.M.E.

Born 1929, Verviers, Belgium.
Current Post Prof. Econ., CORE, Univ. Catholique de Louvain, Louvain-la-Neuve, Belgium, 1968–.
Past Posts Ass Prof., Carnegie Inst. Technology, 1957–8; Chargé de cours, Prof., Univ. Catholique de Louvain, 1958–62, 1962–4; Prof., Univ. Chicago, 1964–8.
Degrees Licence, Univ. de Liège, 1951; PhD Columbia Univ., 1958; Hon. Dr Univs. Essex, 1980, Paris I-Sorbonne, 1980, Montreal, 1982, Liège, 1983.
Offices and Honours Fellow, Vice-Pres., Pres., Em Soc, 1964, 1969, 1970; Hon. Member, AEA, 1976; Foreign Hon. Member, AAAS, 1978; Foreign Member, Royal Netherlands Academy Arts and Sciences, 1980.
Editorial Duties Co-ed. *Em*, 1967–9.
Principal Fields of Interest 021 General Equilibrium Theory; 026 Economics of Uncertainty and Information; Game Theory and Bargaining Theory; 211 Econometric and Statistical Methods and Models.
Publications *Books:* 1. *Conceptions de l'Université* (with J. Debelle), (Fondation Industrie-Université, 1966, Editions Univ., 1969; transl., Italian, 1969); 2. *Allocation under Uncertainty: Equilibrium and Optimality*, ed. (Macmillan, 1974); 3. *Labour Management and Labour Contracts, A General Equilibrium Approach* (Blackwell, 1984); 4. *Essays on Economic Decisions under Uncertainty* (CUP, forthcoming, 1985).
Articles: 1. 'Quelques reflexions sereines sur l'adaption de l'industrie Belge au marché commun', *Comptes Rendus de la Societé d'Econ. Polit. de Belgique,* 275, 1960; 2. 'Some postwar contributions of French economists to theory and public policy', *AER,* 54, pt. 2, 1964; 3. 'Decision and horizon rules for stochastic planning problems: a linear example' (with A. Charmers and M. Miller), *Em,* 34(2), April 1966; 4. 'A *tâtonnement* process for public goods' (with D. de la Vallee Poussin), *REStud,* 38, April 1971; 5. 'Econometrics and decision theory', *Em,* 40(1), Jan. 1972; 6. 'Cores and prices in

an exchange economy with an atomless sector' (with J. J. Gaxzewicz, D. Schmeilder and K. Vind), *Em,* 40(6), Nov. 1972; 7. 'Existence of an exchange equilibrium under price rigidities', *Int ER,* 16(2), June 1975; 8. 'Cooperative games with coalition structures' (with R. Aumann), *Internat. J. Game Theory,* 3(4), June 1975; 9. 'Pricing, spending and gambling rules for non-profit organizations' (with M. Marehand), in *Public and Urban Economics,* ed. R. E. Grieson (D. C. Heath, 1976); 10. 'The trade-off between real wages and employment in an open economy (Belgium)' (with F. Modigliani), *Europ ER,* 15(1), Jan. 1981.

Principal Contributions The main topics in which I have held continued interest over a number of years are: (1) the 'Standard Good Hypothesis' (small industrial countries have a relative advantage in the production of commodities which are not qualitatively differentiated across countries) initially presented and verified for Belgium in Article No. 1 above, and since tested by others on several other small economies; (2) the foundations of decision theory and in particular the extension of the model of Savage (subjectively probability and expected utility) to situations of moral hazard or games and state-dependent preferences; this work, initiated in my PhD dissertation and published in French periodicals, receives a much simpler and more general treatment in my 1985 book, which also includes an application to the value of life and safety; (3) the economics of uncertainty, in particular consumer decisions (about savings, portfolios and occupations), producer decisions (industry equilibrium, sticky prices, investment), labour contracts and decisions of non-profit organisations. Some 15 papers on these topics are collected in my 1985 book; (4) Bayesian analysis of simultaneous equation models – an ongoing project, described in article No. 6 above and more recently in the *Handbook of Econometrics*; (5) the analysis of the core of economies with syndicates or monopolies — see article No. 5 and references there; (6) *tâtonnement* processes for public goods which converge to a Pareto optimum and embody incentives for correct revelation of preferences — see article No. 4; (7) the theory of the second best, first discussed in the work of Boiteux, then applied to discount rates, to non-profit organisations in article No. 9, and recently to economies experiencing disequilibrium; (8) equilibrium theory under price rigidities and quantity constraints, as introduced in article No. 7 and later extended to public goods, second-best policies and economies with increasing returns; (9) the pure theory of labour-managed economies, especially in a general equilibrium framework and in contexts of uncertainty and disequilibrium — see 1984 book; and (10) employment policies in small open economies — article No. 10.

DUESENBERRY, James Stemble

Born 1918.
Current Post Prof. Econ., Harvard Univ., 1957–.
Past Posts Teaching Fellow, Univ. Michigan, 1939–44; Res. Fellow, US SSRC, 1941; Instr., MIT, 1946; Teaching Fellow, Ass. Prof., Assoc. Prof. Econ., Harvard Univ., 1946–8, 1948–53, 1953–7; Fulbright Fellow, Univ. Camb., 1954–5; Member, US President's Council Econ. Advisers, 1966–8.
Degrees BA, MA, PhD Univ. Michigan, 1939, 1941, 1948.
Offices and Honours Chairman, Board Dirs., Fed. Reserve Bank Boston, 1969–74.
Principal Fields of Interest 311 Domestic Monetary Theory.
Publications *Books:* 1. *Income, Saving and the Theory of Consumer Behavior* (Harvard Univ. Press, 1949, OUP, 1967); 2. *Business Cycles and Economic Growth* (McGraw-Hill, 1958); 3. *Cases and Problems in Economics* (with L. E. Preston), (A & U, 1960); 4. *Money and Credit: Impact and Control* (Prentice-Hall, 1964, 1972); 5. *Capital Needs in the Seventies* (with B. Bosworth and A. S. Carron), (US Govt. Printing Office, 1975); 6. *Money, Banking and the Economy* (with T. Mayer and R. Alibers), (Prentice-Hall, 1981).

DÜHRING, Eugen Karl*

Dates and Birthplace 1833–1921, Berlin, Germany.
Posts Held Prof., Univ. Berlin, 1863–77; then independent scholar and writer.
Degrees Dr Philo. Univ. Berlin, 1861.
Publications *Books:* 1. *Carey's Umwälzung der Volkswirtschaftslehre und Socialwissenschaft* (1865); 2. *Capital und Arbeit* (1865); 3. *Kritische Grundlegung der Volkswirtschaftslehre* (1866); 4. *Kritische Geschichte der Nationalökonomie und des Socialismus* (1871); 5. *Cursus* (1873).
Career Though blind from an early age, he sought to master a vast range of intellectual disciplines, and in fact made original contributions to several, including economics. His philosophy of life, which he called 'personalism', and his system of social reform, called 'societary', were unifying elements. His aggressive style of disputation earned him enemies and limited the recognition of his work, whilst analytical weaknesses flawed many of his writings. In economics, his greatest contribution was an anti-Marxist theory which explained many of the property relations of capitalist society by political rather than economic causes. Chiefly remembered today as the subject of one of Engels' popular expositions of Marxism in a book known by its abbreviated title, *Anti-Dühring*.
Secondary Literature G. Albrecht, *Eugen Dühring* 1927).

DUNBAR, Charles Franklin*

Dates and Birthplace 1830–1900, Abington, MA, USA.
Posts Held Journalist, *Boston Daily Advertiser, 1959–69;* Prof. Polit. Econ., Harvard Univ., 1871–1900.
Degrees BA Harvard Univ., 1851.
Offices and Honours Ed., *QJE,* 1886–96.
Publications *Books:* 1. *Theory and History of Banking* (1891); 2. *Economic Essays,* ed. O. M. W. Sprague (1904).
Career As a journalist he wrote in-

fluentially on current financial question — paper currency, a national banking system and the National Debt. His publications during his academic career were mainly on banking, international trade, taxation and finance, but it was through his editorship of *QJE* that he exercised his greatest influence. He was an organiser and a teacher rather than an original theorist.

Secondary Literature F. W. Taussig, (obit.) 'Charles Franklin Dunbar', *EJ*, 10, March 1900.

DUNLOP, John Thomas

Born 1914, Placerville, CA, USA.
Current Post Lamont Univ. Prof., Harvard Univ., Cambridge, MA, USA, 1980–.
Past Posts Acting Instr., Stanford Univ., 1936–7; Instr., Assoc. Prof., Prof., Dean Faculty Arts and Sciences, Harvard Univ., 1938–43, 1945–50, 1950–70, 1969–73; Dir., Cost Living Council, Washington, DC, 1973–4; US Secretary Labor, Washington, DC, 1975–6; Dir., GTE, 1976–83; Chairman, Labor Management Group, 1973–.
Degrees BA, PhD Univ. Cal. Berkeley, 1935; Hon. LLD Univ. Chicago, 1968, Temple Univ. 1975, Boston Coll., 1975, Univ. Akron, 1975, Univ. Penn., 1976, Babson Coll., 1977, Loyola Univ., 1978, Villanova Univ., 1983.
Offices and Honours US SSRC, 1937–8; Member, AAAS, 1957; Pres., IRRA, 1960; Guggenheim Foundation Fellow; American Philo. Soc., 1972; Louis K. Comstock Award, Nat. Electrical Contractors Assoc., 1974; Pres., Internat. Industrial Relations Assoc., 1973–6; Cushing Award Excellence in Labor Management Relations, 1978; US General Accounting Office, Award for Public Service, 1979; Hon. Member, American Hospital Assoc., 1984.
Editorial Duties Ed., *Wertheim Publications in Industrial Relations* (Harvard Univ. Press, 1945–).
Principal Fields of Interest 820 Labour Markets; Public Policy; 830 Trade Unions, Collective Bargaining, Labour-Management Relations; 610 Industrial Organisation and Public Policy.

Publications *Books:* 1. *Wage Determination Under Trade Unions* (Macmillan, 1944, 1950); 2. *Collective Bargaining: Principles and Cases* (Richard D. Irwin, 1949, 1953); 3. *The Wage Adjustment Board* (with A. D. Hill), (Harvard Univ. Press, 1950); 4. *The Theory of Wage Determination*, ed. (Macmillan, 1957); 5. *Industrial Relations Systems* (Henry Holt, 1958); 6. *Industrialism and Industrial Man* (with C. Kerr, F. H. Harbison and C. A. Myers), (Harvard Univ. Press, 1960); 7. *Labor and the American Community* (with D. C. Bok), (Simon & Schuster, 1970); 8. *The Lessons of Wage and Price Controls — The Food Sector* (with K. J. Fedor), (Harvard Univ. Press, 1977); 9. *Business and Public Policy*, ed. (Harvard Univ. Press, 1980); 10. *Dispute Resolution, Negotiation and Consensus Building* (Auburn House, 1984).

Articles: 1. 'The movement of real and money wage rates', *EJ*, 48, Sept. 1938; 2. 'The development of labor organization: a theoretical framework', in *Insights Into Labor Issues*, eds. R. A. Lester and J. Shister (Macmillan, 1948); 3. 'Productivity and the wage structure', in *Income, Employment and Public Policy, Essays in Honor of Alvin H. Hansen* (W. W. Norton, 1948); 4. 'The decontrol of wages and prices', in *Labor in Postwar America*, ed. C. E. Warne (Remsen Press, 1949); 5. 'International comparison of wage structures' (with M. Rothbaum), *Int Lab Rev*, April 1955; 6. 'The task of wage theory', in *New Concepts in Wage Theory*, eds. G. W. Taylor and F. Pierson (McGraw-Hill, 1957); 7. 'Job vacancy measures and economic analysis', in *The Measurement and Interpretation of Job Vacancies* (NBER, 1966); 8. 'Guideposts, wages and collective bargaining', in *Guidelines, Informal Controls and the Market Place* (Univ. Chicago Press, 1966); 9. 'Inflation and incomes policies: the political economy of recent US experience' (Univ. Monash, 1974); 10. 'Industrial relations, labor economics and policy decisions', *ILRR*, 30, April 1977.

Principal Contributions I started my professional career with an intellectual interest in the determination of wages and prices, in labour economics and industrial organisation. The War Labor Board (1943–7) in World War II and the Korean war period dispute settlement and stabilisation agencies (1950–3) provided extensive experience in wage-setting, labour-management dispute resolution and responsibility for decision-making. These perspectives were reinforced by further university and public responsibilities as well as continuing as a labour-management arbitrator in many industries. These experiences were to influence the choice of research and writing, notions of relevance in economics as well as views on the relations between economic analysis and public policy. Living at the margin of a large number of organisations — labour unions, business organisations, government agencies, university administrations at national and local levels — provided an opportunity to introduce many generations of PhD students and junior faculty to data and materials not otherwise available. A number of the volumes of such research appear in the *Wertheim Publications in Industrial Relations*, numbering over 50 volumes, for which I am the editor.

A major companion to this experience has been industrial relations and economic systems in other countries, partcularly in the Third World. *Industrialism and Industrial Man* (with Kerr, Harbison and Myers) and 12 years of conferences with the Soviets and Eastern Europeans are reflected in publications. Thus the continuing themes of my own writing have been wage determination, the influence of product market structures on wage-setting, the operation of labour markets, decision processes within labour organisations and businesses, the negotiation process, regulatory and other public policy decisions and their interaction with private groups, and the relevance of economic analysis to public policy.

DUNNING, John Harry

Born 1927, Sandy, Bedfordshire, England.
Current Post Prof. Internat. Invest-

ment and Bus. Stud., Univ. Reading, Berkshire, England, 1975–.
Past Posts Ass. Lect., Lect., Sr. Lect., Univ. Southampton, 1952–64; Prof. Econ., Univ. Reading, 1964–75; Res. Ass., Univ. Coll. London, 1981–2; Vis. Prof. Econ., Univs. Western Ontario, 1967–9, Univ. Cal. Berkeley, 1969, Boston, 1976, Montreal, 1980.
Degrees BSc Univ. London, 1951; PhD Univ. Southampton, 1957; Hon. PhD Univ. Uppsala, 1975.
Offices and Honours Member, UN Group of Eminent Persons to Study Effects of Multinational Corps on Econ. Devlp., 1973–4; Member, UK Econ. Planning Council, 1965–8.
Editorial Duties Ed. Boards, *Bus. Ratios*, 1966–8; *JI Bus Stud*, 1979–; *J Bus Res*, 1980–; *WD*, 1981.
Principal Fields of Interest 441 International Investment and Capital Markets; 442 International Business.
Publications *Books:* 1. *American Investment in British Manufacturing Industry* (A & U, 1958, repr. Arno Press, 1976); 2. *British Industry* (with C. J. Thomas), (Hutchinson, 1961, 1963); 3. *Economic Planning and Town Expansion* (Workers Educ. Assoc., 1963); 4. *Studies in International Investment* (A & U, 1970); 5. *An Economic Study of the City of London* (with E. V. Morgan), (A & U, 1971); 6. *The Multinational Enterprise*, ed. (A & U, 1971); 7. *Economic Analysis and the Multinational Enterprise* (A & U, 1974); 8. *International Production and the Multinational Enterprise* (A & U, 1981); 9. *The World's Largest Companies* (with R. D. Pearce), (Gower Press, 1981); 10. *Multinational: Company Performance and Global Trends* (with J. Stopford), (Macmillan, 1983).
Articles: 1. 'The determinants of international production', *OEP*, 25(3), Nov. 1973; 2. 'Theories of business behaviour and the distribution of surplus profits', *Kyk*, 31(4), 1978; 3. 'Towards an eclectic theory of international production: some empirical tests', *JI Bus Stud*, 11, Spring-Summer 1980; 4. 'Explaining changing patterns of international production: in support of the eclectic theory', *OBES*, 41(4), Nov. 1980; 5. 'Explaining the international direct investment position of countries:

towards a dynamic approach', *WA*, 117(2), 1981; 6. 'International business in a changing world environment', *BNLQR*, 143, Dec. 1982; 7. 'Changes in the level and structure of international production: the last 100 years', in *Growth of International Business*, (A & U, 1983).

Principal Contributions Early work in the field of regional and industrial economics. Later became a specialist in international direct investment and the multinational enterprise. Since the mid 1960s, all my major writings have been in this field.

DUNOYER, Charles*

Dates and Birthplace 1786–1862, Carennac, France.

Posts Held Prefect, Allier, 1830–2; Somme, 1832–8; Counsellor of State, 1838–51.

Offices and Honours Member, French Inst., 1832; Pres., Soc. d'Econ. Polit., 1845.

Publications *Books:* 1. *L'Industrie et la morale considerées dans leurs rapports avec la liberté* (1825); 2. *Nouveau traité de'économie sociale*, 2 vols (1830); 3. *De la liberté du travail*, 3 vols (1845); 4. *Le second empire et une nouvelle restauration*, 2 vols (1865).

Career Considered during the nineteenth century as a great economist, his ideas are contained in one evolving work which began as a course of lectures at the Paris Athenaeum and appeared successively, though with considerable additions, as *L'Industrie ..., Nouveau traité ...* and *De la liberté ...* His theory of 'immaterial wealth' is perhaps the chief individual element in his ideas.

DUPONT DE NEMOURS, Pierre Samuel*

Dates and Birthplace 1739–1817, Paris, France.

Posts Held Various official posts in France.

Offices and Honours Member, French Estates-General, 1789; Secretary, French Provisional Govt., 1814.

Publications *Books:* 1. *Physiocratie* (1768).

Career One of the ablest of the physiocrats and their chief publicist, editing the *Ephemerides du citoyen* to which he contributed articles, including a history of economics. In addition to writing voluminously, he held a variety of important official posts and eventually emigrated to America where he founded the famous industrial dynasty of Dupont.

Secondary Literature H. W. Spiegel, ed., *Pierre Samuel Dupont de Nemours on Economic Curves* (JHUP, 1955); J. J. McLain, *The Economic Writings of Du Pont de Nemours* (Univ. Delaware Press, 1977).

DUPUIT, Arsène Jules Etienne Juvenal*

Dates and Birthplace 1804–66, Fossano, Piedmont, Italy.

Posts Held Official, Corps des Ponts et Chaussées, Chief Engineer, Paris, 1850; Inspector-general, Corps, 1885.

Degrees Student, l'Ecole Polytechnique, l'Ecole des Ponts et Chaussées;.

Offices and Honours Member, Soc. d'Econ. Polit.

Publications *Books:* 1. *La liberté-commerciale* (1861); 2. *Calcul économique et économie politique*, ed. F. Etnier (1983).

Articles: 1. 'Mémoire sur le tirage de voiture et sur le frottement de roulement', *Annales des ponts et chaussées*, pt. 2, 3, 1842; transl. as 'On tolls and transport charges', *Internat. Econ. Papers*, 1 (1962); 2. 'De la mésure de l'utilité des travaux publics', *Annales des ponts et chaussées*, 13, 1844; transl. as 'On the measurement of the utility of public works', *Internat. Econ. Papers*, 2 (1952); 3. 'De l'utilité et de sa mésure', *J. des Economistes*, 1, 35, July–Sept. 1853.

Career Whilst an enthusiastic supporter of *laissez faire* arguments, he is mostly remembered for his work on public utilities. His engineering career led him to consider the question of the conditions under which the construction of bridges and public works could be justified. He used a rigorous cost-benefit approach and developed the concept of the demand curve in the process. To measure the utility of public works, he examined the benefits discernible over and above the costs or tolls paid by the user. This is the notion which Marshall later named consumer's surplus. Although frequently hailed as the founder of the concept of marginal cost pricing, Dupont did not in fact carry the argument to its logical conclusion.

Secondary Literature W. S. Vickrey, 'Dupuit, Jules', *IESS*, 4; R. B. Ekelund Jr. and R. F. Hébert, 'Public economics at the Ecole des Ponts et Chaussées: 1830–1850', *J Pub E*, 2, July 1973; R. B. Ekelund Jr. and R. F. Hébert, 'Dupuit and marginal utility: context of the discovery', *HOPE*, 8(3), Summer 1976.

DURAND, David

Born 1912, Ithaca, NY, USA.
Current Post Prof. Emeritus, Sloan School Management, MIT, USA, 1973–.
Past Posts Res. Ass., NBER, 1938–40; US Navy, 1942–5; Res. Staff, NBER, 1946–54; Res. Assoc., MIT, 1954–5; Assoc. Prof., MIT, 1955–8; Prof. Management, MIT, 1958–73; Vis. Prof., Technical Univ. Berlin, W. Germany, 1968, 1971–2.
Degrees BA (Maths.) Cornell Univ., 1934; MA, PhD Columbia Univ., 1938, 1941.
Offices and Honours Member, Inst. Advanced Study, Princeton Univ., 1941.
Editorial Duties Assoc. Ed., *J Fin*, 1964–6, *Fin Management*, 1979–.
Principal Fields of Interest 211 Econometric and Statistical Methods and Models; 313 Capital Markets; 521 Business Finance.
Publications *Books:* 1. *Risk Elements in Consumer Instalment Financing* (NBER, 1941); 2. *Basic Yields of Corporate Bonds: 1900–1942* (NBER, 1942); 3. *Basic Yields of Bonds 1926–1947: Their Measurement and Pattern* (with W. J. Winn), (NBER, 1947); 4. *Mortgage Lending Experience in Agriculture* (with L. A. Jones), (Princeton

Univ. Press, 1954); 5. *Bank Stocks and the Bank Capital Problem* (NBER, 1957); 6. *Stable Chaos: An Introduction to Statistical Control* (Gen. Learning Press, 1971).
Articles: 1. 'Some thoughts on marginal productivity, with special reference to Professor Douglas' analysis', *JPE*, 45(6), Dec. 1937; 2. 'Costs of debt and equity funds for business: trends and problems of measurement', in *Conference on Research in Business Finance* (NBER, 1952), repr. in *The Management of Corporate Capital*, ed. E. Solomon (Free Press, 1959), and *The Theory of Business Finance: A Book of Readings*, eds. S. H. Archer and C. A. D'Ambrosio (Macmillan, 1967); 3. 'Bank stocks and the analysis of covariance', *Em*, 23(1), Jan. 1955; 4. 'Growth stocks and the Petersburg paradox', *J Fin*, 12(3), Sept. 1957; repr. in *Modern Developments in Investment Management: A Book of Readings*, eds. J. Lorie and R. Brealey (Praeger, 1972); 5. 'Modifications of the Rayleigh test for uniformity in analysis of two-dimensional orientation data' (with J. A. Greenwood), *J. Geology*, 66(3), May 1958; 6. 'The cost of capital, corporation finance and the theory of investment: comment', *AER*, 49(4), Sept. 1959, repr. in *The Management of Corporate Capital*, ed. E. Solomon (Free Press 1959), and in *The Theory of Business Finance, op. cit.*; 7. 'The cost of capital to the TK corporation is 00.0%: or, much ado about very little', in *Decision-making Criteria for Capital Expenditures* (Eng. Economist, 1966); 8. 'Die Kosten des Kapitals: ein Doppelkriterium für profitable Investitionen' (with E. Durand), *Betriebswirtschaftliche Forschung und Praxis*, 24(1), Jan. 1972; 9. 'Indices of profitability: aids to judgement in capital budgeting', *J Bank Res*, 3(4), Winter 1973; 10. 'Payout period, time spread and duration: aids to judgement in capital budgeting', *J Bank Res*, 5(1), Spring 1974.
Principal Contributions Contributions fall under one or both of two main headings: statistics (not always related to economics) and finance. Under finance the main headings are: credit risk, capital budgeting and the cost of capital, term structure of interest rates,

and time as a dimension of investment. Early work on term structure (books 2 and 3) was fundamental. Early work on cost of capital (articles 2 and 6) was involved in a famous controversy with Modigliani and Miller and was widely reprinted. Later work is concerned mainly with incorporating the theme of time as a dimension of investment with that of capital budgeting.

DURBIN, Evan Frank Mottram*

Dates and Birthplace 1906–48, England.
Posts Held Lect., New Coll., Oxford; Lect., LSE, Civil Servant, World War II; MP (Labour), 1945–8; Parliamentary Secretary, UK Ministry of Works, 1947–8.
Degree BA (Philo., Polit. and Econ.) Univ. Oxford.
Offices and Honours Jr., Sr. Webb Medley Scholar; Ricardo Fellow, LSE.
Publications *Books:* 1. *Purchasing Power and Trade Depression* (1933); 2. *The Problem of Credit Policy* (1935); 3. *Personal Aggressiveness and War* (with J. Bowlby), (1938); 4. *The Politics of Democratic Socialism* (1940); 5. *What Have We To Defend?* (1942); 6. *Problems of Economic Planning* (1949).
Career Coming to economics from the natural sciences, he brought to it a formidable logical ability. His perception of the need for state planning led him into Labour politics, as did the ethical values of his non-conformist family background. He favoured a devolved and responsive planning system, but just when his elevation to ministerial rank made it possible to realise his views, he was killed in a swimming accident.
Secondary Literature E. H. Phelps Brown, 'Evan Durbin 1906–1948', *Ec*, N.S. 18, Feb. 1951.

E

EASTERLIN, Richard Ainley

Born 1926, NJ, USA.
Current Post Prof. Econ., UCLA, CA, USA, 1982–.

Past Posts Instr., Ass. Prof., Assoc. Prof., Prof. Econ., William R. Kenan Jr. Prof., Univ. Penn., 1948–53, 1953–6. 1956–60, 1960–78, 1978–82; Vis. Prof., Stanford Univ., 1960–1, Univ. Warwick, England, 1978.
Degrees ME (Eng.) Stevens Inst. Technology, 1945; MA, PhD Univ. Penn., 1949, 1953.
Offices and Honours Press., Pop. Assoc. Amer., 1978; Pres., EHA, 1980; Fellow, Em Soc, 1983; Fellow, AAAS, 1978; Sherman Fairchild Disting. Scholar, Cal. Inst. Technology, 1980–1; Fellow, Center Advanced Study Behavioral Sciences, Stanford, CA, 1970–1
Editorial Duties Ed. Boards, *AER*, 1965–70, *JEL*, 1968–70, *JEH*, 1965–70, 1974–9, *Explor. Econ. Hist.*, 1973–, *Demograph*, 1965–7, *J Ec Behav*, 1982–; Advisory Board, *Pop. and Devlp. Rev.*, 1980–.
Principal Fields of Interest 840 Demographic Economics; 041 Economic History; General.
Publications *Books:* 1. *Population Redistribution and Economic Growth, United States, 1870–1950*, 2 vols. (with others) (Amer. Philo. Soc., 1957, 1960); 2. *The American Baby Boom in Historical Perspective* (NBER, 1962); 3. *Population, Labor Force, and Long Swings in Economic Growth: The American Experience* (Columbia Univ. Press, 1968); 4. *American Economic Growth: An Economist's History of the United States,* co-ed. (Harper & Row, 1972); 5. *Population and Economic Change in Developing Countries,* ed. (Univ. Chicago Press, 1980); 6. *Birth and Fortune: The Impact of Numbers on Personal Welfare* (Basic Books, 1980); 7. *Immigration* (with D. Ward, W. S. Bernard and R. Ueda), (Belknap Press, 1982); 8. *An Exploratory Study of the 'Synthesis Framework' of Fertility Determination with WFS Core Questionnaire Data* (with E. M. Crimmins), (World Fertility Survey, 1982).
Articles: 1. 'Regional income trends, 1840–1950', in *American Economic History,* ed. S. E. Harris (McGraw-Hill, 1961); 2. 'Towards a socio-economic theory of fertility: a survey of recent research on economic factors in American fertility', in *Fertility and*

Family Planning: A World View, eds. S. J. Behrman, et al. (Michigan Press, 1969); 3. 'Economic growth: an overview', in *International Encyclopedia of the Social Sciences,* ed. D. L. Sills (Macmillan, Free Press, 1968); 4. 'Does economic growth improve the human lot?', in *Nations and Households in Economic Growth: Essays in Honor of Moses Abramovitz,* eds. P. A. David and M. W. Reder (Academic Press, 1974); 5. 'Population change and farm settlement in the northern United States', *JEH,* 36(1), March 1976; 6. 'What will 1984 be like? Socioeconomic implications of the recent twists in age structure', *Demography,* 15(4), Nov. 1978; 7. 'The economics and sociology of fertility: a synthesis', in *Historical Studies of Changing Fertility,* ed. C. Tilly (Princeton Univ. Press, 1978); 8. 'Toward a more general economic model of fertility determination: endogenous preferences and natural fertility' (with R. A. Pollak and M. L. Wachter), in *Population and Economic Change in Developing Countries, op. cit.;* 9. 'Why isn't the whole world developed?', *JEH,* 41(1), March 1981; 10. 'New perspectives on the demographic transition: a theoretical and empirical analysis of an Indian state, 1951–1975' (with E. Crimmins, S. Jejeebhoy and K. Srinivasan), *EDCC,* 32(4), Jan. 1984.

Principal Contributions My basic research motivation has been better understanding of various real world conditions: the limited spread of modern economic growth; the meaning of economic welfare and its relation to economic growth; the transition from high to low fertility that has invariably accompanied modernisation; 'long swings' of 15 to 25 years in population and economic growth in the US and other developed countries; the post World War II American baby boom and bust and associated swings in economic and social conditions relating to women's work, divorce, suicide, crime, etc. Progress on these problems has often involved empirical work to establish more clearly the facts to be explained — from estimation of regional incomes and reconstruction of trends in childbearing behaviour in the US to an attempt to chart the rise of school enrolments in countries throughout the world. It has required the use of economic theory to organise data and formulate hypotheses, and led to new theorising on topics such as childbearing behaviour. It has called for learning new techniques that fall outside the purview of economics, such as demographic methodology.

Finally, the resistance of reality to purely economic interpretation has increasingly led me to recognise the relevance of important theoretical concepts in other social sciences, such as 'relative deprivation' and 'natural' (i.e. unregulated) fertility, and to try to reconcile such concepts with received economic doctrine. I would like to feel that my work has provided some insight into both the long-term trend and post-World War II swing in American fertility; the factors responsible for the demographic transition in today's developing countries; the importance of education in the spread of economic development; the interrelations between social conditions and economic change; and the relativity of economic welfare. Perhaps also it may have contributed to a better economic theory of human fertility, and to the promotion of relative income-type concepts in economic analysis.

EATON, B. Curtis

Born 1943, Price, UT, USA.
Current Post Prof. Econ., Univ. Toronto, Ont., Canada, 1982–.
Past Posts Ass. Prof., Assoc. Prof., Prof. Econ., Univ. British Columbia, 1969–73, 1974–8, 1979–81.
Degrees BA, PhD Univ. Colorado, 1965, 1969.
Offices and Honours Canada Council Leave Fellow, 1974–5, 1979–80.
Editorial Duties Ed. Board, *CJE.*
Principal Fields of Interest 022 Microeconomic Theory; 600 Industrial Organisaton.
Publications *Articles:* 1. 'Spatial competition revisited', *CJE,* 5(2), May 1972; 2. 'The principle of minimum differentiation reconsidered: some new developments in the theory of spatial

competition' (with R. G. Lipsey), *REStud,* 42(1), Jan. 1975; 3. 'Free entry in one-dimensional models: pure profits and multiple equilibria', *J Reg S,* 16(1), 1976; 4. 'Freedom of entry and the existence of pure profit' (with R. G. Lipsey), *EJ,* 88, Sept. 1978; 5. 'The theory of market pre-emption: the persistence of excess capacity and monopoly in growing spatial markets' (with R. G. Lipsey), *Ec,* 46, May 1976; 6. 'Comparison shopping and the clustering of homogeneous firms' (with R. G. Lipsey), *J Reg S,* 19(4), Nov. 1979; 7. 'Exit barriers are entry barriers: the durability of capital as a barrier to entry' (with R. G. Lipsey), *Bell JE,* 11(2), Autumn 1980; 8. 'An economic theory of central places' (with R. G. Lipsey), *EJ,* 92, March 1982; 9. 'Agent compensation and the limits of bonding' (with W. White), *EI,* 26(3), July 1982; 10. 'The economy of high wages: an agency problem' (with W. White), *Ec,* 50, May 1983.

Principal Contributions Choice of plant location and/or the development of differentiated products invariably involves sunk costs. Much of my research, primarily in collaboration with Richard Lispsy, has focussed on the implications of sunk costs in markets where products are differentiated, either spatially or by product characteristics. The implications for static equilibrium in such markets include non-uniqueness of equilibrium and the existence of pure profit in free-entry equilibrium. The existence of sunk costs and the potential for pure profit imply that incumbent firms have the ability and the incentive to choose strategically among the set of possible free-entry equilibria. There are three major implications of strategic choice of product line: one must inevitably expect an oligopolistic market structure: much of the potential profit is dissipated through early, strategic introduction of new products to control entry; there is no presumption that this behaviour necessarily is anti-social.

Another focus of my research, again in collaboration with Lipsey, has been the attempt to understand the gross features of the location of retail activity in space. The facts that transportation is costly and that shoppers are indivisible create the positive demand externalities between firms selling different products and between firms selling similar products when shoppers compare goods. These demand externalities explain the gross features of agglomeration of retail activity in space. The most recent focus of my research, in collaboration with William White, has been on the role which assets play in principal-agent problems. Assets allow individuals to enter into efficient, incentive-compatible contracts. It follows that efficiency and distribution are not separable considerations: the set of attainable allocations is determined by the distribution of assets. Further, principals may find it in their interest to augment agents' assets by paying above market, contingent wages.

ECKAUS, Richard Samuel

Born 1926, Kansas City, MO, USA.
Current Post Ford Internat. Prof. Econ., MIT, Cambridge, MA, 1977–.
Past Posts Instr. Econ., Babson Inst., 1948–50; Ass. Prof., Assoc. Prof. Econ., Brandeis Univ., 1951–4, 1954–62; Assoc. Prof. Econ., Prof. Econ., MIT, 1962–5, 1965–77.
Degrees BS (Electrical Eng.) Iowa State Univ., 1944; MA Washington Univ., 1946; PhD MIT, 1954.
Principal Fields of Interest 112 Economic Development Models; 113 Economic Planning Theory; 121 Less Industrialised Countries.
Publications *Books:* 1. *Planning for Growth* (with K. Parikh), (MIT Press, 1968); 2. *Development and Planning,* co-ed. (with J. Bhagwati), (A & U, 1973); 3. *Appropriate Technologies for Developing Countries* (NAS, 1977). *Articles:* 1. 'The factor proportions problem in economic development', *AER,* 45(4), Sept. 1955, repr. in *L'Industria,* Dec. 1955, and *The Economics of Underdevelopment,* eds. A. A. Agarwal and S. P. Singh (OUP, 1958); 2. 'The north-south differential in Italian economic development', *JEH,* 21(3), Sept. 1961; 3. 'Economic criteria for education and training', *REStat,* 46(2), May 1964; 4. 'Economic criteria for

foreign aid for economic development', in *Foreign Aid*, ed. J. Bhagwati (A & U, 1970); 5. 'The structure of the financiera system in Mexico, 1940–70', *Cemla Boletin Mensual*, 21, May 1975; 6. 'Strategies of development and the international division of work', *Second Conferencia Internacional Sobre Economia Portuguesa*, 1980; 7. 'A social accounting matrix for Egypt, 1976' (with F. D. McCarthy and A. M. Eldin), *J Econ Devlp*, 9(2), Oct. 1981; 8. 'Observations on the conditionality of financial institutions', *WD*, 10(9), Sept. 1982; 9. 'Consequences of changes in subsidy policy in Egypt', in *Economic Structure and Performance*, ed. L. Wesphal (Academic Press, 1983).

Principal Contributions There have been several main strands. One has been mainly microeconomic, suggesting the importance of considering the possibilities and implications of limited technical substitutability of resources used in production. While this hypothesis has remained a controversial one, it has also been fruitful, and has been adopted in many types of theoretical and applied development models. An extension of this microeconomic interest was my work on the economics of education which generated calculations of 'requirements' for labour with different levels of formal education as well as different levels of job training. This produced what was, perhaps, one of the first suggestions of the possibility of imbalances between the numbers of graduates of schools at different levels of schooling and the demand for workers with those levels. The construction of relatively large intertemporal, multisectoral models for analysis of development options has been another area of concentration. This started in a collaborative effort for India, and resulted in one of the first models of its type which had a linear programming structure. The models were extended and elaborated in further collaborative work in a number of other countries: Chile, Egypt and Mexico. In the last case, extensive nonlinearities were embodied in the model overcoming many of the original limitations.

Collaboration in the construction and application of multisector computable general equilibrium models has been an extension of the interest in policy models. The modification of the models to include substitution possibilities for energy sources of various types has been one type of extension of such models. Other nonlinearities have also been embodied. All of this model-building has involved extensive data preparation. The study of the development problems, both general and specific, has resulted in large- and small-scale modelling as well as project and sector studies, and estimation and refinement of data, nearly always with local collaboration. Such work has been undertaken in Chile, Costa Rica, Egypt, India, Jamaica, Mexico, Portugal, Sri Lanka and Turkey.

ECKSTEIN, Otto*

Dates and Birthplace 1926–84, Ulm, W. Germany.

Posts Held Technical Dir., Joint Econ. Comm., US Congress, 1959–60; Paul M. Warburg Prof. Econ., Harvard Univ., 1963–84; Member, US President's Council Econ. Advisers, 1964–6; Pres., Data Resources Inc., Lexington, MA, USA, 1972–84.

Degrees BA Princeton Univ., 1951, 1966; MA, PhD Harvard Univ., 1952, 1955; Hon. degree, Free Univ. Brussels, 1975.

Offices and Honours Fellow, ASA, Em Soc, Nat. Assoc. Bus. Economists; Exec. Comm., Vice-Pres., AEA, 1967–70, 1981.

Publications *Books:* 1. *Water Resource Development: The Economics of Project Evaluation* (Harvard Univ. Press, 1958); 2. *Staff Report on Employment, Growth, and Price Levels* (with others), US Congress, Joint Econ. Comm. (US Govt. Printing Office, 1959); 3. *The Great Recession* (N-H, 1978); 4. *Public Finance* (Prentice-Hall, 1979); 5. *Core Inflation* (Prentice-Hall, 1981).

Articles: 1. 'Investment criteria for economic development and the theory of intertemporal welfare economics', *QJE*, 71, Feb. 1957; 2. 'The determination of money wages in American industry' (with T. A. Wilson), *QJE*, 76,

Aug. 1972; 3. 'A theory of the wage-price process in modern industry', *REStud*, 31, Oct. 1964; 4. 'The price equation' (with G. Fromm), *AER*, 58(5), Dec. 1968; 5. 'The data resources model: uses, structure and the analysis of the US economy' (with E. Green and A. Sinai), *Int ER*, 15(3), Oct. 1974.

Career Research on cost-benefit analysis, public finance and inflation theory but best known for his econometric models of the US economy, regularly employed for forecasting the effects of particular economic policies. He appeared frequently before Congressional committees to testify on economic questions.

EDEN, Frederck Morton*

Dates and Birthplace 1766–1809, England.
Posts Held Founder and Chairman, Globe Insurance Co.
Degrees BA, MA, Univ. Oxford, 1787, 1789.
Publications *Books:* 1. *The State of the Poor*, 3 vols (1797); 2. *Estimate of the Number of Inhabitants in Great Britain and Ireland* (1800); 3. *Address on Maritime Rights* (1808).
Career His *State of the Poor* is the result of a major social investigation involving travel and correspondence on his part and the employment of a full-time researcher. It contains great quantities of factual information, parish by parish, including family budgets. His conclusions were in favour of friendly societies and against poor laws or minimum wages.
Secondary Literature D. W. Douglas, 'Eden, Sir Frederick Morton', *ESS*, 5.

EDGEWORTH, Francis Ysidro*

Dates and Birthplace 1845–1926, Edgeworthstown, Co. Longford, Ireland.
Posts Held Lect. Logic, Tooke Prof. Econ. Science and Stats., King's Coll. London, 1880–89, 1890–1; Drummond Prof. Polit. Econ., Fellow, All Souls Coll. Oxford, 1891–1922.
Degree BA Univ. Oxford, 1869.

Offices and Honours Fellow, BA; Vice-Pres., RES; Pres., RSS; Pres., Econ. Section, BAAS, 1889, 1922; Ed., *EJ*, 1891–1926.
Publications *Books:* 1. *New and Old Methods of Ethics* (1877); 2. *Mathematical Psychics* (1881, 1953); 3. *Metretike* (1887); 4. *Papers Relating to Political Economy*, 3 vols (1891–1921, 1963).
Career His earliest writings are concerned with the application of mathematics to social science questions and in *Mathematical Psychics* he worked out practical aspects of utilitarian ethics in mathematical form. The insights on exchange equilibrium, welfare economics and the theory of barter are still valuable. His chief output was in article form on topics such as taxation, monopoly, index numbers and value of money. His exposition was obscure and his personality was retiring, with the result that his ideas are continually being rediscovered by those who arrive at them in their own way. Though his work was never drawn together into a comprehensive scheme, he is still valued for his various precedents in mathematical economics and statistics. His ideas on the 'contract curve' and the 'core' of an exchange economy have recently attracted considerable attention. His editorship of the *EJ* was of major value to the British economic community.
Secondary Literature J. M. Keynes, 'Frances Ysidro Edgeworth: 1845–1926', in *Essays in Biography* (Macmillan, 1933, 1972); C. Hildreth, 'Edgeworth, Francis Ysidro', *IESS*, 4; J. Creedy, 'F. Y. Edgeworth', in *Pioneers of Modern Economics in Britain*, eds. D. P. O'Brien and J. R. Presley (Macmillan, 1981).

EDWARDS, Richard C.

Born 1944, Minot, NDak, USA.
Current Post Prof. Econ., Univ. Mass.-Amherst, MA, USA, 1982–.
Past Posts Res. Econ., NBER, New York, 1970–1; Res. Assoc., Harvard Grad. School Educ., 1972–4; Ass., Assoc. Econ., Univ. Mass.-Amherst,

1974–82; Vis. Prof. Econ., Univ. di Siena, Italy, 1983.
Degrees BA Grinnell Coll., 1966; PhD Harvard Univ., 1972.
Principal Fields of Interest 820 Labour Markets.
Publications *Books:* 1. *Contested Terrain: The Transformation of the Workplace in the Twentieth Century* (Basic Books, 1979).
Articles: 1. 'A radical approach to economics: basis for a new curriculum' (with A. MacEwan and Staff of Soc. Sciences 125), *AER*, 60(2), May 1970; repr. in *Problems in Political Economy: An Urban Perspective*, ed. D. Gordon (D. C. Heath, 1971); 2. 'Economic sophistication in nineteenth-century congressional tariff debates', *JEH*, 30(4), Dec. 1970; 3. 'A theory of labour market segmentation' (with D. Gordon and M. Reich), *AER*, 63(2), May 1973, repr. in *Industrial Relations Res. Assoc. Series, Proceedings of the Twenty-Fifth Annual Winter Meeting*, Dec. 1972, in *Education in the Corporate World*, ed. M. Carnoy (David McKay, 1975), in *Wealth, Income and Inequality*, ed. A. B. Atkinson (OUP, 1980), in *The Economics of Women and Work*, ed. A. Amsden (Penguin, 1980); 4. 'Stages in corporate stability and the risks of corporate failure', *JEH*, 35(3), June 1975; 5. 'Individual traits and organizational incentives: what makes a "good" worker?', *JHR*, 11(1), Winter 1976; 6. 'Personal traits and "success" in schooling and work', *Educ. and Psychologic Measurement*, Spring 1977; 7. 'The social relations of production at the point of production', *Insurgent Sociologist*, Fall 1978; 8. 'Il terrano conteso', *Quaderni: Ressenga Sindicale*, 98, 99, Sept.–Dec. 1982; 9. 'Work incentives and worker responses in bureaucratic enterprises: an empirical study', *Res. Soc. Stratification and Mobility*, 2(2), Spring 1983.
Principal Contributions My principal contribution has been to develop the theory of how labour processes are organised in large corporations and how labour markets are structured in the modern contemporary economy. Primarily this work has involved extending the ideas and insights of Marx, Weber and Schumpeter to construct a

theoretical basis for developing an institutional historical account of contemporary American capitalism. This research has demonstrated how relations of power (what are termed 'systems of control' in *Contested Terrain*) are constructed to regulate social and conflictual interactions between employers and workers as the former attempt to maximise profits, and how these forces account for such institutional forms as bureaucratic control and internal labour markets. This work has touched on the fields of general economic theory, theories of institutional change, industrial relations, management, industrial organisation, and labour economics. A second contribution has been in the area of economic history. After some early work on diverse topics, this work has focussed on the historical transformation of work and workplaces in the US economy. The principal argument here is how workplace relations have been shaped by social and conflictual (as well as technological) factors. A third contribution is the area of developing a coherent, consistent, and assessible account or 'vision' of economic processes as an alternative to mainstream neoclassical analysis. This effort involves both the construction of a theoretically grounded and empirically plausible explanation of how the modern political economy works and the creation of pedagogical material appropriate to this task.

EHRENBERG, Ronald G.

Born 1946, New York City, NY, USA.
Current Post Prof. Econ. Labor Econ., Cornell Univ., Ithaca, NY, USA, 1977–.
Past Posts Instr., Northwestern Univ., 1970; Staff Econ., US President's Council Econ. Advisers, Washington, DC, 1970; Ass. Prof, Loyola Univ., Chicago, 1970–1; Assoc. Prof., Univ. Mass., 1971–5; Assoc. Prof., Cornell Univ., 1975–7; Vis. Prof., Harvard Univ., 1976–9; Vis. Scholar, NBER, 1980; Vis. Prof., Tel Aviv Univ., 1980; Res. Assoc., NBER, 1981.

Degrees BA Harpur Coll., State Univ. NY Binghamton, 1966; MA PhD Northwestern Univ., 1970.

Offices and Honours NDEA Fellow, 1966–9; Woodrow Wilson Fellow, 1969–70.

Editorial Duties Ed., *Res. Labor Econ.*, 1977; Ed. Board, *J Econ. and Bus.*, 1975–9, *ILRR*, 1977, *Econ. Letters*, 1978, *AER*, 1981–4.

Principal Fields of Interest 820 Labour Markets; Public Policy; 830 Trade Unions and Collective Bargaining; 636 Nonprofit Industries; Theory and Studies.

Publications *Books:* 1. *Fringe Benefits and Overtime Behavior* (D. C. Heath, 1971); 2. *The Demand for State and Local Government Employees* (D. C. Heath, 1972); 3. *Dispute Resolution Under Fact-Finding and Arbitration* (with T. Kochan, *et al.*), (Amer. Arbitration Assoc., 1979); 4. *The Regulatory Process and Labor Earnings* (Academic Press, 1979); 5. *Longer Hours or More Jobs?* (with P. Schumann), (Industrial Labor Relations Press, 1982); 6. *Modern Labor Economics: Theory and Public Policy* (with R. Smith), (Scott Foresman, 1982, 1985); 7. *Labor Economics and Labor Relations* (with R. Flanagan and R. Smith), (Scott Foresman, 1984).

Articles: 1. 'Absenteeism and the overtime decision', *AER*, 60(3), June 1970; 2. 'Heterogeneous labor, the internal labor market and the dynamics of the employment-hours decision', *JET*, 3, March 1971; 3. 'The demand for state and local government employees', *AER*, 63(3), June 1973; 4. 'Household allocation of time and church attendance' (with C. Azzi), *JPE*, 83, Feb. 1975; 5. 'Unemployment insurance, duration of unemployment and subsequent wage gains' (with R. Oaxaca), *AER*, 66(5), Dec. 1976; 6. 'The costs of defined benefit plans and firm adjustments' (with B. Barnow), *QJE*, 83, Nov. 1979; 7. 'Estimating the narcotic effect of public sector impasse procedures' (with R. Butler), *ILRR*, 35, Oct. 1981; 8. 'Cost of living adjustment clauses in union contracts: a summary of results', *J Lab E*, 1, July 1983; 9. 'Optimal financial aid policies for a selective university' (with D. Sherman),

JHR, 18, Spring 1984; 10. 'Public sector labor markets' (with J. Schwarz), in *Handbook of Labor Economics*, eds. O. Ashenfelter and R. Layard (N-H, forthcoming, 1985).

Principal Contributions Throughout my career my interests have focussed on the interaction of government and the labour market. One strand of research has been directed towards public-sector labour markets *per se* and has addressed issues like the demand for labour, the effects of unions on wages and productivity, compensating wage differentials for fringe benefits, and the effects of public-sector dispute resolution procedures. Throughout this research programme I have stressed the applicability of maximising models to the government sector and the value of using sophisticated econometric methods.

A second strand of research has focussed on evaluating the effects of labour market programmes, legislation and institutions on labour market outcomes, with the goal of providing information that would be useful to policy-makers. Among the topics I have studied here are minimum wage laws, the overtime pay premium, the unemployment insurance system, pension reform legislation, the effects of regulation on labour earnings, and anti-discrimination programmes. Throughout this research I have again stressed the need to use rigorous economic and econometric models.

My research led naturally to the writing of two labour economics and labour relations texts that are oriented towards the use of economics in policy analysis. In recent years I have also become interested in using economic theory to explain the form union contract provisions take and to help determine the optimal allocation of resources at universities. My current focus in the latter area is on financial aid policies and this has led me to the study of the effects of these policies on students.

EHRLICH, Issac

Born 1938, Tel Aviv, Israel.
Current Post Melvin H. Baker Prof.

Amer. Enterprise and Prof. Econ., State Univ. NY, Buffalo, NY, USA, 1977–.

Past Posts Instr., Ass. Prof., Assoc. Prof. Bus. Econ., Univ. Chicago, 1969–70, 1971–4, 1974–7; Lect. Econ., Tel Aviv Univ., 1971–2; Vis. Assoc. Prof. Law and Econ., Univ. Virginia, 1973.

Degrees BA (Econ. and Hist. Muslim People) Hebrew Univ., Jerusalem, 1964; PhD Columbia Univ., 1970.

Offices and Honours Ford Foundation Doctoral Fellow; Sr. Res. Assoc., NBER, 1970–1.

Principal Fields of Interest 026 Economics of Uncertainty and Information; 913 Economics of Health; 916 Economics of Crime.

Publications *Books:* 1. *National Health Policy: What Role for Government?* (Hoover Inst. Press, 1982).

Articles: 1. 'Market insurance, self-insurance and self-protection' (with G. S. Becker), *JPE,* 80(4), July–Aug. 1972; 2. 'Participation in illegitimate activities — a theoretical and empirical investigation', *JPE,* 81(3), May–June 1973, repr. in *The Economics of Crime and Law Enforcement,* eds. L. R. McPheters and W. B. Strange (Charles C. Thomas, 1974); 3. 'The deterrent effect of capital punishment – a question of life and death', *AER,* 65(3), June 1975; 4. 'Asset management, allocation of time and returns to savings' (with U. Ben-Zion), *EI,* 14(4), Dec. 1976; 5. 'Capital punishment and deterrence: some further thoughts and additional evidence', *JPE,* 85(4), Aug. 1977, repr. in *Criminology Review Yearbook,* eds. R. Messinger and L. Bittner (Sage, 1979); 6. 'The economic approach to crime — a preliminary assessment', in *Criminology Review Yearbook, op. cit.,* repr. in *Readings in the Economics of Law,* eds. A. I. Ogus and C. G. Veljanovski (OUP, 1984); 7. 'On the usefulness of controlling individuals: an economic analysis of rehabilitation, incapacitation and deterrence', *AER,* 71(3), June 1981; 8. 'On the rationale for national health insurance: where did the private market fail?', in *National Health Policy: What Role for Government?, op. cit.;* 9. 'The optimum enforcement of laws and the concept of justice: a positive analysis', *Internat. Rev. Law and Econ.* 2, June 1982; 10. 'The derived demand for advertising: a theoretical and empirical investigation' (with L. Fisher), *AER,* 72(3), June 1982.

Principal Contributions Applications of general economic theory in the study of diversified human conduct both in the market place and in a variety of nonmarket activities with a particular emphasis on the role of time, information, and uncertainty in influencing that conduct. The most provocative illustration concerns participation in illegitimate activities. Use of optimisation and equilibrium analysis and econometric methodology to explain and measure the rate and direction of all legal infractions, including serious crimes, has challenged received theories in criminology, and opened up a new research frontier: the economics of crime. Work on behaviour under uncertainty has provided a framework for studying time allocation into risky endeavours in general and the joint demand for market insurance, and a variety of self-insurance and self-protection activities that influence risk bearing.

Work on asset management, the derived demand for advertising, and the economics of health and longevity, a more current research focus, has had its origins in earlier work through its links to the economics of time, information and uncertainty. Work on asset management represents a deviation from the perfect market hypothesis in finance in that it allows for the role of individual time and acquired special knowledge in the determination of returns on managed assets, the selection of individual portfolios, and consumption and production decisions over the life-cycle. Work on advertising links firms' use of conventional advertising and all other selling efforts to consumers' search (hence value of time) and need for specific knowledge concerning the attributes of goods and services for which individual knowledge is incomplete. Work on the demand for longevity deals with length of life as a commodity which competes with *quality* of life over allocation of lifetime resources, and analyses investment in health and longevity as an integral part of both human capital theory and the general theory of self-protection against detrimental risks to life.

EINAUDI, Luigi*

Dates and Birthplace 1874–1961, Carrù, Italy.
Posts Held Fellow Polit. Econ., Prof. Fin. Science, 1899, 1907, Univ. Turin; Governor, Bank of Italy, 1945.
Offices Deputy, Italian Constituent Assembly, 1945; Italian Minister Budget, 1947; Senator, 1948; Pres., Italian Republic, 1948–55.
Publications *Books:* 1. *Studi sugli effetti delle imposte* (1902); 2. *La terra e l'imposta* (1924); 3. *Principi di scienza della finanza* (1932, 1948); 4. *I problemi economici della federazione Europea* (1945); 5. *Lezioni di politica sociale* (1949).
Articles: 1. 'Fifty years of Italian economic thought: 1896–1946. Reminiscences', *Cinquant'anni di vita intellectuale Italiana* (1950), repr. in *Internat. Econ. Papers*, 5, eds. A. T. Peacock, *et al.* (Macmillan, 1955)
Career An economist of the classical school, he was also a liberal in politics. In addition to his writings on finance and taxation, he contributed to economic history and history of economic thought. His personal library of economic works was legendary. Probably his outstanding economic work is *Principi ...* (1932) but his editorial and journalistic work with *La riforma sociale* and *Rivista di storia economica* were also important. Forced to flee to Switzerland in 1943, his return to Italy was followed by a period of outstanding achievement as a statesman.

EISNER, Robert

Born 1922, New York City, NY, USA.
Current Post William R. Kenan Prof. Econ., Northwestern Univ., Evanston, IL, USA, 1974–.
Past Posts Econ. and Stat., US Office Price Info., Office War Info., Office Housing Expediter, 1941–7; Jr. Instr. Polit. Econ., Johns Hopkins Univ., 1951; Instr., Res. Ass., Prof. Econ. Univ. Illinois, 1950–2; Ass. Prof., Assoc. Prof., Prof., Northwestern Univ., 1952–4, 1954–6, 1960–74; Vis. Disting Prof., Univ. Binghamton, 1971; Monash Univ., Australia, 1982; Sr. Res. Assoc., NBER, 1969–78.
Degrees BSS City Coll. NY, 1940; MA Columbia Univ, 1942; PhD Johns Hopkins Univ., 1951.
Offices and Honours Guggenheim Foundation Fellow, 1960; Fellow, Center Advanced Study Behavioral Sciences, Stanford, 1968; Member, Exec. Comm., Vice-Pres., Acting Pres.-elect, AEA, 1970–3, 1977, 1977; Pres., MEA, 1982–3; Fellow, Em Soc.
Editorial Duties Ed. Board, *AER*, 1966–8, *JEL*; Assoc. Ed., *REStat*.
Principal Fields of Interest 023 Macroeconomic Theory; 133 General Outlook and Stabilisation Theories and Policies; 221 National Income Accounting.
Publications *Books:* 1. *Determinants of Capital Expenditures: An Interview Study* (Univ. Illinois, 1956); 2. *Some Factors in Growth Reconsidered* (Center Planning and Econ. Res. Athens, 1966); 3. *Factors in Business Investment* (Ballinger, 1978).
Articles: 1. 'Determinants of business investment' (with R. H. Strotz), in *Impacts of Monetary Policy* (Prentice-Hall, 1963), repr. in *Readings in Economic Statistics & Econometrics*, ed. A. Zellner (Little Brown, 1968), and *Readings in Macroeconomics, Theory, Evidence and Policy*, ed. N. F. Keiser (Prentice-Hall, 1970); 2. 'On growth models and the neo-classical resurgence', *EJ*, 68, Dec. 1958; 3. 'The permanent income hypothesis: comment', *AER*, 48(5), Dec. 1958; 4. 'A distributed lag investment function', *Em*, 28, Jan. 1960; 5. 'A permanent income theory for investment: some empirical exploration', *AER*, 57(8), June 1967; 6. 'Investment behavior and neoclassical theory' (with M. I. Nadiri), *REStat*, 50, August 1968, repr. in *Aggregate Investment: Selected Readings*, ed. J. F. Helliwell (Penguin, 1976); 7. 'Fiscal and monetary policy reconsidered', *AER*, 59(5), Dec. 1969; 8. 'Total incomes in the United States, 1946 to 1976: a sum-

mary report', *RIW*, June 1982; 9. 'Tax policy and investment in major U.S. macroeconomic econometric models' (with R. S. Chirinko), *J Pub E*, 20(2), April 1983; 10. 'A new view of the federal debt and budget deficits' (with P. J. Pieper), *AER*, 74(1), March 1984.

Principal Contributions I have made major contributions to the formulation and estimation of the investment function, macroeconomic theory and policy, and extended measures of income and output. My early work on the distributed lag investment function and then my seminal paper with Robert H. Strotz integrated the theory of investment and changing demands for capital in terms of adjustment costs. Traditional dichotomies of long and short run were generalised to paths of capital and investment over time, determined by the increasing cost of more rapid change.

In later work I brought forth the role of expectations and the implications of the permanent income hypothesis for estimation of both consumption and investment functions. With M. I. Nadiri, I offered modifications and generalisations of the 'neoclassical' investment function in terms of unconstrained underlying production functions and elasticities. I carried this forward in important recent work on the implications of accelerated depreciation and other investment tax parameters in major, large-scale econometric models. I have also related determinants of growth and employment to parameters of production, investment and consumption functions and liquidity preference, and noted limitations as well as potential innovations in fiscal and monetary policy. I showed the reduced and sometimes perverse effects on aggregate demand and output to be expected from temporary changes in personal and business income tax rates.

Also I have undertaken significant extensions of existing concepts of national income and product and have recently completed comprehensive estimates of the modified and expanded measures. These have involved nonmarket as well as market output and show traditional net private domestic investment to be a minor fraction of all net human and non-human capital formation by business,

government, and households. Most recently, in adjusting government budget deficits for effects of inflation and other distortions, I have offered important new perceptions of the macroeconomic impacts of fiscal policy.

EKELUND, Robert Burton Jr.

Born 1940, Galveston, TX, USA.
Current Post Lowder Prof. Econ., Auburn Univ., AL, USA, 1983–.
Past Posts Instr., St Mary's Univ., TX, 1962–3; Grad. Ass., Louisiana State Univ., 1963–7; Ass. Prof., Assoc. Prof., Prof., Texas A & M Univ., 1967–70, 1970–4, 1974–9; Prof., Auburn Univ., 1979–83; Cons., US Fed. Trade Commission, 1982–4.
Degrees BBA, MA St Mary's Univ., San Antonio, TX, 1962, 1963; PhD Louisiana State Univ., 1967.
Offices and Honours Exec. Comm., Assoc. Social Econ., 1977–8, SEA, 1982–3.
Editorial Duties Ed. Boards, *RSE*, 1977–, *HOPE*, 1983–.
Principal Fields of Interest 031 History of Economic Thought; 612 Public Policy towards Monopoly and Competition; 613 Public Utilities and Costs of Government Regulation of Other Industries in the Private Sector.
Publications *Books:* 1. *The Evolution of Modern Demand Theory: A Book of Essays*, co-ed. (with E. G. Furubotn and W. P. Gramm), (D. C. Heath, 1972); 2. *A History of Economic Theory and Method* (with R. F. Hébert), (McGraw-Hill, 1975, 1983; Southeast Book Co., 1985); 3. *Mercantilism as a Rent-seeking Society: Economic Regulation in Historical Perspective* (with R. Tollison), (Texas A & M Univ. Press, 1981); 4. *The Essentials of Money and Banking* (with L. Auerheimer), (Wiley, 1982); 5. *Macroeconomics* (with C. DeLorme), (Business Publication, 1983); 6. *Economics* (with R. D. Tollison), (Little Brown, 1985).
Articles: 1. 'Jules Dupuit and the early theory of marginal cost pricing', *JPE*, 76, May–June 1968; 2. 'A reconsideration of advertising expenditures, aggregate demand and economic stabilization' (with W. P. Gramm), *QREB*, 9,

Summer 1969; 3. 'Price discrimination and product differentiation in economic theory: an early analysis', *QJE*, 83, May 1970; 4. 'Advertising and concentration: some new evidence' (with W. P. Gramm), *Antitrust Bull*, 15, Summer 1970; 5. 'Public economics at the École des Ponts et Chaussées, 1830–50' (with R. F. Hébert), *J Pub E*, 2, July 1973; 6. 'A short-run model of capital and wages: Mill's recantation of the wages fund', *OEP*, 28, March 1976; 7. 'Chadwick and Demsetz on competition and regulation' (with M. Crain), *J Law E*, 19, April 1976; 8. 'The new political economy of J. S. Mill: the means of social justice' (with R. D. Tollison), *CJE*, 9, May 1976; 9. 'Mercantile origins of the corporation' (with R. D. Tollison), *Bell JE*, 11, Autumn 1980; 10. 'Capital fixity, innovations and long-term contracting: an intertemporal economic theory of regulation' (with R. S. Higgins), *AER*, 72(1), March 1982.

Principal Contributions Early and continuing interests have centred upon the history of economic theory and policy, the political economy of regulation, and the economics of advertising. A fundamental area of interest related to the economic engineering studies of the members of the French École des Ponts et Chaussées, best remembered in the writings of Jules Dupuit. This tradition represents an advanced corpus of economic analysis rivalling that produced by mainstream neoclassical economists. These developments, along with a general history of economic theory and thought, are described in textbook format in *History of Economic Theory and Method* (1975, 1983). In the mid- to late-1970s, my research interests turned to regulation including the mechanisms of franchise bidding and to intertemporal theories of contracting, regulation and market processes. In addition to these topics, I have been concerned with the advertising process as it relates to competition and economic stabilisation. Most recently, I have co-developed a critique of the contemporary theory of mercantilism. This assessment combines a modern theory of regulation of public choice with the more traditional views of classic interpretations.

EKERN, Steinar

Born 1942, Lillehammer, Norway.
Current Post Prof. Bus., Norwegian School Econ. and Bus. Admin., Bergen, Norway, 1978–.
Past Posts Econ., Norsk Hydro, Oslo, 1966–8; Res. Fellow, Ass. Prof., Assoc. Prof., Norwegian School Econ. and Bus. Admin., Bergen, 1968–78.
Degrees Sivilokonom Norwegian School Econ. and Bus. Admin., 1966; MS (OR), PhD (Bus.) Stanford Univ., 1972, 1973.
Offices and Honours Ford Foundation Doctoral Fellow, 1970–3.
Principal Fields of Interest 520 Business Finance and Investment; 310 Domestic Monetary and Financial Theory and Institutions; 512 Managerial Economics.
Publications *Articles:* 1. 'On the theory of the firm in an economy with incomplete markets' (with R. Wilson), *Bell JE*, 5(1), Spring 1974; 2. 'On the theory of the firm in an economy with incomplete markets: an addendum', *Bell JE*, 6(1), Spring 1975; 3. 'Forecasting with adaptive filtering: a critical re-examination', *Operations Res. Q.*, 27(3), 1976; 4. 'On the inadequacy of a probabilistic internal rate of return', *J. Bus. Fin. Accounting*, 6(2), 1979; 5. 'Stochastic breakeven points', *J. Operations Res. Soc.* 30(3), 1979; 6. 'The new Soviet incentive model: comment', *Bell JE*, 10(2), Autumn 1979; 7. 'Comparative statics and risk aversion', *Econ. Letters*, 5, 1980; 8. 'Increasing nth degree risk', *Econ. Letters*, 6, 1980; 9. 'Time dominance efficiency analysis', *J Fin*, 36(5), Dec. 1981; 10. 'On simulation studies of adaptive forecasts', *Omega*, 10(1), 1982.

Principal Contributions My interest in the economics of uncertainty was nurtured by the seminal works of my senior colleagues (Borch, Mossin and Sandmo) at the Norwegian School of Economics and Business Administration. Early contributions to the 'unanimity approach' to economies with incomplete markets can be found in my dissertation and its derived articles. Later I developed general propositions for simplifying comparative statics analysis using Pratt-Arrow risk aversion measures and extended the Rothschild-Stiglitz 'increasing risk' results. I have repeatedly demonstrated shortcomings in various studies purporting to show complex adaptive forecasting methods outperforming more simple forecasting schemes. The decision relevance of stochastic ratios has been questioned. By transferring stochastic dominance analysis to a temporal context I have provided rules for ranking projects according to net present values without having to quantify discounting factors. My current applied research interests include petroleum economies and the use of recent financial instruments in planning control.

ELLET, Charles Jr.*

Dates and Birthplace 1810–62, Penn's Manor, PA, USA.
Post Held Civil Engineer.
Publications *Books:* 1. *An Essay on the Laws of Trade in Reference to the Works of Internal Improvement in the United States* (1839, 1966); 2. *The Laws of Trade Applied to the Determination of the Most Advantageous Fares for Passengers on Railroads* (1840).

Career His career as a civil engineer was a distinguished one, including the building of a suspension bridge of record length over the Ohio, and many other major works. The question of appropriate tariffs for a canal he was constructing and a period of study at l'Ecole des Ponts et Chaussées in Paris, led to his *Essay....* In this and subsequent works he developed an economic analysis of transportation, involving questions of tariff-fixing and monopoly pricing, in mathematical terms.

Secondary Literature C. D. Calsoyas, 'The mathematical theory of monopoly in 1839: Charles Ellet Jr', *JPE*, 58, April 1950; R. B. Ekelund and D. L. Hooks, 'Joint demand, discriminating two-part tariffs and location theory: an early American contribution', *WEJ*, 10, March 1972.

ELLICKSON, Bryan

Born 1941, New York City, NY, USA.
Current Post Prof. Econ., UCLA, 1983–.
Past Posts Ass. Prof., Assoc. Prof. Econ., UCLA, 1968–73, 1973–83.
Degrees BA (Physics) Univ. Oregon, 1963; PhD MIT, 1970.
Offices and Honours Phi Beta Kappa; Woodrow Wilson Fellow, 1963–4; RAND Fellow Math. Econ., 1965–6; Samuel Stouffer Fellow, Harvard-MIT Joint Center Urban Stud., 1967–8; Resources for the Future Fellow, 1967–8; UCLA Alumni Assoc. Disting. Teaching Award, 1983; WEA Disting. Teaching Award, 1983.
Editorial Duties Ed. Board, *JUE*, 1979–.
Principal Fields of Interest 021 General Equilibrium Theory; 022 Microeconomic Theory; 930 Urban Economics.
Publications *Articles:* 1. 'Jurisdictional fragmentation and residential choice', *AER*, 61(2), May 1971; 2. 'A generalization of the pure theory of public goods', *AER*, 63(3), June 1973; 3. 'The politics and economics of decentralization', *JUE*, 4(2), April 1977; 4. 'Public goods and joint supply', *J Pub E*, 9(3), June 1978; 5. 'Local public goods and the market for neighborhoods', in *The Economics of Neighborhood*, ed. D. Segal (Academic Press, 1979); 6. 'Hedonic theory and the demand for cable television', *AER*, 69(1), March 1979; 7. 'Competitive equilibrium with local public goods', *JET*, 21(1), Aug. 1979; 8. 'An alternative test of the hedonic theory of housing markets', *JUE*, 9(1), Jan. 1981; 9. 'Indivisibility, housing markets and public goods', in *Research in Urban Economics*, ed. J. V. Henderson (JAI Press, 1983); 10. 'Is a local public good different from any other?', in *The Urban Economy and Housing*, ed. R. Greison (D. C. Heath, 1983).
Principal Contributions The unifying theme in my research has been indivisibility and nonconvexity with particular emphasis on hedonic theory and local public goods. My doctoral dissertation at MIT, which dealt with residential

location and local public goods, was an attempt to develop some ideas of Jerome Rothenberg in a general equilibrium setting. The principal contributions of that work, which have had some lasting impact, were the derivation of bid price functions using duality theory and characterisation of sufficient conditions for jurisdictions to stratify by income class in terms of the slopes of bid price functions. Using some relatively simple tools of formal general equilibrium theory, I reached the conclusion that nonconvexity and local public goods were intimately related (No. 2 above). At that juncture I realised that, despite taking 'advanced theory' as my major field at MIT, I was dealing with mathematical issues that were over my head. As a consequence, I spent five years auditing graduate mathematics courses at UCLA. I am now in the process of writing a book on general equilibrium theory, which emphasises applications to indivisibility, nonconvexity and externality.

ELLMAN, Michael John

Born 1942, Ripley, Surrey, England.
Current Post Prof. Econ., Univ. Amsterdam, Amsterdam, Netherlands, 1978–.
Past Posts Lect. Econ., Glasgow Univ., 1967–9; Res. Officer, Sr. Res. Officer, Dept. Applied Econ., Univ. Camb., 1969–75; Reader Econ., Amsterdam Univ., 1975–8; Vis. Prof. Social Stud., The Hague, Netherlands, 1983.
Degrees MA, PhD Univ. Camb., 1966, 1972; MSc LSE, 1965.
Editorial Duties Assoc. Ed., *Camb JE*; Ed. Board, *Matekon*.
Principal Fields of Interest 053 Comparative Economic Systems; 052 Socialist and Communist Economic Systems.
Publications *Books:* 1. *Soviet Planning Today* (CUP, 1971); 2. *Planning Problems in the USSR. The Contribution of Mathematical Methods to Their Solution* (CUP, 1973; transl., Italian, Liguori Editore, 1979); 3. *Socialist Planning* (CUP, 1979; transls., Dutch, Samson, 1980, Brasilian, Zahar Editores, 1980, Italian, Editori Riuniti,

1981, Japanese, Iwanami Shoten, 1982, Mexican, Fondo de cultura economica, 1983); 4. *Collectivisation, Convergence and Capitalism* (Academic Press, 1984); 5. *De Chinese economie*, ed. (Stenfert Kroese, 1980); 6. *De Collectieve Sector in de Crisis*, co-ed. (with others), (Kluwer, 1983).
Articles: 1. 'Individual preferences and the market', *Econ. of Planning*, 3, 1966; 2. 'The use of input-output in regional economic planning: the Soviet experience', *EJ*, 78, Dec. 1968; 3. 'Aggregation as a cause of inconsistent plans', *Ec*, N.S. 36, Feb. 1969; 4. 'The consistency of Soviet plans', *SJPE*, 16(1), Feb. 1969; 5. 'Report from Holland: the economics of North Sea hydrocarbon', *Camb JE*, Sept. 1977; 6. 'The fundamental problem of socialist planning', *OEP*, 30(2), July 1978; 7. 'Changing views on central economic planning: 1958–1983', *ACES Bull*, Spring 1983; 8. 'Agricultural productivity under socialism', *WD*, Sept.–Oct. 1981; 9. 'The crisis of the welfare state — the Dutch experience', in *The Economics of Human Betterment*, ed. K. Boulding (CUP, 1984); 10. 'Monetarism and the state socialist world', in *Monetarism, Economic Crisis and the Third World*, ed. K. Jansen (OUP, 1983), repr. in *Readings in Socialist Economic Development*, ed. K. Martins (A & U, 1985).
Principal Contributions My work has ranged across the whole area of comparative economic systems, from welfare economics to Marxist-Leninist theory, from the Polish crisis of 1979–82 to the crisis of the welfare state. My main contributions have concerned Soviet economic thought, planning techniques, economic reform under State Socialism, Marxist theory, the economics of the collectivisation of agriculture and the convergence theory. In my book and articles on Soviet economic thought (in particular the discussion of the 1960s about the use of mathematical methods), I provided a well documented internalist account of this development. I also provided, however, unlike other Western commentators on this discussion, an externalist critique of the significance of this debate. Furthermore, I related the

theoretical discussions to real planning problems and the ability (or otherwise) of mathematical methods to resolve them. My work on planning techniques made clear what input-output and linear programming can *not* do. It also described where they are being used successfully to raise the efficiency of planning. My contribution to knowledge of economic reform consists of detailed empirical studies of attempted changes plus stress on economic reform as a matter of political and social choice. In my work on the economics of collectivisation, I argued that Soviet industrialisation was *not* financed by an increased transfer of surplus from the peasantry, but was financed mainly by 'the self-exploitation of the working-class'. In a widely referred to paper (and subsequent discussion), I criticised the Tinbergian variant of the convergence theory as misleading and harmful.

ELTIS, Walter Alfred

Born 1933, Warnsdorf, Czechoslovakia.

Current Post Fellow, Tutor Econ., Exeter Coll. Oxford, 1963–.

Past Posts Res. Fellow, Lect. Econ., Exeter Coll., Keble Coll., Oxford, 1959–60, 1960–3; Vis. Reader Econ., Univ. Western Australia, 1970; Vis. Prof. Econ., Univ. Toronto, 1976–7, European Univ. Inst., Florence, Italy, 1979.

Degrees BA Univ. Cambridge, 1956; MA Univ. Oxford, 1960.

Offices and Honours Cons., Nat. Econ. Devlp. Office, London, UK, 1963–6.

Editorial Duties Ed. Board, General Ed., *OEP*, 1974–81, 1975–81.

Principal Fields of Interest 031 History of Economic Thought; 110 Economic Development; 300 Domestic Monetary and Fiscal Theory and Institutions.

Publications Books: 1. *Economic Growth: Analysis and Policy* (Hutchinson, 1966); 2. *Induction, Growth and Trade: Essays in Honour of Sir Roy Harrod*, co-ed. (with M. F. G. Scott and J. N. Wolfe), (OUP, 1970); 3. *Growth and Distribution* (Macmillan, Wiley, 1973); 4. *The Age of US and UK Machinery* (with R. W. Bacon), (Nat. Econ. Devlp. Office, 1974); 5. *Britain's Economic Problem: Too Few Producers* (with R. W. Bacon), (Macmillan, St Martin's Press, 1976, 1978); 6. *The Money Supply and the Exchange Rate*, co-ed. (with P. J. N. Sinclair), (OUP, 1981); 7. *The Classical Theory of Economic Growth* (Macmillan, St Martin's Press, 1984).

Articles: 1. 'Investment, technical progress and economic growth', *OEP*, 15, March 1963; 2. 'Capital accumulation and the rate of industrialization of developing countries', *ER*, 46, June 1970; 3. 'The determination of the rate of technical progress', *EJ*, Sept. 1971; 4. 'Adam Smith's theory of economic growth', in *Essays on Adam Smith*, eds. A. S. Skinner and T. Wilson (OUP, 1975); 5. 'Francois Quesnay: a reinterpretation, 1. The tableau économique, 2. The theory of economic growth', *OEP*, 27 July, Nov. 1975; 6. 'The failure of the Keynesian conventional wisdom', *LBR*, 122, Oct. 1976; 7. 'The true deficits of the public corporations', *LBR*, 131, Jan. 1979; 8. 'The measurement of the growth of the non-market sector and its influence: a reply to Hadjimatheou and Skouras' (with R. W. Bacon), *EJ*, 89, June 1979; 9. 'Malthus's theory of effective demand and growth', *OEP*, 32, March 1980; 10. 'The interconnection between public expenditure and inflation in Britain', *AER*, 73(2), May 1983.

Principal Contributions The first publications are concerned with the relationship between the nature of capital equipment, accumulation and income distribution. This culminates in *Growth and Distribution* in which a model is developed where the rate of profit, the share of investment and the rate of economic growth are simultaneously determined by an investment function, a production function and a technical progress function. The latter has the characteristic (unlike Kaldor's and Arrow's) that a higher share of investment is associated with faster steady-state technical progress and economic growth. The model has several classical features including a close interconnection between profits, capital accumulation and technical progress. The later publications are specifically classical. The theories of economic growth and income distribution of Quesnay, Smith, Malthus, Ricardo and Marx are restated in modern terms, using their original assumptions and arriving at their own principal conclusions. This culminates in *The Classical Theory of Economic Growth*. In *Britain's Economic Problem* a modern growth model is derived from Smith and Quesnay to help explain some of the economic difficulties of the UK (and other economies which have suffered similar trends) in the 1960s and 1970s. Investment and exports must originate from the economy's surplus-producing market sector, and if too high a fraction of its surplus of marketed output is diverted to the surplus-using sector where marketed output is consumed by those who produce none (mainly in the public sector), too little will remain for job-creating investment in the market sector itself. As a result, the employment it provides will decline, and in due course its output also, which will reduce the economy's tax base. Financial collapse may ensue as the employment which the market sector can provide declines, while the welfare needs of the rest of the community which it is obliged to finance continuously increase.

ELTON, Edwin Joel

Born 1939, Milwaukee, WI, USA.
Current Post Prof. Fin., NYU, New York City, NY, USA, 1972–.
Past Posts Ass. Prof., Assoc. Prof. Fin., NYU, 1965–70, 1970–2; Sr. Res. Fellow, Internat. Inst. Management, 1972–4.
Degrees BS (Maths. and Physics) Ohio Wesleyan Univ., 1961; MS, PhD (Industrial Admin.) Carnegie-Mellon Univ., 1965, 1970.
Offices and Honours Dir., AFA, 1980–1.
Editorial Duties Assoc. Ed., *Ed., J Fin.*, 1977–83, 1983; Assoc. Ed., *Management Science*, 1977–82; Ed., *NYU Monograph Series* (NYU Press, 1975–80).

Principal Fields of Interest 521 Business Finance.
Publications *Books:* 1. *Modern Portfolio Theory* (J. Wiley, 1980, 1984); 2. *Portfolio Management: Twenty-Five Years Later* (N-H, 1979); 3. *International Capital Markets* (N-H, 1975); 4. *Finance as a Dynamic Process* (Prentice-Hall, 1975); 5. *Security Evaluation and Portfolio Analysis* (Prentice-Hall, 1972).
Articles: 1. 'Risk reduction and portfolio size: an analytical solution' (with M. J. Gruber), *J Bus*, 50(9), Oct. 1977; 2. 'Simple criteria for optimal portfolio selection: the multi-group case', *J. Fin. Quant. Analysis*, 12(3), Sept. 1977; 3. 'Simple criteria for optimal portfolio selection: the multi-index case', *Management Science*, Sept. 1979; 4. 'Are betas best?', *J Fin*, 34(5), Dec. 1979; 5. 'Taxes and portfolio composition in efficient markets', *J Fin Econ*, 8(4), Dec. 1979; 6. 'Simple rules for optimal portfolio selection in a stable market', *J Fin*, 34(9), Sept. 1979; 7. 'Expectations and share prices', *Management Science*, Sept. 1981; 8. 'Equilibrium returns on assets under inflation', *J Fin*, 38(1), March 1983; 9. 'Professional expectations: accuracy and diagnosis of errors', *J Fin. Quant. Analysis*, 19(2), June 1984; 10. 'Intra-day tests of the efficiency of the treasury bill future markets', *REStat*, 66(1), Jan. 1984.
Principal Contributions Developed a simple algorithm for solving portfolio problems. The algorithm gives exact solutions, is so simple to solve that it does not require computers, and clarifies for the first time why a security is included or excluded. Demonstrated the presence of tax effects in security returns and measured its importance. Pioneered the use of mathematical models for analysing financial problems.

ELY, Richard Theodore*

Dates and Birthplace 1854–1943, Ripley, NY, USA.
Posts Held Lect. Econ., Johns Hopkins Univ., 1881–92; Prof., Univ. Wisconsin, 1892–1922.
Degrees BA Columbia Coll., 1876.

Offices and Honours Founder and Pres., AEA, 1900–2; Founder, Inst. Res. Land Econ. and Public Utility Econ., 1920.

Publications *Books:* 1. *The Past and Present of Political Economy* (1884); 2. *The Labor Movement in America* (1886); 3. *An Introduction to Political Economy* (1889); 4. *Outlines of Economics* (1893, with R. H. Hess, 1937); 5. *Property and Contract in their Relation to the Distribution of Wealth*, 2 vols (1914); 6. *Grounds Under our Feet: An Autobiography* (1938); 7. *Land Economics* (with G. S. Wehrwein), (1940, 1964).

Career His advocacy of reform movements and in particular his account of labour organisations caused him to be embroiled in controversy over strikes and the issue of socialism. The University of Wisconsin 'trial' in 1894 exonerated him and resulted in a classic statement in favour of academic freedom. The school he founded at Wisconsin provided a link between German historical economics and institutionalism, and became famous because of its collaboration with the progressive state government of Wisconsin. *Property and Contract . . .* was his main published contribution, but was only part of a massive output of articles and editorial work. His teaching and founding work for the AEA made him one of the most influential economists of his time.

Secondary Literature A. W. Coats, 'Ely, Richard T.', *IESS*, 5.

ENGEL, Ernst*

Dates and Birthplace 1821–96, Germany.

Posts Held Dir. Stat. Bureaux, Saxony, 1850–8, Prussia, 1861–82.

Degrees Student, l'Ecole des Mines, Paris.

Offices and Honours Founder, Internat. Stat. Inst., 1886.

Publications *Books:* 1. *Der Kostenwerth des Menschen* (1883).

Articles: 1. 'Die productions- und consumtionsverhältnisse des Königsreichs Sachsen', *Zeitschrift des Statistischen Bureaus des Königlich Sächsischen Ministeriums des Innern*, 3, 1857.

Career An official statistician who was involved in social reform movements and devised 'Engel's Law': the proportion of a consumer's budget spent on food tends to decline as the consumer's income rises. The law is remarkable as probably the first quantitative law derived from empirical economic data; moreover it has been confirmed by innumerable surveys around the world. He also wrote on labour, industry, taxation, insurance, banking and war.

Secondary Literature H. S. Houthakker, 'Engle, Ernst', *IESS*, 5.

ENGELS, Friedrich*

Dates and Birthplace 1820–95, Barmen, Germany.

Posts Held Cotton manufacturer and journalist.

Publications *Books:* 1. *The Condition of the Working Class in England* (1845, 1958); 2. *The Holy Family* (with K. Marx), (1845, 1956); 3. *The German Ideology* (with K. Marx), (1845, 1939); 4. *The Peasant War in Germany* (1850, 1956); 5. *Anti-Dühring* (1878, 1959); 6. *Socialism: Utopian and Scientific* (1880, 1935); 7. *The Origin of the Family, Private Property and the State* (1884, 1942); 8. *Ludwig Feuerbach and the Outcome of Classical German Philosophy* (1886, 1941).

Career Revolutionary and Marx's close collaborator and friend. After their first meeting in 1844 to discuss Engels's early economic writings, Engels gradually left theoretical work to Marx and concentrated on polemical and journalistic writing. He wrote extensively on military topics and the military aspects of revolution. After Marx's death, he organised the editing and publication of his works, including the unpublished second and third volumes of *Kapital,* and provided them with important introductions. Because of the close association in which he and Marx worked it is almost impossible to distinguish their individual contributions to any aspect of theory on which they wrote, including the subject of economics.

Secondary Literature G. Mayer,

Friedrich Engels: a Biography (Chapman, 1936); T. Ramm, 'Engels, Friedrich', *IESS*, 5; W. O. Henderson, *The Life of Friedrich Engels*, 2 vols (Frank Cass, 1974).

ENGERMAN, Stanley Lewis

Born 1936, New York City, NY, USA.
Current Post Prof. Econ. and Hist., Univ. Rochester, Rochester, NY, USA, 1971–.
Past Posts Ass. Prof., Yale Univ., 1962–3; Ass. Prof., Assoc. Prof., Univ. Rochester, 1963–6, 1966–71.
Degrees BS, MBA NYU, 1956, 1958; PhD Johns Hopkins Univ., 1962.
Offices and Honours Trustee, Vice-Pres., Pres., EHA; Exec. Council, Social Science Hist. Assoc.; NSF Science Faculty Fellow; Guggenheim Foundation Fellow.
Editorial Duties Assoc. Ed., *Explor. Econ. Hist.*; Ed. Board, *Bus. Hist. Rev.*, 1971–80, *JEH*, 1972–84, *Southern Stud.*, 1977–, *Historical Methods*, 1980–, *EI*, 1981–, *J Amer. Hist.*, 1981–4, *J Family Hist.*, 1983–.
Principal Fields of Interest 041 Economic History — General; 042 North American Economic History; 047 Latin American & Caribbean Economic History.
Publications *Books:* 1. *The Reinterpretation of American Economic History*, co-ed. (with R. W. Fogel), (Harper & Row, 1971); 2. *Time on the Cross* (with R. W. Fogel), (Little Brown, 1974; transls., Spanish, Japanese); 3. *Race and Slavery in the Western Hemisphere*, co-ed. (with E. D. Genovese), (Princeton Univ. Press, 1975).
Articles: 1. 'Exploring the uses of data on height: the analysis of long-term trends in nutrition, labor, welfare and labor-productivity' (with R. W. Fogel and J. Trussel), *Social Science Hist.*, 6, Fall 1982; 2. 'Economic aspects of the adjustments to emancipation in the United States and the British West Indies', *J. Interdisciplinary Hist.*, 13, Autumn 1982; 3. 'Economic growth, 1783–1860' (with R. E. Gallman), in *Res. in Economy Hist.*, 8, ed. P. Useld-

ing (JAI Press, 1983); 4. 'Contract labor, sugar and technology in the nineteenth century', *JEH*, , 43, Sept. 1983; 5. 'The level and structure of slave prices on Cuban plantation in the mid-nineteenth century: some comparative perspectives' (with M. M. Fraginals and H. S. Klein), *Amer. Hist. Review*, 88, Dec. 1983.
Principal Contributions My major research interests have been in the development of alternative forms of labour organisation, most particularly the nature of slave economies. In various works, some joint (most frequently with R. W. Fogel), some alone, I have examined the economic aspects of slavery and of the adjustments to the end of slavery in the US and in the Caribbean. Related to this focus on labour are the studies (joint with Fogel and others) on the relationship of nutrition, height and productivity and (joint with H. S. Klein) on mortality in the transatlantic slave trade.

ENTHOVEN, Alain

Born 1930, Seattle, WA, USA.
Current Post Marriner S. Eccles Prof. Public and Private Management, Grad. School Bus., Prof. Health Care Econ., School Medicine, Stanford Univ., CA; Cons., Kaiser Foundation Health Plan Inc., Oakland, CA, 1973–.
Past Posts Instr. Econ., MIT, 1955–6; Econ., RAND Corp., 1956–60; Cons., Brookings Inst., 1956–60; Vis. Assoc. Prof. Econ., Univ. Washington, 1958; OR Analyst, US Office Dir. Defense Res. and Eng., 1960; Dep. Comptroller, Dep. Ass. Secretary Defense, 1961–5; Ass. Sec. Defense for Systems Analysis, 1965–9; Vice-Pres. Econ. Planning, Litton Industries, 1969–71; Pres., Litton Medical Products, 1971–3.
Degrees BA Stanford Univ., 1952; BPhil Oxford Univ., 1954; PhD MIT, 1956.
Offices and Honours US President's Award Disting. Fed. Civilian Service, 1963; US Dept. Defense Medal Disting. Public Service, 1969; Rhodes Scholar; Phi Beta Kappa; Board Dirs., Georgetown Univ., Medical Center Comm.,

1968–73; Stanford Univ. Computer Science Advisory Comm., 1968–73; Cons., RAND Corp., 1969–; Board Regents, St John's Hospital, Santa Monica, 1971–3; Cal. Inst. Technology, Vis. Comm. Environmental Quality Laboratory, 1972–5; Program Comm., Inst. Medicine, NAS, 1974–6; Vis. Comm., Harvard School Public Health, 1974–80; Vis. Comm., Univ. Health Services, Harvard Univ., 1980–; Special Cons., Secretary, US Dept. Health, Educ. and Welfare, Nat. Health Insurance, 1977–8; Res. Advisory Board, Palo Alto Medical Foundation, 1982–.

Principal Fields of Interest 913 Economics of Health.

Publications *Books:* 1. *How Much is Enough? Shaping the Defense Program 1961–1969* (with K. W. Smith), (Harper & Row, 1971, Kraus, 1980); 2. *Pollution, Resource and the Environment* (with A. M. Freeman III), (W. W. Norton, 1973); 3. *Health Plan: The Only Practical Solution to the Soaring Cost of Medical Care* (Addison-Wesley, 1980).

Articles: 1. 'A theorem of expectations and the stability of equilibrium' (with K. J. Arrow), *Em*, 24(3), July 1956; 2. 'The simple mathematics of maximisation', in *The Economics of Defense in the Nuclear Age*, eds. C. J. Hitch and R. N. McKean (Harvard Univ. Press, 1960); 3. 'A neo-classical model of money, debt and economic growth', in *Money in a Theory of Finance*, eds. J. G. Gurley and E. S. Shaw (Brookings Inst., 1960); 4. 'Economic analysis in the department of defense', *AER*, 53(2), May 1963; 5. 'Introduction', in *A Modern Design for Defense Decision, A McNamara-Hitch-Enthoven Anthology*, ed. S. A. Tucker (Industrial Coll. Armed Forces, 1965); 6. 'The planning, programming, and budgeting system in the department of defense: current status and next steps' (with K. W. Smith), in *The Analysis and Evaluation of Public Expenditures: The PPB System*, Subcomm. on Economy in Government, Joint Econ. Comm., US Congress, 111 (US Govt. Printing Office, 1969); 7. 'Analysis, judgement and computers', *Business Horizons*, 12(4), Aug. 1969, repr. in *Readings in Economics*, ed. P. A.

Samuelson (McGraw-Hill, 1970); 8. 'The planning, programming, and budgeting system in the department of defense: an overview from experience' (with K. W. Smith), in *Public Expenditures and Policy Analysis*, eds. R. Haveman and J. Margolis (Markham, 1970); 9. '1963 nuclear strategy revisited', in *Ethics and Nuclear Strategy?*, eds. H. P. Ford and F. X. Winters (Orbis Books, 1977); 10. 'How interested groups have responded to a proposal for economic competition in health services', *AER*, 70(2), May 1980.

EPPLE, Dennis N.

Born 1946, IN, USA.

Current Post Prof. Econ., Grad. School Industrial Admin., Carnegie-Mellon Univ., Pittsburgh, PA, 1984–.

Past Posts Ass. Prof., Assoc. Prof. Econ., Grad. School Industrial Admin., Carnegie-Mellon Univ., 1974–8, 1978–83.

Degrees BS (Aeronautical Eng.) Purdue Univ., 1968; MS (Public and Internat. Affairs) Woodrow Wilson School Public and Internat. Affairs, Princeton Univ., 1971; MS, PhD Princeton Univ., 1973, 1975.

Offices and Honours Nat. Fellow, Hoover Inst., Stanford Univ., 1984–5.

Principal Fields of Interest 324 State and Local Government Finance; 720 Natural Resources; 610 Industrial Organisation and Public Policy.

Publications *Books:* 1. *Petroleum Discoveries and Government Policy: An Econometric Study of Supply* (Ballinger, 1975).

Articles: 1. 'A search for testable implications of the Tiebout hypothesis' (with A. Zelenitz and M. Visscher), *JPE*, 86(3), June 1978; 2. 'The implications of competition among jurisdictions: does Tiebout need politics' (with A. Zelenitz), *JPE*, 89(6), Dec. 1981; 3. 'Environmental pollution: modelling occurrence, detection and deterrence' (with M. Visscher), *J Law E*, 27(1), April 1984; 4. 'The econometrics of exhaustible resource supply: a theory and an application', *Energy, Foresight and Strategy* (Resources for the Future,

1985); 5. 'Equilibrium among jurisdictions: toward an integrated treatment of voting and residential choice' (with R. Filimon and T. Romer), *JPE*, forthcoming, 1985.

Principal Contributions Observed equilibria among local governments arise from the interaction of two kinds of forces. Collective decisions determine *inter alia* tax rates, spending levels, borrowing and land use controls. Individual households determine the jurisdiction in which they will reside and the amount of housing and other private goods and services that they will consume. The objective of my research on this subject is to understand how competition among jurisdictions (arising from mobility of households) and intra-jurisdictional choice processes affect residential choice, tax and spending levels, housing prices, and other facets of local equilibrium. Econometric modelling of exhaustible resource markets is concerned with modelling the time paths of depletion of one or more such resources and the associated paths of prices. Ideally, an econometric model should be derived from a characterisation of the problem being solved by the resource producer; it should reflect the inherent uncertainty about future prices and costs of extraction; and it should reflect the increase in cost of resource extraction that occurs as the resource is depleted. The objectives of my research on this topic are to use dynamic economic theory to derive such econometric models, and to test the models empirically.

ERHARD, Ludwig*

Dates and Birthplace 1897-1977, Fürth, Germany.

Posts Held Ass., Nuremberg Inst. for Econ. Observation, 1928–42.

Degree Dr Rer. Pol. Univ. Frankfurt-am-Main.

Offices Econ. Minister, Bavaria, 1945–6; Dir., Advisory Comm. Money and Credit, 1947–8; Dir., Econ. Council, Anglo-American Occupation District, 1948–9; Econ. Minister, 1949–63; Vice-Chancellor, 1957–63, Chancellor, 1963–6, Bundesrepublik.

Publications *Books:* 1. *Deutschlands Rückkehr zum Weltmarkt* (1953); 2. *Wohlstand für Alle* (1957); 3. *Deutsche Wirtschaftspolitik* (1962).

Career Professional economist who was entrusted with reconstruction work by the Allies in postwar Germany. The German 'economic miracle' was based on his 'social market system'. His achievement led to his appointment as German Chancellor.

ERICSON, Richard Eric

Born 1949, San Miguel, Mexico.

Current Post Assoc. Prof. Econ., Northwestern Univ., Evanston, IL, USA, 1983–.

Past Posts Fulbright-Hayes Res. Scholar, Moscow State Univ., Moscow, 1977–8; Inst., Ass. Prof., Harvard Univ., 1978, 1978–83; Vis. Ass. Prof., Northwestern Univ., 1981; Vis. Assoc. Prof., Yale Univ., 1983.

Degrees BS (Internat. Affairs) Georgetown Univ., 1971; MIA (Internat. Affairs & Soviet Stud.) Columbia Univ., 1974; PhD Univ. Cal. Berkeley, 1979.

Offices and Honours Fulbright-Hayes Fellow, 1977–8.

Principal Fields of Interest 020 General Economic Theory; 050 Economic Systems; 113 Planning Theory.

Publications *Articles:* 1. 'On the stability of production inventories in a model with random perturbation of supply' (in Russian), in *Probabilistic Models and the Control of Economic Processes* (Russian), ed. V. I. Arkin, (CEMI, 1978); 2. 'Inventory stability and resource allocation under uncertainty in a command economy', *Em*, 50(2), March 1982; 3. 'A difficulty with the command allocation mechanism', *JEI*, 30(1), Oct. 1983; 4. 'Predatory capacity expansion in a deregulated motor carrier industry' (with C. Winston), in *Research in Transportation Economics*, ed. T. Keeler (JAI Press, 1983); 5. 'On an allocative role of the soviet second economy', in *Marxism Planning and the Soviet Economy*, ed. P. Desai (MIT Press, 1983); 6. 'The second economy and resource allocation under central planning', *J Comp E*, 8(1), March 1984.

Principal Contributions My primary research has centred on the question of how economic outcomes are generated in centrally planned economic systems such as that of the Soviet Union. Taking the economic plan as given, I have concentrated on the impact of its inevitable incompleteness and of the structure of authority in such economies on economy performance in an uncertain and ever-changing environment. In general, these characteristics were found to generate inflexibility in response to both opportunities and contingencies and to generate a pervasive microeconomic instability in outcomes. This research focussed in particular on the behaviour of intermediate product inventories in the Soviet Union. This study naturally led to an investigation of various informal, unplanned mechanisms that arise to cope with these unanticipated consequences of planning. In particular, I have concentrated on modelling market-like processes that have arisen in the so-called Second Economy of the Soviet Union.

This research has raised questions about the meaning of 'markets' and their role under central planning, to which I have most recently turned my attention. I have also recently begun to investigate through theoretical modelling the microeconomic interaction between superiors and subordinates in a centrally planned economy under uncertainty and incomplete information. Other research of mine has dealt with questions of industrial organisation in a market economy. In particular I have studied the change in industrial structure under deregulation and worked on models of research and development investment and the accumulation of 'R & D capital'.

ETHIER, Wilfred John

Born 1943, Brockton, MA, USA.
Current Post Prof. Econ., Univ. Penn., Philadelphia, PA, USA, 1980–.
Past Posts Ass. Prof., Assoc. Prof. Econ., Univ. Penn., 1969–73, 1973–80.

Degrees BA (Maths.), PhD Univ. Rochester, 1965, 1970.
Editorial Duties Assoc. Ed., *Int ER, J Int E*.
Principal Fields of Interest 400 International Economics; 410 International Trade Theory.
Publications *Books:* 1. *Modern International Economics* (W. W. Norton, 1983).
Articles: 1. 'International trade and the forward exchange market', *AER*, 63(3), June 1973; 2. 'Some of the theorems of international trade with many goods and factors', *J Int E*, 4(2), May 1974; 3. 'The theory of effective protection in general equilibrium: effective-rate analogues of nominal rates', *CJE*, 10(2), May 1977; 4. 'Internationally decreasing costs and world trade', *J Int E*, 9(1), Feb. 1979; 5. 'Dumping', *JPE*, 90(3), June 1982; 6. 'National and international returns to scale in the modern theory of international trade', *AER*, 72(3), June 1982; 7. 'Higher dimensional issues in trade theory', in *Handbook of International Economics*, 1 (N-H, 1984).

EUCKEN, Walter*

Dates and Birthplace 1891–1950, Jena, Germany.
Posts Held Prof., Univ. Tübingen, 1925–7, Univ. Freiburg, 1927–50.
Publications *Books:* 1. *Kapitaltheoretische Untersuchungen* (1934); 2. *The Foundations of Economics* (1940, 1950).
Articles: 'On the theory of the centrally administered economy: an analysis of the German experiment, Pts I–II', *Ec*, N.S. 15, May–Aug. 1948.
Career A neo-liberal who attempted to integrate the historical school's approach with that of standard, neoclassical theory. In his *Foundations . . .* , he attempted to develop a taxonomic approach to comparative economic systems. He was influential in post-World War II Germany in the movement to liberalise the German economy.
Secondary Literature T. W. Hutchinson, 'Walter Eucken and the German social-market economy', in *The Politics and Philosophy of Economics*

(Blackwell, 1981); F. A. Lutz, 'Eucken, Walter', *Handwörterbuch der Sozialwissenschaften*, 3, eds. E. V. Beckerath, *et al.* (Gustav Fisher, 1959).

EVANS, Griffith Conrad*

Dates and Birthplace 1887–1972, Boston, MA, USA.
Posts Held Lect. Maths. Rice Inst., 1912–34; Prof. Maths., Univ. Cal. Berkeley, 1934–55.
Degrees BA, MA Harvard Univ., 1909, 1911.
Offices and Honours Pres., Amer. Math. Soc.; Fellow, Em Soc.
Publications *Books:* 1. *Mathematical Introduction to Economics* (1930).
Articles: 1. 'A simple theory of competition', *Amer. Math. Monthly*, 29, Dec. 1922; 2. 'The dynamics of monopoly', *Amer. Math. Monthly*, 31, Feb. 1924, repr., as in (1) in *Precursors of Mathematical Economics*, eds. W. J. Baumol and S. M. Goldfeld (1968).
Career Although a professional mathematician, he and his students played an important role in the early development of economic dynamics. His major contribution, *Mathematical Introduction to Economics*, consisted of a series of mathematical treatments of selected economic problems, a few of which were dealt with by unusual and original methods.

EZEKIEL, Mordecai Joseph Brill*

Dates and Birthplace 1899–1974, Richmond, VA, USA.
Posts Held Stat. Ass., US Dept. Agric., 1922–30; Ass. Chief Econ., Fed. Farm Board, 1930–3; Econ. Adviser, US Secretary Agric., 1933–44, US Dept. Agric., 1944–6; Ass. to Exec. Vice-Chairman, US War Production Board, 1942–3; Econ., Deputy Dir. Econ. Div., Head Econ. Div., Ass. Dir. Gen., FAO, 1947–50, 1951–8, 1959–60, 1961–2; Chief, UN Div., Agency Internat. Devlp., US Dept. State, 1962–7; Econ. Cons., 1967–74.
Degrees BS Univ. Maryland, 1918; MS Univ. Minnesota, 1924; PhD

Robert Brookings Grad. School Econ. and Govt., Washington, 1926.
Offices and Honours Guggenheim Foundation Fellow, 1930; Member, FAO Missions to Greece, Poland, 1946, 1947; Fellow, ASA, Em Soc, AFEA.
Publications *Books:* 1. *Methods of Correlation Analysis* (1930); 2. *$2,500 a Year — From Scarcity to Abundance* (1936); 3. *Jobs for All* (1939); 4. *Use of Agricultural Surplus to Finance Economic Development in Underdeveloped Countries — A Pilot Study in India* (1955).
Articles: 1. 'The cobweb theorem', *QJE*, 52, Feb. 1938.
Career After a prewar career in statistics and agricultural economics — a pioneer in curvilinear multiple correlation, one of the drafters of Roosevelt's Agriculture Adjustment Act, and a prominent figure in the debate over methods of farm relief during the Great Depression — he turned after the war to development economics. His fame in economics, however, rests on a single article, which explored the so-called Cobweb Theorem.

F

FABRICANT, Solomon

Born 1906, New York City, NY, USA.
Current Post Retired, 1974–.
Past Posts Member, Res. Staff, Dir. Res., NBER, 1930–72, 1953–65; Chief Econ., US War Production Board, 1942–5, UN Lect., 1946–7; Assoc. Prof., Prof. Econ., NYU, 1947–8, 1948–74; Vis. Prof. Econ., Columbia Univ., 1952.
Degrees BS NYU, 1926; BS Coll. City NY, 1929; MA, PhD Columbia Univ., 1930, 1938.
Offices and Honours Exec. Comm., Vice-Pres., Disting. Fellow, AEA, 1958–60, 1961, 1980; Trustee, EHA, 1952–6; Council, IARIW, 1968–72; Fellow, AAAS, Amer. Philo. Soc.
Editorial Duties Ed. Boards, *JASA*, 1950–1, *JEL*, 1977–9.
Principal Fields of Interest 110 Econ-

omic Growth; 130 Economic Fluctuations; 226 Productivity and Growth.

Publications *Books:* 1. *Economic Principles and Problems* (with others), (Farrar & Rinehart, 1936); 2. *Capital Consumption and Adjustment* (NBER, 1938); 3. *Output of Manufacturing Industries, 1899–1937* (NBER, 1940); 4. *Employment in Manufacturing, 1899–1939* (NBER, 1942); 5. *Trends of Government Activity in the US Since 1900* (NBER, 1952); 6. *War and Defense Economics* (with others), (Rinehart, 1952); 7. *Primer on Productivity* (Random House, 1969); 7. *The Economic Growth of the US: Perspective and Prospective* (Howe Research Inst., 1979); 8. *Studies in Social and Private Accounting* (Garland Publ., 1982).

Articles: 1. 'An appraisal of the US Bureau of labor statistics cost-of-living index' (with D. S. Parady), *JASA*, 39, March 1944; 2, 'Size and efficiency of the American economy', in *Economic Consequences of the Size of Nations*, ed. E. A. G. Robinson (Macmillan, 1960); 3. 'An economist's view of philanthropy', *Proceedings Amer. Philo. Soc.*, 1961; 4. 'Which productivity?', *MLR*, 12, 1962; 5. 'Productivity', in *International Encyclopedia of the Social Sciences*, ed. D. L. Sills (Macmillan, Free Press, 1968); 6. 'Labor productivity under modern capitalism', in *Progress and Planning in Industry* (Hungarian Academy of Sciences, 1970); 7. 'Economics of pollution', in *Economics of Pollution*, ed. K. E. Boulding, *et al.* (NYU Press, 1971); 8. 'Recent economic charges and the agenda of business cycle research', *NBER*, 1971; 9. 'Perspective on productivity research', *RIW*, 20(3), Sept. 1974; 10. 'World economic growth; past, present and future', *RISE*, 23(5), May 1976.

Principal Contributions My main interest has been in the process, causes, and consequences of the larger historical changes that have taken place in economic life over the years. To strengthen the scientific basis of economic policy to deal with these changes has been the objective of my research, whether on social and private accounting, the evolving industrial structure of production and employment, produc- tivity trends and cycles, or the widening role of government. This motive also underlies what I have tried to do in the administration of economic research.

FAIR, Ray C.

Born 1942, Fresno, CA, USA.
Current Post Prof. Econ., Yale Univ., New Haven, CT, USA, 1979–.
Past Posts Ass. Prof. Econ., Princeton Univ., 1968–74; Vis. Assoc. Prof. Econ., MIT, 1977; Assoc. Prof. Econ., Yale Univ., 1974–9.
Degrees BA Fresno State Coll., 1964; PhD MIT, 1968.
Offices and Honours Fellow, Em Soc; Res. Assoc., NBER.
Editorial Duties Assoc. Ed., *REStat, J Ec Dyn.*
Principal Fields of Interest 023 Macroeconomic Theory; 210 Econometric, Statistical and Mathematical Methods and Models; 400 International Economics.

Publications *Books:* 1. *The Short-Run Demand for Workers and Hours* (N-H, 1969); 2. *A Short-Run Forecasting Model of the United States Economy* (D. C. Heath, 1971); 3. *A Model of Macroeconomic Activity*, 2 vols (Ballinger, 1974, 1976); 4. *Specification, Estimation and Analysis of Macroeconometric Models* (Harvard Univ. Press, 1984).

Articles: 1. 'The estimation of simultaneous equation models with lagged endogenous variables and first order serially correlated errors', *Em*, 38(3), May 1970; 2. 'The optimal distribution of income', *QJE*, 85(4), Nov. 1971; 3. 'Methods of estimation for markets in disequilibrium' (with D. M. Jaffee), *Em*, 40(3), May 1972; 4. 'On the solution of optimal control problems as maximization problems', *Annals Econ. and Social Measurement*, 3(1), Jan. 1974; 5. 'The effect of economic events on votes for president', *REStat*, 60(2), May 1978; 6. 'The sensitivity of fiscal-policy effects to assumptions about the behavior of the federal reserve', *Em*, 46(5), Sept. 1978; 7. 'A model of the balance of payments', *J Int E*, 9(1), Feb. 1979; 8. 'Estimating the expected predictive accuracy of econometric models', *Int ER*, 21(2), June 1980; 9.

'Estimated output, price, interest rate, and exchange rate linkages among countries', *JPE*, 90(3), June 1982; 10. 'Solution and maximum likelihood estimation of dynamic rational expectations models' (with J. B. Taylor), *Em*, 51(4), July 1983.

Principal Contributions Although some of my research has been in economic theory and some in the development of econometric techniques, my main interests have always been empirical. Most of my theoretical work and my work on econometric techniques has been motivated by some empirical problem. My work in macroeconomics began with my PhD thesis on the demand for employment and has cumulated in my current model of the US economy and my current multicountry model. In between I have done separate studies of production decisions, labour force participation, and Fed. Reserve behaviour. One of my early models was designed primarily for short-run forecasting. My current macroeconometric model is structural and is based on a theoretical model that I developed in the early 1970s. My multicountry econometric model is based on a theoretical model of the balance of payments that I developed in 1979.

Some of my work on econometric techniques has been for models with autoregressive errors, which are commonly found in macroeconomic models. I have also worked on the robust estimation of econometric models and with John Taylor on the solution and estimation of models with rational expectations. One of my main interests in econometrics is the development of techniques to test models. I have developed a method that can be used to test alternative models and I have applied this method to a number of models.

In 1972 I did work with Dwight Jaffee on methods of estimation for markets in disequilibrium. This study began what is now a large literature on disequilibrium econometrics. In 1971 I did a theoretical study of the optimal distribution of income. This work and independent work of Jim Mirlees spawned a large literature on optimal income taxation. In 1974 I developed a method for solving optimal control problems for

macroeconometric models, and this method has been widely used. I have also done work on the effects of the economy on election outcomes. My current work includes the testing of alternative expectational hypotheses in macroeconometric models.

FALVEY, Rodney Edward

Born 1948, Timaru, New Zealand.

Current Post Assoc. Prof. Econ., Tulane Univ., New Orleans, LA, USA, 1978–.

Past Posts Ass. Prof., Virginia Polytechnic Inst. & State Univ., 1974–6; Ass. Prof., Tulane Univ., 1976–8; Vis. Lect., Univ. Auckland, 1980; Sr. Res. Fellow, ANU, 1983–5.

Degrees BA, MA Univ. Canterbury, New Zealand, 1970, 1971; PhD Univ. Rochester, 1975.

Principal Fields of Interest 410 International Trade Theory; 420 Trade Relations: Commercial Policy: International Economic Integration; 440 International Investment and Foreign Aid.

Publications *Articles:* 1. 'A note on the distinction between tariffs and quotas', *Ec*, N.S. 42, Aug. 1975; 2. 'Quantitative restrictions and the transfer problem', *Int ER*, 17, Feb. 1976; 3. 'A note on quantitative restrictions and capital mobility', *AER*, 66(1), March 1976; 4. 'Transport costs in the pure theory of international trade', *EJ*, 86, Sept. 1976; 5. 'A note on preferential and illegal trade under quantitative restrictions', *QJE*, 92, Feb. 1978; 6. 'Specific factors, comparative advantage and international investment: an extension', *Ec*, N.S. 46, Feb. 1979; 7. 'The composition of trade within import-restricted product categories', *JPE*, 87, Oct. 1979; 8. 'Comparative advantage in a multi-factor world', *Int ER*, 22, June 1981; 9. 'Commercial policy and intra-industry trade', *J Int E*, 11, Nov. 1981; 10. 'Protection and the choice of import-competing production in a multi-product industry', *Int ER*, 24, Oct. 1983.

Principal Contributions Comparisons of the effects of price and quantitative trade restrictions, extending the non-equivalence results to include consideration of the transfer problem, capital mobility and illegal trade. Recent interest involves multiproduct industries, specifically the explanation of import upgrading under trade controls and the analysis of the effects of trade policies on the volume and range of intra-industry trade.

FAMA, Eugene F.

Born 1939, Boston, MA, USA.
Current Post Theodore O. Yntema Disting. Service Prof. Fin., Grad. School Bus., Univ. Chicago, 1984–.
Past Posts Ass. Prof., Assoc. Prof., Prof. Fin., Theodore O. Yntema Prof. Fin., Grad. School Bus., Univ. Chicago, 1963–5, 1966–8, 1968–73, 1973–84; Board Dirs., Dimensional Fund Advisers, 1982–.
Degrees BA Tufts Univ., 1960; PhD Univ. Chicago, 1964.
Offices and Honours Society of Scholars; Phi Beta Kappa; Omicron Chi Epsilon; Class of 1888 Prize Scholar, Tufts Univ.; Beta Gamma Sigma, Univ. Chicago; Fellow, Em Soc.
Editorial Duties Assoc. Ed., *J Fin*, 1971–3, 1977–80; Advisory Ed., *J Fin Econ*, 1974–; Assoc. Ed., *AER*, 1975–7.
Principal Fields of Interest 521 Business Finance.
Publications *Books:* 1. *The Theory of Finance* (with M. Miller), (Holt, Rinehart & Winston, 1972); 2. *Foundations of Finance* (Basic Books, 1976).
Articles: 1. 'Efficient capital markets: a review of theory and empirical work', *J Fin*, 25(2), May 1970; 2. 'Risk, return and equilibrium', *JPE*, 79(1), Jan.–Feb. 1971; 3. 'Ordinal and measurable utility', in *Studies in the Theory of Capital Markets*, ed. M. Jensen (Praeger, 1972); 4. 'The number of firms and competition' (with A. Laffer), *AER*, 62(4), Sept. 1972; 5. 'Inflation uncertainty and expected returns on treasury bills', *JPE*, 84(3), June 1976; 6. 'Human capital and capital market equilibrium' (with G. W. Schwert), *J Fin Econ*, 4(1), Jan. 1977; 7. 'Interest rates and inflation: the message in the entrails', *AER*, 67(3), June 1977; 8. 'Agency problems and the theory of the firm', *JPE*, 88(2),

April 1980; 9. 'Stock returns, real activity, inflation and money', *AER*, 71(4), Sept. 1981; 10. 'Separation of ownership and control' (with M. Jensen), *J Law E*, 26(2), June 1983.

FAN, Liang-Shing

Born 1932, Taiwan.
Current Post Prof. Econ., Colorado State Univ., Fort Collins, CO, USA, 1972–.
Past Posts Instr., Res. Fellow, Univ. Minnesota, 1962–4; Ass. Prof., Kansas State Univ., 1964–8; Vis. Ass., Assoc. Prof., Univ. Minnesota, 1965, 1966; Assoc. Prof., Colorado State Univ., 1968–72; Fulbright Sr. Lect., Nat. Chengchi Univ., Soochow Univ., Taipei, Taiwan, 1977–8.
Degrees BA Nat. Taiwan Univ., Taiwan, 1956; MA, PhD Univ. Minnesota, 1960, 1965.
Offices and Honours AT&T Faculty Fellow; Fulbright-Hays Fellow, 1977–8; Fulbright Award, 1980.
Principal Fields of Interest 023 Macroeconomics; 112 Economic Development Models and Theories; 311 Domestic Monetary and Financial Theory and Institutions.
Publications *Books:* 1. *The International Monetary System* (with R. Carbaugh) (Univ. Press, Kansas, 1976).
Articles: 1. 'A note on the shapes of marginal utility curves', *Kyk*, 21(4), 1968; 2. 'Monetary performances in developing economies: a quantity theoretic approach', *QREB*, 10(2), June 1970; 3. 'Pulling effect and the capacity to follow: the case of Japan in East Asia', *Devlp. Econ.*, 8(2), June 1970; 4. 'Demand for money in Asian countries: empirical evidence' (with Z. R. Liu), *Indian EJ*, 18(4), April 1971; 5. 'Leisure and time elements in consumer behavior', *SEJ*, 38(4), Sept. 1972; 6. 'The economy and the trade of China', *Law and Contemporary Issues*, 38(2), Sept. 1974; 7. 'On the reward system', *AER*, 65(1), March 1975; 8. 'B-efficiency in the theory of firms: a note', *SEJ*, 41(4), April 1975; 9. 'Some recent developments in Chinese incentive schemes in agriculture' (with C. M. Fan), *Canadian J. Agric. Econ.* 28(2), 1980; 10. 'A

developmental strategy: an analysis of Singaporean wage policy' (with C. M. Fan), *RISE*, 29(7), July 1982.

Principal Contributions East Asia has been the major area of my concern, especially the leading role Japan played in the region's economy. The new field of the design of mechanisms, especially the role of the incentive scheme in the developmental process, e.g. in China, attracts my research interest. Since 1980, visits to SE Asian countries, China, and India have rekindled my interest in Asian development.

FARRELL, Michael James*

Dates and Birthplace 1926–75, England.

Posts Held Ass. Lect., Lect. Econ., Univ. Camb., 1953–6, 1956–70; Vis. Prof., Yale Univ., 1962, Univ. Cal. Berkeley, 1966–7; Ford Disting. Vis. Res. Prof., Carnegie-Mellon Univ., 1969; Fellow, Gonville and Caius Coll., Reader Econ., Univ. Camb., 1958–75, 1970–5.

Degrees MA Univ. Oxford, 1953; MA Univ. Camb., 1953.

Offices and Honours Commonwealth Fund Fellow, 1951–3; Fellow, Em Soc, 1962–75.

Editorial Duties Ed., *J Ind E*, 1963–75; Joint Managing Ed., *REStud*, 1965–8.

Publications *Books:* 1. *Fuller Employment* (1965); 2. *Readings in Welfare Economics*, ed. (1973).

Articles: 1. 'In defence of public-utility price theory', *OEP*, 10, Feb. 1958, repr. in *Public Enterprise. Selected Readings*, ed. R. Turvey (Penguin, 1968); 2. 'The convexity assumption in the theory of competitive markets', *JPE*, 67, Aug. 1959; 3. 'The new theories of the consumption function', *EJ*, 69, Dec. 1959.

Career Leading British welfare economist of the 1950s, writing on both theoretical and applied problems.

FAULHABER, Gerald R.

Born 1939.

Current Post Assoc. Prof. Public Pol. and Management; Dir., Fishman-Davidson Center Study of Service Sector, Wharton School, Univ. Penn., Philadelphia, PA, USA, 1983–.

Past Posts Technical Staff, Supervisor, Res. Head Econ. Modeling, Bell Telephone Lab. Inc., NJ, 1962–8, 1968–75, 1975–7; Vis. Instr. Princeton Univ., 1976–7; Dir., Microecon. Stud., Dept. Strategic Planning, Dir. Fin. Management, AT&T, NY, 1978–82, 1982–3, 1983; Res. Assoc. Prof., NYU, 1979–83.

Degrees BA Haverford Coll., 1962; MS NYU, 1964; MA, PhD Princeton Univ., 1974, 1975.

Principal Fields of Interest 100 Quantitive Economic Methods and Data; 210 Econometric, Statistical and Mathematical Methods and Models; 635 Industry Studies, Services and Related Industries.

Publications *Books:* 1. *Telecommunications Access and Public Policy*, co-ed. (with A. Buaghcum), (Ablex, 1984).

Articles: 1. 'Cross subsidization: pricing in public enterprises', *AER*, 65(5), Dec. 1975; 2. 'Optimal two-part tariffs with self selection' (with J. Panzar), *Bell Lab. Econ. Discussion Paper*, 74, 1977; 3. 'Cross-subsidization in public enterprise pricing', in *Pricing in Regulated Industries, Theory and Application II*, ed. J. T. Wenders (Colorado Univ. Press, 1979); 4. 'Peak-load pricing and regulatory accountability', in *Problems in Public Utility Economies and Regulation*, ed. M. A. Crew (D. C. Heath, 1979); 5. 'Regulation and market structure in telecommunications' (with J. H. Rohlfs), *Conference on Economics of Telecommunications* (Northwestern Univ., 1980); 6. 'Subsidy-free prices and anonymous equity', *AER*, 71(5), Dec. 1981; 7. 'A public enterprise pricing primer', in *Economic Analysis of Regulated Markets*, ed. J. Finsinger (Ablex, 1984).

Principal Contributions My early work concentrated in public utility pricing, particularly in cross-subsidization. My 1975 article (No. 1 above) rigorously defended the concept of cross-subsidies in pricing, and explored its welfare, equity and incentive implications. The 1981 article (No. 6 above) completed my PhD research by examining the relationship between cross-subsidy among products and cross-subsidy among groups of consumers. My work in the 1976–80 period was devoted to non-uniform pricing and economic policy issues in telecommunications, an industry in the throes of change at that time. More recently, my interests have broadened to include the entire service sector. My current efforts are in the area of the economics of reputation.

FAWCETT, Henry*

Dates and Birthplace 1833–84, Salisbury, Wiltshire, England.
Posts Held Fellow, Trinity Hall, Prof. Polit. Econ., Univ. Camb., 1856–84, 1863–84.
Degrees BA Univ. Camb., 1856.
Offices and Honours MP Brighton, 1865–74, Hackney, 1874–84; UK Postmaster-General, 1880–4; Fellow, Royal Soc., 1882.
Publications *Books: 1. Manual of Political Economy* (1863).
Career Blinded in a shooting accident at the age of 25, he nevertheless enjoyed a most distinguished career as member of parliament, cabinet minister and professor of economics. His *Manual* ... is in effect a popularisation of the ideas of his friend J. S. Mill, and as such enjoyed great success as a textbook throughout the second half of the nineteenth century. The level of analysis is, however, unremarkable, with a dogmatic presentation of *laissez-faire* and a strict adherence to the wages fund theory. He was the first salaried professor of political economy at Cambridge University, and was Marshall's predecessor in the chair.
Secondary Literature L. Stephen, *Life of Henry Fawcett* (Macmillan, 1885).

FEINSTEIN, Charles Hilliard

Born 1932, Johannesburg, Transvaal, S. Africa.
Current Post Prof. Econ. and Social Hist., Univ. York, York, England, 1978–.
Past Posts Res. Officer, Dept. Appl. Econ., Lect. Econ., Fellow, Clare Coll.,

Univ. Cambridge, 1958–63; Exchange Vis., Univ. Moscow, 1966; Res. Fellow, Russian Res. Centre, Univ. Harvard, 1967–8; Vis. Prof., Univ. Delhi, 1972.
Degrees B.Com Univ. Witwatersrand, S. Africa, 1950; Certified Accountant, S. Africa, 1954; PhD Univ. Camb., 1958.
Offices and Honours Council, RES, 1980–; Council, EHS, 1980–; Econ. Affairs Comm., UK SSRC, 1982–; Fellow, BA, 1983.
Editorial Duties Ass. Ed., *London & Camb Econ. Bull.*, 1962–4; Ed. Board, *Explor. in Econ. Hist.*, 1975–81; Ed., *EJ*, 1980–.
Principal Fields of Interest 040 Economic History; 052 Social and Economic Systems; 221 National Income Accounting.
Publications *Books: 1. Domestic Capital Formation in the United Kingdom, 1920–1938* (CUP, 1965); 2. *Socialism, Capitalism and Economic Growth, Essays presented to Maurice Dobb*, ed. (CUP, 1967); 3. *National Income, Expenditure and Output of the United Kingdom, 1955–1965* (CUP, 1972); 4. *The Relevance of Economic Theories*, co-ed. (with J. Pajeskka), (Macmillan, 1980); 5. *York, 1831–1981*, ed. and contrib. (Sessions of York, 1981); 6. *British Economic Growth, 1856–1973* (with R. C. O. Matthews and J. Odling-Smee), (OUP, 1982); 7. *The Managed Economy, Essays in British Economic Policy and Performance since 1929*, ed. (OUP, 1983).
Articles: 1. 'Income and investment in the United Kingdom, 1856–1914', *EJ*, 71, June 1961; 2. 'Stocks and stock-building', *London & Camb Econ. Bull.*, 44, 45, Dec. 1962, March 1963; 3. 'Production and productivity in the United Kingdom, 1920–1962', *London & Camb. Econ. Bull.*, 48, Dec. 1963, repr. in *Economic Growth in 20th Century Britain*, eds. D. H. Aldcroft and P. Fearon (Macmillan, 1969); 4. 'Evolution of the distribution of the national income in the U.K. since 1860', in *The Distribution of National Income*, eds. J. Marchal and B. Ducros (Macmillan, 1968); 5. 'The compilation of gross domestic fixed capital formation statistics, 1856–1913', in *Aspects of Capital Investment in Great Britain*, eds. J. P.

P. Higgins and S. Pollard (Methuen, 1971); 6. 'Capital accumulation and economic growth in Great Britain, 1760–1860', in *Cambridge Economic History of Europe*, 7, eds. P. Mathias and M. M. Postan (CUP, 1978); 7. 'OPEC surpluses, the world recession and the U.K. economy' (with W. B. Reddaway), *MBR*, Spring 1978, repr. in *Contemporary Problems of Economic Policy — Essays from the Clare Group*, eds. R. C. O. Matthews and J. R. Sargent (Methuen, 1983); 8. 'Capital accumulation and the industrial revolution', in *The Economic History of Britain since 1700*, 1, eds. R. Floud and D. McCloskey (CUP, 1981); 9. 'The timing of the climacteric and its sectoral incidence in the U.K., 1873–1913' (with R. C. O. Matthews and J. C. Odling-Smee), in *Economics in the Long View*, eds. C. P. Kindleberger and G. Di Tella (Macmillan, 1982).

Principal Contributions My initial interest as a graduate student was in the problems of growth and retardation in Britain and the role in this of overseas lending. This led to an attempt to develop more reliable and comprehensive national accounts for the years 1856–1948 including, in particular, series for domestic capital formation. What began as a brief investigation turned into a thirty-year study. This included a major effort to reconcile the separate estimates of GDP I had built up from income, expenditure and output data. The analysis and interpretation of these (and related) series was undertaken in association with Robin Matthews and John Odling-Smee. The work on capital accumulation was also carried back into the preceding period (1760–1860) as part of the debate about the contribution of capital to growth during the industrial revolution.

FELDMAN, Allan M.

Born 1943, Paterson, NJ, USA.
Current Post Assoc. Prof. Econ., Brown Univ., Providence, RI, USA, 1978–.
Past Posts Ass. Prof., Brown Univ., 1971–7; Vis. Assoc. Prof., Univ. Virginia, 1978.

Degrees BS (Maths.), MA (Anthrop.) Univ. Chicago, 1965, 1967; PhD Johns Hopkins Univ., 1972.
Offices and Honours Phi Beta Kappa.
Editorial Duties Ed. Cons, *AER*, 1973–81.
Principal Fields of Interest 022 Microeconomic Theory; 024 Welfare Theory; 025 Social Choice, Bureaucratic Performance.
Publications *Books:* 1. *Welfare Economics and Social Choice Theory* (Martinus Nijhoff, 1980).
Articles: 1. 'Bilateral trading processes, pairwise optimality, and Pareto optimality', *REStud*, 40(4), Oct. 1973; 2. 'Recontracting stability', *Em*, 42(1), Jan. 1974; 3. 'Fairness and envy' (with A. Kirman), *AER*, 42(1), Jan. 1974; 4. 'Manipulating voting procedures', *EI*, 17(3), July 1979; 5. 'Manipulation and the Pareto rule', *JET*, 21(3), Dec. 1979; 6. 'A model of majority voting and growth in government expenditures', *Public Choice*, 1984; 7. 'Sunset for industrial policy', *Pol. Rev.*, 1984.

Principal Contributions My early work was on general equilibrium theory and welfare economics. Thus I showed that in an exchange economy model, bilateral trade could suffice to carry the economy to a Pareto optimal state, and in a game theoretic model, a random recontracting process could in general be used to carry the system to the core. As I studied the fundamental theorems of welfare economics, however, I started to see the importance of judging among Pareto optimal or noncomparable states of the economy, and so my interest gradually turned to Arrow's theorem, fairness, and various issues of manipulability of social decision functions.

FELDSTEIN, Martin

Born 1939, New York City, NY, USA.
Current Post Prof. Econ., Harvard Univ., 1967–; Pres., NBER, Cambridge, Mass., 1977–.
Recent Posts Fellow, Nuffield Coll. Oxford, 1965–7.
Degrees BA Harvard Univ., 1961; BLitt., MA, DPhil Univ. Oxford, 1963, 1964, 1967.

Offices and Honours Fellow, Council Member, Fisher-Schultz Lecture, Em Soc, 1970, 1977–, 1980; John Bates Clark Medal, AEA, 1977; Chairman, US President's Council Econ. Advisers, 1982–4.

Principal Fields of Interest 023 Macroeconomic Theory.

Publications *Books:* 1. *Economic Analysis for Health Service Efficiency* (N-H, 1967); 2. *Hospital Costs and Health Insurance* (Harvard Univ. Press, 1981); 3. *Capital Taxation* (Harvard Univ. Press, 1981); 4. *Inflation, Tax Rules and Capital Formation* (Chicago Univ. Press, 1981); 5. *Behavioral Simulation Methods in Tax Policy Analysis* (Chicago Univ. Press, 1981).

Principal Contributions Quantitative studies in public economics, including tax, transfer and spending programmes. More specifically, the effects of these fiscal programmes on capital formation and employment. Studies of social insurance programmes (social security pensions, unemployment insurance, health insurance). Analyses of the interaction between fiscal structure and macroeconomic policy. Studies of capital formation.

FELLNER, William John*

Dates and Birthplace 1905–83, Budapest, Hungary.

Posts Held Partner, Hungarian family enterprise, 1929–38; Ass. Prof., Assoc. Prof., Univ. Cal. Berkeley, 1939–52; Prof., Sterling Prof. Econ., Yale Univ., 1952–5, 1959–73; Member, US President's Council Econ. Advisers, 1973–5; Res. Scholar, AEI, Washington, DC, 1975–83.

Degrees Diplome (Chem. Eng.) Fed. Inst. Technology, Zurich, 1927; PhD Univ. Berlin, 1929.

Offices and Honours Phi Beta Kappa; Fellow, AAAS; Corresp. Member, Bavarian Academy Sciences; Pres., AEA, 1969; Commander's Cross Order Merit, German Fed. Republic, 1979; Bernard-Harms Prize, Inst. für Weltwirtschaft, Kiel, 1982.

Publications *Books:* 1. *Monetary Policies and Full Employment* (1946); 2. *Competition Among the Few* (1949);

3. *Trends and Cycles in Economic Activity* (1955); 4. *Probability and Profit* (1965); 5. *Towards a Reconstruction of Macroeconomics* (1976); 6. *Corrective Taxes for Inflation* (with K. W. Clarkson and J. H. Moore), (1975).

Articles: 1. 'Prices and wages under bilateral monopoly', *QJE*, 61, Aug. 1947; 2. 'Average-cost pricing and the theory of uncertainty', *JPE*, 56, June 1958; 3. 'Two propositions in the theory of induced innovations', *EJ*, 71, June 1961; 4. 'Lessons from the failure of demand-management policies', *JEL*, 14(1), March 1976; 5. 'The valid core of rationality hypotheses in the theory of expectations', *JMCB*, 12(4), pt. 2, Nov. 1980; 6. 'The bearing of risk aversion on measurements of spot and forward exchange relative to the dollar', in *Flexible Exchange Rates and the Balance of Payments: Essays in Memory of E. Sohmen*, eds. J. S. Chipman and C. P. Kindleberger (1980); 7. 'Economic theory amidst political currents: the spreading interest in monetarism and in the theory of market expectations', *WA*, 118(3), 1982; 8. 'The high-employment budget and potential output', *Survey Current Bus.*, 62(9), Nov. 1982.

Career After a prewar interest in Keynesian economics, he turned after the war to oligopoly theory, growth theory (in particular the theory of induced innovations) profit theory, and an abiding concern with the history of economic thought. The 1970s saw a return to his earlier love, macroeconomics, where he took up a position that might be described as 'critical monetarism' or 'monetarism, but . . . '. Throughout his career he showed an unusual talent for summing up the state-of-the-art in a subject, bringing to it some rigours in reformulating the problem but, above all, wisdom and perspective in placing it in context.

FELS, Rendige

Born 1917, Cincinnati, OH, USA.

Current Post Prof. Econ. Emeritus, Vanderbilt Univ., Nashville, TN, USA, 1982–.

Past Posts Ass. Prof., Assoc. Prof., Prof. Econ., Vanderbilt Univ., 1948–52,

1952–6, 1956–82; Vis. Prof., Stanford Univ., 1955, Salzburg Seminar Amer. Stud., 1963; Cons., Econ. Devlp. Inst., Univ. Nigeria, 1963, NBER, 1964.

Degrees BA, PhD Harvard Univ., 1939, 1948; MA Columbia Univ., 1940.

Offices and Honours Chairman, Comm. Coll. Level Test Econ. Understanding, 1965–8; Pres., SEA, 1967–8; Secretary, Treasurer, AEA, 1970–5, 1970–; Harvie Branscomb Disting. Prof., Vanderbilt Univ., 1980–1; Madison Sarratt Prize, Excellence Undergrad, Teaching, 1981; Pres., Midwest Econ. Assoc. 1984–5.

Editorial Duties Ed. Boards, *SEJ*, 1952–5, *AER*, 1959–61; *J. Econ. Educ.*, 1969.

Principal Fields of Interest 012 Teaching of Economics; 131 Economic Fluctuations; 036 Economic Methodology.

Publications *Books:* 1. *Wages, Earnings and Employment, Nashville, Chattanooga and St. Louis Railway, 1866–1896* (Vanderbilt Univ. Press, 1953); 2. *American Business Cycles, 1865–1897* (Univ. N. Carolina Press, 1959); 3. *Challenge to the American Economy: An Introduction to Economics* (Allyn & Bacon, 1961, 1966); 4. *Forecasting and Recognizing Business-Cycle Turning Points* (with C. E. Hinshaw), (Columbia Univ. Press, 1968); 5. *Casebook of Economic Problems and Policies* (with R. G. Uhler and S. G. Buckles), (West Publishing, 1974, 1981); 6. *Recent Advances in Economics*, co-ed. (with J. J. Siegfried), (Richard D. Irwin, 1974); 7. *Research on Teaching College Economics*, co-ed. (with J. J. Siegfried), (Joint Council Econ. Educ., 1982).

Articles: 1. 'On teaching elementary economics', *AER*, 45(2), May 1955; 2. 'The recognition-lag and semi-automatic stabilizers', *REStat*, 45, Aug. 1963; 3. 'The US downturn of 1948', *AER*, 55(5), Dec. 1965; 4. 'A new "test of understanding in college economics"', *AER*, 57(2), May 1967; 5. 'Multiple choice questions in elementary economics', in *Recent Research in Economics Education*, ed. K. G. Lumsden (Prentice-Hall, 1970); 6. 'Developing independent problem-solving ability in elementary economics', *AER*, 64(2), May 1974; 7. 'The Vanderbilt-JCEE experimental course in elementary eco-

nomics', *J. Econ. Educ.*, Special Issue, 2, Winter 1974; 8. 'What economics is most important to teach: the Hansen committee report', *AER*, 67(2), May 1977; 9. 'What causes business cycles?', *Social Science Q.*, June 1977; 10. 'Research on teaching college economics: a survey' (with J. J. Siegfried), *JEL*, 17(3), Sept. 1979.

Principal Contributions Early work was on business cycles. In particular, I applied existing business-cycle theories to explaining fluctuations in the US in the last third of the nineteenth century. Lost interest as it became apparent that cycles are not (or at least are no longer) endogenous but are dominated by monetary and fiscal policies and other exogenous disturbances. My recent work has been on the teaching of economics. I chaired the committee that developed the Test of Understanding in College Economics, subsequently used, mostly by others, in over 70 published research studies. Along with Bach, Hansen, Kelley, Lumsden, Saunders, Siegfried and others, I have contributed to making research on teaching economics a respectable subject.

FERBER, Robert*

Dates and Birthplace 1922–1981, New York City, NY, USA.

Posts Held Prof. Econ. and Bus. Admin., Dir., Survey Res. Laboratory, Univ. Illinois Urbana-Champaign, IL, 1951–79, 1964–79; Prof. Marketing, Univ. Illinois Chicago Circle, 1979–81.

Degrees BS (Maths.), City Coll., NY, 1942; MA (Econ., Stats.), PhD (Econ. Stats.), Univ. Chicago, 1945, 1951.

Offices and Honours Ford Foundation Master Scholar, 1963; Hall of Fame Distribution, 1964; Pres., Amer. Marketing Assoc., 1969–70; Charles Coolidge Parlin Award, 1972; Chairman Publications Comm., ASA, 1977–81; AEA, 1978–81.

Editorial Duties Ed., *J. Marketing Res.*, 1964–9, *JASA*, 1969–76, *J. Consumer Res.*, 1977–.

Publications *Books:* 1. *A Study of Aggregate Consumption Functions* (1953); 2. *Research Methods in Eco-

nomics and Business (with R. Ferber and P. J. Verdoorn), (1962); 3. *The Reliability of Consumer Reports of Financial Assets and Debts* (1966); 4. *Determinants of Investment Behavior*, ed. (1967); 5. *Consumption and Income Distribution in Latin America: Selected Topics*, ed. (1980).

Articles: 1. 'Measuring the accuracy and structure of businessmen's expectations', *JASA*, 48, Sept. 1953; 2. 'The accuracy of aggregate saving functions in the postwar years', *REStat*, 37, May 1955; 3. 'Consumer economics, a survey', *JEL*, 11(4), Dec. 1973; 4. 'Finding the poor' (with P. Musgrove), *RIW*, 24, Sept. 1978; 5. 'Social experimentation and economic policy: a survey' (with W. Z. Hirsch), *JEL*, 16(4), Dec. 1978.

Career Studies on the reliability of economic data obtained in household surveys and ways of improving these data. Investigations of consumer saving and spending patterns and their determinants in industrialised and in less-developed countries. Studies of the roles of expectations in consumer and business behaviour.

FERGUSON, Adam*

Dates and Birthplace 1723–1816, Perthshire, Scotland.
Posts Held Military Chaplain; Keeper, Advocate's Library, Edinburgh; Prof. Nat. Phil., Prof. Moral Phil., Univ. Edinburgh, 1759–64, 1764–85.
Degree BA Univ. Edinburgh.
Offices and Honours Founder Member, Royal Soc. Edinburgh; Hon. Member, Berlin Academy Sciences.
Publications *Books:* 1. *An Essay on the History of Civil Society* (1767, 1978); 2. *Institutes of Moral Philosophy* (1769, 1800); 3. *History of the Progress and Termination of the Roman Republic*, 3 vols (1783, 1841); 4. *Principles of Moral and Political Science*, 2 vols (1792).

Career Scottish moral philosopher whose *History of Civil Society* has been identified as an early example of sociological method. His work is of interest to economists because of the clear exposition of the principle of the division of labour in economy and society, which

almost certainly had a major influence on Adam Smith.

Secondary Literature D. Kettler, *The Social and Political Thought of Adam Ferguson* (Ohio State Univ. Press, 1965); W. C. Lehmann, 'Ferguson, Adam', *IESS*, 5.

FERGUSON, Charles E.*

Dates and Birthplace 1928–72, Nashville, AR, USA.
Posts Held Instr. Social Science, Nashville High School, 1949–50; Instr., Hendrix Coll., 1951–2; Ass. Prof., Assoc. Prof., Prof., Duke Univ., 1957–60, 1960–2, 1962–7; Prof., Michigan State Univ., 1967–8; Prof. Texas A&M Univ., 1968–72.
Degrees BA Hendrix Coll., 1949; MA, PhD Univ. N. Carolina, 1951, 1957.
Offices and Honours Univ. Fellow, Univ. N. Carolina, 1950–1, 1954–5; Earhart Foundation Fellow, 1955–6; Ford Foundation Doctoral Dissertation Fellow, 1956–7; Ford Foundation Faculty Fellow, 1961–2; US SSRC Fellow, 1964–5; Member, Australian and New Zealand Soc. Econ.; Fellow, Em Soc; Exec-Comm., Vice-Pres., Pres., SEA, 1963–4, 1966–7, 1971–2; Elected Fellow, ASA, AAAS.
Editorial Duties Ed. Boards, *SEJ*, 1964–71, *AER*, 1969–72.
Publications *Books:* 1. *Principles of Economics* (with J. M. Kreps), (Holt, Rinehart & Winston, 1962, 1965; transl., Spanish, 1967); 2. *A Macroeconomic Theory of Workable Competition* (Duke Univ. Press, 1964; transl., German, 1970); 3. *Microeconomic Theory* (Richard D. Irwin, 1966, 1972; transls., Japanese, 1967, Spanish, 1971); 4. *The Neoclassical Theory of Production and Distribution* (CUP, 1969; transl., Japanese, 1971); 5. *Economic Analysis* (with S. C. Maurice), (Richard D. Irwin, 1970).

Articles: 1. 'On theories of acceleration and growth', *QJE*, 74, Feb. 1960; 2. 'A metric general solution of linear difference equations with constant coefficients' (with R. W. Pfouts), *Maths. Magazine*, 33, Feb. 1960; 3. 'Modified Edgeworth phenomena and the nature of related commodities', in *Essays in Economics and Econometrics in Honor of Harold Hotelling*, ed. R. W. Pfouts (Univ. N. Carolina Press, 1960); 4. 'Learning and expectations in dynamic duopoly behavior' (with R. W. Pfouts), *Behavioral Science*, 7, April 1962; 5. 'Cross-section production functions and the elasticity of substitution in American manufacturing industry, 1947–1958', *REStat*, 45, Aug. 1963; 6. 'Time-series production functions and technological progress in American manufacturing industry', *JPE*, 74, April 1965; 7. 'Substitution, technical progress, and returns to scale', *AER*, 55(2), May 1965; 8. 'Production, prices and the theory of jointly-derived input demand functions', *Ec*, N.S. 33, Nov. 1966; 9. '"Inferior factors" and the theories of production and derived demand', *Ec*, N.S. 35, May 1968; 10. 'Long-run scale adjustments of a perfectly competitive firm and industry' (with T. R. Saving), *AER*, 59(4), Sept. 1969.

Career Neoclassical economist who worked widely in both micro- and macroeconomics.

FERRARA, Francesco*

Dates and Birthplace 1810–1900, Palermo, Italy.

Posts Held Dir. Stats., Palermo region, 1834; Prof. Polit. Econ., Univ. Turin 1845–59; Controller Customs, Palermo, 1862; Italian Minister Fin., 1867; Dir., School of Commerce, Venice, 1881.

Publications *Books:* 1. *Esame storico-critico di economisti e dottrine economiche* (1889–92); 2. *Oeuvres économiques choises*, eds. G. H. Bousquet and J. Crisafulli (1938).

Articles: 1. 'Preface on the doctrine of the physiocrats', *Fisiocrati*, 1850, repr. in *Internat. Econ. Papers*, 8, eds. A. T. Peacock, *et al.* (Macmillan, 1958).

Career His varied career in the public service, politics and education included periods of imprisonment and exile as well as periods in government. He founded the *Giornale di Statistica* and was responsible for the *Biblioteca*

dell'Economista (1850–70) which collected translations of notable foreign and Italian economic literature. His doctrinaire free trade liberalism became unfashionable during his later years and he became an increasingly isolated figure.

Secondary Literature A. Loria, 'Francesco Ferrara' (obit.), *EJ*, 10, March 1900; G. H. Bousquet, 'Un grand économiste Italien, Francesco Ferrara', *Revue d'histoire écon. et sociale*, 14, 1926.

FETTER, Frank Albert*

Dates and Birthplace 1863–1949, Peru, IN, USA.

Posts Held Prof., Indiana Univ., 1895–8, Stanford Univ., 1898–1901, Cornell Univ., 1901–11, Princeton Univ., 1911–33.

Degrees BA Indiana Univ., 1891; MPhil Cornell Univ., 1892; PhD Univ. Halle, Germany, 1894.

Offices and Honours Council Member, Amer. Philo. Soc., Pres., AEA, 1912; Karl Menger Medal, Austrian Econ. Soc., 1927.

Publications *Books:* 1. *The Principles of Economics with Applications to Practical Problems*, (1904); 2. *Economic Principles* (1915); 3. *Modern Economic Problems* (1917); 4. *Capital, Interest, and Rent. Essays in the Theory of Distribution*, ed. M. N. Rothbard (1977).

Career His interest in bringing economics into line with new trends in psychology led him to concentrate on theories of value. His work on value theory in turn brought him into friendly contact with Böhm-Bawerk and Wieser, whilst his distaste for the preservation of 'outdated' theory made him an opponent of Marshall. Welfare economics was a major concern and he frequently applied economic theory to public questions; for instance, in 1923–4 he was a member of a group which placed evidence before the Federal Trade Commission on pricing practices in the steel industry. The concept of 'psychic income', taken up by Irving Fisher, was one of his best known contributions.

Secondary Literature S. E. Howard

and E. W. Kemmerer, 'Frank Albert Fetter. A birthday note', *AER*, 33(1), March 1943.

FETTER, Frank Whitson

Born 1899, San Francisco, CA, USA.
Current Post Prof. Econ. Emeritus, Northwestern Univ., Evanston, IL, USA.
Past Posts Instr., Ass. Prof. Econ., Princeton Univ., 1924–34; Assoc. Prof., Prof. Econ., Haverford Coll., 1934–48; Prof. Econ., Northwestern Univ., 1948–67; Vis. Prof. Econ., Dartmouth Coll., 1967–8.
Degrees BA Swarthmore Coll., 1920; MA, PhD Princeton Univ., 1922, 1926; MA Harvard Univ., 1924.
Offices and Honours Phi Beta Kappa, 1920; Guggenheim Foundation Fellow, 1937–8; Exec. Comm., AEA, 1944–6; Pres., MEA, 1932; Dir., Chairman, NBER, 1950–73, 1965–7.
Editorial Duties Ed. Board, *HOPE*, 1969–84.
Principal Fields of Interest 031 History of Economic Thought.
Publications *Books:* 1. *Monetary Inflation in Chile* (Princeton Univ. Press, 1931; transl., Spanish, 1937); 2. *The Irish Pound* (A&U, Northwestern Univ. Press, 1955); 3. *Development of British Monetary Orthodoxy* (Harvard Univ. Press, 1965, Augustus M. Kelley, 1978); 4. *Monetary and Financing Policy in 19th Century Britain* (with D. Gregory), (Irish Univ. Press, 1973); 5. *The Economist in Parliament* (Duke Univ. Press, 1980).
Articles: 1. 'The life and writings of John Wheatley', *JPE*, 50, June, 1942; 2. 'Does America breed depressions?', *Three Banks Rev.*, 27, Sept. 1955; 3. 'Economic controversies in the British reviews', *Ec*, 32, Nov. 1965; 4. 'The transfer problem: formal elegance or historical realism?', in *Essays in Money and Banking in Honour of R. S. Sayers* (OUP, 1968); 5. 'The rise and decline of Ricardian economics', *HOPE*, 1(1), Spring 1969.
Principal Contributions Development of British monetary and banking policy between 1797 and 1875; econ-omic opinion in the British reviews up to 1850; role of an economist in parliament between Adam Smith and J. S. Mill; relation of British economic thought to the spirit of the Enlighten-ment; and the transfer problem.

FINDLAY, Ronald Edsel

Born 1935, Rangoon, Burma.
Current Post Ragnar Nurkse Prof. Econ., Columbia Univ., 1977–.
Past Posts Tutor Econ., Rangoon Univ., 1954–7; Lect., Prof. Econ., Rangoon Univ., 1960–9; Prof. Econ., Columbia Univ., 1969–77; Gunnar Myrdal Vis. Res. Prof. Internat. Econ., Stockholm, 1984.
Degrees BA Rangoon Univ., 1954; PhD MIT, 1960.
Principal Fields of Interest 411 International Trade Theory; 112 Economic Development Models; 020 Economic Theory.
Publications *Books:* 1. *Trade and Specialization* (Penguin, 1970); 2. *International Trade and Development Theory* (Columbia Univ. Press, 1970).
Articles: 1. 'Factor intensities, technological progress and the terms of trade' (with H. Grubert), *OEP*, N.S. 11, Feb. 1959; 2. 'The Robinsonian model of accumulation', *Ec*, N.S. 30, Feb. 1962; 3. 'Factor proportions and comparative advantage in the long run', *JPE*, 78(1), Jan.–Feb. 1970; 4. 'Relative prices, growth and trade in a simple Ricardian system', *Em*, 41, Feb. 1974; 5. 'Slavery, incentives and manu-mission', *JPE*, 83(5), Oct. 1975; 6. 'Project evaluation, shadow prices and trade policy' (with W. Willisz), *JPE*, 84(3), June 1976; 7. 'Relative back-wardness, direct foreign investment and the transfer of technology', *QJE*, 92(1), Feb. 1978; 8. 'An Austrian model of international trade and inter-est rate equaliziation', *JPE*, 86(6), Dec. 1978; 9. 'The terms of trade and equilibrium growth in the world econ-omy', *AER*, 70(3), June 1980; 10. 'In-ternational trade and human capital' (with H. Kierzkowski), *JPE*, 91(6), Dec. 1983.
Principal Contributions The rela-tionships between economic growth

and development and international trade and factor mobility have been the main focus of my work. My first paper was on the effects of technological progress on the terms of trade. My 1973 book put forward a series of interrelated models of trade and development drawn from a variety of sources in neoclassical and 'Cambridge' growth and capital theory, but adapted to apply to the structural conditions of the developing countries. They could perhaps be described as representing the application of 'marginalist' theory to 'structuralist' problems, with Samuelson and Solow as the source of the former and Lewis and Murkse of the latter. These twin sources of inspiration are perhaps best revealed in my recent work on 'North-South' models of asymmetric interdependence in the world economy, involving trade between a Solow-type industrialised 'North' characterised by full employment of a growing labour force and a Lewis-type 'South' characterised by surplus labour, with the terms of trade linking the growth rates of the two regions. Another recent interest has been the attempt to 'endogenise' the stocks of physical and human capital in the Heckscher-Ohlin trade model by combining it with an 'Austrian' view of the production process. I have also been interested in the application of economic theory to economic history, with a 1975 paper on slavery and manumission in antiquity and a 1982 paper on trade and growth in the industrial revolution. Currently I am engaged in what may be called neoclassical political economy, using simple general equilibrium models to analyse the role of the State and the 'rent-seeking' activities of interest groups.

FINGER, Joseph Michael

Born 1939, D'Hanis, TX, USA.
Current Post Chief, Internat. Econ. Res. Div., Devlp. Res. Dept., World Bank, Washington, DC, USA, 1983–.
Past Posts Ass. Prof. Econ., Duke Univ., 1965–9; Assoc. Prof. Econ., Univ. Georgia, 1969–70; Scholar in Residence, US Tariff Commission, 1970–1; Sr. Econ., Res. Div., UN Conf. Trade and Devlp., Geneva, 1971–4; Sr. Internat. Econ., Acting Deputy Ass. Sec., Res. and Planning, Dir., Office Trade Res., US Treasury Dept., 1974–5, 1976, 1975–80; Sr. Econ., Econ. Res. Staff, World Bank, 1980–3.
Degrees BA Univ. Texas, 1960; PhD Univ. N. Carolina, 1967.
Offices and Honours Exec. Comm., Vice-Pres., SEA, 1976–8, 1980–1; Certificate Appreciation, Merit Achievement Award, US Treasury Dept., 1977, 1980.
Principal Fields of Interest 400 International Economics; 610 Industrial Organisation and Public Policy; A00 Political Science.
Publications *Books:* 1. *The Internalization of the American Economy* (with T. D. Willett), (Amer. Academy Polit. & Social Science, 1982).
Articles: 1. 'Substitution and the effective rate of protection', *JPE*, 77(6), Dec. 1969; 2. 'Effects of the Kennedy round tariff concessions on the exports of developing countries', *EJ*, 86, March 1976; 3. 'Trade overlap and intra-industry trade', *EI*, 13(4), Dec. 1975; 4. 'Trade and domestic effects of the offshore assembly provision in the United States tariff', *AER*, 66(4), Sept. 1976; 5. 'A new international economic order: a critical survey of the issues' (with M. E. Kreinin), *J. World Trade Law*, 16(6), Nov.–Dec. 1976; 6. 'The processing of primary commodities: effects of developed country tariff escalation and developing country export taxes' (with S. Golub), *JPE*, 87(2), May–June 1979; 7. 'Trade liberalization: a public choice perspective', in *Challenges to a Liberal International Economic Order*, eds. R. C. Amacher, G. Haberler and T. D. Willett (AEI, 1979); 8. 'Policy research', *JPE*, 89(6), Dec. 1981; 9. 'The political economy of administered protection' (with H. K. Hall and D. R. Nelson), *AER*, 73(3), June 1982; 10. 'Incorporating the gains from trade into policy', *The World Economy*, 5(4), Dec. 1982.
Principal Contributions My first start at a PhD dissertation was abandoned. I had worked for several months on a topic in pure theory but an attempt

to write an introduction led to a long pause reading the philosophy of science and an eventual introduction which argued that what followed was valueless. Convinced by my own argument, I threw away everything but the introduction (from which three papers eventually were published) and did a dissertation on intra-industry trade. Seven years later I published a paper 'out' of this dissertation, which argued a thesis totally opposite to that of the dissertation. By then I had left teaching for the bureaucracy and made a series of studies estimating the effects of various trade policies — the Dillon and Kennedy Round tariff concessions, offshore assembly provisions, etc. These could have been done by anyone with good contemporary training in economics, an awareness that the policies existed, and a willingness to work. Eventually I became more interested in the determinants of trade policy than in its effects, though to make a living I still crank out 'effects of' studies. If there is anything I have written which anyone might benefit from *studying* (not just taking down the results), it is the short essay 'Policy Research' and perhaps 'The Political Economy of Administered Protection'. But too many people stop with the numbers in the latter paper and never get to the ideas.

FINNEGAN, Thomas Aldrich

Born 1929, Long Beach, CA, USA.
Current Post Prof. Econ., Vanderbilt Univ., Nashville, TN, USA, 1970–.
Past Posts Ass. Prof. Econ., Vis. Sr. Res. Econ., Princeton Univ., 1960–4, 1971; Assoc. Prof. Econ., Vanderbilt Univ., 1965–70.
Degrees BA Claremont Men's Coll., 1951; MA, PhD Univ. Chicago, 1953, 1960.
Offices and Honours Exec. Board, Vice-Pres., SEA, 1972–4, 1978; Lawrence R. Klein Award, US Dept. Labor, 1972; Ellen Gregg Ingalls Award Excellence in Teaching, Vanderbilt Univ., 1975; Nominating Comm., AEA, 1983.
Editorial Duties Ed. Board, *SEJ*, 1968–70.

Principal Fields of Interest 813 Labour Force; 824 Labour Market Studies, Wages, Employment; 833 Labour Management Relations.
Publications *Books:* 1. *The Economics of Labor Force Participation* (with W. G. Bowen), (Princeton Univ. Press, 1969).
Articles: 1. 'Hours of work in the United States: a cross-sectional analysis', *JPE*, 70(5), Oct. 1962; 2. 'Educational attainment and labor force participation' (with W. G. Bowen), *AER*, 56(2), May 1966; 3. 'Labour force growth and the return to full employment', *MLR*, 95(2), Feb. 1972; 4. 'Participation of married women in the labor force', in *Sex, Discrimination and the Division of Labor*, ed. C. T. Lloyd (Columbia Univ. Press, 1975); 5. 'Improving our information on discouraged workers', *MLR*, 101(9), Sept. 1978; 6. 'Discouraged workers and economic fluctuations', *ILRR*, 35(1), Oct. 1981.
Principal Contributions Empirical studies of labour supply in the USA, including an early analysis of cross-sectional differences in hours of work, extensive research with W. G. Bowen on the economics of labour force participation, and recent work on the measurement, behaviour, and classification of discouraged workers.

FISCHER, Stanley

Born 1943, Lusaka, Zambia.
Current Post Prof. Econ., MIT, Cambridge, MA, USA, 1977–.
Past Posts Postdoctoral Fellow, Ass. Prof., Univ. Chicago, 1969–70; Vis. Lect., Hebrew Univ. Jerusalem, 1973; Assoc. Prof., MIT, 1973–7; Fellow, Inst. Advanced Stud., Hebrew Univ. 1976–7; Vis. Scholar, Hoover Inst., Stanford Univ., 1981–2; Vis. Prof., Hebrew Univ., 1984.
Degrees BSc, MSc Univ. London, 1965, 1966; PhD MIT, 1969.
Offices and Honours Fellow, Em Soc, AAAS.
Editorial Duties Former Assoc. Ed., *JET, JMCB, JEL, J Mon E*; Assoc. Ed., *Em*; Ed. Board, *J Mon E*.
Principal Fields of Interest 310

Domestic Monetary and Financial Theory and Institutions; 430 Balance of Payments; International Finance; 130 Economic Fluctuations; Forecasting; Stabilisation and Inflation.

Publications *Books:* 1. *Macroeconomics* (with R. Dornbusch), (McGraw-Hill, 1978, 1984; transls., Japanese, 1978, Spanish, 1980, 1981, Portuguese, 1979, 1981; Italian, Il Mulino, 1980, Canadian, with G. Sparks, McGraw-Hill, Ryerson, 1982); 2. *Rational Expectations and Economic Policy*, ed. (Univ. Chicago Press, 1980); 3. *Economics* (with R. Dornbusch), (McGraw-Hill, 1983; with D. Begg, McGraw-Hill, 1984); 4. *Indexing, Inflation, and Economic Policy* (MIT Press, 1986).

Articles: 1. 'Stochastic simulation of monetary rules in two macroeconometric models' (with J. P. Cooper), *JASA*, 67, Dec. 1972; 2. 'Money and the production function', *EI*, 12(4), Dec. 1974; 3. 'The demand for index bonds', *JPE*, 83(3), June 1975; 4. 'Long-term contracts, rational expectations and the optimal money supply rule', *JPE*, 85(1), Feb. 1977; 5. 'Wage indexation and macroeconomic stability', in *Stabilization of the Domestic and International Economy*, eds. K. Brunner and A. Meltzer (N-H, 1977); 6. 'Comparative advantage, trade and payments in a Ricardian model with a continuum of goods' (with R. Dornbush and P. A. Samuelson), *AER*, 67(5), Dec. 1977; 7. 'Towards an understanding of the real effects and costs of inflation' (with F. Modligiani), *WA*, 114(4), 1978; 8. 'Capital accumulation on the transition path in a monetary optimizing model', *Em*, 47(6), Nov. 1979; 9. 'Seigniorage and the case for a national money', *JPE*, 90(2), April 1982.

Principal Contributions Analysis of the actual and potential roles of activist policy in stabilising the economy. Early research (with J. P. Cooper) examined the effects of lags and uncertainty on the effectiveness of policy; subsequent research has concentrated on the role of policy when expectations are rational but prices not immediately flexible. In this context developed a simple macro model with long-term nominal labour contracts that generate price-stickiness, giving short-term Keynesian results and long-term classical results. Analysis of the effects of and reasons for the presence or absence of indexation of wages and asset returns. Showed that indexation of wages is stabilising for output when shocks are nominal but not when they are real; have analysed the view that indexing is itself inflationary, first with exogenous policy, later through its effects on the choice of policy. Showed how index bonds would be priced if they were introduced, and examined welfare economics of their introduction. Analysis of the real effects and costs of inflation (research started jointly with F. Modigliani), showing the role of slowly changing institutions in making inflation costly. Analysis of seigniorage and reasons for use of a national courrency. Education of MIT graduate students, and through *Macroeconomics*, many undergraduates.

FISHBURN, Peter C.

Born 1936, Philipsburg, PA, USA.
Current Post Technical Staff, Math. Sciences Res. Center, AT&T Bell Labs., Murray Hill, NJ, USA, 1978–.
Past Posts Technical Staff, Res. Analysis Corp., McLean, VA, 1964–70; Vis. Lect., Technical Univ. Denmark, 1967; Member, Inst. Advanced Study, Princeton, NJ, 1970–1; Res. Prof. Management Science, Penn. State Univ., 1971–8.
Degrees BA (Industrial Eng.) Penn. State Univ., 1958; PhD (Operations Res.), Case Inst., Technology, 1962.
Offices and Honours Internat. Educ. Award, Amer. Soc. Tool Eng., 1957; Lanchester Prize, ORSA, 1970; Fellow, Em Soc, 1974.
Editorial Duties Ed. Board, *Em*, 1972–8, *Operations Res.*, 1974–8, *Annals Stats.*, 1974–80, *Theory & Decision*, 1974–, *Math. Operations Res.*, 1975–, *SIAM J. Appl. Maths.*, 1976–83, *J. Math. Psychol.*, 1977–, *Discrete Applied Maths.*, 1978–, *JET*, 1978–, *Math. Social Science*, 1979–, *Order*, 1982–, *Social Choice and Welfare*,

1982–, *Naval Res. Logistics Q.*, 1982–, *Annals Operations Res.*, 1983.

Principal Fields of Interest 022 Microeconomic Theory; 025 Social Choice; 026 Economics of Uncertainty and Information.

Publications *Books:* 1. *Decision and Value Theory* (Wiley, 1964); 2. *Utility Theory for Decision Making* (Wiley, 1970); 3. *Mathematics of Decision Theory* (Mouton, 1972); 4. *The Theory of Social Choice* (Princeton Univ. Press, 1973); 5. *The Foundations of Expected Utility* (Reidel, 1982); 6. *Approval Voting* (with S. J. Brams), (Birkhauser, 1983); 7. *Interval Orders and Interval Graphs* (Wiley, 1984).

Articles: 1. 'Independence in utility theory with whole product sets', *Operations Res.*, 13, 1965; 2. 'Utility theory', *Management Science*, 14, 1968; 3. 'A study of independence in multivariate utility theory', *Em*, 37(1), Jan. 1969; 4. 'Intransitive indifference with unequal indifference intervals', *J. Math. Psychol*, 7, 1970; 5. 'Arrow's impossibility theorem: concise proof and infinite voters', *JET*, 2(1), March 1970; 6. 'The theory of representative majority decision', *Em*, 39(2), March 1971; 7. 'Lexicographic orders, utilities and decision rules: a survey', *Management Science*, 20, 1974; 8. 'Unbounded expected utility', *Annals Stats.*, 3, 1975; 9. 'Ordinal preferences and uncertain lifetimes', *Em*, 46(4), July 1978; 10. 'Continua of stochastic dominance relations for unbounded probability distributions', *J Math E*, 7, 1980.

Principal Contributions My early work focussed on expected utility theory (von Neumann & Morgenstern, Savage) and decision theory, including axiomatisations, analyses with incomplete information, and multivariate models. This led naturally to social choice theory in the late 1960s, and during the 1970s my research was divided about evenly between individual decision theory and social choice theory. These interests continue today, and in the early 1980s have involved concentrated efforts on new nonlinear utility theories and the practical assessment of alternative election schemes. Concurrently, I have become more interested in several areas of discrete mathematics, including partially ordered sets and graph theory. These latter interests threaten to dominate the earlier interests but have not yet succeeded in doing so.

FISHER, Franklin Marvin

Born 1934, New York City, NY, USA.

Current Post Prof. Econ., MIT, Cambridge, MA, USA, 1968–.

Past Posts Teaching Fellow, Harvard Univ., 1956–7; Ass. Prof. Econ., Univ. Chicago, 1959–60, MIT, 1962–5; Ford Foundation Faculty Res. Fellow, LSE, Hebrew Univ., Jerusalem, 1966–7; NSF Postdoctoral Fellow, Econometric Inst., Netherlands School Econ., 1968; Vis. Prof. Econ., Hebrew Univ., 1967, 1973, Tel–Aviv Univ., 1973, 1977, Harvard Univ., 1981–2; Erskine Fellow, Univ. Canterbury, New Zealand, 1983.

Degrees BA, MA, PhD Harvard Univ., 1956, 1957, 1960.

Offices and Honours Phi Beta Kappa; Jr. Fellow, Soc. Fellows, Harvard Univ., 1957–9; Em Soc, 1963–; AAAS, 1969–; John Bates Clark Medal, AEA, 1973; Vice-Pres., Pres., Em Soc, 1977–9, 1979; Guggenheim Foundation Fellow, 1981–2.

Editorial Duties Assoc. Ed. *JASA*, 1965–8; Amer. Ed., *REStud*, 1965–8; Ed., *Em*, 1968–77.

Principal Fields of Interest 021 General Equilibrium Theory; 022 Microeconomic Theory; 610 Industrial Organisation and Public Policy.

Publications *Books:* 1. *A Priori Information and Time Series Analysis: Essays in Economic Theory and Measurement* (N-H, 1962); 2. *A Study in Econometrics: The Demand for Electricity in the United States* (with C. Kaysen), (N-H, 1962); 3. *Essays on the Structure of Social Science Models* (with A. Ando and H. Simon), (MIT Press, 1963); 4. *Supply and Costs in the United States Petroleum Industry: Two Econometric Studies* (JHUP, 1964); 5. *The Identification Problem in Econometrics* (McGraw-Hill, 1966); 6. *The Economic Theory of Price Indices* (with K. Shell), (Academic Press, 1972); 7. *Folded, Spindled and Mutilated:*

Economic Analysis and US v. IBM (with J. J. McGowan and J. Greenwood), (MIT Press, 1983); 8. *IBM and the US Computer Industry: An Economic History* (with J. McKie and R. J. Mancke), (Praeger, 1983); 9. *Disequilibrium Foundations and Equilibrium Economics* (CUP, 1983).

Articles: 1. 'On the cost of approximate specification in simultaneous equation estimation', *Em*, 29(2), April 1961; 2. 'The costs of automobile model changes since 1949' (with Z. Griliches and C. Kaysen), *JPE*, 70(5), Oct. 1962, repr. in *Price Theory in Action*, ed. D. S. Watson (Houghton Mifflin, 1965), and in *Readings in Microeconomics*, ed. D. R. Kamerschen (Wiley, 1969), abstract repr. in *Readings in Economics*, ed. P. A. Samuelson (McGraw-Hill, 1970); 3. 'Embodied technical change and existence of an aggregate capital stock', *REStud*, 32(4), Oct. 1965; 4. 'The existence of aggregate production functions', *Em*, 37(4), Oct. 1969; 5. 'Tests of equality between sets of coefficients in the linear regressions: an expository note', *Em*, 38(2), March 1970; 6. 'An econometric model of the world copper industry' (with P. H. Cootner and M. N. Bailey), *Bell JE*, 3, Autumn 1972; 7. 'Diagnosing monopoly', *QREB*, 19(2), Summer 1979; 8. 'Multiple regression in legal proceedings', *Columbia Law Rev.*, 80(4), May 1980; 9. 'Stability, disequilibrium awareness, and the perception of new opportunities', *Em*, 49(2), March 1981; 10. 'On the misuse of accounting rates of return to infer monopoly profits' (with J. J. McGowan), *AER*, 73(1), March 1982.

Principal Contributions I have been fortunate in several times coming on a rich deposit of scholarly ore. The first such deposit was in econometric theory, particularly the theory of identification and of simultaneous equations. My interests here grew out of my early applied econometric work on particular industries and took on a life of its own. About 1970, however, I encountered diminishing returns. Future advances would largely come from those well trained and interested in mathematical statistics rather than from those like me who approached the subject largely from the direction of linear algebra and application-gained insight. Fortunately, there were other deposits. I had already been mining one which combined theory and practice — the production-theoretic basis for the existence of aggregate production functions and — somewhat related — the economic theory of price indices.

Now I moved more squarely into theory and began to examine what I consider to be the central unsolved problem of economic theory, the question of how prices change in disequilibrium. After some early work on search theory, my focus became the disequilibrium foundations of equilibrium economics and I have continued in that area. All through the 1960s, however, I had continued applied work in particular industries, and — also in 1970 — I made a decision of unrealised importance; I agreed to assist the defence attorneys in the IBM antitrust litigation. That decision reawakened my interest in industrial organisation, and led to a considerable effort in that area which did not terminate when the case was dismissed in 1981 and my books were published. These two areas are not unconnected. In application as well as theory, the examination of economic phenomena with the hidden or explicit assumption that long-run equilibria are all that matter is a dangerous practice.

FISHER, Irving*

Dates and Birthplace 1867–1947, Saugerties, NY, USA.

Posts Held Teacher Maths., Prof. Econ., Yale Univ., 1892–5, 1895–1935; Businessman, directorships, including Remington Rand, 1926–47.

Degrees BA, PhD Yale Univ., 1898, 1891.

Offices and Honours Pres., ASA, Internat. Em Soc, Nat. Inst. Social Sciences, Amer. Assoc. Labor Legislation, and active in a host of other societies.

Publications *Books:* 1. *Mathematical Investigations in the Theory of Value and Prices* (1892, 1961); 2. *The Nature of Capital and Income* (1906, 1927); 3. *The Purchasing Power of Money*

(1911, 1920); 4. *Elementary Principles of Economics* (1912); 5. *Stabilizing the Dollar* (1920); 6. *The Making of Index Numbers* (1922, 1927); 7. *The Money Illusion* (1928); 8. *The Theory of Interest* (1930, 1961); 9. *Booms and Depressions* (1932); 10. *Inflation?* (1933).

Career One of the greatest, if not the greatest, and certainly one of the most colourful American economists. A writer and teacher of prodigious scope and output, whose business career included the earning of a fortune from the invention of a visible card index system. He campaigned for a great number of causes, including world peace, prohibition, preventive medicine, eugenics, and 100 per cent deposit reserve money. His works are distinguished by their unusual clarity of exposition and contain major contributions to mathematical economics, the theory of value and prices, capital theory, monetary theory, and statistics. The now familiar distinction between stocks and flows is almost entirely due to his brilliant book on *The Nature of Capital and Income*. His ability in theoretical work was allied to a deep concern with the observation of facts: the Fisher 'ideal index' of prices is only one of his contributions to statistics.

Secondary Literature J. A. Schumpeter, 'Irving Fisher 1867–1947', in *Ten great Economists from Marx to Keynes* (OUP, 1948); M. Allais, 'Fisher, Irving', *IESS*, 5.

FISHLOW, Albert

Born 1935, Philadelphia, PA, USA.
Current Post Prof. Econ., Univ. Cal. Berkeley, CA, USA, 1983–.
Past Posts Acting Ass. Prof., Assoc. Prof., Prof., Univ. Cal. Berkeley, 1961–3, 1963–6, 1966–78; Vis. Res. Assoc., NBER, 1963–4; Dir., Brazil Devlp. Ass. Project, 1965–70; Vis. Fellow, All Souls Coll. Oxford, 1972–3; Dep. Ass. Secretary State Interamer. Affairs, 1975–6; Prof. Econ., Dir., Yale Center Internat. and Area Stud., 1978–83; Vis. Ford Res. Prof. Econ., Univ. Cal. Berkeley, 1982–3.
Degrees BA Univ. Penn., 1956; PhD Harvard Univ., 1963.

Offices and Honours David Wells Prize, Harvard Univ., 1964; Schumpeter Prize, 1971; Guggenheim Foundation Fellow, 1972–3; Vice-Pres., EHA, 1974; Disting. Service Award, US Dept. State, 1976; Chairman, Joint SSRC–ACLS Comm. Latin Amer., 1978–80.
Editorial Duties Chairman, Ed. Board, *Internat. Organization*, 1983–4, *Foreign Pol.*, 1977–.
Principal Fields of Interest 121 Economic Studies Developing Countries; 040 Economic History; 443 International Lending and Aid.
Publications *Books:* 1. *American Railroad and the Transformation of the Ante Bellum Economy* (Harvard Univ. Press, 1965); 2. *Rich and Poor Nations in the World Economy* (with C. Diaz-Alejandro, R. Fagen and R. Hanson), (McGraw-Hill, 1978); 3. *Latin America's Emergence: Toward a US Response* (with A. Lowenthal), (Foreign Pol. Assoc., 1979); 4. *Trade in Manufacturing Products with Developing Countries: Reinforcing North-South Partnership* (with S. Sekiguchi and J. Carriere), (Trilateral Commission Trianole Paper, 1981).

Articles: 1. 'Ante bellum interregional trade reconsidered', *AER*, 54(2), May 1964, repr. in *New Views on American Economic Development*, ed. R. Andrerno (Schenkman, 1965); 2. 'Productivity and technical change in the railroad sector, 1840–1910', *Stud. in Income & Wealth*, 30 (NBER, 1965); 3. 'Brazilian size distribution of income', *AER*, 62(2), May 1972, repr. in *Distribution of Income*, ed. A. Foxley (CUP, 1977; transls., Spanish, Portuguese); 4. 'Origins and consequences of import substitution in Brazil', in *International Economics and Development*, ed. L. Di Marco (Academic Press, 1972; transls., Spanish, Portuguese); 5. 'Some reflections on post-1964 Brazilian economic policy', in *Authoritarian Brazil*, ed. A. Stepan (Yale Univ. Press., 1974); 6. 'The mature neighbor policy: a proposal for a US economic policy for Latin America', in *Latin America and the World Economy*, ed. J. Grunwald (Sage, 1978); 7. 'Latin American external debt: the case of uncertain development', in

Trade, Stability, Technology and Equity in Latin America (Academic Press, 1982); 8. 'The United States and Brazil: the case of the missing relationship', *Foreign Affairs*, Spring, 1982; 9. 'The debt crisis: round two ahead?', in *Adjustment Crisis in the Third World* (Overseas Devlp. Council, 1984); 10. 'Reciprocal trade growth: the Latin American integration experience', in *Economic Structure and Performance* (Academic Press, 1984).

Principal Contributions My initial focus was upon US economic history, and especially the determinants of its highly successful transition from an agricultural to an industrial nation. This interest motivated my studies of infrastructure investment in railroads, technological change in that sector and the contribution of education to US economic growth. A subsequent phase of my career, from the mid-1960s through the mid-1970s, was dominated by issues of Brazilian economic development, both the longer trends of change and the shorter-term effects of public policy. This grew out of a period of residence in Brazil working in the research divisions of the Ministry of Planning and was a logical extension of my academic concerns applied to contemporary problems. I studied not only central aspects of the strategy of import substitution but also the income distribution consequences of the Brazilian developmental pattern and the economic policies of an authoritarian regime.

A third set of interests covering the last decade have been international economic relations and US foreign economic policy. I have worked on North-South economic issues, including trade in manufactured products and the results of economic integration; relations between the US and Latin America; and, especially, the problem of developing country external debt. Most recently, I have been engaged in research emphasising comparative analysis: the nineteenth-century capital market in comparison with the twentieth, the differential response of Latin American countries to development opportunities in the 1960s and 1970s, and their contrast with the East Asian style. These themes reflect a search for political economic generalisations that can illuminate the wide differences in national experiences. As in the past, I have tried to understand the complex workings of market forces, and their limitations. So there has been continuity as well as change during the last 20 years.

FITOUSSI, Jean-Paul Samuel

Born 1942, La Goulette, Tunisia.
Current Post Prof. Econ., Inst. d'Etudes Politiques de Paris; Dir., Res. Dept., Observatoire Français des Conjonctures Econ., Paris, France, 1983–.
Past Posts Ass. Prof., Prof. Econ., Dean Faculty Econ., Dir., Bureau d'Econ. Théoretique et Appliquée, Univ. Louis Pasteur, Strasbourg, 1971–3, 1974–9, 1974–7, 1974–80; Prof. Econ., Europ. Univ. Inst., Florence, 1980–3; Vis. Prof., UCLA, 1984.
Degrees Licencie, Diplome d'Etudes Supérieures, Dr d'Etat, Strasbourg Univ., 1966, 1967, 1971; Agregé, Paris, 1973.
Offices and Honours General Secretary, IEA, 1984–; Cons., EEC, 1978–80, 1981–2; Member High Council, French Univs., 1977–81; Prize, French Econ. Assoc., 1972; Prize, Academie des Sciences Morales et Politiques, 1974; Hon. Member, Internat. Assoc. Applied Econometrics, 1975.
Editorial Duties Corresponding Ed., *MS*; Ed. Boards, *Eurepargne, Econ App*.
Principal Fields of Interest 023 Macroeconomic Theory; 134 Inflation and Deflation; 212 Construction, Analysis and Use of Econometric Models.
Publications Books: 1. *Inflation, équilibre et chomage* (Cujas, 1973); 2. *Le fondement microéconomique de la théorie keynesienne* (Cujas, 1974); 3. *Unemployment in Western Countries*, co-ed. (with E. Malinvaud), (Macmillan, 1980); 4. *Modern Macroeconomic Theory*, ed. (Blackwell, 1983); 5. *Dynamique Economique*, co-ed. (with P. A. Muet), (Presses de la Fondation Nationale des Sciences Politique, 1983).
Articles: 1. 'Inflation d'équilibre et chomage', *Revue Science Financière*,

64, 1972; 2. 'De l'inflation d'équilibre a la staglation: théorie et verification empirique', *Econ. App*, 28(1), 1974; 3. 'Emploi, structure et régulation', *REP*, 89(1), 1979; 4. 'Inflazione e disoccupazione: l'impossible controllo congiunturale di uno squilibrio strutturale', *RISE*, 26(7), 1979; 5. 'Structure and involuntary unemployment' (with N. Georgescue-Roegen), in *Unemployment in Western Countries, op. cit.*; 6. 'Politique monétaire ou politique économique', *Observations et Diagnostic Econ.*, 1, June 1982; 7. 'Modern macroeconomic theory: an overview', in *Modern Macroeconomic Theory, op. cit.*; 8. 'Equilibres de stagflation et indexation des salaires' (with P. Dehez) in *Dynamique Economique, op. cit.*; 9. 'A non-linear model of output fluctuations in a mixed economy' (with K. Velupillai), in *Dynamique Economique, ibid.*

Principal Contributions The study of disequilibrium theories. Developed a theory of stagflation built up from microeconomic foundations and an explicit aggregation procedure. Stagflation was analysed as the result of the interaction of two effects — a global effect, which is the outcome of aggregate disequilibrium, and a structural effect, which works through the dispersion of market disequilibria around their mean. Contributed to the theory and empirical analysis of a consumption function with microeconomic foundations. Recent research concerns the introduction of partial price flexibility and indexation into a macromodel of general equilibrium with rationing, and the construction of a nonlinear model of output and employment fluctuations.

FLEISHER, Belton M.

Born 1935, Hayward, CA, USA.
Current Post Prof. Econ., Ohio State Univ., Columbus, OH, 1969–.
Past Posts Ass. Prof., Univ. Chicago, 1961–5; Ass. Prof., Assoc. Prof., Ohio State Univ., 1965–6, 1966–9.
Degrees BA, MA, PhD Stanford Univ., 1957, 1959, 1961.
Offices and Honours Ford Found-

ation Dissertation Fellow, 1959–60; NSF Postdoctoral Fellow, 1963–4.
Principal Fields of Interest 800 Manpower; Labour; Population.
Publications *Books:* 1. *The Economics of Delinquency* (Quadrangle, 1966); 2. *Labor Economics: Theory Evidence and Policy* (Prentice-Hall, 1970, with T. J. Kneisner, 1980, 1984; transl., Japanese, Sogo Rodo Kenkyusho, 1975); 3. *Minimum Wage Regulation in Retail Trade* (AEI, 1981); 4. *Minimum Wage Regulation in the United States* (National Chamber Foundation, 1983).

Articles: 1. 'The impact of Puerto Rican migration to the United States', in *Human Resources in the Urban Economy*, ed. M. Perlman (JHUP, 1963); 2. 'The effect of unemployment on juvenile delinquency', *JPE*, 71, Dec. 1963; 3. 'The effect of income on delinquency', *AER*, 56(1), March 1966; 4. 'Employment and wage rates in retail trade subsequent to the 1961 amendment of the fair labor standards Act' (with W. J. Shkurti), *SEJ*, 35, July 1968; 5. 'Asset adjustment and labor supply of older workers' (with D. O. Parsons and R. D. Porter), in *Income Maintenance and Labor Supply: Econometric Studies*, ed. G. G. Cain and H. Watts (Rand McNally, 1973); 6. 'Unemployment and the labor force participation of married men and women: a simultaneous model' (with G. Rhodes), *REStat*, 58(4), Nov. 1976; 7. 'Mother's home time and the production of child quality', *Demography*, 14(2), May 1977; 8. 'Fertility, women's wage rates, and labor supply' (with G. F. Rhodes, Jr.), *AER*, 69(1), March 1979; 9. 'Individual labor force decisions and unemployment in local labor markets' (with G. F. Rhodes, Jr.), *REStat*, 61(4), Nov. 1979; 10. 'Husband's health and the wife's labor supply' (with M. C. Berger), *JHE*, April 1984.

FLEMMING, John Stanton

Born 1941, Reading, Berkshire, England.
Current Post Econ. Adviser to Governor, Bank England, London, England, 1984–.

Past Posts Lect., Fellow, Oriel Coll., Oxford, 1963–5; Official Fellow, Nuffield Coll., Oxford, 1965–80; Chief Adviser, Bank England, 1980–4.

Degrees BA (PPE), MA, Univ. Oxford, 1962, 1966.

Offices and Honours Harkness Fellow, 1968–9; Council RES, 1980–; Council, Inst. Fiscal Stud., 1980–; Chairman, Econ. Affairs Comm., UK–SSRC, 1980–4.

Editorial Duties Assoc. Ed. Board, *OEP*, 1964–72; Board Member, Assoc. Ed., *REStud*, 1970–80, 1972–5; Managing Ed., *EJ*, 1975–80.

Principal Fields of Interest 130 Economic Fluctuations; 300 Domestic Monetary & Fiscal Theory & Institutions; 910 Welfare, Health, Education.

Publications *Books:* 1. *Why we need a Wealth Tax* (with I. M. D. Little), (Methuen 1974); 2. *Inflation* (OUP, 1976, transls., Japanese, 1978, Spanish, Huemal, 1978); 3. *The Structure and Reform of Direct Taxation* (with J. E. Meade, and others), (A & U, 1978).

Articles: 1. 'The utility of wealth and the utility of windfalls, *REStud*, 36(1), Jan. 1969; 2. 'The consumption function when capital markets are imperfect', *OEP*, 25(2), July 1973; 3. 'Portfolio choice and liquidity preference: a continuous time treatment', in *Issues in Monetary Economics*, eds. H. G. Johnson and A. R. Nobay (OUP, 1974); 4. 'Wealth effects in Keynesian models', *OEP*, 26(2), July 1974; 5. 'Wage rigidity and employment adjustment', in *Contemporary Issues in Economics*, eds. M. Parkin and A. R. Nobay (Manchester Univ. Press, 1975); 6. 'A reappraisal of the corporation income tax', *J Pub E*, 6(1,2), July–Aug. 1976; 7. 'What discount rate for public expenditure?' in *Public Expenditure*, ed. M. V. Posner (CUP, 1977); 8. 'Optimal payroll taxes and social security funding', *J Pub E*, 7(3), June 1977; 9. 'Aspects of optimal unemployment insurance', *J Pub E*, 10(3), Dec. 1978; 10. 'Effects of earnings inequality, imperfect capital markets, and dynastic altruism on the distribution of wealth in life cycle models', *Ec*, N.S. 46, Nov. 1979.

Principal Contributions Early work, with M. S. Feldstein and J. F. Wright, on investment criteria led to estimating an investment function and considering capital market imperfections (Articles Nos. 1 and 2 above), taxation, expectations and uncertainty. I have found the continuous time uncertainty formulation (Article No. 3) liberating and use stochastic processes (Article No. 9) and in current work on optimal public finance. My book on inflation integrated rational and adaptive aspects of inflation expectations, and also suggested an appropriate UK response to OPEC I.

In 1974, with I. M. D. Little, I advocated replacing the taxation of all income from property by a direct wealth tax. I was a member of the Meade Committee which advocated an expenditure tax topped off with wealth and transfer taxes. I have since questioned the case for these when consumption is adequately taxed. Taxes inhibiting wealth accumulation and transfer discourage equalising transfers and increase the correlation between lifetime consumption and earnings; No. 10 above explores this and the extent to which earnings inequality 'explains' that of wealth. Articles Nos. 6 and 8 represent attempts, under the influence of J. A. Mirrlees, to approach optimal intertemporal and redistributive taxation. Article No. 9 extends the argument to unemployment income.

Inflation gave some weight to unemployment insurance as a determinant of the national rate of unemployment; with A. B. Atkinson, the timing effect of disincentives arising from the interaction of tax and benefit systems was emphasised; see also MBR 1978 — for the CLARE Group — one of several groups of centrist economists with which I became involved about the time of the 1976 crisis in UK economic policy. Continuing macroeconomic concerns related to the effects of capital market imperfections and wage stickiness (Article No. 5 above). I have subsequently explored their relationship, together with appropriate monetary policy, to the stability of employment.

FLORENCE, Philip Sargant*

Dates and Birthplace 1890–1982, Nutley, NJ, USA.
Posts Held Lect., Univ. Camb., 1921–9; Prof. Com., Dean Com. and Social Sciences, Univ. Birmingham, 1929–55, 1947–50.
Offices and Honours Pres., Section F BAAS, 1937; CBE, 1952; Vice-Pres., RES, 1972–82.
Publications *Books:* 1. *Economics of Fatigue and Unrest* (1942); 2. *Overpopulation, Theory and Statistics* (1926); 3. *Economics and Human Behaviour* (1927); 4. *The Statistical Method in Economics and Political Science* (1929); 5. *The Logic of Industrial Organisation* (1933); 6. *Industry and the State* (1957); 7. *Economics and Sociology of Industry* (1964); 8. *The Roots of Inflation* (1975).
Career Applied economist, whose move from Cambridge to Birmingham enabled him to pursue research in the organisation of trade and industry and, as Dean, to foster a broad, interdisciplinary approach in the Faculty of Commerce and Social Sciences. He had an important role in the postwar reconstruction and subsequent planning of the West Midlands region of England.

FLÓREZ ESTRADA, Alvaro*

Dates and Birthplace 1765–1854, Spain.
Posts Held Civil Servant; Attorney General, Asturias, Spain, 1798; Chief Justice, Seville, 1813.
Offices and Honours Corresp. Member, Académie des Sciences Morales et Politiques, 1851.
Publications *Books:* 1. *Examen Imparcial de las Disensiones de América y Medios de Conciliación* (1814); 2. *Efectos Producidos en Europa por la Baja en el Producto de las Minas de Plato* (1824); 3. *Examen de la Crisis Comercial de la Inglaterra en 1826* (1827); 4. *Curso de Economía Política*, 2 vols (1828, 1852, 1980); 5. *La Cuestíon Social; Origin, Latitud, y Efectos del Derecho de Propriedad* (1839).
Career First distinguishing himself by his opposition to Napoleon and his criticism of Spanish colonial administration, much of his writing was done whilst in exile. His *Curso . . .* is the first systematic economic treatise by a Spaniard, and is largely based on Smith and Ricardo, but diverges from orthodoxy in advocating the common ownership of land. In *La cuestión social . . .* he developed a fully-fledged programme for the nationalisation of land. Subsequent Spanish economists built on his work, without, however, accepting his most original contributions.
Secondary Literature G. Bernacer, 'Flórez Estrada, Alvaro,', *ESS*, 6.

FLUX, Alfred William*

Dates and Birthplace 1867–1942, Portsmouth, Hampshire, England.
Posts Held Cobden Lect., Jevons Prof., Manchester Univ., 1893–8, 1898–1901; Fellow, St John's Coll. Camb., 1889–93; Prof., McGill Univ., 1901–8; Civil Servant, UK Stat. Dept., Board Trade, 1908–32.
Degree BA(Maths.) Univ. Camb., 1887.
Offices and Honours Marshall Prize, Univ. Camb.; Knighted; Pres., RSS; Hon. Member, Internat. Inst. Stats.
Publications *Books:* 1. *Economic Principles* (1904); 2. *Swedish Banking System* (1910); 3. *Foreign Exchanges* (1924).
Articles: 1. 'Review of Wicksteed, *Essay on the Co-ordination of the Laws of Distribution*', *EJ*, 6, June 1894, repr. in *Precursors of Mathematical Economics: An Anthology*, eds. W. J. Baumol and S. M. Goldfeld (LSE, 1968).
Career After an academic career which did not quite fulfil expectations, his official work, particularly in directing the Censuses of Production 1912, 1924 and 1930, was of outstanding quality. His published papers in the field of applied economic statistics covered topics such as wholesale price index numbers, the index of production and national income. He was frequently consulted by the government as an economic adviser. Although Wicksteed is usually credited with the introduction of Euler's theorem into economics, it

was Flux, in a review of Wicksteed's *Essay*, who first drew attention to the relevance of Euler.

Secondary Literature S. J. Chapman, 'Sir Alfred Flux (obit.)', *EJ*, 52, Dec. 1942.

FOGEL, Robert William

Born 1926, New York City, NY, USA.

Current Post Charles R. Walgreen Prof. Amer. Insts., Prof. Econ., Grad. School Bus., Univ. Chicago, 1982–.

Past Posts Instr., Johns Hopkins Univ., 1958–9; Ass. Prof., Univ. Rochester, 1960–4, 1968–75; Assoc. Prof., Prof., Univ. Chicago, 1964–5, 1965–75; Dir., Walgreen Foundation, Dir., Center Pop. Econ., Univ. Chicago; Prof., Harvard Univ., 1975–81.

Degrees BA Cornell Univ., 1948; MA Columbia Univ., 1960, Univ. Camb., 1975, Harvard Univ., 1976; PhD Johns Hopkins Univ., 1963.

Offices and Honours Member, Chairman, Hist. Advisory Comm. Math. Social Science Board, 1965–72; Assoc. Columbia Univ. Seminar Econ. Hist., 1969–; Member, Board of Trustees, Pres., EHA, 1972–, 1977–8; Chairman, Ad Hoc Comm. Quant. Methods Hist., Univ. Chicago, 1974–5; Res. Assoc., Program Dir., NBER, 1978–; NAS Comm. Ageing, 1978–81; Pres., Social Science Hist. Assoc., 1980–1.

Editorial Duties Ed. Boards, *Explor. Econ. Hist.*, 1970–; *Social Science Hist.*, 1976–80; *Southern Stud.*, 1977–; General Ed., *Princeton Series Quant. Stud. in Hist.*, 1971–6; General Ed. (with S. Thernstrom), CUP series *Interdisciplinary Perspectives in Modern History*, 1979–.

Principal Fields of Interest 042 North American Economic History.

Publications *Books:* 1. *The Union Pacific Railroad: A Case in Premature Enterprise* (JHUP, 1960); 2. *Railroads and American Economic Growth: Essays in Econometric History* (JHUP, 1964; transl., Spanish, 1972); 3. *The Reinterpretation of American Economic History* (with S. L. Engerman, *et al.*), (Harper & Row, 1971; transl. Italian, 1975); 4. *Time on the Cross: The Economics of American Negro Slavery* (with S. L. Engerman), (Little Brown, 1974; transls. Braille, 1974, Italian, 1978, Japanese, 1980, Spanish, 1981); 5. *Scientific History and Traditional History* (with G. R. Elton), (Yale Univ. Press, 1982).

Principal Contributions The application of economic models and statistical methods to the analysis of long-term trends in economic development. Much of the research has focussed on the retrieval of data capable of illuminating the relationship between the current and past behaviour of households. Data sets linking together up to ten generations have been constructed to analyse the interaction of economic and cultural factors on such variables as the savings rate, the female participation rate, fertility and mortality rates, economic and social mobility, and migration rates.

FOLDES, Lucien Paul

Born 1930, Vienna, Austria.

Current Post Prof. Econ., LSE, London, England, 1979–.

Past Posts Ass. Lect., Lect., Reader Econ., LSE, 1951–55, 1955–61, 1961–79; British Army, 1952–4; Rockefeller Travelling Fellow, USA, 1962.

Degrees BCom, Diploma Bus. Admin., MSc LSE, 1950, 1951, 1952.

Principal Fields of Interest 020 General Economic Theory; 213 Mathematical Methods and Models; 520 Business Finance and Investment.

Publications *Articles:* 1. 'Uncertainty, probability and potential surprise', *Ec*, N.S. 25, Aug. 1958; 2. 'Imperfect capital markets and the theory of investment', *REStud*, 18(3), June 1961; 3. 'Domestic air transport policy', *Ec*, N.S. 28, May–Aug. 1961; 4. 'A determinate model of bilateral monopoly', *Ec*, N.S., 31, May 1964; 5. 'Income redistribution in money and in kind', *Ec*, N.S., 34, Feb., May 1967, 35, May 1968; 6. 'Some comments on the theory of monopoly', in *Essays in Honour of Lord Robbins*, eds. M. Peston and B. Corry (Weidenfeld & Nicholson, 1972); 7. 'Expected utility and continuity', *REStud*, 39(4), Oct.

1972; 8. 'Optimal saving and risk in continuous time', *REStud*, 45(1), Feb. 1978; 9. 'Martingale conditions for optimal saving: discrete time', *J Math E*, 5(1), March 1978; 10. 'Quarterly returns to UK equities 1919–1970' (with P. M. Watson), *Ec*, 49, May 1982.

Principal Contributions My training at LSE in traditional microeconomics and business subjects gave me interests in theoretical problems connected with costs, capital, welfare and uncertainty, as well as in more 'applied' questions of pricing policy, financial control and government regulation of industry. Following a thesis on the theory of costs (which led eventually to No. 2 above), I at first taught and wrote mainly on problems of delegation in budgeting and control of public enterprise, my most substantial effort being No. 3. At the same time I studied mathematics, particularly analysis and probability, and gradually shifted the emphasis of my work in this direction. During the 1960s I published a number of papers on topics in microeconomics and welfare (investment, redistribution, monopoly). Taking over a course on business administration, I reoriented the teaching towards quantitative decision models, particularly models of risk and uncertainty.

My first publication on mathematical decision theory was No. 7 on expected utility, which sorts out systematically the relationships between (1) assumptions of continuity of preferences with respect to alternative topologies in a space of lotteries and (2) analytic properties of the corresponding cardinal utility function. Since completing this paper I have specialised increasingly — in teaching and consulting as well as research — on problems of risk in investment decisions, particularly on applications of stochastic processes. My main publication during this period is No. 8, which considers a continuous-time, stochastic model of optimal accumulation, proving the existence of an optimal plan and characterising this plan by means of martingale properties of the shadow prices. I am continuing to work on models of this type, extending my previous results and investigating the properties of optimal savings functions; this involves the study of certain boundary value problems for a second-order ordinary differential equation.

FOLEY, Duncan Karl

Born 1942, Columbus, OH, USA.
Current Post Prof. Econ., Barnard Coll., Columbia Univ., NY, USA, 1979–.
Past Posts Ass. Prof., Assoc. Prof. Econ., MIT, 1966–73; Assoc. Prof. Econ., Stanford Univ., 1973–9.
Degrees BA Central High School, Philadelphia, PA, 1960; BA (Maths.) Swarthmore Coll., 1964; PhD Yale Univ., 1966.
Offices and Honours Ford Foundation Faculty Res. Prof., 1969–70.
Editorial Duties Ed. Board, *JET*, 1976–81; *JEL*, 1984–7.
Principal Fields of Interest 020 General Economic Theory; 100 Economic Growth; Development; Planning; Fluctuations; 310 Domestic Monetary and Financial Theory and Institutions.
Publications *Books: Monetary and Fiscal Policy in a Growing Economy* (with M. Sidrauski), (Macmillan, 1971).
Articles: 1. 'Resource allocation and the public sector', *YEE*, 7(1), Spring 1967; 2. 'Lindahl's solution and the core of an economy with public goods', *Em*, 38(1), Jan. 1970; 3. 'Portfolio choice, investment and growth', (with M. Sidrauski), *AER*, 60(1), March 1970; 4. 'Economic equilibrium with costly marketing', *JET*, 2(3), Sept. 1970; 5. 'Asset management under trading uncertainty' (with M. F. Hellwig), *REStud*, 42(3), July 1975; 6. 'On two specifications of asset equilibrium in macroeconomic models', *JPE*, 83(2), April 1975, 85(2), April 1977; 7. 'Problems vs. conflicts: economic theory and ideology', *AER*, 65(2), May 1975; 8. 'Realization and accumulation in a Marxian model of the circuit of capital', *JET*, 28(2), Dec. 1982; 9. 'The value of money, the value of labor power, and the Marxian transformation problem', *Rev. Radical Polit. Econ.*, 14(2), Summer 1982; 10.

'On Marx's theory of money', *Social Concept*, 1(1), May 1983.

Principal Contributions My early work involved the extension of the general equilibrium model of resource allocation to economies with public goods, and the investigation of game theoretic solutions in that context. The main research problem that has engaged me has been the problem of the instability of accumulation in capitalist economies, or, in more traditional language, the business cycle, and the role of money in those phenomena. After attempting a synthesis of Keynesian and neoclassical approaches to these problems with Miguel Sidrauski, further investigations of deeper problems in these models led me to conclude that an understanding of these issues would require a fundamental reworking of the bases of economic theory, and in particular the abandonment of the traditional neoclassical paradigm of price determination through universal market clearing. My search for an alternative has led me to study the classical political economists and Marx, with particular attention to their theories of value, money and accumulation. My current project is to formulate these theories in operational and testable terms through the use of modern mathematical techniques, and to discover the relations between these theories and those of neoclassical economics and Keynes.

FORD, Alec George

Born 1926, Leicester, Leicestershire, England.

Current Post Prof. Econ., Univ. Warwick, Coventry, UK, 1970–.

Past Posts Lect. Econ., Sr. Lect., Univ. Leicester, 1953–63, 1963–65; Reader Econ., Univ. Warwick, 1965–70.

Degrees BA, MA DPhil Univ. Oxford, 1951, 1954, 1956.

Offices and Honours George Webb Medley Sr. Scholar, Oxford Univ., 1951–3; Member, Econ. and Social Hist. Comm., UK–SSRC, 1977–81; Pro-Vice-Chancellor, Univ. Warwick, 1971–2, 1977–83, 1983–5.

Principal Fields of Interest 044 European Economic History; 047 Latin American Economic History; 432 International Monetary Arrangements.

Publications *Books:* 1. *The Gold Standard 1880–1914; Britain and Argentina*, (OUP, 1962; transl., Spanish, 1966); 2. *Planning and Growth in Rich and Poor Countries*, co-ed. (with W. B. Birmingham), (A&U, 1966); 3. *Income, Spending and the Price-Level* (Fontana, 1971).

Articles: 1. 'Argentine and the Baring crisis of 1890', *OEP*, 8, June 1956; 2. 'Flexible exchange rates and Argentina, 1885–1900', *OEP*, 10, Oct. 1958; 3. 'The transfer of British foreign lending, 1870–1913', *EHR*, 11(2), 1958; 4. 'Notes on the transfer of overseas lending and grants', *OEP*, 14, Feb. 1962; 5. 'Bank rate, the British balance of payments and the burdens of adjustment, 1870–1914', *OEP*, 16, March 1964; 6. 'Overseas lending and internal fluctuations, 1870–1914', *YBESR*, 17, May 1965, repr. in *The Export of Capital from Britain 1870–1914*, ed. A. R. Hall (Methuen, 1968); 7. 'British economic fluctuations 1870–1914', *MS*, 37(2), June 1969, repr. in *British Economic Fluctuations 1790–1939*, eds. D. H. Aldcroft and P. Fearon (Macmillan, 1972); 8. 'British investment in Argentina and long savings, 1880–1914', *JEH*, 31, Sept. 1971, repr. in *Essays in Quantitative Economic History* ed. R. Floud (OUP, 1974); 9. 'British investment and Argentine economic development, 1880–1914', in *Argentina in the Twentieth Century*, ed. D. Rock (Duckworth, 1975); 10. 'The trade cycle in Britain 1860–1914', in *The Economic History of Britain since 1700*, 2, eds. R. Floud and D. McCloskey (CUP, 1981).

Principal Contributions My interest as an economist in historical problems was first aroused by work on my doctoral dissertation on the gold standard in Argentina before 1914; I came to realise the important role which economic analysis could play in explaining historical episodes. Furthermore, I became sensitive to the distinct feedback from history to the reshaping of economic analysis in terms of appropriate assumptions to make and processes to emphasise as well as the ways economic analysis was constrained in practice by social, political and institutional factors. Besides my contributions to Argentine economic history, I have tackled various problems in international and British economic history before 1914 — how the gold standard *really* worked; how Britain accomplished the transfer of its overseas lending; how British economic fluctuations and crises might be explained. In each of these I found it valuable to adopt a predominantly Keynesian style of analysis but I have come to recognise that, in the long run, the monetary approach has a contribution to offer as well. I have sought to encourage the quantitative approach to economic history in Britain, at the same time emphasising the role of economic analysis (and not only the neoclassical approach!) as well as quantitative techniques.

FORD, James Lorne

Born 1939, Bebington, Cheshire, England.

Current Post Mitsui Prof. Econ., Univ. Birmingham, Birmingham, England, 1980–.

Past Posts Ass. Lect., Lect., Univ. Manchester, 1961–7; Sr. Lect., New Univ. Ulster, 1968–9; Vis. Prof., UCLA; Sr. Res. Fellow, Prof. Econ., Univ. Sheffield, 1970–3, 1973–9.

Degrees BA, MA Univ. Liverpool, 1960, 1962.

Offices and Honours Rockefeller Res. Fellow, Univs. Yale, Stanford and Michigan State, 1964–5.

Editorial Duties Co-ed. (with J. Hey), *Mutsui Lectures Econ. Series on Uncertainty and Expectation in Economics* (Blackwell).

Principal Fields of Interest 020 General Economic Theory; 130 Economic Fluctuations, Forecasting and Inflation; 210 Econometric, Statistical and Mathematical Methods and Models.

Publications *Books:* 1. *The Ohlin-Heckscher Theory of Commodity Trade* (Asia Publishing House, 1965); 2. *Long and Short-Term Interest Rates: An Econometric Study* (with T. Stark),

(Blackwell, A. M. Kelley, 1967); 3. *Uncertainty and Expectations in Economics*, co-ed. (with C. F. Carter), (Blackwell, A. M. Kelley, 1972); 4. *Expectations, Uncertainty and the Term-Structure of Interest Rates* (with J. C. Dodds), (Martin Robertson, Barnes & Nobles, 1974, 1977); 5. *The Portfolio and Debt Behaviour of UK Building Societies* (with G. Clayton, J. C. Dodds and M. J. Driscoll), (*Societé Univ. Européenne de Recherches Financi*, 1975); 6. *Choice, Expectation and Uncertainty* (Martin Robertson, Barnes & Noble, 1983).

Articles: 'Variable returns to scale and the factor-price equalisation theorem', *RISE*, 16, Aug. 1969; 2. 'An econometric model of the UK financial sector: some preliminary findings' (with G. Clayton, J. C. Dodds and D. Ghosh), in *Issues in Monetary Economics*, eds. H. G. Johnson and A. R. Nobay (OUP, 1974); 3. 'The stability of the demand for money function and the predictability of the effects of monetary policy' (with M. J. Driscoll), *EJ*, 90, Dec. 1980; 4. 'The Ricardian and Heckscher-Ohlin explanations of trade patterns: an equivalence theorem and its empirical implications', *OEP*, 34, March 1982; 5. 'Protection, the value of imports and optimal trade-restricting policies' (with M. J. Driscoll), *WA*, 18(2), 1982; 6. Rational expectations, random parameters and the non-neutrality of money' (with D. G. Dickinson and M. J. Driscoll), *Ec*, N.S. 49, Aug. 1982; 7. 'Real sector parameter instability and the optimal choice of monetary policy' (with M. J. Driscoll), *Macroeconomics*, 4, Summer 1982; 8. 'Money, output, rational expectations and neutrality: some econometric results for the UK' (with M. J. Driscoll, A. W. Mullineux and S. Sen), *Ec*, N.S. 50, Aug. 1983; 9. 'Protection and optimal trade-restricting policies under uncertainty' (with M. J. Driscoll), *MS*, 51, March 1983; 10. 'The gains and losses to predicting nominal income by disaggregating via the new classical aggregate supply and rational expectations hypotheses' (with M. J. Driscoll and A. W. Mullineux), *J. Empirical Econ.*, 8, (1), 1983.

Principal Contributions Early work

concentrated on the pure theory of trade, especially on the Heckscher-Ohlin and Ricardian models. General aspects of those models were investigated, the main research contributions being concerned with the effect on the H–O theorems of variable returns to scale and specific factors of production, and the derivation of an equivalence theorem relating to H–O and Ricardian theorems, which has important implications for the existing empirical tests of those theories. Before the end of the 1960s, disenchantment with the general equilibrium, certainty framework of trade theory led me to concentrate on the work in monetary economics which had been proceeding in tandem. Theoretical and econometric research was undertaken on the level and structure of interest rates.

That research led to two innovations: the first attempt (simultaneously with Kane) to derive and use a 'monetary aggregate' or liquidity variable; and the construction of the first disaggregated econometric model of the UK monetary/financial system. The latter also prompted the development of models of the portfolio behaviour of major financial institutions. A main thread in the research on financial markets was 'uncertainty and expectation'. In the last few years my research has been concerned with that theme and has been predominantly theoretical. Amongst the issues considered have been: Shackle's anti-probabilistic theory of behaviour under 'uncertainty' and how it can be transformed into a viable alternative paradigm; the introduction of multiplicative as opposed to additive, uncertainty into macro models, which has challenged established results (for example, that of Friedman on the stability of money demand and that of Poole on choice of monetary policy); and the effect of uncertainty on the choice of commercial policy. On the empirical side research has been conducted on the rational expectations, structural neutrality hypotheses for several countries. It points to some methodological problems with existing literature and suggests that there is little support for those hypotheses.

FOURIER, Charles*

Dates and Birthplace 1772–1837, Besançon, France.

Posts Held Businessman and civil servant until 1816, then private income.

Publications *Books:* 1. *The Social Destiny of Man* (1808, 1840); 2. *Oeuvres complètes de Ch. Fourier*, 6 vols (1841–5); 3. *Design for Utopia: Selected Writings of Charles Fourier*, ed. M. Poster (1971).

Career Socialist thinker who sought to prescribe a social order in harmony with natural order. His decription of the 'phalanstery', a social unit whose numbers and organisation were based on his understanding of the order of the cosmos, led to various Fourierist experiments. His system was non-revolutionary, was believed to be able to flourish within any type of political system, and had some influence on later co-operative movements. Achieved subsequent notoriety as a 'utopian socialist' scorned by the founders of 'scientific socialism', Marx and Engels.

Secondary Literature E. Poulat, 'Fourier, Charles', *IESS*, 5; N. V. Riasanovsky, *The Teaching of Charles Fourier* (Univ. Cal. Press, 1970).

FOXWELL, Herbert Somerton*

Dates and Birthplace 1849–1936, Shepton Mallet, Somerset, England.

Posts Held Fellow, St John's Coll. Camb., 1874–98, 1905–36; Prof., Univ. Coll. London, 1881–1922.

Degrees BA Univ. London, 1867; BA Univ. Oxford, 1870.

Offices and Honours Fellow, BA; Member, Polit. Econ. Club, 1881–1936; Founder, Pres., RES, 1929–31.

Publications *Articles:* 1. 'Introduction' to A. Menger, *The Right of the Whole Produce of Labour* (1899); 2. *Papers on Current Finance* (1919).

Career Played an important role in the fostering of economic studies in Britain through his teaching, his work with the Royal Economic Society and other organisations, and his prodigious book collecting. Foxwell was probably the greatest collector of economic literature and over 70,000 books passed through his possession, most of them to form the present collection of the Goldsmith's Library, London University and the Kress Library, Harvard University. His publications were mainly articles or introductions to books, most notably the masterly article on the 'Ricardian socialists' presented as the introduction to Menger's *Right of the Whole Produce of Labour*.

Secondary Literature J. M. Keynes, 'Herbert Somerton Foxwell', in *Essays in Biography* (Macmillan, 1933).

FRANK, Charles Raphael, Jr.

Born 1937,Pittsburgh, PA., USA.
Current Post Vice-Pres., Salomon Brothers, New York City, NY, USA, 1978–.
Past Posts Prof. Econ. Internat. Affairs, Princeton Univ., 1967–74; Sr. Fellow, Brookings Inst., 1972–4; Sr. Econ., Pol. Planning Staff, US State Dept., 1974–7; Dept. Ass. Secretary State, US State Dept., 1977–8.
Degrees BS(Maths.) Rensselaer Polytechnic Inst., 1959; PhD Princeton Univ., 1963.
Offices and Honours Member, Council Foreign Relations; Res. Advisory Comm., US Agency Internat. Devlp.; Cons., US Agency Internat. Devlp., US Treasury, World Bank, UN, Conference Board.
Principal Fields of Interest 112 Economic Development Models and Theories.
Publications *Books:* 1. *Production Theory and Indivisible Commodities* (Princeton Univ. Press, 1969); 2. *Debt and Terms of Aid* (Overseas Devlp. Council, 1970), repr. in *Assisting Developing Countries, Problems of Debts, Burden Sharing, Jobs and Trade*, ed. C. R. Frank, Jr., *et al.* (Overseas Devlp. Council, 1970); 3. *Foreign Trade Regimes and Economic Development: South Korea* (with K. S. Kim and L. Westphal), (NBER, 1975); 4. *Foreign Trade and Domestic Aid: US Trade Adjustment Assistance and Other Adjustment Programs* (with S. Levinson), (Brookings Inst., 1977); 5. *Income Dis-*

tribution: Problems and Policies in Developing Countries, co-ed. (with R. Webb), (Brookings Inst., 1981).

Articles: 1. 'Urban unemployment and economic growth in Africa', *OEP*, 20(2), July 1968, repr. in *Third World Employment*, ed. R. Jolly, *et al.* (Penguin, 1973), and *The Study of Africa*, eds. P. J. M. McEwan and R. B. Sutcliffe (Methuen, 1974); 2. 'A generalization of the Koopmans-Gale theorem on pricing and efficiency', *Int ER*, 10(4), Oct. 1969; 3. 'Optimal terms of foreign assistance', *JPE*, 78(5), Sept.–Oct. 1970; 4. 'Measurement of debt service capacity: an application of discriminant analysis', *J Int E*, 1(3), Oct. 1971; 5. 'The problem of urban unemployment in Africa', in *Employment and Unemployment Problems of the Near East and South Asia*, 2, eds. R. G. Ridker and H. Lubell (Vikas Publications, 1971).

Principal Contributions Generalisations of welfare theory and theory of production with increasing returns to scale; debt-servicing problems of developing countries, theory and policy; theory and policy concerning unemployment problems and income distribution in less developed countries; analysis of national policies designed to facilitate adjustments required by shifting patterns of international trade; and foreign trade and economic development in S. Korea.

FRANKEL, Sally Herbert

Born 1903, Johannesburg, S. Africa.
Current Post Prof. Emeritus, Univ. Oxford.
Past Posts Prof. Econ. Underdeveloped Countries, Univ. Oxford, 1946–71; Vis. Prof. Econ., Univ. Virginia, 1967, 1969–74.
Degrees MA, Hon. DLitt Rand Univ., Johannesburg, 1926, 1970; PhD, DSc Univ. London, 1928, 1938; MA Univ. Oxford, 1946; Hon. DSc Rhodes Univ., Grahamstown, 1969.
Offices and Honours Member, Mont Pelerin Soc., 1928–, Econ. Soc. S. Africa, 1928, RES, 1930–, Royal Inst. Internat. Affairs, 1930–, Royal African Soc., 1930–; Member, Union SA

Treasury Advisory Council, 1941–2; Member, SA Miners' Phthisis Commission, 1941–2; Chairman, Enquiry Mining Industry Southern Rhodesia, 1945; Member, E. Africa Royal Commission, 1953–5.

Editorial Duties Joint Ed., *SAJE*, 1940–4.

Principal Fields of Interest 221 National Income Accounting; 121 Economic Studies of Less Industrialised Countries.

Publications *Books:* 1. *Capital Investment in Africa: Its Course and Effects* (OUP, 1938); 2. *The Economic Impact on Underdeveloped Societies: Essays on International Investment and Social Change* (OUP, 1953); 3. *Investment and the Return to Equity Capital in the South African Gold-mining Industry, 1887–1965: An International Comparison* (OUP, Harvard Univ. Press, 1967); 4. *Two Philosophies of Money: The Conflict of Trust and Authority* (St Martins Press, Blackwell, 1978); 5. *Money and Liberty* (AEI, 1980).

Articles: 1. 'The position of the native as a factor in the economic welfare of the European population of South Africa', *J Econ. Soc.*, July 1927; 2. 'The tyranny of economic paternalism in Africa', *Optima*, Suppl., Dec. 1960; 3. 'Economic change in Africa in historical perspective', in *Economic Development in the Long Run*, ed. A. J. Youngson (Macmillan, 1972); 4. 'The roots of economic progress', in *Science and Ceremony: The Institutional Economics of C. E. Ayres*, eds. W. Breit and W. P. Culbertson Jr. (Austin, 1975).

Principal Contributions Originated first official calculations of the national income of the Union of South Africa; economic analysis of fundamental factors affecting capital investment and economic growth of African countries; analysis of theories and policies relating to economic growth and decline of underdeveloped societies in relation to advanced economies; analysis of yield to capital investment in gold mining in relation to that obtained on industrial investments and government bonds 1887–1965; analysis of the economic roots of racial conflict; contribution to theory and practice of monetary poli-

cies; and analysis of philosophies of money and the relation of money to liberty.

FRANKLIN, Benjamin*

Dates and Birthplace 1706–90, Boston, MA, USA.

Posts Held Printer and journalist, 1718–36; Official, Colony and State of Penn.; Missions to England, 1757, 1764–75; Diplomat in France, 1776–85.

Offices and Honours Three times Pres. of Penn.; Framer US Declaration of Independence, 1776; Delegate, US Constitutional Convention, 1787.

Publications *Books:* 1. *Modest Inquiry into the Nature and Necessity of Paper Currency* (1729); 2. *Observations Concerning the Increase of Mankind* (1751); 3. *Positions to be Examined Concerning National Wealth* (1769); 4. *Reflections on the Augmentation of Wages* (1771).

Career This great statesman and scientist not only contributed popular treatments of economic topics to periodicals, such as his own *Poor Richard's Almanack*, but also wrote able economic tracts. The position he adopted was broadly that of *laissez faire*.

Secondary Literature W. A. Wetzel, *Benjamin Franklin as an Economist* (1895).

FRECH, Harry Edward III

Born 1946, St Louis, MO, USA.

Current Post Prof. Econ., Univ. Cal. Santa Barbara, CA, USA, 1982–.

Past Posts Econ., US. Dept. Health Educ. and Welfare, 1970–2; Acting Ass. Prof., Ass. Prof., Prof., Univ. Cal. Santa Barbara, 1973–82; Vis. Ass. Prof., Harvard Univ., 1976–7; Vis. Prof., Univ. Chicago 1982.

Degrees BS (Industrial Eng.) Univ. Missouri, 1968; MA, PhD UCLA, 1970, 1974.

Offices and Honours Johnson Foundation Fellow, Harvard Univ., 1976–7.

Editorial Duties Assoc. Ed., *EI*, 1980, 1981; Ed. Board, *AER*, 1981–.

Principal Fields of Interest 022

Microeconomic Theory; 610 Industrial Organisation and Public Policy; 913 Economics of Health.

Publications *Books:* 1. *Public Insurance in Private Markets: Some Problems of National Health Insurance* (AEI, 1978).

Articles: 1. 'Physical pricing: monopolistic or competitive' (with P. B. Ginsburg), *SEJ*, 38(4), April 1972; 2. 'Optimal scale in medical practice: survivor analysis' (with P. B. Ginsburg), *J Bus*, 47(1), Jan. 1974; 3. 'Property rights and the dynamic inefficiency of capitalism: comment', *JPE*, 83 (1), Feb. 1975; 4. 'Imposed health insurance in monopolistic markets: a theoretical analysis' (with P. B. Ginsburg), *EI*, 13(1), March 1975; 5. 'The property rights theory of the firm: empirical results from a natural experiment', *JPE*, 84(1), Jan. 1976; 6. 'The extended Coase theorem and long run equilibrium: the non-equivalence of liability rules and property rights', *EI*, 17(1), April, 1979; 7. 'Advertising as a privately supplied public good' (with C. B. Rochlin), *EI*, 17(2), July 1979; 8. 'The welfare loss of excess nonprice competition: the case of property–liability insurance regulation' (with J. C. Samprone, Jr.), *J Law E*, 23(2), Oct. 1980; 9. 'Strategic behavior and antitrust analysis' (with W. S. Comanor), *AER*, 74(2), May 1984; 10. 'The effects of the California coastal commission on housing prices' (with R. N. Lafferty), *JUE*, 16(1), July, 1984.

Principal Contributions My work can be summarised as using microeconomic theory to explain behaviour and institutions (property rights and contracts) in a wide range of settings and industries. The work is about equally divided between theoretical and empirical contributions. I have tried to use the concept of Pareto optimality as a benchmark, a means of communicating with the profession and a way of keeping my work at least potentially policy relevant. Although much of the work is theoretical, I have been guided by the idea that economics is a science, not a branch of logic. Thus my theoretical work has been disciplined by a reference to the empirical world and has stressed economics rather than technique. I have

been strongly influenced by my teachers, Armen Alchian, Jack Hirshleifer, Earl Thompson and Sam Peitzman at UCLA, and Wayne Leeman at Missouri, although my interests are more empirical and statistical than that list might suggest.

My earliest work was on human capital and the size distribution of income, based on Dutch and American data. I next turned to the economics of health and health care, a lifelong interest. Much of this work deals with industrial organisation issues of the peculiar institutions in health care and imperfect competition in these markets. Later I branched out into the economics of property rights, writing on the Coase Theorem and its extensions and the property rights theory of the firm. My interests then broadened to the regulation of insurance, land use controls, sociobiology and the oil industry. My latest work has been on topics related to antitrust policy, exclusive dealing, advertising as a public good, and strategic behaviour in oligopoly.

FREEMAN, A. Myrick III

Born 1936, Plainfield, NJ, USA.

Current Post Prof. Econ., Bowdoin Coll., Brunswick, ME, USA, 1975–.

Past Posts Res. Assoc., Univ. Washington, Seattle, WA, 1963–4; Ass. Prof., Assoc. Prof., Bowdoin Coll., 1965–70, 1970–5; Vis. Scholar, Resources for the Future, Washington DC, 1969–70; Vis. Assoc. Prof., Univ. Wisconsin-Madison, 1973; Fellow, Resources for the Future, 1976–8; Prof., Univ. Washington, 1982.

Degrees BA Cornell Univ., 1957; MA, PhD Univ. Washington, 1964, 1965.

Offices and Honours Board Dirs., Assoc. Environmental and Resource Econ., 1980–2; Member, Board Toxicology and Environmental Health Hazards, NAS, 1980–3.

Principal Fields of Interest 721 Natural Resources; 022 Microeconomic Theory; 024 Welfare Theory.

Publications *Books:* 1. *International Trade: An Introduction to Method and Theory* (Harper & Row, 1971); 2. *The*

Economics of Environmental Policy (with R. H. Haveman and A. V. Kneese), (Wiley, 1973); 3. *Pollution, Resources and the Environment — A Book of Readings*, co-ed. (with A. C. Enthoven), (W. W. Norton, 1973); 4. *The Benefits of Environmental Improvement: Theory and Practice* (JHUP, 1979); 5. *Air and Water Pollution Control: A Benefit-Cost Assessment* (Wiley, 1982); 6. *Intermediate Microeconomic Analysis* (Harper & Row, 1983).

Articles: 'Income distribution and planning for public investment', *AER*, 57(3), June 1967; 2. 'Income distribution and social choice: a pragmatic approach', *Public Choice*, Fall 1969; 3. 'Option demand and consumer surplus: further comment' (With C. J. Cicchetti), *QJE*, 85(3), Aug. 1971; 4. 'On the economics of mass demonstrations: a case study of the November march on Washington' (with C. J. Cicchetti, H. Haveman and J. L. Knetsch), *AER*, 61(4), Sept. 1971; 5. 'Residuals charges for pollution control: a policy evaluation' (with R. Haveman), *Science*, 28, July 1972; 6. 'On estimating air pollution control benefits from land value studies', *JEEM*, 1(1), Jan. 1974; 7. 'Congestion, quality deterioration and heterogeneous tastes' (with R. H. Haveman), *J Pub E*, 8(2), Oct. 1977; 8. 'The incidence of the costs of controlling automotive air pollution', in *The Distribution of Economic Well Being*, ed. F. T. Juster (Ballinger, 1977); 9. 'On the sign and size of option value', *Land Econ.*, 60(1), Feb. 1984; 10. 'Depletable externalities and Pigouvian taxation', *JEEM*, 11(2), June 1984.

Principal Contributions Most of my work in environmental and resource economics has been concerned with the distributional implications of environmental policy, policy analysis, the design of more efficient and effective policy instruments, and the theory of measuring welfare changes associated with environmental and resource policies.

I have long been interested in the issues surrounding the distribution among income groups of the benefits and costs of various environmental and resource policy decisions. I worked on one aspect of this problem in my doctoral dissertation on public investments in irrigation projects. I also examined approaches to integrating distributional objectives into the economic analysis of resource development projects. In later work I traced the impacts of urban air pollution to different income groups and examined the incidence of the costs of controlling automotive air pollution.

I have been concerned with the development of more rational and effective policies for controlling air and water pollution. This has led me to write about emission charges and other approaches to achieving cost-effective pollution control. I have also written about risk-benefit assessment and decision-making under uncertainty as applied to setting environmental standards with incomplete information.

Finally, as an advocate of greater use of benefit-cost analysis in environmental policy-making, I have had to confront the question of the adequacy of our theoretical and empirical tools for measuring the benefits that would stem from improvements in environmental quality. I have found two questions to be of particular interest. The first is the question of the appropriate measure of the benefits of the future provision of an environmental service for an individual who is uncertain of his future demand for that service (the 'option value' question). The second is the question of the proper interpretation of empirical relationships between property values and air pollution levels within urban residential property markets (the 'hedonic property value method').

FREEMAN, Richard B.

Born 1945, Newburgh, NY, USA.
Current Post Prof. Econ., Harvard Univ., 1979–.
Degrees BA Dartmouth Coll., 1964; PhD Harvard Univ., 1969.
Offices and Honours Dir. Labor Studies, NBER.
Principal Fields of Interest 820 Labour Markets; 830 Trade Unions.

Publications *Books:* 1. *Labor Market for College-trained Manpower* (Harvard Univ. Press, 1971); 2. *Black Elite* (McGraw Hill, 1976); 3. *The Over-educated American* (Academic Press, 1976); 4. *The Youth Joblessness Problem,* co-ed. (with D. Wise), (Univ. Chicago Press, 1981); 5. *What Do Unions Do?* (with J. Medoff), (Basic Books, 1984); 6. *The Black Youth Job Crisis,* co-ed. (with H. Holzer), (Univ. Chicago Press, 1985).

Articles: 1. 'Supply and salary adjustments to the changing science manpower market: physics, 1948–1975', *AER,* 65(1), March 1975; 2. 'Individual mobility and union voice in the labor market', *AER,* 66(2), May 1976; 3. 'The exit-voice trade off in the labor market, unionism, job tenure, quits and separations', *QJE,* 94, June 1980; 4. 'Union wage practices and wage dispersion with establishments', *ILRR,* 35(5), Oct. 1980; 5. 'Analyzing trade union effects with longitudinal data', *J Lab E,* Jan. 1984.

Principal Contributions Empirical findings: students' supply responsiveness is very sizable; high-level job markets are subject to cobweb-type fluctuations; return to college training in the West has dropped in era of educational expansion; minorities have progressed in era of anti-bias activity in US; slow economic progress of Blacks in US is due to loss of voting rights and consequent governmental discrimination at turn of century; trade unions have a sizable non-wage effect, best analysed in 'exit-voice' framework (effects include reduced turnover, greater fringe benefits, reduced inequality); measurement error in longitudinal data biasses estimates considerably; unions reduce profits of concentrated industries; and decline of union representation in US due to severe management opposition.

FRENKEL, Jacob A.

Born 1943, Tel Aviv, Israel.
Current Post David Rockefeller Prof. Internat. Econ., Univ. Chicago, USA, 1982–.
Past Posts Sr. Lect., Tel Aviv Univ.,

1971–3; Ass. Prof. Econ., Assoc. Prof. Econ., Prof. Econ., Univ. Chicago, 1973–4, 1974–8, 1979–82.
Degrees BA, MA Hebrew Univ. Jerusalem, 1966, 1967; MA, PhD Univ. Chicago, 1969, 1970.
Offices and Honours Res. Assoc., NBER, 1978–; Res. Fellow, Lehrman Inst., NY, 1981–2; Fellow, Em Soc, 1982–, Sackler Inst. Advanced Stud., Tel Aviv Univ., 1983–4; Cons., IMF, World Bank, 1981–.
Editorial Duties Ed., *JPE,* 1975–; Ed. Boards, *J Mon E,* 1978–84; Advisory Ed., *Econ. Letters,* 1980–.
Principal Fields of Interest 400 International Economics; 300 Domestic Monetary and Fiscal Theory and Institutions.
Publications *Books:* 1. *The Monetary Approach to the Balance of Payments,* co-ed. (with H. G. Johnson), (A&U, Univ. Toronto Press, 1976); 2. *The Economics of Exchange Rates: Selected Studies,* co-ed. (with H. G. Johnson), (Addison-Wesley, 1978); 3. *International Economic Policy Theory and Evidence,* co-ed. (with R. Dornbusch), (JHUP, 1979); 4. *Exchange Rates and International Macroeconomics,* ed. (Univ. Chicago Press, 1983). 5. *The World Economic System: Performance and Prospects,* co-ed. (with M. Mussa), (Huburn House Publishing, 1984); 6. *Collected Papers of Harry G. Johnson,* co-ed. (with D. Laidler), (MIT Press, 1985).

Articles: 1. 'A theory of money, trade and the balance of payments in a model of accumulation', *J Int E,* 1(2), May 1971; 2. 'Inflation and the formation of expectations', *J Mon E,* 1(4), Oct. 1975; 3. 'Portfolio equilibrium and the balance of payments: a monetary approach' (with C. Rodriquez), *AER,* 65(4), Sept. 1975; 4. 'A monetary approach to the exchange rate', *Scand JE,* 76(2), May 1976, repr. in *Flexible Exchange Rates and Stabilization Policy,* eds. J. Herin, A. Lindbeck and J. Myhrman (Macmillan, 1977), and in *The Economics of Exchange Rates,* eds., J. A. Frenkel and H. G. Johnson (Addison-Wesley, 1978), and in *International Financial Management: Theory and Application,* ed. D. R. Lessard (Warren, Gorham & Lamont,

1979); 5. 'The forward exchange rate, expectations and the demand for money: the German hyperinflation', *AER*, 67(4), Sept. 1977; 6. 'Transaction costs and interest arbitrage: tranquil versus turbulent periods' (with R. Levich), *JPE*, 85(6), Dec. 1977, repr. in *International Financial Management: Theory and Applications*, ed. D. R. Lessard (Warren, Gorham & Lamont, 1979); 7. 'Flexible exchange rates, prices and the role of 'news': lessons from the 1970s', *JPE*, 89(4), Aug. 1981, repr. in *Exchange Rate Policy*, eds. R. Batchelor and G. E. Wood (Macmillan, 1982), and in *Economic Interdependence and Flexible Exchange Rates*, eds. J. S. Bhandari and B. H. Putnam (MIT Press, 1983), and in *Readings in International Financial Management*, ed. D. R. Lessard (Wiley, 1984); 8. 'The collapse of purchasing power parities in the 1970s', *Europ ER*, 16(1), May 1981; 9. 'Aspects of the optimal management of exchange rates' (with J. Aizenmann), *J Int E*, 13(4), Nov. 1982, repr. in *The International Monetary System: Choices for the Future*, ed. M. Connolly (Praeger, 1982), and in *Recent Issues in the Theory of Flexible Exchange Rates*, eds. E. Classen and P. Salin (N-H., 1983); 10. 'International liquidity and monetary control', in *International Money and Credit: The Policy Roles*, ed. G. von Furstenberg (IMF, 1983), repr. in *International Banking and Global Financing*, ed. S. K. Kushik (Pace Univ., 1983).

Principal Contributions Studied the relation between economic growth and the balance of payments and contributed to the developments of the monetary approach to the balance of payments and the asset market theory of exchange-rate determination. Developed a methodology for estimating transactions costs in the market for foreign exchange and studied the operation of covered interest arbitrage. Studied the economics of hyperinflation and analysed the use of forward exchange rates as measures of expectations. Studied the Purchasing Power Parity theory and the relation between spot and forward exchange rates. Contributed to the theory and the empirical research on the demand for international reserves. Analysed the determinants of the optimal management of exchange rates and the interaction between wage indexation and exchange rate policy. Most recently, studied the impact of government spending and budget deficits on world rates of interest and the international transmission of fiscal policies in the interdependent world economy

FREY, Bruno S.

Born 1941, Basel, Switzerland
Current Post Prof. Econ., Univ. Zürich, Zürich, Switzerland, 1977–.
Past Posts Vis. Lect., Wharton School, Univ. Penn., 1967–8; Assoc. Prof., Univ. Basel, 1969–70; Prof., Univ. Konstanz, W. Germany, 1970–7; Vis. Prof., Univ. Stockholm, 1982; Fellow, Inst. Internat. Econ. Stud., Stockholm 1982; Guest Prof., Inst. Advanced Stud., Vienna, 1983; Vis. Fellow, All Souls Coll. Oxford, 1983.
Degrees Ricentiatus Rer. Pol. Dr Rer. Pol., Habilitation Univ. Basel, 1964, 1965, 1969.
Offices and Honours Pres., Theoretical Study Group Swiss Soc. Econ. and Stats., 1972–82; Member, Steering Comm., Internat. Seminar Public Econ., 1976–; Member, Exec. Comm. Europ. Public Choice Soc., 1977–.
Editorial Duties Managing Ed., *Kyk*, 1979–.
Principal Fields of Interest 320 Public Finance; 720 Natural Resources.
Publications *Books:* 1. *Umweltoekonomie* (Vaudenhoeck & Ruprecht, 1972); 2. *Modern Political Economy* (Martin Robertson, 1978, 1980; Halsted-Wiley, 1978; transls., German, Vahlen, 1977, Japanese, Diamond, 1980, Portuguese, Zahar, 1983, French, Presses Univ. de France, 1984); 3. *Democratic Economic Policy. A Theoretical Introduction* (Martin Robertson, 1983, St Martin's Press, 1983; transls., German, Vahlen, 1981, Japanese, Diamond, 1984, French, Bonnet, 1984, Spanish, Alianza, 1984); 4. *Schattenwirtschaft* (with H. Weck and W.W. Pommerehne), (Vahlen, 1984); 5. *International Political Economics* (Blackwell, 1984).

Articles: 1. 'Towards a mathematical model of government behaviour' (with L. J. Lan), *ZN,* 28(3/4), 1968; 2. 'Politico-economic models and cycles', *J Pub E,* 9, April 1978; 3. 'An empirical study of politico-economic interaction in the United States' (with F. Schneider), *REStat,* 60, May 1978; 4. 'A politico-economic model of the United Kingdom' (with F. Schneider), *EJ,* 88, June 1978; 5. 'An economic analysis of the museum' (with W. W. Pommerehne), in *Economic Policy for the Arts,* ed. W. Hudson (Abt Books, 1980); 6. 'Central bank behavior. A positive empirical analysis' (with F. Schneider), *J Mon E,* 7, April 1981; 7. 'Self-interest and collective action: the economics and psychology of public goods' (with W. Stroebe), *British J Social Psychology,* 21, June 1982; 8. 'What produces a hidden economy? An international cross section analysis' (with H. Weck), *SEJ,* 49, Jan. 1983; 9. 'The hidden economy: state and prospect for measurement' (with W. W. Pommerehne), *RIW,* 30, March 1984; 10. 'Consensus and dissension among economists: an empirical inquiry' (with W. W. Pommerehne, F. Schneider and G. Gilbert), *AER,* 74(5), Dec. 1984.

Principal Contributions Early work was in the then fashionable fields of economic growth and income distribution. Since the late 1960s I have increasingly become interested in the application of the economic approach to new fields, among them environmental economics. My main research area has been modern political economy (public choice). I have constructed theoretical models of the interactions of the economy and politics (politico-economic models, sometimes called political business-cycle models), and have econometrically tested them for various representative (US, UK, Germany) and direct (Switzerland) democracies. In addition to voters, government and public bureaucracy, the Central Bank's behaviour has also been taken into account. The research has now shifted to integrating and measuring the shadow (or hidden) economy; to the study of the (far-reaching) consequences of public choice for the theory of economic policy; and to the

application of public choice to international problems (international political economics). Among the other 'non-market' areas, I have contributed to the economics of the arts. While I am convinced that the economic model of behaviour is superior to most others, I endeavour to improve its performance (in collaboration with psychologists and sociologists) by taking new aspects of human behaviour into account.

FRIEDMAN, Benjamin M.

Born 1944, Louisville, KY, USA.
Current Post Prof. Econ., Harvard Univ., Cambridge, MA, USA, 1980–; Program Dir., Fin. Markets and Monetary Econ., NBER, 1983–.
Past Posts Econ., Morgan Stanley & Co., New York City, 1971–2; Ass. Prof., Assoc. Prof. Econ., Harvard Univ., 1972–6, 1976–80;
Degrees BA, MA Harvard Univ., 1966, 1969; MSc King's Coll. Camb., 1970; PhD Harvard Univ., 1971.
Offices and Honours Marshall Scholar, 1966–8; Jr. Fellow, Soc. Fellows, Harvard Univ., 1968–71; Horowitz Prize, Bank Israel, 1982; Trustee, Coll. Retirement Equities Fund, 1978–82.
Editorial Duties Assoc. Ed., *J Mon E,* 1977–.
Principal Fields of Interest 023 Macroeconomic Theory; 311 Domestic Monetary and Financial Theory and Policy; 321 Fiscal Theory and Policy.
Publications *Books:* 1. *Economic Stabilization Policy: Methods in Optimization* (N-H, 1975); 2. *New Challenges to the Role of Profits,* ed. (D. C. Heath, 1976); 3. *Monetary Policy in the United States* (Assoc. Reserve City Bankers, 1981; transl., Japanese, Toyo Keizai, 1982); 4. *The Changing Roles of Debt and Equity in Financing U.S. Capital Formation* (Univ. Chicago Press, 1982).

Articles: 1. 'Targets, instruments and indicators of monetary policy', *J Mon E,* 1, Oct. 1975, repr. in *Monetary Theory and Policy,* ed. R. S. Thorn (Praeger, 1976); 2. 'Financial flow variables and the short-run determination of long-term interest rates', *JPE,* 85,

Aug. 1977; 3. 'Optimal expectations and the extreme information assumptions of "rational expectations" macromodels', *J Mon E*, 5, Jan. 1979; 4. 'Substitution and expectation effects on long-term borrowing behavior and long-term interest rates,' *J Mon E*, 11, May 1979; 5. 'Price inflation, portfolio choice, and nominal interest rates', *AER*, 70(1), March 1980; 6. 'Post-war changes in the American financial markets', in *The American Economy in Transition*, ed. M. Feldstein (Univ. Chicago Press, 1980); 7. 'Debt and economic activity in the United States', in *The Changing Roles of Debt and Equity, op. cit.;* 8. 'The roles of money and credit in macroeconomic analysis', in *Macroeconomics, Prices, and Quantities: Essays in Memory of Arthur M. Okun*, ed. J. Tobin (Brookings Inst., 1983).

Principal Contributions The principal goal of most of my research to date has been, in the first instance, to further understanding of how financial markets work and why what happens in financial markets matters for nonfinancial economic activity, and, secondly, to seek ways of exploiting that understanding for improved policy decision-making. Within this overall objective, the central principle that has influenced my approach has been the belief that observed economic behaviour in general and financial behaviour in particular depend importantly on prevailing institutional structures, including legal and regulatory restrictions as well as aspects of business organisation and practice in the broadest sense. As a result of influences of the institutional environment in which actual businesses and consumers take and execute decisions, many familiar classical propositions, describing the functioning of perfect markets populated exclusively by atomistic traders possessing full information, no longer apply. The resulting, more complex set of relationships connecting financial market phenomena with nonfinancial economic outcomes gives rise in general to opportunities for public actions to affect nonfinancial economic activity, deliberately or inadvertently, and for good or ill.

My earliest work focussed explicitly on aspects of monetary and fiscal policies consistent with this central line of thinking, and work on monetary and fiscal policies continues to be an important part of my research agenda. I next devoted a substantial part of my work to studying the determination of asset returns, especially returns on long-term debt instruments. Most recently, I have been examining more closely the portfolio behaviour of risk-averse investors and borrowers that underlies the determination of asset returns. Finally, a further principle that has also guided much of my work on all of these subjects is the belief that the most interesting questions in the context of these broad concerns are really empirical ones, and that the advances which will ultimately prove most valuable will emerge from careful marshalling and assessment of the relevant evidence.

FRIEDMAN, James W.

Born 1936, Cleveland, OH, USA.

Current Post Prof. Econ., Virginia Polytechnic Inst. and State Univ., Blacksburg, VA, USA, 1983–.

Past Posts Instr. Econ., Ass. Prof. Econ., Res. Staff, Ass. Dir., Cowles Foundation, Yale Univ., 1962–3, 1963–8, 1964–6; Cons., General Electric Co., NY, 1964, RAND Corp., Santa Monica, CA, 1965; Assoc. Prof., Prof. Econ., Univ. Rochester, 1968–72, 1972–83; Vis. Prof., Inst. Math. Econ., Univ. Bielefeld, W. Germany, 1976, Hebrew Univ., Jerusalem, 1973; Prof. Polit. Science, Univ. Rochester, 1980–3.

Degrees BA Univ. Michigan, MA, PhD Yale Univ., 1960, 1963.

Offices and Honours Ford Foundation Dissertation Fellow, 1961–2; Yale Jr. Faculty Fellow, 1966–7; Fellow, Em Soc., 1977.

Editorial Duties Assoc. Ed., *Em*, 1957–81.

Principal Fields of Interest 020 General Economic Theory; 000 General Economics.

Publications *Books:* 1. *Oligopoly and the Theory of Games* (N-H, 1977); 2. *Research in Experimental Economics: An Experiment in Noncooperative Oligopoly* (with A. Hoggatt), (JAI

Press, 1979); 3. *Oligopoly Theory* (CUP, 1983).

Articles: 1. 'An experimental study of cooperative duopoly', *Em*, 35, July-Oct. 1967; 2. 'A non-cooperative equilibrium for supergames', *REStud*, 38, Jan. 1971; 3. 'Duality principles in the theory of cost and production revisited', *Int ER*, 13(1), Feb. 1972; 4. 'Concacity of production functions and non-increasing returns to scale', *Em*, 41(5), Sept. 1973; 5. 'Non-cooperative equilibria in time dependent supergames', *Em*, 42(2), March 1974; 6. 'Reaction functions as Nash equilibria', *REStud*, 43(1), Feb. 1976; 7. 'Oligopoly theory', in *Handbook of Mathematical Economics*, ed. by K. Arrow and M. Intriligator (N-H, 1982); 8. 'Limit price entry prevention when complete information is lacking', *J Ec Dyn*, 5(2–3), May 1983; 9. 'Low information Nash equilibria for oligopolistic markets', *Info. Econ. and Pol.*, 1983; 10. 'Advertising and oligopolistic equilibrium', *Bell JE*, 14(2), Autumn 1983.

Principal Contributions My work has been in oligopoly and game theory. Early work centred on laboratory experimentation, which I believe to be a neglected, a potentially very illuminating method of empirical investigations. Later I concentrated on pure theory in oligopoly and games. This work was interrelated in two respects: first, dynamic models were studied and developed in both areas, second, the game theory work was largely motivated by a desire to develop tools in game theory that would be of particular use for applications in economics.

FRIEDMAN, Milton

Born 1912, New York City, NY, USA.

Current Post Sr. Res. Fellow, Hoover Inst., Stanford, CA, USA, 1983–.

Past Posts Assoc. Econ., Nat. Resources Comm., Washington, DC, 1935–7; Part-time Lect., Columbia Univ., 1937–40; Res. Staff, NBER, 1937–40, 1948–81; Vis. Prof., Univ. Wisconsin, 1940–1; Principal Econ., Division Tax Res., US Dept. Treasury, 1941–3; Assoc. Dir., Stat. Res. Group, Division War Res., Columbia Univ., 1943–5; Assoc. Prof., Univ. Minnesota, 1945–6; Assoc. Prof., Prof., Paul Snowden Russell Disting. Service Prof., Prof. Emeritus, Univ. Chicago, 1946–8, 1948–63, 1963–83, 1983–; Cons., EEC, Paris, 1950; Vis. Fulbright Lect., Univ. Camb., 1953–4; Cons., Internat. Cooperation Admin., India, 1955; Wesley Clair Mitchell Vis. Res. Prof., Columbia Univ., 1964–5; Columnist, Contributing Ed., *Newsweek*, 1966–84; Vis. Prof., UCLA, 1967, Univ. Hawaii, 1972; Vis. Scholar, Fed. Reserve Bank, San Francisco, 1977.

Degrees BA, Hon. LLD Rutgers Univ., 1932, 1968; MA Univ. Chicago, 1933; PhD Columbia Univ., 1946; Hon. LLD St Paul's Univ., Tokyo, 1963, Kalamazoo Coll., 1963, Lehigh Univ., 1969, Loyola Univ., Chicago, 1971, Univ. New Hampshire, 1975, Harvard Univ., 1979, Brigham Young Univ., 1980, Dartmouth Coll., 1980, Gonzaga Univ., 1981; Hon. LLD Rockford Coll., 1969, Roosevelt Univ., 1975, Hebrew Union Coll., LA, 1981; Hon. LittD Bethany Coll., 1971; Hon. DSc Univ. Rochester, 1971; Hon. PhD Hebrew Univ., Jerusalem, 1977; Hon. Doctor en Ciencias Sociales, Francisco Marroquin Univ., Guatemala, 1978.

Offices and Honours John Bates Clark Medal, Exec. Comm., Pres., AEA, 1951, 1955–7, 1967; Fellow, Center Advanced Study Behavioral Sciences, Stanford, 1957–8; Amer. Secretary, Member Council, Vice-Pres., Pres., Vice-Pres., Mont Pelerin Soc., 1957–62, 1962–5, 1967–70, 1970–2, 1972–80; Ford Faculty Res. Fellow, 1962–3; Board Trustees, Philadelphia Soc., 1965–7, 1970–2, 1976–8; Chicagoan of the Year, Chicago Press Club, 1972; Educator of the Year, Chicago United Jewish Fund, 1973; Member, NAS, 1973–; Nobel Prize in Econ., 1976; Scopus Award, Amer. Friends of Hebrew Univ., 1977; Gold Medal, Nat. Inst. Social Sciences, 1978; Private Enterprise Examplar Medal, 1978; Valley Forge Hon. Certificate, 1978; George Washington Honor Medal, Freedoms Foundation at Valley Forge, 1978, 1980; Tuck Media Award Econ. Understanding, Amos Tuck School Bus. Admin., Dartmouth Coll., 1981; New

Perspectives Award, Rouche Ross & Co., Ohio State Award for 'Free to Choose' TV Series, 1981; Statesman of the Year Award, Sales & Marketing Exec. Internat., 1981; Vice-Pres., Pres., WEA, 1982–3; 1984–5.

Editorial Duties Ed. Boards, *AER*, 1951–3, *Em*, 1957–69.

Principal Fields of Interest 020 General Economic Theory; 200 Quantitative Economic Methods and Data; 300 Domestic Monetary and Fiscal Theory and Institutions.

Publications *Books:* 1. *Essays in Positive Economics* (Univ. Chicago Press, 1953; transls., Spanish, Editorial Gredos, 1967, Japanese, Fuji Shobo, 1977); 2. *A Theory of the Consumption Function* (Princeton Univ. Press, 1957; transl., Japanese, Ganshodo, 1961); 3. *Capitalism and Freedom* (Univ. Chicago Press, 1962; transls., Spanish, Ediciones Rialp, 1966, Italian, Vallecchi Editore, 1967, French, Editions Robert Laffont, 1971, German, Seewald Verlag, 1971, Deutscher Taschenbuch Verlag, 1976, Swedish, A. Bonniers Föflag, 1972, Japanese, McGraw-Hill Kogakusha, 1975, Hebrew, Adam Publishers, 1978, Icelandic, Almenna Bokafelagid og Felag Frjalsyggjumanna, 1982, Russian, Khronika Press, Chalidze Publications, 1982, Greek, Helliniki Euroekdotiki, forthcoming); 4. *A Monetary History of the United States, 1867–1960* (with A. J. Schwartz), (Princeton Univ. Press, 1963; transl., Italian, Unione Tipografico Editrice Torinese, 1979); 5. *The Optimum Quantity of Money and Other Essays* (Aldine, 1969; transl., German, Verlag Moderne Industrie, Wolfgang Dummer, 1970, Fischer Taschenbuch Verlag, 1976); 6. *Milton Friedman's Monetary Framework: A Debate with his Critics* (with others), ed. R. J. Gordon (Univ. Chicago Press, 1974; transls., Japanese McGraw-Hill Kogakusha, 1978, Spanish, Premia Editora, 1978); 7. *Price Theory* (Aldine, 1976; transls., German, Verlag Moderne Industrie, Wolfgang Dummer, 1977, French, Economica, 1983); 8. *Free to Choose* (with R. Friedman), (Harcourt Brace Jovanovich, 1980, Avon Books, 1981; transls., French, Pierre Belfond, 1980, German, Ullstein, 1980, Japanese, Nihon Keizai Shimbun, 1980, Nor-wegian, NA Forlag, 1980, Spanish, Ediciones Grijalbo, 1980, Swedish, Liber Läromedel, 1980, Danish, G.E.C. Gads Forlag, 1981, Italian, Longanesi, 1981, Portuguese, Editora Record, 1981, Finnish, Otava, 1982); 9. *Monetary Trends in the United States and the United Kingdom* (with A. J. Schwartz), (Univ. Chicago Press, 1982); 10. *Tyranny of the Status Quo* (with R. Friedman), (Harcourt Brace Jovanovich, 1984).

Articles: 1. 'The use of ranks to avoid the assumption of normality implicit in the analysis of variance', *JASA*, 32, Dec. 1937; 2. 'The utility analysis of choices involving risk' (with L. J. Savage), *JPE*, 56, Aug. 1949; 3. 'The expected utility hypothesis and the measurement of utility' (with L. J. Savage), *JPE*, 60, Dec. 1952; 4. 'Choice, chance and the personal distribution of income', *JPE*, 61 Aug. 1953; 5. 'Leon Walras and his economic system', *AER*, 45(5), Dec. 1955; 6. 'The relative stability of monetary velocity and the investment multiplier in the United States, 1897–1958' (with D. Meiselman), in *Stabilization Policies, Commission on Money and Credit* (Prentice-Hall, 1963); 7. 'Myths that keep people hungry', *Harper's Magazine*, April 1967; 8. 'The role of monetary policy', *AER*, 58(1), March 1968; transls., Spanish, *Cemla Boletin Mensual* (Mexico), 15(4), April 1969, *Informacion Comercial Espanola* (Madrid), 425, June 1969, *Revista del Banco Hipotecario de El Salvador*. 6, Jan.–March 1971; Italian, *Economia Internazionale*, 22, Feb. 1969, and repr. in *Il dibattito sulla moneta*, ed. G. Bellone (Society Editrice il Mulino, 1972), Japanese, Nihon Keizai Shimbunsha, 1972, German, *Geldtheorie*, ed. K. Brunner, *et al.* (Kiepenheur & Witsch, 1974); 9. 'Inflation and unemployment', *JPE*, 85, June 1977 and in *Les Prix Nobel* (Nobel Foundation, 1977); transls., Spanish, *Economicas y Empresariales en la Universidad Nacional de Educacion a Distancia* (Madrid), 3, 1976, *Paro e inflacion* (Union Editorial, 1977), *Los premios Nobel de economia* (Banco de Mexico, Fondo de Cultura Economica, 1978), Italian, *Il Politico* (Padua), 43(1), March 1978, Japanese, *Infureshon to shitsugyo* (McGraw-Hill Kogakusha, 1978); 10. 'Monetary policy for the

1980s', in *To Promote Prosperity: US Domestic Policy in the Mid-1980s*, ed. J. Moore (Hoover Inst. Press, 1984).

Principal Contributions Permanent income theory of consumption; understanding the role of money in determining the course of events, in particular the monetary source of the US Great Depression; analysis of inflation, its sources, consequences, and possible cures; concept of natural rate of unemployment and accelerationist theory of Phillips curve; role and operation of monetary policy; theory of capital; demonstration that Gibson paradox is of very limited applicability and is to be explained much more along the lines of Irving Fisher than of John Maynard Keynes; derivation of a stable demand curve for money covering more than a hundred years and applicable to the US and the UK.

Secondary Literature N. Thygesen, 'The scientific contributions of Milton Friedman', *Scand JE*, 79, 1979, repr. in *Contemporary Economists in Perspective*, eds. H. W. Spiegel and W. J. Samuels (JAI Press, 1984); J. Burton, 'Positively Milton Friedman', in *Twelve Contemporary Economists*, eds. J. R. Shackleton and G. Locksley, (Macmillan, 1981; Wiley, Halsted, 1981).

FRIEND, Irwin

Born 1915, Schenectady, NY, USA.
Current Post Edward J. Hopkinson Prof. Fin. and Econ., Wharton School, Univ. Penn., Philadelphia, PA, USA, 1982–.
Past Posts Ass. Dir., Trading and Exchange Div.; Chief, Econ. and Stats. Subdiv., US Securities and Exchange Commission, 1937–47; Chief, Bus. Structure Div., US Dept. Commerce, 1947–53; Prof. Econ. Fin. and Stats., Univ. Penn., 1953–82.
Degrees BS(Maths.) Coll. City NY, 1935; PhD Amer. Univ., 1953.
Offices and Honours Pres., AFA; Fellow, ASA, Em Soc.
Editorial Duties Ed. Board, *AER, JASA, J Fin, J Bank Fin.*
Principal Fields of Interest 130 Economic Fluctuations, Forecasting, Stabilization and Inflation; 200 Quantitative

Economic Methods and Data; 300 Domestic Monetary and Financial Policy and Institutions.

Publications *Books:* 1. *The Over-The-Counter Securities Markets* (with G. W. Hoffman, *et al*), (McGraw-Hill, 1958); 2. *A Study of Mutual Funds* (with F. E. Brown, *et al*), (US Govt. Printing Office, 1962); 3. *Private Capital Markets* (with H. Minsky, *et al*), (Prentice-Hall, 1964); 4. *Investment Banking and the New Issues Market* (with J. R. Longstreet, *et al*), (World Publishing, 1967); 5. *Study of the Savings and Loan Industry* (with P. J. Dhrymes, *et al*), (US Govt. Printing Office, 1969); 6. *Mutual Funds and Other Institutional Investors: A New Perspective* (with M. E. Blume, *et al*), (McGraw-Hill, 1970); 7. *The Changing Role of the Individual Investor* (with M. E. Blume), (Wiley, 1978); 8. *Financial Effects of Capital Tax Reform* (with M. E. Blume, *et al*), (US Treasury Dept., 1979); 9. *A Study of the US Tax Structure* (with A. Ando, *et al*), (Univ. Penn., 1984).

Articles: 1. 'A short-term forecasting model' (with P. Taubman), *REStat*, 46, Aug. 1964; 2. 'Dividends and stock prices' (with M. Puckett), *AER*, 54(4), Sept. 1964; 3. 'The impact of monetary stringency on business investment' (with J. Crockett, *et al*), *Survey Current Bus.*, 46(2), Aug. 1967; 4. 'Short-run asset effects on household saving and consumption' (with C. Leiberman), *AER*, 65(4), Sept. 1975; 5. 'The demand for risky assets' (with M. E. Blume), *AER*, 65(5), Dec. 1975; 6. 'The demand for risky assets under uncertain inflation' (with Y. Landskroner and E. Losq), *J Fin*, 31(5), Dec. 1976; 7. 'The effect of inflation on the profitability and valuation of US corporations' (with J. Hasbroucky), in *Saving, Investment and Capital Markets in an Inflationary Economy*, eds. M. Sarnat and G. P. Szego (Ballinger, 1982); 8. 'Saving and after-tax rates of return' (with J. Hasbroucky), *REStat*, 65(4), Nov. 1983; 9. 'A critical reexamination of the empirical evidence on the arbitrage pricing theory' (with P. J. Dhrymes, *et al*), *J Fin*, 39(3), June 1984; 10. 'Economic and equity aspects of securities regulation', in *Management under*

Government Intervention: The View from Mt. Scopus, eds. J. Lanzillotti and E. Peles (JAI Press, 1984).

Principal Contributions My work has been devoted largely to the testing and extension of theory in economics and finance. This includes theory for risky assets and capital asset pricing, including pricing under uncertainty, heterogeneous expectations, inflation and taxation: the efficiency of capital markets, including the effect of regulation on such markets; the optimal corporate financial policies, especially relating to capital structure and dividend policy. Part of this work necessitated the development of new statistical measures of highly important, but heretofore unobservable economic and related variables, such as the Pratt-Arrow measure of relative risk aversion for the market as a whole (after demonstrating that constant proportional risk aversion is a tenable approximation to the market's portfolio behaviour); the cost of capital under uncertainty; and anticipated plant and equipment expenditures and related expectations held by the business community. The testing of theory I have carried out has frequently required an extension of existing theory (as indicated for example by the extension of the theory on the demand for risky assets from the micro- to the macro-levels and from the existing no-tax model to one incorporating taxes). It has also frequently required both the use of data not generally used for this purpose (e.g. cross-section as well as time-series data in determining the nature of the demand for risky assets and continuous cross-section data for testing saving and consumption functions) and the collection of new data on investments and their financing directly from corporations and institutional and individual investors.

FRISCH, Ragnar Anton Kittil*

Dates and Birthplace 1895–1973, Oslo, Norway.

Posts Held Lect. at various univs.; Privatdocent, Docent, Prof., Univ. Oslo, 1923, 1928, 1931–65; Rockefeller

Scholar, 1926–8; Vis. Prof., Yale Univ., 1930–1.

Degrees BA, PhD Univ. Oslo, 1919, 1926.

Offices and Honours Founder, Em Soc, 1930; Joint Nobel Prize in Econ., 1969.

Editorial Duties Ed., *Em*, 1933–5.

Publications *Books:* 1. *New Methods of Measuring Marginal Utility* (1932); 2. *Statistical Confluence Analysis by Means of Complete Regression Systems* (1934); 3. *Theory of Production* (1965); 4. *Economic Planning Studies: A Collection of Essays* (1976).

Articles: 1. 'Propagation problems and impulse problems in dynamic economies', in *Economic Essays in Honor of Gustav Cassel* (1933), repr. in *Readings in Business Cycles*, eds. R. A. Gordon and L. R. Klein (1965).

Career A pioneer of the application of mathematical and statistical methods to economics, which he himself named 'econometrics'. Only part of his wide-ranging work has been published, but many of the papers he did publish are regarded as classics. He not only exercised a dominating influence over economic thought, but also over economic policy in Norway. Adviser to developing countries such as Egypt and India. The 'decision models' he developed in the 1940s and other models for government planning were widely used. Consumer behaviour, production theory, macroeconomic problems and a range of other topics occupied him at different times.

Secondary Literature L. Johansen, 'Frisch, Ragnar', *IESS*, 18; L. Johansen, 'Ragnar Frisch's scientific contributions to economics', in *Contemporary Economists in Perspective*, 1, eds. H. W. Spiegel and W. J. Samuels (JAI Press, 1984); J. C. Andvig, 'Ragnar Frisch and business cycle research during the interwar years', *HOPE*, 13(4), Sept. 1981.

FULLARTON, John*

Dates and Birthplace 1780(?)–1849, Scotland.

Posts Held Surgeon and banker, India, 1813–.

Offices and Honours Fellow, Royal Asiatic Soc.

Publications *Books:* 1. *On the Regulation of Currencies* (1844).

Career Wrote on theory and policy of banking in his retirement from business. *Regulation* . . . was a considerable success and frequently drawn on by later writers, including Marx. The book arose from the controversy over Peel's Act of 1844, but the general soundness and accessibility of its argument ensured its long-term success. His argument was that of the 'Banking school', in which convertibility of notes is regarded as the only requirement for stability of the currency.

FURTADO, Celso

Born 1920, Pombal, Paraiba, Brazil.

Current Post Dir. Res., Ecole de Hautes Etudes en Sciences Sociales, Univ. Paris, France, 1979–.

Past Posts Head Devlp. Div., UNECLA, 1950–7; Dir., Brazilian Nat. Devlp. Bank, 1958–9; Head, Agency Devlp. Northeast Brazil, 1958–9; Minister of Plan, Brazilian Govt., 1963–4; Res. Fellow, Yale Univ., 1964–5; Prof. Econ. Devlp., Univ. Paris, 1965–79; Vis. Prof., Univs. Amer., 1972, Camb.; 1973–4, Sao Paulo, 1975, Columbia, 1977.

Degrees BA Univ. Brazil, 1944; Dr Univ. Paris, 1948.

Offices and Honours Pres., Econ. Club, Rio de Janeiro, 1953–6.

Editorial Duties Member, UN Res. Council, 1975–9; Ed. Boards, *Ekonomica Brasileira*, 1954–63, *El Trimestre Economico*, 1965–, *Desarrollo Economico*, 1966–70, *Revista de Economia Politica*, 1981, *Bensamiento Iberoamericano*, 1982.

Principal Fields of Interest 047 Economic History; Latin American and Carribean; 112 Economic Development Methods and Theories; 121 Economic Development of Less Developed Countries.

Publications *Books:* 1. *The Economic Growth of Brazil* (Univ. Cal. Press, 1963, original Portuguese, Fundo de Cultura, 1959; transls., Spanish, Fondo de Cultura, 1962, Polish, Panstwowe

Wydawnictwo Naukowe, 1967, Italian, Einaudi, 1970, Japanese, Shisekaisha, 1972, French, Mouton, 1972, German, Fink Verlag, 1975); 2. *Development and Underdevelopment* (Univ. Cal. Press, 1964; original Portuguese, 1961; transls., Spanish, EUDEBA, 1964, French, Presses Univ. de France, 1966, Persian, 1980); 3. *Diagnosis of the Brazilian Crisis* (Univ. Cal. Press, 1965; original Portuguese, 1964; transl. Spanish, Fondo de Cultura, 1965); 4. *Economic Development of Latin America* (CUP, 1970; original Portuguese, 1969; transls., French, Sirey, 1970, Spanish, Siglo XXI, 1971, Italian, Laterza, 1971, Swedish, Raben and Sjögren, 1972, Japanese, Shinsekaisha, 1975); 5. *Obstacles to Development in Latin America* (Doubleday, 1970; original Portuguese, Civilizacao Brasileira, 1966; transls., French, Calmann-Levy, 1970, Spanish, Edicusa, 1971, Italian, Franco Angeli, 1971); 6. *O Mito do Desenvolvimento Economico* (Paz e Terra, 1974; transls., Spanish, Siglo ZI, 1975, French, Anthropos, 1976, Polish, Panstwowe Wydawnictwo Ekonomiczne, 1982); 7. *Prefacio a nova Economia Politica* (Paz e Terra, 1976; transls., Spanish, Siglo ZI, 1976, Italian, Jaca Book, 1977); 8. *Accumulation and Development* (Martin Robertson, 1983; original Portuguese, 1978; transls., Spanish, Siglo XXI, 1979, French, Presses Univ., 1981); 9. *O Brasil pos-'milagre'* (Paz e Terra, 1981; transl. Spanish, Fondo de Cultura, 1983); 10. *A nova dependencia* (Paz e Terra, 1982; transl. Spanish, Centro Editor, 1984).

Articles: 1. 'Capital formation and economic development', *Internat. Econ. Papers*, 4, (Macmillan, 1954); 2. 'Development and stagnation in Latin America: a structuralist approach', *Stud. Comparative Internat. Devlp.*, 1(11), 1965; 3. 'The Brazilian "Model"', *Social and Econ. Stud.* 22(1), 1973; 4. 'Intra-country discontinuities: towards a theory of spatial structures', *Social Science Info.*, Dec. 1967; 5. 'Development', *Internat. Social Science J.*, 28(4), 1977; 6. 'La dette exterieure bresilienne', *La documentation française*, 693, Nov. 1982; 7. 'Dependence in a unified world', *Alternatives*, 8(2), 1982; 8. 'Las relaciones comerciales entre la Europa

Occidental y la America Latina', *El Trimestre Economico*, 50(3), 199, 1983.

Principal Contributions Early work was concentrated on the history of Brazilian economic development with a methodological innovation consisting of the introduction of macroeconomic models into the analysis of each historical phase from the 16th century. In my *Development and Underdevelopment*, underdevelopment was regarded, not as a stage on the road to development, but as a permanent structural feature. As far as the patterns of consumption of the advanced countries are imitated in countries of much lower levels of productivity, such countries tend to remain 'underdeveloped', namely socially more heterogeneous. More recently, in my *Accumulation and Development*, an interdisciplinary approach was introduced to the study of development, linking the theory of accumulation with the theory of social stratification and the theory of power. Recent work has also concentrated on the social distortions produced by the rapid economic growth of the Brazilian economy in the 1970s.

FURUBOTN, Erik G.

Born 1923, New York City, NY, USA.

Current Post James L. West Prof. Econ., Univ. Texas, Arlington, TX, USA.

Past Posts Prof. Econ., State Univ., 1963–7; Vis. Prof., Tulane Univ., 1965; Prof. Econ., Texas A&M Univ.

Degrees BA Brown Univ., 1948; MA, PhD Columbia Univ., 1951, 1959.

Offices and Honours Francis Wayland Scholar, Brown Univ., 1948; Phi Beta Kappa; Member, AEA, RES, Em Soc, SEA; Exec. Comm., SEA, 1975–7.

Editorial Duties Advisory Board, *Appl. Econ.*, 1971–2; Ed. Boards, *SEJ*, 1979–80, *ZGS*, 1983–.

Principal Fields of Interest 025 Social Choice.

Publications *Books:* 1. *The Evolution of Modern Demand Theory* (with R. B. Ekelund and W. P. Gramm), (D. C. Heath, 1972); 2. *The Economics of Property Rights*, co-ed. (with S. Pejovich), (Ballinger, 1974).

Articles: 1. 'Engineering data and the production function', *AER*, 55(3), June 1965; 2. 'The orthodox production function and the adaptability of capital', *WEJ*, 3(3), 1965; 3. 'Property rights and economic theory: a survey of recent literature' (with S. Pejovich), *JEL*, 10(4), Dec. 1972; 4. 'Property rights, economic decentralization, and the evolution of the Yugoslav firm, 1965–72' (with S. Pejovich), *J Law E*, 16(2), Oct. 1973; 5. 'The long-run analysis of the labor-managed firm: an alternative interpretation', *AER*, 66(1), March 1976.

Principal Contributions Redefining and broadening the concept of the production function and incorporating the behavioural effects of property relations into standard microeconomic theory. By applying 'property-rights' or 'entitlements' approach to problems in the area of comparative systems, it is possible to achieve improved understanding of the behaviour of diverse types of business organisations, including the socialist labour-managed firm, the Soviet firm, the codeterminationist firm, etc.

G

GABOR, André

Born 1903, Budapest, Hungary.

Current Post Pricing Cons., Dir. Pricing Res. Ltd., London, England; Member, Nottingham Univ. Consumer Study Group, 1974–.

Past Posts Sr. Lect., Univ. Nottingham, 1947–69, Univ. Sheffield, 1969–70, Univ. Leeds, 1970–1, Univ. York, 1971–2, Univ. Essex, 1972–3, Univ. Newcastle, 1973–4; Vis. Prof., Univs. Virginia, 1964, Clermont, France, 1980, 1981; Member, Ford Foundation Workshop, Carnegie Inst. Technology, 1965.

Degrees BA School Econ., Berlin, 1928; BSc Univ. London, 1944.

Offices and Honours Fellow, RSS; Leverhulme Emeritus Res. Fellow, 1974–6; Edouard Gaudy Prize, Societé de Géographie Commerciale, Paris, 1977.

Editorial Duties Founder-ed. *Appl. Econ.*; Ed. Board, *J. Econ. Psychology*; Guest Ed., *Europ. J. Marketing*.

Principal Fields of Interest 022 Micro-economic Theory; 229 Micro-data.

Publications *Books:* 1. *Pricing: Principles and Practices* (Heinemann Educ., 1977, 1980); 2. *Issues in Pricing Policy*, ed. (MCB Publications, 1979); 3. *Economics Papers* (MCB Publications, 1979); 4. *Pricing Decisions: Essays* (MCB Publications, 1979).

Articles: 1. 'A new approach to the theory of the firm' (with I. F. Pearce), *OEP*, 4, Oct. 1952, repr. in *Readings in Industrial Economics*, ed. C. K. Rowley (Macmillan, London, 1972); 2. 'An essay on the mathematical theory of freedom' (with D. Gabor), *JRSS*, Series A, 117 (1), 1954; 3. 'Block Tariffs', *REStud*, 23(1), Jan. 1955; 4. 'On the price consciousness of consumers' (with C. W. J. Granger), *Appl. Stats.*, 10(3), 1961, repr. in *Pricing Strategy*, eds. B. Taylor and G. Wills (Staples, London, 1969); 5. 'Price sensitivity of the consumer' (with C. W. J. Granger) , *J. Advertising Res.*, 4(4), Dec. 1964, repr. in *Readings in Market Research*, ed. K. K. Cox (Appleton-Century-Crofts, 1967), and *Readings in Marketing*, eds. C. J. Dirksen, and others (Richard D. Irwin, Wiley 1969); 6. 'The pricing of new products' (with C. W. J. Granger), *Scientific Bus.*, Aug. 1965, repr. in *Price Policies and Practices*, eds. D. F. Mulvihill and S. Paranka (Wiley 1967), and *Pricing Strategy*, eds. B. Taylor and G. Wills (Staples, 1969), and *Creating and Marketing New Products*, eds. G. Wills, *et al.* (Crosby Lockwood Staples, 1973), and *Analytical Marketing Management*, eds. P. Doyle, *et al.* (Harper & Row, 1974), and in Hungarian in *Piac es Vallalati Arpolitika*, ed. R. Hock (Kozgazdasagi es Jogi Konyvkiado, 1968); 7. 'Price as an indicator of quality' (with C. W. J. Granger), *Ec.*, N.S. 33, Feb. 1966; 8. 'The theory of constant arc elasticity functions', *Bull. Econ. Res.*, 26(2), 1974, 27(2), 1975; 9. 'Price and consumer behaviour' and 'Decimalisation and the consumer', in *Economics of Consumer Protection*, ed. D. Morris (Heinemann Educ., 1980); 10. 'The theory and practice of

transfer pricing', in *Demand, Equilibrium and Trade*, eds. A. Ingham and A. Ulph (Macmillan, 1984).

Principal Contributions After obtaining my first degree in Berlin, I worked in industry, commerce and insurance (also, during World War II and for some years after, in the service of the UK Ministry of Agriculture) with the consequence that I re-entered the academic fold about twenty years later in life than most of my fellow economists. I suppose that it was due to my early practical experience that even my essays in pure theory were written with the world outside the ivory tower in mind, but I soon found that my main sphere of interest was that of the problems of pricing, especially (but not exclusively) with regard to consumer behaviour. It is a source of satisfaction to me that the methods developed with the help of my research associates, and to which I gave the name of 'buy-response analysis', have proved to be of practical help to the manufacturers of fast-moving consumer goods and are in widespread use.

GAERTNER, Wulf

Born 1942, Berlin, W. Germany.

Current Post Prof. Econ., Univ. Osnabrück, W. Germany, 1980–.

Past Posts Ass. Lect., Lect., Univ. Bielefeld, W. Germany, 1973–8, 1978–80; Vis. Fellow, All Soul's Coll. Oxford, 1984–5.

Degrees Diploma, Dr rer. pol. Univ. Bonn, 1969, 1973; Habilitation Univ. Bielefeld, 1978.

Editorial Duties Managing Ed., *Social Choice and Welfare*, 1984–.

Principal Fields of Interest 022 Micro-economic Theory: 024 Welfare Theory; 025 Social Choice; Bureaucratic Performance.

Publications *Books:* 1. *Interdependence of Consumer Decisions* (German), (Bonn Univ. Press, 1973); 2. *The Economics of the Shadow Economy,* co-ed. (Springer Verlag, 1984).

Articles: 1. 'A dynamic model of interdependent consumer behavior', *ZN,* 34(3–4), Dec. 1974; 2. 'On two sufficient conditions for transitivity of the social preference relation' (with A. Heinecke), *ZN*, 37(1–2), June 1977; 3. 'An analysis and comparison of several necessary and sufficient conditions for transitivity under the majority decision rule', in *Aggregation and Revelation of Preferences*, ed. J. J. Laffont (N-H, 1979); 4. 'Self-supporting preferences and individual rights' (with L. Krüger), *Ec*, 48, March 1981; 5. 'Rawlsianism, utilitarianism, and profiles of extended orderings', *ZGS*, 137(1), March 1981; 6. 'Procedures d'agrégation avec domaines restreints et theorèmes d'éxistence' (with M. Salles), in *Analyse et agregation des préférences*, eds. P. Batteau, E. Jacquet-Lagreze and B. Monjardet (Economica, 1981); 7. 'Envy-free rights assignments and self-oriented preferences', *Math. Social Sciences,* 2(2), 1982; 8. 'How to reconcile individual rights with collective action' (with L. Krüger), in *Philosophy of Economics*, eds., W. Stegmüller, W. Balzer and W. Spohn (Springer Verlag, 1982); 9. 'Equity- and inequity-type borda rules', *Math. Social Sciences,* 4(1), 1983; 10. 'Alternative libertarian claims and Sen's paradox' (with L. Krüger), *Theory and Decision*, 15(3), Sept. 1983.

Principal Contributions Every economist will agree that preferences (tastes) are not constant over time. Experience and learning, habit formation and the social environment seem to be important factors of influence. My early work concentrated on these phenomena and developed a dynamic model of consumer behaviour where emphasis was on social interdependence. Phenomena such as imitation of other people's consumption behaviour or the desire to be different from others were some of the items discussed within a difference equation model. Very recently, my interest has come back to systems of difference equations and behavioural patterns over time. Nonlinear difference equations can produce highly regular, but also very irregular time paths. These patterns seem to contradict the well-known axioms of choice consistency.

Another subject of interest was and still is the existence of soical welfare functions. As is well known, there are many escape routes from Arrow's impossibility result. Some of my work concentrated on new domain conditions being both necessary and sufficient for an Arrowian welfare function to exist. Some other work in the area focussed on the integration of personal rights into the collective choice process: under what kind of conditions is it possible to grant particular rights to individuals, rights that cannot be overridden by society? Some recent work dealt with the issue of distributive justice, investigating the axiomatic structure behind utilitarianism, the Rawlsian theory of justice and other structurally related justice principles.

GÄFGEN, Gerard Franz Marcel

Born 1925, Luxembourg, Luxembourg.
Current Post Prof. Econ., Univ. Constance, Konstanz, W. Germany, 1969–.
Past Posts Res. Ass., Ass. Prof., Univ. Cologne, 1955–61, 1961–2; Vis. Prof., Univ. Hamburg, 1961–2; Prof. Econ., Univ. Karlsruhe, 1962–5; Prof. Econ., Univ. Hamburg, 1965–9.
Degrees Diplom-Volkswirt, Dr wirtschaftlichen Staatswissenschaften, Dr Rer Pol., Univ. Cologne, 1953, 1955, 1961.
Offices and Honours Academic Council, Vice-Chairman, German Fed. Ministry Econ. Affairs, 1971–, 1976–80; Exec. Comm. Gesellschaft für Wirtschafts- und Sozialwissenschaften, 1983–.
Editorial Duties Ed. Board, *Theory and Decision*, 1970–.
Principal Fields of Interest 020 General Economics; 036 Economic Methodology; 913 Economics of Health.
Publications Books: 1. *Theorie der wirtschaftlichen Entscheidung* (Mohr-Siebeck 1963, 1974); 2. *Grundlagen der Wirtschaftspolitik*, ed. (Kiepenheuer & Witsch, 1966, 1972); 3. *Die Kosten der Mitbestimmung* (with H. Steinmann and W. Blomeyer), (Bibliographisches Inst., 1981); 4. *Stand und Entwicklung der Gesundheitsökonomie* (Pharma-Dialog, 1981).
Articles: 1. 'Quasimonopole und

Pseudomonopole', in *Theoretische und institutionelle Grundlagen der Wirtschaftspolitik,* ed. H. Besters (Duncker & Humblot, 1967); 2. 'Die Marktmacht sozialer Gruppen', *Hamburger Jahrbuch fur Wirtschafts- und Gesellschaftspolitik,* 12, Dec. 1967; 3. 'Entscheidungs- und organisations-theoretische Probleme einer optimalen Infrastrukturplanung', in *Grundfragen der Infrastrukturplanung fur wachsende Wirtschaften* (Duncker & Humblot, 1971); 4. 'On the methodology and political economy of Galbraithian economics', *Kyk,* 27(4), 1974, repr. in *Economics and Social Institutions,* ed. K. Brunner (Martinus Nijhoff, 1979); 5. 'Theorie der Wirtschafts-politik', in *Kompendium der Volkswirtschaftslehre,* 2, eds. W. Ehrlicher, *et al.* (Vandenhoeck & Ruprecht, 1975); 6. 'Politische Ökonomie und Lehre von der Wirtschaftspolitik. Zur Realisierbarkeit Wirtschaftspolitisher Vorschlage', in *Wirtschaftspolitik — Wissenschaft und politische Aufgabe,* eds. H. Korner, *et al.* (Verlag P. Haupt, 1976); 7. 'Zur Eignung soziologischer Paradigmen. Betrachtungen aus der Sicht des Ökonomen' (with H. G. Monissen), *Jahrbuch fur Sozialwissenschaft,* 2, Jan. 1978; 8. 'Ökonomische Implikationen ethischer Prinzipien', in *Politik und Markt,* eds. D. Duwendag and H. Siebert (G. Fischer Verlag, 1980); 9. 'Leistungsmessung in Gesundheitswesen. Ein Beispiel fur die Ökonomie des Dienstleistungssektors', *Hamburger Jahrbuch fur Wirtschafts- und Gesellschaftspolitik,* 25, Dec. 1980; 10. 'Institutioneller Wandel und ökonomische Erklärung', *Jahrbuch für neue politische Ökonomie,* 2, Dec. 1983.

Principal Contributions In the wake of a dissertation on the investment ratio in the West German economy, scepticism about the empirical contents of the micro-foundations of economic theory led to investigations into the logical structure of rational action and its importance for the explanation of economic behaviour. The results bear upon formal decision theory, especially a general strategy of rational decisions and a reformulation of procedures for social choice. Normative aspects were treated in essays on evaluation, relevance, and formal ethics. Interest in methodological questions subsequently extended into conceptual problems of economic theory (as shown in articles on the concept of market power), and a general framework for a 'theory of economic policy', followed later on by critical appraisals of other schools of thought (sociology and neo-institutional economics).

Another issue treated in early work on economic decisions is the possibility of a positive theory of economic behaviour; fields of application — to be seen in connection with the studies in economic policy — were political-economic processes and the formation of ideologies. Under the influence of the property rights paradigm, institutional constraints were incorporated into behavioural theory in essays on institutional change and on the behaviour of hospitals. The last topic points to a growing interest in applying economic theories and concepts as well as methods of measurement and evaluation to actual social issues, e.g. workers' participation, research policy of the State, and lately above all the wide range of health and medical care.

GAITSKELL, Hugh Todd Naylor*

Dates and Birthplace 1906–63, London, England

Posts Held Lect. Econ., Workers' Educ. Assoc.; Reader Polit. Econ., Univ. London, 1938; UK Ministry Econ. Warfare, Board Trade, 1939–45.

Degree BA Univ. Oxford, 1927.

Offices and Honours MP (Labour), 1945–63; UK Minister Fuel and Power, 1946; UK Chancellor of Exchequer, 1950–1; Leader, Labour Party, 1955.

Publications *Books:* 1. *Chartism* (1929); 2. *Money and Everyday Life* (1939); 3. *The Challenge of Co-existence* (1957).

Articles: 1. 'Four monetary heretics', in *What Everybody Wants to Know About Money,* ed. G. D. H. Cole (Victor Gollancz, 1933); 2. 'Notes on the period of production Pts. I–II', *ZN,* 7, Dec. 1936, 9, July 1938.

Career Moving into government service from academic economics during

World War II, he quickly established his practical abilities. Membership of parliament, ministerial office and the leadership of his party followed quickly. His position regarding the economic policy of the Labour Party was that the traditional aim of common ownership of the means of production, distribution and exchange was not sacrosanct. He preferred a version of socialism more adapted to modern society and defended it ably in the Party. His early death frustrated this clarification of economic aims as it did his work on other issues, such as disarmament. In the 1930s he studied in Vienna and published a remarkable draft of an unfinished PhD thesis on the Austrian theory of capital.

Secondary Literature P. Williams, *Hugh Gaitskell: A Political Biography* (Gollancz, 1979).

GALBRAITH, John Kenneth

Born 1908, Iona Station, Ontario, Canada.

Current Post Retired.

Past Posts Instr., Prof., Harvard Univ. 1935, 1946–75; Dep. Admin., US Office Price Admin., 1941–3; Dir., US Strategic Bombing Survey, 1945–6; US Ambassador to India, 1961–3.

Degrees BA Ontario Coll. Agric., Guelph, 1930; PhD (Agric. Econ.) Univ. Cal. Berkeley, 1934.

Offices and Honours Chairman, Amer. Democratic Action, 1967–9; Pres., AEA, 1972.

Principal Fields of Interest 051 Capitalist Economic Systems.

Publications *Books:* 1. *Theory of Price Control* (Harvard Univ. Press, 1952); 2. *American Capitalism: The Concept of Countervailing Power* (Houghton Mifflin, 1952, 1956, 1962); 3. *The Great Crash, 1929* (Houghton Mifflin, 1954, 1961, 1972); 4. *The Affluent Society* (Houghton Mifflin, 1958, 1971, 1976); 5. *The New Industrial State* (Houghton Mifflin, 1967, 1972, 1978; transls., Russian, Hungarian, Polish, German, Croatian); 6. *The Age of Uncertainty* (Houghton Mifflin, 1977); 7. *Economics and the Public Purpose* (Houghton Mifflin, 1973); 8. *Money, Whence It Came, Where It Went* (Hough-

ton Mifflin, 1975); 9. *Almost Everyone's Guide to Economics* (with N. Salinger), (Houghton Mifflin, 1978); 10. *A Life in Our Times* (André Deutsch, 1981).

Secondary Literature M. E. Sharpe, 'Galbraith, John Kenneth', *IESS,* 18; C. H. Hession, *John Kenneth Galbraith and his Critics* (New Amer. Library, 1972); D. G. Fusfeld, 'On Galbraith', *Contemporary Economists in Perspective,* 2, eds. W. H. Spiegel and W. J. Samuels (JAI Press, 1984).

GALE, Douglas Maxwell

Born 1950, Ottawa, Canada.

Current Post Reader Econ., LSE.

Past Posts Res. Fellow, Churchill Coll., Camb., 1975–8; Lect. Econ., LSE, 1978–81.

Degrees BSc Univ. Trent, 1970; MA Carleton Coll., 1972; PhD Univ. Camb., 1975.

Offices and Honours Ass. Ed., *REStud,* 1980–.

Principal Fields of Interest 021 General Equilibrium Theory.

Publications *Books:* 1. *Money in General Equilibrium* (Nisbet, CUP, 1981).

Articles: 1. 'The core of monetary economy without trust', *JET,* 21(3), Dec. 1978; 2. 'Large economies with trading uncertainty', *REStud,* 47(3), April 1980; 3, 'Money, information and equilibrium', *JET,* 23(1), Aug. 1980.

Principal Contributions Initiated the study of general, manipulable and stochastic rationing schemes and the use of the Nash equilibrium of a generalised game to analyse effective demands under trading uncertainty. Principal contributions have been to the foundations of monetary economics, using game theoretic methods to rationalise the theory of sequence economies and the use of money.

GALENSON, Walter

Born 1914, New York City, NY, USA.

Current Post Jacob Gould Schurman Prof., Cornell Univ., Ithaca, NY, 1980–.

Past Posts Econ. US War Dept. Office

Strategic Services, 1942-5; Labor Attaché, US Embassies, Norway, Denmark, 1945–6; Ass. Prof. Econ., Harvard Univ., 1946–51; Prof. Econ., Univ. Cal. Berkeley 1951–65; Cons., ILO, 1961–71; Prof. Econ., Cornell Univ., 1966–80; Pitt Prof., Camb. Univ., 1970–1; Cons., Govt. Indonesia, 1971–2; Member, US Delegation, ILO, 1972, 1976; Vis. Prof., Univ. Gothenburg, 1974.

Degrees BA, MS, PhD Columbia Univ., 1934, 1935, 1940; Hon. MA Camb. Univ., 1971.

Offices and Honours Fellow Amer. Philo. Soc., 1947–9; Fulbright Fellow Norway 1950–1; Guggenheim Foundation Fellow Norway, 1955–6; Pres., Assoc. Comparative Econ. Studs., 1973.

Editorial Duties Ed. Board, *Labor Hist.*, 1962–73, *Industrial Relations*, 1961–6, *ILRR*, 1967–74.

Principal Fields of Interest 824 Labour Market Studies, Wages, Employment; 830 Trade Unions, Collective Bargaining; 120 Economic Growth — Country Studies.

Publications *Books:* 1. *Labor in Norway* (Harvard Univ. Press, 1949); 2. *The Danish System of Labor Relations* (Harvard Univ. Press, 1952); 3. *Labor Productivity in Soviet and American Industry* (Columbia Univ. Press, 1955; transls., Russian, Moscow, 1957, Japanese, Tokyo, 1957); 4. *The CIO Challenge to the AFL* (Harvard Univ. Press, 1960); 5. *Trade Union Democracy in Western Europe* (Univ. Cal. Press, 1962); 6. *The Quality of Labor and Its Impact on Economic Development* (with F. G. Pyatt), (ILO, 1964); 7. *A Primer on Employment and Wages* (Random House, 1966); 8. *The Chinese Economy Under Communism* (with N. R. Chen), (Aldine, 1969); 9. *The International Labor Organization* (Univ. Wisconsin Press, 1981); 10. *The United Brotherhood of Carpenters and Joiners* (Harvard Univ. Press, 1983).

Articles: 1. 'Investment criteria, productivity and economic development' (with H. Leibenstein), *QJE*, 69, August 1955; 2. 'Industrial training in the Soviet Union', *ILRR*, 9, July 1956; 3. 'International comparison of unemployment rates' (with A. Zellner), in *The Measurement and Behavior of Unemployment* (NBER, 1957); 4. 'Economic development and the expansion of employment', *Int Lab Rev*, June 1963; 5. 'Wage structure and administration in Soviet Industry', in *Internal Wage Structure*, ed. J. L. Meij (Macmillan, 1963); 6. 'Earnings and employment in Eastern Europe' (with A. Fox), *QJE*, 81, May 1967; 7. 'Social security and economic development', *ILRR*, 21, July 1968; 8. 'The Japanese labor market', in *Asia's New Giant*, eds. H. Patrick and H. Rosovsky (Brookings Inst., 1976); 9. 'Current problems of Scandinavian trade unions', in *Scandinavia at the Polls*, ed. K. H. Cerny (1977); 10. 'Economic growth, poverty and the international agencies', *J. Econ. Pol. Modeling*, 1(2), 1979.

Principal Contributions In one way or another, all my work has involved the labour market and its institutions. It has also largely been comparative. Out of my experience serving at the US embassies in Oslo and Copenhagen after World War II came books on the labour movements and industrial relations systems of Norway and Denmark. For some time thereafter, my interests switched to the Soviet economy and I worked on various aspects of that nation's labour problems. As a graduate student in the 1930s, I was fascinated by the rapid growth of the American labour movement, and I spent several years writing about this critical period in American history.

My interests then switched to what was on everyone's mind at the time — economic development. I wrote on the labour market problems of developing countries; directed a large Ford Foundation financed project on the Chinese economy; and helped plan and direct the World Employment Program of the International Labour Organization. That experience convinced me that the key to successful economic development was *rapid* growth, and I became involved with Taiwan, out of which came two books that I edited, one dealing with the major economic factors behind Taiwan's growth, and the second extending the analysis to Taiwan's three Pacific neighbours — South Korea, Hong Kong and Singapore. I also did some writing on the Japanese labour market, which has been the source of a great deal of controversy in the West, and arrived at conclusions that varied considerably from those of most Japanese economists. Most recently, I had the opportunity to study the history of one of America's oldest and largest trade unions and its role in the building trades.

GALIANI, Ferdinando*

Dates and Birthplace 1728–87, Chieti, Italy.

Posts Held Secretary, Neapolitan Embassy, Paris, 1759–69; Civil Servant, mainly in econ. depts., 1769–87.

Publications *Books:* 1. *On Money* (1750, 1977); 2. *Dialogue sur le commerce des blés* (1770, 1968).

Career His economic ideas were eclectic, and despite his long residence in France he largely rejected physiocracy. He developed a value theory with a considerable subjective element. His discussion of interest did not concern its morality, but explored the reasons why it is paid; he described it as a payment for the lender's risk in parting with his money. Policy prescriptions are largely confined to his *Dialogue* . . . which recognises the need to adjust economic principle in accordance with historical and geographical circumstances.

Secondary Literature P. R. Toscano, 'Galiani, Ferdinando', *IESS*, 6; W. Weigand, *Der Abbe Galiani* (Ludwig Röhrscheid, 1948); F. Cesarano, 'Monetary theory in Ferdinando Galiani's *Della Moneta*', *HOPE*, 8(3), Fall 1976.

GALLAWAY, Lowell Eugene

Born 1930, Toledo, OH, USA.

Current Post Disting. Prof. Econ., Ohio Univ., Athens, OH, USA, 1974–.

Past Posts Ass. Prof., Colorado State Univ., 1957–9; Ass. Prof., San Fernando Valley State Coll., 1959–62; Vis. Assoc. Prof., Univ. Minnesota, 1962–3; Chief, Analytic Stud. Section, US Social Security Admin., 1963–4; Assoc. Prof., Univ. Penn., 1964–7; Prof., Ohio Univ., 1967–74; Vis. Scholar, Lund Univ., Sweden, 1973; Vis. Prof., Univ. Texas, Arlington, 1976, Univ. New South Wales, Sydney, 1978, Univ. N. Carolina, Chapel Hill, 1980; Staff Econ., Joint Econ. Comm., US Congress, 1982.

Degrees BS Northwestern Univ., 1951; MA, PhD Ohio State Univ., 1955, 1959.

Offices and Honours Ford Foundation Faculty Fellow, 1960; General Electric Foundation Fellow, 1962; Res. Fellow, Ohio Univ., 1972; Fulbright–Hayes Sr. Scholar, Australia, 1978; Liberty Fund Fellow, Inst. Humane Stud., 1983; Pacific Inst. Public Pol. Res. Fellow, 1983–.

Editorial Duties Assoc. Ed., *RSE*.

Principal Fields of Interest 023 Macroeconomic Theory; 042 North American Economic History; 823 Labour Mobility; National and International Migration.

Publications *Books:* 1. *The Retirement Decision: An Exploratory Essay* (US Govt. Printing Office, 1965); 2. *Interindustry Labor Mobility in the United States, 1957–1960* (US Govt. Printing Office, 1967); 3. *Geographic Labor Mobility in the United States, 1957–1960* (US Govt. Printing Office, 1969); 4. *Manpower Economics* (Richard D. Irwin, 1971); 5. *Poverty in America* (Grid, 1973); 6. *Economic Impact of the 1982 'Bull Market'* (US Govt. Printing Office, 1982); 7. *The 'Natural' Rate of Unemployment* (with R. K. Vedder), (US Govt. Printing Office, 1982).

Articles: 1. 'The wage-push inflation thesis, 1950–1957', *AER*, 48(5), Dec. 1958; 2. 'A quarterly econometric model of the United States' (with P. E. Smith), *JASA*, 56, June 1961; 3. 'The North-South wage differential', *REStat*, 45(3), Aug. 1963; 4. 'Labor mobility, resource allocation and structural unemployment', *AER*, 53(4), Sept. 1963; 5. 'The theory of relative shares', *QJE*, 78(4), Nov. 1964; 6. 'The foundations of the war on poverty', *AER*, 55(1), March 1965; 7. 'Mobility of native Americans' (with R. K. Vedder), *JEH*, 31(3), Sept. 1971; 8. 'The neoclassical production function' (with V. Shukla), *AER*, 64(3), June 1974; 9. 'On the specification of the aggregate production function', *RISE*, 29(8), Aug. 1982; 10. 'Wages, prices and employment: von Mises and the "Progressives"' (with R. K. Vedder), *J. Austrian Econ.*, 1(1), 1984.

Principal Contributions In my younger days I had socialist leanings. By the time I left graduate school, these had been refined into a predilection towards Veblenian institutionalism. Once into the world of academe, though, I found these paradigms almost useless from the standpoint of providing meaningful answers to the questions in which I was interested. To my surprise, I found the standard neoclassical notions more capable of generating testable hypotheses and, unexpectedly, the available evidence generally seemed to support the neoclassical reasoning. Thus I started down the path towards becoming a thorough-going neoclassicist. The primary emphasis has been on evaluating the behaviour of labour markets, originally at the microeconomic level, but, more recently, as a macroeconomic phenomenon. The basic thrust of my research findings has been that the world appears to behave in accordance with neoclassical theory, both at the micro- and macro-levels. In the past few years, I, along with R. Vedder, have developed a considerable body of evidence that suggests that the economic profession 'backed the wrong horse', beginning in the 1930s, when it came to accounting for variations in unemployment. Specifically, contrary to the aggregate demand-oriented Keynesian theories, a real wage centred model will explain movements in unemployment quite well during such diverse periods.

GARDNER, Bruce L.

Born 1942, Solon Mills, IL, USA.
Current Post Prof. Agric. and Resource Econ., Univ. Maryland, Coll. Park, MD, USA, 1980–.
Past Posts Ass. Prof., Assoc. Prof. Econ., N Carolina State Univ., 1968–75; Sr. Staff Econ., US President's Council Econ. Advisers, Washington, DC, 1975–7; Prof. Agric. Econ., Texas A&M Univ., 1977–80; Vis. Fellow, Center Study of the Econ. and the State, Univ. Chicago, 1980–1.
Degrees BS Univ. Illinois, 1964; PhD Univ. Chicago, 1968.
Offices and Honours Awards, Outstanding Article, Quality Research,

AAEA, 1975, 1980; Board Dirs., AAEA, 1984–.
Editorial Duties Assoc. Ed, *AJAE*, 1983–5.
Principal Fields of Interest 710 Agriculture.
Publications *Books:* 1. *Optimal Stockpiling of Grain* (D. C. Heath 1979); 2. *The Governing of Agriculture* (Regents Press, Kansas, 1981).
Articles: 1. 'Economics of the size of North Carolina rural families', *JPE*, pt. III, 81(2), March–April 1973; 2. 'Farm population decline and the income of rural families', *AJAE*, 56(3), Aug. 1974; 3. 'The farm-retail price spread in a competitive food industry', *AJAE*, 57(3), Aug. 1975; 4. 'Futures prices in supply analysis', *AJAE*, 58(1), Feb. 1976; 5. 'Commodity options for agriculture', *AJAE*, 59(5), Dec. 1977; 6. 'Schooling and the agricultural minimum wage' (with H. F. Gallasch), *AJAE* 60(2), May 1978; 7. 'Robust stabilization policies for international commodity agreements', *AER*, 69(2), 70(2), 1979; 8. 'Determinants of supply elasticity in interdependent markets', *AJAE* 71(3), Aug. 1979; 9. 'Public stocks of grain and the market for grain storage', in *New Directions in Econometric Modeling and Forecasting in US Agriculture*, ed. G. Rausser (N-H, 1982); 10. 'Efficient redistribution through commodity markets', *AJAE*, 75(2), May 1983.
Principal Contributions My work has been entirely in agricultural economies, broadly defined, but has migrated over time to different areas in this field. The first area involves human resources in agriculture. I have published empirical findings on fertility behaviour and rural family size, the effects of agricultural minimum wages and the bracers programme. The second area is agriculture as an aggregated sector of the economy, where I have published empirical results on off-farm migration, the distribution of income in agriculture and the effects of inflation and recession on the farm sector. Thirdly, I have worked on the construction and evaluation of economic data for agriculture, particularly on economic well-being and on agricultural productivity. Fourthly, I have published conceptual work on the

farm-retail marketing margin and on supply elasticities in interdependent markets. Fifthly, in recent years I have written assessments of several US agricultural commodity programmes, in particular tobacco, grains, sugar and wool. The most extensive such work involved grain storage and price stabilisation programmes. In addition I have been attempting to explain why we get the farm policies that we observe. Finally, I have published works bearing on futures, commodity options, and risk. This has primarily involved using futures to aid in analysing the structure of commodity markets and options to throw light on policy issues.

GAREGNANI, Pierangelo

Born 1930, Milan, Italy.
Current Post Prof. Econ., Univ. Rome, Italy, 1974–.
Past Posts Prof. Econ., Univ. Sassari, Sardinia, Italy, 1962–6, Univ. Pavia, 1966–70, Univ. Florence, 1970–3; Fellow, Trinity Coll. Camb., Vis. Prof., Univ. Camb., 1973–4.
Degrees BA (Polit. Science) Univ. Paris, 1953; PhD Univ. Camb., 1959.
Offices and Honours Rockefeller Fellow, MIT, 1962–3.
Principal Fields of Interest 022 Microeconomic Theory; 031 History of Economic Thought; 111 Economic Growth Theory.
Publications *Books:* 1. *Il Capitale nelle Teorie della Distribuzione* (Giuffre, Milan, 1960, 1982; transls., Japanese, 1966, French, Maspero, 1980, Spanish, Oikos Tatt, 1982); 2. *Il Problema della Domanda Effettiva nello Sviluppo Economico Italiano* (SVIMEZ, 1962); 3. *Valore e Domanda Effettiva*, ed. (Einaudi, 1979); 4. *Marx e gli Economisti Classici* (Einaudi, 1981).
Articles: 1. 'Switching of techniques', *QJE*, 80, Nov. 1966; 2. 'Sulle equazioni walrasiane della capitalizzazione: una risposta', *Giornale degli Economisti*, March–April 1966; 3. 'Heterogeneous capital, the production function and the theory of distribution', *REStud*, 37(3), July 1970, repr. in *A Critique of Economic Theory*, eds. E. K. Hunt and J. C. Schwartz (Penguin, 1972); 4. 'On

a change in the notion of equilibrium in recent work on value: a comment on Samuelson', in *Essays in Modern Capital Theory*, eds. M. Brown, K. Sato and P. Zarembka (N-H, 1976); 5. 'Notes on consumption investment and effective demand', *Camb JE*, 2, Dec. 1978, March 1979, repr. in *Keynes's Economics and the Theory of Value and Distribution*, eds. J. Eatwell and M. Milgate (Duckworth, 1983); 6. 'Notes on consumption, investment and effective demand, a reply to Joan Robinson', *Camb JE*, 3, June 1979, repr. in *ibid.*; 7. 'On Hollander's interpretation of Ricardo's early theory of profits', *Camb JE*, 6, March 1982; 8. 'The classical theory of wages and the role of demand schedules in the determination of relative prices', *AER*, 73(2), May 1983; 9. 'Two routes to effective demand', in *Distribution, Effective Demand and International Economic Relations*', ed. J. A. Kregel (Macmillan, 1983); 10. 'Value and distribution in the classical economists and Marx', *OEP*, 35(2), June 1984.
Principal Contributions In the light of Sraffa's 'Introduction' to Ricardo's *Principles*, my early work was based on the distinction between the rediscovered 'classical' approach to distribution in Quesnay, Smith and Ricardo and later theory. This work was an attempt to trace in both approaches the same unsolved problem of 'measuring' capital independently of distribution. The problem emerged as solvable in the classical analysis, compatible with 'measurement' in terms of a set of magnitudes. However, later theory, examined in Walras's and Wicksell's versions, was found to depend on an unavailable 'measurement' of capital as a single magnitude. From this basis, later work proceeded along three lines. The first pursued the criticism of the conception of capital in modern explanation of distribution by the demand and supply of the factors of production in terms of their reciprocal 'substitutability'. This work dealt with the implications of the 'reswitching' of techniques and 'reverse capital deepening'. It then pointed to the attempts to avoid the difficulty by expressing capital endowment in terms of a set of magnitudes, with the abandonment of the notion of a long-period

general equilibrium characteristic of previous theory, and with a recognised loss of descriptive power of the theory. The second line consisted of a clarification of the alternative classical analysis. This brought into focus its characteristic separation between the determination of distribution and that of outputs. This separation contrasts sharply with modern simultaneous determination. The third line used results from the previous two in order to set Keynes's propositions on the determination of aggregate output on a more solid basis, thus allowing for their application to long-term policy; my interest has focussed of late on the way in which aggregate demand affects the evolution of output as productive capacity changes.

GARNIER, Germain*

Dates and Birthplace 1754–1821, Auxerre, France.

Post Held Prefect, Seine et Oise, France, 1799.

Offices and Honours Created Count, 1804; Pres., Napoleonic Senate, 1809–11; Member, Royal Council of State, 1814; created Marquis.

Publications *Books:* 1. *De la propriété dans ses rapports avec le droit politique* (1792); 2. *Abrégé élémentaire des principes de l'économie politique* (1976); 3. *Théorie des banques d'escompte* (1806); 4. *Appel à tous les propriétaires en Europe* (1818). 5. *Histoire de la monnaie*, 2 vols, (1819).

Career French translator of Smith's *Wealth of Nations*, who emphasised the elements in Smith sympathetic to physiocracy and played down Smith's views on industrialisation. This version of Smith was heartily rejected by Say and his followers, who can be seen as reacting against Garnier almost as much as in favour of Smith. His political career revealed considerable powers of adaptation to the dominant trend of the day.

Secondary Literature E. Teilhac, 'Garnier, Germain', *ESS*, 6.

GARNIER, Joseph Clement*

Dates and Birthplace 1813–81, Beuil, Alpes Maritimes, France.

Posts Held Prof., l'Ecole Supérieure de Commerce, Athenée l'Ecole Nat. des Ponts et Chaussées, Paris.

Offices Founder Soc. d'Econ. Polit., 1842; Ed., *J. des Economistes*, 1845–81; Member, Inst. de France, 1873.

Publications *Books:* 1. *Eléments de l'économie politique* (1845) 2. *Richard Cobden, les ligueurs et la ligue* (1846); 3. *Du principe de la population* (1857); 4. *Traité des finances* (1862).

Career Though not remarkable for any theoretical contribution, he achieved a position of considerable influence in the French economic community, chiefly through his editorship of the *Journal des économistes*. Rigidly orthodox in his *laissez faire* beliefs.

Secondary Literature E. Teilhac, 'Garnier, Joseph Clément', *ESS*, 6.

GASTWIRTH, Joseph Lewis

Born 1938, New York City, NY, USA.

Current Post Prof. Stat. Econ., George Washington Univ., Washington DC, USA, 1978–; Stat. Adviser, US Office Management and Budget, 1982–.

Past Posts Res. Assoc., Stanford Univ., 1963–4; Ass. Prof., Assoc. Prof., Johns Hopkins Univ., 1966–72; Vis. Assoc. Prof., Harvard Univ., 1970–1; vis. Faculty Adviser, Office of Stat. Pol., Exec. Office US President, 1971–2; Vis. Prof., MIT, 1979.

Degrees BS(Maths.) Yale Univ., 1958; PhD (Math. Stats.) Columbia Univ., 1963.

Offices and Honours Fellow, ASA, Inst. Math. Stat., Amer. Assoc. Advancement Science; Washington Stat. Soc. Prize Young Stats., 1969; Pres., Wash. Stat. Soc., 1982–3.

Editorial Duties Assoc. Ed., Book Rev. Ed., *JASA*, 1978–9, 1980–1.

Principal Fields of Interest 200 Quantitative Economic Methods and Data; 826 Labour Markets, and Demographic Characteristics.

Publications *Articles:* 1. 'On robust

procedures', *JASA*, 61, Oct. 1966; 2. 'The estimation of the Lorenz curve and Gini index', *REStat*, 54(3), Aug. 1972; 3. 'On the large sample theory of some measures of income inequality', *Em*, 42(1), Jan. 1974; 4. 'On probabilistic models of consumer search for information', *QJE*, 90(1), Feb. 1976; 5. 'Defining the labour market for equal employment standards' (with S. Haber), *MLR*, 99(3), March 1976, repr. in *Perspectives on Employee Staffing and Selection*, eds. J. Dreher and R. Sackett (Richard D. Irwin, 1983); 6. 'The robustness properties of two tests for serial correlation' (with M. R. Selwyn), *JASA*, 75, March 1980; 7. 'Estimating the demographic mix of the available labor force', *MLR*, 104(4), April 1981; 8. 'Statistical properties of a measure of tax assessment uniformity', *J. Stat. Info. and Planning*, 6, 1982; 9. 'Interpolation from grouped data for unimodal densities' (with A. Krieger), *Em*, 52(2), March 1984; 10. 'Two statistical methods for analyzing claims of employment discrimination', *ILRR*, 38(1), Oct., 1985.

Principal Contributions My major research interest has been the development of robust statistical methods which are useful in the analysis of data arising in economics and public policy. After conducting research in statistical theory and methods I applied these techniques to develop statistical methods for estimating measures of economic inequality. My year as a visiting faculty adviser to the Office of Statistical Policy kindled my interest in labour economics and problems arising in measuring possible discrimination in the labour market. Subsequently, I became involved as an expert witness in a variety of legal cases in the areas of discrimination and consumer protection and am now primarily concerned with the use of statistical and economic arguments in the legal and public-policy arenas. Because many policy decisions, e.g. tax policy and regulation, are often made on the basis of data collected for another purpose, non-parametric and robust statistical methods which are less sensitive to deviations from the assumptions which underlined their original derivation are especially useful.

GAYER, Arthur David*

Dates and Birthplace 1903–51, Poona, India.

Posts Held Lect., Ass. Prof. Econ., Columbia Univ., 1931–40; Assoc. Prof. Econ., Queen's Coll., New York City, 1940–51.

Degrees BA, MA, DPhil Univ. Oxford, 1923, 1924, 1927.

Offices Sr. Medley Res. Fellow Econ., Univ. Oxford, 1925–7; Adviser, US Govt. Comms., 1932–; Sr. Econ., Fed. Reserve Board, 1936.

Publications *Books:* 1. *Monetary Policy and Economic Stabilisation* (1935); 2. *Public Works in Prosperity and Depression* (1935); 3. *Public Works and Unemployment Relief in the United States* (1936); 4. *The Sugar Economy of Puerto Rico* (with P. T. Homan and E. K. James), (1938); 5. *The Growth and Fluctuation of the British Economy 1790–1850,* 2 vols (with W. W. Rostow and A. J. Schwartz), (1953).

Career His work for Roosevelt's Commission on Economic Reconstruction (1932–4) was the ideal complement to his academic study of economic fluctuations. This and the experience of other official work was crystallised in his *Monetary Policy*, his best-known book. He was quick to take up Keynes's message, having arrived at Keynesian policy views well before Keynes. The data and analysis in *Growth and Fluctuation* is also frequently cited by economic historians.

Secondary Literature (Obit.) 'Professor A. D. Gayer: problems of economic stability', *The Times*, 24 Nov. 1951.

GENOVESE, Eugene Dominick

Born 1930, New York City, NY, USA.

Current Post Prof. Hist., Univ. Rochester, Rochester, NY, USA, 1969–.

Past Posts Ass. Prof., Polytechnic Inst. Brooklyn, 1958–63; Ass. Prof., Assoc. Prof., Rutgers Univ., 1963–7; Prof., Sir George Williams Univ., Montreal, 1967–9; Vis. Prof., Columbia Univ, 1967, Yale Univ., 1968; Pitt

Prof. Amer. Civilization, Univ. Camb., 1974–5.

Degrees BA(Hist.) Brooklyn Coll., 1953; MA(Hist), PhD(Hist.) Columbia Univ., 1955, 1959.

Offices and Honours Fellow, AAAS, Center Study Behavioral Sciences, Stanford, CA, 1972–3, 1984–5; Annual Award, Amer. Academy and Inst. Arts, 1975; Bancroft Prize, 1975.

Editorial Duties Ed. Boards, *J. Social Hist., Dialectical Anthrop.*

Principal Fields of Interest 040 Economic History.

Publications *Books:* 1. *The Political Economy of Slavery* (Pantheon, 1965); 2. *Slavery in the New World*, co-ed. (with L. Fower), (Prentice-Hall, 1967); 3. *The Slave Economies*, ed. (Wiley, 1968); 4. *The World the Slaveholders Made* (Pantheon, 1969); 5. *In Red & Black* (Pantheon, 1971); 6. *Roll, Jordan, Roll* (Pantheon, 1974); 7. *From Rebellion to Revolution* (Louisiana State Univ. Press, 1979); 8. *Fruits of Merchant Capital* (with E. Fox-Genovese), (Pantheon, 1983).

Principal Contributions Since an undergraduate student at Brooklyn College, I have primarily been interested in the slave society of the Old South, and secondarily interested in other modern slave societies. More specifically, I have tried to reinterpret the history of the Old South from a Marxist point of view, albeit one not all Marxists accept, and have argued that its economic, political, social, intellectual and legal history must be studied as an integrated whole at the basis of which lay the master-slave relation.

The work in economic history began with *The Political Economy of Slavery*, in which I argued — too schematically, I fear — that the slave economy could not be understood in neoclassical or other discretely economic terms, but, rather, had to be studied in organic relation to a larger culture I described as 'prebourgeois' but might better have described simply as 'non-bourgeois.' Collaboration with Elizabeth Fox-Genovese since 1968 has led to considerable refinement of the basic thesis and to reformulation and even abandonment of some subsidiary theses. In particular, it has led to a much stronger

emphasis on the contradictory role of merchant capital in the development of modern slave societies (see especially our *Fruits of Merchant Capital*).

Simultaneously, together with Ms. Fox-Genovese, I have been attempting to contribute to a reformulation of the Marxist interpretation of history that rejects, on the one side, economic determinism and other forms of mechanical materialism, and, on the other side, the idealism of Marx's philosophy of humanity and its projection of a 'new' and 'liberated' man and woman.

GENOVESI, Antonio*

Dates and Birthplace 1712–69, Salerno, Italy.

Posts Held Teacher Metaphysics, Prof. Commerce, Univ. Naples, 1741–54, 1754–69.

Publications *Books:* 1. *Lezioni di Commercio Ossiadi Economia Civile* (1765).

Career A great teacher and founder of a distinct Neapolitan school. His published lectures have been criticised for lack of rigour and system; however, they cover the range of utilitarian ideas current at the time and present a balanced view of trade questions which gives credit to mercantilist ideas.

Secondary Literature A. Cutolo, *Antonio Genovesi* (1926).

GEORGE, Henry*

Dates and Birthplace 1839–97, Philadelphia, PA, USA.

Posts Held Journalist and political campaigner.

Publications *Books:* 1. *Our Land and Land Policy* (1871); 2. *Progress and Poverty* (1879, 1936, 1960); 3. *The Land Question* (1881); 4. *The Condition of Labor* (1891); 5. *The Science of Political Economy* (1897).

Career Developed the idea that ownership of land by a minority was the chief cause of poverty, and advocated taxation of the 'unearned increment' of rental values. He also favoured public ownership of railways and other monopolies such as telegraphs, but stopped well short of socialism. His arguments at first received some academic acceptance in Europe but later his enormously successful speaking tours in Britain caused Fawcett, Marshall and others forcibly to reject his ideas. In the 1880s he seized on the term 'single tax' as his main object and formed a major political movement in its favour. To this day he has disciples around the world, particularly in Australia and New Zealand, who generally favour 'site value taxation' of land as the kernel of Georgism.

Secondary Literature C. A. Barker, 'George, Henry', *IESS*, 6; *Critics of Henry George*, ed. R. V. Andelson (Farkleigh Dickinson Univ., 1979); C. Collier, 'Henry George's system of political economy', *HOPE*, 11(1), Spring 1979.

GEORGESCU-ROEGEN, Nicholas

Born 1906, Constanta, Romania.
Current Post Disting. Prof. Emeritus, Vanderbilt Univ., Nashville, TN, USA, 1976–.
Past Posts Prof., Univ. Bucharest, School Stats., 1932–46; Ass. Dir., Central Stat. Inst., Bucharest, 1932–8; Econ. Adviser, Romanian Treasury Dept., Bucharest, 1938–9; Delegate, Comm. on Peaceful Change, League of Nations, 1938; Dir., Romanian Board Trade, 1939–44; Secretary, General Romanian Armistice Comm., 1944–5; Lect., Res. Assoc., Harvard Univ., 1948–9; Prof., Vanderbilt Univ., 1949–76; Rockefeller Vis. Prof., Osaka Univ., Hitotsubashi Univ., Japan, 1962–3; Vis. Lect., Inst. Stats., India, 1963; Ford Vis. Lect., Cons., Brazil, 1964, 1966–7; Vis. Prof., US Agency Internat. Devlp., Brazil, 1971; Comm. Mineral Resources and Environment, NAS, 1973–5; Vis. Prof., Florence, Italy, 1974, Ottawa, 1975; Cons., Austrian Social Democratic Party, 1976; Vis. Claude Worthington Benedum Prof., W. Virginia Univ., 1976–8; Prof. Assoc., Univ. Louis Pasteur, Strasbourg, 1977–8; US Office of Technology Task Force, 1977–8; Vis. Prof., Technische Univ., Vienna, 1978, Univ. Texas, Austin, 1979, McGill Univ.,

1979, Inst. Advanced Stud., Vienna, 1982.
Degrees Licence (Math.) Univ. Bucharest, 1926; Dr Diploma (Stats.) Univ. Paris (Sorbonne), 1930; Hon. Dr Univ. Louis Pasteur, Strasbourg, 1976, Univ. Florence, Italy, 1980, Univ. of South, USA, 1983.
Offices and Honours Vis. Rockefeller Fellow, USA, 1934–6; Fellow, Em Soc, 1950; Guggenheim Foundation Fellow, 1958–9; Fellow, Internat. Inst. Sociology, 1960; Harvie Branscomb Award, 1967; Fellow, Internat. Inst. Stats., 1970; Res. Fellow, NSF, 1968–70; Disting. Fellow, AEA, 1971; Fellow, AAAS, 1973; Earl Sutherland Prize, 1976; Hon. Member, Assoc. Appl. Em., 1977; Fellow, Accad. Toscana di Scienzia e. Lett., 1977; Disting. Assoc., Atlantic Econ. Assoc., 1979.
Editorial Duties Assoc. Ed., *Em*, 1951–68; Advisory Board, *Fundamenta Scientiae*, 1976–; Ed. Board, *Metroeconomica*, 1982–.
Principal Fields of Interest 020 General Economic Theory; 213 Mathematical Methods and Models; 700 Agriculture and Natural Resources.
Publications *Books:* 1. *Activity Analysis of Production and Allocation* (with T. C. Koopmans, *et al.*), (Wiley, 1951); 2. *Analytical Economics: Issues and Problems* (Harvard Univ. Press, 1966; transls., French, Dunod, 1970, Italian, Sansoni, 1973); 3. *The Entropy Law and the Economic Process* (Harvard Univ. Press, 1971; transl., Romanian, Editura Politica, 1979); 4. *Energy and Economic Myths: Institutional and Analytical Economic Essays* (Pergamon Press, 1976; transl., Italian, *Energia e miti economici*, Editore Boringheri, 1982); 5. *Demain la decroissance* (Edns. Pierre-Marcel Favre, 1979); 6. *Entropy and Economic Myths* (Science Council Canada, 1980); 7. *Economics of Natural Resources: Myths and Facts* (Toyo Keizai, Tokyo, 1981).
Articles: 1. 'Utility', *IESS* (Macmillan, Free Press, 1968), 16; 2. 'The measure of information: a critique', *Proceedings of the Third International Congress of Cybernetics and Systems*, 3 (Springer Verlag, 1975); 3. 'The steady

state and ecological salvation: a thermodynamic analysis', *BioScience*, 17(4), April 1977; 4. 'Inequality, limits and growth from a bioeconomic viewpoint', *RSE*, 35(3), Dec. 1977; 5. 'Technology assessment: the case of direct use of solar energy', *Atlantic Econ. J.*, 6(4), Dec. 1978; 6. 'Methods in economic science', *JEI*, 13(2), June 1979; 7. 'Structure and involuntary unemployment' (with J–P. Fitoussi), in *Unemployment in Western Countries*, eds. E. Malinvaud and J–P. Fitoussi (Macmillan, 1980); 8. 'Energy, matter and economic valuation: where do we stand?', in *Energy, Economics, and the Environment*, eds. H. E. Daly and A. Umana (Westview Press, 1981); 9. 'The Promethean condition of viable technologies', *Materials and Soc.*, 7(3–4), 1983; 10. 'Herman Heinrich Gossen: his life and work in historical perspective', in *The Laws of Human Relations and the Rules of Human Actions Derived Therefrom*, by H. H. Gossen (MIT Press, 1983).

Principal Contributions At times, it may take a statistician to beget an economist, of some sort. Since in the 1920s business cycles constituted a major problem for economists, for my dissertation in statistics I chose to develop a method for decomposing a time series into *cyclical* components — a novel approach which filled the entire October 1930 issue of *Journal de la Societé de Statistique de Paris*. Believing that work on cycles as that of G. Warren and F. Pearson was still pursued at Harvard, I naturally wanted to spend my Rockefeller fellowhip there. To my great fortune, there was no such work when I arrived: seeking someone interested in cycle analysis, I came to meet professor J. A. Schumpeter (who, symptomatically, later used my method in his *Business Cycles*). His dedication to the young scholars around him guided my path into economics. I thus became a true Schumpeterian, envisioning economics as an evolutionary science. An old habit (some may say, fault) prompted me to probe the epistemological validity of every mathematical representation, a propensity characterising all my endeavours. Here only those contributions of which I am proud should be mentioned (there are plenty of which I am not). In consumer theory, I resolved the non-integrability paradox, following with analyses of stochastic choice, want hierarchy, uncertainty vs. risk, qualitative residual, all demonstrating the difficulty of measurement, even in production theory. Intrigued by the disregard of marginal pricing in Romania's economy, I offered an analytical justification of such economies, with the corollary that Walras's system, although with a solution on paper, cannot always work because of its stringent initial conditions. On this line, I showed that even accretive growth cannot be represented by dynamic systems. My flow-fund model, negating the traditional production function, led me further into environmental economics and, by a Schumpeterian inspiration, into bioeconomics. Dialectics rather than arithmomorphism is my creed.

Secondary Literature N. Wade, 'Nicholas Georgescu-Roegen: entropy the measure of economic man', *Science*, 31, Oct. 1975; S. Zamagni, *Georgescue-Roegen: I fondamenti della teoria del consumatore* (Etas Libri, 1979).

GERSCHENKRON, Alexander*

Dates and Birthplace 1904–78, Odessa, Russia.

Posts Held Assoc., Austrian Inst. Bus. Cycle Res., Vienna; Res. Ass., Lect. Econ., Univ. Cal. Berkeley, 1938–44; Res. Staff, Board Governors, Fed. Reserve System, 1944–8; Prof., Harvard Univ., 1948–74.

Degrees Dr Rer. Pol. Univ. Vienna, 1928.

Publications *Books:* 1. *Bread and Democracy in Germany* (1943); 2. *Economic Relations with the USSR* (1945); 3. *A Dollar Index of Soviet Machinery Output 1927–8 to 1937* (1951); 4. *Economic Backwardness in Historical Perspective* (1962); 5. *Continuity in History and Other Essays* (1968); 6. *Europe in the Russian Mirror* (1970); 7. *An Economic Spurt that Failed* (1977).

Career Originally concentrated on soviet economic history and economics.

Examining the swift movement of indices of industrial growth in Russia, he discovered the 'Gerschenkron effect', whereby the choice of a base year for such indices influences their subsequent progress. Among his many other breakthroughs was his account of how the more backward countries of nineteenth-century Europe were able to develop at much greater speed than the earlier industrial countries.

Secondary Literature A. Ehrlich, 'Gerschenkron, Alexander', *IESS*, 18.

GERVAISE, Isaac*

Dates and Birthplace 1700s, Paris, France.

Publications *Books:* 1. *The System or Theory of the Trade of the World* (1720, 1954).

Career Eighteenth-century Huguenot merchant in London known only for his *System*. This was a general equilibrium treatment of international trade containing an analysis of the various causes of disequilibrium. It is also unusual for its clear statement of the case for free trade at a time when such ideas were almost unheard of. The quality of Gervaise's argument and his intimate practical understanding of economic phenomena are both remarkable.

Secondary Literature J. M. Letiche, 'Gervaise, Isaac', *IESS*. 6.

GESELL, Silvio*

Dates and Birthplace 1862–1930, Belgium.

Posts Held Merchant, Buenos Aires, 1887–1914, Germany after 1914.

Publications *Books:* 1. *Die Verstaatlichung des Geldes* (1891).

Career Monetary writer, considered a crank until Keynes rehabilitated him and others of the 'brave army of heretics' in the *General Theory*. His plan for stamped money was designed to discourage hoarding by requiring that stamps be bought and fixed to money to preserve its value.

Secondary Literature L. Weden, 'Gesell, Silvio', in *Handwörterbuch der Sozialwissenschaften*, 3, eds. E. V. Beckerath, *et al.* (Gustav Fischer, 1959).

GIDE, Charles*

Dates and Birthplace 1847–1932, Uzès, France.

Posts Held Prof., Univs. Bordeaux, Montpellier, Paris.

Offices Founder, *REP*, 1887.

Publications *Books:* 1. *Principes d'économie politique* (1883); 2. *Economie sociale* (1905); 3. *Cours d'économie politique* (1909); 4. *A History of Economic Doctrines* (with C. Rist), (1909, 1948); 5. *Les colonies communistes et co-operatives* (1930).

Career He was one of the professors of economics appointed to the Faculties of Law in French universities in 1876. These appointments broke the hold of the *laissez faire* liberal school in French economics and Gide's 1883 *Principes* ... was a means of spreading a more open-minded attitude towards historical and other approaches. Economics was only part of his general interest in social philosophy and he was an enthusiastic and successful advocate of the co-operative movement.

Secondary Literature C. Rist, 'Charles Gide' (obit.), *EJ*, 42, June 1932; C. Rist, *Charles Gide, sa vie et son oeuvre* (1933).

GIERSCH, Herbert Hermann

Born 1921, Reichenbach, Germany.

Current Post Pres., Inst. World Econ., Kiel, Prof. Econ., Kiel Univ., W. Germany, 1969–.

Past Posts Ass. Lect., Univ. Munster, 1947–8, 1951–5; British Council Fellow, LSE, 1948–9; Administrator, Counsellor, OEEC Secretariat, Paris, 1950–1, 1953–4; Prof. Econ., Univ. the Saar, 1955–69; Vis. Prof., Yale Univ., 1962–3, 1977–8.

Degrees Diplom-Volkswirt, 1942; PhD, Privatdozent Univ. Munster, 1948, 1950; Hon. Dr, Univ. Erlangen, 1977.

Offices and Honours Hon. Fellow, LSE, 1971; Hon. Member, AEA, 1976; Corresp. Fellow, BA, 1983;

Exec. Comm., Treasurer, Pres., IEA, 1971–83, 1974–83, 1983; German Council of Econ. Advisers (Sachverständigenrat), 1964–70; Pres., Assoc. Europ. Business Cycle Res. Inst., 1974–8.

Editorial Duties Ed. Boards, *Kieler Studien, World Economy, Econ. Devlp.*

Principal Fields of Interest 110 Economic Growth; Development; and Planning Theory and Policy; 130 Economic Fluctuations; Forecasting; Stabilisation and Inflation; 400 International Economics.

Publications *Books:* 1. *Der Ausgleich der Kriegslasten vom Standpunkt sozialer Gerechtigkeit* (Bitter, 1948); 2. *Beitrage zur Multiplikatortheorie* (with R. Richter), (Duncker & Humblot, 1954); 3. *Allgemeine Wirtschaftspolitik, 1: Grundlagen* (Gabler, 1960); 4. *Six Annual Reports of the German Council of Economic Advisers 1964–70* (with various co-authors), (Verlag W. Kohlhammer, 1964–70); 5. *Growth, Cycles and Exchange Rates. The Experience of West Germany* (Almqvist & Wiksel, 1970); 6. *Kontroverse Fragen der Wirtschaftspolitik* (Piper, 1971); 7. *Indexklauseln und Inflationsbekampfung* (Inst. fur Weltwirtschaft, 1973; transl., English, AEI, 1974); 8. *Economic Policy for the European Community* (with A. Cairncross, A. Lamfalussy, G. Petrilli and P. Uri), (Holmes & Meier, 1974; transls., German, Piper, 1974, Italian, Rizzoli, 1975, French, Presses Univ. de France, 1976); 9. *Allgemeine Wirtschaftspolitik 2: Konjunktur- und Wachstumspolitik* (Gabler, 1977); 10. *Im Brennpunkt: Wirtschaftspolitik. Kritische Beitrage von 1967 bis 1977*, ed. (Deutsche Verlagsanstalt, 1978).

Articles: 1. 'Economic union betwen nations and the location of industries', *REStud*, 17(2), 1950; 2. 'Akzelerationsprinzip und Importneigung', *WA*, 70(2), 1953; 3. 'Strategien der Wachstumspolitik', *ZGS*, 119(2), 1963; 4. 'Das ökonomische grundproblem der regionalpolitik', *Jahrbuch für Sozialwissenschaft*, 14(3), 1963; 5. 'Episoden und lehren der globalsteurerung', in *Wirtschaftspolitik, Wissenschaft und politische Aufgabe. Festschrift zum 65. Geburtstag von Karl Schiller* (J. B. C.

Mohr, 1976); 6. 'IMF surveillance over exchange rates', in *The New International Monetary System* (IMF, 1977); 7. 'Aspects of growth, structural change and employment. A Schumpeterian perspective', *WA*, 115(4), 1979; 8. 'Towards an explanation of the recent productivity slowdown: an acceleration–deceleration hypothesis', (with F. Wolter), *EJ*, 93, March 1983; 9. 'Arbeit, lohn und produktivität', *WA*, 119(1), 1983; 10. 'The age of Schumpeter', *AER*, 74(2), May 1984.

Principal Contributions My research efforts have been directed at improving economic policies. A straightforward proposal to complement the West German currency reform by a scheme of compensating for war damages (1948) was implicitly based on the principle 'redistribute now, grow later'. In search of more roundabout and hence more effective ways of approaching policy problems, I chose to look at growth in open economies from the angle of location theory and applied the latter to identify some effects of European economic integration (1949) and to understand what transportation costs meant for trade and welfare (1956) and for the regional distribution of incomes (1958). The notion of a region's development potential was introduced as a criterion for evaluating regional policy in a growth context (1963). Concern about demand management in an open economy arose from OEEC experience during the 1950 German balance of payments crisis, which induced me to apply the acceleration principle to evaluate the demand for imports (1953). Work on a textbook (1961) which led me into the methodology of policy advice was perhaps instrumental to becoming a foundling member of the German Council of Economic Advisers, where I was stimulated to develop the concepts of stabilisation without stagnation, cost-neutral wage policy, and demand-neutral exchange rate revaluation. The anticipated breakdown of Bretton Woods made me think about entrepreneurial risk under flexible exchange rates, the event itself about IMF surveillance.

Issues of supply and structural change, summarily dealt with in 1963, were given weight in the Kiel Institute's research programme after 1970 and in later publications. The slowdown of economic growth induced me to adopt a Schumpeterian perspective which appears to me more appropriate for identifying and tackling emerging policy problems. Together with Schumpeter, Thünen helped me in forming a centre-periphery view of the world economy, encompassing growth, resource transfer and trade.

GIFFEN, Robert*

Dates and Birthplace 1837–1910, Strathaven, Scotland.
Posts Held Journalist, 1860–71; Official, Stat. Section, UK Board Trade, 1871–97.
Offices and Honours Founder, RES; Pres., RSS, 1882–4.
Publications *Books:* 1. *Essays in Finance* (1886, 1890); 2. *Economic Inquiries and Studies*, 2 vols (1869–1902); 3. *Stock Exchange Securities* (1877); 4. *The Growth of Capital* (1889).
Career Through his frequent contributions to the press and learned journals he was able to disseminate knowledge of the use of official statistics. He was not a theoretical statistician but nevertheless achieved important progress in difficult fields, such as the measurement of national income. The so-called 'Giffen Paradox' was an exception to the general law of demand for which Marshall gave him credit, apparently without warrant. Giffen also wrote on the quantity theory of money. Despite his official post he was an enthusiastic public campaigner for free trade and against bimetallism.
Secondary Literature G. J. Stigler, 'Notes on the history of the Giffen Paradox', *Essays in the History of Economics* (Univ. Chicago Press, 1965); K. J. Penney, 'Giffen, Robert', *IESS*, 6; W. P. Gramm, 'Giffen's paradox and the Marshallian demand curve', *MS*, 38, March 1970.

GILBERT, Milton*

Dates and Birthplace 1909–79, USA.
Posts Held Ed., *Survey Current Bus.*, 1938–41; Chief, Nat. Income Div., US Dept. Commerce, 1941–51; Dir., Stats. and Nat. Accounts, OEEC, 1951–5; Dir., Econ. and Stats., OEEC, 1955–60; Adviser, Head, Monetary and Econ. Dept., Bank Internat. Settlements, Switzerland, 1960–75, 1975–9.
Degrees MA Temple Univ., 1933; PhD Univ. Penn., 1937.
Offices and Honours Fellow, ASA.
Publications *Books:* 1. *US National Income Supplements* (with others), (US Govt. Printing Office, 1947); 2. *An International Comparison of National Products and the Purchasing Power of Currencies* (with I. B. Kravis), (OECD, 1954); 3. *The Gold Dollar System: Conditions of Equilibrium and the Price of Gold* (Princeton Univ. Press, 1968); 4. *The Discipline of the Balance of Payments and the Design of the International Monetary System* (OECD, 1970); 5. *Quest for World Monetary Order*, eds. P. Oppenheimer and M. G. Dealtry (Wiley, 1980).

GILROY, Curtis Lloyd

Born 1942, Boston, MA, USA.
Current Post US Army Res. Inst., Washington, DC, 1982–4.
Past Posts Instr., Ass. Prof., Wells Coll., Aurora, NY, 1967–9, 1970–2; Econ., US Bureau Labor Stat., Washington, DC, 1972–4; Sr. Econ., US Dept. Labor, Washington, DC, 1975–6; Staff Econ., Nat. Commission Employment and Unemployment Stats., 1977–9; Sr. Econ., Minimum Wage Study Commission, Washington, DC, 1980–2.
Degrees BA Acadia Univ., Nova Scotia, Canada, 1964; MA Univ. Toronto, Ont., Canada, 1966; MBA McMaster Univ., Ont. 1967; PhD State Univ. NY 1973.
Offices and Honours E. M. Saunders Scholar Arts, 1963–4; Province Ont. Fellow, 1965–6; Samuel Bronfman Foundation Scholar, 1966–7; US Bureau Labor Stats., Laurence Klein Award, 1973, 1974.

Principal Fields of Interest 813 Labour Force; 824 Labour Market Studies; 826 Labour Markets.

Publications *Books:* 1. *Women in the Labor Market* (with C. Lloyd and E. Andrews), (Columbia Univ. Press, 1979).

Articles: 1. 'Job losers, leavers and entrants: a cyclical analysis' (with R. J. McIntire), *MLR*, 97(11), Nov. 1974; 2. 'Supplemental measures of labor force underutilization', *MLR*, 98(5), May 1975; 3. 'Investment in human capital and black-white unemployment differences: 1960 and 1970', *MLR*, 98(7), July 1975; 4. 'The relationship between labor force participation and service sector employment: a reformulation' (with R. S. Warren), *J Reg S*, 16(3), Dec. 1976; 5. 'Counting the labor force with the *Current Population Survey*', *AER*, 69(2), May 1979; 6. 'Minimum wages and agricultural employment: a review of the evidence', *Proceedings IRRA*, Dec. 1981; 7. 'The effect of the minimum wage on employment and unemployment' (with C. Brown and A. Kohen), *JEL*, 20(2), June 1982; 8. 'Time-series evidence of the effect of the minimum wage on youth employment and unemployment' (with C. Brown and A. Kohen), *JHR*, 18(1), Winter 1983; 9. 'The effects of the business cycle on the size and composition of the U.S. Army' (with C. Dale), *Atlantic Econ., J.*, 11(1), 1983; 10. 'Determinants of military enlistments: a macroeconomic time-series view' (with C. Dale), *Armed Forces and Soc.*, 10(2), Winter 1984.

Principal Contributions Although my research has focussed on the theory and operation of labour markets, its early emphasis was on the economics of discrimination. Special attention was paid to the labour force status of minorities and women. I was not so much interested in employment and training policy as in empirical investigation and data development. This latter interest led to a real concern with such issues as data accuracy and conceptual measurement. How successful are the labour market surveys in measuring what they purport to measure? I was fortunate to join the research staff of a Presidential Commission mandated to appraise the

nation's labour force statistics — how the government measures employment, unemployment, 'discouraged workers', earnings, etc. This experience and my familiarity with the many government and government-sponsored labour market related surveys provided a background for subsequent empirical research on the economic effects of minimum wage legislation. I joined the research staff of a Congressional Commission on minimum wages and focussed on the employment and unemployment effects of minimum wage legislation under the Fair Labor Standards Act. I have continued to study the operation of labour markets, most recently for the US Army. The inception of the All-Volunteer Force has opened up a new arena for the application of theoretical and empirical labour market models.

GINTIS, Herbert Malena

Born 1940, Philadelphia, PA, USA.
Current Post Prof. Econ., Univ. Massachusetts, Amherst, MA, USA, 1977–.
Past Posts Lect. Econ., Res. Assoc. Educ., Harvard Grad. School Educ., Ass. Prof. Econ., Harvard Univ., 1969–71, 1969–74, 1973–4; Assoc. Prof. Econ., Univ. Mass., 1974–7; Fellow, Inst. Advanced Study, Princeton, 1977–8; Vis. Prof. Econ. and Sociology, Vis. Prof. Econ., Harvard Univ., 1982, 1982–3.
Degrees BA (Maths.) Univ. Penn., 1963; MA(Maths.), PhD Harvard Univ., 1965, 1969.
Editorial Duties Ed. Board, Book Rev. Ed., *Rev. Radical Polit. Econ.* 1969–76, 1980–4; Ed., *Socialist Rev.*, 1979–81.
Principal Fields of Interest 020 General Economic Theory; 220 Economic and Social Statistical Data and Analysis; 820 Labour Markets; Public Policy.
Publications *Books:* 1. *Inequality: A Reassessment of the Effect of Family and Schooling in America* (with C. Jencks, *et al.*), (Basic Books, 1972); 2. *Schooling in Capitalist America* (with S. Bowles), (Basic Books, 1976).

Articles: 1. 'Education, technology and the characteristics of worker productivity', *AER*, 61(2), May 1971; 2. 'A radical analysis of welfare economics and individual development', *QJE*, 86(4), Nov. 1972; 3. 'Welfare criteria with endogenous preferences', *Int ER*, 15(2), June 1974; 4. 'The problem with human capital theory' (with S. Bowles), *AER*, 65(2), May 1975; 5. 'The nature of the labor exchange', *Rev. Radical Polit. Econ.* 8(2), 1976; 6. 'The Marxian theory of value and heterogeneous labour' (with S. Bowles), *Camb JE*, 1(2), 1977; 7. 'Rawlsian justice and economic systems' (with B. Clark), *Philo. & Public Affairs*, Summer 1978; 8. 'The crisis of liberal democratic capitalism' (with S. Bowles), *Politics and Society*, 11(1), 1982; 9. 'The welfare state and long-term economic growth' (with S. Bowles), *AER*, 72(2), May 1982.

Principal Contributions My work has dealt with two major themes. First, that economic behaviour can only be understood by taking preferences as the product as much as the source of economic activity. And second, that labour can be treated properly in economic models only if the incompleteness of the labour contract, and the abiding conflict between employer and employee, are carefully understood and properly modelled. My early efforts in this direction consisted of the critique of neoclassical welfare economics on the grounds that it considered preference satisfaction at the expense of ignoring preference development. At the same time, I argued through the use of quantitative evidence that the returns to education, traditionally considered as human capital of the skill-oriented variety, were in fact largely returns to forms of preference development, broadly conceived. I moved on to reassess the nature of the labour exchange, in an attempt to apply organisational theory, Marxian analysis, and the mocroeconomics of incomplete contracts (then a quite novel field) towards supporting the Marxian labour/labour-power distinction as the basis for an improved theory of the firm. The theory of the firm and the theory of education/economy interaction deriv-

ing from these investigations were then applied in an extended analysis of education, growth, and economic inequality by myself and Samuel Bowles.

My work has since turned to the application of these principles to the area of macroeconomic performance — investment, profit and productivity, in particular. First, the incompleteness of the labour contract implies that the conceptual split between economics as allocation and distribution and the State as politics and power must be abandoned. Thus, I and my colleagues have argued for macro models in which the State/economy interface is explicitly modelled. Second, I have moved towards developing macro models of labour market behaviour which take involuntary unemployment as the cost of labour discipline, and which are capable of explicitly modelling labour productivity changes in response to alterations in unemployment rates and the level of social services. This endeavour is conceived as an alternative to Keynesian treatments of labour market behaviour.

GIRTON, Lance

Born 1942, Brazil, ID, USA.
Current Post Prof. Econ., Univ. Utah, Salt Lake City, USA, 1978–.
Past Posts Instr. Econ., Elmhurst Coll., Elmhurst, IL, 1968–9; Ass. Prof. Econ., Michigan Tech. Univ., Houghton, 1969–71; Econ., Board of Governors, Fed. Reserve System, 1971–8; Assoc. Prof., George Washington Univ., Washington, DC, 1975–6; Vis. Prof. Econ., Penn. State Univ., 1983–4.
Degrees BA Southern Illinois Univ., Carbondale, 1964; MA, PhD Univ. Chicago, 1967, 1976.
Offices and Honours Nat. Inst. Health Fellow, 1966–8.
Principal Fields of Interest 432 International Monetary Arrangement; 311 Domestic Monetary and Financial Theory and Policy; 023 Macroeconomic Theory.
Publications *Articles:* 1. 'SDR creation and the real bills doctrine', *SEJ*, 41, July 1974; 2. 'Central bank opera-

tions in foreign and domestic assets under fixed and flexible exchange rates' (with D. Henderson), in *The Effects of Exchange Rate Adjustments*, eds. P. Clark, *et al.* (US Govt. Printing Office, 1974); 3. 'Financial capital movements and central bank behavior in a two country short-run portfolio balance model' (with D. Henderson), *J Mon E*, 3, Jan. 1976; 4. 'Critical determinants of the effectiveness of monetary policy in the open economy' (with D. Henderson), *Kredit und Kapital*, 3, Dec. 1976; 5. 'A monetary model of exchange market pressure applied to the postwar Canadian experience' (with D. Roper), *AER*, 67(4), Sept. 1977; 6. 'J. Laurence Laughlin and the quantity theory of money' (with D. Roper), *JPE*, 86, Aug. 1978; 7. 'Competitive monies and the monetary standard' (with D. Roper), in *Political Economy of Monetary Policy*, ed. M. Dooley, *et al.* (Sage, 1978); 8. 'Monetary integration in the presence of currency substitution' (with D. Roper), *Econ App*, 33(1), 1980; 9. 'Theory and implications of currency substitution' (with D. Roper), *JMCB*, 13, Feb. 1981; 10. 'Institutional investors and concentration of financial power: Berle and Means revisited' (with D. Farrar), *J Fin*, 36, May 1981.

Principal Contributions My work has been on monetary theory and policy. I have concentrated on the interrelationships between international and domestic monetary policy. My work has been influenced by a belief that institutions are important. Since institutions can change rapidly in response to events, institutional assumptions underlying theory and policy analysis should be carefully identified. My early work with Dale Henderson used portfolio theory to examine the relationships between exchange market policy and domestic monetary policies under international monetary institutions prevailing in the 1970s. Work with Don Roper focussed on international and domestic monetary policy under floating exchange rates and developed the theory of exchange market pressure. In related work, we examined the relationships between the quantity theory of money for a closed economy and the theory of the effect of money on the

balance of payments and exchange rates. In subsequent work with Roper, I developed the theory and implications of having substitutable monies available to money holders. We examined the implications of multiple monies for monetary policy and the stability and determinancy of exchange rates between monies. In recent work, we argue that international monetary factors, in particular the undervaluation of gold in the 1920s, was an important cause of the international and domestic monetary collapse in the 1930s.

GIRVAN, Norman Paul

Born 1941, St Andrew, Jamaica, West Indies.

Current Post Sr. Cons., UN Centre Transnat. Corps., UN, New York City, NY, USA, 1983–.

Past Posts Temp. Lect., Univ. W. Indies, Trinidad, 1966; Secretary, Sr. Lect., Univ. W. Indies, Jamaica, 1966–72, 1972–73; Vis. Fellow, Inst. Internat. Stud., Univ. Chile, 1969, Yale Univ., 1970; Sr. Res. Fellow, UN African Inst. Devlp. and Planning, 1973–5; Co-ord., Caribbean Technical Project, Univ. W. Indies, Univ. Guyana, 1975–7; Chief Technical Dir., Material Planning Agency, Govt. Jamaica, 1977–80; Sr. Officer, UN Centre Transnat. Corps., 1981, 1983; Sr. Cons., Internat. Devlp. Res. Corp., Canada, 1982.

Degrees BSc London Univ., Coll. W. Indies, 1962; PhD LSE, 1966.

Offices and Honours Student of Year, Univ. Coll. W. Indies, 1961; Ford Foundation Fellow, 1969–70; US SSRC Res. Fellow, 1976; Internat. Pres., Caribbean Assoc. Polit. Econ., 1981.

Editorial Duties Ed. Board, *New World Q.*, 1967–71.

Principal Fields of Interest 441 International Investment and Capital Markets; 621 Technological Change: Innovation, Research and Development; 632 Industry Studies: Extractive Industries.

Publications *Books:* 1. *The Caribbean Bauxite Industry* (Univ. W. Indies,

1967); 2. *Foreign Capital and Economic Underdevelopment in Jamaica* (Univ. W. Indies, 1971); 3. *Copper in Chile: A Study in Conflict between Corporate and National Economy* (Univ. W. Indies, 1972); 4. *Corporate Imperialism: Conflict and Expropriation* (M. E. Sharpe, 1976, Monthly Rev., 1978); 5. *The IMF and the Third World: A Case Study of Jamaica* (with R. Bernal and W. Hughes), (Dag Hammarksjold Foundation, 1980); 6. *Technology Policies for Small Developing Economies: A Study of the Caribbean* (Univ. W. Indies, 1983); 7. *Readings in the Political Economy of the Caribbean*, co-ed. (with O. C. Jefferson), (New World Group, 1971): 8. *Dependence and Underdevelopment in the New World and the Old*, ed., (Univ. W. Indies, 1973); 9. *Essays in Science and Technology Policy in the Caribbean*, ed. (Univ. W. Indies, 1979); 10. *Aspects of the Political Economy of Race in the Caribbean and the Americas: A Preliminary Interpretation* (Inst. Black World, 1975, repr. Univ. W. Indies, 1976).

Articles: 1. 'Regional integration vs. company integration in the utilization of Caribbean bauxite', in *Caribbean Integration: Proceedings of the Third Caribbean Scholars Conference*, eds. S. Lewis and T. Mathews (Univ. Puerto Rico, 1968); 2. 'Corporate vs. Caribbean integration' (with O. C. Jefferson), *New World Q.*, 4(2), 1968, repr. in *Readings in the Political Economy of the Caribbean, op. cit.*, and *Desarrolo Economico*, Oct.–Dec. 1967; 3. 'Multinational corporations and dependent underdevelopment in mineral-export economies', *Social and Econ. Stud*, 19(4), Dec. 1970; 4. 'Bauxite: why we need to nationalize, and how to do it' (New World Group, 1971), repr. in *Rev. Black Polit. Econ.*, Fall 1971, and *Readings in the Political Economy of the Caribbean, op. cit.*; 5. 'Making the rules of the game: company-country agreements in the bauxite industry', *Social and Econ. Stud.*, 20(4), Dec. 1971; 6. 'Dependency economics in Latin America and the Caribbean: review and comparison', *Social and Econ. Stud*, 22(1), March 1973; 7. 'Expropriation and compensation from a third world perspective', in *Valuation III*, ed. R. Lillich (Univ. Virginia, 1975); 8. 'Economic nationalism', *Daedalus*, Fall 1975; 9. 'The approach to technology policy studies', *Social and Econ. Stud*, 28(1), March 1979; 10. 'Swallowing IMF medicine in the seventies', *Devlp. Dialogue*, 2, 1980.

Principal Contributions An examination of the impact of foreign capital on the Jamaican economy led to the conclusion that developing countries like Jamaica could not hope to experience sustained development through large-scale foreign investment inflows; and also that a proper analysis of the foreign investment process required an understanding of the behaviour of multinational corporations (MNC). Early post-doctoral work focussed on the effects of vertically integrated, oligopolistic MNCs on distorting the pattern of resource allocation in mineral exporting economies, for example by inhibiting integrated resource development within and between these economies, and more broadly in generating a process of dependent underdevelopment. I have always been as interested in policy as in theory, and one branch of my subsequent work was the study of the nationalisation of MNCs in developing countries as one instrument for promoting a more autonomous, integrated, development pattern. Another branch was the study of transfer of technology, leading to a comprehensive examination of technology policies for small developing economies. My work as Director of Planning in Jamaica led logically to a concern with the theory and practice of the IMF in developing countries, and with the possibility of devising alternative development strategies. A case study of IMF programmes in Jamaica added to the rapidly growing literature critical of stabilisation measures and their theoretical underpinnings. My more recent work has seen a return to the study of the behaviour of MNCs and their effects on developing economies, focussing on transfer of technology relations, and the strategies which developing countries may utilise to facilitate effective transfer and promote their own technological development.

GLAHE, Fred Rufus

Born 1934, Chicago, IL, USA.
Current Post Prof. Econ., Univ. Colorado, Boulder, CO, USA, 1973–.
Past Posts Aeronautical Engineer, Allison Div., General Motors Corp., Indianapolis, 1957–61; Instr., Purdue Univ., W. Lafayette, ID, 1962–4; Vis. Prof., Ohio State Univ., Columbus, 1964–5; Sr. Res. Econ., Battelle Memorial Inst., Columbus, OH, 1964–5; Ass. Prof., Assoc. Prof. Econ., Univ. Colorado, 1965–8, 1968–73.
Degrees BS (Aeronautical Eng.) Purdue Univ., 1957; MA, PhD Purdue Univ., 1962, 1964.
Offices and Honours Ford Foundation Fellow, 1961–2; Board Dirs., Internat. Res. Center Energy and Econ. Devlp., 1973–84; Pres., Econ. Inst. Res. and Educ., 1976–84; Disting Service Award, Omicron Delta Elpsilon, 1981; H. B. Earhart Foundation Res. Fellow, 1982–3.
Editorial Duties Board Advisers, *Austrian Econ.*
Principal Fields of Interest 031 History of Economic Thought; 036 Economic Methodology; 311 Domestic Monetary and Financial Theory and Policy.
Publications *Books:* 1. *Systems Analysis of the Mobil Medium Range Ballistic Missile* (General Motors Co., 1961); 2. *An Empirical Study of the Foreign Exchange Market: Test of a Theory* (Princeton Univ. Press, 1967); 3. *Readings in Econometric Theory*, co-ed. (with J. Malcolm Dowling), (Colorado Assoc. Univ. Press, 1970); 4. *The Collected Papers of Kenneth E. Boulding*, 2 vols, ed. (Colorado Assoc. Univ. Press, 1971, 1972); 5. *Guide to Graduate Study in Economics and Agricultural Economics in the U.S. and Canada*, co-ed. (with W. Owen), (AEA, 1975); 6. *Macroeconomics: Theory and Policy*, (Harcourt, Brace Jovanovich, 1973, 1984; transl., Japanese, Charles E. Tuttle, 1977); 7. *Implications of Regional Development in the Middle East for U.S. Trade, Capital Flows, and Balance of Payments* (with R. El Mallakh, C. McGuire and B. Poulson), (Internat. Res. Center Energy and Econ. Devlp., 1977); 8.

Adam Smith and the Wealth of Nations: Bicentennial Essays 1776–1976, ed. (Colorado Assoc. Univ. Press, 1978); 9. *Microeconomics: Theory and Applications* (with D. Lee), (Harcourt, Brace Jovanovich, 1981); 10. *The American Family and the State*, co-ed. (with J. Peden), (Ballinger, 1984).
Articles: 1. 'Professional and non-professional speculation, profitability and stability', *SEJ*, 33(1), July 1966; 2. 'The small sample properties of simultaneous equation least absolute estimators' (with J. G. Hunt), *Ec*, N.S. 38(5), Sept. 1970; 3. 'Pricing in the American automobile industry and the Galbraith hypothesis' (with P. Burgess), *RISE*, 17(12), Dec. 1970; 4. 'The real-balance effect: a note concerning the confusion surrounding its definition', *RISE*, 19(5), May 1972; 5. 'A permanent restatement of the IS–LM model', *Amer. Econ.*, 17(1), Spring 1973; 6. 'L_1 estimation in small samples with LaPlace error distributions' (with M. Dowling and J. Hunt), *Decision Sciences*, 15(1), Jan. 1974; 7. 'Behavior of professional risk-bearers: a better test of a theory', *JMCB*, 7(4), Nov. 1975; 8. 'Exchange rate policies and financial capital flows' (with F. A. Alburo), *Philippine Econ. J.*, 15(3), 1976; 9. 'Prospects and requirements for world society', in *International Society in Transition. Proceedings 26th Conference on National Affairs* (Texas A&M Univ., 1981).
Principal Contributions Early work was in the survivability of mobile ballistic missile systems. In the 1960s my research centred on the foreign exchange market with special reference to the stability of market equilibrium in flexible exchange rate systems. This work led to a monograph. I next became interested in the bias introduced into least squares estimators when small sample sizes are employed or when the error term is not normally distributed and this led to my papers dealing with the robustness of least absolute estimators.
The monetarist counter-revolution of the 1960s and 70s led to my critical examination of the foundations of the theoretical works of Keynes, Tobin and Friedman. This work has been

synthesised in my advanced text, *Macro-economics: Theory and Policy*, which is currently being prepared for its third edition. Recently I have become interested in the revival of the Austrian school of economics and the philosophy of science. The former results from a growing dissatisfaction with the neoclassical paradigm and the latter is the outgrowth of a general interest in the theory of knowledge and its metaphysical implications.

GLOBERMAN, Steven

Born 1946, New York City, NY, USA.

Current Post Prof. Bus. Admin., Simon Fraser Univ., Burnaby, British Columbia, Canada, 1981–.

Past Posts Ass. Prof., York Univ., Toronto, 1971–7; Sr. Econ. Imperial Oil Ltd., 1975–7; Assoc. Prof., York Univ., 1977–80; Vis. Assoc. Prof., Univ. Cal. Irvine, 1977–8; Univ. British Columbia, 1980–1.

Degrees BA Brooklyn Coll, 1966; MA UCLA, 1967; PhD NYU, 1971.

Offices and Honours Founders Day Award Excellence Grad. Stud., 1971; Res. Staff, Canadian Royal Commission Corp. Concentration, 1976–7; Adviser, Econ. Council Canada Res. Program Technological Change, 1981, Consumer and Corp. Affairs, Canada, Canada's Intellectual Property Legislation, 1981–.

Editorial Duties Ed. Board, *J Cultural Econ.*, 1978–81.

Principal Fields of Interest 442 International Business; 610 Industrial Organisation and Public Policy; 620 Economics of Technological Change.

Publications *Books:* 1. *Tariffs and Science Policies: Applications of a Model of Nationalism* (with D. J. Daly), (Univ. Toronto Press, 1976); 2. *U.S. Ownership of Firms in Canada* (C. D. Howe Res. Inst., 1979); 3. *Cultural Regulation in Canada* (Inst. Res. Public Pol., 1983); 4. *Fundamentals of International Business* (Prentice-Hall, 1985).

Articles: 'The empirical relationship between R & D and industrial growth in Canada', *Appl. Econ.*, 4(3), Sept. 1972; 2. 'Technological diffusion in the Canadian tool and die industry', *REStat*, 57(4), Nov. 1975; 3. 'Formulating cost and output policies for the performing arts,' *Canadian Public Pol.*, 2(1), Winter, 1976; 4. 'The Canadian petroleum industry and delivered pricing revisited', *Antitrust Bull.*, 22(2), Summer 1977; 5. 'Foreign direct investment and spillover efficiency benefits in Canadian manufacturing', *CJE*, 12(1), Feb. 1979; 6. 'The adoption of computer technology in hospitals', *J. Behavioral Econ.*, 11(2), Winter, 1982.

Principal Contributions My early work concentrated on the relationship between market structure and technological change, following work on that topic as a graduate student. A consulting assignment for the Ontario Arts Council in the early 1970s led me to pursue research into the economics of cultural industries. This interest has continued to the present.

In the mid-1970s, I undertook a fairly major study of technological diffusion in Canada. The results suggested that although the sample innovations were well known to Canadian managers, the latter were generally slower than their American and US counterparts to adopt these innovations. Over the latter half of the 1970s, I examined reasons for the slower rate of technological diffusion in Canada and expanded my examination to consider the adoption performances of Canadian service industries. Much of this work was summarised recently in the Economic Council of Canada's 1983 Annual Report, in which the council recommended that more attention be paid to technological diffusion and less to the performance of research and development. More recently, I have concentrated on problems of managing international businesses. This represents an extension of prior research on direct investment policy issues but with a more 'practical' managerial focus.

GODWIN, William*

Dates and Birthplace 1756–1836, Wisbech, Cambridgeshire, England.

Posts Held Nonconformist clergyman, 1777–82; Professional writer and publisher.

Publications *Books:* 1. *Enquiry Concerning Political Justice* (1793, 1946, 1976); 2. *Of Population* (1820); 3. *Godwin Criticism*, ed. B. R. Pollin (OUP, 1969).

Career His *Enquiry* ... was a great success, with its emphasis on the perfectability of man. His vision of a prosperous society in which equality reigned provoked Malthus into raising the difficulty caused by increasing population. Godwin's role in stimulating Malthus' *Essay* is better remembered than his positive contribution. His belated attempt to refute Malthus in *Of Population* was a pathetic failure, despite the good arguments available to him.

Secondary Literature *A Fantasy of Reason: The Life and Thought of William Godwin*, ed. D. Locke (Routledge & Kegan Paul, 1980).

GOLDBERGER, Arthur Stanley

Born 1930, New York City, NY, USA.

Current Post Vilas Res. Prof. Econ., Univ. Wisconsin-Madison, 1979–.

Past Posts Acting Ass. Prof., Stanford Univ., 1956–9; Assoc. Prof., Prof., Groves Prof., Res. Assoc., Inst. Res. Poverty, Univ. Wisconsin, 1960–3. 1963–70, 1970–9, 1972–.

Degrees BS New York Univ., 1951; MA, PhD Univ. Michigan, 1952, 1958.

Offices and Honours Fellow, Council Member, Em Soc, 1964, 1975–80; Fellow, ASA, 1968–; Guggenheim Foundation Fellow, 1972, 1985; Fellow, Center Advanced Study Behavioral Sciences, Stanford, CA, 1976–7, 1980–1; Fellow, AAAS, 1977–.

Principal Fields of Interest 212 Econometric Models.

Publications *Books:* 1. *An Econometric Model of the United States 1929–52* (with L. R. Klein), (N-H, 1955); 2. *Impact Multipliers and Dynamic Properties* (N-H, 1958); 3. *Econometric Theory* (Wiley, 1964); 4. *Topics in Regression Analysis* (Macmillan, 1968); 5. *Structural Equation Models in the Social Sciences*, co-ed. (with O. D. Duncan), (Seminar Press, 1973); 6. *Latent Variables in Socio-economic Models*, co-ed. (with D. J. Aigner), (N-H, 1977).

Articles: 1. 'Best linear unbiased prediction in the generalized linear regression model', *JASA*, 57, 1962; 2. 'Econometrics and psychometrics: a survey of communalities', *Psychometrika*, 36, 1971; 3. 'Structural equation methods in the social sciences', *Em*, 40(6), Nov. 1972; 4. 'The non-resolution of IQ inheritance by path analysis', *Amer. J Human Genetics*, 30, 1978; 5. 'Heritability', *Ec*, 46, Nov. 1979. 6. 'Reverse regression and salary discrimination', *JHR*, 19, Summer 1984.

GOLDFELD, Stephen Michael

Born 1940, New York City, NY, USA.

Current Post Prof. Econ. and Banking, Princeton Univ., Princeton, NJ, USA, 1969–.

Past Posts Ass. Prof., Assoc. Prof., Princeton Univ., 1963–6, 1966–9; Member, Sr. Econ., US President's Council Econ. Advisers, 1966–7, 1980–1; Vis. Prof., Core, Univ. Louvain, Belgium, 1970; Ford Vis. Prof., Univ. Cal. Berkeley, 1975–6; Mendes-France Prof., Technion, Haifa, Israel, 1980.

Degrees BA (Maths.) Harvard Univ., 1960; PhD MIT, 1963.

Offices and Honours Proctor and Gamble Faculty Fellow, 1964; NSF Sr. Post-Doctoral Fellow, 1970–1; Fellow, Em Soc, 1973.

Editorial Duties Assoc. Ed., *Int ER*, 1971–, *J Em*, 1972–, *AER*, 1973–5, *REStat*, 1973–, *JMCB*, 1981–.

Principal Fields of Interest 210 Econometrics; 300 Money and Fiscal Theory and Institutions; 130 Macroeconomics.

Publications *Books:* 1. *Commercial Bank Behavior and Economic Activity: A Structural Study of Monetary Policy in the Postwar United States* (N-H, 1966); 2. *Precursors in Mathematical Economics: An Anthology*, co-ed. (With W. J. Baumol), (LSE, 1968); 3. *Nonlinear Methods in Econometrics* (with R. E. Quandt), (N-H, 1972); 4. *Studies in Nonlinear Estimation*, co-ed (with R. E. Quandt), (Ballinger, 1976);

5. *The Economics of Money and Banking* (with L. V. Chandler), (Harper & Row, 1981).

Articles: 1. 'Some tests for homoscedasticity' (with R. E. Quandt), *JASA*, 60, June 1965; 2. 'Maximization by quadratic hill-climbing' (with R. E. Quandt and H. F. Trotter), *Em*, 34(3), July 1966; 3. 'Some implications of endogenous stabilization policy' (with A. S. Blinder), *Brookings Papers Econ. Activity*, 3, 1972; 4. 'Simulation and aggregation: a reconsideration' (with D. J. Aigner), *REStat*, 55(1), Feb. 1973; 5. 'A Markov model for switching regressions' (with R. E. Quandt), *J Em*, 1(1), March 1973; 6. 'The estimation of structural shifts by switching regressions' (with R. E. Quandt), *Annals Econ. and Social Measurement*, Oct. 1973; 7. 'The demand for money revisited', *Brookings Papers Econ. Activity*, 3, 1973; 8. 'New measures of fiscal and monetary policy, 1958–1973' (with A. S. Blinder), *AER*, 66(5), Dec. 1976; 9. 'The case of the missing money', *Brooking Papers Econ. Activity*, 3, 1976 10. 'A model of FHLBB advances: rationing or market clearing?' (with D. Haffee, R. E. Quant), *REStat*, 62(3), Aug. 1980.

Principal Contributions I have continued to work on the three topics which formed the basis of my doctoral dissertation — money and banking, macroeconomics and econometrics. My interests in macroeconomics and money have been revitalised by serveral stints in government policy positions. These have also served to contrast the 'real world', the textbook world, and the academic-journal world, and I have tried on occasion to bridge these gaps in research. My interests in econometrics have been both applied and methodological. In contrast with the sometimes frustrating experience of empirical work, I find that theoretical econometrics is often refreshingly clean and satisfying. I would put my work in nonlinear methods and disequilibrium econometrics in this category.

GOLDSMITH, Raymond William

Born 1904, Brussels, Belgium.

Current Post Prof. Econ. Emeritus, Yale Univ., New Haven, CT, USA, 1974–.

Past Posts German Stat. Office, Berlin, 1927–9; Inst. für Finanzwesen, Berlin, 1931–3; US Securities and Exchange Commission, Washington, DC, 1934–41; US War Production Board, Washington, DC, 1942–6; Prof. Econ., NYU., 1956–61; Prof. Econ., Yale Univ. 1962–74.

Degrees PhD Univ. Berlin, 1927.

Offices and Honours Fellow, ASA; Council, Chairman, IARIW, 1950–60.

Principal Fields of Interest 224 National Wealth; 314 Financial Intermediaries; 041 Economic History.

Publications *Books:* 1. *Kapitalpolitik* (Junker und Dunnhampt, 1933); 2. *The Changing Structure of American Banking* (G. Routledge & Son, 1933); 3. *A Study of Saving in the United States*, 3 vols. (Princeton Univ. Press, 1955); 4. *Studies in the National Balance Sheet of the United States* (with R. Lipsey and M. Mendelson), (Princeton Univ. Press, 1963); 5. *Financial Structure and Development* (Yale Univ. Press, 1969); 6. *The National Balance Sheet of the United States 1953–80* (Columbia Univ. Press, 1982); 7. *The Financial Development of India 1860–1977* (Yale Univ. Press, 1983); 8. *The Financial Development of Japan, 1868–1977* (Yale Univ. Press, 1983).

Articles: 1. 'Measuring national wealth in a system of social accounting', in *Studies in Income and Wealth* (NBER, 1950); 2. 'The growth of reproducible wealth of the US from 1805 to 1950', in *Income and Wealth of the US*, ed. S. Kuznets (Bowes and Bowes, 1952); 3. 'Financial structure and economic growth in advanced countries', in *Capital Formation and Economic Growth* (NBER, 1956); 4. 'The mobilization of internal financial resources in Latin America', in *The Mobilization of Domestic Resources through the Financial System* (Interamer. Devlp. Bank, 1971). 5. 'The development of financial institutions during the post-war period', *BNLQR*, 97, June 1971; 6. 'A century of financial development in Latin

America', in *Memoria de la Reunion de Tecnicor de Bancor Centraler del Continente Americano* (Bancor Centrale, 1972); 7. 'National balance sheets as tools of international economic comparisons', in *Comparative Development, Perspectives*, eds. G. Ranis and R. L. West (Westview Press, 1984).

Principal Contributions During my service in the Federal Government, I was concerned mainly with securities markets (1934–41), with war finance (1942–45), and with the German currency reform (1946). Since 1948 I have concentrated on statistical and institutional aspects of financial institutions, saving, capital stock and national balance sheets, first for the US, but from the 1960s on an international comparative basis. In these fields I regard as my main innovations (1) the estimation of saving by forms; (2) the development of the perpetual inventory method of estimating capital stocks as cumulated price-adjusted net investment, first applied to the US but then to many other countries; and (3) the introduction of the financial interrelations ratio (financial assets/tangible assets), the financial intermediation ratio (assets of financial institutions/total financial assets) and the development of formulas which identify the main determinants of the financial interrelations ratio.

GOMULKA, Stanislaw

Born 1940, Krezoly, Poland.
Current Post Sr. Lect. Econ., LSE, London, UK, 1980–.
Past Posts Ass. Lect., Lect., Univ. Warsaw, Poland, 1962–5; Vis. Lect., Reader, Univ. Aarhus, Denmark, 1970, 1972–3; Lect., LSE, 1970–80; Fellow, Inst. Advanced Study Humanities and Social Sciences, The Netherlands, 1980–1; Vis. Prof., Univ. Penn., 1984–5.
Degrees MSc (Physics), PhD Univ. Warsaw, 1962, 1966.
Principal Fields of Interest 621 Technological Change; 123 Comparative Economic Studies.
Publications *Books:* 1. *Inventive*

Activity, Diffusion and the Stages of Economic Growth (Inst. Econ., Univ. Aarhus, 1971); 2. *West-East Technology Transfer and its Contribution to East's Economic Growth* (with A. Nove and G. Holliday), (OECD, 1984); 3. *Growth, Innovation and Reforms in Eastern Europe* (Wheatsheaf Books, 1984).

Articles: 1. 'Technical progress and long-run growth' (with A. Chilosi), *Rivista di Politico Economica*, 1970, repr. (Polish), *Ekonomista*, 1, 1969, (Russian), *Ekonometrika Matematica*, 6, 1969; 2. 'Extensions of the "Golden Rule of Research" of Phelps', *REStud*, 37(1), Jan. 1970; 3. 'Technological condition for balanced growth: a criticism and restatement' (with A. Chilosi), *JET*, 9(2), Oct. 1974; 4. 'Technological condition for balanced growth: a note on Professor Whitaker's contribution', *JET*, 11(2), Oct. 1976; 5. 'Testing the realism of five year plans' (with P. Wiles), in *Comparative Economic Systems*, ed. M. Lago (Pittsburgh Univ. Press, 1975); 6. 'Import-led growth: theory and estimation' (with J. D. Sylwestrowicz), in *On the Measurement of Factor Productivities: Theoretical Problems and Empirical Results*, ed. L. Altman, *et al*. (Vandenhoech & Rupprecht, 1976); 7. 'Slowdown in Soviet industrial growth in 1947–75 reconsidered', *Europ. ER*, 10(1), Oct. 1977; 8. 'A simple mathematical model of the world oil cartel' (with J. Gomulka), in *On Stability of Contemporary Economic Systems*, eds. O. Kyn and W. Schrettle (Vandenhoech & Rupprecht, 1978); 9. 'Britain's slow industrial growth: increasing inefficiency versus low rate of technical change', in *Slow Growth in Britain: Causes and Consequences*, ed. W. Beckerman (OUP, 1979); 10. 'The Polish crisis: will it spread and what will be the outcome?', in *Crisis of the East European Economy*, ed. J. Drewnowski (Croom Helm, 1982).

Principal Contributions One group of writings are theoretical and empirical studies of the causes of variation in rates of innovation and economic growth among countries and over time, in particular the factors pertaining to the size of international diffusion of technology, size and dynamics of inventive activities in specific countries, and institutional as well as social factors that influence innovation, diffusion and economic efficiency. Two 'hat-shape' relationships are suggested to operate. One describes how the innovation rate in the world's technology frontier changes over time; it implies that productivity growth will slow down. The other relates the innovation rate to the technological gap for countries behind the technological frontier; it is a cross-country relationship or a growth path for any specific country. Most of my other papers are studies of economic growth, innovation, crises phenomena and institutional reforms in centrally-planned economies of Eastern Europe and the USSR. Specific topics include Soviet growth slowdown in the post-1945 period, growth implications of the West-East technology transfer, price inflexibility and soft budget constraint in explaining the shortage and inefficiency phenomena and crisis and economic reform in Poland.

GONNARD, René*

Dates and Birthplace 1874–1966, Chamay les Maçon, France.
Post Held Prof., Univ. Lyons, 1901–44.
Degree Agrégé Econ. 1901.
Offices and Honours Corresp. Member, Institut de France; Chevalier, Légion d'Honneur, 1935.
Publications Books: 1. L'émigration européenne au XIXe siècle (1906); 2. Histoire des doctrines économiques (1921); 3. Histoire des doctrines de la population (1923); 4. Histoire des doctrines monètaires (1935); 5. La propriété dans la doctrine et dans l'histoire (1943).
Career Distinguished French historian of economic ideas in the inter-war period.

GONNER, Edward Carter Kersey*

Dates and Birthplace 1862–1922, England.

Post Held Prof., Univ. Liverpool, 1891–1922.
Degree MA Univ. Oxford, 1883.
Offices and Honours Pres., Section F BAAS, 1897, 1914; Knighted, 1921.
Publications Books: 1. The Socialist State (1895); 2. The Social Philosophy of Rodbertus (1899); 3. Interest and Saving (1906); 4. Germany in the Nineteenth Century (1912); 5. Common Land and Inclosure (1912).
Career His writings range widely from commercial geography to socialist ideas and economic history. He was a successful wartime civil servant in the Ministry of Food.
Secondary Literature L. L. Price, 'Gonner, Sir Edward Carter Kersey', ESS, 5.

GOODHART, Charles A. E.

Born 1936, London, England.
Current Post Chief Adviser Monetary Policy, Bank of England, 1969–.
Past Posts Ass. Lect., Univ. Camb., 1963–5; Econ. Adviser, UK Dept. Econ. Affairs, 1967–8; Lect. Monetary Econ., LSE, 1967–9.
Degrees BA Univ. Camb., 1960; PhD Harvard Univ., 1963.
Offices and Honours Adam Smith Prize, Univ. Camb., 1959; Prize Fellow, Trinity Coll., Camb., 1963; Dir., UK SSRC Money Study Group, 1979.
Editorial Duties Treasurer, REStud, 1968–75.
Principal Fields of Interest 300 Domestic Monetary and Fiscal Theory and Policy: 023 Macroeconomic Theory; 041 Economic History: General.
Publications Books: 1. The New York Money Market and the Finance of Trade, 1900–13 (Harvard Univ. Press, 1969); 2. The Business of Banking, 1891–1914 (Weidenfeld & Nicolson, 1972); 3. Money, Information and Uncertainty (Macmillan, 1975); 4. Monetary Theory and Practice: The UK Experience (Macmillan, 1984).
Articles: 1. 'Political economy', Polit. Stud., 18, March 1970; 2. 'The importance of money', Bank of England Quarterly Bull., 10, June 1970; 3. 'Monetary policy in the United King-

dom', in *Monetary Policy in Twelve Industrial Countries* (Fed. Reserve Bank Boston, 1973); 4. 'Analysis of the determination of the stock of money', in *Essays in Modern Economics*, eds. M. Parkin and A. R. Nobay (Longman, 1973); 5. 'Problems of monetary management: the UK experience', in *Papers in Monetary Economics* (Reserve Bank Australia, 1975); 6. 'Money, income and causality: the UK experience' (with D. Williams and D. H. Gowland), *AER*, 66(3), June 1976; 7. 'The relationship between yields on short and long-dated gilt-edged stocks' (with D. Gowland), *BER*, 29, Nov. 1977; 8. 'Monetary policy', in *Demand Management*, ed. M. Posner (Heinemann, 1978); 9. 'Money in an open economy', in *Economic Modelling*, ed. P. Ormerad (Heinemann, 1979); 10. 'Monetary trends in the United States and the United Kingdom: a British review', *JEI*, 20(4), Dec. 1982.

Principal Contributions After two books on banking history (USA and UK 1890–1913), concentrated on monetary theory, application and policy, first as an academic, then as adviser to the Bank of England. Closely involved in formulation and implementation of UK monetary policies from 1968 onwards; in debates on methods of monetary control I opposed monetary base control. More widely known for two less serious pieces, first as one of the earliest researchers into the relationship between macroeconomic developments and political popularity, and second as the author of 'Goodhart's law': any statistical regularity, notably in the monetary area, will break down when pressure is placed upon it for control purposes.

GORDON, David M.

Born 1944, Washington, DC, USA.
Current Post Prof. Econ., Grad. Faculty, New School Social Res., New York City, NY, USA, 1983–.
Past Posts Lect. Econ., Yale Univ., 1969–70; Res. Assoc., NBER, 1970–2; Res. Assoc., Center Educ. Pol. Res., Harvard Univ., 1972–3; Ass. Prof., Assoc. Prof., New School Social Res.,

1973–77, 1977–83; Vis., Inst. Advanced Study, Princeton, NJ, 1978.
Degrees BA, PhD Harvard Univ., 1965, 1971.
Offices and Honours NSF Fellow, 1966–9; Exec. Comm., Union Radical Polit. Econ., 1975–7; Nominating Comm., AEA, 1977; C. Wright Mills Award, 1973; Chair, Div. I, Nat. Conf. Social Welfare, 1974; Guggenheim Foundation Fellow, 1984–5.
Editorial Duties Ed. Boards, *Dialectical Anthrop.*, 1977–, *New Polit. Science*, 1980–; Assoc. Ed., *Camb JE*, 1978–.
Principal Fields of Interest 051 Capitalist Economic Systems; 042 North American Economic History; 820 Labour Markets; Public Policy.
Publications *Books:* 1. *Low-Income Labor Markets and Urban Manpower Programs* (with P. Doeringer, *et al.*), (US Dept. Labor, 1971); 2. *Problems in Political Economy: An Urban Perspective*, ed. (D. C. Heath, 1971, 1977); 3. *Theories of Poverty and Underemployment* (D. C. Heath, 1973); 4. *Radical Perspectives on the Economic Crisis*, co-ed. (with others), (Union for Radical Polit. Econ., 1975); 5. *Labor Market Segmentation*, co-ed. (with others), (D. C. Heath, 1976); 6. *US Capitalism in Crisis*, co-ed. (Union for Radical Polit. Econ., 1978); 7. *The Working Poor: Toward a State Agenda* (Duke Univ. Press, 1983); 8. *What's Wrong with the US Economy?* (South End Press, 1982); 9. *Segmented Work, Divided Workers: The Historical Transformation of Labor in the United States* (with R. Edwards and M. Reich), CUP, 1982; partial transl., Italian, *Quaderni Rassegna Sindacale*, 20 Sept.–Dec. 1982); 10. *Beyond the Waste Land: A Democratic Alternative to Economic Decline* (with S. Bowles and T. W. Weisskopf), (Anchor Press, Doubleday, 1983, 1984; transl., French, Maspero, 1984).
Articles: 1. 'Class and the economics of crime', *Rev. Radical Polit. Econ.*, 3, Summer 1971, repr. in *Crime and Delinquency*, 17, April 1973, and *Modern Political Economy*, ed. J. Weaver (Allyn & Bacon, 1973), and *Classes, Conflict and Control*, ed. J. Munro (Anderson Publ., 1975), and

Economic Issues and Policies, eds. J. S. Elliott and A. Grey (Houghton-Mifflin, 1976); 2. 'Taxation of the poor and the normative theory of tax incidence', *AER*, 62(2), May 1971, repr. in *The Second Crisis of Economic Theory*, ed. R. Fels (General Learning Press, 1972); 3. 'A theory of labor market segmentation' (with R. Edwards and M. Reich), *AER*, 63(2), May 1973, repr. in *Wealth, Income and Inequality*, ed. A. B. Atkinson (OUP, 1980), and *Schooling in a Corporate Society*, ed. M. Carnoy (D. McKay, 1975), and *The Economics of Women and Work*, ed. A. Amsden (Penguin, 1980); 4. 'Capitalist efficiency and socialist efficiency', *Monthly Rev.*, 28, July–Aug. 1976, repr. in *Technology, the Labor Process, and the Working Class*, ed. J. Geller (Monthly Rev. Press, 1976); 5. 'Capitalist development and the history of American cities', in *Marxism and the Metropolis*, eds. W. Tabb and L. Sawers (OUP, 1978, 1983), repr. in *The Rise of the Sunbelt Cities*, eds. D. Perry and A. Watkins (Sage, 1978), and *The Political Economy of Ecology*, eds. A. Cockburn and J. Ridgeway (Quadrangle, 1979), and (in German), *Stadtkrise und soziale Bewegungen*, eds. M. Mayer, R. Roth and V. Brandes (Europäische Verlagsanstalt, 1978); 6. 'Stages of accumulation and long economic cycles', in *Processes of the World-System*, eds. T. Hopkins and I. Wallerstein (Sage, 1980), repr. (in Spanish), *Estados Unidos: Perspectiva Latinoamericana*, 71, 1 Sept., 1980; 7. 'The best defense is a good defense; toward a marxian theory of labor union structure and behavior', in *New Directions in Labor Economics and Industrial Relations*, eds. M. Carter and W. Leahy (Notre Dame Univ. Press, 1981); 8. 'Capital-labor conflict and the productivity slowdown', *AER*, 71(2), May 1981; 9. 'Long swings and the nonreproductive cycle' (with S. Bowles and T. E. Weisskopf), *AER*, 73(2), May 1983; 10. 'Hearts and minds: a social model of US productivity growth' (with S. Bowles and T. E. Weisskopf), *Brookings Papers Econ. Activity*, 2, 1983.

Principal Contributions With many others, I've sought since the late 1960s to constitute a coherent and robust 'radical' or neo-Marxist alternative to mainstream economics — not simply to interpret the world through different lenses, as our seminal source might have put it, but also to change it fundamentally.

Analytically, this quest has propelled me through discourses on critical methodology, analyses of labour segmentation and urban transformation, contributions to the theory of long swings and stages of capitalist development, and, most recently, investigations of the dynamics of postwar US capitalism and particularly of declining profitability and the productivity slowdown. Institutionally, we've been forced to devote substantial energy to establishing alternative bases within the economics profession, in my case particularly through efforts at constructing a serious graduate programme in political economy at the New School for Social Research.

Politically, several of us have turned increasingly to formulation of discrete and concrete alternative policy proposals which embody the apparently bizarre notion that we can transcend the alleged trade-off between equity and efficiency, that fairness, decency, equality and democracy actually make good economic sense. *Beyond the Waste Land*, with Bowles and Weisskopf, reflects one major step in this direction. Another is an independent research and educational institute which I founded, the Centre for Democratic Alternatives. We aim to put socialist democracy on the agenda in the US, which is precisely where it belongs.

GORDON, Donald Flemming

Born 1923, Saskatoon, Saskatchewan, Canada.

Current Post Prof., Dir., Center Study Bus. Govt, Baruch Coll., City Univ. NY, USA, 1978–.

Past Posts Ass. Prof., Assoc. Prof., Prof. Econ., Univ. Washington, 1950–66; Prof., Grad. School Management, Univ. Rochester, 1966–74; Prof., Exec. Officer PhD Program Econ.,

City Univ. NY, 1974–6; Prof., Simon Fraser Univ., British Columbia, 1976–8.

Degrees BA Univ. Saskatchewan, 1944; MA Univ. Toronto, 1946; PhD Cornell Univ., 1949.

Offices and Honours Award, Best Article 1974 in *EI*; Vice-Pres., Pres., WEA, 1978–80.

Principal Fields of Interest 022 Microeconomic Theory.

Publications *Articles:* 1. 'Operational propositions in economic theory', *JPE*, 63, April 1955; 2. 'What was the labor theory of value?', *AER*, 49(2), May 1959; 3. 'Primary products and economic growth: an empirical measurement' (with E. Chambers), *JPE*, 74, Aug. 1966; 4. 'On the theory of price dynamics' (with A. Hynes) in *The Microeconomic Foundations of Employment and Inflation Theory*, ed. E. S. Phelps (Norton, 1970); 5. 'A neoclassical theory of Keynesian unemployment', *EI*, 12(4), Dec. 1974.

Principal Contributions A search model of employment with an argument for the invalidity of dynamic equations which depend on expectations (with A. J. Hynes); the distinction between relative and absolute value in classical and Marxian economics: the latter is a definition and not subject to empirical, logical or normative refutation; the methodological position that operational propositions cannot be derived from the maximising calculus, but stem from the hypothesis of stable tastes; a test of the proposition that rapid economic growth in Canada in 1901–10 was primarily due to staple exports (with E. J. Chambers); and an independent development of implicit contracts as an explanation for lay-offs, job-rationing and unemployment.

GORDON, Myron Jules

Born 1920, New York City, NY, USA.

Current Post Prof. Fin., Univ. Toronto, Toronto, Ont., Canada, 1970–.

Past Posts Ass. Prof., Carnegie-Mellon Univ., Pittsburgh, 1947–52; Assoc. Prof. MIT, 1952–62; Prof., Univ. Rochester, 1962–70; Vis. Prof., Univ. Cal. Berkeley, 1966–7, Hebrew Univ., Jerusalem, 1973, Univ. Penn., 1977.

Degrees BA Univ. Wisonsin, 1941; PhD Harvard Univ., 1952.

Offices and Honours Ford Foundation Fellow, 1971; Connaught Fellow, 1982; Pres., AFA 1975; Comm. Member, Amer. Accounting Assoc., AFA, Inst. Management Sciences.

Editorial Duties Ed. Boards, *Accounting Rev.*, *J Fin*, *Fin. Managment*, *J Bank Fin*.

Principal Fields of Interest 130 Economic Fluctuations; 520 Business Finance & Investment. 610 Industrial Organisation & Public Policy.

Publications *Books:* 1. *Accounting : A Management Approach* (with G. Shillinglaw), (Richard D. Irwin, 1951, 1979); 2. *The Investment Financing and Valuation of the Corporation* (Richard D. Irwin, 1962, 1982; transl., Japanese, 1972); 3. *The Cost of Capital to a Public Utility* (Mich. State Univ. Press, 1974); 4. *The Drug Industry: A Case Study in Foreign Control* (with D. Fowler), (Lorimer, 1981).

Articles: 1. 'Cost allocations and the design of accounting systems for control', *Accounting Rev.*, April 1951; 2. 'Scope and method of theory and research in the measurement of income and wealth', *Accounting Rev.*, Oct. 1960; 3. 'Security and a financial theory of investment', *QJE*, 7(4), Aug. 1960; 4. 'Experimental evidence on alternative portfolio decision rules' (with G. E. Paradis and C. A. Rorke), *AER*, 62(1), March 1972; 5. 'A portfolio theory of the social discount rate and the public debt', *J Fin*, 3(2), May 1976; 6. 'The cost of equity capital: a reconsideration' (with L. I. Gould), *J Fin*, 33(3), June 1978; 7. 'Growth and survival in a capitalist system', *J Post Keyn E* 2(4), Summer 1980; 8. 'Corporate bureaucracy, productivity gain and the distribution of revenue in U.S. manufacturing, 1947–77', *J Post Keyn E*, 4(4), Summer 1982;

Principal Contributions From 1947–1960 my research was concerned primarily with two questions in accounting. One was the principles of asset valuation and income measurement that maximise the value and income of a firm. At that time accounting research was devoted to arriving at the true value and income of a firm. The question I posed and the answers I found in paper (No. 2. above) and other articles had a considerable impact on subsequent research in accounting. The other question that concerned me was the design of responsibility accounting systems under alternative delegations of authority to subordinate levels of management for the purpose of maintaining top management control. Standard costs, overhead budgets and other methods of transfer pricing in the accounts were looked at and developed within this theoretical framework. A number of articles and my textbooks on accounting contributed to the early development of the theory of responsibility accounting systems.

During the 1950s I became increasingly interested in the theory of asset valuations under uncertainty and with the investment and financing policies that maximise the value of a corporation. This resulted in my most influential work to date, *The Investment Financing and Valuation of the Corporation*. Part of this work was the discounted cash flow measure of share yield which has become widely used in industry and finance as the expected return on a share of stock.

During the last five years my interest has turned to the macroimplications of my work on investment, financing, growth and survival. Starting with my presidential address (No. 5. above), a number of papers have been concerned with the cyclical and long-run behaviour of a capitalist system in which person and firms are concerned with the security of their income as well as its expected level. These macro-objectives have also been served by my work on the non-production activities of large widely-owned corporations that are employed to maintain and increase their rents.

GORDON, Robert Aaron*

Dates and Birthplace 1908–78, Washington, DC, USA.

Posts Held Instr., Harvard Univ., 1931–8; Ass. Prof., Assoc. Prof., Prof., Prof. Emeritus, Univ. Cal. Berkeley, 1938–40, 1940–7, 1947–76, 1976–8.

Degrees BA Johns Hopkins Univ., 1928; MA, PhD Harvard Univ., 1931, 1934.

Offices and Honours Officer, US Combined Raw Materials Board, 1942–5, Res. Advisory Board, Comm. Econ. Devlp., 1954–8, 1960–3; Guggenheim Foundation Fellow, 1956–7; Board Dirs., NBER, 1961–76; Chairman, US President's Comm. Employment and Unemployment Stats., 1961–2; Member, Nat. Task Force Econ. Educ., 1960–1; Vice-Pres., Disting. Fellow, Pres., AEA, 1950–2, 1972, 1975; Phi Beta Kappa; Beta Gamma Sigma.

Publications *Books:* 1. *Business Leadership in the Large Corporation* (1945); 2. *Business Fluctuations* (1952, 1961); 3. *Readings in Business Cycles*, co-ed. (with L. R. Klein), (1965); 4. *The Goal of Full Employment* (1967); 5. *Economic Instability and Growth: The American Record* (1974).

Career Wrote extensively on industrial organisation and the theory of business cycles in the postwar period.

GORDON, Robert James

Born 1940, Boston, MA, USA.

Current Post Prof. Econ., Northwestern Univ., IL, USA; Res. Assoc., NBER, 1978–.

Past Posts Ass. Prof., Harvard Univ., 1967–8; Ass. Prof., Univ. Chicago, 1968–73.

Degrees BA Harvard Univ., 1962; BA, MA Univ. Oxford, 1964, 1969; PhD MIT, 1967.

Offices and Honours Member, Sr. Adviser, Brookings Panel Econ. Activity, 1970–1; Fellow, Treasurer, Em Soc, 1975; Guggenheim Foundation Fellow, 1980–1; Exec. Comm., AEA, 1981–3.

Editorial Duties Co-ed., *JPE*, 1970–3; Ed. Board, *AER*, 1975–7.

Principal Fields of Interest 123 Comparative Economic Studies; 130 Economic Fluctuations; 226 Productivity and Growth.

Publications *Books:* 1. *Milton Friedman's Monetary Framework: A Debate with his Critics*, ed. (Univ. Chicago Press, 1974; transl., Japanese 1978); 2. *Macroeconomics* (Little Brown, 1978, 1984; transls., Japanese 1981, Italian, 1982, Spanish, 1983); 3. *Challenges to Interdependent Economics: The Industrial West in the Coming Decade* (with J. Pelkmans), (McGraw-Hill, 1979); 4. *The American Business Cycle: Continuity and Change*, ed. (Univ. Chicago Press, 1985); 5. *The Measurement of Durable Goods Prices* (Univ. Chicago Press, 1985).

Articles: 1. 'The incidence of the corporation income tax in US manufacturing', *AER*, 57(4), Sept. 1967; 2. '$45 billion of US private investment has been mislaid', *AER*, 59(3), June 1969; 3. 'The welfare cost of higher unemployment', *Brookings Papers Econ. Activity*, 1, 1973; 4. 'Alternative responses of policy to external supply shocks', *Brookings Papers Econ. Activity*, 6, 1975; 5. 'The demand for and supply of inflation', *J Law E*, 18(3), Dec. 1975; 6. 'Output fluctuations and gradual price adjustment', *JEL*, 19(2), June 1981; 7. 'Why US wage and employment behavior differs from that in Britain and Japan', *EJ*, 92, March 1982; 8. 'Price inertia and policy ineffectiveness in the US, 1890–1980', *JPE*, 90, Dec. 1982; 9. 'The output cost of disinflation in traditional and vector autoregressive models', *Brookings Papers Econ. Activity*, 13, 1982(2); 10. 'The short-run demand for money: a reconsideration', *JMCB*, 16, Nov. 1984.

Principal Contributions Demonstrated that inflation depends both on demand pressure and supply shocks and that excess demand stems from pressures on the central bank to accommodate wage push, supply shocks and fiscal deficits. Have called attention to the greater inertia of inflation in the postwar US than in either the prewar US or in other postwar countries (especially UK and Japan). Have questioned conventional approaches to the econometric specification of fixed investment and money demand functions and suggested a new treatment of each topic. Work on price measurement for durable goods has developed new techniques to adjust for improvements in performance and energy efficiency, as well as 20,000 new data observations that yield radically different estimates of changes in aggregate prices and productivity, and in the industry allocation of productivity gains.

GORMAN, William Moore

Born 1923, Kesh, County Fermanagh, N. Ireland.

Current Post Sr. Res. Fellow, Nuffield Coll. Oxford, UK, 1983–.

Past Posts Ass. Lect., Lect., Sr. Lect. Econometrics, Univ. Birmingham, 1949–62; Prof. Econ., Official Fellow, Nuffield Coll., Oxford, 1962–7, 1979–83; Prof. Econ., LSE, 1967–9; Vis. Prof., Iowa State Coll. Agric. and Mechanic Arts, 1956–7, Stanford Univ., 1967, Univ. N. Carolina, 1970–1, Johns Hopkins Univ., 1979–80.

Degrees BA, BA (Maths.) Trinity Coll., Dublin, 1948, 1949; Hon. Dr Social Sciences, Univ. Birmingham, 1973, Univ. Southampton, 1974.

Offices and Honours Fellow, Pres., Em Soc, 1962, 1972; Sr. Vis. Foreign Scientist, Stanford Univ., 1967; Council, RES, 1968–74; Council, Royal Stat. Soc., 1966; Fellow, BA, 1978.

Editorial Duties Assoc. Ed., *Em*, 1958–; Chairman, Ed. Board, *REStud*, 1963–7.

Principal Fields of Interest 020 General Economic Theory; 210 Econometrics, Statistical and Mathematical Methods and Models; 410 International Trade Theory.

Publications *Articles:* 1. 'Community preference fields', *Em*, 21, June 1953; 2. 'Convex indifference curves and diminishing marginal utility', *JPE*, 65, Feb. 1957; 3. 'Tariffs, retaliation, and the elasticity of demand for imports', *REStud*, 25(3), June 1957, repr. in *Readings in Welfare Economics*, ed. M. J. Farrell (Macmillan, 1973); 4. 'Separable utility and aggregation', *Em*, 27(3), July 1959, repr. in *Selected Readings in Economic Theory from*

Econometrica, ed. K. J. Arrow (MIT Press, 1971); 5. 'Professor Friedman's consumption function and the theory of choice', *Em*, 32, 1–2, Jan.–April 1964; 6. 'Measuring the quantities of fixed factors', in *Value Capital and Growth, Essays in Honour of Sir John Hick*, ed. J. N. Wolfe (OUP, 1968); 7. 'The structure of utility functions', *REStud*, 35, Oct. 1968; 8. 'Tricks with utility functions', in *Essays in Economic Analysis*, ed. M. J. Artis (OUP, 1976); 9. 'A possible procedure for analysing quality differentials in the egg market', *REStud*, 47, Oct. 1980; 10. 'Some Engel curves', in *Essays on the Theory and Measurement of Demand in Honour of Sir Richard Stone*, ed. A. Deaton (OUP, 1981).

Principal Contributions James Davidson at Foyle College, Derry and George Duncan at Trinity College, Dublin taught me to think of mathematics and economics as styles of thought not collections of theorems, and Birmingham taught me to think of the social sciences as a unity with history as one way of holding them together. My research has accordingly been devoted to the end of flexible modelling, that is, to allow economists to immerse themselves in their data and in the opinions of other social scientists, and then to choose forms which seem capable of handling this information. This has been even more true of my teaching, largely through workshops for students beginning research.

GORT, Michael

Born 1923, Russia.
Current Post Prof. Econ., State Univ. NY., Buffalo, NY, USA, 1975–.
Past Posts Lect. Econ., Univ. Cal. Berkeley, 1951–4; Assoc. Prof. Fin., Grad. School Bus., Univ. Chicago, 1957–62; Cons., Office Bus. Econ., US Dept. Commerce, 1962–3; Vis. Prof. Econ., Northwestern Univ., 1967–8; Res. Staff, Sr. Res. Staff, Dir. Res. Program Industrial Organisation, NBER, 1954–7, 1971–5.
Degrees BA Brooklyn Coll., 1943; MA, PhD Columbia Univ., 1951, 1954.
Offices and Honours US SSRC Res. Training Fellow, 1950–1; Res. Assoc. Fellow, NBER, 1954.
Principal Fields of Interest 610 Industrial Organisation and Public Policy; 620 Economics of Technological Change.
Publications *Books:* 1. *Diversification and Integration in American Industry* (Princeton Univ. Press, 1962); 2. *Changes in the Size Structure of Business Firms* (US Small Bus. Admin., 1964).

Articles: 1. 'The analysis of factor shares by industry', *Stud. Income and Wealth*, 27, 1964; 2. 'The analysis of stability and change in market share', *JPE*, 71(1), Feb. 1963; 3. 'Diversification, mergers and profits', in *The Corporate Merger*, eds. W. Alberts and J. Segall (Univ. Chicago Press, 1966); 4. 'Vintage effects and the time path of investment in production relations' (with R. Boddy), *Stud. Income and Wealth*, 31, 1967; 5. 'An economic disturbance theory of mergers', *QJE*, 83(4), Nov. 1969; 6. 'New evidence on mergers' (with T. Hogarty), *J Law E*, 13(1), April 1970; 7. 'The substitution of capital for capital' (with R. Boddy), *REStat*, 53(2), May 1971; 8. 'Concentration and profit rates: new evidence on an old issue' (with R. Singamsetti), *Explor. in Econ. Res.*, 3(1), Winter 1976; 9. 'Time paths in the diffusion of product innovations' (with S. Klepper), *EJ*, 92, Sept. 1982; 10. 'A model of diffusion in the production of an innovation' (with A. Konakayama), *AER*, 72(5), Dec. 1982.

Principal Contributions The common theme in most of my research has been the role of constraints on the choices and behaviour of firms arising from their endowments. These endowments are seen as dependent upon the history of the firm and/or the juncture in the evolution of the industry that the firm finds itself. In my study of product diversification (*Diversification and Integration in American Industry*), the key variable in determining diversification decisions was seen as the requirements for human capital in the form of technological skills needed for entry into new markets. Comparative advantage was then decided by the endowments of the firm with respect to such skills which, in turn, depended upon the industries in which the firm was already active. In a forthcoming sequel to this work, the additional conclusion is drawn that diversification decisions represent an attempt to preserve the firms accumulated organisational (human) capital.

The interdependence between past decisions and present choices is also the central theme in No. 4 above. The power of investment to change output depends not only upon the current technological attributes of the production process, but also upon the accumulated stock of capital goods that firms possess. This is because new investment interacts with old investment in the production process, and the vintage of old investment determines the flexibility of such interactions. In No. 9 above, a central focus is the impact of innovations on entry and on the number of firms in a market. Once again evolutionary factors are seen as decisive. In the early stages of an industry's life-cycle, it is shown that innovation accelerates entry while in the late phases of the cycle it retards entry. A closely related theme, though with respect to a different set of questions, is developed in No. 5. It is shown that the development and, hence, the characteristics of markets determine the degree of uncertainty about the future earnings of firms. This, in turn, generates discrepancies in valuation and, as a result, mergers.

GOSCHEN, George Joachim*

Dates and Birthplace 1831–1907, London, England.

Posts Held Businessman, 1853–66; Dir., Bank of England, 1858.

Degree BA Univ. Oxford, 1853.

Offices and Honours MP, 1863–86, 1887–1900; Cabinet Minister, 1866–74, 1887–92, 1895–1900; Chancellor, Univ. Oxford, 1903–7; Life Peer, 1900.

Publications Books: 1. Theory of the Foreign Exchanges (1861); 2. Reports and Speeches on Local Taxation (1872); 3. Addresses on Educational and Economical Subjects (1885); 4. Essays and Addresses on Economics Questions (1905).

Career Statesman economist, whose early work on foreign exchanges was his only major publication. This was the first systematic theory of international price adjustments and was for long the standard work on the subject. A convinced supporter of laissez faire policies, he followed non-interventionist policies during his long periods of government office. His major achievements are regarded as the reorganisation of local government finance and the conversion of part of the National Debt.

Secondary Literature L. M. Fraser 'Goschen, First Viscount', ESS, 6.

GOSSEN, Hermann Heinrich*

Dates and Birthplace 1810–58, Düren, Germany

Posts Held Civil servant and businessman.

Publications Books: 1. The Laws of Human Relations and the Rules of Human Action Derived Therefrom (1854, 1983).

Career Gossen's only known publication on economics was ignored by his contemporaries both because of the dominance of the views of the historical school and the pretentious presentation of his ideas. Thus, both Jevons and Walras were forced to recognise that their work on marginal utility had been substantially anticipated by Gossen; indeed, Gossen's exact anticipation of Jevons' theory of labour supply is almost uncanny. Gossen's book is, in general, a working out of the hedonistic calculus using mathematical methods.

Secondary Literature H. W. Spiegel, 'Gossen, Hermann Heinrich', IESS, 6; N. Georgescu-Roegen, 'Hermann Heinrich Gossen: his life and work in historical perspective', in Human Relations by H. H. Gossen, transl. R. C. Blitz (MIT Press, 1983).

GOTTL–OTTLILIENFELD, Friedrich von*

Dates and Birthplace 1868–1958, Vienna, Austro-Hungary.
Posts Held Prof., Technical High School, Brünn, 1902–8, Münich, 1908–20; Prof. Theoretical Econ., Univ. Berlin, 1926–41.
HonoursGoethe-Medaille für Kunst und Wissenschaft.
Publications *Books:* 1. *Wirtschaft als Leiben. Eine Sammlung erkenntniskritischer Arbeiten* (1925); 2. *Wirtschaft als Wissen, Tat und Wehr über Volkswirtschaftslehre, Autarkie und Wehrwirtschaft* (1940).
Career As much a sociologist as an economist, Gottl is chiefly known for his constant advocacy and exposition of Weberian 'Verstehen' doctrine in the social sciences.
Secondary Literature G. von Haberler, 'Kritische Bemerkungen zu Gottls Methodologischen Schriften', *ZN*, 1, June 1930; G. Weippert, 'von Gottl-Ottlilienfeld, Friedrich', *Handwörterbuch der Sozialwissenschaften* 4, eds., E. V. Beckerath, *et al.* (Gustav Fisher, 1960).

GOULD, John P.

Born 1939, Chicago, IL, USA.
Current Post Dean, Disting. Service Prof. Econ., Grad. School Bus., Univ. Chicago, 1983–.
Past Posts Special Ass., Econ. Affairs, US Dept. Labor, 1969–70; Cons. Econ. Affairs to Dir., US Office Management and Budget, Exec. Office Pres., 1970; Vis. Prof. Econ., Grad. Inst. Econ., Nat. Taiwan Univ., 1978; Prof. Econ., Grad. School Bus., Univ. Chicago, 1965–83.
Degrees BS Northwestern Univ., 1960; PhD Univ. Chicago, 1966.
Offices and Honours Fellow, Em Soc; Earhart Fellow, 1963–4; Wall Street Journal Award, 1960.
Editorial Duties Ed., *J Bus*; Assoc. Ed., *J Fin Econ, J. Accounting Econ.*
Principal Fields of Interest 022 Microeconomic Theory.
Publications *Books:* 1. *Microeconomic Theory* (with C. E. Ferguson),

(Richard D. Irwin, 1975; transls., Japanese, 1977, Spanish, 1978).
Articles: 1.'Adjustment costs in the theory of investment of the firm', *REStud*, 35, Jan. 1968; 2. 'Diffusion processes and optimal advertising policy', in *Microeconomic Foundations of Employment and Inflation Theory*, ed. E. Phelps (Norton, 1970, 1973, Macmillan, 1971); 3. 'The economics of legal conflicts', *J Legal Stud.*, June 1973; 4. 'Risk, stochastic preference and the value of information', *JET*, 8(1), May 1974; 5. 'Inventories and stochastic demand: equilibrium models of the firm and industry', *J Bus*, 15(1), Jan. 1978.
Principal Contributions Earliest research concentrated on the dynamic theory of the firm with particular reference to the role of adjustment costs in capital accumulation and the effect of diffusion processes in advertising. Subsequent work dealt with the effects of information and uncertainty in a variety of circumstances including the resolution of legal conflicts, the demand for insurance, the effect of risk on the value of information, and the nature of equilibrium in industries facing stochastic demand.

GOULD, Joseph Robert

Born 1927, London, England.
Current Post Reader Econ., LSE, London, England, 1979–.
Past Posts Ass. Lect., Lect., Sr. Lect., LSE, 1957–79; Vis. Assoc. Prof., Univ. Cal. Berkeley, 1963–4; Vis. Prof., Univ. Victoria, BC, 1967.
Degree BSc Univ. London, 1957.
Principal Fields of Interest 022 Microeconomic Theory; 024 Welfare Theory; 610 Industrial Organisation and Public Policy.
Publications *Articles:* 1. 'Internal pricing in firms when there are costs of using an outside market', *J Bus*, 37(1), Jan. 1964, repr. in *Modern Financial Management*, eds. B. V. Carsberg and H. C. Eday (Macmillan, 1969), and in *Contemporary Cost Accounting and Control*, ed. G. J. Benston (Macmillan, 1977); 2. 'Resale price maintenance and retail outlets' (with L. E. Preston),

Ec, 32, Aug. 1965, repr. in *Economics of Retailing*, eds. K. A. Tucker and B. S. Yamey (Macmillan, 1973); 3. 'On investment criteria for mutually exclusive projects', *Ec*, 39, Feb. 1972, repr. in *1972 Benefit-Cost Analysis Annual*, eds. W. Nisnkensen, *et al.* (Aldine, 1973); 4. 'Extinction of a fishery by commercial exploitation: a note', *JPE*, 80(5), Sept.–Oct. 1972; 5. 'Externalities, factor proportions and the level of exploitation of free-access resources', *Ec*, 39, Nov. 1972; 6. 'Professor Meade on external economies: should the beneficiaries be taxed?', *J Law E*, 16(1), April 1973; 7. 'External economies and the production frontier', *JPE*, 82(5), Nov.–Dec. 1974; 8. 'Total conditions in the analysis of external effects', *EJ*, 87, Sept. 1977; 9. 'Price discrimination and vertical control: a note', *JPE*, 87(5), Oct. 1977; 10. 'On the interpretation of inferior goods and factors', *Ec*, 48, Nov. 1981.

Principal Contributions My undergraduate studies were specialised in accounting, which formed the background for early work on the application of microeconomic analysis to accounting information for managerial decisions. My interests then shifted further towards microeconomics, welfare economics, and industrial organisation. Work on externalities led to the development of interest in property rights and transactions costs, the application of these concepts to problems of industrial organisation, and a general interest in the economic analysis of law.

GRABOWSKI, Henry George

Born 1940, Scranton, PA, USA.
Current Post Prof. Econ., Duke Univ., Durham, NC, USA, 1976–.
Past Posts Lect., Ass. Prof., Yale Univ., 1966–7, 1967–71; Res. Assoc., NBER, 1971–2; Assoc. Prof., Duke Univ., 1972–6; Res. Fellow, Internat. Inst. Management, Berlin, 1976; Vis. Scholar, Health Care Financing Admin., US Office of Res., Washington, DC, 1979–80.
Degrees BS (Eng. and Physics) Lehigh Univ., Bethlehem, PA, 1962; MA, PhD Princeton Univ., 1964, 1967.

Offices and Honours US SSRC Res. Fellow, 1968; Member, NAS, Comm. Technology, 1978–9; Adjunct Scholar, AEI, 1980–; Member, Inst. Medicine Comm. Vaccine Innovation, 1983–; Member, Board Dirs., Univ. Rochester Center for Study of Drug Devlp., 1983–.
Editorial Duties Assoc. Ed., *Internat. J. Industrial Organization*, 1980–.
Principal Fields of Interest 610 Industrial Organisation and Public Policy; 620 Economics of Technological Change; 913 Economics of Health.
Publications *Books:* 1. *Drug Regulation and Innovation: Empirical Evidence and Policy Options* (AEI, 1976); 2. *The Impact of Regulation on Industrial Innovation* (with J. Vernon), (NAS, 1979); 3. *The Regulation of Pharmaceuticals: Balancing the Benefits and Risks* (with J. Vernon), (AEI, 1983).
Articles: 1. 'The determinants of effects of industrial research and development expenditures', *JPE*, 76(2), March–April 1968, repr. in *Readings in Managerial Economics*, ed. K. S. Palda (Prentice-Hall, 1973), and *Economics of Industrial Structure: Selected Readings*, ed. B. S. Yamey (Penguin, 1973); 2. 'Demand shifting, optimal firm growth, and rule-of-thumb decision making', *QJE*, 84(2), May 1970; 3. 'Managerial and stockholder welfare models of firm expenditures' (with D. Mueller), *REStat*, 54(1), Feb. 1972; 4. 'The effects of advertising on interindustry distribution of demand', *Explor. Econ. Res.*, 3(1), Winter 1976; 5. 'Estimating the effects of regulation on innovation: an international comparative analysis of the pharmaceutical industry' (with J. Vernon and L. Thomas), *J Law E*, 21(1), April 1978; 6. 'Consumer product safety regulation' (with J. Vernon), *AER*, 68(2), May 1978; 7. 'Industrial research and development, intangible capital stocks, and firm profit rates' (with D. Mueller), *Bell JE*, 9(2), Fall 1978; 8. 'Regulation and the international diffusion of pharmaceuticals', in *The International Supply of Medicines* (AEI, 1980); 9. 'Auto safety regulation: an analysis of market failure' (with R. Arnould), *Bell JE*, 12(1), Spring 1981; 10. 'The Pharmaceutical industry' (with J. Vernon),

in *Government and Technical Progress — A Cross-Industry Analysis* (Pergamon, 1982).

Principal Contributions My research has focussed on the economics of technological change, government regulation of business and related topics in industrial organisation. I have analysed these topics in terms of both specific industry studies as well as from a broader empirical perspective. My initial work investigated industrial research and development activity, analysing its determinants as well as effects. This research was later broadened to a more general analysis of corporate decision-making, which examined the allocation of cash flows across fixed capital investment, advertising, R&D, and other uses. About a decade ago I became interested in the effects of government regulation on innovation and other performance measures. This led to studies of government product safety regulations in several industries, including pharmaceuticals, automobiles, and other consumer-oriented products. Among the principal findings of this research were that (1) regulation has had significant negative effects on innovation in industries subject to pre-market approval (like pharmaceuticals); (2) international comparative studies suggest that the more stringent US regulations have had moderately higher benefits and much higher costs (compared with Western Europe); (3) consumer choice situations involving low probability events often result in significant underprotection against hazards (such as the case of automobile seat belt utilisation). Most recently, I have been examining evolutionary models of technological change to study the effects and interaction between different government policies (regulatory, tax, property rights and industrial competition) on long-run trends in industrial innovation.

GRAHAM, Daniel Arthur

Born 1944, Amarillo, TX, USA.
Current Post Prof. Econ., Duke Univ., Durham, NC, USA, 1977–.

Past Posts Res. Ass., Econometric Systems Simulation Program, Ass. Prof. Econ., Prof. Econ., Duke Univ., 1968–9, 1969–74, 1974–7; Vis. Faculty Res. Fellow, NBER, NY, 1976–7.
Degrees BS W. Texas State Univ., Canyon, TX, 1967; PhD Duke Univ., 1969.
Offices and Honours Nat. Defense Educ. Act Fellow, 1968–9; Phi Beta Kappa, Duke Univ.,
Editorial Duties Ed. Board, *J. Law and Contemporary Problems*, 1983–.
Principal Fields of Interest 022 Microeconomic Theory; 026 Economics of Uncertainty and Information; 213 Mathematical Methods and Models.
Publications *Books:* 1. *Microeconomics: The Analysis of Choice* (D. C. Heath, 1980).
Articles: 1. 'Profitability of monopolization by vertical integration' (with J. Vernon), *JPE*, 79, July-Aug. 1971, repr. in *Economics of Industrial Structure*, ed. B. S. Yamey (Penguin, 1973); 2. 'Multi-sector economic models with continuous adaptive expectations' (with E. Burmeister), *REStud*, 16, July 1974; 3. 'A geometrical exposition of input-output analysis', *AER*, 65(1), March 1975; 4. 'On convergence to Pareto allocations' (with E. R. Weintraub), *REStud*, 42, July 1975; 5. 'The economics of the network-affiliate relationship' (with J. Vernon), *AER*, 65(5), Dec. 1975; 6. 'Trader-commodity parity theorems' (with L. Jennergren, D. Peterson and E. R. Weintraub), *JET*, 12, June 1976; 7. 'Real transactions costs are inessential' (with H. Baligh, E. R. Weintraub and M. Wisefeld), *Kyk*, 29, Fall 1976; 8. 'The demand for insurance and protection: the case of irreplaceable commodities' (with P. J. Cook), *QJE*, 91, Feb. 1977; 9. 'Cost-benefit analysis under uncertainty', *AER*, 71(4), Sept. 1981; 10. 'Contingent damages for products liability' (with E. R. Peirce), *J. Legal Stud.*, 13, Aug. 1984.
Principal Contributions From an early focus upon general equilibrium theory and dynamical systems, my interests have increasingly shifted toward more applied topics involving choices made under uncertainty in the absence

of complete markets. My work on irre-placeable losses, for example, concerns the implications of the inability to re-place commodities lost in accidents upon the *ex ante* demands for insur-ance and protection. My work on cost-benefit analysis provides a procedure for measuring the value of public pro-jects which entail uncertain benefits in the absence of complete contingent claims markets. Most recently, my re-search on product liability involves the contract as a device for providing insur-ance and incentives in the context of irreplaceable accident losses.

GRAHAM, Frank Dunstone*

Dates and Birthplace 1890–1949, Halifax, Nova Scotia, Canada.

Posts Held Instr. Econ., Rutgers Coll., 1917–20; Ass. Prof., Dartmouth Coll., 1920–1; Prof., Princeton Univ., 1921–49.

Degrees MA, PhD Harvard Univ., 1917, 1920.

Publications *Books:* 1. *Exchange, Prices and Production in Hyper-inflation, Germany 1920–3* (1930); 2. *The Abolition of Unemployment* (1923); 3. *Protective Tariffs* (1934); 4. *Golden Avalanche* (with C. R. Whit-tlesey), (1939); 5. *Social Goals and Economic Institutions* (1942); 6. *Plan-ning and Paying for Full Employment* (with A. P. Lerner, *et al.*), (1946); 7. *The Theory of International Values* (1948).

Career Attacked the classical inter-national trade theory, particularly the two-country, two-commodity approach and the assumption of comparative advantage statically conceived. Rejec-tion of Graham's criticisms was for years the litmus-paper test of ortho-doxy in trade theory. Served on the special US War Dept. Commission on the conduct of the war in 1945.

GRAMLICH, Edward Martin

Born 1939, Rochester, NY, USA.
Current Post Prof. Econ. and Public Pol., Univ Michigan, Ann Arbor, MI, USA, 1976–.

Past Posts Res. and Stats. Div., Fed. Reserve Board, Washington, DC, 1965–7; Vis. Prof., Monash Univ., Melbourne, Australia, 1970; Dir., Pol. Res. Div., US Office Econ. Oppor-tunity, Washington, DC., 1970–3; Sr. Fellow, Brookings Inst., 1970–5; Vis. Prof., Cornell Univ., 1975–6.

Degrees BA Williams Coll., 1961; MA, PhD Yale Univ., 1962, 1965.

Offices and Honours Econ. Panel, NSF, 1973–5; Pol. Council, Vice-Pres., Assoc. Public. & Management, 1979–85, 1979–80.

Editorial Duties Ed. Board, *Nat. Tax J.*, 1970–84, *Evaluation Rev.*, 1980–4, *JEL*, 1981, *J Pol. Analysis and Management*, 1982–.

Principal Fields of Interest 321 Fiscal Theory & Policy; 325 Intergovernmen-tal Financial Relationships; 023 Macro-economics.

Publications *Books:* 1. *Savings Deposits, Mortgages and Housing in the FRB-MIT-Penn Econometric Model*, co-ed. (with D. M. Jaffee), (D. C. Heath, 1972); 2. *Educational Perfor-mance Contracting : An Evaluation of an Experiment* (with P. P. Koshel), (Brookings Inst., 1975); 3. *Setting National Priorities: The 1975 Budget* (with B. M. Blechman and R. W. Hartman), (Brookings Inst., 1974); 4. *Setting National Priorities : The 1976 Budget* (with B. M. Blechman and R. W. Hartman), (Brookings Inst., 1975); 5. *Benefit-cost Analysis of Government Programs* (Prentice-Hall, 1981); 6. *Tax Reform : There Must be a Better Way,*, (with P. N. Courant), (Nat. Pol. Ex-change, 1982).

Articles: 1. 'The behavior and ade-quacy of the U.S. Federal budget, 1952–64', *YEE*, 6(1), Spring 1966; 2. 'State and local governments and their budget constraint', *Int ER* 10(2), June 1969; 3. 'The channels of monetary policy: a further report on the FRB-MIT econometric model' (with F. de Leeuw), *J Fin*, 24(2), May 1969, repr. in *Fed. Reserve Bull.*, June 1969, and *Monetary Economics, Readings on Current Issus*, eds. W. E. Gibson and G. C. Kaufman (McGraw-Hill, 1971), and *Monetary Theory and Policy*, ed. T. Havrilesky (AHM Publishing, 1976); 4. 'A statistical analysis of the

OEO experiment in educational performance contracting' (with I. Garfinkel), *JHR*, 8(3), Summer 1973, repr. in *The 1973 Benefit Cost and Policy Analysis Annual*, ed. R. H. Haveman, *et al.* (Brookings Inst., 1974); 5. 'State and local fiscal behavior and federal grant policies' (with H. Galper), *Brookings Papers Econ. Activity*, 1, 1973; 6. 'The impact of minimum wages on other wages, employment and family incomes', *Brookings Papers Econ. Activity*, 2, 1976; 7. 'Macro policy responses to price shocks', *Brooking Papers Econ. Activity* 1, 1979; 8. 'Public employee market power and the level of government spending' (with P. N. Courant and D. L. Rubinfeld), *AER*, 69(5), Dec. 1979, repr. in *Municipal Expenditures, Revenues, and Services*, ed. W. P. Beaton (Rutgers Univ., 1984); 9. 'Using micro data to estimate public spending demand functions and test the Tiebout and median voter hypotheses' (with D. L. Rubinfeld), *JPE*, 90(3), June 1982; 10. 'An econometric analysis of the new federalism', *Brookings Papers Econ. Activity* 2, 1982.

Principal Contributions My early work was in macroeconomics, building a small macro model for my thesis and then being part of a project to build a large one at the Federal Reserve Board. One of the interesting projects I became involved in then was the question of how to model the fiscal behaviour of State and local governments — a framework I developed then and have used since to look at all kinds of questions regarding grant behaviour, conversion of grants to block form, public employment and swings in State and local saving.

Later I became interested in questions of poverty and unemployment and took a job at the Office of Economic Opportunity. Ideas for papers on the distributional impact of the business cycle and minimum wages originated there. In addition, I was introduced to the fascinating question of programme evaluation, first with the performance contracting experiment and later continuing with my benefit-cost text. That focusses particularly on the evaluation of distributional programmes.

These earlier interests continued when I moved to Michigan, and were supplemented by a new one. Tax cut fever was in the air at the time, and I began working on the analytics of government size and growth. Two colleagues (Paul Courant and Daniel Rubinfeld) and I did some theoretical models on this issue, and we also conducted a voter survey to try to get better data on individual spending demands. Unlike previous surveys, we tried to analyse our data within the context of a median voter model, and we also used it to test a number of hypotheses regarding tastes of public employees, the impact of tax limits, and migration. That, in turn, inspired a more intense interest in the underappreciated migration question and I am now trying to establish, from a theoretical and empirical standpoint, how important a constraint on government behaviour that really is.

GRANDMONT, Jean-Michel

Born 1939, Toulouse, France
Current Post Maître de Recherche, CNRS, Paris; Maître de Conf., Ecole Polytechnique, Paris; Res. Assoc., CEPREMAP, Paris.
Past Posts Res. Ass., CEPREMAP, 1970–; Vis. Res. Ass., CORE, Louvain, 1972–3; Vis. Res. Ass., Stanford Univ., 1975, Harvard Univ., 1975; Vis. Prof., Bonn Univ., 1975, Stanford Univ., 1976, 1983, Univ. Penn. 1980, Univ. Lausanne, 1982–3.
Degrees Licence en Sciences Univ. Paris, 1961; Ingénieur Ecole Polytechnique, 1962; Ingenieur Ecole Ponts et Chaussees, 1965; PhD Univ. Cal. Berkeley, 1971.
Offices and Honours Fellow *Em. Soc.* 1974; Member, Europ. Council *Em. Soc.*, 1977–83.
Editorial Duties Assoc. Ed., *Em*, *JET*, *J Math. E.*
Principal Fields of Interest 021 General Equilibrium Theory; 306 Monetary Theory; 131 Economic Fluctuations.
Publications *Books:* 1. *Money and Value : A Reconsideration of Classical*

and Neoclassical Monetary Theories (CUP, 1983);

Articles: 1. 'On the short run equilibrium in a monetary economy', in *Allocation Under Uncertainty, Equilibrium and Optimality*, ed. J. Dréze (Macmillan, 1974); 2. 'On the role of money and the existence of a monetary equilibrium' (with Y. Younès), *REStud*, 39(3), July 1972; 3. 'On the efficiency of a monetary equilibrium' (with Y. Younès), *REStud*, 40(2), April 1973; 4. 'Stochastic Processes of temporary equilibria' (with W. Hildenbrand), *J. Math. E*, 1974; 5. 'Temporary general equilibrium theory', *Em*, 45(3), April 1977; 6. 'Intermediate preferences and the majority rule', *Em*, 46(2), March 1978; 7. 'On endogenous competitive business cycles', *Em*, forthcoming, 1985.

Principal Contributions Introduction of money in general equilibrium theory. Introduction of time and expectation formation in equilibrium theory (temporary general equilibrium theory). Contributions to disequilibrium theory and its relation to macroeconomics. Generalisation of existing results on the aggregation of preferences by the majority rule, using the notion of intermediate preferences. Contribution to the theory of endogenous, deterministic competitive business cycles by using the notion of the bifurcation of nonlinear dynamical systems (transition from periodic to turbulent or chaotic behaviour). Countercyclical policies.

GRANGER, Clive William John

Born 1934, Swansea, Wales.
Current Post Prof. Econ., Univ. Cal. San Diego, CA, USA, 1974–.
Past Posts Ass. Lect. Maths. Lect. Econ., Reader Maths., Prof. Appl. Stats. and Econometrics, Univ. Nottingham, 1955–7, 1958–63, 1964–5, 1965–74; Vis. Prof., Princeton Univ., 1959–60, Stanford Univ., 1963, ANU, 1977.
Degrees BA (Maths.), PhD (Stats.) Univ. Nottingham, 1955, 1959.
Offices and Honours Harkness Fellow, Commonwealth Fund, 1959–60; Fellow, Em Soc.

Editorial Duties Joint Ed., *Appl. Econ.*, 1973–8; Assoc. Ed. *J Fin Econ.*, 1975–9, *J Em*, 1977–84, *JASA*, 1978–80, *Appl. Econ.*, 1979–84, *Energy*, 1981–3, *J. Bus. and Econ. Stats.*, 1982–, *Communication in Stats.* 1983–, *Spectrum*, 1984; Advisory Board, *Theoretical Em*, 1984.

Principal Fields of Interest 211 Econometric and Statistical Methods and Models; 132 Economic Forecasting and Econometric Models; 313 Capital Markets.

Publications *Books:* 1. *Spectral Analysis of Economic Time Series* (with M. Hatanaka), (Princeton Univ. Press, 1964; transl., French, Dunod, 1969); 2. *Predictability of Stock Market Prices* (with O. Morgenstern), (D. C. Heath, 1970); 3. *Speculation Hedging and Forecasts of Commodity Prices* (with W. C. Labys), (D. C. Heath, 1970; transl., Japanese, 1976); 4. *Trading in Commodities*, ed. and contrib. (Woodhead-Faulkner, 1974); *Getting Started in London Commodities* (Investor Publications, 1975, 1983); 5. *Forecasting Economic Time Series* (with P. Newbold), (Academic Press, 1977); 6. *Bilinear Time Series Models*, co-ed. (with A. Anderson), (Vandenhoeck & Ruprecht, 1978); 7. *Forecasting in Business and Economics* (Academic Press, 1980).

Articles: 1. 'The typical spectral shape of an economic variable', *Em*, 34, Jan. 1966; 2. 'Investigating causal relations by econometric models and cross-spectral methods', *Em*, 37(3), July 1969; repr. in *Rational Expectations*, eds. R. E. Lucas and J. T. Sargent (Univ. Minnesota Press, 1981); 3. 'The combination of forecasts' (with J. Bates), *Operational Res. Q.*, 20, 1969; 4. 'Some comments on the evaluation of forecasts' (with P. Newbold), *Appl. Econ.*, 5(1), March 1973; 5. 'Spurious regressions in econometrics' (with P. Newbold), *JRSS*, B, 38, 1976; 6. 'Seasonality; causation, interpretation and implications', in *Seasonal Analysis of Economic Time Series*, ed. A. Zellner (US Bureau of Census, 1979); 7. 'Nearer normality and some econometric models', *Em*, 47(3), May 1979; 8. 'Testing for causality, a personal viewpoint', *J Ec Dyn*, 2(4), 1980; 9.

'Co-integrated variables and error-correcting models', Working Paper Univ. Cal. San Diego, 1983.

Principal Contributions I believe that I have helped introduce time-series models and approaches into economics. My work on spectral analysis was one of the first in the area. I have introduced a definition of causality that many find useful, have discussed the evaluation and combination of forecasts, and have applied time-series techniques to data from speculative markets. I feel that my most significant contribution to date concerns co-integration and error-correction models, as this work brings together economic equilibrium theory ideas, time-series model specification, simultaneity and causality concepts.

GRAY, Alexander*

Dates and Birthplace 1882–1968, Dundee, Scotland.

Posts Held Civil Servant, 1905–21, Prof. Polit. Econ., Univ. Aberdeen, 1921–35, Univ. Edinburgh, 1935–56.

Degree BA Univ. Edinburgh, 1902.

Offices and Honours Council, RES, 1929–55; Knighted, 1947; Pres., Section F BAAS, 1949.

Publications *Books:* 1. *The Development of Economic Doctrine* (1931); 2. *The Socialist Tradition* (1946).

Career Historian of economic thought whose work was authoritative and distinctive for its elegant style.

GRAY, John*

Dates and Birthplace 1799–1883, England.

Posts Held Businessman and publisher.

Publications *Books:* 1. *Lecture on Human Happiness* (1825, 1931); 2. *The Social System, a Treatise on the Principle of Exchange* (1831); 3. *Remedy for the Distress of Nations* (1842); 4. *Money* (1848).

Career His early experiences as a clerk in a London wholesale house led him to become a bitter critic of competition. The first remedy which he proposed was producer-co-operatives, but he later changed his emphasis to planning and monetary reform.

Secondary Literature J. Kimball, *The Economic Doctrines of John Gray* (Catholic Univ. of America Press, 1948).

GRAY, Simon*

Dates and Birthplace c. 18th century, England.

Post Held War Office employee.

Publications *Books:* 1. *The Essential Principles of the Wealth of Nations* (1797); 2. *The Happiness of States: Or an Inquiry Concerning Population* (1815, 1819); 3. [G. Purves], *All Classes Productive of National Wealth* (1817); 4. [G. Purves], *Gray Versus Malthus: The Principles of Population and Production Investigated* (1818); 5. *Remarks on the Production of Wealth* (1820).

Career A virulently anti-Malthusian writer who published two works under the pseudonym George Purves, praising his own work (a practice that was not uncommon in the nineteenth century). His *Happiness of States . . .* contains a clear statement that bread is what has come to be called a 'Giffen good'.

Secondary Literature E. Masuda and P. Newman, 'Gray and Giffen goods', *EJ*, 91, Dec. 1981.

GREEN, Harold Alfred John*

Dates and Birthplace 1923–76, Birmingham, England.

Posts Held Lect. Econ., Univ. Keele, 1955–8; Ass. Prof. Econ., Univ. Cal., Santa Barbara, 1958–9; Ass. Prof. Prof. Econ., 1959–72; Prof. Econ. Theory, Univ. Kent, 1972–6.

Degrees BA, MA, Univ. Oxford, 1947, 1948; PhD MIT, 1954.

Offices Simon Vis. Prof., Univ. Manchester, 1965–6; Vis. Prof., Univ. Essex, 1971–2.

Publications *Books:* 1. *Aggregation in Economic Analysis* (Princeton Univ. Press, 1964); 2. *Consumer Theory* (Penguin, 1971, Macmillan, 1976). *Articles:* 1. 'Some logical relations in revealed preference theory', *Ec*, N.S. 24, Nov. 1957; 2. 'The social optimum in the presence of monopoly and taxation', *REStud*, 29, Oct. 1961; 3. 'Embodied progress, investment and growth', *AER*, 56(1), March 1966; 4. Uncertainty and the "expectations hypothesis"', *REStud*, 34, Oct. 1967; 5. 'Two models of optimal pricing and taxation', *OEP*, 27(3), Nov. 1975.

Career Principal contribution to economics lay in the careful exposition and evaluation of propositions in economic theory. His earlier work was in the theories of growth and distribution, but the majority of his publications, including his well-known book on consumer theory, were largely concerned with aspects of consumer and social choice under various constraints. His final published paper on optimal taxation brought together apparently different results within a single framework, and many of his earlier works were similarly concerned to survey and reconcile different approaches to a topic.

GREENE, Kenneth Vincent

Born 1943, New York City, NY, USA.

Current Post Prof. Econ., State Univ. NY–Binghamton, NY, USA, 1982–.

Past Posts Ass. Prof., Assoc. Prof. Econ., State Univ. NY–Binghamton, 1968–75, 1975–82; Vis. Ass. Prof., Assoc. Prof. Econ., Univ. Colorado, 1969, 1980; Res. Staff, Urban Inst., Washington, DC, 1971, 1972–3;

Degrees BBA St John's Univ., NY, 1965; MA, PhD Univ. Virginia, Charlottesville, 1967, 1968.

Offices and Honours National Defense Education Act Fellow, 1965–8; NY State Faculty Res. Fellow, 1970, 1971, 1972, 1974.

Principal Fields of Interest 320 Public Finance; 324 State and Local Government Finance; 025 Social Choice; Bureaucratic Performance.

Publications *Books:* 1. *Fiscal Interactions in a Metropolitan Area* (with W. B. Neenan and C. D. Scott), (D. C. Heath, 1974).

Articles: 1. 'Some institutional considerations in federal-state fiscal relations', *Public Choice*, 9, Fall 1970, repr. in *Theory of Public Choice: Political Applications of Economics*, eds. R. D. Tollison & J. M. Buchanan (Univ. Michigan Press, 1972); 2. 'Attitudes toward risk and the relative size of the public section', *Public Fin. Q.*, 1, April 1973, repr. in *The Economic Approach to Public Policy*, ed. R. Amacher (Cornell Univ. Press, 1976), and *Democracia Y Economia Politica*, ed. A. Casahuga (Madrid, 1981); 3. 'Collective decision-making models and the measurement of benefits in fiscal incidence studies', *Nat. Tax J.*, 26(2), June 1973; 4. 'Toward a positive theory of intergenerational income transfers', *PF*, 30, 1975, repr. in *Hacienca Publica Espanola*, 1981; 5. 'Fiscal incidence in the Washington metropolitan area' (with W. B. Neenan and C. D. Scott), *Land Econ.*, 52(1), Feb. 1976; 6. 'The role of employee and constituent demand in the growth of public expenditures' (with V. Munley), *Public Fin. Q.*, 7, 1979; 7. 'Goofing off, aging and earnings', *SEJ*, 46(2), Oct. 1979; 8. 'Political externalities, efficiency and the welfare losses from consolidation' (with T. J. Parliment), *Nat. Tax J.*, 33(2), June 1980; 9. 'Sequential referenda and bureaucratic man', *Public Choice*, 42, Fall 1984; 10. 'Municipal employee residency requirements statutes: an economic analysis' (with G. D. Moulton), *Res. Law and Econ.*, 7, 1984.

Principal Contributions Early work concentrated on the applicability of public choice models to fiscal federalism. It demonstrated how this distribution of taxes at different government levels could affect the distribution of expenditures between governments, and explored the logical foundations of benefit incidence in fiscal studies; it was followed by an empirical implementation of fiscal incidence in an urban multigovernment area. The public choice methodology was applied to questions about support for volunteer armies, the social insurance budget and education. The latter led me into a number of topics utilising school finance data, including the role of employee groups in stimulating demand, welfare losses from consolidation, the effects of guaranteed tax bases, the exportability of non-residential property taxes and empirical tests of bureaucratic behaviour by school district administrators. Recently my interests have focussed on applying the public choice methodology to explaining government institutions, such as the use of residency requirements and more or less progressive tax structures.

GREENHALGH, Christine Anne

Born 1946, Crayford, London, England.
Current Post Fellow, St Peter's Coll., Lect., Univ. Oxford, UK, 1979–.
Past Posts Ass. Lect., Univ. Cape Coast, Ghana, 1968–70; Lect., Univ. Ghana, Legon, 1971–2; Temp. Lect., Lect., Univ. Southampton, 1975–9.
Degrees BSc, MSc Univ. London, 1967, 1968; PhD Princeton Univ., 1978.
Offices and Honours Employment Market Res. Consultative Group, UK Dept. Employment, 1983–.
Editorial Duties Ed. Board, *OEP*, 1982–; Advisory Board, *Econ. Rev.*, 1983–.
Principal Fields of Interest 824 Labour Market Studies; Wages; Employment; 851 Human Capital; 917 Economics of Minorities; Economics of Discrimination.
Publications *Books:* 1. *The Causes of Unemployment*, co-ed. (with R. Layard and A. Oswald), (OUP, 1984).
Articles: 1. 'Income differentials in the eastern region of Ghana', *Econ. Bull. Ghana*, Second Series, 2(3), 1972; 2. 'A labour supply function for married women in Great Britain', *Ec*, 44, Aug. 1977; 3. 'Male labour force participation in Great Britain', *SJPE*, 26(3), Nov. 1979; 4. 'Participation and hours of work for married women in Great Britain', *OEP*, 32(2), July 1980; 5. 'Male-female wage differentials in Great Britain: is marriage an equal opportunity?', *EJ*, 90, Dec. 1980; 6. 'The taxation of husband and wife: equity, efficiency and female labour supply', *Fiscal Stud.*, 2(2), July 1981; 7. 'Labour supply in Great Britain: theory

and evidence' (with K. Mayhew), in *The Economics of the Labour Market*, eds. Z. Hornstein, *et al.* (HMSO, 1981); 8. 'The training and experience dividend' (with M. Stewart), *Employment Gazette*, Aug. 1982; 9. 'Work history patterns and the occupational attainment of women' (with M. Stewart), *EJ*, 94, Sept. 1984; 10. 'Occupational status and mobility of men and women' (with M. Stewart), *OEP*, 34(4), March 1985.
Principal Contributions As a teenager I had great plans to change the world, to eliminate poverty and inequality. Four years in West Africa convinced me that I was being a little ambitious and that, in any case, economics can only provide partial solutions. I also discovered that a reputation within the Western world's economics profession and a position in a respectable university are useful prerequisites to being taken seriously as a policy adviser. Since 1972 I have retreated from the world's problems and worked my apprenticeship on the British labour market, focussing on the employment, wages and occupations of women. I have concentrated on empirical analysis with a view to generating useful evidence for policy-makers. With the arrival of my son in Dec. 1982, I have experienced first-hand the problems of combining work and motherhood! Nevertheless, I have ambitions to widen the spectrum of problems addressed in my research. Analysis of the processes of international competition and their impact on labour markets in rich and poor countries is the general field into which I intend to move. I shall be supported in both domestic and academic spheres by my husband, who is not only a good cook, but has expert knowledge of trade and production problems in LDCs.

GREENHUT, Melvin L.

Born 1921, New York City, NY, USA.
Current Post Alumni Disting. Prof. Econ., Texas A&M Univ., USA, 1969–.
Past Posts Ass. Prof., Auburn Univ.,

AL, 1948–52; Chief Econ., US Office Price Stats., Birmingham, 1952; Assoc. Prof., Mississippi State Univ., 1952–3; Prof. Bus. and Econ., Chairman Div., Rollins, 1953–7; Assoc. Dean, School Bus., Univ. Richmond, 1959–62; Prof., Florida State Univ., 1957–9, 1962–6; Vis. Prof. Bus., Michigan State Univ., 1963; Prof. Econ., Texas A&M Univ., 1966–9; Vis. Prof., Univs. Cape Town, 1971, Mannheim, 1973, Pittsburgh, 1976; Adjunct Prof., Univ. Karlsruhe, 1978.

Degrees BA Hofstra Univ., 1940; MA, PhD Washington Univ., 1947, 1951.

Offices and Honours Member, Inter-Univ. Comm. Res. on the South, 1959–64; Nat. Econ. Pol. Comm. and Econ. Advisory Council, US Chamber Commerce, 1961–64; Exec. Comm., Vice-Pres., SEA, 1961–3, 1965–6; Councillor, RSA, 1967–70; Dir., Region VI, Univ. Prof. for Academic Order, 1972–3; Adjunct Scholar, Cato Inst., 1982.

Editorial Duties Consulting Ed., *Industrial Devlp.* 1959–62; Ed., *SEJ*, 1966–8.

Principal Fields of Interest 020 General Economic Theory; 610 Industrial Organisation & Public Policy; 940 Regional Economics.

Publications *Books:* 1. *Plant Location in Theory and in Practice* (Univ. N. Carolina Press, 1956, 1967, Greenwood Press, 1982; transl., Japanese, Taimedo, 1972); 2. *Intermediate Income and Growth Theory* (with F. Jackson), (Prentice-Hall, 1961); 3. *Full Employment, Inflation and Common Stocks* (Public Affairs Press, 1961); 4. *Factors in the Location of Florida Industry* (with M. Colberg), (Florida State Univ. Press, 1962); 5. *Micro-economics and the Space Economy* (Scott Foresman, 1963); 6. *Essays on Southern Economic Development*, ed. (Univ. N. Carolina Press, 1964); 7. *A Theory of the Firm in Economic Space* (Appleton-Century-Crofts, 1970, Lone Star, 1974); 8. *Theory of Spatial Prices and Market Areas* (with H. Ohta), (Duke Univ. Press, 1975); 9. *Economics for the Voter* (with C. Stewart), (Lone Star, 1981); 10. *From Basic Economics to Supply-side Economics* (with C. Stewart), (Texas A&M Univ. Press, 1983).

Articles: 1. 'An empirical model and a survey: new plant locations in Florida', *REStat*, 41, Nov. 1959, repr. in *Factors in Location of Florida Industry*, ed. M. Colberg (Florida State Univ. Press, 1962); 2. 'Needed — a return to the classics in regional economic development theory', *Kyk*, Aug. 1966, transl., Portuguese, *Regional Economic Development Theory* (Brazil Sariva, 1977); 3. 'Monopoly output under alternative spatial pricing techniques' (with H. Ohta), *AER* 62(4), Sept. 1972; 4. 'Observations on the shape and relevance of the spatial demand function' (with M. Hwang and H. Ohta), *Em*, 43(4), July 1975; 5. 'Spatial price discrimination, competition and locational effects' (with J. G. Greenhut), *Ec*, N.S. 42, Nov. 1975; 6. 'Related market conditions and inter-industrial merger' (with H. Ohta), *AER*, 66(3), June 1976; 7. 'Non-linearity of delivered price schedules and predatory pricing' (with J. G. Greenhut), *Em*, 45(8), Nov. 1977; 8. 'Vertical integration of successive oligopolists' (with H. Ohta), *AER*, 69(1), March 1979; 9. 'Spatial pricing patterns in the United States' (with J. G. Greenhut and S. Li), *QJE*, 96(1), 1980; 10. 'Spatial pricing in the U.S.A., West Germany and Japan', *Ec*, 48, Feb. 1981.

Principal Contributions Early work was centred on plant location theory, particularly the demand factor of location. This emphasis stemmed from the writings of Lösch which contrasted sharply with the traditional focus on cost factors, e.g. transport costs, labour costs, taxes. In classical location theory, markets were conceived at a point, a counterpart spatial framework to perfect competition. Via Lösch's market area approach, as evaluated and developed further in my early writings, the theory of plant location was found to involve oligopolistic interdependencies. The premise that industrial location entails substitution among cost and demand factors opens up a Pandora's box since the latter factor finds expression in the effects of different demand curve convexities on pricing systems. The box includes the question of welfare maximisation in a spatial world where competitive firms can discriminate in prices. Indeed, empirical studies in several nations have lent reality to theoretical findings (and expectations) of discriminatory pricing rather than f.o.b. mill (perfectly competitive) pricing.

Besides requiring a determinate theory of oligopoly, resolving short- and long-run locations of firms, and ascertaining the market spaces over which firms sell, the subject of spatial economics extends well beyond that of location theory. In a recent book by L. Philips, pricing over space was viewed as counterpart to pricing over time. The fees of medical doctors, the prices of utility companies, of banks offering unlimited versus limited checking facilities, the bundling of goods, the use of multinational corporations and their impacts on international trade theory, all are part of the analytical techniques (framework) of spatial economics. That a microworld predicated an oligopolistic markets portends a different foundation for evaluating macro-theories and for prescribing policies recently led me to combine my interest in spatial economics with an interest in the Keynesian-Monetarist-Supply-Side controversy.

GREENWOOD, Michael J.

Born 1939, Chicago, IL, USA.
Current Post Prof. Econ., Dir., Center Econ. Analysis, Univ. Colorado, 1980–.
Past Posts Assoc. Prof. Econ., Kansas State Univ., 1965–73; Brookings Econ. Pol. Fellow, 1971–2; Prof. Econ., Arizona State Univ., 1973–80; Sr. Res. Econ., Econ. Devlp. Admin., US Dept. Commerce, 1977.
Degrees BS DePaul Univ., 1962; MA, PhD Northwestern Univ., 1965, 1967.
Offices and Honours Member, ASA, WEA, RSA, WRSA, PAA; Arizona State Univ. Grad. Coll., Disting. Res. Prof., 1977–8.
Editorial Duties Assoc. Ed., *RSE.*, 1976–; *J Reg S*, 1977–.
Principal Fields of Interest 823 Labour Mobility.

Publications *Books:* 1. *Migration and Economic Growth in the United States: National, Regional and Metropolitan Perspectives* (Academic Press, 1981).
Articles: 1. 'An analysis of the determinants of geographic labor mobility in the United States', *REStat*, 51(2), May 1969; 2. 'A regression analysis of migration to urban areas of a less developed country: the case of India', *J Reg S*, 11(2), Aug. 1971; 3. 'Research on internal migration in the United States: a survey', *JEL*, 13(2), June 1975; 4. 'A simultaneous-equations model of urban growth and migration', *JASA*, 70, Dec. 1975; 5. 'Metropolitan growth and the intrametropolitan location of employment, housing, and labor force', *REStat*, 62(3), Aug. 1980; 6. 'Migration and interregional employment redistribution in the United States', *AER*, 74(5), Dec. 1984.
Principal Contributions Assessment of the magnitudes of various influences on inter-regional migration to determine the impacts of origin and destination regions, and to explain intra-urban location patterns of employment, housing and labor force. Other work has focussed on the determinants and consequences of international migration.

GREGORY, Robert George

Born 1939, Melbourne, Australia.
Current Post Prof. Fellow, Res. School Social Sciences, ANU, Canberra, Australia, 1978–.
Past Posts Sr. Tutor Econ., Univ. Melbourne, 1962–3; Ass. Lect., LSE, 1965–7; Vis. Ass. Prof., Vis. Assoc. Prof., Northwestern Univ., IL, 1967–9, 1976; Sr. Res. Fellow, Sr. Fellow, Econ. Res. School Social Sciences, ANU, 1969–78; First Ass. Commissioner, Australian Industries Assistance Commission, 1973–5; Vis. Scholar, Board Governors, Fed. Reserve System, Washington, DC, 1977; Chair Australian Stud., Harvard Univ., 1983.
Degrees BCom Univ. Melbourne, 1961; PhD London Univ., 1965.
Offices and Honours Prize Best Economic Undergrad. of Year, 1958, 1959, 1960, 1961; Commonwealth Scholarship to US, 1962; Editors Prize,

Best Paper in *Australian J. Agric. Econ.*, 1976; Fellow, Australian Academy Social Sciences, 1979; Pres., Section 24, Australian and NZ Assoc. Academies Social Sciences, 1982.

Editorial Duties Assoc. Ed., *J Ind E*, 1978–82; Ed. Board, *Australian J. Management*, 1975–; Joint Ed., *ER*, 1982.

Principal Fields of Interest 420 Commercial Policy; 430 Balance of Payments; 820 Labour Markets.

Publications *Books:* 1. *The Processes of Economic Policy Making in Australia* (with S. Harris and I. Castle), (Royal Commission Australian Govt. Admin. 1975); 2. *Youth Employment, Education and Training* (with C. E. Baird and F. H. Gruen), (Centre Econ. Pol. Res., ANU, 1981).

Articles: 1. 'United States imports and internal pressure of demand: 1948–68', *AER*, 62(1), March 1971; 2. 'Do new factories embody best practice technology?' (with D. James), *EJ*, 83, Dec. 1973; 3. 'An analysis of relationships between import flows to Australia and recent exchange rate and tariff changes' (with L. D. Martin), *ER*, 52, March 1976; 4. 'Some implications of the growth of the mining sector', *Australian J. Agric. Econ.*, 20, Aug. 1976; 5. 'Labour market in the 1970s' (with R. C. Duncan), in *Conference in Applied Economic Research* (Reserve Bank Australia, 1980); 6. 'Teenage unemployment: the role of a typical labour supply' (with R. C. Duncan), *ER*, 56, Dec. 1980; 7. 'Segmented labour market theories and the Australian experience of equal pay for women' (with R. C. Duncan), *J Post Keyn E*, 3(3), Spring 1981; 8. 'The slide into mass unemployment: labour market theories, facts and policies', *Academy Social Sciences Australia*, 1983; 9. 'The contribution of employment separation to teenage unemployment' (with W. F. Foster), *ER*, 58, June 1982; 10. 'Work and welfare in the years ahead', *AEP*, 21, Dec. 1982.

Principal Contributions I was influenced greatly by the positivist methodology that was popular at LSE during the 1960s, although I now believe that as an ideal methodology it imputes too much status to existing theory. I now favour a much more pragmatic approach. A major influence on my writing was the experience associated with two years in the Australian public service during 1973–5, preparing public reports on proposed tariff reform. Since then I have focussed more on Australian problems and writing for a wider audience than the usual readership of an economic journal.

My paper that I like best and learned most from is concerned with equal pay for women (No. 6 above). It taught me the importance of sexual discrimination and segregation in the labour market and how institutions can matter. My most widely quoted paper — professionally and in the public sphere — is concerned with the structural change implications of a booming mineral export sector in Australia (No. 4 above). It was a forerunner of the 'Dutch Disease' literature. Recently I have been interested in macroeconomics viewed from a labour-market perspective.

GREGORY, Theodore Emanuel Gugenheim*

Dates and Birthplace 1893–1971, England.

Posts Held Ass. Lect., LSE, 1913–19; Prof. Econ., Univ. London, 1927–37.

Offices and Honours Knighted, 1942.

Publications *Books:* 1. *Tariffs: A Study in Method* (1921); 2. *An Introduction to Tooke and Newmarch's 'A History of Prices'* (1928, 1962); 3. *Select Statutes, Documents and Reports Relating to British Banking 1832–1928*, 2 vols (1929); 4. *An Introduction to Finance* (1932); 5. *The Westminster Bank Through a Century*, 2 vols (1936).

Career An inspiring though difficult teacher with a deep interest in theory and a strong sense of history. His lectures at LSE on the history of currency and banking carried on a tradition inaugurated by Foxwell. He was frequently called upon as an adviser by overseas governments.

GRIFFIN, Keith Broadwell

Born 1938, Colon, Panama.
Current Post Pres., Magdalen Coll. Oxford, 1979–.
Past Posts Vis. Prof., Inst. Econ., Univ. Chile, 1962–3, 1964–5; Acting Chief, FAO Mission, Algiers, 1963–4; Fellow, Magdalen Coll. Oxford, 1965–76; Chief, Rural Urban Employment Policies Branch, ILO, 1975–6; Warden Dir., Queen Elizabeth House, Inst. Commonwealth Stud., Univ. Oxford, 1978–9; Chief, ILO Employment Advisory Mission, Ethiopia, 1982.
Degrees BA, Hon. DLitt. Williams Coll., Williamstown, MA, USA, 1960, 1980; BPhil., DPhil. Univ. Oxford, 1962, 1965.
Offices and Honours Pres., Devlp. Stud. Assoc., 1978–80; Pres., Oxford, Branch, UN Assoc., 1982–.
Editorial Duties Ed. Board, *Food Pol.*, 1976–9, *OEP*, 1979–; Exec. Ed, *WD*, 1978–9.
Principal Fields of Interest 121 Economic Studies of Less Industrialised Countries; 717 Land Reform and Land Use; 443 International Aid.
Publications *Books:* 1. *Underdevelopment in Spanish America* (A&U, MIT Press, 1969; transl., Spanish, Amorrurtu Editores, 1972); 2. *Planning Development* (with J. Enos), (Addison-Wesley, 1970; transl., Spanish, Fondo de Cultura Economica, 1975); 3. *Financing Development in Latin America*, ed. (Macmillan, 1971); 4. *Growth and Inequality in Pakistan*, co-ed. (with A. R. Khan), (Macmillan, 1972); 5. *The Political Economy of Agrarian Change* (Macmillan, Harvard Univ. Press, 1974, 1979; transls., Spanish, Fondo de Cultura Economica, 1982, Hindi, Macmillan of India, 1983); 6. *Land Concentration and Rural Poverty* (Macmillan, Holmes & Meier, 1976, 1981; transl., Spanish, Fondo de Cultura Economica, 1983); 7. *International Inequality and National Poverty* (Macmillan, Holmes & Meier, 1978); 8. *The Transition to Egalitarian Development* (with J. James), (Macmillan, St Martin's Press, 1981); 9. *Growth and Equality in Rural China* (with A. Saith), (Maruzen, 1981).

Articles: 1. 'A note on wages, prices and unemployment', *OBES*, 24(3), Aug. 1962; 2. 'Customs unions and Latin American integration' (with R. Ffrench-Davis), *J. Common Market Stud.*, 6(1), Oct. 1965; 3. 'An evaluation of Pakistan's third five year plan' (with B. Glassburner), *JDS*, 2(4), July 1966; 4. 'Foreign assistance: objectives and consequences' (with J. Enos), *EDCC*, 18(3), April 1970, repr. in Spanish, *Trimestre Economico*, 60(1), March, 1973; 5. 'Reflections on Latin American development', *OEP*, 18(1), March 1966, repr. in *Latin America: Problems in Economic Development*, ed. C. T. Nisbet (Free Press, 1969), and *The Political Economy of Development*, eds. N. T. Uphoff and W. F. Ilchman (Univ. California Press, 1972); 6. 'The effect of aid and other resource transfers in savings and growth in less-developed countries: a comment', *EJ*, 83, Sept. 1973; 7. 'Rural poverty and development alternative in South and Southeast Asia: some policy issues' (with A. Ghose), *Development and Change*, 2(4), Oct. 1980; 8. 'Institutional change and income distribution in the Chinese countryside' (with K. Griffin), *OBES*, 45(3), Aug. 1983.
Principal Contributions Early work on international economic issues in Latin America, industrialisation within the context of regional integration, and the role of foreign capital. The influence of the 'structuralist' school of thought is evident in my *Underdevelopment in Spanish America* as well as in the publications in Spanish I wrote about the same time. A year with the Planning Commission in Algeria stimulated an interest in planning (which resulted in *Planning Development* and several papers in Spanish and English), in problems of development finance (which resulted in the edited book on *Financing Development in Latin America* and papers on Pakistan) and in problems of rural development. Subsequently I worked on land reform, particularly in Latin America and North Africa (and published *Land Concentration and Rural Poverty*), on the 'green revolution' in Asia and Latin America (which resulted in *The Political Economy of Agrarian Change*), on

trends in rural poverty in Asia (see ILO, *Poverty and Landlessness in Rural Asia*) and on communal tenure systems (particularly in China and Ethiopa).

A period in Geneva with the ILO enabled me to pursue interests in general development strategy with a focus on employment and income distribution and to participate in the drafting of the ILO's *Employment, Growth and Basic Needs*, a document which had much influence on thinking about economic development in the late 1970s. Short-term policy questions and problems of economic management, however, were largely overlooked in the original 'basic needs' literature and consequently I was prompted to turn my attention to *The Transition to Egalitarian Development*. More recently, opportunities to travel and undertake research in China have led me to concentrate my efforts on that country.

GRILICHES, ZVI

Born 1930, Kaunas, Lithuania.
Current Post Prof. Econ., Harvard Univ., Cambridge, MA, 1969–.
Past Posts Ass. Prof. Econ., Univ. Chicago, 1956–9; Vis. Prof. Econ. Res. Center, Catholic Univ., Santiago, Chile, 1959; Res. Assoc., NBER, NY, 1959–60; Assoc. Prof., Prof. Econ., Univ. Chicago, 1960–4, 1964–9; Vis. Prof. Econ. Inst., Netherlands School Econ., Rotterdam, Hebrew Univ., Jerusalem, 1963–4, 1972; Vis. Fellow, Inst. Advanced Stud., Einstein Vis. Fellow, Hebrew Univ., Jerusalem, 1977–8, 1984; Vis. Prof., Ecole des Hautes Etudes en Sciences Sociales, Paris, 1984.
Degrees BS, MS (Agric. Econ.) Univ. Cal. Berkeley, 1953, 1954; MA, PhD Univ. Chicago, 1955, 1957.
Offices and Honours Merit and Prizes, Amer. Farm Econ. Assoc., Best Published Res. Report, 1958, 1959, 1960, 1964; Fellow, Pres., Em Soc., 1964, 1975; AAAS, 1965, ASA, 1965, Amer. Assoc. Advancement Science, 1965; John Bates Clark Medal, Exec. Comm., Vice-Pres. AEA, 1965, 1979–82, 1984; Member, Nat. Academy Sciences, 1975.

Editorial Duties Co-ed., *Em*, 1969–77.
Principal Fields of Interest 211 Econometric Methods; 621 Technological Change; 852 Human Capital.
Publications *Books:* 1. *Economies of Scale and the Form of the Production Function* (with V. Ringstad), (N-H, 1971); 2. *Price Indexes and Quality Change*, ed. (Harvard Univ. Press, 1971); 3. *Patents, Invention and Economic Change, by Jacob Schmookler*, co-ed. (with L. Hurwicz), (Harvard Univ. Press, 1972); 4. *Income Distribution and Economic Inequality*, co-ed. (with W. Krelle, H. Krupp, and O. Kyn), (Campus Verlag, 1978); 5. *Handbook of Econometrics*, 3 vols., co-ed. (with M. Intriligator), (N-H, 1983, 1984, 1984); 6. *R&D, Patents, and Productivity*, ed. (Univ. Chicago Press, 1984).

Articles: 1. 'Hybrid corn: an exploration in the economics of technological change', *Em*, 25(4), Oct. 1957, repr. in *Readings in the Economics of Agriculture*, eds. K. A. Fox and D. G. Johnson (Richard D. Irwin, 1969), and in *Selected Readings in Econometrics from Econometrica*, eds. J. W. Hooper and M. Nerlove (MIT Press, 1970); 2. 'Research, cost and social returns: hybrid corn and related innovations', *JPE*, 66(5), Oct. 1958, repr. in *Agriculture in Economic Development*, eds. J. Eicher and K. Witt (McGraw-Hill, 1964), and transl. Spanish, Limma-Wiley, 1968, German, *Forschungs-ökonomie und Forschungs-Politik*, ed. J. Naumann (Ernst Klett Verlag, 1970); and *Penguin Modern Economic Readings: The Economics of Technological Change*, ed. N. Rosenberg (Penguin, 1971); 3. 'The sources of measured productivity growth: US Agriculture, 1940–1960', *JPE*, 71(4), 1963, repr. in *Penguin Modern Economic Readings, op. cit.*; 4. 'Distributed lags: a survey', *Em*, 35(1), Jan. 1967, repr. in *Readings in Econometric Theory*, eds. J. M. Dowling and F. R. Glahe (Colorado Assoc. Univ. Press, 1970); 5. 'The explanation of productivity change' (with D. Jorgenson), *REStud*, 34(3), July 1967, repr. in *Penguin Modern Economics Readings: Growth Economics*, ed. A. K. Sen (Penguin, 1970), and in

Survey Current Bus., pt. 2, May 1969, pt. 3, May 1972; 6. 'Returns to research and development expenditures in the private sector', in *New Developments in Productivity Measurement*, eds. J. W. Kendrick and B. Vaccara (Univ. Chicago Press, 1980); transl., Russian, in *Proceedings of the First Soviet American Symposium on the Effectiveness of Information Systems* (Council of Ministers USSR, 1976); 7. 'Estimating the returns to schooling: some econometric problems', *Em*, 45(1), Jan. 1977; 8. 'Missing data and self-selection in large panels' (with B. H. Hall and J. A. Hausman), *Annales de L'INSEE*, 30–31, 1978; 9. 'Sibling models and data in economics: beginnings of a survey', *JPE*, 87(5), pt. 2, Oct. 1979; 10. 'Comparing productivity growth: an exploration of French and U.S. industrial and firm data' (with J. Mairesse), *Europ. ER*, 21(1–2), March–April 1983.

Principal Contributions My work has focussed primarily on the economics of technological change and on econometric problems that arise in trying to study this and related topics. One of the first to analyse the diffusion of an innovation (hybrid corn) within an economic framework and to compute rates of return to public R&D investments. Showed that measurement issues are paramount in interpreting productivity growth data and estimated the contribution of education, R&D, and economies of scale to the growth of US agriculture and industry. Revived the 'hedonic' regression method for analysing quality change issues, estimated production functions using firm data in Norway and the US, and analysed the effects of schooling and ability on earnings using individual and sibling data. Data-instigated contributions to econometric methodology include developments in and exposition of specification analysis, statistical aggregation, distributed lag models, sample selection bias, and measurement error and other unobservable variance component models. Recent work has focussed again on the contribution of R&D to productivity growth and on patents as an indicator of inventive activity.

GRONAU, Reuben

Born 1937, Tel Aviv, Israel.
Current Post Prof. Econ., Hebrew Univ. Jerusalem, Israel, 1983–.
Past Posts Res. Supervisor, Maurice Falk Inst. Econ. Res., Israel, 1968–71, 1972–4; Post-doctoral Fellow, Univ. Chicago, 1971–2; Assoc. Prof., Hebrew Univ., 1974–83; Res. Assoc., NBER, 1972–; Vis. Prof., UCLA, 1972, MIT, 1980–1; Vis. Assoc. Prof., Stanford Univ., 1975–6.
Degrees BA, MA Hebrew Univ., Jerusalem, 1960, 1963; PhD Columbia Univ., 1967.
Principal Fields of Interest 821 Theory of Labour Market; 615 Economics of Transportation; 824 Labour Market Studies.
Publications *Books:* 1. *The Value of Time in Passenger Transportations* (Columbia Univ. Press, 1970); 2. *The Supply of Labor and Wages of Israeli Married Women* (Hebrew), (Maurice Falk Inst. Econ. Res., 1979).
Articles: 1. 'The effect of children on the housewife's value of time', *JPE*, 81(2), pt. 2, March–April 1973; 2. 'The intrafamily allocation of time: the value of housewives' time', *AER*, 65(4), Sept. 1973; 3. 'Wage comparisons — a selectivity bias', *JPE*, 82(6), Nov.–Dec. 1974; 4. 'Leisure, home production and work — the theory of the allocation of time revisited', *JPE*, 85(6), Dec. 1977; 5. 'Home production — a forgotten industry', *REStat*, 62(3), Aug. 1980.
Principal Contributions The analysis of the economic activity in the home sector; the analysis and estimation of the value people assign to their time; the analysis of the factors determining the allocation of time in the home sector; and the evaluation of the output of this sector. This analysis led to improved estimates of the factors determining wives' labour force participation and their earnings, allowing for selectivity biasses.

GROSSMAN, Gregory

Born 1921, Kiev, USSR.
Current Post Prof. Econ., Univ. Cal. Berkeley, CA, USA, 1962–.

Past Posts Econ., US Dept. State, Washington, DC, 1948–50; Econ., Board Governors, Fed. Reserve System, Washington, DC, 1948–50; Ass. Prof., Assoc. Prof. Econ., Univ. Cal. Berkeley, 1953–8, 1958–62.

Degrees BS (Commerce), MA Univ. Cal. Berkeley, 1941, 1943; PhD Harvard Univ., 1953.

Offices and Honours Pres., Western Slavic Assoc., 1971–2, Assoc. Comparative Econ. Stud., 1972; Amer. Assoc. Advancement of Slavic Stud., 1980–1; Fulbright Grant, Italy, 1960–1; Guggenheim Foundation Fellow, 1964–5.

Editorial Duties Ed. Boards, *J. Contemporary Econ.*, *Slavic Rev.*

Principal Fields of Interest 052 Social and Communist Economic Systems; 053 Comparative Economic Systems; 124 Economic Studies of Centrally Planned Economies.

Publications *Books:* 1. *Soviet Statistics of Physical Output of Industrial Commodities* (Princeton Univ. Press, 1960); 2. *Value and Plan*, ed. (Univ. Cal. Press, 1960); 3. *Economic Systems* (Prentice-Hall, 1967, 1974); 4. *Essays in Socialism and Planning in Honor of Carl Landauer*, ed. (Prentice-Hall, 1971).

Articles: 1. 'Gold and the sword: money in the Soviet command economy', in *Industrialization in Two Systems*, ed. H. Rosovsky (Wiley, 1966); 2. 'The solidary society: a philosophical issue in communist economic reforms', in *Essays in Socialism and Planning in Honor of Carl Landauer*, *op. cit.*; 3. 'Price control, incentives and innovation in the Soviet economy', in *The Socialist Price Mechanism*, ed. A. Abouchar (Duke Univ. Press, 1977); 4. 'The party as manager and entrepreneur', in *Entrepreneurship in Imperial Russia and the Soviet Union*, eds. G. Guroff and E. V. Carstensen (Princeton Univ. Press, 1983); 5. 'Economics of virtuous haste: a view of Soviet industrialization and institutions', in *Marxism, Central Planning and the Soviet Economy*, ed. P. Desai (MIT Press, 1983); 6. 'Scare capital and Soviet doctrine', *QJE*, 67(3), August 1953, repr. in *Readings on the Soviet Economy*, ed. F. D. Holzman (Richard

D. Irwin, 1962); 7. 'The structure and organization of the Soviet economy', *Slavic Rev.*, 21(2), June 1962; 8. 'Notes for a theory of the command economy', *Soviet Stud.*, 15(2), Oct. 1963, repr. in *Comparative Economic Systems: Models and Cases*, ed. M. Bornstein (Richard D. Irwin, 1965); 9. 'The "second economy" of the USSR', *Problems of Communism*, 26(5), Sept.–Oct. 1977.

Principal Contributions It was by happenstance that I came to a life-long career of study and teaching of the Soviet and Soviet-type economies. Grown up in the interwar years in a Russian-speaking milieu (outside the USSR, thank God), I had as an undergraduate the good fortune of meeting the late Alexander Gerschenkron, who introduced me to the scholarly study of the Soviet economy, and later, after the war, helped steer me into government research, doctoral study, and an academic career. Thanks to him I have tended to see the Soviet economy within its social and historical continua, that is, inseparable from the country's polity and culture, ruling ideology, and history.

This made me somewhat of a generalist in the study of the Soviet economy: I tend to look at it holistically, as a system, as a seamless web (perhaps paradoxically, but defensibily, for an economy chronically characterised by mirco- and macrodisequilibria in the theorist's sense).

Accordingly, I gravitated toward systemic investigation of the 'common economy' and of attempts at reforming it, the influence of doctrine on the system, the place of money in the command economy, and the like. I have been interested in the antinomy between administrative authority and 'economic' forces, a conflict that helps sustain the chronic repressed inflation and its reverse effects on the system. More recently, I've been absorbed in a study of the 'second economy' the aggregate of legal-private and illegal activities, which in large measure is both a creature of and a shaping influence on the command system.

346 GROSSMAN

GROSSMAN, Henryk*

Dates and Birthplace 1881–1950,
Cracow, Austro-Hungary.
Posts Held Prof. Polit. Science, Free
Polish Univ., Warsaw, 1922–5; Inst.
Social Res., Univ. Frankfurt, 1925–30;
Prof., Univ. Frankfurt, 1930–3, Univ.
Leipzig, 1949–50.
Publications *Books:* 1. *Simonde de
Sismondi et ses théories économiques*
(1924); 2. *Das Akkumulations- und
Zusammenbruchsgesetz des Kapitalist-
ischen Systems* (1929).
Articles: 1. 'The evolutionist revolt
against classical economics', *JPE*, 51,
Oct., Dec. 1943.
Career Marxist scholar whose writ-
ings include one of the many attempts
to work out the Marxian theory of busi-
ness cycles. His theory of capitalist
breakdown roused a storm of controv-
ersy among Marxist theorists in the interwar period.
Secondary Literature P. M. Sweezy,
The Theory of Capitalist Development
(OUP, 1942), chap. 11.

GROSSMAN, Herschel I.

Born 1939, Philadelphia, PA, USA.
Current Post Merton P. Stoltz Prof.
Social Sciences, Prof. Econ., Brown
Univ., Providence, RI, USA, 1973–.
Past Posts Ass. Prof., Assoc. Prof.,
Brown Univ., 1964–73; Fellow, Univ.
Essex, England, 1969; Simon Sr. Res.
Fellow, Univ. Manchester, England,
1971; Vis. Scholar, State Univ. NY,
Buffalo, 1978–; Inst. Advanced Stud.,
Vienna, 1979–; European Univ. Inst.,
Florence, 1980; Univ. Louis Pasteur,
Strasbourg, 1982.
Degrees BA Univ. Virginia, 1960;
BPhil Univ. Oxford, 1962; PhD Johns
Hopkins Univ., 1965.
Offices and Honours Guggenheim
Foundation Fellow, 1979–80; Res.
Assoc., NBER, 1979.
Editorial Duties Ed. Board, *J Mon E*
1977–, *AER*, 1980–3; Book Rev. Ed., *J
Mon E*, 1984–.
Principal Fields of Interest 023
Macroeconomic Theory.
Publications *Books:* 1. *Money, Em-
ployment and Inflation* (with R. J.

Barro), (CUP, 1976; transl. Chinese,
Bank Taiwan Classics Econ., 1981,
Japanese, McGraw-Hill Kogakusha,
1982, Italian, Cedam, 1982); 2. *Money,
Expectations and Business Cycles:
Essays in Macroeconomics* (Academic
Press, 1981).
Articles: 1. 'A general disequilib-
rium model of income and employ-
ment' (with R. J. Barro), *AER*, 61(1),
March 1971, repr. in *Revista Espanola
de Economia*, 1975, and *Desequilibrio,
Inflacion Y Desempleo* (Editorial
VicensVives, 1978), and *Modern
Macroeconomics*, eds. P. Korliras and
R. Thorn (Harper & Row, 1979), and
*On the Reappraisal of Keynesian Econ-
omics*, ed. T. Hanawa (Toyo Keizai
Shinposha, 1980), and *Die Neue
Makroökonomik*, eds. J. Hagemann,
L. Kurz, and D. Schafer (Campus
Verlag, 1981); 2. 'Money, interest and
prices in market disequilibrium', *JPE*,
75(5), Sept.–Oct. 1971, repr. in *Revista
Espanola de Economia*, 1975, and *On
the Reappraisal of Keynesian Economics*, ed. T. Hanawa (Toyo Keizai
Shinposha, 1980); 3. 'A choice-theoretic
model of an income-investment accelerator', *AER*, 62(4), Sept. 1972; 4.
'Aggregate demand, job search and
employment', *JPE*, 77(4), Nov.–Dec.
1973; 5. 'Money balances, commodity
inventories, and inflationary expectations' (with A. Policano), *JPE*, Dec.
1975; 6. 'Risk shifting, layoffs and seniority', *J Mon E*, 4(4), Nov. 1978; 7.
'Rational, expectations, business cycles, and government behavior', in
*Rational Expectations and Economic
Policy* ed. S. Fisher (Univ. Chicago
Press, 1980); 8. 'Incomplete information, risk shifting and employment fluctuations', *REStud*, 48(2), April 1981; 9.
'Risk shifting, statistical discrimination, and the stability of earnings' (with
W. T. Trepeta), in *Studies in Labor
Markets*, ed. S. Rosen (Univ. Chicago
Press, 1981); 10. 'Tests of equilibrium
macroeconomics using contemporan-
eous monetary data' (with J. Boschen),
J Mon E, 8(4), Nov. 1982.
Principal Contributions The principal motivation for my research has
been to discover a theory of the connection between money and fluctuations in
economic activity that is consistent with

maximising behaviour by individual economic agents. This effort has involved the study of non-market-clearing models, models of the sharing of risk between workers and employers, and models of incomplete information about monetary disturbances. Although empirically motivated, the content of my early work was largely theoretical. In contrast, stimulated by the integration of theory and econometrics made possible by the postulate of rational expectations, much of my recent work has involved the use of data in formal hypothesis testing. Although the primary goal of understanding observed relations between nominal and real aggregate variables has remained elusive, my efforts have helped to clarify the nature of the mystery that the observed business cycle presents — specifically, the difficulty of reconciling this aspect of reality with the neoclassical postulate of maximisation. These efforts also have led me into a number of lengthy and productive excursions involving research on such diverse problems as the theory of Walrasian models without recontracting, the efforts of suppressed inflation, the relation between money balances and commodity inventories, the nature of implicit labour contracts and the form of fluctuations in employment and earnings, the effects of minimum wages, and the existence of rational asset price bubbles. My current work includes a theoretical and empirical research programme for positive macroeconomic analysis that incorporates choice-theoretic modelling of monetary policy.

GROVES, Theodore Francis, Jr.

Born 1941, Whitehall, WI, USA.
Current Post Prof. Econ., Univ. Cal. San Diego, CA, USA, 1978–.
Past Posts Ass. Prof. Econ., Univ. Wisconsin-Madison, 1969–73; Assoc. Prof., Prof., Managerial Econ. and Decision Sciences, Northwestern Univ., 1973–6, 1976–8; Vis. Prof. Econ., Stanford Univ., 1977–8.
Degrees BA Harvard Univ., 1964; MA, PhD Univ. Cal. Berkeley, 1966, 1970.

Offices and Honours Fellow, Em Soc, 1977.
Editorial Duties Foreign Co-ed., *REStud*, 1976–9.
Principal Fields of Interest 020 General Economic Theory; 511 Organisation and Decision Theory; 053 Comparative Economic Systems.
Publications *Books: Adaptive Economic Models*, co-ed. (with R. Day), (Academic Press, 1975).
Articles: 1. 'Incentives in teams', *Em*, 41(4), July 1973; 2. 'Incentives and public inputs' (with M. Loeb), *J Pub E*, 4(3), Aug. 1975; 3. 'Optimal allocation of public goods: a solution to the "free rider" problem' (with J. Ledyard), *Em*, 45(4), May 1977; 4. 'Incentives in a divisionalized form' (with M. Loeb), *Management Science*, 25(3), March 1977; 5. 'Efficient collective choice when compensation is possible', *REStud*, 46(2), April 1979; 6. 'The existence of efficient and incentive compatible equilibria with public goods', *Em*, 48(6), Sept. 1980; 7. 'Efficiency of resource allocation by uniformed demand' (with S. Hart), *Em*, 50(6), Nov. 1982; 8. 'The usefulness of demand forecasts for team resource allocation in a dynamic environment', *REStud*, 50(3), July 1983.
Principal Contributions Discovery of the general class of mechanisms (Groves mechanisms) with the property that agents have an incentive to reveal truthfully their preferences among collective choices, thus enabling an optimal group choice to be made. Developed (with M. Loeb) a specific member of the class and solved the partial equilibrium 'free rider' problem with public inputs. Co-discovery (with J. Ledyard) of the first general equilibrium mechanism (the Groves–Ledyard mechanism) for solving the general 'free rider' problem with public goods. The mechanism provides consumers with sufficient incentives to reveal their true preferences for public goods at an equilibrium. Recently, have been working on incentive mechanisms for optimal risk sharing, group-incentive compatible mechanisms, and incentives in the theory of planning.

GRUBEL, Herbert Gunter

Born 1934, Frankfurt-am-Main, Germany.

Current Post Prof. Econ., Simon Fraser Univ., Vancouver, British Columbia, Canada, 1972–.

Past Posts Ass. Instr., Yale Univ., 1961–2; Ass. Prof., Stanford Univ., 1962–3; Ass. Prof., Univ. Chicago, 1963–6; Assoc. Prof., Univ. Penn., 1966–70; Res. Fellow, ANU, 1969; Pol. Analyst, US Treasury Dept., 1971; Vis. Res. Fellow, Nuffield Coll. Oxford, 1974–5; Vis. Prof., Univ. Nairobi, Kenya, 1978–9; Univ. Cape Town, S. Africa, 1984.

Degrees Abitur Germany, 1954; BA Rutgers Univ., 1958; PhD Yale Univ., 1962.

Offices and Honours Exec. Comm., *CEA*, 1974–7; Pres. N. Amer. Econ. Stud. Assoc., 1980–1.

Editorial Duties Assoc. Ed, *J Fin*, 1972–4; Ed. Board, *Fraser Inst.*, 1975–.

Principal Fields of Interest 400 International Economics; 300 Domestic Monetary and Fiscal Theory; 910 Welfare, Health & Education.

Publications *Books:* 1. *World Monetary Reform*, ed. (Stanford Univ. Press, 1963); 2. *Forward Exchange* (Stanford Univ. Press, 1966); 3. *The International Monetary System* (Penguin, 1969, 1984); 4. *Effective Tariff Protection*, co-ed. (with H. G. Johnson), (General Agreement on Tariffs and Trade-GATT, 1971); 5. *Intra-Industry Trade* (with P. J. Lloyd), (Macmillan, 1975); 6. *International Economics* (Richard D. Irwin, 1977, 1981); 7. *Brain Drain* (with A. D. Scott), (Wilfred Laurier Univ. Press, 1977); 8. *Unemployment Insurance*, co-ed. (with M. Walker), (Fraser Inst., 1978); 9. *The Real Cost of the BC Milk Board* (Fraser Inst., 1983); 10. *Free Economic Zones* (Fraser Inst., 1983).

Articles: 1. 'Benefits & costs of being the world's banker', *Nat. Banking Rev.*, Dec. 1964; 2. 'The international flow of human capital' (with A. D. Scott), *AER*, 56(2), May 1966; 3. 'Intra-industry specialization and the pattern of trade', *CJE*, 33, Aug. 1967; 4. 'Internationally diversified portfolios: welfare gains and capital flows', *AER*,

58(5), Dec. 1968; 5. 'Risk, uncertainty and moral hazard', *J. Risk and Insurance*, 38(1), March 1971; 6. 'The case for optimum exchange rate stability', *WA*, 100(3), 1973; 7. 'Taxation and rates of return from some US Asset holdings abroad', *JPE*, 82(3), May–June 1974; 8. 'The effects of unemployment insurance on the US rate of unemployment' (with D. R. Maki) *WA*, 112(2), 1976; 9. 'Towards a theory of free economic zones', *WA*, 118(1), 1982; 10. 'A theory of optimum regional associations', in *The Economics of Common Currencies*, eds. H. Grubel, H. G. Johnson and A. Swoboda (A&U, 1973).

Principal Contributions After my thesis work on forward exchange models, I wrote *The International Monetary System*, which has gone through four editions. It represents the only existing attempt to construct a price-theoretic model of an efficient international monetary system and to use it for an evaluation of theoretical prototypes and historical experiences.

In later years I have occupied myself with empirical studies which have had important implications for received theory and current policy issues. These studies covered brain drain (human capital migration), intra-industry trade (trade in differentiated products), international capital flow (diversified portfolios, taxation), effective tariff protection, moral hazard effects (insurance induced unemployment), free economic zones (partial deregulation), and multinational banking. My text *International Economics* contains a comprehensive neoclassical treatment of international trade and finance.

GRUNFELD, Yehuda*

Dates and Birthplace 1930–60, Israel.

Posts Held Ass. Prof., Univ. Chicago, 1957–8; Lect. Econ. and Stats., Sr. Econ., Falk Project Econ. Res., Israel, 1958–60.

Degrees BA, MA Hebrew Univ. Jerusalem, 1953, 1955; PhD Univ. Chicago, 1958.

Offices and Honours McKinsey Award for Best Article in Economics.

Publications *Articles:* 1. 'The effect of the per diem rate on the efficiency and size of the American railroad freight-car fleet', *J Bus*, 32, Jan. 1959; 2. 'The determinants of corporate investment', in *The Demand for Durable Goods*, ed. A. C. Harberger (Univ. Chicago Press, 1960); 3. 'Is aggregation necessarily bad?' (with Z. Griliches), *REStat*, 42, Feb. 1960; 4. 'The interpretation of cross section estimates in a dynamic model', *Em*, 29, July 1961.

Career Empirical econometric work and econometric theory. At the time of his death, he was preparing to study the economic aspects of education in Israel.

GUITTON, Henri

Born 1904, St-Etienne, Loire, France.
Current Post Prof. d'Analyse Econ. et de Statistique, Univ. Paris I, Panthéon-Sorbonne.
Degree Hon. Dr Univ. Liège, 1930.
Offices and Honours Member, l'Inst. de France; Pres., l'Académie des Sciences Morales et Politiques; Member, l'Académie Nationale dei Lincei, Rome; Former member, Section de Conjonctur, Conseil Econ. et Social; Past-Pres., Commission des Etudes Econ. du CNRS.
Principal Fields of Interest 020 General Economic Theory.
Publications *Books:* 1. *Essai sur la loi de King* (Sirey, 1938); 2. *Les fluctuations économiques* (Sirey, 1951); 3. *L'objet de l'économie politique* (Rivière, 1951); 4. *A la recherche du temps économique* (Fayard, 1970); 5. *De l'imperfection en économie* (Calmann Levy, 1979).
Principal Contributions A wide variety of topics of both micro- and macroeconomics.

GUTOWSKI, Armin Ferdinand

Born 1930, Nuremberg, W. Germany.
Current Post Pres., Inst. für Wirtschaftsforschung, Hamburg; Prof. Econ., Univ. Hamburg, 1978–.
Past Posts Res. Assoc., Forschungs-

inst. für Wirtschaftspolitik, Univ. Mainz, 1953–66; Deputy Chief Econ., Chief Econ. Adviser, Kreditanstalt für Wiederaufbau, Frankfurt, 1966–7, 1969–78; Prof. Econ., Dir., Tropeninstitut, Univ. Giessen, 1967–70; Prof. Econ., Univ. Frankfurt, 1970–8.
Degrees Diplom-Volkswirt, Dr Rer. Pol., Habilitation Univ. Mainz, 1952, 1957, 1967.
Offices and Honours Rockefeller Foundation Fellow, Univs. Cal. Berkeley, Princeton, Chicago, 1960–1; Member, Council Econ. Experts Fed. Republic Germany (Sachverständigenrat), 1970–8; Member, Board Advisers, German Econ. Ministry, 1970–; Member, Deutsches Forum fur Entwicklungspolitik, 1970–3; Board Dirs., Mont Pelerin Soc., 1970–4; Adviser, Govt. People's Republic China, 1979–; Member, Joint Comm. Staff Compensation Issues World Bank and IMF, 1977–8, Cons. Group, Internat. Econ. and Monetary Affairs (Group of Thirty), 1978–, Kronberger Kreis, 1981–, Comité de Patronage, Inst. Econ. de Paris, 1982–, Academic Council, *J. Econ. Affairs*, London, 1983–, UN Comm. Devlp. Planning, 1984–, Bundesverdienstkreuz 1. Klasse, W. Germany, 1979.
Editorial Duties Ed. Board, *Wirtschaft und Wettbewerb*, 1973–9; Co-ed., *Hamburger Jahrbuch für Wirtschafts- und Gesellschaftspolitik*, 1980–.
Principal Fields of Interest 130 Economic Fluctuations; Forecasting; Stabilisation; and Inflation; 300 Domestic Monetary and Fiscal Theory and Institutions; 400 International Economics.
Publications *Books:* 1. *Knostruktions- und Entwicklungsaufträge* (Quelle & Meyer, 1960); 2. *Wirtschafgliche Weinbaupolitik* (Quelle & Meyer, 1962); 3. *Pressefreiheit. Entwurf eines Gesetzes zum Schutz freier Meinungsbildung und Dokumentation des arbeitskreises Pressefreiheit* (with H. Armbruster, *et al.*), (Luchterhand, 1970); 4. *Konglomerate Unternehmensgrösse und wirtschaftliche Macht* (J. C. B. Mohr, P. Siebeck, 1971); 5. *International Monetary Problems* (with F. A. Lutz and F. Machlup), (AEI, 1972); 6. *East-West Trade at a Crossroads. Economic Relations with the Soviet Union and*

Eastern Europe (with M. Matsukawa and R. V. Rossa), (NYU Press, 1982; transl., German, Verlag Weltarchiv, 1984); 7. *Währung, Geldwert, Wettbewerb-Entscheidungen für Morgen, Jahresgutachten 1971–2; Gleicher Rang für den Geldwert, 1972–3; Mut zur Stabilisierung, 1973–4; Vollbeschäftigung für Morgen, 1974–5; Vor dem Aufschwung, 1975–6; Zeit zum Investieren, 1976–7; Mehr Wachstum, mehr Beschäftigung, 1977–8* (with O. Sievert, *et al.*), (Verlag W. Kohlhammer, 1971); 8. *Analyse der Subventionspolitik, Ergänzungsband 4 zum HWWA Strukturbericht 1983* (with E. Thiel and M. Weilepp), (Verlag Weltarchiv, 1984); 9. *International Capital Movements Debt and Monetary System*, co-ed. (Hase & Köhler, 1984).

Articles: 1. 'Theoretical approaches to a concept of supplier's power', *German Econ. Rev.*, 11(3), 1973; 2. 'Brauchen wir neue Instrumente der Kreditpolitik?', in *Währungsstabilität in einer integrierten Welt. Beitrage zur Geldtheorie und Geldpolitik* (Verlag Kohlhammer, 1974); 3. 'Chances for price-level stability in various international monetary systems', in *The Phenomenon of Worldwide Inflation*, eds. D. I. Meiselmann and A. B. Laffer (AEI, 1975); 4. 'How can the world afford OPEC oil?' (with K. Farmanfarmaian, *et al.*), *Foreign Affairs*, 53(2), Jan. 1975; 5. 'Statement', in *Issues at the Summit*, Joint Econ. Comm., US Congress, 95th Session, April 1977 (US Govt. Printing Office, 1978); 6. 'Realer Wechselkurs, Wettbewerbsfähigkeit und Beschäftigung — Zur Schlüsselrolle der Geldpolitik', in *Theorie und Politik der internationalen Wirtschaftsbeziehungen*, eds. K. Borchard and F. Holzheu (G. Fischer Verlag, 1980); 7. 'From shock therapy to gradualism — anti-inflationary policy in Germany from 1973 to 1979', in *Shock Therapy or Gradualism? A Comparative Approach to Anti-Inflation Policies*, eds. A. Gutowsky, H. E. Scharrer and H. H. Härtel (Group of Thirty, 1981); 8. 'Entwicklungschancen der Volksrepublik China', *Bankhistorisches Archiv, Zeitschrift zur Bankengeschichte*, Heft 1, 1982; 9. 'Zur Theorie und Praxis der unabhängigen wirt-schaftswissenschaftlichen Politikberatung', in *Hamburger Jahrbuch für Wirtschafts- und Gessellschaftspolitik*, 28 (J. C. B. Mohr, 1983); 10. 'Limits to international indebtedness', in *International Lending in a Fragile World Economy* (Martinus Nijhoff, 1983).

Principal Contributions My first book (1960) was on a very practical matter, namely, how public institutions should procure goods which have not yet been developed or which are of a sophisticated technical nature; I recommended a two-stage-competitive procurement procedure, the first — based on a functional specification — for the procurement of the blueprints including patents and other property rights, the second — based on a constructional specification — for the purchase of the good itself. My second and perhaps main contribution was a new approach to the theory of supply in my unpublished Habilitation thesis (1967), which resulted in several published articles: I derived the necessary and sufficient conditions for the existence of market power from a dynamic theory of market entry. I also contested the prevailing theory of the entry-preventing price, showing that the expected price after entry was decisive. The consequences for economic policy of my theoretical works on workable competition were reflected in the chapter on policies regarding restrictions of competition in the German Council of Economic Experts' report 1971–2.

While I was on that council, the emphasis of my work shifted to monetary policy, international monetary systems and, in general, to cyclical and medium-term stabilisation policies. In particular, I contributed to the development of a production-potential-oriented concept of domestic monetary policy which, by and large, was subsequently applied by the German Central Bank (Council's report 1974–5). I did some work on the long-term economic consequences of the oil-price shock and proposed a possible solution to the problems arising from it. I also dealt with the question of how various international monetary systems compare with pure systems of fixed and flexible exchange rates. Finally, in the last few years, I have devoted a great deal of my research work to the determinants of the capacity of developing countries to service external debts.

H

HABAKKUK, Hrothgar John

Born 1915, Barry, S. Wales, UK.
Current Post Retired.
Past Posts Prof. Econ. Hist., Vice-Chancellor, Univ. Oxford, 1950–67, 1973–7; Principal, Jesus Coll. Oxford, 1968–84; Pres., Univ. Coll. Swansea, Wales, 1975–84.
Degrees MA Univ. Camb., 1938; MA Univ. Oxford, 1950; DLitt Univs., Wales, Camb., Kent, Penn.
Offices and Honours Fellow, BA; Council, RES, 1950–69; Pres., Royal Hist. Soc., 1976–80.
Principal Fields of Interest 040 Economic History.
Publications *Books:* 1. *American and British Technology in the Nineteenth Century: The Search for Labour-saving Inventions* (CUP, 1962); 2. *Industrial Organisation Since the Industrial Revolution* (Univ. Southampton, 1968); 3. *Population Growth and Economic Development since 1750* (Leicester Univ. Press, 1971).
Articles: 1. 'Free trade and commercial expansion 1853–1870', in *Cambridge History of the British Empire*, 2 (CUP, 1940); 2 'English population in the eighteenth century', *EHR*, 6(2), 1953; 3. 'Fluctuations in housebuilding in Britain and the United States in the nineteenth century', *JEH*, 22, June 1962; 4. 'The rise and fall of English landed families, 1600–1800', *Royal Hist. Soc. Transactions*, 29–31, 1979–81.
Principal Contributions A restatement of the hypothesis that fertility changes were a major factor in population growth 1750–1830; an exploration of the hypothesis that differences in technology between Britain and USA during nineteenth century were due to differences in factor proportions; in particular that abundance of natural resources in America (a higher land/labour ratio) stimulated substitution of capital for labour and that this substitution was favourable to invention of new methods of production, especially of more mechanised capital-intensive techniques; an attempt to argue that the long swings in investment in America and Britain before 1914 were not inversely related in a systematic way; and studies in English land ownership 1500–1800.

HABERLER, Gottfried

Born 1900, Purkersdorf (near Vienna), Austro-Hungary.
Current Post Resident Scholar, AEI, 1971–.
Past Posts Lect., Prof. Econ. and Stats., Univ. Vienna, 1928–36; Vis. Lect., Prof. Econ., Harvard Univ., 1931–2, 1936–71; Expert, League of Nations, Geneva, 1934–6; Board Governors, Fed. Reserve System, Washington, DC, 1943–4; Cons., US Dept. Treasury, Washington, DC, 1965–78.
Degrees Dr Rer. Pol., Dr Law Univ. Vienna, 1923, 1925; Hon. Dr, Univs. St Gallen, Switzerland, 1949, Saarland, W. Germany, 1967, Innsbruck, 1970, Vienna, 1980.
Offices and Honours Rockefeller Fellow, 1927–9; Pres., Hon Pres., IEA, 1950–1, 1953–; Pres., NBER, 1955; Pres., AEA, 1963; Bernhard Harms Award, Univ. Kiel, W. Germany, 1974; Antonio Feltrinelli Prize, Accademia Nazionale dei Lincei, Rome, Italy, 1981.
Editorial Duties Ed., *QJE*, *REStat*.
Principal Fields of Interest 410 International Trade Theory; 131 Economic Fluctuations; 010 General Economics.
Publications *Books:* 1. *Der Sinn der Indexzahlen* (J. C. B. Mohr, Paul Siebeck, 1927); 2. *Der Internationale Handel* (Verlag Springler, 1933); 3. *The Theory of International Trade, with its Application to Commercial Policy* (William Hodge, Macmillan, 1936); 4. *Prosperity and Depression* (League of Nations, 1937, Harvard Univ. Press, 1958); 5. *Economic Growth and Stability* (Nash Publishing, 1974).
Articles: 1. 'The market for foreign

exchange and the stability of the balance of payments', *Kyk*, 3(3), 1949; 2. 'Some problems in the pure theory of international trade', *EJ*, 60, June 1950; 3. 'International trade and economic development', *Nat. Bank Egypt, 50th Anniversary Commemoration Lectures* (1959); 4. 'Integration and growth of the world economy in perspective', *AER*, 54(1), March 1964; 5. 'The world economy, money and the great depression 1919–1939' (AEI, 1976).

Principal Contributions Clarification of the concept of the 'price level' (value of money) and the methods of measuring its change by price index numbers. Reformulation of the basic theory of classical international trade, the theory of comparative cost, in terms of the modern general equilibrium theory. Derivation of the welfare implications of the reformulated theory of comparative cost which permits the precise formulation of advantages and disadvantages of free trade and protection. The theory of international transfers of reparations and capital. Clarification of the theory of purchasing power parity. Analysis of the advantages and disadvantages of the systems of fixed and fluctuating exchange rates. Synthesis of the major theories of the business cycle. Theoretical analysis of causes and cures of inflation.

Secondary Literature J. N. Bhagwati and J. S. Chipman, 'Salute to Gottfried Haberler on the occasion of his 80th birthday', *J Int E*, 10(3), Aug. 1980.

HADLEY, Arthur Twining*

Dates and Birthplace 1856–1930, New Haven, CT, USA.

Posts Held Prof., Dean, Grad. School, Pres., Yale Univ., 1879, 1892–5, 1899–1921.

Degree BA Yale Univ., 1876.

Offices and Honours Chairman, various Govt. Commissions and Comms.; Pres., AEA, 1898–9.

Publications *Books: 1. Railroad Transportation: Its History and Laws* (1885); 2. *Economics* (1896); 3. *The Relation Between Freedom and Democracy in the Evolution of Democratic Government* (1903); 4. *Standards of*

Public Morality (1907); 5. *Economic Problems of Democracy* (1923).

Career University administrator whose *Economics* was a very effective introduction to the subject, but also an effective apologia for current economic institutions. He was led to seek justifications for his opposition to social change in ethical and political arguments. His major work on railroads (1885) stands at the forefront of the rich literature on railway rates in the nineteenth century.

Secondary Literature M. Lerner, 'Hadley, Arthur Twining', *ESS*, 7; M. Cross and R. E. Ekelund Jr., 'A. T. Hadley on monopoly theory and railway regulation: an American contribution to economic analysis and policy', *HOPE*, 12(2), June 1980.

HAGEN, Everett Einar

Born 1906, Holloway, MN, USA.

Current Post Econ. Cons. Devlp. Countries, PO Box 426, Cataumet, MA, USA, 1972–.

Past Posts Instr., Michigan State Coll., 1937–42; Econ., US War Agencies, 1942–5; Fiscal Econ., US Bureau Budget, 1946–8; Prof., Univ. Illinois, 1948–51; Cons., Govt. Burma, 1951–3; Vis. Prof., Prof. Econ., Prof. Polit. Science, MIT, 1953–8, 1958–72, 1966–72; Dir., MIT Center Internat. Stud., 1970–2; Cons., US ECA, 1948; President's Task Force Foreign Member, Econ. Assistance, 1961, Agency Internat. Devlp., 1965–72; US Council Internat. Chamber Commerce, 1955; Cons., Govt. Japan, 1956, El Salvador, 1962–3, Saudi Arabia, 1968–; Member, US President's Commission Amer. Indian, 1967–8.

Degrees BA St Olaf Coll., 1927; MA (Hist.), PhD Univ. Wisconsin, 1932, 1941; Hon. LLD Michigan State Univ., 1974.

Offices and Honours Guggenheim Foundation Fellow, 1963–4; Guest, Tavistock Inst., London, 1964–5; Pres., Assoc. Comp. Econ., 1967; Sr. Fellow, East-West Center, Honolulu, 1972–3; Member Phi Beta Kappa, AAAS.

Principal Fields of Interest 112

Economic Development Models and Theories; 121 Economic Studies of Developing Countries; 621 Technological Change; Innovation; Research and Development.

Publications *Books:* 1. *Economic Development of Burma* (Nat. Planning Assoc., 1956); 2. *Handbook for Industry Studies* (Free Press, 1958); 3. *On the Theory of Social Change: How Economic Growth Begins* (Dorsey Press, 1962; transls., Korean, Eulyoo, 1965, German, Kiepenheuer & Witsch, 1969); 4. *Economics of Development* (Richard D. Irwin, 1968, 1980; transls., Portuguese, Editora Atlas, 1971, Spanish, Amorrortu Editores, 1971, French, Economica, 1982); 5. *Planning Economic Development*, ed. (Richard D. Irwin, 1963; transl., Spanish, Fondo de Cultura Economica, 1964).

Articles: 1. 'Capital theory in a system with no agents fixed in quantity', *JPE*, 50, Dec. 1942; 2. 'The national output at full employment in 1950' (with M. B. Kirkpatrick), *JPE*, 50, Dec. 1944; 3. 'The consumption function: a review article', *REStat*, 37(1), Feb. 1955; 4. 'An economic justification of protectionism', *QJE*, 72(4), Nov. 1958, 74(3), June 1960; 5. 'Population and economic growth', *AER*, 49(3), June 1959, 50(3), June 1960; 6. 'The use of analytical models in the social sciences', *Amer. J. Sociology*, 67(2), Sept. 1961; 7. 'Analysis of world income and growth, 1955–1965' (with O. Hawrylyshyn), *EDCC*, 18(1), pt. II, Oct. 1969; 8. 'Why economic growth is slow', *WD*, 8(4), April 1980; 9. 'Technological disemployment and economic growth', *JDE*, 10(2), April 1982.

Principal Contributions Apart from my first article, my early work was relevant to wartime economic planning. My work after two years as adviser on economic development to the government of Burma (the advice did not 'take') has dealt in one way or another with the theory and practice of the economic development of low-income countries and of economic aid to development. Mid-career work in this area dealt with the relationship of noneconomic factors to the initiation and rate of modern economic growth; my expositions had some influence on anthropologists and sociologists but it was of little interest to general economists, who do not deal with inter-individual differences. In general, I have argued that economic growth in the LDCs has been no faster not because of peculiar characteristics of those countries, or special barriers, but because of the sheer difficulty of technical advance, and that differences in growth rates are due largely to differences in interest and effectiveness in attacking that process.

In addition I have made three specific contributions. I have argued the irrelevance of the theory of a low-income population growth trap. I have noted that appropriate protection of manufacturing industry increases national output if factor prices in agriculture and manufacturing differ from shadow prices in the usual ways. (Others then noted that subsidies to industry yield still greater gain.) More recently (No. 9 above) I have resurrected the theory of technological unemployment, a sound theory highly relevant to economic growth that was ejected from economic theory during the 1920s and 1930s out of reaction to the excesses of the technocrats.

HAGUE, Douglas Chalmers

Born 1926, Leeds, Yorkshire, England.

Current Post Chairman, Econ. and Social Res. Council, London, England, 1983–.

Past Posts Ass. Tutor Commerce, Birmingham Univ., 1946; Ass. Lect., Lect., Reader Polit. Econ., Univ. London, 1947–9, 1950–6, 1957; Newton Chambers Prof. Econ., Univ. Sheffield, 1957–63; Vis. Prof., Duke Univ., USA, 1960–1; Prof. Applied Econ., Univ. Manchester, 1963–5; Prof. Managerial Econ., Dept. Dir., Manchester Bus. School, 1965–81, 1978–81; Dir. Econ., Models Ltd., 1970–8, The Laird Group, 1976–9.

Offices and Honours Rapporteur, Ed. General, IEA, 1953–78, 1981–; Cons., Secretariat, Nat. Econ. Devlp. Council, 1962–3; Member, UK Treasury Working Party, Management Training

Civil Service, 1965–7; Working Party, Local Govt. Training Board, 1969–70; Dep. Chairman, UK Price Comm., 1977; Member, Council, Manchester Bus. School, 1964–; Chairman, Manchester Industrial Relations Soc., 1964–6; Pres., North-West OR Group, 1967–9; Econ. Adviser, Mrs Thatcher Govt. Election Campaign, 1979; Adviser, UK Prime Minister's Pol. Unit, 1979–83; CBE, Knighted, 1978, 1982; Professorial Fellow, Oxford Centre Management Stud., 1981–.

Principal Fields of Interest 512 Managerial Economics.

Publications *Books:* 1. *A Textbook of Economic Theory* (with A. W. Stonier), (Longmans 1955, 1980); 2. *The Essential of Economics* (with A. W. Stonier), (Longmans, 1955); 3. *The Economics of Man-Made Fibres* (Longmans, 1957); 4. *The Theory of Capital*, ed. (Macmillan, 1961); 5. *Managerial Economics* (Longmans, 1969); 6. *Pricing in Business* (Longmans, 1971); 7. *Britain in the Common Market: A New Business Opportunity* (with M. E. Beesley), (Longmans, 1971); 8. *Devaluation and Pricing Decisions: A Case Study Approach* (with W. E. F. Oakeshott and A. A. Strain), (Longmans, 1974); 9. *Public Policy and Private Interests: The Institutions of Compromise* (with W. J. M. McKenzie and A. Barker), (Macmillan, 1975); 10. *The IRC: An Experiment in Industrial Intervention* (with G. Wilkinson), (Longmans, 1978).

HAHN, Frank Horace

Born 1925, Berlin, Germany.

Current Post Prof. Econ., Univ. Camb., England, 1972–.

Past Posts Lect., Reader Maths. Econ., Univ. Birmingham, 1948–60; Vis. Prof., MIT, 1956–7, 1972–3, 1982–3; Vis. Prof., Univ. Cal. Berkeley, 1959–60; Lect. Econ. Univ. Camb., 1960–6; Prof. Econ., LSE, 1967–72; Taussig Prof., Harvard Univ., 1973–4; Schumpeter Prof., Vienna, 1984.

Degrees BSc, MA Univ. Camb., 1945, 1945; PhD Univ. London, 1950; Hon. Dr Social Science, Univ. Birmingham, 1981; Hon. Dr Litt., Univ. East Anglia, 1984.

Offices and Honours Fellow, Churchill Coll. Camb., 1960–; Center Advanced Stud. Behavioral Sciences, Stanford, 1966–7; BA, Foreign Hon. Member, AAAS.

Editorial Duties Managing Ed., *REStud*, 1963–6; Assoc. Ed., *JET*, 1971–6.

Principal Fields of Interest 021 General Equilibrium Theory; 022 Microeconomic Theory.

Publications *Books:* 1. *The Share of Wages in National Income* (Weidenfeld & Nicolson, 1972); 2. *General Competitive Analysis* (with K. J. Arrow), (Oliver & Boyd, Holden-Day, 1971); 3. *Money and Inflation* (Blackwell, 1982); 4. *Equilibrium and Macroeconomics* (Blackwell, 1984).

Articles: 1. 'The rate of interest and general equilibrium analysis', *EJ*, 65, March 1955; 2. 'Gross substitutes and the dynamic stability of general equilibrium', *Em*, 26, Jan. 1958; 3. 'The stability of growth equilibrium', *QJE*, 74, May 1960, 76, Aug. 1962; 4. 'On the stability of a pure exchange equilibrium, *Int ER*, 3, May 1962; 5. 'A theorem on non-tâtonnement stability' (with T. Negishi), *Em*, 30, July 1962; 6. 'The theory of economic growth: a survey' (with R. C. O. Matthews), *EJ*, 74, Dec. 1964; 7. 'Equilibrium dynamics with heterogeneous capital goods,' *QJE*, 80, Nov. 1966; 8. 'Equilibrium with transactions costs', *Em*, 39(3), May 1971; 9. 'On non-Walrasian equilibria', *REStud*, 45(1), Feb. 1978.

Principal Contributions My first interest was the theory of income distribution which was the subject of my PhD. dissertation. The approach taken was in some respects similar to the theory later proposed by Kaldor. But it also differed from it in crucial respects since I did not abandon marginal productivity and I did not stipulate full employment.

But my real interest from very early acquaintance with economics was in what I took to be the programme of *Value and Capital*: the construction of a rigorous theory of the economy as a whole from a theory of its individual agents. Quite early on (1952) I considered the proper equilibrium notion for an economy with sequential markets, a subject to which I returned some twenty years later (1974). Debreu's splendid book made it clear that such sequential economics had to be considered by any monetary theory. Patinkin's work did not quite provide what was required and I showed that his model always possessed non-monetary equilibria. This direction eventually led me to consider general equilibrium with transaction costs.

At the same time I was active in the 'stability' research of the 1960s. I am most pleased with my joint work with Negishi on stability when trading at 'false' prices is allowed.

The stability interest led to my study of economics with heterogeneous capital goods which showed that finite perfect foresight equilibria had bad properties. Recently I have studied similar problems with overlapping generations. My recent work has been on conjectural equilibria (to get away from perfect competition) and on employment theory and contracts. In between I have tried to show why neo-Ricardian economics and monetarist 'theories' are aberrations.

HAITOVSKY, Yoel

Born 1933, Kovno, Lithuania.
Current Post Prof. Econ. and Stats., Hebrew Univ. Jerusalem, Jerusalem, Israel, 1980–.
Past Posts Teaching Fellow, Harvard Univ., 1961, 1963–4; Stat. Cons., Harvard Computer Center, 1965; Lect., Sr. Lect., Technion, Haifa, Israel, 1965–7; Sr. Lect., Haifa Univ., 1966–7; Res. Fellow, NBER, New York City, 1967–74; Vis. Prof., City Coll. NY, 1968; Sr. Lect., Assoc. Prof., Hebrew Univ., 1969–73; Cons., Bank Israel, 1969–; Res. Fellow, Falk Inst. Econ. Res. in Israel, 1970–1; Vis. Res. Fellow, Univ. Coll. London 1971, 1972–3; Dir., Data Bank Devlp. Div., Israeli Central Bureau Stats., 1973–8; Vis. Prof., CORE, Catholic Univ. Louvain, Belgium, 1974; Dir., Social Science Data Archive, Hebrew Univ., 1973–8; Vis. Chief Scientist, Erasmus Univ.,

Rotterdam, 1977; Vis. Prof., UCLA, 1978–80; Dir., Empirical Res. Unit, Hebrew Univ., 1980–2; Vis. Scholar, Univ. British Columbia, Canada, 1980; Vis. Scientist, Nat. Res. Inst. Math. Sciences, CSIR, Pretoria, S. Africa, 1982.
Degrees BS N. Carolina State Coll., 1961; MA, PhD Harvard Univ., 1963, 1966.
Offices and Honours C. Osward George Annual Award Applied Stats., Inst. Stats. for Young Scientists, 1968; Belgium-Israeli Scientific Exchange Program Fellow, 1974; Erasmus Univ. Res. Fellow, 1974.
Principal Fields of Interest 211 Econometric and Statistical Methods and Models; 212 Construction, Analysis and Use of Econometric Models; 132 Economic Forecasting and Econometric Models.
Publications *Books:* 1. *Regression Estimation from Grouped Observations* (Griffin, 1973); 2. *Forecasts with Quarterly Macro-Econometric Models* (with G. Treyz and V. Su), (Columbia Univ. Press, 1974).
Articles: 1. 'Multicollinearity in regression analysis: a comment', *REStat*, 51(9), Nov. 1969; 2. 'An analysis of the forecasting properties of US econometric models' (with M. K. Evans and G. I. Treyz), in *Econometric Models of Cyclical Behavior*, ed. S. G. Hickman (Columbia Univ. Press, 1972); 3. 'A study of discretionary and non-discretionary fiscal and monetary policies in the context of stochastic macroeconometric models' (with A. Wallace), in *The Business Cycle Today*, ed. V. Zarnowitz (Columbia Univ. Press, 1972); 4. 'On errors of measurement in regression analysis in economics', *Rev. Internat. Stat. Inst.*, 1972; 5. 'Forecasts with quarterly macroeconomic models, equation adjustments and benchmark predictions: the US experience' (with G. Treyz), *REStat*, 54(3), Aug. 1972; 6. 'A Bayesian simultaneous equation theory applied to underidentified econometric models' (with A. O'Hagan), in *Modelling for Government and Business*, eds. C. A. von Bochove, *et al.* (Martinus Nijhoff, 1977); 7. 'Generalized ridge regression, least squares with stochastic prior information and

Bayesian estimators' (with Y. Wax), *Appl. Maths. & Computation*, 7, 1980; 8. 'Grouped data', in *Encyclopedia of Statistical Sciences*, 3, eds., S. Kotz, N. L. Johnson and C. B. Head (Wiley, 1983); 9. 'The linear hierarchical model and its application in econometric analysis', in *Bayesian Inference and Decision Techniques with Applications: Essays in Honor of Bruno di Finetti*, eds. P. K. Goel and A. Zellner (Wiley, 1983); 10. 'Approximating hierarchical normal priors using a vague component' (with J. V. Zidek), *J. Multivariate Analysis*, forthcoming, 1985.

Principal Contributions Early work was concerned with the problem of estimating regression models with insufficient data. One type of insufficiency is when only grouped observations are available, but the cross-classifications, necessary for efficient estimation of multiple regression coefficients, are not and hence the available grouped data must be combined in a particular fashion to yield alternative estimates. Another type of insufficiency is when some data, either random or a whole block of, say, time-series data, are missing. A third type is the so-called 'error of measurement in regression' problem, where in my work the errors are not assumed to be uncorrelated with the true quantities, as it is normally assumed. A related problem is that of multicollinearity. Later work was concerned with macroeconometric models, their estimation (Bayesian method) and their use as a forecasting tool and policy evaluation. More recently, I have worked on the development of the Linear Hierarchical Model — a generalisation of the statistical linear model (or regression model) — and its application in various economic areas such as household demand for electricity, firm's production and investment function, returns to schooling, etc. Another area of interest is the use of first differencing in econometric analyses and forecasts.

HAKANSSON, Nils H.

Born 1937, Marby, Sweden.
Current Post Sylvan C. Coleman Prof. Fin. and Accounting, School Bus.

Admin., Univ. Cal. Berkeley, USA, 1976–.

Past Posts Staff Accountant, CPA, Cons., Arthur Young & Co., 1960–3; Ass. Prof., UCLA, 1966–7; Ass. Prof., Yale Univ., 1967–9; Assoc. Prof., Univ. Cal. Berkeley, 1969–71; Hoover Fellow, Univ. New South Wales, Sydney, 1975; Vis. Scholar, Bell Labs., Murray Hill, 1980–1; Vis. Prof., Stockholm School Econ., 1984.

Degrees BS Univ. Oregon, 1958; MBA, PhD (Bus. Admin.) UCLA, 1960, 1966; Hon. Dr Stockholm School Econ., 1984.

Offices and Honours Pres., Western Fin. Assoc., 1983–4; Graham & Dodd Award, 1977, 1983; Fellow, Accounting Res. Internat. Assoc., 1980.

Editorial Duties Advisory Board, *Midland Corp. Fin. J.*, 1983–, *Chase Fin. Q.*, 1981–3; Cons. Ed., *J Accounting & Econ.*, 1978–81, *Accounting Rev.*, 1977–80; Assoc. Ed., *J. Accounting & Econ.*, 1981–; *J Fin Econ.*, 1973–81; *J. Fin. Quant. Analysis*, 1969–74; *Management Science*, 1979–82.

Principal Fields of Interest 026 Economics of Uncertainty and Information; 521 Business Finance; 540 Accounting.

Publications *Articles:* 1. 'Friedman-Savage utility functions consistent with risk aversion', *QJE*, 84(4), Aug. 1970; 2. 'Optimal investment and consumption strategies under risk for a class of utility functions', *Em*, 38(5), Sept. 1970, repr. in *Stochastic Optimization Models in Finance*, eds. W. T. Ziemba and R. G. Vickson (Academic Press, 1975); 3. 'Convergence to isoelastic utility and policy in multiperiod portfolio choice', *J Fin Econ*, 1, Sept. 1974; 4. 'The purchasing power fund: a new kind of financial intermediary', *Fin. Analysts J.*, 32, Nov.–Dec. 1976; 5. 'The superfund: efficient paths toward efficient capital markets in large and small countries', in *Financial Decision Making Under Uncertainty*, eds. H. Levy and M. Sarnat (Academic Press, 1977); 6. 'On the politics of accounting disclosure and measurement: an analysis of economic incentives', *J. Accounting Res.*, 19, Suppl. 1981; 7. 'To pay or not to pay dividends', *J Fin*, 37, May 1982; 8. 'Changes in the financial market: welfare and price effects and the basic theorems of value conservation', *J Fin*, 37, Sept. 1982; 9. 'Sufficient and necessary conditions for information to have social value in pure exchange' (with G. Kunkel and J. Ohlson), *J Fin*, 37, Dec. 1982.

Principal Contributions Early research efforts were among the first to focus on multi-period portfolio theory, with particular emphasis on optimal allocations to investment and consumption under uncertainty; dissertation (June 1966, unpublished but widely circulated) originated the modern approach to intertemporal consumption and investment decisions under risk. More recent activities have been concerned with the welfare implications of different financial market structures (i.e., the set of securities available in the market) and the economics of public and private information. The specific fallout from this work includes: (1) a statement (for the taxless, two-period case) of the conditions under which value conservation occurs in financial markets, and an extension of the theory of firms' capital structures to arbitrary securities, (2) an extension of Ross's efficiency analysis of option markets, (3) the concept of 'supershares' and a statement of the latter's efficiency properties (the options and futures on broadly-based stock indexes recently introduced are approximate composites of supershares), (4) a comprehensive theory of dividend policy (with and without taxes), and (5) an analysis of the conflicting incentives that surround financial reporting and other disclosures by firms and their likely effects on productive efficiency.

HALDI, John

Born 1931, Ann Arbor, MI, USA.
Current Post Pres., Haldi Assoc. Inc., New York City, NY, USA.
Degrees BA Emory Univ., 1952; MA, PhD Stanford Univ., 1953, 1957.
Principal Fields of Interest 513 Business and Public Administration; 720 Natural Resources; 913 Economics of Health.
Publications *Books:* 1. *Simulated Economic Models — A Laboratory*

Guide to Economic Principles of Market Behavior (with H. Wagner), (Richard D. Irwin, 1963); 2. *A Study of Hawaii's Motor Vehicle Insurance Program* (Hawaii Office Auditor, 1972); 3. *The Medical Malpractice Insurance Market*, App. to *Report of Secretary's Commission on Medical Malpractice* (US Dept. Health, Educ. & Welfare, 1973); 4. *Postal Monopoly: An Assessment of the Private Express Statutes* (AEI, 1974); 5. *Financing the New Jersey Unemployment Insurance Program* (US Dept. Labor & Industry, 1975); 6. *Social Decision-Making for High Consequence, Low Probability Occurrences* (US Environmental Protection Agency, 1978); 7. *Study of the Workers' Compensation Program of the State of Hawaii* (Hawaii Office Auditor, 1984).

Articles: 1. 'Applications of program budgeting to environmental problems', in *Social Sciences and the Environment* (Univ. Colorado Press, 1967); 2. 'Promises and pitfalls of PPB', in *Analysis for Planning-Programming-Budgeting* (Washington Operations Res. Council, 1968).

Principal Contributions The role of economies of scale in investment decisions and economic development; application of economic principles to governmental budgeting; and evaluation of public programmes.

HALEVY, Elie*

Dates and Birthplace 1870–1937, Etretat, France.
Posts Held Prof., l'Ecole Libre des Sciences Polit., Paris.
Degree Agrégé de Philo. Sorbonne, 1900.
Publications *Books:* 1. *La théorie platonicienne des sciences* (1896); 2. *The Growth of Philosophical Radicalism*, 3 vols (1901–4, 1928, 1949); 3. *Thomas Hodgskin* (1903, 1956); 4. *History of the English People in the Nineteenth Century*, 3 vols (1913–23), 5 vols (1926, 1961); 5. *Sismondi* (1933); 6. *Histoire du socialisme européen* (1948).

Career Historian of England whose work is best known for its emphasis on the role of Methodism as the reason why England escaped the French Revolution. His account of philosophical radicalism is a major contribution to the history of the utilitarian idea and his account of Thomas Hodgskin rescues an important early socialist writer from undeserved obscurity.

HALL, Charles*

Dates and Birthplace c. 1740–c. 1820, England.
Posts Held Physician.
Degree Medical Grad., Univ. Leiden, The Netherlands.
Publications Books: 1. The Effects of Civilisation (1805).
Career Early critic of capitalism whose estimate that the poor retained only the product of one hour's work out of eight made a considerable impression on pre-Marxist socialist writers.
Secondary Literature M. Beer, 'Hall, Charles', ESS, 7.

HALL, Robert Ernest

Born 1943, Palo Alto, CA, USA.
Current Post Prof. Econ., Sr. Fellow, Hoover Inst., Stanford Univ., Stanford, CA, USA, 1978–.
Past Posts Ass. Prof., Acting Assoc. Prof., Univ. Cal. Berkeley, 1967–70; Assoc. Prof., Prof., MIT, 1970–4, 1974–8; Fellow, Center Advanced Study Behavioral Sciences, Stanford, CA, 1977–8.
Degrees BA Univ. Cal. Berkeley, 1964; PhD MIT, 1967.
Offices and Honours Fellow, Em Soc, 1973.
Editorial Duties Assoc. Ed., JASA, 1968–70; Ed. Board, AER, 1972–5; Assoc. Ed., Em, 1970–4.
Principal Fields of Interest 131 Economic Fluctuations; 824 Labour Market Studies, Wages, Employment; 211 Econometric and Statistical Methods and Models.
Publications Books: 1. Inflation: Causes and Effects, ed. (Univ. Chicago Press, 1982); 2. Low Tax, Simple Tax, Flat Tax (With A. Rabushka), (McGraw-Hill, 1983).

Articles: 1. 'Tax policy and investment behavior' (with D. Jorgenson), AER, 57(3), June 1967; 2. 'Why is the unemployment rate so high at full employment?', Brookings Papers Econ. Activity, 3, 1970; 3. 'The dynamic effects of fiscal policy in an economy with foresight', REStud, 38, April 1971; 4. 'The specification of technology with several kinds of ouput', JPE, 81, July 1973; 5. 'Stochastic Implications of the life-cycle permanent income hypothesis', JPE, 86, Dec. 1978; 6. 'Efficient wage bargains under uncertain supply and demand' (with D. Lilien), AER, 69(5), Dec. 1979; 7. 'Labor supply and aggregate fluctuations', J Mon E, Suppl., 12, 1980; 8. 'The importance of lifetime jobs in the US Economy', AER, 72(4), Sept. 1982.
Principal Contributions As an undergraduate, I worked with D. Jorgenson; this led to our 1967 joint paper on taxes and investment. This paper is most famous for the 'Hall-Jorgenson formula' which shows how tax considerations affect the user cost of capital. I have pursued this line of thought on several subsequent occasions, most recently in the tax reform book (1983), which argues for a straightforward consumption tax. During the early 1970s I worked mainly on labour issues from a macro point of view. I published quite a number of papers that stressed the importance of turnover in understanding unemployment and related issues. In 1976 I came up with my single best idea, in thinking about the implications of rational expectations for consumption. The essence of the idea is that consumption is the personal equivalent of a security valuation — it embodies all current information about an individual's well-being. Like a security valuation, consumption should evolve as a random walk, loosely speaking. My paper on this point stimulated dozens of responses and extensions. Starting in 1980, I have worked extensively on issues in monetary and fiscal policy. Recently I have developed a characterisation of the class of monetary policies that concern themselves with both employment and price stability. I have argued for this type of policy at both a practical and theoretical level. As for

fiscal policy, I have become something of a public figure as an advocate of a flat-rate consumption tax.

HAMADA, Koichi

Born 1936, Tokyo, Japan.
Current Post Prof. Econ., Univ. Tokyo, Tokyo, Japan, 1980–.
Past Posts Res. Assoc., Assoc. Prof. Econ., Univ. Tokyo, 1965–9, 1969–79; Vis. Scholar, MIT, 1971–3; Vis. Lect., LSE, 1977–8; Luce Vis. Prof. Japanese Econ., Univ. Chicago, 1984.
Degrees LLB, BA, MA Univ. Tokyo, 1958, 1960, 1962; PhD Yale Univ., 1965.
Offices and Honours Nikkei Tosho Bunka-sho (Prize, Best Book of Year in Econ.), 1968; Economisuto sho (Prize, Best Empirical Work of Year on Japanese Economy), 1981; Fulbright Fellow, 1962–3; Ford Dissertation Fellow, 1964–5; ACLS Fellow, 1971–3; Japan Foundation Fellow, 1977–8; Fellow, Council Member, Em Soc, 1978, 1980–5; Exec. Comm., Riron Keiryo Keizai Gakkai, 1978–84.
Editorial Duties Assoc. Ed., JET, 1969–71, J Int E, 1973–9; J Pub E, 1982–; Co-ed., Econ. Stud. Q., 1974–7.
Principal Fields of Interest 023 Macroeconomic Theory; 432 International Monetary Arrangement; 441 International Investment and Capital Market.
Publications Books: (all in Japanese) 1. An Introduction to the Programming Theory (with T. Negishi), (Nihon Noritsu Kyokai, 1962); 2. Economic Growth and Capital Movements (Toyokeizai, 1967); 3. Intermediate Monetary Theory (with R. Tachi), (Iwanami, 1972); 4. An Economic Analysis of Liability Rules in Tort in Japan (Univ. Tokyo Press, 1977); 5. Economic Policy and Banking Behavior in Japan (with K. Iwata), (Toyokeizai, 1980); 6. The Political Economy of International Monetary Relations: A Strategic Approach (Sobunsha, 1982); 7. Macroeconomics and the Japanese Postwar Experience (with Y. Kurosaka), (Nihon Hyoronsha, 1984); 8. Monetary Mechanism in Japan, co-ed. (with T. Shimano), (Iwanami, 1971); 9. Proceedings of Conference on Japanese Economy co-ed. (with R. Tachi, et al.), (Univ. Tokyo Press, 1976); 10. Proceedings of the Conference on The Third World, co-ed. (with A. Takahashi, et al.), (Univ. Tokyo Press, 1982).

Articles: 1. 'Economic growth and long-term international capital movements', YEE, 6(1), Spring 1966; 2. 'Strategic aspects of taxation on foreign investment income', QJE, 80(3), Aug. 1966; 3. 'Optimal capital accumulation by an economy facing an international capital market', JPE, 77(4), pt. 2, July–Aug. 1969; 4. 'A simple majority rule on the distribution of income', JET, 6(3), June 1973; 5. 'Alternative exchange rate systems and the interdependence of monetary policies', in National Monetary Policies and the International Financial Systems, ed. R. Z. Aliber (Univ. Chicago Press, 1974); 6. 'An economic analysis of the duty free zone', J Int E, 4, Aug. 1974; 7. 'Liability rules and income distribution in product liability', AER, 66(1), March 1976; 8. 'A strategic analysis of monetary inderdependence', JPE, 84(4), pt. 1, Aug. 1976; 9. 'International transmission of stagflation under fixed and flexible exchange rates' (with M. Sakurai), JPE, 86(5), Oct. 1978; 10. 'National income, terms of trade and economic welfare' (with K. Iwata), EJ, 94, Dec. 1984.
Principal Contributions I have kept myself interested not only in the analytical structure of economic models but in their relationship to actual policy issues. I started in my dissertation at Yale with an attempt at dynamic analysis of international capital movements in which I applied tools of optimal control to international economics. My major concern in the theoretical field for the past twenty years has been the strategic or game theoretic analysis of international monetary (as well as trade) co-ordination and conflict. I studied how nonco-ordinated macroeconomic policy actions and reactions lead to a situation like the Cournot–Nash equilibrium that diverges from the Pareto optimum frontier. Also I studied how an international monetary regime can contribute to reducing this divergence and if there are incentives

to agree to such a regime on the part of participating actions.

Aside from this main line of research, I was interested in various topics in international trade, public economics, law and economics, monetary theory and macroeconomics. Radical economics in the early 1960s directed my attentions to social issues such as income distributions, external diseconomies and the economic analysis of law, though I carried out most analyses within the framework of the neoclassical discipline. Recently, I have become interested in the macroeconomic analysis of the postwar experience of the Japanese economy. I study such questions as: how could the Japanese economy have grown so fast? How does Okun's law and the Phillips curve look in the Japanese economy? How can we evaluate the Keynesian-monetarist-rationalist controversy in terms of data from Japanese experience? and so forth.

HAMADA, Robert S.

Born 1937, San Francisco, CA, USA.

Current Post Prof. Fin., Dir., Center Res. Security Prices, Grad. School Bus., Univ. Chicago, Chicago, IL, USA, 1976–.

Past Posts Econ. and Fin. Analyst, Sun Oil Co., Philadelphia, PA, 1961–3; Instr., Assoc. Prof. Fin., Grad School Bus., Univ. Chicago, 1966–76; Vis. Assoc. Prof. Fin., UCLA, 1971, Univ. Washington, Seattle, 1971–2; Vis. Sr. Lect. Fin., London Grad. School Bus. Stud., 1973; Leslie Wong Disting. Faculty Res. Fellow, Univ. British Columbia, Vancouver, 1976; Baring Brothers Vis. Prof. Fin., London Grad. School Bus. Stud., 1979–80.

Degrees BE (Chemical Eng.) Yale Univ., 1959; SM (Industrial Management), PhD MIT, 1961, 1969.

Offices and Honours Board Dirs., AFA, A. M. Castle & Co., Van Straaten Chemical Co.; Ford Foundation Fellow; Standard Oil Fellow; McKinsey Award Excellence in Teaching, 1981.

Editorial Duties Assoc. Ed., *J Fin, J. Fin. and Qunt. Analysis*; Advisory Board, *Midland Corporate Fin. J.*; Cons. Ed., *Fin. Series* (Scott, Foresman & Co.).

Principal Fields of Interest 520 Business Finance and Investment; 313 Capital Markets; 206 Economics of Uncertainty and Information.

Publications *Articles:* 1. 'Portfolio analysis, market equilibrium and corporation finance', *J Fin*, 24(1), March 1969, repr. in *The Theory of Business Finance: A Book of Readings*, eds. S. Archer and C. D'Ambrosio (Macmillan, 1976); 2. 'The effects of leverage and corporate taxes on the shareholders of regulated utilities', in *Rate of Return Under Regulation: New Directions and Perspectives*, eds. H. M. Trebbing and R. Howard (Michigan State Univ. Press, 1979); 3. 'Investment decision with a general equilibrium mean-variance approach', *QJE*, 85(4), Nov. 1971; 4. 'The effect of the firm's capital structure on the systematic risk of common stocks', *J Fin*, 27(2), May 1972, repr. in *Capital Market Equilibrium and Efficiency: Implications for Accounting, Financial and Portfolio Decision-Making*, ed. J. Bicksler (D. C. Heath, 1975), and in *Modern Developments in Financial Management*, ed. S. Myers (Dryden Press, 1976); 5. 'Financial theory and taxation in an inflationary world: some public policy issues', *J Fin*, 34(2), May 1979; 6. 'Taxes and corporate financial management' (with M. Scholes), in *Recent Advances in Corporate Finance*, eds. E. Altman and M. Subrahmanyan (Richard D. Irwin, 1984).

Principal Contributions Past and current research, both theoretical and empirical, on the many effects of the firm's decision to change its capital structure and dividend policies. Incorporated in these investigations are the effects of risk, taxes and inflation. Research into the interrelation between the financing and capital budgeting decisions within the firm, on portfolio and security selection by individuals, and on the equilibrium pricing of multiperiod risky securities has been an abiding interest. Some past interests included the incidence and risk-taking effects of various taxes from a public policy point of view and on the financing of nonprofit and government organisations. Current research interests are centred on how the myriad of US tax provisions interact with the many potential participants in the capital markets (including the implications of the fast developing futures and options markets) to result in a set of equilibrium relative rates of return confronting an investor or supplier of securities.

HAMBERG, Daniel

Born 1924, Philadelphia, PA, USA.
Current Post Prof. Econ., State Univ. NY Buffalo, Buffalo, NY, USA, 1961–.
Past Posts Instr., Univ. Delaware, 1946–7, 1948–51; Instr., Princeton Univ., 1947–8; Ass. Prof., Assoc. Prof., Prof., Univ. Maryland, 1952–8, 1958–61; US Secretary Labor, 1962–4; Guest Prof., Netherland School Econ., 1956–7; Vis. Prof., Johns Hopkins School, Advanced Internat. Stud., Bologna, Italy, 1965–6.
Degrees BS, MA, PhD Univ. Penn., 1945, 1947, 1952.
Offices and Honours Pi Gamma Mu; Phi Kappa Phi; US SSRC Fellow, 1951–2; Lifetime Fellow, RES, 1952; Fulbright Award, 1956–7, 1965–6; Ford Faculty Res. Fellow, 1961–2.
Principal Fields of Interest 310 Domestic Monetary and Financial Theory and Institutions; 020 General Economic Theory; 111 Economic Growth Theory and Models.
Publications *Books:* 1. *Business Cycles* (Macmillan, 1951); 2. *Economic Growth and Instability* (W. W. Norton, 1956, Greenwood Press, 1978; transl., Japanese, Toyo-Keizai, 1960, Asian ed. English, Kinokuniya Book Store, 1960); 3. *Principles of a Growing Economy* (W. W. Norton, 1961); 4. *Essays in the Economics of Research and Development* (Random House, 1966); 5. *Models of Economic Growth* (Harper & Row, 1971); 6. *The U.S. Monetary System* (Little Brown, 1981).
Articles: 1. 'The recession of 1948–9 in the United States', *EJ*, 62, March 1952; 2. 'Full capacity vs. full employment growth', *QJE*, 66(3), Aug. 1952; 3. 'Production functions, innovations,

and economic growth', *JPE*, 67, June 1959; 4. 'Size of firm, monopoly and economic growth', in *Hearings of the Joint Economic Committee on Employment, Growth and Price Levels: Part 7, The Effects of Monopolostic and Quasi-Monopolistic Practices* (US Govt. Printing Office, 1959, repr. in *Economic Issues*, eds. C. R. McConnell and R. C. Bingham, McGraw-Hill, 1969, and *Readings and Problems*, eds. M. Silver and A. Ginsburg, Appleton-Century-Crofts, 1968); 5. 'Fiscal policy and stagnation since 1957', *SEJ*, 29(1), Jan. 1963, repr. in *Macroeconomic Readings*, ed. J. H. Landauer (Free Press, 1968); 6. 'Liquidity preference as behavior toward risk is a demand for short-term securities — not money', *AER*, 73(3), June 1983; 7. 'Federal reserve policy since 1979', *BNLQR*, 36, Dec. 1983.
Principal Contributions My first book was written before my PhD dissertation. It began as a co-authored work inspired by a desire to impose a common language and set of analytical tools (Keynesian theory) on the extant theories of the business cycle. When my half of the book was completed, my co-author had written nothing. Rather than see this intellectual capital wasted, I wrote the second half — all in eighteen months. The work on business cycles then evolved naturally into research on growth and business cycles, culminating eventually in my second book.

By this time I had become unhappy with the treatment of technical change as an exogenous variable and resolved on a long-term programme to fill those 'empty boxes'. By chance, the Joint Economic Committee asked me to contribute a paper on the implications of company size and industry concentration for invention and innovation. The investigations for this paper focussed my interest on the economics of research and development and led to a series of studies that comprised the contents of my fourth book. In the process, however, disenchantment set in over the absence of decent data with which to do empirical research. If I had to do pure theory, I decided, I might as well return to my earlier 'love', growth theory. This work evolved into my fifth book. This one finally exhausted my interest in growth theory. Shortly after, I happened to return to teaching courses in monetary economics, a subject that had (avocationally) held my interest since graduate school. Before long, I was at work on my sixth book. Monetary economic continues to dominate my interests, and I am now pursuing a long-term study of the conduct of US monetary policy since 1970.

HAMERMESH, Daniel

Born 1943, Cambridge, MA, USA.
Current Post Prof. Econ., Michigan State Univ., USA, Sr. Res. Assoc., NBER, 1975–.
Past Posts Ass. Prof., Princeton Univ., 1969–73; Dir. Res., Office US Secretary Labor, 1974–5; Vis. Prof., Harvard Univ., 1981.
Degrees BA Univ. Chicago, 1965; PhD Yale Univ., 1969.
Offices and Honours Phi Beta Kappa; Ford Dissertation Fellow, 1967; Vice-Pres., *MEA*, 1982.
Editorial Duties Ed. Board, *QREB, J Econ. and Bus.*
Principal Fields of Interest 820 Labour Markets; Public Policy; 910 Welfare, Health and Education; 840 Demographic Economics.
Publications *Books:* 1. *Economic Aspects of Manpower Training Programs* (D. C. Heath, 1971); 2. *Labor in the Public and Nonprofit Sectors* (Princeton Univ. Press, 1975); 3. *Jobless Pay and the Economy* (JHUP, 1977); 4. *Economics of Work and Pay* (with A. Rees), (Harper & Row, 1984).
Articles: 1. 'Wage bargains, threshold effects and the Phillips curve', *QJE*, 84(3), Aug. 1970; 2. 'An economic theory of suicide' (with N. M. Soss), *JPE*, 82(1), Jan.–Feb. 1974; 3. 'Interdependence in the labour market', *Ec*, 42, Nov. 1975; 4. 'Econometric studies of labor demand and their application to policy analysis', *JHR*, 11(4), Fall 1976; 5. 'Econometric studies of labor-labor substitution and their implications for policy' (with J. Grant), *JHR*, 14(4), Fall 1979; 6. 'Factor market dynamics and the incidence

of taxes and subsidies', *QJE*, 95(4), Dec. 1980; 7. 'Labor-market competition among youths, white women and others', *REStat*, 63(3), Aug. 1981; 8. 'Social insurance and consumption', *AER*, 72(1), March 1982; 9. 'Minimum wages and the demand for labor', *EI*, 20(3), July 1982; 10. 'Consumption during retirement', *REStat*, 66(1), Feb. 1984.

Principal Contributions Since my dissertation, work on various aspects of the demand for labour, including: studies of substitution among workers of different demographic groups; attempts to provide better estimates of the aggregate labour demand elasticity; examination of how the minimum wage affects labour demand; and applications of these and other estimates to the evaluation of current and proposed labour-market policies.

Beginning in the mid-1970s substantial work on the economics of social insurance, including: studies of labour-force participation induced by unemployment insurance; analysis of effects of unemployment insurance and social security on consumption and wealth holdings; and examination of the effect of increased life span on the success of social security in maintaining consumption. In general, attempts to understand the institutional details of these programmes in order to model and estimate their effects more carefully, especially their ability to meet their original goal of maintaining consumption.

HAMMOND, Peter J.

Born 1945, Marple, Cheshire, England.
Current Post Prof. Econ., Stanford Univ., Stanford, CA, USA, 1976–.
Past Posts Jr. Res. Fellow, Nuffield Coll., Oxford, 1969–71; Lect., Prof., Univ. Essex, England, 1971–9; Res. Fellow, ANU, Canberra, 1974–5; J. A. Schumpeter Vis. Prof., Univ. Graz, Austria, 1983.
Degrees BA (Maths.), PhD Univ. Camb., 1967, 1974.
Offices and Honours Fellow, Em.

Soc., 1977; Fellow, Inst. Advanced Stud., Hebrew Univ., Jerusalem, 1983.

Editorial Duties Ed. Board, Joint Managing Ed., *REStud*, 1971–5, 1975–9.

Principal Fields of Interest 024 Welfare Theory; 026 Economics of Uncertainty and Information; 021 General Equilibrium Theory.

Publications *Articles:* 1. 'Agreeable plans with many capital goods', *REStud*, 42(1), Jan. 1975; 2. 'Charity: altruism or cooperative egotism?', in *Altruism, Morality and Economic Theory*, ed. E. S. Phelps (Russell Sage, 1975); 3. 'Changing tastes and coherent dynamic choice', *REStud*, 43(1), Feb. 1976; 4. 'Dynamic restrictions on metastatic choice', *Ec*, N.S. 44, Nov. 1977; 5. 'Equity, Arrow's conditions, and Rawls' difference principle', *Em*, 44(4), July 1976, repr. in *Philosophy and Economic Theory*, eds. F. H. Hahn, and M. Hollis (OUP, 1979); 6. 'Straightforward individual incentive compatibility in large economies', *REStud*, 46(2), April 1979; 7. 'The implementation of social choice rules: some general results in incentive compatibility' (with P. S. Dasgupta and E. S. Maskin), *REStud*, 46(2), April 1979; 8. 'Liberalism, independent rights and the Pareto principle', in *Logic, Methodology and the Philosophy of Science*, VI, eds. L. J. Cohen, *et al.* (N-H, 1982); 9. 'Overlapping expectations and Hart's conditions for equilibrium in a securities model', *JET*, 31(1), Oct. 1983; 10. 'Ex-post optimality as a dynamically consistent objective for collective choice under uncertainty', in *Social Choice and Welfare*, eds. P. K. Pattanaik and M. Salles (N-H, 1983).

Principal Contributions Early research for my PhD thesis 'Consistent Planning and International Welfare Economics' was on optimal growth and 'agreeable' plans for infinite time horizons. The thesis also included results on dynamic choice. A related early interest was consistent (or 'perfect') co-operative solutions to extensive games.

Later work was in static welfare economics. In social choice theory a way was found to satisfy the essential conditions of Kenneth Arrow's Impossibility Theorem without a dictatorship by incorporating interpersonal comparisons of utility. In welfare economics proper, the incentive constraints which arise because individuals' personal characteristics are unobservable were explored for economies with many consumers. Such constraints were shown generally to exclude the lump-sum transfers which could otherwise be used to optimise the distribution of income. This work implies that commodity taxes, income taxes, and other 'distortions' are not necessarily truly inefficient after all, once such incentive constraints are recognised. More recently some work has been done on cost-benefit analysis and its integration with a general theory of policy reform.

In normative theory, it is natural to assume that behaviour can be entirely explained by its consequences. This apparently very weak condition, appropriately formulated, has recently been shown to imply many of the usual properties of 'rational' choice, including expected utility maximisation in the face of uncertainty. In collective choice theory, this 'consequentialist' approach appears to justify utilitarianism.

My latest interests include sequence economies, starting with existence of temporary Walrasian equilibrium, properties of incentive-compatible allocation rules, and welfare questions arising when there is uncertainty and incomplete information. Ultimately I intend working toward a welfare economic theory rich enough to incorporate macroeconomic phenomena and to allow more realistic microeconomic analysis of macroeconomic policies.

HANCOCK, William Neilson*

Dates and Birthplace 1820–88, Lisburn, Co. Antrim, Ireland.

Posts Held Lawyer; Prof., Trinity Coll., Dublin, 1846–51, Queen's Coll., Belfast, 1849–51.

Degrees BA, LLB, LLD Trinity Coll., Dublin, 1843, 1846, 1849.

Offices Secretary Various Govt. Comms; Founder, Pres., Stat. and Social Inquiry Soc. Ireland, 1847, 1881–2.

Publications *Books:* 1. *Tenant-right of Ulster Considered Economically* (1845); 2. *On Laissez-faire and the Economic Resources of Ireland* (1848); 3. *Impediments to the Prosperity of Ireland* (1850).

Career Economist and reformer, whose Statistical and Social Inquiry Society was a means for both investigation and the propagation of reformist ideas. He regarded the problem of Irish agricultural distress as arising from restrictions on the free exchange of land imposed by existing laws. He also wrote on the Poor Laws and published statistical reports in connection with his work for government commissions.

Secondary Literature G. O'Brien, 'Hancock, William Neilson', *ESS*, 7.

HANNAH, Leslie

Born 1947, Oldham, Lancashire, England.

Current Post Prof. Bus. Hist., LSE, 1982–.

Past Posts Jr. Res. Fellow Hist., Univ. Oxford, 1969–73; Lect. Econ., Univ. Essex, 1973–5; Lect. Recent British Econ. and Social Hist., Fellow, Emmanuel Coll. Camb., 1975–8; Dir., Bus. Hist. Unit., LSE, Imperial Coll. Science and Technology, London, 1978–; Thomas Carroll Ford Foundation Vis. Prof., Harvard Grad. School Bus. Admin., 1984–5.

Degrees BA (Hist.), DPhil, MA Univ. Oxford, 1968, 1972, 1972; MA, PhD Univ. Camb., 1975, 1975.

Editorial Duties Ed., *Bus. Hist.*; Chairman, Ed. Advisory Board, *Dictionary of Bus. Biography*.

Principal Fields of Interest 040 Economic History; 600 Industrial Organisation.

Publications *Books:* 1. *The Rise of the Corporate Economy* (Methuen, JHUP, 1976, 1983); 2. *Management Strategy and Business Development. An Historical and Comparative Study*, ed. (Macmillan, 1976); 3. *Concentration in Modern Industry: Theory Measurement and the U.K. Experience* (with J. A. Kay), (Macmillan, 1977); 4. *Electricity Before Nationalisation: A Study of the Electricity Supply Industry in Britain to 1948* (Macmillan, JHUP, 1979); 5. *New Horizons for Business History* (UK-SSRC, 1981); 6. *Engineers, Managers and Politicians: The First Fifteen Years of Nationalised Electricity Supply in Britain 1948–62* (Macmillan, JHUP, 1982); 7. *From Family Firm to Professional Management*, ed. (Budapest Internat. Congress Econ. Hist., 1982); 8. *Entrepreneurs and the Social Sciences* (LSE, 1983).

Articles: 1. 'Takeover bids in Britain before 1950', *Bus. His.*, 16(1), 1974; 2. 'Mergers in British manufacturing industry 1880–1918', *OEP*, 26(1), Jan. 1974; 3. 'A pioneer of public enterprise: the central electricity board and the national grid, 1927–1940', in *Essays in British Business History*, ed. B. Supple (OUP, 1977); 4. 'Public policy and the advent of large-scale technology: the case of the electricity supply industry in the USA, Germany and Britain', in *Recht und Entwicklung der Grossunternehemen im 19, und frühen 20. Jahrhundert*, eds. N. Horn and J. Kocka (Vandenhoeck & Ruprecht, 1979); 5. 'Visible and invisible hands in Great Britain', in *Managerial Hierarchies: Comparative Perspectives on the Rise of the Modern Industrial Enterprise* eds. A. D. Chandler and H. Daems (Harvard Univ. Press, 1980); 6. 'Mergers', in *Dictionary of American Economic History*, ed. G. Porter (Scribners, 1980); 7. 'Government and business in Britain: the evolution of the modern relationship', in *Government and Business* ed. K. Nakagawa (Univ. Tokyo Press, 1980); 8. 'The contribution of mergers to concentration growth' (with J. A. Kay), *J Ind E*, 29, March 1981; 9. 'Gibrat's law, deterministic theories of the growth of large enterprise and the conditions for the survival of small enterprise', in *Entreprises et Entrepreneurs XIX-XXème siècles*, eds. F. Caron, *et al.* (Presses de l'Univ. de Paris, 1983); 10. 'New issues in British business history', *Bus Hist. Rev.*, 57, Summer 1983.

Principal Contributions My central research interest has been and remains the microeconomic roots of Britain's poor economic performance in the twentieth century. I have tried to bring together some of the empirical work by historians and theoretical work by economists, initially in the area of mergers and concentration, then in studies of a major 'new industry', the electricity industry under private and public ownership. In the latter, international comparisons made me more and more aware of the 'noneconomic' sources of poor performance. Currently I am working on the empirical analysis of entrepreneurial quality differences and on the development of occupational pension schemes (US/UK comparisons).

HANOCH, Giora

Born 1932, Haifa, Israel.
Current Post Prof. Econ., Hebrew Univ. Jerusalem, Israel.
Past Posts Vis. Lect., Harvard Univ., 1970, 1974; Vis. Prof., UCLA, 1975; Cons., Rand Corp., 1975-6, Sr Res. Assoc., Center Social Sciences, Columbia Univ., 1977-80, 1980-1.
Degrees BA, MA Hebrew Univ., 1960, 1961; PhD Univ. Chicago, 1965.
Offices and Honours Res. Assoc., Maurice Falk Research Inst., Israel, 1959-61, 1966-72; Bareli Award, Israel Labour Org., 1960; Univ. Fellow, Univ. Chicago, 1964; Cons., Bank Israel Res. Dept, 1972-; Fellow, Em Soc, 1975-; Member, Israeli Commission Wages Public Sector, 1977-80.
Principal Fields of Interest 820 Labour Markets; Public Policy.
Publications *Articles:* 1. 'An economic analysis of earnings and schooling', *JHR*, 2(3), Summer 1967; 2. 'Testing the assumptions of production theory: a non-parameter approach' (with M. Rothschild), *JPE*, 80(2), March/April 1972; 3. 'The labor supply curve under income maintenance programs' (with M. Honig), *J Pub E*, 9(1), Feb. 1978; 4. 'Symmetric duality and polar production functions', in *Production Economics: A Dual Approach to Theory and Applications*, eds. M. Fuss and D. McFadden (N-H, 1978); 5. 'Hours and weeks in the theory of labor supply', in *Female Labor Supply*, ed. J. P. Smith (Princeton Univ. Press, 1980).
Principal Contributions Topics in the fields of human resources, income distribution, production theory and

duality, portfolio selection and uncertainty, panel data analysis, and theory and estimation of labour supply and retirement. Recently been engaged in a research project on labour market behaviour of older persons in the US, using panel data, and a multivariate model of participation, wages, hours and weeks of work, with emphasis on separating age, period and cohort effects.

HANSEN, Alvin Harvey*

Dates and Birthplace 1887-1975, Viborg, SD, USA.
Posts Held Schoolteacher and Headmaster, 1910-13; Instr. Econ., Univ. Wisconsin, 1915-16, Brown Univ., 1916-19, Univ. Minnesota, 1919-27; Prof. Polit. Econ., Harvard Univ., 1937-62.
Degrees BA Yankton Coll., 1910; MA, PhD Univ. Wisconsin, 1915, 1918.
Offices Vice-Pres., ASA, 1937; Pres., AEA, 1938.
Publications *Books:* 1. *Business-cycle Theory* (1927); 2. *Economic Stabilisation in an Unbalanced World* (1932); 3. *Full Recovery or Stagnation?* (1938); 4. *Fiscal Policy and Business Cycles* (1941); 5. *State and Local Finance in the National Economy* (with H. S. Perloff), (1944); 6. *Monetary Theory and Fiscal Policy* (1949); 7. *Business Cycles and National Income* (1951, 1964); 8. *A Guide to Keynes* (1953); 9. *The Dollar and the International Monetary System* (1965).
Career The chief propagator of Keynesian ideas in America, he was also very frequently called on as a government adviser. Advisory posts held included Dir. of Research for the 1933-4 Committee on Policy in International Economic Relations, membership of the Advisory Council on Social Security, 1941-3 and special economic adviser to the Federal Reserve Board, 1940-5. From an early preference for deflationary policies, he came to favour policies based on the stimulation of demand. It was in this context that he worked out aspects of Keynes's ideas and presented them in more

acceptable form for students' consumption. He also made a number of original contributions, for instance, to the theory of the multiplier.

Secondary Literature S. E. Harris, 'Hansen, Alvin', *IESS*, 6; P. A. Samuelson, 'Alvin Hansen as a creative economic theorist', *QJE*, 90, Feb. 1976.

HANSEN, Bent

Born 1920, Ildved, Denmark.
Current Post Prof. Econ., Univ. Cal. Berkeley, USA, 1966–.
Past Posts Ass. Prof., Göteborg Handelsehogeskola, 1948–50; Ass. Prof., Assoc. Prof., Uppsala Univ., 1947–51, 1951–5; Prof., Chief, Nat. Inst. Econ. Res., Stockholm, 1955–64; Adviser, Inst. Planning, Cairo, 1962–5; Prof., Univ. Stockholm, 1966.
Degrees Cand. Pol. Univ. Copenhagen, Denmark, 1946; Fil. Lic., Fil. Dr Uppsala Univ., Sweden, 1950, 1951.
Offices and Honours Fellow, Em Soc., 1953; Prize, Vetenshapsakademien, Stockholm, 1957; Fellow, Assoc. Middle East Stud. North Amer., 1975.
Editorial Duties Ed., *Swed JE*, 1955–62; Advisory Board, *Int ER*, 1955–72, 1975–82; Ed. Board, *AER*, 1973–7, *PDR*, 1979–83; Advisory Ed., *PF*, 1972–82.
Principal Fields of Interest 110 Economic Growth, Development, Planing Theory and Policy; 300 Monetary and Fiscal Theory and Institutions.
Publications *Books:* 1. *A Study in the Theory of Inflation* (A&U, 1951; transl., Japanese, 1953); 2. *The Economic Theory of Fiscal Policy* (A&U, 1958, 1971); 3. *Foreign Trade Credits and Foreign Exchange Reserves* (N-H, 1961); 4. *The Problem of Rising Prices* (with W. Fellner, *et al.*), (OECD, 1961); 5. *Development and Economic Policy in the UAR* (with G. Marzouk), (N-H, 1965); 6. *Lectures in Economic Theory* (INP, 1963, 1976, Lund, 1966); 7. *Fiscal Policy in Seven Countries, 1955–65* (with W. W. Synder), (OECD, 1969); 8. *Long and Short-Term Planning in Underdeveloped Countries* (N-H, 1967; transl., Japanese, 1973, Spanish, 1976, Portuguese, 1978); 9. *A Sur-*

vey of General Equilibrium Systems (McGraw-Hill, 1970; Krieger, 1982; transls., Japanese, 1972, Polish, 1976); 10. *Foreign Exchange Regimes and Economic Development: Egypt* (with K. Nashashibi), (Columbia Univ. Press, 1975).

Articles: 1. 'Theoretical analysis of smuggling' (with J. N. Bhagwati), *QJE*, 87(2), May 1973, repr. in *Illegal Trade*, ed. J. Bhagwati (N-H, 1974); 2. 'Income and consumption in Egypt, 1886/87–1937', *Internat. J. Middle East Stud.*, 1, 1979; 3. 'Colonial economic development with unlimited supply of land: a Ricardian case', *EDCC*, 27(4), July 1979; 4. 'Unemployment, Keynes and the Stockholm school', *HOPE*, 13(2), Summer 1981; 5. 'An economic model for Ottoman Egypt: the economics of collective tax responsibility', in *Middle East Economics from 1100–1900*, ed. A. Udovich (Princeton Univ. Press, 1981); 6. 'Employment planning in Egypt: and insurance policy for the future', *Int Lab Rev*, 121(5), Sept.–Oct., 1982; 7. 'Wage theory for LDCs', *ILRR*, May 1983; 8. 'LDC Labor markets: applications of internal labor market theory', *Industrial Relations*, 22(2), Spring 1983; 9. 'Interest rates and foreign capital in Egypt under British occupation', *JEH*, 42, Dec. 1983; 10. 'On the accuracy of index numbers' (with E. Lucas), *RIW*, 30(1), March 1984.

Principal Contributions Developed inflation theory in terms of excess demand analysis and the nation of quasi-equilibrium. An early example of disequilibrium theory. Developed fiscal theory in terms of target instrument analysis and suggested use of tax policy for wage control. Initiated studies of wage-drift as a function of excess demand for labour. Studied rural wages in Egypt and used results as evidence against the surplus labour hypothesis.

HANSEN, W. Lee

Born 1928, Racine, WI, USA.
Current Post Prof. Econ. and Educ. Pol. Stud., Dir. Industrial Relations Res. Inst., Univ. Wisconsin-Madison, WI, USA, 1976–.

Past Posts Staff, UCLA, 1958–65; Sr. Staff Econ., US President's Council Econ. Advisers, 1964–5; Vis. Prof., Univ. Minnesota, 1975; Academic Vis., LSE, 1982.

Degrees BA (Internat. Relations), MA Univ. Wisconsin-Madison, 1950, 1955; PhD Johns Hopkins Univ., 1958.

Offices and Honours Earhart Fellow, Johns Hopkins Univ, 1956–7; Fellow, Brookings Inst., 1957–8; Postdoctoral Fellow Polit. Econ., Univ. Chicago, 1961–2; Guggenheim Foundation Fellow, 1969–70; Chancellor's Teaching Award, Univ. Wisconsin, 1982; Chair., AEA Comm. Econ. Educ., 1983–.

Editorial Duties Ed., *JHR*, 1981–.

Principal Fields of Interest 820 Labour Markets: Public Policy; 810 Manpower Training and Allocation: Labour Force and Supply; 912 Economics of Education.

Publications *Books:* 1. *Markets for California Products: An Analysis of the Sources of Demand* (with C. M. Tiebout and R. T. Robson), (State of Cal., 1961); 2. *Benefits, Costs and Finance of Public Higher Education* (with B. A. Weisbrod), (Markham, 1969); 3. *Education, Income and Human Capital*, ed. (NBER, 1970); 4. *The Labor Market for Scientists and Engineers* (with G. C. Cain and R. B. Freeman), (JHUP, 1973); 5. *Perspectives on Economic Education: Conference Proceedings*, co-ed. (with D. R. Wentworth and S. Hawke), (Joint Council Econ. Educ., 1977); 6. *Basic concepts in Economics: A Framework for Teaching Economics in the Nation's Schools* (with G. L. Bach, J. D. Calderwood and P. Saunders), (Joint Council Econ. Educ., 1977, 1984); 7. *Resource Manual for Teacher Training Programs in Economics* (with P. Saunders and A. L. Welsh), (Joint Council Econ. Educ., 1978).

Articles: 1. 'Total and private rates of return to investment in schooling', *JPE*, 81, April 1963, repr. in *Economics of Education, 1*, ed. M. Blaug (Penguin, 1968); 2. 'An income new worth measure of economic position' (with B. A. Weisbrod), *AER*, 67(5), Dec. 1968; 3. 'A new approach to higher education finance' (with B. A. Weisbrod), in *Financing Higher Education*, ed. M. Orwig (Amer. Coll. Testing Program, 1971); 4. 'Prediction of graduate success in economics', *J. Econ. Educ.,* 3, Fall 1971; 5. 'Modelling the earning and research productivity of academic economists' (with R. P. Strauss and B. A. Weisbrod), *JPE*, 86(4), Aug. 1978; 6. 'Forecasting the market for new PhD economists' (with H. B. Newburger, *et al.*), *AER*, 70(1), March 1980; 7. 'Improving classroom discussion in economics', *J. Econ. Educ.*, 14, Winter 1983; 8. 'Good intentions and mixed results: an update on the BEOG program 8 years later' (with R. J. Lampman), in *Public Expenditure and Policy Analysis*, eds. R. Haveman and J. Margolis (Rand McNally, 1983); 9. 'Economic growth and equal educational opportunity: conflicting or complementary goals in higher education', in *Education and Economic Growth*, ed. E. Dean (Ballinger, 1984); 10. 'Is there a shortage of engineers: a review of four studies', in *Labor Market Conditions for Engineers: Is There a Shortage?*, ed. Office of Scientific and Eng. Personnel (Nat. Res. Council, 1984).

Principal Contributions My interests in economics have been and continue to be wide-ranging. Basically, I am a labour economist. Early in my career I got caught up in the interest in human capital. This led to a growing and indeed continuing interest in the economics of education, with particular attention to the costs, benefits, and finance of higher education. At the same time I maintained a strong interest in the operation of labour markets for highly-educated personnel, such as scientists, engineers, and academics. While my research interests always dominated, I have over the years become increasingly interested in economic education — how to enhance general economic literacy and how to improve the effectiveness of economics instruction at the college level. All of these interests are reflected in the selection of publications listed above. What it all adds up to is for others to judge.

HANUSHEK, Erick Alan

Born 1943, Lakewood, OH, USA.
Current Post Dep. Dir., US Congressional Budget Office, Washington, DC, USA; Prof. Econ., Univ. Rochester, Rochester, NY, USA, 1984–.
Past Posts Instr., Ass. Prof. Econ., US Air Force Academy, 1968–9, 1969–71; Sr. Staff Econ., US President's Council Econ. Advisers, Washington, DC, 1973–4; Assoc. Prof. Econ. and Inst. for Social and Policy Stud., Yale Univ., 1975–8; Dir., Public Pol. Analysis Program, Univ. Rochester, 1978–84.
Degrees BS US Air Force Academy, Colorado, 1965; PhD MIT, 1968.
Offices and Honours Member, Pol. Council, Assoc. Public Pol. Analysis and Management, 1981–.
Editorial Duties Ed. Boards, *Social Science Res.*, 1978–, *Econ. Educ. Rev.*, 1980–.
Principal Fields of Interest 320 Public Finance; 820 Labour Markets; 900 Welfare Programmes; Urban.
Publications *Books:* 1. *Education and Race — An Analysis of the Educational Production Process* (D. C. Heath, 1972); 2. *Statistical Methods for Social Scientists* (with J. E. Jackson), (Academic Press, 1977).
Articles: 1. 'Teacher characteristics and gains in student achievement: estimation using micro-data', *AER*, 61(2), May 1971; 2. 'On the value of "equality of educational opportunity" as a guide to public policy' (with J. F. Kain), in *On Equality of Educational Opportunity*, eds. F. Mosteller and D. P. Moynihan (Random House, 1972); 3. 'Regional differences in the structure of earnings', *REStat*, 55(2), May 1973; 4. 'Implicit investment profiles and intertemporal adjustments of relative wages' (with J. M. Quigley), *AER*, 68(1), March 1978; 5. 'The dynamics of postwar industrial location' (with B. N. Song), *REStat*, 60(4), Nov. 1978; 6. 'The dynamics of the housing market: a stock adjustment model of housing consumption' (with J. Quigley), *JUE*, 6(1), Jan. 1979; 7. 'Conceptual and empirical issues in the estimation of educational production functions', *JHR*, 14(3), Summer 1979, repr. in *Research on Teaching College Economics*, eds. R. Fels and J. J. Siegfried (Joint Council Econ. Educ., 1982); 8. 'What is the price elasticity of housing demand?' (with J. M. Quigley), *REStat*, 42(3), Aug. 1980; 9. 'Alternative models of earnings determination and labor market structure', *JHR*, 16(2), Spring 1981; 10. 'Throwing money at schools', *J. Pol. Analysis and Management*, 1(1), Fall 1981.

Principal Contributions Research and teaching have touched a variety of applied economics areas, beginning with early work in the economics of education and carrying through into topics in labour economics, urban and regional economics, and public finance. Related work has dealt with econometric theory, particularly as motivated by applied problems. The education work has built upon analyses of production functions and the determinants of scholastic performance. This relates quite directly to policy concerns in the financing of schooling, desegregation of schools, and changes in work behaviour and family structure. The education analyses extend naturally into wage determination and labour economics where human capital perspectives have been considered more broadly. The urban analyses have considered individual and firm locational decisions, housing demand and policies, and urban mobility. The academic work has been complemented by periods of work in government at the Council of Economic Advisers, the Cost of Living Council, and most recently the Congressional Budget Office.

HARBERGER, Arnold Carl

Born 1924, Newark, NJ, USA.
Current Post Gustavus F. and Ann M. Swift Disting. Service Prof. Econ., Univ. Chicago, 1977–; Prof. Econ., UCLA, 1984–.
Past Posts Res. Ass., Cowles Commission Res. Econ., 1949; Ass. Prof. Polit. Econ., Johns Hopkins Univ., 1949–53; Assoc. Prof., Prof. Econ., Univ. Chicago, 1953–9, 1959–76; Vis. Prof., MIT Center Internat. Stud., New Delhi, 1961–2, Harvard Univ.,

1971–2, Princeton Univ., 1973–4, UCLA, 1983–4.

Degrees MA (Internat. Relations), PhD Univ. Chicago, 1947, 1950; Hon. DHC Univ. Tucuman, 1979.

Offices and Honours US SSRC Faculty Res. Fellow, 1951–3, 1954–5; Guggenheim Foundation Fellow, 1958; Ford Foundation Faculty Res. Fellow, 1968–9; Fellow, Em Soc, AAAS; Member, Exec. Comm., AEA, 1970–2.

Editorial Duties Ed. Boards, *AER*, 1959–61, *JEL*, 1969–70.

Principal Fields of Interest 320 Fiscal Theory & Policy, Public Finance; 121 Economic Studies of Developing Countries; 400 International Economics.

Publications *Books:* 1. *The Demand for Durable Goods*, ed. (Univ. Chicago Press, 1960); 2. *The Taxation of Income from Capital*, co-ed. (with M. Bailey), (Brookings Inst., 1969); 3. *Key Problems of Economic Policy in Latin America*, ed. (*JPE*, Suppl. 78(4), July–Aug. 1970); 4. *Project Evaluation* (Macmillan, 1972); 5. *Taxation and Welfare* (Little Brown, 1974, Univ. Chicago Press, 1978); 6. *World Economic Growth*, ed. (Inst. Contemporary Stud., 1984).

Articles: 1. 'Currency depreciation, income, and the balance of trade', *JPE*, 58, Feb. 1950; 2. 'Projection of 1975 materials demand', in *The Outlook for Key Commodities: Resources for Freedom* (US Govt. Printing Office, 1952); 3. 'Monopoly and resource allocation', *AER*, 44(2), May 1954; 4. 'The taxation of mineral industries', in *Federal Tax Policy for Economic Growth and Stability* (US Govt. Printing Office, 1955); 5. 'The incidence of the corporation income tax', *JPE*, 70, June 1962, repr. in *Bobbs-Merrill Reprint Series in Economics*, 137 (Bobbs-Merrill, 1971–2); 6. 'The dynamics of inflation in Chile', in *Measurement in Economics*, eds. C. Christ, *et al.* (Stanford Univ. Press, 1963); 7. 'The measurement of waste', *AER*, 54(3), May 1964; 8. 'Three basic postulates for applied welfare economics', *JEL*, 9(3), Sept. 1971; 9. 'Basic needs versus distributional weights in social cost-benefit analysis', *EDCC*, 32(3), April 1984.

Principal Contributions The princi-pal influences on my graduate educa-tion came, in alphabetical order, from Friedman (price theory), Marschak (macro-theory), Metzler (international trade) and T. W. Schultz (policy econ-omics). My first major paper applied macro-theory model-building to the problem of currency devaluation. Shortly after receiving my degree I joined the staff of Truman's President's Materials Policy Commission. There I made one of the earliest 'general equil-ibrium' sets of long-term projections for the US economy, ultimately projec-ting (in 1951–2) the US demand (under specified assumptions) for all major mineral-type raw materials for the year 1975. That exercise further stimulated an already strong interest in policy economics.

When I moved to Chicago in 1953, my major teaching area became public finance, and there ensued a substantial series of writings in this area. On the tax side, my interest concentrated on the applied welfare economic aspects of taxation, and on tax incidence theory. On the expenditure side, it focussed on project evaluation. In nearly all this work a general-equilibrium focus was maintained, but in the tradition of trade theory (Metzler), of relatively simple macro models (Marschak), and of interacting micro markets (Friedman), not in the n-equation, n-unknown Walrasian tradition. In my early incidence work I 'brought' trade-type general equilibrium models into public finance; in my project evaluation and much tax work I focussed on ana-lysing the costs and benefits of particu-lar policies, projects or other actions, given the presence of a set of pre-existing distortions (taxes, subsidies, externalities, etc.). My policy and wel-fare interests also carried me into much work in and on developing countries — including the study of inflation and of trade and exchange-rate policies. Per-haps my greatest professional pride is the group of 400 or more graduate stu-dents from developing countries, in whose training and subsequent devel-opment as professionals, scholars, edu-cators and policy-makers, I may have played an important role.

HARCOURT, Geoffrey Colin

Born 1931, Melbourne, Victoria, Australia.

Current Post Fellow, Lect. Econ., Jesus Coll. Camb., 1982–.

Past Posts Lect., Sr. Lect., Reader, Prof. Econ., Univ. Adelaide, 1958–62, 1962–5, 1965–7, 1967–82; Univ. Lect., Fellow, Trinity Hall Camb., 1963–6; Leverhulme Exchange Fellow, Keio Univ., Tokyo, 1969–70; Vis. Fellow, Clare Hall, Camb., 1972–3; Vis. Prof., Scarborough Coll., Univ. Toronto, 1977, 1980.

Degrees BCom, MCom Univ. Melbourne, 1954, 1956; PhD Univ. Camb., 1960.

Offices and Honours Fellow, Academy Soc. Sciences Australia, 1971; Exec. Comm, Pres., Econ. Soc. Australia and NZ, 1974–77.

Editorial Duties Joint Ed., *AEP*, 1967–; Assoc. Ed., Joint Ed., *Camb JE*, 1975–83, 1983–; Academic Board, *J Post Keyn E*, 1978–; Corresp. Ed., *MS*, 1982–; Ed. Board, Library Polit. Econ., Univ. Oxford, 1982–.

Principal Fields of Interest 010 General Economics; 023 Macroeconomic Theory; 031 History of Economic Thought.

Publications *Books:* 1. *Economic Activity* (with P. H. Karmel and R. H. Wallace), (CUP, 1967; transl., Italian, 1969); 2. *Readings in the Concept and Measurement of Income* co-ed. (with R. H. Parker), (CUP, 1969); 3. *Capital and Growth, Selected Readings,* co-ed (with N. F. Laing), (Penguin, 1971, 1973; transl., Spanish, 1977); 4. *Some Cambridge Controversies in the Theory of Capital* (CUP, 1972, 1977; transls., Italian, 1973, Polish, 1975, Spanish, 1975, Japanese, 1980); 5. *Theoretical Controversy and Social Significance: An Evaluation of the Cambridge Controversies* (Univ. Western Australia Press, 1975); 6. *The Microeconomic Foundations of Macroeconomics,* ed. (Macmillan, 1977); 7. *The Social Science Imperialists: Selected Essays,* ed. P. Kerr (Routledge & Kegan Paul, 1982).

Articles: 1. 'The accountant in a golden age', *OEP*, 17, March 1965, repr. in *Readings in the Concept and Measurement of Income, op. cit.*; 2. 'A two-sector model of the distribution of income and the level of employment in the short run', *ER*, 41, March 1965; 3. 'Biases in empirical estimates of the elasticities of substitution of C.E.S. production functions', *REStud*, 33(3), July 1966; 4. 'Investment decision criteria, investment incentives and the choice of technique', *EJ*, 78, March 1968; 5. 'Some Cambridge controversies in the theory of capital', *JEL*, 7(2), June 1969, repr. in Italian in *Teori dello Sviluppo Economico,* eds. G. Nargozzi and V. Valli (Etas Kompass, 1971); 6. 'The Cambridge controversies: old ways and new horizons — or dead end?', *OEP*, 28(1), March 1976; 7. 'Pricing and the investment decision' (with P. Kenyon), *Kyk*, 29(3), 1976; 8. 'Robinson, Joan', in *IESS, Biographical Supplement,* 18 (Free Press, 1979); 9. 'Notes on an economic queriest: G. L. S. Shackle', *J Post Keyn E*, 4(1), Fall, 1981; 10. 'On Piero Sraffa's contributions to economics', in *Altro Polo: Italian Economics/Past and Present,* eds. P. Groenwegen and J. Halevi (Univ. Sydney, 1983).

Principal Contributions Tried to make clear in a fair and good-humoured way to students and colleagues alike the issues involved in the Cambridge controversies over capital theory. Also made contributions to post-Keynesian theory, especially to the theory of pricing and the investment decision, and to the theory of the distribution of income and the level of activity in the short run. Finally, by sketching the intellectual biographies of some leading economists, tried to make the subject more alive and humane.

HARDY, Charles Oscar*

Dates and Birthplace 1884–1948, Island City, MO, USA.

Posts Held Prof., Univ. Ottawa, KS, 1910–18; Lect., Univ. Chicago, 1918–22; Prof., Univ. Iowa, 1922–4; Member, Res. Staff, Brookings Inst.

Degrees BA Univ. Ottawa, 1904; PhD Univ. Chicago, 1916.

Offices and Honours Vice-Pres., Fed. Reserve Bank, Kansas City.

Publications *Books:* 1. *Risk and Risk*

Bearing (1923); 2. *Credit Policies of the Federal Reserve System* (1932); 3. *Is There Enough Gold?* (1936); 4. *Wartime Control of Prices* (1940).

Career Mathematician who brought a meticulous concern for accuracy to economic questions. His best-known contribution was on the question of gold, where he argued that there was too much gold available, and that this permitted an undue volume of credit expansion. Whilst at Brookings he was a frequent adviser to government.

HARRIS, Donald J.

Born 1938, Jamaica.
Current Post Prof. Econ., Stanford Univ., Stanford, CA, USA, 1975–.
Past Posts Ass. Prof. Econ., Univ. Illinois, Urbana, 1965–7; Ass. Prof. Econ., Northwestern Univ., 1967–8; Cons., UN Conference on Trade and Devlp., NY, 1966–7; Assoc. Prof. Econ., Univ. Wisconsin-Madison, 1968–72; Assoc. Prof., Stanford Univ., 1972–4.
Degrees BA London Univ., 1960; PhD Univ. Cal. Berkeley, 1966.
Offices and Honours Internat. Fellow, Res. Division, UN, NY, 1963; Vis. Fellow, Delhi School Econ., India, 1968; Faculty Fellow, Assoc. Fellow, Clare Hall, Camb., 1966, 1969; Assoc. Fellow, Trinity Coll., Camb., 1971, 1982; Nat. Res. Council Fellow, 1984–5.
Editorial Duties Ed. Board, *JEL*, 1979–83.
Principal Fields of Interest 111 Economic Growth Theory and Models.
Publications *Books:* 1. *Capital Accumulation and Income Distribution* (Stanford Univ. Press, 1978; transl., Japanese, Nihon-Keizai-Hyoron-Sha, 1982).
Articles: 1. 'Econometric analysis of household consumption in Jamaica', *Social and Econ. Stud.*, 13(4), Dec. 1964; 2. 'Inflation, income distribution, and capital accumulation in a two-sector model of growth', *EJ*, 77, Dec. 1967; 3. 'Income, prices and the balance of payments in underdeveloped economies: a short-run model', *OEP*, 22(2), July 1970; 4. 'On Marx's scheme of repro-duction and accumulation', *JPE*, 80(3), pt. 1, May–June 1972; 5. 'The black ghetto as "internal colony": a theoretical critique and alternative formulation', *Rev. Black Polit. Econ.*, 2(4), Summer 1972; 6. 'Capital, distribution, and the aggregate production function', *AER*, 63(1), March 1973; 7. 'The theory of economic growth: a critique and reformulation', *AER*, 65(2), May 1975; 8. 'Profits, productivity, and thrift: the neoclassical theory of capital and distribution revisited', *J Post Keyn E*, 3(3), Spring 1981; 9. 'On the timing of wage payments', *Camb JE*, 5, Dec. 1981; 10. 'Accumulation of capital and the rate of profit in Marxiam theory', *Camb JE*, 7, Sept.–Dec. 1983.

Principal Contributions The overriding concern in my work is with analysis of the process of expansion and development of capitalist economies and the specific mechanisms through which this process occurs. This interest has taken me into a detailed critical investigation of the substantive content of existing economic theories as concerns their treatment of this problem at the most abstract as well as concrete level. In addition, I have sought to grapple with the problem in its historical and contemporary dimensions. I am seeking now to formulate my own conception of the process in terms of 'a theory of uneven development'.

HARRIS, John Rees

Born 1934, Rockford, IL, USA.
Current Post Dir., African Stud. Center, Prof. Econ., Boston Univ., MA, USA, 1975–.
Past Posts Instr. Econ., Northwestern Univ., 1964–6; Ass. Prof. Econ., 1966–70, Assoc. Prof. Econ. Urban Planning, MIT, 1970–4.
Degrees BA Wheaton Coll., IL, 1955; MA PhD, Northwestern Univ., 1964, 1967.
Offices and Honours African Stud. Assoc., 1964–.
Principal Fields of Interest 823 Labour Mobility.
Publications *Articles:* 1. 'Migration, employment and development: a two-sector analysis' (with M. Todaro),

AER, 60(2), March 1970; 2. 'Urban and industrial deconcentration in developing economies: an analytical framework', *Regional Urban Econ.*, 1, Aug. 1971; 3. 'Migration, employment and earnings' (with B. Aklilu), in *The Indonesian Economy*, ed. G. F. Papanek (Praeger, 1980); 4. 'Urban unemployment in developing countries: towards a more general search model' (with R. Sabot), in *Essays on Migration and the Labor Market in Developing Countries*, ed. R. Sabot (Westview Press, 1981).

Principal Contributions Understanding rural-urban migration in developing countries in terms of expected incomes (the Harris-Todaro model). Recently, incorporated more understanding of the role of labour-market institutions and social networks (particularly extended families) in affecting the pace and selectivity of migration.

HARRIS, Joseph*

Dates and Birthplace 1702–64, England.

Post Held Assay master, 1748.

Publications *Books:* 1. *Essay upon Money and Coins*, 2 pts (1757, 1758).

Career Monetary writer who placed his theory of money firmly in a framework of economic principles, in contrast to the common practice of divorcing discussions of money from the analysis of prices. He advocated monometallism, and held views on foreign trade on which Adam Smith may have drawn.

Secondary Literature A. E. Monroe, 'Harris, Joseph', *ESS*, 7.

HARRIS, Seymour Edwin*

Dates and Birthplace 1897–1975, New York City, NY, USA.

Posts Held Instr., Lect., Prof., Harvard Univ., 1922–64; Vis. Prof., Univ. Cal. San Diego, 1964–73.

Degrees BA, PhD Harvard Univ., 1920, 1926.

Offices and Honours Member of numerous official commissions and comms.; Ed., *REStat*, 1943.

Publications *Books:* 1. *The New*

Economics. Keynes' Influence on Theory and Public Policy, ed. (1947); 2. *Keynes: Economist and Policy Maker* (1955); 3. *Higher Education in the United States: The Economic Problem* (1960); 4. *Higher Education: Resources and Finance* (1962); 5. *Economics of the Kennedy Years* (1964).

Career Prolific author and editor of whom F. A. Lutz once said that he 'couldn't hold his ink'. His chief concern was with the practical relevance of what he wrote or edited. During his tenure of office, *REStat* increased its circulation greatly and published large numbers of papers of immediate relevance. Along with Hansen and Samuelson, he was one of the chief disseminators of Keynesian ideas in America. His publications included books on the economics of health care, education, social security, international monetary policy, central bank policy, monetary history and various other subjects.

HARRISON, Bennett

Born 1942, Jersey City, NJ, USA.

Current Post Prof. Polit. Econ. and Planning, MIT, USA., 1983–.

Past Posts Lect. Econ., New School Social Res., NY, 1967–8; Ass. Prof. Econ., Univ. Maryland, 1968–72; Vis. Prof. Urban Stud., Univ. Penn. 1972; Assoc. Prof. Econ. and Urban Stud., MIT, 1972–82; Vis. Prof. Econ., Boston Univ., 1975; Vis. Prof. City and Regional Planning, Univ. Cal. Berkeley, 1983.

Degrees BA (Polit. Science) Brandeis Univ. 1965; MA; PhD Univ. Penn., 1966, 1970.

Offices and Honours Honors Polit. Science, Brandeis Univ., 1965; Carey Prize Econ., Univ. Penn., 1970; US SSRC Fulbright Fellow, 1983; Hon. Mention, C. Wright Mills Prize, 1983.

Editorial Duties Ed. Board, *Social Pol.*

Principal Fields of Interest 110 Economic Growth, Development, Planning Theory; 820 Labour Markets, Public Policy; 941 Regional Economics.

Publications *Books:* 1. *The Economic Development of Harlem* (with T. Vietorisz), (Praeger, 1970); 2. *Educa-*

tion, Training and the Urban Ghetto (JHUP, 1972); 3. *The Political Economy of Public Service Employment*, co-ed, (with H. Shephard and W. Spring), (D. C. Heath, 1972); 4. *Urban Economic Development* (Urban Inst. 1974); 5. *Patterns of Racial Discrimination*, co-ed. (with G. M. von Furstenberg), (D. C. Heath, 1974); 6. *The Deindustrialization of America* (with W. B. Bluestone), (Basic Books, 1982).

Articles: 1. 'Education and under-employment in the urban ghetto', *AER*, 62(5), Dec. 1972., repr. in *Schooling in a Corporate Society*, ed. M. Carnoy (McKay, 1975), and *Problems in Political Economy*, ed. D. Gordon (D. C. Heath, 1978); 2. 'Labor market segmentation : postitive feedback and divergent development' (with T. Vietorisz), *AER*, 63(2), May 1973; 3. 'Ghetto employment and the model cities program', *JPE*, 82(2), March–April, 1974; 4. 'Ghetto economic development', *JEL*, 12(1), March 1974; 5. 'The political economy of state job-creation business incentives' (with S. Kanter), *J. Amer. Inst. Planners*, 44(4), Oct. 1978, repr. in *The Revitalization of the Northeast*, eds. G. Sternlieb and J. Hughes (Transaction, 1978); 6. 'The changing structure of jobs in older and younger cities' (with E. Hill), in *Central City Economic Development*, ed. B. Chinitz (ABT Assoc. 1979); 7. 'Welfare payment and the reproduction of low-wage workers and secondary jobs', *Rev. Radical Polit. Econ.*, 11(2), Summer 1979; 8. 'The incidence and regulation of plant closings' (with B. Bluestone), *Pol. Stud. J.*, 10(2), Dec. 1981, repr. in *Public Policies for Distressed Communities*', eds. S. Redburn and T. Buss (D. C. Heath, 1982), and in *Sunbelt-Snowbelt : Urban Growth and Regional Restructuring* eds. L. Sawers and W. Tabb (OUP 1984); 9. 'The tendency towards increasing instability and inequality underlying the revival of New England', *Reg. Science Assoc. Proceedings*, 28, 1982, repr. in *The Economic Prospects for the Northeast*, ed. H. Richardson (Temple Univ. Press, 1984); 10. 'Regional restructuring and good business climates: the economic transformation of New England since World War II', *Sunbelt-Snowbelt, op. cit.*

Principal Contributions I have always been interested in the spatial aspects of industrial and employment change: how they affect workers of different races and genders, and the economic vitality of local communities. My first book was a study of the Black ghetto in New York City called Harlem. Two years later, my doctoral dissertation was published, which extended my researches on the social and economic organisation of the urban ghetto to comparative analyses of twelve such areas located across the country

I came to the Urban Planning Department of MIT in 1973 to develop a new curriculum in the field of 'community economic development'. Studying the poor, their neighbourhoods, and even their cities as a way of trying both to understand and to remedy their condition seemed increasingly inadequate; the problem lay in the development and functioning of broader, more fundamental social and political institutions. In 1974 and 1975, I became a consultant to the Massachusetts Legislature and helped to formulate a series of recommendations on State economic policy designed to facilitate the rebuilding of a balanced economic base. I then obtained a research grant to conduct more extensive inquiries into the changing economic structure of the Massachusetts and New England economies. During the course of the New England research, Barry Bluestone and I were approached by a consortium of major unions (principally the United Auto Workers) and public policy organisations and asked to conduct an investigation of the magnitude and consequences of plant shutdowns in the US. This led to the most exciting research effort of my life, which culminated in the publication in 1982 of our book, *The Deindustrialization of America*.

HARROD, Roy Forbes*

Dates and Birthplace 1900–78, Norfolk, England.
Posts Held Lect., Fellow, Christ Church Coll. Oxford, 1922.
Degree BA Univ. Oxford.
Offices Co-ed., *EJ*.

Publications *Books:* 1. *The Trade Cycle* (1936); 2. *Towards a Dynamic Economics* (1948); 3. *Life of John Maynard Keynes* (1951); 4. *Economic Essays* (1952); 5. *Foundations of Inductive Logic* (1956); 6. *Reforming the World's Money* (1965); 7. *Money* (1969); 8. *Economic Dynamics* (1973).

Career Made major contributions to the conceptualisation of imperfect competition theory, international trade and business cycle theory. His model of economic growth, demonstrating the conditions under which growth is possible at a steadily sustained rate, was his major achievement. Because Evsey Domar produced a later but similar version of the same theory, it has come to be known as 'Harrod-Domar Growth Theory'. He was also the first biographer of Keynes and a major promoter of Keynesian economics. He was a frequent adviser to government and international organisations.

Secondary Literature I. C. Johnson, 'Harrod, Roy F.', *IESS*, 18; H. Phelps-Brown, 'Sir Roy Harrod: A Biographical Memoir', *EJ*, 30. March 1980; G. L. S. Shackle, 'On Harrod', *Contemporary Economists in Perspective*, eds. H. W Spiegel and W. J. Samuels (JAI Press, 1984).

HARSANYI, John Charles

Born 1920, Budapest, Hungary.

Current Post Flood Res. Prof. Bus. Admin., Prof. Econ., Univ. Cal. Berkeley, 1983–.

Past Posts Univ. Ass., Univ. Budapest, Hungary, 1947–8; Pharmacy Manager, Budapest, 1948–50; Factory Worker, Sydney, Australia, 1951–3; Lect., Univ. Queensland, Brisbane, 1953–6; Res. Assoc., Cowles Foundation, Yale Univ., 1957; Vis. Ass. Prof., Stanford Univ., 1958; Sr. Fellow, ANU, 1959–61; Prof. Econ., Wayne State Univ., Detroit, 1961–3; Prof. Bus. Admin., Univ. Cal. Berkeley, 1964–83; Vis. Prof., Univs., Bielefeld, W. Germany, 1973–4, 1978–9, Bonn, W. Germany, 1978, Paris XII, 1979, Sydney, 1983.

Degrees M Pharmacy, PhD (Philo. and Sociology) Univ. Budapest, Hungary, 1944, 1947; MA Univ. Sydney, 1951; PhD Stanford Univ., 1959.

Offices and Honours First Prize Maths., Nat. Competition High School Students, Hungary, 1937; Rockefeller Fellow, 1956; Fellow, Center Advanced Study Behavioral Sciences, Stanford, CA, 1965–6; Fellow, Em Soc, 1968–, AAAS, 1984–.

Editorial Duties Ed. Boards, *Internat. J. Game Theory, J. Conflict Resolution, Math. Social Sciences*; Assoc. Ed., *Maths. Operations Res.*

Principal Fields of Interest 022 Microeconomic Theory; 026 Game Theory and Decision Theory; 024 Utilitarian, Welfare Economics and Ethics.

Publications *Books:* 1. *Essays in Ethics, Social Behaviour and Scientific Explanation* (Reidel, 1976); 2. *Rational Behaviour and Bargaining Equilibrium in Games and Social Situations* (CUP, 1977); 3. *Papers in Game Theory* (Reidel, 1982).

Articles: 1. 'Solutions for some bargaining games under the Harsanyi-Selten solution theory, Parts I and II', *Maths. Social Sciences*, 3(2–3), Sept.–Oct. 1982; 2. 'Mathematics, the empirical facts and logical necessity', *Erkenntnis*, 19(1–3), May 1983.

Principal Contributions I was attracted to economics by the elegance and the analytical power of economic theory. But I soon concluded that this power could be significantly increased by theoretical innovations based on modern decision theory and game theory. For instance, the old welfare economics, based on ordinal and interpersonally noncomparable utilities, could seldom supply clear policy recommendations. I showed how we can use decision theory as a logical foundation for a much more powerful utilitarian welfare economics, provided that we admit interpersonal utility comparisons, for which there are compelling philosophical reasons in any case.

In positive economics, conventional theory fails to supply unique predictions for bargaining, oligopoly, and many other cases. This led me to study game-theoretical solution concepts that do supply unique predictions. Thus, I showed the equivalence of Nash's and Zeuthen's bargaining solutions; and defined a generalised Shapley value, which was a generalisation of both the Shapley value and of the Nash-Zeuthen solution. I also proposed game-theoretical models for political power and for social status. Then, I showed how to extend game theory itself to games with incomplete information. This work greatly increased the use of game-theoretical models in economics, particularly in the study of bargaining, auctions, public tenders and oligopoly, as was pointed out by Reinhard Selten and myself and is now gaining increasing acceptance: nonco-operative-game models, including nonco-operative bargaining models, are often much more informative than cooperative-game models. But this raises the question of how to select *one* specific equilibrium point of each nonco-operative game as the solution. I first proposed the 'tracing procedure' as a partial answer and later, jointly with Selten, proposed a 'general theory of equilibrium-point selection'. I have also written several papers in the philosophy of science, including one on the foundations of mathematics.

HART, Albert Gailord

Born 1909, Oak Park, IL, USA.
Current Post Prof. Emeritus, Econ., Columbia Univ., 1978–.
Past Posts Teaching Ass., Instr., Univ. Chicago, 1932–4, 1934–9; Econ. Analyst, US Treasury, 1934; Vis. Lect., Univ. Cal. Berkeley, 1936; Project Dir., Debt Adjustment, Twentieth Century Fund, 1937–8; Assoc. Prof., Prof., Iowa State Coll., Ames, IW, 1939–45; Principal Econ., US Treasury, 1943–4; Res. Econ., Comm. Econ. Devlp., Chicago, 1944–6; Prof., Columbia Univ., 1946–78; Project Dir., Econ. Stabilization, Twentieth Century Fund, 1949–53; Fulbright Res. Prof., Institut de Science Econ. Appl., Paris, 1952–3; Fiscal Econ., Bureau Technical Assistance, UN, 1961–2; Fiscal Econ., Organisation Amer. States, 1963; Fiscal Econ., Technical Assistance Argentina, UN, 1964; Fulbright Prof., Goethe Univ., Frankfurt am Main, 1967; Vis. Prof., Univ. Central De Venezuela, 1978,

Grad. School Econ., Banco Central de Uruguay, Montevideo, 1980; Cons. Econ., Comision de Estudio y Reforma Fiscal, Venezuela, 1982–3.
Degrees BA Harvard Univ., 1930; PhD Univ. Chicago, 1936.
Offices and Honours Sheldon Travelling Fellow, Harvard Univ., 1930–1; Member Exec. Comm., Conference Res. Nat. Income and Wealth, 1938–44; Ford Faculty Fellow, 1956–7; Vice-Pres., AEA, 1963.
Editorial Duties Ed. Board, *AER*, 1946–8.
Principal Fields of Interest 026 Economic Theory: Uncertainty; 310 Domestic Monetary Policy; 123 Comparative Economic Studies.
Publications *Books:* 1. *Debts and Recovery* (Twentieth Century Fund, 1938); 2. *Anticipations, Uncertainty and Dynamic Planning* (Univ. Chicago Press, 1940, Augustus M. Kelley, 1951, 1965); 3. *Paying for Defense* (with E. D. Allan, *et al.*), (Blakiston, 1941); 4. *Social Framework of the American Economy* (with J. R. Hicks), (OUP, 1945, with J. Ford, 1955; transls., Spanish, Fondo de Cultura Economica, 1950, Greek, Hellenic Econ. Assoc., 1955); 5. *Money, Debt and Economic Activity* (Prentice-Hall, 1948, with P. B. Kenen, 1953, 1961, with A. E. Entine, 1969); 6. *Defense Without Inflation* (Twentieth Century Fund, 1951); 7. *Appraisal of Data and Research on Business Men's Expectations* (with M. Gainsbrugh, *et al.*), (Fed. Reserve Board, 1955); 8. *Quality and Economic Significance of Anticipations Data*, co-ed. (Princeton Univ. Press, 1960); 9. *International Compensation for Fluctuations in Commodity Trade* (with L. Abdel-Rahman, *et al.*), (UN, 1961); 10. *Issues in Banking and Monetary Analysis*, co-ed. (Holt Rinehard Winston, 1967).
Articles: 1. 'Risk, uncertainty and the unprofitability of compounding probabilities', in *Studies in Mathematical Economics and Econometrics*, eds. O. Lange, *et al.* (Univ. Chicago Press, 1942), repr. in *Readings in Income Distribution*, ed. W. Fellner (Blakiston, 1946); 2. 'Model building and fiscal policy', *AER*, 35(4), Sept. 1945; 3. 'The problem of economic instability'

(with E. Desprès, *et al.*), *AER*, 40(4), Sept. 1950; 4. 'Experimental verification of a composite indifference map' (with S. Rousseas), *JPE*, 59(4), Aug. 1951; 5. 'Public management of private employment' (with R. Hazelett), *AER*, 47(1), March 1957; 6. 'The case as of 1976 for commodity reserve currency', *WA*, 112(1), 1976; 7. 'Taxation in the management of primary commodity markets', in *Taxation and Development*, ed. N. T. Wang (Praeger, 1976); 8. 'The multiple futures', in *Frontiers in Social Thought*, ed. M. Pfaff (N–H, 1976); 9. 'Regaining control over an open-ended money supply', in *Stagflation Compendium*, Joint Econ. Comm., US Congress (US Govt. Printing Office, 1980).

Principal Contributions 'Flexibility' as decision-response to uncertainty, dating from 1936; persuading Congress of merits of current taxation of income, 1941; abatement of 'linkage of risk' as motive for cash-balance demand and insurance (substance of 'factor-of-production' view of money) from 1946; and reformulation of national accounts to show, for example, Venezuelan private economy ex-petroleum.

HART, Oliver Simon D'Arcy

Born 1948, London, England.
Current Post Prof. Econ., LSE, London, England, 1982–.
Past Posts Lect., Univ. Essex, England, 1974–5; Ass. Lect., Lect., Univ. Camb., 1975–81; Vis. Sr. Lect., Wharton School, Univ. Penn., 1979; Programme Dir., Centre Econ. Pol. Res., London, 1984–; Vis. Prof., MIT, 1984–5.
Degrees BA(Maths.) Univ. Camb., 1969; MA Univ. Warwick, 1972; PhD Univ. Princeton, 1974.
Offices and Honours Fellow, Council Member, Exec. Comm., Em Soc, 1979, 1983–, 1984–.
Editorial Duties Assoc. Ed., *JET*, 1976–9, *Em*, 1984–; Managing Ed., *REStud*, 1979–83; Ed. Board, *REStud*, 1975–.
Principal Fields of Interest 022 Microeconomic Theory; 023 Macroeconomic Theory; 026 Economics of Uncertainty

and Information; Game Theory and Bargaining Theory.

Publications *Articles:* 1. 'On the optimality of equilibrium when the market structure is incomplete', *JET*, 11(2), Dec. 1975; 2. 'Monopolistic competition in a large economy with differentiated commodities', *REStud*, 46(1), Jan. 1979; 3. 'On shareholder unanimity in large stock market economies', *Em*, 47(5), Sept. 1979; 4. 'Take-over bids, the free rider problem, and the theory of the corporation' (with S. Grossman), *Bell JE*, 11(1), Spring 1980; 5. 'Implicit contracts, moral hazard and unemployment' (with S. Grossman), *AER*, 74(2), May 1981; 6. 'A model of imperfect competition with Keynesian features', *QJE*, 97(1), Feb. 1982; 7. 'An analysis of the principal-agent problem' (with S. Grossman), *Em*, 51(1), Jan. 1983; 8. 'Optimal labour contracts under asymmetric information: an introduction', *REStud*, 50(1), Jan. 1983; 9. 'The market mechanism as an incentive scheme', *Bell JE*, 14(2), Autumn 1983; 10. 'Unemployment with observable aggregate shocks' (with S. Grossman and E. Maskin), *JPE*, 91(5), Dec. 1983.

Principal Contributions I have worked in the areas of the theory of the firm (with particular emphasis recently on incentive problems), the theory of monopolistic competition, and the theory of contracts. A continuing area of interest for me is the microfoundations of macroeconomics — an area I have worked in and hope to continue to work in in the future.

HART, Peter E.

Born 1928, London, England.
Current Post Freelance Econ. Cons.
Past Posts Lect., Sr. Lect., Univ. Bristol, 1961–7; Prof. Econ., Univ. Reading, 1967–83.
Degrees BSc LSE, 1949.
Offices and Honours Fellow, RSS, Em Soc; Cons., NIESR, 1965–80; Council, RES, 1980; Member, UK SSRC, Econ. Comm., 1980, Industry Panel, 1981.
Editorial Duties Ed. Board, *REStud*, 1963–73; Ed., *J Ind E*, 1975–.

Principal Fields of Interest 122 Economic Studies of Industrialised Countries.

Publications *Books:* 1. *Studies in Profit, Business Saving and Investment in the United Kingdom, 1920–62*, 2 vols. (A&U, 1965, 1968); 2. *Mergers and Concentration in British Industry* (with M. A. Utton and G. Walshe), (CUP, 1973); 3. *Concentration in British Industry 1935–75* (with R. Clarke), (CUP, 1980).

Articles: 1. 'Population densities and optimal aircraft flight paths', *Regional Stud.*, 6, 1973; 2. 'Moment distributions in economics: an exposition', *JRSS*, pt. 2, 138, 1975; 3. 'The comparative statics and dynamics of income distributions', *JRSS*, pt. 3, 139, 1976; 4. 'The dynamics of earnings, 1963–73', *EJ*, 86, Dec. 1976; 5. 'The statics and dynamics of income distributions: a survey', in *The Statics and Dynamics of Income*, eds. N. A. Klevmarken and J. A. Lybeck (Tieto, 1981); 6. 'On bias and concentration', *J Ind E*, 27(3), March 1979; 7. 'Lognormality and the principle of transfers', *BOIS*, 42(3), Aug. 1980; 8. 'The effects of mergers on industrial concentration', *J Ind E*, 29(3), March 1981; 9. 'Entropy, moments and aggregate business concentration', *BOIS*, 44(2), May 1982; 10. 'Experience curves and industrial policy', *Internat. J. Industrial Organization*, 1, Feb. 1983.

Principal Contributions Compiled and explained time series of the factor distribution of income in the UK 1870–1962 and the rate of return on capital 1920–62. Analysed the comparative statics and dynamics of personal income distributions, including life-cycles of income, and changes in business concentration in individual industries and in manufacturing as a whole. Other work includes spatial economics (regional and international differences in productivity, population densities and optimal aircraft flight paths) and statistical measurements in inequality (the reduction of general entropy measures to moments-of-moment distributions).

HAUSMAN, Jerry Allen

Born 1946, Weinton, VA, USA.
Current Post Prof. Econ., MIT, Cambridge, MA, 1979–.
Past Posts Ass. Prof., Assoc. Prof., MIT, 1973–6, 1976–9; Res. Assoc., NBER, 1979–; Vis. Prof., Harvard Univ., 1982–3.
Degrees BA(Hist.) Brown Univ., 1968; BPhil, DPhil Univ. Oxford, 1972, 1973,
Offices and Honours Marshall Scholar, 1970–2; Fellow, Em Soc, 1979; Frisch Medal Em Soc, 1980; JB Clark Award, AEA, 1985.
Editorial Duties Ed. Boards, *Bell JE*, 1974–83, *Rand J.*, 1984–, *Em*, 1978–, *Math. Rev.*, 1978–80, *REStud*, 1979–82, *J Pub E*, 1982–.
Principal Fields of Interest 022 Microeconomics; 211 Econometrics; 321 Fiscal Theory and Policy.

Publications *Books:* 1. *Social Experimentation*, co-ed. (with D. Wise), (Univ, Chicago Press, 1985).

Articles: 1. 'An instrumental variable approach to full-information estimators in linear and certain non-linear econometric models', *Em*, 43, May 1975; 2. 'A conditional probit model for qualitative choice' (with D. Wise), *Em*, 46, March 1978; 3. 'Specification tests in econometrics', *Em*, 46, May 1978; 4. 'Attrition bias in experimental and panel data: the Gary income maintenance experiment' (with D. Wise), *Em*, 47, Jan. 1979; 5. 'Individual discount rates and the purchase and utilization of energy using durables', *Bell JE*, Spring 1979; 6. 'The effect of taxes on labor supply', in *How Taxes Affect Economic Behavior* (Brookings Inst., 1981); 7. 'Exact consumers' surplus and deadweight loss', *AER*, 71(2), May 1981; 8. 'Panel data and unobservable individual effects' (with W. Taylor), *Em*, 49, Nov. 1981; 9. 'The econometrics of nonlinear budget sets', *Em*, forthcoming, 1985; 10. 'Seasonal adjustment with measurement error present' (with M. Watson), *JASA*, forthcoming, 1985.

Principal Contributions My major research activity has been the methodological development and application of econometrics. I have done research into the simultaneous equations model, the discrete choice model, and in panel data to develop new econometrics models and methods to overcome problems which existed in each of these areas. I have also been interested in tests of the adequacy of the specification of econometric models. I have developed specification tests which can be used in a variety of circumstances to test for correct specifications. Recently I have been doing research on the effects of errors in variables on econometric estimators. I have been engaged in the development of estimation techniques which overcome or alleviate this problem.

Another area of methodological and applied interest has been the design and analysis of social and economic experiments. I have done research on the negative income tax experiments and also experiments in electricity and telephone pricing and electricity conservation activities. One primary area of applied research has been in public finance. I have estimated models of labour supply which explicitly take account of the tax system which creates nonlinear budget sets. My research has indicated the potential of large deadweight loss from the current US income tax system. I have also considered the effects of the welfare system in the US and social security on economic activity including labour-force participation, retirement behaviour, and savings behaviour. My applied research has also led to the development of empirical methods to calculate exact consumers' surplus and deadweight loss to make welfare calculations. The research indicates that approximate methods are inadequate for empirical measurement of deadweight loss.

HAVEMAN, Robert H.

Born 1936, Grand Rapids, MI, USA.
Current Post Prof. Econ., Univ. Wisconsin-Madison, USA, 1970–.
Past Posts John Bascom Prof. Econ., Grinnel Coll., IA, 1965–70; Fellow, Netherlands Inst. Advanced Study, 1975–6; Tinbergen Prof., Erasmus Univ., Rotterdam, 1984–5.

Degrees BA Calvin Coll., 1958; PhD Vanderbilt Univ., 1963.
Principal Fields of Interest 911 General Welfare Programmes.
Publications Books: 1. *Unemployment, Idle Capacity and the Evaluation of Public Expenditures* (with J. V. Krutilla), (JHUP, 1968); 2. *The Economics of the Public Sector* (Wiley, 1970, 1976); 3. *The Economic Impacts of Tax-transfer Policy: Regional and Distributional Effects* (with F. Golladay), (Academic Press, 1977); 4. *Earnings Capacity, Poverty, and Inequality* (with I. Garfinkel), (Academic Press 1978); 5. *Microeconomic Simulation Models for Public Policy Analysis*, co-ed. (with K. Hollenbeck), (Academic Press, 1980); 6. *Public Policy Towards Disabled Workers* (with V. Halberstadt and R. Burkhauser), (Cornell Univ. Press, 1985).
Articles: 1. 'Unemployment excess capacity, and benefit-cost investment criteria' (with J. V. Krutilla), *REStat*, 49, Aug., Nov. 1967; 2. 'Common property, congestion, and environmental pollution', *QJE*, 87(2), May 1973; 3. 'Regional and distributional effects of a negative income tax' (with F. Golladay), *AER*, 66(4), Sept. 1976; 4. 'Congestion, quality deterioration, and heterogenous tastes' (with A. M Freeman III), *J Pub E*, 8(2), Oct. 1977; 5. 'Earnings capacity and its utilization' (with I. Garfinkel), *QJE*, 42, Aug. 1978; 6. 'Disability transfers and early retirement: a causal relationship' (with B. Wolfe), *J Pub E*, 24(2), Oct. 1984; 7. 'Schooling and economic well-being: the role of non-market effects' (with B. Wolfe), *JHR*, 19(3), Summer, 1984.
Principal Contributions Applied welfare economics (benefit-cost analysis), micro-data simulation modelling, regional modelling, measuring economic well-being, analysis of income distribution, poverty and its determinants, and analysis of social policy.

HAWLEY, Frederick Barnard*

Dates and Birthplace 1843–1929, USA.
Post Held Cotton broker.

Degrees Grad. Williams Coll.

Publications *Books:* 1. *Capital and Population* (1882); 2. *Enterprise and the Productive Process* (1907).

Career Businessman whose economics concentrates on the significance of the entrepreneur. His methodology was the deductive one of the English classics but his material was confined to activities in which motivation was individualistic.

Secondary Literature K. W. Bigelow, 'Hawley, Frederick Barnard', *ESS*, 7.

HAWTREY, Ralph George*

Dates and Birthplace 1879–1971, England.

Posts Held Civil Servant, UK Treasury, 1904–45; Price Prof. Internat. Econ., Royal Inst. Internat. Affairs, 1947–52.

Degree BA (Maths.) Univ. Camb.

Offices and Honours Fellow, BA; Pres., RES, 1946–8; Knighted, 1956.

Publications *Books:* 1. *Good and Bad Trade* (1913, 1962); 2. *Currency and Credit* (1919, 1950); 3. *The Art of Central Banking* (1932, 1962); 4. *Capital and Employment* (1937, 1952); 5. *A Century of the Bank Rate* (1938, 1962); 6. *Economic Destiny* (1944); 7. *The Pound At Home and Abroad* (1961).

Career One of the British economists responsible for the rethinking of monetary theory after 1919, he also pioneered the 'income' approach in Britain. The value of his contribution was in clarifying the operation of the banking system and the role of money in the twentieth-century economy. His views on topics, such as the futility of public works as a method of avoiding slumps, underwent considerable modification as circumstances changed, but the fundamental ideas on the role of the Bank Rate and the influence of the credit system remained consistent.

Secondary Literature C. W. Guillebaud, 'Hawtrey, R. G.', *IESS*, 6; E. G. Davis, 'R. G. Hawtrey', *Pioneers of Modern Economics in Britain*, eds. D. P. O'Brien and J. R. Presley (Macmillan, 1981).

HAYAMI, Yujiro

Born 1932, Tokyo, Japan.

Current Post Prof. Econ., Tokyo Metropolitan Univ., Tokyo, Japan, 1972–.

Past Posts Res. Assoc., Nat. Res. Inst. Agric. Econ., Japanese Ministry Agric. Forestry, 1956–66; Assoc. Prof., Tokyo Metropolitan Univ., 1966–72; Vis. Assoc. Prof., Univ. Minnesota, 1968–70; Agric. Econ., Internat. Rice Res. Inst., Philippines, 1974–6; Vis. Prof. Econ., Univ. Philippines, 1975–6; Inst. Econ. Growth, Delhi, India, 1981.

Degrees BA Tokyo Univ. 1956; PhD Iowa State Univ., 1960.

Offices and Honours Dist. Res. Award, Agric. Econ. Soc. Japan, 1967; Outstanding Article Award Inst. Developing Economies, Japan, 1968; Outstanding Econ Book Award, Nikkei Shinbun (Japan Econ. Newspaper), 1973; Outstanding Published Res. Award, Outstanding Journal Article Award, AAEA, 1971, 1976, 1978.

Editorial Duties Ed. Council, *AJAE*, 1972–4, 1984–.

Principal Fields of Interest 710 Agriculture; 620 Economics of Technological Change; 110 Economic Growth.

Publications *Books:* 1. *Agricultural Development: An International Perspective* (with V. W. Ruttan), (JHUP, 1971); 2. *A Century of Agricultural Growth in Japan: Its Relevance to Asian Development* (Univ. Tokyo Press, Univ. Minnesota Press, 1975); 3. *Anatomy of a Peasant Economy: A Rice Village in the Philippines* (Internat. Rice Res. Inst., 1978); 4. *Agricultural Growth in Japan, Taiwan, Korea and the Philippines*, co-ed. (with V. W. Ruttan and H. M. Southworth), (Univ. Press Hawaii, 1979); 5. *Asian Village Economy at the Crossroads* (with M. Kikuchi), (Univ. Tokyo Press, JHUP, 1981).

Articles: 1. 'Technological progress in agriculture' (with S. Yamada), in *Economics Growth: the Japanese Experience since the Meiji Era*, eds. L. R. Klein and K. Ohkawa (Richard D. Irwin, 1968); 2. 'Factor prices and technical changes in agricultural development: the United States and Japan, 1880–1960' (with V. W. Ruttan), *JPE*,

78(5), Sept.–Oct. 1970; 3. 'Korean rice, Taiwan rice and Japanese agricultural stagnation: an economic consequence of colonialism' (with V. W. Ruttan), *QJE*, 84, Nov. 1970; 4. 'Agricultural productivity differences among countries' (with V. W. Ruttan), *AER*, 60(5), Dec. 1970; 5. 'Elements of induced innovation: an historical perspective for the green revolution', *Explor. Econ. Hist.*, 8(4), Summer 1971; 6. 'Rice policy in Japan's economic development', *AJAE*, 54(1), Feb. 1972; 7. 'Social returns to public information services: statistical reporting of U.S. farm commodities' (with W. L. Peterson), *AER*, 62(1), March 1972; 8. 'Economics of community work programs: a communal irrigation project in the Philippines' (with M. Kikuchi and G. Dozina), *EDCC*, 26(2), Jan. 1978; 9. 'Price incentive versus irrigation investment to achieve food self-sufficiency in the Philippines' (with R. Barker and E. Bennagen), *AJAE*, 59(4), Nov. 1977; 10. 'Investment inducements to public infrastructure: irrigation in the Philippines' (with M. Kikuchi), *REStat*, 60(1), Feb. 1978.

HAYEK, Friedrich A. von

Born 1899, Vienna, Austro-Hungary.
Current Post Prof. Emeritus Univs., Chicago, Freiburg im Breisgau, W. Germany.
Degrees Dr Jur., Dr Rer. Pol., Univ. Vienna, 1921, 1923; DSc Univ. London, 1940.
Offices and Honours FBA, 1945; Joint Nobel Prize in Econ., 1974.
Principal Fields of Interest 020 General Economic Theory; 031 History of Economic Thought.
Publications *Books:* 1. *Prices and Production* (Routledge & Kegan Paul, 1931, 1935); 2. *Profits, Interest and Investment* (Routledge & Kegan Paul, 1939); 3. *The Pure Theory of Capital* (Macmillan, Routledge & Kegan Paul, Univ. Chicago Press, 1941); 4. *The Road to Serfdom* (Routledge & Kegan Paul, Univ. Chicago Press, 1944); 5. *Individualism and Economic Order* (Routledge & Kegan Paul, Univ. Chicago Press, 1949); 6. *The Constitution of Liberty* (Rout-

ledge & Kegan Paul, Univ. Chicago Press, 1960); 7. *Studies in Philosophy, Politics and Economics* (Routledge & Kegan Paul, Univ. Chicago Press, 1967); 8. *Law, Legislation and Liberty*, 3 vols. (Routledge & Kegan Paul, Univ. Chicago Press, 1973, 1976, 1979); 9. *New Studies in Philosophy, Politics, Economics and the History of Ideas* (Routledge & Kegan Paul, Univ. Chicago Press, 1978); 10. *Money, Capital & Fluctuations* (Routledge & Kegan Paul, 1984).
Principal Contributions Exploration of the guiding function of prices in determining the accumulation of capital, industrial fluctuations, and the productivity of the economy generally, making a free competitive order the essential condition for the sustenance of the present numbers of mankind.
Secondary Literature F. Machlup, 'Friedrich von Hayek's contributions to economics', *Swed JE* 76(4), Dec. 1974, repr. in *Contemporary Economists in Perspective*, eds. H. W. Spiegel and W. J. Samuels (JAI Press, 1984); N. P. Barry, *Hayek's Economic and Social Philosophy* (Macmillan, 1979); J. Gray, *Hayek on Liberty* (Blackwell, 1984).

HAZELL, Peter Brian Reginald

Born 1944, Essex, England.
Current Post Res. Fellow, Internat. Food Policy Res. Inst, Washington, DC, 1979–.
Past Posts Res. Ass., Cornell Univ., 1965–70; Sr. Res. Assoc., Agric. Adjustment Unit, Univ. Newcastle, England, 1970–2; Econ., World Bank, Washington, DC, 1973–9; Cons., Inter-Amer. Agric. Salina, San José, Costa Rica, 1979.
Degrees Nat. Diploma Agric., Diploma Farm Management, Seale-Hayne Agric. Coll., Newton Abbot, Devon, 1964, 1965.
Principal Fields of Interest 710 Agriculture.
Publications *Books:* 1. *Instability in Indian Foodgrain Production* (Internat. Food Pol. Res. Inst., 1982); 2. *Project Evaluation in Regional Perspective: A Study of an Irrigation Project in Northwest Malaysia* (with C. Bell and R.

Slade), (JHUP, 1982); 3. *Rural Growth Linkages: Household Expenditure Patterns in Malaysia and Nigeria* (with A. Roell), (Internat. Food Pol. Res. Inst., 1983); 4. *Risky Agricultural Markets: Expectations, Welfare and Intervention* (with P. L. Scandizzo and J. R. Anderson), (Westview, 1984); 5. *Agricultural Risks and Insurance: Issues and Policies*, co-ed. (with C. Pomareda and A. Valdes), (Internat. Food Pol. Res. Inst., 1984).
Articles: 1. 'Implications of aggregation bias for the construction of static and dynamic linear programming supply models' (with A. E. Buckwell), *J Agric. Econ.* 23, May 1972; 2. 'Competitive demand structures under risk in agricultural linear programming models', *AJAE*, 56, May 1974; 3. 'Market intervention policies when production is risky' (with P. L. Scandizzo), *AJAE*, 57, Nov. 1975; 4. 'Adjustment in British farm production' (with B. Davey), in *Agriculture and the State*, eds. B. Davey, T. Josling and A. McFarquhar (Macmillan, 1976); 5. 'Farmers' expectations, risk aversion and market equilibrium under risk' (with P. L. Scandizzo), *AJAE*, 59, Feb. 1977; 6. 'Endogenous input prices in linear programming models', *AJAE*, 61, Aug. 1979; 7. 'Optimal price intervention policies when production is risky' (with P. L. Scandizzo), in *Risk, Uncertainty and Agricultural Development*, eds. J. A. Roumasset, J. M. Boussard and I. Singh (Agric. Dev. Council, 1979); 8. 'Measuring the indirect effects of an agricultural investment project on its surrounding region' (with C. L. G. Bell), *AJAE*, 62, Feb. 1980, repr. in *Agricultural Sector Analysis in Asia*, eds. M. Langham and R. Retzlaff (Singapore Univ. Press, 1982), and *Further Readings on Malaysian Economic Development*, ed. D. Lim (*OUP*, 1983); 9. 'Evaluating price stabilization schemes with mathematical programming' (with C. Pomareda), *AJAE*, 63, Aug. 1981; 10. 'Applications of risk preference estimates in firm-household and agricultural sector models', *AJAE*, 64, May 1982.

HAZLEDINE, Tim

Born 1947, Dunedin, New Zealand.
Current Post Assoc. Prof., Agric. Econ., Univ. British Columbia, Vancouver, Canada, 1982–.
Past Posts Ass. Lect., Otago Univ., NZ, 1969–72; Lect., Warwick Univ., 1973–4, Balliol Coll. Oxford, 1974–5; Res. Econ., Agric., Canada, 1975–7; Econ. Council Canada, Ottawa, 1977–8; Econ. Cons., 1979–83; Vis. Assoc. Prof., Queen's Univ., Ont., 1979–80, 1981–2.
Degrees BA, MA (Econ. and Maths.) Univ. Canterbury, NZ, 1968, 1969; MA Univ. Otago, NZ, 1972; PhD Univ. Warwick, England, 1978.
Offices and Honours P.W.S. Andrews Memorial Prize, 1973; Vis. Fellow, NZ Inst. Econ. Res., Wellington, 1979; Hon. Res. Fellow, Univ. Coll., London, 1983–4; Vis. Fellow, Warwick Univ., 1984.
Principal Fields of Interest 134 Inflation and Deflation; 612 Public Policy towards Monopoly and Competition; 616 Industrial Policy.
Publications *Books:* 1. *Full Employment without Inflation: Manifesto for a Governed Economy* (Macmillan, St Martins Press, 1984).
Articles: 1. 'Employment and output functions for New Zealand manufacturing industries', *J Ind E*, 22(3), March 1974; 2. 'Unbalanced growth and the welfare state', *SJPE*, 23(3), Nov. 1976; 3. 'Population and economic growth: a world cross-section model' (with R. S. Moreland), *REStat*, 59(3), Aug. 1977; 4. 'New specifications for employment and hours functions', *Ec*, N.S. 45, May 1978; 5. 'Constraints limiting the demand for labour in Canadian manufacturing industry', *AEP*, June 1979; 6. 'The regional implications of the Canadian tariff structure', *AJAE*, 60(5), Dec. 1978; 7. 'Testing models of pricing and tariff protection with Canadian data', *J Ind E*, 24(2), Dec. 1980; 8. 'The nature of industrial market power in the UK', in *Microeconomic Analysis*, eds. D. Currie and D. Piel (Croom Helm, 1981); 9. 'Employment functions and the demand for labour in the short-term', in *Essays on the Labour Market*, eds. J Hornstein, *et al.* (HMSO,

1981); 10. 'The possibility of price umbrellas in Canadian manufacturing industries', *Internat. J. Industrial Organisation*, 1985.

Principal Contributions My research deals with economies in which output is predominantly produced and sold under conditions of imperfect competition. I began by studying the demand for labour in manufacturing industries and found that the puzzling phenomenon of pro-cyclical productivity ('Okun's Law') is not due, as had been believed, to adjustment costs, but is a permanent characteristic of the cost curves on which firms operate. This appears to rule out the existence of a price-taking competitive equilibrium, and my subsequent work has focussed on the implications of firms facing less than perfectly elastic demand for their output. My research is proceeding at three levels. At the micro or 'industrial organisation' level, I am studying profitability and productivity behaviour in Canadian manufacturing industries, using a newly available panel database which permits us to go below the surface of the usual industry-level published data to track individual firms and groups of firms over time. Secondly, I have built empirical general equilibrium models of the Canadian economy in which 'lumpiness' matters. That is, the models are built from blocks of sectors — manufacturing, primary energy, etc. — which have distinct market characteristics. Then, at the 'macro' level, I have studied the problem of achieving non-inflationary full employment in imperfectly competitive economies. This had led to my proposal for a new species of permanent high-level price controls in effect to simulate competitive conditions by forcing firms to act as price-taker rather than price-makers, and so turn their attention to increasing output and employment as the means of increasing profits. These ideas are developed in my recent book.

HEAL, Geoffrey Martin

Born 1944, Bangor, Wales.
Current Post Prof. Econ., Univ. Essex, England, 1981–.

Past Posts Prof. Econ., Univ. Sussex, 1973–80; Vis. Prof., Yale Univ., 1975, Stanford Univ., 1976; Wesley Mitchell Vis. Prof., Columbia Univ., 1979.
Degrees BA, PhD Univ. Camb., 1966, 1969.
Offices and Honours Pres. Assoc. Environmental Resource Econ.; Fellow, Em Soc.
Editorial Duties Assoc. Ed., *Em*, *Econ. Letters*, *Energy Resources*; Managing Ed., *REStud*, 1969–74.
Principal Fields of Interest 723 Energy.
Publications Books: 1.*The Theory of Economic Planning* (N-H, 1973; transls., Spanish, Italian); 2. *Linear Algebra and Linear Economics* (with J. Hughes and R. Tarling), (Macmillan, Elsevier, 1977); 3. *Economic Theory and Exhaustible Resources* (with P. Dasgupta), (Nisbet, CUP, 1979); 4. *Public Policy and the Tax System*, co-ed. (with J. Hughes), (A&U, 1980).

Articles: 1. 'Planning, prices and increasing returns', *REStud*, 38(3), July 1971; 2. 'Optimal depletion of exhaustible resources' (with P. S. Dasgupta), *REStud*, Symposium 1974; 3. 'Equity efficiency and increasing returns', *REStud*, 46(4), Oct. 1979; 4. 'Metal price movements and interest rates', *REStud* 47(1), Jan. 1980; 5. 'Marginal cost pricing, two part tariffs and increasing returns in a general equilibrium framework', *J Pub E*, 13, Feb. 1980.

Principal Contributions Development of a theoretical basis for the study of alternative economic systems; bringing the study of economics with increasing returns to scale in production within the scope of formal resource allocation theory; and the development of theoretical and empirical frameworks for the analysis of economic issues relating to extractive resources.

HEARN, William Edward*

Dates and Birthplace 1826–88, Co. Cavan, Ireland.
Posts Held Prof. Greek, Queen's Coll., Univ. Galway, 1849–54; Prof., Dean, Chancellor, Univ. Melbourne, 1854–86.
Degrees BA Trinity Coll., Dublin.

Offices and Honours Member, Australian Legislative Council, 1878–88.

Publications *Books:* 1. *Plutology: The Theory of the Efforts to Satisfy Human Wants* (1863).

Career Hearn's *Plutology* . . . is one of those major contributions to economics which have sometimes come from Australia. It is notable for its emphasis on the demand side, its biological analogies, and its capable treatment of capital and production. Hearn had read unusually widely and incorporated the ideas of Longfield and Rae.

Secondary Literature J. A. La Nauze, 'Hearn and economic optimism', in *Political Economy in Australia* (1949).

HEATON, Herbert*

Dates and Birthplace 1890–1972, Silsden, Yorkshire, England.

Posts Held Lect., Univs. Birmingham, 1912–14, Tasmania, 1914–7, Adelaide, 1917–25; Prof. Econ., Queen's Univ., Canada, 1925–7; Prof. Econ. Hist., Univ. Minnesota, 1927–57.

Degrees MA, D Litt Univ. Leeds; MCom Univ. Birmingham.

Offices and Honours Pres., EHA, 1948–50.

Publications *Books:* 1. *The Yorkshire Woollen and Worsted Industries* (1920); 2. *Modern Economic History with Special Reference to Australia* (1920); 2. *History of Trade and Commerce with Special Reference to Canada* (1928); 4. *The British Way to Recovery* (1934); 5. *Economic History of Europe* (1936).

Articles: 1. 'Heckscher on mercantilism: review', *JPE*, 45, June 1937.

Career British economic historian, specialising in the seventeenth and eighteenth centuries and in the colonial history of Australia and Canada. His masterly review of Heckscher's great book on mercantilism displays his powers to best advantage.

HECKMAN, James J.

Born 1944, Chicago, IL, USA.
Current Post Prof. Econ., Univ. Chicago, 1980–.

Past Posts Ass. Prof., Assoc. Prof., Columbia Univ., 1970–2, 1972–4; Assoc. Prof., Univ. Chicago, 1974–80; Vis. Prof., UCLA, 1976, Univ. Wisconsin, 1977, LSE, 1977, Yale Univ., 1984.

Degrees BA(Maths.) Colorado Coll., 1965; MA, PhD Princeton Univ., 1968, 1971.

Offices and Honours Guggenheim Foundation Fellow, 1978–9; Fellow, Em Soc, 1980; Fellow, Center Advanced Stud. Behavioral Sciences, Stanford, CA 1982; John Bates Clark Medal, AEA, 1983.

Editorial Duties Co-Ed., *JPE*, 1981–; Amer. Ed., *REStud*, 1982–5; Assoc. Ed., *J Labor E*, 1983–.

Principal Fields of Interest 211 Econometrics; 800 Manpower, Labour, Population.

Publications *Books:* 1. *Longitudinal Analysis of Labor Market Data*, co-ed. (with D. Singer), (CUP, 1985); 2. *Lecture Notes on Longitudinal Data* (with B. Singer), (Springer-Verlag, 1985).

Articles: 1. 'Shadow prices, market wages and labor supply', *Em*, 42(4), July 1974; 2. 'Effects of child-care programs on woman's work effort', *JPE*, 82(2), pt. 2, March-April 1974; 3. 'A life cycle model of earnings, learning and consumption', *JPE*, 84(4), Aug. 1976; 4. 'The government's impact on the labor market status of black Americans', in *Equal Rights and Industrial Relations*, ed. F. E. Bloch, *et al.* (IRRA, 1977); 5. 'Dummy endogenous variables in a simultaneous equal system', *Em*, 46(4), July 1978; 6. 'Sample selection bias as a specification error', *Em*, 47(1), Jan. 1979; 7. 'Econometric duration analysis', *JEm*, 24(1), Jan. 1984; 8. 'Alternative methods for estimating the impact of interventions', in *Longitudinal Analysis of Labour Market Data, op. cit.*

Principal Contributions I have attempted to explore the consequences of sample design on empirical estimates obtained from those samples. Sample selection and self-selection are pervasive phenomena that critically affect the interpretation placed on social statistics. I have helped direct the attention of the profession to this topic. In addition, I have explored the consequences of failing to account for unobservables in dynamic models of labour supply and fertility. Such unobservables — termed 'heterogeneity' — seriously affect the inferences one can draw from dynamic data. The hypothesis that people are different can account for a wide variety of empirical regularities in social science. Economic models that rationalise statistical artefacts are a pernicious waste of time. My principal goal — but perhaps not my principal contribution—is to provide a factual basis for economics, to free it of metaphysical or political bias and to sort out the empirically testable from the huge corpus of economics that is not empirically founded. All of my work is directed toward producing testable economic models and to separating the knowable (in an empirical source) from the conjecture, however fashionable or widely held. By placing economics on an empirical basis and eliminating the subjective element which currently dominates the field, it may be possible to make progression in a subject that is widely perceived to be discredited because it has so little empirical content and cares so little about developing it.

HECKSCHER, Eli Filip*

Dates and Birthplace 1879–1952, Sweden.

Posts Held Prof. Econ. Stats. Stockholm Bus. School, 1909–29; Prof., Stockholm Inst. Econ. Hist., 1929.

Publications Books: 1. The Continental System: An Economic Interpretation (1918, 1922); 2. Mercantilism, 2 vols. (1931, 1955); 3. An Economic History of Sweden (1941, 1954).

Career His work on economic history was that of an economist and statistician. His only real contribution to economic theory was an argument in favour of free trade, which, elaborated as it was by Ohlin, has become known as the 'Heckscher-Ohlin theorem'. However, his prodigious output of articles and pamphlets led him into many historical fields. His work on Swedish population movements and his masterly treatment of mercantilism are perhaps his best-known achievements.

Secondary Literature G. Ohlin, 'Heckscher, Eli', IESS, 6.

HEERTJE, Arnold

Born 1934, Breda, The Netherlands.

Current Post Prof. Econ., Faculty of Law, Univ. Amsterdam, 1961–.

Past Posts Fellow, Netherlands Inst. Advanced Study Humanities and Social Sciences, 1974–5; Vis. Prof. Econ., Univ. Cal. Berkeley, 1982, 1983.

Degree PhD Univ. Amsterdam, 1960.

Principal Fields of Interest 020 General Economic Theory; 030 History of Economic Thought; 620 Economy of Technological Change.

Publications Books: 1. Economics of Technical Change (Weidenfeld & Nicholson, 1977); 2. Economie et progrès technique (Aubien, 1979); 3. Basic Economics (with B. R. G. Robinson), (Holt, Rinehart & Winston, 1979, 1982); 4. Economics (with F. Rushing and F. Skidmore), (Dryden Press, 1983); 5. Schumpeter's Vision, Capitalism, Socialism and Democracy after 40 Years, ed. (Praeger, 1981); 6. Investing in Europe's Future, ed. (Blackwell, 1983; transl., French, German and Italian); 7. The Black Economy (with M. Allen and H. Cohen), (Pan Books, 1982); 8. L'économie souterraine, (with M. Allen), (Economica, 1983).

Articles: 1. 'Die theoretische und empirische Bedeutung der Patinkin-kontroverse', Kyk, 17(2), 1967; 2. 'Preferences and economic growth', Kyk, 20(2), 1967; 3. 'Two letters from James Mill to Jean-Baptiste Say', HOPE, 3(2), Fall, 1971; 4. 'An essay on Marxian economics', Schweizerische Zeitschrift für Volkswirtschaft und Statistik, 108(1), March 1972, repr. in Penguin Modern Economics Readings: The Economics of Marx, eds. M. C. Howard and J. E. King (Penguin, 1976); 5. 'On David Ricardo', Jewish Hist. Soc. of England, Trans., Sessions 1970–3, 24, 1975; 6. 'The Cambridge controversy and welfare', in Relevance and Precision in Economics. Essays in Honour of Pieter de Wolff (Elsevier, 1976); 7. 'On Marx's theory of unemployment' (with D. Furth and R. J. van der Veen), OEP, 30(2), July 1978; 8. 'An unpublished letter of David Ricardo: to Thomas Smith of Easton Grey, 27 April 1819', EJ, 88, Sept. 1978; 9. 'An important letter from W. S. Jevons to L. Walras', MS,

50(4), Dec. 1982; 10. 'G. L. S. Shackle as historian of economic thought', in *Research in the History of Economic Thought and Methodology*, 1, ed. W. Samuels (JAI Press, 1983).

Principal Contributions Early work was concentrated on the theory of oligopoly including a new approach to the problem of price setting in oligopolistic markets. Later I turned to problems of economic growth and welfare economics as may be seen from a paper on the optimal savings ratio. In the 1970s my main contribution has been to the economics of technical change, which is still a topic I am highly interested in. In the field of the history of economic thought, I published letters of Mill, Ricardo and Jevons, which I happened to discover.

HEGGESTAD, Arnold Andersen

Born 1943, Madison, WI, USA.

Current Post William H. Dial Prof. Banking, Coll. Bus. Admin., Univ. Florida, Gainesville, FL, USA, 1977–.

Past Posts Econ., US Federal Trade Commission, 1965–7; Econ. Board of Governors, Fed. Reserve System, 1970–4; Ass. Prof. Econ., Univ. Florida, 1974–6; Sr. Analyst, Abt Assoc., Washington, DC, 1976–7; Vis. Prof., Univ. Uppsala, Sweden, 1979; Dir., Fin. Inst. and Monetary Pol. Center, Univ. Florida, 1979–; Vis., Fed. Reserve Bank Atlanta, 1980–1; Sr. Econ., Board of Governors, Fed. Reserve System, 1983.

Degrees BA Univ. Maryland, 1965; MA, PhD Michigan State Univ., 1970, 1973.

Editorial Duties Advisory Board, *Bank Acquisition Report*.

Principal Fields of Interest 310 Domestic Monetary and Financial Theory and Institutions; 620 Industrial Organisation and Public Policy; 520 Business Finance and Investment.

Publications *Books:* 1. *Regulation of Consumer Financial Services*, ed. (Abt Books, 1981); 2. *Studies in Public Regulation of Financial Services: Cost and Benefits to Consumers — A Bibliography* (Westview, 1978).

Articles: 1. 'Uncertainty, market structure, and performance: the Galbraith-Caves hypothesis and managerial motives in banking' (with F. R. Edwards), *QJE*, 77, Aug. 1973; 2. 'Prices, nonprices, and concentration in banking markets' (with J. J. Mingo), *JMCB*, 7(1), Feb, 1976; 3. 'Concentration and firm stability in commercial banking' (with S. A. Rhoades), *REStat*, 58(4), Nov. 1976; 4. 'The competitive condition of US Banking markets and the impact of structural reform' (with J. J. Mingo), *J Fin*, 33(3), June 1977; 5. 'Industry', *J Fin*, 32(4), Sept. 1977; 6. 'Bank portfolio regulation and the probability of bank failure' (with R. Blair), *JMCB*, 10(1), Feb. 1978; 7. 'Multi-market interdependence and local market competition in banking' (with S. A. Rhoades), *REStat*, 60(4), Nov. 1978; 8. 'Bank market structure and competition: A survey: Comment', *JMCB*, 16(4), pt. 2, Nov. 1984; 9. 'Multi-market interdependence and market performance in banking: a note' (with S. A. Rhoades), *Antitrust Bull*. 29(4), Winter 1984; 10. 'Mergers and acquisitions: financial and economic aspects', in *The Banking Handbook*, eds. R. C. Aspinwall and R. Eisenbeis (Wiley, 1984).

Principal Contributions My work has concentrated on the analysis of microeconomic issues in financial intermediation with particular emphasis on the US commercial banking industry. My early work focussed on the impact of market structure on performance of commercial banking markets. My particular interest was in the impact of monopoly power on interest rates, profitability, and on managerial objectives. In recent years, the greatest emphasis has been on the effect of deregulation on the financial services industry. Deregulation has important consequences for competition and antitrust policy. I have also studied the implications of deregulation for strategic planning and financial management.

HEILBRONER, Robert Louis

Born 1919, New York City, NY, USA.

Current Post Norman Thomas Prof.

Econ., Grad. Faculty, New School Social Res., NYC, NY, USA, 1973–.

Past Posts Prof. Econ, New School Social Res., 1968–73.

Degrees BA Harvard Univ., 1940; PhD New School Social Res., 1963; Hon. LLD, La Salle Univ., 1968, Ripon Coll., 1977, Long Island Univ., 1980, Wagner Coll., 1983.

Offices and Honours Exec. Comm., Comm. Honors and Awards, Vice-Pres., AEA, 1973–5, 1966–72, 1983–4; Advisory Board, Nat. Endowment Humanities, 1974–6; Fellow, AAAS, 1980; Guggenheim Foundation Fellow, 1983.

Editorial Duties Ed. Board, *Social Res.*, 1963, *Challenge*, 1970–, *Dissent*, 1970–.

Principal Fields of Interest 010 General Economics; 031 History of Economic Thought; 050 Economic Systems.

Publications *Books:* 1. *The Worldly Philosophers* (Simon & Schuster 1952, 1980; transls., 15 languages); 2. *The Future as History* (Harper & Row, 1959); 3. *The Great Ascent* (Harper & Row, 1963); 4. *The Limits of American Capitalism* (Harper & Row, 1966); 5. *The Economic Problem* (with L. Thurow), (Prentice Hall, 1968, 1983); 6. *Between Capitalism and Socialism* (Random House, 1970); 7. *An Inquiry into the Human Prospect* (W. W. Norton 1974, 1980); 8. *Business Civilization in Decline*, (W. W. Norton, 1976); 9. *Beyond Boom and Crash* (W. W. Norton, 1978); 10. *Marxism: For and Against* (W. W. Norton, 1980).

Articles: 1. 'Was Schumpeter right?', *Social Res.*, 85(3), Summer 1981; 2. '"The paradox of progress", decline and decay in the *Wealth of Nations*', in *Essays on Adam Smith*, ed. A. T. Wilson and A. S. Skinner (OUP, 1975); 3. 'Adam Smith', *Encyclopedia Britannica* (Helen Hemingway Beaton, 1974); 4. 'Modern economics as a chapter in the history of thought', *HOPE*, 11(2), Summer 1979; 5. 'The socialization of the individual in Adam Smith', *HOPE*, 14(3), Fall 1982; 6. 'The problem of value in the constitution of economic thought', *Social Res.*, 50(2), Summer 1983; 7. 'Economics and political economy: Marx, Keynes and Schumpeter', *JEI*, 18(3), Sept. 1984.

Principal Contributions My work began with an interest in the evolution of economic thought, not considered as an exercise in analysis, but as an aspect of intellectual history, and has continued in that vein. Gradually my focus of interest has shifted, however, from the 'scenarios' of the great economists to a consideration of the nature and logic of capitalism. This change in emphasis perhaps reflects my evolution from a naive Keynesian (graduated amid the early debates about the *General Theory* in 1940), through a second education in the classical economists, largely received at the hands of Adolph Lowe, my mentor at the New School, to a deep interest in Marx, the result of my exposure to the critical thought of students and colleagues during the last decade at the New School. I now see my life career as an effort to come to grips with, make my peace with, and finally to venture beyond Marx. The degree to which I have succeeded is of course for others to say but the direction of my impetus should at least be made clear. I have always been interested in writing as clearly and nontechnically as possible in the belief that scholarly efforts should not preclude communication with other educated readers.

HELLEINER, Gerald Karl

Born 1936, St Polten, Austria.

Current Post Prof. Econ., Univ. Toronto, Toronto, Ont., Canada, 1968–.

Past Posts Instr., Ass. Prof, Yale Univ., 1961–2, 1962–5; Assoc. Res. Fellow, Nigerian Inst. Social and Econ. Res., Univ. Ibadan, Nigeria, 1962–3; Assoc. Prof., Univ. Toronto, 1965–8; Dir., Econ. Res. Bureau, Univ. Coll, Dar es Salaam, Tanzania, 1966–8; Vis. Fellow, Inst. Devlp. Stud., Univ. Sussex, 1961–2, 1975, Queen Elizabeth House, Univ. Oxford, 1979; Res. Fellow, Internat, Devlp. Res. Centre, 1975–6.

Degrees BA (Polit. Science & Econ.) Univ. Toronto, 1958; MA, PhD Yale Univ., 1960, 1962.

Offices and Honours Guggenheim Foundation Fellow, 1971–2; Fellow,

Royal Soc. Canada, 1979; Vice-Chairman NS Inst., Ottawa, 1976–; Pres., Canadian Assoc. African Stud., 1969–71; UN Comm. Devlp. Planning, 1984.

Editorial Duties Ed. Board, *Internat. Organization, Devlp. and Change.*

Principal Fields of Interest 400 International Economics; 112 Economic Development; 121 Economic Studies of Less Industrialised Countries.

Publications *Books:* 1. *Peasant Agriculture, Government and Economic Growth in Nigeria* (Richard D. Irwin, 1966); 2. *Agricultural Planning in East Africa*, ed. (E. Africa Publ. House, 1968); 3. *International Trade and Economic Development* (Penguin, 1972; transl., Spanish, Alianza Universidad, 1975); 4. *A World Divided: The Less Developed Countries in the International Economy*, ed. (CUP, 1976; transl., Spanish, Signo Veintiuno Editores, 1979); 5. *International Economic Disorder: Essays in North South Relations* (Macmillan, Univ. Toronto Press, 1980); 6. *Intra-firm Trade and the Developing Countries* (Macmillan, St Martins, 1980); 7. *For Good or Evil, Economic Theory and North-South Negotiations* (Universitetsforlaget, Univ. Toronto Press, 1982); 8. *Handmaiden in Distress: World Trade in the 1980s* (with C. F. Diaz-Alejandro), (North-South Inst., Overseas Devlp. Inst., 1982); 9. *Protectionism, Threat to International Order* (with A. Cairncross, *et al.*), (Commonwealth Secretariat, 1982); 10. *Towards a New Bretton Woods, Challenges for the World Financial and Trading System* (with others), (Commonwealth Secretariat, Longman, 1983).

Articles: 1. 'Socialism and economic development in Tanzania', *J Dev Stud*, 8(1), Jan. 1972; 2. 'Manufactured exports from less developed countries and multinational firms', *EJ*, 83, March 1973; 3. 'The role of multinational corporations in the less developed countries' trade in technology', *WD*, 3(4), April 1975; 4. 'Smallholder decisionmaking: tropical African evidence', in *Agriculture in Development Theory* ed. L. G. Reynolds (Yale Univ. Press, 1975); 5. 'Industry characteristics and the competitiveness of manufacturers from less developed countries', *WA*, 112, 3,

1976; 6. 'Multinationals, manufactured exports and employment in the less developed countries', in *L'Actualité Economique*, April–June 1977; 7. 'The political economy of Canada's tariff structure: an alternative model, *CJE*, 10(2), May 1977; 8. 'International technology issues: southern needs and northern responses', in *The New International Economic Order: The North South Debate*, ed. J. Bhagwati (MIT Press, 1977); 9. 'Lender of early resort: the IMF and the poorest', *AER*, 73(2), May 1983; 10. 'The IMF and Africa in the 1980s', *Princeton Essays Internat. Fin.*, 173, July 1983;

Principal Contributions I began my career with primary concern for the development problems of tropical Africa. Inevitably that led me to research on agricultural economics and the performance of government-owned marketing boards in Nigeria. Later, in Tanzania I was similarly motivated but now within the context of a State with socialist aspirations. My interest in African economic development has remained firm but, from a Canadian base, it made more sense to shift my primary focus to broader questions of international and development economics.

I have sought to elucidate aspects of the interrelationships between industrialised countries and the developing ones, and to do so without the theoretical preconceptions and patronising tones of much of the current literature in the 'North' or the shrill rhetoric of some of that of the 'South'. Facts and logic are likely to generate the 'best' policy outcomes for both the developing countries and the world. In this connection I have consulted for the World Bank, UNCTAD, ILO, the UN Centre on Transnational Corporations, the UNDP, the Commonwealth Secretariat, the Brandt Commission, and the governments of individual developing countries.

In recent years my work has encompassed analysis of transnational corporate productivity, international financial flows and the role of the IMF. I have been particularly concerned with the wider implications of the growth of intra-firm international trade. In an approach to a more equitable, efficient and sustainable world it now seems to me that an understanding of politics is at least as important as economic analysis. Accordingly, I have developed a new interest in theories of public policy and in the role of information.

HELLER, Walter W.

Born 1915, Buffalo, NY, USA.
Current Post Regents' Prof. Econ., Univ. Minnesota, Minneapolis, MN, USA 1957–.
Past Posts Instr., Univ. Wisconsin, 1941–2; Econ., US Treasury, 1942–6; Ass. Prof., Assoc. Prof. Econ., Univ. Minnesota, 1946–57; Chief Internal. Fin., US Military Govt., W. Germany, 1947–8; Tax Adviser, King Hussein and Royal Commission Jordan, 1960; Chairman, US President's Council Econ. Advisers, Washington, DC, 1961–4; Cons., Exec. Office, US President, 1965–9, 1974–7, US Congressional Budget Office, 1975–; Chairman, Group Fiscal Experts, OECD, 1966–8; Vis. Prof., Univ. Washington, Univ. Wisconsin, Univ. Harvard, 1966, 1969, 1978.
Degrees BA Oberlin Coll., 1935; MA, PhD Univ. Wisconsin, 1938, 1941; Hon. LLD, LHD, Univs., Oberlin, 1964, Kenyon 1965, Ripon 1967, Coe, 1967, Long Island, 1968, Wisconsin, 1969, Loyola, 1979;, Roosevelt, 1976.
Offices and Honours Phi Beta Kappa; Beta Gamma Sigma; Ford Foundation Fellow, 1965–6; Carnegie Fellow, 1967–8; Vice-Pres., Pres., Disting. Fellow, AEA, 1967–8, 1974, 1975; Dir. Chairman, NBER, 1955, 1971–4, 1982–3; Fellow, Amer. Philo. Soc., 1975–; Fellow, AAAS, 1963; US Treasury Disting. Service Award, 1968; Member, *TIME*; Board Econ., Board Contrib., *Wall Street Journal*; Advisory Board, Banco del Lavoro, Rome, 1984–.
Principal Fields of Interest 010 General Economics; 310 Domestic Monetary and Fiscal Theory and Institutions.
Publications *Books:* 1. *Savings in the Modern Economy*, co-ed. (Univ. Minnesota Press, 1953); 2. *State Income Tax Administration* (with C. Penniman), (Public Admin. Service, 1959); 3. *New Dimensions of Political Economy* (Harvard Univ. Press, 1966); 4. *Revenue Sharing and the City* (with R. Ruggles, *et al.*), (JHUP, 1968); 5. *Prespectives on Economic Growth*, ed. (Random House, 1968); 6. *Monetary vs. Fiscal Policy, a Dialogue with Milton Friedman* (with M. Friedman), (W. W. Norton, 1969); 7. *Collision or Co-Existence?* (General Learning Press, 1973); 8. *The Economy : Old Myths and New Realities* (W. W. Norton, 1976).

Articles: 1. 'The anatomy of investment decision', *Harvard Bus. Rev.*, March 1951; 2. 'Limitations of the federal individual income tax', *J Fin*, May 1952; 3. 'Fiscal policies for under-developed countries' (UN, 1952), repr. in *Readings on Taxation in Developing Countries*, eds. R. M. Bird and O. Oldman (JHUP, 1967); 4. 'CED's stabilizing budget policy after ten years', *AER*, 47(4), Sept. 1957; 5. 'Economics and the applied theory of government expenditures', in Congressional Joint Econ. Comm. Compendium, *Federal Expediture Policy for Economic Growth and Stability* (US Govt. Printing Office, 1957); 6. 'Battle against inflation : an appraisal', *AER*, 60(1), Jan. 1970; 7. 'Economics of the race problem', *Social Res.*, 74(4), Winter 1970; 8. 'What's right with economics?', *AER*, 65(1), March 1975; 9. 'Economic policy for inflation' in *Reflections of America* (US Bureau of the Census, 1981), repr. in *Challenge*, Jan.–Feb. 1981; 10. 'Kennedy economics revisited', in *Economics in the Public Service, Papers in Honor of Walter W. Heller* (W. W. Horton, 1982).

Principal Contributions I am one of those fortunate individuals who has been able to realise his youthful professional ambitions, namely, a combined career of teaching, research and public service. Teaching and research, especially in taxation and public finance, dominated the first couple of decades of my career. My research was largely concentrated in federal and State income taxation and intergovernmental relations. Early on, the opportunity to apply some of my training and experience to public policy questions came, first, as an economic analyst for the US Treasury Department, working on war finance with Roy Blough, Milton Friedman, Albert G. Hart, Joseph Pechman and others, and second, as Chief of Internal Finance and tax adviser to General Lucius Clay, US Military Governor of Germany 1947–8. For a time in the early–1950s, working as a consultant with the UN and as a summer teacher and researcher at Harvard, I worked and wrote on fiscal policy for less developed countries, with special applications in the field of general taxation and agricultural taxation. Serving as tax adviser to King Hussein and the Royal Commission of Jordan in 1960 and later as Chairman of the Group of Fiscal Experts for OECD gave me an opportunity to apply some of these and other 'lessons' in public finance to practical policy problems.

Since serving as Chairman of the President's Council of Economic Advisers under Presidents Kennedy and Johnson in 1961–4, my career interests have shifted even more to the translation of economic analysis and research into public policy. Coupled with that has been an emphasis on the wider dissemination of economic ideas and findings to the informed lay public and policy-makers in business, finance and the government.

HELLWIG, Martin Friedrich

Born 1949, Düsseldorf, W. Germany
Current Post Prof. Econ., Univ. Bonn, Bonn, W. Germany, 1979–.
Past Posts Res. Assoc., Stanford Univ., 1973–4; Ass. Prof., Princeton Univ., 1974–7; Assoc. Prof., Univ. Bonn, 1977–9;
Degrees Diplom-Volkswirt Univ. Heidelberg 1970; PhD MIT, 1973.
Offices and Honours Fellow, Em Soc., 1981.
Editorial Duties Foreign Ed., *REStud*, 1982.
Principal Fields of Interest 026 Uncertainty and Information; 311 Domestic Monetary and Financial Theory; 315 Credit.
Publications *Articles:* 1. 'Asset management with trading uncertainty' (with D. K. Foley), *REStud*, 42(3), July 1975; 2. 'A model of borrowing and lending with bankruptcy', *Em*, 45(8), Nov. 1977; 3. 'On the aggregation of information in competitive markets', *JET*, 22(3), June 1980; 4. 'Bankruptcy, limited liability and the Modigliani-Miller theorem', *AER*, 71(1), March 1981; 5. 'Rational expectations equilibrium with conditioning on past prices : a mean-variance example', *JET*, 26(2), April 1982; 6. 'Moral hazard and monopolistically competitive insurance markets', *Geneva Papers Risk and Insurance*, 8, 1983.

Principal Contributions Research interests involve the microeconomic foundations of monetary theory, the economics of information and capital markets. Work on monetary theory concerns the development and analysis of equilibrium models of money, based on precautionary money holding or transactions. Work in the other areas concerns rational expectations equilibria — with and without communication through prices — insurance markets with moral hazard, and the economics of credit and bankruptcy.

HELMSTÄDTER, Ernst

Born 1924, Mannheim, W. Germany.
Current Post Prof. Econ., Univ. Münster, 1970–.
Past Posts Prof. Econ., Univ. Bonn, 1965–9; Dean, Faculty Econ. and Social Sciences, Univ. Münster, 1974–5; Expert Cons., Deutsche Forschungsgemeinschaft, 1976–84.
Degrees Dr Rer. Pol. Univ. Heidelberg, 1956; Habilitation Univ. Bonn, 1965.
Offices and Honours Board Member, List Soc, 1975–; Member, Pres., Verein für Sozialpolitik, 1978–82, 1983; Member, Sachverständigenrat zur Begutachtung der gesamtwirtschaftlichen Entwicklung, 1983.
Editorial Duties Co-ed., *Kyk, Internat. Zeitschrift für Sozialwissenschaften*.
Principal Fields of Interest 010 General Economics; 100 Economic Growth; Development; Planning; Fluctuations.
Publications *Books:* 1. *Der Kapitalkoeffizient. Eine Kapitaltheoretische Untersuchung* (Gustav Fischer, 1969);

2. *Wirtschaftstheorie*, I, II (Verlag F. Vahlen, 1974, 1983; 1976, 1981); 3. *Die Bedingungen des Wirtschaftswachstum in Vergangenheit und Zukunft*, ed. (J. C. B. Mohr, 1984).
Articles: 1. 'Produktionsstruktur und Wachstum', *JNS*, 169, 1957–8; 2. 'Linearität und Zirkularität des volkswirtschaftlichen Kreislaufs', *WA*, 94(1), 1965; 3. 'Investitionsquote und Wachstumsrate bei Harrod-neutralem Vorschritt', *JNS*, 178, 1965; 4. 'Wachstumstheorie I: Uberblick', in *Handwörterbuch der Wirtschaftswissenschaft*, 18 (Gustav Fischer, 1979); 5. 'Quesnays Multiplikatortableau als kreislaufanalytisches Instrument', in *Studien zur Entwicklung der Ökonomischen Theorie*, III, ed. H. Scherf (Gustav Fischer, 1983).
Principal Contributions Input-output analysis: triangulation. Theory of technical progress. Theory of income distribution.

HELPMAN, Elhanan

Born 1946, Dz Alabad, USSR.
Current Post Prof. Econ., Tel Aviv Univ., Tel Aviv, Israel, 1981–.
Past Posts Lect., Sr. Lect., Tel Aviv Univ., 1974–6, 1976–8; Vis. Assoc. Prof., Univ. Rochester, USA, 1977–9; Assoc. Prof., Tel Aviv Univ., 1978–81; Vis. Res. Fellow, Inst. Internat. Econ. Stud., Stockholm, 1979; Vis. Prof., Harvard Univ., 1982–3, MIT, 1983–4.
Degrees BA, MA (Econ. Stats.), Tel Aviv Univ., 1969, 1971; PhD Harvard Univ., 1974.
Offices and Honours Fulbright Award, 1983.
Editorial Duties Advisory Ed., *Econ. Letters*, 1978; Assoc. Ed. Co-ed., *J Int E*, 1981–2.
Principal Fields of Interest 022 Microeconomic Theory; 023 Macroeconomic Theory; 300 Domestic Monetary and Fiscal Theory and Institutions.
Publications *Books:* 1. *A Theory of International Trade under Uncertainty* (with A. Razin), (Academic Press, 1978); 2. *Social Policy Evaluation: an Economic Perspective*, co-ed. (with A. Razin and E. Sadka), (Academic Press, 1983).

Articles: 1. 'Optimal income taxation for transfer payments under different social welfare criteria' (with R. Cooter), *QJE*, 88(4), Nov. 1974; 2. 'Nontraded goods and macroeconomic policy under a fixed exchange rate', *QJE*, 91(3), Aug. 1977; 3. 'The optimal income tax' (with E. Sadka), *J Pub E*, 9(3), Aug. 1978; 4. 'Optimal public investment and dispersion policy in a system of open cities' (with D. Pines), *AER*, 70(3), June 1980; 5. 'International trade in the presence of product differentiation, economies of scale and monopolistic competition', *J Int E*, 11(3), Aug. 1981; 6. 'An exploration in the theory of exchange rate regimes', *JPE*, 89(5), Oct. 1981; 7. 'Optimal spending and money holdings in the presence of liquidity constraints', *Em*, 49(6), Nov. 1981; 8. 'Dynamics of a floating exchange rate regime' (with A. Razin), *JPE*, 90(4), Aug. 1982; 9. 'Increasing returns, imperfect markets and trade theory', in *Handbook of International Economics* (N-H, 1984); 10. 'The factor content of foreign trade', *EJ*, 94, March 1984.
Principal Contributions In the earlier years the work was concerned with macroeconomic and fiscal policy. The latter interest led to the study of urban economic problems related to taxation and local public goods. Later on the focus was shifted to microeconomic foundations of exchange-rate regimes plus uncertainty and imperfect competition in foreign trade. The study of exchange-rate regimes has been directed towards a better understanding of the interaction between financial systems and the real structure of economies in affecting macroeconomic variables. The interaction between the financial system and the real structure was also the focus of the study of trade under uncertainty. However, the work on exchange-rate regimes has focussed mainly on monetary arrangements while the work of trade under uncertainty has focussed on the role of risk-sharing arrangements via trade in securities on trade performance. International trade under imperfect competition has been studied in order to provide a better explanation of trade structure in the industrial countries, the emphasis being on the volume of trade, its composition

in terms of intra versus intersectoral trade and the intersectoral pattern of trade.

HENDERSON, Hubert Douglas*

Dates and Birthplace 1890–1952, Beckenham, Kent, England.
Posts Held Stat. UK Board Trade, 1914–18; Lect. Econ., Univ. Camb., 1918–23; Ed., *Nation*, 1923–30; Secretary, UK Econ. Advisory Council, 1930–4; Res. Fellow, All Souls Coll., Drummond Prof., Univ. Oxford, 1934–52, 1945–52.
Degrees BA Univ. Camb., 1912.
Offices and Honours Member, UK Commissions on the West Indies, Unemployment, Insurance, Population; Knighted, 1942; Pres., Section F BAAS, 1948–9; Pres., RES, 1950–2.
Publications *Books:* 1. *Supply and Demand* (1922); 2. *The Agricultural Dilemma* (1935); 3. *The Inter-war Years* (1955).
Career Deeply involved in public affairs through his membership of various official commissions and committees, his economic writings were invariably directed towards contemporary practical questions. His early experience as editor of the *Nation* involved him in political issues on the side of Keynes, though he later rejected much of Keynes's *General Theory*. Though in many ways an old-fashioned orthodox economist, his teaching at Oxford was successful in an era during which Keynes's ideas and other more recent developments were dominant.
Secondary Literature D. H. Robertson 'Obit. Sir Hubert Henderson 1890–1952', *EJ*, 63, Dec. 1953.

HENDERSON, John Vernon

Born 1947, Vancouver, British Columbia, Canada.
Current Post Prof. Econ. and Urban Stud., Brown Univ., Providence, RI, USA.
Past Posts Ass. Prof., Queen's Univ., Canada, 1972–4; Vis. Ass. Prof., Univ. Chicago, 1974; Ass. Prof., Assoc. Prof., Brown Univ., 1974–9, 1979–82; Vis.

Lect., Tribhuvai Univ., Nepal, 1976; Cons. Federalism, Eginai, Bilbao, Spain, 1976, World Bank Res. Projects and Missions, Brazil, China, 1979; Res. Assoc., NBER, 1982–.
Degrees BA Univ. British Columbia, Canada, 1968; MA, PhD Univ. Chicago, 1969, 1972.
Offices and Honours Guggenheim Foundation Fellow, 1984.
Editorial Duties Ed. Board, *JUE*, 1978–, *Public Fin. Q.*, 1981–, *Regional Science and Urban Econ.*, 1983; Ed., *Res. Urban Econ: A Res. Annual* (JAI Press).
Principal Fields of Interest 026 Economics of Uncertainty and Information; 930 Urban Economics; 940 Regional Economics.
Publications *Books:* 1. *Peer Group Effects and Educational Production Functions* (with P. Mieszkowski and Y. Sauvageau), (Econ. Council Canada, 1976); 2. *Economic Theory and the Cities* (Academic Press, 1977, 1984).
Articles: 1. 'Optimum city size: the external diseconomy question', *JPE*, pt. 1, 82(2), March–April 1974, repr. in *Urban Growth Policy in a Market Economy*, eds. J. Gardner, P. Graves and G. Tolley (Academic Press, 1979); 2. 'Public goods, efficiency and regional fiscal equilization' (with F. Flatters and P. Mieszkowski), *J Pub E*, 3(2), May 1974, repr. in *The Economics of Federalism*, eds. B. G. Brewai, *et al.* (ANU Press, 1980); 3. 'The sizes and types of cities', *AER*, 64(4), Sept. 1974; 4. 'Externalities in a spatial context: the case of air pollution', *J Pub E*, 7(1), Feb. 1977; 5. 'Community development: the effects of growth and uncertainty', *AER*, 70(2), May 1980; 6. 'The economics of staggered work hours', *JUE*, 9(3), May 1981; 7. 'Aspects of growth in a system of cities' (with Y. Ioannides), *JUE*, 10(8), Feb. 1981; 8. 'The impact of government policies on urban concentration', *JUE*, 12(3), Nov. 1982; 9. 'A model of housing tenure choice' (with Y. Ioannides), *AER*, 73(1), March 1983; 10. 'Industrial bases and city size', *AER*, 73(2), May 1983.
Principal Contributions My early work presented the first general equilibrium model of a system of cities with endogenous number of cities, city sizes

and prices. Following this, I worked on the welfare economics aspects of a system of cities but then I laid the general topic aside for almost five years. Over that time, I worked on theoretical topics, such as peaking load pricing in transportation, clubs and provisions of local public services, and growth and uncertainty in community development. During that five years I also wrote a book, *Economic Theory and the Cities*, presenting the state of middle-brow theory in urban economics at that time.

Starting in 1978, I returned to working on systems of cities. First, I developed the original model to include multiple types of cities, international trade and growth and technological change. Then I did econometric work estimating the properties of the system of cities in both the USA and Brazil, documenting the nature of urban scale economies, the extent of urban specialisation, the nature of manufacturing production technology, and the determinants of urban population composition. Currently, I am doing theoretical and econometric work on housing consumption and investment demand applying portfolio models and developing an econometric model of tenure spells and durable goods demand for panel data. Secondly I am doing theoretical work on property tax incidence, heterogeneity in Tiebout models, and long-run equilibrium in Tiebout models under consistent solutions. Finally, a second edition of *Economic Theory and the Cities* is currently in press.

HENDRICKS, Wallace

Born 1945, Vallejo, CA, USA.
Current Post Prof. Econ., and Lab. and Industrial Relations, Univ. Illinois, Urbana Champaign, IL, USA, 1982–.
Past Posts Ass. Prof., Assoc. Prof., Univ. Illinois, 1973–8, 1978–82.
Degrees BA, PhD Univ. Cal. Berkeley, 1967, 1971.
Principal Fields of Interest 824 Labour Market Studies; 832 Collective Bargaining; 613 Public Utilities and Government Regulation.
Publications *Books:* 1. *Wage In-*

dexation in the U.S. (with L. Kahn), (Ballinger, 1984).
Articles: 1. 'The effect of regulation on collective bargaining in electric utilities', *Bell JE*, 6(2), Autumn 1975; 2. 'Labor market structure and union wage levels', *EI*, 13(3), Sept. 1975; 3. 'Consumption patterns for electricity' (with R. Koenker and R. Podlasek), *J Em*, 5(2), March 1977; 4. 'Regulation and labor earnings', *Bell JE*, 8(2), Autumn 1977; 5. 'Residential demand for electricity: an econometric approach' (with R. Koenker and D. Poirier), *J Em*, 9(1), Jan. 1979; 6. 'A stochastic parameter model for panel data: an application to the Connecticut peak pricing experiment' (with R. Koenker and D. Poirier), *Int ER*, 20(3), Oct. 1979; 7. 'Regulation, deregulation and collective bargaining in airlines' (with R. Feuille and C. Szerszen), *ILRR*, 34(11), Oct. 1980; 8. 'Unionism, oligopoly and rigid wages', *REStat*, 63(2), May 1981; 9. 'The determinants of bargaining structure in U.S. manufacturing' (with L. Kahn), *ILRR*, 35(2), Jan. 1982; 10. 'Determinants and effects of cost of living allowances in U.S. collective bargaining agreements' (with L. Kahn), *ILRR*, 36(3), April 1983.
Principal Contributions During my student days at Berkeley, I became interested in both labour and industrial organisation as applied fields. Unlike many of my colleagues, however, I was never really able to make a total choice between the two. This is now reflected in a somewhat unusual combination of interests. At first, I was able to combine my interests under the general theme of the impact of market structure on outcomes in the labour market. This area of study included the impact of bargaining structure and the impact of regulation of the product market. Studying labour market outcomes of regulation led me to concentrate on regulation within the field of industrial organisation. At the time, some very interesting work was being started on the application of time-of-use pricing to electricity pricing in the USA. Along with several colleagues, I became actively involved in the analysis of the data which were being generated by time-of-use pricing experiments funded by the federal

government. These experiments posed interesting methodological problems in dealing with the individual demand data generated by the experiments. The same experimental data also provided the opportunity to design analyses of the costs and benefits of introduction of these pricing schemes.

At the same time, my interests in labour market structure and unions in particular remained. My earlier work using individual union contract data had yielded valuable results, and I continue to work in that area. More recently this has led to an interest in wage indexation within the union sector (both the reasons for its existence and its impacts) as well as an interest in attempting to measure the impact of unions on productivity.

HENDRY, David Forbes

Born 1944, Nottingham, Nottinghamshire, England.

Current Post Prof. Econ., Fellow, Nuffield Coll. Oxford, England, 1981–.

Past Posts Lect., Reader, Prof., LSE, 1969–81; Vis. Prof., Cowles Foundation, Yale Univ., 1975, Univ. Cal. Berkeley, 1976; Vis. Res. Fellow, ANU, 1976; Vis. Res. Prof., CORE, Louvain, Belgium, 1980; Vis. Prof., Univ. Cal. San Diego, 1981.

Degrees MA Aberdeen Univ. 1966; MSc, PhD Univ. London, 1967, 1970.

Offices and Honours Member, Econ. Comm., UK SSRC, 1977–82; Fellow, Em Soc., 1975–; Member, Academic Panel, UK Treasury, 1976–; Council Member, RES, 1978–83; Chairman, Soc. Econ. Analysis, 1981–; Acting Dir., Oxford Inst. Econ. and Stats., 1982–4.

Editorial Duties Joint Managing Ed., *REStud*, 1971–5; Em Ed., *EJ*, 1976–80; Joint Ed., *BOIS*, 1982–; Ed. Board, *REStud*, 1976–; Assoc. Ed., *Em*.

Principal Fields of Interest 211 Econometric and Statistical Methods.

Publications *Articles:* 1. 'Maximum likelihood estimation of systems of simultaneous regression equations with errors generated by a vector autoregressive process', *Int ER*, 12(2), June 1971; 2. 'Maximum likelihood estimation of difference equations with moving-average errors: a simulation study' (with P. K. Trivedi), *REStud*, 32(2), April 1972; 3. 'Stochastic specification in an aggregate demand model of the United Kingdom', *Em*, 42(3), May 1974; 4. 'The structure of simultaneous equations estimators', *J Em*, 4(1), Jan. 1976; 5. 'Testing dynamic specification in small simultaneous systems: an application to a model of building society behaviour in the United Kingdom' (with G. J. Anderson), in *Frontiers of Quantitative Economics* III, ed. M. D. Intriligator (N-H, 1977); 6. 'Econometric modelling of the aggregate time series relationship between consumers, expenditure and income in the United Kingdom' (with J. E. H. Davidson, F. Srba and S. Yeo), *EJ*, 88, Dec. 1978; 7. 'Predictive failure and econometric modelling in macroeconomics: the transactions demand for money', in *Economic Modelling*, ed. P. Ormerod (Heinemann, 1979); 8. 'Econometrics: alchemy or science?', *Ec*, N.S. 47, Nov. 1980; 9. 'Exogeneity' (with R. F. Engle and J-F. Richard), *Em*, 51(2), March 1983; 10. 'The econometric analysis of economic time series' (with J-F. Richard), *Internat. Stat. Rev.*, 51(2), May 1983.

Principal Contributions My research since 1970 has been directed towards writing *Dynamic Econometrics*, which seeks an integrated approach to the empirical modelling of economic time series. There are six main strands to this effort: firstly, deriving and analysing methods of estimation and inference relevant to time-series data; next, developing Monte Carlo techinques for investigating the small sample properties of possible methods; thirdly, implementing the various tools in appropriate computer programs (the AUTOREG library, summarised in *J Em*, 1980); fourthly, exploring the practical usefulness of alternative modelling strategies and 'methodologies'; fifthly, analysing concepts and criteria which would provide a viable basis for modelling; and finally, testing out all of these developments in a series of simulation and empirical investigations of consumption, money demand and the housing market to ascertain what (if anything) actually works. Although the text is still incomplete, the attempts to write it and to implement the approach continue to highlight the gaps most in need of filling.

At present, the emphasis is on the critical, evaluative role of econometrics rather than its uses as a 'constructive' method for obtaining models. Much of this recent work is jointly with Jean-François Richard and is summarised in No. 9 noted above. My other main interest is the history of econometric thought because of the insights available from thoughtful earlier analyses when technique was less dominant; joint research with Mary S. Morgan documenting the progress of the discipline prior to 1950 is nearing completion.

HENNIPMAN, Pieter

Born 1911, Leiden, The Netherlands.
Current Post Emeritus Prof. Econ., Univ. Amsterdam, Amsterdam, The Netherlands, 1973–.
Past Posts Econ., Twentsche Bank, Amsterdam, 1934–6, Bureau Econ. Res., Dutch Ministry Econ. Affairs, The Hague, 1936–8; Reader Econ. (dismissed by German authorities), Prof. Econ., Univ. Amsterdam, 1938–45, 1945–73; Simon Vis. Prof., Univ. Manchester, England, 1953; Fellow, Netherlands Inst. Advanced Stud., 1971–2.
Degrees Candiaat, Doctorandus, Dr Econ. Univ. Amsterdam, 1932, 1934, 1940; Hon. Dr Econ. Science State Univ. Ghent, Belgium, 1971.
Offices and Honours Member, Board Vereniging voor de Staathuishoudkunde (Soc. Econ.), 1946–9; F. de Vries Foundation, 1954–; N. G. Pierson Foundation, 1959–; Member, Netherlands Academy Science and Letters, 1958; N. G. Pierson Medal, 1959; Knight, Order Netherlands Lion, 1960.
Editorial Duties Ed. Boards, *Openbare Financiën* (Public Fin.), 1946–64, *DE*, 1973–; Managing Ed., *DE*, 1946–73.
Principal Fields of Interest 024 Welfare Theory; 031 History of Economic Thought; 036 Economic Methodology.
Publications *Books:* 1. *Enkele prob-*

lemen der economische dynamics (Scheltema en Holkema, 1938); 2. *Economisch moteif en economisch principe* (Noord-Hallandsche Uitgevers, 1945); 3. *De theoretische economie en de wederopbouw* (Noord-Hollandsche Uitgevers, 1945); 4. *De taak van de mededinginspolitiek* (De Erven F. Bohn, 1966).

Articles: 1. 'De norm der geldpolitiek', *Maandschrift Econ.*, 9(1–2), Oct.–Nov. 1943; 2. 'Werkgelegenheidspolitiek en internationale handel', *DE*, 95(11), Nov. 1947; 3. 'Monopoly: impediment or stimulus to economic progress?', in *Monopoly and Competition and Their Regulation*, ed. E. H. Chamberlin (Macmillan, 1954); 4. 'De economische problematiek van het saprent', in *Verbruik en sparen in theorie en parktijk*, eds. P. Hennipman, *et al.* (H. D. Tjeenk Willink & Zoon, 1956); 5. 'Recente kritiek op de economische wetenschap', *Tijdschrift voor Documentatie en Voorlichting van de Nationale Bank van België*, 33(1–4), April 1958, repr. (Spanish) *En Trimestro Economico*, 26(2), April–June 1958; 6. 'Pareto optimality: value judgement or analytical tool?', in *Relevance and Precision, Essays in Honour of Pieter de Wolff*, eds. J. S. Cramer, *et al.* (Samsom Publishers, 1976); 7. 'Some notes on Pareto optimality and Wicksellian unanimity', in *Wandlungen in Wirtschaft und Gesellschaft, Essays in Honour of W. A. Jöhr*, ed. E Küng (J. C. B. Mohr, 1980); 8. 'De verdeling in de Paretiaanse welvaartstheorie', in *Inkomensverdeling en openbare financiën. Opstellen voor Jan Pen*, eds. P. J. Eijgelshoven and L. J. van Gemerden (Uitgeverij Het Spectrum, 1981); 9. 'Wicksell and Pareto: their relationship in the theory of public finance', *HOPE*, 14(1), Spring 1982; 10. 'Normative or positive: Mishan's half-way house', *DE*, 132(1), 1984.

Principal Contributions My writings are almost entirely in the field of economic theory; they are innocent of mathematics and for the greater part they are in Dutch. There is no empirical research and little on topical issues. They cover quite a large diversity of subjects, mostly of broad or even fundamental significance. A lifelong interest in the history of economic thought and methodlogy is particularly apparent in an early magnum opus (1945), which dissects in minute details the manifold varieties of *Homo oeconomicus*, concluding that the scope of economics is not restricted to the behaviour of such an animal. It is argued that the concept of economic welfare is devoid of specific content and that economics cannot be normative; also the connection between economics and psychology is considered. It shows the influence of the Austrian subjectivist way of thinking and of Robbin's *Essay*.

Later works likewise contain comprehensive critical surveys of a mass of historical and contemporary materials: a book-length study of the economics (micro and macro) of saving, attempting to reconcile the classical and Keynesian positions, and a review of the theory of economic policy. Several articles deal with special policy areas: the tension between employment and optimal trade policies, monetary policy (neutral money, 100% plan) and competition policy. A related IEA paper on the effect of monopoly on innovation is my best known contribution outside the Netherlands. Further categories are book reviews (nearly 100) and portrayals of economists, among them N. G. Pierson (in German), Pigou and William Jaffe. Publications during the last decade mainly concern welfare economics, e.g. twin articles exploring the historical and analytical relations between Pareto optimality and Wicksellian unanimity. A major theme is the contention that welfare economics is a non-normative theory. Interpersonal comparisons of utility and Pareto optimal redistribution are discussed from this point of view.

HERMANN, Friedrich Benedict Wilhelm von*

Dates and Birthplace 1795–1868, Dinkelsbühl, Germany.
Posts Held Prof. Kameralwissenschaften, Univ. Münich, 1827; Dir., Bavarian Stat. Bureau, 1839.
Offices and Honours Member, Frankfurt parliament, 1848.

Publications *Books:* 1. *Staatswirtschaftliche Untersuchungen* (1832).
Career Author of one of the few non-Smithian economic works of the period in Germany. His thought is uncluttered by methodological preoccupations and his analysis was both able and influential.
Secondary Literature M. Palyi, 'Hermann, F. B. W. von', *ESS*, 7.

HESSE, Helmut Siegfried

Born 1934, Gadderbaum, W. Germany.
Current Post Prof. Econ., Univ. Göttingen, Göttingen, W. Germany; Dir., Ibero-America Inst. Econ. Res., Univ. Göttingen, 1966–.
Past Posts Ass. Prof., Univ. Münster, W. Germany, 1965–6; Cons., World Bank, Washington, DC, 1971; Konrad-Adenauer Prof., Georgetown Univ., Washington, DC, 1983–4.
Degrees BA Univ. Kiel, 1955; MA, PhD Univ. Münster, 1956, 1958.
Offices and Honours Chairman, Comm. Internat. Trade and Trade Pol. Pres., Verein für Sozialpolitik, 1977–8, 1979–82; Member, Club of Rome; Member, Chairman, Scientific Advisory Council, W. Germany Fed. Ministry Econ., 1980–2; Member W. Germany Fed. Council Scientific Affairs (Deutscher Wissenschaftsrat), 1984–.
Editorial Duties Co-ed., *Schriften zur angewandten Wirtschaftsforschung* (Publication Series Appl. Econ.), 1972–; Co-ed., *Handwörterbuch der wirtschaftswissenschaften* (J. C. B. Mohr, Paul Siebeck, F. Vandenkoet und Ruprecht).
Principal Fields of Interest 400 International Economics; 010 General Economics.
Publications *Books:* 1. *Der Aussenhandel in der Entwicklung unterentwickelter Länder unter besonderer Berücksichtigung Lateinamerika* (J. C. B. Mohr, Paul Siebeck, 1961); 2. *Das Wachstum der Deutschen Volkswirtschaft seit der Mitte des 19, Jahrhunderts* (with W. G. Hoffmann and F. Grumbach), (Springer-Verlag, 1965); 3. *Strukturwandlungen im Welthandel 1950–1960/61* (J. C. B. Mohr, Paul Siebeck, 1967); 4. *Sustitución de*

Importaciones y Politíca del Desarollo (1969); 5. *Gesamtwirtschaftliche Produktionstheorie,* 2 vols (with R. Linde), (Physica-Verlag, 1976); 6. *Einführung in die Entwicklungstheorie und politik* (with H. Sautter), (Werner-Verlag 1977), 7. *Angewandte Mikroökonomik* (J. C. B. Mohr, Paul Siebeck, 1980); 8. *Theoretische Grundlagen der 'Fiscal Policy'* (Vahlen-Verlag, 1983). *Articles:* 1. 'Die Industrialisierung der Entwicklungsländer in ihren Auswirkungen auf den internationalen Handel', *Jahrbuch fur Sozialwissenschaft,* 14(3), 1963; 2. 'Die Bedeutung der reinen Theorie des internationalen Handels für die Erklärung des Aussenhandels in der Nachkriegszeit', *ZFS,* 122(2), April 1966; transl., English 'The significance of the pure theory of international trade in explaining foreign trade in the post-war period', *German Econ. Rev.,* 2, 1966; 3. 'Nutzen-Kosten-Analyse für städtische Verkehrsprojekte — Dargestellt am Beispiel der Unterpflasterstrassenbahn in Hannover', *Kyk,* 33, 1970; 4. 'Der Einfluss des Staates auf die wirtschaftliche Entwicklung', *ZGS,* 117(4), Oct. 1971; 5. 'Promotion of manufactured exports as development strategy of semi-industrialized countries: the Brazilian case', *WA,* 108(2), 1972; 6. 'Hypothesis for the explanations of trade between industrial countries, 1952–70', in *The International Division of Labour: Problems and Perspectives,* ed. H. Giersch (J. C. B. Mohr, Paul Siebeck, 1974); 7. 'Zum konzept einer Handelsanpassungspolitik', in *Probleme der Wettbewerbstheorie und — politik,* eds. G. Bombach und B. Gahlen (J. C. B. Mohr-Verlag, 1976); 8. 'Aussenhandel, I: Determinanten', *Handwörterbuch der Wirtschaftswissenschaften* (Vandenkoek und Ruprecht, 1977); 9. 'Industrial redeployment: opportunity, threat, or illusion?', *The Role of Europe in the New International Economic Order* (Ed. de l'Univ. Bruxelles, 1979); 10. 'Exportbeschränkungen zur Vermeidung eines "kritischen Mangels"', in *Zur Theorie und Politik Internationaler Wirtschaftsbeziehungen,* eds. G. Bombach und B. Gahlen (J. C. B. Mohr-Verlag, 1981).

Principal Contributions Work has been concentrated on the international division of labour in all its aspects: trade, trade policy, world trade order, structural changes, and adjustment problems. Most publications can be attributed to applied theory, among them the PhD thesis (1966) which elaborated intra-industrial trade between industrial countries. In most articles, political conclusions have been drawn from the findings. Thus, the concept of a trade ajustment policy has been worked out, development strategies (inward and outward looking strategies) have been commented upon, export restrictions have been dealt with, and problems of reshaping the economic order have been discussed. Because applied theory and political considerations necessitate a firm theoretical basis, some articles and most of the textbooks focus on theoretical issues. Some of these issues are not directly linked with international trade. However, the corresponding publications cannot be judged as deflections from the main topic of interest; in view of the general interdependence of all economic affairs, analyses of foreign trade have to shored up by a general economic theory. Recent articles concentrate on the increasing degree of international economic interconnectedness and the evolving integrated world economy in which independent national economic policy can hardly be pursued.

HEWINS, William Albert Samuel*

Dates and Birthplace 1865–1931, Wolverhampton, W. Midlands, England.

Posts Held Univ. Extension Lect., 1887–95; Dir., LSE, 1895–1903; Secretary, UK Tariff Commission, 1903–17.

Degrees BA Univ. Oxford, 1887.

Offices and Honours MP Hereford, 1912–18; UK Under-Secretary State Colonies, 1917–19.

Publications *Books:* 1. *English Trade and Finance in the 17th Century* (1892); 2. *Imperialism and its Probable Effects on the Commercial Policy of the UK* (1901); 3. *Trade in the Balance* (1924); 4. *Empire Restored* (1927); 5. *Apologia of an Imperialist* (1929).

Career Apart from his successful directorship of the LSE, the chief reason Hewins is remembered is for his advocacy of trade protection. He maintained this thoroughly unfashionable line in lectures, articles and through his association with Joseph Chamberlain's Tariff Commission.

HICKMAN, Bert George

Born 1924, Los Angeles, CA, USA.
Current Post Prof. Econ., Stanford Univ., CA, USA, 1966–.
Past Posts Instr., Stanford Univ. 1949–51; Ass. Prof., Northwestern Univ., 1952–4; Sr. Staff, US President's Council Econ. Advisers, 1954–6; Sr. Staff, Brookings Inst., 1956–66; Vis. Prof., Univ. Cal. Berkeley, 1960–1; NSF Sr. Fellow, Netherlands School Econ., 1964–5; Vis. Prof., London Bus. School, 1972–3; Inst. Advanced Stud., Vienna, 1974, 1975, Kyoto Univ., 1977; Scientific Staff, Internat. Inst. Appl. Systems Analysis, Laxenburg, Austria, 1979, 1980.
Degrees BS (Bus. Admin.), PhD Univ. Cal. Berkeley, 1947, 1951.
Offices and Honours Fellow, Em. Soc.; Chairman, Comm. Econ. Stability and Growth, US–SSRC, 1962–; Member, Chairman, Census Advisory Comm. AEA, 1962–6, 1968–71; Chairman, Exec. Comm. Project LINK, 969–; Chairman, CEME Seminar Global Modelling, 1975–82.
Principal Fields of Interest 110 Economic Growth; 130 Economic Fluctuations; 210 Econometric Models.
Publications *Books:* 1. *Growth and Stability of the Postwar Economy* (Brookings Inst., 1960); 2. *Investment Demand and U.S. Economic Growth* (Brookings Inst., 1965); 3. *Quantitative Planning of Economic Policy*, ed. (Brookings Inst., 1965); 4. *Econometric Models of Cyclical Behavior*, ed. (Columbia Univ. Press, 1972); 5. *An Award Growth Model of the U.S. Economy* (with R. M. Coen), (N-H, 1976); 6. *Global International Economic Models*, ed. (N-H, 1983); 7. *Global Econometrics: Essays in Honor of Lawrence R. Klein*, co-ed. (with F. G. Adams), (MIT Press, 1983).

Articles: 1. 'Diffusion, acceleration and business cycles', *AER*, 49(4), Sept. 1959; 2. 'The postwar retardation, another long swing in the rate of growth?', *AER*, 53(2), May 1963; 3. 'On a new method of capacity estimation', *JASA*, June 1967; 4. 'Constrained joint estimation of factor demand and production functions' (with R. M. Coen), *REStat*, 52(3), Aug. 1970; 5. 'Elasticities of substitution and export demand in a world trade model' (with L. J. Lau), *Europ ER*, 4(4), Dec. 1973; 6. 'A general linear model of world trade', in *International Linkage of National Economic Models*, ed. R. J. Ball (N-H, 1973); 7. 'What became of the building cycle?', in *National Households in Economic Growth: Essays in Honor of Moses Abramovitz*, eds. P. A. David and M. W. Reder (Academic Press, 1974); 8. 'The interdependence of national economies and the synchronization of economic fluctuations: evidence from the LINK Project' (with S. Schleicher), *WA*, 114, 1978; 9. 'Investment and growth in an econometric model of the United States' (with R. M. Coen), *AER*, 70(2), May 1980; 10. 'A decomposition of international income multipliers' (with V. Filator), in *Global Econometrics, op. cit.*

Principal Contributions Early contributions were to the quantitative–historical analysis of business cycles, long swings in growth, and the relationships between cyclical diffusion and the acceleration principle (1957–63). Turned next to econometric analyses of investment behaviour, capacity utilisation and systems of factor demand and production functions (1964–70). Thereafter pursued two parallel and continuing lines of research: (1) the Hickman–Coen annual growth model of the US economy (combining neoclassical growth theory and Keynesian effective demand theory); (2) the international transmission of economic fluctuations, as a founding member of Project LINK and through specific studies of matrix models of world trade and international income and price multipliers (1970–83). Finally, have organised several comparative studies of structures and properties of US national and of global multinational econometric models.

HICKS, John R.

Born 1904, Warwick, Warwickshire, England.

Current Post Prof. Emeritus, Univ. Oxford, 1965–; Fellow, Nuffield Coll. Oxford, 1946–.

Past Posts Lect., LSE, 1929–35; Fellow, Univ. Camb., 1935–8; Prof. Polit. Econ., Univ. Manchester, 1938–46; Drummond Prof., Univ. Oxford, 1950–65.

Degrees BA Univ. Oxford, 1925.

Offices and Honours Fellow, BA, 1943; Knighted, 1966; Nobel Prize in Econ., 1972.

Principal Fields of Interest 010 General Economics.

Publications *Books:* 1. *Theory of Wages* (Macmillan, 1932, 1963); 2. *Value and Capital* (OUP, 1939); 3. *A Contribution to the Theory of the Trade Cycle* (OUP, 1950); 4. *Capital and Growth* (OUP, 1965); 5. *The Crisis in Keynesian Economics* (Blackwell, 1975); 6. *Collected Essays on Economic Theory*, 3 vols (Blackwell, 1981, 1982, 1983).

Secondary Literature G. C. Reid and J. N. Wolfe 'Hicks, John R.', *IESS*, 18; W. J. Baumol 'John R. Hicks' contribution to economics', *Swed JE* 74, Dec., 1972; repr. in *Modern Economists in Perspective*, eds. H. W. Spiegel and W. J. Samuels (JAI Press, 1985); B. Morgan 'Sir John Hicks' contributions to economic theory', *Twelve Contemporary Economists*, eds. J. R. Shackleton and G. Locksley (Macmillan, 1981).

HIGGINS, Benjamin Howard

Born 1912, London, Ont,. Canada.

Current Post Dir., Centre Appl. Stud. Devlp., Univ. S. Pacific, UN Centre Regional Devlp.; Cons. Nagoya, Japan.

Past Posts Vis. Fellow, Centre Res. Fed. Fin. Relations, Devlp. Stud. Centre, ANU, Canberra; Devlp. Econ., CIDA/Lower Uva Project, Sri Lanka, 1980–1.

Degrees BA Univ. Western Ontario, 1933; MSc LSE, 1935; MPA Harvard Univ., 1939; PhD Univ. Minnesota, 1941; MA (Hon.) Univ. Melbourne, 1948.

Offices and Honours Fellow, Royal Soc. Canada; Member, Chairman Exec. Comm., AEA Econ. Devlp. Inst., Boulder, CO, 1965–7; Chairman, Advisory Comm., UNCRD, 1979–.

Principal Fields of Interest 112 Economic Development.

Publications *Books:* 1. *What Do Economists Know?* (Melbourne Univ. Press, 1954); 2. *Indonesia's Economic Stabilisation and Development* (Inst. Pacific Relations, 1957); 3. *Social Aspects of Economic Development of Latin America* (with J. M. Echavarria), (UNESCO, 1959); 4. *Economic Development: Principles, Problems, Policies* (Norton, 1959, 1968); 5. *Economic Development of a Small Planet* (with J. D. Higgins), (Norton, 1979).

Articles: 1. 'Interactions of cycles and trends', *EJ*, 65, Dec. 1955; 2. 'Economic development and cultural change: seamless web or patchwork quilt?', in *Essays on Economic Development and Cultural Change in Honour of Bert Hoselitz*, ed. M. Nash (Univ. Chicago Press, 1977); 3. 'The disenthronement of basic needs? Twenty questions', in *Regional Development Dialogue*, 1(1), Spring 1980; 4. 'Growth and stagnation in a world of shifting trade-off curves: homage to Alvin Hansen', in *Développement, croissance, progrès, economies et sociétés*, Série F, special issue (Dunod, 1981); 5. 'Multilevel planning: a new liberal philosophy', in *Humanizing Development. Essays on People, Space and Development in Honour of Masahiko Honjo*, ed. R. P. Misra (Maruzen, 1981).

Principal Contributions Combined academic research and advisory services to governments. Taught at McGill, Melbourne, Texas, MIT, Montreal, Ottawa, California-Berkeley, Yale, Monash, Murdoch and ANU. Served as adviser to the governments of Australia, Canada, the US and some two dozen countries in Asia, Africa and Latin America. Began career in microeconomics and methodology, moved to macroeconomics, and recent years have concentrated on economic development and urban and regional development and planning.

HIGGS, Henry*

Dates and Birthplace 1864–1940, Cornwall, England.
Posts Held UK Civil Servant, 1881–1921, including Private Secretary, Prime Minister Campbell-Bannerman.
Degrees LLB Univ. London, 1890.
Offices and Honours Founder Member, Secretary, RES, 1890, 1892–1905.
Principal Fields of Interest Founder Member, Secretary, RES, 1890, 1892–1905.
Publications *Books:* 1. *The Physiocrats* (1897); 2. *The Financial System of the United Kingdom* (1914); 3. *Financial Reform* (1926).
Career His long and devoted service to RES in various offices makes him an important figure in the history of the British economics profession. His research on Cantillon and French economics was a result of Foxwell's lectures at University Coll., London, which also first aroused his interest in economics. His publications on financial matters gained from his intimate acquaintance with their management at the highest levels, but it is not for his writings but for his more general services to economics that he is remembered.
Secondary Literature C. E. Collet and J. M. Keynes, 'Henry Higgs' (obit.), *EJ*, 50, Dec. 1940.

HILDEBRAND, Bruno*

Dates and Birthplace 1812–78, Naumburg, Germany.
Posts Held Prof. Hist., Univ. Breslau, 1839–41; Prof. Govt. Univs. Marburg, Zürich, Bern, Jena.
Degrees PhD Univ. Breslau, 1836.
Offices Deputy in the Frankfurt Nat. Assembly, 1848; Founder, *JNS*, 1863.
Publications *Books:* 1. *Die National-ökonomie der Gegenwart und Zukunft* (1848, 1922); 2. *Stastiche Mitteilungen über die volkswirtschaftlichen Zustände Kurhessens* (1853); 3. *Statistik Thüringens*, 2 vols (1866–78).
Career Originally an historian and political radical, he turned increasingly to economic and then statistical questions. His economics was analytically unremarkable but his teaching, particularly his Jena seminar, inspired many economists of the historical school. His achievements in the statistical field include the founding of the Thuringian Statistical Office in 1864.
Secondary Literature H. Kisch, 'Hildebrand, Bruno', *IESS*, 6.

HILDENBRAND, Werner

Born 1936, Göttingen, W. Germany.
Current Post Prof. Econ., Univ. Bonn, Bonn, W. Germany, 1969–.
Past Posts Teaching Ass., Univ. Heidelberg, 1958–61; Res. Fellow, Univ. Bonn, 1961–2; Research Ass. Project Leader, Lect., Univ. Heidelberg, 1962–4, 1965–8; Vis. Ass. Prof., Univ. Cal. Berkeley, 1966–8; Res. Prof., Univ. Louvain, Belgium, 1968–76; Vis. Prof., Univ. Cal. Berkeley, Stanford Univ., 1970, 1973–4.
Degrees Dipl. (Maths.), Dr Rer. Nat., Habilitation, Univ. Heidelberg, 1961, 1964, 1968.
Offices and Honours Fellow, Council, Em Soc, 1971, 1973–8, 1982; Member, Rheinisch-Westfalische Akademie der Wissenschaften, 1981.
Editorial Duties Ass. Ed., *JET, Int ER*; Ed., *J. Math. E, Int. Econ. Rev.*
Principal Fields of Interest 020 General Economic Theory; 021 General Equilibrium Theory.
Publications *Books:* 1. *Core and Equilibria of a Large Economy* (Princeton Univ. Press, 1974); 2. *Lineare Ökonomische Modelle* (with K. Hildenbrand), (Springer-Verlag, 1975); 3. *Introduction to Equilibrium Analysis* (with A. Kirman), (CUP, 1979); 4. *Advances in Economic Theory*, ed. (CUP, 1982): 5. *Advances in Econometrics*, ed. (CUP, 1982).
Articles: 1. 'On the core of an economy with a measure space of economic agents', *REStud*, 35, Oct. 1968; 2. 'Pareto optimality for a measure space of economic agents', *Int ER*, 10(3), Oct. 1969; 3. 'On economies with many agents', *JET*, 2(2), June 1970; 4. 'Existence of equilibria for economies with production and a measure space of consumers', *Em*, 38(5), Sept. 1970; 5. 'Stochastic processes of temporary equilibria' (with J. M. Grandmont), *J*

Math E, 1, 1974; 6. 'Distributions of agents' characteristics', *J Math E*, 2, 1975; 7. 'On Keynesian equilibria with unemployment and quantity rationing' (with K. Hildenbrand), *JET*, 18(2), Aug. 1978; 8. 'Short-run production functions based on microdata', *Em*, 49(5), Sept. 1981; 9. 'On the law of demand', *Em*, 51(4), Aug. 1983; 10. 'Core of an economy', in *Handbook of Mathematical Economics*, eds. K. J. Arrow and M. D. Intriligator (N-H, 1982).

Principal Contributions Most of my research is concentrated on equilibrium analysis of 'large economies', i.e., economies with a large number of economic agents. In my early work I studied the relationship between the core of an economy and the set of competitive equilibria for pure exchange economies as well as for economies with production. The concept of 'competitive sequences of economies', which generalises the well-known 'replica-sequences' is defined in terms of the 'distributions of agents' characteristics', a concept which played a central role in the analysis of limit theorems of the core but also in my later work. My main aim is to derive some useful structure of general equilibrium models (for example, a structure which allows one to do comparative statics) by making assumptions on the distributions of agents' characteristics. In the production sector of an economy, this approach led to my paper on short-run production functions and, in the consumption sector, the approach of making an assumption about the distribution of expenditure led to my paper on the law of demand. In both papers the concept of the distribution of agents' characteristics (i.e. micro-data) played a crucial role.

HILFERDING, Rudolf*

Dates and Birthplace 1877–1941, Vienna, Austro-Hungary.
Posts Held Practised as doctor, 1901–6, 1915–19; Lect. and Ed., German Social Democratic Party.
Degrees Dr Medicine, Vienna, 1901.
Offices German Minister Fin., 1923, 1928–9; Member, Reichstag, 1924–33.

Publications *Books:* 1. *Böhm-Bawerk's Criticism of Marx* (1904, 1949); 2. *Finance Capital* (1910, 1981).
Career A Marxist and leader of the German Social Democratic Party. His *Finanzkapital* is a classic of Marxist economics; Bukharin and Lenin were both influenced by his analysis of imperialism. The book concentrates on capitalist production in the twentieth century with particular attention to questions of money. He was kidnapped by the Nazis from unoccupied territory in Vichy France and died in unexplained circumstances.
Secondary Literature T. Bottomore, 'Introduction' to R. Hilferding, *Finance Capital* (Routledge & Kegan Paul, 1981); T. Bottomore and P. Goode, eds. *Austro-Marxism* (OUP, 1978).

HINES, Albert G.

Born 1935, Milk River, Clarendon, Jamaica.
Current Post Retired.
Past Posts Ass. Lect., Univ. Bristol, 1962–4; Lect., Univ. Coll. London, 1964–8; Prof., Univ. Durham, 1968–71; Vis. Prof., MIT, 1971–2; Prof. Econ., Birkbeck Coll., Univ. London, 1971–82.
Degrees BSc LSE, 1961.
Offices and Honours Chairman, Commission Econ. Stabilisation, Jamaica, 1975–6; Council Member RES, 1977–.
Principal Fields of Interest 023 Macroeconomic Theory.
Publications *Books:* 1. *On the Reappraisal of Keynesian Economics* (Martin Robertson, 1971).
Articles: 1. 'Trade unions and wage inflation in the United Kingdom: 1893–1961', *REStud*, 31, Oct. 1964; 2. 'Unemployment and the rate of change of money wage rates in the United Kingdom 1862–1963: a reappraisal', *REStat*, 50, Feb. 1968; 3. 'Investment in UK manufacturing industry 1956–67' (with G. Catephores), in *The Econometric Study of the United Kingdom*, eds. K. Hilton and D. Heathfield (Macmillan, 1970); 4. 'The determinants of the rate of change of money wage rates and the effectiveness of incomes policy', in *The Current Inflation*, eds. H. G. Johnson

and R. Nobay (Macmillan, 1971); 5. 'Involuntary unemployment', in *Unemployment in Western Countries*, eds. E. Malinvaud and J. Fitoussi (Macmillan, 1980).

Principal Contributions Empirical and theoretical analyses of the part trade unions play in the process of inflation, seen as the outcome of their role in the labour process, in the distribution of income and in the determination of output and employment; in particular, there is the demonstration that trade unions influence wages independently of the demand for labour. Interpretation and development of the reappraisal of Keynesian economics, including the theory of interest rates and the theory of unemployment.

HINSHAW, Randall

Born 1915, La Grange, IL, USA.

Current Post Dir., Bologna-Claremont-Hamburg Series Biennial Monetary Confs., Claremont Grad. School, Claremont, CA, USA, 1982–.

Past Posts Econ., Bureau Foreign Domestic Commerce, US Dept. Commerce, 1942; Teaching Fellow Econ., Harvard Univ., 1942–3; Econ., Div. Internat. Fin., Fed. Reserve Board, 1943–6, 1947–52; Ass. Prof. Econ., Amherst Coll., 1946–7; Special Adviser, Internat. Monetary Problems, US Mission NATO and Europ. Regional Orgs., Paris, 1952–7; Deputy US Representative, European Payments Union, Paris, 1952–3; Adviser, US Delegation UN Meetings East-West Payments Problems, Geneva, 1955–7; Vis. Prof. Econ., Yale Univ., 1957–8, Oberlin Coll., 1958–9, Univ. S. Cal., 1963–4, Johns Hopkins Univ., Bologna Center, 1965–8, 1971, UCLA, 1968; Prof. Econ., Claremont Grad. School, 1960–82.

Degrees BA, MA Occidental Coll., 1937, 1938; PhD Princeton Univ., 1944.

Offices and Honours Phi Beta Kappa; Club Fellow, Princeton Univ., 1940–1; Vis. Fellow, Council Foreign Relations, NY, 1959–60.

Editorial Duties Ed., *Bologna-Claremont-Hamburg Series Biennial Monetary Conferences*, 1967–.

Principal Fields of Interest 410 International Trade Theory; 420 Trade Relations: Commercial Policy; International Economic Integration; 430 Balance of Payments; International Finance.

Publications *Books:* 1. *The European Community and American Trade: A Study in Atlantic Economics and Policy* (Praeger, 1964); 2. *Monetary Reform and the Price of Gold: Alternative Approaches*, ed. and contrib. (JHUP, 1967; transls., Japanese, Toyo Keizai Shimpo Sha, 1968, Italian, Societa editrice Il Mulino, 1968); 3. *The Economics of International Adjustment*, ed. and contrib. (JHUP, 1971); 4. *Inflation as a Global Problem*, ed. and contrib. (JHUP, 1972); 5. *Key Issues in International Monetary Reform*, ed. and contrib. (Marcel Dekker, 1975); 6. *Stagflation: An International Problem*, ed. and contrib. (Marcel Dekker, 1977); 7. *Domestic Goals and Financial Interdependence: The Frankfurt Dialogue*, ed. and contrib. (Marcel Dekker, 1980); 8. *Global Monetary Anarchy: Perspectives on Restoring Stability*, ed. and contrib. (Sage, 1981; transl., Japanese, Sankei, 1983); 9. *Global Economic Priorities: The Hamburg Dialogue*, ed. and contrib. (Hamburg Inst. Econ. Res., 1983).

Articles: 1. 'American prosperity and the British balance-of-payments problem', *REStat*, 27(1), Feb. 1945; 2. 'Foreign investment and American employment', *AER*, 36(2), May 1946; 3. 'Keynesian commercial policy', in *The New Economics: Keynes' Influence on Theory and Public Policy*, ed. E. Harris (A. A. Knopf, 1947); 4. 'Professor Frisch on discrimination and multilateral trade', *REStat*, 30(4), Nov. 1948; 5. 'Currency appreciation as an anti-inflationary device', *QJE*, 65(4), Nov. 1951, 66(1), Feb. 1952; 6. 'The effect of devaluation on the price level: comment', *QJE*, 72(4), Nov. 1958; 7. 'Elasticity pessimism, absorption, and flexible exchange rates', in *International Trade and Finance: Essays in Honour of Jan Tinbergen*, ed. W. Sellekaerts (Macmillan, 1973); 8. 'Non-traded goods and the balance of payments: further reflections', *JEL*, 13(2), June 1975; 9. 'Devaluation and absorption:

an alternative analysis', in *Inflation, Trade and Taxes: Essays in Honor of Alice Bourneuf*, eds. A. Belsley, *et al.* (Ohio State Univ. Press, 1976); 10. 'Sir Roy Harrod', *J Int E*, 8(3), Aug. 1978, repr. *J Int E*, Suppl., 12(1), Jan. 1982.

Principal Contributions The first to make an estimate of the average price elasticity of the US demand for (merchandise) imports; low figure of −0.5, published in 1945, led to a considerable body of literature on 'elasticity pessimism'. Have made various contributions to exchange-rate-theory — particularly to the effect of exchange-rate changes on the domestic price level, on the terms of trade, on nominal and real absorption, and on other aspects of international adjustment. Like others who first studied economics during the Great Depression, my interests are strongly policy-oriented. My early work was greatly influenced by Frank D. Graham; other important intellectual influences have been Lloyd Metzler, Gottfried Haberler, Roy Harrod and, more recently, Robert Mundell.

HIRSCH, Werner Z.

Born 1920, Linz, Germany.
Current Post Prof. Econ., UCLA, CA, USA, 1963–.
Past Posts Ass. Prof., Univ. Cal. Berkeley, 1949–51; Econ., UN, 1951–2; Res. Fellow, Brookings Inst., Washington, DC, 1952–3; Assoc. Prof., Washington Univ., St Louis, 1953–63.
Degrees BS, PhD Univ. Cal. Berkeley, 1947, 1949.
Offices and Honours Phi Beta Kappa; Sigma Xi; Vice-Pres., MEA, 1960–1; Citation, Senate, 1970; Pres., Town Hall West, CA, 1978–9; Pres., WRSA.
Editorial Duties Assoc. Ed., *JASA*; Ed. Board, *Pakistan J Appl. Econ., Internat. Rev. Law & Econ.*
Principal Fields of Interest 321 Fiscal Theory and Policy; 325 Inter-governmental Finance; 931 Urban Economics.
Publications *Books:* 1. *Introduction to Modern Statistics* (Macmillan, 1957); 2. *Elements of Regional Accounts*, ed. (JHUP, 1964); 3. *Spillover of Public Education Costs and Benefits* (with E. W. Segelhorst and M. J. Marcus),

(Inst. Govt. and Public Affairs, UCLA, 1969); 4. *The Economics of State and Local Government* (McGraw-Hill, 1970); 5. *Urban Economic Analysis* (McGraw-Hill, 1973); 6. *Recent Experiences with National Planning in the United Kingdom* (US Govt. Printing Office, 1977); 7. *Law and Economics: An Introductory Analysis* (Academic Press, 1979); 8. *Social Experimentation and Economic Policy* (with R. Ferber), (CUP, 1981); 9. *The Economics of Municipal Labor Markets*, co-ed. (with A. Rufolo), (Inst. Industrial Relations, UCLA, 1983); 10. *Urban Economics* (Macmillan, 1984).

Articles: 1. 'Manufacturing progress functions', *REStat*, 34(2), May 1952; 2. 'Expenditure implications of metropolitan growth and consolidation', *REStat*, 41(3), Aug. 1959; 3. 'Inter-industry relations of a metropolitan area', *REStat*, 41(4), Nov. 1959; 4. 'A model of municipal labor markets', *JUE*, 2, 1975; 5. 'The efficiency of restrictive land use instruments', *Land Econ.*, 53(2), May 1977; 6. 'Habitability laws and the shrinkage of substandard rental housing stock' (with C. K. Law), *Urban Stud.*, 16, 1979; 7. 'Exclusionary zoning: local property taxation and the unique-ubiquitous research distinction', *Southern Cal. Law Rev.* 52(6), Sept. 1979; 8. 'Habitability laws and the welfare of indigent tenants', *REStat*, 63(2), May 1981; 9. 'Effects of prevailing wage laws on municipal government wages' (with A. M. Rufolo), *JUE*, 13, Jan. 1983; 10. 'The changing landlord-tenant relationship in California: an economic analysis of the swinging pendulum' (with J. G. Hirsch), *Southwestern Univ. Law Rev.*, 14, 1983.

Principal Contributions Application of microeconomic theory and econometrics to the development and estimation of progress functions, production and cost functions of urban governments, the process of metropolitan consolidation, and the effects of habitability laws and speedy eviction laws on the welfare of indigent tenants. Contributed to the emerging fields of regional input-output analysis, urban economic analysis, and law and economics. Also, analysis of the efficiency and distributional effects of revenue limitation measures.

HIRSCHMAN, Albert Otto

Born 1915, Berlin, W. German.
Current Post Prof. Social Science,
Inst. Advanced Study, Princeton Univ.,
NJ, USA, 1974–.
Past Posts Econ., Inst. Recherches
Economiques et Sociales, Inst. Inter-
nat. de Coopération Intellectuelle,
Paris, 1938–9; Res. Fellow Internat.
Econ., Univ. Cal. Berkeley, 1941–3;
Econ., Fed. Reserve Board, Washing-
ton, DC, 1946–52; Econ. Adviser,
Cons., Bogotá, Colombia, 1952–6; Vis.
Res. Prof., Yale Univ., 1956–8; Prof.
Internat. Econ. Relations, Columbia
Univ., 1958–64; Lucius N. Littauer
Prof. Polit. Econ., Harvard Univ.,
1964–7, 1967–74; Fellow, Center Ad-
vanced Study Behavioral Sciences,
Stanford, CA, 1968–9; Vis. Member,
Inst. Advanced Study, Princeton Univ.,
1972–3.
Degrees Certificat. Inst. Statistique,
Sorbonne, Paris, 1934; Diplôme, Ecole
des Hautes Etudes Commerciales,
Paris, 1935; Dottore di Scienze Econo-
miche, Univ. Trieste, Italy, 1938; Hon.
LLD, Rutgers Univ., 1978.
Offices and Honours Member,
AAAS; Fellow, Internat. Student Ser-
vice, LSE, 1935–6; Rockefeller Found-
ation Fellow, Univ. Cal. Berkeley,
1941–3; Ford Foundation Faculty Res.
Fellow, 1964–5; Frank E. Seidman Dis-
ting. Award Polit. Econ., 1980; Talcott
Parsons Prize, Social Science, AAAS,
1983; Disting. Fellow, AEA, 1984.
Principal Fields of Interest 010
General Economics; 110 Economic
Growth; Development; and Plann-
ing Theory and Policy; 031 History of
Economic Thought.
Publications *Books:* 1. *National
Power and the Structure of Foreign
Trade* (Univ. Cal. Press, 1945, 1980;
transl., Spanish, Aguilar, 1950); 2.
*The Strategy of Economic Develop-
ment* (Yale Univ. Press, 1959, Norton
Library, 1978; transls., Spanish, Fondo
de Cultura Economica, 1961, Portuguese, Editora Fundo de Cultura,
1961, French, Les Eds. Ouvrières,
1964, Korean, 1965, German, Gustav
Fischer, 1967, Italian, La Nuova Italia,
1968, Swedish, Raben & Sjorgren
1971, Japanese, Bengali); 3. *Journeys*

*Toward Progress: Studies of Economic
Policy-Making in Latin America*
(Twentieth-Century Fund, 1963,
Anchor, 1965, Norton Library, 1973;
transls., Spanish, Aguilar, 1964, Portu-
guese, Editora Fundo de Cultura,
1965); 4. *Development Projects Ob-
served* (Brookings Inst., 1967; transls.,
Spanish, Siglo Veintiuno,1969, Portu-
guese, Zahar, 1969, Italian, Franco
Angeli, 1975, Japanese); 5. *Exit, Voice
and Loyalty: Responses to Decline in
Firms, Organizations and States* (Har-
vard Univ. Press, 1970; transls., French,
Les Eds. Ouvrières, 1972, Swedish,
Rabén & Sjogren, 1972, Portuguese,
Editora Perspectiva, 1973, German, J.
C. B. Mohr, 1974, Japanese, 1975,
Spanish, Fondo de Cultura Econó-
mica, 1977, Italian, Bompiani, 1982);
6. *A Bias for Hope: Essays on Devel-
opment and Latin America* (Yale Univ.
Press, 1971; transl., Spanish, Fondo de
Cultura Economica, 1973); 7. *The Pas-
sions and the Interests: Political Argu-
ments for Capitalism before its Triumph*
(Princeton Univ. Press, 1977; transls.,
Spanish, Fondo de Cultura Economica,
1978, Italian, Feltrinelli, 1979, Portu-
guese, Paz e Terra, 1979, French,
Presses Univ. de France, 1980, Ger-
man, Suhrkamp, 1980); 8. *Essays in
Trespassing: Economics to Politics and
Beyond* (CUP, 1981; transl., Spanish,
Fondo de Cultura Economica, 1984);
9. *Shifting Involvements: Private Inter-
est and Public Action* (Princeton Univ.
Press, 1982; transls., French, Fayard,
1983, Italian, Il Mulino, 1983, German,
Suhrkamp, 1984, Portuguese, Editora
Brasiliense, 1984, Spanish, Fondo de
Cultura Economica, 1984); 10. *Getting
Ahead, Collectively: Grassroots Experiences in Latin America* (Pergamon,
1984).
Articles: 1. 'Inflation and deflation
in Italy', *AER*, 38(4), Sept. 1948; 2.
'Devaluation and the trade balance: a
note', *REStat*, 31(1), Feb. 1949; 3. 'The
European payment union — negotiations and issues', *REStat*, 33(1), Feb.
1951; 4. 'The principle of the hiding
hand', *Public Interest*, 6, Winter 1967; 5.
'Rival interpretations of market society;
civilizing, destructive or feeble?', *JEL*,
20(4), Dec. 1982; 6. 'The principle of
conservation and mutation of social

energy', *Grassroots Devlp.*, 7(2), 1983; 7. 'A dissenter's confession: revisiting *The Strategy of Economic Development*', in *Pioneers in Development*, eds. G. M. Meier and D. Seers, (OUP, 1984); 8. 'Against parsimony: three easy ways of complicating some categories of economic discourse', *AER*, 74(2), May 1984.

Principal Contributions Early interest was in structure of world trade and political implications of its asymmetries and patterns of concentration (Book No. 1 above). In the immediate postwar years I turned to problems of 'dollar shortage' and European reconstruction, particularly in France and Italy, and integration. Subsequent advisory work in Colombia led to elaboration of a theory of 'unbalanced growth' that assigned an important role to nonmarket forces (Book No. 2). This was followed by detailed examination of policy-making and problem-tackling sequences in Latin America (Book No. 3) and of dynamics of World-Bank-financed projects in Latin America, Asia and Africa (Book No. 4). The interaction of market and nonmarket processes, or between economics and politics, was then explored at a more theoretical level, for firms and for other organisations in *Exit, Voice, and Loyalty*.

With repressive authoritarian regimes on the rise in Latin America after a period of economic growth, I looked to the history of ideas for clues to the likely political effects of economic expansion and wrote about the hopeful, beautiful and flawed 17th- and 18th-century speculations about this matter (in Book No. 7), whose story is brought up to date in Article No. 5. Next I contrasted the pursuit of one's private interests with that of the public interest and attempted to understand oscillations — of persons, generations, or entire societies — between these two pursuits (Book No. 9). Finally I felt that private and group interests are often conjoined among economically deprived groups and this thought led me back to Latin America for a close look at grassroots development (Book No. 10). Thus my principal interests have been economic and social change and the interaction of economics, politics and ideology.

HIRSHLEIFER, Jack

Born 1925, New York City, NY, USA.

Current Post Prof. Econ., UCLA, USA, 1962–.

Past Posts US Naval Reserve (active duty), 1943–5; Ass. Social Scientist, Assoc. Social Scientist, Cons., Rand Corp., 1949–55; 1955–; Ass. Prof., Assoc. Prof., School Bus., Univ. Chicago, 1955–8, 1958–60; Assoc. Prof. Econ., UCLA, 1960–2; Cons., US President's Scientific Advisory Comm., 1961–3, Hudson Inst., 1962–.

Degrees BA, MA, PhD Harvard Univ., 1945, 1948, 1950.

Offices and Honours Fellow, Center Advanced Study Behavioral Sciences, Stanford, CA, 1961–2; Guggenheim Foundation Fellow, 1962; Ford Faculty Fellow, 1964–5; NSF Sr. Postdoctoral Fellow, 1967–8; Fellow, AAAS, 1975; Vice-Pres., AER, 1979.

Editorial Duties Co-ed., *J Bus*, 1957–60; Ed. Boards, *AER*, 1971–4, 1983–, *J Ec Behav*, 1980–, *JEL*, 1984–.

Principal Fields of Interest 022 Microeconomic Theory; 026 Economics of Uncertainty and Information; Game Theory and Bargaining Theory; 010 General Economics.

Publications *Books:* 1. *Water Supply: Economics, Technology and Policy* (with J. C. DeHaven and J. W. Milliman), (Univ. Chicago Press, 1960, 1969); 2. *Investment, Interest and Capital* (Prentice-Hall, 1970; transls., German, as *Kapitaltheorie*, Studien-Bibloitek Keipenhauer & Witsch, 1974, Chinese, 1971); 3. *Price Theory and Applications* (Prentice-Hall, 1976, 1984; transls., Japanese, McGraw-Hill Kogakuska, 1980, Spanish, Prentice-Hall Internat., 1980).

Articles: 1. 'On the economics of transfer pricing', *J Bus*, 29, July 1956; 2. 'On the theory of optimal investment decision', *JPE*, 65, Aug. 1958; 3. 'Investment decision under uncertainty: choice-theoretic approaches', *QJE*, 79, Nov. 1965; 4. 'The private and social value of information and the reward to inventive activity', *AER*, 61(4), Sept. 1971; 5. 'Liquidity, uncertainty and the accumulation of information', in *Uncertainty and Expectations in Economics: Essays in Honour of G. L. S. Shackle*, eds. C. F. Carter and J. L. Ford (Blackwell, 1972); 6. 'Economics from a biological viewpoint', *J Law E*, 20(1), April 1977; 7. 'The theory of speculation under alternative regimes of markets', *J Fin*, 32, Sept. 1977; 8. 'The analytics of uncertainty and information: an expository survey' (with J. G. Riley), *JEL*, 17, Dec. 1979; 9. 'Evolutionary models in economics and law: cooperation versus conflict strategies', *Res. in Law and Econ.*, 4 (JAI Press, 1982); 10. 'From weakest-link to best-shot: the voluntary provision of public goods', *Public Choice*, 41(3), 1983.

HOBSON, John Atkinson*

Dates and Birthplace 1858–1940, Derby, Derbyshire, England.

Posts Held Schoolmaster, 1880–7; Univ. Extension Lect., 1887–97; Journalist and professional writer.

Degrees MA Univ. Oxford.

Publications *Books:* 1. *The Physiology of Industry* (with A. F. Mummery), (1889, 1956); 2. *The Evolution of Modern Capitalism* (1894, 1949); 3. *Imperialism: A Study* (1902, 1948); 4. *The Industrial System* (1909, 1910); 5. *Work and Wealth* (1914, 1933); 6. *Confessions of an Economic Heretic* (1938).

Career Hobson was essentially a humanistic critic of current economics, rejecting exclusively materialistic definitions of value. With A. F. Mummery he developed the theory of over-saving which was given a generous tribute by Keynes. His second major contribution was his analysis of capitalism on which Lenin drew freely. Critics have pointed to the technical inadequacies of his arguments but his influence was significant in at least the two examples cited.

Secondary Literature H. N. Brailsford, *The Life-work of J. A. Hobson* (OUP, 1948); R. Lekachman, 'Hobson, John A.', *IESS*, 6.

HOCH, Irving

Born 1926, Chicago, IL, USA.

Current Post Sr. Fellow, Resources for the Future, Washington, DC, 1967–.

Past Posts Econ., Chicago Area Transportation Study, Chicago, 1956–9; Ass. Prof., Assoc. Prof. Agric. Econ., Univ. Cal. Berkeley, 1959–67; Sr. Lect., Fulbright-Hays Program, Autonomous Univ., Madrid, Spain, 1970.

Degrees BPhil (Liberal Arts), MA, PhD Univ. Chicago, 1945, 1951, 1957.

Offices and Honours Member, NATO Rev. Panel, Council Internat. Exchange Scholars, 1975–80; Res. Scholar, Agric. Econ., Penn. State Univ., 1978; Advisory Comm., Advisory Board Built Environment, Nat. Res. Council, 1983.

Editorial Duties Ed. Board, *JUE*.

Principal Fields of Interest 710 Agriculture; 930 Urban Economics; 200 Quantitative Economics and Data.

Publications *Books:* 1. *Forecasting Economic Activity for the Chicago Region: Final Report* (Chicago Area Transportation Study, 1959); 2. *Resource and Capital Requirement Matrices for the California Economy* (with P. Zusman), (Giannini Foundation, Univ. Cal., 1965); 3. *Estimates of Value and Agricultural Land, by State* (Univ. Cal., 1966); 4. *Analyses of California Farm Income Relationships* (with G. Elsner), (Giannini Foundation, Univ. Cal., 1966); 5. *A Study of the Economy of Napa County, California* (with N. Tryphonopoulos), (Giannini Foundation, Univ. Cal., 1969); 6. *Progress in Urban Economics* (Resources for the Future, 1969); 7. *Production Functions and Supply Applications for California Dairy Farms* (Giannini Foundation, Univ. Cal., 1976); 8. *Energy Use in the United States by State and Region* (Resources for the Future, 1978, 1979); 9. *The Economics of Managing Chlorofluorocarbons: Stratospheric Ozone and Climate Issues*, co-ed. (with J. Cumberland and J. Hibbs), (Resources for the Future, 1982); 10. *An Energy Oriented Input-Output Model* (with R. Carson), (Resources for the Future, 1984).

Articles: 1. 'Simultaneous equation bias in the context of the Cobb-Douglas production function', *Em*, 26(4), Oct. 1958; 2. 'Economic analysis of wilderness areas', in *Wilderness and Recreation* (US Outdoor Recreation Resources Rev. Commission, 1962, Sierra Club, 1963); 3. 'Estimation of production function parameters combining time series and cross-section data', *Em*, 30(1), Jan. 1962; 4. 'The three-dimensional city: contained urban space', in *The Quality of Urban Environment*, ed. H. S. Perloff (JHUP, 1969); 5. 'Income and city size', *Urb Stud*, 21(1), Oct. 1972, repr. in *Cities, Regions and Public Policy*, eds. G. C. Cameron and L. Wingo (Oliver & Boyd, 1973); 6. 'Urban scale and environmental quality', in *Research Reports, 3, Population, Resources and the Environment*, ed. R. Ridker (US Commission Pop. Growth and the Amer. Future, 1972); 7. 'Wages, climate and the quality of life' (with J. Drake), *JEEM*, 1(4), Dec. 1974; 8. 'City size effects, trends and policies', *Science*, 193, Sept. 1976; 9. 'Energy and location', in *Nonmetropolitan America in Transition*, eds. A. H. Hawley and S. M. Mazie (Univ. N. Carolina Press, 1981); 10. 'Farm real estate price components, 1920–78', *AJAE*, 64(1), Feb. 1982.

Principal Contributions I usually operate by applying the theory of the firm. Among those applications, I helped pioneer the use of analysis of covariance in estimating production functions, which include time and firm effects (shifters). I examined simultaneous equation bias in Cobb-Douglas functions, demonstrating that usual single equation estimates tend to yield the erroneous inference of constant returns to scale, which might be avoided by including firm effects. Empirical studies by myself and others support that conclusion.

I also applied the theory of the firm to city size, viewing cities as analogous to firms. I hypothesised that large cities have become large because they are relatively more productive, and that workers must receive higher wage rates as cities grow larger to compensate for corresponding higher costs-of-living, including psychic costs. Generalising from city to settlement ties together

work in urban economics and rural development. I then made empirical studies which related wage rates to settlement size and climate, hypothesising that wage differentials also reflect better or worse climate. Results have been encouraging.

Much of my work fits under the heading of land use and population distribution, including such varied topics as the allocation of wilderness land, the optimal spacing of urban highways, the determinants of farm real estate value and the effect of increased energy prices on the distribution of population. I have been an input-outputer, using that technique in projecting regional economic growth and in examining the effects of higher energy prices on the composition of industrial production. In the first instance, I innovated by treating the household sector as endogenous; the estimation of the energy embodied in US imports and exports was an innovative feature of the latter case.

HOCHMAN, Harold M.

Born 1936, New Haven, CT, USA.
Current Post Prof. Econ. and Public Admin., Baruch Coll. and Grad. Center, City Univ., NY, 1975–; Dir., Center Study Bus. and Govt., Baruch Coll., 1981–.
Past Posts Dir. Stud. Urban Public Fin., Sr. Res. Assoc., Urban Inst., Washington, DC, 1969–75; Vis. Lect., Grad. School Public Pol., Univ. Cal. Berkeley, 1973–4; Lady Davis Vis. Prof. Econ., Hebrew Univ., Jerusalem, 1980–1.
Degrees BA, MA, PhD Yale Univ., 1957, 1959, 1965.
Offices and Honours Phi Beta Kappa, 1957; Gerard Swope Fellow, General Electric Foundation, 1960–1.
Editorial Duties Ed. Boards, *Nat. Tax J.*, 1972–83, *Public Fin. Q.*, 1972–, *Pol. Rev.*, 1977–.
Principal Fields of Interest 320 Fiscal Theory and Policy; Public Finance; 900 Welfare Programmes; Consumer Economics; Urban and Regional Economics; 020 General Economic Theory.
Publications *Books:* 1. *Reading*

in Microeconomics, co-ed. (with W. Breit), (Holt, Rinehart & Winston, 1968, 1971; transls., Italian, 1976, Spanish, 1979); 2. *Redistribution Through Public Choice*, co-ed. (with G. E. Peterson), (Columbia Univ. Press, 1974); 3. *The Urban Economy*, ed. (W. W. Norton, 1976).

Articles: 1. 'Some aggregative implication of depreciation acceleration', *YEE*, 6(1), Spring 1966; 2. 'Pareto optimal redistribution' (with J. D. Rodgers), *AER*, 59(4), Sept. 1969; 3. 'Social problems and the urban crisis: can public policy make a difference?' (with W. Bateman), *AER*, 61(2), May 1971; 4. 'Utility interdependence and income transfers through charity' (with J. D. Rodgers), in *Transfers in an Urbanized Economy: Theories and Effects*, eds. K. Boulding and M. Pfaff (Wadsworth, 1973); 5. 'Rule change and transitional equity', in *Redistribution Through Public Choice, op. cit.*; 6. 'The simple politics of distributional preference' (with J. D. Rodgers), in *The Distribution of Economic Well-being*, ed. T. Juster (NBER, 1977); 7. 'The optimal tax treatment of charitable contributions' (with J. D. Rodgers), *Nat. Tax J.*, March 1977; 8. 'The over-regulated city: a perspective on regulatory procedures in the city of New York', *Public Fin. Q.*, 9, April 1981; 9. 'Contraction theories of redistribution', in *Social Policy Analysis*, eds. E. Helpman, A. Razin and E. Sadka (Academic Press, 1983); 10. 'Tiebout and sympathy' (with S. Nitzan), *J. Math. Social Science*, forthcoming, 1985.

Principal Contributions Principal contributions in public sector and urban economics. A series of papers (many co-authored with J. D. Rodgers) traced out the relationship between utility interdependence and the logic of redistribution, indicating the conditions under which transfers are required to achieve a Pareto optimum (in contrast to the then-prevailing view that redistribution must be justified by an external value judgement). Subsequent papers examined the empirical underpinnings of redistribution through public choice, examining charitable contributions and voter atti-

tudes toward welfare spending, and developed the concept of transitional equity, which is central to the problem of sustaining fairness in rule change. Research in progress defines the economic content and implications of patterns of extended preference, including concepts of antipathy (with S. Nitzan); examines the relationship between attitudes toward risk and distributional choice (with E. Kleiman); and develops a model of addictive behaviour (with T. Barthold).

HODGSKIN, Thomas*

Dates and Birthplace 1787–1869, England.

Posts Held Naval Officer; Journalist.

Publications *Books:* 1. *An Essay on Naval Discipline* (1813); 2. *Travels in the North of Germany* (1820); 3. *Labour Defended Against the Claims of Capital* (1825, 1964); 4. *Popular Political Economy* (1827); 5. *The Natural and Artifical Right of Property Contrasted* (1832).

Career Disgusted by the horrors of naval discipline, he first made a name by his attack on the navy, and established what was essentially an anarchist criticism of society. Turning to writing, he travelled extensively in Germany for the purpose of his book on that country. His economic writings were based on the idea that labour is the sole source of wealth, and that the workers were deprived of their true share of the wealth they produced. His *Popular Political Economy* was derived from his controversial lectures to the London Mechanics Institute and constituted the first textbook of socialist economics. In later life he was a frequent contributor to the *Economist*.

Secondary Literature E. Halévy, *Thomas Hodgskin 1787–1869* (Ernest Benn, 1903, 1956).

HOLLANDER, Jacob Harry*

Dates and Birthplace 1871–1940, Baltimore, MD, USA.

Posts Held Assoc. Prof., Prof., Johns Hopkins Univ., 1894–1940.

Degrees BA, PhD Johns Hopkins Univ., 1881, 1894.

Offices and Honours Pres., AEA, 1921.

Publications *Books:* 1. *Studies in State Taxation* (1900); 2. *Report on the Debt of Santo Domingo* (1906); 3. *David Ricardo: A Centenary Estimate* (1911); 4. *The Abolition of Poverty* (1914); 5. *War Borrowing* (1919); 6. *Economic Liberation* (1925); 7. *Want and Plenty* (1932).

Career A great collector and publisher of material on the history of economics, he also served in numerous official positions and wrote on economic theory. His government work included reforming the revenue system of Puerto Rico and advising the government of Santo Domingo on its public debt. He also was an official arbitrator in various labour disputes. His contributions to Ricardo scholarship are considerable and he initiated a famous series of *Reprints of Economic Tracts* in 1903.

Secondary Literature Anon., 'Jacob Henry Hollander', *AER*, 38(5), June 1948.

HOLLANDER, Samuel

Born 1937, London, England.

Current Post Prof. Econ., Univ. Toronto, Toronto, Ont., Canada, 1970–.

Past Posts Ass. Prof., Assoc. Prof., Univ. Toronto, 1963–7, 1967–70; Vis. Lect., McMaster Univ., Ont., 1966–8, Univ. Florence, 1973–4, Univ. London, 1974–5, Hebrew Univ., Jerusalem, 1979–80.

Degrees BSc LSE, 1959; MA, PhD Princeton Univ., 1961, 1963.

Offices and Honours Sir Edward Gonner Prize, Univ. London, 1959; Fulbright Travel Award, 1959; Ford Foundation Patent Fellow, 1961–3; Guggenheim Foundation Fellow, 1968–9; Sr. Canada Council Fellow, 1969–71; Killam Res. Fellow, 1973–5; Fellow, Royal Soc. Canada, 1976; Lady Davis Professorial Fellow, 1979–80; Canada Social Sciences and Humanities Res. Council Fellow, 1981–4; Vice-Pres., Hist. Econ. Soc., USA, 1983–4.

Editorial Duties Ed. Boards, *HOPE*, 1970, *CJE*, 1983, *Collected Works of J. S. Mill* (Univ. Toronto Press, 1967).

Principal Fields of Interest 031 History of Economic Thought; 036 Economic Methodology.

Publications *Books:* 1. *The Sources of Increased Efficiency: A Case Study of Du Pont Rayon Plants* (MIT Press, 1965); 2. *The Economics of Adam Smith* (Univ. Toronto Press, Heinemann Educational Books, 1973; transls., Italian, Feltrinelli, 1976, Japanese, Toyo Keizai, 1976); 3. *The Economics of David Ricardo* (Univ. Toronto Press, Heinemann Educ., 1979); 4. *The Economics of John Stuart Mill* (Univ. Toronto Press, Blackwell, 1985).

Articles: 1. 'The reception of Ricardian economics', *OEP*, 29(2), July 1977; 2. 'Adam Smith and the self-interest axiom', *J Law E*, 20(1), April 1977; 3. 'Mr Ricardo and the moderns' (with J. Hicks), *QJE*, 41(3), Aug. 1977; 4. 'On Prof. Samuelson's canonical classical model', *JEL*, 18(2), June 1980; 5. 'The post-Ricardian dissension: a case study in economics and ideology', *OEP*, 32(4), Nov. 1980; 6. 'Marxian economics as general-equilibrium theory', *HOPE*, 13(1), Spring 1981; 7. 'On the substantive identity of the classical and neo-classical conceptions of economic organization', *CJE*, 15(4), Nov. 1982; 8. 'William Whewell and J. S. Mill on the methodology of political economy', *Stud. in Hist. and Philo. of Science*, 14(2), 1983; 9. 'Professor Garegnani's "Defence of Sraffa on the material rate of profit"', *Camb J Econ*, 7, May 1983; 10. 'Marx and Malthusianism: Marx's secular path of wages', *AER*, 71(1), March 1984.

Principal Contributions The primary outcome of my research on eighteenth- and nineteenth-century economics is the demonstration of the existence of a 'core' of analytics — essentially allocation via the price mechanism in terms of general equilibrium — common to various representations of the capitalist exchange system. This holds true of works of the most disparate ideological intent — those of Marx and Ricardo as well as of Adam Smith and the late 'neoclassical' economists. Any notion of a dual development of nineteenth-century analysis, involving systems centred upon demand–supply or embryonic general equilibrium versus systems wherein distribution is solved prior to pricing, is suspect.

HOLT, Charles A

Born 1948, Richmond, VA, USA.
Current Post Assoc. Prof. Econ., Univ. Virginia, Charlottesville, VA, USA, 1983–.
Past Posts Ass. Prof., Assoc. Prof. Econ., Univ. Minnesota, Minneapolis, MN, 1976–82, 1982–3.
Degrees BA Washington and Lee Univ., 1970; MS, PhD Carnegie-Mellon Univ., 1974, 1977.
Offices and Honours L. J. Savage Award, 1977; Alexander Henderson Dissertation Award, 1977.
Editorial Duties Ed. Board, *Atlantic Econ. J.*, 1982–.
Principal Fields of Interest 022 Microeconomic Theory; 213 Mathematical Methods and Models; 610 Industrial Organisation.
Publications *Articles:* 1. 'Bidding for contracts' (with R. W. Shore), in *Bayesian Analysis in Economic Theory and Time Series Analysis* eds. A. Zellner and J. B. Kadane (N-H, 1980); 2. 'A note on first degree stochastic dominance' (with L. P. Hansen and D. Peled), *Econ. Letters*, 1(4), 1979; 3. 'Uncertainty and the bidding for incentive contracts', *AER*, 69(4), Sept. 1979; 4. 'Capital allocation within a firm' (with R. M. Cyert and M. H. DeGroot), *Behavioral Science*, 24(5), Sept. 1979; 5. 'Forecasting rules as equilibrium strategies in duopoly models', *Amer. Econ.*, 23(2), Fall 1979; 6. 'Competitive bidding for contracts under alternative auction procedures', *JPE*, 88(3), June 1980; 7. 'Waiting-line auctions' (with R. Sherman), *JPE*, 90(2), April 1982; 8. 'On the use of profit data to estimate the social cost of monopoly power in an oligopoly', *J. Econ. and Bus.*, 34, 1982; 9. 'When a queue is like an auction' (with R. Sherman), in *Auctions Bidding and Contracting: Uses and Theory*, ed. M. Shubik, R. Englebrecht-Wiggans, and R. Start (NYU Press, 1983); 10. 'Scoring rule proced-

ures for the elicitation of subjective probability distributions and von Neumann-Morgenstern utility functions', in *Bayesian Inference and Decision Techniques: Essays in Honor of Bruno de Finetti*, eds. P. K. Goel and A. Zellner (N-H, 1984).
Principal Contributions Early work was mainly concerned with game theoretic models of bidding behaviour in auctions. The initial results pertaining to the effects of procurement contract provision on bidding behaviour are contained in No.1 above, which received the 1977 Savage Dissertation Award. The effects of alternative auction institutions were considered in subsequent papers. The analysis of the effect of bidder risk aversion on expected procurement costs in the 1980 *JPE* paper was a generalisation of Vickrey's earlier work on this topic.

Most recent work has focussed on behaviour in laboratory experiments. Current experimental research involves an analysis of factors that facilitate tacit collusion in oligopoly markets and reconsideration of convergence of prices to competitive levels in oral double auctions.

HOMAN, Paul Thomas*

Dates and Birthplace 1893–1969, Indianola, IA, USA.
Posts Held Prof., Cornell Univ., 1929–47, UCLA, 1950–69, Southern Methodist Univ., Dallas, TX, 1953–63; US President's Council Econ. Advisers, 1947–50.
Degrees BA Williamette Univ., 1914; BA Univ. Oxford, 1919; PhD Brookings Inst., 1926.
Offices UNRRA, Adviser UNESCO, etc.
Editorial Duties Ed. *AER*, 1941–52.
Publications *Books:* 1. *Contemporary Economic Thought* (1928); 2. *Current Economic Problems*, ed. (1932–); 3. *The Sugar Economy of Puerto Rico* (with A. D. Gayer and E. K. James), (1938).
Career A student of Herbert Davenport at Cornell where he later held a chair of economics. His discussion of current theory in *Contemporary Economic*

Thought was sympathetic both to heterodoxy and to the current orthodox school. His editorship of *AER* was instrumental not only in raising its own standards but those of economic journals in the US generally. His work on public policy involved membership at various times of the Brookings Institute, the War Production Board, UNRRA, UNESCO, and the President's Council of Economic Advisers.

HORNER, Francis*

Dates and Birthplace 1778–1817, Edinburgh, Scotland.
Posts Held Lawyer and politician.
Offices Co-founder, *Edinburgh Rev.*, 1802; MP St Ives, 1806–7, Wendover, 1807–12, St Mawes, 1813–17; Chairman, UK Bullion Comm., 1810–11.
Publications *Books:* 1. *The Economic Writings of Francis Horner in the 'Edinburgh Review' 1802–6*, ed. F. W. Fetter, (LSE, 1957).
Career Whig politician whose association with the Bullion Committee made his name as an economic expert, despite the committee's recommendation for the resumption of cash payments by the Bank of England failing to gain legislative support. He was an opponent of the corn duties and spoke tellingly in parliament on a number of other issues.

HORTON, Samuel Dana*

Dates and Birthplace 1844–95, USA.
Posts Held Lawyer.
Offices Secretary, Internat. Monetary Congress, Paris, 1878; Amer. Representative, Paris Conf., 1881.
Publications *Books:* 1. *Silver and Gold and their Relation to the Problem of Resumption* (1876); 2. *Silver: An Issue of International Politics* (1886), 3. *The Silver Pound and England's Monetary Policy since the Restoration* (1887); 4. *Silver in Europe* (1890); 5. *Confidential Notes on Silver Diplomacy* (1891).
Career With F. A. Walker, one of the leading advocates of an international bimetallic coinage. He argued the effectiveness of bimetallism from historical evidence and disregarded the success of Britain with its single standard as an exceptional example. In his later years he abandoned his legal practice and devoted himself entirely to the cause of bimetallism.
Secondary Literature H. L. Reed, 'Horton, Samuel Dana', *ESS*, 7.

HORVITZ, Paul Michael

Born 1935, Providence, RI, USA.
Current Post Judge James A. Elkins Prof. Banking and Fin., Univ. Houston, Houston, TX, USA, 1977–.
Past Posts Fin. Econ. Fed. Reserve Bank Boston, 1956–60; Ass. Prof., Boston Univ, 1960–2; Econ. Analyst, Mitre Corp., Bedford, MA, 1962–3; Sr. Econ. US Office Comptroller of Currency, Washington, DC, 1963–6; Ass. Dir. Res., Dir. Res., Asst. Chairman, Fed. Deposit Insurance Corp., 1967, 1968–76, 1976–7.
Degrees BA Univ. Chicago, 1954; MBA Boston Univ. 1956; PhD MIT, 1958.
Offices and Honours Ford Foundation Scholar, 1951–3; NSF Fellow, 1957–8.
Editorial Duties Ed. Board, *Fin. Rev.*, *J. Bank Res.*, 1972–81; Assoc. Ed., *Nat. Banking Rev.*, 1963–6, *Fin. Management*, 1972–4, *J. Fin. Res.*, 1981–.
Principal Fields of Interest 311 Domestic Monetary and Financial Theory and Policy; 312 Commercial Banking; 314 Financial Intermediaries.
Publications *Books:* 1. *Concentration and Competition in New England Banking* (Fed. Reserve Bank Boston, 1958); 2. *Monetary Policy and the Financial System* (Prentice-Hall, 1963, 1981); 3. *Federal Reserve Membership* (with P. Merrill), (Amer. Bankers Assoc., 1979); 4. *The Management of Commercial Bank Funds* (with G. McKinney and W. Brown), (Amer. Inst. Banking, 1980); 5. *The Future Development of Foreign Banking Organizations in the U.S.* (with B. Shull), (Amer. Bankers Assoc., 1981); 6. *The Changing Environment of Non-Local Competition in U.S. Banking* (with P. Merrill), (Amer. Bankers Assoc., 1981); 7. *Problems in the Financing of Small Business*, co-ed. (with R. Pettit), (JAI Press,

1983); 8. *Sources of Financing for Small Business*, co-ed. (with R. Pettit), (JAI Press, 1984).

Articles: 1. 'Bank earnings and the competition for savings', *JPE*, 70, Feb. 1962; 2. 'The impact of branch banking on bank performance' (with B. Shull), *Nat. Banking Rev.*, Dec. 1964, repr. in *Banking Competition and the Banking Structure* (US Comptroller of the Currency, 1966); 3. 'Stimulating bank competition through regulatory action', *J Fin*, 20, March 1965, repr. in *Banking Markets and Financial Institutions* (Richard D. Irwin, 1971); 4. 'A note on textbook pricing', *AER*, 55(4), Sept. 1965; 5. 'The pricing of textbooks and the remuneration of authors', *AER*, 56(2), May 1966, repr. in *The Daily Economist*, ed. H. G. Johnson (Prentice-Hall, 1973); 6. 'Failures of large banks: implications for banking supervision and deposit insurance', *J. Fin. and Quant. Analysis*, 10(4), Nov. 1975; 7. 'A reconsideration of the role of bank examination: a note', *JMCB*, 12(4), pt. 1, Nov. 1980; 8. 'Regulation of the money order industry', *Fin. Management*, Winter 1980; 9. 'The case against risk-related deposit insurance premiums', *Housing Fin. Rev.*, Sept. 1983; 10. 'Reorganization of the financial regulatory agencies', *J. Bank Res.*, 14(4), Winter 1983.

Principal Contributions My early research focussed on issues related to the structure of the banking industry (mergers, branch banking, entry, etc). There had been a fair amount of literature in this area in the 1930s, and Chandler set forth a research agenda in a 1938 article, but very little was done until work by Alhadeff in the 1950s. Interest in this subject increased rapidly, due in part to the efforts of the Federal Reserve, the office of the Comptroller of the Currency and FDIC. While at the FDIC my interests shifted to an emphasis on regulation on financial institutions. The trend toward deregulation of several industries, including financial services, has increased interest in the question of the extent to which market forces can replace regulation and supervision in assuring efficiency and stability of the financial system. Federal deposit insurance plays a key role in this, and much of my recent research has focussed on the problem of deposit insurance.

HOSELITZ, Bert F.

Born 1913, Vienna, Austro-Hungary
Current Post Prof. Emeritus Econ. Social Science, Univ. Chicago, 1978–.

Past Posts Instr. Econ., Manchester Coll., IN, 1940–1; Res. Ass. Econ. Internat. Relations, Inst. Internat. Stud., Yale Univ., 1943; Instr. Social Sciences, Ass. Prof. Econ., Assoc. Prof. Social Science, Prof. Econ. Social Science, Univ. Chicago, 1945–6, 1946–7, 1948–53, 1954–78; Assoc. Prof. Econ., Carnegie Inst. Technology, 1947–8; Vis. Prof. Econ., Univ. Frankfurt, 1953–4, MIT, 1963–4, Univ. Cal. Santa Cruz, 1967, Univ. Hawaii, East-West Center, 1971.

Degrees Dr Juris Univ. Vienna, 1936; MA Univ. Chicago, 1945.

Offices and Honours Member, RES, EHA, Royal Econ. Hist. Soc., Univ. Chicago; Cowles Commission Fellow, 1942; Encyclopedia Britannica Fellow, 1943–5; Dir. Stud. Comm. Internat. Relations, 1948–58; Founder, Dir. Res. Center Econ. Devlp. Cultural Change, 1951–74; Acting Dir., RADIR Project, Hoover Library, Stanford Univ., 1949; Cons., UNESCO, 1954, 1960–1; US Senate Comm. Foreign Relations, 1956; Internat. Social Science Council, 1960–1; Fellow, Center Advanced Study Behavioral Science, Stanford, CA, 1955–6; Guggenheim Foundation Fellow, 1961–2.

Editorial Duties Ed., *EDCC*, 1953–61, 1966–, *ESS*, 1961.

Principal Fields of Interest 112 Economic Development Theories and Models.

Publications *Books:* 1. *The Economics of Military Occupation* (with H. S. Bloch), (Univ. Chicago Press, 1944); 2. *The Progress of Underdeveloped Areas*, ed. (Univ. Chicago Press, 1952); 3. *Reader's Guide to the Social Sciences*, co-ed. (Free Press, 1959, 1970); 4. *Sociological Aspects of Economic Growth* (Free Press, 1960; transls. into approximately 25 languages).

Articles: 1. 'Socialist planning and

international economic relations', *AER*, 33(4), Dec. 1943; 2. 'The role of cities in the economic growth of under-developed countries', *JPE*, 56(3), June 1953; 3. 'Non-economic factors in economic development', *AER*, 47(2), May 1957; 4. 'Tradition and economic growth', in *Tradition, Values, and Socio-economic Development*, eds. R. Braibanti and J. J. Spengler (Duke Univ. Press, 1961); 5. 'Entrepreneur-ship and traditional élites', *Explor. Entrepreneurial Hist.*, 2nd series, 1(1), Fall 1963.

Principal Contributions As writer, researcher, and teacher, I am most proud of teaching skills from 1940–63. Many students of that period have done and are still doing important work in the field of international relations and economic development.

HOTELLING, Harold*

Dates and Birthplace 1895–1973, Fulda, MN, USA.
Posts Held Journalist and school-teacher; Math. Cons., Food Res. Inst., Stanford, 1924–6; Lect., Math., Stan-ford Univ., 1927–3; Prof. Econ., Colum-bia Univ., 1931–46; Prof. Math. Stats., Univ. N. Carolina, 1946–66.
Degrees BA, MA Univ. Washington, 1919, 1921; PhD Princeton Univ., 1924.
Offices and Honours Disting. Fellow, AEA; Pres., Em Soc, 1936–7.
Publications *Articles:* 1. 'Stability in competition', *EJ*, 39, March 1929, repr. in *Readings in Price Theory*, eds. G. J. Stigler and K. E. Boulding (Richard D. Irwin, 1953); 2. 'Economics of exhaustible resources', *JPE*, 39, April 1931; 3. 'Edgeworth's taxation paradox and the nature of demand and supply functions', *JPE*, 40, Oct. 1932, repr. in *Precursors in Mathematical Economics: An Anthology*, eds. W. J. Baumol and S. M. Goldfeld (LSE, 1968); 4. 'Demand functions with limited budgets', *EM*, 3, Jan. 1935; 5. 'The general welfare in relation to problems of taxation and of railway and utility rates', *Em*, 6, July 1938, repr. in *Read-ings in Welfare Economics*, eds. K. J. Arrow and T. Scitovsky (Richard D.

Irwin, 1969); 6. 'Multivariate analysis: III Correction', *IESS*, 10.

Career A pioneer of mathematical economics and statistical theory whose fame rests on a comparatively small number of published papers, and on his success as a teacher. His contributions were mainly in the areas of demand theory, welfare economics, optimisation over time, location theory under con-ditions of monopolistic competition, and the incidence of taxation.

Secondary Literature P. A. Samuel-son, 'Harold Hotelling as mathematical economist', *Amer. Stat.*, 14(3), 1960; R. W. Pfouts and M. R. Leadbetter, 'Hotelling, Harold', *IESS*, 18.

HOUTHAKKER, Hendriks

Born 1924, Amsterdam, The Nether-lands.
Current Post Henry Lee Prof. Econ., Harvard Univ., 1980–.
Past Posts Prof. Econ., Harvard Univ., 1960–80; Member, US Presi-dent's Council Econ. Advisers, 1969–71.
Degrees Doctorandus, Univ. Amster-dam, 1949; Hon. Dr Univ. Amsterdam, Univ. Freibourg.
Offices and Honours Member, NAS, AAAS, Internat. Stat. Inst.; John Bates Clark Medal, Vice-Pres., AEA, 1963, 1972; Fellow, Pres., Em Soc, 1967; Corresp. Member, Netherlands Academy Sciences.
Principal Fields of Interest 022 Micro-economic Theory.
Publications *Books:* 1. *The Analysis of Family Budgets* (with S. J. Prais), (CUP, 1955, 1971); 2. *Consumer De-mand in the United States* (with L. D. Taylor), (Harvard Univ. Press, 1966, 1970); 3. *Economic Policy for the Farm Sector* (AEI, 1967); 4. *The World Price of Oil: A Medium-term Analysis* (AEI, 1976).
Articles: 1. 'Revealed preference and the utility function', *Ec*, N.S. 17, May 1950; 2. 'The Pareto distribution and the Cobb-Douglas production function in activity analysis', *REStud*, 23(1), 1955; 3. 'Income and price elasticities in world trade' (with S. P. Magee), *REStat*, 51(2), May 1969; 4. 'Growth

and inflation: analysis by industry', *Brookings Papers Econ. Activity*, 1, 1979; 5. 'The use and management of North Sea oil', in *Britain's Economic Performance*, eds. R. E. Caves and L. B. Krause (Brookings Inst., 1980).

Principal Contributions Empirical research on consumption directed at the forms of Engel curves and at dynamic phenomena; theoretical research on that subject dealing with axiomatics and with special assumptions to improve applicability. Suggested a novel microfoundation for the production function; also explored the price-output behaviour of industries. In international economics demonstrated the importance of income elasticities and presented a computerised extension of the Ricardian model. Publications on commodity markets dealt with the theory of 'normal backwardation' with the efficiency of futures markets and with the conditions under which futures markets can exist. In energy, participated in the development of worldwide models and in research on mineral economics. In addition, contributed to various areas of economic policy, particularly regulation.

HOWITT, Peter Wilkinson

Born 1946, Toronto, Ontario., Canada.
Current Post Prof. Econ., Univ. Western Ontario., London, Ont., Canada, 1982–.
Past Posts Ass. Prof., Assoc. Prof., Univ. Western Ont., 1972–82; Vis. Prof., Hebrew Univ., Jerusalem, 1980.
Degrees BA McGill Univ., 1968; MA Univ. Western Ontario, 1969; PhD Northwestern Univ., 1973.
Editorial Duties Assoc. Ed., *CJE*, 1978–81; Ed. Board, *AER*, 1980–3.
Principal Fields of Interest 023 Macroeconomic Theory; 131 Economic Fluctuations; 311 Domestic Monetary and Financial Theory and Policy.
Publications *Articles:* 1. 'Stability and the quantity theory', *JPE*, 82, Jan.–Feb. 1974; 2. 'The transaction theory of the demand for money: a reconsideration' (with R. Clower), *JPE*, 86, June 1978; 3. 'The limits to stability of a full-employment equil-

ibrium', *Scand JE*, 80, Sept. 1978; 4. 'Credit rationing and implicit contract theory' (with J. Fried), *JMCB*, 12, Aug. 1980; 5. 'Activist monetary policy under rational expectations', *JPE*, 89, April 1981; 6. 'The effects of inflation on real interest rates' (with J. Fried), *AER*, 73(5), Dec. 1983.

Principal Contributions Most of my work has been aimed at furthering our understanding of monetary phenomena by examining the nature of market interactions in idealised settings where transacting and communicating are costly activities. Monetary dynamics are studied by means of non-*tâtonnement* stability theory. The demand for money is modelled in terms of the optimal sequencing of transactions by a trader in a world with set-up cost of transactions. The role of monetary policy is examined in a setting where price-setting decisions cannot be perfectly co-ordinated. Price-adjustment is modelled as if undertaken by specialised middlemen who help to defer the costs of trading. Recent work has been aimed at understanding unemployment as a manifestation of transaction costs.

HOXIE, Robert Franklin*

Dates and Birthplace 1868–1916, Edmeston, NY, USA.
Posts Held Prof., Econ., Univ. Chicago.
Publications *Books:* 1. *Scientific Management and Labor* (1915); 2. *Trades Unionism in the United States* (1917).
Articles: 1. 'On the empirical method of economic instruction', *JPE*, 9, Sept. 1901.
Career Labour economist who sought to instil general economic theory with a more accurate vision of the complexity of industrial life. Thus his studies of trade unionism stress its diversity. An outstanding teacher, much of whose best work was heard in the classroom rather than appearing in print.
Secondary Literature C. Goodrich, 'Hoxie, Robert Franklin', *ESS*, 7.

HUDSON, Edward Allan

Born 1946, Wellington, New Zealand.
Current Post Pres., Cambridge Planning and Analytics, Inc., Cambridge, MA, USA, 1982–.
Past Posts Jr. Lect., Sr. Lect., Victoria Univ., Wellington, NZ, 1968–9, 1975–7; Sr. Econ., Data Resources Inc., Lexington, MA, 1973–5; Dir., Dale Jorgenson Assoc., Cambridge, MA, 1977–82.
Degrees BA Victoria Univ., Wellington, NZ, 1968; MA, PhD Harvard Univ., 1971, 1973.
Offices and Honours Fulbright Scholar, 1969–73.
Principal Fields of Interest 021 General Equilibrium Theory; 132 Economic Forecasting and Econometric Models; 723 Energy.
Publications *Books:* 1. *Solar Energy and the US Economy* (with C. J. Pleatsikas and R. J. Goettle), (Westview, 1982).
Articles: 1. 'US energy policy and economic growth, 1975–2000' (with D. Jorgenson), *Bell JE*, 5(2), Autumn 1974; 2. 'Tax policy and energy conservation' (with D. Jorgenson), in *Econometric Studies of US Energy Policy* (N-H, 1976); 3. 'Optimal extraction of energy resources', *New Zealand Econ. Papers*, 11, 1977; 4. 'New Zealand general elections: a formal analysis' (with M. L. Wevers), *Polit. Science*, 29(1), July 1977; 5. 'Energy policy and US economic growth' (with D. Jorgenson), *AER*, 68(2), May 1978; 6. 'Energy prices and the US economy, 1972–1976, (with D. Jorgenson), *Natural Resources J.*, Oct. 1981, repr. in *US Energy Policy*, eds. W. Mead and A. Utton (Ballinger, 1979); 7. 'Economic effects of increased penetration of solar energy', *The Energy J.*, 1(3), July 1980; 8. 'The impact of restrictions on the expansion of electric generating capacity' (with D. Jorgenson and D. O'Connor), in *Advances in the Economics of Energy and Resources*, 3 (JAI Press, 1980); 9. 'US energy price decontrol: energy, trade and economic effects', *Scand JE*, 83(2), 1981, repr. in *The Impact of Rising Oil Prices on the World Economy*, ed. L. Mathiessen (Macmillan, 1982); 10. 'Macroeconomic effects of natural gas price decontrol' (with R. Goettle), in *Energy Models and Studies* (N-H, 1983).

Principal Contributions My central professional objective has been to use economic analysis to generate useful information for policy and management decisions. My early work involved decision rules for engineering projects such as formulating strategies for highway design, construction and maintenance. My dissertation was a numerical application of optimal control to examine US growth possibilities and tax policies. Then I worked for several years in collaboration with Dale Jorgenson on applied general equilibrium analysis. The centrepiece of this work was an econometric general equilibrium simulation model of US economic structure and growth. The model also featured flexible coefficient consumer and producer models and consistent micromacro aggregation. This framework proved most useful in analysing several economy-wide problems and concerns of the 1970s — energy price increases and supply disruptions, energy policy, productivity growth, the supply possibilities of the economy, and longer-run growth processes and prospects. My work also included the examination of energy policy issues such as energy pricing, contingency planning, new supply technologies, and the two strategic debates — demand- vs. supply-focussed energy policies, and government- vs. market-based policies. More recently, I have moved towards management and providing information for management. I led the construction of an econometric macro model, based on credit-spending-income interactions, and integrating the flow of funds into a demand-based forecasting model. My company has been applying this model and forecasts to corporate planning. Related work has involved market studies, project and technology evaluations, and other analyses for corporate decision-making. Most recently, I have been directing the production and marketing of economic information systems on personal computers for corporate and government managers.

HUFBAUER, Gary Clyde

Born 1939, San Diego, CA, USA.

Current Post Sr. Fellow, Inst. Internat. Econ., Washington, DC, USA, 1982–; Counsel, Chapman, Duff and Paul, Washington, DC, USA, 1980–.

Past Posts Ass. Prof., Assoc. Prof., Univ. New Mexico, Albuquerque, NM, 1963–7; Econ. Adviser, Govt. W Pakistan, Harvard Devlp. Advisory Service, Lahore, Pakistan, 1976–9; Prof. Econ., Univ. New Mexico, 1970–4; Dir., Internat. Tax Staff, US Treasury, Washington, DC, 1974–6; Deputy Ass. Secretary, Internat. Trade and Investment Pol., US Treasury, 1977–80; Dep. Dir., Internat. Law Inst., Georgetown Univ. Law Center, Washington, DC, 1980–2.

Degrees BA Harvard Univ., 1960; PhD Univ. Camb. 1963; JD Georgetown Univ. Law School, 1980.

Offices and Honours Phi Beta Kappa, 1960; Marshall Scholar, 1960–3; Ford Foundation Faculty Fellow, 1966–7; Fulbright Res. Fellow, Univ. Camb., 1973.

Editorial Duties Ed., Office of Tax Analysis Papers, US Treasury, 1979.

Principal Fields of Interest 400 International Economics

Publications *Books:* 1. *Synthetic Materials and the Theory of International Trade* (Duckworth, 1966); 2. *Overseas Manufacturing Investment and the Balance of Payments* (with F. M. Adler), (US Govt. Printing Office, 1968); 3. *The International Framework for Money and Banking in the 1980s*, ed. (Internat. Law Inst., 1981); 4. *US International Economic Policy, 1981: A Draft Report*, ed. (Internat. Law Inst., 1982); 5. *Emerging Standards for International Trade and Investment*, co-ed. (Rowman & Allanheld, 1984); 6. *Subsidies in International Trade* (with J. Shelton-Erb), (Inst. Internat. Econ., 1984).

Articles: 1. 'The impact of national characteristics and technology on the commodity composition of trade in manufactured goods', in *The Technology Factor in International Trade*, ed. R. Vernon (Columbia Univ. Press, 1970); 2. 'The GATT Codes and the unconditional   most-favored-nation

principle' (with J. S. Erb and H. P. Starr), *Law and Pol. in Internat. Bus.*, 1, 1980.

Principal Contributions My career in economics has had three phases. In the first period (1960–7) as befits a young scholar, I was principally concerned with uncovering empirical relations in the international economy. My works on technology and trade, and the impact of foreign investment on the balance of payments were highlights. During this period, I had the joy of living in New Mexico, a place of great charm and beauty, most conducive to scholarship.

The second period began with an assignment in Pakistan with the Harvard Development Advisory Service (1967–9) and continued through six years of service in the US Treasury Department (1974–80). During this phase my concern was to shape government policies in sensible directions — but aspirations often exceed achievements! My writings reflected my policy responsibilities: the Pakistan exchange-rate system, US international tax policy, and the Tokyo Round of trade negotiations. Negotiating the GATT Code on Subsidies and Countervailing Duties was the high point of my Treasury years.

In the third phase of my career (since 1980), I have pursued an interest in international economic policy from the safety of Washington 'think tanks', initially the International Law Institute and now the Institute for International Economics. I try to keep a foot in the real world by practising law and managing investments on the side.

HUFFMAN, Wallace Edgar

Born 1943, Batavia, IA, USA.

Current Post Prof. Econ., Iowa State Univ., Ames, IA, USA, 1982–.

Past Posts Lect., Univ. IL, Chicago Circle, Chicago, 1970–2; Ass. Prof., Oklahoma State Univ., 1972–4; Ass. Prof., Assoc. Prof., Iowa State Univ., 1974–8, 1978–82; Vis. Fellow, Res. Assoc., Yale Univ., 1980–1.

Degrees BS (Agric.) Iowa State Univ., 1966; MA, PhD Univ. Chicago, 1971, 1972.

Offices and Honours Award Quality

of Res. Discovery, AAEA, 1978; Ingersoll Econ. Fellow; Rockefeller Foundation Agric. Econ. Fellow; Ford Foundation Fellow.

Editorial Duties Ed. Board, *N. Central J. Agric. Econ.*, 1978–81; Assoc. Ed., *AJAE*, 1983–.

Principal Fields of Interest 210 Econometrics; 713 Agricultural Policy; 850 Human Capital.

Publications *Articles:* 1. 'Decision making: the role of education', *AJAE*, 56(1), Feb. 1974; 2. 'Productive value of human time in US agriculture', *AJAE*, 58(4), Nov. 1976; 3. 'The value of the productive time of farm wives: Iowa, North Carolina and Oklahoma', *AJAE*, 58(5), Dec. 1976; 4. 'Allocative efficiency: the role of human capital', *QJE*, 91(1), Feb. 1977; 5. 'Farm and off-farm work decisions: the role of human capital', *REStat*, 52(1), Feb. 1980; 6. 'Money in the United Kingdom, 1833–1880', *JMCB*, 12(2), May 1980; 7. 'An economic analysis of state expenditures on experiment station research', *AJAE*, 63(1), Feb. 1981; 8. 'Black-white human capital differences: impact on agricultural productivity in the US south', *AER*, 71(1), March 1981; 9. 'International trade in labor versus commodities: US-Mexican agriculture', *AJAE*, 64(5), Dec. 1982.

Principal Contributions Early research provided initial econometric evidence that farmers' schooling and agricultural extension enhance allocative performance, farmers' responses to relative price changes, adoption of new technology and cultural practices. The results produced valuable evidence against the hypothesis that schooling only signals innate ability. Next, production functions fitted to agricultural data yielded estimates of marginal products of agricultural extension, labour, and other inputs. The estimates of the marginal product of extension were a new contribution. Subsequent work, which treated research and extension as endogenous variables, has provided pioneering econometric estimates of demand functions for these publicly provided services. Analogous to decisions of firms, models of households' choices have been developed on a range of resources, contributing to the development of the new home economics. Research has focussed upon modelling and providing econometric evidence for the demand for household capital services, and the supply of husband's and wife's off-farm work. New estimates of off-farm labour-supply functions and of substitution possibilities between physical capital and labour in household production were obtained. The research applies multiple-sample selection techniques to multiple-equation econometric models. Current research focusses upon US-Mexican trade in fresh agricultural commodities and illegal immigrants. Included are theoretical and empirical modelling of endogenous regulation of illegal immigration and commodity trade, and of trade equations for fresh vegetables and labour services. Other work concerns the historical support and performance — intermediate and final products — of the US agricultural experiment station system and the market for new agricultural scientists. Another interest is econometric exploration of US and UK monetary history.

HULTEN, Charles Reid

Born 1942, Eugene, OR, USA.

Current Post Sr. Res. Assoc., Urban Inst., Washington, DC, USA, 1978–.

Past Posts Teaching Ass., Harvard Univ., 1970; Ass. Prof., Johns Hopkins Univ., 1971–8.

Degrees BA (Stats.), PhD Univ. Cal. Berkeley, 1965, 1973.

Offices and Honours Nat. Defense Educ. Act Fellow, 1966–8.

Principal Fields of Interest 111 Economic Growth Theory and Models; 226 Productivity and Growth Indicators; 323 National Taxation and Subsidies.

Publications *Books:* 1. *Depreciation, Inflation and the Taxation of Income from Capital* , ed. (Urban Inst. Press, 1981); 2. *The Legacy of Reaganomics: Prospects for Long-Run Growth*, co-ed. (with I. V. Sawhill), (Urban Inst. Press, 1984).

Articles: 1. 'Divisia index numbers', *Em*, 41(6), Nov. 1973; 2. 'Technical change and the reproducibility of capital', *AER*, 65(5), Dec. 1975; 3. 'The sources of Japanese economic growth, 1955–71' (with M. Nishimizu), *REStat*, 60(3), Aug. 1978; 4. 'Growth accounting with intermediate impacts', *REStud*, 45(3), Oct. 1978; 5. 'On the "importance" of productivity change', *AER*, 69(1), March 1979; 6. 'The estimation of economic depreciation using vintage asset prices: an application of the box-cox power transformation' (with F. Wykoff), *J Em*, 15, 1981; 7. 'Economic depreciation and accelerated depreciation: an empirical analysis of the Conable-Jones 10–5–3 proposal' (with F. Wykoff), *Nat. Tax J.*, 34(1), March 1981; 8. 'Regional productivity growth in US manufacturing: 1951–1978' (with R. Schwab), *AER*, 74(1), March 1984; 9. 'Productivity change in state/local governments', *REStat*, 66(2), May 1984; 10. 'Tax policy and the investment decision', *AER*, 74(2), May 1984.

Principal Contributions Early work was devoted to the theoretical aspects of productivity measurement with particular emphasis on index number theory. Early research also focussed on the problem of measuring rates of economic depreciation, using data on the market prices of used structures and equipment. This line of research led to an interest in business tax policy and its relationship to economic growth. Specific studies have examined how various aspects of tax policy have changed the incentives to invest in various types of assets. Other research interests include the comparison of international productivity trends, with particular emphasis on US–Japan economic relationships, the measurement of regional productivity trends within the US and developing methods for measuring public sector productivity, where explicit measures of real output are unreliable or unavailable.

HUME, David*

Dates and Birthplace 1711–76, Edinburgh, Scotland.

Posts Held Tutor, 1745; Diplomat, 1746, 1763–6; Keeper, Advocate's Library, Edinburgh, 1752; Under-Secretary State, Home Dept., 1767–8.

Publications *Books:* 1. *A Treatise on Human Nature* (1739–40, 1958, 1969); 2. *Essays Moral and Political*, 2 vols (1741–2, 1912, 1963); 3. *An Inquiry Concerning Human Understanding* (1748); 4. *Political Discourses* (1752); 5. *History of England*, 3 vols (1754–62, 1894); 6. *Writings on Economics*, ed. E. Rotwein (1955).

Career Primarily known as a philosopher, he also wrote substantial histories, and in his essays dealt with political, sociological and economic topics. All these fields were illuminated by his basic philosophy which involved the analysis of human nature and the examination of the way in which environmental forces act on that nature to produce particular forms of behaviour. The economic essays chiefly deal with money, trade and taxes and have a quality that still makes them refreshing to read. On such topics as monetary theory, international trade and population growth, he was not equalled even by Adam Smith, a close friend on whom he had an enormous influence.

Secondary Literature E. C. Mossner, *Life of David Hume* (Univ. Texas Press, 1954); E. Rotwein, 'Hume, David', *IESS*, 6.

HURTER Jr., Arthur Patrick

Born 1934, Chicago, IL, USA.

Current Post Prof., Industrial Eng. and Management Sciences, Northwestern Univ., Evanston, IL, USA, 1970–.

Past Posts Res. Assoc., Transportation Center, Northwestern Univ., 1961–5; Ass. Prof., Assoc. Prof., Industrial Eng. and Management Sciences, Northwestern Univ., 19672–6, 1966–70.

Degrees BS (Chemical Eng.), MS (Chemical Eng.), MA, PhD Northwestern Univ., 1955, 1956, 1958, 1962.

Offices and Honours Phi Lambda Upsilon; Sigma Xi; Tau Beta Pi (Disting. Engineer); Fellow, US SSRC; National Nominating Comm., OR Soc. Amer.; Science and Technological Advisory Comm., Illinois Inst. Natural Resources.

Editorial Duties Assoc. Ed., *Amer. Inst. Industrial Eng. Transaction*, 1975–81.

Principal Fields of Interest 022 Microeconomic Theory; 522 Business Investment; 941 Regional Economics.

Publications *Books:* 1. *The Economics of Private Truck Transportation* (with W. Oi), (Brown, 1965); 2. *Inland Waterway Transportation: Studies in Public and Private Management and Investment Decisions* (with C. Howe, *et al.*), (JHUP, 1969).

Articles: 1. 'Transportation investment and regional development' (with L. Moses), in *Readings in Comprehensive Logistics: Aspects of Planned Transportation* (Univ. Texas Press, 1969); 2. 'Decision making mechanisms for research project selection in the private sector' (with A. Rubenstein), in *Resource Allocation in Agricultural Research* (Univ. Minnesota Press, 1971); 3. 'A theory of vertical integration in road transport services' (with W. Oi), in *Economics of Industrial Structure* (Penguin, 1973); 4. 'An input-output analysis of the costs of air pollution control' (with A. Cohen), *Management Science*, 21(4), Dec. 1974; 5. 'Minimization of a nonseparable objective function subject to disjoint constraints: location-allocation problems' (with R. Wendell), *Operations Res.*, 24(4), July–Aug. 1976; 6. 'The generalized market area problem' (with T. Lowe), *Management Science*, 22(10), June 1976; 7. 'A note on the separability of production and location', *AER*, 70(5), Dec. 1980; 8. 'Benefit-cost analysis and the common sense of environmental policy', in *Environmental Policy Elements of Environmental Analysis* (Ballinger, 1981); 9. 'Price uncertainty and the optimal production-location decision' (with J. Martinich), *Regional Science and Urban Econ.*, 12(1), Nov. 1982; 10. 'Regional investment and interregional programming' (with L. Moses), in *Transport and the Spatial Structure of Cities and Regions* (Northwestern Univ. Transportation Center, 1982).

Principal Contributions Through the years, I have attempted to combine my interest and training in economics and operations research. Certain topics such as transportation, plant and equipment investment, facility location, regional, and environmental economics form the focus of my work. This is manifest in over fifty publications, in my classroom lectures, and in the training of more than twenty PhD students. Recently, I have been particularly concerned with developing models of individual decision-making units which include facility design (productive-investment) and facility location. These considerations are not treated in an integrated manner in either the economics or the operations research literature. The integration of production-investment location considerations leads to a complex model, making solution difficult. I have contributed to methods for the solution of these problems, and continue to work on better methods. The concept of input substitutability in the design problem is central to this effort whether in a stock-flow production function or in activity analysis representation. Uncertainty in prices and in the production process has been introduced along with von Neumann-Morgenstein utility functions. These models and solution techniques are currently under development. The models of production-investment-location decisions are appropriate for the evaluation of the regional or locational effects of tax policies and regulations (eg. environmental). For example, certain kinds of taxes may lead strongly risk-averse firms to choose a location for a new plant different from one they would choose under an alternative tax yielding the same revenue. Finally, my work on production-investment-location models has led me again to pursue one of my major interests, environmental economics. In this instance, investigation of multi-attribute production-investment-location models has led naturally to a consideration of location decisions for hazardous or toxic facilities.

HURWICZ, Leonid

Born 1917, Moscow, Russia.

Current Post Regents' Prof. Econ., Univ. Minnesota, MN, USA.

Past Posts Res. Assoc., Cowles Commission, Univ. Chicago, 1944–6; Assoc. Prof., Prof., Iowa State Coll., 1946–9; Prof Econ., Maths., Stats., Univ. Illinois, 1949–51; Univ. Minnesota, 1951–;

Vis. Prof., Stanford Univ., 1955–6, 1958–9, Harvard Univ., 1969–71, Univ. Cal. Berkeley, 1976–7.

Degrees LLM Univ. Warsaw, 1938; Hon. Dr Science Northwestern Univ., 1980.

Offices and Honours Fellow, Pres., Em Soc, 1949, 1969; Fisher (Em Soc) Lect., Univ. Copenhagen, 1963; Member, AAAS, 1965; Ely (AEA) Lect. Univ. Toronto, 1972; Member, NAS, 1974; Disting. Fellow, AEA, 1977.

Principal Fields of Interest 050 Economic Systems.

Publications *Books:* 1. *Studies in Linear and Non-linear Programming* (with K. J. Arrow and H. Uzawa), (Stanford Univ. Press, 1958); 2. *Preferences, Utility and Demand* (with J. S. Chipman, *et al.*), (Harcourt, Brace Jovanovich, 1971); 3. *Studies in Resource Allocation Processes* (CUP, 1977).

Articles: 1. 'The theory of economic behavior', *AER*, 35, Dec. 1945; 2. 'On the stability of the competitive equilibrium I–II' (with K. J. Arrow and H. D. Block), *Em*, 26–7, Oct. 1958, Jan. 1959; 3. 'Optimality and informational efficiency in resource allocation processes', in *Mathematical Methods in the Social Sciences*, eds. K. J. Arrow, *et al.* (Stanford Univ. Press, 1960); 4. 'Outcome functions yielding Walrasian and Lindahl allocations at Nash equilibrium points', *REStud*, 46(2), April 1979; 5. 'On allocations attainable through Nash equilibria', *JET*, 21, Aug. 1979.

Principal Contributions Looking at economic systems from a 'designer's point of view', regarding the economic mechanism as the unknown of the problem rather than a datum, the problem being to construct mechanisms satisfying specified desiderata (e.g. informational decentralisation, efficiency, individual rationality). Constructing formal models useful in analysing and designing economic systems; formulating rigorous definitions of informational decentralisation and incentive-compatibility. Using the framework of noncooperative game theory to study the incentive-compatibility properties of economic mechanisms. Results on stability of competitive equilibrium (with K. J. Arrow and H. D. Block), programming in infinite-dimensional spaces, least squares bias in autoregressive time series. Analysis of the concept of causality.

HUTCHESON, Francis*

Dates and Birthplace 1694–1746, Co. Down, Ireland.

Posts Held Presbyterian Minister; Prof. Moral Philo., Univ. Glasgow, 1729–46.

Publications *Books:* 1. *Inquiry into the Origin of our Ideas of Beauty and Virtue* (1720); 2. *Essay on the Nature and Conduct of the Passions* (1728); 3. *Introduction to Moral Philosoophy* (1753); 4. *A System of Moral Philosophy* (1755).

Career Adam Smith's teacher, whose philosophy had a basis in utilitarian ideas. To him virtue and natural law were both grounded in utility. His *System . . .* incorporates material which was given in his lectures, and the divisions of the subject he used are very similar to those later adopted by Smith. He laid great stress on the division of labour, and his ideas on the value of money and whether corn or labour afforded the most stable standard of value resemble those of Smith.

Secondary Literature W. L. Taylor, *Francis Hutcheson and David Hume as Predecessors of Adam Smith* (Duke Univ. Press, 1965).

HUTCHESON, Thomas Lee

Born 1942, Jacksonville, TX, USA.

Current Post Adviser, Trade & Industry Reform Program., Harvard Inst. Internat. Devlp., Dhaka, Bangladesh, 1983–.

Past Posts Peace Corps., Bolivia, 1964–6; Adviser, Harvard Devlp. Advisory Service, Bogotá, Colombia, 1969–71; Country Econ., World Bank, 1972–5; Econ., Industrial Devlp. and Fin., World Bank, 1975–83.

Degrees BS Univ. Texas, 1964; MA, PhD Univ. Michigan, 1969, 1972.

Offices and Honours Phi Beta Kappa.

Principal Fields of Interest 121 Economic Studies of Less Industrialised

Countries; 314 Financial Intermediaries; 423 Economic Integration.

Publications *Books:* 1. *The Cost of Tying Aid: A Methodology and Some Colombian Estimates* (with R. C. Porter), (Princeton Univ. Press, 1969); 2. *Incentives for Industrialization in Colombia* (Univ. Microfilms, 1972).

Articles: 1. 'Factor intensity and the CES production function', *REStat*, 51(4), Nov. 1969; 2. 'Colombia' (with D. Schydlowsky) in *Development Strategies in Semi-Industrial Countries*, ed. B. Baksan, *et al.* (JHUP, 1982).

Principal Contributions I am a development economist who does not believe in development economics. I rather try to apply standard economics to the problem of making people in poor countries richer. Since most people in poor countries want to be richer, governments usually try to satisfy this demand. Unfortunately it is easy for governments to adopt 'development' policies that make a few easily identified people richer while making the country poorer. If these development policies are spread widely enough, almost no one (except those who administer them) will be better off than if there were no 'development' policies at all. I see my task as identifying the worst policies, marshalling evidence and arguments against them, and suggesting ways of starting to untie the knot.

My professional career began in Colombia where my thesis described the structure of protection that was severely retarding growth in the late 1960s near the beginning of Colombia's significant but partial and short-lived liberalisation. Among various assignments for the World Bank I have worked on: (1) export subsidies and interest rates in Mexico (both too low in the early 1970s), (2) changes in the level of protection (lower and more uniform), the real exchange rate (higher) and interest rates (higher then lower) to ameliorate the Dutch Disease in Colombia brought on by the mid-1970s coffee and drug booms, (3) industrial incentives given through tariff exemptions in Ecuador and Panama (exemptions below a minimum tariff are mistaken), and (4) integration strategy in the Andean Group (think of it as a single country and apply standard trade theory).

In practical policy work I have tried to show that the Lerner Theorem is the most powerful tool we have for analysing tariffs and export subsidies. Unfortunately its implications are largely unrecognised by trade policy-makers and still officially undiscovered by GATT. There are interesting parallels in interest-rate policy.

HUTCHISON, Terence W.

Born 1912, Bournemouth, Hampshire, England.
Current Post Retired.
Past Posts Mitsui Prof. Econ., Univ. Birmingham, 1956–78; Vis. Prof., Columbia Univ., 1954–5, Univ. Virginia, 1960, Univ. Saarland, 1962, 1980, Yale Univ., 1963–4, ANU, 1967, Dalhousie Univ., 1970, Univ. Western Australia, 1975, Univ. Cal. Davis, 1978.
Degrees BA, MA Univ. Camb., 1934, 1937.
Principal Fields of Interest 030 History of Economic Thought; Methodology.
Publications *Books:* 1. *The Significance and Basic Postulates of Economic Theory* (Macmillan, 1938, Kelley, 1960); 2. *A Review of Economic Doctrines 1870–1929* (OUP, 1953, Greenwood Press, 1975); 3. *Economics and Economic Policy 1946–1966* (A&U, 1968); 4. *Positive Economics and Policy Objectives* (A&U, 1964); 5. *Markets and the Franchise* (INEA, 1966); 6. *Knowledge and Ignorance in Economics* (Blackwell, 1977); 7. *Revolutions and Progress in Economic Knowledge* (CUP, 1978); 8. *The Politics and Philosophy of Economics* (Blackwell, 1982).

Articles: 1. 'A note on tautologies and the nature of economic theory', *REStud*, 2(2), Feb. 1935; 2. 'Theoretische Ökonomie als Sprachsystem', *ZN*, 8(1), 1937; 3. 'Methodological prescriptions in economics: a reply', *Ec*, N.S. 27, May 1960.

Principal Contributions Areas of the method and history of economics.

HUTT, William Harold

Born 1899, London, England.
Current Post Retired, freelance author.

Past Posts Ernest Benn Ltd., The Individualist Bookshop Ltd., 1924–6; Sr. Lect., Prof., Univ. Cape Town, S. Africa, 1927–65, 1966–81; Vis. Prof., Univs. Virginia, Rockford Coll., Wabash Coll., Cal. State Univ., Hayward, Texas A&M Univ., Univ. Dallas, 1966–81; Vis. Res. Fellow, Hoover Inst., Stanford, CA, 1980–1.

Degrees BCom Univ. London, 1924; Hon. LLD Univ. Cape Town, 1977; Hon. Dr Social Sciences, Univ. Francisco Marroquin, Guatemale, 1979; Hon. Dr Humane Letters, Univ. Dallas, 1984.

Principal Fields of Interest 031 History of Economic Thought; 820 Labour Markets.

Publications *Books:* 1. *The Theory of Collective Bargaining* (King, 1930; Hobart & Cato, 1975); 2. *Economists and the Public* (Jonathan Cape, 1936); 3. *The Theory of Idle Resources* (Jonathan Cape, 1939, Liberty Press, 1975); 4. *Plan for Reconstruction* (Routledge & Kegan Paul, 1944); 5. *Keynesianism, Retrospect and Prospect* (Regenery, 1963); 6. *The Economics of the Color Bar* (INEA, 1964); 7. *Politically Impossible . . .?* (INEA, 1971); 8. *The Strike-Threat System* (Arlington House, 1973); 9. *A Rehabilitation of Say's Law* (Ohio Univ. Press, 1974); 10. *The Keynesian Episode* (Liberty Press, 1979).

Articles: 1. 'The factory system of the early nineteenth century', *Ec*, 6, March 1966; 2. 'Economic method and the concept of competition', *SAJE*, 2, March 1934; 3. 'Co-ordination and the size of the firm', *SAJE*, 2, Dec. 1934; 4. 'The nature of aggressive selling', *Ec*, N.S. 2, Aug. 1935; 5. 'Natural and contrived scarcities', *SAJE*, 3, Sept. 1935; 6. 'Discriminating monopoly and the consumer', *EJ*, 46, March 1936; 7. 'The price mechanism and economic immobility', *SAJE*, 4, Sept. 1936; 8. 'Pressure groups and laissez-faire', *SAJE*, 6, March 1938; 9. 'Privacy and private enterprise', *SAJE*, 7, Dec. 1939; 10. 'The concept of consumers' sovereignty', *EJ*, 50, March 1940.

Principal Contributions After entering academic life, I decided early that the concept of 'competition' needed rigorous definition. I eventually offered the following: 'Competition is the pro-cess of substituting a lower priced method of achieving any objective, material or non-material, including the production and marketing of any product'. Every economic society was, I perceived, co-ordinated through competition in this sense. The productive services of assets and men are priced, and the magnitude of aggregate income and its distribution among the owners of assets, and among men (as workers or entrepreneurs), are determined through the pricing system. 'Consumers' sovereignty', a term I believe I coined in the early 1930s can, when unconstrained, be shown to secure the ideal composition of the flow of aggregate output. I eventually concluded that aggregate income is maximised and the degree of inequality in its distribution minimised when, in every pursuit, each person is offered and accepts the *minimum* necessary to attract and retain the services of his assets or of his labour. The nonmarket determination of prices via the coercive power of special interest groups (e.g. labour unions) or via the State in the interest of such groups, always constrains the magnitude of society's real income and renders the distribution of that income more unequal. Crucial to the problem of pricing is the role of the money unit. Very early in the 1930s I defended the gold standard or any other device under which society's decision-makers can rely on a money unit of unchanging purchasing power. I was accordingly led to a critical opposition to the notions of Lord Keynes several years before his famous exposition in *The General Theory* appeared in 1936.

HYMER, Stephen Herbert*

Dates and Birthplace 1934–74, Montreal, Quebec, Canada.

Posts Held Res. Assoc., Ghanaian Planning Board, 1961–2; Ass. Prof., MIT, 1962–3; Ass. Prof. Econ., Yale Univ., 1963–70; Prof. Econ., New School Social Res., 1970–6.

Degrees BA McGill Univ., Montreal, 1955; PhD MIT, 1960.

Offices and Honours Council Foreign Relations Fellow, 1968–9; Member, Union Radical Polit. Econ.

Publications *Books:* 1. *The International Operations of National Firms: A Study of Direct Foreign Investment* (MIT Press, 1976).

Articles: 1. 'Firm size and rate of growth' (with P. Pashigian), *JPE*, 70, Dec. 1962; 2. 'A model of an agrarian economy' (with S. A. Resnick), *AER*, 59(4), Sept. 1969; 3. 'Economic forms in pre-colonial Ghana', *JEH*, 30(1), March 1970; 4. 'Multinational corporations and international oligopoly', in *The International Corporation*, ed. C. P. Kindleberger (MIT Press, 1970); 5. 'International trade and uneven development' (with S. A. Resnick), in *Trade, Balance of Payments and Growth*, eds. J. Bhagwati, *et al.* (N-H., 1971); 6. 'The multinational corporation and the problem of uneven development', in *Economics and World Order*, ed. J. Bhagwati (Macmillan, 1971).

Career Stephen Hymer's principal contribution was to turn the theory of the multinational corporation away from an international trade context into one of industrial organisation with an emphasis on rent-seeking based on the advantage that the corporation has over those in the foreign country. The thesis was written in 1960, circulated by inter-library loan in typed form for a number of years, and was finally published after Hymer's death. It gave rise to a torrent of derivative literature, some claiming originality, emphasising transactions costs, internalisation, appropriability, etc. In addition to his work on the multinational corporation, Hymer had a deep interest in economic development, especially in the context of Africa.

Secondary Literature C. P. Kindleberger, *Multinational Excursions* (MIT Press, 1984), chapt. 13; V. H. Dunning, *et al.*, 'In Honor of Stephen H. Hymer: The first quarter century of the theory of foreign direct investment', *AER*, 75(2), May 1985.

HYNDMAN, Henry Mayers*

Dates and Birthplace 1842–1921, London, England.
Posts Held Journalist and political leader.

Degrees BA Univ. Camb. 1863.
Offices and Honours Founder, Social Democratic Federation, 1881, Nat. Socialist Party, 1916; Founder and Ed., *Justice*, 1884.
Publications *Books:* 1. *England For All* (1881); 2. *The Historical Basis of Socialism* (1883); 3. *A Summary of the Principles of Socialism* (with W. Moris), (1884); 4. *Commercial Crises of the Nineteenth Century*(1892); 5. *Economics of Socialism* (1896); 6. *Record of an Adventurous Life* (1911); 7. *Further Reminiscences* (1912).

Career Converted to socialism whilst a wealthy young man by his reading of Marx's *Capital*, he became Britain's first important socialist political leader. His various books expounded Marxism in a readable style to the British public. He was a determined advocate of Indian self-government and an opponent of British imperialist policy.

I

IJIRI, Yuji

Born 1935, Kobe, Japan.
Current Post Robert M. Trueblood Prof. Accounting and Econ., Carnegie-Mellon Univ., Pittsburgh, PA, 1967–.
Past Posts Ass. Prof., Assoc. Prof. Bus. Admin., Stanford Univ., Grad. School Bus., 1963–7.
Degrees CPA Japan, 1956; LLB Ritsumeikan Univ., Japan, 1956; MS Univ. Minnesota, 1960; PhD Carnegie-Mellon Univ., 1963.
Offices and Honours Member, Vice-Pres., Pres., AAA, 1963, 1974–5, 1982–3.
Principal Fields of Interest 214 Computer Programs; 512 Managerial Economics.
Publications *Books:* 1. *Management Goals and Accounting for Control, Studies in Mathematical and Managerial Economics*, ed. H. Theil, 3 (N-H, 1965; transls., Japanese, 1970, French, 1970, Spanish, 1976); 2. *The Foundations of Accounting Measurement: A Mathematical, Economic and Behavioral Inquiry* (Prentice-Hall, 1967, Scholars Book, 1978; transl., Japanese, 1968); 3.

Theory of Accounting Measurement (Amer. Accounting Assoc., 1975; transl., Japanese, 1976); 4. *Skew Distributions and the Sizes of Business Firms* (with H. A. Simon), (N-H, 1977); 5. *Recognition of Contractual Rights and Obligations: An Exploratory Study of Conceptual Issues* (Fin. Accounting Standards Board, 1980); 6. *Triple-Entry Book-keeping and Income Momentum* (AAA, 1982); 7. *Accounting Structured in APL* (AAA, 1984).

Articles: 1. 'The linear aggregation coefficient as the dual of the linear correlation coefficient', *Em*, 36(2), April 1968; 2. 'Fundamental queries in aggregation theory', *JASA*, 66(336), Dec. 1971; 3. 'Interpretations of departures from the Pareto curve in firm-size distributions' (with H. A. Simon), *JPE*, 82(2), March–April 1974; 4. 'Distributions associated with Bose-Einstein statistics' (with H. A. Simon), *NAS Proceedings*, 72(5), May 1975; 5. 'Cost flow networks and generalized inverses', in *Extremal Methods and Systems Analysis*, eds. A. V. Fiacco and K. O. Kortanek (Springer-Verlag, 1980).

Principal Contributions Aggregation theory, firm size distributions, accounting measurement theory, computer languages, and quantitative models in business and economics.

ILCHMAN, Warren F.

Born 1933, Denver, CO, USA.
Current Post Provost, Rockefeller Coll. Public Affairs; Dir., Rockefeller Inst. Govt., State Univ., New York, NY, USA, 1982–.
Past Posts Prof. Polit. Science, Univ. Cal. Berkeley, 1965–73; Dean, Coll. Liberal Arts, Grad. School, Prof. Polit. Sciences Econ., Boston Univ., 1974–6; Program Adviser, Internat. Div., Ford Foundation, 1976–80.
Degrees BA Brown Univ., 1955; PhD Univ. Camb., 1959.
Offices and Honours Phi Beta Kappa; Marshall Scholar; Contributing Author White House Library; Amer. Soc. Public Admin. Burchfield Award, 1965; Fulbright-Hays Sr. Res. Prof., India, 1968–9; Danforth Foundation Harbison Prize Outstanding Teaching, 1969–70;

Danforth Nat. Academy Public Admin., 1984.
Principal Fields of Interest 112 Economic Development Models; 511 Organisation and Decision Theory.
Publications *Books:* 1. *New Men of Knowledge and the New States: Planners and the Polity* (with A. S. Ilchman), (Univ. Cal. Press, 1968); 2. *The Political Economy of Change* (with N. T. Uphoff), (Univ. Cal. Press, 1969); 3. *The Political Economy of Development: Theory and Contributions* (with N. T. Uphoff), (Univ. Cal. Press, 1972); 4. *Policy Sciences and Population* (with H. D. Lasswell, et al.), (D. C. Heath, 1975); 5. *Employment and Education: The Policy Nexus* (with A. S. Ilchman and T. N. Dhar), (S. Asia Books, 1976).

Articles: 1. 'Balanced thought and economic growth', *EDCC*, 14(4), July 1966; 2. 'The political economy of foreign aid: the case of India', *Asian Survey*, Oct. 1967; 3. 'People in plenty: educated unemployment in India', *Asian Survey*, Oct. 1969; 4. 'Beyond the economics of labor-intensive development: politics and administration', *SEADAG Occasional Papers*, 1973; 5. 'Preserving the cosmopolitan research university in the United States', *Annals AAAS*, 449, May 1980.

Principal Contributions Early work applied to developing a theoretical capacity to consider political and economic resources in the same calculus. Thereafter, worked increasingly on applying this perspective to the public policy issues of employment, education, land reform and population, and to evaluating the productivity of social science knowledge for public choice.

INGHAM, Alan

Born 1948, Fleetwood, Lancashire, England.
Current Post Lect., Univ. Southampton, England, 1971–.
Past Posts Vis. Res. Fellow, IRES, Univ. Catholique de Louvain, 1977; Vis. Prof., J. W. Goethe Univ., Frankfurt, 1978; Vis. Assoc. Prof., Univ. British Columbia, Vancouver, 1981–2.
Degrees BSc, MSc Univ. London, 1969, 1971.

Principal Fields of Interest 020 General Economic Theory; 210 Econometric, Statistical and Mathematical Methods and Models; 720 Natural Resources.

Publications *Books:* 1. *Demand, Equilibrium and Trade, Essays in Honour of I. F. Pearce*, co-ed. (with A. Ulph), (Macmillan, 1984); 2. *Participation and Risk in Economics of Codetermination* (Macmillan, 1977).

Articles: 1. 'Natural resources and growing population' (with P. Simmons), *REStud*, 42, April 1975; 2. 'Projecting input output coefficients for the Southampton econometric model', in *Medium Term Dynamic Forecasting* (Input-Output Publishing, 1977); 3. 'A discontinuous investment model for the US', in *Selected Papers on Contemporary Econometric Problems* (Athens School Econ., 1982); 4. 'Unemployment equilibria in a small resource importing economy', in *Economic Theory of Natural Resources* (Physica Verlag, 1983); 5. 'Balanced growth in a macro economic natural resource model', in *The Employment Consequences of Technological Change* (HMSO, 1983).

Principal Contributions My interests have included many topics in economics which have as theme a concern for public policy and a quantitative methodology. I have tried to take a broad approach to questions and not be limited by current models or approaches. A constant theme in my work has been the economics of natural resources. Starting with considerations of optimal plans for depletion policies, in particular the consequences of using various models and social objectives for the possibility of existence of optimal plans and their nature, I have moved on to consider models with a greater degree of historical realism in terms of how natural resources entered into the production system. This led to consideration of learning by doing, and a vantage structure of production. My interests in this area have moved to an econometric analysis, in particular the demand for energy by the manufacturing sector in Britain, and it is hoped to be able to use the results of the empirical analysis in considering the employment consequences of various depletion and resource pricing policies. Another important interest has been whether the assumption of continuity of dynamic processes almost universally accepted by applied econometricians is a valid one. My paper on investment suggests that approximations to small-scale dynamic models may necessarily have to be discontinuous and that this can be supported at both an empirical and a theoretical level. Other work related to discontinuity of the evolution of economic systems has been a study of the enclosure of common lands and the end of the open-field system in English agriculture.

INGRAM, John Kells*

Dates and Birthplace 1823–1907, Temple Carne, Donegal, Ireland.

Posts Held Fellow, Prof. Oratory, Regius Prof. Greek, Librarian, Vice-Provost, Trinity Coll., Univ. Dublin, 1846, 1852, 1866–77, 1879–87, 1898–9.

Degrees BA Trinity Coll., Univ. Dublin, 1843.

Offices Founder, Stat. and Social Enquiry Soc. Ireland; Ed., *Hermathena*.

Publications *Books:* 1. *A History of Political Economy* (1888, 1967).

Career A firm adherent of Comte and spokesman for historical economics in Britain, who also shone in the fields of law, literature, the classics and mathematics. His attack on classical economics encompassed its methodology and its conclusions. The latter he characterised as apologies for the employing classes. His *History* ... was extremely successful, being frequently translated and serving as a textbook till the 1920s. Its polemical Comtist tone now renders it obsolete. In it Ingram is drawn into extreme positions, such as his condemnation of mathematical economics as completely sterile.

Secondary Literature C. L. Falkiner, *Memoir of John Kells Ingram* (1907).

INMAN, Robert Paul

Born 1942, Evanston, IL, USA.

Current Post Prof. Fin. Econ. Public Pol. and Management, Wharton School, Univ. Penn., Philadelphia, PA, USA, 1980–.

Past Posts Ass. Prof. Econ. and Public Pol., Assoc. Prof. Fin. and Econ., Wharton School, Univ. Penn., 1972–6, 1976–80; Vis. Sr. Scholar, Fed. Reserve Bank, Philadelphia, 1980; Vis. Scholar, Birkbeck Coll., London, 1980.

Degrees BA, MEd, PhD Harvard Univ., 1964, 1967, 1972.

Offices and Honours Nat. Tax Assoc., Dissertation Award, 1971; Robert Wood Johnson Faculty Fellow, Harvard Univ., 1976.

Editorial Duties Assoc. Ed., *PF Q*.

Principal Fields of Interest 320 Fiscal Theory and Policy; 910 Welfare, Health, Education; 930 Urban Economics.

Publications *Books:* 1. *Economics of Public Services*, co-ed. (with M. S. Feldstein), (Macmillan, 1974); 2. *Managing the Service Economy: Problems and Prospects* (CUP, 1984).

Articles: 1. 'The family's provision of children's health', in *The Role of Health Insurance in the Health Service Sector* (NBER), 1976); 2. 'Micro-fiscal planning in the regional economy: a general equilibrium approach', *JPE*, 7(2), April 1977; 3. 'A generalized congestion function for highway travel', *JIE*, 5(1), Jan. 1978; 4. 'Optimal fiscal reform of metropolitan schools: some simulation results', *AER*, 68(1), March 1978; 5. 'Testing political economy's "as if" proposition: is the median income voter really decisive?', *Public Choice*, 33(1), Winter 1978; 6. 'The indicial pursuit of local fiscal equity', *Harvard Law Rev.*, 92(8), June 1979; 7. 'The economic care for limits to government', *AER*, 72(2), May 1982; 8. 'Public employee pensions and the local labor budget', *J Pub E*, 19(1), Oct. 1982; 9. 'Federal aid and public education: an empirical look at the new fiscal federalism', *REStat*, 64(4), Nov. 1982; 10. 'Markets, government and the new political economy', in *Handbook of Public Economics* (N-H, 1984).

Principal Contributions The central focus of my research has been and remains the analysis of the processes for allocating societal resources through non-market mechanisms. My early work focussed on the theory and estimation of government budgeting, applied to local governments because of the rich institutional variation across observa-

tions. This early work was an extension of well-known economic models of political allocations. More recent work has attempted to test the validity of this procedure (No. 5 above) as well as to develop alternative models of political allocations based on the theory of efficient bargains (No. 8 above) and the theory of structure-induced, majority-rule equilibrium (No. 10 above). In addition to constructing and testing predictive (positive) models of government allocation, my work has proposed and examined alternative reforms of the process of public-sector allocations. Judicial reform of government performance, constitutional reform, and fiscal (i.e., grants-in-aid) reform have all been examined in various research papers. I retain a secondary, but active research interest in health care policy and in urban economics and policy. I am currently completing a major study on the economic consequences of disabling illnesses (and the use of social insurance for the disabled) as well as a book-length manuscript on urban economic development and urban fiscal crises. I anticipate continued research in these areas.

INNIS, Harold Adams*

Dates and Birthplace 1894–1952, Otterville, Ont., Canada.

Posts Held Prof., Dean, Univ. Toronto.

Degrees BA, MA McMaster Univ., 1916, 1918; PhD Univ. Chicago, 1923.

Offices and Honours Pres., Canadian Polit. Science Assoc., 1937, EHA, 1942, Royal Soc. Canada, 1946, AEA, 1951.

Publications *Books:* 1. *The Fur Trade in Canada: An Introduction to Canadian Economic History* (1930); 2. *The Cod Fisheries: The History of an International Economy* (1940); 3. *Political Economy in the Modern State* (1946); 4. *Empire and Communications* (1950); 5. *The Bias of Communications* (1951); 6. *Changing Concepts of Time* (1952).

Career Canada's most famous economic historian who sought a distinctively New World approach. His books on the fur and fishery trades of Canada re-oriented opinions on Canadian history in dramatic fashion. His later work concentrated on the economics and political aspects of communications media. Though not fully worked out at the time of his death, this was intended to combat the anti-cultural implications of modern communications monopolies.

Secondary Literature J. B. Brebner, 'Obit. Harold Adams Innis', *EJ*, 63, Sept. 1953.

INTRILIGATOR, Michael David

Born 1938, New York City, NY, USA.

Current Post Prof. Econ., UCLA, Prof. Polit. Science, Dir., Center Internat. and Strategic Affairs, UCLA, 1973–.

Past Posts Ass. Prof., Assoc. Prof., UCLA, 1963–6, 1966–72; Prof., Univ. Southern Cal., 1972–3.

Degrees SB MIT, 1959; MA Yale 1960; PhD MIT, 1963.

Offices and Honours Woodrow Wilson Fellow, 1959–60; MIT Fellow, 1960–1; Ford Foundation Faculty Res. Fellow, 1967–8; Fellow, Em Soc, 1982; Member, Internat. Inst. Strategic Stud., 1983.

Editorial Duties Co-ed. *Handbooks in Economics, Advanced Textbooks in Economics* (N-H, 1972); Ed. Board, *Math. Social Science*, 1983–, *Info. Econ. and Pol.*, 1982, *J. Optimal Theory and Appl.*, 1979, *Pol. Analysis and Info. Systems*, 1979, *J. Ec Dyn*, 1978–83, *Internat. J. Appl. Analysis*, 1977–, *J. Bus. and Econ. Stat*, 1981–, *J. Interdisciplinary Modeling and Simulation*, 1977–, *Conflict Management and Peace Science*, 1980–, *Comparative Strategy*, 1980–.

Principal Fields of Interest 020 General Economic Theory; 210 Econometric, Statistical and Mathematical Methods and Models.

Publications *Books:* 1. *Mathematical Optimization and Economic Theory* (Prentice-Hall, 1971; transls., Spanish, Editorial Prentice-Hall Internacional, 1973, Russian, Progress, 1975); 2. *Frontiers of Quantitative Economics*, ed. (N-H, 1971); 3. *Frontiers of Quantitative Economics, II*, co-ed. (with D. Kendrick), (N-H, 1974); 4. *Frontiers*

Quantitative Economics, III, ed. (N-H, 1977); 5. *Econometric Models, Techniques and Applications* (Prentice-Hall, N-H, 1978; transl., Greek, Gutenberg, 1983); 6. *A Forecasting and Policy Simulation Model of the Health Care Sector: The HRRC Prototype Microeconometric Model* (with D. E. Yett, L. J. Drabek, and L. Kimbell), (D. C. Heath, 1979); 7. *Handbook of Mathematical Economics*, co-ed. (with K. J. Arrow), (N-H, 1981, 1982, 1984); 8. *Handbook of Econometrics*, 3 vols co-ed. (with Z. Griliches), (N-H, 1983, 1984, 1985); 9. *Strategies for Managing Nuclear Proliferation — Economic and Political Issues*, co-ed. (with D. L. Brito and A. E. Wick), (D. C. Heath, 1983); 10. *National Security and International Stability*, co-ed. (with B. Brodie and R. Kolkowicz), (Oelgeschlager, Gunn & Hain, 1983).

Articles: 1. 'Embodied technical change and productivity in the United States, 1929–1958', *REStat*, 47(1), Feb. 1965; 2. 'Generalized comparative statics, with applications to consumer and producer theory' (with P. J. Kalman), *Int ER*, 14(2), June 1973; 3. 'A probabilistic model of social choice', *REStud*, 40(4), Oct. 1973; 4. 'Strategic considerations in the Richardson model of arms races', *JPE*, 83(2), April 1975; 5. 'A microeconometric model of the health care system in the United States' (with D. E. Yett, L. J. Drabek and L. Kimbell), *Annals Econ. and Social Measurement*, 4, July 1975; 6. 'A new approach to the Nash bargaining problem' (with D. L. Brito and A. M. Buoncristiani), *Em*, 45(5), July 1977; 7. 'Income redistribution: a probabilistic approach', *AER*, 69(1), March 1979; 8. 'Nuclear proliferation and the probability of nuclear war' (with D. L. Brito), *Public Choice*, 37, 1981; 9. 'Research on conflict theory: analytic approaches and areas of application', *J. Conflict Resolution*, 26, June 1982; 10. 'Can arms races lead to the outbreak of war?' (with D. L. Brito), *J. Conflict Resolution*, 28, March 1984.

Principal Contributions The common theme running through my work has been the development of models using the analytic approaches of decision theory, control theory, game theory, and econometrics in order to analyse, predict and control aspects of some of the fundamental problems of our economy and society, including technical change, individual structure, health care delivery, and arms races and arms control. In particular, my principal contributions are in four fields:

(1) *Economic Theory and Mathematical Economics*: Early contributions were in applications of control theory to economics, including optimal savings, regional allocations of investment, and allocation of scientific effort. My advanced text (Book No. 1) discusses programming and control theory and their applications in economics. Later contributions were to generalised comparative statics, probabilistic social choice and the Nash bargaining problem.

(2) *Econometrics*: Early contributions were in estimation of embodied technical change and productivity, while later work involved the specification and estimation of econometric models of industrial organisations and alcoholism. My advanced text (Book No. 5) treats econometric techniques of estimation but also such pre-estimation issues as the uses of estimated econometric models for structural analysis, forecasting and policy evaluation.

(3)*Health Economics*: Early contributions were as a member of a team involved in estimating a microsimulation model of the health care system in the US. Later contributions involved an analysis of the major policy issues in the economics of health care in the US.

(4)*Strategy Arms and Control*: Early contributions involved the development of models of arms races and strategy in a missile war, while later work involved analysis of the strategy of an arms race, arms control, nuclear proliferation, strategic arms limitation treaties, and the outbreak of war.

ISARD, Walter

Born 1919, Philadelphia, PA, USA.
Current Post Prof. Econ., Regional Science and Peace Science, Cornell Univ., Ithaca, NY, USA, 1979–.
Past Posts Assoc. Prof. Econ., Assoc. Dir. Teaching Instr. Econ., Amer.

Univ., 1948–9; Res. Fellow, Lect., Harvard Univ., 1949–53; Assoc. Prof. Regional Econ., Dir. Urban Regional Stud., MIT, 1953–6; Vis. Prof., Regional Science, Yale Univ., 1960–1; Prof. Econ. Regional Science and Peace Science, Univ. Philadelphia, 1956–79; Vis. Prof., Landscape Architecture and Regional Science, Harvard Univ., 1966–71; Sr. Res. Assoc., Vis. Prof. Econ., Cornell Univ., 1971–9; Disting. Vis. Prof. Inst. für Regionalwissenschaft, Univ. Karlsruhe, 1972; Hon. Res. Assoc., Center Internat. Affairs, Harvard Univ., 1974; Faculty Assoc. Center Transp., Northwestern Univ., 1975–7.
Degrees BA Temple Univ., 1939; MA, PhD Harvard Univ., 1941, 1943; Hon. MA Univ. PA, 1970; Doctoris Honoris Causa Poznan Academy Econ., 1976, Erasmus Univ., Rotterdam, 1978; Univ. Karlsruhe, 1979, Umea Univ., IL, 1980, Univ. Illinois, 1982.
Offices and Honours Edward Hillman Fellow, Univ. Chicago, 1941–2; US SSRC Pre-doctoral Fellow, 1942–3; USSR Post-doctoral Fellow, 1946–8; Ford Foundation Fellow Econ. and Bus. Admin., 1959–60; Founder's Medal, Regional Science Assoc., 1978; Fellow, Southern Regional Science Assoc., 1979; Founder, Regional Science Assoc., 1954, Peace Science Soc. (Internat.), 1968.
Editorial Duties Ed., Co-ed., *Papers, Regional Science Assoc.*, 1954–68, *Papers, Peace Science Soc. (Internat.)*, 1963; Assoc. Ed., *QJE*, 1968–71; Ed. Boards, *J. Conflict Resolution*, 1972–84; Co-ed., *J. Peace Sciences*, 1973–, *Regional Science & Urban Econ.*, 1974–; Ed., *Regional Science Stud. Series* (MIT Press, 1958–73).
Principal Fields of Interest 941 Regional Economics.
Publications Books: 1. *Location and Space Economy* (Wiley, 1962); 2. *Regional Econ. Planning*, co-ed. (with J. Cumberland), (OECC, 1961; transl., French, 1961); 3. *General Theory: Social, Political, Economic and Regional* (with T. E. Smith, *et al.*), (MIT Press, 1969); 4. *Regional Input Output Study* (with T. Langford), (MIT Press, 1971); 5. *Ecologic Economic Analysis for Regional Planning* (with Choguill, Kissin, *et al.*), (Free Press, 1971); 6.

The Middle East: Some Issues and Alternatives, co-ed. (Schenkman, 1972); 7. *Introduction to Regional Science* (Prentice-Hall, 1975); 8. *Spatial Dynamics and Optimal Space-Time Development* (with P. Liossatos, *et al.*), (N-H, 1978); 9. *Conflict Management Analysis and Practical Procedures* (with C. Smith), (N-H, 1982); 10. *International and Intranational Conflict: Some Analytic Approaches* (with Y. Nagao), (Ballinger, 1983).

Principal Contributions Pioneered and developed fields of urban and regional economics, regional science and peace science.

ISNARD, Achylle-Nicolas*

Dates and Birthplace 1749–1803, Paris, France.

Posts Held Civil engineer, Arbois, Evreux, Le Havre, Carcassonne, Lyons.

Degrees Grad. L'Ecole des Ponts et Chauseés, Paris.

Offices and Honours Member of the Tribunate, 1800.

Publications *Books:* 1. *Traité des richesses*, 2 vols (1781); 2. *Catéchisme sociale ou instructions élémentaires sur la morale sociale et l'usage de la jeunesse* (1784); 3. *Observations sur le principe qui a produit les révolutions* (1789); 4. *Les devoirs de la deuxième legislature*, 4 vols (1791); 5. *Considerations théoriques sur les caisses d'amortissement de la dette publique* (1801).

Career Engineer-economist whose chief work is his *Traité*.... Whilst having some affinity to the physiocratic philosophy, this work rejected the doctrine that the soil alone produces a 'produit net'. His book is remarkable for its mathematical treatment of production, capital, money and the theory of exchange. The latter is sufficiently similar to that of Walras to suggest that Walras was influenced by Isnard.

Secondary Literature W. Jaffé, 'A. N. Isnard, progenitor of the Walrasian general equilibrium model', *HOPE*, 1(1), Spring 1969; repr. in *William Jaffé's Essays on Walras*, ed. D. A. Walker (CUP, 1983).

IWAI, Katsuhito

Born 1947, Tokyo, Japan.

Current Post Assoc. Prof. Econ., Univ. Tokyo, Tokyo, Japan, 1981–.

Past Posts Ass. Prof. Econ., Sr. Res. Assoc., Cowles Foundation Res. Econ., Yale Univ., 1973–9, 1979–81.

Degrees BE Univ. Tokyo, 1969; PhD MIT, 1972.

Offices and Honours Grand Prix Nikkei Econ. Books Award, 1982.

Principal Fields of Interest 020 General Economic Theory; 023 Macroeconomic Theory; 620 Economics of Technological Change.

Publications *Books:* 1. *Disequilibrium Dynamics — A Theoretical Analysis of Inflation and Unemployment* (Yale Univ. Press, 1981); 2. *Venice no Shoninno Shihonron* (Japanese), (Chikuma Shobo, 1985).

Articles: 1. 'Optimal economic growth and stationary ordinal utility — a Fisherian approach', *JET*, 5(1), Aug. 1972; 2. 'The firm in uncertain markets and its price, wage and employment adjustments', *REStud*, 41(2), April 1974; 3. 'Schumpeterian dynamics: an evolutionary model of innovation and imitation', *J Ec Behav*, 5(2), June 1984; 4. 'Schumpeterian dynamics, Part II: technological progress, firm growth and "economic selection"', *J Ec Behav*, 5(3), Aug.–Dec. 1984.

Principal Contributions Developed a theory of disequilibrium dynamics which integrates a Wicksellian model of the cumulative process and the Keynesian principle of effective demand. Its major theses are that (1) decentralised price-formation process in the monetary economy has an intrinsically unstable character; (2) inflexibility rather than flexibility of money wages is what stabilises the monetary economy; and (3) Keynesian features will never disappear from the economy even in the long run. Also developed a Schumpeterian theory which analyses the evolution of industry structure as a dynamic outcome of interactions among innovation, imitation and capacity growth of individual firms.

J

JACQUEMIN, Alexis Pierre

Born 1938, Liège, Belgium.
Current Post Prof. Écon., Univ.
Louvain, Louvain-La-Neuve, Belgium,
1971–.
Past Posts Res. Ass., Univ. Liège,
1962–4; Assoc. Prof., Univ. Louvain,
1967–71; Dir. Cabinet, Belgian Ministry
of Science Pol., 1974–5; Vis. Prof.,
Univs., Laval, Canada, 1970, Paris IX,
1972, Michigan, 1974, Paris-Sorbonne,
1979, Montreal, 1980, Ecole Polytech-
nique, Paris, 1981, European Univ.
Inst. Florence, 1984.
Degrees Doctorat en Droit Univ.
Liège, 1961; Licencie, Doctorat Univ.
Louvain, 1964, 1967; MA Univ. Cal.
Berkeley, 1966.
Offices and Honours Bernheim
Europ. Award, 1965; Award Belgian
Univ., Foundation for Social Science,
1974; P. H. Spaak Award, 1976; Prix
Francqui, 1983; Pres., Europ. Assoc.
Res. Industrial Organisation, 1981–3;
Vice-Pres., Assoc. Internat. Droit
Econ., 1982–.
Editorial Duties Assoc. Ed., *J Ind E,
Europ ER*, 1975–6; Ed., *Internat. J.
Industrial Organization*, 1982–.
Principal Fields of Interest 600 Indus-
trial Organisation; 022 Microeconomic
Theory.
Publications *Books:* 1. *L'entreprise et
son pouvoir de marché* (Presses Univ.
de France, 1967; transl., Spanish,
Hispano European, 1969); 2. *Le droit
économique* (with G. Schrans), (Presses
Univ. de France, 1970; transl., Portuguese, Varga, 1974); 3. *Fondements
d'économie politique* (with H. Tulkens),
(Renaissance du Livre, 1970); 4. *Economie industrielle Européen* (Dunod,
1975; transls., Spanish, Hispano
Europea, 1982, Portuguese, Edicoes
70, 1984); 5. *Market Structure, Corporate Behavior and the State*, co-ed. (with
H. de Jong), (Nijhoff, 1976); 6. *European Industrial Organization* (with H.
de Jong), (Macmillan, Wiley, 1977;
transls., Italian, Il Mulino, 1979,
Hungarian, 1981); 7. *Welfare Aspects
of Industrial Markets*, co-ed. (with H.
de Jong), (Nijhoff, 1976); 8. *Selection*

*et pouvoir dans la nouvelle économie
industrielle* (Economica, 1984).
Articles: 1. 'Strategy of the firm and
market structure: an application of
optimal control theory' (with J. Thisse),
in *Market Structure and Corporate Behaviour*, ed. K. Cowling (Gray-Mills,
1972); 2. 'Optimal control and advertising policy', *Metroec.*, 25, May 1973; 3.
'A comparison of the performance
of the largest European and Japanese
firms' (with W. Säez), *OEP*, 28, July
1976; 4. 'Degree of concentration,
monopoly power and threat of entry'
(with D. Encaova), *Int ER*, 21, Feb.
1980; 5. 'Exports in an imperfect competition framework' (with H. Glesjer),
QJE, 94, May 1980; 6. 'Export-cartels
and stability: the Japanese case' (with
T. Nambu), *EJ*, 91, Sept. 1981; 7.
'Organizational efficiency and monopoly power: the case of French industrial groups' (with D. Encaova), *Europ
ER*, 19(1), Sept. 1982; 8. 'Imperfect
market structure and international
trade', *Kyk*, 35, Jan. 1982; 9. 'On the
stability of collusive price leadership'
(with C. d'Aspremont, R. Galisewiez
and J. Weymark), *CJE*, 16, Feb. 1983;
10. 'Dominant firms and their alleged
decline' (with P. Geroski), *Internat. J.
Industrial Organization*, 2, March 1984.
Principal Contributions My works
have concentrated on two main subjects.
The first one is the analysis of market
power in decentralised economies. A
main aspect has concerned the dynamic
process through which market performance interacts with market structure,
so that current performances can become embedded in future market structure through strategic investments
made by firms. This has been an occasion for one of the first applications of
optimal control theory to industrial
organisation. The second subject is the
interaction between law, institutions
and economics in the functioning of our
mixed economies. This is not limited
to an economic analysis of law but includes broader research on the changing
roles of the legislature and the judiciary
in modern 'welfare' societies.

JAFFÉ, William*

Dates and Birthplace 1898–1980, New York City, NY, USA.

Posts Held Ass. Prof., Assoc. Prof., Prof. Econ., Prof. Emeritus, North-western Univ., 1928–36, 1936–56, 1956–66, 1966–80; Prof. Econ., York Univ., Ont., 1970–80.

Degrees BA City Coll., New York, 1918; MA Columbia Univ., 1919; Dr Droit et Sciences Econ. et Polit. Univ. Paris, 1924; Hon. LLD York Univ., 1974.

Offices and Honours Fellow, Em Soc, Res. Fellowships, Guggenheim Foundation, 1958–9, Ford Foundation, 1963–4, NSF, 1965–9, Canada Council, 1972–80, Killam Foundation 1975–7; Foreign Member, Royal Netherlands Academy Sciences Letters, 1968; Corresp. Fellow, BA, 1977; Chevalier, Legion d'Honneur, 1978; Fellow, Royal Soc. Canada, 1979, Hist. Econ. Soc. Disting. Fellow, 1980.

Publications *Books:* 1. *Les théories économiques et sociales de Thorstein Veblen* (1924); 2. *The Economic Development of Post-War France* (with W. F. Ogburn), (1929); 3. *L. Walras, Elements of Pure Economics*, transl. and annotated (1954); 4. *Correspondence of Leon Walras and Related Papers*, 3 vols, ed. and annotated (N-H, 1965); 5. *William Jaffé's Essays on Walras*, ed. D. A. Walker (1983).

Career First, in his translation of Walras' *Elements d'économie politique pure*, Jaffé furnished English-speaking economists with access to Walras' major theoretical work. Second, in his edition of Walras' *Correspondence*, he provided a sourcebook of bibliographical, biographical, scientific, social and economic information about Walras and his century that is relevant for understanding the genesis of Walras' work and the development of neoclassical economics. Third, in his many essays on Walras, he treated most of the themes that are important in Walras' work, and many of the questions that can be asked about his life and impact on economic thought. Thus, he provided an exposition and evaluation of Walras' theories, as well as a history of the circumstances and sources that were important in their development.

Secondary Literature D. A. Walker, 'William Jaffé, historian of economic thought, 1898–1980', *AER*, 71(5), Dec. 1981; V. J. Tarascio, 'William Jaffé, 1898–1980', *HOPE*, 13(2), Summer 1981; D. A. Walker, 'William Jaffé, officier de liaison intellectual', *Research in the History of Economic Thought and Methodology*, 1, ed. W. J. Samuels (JAI Press, 1983).

JAFFEE, Dwight M.

Born 1943, Chicago, IL, USA.

Current Post Prof. Econ., Princeton Univ., Princeton, NJ, USA, 1968–.

Past Posts Lect. Econ., MIT, 1968.

Degrees BA Northwestern Univ., 1964; PhD MIT, 1968.

Offices and Honours Phi Beta Kappa, 1968; Public Interest Dir., Fed. Home Loan Bank, NY, 1983–; Member, NJ Econ. Pol. Council, 1976–83; Member, Academic Advisory Board, Nat. Assoc. Savings Inst., 1981–.

Editorial Duties Assoc. Ed. *JMCB*, 1973–5, *J Mon E*, 1975–8, *J Fin*, 1974–8, *Housing Fin. Rev.*, 1980–, *J Bank Fin*, 1981–.

Principal Fields of Interest 200 Quantitative Economic Methods and Data; 310 Domestic Monetary and Financial Theory and Institutions; 932 Housing Economics.

Publications *Books:* 1. *Credit Rationing and the Commercial Loan Market* (Wiley, 1971); 2. *Savings Deposits, Mortgages and Residential Construction*, ed. (with E. Gramlich), (D. C. Heath, 1972); 3. *Economic Implications of an Electronic Monetary Transfer System* (with M. Flannery), (D. C. Heath, 1973).

Articles: 1. 'A theory and test of credit rationing' (with F. Modigliani), *AER*, 59(5), Dec. 1969; 2. 'The determinants of deposit-rate setting by savings and loan associations' (with S. Goldfeld), *J Fin*, 25, June 1970; 3. 'Methods of estimation for markets in disequilibrium' (with R. C. Fair), *Em*, 40(3), May 1972; 4. 'On the application of portfolio theory to depository financial intermediaries' (with O. D. Hart), *REStud*, 41(1), Jan. 1974; 5. 'Cyclical variations in the risk structure of interest rates', *J Mon E*, 1,

July 1975; 6. 'Imperfect information, uncertainty, and credit rationing' (with T. Russell), *QJE*, 40(4), Nov. 1976; 7. 'Mortgage credit availability and residential construction activity' (with K. Rosen), *Brookings Papers Econ. Activity*, 2, 1979; 8. 'The extension of futures trading to the financial sector', *J Bank Fin*, 6, 1982; 9. 'New residential constructions and energy costs', in *Energy Costs, Urban Development and Housing*, eds. A. Downs and K. L. Bradbury (Brookings Inst., 1984); 10. 'Interest rate hedging strategies for savings and loan associations', in *Managing Interest Rate Risk in the Thrift Industry* (Fed. Home Loan Bank San Francisco, 1982).

Principal Contributions Most of the research effort has focussed on the behaviour of financial intermediaries, including both theoretical models and empirical testing. Specific studies have been divided about equally among topics relating to lending behaviour, liability and deposit issues, and integrated models of intermediary behaviour. Research on loan markets has covered business, mortgage, and consumer loan markets. A critical and continuing theme of loan market research concerns models and tests of nonprice credit rationing. Current research projects in this area study the role of moral hazard and adverse selection as they impact lender and credit rationing behaviour. Research on deposit markets has considered the rate-setting behaviour of depository institutions, the impacts of Regulation Q ceilings on their behaviour and its macroeconomic consequence, and alternative sources of funds. Research on integrated models of intermediary behaviour have included the application of portfolio theory to intermediary behaviour, and more recently has focussed specifically on the risk associated with balance sheets of unmatched asset and liability maturities. Current research projects centre on the alternative strategies available to the institutions for hedging their interest-rate exposure, including variable rate loans and futures market hedging. This in turn has led to a series of research projects concerned directly with the newly developed futures markets for financial instruments. Other areas of more than passing research interest have included models of disequilibrium markets and econometric estimation methods for them, the market for residential construction including the demographic component of housing demand, and electronic funds monetary systems.

JASKOLD-GABSZEWICZ, Jean

Born 1936, Buta, Zaire.
Current Post Prof. Econ., Univ. Catholique de Louvain, Louvain-la-Neuve, Belgium, 1978–.
Degrees Dr en Droit, Dr en Sciences Econ. Univ. Catholique de Louvain, 1963.
Offices and Honours Fellow, Em Soc.
Editorial Duties Assoc. Ed., *JET*, 1977–80.
Principal Fields of Interest 022 Microeconomics; 213 Mathematical Methods.
Publications *Articles:* 1. 'Syndicates of traders in an exchange economy' (with J. Drèze), in *Differential Games and Related Topics* (N-H, 1971); 2. 'An equivalence theorem for the core of an economy whose atoms are not "too" big' (with J. F. Mertens), *Em*, 39(5), Sept. 1971; 3. 'Collusion of factor owners and distribution of social output' (with T. Hansen), *JET*, 4(1), Feb. 1972; 4. 'Oligolopy "à la Cournot" in a general equilibrium analysis' (with J-P. Vial), *JET*, 4(3), June 1972; 5. 'On disequilibrium savings and public consumption' (with P. Dehez), *ZN*, 39(1,2), Jan.–Feb. 1979; 6. 'Price competition, quality and income disparities' (with J-F. Thisse), *JET*, 20(3), June 1979; 7. 'On Hotelling's "Stability in competition"' (with C. d'Aspremont and J-F. Thisse), *Em*, 47(5), Sept. 1979; 8. 'Entry (and exit) in a differentiated industry' (with J-F. Thisse), *JET*, 22(2), April 1980; 9. 'International trade with differentiated products' (with A. Shaked, J. Sutton and J-F. Thisse), *Int ER*, 22(3), Oct. 1981.

Principal Contributions My research interests are mainly centred around the theme of imperfect competition. I was attracted by this topic when writing my doctoral dissertation which dealt with the relationship between the concepts of core and competitive equilibrium. It was proved by R. V. Aumann (*Em*, Jan. 1964) that, in atomless exchange economies, the core coincides with the set of competitive allocations. For years I have studied the nature of the relationship between these two concepts when the exchange economy embodies 'atoms' (an atom in a measure space is any subset of positive measure which does not include another subset of positive measure; if this subset is interpreted as coalition of economic agents, it means that this coalition cannot 'split'; the participants have to act in unison). Among other results (see Nos. 1 and 3 above), sufficient conditions on the size of cartels have been derived under which Aumann's result is preserved in spite of the existence of atoms.

Another research area in which I have been involved is the extension of the nonco-operative Cournot model to general equilibrium analysis. In my work with J. P. Vial (see No. 4), a general equilibrium model embodying a consumption and a production sector is considered, and a concept of Cournot-Nash equilibrium is derived. More recently, I have been much interested in analysing models with product differentiation 'à la Hotelling'. Starting from my paper with d'Aspremont and Thisse (No. 7), where it was noticed that the 'Principle of Minimum Differentiation' does not hold, I have pursued my work in this area with my colleague, J-F. Thisse. An interesting output of this analysis is the result according to which entry of new firms via differentiated products does not necessarily lead to the competitive outcome: low-quality products are driven out of the market by the entry of higher-quality products, so that only few firms can remain simultaneously in the market (No. 8).

JASZI, George

Born 1915, Budapest, Hungary.

Current Post Dir., Bureau Econ. Analysis, US Dept. Commerce, Washington, DC, 1963–.

Degrees BSc LSE, 1936; PhD Harvard Univ., 1946.

Offices and Honours Chairman, Conf. Res. Income and Wealth, 1955–6; Chairman, Internat. Assoc. Res. Income and Wealth, 1973; Fellow, ASA, 1965; Fellow, Nat. Assoc. Bus. Econs. 1972; Rockefeller Public Service Award, 1974; Disting. Exec., Sr. Exec. Service, 1980; Hon. Fellow, LSE, 1980.

Principal Fields of Interest 221 National Income Accounting.

Publications *Articles:* 1. 'The conceptual basis of the accounts', *Income and Wealth*, 22, 1958; 2. 'The measurement of aggregate economic growth: a review of key conceptual and statistical issues as suggested by the United States experience', *REStat*, 63(4), Nov. 1961; 3. 'An improved way of measuring quality change', *REStat*, 64(3), Aug. 1962; 4. 'Taking care of soft figures: reflections on improving the accuracy of the GNP', *Stat. News*, 18, Aug. 1972; 5. 'A framework for the measurement of economic and social performance', in *The Measurement of Economic and Social Performance*, ed. M. Moss (Columbia Univ. Press, 1973).

Principal Contributions Contributed to the development of macroeconomic accounts: national income and products, input-output, saving and investment, etc., and their use in economic analysis.

JENKIN, Henry Charles Fleeming*

Dates and Birthplace 1833–85, Kent, England.

Posts Held Engineer; Prof. Eng., Univ. Coll., London, 1866–8, Univ. Edinburgh, 1868–85.

Degrees MA Univ. Genoa, 1850.

Offices and Honours Fellow, Royal Soc., 1865.

Publications *Books:* 1. *Graphic Representation and other Essays on Political Economy* (1887, 1931).

Career A successful engineer, inventor, and scientific journalist, he turned to economics in 1868 with an article on trade unions. Two subsequent published papers on 'The graphic representation of the laws of supply and demand' (1870) and 'Principles which regulate the incidence of taxes' (1871) constitute the sum of his economic publications. His application of mathematics was related to the partial equilibrium analysis of individual markets which Marshall later developed. His work was little noticed, even by Jevons and Marshall, and had little effect on the subsequent course of economic thought despite its striking quality and originality.

Secondary Literature A. D. Brownlie and M. F. Lloyd Prichard, 'Professor Fleeming Jenkin, 1833–1885; pioneer in engineering and political economy', *OEP*, 15, Nov. 1963.

JENKS, Jeremiah Whipple*

Dates and Birthplace 1856–1929.

Posts Held Teacher Classics, Mt. Movis College, 1879–80, 1881–3; Prof. Polit. Science, Knox Coll., 1886–9; Prof. Polit. Econ., Indiana Univ., 1889–91; Prof. Polit. Econ., Cornell Univ., 1891–1912; Prof. Govt. and Public Admin., NYU, 1917–29.

Degrees BA, MA, LLD Michigan, 1878, 1879, 1903; PhD Univ. Halle, Germany, 1885.

Offices and Honours Expert Agent, US Industrial Comm. Investigation of Trusts in US and Europe, 1899–1901; Special Expert, Questions of Currency, Labor, Internal Taxation and Pol. in the Orient, 1901–2, Currency Reform, Govt. Mexico, 1903; Member, US Commission Reform of Currency in China, 1903–4; Member, US Inauguration Commission, 1907–10; Dir., Pacific Railways of Nicaragua, 1918–29; Pres., Alexander Hamilton Inst., 1913–21; Pres., AEA, 1906–7; Pres., Nat. Council Religion in Higher Educ., 1917–18; Member, Exec. Board, Boy Scouts of Amer.

Publications *Books:* 1. *Henry C. Carey als Nationalökonom* (1885); 2. *The Trust Problem* (1900, with W. E. Clark, 1917); 3. *Certain Economic Questions in the English and Dutch Colonies in the Orient* (1902); 4. *Principles of Politics* (1909); 5. *The Inauguration Problem* (with W. J. Lauck), (1913).

Career Jenks was perhaps the first American academic economist to devote a large part of his career to service on central government boards and commissions, chiefly on questions of trusts and immigration but also on currency and taxation problems in China, Mexico and the Philippines. At the age of 56, he switched fields from economics to politics and began a second career as academic and government consultant. He was a voluminous writer who published almost as many books on the readings of Vesus as on economic and political subjects.

JENSEN, Michael C.

Born 1939, Rochester, MN, USA.

Current Post LaClare Prof. Fin. and Bus. Admin., Dir., Managerial Econ. Res. Center, Grad. School Management, Univ. Rochester, 1983–.

Past Posts Instr., Northwestern Univ., 1967; Ass. Prof., Assoc. Prof., Univ. Rochester, 1967–71, 1972–9; Vis. Prof., Grad. School Bus. Admin., Univ. Harvard, 1984–5.

Degrees BA Macalester Coll., 1962; MA, PhD Univ. Chicago, 1964, 1968.

Offices and Honours Recipient Leo Melamed Prize (with W. H. Meckling), 1978; Recipient Graham and Dodd Plaque (with W. H. Meckling), 1978; Member, Exec. Comm., WEA, 1981–4; Board Dirs., AFA, 1983–6; Board Advisers, Pacific Inst., 1983–; Board Advisers, Eller Center, 1984–.

Editorial Duties Founding Ed., *J Fin Econ.*, 1978–; Advisory Ed., *Econ. Letters*, 1978–.

Principal Fields of Interest 512 Managerial Economics; 521 Business Finance.

Publications *Books:* 1. *The Modern Theory of Corporate Finance*, co-ed. (with C. Smith, Jr.), (McGraw-Hill, 1984); 2. *Studies in the Theory of Capital Markets*, ed. (Praeger, 1972).

Articles: 1. 'The adjustment of stock prices to new information' (with E. Fama, *et al.*), *Int ER*, 10, Feb. 1969; 2. 'Risk, the pricing of capital assets, and the evaluation of investment portfolios', *J Bus*, 42(2), April 1969; 3. 'The capital asset pricing model: some empirical tests' (with F. Black and M. Scholes), in *Studies in the Theory of Capital Markets*, ed. M. C. Jensen (Praeger, 1972); 4. 'Capital markets: theory and evidence', *Bell JE*, 3(2), Autumn 1972; 5. 'Theory of the firm: managerial behavior, agency costs and ownership structure' (with W. H. Meckling), *J Fin Econ*, 3(4), Oct. 1976; 6. 'Rights and production functions: an application to labor-managed firms and codetermination' (with W. H. Meckling), *J Bus*, 52(4), Oct. 1979; 7. 'The market for corporate control: the scientific evidence' (with R. Rubock), *J Fin Econ*, 11(2), April 1983; 8. 'Separation of ownership and control' (with E. Fama), *J Law E*, 26(2), June 1983; 9. 'Agency problems and residual claims', *J Law E*, 26(2), June 1983; 10. 'Takeovers: folklore and science', *Harvard Bus. Rev.*, Nov.–Dec. 1984.

Principal Contributions In finance, primarily to asset pricing theory, portfolio theory, efficient market theory and the measurement of portfolio performance. In economics, primarily to the theory of property rights, agency theory, corporate control and organisation theory, and law and economics.

JEVONS, Herbert Stanley*

Dates and Birthplace 1875–1955.
Posts Held Lect., Prof. Econ., Univ. Wales, Cardiff, 1905–11; Prof. Econ., Univ. Allahabad, India, 1914–23, Univ. Rangoon, Burma, 1923–30.
Degrees BSc, MA Univ. London.
Offices and Honours Ed., *Indian J. Econ.*, 1916–22; Council Member, RSS, 1932–7.
Publications *Books:* 1. *Essays on Economics* (1905); 2. *The British Coal Trade* (1915); 3. *Economics of Tenancy Law and Estate Management* (1921); 4. *Money, Banking and Exchange in India* (1922); 5. *The Future of Exchange and the Indian Currency* (1922); 6. *Economic Equality in the Co-operative Commonwealth* (1933).
Career Originally a geologist (like his father), his switch to economics at Cardiff also brought him involvement in housing reform. Temporarily abandoning his academic career, he spent the years 1911–14 directing various housing schemes. In India, too, he was involved in practical matters, particularly on behalf of the cotton industry. His work on the coal trade and economics of tenancy law was well received and influential. In his later years, he was

an adviser to the Emperor of Ethiopia and organised the Abyssinian Association and the Anglo-Ethiopian Society.
Secondary Literature (Obit.) 'Prof. Stanley Jevons: friend of Ethiopia', *The Times*, 29 June 1955.

JEVONS, William Stanley*

Dates and Birthplace 1835–82, Liverpool, England.
Posts Held Assayer Australian Mint, 1854–8; Tutor, Lect., Prof. Logic and Moral Philo., Owens Coll., Manchester, 1863–76; Prof. Polit. Econ., Univ. Coll. London, 1876–81.
Degrees BA, MA Univ. London, 1860, 1862.
Offices and Honours Pres., BAAS, 1870.
Publications *Books:* 1. *Investigations in Currency and Finance* (1863–84); 2. *The Coal Question* (1865, 1906); 3. *The Theory of Political Economy* (1871, 1957, 1970); 4. *The State in Relation to Labour* (1888, 1972); 5. *Principles of Economics* (1905); 6. R. D. Collison Black, ed. *Papers and Correspondence of William Stanley Jevons*, 7 vols (1972–81).
Career With Menger and Walras he was one of the three co-discoverers of marginal utility theory, but was also widely known for his textbooks on logic and his applied economic studies. In *The Coal Question*, he treated coal as the essential resource for the British industrial economy and argued that it was an exhaustible resource. His other quantitative studies, collected posthumously in *Investigations*, were largely concerned with economic fluctuations, which he examined through statistics on seasonal movements, business cycles and secular trends. His later work included the heroic but doomed attempts to trace business cycles to sunspot activity. His discovery of the marginal utility concept in 1862 aroused no interest, and not until *Theory of Political Economy* was published in 1871 was it properly made public. The root of his inspiration was Bentham's 'felicific calculus' of pleasure and pain. Although *Theory of Political Economy* provides only half the entire field of microecon-

omics — the theory of consumer behaviour — the book, along with the treatises of Menger and Walras, must be considered as opening up a new period in economic theorising. The preface to the second edition, together with a bibliography of works on mathematical economics dating back to 1711, did much to teach the generation that came after him about the long history of marginal analysis and utility theory in the century before 1871.

Secondary Literature J. M. Keynes, *Essays in Biography* (Macmillan, 1933, 1972); T. W. Hutchison, 'Jevons, William Stanley', *IESS*, 8; R. D. Collison Black, 'W. S. Jevons', in *Pioneers of Modern Economics in Britain*, eds. D. P. O'Brien and J. R. Presley (Macmillan, 1981).

JOHANNSEN, Nicolaus August Ludwig Jacob*

Dates and Birthplace 1844–1928, Germany.

Posts Held Businessman.

Publications *Books:* 1. *Cheap Capital* (pseud. A. Merwin), (1878); 2. *Depressions-Perioden* (pseud. J. J. O. Lahne), (1903); 3. *A Neglected Point in Connection with Crises* (1908); 4. *Die Steuer der Zukunft* (1913); 5. *The True Way for Deflation* (1920) 6. *Business Depressions* (1925).

Career German-American economic 'crank' whose theories were taken seriously by Hobson, Mitchell and other unorthodox economists. His earlier works were pseudonymous but the *Neglected Point . . .* appeared under his own name, and argued that depressions were caused by an 'impaired' form of savings. His subsequent works put forward various methods by which depressions might be avoided, including a form of taxed currency similar to Gesell's stamped money.

Secondary Literature J. Dorfman 'N. A. L. J. Johannsen: the "amateur economist"', in *The Economic Mind in American Civilisation*, 3 (Viking, 1949).

JOHANSEN, Leif*

Dates and Birthplace 1930–82, Eidsvoll, Norway.

Posts Held Assoc. Prof. Public Fin., Univ. Oslo, 1959–65; Prof. Econ., Inst. Econ., Univ. Oslo, 1965–82.

Degrees Candidate Econ., PhD Univ. Oslo, 1954, 1962.

Offices and Honours Member, Norwegian Academy Sciences, Royal Swedish Academy Sciences; Foreign Hon. Member, AEA; Fellow, Council, Em Soc, 1966–82; Co-ed Assoc. Ed., *J Pub E*; Member Ed. Boards of various scientific journals; Fridtjof Nansen Award Sciences, Norwegian Academy Sciences, 1979.

Publications *Books:* 1. *A Multisectoral Study of Economic Growth* (1960, 1974); 2. *Public Economics* (1965); 3. *Production Functions. An Integration of Micro- and Macro-, Short-run and Long-run Aspects* (1972); 4. *Lectures on Macro-economic Planning*, 2 vols (1977–8).

Articles: 1. 'Substitution versus fixed production coefficients in the theory of economic growth: a synthesis', *Em*, 27, April 1959; 2. 'Rules of thumb for the expansion of industries in a process of economic growth', *Em*, 28, April 1960; 3. 'Some notes on the Lindahl theory of determination of public expenditures', *Int ER*, 4, Sept. 1963; 4. 'On the theory of dynamic input-output models with different time profiles of capital construction and finite life-time of capital equipment', *JET*, 19(2), Dec. 1978; 5. 'The bargaining society and the inefficiency of bargaining', *Kyk*, 32(3), 1979; 6. 'Cores, aggressiveness and the breakdown of co-operation in economic games', *J Ec Behav*, 3(1), March 1982; 7. 'Some notes on employment and unemployment with heterogeneous labour', *Nationaløkonomisk Tiddsskrift*, Suppl., 1982; 8. 'On the status of the Nash types of noncooperative equilibrium in economic theory', *Scand JE*, 84(3), 1982.

Career Development of a fairly large multi-sectoral growth model (the MSG-model), which includes input-output relationships, factor substitution in production, income generation, price-dependent consumer-demand relations, and other relations for the Norwegian economy. The model was extensively used in Norwegian long-term planning and projections, and was probably the first empirical elaboration and application of a general equilibrium model (for a moving equilibrium) with endogenous prices and substitution effects. Various contributions to public economics, especially the formal elaboration of the Lindahl theory of public expenditure and the interpretation of this theory on the basis of modern welfare theory. The synthesising of various approaches to the theory and methodology of economic policy and planning; more special contributions in such fields as complete systems of demand functions, dynamic input-output analysis, etc.

Secondary Literature R. M. Solow, 'Leif Johansen (1930–82): a memorial', *Scand JE*, 85(4), 1983.

JOHNSON, David Gale

Born 1916, Vinton, IA, USA.
Current Post Prof. Econ., Univ. Chicago, Chicago, IL, USA, 1980–.
Past Posts Ass. Prof., Iowa State Coll., Ames, 1941–4; Res. Assoc., Ass. Prof., Assoc. Prof., Prof., Eliakim Hastings Moore Disting. Service Prof. Econ., Univ. Chicago, 1944–80.
Degrees BS, PhD Iowa State Coll., 1938, 1945; MS Univ. Wisconsin, 1939.
Offices and Honours Dir., US SSRC, 1953–6; Vice-Pres., Pres., Fellow, Amer. Farm Econ. Assoc., 1953–4, 1964–5, 1968–; Assoc. Dean, Dean, Division Social Sciences, Provost, Univ. Chicago, 1957–60, 1960–70, 1975–80; Pres., Nat. Opinion Res. Center, 1962–75, 1979–; Member, Exec. Comm., Div. Behavioral Sciences, Nat. Res. Council, 1969–73; Pres., S. E. Chicago Commission, 1980–; Council Academic Advisers, AEI, 1974–.
Principal Fields of Interest 420 Trade Relations, Commerical Policy, International Economic Integration; 710 Agriculture.
Publications *Books:* 1. *Agriculture and Trade* (Wiley, 1950); 2. *Grain Yields and the American Food Supply: An An-*alysis of Yield Changes and Possibilities (with R. Gustafson), (Univ. Chicago Press, 1962); 3. *Forward Prices for Agriculture* (Univ. Chicago Press, 1976); 4. *The Struggle Against World Hunger* (Foreign Pol. Assoc., 1967); 5. *World Agriculture in Disarray* (Macmillan, St Martin's Press, 1973); 6. *Farm Commodity Programs: An Opportunity for Change* (AEI, 1973); 7. *The Sugar Program: Large Costs and Small Benefits* (AEI, 1974); 8. *World Food Problems and Prospects* (AEI, 1975); 9. *Progress of Economic Reform in the People's Republic of China* (AEI, 1982); 10. *Prospects for Soviet Agriculture in the 1980s* (with K. Brooks), (Indiana Univ. Press, 1983).

Articles: 1. 'Contribution of price policy to income and resource problems in agriculture', *JFE*, 26, Nov. 1944; 2. 'Resource allocation under share contracts', *JPE*, 58, April 1950; 3. 'The nature of the supply function for agricultural products', *AER*, 40(4), Sept. 1950; 4. 'Some effects of region, community size, color, and occupation on family and individual income', *Stud. in Income and Wealth*, 15 (NBER, 1952); 5. 'Comparability of labor capacities of farm and nonfarm labor', *AER*, 43(3), June 1953; 6. 'Competition in agriculture: fact or fiction?', *AER*, 44(2), May 1954; 7. 'World agriculture, commodity policy, and price variability', *AJAE*, 57(5), Dec. 1975; 8. 'Resource adjustment in American agriculture and agricultural policy', in *Contemporary Economic Problems, 1977*, ed. W. Fellner (AEI, 1977); 9. 'International trade and agricultural labor markets: farm policy as quasi-adjustment policy', *AJAE*, 64(2), May 1982.

Principal Contributions My first work was an analysis of the effects of agricultural price policies upon resource use and income distribution. I showed that price policies that reduced risk and uncertainty could increase productivity in agriculture. If prices were set above equilibrium levels, the distribution of income became more unequal within agriculture. Subsequent work showed that high farm prices transferred income from low-income urban consumers to high-income rural families. Related work was my analysis of the inconsistencies between the domestic farm policies of the industrial countries and liberal trade policies that most espoused. My work on share cropping showed that resource efficiency could be and probably was achieved under this form of tenure, contrary to widely held views.

I analysed the long-term trends in world supply and demand for food and showed that the trend was for lower real prices of the cereals, the major source of calories for low-income people. In that work I found that much of the price variability in international markets for farm products resulted from numerous governments stabilising their domestic farm and consumer prices by varying net trade and forcing others to bear the costs of their variability. My students and I undertook research on optimal grain reserves and showed that if there were free trade in the world, there would be little need for reserve stocks. The general subject of my book *World Agriculture in Disarray* (1973) has guided much of my research during the past decade. In particular, I have shown that high levels of price supports are insufficient to have a long-run effect upon the return to farm labour; alternative employment opportunities and the amount of human capital are the primary determinants of labour returns in agriculture.

JOHNSON, George Edwards

Born 1940, Boston, MA, USA.
Current Post Prof. Econ., Univ. Michigan, Ann Arbor, MI, 1974–.
Past Posts Res. Fellow, Univ. Nairobi, Kenya, 1970–1; Dir., Office Evaluation, US Dept. Labor, 1971–4; Sr. Econ., US President's Council Econ. Advisers, 1977–8; Vis. Fellow, LSE, 1979; Res. Assoc., NBER, Cambridge, MA, 1983–.
Degrees MA, PhD Univ. Cal. Berkeley, 1964, 1968.
Principal Fields of Interest 800 Manpower Labour; 900 Welfare Programmes.
Publications *Articles:* 1. 'Bargaining theory, trade unions and industrial strike activity' (with O. Ashenfelter), *AER*, 59(1), March 1969; 2. 'The de-

mand for labor by educational category', *SEJ*, 37, Oct. 1970; 3. 'Earnings and promotion of women faculty' (with F. Stafford), *AER*, 64(5), Dec. 1974; 4. 'Fiscal substitution effect' (with J. Tomola), *JHR*, 12, Winter 1977; 5. 'Theory of labour market intervention', *Ec*, 47, Aug. 1980; 6. 'Subsidies for higher education', *J Labor E.*, 2, July 1984.

Principal Contributions In the first part of my career I was interested in straightforward questions about how labour markets work and also in how to integrate unionism into an economic framework. In the 1970s I became interested in how government policies influence labour market outcomes. During the 1980s I have been working on the question of why relative wage rates do not adjust as rapidly as they 'should' and what this implies about macroeconomic adjustment.

JOHNSON, Harry G.*

Dates and Birthplace 1923–79, Toronto, Ont., Canada.
Posts Held Acting Prof., St Francis Xavier Univ., Ont., Canada, 1943–4; Instr., Univ. Toronto, 1946–7; Ass. Lect., Lect., Univ. Camb. 1949, 1950–6; Prof., Univ. Manchester, 1956–9; Prof., Charles F. Grey Disting. Service Prof., Univ. Chicago, 1959–74, 1979; Prof., LSE, 1966–74; Prof., Grad. Inst. Internat. Stud., Geneva, 1976–9.
Degrees BA, MA Univ. Toronto, 1943, 1947; BA, MA Univ. Camb., 1946, 1951; MA, PhD Harvard Univ., 1948, 1958; MA, DSc Univ. Manchester, 1960, 1972; Hon. LLD Univs. St Francis Xavier, 1965, Windsor, 1966, Queen's Ont. 1967, Sheffield, 1969, Carleton, 1970, Western Ontario, 1973.
Offices and Honours Fellow, AAAS, 1962, BA, 1969, Em Soc, 1972, Royal Soc. Canada, 1976; Pres., Canadian Polit. Science Assoc., 1965–6, Chairman, UK AUTE 1968–71; Pres., Section F BAAS, 1972–3; Pres., EEA, 1976–7; Vice-Pres., AEA, 1976; Officer, Order Canada, 1976.
Publications *Books:* 1. *International Trade and Economic Growth: Studies in Pure Theory* (1958); 2. *Economic*

Policies Toward Less Developed Countries (1967); 3. *Essays in Monetary Economics* (1967, 1969); 4. *Aspects of the Theory of Tariffs* (1971); 5. *On Economics and Society* (1975).

Career As one of the most prolific economists of his generation, he contributed to the formulation and development of the theory of effective protection, the concept of the 'scientific' tariff, the monetary approach to balance-of-payments problems, and the two-factor, two-sector model of general equilibrium, both in the context of comparative statics and economic growth. Also his writings helped to lead macroeconomists to a new and continually evolving synthesis of Keynesian thinking with the neoclassical tradition of microeconomics. Finally, he wrote expertly on a wide variety of special topics, such as brain drain, the economics of R&D, and the economics of higher education.

Secondary Literature J. N. Bhagwati and J. A. Frankel, 'Johnson, Harry G.', *IESS*, 18.

JOHNSON, Robert W

Born 1921, Denver, CO, USA.

Current Post Prof. Management, Krannert Grad. School Management, Purdue Univ., W. Lafayette, IND, USA.

Past Posts Lect., Prof. Fin., Univ. Buffalo, 1950–9; Prof. Fin. Admin., Michigan State Univ., 1959–64.

Degrees MBA Harvard Bus. School, 1946; PhD Northwestern Univ., 1950.

Offices and Honours Vice-Pres., Dir., AFA, 1969; Pres., Fin. Management Assoc., 1971.

Principal Fields of Interest 521 Business Finance.

Publications *Books:* 1. *Financial Management* (Allyn & Bacon, 1959, 1971, with R. Melicher, 1982); 2. *Self-correcting Problems in Finance* (with R. I. Robinson), (Allyn & Bacon, 1971, 1976); 3. *Capital Budgetting* (Kendall/Hunt Publ. Co., 1977).

Articles: 1. 'Regulation of finance charges on consumer instalment credit', *Michigan Law Rev.*, 66, 1967; 2. 'Better ways to monitor accounts receivable', *Harvard Bus. Rev.*, 50, 1972; 3. 'Denial

of self-help repossession: an economic analysis', *Southern Cal. Law Rev.*, 47, 1973; 4. 'Consumer credit regulation: illusion or reality', *Bus. Lawyer*, 33, 1978; 5. 'Pricing of bank card services', *J. Retail Banking*, 1, 1979.

Principal Contributions Research on the costs and benefits of various types of government regulations in the area of consumer and mortgage credit. Studies of pricing policies, industry structure, and anti-trust issues in the consumer credit field. In the area of finance, most research and publication has been in the area of capital investment and financial management.

JOHNSON, Thomas

Born 1936, Halletsville, TX, USA.

Current Post Prof. Econ., Bus. and Stats., N. Carolina State Univ., Raleigh, NC, USA, 1977–.

Past Posts Nuclear Engineer, Convair-Fort Worth, TX, USA, 1957–61; Eng. Specialist, LTV-Vought, Dallas, TX, 1961–4; Operations Analyst, Res. Triangle Inst., NC, 1964–9; Res. Assoc., N. Carolina State Univ., 1969; Ass. Prof., Assoc. Prof. Econ. and Stats., Southern Methodist Univ., Dallas, 1969–74; Assoc. Prof. Econ. and Bus. and Stats., N. Carolina State Univ., 1974–7.

Degrees AA(Maths.) Navarro Coll., TX, 1955; BA(Maths.) Univ. Texas, 1957; MA(Maths.) Texas Christian Univ., 1962; MES(Stats.), PhD(Econ. and Stats.) N. Carolina State Univ., 1969, 1969.

Offices and Honours Phi Kappa Phi; Pi Mu Epsilon; Phi Theta Kappa; Gamma Sigma Delta.

Principal Fields of Interest 210 Econometric, Statistics and Mathematical Models and Methods; 720 Natural Resources; 850 Human Capital.

Publications *Books:* 1. *Towards Economic Understanding* (with P. Heyne), (Science Res. Assoc., 1976); 2. *A Student's Guide to Economic Understanding* (Science Res. Assoc., 1976); 3. *Toward Understanding Microeconomics* (with P. Heyne), (Science Res. Assoc., 1976); 4. *Towards Understand-*

ing Macroeconomics (with P. Heyne), (Science Res. Assoc., 1976).

Articles: 1. 'A model for returns from investment in human capital', *AER*, 60(4), Sept. 1970; 2. 'Qualitative and limited dependent variables in economic relationships', *Em*, 40(3), May 1972; 3. 'Investment in human capital and growth in personal income 1956–1966' (with F. J. Hedein), *AER*, 64(4), Sept. 1974; 4. 'Zealots and malingerers: results from firm-specific human capital investments', *SEJ*, 41(4), April 1975; 5. 'Selection without (unfair) discrimination', *Communications in Stats.*, A7(11), 1978; 6. 'Time in school: the case of the prudent patron', *AER*, 68(5), Dec. 1978; 7. 'Allocation of time by married couples approaching retirement' (with R. L. Clark and A. A. McDermed), *Social Security Bull.*, April 1980.

Principal Contributions After my BA I began my career working as a nuclear engineer on the Nuclear Powered Airplane Project and then on the Nuclear Power Ram Jet Project. In this period, I worked on problems of shielding against radiation, safety, reliability and environmental effects. In this work, I became interested in problems of statistics and operations research, so I changed jobs and began work on a PhD in statistics. To take the course I wanted in econometrics, I had to take some graduate economics courses and I became so interested in economics that I co-majored it for my PhD. I was drawn to problems of human capital and the challenges they hold for modelling and estimation. In this work I included questions of schooling, on-the-job training, selection, and, eventually, retirement. In the study of retirement, I tackled my most difficult problems in using optimal control to model economic relationships. Since 1980 I have turned my attention more to questions of natural and agricultural resources. But my focus is still on problems of dynamics, especially in modelling systems. My most recent work has included models of the scallop fishery and the growth of cattle in the context of dynamic models of a firm.

JOHNSON, William Ernest*

Dates and Birthplace 1859–1931, Cambridge, England.
Posts Held Sidgwick Lect., Fellow, King's Coll. Camb., 1886–1931, 1902–31.
Degrees BA, MA Univ. Camb., 1882, 1885.
Offices and Honours Fellow, BA, 1926.
Publications *Books:* 1. *Logic*, 3 vols (1921–4).
Articles: 1. 'Exchange and distribution', *Camb. Econ. Club*, 1891; 2. 'On certain questions connected with demand' (with C. P. Sanger), *Camb. Econ. Club*, 1894; 3. 'The pure theory of utility curves', *EJ*, 23, Dec. 1913; all three repr. in *Precursors in Mathematical Economics: An Anthology*, eds. W. J. Baumol and S. M. Goldfeld (1978).

Career Logician who, seemingly unaware of Fisher and Pareto, took the indifference curves in Edgeworth's *Mathematical Psychics* and turned them upside down. He called these 'iso-utility' curves, and they have been used in this form ever since. However, Johnson's work, and that of Slutsky, was independently rediscovered by Hicks and Allen to whom its use must be attributed.

JOHNSTON, Bruce Foster

Born 1919, Lincoln, NB, USA.
Current Post Prof., Food Res. Inst., Stanford Univ., Stanford, CA, USA, 1959–.
Past Posts Agric. Marketing Admin., US Dept. Agric., 1941–2; US Army School Military Govt., Charlottesville, VA, and Far Eastern Civil Affairs Training School, Stanford Univ., 1944–6; Chief, Food Branch, Econ. Scientific Section, GHQ, Southern Command Asia and the Pacific, Tokyo, 1945–8; Agric. Econ., Food and Agric. Div., US Mission NATO and Europ. Regional Organisation, Paris, 1952–4; Assoc. Prof., Food Res. Inst., Stanford Univ., 1954–9; Cons., FAO, 1961–, Harvard Advisory Group, Govt. Ghana, 1967, Pakistan Inst. Devlp. Econ., 1968, World Bank Mission Ghana, 1970,

Asian Devlp. Bank 1976; Member, Steering Comm., Res. and Action Programme, ILO, 1972; ILO Employment Mission, Tanzania, 1977.

Degrees BA Cornell Univ., 1941; MA, PhD Stanford Univ., 1950, 1953.

Offices and Honours Guggenheim Foundation Fellow, 1962; Fellow, Board Dirs., African Stud. Assoc., 1962–5; Member, US SSRC Comm. Agric. Econ., 1962–6; Advisory Board, Foreign Area Fellowship Program, 1963–6; Member, Advisory Panel Devlp. Problems, US Dept. State, 1966–7; Vis. Prof., Inst. Devlp. Stud., Univ. Nairobi, Kenya, 1974–5; Res. Fellow, Internat. Inst. Appl. Systems Analysis, Laxenberg, Austria, 1978–9.

Editorial Duties Ed. Boards, *AJAE*, 1972–4, *Agric. Admin.*, 1975–.

Principal Fields of Interest 112 Teaching of Economics; 713 Agricultural Policy; 826 Labour Markets, Demographic Characteristics.

Publications *Books:* 1. *Japan's Food Management During World War II* (with M. Hosoda and Y. Kusumi), (Stanford Univ. Press, 1953); 2. *Manual on Food and Nutrition Policy* (with P. Greaves), (FAO, 1969); 3. *Food and Nutrition Strategies in National Development* (with others), (FAO, WHO, 1976); 4. *The Staple Food Economies of Western Tropical Africa* (Stanford Univ. Press, 1958); 5. *Agricultural Development and Economic Growth*, co-ed. (with H. M. Southworth), (Cornell Univ. Press, 1967); 6. *Agriculture and Economic Growth: Japan's Experience*, co-ed. (with K. Ohkawa and H. Kaneda), (Tokyo Univ. Press, 1969; transl., Japanese, 1979, Indonesian, Gadjah Mada Univ. Press, 1983); 7. *Agricultural and Structural Transformation: Economic Strategies in Late-Developing Countries* (with P. Kilby), (OUP, 1975; transls., Portuguese, Zahar Editores, 1977, Japanese, Agric. Pol. Res. Comm., 1978, Spanish, Fondo de Cultura Economica, 1980); 8. *Agricultural Change in Tropical Africa* (with K. R. M. Anthony, W. O. Jones, and V. C. Uchendu), (Cornell Univ. Press, 1979); 9. *Redesigning Rural Development: A Strategic Perspective* (with W. C. Clark), (JHUP., 1982).

Articles: 1. 'The role of agriculture in economic development' (with J. W. Mellor), *AER*, 51(4), Sept. 1961; 2. 'Agriculture and structural transformation in developing countries: a survey of research', *JEL*, 8(2), June 1970; 3. 'Interrelations between agricultural and industrial growth', in *Agricultural Policy in Developing Countries* ed. N. Islam (Macmillan, 1974); 4. 'Agricultural strategy and industrial growth', in *Economic Growth in Developing Countries: Material and Human Resources*, ed. Y. Ramati (Praeger, 1975); 5. 'Food, health and population in development', *JEL*, 15(3) Sept. 1977; 6. 'Socioeconomic aspects of improved animal-drawn implements and mechanization in semi-arid East Africa', in *Proceedings of the International Workshop on Socioeconomic Constraints to Development of Semi-Arid Tropical Agriculture, 19–23 February 1979, Hyderabad, India* (ICRISAT, 1980); 7. 'The design and redesign of strategies for agricultural development: Mexico's experience revisited', in *U.S.-Mexico Relations: Economic and Social Aspects*, eds. C. W. Reynolds and C. Tello (Stanford Univ. Press, 1983); 8. 'Integrated multi-sectoral interventions at the village level', in *Nutrition Policy Implementation: Issues and Experience*, eds. N. S. Scrimshaw and M. B. Wallerstein (Plenum Press, 1982); 9. 'Rural development programmes: a critical review of past experience' (with W. C. Clark), in *Growth and Equity in Agricultural Development*, eds. A. Maunder and K. Okhawa (Gower, 1983); 10. 'The world food equation: interrelations among development, employment, and food consumption' (with J. W. Mellor), *JEL*, 22(2), June 1984.

Principal Contributions An early interest in agriculture's role in the economic development of Japan and Taiwan led to more general analysis of agriculture's role in economic development. More recent work has combined a concern with agricultural strategies with a focus on rural development, with emphasis on interrelated health, nutrition, and family planning programmes that directly increase human welfare, enhance the effectiveness of a country's labour force, and slow its rate of growth. An extended period of concentration on the food and agriculture problems of tropical Africa was followed by research with Peter Kilby on agriculture and structural transformation in Taiwan, India and Pakistan and by study of agriculture and rural development in Mexico.

JOHNSTON, Jack

Born 1923, Belfast, N. Ireland.

Current Post Prof. Econ., Univ. Cal., Irvine, USA, 1978–.

Past Posts Prof. Econometrics, Stanley Jevons Prof. Econometrics, Univ. Manchester, England, 1959–67, 1967–78.

Degrees BComSc Queen's Univ., Belfast, 1947; PhD Univ. Wales, 1957; Hon. MA Univ. Manchester, 1962.

Offices and Honours Fellow, Em Soc., 1963; Disting. Faculty Lect., Univ. Cal., Irvine, 1984.

Editorial Duties Ed. Board, *J. Macroecon*, 1979.

Principal Fields of Interest 210 Econometric, Statistical and Mathematical Methods and Models; 130 Economic Fluctuations; Forecasting; Stabilisation and Inflation; 220 Economic and Social Statistical Data and Analysis.

Publications *Books:* 1. *Statistical Cost Analysis* (McGraw-Hill, 1960; transl., Spanish, 1961); 2. *Econometric Methods* (McGraw-Hill, 1963, 1984; transl., Japanese, Spanish, Portuguese, Italian, and Malaysian).

Articles: 1. 'An econometric study of the production decision', *QJE*, 75, May 1961; 2. 'The productivity of management consultants', *JRSS*, 125(2), 1963; 3. 'A model of wage determination under bilateral monopoly', *EJ*, 82 Sept. 1972; 4. 'A macro-model of inflation', *EJ*, 85, June 1975; 5. 'The elusive Phillips curve', *J. Macroecon.*, 2(4), Fall 1980.

Principal Contributions A series of studies in applied econometrics, especially in the areas of statistical cost functions and labour productivity; the clarification and exposition of econometric methods; and theoretical and empirical studies of wage and price inflation.

JONES, Richard*

Dates and Birthplace 1790–1855, Tunbridge Wells, Kent, England.

Posts Held Clergyman; Prof. Polit. Econ., King's Coll., Univ. London, 1833–5, Haileybury Coll., 1835–55.

Degree MA Univ. Camb., 1819.

Offices and Honours Member, UK Tithe Commission and Charity Commission.

Publications *Books:* 1. *Essay on the Distribution of Wealth and on the Sources of Taxation* (1831, 1964); 2. *Literary Remains*, ed. W. Whewell (1859, 1964).

Career As a member of the Cambridge circle, which included Whewell and Herschel, he became a devotee of the inductive methods in the sciences and was determined to apply it to political economy. His volume on rent was the only part of his *Essay* . . . which he completed, and consisted of a categorisation of forms of rent extending much beyond that described by Ricardo. This form of attack on Ricardian economics met with little success, but he is now widely looked on as a precursor of the historical school in Britain.

Secondary Literature M. L. Miller, 'Richard Jones's contributions to the theory of rent', *HOPE*, 9(3), Fall 1977.

JOPLIN, Thomas*

Dates and Birthplace 1790(?)–1847, Newcastle-upon-Tyne, England.

Posts Held Timber Merchant and banker.

Publications *Books:* 1. *An Essay on the General Principles and Present Practices of Banking in England and Scotland* (1822); 2. *Outline of a System of Political Economy* (1823); 3. *Views on the Subject of Corn and Currency* (1826); 4. *An Analysis and History of the Currency Question* (1832); 5. *The Cause and Cure of Our Commercial Embarrassments* (1841).

Career His *Essay* . . . attacked the monopoly of the Bank of England and proposed the setting up of joint stock banks. This attracted considerable notice and his ideas were at the root of the system initiated in 1828. Joplin's own banking ventures brought him little profit and he died in some obscurity. His subsequent writings were largely ignored.

JORGENSON, Dale W.

Born 1933, Bozeman, MT, USA.
Current Post Frederic Eaton Abbe Prof. Econ., Harvard Univ., 1981–.
Past Posts Ass. Prof., Assoc. Prof., Prof. Econ., Univ. Cal. Berkeley, 1959–61, 1963–9; Prof. Econ., Harvard Univ., 1969–80; Vis. Prof. Econ., Univ. Chicago, 1962–3, Oxford Univ. 1968, Hebrew Univ., Jerusalem, 1967, Stanford Univ., 1973.
Degrees BA Reed Coll., 1955; MA, PhD Harvard Univ., 1957, 1959.
Offices and Honours Fellow, Em Soc, 1964; Fellow, ASA, 1965; NSF Sr. Post-Doctoral Fellow, Netherlands School Econ., Rotterdam, 1967–8; Member, Conf. Res. Income and Wealth, 1967; Guggenheim Memorial Fellow, 1968; Fellow, AAAS, 1969; John Bates Clark Medal, AEA, 1971; Fellow, Center Advanced Study Behavioural Sciences, Stanford, 1975; Member, NAS, 1978; Fellow, Amer. Assoc. Advancement Science, 1982; John R. Commons Award, Omicron Delta Epsilon, Internat. Honor Soc. Econ., 1983.
Editorial Duties Assoc. Ed., *JASA*, 1962–5; Amer. Ed., *REStud.*, 1963–7; Ed., *AER*, 1967–9; Assoc. Ed., *QJE*, *RES*, 1969–; Board of Syndics, Harvard Univ. Press, 1984.
Principal Fields of Interest 023 Macroeconomic Theory; Investment; 211 Econometric and Statistical Methods and Models.
Publications *Books:* 1. *Optimal Replacement Policy* (with J. J. McCall and R. Radner), (N-H, 1967; transl., Italian, *Politiche Ottimali di Sostituzione e Manuetezione dei Maccinari*, Franco Angeli Editorie, 1969); 2. *Econometric Studies of US Energy Policy*, co-ed. (with E. A. Hudson), (N-H, 1976).
Articles: 1. 'The development of a dual economy', *EJ*, 71, June 1961; 2. 'Capital theory and investment behavior', *AER*, 53(2), May 1963, repr. in *Readings in Business Cycles*, eds. R. A. Gordon and L. R. Klein (Richard

D. Irvin, 1965), and *Reprint Series in Economics* (Bobbs-Merrill, 1967); 3. 'Rational distributed lag functions', Em, 34(1), Jan. 1966; 4. 'Tax policy and investment behavior' (with R. E. Hall), *AER*, 57(3), June 1967, repr. in *Reprint Series in Economics*, (Bobbs-Merrill, 1969); 5. 'Econometric studies of investment behaviour: a review', *JEL*, 9(4), Dec. 1971; 6. 'Transcendental logarithmic production frontiers' (with L. R. Christensen and L. J. Lau), *REStat*, 55(1), Feb. 1973; 7. 'US energy policy and economic growth, 1975–2000' (with E. A. Hudson), *Bell JE*, 5(2), Autumn 1974, repr. in *International Inst. Appl. Systems Analysis, Proceedings of IIASA Working Seminar on Energy Modelling* (IIASA, 1974), and *Energy Systems Forecasting, Planning and Pricing*, eds. C. J. Ciccheti and W. K. Foell (Univ. Wisconsin, 1975); 8. 'Trancendental logarithmic utility functions' (with L. R. Christensen and L. J. Lau), *AER*, 65(3), June 1975; 9. 'The transcendental logarithmic model of aggregate consumer behavior' (with L. J. Lau and T. M. Stoker), in *Advances in Econometrics*, 1, eds. R. L. Basmann and G. Rhodes (JAI Press, 1982); 10. 'Econometric methods for applied general equilibrium analysis', in *Applied General Equilibrium Analysis*, eds. H. Scarf and J. Shoven (CUP, 1984).

Principal Contributions Contributions through 1971 are summarised as follows in the citation for the John Bates Clark Medal; 'Dale Jorgenson has left his mark with great distinction on pure economic theory (with, for example, his work on the growth of a dual economy); and equally on statistical method (with for example, his development of estimation methods for rational distributed lags). But he is preeminently a master of the territory between economics and statistics, where both have to be applied in the study of concrete problems. His prolonged exploration of the determinant of investment spending, whatever its ultimate lessons, will certainly long stand as one of the finest examples in the marriage of theory and practice in economics.' Since 1971 I have concentrated on the development of econometric methods for implementing general equilibrium models. This research has led to the introduction of the transcendental logarithmic functional forms for modelling producer behaviour and consumer demand. It has also led to the origination of econometric methods for estimating systems of nonlinear simultaneous equations. Modelling of consumer behaviour has resulted in the introduction of new methods for measuring economic welfare. These methods have been applied to assessments of the impact of changes in economic policy, measurement of inequality in the distribution of individual welfare, and a new approach to cost of living measurement. Modelling of producer behaviour has resulted in the introduction of new methods for analysing productivity and for making international productivity comparisons.

JOSKOW, Paul L.

Born 1947, New York City, NY, USA.

Current Post Prof. Econ., MIT, Camb., MA, USA, 1978–.

Past Posts Ass. Prof., Assoc. Prof. Econ., MIT, 1972–5, 1975–8; Vis. Prof. John F. Kennedy School Govt., Harvard Univ., 1979–80.

Degrees BA Cornell Univ. 1968; MPhil, PhD Yale Univ., 1971, 1972.

Offices and Honours Phi Beta Kappa; Woodrow Wilson Fellow; NSF Grad. Fellow.

Editorial Duties Co-ed., *Bell JE*; Ed. Boards, *Bell JE*, *Rand JE*, *Land Econ.*, *Energy J.*, *J Ec Behav*.

Principal Fields of Interest 610 Industrial Organisation and Public Policy; 630 Industrial Studies; 720 Natural Resources.

Publications *Books:* 1. *Electric Power in the United States: Models and Policy Analysis* (with M. Baughman and D. Kamat), (MIT Press, 1979); 2. *Controlling Hospital Costs: The Role of Government Regulation* (MIT Press, 1981); 3. *Markets for Power: An Analysis of Electric Utility Deregulation* (with R. Schmalensee), (MIT Press, 1983).

Articles: 1. 'Pricing decisions of regulated firms: a behavioural approach', *Bell JE*, 2(1), Spring, 1972; 2. 'Inflation

and environmental concern: change in the process of public utility price regulation', *J Law E*, 17(2), Oct. 1974; 3. 'Cartels, competition and regulation in the property–liability insurance industry', *Bell JE*, 4(2), Autumn, 1973; 4. 'Electric utility fuel choice behavior' (with F. S. Mishkin), *Int ER*, 18(3), Oct. 1977; 5. 'Commercial impossibility, the uranium market and the Westinghouse case', *J. Legal Stud.*, Jan. 1977, repr. in *Corporate Counsel's Annual*, 1978; 6. 'The effects of learning by doing on nuclear power plant operating reliability' (with G. Rozanski), *REStat*, 61(2), May 1979; 7. 'A framework for analyzing predatory pricing policy' (with A. Klevorick), *Yale Law J.*, Dec. 1979, repr. in *Corporate Counsel's Annual, 1981*; 8. 'The effects of competition and regulation on hospital bed supplies and the reservation quality of the hospital', *Bell JE*, 11(2), Autumn, 1980; 9. 'The simple economics of industrial cogeneration', *Energy J.*, Jan. 1983; 10. 'Regulation in theory and practice: a current overview' (with R. Noll), in *Studies of Public Regulation*, ed. G. Fromm (MIT Press, 1981).

Principal Contributions My primary interest is in exploring the causes and consequences of government regulation of industrial markets. Many years ago it was convenient to categorise industries as being either 'regulated' or 'unregulated'. This categorisation is no longer valid, if it ever was. Virtually all firms are subject to some form of regulation whether of price, product quality, environmental hazards, or health and safety. I believe that to understand the causes and effects of government regulation one must have a detailed understanding of the industries being regulated and the institutional arrangements that have evolved for regulating them. Thus, my work involves both detailed studies of demand, supply and pricing in regulated industries and the application of regulatory constraints to these industries. My work in the electric utility industry, the insurance industry, the hospital sector and the nuclear energy industry all fits into this framework. In the last few years I have also become interested in the development of normative regulatory rules for application in different industries. My work on predatory pricing and my current research on incentive regulation reflect this interest.

JUGLAR, Clement*

Dates and Birthplace 1819–1905, France.
Posts Held Physician; Teacher Stats., L'Ecole Libre des Sciences Polit.
Offices and Honours Founder, Soc. de Stat. de Paris; Pres., Soc. d'Econ. Sociale.
Publications *Books:* 1. *Des crises commerciales et de leur retour périodique* (1862); 2. *Du change et de la liberté d'émission* (1868); 3. *Les banques de dépot, d'escompte et d'émission* (1884).
Articles: 1. 'Des crises commerciales', *Annuaire de l'écon. polit.*, 13, 1856.
Career From his early background in medicine he brought to the study of economics a scientific training and an interest in demographic phenomena. He turned immediately to the question of commercial crises, becoming in fact the first noted theorist of the business cycle. He viewed business cycles of 7–11 years' duration as occurring naturally and unavoidably. His use of statistics was able and imaginative and he proved to be a remarkably accurate predictor of the turning points in business cycles.
Secondary Literature A Marchal, 'Juglar, Clement', *IESS*, 8.

JUST, Richard E.

Born 1948, Tulsa, OK, USA.
Current Post Prof. Agric. and Resource Econ., Univ. Cal. Berkeley, CA, USA, 1980–.
Past Posts Assoc. Prof. Agric. Econ and Stat., Oklahoma State Univ., 1972–5; Prof. Econ., Brigham Young Univ., Provo, UT, 1979–80.
Degrees BS Oklahoma State Univ., 1969; MA (Stats.), PhD Univ. Cal. Berkeley, 1971, 1973.
Offices and Honours Giannini Fellow, 1969–71; Outstanding Published Res. Award, Western Agric Econ. Assoc., 1975; Outstanding Published Res.

Award, AAEA, 1977, 1980; Outstanding Journal Article Award, AJAE, 1981.
Editorial Duties Ed., Council, *AJAE*, 1978–80, 1984–6; Ed., Council, *Western J. Agric. Econ.*, 1982–4.
Principal Fields of Interest 710 Agriculture; 022 Microeconomic Theory; 024 Welfare Theory.
Publications *Books:* 1. *Applied Welfare Economics and Public Policy* (with D. Hueth and A. Schmitz), (Prentice-Hall, 1982); 2. *Econometric Analysis of Production Decisions with Government Intervention* (Univ. Cal. Press, 1974); 3. *Econometric Analysis of Supply Response and Demand for Processing Tomatoes in California* (with W. Chern), (Univ. Cal. Press, 1978).
Articles: 1. 'An investigation of the importance of risk in farmers' decisions', *AJAE*, 56(1), Feb. 1974; 2. 'A study of debt servicing capacity applying logit analysis' (with G. Feder), *JDE*, 4(1), March 1977; 3. 'Estimation of an adaptive expectations model', *Int ER*, 18(3), Oct. 1977; 4. 'Existence of stable distributed lags', *Em*, 45(6), Sept. 1977; 5. 'Storage with price uncertainty in international trade' (with G. Feder and A. Schmitz), *Int ER* 18(3), Oct. 1977; 6. 'Stochastic specification of production functions and economic implications' (with R. D. Pope), *J Em*, 7(1), Feb. 1978; 7. 'Welfare measures in a multi-market framework' (with D. L. Hueth), *AER*, 69(5), Dec. 1979; 8. 'Price controls and optimal export policies under alternative market structures' (with A. Schmitz and D. Zilberman), *AER*, 69(4), Sept. 1979; 9. 'Tomatoes, technology and oligopsony' (with W. S. Chern), *Bell JE* 11(2), 1980; 10. 'Stochastic structure, farm size, and technology adoption in developing agriculture' (with D. Zilberman), *OEP*, 35, May 1983.
Principal Contributions My most innovative accomplishments include: (1) developing an econometric approach for estimation of the importance of risk in aggregate supply; (2) pioneering the application of proper quantitative tools for the analysis and prediction of debt-servicing capacity by developing countries in international credit markets; (3) development of a flexible stochastic production function specification that can

allow treatment of both risk-reducing and risk-increasing inputs; (4) development of a method for efficiently estimating multi-output production functions in agriculture; (5) development of the method for measuring welfare effects on producers and consumers from changes in uncertainty; (6) development of techniques for measuring welfare effects that impact on many markets through equilibrium approaches; (7) analytical analysis of the role of discrete-continuous technology adoption choices in agriculture and the impact of such choices on the distributional effects of agricultural policy; (8) various other analytical analyses of the role of uncertainty in microproduction models with emphasis on agricultural application; and (9) theoretical and empirical work that shows the role of exchange rates in agricultural trade.

JUSTER, F. Thomas

Born 1926, Hollis, NY, USA.
Current Post Dir., Inst. for Social Res., Prof. Econ., Univ. Michigan, Ann Arbor, MI, USA, 1973–.
Past Posts Sr. Res. Analyst, CIA, 1951–3; Ass. Prof., Amherst Coll., 1953–9; Res. Staff, Sr. Res. Staff, NBER, 1959–64, 1964–73; Joel Dean Associates, 1964–6.
Degrees BS(Educ.) Rutgers Univ., 1949; PhD Columbia Univ., 1956.
Offices and Honours Fellow, ASA; Secretary, Chairman, Bus. and Econ. Section, ASA, 1969–71, 1971; Dir. AFA, 1970–1.
Editorial Duties Ed., *Econ. Outlook*, USA, 1973.
Principal Fields of Interest 229 Microdata.
Publications *Books:* 1. *Consumer Expectations, Plans and Purchases: A Progress Report* (Princeton Univ. Press, 1959); 2. *Anticipations and Purchases: An Analysis of Consumer Behavior* (Princeton Univ. Press, 1964); 3. *Consumer Sensitivity to Finance Rates: An Empirical and Analytical Investigation* (with R. Shay), (Columbia Univ. Press, 1964); 4. *Household Capital Formation and Financing: Growth and Cyclical Behavior,1897–1962* (Columbia Univ.

Press, 1966); 5. *Education, Income and Human Behavior*, ed. (Columbia Univ. Press, 1975); 6. *The Economic and Political Impact of General Revenue Shared*, ed. (Survey Res. Center, Univ. Michigan, 1977); 7. *The Distribution of Economic Well-being*, ed. (Columbia Univ. Press, 1978); 8. *Social Accounting Systems: Essays on the State of the Art*, co-ed. (with K. Land), (Academic Press, 1981).
Articles: 1. 'Consumer buying intentions and purchase probabilities: an experiment in survey design', *JASA*, 61, Sept. 1966; 2. 'Consumer asset formation in the United States' (with R. E. Lipsey), *EJ*, 77, Dec. 1967; 3. 'Microdata, economic research, and the production of economic knowledge', *AER*, 60(2), May 1970; 4. 'Uncertainty, expectations and durable goods demand models', in *Human Behavior in Economic Affairs – Essays in Honor of George Katona* (Univ. Michigan Press, 1972); 5. 'Inflation and the consumer' (with P. Wachtel), *Brookings Papers Econ. Activity*, 1, 1972; 6. 'Microdata requirements and public policy decision', *Annals Econ. and Social Measurement*, 1(1), Jan. 1972; 7. 'Anticipator and objective models of goods demand' (with P. Wachtel), *AER*, 62(4), Sept. 1972; 8. 'Toward a theory of saving behavior' (with L. Taylor), *AER*, 65(2), May 1975; 9. 'A theoretical framework for the measurement of well-being', *RIW*, 1, Series 27, March 1981; 10. 'The theory and measurement of well-being: a suggested framework for accounting and analysis' (with P. Courant and G. K. Dow), *Social Accounting Systems*, 1981.
Principal Contributions Much of my professional career has been spent in studying the behaviour of households, initially in its cyclical aspects with respect to purchase decisions and saving rates, more recently in its secular aspects with respect to the use of resources to produce well-being. In analysis of cyclical behaviour, much of the work has focussed on the role of expectational or anticipatory phenomena in explaining consumer decisions. This interest leads naturally to the use of survey data of one kind or another in analysis of purchase and saving decisions. My more recent interest in secular

trends in household behaviour, which is focused on the generation of well-being, had its original roots in a concern with the degree to which conventional national income measurements misrepresented both the distribution and the change over time in household income. My current interest in household allocation of time, and the development of micro-oriented social accounting systems based on time allocation, grows naturally out of an interest in the development of comprehensive measures of well-being that go well beyond conventional monetary transaction flows. There is thus a natural progression in this work from a concern over the deficiencies of the conventional transactions-based GNP measures of output and income to the development of a comprehensive framework for the measurement of well-being, where the ultimate resource constraints are represented by the stock of wealth accumulated in the past and available time. Virtually all of my scientific interests reflect a concern with measurement issues related to the behavioural responses of economic units. Those convictions lead naturally to a concern with a generation of relevant behavioural measurements, typically obtained from surveys of economic units, and to a concern with building behavioural models that seem relevant to decision processes rather than to an interest in models characterised by consistency, completeness, or structural elegance.

K

KAHN, Alfred E.

Born 1917, Paterson, NY, USA.

Current Post Robert Julius Thorne Prof. Polit. Econ., Cornell Univ., Ithaca NY, USA; Special Cons., Nat. Econ. Res. Assoc., White Plains, NY, USA, 1976–.

Past Posts Ass. Prof., Assoc. Prof., Prof. Polit. Econ., Cornell Univ., 1947–76; Sr. Staff, US President's Council Econ. Advisers, 1968–72; Board Econ. Advisers, AT&T, 1968–74; Chairman, NY State Public Service Commission, 1974–7; Chairman, Civil Aeronautics Board, 1977–8; Chairman, Council Wage and Price Stability, 1978–80; Adviser to Pres. Reagan on Inflation, 1978–80.

Degrees BA, MA NYU, 1936, 1937; Grad Study, Univ. Missouri, 1937–8; PhD Yale Univ., 1942; Hon. LLDs Colby Coll., 1978, Univ. Mass., 1979, Ripon Coll., 1980, Northwestern Univ., 1981, Colgate Univ., 1983.

Offices and Honours Fellow, AAAS; NYU Alumni Achievement Award; Exec. Comm., Nat. Assoc. Regulatory Utility Commissioners, 1974–8; Vice-Pres., AEA, 1981–2.

Editorial Duties Ed. Board, *AER*, 1961–4.

Principal Fields of Interest 320 Fiscal Theory and Policy; 610 Industrial Organisation and Public Policy; 630 Industry Studies.

Publications *Books:* 1. *Great Britain in the World Economy* (Columbia Univ. Press, 1946, 1968); 2. *Fair Competition: The Law and Economics of Antitrust Policy* (with J. B. Dirlam), (Cornell Univ. Press, 1954, 1970); 3. *Integration and Competition in the Petroleum Industry* (with M. G. DeChazeau), (Yale Univ. Press, 1959, Kennikat Press, 1973); 4. *The Economics of Regulation*, 2 vols. (Wiley, 1970, 1971); 5. *Must We Live with Inflation Through the 1980s? Major Issues of the 1980s Lecture Series* (Lowell Inst. Boston, Harvard Univ. Extension, 1981); 6. *The Airline Industry: Is It Time to Reregulate?* (Transportation Center, Northwestern Univ., Nat. Econ. Res. Assoc., 1982).

Articles: 1. 'Fundamental deficiencies of American patent law', *AER*, 30(4), Sept. 1940; 2. 'The chemical industry', in *The Structure of the American Industry*, ed. W. Adams (Macmillan, 1948, 1961); 3. 'Investment criteria in development programs', *QJE*, 65, Feb. 1951; 4. 'Standards for antitrust policy', *Harvard Law Rev.*, 67, Nov. 1953, repr. in *Readings in Industrial Organization and Public Policy*, eds. R. F. Heflebower and G. W. Stocking (Richard D. Irwin, 1958); 5. 'The role of patents', in *Competition, Cartels and their Regulation*, ed. J. P. Miller (N-H, 1962); 6. 'The depletion allowance in context of carelization', *AER*, 54(3), June 1964; 7.

'Tyranny of small decisions: market failures, imperfections, and the limits of economics', *Kyk*, 19, Feb. 1966; 8. 'Market power inflation: a conceptual framework', in *The New Inflation in Industrial Economies*, ed. J. Blair (Lenox Hill, 1974); 9. 'Applications of economics to an imperfect world',*AER*, 69(2), May 1979; 10. 'The passing of the public utility concept: a reprise', in *Telecommunications Today and Tomorrow*, ed. E. Noam (Harcourt Brace Jovanovich, 1983).

KAHN, Richard Ferdinand.

Born 1905, London, England.
Current Post Retired Prof. Econ., Univ. Camb., 1972–; Fellow, King's Coll., Camb., 1930–.
Past Posts Lect., Prof. Econ., Univ. Camb. 1933–51, 1951–72; Second Bursar, First Bursar, King's Coll. Camb., 1935–46; 1946–51; Wartime, UK Civil Servant, 1939–46.
Degrees BA, MA, Univ. Camb. 1927, 1931.
Offices and Honours Fellow, BA; Created Life Peer, 1974.
Principal Fields of Interest 020 General Economic Theory.
Publications *Books:* 1. *Selected Essays on Employment and Growth*, (CUP, 1972); 2. *L'Economia del Breve Periodo.* (Editore Boringhieri, 1983); 3. *The Making of Keynes' General Theory* (CUP, 1984).
Articles: 1. 'Theory of display', *EJ*, 48, March 1938; 2. 'Historical origin of the international monetary fund, in *Keynes and International Monetary Relations*, ed. A. P. Thirlwall (Macmillan, 1976); 3. 'Some aspects of the development of Keynes' theory', *JEL*, 16(3), June, 1978.
Principal Contributions I was closely associated with Keynes from 1928 until his death in April, 1946 — as pupil, as collaborator on his economic writings, and in his stock exchange ventures on account of King's College; on his death I succeeded him as First Bursar. As a war-time civil servant from Dec. 1939 until Sept. 1946, I received administrative experience over a number of different fields, including 14 months in the

Middle East as Economic Adviser to the Minister of State. After the war my range of interests was further widened by work for the Treasury and three years as a part-time member of the National Coal Board in whose problems I became deeply interested.

I spent a year (1955) in Geneva as a member of the Research Division of EEC (of the UN). Co-operating in the preparation of their *Economic Survey of Europe in 1955* (1956), my particular concern was with obstacles to industrial investment in Western Europe. In 1959 I was appointed a member of a group of experts of the OEEC (predecessor of the OECD) to study a problem of rising prices. The group introduced the idea of the wage spiral via 'leap frogging'. In the course of the years 1965–9, I served as a member of four groups of experts of UNCTAD.

KAIN, John F.

Born 1935, Fort Wayne, IN, USA.
Current Post Prof. Econ., Prof. City Regional Planning, Kennedy School Govt., Harvard Univ., 1969–, 1980–.
Past Posts Sr. Staff Member, Rand. Corp., Santa Monica, CA, 1961–2; Assoc. Prof., Dept. Econ., US Air Force Academy, 1962–4.
Degrees BA Bowling Green State Univ., 1957; MA, PhD Univ. Cal. Berkeley, 1961, 1961; Hon. MA Harvard Univ., 1964.
Offices and Honours Em Soc; Amer. Planning Assoc.; Amer. Inst. Certified Planners; Urban Land Inst.
Principal Fields of Interest 933 Urban Transportation Economics.
Publications *Books:* 1. *The Urban Transporation Problem* (with J. R. Meyer and M. Wohl), (Harvard Univ. Press, 1965); 2. *Empirical Models of Urban Land Use* (with H. J. Brown, *et al.*), (NBER, 1971); 3. *The Detroit Prototype of the NBER Urban Simulation Model* (with G. K. Ingram and J. R. Ginn), (NBER, 1972); 4. *Housing Markets and Racial Discrimination: A Micro-economic Analysis* (with J. M. Quigley). (NBER, 1975); 5. *Essays on Urban Spatial Structure* (Ballinger, 1975). 6. *Housing and Neighborhood*

Dynamics: A Simulation Study (with W. C. Argar, Jr.), (Harvard Univ. Press, 1985).

Articles: 1. 'Housing segregation, Negro employment, and metropolitan decentralization', *QJE*, 82(2), May 1968; 2. 'How to improve transportation at practically no cost', *Public Pol.*, 20(3), Summer 1972; 3. 'Housing market discrimination, homeownership, and savings behaviour' (with J. M. Quigley), *AER*, 62(3), June 1972; 4. 'Cumulative urban growth and urban density functions' (with D. Harrison Jr.), *JUE*, Jan. 1974; 5. 'Simulation of housing market dynamics' (with W. C. Apgar), *Amer. Real Estate Urban Econ. Assoc. J.*, 7(4), Winter 1980; 6. 'America's persistent housing crises: error in anaylsis and policy', *Annals AAPSS*, 465, Jan. 1983; 7. 'Impacts of higher petroleum prices on transportation patterns and urban development', in *Research in Transportation Economics*, ed. T. E. Keeler (JAI Press, 1984).

Principal Contributions Author of several papers identifying links between housing market segregations, discrimination and low levels of Black homeownership and wealth. Head of 10-year project to develop NBER Urban Simulation Model and to apply it to the analysis of housing and urban development programmes and policies.

KALDOR, Nicholas

Born 1908, Budapest, Hungary.
Current Post Prof. Emeritus, Fellow, King's Coll., Camb., 1975–.
Past Posts Ass. Lect., Reader Econ., LSE, 1932–47; Res. Assoc. NIESR, 1943–5; Chief, Econ. Planning Staff, US Strategic Bombing Survey, 1945; Dir., Res. and Planning Div., ECE, Geneva, 1947–9; Member, UN Group Experts, Internat. Measures for Full Employment, 1949; Fellow, King's Coll. Camb., 1949–; Reader Econ., Prof. Econ., Univ. Camb., 1952–65; 1966–75; Member UK Royal Commission Taxation of Profits and Income, 1951–5; Adviser Tax Reform, Govt. India, 1956; Econ. Adviser, UNECLA, Santiago, Chile, 1956; Fiscal Adviser,

Govts.: Ceylon, 1958, Mexico, 1960, British Guiana, 1961, Turkey, 1962, Iran, 1966, Venezuela, 1976; Ford Vis. Res. Prof., UCLA, 1959–60; Econ. Adviser, Govt. Ghana, 1961; Vis. Econ., Reserve Bank Australia, 1963; Special Adviser, UK Chancellor Exchequer, 1964–8, 1974–6.
Degrees BSc LSE, 1930; Hon. Dr Univ. Dijon, 1970.
Offices and Honours Fellow, BA, 1963; Hon. Fellow, LSE, 1970; Pres., Section F, BAAS, 1970, RES, 1974–6; Created Life Peer, 1974; Hon. Member, AAAS, AEA, RES of Belgium, Hungarian Academy Sciences.
Principal Fields of Interest 023 Macroeconomic Theory; 111 Economic Growth; 323 National Taxation.
Publications *Books:* 1. *National and International Measures for Full Employment* (with others), (UN, 1949); 2. *An Expenditure Tax* (A&U, 1955, 1965); 3. *Essays on Value and Distribution* (Duckworth, Free Press, 1960); 4. *Essays on Economic Stability and Growth* (Duckworth, Free Press, 1960); 5. *Essays on Economic Policy*, 2 vols (Duckworth, W. W. Norton, 1964, 1965); 6. *Further Essays on Economic Theory* (Duckworth, 1978); 7. *Further Essays on Applied Economics* (Duckworth, 1978); 8. *Reports on Taxation*, 2 vols (Duckworth, 1979); 9. *The Scourge of Monetarism* (OUP, 1982); 10. *The Economic Consequences of Mrs. Thatcher* (Duckworth, 1983).
Principal Contributions See my introductions to *Collected Economic Essays*, particularly vols 1, 3, and 5.
Secondary Literature L. L. Pasinetti, 'Kaldor, Nicholas', *IESS*, 18; A. P. Thirlwall, *et al.*, 'Symposium: Kaldor's growth laws', *J Post Keyn E*, 5(3), Spring, 1983.

KALECKI, Michal*

Dates and Birthplace 1899–1970, Lodz, Russia (now Poland).
Posts Held Econ. Journalist; Employee, Polish Res. Inst. Bus. Cycles and Prices, 1929–37; Oxford Inst. Stats, 1940–5; Econ., UN, 1946–54; Govt. Econ., Teacher Econ., Poland, 1955–67.

Degree Student Gdansk Polytechnic.
Offices and Honours Member, Polish Academy Sciences, 1966.

Publications *Books:* 1. *Essays in the Theory of Economic Fluctuations* (1939); 2. *Studies in Economic Dynamics* (1943); 3. *Studies in the Theory of Business Cycles 1933–9* (1966); 4. *Introduction to the Theory of Growth in a Socialist State* (1969); 5. *Selected Essays on the Dynamics of the Capitalist Economy 1933–70* (1971); 6. *The Last Phase in the Transformation of Capitalism* (1972); 7. *Selected Essays on the Economic Growth of the Socialist and Mixed Economy* (1972).

Career Acknowledged posthumously as an independent creator of many of the elements of the 'Keynesian' system. A Marxist of an individual kind, he worked in capitalist and socialist countries and was critical of both economic systems. He used statistics and mathematical methods extensively, first to make his theorising congruent with current circumstances and second, to give it the quality of precision. Along with Oskar Lange, he was responsible for the introduction of modern Western methods in economics into the Eastern bloc. He did not undertake broad economic surveys but concentrated on a number of precise and detailed studies. His outstanding contributions were in the theory of macroeconomic dynamics.

Secondary Literature G. R. Feiwel, 'Kalecki, Michal', *IESS*, 18; G. R. Feiwel, *The Intellectual Capital of Michal Kalecki* (Univ. Tenn. Press, 1975).

KAMERSCHEN, David R.

Born 1937, Chicago, IL, USA.
Current Post Disting Prof. Econ., Jasper N. Dorsey Prof., Public Utilities, Univ. Georgia, USA, 1980.
Past Posts Grad. Ass., Instr., Miami (Ohio) Univ., 1959–60; Ass. Instr., Michigan State Univ., 1962–4; Ass. Prof., Washington Univ., 1964–6; Assoc. Prof., Prof., Univ. Missouri, 1966–8, 1968–74; Prof. Econ., Univ. Georgia, 1974–80.
Degrees BS, MA Miami (Ohio) Univ.,

1959, 1960; PhD Michigan State Univ., 1964.
Offices and Honours Exec. Comm., SEA, 1974–6; Grad. Council Fellow, NSF Co-op. Fellow, Michigan State Univ., 1961–2, 1962–3; Outstanding Grad. Teachers Award, Outstanding Educ. Amer. Award, 1973, 1974, 1975; Superior Teaching, Univ. Georgia, 1978–9, 1980.
Editorial Duties Ed. Board, Advisory Board, Co-Ed., eight professional journals.
Principal Fields of Interest 600 Industrial Organisation; 000 General Economics; 100 Economic Growth.
Publications *Books:* 1. *Readings in Microeconomics*, ed. (World Publishing, 1967, Wiley, 1969); 2. *Macroeconomics: Selected Readings*, co-ed. (with W. L. Johnson), (Houghton Mifflin, 1970); 3. *Readings in Economic Development*, co-ed. (with W. L. Johnson), (South-Western Publishing, 1972); 4. *Economics* (with G. E. Vredeveld), (Cliffs Notes, 1975); 5. *Money and Banking* (South-Western Publishing, 1980, 1984); 6. *Intermediate Microeconomic Theory* (with L. M. Valentine), (South-Western Publishing, 1981); 7. *Current Issues in Public Utility Economics: Essays in Honor of James C. Bonbright*, co-ed. (with A. L. Danielsen), (D. C. Heath, 1983).

Articles: 1. 'An estimation of the "welfare losses" from monopoly in the American economy', *WEJ*, 4(3), Summer 1966; 2. 'Market growth and industry concentration', *JASA*, 63, March 1968; 3. 'The influence of ownership and control on profit rates', *AER*, 58(3), June 1968, 58(4), Dec. 1968; 4. 'An empirical test of oligopoly theories', *JPE*, 76(4), pt. 1, July–Aug. 1968, repr. in *J. Reprints for Antitrust Law and Econ.*, 1, pt. 2, Winter 1969; 5. 'The determination of profit rates in "oligopolistic" industries', *J Bus*, 42(3), July 1969; 6. 'The return of target pricing?', *J Bus*, 48(2), April 1975; 7. 'The economic effects of monopoly: a lawyer's guide to antitrust economics', *Mercer Law Rev.*, 27(4), Summer 1976, repr. in *Economic Analysis and Antitrust Law*, eds. R. Calvani and J. J. Siegfried (Little, Brown, 1979); 8. 'An economic approach to the detection and proof of collusion', *Amer. Bus. Law J*, 17(2), Summer 1979; 9. 'The economics expert in antitrust litigation: an interview', *Antitrust Law and Econ. Rev.*, 13(4), 1981, 14(1), 1982.

Principal Contributions My early work was concentrated in the areas of economic growth and development, population economics, price theory and applied microeconomics, especially industrial organisation, including antitrust economics, public utility economics and the history of economic thought. Later on my interest began to focus on augmenting and incorporating microeconomics in the field of industrial organisation so as to explain and predict market structure, conduct (behaviour), performance and their interrelationships. I have been particularly active in recent years in theory formulation and hypotheses testing in a wide variety of antitrust and public utility economics areas so as to aid society in using its scarce resources more effectively in the formulation of public policy, In addition to writing numerous articles for professional economists, I have tried to keep non-specialists and non-economists informed about what is happening in antitrust, public utility, etc. areas.

KAMIEN, Morton Issac

Born 1938, Warsaw, Poland.

Current Post Harold L. Stuart Prof. Managerial Econ., J. L. Kellogg Grad. School Management, Northwestern Univ., Evanston, IL, USA, 1979–.

Past Posts Ass. Prof., Assoc. Prof. Econ., Grad. School Industrial Admin., Carnegie-Mellon Univ., Pittsburgh, 1963–7, 1967–70; Prof. Managerial Econ., J. L. Kellogg Grad. School Management, Northwestern Univ., 1970–9.

Degrees BA City Coll. NY, 1960; PhD Purdue Univ., 1964.

Principal Fields of Interest 022 Microeconomic Theory; 611 Market Structure; Industrial Organisation and Corporate Strategy; 621 Technological Change; Innovation; Research and Development.

Publications *Books:* 1. *Dynamic Optimization: The Calculus of Varia-*

tions and Optimal Control in Economics and Management (with N. L. Schwartz), (N-H, 1981); 2. *Market Structure and Innovation* (with N. L. Schwartz), (CUP, 1982).

Articles: 1. 'The paradox of voting probability calculations' (with M. B. Garman), *Behavioral Science*, 13, July 1968; 2. 'Optimal induced-technical change' (with N. L. Schwartz), *Em*, 36(1), Jan. 1968; 3. 'Induced factor augmenting technical progress from a microeconomic viewpoint' (with N. L. Schwartz), *Em*, 37(4), Oct. 1969; 4. 'Limit pricing and uncertain entry' (with N. L. Schwartz), *Em*, 39(3), May 1971; 5. 'Optimal maintenance and sale age of a machine subject to failure' (with N. L. Schwartz), *MS*, 17, April 1971; 6. 'Timing of innovations under rivalry' (with N. L. Schwartz), *Em*, 40(1), Jan. 1972; 7. 'Market structure and innovative activity' (with N. L. Schwartz), *JEL*, 13(1), March 1975; 8. 'On the degree of rivalry for maximum innovative activity' (with N. L. Schwartz), *QJE*, 90(2), May 1976; 9. 'Optimal exhaustible resource depletion with endogenous technical change' (with N. L. Schwartz), *REStud*, 45(1), Feb. 1978; 10. 'Conjectural variations' (with N. L. Schwartz), *CJE*, 16(2), May 1983.

Principal Contributions My interest in the economics of technical change stems from the claim in the popular press in the late 1950s and early 1960s that automation was reducing job opportunities for the unskilled. Technological advance was thought to be the source of structural unemployment with a bias against the unskilled. I sought to analyse this question by determining the profit-maximising behaviour of a firm through time when its production function was endogeneous and subject to change. My interest then turned to the question of whether a competitive market system led to over- or under-investment in technical advance. On the one hand the inability of firms to capture all the rewards from a technical advance suggested under-investment while on the other hand, the race to be first suggested over-investment. I and N. L. Schwartz attempted to analyse this question by determining how rapidly a firm would develop an innovation when faced by the prospect that rivals were also attempting to achieve the same innovation. This model was extended in several directions culminating in an effort to use it to explain the empirically observed phenomenon that a market structure intermediate between monopoly and perfect competition led to the most rapid rate of technical advance. My interest in limit pricing stemmed from the belief that previous work on this subject was not founded on profit-maximising behaviour of the firm and required an unrealistic amount of information by the incumbent firm. Specifically, in the previous work it was assumed that the incumbent firm set its price so as to prevent entry forever. It was not clear that this was a long-run, profit-maximising strategy. Moreover, the incumbent firm was assumed to know exactly the cost function of any potential entrant. This assumption appeared too severe. My interest at present has turned to interaction among firms through time.

KANTOROVICH, Leonid Vitalievicz

Born 1912, Leningrad (St Petersburg), USSR.
Current Post Chief Dept., Inst. Systems Analysis, Academy Sciences, Moscow, USSR, 1976–.
Past Posts Instr., Prof., Leningrad Inst. Construction Eng., 1930–2, 1932–9; Prof., Leningrad Univ., 1934–60; Head, Dept. Maths., Inst. Academy Sciences, Leningrad, 1948–60; Vice-Dir., Siberian Inst. Maths., Novosibirsk, 1960–71; Chief, Laboratory Inst. Nat. Econ. Management, Moscow, 1971–6.
Degrees BS, Dr (Sciences) Leningrad State Univ., 1930, 1935; Hon. Dr, Univs. Glasgow, 1966, Grenoble, 1967, Nice, 1968, Warczawa, 1969, Munich, 1969, Helsinki, 1971, Paris (Sorbonne), 1975, Cambridge, 1976, Philadelphia, 1976, Calcutta, 1978.
Offices and Honours Corresp. Member, Leningrad Univ., 1956–64; Member, Academy Sciences USSR, 1964; Order of Lenin (Maths.), 1949, (Econ.), 1965; Foreigner Member, Academy

Sciences, 1966, AAAS, 1969, Jugoslav. Academy Art and Sciences, 1979, Corresp. Member, Eng. Academy, Mexico, 1976; Fellow, Em Soc., 1973–; Joint Nobel Prize in Econ., 1975.
Editorial Duties Ed. Boards, *Mathematical Programming*, 1970, *Operations Researches* (Paris), 1975, *Siberian Math. J.*, 1962, *Econ. and Maths. Methods* (Moscow), 1964, *Quanta* (Moscow), 1981.
Principal Fields of Interest 052 Socialist and Communist Economic Systems; 113 Economic Planning; 213 Mathematical Methods and Models.
Publications *Books:* (all in Russian, except No. 7) 1. *Numerical Method of Higher Analysis* (with V. Krylof), (State Publ., 1936, 1949; transl., English, Nordhoff, 1958). 2. *The Mathematical Methods of Production Planning Organisation* (Leningrad State Univ., 1939; transl., English as *Management Science*, 1960); 3. *Functional Analysis in Semi-ordered Spaces* (with B. Vulich and A. Pinscer), (USSR State Publ., 1950); 4. *Rational Cutting of Materials* (with V. Zalgaller), (USSR State Publ., 1951, 1971); 5. *The Best Use of Economic Resources* (USSR Academic Publ., 1959; transl., English, Pergamon, 1965); 6. *Optimal Solutions in Economics* (with A. Gorstko), (USSR Publ. House Nauka, 1972); 7. *Essays in Optimal Planning*, ed. J. Smolinsky (Wiley, 1976); 8. *Functional Analysis* (with G. Akiloff), (USSR State Publ. 1977; transl., English, Pergamon, 1981).
Articles: 1. 'Memoire on the analytical operations and the projective sets (with E. Livenson), *Fundamenta Mathematicae*, 20, 1931, 1933; 2. 'On the translocation of masses' (in Russian), *Reports USSR Academy Sciences*, 1942; transl., English, *Management Science*, 1, 1958; 3. 'Functional analysis and applied mathematics' (in Russian), *Uspechi Math. Nauk*, 1948; 4. 'Optimal models of perspective planning' (in Russian) (with V. Makarov), *Primenenie Mathematiki v economocheskich issledovanijach* 3, 1965; 5. 'Mathematical optimal methods in planning development branch of industry' (in Russian), *Voprosii Ekonomiki*, 10, 1967; 6. 'Estimating the effectiveness of capital expenditures' (with V. Bogachev,

V. Makarov), *Mathecon.*, 8(1), Fall 1971; 7. 'Economic problems of science and technical progress', *Scand JE*, 78(5), 1976; 8. 'Mathematics in economics: achievements, difficulties, perspectives', *Math. Programming*, 11, 1976; 9. 'On the use of optimal calculations in the branch systems of automatic control' (with J. Zorin and others), *Econ. and Math. Methods*, 5, 1978.

Principal Contributions From 1929 in many branches of mathematical analysis; set theory, function theory, functional analysis, numerical mathematics, and computer technique. Developed the outlines of linear programming in 1939; effective algorithms, objectively determined valuations (shadow prices), many fields of applications. Particularly potential method for transportation problem. Introduced static and dynamic models of current and perspective planning. Considered general problem of optimal use of resources. Applied the optimisation models in the problem of planning, price theory, theory of rent, effectiveness theory of investments, amortisation theory, technical progress, and other problems of socialist economy.

Secondary Literature 1. I Johansen, 'L. V. Kantorovich's contributions to economics', in *Contemporary Economists in Perspective*, eds. H. W. Spiegel and W. J. Samuels (JAI Press, 1984).

KATONA, George*

Dates and Birthplace 1901–81, Budapest, Hungary.
Posts Held Assoc. Ed., *Der Deutsche Volkswirt*, Berlin, 1926–33; Investment Adviser, NYC, 1933–6; Lect. Econ., New School Social Res., NY, 1932–42; Res. Dir., Comm. Price Control, Univ. Chicago, 1943–5; Study Dir., Dir., Program Surveys, US Dept. Agric., 1945–6; Prof. Econ. and Psychology, Dir., Inst. Social Res., Univ. Michigan, 1946–72; Vis. Prof., MIT, 1961, NYU, 1964.
Degrees PhD (Psychology) Univ. Göttingen, 1921; Hon. Dr Univ. Amsterdam, 1977, Free Univ., Berlin, 1981.
Offices and Honours Guggenheim Foundation Fellow, 1940–2; Forst

Hegemann Prize, Düsseldorf, 1963; Award Disting. Contrib., Amer. Psychological Assoc., 1977.
Publications *Books:* 1. *Organizing and Memory* (1940); 2. *War Without Inflation* (1942); 3. *Price Control and Business* (1945); 4. *Psychological Analysis of Economic Behavior* (1951); 5. *Consumer Attitudes and Demand* (1953); 6. *Consumer Expectations* (1956); 7. *The Powerful Consumer* (1960); 8. *The Mass Consumption Society* (1964); 9. *Aspirations and Affluence* (1971); 10. *Psychological Economics* (1975).
Career Pioneered the measurement of expectations, first in quarterly *Surveys of Consumer Attitudes*, and later in special panel studies annually undertaken by the Institute for Social Research at Ann Arbor, Michigan. A prolific writer, he never tired of attacking the prevailing disdain of economists towards psychological research.
Secondary Literature R. Curtin, 'On Katona', in *Contemporary Economists in Perspective*, eds. H. W. Spiegel and W. J. Samuels (JAI Press, 1984).

KATZNER, Donald Wahl

Born 1938, Baltimore, MD, USA.
Current Post Prof. Econ., Univ. Mass.-Amherst, USA, 1975–.
Past Posts Ass. Prof., Univ. Penn., 1965–71; Vis. Prof., Inst. Social Econ. Res., Osaka Univ., Osaka, Japan, 1967–8; Assoc. Prof., Prof., Univ. Waterloo, Ont., 1970–1, 1971–3; Lect., Univ. Cal. San Diego, 1973–5; Vis. Scholar, MIT, 1981–2.
Degrees BA (Maths.), Oberlin Coll., 1959; MA (Maths.), PhD Univ. Minnesota, 1962, 1965.
Offices and Honours Ford Foundation Doctoral Dissertation Fellow, 1964–5;
Editorial Duties Ed. Board, *J Post Keyn E*, 1977.
Principal Fields of Interest 022 Microeconomic Theory; 036 Economic Methodology.
Publications *Books:* 1. *Static Demand Theory* (Macmillan, 1970); 2. *Choice and the Quality of Life* (Sage, 1979); 3. *Analysis without Measurement* (CUP, 1983).

Articles: 1. 'A note on the differentiability of consumer demand functions', *Em*, 36(2) April 1968; 2. 'A general approach to the theory of supply', *Econ. Stud. Q*, 19(2), July 1968; 3. 'On the possibility of the general linear economic model' (with L. R. Klein), in *Economic Models, Estimation and Risk Programming*, ed. K. Fox, *et al.* (Springer, 1969); 4. 'Political structure and system and the notion of logical completeness', *General Systems*, 14, 1969; 5. 'Demand and exchange analysis in the absence of integrability conditions', in *Preferences, Utility and Demand*, ed. J. S. Chipman, *et al.* (Harcourt, Brace, Jovanovich, 1971); 6. 'A simple approach to existence and uniqueness of competitive equilibria', *AER*, 62(3), June 1972; 7. 'An approach to a unified micro-macro economic model' (with S. Weintraub), *Kyk*, 27(3), 1974; 8. 'On not quantifying the non-quantifiable', *J Post Keyn E*, 1(2), Winter, 1978–9; 9. 'Profits, optimality and the social division of labor in the firm' (with H. Gintis), in *Sociological Economics*, ed. L. Levy-Garboua (Sage Publ., 1979); 10. 'The formal structure of argument in Professor Apter's *Choice and the Politics of Allocation*', *Polit. Methodology*,7(2), 1979.

Principal Contributions Early work was concerned with the organisation, unification and extension of the theory of demand. Subsequent efforts have branched off in two directions. On one hand the early work was continued in the area of microeconomic, general equilibrium. On the other, a methodology was developed to enable scientists to deal with (i.e. construct and empirically test models of) phenomena in which the variables involved seem incapable of measurement. Rather than attempting to 'quantify the unquantifiable', the question of how such phenomena can be understood and analysed in the absence of numerical gauges was investigated. This methodology was then applied in examining a variety of specific problems in economics, political science and sociology.

KAUTSKY, Karl*

Dates and Birthplace 1854–1938, Prague, Austro-Hungary.
Offices and Honours Founder, Ed., *Die Neue Zeit*, 1883–1917; German Secretary State Foreign Affairs, 1918.
Publications *Books:* 1. *Economic Doctrines of Karl Marx* (1887, 1936); 2. *The Class Struggle* (Erfurt Program), (1892, 1910, 1971); 3. *Die Agrarfrage* (1899); 4. *The Road to Power* (1909); 5. *The Dictatorship of the Proletariat* (1918); 6. *Die Materialistische Geschichtsanfassung*, 2 vols., (1927); 7. *War and Democracy* (1932); 8. *Socialists and the War* (1937).

Career Socialist theorist who in his early career was closely associated with Engels, and was later involved in all the major theoretical and political debates within the German Social Democratic Party and the socialist movement generally. His journalism spread Marxist ideas, he drafted political programmes, opposed Soviet Bolshevism and in later life did non-Marxian social science research. His considerable output includes historical works, polemical tracts and a major examination of the materialist conception of history.

Secondary Literature J. H. Kautsky, 'Kautsky, Karl', *IESS*,8; G. P. Steenson, *Karl Kautsky 1851–1938* (Univ. Pittsburgh Press, 1978).

KAYSEN, Carl

Born 1920, Philadelphia, PA, USA.
Current Post David W. Skinner Prof. Polit. Econ., Dir., Program Science, Technology and Society, MIT, 1976–.
Past Posts Res. Asst., NBER, 1940–2; Econ., US Office Strategic Services, Washington, DC, 1942; Ass. Prof., Assoc. Prof., Prof. Econ., Lucius N. Littauer Prof. Polit. Econ., Harvard Univ., 1950–66; Fulbright Vis. Scholar, LSE, 1955–6; Ford Foundation Fellow, Greece, 1959–60; Deputy Special Ass. to US President for Nat. Security Affairs, White House, Washington, DC, 1961–3; Dir., Prof. Social Science, Inst. Advanced Studies, Princeton, NJ, 1966–76.
Degrees BA Univ. Penn., 1940; MA, PhD Harvard Univ., 1947, 1953.

Offices and Honours Member, AAAS, 1955; Guggenheim Foundation and Fulbright Fellow, 1956; Amer. Philo. Soc., 1967.

Editorial Duties Ed. Boards, *AER*, 1952–5, *Foreign Affairs*, 1974–.

Principal Fields of Interest 610 Industrial Organisation; 620 Economics of Technological Change; 850 Human Capital.

Publications *Books:* 1. *United States v. United Shoe Machinery Corporation, an Economic Analysis of an Anti-Trust Case* (Harvard Univ. Press, 1956); 2. *The American Business Creed* (with others), (Harvard Univ. Press, 1956, 1962); 3. *Anti-Trust Policy* (Harvard Univ. Press, 1959); 4. *The Demand for Electricity in the United States* (with F. M. Fisher), (N-H, 1962); 5. *Higher Learning, the Universities and the Public* (Princeton Univ. Press, 1969); 6. *Nuclear Power, Issues and Choices* (with others), (McGraw-Hill, 1977); 7. *A Debate on a Time to Choose* (with others), (Ballinger, 1977); 8. *Review of US-USSR Interacademy Exchanges and Relations*, ed. (NAS, 1977); 9. *A Program for Renewed Partnership: The Report of the Sloan Commission on Government and Higher Education*, Vice Chairman and Dir. of Res. (Ballinger, 1980).

Articles: 1. 'A revolution in economic theory?', *REStud*, 14(1), 1946; 2. 'A dynamic aspect of the monopoly problem', *REStat*, 31(2), May 1949; 3. 'Basing point pricing and public policy', *QJE*, 63(3), Aug. 1949; 4. 'Collusion under the Sherman Act', *QJE*, 65(2), May 1951; 5. 'Dynamic aspects of oligopoly price theory', *AER*, 42(2), May 1952; 6. 'The social significance of the modern corporation', *AER*, 47(2), May 1957; 7. 'Another view of corporate capitalism', *QJE*, 79, Feb. 1965; 8. 'Federal support of basic research', in *Report to the Committee on Sciences and Astronautics, US House of Representatives* (NAS, 1965); 9. 'Higher education: for whom? at whose cost?', in *Proceedings of the 1970 Invitational Conference on Testing Problems* (Educ. Testing Service, 1971); 10. 'Government and scientific research — some unanswered questions', *Public Interest*, Summer 1971.

Principal Contributions My work in economics contains three elements. The first is the study of public policy in relation to monopoly and competition, especially the antitrust laws. My contribution has been to elaborate and refine the idea of market power, apply it to the study of specific markets and also use the concept as a basis for analysis of the US laws on competition and monopoly and their administration. My books on the shoe-machinery industry and antitrust laws, and nearly half my published articles in economic journals, deal with this area. They include several relating the concept of market power to more theoretical models of monopoly, oligopoly, and competition, especially in a dynamic context. The second area of contribution is the study of business institutions from a socio-political, as well as an economic, point of view. In this area falls the book of which I was a co-author, *The American Business Creed*, and several articles on the modern corporation and corporate capitalism.

Finally, I have looked at the activities of basic research and higher education from both an economic and broader point of view. I have argued that the economists' traditional perspective on higher education as an investment in human capital is too narrow to capture many important features of the educational system. To understand the structure and functioning of higher education and see the interplay between its social and private benefits and costs it must also be seen as a consumption activity, a class and status marker, and an institutional structure with its own politics. Similar problems of social versus individual benefits and costs arise in the economics of basic research, and I have examined how far economics goes and fails to go in explaining what a society spends on research, how the activities are performed, and the fruits distributed.

KEELEY, Michael Clark

Born 1947, Kearney NB, USA.

Current Post Econ., Fed. Reserve Bank San Francisco, San Francisco, CA, 1983–.

Past Posts Econ., General Electric

Tempo, Center Advanced Stud., Washington, DC, 1973–5; Sr. Econ., Manager, Antitrust Econ. Consulting Group, SRI Internat., Menlo Park, Cal., 1975, 1981–3; Vis. Assoc. Prof., Univ. Santa Clara, CA, 1982–3.

Degrees BS MIT 1969; MA, PhD Univ. Chicago, 1971, 1974.

Offices and Honours NIH Fellow, Univ. Chicago, 1969–73.

Editorial Duties Ed. Board, *Internat. Program Pop. Analysis*, (Smithsonian Inst.).

Principal Fields of Interest 800 Manpower; Labour; Population; 600 Industrial Organisation; 210 Econometric, Statistical and Mathematical Models.

Publications *Books:* 1. *Population, Public Policy and Economic Development*, ed. (Praeger, 1976); 2. *Labor Supply and Public Policy: A Critical Review* (Academic Press, 1981); 3. *Monetary Incentives: A Practical Guide to the Use of Fees, Subsidies and Cost Internalization as Regulatory Techniques* (with J. Daly), (US Govt. Printing Office, 1981); 4. *Marketable Rights in Regulatory Programs: A Practical Guide* (with D. Downing), (US Govt. Printing Office, 1981).

Articles: 1. 'A comment on an interpretation of the economic theory of fertility', *JEL*, 13(2), June 1975; 2. 'The economics of family formation: an investigation of the age of first marriage', *EI*, 15(2), April 1977; 3. 'The estimation of labor-supply models using experimental data' (with P. K. Robins, R. G. Spiegelman, and R. W. West), *AER*, 68(5), Dec. 1978; 4. 'The labor-supply effects and costs of alternative negative income tax programs', (with P. K. Robins, R. G. Spiegelman, and R. W. West), *JHR*, 13(5), Winter 1978; 5. 'Work incentives and the negative income tax' (with P. Robins), *Challenge*, 22(1), March–April 1979; 6. 'An analysis of the age pattern of first marriage', *Int ER*, 20(2), June 1979; 7. 'Migration as consumption: the impact of alternative negative income tax programs', in *Research in Population Economics*, 2, eds. J. Simon and J. DeVanzo (JAI Press, 1979); 8. 'Experimental design, the Conlisk-Watts assignment model, and the proper estimation of behavioral response' (with P. K. Robins), *JHR*,

15(4), Fall 1980; 9. 'The effects of a negative income tax on fertility', *JHR*, 15(4), Fall, 1980; 10. 'The economics of firm size: implications from labor-market studies', *Econ. Rev., San Francisco Fed. Reserve Bank*, Winter 1984.

Principal Contributions Gary Becker at the University of Chicago introduced me to the application of economics to the analysis of nonmarket behaviour. My early research applied this approach to the analysis of marriage and fertility. This approach also proved to be useful in many areas of demographic economics, including problems in economic development and the relationship between demographics and development. This research culminated in my book, *Population, Public Policy*. Later, my work at SRI International turned to the analysis of the effects of an experimental negative income tax (NIT) programme on labour supply, fertility, migration and divorce. This research was among the first to exploit the exogenous variations in budget constraints caused by the experimental NIT programme to estimate effects on a variety of behaviour. Much of this research on labour supply is summarised in my book, *Labor Supply and Public Policy*. My research interests then turned to regulation and antitrust and I have worked on such issues as price-fixing, price discrimination, analysis of the competitive effects of mergers, and various competitive aspects of vertical integration. This work was performed as a consultant to various law firms. Most recently I have been studying the regulation (and deregulation) of the financial sector.

KEENEY, Ralph Lyons

Born 1944, Lewistown, MT, USA.

Current Post Prof. Systems Science, Univ. Southern Cal. Los Angeles, USA, 1983–.

Past Posts Ass. Prof., Assoc. Prof. Civil Eng. Management, MIT, 1969–74; Res. Scholar, Internat. Inst. Appl. Systems Analysis, Laxenburg, Austria, 1974–6; Head, Decision Analysis Group, Woodward-Clyde Consultants, San Francisco, 1976–83.

Degrees BSc (Eng.) UCLA, 1966;

SM (Electrical Eng.) 1967, EE (Electrical Eng.), PhD (OR.) MIT, 1968, 1969.

Offices and Honours Lanchester Prize Best English Language Publication OR., 1976; Council Member, ORSA, 1979–82.

Principal Fields of Interest 511 Organisation and Decision Theory; 512 Managerial Economics.

Publications *Books:* 1. *Decisions with Multiple Objectives* (with H. Raiffa), (Wiley, 1976); 2. *Conflicting Objectives in Decisions*, ed. (with D. Bell and H. Raiffa), (Wiley, 1977); 3. *Decision Analysis. A Videotape Course with Study Guide for Decision Analysis* (with A. Drake), (MIT Center Advanced Eng. Study, 1978); 4. *Siting Energy Facilities* (Academic Press, 1980); 5. *Acceptable Risk* (with B. Fischhoff *et al.*), (CUP, 1981).

Articles: 1. 'Multiplicative utility functions', *Operations Res.*, 22, 1974; 2. 'A group preference axiomatization with cardinal utility', *Management Science*, 23, 1976; 3. 'The art of assessing multiattribute utility functions', *Organizational Behavior Human Performance*, 19, 1977; 4. 'Decision analysis: how to cope with increasing complexity', *Management Rev.*, 68, 1979; 5. 'Evaluating alternatives involving potential fatalities', *Operations Res.*, 28, 1980; 6. 'Decision anaylsis: an overview', *Operations Res.*, 30, 1982.

Principal Contributions Structuring models of value-judgements for complex situations. Specifically, von Neumann-Morgenstern utility functions are derived from various assumptions. Many applications of these utility functions have been illustrated and used in practical decision situations. Contributions to structuring preferences for groups.

KEESING, Donald

Born 1933, London, England.

Current Post Sr. Econ., World Bank, Washington, DC, 1976–.

Past Posts Econ., Harvard Defense Stud. Program, 1956–7; Econ., US Air Force, Cambridge Res. Center, Bedford, MA, 1957–9; Teaching Fellow, Tutor Econ., Res. Ass., Econ. Res. Project, Harvard Univ., 1959–61; Econ., Inst. Defense Analyses, Washington, DC, 1961–4; Ass. Prof. Econ., Columbia Univ., 1964–8; Vis. Scholar, Stanford Univ., 1966–7, El Colegio de Mexico, 1967–8; Assoc. Prof. Econ., Stanford Univ., 1968–72; Prof. Econ., Univ. N. Carolina, 1972–5; Vis. Prof. Econ., Williams Coll., 1974–5; Econ., World Bank, 1975–6.

Degrees BA (Hist.), MA, PhD Harvard Univ., 1954, 1956, 1961.

Offices and Honours Harvard Coll. Scholar., 1950–4; Magna cum laude, Phi Beta Kappa, 1954; Upham Scholar, 1954–6; US SSRC Amer. Council Learned Socs. Foreign Area Fellow Latin Amer. Stud., 1966–8.

Editorial Duties Ed. Board, *Internat. Stud. Q.*, 1972–80, *SEJ*, 1972–3.

Principal Fields of Interest 411 International Trade Theory; 121 Economic Studies of Less Industrialised Countries.

Publications *Books:* 1. *Textile Quotas Against Developing Countries* (with M. Wolf), (Trade Pol. Res. Centre, 1980); 2. *China: Socialist Economic Development* (with P. Hasan, *et al.*), (World Bank, 1983).

Articles: 1. 'Labor skills and comparative advantage', *AER*, 56(2), May 1966; 2. 'The impact of research and development on United States trade', *JPE*, 75, Feb. 1967; 3. 'Outward-looking policies and economic development', *EJ*, 77, June 1967; 4. 'Structural change early in development: Mexico's changing industrial and occupational structure from 1895 to 1950', *JEH*, 29(4), Dec. 1969; 5. 'Different countries' labor skill coefficients and the skill intensity of international trade flows', *J Ind E*, 1(4), Nov. 1971; 6. 'Population density in patterns of trade and development' (with D. R. Sherk), *AER*, 61(5), Dec. 1971; 7. 'Economic lessons from China', *JDE*, 2(1), March 1975; 8. 'National diversity and world progress', *WD*, 3(4), April 1975; 9. 'Linking up to distant markets: south to north exports of manufactured consumer goods', *AER*, 73(2), May 1983.

Principal Contributions Pioneered empirical analysis of the influence on international trade of labour skills and R&D. For better or worse, was first to use technical coefficients of one country to evaluate trade of a whole set of countries. Demonstrated strong effects of country size or scale effects and population density in cross-country patterns of trade and development. At an early date summarised advantages of outward-looking development policies. Have also contributed fresh insights on many other policy-related matters, ranging from the Chinese economic system to political corollaries of trade policies and feasible sequences of policy changes in developing countries. Played an influential role at the World Bank in analysing manufactured exports from developing countries and associated policy issues. Also put together pictures of surrounding institutional, business and marketing arrangements, the role of the buyer and its implications, and the realities and effects of textile quotas. Recently have been trying to provide industrial policy advice in various countries of Africa and the Indian subcontinents, and to draw lessons from what has happened to industry in Africa.

KELLEY, Allen Charles

Born 1937, Everett, WA, USA.
Current Post James B. Duke Prof. Econ., Duke Univ., Durham, NC, USA, 1973–.
Past Posts Ass. Prof, Stanford Univ., 1963–4; Ass., Assoc. Prof., Prof., Univ. Wisconsin-Madison, 1964–73; Vis. Prof., Monash Univ., Melbourne, Australia, 1970–1; Esmee Fairbairn Res. Prof, Heriot-Watt Univ., Edinburgh, 1978–9; Res. Scholar, Internat. Inst. Appl. Systems Analysis, Laxenburg, Austria, 1979–80.
Degrees BA, PhD Stanford Univ., 1964.
Offices and Honours Kazanjian First Prize Teaching Econ., 1972; Arthur Cole Prize Econ. Hist. (with J. G. Williamson), 1972.
Editorial Duties Ed. Board, *J. Econ. Educ.*
Principal Fields of Interest 840 Demographic Economics; 110 Economic Development; 012 Economic Education.
Publications *Books:* 1. *Dualist Economic Development: Theory and History* (with R. J. Cheetham and J. G. Williamson), (Univ. Chicago Press, 1972); 2.

Lessons from Japanese Development: An Analytical Economic History (with J. G. Williamson), (Univ. Chicago Press, 1974); 3. *Modeling Growing Economies in Equilibrium and Disequilibrium* (with W. Sanderson and J. G. Williamson), (Duke Univ. Press, 1983); 4. *Population and Development in Rural Egypt* (with A. M. Khalifa and N. M. El-Khorazaty), (Duke Univ. Press, 1982); 5. *What Drives Third World City Growth? A Dynamic General Equilibrium Analysis* (with J. G. Williamson), (Princeton Univ. Press, 1984).

Articles: 1. 'Markov processes and economic analysis: the case of migration' (with L. W. Weiss), *Em*, 37(2), April 1969; 2. 'Writing history backwards: Meiji Japan revisited' (with J. G. Williamson), *JEH*, 31(4), 1971; 3. 'TIPS and technical change in classroom instruction', *AER*, 62(2), May 1972; 4. 'Population growth, the dependency rate, and the pace of economic development', *Pop. Stud.*, 27(3), Nov. 1973; 5. 'The role of population in models of economic growth', *AER*, 64(2), May 1974; 6. 'Savings, demographic change and economic development', *EDCC* 24(4), July 1976; 7. 'Demographic change and the size of the government sector', *SEJ*, 43(2), Oct. 1976; 8. 'Demographic impacts and demand patterns in the low-income setting', *EDCC*, 30(1), Oct. 1981; 9. 'Improving the teaching of economics; achievements and aspirations' (with G. L. Bach), *AER*, 74(2), May 1984; 10. 'Population growth, industrial revolutions and the urban transition' (with J. G. Williamson), *Pop. and Devlp. Rev.*, 10(3), Sept. 1984.

Principal Contributions My research has been about equally divided among three fields: economic development, economic demography, and economic education. The focus of the research in economic development has been the construction of computable general equilibrium models of the economy. Simulations of the modelled economy are then compared with reality and if the resulting empirical paradigm passes tests of validation, it is used to analyse the sources of economic growth. Some of the studies have dealt with specific countries (Meiji Japan); some have highlighted particular facets of development (Third-World urbanisation); and some have examined the development process in general (a 'Representative Developing Economy'). The general theme of this research is that models of development in which prices are endogenous are likely to give a much more realistic representation of economic development than the planning models so common in the literature.

KEMMERER, Edwin Walter*

Dates and Birthplace 1875–1945, Scranton, PA, USA.
Posts Held Prof. Econ., Cornell Univ., 1906–12; Prof., Princeton Univ., 1912–43.
Degrees BA Wesleyan Univ., 1899; PhD Cornell Univ., 1903.
Offices and Honours Adviser on currency systems to the Govts. of Philippines, Mexico, Guatemala, Colombia, South Africa, Chile, Poland, Ecuador, Bolivia, Peru, China and Turkey.
Publications *Books:* 1. *Money and Credit Instruments in their Relation to General Prices* (1907); 2. *Modern Currency Reforms* (1916); 3. *The ABC of the Federal Reserve* (1919); 4. *The Principles of Money* (1935); 5. *ABC of Inflation* (1942); 6. *Gold and the Gold Standard* (1944).
Career A tenacious defender of the gold standard who first made his name as an international economist. He gave frequent service to foreign governments on questions of currency. His interest in money problems began with his Cornell thesis and ended with his determined attacks on the Bretton Woods Agreement. His attachment to the gold standard strengthened with his advancing years and is the theme of most of his writings.
Secondary Literature G. F. Shirras, 'Obit.: Edwin Walter Kemmerer (1875–1945)', *EJ*, 56, June 1946.

KEMP, Murray C.

Born 1926, Melbourne, Victoria, Australia.
Current Post Res. Prof. Econ., Univ. New South Wales, Australia, 1962–.

Past Posts Vis. Prof., Univs. Cal. Berkeley, 1969–70, Paris, 1976–7, Western Ontario, 1977.
Degrees BCom, MA Univ. Melbourne, 1947, 1949; PhD Johns Hopkins Univ., 1955.
Offices and Honours Fellow, Em Soc, 1964; Keynes Prof., Univ. Essex, 1967–8.
Principal Fields of Interest 411 International Trade Theory.
Publications *Books:* 1. *The Pure Theory of International Trade* (Prentice-Hall, 1964); 2. *A Contribution to the General Equilibrium Theory of Preferential Trading* (N-H, 1969); 3. *Variational Methods in Economics* (with G. Hadley), (N-H, 1971); 4. *Three Topics in the Theory of International Trade* (N-H, 1976); 5. *Exhaustible Resources, Optimality, and Trade*, co-ed. (with N. V. Long), (N-H, 1980); 6. *Production Sets*, ed. (Academic Press, 1982); 7. *Essays in the Economics of Exhaustible Resources*, ed. (N-H, 1984).
Principal Contributions Contributed to the pure theory of international trade, to the economic theory relating to exhaustible resources and to the interrelationships between the two.

KENEN, Peter Bain

Born 1932, Cleveland, OH, USA.
Current Post Walker Prof. Econ. and Internat. Fin., Dir., Internat. Fin. Section, Princeton Univ., Princeton, NJ, USA, 1971–.
Past Posts Instr. Econ., Ass. Prof., Assoc. Prof., Prof., Provost, Columbia Univ., 1957–8, 1958–61, 1961–64, 1964–71, 1969–70; Vis. Prof., Hebrew Univ., Jerusalem, 1967, Stockholm School of Econ., 1967, Tel Aviv Univ., 1977, Univ. Cal. Berkeley, 1980, ANU, 1983–4; Fellow, Center Advanced Stud. Behavioral Sciences, Stanford, CA, 1971–2; Cons., US President's Council Econ. Advisers, 1961, US Treasury, 1961–8, US Bureau Budget, 1964–8, UNCTAD, 1972, Pol. Planning Group, US Treasury, 1978–80; Member, Rev. Comm., Balance of Payments Stats., 1963–4; UN Group Experts, Payments Arrangements Developing Countries, 1966; Advisory Comm., Reform Inter-

nat. Monetary System, 1977; Member, Council Foreign Relations, Group of Thirty.

Degrees BA Columbia Univ., 1954; MA, PhD Harvard Univ., 1956, 1958.

Offices and Honours David A. Wells Prize, Harvard Univ., 1958–9; Columbia Univ. Medal Excellence, 1977; Woodrow Wilson Fellow, 1954–5; Earhart Foundation Fellow, 1955–6; US SSRC Dissertation Fellow, 1956–7; Ford Faculty Res. Fellow, 1962–3; US SSRC Faculty Res. Fellow, 1966–7; Guggenheim Foundation Fellow, 1975–6.

Editorial Duties Ed. Board, *Polit. Science Q.*, 1963–71, *JMCB*, 1969–70; *JEL*, 1969–71; Assoc. Ed., *J Int. E*, 1977–80.

Principal Fields of Interest 430 Balance of Payments and International Finance; 410 International Trade Theory; 023 Macroeconomic Theory.

Publications *Books:* 1. *British Monetary Policy and the Balance of Payments 1951–7* (Harvard Univ. Press, 1957); 2. *Giant Among Nations* (Harcourt Brace Jovanovitch, 1960); 3. *International Economics* (Prentice-Hall, 1964, 1971; transls., Dutch, Italian, Japanese, Portuguese, Spanish, Swedish); 4. *The Open Economy*, co-ed. (with R. C. Lawrence), (Columbia Univ. Press, 1968); 5. *A Model of the U.S. Balance of Payments* (D. C. Heath 1978); 6. *Asset Markets, Exchange Rates and Economic Integration* (with P. R. Allen), (CUP, 1980); 7. *Essays in International Economics* (Princeton Univ. Press, 1982); 8. *The International Economy* (Prentice-Hall, 1984); 9. *International Trade and Finance*, ed. (CUP, 1975); 10. *Handbook of International Economics*, co-ed. (with R. W. Jones), (N-H, 1984).

Articles: 1. 'Intervention and sterilization in the short run and the long run', in *The International Monetary System*, eds. R. N. Cooper, *et al.* (Ballinger, 1981).

Principal Contributions Three themes run through my professional work. My contributions to the real side of trade theory have been concerned to state as clearly and simply as possible the 'cosmopolitan' case for free trade; my very first paper dealt with this issue, and I have returned to it frequently, in papers on human capital and trade, and my note on tariff changes and world welfare. My contributions to the monetary side of trade theory have been concerned with two quite different themes. On the one hand, I have been concerned with 'positive' aspects of interactions among national economies — an interest exemplified by my joint work with Polly Reynolds Allen. On the other hand, I have been concerned with 'normative' aspects and institution building — an interest exemplified by papers on comparisons among exchange-rate regimes, the role of Special Drawing Rights in the monetary system, and the problems of policy co-ordination.

KENNEDY, Charles Marius

Born 1923, London, England.

Current Post Self-employed; Hon. Prof. Econ. Theory, Univ. Kent, Canterbury, England, 1970–.

Past Posts Ass. Stat., UK Prime Minister's Stat. Section 1942–5; Ass. Lect., ⸱Univ. Coll. London 1946–7; Lect., Balliol Coll. Oxford, 1947–8; Fellow, Praelector, Queen's Coll. Oxford, 1948–61; Prof., Univ. W. Indies, Kingston, Jamaica, 1961–6; Prof. Econ. Theory, Univ. Kent, Canterbury, 1966–70.

Degrees BA (Polit., Philo. and Econ.), MA Univ. Oxford, 1942, 1948.

Offices and Honours Dir., Bank Jamaica, 1963–6.

Principal Fields of Interest 111 Economic Growth Theory and Models; 024 Welfare Theory; 521 Business Finance.

Publications *Articles:*1. 'The economic welfare function and Dr Little's criterion', *REStud*, 20(2), 1952–3; 2. 'Concerning utility', *Ec*, N.S. 21, Feb. 1954; 3. 'The character of improvements and of technical progress', *EJ*, 72, Dec. 1962; 4. 'Induced bias in innovation and the theory of distribution', *EJ*, 74, Sept. 1964; 5. 'Keynesian theory in an open economy', *Social and Econ. Stud.*, 15(1), March 1966; 6. 'Time, interest and the production function', in *Value, Capital and Growth*, ed. J. N. Wolfe (Edinburgh Univ. Press, 1968); 7. 'A generalisation of the theory of induced bias in technical progress', *EJ*,

83, March 1973; 8. 'Inflation accounting, profits, profitability and share valuation', *J. Bus. Fin. and Accounting*, 3(1), 1976; 9. 'Inflation accounting: retrospect and prospect', *Econ. Pol. Rev.*, 4, March 1978; 10. 'Fixed assets and the Hyde Gearing adjustment', *J. Bus. Fin. and Accounting*, 5(4), 1978.

Principal Contributions I have not worked in any settled field of specialisation but have made contributions in many areas of economic theory, including welfare economics, the macroeconomic analysis of open economies, monetary theory, growth theory and technical progress; my most widely recognised contribution has been the development of the theory of induced bias in technical progress. More recently, my interest has shifted away from mainstream economics towards business finance, especially the theory of options, warrants and convertibles. I have made a number of contributions to the debate leading to the development of inflation accounting in the UK.

KESSEL, Reuben A.*

Dates and Birthplace 1923–75, Chicago, IL, USA.

Posts Held Instr. Econ., Univ. Missowa, 1948–9; Econ., Rand Corp., Santa Monica, CA, 1950–4; Instr. Econ., Assoc. Prof., Prof., Grad. School Bus., Univ. Chicago, 1957, 1962–5; 1965–75; Cons., Dir., Bell Fed. Savings and Loan Assoc.

Degrees MBA, PhD Grad. School Bus., Univ. Chicago, 1948, 1952.

Offices and Honours Dir. Res., Grad. School Bus., Univ. Chicago, 1963–5.

Publications *Books:* 1. *The Cyclical Behavior of the Term Structure of Interest Rates* (Columbia Univ. Press, 1965); 2. *Essays on Applied Price Theory*, eds. R. H. Coase and M. H. Miller (Univ. Chicago Press, 1980).

Career Wrote brilliant articles on health economics, particularly the role of the AMA in the professionalisation of American medicine, the functioning of capital markets, with particular reference to the term structure of the

interest rate, industrial economics, and the traditional theory of inflation (jointly with A. A. Alchian).

KEYNES, John Maynard*

Dates and Birthplace 1883–1946, Cambridge, Cambridgeshire, England.

Posts Held Civil Servant, UK India Office, 1906–8, UK Treasury, 1915–19, 1940–5; Teacher Econ., Univ. Camb., 1908–42; Businessman, including Chairman, Nat. Mutual Life Insurance Co., 1921–38; Journalist for various papers including *The Nation* (Chairman, 1923–9).

Degree MA Univ. Camb., 1905.

Offices and Honours Fellow, BA; Pres., RES; Governor, IBRD; Dir., Bank of England; Ed., *EJ*, 1911–44; created Viscount, 1942.

Publications *Books:* 1. *Indian Currency and Finance* (1913), *Collected Writings of John Maynard Keynes*, eds. E. Johnson and D. Moggridge, vol. 1 (1971); 2. *The Economic Consequences of the Peace* (1919), *Collected Writings*, vol. 2 (1971); 3. *A Treatise on Probability* (1921), *Collected Writings*, vol 8 (1973); 4. *A Tract on Monetary Reform* (1923), *Collected Writings*, vol. 4 (1971); 5. *A Treatise on Money*, 2 vols (1930), *Collected Writings*, vols 5, 6 (1971); 6. *Essays in Biography* (1933), *Collected Writings*, vol. 10 (1972); 7. *The General Theory of Employment, Interest and Money* (1936), *Collected Writings*, vol. 7 (1973).

Career Unquestionably the major figure in twentieth-century British economics. His reputation does not rest purely on the *General Theory*, which initiated the so-called 'Keynesian revolution', but also on his other writings, most notably the *Treatise on Money*, his immensely influential work for government, and on his prominent place in the cultural and intellectual life of his day. His trenchant criticism of the 1919 treaty with Germany first raised him to national prominence and effectively undermined support for the treaty. During World War II, he was the chief architect of British economic policy and made a major contribution to post-war economic reconstruction through his participation in the Bretton Woods Conference and the founding of the IMF. His early economic work was very much within the Marshallian tradition, but during the crises of the 1920s he increasingly came to identify deflationary policies as the cause of much of the problem. From this beginning he developed his new theory of employment and his theories of interest, wages and money. The gradual but increasingly widespread acceptance of all or part of his views raised Keynesianism for a while to the position of a prevailing orthodoxy. In recent years, his star has begun to wane. Even so he remains to this day one of the three or four most influential economists that ever lived.

Secondary Literature R. F. Harrod, *The Life of John Maynard Keynes* (Macmillan, 1951); 'Keynes, John Maynard', *IESS*, 8; D. E. Moggridge, *Keynes* (Fontana, 1976); R. Skidelsky, *John Maynard Keynes, 1 — Hopes Betrayed 1883–1920* (Macmillan, 1983); *John Maynard Keynes — Critical Assessments*, 4 vols, ed. J. C. Wood (Croom Helm, 1983).

KEYNES, John Neville*

Dates and Birthplace 1852–1949, Salisbury, Wiltshire, England.

Posts Held Fellow, Pembroke Coll., Registrar, Univ. Camb., 1876, 1910–25.

Degrees BSc, MA, DSc Univ. Camb., 1876, 1891, 1891.

Publications *Books:* 1. *Studies and Exercises in Formal Logic* (1884); 2. *The Scope and Method of Political Economy* (1891, 1955).

Career Logician and political economist who first made his name with his textbook on logic, which remained much-used both because of the clarity of its exposition and its avoidance of mathematical symbolism. His influential methodological book on economics followed Marshall in somehow reconciling the historical and the abstract deductive method. He was the father of John Maynard Keynes and outlived his son.

Secondary Literature D. Dillard, 'Keynes, John Neville', *IESS*, 8.

KEYSERLING, Leon H.

Born 1908, Charleston, SC, USA.

Current Post Self-employed Cons, 1971–.

Past Posts Ass. Econ, Columbia Univ., 1931–3; Legislative Ass. Adviser, US Senator R. F. Wagner, 1933–7, 1937–46; Expert, US Senate Comm. Banking & Currency, 1935–7; Pres., Conf. Econ. US Housing Authority, 1937–46; Vice-Chairman, Chairman, US President's Council Econ. Advisers, 1946–9, 1949–53; Cons., US Congress, 1937–46, 1953–; Econ. Cons., Govts. France, India, Israel, and Puerto Rico, 1953–71.

Degrees BA Columbia Univ., 1928; LLB Harvard Law School, 1931; Hon. Dr Bus. Science, Bryant Coll., 1965; Hon. Dr Humane Letters, Univ. Missouri, 1978.

Offices and Honours Phi Beta Kappa, 1928; $10,000 Prize Pabst Employment Contest, 1944; Pres., Nat. Conf. Labor, Israel, 1969–73; Man-of-Year-Award, Amer. Jewish Congress; Hon. Faculty, Industrial Coll., Armed Forces, 1966–; Ed. Board, US Center Study of Presidency, 1980–.

Principal Fields of Interest 130 Economic Fluctuations; Forecasting; Stabilisation.

Publications *Books:* 1. *Progress or Poverty* (Conf. Econ. Progress, 1964); 2. *Achieving Nationwide Educational Excellence* (Conf. Econ. Progress, 1968); 3. *Taxation of Whom & for What?* (Conf. Econ. Progress, 1969); 4. *Wages, Prices and Profits* (Conf. Econ. Progress, 1971); 5. *The Coming Crisis in Housing* (Conf. Econ. Progress, 1972); 6. *The Scarcity School of Economics* (Conf. Econ. Progress, 1973); 7. *Full Employment Without Inflation* (Conf. Econ. Progress, 1975); 8. *'Liberal' and 'Conservative' National Money, Credit and Interest Rates; Their Gross Mismanagement by the Federal Reserve System* (Conf. Econ. Progress, 1981); 9. *Economic Policies and Their Consequences, 1919–1979* (Conf. Econ. Progress, 1980); 10. *How to cut Unemployment and end Inflation and Deficits by 1987* (Conf. Econ. Progress, 1983).

Principal Contributions During

more than half a century in public office and private consulting, my work has concentrated upon efforts to increase the economic security and, through real economic growth and improve income distribution, (coupled with full employment and reasonable price stability) to lift the real incomes and living standards of the American people. Throughout this effort, the primary lifelong influences upon my work have been my father, William Keyserling, my old teacher, Rexford Guy Tugwell, and my long-time employer, US Senator Robert F. Wagner.

KHAN, Mohsin Said

Born 1946, Lahore, Pakistan.
Current Post Adviser, Res. Dept., IMF, Washington, DC., USA, 1982–.
Past Posts Econ., IMF, 1972–8; Res. Fellow, LSE, 1975–6; Adviser, Central Bank Venezuela, 1975–6; Ass. Div. Chief, Ass. Dir. Res., IMF, 1978–81, 1981–2.
Degrees BA Punjab Univ., Lahore, Pakistan, 1966; BSc, PhD LSE,1969, 1975; MA Columbia Univ., 1971.
Offices and Honours Univ. Fellow, Columbia Univ., 1969–70; Student, Univ. London, 1971–2.
Editorial Duties Assoc. Ed., *JMCB*, 1980–, *Pakistan J. Appl. Econ.*, 1980–; Internat. Ed. Board *PDR*, 1980–.
Principal Fields of Interest 310 Domestic Monetary and Financial Theory and Institutions; 410 International Trade Theory; 430 Balance of Payments; International Finance.
Publications *Books:* 1. *The Dynamics of Money and Prices and the Role of Monetary Policy in Seacen Countries* (Seacen Res. Centre, 1980); 2. *Effects of Slowdown in Industrial Countries on Growth in Non-Oil Developing Countries* (with M. Goldstein), (IMF, 1982); 3. *The Macroeconomic Effects of Changes in Barriers to Trade and Capital Flows: A Simulation Analysis* (with R. Zahler), (UNECLA, 1982).
Articles: 1. 'Import and export demand in developing countries', *IMF Staff Papers*, 21(3), Nov. 1974; 2. 'The stability of the demand-for-money function in the United States', *JPE*,

82(6), Nov.–Dec. 1974; 3. 'A monetary model of balance of payments adjustment: the case of Venezuela', *J Mon E*, 2, July 1976; 4. 'Inflationary finance and the dynamics of inflation: Indonesia 1954–1972' (with B. Aghevli), *AER*, 67(3), June 1977; 5. 'The variability of expectations in hyperinflations', *JPE*, 85(4), Aug. 1977; 6. 'The supply and demand for exports: a simultaneous approach' (with M. Goldstein), *REStat*, 60(2), May 1978; 7. 'The demand for money and the term structure of interest rates' (with H. R. Heller), *JPE*, 87(1), Feb. 1979; 8. 'Dynamic stability in the Cagan model of hyperinflation', *Int ER*, 21(3), Oct. 1980; 9. 'Stabilization programs in developing countries: a formal framework' (with M. D. Knight), *IMF Staff Papers*, 28(1), March 1981; 10. 'Unanticipated monetary growth and inflationary finance' (with M. D. Knight), *JMCB*, 14(3), Aug. 1982.
Principal Contributions Research has focussed mainly on the theory and estimation of the demand for money and foreign trade relationships. In the money demand area, studied issues of parameter stability and proposed alternative methods for specifying and testing regression equations involving variable parameters. These approaches were utilised extensively in the modelling of the inflationary process, including hyperinflations. Work on estimating import and export functions for both developed and developing countries showed that price responsiveness was much larger than had earlier been thought. Recent research has been directed towards formulating small-scale open-economy models which integrate the real and monetary sectors through emphasising the role of monetary disequilibrium in the behaviour of key macroeconomic variables.

KINDLEBERGER, Charles Poor

Born 1910, New York City, NY., USA.
Current Post Ford Internat. Prof. Econ. Emeritus, MIT, 1976–, Vis. Prof. Econ., Brandeis Univ., Waltham, MA, 1983–4.

Past Posts Res. Econ., US Treasury Dept., 1936, Fed. Reserve Bank NY, 1936–9, Fed. Reserve Board, 1940–2; US Army, 1942–5; Econ., US Dept. State, 1945–8; Prof. Econ., MIT, 1948–76; Vis. Prof., Atlanta Univ., 1967–8, Inst. Advanced Stud., Univ. Princeton, 1977; Fellow Center Advanced Study Behavioral Science, Stanford, 1980; Gunnar Myrdal Prof. Econ., IIES, Stockholm, 1982.

Degrees BA Univ. Penn., 1932; MA, PhD Columbia Univ., 1934, 1937; Hon. Dr Univ. Paris, 1966, Univ. Ghent, 1971.

Offices and Honours Exec. Comm., Vice-Pres., Pres., Disting. Fellow, AEA, 1961–3, 1966, 1985, 1980; AAAS; Bernard Harms Prize, Inst. für Weltwirtschaft, Kiel, 1978.

Editorial Duties Ed. Board, *AER*, 1956–8.

Principal Fields of Interest 430 Balance of Payments, International Finance; 440 International Investment and Foreign Aid; 040 Economic History.

Publications *Books:* 1. *International Short-Term Capital Movements* (Columbia Univ. Press, 1937); 2. *Interational Economics* (Richard D. Irwin, 1953, 1973); 3. *Economic Growth in France and Britain, 1851–1950* (Harvard Univ. Press, 1964); 4. *The World in Depression, 1929–39* (Allen Lane, Penguin, 1973); 5. *Economic Response* (Harvard Univ. Press, 1978); 6. *Manias, Panics and Crashes* (Basic Books, 1978); 7. *International Money* (A&U, 1981); 8. *A Financial History of Western Europe* (A&U, 1984); 9. *Economic Laws and Economic History* (CUP, 1984); 10. *Multilateral Excursions* (MIT Press, 1984).

Articles: 1. 'Group behavior and international trade', *JPE*, 59, Feb. 1951; 2. 'The formation of single financial centers', *Princeton Studies in International Finance, No. 34* (Princeton Univ., 1974); 3. 'Keynesianism vs monetarism in eighteenth- and nineteenth-century France', *HOPE*, 12(4), Winter 1980; 4. 'The rise and fall of the United States in the world economy', in *The Business Cycle and Public Policy, 1929–80, Papers Submitted to the Joint Economic Committee, Congress of the United States* (US Govt. Printing

Office, 1980); 5. 'The life of an economist', *BNLQR*, 134, Sept, 1980.

Principal Contributions Textbook on international economics, now in sixth edn (with E. Despres and W. S. Salant). Developed theory of US as a bank, conducting international financial intermediation to provide world with liquidity. Interested in hierarchical structure of world financial system, with leading country as lender of last resource. Contributed to the theory of financial crises, their propagation and halting by last-resort lending. In addition, *Europe's Postwar Growth* applies the Lewis model of growth with unlimited supplies of labour to Europe after World War II. Currently engaged in work on a financial history of Western Europe.

KING, Mervyn Allister

Born 1948, Chesham, Buckinghamshire, England.

Current Post Prof. Econ., LSE, England, 1984–.

Past Posts Jr. Res. Officer, Dept. Appl. Econ., Univ. Fellow, St Johns Coll. Camb., 1969–73, 1973–6, 1972–77; Vis. Prof. Econ., Harvard Univ., 1982, MIT, 1983–4; Esmée Fairbairn Prof. Investment, Univ. Birmingham, 1977–84.

Degree BA Univ. Cambridge, 1969.

Offices and Honours Council, Exec. Comm., RES, 1981–; Richards Prize, King's Coll. Camb., 1969; Wrenbury Scholar, Stevenson Prize, Univ. Camb., 1969, 1970; Kennedy Scholar, Harvard Univ., 1971; Medal, Univ. Helsinki, 1982.

Editorial Duties Ed., *REStud*, 1978–83; Assoc. Ed., *J Pub E*, 1982–; Ed. Board, *J Ind E*, 1977–83; Ass. Ed., *EJ*, 1974–5.

Principal Fields of Interest 323 National Taxation.

Publications *Books:* 1. *Public Policy and the Corporation* (Chapman & Hall, 1977); 2. *The British Tax System* (with J. A. Kay), (OUP, 1978, 1983); 3. *Indexing for Inflation*, co-ed. (with T. Liesner), (Heinemann, 1975); 4. *The Taxation of Income from Capital: A Comparative Study of the US, UK,*

Sweden and W. Germany (with D. Fullerton, *et al.*), (Univ. Chicago Press, 1984).

Articles: 1. 'Taxation and investment incentives in a vintage investment model', *J Pub E*, 1, April 1972, repr. in *Aggregate Investment* (with J. F. Helliwell), (Penguin, 1976); 2. 'Taxation and the cost of capital', *REStud*, 41(1), Jan. 1974; 3. 'The UK profits crisis: myth or reality?', *EJ*, 85, March 1975; 4. 'Savings and taxation', in *Public Policy and the Tax System*, eds. G. A. Hughes and G. M. Heal (A&U 1980); 5. 'An econometric model of tenure choice and the demand for housing as joint decision', *J Pub E*, July 1980; 6. 'Corporate financial policy with personal and institutional investors' (with A. Auerbach), *J Pub E*, 17(2), July 1982; 7. 'Asset holdings and the life cycle' (with L. Dicks-Mireaux), *EJ*, 92, June 1982; 8. 'An index of inequality: with applications to horizontal equity and social mobility', *Em*, 51, Jan. 1983; 9. 'Welfare analysis of tax reforms using household data', *J Pub E*, 21(2), July 1983; 10. 'Taxation, portfolio choice and debt-equity ratios: a general equilibrium model' (with A. Auerbach), *QJE*, 98, Nov. 1983.

Principal Contributions Study of the economics of capital markets has been divided between economics departments and finance groups in business schools. Interaction between the two has been less than one might have hoped (as a glance at the references to each other's literature demonstrates). I see my own work as an attempt to bridge the gap between the two traditions of public and private finance. This was not my goal when I started research. After I took the Cambridge Tripos, Richard Stone invited me to join his Growth Project, a group concerned with the empirical analysis of the UK economy. My initial interest was in investment but this later broadened into a general concern with public policy and the capital market. Early papers related to dividends, investment, taxation, unanimity of shareholders and corporate financial policy, and culminated in my book *Public Policy and the Corporation*. The systematic analysis of the effects of taxa-

tion on corporate financial policy and investment decisions developed by Joseph Stiglitz and myself showed that the traditional view of the incidence of corporate taxation was inadequate. Financial policy was crucial in determining effective tax rates. This led to the so-called 'new view' of corporate taxation (associated with the names of Auerbach, Bradford and myself), according to which the differential taxation of dividends and capital gains was capitalised in lower stock market values with no consequence for the incentive to invest out of retained earnings. Empirical studies showed that effective tax rates on investment were much lower than previously thought, and that in the UK the tax was virtually non-existent. It is clear that many policies have effects rather different from those believed to result by the government that instituted them, a lesson reinforced by my experience as a member of the Meade Committee and co-author (with John Kay) of a book on *The British Tax System*, and that economic analysis can help to determine the climate of opinion within which policies are formed.

KISLEV, Yoav

Born 1932, Haifa, Israel.
Current Post Assoc. Prof. Agric. Econ., Hebrew Univ., Rehovot, Israel, 1974–.
Past Posts Lect., Hebrew Univ., 1966–73; Sr. Lect., 1973–6; Vis. Scholar, Econ. Growth Centre, Yale Univ., 1970–2; Vis. Assoc. Prof., Univ. Minnesota, 1978–9.
Degrees BSc (Agric.), MSc (Agric.) Hebrew Univ., 1960, 1961; PhD Univ. Chicago, 1965.
Principal Fields of Interest 710 Agriculture; 112 Economic Development Models; 431 Balance of Payments.
Publications *Books:* 1. *Agricultural Research and Productivity* (with R. E. Evenson), (Yale Univ. Press, 1975); 2. *An Economic Analysis of Flood Control Projects in the Hula Valley* (in Hebrew), (with B. Nadel and I. Nun), (Center for Agric. Econ. Res., 1975).
Articles: 1. 'Research and produc-

tivity in wheat in Israel' (with M. Hoffman), *J Dev Stud*, 14(2), Jan. 1978; 2. 'Economic aspects of selection in the dairy herd in Israel' (with U. Rabiner), *Australian J. Agric. Econ.*, 23, 1979; 3. 'Prices, technology and farm size' (with W. Peterson), *JPE*, 90(3), June 1982.

Principal Contributions My main interest has been the economics of technical change. I started by studying the diffusion of innovations in agriculture and developed the notion of an innovation cycle — from the better to the less skilled farmer. Later I worked (with R. E. Evenson) on the economics of agricultural research, both theoretically and empirically. My latest interest has been in the changing structure of the farm as a result of technical progress.

Also interested in inflation and balance of payment questions, I have attempted to apply the monetary approach to the balance of payments to Israel's experience.

KLEIN, Lawrence Robert

Born 1920, Omaha, NB, USA.
Current Post Benjamin Franklin Prof. Econ. and Fin., Univ. Penn., USA, 1968–.
Past Posts Res. Assoc., Cowles Commission, Univ. Chicago, 1947; Res. Assoc., NBER, 1948–50, Survey Res. Center, Univ. Michigan, 1948–50, 1948–54; Ass. Prof., Univ. Michigan, 1949–54; Oxford Inst. Stats., 1954–8; Prof., Univ. Penn., 1958–68; Vis. Prof., Univ. Osaka, 1960, Univ. Colorado, 1962, City Univ., NY, 1962–3, Hebrew Univ., 1964, Princeton Univ., 1964, Stanford Univ., 1966, Univ. Copenhagen, 1942; Ford Vis. Prof., Univ. Cal. Berkeley, 1968, Inst. Advanced Stud., Vienna, 1970, 1974; Cons., Canada Govt., 1947, UNCTAD, 1966, 1967, 1975, 1977, 1980; Fed. Res. Board, 1973, US President's Council Econ. Advisers, 1977–80.
Degrees BA Univ. Cal. Berkeley, 1942; PhD MIT, 1944; MA Univ. Oxford, 1957; Hon. degrees, DHC Bonn, 1974, LLD Michigan, 1977, Dr Hon Causis, Vienna, 1977, Villanon, 1978, Brussels, 1979, Paris, 1979; DSc

Elizabeth House, Univ. Oxford, 1981, Durham, 1981, Technion, Haifa, 1982, Nebraska, 1983.
Offices and Honours Phi Beta Kappa, 1942; Fellow, Pres., Em Soc, 1948, 1960; John Bates Clark medal, AEA, 1959; Member, AAAS, 1961, Amer. Philo. Soc., 1970, NAS, 1973; William Butler Award, 1975; Pres., EEA, 1975; Pres., AEA, 1977; Fellow, Nat. Assoc. Bus. Economists, 1979; Nobel Prize in Econ., 1980.
Editorial Duties Ed. Boards, *IER*, *Empirical Econ.*, *Em*.
Principal Fields of Interest 211 Econometric and Statistical Methods; 131 Economic Fluctuations; 132 Economic Forecasting.
Publications *Books:* 1. *The Keynesian Revolution* (Macmillan, 1947, 1966); 2. *Economic Fluctuations in the United States, 1921–1941* (Wiley, 1950); 3. *A Textbook of Econometrics* (Row, Peterson, 1953, 1974); 4. *An Econometric Model of the United States, 1929–1952* (with A. S. Goldberger), (Wiley, 1955); 5. *An Introduction to Econometrics* (Row, Peterson, 1962).
Articles: 1. 'Macroeconomics and the theory of rational behavior', *Em*, 14, April 1946; 2. 'Theories of effective demand and employment', *JPE*, 55, April 1947; 3. 'A comparison of eleven econometric models of the United States' (with G. Fromm), *AER*, 63(2), May 1973; 4. 'Research contributions of the SSRC-Brookings econometric model project — a decade in review', in *The Brookings Model*, eds. G. Fromm and L. R. Klein (N-H, 1975).
Principal Contributions Mathematical modelling of economic systems based on received economic doctrine, with empirical estimation from live data of the actual economy, application of estimated systems to problems of theoretical economic analysis and public policy, including cyclical studies, stochastic fluctuations, dynamic multiplier response, scenario analysis, and prediction. Models studied include developing and centrally planned economies, as well as industrial market economies, together with their international trade and financial interrelationships.
Secondary Literature R. J. Ball, 'L.

R. Klein's contributions to economics', *Swed JE*, 83(1), Jan. 1981, repr. in *Contemporary Economists in Perspective*, eds. J. J. Spiegel and W. J. Samuels (JAI Press, 1984).

KLOTEN, Norbert Wilhelm

Born 1926, Sinzig, Rhein, Germany. **Current Post** Pres., Landeszentralbank Baden-Württemberg, Stuttgart, W. Germany, Member, Central Bank Council, Deutsche Bundesbank, 1976–. **Past Posts** Prof. Econ., Univ. Tübingen, 1960–76; Scholarly Experts, Planning Staff, Fed. Chancellory, W. Germany, 1967–9; Chairman, German Council Econ. Experts, 1969–76. **Degrees** Diploma, Dr Rer. Pol., Univ. Bonn, 1948, 1951; Dr Rer. Pol.h.c., Univ. Karlsruhe, 1980; Hon. Prof. Econ., Univ. Tübingen, 1976. **Offices and Honours** Member Board, List Gesellschaft; Advisory Council, W. German Fed. Econ. Ministry; Kuratorium, Fritz Thyssen Foundation; Board Dirs., Adolf Weber Foundation, Assoc., Econ. and Social Res. Soc. of Social Politics, Internat. Inst. Public Fin. **Principal Fields of Interest** 031 History of Economic Thought; 311 Domestic Monetary and Financial Theory and Policy; 432 International Monetary Arrangements. **Publications** *Books:* 1. *Die Eisenbahntarife in Güterverkehr. Versuch einer theorethischen Grundlegung* (J. C. B. Mohr, P. Siebeck, 1959); 2. *Annual Reports, German Council of Economic Experts* (1969–76); 3. *Zur Entwicklung des Geldwertes in Deutschland. Wirtschaft und Gesellschaft 15*, (with J. H. Barth. K. H. Ketterer and R. Vollmer), (J. C. B. Mohr, P. Siebeck, 1980); 4. *Beiträge zur Geldtheorie und Geldpolitik* (with W. Krelle and M. Meier-Preschany), (Athanäum, 1980). *Articles:* 1. 'Wirtschaftswissenschaft: Methodenlehre, teil II', in *Handwörterbuch der Sozialwissenschaften* (Vandenhoek & Ruprecht, 1952); 2. 'Der Methodenpluralismus und das Verstehen', in *Systeme und Methoden in den Wirtschafts- und Sozialwissen-*

schaften. Erwin von Beckerath zum 75. Geburtstag, eds. N. Kloten, *et al.* (J. C. B. Mohr, P. Siebeck, 1964); 3. 'Utopie und Leitbild im wirtschaftspolitischen Denken', *Kyk*, 20, 1967; 4. 'Wissenschaftliche Erkenntnis — politische Entscheidung', *Verhandlungen auf der Arbeitstagung des Vereins für Sozialpolitik* (Gesellscaft für Sozialwissenschaften, 1977); 5. 'Wirtschaftsdemokratie — eine ordnungs-politische Alternative?', in *Die Demokratie im Spektrum der Wissenschaften*, ed. K. Hartmann (Freiburg, 1978); 6. 'Das Europäische Währungssystem, eine europa-politische Grundentscheidung in Rückblick', *Rheinisch-Westfälische Akademie der Wissenschaften*, 1980; 7. 'Theorien der Geldwirkungen, Geldversorgung und Notenbankpolitik', in *Obst/Hintner: Geld-, Bank- und Börsenwesen, 37. Völlig neu gestaltete Auflage*, eds. N. Kloten and J. H. von Stein (J. C. B. Mohr, P. Siebeck, 1980); 8. 'Zur "Endphase" des europäischen Währungssystems', in *Schriften des Vereins für Sozialpolitik*, 114 (Internat. Anpassungsprozesse, 1981); 9. 'Informationsbedarf der Wirtschaftspolitik', in *Schriften des Vereins für Sozialpolitik*, 126, (Info. Wirtschaft, 1982). **Principal Contributions** Contributions to the theory of economic order, the theory of transport, especially of railroad tariffs, major aspects of the history and the methods of economic thought, decision-making and planning in economic policy, and monetary and fiscal policy.

KMENTA, Jan

Born 1928, Prague, Czechoslovakia. **Current Post** Prof. Econ. and Stats., Univ. Michigan, MI, USA, 1973–. **Past Posts** Lect., Univ. New S. Wales, Australia, 1956–60; Lect., Univ. Sydney, 1960–3; Ass. Prof. Econ., Univ. Wisconsin, 1963–5; Assoc. Prof., Prof. Econ., Michigan State Univ., 1965–8, 1968–73; Vis. Prof., Univ. Bonn, 1971–2, 1979–80, Univ. N. Carolina, 1973, Univ. New S. Wales, 1979, Univ. Saarbrücken, W. Germany 1984. **Degrees** BEc Sydney Univ., 1955; MA, PhD Stanford Univ., 1959, 1964.

Offices and Honours Fellow, ASA, 1970–, Em Soc., 1980–; Alexander von Humboldt Prize, Fed. Republic Germany, 1979.

Editorial Duties Assoc. Ed., *JASA*, 1973–9, *REStat*, 1975–, *Metrika*, 1980–, *Stat. Hefte*, 1984–; Assoc. Book Rev. Ed., *JASA*, 1973–.

Principal Fields of Interest 211 Econometric Methods; 212 Econometric Models.

Publications *Books:* 1. *Elements of Econometrics* (Macmillan, 1971; transls., Spanish, Vicens Universidad, 1977, Portuguese, Editora Atlas, 1978); 2. *Evaluation of Econometric Models*, co-ed. (with J. B. Ramsey) (Academic Press, 1980); 3. *Large-Scale Macro-Econometric Models*, co-ed. (with J. B. Ramsey) (N-H, 1981).

Articles: 1. 'Some properties of alternative estimators of the Cobb-Douglas production function', *Em*, 32, Jan.–April 1964; 2. 'An econometric model of Australia, 1948–61', *AEP*, 5, Dec. 1966; 3. 'Formulation and estimation of Cobb-Douglas production function models' (with A. Zellner and J. Drèze), *Em*, 37, Oct. 1966, repr. in *Readings in Economic Statistics and Econometrics*, ed. A. Zellner (Little, Brown, 1968); 4. 'On estimation of the CES production function', *Int ER*, 8, June 1967; 5. 'Small sample properties of alternative estimators of seemingly unrelated regressions' (with R. F. Gilbert), *JASA*, 63, Dec. 1968; 6. 'Autonomous expenditures versus money supply: an application of dynamic multipliers' (with P. E. Smith), *RE Stat*, 55(3), Aug. 1973; 7. 'A general procedure for obtaining maximum likelihood estimates in generalized regression models' (with W. Oberhofer), *Em*, 42, May 1974; 8. 'The dynamics of household budget allocation to food expenditures' (with J. Benus and H. Shapiro), *REStat*, 58(2), May 1976; 9. 'On the problem of missing measurements in the estimation of economic relationships', in *Proceedings of the Econometric Society European Meeting 1979*, ed. E. G. Charatsis (N-H, 1981); 10. 'Ridge regression under alternative loss criteria' (with K. Lin), *REStat*, 64(3), Aug. 1982.

Principal Contributions Earlier work focussed mainly on formulation and estimation of production models and included the development of a simple approximation to the CES production function. Other efforts involved a construction and estimation of an econometric model of Australia, the purpose of which was to determine the economic effects of immigration. Later work dealt with a variety of theoretical and applied econometric problems in both micro and macro areas. The textbook, *Elements of Econometrics*, was designed for the second and further generations of the post-scientific-revolution students of economics whose mathematical sophistication was matched by few in the preceding generation. Most of the writing — and teaching — has been characterised by an emphasis on a careful and thoughtful specification of the *stochastic* properties of models, and by a strong attempt to avoid 'mindless mathematics' and to achieve simplicity through a systematic development of thought and a clarity of exposition.

KNAPP, George Friedrich*

Dates and Birthplace 1842–1926, Giessen, Germany.

Posts Held Head, Leipzig City Stat. Office; Teacher, Univ. Leipzig, 1867–74, Univ. Strassburg, 1874–1919.

Publications *Books:* 1. *Über die Ermittlung der Sterblichkeit aus den Aufzeichnungen der Bevölkerungsstatistik* (1868); 2. *Die neueren Ansichten über Moralstatistik* (1871); 3. *Theorie des Bevölkerungs-wechsels* (1874); 4. *Die Bauernbefreiung und der Ursprung der Landarbeiter*, 2 vols (1887); 5. *The State Theory of Money* (1905).

Career Statistician, economic historian and economic theorist whose first published work was a systematic theory of mortality measurement. He developed his application of mathematical methods to demographic problems in later publications. At Strassburg he switched his attention to agricultural history, identifying landed estates as a special form of capitalism. His final phase produced his controversial work on money which emphasised the role of the state in preserving the value of money.

Secondary Literature J. A. Schumpeter, 'Georg F. Knapp', *Ten Great Economists from Marx to Keynes* (OUP, 1951).

KNEESE, Allen V.

Born 1930, Fredricksburg, TX, USA.
Current Post Sr. Fellow, Resources for the Future, Washington, DC, 1978–.
Past Posts Royer Vis. Prof. Polit. Econ., Univ. Cal. Berkeley, 1971; Dir., Quality Environmental Program, Resources for the Future, 1967–74; Prof. Econ., Univ. New Mexico, 1974–8.
Degree PhD Indiana Univ., 1956.
Offices and Honours Member, US Commission Natural Resources, Chairman, Board Minerals and Energy, NAS, 1974–80, 1975–80; Pres., Assoc. Environmental and Resource Econs., 1978.
Principal Fields of Interest 721 Natural Resources.
Publications *Books:* 1. *Managing Water Quality: Economics, Technology, Institutions* (with B. T. Bower), (JHUP, 1968; transl., German, 1972); 2. *Economic Theory of Natural Resources* (with O. C. Herfindahl), (Charles E. Merrill, 1974); 3. *Pollution, Prices, and Public Policy* (with C. L. Schultze), (Brookings Inst., 1975; transl., Spanish, 1976); 4. *Economics and the Environment* (Penguin, 1976); 5. *Environmental Quality and Residuals Management: Report of a Research Program on Economic, Technological, and Institutional Aspects* (with B. T. Bower), (JHUP, 1979); 6. *Measuring the Benefits of Clean Air and Water* (Resources for the Future, 1984); 7. *Handbook of Natural Resources and Energy Economics*, co-ed. (with J. L. Sweeney), (N-H., 1984).
Articles: 1. 'Production, consumption, and externalities' (with R. Ayres), *AER*, 59(3), June 1969; 2. 'Environmental pollution: economics and policy', *AER*, 61(2), May 1971; 3. 'Natural resources policy 1975–1985', *JEEM*, 3(4), Dec. 1976; 4. 'Environment, health, and economics — the case of cancer' (with W. Schulze),

AER, 67(1), Feb. 1977; 5. 'The Southwest — a region under stress' (with F. L. Brown), *AER*, 68(2), May 1978.
Principal Contributions One of the first economists to undertake a sustained programme of research on environmental economics. Helped to establish this area as a legitimate field of economic enquiry which is now taught in most universities.

KNETSCH, Jack Louis

Born 1933, Kalamazoo, MI, USA.
Current Post Prof. Econ., Simon Fraser Univ., Burnaby, British Columbia, Canada, 1974–.
Past Posts Econ., Tennessee Valley Authority, 1956–61; Res. Assoc., Resources for the Future, Washington, DC, 1961–6; Prof. Econ., George Washington Univ., 1967–70; Sr. Staff Econ., US Council Environmental Quality, Washington, DC, 1970–1; Adviser, Malysia Govt., Harvard Univ. Devlp. Advisory Service, 1971–3; Fulbright Scholar, Vis. Prof., Univ. Newcastle, Australia, 1973; Vis. Prof., Univ. Toronto, 1977–8, Univ. New England, Australia, 1981, Oxford Univ., 1983.
Degrees BS (Soil Science), MS (Agric. Econ.) Mich. State Univ., 1955, 1956; MPA, PhD Harvard Univ., 1960, 1963.
Offices and Honours Pres., Western Regional Science Assoc.
Editorial Duties Ed. Board, *Land Econ*; Ed. Council, *Annals Regional Science*.
Principal Fields of Interest 722 Conservation and Pollution; 025 Social Choice.
Publications *Books:* 1. *Property Rights and Compensation: Compulsory Acquisitions and Other Losses* (Butterworths, 1983); 2. *Land Policy and Economic Development in Papua New Guinea* (with M. J. Trebilcock), (Inst. Nat. Affairs, 1981); 3. *Outdoor Recreation and Water Resources Planning* (Amer. Geophysical Union, 1974); 4. *Economics of Outdoor Recreation* (with M. Clawson), (JHUP, 1967, 1974).
Articles: 1. 'Outdoor recreation

demands and benefits', *Land Econ.*, 39, Nov. 1963; 2. 'The influence of reservoir projects on land values', *JFE*, 46, Feb. 1964; 3. 'On the economics of mass demonstrations: a case study of the November 1969 march on Washington' (with C. J. Cicchetti, A. M. Freeman and R. H. Haveman), *AER*, 61(4), Sept. 1971; 4. 'A recreation site demand and benefit model' (with F. J. Cesario), *Regional Stud.*, 1976; 5. 'Displaced facilities and benefit calculations', *Land Econ.*, 53, Feb. 1977; 6. 'Expropriation of private property and the basis for compensation' (with T. E. Borcherding), *Univ. Toronto Law J.*, 29, 1979; 7. 'Property rights, land use conflicts and compensation', *Canadian J. Agric. Econ.*, 1980; 8. 'Legal rules and the basis for evaluating economic losses', *Internat. Rev. Law and Econ.*, June 1984; 9. 'Some economic implications of matrimonial property rules', *Univ. Toronto Law J.*, 34, 1984; 10. 'Willingness to pay and compensation demanded: experimental evidence of an unexpected disparity in measures of value' (with J. A. Sinden), *QJE*, 99(3), Aug. 1984.

Principal Contributions One early study was among the first to use land value changes as an indirect measure of the benefit provided by an amenity resource. Further contributions have been made in the assessment of nonpecuniary values in such areas as recreation, environmental quality, and time devoted to household production. More recent work has centred on alternative techniques of assessing changes in economic welfare. This has included the issue of appropriate choice of bases for measurement as well as observed differences between them. Another major area of research has been the economic analysis of various legal rules and institutions. This has included compulsory acquisition, assignments of entitlements, compensation claims, matrimonial property and regulatory change.

KNIES, Karl*

Dates and Birthplace 1821–98, Marburg, Germany.

Posts Held Docent, Univ. Marburg, 1846; Prof. Politics, Univ. Freiburg, 1855; Dir., Board Educ., Baden, 1862–5; Prof., Univ. Heidelberg, 1865–96.

Degree Dr Univ. Marburg, 1846.

Publications *Books:* 1. *Die Statistik als selbständige Wissenschaft* (1850); 2. *Die Eisenbahnen und ihre Wirkungen* (1853); 3. *Die politische Ökonomie von geschichtlichen Standpunkte* (1853); 4. *Der Telegraph als Verkehrsmittel* (1857); 5. *Geld und Credit*, 3 vols, (1873–9, 1931).

Career Historical economist, whose early political involvement forced his exile in Switzerland after 1848. He returned to academic success at Freiburg and Heidelberg. His economics was essentially nationalistic and a source of his objection to the cosmopolitanism of the classical school. Knies was an able teacher and his Heidelberg seminar achieved a pre-eminent position in Austro-German economics.

Secondary Literature H. Kisch, 'Knies, Karl', *IESS*, 8.

KNIGHT, Frank Hyneman*

Dates and Birthplace 1885–1972, McLean County, IL, USA.

Posts Held Taught Univs. Cornell, Chicago, Iowa, (and again) Chicago, 1928–55.

Degrees BA Milligan Coll., 1911; BA, MA Univ. Tennessee, 1913; PhD Cornell Univ., 1916.

Offices and Honours Pres., Francis Walker Medal, AEA, 1950, 1957.

Publications *Books:* 1. *Risk, Uncertainty and Profit* (1921, 1965); 2. *The Economic Organisation* (1933, 1951); 3. *The Ethics of Competition* (1935); 4. *The Economic Order and Religion* (with T. W. Merriam), (1945); 5. *Freedom and Reform* (1947); 6. *The Ethics of Competition and Other Essays* (1951); 7. *On the History and Method of Economics* (1956); 8. *Intelligence and Democratic Action* (1960).

Career His published work is chiefly in article form and is usually concerned with clarifying some particular problem and assessing possible solutions. This remained at the level of analysis and he was loath to propose specific social reforms. His earliest and most fundamental contribution was a clarification of profit theory, developing the crucial distinction between risk and uncertainty. He then turned to capital theory and in the process launched a vigorous attack on the Austrian theory of capital. Other writings concern methodological and philosophical questions in relation to economics. His unwillingness to commit himself wholly to any single approach or answer deprived him of disciples but his deep effect on students and readers is well documented.

Secondary Literature J. M. Buchanan, 'Knight, Frank H.', *IESS*, 8.

KOMIYA, Ryutaro

Born 1928, Kyoto, Japan.
Current Post Prof. Econ., Univ. Tokyo, 1978–.
Past Posts Vis. Prof. Econ., Stanford Univ., 1964–5; Vice-Pres., Univ. Tokyo, 1981–3.
Offices and Honours Pres., Japan Assoc. Econ. Theory and Em, 1983.
Principal Fields of Interest 023 Microeconomics; 420 Trade Relations; 430 Balance of Payments.
Publications *Books:* (all in Japanese except 1) 1. *Postwar Economic Growth in Japan*, ed. (Univ. Cal. Press, 1966); 2. *International Economics* (with A. Amano), (Iwanami-Shoten, 1972); 3. *Theory of Corporate Finance* (with K. Iwata), (Nihon Keizai Shimbunsha, 1973); 4. *Studies on the Contemporary Japanese Economy* (Iwanami-Shoten, 1975); 5. *Studies in International Economics* (Iwanami-Shoten, 1975); 6. *Contemporary International Finance: Theory, History and Policy* (with M. Suda), (Nihon Keizai Shimbunsha, 1983).
Articles: 1. 'Monetary assumptions, currency depreciation and the balance of trade', *ESQ*, 17(2), Dec. 1966; 2. 'Non-traded goods and the pure theory of international trade', *Int ER*, 8(2), June 1967; 3. 'Economic growth and the balance of payments: a monetary approach', *JPE*, 77(1), Jan.–Feb. 1969; 4. 'Planning in Japan', in *Economic Planning East and West*, ed. M. Bornstein (Ballinger, 1975), repr. in *Comparative Economic Systems: Models and Cases*, ed. M. Bornstein (Richard D. Irwin, 1975); 5. 'Inflation in Japan' (with Y. Suzuki), in *World-wide Inflation: Theory and Recent Experience*, eds. L. Krause and W. S. Salant (Brookings Inst., 1977); 6. 'Is international co-ordination of national economic policies necessary?', in *Issues in International Economics*, ed. P. Oppenheimer (Oriel Press, 1980); 7. 'The officer in charge of economic affairs in the Japanese government' (with K. Yamamoto), *HOPE*, 13(3), Fall 1981; 8. 'Japan's macroeconomic performance since the first oil crisis' (with K. Yasui), *Carnegie-Rochester Conf. Series on Public Pol.*, 20, 1984.
Principal Contributions Analysis of various aspects of contemporary Japanese economy and policy issues. In international economics, monetary or general equilibrium approach to the balance of payments theory and the theory of direct investment. Recently, theoretical and historical analysis of developments in the yen-dollar exchange market. Japanese government's foreign exchange policies, and short-term capital movements under the floating exchange rate system since 1973.

KONDRATIEFF, Nikolai Dmitrievich*

Dates and Birthplace 1892–(?), Russia.
Posts Held Founder, Dir., Moscow Bus. Conditions Inst., 1920–8.
Offices and Honours Dep. Minister Food, Russian Provisional Govt., 1917.
Publications (all in Russian) *Books:* 1. *The World Economy and its Condition During and After the War* (1922); 2. *Major Economic Cycles* (1928, transl. English as *The Long Wave Cycle*, E. P. Dutton, 1984).
Articles: 1. 'The long waves in economic life', (1926), *REStat*, 17, pt. 2, Nov. 1935; 2. 'The major economic cycles', *The Review*, 4, Spring 1979.
Career Russian economist and statistician whose work on agricultural statistics included the devising of the

so-called 'peasant indices' of the products bought and sold by farmers. He was one of the authors of the first Soviet five-year plan for agriculture. His analysis of the phenomenon of 'long-cycles' (or as he called them, 'long-waves') is the work with which his name is most usually associated. Coming into conflict with official policies on the question of planning he was imprisoned and died at some unknown date in the 1930s.

Secondary Literature G. Garvy, 'Krondratieff, N. D.', *IESS*, 8; J. Schuman and D. Roseman, *The Kondratieff Wave* (World Publ., 1972); N. Jasny, *Soviet Economists of the 20s: Names to be Remembered* (CUP, 1972).

KOOPMANS, Tjalling C.*

Dates and Birthplace 1910–84, 's Graveland, The Netherlands.

Posts Held Res. Assoc., Cowles Comm., 1944–54; Assoc. Prof., Dir. Res., Cowles Commission, Prof. Econ., Univ. Chicago, 1946–8, 1948–54, 1948–55; Prof. Econ., Dir., Cowles Foundation Res. Econ., Prof. Emeritus Econ., Yale Univ., 1955–80, 1961–7, 1981–4; Frank W. Taussig Prof. Econ., Harvard Univ., 1960–1; Res. Scholar, Head of Methodology Project, Internat. Inst. Appl. Systems Analysis, Laxenberg, Austria, 1974; Vis. Prof., Univ. Cal. Irvine, 1980, 1981, 1982.

Degrees MA (Physics, Maths.) Univ. Utrecht, 1933; PhD Univ. Leiden, 1936; Hon. PhD Netherlands School Econ., 1964, Catholic Univ. Louvain, 1967; Hon. PhD (Science) Northwestern Univ., 1975; Hon. PhD (Law) Univ. Penn., 1976.

Offices and Honours Fellow, Vice-Pres., Pres., Council Member, Em Soc, 1940–84, 1949, 1950, 1966–71; Pres., AEA, 1978; Correspondent, Royal Netherlands Academy Sciences; Member, Amer. Math. Soc., Inst. Management Sciences, ORSA, AAAS, NAS, Math Programming Soc.; Chairman, Group Energy Modelers, Comm. Nuclear Alternative Energy System, Nat. Res. Council, 1976–8; Internat.

Assoc. Energy Economists, 1979; Nobel Prize in Econ., 1975.

Publications *Books:* 1. *Linear Regression Analysis of Economic Time Series* (Netherlands Econ. Inst., 1937); 2. *Tanker Freight Rates and Tankship Building* (Netherlands Econ. Inst., 1939); 3. *Statistical Inference in Dynamic Economic Models*, co-ed. (Yale Univ. Press, 1950); 4. *Activity Analysis of Production and Allocation*, co-ed. (Yale Univ. Press, 1951); 5. *Studies in Econometric Method*, co-ed. (Yale Univ. Press, 1953); 6. *Three Essays on the State of Economic Science* (McGraw-Hill, 1957); 7. *Scientific Papers of Tjalling C. Koopmans* (Springer-Verlag, 1970); 8. *Energy Modeling for an Uncertain Future* (with others), (NAS, 1978).

Career After an early interest in mathematical statistics and econometrics, he made his reputation by his application of linear programming techniques to transportation problems. The first of his *Three Essays ...* is a classic exposition of price theory in terms of 'activity analysis'. Subsequently, he worked on the choice of criteria for the allocation of resources over time with particular reference to the problem of exhaustible resources.

Secondary Literature L. Werin and K. G. Jugenfelt, 'Tjalling Koopmans' contribution to economics', *Scand JE*, 78(1), 1976; repr. in *Contemporary Economists in Perspective*, eds. H. W. Spiegel and W. J. Samuels, 1 (JAI Press, 1984).

KOOT, Ronald S.

Born 1937, Windber, PA, USA.

Current Post Prof. Management Science, Penn. State Univ., Univ. Park, PA, USA, 1973–.

Past Posts Ass. Prof. Quant. Bus. Analysis, Assoc. Prof. Management Science, Penn. State Univ., 1966–70, 1970–3.

Degrees BS Penn. State Univ., 1962; MA, PhD Univ. Oregon, 1967.

Offices and Honours Phi Kappa Phi; Beta Gamma Sigma; Omicron Delta Kappa; Nat. Leadership Soc.

Editorial Duties Assoc. Ed., *J. Fin. Res.*, 1980.

Principal Fields of Interest 211 Econometric and Statistical Methods and Models; 512 Managerial Economics; 310 Domestic Monetary and Financial Theory and Institutions.

Publications *Books:* 1. *Wage Determination and the Role of Wages in the Inflationary Process in Mexico and Chile* (Penn. State Univ., 1969); 2. *Analysis of Railroad Track Maintenance Expenditures for Class I Railroads, 1962–77* (with J. E. Tyworth, *et al.*), (Transportation Systems Center, US Dept. Transportation, 1980); 3. *Track Quality Measurement by Factor Analysis: An Exploratory Study* (with J. E. Tyworth), (Transportation Systems Center, US Dept. Transportation, 1984).

Articles: 1. 'Wages, unemployment and inflation in Chile', *ILRR*, 22(4), July 1969; 2. 'Short-run cost curves of a multi-product firm' (with D. A. Walker), *J Ind E*, 18(2), April 1970, repr. in *Readings in Managerial Economics*, eds. T. J. Coyne, W. W. Haynes and D. K. Osborne (Bus. Pub, 1977); 3. 'An analysis of income stability and the money supply, 1952–1968' (with D. A. Walker), *Appl. Econ.*, 3(1), Jan. 1971; 4. 'Rules versus authority: an analysis of income stability and the money supply 1952–68' (with D. A. Walker), *JMCB*, 6(2), May 1974; 5. 'Non-constant coefficients of expectation and recent demand for money', *J Mon E*, 1, Aug. 1975; 6. 'A factor analytic approach to an empirical definition of money', *J Fin*, 30(4), Sept. 1975; 7. 'The demand for credit union shares', *J Fin and Quant. Analysis*, 11(1), March 1976; 8. 'On the St. Louis equation and an alternative definition of money', *J Fin*, 32(3), June 1977; 9. 'On economies of scale in credit unions', *J Fin*, 33(4), Sept. 1978; 10. 'The determinants of railroad track maintenance expenditures: a statistical analysis' (with J. E. Tyworth), *Transportation J.*, 17(3), Autumn 1981.

Principal Contributions My original research interests lay in the area of applied econometrics, but, having conducted research in South America, I developed a parallel interest in problems of economic development. Thus the former interest led to papers on a firm's cost functions, on growth and market shares, on job flow-time models, and on firm performance evaluation by Pearson-curve fitting. The latter interest led to a series of articles on tests for demand-pull or wage-push inflation, income stabilisation models, and price expectations and monetary adjustments.

Because of the nature of the research topics in the development area, my interests evolved toward macroeconomic models of the US, and of US financial institutions. The result was a series of articles on income stability and the money supply, demand for money and non-constant coefficients of expectation, empirical definitions of money, the pricing of Federal Reserve services, the impact of monetary policy on lending by financial intermediaries, and economic analyses of credit unions. While maintaining interest in these research areas, most recently I have also become interested in the area of railroad transportation and related problems. This interest has led to studies and articles in such topic areas as railroad maintenance-of-way expenditures, construction of indexes of track performance capability, and the impact of general rail rate increases on penetration of Midwestern markets by Pacific coast lumber producers.

KORNAI, Janos

Born 1928, Budapest, Hungary.

Current Post Prof. Econ., Inst. Econ. Hungarian Academy Sciences, Budapest, Hungary, 1967–.

Past Posts Res. Assoc., Inst. Econ. Hungarian Academy Sciences, 1955–8; Head Econ. Res. Dept., Inst. Textile Industry, Budapest, 1958–63; Head Econ. Res. Dept., Computing Centre, Hungarian Academy Sciences, 1963–7; Vis. Prof., Univs., LSE, 1964, Sussex, 1966, Stanford, 1968, Yale, 1970, Princeton, 1971, Stanford, 1972–3, Stockholm, 1976–7; Member, Inst. Advanced Study, Princeton Univ., 1983–4.

Degrees Candidate Sciences, Dr

Sciences Hungarian Academy Science, 1956, 1966; Dr Econ., Karl Marx Univ. Econ., Budapest, 1961; Hon. Dr Univ. Paris, 1978, Univ. Posnan, Poland, 1978.

Offices and Honours Fellow, Pres., Em Soc, 1968, 1978; Hon. Member, AAAS, 1972; Corresp. Member, Ordinary Member, Hungarian Academy Sciences, 1976, 1982; Hon. Member, AEA, 1976; Corresp. Member, BA, 1978; Foreign Member, Royal Swedish Academy, 1980; Frank E. Seidman Disting. Award Polit. Econ., USA, 1982; Hungarian State Prize, 1983; Alexander von Humboldt Prize, W. Germany, 1983.

Editorial Duties Ed. Boards, *Közgazdasagi Szemle*, *Acta Oeconomica*, *J Ec Behav*, *WD*.

Principal Fields of Interest 020 General Economic Theory; 050 Economic Systems; 110 Economic Growth; Development, Planning Theory and Policy.

Publications *Books:* 1. *Overcentralization of Economic Administration* (OUP, 1959, Hungarian original, 1957); 2. *Mathematical Planning of Structural Decisions* (N-H, 1967, 1975, Hungarian orig., 1965, 1973; transls., Slovak, Slovenske Vydavatelstro Technickej Literatura, 1966, German, Wirtschaft, 1967, Polish, PWN, 1969); 3. *Anti-Equilibrium* (N-H, 1971, Hungarian orig., 1971; transls., Polish, PWN, 1973, 1977, Rumanian, Editura Stiintifica, 1974, German, Springer, 1975, Japanese, Nihonkezai Shinbusa, 1975, Serbo-Croatian, 1982); 4. *Rush versus Harmonic Growth* (N-H, 1972, Hungarian orig., 1972; transls., Czech, Ek. Ustav, 1977, Spanish, Saltes, 1977); 5. *Economics of Shortage* (N-H, 1980, Hungarian orig., 1980; transl., French, Economica, 1984); 6. *Non-Price Control*, co-ed. (with B. Martos), (N-H, 1981, Hungarian orig., Akademiai Kiado, 1981); 7. *Growth, Shortage and Efficiency* (Blackwell, Univ. Cal. Press, 1982, Hungarian orig., 1982); 8. *Economics of Anti-Equilibrium and Shortage* (in Japanese), (Nikon Hyoron, 1983); 9. *Ellentmondasok es dilemmak* (in Hungarian), (Magvetö, 1983).

Articles: 1. 'Two-level planning'

(with T. Liptak), *Em*, 33(1), Jan. 1965, repr. in Russian, *Primenenie Matematiki v Ekonomicheskiy Islodowaniah*, ed. V. S. Nemchinov (ISESL, 1965), and *Selected Readings in Economic Theory*, ed. K. J. Arrow (MIT Press, 1971), and in Hungarian, *MTA Matematikai Kutato Intezetenek Közlemenyei*, 7(4), 1962, and in Polish, *Biuletyn Wewnetrzny*, 13, 1963; 2. 'Multi-level programming — a first report on the model and the experimental computations', *Europ ER*, 1(2), 1969, repr. in Hungarian, *Közgazdasagi Szemle*, 15, (1–2), 1968; 3. 'Autonomous control of the economic system' (with B. Martos), *Em*, 41(3), May 1973, repr. in Hungarian, *Szigma*, 4, (1–2), 1971; 4. 'Decentralized control problems in Neumann-economies', *JET*, 14(1), Jan. 1977, repr. in Hungarian, *Szigma*, 8, (2–3, 4), 1975; 5. 'Resource-constrained versus demand-constrained systems', *Em*, 47(4), July 1979, repr. in Hungarian, *Közgazdasagi Szemle*, 25(9), 1978, in Japanese, *Nihon Dizai Shimbun*, 37, 1979, in Portuguese, *Etudos de Economia*, 1(2), 1981, in Estonian, *Sirp ja Vasar*, 20(22), 1981; 6. 'The dilemmas of a socialist economy: the Hungarian experience', *Camb JE*, 4(2), April 1980, repr. in Hungarian, *Valosag*, 23(5), 1980, in German, *Budapester Rundschau*, 14(29–32), 1980, in Polish, *Zycie Gospodarske*, 36(3), 1981, in Japanese, *Keizaihyron*, 11, 1981, in Estonian, *Sirp ja Vasar*, 41(48–9), 1981; 7. '"Hard" and "soft" budget constraint', *Acta Oecon.*, 25(2), 1980, repr. in Hungarian, *Gazdasag*, 13(4), 1980, in Portuguese, *Estudos de Economia*, 3(2), 1983; 8. 'Comments on the present state and the prospects of the Hungarian economic reform', *J Comp E*, 7(3), Sept. 1983, repr. in Hungarian, *Gazdasag*, 15(3), 1982; 9. 'The health of nations: reflections on the analogy between the medical science and economics', *Kyk*, 36(2), 1983, repr. in Hungarian, *Valosag*, 26(1), 1983; 10. 'Paternalism, buyer's and seller's market' (with J. W. Weibull), *Math. Social Sciences*, 5(6), 1983.

Principal Contributions First book written in 1955–6 was a critique of the overcentralised socialist system; one of the first works suggesting decentralisation reforms. In the late 1950s, I was among those initiating the use of mathematical methods in socialist planning. Elaborated the theory of two-level planning with T. Lipták and directed the first large-scale economy-wide multi-level planning project. Experiencing the limits of centralised planning based on the idea of the planner as *homo oeconomicus*, and finding that conventional economics inadequately explained contemporary socio-economic systems, led to an increasing interest in theoretical foundations. *Anti-Equilibrium* (1971), a controversial essay criticising Walrasian neoclassical economics, suggested new approaches to studying chronic non-Walrasian states, price- and non-price signals. In my personal intellectual development, this book was a preparation for the task that followed: enquiry into the nature of socialist systems. Unlike previous so-called theories of socialism or theories of planning which were in the normative domain, this inquiry shifted the focus of research to the positive aspects of existing socialist economies, discovering their regularities, appreciating their achievements, but also facing their systemic contradictions and inefficiencies. Issues like chronic shortage, forced growth, bureaucratisation, and conflicts between socialist principles and efficiency became the main concern. Extensive research on these topics was carried out in collaboration with a group of other economists, mainly Hungarians. The approaches applied included: (1) verbal formulation of general positive theories (e.g., theory of shortage); (2) formal mathematical models (e.g., models of non-price control, queuing, a seller's market, growth with chronic shortage, paternalism); (3) empirical testing of hypotheses (e.g., hypotheses concerning the phenomenon of a 'soft budget constraint' or non-standard supply and demand responses under chronic shortages).

KOSTERS, Marvin H.

Born 1933, Corsica, SDak, USA.
Current Post Res. Scholar, Dir. Govt. Regulation Stud., AEI, Washington, DC, USA, 1975–.
Past Posts Econ., Rand Corp., 1965–9; Sr. Staff Econ., US President's Council Econ. Advisers, 1969–71; Assoc. Dir. Econ. Pol., US Cost Living Council, 1971–4; Dep. Asst. US President, Econ. Affairs, White House, Washington, DC, 1974–5.
Degrees BA Calvin Coll., Grand Rapids, MI, 1960; PhD Univ. Chicago, 1966.
Offices and Honours Ingersoll Foundation Fellow, 1960–1; Earhart Foundation Fellow, 1962–3; Ford Foundation Fellow, 1964–5.
Editorial Duties Ed. Board, *Regulation, AEI Econ.*
Principal Fields of Interest 010 General Economics; 820 Labour Markets, Public Policy; 130 Economic Fluctuations, Forecasting and Inflation.
Publications *Books:* 1. *Controls and Inflation* (AEI, 1975); 2. *Reforming Regulation*, co-ed. (AEI, 1975).
Articles: 1. 'Effects of an income tax on labor supply', in *The Taxation of Income from Capital*, eds. A. C. Harberger and M. J. Bailey (Brookings Inst. 1969); 2. 'Income guarantees and the working poor: the effect of income maintenance programs on hours of work of male family heads' (with D. Greenburg), (Rand Corp. 1981), repr. in *Income Maintenance and Labor Supply: Econometric Studies*, eds. G. C. Cain and H. W. Watts (Markham, 1973); 3. 'The effects of minimum wages on the distribution changes in aggregate employment' (with F. Welch), *AER*, 57(3), June 1972, repr. in part in *Economics of Labor Relations*, ed. H. R. Northrup (Richard D. Irwin, 1972); 4. 'Collective bargaining settlements and the wage structure' (with K. Fedor and A. Eckstein), *Labor Law J.*, 24(8), Aug. 1973; 5. 'The nature of the inflationary process', in *Analysis of Inflation*, ed. P. H. Earl (D. C. Heath, 1975); 6. 'Relative wages and inflation', *Proceedings of the Thirtieth Annual Winter Meeting* (IRRA, 1978); 7. 'Counting the costs', *Regulation: AEI J.*

Govt. and Soc., 1979; 8. 'Government regulation', in *Toward a New Industrial Policy*, eds. M. L. and S. M. Wachter (Univ. Penn. Press, 1981); 9. 'Government regulation: an overview of developments and reform policies', in *The Political Economy of the United States* ed. C. Stoffaes (N-H, 1982); 10. 'Disinflation and the labor market', in *Contemporary Economic Problems*, ed. W. J. Fellner (AEI, 1984).

Principal Contributions My initial research on labour supply issues was followed by research on economic aspects of nuclear poliferation (resource requirements for development of nuclear weapons capabilities). During a period of service with the federal government the main focus of policy analysis was, first, on labour market analysis and inflation, and second, on wage and price controls and related government policies intended to restrain inflation. More recently I have maintained an interest in labour market developments, how labour costs have been influenced by changes in competitive conditions, and relationships between inflation and labour costs trends. I have also studied issues in the analysis and management of government regulation and developed research projects to analyse government regulatory policy and evaluate the performance of regulatory programmes.

KOTLIKOFF, Laurence J.

Born 1951
Current Post Prof. Econ., Boston Univ., Boston, MA, 1984–.
Past Posts Cons., US Dept. Labor, Bureau Internat. Labor Affairs, 1978–81; Post-doctoral Fellow, UCLA, 1977–80; Res. Assoc., Vis. Scholar, NBER, 1977–, 1978, 1983; Assoc., Cowles Foundation, Ass. Prof., Assoc. Prof., Yale Univ., 1980–, 1980–1, 1981–4; Sr. Econ., US President's Council Econ. Advisers, 1981–2; Res. Vis., IMF, 1983.
Degrees BA Univ. Penn., 1973; MA, PhD Harvard Univ., 1976, 1977.
Offices and Honours Phi Beta Kappa, 1977; Harvard Univ. Scholar, 1977; Student Intern, Internat. Fin.;

Board Governors, Fed. Reserve System, 1975; Hoover Foundation Fellow, 1976–7; Foundation Res. Econ., 1977–80.
Editorial Duties Assoc. Ed., *AER*, 1981–4.
Principal Fields of Interest 915 Social Security.
Publications *Books:* 1. *Pensions in the American Economy* (with D. Smith), (Univ. Chicago Press, 1983). *Articles:* 1. 'Testing the theory of social security and life cycle accumulation', *AER*, 69(3), June 1979; 2. 'Social security and equilibrium capital intensity', *QJE*, 93(2), May 1979; 3. 'The family as an incomplete annuities market' (with A. Spivak), *JPE*, 89(3), April 1981; 4. 'The role of intergenerational transfers in aggregate capital formation' (with L. Summers), *JPE*, 89(4), Aug. 1981; 5. 'The adequacy of savings' (with L. Summers and A. Spivak), *AER*, 72(5), Dec. 1982; 6. 'The efficiency gains from dynamic tax reform' (with A. Auerbach and J. Skinner), *Int ER*, 24, May 1983; 7. 'National savings, economic welfare and the structure of taxation' (with A. Auerbach), in *Behavioral Simulation Methods in Tax Policy Analysis* (Univ. Chicago Press, 1983); 8. 'Savings versus investment incentives — the size of the bang for the buck and the potential for self-financing business tax cuts' (with A. Auerbach), in *The Economic Consequences of Government Deficits*, ed. L. H. Meyer (Kluwer Nijhoff, 1983); 9. 'Taxation and savings — a neoclassical perspective', *JEL*, 22(4), Dec. 1984; 10. 'Annuity markets, savings, and the capital stock' (with J. Shoven and A. Spivak), in *Pensions and Retirement in the United States* (Chicago Univ. Press, 1985).

KOUTSOYIANNIS, Anna

Born 1932, Athens, Greece.
Current Post Prof. Econ., Univ. Ottawa, Ont., Canada, 1983–.
Past Posts Lect., Univ. Manchester, 1960–2; Lect., Grad. School Bus. Stud., Athens, 1962–4; Ass. Prof., Assoc. Prof., Univ. Thessaloniki, Greece, 1964–5, 1965–8; Sr. Lect.,

Reader Econ. and Em., Univ. Lancaster, 1968–73, 1974–5; Prof., Univ. Waterloo, Waterloo, Ont., Canada, 1975–83.

Degrees BA Athens School Econ., 1954; PhD Univ. Manchester, 1962.

Offices and Honours Disting. Student Award, Athens School Econ., 1954; Disting. Teacher Award, Univ. Waterloo, 1978.

Editorial Duties Assoc. Ed., *J. Forecasting*, 1983–.

Principal Fields of Interest 022 Microeconomic Theory; 211 Econometric and Statistical Methods and Models; 611 Industrial Organisation and Market Structure.

Publications *Books:* 1. *An Econometric Study of the Leaf Tobacco Market of Greece* (Papadimitropoulos Press, 1963); 2. *Production Functions of the Greek Manufacturing Industry* (Center Planning and Econ. Res., 1964); 3. *Theory of Econometrics* (Macmillan, 1973, 1977); 4. *Modern Microeconomics* (Macmillan, 1975, 1979; transl., Italian, Etas Libri, 1981); 5. *Non-Price Decisions: The Firm in a Modern Context* (Macmillan, 1982).

Articles: 1. 'Demand functions for tobacco', *MS*, 33(1), Jan. 1963; 2. 'Managerial job security and the capital structure of firms', *MS*, 46(1), March 1978; 3. 'The impact of multinational corporations on prices and costs in host-country markets: the case of Canadian manufacturing industry', *Econ. Int.*, 34(4), Nov. 1981; 4. 'A short-run pricing model for a speculative asset, tested with data of the gold bullion market', *Appl. Econ.*, 15(5), Oct. 1983; 5. 'Goals of oligopolistic firms: an empirical test of competing hypothesis', *SEJ*, 5(4), April 1984.

Principal Contributions Major contributions have been the simplification of econometric techniques, and the propagation of recent developments in the field of the theory of the firm. First publication dealt with applications of econometric methods to particular microeconomic aspects (demand, supply, production). Concerned with the complexity of presentation of econometric techniques in established textbooks, I wrote *Theory of Econometrics* using summations instead of

linear algebra, thereby rendering the powerful tools of econometrics accessible to professional economists and students of economics who are averse to mathematics and statistics. In later years, I became increasingly preoccupied with the content of standard microeconomics textbooks, which largely ignore the changed economic conditions of the countries of the Western world, dominated as they are by large oligopolistic conglomerates. In *Modern Microeconomics* and *Non-Price Decisions*, oligopoly is treated as the general case rather than the exception in the contemporary business world. Students of economics are exposed to the recent developments on the oligopoly front, thus being equipped with knowledge that will hopefully enable them to contribute to the solution of current economic problems. Recent research involves tests of alternative hypotheses regarding the goals of firms, assessment of some economics effects of multinational corporations, and development of a novel approach to the measurement of risk.

KRAVIS, Irving Bernard

Born 1916, Philadelphia, PA, USA.

Current Post Prof. Econ., Univ. Penn., Philadelphia, PA, USA, 1961–.

Past Posts Ass. Prof., Assoc. Prof. Econ., Univ. Penn., 1949–61; Assoc. Dean, Wharton School, Univ. Penn., 1958–60; Res. Staff, NBER, 1962–; Dir., UN Internat. Comparison Project, 1968–82; Cons., OECD, US Dept. State, US Dept. Labor, Fed. Reserve Board, World Bank, UN.

Degrees BS, MA, PhD Univ. Penn., 1938, 1939, 1949.

Offices and Honours Guggenheim Foundation Fellow, 1967–8; Fellow, Em Soc, 1979; AAAS, 1978; Ford Foundation Faculty Res. Fellow, 1960–1; Fellow, Amer. Assoc. Advancement Science, 1984; Council, IARIW, 1975–83.

Editorial Duties Chairman, Comm. Publications, *AEA*, 1962–5.

Principal Fields of Interest 227 Prices; 226 Productivity and Growth; 421 Trade Relations.

Publications *Books:* 1. *An International Comparison of National Products and the Purchasing Power of Currencies* (with M. Gilbert), (OEEC, 1954); 2. *Price Competitiveness in World Trade* (with R. Lipsey), (NBER, 1971); 3. *A System of International Comparisons of Gross Product and Purchasing Power* (with Z. Kenessey, A. Heston and R. Summers), (JHUP, 1975); 4. *International Comparisons of Real Product and Purchasing Power* (with A. Heston and R. Summers), (JHUP, 1978); 5. *World Product and Income: International Comparisons of Real Gross Product* (with A. Heston and R. Summers), (JHUP, 1982).

Articles: 1. 'The location of overseas production and production for export by US multinational firms' (with R. Lipsey), *J Int E*, 21(3/4), May 1982; 2. 'The share of services in economic growth' (with A. Heston and R. Summers), in *Global Econometrics: Essays in Honor of Lawrence R. Klein*, eds. F. G. Adams and B. Hickman (MIT Press, 1983); 3. 'Price behavior in the light of balance of payments theories' (with R. Lipsey), *J Int E*, 17(3), May 1978; 4. 'Towards an explanation of national price levels' (with R. Lipsey), *Princeton Stud. in Internat. Fin.*, 52, Nov. 1983; 5. 'Comparative studies of national income and prices', *JEL*, 22(1), March 1984.

Principal Contributions Much of my work has dealt with comparative economic structures, particularly of quantities and prices. I have also been interested in the role of prices in international trade and in the role of multinational enterprises in world trade. A large part of the comparative economic structure work was represented by two major projects aimed at international comparisons of GDP and of the purchasing power of currencies. The first was the comparisons involving developed European countries carried out at the OECD and resulting in the Gilbert-Kravis volume. The second was the UN International Comparison Project which I directed through the first three phases starting in 1968 and ending in 1982. This resulted in three reports and a number of papers authored jointly with A. Heston and R. Summers. The methodology of such comparisons was established and comparisons made for 34 varied countries with means of extending the results to other countries worked out. Also, in conjunction with Heston and Summers and with R. Lipsey, a start has been made in exploring the substantive content of the data. The comparisons open up the possibility, for example, of investigating differences in the level of prices, work that I have started in collaboration with Lipsey. In the trade field, I produced some early studies of US trade patterns showing that US exports depended to a substantial extent on successive innovations. Later, my work concentrated more on the role of prices. Both the GDP price comparisons and those made in connection with trade flows indicate a diversity of prices and pricing practices even for similar or highly competitive goods. The explanation of these differences in prices remains on the agenda for research.

KREGEL, Jan Allen

Born 1944, Dallas, TX, USA.
Current Post Prof. Econ. Special Reference Monetary Theory, Univ. Groningen, The Netherlands, 1982–.
Past Posts Lect. Econ., Univ. Bristol, 1969–72; Chargé de cours invité, Prof. invité, Univ. Catholique de Louvain, Belgium, 1972–3, 1974; Prof. Incaricato, Univ. Bologna, 1973; Lect., Sr. Lect., Univ. Southampton, 1973–9; Prof. Econ., Livingston Coll., New Brunswick, NY, 1977–81; Adjunct Prof. Monetary Theory, New School Social Res., NY, 1978–80; Vis. Res. Prof., Inst. Econ., Univ. Rome, 1982; Netherlands–Germany Cultural Exchange Prof., Univ. Bremen, 1982.
Degrees BA Beloit Coll., WI, 1966; PhD Rutgers Univ., 1970.
Editorial Duties Ed. Boards, *J Post Keyn E*, 1977–, *Metroec.*, 1983–, *Monnaie et Production series*, *Economies et Sociétés*, 1983–.
Principal Fields of Interest 020 General Economic Theory; 030 History of Economic Thought; Method-

ology; 310 Domestic Monetary and Financial Theory and Policy.

Publications *Books:* 1. *Rate of Profit, Distribution and Growth: Two Views* (Macmillan, Aldine, 1971; partially transl., French, 1974); 2. *The Theory of Economic Growth* (Macmillan, 1972; transls., Italian, Spanish, Greek and Turkish); 3. *The Reconstructions of Political Economy* (Macmillan, Halsted, 1973, 1975); 4. *Theory of Capital* (Macmillan, 1976; transls., Italian, Spanish, Greek, and Turkish); 5. *Distribution, Effective Demand, and International Economic Relations*, ed. (Macmillan, 1983).

Articles: 1. 'Economic methodology in the face of uncertainty: the modelling methods of Keynes and the post-Keynesians', *EJ*, 86, June 1976; 2. 'On the existence of expectations in English neo-classical economics', *JEL*, 15(2), June 1977; 3. 'Economic dynamics and the theory of steady growth: an historical essay on Harrod's knife-edge', *HOPE*, 12(1), Spring 1980; 4. 'I fondamenti Marshalliani del principio della domanda effettiva di Keynes', *Giornale degli Economisti e Annali di Econ*, March–April, 1980; transl., Japanese, *Keizai Hyoron*, April 1981; 5. 'Markets and institutions as features of a capitalistic production system', *J Post Keyn E*, 3(1), Fall 1980; 6. 'Money, expectations and relative prices in Keynes' monetary equilibrium', *Econ App*, 36(3), 1982; 7. 'Microfoundations and Hicksian monetary theory', *DE*, 130(4), 1982; 8. 'Terms of trade and Italian economic growth: accounting for miracles' (with E. Grilli and P. Savona), *BNLQR*, 35, Dec. 1982; transl., Italian, *Moneta e Credito*, 140, Dec. 1982; 9. 'The microfoundations of the "generalisation of the general theory" and "bastard Keynesianism"': Keynes theory of employment in the long and short period', *Camb JE*, 7(3–4), Sept.–Dec. 1983; 10. 'Effective demand — origins and development of the notion', in *Distribution, Effective Demand and International Economic Relations*, *op. cit.*

Principal Contributions Study of Keynes's economics and subsequent exposure to the Anglo-Italian theories of value and distribution in Cambridge in the 1960s created an interest in the possibilities for an integration of Keynes's theory of monetary production and these new explanations of value and distribution. Early work on the reconstruction of political economy attempts to formulate a coherent framework for economic analysis on the basis of the work of Keynes, Kalecki, and the classical economists, which has come to be called the 'post-Keynesian' approach. Response to this work made it clear that Keynes's monetary theory should be made more explicit. Recent work attempts to provide an explanation of the level of activity presumed in Sraffa's theory of prices and distribution via Keynes's theory of effective demand in a monetary production framework. I have investigated the compatibility of Sraffa's commodity rates of interest, which in equilibrium yield Sraffa prices, and Keynes's theory of money prices based on own rates of own interest, which in equilibrium equal the money rate of interest as established by liquidity preference.

KREININ, Mordechai E.

Born 1930, Tel Aviv, Israel.

Current Post Prof. Econ., Michigan State Univ., East Lansing, MI, USA, 1961–.

Past Posts Ass. Study Dir., Study Dir., Survey Res. Center, Univ. Michigan, 1954–5, 1955–7; Lect. Econ., Ass. Prof., Assoc. Prof., Univ. Michigan, 1956–7, 1957–9, 1959–61; Vis. Prof., Univs. UCLA, 1969, Southern Cal., 1974, NYU, 1975, Hawaii, 1977, Toronto, 1978, British Columbia, 1983; Special Adviser, UNCTAD, Geneva, 1971–5; Res. Cons., IMF, Washington, 1976; Vis. Scholar, Inst. Internat. Econ. Stud., Univ. Stockholm, 1978–81.

Degrees BA Tel Aviv Univ., 1951; MA, PhD Univ. Michigan, 1952, 1955.

Offices and Honours Horace H. Rackham Pre-doctoral Fellow, Univ. Michigan, 1954; Phi Kappa Phi; Phi Beta Kappa; Faculty Res. Fellow, US SSRC, 1959; Ford Foundation Faculty Res. Fellow, 1960–1; Research Fellow, Israel's Technical Aid Africa and Asia,

1961–2; Rockefeller Foundation Fellow, 1966; Nat. Science Foundation Fellow, 1967; Golden Key, Nat. Scholastic Soc.; Disting. Faculty Award, Michigan State Univ., 1968; Faculty Award, Michigan Assoc. Governing Boards, 1984.

Principal Fields of Interest 410 International Trade Theory; 420 Trade Relations; 430 Balance of Payments; International Finance.

Publications *Books:* 1. *Israel and Africa: A Study in Technical Cooperation* (Praeger, 1964); 2. *Alternative Commercial Policies — Their Effects on the American Economy* (Michigan State Univ. Bureau Bus. Econ. Res., 1967); 3. *International Economics — A Policy Approach* (Harcourt, Brace Jovanovich, 1971, 1983). 4. *Trade Relations of the EEC — An Empirical Investigation* (Praeger, 1974); 5. *The Monetary Approach to the Balance of Payments: A Survey* (with L. H. Officer), (Internat. Fin. Section, Princeton Univ., 1978); 6. *Economics* (Prentice-Hall, 1983).

Articles: 1. 'Factors associated with stock ownership', *REStat*, 41, Feb. 1959; 2. 'European integration and American trade', *AER*, 49(4), Sept. 1959; 3. 'Effect of tariff changes on the prices and volume of imports', *AER*, 51(3), June 1961; 4. 'On the dynamic effects of a customs union', *JPE*, 72, April 1964; 5. 'Freedom of trade and capital movements', *EJ* 75, Dec. 1965; 6. 'Israel and the EEC', *QJE*, 82, May 1968; 7. 'Disaggregated import demand functions', *SEJ*, 40(1), July 1973; 8. 'A new international economic order? — a critical survey of the issues' (with others), *J. World Trade Law*, Dec. 1976, repr. in *World Trade and Payments*, ed. B. Belassa (W. W. Norton, 1978), and *International Business — 1977*, ed. D. Hanley (Michigan State Univ. Bus. Econ. Res., 1977); 9. 'Determinants of international trade flows' (with D. Warner), *REStat*, 65(1), Feb. 1983; 10. 'Wage competitiveness in steel and motor vehicles', *EI*, Jan. 1984.

Principal Contributions Early work centred on utilising data from the Survey Research Center to glean insights into consumer behaviour in a variety of economic areas. Concommitantly, several papers were published on the Israeli economy. At a subsequent stage, most of my work shifted to international economics (broadly conceived), with several major forays into such areas as taxes, macroeconomics, and university finances. Within international economics, contributions were made in the following areas: the theory and empirical measurement of regional integration; tariff theory and measurement of its effects; balance of payments theory; import-demand functions and their measurements; testing (empirically) various trade theories, including comparative cost and the H–O model; theoretical and policy issues in the trade-development nexus; the trade-capital movement nexus; foreign investments; international liquidity; the theory and measurement of price elasticities; the equivalence of tariffs and quotas; optimum currency areas; effective protection; preferences and reverse preferences; new international economic order; technical assistance to LDCs; institutional arrangements in international trade and finance; the transfer problem; exchange-rate changes and their effects; trade liberalisation; comparative advantage measurement in autos and steel; and the monetary approach to the balance of payments.

KRUEGER, Anne O.

Born 1934, Endicott, NY, USA.

Current Post Vice-Pres., Econ. and Res., World Bank, Washington, DC., USA, 1982.

Past Posts Fellow, Teaching Ass., Ford Foundation Doctoral Dissertation Fellow, Instr., Univ. Wisconsin, 1955–6, 1956–7, 1957–8, 1958–9; Ass. Prof., Assoc. Prof. Econ., Univ. Minnesota, 1959–63, 1963–6, 1966–82; Vis. Prof., Monash Univ., 1973–4, Centre Pol. Stud., Clayton, Australia, 1973, 1976, 1978, 1981, ANU, 1977, Northwestern Univ., 1977, Univ. Aarhus, Denmark, 1979, Univ. Paris, 1980, Inst. Internat. Econ. Stud., Industrial Inst. Econ. Social Res., Stockholm, 1982, Univ. Maryland Coll. Park, 1983.

Degrees BA Oberlin Coll, 1953; MS, PhD Univ. Wisconsin, 1956, 1958.

Offices and Honours Pres., Minnesota Econ. Assoc., 1971–2, MEA, 1974–5; Vice-Pres., AEA, 1977–8; Fellow, Em Soc., 1981, AAAS, 1983; Robertson Award, NAS, 1984.

Editorial Duties Ed. Board, *JEL*, 1973–6; Book Rev. Ed., Assoc. Ed., *J Int E*, 1973–6, 1980; Cons. Ed., *Portfolio*, 1974–82; Ed. Boards, *Econ. Letters*, 1979–, *PDR*, 1979–, *AER*, 1980–1; Co-ed., Devlp. Series (JHUP, 1981–2).

Principal Fields of Interest 123 Comparative Economic Studies; International Statistical Comparisons; 410 International Trade Theory; 421 Trade Relations.

Publications *Books:* 1. *Foreign Trade Regimes and Economic Development: Turkey* (Columbia Univ. Press, 1974); 2. *The Benefits and Costs of Import Substitution in India: A Microeconomic Study* (Univ. Minnesota Press, 1975); 3. *Trade and Development in Korea*, co-ed. (with W. Hong), (Korea Devlp. Inst., 1975); 4. *Growth, Distortions and Patterns of Trade Among Many Countries* (Princeton Stud. Internat. Fin., Princeton Univ., 1977); 5. *Foreign Trade Regimes and Economic Development: Liberalization Attempts and Consequences* (Ballinger, 1978); 6. *The Developmental Role of the Foreign Sector and Aid* (Harvard Univ. Press, 1979, 1982); 7. *The Developmental Role of the Foreign Sector and Aid. Studies in the Modernization of the Republic of Korea: 1945–75* (Harvard Univ. Press, 1979, 1982); 8. *Trade and Employment in Developing Countries, 3: Synthesis and Conclusions* (Univ. Chicago Press, 1983); 9. *Exchange Rate Determination* (CUP, 1983).

Articles: 1. 'Problems and prospects of the international economy for the 1980s', *Ejecutivos de Finanzas*, April 1980; 2. 'Protectionist pressures, imports and employment in the United States', *Scand JE*, 82(2), 1980; 3. 'The political economy of the rent-seeking society', *AER*, 64(3), June 1974, repr. in *Towards a Theory of the Rent-seeking Society*, eds. J. Buchanan, R. Tollison and G. Tullock (Texas A&M Univ. Press, 1980); 4. 'Loans to assist

the transition to outward-looking policies', *The World Economy*, 4(3), Sept. 1981; 5. 'Opening up: the case for cutting tariffs and eliminating quotas', *Econ. Papers*, 68, Oct. 1981; 6. 'Alternative trade strategies and employment in LDCs: an overview,' *PDR*, 20(3), Autumn 1981; 7. 'An empirical test of the infant industry argument' (with B. Tuncer), *AER*, 72(5), Dec. 1982; 8. 'Growth of factor productivity in Turkish manufacturing industries' (with B. Tuncer), *JDE*, 11(3), Dec. 1982; 9. 'Analyzing disequilibrium exchange-rate systems in developing countries', *WD*, 10(12) Dec. 1982; 10. 'Protectionism, exchange rate distortions and agricultural trading patterns', *AJAE*, 65, Dec. 1983.

Principal Contributions My early work was focussed on international trade and payments theory and its relevance for the understanding of the international economy. This led to asking how much of income differentials were accounted for by differences in factor endowments, whether racial discrimination could be explained in terms of a trade model and how highly restrictionist trade regimes really functioned. This led, first, to the effort to quantify domestic resource costs, and second, to a concern with the broader costs of individual restrictions, encompassed in part by the concept of rent-seeking. An opportunity to analyse the Korean experience with trade and growth then led to questions about that interrelationship, on which I continue to work.

KRUTILLA, John Vasil

Born 1922, Tacoma, WA, USA.

Current Post Sr. Fellow, Resources for the Future, Washington, DC, USA, 1975–.

Past Posts Industrial Econ., Principal Econ., Tennessee Valley Authority, 1952–4, 1954–5; Fellow, Assoc. Dir., Water Resources Program, 1955–7, 1960–7; Dir., Natural Environments Program, Resources for the Future, 1968–75.

Degrees BA Reed Coll., 1949; MA,

PhD Harvard Univ., 1951, 1952; Hon. LLD Reed Coll., 1978.

Offices and Honours Phi Beta Kappa; Vice-Pres., Pres., Assoc. Environmental and Resource Econs., 1978, 1980; Amer. Motors Conservation Award, 1977; Governing Council, Treasurer, Wilderness Soc., 1973–6; Board Dirs., Environmental Defense Fund, 1971–4; Public Member, Comm. Educ. Pol., Soc. Amer. Foresters, 1977–.

Editorial Duties Ed. Board, *JEEM*.

Principal Fields of Interest 721 Natural Resource Economics; 024 Welfare Theory.

Publications *Books:* 1. *Multiple Purpose River Development Studies in Applied Economics Analysis* (with O. Eckstein), (JHUP, 1958); 2. *The Columbia River Treaty: The Economics of an International River Basin Development* (JHUP, 1967; transl. Czech, 1969); 3. *Natural Environments: Studies in Theoretical and Applied Analysis*, ed. (JHUP, 1972); 4. *The Economics of Natural Environments: Studies in the Valuation of Commodity and Amenity Resources* (with A. C. Fisher), (JHUP, 1975); 5. *The Structure and Properties of a Wilderness Travel Simulator* (with V. K. Smith), (JHUP, 1976); 6. *The Regional Economic and Fiscal Impacts of Energy Resource Development: A Case Study of Northern Great Plains Coal* (with A. C. Fisher), (JHUP, 1978); 7. *Water Rights and Energy Development in the Yellowstone River Basin: An Integrated Analysis* (with C. M. Boris), (JHUP, 1980); 8. *Explorations in Natural Resource Economics* (with V. K. Smith), (JHUP, 1982).

Articles: 1. 'Criteria for evaluating regional development programs', *AER*, 45(2), May 1955; 2. 'Welfare aspects of benefit-cost analysis', *JPE*, 69(3), June 1961; 3. 'Unemployment, excess capacity and benefit-cost investment criteria' (with R. H. Haveman), *REStat*, 49, Aug. 1967; 4. 'Conservation reconsidered', *AER*, 54(4), Sept. 1967; 5. 'The economics of environmental preservation: a theoretical and empirical analysis' (with C. J. Cicchetti and A. C. Fisher), *AER* 62(4), Sept. 1972; 6. 'Valuing long-run ecological

consequences and irreversibilities (with A. C. Fisher), *JEEM*, 1(2), Aug. 1974; 7. 'Resource conservation, environmental preservation and the rate of discount' (with A. C. Fisher), *QJE*, 89(3), Aug. 1975; 8. 'Toward a responsible energy policy' (with R. T. Page), *Pol. Analysis*, 1(1), Winter 1975; 9. 'An integrated approach to national forest management' (with J. A. Haigh), *Environmental Law*, 8(2), Spring 1978; 10. 'Resource and environmental constraints to growth' (with V. K. Smith), *AJAE*, 61(3), Aug. 1979.

Principal Contributions Undertook to place natural resource management in an economic framework, applying relevant concepts from welfare economics for the valuation of non-priced resource services. This work led naturally to encompass some areas of environmental economics in which the interrelation between private and common property resources provided opportunities to treat provision of environmental services as resource-allocative issues.

KUENNE, Robert Eugene

Born 1924, Saint Louis, MI, USA.

Current Post Prof. Econ., Princeton Univ., Princeton, NJ, USA, 1972–.

Past Posts Vis. Ass. Prof., Univ. Virginia, 1955–6; Vis. Prof. Military Systems Analysis, US Army War Coll., 1967–.

Degrees BJ (Journalism) Univ. Missouri, 1947; BA, MA Washington Univ., 1948, 1949; MA, PhD Harvard Univ., 1951, 1953.

Offices and Honours Oliver Ellsworth Bicentennial Preceptor, Princeton Univ., 1957–60; Sr. Fellow, Council Humanities, Princeton Univ., 1962–5; Res. Fellow, Nat. Inst. Health, 1965–9; Ford Foundation Faculty Res. Fellow, 1965–6; Member, Scientific and Management Advisory Comm., US Army Computer Systems Command, 1971–4.

Editorial Duties Ed. Boards: *J Reg S*, 1967, *Energy Econ.*, 1976, *Econ. Modelling*, 1984–.

Principal Fields of Interest 021 General Equilibrium Theory; 213

Mathematical Method and Models; 941 Regional Economics.

Publications *Books:* 1. *The Theory of General Economic Equilibrium* (Princeton Univ. Press, 1963); 2. *The Attack Submarine: A Study in Strategy* (Yale Univ. Press, 1965); 3. *The Polaris Missile Strike: A General Economic Systems Analysis* (Ohio State Univ. Press, 1967); 4. *Monopolistic Competition Theory: Studies in Impact*, ed. (Wiley, 1968); 5. *Microeconomic Theory of the Market Mechanism: A General Equilibrium Approach* (Macmillan, 1968); 6. *Eugen von Böhm-Bawerk* (Columbia Univ. Press, 1971).

Articles: 1. 'The impact of steel upon the greater New York-Philadelphia industrial region' (with W. Isard), *REStat*, 35, Nov. 1953; 2. 'Walras, Leontief, and the interdependence of economic activities', *QJE*, 68, Aug. 1954; 3. 'On the existence and role of money in a stationary state', *SEJ*, 25, July, 1958; 4. 'On Hicks's concept of perfect stability in multiple exchange', *QJE*, 73(4), May 1959; 5. 'An efficient algorithm for the numerical computation of the minimum-transport cost point in a generalized Weber problem in spatial economics' (with H. Kuhn), *J Reg S*, 4, 1962; 6. 'Exact and approximate solutions to the multisource Weber problem' (with R. Soland), *Math. Programming*, 3, 1972; 7. 'Toward a usable general theory of oligopoly', *DE*, 122(6), 1974; 8. 'Rivalrous consonance and the power structure of OPEC', *Kyk*, 32(4), 1979; 9. 'Duopoly reaction functions under crippled optimization regimes', *OEP*, 32(2), June 1980; 10. 'The Genesys model of OPEC: 1974–1980', *Energy Econ.*, 4(3), July 1982.

Principal Contributions Over my career my interests have drawn me toward the large-scale interdependent microeconomic system in both my theoretical and applied research. That interest began in graduate student days by a fascination with the Walrasian general equilibrium structure when that approach received little attention in Anglo-American economics. I feel that my *Theory of General Economic Equilibrium* and some prior articles may have played some small role in the popularity now enjoyed by general as opposed to partial frameworks.

From the beginning, however, I shared with most scholars the essential barrenness of the Walrasian model in its inability to yield qualitative theorems. This led me to input–output analysis as one operational alternative for the derivation of theorems, but its lack of true economic dimension did not completely satisfy my theoretical conscience.

The modern work in general equilibrium theory that began in the 1950s and exploited point-set topology and real analysis has led the field in precisely the wrong directions. Its misguided fascination with the 'newer' mathematical techniques has led the field to concerns of secondary and tertiary economic significance and permitted it, by instilling it with a misplaced sense of achievement in deriving existence or uniqueness proofs, to ignore its central deficiencies. It has reinforced the attachment of modelling to purely competitive market structures despite universal recognition of the inappropriateness of that assumption, and it has actually reduced the capability of general economic systems to yield realistically worthwhile theorems.

My current research continues, therefore, to pursue paths that will make micro-general economic analysis operationally useful. I have recently completed work which attempts to construct an operational approach to general oligopolistic equilibrium, using nonlinear programming.

KUH, Edwin

Born 1925, Chicago, IL, USA.

Current Post Prof. Econ. Fin., Dir., Center Computational Res. Econ. Management Science, MIT, USA, 1962–.

Past Posts Lect., Johns Hopkins Univ., 1953–5; Ass. Prof., Sloan School Management, MIT, 1955–9; Assoc. Prof. Fin., MIT, 1959–62.

Degrees BA Williams Coll., 1949; PhD Harvard Univ., 1955.

Offices and Honours David A. Wells

Prize, Harvard Univ., 1955; Fellow, Em. Soc., 1965, AAAS, 1968.

Principal Fields of Interest 210 Econometric, Statistical and Mathematical Methods and Models; 130 Economic Fluctuations; Forecasting Stabilisation and Inflation.

Publications *Books:* 1. *The Investment Decision: An Empirical Study* (with J. R. Meyer), (Harvard Univ. Press, 1957); 2. *Capital Stock Growth: A Microeconometric Approach* (N-H, 1963); 3. *The Brookings Quarterly Econometric Model of the United States* co-ed. (with J. S. Duesenberry, *et al.*), (Rand McNally, N-H, 1965); 4. *An Introduction to Applied Macroeconomics* (with R. Schmalensee), (N-H, 1972); 5. *Diagnostics in the Linear Regression Model: Identifying Influential Data and Sources of Collinearity* (with D. Belsley and R. Welsch), (Wiley, 1980).

Articles: 1. 'Income distribution and employment over the business cycle', in *The Brookings Quarterly Econometric Model of the United States*, *op. cit.*; 2. 'Unemployment, production functions, and effective demand', *JPE*, 74, June 1966; 3. 'A productivity theory of wage levels — an alternative to the Phillips curve', *REStud*, 34(4), Oct. 1967; 4. 'An essay on aggregation theory and practice', in *Essays in Honour of Jan Tinbergen*, ed. W. Sellekaerts (Macmillan, 1974); 5. 'The variances of regression coefficient estimates using aggregate data' (with R. Welsch), *Em*, 44(2), March 1976; 6. 'Econometric model diagnostics' (with J. Neese), in *International Symposium on Criteria for Evaluating the Reliability of Macroeconomic Models*, eds. G. Chow and P. Corsi (Wiley, 1982); 7. 'Parameter sensitivity, dynamic behavior and model reliability: an initial exploration with the MOEM monetary sector' (with J. Neese), in *Proceedings Em Soc. European Meetings 1979. Selected Econometric Papers — In Memory of Stefan Valavanis*, ed. E. G. Charatsis (N-H, 1982); 8. 'Estimation for dirty data and flawed models' (with W. S. Krasker and R. E. Welsch), in *Handbook of Econometrics*, eds. Z. Grilliches and M. D. Intriligator (N-H, 1982).

Principal Contributions Worked on three principal topics: investment behaviour, cyclical productivity and income distribution, and diagnostics for econometric model reliability. Early endeavour was sorting out the influence of (*ex-post*) profits and output on investment; later, studied observed regularities in cyclical income arising from labour demand function dynamics. More recently, work on model reliability has been on aggregation conditions under which aggregates improve estimation efficiency. Work on diagnostics concerns detection of influential subsets of data in regressions that can dominate and contaminate estimates, and parameter sensitivity analysis for complete econometric models. Interest in 'guided computing' that uses artificial intelligence concepts to devise systematic ways to capitalise on useful model-building heuristics.

KURZ, Mordecai

Born 1934, Nethanya, Israel.
Current Post Prof. Econ., Stanford Univ., Stanford, CA, USA; Dir. Econ., Inst. Math. Stud. in Social Sciences, Stanford Univ., Stanford, CA, USA, 1969–.
Past Posts Res. Assoc., Inst. Math. Stud. in Social Sciences; Ass. Prof. Econ., Vis. Assoc. Prof., Assoc. Prof. Econ., Stanford Univ., 1961–2, 1962–3, 1966–7, 1967–8; Lect., Sr. Lect. Econ., Hebrew Univ., Jerusalem 1963–4, 1964–6.
Degrees BA (Econ. and Polit. Science) Hebrew Univ., Jerusalem, 1957; MA, PhD Yale Univ., 1958, 1961; MS (Stats.) Stanford Univ., 1960.
Offices and Honours Ford Faculty Res. Fellow, 1973, Guggenheim Foundation Fellow, 1977–8, Fellow, Em Soc, Inst. Advanced Stud., Hebrew Univ., Jerusalem, 1979–80; Special Econ. Adviser, Govt. Canada, 1977–9; US President's Commission on Pension Pol., 1978–9.
Editorial Duties Assoc. Ed., *JET*.
Principal Fields of Interest 020 General Economic Theory; 100 Economic Growth, Development; and Planning Theory and Policy; 910 Welfare, Health and Education.

Publications *Books:* 1. *Public Investment, the Rate of Return, and Optimal Fiscal Policy* (with K. J. Arrow), (JHUP, 1970).
Articles: 1. 'Technology and scale in electricity generation' (with P. Dhrymes), *Em*, 32(4), July 1964; 2. 'Optimal paths of capital accumulation under the minimum time objective', *Em*, 33(1), Jan. 1965; 3. 'The general instability of a class of growth processes', *REStud*, 35, April 1967; 4. 'Optimal public investment policy and controllability with fixed private savings ratio' (with K. J. Arrow), *JET*, 2(5), Aug. 1969; 5. 'Equilibrium with transaction cost and money in a single market exchange economy', *JET*, 7(4), April 1974; 6. 'Altruistic equilibrium', in *Economic Progress, Private Values and Public Policy, Essays in Honor of William Fellner*, eds. B. Ballasa and R. R. Nelson (N-H, 1977); 7. 'Power and taxes' (with R. Aumann), *Em*, 45(4), July 1977; 8. 'Unemployment equilibrium in an economy with linked prices', *JET*, 26(1), Feb. 1982; 9. 'Endogenous formation of coalitions' (with S. Hart), *Em*, 51(4), July 1983; 10. 'Capital accumulation and the characteristics of private intergenerational transfers', *Em*, 51, Feb. 1984.

Principal Contributions My early work concentrated on problems of economic growth where both theoretical and empirical projects were undertaken. These studies examined the relations between technology and social institutions. Also, an extensive amount of work was dedicated to investigating the scope for public policy which aims at efficient growth. Later I worked on problems in general equilibrium theory with emphasis on equilibria with transaction cost and price rigidities. In recent years my interests have focussed on the process in which public policy is formed and the role of political power in determining both tax structures and income distribution. As part of this general interest, I completed empirical investigations of some aspects of negative income taxation and social security, while my theoretical work concentrated on the analysis of tax structures and income distribution as an endogenous outcome of a social bargaining process.

KUSKA, Edward Arthur

Born 1937, Alliance, NB, USA.
Current Post Sr. Lect., LSE, London, England, 1982–.
Past Posts Ass. Lect., Lect., LSE, 1961–4, 1964–82.
Degrees BA Idaho State Univ., 1959; PhD Univ. London, 1970.
Offices and Honours Secretary, UK SSRC, Internat. Econ. Res. Seminar.
Principal Fields of Interest 010 General Economics; 310 Domestic Monetary and Financial Theory and Institutions; 400 International Economics.
Publications *Books:* 1. *Maxima, Minima and Comparative Statics* (Weidenfeld & Nicolson, 1973).
Articles: 1. 'The simple analytics of the Phillips curve', *Ec*, N.S. 33, Nov. 1966; 2. 'The pure theory of devaluation', *Ec*, N.S. 39, Aug. 1972; 3. 'The long run behaviour of the Patinkin model', *Ec*, N.S. 42, Aug. 1975; 4. 'Devaluation, equi-proportional export subsidies and import tariffs, and transfer payments', *Ec*, N.S. 43, May 1976; 5. 'The post devaluation time profile of reserves and prices under neoclassical assumptions', *Ec*, N.S. 44, Aug. 1977; 6. 'On the almost total inadequacy of Keynesian balance-of-payments theory', *AER*, 68(4), Sept. 1978; 7. 'Growth and the balance-of-payments; the Mundell and Wein theorems', *EJ*, 88, Dec. 1978; 8. 'On the adequacy or inadequacy of Keynesian balance-of-payments theory: a reply', *AER*, 72(4), Sept. 1982.

Principal Contributions My early interests were in macroeconomics and general equilibrium models, but as the international monetary system began exhibiting signs of stress in the latter 1960s I became concerned with issues in international economics, especially those related to the balance of payments. In my work in this area, I attempted to take full account of general equilibrium requirements and this led to a number of monetary approach results and to a reconsideration of the two-country Keynesian and asset-approach models.

KUZNETS, Simon*

Dates and Birthplace 1901–85, Russia.

Posts Held Prof. Polit. Econ., Johns Hopkins Univ., 1954–60; Prof. Econ., Harvard Univ., 1960–71. Retired, 1971.

Degrees BSc, MA, PhD Columbia Univ., 1923, 1924, 1926.

Offices and Honours Pres., ASA, 1949, AEA, 1954; Nobel Prize in Econ., 1971.

Principal Fields of Interest 111 Economic Growth Theory; 221 National Income Accounting.

Publications *Books:* 1. *Secular Movements in Production and Prices* (Houghton-Mifflin, 1930); 2. *Seasonal Variations in Industry and Trade* (NBER, 1933); 3. *National Income since 1869* (NBER, 1946); 4. *Modern Economic Growth* (Yale Univ. Press, 1966); 5. *Economic Growth of Nations* (Harvard Univ. Press, 1971).

Articles: 1. 'Equilibrium economics and business cycle theory', *QJE*, 44, May 1930; 2. 'National income: a new version', *REStat*, 30, Aug. 1948; 3. 'Long swings in the growth of populations and in related economic variables', *Amer. Philo. Soc. Proceedings*, 102, Feb. 1952; 4. 'Economic growth and income inequality', *AER*, 45(1), March 1955; 5. 'Demographic aspects of the size distribution of income', *EDCC*, 25, Oct. 1976.

Principal Contributions Study of types of economic change (cyclical fluctuations, secular movements, seasonal variations); clarification and quantification of the concepts of national economic product and its structure; attempt to apply the concepts and measures of national economic product to the study of economic growth of nations; and the bearing of demographic trends and structures on economic growth and income distribution.

Secondary Literature R. A. Easterlin, 'Kuznets, Simon', *IESS*, 18; E. Lundberg, 'Simon Kuznets' contributions to economics', *Swed. JE*, 73(1), Jan. 1971, repr. in *Contemporary Economists in Perspective*, eds. H. W. Spiegel and W. J. Samuels, 22 (JAI Press, 1984).

KYDLAND, Finn E.

Born 1943, Norway.

Current Post Prof. Econ., Carnegie-Mellon Univ., Pittsburgh, PA, USA, 1982–.

Past Posts Ass. Prof. Econ., Norwegian School Econ. Bus. Admin., 1973–6; Vis. Scholar, Univ. Minnesota, Minneapolis, 1976–7; Vis. Fellow, Assoc. Prof. Econ., Carnegie-Mellon Univ., 1977–8, 1978–82.

Degrees Siviløkonom (Bus. Admin.) Norwegian School Econ., 1968; MS, PhD Carnegie-Mellon Univ., 1972, 1973.

Offices and Honours John Stauffer Nat. Fellow Public Pol., Hoover Inst., Stanford, CA, USA.

Principal Fields of Interest 131 Economic Fluctuations; 300 Domestic Monetary and Fiscal Theory and Institutions; 821 Theory of Labour Markets and Leisure.

Publications *Articles:* 1. 'Hierarchical decomposition in linear economic models', *Management Science*, 21, May 1975; 2. 'Noncooperative and dominant player solution in discrete dynamic games', *Int ER*, 16, June 1975; 3. 'Decentralized stabilization policies: optimization and the assignment problem', *Annals Econ. Social Measurement*, 5, 1976; 4. 'Rules rather than discretion: the inconsistency of optimal plans' (with E. C. Prescott), *JPE*, 85, June 1977, repr. in *Rational Expectations and Econometric Practice*, eds. R. E. Lucas, Jr. and T. J. Sargent (Univ. Minnesota Press, 1981); 5. 'Equilibrium solutions in dynamic dominant-player models', *JET*, 15, Aug. 1977; 6. 'A dynamic dominant firm model of industry structure', *Scand JE*, 81(3), 1979; 7. 'Dynamic optimal taxation, rational expectations and optimal control' (with E. C. Prescott), *J Ec Dyn*, 2, Feb. 1980; 8. 'A competitive theory of fluctuations and the feasibility and desirability of stabilization policy' (with E. C. Prescott), in *Rational Expectations and Economic Policy*, ed. S. Fischer (Univ. Chicago Press, 1980); 9. 'Time to build and aggregate fluctuations' (with E. C. Prescott), *Em*, 50, Nov. 1982; 10. 'Labor-force heterogeneity and the business cycle', in

Carnegie-Rochester Conf. Series in Public Pol., eds. K. Brunner and A. H. Meltzer (N-H, 1984).

Principal Contributions Theoretical and empirical research on business cycles. Emphasis on determining what propagation mechanisms for shocks are important for understanding aggregate fluctuations. Discipline is imposed through the use of explicit dynamic optimisation models of economic behaviour and the assumption that markets clear. Examples of model elements are inter-temporally nonseparable utility in leisure and a multiple-period investment technology. Have emphasised the role of labour markets, including skill differences, for aggregate fluctuations. Pointed out in an early article the time-inconsistency of optimal government policy, and have explored its implications. Did early work on dynamic games, with emphasis on determining what equilibrium concepts make economic sense and applications in decentralised policy-making and oligopoly theory.

L

LAFFONT, Jean-Jacques Marcel

Born 1947, Toulouse, France.
Current Post Prof. Econ., Univ. Sciences Sociales, Toulouse, France, 1980–.
Past Posts Res. Assoc., CNRS, Paris, 1974–8; Prof. Econ., Amiens, France, 1978–80.
Degrees Diplôme Eng., Paris, 1970; Doctorat Trois-cycle (Maths.), Paris, 1972; PhD Harvard Univ., 1975.
Offices and Honours David A. Wells Prize, Harvard Univ.; Council, Chairman, Europ. Symposia Comm.; Fellow, Em Soc; Membre, Comité Dir. de l'Assoc. Française De Science Econ., Conseil Superieur des Univs. Françaises.
Editorial Duties Assoc. Ed., *REStud*, *JET*, *J Math E*, *Econ. Letters*, *REP*.
Principal Fields of Interest 020 General Economic Theory; 200 Quantitative Economic Methods.
Publications *Books:* 1. *Effets externes et théorie economique* (CNRS,

1977); 2. *Incentives in Public Decision Making* (with J. Green), (N-H, 1979); 3. *Aggregation and Revelation of Preferences*, ed. (N-H, 1979); 4. *Essays in the Economics of Uncertainty* (Harvard Univ. Press, 1980); 5. *Cours de théorie microéconomique*, 1, *Fondements de l'economie publique* (Economica, 1982).

Articles: 1. 'Optimism and experts against adverse selection in a competitive economy', *JET*, 10(3), June 1975; 2. 'On moral hazard in general equilibrium theory' (with E. Helpman), *JET*, 10(1), Feb. 1975; 3. 'Existence d'un équilibre général de concurrence imparfaite' (with G. Laroque), *Em*, 44(2), March 1976; 4. 'Efficient estimation of nonlinear simultaneous equations with additive disturbances' (with D. W. Jorgenson), *Annals Social and Econ. Measurement*, 3(4), Oct. 1974; 5. 'Characterization of satisfactory mechanisms for the revelation of preferences for public goods' (with J. Green), *Em*, 45(2), March 1977; 6. 'More on prices versus quantities', *RES*, 44(1), Feb. 1977; 7. 'Disequilibrium econometrics for business loans' (with R. Jancia), *Em*, 45(5), July 1977; 8. 'A differentiable approach to dominant strategy mechanisms' (with E. Maskin), *Em*, 48(6), Sept. 1980; 9. 'Disequilibrium econometrics in simultaneous equation systems' (with A. Monfort and C. Gowrieroux), *Em*, 48(1), Jan. 1980; 10. 'The non-existence of a free entry Cournot equilibrium in labor-managed economies' (with M. Moneaux), *Em*, 51(2), March 1983.

Principal Contributions Contributions to the theory of incentives, to general equilibrium theory and to the methods of econometrics.

LAIDLER, David Ernest William

Born 1938, Tynemouth, England.
Current Post Prof. Econ., Univ. Western Ont., Canada, 1975–.
Past Posts Temp. Ass. Lect., LSE, 1951–2; Ass. Prof. Econ., Univ. Cal. Berkeley, 1963–6; Acting Ass. Prof., Stanford Univ., 1964; Lect. Econ., Univ. Essex, 1966–9; Part-time Econ. Adviser, UK Ministry Housing and Local Govt., 1968–70; Prof. Econ.,

Univ. Manchester, 1969–75; Vis. Prof., Brown Univ., 1973; Vis. Econ., Reserve Bank Australia, 1977; Vis. Prof., Stockholm School Econ., 1978, Univ. Konstanz, 1980; Vis. Special Lect., Monash Univ., 1980.

Degrees BSc LSE, 1959; MA Univ. Syracuse, 1960; PhD Univ. Chicago, 1964; MA Univ. Manchester, 1973.

Offices and Honours Lister Lect. BAAS, 1972; Fellow, Royal Soc. Canada, 1982; Exec. Com., AUTE, 1970–5; Member, Secretary, Soc. Econ. Analysis, 1971–5; Exec. Com., CEA, 1980–3.

Editorial Duties Ed. Boards, *MS*, 1969–75, *REStud*, 1970–5, *AER*, 1976–8, *CJE*, 1977–9, *JEL*, 1978–; Assoc. Ed., *JMCB*, 1979–; North Amer. Corresp. Ed., *MS*, 1982–; Gen. Ed. (with J. M. Parkin), Inflation Series (Manchester Univ. Press); Ed. Adviser, Philip Allan Publishers.

Principal Fields of Interest 030 History of Economic Thought, Methodology; 130 Economic Fluctuations; Forecasting; Stabilisation and Inflation; 430 Balance of Payments; International Finance.

Publications *Books:* 1. *The Demand for Money — Theories and Evidence* (Internat. Textbook, 1969, T. Y. Crowell, 1977, Harper & Row, 1984); 2. *Readings in British Monetary Economics*, co-ed. (with H. G. Johnson, *et al.*), (OUP, 1972); 3. *Labour Markets and Inflation*, co-ed. (with D. Purdy), (Manchester Univ. Press, Univ. Toronto Press, 1974); 4. *Introduction to Microeconomics* (Philip Allan, 1974, 1981); 5. *Essays on Money and Inflation* (Manchester Univ. Press, Univ. Chicago Press, 1975); 6. *Report on the Role of Primary Non-Labour Incomes in the Inflationary Process in the United Kingdom*, ed. (EEC Commission, 1976); 7. *Monetarist Perspectives* (Philip Allan, Harvard Univ. Press, 1982).

Articles: 1. 'The rate of interest and the demand for money — some empirical evidence', *JPE*, 68(6), Dec. 1969; 2. 'The definition of money — theoretical and empirical problems', *JMCB*, 1(3), Aug. 1969; 3. 'Money, wealth and time preference in a stationary economy', *CJE*, 2(4), Nov. 1969; 4. 'Inflation — a survey' (with J. M. Parkin), *EJ*, 85,

Dec. 1975; 5. 'The welfare costs of inflation in neoclassical theory — some unsettled questions', in *Inflation Theory and Anti-Inflation Policy*, ed. E. Lundberg (Macmillan 1978); 6. 'An empirical model of an open economy under fixed exchange rates — the United Kingdom 1954–70' (with P. O'Shea), *Ec*, N.S. 47, May 1980; 7. 'The demand for money in the United States yet again', in *The State of Macroeconomics*, eds. K. Brunner and A. H. Meltzer (N-H, 1980); 8. 'Adam Smith as a monetary economist', *CJE*, 14(2), May 1981; 9. 'Jevons on money', *MS*, 50(4), Dec. 1982; 10. 'The "buffer stock notion" in monetary economics', *EJ*, 94, Suppl., 1984.

Principal Contributions My first published papers were empirical studies of the US demand for money function, concerned with establishing the importance of the interest rate and some wealth or permanent income measure in the function. Later my interest turned to inflation, and I became involved in integrating hypotheses about inflation-output (or unemployment) interaction into macroeconomic systems, thereby producing what are essentially dynamic IS/LM models capable of dealing with simultaneous price and output fluctuations. I have constructed both analytic and small econometric models of closed and open economies which, involving as they do notions of excess demand and supply, represent alternatives to so-called New Classical models of the business cycle, even though both classes of models have their roots in the monetarist analysis of the 1960s.

Recently, I have been investigating the links between the adjustment lags frequently found in single equation studies of the demand for money, and the lags in the transmission mechanism linking money supply changes with output and prices. I am becoming convinced that these two apparently different types of lags are, in fact, one and the same phenomenon. If true, this would imply that there is no such structural relationship as a short-run aggregate demand for money function. I conjecture that it will also be found to imply that the hypothesis of clearing competitive markets cannot be sustained as a basis for empirical macro-economic analysis.

In addition to the above, I have also written from time to time on current issues of policy in the UK, the US and Canada, and I have undertaken a number of studies of particular aspects of the history of monetary economics.

LAL, Deepak Kumar

Born 1940, Lahore, India.
Current Post Reader Polit. Econ., Univ. Coll., London, England.
Past Posts Lect., Christ Church, Oxford, 1966–8; Res. Fellow, Nuffield Coll. Oxford, 1968–70; Lect., Polit Econ., Univ. Coll., 1970–9.
Degrees BA Delhi School Econ., 1959; BA BPhil., MA Univ. Oxford, 1962, 1965, 1966.
Offices and Honours Cons., OECD Devlp. Centre, 1967–8, World Bank, 1971–, ILO, 1973–4, UNIDO, 1975–7, OECD, 1975–7, LADB, 1976–7; Full-time Cons., Indian Planning Commission, New Delhi, 1973–4; Adviser, Ministry Planning, S. Korea, 1977, Ministry Fin. Planning, Sri Lanka, 1978; Vis. Fellow, Res., School Pacific Stud., ANU, 1978.
Principal Fields of Interest 112 Economic Development Models.
Publications *Books:* 1. *Wells and Welfare — An Exploratory Cost-benefit Study of Small-scale Irrigation in Maharashtra* (OECD Devlp. Centre, 1972); 2. *Methods of Project Appraisal* (JHUP, 1974); 3. *Appraising Foreign Investment in Developing Countries* (Heinemann Educ., 1975); 4. *Unemployment and Wage Inflation in Industrial Economics* (OECD, 1977); 5. *Prices for Planning — Towards the Reform of Indian Planning* (Heinemann Educ., 1980); 7. *The Poverty of 'Development Economics'* (INEA, 1983).
Articles: 1. 'The foreign exchange bottleneck revisited: a geometric note', *EDCC*, 20(4), July 1972; 2. 'Disutility of effort, migration and the shadow wage rate', *OEP*, 25(1), March 1973; 3. 'Distribution and development', *WD*, 4(9), Sept. 1976; 4. 'Poverty, power and prejudice — the North–South confrontation', *Fabian Res. Series*, No.

340, Dec. 1978; 5. 'A liberal international economic order: the international monetary system and economic development', *Princeton Essays in Internat. Fin.*, No. 139 (Princeton Univ., 1980).
Principal Contributions Development and application of modern 'second best' welfare economics, in the form of cost-benefit analysis, in the design of public policies, particularly in developing countries; the theory of trade and development, and the political economy of both real and monetary international economics; a critical examination of the philosophical, political and economic bases of alternative policies concerning poverty, distribution and growth in developing countries, and critical appraisals of the new macroeconomics, including an ongoing study of labour market evolution during different stages of development.

LALL, Sanjaya

Born 1940, Patna, Bihar, India.
Current Post Sr. Res. Officer, Inst. Econ. and Stats., Fellow, Green Coll. Oxford, England, 1979–.
Past Posts Econ., World Bank, Washington, DC, 1965–9; Res. Officer, Inst. Econ. and Stats., Oxford, 1968–79; Dir. Studies, Indian Council Res. Internat. Econ. Relations, New Delhi, 1981–4; Cons., UN Conf. Trade and Develp., Geneva, ILO, Geneva, UN Industrial Devlp. Organisation, Vienna, World Bank, Washington, DC, OECD, Paris, UN Centre Transnat. Corp., NY, Commonwealth Secretariat, London, FAO, Rome, Inst. Res. on Multinat., Paris, Geneva, Ford Foundation, NY, NEDO, London, 1973–.
Degrees BA Patna Univ., India, 1960; BA MPhil Univ. Oxford, 1963, 1965.
Offices and Honours Gold Medal, Patna Univ.; Book Prize, St John's Coll. Oxford.
Editorial Duties Ed. Boards, *WD, Political Economy of World Poverty* (Univ. Toronto Press).
Principal Fields of Interest 121 Economic Studies of Less Industrialised Countries; 442 International Business;

621 Technological Change, Innovation: Research and Development.

Publications *Books:* 1. *Private Foreign Manufacturing Investment and Multinational Corporations: An Annotated Bibliography* (with P. Streeten), (Praeger, 1975); 2. *Foreign Investment, Transnationals and Developing Countries* (with P. Streeten), (Macmillan, 1977, 1980); 3. *The Growth of the Pharmaceutical Industry in Developing Countries* (UN, 1979; transl., French, 1980); 4. *The Multinational Corporation: Nine Essays* (Macmillan, 1980, 1983); 5. *Developing Countries in the International Economy* (Macmillan, 1981, 1985); 6. *Developing Countries as Exporters of Technology* (Macmillan, 1982); 7. *The New Multinationals* (with E. Chen, and others), (Wiley, 1983; transls., French, Presses Univ. de France, 1984, German, Campus, 1984); 8. *Multinationals, Technology and Exports* (Macmillan, 1985); 9. *Theory and Reality in Development: Essays in Honour of Paul Streeten*, co-ed. (With F. Stewart), (Macmillan, 1985).

Articles: 1. 'Transfer pricing by multinational manufacturing firms', *OBES*, 35(3), Aug. 1973, repr. in *Frontiers of International Financial Management*, ed. D. Lessard (Warren Gorham & Lamont, 1981), and *International Accounting and Transnational Decisions*, ed. S. J. Gray (Butterworths, 1983); 2. 'The international pharmaceutical industry and less-developed countries', *OBES*, 36(3), Aug. 1974; 3. 'Is "dependence" a useful concept in analysing underdevelopment?', *WD*, 3(11–12), Nov.–Dec. 1975; 4. 'The political economy of controlling transnationals: the pharmaceutical industry in Sri Lanka' (with S. Bibile), *WD*, 5(8), Aug. 1977, repr. in *Imperialism, Health and Medicine,* ed. V. Navarro (Baywood, 1981); 5. 'Transnationals, domestic enterprises and industrial structure in LDCs: a survey', *OEP*, 30(2), July 1978, repr. in *Development Economic and Policy*, ed. T. Livingstone (A&U, 1981), and *Leading Issues in Economic Development*, ed. G. Meier (OUP, 1984); 6. 'The pattern of intra-firm trade by US multinationals', *OBES*, 40(3), Aug. 1978; 7. 'Monopo-

listic advantages and foregoing involvement by US manufacturing industries', *OEP*, 32(1), Mar. 1980; 8. 'Vertical interfirm linkages in LDCs: an empirical study', *OBES*, 42(3), Aug. 1980; 9. 'The monopolistic advantages of multinationals: lessons from foreign investment in the US' (with N. S. Siddharthan), *EJ*, 92, Sept. 1982; 10. 'South economic cooperation and global negotiations', in *Power, Passions and Purposes*, eds. J. N. Bhagwati and J. G. Ruggie (MIT Press, 1984).

Principal Contributions One of the pioneers of rigorous economic analysis of impact of multinational corporations on less-developed countries. Studied MNCs balance-of-payments effects, transfer pricing, transfer of technology and the provision of medicines. Started with a critical approach, realised weaknesses of 'dependency' school, and moved to mainstream economic analysis. Then contributed several publications to international investment literature, extending knowledge of MNC theory, intra-firm trade, impact of MNCs on market structure, R&D allocation by MNCs, vertical linkages and exports by MNCs, and the emergence of Third World multinationals. Published a number of detailed empirical studies of the international pharmaceutical, automotive and food-processing industries, finding that MNCs could play a positive and important role in less-developed countries if permitted to operate in liberal, outward-looking regimes. In past four years launched research into technological development in and exports of technology by the more industrialised LDCs. Under World Bank auspices, conducted exhaustive analysis of technological progress in selected Indian firms; discovered a paradoxical mixture of considerable capability with the inability to exploit it effectively in domestic and foreign markets. This study supports and enriches, at the micro-technological level, the various findings about the costs of highly protected, inward-looking policies. Extended understanding of determinants of intra-developing country trade and its possible benefits and costs. The 'revealed comparative advantage' of all the leading developing countries has been analysed over time, with reference to the direction of trade.

LAMPMAN, Robert James

Born 1920, Plover, WI, USA.
Current Post Vilas Prof. Econ., Univ. Wisconsin-Madison, WI, USA, 1974–.
Past Posts Ass. Prof., Assoc. Prof., Univ. Washington, Seattle, 1948–58; Vis. Assoc. Prof., Amer. Univ. Beirut, 1951–2; Vis. Prof., Univ. Wisconsin, 1955–6; Res. Assoc., NBER, 1957–8; Prof., Univ. Wisconsin, 1958–74; Staff, US President's Council Econ. Advisers, 1962–3; Vis. Prof., Univ. Philippines, 1966–7, Cornell Univ., 1973–4; Res. Fellow, Univ. Melbourne, 1981.
Degrees BA, PhD Univ. Wisconsin-Madison, 1942, 1950.
Offices and Honours Exec. Comm., Conf. Res. Income and Wealth, 1963–6; Board of Dirs., NBER, 1968–79; Exec. Comm., AEA, 1976–9.
Editorial Duties Ed., *JHR*, 1968–73; Ed. Board, *JEL*, 1978–81.
Principal Fields of Interest 320 Fiscal Theory and Policy; 910 Welfare Programmes; 220 Economics and Social Status.
Publications *Books:* 1. *The Low-income Population and Economic Growth* (US Govt. Printing Office, 1959); 2. *The Share of Top Wealthholders in National Wealth* (NBER, 1962); 3. *Washington Medical Service Corporations* (with G. A. Shipman and S. F. Miyamoto), (Harvard Univ. Press, 1962); 4. *Ends and Areas of Reducing Income Poverty* (Academic Press, 1971); 5. *Social Welfare Spending: Accounting for Changes from 1950 to 1979* (Academic Press, 1984); *Articles:* 1. 'Income, ability and family size' (with D. A. Worcester), *JPE*, 58, Oct. 1950; 2. 'Recent changes in income inequality reconsidered', *AER*, 44(3), June 1954; 3. 'On choice in labor markets', *ILRR*, 9, July 1956; 4. 'Recent thought on egalitarianism , *QJE*, 71, May 1957; 5. 'Paying the price of higher fertility', in *Problems of US Economic Development* (Comm. Econ. Devlp., 1958); 6. 'Approaches to the reduction of poverty', *AER*, 55(2), May 1965; 7. 'Sources of post-war economic growth in the Philippines', *Philippine EJ*, 6, Winter 1967; 8. 'Transfer approaches to distribution policy', *AER*, 60(2), May 1970; 9. 'What does it do for the poor?', *Public Interest*, Jan. 1974; 10. 'Basic opportunity grants for higher education' (with W. Lee Hansen), *Challenge*, Nov. 1974.
Principal Contributions My graduate training was in labour economics with a minor in law. However, I soon drifted into the study of income and wealth distributions and of policies related thereto. This drift led me to work in social accounting and what I call economics of health, education and welfare. A considerable part of what I have written could be classified as policy analysis and is related to my advisory role with government agencies. Most of my writing relates to the US, but some of it reflects a secondary and recurring interest in developing nations stemming from teaching in Lebanon and the Philippines.

LANCASTER, Kelvin John

Born 1924, Sydney, New S. Wales, Australia.
Current Post John Bates Clark Prof. Econ., Columbia Univ., NYC, USA 1978–.
Past Posts Ass. Lect., Lect., LSE, 1954–9; Reader Econ., Univ. London, 1959–62; Prof. Polit. Econ., Johns Hopkins Univ., 1962–6; Prof. Econ., Columbia Univ., 1966–78; Vis. Prof., Europ. Inst. Advanced Management Stud., Inst. Advanced Stud., Hebrew Univ., Jerusalem, Ottawa Univ., ANU, NYU, Brown Univ., Univ. Birmingham.
Degrees BSc (Maths. & Geology), BA (English Literature), MA (English Literature) Univ. Sydney, 1948, 1949, 1953; BSc (External) PhD Univ. London, 1953, 1958.
Offices and Honours Member, AAAS; Fellow, Em Soc.
Principal Fields of Interest 020 General Economic Theory; 210 Mathematical Methods and Models; 410 International Trade Theory.

Publications *Books:* 1. *Mathematical Economics* (Macmillan, 1968); 2. *Introduction to Modern Microeconomics* (Rand McNally, 1969, 1974); 3. *Consumer Demand: A New Approach* (Columbia Univ. Press, 1971); 4. *Modern Economics: Principles and Policy* (Rand McNally, 1973); 5. *Variety, Equity and Efficiency* (Columbia Univ. Press, 1979).

Articles: 1. 'The general theory of second best' (with R. G. Lipsey), *REStud*, 24(1), 1956; 2. 'The scope of qualitative economics', *REStud*, 29, Feb. 1962; 3. 'A new approach to consumer theory', *JPE*, 74, April 1966; 4. 'The dynamic inefficiency of capitalism', *JPE*, 81(5), Sept.–Oct. 1973; 5. 'Socially optimal product differentiation', *AER*, 65(4), Sept. 1975; 6. 'Intra-industry trade under perfect monopolistic competition', *J Int E*, 10(4), Nov. 1980; 7. 'Innovative entry: profit hidden beneath the zero', *J Ind E*, 31(1–2), Sept.–Oct. 1982.

Principal Contributions My main contributions to economics would undoubtedly be described as theoretical, but I would like to modify that rather loose term somewhat. I regard myself as a *modeller*, one trying to model reality as accurately as possible but yet retain a general form. The most widely cited of my papers (No. 3 above) was an attempt to expand the modelling of the consumer's decision process in order to account for the ability of consumers to handle decision processes involving new products. The conventional model, taken at face value, provided no clue as to what a consumer would do when confronted by a new product, no matter how much information was available about its properties and capabilities. Thus I see my contribution as adding to realism. One of the predictions of this model was that any one consumer would purchase only a small number of the many varieties of available goods and that observed market demand could be described adequately only by taking account of the variety and heterogeneity of consumer preferences. A natural development from this has been my more recent work on the market structures and welfare problems associated with product vari-

ety and with preference heterogeneity, as in No. 5 above and *Variety, Equity and Efficiency*, work which has been extended into the international trade area and is continuing. Although the above is the most consistent single theme, I have worked on a wide variety of conventional problems and some less conventional, including qualitative methods in economics and differential game aspects of growth and distribution. My predilection has been to search out neglected weak points in our picture of how the economy works, rather than to join the mass attack on problems catching current attention.

LANDES, David S.

Born 1924, New York City, NY, USA.

Current Post Coolidge Prof. Hist., Prof. Econ., Harvard Univ., 1981–.

Past Posts Jr. Fellow, Soc. Fellow, Harvard Univ., 1950–3; Ass. Prof., Assoc. Prof. Econ., Columbia Univ., 1952–5, 1955–8; Prof. Hist. and Econ., Univ. Cal. Berkeley, 1958–64; LeRoy B. Williams Prof. Hist. and Polit. Science, Robert Walton Goelet Prof. French Hist., Prof. Econ., Chairman, Faculty Comm. Degrees Social Stud., Harvard Univ., 1964–72, 1972–5, 1975–81, 1977–, 1981–; Overseas Fellow, Churchill Coll. Camb., 1968–9; Professeur Associé, Univ. Paris–IV, 1972–3; Vis. Prof., Univ. Zürich and Eidgenossische Technische Hochschule, Zürich, 1978.

Degrees BA City Coll., NY, 1942; MA, PhD Harvard Univ., 1943, 1953; Dr h.c. Univ. de Lille, 1973.

Offices and Honours Fellow, Center Advanced Study Behavioral Sciences, Stanford, 1957–8; Res. Fellow, Rockefeller Foundation and US SSRC, 1960–1; Fellow, AAAS, BA, Royal Hist. Soc.; Member, Nat. Academy Sciences, Amer. Philo. Soc.; Membre Associé, Fondation Royaumont pour le Progrès des Sciences de l'Homme; Member, EHA, British Econ. Hist. Soc., Soc. French Hist. Stud., Societé d'Histoire Modèrne; Pres., Council Res. Econ. Hist., 1963–6; Dir., Center Middle Eastern Stud., Harvard Univ., 1966–8;

Acting Dir., Center West Europ. Stud., Harvard Univ., 1969–70; Pres., EHA, 1976–7.

Editorial Duties Board of Syndics., Harvard Univ. Press, 1980–3; Ed. Boards, *Kyk, JEH, J. Social Hist, J. Interdisciplinary Hist, Technology and Hist.*

Principal Fields of Interest 044 European Economic History.

Publications *Books:* 1. *Bankers and Pashas: International Finance and Economic Imperialism in Egypt* (Heinemann, Harvard Univ. Press, 1958); 2. *The Rise of Capitalism*, ed. (Macmillan, 1965); 3. *The Unbound Prometheus: Technological Change and Industrial Development in Western Europe from 1750 to the Present* (CUP, 1968); 4. *History as Social Science*, co-ed. (Prentice-Hall, 1971); 5. *Der entfesselte Prometheus* (Kiepenheuer & Witsch, 1973); 6. *L'Europe technicienne* (Gallimard, 1975); 7. *Western Europe: The Trials of Partnership, Critical Choices for Americans*, 8, ed. (D. C. Heath, 1977); 8. *Revolution in Time: Clocks and the Making of the Modern World* (Harvard Univ. Press, 1983).

Articles: 1. 'Technological change and industrial development in western Europe, 1750–1914', *Cambridge Econ. Hist.*, VI (CUP, 1965); 2. 'Japan and Europe: contrasts in industrialization', in *The State and Economic Enterprise in Japan: Essays in the Political Economy of Growth*, ed. W. Lockwood (OUP, 1965); 3. 'Bleichreders and Rothschilds: the problem of continuity in the family firm', in *The Family in History*, ed. C. E. Rosenberg (Univ. Penn. Press, 1975); 4. 'Religion and enterprise: the case of the French textile industry', in *Enterprise and Entrepreneurs in Nineteenth- and Twentieth-Century France*, eds. C. Carter II, R. Forster and J. Moody (JHUP, 1976); 5. 'Watchmaking: a case study in enterprise and change', *Bus. Hist. Rev.*, 53, 1979; 6. 'Palestine before the Zionists', *Commentary*, 61(2), Feb. 1976; 7. 'On being Bernard Berenson', *Moment*, 1980.

LANDES, Elisabeth

Born 1945, Chicago, IL, USA.

Current Post Sr. Econ., Lexecon Inc., Chicago, IL, USA, 1981–.

Past Posts Res. Assoc., Barnard Coll., NY, 1973; Vis. Instr., NBER, 1974–6; Vis. Ass. Prof., Res. Fellow, Grad. School Bus., Univ. Chicago, 1977, 1978, 1978–80.

Degrees BA (Maths.) Radcliffe Coll., Cambridge, MA, 1967; PhD Columbia Univ., 1974.

Offices and Honours NSF Fellow, 1970–1, 1971–2; John W. Burgess Disting. Fellow, Columbia Univ., 1972–3; Charles R. Walgreen Post-doctoral Fellow, Grad. School Bus., Univ. Chicago, 1976–8.

Principal Fields of Interest 610 Industrial Organisation; 820 Labour Economic.

Publications *Articles:* 1. 'Sex differences in wages and employment: a test of the specific hypothesis', *EI*, 14(4), Oct. 1977; 2. 'An economic analysis of marital instability' (with G. S. Becker and R. T. Michael), *JPE*, 84(6), Dec. 1977; 3. 'The economics of alimony', *J Legal Stud*, 7(1), Jan. 1978; 4. 'The economics of the baby shortage' (with R. A. Posner), *J Legal Stud*, 7(2), June 1978; 5. 'The effect of state maximum-hours on the employment of women in 1920', *JPE*, 88(3), June 1980; 6. 'Insurance, liability and accidents: a theoretical and empirical investigation of the effect of no-fault accidents', *Univ. Chicago Working Paper*, 017, 1980; 7. 'Insurance, liability and accidents: a theoretical and empirical investigation of the effect of no-fault accidents', *J Law E*, 25(1), April 1982; 8. 'Compensation for automobile accident injuries: is the tort system fair?', *J. Legal Stud.*, 11(2), June 1982.

Principal Contributions My early interest in human capital and the economics of the family led to an interest in the interaction between the family and the State. I wrote three articles concerning government regulation of family activities — adoption, alimony and the hours of working women. These led in turn to a more general interest in government regulation and industrial organisation and to two articles on the regulation of automobile insurance. These interests continue; in my current position I have studied regulation of entry into health care, competition in the computer industry, and State regulation of natural gas prices.

LANDES, William Martin

Born 1939, New York City, NY, USA.
Current Post Clifton R. Musser Prof. Econ., Univ. Chicago Law School, 1974–; Founder, Lexecon Inc., Chicago, IL, 1974–.
Past Posts Ass. Prof., Stanford Univ., 1965–6; Ass. Prof., Univ. Chicago, 1966–9; Assoc. Prof., Columbia Univ., 1969–72; Assoc. Prof., City Univ. NY, Grad. Center, 1972–4; Res. Staff, NBER, 1966–.
Degrees BA, PhD Columbia Univ., 1960, 1966.
Offices and Honours President's Fellow, Columbia Univ., 1962–3; Ford Foundation Doctoral Dissertation Fellow, 1963–4; IBM Watson Fellow, 1964–5; Ansley Award Nomination, Columbia Univ., 1966.
Editorial Duties Ed., *J Law E*, 1975–.
Principal Fields of Interest 600 Industrial Organisation; 916 Economics of Crime; 950 Law and Economics.
Publications *Books:* 1. *Essays in the Economics of Crime and Punishment*, co-ed. (with G. S. Becker), (Univ. Chicago Press, 1974).
Articles: 1. 'The economics of fair employment laws', *JPE*, 76(4), July–Aug. 1968; 2. 'An economic analysis of the courts', *J Law E*, 14(2), April 1971, repr. in *Essays in the Economics of Crime and Punishment, op. cit.*; 3. 'The private enforcement of law' (with R. A. Posner), *J. Legal Stud.*, Jan. 1975; 4. 'An economic study of US aircraft hijacking, 1961–76', *J Law E*, 21(2), April 1978; 5. 'Joint and multiple tort-feasors: an economic analysis' (with R. A. Posner), *J. Legal Stud.*, June 1980; 6. 'Market power in antitrust cases' (with R. A. Posner), *Harvard Law Rev.*, March 1981; 7. 'The positive economic theory of tort law' (with R. A. Posner), *Georgia Law Rev.*, Summer 1981; 8. 'An economic theory of

intentional torts' (with R. A. Posner), *Internat. Rev. Law Econ.*, Dec. 1981; 9. 'Optimal sanctions for antitrust violations', *Univ. Chicago Law Rev.*, Spring 1983.
Principal Contributions The application of economic theory and quantitative methods of law. Early work concerned the impact of laws (e.g. fair employment laws) and legal institutions (e.g. courts) on behaviour. More recently, developed models to test the hypothesis that common law rules in torts, contracts and property are best explained as efforts by courts to promote efficient resource allocation.

LANDRY, Michel Auguste Adolphe*

Dates and Birthplace 1874–1956, Ajaccio, Corsica.
Posts Held Prof., l'Ecole Pratique des Hautes Etudes, 1907; Conseiller, Generale de Calvi, 1920–51.
Degrees Agrégé de philo., Dr de lett., l'Ecole Normale Supérieure, Paris.
Offices and Honours French Deputy, 1910–46; Senator, Corsica, 1946; Minister, Marine et Travail.
Publications *Books:* 1. *L'utilité sociale de la propriété individuelle* (1901); 2. *L'interêt du capital* (1904); 3. *Manuel d'économique* (1908); 4. *Les mutations des mannaies dans l'ancienne France* (1910); 5. *La revolution démographique* (1934); 6. *Traite de démographie* (1945).
Career *L'interêt* ... is still remembered as a restatement of Böhm-Bawerk's theory of time-preference in the language of utility theory. Subsequent work was largely in economic and particularly in demographic history.
Secondary Literature R. Courtin, 'Necrologie: Adolphe Landry', *REP*, Jan.–Feb. 1957.

LANDSKRONER, Yoram

Born 1944, Urbach, USSR.
Current Post Sr. Lect., Hebrew Univ., Jerusalem, Israel, 1976–.
Past Posts Instr., Baruch Coll., NY, 1974–5; Ass. Prof., Univ. Penn., 1975–6; Vis. Ass. Prof., Univ. Illinois, 1979;

Vis. Assoc. Prof., Boston Univ., 1980; Vis. Lect., Univ. Cal. Berkeley, 1980–1; Vis. Assoc. Prof., NYU, 1983.

Degrees BA, MSS Hebrew Univ., 1969, 1970; PhD Univ. Penn., 1975.

Offices and Honours R. L. White Fellow, 1974–5.

Principal Fields of Interest 520 Business Finance and Investments; 026 Economics of Uncertainty; 441 International Investment and Capital Markets.

Publications *Articles:* 1. 'The demand for risky assets under uncertain inflation' (with E. Losq and I. Freud), *J Fin*, 31(5), Dec. 1976; 2. 'Nonmarketable assets and the determinants of the market price of risk', *REStat*, 59(4), Nov. 1977; 3. 'Intertemporal determination of the market price of risk', *J Fin*, 32(5), Dec. 1977; 4. 'Effects of interest rate policy on external balances', *J Bank Fin*, Oct. 1978; 5. 'Inflation, depreciation and optimal production', *Europ ER*, 12(4), Oct. 1979; 6. 'Index-linked bond and the pricing of capital assets', *J. Econ. and Bus.*, Winter 1981; 7. 'Risk premia and the sources of inflation', *JMCB*, 13(2), May 1981; 8. 'Lease financing: cost vs liquidity', *Eng. Econ.*, 27(1), Fall 1981; 9. 'Inflation uncertainties and returns on bonds', *Ec*, 51, Nov. 1984; 10. 'The impact of the government sector on financial equilibrium and corporate financial decisions', *J. Bus. Fin. and Accounting*, 1984.

LANGE, Oskar*

Dates and Birthplace 1904–65, Tomaszow, Poland.

Posts Held Lect., Krakow Univ., 1931–5, Univ. Michigan, 1936–43; Prof., Univ. Chicago, 1943–5; Prof., Univ. Warsaw, 1955–65.

Degrees LIM, LLD Univ. Krakow, 1927, 1928.

Offices and Honours Polish Ambassador to USA, 1945, UN, 1946–9; Chairman, Polish State Econ. Council.

Publications *Books:* 1. *On the Economic Theory of Socialism*, ed. B. E. Lippincott (1938); 2. *Price Flexibility and Employment* (1944, 1952); 3. *The Political Economy of Socialism* (1958); 4. *Introduction to Econometrics* (1959,

1963); 5. *Political Economy* (1959, 1963); 6. *Economic and Social Essays 1930–1960*, (1961, 1970); 7. *Essays on Economic Planning* (1963); 8. *Political Economy*, 1 (1963); 9. *Wholes and Parts: A General Theory of Systems Behavior* (1965); 10. *Introduction to Economic Cybernetics* (1970).

Articles: 1. 'Say's law: a reinstatement and critique', in *Studies in Mathematical Economics and Econometrics in Memory of Henry Schultz*, eds. O. Lange, F. McIntyre and T. O. Yntema (1942); 2. 'The economic laws of socialist society in the light of Joseph Stalin's last work', *Nanka Polska*, 1953, repr. in *Internat. Econ. Papers*, 4, eds. A. T. Peacock, *et al.* (Macmillan, 1954); 3. 'Outline of a reconversion plan for the Polish economy', *Zycie Godspodarcze*, 1956, repr. in *Internat. Econ. Papers*, 7, eds. A. T. Peacock, *et al.* (Macmillan, 1957); 4. 'Marxian economics and modern economic theory', *REStud*, 2, June 1935, repr. in D. Horowitz, ed., *Marx and Modern Economics* (1968).

Career His economic work can be divided between his early period and his return to Poland. During the former his main concern was with analytical questions, and during the latter his interest lay in propagating an undogmatic version of Marxism. His paper 'On the economic theory of socialism', first published in 1936–7, not only made a major contribution to the bourgeois theory of socialism but also influenced the 'new' welfare economics emerging at the time. His war-time book, *Price Flexibility and Employment*, was one of the first of many later attempts to provide a microeconomic underpinning to Keynesian macroeconomics. His post-war *Political Economy* was an important event in the communist countries, accepting as it did basic Marxian premises, but incorporating modern economic techniques. His personal contributions to the fields of econometrics and growth theory are minor in comparison to this introduction of modern economics to Poland and the other countries of the Soviet bloc.

LARDNER, Dionysius*

Dates and Birthplace 1793–1859, Dublin, Ireland.
Posts Held Ed. of encyclopaedic works and miscellaneous writer; Prof. Natural Philo., Univ. London, 1827.
Degrees BA, MA, LLB, LLD Trinity Coll., Dublin, 1817, 1819, 1827, 1827.
Offices Fellow, Royal Soc.; Hon. Fellow, Stat. Soc., Paris.
Publications *Books: Railway Economy* (1850, 1968).
Career As a scientific populariser and editor, his greatest achievement was probably the *Cabinet Cyclopaedia*, 133 vols (1829–49), which included numerous distinguished contributors. Only *Railway Economy* from amongst his many writings is a contribution to economics. In this work he examined various economic questions both mathematically and graphically in a way which Jevons acknowledged as an influence on his own thinking. This included hints of a profit-maximising theory of the firm and an account of monopoly price discrimination. Marshall labelled Lardner's conjecture that reductions in the costs of transport per unit of distance are likely to increase by the square of the distance of the sales area of the goods transported as 'Lardner's Law of Squares'.
Secondary Literature D. L. Hooks, 'Monopolistic price discrimination in 1850: Dionysius Lardner', *HOPE*, 3(1), Spring 1971.

LAROQUE, Guy Raymond

Born 1946, Paris, France.
Current Post Head, Div. Q. Nat. Accounts, INSEE, Paris, France, 1982–.
Past Posts Ass. Prof., Ecole Nat. de la Statistique et de l'Admin. Econ., 1970–3; Vis. Res. Fellow, Harvard Univ., 1975–6; Member, Unité de Récherche, 1976–9.
Degrees Ecole Polytechnique, 1965; DES, Univ. Paris I, 1971; DEA (Maths. l'Econ.), Univ. Paris VI, 1971.
Offices and Honours Fellow, Em Soc, 1979.
Editorial Duties Ass. Ed., *REStud*, 1976–81.

Principal Fields of Interest 021 General Equilibrium Theory; 023 Macroeconomic Theory; 131 Economic Fluctuations.
Publications *Books:* 1. *Collections de l'INSEE* (with B. Le Calvez and P. Nasse), (INSEE, 1975); 2. *Collections de l'INSEE* (with J. Bournay and O. Maigne), (INSEE, 1979).
Articles: 1. 'On money and banking' (with J. M. Grandmont), *REStud*, 42(2), April 1975; 2. 'Dynamics of temporary equilibria and expectations' (with G. Fuchs), *Em*, 44(6), Nov. 1976; 3. 'The liquidity trap' (with J. M. Grandmont), *Em*, 44(1), Jan. 1976; 4. 'On temporary Keynesian equilibria' (with J. M. Grandmont), *REStud*, 43(1), Feb. 1976; 5. 'Existence d'un équilibre general de concurrence imparfaite' (with J-J. Laffont), *Em*, 44(2), March 1976; 6. 'On the structure of the set of fixed price equilibria' (with H. Polemarchakis), *J Math E*, 5(1), March 1978; 7. 'The fixed price equilibria: some results in local comparative statics', *Em*, 46(5), Sept. 1978; 8. 'On the local uniqueness of the fixed price equilibria', *REStud*, 48(1), Jan. 1971; 9. 'Fair allocations in large economies' (with P. Champsaur), *JET*, 25(2), Oct. 1981; 10. 'Strategic behavior in decentralized planning procedures' (with P. Champsaur), *Em*, 50(2), March 1982.

LASPEYRES, Etienne*

Dates and Birthplace 1834–1913, Germany.
Posts Held Teacher, Univ. Giessen, 1874–1900.
Degrees BA Univ. Heidelberg.
Publications *Books:* 1. *Geschichte der volkswirtschaftlichen Anschauungen der Niederländer* (1863); 2. *Der Einfluss der Wohnung auf die Sittlichkeit* (1869).
Articles: 1. 'Die Kathedersocialisten und die statistischen Congresse', *Deutsche Zeit- und Streit-Fragen*, 52, 1875; 2. 'Statistischen Untersuchungen zur Frage Steuerüberwälzung', *Fin. Archiv*, 18, 1901.
Career Statistician and advocate of quantitative economics, chiefly known for his work on index numbers. He published various comprehensive price

studies based on German data. Lack of statistical data prevented him from testing his important ideas on index numbers.

Secondary Literature R. Meerworth, 'Laspeyres, Etienne', *ESS*, 9.

LASSALLE, Ferdinand*

Dates and Birthplace 1825–64, Breslau, Germany.

Posts Held Journalist and politician.

Degrees Student at Breslau, Berlin and Paris.

Publications *Books:* 1. *Gesammelte Reden und Schriften*, 12 vols (1919–20).

Career Prussian socialist leader who organised the first German workers' party, the *Allgemeiner Deutscher Arbeiterverein*, in 1863. Joined with Marx in 1848 but retained his Hegelian belief that ideas were to some extent independent of economic circumstances. His version of socialism was one in which the State would grant workers capital or credit to form co-operatives; the co-ops would enable the workers to enjoy profits as well as wages and thus escape what he called 'the iron law of wages', i.e. subsistence wages. His opposition to *laissez faire* liberalism led him into an unlikely alliance with Bismarck, which he hoped would result in the granting of universal suffrage. He was killed in a duel before this alliance came to fruition.

Secondary Literature G. Mayer, 'Lassalle, Ferdinand', *ESS*, 9; D. Footman, *Ferdinand Lassalle: Romantic Revolutionary* (Yale Univ. Press, 1947).

LASUEN, Jose-Ramon

Born 1932, Alcaniz (Teruel), Spain.

Current Post MP, Econ. Spokesman Liberal-Conservative Coalition, Congreso de los Diputados, Madrid, Spain, 1983–.

Past Posts Ass. Prof., Madrid Univ., 1958–60; Prof., Univ. Barcelona, 1960–6; Res. Assoc., Resources for the Future, Washington, DC, 1967–9; Prof., Dean, School Econ. and Bus. Admin., Autonomous Univ. Madrid, 1970–83, 1970–3; MP, 1977–9; Econ. Adviser Pres. of Spain, 1977–8.

Degrees BA, PhD Madrid Univ., 1954, 1959; MA Stanford Univ., 1957; Hon. PhD World Academy Scholars, 1965.

Offices and Honours Fulbright Fellow, 1956–7; March Fellow, 1958–9; Ekistics, 1965; Club of Rome, 1977.

Editorial Duties Ed. Board, *Europ ER*, 1977.

Principal Fields of Interest 941 Regional Economics; 112 Economic Development Models and Theories; 023 Macroeconomic Theory.

Publications *Books:* 1. *España ante la Intergracion Economica Europea* (with A. Garcia, *et al.*), (Ariel, 1966); 2. *Estudios de Economia Urbana* (with M. Ribas, *et al.*), (Inst. Estudios Politicos, 1974); 3. *Sectores Prioritarios del Desarrollo Español* (Guadiana, 1973); 4. *Miseria y Riqueza* (Alianza Editorial, 1974); 5. *Ensayos de Economia Regional y Urbana* (Ariel, 1976); 6. *La Espãna Mediocratica* (Planeta, 1979).

Articles: 1. 'Development regional and national', *Cahiers de L'ISEA*, June 1960; 2. 'Regional income inequalities and the problems of growth in Spain', *J Reg S*, 8, 1962; 3. 'Desarrollo economico y distribucion de caucaces por tamano', *Arquitectura*, 101, 1967; 4. 'On growth roles', *Urb. Stud*, 6(2), 1969; 5. 'Quelques aspects du processus de développement des systèmes des nations: stabilité, polarisation, diffusion' (with F. Wasservogel, *et al.*), *REP*, 2, 1970; 6. 'Multi-regional economic development. An open systems approach', in *Information Systems for Regional Development*, *Lund Stud*, Series B, 37, 1971; 7. 'Urbanisation and development', *Urb Stud*, 10(1), 1973; 8. 'Spain's regional growth', in *Public Policy and Regional Economic Development*, ed. N. M. Hansen (CUP, 1974); 9. 'Perspectivas regionales de España' (with A. Pastor), in *la España de las Autonomias* (Espasa Calpe, 1981); 10. 'The multi-regional state', in *Regional Development in Spain. Experiences and Prospects* (Mouton, 1984).

Principal Contributions My main interest is the study of the interaction between regional and national development processes. First works in the 1960s dealt with the effects of regional income disparities on national growth. They showed that regional inequalities were inimical to national development because they segmented aggregate demand into too large a number of internal sectors. Later works showed that indiscriminate regional incomes equalisation policies were also unfavourable to development because national growth results from the adaptation of international growth patterns in certain regions, which must register faster growth than the rest of the country. Both excessive regional divergence and convergence can be hostile to growth.

In the 1970s my attention focussed on how to maximise the benefits and minimise the costs of regional differentiation. I found that nations are structured around a stable and hierarchical system of 'growth poles', which act as adaptors and diffusors of international innovations. In consequence, maximum national growth can be attained through long-term policies which induce the higher-order poles faster to adopt international innovations and also to diffuse them faster to lower-order poles. By the end of the decade I showed that these policies, which are natural in 'normal' countries, where the higher-order growth poles are also the dominant political centres, are very difficult to apply in other 'inverted' countries, where the political centres are the economic peripheries. In the 1980s, as a consequence, my research was addressed to find out which political instruments, decentralisation schemes, inter-party alliances, etc., can be used to make 'inverted' countries behave 'normally', using regional policies conducive to national growth, and vice versa.

LATANE, Henry Allen

Born 1907, Buchanan, VA, USA.
Current Post Chairman, Latane Morris Investment Assoc., N. Carolina; Willis Prof. Investment Banking Emeritus, Univ. N. Carolina, Chapel Hill, 1980–.
Past Posts Fin. Analyst, Bankers Trust Co., NYC, 1930–41, Lionel Edie & Co., NYC, 1941–50; Prof. Econ. and Fin., Univ. N. Carolina, Chapel Hill, 1959–80; Cons., Indian Capital Market Study, Nat. Bureau Appl. Econ. Res., New Delhi, India, 1965.
Degrees BA Univ. Richmond, 1928; MBA Harvard Univ., 1930; PhD Univ. N. Carolina, 1959.
Editorial Duties Ed. Boards, *SEJ*, 1965–80, *J Fin*, 1960–76; *J. Quant. and Fin. Res.*, 1969–80, *Fin. Rev.*, 1980–.
Principal Fields of Interest 132 Economic Forecasting; 311 Domestic Monetary and Financial Theory and Policy; 521 Business Finance.
Publications *Books:* 1. *Security Analysis and Portfolio Management* (with D. L. Tuttle), (Ronald Press, 1970, 1975).
Articles: 1. 'Seasonal factors determined by difference from average of adjacent months', *JASA*, 37, Dec. 1942; 2. 'Cash balances and the interest rate — a pragmatic approach', *REStat*, 36(4), Nov. 1954; 3. 'Criteria for choice among risky ventures', *JPE*, 67(2), April 1959; 4. 'Investment criteria: a three asset portfolio balance model', *REStat*, 45(4), Nov. 1963; 5. 'Standardized unexpected earnings — a progress report' (with C. P. Jones), *J Fin*, 32(5), Dec. 1977.
Principal Contributions My principal contributions revolve around the twin themes of forming probability beliefs about the future and making rational decisions based on these beliefs. My first published contribution was a seasonal adjustment to minimise the difference of each period from the average of the two adjacent periods (the Census XII model was based on this approach). Work on the relationship of interest rates and income velocity, or rather, their reciprocals — bond prices and proportionate cash balances — followed. Models developed in the 1950s still hold with no change in parameters. Based strictly on model parameters estimated in the 1950s, a velocity of 6.7 as in 1984 should be accompanied by high grade interest rates of 13.5% as compared to actual 13.4% yields on Triple A bonds in August.

More recently, I have investigated capital market anomalies indicating imperfect use of information by investors, and developed the concept of Standardized Unexpected Earnings which has been useful in predicting stock price behaviour. Shares of companies whose announced earnings deviate significantly above or below their historic trend tend to show price changes in the appropriate direction even several months after this information is made public.

The second theme justified the geometric mean as a criterion for choosing among risky ventures to maximise the likelihood of long-run success and led to the development of a portfolio balance strategy including money, bonds and stocks.

LAUDERDALE, James Maitland 8th Earl of*

Dates and Birthplace 1759–1839, Scotland.

Posts Held Landowner; Member, House of Lords.

Publications *Books:* 1. *An Inquiry into the Nature and Origin of Public Wealth* (1804, 1819, 1962); 2. *Thoughts on the Alarming State of the Circulation* (1805); 3. *Three Letters to the Duke of Wellington* (1829, 1965).

Career His major economic work was the *Inquiry* . . . , a work cast in the Smithian mould, which nevertheless deviated from classical orthodoxy in several ways. He emphasised the role of utility in determining relative prices and also argued that oversaving was a possibility. His later works are on monetary questions and, paradoxically for a writer who feared underconsumption, took the Bullionist position.

Secondary Literature B. Corry, 'Lauderdale, James Maitland', *IESS*, 9.

LAUGHLIN, James Laurence*

Dates and Birthplace 1850–1933, USA.

Posts Held Taught at Harvard Univ. and Cornell Univ., 1873–92; Prof. Polit. Econ., Univ. Chicago, 1892–1916.

Offices and Honours Founder, *JPE*, 1892.

Publications *Books:* 1. *The Study of Political Economy* (1885); 2. *History of Bimetallism in the United States* (1886); 3. *Principles of Money* (1903); 4. *Credit of the Nations* (1918); 5. *Money and Prices* (1919); 6. *A New Exposition of Money, Credit and Prices*, 2 vols (1931); 7. *The Federal Reserve Act* (1933).

Career As the founder of the Chicago department, he made a major contribution to American economics as a teacher and colleague. His career included enthusiastic campaigning against the free-silver agitation and in favour of the federal reserve system. His publications chiefly concern monetary topics: *Money, Credit and Prices* is his major achievement in this field.

Secondary Literature J. U. Nef, 'James Laurence Laughlin (1850–1933)', *JPE*, 42, Feb. 1934; A. Borneman, *J. Laurence Laughlin* (Amer. Council Public Affairs, 1940).

LAUNHARDT, Carl Friedrich Wilhelm*

Dates and Birthplace 1832–1918, Hannover, Germany.

Posts Held Prof. Eng. Science, Rector, Polytechnic Coll., Hannover, Germany, 1869–1918.

Honours Hon. Dr Dresden Inst. Technology, 1903.

Publications *Books:* 1. *The Theory of the Trace: Being a Discussion of the Principles of Location* (1872, 1900); 2. *Mathematische Begründung der Volkswirtschaftslehre* (1885, 1976). *Articles:* 1. 'Die Bestimmung des zweckmässigsten Standortes einer gewerblichen Anlage', *Zeitschrift des Vereines Deutscher Ingenieure*, 26, 1882.

Career A civil engineer who applied mathematical techniques to economic problems. His writing on railway pricing virtually discovered the theory of marginal cost pricing as well as its implication of deficits for decreasing-cost industries, and continues to influence current thinking on railway tariffs. He also made significant contributions to industrial location theory, particularly market area analysis. A version of the pole principle for finding plant locational equilibrium points is to be found in the seminal 1882 article. His *Mathe-*

matische Begründung is, among other things, the first ever text of mathematical economics; in addition to original results on location, it taught the doctrines of Jevons and Walras.

Secondary Literature E. M. Fels, 'Launhardt, Wilhelm', *IESS*, 9; J. V. Pinto, 'Launhardt and location theory: rediscovery of a neglected book', *J Reg S*, 17(1), 1977.

LAVELAYE, Emile Louis Victor de*

Dates and Birthplace 1822–92, Bruges, Belgium.

Posts Held Lawyer and writer; Prof., Univ. Liège, 1864.

Publications *Books:* 1. *Etudes historiques et critiques sur le principe et les conséquences de la liberté du commerce international* (1857); 2. *De la propriété et de ses formes primitives* (1873); 3. *Le socialisme contemporaine* (1880); 4. *Eléments d'économie politique* (1882); 5. *La monnaie et le bimétallisme international* (1891).

Career Belgian academic socialist whose prolific writings made many contributions to the journals, in addition to his books. His topics included money, international law, agricultural economics and many others, economic and non-economic. He saw political economy as an art not a science, accepted the role of the State in economic life, and judged economic questions in terms of moral standards.

Secondary Literature E. Mahaim, 'Obit.: Emile de Lavelaye', *EJ*, 2, March, 1892.

LAVIGNE, Marie

Born 1935, Strasbourg, France.

Current Post Prof. Econ., Univ. of Paris I Panthéon-Sorbonne, France, 1974–.

Past Posts Ass. Prof., Univ. Strasbourg, 1959–69, Univ. Paris I, 1969–73; Assoc. Prof., Univ. Paris XII, 1973–4; Vis. Prof., Univ. Rennes, Belgium, 1969–70, Liège, Belgium, 1972–3.

Degrees MA (law), MA (Russian Language and Lit.), PhD Univ. Strasbourg, 1955, 1956, 1960.

Offices and Honours Secretary General, Res. Centre, USSR and Eastern Europ. Countries, Univ. Strasbourg, 1959–69: Dir., Centre Internat. Econ. Socialist Countries, Univ. Paris I, 1973–; Exec. Member, Internat. Comm. Soviet and East European Stud., 1980–; Silver Medal (Econ.), CNRS, 1963.

Editorial Duties Ed. Boards, *Le Courrier des Pays de l'Est*, 1975, *Soviet and E. Europ. Foreign Trade*, 1978, *J Comp. E*, 1982; Co-ed., *Economies et Sociétés serie G (Economie planifiée)* (with H. Chambre), 1978.

Principal Fields of Interest 052 Socialist and Communist Economic Systems; 113 Economic Planning Theory and Policy; 420 Trade Relations, Commercial Policy, International Economic Integration.

Publications *Books:* 1. *Le capital dans l'économie soviétique* (SEDES, 1962); 2. *Le problème des prix en Union Soviétique* (with H. Denis), (Cujas, 1965); 3. *Les économies socialistes soviétique et européenes* (Armand Colin, 1970, 1983; transl., English as *The Socialist Economies of USSR and Eastern Europe*, Martin Robertson, 1974); 4. *Le Comecon* (Cujas, 1974); 5. *Economie politique de la planification en système socialiste*, ed. (Economica, 1978); 6. *Les relations économiques Est-Ouest* (Presses Univ. de France, 1979); 7. *Stratégies des pays socialistes dans l'échange international*, ed. (Economica, 1980); 8. *Travail et monnaie en système socialiste*, ed. (Economica, 1981).

Articles: 1. 'The problem of the multinational state enterprise', *ACES Bull.*, 17(1), Summer 1975; 2. 'Economic reforms in Eastern Europe: ten years after', in *Economic Development in Soviet Union and Eastern Europe*, I, ed. Z. Fallenbuchl (Praeger, 1975); 3. 'The creation of money by the State Bank of the USSR', *Econ. and Soc.*, 7(1), Feb. 1978; 4. 'The international monetary fund and the Soviet Union', in *Internationale Wirtschaftsvergleiche und Interdependenzen, Festschrift für Franz Nomschak*, ed. F. Levcik (Springer, 1978); 5. 'The Soviet Union inside Comecon', *Soviet Stud.*, 2(35), 1983.

Principal Contributions Early work was concentrated on the renaissance of the post-Stalin economic thought in the Soviet Union: investment theory and price theory. Along with the growing differentiation between the Soviet and Eastern European forms of economic management, I have attempted to develop a synthetic approach to the socialist economies of Eastern Europe. Recently my work has been devoted to the international relations of the Eastern European countries (East-East, East-West and East-South).

LAVINGTON, Frederick*

Dates and Birthplace 1881–1927, England.
Posts Held Bank employee, 1897–1908; UK Board of Trade, 1912; Fellow, Emmanuel Coll. Camb., 1922.
Degrees BA Univ. Camb., 1911.
Honours Adam Smith Prize, Univ. Camb., 1912.
Publications *Books:* 1. *The English Capital Market* (1921, 1984); 2. *The Trade Cycle* (1922).
Career An economist of the most orthodox, classical kind, seeing his work on the capital market as a mere application of Marshall's ideas to an individual case. This reliance on authority disguised the considerable originality of his major study of the British capital market.
Secondary Literature 'Frederick Lavington (obit.)', *EJ*, 37, March 1927.

LAW, John*

Dates and Birthplace 1671–1729, Edinburgh, Scotland.
Posts Held Banker, merchant and statesman.
Offices French Minister Fin., 1720.
Publications *Books:* 1. *Money and Trade Considered* (1705, 1966); 2. *Oeuvres complètes*, ed. P. Harsin, 3 vols (1934).
Career Promoted various schemes for banks, beginning in 1702 with a proposal for a Bank of France. The schemes involved the creation of paper money backed by land holdings, which he argued would stimulate economic activity. In 1716 he was permitted to set up

his General Bank in France, and in the following year his company of the West began to sell stock in France's North American possession of Louisiana and Mississippi, His financial influence grew to a peak with his appointment as Minister of Finance in 1720. His belief that shares of stock were identical with money led to mistakes in the management of the speculative 'bubble' which followed. Law's system collapsed and he was permanently discredited, his name becoming almost synonymous with cranky monetary panaceas.
Secondary Literature E. J. Hamilton, 'Law, John', *IESS*, 9.

LAYARD, Peter Richard Grenville

Born 1934, Welwyn Garden City, Hertfordshire, England.
Current Post Prof. Econ., Head, Centre Labour Econ., LSE, 1980–.
Past Posts Hist. Teacher, Woodberry Down School, Forest Hill School, London, 1958–61; Sr. Res. Officer, Robbins Comm. Higher Educ., 1961–3; Dep. Dir., Higher Educ. Res. Unit, LSE, Lect., Reader Econ., LSE, 1964–74, 1968–75, 1975–80; Econ. Cons., UK Treasury, 1968–71; Dir., Ford Foundation UK–US Econ. of Educ. Exchange Programme, 1976–80; Res. Assoc., NBER, USA, 1978–80; Cons., Centre Europ. Pol. Stud., Brussels, 1982–.
Degrees BA (Hist.) King's Coll. Camb., 1957; MSc LSE, 1967.
Principal Fields of Interest 820 Labour Markets; 321 Fiscal Theory and Policy; 624 Welfare Theory.
Publications *Books:* 1. *Report of the Robbins Committee on Higher Education*, App. 1, *The Demand for Places in Higher Education*, App. 2(A), 2(B), *Students and their Education*, App. 3, *Teachers in Higher Education* (HMSO, 1963); 2. *Manpower and Educational Development in India, 1961–86* (with T. Burgess and P. Pant), (Oliver & Boyd, 1968); 3. *The Causes of Graduate Unemployment in India* (with M. Blaug and M. Woodhall), (Allen Lane/Penguin, 1969); 4. *The Impact of Robbins: Expansion in Higher Education* (with J. King and C. Moser), (Penguin, 1969);

5. *Qualified Manpower and Economic Performance: An Inter-plant Study in the Electrical Engineering Industry* (with J. Sargan, M. Ager and D. Jones), (Allen Lane/Penguin, 1971); 6. *Cost-Benefit Analysis*, ed. (Penguin, 1973); 7. *Microeconomic Theory* (with A. A. Walters), (McGraw-Hill, 1978; transl., Japanese, Sobunsha Inc., 1982); 8. *The Causes of Poverty* (with D. Piachaud and M. Stewart), (HMSO, 1978); 9. *More Jobs, Less Inflation* (Grant McIntyre, 1982); 10. *The Causes of Unemployment*, co-ed. (with C. Greenhalgh and A. Oswald), (OUP, 1984).
Articles 1. 'The screening hypothesis and returns to education' (with G. Psacharopoulos), *JPE*, 82(5), Sept.–Oct. 1974; 2. 'Capital-skill complementarity, income distribution and output accounting' (with P. Fallon), *JPE*, 83(2), April 1975; 3. 'On measuring the redistribution of lifetime income', in *The Economics of Public Services*, eds. M. S. Feldstein and R. P. Inman (Macmillan, 1977); 4. 'Family income distribution: explanation and policies' (with A. Zabalza), *JPE*, 87(5), pt. 2, Oct. 1979; 5. 'The efficiency case for long-run labour market policies' (with R. Jackman), *Ec*, N.S. 47, Aug. 1980; 6. 'Human satisfactions and public policy', *EJ*, 90, Dec. 1980; 7. 'Youth unemployment in Britain and the U.S. compared', in *The Youth Labor Market Problem*, eds. R. Freeman and D. Wise (Univ. Chicago Press, 1982); 8. 'Causes of the current stagflation' (with D. Grubb and R. Jackman), *REStud*, 49, Oct. 1982; 9. 'Is incomes policy the answer to unemployment?', *Ec*, N.S. 49, Aug. 1982; 10. 'Wage rigidity and unemployment in OECD countries' (with D. Grubb and R. Jackman), *Europ. ER*, 21 (1–2), 1983.

Principal Contributions I have tried to use theory and evidence to throw light on issues of public policy — first education, then income distribution and now unemployment. For example, on education, I illustrated how one might evaluate policy changes using current wage data together with an explicit social welfare function. On income distribution, I confirmed that any conceivable minimum wage would have a very small effect on the inequality of income per household member. I also argued that the efficiency costs of taxes on earnings were less than is supposed because envy may lead people to work more than is efficient. On unemployment, I have been trying to understand its secular increase in Europe. Two papers have traced the inflationary impact of lower productivity growth and higher real input prices, and the role of higher unemployment in combating this. I now hope to show how vacancy data can throw light on unemployment trends. On policies to combat unemployment, I have advocated a tax-based incomes policy and tried to provide a proper general equilibrium treatment of how this might work. I have also analysed the advantages of employment subsidies, especially if they are *per capita* and (in a contracyclical context) marginal.

LAZEAR, Edward Paul

Born 1948, New York City, NY, USA.
Current Post Prof. Industrial Relations, Univ. Chicago, Grad. School Bus., Chicago, Res. Assoc., NBER, 1981–.
Past Posts Res. Assoc., NORC; Ass. Prof. Econ., Assoc. Prof. Industrial Relations, Univ. Chicago, 1974–8, 1978–81.
Degrees BA, MA UCLA, 1971; PhD Harvard Univ., 1974.
Offices and Honours Em Soc; Grad. Fellow, Fellow, NSF, 1971–4, 1979–81; Fellow, Inst. Advanced Study, Hebrew Univ., Jerusalem, 1978–9.
Principal Fields of Interest 820 Labour Markets; Public Policy.
Publications *Articles:* 1. 'Education: consumption or production?', *JPE*, 85(2), June 1977; 2. 'Why is there mandatory retirement?', *JPE*, 87(6), Dec. 1979; 3. 'The narrowing of black-white wage differentials is illusory', *AER*, 69(4), Sept. 1979; 4. 'Family background and optimal schooling decisions', *REStat*, 62(1), Feb. 1980; 5. 'Agency, earnings profiles, productivity and hours restrictions', *AER*, 71(4), Sept. 1981; 6. 'Rank-order tournaments as optimum labor contracts' (with S.

Rosen), *JPE*, 89(5), Oct. 1981; 7. 'A competitive theory of monopoly unionism', *AER*, 73(4), Sept. 1983; 8. 'Pensions as severance pay', in *Financial Aspects of the U.S. Pension System*, eds. Z. Bodie and J. Shoven (Univ. Chicago Press, 1983); 9. 'The excess sensitivity of layoffs and quits to demand' (with R. Hall), *JLabor E*, 2(2), April 1984; 10. 'Incentives, productivity, and labor contracts' (with R. L. Moore), *QJE*, 99(2), May 1984.

Principal Contributions Analysis of the effect of compensation schemes on productivity; a general theory of labour union behaviour; work on income distribution, analysis of wage differentials by race and sex, and the cause of such differentials; general studies on the relationship between wages and schooling, productivity, and demographic characteristics; and examination of labour institutions such as pensions, severance pay, and mandatory retirement.

LAZONICK, William Harold

Born 1945, Toronto, Ont., Canada.
Current Post Harvard-Newcomen Res. Fellow, Grad. School Bus. Admin., Harvard Univ., Boston, MA, 1984–.
Past Posts Ass. Prof., Assoc. Prof. Econ., Harvard Univ., 1975–80, 1980–4; Vis. Assoc. Prof. Econ., Univ. Toronto, 1982–3.
Degrees BCom Univ. Toronto, 1968; MSc Univ. London, 1969; PhD Harvard Univ., 1975.
Offices and Honours Newcomen Award, Outstanding Article *Bus. Hist. Rev.*, 1983; German Marshall Fund USA Res. Fellow, 1985–6.
Editorial Duties Ed. Boards, *Rev. Radical Polit. Econ., Dollars & Sense, JEH*, 1983–.
Principal Fields of Interest 030 History of Economic Thought; 040 Economic History; 620 Economics of Technological Change.
Publications *Books:* 1. *The Decline of the British Economy*, co-ed. (with B. Elbaum), (OUP, 1985).
Articles: 1. 'Karl Marx and enclosures in England', *Rev. Radical Polit. Econ.*, 6(2), Summer 1974; 2. 'Industrial relations and technical change: the case of

the self-acting mule', *CJE*, 3(3), Sept. 1979; 3. 'Production relations, labor productivity and choice of technique — US & British cotton spinning', *JEH*, 41(3), Sept. 1981; 4. 'Technological change and the control of work: the development of capital-labor relations in US mass production industries', in *Managerial Strategies and Industrial Relations*, eds. H. Gospel and C. Littler (Heinemann, 1983); 5. 'Factor costs and the diffusion of ringspinning in Britain prior to World War I', *QJE*, 96(1), Feb. 1981; 6. 'Industrial organization and technological change: the decline of the British cotton industry', *Bus. Hist. Rev*, 57(2), Summer 1983; 7. 'The performance of the British cotton industry, 1870–1913' (with W. Mass), in *Res. in Econ. Hist.*, 9, 1984; 8. 'The decline of the British economy: an institutional perspective' (with B. Elbaum), *JEH*, 44(2), June 1984; 9. 'The "Horndal effect" in early US manufacturing' (with J. Brush), *Explor. Econ. Hist.*, Jan. 1985; 10. 'Strategy, structure and management development in the United States and Britain', in *The Development of Managerial Enterprises*, ed. K. Kobayashi (Univ. Tokyo Press, 1985).

Principal Contributions My work on the history and theory of capitalist development is both critical and constructive. It criticises neoclassical orthodoxy for positing that the essential feature of a well-functioning free-enterprise economy is the subordination of firms to market forces. The basis of the critique is the construction of an analysis that combines in-depth case study research with broad historical synthesis to show that a more accurate depiction of a successful capitalist economy is one in which market forces are subordinate to internal organisation. By placing the firm at the centre of the analysis of the capitalist economy, I have begun to develop an alternative microeconomics that uses theory as a guide to empirical analysis as opposed to the orthodox tendency to regard theory *per se* as a scientific engine of inquiry. Using this methodological approach, I argue that rigour in economics derives much more from a solid understanding of the economic history that is relevant to a problem than from the construction of ever more sophisticated models that often bear little relation to real-world phenomena. My historical methodology has been influenced greatly by my assessment of the strengths and weaknesses of Karl Marx's analysis of capitalist development as well as by my interpretation of Alfred Chandler's institutional analysis of the rise of the modern capitalist enterprise. I have developed his analysis of the relation between firms and markets by means of detailed historical research on the relative decline of the British cotton industry as well as more general analyses of the influences of the organisation of work and management structures on economic development. With Bernard Elbaum, I have elaborated a broad institutional perspective on the long-run decline of the British economy.

LEAMER, Edward Emery

Born 1944, La Crosse, WI, USA.
Current Post Prof. Econ., UCLA, Los Angeles, CA, USA, 1975–.
Past Posts Ass. Prof., Wayne State Univ., 1970; Ass. Prof., Harvard Univ., 1970–3; Assoc. Prof., Harvard Univ., 1973–5; Vis. Prof., Univ. Southern Cal., 1979–80.
Degrees BA (Maths.) Princeton Univ., 1966; MA (Maths.), PhD Univ. Michigan, 1969, 1970.
Offices and Honours Soc. Sigma Xi; Fellow, Em Soc.
Editorial Duties Ed. Boards, *REStat*, 1970–, *QJE*, 1970–5, *JASA*, 1975–9, *Em*, 1975–9; *J Int E*, 1980.
Principal Fields of Interest 210 Econometric, Statistical and Mathematical Methods and Models; 410 International Trade Theory.
Publications *Books:* 1. *Quantitative International Economics* (with R. H. Stern), (Allyn & Bacon, 1970); 2. *Specification Searches: Ad Hoc Inference with Non Experimental Data* (Wiley, 1978); 3. *Sources of International Comparative Advantage: Theories and Evidence* (MIT Press, 1984).
Articles: 1. 'False models and post-data model construction', *JASA*, 69, March 1974; 2. 'Multicollinearity: a Bayesian interpretation', *REStat*, 55,

Aug. 1973; 3. 'Matrix weighted averages and posterior bounds' (with G. Chamberlain), *JRSS*, Series B, 38(1), 1976; 4. 'The Leontief paradox, reconsidered', *JPE*, 88(3), June 1980; 5. 'Is it a supply curve or is it a demand curve: partial indentification through inequality constraints', *REStat*, 58(3), Aug. 1981; 6. 'Sets of posterior means with bounded variance priors', *Em*, 50, May 1982; 7. 'Robust sets of estimates for regression' (with C. Z. Gilstein), *Em*, 51(2), March 1983; 8. 'Lets take the con out of econometrics', *AER*, 73(1), March 1983; 9. 'Reporting the fragility of regression estimates' (with H. Leonard), *REStat*, 65, May 1983; 10. 'Sets of maximum likelihood estimates for regression with all variables measured with error' (with S. Klepper), *Em*, 52(1), Jan. 1984.
Principal Contributions In a series of papers, and most especially in my book (No. 2), I have offered a distinctive perspective on econometric methodology. The wellspring of these ideas is the intellectual discord between econometric theory and econometric practice. In a general sense, econometric theory assumes a fully specified model, but the extensive model searching that is a characteristic of almost all applications constitutes a clear rejection of this assumption. Initially, I sought to identify the reasons for these specification searches, and to construct proper statistical theory to carry out the legitimate intentions of practitioners. Since the publication of my book I have concentrated on what I call global sensitivity analysis. A statistical inference requires a list of assumptions that identify a sampling distribution and possible *a priori* distributions. Because it is impossible to select these assumptions with complete confidence, it is necessary to perform a sensitivity analysis and to discard inferences that are excessively fragile. In a global sensitivity analysis a range of assumptions is selected, and the corresponding range of inferences is identified. If, in order to obtain a usefully narrow range of inferences, it is necessary to select an incredibly narrow range of assumptions, then inference from the given data set is suspended.

I have also had continuing interest in empirical work on the micro side of international trade which began when I was writing *International Economics* with Robert Stern. I have written a couple of papers that point out the lack of a foundation in economic theory of empirical testing of the Heckscher-Ohlin model. Most notably I have shown that the Leontif paradox is a simple conceptual misunderstanding. In addition, my book (No. 3) contains an empirical analysis of international trade dependence. This book illustrates my main message: convincing empirical work requires a solid theoretical foundation and extensive sensitivity analysis.

LEDERER, Emil*

Dates and Birthplace 1882–1939, Pilsen, Austro-Hungary.
Posts Held Prof., New School Social Res., New York City, USA, 1933–9.
Publications *Books:* 1. *Die Privatan-gestellen in der modernen Wirtschafts-entwicklung* (1912); 2. *Die wirtschaft-lichen Organisationen* (1913); 3. *Grundzüge der okonomischen Theorie* (1922); 4. *Aufriss der theoretischen Oekonomie* (1933); 5. *Technical Progress and Unemployment* (1938); 6. *The State of the Masses: The Threat of the Classless Society* (1939).
Career A leading academic socialist in the Weimar Republic. Emigrated to the USA in early 1930s where he continued to work on problems of business cycles and technological unemployment at the New School with Adolph Lowe and Hans Neisser.
Secondary Literature H. Neisser, 'Emil Lederer 1882–1939; I The sociologist', 'II The economist', *Social Res.*, 7, 1940, 8, 1941.

LEE, Tong Hun

Born 1931, Seoul, Korea.
Current Post Prof. Econ., Univ. Wisconsin-Milwaukee, USA, 1967–.
Past Posts Res. Assoc., Social Systems Res. Inst., Univ. Wisconsin-Madison, 1960–2; Ass. Prof., Assoc. Prof. Econ., Univ. Tennessee, 1962–4, 1964–7; UNDP Mission, Korea, 1972.
Degrees BS (Bus. Admin.) Yonsei

Univ., Seoul, 1955; BA Northeast Missouri State Univ., Kirksville, 1956; MA, PhD Univ. Wisconsin-Madison, 1958, 1961.
Principal Fields of Interest 200 Quantitative Economic Methods and Data; 300 Domestic Monetary and Fiscal Theory and Institutions; 900 Welfare Programmes; Consumer Economics; Urban and Regional Economics.
Publications *Books:* 1. *Regional and Interregional Intersectoral Flow Analysis* (with J. R. Moore and D. P. Lewis), (Univ. Tennessee Press, 1973); 2. *A Discussion with Nobel Laureate James Tobin* (Maeil Kyungje Press, 1983).
Articles: 1. 'Demand for housing: a cross-section analysis', *REStat*, 45, May 1963; 2. 'The stock demand elasticities of non-farm housing', *REStat*, 46, Feb. 1964; 3. 'Income, wealth and the demand for money: some evidence from cross-section data', *JASA*, 59, Sept. 1964; 4. 'Joint estimation of relationships involving discrete random variables' (with A. Zellner), *Em*, 33, April 1965; 5. 'Substitutability of non-bank intermediary liabilities for money: the empirical evidence', *J Fin*, 21, Sept. 1966; 6. 'Alternative interest rates and the demand for money: the empirical evidence', *AER*, 57(5), Dec. 1967; 7. 'Housing and permanent income: tests based on a three-year reinterview survey', *REStat*, 50, Nov. 1968; 8. 'Multiregion intersectoral flow analysis' (with D. P. Lewis and J. R. Moore), *J Reg S*, 11(1), April 1971; 9. 'More on windfall income and consumption', *JPE*, 83, April 1975; 10. 'Elasticities of housing demand' (with C. M. Kong), *SEJ*, 44, Oct. 1977.
Principal Contributions Contributed in several areas of economics and quantitative methods. In quantitative methods, developed (with A. Zellner) a joint estimation procedure for a system of equations involving discrete random variables, which would yield efficient estimators by taking account of heteroscedasticity as well as the correlations existing between the random variables. Extended the instrumental variable method for testing the permanent income hypothesis where a lagged or future income is not the perfect instrument for permanent income. Developed

an interregional interindustry model which requires data only on interregional interindustry sales flows rather than interregional input-output structures. Extended the regression method for correcting heteroscedasticity which is related to the exponential function of the expected value of the dependent variable. In monetary economics, contributed the first empirical evidence supporting the Gurley-Shaw hypothesis that non-bank financial intermediary liabilities are close substitutes for cash balances, revealing important implications for monetary theory and policy. Provided initial empirical results that supported the Baumol-Tobin-Whalen hypothesis on economies of scale in holding cash balances. In the theory of the consumption function, produced evidence contradicting Friedman's permanent income hypothesis while showing the important influence of transitory income such as windfall income obtained from a temporary income-tax reduction. Also provided a set of definitive empirical results indicating that, although long-run income has a unique role in housing demand, its effect had been exaggerated for over a decade and its elasticity is, in fact, less than unity. This finding has an important implication for the theory of urban economics, indicating that the population flight from an urban centre cannot simply be explained by the rising standard of living. In regional economics, demonstrated that linking economies among multi-regions empirically provided the optimal location of an industry and measured the impact of one region on another.

LEEUW, Frank de

Born 1930, Amsterdam, The Netherlands.
Current Post Chief Stat., Bureau Econ. Analysis, US Dept. Commerce, Washington, DC, USA, 1977.
Past Posts Ass. Econ., Fed. Reserve Bank San Francisco, 1953–6; Econ., Section Chief, Fed. Reserve Board, 1956–69, Buffalo, 1967–8; Vis. Prof., State Univ. NY Buffalo, 1967–8; Sr. Analyst, Urban Inst., 1969–75; Lect.,

Howard Univ., 1969–71; Ass. Dir., Congressional Budget Office, 1975–7.
Degrees BA, MBA, PhD Harvard Univ., 1951, 1953, 1965.
Offices and Honours Phi Beta Kappa; Chairman, Exec. Comm., Conf. Res. Income and Wealth, NBER, 1972–4; US Dept. Commerce Gold Medal, 1982.
Editorial Duties Ed. Board, *JUE*, 1973–8.
Principal Fields of Interest 300 Monetary and Fiscal Theory and Institutions; 200 Quantitative Economic Methods and Data; 930 Urban Economics.
Publications *Books:* 1. *Operating Costs in Public Housing: A Financial Crisis* (Urban Inst., 1970); 2. *The Web or Urban Housing* (with R. Struyk), (Urban Inst., 1975).
Articles: 1. 'A model of financial behavior', in *The Brookings Quarterly Econometric Model of the United States*, eds. J. Duesenberry, *et al*. (Rand McNally, 1965); 2. 'The channels of monetary policy' (with E. Gramlich), *Fed. Reserve Bull.*, 55(6), June 1969; 3. 'The demand for housing: a review of cross-section evidence', *REStat*, 53(1), Feb. 1971; 4. 'The supply of rental housing' (with N. F. Ekanem), *AER*, 61(5), Dec. 1971; 5. 'The realisation of plans reported in the BEA plant and equipment survey' (with M. McKelvey), *Survey Current Bus.*, 61(9), Oct. 1981; 6. 'Inventory investment and economic instability', *Survey Current Bus.*, 61(12), Dec. 1982; 7. 'A "true" time-series and its indicators' (with M. J. McKelvey), *JASA*, 78, March 1983; 8. 'Cyclical adjustment of the federal budget and federal debt' (with T. Holloway), *Survey Current Bus.*, 63(12), Dec. 1983; 9. 'Price expectations of business firms: bias in the short and long run' (with M. McKelvey), *AER*, 13(1), March 1984.
Principal Contributions Empirical implementation and testing of economic theories has been my principal interest. Early contributions brought this interest to bear on financial markets and urban housing markets. Recent contributions have applied the same interest to investment in plant and equipment and inventories, price expectations, and fiscal policy.

LEFF, Nathaniel H.

Born 1938, New York City, NY, USA.

Current Post Prof. Bus. Econ. and Internat. Bus., Grad. School Bus., Columbia Univ., NY, USA, 1973–.

Past Posts Res. Assoc., Center Stud. Educ. and Devlp., Center Internat. Affairs, Harvard Univ., 1965–7; Ass. Prof., Assoc. Prof., Columbia Bus. School, 1967–70, 1970–3; Assoc. Prof., Tel Aviv Univ., 1972–3; Vis. Prof., Princeton Univ., 1977.

Degrees BA Harvard Univ., 1959; MA Columbia Univ., 1962; PhD (Polit. Science) MIT, 1966.

Offices and Honours Phi Beta Kappa, Magna Cum Laude, Harvard Coll.; Seager Fellow, Internat. Fellow, Columbia Univ.; NDFL Fellow, MIT; IBM Fellow Internat. Bus. Stud., 1976; Tinker Res. Fellow, 1978; Book Award, AHA, 1983.

Principal Fields of Interest 112 Economic Development; 130 Macroeconomics; 442 International Business.

Publications *Books:* 1. *The Brazilian Capital Goods Industry, 1929–64* (Harvard Univ. Press, 1968); 2. *Economic Policy-Making and Development in Brazil, 1947–64* (Wiley 1968; transl., Portuguese, Editora Perspectiva, 1977); 3. *Underdevelopment and Development in Brazil, 1822–1947*, 2 vols (A&U, 1982).

Articles: 1. 'Export stagnation and autarkic development in Brazil', *QJE*, 80, May 1967, repr. in *Latin American Economic Development* (Free Press, 1970), and Spanish, *El Trimestre Economico*, 1969; 2. 'Import constraints and development; causes of the recent decline of Brazilian economic growth', *REStat*, 49, Nov. 1967, repr., Spanish, *El Trimestre Economico*, 1970; 3. 'Marginal savings rates in the development process: the Brazilian experience', *EJ*, 78, Sept. 1968; 4. 'Dependency rates and aggregate saving rates', *AER*, 79(5), Dec. 1969, repr., Spanish, *Demografia y Economia*, 1969, and *Devlp. Digest*, 1971; 5. 'Economic development and regional inequality: origins of the Brazilian case', *QJE*, 85, May 1972, repr., Spanish, *Revista Brasileira de Economia*, 1972; 6. 'Industrial organization and entrepreneurship in the developing countries', *EDCC*, 26(4), July 1978, repr., Spanish, *El Trimestre Economico*, 1979, Portuguese, *Estudos Economicos*, 1983; 7. 'Entrepreneurship and economic development: the problem revisited', *JEL*, 17(1), March 1979; 8. 'U.S. foreign policy and transfer of technology to the third world', *Orbis*, Spring 1979; 9. 'Macroeconomic adjustment in developing countries: instability, short-run growth and external dependency' (with K. Sato), *REStat*, 62, May 1980, repr., Portuguese, *Pesquisa e Planejamento Economico*, 1981, Spanish, *El Trimestre Economico*, March 1980; 10. 'Optimal investment choice for developing countries: rational theory and rational decision-making', *JDE*, 16(3–4), Nov.–Dec. 1984.

Principal Contributions I am interested in the economics of the less developed countries, and have focussed mainly on positive analysis. Preferring to work within a well-specified framework, I did much of my early work in the context of a single country, Brazil. That research included an industry study (on an industry whose rapid development raised questions concerning some accepted assumptions in the field of development economics), and a book on economic policy-making. That work led to research on macroeconomic and trade problems. Subsequent papers have focussed on savings behaviour, macroeconomic adjustment, transfer of technology, industrial organisation and entrepreneurship. I have found economic theory a very useful tool for understanding less developed economies. In addition, I have found historical studies valuable for clarifying the analytics of long-term development. In that vein, I have done a two-volume study of Brazil's economic experience in the 125 years between Independence and World War II. This time span raises interesting analytical questions, for it includes both a long period of relative stagnation and the shift (circa 1900) to sustained, rapid development. More recently, I have been working on macroeconomic adjustment, on approaches to investment choice and on the use of research.

LEFTWICH, Richard Henry

Born 1920, Burden, KS, USA.
Current Post Regents Prof. Econ., Oklahoma State Univ., Stillwater, OK, USA, 1975–.
Past Posts Ass. Prof., Assoc. Prof., Prof. Econ., Oklahoma State Univ., 1948–51, 1951–5, 1955–75; Vis. Prof., Univ. Chicago, 1962–3; Disting. Vis. Prof., Tunghai Univ., Taichung, Taiwan, 1981.
Degrees BA Southwestern Coll., KS, 1941; MA, PhD Univ. Chicago, 1948, 1950.
Offices and Honours Pres., SEA, 1965–6, Western Social Science Assoc., 1972–3, MEA, 1977–8, Southwestern Econ. Assoc., 1984–5; Beta Gamma Sigma Disting. Scholar, 1976–7; Hon. Lect., Mid-Amer. State Univs. Assoc., 1977–8; Leavey Award, Excellence Teaching Private Enterprise, Freedoms Foundation Valley Forge, 1982.
Editorial Duties Ed. Board *SEJ*, 1957–60.
Principal Fields of Interest 020 General Economic Theory; 310 Domestic Monetary and Financial Theory and Institutions; 820 Labour Markets, Public Policy.
Publications *Books:* 1. *The Price System and Resource Allocation* (Rinehart, 1955, Holt, Rinehart & Winston, 1960, 1970, Dryden Press, 1973, 1979 (with R. Eckert), 1982, 1985; transls., Portuguese, Livraria Pioneira Editora, 1971, Spanish, Interamericana, 1975, French, Les Eds HRW Ltee, 1975, German, Gustav Fischer, 1972, Thai, Hindi, Arabic); 2. *An Introduction to Economic Thinking* (Holt, Rinehart & Winston, 1969); 3. *Introduction to Microeconomics* (Holt, Rinehart & Winston, 1969, 1970; transl., Spanish, Interamericana, 1972); 4. *Economic Thinking in a Canadian Context* (with G. F. Boreham), (Holt, Rinehart & Winston Canada, 1970); 5. *Elementary Analytics of a Market System* (General Learning Press, 1972); 6. *Economics of Social Issues* (with A. M. Sharp), (Bus. Publs, 1974, 1984); 7. *A Basic Framework for Economics* (Bus. Publs, 1980, 1984).
Articles: 1. 'Diseconomies', in *A Dictionary of the Social Sciences* (UNESCO, 1964); 2. 'Organized labor and national economic objectives', *SEJ*, 32, April 1966; 3. 'Exchange rates, balance of payments, and trade restrictions in Chile', *EDCC*, 14, July 1966; 4. 'Some obstacles to economic development — the Chilean case', *Econ. and Bus. Bull. Temple Univ*, Dec. 1966; 5. 'Syllabus for an "issues approach" to teaching economic principles' (with A. M. Sharp), *J. Econ. Educ.*, Winter 1974; 6. 'Productivity', in *Encyclopedia Americana* (Encyclopedia Americana, 1981); 7. 'Efficiency versus equity — false dilemma?', *Midsouth J. Econ.*, 1978.
Principal Contributions As a graduate student in the late 1940s my primary interest was in labour economics. Because of the institutional nature of that field at the time, I soon turned my attention to price theory where my main interest has remained up to the present. I have also been concerned with lesser-developed economies, this interest stemming from World War I experiences in India and China, from extended periods of Chile and Taiwan, and from shorter visits to various other lesser-developed countries. Since the early 1970s, I have spent much time on unconventional approaches to the teaching of elementary economics, believing that we attempt to do too much and succeed in doing too little. Through public lectures, newspaper columns, radio and television lectures I have made some attempt to convey basic economic principles to the non-university public, a segment of the population that we economists have long neglected.

LEHFELDT, Robert Alfred*

Dates and Birthplace 1868–1927, Birmingham, W. Midlands, England.
Posts Held Prof. Physics, East London Coll., S. Africa, 1896; Prof. Physics, Prof. Econ., S. African School of Mines and Technology, 1906, 1916–27.
Degrees BSc Univ. London, 1889; BA Univ. Camb., 1890.
Offices and Honours Pres., Section F, South African Assoc. Advancement Science, 1920; Founder, Vice-Pres., Econ. Soc. South Africa.
Publications *Books:* 1. *Economics in the Light of War* (1916); 2. *Gold Prices*

and the Witwatersrand (1919); 3. *The National Resources of South Africa* (1922); 4. *Restoration of the World's Currencies* (1923); 5. *Money* (1926); 6. *Controlling the Output of Gold* (1926); 7. *Descriptive Economics* (1927).

Career After an early successful career as a physicist, began to turn his mathematical skills to economic and sociological problems. Many of his studies were of South African questions and his appointment in 1917 to the Statistical Council of South Africa enabled him to encourage the national collecting of statistics. He was convinced that economic pressures would eventually oblige South Africa to recognise the non-white population as full citizens. Outside South Africa he was chiefly known for his work on currency, particularly in the light of South African gold production.

Secondary Literature S. H. Frankel, 'Obit., Professor Robert Alfred Lehfeldt', *EJ*, 38, March 1928.

LEIBENSTEIN, Harvey

Born 1922, USA.
Current Post Andelot Prof. Econ. Pop., Harvard Univ., 1967–.
Past Posts Ass. Prof., Prof., Univ. Cal. Berkeley, 1951–60, 1960–7; Vis. Prof., Harvard Univ., 1966–7.
Degrees BS, MA Northwestern Univ., 1945, 1946; PhD Princeton Univ., 1951.
Offices and Honours Social Affairs Officer, Pop. Div., UN, 1949; US SSRC Fellow, 1950–1; Cons., Rand Corp., 1954–5; Faculty Res. Fellow, Univ. Cal. Berkeley, 1956–9; Guggenheim Foundation Fellow, 1963; Member, Inst. Advanced Stud., Princeton Univ., 1978–9.
Principal Fields of Interest 840 Demographic Economics; 610 Industrial Organisation.
Publications *Books:* 1. *Economic Backwardness and Economic Growth: Studies in the Theory of Economic Development* (Wiley, 1957); 2. *Economic Theory and Organisational Analysis* (Harper, 1960); 3. *Beyond Economic Man* (Harvard Univ. Press, 1976); 4. *General X-efficiency Theory and Economic Development* (OUP, 1978); 5. *Inflation, Income Distribution and X-efficiency Theory* (Croom Helm, 1980).

Articles: 1. 'Bandwagon, snob and Veblen effects in the theory of consumers' demand', *QJE*, 64, May 1950, repr. in *Readings in Microeconomics*, ed. D. R. Kamerschen (World Publ., 1967); 2. 'Allocative efficiency vs "X-efficiency"', *AER*, 56(3), June 1966; 3. 'Allocative efficiency, X-efficiency, and the measurement of welfare losses' (with W. S. Comanor), *Ec*, N.S. 36, Aug. 1969; 4. 'An interpretation of the economic theory of fertility: promising path or blind alley?', *JEL*, 12(2), June 1974; 5. 'A branch of economics is missing: micro-micro theory', *JEL*, 17(2), June 1979. 6. 'The prisoner's dilemma in the invisible hand: an analysis of intrafirm productivity', *AER*, 72(2), May 1982; 7. 'On the economics of conventions and institutions: an exploratory essay', *ZGS*, 140(1), March 1984.

Principal Contributions The microeconomics of human fertility, and X-efficiency theory (the non-allocative aspects of inefficiency). The latter attempts to develop a mode of analysis which relaxes the maximisation assumption of conventional micro-theory and substitutes postulates under which individuals are non-maximisers when there is little pressure on them, approaching maximising behaviour as external pressure increases. Behaviour according to convention is an important aspect of this approach. Also, current research involves the application of the prisoner's dilemma paradigm to normal economic behaviour.

LEIBOWITZ, Arleen

Born Binghamton, NY, USA.
Current Post Econ., Rand Corp., Santa Monica, CA, USA, 1977–.
Past Posts Res. Assoc., NBER, 1971–4; Vis. Ass. Prof., Brown Univ., 1972–5; Res. Prof., Law and Econ. Center, Univ. Miami, Miami, FL, 1976–7.
Degrees BA Smith Coll., 1964; MA, PhD Columbia Univ., 1965, 1974.
Principal Fields of Interest 826 Labour Markets: Demographic Characteristics; 913 Economics of Health.

Publications *Books:* 1. *Wealth Redistribution and the Income Tax*, ed. (D. C. Heath, 1978).

Articles: 1. 'Education and home production', *AER*, 64(2), May 1974; 2. 'Home investments in children', *JPE*, 82, pt. 2, March–April 1974; 3. 'Parental inputs and children's achievement', *JHR*, 12(2), Spring 1977; 4. 'Family background and economic success: a review of the evidence', in *Kinometrics: Determinants of Socioeconomic Success Within and Between Families* (N-H, 1977); 5. 'Learning and earning in law firms' (with R. Tollison), *J. Legal Stud.*, 7(1), Jan. 1978; 6. 'Family bequests and the derived demand for health inputs' (with B. Friedman), *EI*, 17(3), July 1979; 7. 'A theory of legislative organization: making the most of your majority' (with R. Tollison), *QJE*, 94(2), March 1980; 8. 'Free riding, shirking, and team production in legal partnerships' (with R. Tollison), *EI*, 18(3), July 1980; 9. 'Factors discriminating pregnancy resolution decisions of unmarried adolescents' (with M. Eisen and G. Zellman), *General Psychology Monographs*, 108, 1983.

Principal Contributions My early work focussed on the relationship between women's labour force participation and human capital investments in children. Following up on this work, I attempted to see what parental time inputs yielded for children's abilities, schooling, income and health. My master's essay was an economic analysis of crime. Returning to law and economics, I used human capital theory to analyse the lifetime earnings patterns of lawyers who enter solo or group practice. A related paper concerned the optimal size and legal organisation of law firms. Since 1977 I have analysed health care expenditures as a part of the Rand Health Insurance Study. My particular interests are the effects of provider incentives on health care use, paediatric and maternity expenditures, the demand for drugs, and the time costs of medical care.

LEIJONHUFVUD, Axel Stig Bengt

Born 1933, Stockholm, Sweden.
Current Post Prof. Econ., UCLA, Los Angeles, CA, USA, 1971–.
Past Posts Act. Ass. Prof., Assoc. Prof., UCLA, 1964, 1967–71; Vis. Prof. Econ., Stockholm School Econ., 1969, Inst. Advanced Stud., Vienna, 1976, Inst. Advanced Stud., Jerusalem, 1978, Nihon Univ. Tokyo, 1980, European Univ. Inst., Florence, 1982, Handelschochschule, St Gallen, Switzerland, 1983; Permanent Vis. Prof., Univ. Konstanz, W. Germany, 1982–7.
Degrees Fil. Kand., Univ. Lund, 1960; MA Univ. Pittsburgh, 1961; PhD Northwestern Univ, 1967; Fil. Dr Causa, Univ. Lund, 1983.
Offices and Honours Brookings Fellow, Brookings Inst., 1963–4; Overseas Fellow, Churchill Coll. Cambridge, 1974; Member, Inst. Advanced Study, Princeton Univ., 1983–4.
Principal Fields of Interest 020 General Economic Theory; 311 Domestic Monetary Theory; 031 History of Economic Thought.
Publications *Books:* 1. *On Keynesian Economics and the Economics of Keynes: A Study in Monetary Theory* (OUP, 1968; transls., German, 1973, Italian, Biblioteca Moderna di Economia, 1976, Spanish, Vicens Vives, 1976, Japanese, Toyo Keizai Shimposa, 1978); 2. *Keynes and the Classics: Two Lectures* (INEA, 1969; transl., Spanish, Editorial Saltes, 1976); 3. *Information and Coordination: Essays in Macroeconomic Theory* (OUP, 1981; transl., Japanese, Toyo Keizai Shimposa, 1983).

Articles: 1. 'The coordination of economic activities: a Keynesian perspective' (with R. W. Clower), *AER*, 65(2), May 1975; transl., Japanese in *Reappraisal of Keynesian Economics* (1981); 2. 'Theories of stagflation', *Rev. de L'Assoc. Française de Fin.*, Dec. 1980; 3. 'What was the matter with IS-LM?', in *Modern Macroeconomic Theory*, ed. J. P. Fitoussi (Blackwell, 1983); 4. 'Inflation and economic performance', *Kieler Vortraege*, 101 (J. C. B. Mohr, 1983); 5. 'Keynesianism, monetarism, and rational expectations: some reflections and conjectures', in *Individual Forecasting and Aggregate*

Outcomes: 'Rational Expectations' Examined, eds. R. Frydman and E. S. Phelps (CUP, 1983); 6. 'What would Keynes have thought of rational expectations?', in *Keynes and the Modern World*, eds. G. D. N. Worswick and J. S. Trevithick (CUP, 1983); 7. 'Rational expectations and monetary institutions', in *Monetary Theory and Monetary Institutions*, eds. M. de Cecco and J. P. Fitoussi (1985); 8. 'Constitutional constraints on the monetary powers of government', *Scelte Economiche*, 1985; 9. 'Hicks and Keynes', *OEP*, 1985.

Principal Contributions My early work was concerned with unemployment and with business fluctuations. Concern with inflation came later. I see these macroeconomic problems as problems of co-ordination in large, complex systems. Co-ordination should be treated as problematic: we deal with systems that sometimes do very well and sometimes do very badly at it. Yet, in trying to develop this conception, one finds that inherited theories are of little help — 'Keynesian' ones portray economies that cannot succeed, 'neo-classical' ones economies that cannot fail to co-ordinate activities. This conception of the theoretical situation was argued in my 1968 book and also informs most of the essays in the 1981 collection.

The 1968 book already makes use of the history of economics in a way that I have often adopted more self-consciously later. One way to understand the relationship between two branches of economics such as neo-classical and Keynesian theory, or between two schools in some interminable controversy such as the monetarist one, is to construct a mathematical model general enough to feature the contestants as special cases. Alternatively, one may think of the history of the subject as a decision-tree with the current contestants querously twittering away from different twigs and branches. By backtracking down the tree one can understand current differences as the product of sequences of decisions (e.g. to assume A rather than B) stemming from the influential contributions of the past. The latter method can some-

times get it right when the fomer has failed.

Since about 1974 ('Costs and Consequences of Inflation' in the 1981 collection), my main concern has been inflation and other problems of monetary instability. Mostly I have tried to understand better the consequences (as opposed to the causes) of inflation. I am more of an 'alarmist' on this subject than most American macroeconomists.

LEKACHMAN, Robert

Born 1920, New York City, NY, USA.

Current Post Disting. Prof., City Univ., New York City, NY, USA.

Past Posts Prof., Barnard Coll., Columbia Univ., 1948–65; Prof., State Univ. NY-Stonybrook, 1965–73.

Degrees BA, PhD Columbia Univ., 1942, 1954.

Principal Fields of Interest 031 History of Economic Thought.

Publications *Books:* 1. *History of Economic Ideas* (Harper, 1959); 2. *Ages of Keynes* (Random, 1966); 3. *Inflation* (Vintage, 1973); 4. *Economists at Bay* (McGraw-Hill, 1976); 5. *Capitalism for Beginners* (Pantheon, 1981).

Principal Contributions Contained in *History of Economic Ideas*, published in 1959, and still in print.

LELAND, Hayne E.

Born 1941, Boston, MA, USA.

Current Post Prof., School Bus. Admin., Univ. Cal. Berkeley, USA, 1978–.

Past Posts Ass. Prof., Stanford Univ., 1968–74; Assoc. Prof., Univ. Cal. Berkeley, 1974–8.

Degrees BA, PhD Harvard Univ., 1964, 1968; MSc LSE, 1965.

Offices and Honours Dir., AFA; Dir., LDR Assoc. Inc.

Editorial Duties Assoc. Ed., *Int ER*, 1973–8, *JET*, 1976–9.

Principal Fields of Interest 521 Business Finance; 522 Business Investment.

Publications *Articles:* 1. 'Savings and uncertainty: the precautionary demand for saving', *QJE*, 82, Aug. 1968, repr. in *A Book of Readings*, eds. P. Diamond and M. Rothschild (Univ. Chicago Press, 1979); 2. 'Theory of the firm facing uncertain demand', *AER*, 62(3), June 1972; 3. 'Production theory and the stock market', *Bell JE*, 5(1), Spring 1974; 4. 'Information asymmetries, financial structure and financial intermediation' (with D. Pyle), *J Fin*, 31(2), May 1976; 5. 'Quacks, lemons, and licensing: a theory of minimum quality standards', *JPE*, 87(6), Dec. 1979.

LENIN, Vladimir Illich*

Dates and Birthplace 1870–1924, Simbirsk, Russia.

Posts Held Organiser of the Russian Communist Party; Leader of Russia after the 1917 Revolution.

Degrees Grad. Law Univ. St Petersburg, 1891.

Publications *Books:* 1. *The Development of Capitalism in Russia* (1899, 1960); 2. *What is to be Done?* (1901, 1961); 3. *Imperialism, the Highest Stage of Capitalism* (1916, 1964); 4. *The State and Revolution* (1917, 1964); 5. *Selected Works*, 12 vols (1935–8).

Career His writings, though revered in Soviet Russia, are not remarkable for their originality. *Imperialism . . .* owes much to the writings of Hobson, Bukharin, and Hilferding, and even the earlier *Development of Capitalism in Russia*, his only genuine contribution to economics, is derivative. This latter work, while presented as an application of the theory of Marx's *Capital* to Russian conditions, is in fact a radically unorthodox work which abandons many of the central indeas of Marxism, such as the progressive role of industrialisation in the countryside.

Secondary Literature A. Nove, 'Lenin as an economist', in *Lenin: the Man, the Theorist, the Leader*, eds. L. Shapiro and P. Reddaway (Stanford Univ. Press, 1967); J. D. Clarkson, 'Lenin', *IESS*, 9.

LEONTIEF, Wassily

Born 1906, St Petersburg, Russia.

Current Post Prof. Econ., NYU, 1975–; Dir., Inst. Econ. Analysis, NYU, 1976–.

Past Posts Res. Assoc., Inst. World Econ., Univ. Kiel, 1927–8; Econ. Adviser, Chinese Govt., Nanking, 1928–9; Res. Assoc., NBER, 1931; Instr., Ass. Prof., Assoc. Prof., Prof. Econ., Henry Lee Chair Political Econ., Harvard Univ., 1932–3, 1933–9, 1939–46, 1946–53, 1953–75; Gen. Cons., US Dept. Labor, 1941–7, 1961–5; Part-time Econ. Cons., Chief, Russian Econ. Sub-Division, US Office Strategic Services, 1943–5; Cons., UN Secretary General's Consultative Group Econ. and Social Consequences of Disarmament, 1961–2; Part-time Gen. Cons., US Dept. Commerce, 1966–; Member, Exec. Board, Environmental Protection Agency, 1975–80; Part-time Gen. Cons., Office Technology Assessment, 1980–; Cons., UNDP, 1980–.

Degrees MA (Social Sciences) Univ. Leningrad, 1921–5; PhD Univ. Berlin, 1925–8; Hon. degrees, Univs., Pisa, 1953, Brussels, 1962, York, 1967, Louvain, 1971, Paris Sorbonne, 1972, Penn., 1976, Lancaster, 1976, Toulouse, 1980, Louisville, 1980, Vermont, 1980, C. W. Post Center, Long Island, 1980.

Offices and Honours Amer. Philo. Soc., Internat. Stat. Inst.; Hon. Member, Japan Econ. Res. Center, Tokyo; Hon. Fellow, RSS; Corresp. Fellow, Inst. de France, 1968; Officer, French Légion d'Honneur, 1968; Corresp. Fellow, BA, 1970; Bernard Harms Prize Econ., W. Germany, 1970; Pres., AEA, 1970; Nobel Prize in Econ., 1973; Member, NAS, 1974; Accademia Nazionale dei Lincie, Italy, 1975; American Comm. East-West Accord, 1975; Hon. Member, Royal Irish Academy, 1976; Pres., Section F, BAAS, 1976; Fellow, AAAS, 1977; Commission to Study Organization of Peace, 1978; Comm. Nat. Security, 1980; Russian-Amer. Hall of Fame, 1980; Order Rising Sun (2nd Rank), Japan, 1984.

Principal Fields of Interest 222 Input-Output.

Publications *Books:* 1. *The Structure*

of the American Economy, 1919–1929 (OUP, 1941, 1953); 2. *Studies in the Structure of the American Economy* (OUP, 1953); 3. *Input-output Economics* (OUP, 1966, 1985); 4. *Essays in Economics* (OUP, 1966, 1985); 5. *The Future of the World Economy* (OUP, 1977).

Principal Contributions Input-output analysis. Theory of international trade and its empirical implementation.

Secondary Literature W. H. Miernyk, 'Leontief, Wassily', *IESS*, 18; R. Dorfman, 'Wassily Leontief's contributions to economics', *Swed JE*, 79, 1977; repr. in *Contemporary Economists in Perspective*, eds. H. W. Spiegel and W. J. Samuels (JAI Press, 1984).

LERNER, Abba P.*

Dates and Birthplace 1903–1982, Russia.

Posts Held Ass. Lect., LSE, 1935–7; Ass. Prof., Univ. Kansas City, 1940–2; Assoc. Prof., Prof. Econ., New School Social Res., NY, 1942–6, 1946–7; Prof. Econ., Roosevelt Univ., 1947–59, Michigan State Univ., 1959–65, Univ. Cal. Berkeley 1965–71; Disting. Prof. Econ., Queen's Coll., NY, 1971–8, Florida State Univ., 1978–80.

Degrees BSc, PhD Univ. London, 1932, 1943; Hon. DSc Northwestern Univ., 1978.

Offices and Honours Tooke Scholarship, LSE, 1930; Gonner Prize, LSE, 1932; Gladstone Memorial Prize, LSE, 1932; LSE Res. Fellow, 1932–4; Leon Fellow, Univ. London, 1934–5; Rockefeller Fellow, US, 1938–9; Cons., Rand Corp., 1949, UNECE, Geneva, 1950–1, Econ. Advisory Staff, Jerusalem, 1953–5; Adviser, Treasury, Govt. Israel, Bank Israel, 1955–6; Fellow, Center Advanced Study Behavioral Sciences, Stanford, CA, 1960–1; Vice-Pres., Disting. Fellow, AEA, 1963, 1966; Hon. Fellow, LSE, 1970–82; Fellow, AAAS, 1971–82; Pres., Univ. Center Rational Alternatives, 1973–82; Member, NAS, 1974–82; Pres., Atlantic Econ. Soc., 1980.

Publications *Books:* 1. *The Economics of Control* (1944); 2. *The Economics of Employment* (1951); 3. *Essays in Economic Analysis* (1953); 4. *Flation* (1972, 1973); 5. *MAP — A Market Anti-inflation Plan* (with D. Colander), (1980).

Career An early and enthusiastic convert to Keynesian economics, he soon turned to the 'economics of socialism' and in his major work, *The Economics of Control*, provided a sustained defence of a liberal economic order grounded in cost-benefit analysis and the 'new' welfare economics of Hicks, Kaldor and Bergson. Similarly, his exposition of the principles of 'functional finance' married the 'new' welfare economics to a radical version of Keynesian economics to furnish a complete 'economics of control' for any economic order, whether capitalist or socialist. In later years he became a vigorous advocate of MAP, a scheme for controlling inflation in a mixed economy by the sale of tradeable 'permits', the possession of which would be required for any business firm that wanted to raise the wages of its staff.

Secondary Literature T. Scitovsky, 'Lerner's Contribution to Economics', *JEL*, 22(4), December 1984.

LEROY, Stephen Francis

Born 1943, Philadelphia, PA, USA.

Current Post Prof., Univ. Cal. Santa Barbara, Santa Barbara, CA, USA, 1982–.

Past Posts Econ., Fed. Reserve Bank Kansas City, 1970–3; Econ., Fed. Reserve Board, 1973–7; Assoc. Prof., Inst. Internat. Econ. Stud., Stockholm, 1977; Ass. Prof., Assoc. Prof., Univ. Cal. Santa Barbara, 1977–80; Vis. Ass. Prof., Univ. Chicago, 1979–80.

Degrees BA Cornell Univ., 1965; PhD Univ. Penn., 1971.

Editorial Duties Advisory Ed., *Econ. Letters*, 1981–3.

Principal Fields of Interest 023 Macroeconomic Theory; 313 Capital Markets; 311 Monetary Theory.

Publications *Articles:* 1. 'Risk aversion and the martingale property of stock prices', *Int ER*, 13(2), June 1973; 2. 'Urban land rent and the incidence of property taxes', *JUE*, 3(4), Oct. 1976; 3. 'Entry and equilibrium under adjustment costs', *JET*, 23(3), May 1980; 4. 'The present-value relation: tests based on implied variance bounds' (with R. D. Porter), *Em*, 49(3), May 1981; 5. 'Identification and estimation of money demand' (with T. F. Cooley), *AER*, 71(5), Dec. 1981; 6. 'Risk aversion and the dispersion of asset prices' (with C. J. LaCivita), *J Bus*, 54(4), 1981; 7. 'Expectations models of asset prices: a survey of theory', *J Fin*, 27(1), March 1982; 8. 'Paradise lost and regained: American cities in the 1970s' (with J. Sonstelie), *JUE*, 13(1), Jan. 1983; 9. 'Keynes' theory of investment', *HOPE*, 15(3), Fall 1983; 10. 'Nominal prices and interest rates in general equilibrium: money shocks', *J Bus*, 57(2), April 1984.

Principal Contributions My PhD dissertation, published subsequently as No. 1 above, presented the first analysis of financial asset pricing in a context of stochastic steady-state rational-expectations equilibrium. The substantive point was to argue against the then prevailing idea that asset prices necessarily follow martingales in efficient capital markets if agents are risk-averse. My interest in finance has continued throughout; the question of whether financial asset prices are more volatile than is consistent with received finance theory became a focus for much of my subsequent research. The first contribution, suggesting that stock prices are in fact too volatile, was (No. 3). A later paper (No. 6) argued that in some settings risk-aversion would increase stockprice volatility, hence possibly biassing volatility tests towards rejection of risk-neutrality. I also worked on aspects of financial asset pricing not connected with volatility (No. 7, for example). Macroeconomics and monetary theory have been a major focus. Here much of the work, such as No. 10, has been oriented towards extending results on real asset prices in nonmonetary economies to nominal asset prices and nominal interest rates in monetary economies. Some of my macroeconomics work has been in a critical vein, such as No. 5 and several recent unpublished papers. Investment theory has also interested me (Nos. 3 and 9). Topics of secondary interest are urban economics (Nos. 2 and 8) and the history of economic thought (No. 9).

LEROY-BEAULIEU, Paul*

Dates and Birthplace 1843–1916, France.

Posts Held Journalist, Ed., 1867–72; Prof. Public Fin., Ecole Libre des Sciences Polit., 1872; Prof. Polit. Econ., Collège de France, Paris, 1880.

Degrees Studied in Paris.

Offices and Honours Ed., *J des débats*, 1871; Founder, Ed., *Economiste Française*, 1873.

Publications *Books:* 1. *L'etat moral et intellectual des classes ouvrières* (1868); 2. *Traité de la science des finances*, 2 vols (1877); 3. *Essai sur la répartition des richesses* (1881); 4. *Traité théoretique et pratique d'économie politique*, 4 vols (1895).

Career Liberal economist who largely followed the principles of classical economics. However, he rejected Ricardo's rent theory and Lassalle's 'iron law of wages' in favour of a more optimistic view. He modified his opposition to State intervention in the case of State encouragement of large families. He was a large landowner and his success in agricultural management led to his frequent consultation as an adviser by firms.

Secondary Literature E. R. A. Seligman, 'Leroy-Beaulieu, Paul', *ESS*, 9; *Classics in the Theory of Public Finance*, eds. R. A. Musgrave and A. T. Peacock (Macmillan, 1958).

LESCURE, Jean*

Dates and Birthplace 1882–1947, France.

Posts Held Prof., Univs. Poitiers, Bordeaux, Paris.

Degrees Agrégé, 1910.

Publications *Books:* 1. *Des crises générales et périodiques de surproduction* (1906); 2. *L'épargne en France* (1914); 3. *Hausses et baisses des prix de longue durée* (1933); 4. *Etude sociale comparée des régimes de liberté et des régimes authoritaires* (1939); 5. *Principes d'économie rationelle* (1947).

Career Writer on cycles whose methodology was derived from that of Juglar. His emphasis was on the role of cost items in creating losses for manufacturers newly entering a buoyant market, as well as the time-lags resulting from the manufacture and setting up of new plant and equipment.

LESLIE, Thomas Edward Cliffe*

Dates and Birthplace 1827–82, Wexford, Ireland.

Posts Held Prof. Jurisprudence and Polit. Econ., Queen's Univ., Belfast, 1853–82.

Degrees BA Trinity Coll., Dublin.

Publications *Books:* 1. *Land Systems and Industrial Economy of Ireland, England and Continental Countries* (1870); 2. *Essays in Political and Moral Philosophy* (1879); 3. *Essays in Political Economy* (1879, 1888).

Career Leslie's published work was entirely in the form of essays, most of which were later collected in book form. Much of his work concerned the problems of Ireland. He rejected Home Rule as a solution, preferring land reform in favour of small proprietorship. The different circumstances he observed in his studies of land systems led him to reject classical methodology in favour of an emphasis on the historical approach and the importance of economic institutions. He was, however, an independent critic and not part of an organised historical school such as that of Germany.

Secondary Literature F. W. Fetter, 'Leslie, T. E. Cliffe', *IESS*, 2.

LESLIE, Derek Gascoigne

Born 1948, Belfast, N. Ireland.

Current Post Lect. Econ., Manchester Univ., Manchester, UK, 1975–.

Past Posts Lect. Econ., Swansea Univ., Wales, 1971–5; Vis. Res. Assoc., Boston Univ., 1983.

Degrees BA Univ. Oxford, 1970; MA Univ. Essex, 1971; PhD Univ. Manchester, 1979.

Principal Fields of Interest 820 Labour Markets; Public Policy.

Publications *Books:* 1. *Demand Management Supply Constraints and Inflation*, co-ed. (with M. J. Artis, C. J.

Green and G. Smith), (Manchester Univ. Press, 1982).

Articles: 1. 'The productivity of hours in UK manufacturing and production industries' (with J. Wise), *EJ*, 90, March 1980; 2. 'A two class model of Keynesian unemployment' (with T. Fujimoto), *Metroec.*, Feb.–June 1983; 3. 'Productivity growth in UK manufacturing and production industries', *Appl. Econ.*, 17(1), Feb. 1985; 4. 'The productivity of hours of work in United States manufacturing', *REStat*, 1985.

Principal Contributions My early work and a continuing interest is the productivity of hours of work. My recent contribution has been to show the difficulty of measuring the productivity effects of hours changes using an aggregate production function. Recently my work has broadened into a wider consideration of productivity growth. Another field of interest is the question of real wage rigidity. I have recently completed a paper on the economics of cash limits and how they impinge on pay negotiations. My hope is that this study may lead to a better understanding of why quantity rather than price adjustments dominate in actual economies.

LESOURNE, Jacques François

Born 1928, La Rochelle, France.

Current Post Prof. Econ., Conservatoire Nat. des Arts et Métiers, Paris, France, 1974–.

Past Posts Chief Econ., Charbonnages de France, 1954–7; Dir. General, Pres., Sema and Metra Internat., 1958–75; Dir., Interfutures Project, OECD, 1976–9; Prof. Econ., Ecole des Mines, Saint-Etienne, 1958–61; Prof. Industrial Econ., Ecole National Supérieur de la Statistique, 1960–3; Dir. d'Enseignement, Inst. August Comte, 1979–81.

Degrees Ingenieur Dipl. Ecole Polytechnique, 1951; Ingenieur Dipl. Ecole des Mines, Paris, 1953.

Offices and Honours Fellow, *Em Soc*, 1967; Chairman, Assoc. Française Informatique et Recherches Operationnelle, 1964–7; Council, Inst. Management Science, 1976–9; Vice-Chairman, Internat. Inst. Appl. Systems Analysis, Laxenburg, Austria, 1973–9; Member,

Comm. Comptes et Budgets Econ., France, 1975–9; Pres., Comm. Emploi 8ème Plan, France, 1979–81; Member, Comm. du Bilan, 1981–2; Chairman, Assoc. Française Science Econ., 1981–3; Member, Internat. Stat. Inst., 1974. **Editorial Duties** Ed. Board, *J Pol. Modeling, Internat. J. Industrial Organization.*

Principal Fields of Interest 022 Microeconomy Theory; 110 Economic Growth; Development; and Planning Theory and Policy; 600 Industrial Organisation; Technological Change; Industries Studies.

Publications *Books:* 1. *Technique economique et gestion industrielle* (Dunod, 1958; transls., English, Prentice-Hall, 1963, German, Oldenburg, 1964, Italian, Zanichelli, 1964, Spanish, Aguilar, 1964); 2. *Le calcul économique* (Dunod, 1964; transl., Italian, Franco Angeli, 1964); 3. *Matière grise année* (with R. Lattes and R. Armand), (Denoel, 1970; transls., English, Macdonald, 1972, German, Molden, 1972); 4. *Le calcul économique, théorie et applications* (Dunod, 1972; transl., English, N-H, 1975); 5. *Modèles de croissance de l'entreprise* (Dunod, 1972); 6. *Les systèmes du destin* (Dalloz, 1976); 7. *A Theory of the Individual for Economic Analysis* (N-H, 1977); 8. *L'analyse des décisions d'aménagement du territoire* (with R. Loué), (Dunod, 1973); 9. *Face aux futurs: pour une maîtrise du vraisemblable et une gestion de l'imprévisible* (with Interfutures team), (OECD, 1979; transls., Spanish, Inst., Nat. Prospectiva, 1980, Japanese, Japan Productivity Center, 1980, Dutch, Weltarchiv, 1981); 10. *Les mille sentiers de l'avenir* (Seghers, 1981; transl., Japanese, Tokay Univ. Press, 1983).

Articles: 1. 'A la recherche d'un critère de rentabilité pour les investissements importants', *Cahier du Séminaire d'Econométrie*, 1959; 2. 'Esquisse d'une théorie de l'individu', *REP*, 3, May–June 1975; 3. 'The optimal growth of the firm in a growing environment', *JET*, 13(1), Aug. 1976; 4. 'Managers' behaviour and perfect competition, *Europ ER*, 9, Jan. 1977; 5. 'External diseconomies in consumption and monopoly pricing: a comment', *Em*, 45(2), March 1977; 6. 'Business strate-gies in inflationary economies,' *REStud*, 44(2), June 1977; 7. The firm's investment and employment policy through a business cycle' (with R. Leban), *Europ ER*, 13, Jan. 1980; 8. 'Adaptive strategies of the firm through a business cycle (with R. Leban), *J Ec Dyn*, 5, 1983; 9. 'L'avenir des économies europées: évolutions autonomes et pressions extérieures,' *Communication a l'Académie des Sciences Morales et Politiques*, 27, Sept. 1982.

Principal Contributions At the beginning of my career my main concern was the development of industrial economics, both at the theoretical and at the applied level (in relation to operations research). Hence my first book, *Economic Technique and Industrial Management*. But, having become the president of an international consulting group, I realised that progress had to be made to extend the analysis from a static to a dynamic environment and to integrate better the financial and the social dimensions with the productive one. The book on *Modèles de croissance l'entreprise* and several other papers have been the result of this research. Simultaneously, I had to study the social profitability of many projects in the fields of energy, transportation, urban and regional planning, which led me to look at the foundations of cost-benefit analysis and to present them in various papers and in a book, *Cost-benefit Analysis: Theory and Applications.*

Forecasting and prospective research was an important activity of the consulting firm I was involved in. It may have been the reason why I was appointed in 1976 Director of the Interfutures project at OECD. This was an opportunity to deepen my interest in global modelling and long-term international prospective analysis. My book (No. 10, above) has been the product of several years of research in that direction.

Since the early 1960s I had been convinced of the fruitfulness of a system approach in the social sciences. In 1976, I published on this subject a book (No. 6, above) which is more an essay than a scientific text, but the views expressed in that book have inspired my research in prospective analysis and in economic theory in the last years. I am working now on self-organisation in economic systems (for instance on market processes). One of my next books will be devoted to this topic.

LESSARD, Donald

Born 1943, San Jose, CA, USA.
Current Post Prof. Internat. Management, Sloan School Management, MIT, Cambridge, MA, USA, 1984–.
Past Posts Ass. Prof., Amos Tuck School, Dartmouth Coll., NH, 1969–74; Ass. Prof., Assoc. Prof., Sloan School Management, MIT, 1973–7, 1977–84; Nat. Westminster Vis. Prof. Internat. Fin., London Bus. School, 1981.
Degrees BA, MBA, PhD Stanford Univ., 1965, 1969, 1970.
Offices and Honours Graham and Dodd Award, Fin. Analysts Federation, 1976; Vis. Scholar, Harvard Inst. Internat. Devlp., 1980.
Editorial Duties Assoc. Ed., *J Fin*, 1979–81; Ed. Board, Ed., *Fin, J. Internat. Bus. Stud.*, 1980–4, 1983–4.
Principal Fields of Interest 441 International Investment and Capital Markets; 442 International Business; 521 Business Finance.
Publications *Books:* 1. *New Mortgage Designs for Stable Housing in an Inflationary Environment*, co-ed. (Fed. Reserve Bank Boston, 1975); 2. *International Financial Management: Theory and Application*, ed. (Warren, Gorham & Lamont, 1979, Wiley, 1985).
Articles: 1. 'International diversification for developing countries: a multivariate analysis for a group of Latin American countries', *J Fin*, 28(3), June 1973; 2. 'En defensa de una union latinoamericano de inversiones', *El Trimestre Economico*, Jan.–Mar. 1975; 3. 'World, country, and industry factors in equity returns: implications for risk reduction through international diversification', *Fin. Analysts J.*, Jan.–Feb. 1976; 4. 'Risk efficient external financing strategies for commodity producing countries', *Cuadernos de Economia*, Aug. 1977; 5. 'Transfer prices, taxes, and financial markets: implications of internal financial transfers within the multinational firm', in *Economic Issues of the Multinational*

Firm, ed. R. Hawkins (JAI Press, 1979); 6. 'Evaluating international projects — an adjusted present value approach', in *Capital Budgeting Under Conditions of Uncertainty*, eds. R. Crum and F. Derkinderen (Martinus Nijhoff, 1980), repr. in *International Financial Management, op cit.*; 7. 'Public enterprise finance: towards a synthesis', in *Public Enterprises in Less Developed Countries*, eds. L. Jones, *et al.* (CUP, 1982); 8. 'North-south: the implications for banking', *J Bank Fin*, Dec. 1983; 9. 'Risk bearing and the choice of contract forms for oil exploration and development' (with C. Blitzer and J. Paddock), *Energy J*, Jan. 1984; 10. 'Finance and global competition', in *Competition in Global Enterprises*, ed. M. Porter (Harvard Bus. School Press, 198–).

Principal Contributions My research interests have been concentrated in three general areas: international corporate finance, finance for developing countries, and international portfolio diversification. A theme running throughout much of this work, beginning with my doctoral dissertation which analysed the potential benefits of and obstacles to portfolio diversification across less developed countries, is the limited extent of cross-border risk shifting through financial transactions given the potential welfare gains due to relatively low correlations in asset returns and underlying economic activity. In recent years I have focussed on identifying barriers to cross-border contracting, both at an aggregate and enterprise level, and have tried to identify ways to circumvent these limits and increase risk-sharing. Within corporate finance, I have looked at investment, financing, and financial logistics within multinational firms facing multiple tax jurisdictions, currencies and, in many cases, barriers to capital movements. Most recently, I have extended this work to interactions between finance and operations in the context of volatile real exchange rates and to a new class of hedging transactions relevant to this environment.

LESTER, Richard Allen

Born 1908, Blasdell, NY, USA.
Current Post Faculty Assoc. Emeritus, Industrial Relations Section, Princeton Univ., 1974–.
Past Posts Instr. Econ., Princeton Univ., 1931–2, 1934–8; Ass. Prof. Labor, Univ. Washington, Seattle, 1938–40; Ass. Prof., Assoc. Prof. Econ., Duke Univ., 1940–5; Fed. Wartime Agencies, 1941–4; Assoc. Prof., Prof. Econ., Dean, Princeton Univ., 1945–8, 1948–74.
Degrees PhB Yale Univ., 1929; MA, PhD Princeton Univ., 1930, 1936.
Offices and Honours Vice-Pres., AEA, 1951–3, 1961; Pres., IRRA, 1956.
Principal Fields of Interest 820 Labour Market, Public Policy; 830 Trade Union, Collective Bargaining, Labour-Management Relations; 810 Manpower Training and Allocation, Labour Force and Supply.
Publications *Books:* 1. *Monetary Experiments: Early American and Recent Scadinavian* (Princeton Univ. Press, 1939); 2. *Economics of Labor* (Macmillan, 1941, 1964); 3. *Hiring Practices and Labor Competition* (Industrial Relations Section, Princeton Univ., 1954); 4. *As Unions Mature* (Princeton Univ. Press, 1958; transls., Spanish, Japanese); 5. *The Economics of Unemployment Compensation* (Industrial Relations Section, Princeton Univ., 1962); 6. *Manpower Planning in a Free Society* (Princeton Univ. Press, 1966); 7. *Reasoning about Discrimination: An Analysis of Professional and Executive Work in Federal Antibias Programs* (Princeton Univ. Press, 1980); 8. *Labor Arbitration in State and Local Government* (Industrial Relations Section, Princeton Univ., 1984).
Articles: 1. 'Shortcomings of marginal analysis for wage-employment problems', *AEA*, 36(1), March 1946; 2. 'Marginalization, minimum wages and labor markets, *AEA*, 37(1), March 1947; 3. 'Southern wage differentials: developments, analysis and implications', *SEJ*, 13(2), April 1947; 4. 'Reflections on the "labor monopoly" issue', *JPE*, 55(4), Dec. 1947; 5. 'A range theory of wage differentials', *ILRR*, 5(2), July 1952; 6. 'Economic adjustments to changes in wage differentials', in *New Concepts in Wage Differentials* (McGraw-Hill, 1957); 7. 'Manipulation of the labor market', in *The Next Twenty Five Years of Industrial Relations* (IRRA, 1973).
Principal Contributions My research in the 1930s developed a new set of conclusions concerning the effects of the issuance of paper money in the American colonies. In the 1940s and 1950s, my studies of company policies and practices with respect to wages, employment and personnel management showed the market limitations that the traditional theory of the firm and marginal productivity theory of wage determination have for explaining actual operations in much of modern industry. I suggested an alternative approach and method of analysis for a realistic understanding of developments and adjustments to cost changes in sizeable companies. That challenge helped to stimulate others to study and develop different theories concerning the set of aims and actual behaviour of business management. Several labour economists including myself made systematic studies of individual local labour markets, indicating the extent to which wages and other aspects of employment were administered and varied by company and occupation within companies (see *Economics of Labour*, 1964, pp. 192–221, 255–91).

Additional contributions with respect to employment practices and wage determination were made in the 1950s and 1960s from my studies of: (1) experience with general application of Federal-agency, anti-discrimination regulations (especially the requirement of calculation and enforcement of numerical hiring and promotion goals for professional and managerial employment) and (2) experience of professional neutrals in mediating and arbitrating union-management conflicts over the terms and conditions of employment in a new collective agreement for State and local government units under State, public-sector, labour-relations legislation.

LETICHE, John Marion

Born 1918, Uman, Kiev, USSR.
Current Post Prof. Econ., Univ. Cal. Berkeley, USA, 1960–.
Past Posts Res. Econ., Cowles Commission, Univ. Chicago, 1943–4; Econ., US President's Emergency War Recovery Board, 1945; Econ., US Council on Foreign Relations, NY, 1945–6; Lect., Ass. Prof., Assoc. Prof., Univ. Cal. Berkeley, 1946–60; Cons., US President's Council Econ. Advisers, 1956, Comm. Foreign Trade Pol., Washington, DC, 1960, UNECA, Africa, 1961–2, US Depts. State, Labor, Treasury, 1962–, Econ. Devlp. Inst., Univ. Nigeria, 1963–5, Foreign Service Inst., US Dept. State, 1965–71, Inst. Internat. Educ., NY, 1965–9, Fed. Govt. Nigeria, 1968, Emissary to Japan and S. Korea, US Dept. State, 1971, Econ. Council Canada, 1972–5, Council Pol. Alternatives, MIT, 1975–6, World Bank, 1981.
Degrees BA, MA McGill Univ., Montreal, Canada, 1940, 1941; PhD Univ. Chicago, 1951.
Offices and Honours Allen Oliver Fellow, McGill Univ., 1940; Univ. Fellow, Marshall Field Fellow, Univ. Chicago, 1941–3; Rockefeller Fellow, 1945–6; Smith-Mundt-Fulbright Fellow, Denmark, 1951–2; Guggenheim Foundation Fellow, 1956–7; Amer. Council Learned Soc. Fellow, 1973; Certificate Merit, Encyclopaedia Britannica, 1976; Internat. Legal Center, Univ. Mich., 1977; Adam Smith Medal, Univ. Verona, 1977; Board, Amer. Soc. Internat. Law, 1969–73; Nomination Comm., AEA, 1968–9; Disting. Standing Member, Nat. Educ. Advisory Board, 1984–.
Editorial Duties Ed. Boards, *J. African Stud.*, 1979–, *Internat. Social Science Rev.*, 1982–, *Nat. Educ. Biographical Rev.*, 1984–; Gen. Ed., Royer Lectures (Univ. Cal. Berkeley), 1981–.
Principal Fields of Interest 400 International Economics; 030 History of Economic Thought; 100 Economic Growth, Development, Fluctuations.
Publications *Books:* 1. *Reciprocal Trade Agreements in the World Economy* (King's Crown Press, 1948, OUP, 1948; transl., Japanese, 1956); 2. *The System or Theory of the Trade of the World by I. Gervaise*, ed. (JHUP, 1954, 1957); 3. *Balance of Payments and Economic Growth* (Harper, 1959, A. M. Kelley, 1975); 4. *A History of Russian Economic Thought: Ninth Through Eighteenth Centuries*, co-ed. and transl. (with B. Dmytryshyn and R. A. Pierce), (Univ. Cal. Press, 1964, CUP, 1964, Greenwood Press, 1977); 5. *The Key Problems of Economic Reconstruction and Development in Nigeria* (Nigerian Inst. Internat. Affairs, 1969); 6. *International Economic Policies and Their Theoretical Foundations*, ed. (Academic Press, 1982); 7. *Russian Statecraft: The Political Economy of Jurii Krizhanich* (with B. Dmytryshyn), (Blackwell, 1984).
Articles: 1. 'Isaac Gervaise on the international mechanism of adjustment', *JPE*, 60, Feb. 1952; 2. 'Balance of payments', in *Encyclopaedia Britannica* (1954, 1958), revised as 'International Payments' (1969); 3. 'Differential rates of productivity growth and international imbalance', *QJE*, 69, Aug. 1955; 4. 'The relevance of classical and contemporary theories of growth to economic development', *AER*, 49(2), May 1959, repr. in Italian, *La Scuola in Azione*, Sept. 1965; 5. 'Adam Smith and David Ricardo on economic growth', in *Theories on Economic Growth*, ed. B. F. Hoselitz (Glencoe Press, 1960), repr. in *The Punjab Univ. Economist*, Jan. 1960; transl., Spanish, *Herrero Hermanos Sucesores* (SA of Mexico, 1964); 6. 'African monetary systems: their impact on trade and development', in *Africa and Monetary Integration*, ed. R. Tremblay (Holt Rinehart & Winston, 1972), and in *International Economics and Development*, ed. L. E. di Marco (Academic Press, 1972); transl., Portuguese, *Economia Internacional Y Desarrollo* (Depalma Press, 1974); 7. 'The history of economic thought in the international encyclopedia of the social sciences', *JEL*, 7(2), June 1969, transl., Italian, *RISE*, 44, 1970; 8. 'Soviet views on Keynes', *JEL*, 9(2), June 1971, repr. in *J. M. Keynes: Critical Assessments*, ed. J. C. Wood (Croom Helm, 1984); 9. 'Dependent monetary systems and economic development: the case of sterling East Africa', in *Economic*

Development and Planning, Essays in Honour of Jan Tinbergen, ed. W. Sallekaerts (Macmillan, 1974); 10. 'The development of gains from trade theory: classical to modern literature' (with R. G. Chambers and A. Schmitz), in *Economic Prospectives: An Annual Survey of Economic Theory*, 1, 1979, repr. in *International Trade and Agriculture*, ed. S. Hillman (Harwood Press, 1979), and in *International Economic Policies and Their Theoretical Foundations, op. cit.*

Principal Contributions Throughout my career it has been my objective to put economic analysis and the history of economic thought to the quantitative and practical test. Toward that end I began my research by showing that the level of protection in the US was related to the degree of inefficiency of American industries. Under conditions of normal economic growth and without inflation, it was demonstrated that the US underwent striking adaptions in industrial fields. The evidence showed that it was archaic to maintain that American industry required protection from the competition of the newly developing countries. However, it was also demonstrated that under inflation, followed by major recessions, the foundations of US freer trade policies and those of the IMF would be seriously undermined. This research was followed by the formulation of a more general theory of the balance of payments and its application to specific issues of economic development. The role of factoral terms of trade in the time sequence of economic growth and trade patterns was demonstrated to be of primary significance. Differential rates of productivity growth and international imbalance were proved to be caused primarily by monetary and institutional disturbances rather than structural ones.

As regards the history of economic thought, I discovered the true identity of Isaac Gervaise and the nature of his business career, rendering it possible for the first time to place his remarkable *Essay* in its historical setting. Similarly, I have endeavoured to examine the history of economic thought of numerous countries to enlighten our understanding of their objectives and actions.

Recently, my research has turned toward linking mainstream macroeconomics, microeconomics, and Keynesian economics with the aim of integrating key monetary and real variables in balance-of-payments disequilibrium.

LEVASSEUR, Emile*

Dates and Birthplace 1828–1911, Paris, France.

Posts Held Teacher Rhetoric, Alençon, Besançon; Teacher Econ. Hist., Collège de France, Paris, 1868–71; Prof., Conservatoire des Arts et Métiers, Paris, 1871; Teacher, L'Ecole Libre des Sciences Polit., 1871–1911.

Degrees Agrégé des Lettres, L'Ecole Normale Supérieure.

Publications *Books:* 1. *Recherches historiques sur le système de Law* (1854); 2. *Histoire des classes ouvrières et de l'industrie en France avant 1789* (1859, 1901); 3. *Histoire des classes ouvrières et de l'industrie en France de 1789 à 1870* (1867, 1904); 4. *Rapport sur le commerce et le tonnage relatifs au canal interocéanique* (1879); 5. *La population française*, 3 vols (1889–92); 6. *The American Workman* (1898, 1900).

Career The founder of modern economic history in France, who introduced the historical method into the largely abstract world of French political economy. He described his own area of work as 'economic art' in contrast to pure theory, which he labelled as 'economic science'.

Secondary Literature C. Fohlen, 'Levasseur, Emile', *IEES*, 9.

LEVHARI, David

Born 1935, Ramat-Gan, Israel.

Current Post Prof. Econ., Hebrew Univ. Jerusalem, 1964–.

Past Posts Vis. Prof., Univs., Stanford, Penn., Illinois, Amsterdam.

Degrees BA (Econ. Stats.), MA Hebrew Univ., 1959, 1961, PhD MIT, 1964.

Offices and Honours Fellow, Em Soc, 1970–.

Principal Fields of Interest 111 Economic Growth Theory.

Publications *Articles*: 1. 'Extension of Arrow's "learning by doing"', *REStud*, 32(2), Jan. 1966; 2. 'Optimal savings under uncertainty' (with T. Srinivasan), *REStud*, 36, April 1969; 3. 'The relation between the rate of return and the rate of technical progress' (with E. Sheshinski), *REStud*, 36, July 1969; 4. 'Risk and the theory of indexed bonds' (with N. Liviatan), *AER*, 67(3), June 1977; 5. 'The great fish war: an example using a dynamic Cournot-Nash equilibrium' (with L. Mirman), *Bell JE*, 11(1), Spring 1980; 6. 'The internal organization of the firm and the shape of average costs', *Bell JE*, 14(1), Spring 1983.

Principal Contributions The fields of capital theory, growth models, and dynamic models of optimisation. Studied growth models with various kinds of technological change and their economic implications. More recently studied exploitation of exhaustible or renewable resources, optimal accumulation under uncertainty, inflation and indexed bonds markets.

LEVI, Maurice David

Born 1945, London, England.

Current Post Bank of Montreal Prof. Internat. Fin., Univ. British Columbia, Vancouver, British Columbia, Canada, 1982–.

Past Posts Lect., Roosevelt Univ., Chicago, IL, 1971; Indiana Univ., E. Chicago, 1971; Ass. Prof., Assoc. Prof., Univ. British Columbia, 1974–7, 1979–82; Vis. Prof., Hebrew Univ., Israel, 1978; Vis. Assoc. Prof., Univ. Cal. Berkeley, 1979.

Degrees Hon. BA, MA Univ. Manchester, 1967, 1968; PhD Univ. Chicago, 1972.

Offices and Honours T. S. Ashton Prize, R. Cobden Prize, Univ. Manchester; Ford Foundation Fellow, Univ. Chicago; J. S. Perry Award; Killam Post-doctoral Fellow; Leslie Wong Fellow; Canada Council Fellow.

Editorial Duties Ed. Board, *J Internat. Money and Fin.*

Principal Fields of Interest 023 Macroeconomic Theory; 442 International Business; 212 Construction, Analysis and Use of Econometric Models.

Publications *Books:* 1. *Economics Deciphered* (Basic Books, 1981; transls., German, Birkhauser, 1982, Japanese, 1982, Spanish, El Aleneo, 1982); 2. *International Finance* (McGraw-Hill, 1983).

Articles: 1. 'Errors in variables bias in the presence of correctly measured variables', *Em*, 4(5), Sept. 1973; 2. 'Effectiveness of monetary and fiscal policy as implied by the behavior of inventory stocks', *J Mon E*, 1(2), April 1975; 3. 'World-wide effects and import elasticities', *J Int E*, 6(2), May 1976; 4. 'Taxation and abnormal international capital flows', *JPE*, 85(3), June 1976; 5. 'Measurement errors and bounded OLS estimates', *J Em*, 6(4), Sept. 1977; 6. 'Anticipated inflation and interest rates' (with J. Makin), *AER*, 68(5), Dec. 1978; 7. 'Inflation uncertainty and the Phillips curve' (with J. Makin), *AER*, 70(5), Dec. 1980; 8. 'Phillips, Friedman and the measured impact of inflation' (with J. Makin), *J Fin*, 34(1), March 1979; 9. 'Weekend effects on stock returns' (with J. LaKouishok), *J Fin*, 37(3), June 1982; 10. 'Spot vs forward speculation and hedging', *J. Internat. Money and Fin.*; 3(1), April 1984.

Principal Contributions The broad applicability of economic and statistical principles allows the economist to tackle the problems of the day. Since the problems keep changing, so have my research topics, which read like a summary of contemporary problems, albeit with a lag. With the debate over monetary vs fiscal policy still raging in the 1970s, I began by looking at policy effectiveness. In particular, my concern was that successfully applied stabilisation policy would not correlate with what was stabilised. For example, if tax cuts prevented an incipient recession and GNP was stabilised, we would have tax cuts and no change in GNP. The only way to get unbiassed estimates is to include all exogenous variables, but since this is difficult I use an indirect estimation method via inventories. The buffer stock motive means that inventories should show effects of policy, especially if the policy itself was unanticipated.

With inflation accelerating during the 1970s the relationship of inflation to interest ratio became a hot topic of debate. With J. Makin, I developed a macroeconomic model showing how the relationship between inflation and interest rates depended upon the effect of inflation on employment, taxes and uncertainty about inflation. Other current problems which have attracted my attention include the reasons for capital to flow two ways between nations and why exchange rates reveal 'seasonality'. I have also looked at national debt in macroeconomic adjustment, the effect of administered prices on the measured relation between monetary policy and inflation, the effect of economic performance on Presidential popularity, biases in measuring import elasticities, and a number of measurement and specification problems in econometrics. My current interests concern the effects of real changes in exchange rates on firms, and the effect of differential tax treatment of investment on the rate of growth. The latter work involves the cost of interfering with evolution in economies via innovation, and is connected to mutation theory in biology and the development of cells.

LEVIN, Henry M.

Born 1938, New York City, NY, USA.

Current Post Prof. Educ. and Econ., Stanford Univ., Stanford, CA, 1975–.

Past Posts Instr. Econ., Rutgers Univ., 1964–5; Assoc. Res. Scientist, NYU, 1965–6; Res. Assoc., Brookings Inst., 1966–8; Ass. Prof., Assoc. Prof., Univ. Stanford, 1968–9; Fellow, Center Advanced Study Behavioral Sciences, Stanford, 1976–7.

Degrees BS NYU, 1960; MA, PhD Rutgers Univ., 1962, 1967.

Offices and Honours Founders Day Award, NYU; Pres., Evaluation Res. Soc., 1982; Vice Pres., Amer. Educ. Res. Assoc., 1971–3.

Editorial Duties Ed. Boards, *Public Fin. Q.*, 1973–, *Econ. and Industrial Democracy*, 1980–, *Evaluation Rev.*, 1979–82, *New Directions Program Evaluation*, 1972–, *Amer. JE*, 1978–83, *Econ. Educ. Rev.*, 1980–, *Educ. Res.*, 1972–6, 1979–83, *Rev. Educ. Res.*, 1980–3.

Principal Fields of Interest 810 Manpower Training and Allocation: Labour Force and Supply; 820 Labour Markets: Public Policy; 850 Human Capital.

Publications *Books:* 1. *Community Control of Schools*, ed. (Brookings Inst., 1970); 2. *Schools and Inequality* (with others), (MIT Press, 1971); 3. *Limits of Educational Reform* (with M. Carnoy), (Longmans, 1976); 4. *Cost-Effectiveness: A Primer* (Sage, 1983); 5. *Financing Recurrent Education*, ed. (Sage, 1983); 6. *Public Dollars for Private Schools*, ed. (Temple Univ. Press, 1983); 7. *Worker Cooperatives in America* (with R. Jackall), (Univ. Cal. Press, 1984); 8. *Schooling and Work in the Capitalist State* (with M. Carnoy), (Stanford Univ. Press, 1985).

Articles: 1. 'The determinants of scholastic achievement — an appraisal of some recent evidence' (with S. Bowles), *JHR*, 3(1), Winter 1968; 2. 'A cost-effectiveness analysis of teacher selection', *JHR*, 5(1), Winter 1970; 3. 'Measuring efficiency in educational production', *Public Fin. Q.*, 2(1), Jan. 1974; 4. 'Cost-effectiveness in evaluation research', in *Handbook of Evaluation Research*, 2, eds. M. Guttentag and E. Struening (Sage, 1975); 5. 'Concepts of economic efficiency and educational production', in *Education as an Industry*, eds. J. Froomkin, D. Jamison and R. Radner (Ballinger, 1976); 6. 'A decade of policy development in improving education and training for low-income populations', in *A Decade of Federal Anti-Poverty Policy: Achievements, Failures and Lessons*, ed. R. Haverman (Academic Press, 1977); 7. 'An evaluation of the costs of computer-assisted instruction' (with L. Woo), *Econ. Educ. Rev.*, 1(1), Winter 1981; 8. 'Raising employment and productivity with producer co-operatives', in *Human Resources, Employment and Development*, 2, eds. P. Streeten and H. Maier (Macmillan, 1983); 9. 'Education and organizational democracy', in *International Yearbook of Organizational Democracy*, 1, eds. C. Crouch and F. Heller (Wiley, 1983); 10. 'Assessing the equalization potential of education', *Comp. Educ. Rev.*, 28(1), Feb. 1984.

Principal Contributions After a short

career in business, I chose my local university, Rutgers, to pursue graduate study. Under Professor C. Harry Kahn I wrote a thesis that used the Tiebout hypothesis on 'voting with one's feet' as a basis for estimating the demand for public recreational land. In 1965 I joined the research staff of the Mayor's Temporary Commission for the Study of New York City's Finances under its Chairman, Dick Netzer. I studied the New York City sales tax, finding very serious sales and employment losses from the tax because of the 'border' problem.

In 1966 I went to the Brookings Institution to specialise in the economics of education. About that time I met Sam Bowles at Harvard, and we wrote a widely circulated critique of the Coleman report on school effectiveness. In 1968 I joined the faculty of the Stanford University School of Education with a joint appointment in economics. From 1968 to the early 1970s I did substantial work estimating educational production functions, earnings functions for teachers, and cost-effectiveness studies in education.

By the early 1970s I had become disappointed with the ostensible failure of the education and training programme of the War on Poverty to improve the distribution of income. This led to my study of labour market issues and especially the structure of ownership and productive organisation on education and work. Although I have continued to do studies in educational productivity, educational finance, and cost-effectiveness analysis, much of my work in recent years has focussed on economic democracy and especially the economics of worker co-operatives. I have found both theoretical and empirical evidence for the propositions that worker participation can increase productivity and employment. My present focus is on estimating production losses from the underutilisation of educated labour, and applying concepts from producer co-operatives to increase productivity and employment.

LEVIN, Richard C.

Born 1947, San Francisco, CA, USA.

Current Post Prof. Econ. and Management, Yale Univ., New Haven, CT, USA, 1982–.

Past Posts Ass. Prof., Assoc. Prof., Yale Univ., 1974–9, 1979–82.

Degrees BA (Hist.) Stanford Univ., 1968; BLitt (Polit.) Univ. Oxford, 1971; MPhil, PhD Yale Univ., 1972, 1974.

Offices and Honours Member, NAS Comm. Very High Speed Integrated Circuits.

Editorial Duties Co-ed., *Res. Pol.*, 1982–.

Principal Fields of Interest 610 Industrial Organisation and Public Policy; 620 Economics of Technological Change; 615 Economics of Transportation.

Publications *Articles:* 1. 'Technical change and optimal scale: some evidence and implications', *SEJ*, 44, Oct. 1977; 2. 'Technical change, barriers to entry and market structure', *Ec*, 45, Nov. 1978; 3. 'Allocation in surface freight transportation: does rate regulation matter?', *Bell JE*, 8, Spring 1978; 4. 'Alternatives for restructuring the railroads: end-to-end or parallel mergers?' (with D. Weinberg), *EI*, 17, July 1979; 5. 'Railroad rates, profitability and welfare', *Bell JE*, 11, Spring 1981; 6. 'Railroad regulation, deregulation and workable competition', *AER*, 7(2), May 1981; 7. 'Vertical integration and profitability in the oil industry', *J Ec Behav*, 2, Sept. 1981; 8. 'The semiconductor industry', in *Government and Technical Progress: A Cross-Industry Analysis*, ed. R. R. Nelson (Pergamon, 1982); 9. 'Tests of a Schumpeterian model of R & D and market structure' (with P. Reiss), in *R & D, Patents and Productivity*, ed. Z. Griliches (Univ. Chicago Press, 1984); 10. 'A welfare analysis of constraints on pricing to deter entry' (with A. Klevorick), in *Research in Finance: Supplement 1*, eds. R. Lenzillotti and Y. Peles (JAI Press, 1984).

Principal Contributions My earliest work focussed on the relationship between technological change and industrial market structure, emphasising the endogenous determination of seller concentration in contrast to the prevailing structure-conduct-performance paradigm in industrial organisation. This work highlighted the role of technological change in extending the range of output over which scale economies are realised. My interest turned next to the consequences of economic regulation in the US freight transportation industry. In a series of econometric papers I studied the effects of regulating railroad rates, mergers and route abandonments. In a subsequent pair of papers I simulated the effects of partial and complete deregulation on railroad rates, profitability and welfare. Recently I have returned to the economics of technological change, concentrating on three subjects: (1) the impact of government policy on the evolution of the US semiconductor industry, (2) inter-industry differences in R & D appropriability and technological opportunity, and (3) simultaneous equations models of industrial R & D and market structure. I have also studied the effects of vertical integration in the oil industry and, more recently, the welfare consequences of alternative antitrust rules constraining the behaviour of dominant firms.

LEVITAN, Sar A.

Born 1914, Shiauliai, Lithuania.
Current Post Res. Prof. Econ., Dir. Center Social Pol. Stud., George Washington Univ., Washington, DC, 1967–.
Past Posts Chairman, US Nat. Commission Employment and Unemployment Stats., 1977–9.
Degrees BS Coll. City NY, 1937; MA, PhD Columbia Univ., 1939, 1949.
Offices and Honours Chairman, Exec. Comm., US Nat. Council Employment Pol., Center Employment Pol. Stud.
Principal Fields of Interest 914 Economics of Poverty; 810 Manpower Training and Allocation.
Publications *Books:* 1. *Antipoverty Work and Training Efforts* (Inst. Labor & Industrial Relations, 1967); 2. *The Great Society's Poor Law* (JHUP, 1969); 3. *The Promise of Greatness* (Harvard Univ. Press, 1976); 4. *Programs in Aid*

of the Poor for the 1980s (JHUP, 1980); 5. *What's Happening to the American Family?* (JHUP, 1981); 6. *Second Thoughts on Work* (Upjohn Inst. Employment Res., 1982); 7. *Business Lobbies: The Public Good and the Bottom Line* (JHUP, 1983); 8. *Human Resources and Labor Markets* (Harper & Row, 1981).
Articles: 1. 'Evaluating social programs', *Society*, May–June 1977; 2. 'Work and the welfare state', *Challenge*, July–Aug. 1977; 3. 'The great society did succeed', *Polit. Science Q.*, Winter 1976–7; 4. 'The unemployment number is the message', Center for Vocational Educ., Occasional Paper 38; 5. 'The work ethic lives!', *Across the Board*, Aug. 1979; 6. 'Labor force statistics to measure full employment', *Society*, Sept.–Oct. 1979; 7. 'Doing the impossible — planning a human resource policy', in *The Future of Vocational Education* (Amer. Vocational Assoc., 1982); 8. The future of work: does it belong to us or the robots?', *MLR*, 105(9), Sept. 1982.
Principal Contributions Major interest has been to assess the impact of government policies in the field of employment and social welfare. As an institutional economist, work has drawn on the insights of other disciplines in examining major policy issues concerning labour market operations and measurements, poverty and manpower programme, and the status of minorities.

LEWIS, William Arthur

Born 1915, St Lucia, W. Indies.
Current Post Prof. Econ., Princeton Univ., Princeton, NJ, 1973–.
Past Posts Lect., LSE, 1938–48; UK Board Trade, UK Colonial Office, 1940–5; Prof. Econ., Univ. Manchester, England, 1948–58; Principal, Univ. Coll., W. Indies, 1958–62; Vice-Chancellor, Univ. W. Indies, 1962–3; Prof. Econ., Princeton Univ., 1963–70; Pres., Caribbean Devlp. Bank, 1970–3; Cons., Govt. Gold Coast, 1953, Western Nigeria, 1955; Econ. Adviser, Prime Minister Ghana, 1957–8.
Degrees BA LSE, 1937; MA Univ.

Manchester, 1940; PhD Univ. London, 1942; Hon. degrees 20 universities.

Offices and Honours Member, UN Group Experts Underdeveloped Countries, 1950–2; Knighted, 1963; Nobel Prize in Econ., 1979; Pres., AEA, 1982.

Principal Fields of Interest 110 Economic Growth; Development; and Planning Theory and Policy

Publications *Books:* 1. *Economic Survey, 1918–1939* (A&U, 1949); 2. *Overhead Costs* (A&U, 1949); 3. *The Principles of Economic Planning* (A&U, 1950, 1969); 4. *The Theory of Economic Growth* (A&U, 1955); 5. *Development Planning: The Essentials of Economic Planning* (A&U, 1966); 6. *Some Aspects of Economic Development* (Ghana Univ., 1969); 7. *Tropical Development 1880–1913 (A&U, 1971); 8. The Evolution of the International Economic Order* (A&U, 1977); 9. *Growth and Fluctuations 1870–1913* (A&U, 1978); 10. *Selected Economic Writings of W. Arthur Lewis,* ed. M. Gersovitz (Columbia Univ. Press, 1980).

Secondary Literature R. Findlay, 'W. A. Lewis' contributions to economics', *Scand JE*, 82(1), Jan. 1980, repr. in *Contemporary Economists in Perspective*, eds. H. W. Spiegel and W. J. Samuels (JAI Press, 1984).

LEXIS, Wilhelm*

Dates and Birthplace 1837–1914, Eschweiler, Germany.

Posts Held Res. Chemistry, Univ. Heidelberg, 1859–61; Prof., Univs. Strassburg, 1872, Dorpat, 1874, Freiburg, 1876, Breslau, 1884, Göttingen, 1887.

Degrees Grad. Univ. Bonn, 1859.

Publications *Books:* 1. *Die französischen Ausfuhrprämien im Zusammenhange mit der Tarifgeschichte und Handelsentwicklung Frankreichs* (1870); 2. *Einleitung in die Theorie der Bevölkerungsstatistik* (1875); 3. *Erörterungen über die Währungsfrage* (1881); 4. *Abhandlungen zur Theorie der Bevölkerungs- und Moralstatistik* (1903); 5. *Das Kredit- und Bankswesen* (1914, 1929).

Articles: 1. 'The concluding volume of Marx's *Capital*', *QJE*, 10, Oct. 1895.

Career Having studied a wide range of subjects, he turned to the social sciences and brought his statistical expertise to economic questions. He was a strong critic of contemporary mathematical economics as having an inadequate quantitative base. His considerable contributions to population theory and economic time series are probably less well-known than his achievements in the theory of statistics and its application. In an interesting critique of the second volume of Marx's *Capital* in 1885, he correctly predicted the 'transformation problem' that emerged in vol. 3 of *Capital* (not published until 1894); Engels commented extensively on Lexis' solution in his preface to *Capital,* vol. 3.

Secondary Literature K-P. Heiss, 'Lexis, Wilhelm', *IESS*, 9.

LIEBEN, Richard*

Dates and Birthplace 1842–1919, Austro-Hungary.

Posts Held Banker.

Offices Vice-Pres., Handels-Akademie and Court Arbitration, Stock Exchange.

Publications *Books:* 1. *Untersuchungen über die Theorie des Preises* (with R. Auspitz), (1889).

Career He advocated the adoption of the gold standard to the inquiry into the reform of the Austrian currency in 1892. For an account of his writings, see Auspitz, Rudolf.

Secondary Literature O. Weinberger, 'Lieben, Richard', *ESS*, 9.

LIEBHAFSKY, Herbert Hugo

Born 1919, Shiner, TX, USA.

Current Post Prof. Econ., Univ. Texas Austin, Austin, TX, USA, 1961–.

Past Posts US Army, 1942; Econ., US Dept. State, Washington, DC, 1949–53; Instr., Univ. Michigan, 1953–6; Ass. Prof., Univ. Texas-Austin, 1956–61.

Degrees BA, MS Texas A&M Univ., 1940, 1941; Juris Dr Univ. Michigan Law School, 1949; PhD Univ. Michigan, 1956.

Offices and Honours Member, Michigan Bar, 1949; Fred. M. Taylor Award Econ. Theory, Univ. Michigan, 1955; Life Member, Board Supervisors, Indian Inst. Econ. Res. (Shartiya Arthik Shedth Dansthan), 1980.

Editorial Duties Ed. Boards, *SEJ*, 1962–6, *Amer. Econ.*, 1964–9, *Varta*, 1980.

Principal Fields of Interest 020 General Economic Theory; 036 Economic Methodology; 610 Industrial Organisation and Public Policy.

Publications *Books:* 1. *The Nature of Price Theory* (Dorsey Press, 1963, 1968; transls., Indonesian, Bhratra Press, 1969, Hindi, Hindi Granth Academy, 1977, Chinese, Bank of Taiwan, 1983); 2. *American Government and Business* (Wiley, 1971).

Articles: 1. 'Marshall's industry & trade: a curious case of neglect', *CJE*, 21(3), Aug. 1955; 2. 'The international materials conference in retrospect', *QJE*, 71(2), May 1957; 3. 'Ten years of GATT', *SEJ*, 25(1), July 1958; 4. 'Institutions and technology in economic progress', *Amer. J Econ. and Sociology*, 19(2), Jan. 1960; 5. 'The origin of Slutsky's "well-known formula" in the theory of determinants', *ZGS*, 125(2), April 1969; 6. 'New thoughts about inferior goods', *AER*, 59(5), Dec. 1969; 7. 'Example of a preference function generating a perfectly inelastic demand function', *JPE*, 80(4), July–Aug. 1972; 8. 'The problem of social cost — an alternative approach', *Natural Resources J*, 13(4), Oct. 1973; 9. 'Price theory as jurisprudence: law and economics, Chicago style', *JEI*, 10(1), March 1976; 10. 'Commons and Clark on law and economics', *JEI*, 10(4), Dec. 1976.

Principal Contributions My early work was concerned primarily with various interpretations and implications of the Slutsky Equation and microeconomic theory generally, with some work also in the area of international economics based on my experience in the US Dept. of State. I became particularly interested in the restrictions imposed upon the demand functions by various interpretations of the Marshallian constancy assumption. With the rise of the Chicago school's price-theory-is-jurisprudence notions, I turned my interest as a lawyer to a critical evaluation of these notions. More recently, my interest has turned to a further probing of John Dewey's 'experimentalism' as an approach to social science and, in particular, to a study of the literature of three generations of institutionalist economic literature, ranging from Veblen, Commons and Mitchell to the present day.

LILLARD, Lee A.

Born 1943, Fort Worth, TX, USA.

Current Post Sr. Econ., Rand Corp., Santa Monica, CA, USA, Adjunct Assoc. Prof. Econ., Univ. Southern Cal., 1977–.

Past Posts Res. Assoc. NBER, NY, Stanford, CA, 1972–7; Vis. Prof., Grad. Center City Univ., NY, 1972–4; Vis. Scholar, US Dept. Labor, 1976–7.

Degrees BA Univ. Texas, Arlington, 1966; MA Southern Methodist Univ., TX, 1968; MS, PhD N. Carolina State Univ., 1970, 1972.

Offices and Honours Kellogg Fellow, 1968–70; Manpower Fellow, 1970–1.

Editorial Duties Assoc. Ed., *Annals Econ. and Social Measurement*, 1974–8.

Principal Fields of Interest 824 Labour Market Studies, Wages and Employment; 211 Econometric and Statistical Methods and Models; 913 Economics of Health.

Publications *Articles:* 'The distribution of earnings and human wealth in a life cycle context', in *The Distribution of Economic Well-Being*, ed. F. T. Juster (NBER, 1977); 2. 'Inequality: earnings versus human wealth', *AER*, 67(2), May 1977; 3. 'Dynamic aspects of earning mobility' (with R. J. Willis), *Em*, 46(5), Sept. 1978; 4. 'Experience, vintage and time effects in the growth of earnings: American scientists 1960–70' (with Y. Weiss), *JPE*, 86(3), June 1978; 5. 'Seasonal electricity demand and pricing analysis with a variable response model' (with J. P. Acton), *Bell JE*, 12(1), Spring 1981; 6. 'Promotion standards, productivity, and the waiting time to promotion for academic scientists' (with Y. Weiss), in *Research in Labor Economics*, ed. R. Ehrenberg (JAI Press, 1982); 7. 'Determinants of schooling attainment: enrollment and continuation probabilities: the Philippines' (with E. King), (Rand Corp., 1983); 8. 'Settlement out of court: the disposition of medical malpractice claims' (with P. Danzon), *J. Legal Stud.*, 12, June 1983; 9. 'Measuring peak-load pricing response experimental data: and exploratory analysis' (with D. Ainger), *J. Bus. and Econ. Stats.*, Jan. 1984.

Principal Contributions Early work concentrated on models of human capital investment and the use of panel or longitudinal data for the analysis of earnings determination. These works developed the notion of individual differences in lifetime wage patterns and the implications of poverty dynamics and labour supply. Subsequent research focussed on the effects of local labour market conditions over time and on the effects of this on earnings. Contributions to applied microeconometric modelling include research on energy demand, time-of-day pricing of electricity, legal decision-making, dispute resolution in medical malpractice cases, educational investments in developing countries, the demand for medical care, the efficacy of preventive medical care, and academic promotion of scientists.

LIM, Chin

Born 1947, Malaysia.
Current Post Assoc. Prof., Univ. Western Ont., London, Ont., Canada, 1983–.
Past Posts Lect., Ass. Prof., Univ. Western Ont., 1977–8, 1978–83.
Degrees B Agric. Science Univ. Malaya, 1970; MSc Univ. British Columbia, 1972; PhD Queen's Univ., Canada, 1978.
Offices and Honours Univ. British Columbia Fellow, 1971; Queen's Univ. Fellow, 1972; DaFoe Foundation Fellow, 1973; Ontario Grad. Fellow, 1974; Canada Council Fellow, 1975; Samuel McLaughlin Fellow, 1976.
Principal Fields of Interest 022 Microeconomic Theory; 320 Public Finance.
Publications *Books:* 1. *Copyright, Competition and Canadian Culture: The Impact of Alternative Copyright Act Import Provisions on the Book and*

Sound Recording Industries (with A. Blomqvist), (Canadian Dept. Consumer and Corp. Affairs, 1981).
Articles: 1. 'The ranking of behavioral modes of the firm facing uncertain demand', *AER*, 70(1), March 1980; 2. 'Risk pooling and intermediate trading agents', *CJE*, 14(2), May 1981; 3. 'Theory of the firm: uncertainty and choice of experiments', *JET*, 24(3), June 1981; 4. 'Monopoly versus competition under uncertainty' (with E. Appelbaum), *CJE*, 15(2), May 1982; 5. 'Long run industry equilibrium with uncertainty' (with E. Appelbaum), *Econ. Letters*, 9(2), 1982; 6. 'Employment insurance and competitive equilibrium labor contracts', *Ec*, 50, Aug. 1983.

Principal Contributions Initial published works were on the economics of uncertainty, especially regarding the theory of the firm and its choice of behavioural modes in a stochastic environment. This work has led to other published works on risk-shifting and risk-sharing between firms and intermediate trading agents, and between firms and employees in labour contracts. At present, my work concentrates on the question of equilibrium entry. One piece deals with the question of how incumbents would optimally choose various strategies to affect the probability of entry in a perfectly contestable market; and another piece studies the question of the equilibrium timing of entry in a rational expectations model of a fully contestable market. In addition to these market models, present interests include the modelling of moral incentives.

LIND, Robert Clarence

Born 1937, Seattle, WA, USA.
Current Post Prof. Econ., Management and Public Pol., Grad. School Management, Cornell Univ., Ithaca, NY, USA, 1974–.
Past Posts Ass. Prof. Econ., Univ. Washington, 1966–7; Ass. Prof., Assoc. Prof. Eng.-Econ. Systems, Assoc. Prof., Grad. School Bus., Stanford Univ., 1967–70, 1970–1, 1971–4; Dir., Public Admin Program, Dir., Energy Pol. Stud., Cornell Univ., 1976–9; Pres.,

Washington Campus, Washington, DC, 1979–.

Degrees BA Yale Univ., 1960; PhD Stanford Univ., 1966.

Principal Fields of Interest 020 General Economic Theory; History Systems; 300 Domestic Monetary and Fiscal Theory and Institutions; 600 Industrial Organisation; Technical Change; Industry Studies.

Publications *Books:* 1. *Discounting for Time and Risk in Energy Policy* (with K.J. Arrow, *et al.*), (JHUP, 1982).

Articles: 1. 'Social rate of discount and the optimal rate of investment: further comment', *QJE*, 78, May 1964; 2. 'Flood control alternatives of the economics of flood protection', *Water Resource Res.*, 3(2), 1967; 3. 'Benefit-cost analysis: a criterion for social investment', in *Water Resources Management* (Univ. Washington Press, 1968); 4. 'Uncertainty and the evaluation of public investment decisions' (with K.J. Arrow), *AER*, 62(1), March 1972, repr. in *Essays in the Theory of Risk Bearing*, ed. K.J. Arrow (Markham, 1971), and *Cost-Benefit Analysis*, ed. R. Layard (Penguin, 1974), and *Uncertainty in Economics, Reading and Exercises*, eds. P. Diamond and M. Rothchild (Academic Press, 1978); 5. 'Spatial equilibrium, the theory of rents, and the measurement of benefits from public programs', *QJE*, 87(2), May 1973, repr. in *Benefit-cost Analysis and Public Policy*, ed. R. Haveman (Adeline, 1974); 6. 'Crime and punishment reconsidered' (with M. Block), *J. Legal Stud.*, Jan 1975; 7. 'A choice theoretic analysis of crime punishable by imprisonment' (with M. Block), *J. Legal Stud.*, June 1975.

Principal Contributions The major thrust of my research, publication, consulting, and teaching up until six or seven years ago dealt with the analysis of public investment and policy discussions. This work included theoretical pieces dealing with the treatment of uncertainty, the choice of the appropriate rate of discount, and methods for correctly measuring benefits and costs, and it also included many applications of this framework of analysis to the fields of energy, water resources, health care, criminal justice, and employment

policy. Over the past five or six years, however, my interests have expanded to include macroeconomic theory and policy and the policy-related aspects of industrial organisation such as antitrust and regulatory policy. This has been coupled with a growing conviction that you cannot analyse economic policy without including a fundamental analysis of the political process and environment in which that policy is formulated, enacted, and implemented.

My interest in macroeconomic theory and policy grew out of my work on the social rate of discount and the fact that one cannot separate individual public investment decisions from the overall macroeconomic environment which in most cases is the driving economic force in budgetary decisions. My interest and work on antitrust and regulatory issues stems both from my extensive involvement as an expert in litigation and from the fact that the many sectors of the US economy are being reshaped by antitrust and regulatory policy, including deregulation.

A final area of current research, teaching, and consulting, addresses the broad question of how corporate management can participate in the political process on economic issues. This involves the entire field of study of the relationship of business to government and the public policy process.

LINDAHL, Erik Robert*

Dates and Birthplace 1891–1960, Stockholm, Sweden.

Posts Held Ass. Prof., Univs. Lund, 1920–4, Uppsala, 1924; Prof., Univs. Göteborg, 1932, Lund, 1939–58.

Degrees Dr Univ. Lund, 1919.

Publications *Books:* 1. *Die Gerechtigkeit der Besteuerung* (1919); 2. *Scope and Means of Monetary Policy* (1929); 3. *Studies in the Theory of Money and Capital* (1939).

Articles: 'Some controversial questions in the theory of taxation' (1928), repr. in *Classics in the Theory of Public Finance*, eds R. A. Musgrave and A. T. Peacock (1958).

Career One of the so-called 'Stockholm School' of Swedish economists who, along with Myrdal and Ohlin, developed Wicksell's monetary theory by applying it to conditions of less than full employment. He began in the field of public finance using marginalist principles to produce a value-of-service theory. His work was essentially an attempt to reconcile economic analysis with the concept of equity. The result was to be an economic policy which could anticipate threats to equilibrium and avert them by appropriate monetary adjustments.

Secondary Literature B. B. Seligman, 'Erik Lindahl: money and capital', in *Main Currents in Modern Economics* (Free Press, 1962).

LINDBECK, Assar, Carl Eugen

Born 1930, Umea, Sweden.
Current Post Prof., Dir., Inst. Internat. Econ. Studies, Univ. Stockholm, Sweden, 1971–.
Past Posts Swedish Treasury Dept., 1953–6; Vis. Ass. Prof., Univ. Michigan, 1958; Lect., Reader, Univ. Stockholm, 1959–60, 1962–3; Prof., Stockholm School Econ., 1964–71; Wesley Clair Mitchell Res. Prof., Columbia Univ., 1968–9; Ford Rotating Res. Prof., Univ. Cal., 1969; Vis. Fellow, Nat. Univ. Canberra, 1970; Irving Fisher Vis. Prof., Yale Univ., 1976–7; Vis. Scholar, Simon Fraser Univ., 1981; Chairman, Nobel Prize Comm. Econ.; Expert Cons. Swedish Govt., Sveriges Riksbank, OECD, World Bank, UNCTAD, UNIDO.
Degrees MS (Social Sciences) Uppsala Univ., 1953; PhD Univ. Stockholm, 1963.
Offices and Honours Rockefeller Fellow, 1957–8; Erik Lindahl Prize, 1963; Ahrnberg Prize, Swedish Royal Academy Sciences, 1964; Herbert Tingsten Prize, 1977; Albert Bonnier Popular Science Writing Award, 1978; Olle Engkvist Prize Scholarly Work, 1980; Natur och Kultur Cultural Prize, 1981; Member, Swedish Royal Academy Sciences, Swedish Academy Eng. Sciences, Finnish and Danish Academies Sciences; Fellow, Em Soc; Hon. Member, AEA.
Editorial Duties Ed. Board, *J. Econ.*

Systems, 1977–81, *J Int E*, 1971–, *Ekonomisk Debatt*, 1973.
Principal Fields of Interest 023 Macroeconomic Theory; 822 Public Policy; Role of Government; 053 Comparative Economic Systems.
Publications *Books:* 1. *The Short-run Effects of the Government Budget* (Swedish) (Treasury Dept., 1956); 2. *The 'New' Theory of Credit Control in the United States* (Almqvist & Wiksell, 1959); 3. *The Housing Shortage. A Study of the Price System in the Housing Market* (Swedish) (with R. Bentzel and I. Stahl), (Almqvist & Wiksell, 1963); 4. *A Study in Monetary Analysis* (Almqvist & Wiksell, 1963; transls., Italian, Unione Tipografico-Editrice Torinese, 1971, Japanese, 1968); 5. *Monetary-Fiscal Analysis and General Equilibrium* (Yrjo Jahnsson Lectures, 1967); 6. *The Economics of the Agricultural Sector* (with O. Gulbrandsen), (Industriens Utredningsinst, 1973); 7. *The Political Economy of the New Left* (Harper & Row, 1971; transl. 14 languages); 8. *Inflation and Unemployment in Open Economies*, ed. (N-H, 1979); 9. *Swedish Economic Policy* (Univ. California Press, 1974, Macmillan, 1975; transls., Swedish, 1968, 1975, Italian, Liguori Editore, 1976, Japanese, Tokai Univ. Press, 1981); 10. *Inflation — Global, International and National Aspects* (Leuven Univ. Press, 1980).

Articles: 1. 'The method of isolation in economic statics', *Swed. JE*, 68, Sept. 1966; 2. 'Is stabilization policy possible? — time lags and conflicts of goals', in *Public Finance and Stabilization Policy in Honor of Richard Musgrave* (N-H, 1974); 3. 'Economic systems and the economics of the new left', in *Der Streit um die Gesellschaftsordnung* (Schulthess Polygraphischer Verlag, 1975); 4. 'Stabilization Policy in open economies with endogenous politicians', *AER*, 66(2), May 1976; 5. 'Economic dependence and interdependence in the industrialized world', in *From Marshall Plan to Global Interdependence* (OECD, 1978); 6. 'Emerging arteriosclerosis of the Western economies — consequences for the less developed countries', *India Internat. Centre Q.*, 1(9), March 1982; 7. 'Work incentives in the welfare state', *National-*

ökonomische Gesellschaft Lectures 1979–80 (Manz, 1981); 8. 'Tax effects versus budget effects on labor supply', *EI*, 20(4), Oct. 1982; 9. 'The recent slowdown of productivity growth', *EJ*, 93, March 1983; 10. 'Competing wage claims, cost inflation and capacity utilization' (with T. Gylfason), *Europ ER*, 26(3), Dec. 1984.

Principal Contributions Development and empirical application on Swedish data of methods to analyse direct (impact) effects on aggregate demand of discretionary and automatic fiscal policies without using complete econometric model — a simplified version (with unweighted effects) being estimates of 'full employment budget surpluses' (1956). Early demonstration, in *A Study in Monetary Analysis*, of how demand functions in terms of relative prices are transformed into a Keynesian-type aggregate demand function in terms of disposable income if income is constrained by involuntary unemployment. Explanation of credit rationing as the consequence of the attitudes of lenders towards risk as there is risk associated not only with the principal of a loan but also with the interest. Demonstration that changes in initial wealth holdings exert a weaker influence on demand for products than do changes in income (both with the same capital value) if preferences between consumption and wealth are endogenous in the sense that the marginal evaluation of wealth relative to consumption rises by higher initial wealth holdings. Analysis of the effects of alternative mixes of monetary-fiscal policy in two-period models, emphasising the distinction between temporary and permanent changes in various parameters and variables. Treatment of economic systems as a multidimensional phenomenon, and within that framework an analysis of changes over time in the functioning of the Western economic system, as well as of the political economy of the New Left. Economic problems of the national State in a strongly internationalised world economy. Study of theories and problems of Swedish economic development and policy, in particular after World War II. Attempts to endogenise the behaviour of economic policy ('endogenous politicians') in the context of stabilisation policy ('political business cycles') and distribution policy. Currently working on wage formation, involuntary unemployment, macroeconomic deficits and welfare-state problems.

LINDBLOM, Charles Edward

Born 1917, Turlock, CA, USA.
Current Post Sterling Prof. Econ. and Polit. Science, Yale Univ., New Haven, CT, USA, 1978–.
Past Posts Ass. Prof., Assoc. Prof. Econ., Univ. Minnesota, 1938–46; Assoc. Prof., Prof., Dir., Inst. Social and Pol. Stud., Yale Univ., 1946–78, 1974–81; Econ. Adviser, American Ambassador, Dir., US Agency Internat. Devlp. Mission India, 1963–5.
Degrees BA (Econ. and Polit. Science) Stanford Univ., 1937; PhD, Hon. Dr Univ. Chicago, 1945, 1973.
Offices and Honours Fellow, Center Advanced Study Behavioral Sciences, Stanford, 1954–5; Guggenheim Foundation Fellow, 1960–1; Pres., Assoc. Comp. Econ. Stud., 1975–6; Pres., Amer. Polit. Science Assoc., 1981.
Principal Fields of Interest 053 Comparative Economic Systems.
Publications *Books:* 1. *Unions and Capitalism* (Yale Univ. Press, 1949); 2. *Politics, Economics and Welfare* (with R. A. Dahl), (Harper & Bros., 1953); 3. *A Strategy of Decision* (with D. Braybrooke), (Free Press, 1963); 4. *The Intelligence of Democracy* (Free Press, 1965); 5. *The Policy-Making Process* (Prentice-Hall, 1968, 1980); 6. *Politics and Markets: The World's Political-Economic Systems* (Basic Books, 1977); 7. *Usable Knowledge: Social Science and Social Problem Solving* (with D. K. Cohen), (Yale Univ. Press, 1979).
Articles: 1. 'In praise of political science', *World Politics*, Jan. 1957; 2. 'The science of "muddling through"', *Public Admin. Rev.*, Spring 1959; 3. 'The sociology of planning: thought and social interaction', in *Economic Planning, East and West*, ed. M. Bornstein (Ballinger, 1975); 4. 'Still muddling, not yet through', *Public Admin. Rev.*, Winter 1979.

LINDERT, Peter Harrison

Born 1940, Minneapolis, MN, USA.
Current Post Prof. Econ., Univ. Cal. Davis, 1978–.
Past Posts Management Intern, Office Internat. Affairs, US Treasury, 1963, 1964; Ass. Prof., Assoc. Prof. Econ., Univ. Wisconsin, 1966–78; Vis. Lect., Univ. Essex, England, 1969–70, Univ. Camb., 1978.
Degrees BA Princeton Univ, 1962; PhD Cornell Univ, 1967.
Offices and Honours NDEA Fellow Econometrics and Quant. Techniques, 1963–5; Ford Doctoral Fellow, 1965–6; Scholar, Brookings Inst., 1965–6; Disting. Speaker Exchange Program, People's Republic China.
Editorial Duties Ed., *Explor. Econ. Hist.*, 1971–3; Ed. Board, *JEH*, 1979; Co-ed., *Res. Popular Econ.*, 1980–2.
Principal Fields of Interest 040 Economic History; 400 International Economics; 840 Demographic Economics.
Publications Books: 1. *Key Currencies and Gold, 1900–1913* (Princeton Univ. Press, 1969); 2. *Prices, Jobs and Growth* (Little Brown, 1976); 3. *Fertility and Scarcity in America* (Princeton Univ. Press, 1978); 4. *International Economics* (with C.P. Kindleberger), (Richard D. Irwin, 1978–1982; transls., French, Indonesian, and Chinese); 5. *American Inequality: A Macroeconomic History* (with J.G. Williamson), (Academic Press, 1980).
Articles: 1. 'Yardsticks of Victorian entrepreneurs' (with K. Trace), in *Essays on a Mature Economy*, ed. D.N. McCloskey (Princeton Univ. Press, 1971); 2. 'The payments impact of foreign investment controls', *J Fin*, 26(5), Dec. 1971; 3. 'Land scarcity and American growth', *JEH*, 34(4), Dec. 1974; 4. 'Sibling position and achievement', *JHR*, 12(2), Spring 1977; 5. 'Child costs and economic development', in *Population and Economic Change in Developing Countries*, ed. R.A. Easterlin (Chicago Univ. Press, 1980); 6. 'English occupations, 1670–1811', *JEH*, 40(4), Dec. 1980; 7. 'English workers' living standards during the industrial revolution: a new look' (with J.G. Williamson), *EHR*, 2nd Series, 36(5), Feb. 1983, repr. in *Economic*

History and the Industrial Revolution, ed. J. Mokyr (A&U, 1984); 8. 'Revising Britain's social tables, 1688–1913' (with J.G. Williamson), *Explor. Econ. Hist.*, 19(4), Oct. 1982, 20(1), Jan. 1983; 9. 'English living standards, population growth and Wrigley-Schofield', *Explor. Econ. Hist.*, 20(2), April 1983.
Principal Contributions International monetary problems were the focus of my doctoral thesis and an early article. By 1978 the interest in international economics had been channelled into revising editions of the leading texts in this field, jointly with C. P. Kindleberger, until the forthcoming solo 1986 edition. Meanwhile, the joy of economic history brought forays into a wide range of topics, including the appraisal of industrial entrepreneurship and the determinants of land scarcity. A large project on the economic dimensions of fertility in the mid–1970s brought reinterpretations of the fertility-inequality link and a new method for defining and measuring the relative cost of an extra child.

Since the late 1970s, two large projects on the history of inequality, in collaboration with J. G. Williamson, have produced books and articles on American and British inequality trends since the 17th century. These combined fresh data-mining and basic reinterpretations of the timing and causes of inequality movements. One byproduct of the British inequality project was a recasting of the long debate over English workers' well-being during the industrial revolution. Research interests are now shifting toward more contemporary macroeconomic policy issues, though past wanderlust will surely continue.

LINDSAY, Cotton Mather

Born 1940, Atlanta, GA, USA.
Current Post J. Wilson Newman Prof. Managerial Econ., Clemson Univ., Clemson, SC, USA, 1984–.
Past Posts Ass. Prof., Assoc. Prof., Prof. Econ., UCLA, 1969–74, 1974–80, 1980–1; Fellow, Hoover Inst., Stanford Univ., 1975–6; Disting. Vis. Prof. Econ., Arizona State Univ., 1977; Vis. Prof.

Econ., Prof. Econ., Emory Univ., Atlanta, GA, 1980–1. 1981–4.

Degrees BBA Univ. Georgia, 1962; PhD Univ. Virginia, 1968.

Offices and Honours Raven Soc., Univ. Virginia, 1968; NATO Post-doctoral Fellow in Science, LSE, 1968–9.

Principal Fields of Interest 020 General Economic Theory; 820 Labour Markets; 025 Social Choice; Bureaucratic Performance.

Publications Books: 1. *Why the Draft? The Case for Volunteer Army* (with J.C. Miller III, *et al.*), (Penguin, 1968); 2. *Veterans Administration Hospitals: An Economic Analysis of Government Enterprise* (AEI, 1975); 3. *The Pharmaceutical Industry: Economics, Performance and Government Regulation* (Wiley, 1978); 4. *Equal Pay for Comparable Worth: An Economic Analysis of a new Antidiscrimination Doctrine* (Law & Econ. Center, 1980); 5. *National Health Issues: The British Experience* (Roche Laboratories, 1980); 6. *Applied Price Theory* (Dryden Press, 1984).

Articles: 1. 'Medical care and the economics of sharing', *Ec*, N.S. 36, Nov. 1969; 2. 'Measuring human capital returns', *JPE*, 79(6), Nov.–Dec. 1971; 3. 'Two theories of tax deductibility', *Nat. Tax J.*, 25(1), March 1972; 4. 'A theory of government enterprise', *JPE*, 84(5), Oct. 1976; 5. 'Medical schools: producers of what? sellers to whom?' (with T.B. Hall), *J Law E*, 24(1), April 1981; 6. 'Student discount rates, consumption loans and subsidies to professional education' (with K.B. Leffler), *JHR*, 15(3), Summer 1981; 7. 'Markets for medical care and medical education: an integrated long-run structural approach' (with K.B. Leffler), *JHR*, 16(4), Winter 1981; 8. 'Robert Giffen and the Irish potato' (with G.P. Dwyer), *AER*, 74(1), March 1984; 9. 'Substitution in public spending: who pays for Canadian national health insurance?' (with B. Zycher), *EI*, 22(3), July 1984; 10. 'Rationing by waiting list' (with B. Feigenbaum), *AER*, 74(3), June 1984.

Principal Contributions The focus of my earliest work reflected the active development at the University of Virginia in the 1960s of theories seeking to derive normative implications from public choice models. Papers on such varied topics as option demand, tax deductions and nonmarket distribution of medical care sought to explain government behaviour in terms of Pareto-preferred interventions seeking to avoid or internalise market tendencies toward inefficiencies. The observation that it was difficult to interest anyone (especially law-makers) in conclusion of this type led me away from this work toward strictly positive analysis of government behaviour, stressing self-interest and rent-seeking as the motivating forces.

An early product of this stage was the publication of my 'government enterprise' paper in 1976. This paper sought to illuminate the internal consistencies of the 'budget maximisation' paradigm of the time and to replace it with a more logically appealing foundation. This work continues to interest me, and more recent work in this line includes the paper with Tom Hall on the behaviour of medical schools and the paper written with Ben Zycher on the distributional implications of the adoption of national health insurance in Canada. The topic of physician supply led to a number of papers seeking explicitly to develop and incorporate institutional behaviour into what had until this time been treated as being stricly determined by entrant decisions. Several papers written with Keith Leffler sought to develop empirically medical school capacity as endogenous to the problem. My paper on the measurement of human capital returns not only improved the performance of the forecasting models developed in this connection, but helped to explain the apparent continuing high returns to human capital in occupations requiring high levels of this investment.

LINTNER, John*

Dates and Birthplace 1916–84, Lone Elm, KS, USA.

Posts Held George Gund Prof. Econ. Bus. Admin., Harvard Univ., 1964–84.

Degrees BA Univ. Kansas, 1939; MA, PhD Harvard Univ., 1942, 1946.

Offices and Honours Amer. Assoc. Advancement Science; Harvard Soc.

Fellows, 1942–5; Fellow, AAAS; Fellow, Em Soc; Disting. Service Citation, Univ. Kansas, 1973; Pres., AFA, 1974.

Publications *Books:* 1. *Effects of Federal Taxes on Growing Enterprises* (with J.K. Butters), (Harvard Univ. Press, 1945); 2. *Mutual Savings Banks in the Savings and Mortgage Markets* (Harvard Univ. Press, 1948); 3. *Effects of Taxation on Corporate Mergers* (with J.K. Butters and W.L. Cary), (Harvard Univ. Press, 1951).

Articles: 1. 'Distribution of incomes of corporations among dividends, retained earnings, and taxes', *AER*, 46(2), May 1956; 2. 'The valuation of risk assets and the selection of risky investments in stock portfolios and capital budgets', *REStat*, 47, Feb. 1965; 3. 'The aggregation of investors' diverse judgements and preferences in purely competitive securities markets', *J Fin. Quant. Analysis*, 4(4), Dec. 1969; 4. 'The market price of risk, size of market, and investor's risk aversion', *REStat*, 52, Feb. 1970; 5. 'Inflation and security returns', *J Fin*, 30(2), May 1975.

Career Early work on the development of modern portfolio theory, and the so-called 'capital asset pricing model'. Later work incorporated diverse information sets and probability assessments, restrictions on short selling and the absence of a riskless asset. Also identified an important risk-eliminating as well as a risk-sharing function of capital markets. Earlier work on corporate savings behaviour developed the model of dividend policy which is still standard, and examined the effects of taxes on corporate growth and merger activity. Later work includes both theoretical and empirical studies of inflation on security returns.

LIPPMAN, Steven A.

Born 1943, Los Angeles, CA, USA.
Current Post Prof., Grad. School Management, UCLA, 1967–.
Degrees BA Univ. Cal. Berkeley, 1964; MS, PhD Stanford Univ., 1967, 1968.
Editorial Duties Assoc. Ed., *Management Science*, 1972–81.

Principal Fields of Interest 026 Economics of Uncertainty and Information.

Publications *Books:* 1. *Elements of Probability and Statistics* (Holt, Rinehart & Winston, 1971); 2. *Studies in the Economics of Search* (with J.J. McCall), (N-H, 1979).

Articles: 1. 'On dynamic programming with unbounded rewards', *Management Science*, 21, 1975; 2. 'Applying a new device in the optimization of exponential queuing systems', *Operations Res.*, 23, 1975; 3. 'The economics of job search: a survey, Pts I–II' (with J.J. McCall), *EI*, 14(2, 3), June, Sept. 1976; 4. 'The economics of uncertainty: selected topics and probabilistic methods' (with J.J. McCall), in *Handbook of Mathematical Economics*, eds K.J. Arrow and M. Intriligator (N-H, 1981); 5. 'Investment selection with imperfect capital markets' (with D.G. Cantor), *Em*, 52(3), July, 1983.

Principal Contributions Introduced the most useful conditions in the theory underlying Markov decision processes with unbounded rewards. Introduced the idea of phantom transitions in continuous time, finite horizon dynamic programming. Wrote the most up-to-date survey of work on job search (with J.J. McCall). Many results in the economics of uncertainty.

LIPSEY, Richard George

Born 1928, Victoria, British Columbia, Canada.
Current Post Sir Edward Peacock Prof. Econ., Queen's Univ., Kingston, Ont., 1970–; Sr. Res. Adviser, C.D. Howe Inst., Toronto, Canada, 1983–.
Past Posts Res. Ass., British Columbia Provincial Govt., 1950–3; Ass. Lect., Lect., Reader, Prof., LSE, 1955–64; Vis. Prof., Univ. Cal. Berkeley, 1963–4, Univ. Wisconsin, 1964, Univ. British Columbia, 1969–70; Prof. Econ., Dean School Social Stud., Univ. Essex, 1964–70; Vis. Prof., Univ. Manchester, 1973, Univ. Colorado, Boulder, 1974–5, City Univ., London, 1979; Irving Fisher Vis. Prof., Yale Univ., 1979–80.
Degrees BA Univ. British Columbia, 1950; MA Univ. Toronto, 1953; PhD

Univ. London, 1958; Hon Dr (Law) McMaster Univ., 1983.

Offices and Honours W.L. MacKenzie King Fellow, 1952–3; Sir Arthur Sims Fellow, 1953–6; Lister Lect., BAAS, 1961; Council, US SSRC, 1966–9; Council, RES, 1967–71; Council UK AUTE, 1967–70; Res. Advisory Comm., Council, NIESR, 1962–72; Fellow, Em Soc, 1973; Killam Sr. Fellow, 1974–5; Fellow, Royal Soc. Canada, 1979; Pres., CEA, 1980–1; Inaugural Univ. Wide Prize Excellence in Res., Queen's Univ., 1983; National Bus. Writing Award (Best Fin. Writing by Non-professional Journalist), 1983.

Editorial Duties Ed., *REStud*, 1961–4; Ed. Boards, *Ec*, 1961–4, *CJE*, 1975–8.

Principal Fields of Interest 133 Stabilisation and Inflation; 311 Monetary Theory; 611 Market Structure.

Publications *Books:* 1. *An Introduction to Positive Economics* (Weidenfeld & Nicholson, 1963, 1983; transls., Spanish, Portuguese, German, Italian, Greek, Hebrew, Iavancese, Malay, Gujurati, Sinhali, Tamil; Australian edn. with P. Langley and D. Mahoney, Hodder & Stoughton, 1981); 2. *Economics* (with P.O. Steiner), (Harper & Row, 1966, 1983; transls., Spanish, French; Canadian edn. with D. D. Purvis, 1973, 1984); 3. *An Introduction to a Mathematical Treatment of Economics* (with G.C. Archibald), (Weidenfeld & Nicholson, 1967, 1977; transls., Portuguese, Spanish); 4. *Mathematical Economics: Methods and Applications* (with G.C. Archibald), (Harper & Row, 1976; transl., Japanese, 1983); 5. *The Theory of Customs Unions: A General Equilibrium Analysis* (Weidenfeld & Nicholson, 1973); 6. *An Introduction to the UK Economy* (with C. Harbury), (Pitmans, 1983); 7. *Common Ground for the Canadian Common Market* (Inst. Econ. Analysis, 1983); 8. *The Great Anti-Inflationary War 1975–1983?* (Univ. British Columbia Press, 1984).

Articles: 1. 'The general theory of second best' (with K. Lancaster), *REStud*, 24(1), June 1956; 2. 'Monetary and value theory: a critique of Lange and Patinkin' (with G.C. Archibald), *REStud*, 26(2), Oct. 1958; 3. 'The relation between unemployment and the rate of change of money wages in the United Kingdom 1862–1957: a further analysis', *Ec*, N.S. 27, Feb. 1960; 4. 'Trade credit and monetary policy' (with F. Brechling), *EJ*, 73, Dec. 1963; 5. 'Structural and deficient demand unemployment reconsidered', in *Employment Policy and the Labor Market*, ed. A.M. Ross (Univ. Cal. Press, 1965); 6. 'Foundations of the theory of national income: an analysis of some fundamental errors', in *Essays in Honour of Lord Robbins*, eds. M.B. Corry and M. Peston (Weidenfeld & Nicholson, 1972); 7. 'Freedom of entry and the existence of pure profit' (with B.C. Eaton), *EJ*, 88, Sept. 1978; 8. 'The understanding and control of inflation: is there a crisis in macroeconomics?', *CJE*, 14, Nov. 1981; 9. 'An economic theory of central places' (with B.C. Eaton), *EJ*, 92, March 1982; 10. 'Address models of value theory' (with G.C. Archibald and B.C. Eaton), in *The New Industrial Organization*, eds. F. Mathewson and J. Stigliz (MIT Press, 1984).

Principal Contributions Earliest work was on welfare economics. Studies of the ambiguous welfare effects of customs unions led to the *General Theory of Second Best*. Early interest in value theory led to a sorting out of stocks and flows and temporary and full equilibrium in Patinkin's first edition model. Interest in micro-behavioural models led to the first attempt to provide micro underpinnings of the Phillips curve as well as the first empirical tests of some of Phillips' hypotheses and later articles on the micro underpinnings of the Phillips curve and the place of the Phillips curve in macroeconomic models. A continued interest in inflation has led to a series of articles starting with Phillips curve work, including a supply-side survey in the early 1980s and going through a series of contributions to the debate over the cause of and cures of inflation in the 1980s, mainly published in Canada. An early interest in methodology led to the introduction of some of Popper's ideas of testability and a critique of Robbins' views in the *Nature and Significance of Economic Science* into a textbook (No. 1, above) that has been a best-seller (not sold in the US) since 1963. Work on spatial economics with B.C. Eaton began seriously in 1970 and has led to a series of over a dozen articles on spatial aspects of value theory and industrial organisation. Among other things this work has shown that Hotelling's model does not provide a consistent explanation of the clustering of firms, while comparison and multi-purpose shopping does. Much of this work is summarised and placed in a general context in No. 10 above.

LIST, Friedrich*

Dates and Birthplace 1789–1846, Reutlingen, Germany.
Posts Held Prof. Polit. Econ., Univ. Tübingen, 1817–9; Journalist, businessman, USA, 1825–32; Amer. Consul, Leipzig and Baden.
Offices Member, Legislature of Württemberg, 1820; Founder, *Das Zollvereinsblatt*, 1843.
Publications Books: 1. *Outlines of Political Economy* (1827, 1931); 2. *The Natural System of Political Economy* (1837, 1983); 3. *The National System of Political Economy* (1841, 1928); 4. *Schriften, Reden, Briefe*, 10 vols (1927–36).
Career Whilst a political exile in US, he was encouraged by a protectionist organisation to write the *Outlines* . . . in which he drafted the national system of political economy that was more completely realised in his 1841 book. His emphasis was on political factors and particularly the significance of the nation. His enthusiastic promotion of railways was partially because of their role in the economic integration of the German states of the Zollverein. His advocacy of protection has been treated as if it were general, rather than a recognition of the need for protection in certain stages of political and economic development; he was in fact no doctrinaire protectionist.
Secondary Literature E. Salin and R.L. Frey, 'List, Friedrich', *IESS*, 9; W.O. Henderson, *Friedrich List. Economist and Visionary 1789–1846* (Frank Cass, 1983).

LITTLE, Ian Malcolm David

Born 1918, Rugby, Warwickshire, England.
Current Post Retired, 1983.
Past Posts Fellow, All Souls Coll., Trinity Coll., Nuffield Coll., Prof. Econ., Univ. Oxford, 1948–50, 1950–2, 1952–76, 1971–8; Dep. Dir., Econ. Section, UK Treasury, London, 1953–5; Member, MIT Mission India, Delhi, 1958–9, 1965; Vice Pres., OECD Devlp. Centre, Paris, 1965–7; Special Adviser, Cons., World Bank, Washington, 1976–8, 1983–4; Project Dir., Twentieth Century Fund, NY, 1978–81; Vis. Prof., Univs. Boston, 1979, Princeton, 1980, Columbia, 1982.
Degrees MA, DPhil Univ. Oxford, 1947, 1949; Hon. DSc Univ. Edinburgh, 1976.
Offices and Honours Fellow, BA, 1973; Board Member, British Airports Authority, 1969–74; Member, UN Comm. Devlp. Planning, 1972–5.
Principal Fields of Interest 010 General Economics; Theory; 100 Economic Growth; 400 International Economics.
Publications Books: 1. *A Critique of Welfare Economics* (OUP, 1950); 2. *The Price of Fuel* (OUP, 1953); 3. *Concentration in British Industry* (with R. Evely), (OUP, 1960); 4. *Aid to Africa* (Pergamon, 1964); 5. *International Aid* (with J. Clifford), (A&U, 1965); 6. *Higgledy Piggledy Growth Again* (with A.C. Rayner), (Blackwell, 1966); 7. *Manual of Industrial Project Analysis in Developing Countries* (with J. Mirrlees), (OECD, 1969); 8. *Industry and Trade in Some Developing Countries* (with R. Scitovsky and M.F.G. Scott), (OUP, 1970); 9. *Project Analysis and Planning* (with J. Mirrlees), (Heinemann, 1974); 10. *International Development — Theory, Policy and International Relations* (Basic Books, 1982).
Articles: 1. 'A reformulation of the theory of consumers' behaviour', *OEP*, N.S. 1, Jan. 1949; 2. 'Direct versus indirect taxes', *EJ*, 61, Sept. 1951, repr. in *Readings in Welfare Economics*, eds. K. Arrow and T. Scitovsky (Richard D. Irwin, 1969), and in *Readings in the Economics of Taxation*, eds. R.A. Musgrave and C.S. Shoup (Richard D.

Irwin, 1959); 3. 'Social choice and individual values', *JPE*, 60, Oct. 1952, repr. in *Rational Man and Irrational Society*, eds. B.M. Berg and R. Hasdin (Sage, 1982); 4. 'The real cost of labour and the choice between consumption and investment', *QJE*, 75, Feb. 1961, repr. in *Pricing and Fiscal Policies*, ed. P.N. Rosenstien-Rodan (A&U, 1964); 5. 'Higgledy piddledy growth', *BOIS*, 24, Nov. 1962; 6. 'Further reflections on the OECD manual of project analysis, in developing countries', in *Development and Planning*, ed. J. Bhagwati (A&U, 1972); 7. 'An economic reconnaissance', in *Economic Growth and Structural Change in Taiwan*, ed. W. Galenson (Cornell Univ. Press, 1979); 8. 'Indian industrialization before 1945', in *The Theory and Experience of Economic Development*, eds. M. Gessovits, *et al.* (A&U, 1982).

Principal Contributions My 1950 book first examined the ethical basis of welfare economics, relating this to its typical use of persuasive or emotive language. Secondly, it laid the basis for 'second best' theory by emphasising *ad nauseam* that realising one marginal equivalence was insufficient for an improvement. Thirdly it insisted that 'an increase in welfare' required a distributional value judgement, and presented 'Little's Criterion' which provoked much misunderstanding before A.K. Sen cleared the muddied waters. The criterion has recently been rehabilitated (notably by Ng), and I have claimed that it has long been used by cost-benefit analysts (see my chapter in *Economics and Human Welfare*, ed. M.J. Boskin, Academic Press, 1979).

From 1950–8 my work was institutional (the Treasury) or dull. In 1958 I went to India and became a 'development economist'. In the early 1960s I worked mainly on aid. In early 1965, I again went to India, and had the idea of using border prices as the base of a shadow pricing system, after observing the low or negative social returns on some industrial projects. On going to the OECD in late 1965, I organised a major research programme into the failing of industrialisation policies in LDCs. The OECD had already commissioned a manual of Industrial Project Analysis for Developing Countries. With the indispensable help of J.A. Mirrlees, I was able to reconstruct it root and branch. By 1965 I had no faith in structural/planning approaches to development (*Experientia docet!*). In the 1970s work on shadow pricing was extended, until I again became institutionalised at the IBRD. After leaving it in the late 1970s I wrote a major survey of development economics and North/South relations.

LITTLECHILD, Stephen Charles

Born 1943, Wisbech, Cambridgeshire, England.

Current Post Prof. Commerce, Univ. Birmingham, England, 1975–.

Past Posts Temp. Asst. Lect. Industrial Econ., Univ. Birmingham, 1964–5; Sr. Res. Lect. Econ., Grad. Centre Management Studies, Birmingham, 1970–2; Prof. Applied Econ., Univ. Aston Management Centre, Birmingham, 1972–5; Vis. Prof., Res. Fellow, NYU, Stanford Univ., Univ. Chicago, VA Polytechnic Inst. and State Univ., 1979–80.

Degrees BCom Univ. Birmingham, 1964; PhD (Bus. Admin., Computer Science, Maths.), Univ. Texas, 1969.

Offices and Honours Harkness Fellow Commonwealth Fund, 1965–7; Foundation for Management Educ. Fellow, 1968–9; AT&T Post-doctoral Fellow Public Utility Econ., 1969; Member, UK Monopolies and Mergers Commission, 1983.

Principal Fields of Interest 610 Industrial Organisation and Public Policy.

Publications Books: 1. *Operational Research for Managers*, ed. and contrib. (Philip Allan, 1976); 2. *The Fallacy of the Mixed Economy* (INEA, 1978, repr. as *Elements of Telecommunications Economics*, Peter Peregrinus, 1979; transl., Japanese, 1982). 3. *Energy Strategies of the UK* (with K.G. Vaidya), (A&U, 1982); 4. *Regulation of British Telecommunications' Profitability* (UK Dept. Industry, 1983).

Articles: 1. 'Marginal cost pricing with joint costs', *EJ*, 80, June 1970; 2. 'Peak load pricing of telephone calls', *Bell JE*, 2, Autumn 1970; 3. 'A simple expression for the Shapley value in a special case' (with G. Owen), *Management Science*, 20(3), Nov. 1973; 4. 'Weather-dependent pricing for water resources in the high plains of Texas' (with M.N. Lane), *Water Resources Res.*, 12(4), Aug. 1976; 5. 'Aircraft landing fees: a game theory approach' (with G.F. Thompson), *Bell JE*, 8(1), Spring 1977; 6. 'Misleading calculations of the social costs of monopoly power', *EJ*, 91, June 1981; 7. 'Privatization: principles, problems and priorities' (with M.E. Beesley), *LBR*, 149, July 1983.

Principal Contributions Mathematical programming characterisations and calculations of public utility pricing structures, with applications to telephone calls, water resources and energy. Qualitative and quantitative analysis of common cost-sharing using co-operative game theory, with introduction of the Birmingham Airport game. Industrial organisation and public policy from an 'Austrian' perspective. Privatisation of UK nationalised industries, especially telecommunications.

LIU, Ben-Chieh

Born 1938, Chungking, Szechwan, China.

Current Post Prof. Management, Marketing and Info. Systems, Chicago State Univ., Chicago, IL, USA; Pres, L & A Lisle, IL, USA, 1982–.

Past Posts Adjunct. Prof. Econ., Univ. Missouri System, Rockhurst Coll., Illinois Benedictine Coll., 1967–78; Principal Sr. Econ. Adviser, Midwest Res. Inst. Kansas City, MO, 1972–80; Manager, Energy & Environmental Econs. Projects, Argonne Nat. Lab., 1980–1; Prof. Econ. and Bus., Dep. Dir. Res., Oklahoma City Univ., 1981–2; Econ. Adviser, Nat. Planning Council, Jordan, 1982.

Degrees BA Nat. Taiwan Univ., Taiwan, 1961; MA Memorial Univ. Newfoundland, 1965; MA, PhD Washington Univ., St Louis, 1968, 1971.

Offices and Honours Certified Econ., Chinese Professionalist Exam. Board, 1961; Korean-Chinese Scholarship, 1963; World Univ. Scholarship, 1963;

Fellow, US EDA, 1966–8; Amer. Industrial Develp. Council Study Award, 1969; Adviser, NSF 1974; Chinese Central Daily News Essay Awards, 1977; Pres. Organization Chinese Ams, Kansas City Chapter, 1976; Comm. Member, ASA, 1977; Assoc. Social Econs., 1978–; Vice Pres., Chinese Academic & Professional Assoc. Mid-Amer., 1983–.

Editorial Duties Ed. Board, *Amer. J Econ. and Sociology*, 1976–; *Internat. J. Math. Social Sciences*, 1980–.

Principal Fields of Interest 200 Quantitative Economic Methods and Data; 110 Economic Growth and Development; 800 Manpower, Labour and Demographic Economics.

Publications Books: 1. *Quality of Life Indicators in US by State* (Midwest Res. Inst., 1972); 2. *Quality of Life Indicators in US in Metropolitan Areas* (US Govt. Printing Office, 1976, Praeger, 1977); 3. *Air Pollution Damage Functions and Regional Damage Estimates* (with E.Yu), (Technomic, 1978); 4. *Earthquake Risk and Damage Functions* (with C. Hsieh, et al.), (Westview Press, 1981); 5. *Income, Energy Consumption and Quality of Life in USA* (with C. Anderson), (Westview Press, 1984).

Articles: 1. 'An integrated model for earthquake risk and damage assessment', *Internat. Math. Social Sciences*, 1(2), 1981; 2. 'Productivity and thermal energy storage technology', in *Environmental and Economic Considerations in Energy Utilization*, ed. J. P. Reynolds (Amer. Arbor Science, 1981); 3. 'Sulphur dioxide and mortality damage: a benefit/cost analysis', *Internat. Math. Social Sciences*, 1(4), 1981; 4. 'Environmental quality indicators for large metropolitan areas: a factor analysis', *JEEM*, 14(2), 1982; 5. 'Helium conservation and supply and demand projections in USA', *Energy Econ.*, 5(1), Jan. 1983; 6. 'Migration and social life', *Amer. J. Econ. and Sociology*, 42(3), July 1983; 7. 'Variations in economic quality of life indicators by state', *Internat. Math. Social Sciences*, 4(3), 1983; 8. 'Variations in natural gas price elasticity in US, by region and sector', *Energy Econ.*, 5(3), July 1983; 9. 'Quality of life in USA:

an interstate comparison over time', in *Proceedings of the 44th session, International Statistical Institute* (ISI, 1983); 10. 'Evaluating a hospital cost-containment program in a paired experiment', *JASA*, 78(2), 1983.

Principal Contributions Early work was concentrated on urban and regional economics, with statistical and econometric applications to forecasting, resource allocation and manpower utilisation. Completed the first major research study for St Louis' economic structure, entitled *An Interindustrial Structure Analysis: An Input-Output Model for St. Louis SMSA*. This study received the study award from the American Industrial Development Council in 1969 and later it has been used for regional planning, economic impact assessment, manpower needs forecasting, and other purposes in the region. My interest in the quality of life production and social indicator development began in 1972 when I joined the Midwest Research Institute and received a grant from the Kerr Foundation for an inter-state comparison study on the inter-regional inequality of social well-being. Based on the national goals and objectives set forth by the President Eisenhower's Commission, I developed a relatively sophisticated Quality of Life Production (QOL) Model with inputs from psychological and physiological considerations on components affecting our perceived happiness and satisfaction. The QOL model was further modified and expanded in 1975 with the publication of *Quality of Life Indicators in U.S. Metropolitan Areas* and a score of journal articles later for intertemporal and international QOL comparative analysis.

Applied econonometrics to energy and environmental issues and studies and published books, Nos. 3 and 4, above. Both are pioneer work in the field of energy and environmental economics. Empirical work and research studies concerning water pollution and health cost-containment were also launched for public and private agencies. Developed benefit/cost cross-impact probabilistic approach for risk or impact analyses and consulted on management information systems for UN member countries and international agencies. More recently, efforts have been given to academic institutions in programme development and curriculum assignment.

LIU, Ta-Chung*

Dates and Birthplace 1914–75, China.

Posts Held Ass. Commercial Counsellor, Chinese Embassy, Washington, DC, 1942–5; Econ., IMF, 1945–55; Prof. Econ., Cornell Univ., 1955–75.

Degrees BS, MS(Eng.), PhD Cornell Univ., 1936, 1937, 1940.

Offices and Honours Secretary, Chinese Delegation, Bretton Woods Conf., 1946; Chairman, Taiwan Commission Tax Reform, 1968–70; Order Bright Star with Grand Cordon, 2nd class, Republic of China, 1970.

Publications *Books:* 1. *China's National Income, 1931–36* (1946); 2. *Measuring Production Functions in the United States, 1957: An Inter-industry and Interstate Comparison of Productivity* (with G. H. Hildebrand), (1965); 3. *The Economy of the Chinese Mainland: National Income and Economic Development, 1933–39* (with K. C. Yeh), (1965); 4. *Economic Trends in Communist China*, co-ed. (with W. Galenson and A. Eckstein), (1968); 5. Statement in *Economic Development in Mainland China: Hearings Before the Joint Economic Committee* (1972).

Career First attempt to construct national accounts for China. First monthly econometric model of the US economy. Estimates of manufacturing production functions using cross-section data (with G. Hildebrand). Theoretical analysis of the econometric problems of underidentification, structural estimation and forecasting, and the effects of aggregation over time.

Secondary Literature L. R. Klein, *et al.*, 'Ta-Chung Liu, 1914–75', *Em*, 45(2), March 1977.

LLOYD, Cynthia Brown

Born 1943, New York City, NY, USA.

Current Post Chief, Fertility and Family Planning Stud. Section, Pop. Division, UN, New York, NY, USA, 1982–.

Past Posts Part-time Instr., Ass. Prof., Barnard Coll., 1970–2, 1972–9; Co-Dir., Program in Sex Roles and Social Change, Res. Assoc., Center Social Sciences, Columbia Univ., 1977–9, 1979–82; Pop. Affairs Officer, Pop. Div., UN, 1979–82.

Degrees BA Bryn Mawr Coll., 1964; MA, PhD Columbia Univ., 1967, 1972.

Offices and Honours Spivack Grant, Barnard Coll., 1978; Pres. Fellow, Columbia Univ., 1967–8, 1968–9, 1969–70.

Principal Fields of Interest 813 Labour Force; 840 Demographic Economics; 917 Economics of Discrimination.

Publications *Books:* 1. *Sex Discrimination and the Division of Labor*, ed. (Columbia Univ. Press, 1975); 2. *Women in the Labor Market*, co-ed. (with E. Andrews and C. Gilroy), (Columbia Univ. Press, 1979); 3. *The Economics of Sex Differentials* (with B. Niemi), (Columbia Univ. Press, 1979); 4. *Fertility Levels and Trends as Assessed from Twenty World Fertility Surveys* (with others), (UN, 1984).

Articles: 1. 'Recent trends in socio-economic fertility differentials in Japan and the United States', *Internat. Pop. Conf.*, III (Internat. Union Scientific Study Pop., 1971); 2. 'An economic analysis of the impact of government on fertility: some examples from the developed countries', *Public Pol.*, 22(4), Fall 1974; 3. 'Sex differentials in earnings and unemployment rates' (with B. Niemi), *Feminist Stud.*, Spring 1975; 4. 'The division of labor between the sexes; a review', in *Sex, Discrimination and the Division of Labor, op cit.*; 5. 'Sex differentials in labor supply elasticity: the implications of sectoral shifts in demand' (with B. Niemi), *AER*, 68(2), May 1978; 6. 'Do women earn less under capitalism? Comments', in *Income Inequality: Trends and International Comparisons*, ed. J.

R. Moroney (D. C. Heath, 1979); 7. 'Inflation and female labor force participation', in *Inflation Through the Ages: Economic, Social, Psychological and Historical Aspects*, eds. S. N. Schmukler and E. Marcus (Brooklyn Coll. Press, 1983).

Principal Contributions My PhD dissertation was on the effect of child subsidies on fertility. The study looked not only at the impact of a change in the effective price of children on a nation's fertility rate but also at the factors determining the design of government policy. This research laid the groundwork for a continuing interest in population questions. From 1972–9, I devoted my energies to the study of the economics of sex differentials. At an early stage in the development of the field, I brought together a group of scholars doing innovative work on women in the field of labour and selected, edited and published their work in a book titled, *Sex Discrimination and the Division of Labor* (1975). This was at a time when the number of women's studies courses was growing and practically no course material was available in the economics field. This book provided an impetus to further work in the field. One of the books' contributors, Beth Niemi, and I then co-authored a book on *The Economy of Sex Differentials* which provided a thorough analysis of the evolution of the division of labour and the division of rewards between the sexes in the US labour market. During this same period I headed a major US Labor Department Conference on *Women in the Labor Market* and co-edited a book of the same title. Since 1979 my interest has returned to the population field, in particular fertility and family planning with a focus on the developing country context and a special concern for women's work and fertility relationships.

LLOYD, William Forster*

Dates and Birthplace 1795–1852, Bradenham, England.

Posts Held Student, Christ Church Coll., Oxford, 1812–37; Drummond Prof., Univ. Oxford, 1832–7.

Degree MA Univ. Oxford, 1818.
Offices Fellow, Royal Soc., 1834.
Publications *Books:* 1. *Prices of Corn in Oxford* (1830); 2. *Lectures on Population, Value, Poor Laws and Rent* (1837).

Career During his tenure of the Drummond chair, he published some of his lectures (1837), as provided for under the terms attached to the appointment. The lectures generally have a policy orientation, except in the case of the one of 1833 on value. This more purely theoretical lecture contains a very clear description of the principle of diminishing marginal utility. Lloyd's work was largely forgotten until this early statement of the principle was rediscovered by Seligman in 1903.

Secondary Literature R. M. Romano, 'William Forster Lloyd – a non-Ricardian?', *HOPE*, 9(3), Fall 1977.

LOASBY, Brian John

Born 1930, Kettering, Northamptonshire, England.
Current Post Vis. Prof. Econ., Univ. Stirling, Stirling, Scotland, 1984–.
Past Posts Ass. Polit. Econ., Bournville Res. Fellow, Univ. Aberdeen, 1955–8, 1958–61; Tutor, Management Stud., Univ. Bristol, 1961–7; Arthur D. Little Management Fellow, Arthur D. Little Inc., Cambridge, MA, USA, 1965–6; Lect., Sr. Lect., Econ., Prof. Management Econ., Univ. Stirling, 1967–8, 1968–71, 1971–84; Vis. Fellow, Oxford Centre Management Stud., 1974.
Degrees BA, MLitt Univ. Camb., 1952, 1957.
Offices and Honours Council, Scottish Econ., Soc., 1977–; Council, RES, 1981–.
Editorial Duties Advisory Board, *Managerial and Decision Econ.*, 1980–; Advisory Board, *J. Econ. Stud.*, 1984–.
Principal Fields of Interest 030 History of Economic Thought; Methodology; 510 Administration; 620 Economics of Technological Chance.
Publications *Books:* 1. *The Swindon Project* (Pitman, 1973); 2. *Choice, Complexity and Ignorance* (CUP, 1976); 3. *Technological Change and*

Business Policy (with F. R. Bradbury), (Inst. Electrical Engineers, 1980).

Articles: 1. 'Long range formal planning in perspective', *JMS*, 4(3), Oct. 1967, repr. in *Economics of Information and Knowledge*, ed. D. M. Lamberton (Penguin, 1971); 2. 'The decision maker in the organisation', *JMS*, 5(3), Oct. 1968; 3. 'Hypothesis and paradigm in the theory of the firm', *EJ*, 81, Dec. 1971, repr. (French) in *Concurrence monopolistique, concurrence imparfaite* (with C. Geffroy), (Mame, 1972); 4. 'An analysis of decision processes', *R&D Management*, 4(3), June 1974; 5. 'Whatever happened to Marshall's theory of value?', *SJPE*, 25(1), Feb. 1978, repr. in *Alfred Marshall: Critical Assessments*, ed. J. C. Wood (Croom Helm, 1982); 6. 'The entrepreneur in economic theory', *SJPE*, 29(3), Nov. 1982; 7. 'Economics of dispersed and incomplete information', in *Method, Process and Austrian Economics*, ed. I. M. Kirzner (D. C. Heath, 1982); 8. 'Knowledge, learning and enterprise', in *Beyond Positive Economics?*, ed. J. Wiseman (Macmillan, 1983); 9. 'G. L. S. Shackle as historian of economic thought', in *The Craft of the Historian of Economic Thought*, ed. W. J. Samuels (JAI Press, 1983); 10. 'On scientific method', *J Post Keyn E*, 6(3), Spring 1984.

Principal Contributions After an excursion into economic history, I investigated the location decisions of firms moving out of Birmingham, and some years later made a more detailed study of a major transfer from London (*The Swindon Project*). This work convinced me that managerial decisions should be analysed as processes: the identification (possibly incorrect) and the (restricted) search for solutions condition choice, and unexpected outcomes often generate new problems in a continuing cycle. Conventional theories of the firm addressed other questions. On moving to Stirling I began to work with scientists who had experience of managing innovation, which they envisaged as a cyclic process, and heard of T. S. Kuhn from a research student who identified the current paradigms of influential groups (within or outside the innovating organisation) as major barriers to some innovations. A comparable barrier to the acceptance of non-optimising theories of the firm was obvious. Since then my primary twin interests have been in applying theories of the growth of knowledge to the history of economic thought (especially theories of the firm) and to decision-making in organisations. My most recent work (still mostly unpublished) tries to use the concept of research programmes (or construction systems, from the American psychologist George Kelly) as a means of analysing development and the problems of coherence and breakdown within schools of thought, organisations, and economies.

LOCKE, John*

Dates and Birthplace 1632–1704, Somerset, England.

Posts Held Sr. Student, Christ Church Coll., Oxford, 1658–83; Political Adviser, Lord Shaftesbury and other Whig politicians; Held various minor official positions after 1689.

Offices Member, Council of Trade and Plantations; Fellow, Royal Soc., 1688.

Publications *Books:* 1. *Two Treatises of Government* (1690, 1960); 2. *An Essay Concerning Human Understanding*, 2 vols (1690, 1959); 3. *Some Considerations of the Consequences of the Lowering of Interest and Raising the Value of Money* (1691); 4. *Further Considerations* (1695).

Career One of England's greatest political theorists whose wide interests included economics. His two specifically economic publications of 1691 and 1695 advocate maintaining the interest rate and not devaluing the currency. He distinguished between value and price, related market value to supply and demand, and saw price as determined by the amount of money available in relation to supply and demand.

Secondary Literature R. L. Colie, 'Locke, John', *IESS*, 9; K. I. Vaughn, *John Locke Economist and Social Scientist* (Univ. Chicago Press, 1980).

LOMBRA, Raymond E.

Born 1946, New Haven, CT, USA.

Current Post Prof. Econ., Penn. State Univ., Univ. Park, PA, USA, 1977–.

Past Posts Sr. Staff Econ., Board Governors, Fed. Reserve System, Washington, DC, 1971–7; Vis. Scholar, Fed. Reserve Bank Kansas City, 1983.

Degrees BA Providence Coll., RI, 1967; MA, PhD Penn. State Univ., 1968, 1971.

Offices and Honours Nat. Defense Educ. Act Fellow, 1967.

Principal Fields of Interest 311 Domestic Monetary and Financial Theory and Policy; 313 Capital Markets; 314 Financial Intermediaries.

Publications *Books:* 1. *The Political Economy of Policymaking*, co-ed. (with H. Kaufman and M. Dooley), (Sage, 1979); 2. *Money and the Financial System* (with J. Herendeen and R. Torto), (McGraw-Hill, 1980); 3. *The Political Economy of International and Domestic Monetary Relations*, co-ed. (with W. Witte), (Iowa State Press, 1982).

Articles: 1. 'Federal reserve "defensive" behavior and the reserve causation argument' (with R. Torto), *SEJ*, 40(1), July 1973; 2. 'Measuring the impact of monetary and fiscal actions: a new look at the specification problem' (with R. Torto), *REStat*, 56(1), Feb. 1974, repr. in *Current Issues in Monetary Theory and Policy*, eds. T. Havrilesky and J. Boorman (AHM, 1976, 1980); 3. 'The strategy of monetary policy' (with R. Torto), *Econ. Rev. Fed. Reserve Bank Richmond*, Sept. 1975, repr. in *Current Issues in Monetary Theory and Policy, op cit.*; 4. 'Discount rate changes and announcement effects' (with R. Torto), *QJE*, 91(1), Feb. 1977; 5. 'Monetary control: consensus or confusion', in *Controlling Monetary Aggregates III* (Fed. Reserve Bank Boston, 1980); 6. 'Policy advice and policymaking at the federal reserve' (with M. Moran), in *Monetary Institutions and the Policy Process*, 13, Carnegie-Rochester Conf. Series Public Pol., Autumn 1980, repr. in *Theory, Policy, Institutions*, eds. K. Brunner and A. Meltzer (N-H, 1983);

7. 'Rational expectations and short-run neutrality: a reexamination of the role of anticipated money' (with F. Carns), *REStat*, 65(4), Nov. 1983; 8. 'Aggregate demand, food prices, and the underlying rate of inflation' (with Y. Mehra), *J. Macroecon.*, 5(4), Fall 1983; 9. 'The changing role of real and nominal interest rates', *Econ. Rev. Fed. Reserve Bank Kansas City*, Feb. 1984; 10. 'The money supply process: identification, stability and estimation' (with H. Kaufman), *SEJ*, 50(4), April 1984.

Principal Contributions During the preparation of my thesis on Federal Reserve behaviour, it increasingly became obvious that the widespread practice of assuming an exogenous money stock represented a fundamental and potentially serious flaw in received theoretical and empirical work. Accordingly, assessing the sources and consequences of an endogenous money stock (and interest rates) has been a central focus and unifying theme of much of my work. Early work on the effectiveness of monetary and fiscal policy emphasised how the actual conduct of policy influenced causal relationships and the dynamic adjustment of the real and financial sectors of the economy. Subsequently, more intensive examination of the actual formulation and implementation of policy developed the costs and benefits of alternative policy strategies, the role of international openness in the conduct of policy, and the political economy of policy-making. Most recently, my research has focussed on the effects of financial innovation, deregulation, and changing policy procedures on the causal role of real and nominal interest rates, and the effects of such ongoing changes on the identification and estimation of money supply and money demand functions. The ultimate goal of such research is a better understanding of how policy can contribute to economic stability.

LONGE, Francis Davy*

Dates and Birthplace 1831–1910, Suffolk, England.

Posts Held Ass. Commissioner, UK Children's Employment Commission: Inspector, Local Govt. Board.

Degrees BA Univ. Oxford.

Publications *Books:* 1. *An Inquiry into the Law of Strikes* (1860); 2. *A Refutation of the Wage-Fund Theory* (1866, 1903).

Career Author of the first decisive refutation of the wages fund theory which was, however, ignored by Mill whose recantation seems to have been entirely due to Thornton's independent treatment of the doctrine.

Secondary Literature J. H. Hollander, 'Longe, Francis Davy', *ESS*, 9.

LONGFIELD, Samuel Mountifort*

Dates and Birthplace 1802–84, Ireland.

Posts Held Barrister and Judge; Prof. Polit. Econ., Regius Prof. Law, Trinity Coll., Dublin, 1832–6, 1834–84.

Degrees BA, MA, LLD Trinity Coll., Dublin, 1823, 1829, 1831.

Offices and Honours Pres., Stat. Social Enquiry Soc., Ireland, 1863–7.

Publications *Books:* 1. *Four Lectures on Poor Laws* (1834); 2. *Lectures on Political Economy* (1834, 1931); 3. *Three Lectures on Commerce and One on Absenteeism* (1835, 1938).

Career Better known for his legal career, he nevertheless published various lectures, during his period as first holder of the Whately Chair, which included remarkable economic insights. His analysis of the determinants of value, distribution of income and nature of capital are all in advance of contemporary thinking. The marginalist aspects of his writings possibly owe something to his considerable ability as a mathematician.

Secondary Literature E. McKinley, 'Longfield, Samuel Mountifort', *IESS*, 9; L. S. Moss, *Mountifort, Longfield: Ireland's First Professor of Political Economy* (Green Hill Publ., 1976).

LORIA, Achille*

Dates and Birthplace 1857–1943, Mantua, Italy.

Posts Held Prof. Polit. Econ., Univ. Siena, 1881–91, Univ. Padua, 1891–1903, Univ. Turin, 1903–22.

Degree Laurea Law, Univ. Bologna, 1877.

Offices and Honours Member, Academia dei Lincei, 1901; Italian Senator, 1919.

Publications *Books:* 1. *La Legge di Popolazione ed il Sistema Sociale* (1882); 2. *The Economic Foundations of Society* (1886, 1904); 3. *Contemporary Social Problems* (1894, 1911); 4. *Il Movimento Operaio: Origine, Forme, Sviluppo* (1903); 5. *The Economic Synthesis: A Study of the Laws of Income* (1909, 1914); 6. *The Economic Causes of War* (1912, 1918); 7. *Dinamica Economica* (1935).

Career Developed his own quasi-Marxian, deterministic theory of economic development based on the relationship of the productivity of land to the density of population: land scarcity leads to the subjugation of some parts of society by others, this subjugation taking such forms as feudalism or high capitalism. His interest in land-labour ratios encouraged him to develop some ideas on the location of industry independently of Alfred Weber. Frequent use of data from the Americas and the relevance of some of his ideas of American circumstances gave his writings a certain currency in the US.

Secondary Literature L. Einaudi, 'Achille Loria 1857–1943', *EJ*, 56, March, 1946; S. B. Clough, 'Loria Archille', *IESS*, 9.

LÖSCH, August*

Dates and Birthplace 1906–45, Öhringen, Württemberg, Germany.

Posts Held Studied Univs. Tübingen, Kiel, Freiburg, Bönn.

Publications *Books:* 1. *Bevölkerungswellen und wechsel Pagen* (1936); 2. *The Economics of Location* (1940, 1954).

Articles: 1. 'Population cycles as a cause of business cycles', *QJE*, 51, Aug. 1937; 2. 'The nature of economic regions', *SEJ*, 5, July 1938; 3. 'A new theory of international trade', *WA*, 1939, repr. in *Internat. Econ. Papers*, 6, eds. A. T. Peacock, *et al.* (Macmillan, 1956); 4. 'Um eine neue Standorttheorie: Eine Auseinandersetzung mit Ritschl', *WA*, 54, 1941; 5. 'Theorie der Währung. Eine Fragment', *WA*, 62, 1949.

Career His *Economics of Location* is generally regarded as one of the masterpieces of spatial economics, weaving together the classical location theory of Thünen and Weber with the newer emphasis on demand inspired by the monopolistic competition of revolution.

Secondary Literature A. Zottmann, 'August Lösch', *WA*, 62, 1949.

LOVELL, Michael

Born 1930, Cambridge, MA, USA.

Current Post Prof. Econ., Wesleyan Univ., Middletown, CT, USA, 1969–.

Past Posts Jr. Management Ass., US Census Bureau, 1952–3; Teaching Ass., Stanford Univ., 1952–3; Res. Ass. Econ., Military Govt. Dept., US Army, 1953–5; Instr., Ass. Prof., Yale Univ., 1958–9, 1959–63; Vis. Lect., Wesleyan Univ., 1960–2; Assoc. Prof., Prof., Industrial Admin., Carnegie-Mellon Univ., 1963–9; Vis. Prof., Yale School Organization and Management, 1981–2.

Degrees BA Reed Coll., 1952; MA Stanford Univ., 1954; PhD Harvard Univ., 1959.

Offices and Honours W. H. Robinson Fellow, Stanford Univ., 1952–3; Harvard Grad. School Fellow, 1955–6; Earhart Foundation Fellow, 1956–7; US SSRC Training Fellow, 1957–8; Ford Faculty Res. Fellow, 1964–5; First Prize, Joint Council Econ. Educ., Kazanjian Foundation Awards Program Teaching Econ., 1973–4; Fellow, Em Soc, 1980.

Editorial Duties Assoc. Ed., *Em*, 1965–8; *JASA*, 1975–7; Foreign ed., *REStud*, 1968–70.

Principal Fields of Interest 022 Microeconomics; 023 Macroeconomics; 211 Econometric and Statistical Methods.

Publications *Books:* 1. *Sales Antici-*

pations and Inventory Behavior (with A. Hirsch), (Wiley, 1969); 2. *Macroeconomics: Measurement, Theory and Policy* (Wiley, 1975; transl., Spanish, Editorial Limusa, 1979).

Articles: 1. 'The role of the Bank of England as lender of last resort in the crises of the 18th century', *Explor. Entrepreneurial Hist.*, 10, Oct. 1957; 2. 'Maufacturers' inventories, sales expectations and the acceleration principle', *Em*, 29, July 1961, repr. Joint Econ. Comm., *Inventory Fluctuations and Economic Stabilization, II* (US Govt. Printing Office, 1961); 3. 'A Keynesian analysis of forced saving', *Int ER*, 4, Sept. 1963; 4. 'Seasonal adjustment of economic time series and multiple regression analysis', *JASA*, 58, Dec. 1963, repr. in *Readings in Economic Statistics and Econometrics*, ed. A. Zellner (Little, Brown, 1968); 5. 'Inventories, production smoothing and the flexible accelerator' (with P. Darling), *QJE*, 85(2), May 1971; 6. 'The minimum wage, teenage unemployment and the business cycle', *WEJ*, 10(4), Dec. 1972; 7. 'The collective allocation of commodities in a democratic society', *Public Choice*, 24, Winter 1975, repr. in *Essays in Regional Economic Studies*, eds. M. Dutta, J. Harline and D. Loeb (Acorn, 1983); 8. 'Spending for education: the exercise of public choice', *REStat*, 60(4), Nov. 1978; 9. 'Aggregation in a multi-sector model of the inventory cycle', in *Economics and Management of Inventories*, ed. A. Chikan (N-H, 1981); 10. 'Data mining', *REStat*, 65(1), Feb. 1983.

Principal Contributions My research shows more breadth than depth. I have undertaken econometric studies of the early history of the Bank of England and of the history of economic thought; I have studied the methodological problems of pretesting bias, seasonal adjustment and data grubbing; I have investigated the determinants of inventory investment using individual firm data as well as industry and GNP aggregates and have tested whether sales expectations are rational; I have examined the effects of the minimum wage and demographic shifts on teenage unemployment; I have theorised on the effects of an endogenous money supply on both the business cycle and the process of forced saving; I have studied the economics of product differentiation, the economics of public choice, and the financing of education. I believe that the range of topics reflects in large measure the inquiring nature of the students whom I have been privileged to teach but from whom I have learned more than I have taught.

LOWE, Adolph

Born 1893, Stuttgart, Germany.
Current Post Retired, 1963.
Past Posts Prof. Econ. Theory Sociology, Univ. Kiel, 1926–31; Prof. Polit. Econ. Emeritus, Goethe Univ., Frankfurt-am-Main, 1931–3; Hon. Special Lect., Econ. Polit. Science, Univ. Manchester, 1933–40; Alvin Johnson Prof. Econ. Emeritus, Grad. Faculty New School Social Res., New York City, 1941–63.
Degrees LLB, LLD Univ. Tübingen, 1915, 1918; DLitt. (h.c.) New School Social Res., 1964; Dr Rer. Pol. (h.c.) Univ. Bremen, 1983.
Offices and Honours Dir. Res., Inst. World Econ., Univ. Kiel, 1926–30; Dir. Res., Inst. World Affairs, New School Social Res., 1942–51; Hon. Member, German Soc. Sociology, 1975; Veblen-Commons Award, 1979; Grosses Verdienstkreuz der Bundesrepublik Deutschlands, 1984.
Principal Fields of Interest 023 Macroeconomic Theory; 111 Economic Growth Theory.
Publications *Books:* 1. *Economics and Sociology* (A&U, 1913); 2. *The Price of Liberty* (Hogarth Press, 1937); 3. *On Economic Knowledge* (Harper & Row, 1965, M. E. Sharpe, 1977, 1983); 4. *The Path of Economic Growth* (CUP, 1977).
Articles: 1. 'A structural model of production', *Social Res.*, 19(2), 1952; 2. 'The classical theory of economic growth', *Social Res.*, 21(2), 1954; 3. 'Structural analysis of real capital formation', in NBER, *Capital Formation and Economic Growth* (Princeton Univ. Press, 1955); 4. 'Technological unemployment reexamined', in *Wirtschaft und Kultursystem* (Eugen Rentsch

Verlag, 1955); 5. 'Toward a science of political economics', in *Economic Means and Social Ends*, ed. R. L. Heilbroner (Prentice-Hall, 1969); 6. 'Is economic value still a problem?', *Social Res.*, 48(4), Winter 1981.

Principal Contributions Main interest: elaboration of a political economics. In contrast with traditional approaches — classical, neoclassical, Marxian, which base their explanatory and predictive analyses on some maximisation hypothesis — political economics tries to derive the means — behaviour, motivations, public controls — suitable to attain one or more politically stipulated macro-goals. Other concerns: a theory of growth with emphasis on disequilibrium paths; a theory of process innovations; a three-sector model as basis of capital theory; and spontaneous conformity on political essentials as a precondition of political liberty.

LOWE, Joseph*

Dates and Birthplace N.e.
Publications *Books:* 1. *An Inquiry into the State of the British West Indies* (1807); 2. *The Present State of England in Regard to Agriculture, Trade and Finance* (1822, 1823).

Career Improved the technique of index numbers and recommended their use for measuring the variations of money over time. The 'tabular standard' as he called it was intended for voluntary use in stabilising long-run contracts. It constitutes a major step forward in monetary analysis.

LUCAS, Robert E., Jr.

Born 1937, Yakima, WA, USA.
Current Post John Dewey Disting. Service Prof. Econ., Univ. Chicago, 1980–.
Past Posts Lect., Univ. Chicago, 1962–3; Ass. Prof., Assoc. Prof., Prof., Econ., Carnegie-Mellon Univ., 1963–7, 1967–70, 1970–4; Ford Foundation Vis. Res. Prof., Prof., Univ. Chicago, 1974–5, 1975–80; Vis. Prof. Econ., Northwestern Univ., 1981–2.

Degrees BA(Hist.), PhD Univ. Chicago, 1959, 1964.
Offices and Honours Proctor & Gamble Scholar, 1955–9; Phi Beta Kappa, 1959; Woodrow Wilson Fellow, 1959–60; Brookings Fellow, 1961–2; Woodrow Wilson Dissertation Fellow, 1963; Ford Foundation Faculty Fellow, 1966–7; Fellow, AAAS, 1980; Member, Exec. Comm., AEA, 1979–82; Member, NAS, 1981; Guggenheim Foundation Fellow, 1981–2; Council Em Soc, 1982–4.
Editorial Duties Assoc. Ed., *JET*, 1972–8, *J Mon E*, 1977–; Ed., *JPE*, 1978–81.
Principal Fields of Interest 023 Macroeconomics.
Publications *Books:* 1. *Rational Expectations and Econometric Practice*, co-ed. (with T. J. Sargent), (Univ. Minnesota Press, 1981); 2. *Studies in Business-Cycle Theory* (MIT Press, 1981).

Articles: 1. 'Adjustment costs and the theory of supply', *JPE*, 75(4), pt. 1, Aug. 1967; 2. 'Capital-labor substitution in US manufacturing', in *The Taxation of Income from Capital*, eds. A. C. Harberger and M. J. Bailey (Brookings Inst., 1969); 3. 'Real wages, employment and inflation' (with L. A. Rapping), in *The New Microeconomics in Employment and Inflation Theory*, ed. E. S. Phelps, *et al.* (W. W. Norton, 1970); 4. 'Expectations and the neutrality of money', *JET*, 4(2), April 1972, repr. in *Uncertainty in Economics*, eds. P. Diamond and M. Rothschild (Univ. Chicago Press, 1974); 5. 'Econometric policy evaluation: a critique', in *The Phillips Curve and Labor Markets*, eds. K. Brunner and A. Meltzer (N-H, 1975).

Principal Contributions Econometric studies of capital-labour substitution and variations in capacity utilisation; theory of investment and technological change at the firm and industry level; theoretical and econometric work on labour supply; business-cycle theory and capital theory, motivated by the concept of rational expectations.

LUMSDEN, Keith Grant

Born 1935, Bathgate, W. Lothian, Scotland.

Current Post Prof. Econ., Dir., Esmée Fairbairn Res. Centre, Heriot-Watt Univ., Edinburgh, Scotland, 1970–; Affiliate Prof. Econ., INSEAD Fontainebleau, France, 1974–.

Past Posts Instr., Ass. Prof., Assoc. Prof., Res. Assoc., Stanford Univ., 1960–3, 1964–70, 1970–5, 1965–71; Vis. Prof., Stanford Univ., Florence, Italy, 1967, Heriot-Watt Univ., 1969–70; Cons., Nat. Inst. Educ., USA, 1973, Diagramma, Sao Paulo, Brazil, 1974–6, P. Rowe Consultants, Sydney, 1975, Hewlett-Packard, CA, 1975–80.

Degrees MA Univ. Edinburgh, 1959; PhD Stanford Univ., 1968.

Offices and Honours Member, Econ. Educ. Comm., AEA, 1974–6.

Principal Fields of Interest 012 Teaching of Economics; 621 Technological Change; Innovation, Research and Development; 912 Economics of Education.

Publications *Books:* 1. *The Free Enterprise System* (McGraw-Hill, 1963); 2. *International Trade* (Behavioral Res. Lab, 1965); 3. *Microeconomics: A Programmed Book* (with R. Attiyeh and G.L. Bach), (Prentice-Hall, 1966, 1981); 4. *Macroeconomics: A Programmed Book* (with R. Attiyah and G.L. Bach), (Prentice-Hall, 1966, 1981); 5. *New Development in the Teaching of Economics*, ed. (Prentice-Hall, 1967); 6. *Excess Demand and Excess Supply in World Tramp Shipping Markets* (Stanford Univ. Press, 1968); 7. *Recent Research in Economics Education*, ed. (Prentice-Hall, 1970); 8. *Basic Economics: Theory and Cases* (with R. Attiyeh and G. L. Bach), (Prentice-Hall, 1973, 1977); 9. *Efficiency in Universities: The La Paz Papers*, ed. (Elsevier, 1974); 10. *Economics Education in the United Kingdom* (with R. Attiyeh and A. Scott), (Heinemann Educ., 1980).

Articles: 1. 'The effectiveness of programmed learning in economics (with R. Attiyeh), *AER*, 55(2), May 1965; 2. 'The efficiency of programmed learning in economics: the results of a nationwide experiment' (with R. Attiyeh and G. L. Bach), *AER*, 59(2), May 1969; 3. 'University students' initial understanding of economics: the contribution of the A Level Economics course and of other factors' (with R. Attiyeh), *Ec*, N.S. 38, Feb. 1971; 4. 'The core of basic economics' (with R. Attiyeh), *Econ.*, 9(1), Summer 1971; 5. 'Some modern myths in teaching economics: the UK experience' (with R. Attiyeh), *AER*, 62(2), May 1972; 6. 'The Open University: a survey and analysis' (with C. Ritchie), *Instructional Science* 1975; 7. 'Television and efficiency in higher education' (with D. Jamison), *Management Science*, 1, April 1975; 8. 'The effects of right-to-work laws on unionization in the United States' (with C. N. Petersen), *JPE*, 83(6), Dec. 1975; 9. 'An output comparison of Open University and conventional university students' (with A. Scott), *Higher Educ.*, 2, 1982; 10. 'The efficacy of innovative teaching techniques in economics: the UK experience' (with A. Scott), *AER*, 72(2), May 1983.

Principal Contributions Most of my work has been concerned with improving economics education. From an early naive view of proposing advanced mathematics as a prerequisite for studying the subject, I progressed from writing programmed texts to teach basic theory more efficiently, to developing case materials to teach the application of theory to real world problems. The introduction of time-sharing computers led to my involvement in macrosimulations. My other research interests at this time were investigating the effect of right to work laws on unionisation and the economics of shipping.

In 1975 I returned to the UK to head the Esmée Fairbairn Res. Centre concerned with the development and assessment of the efficacy of innovative teaching techniques on different types of students in various institutional settings. The advent of microcomputers persuaded me to devote resources to the software market and we have developed (1) a series of macrosimulations of which *Running the British Economy* (1981) now has a cult followng in the UK and is used by thousands of students; (2) a macroeconomic data base, containing national income related statistics for 25 countries from 1959 to the present (an annual update service is available) plus a series of utility programs for analysing the data; and (3) simulations of companies for management training. Many of the above techniques are being combined into distance learning business packaged courses. Current activities include assessing general linear modelling as a superior technique to regression analysis for analysing large heterogeneous data sets, and research on the care of the mentally handicapped.

Occasionally I teach economics to keep in touch with the student population, but most of my teaching is confined to management programmes at the executive level; it is both stimulating and rewarding but has the disadvantage of a heavy international travel schedule.

LUNDBERG, Erik, Filip

Born 1907, Stockholm, Sweden.
Current Post Scientific Adviser, Skandinaviska Enskilda Banken, Stockholm, 1971–.
Past Posts Dir., Govt Econ. Res. Inst. (Konjunkturinstitutet), 1937–55; Member, State Power Board, 1946–77; Prof. Univ. Stockholm, 1946–65; Member, Govt Planning Council, 1961–; Prof. Stockholm School Econ., 1965–70.
Degree PhD (Econ.) Univ. Stockholm, 1937.
Offices and Honours Pres., Royal Swedish Academy Science, 1973–6; Chairman, Nobel Comm. Econ., 1975–80; Söderström's Medal Econ. Science, 1980; Berhnard Harms Prize, Weltwirtschaftliches Inst., Kiel, 1980.
Principal Fields of Interest 131 Economic Fluctuations.
Publications *Books:* 1. *Studies in the Theory of Economic Expansion* (P. S. Kinga Son, 1937, 1956); 2. *Business Cycles and Economic Policy* (A&U, 1957); 3. *Produktivitet och Räntabilitet* (Productivity and profitability) (Norstedt & Söner, 1961); 4. *Instability and Economic Growth* (Yale Univ. Press, 1968); 5. *Inflation och Arbetslöshet* (Inflation and unemployment) (with L. Calmfors), (SNS, 1974).
Articles: 1. 'The profitability of investment', *EJ*, 69, Dec. 1959; 2. 'Studier

i monetär analys' (Studies in monetary analysis'), *Ekon Tids*, 2, 1963; 3. 'Productivity and structural change - a policy issue in Sweden', *EJ*, Suppl. 82, March 1972; 4. 'World inflation and national policies', Inst. Internat. Econ. Stud. Stockholm, Seminar paper No. 80, 1977; 5. 'Fiscal and monetary policies in Taiwan', Inst. Internat. Econ. Stud., Stockholm, Seminar paper No. 90, 1977.
Principal Contributions Theory of business cycles, particularly models of unstable growth based on the multiplier and acceleration principles. Studies of inflation based on excess demand gaps for goods and labour. Analysis of wage inflation, including effects of marginal and other taxes (tax multiplier effects). Analysis of relations between capital investment and productivity growth in Swedish industry. Discovery of the 'Horndal effect': how labour productivity can go on rising over a long period without new investment. In this connection carried out some empirical analysis of relations between *ex-ante* and actual *ex-post* returns on investment. Comparative studies of stabilisation policies in Sweden from 1920–80.

LUTZ, Friedrich August*

Dates and Birthplace 1901–75, Sarrebourg, France.
Posts Held Privatdozent, Univ, Freibourg 1932–8; Instr., Prof., Princeton Univ., 1938–53; Prof., Univ. Zürich, 1953.
Degree Dr sc. pol.
Offices and Honours Member, Mont. Pélerin Soc.
Publications *Books:* 1. *Das Konjunkturproblem in der nationalökonomie* (1932); 2. *Rebuilding the World Economy* (with N. S. Buchanan), (1947); 3. *Theory of Investment of the Firm* (with V. Lutz), (1951); 4. *Zinstheorie* (1956).
Career Writer in the Austrian tradition, whose *Zinstheorie* was a masterful survey of the history of interest theory and whose *Theory of Investment of the Firm* was a major modern restatement of Austrian capital theory in microeconomic terms.

LUXEMBOURG, Rosa*

Dates and Birthplace 1870–1919, Zamosc, Russia.

Posts Held Polit. Leader, German Social Democratic Party; Lect., Party School, Berlin, 1907–.

Degree Dr Univ. Zürich, 1898.

Publications *Books:* 1. *Die Industrielle Entwicklung Polens* (1898); 2. *The Accumulation of Capital* (1913, 1951); 3. *Gesammelte Werke*, vols 3, 4 and 6 only (1922–8); 4. *Ausgewählte Reden und Schriften*, 2 vols (1951).

Career A founder of the Social Democratic Party of Poland, the leader of the Left Wing of the German Social Democrats and a prominent Marxist economic theoretician. In *Accumulation of Capital* she argued that capitalism must expand into underdeveloped countries and non-capitalist areas because of an inherent insufficiency of aggregate demand. In this way capitalism is an essential cause of the international tensions and instabilities that characterise the modern world. She was murdered whilst in military custody during the 1919 German Revolution.

Secondary Literature J. P. Nettle, *Rosa Luxemburg*, 2 vols (OUP, 1966); T. Kowalik, 'Luxemburg, Rosa', *IESS*, 9.

LYDALL, Harold French

Born 1916, Pretoria, S. Africa.

Current Post Emeritus Prof. Econ., Univ. E. Anglia, Norwich, England, 1978–.

Past Posts Sr. Res. Officer, Inst. Stats., Univ. Oxford, 1950–9; Reader, Prof., Univ. Western Australia, 1960–1; Prof., Univ. Adelaide, 1962–7; Econ., UN, Geneva, 1967–9; Prof., Univ. E. Anglia, 1969–78.

Degrees BA Univ. S. Africa, 1936; MA Univ. Oxford, 1950.

Offices and Honours Rhodes Scholar, 1936–9; Fellow, *Em Soc.*

Editorial Duties Ed. Board, *AEP*, 1964–.

Principal Fields of Interest 020 General Economic Theory; 050 Economic Systems; 820 Labour Markets; Public Policy.

Publications *Books:* 1. *British Incomes and Savings* (Blackwell, 1955); 2. *The Role of Small Enterprises in Indian Economic Development* (with P. N. Dhar), (Asia Publ. House, 1961); 3. *The Structure of Earnings* (OUP, 1968; transl., Italian, Franco Angeli Editore, 1975); 4. *Trade and Employment* (*ILO*, 1975); 5. *A Theory of Income Distribution* (OUP, 1979); 6. *Yugoslav Socialism: Theory and Practice* (OUP, 1984).

Articles: 1. 'The life cycle in income, saving, and asset ownership', *Em*, 23(2), Apr. 1955; 2. 'Income, assets, and the demand for money', *REStat*, 40(1), Feb. 1958; 3. 'A comparison of the distribution of income and wealth in Britain and the United States' (with J. B. Lansing), *AER*, 49(1), Mar. 1959; 4. 'The long-term trend in the size distribution of income', *JRSS*, Series A, 122, pt.1, March 1959; 5. 'The distribution of employment incomes', *Em*, 27(2), April 1959; 6. 'The inequality of Indian incomes', *Econ. Weekly*, June 1960; 7. 'The distribution of personal wealth in Britain' (with D. G. Tipping), *BOIS*, 23(1), Feb. 1961; 8. 'Technical progress in Australian manufacturing', *EJ*, 78(4), Dec. 1968; 9. 'Theories of the distribution of earnings', in *The Personal Distribution of Incomes*, ed. A. B. Atkinson, (A&U, 1976); 10. 'Some problems in making international comparisons of inequality', in *Income Inequality*, ed. J. R. Moroney (D. C. Heath, 1979).

Principal Contributions When, after the war and five years postwar work in business, I returned to Oxford, my first research project was to organise the first British national survey of incomes and savings. The results are given in *British Incomes and Savings*. Subsequently I organised a survey of small manufacturing businesses. In 1959 I made a study from tax statistics of the long-term trend in personal income inequality. Later in the same year I joined the MIT Center for International Studies project in India, and collaborated with P. N. Dhar in a short book on small enterprise policy. In 1960 I moved to Australia and later began to use Australian tax statistics on wages and salaries to analyse the inequality of wage income in that country. This led on to my study of *The Structure of Earnings*, which attempted to compare and to account for earnings inequality in a wide range of countries.

In 1972 the ILO asked me to make estimates of the effects of changes in the pattern of trade in manufactures on employment in rich and poor countries. This report was published as *Trade and Employment*. Meanwhile, I was beginning to formulate a new approach to the theory of income distribution, which appeared in 1979 as *A Theory of Income Distribution*. Later, I started to give serious attention to problems of alternative economic systems, one of the most interesting of which is that of Yugoslavia. My conclusions on that subject are given in *Yugoslav Socialism: Theory and Practice*.

M

MACAVOY, Paul Webster

Born 1934, Haverhill, MA, USA.
Current Post Dean, Prof. Management, Grad. School Management, Prof. Econ., Univ. Rochester, Rochester, NY, USA, 1983–.
Past Posts Ass. Prof. Bus. Econ., Grad. School Bus., Univ. Chicago, 1960–3; Ass. Prof. Econ., Assoc. Prof. Econ., Prof. Management, Henry R. Luce Prof. Public Pol., Sloan School Management, 1963–5, 1966–9, 1969–74, 1974–5; Member, US President's Council Econ. Advisers, 1975–6; Prof. Organization and Management, Frederick William Beinecke Prof. Econ., Yale Univ., 1977–81, 1981–3.
Degrees BA (Econ., Hist., Maths.) Bates Coll., 1955; MA, PhD Yale Univ., 1956, 1965; Hon LLD Bates Coll., 1976.
Offices and Honours Fellow, AAAS, 1982.
Editorial Duties Ed., *Bell JE*, 1970–5; Advisory Ed., *Resources & Energy*, 1977, 1984, *Energy J.*, 1980–4.
Principal Fields of Interest 822 Public Policy; Role of Government; 723 Energy; 613 Public Utilities and Costs of Government Regulation of Other Industries in the Private Sector.

Publications *Books:* 1. *The Crisis of the Regulatory Commissions*, ed. (W. W. Norton, 1970); 2. *Energy Regulation by the Federal Power Commission* (with S. Breyer), (Brookings Inst., 1974); 3. *The Economics of the Natural Gas Shortage 1960–1980* (with R. S. Pindyck), (N-H, 1975); 4. *Price Controls and the Natural Gas Shortage* (with R. S. Pindyck), (AEI, 1975); 5. *Economic Perspective on the Politics of International Commodity Agreement* (Univ. Arizona Press, 1977); 6. *The Regulated Industries and the Economy* (W. W. Norton, 1979); 7. *The Decline of Service in the Regulated Industries* (with S. Carron), (AEI, 1981); 8. *Crude Oil Prices: As Determined by OPEC and Market Fundamentals* (Ballinger, 1982); 9. *Energy Policy: An Economic Analysis* (W. W. Norton, 1983); 10. *The Record of EPA Regulation in Controlling Industrial Air Pollution* (AEI, 1984).
Articles: 1. 'Regulation and the financial condition of the electric power companies in the 1970s' (with P. L. Joskow), *AER*, 65(2), May 1975; 2. 'A hard look at prospects for commodity agreements' (with H. B. Junz), in *Stabilizing World Commodity Markets*, eds. F. G. Adams and A. Klein (D. C. Heath, 1978); 3. 'Conserving energy in the production of aluminum' (with R. Charpie), *Resources and Energy*, 1, 1978; 4. 'A sample of observations on pricing in public and private enterprises' (with N. Funkhouser), *J Pub E*, 18(1), Fall 1979; 5. 'The natural gas policy act of 1978', *Natural Resources J.*, Dec. 1979; 6. 'The impact of regulation on the performance of industry' (with D. Tella), in *Government Regulation of Business: Its Growth, Impact and Future* (Chamber Commerce USA, 1979); 7. 'Corporate philanthropy vs. corporate purpose' (with I. Millstein), in *Corporate Philanthropy* (Council on Foundations, 1982); 8. 'Winning by losing: the AT&T settlement and its impact on telecommunication' (with K. Robinson), *Yale J. Regulation*, Nov. 1983; 9. 'Standards: the experience in the United States', in *Safety and Law*, ed. P. C. Compes (Gesellschaft für Sicherheitswissenschaft, 1984); 10. 'Prolonging federal control of natural gas prices in the 1980s', in *Government-Business*

Relations in the '80s, ed. W. Tolo (Univ. Texas at Austin, 1984).

Principal Contributions Throughout my career, my goal has been to produce stylised facts in the systematic behaviour of private-sector organisations subject to regulation and other governmental policies. While searching fairly widely for testable propositions designed to produce such findings, my work nevertheless has tended to utilise classical price theory and comparative statics. The findings from my dozen books encompass price and quantity changes, and also profitability, productivity, and quality of service from American corporations. Most relate to the natural resource industries and thus necessarily deal with perceived public trade-offs of shortages, deteriorating service quality and declining productivity for price controls that provide ephemeral gains in the form of income redistribution. The value of this work should eventually be realised in the development of an empirical theory of the regulatory agency imposing controls on private organisations.

MACCINI, Louis John

Born 1942, Cambridge, MA, USA.
Current Post Assoc. Prof. Econ., Johns Hopkins Univ., Baltimore, MD, USA, 1975–.
Past Posts Ass. Prof., Johns Hopkins Univ., 1969–75.
Degrees BS Boston Coll., 1965; PhD Northwestern Univ., 1970.
Principal Fields of Interest 023 Macroeconomic Theory; 210 Econometric, Statistical and Mathematical Methods and Models; 130 Economic Fluctuations; Forecasting; Stabilisation and Inflation.
Publications *Articles:* 1. 'On optimal delivery lags', *JET*, 6(2), April 1973; 2. 'Delivery lags and the demand for investment', *REStud*, 40(2), May 1976; 3. 'The dynamic behavior of prices, output and inventories,' *QJE*, 90(2), May 1976; 4. 'The impact of demand and price expectations on the behavior of prices', *AER*, 68(1), March 1978; 5. 'Adjustment lags, economically rational expectations and price behavior', *REStat*, 63(2), May 1981; 6. 'On the theory of the firm underlying empirical models of price behavior', *Int ER*, 22(3), Oct. 1981; 7. 'The interrelationship between price and output decisions and investment decisions: microfoundations and aggregate implications', *J Mon E*, 13(1), Jan. 1984; 8. 'Joint production, quasi-fixed factors of production, and investment in finished goods inventories' (with R. Rossana), *JMCB*, 16(2), May 1984.

Principal Contributions My research has focussed on the microfoundations of macroeconomic behavioural relationships and includes work at both the theoretical and empirical level. Early work introduced delivery lags into the analysis of investment behaviour. Theoretical work was done on both the demand and supply sides of the market for capital goods. An ongoing interest has been the attempt to provide a microeconomic basis for the price and output relationships commonly used in macroeconomic models. I have developed dynamic models of firm behaviour to capture the effects of buffer stocks (inventories, unfilled orders), quasi-fixed factors of production (capital stocks, stocks of workers), and the expectations of demand and factor input prices on price and output decisions. These models study the interaction between price and output decisions and investment decisions, and provide a theory of optimal mark-up pricing. I have used these models as a basis for empirical work to explain movements in prices. A major finding, in contrast to previous literature, is that demand forces exert a strong influence on movements in prices. More recent work has investigated the adjustments of firms to cyclical fluctuations in demand. This work began with empirical studies of the determinants of inventory investment. It is continuing with the development of theoretical models designed to study the interaction of inventories and layoffs over the business cycle.

MacDOUGALL, George Donald Alastair

Born 1912, Glasgow, Scotland.
Current Post Retired, 1984.
Past Posts Ass. Lect., Univ. Leeds, 1936–9; Prime Minister Churchill's Stat. Branch, 1939–45, 1951–3; Fellow, Wadham Coll., Nuffield Coll. Oxford, 1945–50, 1947–60; Econ. Dir., OEEC, Paris, 1948–9; Member, Commission on Fiscal System, Venezuela, 1958; Vis. Prof., ANU, 1959, MIT Center Internat. Stud., New Delhi, 1961; Econ. Dir., UK Nat. Econ. Devlp. Office, 1962–4; Member, Turnover Tax Comm., 1963–4; Dir. General, UK Dept. Econ. Affairs, 1964–8; Head, UK Govt. Econ. Service, Chief Econ. Adviser, UK Treasury, 1969–73; Chief Econ. Advisory Confederation British Industry, London, 1973–84; Chairman, EEC Study Group, Role of Public Finances in Europ. Integration, 1975–7.
Degrees BA, MA Univ. Oxford, 1935, 1938; Hon. LLD Univ. Strathclyde, 1968; Hon. DLitt Leeds, 1971; Hon. DSc Univ. Aston, Birmingham, 1979.
Offices and Honours OBE, 1942; CBE, 1945; Knighted, 1953; Fellow, BA, 1966; Hon. Fellow, Wadham Coll., Nuffield Coll., Oxford, 1964–, 1967–; Pres., RES, 1972–4; Chairman, Exec. Comm., NIESR, 1974–; Pres., Soc. Strategic and Long Range Planning, 1977–; Vice-Pres., Soc. Bus. Econ., 1978–.
Principal Fields of Interest 010 General Economics; 300 Domestic Monetary and Fixed Theory and Institutions; 400 International Economics.
Publications *Books*: 1. *Measures for International Economic Stability* (with J. W. Angell, *et al.*), (UN, 1951); 2. *The World Dollar Problem* (Macmillan, 1957); 3. *The Fiscal System of Venezuela* (with C. S. Shoup, *et al.*), (JHUP, 1959); 4. *The Dollar Problem: A Reappraisal* (Princeton Univ. Press, 1960); 5. *Report of the Committee on Turnover Taxation* (with G. Richardson and H. Benson), (HMSO, 1964); 6. *Studies in Political Economy, 1, The Interwar Years, and the 1940s, 2, International Trade and Domestic Economic*
Policy (Macmillan, 1975); 7. *Economic and Monetary Union 1980* (with R. Marjolin, *et al.*), (EEC, 1975); 8. *The Role of Public Finance in European Integration* (with D. Biehl, *et al.*), (EEC, 1977).
Articles: 1. 'The definition of prime and supplementary costs', *EJ*, 46, Sept. 1936; 2. 'Economic growth and social welfare', *SJPE*, 24(3), Nov. 1977; 3. 'The machinery of economic government: some personal reflections', in *Policy and Politics: Essays in Honor of Norman Chester'*, eds. D. Butler and A. Halsey (Macmillan, 1978).
Principal Contributions The use of economic analysis, and usually a quantitative approach, to illuminate real problems of policy that have arisen during the past half-century in the UK and elsewhere, including Western Europe, the US, Venezuela, India and Australia. The attempt to educate students, civil servants, politicians, businessmen and others.

MACHLUP, Fritz*

Dates and Birthplace 1902–83, Wiener Neustadt, Austro-Hungary.
Posts Held Goodyear Prof. Econ., Univ. Buffalo, 1935–47; Hutzler Prof. Polit. Econ., Johns Hopkins Univ., 1947–60; Walker Prof. Econ. Internat. Fin., Princeton Univ., 1960–71; Prof. Econ., NYU, 1971–83.
Degrees Dr Rer. Pol., Dr Rer. Pol. 50 year Renewal, Univ. Vienna, 1923, 1973; Hon. LLD Lawrence Coll., 1956, Lehigh Univ., 1967, LaSalle Coll., 1968; Hon. Dr Sc. Pol. Univ. Kiel, W. Germany, 1965; Hon. Dr oecon. Univ. St Gallen, Switzerland, 1972; Hon. LHD Case Inst. Technology, 1967.
Offices and Honours Hon. Member, Phi Beta Kappa, 1937; Pres., SEA, 1959–60; AAAS, 1961; Pres., AAUP, 1962–4; Pres., AEA, 1966; Pres., Hon. Pres., IEA, 1971–4, 1974–83; Amer. Philo. Soc., 1963; Nat. Academy Educ., 1965; Fellow, Amer. Assoc. Advancement Science, 1966; Hon. Senator, Univ. Vienna, 1971; Bernhard Harms Prize, Univ. Kiel, 1974; Foreign Member, Academia Nazionale dei Lincei, Rome, 1974.

Publications *Books:* 1. *International Trade and the National Income Multiplier* (1943); 2. *The Economic of Sellers' Competition* (1952); 3. *Essays on Economic Semantics* (1963, 1967); 4. *Methodology of Economic and Other Social Sciences* 1978); 5. *Knowledge: Its Creation, Distribution, and Economic Significance*, vols 1, 2, 3 (1984).

Articles: 1. 'My early work on international monetary problems', *BNLQR*, 133, June 1980; 'My work on international monetary problems, 1940–64', *BNLQR*, 140, March 1982.

Career Work in international economics in 17 books and nearly 100 articles. In the field of economic organisation, major work on competition and monopoly embodied in a 1952 book and, especially, work on knowledge production in the book of 1962 and the series started in 1980. Also work in methodology, most of which is collected in the 1978 volume.

Secondary Literature J. S. Chipman, 'Machlup, Fritz', *IESS*, 18; *Breadth and Depth in Economics: Fritz Machlup — The Man and His Ideas*, ed. J. S. Dreyer (D. C. Heath, 1978).

MACKAY, Ronald Ross

Born 1940, Delhi, India.
Current Post Sr. Lect., Univ. Coll. N. Wales, Bangor, Wales, 1979–.
Past Posts Lect. Econ., Univ. Newcastle, 1965–79; Cons., UNDP Regional Plan Suez Canal Zone, 1983; Special Adviser, Select Comm. Welsh Affairs, 1984; Adviser, Econ. and Social Affairs Comm., EEC, 1984.
Degrees MA Univ. Aberdeen, 1963.
Editorial Duties Ed. Board, *Regional Stud.*
Principal Fields of Interest 941 Regional Economics; 800 Manpower, Labour, Population; 000 General Economics; Theory.
Publications *Books:* 1. *Economic Outlook for Wales* (with S. P. Chakravarty and D. R. Jones), (Inst. Econ. Res., 1982).

Articles: 1 'Employment creation in the development areas', *SJPE*, 19(3), Nov. 1972; 2. 'Employment creation: a resurrection', *SJPE*, 20(2), June 1973;

3. 'Evaluating the effects of British regional economic policy — a comment', *EJ*, 84, June 1974; 4. 'The impact of the regional employment premium', in *The Economics of Industrial Subsidies*, ed. A. Whiting (HMSO, 1976); 5. 'Regional policy for an independent Scotland', in *Economic Options for an Independent Scotland*, ed. D. I. MacKay (HMSO, 1978); 6. 'Important trends in regional policy and regional employment — a modified interpretation' (with L. Thomson), *SJPE*, 26(3), Nov. 1979; 7. 'The death of regional policy — or resurrection squared', *Regional Stud.*, 13(3), 1979; 8. 'Regional policy and regional employment — the UK experience', in *Planning under Regional Stagnation*, eds. W. Buhr and P. Friedrick (Nomos Verlagsgesellschaft, 1982); 9. 'The returns to manpower policy against a background of national economic decline: the Welsh example' (with S. P. Chakravarty and D. R. Jones), *Regional Stud.*, 17(2), April 1983.

Principal Contributions The early articles concentrate on the identification of a regional policy impact in the UK. The underlying theme is that the essential concern of economics with imprecise and uncertain quantification has to be explicitly acknowledged. The measurement procedure has to compensate for the imperfections of the data and for the inability of any one set of statistics to measure what we seek to identify. A useful practical rule is to compare and contrast the returns from different types of measure. Not only does this procedure provide consistency checks, but by identifying different forms of response it provides insight into the nature of the response to regional policy. The approach also illustrates the time-lags involved. The later articles contrast the Keynesian and the monetarist approach to structural intervention. Given the Keynesian approach the return to regional policy depends on the underlying level of demand. Regional policy, employment counselling, retraining are ineffective when unemployment is high and general. In the monetarist approach there is a natural tendency to full employment, and the 'natural' level can be reduced by structural measures which reduce mismatch and improve efficiency in the labour market. At the heart of the conflict are two different views of the market process. In the monetarist approach, price contains all the important information and contracting and recontracting are essentially straightforward. Given the Keynesian approach, an exaggeration of the power and reach of the market withdraws the background conditions on which an effective mixed economy depends.

MACLEOD, Henry Dunning*

Dates and Birthplace 1821–1902, Edinburgh, Scotland.
Posts Held Lawyer; employed by Govt. to prepare digest of laws on bills of exchange, 1868–70.
Degrees BA, MA Univ. Camb., 1843, 1863.
Publications *Books:* 1. *The Theory and Practice of Banking*, 2 vols (1855); 2. *The Elements of Political Economy* (1858); 3. *On the Modern Science of Economics* (1887); 4. *The Theory of Credit*, 2 vols (1889–91); 5. *Bimetallism* (1894); 6. *History of Economics* (1896).
Career Whilst his work on banking was widely appreciated in his day, as an economist he was shunned by the establishment and failed to obtain a university chair. (His implication in the failure of the Royal British Bank had brought him a conviction for conspiracy to defraud, which partially explains his isolation.) Though an original thinker, particularly on the theory of value, his frequently restated views failed to be accepted as the new departure which he claimed them to be. He was responsible for the invention of the term 'Gresham's Law'.
Secondary Literature F. A. Hayek, 'Macleod, Henry Dunning', *ESS*, 10.

MACVANE, Silas Marcus*

Dates and Birthplace 1842–1914, Prince Edward Island, Canada.
Posts Held Instr., Ass. Prof., Prof., Harvard Univ., 1875–1911.

Degrees BA Acadia Coll., Canada., 1865; Harvard Univ., 1873.
Publications *Books:* 1. *The Working Principles of Political Economy* (1890). *Articles:* 1. 'The Austrian theory of value', *Amer. Academy Polit. and Social Science Annals*, 4, 1893–4.
Career Teacher of history, law, politics and government and writer of able works on economics. His criticisms of the writings of F. A. Walker in *QJE* were effective in identifying weaknesses in Walker's ideas. His *Working Principles . . .* achieved some success as a textbook and was a clear exposition of current orthodoxy.
Secondary Literature F. W. Taussig, 'MacVane, Silas Marcus', *ESS*, 10.

MADDALA, Gangaddharrao S.

Born 1933, Hyderabad, India.
Current Post Grad. Res. Prof. Econ., Dir., Center Econometrics and Decision Sciences, Univ. Florida, Gainesville, FL, USA, 1975–.
Past Posts Ass. Prof., Stanford Univ., 1963–7; Assoc. Prof., Prof., Univ. Rochester, 1967–75; Vis. Prof., Cornell Univ., 1969, 1972.
Degrees BA (Maths.) Andhra Univ., India 1955; MA (Stats.) Bombay Univ., India, 1957; PhD Univ. Chicago, 1963.
Offices and Honours Fairchild Disting. Scholar, Caltech., Pasadena, CA, 1979–80; Vice-Pres, Atlantic Econ. Assoc., 1982; Fellow, Em Soc.
Editorial Duties Assoc. Ed., *Em*, 1970–9.
Principal Fields of Interest 211 Econometric, Statistical and Mathematical Methods and Models; 022 Microeconomic Theory; 023 Macroeconomic Theory.
Publications *Books:* 1. *Econometrics* (McGraw-Hill, 1977); 2. *Limited Dependent and Qualitative Variables in Econometrics* (CUP, 1983). *Articles:* 1. 'International diffusion of technical change — a case study of the oxygen steelmaking process' (with P. T. Knight), *EJ*, 77, Sept. 1976; 2. 'On the use of variance component models in pooling cross-section and time-series data', *Em*, 39(2), March 1971; 3. 'Simultaneous equation meth-

ods for large and medium-size econometric models', *REStud*, 38(4), Oct. 1971; 4. 'Some small sample evidence on tests of significance in simultaneous equation models' *Em*, 42(5), Sept. 1974; 5. 'Maximum likelihood methods for models of markets is disequilibrium' (with F. D. Nelson), *Em*, 42(6), Nov. 1974; 6. 'Weak priors and sharp posteriors in simultaneous equation models', *Em*, 44(2), March 1976; 7. 'A function for size distribution of incomes', *Em*, 44(5), Sept. 1976; 8. 'Self-selectivity problems in econometric models', in *Applications in Statistics*, ed. P. R. Krishniah (N-H, 1977); 9. 'Asymptotic covariance matrices of two-stage probit and two-stage tobit methods for simultaneous equations with selectivity' (with L. F. Lee and R. P. Trost), *Em*, 48(2), March 1980; 10. 'Methods of estimation for models of markets with bounded price variation', *Int ER*, 24(2), June 1983.

Principal Contributions Initially worked on technological change in the coal industry when no one was interested in coal. Wrote the first pioneering paper on international diffusion of technical change but somehow left that area to others and moved to econometrics. Worked on the use of variance components models in pooling cross-section and time-series data. Studied Bayesian inference in econometrics and wrote a paper on weak prior and sharp posteriors that brings out some anomolies in Bayesian inference in simultaneous equations. Later worked on econometric models involving disequilibrium and self-selection; also estimation of econometric models with controlled prices. Currently examining critically all the econometric work on rational expectations in macroeconomic and models of expectations based on survey data.

MADDISON, Angus

Born 1926, Newcastle-upon-Tyne, England.
Current Post Prof. Econ., Univ. Groningen, The Netherlands, 1978–.
Past Posts Lect. Econ. Hist., St Andrews Univ., Scotland, 1951–2; Cons., FAO, Rome, 1952; Head, Econ. Div., OEEC, Paris, 1958–62; Ass. Dir., Devlp. Dept., OECD, Paris, 1963; Fellow, OECD Devlp. Centre, 1964–6; Dir., Twentieth-Century Fund Res. Project on Devlp., 1967–9; Centre Internat. Affairs, Harvard Univ., 1969–71; Head, Central Analysis Div., OECD, 1971–8.
Degrees BA, MA, Dr d'état (français) Univ. Camb., 1947, 1951, 1980.
Offices and Honours Exhibitioner, Selwyn Coll. Camb., 1945–8; Bronsman Fellow, McGill Univ., 1949–50; Univ. Fellow, Johns Hopkins Univ., 1950–1; NATO Fellow, Washington, 1958; Member, UN Expert Group Planning Techniques, Bangkok, 1962; Vis. Fellow, ANU, 1982.
Principal Fields of Interest 041 Economic History: General; 123 Comparative Economic Studies; 226 Productivity and Growth.
Publications *Books:* 1. *Economic Growth in the West* (A&U, W. W. Norton, 1964; transls., Japanese, Kino Kuniya, 1965, Spanish, Fondo de Cultura, 1966, Russian, Progress, 1967); 2. *Foreign Skills and Technical Assistance in Economic Development* (OECD 1965, transl., French, OECD, 1965; 3. *Economic Growth in Japan and the USSR* (A&U, W. W. Norton, 1969; transl., Swedish, Prisma, 1971, Japanese, Nihon Keizei Shimbun, 1971; Dutch, Spectrum, 1971, Spanish, Fondo de Cultura, 1971, Italian, Giannini, 1972, German, Lubbe, 1972). 4. *Economic Progress and Policy in Developing Countries* (A&U, W. W. Norton, 1964; transl., Spanish, Fondo de Cultura, 1973); 5. *Class Structure and Economic Growth: India and Pakistan Since the Moghols* (A&U, W. W. Norton, 1971); transl., Spanish, Fondo de Cultura, 1974; 6. *Economic Policy and Performance in Europe 1913–1970, Fontana Economic History of Europe*, 5(2) (Collins, 1976); 7. *Phases of Capitalist Development* (OUP 1982; transls., French, Economica, 1981, Dutch, Spectrum, 1982; Spanish, Fondo de Cultura, 1984); 8. *Foreign Skills and Technical Assistance in Greek Development* (with A. D. Stavrianopoulos and B. Higgins), (OECD 1966; transl., French, OECD, 1966); 9. *Mydral's*

Asian Drama: An Interdisciplinary Critique, ed. (CIRIEC, 1971); 10. *Unemployment: The European Perspective*, ed. (Croom Helm, 1982).

Articles: 1. 'Productivity in an expanding economy', *EJ*, 62, Sept. 1952; 2. 'Growth and fluctuation in the world economy 1870–1960', *BNLQR*, 15, June 1962; 3. 'Explaining economic growth', *BNLQR*, 25, Sept. 1972; 4. 'What is education for?', *LBR*, April 1974; 5. 'Education, inequality and life chances: the major policy issues', in *Education, Inequality and Life Chances*, 2 vols., ed. A. Maddison, (OECD, 1975); 6. 'Monitoring the labour market', in *A Proposal for a Comprehensive Approach in Official Strategies*, *RIW*, 26(2), June 1980; 7. 'Economic growth and structural change in the advanced countries', in *Western Economics in Transition*, eds. I. Leveson and J. W. Wheeler (Croom Helm 1980); 8. 'A comparison of levels of GDP per capita in developed and developing countries', *JEH*, 43(1), March 1983; 9. 'Leading countries in capitalist development: the secrets of success', *Beihefte der Konjunkturpolitik*, Heft 29 (Duncker & Humblot, 1983); 10. 'Economic stagnation since 1973. Its nature and causes. A six county survey', *DE*, 131(4), Dec. 1983.

Principal Contributions My major research interest has been in assessment of forces affecting the economic growth performance of nations. I have devoted a good deal of effort to quantification of output levels and growth, of labour and capital inputs, of productivity, structural change and international trade in an articulate growth-accounting framework in the Clark, Kuznets, Kendrick, Denison tradition. I have emphasised the usefulness of the comparative dimension in such analyses in the Gilbert and Kravis tradition, and by training and inclination attach importance to tracing the relevant historical dimensions. In addition to the more readily measurable technocratic supply-side influences, I have tried to analyse the impact of national policy and degree of international co-operation or conflict on demand and resource allocation. For developing countries, I have also tried to analyse the interaction of indigenous institutions, social structure and colonialism in explaining economic backwardness.

MAHALANOBIS, Prasanta Chandra*

Dates and Birthplace 1893–72, Calcutta, India.

Posts Held Indian Educ. Service. 1915–48; Prof. Physics, Principal, Presidency Coll., India, 1922–45, 1945–8; Lect. Stats., Calcutta Univ., 1917–45; Meteorologist, Alipore Observatory, Calcutta, 1922–6; Secretary, Dir., Stat. Adviser, Indian Stat. Inst., Indian Govt., Calcutta, 1931–72, 1949–72; Member, Indian Planning Commission, 1955–67.

Degrees BSc (Physics) Univ. Calcutta, 1912, MA Univ. Camb., 1915; Hon. DSc Univs. Sofia State, 1961, Delhi, 1964, Stockholm, 1965.

Offices and Honours Vice-Pres., Internat. Biometric Soc., 1947; Pres., Indian Science Congress, 1950; Hon. Pres., Internat. Stat. Inst., 1957; Chairman, UN Subcomm. Stat. Sampling, 1947–51; Pres., Indian Nat. Science Academy, 1957–8; Devad Prasad Sarbahikarn Gold Medal, Czechoslovak Academy Sciences, 1964; Durga Prasad Khaitan Memorial Gold Medal, Asiatic Soc., 1968.

Editorial Duties Ed, *Sankya: Indian J. Stats.*, 1933–72.

Publications *Books:* 1. *Experiments in Statistical Sampling in the Indian Statistical Institute* (1961); 2. *Talks on Planning* (1961); 3. *An Approach of Operational Research to Planning in India* (1963).

Career A notable statistician with a worldwide reputation as an expert on sampling methods, he became in his later years a leading spokesman of India's strategy of development, writing and lecturing in both India and abroad in defence of Soviet-style central planning, emphasising investment goods at the expense of consumer goods. He was also one of the first in the postwar period to seize on Harrod-Domar models as the basis of development planning.

MAIN, Brian G. M.

Born 1947, St Andrews, Scotland.
Current Post Reader Econ., Univ. Edinburgh, Scotland, 1983–.
Past Posts Prod. Planning Manager, Eli Lilly Corp., Liverpool, England, 1970–2; Lect. Econ., Univ. Edinburgh, 1976–83; US Assoc. Prof., Grad. School Bus., Univ. Cal. Berkeley, 1980–1.
Degrees BSc (Physics) St Andrews Univ, 1969; MBA, MA, PhD Univ. Cal. Berkeley, 1970, 1974, 1976.
Offices and Honours Phi Beta Kappa; Assoc. Fellow, Inst. Employment Res., Univ. Warwick, 1981–.
Principal Fields of Interest 810 Manpower Training and Allocation; 820 Labour Markets; Public Policy; 520 Business Finance and Investment.
Publications *Books: 1. Women's Working Lives: Evidence from the National Training Survey* (with P. Elias), (Inst. Employment Res., Univ. Warwick, 1982).
Articles: 1. 'Unemployment spells and unemployment experience' (with G. Akerlof), *AER*, 70(5), Dec. 1980; 2. 'An Engel curve for the direct and indirect consumption of oil', *REStat*, 63(1), Feb. 1981; 3. 'The length of employment and unemployment in great Britain', *SJPE*, 18(2), June 1981; 4. 'Pitfalls in Markov modeling of labor market stocks and flows' (with G. Akerlof), *JHR*, 16(1), Winter 1981; 5. 'An experience-weighted measure of employment and unemployment durations' (with G. Akerlof), *AER*, 71(5), Dec. 1981; 6. 'The firm's insurance decision: some questions raised by the capital asset pricing model', *Managerial and Decision Econ.*, 3(1), March 1982; 7. 'The length of a job in Great Britain', *Ec*, 49(2), Aug. 1982; 8. 'Determinants of employment and unemployment among school leavers: evidence from the 1979 survey of Scottish school leavers' (with D. Raffe), *SJPE*, 30(1), Feb. 1983; 9. 'Corporate insurance purchases and taxes', *J. Risk and Insurance*, 50(2), June, 1983.
Principal Contributions Work in labour economics concentrated at first on unemployment and on the duration and measurement of unemployment spells. Later work on unemployment has extended to the study of the effectiveness of government 'special programmes' in improving the employment prospects of participants. I have also started work on the analysis of women's working lives. This work, to date, has involved the re-analysis of the UK National Training Survey and of the Women and Employment Survey. In a completely different vein I have also investigated the corporate purchase of property and liability insurance. Financial economic theory suggests that such behaviour should not occur but it can be shown that certain common tax treatments of insured losses make insurance purchase rational.

MAITAL, Shlomo

Born 1942, Regina, Saskatchewan, Canada.
Current Post Assoc. Prof. Econ., Technion-Israel Inst. Technology, Haifa, Israel, 1979–.
Past Posts Lect. Econ., Tel Aviv Univ., 1967–79; Vis. Lect., Woodrow Wilson School of Public & Internat. Affairs, Princeton Univ., 1977–80; Vis. Prof., Applied Econ., Sloan School Management, MIT, 1984.
Degrees BA, MA Queen's Univ., Kingston, Ont., Canada, 1963, 1964; MA Univ. Manchester, 1965; PhD Princeton Univ., 1967.
Offices and Honours General Motors Scholar, 1960–4; Commonwealth Scholar, 1964–5; Frank Fetter Fellow, 1967; Member, Soc. Advancement of Behavioral Econ.
Editorial Duties Ed. Board, *Public Fin Q*.
Principal Fields of Interest 213 Mathematical Methods; 320 Public Finance.
Publications *Books: 1. Lagging Productivity Growth* (with N.M. Meltz), (Ballinger, 1980); 2. *Minds, Markets & Money* (Basic Books, 1982); 3. *Economic Games People Play* (with S.L. Maital), (Basic Books, 1984).
Articles: 1. 'Inflation, taxation and equity: how to pay for the war revisited', *EJ*, 82, March 1972; 2. 'Public goods and income distribution: some further results', *Em*, 41(3), May 1973, repr. in *Budgetwirkungen und Budgetpolitik*,

ed. K. Mackscheidt (Fischer Verlag, 1974); 3. 'Multidimensional scaling: some econometric applications', *J Em*, 8(1), Aug. 1978; 4. 'Inflation expectations in the monetarist black box', *AER*, 69(3), June 1979; 5. 'Inflation as prisoner's dilemma' (with Y. Benjamini), *J Post Keyn E*, 2(4), Summer 1980; 6. 'Individual-rational and group-rational inflation expectations: theory and cross-section evidence' (with S.L. Maital), *J Ec Behav*, 2, 1981; 7. 'What do economists know? An empirical study of experts' expectations' (with B.W. Brown), *Em*, 49(2), March 1981; 8. 'Job attitudes as intervening variables between situational factors and economic behavior' (with A. Schwartz and S.L. Maital), *J. Behavioral Econ.*, 12(1), Spring 1983; 9. 'Psychology and economics' (with S.L. Maital), in *Cross-currents in Contemporary Psychology 3, Psychology and Its Allied Disciplines: Social Sciences*, ed. M.L. Bornstein (Lawrence Erlbaum, 1983); 10. 'Voluntary provision of a pure public goods as the game of "chicken"' (with I. Lipnowski), *JPE*, 20(3), April 1983.

Principal Contributions As a young lecturer, I became dissatisfied with the dry, technical material that I both wrote and taught. I felt that human behaviour was largely absent. My wife, a school psychologist, helped me figure out how people could be reintroduced into economic theory. We began by writing an article on what psychologists call 'ability to defer gratification' (in economic jargon, time preference), in 1972. This article led to a decision to write a book on the psychological foundations of economic behaviour, which would analyse each aspect of economic decision-making (consumption, saving, investing, risk-taking, labour supply, productivity, tax evasion, etc.) from the vantage point of social psychology. This ultimately became *Minds, Markets & Money*. This book tried to show how both the models and methods of psychology could be extremely useful in understanding both microeconomics — individual behaviour — and macroeconomics — the national economy — and in particular, could help us link micro and macro in an integrated manner.

Recently I have been trying to reverse my original causal arrow, asking not what psychology can contribute to economics, but what economics might contribute to a synthesis of all the social sciences, including psychology and sociology. The vehicle I chose for this was game theory. *Economic Games People Play* (written with my wife, Sharone, as co-author), analyses economic games played by individuals, families, small and large groups, and entire nations, and uses psychology to understand how people behave in game situations (as opposed to how mathematicians think they *ought* to behave). Our study led us to the claim that a new social contract must be constructed. We contend that much mischief is wrought by the social norm of competitive behaviour. When society plays non-zero-sum games, in which large positive increments accrue to *co-operative* behaviour, competitive behaviour causes waste and harm. Such behaviour is unlikely to change unless a wide consensus to alter it can be built by means of a social contract. Our current research involves canvassing business and labour leaders to determine how such a consensus can best be constructed in both the US and Canada, as well as in our home country, Israel.

MAKAROV, Valery Leonid

Born 1937, Novosibirsk, USSR.

Current Post Dir., Nat. Res. Inst. Organisation and Management Problems, Moscow, USSR, 1980–.

Past Posts Scientific Worker, Chief Lab., Dep. Dir., Inst. Maths., Siberian Branch Academy of Sciences, Novosibirsk, 1960–6, 1967–73, 1973–80; Prof. Math. Econ., Novosibirsk State Univ., 1973–80.

Degrees PhD, Dr (Maths.) Univ. Moscow, 1965, 1968.

Offices and Honours Fellow, Em Soc, 1979.

Editorial Duties Ed. Board, *Siberian Math. J.*

Principal Fields of Interest 213 Mathematical Methods; 621 Technical Progress; 521 Organisation; Decision Theory.

Publications *Books* (all in Russian):

1. *Mathematical Theory of Economic Dynamics and Equilibria* (with A.M. Rubinov), (Nauka, 1973; transl., English, Springer Verlag, 1973); 2. *Models and Computers in Economics* (Znanie, 1979); 3. *Models of Optimal Functioning in Industries* (with V. Marshak), (Economica, 1979).

Articles: 1. 'Models of optimal economic growth' (Russian), *J. Economica i math. methods*, 4, 1969; 2. 'Growth models and their application to long-term planning and forecasting', in *Methods of Long-term Planning and Forecasting* (Macmillan, 1976); 3. 'Economic incentives in innovation's implementation process' (Russian), *Voprosy Ekonomiki*, 3, 1979; 4. 'Some results on general assumptions about the existence of economic equilibrium', *J. Math. Econ.*, 8, 1981; 5. 'Mathematical models of pricing' (with L.V. Kantorovich), in *The Economics of Relative Prices*, eds. B. Csikos-Nazy, D. Hagul and G. Hall (Macmillan, 1984).

Principal Contributions Early investigations were connected mostly with standard mathematical economics' problems: structure of non Neuman and Leontief models, turnpike theorems in growth theory, existence of an economic equilibrium in a general model of a competitive economy, etc. Later, more realistic situations were investigated: multiple price and currency systems, rationing in production and consumption especially for a socialist economy, and co-existence between central planning, rationing and market mechanism in an actual economic system. In economics of innovations, I introduced the value of an innovation as such and studied the consequences of the notion.

MAKIN, John Holmes

Born 1943, Brattleboro, VT, USA.
Current Post Prof. Econ., Dir. Inst. Econ. Res., Univ. Washington, Seattle, WA, USA, 1978–, 1983–; Res. Ass., NBER, 1980–.
Past Posts Instr., Ass. Prof., Assoc. Prof. Econ., Univ. Wisconsin-Milwaukee, 1969–70, 1970–1, 1972–6; Vis.

Assoc. Prof Econ., Univ. Virginia, 1973, Univ. British Columbia, 1975–6; Assoc. Prof. Econ., Univ. Washington, 1976–8; Sr. Internat. Econ., US Dept. Treasury, 1971–2; Vis. Scholar, Fed. Reserve Bank San Francisco, 1977; Cons., US Dept. Treasury, 1972–80, IMF, 1981, 1982–3.
Degrees BA Trinity Coll., Hartford, CT, 1965; MAM, PhD Univ. Chicago, 1969, 1970.
Offices and Honours Fed. Reserve Bank Chicago Fellow, 1968–9; Advisory Board, Center Study Banking and Fin. Markets, Univ. Washington, 1983–.
Editorial Duties Ed. Board, *J Econ. and Bus.*, 1979–82.
Principal Fields of Interest 300 Domestic Monetary and Fiscal Theory and Institutions; 430 Balance of Payments; International Finance; 520 Business Finance and Investment.
Publications *Books:* 1. *Elements of Money* (Dryden Press, 1971); 2. *Theory of Money* (Dryden Press, 1972); 3. *Theory of Macroeconomics* (Dryden Press, 1972); 4. *Theory of Economic Policy* (Dryden Press, 1972); 5. *Macroeconomics* (Dryden Press, 1975); 6. *Eurocurrencies and National Financial Policies*, co-ed. (with C.H. Stems and D. Logue), (AEI, 1976); 7. *World Debt Crisis* (Basic Books, 1984).

Articles: 1. 'The composition of international reserve holdings: a problem of choice involving risk', *AER*, 61(5), Dec. 1971; 2. 'On the success of the reserve currency system in the crisis zone', *J Int E*, 2(1), Feb. 1972; 3. 'Demand and supply functions for stocks and Euro-dollar deposits: an empirical study', *REStat*, 54(4), Nov. 1972; 4. 'Portfolio theory and the problem of foreign exchange risk', *J Fin*, 33(2), May 1978, repr. in *International Financial Management*, ed. D.R. Lessard (Warren, Gorham & Lamont, 1979); 5. 'Anticipated inflation and interest rates: further interpretation of findings on the Fisher equation' (with M.D. Levi), *AER*, 68(5), Dec. 1978; 6. 'Anticipated inflation and interest rates in an open economy', *JMCB*, 10(3), Aug. 1978; 7. 'Fisher, Phillips, Friedman and the measured impact of inflation on interest' (with M.D. Levi), *J Fin*, 34(1), March 1979; 8. 'Inflation uncertainty and the

Phillips curve: some empirical evidence' (with M.D. Levi), *AER*, 70(5), Dec. 1980; 9. 'Anticipated money, uncertainty and real economic activity', *REStat*, 64(1), Feb. 1982; 10. 'Real interest, money surprises, anticipated inflation and fiscal deficits', *REStat*, 65(3), Aug. 1983.

Principal Contributions Early work concentrated on functioning of the failing Bretton Woods international monetary system. Major contributions included: estimation of asset demand equations for central banks showing sensitivity to expected returns on dollars and gold in reserve holding decisions by central banks; implications of central bank switching between holdings of dollars and gold for the viability of the dollar-exchange standard; and analysis of the ability of Special Drawing Rights to coexist with other reserve assets that accurately predicted their lack of widespread acceptance in subsequent years.

A series of empirical articles on the Eurodollar market helped to dispel the 'mystery' surrounding that new phenomenon by showing that the Eurodollar system operated much like a fractional reserve system of financial intermediaries already familiar to students of money and banking. This body of work led to investigation of the effect of increased exchange rate flexibility on demand for reserves by central banks. Further investigation of the effects of exchange-rate flexibility on real trade volume suggested that no systematic link existed.

In a series of articles applying standard portfolio theory to the management of foreign-exchange risk, it was shown that financial managers can deal with such risk by altering payables and receivables in different currencies to achieve an optimal set of long and short positions in various major currencies. Viewed in this way the forward market is only a residual means to adjust exposure, not the only means, as suggested by some analysts.

A series of articles, begun with Maurice Levi and completed on my own, investigated behaviour of real and nominal interest rates employing reduced-form equations derived from an articulated structure of both closed and open economies. The procedure shows that the popular Fisher equation really should be viewed as a reduced-form equation, and this paved the way for interpreting results of estimated equations for interest rates in a way that explains why — despite taxes on interest earnings — most estimated coefficients attached to expected inflation lie below unity.

MALCOMSON, James Martin

Born 1946, Staunton-on-Wye, Herefordshire, England.
Current Post Prof. Econ., Univ. Southampton, Southampton, England, 1985–.
Past Posts Teaching Fellow Econ., Harvard Univ., 1969–71; Ellis Hunter Memorial Fellow Econ., Lect., Sr. Lect. Econ., Univ. York, 1971–2, 1972–3, 1983–5; Vis. Fellow Econ., Univ. Catholique de Louvain, 1983–4.
Degrees BA, MA Univ. Camb., 1967, 1971; MA, PhD Harvard Univ., 1969, 1973.
Principal Fields of Interest 026 Economics of Uncertainty and Information; Game Theory and Bargaining Theory; 210 Econometric, Statistical and Mathematical Methods and Models; 800 Manpower; Labour Population.
Publications *Articles*: 1. 'Replacement and the rental value of capital equipment subject to obsolescence', *JET*, 10(1), Feb. 1975; 2. 'Prices vs. quantities: a critical note on the use of approximations', *REStud*, 45(1), Feb. 1978; 3. 'The estimation of a vintage model of production for UK manufacturing' (with M.J. Prior), *REStud*, 46(4), Oct. 1979; 4. 'The measurement of labour cost in empirical models of production and employment', *REStat*, 62(4), Nov. 1980; 5. 'Corporate tax policy and the service life of capital equipment', *REStud*, 48(2), April 1981; 6. 'Unemployment and the efficiency wage hypothesis', *EJ*, 91, Dec. 1981; 7. 'Tax policy and investment demand: a vintage approach', *J Pub E*, 19(2), Nov. 1982; 8. 'Trade unions and economic efficiency', *EJ*, 93, Suppl., March 1983; 9. 'Work incentives, hierarchy, and internal labor markets', *JPE*, 92(3),

June 1984; 10. 'Dynamic inconsistency, rational expectations, and optimal government policy' (with B. Hillier), *Em*, 52(6), Nov. 1984.

Principal Contributions My early research was concerned with vintage models of production, especially the implications of these models for the understanding of obsolescence, replacement and utilisation of capital equipment, and the impact of tax policy on these. This research involved theoretical explorations of the nature of vintage models. It also involved empirical investigations in which I was particularly concerned to avoid an assumption either that the service life time of capital equipment was given technologically or that it was constant through time. Only in this way can one satisfactorily explore the effects of tax policy on replacement and hence on investment. My empirical research on production led me to the view that it is crucial to develop a better insight into the labour side of the production process if economists are to understand the working of economies. This has influenced the direction of my recent research. My interest here has been to provide a better theoretical understanding of the role of such organisational structures as hierarchies and internal labour markets, the impact of trade unions, and the reasons for unemployment of a genuinely involuntary nature. In this work I have been particularly concerned with issues of incentives and control in an environment in which crucial pieces of information are not common knowledge and hence with the analysis of employment contracts with informal or implicit elements, the legal enforcement of which is difficult or impossible.

MALINVAUD, Edmond Camille

Born 1923, Limoges, France.
Current Post Dir. Général, INSEE, Paris, France, 1974–.
Past Posts Stat., INSEE, 1948–56; Guest, Cowles Commission, Univ. Chicago, 1950–1; Econ., UN Geneva, 1957; Prof. Dir., Ecole Nationale de la Stat. et de l'Admin. Econ., 1957–66;
Vis. Prof., Univ. Cal. Berkeley, 1961, 1967; Res. Adviser, INSEE, 1967–71; Dir., Direction de la Prévision, 1972–4.
Degrees Diplôme Ecole Polytechnique, Diplôme Ecole Nat. de la Stat. et de l'Admin. Econ., 1946, 1948.
Offices and Honours Pres., Em Soc, 1963, IEA, 1974–7, Internat. Stat. Inst., 1979–82; Hon Foreign Member, AEA.
Editorial Duties Co.ed., *Em J*, 1954–64; Assoc. Ed., *JET*.
Principal Fields of Interest 020 General Economic Theory; 113 Economic Planning; 133 Stabilization Theories and Policies.
Publications *Books:* 1. *Méthodes statistiques de l'économétrie* (Dunod, 1964, 1981; transls., English, N-H, 1966, 1980, Spanish, 1967, Italian, 1971, Hungarian, 1974, Russian, 1975); 2. *Leçons de théorie macroéconomique* (Dunod 1969, 1982; transls., English, N-H, 1970, Spanish, 1974, Japanese, 1981); 3. *La croissance française* (with P. Dubois and J.J. Carré), (Le Seuil, 1972; transls., English, Stanford Univ. Press, 1975, and Polish); 4. *The Theory of Unemployment Reconsidered* (Blackwell 1977; transl., French, Calmann Lévy, 1980); 5. *Profitability and Unemployment* (CUP, 1980; transl., French, Calmann Lévy, 1983); 6. *Théorie macroéconomique*, 2 vols. (Dunod 1981, 1982); 7. *Mass Unemployment* (Blackwell, 1984).
Articles: 1. 'Capital accumulation and efficient allocation of resources', *Em*, 21(2), April 1953; 2. 'Programme d'expansion et taux d'intérêt', *Em*, 27(2), April 1959; 3. 'Decentralized procedures for planning', in *Activity Analysis in the Theory of Growth and Planning*, eds. E. Malinvaud and M O.L. Bacharach (Macmillan, 1967); 4. 'First-order certainty equivalence', *Em*, 37(4), Oct. 1969; 5. 'The consistency of non linear regressions', *Annals Math. Stats.*, 41, June 1970; 6. 'A planning approach to the public good problem', *Swed JE*, 73(1), March 1971; 7. 'The allocation of individual risks in large markets', *JET*, 4, April 1972; 8. 'Macroeconomic rationing of employment', in *Unemployment in Western Countries*, eds. J.P. Fitoussi and E. Malinvaud (Macmillan, 1980); 9. 'Wages and unemployment', *EJ*, 92,

March 1982; 10. 'La science économique aujourd'hui', *Revue économique et sociale*, Jan. 1984.

Principal Contributions My main concern has been the building of positive theories from systematic observation. But for twenty years, my contributions dealt with easier subjects at the periphery of this concern. Firstly, regarding the normative theory of optimal resources allocation, I worked on the characterisation of price systems supporting efficient infinite horizon programmes, and decentralised planning procedures, in particular for the provision of public goods. Secondly, regarding the methodology of quantitative economics, I concentrated on the determination of proper rules for the definition of economic statistics and national accounts, unification of econometric methods, asymptotic properties of time series regressions with lagged endogenous variables and serial correlation of errors, proof of consistency of nonlinear regressions, and historical analysis of contemporary French economic growth.

Recent contributions have concerned positive macroeconomic theory: the derivation of the relationship between aggregates from microeconomic specifications; general macroeconomic equilibrium with involuntary unemployment; dynamic models of unemployment; the effect of profitability on investment; and the theory of macroeconomic policy formation.

MALKIEL, Burton G.

Born 1932, Boston, MA, USA.

Current Post Dean, Yale School Organization and Management, New Haven, CT, USA, 1984–.

Past Posts US Army Fin. Corps, 1955–8; Assoc. Fin. Dept., Smith, Barney and Co., NY, 1958–60; Ass. Prof., Dir., Fin. Res. Center, Assoc. Prof., Prof., Princeton Univ., 1964–6, 1966–81, 1966–8, 1968–81; Member, US President's Council Econ. Advisers, 1975–7.

Degrees BA Harvard Univ., 1953; MBA Harvard Grad. School Bus. Admin, 1955; PhD Princeton Univ., 1958; Hon. Dr Univ. Hartford, CT, 1971.

Offices and Honours Phi Beta Kappa.
Editorial Duties Past Assoc. Ed., *J Fin*.
Principal Fields of Interest 310 Domestic Monetary and Financial Theory and Institutions; 521 Business Finance; 522 Business Investment.

Publications *Books:* 1. *International Monetary Arrangements: The Problem of Choice*, co-ed. (with F. Machlup), (Princeton Univ. Press, 1964); 2. *The Term Structure of Interest Rates: Expectations and Behavior Patterns* (Princeton Univ. Press, 1966); 3. *Strategies and Rational Decisions in the Securities Options Market* (with R.E. Quandt), (MIT Press, 1969); 4. *A Random Walk Down Wall Street* (W.W. Norton, 1973, 1981); 5. *Managing Risk in an Uncertain Era: An Analysis for Endowed Institutions* (with P.B. Firstenberg), (Princeton Univ. Press, 1976); 6. *The Inflation-Beater's Investment Guide* (W.W. Norton, 1980; revised as *Winning Investment Strategies*, 1982); 7. *Expectations and the Structure of Share Prices* (with J.G. Cragg), (Univ. Chicago Press, 1982).

Articles: 1. 'Expectations, bond prices and the term structure of interest rates', *QJE*, 76, May 1962, repr. in *Frontiers of Investment Analysis*, ed. E.B. Fredrikson (Wiley, 1971); 2. 'Equity yields, growth and the structure of share prices', *AER*, 53(5), Dec. 1963; 3. 'Bank portfolio allocation, deposit variability and the availability doctrine' (with E.J. Kane), *QJE*, 79, Feb. 1965; 4. 'The valuation of convertible securities' (with W.J. Baumol and R.E. Quandt), *QJE*, 80, Feb. 1966, repr. in *Frontiers of Investment Analysis, op cit.*; 5. 'Expectations and the structure of share prices' (with J.G. Cragg), *AER*, 60(4), Sept. 1970; 6. 'Male-female pay differentials in professional employment' (with J.A. Malkiel), *AER*, 63(4), Sept. 1973; 7. 'Autoregressive and nonautoregressive elements in cross-section forecasts of inflation' (with E.J. Kane), *Em*, 44(1), Jan. 1976; 8. 'The capital formation problem in the United States', *J Fin*, 34(2), May 1979; 9. 'The distribution of investment between industries: a microeconomic application of the "q" ratio' (with G.M. von Furstenburg and H.S. Watson), in *Capital Investment and Saving*, ed. G.M. von Furstenburg, (Ballinger, 1980); 10. 'Risk and return: a new look', in *The Changing Roles of Debt and Equity in Financing US Capital Formation*, ed. B. Friedman (Univ. Chicago Press, 1982).

Principal Contributions My work has concentrated on learning more about how financial markets behave, and exploring the implications of that behaviour on the real economy. I have tried to write not only for my professional colleagues, but also for the public at large. I am pleased that I have also had an opportunity to practise my trade as a professional corporate director, a Presidential adviser, and as an academic administrator.

MALTHUS, Thomas Robert*

Dates and Birthplace 1766–1834, Surrey, England.

Posts Held Clergyman, 1797–1834; Prof. Polit. Econ., E. India Coll., Haileybury, 1805–34.

Degrees BA Univ. Camb., 1788.

Offices Fellow, Jesus Coll., Camb., 1793.

Publications *Books:* 1. *An Essay on the Principle of Population* (1798, 1976); 2. *An Inquiry into the Nature and Progress of Rent* (1815, 1970); 3. *Principles of Political Economy* (1820, 1834, 1964); 4. *Definitions in Political Economy* (1827, 1963); 5. *Five Papers on Political Economy by T.R. Malthus*, ed. C. Renwick (1953); 6. *Occasional Papers of T.R. Malthus*, ed. B. Semmel (1963); 7. *The Travel Diaries of T.R. Malthus*, ed. P. James (1966).

Career His *Essay* . . . was conceived as a reply to the optimistic view of society put forward by Godwin, Condorcet and others. The essential argument that population growth can and will outstrip the food supply has led to 'Malthusian' entering the language to express this and related concepts. The *Essay* in its first edition was a closely-argued tract of 50,000 words, but in its second (1803) and subsequent editions Malthus added a great deal of extra material from his reading and travels, developing it into a full-scale demographic treatise. In his *Principles* . . . he

revealed the differences with Ricardo on questions of theory which had already been closely examined in their private correspondence with each other. His stress on the inadequacy of aggregate demand, the theory of 'general gluts', is his chief divergence from Ricardo. This first received a sympathetic reception in the twentieth century, largely as a result of Keynes's favourable comments. Such was Malthus's fame in his own lifetime, and indeed throughout the nineteenth and twentieth centuries, that he may well be described as the most famous social scientist that ever lived.

Secondary Literature J.M. Keynes, *Essays in Biography* (Macmillan, 1933, 1972); D.V. Glass, ed., *Introduction to Malthus* (Watts, 1953); G.F. McCleary, *The Malthusian Population Theory* (Faber & Faber, 1953); M. Blaug, 'Malthus, Thomas Robert', *IESS*, 9; P. James, *Population Malthus: His Life and Times* (Routledge & Kegan Paul, 1979).

MANDEVILLE, Bernard*

Dates and Birthplace 1670(?)–1733, Rotterdam, The Netherlands.

Posts Held Physician, England, 1699.

Degrees MD Univ. Leyden, 1691.

Publications *Books:* 1. *The Grumbling Hive: Or Knaves Twin'd Honest* (1705); 2. *The Fable of the Bees: Or, Private Vices, Publick Benefits* (1714, 1970); 3. *Free Thoughts on Religion, the Church and National Happiness* (1720); 4. *An Enquiry into the Origin of Honour* (1732); 5. *A Letter to Dion* (1732, 1953).

Career Satirical writer whose doggerel poem, *Grumbling Hive* . . . , introduced the concept of public benefit which was derived from the sum of what might be regarded as private vices. He developed this into the more substantial *Fable of the Bees* . . . The vices he describes — luxury, pride, greed, envy, avarice — all stimulate commercial and manufacturing activity. This amounts to a description of a *laissez faire* economic system, though Mandeville also favoured judicious State management to promote trade, agriculture, etc. His paradox offended many, but his book was widely read and its lesson was taken by Hume and Smith.

Secondary Literature M.M. Goldsmith, 'Mandeville, Bernard', *IESS*, 9; H. Monro, *The Ambivalence of Bernard Mandeville* (OUP, 1975); T.A. Home, *The Social Thought of Bernard Mandeville* (Columbia Univ. Press, 1977).

MANGOLDT, Hans Karl Emil Von*

Dates and Birthplace 1824–68, Dresden, Germany.
Posts Held Official, German Ministry Foreign Affairs, 1847–50; Ed., *Weimarer Zeitung*, 1852; Teacher, Polit. Econ., Univ. Göttingen, 1858–62; Prof. Polit. Econ., Univ. Freibourg (Breisgau), 1862–8.
Degrees Dr Polit. Science, Univ. Tübingen.
Publications *Books:* 1. *Die Lehre vom Unternehmergewinn* (1855); 2. *Grundriss der Volkswirtschaftslehre* (1863, 1871).
Articles: 1. 'The exchange ratio of goods', *Grundrisse der Volkswirtschaftslehre* (1863), repr. in *Internat. Econ. Papers*, 11, eds. A.T. Peacock, *et al.* (Macmillan, 1963).

Career His theoretical achievements were much better appreciated in Britain than in Germany during his own lifetime. His theory of international values was discussed by Edgeworth, and Marshall approved of his theory of entrepreneurial profit. His price theory is probably his greatest contribution, going beyond the determination of an equilibrium price to show that there could be several equilibrium prices, He also analysed price formation in the case of joint demands, joint supplies, or both; this last achievement was taken up by Marshall.

Secondary Literature E. Schneider, 'Mangoldt, Hans Karl Emil von', *IESS*, 9; K.H. Hennings, 'The transition from classical to neoclassical economic theory: Hans von Mangoldt', *Kyk*, 33(4), 1980.

MANN, H. Michael*

Dates and Birthplace 1934–85, Camden, NJ, USA.

Posts Held Special Econ. Ass., Ass. Attorney-General, Anti-Trust Div., US Dept. Justice, 1968–9; Dir., Bureau Econ., US Fed. Trade Commission, 1971–3; Prof., Boston Coll., USA, 1973–85.
Degrees BA Haverford Coll., 1956; PhD Cornell Univ., 1962.
Editorial Duties Managing Ed., *J Ind E*, 1977–85.
Publications *Books:* 1. *Industrial Concentration: The New Learning*, co-ed. (with H.J. Goldschmid, *et al.*), (Little Brown, 1974).
Articles: 1. 'Seller-concentration, barriers to entry, and rates of return in 30 industries, 1950–1960', *REStat*, 48, Aug. 1966; 2. 'Advertising and concentration: an empirical investigation' (with J.A. Henning and J.W. Meehan, Jr.), *J Ind E*, 16, Nov. 1967; 3. 'Asymmetry, barriers to entry, and rates of return in twenty-six concentrated industries, 1948–1957', *WEJ*, 8(1), March 1970; 4. 'Advertising and oligopoly: correlations in search of understanding' (with J.A. Henning), in *Issues in Advertising: The Economics of Persuasion*, ed. D.G. Tuerck (AEI, 1978); 5. 'An appraisal of model building in industrial organisation' (with J.A. Henning), *Res. Law Econ.*, 3, 1981.

Career Established, through replication, the consistency of Bain's findings that entry barriers matter importantly in affecting the ability of firms to price persistently in a monopolistic fashion. As part of ongoing research with J.A. Henning, he attempted to demonstrate that the notion of causal priority provides a potentially significant means by which to uncover causal relationships among industrial organisation variables.

MANNE, Alan Sussmann

Born 1925, New York City, NY, USA.
Current Post Prof. OR., Stanford Univ., Stanford, CA, USA, 1976–.
Past Posts Instr. Econ., Harvard Univ., 1950–2; Econ. Analyst, Rand Corp., 1952–6; Assoc. Prof. Econ., Yale Univ., 1956–61; Prof. Bus. Econ. and OR, Stanford Univ., 1961–74; Prof. Polit. Econ., Harvard Univ., 1974–6;

Res. Assoc., MIT Center Internat. Stud., New Delhi, India, 1963–4; Econ. Adviser, USAID, New Delhi, India, 1966–7; Fellow, Center Advanced Study Behavioral Sciences, Stanford, CA, 1970–1; Econ., Internat. Inst. Appl. Systems Analysis, Laxenberg, Austria, 1974.

Degrees BA, MA, PhD Harvard Univ., 1943, 1948, 1950.

Offices and Honours Phi Beta Kappa; Fellow, Em Soc; Lanchester Prize, OR Soc. Amer.

Editorial Duties Ed., *JDE*, 1974–6.

Principal Fields of Interest 723 Energy Economics; 112 Development Economics; 021 General Equilibrium Theory.

Publications *Books:* 1. *Scheduling of Petroleum Refinery Operations* (Harvard Univ. Press, 1956); 2. *Economic Analysis for Business Decisions* (McGraw-Hill, 1961); 3. *Studies in Process Analysis: Economy-Wide Production Capabilities* (with H. Markowitz), (Wiley, 1963); 4. *Investments for Capacity Expansion: Size, Location and Time-Phasing* (A&U, 1967); 5. *Multi-level Planning: Case Studies in Mexico* (with L. Goreux), (N-H, 1973).

Articles: 1. 'Some notes on the acceleration principle', *REStat*, 27(2), May 1945; 2. 'Oil refining: yield coefficients and actual prices', *QEJ*, 65, Aug. 1951; 3. 'Multiple purpose public enterprises: criteria for pricing', *Ec*, N.S. 19, Aug. 1952; 4. 'Linear programming model of the US petroleum refining industry', *Em*, 26(1), Jan. 1958; 5. 'Programming of economic lot sizes', *Management Sciences*, 4(2), Jan. 1958; 6. 'Capacity expansion and probabilistic growth', *Em*, 29(4), Oct. 1961; 7. 'A consistency model of India's fourth plan' (with A. Rudra), *Sankhya*, Series B, 27, pts. 1, 2, 1965; 8. 'Key sectors of the Mexican economy, 1962–72', in *The Theory and Design of Economic Development*, eds. I. Adelman and E. Thorbecke (JHUP, 1966); 9. 'Waiting for the breeder', *REStud*, Symposium, 1974; 10. 'Energy-economy interactions: the fable of the elephant and the rabbit?' (with W. Hogan), in *Modeling Energy-Economy Interactions, Resources for the Future*, ed. C.J. Hitch (Wiley, 1977).

Principal Contributions During the past three decades I have worked successively in industrial planning, economic development and energy economics. I was fortunate to have been a student of Wassily Leontief, and he taught me the importance of quantitative analysis. I was also fortunate to have been a junior colleague of George Dantzig at Rand. He, together with Harry Markowitz, stimulated my interest in linear programming as a method of analysing large-scale economic systems. At Cowles, Jacob Marschak and Tjalling Koopmans taught me the importance of simplicity in writing. The key ideas can usually be communicated without need for a great deal of jargon. This is especially important when one is attempting to communicate across discipline boundaries — and I find that I have been doing this for much of my career.

In India I found two role models. One was Pitambar Pant, perspective planner. We enjoyed many good arguments over this or that aspect of India's plans. John Lewis, Director of the India Mission of US Agency of Internat. Devlp., taught me whatever I know about being an administrator. I hesitate to list the colleagues who have had a major influence upon me, and hope that those omitted will forgive me: Robert Dorfman, Hollis Chenery, Sukhamoy Chakravarty, Wolf Haefele, Herbert Scarf, Thomas Schelling, William Hogan, William Nordhaus, Gerard Debreu, Kenneth Arrow, Arthur F. Veinoot, Jr., Richard Cottle and Curtis Eaves. As one gets older, one depends increasingly upon one's students (or ex-students) for ideas. In the interest of brevity, let me name only a few: T.N. Srinivasan, Donald Erlenkotter, David Hopkins, Scott Rogers, Richard Richels, John Weyant and Hung-po Chao. It has been a pleasure to work with them over the years.

MANSFIELD, Edwin

Born 1930, Kingston, NY, USA.

Current Post Prof. Econ., Univ. Penn., Philadelphia, PA, USA, 1963–.

Past Posts Ass. Prof. Econ., Grad. School Industrial Admin., Carnegie-Mellon Univ., 1955–60; Vis. Assoc. Prof., Yale Univ., 1961–2; Assoc. Prof.,

Carnegie-Mellon Univ., 1960–3; Vis. Prof., Harvard Univ., 1963–4; Vis. Prof., Cal. Inst. Technology, 1967–8; Fellow, Center Advanced Study Behavioral Sciences, Stanford, 1971–2; Cons., Rand Corp., 1962–76, White House Panel Technology, US Army, 1964–8, US President's Office Science and Technology, 1964, Small Bus. Admin., 1967–8, NSF, 1967–, Ford Foundation, 1972–3, US Dept. Labor 1975, US Fed. Trade Commission, 1979–81, Nat. Inst. Educ., 1981–2.

Degrees BA Dartmouth Coll., 1951; MA, PhD Duke Univ., 1953, 1955, Diploma RSS, 1955; Hon. MA Univ. Penn., 1971.

Offices and Honours Fellow, AAAS, Em Soc; Certificate Appreciation, US Secretary Commerce; 1982 Publication Award, Patent Law Assoc.; Chairman, US-USSR Working Group Econ. Science and Technology; Ford Foundation Faculty Res. Fellow; Fulbright Fellow.

Editorial Duties Assoc. Ed., *JAS*, *Amer. Econ.*, 1964–7, 1969–; *J Econ. Educ.* 1982–; Advisory Ed., W.W. Norton, 1970–81.

Principal Fields of Interest 620 Economics of Technological Change; 610 Industrial Organisation and Public Policy; 210 Econometric, Statistical Methods and Models.

Publications *Books:* 1. *Monopoly Power and Economic Performance*, ed. (W.W. Norton, 1963, 1978; transl., Italian); 2. *Industrial Research and Technological Innovation* (W.W. Norton, Longman Green, 1968; transls., French, Japanese, and Russian); 3. *Managerial Economics and Operations Research*, ed. (W.W. Norton, Macmillan, 1966, 1980); 4. *The Economics of Technological Change* (W.W. Norton, Longman Green, 1968; transls., French, Chinese, Japanese and Russian); 5. *Microeconomics: Theory and Applications* (W.W. Norton, 1970, 1985; transls., Italian, and Portuguese); 6. *Research and Innovation in the Modern Corporation* (W.W. Norton, Macmillan, 1971; transl., French); 7. *Economics: Principles, Problems, Decisions (W.W. Norton, 1974, 1983); 8. The Production and Application of New Industrial Technology* (W.W.

Norton, 1977); 9. *Statistics for Business and Economic: Methods and Applications* (W.W. Norton, 1980, 1983); 10. *Technology Transfer, Productivity and Economic Policy* (W.W. Norton, 1982).

Articles: 1. 'Technical change and the rate of imitation', *Em*, 29, Oct. 1961, repr. in *Penguin Modern Economic Readings: The Economics of Technological Change*, ed. N. Rosenberg (Penguin, 1973); 2. 'Size of firm, market structure and innovation, *JPE*, 73(5), Dec. 1963; 3. 'Entry, Gibrat's law, innovation and the growth of firms', *AER*, 52(5), Dec. 1962; 4. 'Contribution of R&D to economic growth in the United States', *Science*, 4, Feb. 1972; 5. 'Social and private rates of return from industrial innovation' (with J. Racafort, *et al.*) *QJE*, 91(2), May 1977; 6. 'Basic research and productivity increase in manufacturing', *AER*, 70(5), Dec. 1980; 7. 'Technology transfer to overseas subsidiaries by US based firms', *QJE*, 94(4), Dec. 1980; 8. 'Imitation costs and patents: an empirical study' (with M. Schwartz and S. Wagner), *EJ*, 91, Dec. 1981; 9. 'Technological Change and market structure', *AER*, 73(2), May 1983; 10. 'Public policy toward industrial innovation: an international study of direct tax incentives for R and D', in *75th Anniversary Colloquium on Productivity and Technology* (Harvard Bus. School, 1984).

Principal Contributions After some early work concerning the income distribution and the specification of optimal operating procedures for railroads, I became interested in the economics of technological change, the topic which has been the focus of my research interests for the past 25 years. My work has been of several types. Firstly, I have done a considerable number of empirical and econometric studies of the R&D and innovation processes in firms, the diffusion of innovations, the effects of technological change on productivity increase, and the international transfer of technology. Secondly, I have been concerned with public policy toward technological change and have carried out studies of R&D tax credits, government R&D programmes, social returns to industrial innovation, effects of new technology on employment, R&D price deflators, and other aspects of policy in this area. In the course of this work I have been an adviser to many government agencies. Thirdly, I have been interested in modelling and helping to improve ways in which firms develop and react to new technologies. I have done studies of decision-making within firms, and at various times have been a consultant to firms interested in applying the theoretical and econometric results.

MANTOUX, Paul Joseph*

Dates and Birthplace 1877–1956, Paris, France.
Posts Held Prof. French Hist., London, 1913; League of Nations Secretariat, 1920–7; Founder, Dir., Inst. des Hautes Etudes Internat., Geneva, 1927; Prof., Conservatoire Nat. des Arts et Métiers, Univ. Paris, 1934–44.
Degrees Dr Lett. Univ. Paris, 1906.
Honours Officer, Légion d'Honneur.
Publications *Books:* 1. *La crise du trade-unionisme* (with M. Alfassa), (1903); 2. *The Industrial Revolution of the Eighteenth Century* (1906, 1961); 3. *Notes sur les comptes rendus des séances du parlement anglais au XVIII siècle* (1906).
Career His work as an economic historian was largely in the earlier part of his career. After World War I, he was concerned first with the affairs of the League of Nations and then with the Institut des Hautes Etudes Internationales. He was instrumental in founding the latter as a means of fostering world co-operation to fill the gap created by the inadequacies of the League.
Secondary Literature (Obit.), 'M. Paul Mantoux: worker for world peace', *The Times*, 18 December 1956.

MARCET, Jane*

Dates and Birthplace 1769–1858, London, England.
Posts Held Writer.
Publications *Books:* 1. *Conversations in Political Economy* (1816); 2. *John Hopkins' Notions on Political Economy* (1833); 3. *Rich and Poor* (1851).

Career Writer of popular educational works on a range of topics which included political economy. These were widely read and raised by various distinguished economists. *Conversations . . .* sums up the economic doctrines current before the publication of Ricardo's *Principles*, including the just discovered theory of differential rent. Ricardo was a personal friend and so was Malthus, who looms larger in the *Conversations . . .* than Adam Smith.
Secondary Literature L.M. Fraser, 'Marcet, Jane', *ESS*, 10.

MARCHAL, Jean

Born 1905, Colombey-les-Belles, Mewithe et Moselle, France.
Current Post Member, l'Inst. de France, l'Académie des sciences morales et politique, France, 1980–.
Past Posts Prof. honoraire, Faculté de Droit de Nancy, 1947–; Prof., d'Econ. Politique, Univ. Geneva, 1972–5; Prof. honoraire, Univ. Paris Pantheon Sorbonne, 1973–7.
Degrees Dr Droit, Prof. titulaire, Univ. de Nancy, 1929, 1935; Dr H.C. Univs., Geneva, 1959, Liège, 1965, Thessalonika, 1969.
Offices and Honours Prix Joseph Dutens de l'Académie des sciences morales et solique, 1944; Hon. Member, Societé d'Econ. Politique de Belgique, 1953–; Corresp. Member, l'Académie de Stanislas à Nancy, 1957–; Commandeur de la Legion d'Honneur, 1977; Vice-Pres., Exec. Comm., IEA, 1968–71.
Editorial Duties Ed. Boards, *RE*, 1950–, *ZN*, 1957–, *REP*, 1963–6.
Principal Fields of Interest 221 National Income Accounting; 322 National Government Expenditures and Budgeting; 023 Macroeconomic Theory.
Publications *Books:* 1. *Rendements fiscaux et conjoncture. Contribution a la théorie de la sensibilité des impôts* (Lib. de Medicis, 1942, 1944); 2. *Le mécanisme des prix et la structure de l'économie* (Lib. de Medicis, 1946, 1966); 3. *Cours d'économie politique* (Lib. de Medicis, 1950, 1957; transl., Italian, Cedam, 1965); 4. *La repartition du revenu national* (with J. Lecaillon),

4 vols (M.T. Genin, 1958–70); 5. *La comptabilité nationale française* (Cujas, 1959, 1967; transl., Russian, Ed. Statistika, 1967, Japanese, Ed. Shiseido, 1970); 6. *Expansion et recession* (Cujas, 1963, 1965; transl., Awanami, Tokyo, 1966); 7. *Monnaie et credit*, 3 vols (Cujas, 1964, 1984); 8. *Théorie des flux monétaires. Evolution des idées et principes generaux d'analyse* (with J. Lecaillon), (Cujas, 1967); 9. *Analyse monétaire* (with J. Lecaillon), (Cujas, 1971); 10. *Le système monétaire international de Bretton Woods aux changes flottants, 1944–75* (Cujas, 1975, 1979).

Articles: 1. 'Contribution a une théorie moderne de la repartition', *RE*, July 1951; 2. 'The construction of a new theory of profit', *AER*, 41(4), Sept. 1951; 3. 'Die Theorie der Verteilung bei den englischen Klassikern', *ZN*, 14(2–4), 1954; 4. 'Wage theory and social groups', in *The Theory of Wage Determination*, ed. J. Dunlop (Macmillan, 1957); 5. 'Is the income of the "cadres" a special class of wages?' (with J. Lecaillon), *QJE*, 72, May 1958; 6. 'Les modèles macroéconomiques de la repartition du revenu national de K.E. Boulding', *REP*, May–June 1960; 7. 'La théorie de la repartition du revenu national chez N. Kaldor', in *Money, Growth and Methodology*, ed. H. Hegeland (Lund, 1961); 8. 'Wage structure and the theory of the distribution of income: the French pattern' (with J. Lecaillon), in *Wage Structure in Theory and Practice*, ed. E.M. Hugh-Jones (N-H, 1966); 9. 'The spreading progress of incomes in an economy: a reassessment of the multiplier theory through the probabilistic approach' (with F. Poulon), in *Pioneering Economics*, eds. T. Bagiotti and G. Frances (Cedam, 1978).

Principal Contributions Research has been orientated towards price theory, public finance, evolution of the French system of national accounting, distribution of national income, wage and profit theory, money and banking problems, credit multipliers, and the international monetary system.

MARCZEWSKI, Jan Witold

Born 1908, Warsaw, Poland.
Current Post Retired Hon. Prof. Econ., Univ. Paris I, Pantheon-Sorbonne, France, 1977–.
Past Posts Polish Diplomatic Service, Strasbourg, 1926–32, Bucharest, 1933–6, Warsaw, 1937, Brussels, 1937–40; Polish Army, France, 1940–5; Research Dir., Inst. Appl. Econ., Paris, 1946–50; Cons., OECD, Paris, 1949–50; Prof., Univ. Caen, France, 1950–9; Prof., Univ. Saarbrücken, France, 1950–2; Prof., Inst. Polit. Sciences, Paris, 1950–8; Res. Dir. Eastern Europe, Foundation Polit. Sciences, Paris, 1950–8; Prof., Univ. Paris I, 1959–77; Dir., Planning and Nat. Accounts Lab., Univ. Paris I, 1959–77.
Degrees Baccalauréat (Maths. and Philo.) Nancy, France, 1926; Licence Law, Strasbourg Univ., 1929; Dr Law, Univ. Paris, 1941; Agrégation, Paris, 1950.
Offices and Honours Prizes, Faculty Paris, 1941; Académie des sciences morales et politiques prize, 1973; Pres., Société d'économie politique, 1972–6; Assoc. Française de science econ., 1973, Académie de comptabilité, 1976; Jury du concours d'Agrégation Écon., 1969; Chevalier de la Légion d'Honneur; Medaille Militaire; Croix de Guerre; Krzyz Salecznych (Polish).
Editorial Duties Ed., *Europe de l'Est et Union Soviétique*, 1957–8; Internat. Cons., *Soviet Stud.*, 1976.
Principal Fields of Interest 221 National Income Accounting; 110 Economic Growth, Development and Planning Theory and Policy; 134 Inflation and Deflation.
Publications *Books:* 1. *Politique monétaire et financieu du IIIc. reich* (Sirey, 1941); 2. *Planification et croissance economique des démocraties populaires* (Presses Univ. de France, 1956); 3. *La rationalité economique du socialisme* (ISEA, 1956); 4. *La comptabilité nationale* (Dalloz, 1960); 5. *Comptabilité nationale* (with R. Grainer), (Dalloz, 1965, 1978; transl., Turkish, Turkiye Ticaret Odalari, 1975); 6. *Planification et aménagement du territoire* (Cours de Droit, 1965, 1969); 7. *Crise de la planification socialiste?* (Presses Univ. de

France, 1973; transls., English, Praeger, 1974, 1976, Spanish, Fondo de Cultura Economica, 1975, 1979, Iranian, 1983); 8. *Introduction à l'histoire quantitative* (Librarie Droz, 1965); 9. *Inflation et chômage en France, Explication quantitative* (Economica, 1977; transl., English, Praeger, 1977); 10. *Vaincre d'inflation et le chômage* (Economica, 1978).

Articles: 1. 'Le rôle des comptes nationaux daus les économies planifiées de type soviétique', *Income and Wealth*, 4 (Bowes & Bowes, 1955); 2. 'Le Take-Off en France', *Econ App*, 1, March 1961; transl., English, *EDCC*, 9(3), April 1961, and in *The Economics of Take-Off into Sustained Growth*, ed. E.A.G. Robinson (Macmillan, 1963), German, in *Wirtschaft und Gesellschaft in Frankreich seit 1789* (Kiepenheuer & Witsch, 1975); 3. 'Histoire quantitative — buts et méthodes', *Econ App*, 1, July 1961, repr. in *Cahiers Vilfredo Pareto, Revue Européenne d'Histoire des Sciences Sociales*, 3, March 1964, *Cahiers pédagogiques*, Jan. 1967, and German, in *Geschichte und Oekonomie* (Kiepenheuer & Witsch, 1973) Spanish, *Oue es la historia cuantitativa?* (E diciones Nuera Vision, 1973); 4. 'Le rôle des prix dans un systeme planifié', *Econ App*, 19(1), Jan.–March 1966, 20(3), July–Sept. 1967; transls., Italian, in *Le Reforme Economiche nei Paes dell'Est* (Vallechi, 1966), English, *Soviet Stud.*; 23(1), July 1971, Italian, in *Il sistema dei Prezzi nell'Est Europeo* (Franco Angeli Edit., 1967); 5. 'Comptabilité Nationale', in *Encyclopaedia Universalis* (Encyclopedia Universalis, 1969, 1983); 6. 'World stagflation and east-west relations', in *East-West Relations, Prospects for the 1980s*, ed. G. Schiavone (Macmillan, 1982), repr. *Revue d'Economie Comparée Est-Ouest*, 12(2), June 1981; 7. 'National accounts as an instrument for the analysis of the sources of stagflation, an example: France and Germany, 1971–79', *RIW*, 28(1), March 1982; transls., French, *Econ. App*, 34(4), 1981, Italian, *Bancaria*, 38(8), Aug. 1982; 8. 'On remodelling of the Polish economic system: a contribution', *Soviet Stud.*, 31(3), July 1979, repr. *Revue d'Etudes Comparatives Est-Ouest*, 13(4), Dec. 1982; 9. 'Il concetto di costo in presenza dell'inflazione', *Rivista di Politica Economica*, 73(12), Dec. 1983; 10. 'La récession: causes et remèdes', in *Récession et Relance*, ed. T. Grjeline (Economica, 1984).

Principal Contributions As one of the founders of the French National Accounts System, *Le Revenu National*, and a member of the National Income Unit of the OECD in Cambridge, I tried to take the advantage of the double-entry accounting relations for research in economic history. Contrary to Simon Kuznets, who as far as possible tended to convert the historically observed relations into 'economic laws', I stressed the importance of 'historical variables', which are exogeneous to the economic system and contribute to determine its historically observable results.

Despite the spectacular advance of mathematical programming, centralised economic planning is unable to solve the contradiction between the need for the maximal adaptability to the changing conditions of the world economy and the unavoidable rigidity of a centralised system of command. Considered as a system of economic circuits (monetary and real), world economic development is limited by the constraints of solidarity, liquidity and profitability, which cannot be altered without a radical change in the reciprocal East-West and North-South relations and in the monetary and economic policies of particular countries.

MARGET, Arthur William*

Dates and Birthplace 1899–1962, Chelsea, MA, USA.
Posts Held Instr., Econ., Harvard Univ., 1932–7; Assoc. Prof., Prof. Econ., Univ. Minnesota, 1927–30, 1930–48; Vis. Prof., Univ. Cal. Berkeley, 1936; Chief Fin. Div., US Element Allied Comm. Austria, 1945–8; Chief, Econ. Div., Council Foreign Ministers, London, Moscow, 1947–8; Cons., US Treasury, 1948; Dir., Div. Internat. Fin. Board Governors, Fed. Reserve System, 1950–61; US Econ. Adviser, Comm. Central Amer. Integration, 1961–2.
Degrees BA, MA PhD Harvard Univ., 1920, 1921, 1927.

Offices and Honours Legion of Merit, 1946; Phi Beta Kappa.

Publications *Books:* 1. *The Theory of Prices*, 2 vols. (1938, 1941).

Career Expert on monetary theory and policy, whose *Theory of Prices* represented a lifetime's work of scholarship in the history of monetary theory, achieving a monumental grasp of the material combined with an eye for detail that has never been equalled before or since.

MARGOLIS, Julius

Born 1920, New York City, NY, USA.

Current Post Prof. Econ., Univ. Cal. Irvine, CA, USA, 1976–.

Past Posts Econ. Instr., Tufts Coll., 1947–8; Ass. Prof. Econ. and Planning, Univ. Chicago, 1948–51; Ass. Prof. Econ., Stanford Univ., 1951–4; Prof. Bus. Admin., Univ. Cal. Berkeley, 1954–64; Prof. Econ. and Eng. Econ., Stanford Univ., 1964–9; Dir., Fels Center Govt., Prof. Econ. and Public Pol., Univ. Penn., 1969–75, 1969–76.

Degrees BSS Coll. City NY, 1941; MPh Univ. Wisconsin, 1949; PhD Harvard Univ., 1949.

Offices and Honours Res. Fellow, US SSRC, 1961–2; Exec. Comm., Internat. Seminar Public Econ., 1971–7.

Editorial Duties Econ. Ed., Markham Publishers, 1963–73; Ed. Boards, *Water Resources Res.*, 1959–64, *Amer. Behavioral Scientist*, 1970–, *J Pub E*, 1972–80.

Principal Fields of Interest 025 Social Choice; Bureaucratic Performance; 114 Economics, War, Defence, Disarmament; 325 Intergovernmental Financial Relations.

Publications *Books:* 1. *Standards and Criteria for Formulating and Evaluating Federal Water Resources Development* (with M. Hufschmidt and J. Krutilla), (US Bureau Budget, 1961); 2. *The Public Economy of Urban Communities*, ed. (JHUP, 1965); 3. *The Northern California's Water Industry* (with J. Bain and R. Caves), (JHUP, 1966); 4. *Public Economics*, ed. (St Martin's Press, 1969); 5. *Public Expenditures and Policy Analysis*, co-ed. and contrib. (with R.H. Haveman), (Markham, 1970, Rand McNally, 1977, Houghton Mifflin, 1983); 6. *The Analysis of Public Output*, ed. (Columbia Univ. Press, 1977).

Articles: 1. 'Public works and economic stability', *JPE*, 52(4), Aug. 1949; 2. 'A comment on the pure theory of public expenditure', *REStat*, 32, Nov. 1955, repr. in *Readings in Public Finance*, ed. R.W. Houghton (Penguin, 1971); 3. 'Municipal fiscal structure in a metropolitan region', *JPE*, 65, June 1957, repr. in *Urban Economics*, ed. R. Greison (Little Brown, 1973); 4. 'Secondary benefits, external economics and the justification of public investment', *REStat*, 39, Aug. 1957, repr. in *Readings in Welfare Economics*, eds. K.J. Arrow and T. Scitovsky (Richard D. Irwin, 1969); 5. 'Welfare criteria, pricing and decentralization of public services', *QJE*, 71, Aug. 1957; 6. 'Problems of metropolitan area finance: territorial, functional and growth', in *Public Finances: Needs Sources and Utilization* (Princeton Univ. Press, 1961); 7. 'Multilevel planning and decision-making' (with W. Trzeciakowski), in *Multi-Level Planning and Decision-Making* (UN, 1970); 8. 'Public policies for private profits', in *Redistribution Through Public Choice*, ed. H. Hochman (Columbia Univ. Press, 1974); 9. 'The public investment model and the public choice process', in *Public Choice and Public Finance*, ed. K. Roskamp (Cujas, 1980); 10. 'Fiscal problems of political boundaries', in *Management Policies in Local Government Finance*, eds. J.R. Aronson and E. Schwartz (ICMA, 1981).

Principal Contributions My work has been focussed on the analysis of government behaviour. The first papers dealt with stabilisation policy: the ineffectiveness of counter-cyclical public expenditure programmes and the flaws in national economic accounts as policy tools. Subsequently, most of my research has fallen into two tracks: the development of operational criteria by which to evaluate public programmes (benefits-costs measurements) and the study of the behaviour of governments. Occasionally the two strands have overlapped in policy studies of specific public-sector activities. Some studies dealt with particular public functions while others analysed changes in incentives and constraints to improve behaviour. Benefits-costs tools were initially designed for resources development programmes and my first applied studies were in the area of water resources, terminating in books 1 and 3 above. My research shifted to the urban public sector and to the functioning of the complex of competitive and overlapping governments which comprise a Federal fiscal system. Though the central concern was the behavioural properties of governments, my research extended to private firms and to planning. In recent years my attention has shifted to the political economy of the national defence sector.

MARKHAM, Jesse William

Born 1916, Richmond, VA, USA.
Current Post Charles Wilson Prof. Emeritus, Harvard Univ., Res. Prof. Law and Econ. Center, Emory Univ., Atlanta, GA, 1982.
Past Posts Teaching Fellow, Harvard Univ., 1946, 1948; Ass. Prof., Assoc. Prof., Vanderbilt Univ., 1948–52, 1952–3; Assoc. Prof., Prof., Princeton Univ., 1953–7, 1957–68; Chief Econ., US Fed. Trade Commission, 1953–5; Vis. Prof., Columbia Univ, 1957–8, Harvard Univ., 1961–2, Harvard Bus. School, 1965–6; Prof., Harvard Bus. School, 1968–72; Charles Wilson Prof., Harvard Univ., 1972–82.
Degrees BA Univ. Richmond, VA, 1941; MA, PhD Harvard Univ., 1947, 1949.
Offices and Honours Phi Beta Kappa, 1941; Julius Rosenwald Fellow, 1942, 1945–6; Ford Foundation Res. Prof., Geneva, 1958–9; Member, Amer. Bar Assoc. Commission to Study the US Fed. Trade Commission, 1969; Member Advisory Comm., US Secretary Commerce, 1967–71; US Delegate OECD, Paris, 1956–9, 1961.
Editorial Duties Ed. Board, *Anti-Trust Bull.*, 1962–8, *Patent Trademark and Copyright*, 1955–65.
Principal Fields of Interest 022 Microeconomic Theory; 610 Industrial Organisation and Public Policy: 620 Economics of Technical Change.

Publications *Books:* 1. *Competition in the Rayon Industry* (Harvard Univ. Press, 1952; transl., Japanese, Tokyo Univ. Press, 1955); 2. *Workbook in Modern Economics* (with R. Fels), (Harcourt & Brace, 1953); 3. *The Fertilizer Industry: Study of an Imperfect Market* (Vanderbilt Univ. Press, 1958); 4. *The American Economy*, ed. & contrib. (George Braziller, 1963); 5. *The Common Market: Friend or Competitor* (with C. Ficro and H. Piquet), (New York Univ. Press, 1964); 6. *Industrial Organization and Economic Development*, co-ed. (with G. V. Papanek), (Houghton Mifflin 1970); 7. *Conglomerate Enterprise and Public Policy* (Grad. School Bus. Admin., Harvard Univ., 1973); 8. *Horizontal Divestiture and the Petroleum Industry* (with T. Hourihan and F. Sterling), (Ballinger, 1977); 9. *Compulsory Licensing and the Energy Industry* (Nat. Energy Res. Admin., 1977); 10. *Baseball Economics and Public Policy* (with P. Teplitz), (D.C. Heath, 1981).
Articles: 1. 'An alternative approach to the concept of workable competition', *AER*, 40(3), June 1950, repr. in *Readings in Industrial Organization*, ed. G.W. Stocking and R. Heflebower (Richard D. Irwin, 1958); 2. 'The nature and significance of price leadership', *AER*, 41(5), Dec. 1951, repr. in *Reading in Industrial Organization, op. cit.*; 3. 'The Per Se Doctrines and the new rule of reason', *SEJ*, 22, July 1955; 4. 'Changing structure of the American economy: its implications for performance of industrial markets', *JFE*, 41, May 1959; 5. 'United States antitrust policies: how effective have they been?', *SEJ*, 26, July 1959; 6. 'Oligopoly', *IESS*, 11, ed. D.L. Shills (Macmillan, 1968); 7. 'Horizontal divestiture in the petroleum industry' (with A. Hourihan), *Vanderbilt Law J.*, 31, March 1978; 8. 'The role of competition in the American economy', *ZGS*, 36(3), Sept. 1980; 9. 'Inflation and the wage price issue: a reappraisal', in *Comparative Development Perspectives* (Westview Press, 1984).
Principal Contributions As an admiring student of Joseph Schumpeter, I have tried in my earlier published works to synthesise his concepts of innova-

tional activity and the dynamics of creative destruction on the one hand and static models of competition on the other. My *Competition in the Rayon Industry* and *The Fertilizer Industry* were attempts to effect this type of synthesis through the instrument of specific industry studies. Later I centred my attention more directly on the public policy implications of the structure-conduct-performance model of industrial organisation, especially the extent of which business conduct could in a statistical sense be predicted from measures of market structure. My conclusions on this matter in view of the available information at the time were summarised in article 6 above. As it became clearer to me that so many factors conditioned the structure-conduct relationship, I directed my research toward the measurable importance of these factors, especially the technological horizon, the opportunity for product innovation, and what might broadly be defined as creative competitive strategies. A book-length manuscript setting forth this analysis is near completion, and given the tentative title *Oligopolistic Competition: Studies in Structure and Business Conduct*.

MARKOWITZ, Harry Max

Born 1927, Chicago, IL, USA.
Current Post Marvin Speiser Disting. Prof. Econ. and Fin., Rutgers Univ., 1982–.
Past Posts Res. Assoc., Rand Corp., 1952–60, 1961–3; Cons., General Electric Corp., 1960–1; Chairman Board, Technical Dir., Consolidated Analysis Centers Inc., 1963–8; Prof. Fin., UCLA, 1968–9; Pres., Arbitrage Management Co., 1969–72; Cons., 1972–4; Prof. Fin., Wharton School, Univ. Penn., 1972–4; Res. Staff, IBM Corp., 1974–83; Adjunct Prof. Fin., Rutgers Univ., 1980–2.
Degrees BPh (Liberal Arts), MA, PhD Univ. Chicago, 1947, 1950, 1954.
Offices and Honours Cowles Commission Fellow; US SSRC Fellow; Fellow, Em Soc; Board Dirs., Inst. Management Sciences; Pres., AFA.
Principal Fields of Interest 026 Econ-

omics of Uncertainty and Information; 640 Economic Capacity; 213 Mathematical Methods and Models.

Publications *Books:* 1. *Portfolio Selection: Efficient Diversification of Investments* (Wiley, 1959, Yale Univ. Press., 1970); 2. *Simscript: A Simulation Programming Language* (with B. Hausner and H. Kerr), (Prentice-Hall, 1963); 3. *Studies in Process Analysis: Economy-wide Production Capabilities* (with A.S. Manne, *et al.*), (Wiley, 1963); 4. *The Simscript II Programming Language* (with P. Kiviat and R. Villaneueva), (Prentice-Hall, 1969); 5. *The EAS-E Programming Language* (with A.H. Malhotra and D.P. Pazel), (IBM Thomas J. Watson Res. Center, 1981).

Articles: 1. 'Portfolio selection', *J Fin*, 7(1), March 1952; 2. 'The utility of wealth', *JPE*, 60, April 1952; 3. 'Industry-wide, multi-industry and economy-wide process analysis', in *The Structural Interdependence of the Economy*, ed. T. Barna (Wiley, 1954); 4. 'The optimization of a quadratic function subject to linear constraints', *Naval Res. Logistics Q.*, 3, 1956; 5. 'The elimination form of the inverse and its application to linear programming', *Management Science*, 1957; 6. 'Investment for the long run: new evidence for an old rule', *J Fin*, 31(5), Dec. 1976; 7. 'Approximating expected utility by a function of mean and variance' (with H. Levy), *AER*, 69(3), June 1979; 8. 'Simscript', in *Encyclopedia of Computer Science and Technology*, 13, eds. J. Belzer, A.G. Holzman and A. Kent (Marcel Dekker, 1979); 9. 'Mean variance versus direct utility maximization' (with H. Levy and Y. Kroll), *J Fin*, 39(1), March 1984; 10. 'The EAS-E application development system: principles and language summary' (with A.H. Malhotra and D.P. Pazel), in *Communications of the ACM*, forthcoming, 1985.

Principal Contributions A principal professional interest of mine has been the theory of the rational behaviour under uncertainty in general and portfolio theory in particular. Contributions to the latter include: the concept of portfolio selection as distinguished from security selection, and mean- variance efficiency as a criterion for portfolio selection (1952); the 'critical line' algorithm for finding all efficient portfolios, without groping through any inefficient portfolios (1956); and the reconciliation of single-period mean-variance analysis with many-period utility analysis under uncertainty (1959; supplemented later with Levy and Kroll). Portfolio theory was used by Tobin, Sharpe, Lintner and Mossin in the widely cited Capital Asset Pricing Model.

Problems of portfolio theory yielded to analytic methods. Other areas, such as production control, required simulation analysis to evaluate alternatives subject to randomness and uncertainty. Originally, complex simulations took excessively long to program using conventional programming languages. With Hausner and Karr, I designed and helped develop the SIMSCRIPT programming language which reduces this time severalfold. The latest SIMSCRIPT is still widely used.

Business decision-making requires data, including access to data which runs business operations. With Malhotra and Pazel, I designed and helped develop the EAS-E database and business system programming language: efficient enough to support day-to-day operations, yet capable of satisfying advanced analysis needs. EAS-E is based on the entity-attribute-set view of system description originally developed for SIMSCRIPT.

Other research contributions include: models of economic capabilities based on a 'process analysis' approach as opposed to the interindustry hypothesis (with A. Manne and others); and a technique for inverting extremely large but 'sparse' matrices, currently used in modern linear programming codes.

MARQUEZ, Jaime R.

Born 1954, Caracas, Venezuela.
Current Post Econ., Quant. Stud., Internat. Fin. Division, Board of Governors, Fed. Res. System, USA, 1983–.
Past Posts Res. Fellow, Econ. Res. Unit, Univ. Penn., USA, 1979–83.
Degrees BA Univ. Catolica Andres Bello, Caracas, Venezuela, 1978; PhD Univ. Penn., 1983.
Principal Fields of Interest 134 Inflation and Deflation; 212 Construction, Analysis and Use of Econometric Models; 723 Energy.
Publications *Books:* 1. *Oil Price Effects and OPEC's Pricing Policy* (D.C. Heath, 1984); 2. *Econometrics and Economic Theory* (Blackwell, 1984).

Articles: 1. 'A proposition on short-run departures from the-law-of-one-price: an extension', *Europ ER*, 23(1), 1983; 2. 'A note on the variability of inflation and the dispersion of relative price changes' (with D. Vining), *Econ. Letters*, 12, (3–4), 1983; 3. 'A global model of oil price impacts' (with F.G. Adams), in *Essays in Honor of Lawrence Klein* (MIT Press, 1983); 4. 'The impact of petroleum and commodity prices in a model of the world economy' (with F.G. Adams), in *Global International Economic Models* (N-H, 1983); 5. 'Industrial policy in Venezuela', in *Industrial Policies for Growth and Competitiveness* (D.C. Heath, 1983); 6. 'Inflation and relative price behavior: a survey of the literature' (with D. Vining), in *Econ. Perspectives* (Hardwood Academic Publs., 1984); 7. 'Foreign exchange constraints and growth possibilities in the LDCs', *JDE*, 16(3–4), Nov.–Dec. 1984; 8. 'OPEC's pricing policy and the international transmission of oil price effects' (with P. Pauly), *Energy Econ.*, 6(4), Oct. 1984.

Principal Contributions My main research interest has been the determination of optimal price strategies for nonrenewable resources in a general equilibrium framework, allowing for the effects that changes in these prices have on the macroeconomy. In particular, it is possible to demonstrate that not recognising these macroeffects results in an underestimation of the demand price elasticity and an overestimation of the optimal price path. This framework is applied to the international oil market where I model international trade flows (in oil, raw materials, and manufactures), income, and price determination among developed countries, OPEC, and non-OPEC developing countries. In this context one can study the effects of (exogenous) oil price changes on international trade, price, and income. Using optimal control theory, I then determine the optimal price of oil from OPEC's viewpoint, but recognising that oil price changes affect real income of oil importers and that changes in real income of oil importers affect oil prices. This analysis has been extended to allow for the existence of an (uncertain) upper limit to prices and uncertainty with respect to the magnitude of the macro-effects. In this context, producers learn about the underlying stochastic structure by changing their prices. The information acquired is used to update the initial distribution of backstop prices and of oil price effects, which then leads to a recalculation of the optimal price strategy.

A second line of research interest has been the relationship between relative prices and inflation. According to neo-classical general equilibrium analysis, relative prices are determined by 'real' forces only and not by the money supply, which determines the price level. However, an enormous amount of empirical evidence has indicated a positive association between movements in relative price changes and movements in the inflation rate. The questions that I have addressed in this context are: What kind of theoretical explanation can be offered for such a relationship? To what extent does this relationship between relative price changes apply to developing countries? What are the implications for existing theories of the inflationary process?

MARSCHAK, Jacob*

Dates and Birthplace 1898–1977, Kiev, Russia.

Posts Held Privatdozent, Univ. Heidelberg, 1930–3; Lect., Reader Stats., Dir., Oxford Inst. Stats, 1933–5, 1935–9, 1935–9; Univ. Oxford Prof., Grad. Faculty, New School Social Res., NY, 1940–2; Dir., Cowles Commission Res. Econ., Chicago, 1943–8; Prof. Econ., Univ. Chicago, 1943–55, Yale Univ., 1955–60; Prof. Econ., Dir., Western Management Science Inst., UCLA, 1960–77.

Degrees PhD Univ. Heidelberg, 1922; Hon. degrees Univs. Bonn, 1968, Cal., 1971, Heidelberg, 1972, Northwestern Univ., 1977.

Offices and Honours Fellow, NAS, AAAS; Council Member, Inst. Management Science; Pres., Em Soc, 1946; Vice-Pres., ASA, 1947; Fellow, Inst. Math. Stats., 1953; Fellow, Center Advanced Study Behavioral Sciences, 1955–6; Hon. Foreign Fellow, RSS, 1963; Disting. Fellow, Pres., AEA, 1967, 1977.

Publications Books: 1. Elaztizität der Nachfrage (1931); 2. Economic Theory of Teams (with R. Radner), (1972); 3. Economic Information, Decision, and Prediction (1974).

Articles: 1. 'Random simultaneous equations and the theory of production' (with W.H. Andrews), Em, 12, July–Oct. 1944, 13, Jan. 1945; 2. 'Role of liquidity under complete and incomplete information', AER, 39(1), May 1949; 3. 'Towards an economic theory of organization and information', in Decision Processes, eds. R.M. Thrall, et al. (Wiley, 1954); 4. 'Binary-choice constraints and random utility indicators', in Mathematical Methods in the Social Sciences, eds. K.J. Arrow, et al. (N-H, 1959); 5. 'Economics of information systems', in Frontiers of Quantitative Economics, ed. M. Intriligator (N-H, 1971).

Career Pioneered the development of economic theories of information, organisation and decision under uncertainty. Starting with studies of money and liquidity, he gradually edged towards a systematic theory of the economic value of information. With R. Radner, he developed the theory of teams, concerning efficient use of information in decentralised organisations, and proposed and elaborated the theory of stochastic decision. This latter work (done partly with Block, Davidson, Becker and DeGroot) linked theories of rational economic choice to psychological measurement in the attempt to provide a basis of statistical studies for individual choice.

Secondary Literature K.J. Arrow, 'Marschak, Jacob', IESS, 18; R. Radner, 'On Marschak', in Contemporary Economists in Perspective, eds. H.W. Spiegel and W.J. Samuels (JAI Press, 1984).

MARSHALL, Alfred*

Dates and Birthplace 1842–1924, London, England.

Posts Held Fellow, St John's Coll. Camb., 1865–77, 1885–1908; Principal, Univ. Coll., Bristol, 1877–82; Lect., Fellow, Balliol Coll. Oxford, 1883–4; Prof. Polit. Econ., Univ. Camb., 1885–1908.

Offices and Honours Fellow, BA; Vice-Pres., RES.

Publications *Books:* 1. *The Economics of Industry* (with M.P. Marshall), (1879); 2. *Principles of Economic* (1890), Ninth variorum edn. C.W. Guillebaud, 2 vols (1961); 3. *Industry and Trade* (1919); 4. *Money Credit and Commerce* (1923); 5. *Official Papers* (1926). 6. *Early Economic Writings of Alfred Marshall, 1867–1890*, ed. J.K. Whitaker (1980).

Career The dominant figure in British economics of the late nineteenth and early twentieth centuries, whose *Principles* . . . still has the power to fascinate and excite the reader. Though he wrote infrequently, his teaching at Cambridge was a major source of influence on his contemporaries. An able mathematician, he sought to express himself in the simplest language possible, adding the mathematical and quantitative material as appendices and footnotes. His partial equilibrium analysis — the chief element of his method — was designed to be appropriate to a dynamic or biological view of economic life. The chief achievement of the *Principles* is his working out of the economics of the stationary State. He claimed to have independently discovered the marginal utility theory, though typically he did not publish until he had fully integrated this into his system. His welfare economics was of central importance since his decision to take up economics originated in a moral purpose, and his general conclusion was that a redistribution of income from rich to poor would increase total satisfaction. Keynes was among his pupils and the 'Keynesian revolution' can be seen as remaining within the Marshallian tradition.

Secondary Literature J.M. Keynes, 'Alfred Marshall', in *Essays in Biography* (Macmillan, 1933, 1972); B. Corry, 'Marshall, Alfred', *IESS*, 10; D.P. O'Brien, 'A. Marshall' *Pioneers of Modern Economics in Britain*, eds. D.P. O'Brien and J.R. Presley (Macmillan, 1981); *Alfred Marshall: Critical Assessments*, 4 vols, ed. J.C. Wood (Croom Helm, 1983).

MARSHALL, Mary Paley*

Dates and Birthplace 1850–1944, Stamford, Lincolnshire, England.

Posts Held Lect., Univ. Camb., 1875, then Univs. Bristol, Oxford and Camb.

Publications *Books:* 1. *The Economics of Industry* (with A. Marshall), (1879); 2. *What I Remember* (1947).

Career Great-granddaughter of William Paley and wife of Alfred Marshall, her abilities as an economist deserve mention in their own right. As the first woman lecturer in economics at Cambridge and joint-author of a good economic text, she might have had an outstanding career. However, on marriage to Marshall she submerged her career in his.

Secondary Literature J. M. Keynes, 'Mary Paley Marshall', in *Essays in Biography* (Macmillan, 1933, 1972).

MARTIN, Henry*

Dates and Birthplace ?–1721, Wiltshire, England.

Posts Held Lawyer and journalist, *Spectator and British Merchant*, 1713–14; Inspector-general imports exports, 1715.

Publications *Books:* 1. *Considerations on the East India Trade* (1701), repr. in *Early English Tracts on Commerce*, ed. J.R. McCulloch (1856, 1954).

Career *Consideration* . . . was published anonymously; sometimes attributed to Sir Dudley North, it was attributed to Martin by McCulloch. The tract is one of the first to espouse wholeheartedly a free trade system, justified on grounds of the benefits to be derived from international specialisation. The monopolistic chartered trading companies are attacked on the basis of this principle. His articles in the *British Merchant* are credited with causing the rejection of the commercial treaty with France at the Treaty of Utrecht.

Secondary Literature M. Arkin, 'A neglected forerunner of Adam Smith', *SAJE*, 23, Dec. 1955.

MARTINEAU, Harriet*

Dates and Birthplace 1802–76, Norwich, England.
Posts Held Writer.
Publications *Books:* 1. *Illustrations of Political Economy*, 9 vols (1832–4); 2. *Poor Laws and Paupers Illustrated* (1833); 3. *Illustrations of Taxation* (1834); 4. *Society in America* (1837); 5. *History of England during the Thirty Years Peace* (1849); 6. *The Philosophy of Comte, Freely Translated and Condensed* (1853).
Career Wrote on various subjects to earn a living. Mrs Marcet's *Conversations* inspired her to try stories to illustrate principles of political economy. These sold in tens of thousands, provided her with literary celebrity, and probably introduced more early nineteenth-century readers to basic economic ideas than any other contemporary source. Their content was based on a journalistic interpretation of the classical economists, chiefly Smith and Malthus. She also played a major part in popularising the ideas of Comte in Britain.
Secondary Literature R.K. Webb, *Hariet Martineau. A Radical Victorian* (Heinemann, 1960).

MARX, Karl*

Dates and Birthplace 1818–83, Trier, Germany.
Posts Held Writer and political leader; lived in exile in France, Belgium and England, with financial support from Friedrich Engels.
Degrees PhD Univ. Jena, 1841.
Publications *Books:* 1. *The Poverty of Philosophy* (1847, 1956); 2. *Communist Manifesto* (1848, 1972); 3. *The Class Struggles in France* (1850, 1976); 4. *A Contribution to the Critique of Political Economy* (1859, 1971); 5. *Capital*, vol 1, (1867, 1976), vols 2 and 3, ed. F. Engels (1885–94, 1909, 1978);

6. *Theories of Surplus Value*, 3 vols (1905–10, 1963); 7. *Collected Works*, 12 vols (1927–35); 8. *Foundation of the Critique of Political Economy* (1939–41, 1973).
Career Best known as the founder of international communism, he was a philosopher, social scientist and one of the major economists of his or any other age. Already deeply involved in socialist politics, his *Communist Manifesto* may be described as the most important political pamphlet of the nineteenth century. His life was spent in London, writing and organising, the former taking increasing precedence over the latter. The comprehensiveness of his studies and the difficulties of his personal circumstances meant that many of his major projects remained unfinished at his death. His masterpiece *Das Kapital* is only partially complete; the first volume appeared during his lifetime; and further material was edited by Engels. Much other material has been published posthumously including the important *Grundrisse* and *Theorien über den Mehrwert*. Using Hegel's dialectical method, but abandoning his political philosophy, he attempted to show both how society was progressing through successive stages towards the ultimate goal of communism and how that process might be accelerated. To this end he absorbed as much as possible of the existing social and economic thought; for example, his knowledge of previous writings in political economy was as nearly comprehensive as was possible at the time. His ideas have inspired both political Marxism and a very large body of social science grounded in his theoretical schema.
Secondary Literature E. Mandel, *Marxist Economic Theory* (Merlin Press, 1962); M. Rubel, 'Marx, Karl', *IESS*, 10; D. McLellan, *Karl Marx. His Life and Thought* (Macmillan, 1973); L. Kolakowski, *Main Currents of Marxism*, 3 vols (OUP, 1978).

MAS-COLELL, Andrew

Born 1944, Barcelona, Spain.
Current Post Prof. Econ., Harvard Univ., USA, 1981–.
Past Posts Ass. Prof. Econ. Maths., Assoc. Prof. Econ. Maths., Prof. Econ. Maths., Univ. Cal. Berkeley, 1975–7, 1977–9, 1979–81.
Degrees Licenciado en Ciencias Econ. Univ. Bilbao, 1967; PhD Univ. Minnesota, 1972.
Offices and Honours Fellow, Em Soc, 1978–; Sloan Fellow, 1978–80.
Editorial Duties Assoc. Ed., *JET*, 1975–80; *SIAM J. Appl. Maths.*, 1976–9; *J Math E*, 1977–; *Em*, 1978–.
Principal Fields of Interest 021 General Equilibrium Theory; 213 Mathematical Methods.
Publications *Articles*: 1. 'Continuous and smooth consumers: approximation theorems', *JET*, 8(3), July 1974; 2. 'An equilibrium existence theorem without complete or transitive preference', *J Math E*, 1(3), June, 1974; 3. 'A model of equilibrium with differentiated commodities', *J Math E*, 2(1), Sept. 1975; 4. 'The recoverability of consumers' preferences from market demand behavior', *Em*, 45(6), Sept. 1977; 5. 'Notes on the smoothing of aggregate demand' (with A. Aravjo)., *J Math E*, 5(2), Sept. 1978.
Principal Contributions General field of research: mathematical economics and economic theory. Main contributions have been to several foundational aspects of demand and general equilibrium theory. In particular extension of the Walras-Arrow-Debreu-McKenzie model to situations with differentiated commodities or with agents not satisfying some of the traditional rationality or convexity postulates; use and development of calculus and differential topological tools for the examination of the structure of price equilibria (uniqueness, local uniqueness, comparative statics, index of equilibria, etc.); relationships between the notion of price-taking equilibrium and a variety of solution concepts (descendant from Cournot and Edgeworth) incorporating strategic interdependences.

MASON, Edward Sagendorph

Born 1899, Clinton, IA, USA.
Current Post Thomas S. Lamont Univ. Prof. Emeritus, Harvard Univ., Cambridge, MA, USA, 1969–.
Past Posts Instr., Ass. Prof., Assoc. Prof., Prof. Econ., Harvard Univ., 1923–8, 1928–32, 1932–6, 1936–69; Washington Office of Production Management, Office Strategic Services, US Dept. State, 1941–5; Econ. Adviser US Secretary of State, Moscow Conf., 1947; Cons., World Bank, 1961.
Degrees BA Univ. Kansas, 1919; MA, PhD Harvard Univ., 1920, 1925; B. Litt Univ. Oxford, 1923; Litt. D Williams Coll., Williamstown, 1948; LLD Harvard Univ., 1956, Yale Univ., 1964, Concord Coll., Concord, WV, 1971.
Offices and Honours Pres., AEA, 1962; Hon. Fellow, Lincoln Coll. Oxford; AAAS; Philo. Soc.; US Medal Freedom; Star Pakistan.
Principal Fields of Interest 600 Industrial Organisation; 110 Economic Development.
Publications *Books:* 1. *The Paris Commune* (Macmillan, 1930); 2. *The Street Railway in Massachusetts* (Harvard Univ. Press, 1933); 3. *Controlling World Trade* (McGraw-Hill, 1946); 4. *Economic Planning in Underdeveloped Areas* (Fordham Univ. Press, 1955); 5. *Promoting Economic Development: The United States and Southern Asia* (Claremont Press, 1955); 6. *Economic Concentration and the Monopoly Problem* (Harvard Univ. Press, 1959); 7. *Foreign Aid and Foreign Policy* (Harper & Row, 1964); 8. *The World Bank since Bretton Woods* (with R. Asher), (Brookings Inst., 1973); 9. *The Economic and Social Modernization of the Republic of Korea*, co-ed. (with others), (Harvard Univ. Press, 1980).
Articles: 1. 'Resources in the past and for the future', in *Resources for an Uncertain Future*, ed. C. Hitch (JHUP, 1977); 2. 'On the appropriate size of a development program', *Harvard Univ. Center Internat. Affairs*, 1964; 3. 'Economic development in India and Pakistan', *Harvard Univ. Center Internat. Affairs*, 1966; 4. 'Corruption and Development', *Harvard Inst. Internat Devlp.*, 1978.

Principal Contributions I came into economics largely through the influence of a teacher at the University of Kansas, John Ise. He persuaded me to go to Harvard for graduate work and I spent one year there before going on to Oxford as a Rhodes Scholar. At Oxford my supervisor was Francis Y. Edgeworth. I came back to Harvard to get a PhD and started teaching there in 1923. I finished my teaching career at Harvard in 1969, after 46 years, but with many interruptions for government service, consulting and administrative assignments. Early in my career I had a great deal of difficulty in deciding where my interests lay. I was interested both in the European socialist movement and in the relations of government to business. The latter interest won out and from 1930 to the early 1950s most of my teaching and writing was in industrial organisation, the structure of firms, regulation and, in general, government-business relations. I would say that my contributions, if any, dealt with the relations between the structure of industrial markets and the behaviour of firms, and in the roles of law and economics in shaping public policy.

The war years also turned my attention away from industrial organisations and toward international affairs. From the early 1950s on I spent a good deal of time as a member of Presidential commissions dealing with foreign aid, and as a consultant to the Agency for Internat. Devlp. and the World Bank. Although I have written and published extensively in the field of economic development, I don't think I can say that I have made significant contributions to the theory of the subject. Most of my writing was concerned with the analysis of economic policies and with the institutional and organisational characteristics of development. And as an entrepreneur and administrator, my influence has probably been more important than as a scholar. As Dean of Harvard's Graduate School of Public Administration, I organised advisory missions to the Planning Commission of Pakistan and to the Plan Organisation of Iran. This led to the formation of the Harvard Devlp. Advisory Service

which later became the Harvard Inst. for Internat. Devlp. I also began the closely associated Public Service Training Program for government officials from less developed countries which was given my name when I retired. I regard my contribution to the Harvard Trust and to the Edward S. Mason Program as perhaps my most important contribution to the field of economic development.

MASSON, Robert Tempest

Born 1944, Oakland, CA, USA.
Current Post Prof., Cornell Univ., Ithaca, NY, USA, 1983–.
Past Posts Ass. Prof., Northwestern Univ., 1969–74; Econ., US Dept. Justice, 1974–6; Assoc. Prof., Cornell Univ., 1976–83; Vis. Prof., Katholiek Univ., Leuven, 1983–4.
Degrees BA Univ. Cal. Santa Barbara, 1966; MA PhD Univ. Cal. Berkeley, 1967, 1969.
Editorial Duties Ed. Board, *Rev. Industrial Organisation.*
Principal Fields of Interest 600 Industrial Organisation.
Publications Books: 1. *Milk Marketing, a Report of the US Department on Justice to the Task Group of Antitrust Immunities* (with R. Fones and J. Hall), (US Govt. Printing Office, 1977); 2. *Federal Milk Marketing Orders and Price Supports* (with R. Fones and J. Hall), (AEI, 1977).
Articles: 1. 'Executive motivations, earnings, and consequent equity performance', *JPE*, 79(6), Nov.–Dec. 1971; 2. 'The creation of risk aversion by imperfect capital markets', *AER*, 62(1), March 1972; 3. 'Costs of search and racial price discrimination', *Western EJ*, 11(2), June 1973; 4. 'Price discrimination for physicians' services' (with S.Y. Wu), *JHR*, 9(1), Winter 1974; 5. 'Utility functions with jump discontinuities: some evidence and implications from peasant agriculture', *EI*, 12(4), Dec. 1974; 6. 'The social cost of government regulation of milk' (with R.A. Ippolito), *J Law E*, 21(1), April 1978; 7. 'The structural effects of state regulation of retail fluid milk prices' (with L.M. DeBrock), *REStat*, 62(2), May

1980; 8. 'Stochastic-dynamic limit pricing: an empirical test' (with J. Shaanan), *REStat*, 62(3), Aug. 1982; 9. 'Social costs of oligopoly and the value of competition' (with J. Shaanan), *EJ*, 94, Sept. 1984; 10. 'Preying for time' (with D. Easley and R.J. Reynolds), *J Ind E*, forthcoming, 1985.

MATTHEWS, Robert Charles Oliver

Born 1927, Edinburgh, Scotland.
Current Post Prof. Polit. Econ., Master, Clare Coll. Camb., England 1975–.
Past Posts Lect., Merton Coll. Oxford, 1948–9; Univ. Ass. Lect., Univ. Lect. Econ., Fellow, St John's Coll. Camb., 1949–51, 1951–65, 1950–65; Vis. Prof., Univ. Cal. Berkeley, 1961–2; Drummond Prof. Polit. Econ., Fellow, All Souls Coll. Oxford, 1965–75.
Degrees BA, MA Univ. Oxford, 1947, 1958; Hon. DLitt Univ. Warwick, 1980.
Offices and Honours FBA, 1969; Member, Chairman, Econ. Comm., Chairman, Council, UK SSRC, 1969–72, 1970–2, 1972–5; CBE, 1975; Hon. Fellow, Corpus Christi Coll. Oxford, 1976; Trustee, Nuffield Foundation, 1975–, Urwick, Orr & Partners, 1978–; Chairman, CLARE Group Econs., 1976–; Chairman, Bank of England Panel Academic Cons., 1977–; Trustee, Social Sciences Res. Trust, 1984–; Exec. Comm., NIESR, 1975–, Econ. Comm., Social Democratic Party, 1983; Council, Pres., RES, 1973–82, 1984–; British Assoc. Section F, 1984; Member, Council BA, 1972–5; Central Advisory Comm. Science and Technology, 1967–70; OECD Expert Group Noninflationary Growth, 1975–7; Internat. Master Chess Composition, 1965.
Editorial Duties Ass. Ed., Assoc. Ed., Ed., *EJ*, 1951–63, 1964–7, 1968–70.
Principal Fields of Interest 122 Economic Studies of More Industrialised Countries; 131 Economic Fluctuations; 511 Organisation and Decision Theory.
Publications *Books:* 1. *A Study in Trade Cycle History* (CUP, 1954); 2. *The Trade Cycle* (Nisbet, 1958; as *The*

Business Cycle, Chicago Univ. Press, 1958); 3. *La Croissance Economique* (with F.H. Hahn), (Economica, 1972); 4. *Economic Growth and Resources; Trends and Factors*, ed. (Macmillan, 1981); 5. *British Economic Growth 1856–1973* (with C.H. Feinstein and J.C. Odling-Smee), (Stanford Univ. Press, 1982); 6. *The Grants Economy and Collective Consumption*, co-ed. (with G.B. Stafford), (Macmillan, 1982); 7. *Slower Growth in the Western World*, ed. (Heinemann, 1982); 8. *Contemporary Problems of Economic Policy*, co-ed. (with J.R. Sargent), (Methuen, 1983); 9. *Economy and Democracy*, ed. (Macmillan, 1985).

Articles: 1. 'Reciprocal demand and increasing returns', *REStud*, 17(2), 1949–50; 2. 'The trade cycle in Britain, 1790–1850', *OEP*, 6(1), Feb. 1954; 3. 'The saving function and the problem of trend and cycle', *REStud*, 22(2), 1955; 4. 'Expenditure plans and the uncertainty motive for holding money', *JPE*, 71(3), June 1963; 5. 'The theory of economic growth: a survey' (with F. Hahn), *EJ*, 74, Dec. 1964; repr. in AER-RES, *Surveys of Economic Theory*, 2 (Macmillan, St Martin's Press, 1965); 6. 'Why has Britain had full employment since the war?', *EJ*, 78, Sept. 1968; 7. 'Post-war business cycles in the United Kingdom', in *Is the Business Cycle Obsolete?*, ed. M. Bronfenbrenner (Wiley, 1969); 8. 'Morality, competition and efficiency', *MS*, 4, Dec. 1981; 9. 'Darwinism and economic change', *OEP*, N.S. 36, Suppl. 1983, repr. in *Economic Theory and Hicksian Themes*, ed. D.A. Collard, *et al.*, OUP, 1984; 10. 'Animal spirits', in *Proceedings British Academy*, 1984.

Principal Contributions A large part of my empirical work has been on the history of growth and fluctuations — economic history in the style written by economists. The historical slant (regrettably absent in much present-day economics) has also affected my writing in other fields, including theory and stabilisation policy. In the course of the writing of the largest piece of work on which I have been engaged, *British Economic Growth 1856–1973*, I came to feel that straightforward economic analysis, applied in conjunction with careful and wide-ranging scrutiny of the statistical and other evidence, is capable of explaining a great deal about the course of economic change, but at the same time that the conventional model of rational individualistic utility-maximisation has inadequacies that matter. This last conclusion was reinforced by my personal experiences in practical administration and decision-making, academic and other. My more recent interests have therefore moved towards the institutional and psychological underpinnings of economic behaviour.

MAYER, Thomas

Born 1927, Vienna, Austria.
Current Post Prof. Econ., Univ. Cal. Davis, CA, USA, 1962–.
Past Posts Econ., Tax Advisory Staff, Secretary US Treasury Dept., 1951–2; Econ., Office Econ. Pol., US Office Price Stabilization, 1952; Econ., Inter-industry Analysis Branch, US Bureau Mines, 1953; Vis. Ass. Prof., Virginia Univ., 1953–4, Univ. Notre Dame, 1954–6; Ass. Prof., Assoc. Prof., Michigan State Univ., 1956–61; Vis. Assoc. Prof., Univ. Cal. Berkeley, 1961–2.
Degrees BA Queens Coll. NY, 1948; MA, PhD Columbia Univ., 1948, 1953.
Offices and Honours Vice-Pres., Pres., Western Econ. Assoc., 1976–9.
Editorial Duties Ed. Boards, *J Fin*, 1967–70, *WEJ*, 1969–72, *JMCB*, 1970–74, *JEL*, 1975–77, *J Mon E*, 1974–80, *J. Macroecon.*, 1977–, *Stud. Monetary Econ.*, 1976–81, *Cambridge Surveys Econ. Lit.* (CUP, 1977–).
Principal Fields of Interest 310 Domestic Monetary and Financial Theory and Institutions; 130 Economic Fluctuations, Forecasting and Inflation; 023 Macroeconomic Theory.
Publications *Books:* 1. *Monetary Policy in the United States* (Random House, 1968); 2. *Intermediate Macroeconomics* (with D.C. Rowan), (W.W. Norton, 1972); 3. *Permanent Income, Wealth and Consumption* (Univ. Cal. Press, 1972); 4. *The Structure of Monetarism* (with others), (W.W. Norton, 1978); 5. *Money, Banking and the Economy* (with J. Duesenberry and R. Aliber), (W.W. Norton, 1981, 1984).

Articles: 1. 'The inflexibility of monetary policy', *REStat*, 40, Nov. 1958, repr. in *Contemporary Monetary Theory and Policy*, ed. R. Thorn (Random House, 1966); 2. 'The distribution of ability and earnings', *REStat*. 42, May, 1960, repr. in *Wealth, Income and Inequality*, ed. A.B. Atkinson (Penguin, 1973); 3. 'Liquidity functions in the American economy' (with M. Bronfenbrenner), *Em*, 28, Oct. 1960, repr. in *Readings in Macroeconomics*, ed. G. Mueller (Holt, Rinehart & Winston, 1966); 4. 'An extension of Sidgwick's equity principle' (with S. Johnson), *QJE*, 76(4), Aug. 1962; 5. 'Tests of the relative importance of autonomous expenditures and money' (with M. DePrano), *AER*, 55(4), Sept. 1965; 6. 'A graduated deposit insurance plan', *REStat*, 47, Feb. 1965, repr. in *Innovations in Bank Management*, ed. P. Jessup (Wiley, 1979); 7. 'Economics as an exact science', *EI*, April 1980, repr. in *How Economists Explain*, eds. W. Marr and B. Raj (Univ. Press Amer., 1983); 8. 'David Hume and monetarism', *QJE*, 94, Aug. 1980; 9. 'Federal reserve policy in the 1973–5 recession', in *Crises in the Economic and Financial Structure*, ed. P. Wachtel (D.C. Heath, 1982); 10. 'The government budget constraint and standard macrotheory', *J Mon E*, 12, May 1984.

Principal Contributions Although I have sometimes worked in other fields, such as microeconomics and regulation of financial institutions, my main interest has been in applied macroeconomics and in particular in monetary policy. Much of my work has centred on the dispute between Keynesians and monetarists. (My position can be described as a very moderate monetarist or as fellow-traveller of monetarism.) On this issue, as well as on the debate about the permanent income theory, I have tried to synthesise previous work as well as presenting new tests, though I am sceptical of 'tests' that try to mimic time-series data.

I have also worked on the question of whether our standard econometric tests are likely to lead to valid results. My work has been marked by the applications of simple techniques to a variety of problems, frequently with an institutionalist approach. (For example, I have started to work on the question *why* the Federal Reserve System adopts certain policies.) Economists can be divided into those who are concerned mainly with the development of theorems, and those whose main concern is the explanation of observed events. Belonging to the latter group, I have tried to provide plausible, though far from conclusive evidence, on some problems about which little is known rather than to provide more elegant or general solutions to problems that are more nearly solved.

MAZZOLA, Ugo*

Dates and Birthplace 1863–99, Italy.
Posts Held Teacher, Univ. Camerino; Prof. Public Fin., Polit. Econ., Univ. Padua, 1887, 1896.
Degrees Grad. Law Univ. Naples.
Publications *Books:* 1. *L'Assicurazione degli Operaî Nella Scienza e Nella Legislazione Germanica* (1885); 2. *I Dati Scientifici Della Finanza Pubblica* (1890); 3. *L'Imposta Progressiva in Economia Pura e Sociale* (1895); 4. *La Colonizzazione Interna in Prussia* (1900).
Career Specialised in the study of public finance, seeing the State as a co-operative and the finances of the State as a co-operative activity on the part of the citizens. This co-operation is to enable citizens to purchase certain services at a lower cost than if they were obtained privately. He saw no clash between public and private needs, both equally needing to be satisfied for the sake of the general welfare. In his *I Dati Scientifici . . .* , he described for the first time the characteristics of what is now known as 'public goods'.
Secondary Literature C. Pagin, 'Mazzola, Ugo', *ESS*, 10; *Classics in the Theory of Public Finance*, eds. R.A. Musgrave and A.T. Peacock (Macmillan, 1958).

McCall, John Joseph

Born 1933, Chicago, IL, USA.
Current Post Prof. Econ., UCLA, Los Angeles, CA, USA, 1969–.
Past Posts Econ., Rand Corp., 1959–63, 1964–6, 1976–8; Assoc. Prof., Univ. Chicago, 1966; Prof. Econ., Univ. Cal. Irvine, 1968–9; Vis. Walgreen Prof., Univ. Chicago, 1977–8, Univ. Konstanz, W. Germany, 1981.
Degrees BA (Philo.) Univ. Notre Dame, 1955; MBA, PhD Univ. Chicago, 1957, 1959.
Offices and Honours NSF Postdoctoral Fellow, 1963, 1968; Walgreen Scholar, 1977.
Editorial Duties Ed. Board, *Info. Econ. and Pol.*
Principal Fields of Interest 022 Microeconomic Theory; 026 Economics of Uncertainty and Information; 800 Manpower; Labour; Population.
Publications *Books:* 1. *Optimal Replacement Policy* (with D.W. Jorgenson and R. Radner), (N-H, 1967); 2. *Income Mobility, Racial Discrimination and Economic Growth* (D.C. Heath, 1973); 3. *Studies in the Economics of Search*, co-ed. (with S.A. Lippman), (N-H, 1979); 4. *The Economics of Information and Uncertainty* (Univ. Chicago Press, 1982).
Articles: 1. 'The economics of information and optimal stopping rules', *J Bus*, July 1965; 2. 'Competitive production for constant risk utility functions', *REStud*, 34, Oct. 1967; 3. 'Economics of information and job search', *QE*, 84(1), Feb. 1970; 4. 'The simple economics of incentive contracting', *AER*, 60(5), Dec. 1970; 5. 'A Markovian model of income dynamics', *JASA*, 66, Sept. 1971; 6. 'Probalistic microeconomics', *Bell JE*, 2, Spring 1971; 7. 'The economics of job search: a survey, I, II' (with S.A. Lippman), *EI*, 14(2), June, 14(3), Sept. 1976; 8. 'Job search in a dynamic economy' (with S.A. Lippman), *JET*, 12(3), June 1976; 9. 'The economics of belated information' (with S.A. Lippman), IER, 22(4), Dec. 1981; 10. 'A dynamic retention model for air force officers: theory and estimates' (with G.A. Gotz), (Rand, 1984).
Principal Contributions Most of my research has been on the economics of

uncertainty. Early on I recognised that many of these uncertainty problems could be formulated as optimal stopping rules. Much theoretical and empirical work has been stimulated by this observation.

McCALLUM, Bennett Tarlton

Born 1935, Poteet, TX, USA.
Current Post Prof. Econ., Grad. School Industrial Admin., Carnegie-Mellon Univ., Pittsburgh, PA, USA, 1981–.
Past Posts Ass. Prof., Assoc. Prof., Prof. Econ., Univ. Virginia, 1967–71, 1971–4, 1974–81; Cons., Board of Governors, Fed. Reserve System, 1974; Vis. Prof., Carnegie-Mellon Univ., 1980; Adviser, Fed. Reserve Bank Richmond, VA, 1981–.
Degrees BA, BSc (Chemistry), PhD Rice Univ., Houston, TX, 1957, 1958, 1969; MBA Harvard Univ., 1963.
Offices and Honours Res. Assoc., NBER, 1979–; Grad. Record Exams Comm., Examiners Advanced Econ. Test, 1980–2.
Editorial Duties Ed. Boards, *SEJ*, 1975–77, *J Mon E*, 1977–, *Econ. Letters*, 1978–, *JMCB*, 1983–; Advisory Board, *Carnegie-Rochester Conf. Series Public Pol.*, 1980–.
Principal Fields of Interest 023 Macroeconomic Theory; 211 Econometric and Statistical Methods and Models; 311 Domestic Monetary and Financial Theory and Policy.
Publications *Articles:* 1. 'A note concerning asymptotic covariance expressions', *Em*, 41(3), May 1973; 2. 'Rational expectations and the natural rate hypothesis: some consistent estimates', *Em*, 44(1), Jan. 1976; 3. 'Topics concerning the formulation, estimation and use of macroeconometric models with rational expectations', *1979 Proceedings, Business and Economic Statistics Section* (ASA, 1979); 4. 'Rational expectations and macroeconomic stabilization policy: an overview', *JMCB*, 12(4), pt. 2, Nov. 1980; 5. 'Monetarist principles and the money stock growth rule', *AER*, 71(2), May 1981; 6. 'Macroeconomics after a decade of rational expectations: some critical issues', *Fed. Reserve Bank*

Richmond Econ. Rev., 68(6), Nov.–Dec. 1982; 7. 'On non-uniqueness in rational expectations models: an attempt at perspective', *J Mon E*, 11(2), March 1983; 8. 'The role of overlapping-generations models in monetary economics', *Carnegie-Rochester Conf. Series on Public Pol.*, 18, Spring 1983, repr. in *Theory, Policy, Institutions*, eds. K. Brunner and A.H. Meltzer (N-H, 1983); 9. 'A linearized version of Lucas's neutrality model', *CJE*, 17(1), Feb. 1984; 10. 'Are bond-financed deficits inflationary? A Ricardian analysis', *JPE*, 92(1), Feb. 1984.
Principal Contributions Initial research efforts were in the area of applied econometrics and, to a lesser extent, econometric theory. Several empirical studies involved the formulation and estimation of relationships describing dynamic adjustments of nominal wages and prices — i.e., 'Phillips curves'. As such relationships include ubobservable expectational variables, these studies motivated consideration of hypotheses more plausible than the then-prevalent adaptive-expectations theory. This led in turn to an interest in the hypotheses of rational expectations and to the development of techniques appropriate for estimation and testing that hypothesis. In response to the profession's concern with the macroeconomic 'policy effectiveness' proposition, several papers were devoted to the discussion and refinement of that proposition and to the description of structures in which it is theoretically valid, despite the absence of perfect price flexibility. More recent work has involved a wide range of issues in macro and monetary economics. Four of these are the multiplicity of solution paths that obtains in many macroeconomic models with rational expectations, the proper role of overlapping-generations models in monetary economics, the alleged destabilising effect of monetarist policy rules, and the implications of the Ricardian debt hypothesis for the feasibility of an unending sequence of government budget deficits financed by bond sales. Topics of ongoing interest include aggregate supply behaviour, the role of equilibrium and disequilibrium approaches to macroeconomic analysis,

and the possibility of drawing structural inferences by means of relatively model-free statistical techniques.

McCLOSKEY, Donald Nansen

Born 1942, Ann Arbor, MI, USA.
Current Post Prof. Econ. and Hist., Univ. Iowa, Iowa City, IA, USA, 1980–.
Past Posts Ass. Prof., Univ. Chicago, 1968–73; Econ. Vis. Ass. Prof., Stanford Univ., 1972; Assoc. Prof., Assoc. Prof. Hist., Univ. Chicago, 1973–80, 1979–80; Vis. Fellow, ANU, 1982; Member, Inst. Advanced Study, Princeton, 1983–4; Vis. Prof., Univ. York, Canada, 1985–.
Degrees BA, MA, PhD Harvard Univ., 1964, 1967, 1970.
Offices and Honours David A. Wells Prize, Harvard Univ., 1970–1; Guggenheim Foundation Fellow, 1983.
Editorial Duties Ed. Boards, *JEH*, 1974–80, *Explor. Econ. Hist.*, 1974–9, *Econ. and Philo.*, 1983–, *J. British Stud.*, 1983–.
Principal Fields of Interest 044 European Economic History; 036 Economic Methodology; 041 Economic History: General.
Publications *Books:* 1. *Economic Maturity and Entrepreneurial Decline: British Iron and Steel 1870–1913* (Harvard Univ. Press, 1973); 2. *Essays on a Mature Economy: Britain After 1840*, ed. and contrib. (Methuen, Princeton Univ. Press, 1971); 3. *Enterprise and Trade in Victorian Britain* (A&U, 1981); 4. *The Economic History of Britain, 1700-present* (with R. Floud), 2 vols, ed. and contrib. (CUP, 1981); 5. *The Applied Theory of Price* (Macmillan, 1982, 1985; transl., Spanish, 1984); 6. *The Rhetoric of Economics* (University of Wisconsin Press, 1985).

Articles: 1. 'Productivity change in British pig iron, 1870–1939', *QJE*, 82, May 1969; 2. 'The new economic history: an introduction', *Rivista Storica Italiana*, 83, March 1971; 3. 'New perspectives on the old poor law', *Explor. Econ. Hist.*, 10, Summer 1973; 4. 'The persistence of English common fields', in *European Peasants and Their Markets*, eds. E.L. Jones and W. Parker (Princeton Univ. Press, 1975); 5. 'The economics of enclosure: a market analysis', in *European Peasants, op. cit.*; 6. 'English open fields as behavior towards risk', *Res. Econ. Hist.*, 1, Fall 1976; 7. 'Magnanimous Albion: free trade and British national income, 1841–1881', *Explor. Econ. Hist.*, 17, Spring 1980; 8. 'The rhetoric of economics', *JEL*, 21(2), June 1983, 22(2), June 1984; 9. 'Corn at interest: the cost and extent of grain storage in medieval England' (with J. Nash), *AER*, 74(1), March 1984; 10. 'The success of purchasing power parity' (with J.R. Zecher), in *Retrospective on the Classical Gold Standard*, eds. M. Bordo and A.J. Schwartz (Univ. Chicago Press, 1984).

Principal Contributions A second-generation cliometrician, my dissertation work with Alexander Gerschenkron applied quantitative tools to the hypothesis of British entrepreneurial failure in the late 19th century. I was among the co-discoverers of the failure of the hypothesis and of the success of neoclassical economics in British economic history. By a small extension, encouraged by the intellectual turmoil in trade theory at Chicago in the late 1960s, it proved possible to show its success in retelling the story of British foreign trade in the twentieth century. Extension of economics was much in the air at Chicago c. 1970, suggesting its use to illumine the Old Poor Law, *contra* Blaug, and the Gold Standard, *contra* the received wisdom.

The extension into the new institutional economics was the occasion for a study of the enclosures in British agriculture during the eighteenth century, which led to a ten-year project on the economics of the system that replaced medieval open fields. The attempt to communicate these wonders to students, historians, and other incognoscenti led in two directions: on the one hand, the writing of a problem-oriented textbook in economics, an economically-oriented textbook in British economic history, and various other projects of instructing the young and, on the other, it led to unease about the way adults in economics communicate. Beginning with the rhetoricians at Chicago and the University of Iowa, this in turn led to a project of applying literary criticism to economics, examining the fairy tale that economists persuade themselves by scientific methods. The longer-term purpose is to reunify economics with history, and mathematical with literary ways of thinking.

McCULLOCH, John Ramsay*

Dates and Birthplace 1789–1864, Scotland.
Posts Held Journalist and Ed., *The Scotsman*, 1818–20; Private Tutor Econ., 1820–8; Prof. Polit. Econ., Univ. Coll., London, 1828–32; Comptroller, HMSO, 1838–64.
Offices Chief reviewer econ. books, *Edinburgh Rev.* 1817–; Delivered Ricardo Memorial Lectures, 1823–4.
Publications *Books:* 1. *A Discourse on the Rise, Progress, Peculiar Objects and Importance of Political Economy* (1824); 2. *Principles of Political Economy* (1825, 1886); 3. *A Dictionary, Practical, Theoretical and Historical of Commerce and Commercial Navigation* (1832, 1882); 4. *Descriptive and Statistical Account of the British Empire*, 2 vols (1837, 1854); 5. *The Literature of Political Economy* (1845, 1938); 6. *A Treatise on the Principles and Practical Influence of Taxation and the Funding System* (1845, 1975).
Career Traditionally regarded as the most loyal and dogmatic of Ricardo's followers, recent examination of his writings has shown more clearly the Smithian flavour of many of his views, and the shifts in his opinions over time. He was, however, a tireless propagandist for his version of Ricardo's ideas and for political economy generally, both of which he tended to identify with each other. His statistical, encyclopaedic and bibliographical works were extremely successful and were better suited to his abilities than questions of pure theory. He also contributed in *A Discourse . . .* the first serious history of economic thought anywhere.
Secondary Literature M. Blaug, 'McCulloch, John Ramsay', *IESS*, 9; D.P. O'Brien, *J.R. McCulloch: A Study in Classical Economics* (A&U, 1970).

McFADDEN, Daniel L.

Born 1937, Raleigh, NC, USA.
Current Post Prof. Econ., MIT, Camb. MA, USA, 1979–.
Past Posts Vis. Assoc. Prof., Univ. Chicago, 1966–7; Prof. Econ., Univ. Cal. Berkeley, 1968–79; Vis. Scholar, MIT, 1970–1; Vis. Prof., Yale Univ., 1977–8.
Degrees BS (Physics), PhD Univ. Minnesota, 1957, 1962.
Offices and Honours Mellon Post-doctoral Fellow, 1962–3; Ford Faculty Res Fellow 1966–7; Fellow, Em Soc, 1969; John Bates Clark Medal, AEA, 1975; AAAS, 1977; Irving Fisher Res. Prof., 1977–8; Outstanding Teacher Award, MIT Econ. Dept., 1981; NAS, 1981.
Principal Fields of Interest 022 Microeconomic Theory.
Publications *Books:* 1. *Urban Travel Demand: A Behavioral Analysis* (with T. Domencich), (N-H, 1975); 2. *Production Economics: A Dual Approach to Theory and Applications*, ed. (with M. Fuss), (N-H, 1978); 3. *Structural Analysis of Discrete Data with Econometric Applications*, ed. (with C.F. Manski), (MIT Press, 1981).
Articles: 1. 'Conditional logit analysis of qualitative choice behavior', in *Frontiers of Econometrics*, ed. P. Zarembka (Academic Press, 1973); 2. 'On the existence of optimal development programs in infinite horizon economies', in *Models of Economic Growth*, eds. J. Mirrlees and H. Stern (N-H, 1973); 3. 'Modelling the choice of residential location', in *Proceedings of the Conference on Spatial Interaction Theory and Planning Models* (N-H, 1978); 4. 'Determinants of the long-run demand for electricity' (with C. Puig and D. Kirshner), *ASA Proceedings*, 1978; 5. 'Pareto optimality and competitive equilibrium in infinite horizon economies' (with M. Majumdar and T. Mitra), *J Math E*, 7(1), March 1980.
Principal Contributions Primary concern of research is integration of the theory and measurement of economic behaviour. One research area is the reformulation of production theory, using duality, in terms of market data; a second is the development of empirical

consumer theory for unconventional budget sets, such as discrete alternatives, with applications in the demand for transportation and the demand for energy-using appliances.

McKENZIE, Lionel Wilfred

Born 1919, Montezuma, GA, USA.
Current Post Wilson Prof. Econ., Univ. Rochester, Rochester, NY, USA, 1967–.
Past Posts Jr. Econ., US War Production Board, 1946; US Navy, 1943–5; Instr., MIT 1946; Assoc. Prof., Ass. Prof., Duke Univ., 1948–57; Res. Assoc., Yale Univ., 1956; Vis. Assoc. Prof., Univ. Michigan, 1957, Prof. Econ., Univ. Rochester, 1957–66, John Munro Prof. Econ., Univ. Michigan, 1964–7; Taussig Res. Prof., Harvard Univ., 1980–1.
Degrees BA Duke Univ., 1939; MA, PhD Princeton Univ., 1942, 1956; BLitt. Univ. Oxford, 1949.
Offices and Honours Rhodes Scholar, 1939; Fellow, Pres., Em Soc, 1958, 1977; Guggenheim Foundation Fellow, 1973–4; Fellow, AAAS, 1967; Member NAS, 1978; Fellow, Center Advanced Study Behavioral Sciences, Stanford, 1973–4.
Editorial Duties Assoc. Ed., *Int ER*, 1964, *JET*, 1970–3, *J Int E*, 1971–.
Principal Fields of Interest 021 General Equilibrium Theory; 411 International Trade Theory; 111 Economic Growth Theory and Models.
Publications *Books:* 1. *Selected Readings in Macroeconomics and Capital Theory from Econometrics*, co-ed. (with D. Cass), (MIT, 1974).
Articles: 1. 'On equilibrium in Graham's model of world trade and other competitive systems', *Em*, 22, April 1954; 2. 'Specialisation and efficiency in world production', *REStud*, 21(3), June 1954; 3. 'Equality of factor prices in world trade', *Em*, 23, July 1955; 4. 'Demand theory without a utility index', *REStud*, 24(8), June 1957; 5. 'On the existence of general equilibrium for a competitive market', *Em*, 27, Jan. 1959; 6. 'Matrices with dominant diagonals and economic theory', *Math. Methods in Social Science* (Stanford Univ., 1959), repr. in *Selected Read-*

ings in Economic Theory from Econometrica, ed. K.J. Arrow (MIT, 1971); 7. 'Stability of equilibrium and the value of positive excess demand', *Em*, 28, July 1960; 8. 'Turnpike theory', *Em*, 44, Sept. 1976, repr. in *Selected Readings from Econometrica, op. cit.*; 9. 'The classical theorem on existence of competitive equilibrium, *Em*, 41, July 1981.
Principal Contributions On existence of competitive equilibrium: one of the two first rigorous proofs of existence under general conditions, followed by several generalisations of the theorem to include external economies and weaker assumptions of interiority. On stability of equilibrium: a theorem on stability with weak gross substitutes and the weakest form of *tâtonnement*. On international economics: a general theorem on factor price equalisation, a general theorem on specialisation in production in the Graham model of world trade. On optimal growth: various turnpike theorems in the context of Von Neumann's model and a multi-sector Ramsey model, with and without a discount factor.

McKINNON, Ronald Ian

Born 1945, Edmonton, Alberta, Canada.
Current Post Prof. Econ., Stanford Univ., CA, USA, 1961–.
Past Posts Royal Canadian Air Force, 1952–6; Instr. Bus. Admin., Univ. Minnesota, 1957–9; Lect. Econ., Syracuse Univ., 1960–1; Ass. Prof., Assoc. Prof., Stanford Univ., 1961–6, 1966–9; Vis. Res. Prof. Internat. Econ., Brookings Inst., 1970–1; Cons., US Agency Internat. Devlp. Korea, 1967, 1973, Stanford Res. Inst., 1965, IBRD Ethiopia, 1971, Govt. Colombia, 1973, Organization Amer. States on Latin Amer. Capital Markets, 1974, Govt. Kuwait, 1974, Govt. Chile, 1977, Govt. Uruguay, 1979, Govt. Peru, 1981, IMF, 1981, World Bank Korea, 1984.
Degrees BA Univ. Alberta, 1956; PhD Univ. Minnesota, 1960.
Offices and Honours Gold Medal Econ., Univ. Alberta, 1956; Earhart Foundation Grant, 1959–60; Fellow

Univ. Singapore, 1966; Fellow, Center Advanced Study Behavioral Sciences, Stanford Univ., CA, 1974–5; Vis. Scholar, Hoover Inst., Stanford Univ., 1982–3.

Principal Fields of Interest 430 Balance of Payments; International Finance.

Publications *Books:* 1. *Money and Capital in Economic Development* (Brookings Inst., 1973; transls., Korean, 1974, Spanish, 1974, Portuguese, 1978); 2. *Money and Finance in Economic Growth and Development: Essays in Honor of Edward D. Shaw*, ed. (Marcel Dekker, 1976); 3. *Money in International Exchange: The Convertible Currency System* (OUP, 1979; transls., French, 1982, Japanese, forthcoming); 4. *An International Standard for Monetary Stabilization* (Inst. Internat. Econ., 1984).

Articles: 1. 'America's role in stabilizing the world's monetary system', *Daedalus*, 107(1), Winter 1978; 2. 'Commodity reserve money, special drawing rights and the link to less developed countries', in *Economics and Human Welfare: Essays in Honor of Tibor Scitovsky*, ed. M.J. Boskin (Academic Press, 1979); 3. 'Dollar stabilization and American monetary policy', *AER*, 70(2), May 1980; 4. 'Exchange-rate instability, trade imbalances and monetary policies in Japan and the United States', in *Issues in International Economics*, ed. P. Oppenheimer (Oriel Press, 1980); 5. 'Financial policies', in *Policies for Industrial Development*, eds. J. Cody, H. Hughes and D. Wall (OUP, 1980); 6. 'Financial repression and the liberalization problem with less developed countries', in *The Past and Prospects for the World Economic Order*, eds. S. Grossman and E. Lundberg (Macmillan, 1981); 7. 'The exchange rate and macroeconomic policy: changing postwar perceptions', *JET*, 19(2), May 1981; 8. 'Dollar overvaluation against the yen and mark in 1983: How to co-ordinate central bank policies', *Aussenwirtschaft*, 38, Heft 4, 1983, 9. 'Why US monetary policy should be internationalized', in *To Promote Peace: US Foreign Policy in the mid-1980s*, ed. D. Bark (Hoover Inst., 1984); 10. 'A program for international monetary stability', in *The Future of the International Monetary System*, ed. R. Levich (NYU Press, 1984).

Principal Contributions Working out the logic of the international dollar standard. Exchange-rate policies for large and small countries including the US itself. Establishing the importance of financial liberalisation in less developed countries in parallel with liberalising foreign trade. How to maintain monetary control during the liberalisation processes.

McLURE, Charles E., Jr.

Born 1940, Sierra Blanca, TX, USA.

Current Post Dept. Ass. Secretary, Tax Analysis, US Treasury Dept., Washington, DC, USA, 1983–.

Past Posts Ass. Prof., Assoc. Prof., Prof., Allyn R. and Gladys M. Cline Prof., Rice Univ., 1965–9, 1969–72, 1972–9, 1973–9; Cons., US Treasury Dept., 1967–76; Staff Member, Colombian Tax Reform Mission, 1968; Vis. Lect., St Thomas Univ., Houston, 1968–70; Adviser, Govt. Malaysia, 1969; Sr. Staff Econ., US President's Council Econ. Advisers, 1969–70; Cons., Govt. Panama, 1971; John S. Bugas Vis. Disting. Lect., Univ. Wyoming, 1972; Cons., World Bank, 1972 Colombia, 1975–7 Colombia and Kenya, 1982 (Colombia); Vis. Prof., Stanford Univ., 1973; Cons., UN, 1973; Adviser, Govt. Jamaica, 1973–4, 1983; Cons., US Dept. Labor, 1975; Staff Member, Bolivian Tax Reform Mission, 1976; Cons., IMF Venezuela, 1981–2; Cons., Govt. Indonesia, 1982; Adviser, Govt. Colombia, 1982; Vice-Pres., NBER, 1977–81; Sr. Fellow, Hoover Inst., Stanford Univ., 1981–3.

Degrees BA Kansas Univ., 1962; MA, PhD Princeton Univ., 1964, 1966.

Offices and Honours Woodrow Wilson Fellow, 1962–3; H.B. Earhart Fellow, 1963–4; Ford Foundation Fellow, 1964–5; Ford Foundation Faculty Res. Fellow, 1967–8; Hon. Res. Assoc., Harvard Univ., 1967–8, 1977–9; Res. Assoc., NBER, 1978–83.

Editorial Duties Ed. Boards, *Nat. Tax Assoc.* 1972–83, *Public Fin. Q.*, 1975–7, *SEJ*, 1977–9, *Texas Bus. Rev.*, 1982–3.

Principal Fields of Interest 323 National Taxation and Subsidies; 324 State and Local Government Finance; 325 Intergovernmental Financial Relationships.

Publications *Books:* 1. *Fiscal Failure: Lessons of the Sixties* (AEI, 1972); 2. *Value Added Tax: Two Views*, co-ed. (with N.B. Ture), (AEI, 1972); 3. *A New Look at Inflation*, co-ed. (with P. Cagan, *et al.*), (AEI, 1973); 4. *La Reforma Tributaria de 1974* (with M. Gillis), (Biblioteca Banco Popular, 1977); 5. *Once is Enough: The Taxation of Corporate Equity Income* (Inst. Contemporary Stud., 1977); 6. *Must Corporate Income be Taxed Twice?* (Brookings Inst., 1979); 7. *Fiscal Federalism and the Taxation of Natural Resources*, co-ed. (with P. Mieskowski), (D.C. Heath, 1983); 8. *Tax Assignment in Federal Countries*, ed. (Center for Res. on Fed. Fin. Relations, 1983); 9. *The State Corporation Income Tax: Issues in Worldwide Unitary Combination*, ed. (Hoover Inst. Press, 1984).

Articles: 1. 'The interstate exporting of state and local taxes: estimates for 1962', *Nat. Tax J.*, 20(1), March 1967; 2. 'Tax incidence, absolute prices, and macroeconomic policy', *QJE*, 84, May 1970; 3. 'A diagrammatic exposition of the Harberger model with one immobile factor', *JPE*, 82(1), Jan.–Feb. 1974; 4. 'The proper use of indirect taxation in developing nations: the practice of economic marksmanship', *PF*, 30(1), 1975; 5. 'Integration of the personal and corporate income taxes: the missing element in tax reform proposals', *Harvard Law Rev.*, 88, Jan. 1975; 6. 'General equilibrium incidence analysis: the Harberger model after ten years', *J Pub E*, 4(2), Feb. 1975; 7. 'The incidence of Colombian taxes: 1970', *EDCC*, 24(1), Oct. 1975; 8. 'A status report on tax integration in the United States', *Nat. Tax J.*, 31, Dec. 1978; 9. 'Incidence analysis and the courts: an analysis of four 1981 cases', *Supreme Court Econ. Review: The 1980 Term*, 1, 1982 (Macmillan, 1983); 10. 'Defining a unitary business: an economist's view', in *The State Corporation Income Tax, op. cit.*

Principal Contributions My work has occurred in roughly a dozen interrelated areas of research and policy analysis. My earliest work on interstate tax exporting and the general equilibrium theory of tax incidence continues to provide insights for my more recent analysis of tax incidence in developing countries, the incidence of taxes on natural resources, and the incidence of corporate income taxes and property taxes. Similarly, my early interest in State and local finance and fiscal federalism continues in my work on uniformity of State corporate income taxes, assignment of revenue sources in a federal system, and fiscal federalism and the taxation of natural resources. Interest in taxation in open economies has also informed my research on value-added taxes, tax integration, taxation in developing countries, and State corporate income taxation. Over time, I have moved from economic research to the interstices between the economics of taxation and tax law. Following the lead of Richard Musgrave, I have devoted much of my career to policy analysis. Besides writing on federal tax policy in the US, I have been an adviser to a number of foreign governments and international organisations. In my capacity as Deputy Assistant Secretary for Tax Analysis, I am drawing on my previous research in two ways: as Staff Director for the Treasury Department's Working Group on Worldwide Unitary Taxation and as leader of the Treasury Department team studying fundamental tax reform at the direction of the President.

McVICKAR, John*

Dates and Birthplace 1787–1868, New York City, NY, USA.

Posts Held Ordained Clergyman, 1812; Teacher, Columbia Coll., New York City, 1817–64.

Degrees BA Columbia Coll., 1804.

Publications *Books:* 1. *Outlines of Political Economy* (1825); 2. *Hints on Banking* (1827); 3. *First Lessons in Political Economy* (1837).

Career He was one of the earliest, if not the earliest, professors of political economy in US, treating the subject as a branch of moral philosophy. Whilst on a year's sabbatical he was enrolled as a member of the Political Economy Club in London, and met many of the leading economists of the day.

Secondary Literature J.B. Langstaff, *The Enterprising Life: John McVickar 1787–1868* (Columbia Univ. Press, 1961).

MEAD, Walter Joseph

Born 1921, Nehalem, OR, USA.
Current Post Prof. Econ., Univ. Cal. Santa Barbara, CA, USA, 1966–.
Past Posts Ass. Prof. Econ., Lewis and Clark Coll., Portland, Oregon, 1956; Ass. Field Dir., Comm. Econ. Devlp., NYC, 1956–7; Assoc. Prof. Econ., Univ. Cal. Santa Barbara, 1957–66; Cons., Ford Foundation Energy Pol. Project, 1972–3.
Degrees BA, PhD Univ. Oregon, 1948, 1952; MA Columbia Univ., 1950.
Offices and Honours Pres., *WEA*, 1968–9; Chairman, Academic Senate, Univ. Cal. Santa Barbara, 1978–80.
Editorial Duties Advisory Council, *Natural Resources J.*, 1968–; Ed. Board, *Industrial Organization Rev.*, 1973–.
Principal Fields of Interest 610 Industrial Organisation and Public Policy; 723 Energy; 720 Natural Resources.
Publications *Books:* 1. *Competition and Oligopsony in the Douglas-Fir Lumber Industry* (Univ. Cal. Press, 1966); 2. *Transporting Natural Gas from the Arctic: The Alternative System* (AEI, 1978); 3. *Energy and the Environment: Conflict in Public Policy* (AEI, 1978); 4. *US Energy Policy: Errors of the Past, Proposals for the Future*, co-ed. (with A.E. Utton), (Ballinger, 1978).
Articles: 1. 'A cost-benefit analysis of ocean mineral resource development: the case of manganese nodules' (with G.E. Sorensen), *AJAE*, Dec. 1968; 2. 'The system of government subsidies to the oil industry', in *Political Economy of Federal Policy*, eds. R. Haveman and R. Hamlin (Harper & Row, 1973); 3. 'Instantaneous merger profit as a conglomerate merger motive', *WEJ*, 7, Dec. 1969; 4. 'Petroleum: an unregulated industry?', in *Energy Supply and Government Policy*, eds. R.J. Kalter and W.A. Vogely (Cornell Univ. Press, 1976); 5. 'Social cost-benefit analysis of offshore drilling', in *The Question of Offshore Oil*, ed. E.J. Mitchell (AEI, 1976); 6. 'An economic appraisal of President Carter's energy program', *Science*, 197, July 33, 1977, repr. in *Editorial Magazine*, Nov. 1977, and *Energy Rev.*, 5(2), 1978; 7. 'Political-economic problems of energy: a synthesis', *Natural Resources J.*, Oct. 1978; 8. 'The performance of government in energy regulations', *AER*, 69(2), May 1979; 9. 'An economic analysis of crude oil price behavior in the 1970s,' *J. Energy and Econ. Devlp.*, Spring, 1979, repr. in *OPEC: Twenty Years and Beyond*, ed. R.E. Mallakh (Ballinger, 1982); 10. 'A skeptical view of OPEC as a cartel', in *Energy: Coping in the 1980s*, ed. D.L. McLachlan (Univ. Calgary Press, 1981).

MEADE, James Edward

Born 1907, Swanage, Dorset, England.
Current Post Retired, 1974–.
Past Posts Fellow, Hertford Coll. Oxford, 1930–7; Member, Econ. Section League of Nations, 1938–40; Econ. Ass., Dir. Econ. Section, UK Cabinet Office, 1940–5, 1946–7; Prof. Commerce, LSE, 1947–57; Professorial Fellow, Nuffield Res. Fellow, Christ's Coll. Camb., 1959–69, 1969–74; Prof. Polit. Econ., Univ. Camb., 1957–68.
Degrees BA (by incorporation), MA Univ. Camb., 1930, 1957; BA, MA Univ. Oxford, 1930, 1933; Hon. Dr Univs., Basle, Bath, Essex, Hull, Oxford.
Offices and Honours Hon. Fellow, LSE, Oriel Coll., Hertford Coll. Oxford, Christ's Coll. Camb.; Pres., Section F, BAAS, 1957; Hon. Member, Soc. Royale d'Econ. Polit. de Belgique, 1958, AEA, 1962, AAAS, 1966; Foreign Assoc., NAS, 1981; Chairman, Econ. Survey Mission, Mauritius, 1960; Pres., Vice-Pres., RES, 1964–6, 1966; Chairman, Comm. Inst. Fiscal Stud., 1975–7; Nobel Prize in Econ., 1977.
Principal Fields of Interest 020 General Economic Theory.

Publications *Books:* 1. *Economic Analysis and Policy* (OUP, 1936, 1937); 2. *The Economic Basis of a Durable Peace* (A&U, 1940); 3. *National Income and Expenditure* (with R. Stone), (OUP, 1944); 4. *Planning and the Price Mechanism* (A&U, 1948); 5. *Theory of International Economic Policy*, (OUP) 1, *The Balance of Payment*, (1951), 2, *Trade and Welfare* (1955); 6. *A Neo-Classical Theory of Economic Growth* (A&U, 1960, 1962); 7. *Efficiency, Equality and the Ownership of Property* (A&U, 1964, 1969); 8. *Principles of Political Economy*, (A&U), 1, *The Stationary Economy* (1965), 2, *The Growing Economy* (1968), 3, *The Controlled Economy* (1972), 4, *The Just Economy* (1976); 9. *The Intelligent Radical's Guide to Economic Policy* (A&U, 1975); 10. *Stagflation*, (A&U), 1, *Wage-Fixing* (1982), 2, *Demand-Management* (with D. Vines and J. Maciejowski), (1983).

Principal Contributions Mainly concerned with applying economic theory to the formulation of economic policies.

Secondary Literature W.M. Corden and A.B. Atkinson, 'Meade, James E.', *IESS*, 18; H.G. Johnson, 'James Meade's contribution to economics', *Scand JE*, 80(1), 1978, repr. in *Contemporary Economists in Perspective*, eds. H.W. Spiegel and W.J. Samuels (JAI Press, 1984).

MEANS, Gardiner Coit

Born 1896, Windham, CT, USA.
Current Post Self-employed Author and Cons., 1959–.
Past Posts Staff, Near East Relief, Turkey in Asia, 1919–20; Textile Manufacturer, Lowell, MA, 1922–9; Res. Econ., Assoc. Law, Colombia Law School, 1927–33; Econ. Adviser Finance, US Secretary Agric., 1933–5; Member, Consumer Advisory Board, NRA, 1933–5; Dir., Industrial Section, Nat. Resources Comm., 1935–9; Econ. Adviser, Nat. Resources Planning Board, 1939–40; Fiscal Analyst, US Bureau Budget, 1940–1; Assoc. Dir. Res., Advisory Board Cons., Comm. for Econ. Devlp., Washington, DC, 1943–9, 1949–54, 1954–8; Econ. Cons., Fund for Republic, 1957–9; Partner,

Lawn Grass Devlp. Co., 1951–63; Member, Maine State Planning Council, 1968–72.
Degrees BA (Chemistry), MA, PhD Harvard Univ., 1918, 1927, 1933.
Offices and Honours Phi Beta Kappa, Harvard Univ., 1968; Assoc. Evolutionary Econ., Veblen-Commons Award, 1974.
Principal Fields of Interest 611 Market Structure.
Publications *Books:* 1. *The Holding Company: Its Public Significance and its Regulation* (with J.C. Bonbright), (McGraw-Hill, 1932); 2. *The Modern Corporation and Private Property* (with A.A. Berle, Jr.), (Commerce Clearing House, 1932, Macmillan, 1933, Harcourt Brace & World, 1967; transls., Japanese, Bungado Shoten, 1958, Portuguese, Editora Ipanema, 1957, Italian, Giulio Einaudi, 1966); 3. *Industrial Prices and their Relative Inflexibility* (US Govt. Printing Office, 1935); 4. *The Modern Economy in Action* (with C.F. Ware), (Harcourt, Brace, 1936); 5. *Patterns of Resource Use* (US Govt. Printing Office, 1938); 6. *The Structure of the American Economy* (with others), (US Govt. Printing Office, 1939); 7. *Administrative Inflation and Public Policy* (A. Kramer Assoc., 1959, repr. in Senate Banking and Currency Comm., *Hearings on Employment Act Amendments*, US Govt. Printing Office, 1961); 8. *Pricing Power and the Public Interest: A Study on Steel* (Harper, 1962; transl., Japanese, Daiyamond-sha, 1962); 9. *The Corporate Revolution in America* (Collier Books, 1964); 10. *The Roots of Inflation* (with J. Blair, *et al.*), (Burt Franklin, 1975).
Articles: 1. 'The consumer and the new deal', *Annals Amer. Academy Polit. and Social Sciences*, 173, May 1934; 2. 'Price inflexibility and the requirements of a stabilizing monetary policy', *JASA*, 30, June 1935; 3. 'Big business, administered prices, and the problem of full employment', *J. Marketing*, 4, April 1940; 4. 'Monetary institutions to serve the modern economy', in *Institutional Adjustments: A Challenge to a Changing Economy*, ed. C.C. Thompson (Univ. Texas Press, 1967); 5. 'Government policy toward the large corporation', in *Big Business in Australia*

(Australian Inst. Polit. Science, 1970, repr. in *The Oriental Economist*, 1970); 6. 'The administered price theory reconfirmed', *AER*, 62(3), June 1972; 7. 'Acknowledgement of Veblen-Commons award', *JEI*, 9(2), June 1975; 8. 'Corporate power in the marketplace', *J Law E*, 26(2), June 1983.

Principal Contributions Trained as a chemist, my contribution to economics came after I had experienced productive activity in two quite different types of economy. After World War I, the Near East Relief sent me to the pre-industrial economy of Turkey to run a complex of small shops (weaving, shoe-making, carpentry, etc.) to train and supply the needs of Armenian orphans. Then, in the highly industrial US economy, I successfully ran my own small textile enterprise. Curiosity over the great difference between these two economies led me to enter the Harvard Graduate School where I learned how little economic theory had adjusted to the basic structural changes brought to Adam Smith's economy by the modern corporation. My doctoral thesis in 1933 was entitled 'The Corporate Revolution'.

My principal contributions to economics have been: (1) showing the dominant role of the modern corporation; (2) showing the separation of ownership and control which facilitated economic concentration; (3) showing the inflexibility of administered prices which undermined the automatic mechanism traditionally relied on to maintain full employment; (4) delineating the structure of the American economy; and (5) developing a method for projecting 'Patterns of Resource Use' at full employment used successfully in averting a depression at the end of World War II. In 1959, my pamphlet, *Administrative Inflation and Public Policy*, reported the discovery of a wholly new kind of inflation in which prices increase perversely in response to a fall in demand, thus producing simultaneous inflation and recession, an impossibility under traditional theories. Study of this finding showed that the new inflation does not arise from too much money chasing too few goods but from normal administrative decisions which carry an infla-

tionary bias and that it cannot be controlled by monetary and fiscal measures. Only recently have I discovered a practical way of avoiding this inflationary bias in a manner consistent with the market system. This I hope will be my final contribution.

Secondary Literature T.G. Moore, ed., 'Corporations and private property: commemorative issue on *The Modern Corporation and Private Property* by A.A. Berle Jr. and G.C. Means', *J Law E*, 26(2), June 1983.

MEEK, Ronald Lindley*

Dates and Birthplace 1917–78, New Zealand.

Posts Held Lect., Univ. Glasgow, 1948–63; Prof. Econ., Univ. Leicester, 1963–78.

Degrees BA, MA New Zealand, 1939, 1946; PhD Univ. Camb., 1949.

Publications *Books:* 1. *Studies in the Labour Theory of Value* (1956); 2. *Economics of Physiocracy* (1962); 3. *Economics and Ideology* (1967); 4. *Turgot on Progress, Sociology and Economics* (1973); 5. *Social Sciences and the Ignoble Savage* (1976); 6. *Smith, Marx and After* (1977).

Career Outstanding scholar of physiocracy, Turgot, and Adam Smith, whose work on the eighteenth century culminated in his painstaking edition of Smith's *Lectures on Jurisprudence* (1977). He also made a major contribution to the recent revival of Marxian economics by his patient and undogmatic exposition of Marx's ideas during the cold-war period of the 1940s and 1950s.

Secondary Literature I. Bradley and M. Howard, eds., *Classical and Marxian Poltical Economy. Essays in Honour of Ronald L. Meek* (Macmillan, 1982).

MEIER, Gerald Marvin

Born 1923, Tacoma, WA, USA.

Current Post Prof. Internat. Econ., Stanford Univ., Stanford, CA, USA, 1963–.

Past Posts Instr., Williams Coll.,

1952–4; Ass. Prof., Prof. Econ., Chester D. Hubbard Prof. Econ., Wesleyan Univ., 1954–9, 1959–63; Vis. Assoc. Prof., Vis. Prof., Yale Univ., 1956–7, 1958–9, 1959–61; Vis. Prof., Inst. Devlp. Stud., Univ. Sussex, 1968, Univ. W. Indies, 1969–70, Nuffield Coll. Oxford, 1974, Econ. Devlp. Inst., World Bank, 1979–80; Cons., World Bank, 1979–.

Degrees BA (Social Science) Reed Coll., 1947; BLitt. Univ. Oxford, 1952; PhD Harvard Univ., 1953; MA (h.c.) Wesleyan Univ., 1958.

Offices and Honours Phi Beta Kappa, 1947; Rhodes Scholar, 1948–50, 1951–2; Res. Student, Nuffield Coll. Oxford, 1949–52; Guggenheim Foundation Fellow, 1957–8; Brookings Nat. Res. Prof. Econ., 1961–2; Russell Sage Res. Fellow, Law/Social Science, Yale Univ., 1976–7; Res. Scholar, Rockefeller Foundation Study Center, Bellagio, 1981.

Editorial Duties Gen. Ed., *Econ. Devlp. Series* (OUP, 1971–8); Ed. Boards, *Econ. Abstracts*, *WD*.

Principal Fields of Interest 112 Economic Development Models and Theories; 400 International Economics: 121 Economic Studies of Less Industrialised Countries.

Publications *Books:* 1. *Economic Development* (with P.E. Baldwin), (Wiley, Chapman & Hall, 1957; transls., Spanish, Japanese, Arabic, Indian, Vietnamese, Polish); 2. *International Trade & Development* (Harper & Row, 1963, 1978, USIA, 1965; transl., Japanese, 1978); 3. *Leading Issues in Economic Development* (OUP, 1964, 1984); 4. *International Economic Reform, Collected Papers of Emile Després*, ed. (OUP, 1973); 5. *Problems of a World Monetary Order* (OUP, 1971, 1982); 6. *Problems of Cooperation for Development* (OUP, 1976; transl., Japanese, 1976); 7. *Employment, Trade, and Development* (Sijthoff, 1977; transl., Japanese, 1982); 8. *International Economics: Theory of Policy* (OUP, 1980); 9. *Pioneers in Development*, co-ed. (World Bank, 1984); 10. *Emerging from Poverty: The Economics that Really Matters* (OUP, 1984).

Articles: 1. 'The trade matrix: a further comment on Professor Fusch's paper', *AER*, 38(4), Sept. 1948; 2.

'Economic development and the transfer mechanism: Canada, 1895–1913', *CJE*, 19, Feb. 1953; 3. 'Legal-economic problems of private foreign investment in developing countries', *Univ. Chicago Law Rev.*, 33, Spring 1966; 4. 'Free trade and development economics', in *Value Capital and Growth: Essays in Honor of Sir John Hicks*, ed. C. Feinstein (Edinburgh Press, Aldine Press, 1968); 5. 'Development without employment', *BNLQR*, 90, Sept. 1969; 6. 'The Bretton Woods agreement — twenty-five years after', *Stanford Law Rev.*, 23, Jan. 1971; 7. 'International trade and African development: 1870–1960', in *Economics of Colonialism in Africa*, eds. P. Duignan and L.H. Gann (CUP, 1975); 8. 'Export substitution and multinational enterprise', in *Essays in Honour of Hans Singer*, ed. A. K. Cairncross (Macmillan, 1976); 9. 'On appropriate policy technology', in *Festschrift in Honor of Bert F. Hoselitz*, ed. M. Nash (Univ. Chicago Press, 1977); 10. 'Externality law and market safeguards: applications in the GATT multilateral trade negotiations', *Harvard Internat. Law J.*, 18, Summer 1977.

Principal Contributions While a graduate student, reconsidered comparative costs in terms of new welfare economics (1949), and reconsidered Viner's Canadian transfer problem in terms of Keynesian analysis (1953). Early interest in international economics aroused concern over inattention to relations between rich and poor countries. Attempted to establish economic development as a standard course for undergraduates by writing first textbook in the subject (1957). Later emphasised the relations between international trade and economic development, with particular attention to issue of 'gains from trade' versus 'gains from growth'. More recently, attention to interplay between development experience, changing views of economists, and policy. Currently, research on trade and development issues in Pacific basin. Special focus on theory of policy, with effort to integrate some of the older questions of political economy with modern techniques of policy analysis.

MEISELMAN, David I.

Born 1924, Boston, MA, USA.
Current Post Prof. Econ., Dir., Grad. Econ. Program Northern Virginia, Virginia Polytechnic Inst., State Univ., Falls Church, VA, 1971–.
Past Posts Ass. Prof. Econ., Univ. Chicago, 1958–62; Sr. Econ., US Treasury, 1964–6; Sr. Cons., World Bank, 1966; Vis. Prof. Econ., Univ. Minnesota, 1966–8; Prof. Econ., Macalester Coll., 1966–71.
Degrees BA Boston Univ., 1947; MA, PhD Univ. Chicago, 1951, 1961.
Offices and Honours Winner, Ford Foundation Doctoral Dissertation Competition, 1962; Member, Mont Pelerin Soc., 1964–; Miles B. Lane Lecturer, Georgia Inst. Technology, 1969; Pres., Philadelphia Soc., 1974; Vice-Pres., SEA, 1981–2; Fin. Standards Advisory Council, 1983–.
Editorial Duties Ed. Board, *JMCB*, 1968–72; Chairman, Ed. Board, *Pol. Rev.*, 1978–.
Principal Fields of Interest 311 Domestic Monetary Theory.
Publications *Books:* 1. *The Term Structure of Interest Rates* (Prentice-Hall, 1962); 2. *The Measurement of Corporate Sources and Uses of Funds* (with E. Shapiro), (NBER, 1964); 3. *Varieties of Monetary Experience*, ed. (Univ. Chicago Press, 1970); 4. *The Phenomenon of Worldwide Inflation*, co-ed. (AEI, 1975); 5. *Welfare Reform and the Carter Public Service Employment Program: A Critique* (Law Econ. Center, Univ. Miami School Law, 1978).
Articles: 1. 'The relative stability of monetary velocity and the investment multiplier in the United States, 1897–1958' (with M. Friedman), in *Stabilization Policies*, Commission Money and Credit (Prentice-Hall, 1963); 2. 'Bond yields and the price level: the Gibson paradox regained', in *Banking and Monetary Essays in Commemoration of the Centennial of the National Banking System* (Prentice-Hall, 1963); 3. 'More inflation — more unemployment', *Tax Rev.*, Jan. 1976; 4. 'Money, factor proportions, and real interest rates', in *Hearings on the Impact of the Federal Reserve's Money Policies on the Economy*, 94th Congress, 2nd Session, 9 June 1976 (US Govt. Printing Office, 1976).
Principal Contributions Demonstrated that markets reflect anticipations and the discounting of future events (such as interest rates and inflation); that the quantity of money is the main actor in the inflation drama; that mismanagement of money is the principal cause of economic fluctuations; and that market participants are systematically more astute than central bankers and government officials because they are motivated to be so by property rights and the lure of private gains.

MELLOR, John Williams

Born 1928, Paris, France.
Current Post Dir., Internat. Food Pol. Res. Inst., Washington, DC, 1977–.
Past Posts Prof. Agric. Econ., Econ., Asian Stud., Cornell Univ., 1952–76; Chief Econ., Agency Internat. Devlp., US Dept. State, 1976–7.
Degrees BSc, MSc (Agric. Econ.) Cornell Univ., 1950, 1951; Diploma (Agric. Econ.) Univ. Oxford, 1952; PhD Cornell Univ., 1954.
Offices and Honours AAEA Award Best Published Res., 1967; Fellow, AAAS, 1977; AAEA Award Publication of Enduring Quality, 1978; Fellow, AAEA, 1980.
Principal Fields of Interest 710 Agriculture.
Publications *Books:* 1. *The Economics of Agricultural Development* (Cornell Univ. Press, 1966); 2. *Developing Rural India: Plan and Practice* (with T.F. Weaver, *et al.*), (Cornell Univ. Press, 1968); 3. *The New Economics of Growth — A Strategy for India and the Developing World* (Cornell Univ. Press, 1976); 4. *India: a Rising Middle Power*, ed. (Westview Press, 1979).
Articles: 1. 'The role of agriculture in economic development' (with B.F. Johnston), *AER*, 51(4), Sept. 1961; 2. 'The use and productivity of farm family labor in early stages of agricultural development', *JFE*, 45(3), Aug. 1963; 3. 'Accelerated growth in agricultural production and the intersectoral transfer of resources', *EDCC*, 22(1), Oct.

1973; 4. 'Food price policy and income distribution in low income countries', *EDCC*, 27(1), Oct. 1978; 5. 'Technological change, distributive bias and labor transfer in a two sector economy (with U. Lele), *OEP*, 34(3), Nov. 1982.

Principal Contributions Delineation of the role of the agricultural sector in the economic growth of low-income countries. Particular emphasis given to documenting and conceptualising the level and composition of intersectoral resource transfers. For these purposes two sector models have been explored: critiques of standard growth theory drawn and social accounting methods applied. A variant of this work has been analysis of the links between growth in agricultural production and income and small-scale non-agricultural activities in rural market towns. Work on labour transfers has conceptualised the basis of peasant labour allocations, the role of marketing of food in determining inter-sectoral labour transfers, and the interaction of change in technology with these processes. Work on agricultural price policy has dealt with the interaction of income distribution and production effects.

MELMAN, Seymour

Born 1917, New York City, NY, USA.
Current Post Prof. Industrial Eng., Columbia Univ., NY, USA, 1963–.
Past Posts Res. Staff, Nat. Industrial Conf. Board, 1944–5; Instr., Ass. Prof., Assoc. Prof., Columbia Univ., 1948–51, 1951–6, 1956–63; Cons., UN on Economic Conversion, 1979–80; Eugene Lan Vis. Prof. Social Change, Swarthmore Coll., PA, 1984.
Degrees BSS City Coll. NY, 1939; PhD Columbia Univ., 1949.
Offices and Honours Vice-Pres., Sarah L. Poiley Memorial Award, NY Academy Sciences, 1974–5, 1980; Pres., Assoc. Evolutionary Econ., 1975; Great Teacher Award, Soc. Older Grads. Columbia Univ., 1981; Hon. Member Faculty, Industrial Coll. Armed Forces, 1981; Rolex Award for Enterprise, 1981.
Principal Fields of Interest 051 Capitalist Economic Systems; 114 Econ-

omics of War, Defence, and Disarmament; 226 Productivity and Growth; Theory and Data.

Publications *Books:* 1. *Dynamic Factors in Industrial Productivity* (Wiley, 1956); 2. *Inspection for Disarmament*, ed. (Columbia Univ. Press, 1958); 3. *Decision-Making and Productivity* (Wiley, 1958); 4. *The Peace Race* (Ballantine, 1961); 5. *Our Depleted Society* (Holt, Rinehart & Winston, 1965); 6. *Pentagon Capitalism: The Political Economy of War* (McGraw-Hill, 1970); 7. *Conversion of Industry from a Military to Civilian Economy*, 6 vols, ed. (Praeger, 1970); 8. *The Permanent War Economy: American Capitalism in Decline* (Simon & Schuster, 1974); 9. *Profits Without Production* (Knopf, 1983).

Articles: 1. 'The rise of administrative overheads in the manufacturing industries of the United States 1899–1947', *OEP*, 3, Feb. 1951; 2. 'Administration and production cost in relation to size of firms', *Appl. Stats.*, 3, March 1954; 3. 'Industrial productivity in relation to the cost of management', *Productivity Measurement Rev.*, 3, May 1956; 4. 'Are there economic alternatives to arms prosperity?', *Annals Amer. Academy Polit. and Social Science*, 14, Jan. 1964, repr. in *Blatter für Deutsche und Internationale Politik*, Feb. 1964; 5. 'The peaceful world of economics I', *JEI*, 6(1), March 1972; 6. 'The impact of economics on technology', *JEI*, 9(1), March 1975; 7. 'Decision-making and productivity as economic variables', *JEI*, 10(1), June 1976; 8. 'Alternative criteria for the design of means of production', *Theory and Soc.*, 10, 1981; 9. 'Conversion from military to civilian economy', *Annals New York Academy Sciences*, 368, 1981; 10. 'Alternatives for the organization of work in computer-assisted manufacturing', *Annals New York Academy Sciences*, 371, 1984.

Principal Contributions I have explored the dynamics of production decision-making in industry and the determinants of industrial productivity. My early work on management methods (1949–58) defined the growing cost of managing in American industry. That growth has been a function of enlarged scope and intensity of administrative functions, and has been independent of productivity. Studies of machinery-producing industries (1958–9) gave an early warning of the breakdown of cost-minimising in US industry under the impact of the military economy and the declining rate of productivity growth in US manufacturing after 1965.

After 1958 a series of books, monographs, and articles on military economy disclosed the following characteristics: firms in the US military economy operate to maximise cost and subsidy; engineering design, production methods and administrative methods are shaped by this unique microeconomy. The structure of US military economy was found to be that of a multidivision firm (of contractors) operating under a central administrative office (the Pentagon). Major macroeconomic effects include depressing the aggregate rate of productivity growth and depleting effects on infrastructure. These investigations disclosed requirement for carrying out the conversion of enterprises, manufacturing facilities, and military bases from military to civilian work. Recent studies disclosed that top managers have abandoned their 200-year-old interest and competence in the organisation of work. These competences have been displaced in favour of making money rather than making goods. This transformation, together with the inefficient military system, has depressed the economic and technical competence of US industry and given rise to a new problem of industrial stagnation.

MELTZER, Allan H.

Born 1928, Boston, MA, USA.
Current Post John M. Olin Prof. Polit. Econ. and Public Pol., Carnegie-Mellon Univ., Pittsburgh, PA, USA, 1980–.
Past Posts Lect., Wharton School, Univ. Penn., 1956–7; Ass. Prof., Assoc. Prof., Grad. School Industrial Admin., Carnegie Inst. Technology, 1957–61, 1961–4; Ford Foundation Vis. Prof., Univ. Chicago, 1964–5; Prof., Carnegie Inst. Technology (now Carnegie-Mellon Univ.), 1964–80; Vis. Prof. Econ.,

Harvard Univ., 1967–8, Yugoslav Inst. Econ. Res., Belgrade, Yugoslavia, 1968; Ford Disting. Res. Prof., Maurice Falk Prof. Econ. and Social Science, Carnegie-Mellon Univ., 1967–70, 1970–80; Vis. Prof., Fundacao Getulio Vargas, Rio de Janeiro, Brazil, 1976–9; Vis. Fellow, Hoover Inst., Stanford Univ., 1977–8; Vis. Prof., City Univ., London, England, 1980.
Degrees BA Duke Univ., Durham, NC, 1948; MA, PhD UCLA, 1955, 1958.
Offices and Honours Fulbright Fellow, 1955–6; Ford Faculty Res. Fellow, 1962–3; Vice-Pres., AFA, WEA, 1983–4; Disting. Professional Achievement Award, UCLA, 1983.
Editorial Duties Advisory Board, *J Mon E*; Ed. Board, *Pol. Rev.*; Co-ed., *Carnegie Rochester Conf. Series on Public Pol.*, *Carnegie Papers on Polit. Econ.*.
Principal Fields of Interest 023 Macroeconomic Theory; 025 Social Choice; Bureaucratic Performance; 310 Domestic Monetary and Financial Theory and Institutions.
Publications *Books:* 1. *A Study of the Dealer Market for U.S. Government Securities* (with G. von der Linde), (US Govt. Printing Office, 1960); 2. *Federal Tax Treatment of State and Local Securities* (with D. Ott), (Brookings Inst., 1963); 3. *An Analysis of Federal Reserve Monetary Policymaking* (with K. Brunner), (US Govt. Printing Office, 1964); 4. *International Lending and the IMF*, ed. (Heritage Foundation, 1983); 5. *Theory, Policy, Institutions: Papers from the Carnegie-Rochester Conferences on Public Policy*, co-ed. (with K. Brunner), (N-H, 1983); 6. *Keynes on Monetary Reform and the International Economic Order* (Univ. London, 1984).
Articles: 1. 'The demand for money: the evidence from the time series', *JPE*, 71, June 1963; 2. 'The place of financial intermediaries in the transmission of monetary policy', *AER*, 53(2), May 1963; 3. 'A credit market theory of the money supply and an explanation of two puzzles in US monetary policy' (with K. Brunner), *RISE*, 13(5), May 1966; repr. in *Essays in Honor of Marco Fanno*, II (Padova Cedam, 1966); 4. 'The meaning of monetary indicators'

(with K. Brunner), in *Monetary Process and Policy: A Symposium*, ed. G. Horwich (Richard D. Irwin, 1967); 5. 'Liquidity traps for money, bank credit, and interest rates' (with K. Brunner), *JPE*, 76, Jan.–Feb. 1968; 6. 'The uses of money: money in the theory of an exchange economy' (with K. Brunner), *AER*, 61(5), Dec. 1971; 7. 'An aggregative theory for a closed economy' (with K. Brunner), in *Monetarism*, ed. J. Stein (N-H, 1976); 8. 'Discussion: interwar economics from the perspective of the 1970's', *AER*, 70(2), May 1980; 9. 'Comment on "monetarist interpretations of the great depression"', in *The Great Depression Revisited*, ed. K. Brunner (Martinus Nijhoff, 1981); 10. 'Principles que orientan a politica monetaria braxileira', *Edicoes Multiplic.*, April 1981.

Principal Contributions Early work concentrated on the supply and demand for money. A series of studies of money supply included a study of Federal Reserve policy-making (with Karl Brunner), and analysed the basis of Federal Reserve actions and their reason for concentrating attention on free reserves or interest rates. The study showed that Federal Reserve actions from the 1920s to the early 1960s were directed at the control of borrowing of free reserves and the neglect of money, output and price level. Subsequent work on financial markets and intermediation led to the development of a general equilibrium model of credit, money interest rates, asset prices, output and the price level. Recent work is in two areas. Scott Richard and I have developed and tested models of the size of government and other aspects of public choice. I have become interested in the effects of government policies on variability. This has led to an examination of Keynes's major works and a reinterpretation of the *General Theory*. I see these recent interests as part of a broader interest in the role of institutions in relation to economic theory.

MENGER, Anton*

Dates and Birthplace 1841–1906, Maniow, Austro-Hungary.

Posts Held Prof. Civil Procedure, Univ. Vienna, 1877.

Degrees Grad. Law Univ. Vienna, 1872.

Publications *Books:* 1. *The Right to the Whole Produce of Labour* (1886, 1889); 2. *Das bürgerliche Recht und die besitzlosen Volksklassen* (1890); 3. *Uber die sozialen Aufgaben der Rechtswissenschaft* (1895); 4. *Neue Staatslehre* (1903).

Career Brother of Carl Menger. As a lawyer, he examined the juridical theory of socialism as a counterpart to the more usual interest in its economic theory. He detected antecedents of Marx in the early socialists and criticised Marxism as an ethical theory about entitlements to a larger share in the national product. He influenced the compilers of the German Civil Code (1896) to reflect the needs of poorer citizens, advocating a form of State socialism in which the rights of consumers are to be defended against those of producers.

Secondary Literature G. Gurvitch, 'Menger, Anton', *ESS*, 9.

MENGER, Carl*

Dates and Birthplace 1840–1921, Neu Sandec, Austro-Hungary.

Posts Held Member, Press Section, Austrian Prime Minister's Office: Lect., Extraordinary Prof., Full Prof., Univ. Vienna, 1873, 1879–1903; Tutor, Archduke Rudolf, 1876.

Degrees Dr Law Univ. Cracow, 1867.

Publications *Books:* 1. *Principles of Economics* (1871, 1934, 1950); 2. *Problems of Economics and Sociology*, ed. L. Schneider (1883, 1963); 3. *Investigations into the Method of the Social Sciences with Special Reference to Economics* (1884, 1985); 4. *Collected Works of Carl Menger*, 4 vols (1933–6).

Career The founder of the Austrian school of marginal analysis whose international influence was wider than that of his co-discoverers, Walras and Jevons. The *Principles* is a detailed account of the relations between utility, value and price. He was also the initiator and a major participant in the 'Methodenstreit' with the German Historical School. He argued that a 'compositive method' of analysing society was more effective than the use of history to discover empirical laws about society. His contribution to the 1892 dispute on the reform of the Austrian currency was the basis of later Austrian theory on the value of money.

Secondary Literature F.A. von Hayek, 'Menger, Carl', *IESS*, 10; J.A. Schumpeter, 'Carl Menger, 1840–1921', in *Ten Great Economists from Marx to Keynes* (OUP, 1951); J.R. Hicks and W. Weber, eds. *Carl Menger and the Austrian School of Economics (OUP, 1973)*.

MERCIER DE LA RIVIÈRE, Pierre Paul*

Dates and Birthplace 1720–93, Saumur, France.

Posts Held Member, Parlement de Paris, 1747–59, 1764–.

Publications *Books:* 1. *L'ordre naturel et essentiel des sociétés politiques* (1767); 2. *L'intérêt général de l'état* (1770); 3. *De l'instruction publique* (1775); 4. *Essais sur les maximes et loi fondamentales de la monarchie françoise* (1789); 5. *Palladium de la constitution politique* (1790).

Career His *Ordre naturel* . . . concentrated on the political aspects of physiocracy in which he argued that there is a natural law of property which is based on the physical order of nature, and which underlies all other laws. Taxation and the use of public revenue by the ruler are both governed by the natural law of property. His *De l'instruction publique* outlined the system of education which would eventually bring about the ideal society in which nations are at peace, and men cease to profit at the expense of others.

Secondary Literature F. Mauro, 'Mercier de la Rivière', *IESS*, 10.

MERTON, Robert C.

Born 1944, New York City, NY, USA.

Current Post J.C. Penney Prof. Management, A.P. Sloan School Management, MIT, Cambridge, MA, USA, 1980–.

Past Posts Instr. Econ., MIT, 1969–70; Ass. Prof. Fin. and Management, Assoc. Prof. Fin., Prof. Fin., MIT, 1970–3, 1973–4, 1974–80.

Degrees BS (Eng., Maths.) Columbia Univ., 1966; MS (Appl. Maths.) Cal. Inst. Technology, 1967; PhD MIT, 1970.

Offices and Honours Res. Assoc., NBER, 1979–. Dir., Vice-Pres., Pres., AFA, 1982–4, 1985; Fellow, Em Soc, 1983–; Leo Melamed Prize, Univ. Chicago, 1983.

Editorial Duties Assoc. Ed., *Int ER*, 1972–7, *J Fin*, 1973–7, *JMCB*, 1974–9, *J Bank Fin*, 1977–9, *J Fin. Econ.*, 1977–83; Co-ed., *J Fin. Econ.*, 1974–7.

Principal Fields of Interest 026 Economics of Uncertainty and Information; 210 Econometric, Statistical and Mathematical Methods and Models; 520 Business Finance and Investment.

Publications *Books:* 1. *The Collected Scientific Papers of Paul A. Samuelson*, 3, ed. (MIT Press, 1972).

Articles: 1. 'Lifetime portfolio selection under uncertainty: the continuous-time case', *REStat*, 51(3), Aug. 1969; 2. 'Optimum consumption and portfolio rules in a continuous-time model', *JET*, 3(4), Dec. 1971, repr. in *Stochastic Optimization Models in Finance*, eds. W.T. Ziemba and R.G. Vickson (Academic Press, 1975); 3. 'Theory of rational option-pricing', *Bell JE*, 4, Spring 1973; 4. 'An intertemporal capital asset pricing model', *Em*, 41(5), Sept. 1973, repr. in *Studies in Risk and Return*, eds. J. Bicksler and I. Friend (Ballinger, 1975); 5. 'On the pricing of corporate debt: the risk structure of interest rates', *J Fin*, 29(2), May 1974; 6. 'An asymptotic theory of growth under uncertainty', *REStud*, 42(3), July 1975; 7. 'On the pricing of contingent claims and the Modigliani-Miller theorem', *J Fin. Econ.*, 5(2), Nov. 1977; 8. 'On market timing and investment performance part 1: an equilibrium theory of value for market forecasts', *J Bus*, 54, July 1981; 9. 'On the microeconomic theory of investment under uncertainty', in *Handbook of Mathematic Economics*, 2, eds. K. Arrow and M. Intriligator (N-H, 1982); 10. 'On the role of social security as a means for efficient risk-bearing in an economy where human capital is not tradeable', in *Financial*

Aspects of the US Pension system, eds. Z. Bodie and J. Shoven (Univ. Chicago Press, 1984).

MEYER, John Robert

Born 1927, Pasco, WA, USA.
Current Post James W. Harpel Prof. Capital Formation and Econ. Growth, Kennedy School Govt., Harvard Univ., Cambridge, MA, USA, 1983–.
Past Posts Prof. Econ., Prof. Transportation, Logistics and Distrib., Harvard Bus. School, Harvard Univ., 1959–68, 1973–83; Pres., NBER, 1967–77; Prof. Econ., Yale Univ., 1968–73; Vice-Chairman Board, Union Pacific Corp., 1981–3.
Degrees BA Univ. Washington, 1950; PhD Harvard Univ., 1955; Hon. Dr Science, Lowell Technological Inst., 1973.
Offices and Honours Univ. Washington Memorial Scholar, 1949; Jr. Fellow, David A. Wells Prize, Harvard Univ., 1953–5, 1955; Guggenheim Foundation Fellow, 1958–9; Ford Foundation Faculty Res. Fellow, 1962–3; Exec. Comm. AEA, 1971–3; Fellow, AAAS, Em Soc; Phi Beta Kappa.
Editorial Duties Assoc. Ed., *REStat*, 1973–; Ed. Board, *Socio-Econ. Planning Sciences*, 1973–, *Regional Science and Urban Econ.*, 1975–8, *QREB*, 1973–, *Internat. J. Transport Econ.*, 1976–.
Principal Fields of Interest 042 North American (excluding Mexican) Economic History; 615 Economics of Transportation; 520 Business Finance and Investment.
Publications *Books:* 1. *The Investment Decision: An Empirical Inquiry* (with E. Kuh), (Harvard Univ. Press, 1957); 2. *The Economics of Competition in the Transportation Industries* (with M.J. Peck, C. Zwick and J. Stenason), (Harvard Univ. Press, 1959); 3. *The Economics of Slavery and Other Essays on the Quantitative Study of Economic History* (with A.H. Conrad), (Aldine Press, 1964); 4. *The Urban Transportation Problem* (with J.F. Kain and M. Wohl), (Harvard Univ. Press, 1965); 5. *Techniques of Transport Planning*, 2 vols (with D. Kresge, M. Straszheim

and P. Roberts), (Brookings Inst. 1970); 6. *Managerial Economics* (with D. Farrar), (Prentice-Hall, 1970); 7. *Essays in Regional Economics*, co-ed. (with J.F. Kain), (Harvard Univ. Press, 1971); 8. *The Economics of Competition in the Telecommunications Industry* (with others), (Charles River Assoc., 1979); 9. *Autos, Transit and Cities* (with J.A. Gomez-Ibanez), (Harvard Univ. Press, 1981); 10. *Airline Deregulation: The Early Experience* (with C.V. Oster, et al.), (Auburn House, 1981).

Articles: 1. 'Acceleration and related theories of investment: an empirical inquiry' (with E. Kuh), *REStat*, 37(5), Aug. 1955; 2. 'An input-output approach to evaluating the influence of exports on British industrial production in the late 19th century', *Explor. Entrepreneurial Hist.*, Fall 1955; 3. Correlation and regression estimates when data are ratios' (with E. Kuh), *Em*, 23, Oct. 1955; 4. 'Economic theory, statistical inference and economic history' (with A.H. Conrad), *JEH*, 17, Dec. 1957; 5. 'How extraneous are extraneous estimates?' (with E. Kuh), *REStat*, 39(6), Nov. 1957; 6. 'The economics of slavery in the ante-bellum south' (with A.H. Conrad), *JPE*, 66, April 1958; 7. 'The urban disamenity revisited' (with R.A. Leone), in *Public Economics and the Quality of Life*, eds. L. Wingo and A. Evans (JHUP, 1977); 8. 'The New England states and their economic future: some implications of a changing industrial environment' (with R.A. Leone), *AER*, 68(2), May 1978; 9. 'Measurement and analysis of productivity in transportation industries' (with J.A. Gomez-Ibanez), in *New Developments in Productivity Measurement and Analysis* (Univ. Chicago Press, 1980); 10. 'Toward a better understanding of deregulation: some hypotheses and observations', *Internat. J. Transport Econ.*, 10(1–2), April–Aug. 1983.

Principal Contributions The constant concern in my professional work has been the empirical measurement and evaluation of hypotheses concerning behavioural phenomena in economics, with particular emphasis on the use of large microdata sets to test hypotheses previously tested only against highly aggregated national or industry data. Methodologically, this has also led me to be interested in the compatibility and comparability of macro and micro data sets.

Some of my earliest research was concerned with historical applications, testing hypotheses concerning the profitability of slavery in the Southern US prior to the Civil War, and the hiatus in English industrial development of the second half of the nineteenth century. From these I proceeded to evaluate different hypotheses about the determinants of business investment decisions in the US and, in particular, how those determinants might vary at different stages of the business cycle. Finally, I have been interested in achieving a better understanding of the behaviour of so-called 'regulated industries' under different regulatory regimes and, most recently, in the transition away from regulation.

MIESZKOWSKI, Peter Michael

Born 1936, Pelplin, Poland.
Current Post Cline Prof. Econ. Fin., Rice Univ., Houston, TX, 1982–.
Past Posts Ass. Prof., Assoc. Prof., Yale Univ., 1962–7, 1967–71; Prof. Econ., Queen's Univ., Ont., Canada, 1971–4; Prof. Econ, Univ. Houston, 1974–81.
Degrees BSc, MA McGill Univ., 1957, 1959; PhD Johns Hopkins Univ., 1963.
Offices and Honours Post-doctoral fellow, Univ. Chicago, 1964–5.
Editorial Duties Assoc. Ed., *J Pub E*, *JUE*.
Principal Fields of Interest 320 Fiscal Theory and Policy; 931 Urban Economics.
Publications *Books:* 1. *Current Issues in Urban Economics*, co-ed. (with M. Straszhem), (JHUP, 1979); 2. *Fiscal Federalism and Grants-in-aided*, co-ed. (with W. Oakland), (Urban Inst., 1979).
Articles: 1. 'On the theory of tax incidence', *JPE*, 74, June 1967; 2. 'Is a negative income tax practical?' (with J. Tobin and J. Pechman), *Yale Law J.*, 77(1), Nov. 1967; 3. 'The effects of unionization of the distribution of in-

come: a general equilibrium approach' (with H.G. Johnson), *QJE*, 84(4), Nov. 1970; 4. 'The property tax: excise tax or profits tax?', *J Pub E*, 1(1), April 1972; 5. 'Public goods, efficiency, and regional fiscal equilization' (with F. Flatters and V. Henderson), *J Pub E*, 3(2), May 1974; 6. 'The taxation of expenditure rather than income', in *The Economics of Taxation*, eds. H. Aaron and M.J. Boskin (Brookings Inst., 1980); 7. 'The new view of the incidence of the property tax: a reappraisal', in *Local Provision of Public Services: The Tiebout Model After Twenty-Five Years*, eds. P. Mieszkowski and G.R. Zodrow (Academic Press, 1983).
Principal Contributions Applied income distribution problems with special emphasis on tax incidence theory. Also, general equilibrium effects of trade unions on income distribution. In urban economics, analysis of racial discrimination in housing, related work on the determinants of real estate values and the effects of externalities on property values. Also contributions on the theory of local public goods, and the theory of capitalisation. Work on the theory of taxation includes analysis of the implementation of an expenditure tax system and foreign trade aspects of taxation.

MIKESELL, Raymond Frech

Born 1913, Eaton, OH, USA.
Current Post W.E. Miner Prof. Econ., Univ. Oregon, Eugene, OR, USA, 1974–.
Past Posts Ass. Prof., Univ. Washington, Seattle, 1937–46; Prof. Univ. Virginia, Charlottesville, 1946–56; Econ., US Office Price Admin., Washington, DC, 1941–2; Sr. Econ, US Dept. Treasury, 1942–6; Staff, US President's Materials Pol. Comm., 1951; Staff, US President's Council Econ. Advisers, 1955–6; Sr. Res. Assoc., NBER, 1970.
Degrees BA, MA, PhD Ohio State Univ. 1935, 1937, 1939.
Offices and Honours Adviser, Bretton Woods Internat. Monetary and Fin. Conf., 1944; US Delegation, UNCTAD,

Geneva, 1964; Vice-Pres., Fellow, Academy Internat. Bus., 1971–2, 1981–; Member, Advisory Council, Overseas Private Investment Corp., 1971–4; Co-Chairman, Res. Council, Center for Strategic and Internat. Stud., Georgetown Univ., 1973–81; Member, Board Visitors, Amer. Grad. School Internat. Management, 1977–80; Member, Nat. Materials Advisory Board, US Nat. Academy Sciences, 1981–4; Cons., US Dept. State, 1947–53, 1961–83, Organization Amer. States, 1954–75, US Office Technical Assessment, 1978–80.

Editorial Duties Ed. Board, *AER*, 1953–5, *J. Internat. Bus.*, 1977, *J. Resource Management and Technology*, 1983–.

Principal Fields of Interest 721 Natural Resources; 440 International Investment and Foreign Aid; 430 Balance of Payments: International Finance.

Publications *Books:* 1. *United States Economic Policy and International Relations* (McGraw-Hill, 1952); 2. *Foreign Exchange in the Postwar World* (Twentieth-Century Fund, 1954); 3. *Foreign Investment in the Petroleum and Mineral Industries* (JHUP, 1971); 4. *Foreign Dollar Balances and the International Role of the Dollar* (with H. Furth), (*NBER*, 1974); 5. *Rules for Floating Exchange Rates* (with H. Goldstein), (Internat. Fin. Section, Princeton Univ, 1975); 6. *Rate of Discount for Evaluating Public Projects* (AEI, 1978); 7. *The World Copper Industry* (JHUP, 1979); 8. *US Export Competitiveness in Manufactures in Third World Markets* (with M. Farah), (Georgetown Univ. Press, 1980); 9. *Foreign Investment in Mining Projects* (OGH, 1983); 10. *Petroleum Company Operations and Agreements in Developing Countries* (JHUP, 1984).

Articles: 1. 'Oligopoly and the short-run demand for labor', *QJE*, 55(5), Nov. 1940; 2. 'The role of the international monetary agreements in a world of planned economies', *JPE*, 55(6), Dec. 1947, repr. in *Readings in the Theory of International Trade*, eds. H. Ellis and L. Metzler (Blakiston, 1949); 3. 'Regional multilateral payments arrangements', *QJE*, 57(4), Aug. 1948; 4. 'The effectiveness of monetary policy: recent British experi-

ence', (with W.L. Smith), *JPE*, 65(1), Feb. 1957; 5. 'International commodity stabilization schemes and export problems of developing countries', *AER*, 53(2), May 1963; 6. 'The theory of common markets as applied to regional arrangements among developing countries', in *International Trade Theory in a Developing World*, eds. R.F. Harrod and D. Hague (Macmillan, 1964), repr. in *International Economic Policies and their Theoretical Foundations*, ed. J. Letiche (Academy Press, 1982); 7. 'The emergence of the world bank as a development institution', in *Bretton Woods Revisited*, eds. A.L.K. Acheson, et al. (Univ. Toronto Press, 1972); 8. 'The Eurodollar market and the foreign demand for liquid dollar assets', *JMCB*, 4(3), Aug. 1972; 9. 'The nature of the savings function in developing countries: a survey of the theoretical empirical literature' (with J.E. Zinser), *JEL*, 11(1), March 1973; 10. 'The rate of exploitation of exhaustible resources: the case of an export economy', *Natural Resources Forum*, 1, Oct. 1976.

Principal Contributions My pre-World War II research concentrated on ideas in my dissertation on marginal productivity theory and unemployment and resulted in theoretical publications on the demand for labour in the *QJE* and the *AER*. During the war, my work with the US Treasury Department in Washington and the Middle East, followed by participation in the Bretton Woods Conference in 1944, resulted in a number of publications on international financial institutions and foreign exchange, including *Foreign Exchange in the Postwar World*. My association with the President's Materials Policy Commission together with my interest in foreign direct investment led to a series of case studies on foreign investment in nonfuel minerals and petroleum. The material for these case studies was derived from a number of missions to Third World countries for the UN and private mining companies plus research abroad financed by Resources for the Future. This work has resulted in several books on foreign investment in the resource industries and on the economics of the copper industry, which subjects constitute my most significant contributions to the literature. At the same time I continued my research on international finance and foreign exchange with a special interest in the Eurodollar market, and operations of which I studied in the course of visits to the Bank of International Settlements and leading multinational banks. This led to several publications, including two by NBER. Currently I am conducting research on mineral issues, including the economics of stockpiling, but am also engaged, with former graduate students, in joint research projects on international trade and foreign exchange.

MILL, James*

Dates and Birthplace 1773–1836, Forfar, Scotland.

Posts Held Preacher, 1798–1802; Professional writer, 1802–19; Officer, East India Company, 1819–36.

Degrees BA Univ. Edinburgh.

Publications *Books:* 1. *History of British India*, 3 vols (1817, 1968); 2. *Elements of Political Economy* (1821); 3. *Analysis of the Phenomena of the Human Mind*, 2 vols (1828).

Career The disciple and promotor of Jeremy Bentham, he developed the economic side of utilitarian analysis and incorporated the ideas of Malthus and Ricardo. It was through James Mill that a group of followers of Bentham, the so-called 'philosophical radicals' was formed. His *Elements* ... is the first English-language textbook of economics.

Secondary Literature A. Bain, *James Mill* (Macmillan, 1882); D. Winch, *Selected Economic Writings of James Mill* (Oliver & Boyd, 1966); W.J. Barber, *British Economic Thought and India, 1600–1858* (OUP, 1975); W.O. Thweatt, 'James Mill and the early development of comparative advantage', *HOPE*, 8(2), Summer 1976.

MILL, John Stuart*

Dates and Birthplace 1806–73, London, England.

Posts Held Officer, East India Company, 1823–58.

Offices and Honours MP Westminster, 1865–8.

Publications *Books:* 1. *A System of Logic* (1843); 2. *Essays on Some Unsettled Questions of Political Economy* (1844, 1948); 3. *Principles of Political Economy* (1848, 1903); 4. *On Liberty* (1859); 5. *Utilitarianism* (1861); 6. *Autobiography* (1873, 1924); 7. J.S. Mill, *Collected Works*, 9 vols, ed. J.M. Robson (Univ. Toronto Press, 1963–74).

Career The dominant figure of mid-nineteenth-century British political economy, he was educated by his father James as an ardent Benthamite utilitarian, but his mental crisis of 1826 induced serious modifications of his views. Saint-Simon, Comte and other writers can be counted as influences subsequent to this period, as can his friendship with his future wife, Harriet Taylor. His *System of Logic* established his reputation as a major thinker, and it is his philosophical and political writings, most notably *On Liberty*, that are the chief source of his continuing fame. However, the *Principles* is almost equally remembered, becoming the leading economic textbook in the English-speaking world for the rest of the century. It was intended to modify the abstract and sometimes cold-hearted classical political economy. Though his introduction of an historical method did not advance the subject greatly, his perception of the limits to the applicability of abstract-deductive analysis was important. His attacks on the cult of wealth, his concern with the problems of growth and development, his treatment of the question of population and his sympathy with the working man all reflect his humanitarian approach. His analytical ideas on money, international trade and the dynamics of distribution have all been highly praised. On the role of the State in economic life, he struck a judicious balance between his defence of individual freedom and the recognition of a need for some State intervention, in cases such as that of infant industries. The dominance of Mill in subsequent years was such that Jevons felt it necessary to attack him in order to win a favourable hearing for marginal utility economics.

Secondary Literature M. St John Packe, *The Life of John Stuart Mill* (Secker & Warburg, 1954); J.M. Robson, *The Improvement of Mankind: The Social and Political Thought of J.S. Mill* (Univ. Toronto Press, 1968); V.W. Bladen, 'Mill, John Stuart: economic considerations', *IESS*, 10; P. Schwartz, *The New Political Economy of J.S. Mill* (Weidenfeld & Nicolson, 1972); S. Hollander, *The Economics of John Stuart Mill* (University of Toronto Press, Blackwell, 1985).

MILLER, Herman P.

Born 1921, New York City, NY, USA.
Current Post Pres., H. P. Miller Inc., Econ. Cons., Silver Spring, MD, USA, 1972–.
Past Posts Chief, Consumer Income, Proj. Dir., Hist. Stats. US, Special Ass. Dir., Chief Pop. Division, US Bureau of Census, 1947–72; Adjuct. Prof. Econ., American Univ., 1959–64, UCLA, 1964–5, Temple Univ., 1967–74, George Washington Univ. 1971.
Degrees BSS City Coll. NY, 1942; MA George Washington Univ., 1950; PhD American Univ., 1954.
Offices and Honours Fellow, ASA; Gold Medal for Meritorious Service, US Dept. Commerce.
Principal Fields of Interest 220 Economic and Social Statistics; 840 Demographic Economics; 850 Human Capital.
Publications *Books:* 1. *Income of American People* (Wiley, 1954); 2. *Colonial Times to 1957* (US Govt. Printing Office, 1957); 3. *Income Distribution in the United States* (US Govt. Printing Office, 1966); 4. *Present Value of Estimated Lifetime Earnings* (with R. Horsneth), (Census Bureau, 1967); 5. *Rich Man, Poor Man* (T. Y. Crowell, 1971).
Articles: 1. 'Annual and lifetime income in relation to education', *AER*, 50(5), Dec. 1960; 2. 'Lifetime income and economic growth', AER, 55(4), Sept. 1965; 3. 'State differentials in income concentration' (with A. Al-Samarrie), AER, 57(1), March 1967; 4.

'Some determinants of variation in earnings of college men' (with R. H. Reed), *JHR*, 5(2), Spring 1970.
Principal Contributions During the first 30 years of my career (from 1942–72) my efforts were largely devoted to research pertaining to income distribution in the US. During this period I worked on the development of household surveys of income data at the Bureau of Census. I developed procedures for collecting, processing and tabulating these data and wrote books and articles appraising the results and interpreting the findings. These surveys are now an established part of the statistical tools in the US and abroad. Since 1972 I have been working largely as a self-employed consulting, forensic economist, who applies economic theories and data to the courtroom in cases involving loss of income due to death, injury, discrimination and other factors. My conclusions have been incorporated in the findings of appellate courts in several jurisdictions, thereby exerting a significant influence on the case law in the US involving wrongful death and personal injury.

MILLER, Marcus May

Born 1941, Darjeeling, India.
Current Post Prof. Econ., Univ. Warwick, Coventry, England, 1978–.
Past Posts Lect. Econ., LSE, 1967–76; Econ. Ass., Bank of England, 1972–3; Vis. Assoc. Prof. Internat. Fin., Grad School Bus., Univ. Chicago, 1976; Prof. Econ., Univ. Manchester, 1976–8; Houblon-Norman Fellow, Bank of England, 1981–2; Vis. Prof. Public and Internat. Affairs, Woodrow Wilson School, Princeton Univ., 1983–4.
Degrees BA (Philo., Polit. & Econ.), MA Univ. Oxford, 1965, 1982; MA, PhD Yale Univ., 1964, 1971.
Offices and Honours Exec. Comm., AUTE, 1975–80; Chairman, Academic Panel UK Treasury, 1975–80; Specialist Adviser, UK House of Commons Treasury and Civil Service Comm., 1980–1; Exec. Comm., NIESR, 1980–.
Editorial Duties Joint Ed., *Ec*, 1973–6; Ed. Board, *REStud*, 1971–6.

Principal Fields of Interest 300 Domestic Monetary and Fiscal Theory.

Publications *Books:* 1. *Monetary Policy and Economic Activity in West Germany*, co-ed. (with A. S. Courakis and S. Frowen), (Intertext, 1977); 2. *Essays on Fiscal and Monetary Policy*, co-ed. (with M. J. Artis), (OUP, 1981, repr. in *Contemporary Problems of Economic Policy*, eds. R. C. O. Matthews and J. R. Sargent (Methuen, 1983).

Articles: 1. 'Can a rise in import prices be inflationary and deflationary? Economists and UK inflation', *AER* 66(4), Sept. 1976; 2. 'The Precautionary demand for narrow and broad money' (with C. Sprenkle), *Ec*, N.S., 47, Nov. 1980; 3. 'The static economic effects of the UK joining the EEC' (with J. Spencer), *REStud*, 44(1), Feb. 1977; 4. 'Monetary control in the UK', *Camb JE*, 5(1), March 1981; 5. 'Monetary policy and international competitiveness' (with W. Buiter), *OEP*, 33, Suppl., July 1981, repr. in *The Money Supply and the Exchange Rate*, eds. W. Eltis and P. Sinclair (OUP, 1981); 6. 'Real exchange rate overshooting and the output cost of bringing down inflation' (with W. Buiter), *Europ ER*, 18(1–2), May–June 1982; 7. 'Inflation adjusting the public sector financial deficit', in *The 1982 Budget*, ed. J. Kay (Blackwell, 1982); 8. 'Changing the rules: economic consequences of the Thatcher regime' (with W. Buiter), *Brookings Papers Econ. Activity*, 2, 1983; 9. 'The effects of government expenditure on the term structure of interest rates' (with S. J. Turnovsky), *JMCB*, 16(1), Feb. 1984.

Principal Contributions My Yale dissertation on monetary policy in the UK 1954–65 treated the determination of monetary aggregates and asset prices as a financial general equilibrium, an approach also used later to study the impact of monetary reform in the UK. Went on to develop a 'computable general equilibrium' trade model in order to examine the static economic costs and benefits of UK entry into the Common Market. The impact of 'supply-side shocks' on inflation in Britain was treated along lines reflecting empirical work at LSE by Phillips and Sargan. The operation of monetary policy under floating exchange rates has been a major focus of interest. A framework combining rational expectations with 'auction-price' financial markets and non-clearing labour markets has been developed and used to analyse the evolution of macroeconomic policy in the UK since 1979, in work for the Treasury Committee of the House of Commons and in reports for the Brookings Institution, USA. Current research has focussed on combining forward-looking and strategic behaviour under floating exchange rates. In general I have sought to draw upon recent developments in macro- and microeconomic theory to analyse comtemporary problems besetting the British economy. I am happy to acknowledge the influence of mentors such as J. Tobin, H. Scarf, F. Hahn and H. Johnson and of those contemporaries, at LSE and elsewhere, with whom I have published joint work.

MILLER, Merton H.

Born 1923, Boston, MA, USA.

Current Post Leon Carroll Marshall Disting. Service Prof., Grad. School Bus., Univ. Chicago, USA, 1981–.

Past Posts Edward Eagle Brown Prof. Banking Fin., Grad. School Bus., Univ. Chicago, 1965–81.

Degrees BA Harvard Univ., 1944; PhD Johns Hopkins Univ., 1952.

Offices and Honours Fellow, Em Soc; Pres., AFA, 1976.

Principal Fields of Interest 521 Business Finance.

Publications *Books:* 1. *The Theory of Finance* (with E. Fama), (Holt, 1972); 2. *Macro-economics: A Neoclassical Introduction* (with C. Upton), (Richard D. Irwin, 1974).

Articles: 1. 'The cost of capital, corporation finance and the theory of investment' (with F. Modigliani), *AER*, 48, June 1958, 49, Sept. 1959; 2. 'Dividend policy, growth and the valuation of shares' (with F. Modigliani), *J Bus*, 34, Oct. 1961, 36, Jan. 1963; 3. 'Debt and taxes', *J Fin*, 32(2), May 1977.

Principal Contributions Co-author of the Modigliani-Miller theorems and other applications of economic theory to the field of finance.

MILLS, Edwin Smith

Born 1928, Collingswood, NJ, USA.
Current Post Prof. Econ., Princeton Univ., Princeton, NJ, 1970–.
Past Posts Prof. Polit. Econ., Johns Hopkins Univ., 1963–70.
Degrees BA Brown Univ., 1951; PhD Univ. Birmingham, 1956.
Offices and Honours Member, Em Soc.
Principal Fields of Interest 721 Natural Resources; 931 Urban Economics.
Publications *Books:* 1. *Studies in the Structure of the Urban Economy* (JHUP, 1972); 2. *Urban Economics* (Scott, Foresman, 1972, 1980); 3. *The Economics of Environmental Quality* (W. W. Norton, 1978); 4. *Urbanization and Urban Problems, Studies in the Modernization of the Republic of Korea: 1945–1975* (with B. N. Song), (Harvard Univ. Press, 1979); 5. *Measuring the Benefits of Water Pollution: A Statement* (with D. Freenberg), (Academic Press, 1980).
Articles: 1. 'An aggregative model of resource allocation in a metropolitan area', *AER*, 57(2), May 1967, repr. in *Urban Analysis*, eds. A. Page and W. Seyfried (Scott, Foresman, 1970), and *Readings in Urban Economics*, eds. M. Edel and J. Rothenberg (Macmillan, 1972), and *Urban Economic Readings and Analysis*, ed. R. Grieson (Little Brown, 1973); 2. 'The Tiebout hypothesis and residential income segregation' (with B. Hamilton and D. Puryear), in *Fiscal Zoning and Land Use Controls*, eds. E. S. Mills and W. E. Oates (D. C. Heath, 1975); 3. 'Urbanization and urban problems' (with K. Ohta), in *Asia's New Giant*, eds. H. Patrick and H. Rosovsky (Brookings Inst., 1976); 4. 'Planning and market processes in urban models', in *Public and Urban Economics: Essays in Honor of William S. Vickrey*, ed. R. Grieson (D. C. Heath, 1976); 5. 'Economic analysis of urban land-use controls', in *Current Issues in Urban Economics*, eds. P. Mieszkowski and M. Straszheim (JHUP, 1979).

Principal Contributions Interactions among price, output and inventory movements in firms and markets; market processes in urban areas; benefits, costs and government intervention in presence of polluting discharges; and industrial organisation and antitrust programmes.

MINCER, Jacob

Born 1922, Tomaszow, Poland.
Current Post Buttenwieser Prof. Econ., Columbia Univ., NYC, USA, 1979–.
Past Posts Instr., Ass. Prof., City Coll. NY, 1954–6, 1958–60; Assoc. Prof., Prof., Columbia Univ., 1960–2, 1962–79; Res. Staff, NBER, 1960–; Vis. Prof., Hebrew Univ., Jerusalem, 1964; Stockholm School Econ., 1971, Univ. Chicago, 1973–4.
Degrees BA Emory Univ., Atlanta, GA, 1950; PhD Columbia Univ., 1957.
Offices and Honours Phi Beta Kappa, Emory Univ., 1950; Post-doctoral Fellow, Univ. Chicago, 1957–8; Fellow, ASA, 1967–; Guggenheim Foundation Fellow, 1970–1; Fellow, Em Soc, 1973; Member, Nat. Academy Educ., 1974; Member, AAAS, 1974.
Editorial Duties Ed. Boards, *REStat*, 1977–81, *Econ. Educ. Rev.*, 1980–, *J. Labor Econ.*, 1983–.
Principal Fields of Interest 010 General Economics; 800 Labour Economics; 912 Economics of Education.
Publications *Books:* 1. *Economic Forecasts and Expectations*, ed. (Columbia Univ. Press, 1969); 2. *Schooling, Experience and Earnings* (Columbia Univ. Press, 1974).
Articles: 1. 'Investment in human capital and personal income distribution', *JPE*, 66, Aug. 1951; 2. 'Labor force participation of married women — a study of labor supply', in *Aspects of Labor Economics*, ed. H. G. Lewis (Princeton Univ. Press, 1962); 3. 'Market prices, opportunity costs and income effects', in *Measurement in Economics*, ed. C. Christ (Stanford Univ. Press, 1963); 4. 'Labor force participation and unemployment', in *Prosperity and Unemployment*, eds. B. J. Gordon and M. Gordon (Wiley, 1966);

5. 'The distribution of labor incomes', *JEL*, 8(1), March 1970; 6. 'Family investment in human capital: earnings of women' (with S. Polachek), *JPE*, 828(2), pt. 2, March–April 1974; 7. 'Unemployment effects of minimum wages', *JPE*, 84(4), pt. 2, Aug. 1976; 8. 'Family migration decisions', *JPE*, 86(5), Oct. 1978; 9. 'Labor mobility and wages' (with B. Jovenovic), in *Studies in Labor Markets*, ed. S. Rosen (Univ. Chicago Press, 1981); 10. 'Union effects: wages, turnover and training', in *Research in Labor Economics*, Suppl. 2, ed. J. Reid (JAI Press, 1983).

Principal Contributions In my earliest work I formulated and applied human capital analysis to the structure of labour incomes. This work, which focussed on investments in education and in job training, culminated in my 1974 book, in which the human capital earnings or wage function was developed into a simple and popular econometric tool. The human capital approach to the wage structure was further applied to sex differentials in wages in several of my articles. The 1962 article in *Aspects of Labor Economics* was the starting point of the modern developments of labour supply analysis. The formulation of labour supply decisions within the family context permitted an empirical separation of income and substitution effects and an application to the study of trends in the labour force. The concept of opportunity cost of time was generalised and applied to both labour force and fertility behaviour, as well as to cyclical fluctuation in work decisions. The work on human capital and labour supply described above basically integrates non-market (household) behaviour with behaviour in the labour market, extending the same economic analysis to both.

More recently, my research was extended to labour mobility phenomena. This research explores a duality between wage movements and probabilities of job changes on the job and over the life-cycle. This duality is attributable, in large measure to human capital specification in job experience and training. The findings provide insights into some aspects of so-called 'implicit labour contracts', into lifetime wage trajectories, and into the nature of differential unemployment. A part of this work also applies to migration, especially in the family context, which was previously neglected. More recent is my work on the economics of wage floors, analysing the effects of minimum wages and of union wage setting on employment, unemployment, fringes, turnover, and training under alternative models of probabilistic and systematic rationing of excess supply.

MINFORD, Anthony Patrick Leslie

Born 1943, Shrewsbury, Shropshire, England.

Current Post Edward Gonner Prof. Applied. Econ., Univ. Liverpool, Liverpool, England, 1975–.

Past Posts Econ. Ass., UK Ministry Overseas Devlp., 1965–7; Econ. Adviser, Malawi Ministry Fin., 1967–9; Ass. Econ. Matters to Fin. Dir., Courtaulds Co., 1970–1; Econ. Adviser, Balance of Payments Div., UK Treasury, 1971–3; UK Treasury Delegation, British Embassy, Washington, DC, 1973–4.

Degrees BA Univ. Oxford 1964; MSc, PhD Univ. London, 1970, 1973.

Offices and Honours Hallsworth Res. Fellow, Univ. Manchester, 1974–5.

Editorial Duties Ed. Board, *J. Internat. Money and Fin.*; Academic Council, *J. Econ. Affairs*; Ed., *NIESR Econ. Rev.*, 1975–6.

Principal Fields of Interest 132 Economic Forecasting and Econometric Models; 431 Balance of Payments: Mechanisms of Adjustment, Exchange Rates; 824 Labour Market Studies, Wages, Employment.

Publications *Books:* 1. *Substitution Effects, Speculation and Exchange Rate Stability* (N-H, 1978); 2. *Unemployment: Cause and Cure* (with D. H. Davies, M. J. Pell and A. Sprague), (Martin Robertson, 1983); 3. *Rational Expectations and the New Macroeconomics* (with D. A. Pell), (Martin Robertson, 1983).

Articles: 1. 'The costs of variable inflation' (with G. Hilliard), in *Contemporary Economic Analysis*, eds. M.

Artis and A. R. Nobay (Croom-Helm, 1978); 2. 'Asset acquisition — an integrated portfolio approach to private sector expenditure and financial asset accumulation' (with K. Matthews), *JMCB*, 12(4), pt. 1, Nov. 1980; 3. 'A rational expectations model of the UK under fixed and floating exchange rates', in *The State of Macroeconomics*, eds. K. Brunner and A. Meltzer (Carnegie-Rochester Conf. Series Public Pol., 1980); 4. 'The role of monetary stabilisation policy under rational expectations' (with D. A. Peel), *MS*, 49(1), March 1981; 5. 'The exchange rate and monetary policy', *OEP*, 33, July 1981; Suppl. repr. in *The Money Supply and the Exchange Rate*, eds. W. Eltis and P. Sinclair (OUP, 1981); 6. 'The political theory of the business cycle' (with D. A. Peel), *Europ ER*, 17(2), 1981; 7. 'The microfoundations of the Phillips curve with rational expectations' (with D. Peel), *OEP*, 34(3), Nov. 1982; 8. 'Floating exchange rates in a multilateral macro model' (with C. Ioannidis and S. Marwaha), in *Exchange Rates in Multicountry Econometric Models*, eds. P. de Grauwe and T. Peeters (Macmillan, 1983); 9. 'Some implications of partial current information sets in macroeconomic models embodying rational expectations' (with D. A. Peel), *MS*, 51(3), Sept. 1983; 10. 'The Liverpool macroeconomic model of the United Kingdom' (with S. Marwaha, K. Matthews and A. Sprague), *Econ. Modelling*, 1(1), Jan. 1984.

Principal Contributions My work has usually been stimulated by having to give economic advice. The main problems with which I first had to deal concerned the floating exchange rate and the balance of payments; my first book contains my efforts at modelling the UK floating exchange rate in the early 1970s for the Treasury model. In doing this I became convinced that expectations must be modelled as rational, and that this in turn required a complete macroeconomic model for the UK. My work with large-scale models at the Treasury and NIESR made me realise that their complexity and size concealed serious theoretical gaps and gave no advantages in forecasting per-

formance. I resolved to build a new model based on a few key hypotheses (rational expectations, market-clearing, and intertemporal optimisation) and with the minimum of complexity necessary for accurate forecasting. A prototype of this model (the 'Liverpool Model' of the UK) was first used in forecasting in March 1980, and regular forecasts have been published since then, partly in order to establish a track record for evaluation of this 'new classical' approach in practice. I have also been building similar models for other major OECD countries and have linked these in a world model. I am starting to use these models in a similar way. The inexorable rise in unemployment has however led me to supplement these models with work on the 'natural rate'; I have modelled UK (and some other countries') equilibrium unemployment as the result of government intervention in the labour market, notably in setting unemployment benefit and tax rates as well as protecting or encouraging union power. In all this work, the policy implications have also been my major interest, and I have written extensive topical commentary as well as a number of theoretical articles on these implications.

MINSKY, Hyman Philip

Born 1919, Chicago, IL, USA.
Current Post Prof. Econ., Washington Univ., St Louis, MO, USA, 1965–.
Past Posts Instr., Carnegie Inst. Technology, 1947; Teaching Fellow, Harvard Univ., 1947–9; Ass. Prof., Assoc. Prof., Brown Univ., 1949–58; Vis. Assoc. Prof., Assoc. Prof., Univ. Cal. Berkeley, 1956–7, 1958–65; Vis. Prof., Harvard Univ., 1966; Vis. Scholar, St John's Coll. Camb., 1969–70; Vis. Prof., Univ. Cal. Berkeley, 1964; Faculty Centro di Studi Economici Avanzanti, Triest, Italy, 1980.
Degrees BS Univ. Chicago, 1941; MPA, PhD Harvard Univ., 1947, 1954.
Editorial Duties Ed. Board, *J Post Keyn. E*, 1977, *SEJ*, 1973–5; Assoc. Ed., *Transaction Magazine*, 1967–8.
Principal Fields of Interest 310 Domestic Monetary and Financial

Theory and Institutions; 131 Economic Fluctuations; 023 Macroeconomic Theory.

Publications *Books:* 1. *Labor and the War Against Poverty* (Univ. Cal. Inst. Industrial Relations, 1965); 2. *Commercial Banking and Rapid Economic Growth in California* (Univ. Cal. Inst. Bus. and Econ. Res., 1965); 3. *John Maynard Keynes* (Columbia Univ. Press, 1975; transl., Italian, 1981); 4. *The Financial Instability Hypothesis: A Restatement* (Thames Papers Polit. Econ., 1981); 5. *Can 'It' Happen Again?* (M. E. Sharpe, 1982; in UK as *Inflation Recession and Economic Policy*, Wheatsheaf Books, 1982).

Articles: 1. 'Central banking and money market changes' *QJE*, 71(2), May 1957; 2. 'Monetary systems and acceleration models', *AER*, 47(5), Dec. 1957; 3. 'A linear model of cyclical growth', *REStat*, 41(2), May 1959, repr. in *Readings in Business Cycles*, eds. R. A. Gordon and L. R. Klein (Richard D. Irwin, 1965); 4. 'Comment on Friedman and Schwartz "Money and Business Cycles"', *REStat*, 45(1), Feb. 1963; 5. 'Financial crisis, financial systems and the performance of the economy', in *Private Capital Markets* (Prentice Hall, 1964); 6. 'A theory of systemic fragility', in *Financial Crises*, eds. E. D. Altman and A. W. Sametz (Prentice-Hall, 1977); 7. 'Financial interrelations, the balance of payments and the dollar crises', in *Debt and the Less Developed Countries* (Westview Press, 1979); 8. 'Money, financial markets and the coherence of a market economy', *J Post Keyn E*, 3(1), Fall 1980; 9. 'The financial instability hypothesis: capitalist processes and the behavior of the economy', in *Financial Crises: Theory, History and Policy*, eds. C. P. Kindleberger and J. P. Laffargue (CUP, Eds de la Maison des Sciences d l'Hommes, 1982); 10. 'Debt deflation processes in today's institutional environment', *QREB*, 143, Dec. 1982.

Principal Contributions A professional's career starts with teachers. Mine started at the University of Chicago; my principal teachers were Henry Simons, Paul Douglas, Jacob Viner and Oscar Lange: Simons and Lange were the greatest influences. The problems they posed which to this day guide my work are 'What are the flaws in capitalism?' and 'Can systems of intervention be devised to remove or offset these flaws?' World War II interrupted my training. After the war I studied at Harvard; the principal influences were Joseph Schumpeter, Wassily Leontief and Alvin Hansen. My thinking on the importance of institutional evolution in determining system behaviour, and evidence from history in testing theories, can be traced to Schumpeter's influence.

My publications and research have centred on money, banking and finance and how financial instability emerges in a capitalist economy. The 1966 credit crunch focussed my thinking. My 'financial instability hypothesis' interpretation of Keynes is an outgrowth of my dissatisfaction with the banality of orthodox Keynesianism, my study of institutional evolution, and my interest in monetary phenomena.

Further influences resulted from spending 1968–9 in Cambridge. Joan Robinson was particularly important. Aubrey Silberston, Jan Kregel, Victoria Chick, Tony Cramp and Maurice Townsend also influenced me. In recent years the group around the Centro di Studi Economici Avanzati has played a major role in my development.

MIRABEAU, Victor Riquetti, Marquis De*

Dates and Birthplace 1715–89, France.
Posts Held Army officer and landowner.
Publications *Books:* 1. *Mémoire concernant l'utilité des états provinciaux* (1750); 2. *L'ami des hommes, ou traité de la populâtion* (1756); 3. *Théorie de l'impôt* (1760); 4. *Lettres sur les corvées* (1760); 5. *Philosophie rurale*, 3 vols (with F. Quesnay), (1764).

Career From 1765 his Paris salon was the meeting place for the 'économistes'. Mirabeau came to be known as 'l'ami des hommes' after his 1756 publication in which he anticipated much of Quesnay's system. His starting point is the dependence of all aspects of the State on agriculture; he then prescribes reforms which would both revive agriculture and the State itself. His son, Honoré Gabriel, was a major figure in the early years of the Revolution, and also wrote on economic questions.

Secondary Literature P. Sagnac, 'Mirabeau, Marquis de', *ESS*, 10.

MIRRLEES, James A.

Born 1936, Minnigaff, Scotland.

Current Post Edgeworth Prof. Econ., Univ. Oxford, England, 1969–.

Past Posts Adviser, MIT Center Internat. Stud., India Project, New Delhi, 1962–3; Ass. Lect., Lect. Econ., Fellow, Trinity Coll., Camb., 1963–8; Adviser, Pakistan Inst. Devlp. Econ., Karachi, 1966–8; Vis. Prof., MIT, 1968, 1970, 1976.

Degrees MA (Maths.) Univ. Edinburgh, 1957; Maths. Tripos, PhD Univ. Camb., 1959, 1963; Hon. DLitt Warwick Univ., 1982.

Offices and Honours Stevenson Prize Econ., Univ. Camb., 1962; Member, UK Treasury Comm. Pol. Optimization (Ball Comm.), 1976–8; Vice-Pres., Pres., Em Soc, 1980–1, 1982; Hon. Member, AAS, 1981, AEA, 1982, FBA, 1984.

Editorial Duties Ass. Ed., *REStud*, 1969–74; Co-ed., *Em*, 1981–4; Assoc. Ed., *JET, OEP, JPE, Econ. Letters*.

Principal Fields of Interest 010 General Economics; Theory; History; Systems; 300 Domestic Monetary and Fiscal Theory and Institutions.

Publications *Books:* 1. *Models of Economic Growth*, co-ed. (with N. H. Stern), (Macmillan, 1973); 2. *Project Appraisal and Planning for Developing Countries* (with I. M. D. Little), (Heinemann, Basic Books, 1974).

Articles: 1. 'An exploration in the theory of optimum income taxation', *REStud*, 38, April 1971; 2. 'Optimal taxation and public production I: production efficiency', and 'II: tax rules' (with P. A. Diamond), *AER*, 61(1–2), March, June 1971; 3. 'The optimum town', *Swed JE*, 71(1), March 1972; 4. 'Notes on welfare economics, information and uncertainty', in *Essays in Equilibrium Behavior under Uncertainty*, eds. M. Balch, D. McFadden and S. Wu (N-H, 1974); 5. 'Optimum saving with economies of scale' (with A. K. Dixit and N. H. Stern), *REStud*, 42(3), July 1975; 6. 'A pure theory of underdeveloped economies, using a relationship between consumption and productivity', in *Agriculture in Development Theory*, ed. L. A. Reynolds (Yale Univ. Press, 1975); 7. 'Optimal tax theory; a synthesis', *JPE*, 6(4), Dec. 1976; 8. 'A model of optimal social insurance with variable retirment' (with P. Diamond), *JPE*, 10(3), Dec. 1978; 9. 'The theory of optimal taxation', in *Handbook of Mathematical Economics*, eds. K. J. Arrow and M. Intriligator (N-H, 1981); 10. 'The economic uses of utilitarianism', in *Utilitarianism and Beyond*, eds. A. K. Sen and B. Williams (Blackwell, 1982).

Principal Contributions As a doctoral student and, subsequently, worked on the theory of economic planning, identifying as major issues (1) estimation of the quantitative importance of ignoring uncertainty when taking decisions, (2) developing a theory of optimal investment decisions in an economy with constraints on tax rates. The first gave rise to work on optimum growth under uncertainty, both in discrete time and with diffusion processes, which raised difficult existence problems as yet unsolved. Conclusion: uncertainty is of surprisingly small importance at the aggregate level. This and (2) led to work with Little on cost-benefit; and also work on sensitivity and optimal growth with Hammond, Stern, and Dixit.

Went on to study welfare economics under the realistic assumption that government cannot use information individuals would not choose to reveal; developed implications for production rules and taxes with Diamond in the 1960s. Possibilities of nonlinear income taxation were explored numerically in 1969–71. A series of papers on other taxes — on family size, location, foreign incomes — and on assessing public expenditures followed. Thinking out the general structure of welfare economics led to papers on the central technical difficulties, for this and similar problems, of handling the privately rational decisions of individuals in a population as a constraint on welfare maximisation. These studies also led to work, with Diamond, in the mid 1970s on moral-hazard models, both general methods, and special cases for application to pensions and social insurance. Looking always for ways of capturing the important uncertainties of economies, I am now working on decisions in highly distorted economies, on research and enterprise, and on the welfare economics of developing economies.

MISES, Ludwig Edler Von*

Dates and Birthplace 1881–1973, Lemberg, Austro-Hungary.
Posts Held Prof., Univ. Vienna, 1913–38; Prof., Grad. Inst. Internat. Stud., Geneva, 1934–40; Prof., NYU, 1945–69.
Degrees Dr Univ. Vienna, 1906.
Offices and Honours Founder, Mont Pelerin Soc.; Adviser, Austrian Chamber of Commerce, 1909–34; Founder, Austrian Inst. Bus. Cycle Res., 1926.
Publications *Books:* 1. *The Theory of Money and Credit* (1912, 1953, 1981); 2. *Socialism: An Economic and Sociological Analysis* (1922, 1959); 3. *The Free and Prosperous Commonwealth* (1927, 1962); 4. *Die Ursachen der Wirtschaftskrise* (1931); 5. *Epistemological Problems of Economics* (1933, 1960); 6. *Nationalökonomie: Theorie des Handelns und Wirtschaftens* (1940); 7. *Human Action* (1949, 1966); 8. *Theory and History* (1957); 9. *The Ultimate Foundation of Economic Science* (1962).

Career The leading twentieth-century figure of the Austrian School, he developed a once widely accepted theory of business cycles in which booms result from bank credit expansion. His other main contribution was the demonstration that socialist planning could not achieve a rational allocation of resources because of its lack of a true price system. He extended this argument to a general critique of government intervention in a private enterprise economy. He was deeply interested in epistemological questions and developed his own methodology, known as praxeology, which laid heavy stress on individual choices and purposive human action as the *a priori* foundation of valid economic reasoning. He is today hailed as the founding father of the 'new' Austrian School.

Secondary Literature M. N. Rothbard, 'Von Mises, Ludwig', *IESS*, 16; L. S. Moss, ed., *The Economics of Ludwig von Mises* (Sheed & Ward, 1974); M. N. Rothbart, 'On Mises', in *Contemporary Economists in Perspective*, eds. W. H. Spiegel and W. J. Samuels (JAI Press, 1984).

MISHAN, Ezra Joshua

Born 1917, Manchester, England.
Current Post Vis. Prof., various univs., UK, USA, 1977–.
Past Posts Lect., Sr. Lect., Reader, Prof., LSE, 1956–77.
Degrees BA Univ. Manchester, 1964; MSc Univ. London, 1949; PhD Univ. Chicago, 1952.
Offices and Honours Hon. Fellow, City Univ., London, England, 1978–.
Principal Fields of Interest 024 Welfare Theory; 613 Public Utilities; 722 Conservation and Pollution.
Publications *Books:* 1. *The Costs of Economic Growth* (Penguin, 1967); 2. *21 Popular Economic Fallacies* (Penguin, 1969); 3. *Welfare Economics: An Appraisal* (N-H, 1969) 4. *Cost-Benefit Analysis* (A&U, 1971, 1982); 5. *Introduction to Normative Economics* (OUP, 1982); 6. *Economic Efficiency and Social Welfare* (A&U, 1981); 7. *Pornography, Psychedelics and Technology* (A&U, 1981).
Articles: 1. 'Survey of welfare economics: 1939–1959', *EJ*, 70, June 1960; 2. 'Theories of consumer behaviour: a cynical view', *Ec*, N.S. 28, Feb. 1961; 3. 'Second thoughts on second best', *OEP*, N.S. 14, Oct. 1962; 4. 'How to make a burden of the public debt', *JPE*, 71, Dec. 1963; 5. 'What is producer's surplus?', *AER*, 58(5), Dec. 1968; 6. 'The postwar literature of externalities', *JEl*, 9(1), March 1971; 7. 'Evaluation of life and limb: a theoretical approach', *JPE*, 79(4), July–Aug. 1971; 8. 'Welfare criteria: resolution of a paradox', *EJ*, 83, Sept. 1973; 9. 'The

folklore of the market: an inquiry into the economic doctrines of the Chicago school', *JEL*, 9(4), Dec. 1975; 10. 'Choices involving risk: simple steps towards an ordinalist approach', *EJ*, 86, Dec. 1976.

Principal Contributions The bulk of my contributions to the professional journals are in the area of resource allocation and evaluation with emphasis on basic concepts. This interest continues and is supplemented by a growing concern with topics of increasing controversy, which finds expression in the more popular journals such as *Encounter*. Topics include pollution, economic growth, inflation, multi-racialism, immigration, psychedelics, pornography, feminism and the pretensions of economists.

MISHKIN, Frederic S.

Born 1951, New York City, NY, USA.

Current Post Prof., Grad. School Bus., Columbia Univ., NY, 1983–.

Past Posts Ass. Prof., Assoc. Prof., Univ. Chicago, 1976–81, 1981–83; Res. Assoc., NBER, Cambridge, MA, 1980–; Brookings Panel Econ. Activity, 1977–8; Econ., Board Governors, Fed. Reserve System, 1977; Vis. Assoc. Prof., Kellogg Grad. School Management, Northwestern Univ., 1982–3.

Degrees BS, PhD MIT, 1973, 1976.

Offices and Honours Soc. Sigma Xi; 1973; Phi Beta Kappa, 1973; NSF Grad. Fellow, 1973–6; Sloan Foundation Fellow, 1982–.

Editorial Duties Ed. Board, *AER*.

Principal Fields of Interest 023 Macroeconomic Theory; 131 Economic Fluctuation.

Publications Books: 1. *Illiquidity, the Demand for Consumer Durables, and Monetary Policy* (Fed. Reserve Bank Boston, 1977); 2. *A Rational Expectations Approach to Macroeconomics: Testing Policy Ineffectiveness and Efficient Market Models* (Univ. Chicago Press, 1983).

Articles: 1. 'Illiquiity, consumer durable expenditure, and monetary policy', *AER*, 66(4), Sept. 1976; 2. 'What depressed the consumer? The household balance-sheet and the 1973–5 recession', *Brookings Papers Econ. Activity*, 1, 1977; 3. 'The household balance-sheet and the great depression', *JEH*, 38, Dec. 1978; 4. 'Efficient markets theory: implications for monetary policy', *Brookings Papers Econ. Activity*, 3, 1978; 5. 'Monetary policy and long-term interest rates: an efficient markets approach', *J Mon E*, 7, Jan. 1981; 6. 'The real rate of interest: an empirical investigation', *Carnegie-Rochester Conf. Series on Public Pol., The Cost and Consequences of Inflation*, 15, Autumn 1981; 7. 'Does anticipated monetary policy matter? an econometric investigation', *JPE*, 90(1), Feb. 1982; 8. 'Monetary policy and short-term interest rates: an efficient markets-rational expectations approach', *J Fin*, 37, March 1982; 9. 'The sensitivity of consumption to transitory income: estimates from panel data on households' (with R. E. Hall), *Em*, 50, March 1982; 10. 'The real interest rate: a multi-country empirical study', *CJE*, 17(2), May 1984.

Principal Contributions My research has been motivated by the desire to better understand the sources of business-cycle fluctuations and how monetary policy affects aggregate economic activity. My early work focussed on the transmission mechanisms of monetary policy. I explored the impact of changes in household balance-sheets on the demand for illiquid assets, such as consumer durables and residential housing, and found that this could be a potent channel for monetary policy effects on the economy. I then used this analysis to see if this would provide a better understanding of some important business-cycle episodes, in particular the Great Depression and the 1973–5 recession. Because monetary policy has important effects on the economy my affecting financial markets, I next looked at the implications of the theory of efficient capital markets to see how monetary policy should be conducted. This led naturally to my use of this theory (or equivalently the theory of rational expectations) to analyse such topics as the relationship of monetary policy and interest rates. The resulting empirical analysis required the development of econometric techniques which could distinguish between the effects of anticipated versus unanticipated policy. My work on these techniques led to my also pursuing the question of whether anticipated monetary policy matters to business-cycle fluctuations. My most recent work has focussed on the measurement of real interest rates on many different kinds of assets using rational expectations techniques. Since some of these assets are traded internationally, this has also led to work on international financial markets and to the exploration of certain international parity conditions.

MITCHELL, Wesley Clair*

Dates and Birthplace 1874–1948, Rushville, IL, USA.
Posts Held Prof., Univ. Cal., 1903–13, Columbia Univ., 1913–19, 1922–44; Dir., New School Social Res., 1919–31.
Degrees BA, PhD Univ. Chicago, 1896, 1899.
Offices and Honours Dir., NBER, 1920–45; Member, Res. Comm. Social Trends, 1929–33; Member, Nat. Planning Board, 1933.
Publications *Books:* 1. *A History of the Greenbacks* (1903); 2. *Gold Prices and Wages Under the Greenback Standard* (1908); 3. *Business Cycles* (1913, 1959); 4. *The Making and Using of Index Numbers* (1915, 1938); 5. *Business Cycles: The Problem and Its Setting* (1927); 6. *The Backward Art of Spending Money (1937, 1950); 7. Measuring Business Cycles* (with A. F. Burns), (1946); 8. *What Happens During Business Cycles* (1951)
Career Leading authority on business cycles, who devoted himself chiefly to economic research. He helped to found NBER in 1920 to further the development of quantitative studies of the US economy. He regarded his central task as the study of the 'money economy' and consistently sought a dynamic theory of social change. Though other contemporaries, such as Aftalion and Spiethoff, achieved similar results in business-cycle theory, his work on cycles was unique in its breadth and continuity.
Secondary Literature V. Zarnowitz, 'Mitchell, Wesley C.', *IESS*, 10.

MIZON, Grayham Ernest

Born 1942, Rochdale, Lancashire, England.
Current Post Leverhulme Prof. Em., Univ. Southampton, Southampton, England, 1978–.
Past Posts Econ., Unilever Ltd., UK, 1968–70; Econ., Commodities Res. Unit Ltd., UK, 1970–1; Rio Tinto Zinc Res. Fellow, St Catherine's Coll. Oxford, 1971–4; Lect. Stats., LSE, 1974–7; Cons. Stats., Canada, 1974, 1975; Vis. Prof. Univ. Cal. San Diego, 1977; Vis. Fellow, Stats. Dept., ANU, Canberra, 1977, 1982.
Degrees BSc, MSc (Math. Econ. and Econometrics), PhD LSE, 1965, 1966, 1972; MA Univ. Oxford, 1971.
Offices and Honours State Scholarship, UK, 1962–5; Leverhulme Entrance Scholar, LSE, 1962–5; Courtaulds Grad. Student, LSE, 1965–8; Chairman, Steering Comm., UK SSRC Em Study Group, 1978–84; Member, Econ. Comm., UK SSRC, 1979–83; Secretary, Europ. Standing Comm., Em Soc, 1980–3; Res. Programme Dir., Centre Econ. Pol. Res., UK, 1983–.
Editorial Duties Ass. Ed., Managing Ed., *REStud*, 1980–3, 1983–6.
Principal Fields of Interest 130 Economic Fluctuations; Forecasting; Stabilisation; and Inflation; 211 Econometric and Statistical Methods and Models; 212 Construction, Analysis and Use of Econometric Models.
Publications *Articles:* 1. 'The estimation of nonlinear econometric equations: an application to the specification and estimation of an aggregate putty-clay production relation for the UK', *REStud*, 41(3), July 1974; 2. 'Factor substitution and returns to scale in a cross-section of UK industries: an exercise of nonlinear inference', *Em*, 45(5), July 1977; 3. 'Model selection procedures in dynamic models', in *Studies in Modern Economic Analysis*, eds. M. J. Artis and A. R. Nobay (Blackwell, 1977); 4. 'Serial correlation as a convenient simplification, not a nuisance: a comment on a study of the demand for money by the Bank of England' (with D. F. Hendry), *EJ*, 88, Sept. 1978; 5. 'An empirical application and Monte Carlo analysis of tests of dynamic speci-

fication' (with D. F. Hendry), *REStud*, 47(1), Jan. 1980; 6. 'Recent developments in the statistical analysis of causal models', in *Seminario Due Temi Statistica Multivariata* (Univ. degli Studi di Padova, 1979); 7. 'Vintage capital models of production in UK manufacturing industry' (with S. J. Nickell), *Scand JE*, 85(2), 1983, repr. in *Topics in Production Theory*, ed. F. Forsund (Macmillan, 1984); 8. 'Model specification tests against non-tested alternatives: a comment' (with J-F. Richard), *Em Rev.*, 2(1), 1983; 9. 'The encompassing approach in econometrics', in *Econometrics and Quantitative Economics*, eds. D. F. Hendry and K. F. Wallis (Blackwell, 1984); 10. 'Tests of specification in econometrics: a comment' (with T. S. Breusch), *Em Rev.*, 4(2), 1985.

Principal Contributions After six years as an econometrics student at the LSE, I joined the Head Office economics staff of a large multinational company at a time when companies in the UK were beginning tentatively to employ econometric techniques. I spent three rewarding and exciting years in commercial companies, explaining and promoting the use of econometrics, but eventually decided to devote more time to evaluating and developing techniques, and so returned to academia. A constant theme of my research has been the systematic analysis of econometric problems arising in applied work. The poor performance of static putty-putty production relations for time series data led me to consider more general dynamic models of the putty-clay type. These models necessitated analysis of estimation and testing problems in nonlinear models. I employed methods for testing sequences of hypotheses in discriminating between alternative functional forms for production functions, and for the naturally ordered sequences that occur in time series, especially autoregressive distributed lag models. The need to be able to compare statistically non-nested models led to work on testing non-nested hypotheses and the role of the encompassing principle in unifying nested and non-nested hypothesis testing.

The relationships between these dif-ferent hypothesis testing problems, and the value of considering them jointly in an overall approach to econometric modelling, has been the focus of much of my recent research. The demonstration of the advantages of starting from general models, and searching for economically meaningful, yet parsimoniously parameterised, models using hypothesis testing, and the need to carefully and extensively evaluate econometric models, rather than simply use econometric methods to confirm economic theories, has characterised my research. Areas of application include aggregate production and consumer behaviour, money demand, relative price variability and inflation.

MIYAZAKI, Hajime

Born 1948, Naruto, Tokushima, Japan.

Current Post Assoc. Prof. Econ., Ohio State Univ., Columbus, OH, USA, 1984–.

Past Posts Ass. Prof. Econ., Stanford Univ., 1977–84; Vis. Ass. Prof., Inst. Econ. Res., Kyoto Univ., Kyoto, Japan, 1981; Vis. Assoc. Prof. Econ., Univ. Cal. Davis, 1982.

Degrees BA (Econ. and Maths.), PhD Univ. Cal. Berkeley, 1972, 1977.

Principal Fields of Interest 022 Microeconomics; 600 Industrial Organisation; Technological Change; Industry Studies; 830 Trade Unions; Collective Bargaining; Labour-Management Relations.

Publications *Articles:* 1. 'The rat race and internal labor markets', *Bell JE*, 8(2), Autumn 1977; 2. 'The implicit contract theory of unemployment meets the wage bill argument' (with G. A. Akerlof), *REStud*, 47(2), Jan. 1980; 3. 'The Illyrian firm revisited' (with H. M. Neary), *Bell JE*, 14(1), Spring 1983; 4. 'Work norms and involuntary unemployment', *QJE*, 99(2), May 1984; 5. 'Internal bargaining, labor contracts and a Marshallian theory of the firm', *AER*, 74(3), June 1984; 6. 'On success and dissolution of the labor-managed firm in the capitalist economy', *JPE*, 92(5), Oct. 1984.

Principal Contributions I have been interested in the use of labour contracts to analyse the internal organisation of a firm including that of a labour-managed firm. I think that the confluence of labour contract models and the theory of 'firm-specific organisational capital' can provide a better microeconomic basis for the theory of the firm than standard neoclassical models. Recently I have become more involved in the microeconomic analysis of the Japanese economy from the viewpoint of comparative industrial organisations.

MODIGLIANI, Franco

Born 1918, Rome, Italy.
Current Post Prof. Econ. and Fin., MIT, Cambridge, MA, USA, 1962–.
Past Posts Instr., Assoc. Econ. and Stats., Barnard Coll., Columbia Univ., 1942–4; Lect., Ass. Prof., Math. Econ. and Econometrics, New School Social Res., NY, 1943–4, 1946–8; Assoc. Prof., Prof. Econ., Univ. Illinois, 1949, 1950–2; Prof. Econ. Industrial Admin., Carnegie Inst. Technology, 1952–60; Prof. Econ., Northwestern Univ., 1960–2.
Degrees Dr (Jurisprudence) Univ. Rome, 1939; Dr (Social Science) New School Social Res., 1944; LLD (Ad Hon.), Univ. Chicago, 1967; Dr (H.C.), Univ. Catholique de Louvain, 1974, Instituto Univ. di Bergamo, 1979.
Offices and Honours Pres., Em Soc, 1962, AEA, 1976, AFA, 1981; Academic Cons., Board Governors, Fed. Reserve System, 1966–; Sr. Adviser, Brookings Panel Econ. Activity, 1971–; Member, NAS, 1973–; Vice-Pres., Hon. Pres., IEA, 1976–81, 1983; Nobel Prize, 1985.
Principal Fields of Interest 020 General Economic Theory.
Publications *Books:* 1. *National Incomes and International Trade* (with H. Neisser), (Univ. Illinois Press, 1953); 2. *Planning Production, Inventories and Work Forces* (with others), (Prentice-Hall, 1960); 3. *New Mortgage Designs for Stable Housing in Inflationary Environment*, ed. (with D. Lessard), (Fed. Reserve Bank Boston, 1975); 4. *Collected Papers of Franco Modigliani*: vol. 1, *Essays in Macroeconomics*; vol. 2, *Life Cycle Hypothesis of Saving*; vol. 3, *Theory of Finance and Other Essays* (MIT Press, 1980).
Articles: 1. 'Towards an understanding of the real effects and costs of inflation' (with S. Fischer), *WA*, 114(4), 1978; 2. 'Optimal demand policies against stagflation' (with L. Papademos), *WA*, 114(4), 1978; 3. 'Inflation, rational valuation and the market' (with R. C. Cohn), *Fin. Analysis J.*, March-April 1979; 4. 'The trade-off between real wages and employment in an open economy (Belgium)' (with J. Drèze), *Europ ER*, 15(2), 1981; 5. 'Determinants of private saving with special reference to the role of social security — cross-country tests' (with A. Sterling), in *The Determinants of National Saving and Wealth*, eds. F. Modigliani and J. Hemming (Macmillan, 1983); 6. 'Inflation, financial and fiscal structure, and the monetary mechanism' (with L. Papademos), *Europ ER*, 21(1–2), March-April, 1983; 7. 'Government deficits, inflation and future generations', in *Deficits: How Big and How Bad?*, eds. E. Conklin and J. Courchene (Ont. Econ. Council, 1983).
Principal Contributions Contributed to clarifying the relation between the Keynesian 'revolution', classical economics and monetarism, and implication for monetary and fiscal stabilisation policies. Had major responsibility for building model of US economy (MPS) for Federal Reserve System. Originated the life-cycle hypothesis of saving which has found wide applications in the study of family and national saving. Author (with M. Miller) of two theorems basic to modern finance to the effect that under efficient, rational markets, and abstracting from tax effects, the market value of a firm and its costs of capital are independent of both the debt-equity ratio and the dividend-payout ratio.
Secondary Literature E. Schwartz, 'On Modigliani', *Contemporary Economists in Perspective*, eds. H. W. Spiegel and W. J. Samuels (JAI Press, 1984).

MOGGRIDGE, Donald Edward

Born 1943, Windsor, Ont., Canada.
Current Post Prof. Econ., Univ. Toronto, Ont., Canada, 1982–.

Past Posts Jr. Res. Officer, Dept. Appl. Econ., Ass. Lect. Econ., Lect. Econ., Fellow, Vis. Fellow, Clare Coll. Camb., 1968–9, 1971–2, 1973–5, 1971–81, 1977–8, 1980–1.

Degrees BA (Polit. Science and Econ.) Univ. Toronto, 1965; MA, PhD Univ. Camb., 1968, 1970.

Offices and Honours Res. Fellow, Clare Coll., Camb., 1967–71; Treasurer, Conf. Ed. Problems, 1984–.

Principal Fields of Interest 031 History of Economic Thought; 041 Economic History: General; 432 International Monetary Arrangements.

Publications Books: 1. The Return to Gold, 1925 (CUP, 1969); 2. British Monetary Policy 1924–1931 (CUP, 1972); 3. The Collected Writings of John Maynard Keynes, vols 3–14, 19–29, ed. (Macmillan, 1972–83); 4. Keynes: Aspects of the Man and his Work, ed. (Macmillan, 1974); 5. Keynes (Macmillan, Fontana, 1975, 1980; transls., German, Taschenbuch Verlag, 1977, Italian, Biblioteca Universale Rizzioli, 1978, Dutch, Heureka, 1978, Japanese, Toyo Keizai Shinpoia, 1980, Portuguese, Editoria Clutrix, 1981).

Articles: 1. 'British controls on long-term capital movements, 1924–1931', in Essays on a Mature Economy, ed. D. N. McCloskey (Princeton Univ. Press, 1971); 2. 'From The Treatise to The General Theory: an exercise in chronology', HOPE, 6(1), Spring 1973; 3. 'Keynes on monetary policy, 1910–1946' (with S. Howson), OEP, 25(2), July 1974; 4. 'Cambridge discussion and criticism surrounding the writing of The General Theory', in Keynes, Cambridge and the 'General Theory', eds. D. Patinkin and J. C. Leith (Macmillan, 1978); '5. 'Financial crises and lenders of last resort: policy in the crises of 1920 and 1929', JEH, 10(1), Spring 1981; 6. 'Policy in the crises of 1920 and 1929', in Financial Crises: Theory, History and Policy, eds. C. P. Kindleberger and J. P. Laffargue (CUP, 1982); 7. 'The gold standard and national economic policies, 1919–1939', in The Cambridge Economic History of Europe, eds. P. Mathias and S. Pollard (CUP, 1984).

Principal Contributions My professional contributions have been twofold. Firstly I played a part in the revival in the historical discussion of financial policy by economists and economic historians on the basis of the available primary documentary evidence — a revival that has resulted in a number of books, articles and dissertations since 1969. Secondly, I have provided economists and others with raw materials in the form of the Collected Writings of John Maynard Keynes, so that they can reassess the work and the contributions of Keynes to modern economic theory and policy.

MOHRING, Herbert

Born 1928, Buffalo, NY, USA.
Current Post Prof. Econ., Univ. Minnesota, Minneapolis, MN, USA, 1967–.

Past Posts Res. Assoc., Univ. Michigan, Willow Run Res. Center, 1951–2; Teaching Fellow, MIT, 1952–4; US Air Force, 1953; Ass. Study Dir., Study Dir., Survey Res. Center, Univ. Michigan, 1954–7; Res. Assoc., Resources for the Future, Washington, DC, 1957–8; Res. Econ., Transport Center, Northwestern Univ., 1958–61; Cons., Econ. Survey Liberia, Northwestern Univ., 1961; Assoc. Prof. Econ., Adjunct. Prof. Law, Univ. Minnesota, 1961–7, 1969–71; Vis. Prof. Econ., York Univ., Downsview, Canada, 1972–3, Johns Hopkins Univ., 1974, Nat. Univ. Singapore, 1982–3, Faculty Commerce, Univ. British Columbia, 1983.

Degrees BA, Williams Coll. Williamstown, MA, 1950; PhD MIT, 1959.

Editorial Duties Ed. Board, AER, 1971–3, JUE, 1979.

Principal Fields of Interest 020 General Economic Theory; 600 Industrial Organisation; Technological Change; Industry Studies; 930 Urban Economics.

Publications Books: 1. Highway Benefits: An Analytical Framework (with M. Harwitz), (Northwestern Univ. Press, 1962; transl., Japanese, Kajima Inst. Publ., 1968); 2. Transportation Economics (Ballinger, 1976).

Articles: 1. 'Land values and the measurement of highway benefits', JPE, 69(3), June 1961; 2. 'Urban highway investments', in Measuring Benefits *of Government Investments*, ed. R. Dorfman (Brookings Inst., 1965); 3. 'The peak load problem with increasing returns and pricing contraints', *AER*, 60(4), Sept. 1970; 4. 'Analyzing externalities: "direct interaction" vs. "asset utilization" frameworks', *Ec*, N.S. 38, Nov. 1971; 5. 'Optimization and scale economies in urban bus transportation', *AER*, 62(4), Sept. 1972; 6. 'Alternative welfare gain and loss measures', *WEJ*, 9(4), Dec. 1971, repr. in *Benefit-Cost and Policy Analysis, 1972*, eds. W. A. Niskanen, *et al.* (Aldine, 1973); 7. 'The benefits and costs of rate of return regulation' (with J. Callen and G. F. Mathewson), *AER*, 66(3), June 1976; 8. 'The welfare costs of non-optimal pricing and investment policies in highway transportation' (with M. Kraus and T. Pinfold), *AER*, 66(4), Sept. 1976; 9. 'Traffic congestion and the benefits of reserved lanes, mass transit subsidies, and marginal cost pricing', in *Current Issues in Urban Economics*, eds. P. Mieszkowski and M. Straszheim (JHUP, 1979); 10. 'Minibuses in urban transportation', *JUE*, 14(3), Nov. 1983.

Principal Contributions I consider myself to be primarily an applied microeconomist — someone who uses the tools of static price theory to explain and to quantify the supply and demand sides of real-world markets. My research has concentrated heavily on transportation markets — as examples, benefits/cost analysis of transportation improvement, the structure of mass-transit costs when traveller time is considered to be an input to trip production, optimal pricing and subsidy rules for transportation systems, and quantification of the social costs of failure to price transportation systems efficiently. My attention has occasionally strayed to other areas, however. These include the efficiency implications of the antitrust laws, the foundations of benefits/cost analysis, externalities, and renewable resources. My major current interest is in using consumer choices of, for example, travel modes to infer the values they attach to travel time.

MOLINARI, Gustave de*

Dates and Birthplace 1819–1912, Liège, Belgium.

Posts Held Journalist, Propagandist, Paris, 1840–52; Prof. Polit. Econ., Royal Brussels Museum Industry, 1852–60; Ed., *Journal des Débats*, 1867–76; Ed., *Journal des Economistes*, 1881–1909.

Offices and Honours A founder and later Hon. Pres., Soc. d'Econ. Polit.

Publications *Books:* 1. *L'organisation de la liberté industrielle* (1846); 2. *Les soirées de la rue St Lazare* (1849); 3. *Le mouvement socialiste et les réunions publiques* (1870); 4. *Les problèmes du XXᵉ siécle* (1901); 5. *L'économie de l'histoire, théorie due progrès* (1908).

Career Determined advocate of free trade liberalism and opponent of socialism, first as a journalist in Paris and then in academic and editorial capacities. He related liberty and property to the economic phenomena of value, arguing that the object of liberty is value and that value is the substance of property.

Secondary Literature Y. Guyot, 'Obit. Gustave de Molinari', *EJ*, 22, March 1912.

MÖLLER, Hans Otto

Born 1915, Berlin, Germany.

Current Post Prof. Emeritus, Ludwig-Maximilians Univ., Munich, W. Germany, 1983–.

Past Posts Econ., Bank deutscher Länder, Frankfurt, Main, 1948–50; Member, Germany Delegation, OEEC, Paris, 1950–4; Prof., Univ. Frankfurt, 1954–8; Prof., Ludwig-Maximilians Univ., Munich, 1958–83; Vis. Prof., Coll. Europe, Bruges, 1955–6, Univ. Basel, 1957; Part-time Cons., EED, Brussels, 1958–70.

Degrees Dipl. Volkswirt, Dr Rer. Pol., Dr Rer. Pol. Habil. Univ. Berlin, 1936, 1938, 1942; Hon. Dr Univ. Kiel, 1983.

Offices and Honours Member, Bayerische Akademie Wissenschaften; Chairman, Advisory Council, German Ministry Econ., 1970–7.

Editorial Duties Ed. Boards, *Kyk, ZN*.

Principal Fields of Interest 020 General Economic Theory; 310 Domestic Monetary and Finance Theory and Institutions; 400 International Economics.

Publications *Books:* 1. *Kalkulation, Absatzpolitik und Preisbildung* (Springer, 1941, Mohr, 1962); 2. *Internationale Wirtschaftsorganisationen* (Gabler, 1960); 3. *Aussenwirtschaftspolitik* (Gabler, 1961); 4. *Zur Vorgeschichte der deutschen Mark* (Mohr, 1961); 5. *Das Ende einer Weltwährungsordnung?* (Piper, 1972); 6. *Die Europäische Union als Währungsunion?* (with W. Cezanne), (Nomos, 1979); 7. *Umweltötonomik* (with R. Osterkamp and W. Schneider), (Athenäum, 1981).

Articles: 1. 'Die Formen und Grundlagen einer Theorie der regionalen Preisdifferenzierung', *WA*, 57, 1943; 2. 'Das Konkurrenzsystem im Versicherungswesen', *JNS*, 159, 1944; 3. 'H.v. Stackelberg und sein Beitrag für die Wirtschaftswissenschaft', *ZGS*, 105, 1949; 4. 'Probleme der Geld-und Kreditpolitik bei Währungskonvertierbarkeit', in *Wirstschaftsfragen der freien Welt. Festgabe zum 60. Geb. v. Bundeswirtschaftsminster Erhard* (Mohr, 1957); 5. 'The role of international organizations in promoting price stability', in *Inflation*, ed. D. C. Hague (Macmillan, 1962); 6. 'Ursprungs-und bestimmungslandprinzip', *Finanzarchiv*, 27, 1968; 7. 'The reconstruction of the international economic order after the second world war and the integration of the federal republic of Germany into the world economy', *ZGS*, 137, 1981; 8. 'Europäische gemeinschaften', in *Handwörterbuch die Wirtschaftswissenschaften*, 2 (Mohr, Siebeck, 1979); 9. 'Volkswirtschaftslehre', in *Handwörterbuch die Wirtschaftswissenschaften*, 9 (Mohr, Siebeck, 1981).

Principal Contributions Dissemination of neoclassical economies in Germany during and after World War II, in particular the development of modern price theory along the lines set by Chamberlin, Robinson and von Stackelberg; integration of real and monetary theory with special reference to international economics; and, in the economic policy field, promotion of applications of regional and environmental economics, as well as work on international economic organisations and the world economic order.

MONSEN, Raymond Joseph

Born 1931, Payson, UT, USA.

Current Post Prof. Bus., Govt. and Soc., School Bus. Admin., Univ. Washington, Seattle, WA, USA, 1966–.

Past Posts Ass. Prof. Econ., Brigham Young Univ., USA, 1960–3; Assoc. Prof. Bus. Govt. and Soc., Univ. Washington, 1963–6; Hon. Fellow, Econ. and Grad. School Bus., Harvard Univ., 1968–9; Vis. Prof. Public Pol. Grad. School Bus., Stanford Univ., 1971–2.

Degrees BS Univ. Utah;, 1953; MA Stanford Univ. 1954; PhD Univ. Cal. Berkeley, 1960.

Offices and Honours Annual Res. Award., Land Econ. Foundation, 1958; Res. Award, Univ. Cal. Berkeley, 1959; Research Awards, Brigham Young Univ., 1962–3; Guggenheim Foundation Fellow, 1968–9; General Electric Foundation Res. Award, 1976, 1977, 1978, 1979.

Editorial Duties Series Ed.. *Business and Soc.* (Holt, Rinehart & Winston); Ed. Cons., McGraw-Hill, Houghton Mufflin, Wadsworth, Prentice-Hall; Ed. Board, *Bus. Forum*.

Principal Fields of Interest 051 Capitalistic Economic Systems; 052 Socialist and Communist Economic Systems; 442 International Business;.

Publications *Books:* 1. *Modern American Capitalism: Ideologies & Issues* (Houghton-Mufflin, 1963); 2. *The Makers of Public Policy* (with M. W. Cannon), (McGraw-Hill, 1965); 3. *The Business World*, ed. (with B. O. Saxberg), (Houghton Mufflin, 1967, 1972); 4. *Business and the Changing Environment* (McGraw-Hill, 1973); 5. *Management, Systems & Society* (with B. O. Saxberg, R. Johnson, and H. P. Knowles), (Goodyear, 1976); 6. *Nationalized Companies: Capitalism Challenged* (with K. D. Walters), (McGraw-Hill, 1983).

Articles: 1. 'A theory of large management firms' (with A. Downs), *JPE*,

73, June 1965; 2. 'The effect of separating ownership and control on the performance of the large firm' (with J. S. Chiu and D. E. Cooley), *QJE*, 82, Aug. 1968; 3. 'Public goods and private status: the law of consumer differentiation (with A. Downs), *Public Interest*, Spring 1971; 4. 'The unrecognized social revolution: the rise of the new business elite in America', *Cal. Management Rev.*, Winter 1971; 5. 'Bureaucracy and polyarchy as predictors of performance; a cross-national examination' (with B. Russet), *Comp. Polit. Stud.*, April 1975; 6. 'The future of American capitalism', *Cal. Management Rev.*, 21(4), Spring 1979; 7. 'State-owned business abroad: new competitive threat' (with K. D. Walters), *Harvard Bus. Rev.*, March-April 1979; 8. 'The state-owned firm: a review of the data and issues' (with K. D. Walters), in *Research in Corporate Social Performance-Policy*, 2, ed. (JAI Press, 1980); 9. 'The spreading nationalization of European industry' (with K. D. Walters), *Columbia J. World Bus*, Winter 1981; 10. 'Who should control nationalized companies?', *Cal. Management Rev.*, 25(4), Summer 1983.

Principal Contributions My work has been an exploration of the various assumptions of capitalism. My very first article (when still in graduate school) was a study of ownership in San Francisco. Thereafter, in books and articles, I pursued a study of ideologies of American capitalism, the theory of the modern firm and later a study on the consumer in a capitalist society. Thus my attempts were to build more realistic theories of behaviour of the principal microactors — the business manager and the consumer — as well as to study the ideologies they used to legitimise their actions.

Most recently I have been studying Western European firms that have been nationalised, looking at their performance and behaviour when ownership is no longer private. This has resulted in numerous articles and a book published in 1983. Currently, I am continuing my basic interest in capitalism with a study of theories of capitalism.

MOORE, Henry Ludwell*

Dates and Birthplace 1869–1958, Chales County, MD, USA.

Posts Held Prof., Smith Coll., Northampton, MA, 1896–1902; Columbia Univ., 1902–29.

Degrees BA, Ralph-Macon Coll., 1982; PhD Johns Hopkins Univ., 1896.

Publications *Books:* 1. *Laws of Wages: An Essay in Statistical Economics* (1911); 2. *Economic Cycles: Their Law and Cause* (1914); 3. *Forecasting the Yield and Price of Cotton* (1917); 4. *Generating Economic Cycles* (1923); 5. *Synthetic Economics* (1929).

Career A pioneer of econometrics who produced quantitative estimates of elasticities of demand and supply of productivity changes, of cost curves and the determinants of wage rates. After his early work on wages, he turned to the search for a fundamental explanation of economic fluctuations. His explanation was that 8-year cycles of rainfall governed cycles of the whole economy. Later attempts to relate cycles to the transits of Venus failed by his own admission. His final book was an attempt to devise a research programme to estimate Walras' equations of general equilibrium.

Secondary Literature G. J. Stigler, 'Henry L. Moore and statistical economics', in *Essays in the History of Economics* (Univ. of Chicago Press, 1965), 'Moore, Henry L.', *IESS*, 10.

MOORE, James Clark

Born 1936, Dow City, IA, USA.

Current Post Prof. Econ., Krannert School Management, Purdue Univ., IN, 1976–.

Past Posts Ass. Prof. Econ., Univ. Missouri, Columbia, MO, 1965–9; Assoc. Prof. Econ., Purdue Univ., 1969–76; Vis., Center Math. Stud. Econ. and Management Science, Northwestern Univ., 1975.

Degrees BA Univ. Nebraska, Omaha, 1960; PhD Univ. Minnesota, 1968.

Principal Fields of Interest 022 Microeconomic Theory; 024 Welfare Theory; 026 Economics of Uncertainty and Information.

Publications *Articles:* 1. 'Some extensions of the Kuhn-Tucker results in concave programming', in *Papers in Quantitative Economics*, 1, eds. J. P. Quirk and A. M. Zarley (Univ. Press Kansas, 1968); 2. 'The compensation principle in welfare economics' (with J. S. Chipman), in *Papers in Quantitative Economics*, 2, ed. A. M. Zarley (Univ. Press Kansas, 1971); 3. 'Resource allocation in a non-convex economy' (with A. B. Whinston and J. S. Wu), *REStud*, 39(3), July 1972; 4. 'Aggregate demand, real national income, and the compensation principle' (with J. S. Chipman), *Int ER*, 14(1), Feb. 1973; 5. 'The existence of "compensated equilibrium" and the structure of the Pareto efficiency frontier', *Int ER*, 16(2), June 1975; 6. 'The scope of consumers' surplus' (with J. S. Chipman), in *Evolution, Welfare and Time in Economics*, eds. A. M. Tang, *et al.* (D. C. Heath, 1976); 7. 'On social welfare functions and the aggregation of preferences' (with J. S. Chipman), *JET*, 21(1), Aug. 1979; 8. 'Real national income with homothetic preferences and a fixed distribution of income' (with J. S. Chipman), *Em*, 48(2), March 1980; 9. 'Compensating variation, consumer's surplus, and welfare' (with J. S. Chipman), *AER*, 70(5), Dec. 1980; 10. 'Measurable triples and cardinal measurement', *JET*, 29(1), Feb. 1983.

Principal Contributions An early interest in the theory of constrained maximisation evolved into an interest in the theory of welfare criteria used in economics. This resulted (in collaboration with J. S. Chipman) in the analysis, in a general equilibrium context, of the compensation principle, real national income, and social welfare functions. Also with J. S. Chipman, I developed a general framework for the analysis of consumers' surplus concepts. In the area of general equilibrium, have analysed the extent to which non-convexities are consistent with the existence of general competitive equilibrium, and have established what is apparently the only known set of sufficient conditions for the existence of general competitive equilibrium when exchange is necessitated by specialisation (individual consumer endowments are not necessarily elements of the respective consumption sets). More recently, have been working on the theory of measurement and its applications to economics, and on the economics of information.

MORELLET, André*

Dates and Birthplace 1727–1819, Lyons, France.
Posts Held Abbé of the Catholic Church.
Offices and Honours Member, Napoleonic Corps Législatif.
Publications *Books:* 1. *Réflexions sur les avantages de la libre fabrication et de l'usage des toiles peintes en France* (1758); 2. *Manuel des inquisiteurs* (1762); 3. *Fragment d'une lettre sur la police des grains* (1764); 4. *Mèmoire sur la situation actuelle de la Compagnie des Indes* (1769); 5. *Réfutation d'un ècrit intitulé Dialogues sur le commerce des blés* (1770).

Career One of the *encyclopaedistes* and a contributor to Peuchet's *Dictionnaire universel de la géographie commercante* (1799–1800). He was an ardent free trader, arguing that since man is naturally free, any interference with his buying and selling is a violation of natural law. His *Mémoire ...* was responsible for the suspension of the Compagnie des Indes (1769). His translation of the *Wealth of Nations* into French remained unpublished.
Secondary Literature L. Strachey, *Portraits in Miniature* (1931); H. Hauser, 'Morellet, Abbé André', *ESS*, 11.

MORGAN, James N.

Born 1918, Croydon, IN, USA.
Current Post Res. Scientist, Inst. Social Res., Prof. Econ., Univ. Michigan, Ann Arbor, MI, USA, 1979–.
Past Posts Ass. Prof., Brown Univ., 1947–9; Vis., Center Advanced Study, Berlin, W. Germany, 1983–4.
Degrees BA Northwestern Univ., 1939; PhD Harvard Univ., 1947.
Offices and Honours Member, NAS;

Fellow, ASA, AAAS; Member, Gerontological Soc., Board Dir., Consumers Union, USA.

Principal Fields of Interest 229 Microdata.

Publications *Books:* 1. *Income and Welfare in the United States* (with M. David, *et al.*), (McGraw-Hill, 1962); 2. *The Economic Behaviour of the Affluent* (with R. Barlow and H. Brazer), (Brookings Inst., 1966); 3. *Productive Americans* (with I. Siragel-din and L. Baerwaldt), (Inst. Social Res., 1966); 4. *The Economics of Personal Choice* (with G. Duncan), (Univ. Michigan Press, 1980); 5. *Five Thousand American Families: Patterns of Economic Progress* 10 vols, ed. and co-author (Inst. Social Res., 1972–83).

Articles: 1. 'The anatomy of income distribution', *REStat*, 44, Aug. 1962; 2. 'Problems in the analysis of survey data, and a proposal' (with J. Sonquist), *JASA*, 58, June 1963; 3. 'Education and income' (with M. David), *QJE*, 77, Aug. 1963; 4. 'Some pilot studies on communication and consensus in the family', *Public Opinion Q.*, Spring 1968; 5. 'Trends in planned early retirement and trends in satisfaction with retirement' (with R. Barfield), *The Gerontologist*, 1978; 6. 'The role of time in the measurement of transfers and well-being', in *Economic Transfers in the U.S.*, ed. M. Moon (Univ. Chicago Press, 1984).

Principal Contributions Consumer behaviour studied through survey research, survey data collection and analysis methods. Survey research on the poor, the wealthy, car accident victims, injured workers, and businessmen. A major study for two decades has followed all the members of an original sample of families, forming a self-replacing panel and allowing studies of the dynamics of change in income and in family composition.

MORGENSTERN, Oskar*

Dates and Birthplace 1902–77, Goerlitz, Germany.

Posts Held Privatdozent, Prof., Univ. Vienna, 1929–38; Prof., Univ. Princeton, 1938–70.

Degrees Dr Univ. Vienna, 1925.

Offices and Honours Disting. Fellow, AEA, 1976.

Publications *Books:* 1. *Wirtschafts-prognose* (1928); 2. *Die Grenzen der Wirtschaftspolitik* (1934); 3. *Theory of Games and Economic Behaviour* (with J. von Neumann), (1944, 1964); 4. *On the Accuracy of Economic Observations* (1950); 5. *The Question of National Defense* (1959); 6. *Predictability of Stock Market Prices* (with C. W. J. Granger), (1970); 7. *Mathematical Theory of Expanding and Contracting Economies* (with G. L. Thompson), (1976).

Articles: 1. 'Ten critical points in contemporary economic theory: an interpretation', *JEL*, 10(4), Dec. 1972.

Career With von Neumann, introduced games theory into economics. The problem of prediction was his starting point, and the use of formal mathematical models of games was merely suggested as a helpful approach. The burgeoning popularity of games theory has, however, resulted in a rich literature, spanning economics, sociology, and political science. Also wrote on the economics of defence and developed von Neumann's ideas on growth theory.

Secondary Literature M. Shubik, 'Morgenstern, Oskar', *IESS*, 18; A. Schotter, 'On Morgenstern', *Comtemporary Economists in Perspective*, eds. H. W. Spiegel and W. J. Samuels (JAI Press, 1984).

MORISHIMA, Michio

Born 1923, Osaka, Japan.

Current Post Sir John Hicks Prof. Econ., LSE, London, England, 1970–.

Past Posts Ass. Prof., Univ. Kyoto, 1950–1; Ass. Prof., Prof., Univ. Osaka, 1951–69; Rockefeller Foundation Fellow, Univs. Oxford and Yale, 1956–8; Vis. Sr. Fellow, All Souls Coll., Oxford, 1963–4; Prof., Univ. Essex, 1968–70; Chairman, Internat. Centre Econ. and Related Disciplines, LSE, 1978–81.

Degrees BA Univ. Kyoto, 1946.

Offices and Honours Vice-Pres., Pres., Em. Soc, 1964– 1965; Hon.

Member, AEA, 1976–; Foreign Hon. Member, AAAS 1975–; Fellow, BA, 1981–; Bunka Kunsho (Cultural Order of Japan), 1976.

Editorial Duties Assoc. Ed., *Em*, 1960–9; Co-ed., Ed., *Int ER*, 1960–70; Ed. Boards, *JEL*, 1976–8, *Ec*, 1975–.

Principal Fields of Interest 021 General Equilibrium Theory; 031 History of Economic Thought; 051 Capitalist Economic Systems.

Publications *Books:* 1. *Equilibrium, Stability and Growth* (OUP, 1964, 1978; transl., Russian, Nawka, 1972); 2. *Theory of Economic Growth* (OUP, 1969, 1970; transls., Spanish, Editorial Technos, 1973, Italian, Etas Libri, 1974); 3. *The Working of Econometric Models* (with M. Saito, *et al.*), (CUP, 1972); 4. *The Demand for Money: Real and Monetary* (with M. Allingham, *et al.*), (OUP, 1973); 5. *Marx's Economics* (CUP, 1973, 1977; transls., Italian, ISEDI, 1976, Japanese, Toyokeizai, 1974, Spanish, Editorial Technos, 1977); 6. *Kindia Shakai no Keizai Riron* (Sobunsha, 1973, 1975; transls., English, *The Economic Theory of Modern Society*, CUP, 1976, Spanish, Antoni Bosch, 1981); 7. *Walras' Economics* (CUP, 1977, 1981, transls., French, Economica, 1979, Italian, Liquori Editore, 1983, Japanese, Toyokeizai, 1983); 8. *Value, Exploitation and Growth* (with G. Catephores), (McGraw-Hill, 1978; transls., Portuguese, Zahar Editores, 1980, French, 1980); 9. *Why Has Japan 'Succeeded'?* (CUP, 1982, 1984; transls., Korean, Icho-kaku, 1982, Japanese, TBS Britanica, 1984, Italian, Mulino, 1984); 10. *The Economics of Industrial Society* (CUP, 1984; transl., Japanese, Iwanami, 1984).

Articles: 1. 'On the laws of change of the price-system in an economy which contains complementary commodities', *Osaka Econ. Papers*, 1, May 1952; 2. 'The Hicksian Micro-dynamics and the Keynesian macro-dynamics', *Osaka Econ. Papers*, 2, (1), March 1953; 3. 'An analysis of the capitalist process of reproduction', *Metroec.*, 8, Dec. 1956; 4. 'Aggregation in Leontief matrices and the labour theory of value' (with F. Seton), *Em*, 29, April 1961; 5. 'On the two theorems of growth economics: a mathematical exercise', *Em*, 33, Oct. 1965; transl., German in *Mathematische Wirtschaftstheorie*, eds. M. J. Beckman and R. Sato (Keipenheuer & Witsch, 1975); 6. 'A generalisation of gross substitute system', *REStud*, 27(2), April 1970; 7. 'Consumption-investment frontier, wage-profit frontier and the von Neumann growth equilibrium', *ZN*, Suppl. 1, 1971; 8. 'Marx in the light of modern economic theory', *Em*, 42(4), July 1974; transl., *Econ. App*, 28, 1975; 9. 'W. Jaffé on Léon Walras: a comment', *JEL*, 18(2), June 1980; 10. 'The good and bad uses of mathematics', in *Economics in Dissarray*, eds. P. Wiles and G. Routh (Blackwell, 1984).

Principal Contributions My economics research began with the mathematisation of Hicks' *Value and Capital* model published in my first book (Dogakuteki Keizai Riron, 1951). This demonstrated that Samuelson-Lange type conditions will assure the stability of temporary equilibrium, but that totally different stability conditions obtain for moving equilibria (not conditions in terms of prices but conditions in terms of quantities). This research used Frobenius' theorem while also introducing the Liapounoff-like function based on an article by Sono. I subsequently attempted to develop Frobenius' theorem so as to be able to include complementary goods. However, the early *Value and Capital* model later developed into a growth model. My theory has been consistently multisectoral; its focal concern is the accommodation of von Neumann's growth model to general equilibrium models. It is from this perspective that I have attempted to review the works of Marx and Walras. It is my belief that both were Ricardian and when modified along von Neumann lines, the similarities and differences in the theories of the two men became far clearer.

I have recently been looking at the workability of economic systems using a far broader perspective which takes into account social factors (e.g. Max Weber's theory that the development of an economy is on a knife-edge with respect to minute differences in ethos).

MORRIS, Cynthia Taft

Born 1928, Cincinnati, OH, USA.
Current Post Prof. Econ., Smith Coll., Northampton, MA, USA, 1983–.
Past Posts Econ. Analyst, Info. Section, Mutual Security Agency, Paris, 1951–3; Res. Ass. Econ., Yale Univ., 1953–5; Teaching Fellow Econ., Harvard Univ., 1955–7; Res. Fellow, Amer. Assoc. Univ. Women, 1958–9; Cons., Electricity Power Comm., EEC, Geneva, 1960; Ass. Prof. Econ., Amer. Univ. Beirut, 1961–2; Cons., Office Program and Pol. Coordination, Agency Internat. Devlp., 1962–9; Assoc. Prof., Prof. Econ., Amer. Univ., Washington, DC, 1964–9, 1969–83.
Degrees BA (Internat. Relations) Vassar Coll., 1949; MSc LSE; PhD Yale Univ., 1959.
Offices and Honours Phi Beta Kappa.
Principal Fields of Interest 040 Economic History; 110 Economic Growth; 220 Economic and Social Statistical Data.
Publications *Books:* 1. *Evolution of Wage Structure* (with L. G. Reynolds), (Yale Univ. Press, 1956); 2. *Society, Politics, and Economic Development* (with I. Adelman), (JHUP, 1967); 3. *Economic Growth and Social Equity in Developing Countries* (with I. Adelman), (Stanford Univ. Press, 1973); 4. *Comparative Development Perspectives — Essays in Honor of Lloyd Reynolds*, co-ed. (with G. Ranis, *et al.*), (Westview Press, 1983).
Articles: 1. 'Some neglected aspects of sixteenth-century economic thought', *Explor. in Entrepreneurial Hist.*, 9(3), 1957; 2. 'A factor analysis of the interrelationship between social and political variables and per capita gross national product' (with I. Adelman), *QJE*, 74, Nov. 1965; 3. 'An econometric model of socio-economic and political change in underdeveloped countries' (with I. Adelman), *AER*, 58(5), Dec. 1968; 4. 'The measurement of institutional characteristics of nations: methodological considerations' (with I. Adelman), *J Dev Stud*, 8, April 1972; 5. 'Growth and impoverishment in the middle of the nineteenth century'

(with I. Adelman), *WD*, 6(3), 1978; 6. 'The role of institutional influences in patterns of agricultural development in the nineteenth and early twentieth centuries: a cross-section quantitative study' (with I. Adelman), *JEH*, 39, March 1979; 7. 'Patterns of industrialization in the latter nineteenth and early twentieth centuries: a cross-section quantitative study', in *Research in Economic History*, ed. P. Uselding, 5 (JAI Press, 1980); 8. 'Social weighted real income comparisons: an application to India' (with I. Broder), *WD*, 10, 1982; 9. 'Institutional influences on poverty in the nineteenth century: a quantitative comparative study' (with I. Adelman), *JEH*, 43, March 1983; 10. 'The measurement of economic development: quo vadis?' in *Comparative Development Perspectives, op. cit.*

Principal Contributions Throughout my career my major interest has been in the relationship between institutional influences and economic change. In my work with Lloyd Reynolds and in my studies of workers' standards of living for the Marshall Plan, I focussed on the determinants of wage structures and changes in wage levels. When I shifted to the field of development economics in the 1960s, I continued my interest in the many ways in which institutional constraints and changes affected the outcome of economic developments. As I gained familiarity with a wide range of econometric techniques through my work with Irma Adelman, I became fascinated by the challenge of measuring institutional structure and change. This interest in theory and practice of measurement in the broadest sense had a strong influence on both my research and my teaching. My current research work on the long-term evolution of societies in the modern historical epoch of rapid economic growth represents the culmination of two decades of work on the nineteenth and early twentieth centuries, which I undertook with my colleague Irma Adelman in the late 1960s. In this work we investigate the nature and causes of often striking differences in paths of change among different types of countries. Our focus is on the way in which initial resources and institutional conditions have interacted with dynamic economic forces and institutional transformations to influence the processes of economic growth and development. This work will be published as *Where Angels Fear to Tread: Quantitative Studies in History and Development.*

MORTENSEN, Dale T.

Born 1939, Enterprise, OR, USA.
Current Post Prof. Econ., Northwestern Univ., Evanston, IL, USA, 1975–.
Past Posts Ass. Prof., Assoc. Prof., Northwestern Univ., 1965–71, 1971–5; Vis. Scholar, Univ. Essex, England, 1970–1; Fellow, Inst. Advanced Stud., Hebrew Univ., Jerusalem, 1977–8.
Degrees BA Willamette Univ., Salem, OR, 1961; PhD Carnegie-Mellon Univ., 1967.
Offices and Honours Fellow, Em Soc, 1979.
Principal Fields of Interest 020 General Economic Theory; 026 Economics of Uncertainty and Information; 821 Theory of Labour Markets and Leisure.
Publications *Articles:* 1. 'A theory of wage and employment dynamics', in *The Microeconomic Foundations of Employment and Inflation Theory*, ed. E. S. Phelps, *et al.* (W. W. Norton, 1970); 2. 'Job search, the duration of unemployment, and the Phillips curve', *AER*, 60(5), Dec. 1970; 3. 'Generalized costs of adjustment and dynamic factor demand theory', *Em*, 41, July 1973; 4. 'Job matching and under imperfect information', in *Evaluating the Labor Market Effects on Social Programs*, eds. O. Ashenfelter and J. Blum (Princeton Univ. Press, 1976); 5. 'Labor supply under uncertainty' (with K. Burdett), in *Research in Labor Economics*, 2, ed. R. G. Ehrenberg (JAI Press, 1978); 6. 'Specific capital and labor turnover', *Bell JE*, 9(2), Autumn 1978; 7. 'Search, layoffs, and labor market equilibrium' (with K. Burdett), *JPE*, 88(4), Aug. 1980; 8. 'Testing for ability in a competitive labor market' (with K. Burdett), *JET*, 25, June 1981; 9. 'The matching process as a non-cooperative bargaining game', in *The Economics of Information and Uncertainty*, ed. J. J. McCall (Univ. Chicago Press, 1982); 10. 'Property rights and efficiency in mating, racing and related games', *AER*, 72(5), Dec. 1982.

Principal Contributions An interest in dynamic phenomena in economics, not readily explained by existing theory, has marked my research from its beginning. Early work includes papers on the development of formal job search models and their implications for unemployment and wage dynamics, and papers on the theory of dynamic factor demand when adjustment costs are present. Although these were intended as contributions to the microeconomic foundations of macroeconomics, my research interests shifted to applications of the economics of imperfect information and uncertainty. A subsequent series of papers was focussed on the study of job separation behaviour, testing for ability in the labour market, labour supply dynamics, and contract equilibrium in the context of models that account for imperfect information and uncertainty. My recent theoretical contributions have dealt with dynamic models of job-worker matching in a game theoretic context, the effects and design of unemployment insurance schemes, and mobility in labour markets characterised by long-term contracts. Currently, I am interested in the development of empirical models of individual-worker labour market experience over time designed for estimation and testing using panel data. A book on recent contributions of the economics of information and uncertainty to labour economic analysis is in progress.

MOSES, Leon N.

Born 1924, New York City, NY, USA.
Current Post Prof. Econ., Assoc. Transporation Center, Northwestern Univ., Evanston, IL, 1963–, 1979–,
Past Posts Teaching Fellow, Univ. Buffalo, NY, 1945–6; Instr., Univ. Miami, FL, 1946–7; Instr., Northwestern Univ., 1950–1; Industrial

Econ., TVA, 1951–2; Res. Assoc., Ass. Prof., Harvard Univ., 1952–9; Assoc. Prof. Econ. Dir. Res., Dir., Transportation Center, Northwestern Univ., 1959–62; 1974–9; Lect., Amer. Stud. Program, Kyoto Univ. Japan 1973.

Degrees BA Ohio State Univ., 1945; MA, PhD Harvard Univ., 1945, 1953.

Offices and Honours Ford Foundation Prof., 1965; Rockefeller Foundation Award, 1969; Pres, RSA.

Editorial Duties Book Review Ed., *JRS*, 1978–80.

Principal Fields of Interest 930 Urban Economics; 940 Regional Economics; 615 Economics of Transportation.

Publications *Books:* 1. *Cost Benefit Analysis for Inland Navigation Projects*, 3 vols (with L. Lave and R. H. Strotz), (Inst. Water Resources, Dept. US Army, 1974); 2. *Regulatory Reform and the Federal Aviation Act of 1975*, ed. (US Dept. Transporation, 1976); 3. *Motor Carrier Economic Regulation*, ed. (Transportation Center, Northwestern Univ., 1978); 4. *In Search of a Rational Liner Shipping Policy*, ed. (Transportation Center, Northwestern Univ., 1979); 5. *Corporate Planning Under Deregulation: The Case of the Airlines*, ed. (Transportation Center, Northwestern Univ., 1979).

Articles: 1. 'The stability of interregional trading patterns and input-output analysis', *AER*, 45(5), Dec. 1955; 2. 'Location and the theory of production', *QJE*, 72(2), May 1958; 3. 'A general equilibrium model of production, interregional trade and location of industry', *REStat*, 42, Nov. 1960; 4. 'Towards a theory of intra-urban wage differentials and their influence on travel patterns', *Papers and Proceedings* (RSA, 1962); 5. 'Value of time, choice of mode and the subsidy issue in urban transportation' (with H. F. Williamson, Jr.), *JPE*, 71, June 1963; 6. 'The location of economic activity in cities' (with H. F. Williamson, Jr.), *AER*, 57(2), May 1967; 7. 'Thünen, Weber and the spatial structure of the nineteenth-century city' (with R. Fales), in *Spatial, Regional and Population Economics: Essays in Honor of E. M. Hoover*, eds. M. Perl-

man, C. Leven and B. Chinitz (Gordon & Breach Science, 1973); 8. 'Interdependence and the location of economic activities' (with G. S. Goldstein), *JUE*, Jan. 1975; 9. 'Dynamics and land use: the case of forestry' (with J. Ledyard), in *Public and Urban Economics, Essays in Honor of William S. Vickery*, ed. R. E. Griecson (D. D. Heath, 1976); 10. 'Qualitative choice and the blending of discrete alternatives' (with A. Anas), *REStat*, 66(4), Nov. 1984.

Principal Contributions Nowadays, economists generally agree on the need to incorporate spatial considerations into economic reasoning: the influence of transportation and communication costs on the performance and organisation of economic activity are now broadly recognised as involving challenging theoretical and important public policy issues. This was not true thirty years ago. My papers my have contributed to the change, because in them I tried to show that economic theory could be adapted and extended in ways providing significant insight into spatial aspects of economic behaviour. Thus No. 2 above extended the traditional theory of the firm in ways that permitted the relationship between transportation costs and production decisions to be understood. No. 3 demonstrated how the introduction of transportation costs changes the basic conception of comparative advantage, adding an access cost dimension to it. It presented an approach in which the optimal patterns of production and interregional trade of industries are determined simultaneously. The approach also provided insight into the locational question of which industries are candidates for expansion in which regions. The two papers on urban economics (Nos. 6 and 7) contained an approach in which transportation costs influence the structure of factor prices in an urban area and thereby determine patterns of location and land use. The papers' logic also offered insights into the rise of the great mononucleated cities in the 19th century and their decline in the 20th.

An inportant need today is the development of models in which spatial and temporal reasoning are joined. Such models offer promise of providing deeper understanding of the behaviour of firms and households. The development and testing of models in which firms make decisions over both space and time is one of the areas in which I am currently working.

MUELLBAUER, John N. J.

Born 1944, Kempten, Allgäu, W. Germany.
Current Post Official Fellow Econ., Nuffield Coll. Oxford, England, 1981–.
Past Posts Lect., Warwick Univ., 1969–72; Lect., Reader, Prof., Birkbeck Coll., London, 1972–5, 1975–7, 1977–81.
Degrees BA Univ. Camb., 1965; PhD Univ. Cal. Berkeley, 1975.
Offices and Honours Wrenbury Fellow Polit. Econ., Univ. Camb., 1964–5; Flood Fellow Econ., Univ. Cal. Berkeley, 1965–6, 1967–8; Medallion, Helsinki Univ., 1979; Fellow, Em Soc, 1979.
Editorial Duties Board Member, *REStud*, 1973–83; Assoc. Ed., *Em*, 1979–84.
Principal Fields of Interest 022 Microeconomic Theory.
Publications *Books:* 1. *Economics and Consumer Behaviour* (with A. Deaton), (CUP, 1980).
Articles: 1. 'Household production theory, quality and the "hedonic technique"', *AER*, 64(6), Dec. 1974; 2. 'The cost of living and taste and quality change', *JET*, 10(3), June 1975; 3. 'Aggregation, income distribution and consumer demand', *REStud*, 42(4), Oct. 1975; 4. 'Community preferences and the representative consumer', *Em*, 44(5), Sept. 1976; 5. 'Testing the Barten model of household composition effects and the cost of children', *EJ*, 87, Sept. 1977; 6. 'Macroeconomic models with quantity rationing' (with R. Portes), *EJ*, 88, Dec. 1978; 7. 'The estimation of the Prais-Houthakker model of equivalence scales', *Em*, 48(1), Jan. 1980; 8. 'Unemployment, employment, and exports in British manufacturing: a non-clearing markets approach' (with D. Winter), *Europ*

ER, 13(3), May 1980; 9. 'An almost ideal demand system' (with A. Deaton), 70(3), *AER*, June 1980; 10. 'Surprises in the consumption function', *EJ*, Suppl., 93, 1983.
Principal Contributions The relationship of theory to applied economics: thus each theoretical contribution arises out of a problem in applied economics; and conversely, each applied piece is placed within a tight theoretic framework. The main areas are: aggregation theory, particularly in the context of consumer demand and labour supply; index numbers and quality measurement with applications to consumer and producer durables; prices and inequality; the distributional impact of different structures of relative prices; theory and measurement of equivalence scales and hence welfare comparisons across households; non-Walrasian macroeconomics; employment functions; productivity measurement; and aggregate production functions.

MUELLER, Dennis Cary

Born 1940, Milwaukee, WI, USA.
Current Post Prof. Econ., Univ. Maryland, USA, 1977–.
Past Posts Ass. Prof., Simon Fraser Univ., 1964–6; Res. Assoc., Brookings Inst., 1966–8; Ass. Prof., Assoc. Prof., Cornell Univ., 1968–70, 1970–6; Post-doctoral Fellow, Center Study Public Choice, Virginia Polytechnic Inst. and State Univ., 1972–3; Res. Fellow, Dir., Internat. Inst. Management, 1974–8, 1981–3, 1982–3.
Degrees BS (Maths.) Colorado Coll., 1962; PhD Princeton Univ., 1966.
Offices and Honours NSF Grad. Fellow, 1962–5; Pres., Public Choice Soc., 1984–6.
Editorial Duties Co-ed., *Internat. J. Industrial Organization*.
Principal Fields of Interest 025 Social Choice; Brueaucratic Performance; 610 Industrial Organisation and Public Policy; 620 Economics of Technological Change.
Publications *Books:* 1. *Public Choice* (CUP, 1972); 2. *The Determinants*

and Effects of Mergers — An International Comparison, ed. & contrib. (Oelgeschlager, Gunn & Hain, 1980); 3. *The Political Economy of Growth*, ed. and contrib. (Yale Univ. Press, 1983); 4. *The Determinants of Persistent Profits* (Fed. Trade Commission, 1983).

Articles: 1. 'The firm decision process: an econometric investigation', *QJE*, 81, Feb. 1967, repr. in *Readings in the Economics of Industrial Organization*, ed. D. Needhan (Holt, Rinehart & Winston, 1970), and *Readings in Managerial Economics*, ed. K. S. Palada (Prentice-Hall, 1973); 2. 'A theory of conglomerate mergers', *QJE*, 83, Nov. 1969; 3. 'Managerial and stockholder welfare models of firm expenditures' (with H. G. Grabowski), *REStat*, 54(1), Feb. 1972; 4. 'A life cycle theory of the firm', *J Ind E*, 20, July 1972; 5. 'Constitutional democracy and social welfare', *QJE*, 87, Feb. 1973; 6. 'Life-cycle effects on corporate returns on retentions' (with H. G. Grabowski), *REStat*, 57(4), Nov. 1975; 7. 'The persistence of profits above the norm', *Ec*, N.S. 44, Nov. 1977; 8. 'The effects of conglomerate mergers: a survey of the empirical evidence', *J Bank Fin*, 1, Dec. 1977, repr. in *Financial Analysis and Planning: Theory and Application: A Book of Readings*, ed. C. F. Lee (Addison-Wesley, 1984); 9. 'Voting by veto', *J Pub E*, 10, Aug. 1978, repr. in *Aggregation and the Revelation of Preferences*, ed. J. J. Laffont (N-H, 1979), and *The Theory of Public Choice*, 2, ed. J. M. Buchanan (Univ. Michigan Press, 1984); 10. 'The social costs of monopoly' (with K. Cowling), *EJ*, 88, Dec. 1978, repr. in *Towards a Theory of the Rent-Seeking Society*, eds. J. M. Buchanan, R. D. Tollison and G. Tullock (Texas A&M Univ. Press, 1980).

Principal Contributions My first 'love' in economics was the field of public finance, and my decision to go to Princeton to do graduate work was predicated in part on Richard Musgrave's presence on the faculty. One of the fields I chose to study there besides public finance was industrial organisation, taught then by Jesse Markham. I became interested in R&D and technological change, a hot topic at the time,

and this interest turned into a thesis topic and a career in industrial organisation.

A couple of years later I read James Coleman's paper 'The Possibility of a Social Welfare Function', and my original interest in public finance was rekindled, this time, however, under the guise of public choice. While I did write a short comment on the Coleman piece, my main research effort at the time was still in industrial organisation and it wasn't until a couple of years later that I was actually able to devote a substantial amount of effort to the public choice area.

Over the last decade or so I have tried to divide my time roughly equally between the industrial organisation and public choice areas. While some find this division unusual if not schizophrenic, I find that the two areas complement each other nicely. Industrial organisation deals with the aggregation of individual choices in the market, the imperfections in these markets, and that peculiar heirarchical bureaucracy for displacing the market which we call the corporation. Public choice is concerned with the aggregation of preferences through nonmarket mechanisms, the imperfections of these mechanisms as aggregation devices, and the mysterious workings of government bureaucracies. Both share an orientation toward asking important, real-world questions and deriving answers in cognizance of the institutional environment in which the subject matter is grounded. Both fields seem capable of making use of the advantages economic methodology offers without becoming a slave to technique. My hope is to have the time and energy to maintain a foot in each field without having the growth in their respective literatures pull my feet from under me.

MÜLLER, Adam Heinrich*

Dates and Birthplace 1779–1829, Berlin, Germany.

Posts Held Tutor, Prince Bernhard of Saxe-Weimar, Dresden, 1806–9; Civil servant, Austria, 1813.

Publications *Books:* 1. *Die Elemente der Staatskunst*, 2 vols (1809, 1922); 2.

Ausgewählte Abhandlungen (1812, 1931); 3. *Die Theorie der Staatshaushaltung und Ihre Fortschritte* (1812); 4. *Versuche einer neuen Theorie des Geldes* (1816, 1922); 5. *Zwölf Reden uber die Beredsamkeit und deren Verfall in Deutschland* (1817, 1920).

Career German Catholic economist of the Romantic school, who rejected the individuality and emphasis on material values of contemporary political economy. He was closely associated with Metternich and the reactionary politics of the post-Napoleonic period. He favoured an organic view of society in which the State would act to unite all social elements. The implications of this were nationalist and protectionist. He had some influence on the Historical School and inspired Spann's 'universalism'.

Secondary Literature J. Baxa, *Adam Müller* (Fischer, 1930); H. R. Bowen, 'Müller, Adam Heinrich', *IESS*, 10.

MUNDLAK, Yair

Born 1927, Pinsk, Poland.
Current Post Ruth Ochberg Prof. Agric. Econ., Hebrew Univ., Jerusalem, Israel, 1956–.
Past Posts Vis. Assoc. Prof. Agric. Econ., Univ. Cal. Berkeley, 1961–3; Res. Assoc. Econ., MIT, 1963; Vis. Prof. Econ., F. H. Prince Vis. Prof. Econ., Univ. Chicago, 1966–7, 1978–; Dir. Res. Center Agric. Econ. Res., Rehovot, Israel, 1968–83; Cons., Devlp. Res. Center, World Bank, Washington, DC, 1972; Dean, Faculty Agric., Hebrew Univ., Jerusalem, 1971–4; Vis. Prof. Econ., Harvard Univ., 1974–6; Vis. Res., Internat. Food Pol. Res. Inst., Washington, DC, 1976–83.
Degrees BS Univ. Cal. Davis, 1953; MA (Stats.), PhD Univ. Cal. Berkeley, 1956, 1957.
Offices and Honours Phi Beta Kappa, 1953; Best Grad. Paper, Outstanding PhD Dissertation, Best Published Res., Quality Res. Discovery, AAEA, 1956, 1957, 1965, 1980; Bareli Prize, Israel, 1965; Ford Foundation Res. Fellow, 1966–7; Rothschild Prize, Israel, 1972; Pres., Israel Foundation Trustees, 1977–; Fellow, Em Soc.

Editorial Duties Assoc. Ed., *J Em*, 1973–7.
Principal Fields of Interest 100 Economic Growth; 710 Agricultural Economics; 200 Econometrics.
Publications *Books:* 1. *Economic Analysis of Established Family Farms in Israel* (Falk Project Econ. Res. Israel, 1964); 2. *Long Term Projections of Supply and Demand for Agricultural Products in Israel* (Falk Project Econ. Res. Israel, 1964); 3. *The West Bank and Gaza Strip — Economic Structure and Development Prospects* (with Ben-Shahar, E. Berglas and Sadan), (Rand Corp., 1971); 4. *The Effect of Free Trade with the Territories on Israel Agriculture* (Hebrew) (with H. Avni), (Center Agric. Econ. Res., 1974); 5. *Research in Agricultural Economics* (Hebrew), ed. (Center Agric. Econ. Res., 1976); 6. *Arid Zone Development*, co-ed. (with F. Singer), (Ballinger, 1977); 7. *Intersectoral Factor Mobility and Agricultural Growth* (Internat. Food Pol. Res. Inst., 1979); 8. *Agricultural Growth and Economic Growth in an Open Economy — The Case of Argentine* (with D. Cavallo), (Internat. Food Pol. Res. Inst., 1982).

Articles: 1. 'Statistical analysis of supply response in late spring potatoes in California' (with C. O. McCorkle, Jr.), *Hilgardia*, 24(16), April 1956, and *JFE*, 38(2), May 1956; 2. 'Empirical production function free of management bias', *JFE*, 43(1), Feb. 1961, repr. in *Readings in Economics, Statistics and Econometrics*, ed. A. Zellner (Little Brown, 1968); 3. 'Aggregation over time in distributed lag models', *Int ER*, 2(2), May 1961; 4. 'On the micro economic theory of distributed lags', *REStat*, 48(1), Feb. 1966; 5. 'Elasticities of substitution and the theory of derived demand', *REStud*, 35(2), April 1968; 6. 'The correspondence of efficiency frontiers as a generalization of the cost function' (with Z. Volcani), *Int ER*, 14(1), Feb. 1973; 7. 'On the pooling of time series and cross section data', *Em*, 46(1), Jan. 1978; 8. 'On the concept of non-significant functions and its implications for regression analysis', *J Em*, 16(2), May 1981; 9. 'Random effects, fixed effects, convolution and separation' (with J. Yahav), *Em*, 49(6), Nov.

1981; 10. 'Elements of a pure theory of forecasting and Keynesian macroeconometrics', in *Development in an Inflationary World*, eds. J. Flanders and A. Razin (Academic Press, 1981).

Principal Contributions My main interest has been to understand and to quantify the economic performance of the agricultural sector. It started with empirical analysis of supply response in California and later on continued with the analysis of family farms in Israel. This work brought out the quantitative effect of the distribution of entrepreneurial capacity on that of income as well as the estimation of production and behavioural functions. Consequently it led to a formulation of the behavioural functions of the firms within a recursive framework which was to modify, and in parts to replace, the distributed lag analysis. It was also indicated that some of the then reported results on distributed lag analysis were misinterpreted due to negligence on the effect of aggregation over time of dynamic processes. The upshot of this analysis was that in empirical analysis we should endogenise the dynamic pattern of supply response. This framework has been applied in my current work on sectoral growth as described below. The statistical aspects of this work required the correct formulation of pooling cross-section and time series data, which also placed the relationships between fixed and random effect within an appropriate framework. In another direction, I showed how the problems arising from multicollinearity can be overcome by combining principal components and multiple comparisons.

The other major aspect of my work has dealt with the agricultural sector and its relation to the rest of the economy. In order to submit this relationship to empirical analysis, it is necessary to modify the neoclassical framework so as to endogenise the process of resource allocation and the selection of production techniques as well as to integrate in a meaningful way short-term macro analysis with the long-run growth processes. My recent monographs report preliminary results on the applications of this approach to sectoral growth in Japan and Argentina.

MUSGRAVE, Richard Abel

Born 1910, Königstein, Germany.
Current Post Prof. Emeritus, Harvard Univ., Adjunct Prof. Econ., Univ. Cal. Santa Cruz, CA, 1981–.
Past Posts Prof. Econ., Univ. Michigan, 1948–58; Prof. Econ., Johns Hopkins Univ., 1958–61; Prof. Econ., Princeton Univ., 1962–5; H. H. Burbank Prof. Polit. Econ., Harvard Univ., 1965–80.
Degrees Diplom Volkswirt Univ. Heidelberg, 1933; PhD Harvard Univ., 1937; Dr Laws (H.C.) Allegheny Coll, 1979; Dr (H.C.) Univ. Heidelberg, 1981.
Offices and Honours Member, AAAS; Vice-Pres., Disting. Fellow, AEA, 1962, 1978; Hon. Vice-Pres., IIPF, 1978; Pres., Internat. Seminar Public Econ., Frank W. Seidman Award, 1981.
Editorial Duties Ed., *QJE*, 1969–75.
Principal Fields of Interest 320 Fiscal Theory and Policy.
Publications *Books:* 1. *The Theory of Public Finance* (McGraw-Hill, 1958); 2. *Classics in the Theory of Public Finance* (with A. T. Peacock), (Macmillan, 1958); 3. *Fiscal Systems* (Yale Univ. Press, 1969); 4. *Public Finance in Theory and Practice* (with P. Musgrave), (McGraw-Hill, 1973); 5. *Fiscal Reform in Colombia* (Harvard Univ. Press, 1979).
Articles: 1. 'The voluntary exchange theory of public economy', *QJE*, 53(1), Feb. 1939; 2. 'Proportional income taxation and risk taking' (with E. Domar), *QJE*, 58(2), May 1944; 3. 'Distribution of tax payments by income groups: a case study for 1948', *Nat. Tax J.*, 5, March 1951, 5, March 1952; 4. 'Tax reform: growth with equity', *AER*, 53(2), May 1963; 5. 'Maximin, uncertainty, and the leisure trade-off', *QJE*, 88(4), Nov. 1974.
Principal Contributions Incorporation of the economics of public finance into the larger body of economic theory, with special concern for the role of the public sector in a democratic society.

MUSHKIN, Selma*

Dates and Birthplace 1913–79, Centerville, NY, USA.

Posts Held Chief, Div. Fin. Stud., US Social Security Admin., 1937–49; Econ., US Public Health Service, 1949–60; Res. Prof., George Washington Univ., 1963–8; Dir. Res., Stud. State and Local Fin., Urban Inst., Washington, DC, 1968–70; Prof. Econ., Dir., Public Service Lab., 1970–9.

Degrees BA Brooklyn Coll., 1934; MA Columbia Univ., 1935; PhD New School Social Res., NY, 1956.

Publications *Books:* 1. *Consumer Incentives for Health Care*, ed. (1974); 2. *Sharing Federal Funds for State and Local Needs: Grant-in-aid and PPB Systems*, co-ed. (with J. F. Cotton), (1969).

Articles: 1. 'Health as an investment', *JPE*, 70(5), pt. 2, Oct. 1962, repr. in *Investment in Human Capital*, ed. B. F. Kiker (Univ. S. Carolina Press, 1971); 2. 'Investment in health: lifetime health expenditure on the 1960 work force', *Kyk*, 16(4), 1963, repr. in *Human Capital Formation and Manpower Development*, ed. R. A. Wykstra (Free Press, 1971); 3. 'Financing secondary school expansion', in *Financing of Education for Economic Growth* (OECD, 1966); 4. 'Resource requirements and educational obsolesence', in *Economics of Education*, eds. E. A. G. Robinson and J. Vaizey (Macmillan, 1966); 5. 'Education policies for the culturally disadvantaged child', in *Social Objectives in Education* (OECD, 1967).

Career A leading writer on health economics in the 1960s, who also worked extensively on the economics of education and intergovernmental fiscal relations in general.

MUTH, John Fraser

Born 1930, Chicago, IL, USA.

Current Post Prof. Production Management, School Bus., Indiana Univ., Bloomington, IN, USA, 1969–.

Past Posts Sr. Res. Fellow, Ass. Prof., Assoc. Prof., Carnegie-Mellon Univ., 1956–64; Prof. Management, Michigan State Univ., 1964–9; Vis. Lect., Univ. Chicago, 1957–8, Cowles Foundation, Yale Univ., 1961–2.

Degrees BS (Ind. Eng.) Washington Univ., St Louis, MO, 1952; MS, PhD Carnegie-Mellon Univ., 1954, 1962.

Offices and Honours Fellow, Em Soc; Member, Inst. Management Sciences, OR Soc. Amer., Inst. Ind. Engineers.

Principal Fields of Interest 020 General Economic Theory; 210 Econometric, Statistical and Mathematical Methods and Models; 510 Administration.

Publications *Books:* 1. *Planning Production, Inventories and Work Force* (with C. C. Holt, F. Modigliani and H. A. Simon), (Prentice-Hall, 1960); 2. *Industrial Scheduling*, co-ed. (with G. L. Thompson), (Prentice-Hall, 1963); 3. *Operations Management: Analysis for Decisions* (with G. K. Groff), (Richard D. Irwin, 1972).

Articles: 1. 'Optimal properties of exponentially weighted forecasts', *JASA*, 55, 1960; 2. 'Rational expectations and the theory of price movements', *Em*, 29, July 1961; 3. 'Estimation of economic relationships containing latent expectations variables', in *Rational Expectations and Econometric Practice*, eds. R. E. Lucas and T. J. Sargent (Univ. Minnesota Press, 1981).

Principal Contributions Although my interests are primarily in production management and operations research, certain fundamental concepts in economics have interested me for a long time. The first of these concerns expectations modelling. Various naive hypotheses had generally been used in dynamic models through the 1950s, contrasting with rational, optimising hypotheses used for static equilibrium analysis. As a modelling tool, rational expectations, or some variation thereof, has potential relevance in a number of applied areas of economic analysis. The second concerns the use of search theory and the statistical theory of extreme values to explain technological change, human learning, manufacturing progress functions, production and cost functions. This is a tool capable of explaining phenomena, such as productivity improvement, that classical theory is incapable of dealing with. A final area is the logical analysis of theories purporting to explain human behaviour in the context of organisations. This area uses standard tools of economic analysis in an unusual context, and has additional significance in understanding performance incentives.

MUTH, Richard F.

Born 1927, Chicago, IL, USA.
Current Post Prof. Econ., Stanford Univ., USA, 1970–.
Past Posts Assoc. Prof., Grad. School Bus., Univ. Chicago, 1959–64; Economist, Inst. Defense Analyses, 1964–6; Prof. Econ., Washington Univ., 1966–70.
Degrees BA, MA Washington Univ., 1949, 1950; PhD Univ. Chicago, 1958.
Offices and Honours AEA; Em Soc; Vice-Pres., RSA, 1975–6.
Principal Fields of Interest 930 Urban Economics.
Publications *Books:* 1. *Regions, Resources and Economic Growth* (with others), (JHUP, 1960); 2. *Cities and Housing* (Chicago Univ. Press, 1969); 3. *Public Housing* (AEI., 1974); 4. *Urban Economic Problems* (Harper & Row, 1975).
Articles: 1. 'The demand for non-farm housing', in *The Demand for Durable Goods*, ed. A. C. Harberger (Chicago Univ. Press, 1960); 2. 'Household production and consumer demand functions', *Em*, 34, July 1966; 3. 'A vintage model of the housing stock', *RSA Papers*, 1973; 4. 'Numerical solution of urban residential land-use models', *JUE*, 2, 1975; 5. 'The allocation of households to dwellings', *J Reg S*, 18(2), Aug. 1978.
Principal Contributions Principal work in housing, especially housing demand, and spatial pattern of urban housing markets, and government housing programmes.

MYINT, Hla

Born 1920, Bassein, Burma.
Current Post Prof. Emeritus Econ., LSE, England, 1985–.
Past Posts Lect. Econ. Underdevlp. Countries, Univ. Oxford, 1950–65; Rector, Rangoon Univ., 1958–61; Prof. Econ., LSE, 1965–85.
Degrees BA Rangoon Univ., 1939;

PhD Univ. London, 1943; MA Univ. Oxford, 1950.
Principal Fields of Interest 112 Economic Development.
Publications *Books:* 1. *Theories of Welfare Economics* (Longmans, Harvard Univ. Press, 1948); 2. *The Economics of the Developing Countries* (Hutchinson, 1964, Praeger, 1980); 3. *Economic Theory and the Underdeveloped Countries* (OUP, 1971); 4. *Southeast Asia's Economy, Development Policies in the 1970s* (Penguin, Praeger, 1972).
Articles: 1. 'An interpretation of economic backwardness', *OEP,* N.S. 6, June 1954, repr. in *The Economics of Underdevelopment*, eds. A. N. Agarwala and S. P. Singh (OUP, 1958); 2. 'The "classical theory" of international trade and the underdeveloped countries', *EJ*, 68, June 1958, repr. in *Development Economics and Policy Readings*, ed. I. Livingstone (A&U, 1981); 3. 'Economic theory and the underdeveloped countries', *JPE*, 73, Oct. 1965; 4. 'Dualism and the internal integration of underdeveloped economies', *BNLQR* 93, June 1970; 5. 'Adam Smith's theory of international trade in the perspective of economic development', *Ec*, N.S. 44, Aug. 1977.
Principal Contributions The theory of underdeveloped economies especially the effect of external economic forces on the internal economic organisation of these countries; the relationship between economic theory including the history of economic thought and development economics; the development and application of a theory of economic organisation and institutions to the underdeveloped countries.

MYRDAL, Gunnar

Born 1898, Gustafs Parish, Sweden.
Current Post Prof. Emeritus, Univ. Stockholm, Sweden, 1965–.
Past Posts Assoc. Prof., Post-Grad. Inst. Internat. Stud., Univ. Geneva, 1931–2; Lars Hierta Chair Polit Econ., Univ. Stockholm, 1933–9; Exec. Secretary, UNECE, 1947–57; Prof. Internat. Econ., Univ. Stockholm, 1961–5; Disting. Vis. Prof., NY City Univ., 1974–5.

Degrees Dr Juris Econ., Univ. Stockholm, 1927; Hon. degrees: Harvard Univ., 1938, and 30 others.

Offices and Honours Senator, Swedish Parliament, 1934–6, 1942–6; Chairman, Post-War Planning Commission, Sweden, 1945–7; Minister of Commerce, Sweden, 1945–7; Malinowsky Award, Soc. Applied Anthrop., 1950; Dir., Inst. Internat. Econ. Stud., Univ. Stockholm, 1961–; Chairman, Board, Stockholm Internat. Peace Res. Inst., 1962; Joint Nobel Prize in Econ., 1974; Member, Amer. Philo. Soc., 1982; Jawaharlar Nehru Award Internat. Understanding, 1981.

Principal Fields of Interest 112 Economic Development Models.

Publications *Books:* 1. *Monetary Equilibrium* (William Hodge, 1939); 2. *The Political Element in the Development of Economic Theory* (Routledge & Kegan Paul, 1953); 3. *Economic Theory and Underdeveloped Regions* (Duckworth, Methuen, 1957, 1963); 4. *Asian Drama. An Inquiry into the Poverty of Nations*, 3 vols (Twentieth-Century Fund, Pantheon, 1968); 5. *The Challenge of World Poverty. A World Anti-poverty Program in Outline* (Random House, 1972); 6. *Against the Stream. Critical Essays on Economics* (Pantheon, 1973); 7. *Hur styrs landet?* (How is the Country Governed?) (Raben & Sjogren, 1982).

Articles: 1. 'International inequality and foreign aid in retrospect', in *Pioneers in Development* (World Bank, 1984).

Secondary Literature E. Lundberg, 'Gunnar Myrdal's contribution to economics', in *Contemporary Economists in Perspective*, 2, eds. H. W. Spiegel and W. J. Samuels (JAI Press, 1984).

N

NEARY, James Peter

Born 1950, Drogheda, Ireland.

Current Post Prof. Polit. Econ., Univ. Coll. Dublin, Ireland, 1980–.

Past Posts Res. Ass., Econ. Social Res. Inst., Dublin, 1970–2; J. Lect., Trinity Coll. Dublin, 1972–4; Heyworth Res. Fellow, Nuffield Coll. Oxford, 1976–8; Lect., St Catherine's Coll. Oxford, 1977–8; Vis. Scholar, NSF Res. Assoc., MIT, 1978; Lect., Trinity Coll. Dublin, 1978–80; Vis. Scholar, Inst. Internat. Econ. Stud., Univ. Stockholm, 1979; Vis. Prof., Princeton Univ., 1980; Res. Scholar, Internat. Inst. Appl. Systems Analysis, Laxenburg, Austria, 1981; Ford Vis. Res. Prof., Univ. Cal. Berkeley, 1982.

Degrees BA, MA Univ. Coll. Dublin, 1970, 1971; BPhil, DPhil Univ. Oxford 1976, 1978.

Offices and Honours Dir., Res. Programme Internat. Trade, Centre Econ. Policy Res., London, 1983–; Econ. Programme Comm., Em Soc. Europ. Meetings, Pisa, 1983; Chairman, Econ. Programme Comm., Em Soc Europ. Meetings, Madrid, 1984.

Editorial Duties Co-ed. *J Int E*, 1980–3; Assoc. Ed., *EJ*, 1981–; Ed. Board, *REStud*, 1984.

Principal Fields of Interest 400 International Economics; 320 Domestic Fiscal Policy and Public Finance; 110 Economic Growth, Development and Planning Theory and Policy.

Publications *Books:* 1. *An Econometric Study of the Irish Postal Services* (Econ. Social Res. Inst., 1975).

Articles: 1. 'Short-run capital specificity and the pure theory of international trade', *EJ*, 88, Sept. 1978; 2. 'Dynamic stability and the theory of factor-market distortions', *AER*, 68(4), Sept. 1978, repr. in *Readings in International Trade*, ed. J. Bhagwati (MIT Press, 1981); 3. 'The theory of household behaviour under rationing' (with K. W. S. Roberts), *Europ ER*, 13, 1980; 4. 'Non-traded goods and the balance of trade in a neo-Keynesian temporary equilibrium', *QJE*, 94, Nov. 1980; 5. 'Intersectoral capital mobility, wage stickiness and the case for adjustment assistance', in *Import Competition and Response*, ed. J. Bhagwati (Chicago Univ. Press, 1982); 6. 'Booming sector and de-industrialization in a small open economy' (with W. M. Corden), *EJ*, 92, Dec. 1982; 7. 'Towards a reconstruction of Keynesian economics: expectations and constrained equilibria' (with J. E. Stiglitz), *QJE*, 98, Suppl. 1983; 8. 'Real adjustment and exchange-rate dynamics' (with D. D. Purvis), in *Exchange Rates and International Macroeconomics*, ed. J. A. Frenkel (Univ. Chicago Press, 1983); 9. 'The positive theory of international trade' (with R. W. Jones), in *Handbook of International Economics, I*, eds. R. W. Jones and P. B. Kenen (N-H, 1984); 10. 'Real and monetary aspects of the "Dutch disease"', in *Sectoral Adjustment in Advanced Open Economics*, ed. K. Jugenfeld (Macmillan, 1984).

Principal Contributions Much of my work derives from a continuing fascination with the process of structural change, usually modelled as a transition from one equilibrium to another. Early work on adjustment mechanisms in simple trade models led to a focus on the specific-factors model and to attempts (with Ron Jones) to synthesise and extend the range of applicability of simple general equilibrium models. In trade theory, I have also worked on factor-market distortions, problems of aggregation in models with many goods and factors, international factor mobility, and aspects of the 'Dutch Disease' (with Max Corden and Doug. Purvis). While this work was conducted in an equilibrium framework, I have also been interested for some time in the disequilibrium adjustments of the fix-price approach as a framework for short-run analysis. As well as exploring the relevance of this approach to open economies, I have tried (with Joe Stiglitz) to investigate how it can deal with expectations (especially rational expectations) and asset accumulation. Spin-offs from this include work on the theory of household behaviour under rationing (with Kevin Roberts) and attempts to integrate real and monetary aspects of structural change.

NEGISHI, Takashi

Born 1933, Tokyo, Japan.
Current Post Prof. Econ., Univ. Tokyo, Tokyo, Japan, 1976–.
Past Posts Res. Ass., Res. Assoc., Stanford Univ., 1958–9, 1959–60; Ass., Ass. Prof., Univ. Tokyo, 1965–7, 1967–76; Vis. Prof., Univ. New South Wales, 1968; Univ. Minnesota, 1969; Vis. Lect.,

LSE, 1975; Canadian Council Vis. Prof., Univ. British Columbia, 1977.
Degrees BA, MA, PhD Univ. Tokyo, 1956, 1958, 1965.
Offices and Honours Fellow, Council, Em Soc, 1974–9, 1983–; Nikkei Prize Best Books Econ., 1973; Matsunaga Science Foundation Prize Social Science, 1977; Vice-Pres., Japanese Assoc. Theoretical Econ., 1984.
Editorial Duties Assoc. Ed., *Em*, 1969–75, 1978–; *Int ER*, 1964–71; *J Int E*, 1973.
Principal Fields of Interest 021 General Equilibrium Theory; 031 History of Economic Thought; 411 International Trade Theory.
Publications *Books:* (all in Japanese except 3 and 4) 1. *Kakaku to Haibun no Riron* (Theory of Price and Allocation), (Tokokeizai, 1965); 2. *Boekirieki to Kokusaishushi* (Gains from Trade and Balance of Payments), (Sobunsha, 1971); 3. *General Equilibrium Theory and International Trade* (N-H, 1972); 4. *Micro-economic Foundation of Keynesian Macroeconomics* (N-H, 1979); 5. *Keynes Keizaigaku no Micro Riron* (Micro Theory of Keynesian Economics), (Nihonkeizai Shinbun, 1980); 6. *Kotenha Keizaigaku to Kindai Keizaigaku* (Classical Economics and Modern Economics), (Iwanami, 1981); 7. *Keizaigaku no Rekishi* (History of Economics), (Toyokeizai, 1983).
Articles: 1. 'Welfare economics and existence of an equilibrium for a competitive economy' *Metroec.*, 12(2–3), Aug.–Dec. 1960; 2. 'A theorem on non-*tâtonnement* stability' (with E. H. Hahn), *Em*, 30(3), July, 1962; 3. 'The stability of a competitive economy', *Em*, 30(4), Oct. 1962; 4. 'Stability and rationality of extrapolative expectations', *Em*, 32(4), Oct. 1964; 5. 'Approaches to the analysis of devaluation', *Int ER*, 9(2), June 1968; 6. 'The excess of public expenditures on industries', *J Pub E*, 2(3), July 1973; 7. 'Existence of an under-employment equilibrium', in *Equilibrium and Disequilibrium in Economic Theory*, ed. G. Schwoediauer (D. Reidel, 1977); 8. 'Foreign exchange gains in a Keynesian model of international trade', *Econ App*, 32(4), May 1979; 9. 'The labor theory of value in the Ricardian theory of international

trade', *HOPE*, 14(2), Summer 1982; 10. 'A note on Jevon's law of indifference and competitive equilibrium', *MS*, 50(3), Sept. 1982.

Principal Contributions I started with the study of general equilibrium theory, proved the existence of a competitive equilibrium by using its optimality properties, considered the introduction of monopolistic competition, proved the stability of equilibrium under the assumption of gross-substitutability, considered the non-*tâtonnement* process, and clarified the implications of the dichotomy of real and monetary theories. I then applied general equilibrium theory to the study of international economics, i.e., gains from trade under increasing returns, infant industry protection, customs union and the second best, and the stability of foreign exchange markets, and to the study of public economics, i.e., the over-supply of public goods, second-best pricing in public utilities, and the solutions of externality problems.

I always tried, not so much to generalise theory mathematically, as to enrich it with economic significance, so that it can be applied to the problems of the real world economy. In the 1970s, my interests shifted from the theory and application of Walrasian economics to the consideration of the possibility of non-Walrasian economics. Particularly, I developed a model with kinked demand curves to give a microeconomic foundation to Keynesian macroeconomics. My recent interest is in the study of the history of economics theories which are not related to the Walrasian mainstream, so that I can use them in my study of non-Walrasian economics. Some results of this study will be published soon as a book, entitled *Traditions of Non-Walrasian Economic Theory*, which includes studies of classical and Marxian and non-Walrasian modern economic theories.

NEISSER, Hans Philip*

Dates and Birthplace 1895–1975, Breslau, Germany.

Posts Held Res. Officer, Econ. Commission, German Govt., Berlin, 1922–7; Ed., *Wirtschaft*, 1925–6; Instr., Lect., Res. Principal, Inst. World Economy, Kiel, 1927–33; Prof. Monetary Theory, Univ. Penn., 1933–43; Principal Econ., Div. Res., US Office Price Admin., Washington, DC, 1942–3; Prof. Econ., New School Social Res., NY, 1943–65; Res. Principal, Inst. World Affairs, 1943–51.

Degrees Dr Jurisprudence, DSS Univ. Breslau, 1919, 1921.

Offices and Honours Fellow, Em Soc.

Publications *Books:* 1. *The Exchange Value of Money* (1927); 2. *Some International Aspects of the Business Cycle* (1936); 3. *National Income and International Trade* (with F. Modigliani), (1954); 4. *On the Sociology of Knowledge* (1965).

Articles: 1. 'General overproduction: A study of Say's law of markets', *JPE*, 42, Aug. 1934, repr. in *Readings in Business Cycle Theory*, ed. G. Haberler, *et al.* (Richard D. Irwin, 1951).

Career Wrote widely and sometimes brilliantly on monetary theory, business-cycle theory and Keynesian economics.

NELSON, Charles Rowe

Born 1942, Milwaukee, WI, USA.

Current Post Prof. Econ., Univ. Washington, Seattle, WA, 1975–.

Past Posts Ass. Prof., Assoc. Prof., Grad. School Bus., Univ. Chicago, 1971–5; Res. Fellow Stats., LSE; Vis. Fellow, Trinity Coll. Camb., 1984–5.

Degrees BA Yale Univ., 1963; MA, PhD Univ. Wisconsin, 1967, 1969.

Offices and Honours Irving Fisher Grad. Monograph Award, 1969.

Editorial Duties Ed. Boards, *J Mon E*, *J Bus. and Econ. Stats.*

Principal Fields of Interest 211 Econometric and Statistical Methods and Models; 311 Domestic Monetary and Financial Theory and Policy; 313 Capital Markets.

Publications *Books:* 1. *The Term Structure of Interest Rates* (Basic Books, 1972); 2. *Applied Time Series Analysis for Managerial Forecasting* (Holden-Day, 1973).

Articles: 1. 'Estimation of term premiums from average differentials in the term structure of interest rates', *Em*,

40(2), March 1972; 2. 'The prediction performance of the FRB-MIT-Pen model of the US economy', *AER*, 62(5), Dec. 1972; 3. 'The stochastic structure of the velocity of money' (with V. P. Gould), *AER*, 64(3), June 1974; 4. 'Rational expectations and the estimation of econometric models', *Int ER*, 16(3), Oct. 1975; 5. 'Inflation and rates of return on common stocks', *J Fin*, 31(2), May 1976; 6. 'On testing the hypothesis that the real rate of interest in constant' (with G. W. Schwer), *AER*, 67(3), June 1977; 7. 'Granger causality and the natural rate hypothesis', *JPE*, 87(2), April 1979; 8. 'Recursive structure in US income, prices and output', *JPE*, 87(6), Dec. 1979; 9. 'Adjustment lags vs. information lags: a test of alternative explanations of the Phillips curve phenomenon', *JMCB*, 13(1), Feb. 1981; 10. 'Trends and random walks in macroeconomic time series' (with C. I. Plosser), *J Mon E*, 10(2), Sept. 1982.

Principal Contributions I became interested in time series analysis because it seemed the natural framework in which to test models involving expectations. Model specification based on sample characteristics of data along lines suggested by Box and Jenkins seemed much more sensible to me than the *ad hoc* approach to specification of expectations mechanisms prevalent in econometric practice at the time, and the term structure of interest rates was an obvious area in which to apply these tools. Interest in general methodological issues followed: implications of rational expectations for model testing, evaluation of prediction performance, and the power of tests based on sample autocorrelations.

With the advent of rational expectations macro models, I became interested in Granger causality (predictability) and used it to test the notion that real GNP can be thought of as the residual from a recursive system determining nominal GNP and the price level; I also compared the power of various tests for the presence of Granger-causal relationships. Most recently, the treatment of trend in macroeconometric models has intrigued me; in particular, the distinction between deterministic trend and stochastic growth. I have looked at the consequences of assuming the presence of a deterministic trend when growth is in fact stochastic (for example, a random walk with trend); spurious periodicity appears in inappropriately detrended data, and standard regression statistics, such as R square, become misleading or meaningless. Work with C. Plosser tested historical macroeconomic series for the presence of deterministic trends and concluded that they are characterised instead by stochastic growth. One implication of this is that models using time trends to account for growth may greatly overestimate the amplitude and duration of business cycles.

NELSON, Richard R.

Born 1930, New York City, NY, USA.

Current Post Prof. Econ., Dir., Inst. Social and Pol. Stud., Yale Univ., 1968–.

Past Posts Ass. Prof. Econ., Oberlin Coll., 1956–7; Econ. Sr. Econ., Rand Corp., 1957–60, 1963–8; Assoc. Prof. Econ., Carnegie Technology Univ., 1960–1; Staff Econ., US President's Council Econ. Advisers, 1961–3.

Degrees BA Oberlin Coll, 1952; MA, PhD Yale Univ., 1954, 1956.

Offices and Honours US SSRC, Postdoctoral Fellow, 1956; German Marshall Fund Fellow, 1968.

Principal Fields of Interest 010 General Economics; 600 Industrial Organisation; 300 Domestic Monetary and Fiscal Theory and Policy.

Publications *Books:* 1. *Technology, Economic Growth and Public Policy* (with M. J. Peck and E. D. Kalachek), (Brookings Inst., 1967); 2. *Structural Change in a Dual Economy — A Study of Colombian Economic Development* (with C. P. Schultz and R. M. Slighton), (Princeton Univ. Press, 1971); 3. *Public Policy for Day Care of Young Children* (with D. R. Young), (D. C. Heath, 1973); 4. *The Moon and the Ghetto: An Essay on Policy Analysis* (W. W. Norton, 1977); 5. *An Evolutionary Theory of Economic Change* (with S. Winter), (Harvard Univ. Press, 1982); 6. *Government and Technical Advance:*

A Cross Industry Analysis (Pergamon, 1982).

Articles: 1. 'The simple economics of basic scientific research — a theoretical analysis', *JPE*, 67, June 1959; 2. 'Aggregate production functions and medium-range growth projections', *AER*, 54(4), Sept. 1964; 3. 'The CES production function and economic growth projections', *REStat*, 47(4), Aug. 1965; 4. 'A theory of the low level equilibrium trap in underdeveloped economies', *AER*, 32(5), Dec. 1965; 5. 'A "diffusion" model of international productivity differences in manufacturing industry', *AER*, 58(5), Dec. 1968; 6. 'Neo-classical versus evolutionary theories of economic growth: critique and prospectus' (with S. Winter), *EJ*, 84, Dec. 1974; 7. 'Assessing private enterprise: an exegisis of tangled doctrines', *Bell JE*, 12(1), Spring 1981; 8. 'Research on productivity growth and differences', *JEL*, 19(3), Sept. 1981; 9. 'The Schumpeterian trade-offs revisited' (with S. G. Winter), *AER*, 72(1), March 1982; 10. 'The role of knowledge in R&D efficiency', *QJE*, 97(3), Aug. 1982.

Principal Contributions My research has been concerned with the processes of long-run economic change, the character of economic institutions, and the interactions between economic change and economic institutions. I have focussed intensively, but not exclusively, on technical change. My research on this topic has been done in a number of different styles, from development and implementation of the production function framework, to detailed studies of particular inventions, to examinations of the public policies which have influenced technological advances in different industries. My research has been concerned both with the processes of catching up in developing countries and with Schumpeerian competition in the high-technology industries of advanced economies. Increasingly I have argued that neoclassical theory is at best helpful and more often misleading in dealing with technological advance. Over the last decade a large portion of research has been directed towards developing a theoretical framework better capable of encompassing the central phenomena involved in techni-

cal advances. My work on evolutionary theory has been conducted jointly with Sidney Winter.

NERLOVE, Marc Leon

Born 1933, Chicago, IL, USA.

Current Post Prof. Econ., Univ. Penn., Philadelphia, PA, USA, 1982–.

Past Posts Assoc. Prof. Econ. and Agric. Econ., Univ. Minnesota, 1959–60; Prof. Econ., Stanford Univ., 1960–5; Prof. Econ., Yale Univ., 1965–9; Prof. Econ., Univ. Chicago, 1969–74; Cook Prof., Northwestern Univ., 1974–82.

Degrees BA Univ. Chicago, 1952; MA, PhD Johns Hopkins Univ., 1955, 1956; Hon. Dr, Univ. Mannheim, 1982.

Offices and Honours Fellow, Pres., Em Soc, 1960, 1981; Fellow, ASA, 1964; John Bates Clark Medal, Exec. Comm., AEA, 1969, 1977–9; Fellow, AAAS, 1978; Mahalanobis Memorial Medal, Internat. Award, Indian Em Soc, 1975; Guggenheim Foundation Fellow, 1962–3, 1978–9; Member, NAS, 1979.

Editorial Duties Assoc. Ed., *JASA*, 1960–2; Ed. Boards, *AER*, 1970–2, *JEL*, 1969–71.

Principal Fields of Interest 211 Econometric Methods: 711 Agricultural Supply and Demand; 841 Demographic Economics.

Publications *Books:* 1. *The Dynamics of Supply: Estimation of Farmers' Response to Price* (JHUP, 1958); 2. *Distributed Lags and Demand Analysis* (US Govt. Printing Office, 1958); 3. *Estimation and Identifications of Cobb-Douglas Production Functions* (Rand McNally, N-H, 1965); 4. *Love and Life between the Censuses: A Model of Family Decision-Making in Puerto-Rico, 1950–1960* (with T. P. Schultz), (Rand Corp., 1970); 5. *Univariate and Multivariate Log-Linear and Logistic Model* (with S.J. Press), (Rand Corp., 1973); 6. *Analysis of Economic Time Series: A Synthesis* (with D. Grether and J. L. Carvalho), (Academic Press, 1979).

Articles: 1. 'The dynamics of supply: retrospect and prospect', *AJAE*, 61(2), Dec. 1979; 2. 'Household and economy: toward a new theory of population and economic growth', *JPE*, 82(2), pt. 2, March–April 1974; 3. 'On tuition and the costs of higher education: prolegomena to a conceptual framework', *JPE*, 80(3), pt. 2, May–June 1972; 4. 'Lags in economic behaviour', *Em*, 40(2), March 1972; 5. 'Pooling cross-section and time-series data in the estimation of a dynamic model: the demand for natural gas' (with P. Balestra), *Em*, 34(3), July 1966; 6. 'Spectral analysis of seasonal adjustment procedures', *Em*, 32(3), July 1964; 7. 'Returns to scale in electricity supply', in *Measurement in Economics*, eds. C. Christ, *et al.* (Stanford Univ. Press, 1961); 8. 'Expectations, plans and realizations in theory and practice', *Em*, 51(4), Sept. 1983; 9. 'Bequests and the size of population when population is endogenous' (with A. Razin and E. Sadka), *JPE*, 92(3), June 1984; 10. 'The security hypothesis reconsidered' (with A. Razin and F. Sadka), *J. Econ. Devlp.*, forthcoming, 1985.

Principal Contributions My concern has been with the understanding of dynamic economic behaviour with its quantification by appropriate econometric methods. I have examined agricultural supply response, household decision-making and firms' responses to demand shocks and have developed distributed lag models, methods of time series, components of variance models and techniques for analysing categorical data to this end.

NEUBERGER, Egon

Born 1925, Zagreb, Yugoslavia.
Current Post Dean, Social and Behavioural Sciences, 1982–, Prof. Econ., State Univ. NY, Stony Brook, NY, USA, 1967–.
Past Posts Econ. Analyst, US Dept. State, 1949–54; Econ. Officer, Amer. Embassy, Moscow, 1952–3; Ass. Prof., Amherst Coll., MA, 1957–60; Econ., Rand Corp., 1961–6; Adjunct Assoc. Prof., UCLA, 1963–5; Vis. Prof., Univ. Michigan, 1965–6; Vis. Scholar, LSE, 1982, Birkbeck Coll. London, 1982, Centre d'Economie Quant. et Comp., Ecole des Haute Etudes en Sciences Sociales, Paris, 1982, Columbia

Univ., 1967–8, 1975, Indiana Univ., 1969–75.
Degrees BA Cornell Univ., 1947; MA (Internat. Affairs), PhD Harvard Univ., 1949, 1957.
Offices and Honours Joint Comm. Eastern Europe, US SSRC, 1970–4; Winner, Ford Foundation Internat. Competition, Res. on Soviet Union and Eastern Europe, 1975; Exec. Comm., Assoc. Comp. Econ. Stud., 1974–6; Disting. Award Outstanding Service, Omcron Delta Epsilon, 1980–1, 1981.
Editorial Duties Ed., Irving Fisher and Frank W. Taussig Competitions, Omicron Delta Epsilon, 1969–83.
Principal Fields of Interest 053 Comparative Economic Systems; 400 International Economics; 120 Country Studies.
Publications *Books:* 1. *International Trade and Central Planning: An Analysis of Economic Interactions*, co-ed. (with A. Brown), (Univ. Cal. Press, 1968); 2. *Perspectives in Economics: Economists Look at their Fields of Study*, co-ed. (with A. Brown and M. Palmatier), (McGraw-Hill, 1971); 3. *Urban and Social Economics in Market and Planned Economies*, co-ed. (with A. Brown and J. Licaro), (Univ. Windsor Press, Praeger, 1974); 4. *Comparative Economic Systems: A Decision-Making Approach* (with W. Duffy), (Allyn & Bacon, 1976); 5. *Internal Migration: A Comparative Perspective*, co-ed. (with A. Brown), (Academic Press, 1977); 6. *The Foreign Trade Practices of Centrally Planned Economies and Their Impact on US International Competitiveness* (with J. Lara), (Nat. Planning Assoc., 1977); 7. *The Impact of International Economic Disturbances on the Soviet Union and Eastern Europe: Transmission and Response*, co-ed. (with L. D. Tyson), (Pergamon, 1980).
Articles: 1. 'The Yugoslave investment auctions', *QJE*, 73, Feb. 1959; 2. 'International division of labor in CEMA: limited regret strategy', *AER*, 54(2), May 1964, repr. in *Economia 1964–6*, ed. P. M. Mayor (Aguilar, 1966); 3. 'Is the USSR superior to the West as a market for primary products?', *REStat*, 46, Aug. 1964; 4. 'Central planning and its legacies: implications for foreign trade', in *International Trade*

and Central Planning, op.cit.; 5. 'Production function approach to Hungarian economic growth' (with A. Brown and A. Licari), *Acta Oeconomia*, 11, 1973; 6. 'The Yugoslave self-managed enterprise: a systemic approach' (with E. James), in *Plan and Market: Reform in Eastern Europe*, ed. M. Bornstein (Yale Univ. Press, 1973); transl., Russian, *Ekonomska Misao*, 3, 1972; 7. 'Productivity measurement in socialist economies using Divisia indexes and adjusted factor shares' (with A. Brown and J. Licari), *SEJ*, 42, Jan. 1976; 8. 'On the economics of self-management: The Israeli kibbutz and the Yugoslav enterprise' (with A. Ben-Ner), *Econ. Analysis and Workers' Management*, 13, 1979; 9. 'The impact of external economic disturbances on Yugoslavia: theoretical and empirical explorations' (with L. D. Tyson), *J Comp E*, 3, Dec. 1979; 10. 'The university department as a non-profit labor cooperative' (with E. James), *Public Choice*, 36, 1981, repr. in *Collective Choice in Education*, ed. M. J. Bowman (Martinus Nijhoff, 1981).

Principal Contributions My career has been devoted to developing various areas of comparative economic systems in an attempt to bring the field into the mainstream of economics. My basic approach has been inductive — study institutions, develop appropriate analytical instruments, and then generalise from the specific cases. My most important contribution has been the development of a systems theoretic conceptual framework for analysing economic systems, the DIM (decision-making, information, motivation) approach. This was presented in several articles but its simplest and yet most comprehensive treatment was in *Comparative Economic Systems: A Decision-Making Approach*. I taught this approach to a generation of Stony Brook students and they and I have used it to analyse economic systems of many countries, of both the Catholic and Mormon Churches, the East German kombinati, the Israeli kibbutz, and Yugoslav self-managed enterprise, and others. I provided seminal contributions to the study of several institutions, including Yugoslav investment auctions, The Council of Mutual Economic Assist-ance, and self-managed organisations. In addition, I contributed to the analysis of centrally planned foreign trade, the transmission of economic disturbances, the analysis of growth patterns in socialist economies, and internal migration.

Thus, I ranged broadly over the field but always isolated the economic system as the variable for study and have approached it by generalising and abstracting from the real world. My other major contribution to the field of economics was the founding in 1969 of the Irving Fisher Award competition for PhD dissertations, and the Frank W. Taussig Award competition for undergraduate papers, under the sponsorship of Omicron Delta Epsilon. With quality standards set by the first final selection board, composed of Kenneth Arrow, Kenneth Boulding, Milton Friedman and Paul Samuelson, the competitions have stimulated student excellence and some of today's leading young economists have won these coveted awards.

NEUMANN, John Von*

Dates and Birthplace 1903–57, Budapest, Austro-Hungary.

Posts Held Privatdozent, Univ. Berlin, 1927–30, Univ. Hamburg, 1929–30; Prof., Princeton Univ., 1931–3; Prof., Inst. Advanced Study, Princeton Univ., 1933–57.

Degrees PhD Univ. Budapest, 1926; Diploma Zürich Technische Hochschule, 1926.

Offices and Honours Member, NAS; Enrico Fermi Award, 1956.

Publications *Books:* 1. *Theory of Games and Economic Behavior* (with O. Morgenstern), (1944, 1964); 2. *Collected Works*, 6 vols, ed. A. H. Taub (1961–3).

Articles: 1. 'A model of general economic equilibrium' (1938), repr. in *REStud*, 13(1), 1945, and *Precursors in Mathematical Economics: An Anthology*, eds. W. J. Baumol and J. M. Goldfeld (1968), and *Readings in the Theory of Growth*, ed. F. Hahn (1971).

Career Outstanding creative mathematician whose interest ranged from pure mathematics to computing and mathematical physics. He also introduced innovations in mathematical economics, using game theory to model economic and social phenomena. His book on game theory (with Oskar Morgenstern) is one of the classics of the twentieth-century social science. In 1937 he analysed the steady-state equilibrium properties of a uniformly-expanding closed economy under conditions of constant returns to scale in production, an unlimited supply of natural resources, and reproducible labour. This amazingly early article, which only became famous when it was translated in 1945, initiated an entire era in modern growth theory.

Secondary Literature O. Morgenstern, 'Von Neumann, John', *IESS*, 16; O. Morgenstern, 'Collaborating with von Neumann', *JEL*, 14(3), Sept. 1976.

NEVIN, Edward Thomas

Born 1925, Pembroke Dock, Wales.
Current Post Prof. Econ., Univ. Coll. Swansea, Swansea, Wales, 1968–.
Past Posts Temp. Ass. Lect. Econ., Lect. Econ., Prof. Econ., Univ. Coll. Wales, Aberystwyth, 1949–53, 1957–9, 1961–3; Houblon-Norman Res. Fellow, 1952–3; Sr. Admin. Officer, OEEC, 1954–7; Head, External Fin. Div., Ministry Fin., Jamaica, 1959–61; Sr. Res. Officer, Econ. Res. Inst., Dublin, 1963–8.
Degrees BA, MA Univ. Wales, 1949, 1951; PhD Univ. Camb. 1952.
Offices and Honours Member, Welsh Council, 1969–; Council, RES, 1972–4; Chairman, AUTE, 1972–; Governor, NIESR, 1977–; Pres., Section F, BAAS, 1977–; Econ. Adviser, Police Federation England and Wales, 1976–.
Principal Fields of Interest 311 Domestic Monetary Theory; 321 Fiscal Theory and Policy; 941 Regional Economics.
Publications *Books:* 1. *The Problem of the National Debt* (Univ. Wales Press, 1954); 2. *The Mechanism of Cheap Money* (Univ. Wales Press, 1955); 3. *Textbook of Economic Analysis* (Macmillan, 1958, 1981); 4. *Capital Funds in Underdeveloped Countries* (Macmillan, 1961; transls., Japanese, 1962, Spanish, 1963); 5. *A Workbook of Economic Analysis* (Macmillan, 1966, 1969); 6. *The London Clearing Banks* (with E. W. Davis), (Elek Books, 1970); 7. *Regional Policy and the Role of Banking* (Fed. Reserve Bank Minneapolis, 1972); 8. *An Introduction to Micro-economics* (Croom Helm, 1973); 9. *The Economics of Devolution*, ed. and contrib. (Univ. Wales Press, 1978).

Articles: 1. 'Some reflections on the New York new issue market', *OEP*, 13(1), Feb. 1961; 2. 'Debt management: a general survey', *PF*, 16(3), Sept. 1961; 3. 'British debt management policy', *PF*, 16(3), Sept. 1961; 4. 'The life of capital assets: an empirical approach', *OEP*, 15(3), Nov. 1963; 5. 'The cost structure of British manufacturing', *EJ*, 73, Dec. 1963; 6. 'The case for regional development policy', *Three Banks Rev.*, 72, Dec. 1966; 7. 'How not to get a First', *EJ*, 82, June 1972; 8. 'Europe and the regions', *Three Banks Rev.*, 94, June 1972; 9. 'The economics of tribology', *UK SSRC Newsletter*, 23, May 1974; 10. 'Regional policy', in *The Economics of the Common Market* (Philip Allan, 1980).

Principal Contributions Pure chance pushed me initially into the area of monetary policy in general and the public debt in particular. Starting with an MA by research on the postwar monetary policy in the UK, and a Cambridge PhD on the cheap money policy of the 1980s, I was led to social accounting in general and to the arcane topic of regional social accounts and input-output analysis. This in turn led, with a certain inherent logic, to a continuing interest in regional economics in general, and, more recently, regional policy in the EEC. Since regional policy has in practice turned out to be rather low in operational content, this interest has somewhat waned in recent years. A number of years as economic adviser to the Police Federation of England and Wales has however resulted in a great deal of work on the manpower problems of the British police service and the factors determining recruitment and wastage. In the nature of the case little of this work has so far seen the light of published day: this has made it especially rewarding.

NEWBERY, David Michael Garrood

Born 1943, Fulmer Chase, England.
Current Post Lect., Econ., Univ. Camb., 1971–.
Past Posts Fellow, Churchill Coll. Camb., 1965; Nuffield Fellow, Treasury, Govt. Tanzania, 1965–6; Ass. Lect., Univ. Camb., 1966–71; Res. Assoc. Cowles Foundation, Yale Univ., 1969; Assoc. Prof., Stanford Univ., 1977; Econ., World Bank, 1981; Div. Chief, Res. Dept., World Bank, 1982–3.
Degrees BA (Maths. and Econ.), MA, PhD Univ. Camb., 1964, 1968, 1976.
Editorial Duties Ed. Board, *REStud*, 1968–79; Co-ed., *EJ*, 1977–; Co-ed., African Stud. Series (CUP, 1975–83).
Principal Fields of Interest 020 General Economic Theory; 321 Fiscal Theory and Policy; 720 Natural Resources.
Publications *Books:* 1. *Project Appraisal in Practice* (with M. F. G. Scott and J. D. MacArthur), (Heinemann, 1976); 2. *An Overview of the Economic Theory of Uncertainty and its Implications for Energy Supply* (with R. Gilbert and J. E. Stiglitz), (EPRI, 1978); 3. *The Theory of Commodity Price Stabilization* (with J. E. Stiglitz), (OUP, 1981).
Articles: 1. 'Public policy in the dual economy', *EJ*, 82, June 1972; 2. 'Congestion and over-exploitation of free access resources', *Ec*, N.S. 42, Aug. 1975; 3. 'The choice of rental contract in peasant agriculture', in *Agriculture in Development Theory*, ed. L. A. Reynolds (Yale Univ. Press, 1975); 4. 'The social value of private investment in Kenya', in *Using Shadow Prices*, eds. I. M. D. Little and M.Scott (CUP, 1976); 5. 'Risk sharing, sharecropping and uncertain labour markets', *REStud*, 44(3), Oct. 1977; 6. 'Stochastic limit pricing', *Bell JE*, 9(1), Spring 1978; 7. 'Externalities; the theory of environmental policy', in *Public Policy and the Tax System*, eds. G. Heal and G. Hughes (A&U, 1981); 8. 'Oil prices, cartels and the problems of dynamic inconsistency', *EJ*, 9(1) Sept. 1981; 9. 'Optimal commodity stock-piling rules' (with J. E. Stiglitz), *OEP*, 34(3), Nov. 1982; 10. 'Commodity price stabilization in imperfect or cartelized markets', *Em*, 52(2), March 1984.

Principal Contributions On my return from working in the Tanzanian Treasury, I continued my work on social cost-benefit analysis in developing countries, concentrating on the pricing of labour and investment, and using optimal growth theory as a framework. This led to wider interest in public finance and the problems of market failure — of public goods and externalities. I became interested in risk and worked on share cropping, and later on the theory of commodity price stabilisation. If relative prices are risky, then competitive markets are typically not even constrained efficient, and it is interesting to examine the efficiency of various market institutions which evolve to handle risk, notably futures markets, credit markets, and intertemporal storage.

Part of my work on energy explored other responses to risk, such as vertical integration, but the prime focus here was the role of market power for exhaustible resources, where I showed that many of the standard solutions proposed were dynamically inconsistent. On my recent visit to the World Bank I returned to issues of public finance, and to transport pricing and taxation, whilst continuing my interest in commodities and energy pricing. Throughout I have been interested in applying economic theory, often in the form of simple models, to problems of practical importance.

NEWCOMB, Simon*

Dates and Birthplace 1835–1909, Nova Scotia, Canada.
Posts Held Prof. Maths. US Navy, 1861–97; Prof. Maths. Astronomy, Johns Hopkins Univ., 1884–93.
Degrees BS Univ. Harvard, 1858.
Offices and Honours Member, NAS, 1869.
Publications *Books:* 1. *A Critical Examination of our Financial Policy during the Southern Rebellion* (1865); 2. *ABC of Finance* (1878); 3. *Principles of Political Economy* (1885); 4. *Plain Man's Talk on the Labor Question* (1886).
Career Scientist and astronomer,

and America's first mathematical economist. He was an opponent of labour unions, attacked inconvertible paper money and generally adhered to an orthodox political economy. However, his *Principles* ... contains a number of original mathematical contributions.

Secondary Literature A. W. Coates, 'Newcomb, Simon', *IESS*, 11.

NEWHOUSE, Joseph Paul

Born 1942, Waterloo, IA, USA.

Current Post Head, Econ. Dept., Rand Corp., Santa Monica, CA, USA; Adjuct Prof., School Public Health, UCLA; Faculty Rand Grad. Inst., Santa Monica, CA, 1981–.

Past Posts Econ., Rand Corp., 1968–81.

Degrees BA, PhD Harvard Univ., 1963, 1969.

Offices and Honours David N. Kershaw Award, Assoc. Public Pol. and Management, 1983; Fulbright Scholar, 1963–4.

Editorial Duties Ed., *JHE*, 1982; Ed. Board, *Evaluation Rev.*, 1979–82, *Health Scan: The Report of Health Bus. and Law*, 1984.

Principal Fields of Interest 913 Economics of Health; 026 Economics of Uncertainty and Information; 211 Econometric and Statistical Methods and Models.

Publications *Books:* 1. *An Economic Analysis of Public Library Services* (with A. J. Alexander), (D. C. Heath, 1972); 2. *The Economics of Medical Care: A Policy Perspective* (Addison-Wesley, 1978).

Articles: 1. 'Toward a theory of nonprofit institutions: an economic model of a hospital', *AER*, 60(1), March 1970, repr. in *Health Economics*, eds. M. Cooper and A. Culyer (Penguin, 1973); 2. 'The economics of group practice', *JHR*, 8(1), Winter 1973; 3. 'Deductibles and demand: a theory of the consumer facing a variable price schedule under uncertainty' (with E. B. Keeler and C. E. Phelps), *Em*, 45(3), April 1977; 4. 'The demand for supplementary health insurance, or are deductibles relevant?' (with E. B. Keeler and D. Morrow), *JPE*, 85(4), Aug. 1977; 5.

'On having your cake and eating it too: econometric problems in estimating the demand for health services' (with C. E. Phelps and M. S. Marquis), *J Em*, 13(3), Aug. 1980; 6. 'The effect of deductibles on the demand for medical care services' (with J. E. Rolph, B. Mori, and M. Murphy), *JASA*, 75(371), Sept. 1980; 7. 'Some interim results from a controlled trial of cost sharing in health insurance' (with W. G. Manning, Jr., *et al.*), *New England J Medicine*, 305(25), Dec. 1981; 8. 'Does the geographical distribution of physicians reflect market failure?' (with A. P. Williams, B. Bennett, and W. B. Schwartz), *Bell JE*, 13(2), Autumn 1982; 9. 'A comparison of alternative models of the demand for medical care' (with N. Duan, W. G. Manning, Jr., and C. N. Morris), *J Bus. Econ. Stats.*, 1(2), April 1983; 10. 'How many miles to the doctor?' (with A. P. Williams, W. B. Schwartz and B. Bennett), *New England J Medicine*, 309(16), Oct. 1983.

Principal Contributions Most of my research has centred on the economics of health. At a theoretical level I have tried to make sense of the medical-care sector through extensions of neoclassical theory to encompass the phenomena of the medical market place. These applications have included: the theory of nonprofit firms, especially hospitals; group practice; supplementary insurance; demand response to nonlinear price schedules (e.g. a deductible); and the geographic distribution of physicians.

At an empirical level I have focussed most of my energies on estimating demand functions for medical-care services, especially price or insurance elasticities. I have spent 13 years designing and analysing the data from a social experiment in health-care financing. 7706 individuals in 2756 families participated in this experiment, 70 per cent of them for three years and the remainder for five. Most were randomised to insurance plans that varied the co-insurance rate; some were randomly assigned to a health maintenance organisation. The experiment sought to measure the insurance elasticity of demand, its interaction with income, if any, and the consequences for the health status of the participants (i.e. the marginal product of the induced increase in demand). The sample assigned to the health maintenance organisation was used to test the effect of this form of organisation on the use of services and health status; additionally a comparison of those randomised in with those already enrolled affords a measure of adverse selection. This experiment has also contributed to developments in the technology of social experimentation, especially in the method for optimally allocating families to experimental treatments.

NEWMAN, Peter Kenneth

Born 1928, Mitcham, Surrey, England.

Current Post Prof. Polit. Econ., Johns Hopkins Univ., Baltimore, MD, USA, 1966–.

Past Posts Res. Ass., Univ. Coll. London, 1949–51; Ass. Res. Officer, Inst. Stats., Univ. Oxford, 1953–4; Scientific Officer, UK Admiralty, London, 1954–5; UN Technical Ass. Admin., Colombo, Sri Lanka, 1956–7; Lect., Sr. Lect., Univ. Coll., W. Indies, Kingston, Jamaica, 1957–9, 1959–61; Prof. Econ., Univ. Michigan, 1961–3; UN Technical Ass. Admin., Nairobi, 1963–4; Vis. Prof., Johns Hopkins Univ., 1964–5; Sr. Assoc., Robert R. Nathan Assoc., San José, Costa Rica, 1965–6.

Degrees BS, MSc, PhD Univ. London, 1949, 1951, 1962.

Editorial Duties Ed. Boards, *REStud*, 1952–5; Joint Ed., *The New Palgrave: A Dictionary of Economic Theory and Doctrine* (Macmillan, forthcoming, 1986).

Principal Fields of Interest 020 General Economic Theory; 031 History Economic Thought; 940 Demographic Economics.

Publications *Books:* 1. *Costs in Alternative Locations* (with D. C. Hague), (CUP, 1952); 2. *Studies in the Import Structure of Ceylon* (Ceylon Govt., 1958); 3. *British Guiana* (OUP, 1964); 4. *Malaria Eradication and Population Growth* (School of Public Health, Univ. Michigan, 1965); 5. *The Theory of Ex-*change (Prentice-Hall, 1965; transl., Spanish, 1972); 6. *Readings in Mathematical Economics*, 2 vols, ed. (JHUP, 1968).

Articles: 1. 'The early London clothing trades', *OEP*, N.S. 4, Oct. 1952; 2. 'Some calculations on least-cost diets, using the simplex method', *BOIS*, 17, Aug. 1955; 3. 'On a theorem of urbanik', *Fundamenta Mathematica*, 46, 1959; 4. 'The erosion of Marshal's theory of value', *QJE*, 74, Nov. 1960; 5. 'Approaches to stability analysis', *Ec*, N.S. 28, Feb. 1961; 6. 'A model for the long-run theory of value' (with J. N. Wolfe), *REStud*, 29, Oct. 1961; 7. 'Production of commodities by means of commodities', *SZ*, 98, March 1962; 8. 'Some properties of concave functions', *JET*, 1(3), Oct. 1969; 9. 'Malaria and mortality', *JASA*, 72, June 1977; 10. 'Mirrored parts of optimization problems', *Ec*, 49, May 1982.

NEWMARCH, William*

Dates and Birthplace 1820–82, Thirsk, Yorkshire, England.

Posts Held Employee, Dir., insurance and banking houses.

Offices and Honours Pres., RSS, 1869–71.

Publications *Books:* 1. *The New Supplies of Gold (1853); 2. On the Loans Raised by Mr Pitt During the First French War* (1855); 3. *History of Prices* (with W. Tooke), vols 5 and 6 (1857).

Career Statistician and economist, and leading critic of Peel's Bank Act, 1844. His continuation of Tooke's *History of Prices* to cover the period 1847–56 was designed to refute the theories of the currency school which lay behind Peel's Act. He denied that an increase in the volume of money in circulation had the effects that were alleged.

Secondary Literature L. M. Fraser, 'Newmarch, William', *ESS*, 11.

NG, Yew-Kwang

Born 1942, Kedah, Malaysia.

Current Post Reader Econ., Monash Univ., Melbourne, Victoria, Australia, 1974–.

Past Posts Lect., Sr. Lect., Univ. New England, Australia, 1970–1, 1972–3; Vis. Prof., Virginia Polytechnic Inst. and State Univ., 1978–9.

Degrees BCom Nanyang Univ., Singapore, 1966; PhD Sydney Univ., 1971.

Offices and Honours Commonwealth Bank Grad. Scholar, Sydney Univ., 1967–9; Vis. Nuffield Foundation Fellow, Nuffield Coll. Oxford, 1973–4; Vis. Simon Sr. Res. Fellow, Manchester Univ., 1979; Fellow, Academy Social Sciences, Australia.

Editorial Duties Ed. Board, *Maths. Social Sciences, Social Choice & Welfare*; Corresp. Ed., *MS*.

Principal Fields of Interest 022 Microeconomic Theory; 024 Welfare Theory; 025 Social Choice.

Publications *Books:* 1. *Welfare Economics: Introduction and Development of Basic Concepts* (Macmillan, 1979, 1983); 2. *Mesoeconomics: A Micro-Macroeconomic Analysis* (Wheatsheaf Books, 1986).

Articles: 1. 'Why do people buy lottery tickets? Choices involving risk and the indivisibility of expenditure', *JPE*, 73, Oct. 1965; 2. 'Monopoly, X-efficiency, and the measurement of welfare loss' (with R. Parish), *Ec*, N.S. 39, Aug. 1972; 3. 'Value judgements and economists' role in policy recommendation', *EJ*, 82, Sept. 1972, repr. in *How Economists Explain — A Reader in Methodology*, eds. W. Marr and B. Raj (Univ. Press Amer., 1983); 4. 'Optimal pricing with budgetary constraints: the case of the two-part tariff' (with M. Weisser), *REStud*, 71(3), July 1974; transl., Japanese, Tokyo Gas Co., 1974; 5. 'Bentham or Bergson? Finite sensibility, utility functions and social welfare functions', *REStud*, 42(4), Oct. 1975; 6. 'On the existence of social welfare functions, social orderings and social decision functions' (with M. C. Kemp), *Ec*, N.S. 43, Feb. 1976; 7. 'Towards a theory of third-best', *PF*, 32(1), 1977; 8. 'Macroeconomics with non-perfect competition', *EJ*, 90, Sept. 1980; 9. 'A micro-macroeconomic analysis based on a representative firm', *Ec*, N.S. 49, May 1982; 10. 'Quasi-Pareto social improvements', *AER*, 74(5), Dec. 1984.

Principal Contributions Contributions mainly in welfare economics, social choice, and aspects of microeconomics (including the economic theory of clubs, capital theory and consumer choice). In particular, the theory of third-best (No. 7 above) provides a useful policy guide; with informational poverty, first-best rules remain optimal despite second-best complications; when applied to distributional issues, this becomes the rule of treating a dollar as a dollar to whomsoever it goes, leaving the distributional objective to be achieved through taxation. In a world of diverse individual preferences, this can be shown to be a quasi-Pareto improvement with every income group being made better off (No. 10).

The joint article with Kemp (No. 6) establishes Arrow-type impossibility theorems in the framework of a fixed set of individual preferences, freeing Arrow's theorem from the argument of Little and Samuelson that it is irrelevant to welfare economics, and pointing to the necessity of interpersonal comparison of cardinal utilities. Such a comparison is not a value judgement (No. 3) and is made objectively possible by the recognition of finite sensibility which supports a Benthamite social welfare function (No. 5).

More recently, a method of economic analysis has been developed which incorporates elements of micro, macro and general equilibrium by focussing on the microeconomics of a representative firm but taking account of the effects of aggregate demand, aggregate output and average price (No. 9). The method can be used to examine the effects of economy-wide (No. 8) or industry-wide changes on the average price and aggregate output, with implications of economic recovery without aggravated inflation.

NICHOLLS, William Hord*

Dates and Birthplace 1914–78, Lexington, KY, USA.

Posts Held Instr., Ass. Prof., Assoc. Prof., Iowa State Coll., 1938–44; Cons., US Office Price Admin., 1941–2; Ass. Prof., Univ. Chicago, 1945–8; Prof. Econ., Dir., Grad. Center Latin Amer.

Stud., Vanderbilt Univ., Nashville, TN, 1948–78, 1965–77; Vis. Lect., Rio de Janeiro, 1947; Vis. Prof., Salzburg Seminar Amer. Stud., 1949; Econ., Turkish Mission, IBRD, 1950; Staff Econ., US President's Council Econ. Advisers, 1953–4; Cons., Ford Foundation, Brazil, 1960–4; Vis. Prof., Harvard Univ., 1961–2; Agric. Econ., Vargas Foundation, Brazil, 1963–4; Membeı, Agric. Comm., Nat. Planning Assoc., 1950; US SSRC Comm. Agric Econ., 1953–5, 1954–7; Board Dirs., US SSRC, 1957–60; Fed. Advisory Council Employment Security, Nat. Advisory Comm. Manpower Devlp., US Dept. Labor, 1960–2, 1962–3; Agric. Econ. Res. Comm., US Dept. Agric., 1963–8; Member, US Nat. Comm. UNESCO, US Dept. State, 1966–9; Member-at-Large, Nat. Res. Council, Div. Behavioral Sciences, 1973–7; Guest Cons., Ministry Planning, Brazil, 1972–3.

Degrees BA Univ. Kentucky, 1934; MA, PhD Harvard Univ., 1938, 1941.

Offices and Honours First Prize, Farm Price Pol. Essay Competition, AAEA, 1935; Phi Beta Kappa, Omicron Delta Kappa, 1934; US SSRC Postdoctoral Fellow, 1941–2; Pres., SEA, 1958–9; Pres., Fellow, AAEA, 1960–7; Centennial Disting. Alumni Award, Univ. Kentucky, 1956; Harvey Branscomb Disting. Prof. Award, Vanderbilt Univ., 1973–4.

Editorial Duties Managing Ed., *JPE*, 1964–8; Ed. Boards, *EDCC*, 1947–78, *AER*, 1948–51, *AJAE*, 1958–60.

Publications *Books:* 1. *Imperfect Competition within Agricultural Industries* (with J. A. Vieg), (1941); 2. *Wartime Government in Operation* (1943); 3. *Labor Productivity Functions in Meat Packing* (1948); 4. *Price Policies in the Cigarette Industry: A Study of 'Concerted Action' and its Social Control* (1951); 5. *The Economy of Turkey: An Analysis and Recommendations for a Development Program* (with B. U. Ratchford, *et al.*), (1951); 6. *US Agriculture: Perspectives and Prospects*, ed. (1955); 7. *Southern Tradition and Regional Progress* (1960); 8. *The Importance of an Agricultural Surplus in Underdeveloped Countries* (1962); 9. *Ninety-Nine Fazendas: The Structure and Productivity of Brazilian Agriculture* (with R. Miller Paiva), (1975).

Articles: 1. 'A price policy for agriculture, consistent with economic progress, that will promote adequate and more stable income from farming', *AJAE*, 27(4), Nov. 1945, repr. in *Readings in Agricultural Policy*, ed. O. B. Jesness (Blakiston, 1949), and in *Contemporary Readings in Agricultural Economics*, ed. H. G. Halcrow (Prentice-Hall, 1955); 2. 'The tobacco case of 1946', *AER*, 39(2), May 1949, repr. in *Industrial Organization and Public Policy*, eds. R. Heflebower and G. Stocking (Richard D. Irwin, 1958); 3. 'Domestic trade in an underdeveloped country: Turkey', *JPE*, 59(6), Dec. 1951; 4. 'Investment in agriculture in underdeveloped countries', *AER*, 45(6), May 1955; 5. 'Some foundations of economic development in the upper East Tennessee valley', *JPE*, pt. 1, 65(3), March 1956, pt. 2, 65(4), July 1956; 6. 'Southern tradition and regional economic progress', *SEJ*, 26(3), Jan. 1960, repr. in *Regional Development and Planning: A Reader*, eds. A. Fox and D. Gale Johnson (Richard D. Irwin, 1969); 7. 'The Brazilian food supply: problems and prospects', *EDCC*, 19(3), April 1971; 8. 'Agriculture and economic development of Brazil', in *Modern Brazil: New Patterns and Development*, ed. J. Saunders (Univ. Florida Press, 1971).

Career The first to apply the theory of imperfect competition to the buying side represented by agricultural processing industries *vis-à-vis* farmers. On the occasion, he devised several novel diagrammatical tools for duopoly and bilateral monopoly. Concentrating on cigarettes and meat-packing industries, he subjected the production and industrial organisation of agricultural industries to a detailed analysis. In a first departure from the conventional production function, he included the working day among the ordinary variables of that function. As a member of the dissenting 'Ames Group', he wrote a prize-winning critical analysis of the US farm policy and formulated economically efficient policy alternatives. At Vanderbilt he founded a school of thought characterised by an abiding interest in the economic development of the South with special reference to agriculture. In the latter part of his career he shifted the focus of his research to agriculture in the world, with particular attention to agricultural development in low-income countries. His model involving the 'agricultural surplus' has become a frequent tool of research.

NICHOLS, Donald Arthur

Born 1940, New Haven, CT, USA.
Current Post Prof. Econ., Univ. Wisconsin, Madison, WI, USA, 1977–; Econ. Adviser, Governor State Wisconsin, 1983–.
Past Posts Student Intern., US President's Council Econ. Advisers, 1963; Acting Instr., Yale Univ., 1965–6; Ass. Prof., Assoc. Prof., Univ. Wisconsin, 1966–70, 1970–1; Vis. Lect., Yale Univ., 1970–1; Academic Vis., LSE, 1971; Sr. Econ., Comm. on Budget, US Senate, 1975–6; Deputy Ass. Secretary, Econ. Pol. and Res., US Dept. Labor, 1977–9.
Degrees BA, MA, PhD Yale Univ., 1962, 1963, 1968.
Principal Fields of Interest 110 Economic Growth; 130 Economic Fluctuations; 310 Domestic Monetary and Fiscal Theory.
Publications *Books:* 1. *Principles of Economics* (with C. W. Reynolds), (Holt, Rinehart & Winston, 1971); 2. *The Economical Use of Exhaustible Resources* (MSS Modular Publications, 1974); 3. *Monetarism: A Time for Retreat* (Nat. Pol. Exchange, 1982).
Articles: 1. 'A note on inflation and common stock values', *J Fin*, 23, Sept. 1968; 2. 'Market clearing for heterogeneous capital goods', in *Microeconomic Foundations of Employment and Inflation Theory*, eds., E.S. Phelps, *et al.* (W. W. Norton, 1970); 3. 'Land and economic growth', *AER*, 60(3), June 1970; 4. 'Discrimination by waiting time in merit goods' (with E. Smolensky and T. N. Tideman), *AER*, 61(3), June 1971; 5. 'Some principles of inflationary finance', *JPE*, 79(2), March-April 1974; 6. 'The investment income formula of the AEA', *AER*, 64(2), May 1974; 7. 'Comparing tax-based incomes policies

to wage subsidies', *AER*, 69(2), 8. 'Macroeconomic determinants of wage adjustments in white-collar occupations', *REStat*, 65(2), May 1983; 9. 'Why interest rates rise when an unexpectedly large money stock is announced' (with D. Small and C. E. Webster), *AER*, 73(3), June 1983; 10. 'Wage measurement questions raised by an incomes policy', in *The Measurement of Labor Cost*, ed. J. E. Triplett (Univ. Chicago Press, 1983).
Principal Contributions My work is devoted to the improvement of economic policy-making. It reflects the interaction between real-world policy problems and economic research. In the mid-1960s, I was taught separate models for inflation, growth and fluctations, and I started my career by trying to understand how best to integrate these models. I participated in the early efforts to apply dynamic methods and neoclassical theory to the problem of inflation. Back then, a major problem was how to convince policy-makers and academics that there were limits to how far unemployment could be reduced on a permanent basis through the use of demand stabilisation instruments alone. Both the academic and policy community bought that argument only too well. Now, the problem is the reverse, namely, how to convince both policy-makers and academics that a more ambitious pursuit of policy goals makes sense. My recent research has been directed towards furthering our understanding of new policy tools, of the institutions that inhibit price adjustment, and of the implications for policy of a decade of turbulence in macroeconomics. I have spent fully half of my time in the last decade in what has become a second career, namely, as a policy-maker in government. Because of this role, I have also been called on to write synthetic pieces summarising what is known about various issues of interest to the policy community.

NICHOLSON, Joseph Shield*

Dates and Birthplace 1850–1927, Wrawby, Lincolnshire, England.

Posts Held Prof. Polit. Econ., Univ. Edinburgh, 1880–1925.

Degrees MA Univ. London; DSc Univ. Camb.

Offices and Honours Fellow, BA.

Publications *Books:* 1. *Money and Monetary Problems* (1888); 2. *Principles of Political Economy*, 3 vols (1893–1901); 3. *Strikes and Social Problems* (1896); 4. *History of the English Corn Laws* (1904); 5. *War Finance* (1918); 6. *Inflation* (1919); 7. *The Revival of Marxism* (1920).

Career His published work was largely directed at students, while his articles, collected in volumes such as *War Finance*, were directed at the general public. His economics was inspired by Adam Smith and by moral and philosophical considerations. His later works make use of statistical and historical data and are mainly concerned with contemporary issues.

Secondary Literature W. R. Scott, 'Obit.: Joseph Shield Nicholson', *EJ*, 37, Sept. 1927.

NISKANEN, William Arthur

Born 1933, Bend, OR, USA.

Current Post Member, US President's Council Econ. Advisers, Washington, D. C., 1983–.

Past Posts Dir. Special Stud., US Office Secretary Defense, 1962–4; Dir. Econ., Inst. Defense Analysis, 1964–70; Ass. Dir., US Office Management and Budget, 1970–2; Prof., Grad. School Public Pol., Univ. Cal. Berkeley, 1972–5; Dir. Econ., Ford Motor Co., 1975–80; Prof. Grad. School Management, UCLA, 1980–1.

Degrees BA Harvard Coll., 1954; MA, PhD Univ. Chicago, 1955, 1962

Offices and Honours Founder, Nat. Tax Limitation Comm., 1976; Member, Census Advisory Comm., AEA, 1977–81.

Principal Fields of Interest 513 Business and Public Administration.

Publications *Books:* 1. *Bureaucracy and Representative Government* (Aldine-Atherton, 1971); 2. *Structural Reform of the Federal Budget Process* (AEI., 1973).

Articles: 1. 'The defense resource allocation process', *Defense Management*, 1966; 2. 'The peculiar economics of bureaucracy', *AER*, 58(2), May 1968; 3. 'Bureaucrats and politicians', *J Law E*, 18(3), Dec. 1975; 4. 'The prospect for liberal democracy', *Fiscal Responsibility in Constitutional Democracy* (1978); 5. 'Economic and fiscal effects on the popular vote for the President', in *Public Policy and Public Choice* (1979).

Principal Contributions The economics of bureaucracy. Early contributions to demand for alcoholic beverages, defence analysis, and government management; recent contributions to structure of local government, economics of car industry, and selected topics in public choice.

NORDHAUS, William D.

Born 1941, Albuquerque, NM, USA.

Current Post John Musser Prof. Econ., Yale Univ., 1979–.

Past Posts Ass. Prof., Assoc Prof., Prof. Econ., Yale Univ., 1967–70, 1970–3, 1973–9; Member, US President's Council Econ. Advisers, 1977–9.

Degrees Certificat, Inst. d'Etudes Polit., Paris, 1962; BA Yale Univ., 1963; PhD MIT, 1967.

Editorial Duties Assoc. Ed. *AER*, *J Conflict Resolution*, *Energy Econ.*

Principal Fields of Interest 723 Energy.

Publications *Books:* 1. *Invention, Growth and Welfare: A Theoretical Treatment of Technological Change* (MIT Press, 1969); 2. *Industrial Pricing in the United Kingdom* (with W. Godley and K. Coutts), (CUP, 1978); 3. *International Studies in the Demand for Energy*, co-ed. (with others), (N-H, 1978); 4. *The Efficient Use of Energy Resources* (Yale Univ. Press, 1979).

Articles: 1. 'Some sceptical thoughts on the theory of induced innovations', *QJE*, 87(2), May 1973; 2. 'World dynamics: measurement without data', *EJ*, 83, Dec. 1973; 3. 'Resources as a constraint on growth', *AER*, 64(2), May 1974; 4. 'The political business cycle', *REStud*, 42(2), April 1975; 5. 'Thinking about carbon dioxide: theoretical and empirical aspects of optimal control strategies' (US Dept. of Energy, 1980).

Principal Contributions Major research has been in economic growth and natural resources, including studies of the long-run efficient allocation of resources (especially energy), as well as the question of the extent to which resources constrain economic growth. Also research in wage and price behaviour, stressing the behavioural aspects of corporate pricing.

NORMAN, George Warde*

Dates and Birthplace 1793–1882, Bromley, Kent, England

Posts Held Member Family Timber Firm, 1810–30; Dir., Bank England, 1821–72; Dir., Sun Insurance Office, 1830–64.

Offices and Honours Gave evidence before numerous official commissions; Member, Polit. Econ. Club, 1821.

Publications *Books:* 1. *Remarks upon some Prevalent Errors with respect to Currency and Banking* (1833); 2. *Letter to Sir C. Wood, Bart., on Money and the Means of Economising the Use of It* (1841); 3. *An Examination of Some Prevailing Opinions as to the Pressure of Taxation* (1849); 4. *Remarks on the Incidence of Import Duties* (1860); 5. *Papers on Various Subjects* (1869).

Principal Contributions·His *Remarks . . .* , which produced criticism from Torrens and Overstone, developed his theory of cycles, which came close to being a purely monetary one, but he did admit other causal factors. He gave extensive evidence to the committee inquiring into the working of the Bank Charter Act; his *Letter to Sir C. Wood . . .* also deals with this.

NORTH, Douglass Cecil

Born 1920, Cambridge, MA, USA.
Current Post Henry R. Luce Prof. Law and Liberty, Washington Univ., St Louis, MO, USA, 1982–.
Past Posts Grad. Teaching Fellow, Univ. Cal. Berkeley, 1946–9; Prof. Econ., Dir., Chairman, Inst. Econ. Res., Univ. Washington, 1950–61,

1961–6, 1967–9; Peterkin Prof. Polit Econ., Rice Univ., Houston, TX, 1979; Pitt Prof., Univ. Camb., 1981–2.

Degrees BA, PhD Univ. Cal. Berkeley, 1942, 1952.

Offices and Honours Board Dirs., NBER, 1967–; Board Trustees, Econ. Inst., 1968, 1971, 1978; Pres., EHA, 1972–3; Vis. Assoc. Dir., Centre de Recherche Historique, Ecole Pratique des Hautes Etudes, Paris, 1973; Pres., WEA, 1975–6.

Editorial Duties Co-ed., *JEH*, 1960–6.
Principal Fields of Interest 040 Economic History.

Publications *Books:* 1. *The Economic Growth of the United States, 1790–1860* (Prentice-Hall, 1961); 2. *Growth and Welfare in the American Past: A New Economic History* (Prentice-Hall, 1966); 3. *A Documentary History of American Economic Growth, 1607–1860*, co-ed. (with R. L. Miller), (Harper & Row, 1968); 4. *The Economics of Public Issues* (with R. L. Miller), (Harper & Row, 1971); 5. *Institutional Change and American Economic Growth* (with L. E. Davis), (CUP, 1971); 6. *The Rise of the Western World: A New Economic History* (with R. P. Thomas), (CUP, 1973); 7. *Structure and Change in Economic History* (W. W. Norton, 1981).

Articles: 1. 'Economic history', *IESS*, 4, 1968; 2. 'Sources of productivity change in ocean shipping, 1600–1850', *JPE*, 76, Oct. 1983; 3. 'An economic theory of the growth of the western world' (with R. P. Thomas), *EHR*, 23(1), April 1970. 4. 'The first economic revolution' (with R. P. Thomas), *EHR*, 30(2), May 1977; 5. 'Structure and performance: the task of economic history', *JEL*, 16(3), Sept. 1978; 6. 'A framework for analyzing the state in economic history', *Explor. Econ. Hist.*, 16(3), July 1979; 7. 'American government expenditures: an historical perspective' (with J. Wallis), *AER*, 72(2), May 1982; 8. 'Government and the costs of exchange in history', *JEH*, 44(2), June 1984.

Principal Contributions Discussion of the increase in transactions costs in the US (resources devoted to political and economic organisation) reflected in the growth of government and the parallel institutional and market responses.

Development of a model of the growth of the American economy from 1790–1860; discussion of the usefulness of applying simple neoclassical theory to problems in American economic history; and development of a general model of institutional change, and its application to the economic history of the Western world. Empirical contributions have included development of the balance of payments from 1790–1860; the export/import price indices of the US from 1790–1860; and an index of the productivity of ocean shipping from 1600–1914.

NOVE, Alexander

Born 1915, Petrograd, Russia.
Current Post Prof. Emeritus, Hon. Sr. Res. Fellow, Univ. Glasgow, 1982–.
Past Posts Reader, Russian Social Econ. Stud., Univ. London, 1958–63; Dir., Inst. Soviet E. European Stud., Bonar Prof. Econ., Univ. Glasgow, 1963–79, 1963–82.
Degrees BSc Univ. London, 1936; DAg (*H.C.*) Giessen, Germany, 1977.
Offices and Honours Fellow, BA, 1978, RSE, 1981; Hon. Fellow, LSE, 1982.
Principal Fields of Interest 052 Socialist and Communist Economic Systems.
Publications *Books:* 1. *The Soviet Economy* (A&U, 1961, many transls.); 2. *Was Stalin Really Necessary?* (A&U, 1963); 3. *Economic History of the USSR* (Allen Lane/Penguin, 1969); 4. *Efficiency Criteria for Nationalized Industries* (A&U, 1973); 5. *The Soviet Economic System* (A&U, 1977, 1981); 6. *Political Economy and Soviet Socialism* (A&U, 1979); 7. *The Economics of Feasible Socialism* (A&U, 1983).
Principal Contributions The evolution of the USSR and of Soviet-type economies; economies of socialism; efficiency criteria of nationalised industries in East and West; the USSR as a model of development; planning methods in the USSR and in developing countries; socialist agriculture; Russian and Soviet economic thought; comparative systems; the interaction of political, economic and historical factors in Soviet history.

NOVOZHILOV, Viktor Valentinovich*

Dates and Birthplace 1892–1970, Kharkov, Russia.
Degrees Grad. Univ. Kiev, 1915.
Offices and Honours Honoured scientist of the USSR, 1957; Lenin Prize, 1965.
Publications *Books:* 1. *The Use of Mathematics in Economics*, ed. J. S. Nemchinov (Oliver & Boyd, 1964).
Articles: 1. 'On choosing between investment projects', *Trans. Leningrad Industrial Inst.*, 1946, repr. in *Internat. Econ. Papers*, 6, eds. A. T. Peacock, *et al.* (Macmillan, 1956).
Career His work was mainly concerned with the balance between expenditure and performance in the Soviet economy. In this he used mathematical methods and was largely responsible for making mathematical economics quasi-respectable in the USSR after World War II. His later work included a model for the optimisation of resources of production.
Secondary Literature A. Zauberman, *The Mathematical Revolution in Soviet Economics* (OUP, 1975); A. Katselinboigen, *Soviet Economic Thought and Political Power in the USSR: The Development of Soviet Mathematical Economics* (Pergamon, 1979)

NURKSE, Ragnar*

Dates and Birthplace 1907–59, Estonia.
Posts Held Econ., League Nations, 1934–45; Vis. Lect. Econ., Prof. Econ., Univ. Columbia, 1945–6, 1947–59, Inst. Advanced Study, Princeton Univ., 1946–8; Ford Foundation Res. Prof., 1958–9.
Publications *Books:* 1. *Internationale Kapitalbewegungen* (1935); 2. *International Currency Experience* (1954); 3. *Conditions of International Monetary Equilibrium* (1945); 4. *Course and Control of Inflation* (1946); 5. *Problems of Capital Formation in Underdeveloped Countries* (1953).
Career After establishing a reputation in international finance, he turned in his last book to the problem of

development and, besides adding a new term (the 'demonstration effect') to the vocabulary of economists, was a powerful advocate of the 'big push' conception of development.

NUTI, Domenico Mario

Born 1937, Arezzo, Italy.
Current Post Prof. Econ., Europ. Univ. Inst., Florence, Italy, 1982–.
Past Posts Fellow, King's Coll., Res. Fellow, Tutor, Ass. Lect., Lect. Econ. Polit., Univ. Camb., 1966–79, 1966–9, 1969–73, 1971–3, 1976–9; Prof. Polit. Econ., Dir., Centre Russian E. European Stud., Univ. Birmingham, 1980–2.
Degrees Dottore Giurisprudenza Univ. Rome, 1962; MA, PhD Univ. Camb., 1966, 1970.
Offices and Honours Stevenson Prize, Univ. Camb., 1965; Exec., British Nat. Assoc. Soviet E. Europ. Stud., 1980–4; Exec., Italian Assoc. Comp. Econ. Systems, 1984–.
Editorial Duties Ed. Boards, *Camb JE*, 1977–, *Econ. Planning* 1980–3, *Soviet Stud.*, 1980–4, *Econ. Modelling*, 1983–, *Communist Affairs*, 1980–.
Principal Fields of Interest 020 General Economic Theory; 053 Comparative Economic Systems; 052 Socialist Economic Systems.
Publications *Books:* 1. *Socialist Economics*, co-ed. (with A. Nove), (Penguin, 1972, 1976); 2. V. K. Dmitriev, *Economic Essays on Value Competition and Utility*, ed. (CUP, 1974).
Articles: 1. 'Capitalism, socialism and steady growth', *EJ*, 80, March 1970; repr. in *Capital and Growth*, eds. G. C. Harcourt and N. F. Laing (Penguin, 1972); 2. 'On the truncation of production flows', *Kyk*, 26(3), 1973; 3. 'The evolution of Polish investment planning', *Jahrbuch Wirtschaft Osteuropas* 3, 1973; 4. 'The transformation of labour values into production prices and the Marxian theory of exploitation', (Polish), *Ekonomista*, 1, 1974; transl. in *The Subtle Anatomy of Capitalism*, ed. J. Schwartz (Goodyear, 1977); 5. 'On the rates of return on investment', *Kyk*, 27(2), 1974, repr. in *Essays in Modern Capital Theory*, eds. M. Brown, K. Sato and P. Zarembka (N-H., 1976; transl., *Cahiers*

d'Economie Politique, 1976); 6. 'Price and composition effects and the pseudo-production function', in *On the Measurement of Factor Productivities*, eds. F. L. Altmann, O. Kyn and H. J. Wagener (Vandenhoek & Ruprecht, 1976, repr. *Revue d'Economie Politique*, 2, March-April 1977); 7. 'The contradictions of socialist economies — a Marxian interpretation', in *The Socialist Register 1979*, eds. R. Miliband and J. Saville (Merlin Press, 1979, transl. in *Dissenso e Democrazia nei Paesi dell'Est* (Vallecchi, 1980), and *Motsättningar i de Socialistiska Ekonomierma* (Zenit Häften, 1981); 8. 'The Polish crisis: economic factors and constraints', in *The Socialist Register 1981*, eds. R. Miliband and J. Saville (Merlin Press, 1981), repr. in *The Polish Disease*, ed. J. Drewnowski (Croom Helm, 1982); 9. 'Socialism on Earth', *Camb JE*, 5, Dec. 1981; 10. 'Mergers and disequilibrium in labour-managed economies', *Jahrbuch Wirtschaft Osteuropas*, 4, 1984.
Principal Contributions An exploration and development of the Austrian theory of capital and time (steady-state relationships between wage, interest, consumption and growth: valuation of capital and income per man) leading to criticism of aggregate production functions. A detailed investigation of official instructions for the selection of investment projects in the Soviet Union and East European countries. An analysis of recent reforms of industrial organisation in Eastern Europe, their connection with macroeconomic policies and in particular with over-accumulation bias of socialist economies, with special reference to Poland. A model of political-economic fluctuations and crises in Soviet-type economies.

O

OATES, Wallance Eugene

Born 1937, Los Angeles, CA, USA.
Current Post Prof. Econ., Univ. Maryland, Coll. Park, MD, USA, 1979–.
Past Posts Prof. Econ., Princeton Univ., 1965–79; Vis. Fellow, Linacre Coll. Oxford, 1971, LSE, 1974–5.

Degrees MA, PhD Stanford Univ. 1959, 1965.

Offices and Honours NSF Fellow, 1963–5; Guggenheim Foundation Fellow, 1974–5; Fulbright-Hays Res. Scholar, 1974–5; Board of Dirs., Assoc. of Environmental and Resource Econ., 1983.

Editorial Duties Ed. Board, *Nat. Tax J.*, 1972–, *Public Fin. Q.*, 1973–.

Principal Fields of Interest 321 Fiscal Theory and Policy; 324 State and Local Government Finance; 722 Conservation and Pollution.

Publications *Books:* 1. *The Implications of International Economic Integration for Monetary, Fiscal and Exchange-Rate Policy* (with R. Mckinnon), (Princeton Univ. Press, 1966); 2. *Fiscal Federalism* (Harcourt, Brace, Jovanovich, 1972; transl., Spanish, Istituto de Estudios de Admin., 1977); 3. *The Theory of Environmental Policy* (with W. Baumol), (Prentice-Hall, 1975; transl., Spanish, St Pere Claver, 1972); 4. *An Introduction to Econometrics* (with H. Kelejian), (Harper & Row, 1974; transl., Portuguese, Elsevier, 1978); 5. *Fiscal Zoning and Land-Use Controls*, co-ed. (with E. Mills), (D. C. Heath, 1975); 6. *Financing the New Federalism*, ed. (JHUP, 1975); 7. *The Political Economy of Fiscal Federalism*, ed. (D. C. Heath, 1977); 8. *Essays in Labor Market Analysis*, co-ed. (with O. Ashenfelter), (Wiley, 1977); 9. *Economics, Environmental Policy and the Quality of Life* (with W. Baumol), (Prentice-Hall, 1979).

Articles: 1. 'The theory of public finance in a federal system', *CJE*, 1, Feb. 1968; 2. 'The rising cost of local public services: some evidence and reflections' (with D. Bradford and R. Matt), *Nat. Tax J*, 22, June 1960, repr. in *Municipal Needs, Services, and Financing*, ed. P. Beaton (Rutgers Univ. Press, 1974); 3. 'The effect of property taxes and local public spending on property values: an empirical study of tax capitalisation and the Tiebout hypothesis', *JPE*, 77(6), Nov.–Dec. 1969; 4. 'The use of standards and prices for protection of the environment' (with W. Baumol), *Swed JE*, 73(1), March, 1971, repr. in *The Economics of the Environment*, eds. P. Bohm and A.

Kneese (St Martins, 1972); 5. 'Towards a predictive theory of intergovernmental grants' (with D. Bradord), *AER*, 61(2), May, 1971, repr. in *The Economics of Federalism*, ed. B. Grewal, *et al.* (ANU Press, 1980); 6. 'The analysis of revenue sharing in a new approach to collective fiscal decisions' (with D. Bradford), *QJE*, 85(3), Aug. 1971, repr. in *Financiacion de las Autonomias*, ed. A. Gimenez (H. Blume Eds, 1979); 7. 'Suburban exploitation of central cities and governmental structure' (with D. Bradford), in *Redistribution Through Public Choice*, eds. H. Hochman and G. Peterson (Columbia Univ. Press, 1975); 8. 'On local finance and the Tiebout model', *EAR*, 71(2) May, 1981; 9. 'Efficiency in pollution control in the short and long runs: a system of rental emission permits' (with R. Collinge), *CJE*, 15, May 1982; 10. 'On marketable air-pollution permits: the case for a system of pollution offsets' (with A. Krupnick and E. Van De Verg), *JEEM*, 10, Sept. 1983.

Principal Contributions My early work in fiscal federalism attempted to provide a systematic and comprehensive view of the vertical structure of the public sector. *Fiscal Federalism* explores the basic issues of the assignment of functions to different levels of government, the use of fiscal instruments including intergovenmental grants to achieve public-sector objectives, and the empirical testing of a series of hypotheses concerning federal fiscal structure. My subsequent work in this area has examined various issues in State and local finance: theoretical and empirical studies of local government behaviour, studies of State-local tax structure, and the analysis of urban fiscal problems.

More recently, I have devoted much of my research effort to environmental economics with a primary interest in the design and implementation of economic incentives for protection of the environment. This work includes the theoretical analysis of externalities and more policy-oriented studies of systems of effluent fees and of marketable pollution rights for environmental management.

O'BRIEN, Denis Patrick

Born 1939, Knebworth, Hertfordshire, England.

Current Post Prof. Econ., Univ. Durham, England, 1972–.

Past Posts Ass. Lect., Lect., Reader, Queen's Univ. Belfast, N. Ireland, 1963–4, 1965–70, 1970–2.

Degrees BSc Univ. London, 1960; PhD Queen's Univ. Belfast, 1969.

Offices and Honours Council Member, RES, 1978–83.

Principal Fields of Interest 031 History of Economic Thought; 036 Methodology; 612 Public Policy Towards Monopoly and Competition.

Publications *Books:* 1. *Information Agreements, Competition and Efficiency* (with D. Swann), (Macmillan, 1969); 2. *J. R. McCulloch: A Study in Classical Economics* (A&U, 1970); 3. *The Correspondence of Lord Overstone*, 3 vols (CUP, 1971); 4. *Competition in British Industry* (with D. Swann, P. Maunder and W. S. Howe), (A&U, 1974); 5. *The Classical Economists* (Clarendon Press, 1975, 1978; transl., Italian, 1983); 6. *J. R. McCulloch: A Treatise on the Principles and Practical Influence of Taxation and the Funding System*, ed. (Scottish Academic Press, 1975); 7. *Competition Policy, Profitability and Growth* (with W. S. Howe, D. M. Wright and R. J. O'Brien), (Macmillan, 1979); 8. *Pioneers of Modern Economics in Britain*, co-ed. and contrib. (with J. R. Presley), (Macmillan, 1981); 9. *Authorship Puzzles in the History of Economics: A Statistical Approach* (with A. C. Darnell), (Macmillan, 1982); 10. *Economic Analysis in Historical Perspective*, co-ed. and contrib. (with J. Creedy), (Butterworths, 1984).

Articles: 1. 'Patent protection and competition in polyamide and polyester fibre manufacture', *J Ind E*, 12, July 1964; 2. 'The transition in Torrens' monetary thought', *Ec*, N.S. 32, Aug. 1965; 3. 'Information agreement — a problem in search of a policy' (with D. Swann), *MS*, 24, Sept. 1966, repr. in *Readings in the Economics of Industrial Organization*, ed. L. Needham (Holt Rhinehart, 1970); 4. 'J. R. McCulloch and the theory of value', *SJPE*, 24, June 1977; 5. 'Customs unions: trade creation and trade diversion in historical perspective', *HOPE*, 8(4), Winter 1976; 6. 'Torrens, McCulloch and Disraeli', *SJPE*, 24, June 1977; 7. 'Competition policy: the silent revolution', *Antitrust Bull.*, 27(1), Spring 1982; 8. 'Theories of the history of science: a test case', in *Methodological Controversy in Economics*, ed. A. W. Coats. (JAI Press, 1983); 9. 'The evolution of the theory of the firm', in *Firms, Organisation and Labour: Approaches to the Economics of Work Organisation*, ed. F. H. Stephen (Macmillan, 1984); 10. 'Research programmes in competitive structure', *J. Econ. Stud.*, 10(4), 1983.

Principal Contributions Re-evaluation of the work of the 19th-century Scottish economist and statistician J. R. McCulloch, previously ofter regarded in the secondary literature as a slavish follower of Ricardo. Begun in 1963, this involved drawing upon extensive published and unpublished work by McCulloch. The search for the latter led to the discovery of the papers of the leading 19th-century monetary economist and banker S. J. Loyd, Lord Overstone, which had previously been thought to be destroyed. The preparation of a three-volume edition of these papers, with critical and biographical discussion, was conducted alongside the continuation and completion of the McCulloch study.

At the same time, a continuing interest in industrial economics, deriving in part from a spell as a business economist before entering academic life, led to work with D. Swann on the problem of information agreements, including the publication of a book-length study. During the 1970s these research interests broadened into more general work on classical economics (including an edition of McCulloch's *Taxation* and a general study *The Classical Economists*), methodology, and to empirical work on the impact of competition policy. The latter took the form of one large-scale series of case studies (made in conjunction with D. Swann and others) and one large-scale statistical study (with W. S. Howe and others) involving the construction of a special data base and the systematic employment of non-parametric methods.

More recently the two lines of interest have converged; the history of economic thought interest has shifted to the period 1870–1950, with particular emphasis on the treatment of the firm and of competitive structure by writers like Marshall, Chamberlin, and Robinson, and including methodological considerations, while non-parametric statistical technique has been employed in investigating some problems of anonymous authorship in economics.

O'BRIEN, George Augustine Thomas*

Dates and Birthplace 1892–1973, Dublin, Ireland.
Posts Held Barrister, 1913–16; Journalist, 1916–26; Prof., Univ. Coll., Dublin, 1926–61.
Degrees BA, DLitt. Univ. Coll., Dublin, 1912, 1919.
Offices and Honours Member of Seanad of Ireland, 1948–65; Pres., Stat. Soc. Ireland, 1942.
Publications *Books: 1. The Economic History of Ireland in the Eighteenth Century* (1918); 2. *The Economic History of Ireland in the Seventeenth Century* (1919); 3. *The Economic History of Ireland from the Union to the Famine* (1921); 4. *Agricultural Economics* (1929); 5. *Notes on the Theory of Profit* (1929); 6. *The Four Green Fields* (1936); 7. *The Phantom of Plenty* (1948).
Career Perhaps best known outside Ireland for his discovery of Ricardo's letters to James Mill, he was Ireland's major economic historian and most influential teacher of economics during his long tenure of the University College chair. He also sat on numerous commissions of inquiry, and wrote at length on current economic matters in the British and Irish periodical press. His economics, though avowedly taking the conventional deductive, non-mathematical form he learnt in his youth, was non-doctrinaire and responsive to trends. He held a place of unique respect and influence in Irish economics.
Secondary Literature J. Meenan, *George O'Brien: A Biographical Memoir* (1980).

OFFICER, Lawrence Howard

Born 1940, Montreal, Quebec, Canada.
Current Post Prof. Econ., Michigan State Univ., East Lansing, MI, USA, 1970–.
Past Posts Ass. Prof. Econ., Harvard Univ., 1965–70; Cons., IMF 1975; Vis. Prof. Econ., Grad. School Bus., Univ. Chicago, 1980–.
Degrees BA (Econ and Polit. Science) McGill Univ., Montreal, Canada, 1960; MA, PhD Harvard Univ., 1962, 1965.
Offices and Honours Hon. Mention, Coll. and Univ. Div., 18th Annual Nat. Awards Program Teaching Econ., Joint Council Econ. Educ., 1980.
Editorial Duties Assoc. Ed., *REStat*, 1968–, *QJE*, 1966–71; Ed. Board, *CJE*, 1971–4.
Principal Fields of Interest 430 Balance of Payments; International Finance; 420 Trade Relations and Commercial Policy; International Economic Integration.
Publications *Books: 1. An Econometric Model of Canada Under the Fluctuating Exchange Rate* (Harvard Univ. Press, 1968); 2. *The International Monetary System: Problems and Proposals*, co-ed. (with T. D. Willett), (Prentice-Hall, 1969); 3. *Canadian Economic Problems and Policies*, co-ed. (with L. B. Smith), (McGraw-Hill, 1970); 4. *Supply Relationships in the Canadian Economy: An Industry Comparison* (with P. R. Andersen and D. A. Wilton), (Div. Res., Grad. School Bus. Admin., Michigan State Univ., 1972); 5. *Issues in Canadian Economics*, co-ed. (with L. B. Smith), (McGraw-Hill Ryerson, 1974); 6. *The Monetary Approach to the Balance of Payments: A Survey* (with M. E. Kreinin), (Internat. Fin. Section, Princeton Univ., 1978); 7. *So You Have to Write an Economics Term Paper . . .* (with D. H. Saks and J. A. Saks), (Div. Res., Grad School Bus. Admin., Michigan State Univ., 1980, Michigan State Univ. Press, 1981); 8. *Purchasing Power Parity: Theory, Evidence and Relevance* (JAI Press, 1982).
Articles: 1. 'The effect of monopoly in commodity markets upon the foreign exchange market', *QJE*, 80(2), May 1966; 2. 'The optimality of pure

competition in the capacity problem', *QJE*, 80(4), Nov. 1966; 3. 'Monopoly and monopolistic competition in the international transportation industry', *WEJ*, 9(2), June 1971; 4. 'Discrimination in the international transportation industry', *WEJ*, 10(2), June 1972; 5. 'Reserve-asset preferences in the crisis zone, 1958–67', *JMCB*, 6(2), May 1974; 6. 'The purchasing-power-parity theory of exchange rates: a review article', *IMF Staff Papers*, 23(1), March 1976; 7. 'The relationship between absolute and relative purchasing power parity', *REStat*, 60(4), Nov. 1978; 8. 'The floating dollar in the Greenback period: a test of theory of exchange-rate determination', *JEH*, 41(3), Sept. 1981; 9. 'The differential use of IMF resources by industrial, other developed, and less developed countries: a historical approach', *J. Developing Areas*, 16(3), April 1982; 10. 'Dollar-sterling mint parity and exchange rates, 1791–1834', *JEH*, 43(3), Sept. 1983.

Principal Contributions My first published work dealt with theoretical issues in the foreign exchange market and in peak-load pricing. Then I turned to a wide variety of problems, including reciprocity in Canada-US 19th-century trade, labour force participation, import-demand functions, large scale econometric model building, and various aspects of the international monetary system. For a while, the issue of discrimination in oceanic shipping rates fascinated me. Subsequently, with sidelines such as the demand for international liquidity and operations of the IMF, my principal interest became purchasing power parity. (For some time, people would ask me: 'How many PPPs did you fit today?') Fortunately, a general disenchantment with purchasing power parity has arisen — although I dare say the virtues of purchasing power parity will be 'rediscovered' in the future, say, the 21st century, as it has been several times in the past — and I was able to turn to another topic in good conscience.

I think economic history is 'where it's at' — the present being so confusing, one must learn from the past — and the dollar-sterling foreign exchange market in the 19th century has occupied my most recent attention. In summary, apart from purchasing power parity, my writings cover so many fields that some might say I know 'nothing about everything'. Some ne'er-do-wells might reverse that remark to 'everything about nothing' and apply it to my knowledge of purchasing power parities (these people, of course, will not have read Gustav Cassel's works in the original).

OHLIN, Bertin Gotthard*

Dates and Birthplace 1899–1979, Klippan, Sweden.

Posts Held Prof. Econ., Univ. Copenhagen, 1925–30; Prof., Stockholm School Econ. Bus., 1930–65.

Degrees BA, Dr Univ. Stockholm, 1919, 1924.

Offices and Honours Member, Swedish Parliament, 1938–70; Leader, Folkpartiet, 1944–67; Swedish Minister Trade, 1944–5; Nobel Prize in Econ., 1977.

Publications *Books:* 1. *Handelns Teori* (1924); 2. *The Course and Phases of the World Economic Depression* (1931, 1972); 3. *Interregional and International Trade* (1933, 1967); 4. *The Problem of Employment Stabilisation* (1949, 1977).

Career A successful political career as leader of Sweden's main opposition party probably limited the quantity of his output. International trade was his main subject from his published dissertation of 1924 onwards, and *Interregional and International Trade* was his masterpiece. In this he developed Cassel's simplified Walrasian equilibrium model in a manner similar to Heckscher's 1919 article and produced what is nowadays known as the 'Heckscher-Ohlin theorem', which accounts for the commodity composition of international trade entirely by the relative factor endowments of countries. He also made major contributions to theory of money, employment and economic fluctuations, though much of this work has not appeared in English. In his application of the concept of aggregate demand, and his distinction between expected and realised saving and investment, Ohlin anticipated some aspects of Keynes's *General Theory*.

Secondary Literature H. Dickson, 'Ohlin, Bertil', *IESS* 18; R. E. Caves, 'Bertil Ohlin's contribution to economics'; *Scand JE*, 80(1), 1978, repr. in *Contemporary Economics in Perspective*, eds. H. W. Spiegel and W. J. Samuels (JAI Press, 1984); O. Steiger, 'Bertil Ohlin, 1899–1979', *HOPE*, 13(2), Summer 1981.

OI, Walter Yasuo

Born 1929, Los Angeles, CA, USA.
Current Post Elmer B. Milliman Prof. Econ., Univ. Rochester, Rochester, NY, US, 1978–.

Past Posts Instr. Econ., Iowa State Univ., Ames, IA, 1957–8; Res. Econ., Transportation Center, Northwestern Univ. Evanston, IL, 1958–62; Assoc. Prof., Prof. Econ., Univ. Washington, Seattle, 1962–5, 1965–7; Prof., Grad. School Management, Prof. Econ., Univ. Rochester, 1967–75, 1975–8; Vis. Scholar, Hoover Inst., Stanford Univ., 1970–1; Vis. Res. Econ., Industrial Relations Section, Princeton Univ., 1973–4.

Degrees BA (Bus. Stats.), MA UCLA, 1952; PhD Univ. Chicago, 1961.

Offices and Honours Vice-Chairman, US President's Comm. Employment of the Handicapped; Fellow, Em Soc.

Principal Fields of Interest 020 General Economic Theory; 610 Industrial Organisation; 820 Labour Markets.

Publications *Books:* 1. *The Economic Value of the United States Merchant Marine* (with A. R. Ferguson, *et al.*), (Transportation Center, 1961); 2. *An Analysis of Urban Travel Demands* (with P. W. Suldiner), (Northwestern Univ. Press, 1962); 3. *Economics of Private Truck Transportation* (with A. P. Hurter Jr.), (William C. Brown, 1965); 4. *Demand Analysis for Air Travel by Supersonic Transport* (with N. S. Asher, *et al.*), (Inst. Defense Analyses, 1966).

Articles: 1. 'Labor as a quasi-fixed factor', *JPE*, 70(6), Dec. 1962; 2. 'The economic cost of the draft', *AER*, 57(2), May 1967; 3. 'The neoclassical foundations of progress functions', *EJ*, 77, Sept. 1967; 4. 'On the relationship among different members of the k-class', *Int ER*, 10(1), Feb. 1969; 5. 'A Disney-land dilemma: two-part tariffs for a Mickey Mouse monopoly', *QJE*, 85(1), Feb. 1971; 6. 'The economics of product safety', *Bell JE*, 4(1), Spring 1973; 7. 'On the economics of industrial safety', *Law and Contemporary Problems*, 38(4), Summer-Autumn 1974; 8. 'Residential location and labor supply', *JPE*, 84(4), pt. 2, Aug. 1976; 9. 'Heterogeneous firms and the organization of production', *EI*, 21(2), April 1983; 10. 'The fixed employment costs of specialized labor', in *The Measurement of Labor Costs*, ed. J. E. Triplett (Univ. Chicago Press, 1983).

Principal Contributions My first major paper (No. 1 above) tried to develop a coherent explanation for the observed cyclical behaviour of wages and employment. I try in my research to use economic theory to explain observed economic phenomena and to evaluate the merits of policy proposals. My mentors at Chicago and UCLA, H. G. Lewis, A. C. Harberger, A. A. Alchian and others, are responsible for the way in which I attack economic issues but they cannot be held accountable for the resulting products. After the quasi-fixity of labour, I turned my attention to transportation, applied price theory, and a brief foray into econometrics. If I must choose my favourites from this list, they would include the theory in the private trucking book (with A. P. Hurter Jr.), the Disneyland Dilemma, the k-class estimators, and the economics of product safety. Over the period 1964–70 I devoted some 30 months or more to research on military manpower. I have written several papers on the economics of the military draft and I hope that these had some effect on the decision to end conscription. I like to think that they did but I also believe that the work of the President's Commission on an All-Volunteer Force (directed by W. H. Meckling) deserves much of the credit for the final policy decision.

In the last decade, my work has returned to labour economics and the theory of the firm. The papers on workmen's compensation, industrial safety, and residential location have benefited from my study of the articles written by G. S. Becker. Recent papers (Nos. 9

and 10 above) represent my initial attempts to understand the structure of labour and product markets. It seems that if we are to understand labour and product markets, we must explicitly acknowledge and model the heterogeneity of firms as well as of goods and workers.

OLSON, Mancur Lloyd

Born 1932, Grand Forks, N. Dak., USA.
Current Post Disting. Prof. Econ., Univ. Maryland, Coll. Park, MD, USA, 1979–.
Past Posts Teaching Fellow, Harvard Univ. 1956–8; Lect., Princeton Univ., 1960–1; US Air Force, 1961–3; Ass. Prof., Princeton Univ., 1963–7; Deputy Ass. Secretary, US Dept. Health, Educ. & Welfare, 1967–9; Prof. Econ., Univ. Maryland, 1970–9.
Degrees BS, PhD N. Dakota State Univ., 1954; BA, MA Oxford Univ., 1956, 1960; PhD Harvard Univ., 1963.
Offices and Honours Rhodes Scholar, 1954–6; Fellow, Woodrow Wilson Internat. Center for Scholars, 1974; Fellow, Lehrman Inst., 1977–8; Pres., Public Choice Soc., 1972–4; Pres., SEA, 1981–2; Co-winner, Gladys W. Kammerer Award for Best Book US Pol., 1983.
Editorial Duties Ed. Boards, *Public Choice*, 1972–; *Internat. Stud. Q.*, 1975–; *Science*, 1980–1.
Principal Fields of Interest 010 General Economics; 025 Social Choice, Bureaucratic Performance; 320 Fiscal Theory and Policy; Public Finance.
Publications *Books:* 1. *The Economics of Wartime Shortage* (Duke Univ. Press, 1963); 2. *The Logic of Collective Action* (Harvard Univ. Press, 1965; transls., German, J. C. B. Mohr, 1968, French, Presses Univ. de France, 1978, Italian, Feltrinelli, 1983, Japanese, Minerva Shobo, 1983, Portuguese, Univ. of Brasilia Press, 1985); 3. *Toward a Social Report* (with staff US Dept. Health, Educ. and Welfare), (US Govt. Printing Office, 1969); 4. *The No-Growth Society*, co-ed. (W. W. Norton, 1974, Woburn, 1975); 5. *A New Approach to the Economics of Health Care*,

ed. (AEI, 1982); 6. *The Rise and Decline of Nations* (Yale Univ. Press, 1982).
Articles: 1. "Rapid growth as a destabilizing force', *JEH*, 23, Dec. 1963; 2. 'An economic theory of alliances' (with R. Zeckhauser), *REStat*, 47, Aug. 1966; 3. 'The plan and purpose of a social report', *Public Interest*, Spring 1969; 4. 'The efficient production of external economies' (with R. Zeckhauser), *AER*, 60(3), June 1970; 5. 'The treatment of externalities in national income statistics', in *Public Economics and the Quality of Life*, eds. L. Wingo and A. Evans (JHUP, 1977); 6. 'The marginal utility of income does not increase: borrowing, lending and Friedman-Savage gambles' (with M. J. Bailey and P. Wonnacott), *AER*, 70(3), June 1980; 7. 'Positive time preference' (with M. J. Bailey), *JPE*, 89(1), Feb. 1981; 8. 'Environmental indivisibilities and information costs: fanaticism, agnosticism and intellectual progress', *AER*, 72(2), May 1982; 9. 'The South will fall again; the South as leader and laggard in economic growth', *SEJ*, 49(4), April 1983; 10. 'A less ideological way of deciding how much should be given to the poor', *Daedalus*, Fall 1983.
Principal Contributions My PhD thesis, published as *The Logic of Collective Action*, generalised the theory of public goods, showing that private associations and collusions as well as governments provide services that automatically go to everyone in some category, so that voluntary market behaviour cannot explain the support for them, except when the number of beneficiaries is small. My secondary work at this time focussed on how substitution throughout economies that must be viewed as general equilibrium systems had made various wartime shortages much less serious than expected and rendered strategic bombing in World War II relatively ineffective. Then I worked on the efficient production of external economies, the puzzling frequency of discontent and upheaval during periods of rapid economic growth and the unmeasured and often-neglected 'goods' produced by stable social units such as familes.

This was followed by a period of government service with responsibility for an effort to supplement the national income statistics with additional measures of welfare ('social indicators') and broader evaluations of both favourable and unfavourable side-effects of economics growth; these measures and evaluations were embodied in *Toward A Social Report*. Later, I was puzzled by the striking differences in postwar rates of economic growth in different countries, and this led ultimately to the theory and the observations in *The Rise and Decline of Nations*. This book closes with an examination of the incentives that bring about involuntary unemployment, and this had led to an ongoing effort to develop a macroeconomic theory derived entirely from rational individual behaviour. Some recent theoretical work done with others has focussed on positive time preference and on the nonexistence of Friedman-Savage gambles. A final ongoing project attempts to explain why some phenomena, in the words of Marshall and Pigou, fall 'beyond the measuring rod of money'.

ONCKEN, August*

Dates and Birthplace 1844–1911, Heidelberg, Germany.
Posts Held Farmer, 1865–71; Lecturer, Agric. Coll., Vienna; Prof. Econ., Univ. Berne, 1910.
Degrees Studied at Heidelberg, Berlin and Munich.
Publications *Books:* 1. *Adam Smith in der Kulturgeschichte* (1874); 2. *Adam Smith und Immanuel Kant* (1877); 3. *Der altere Mirabeau und die okonomische Gesellschaft in Bern* (1886); 4. *Die Maxime: Laissez-faire et Laissez-passer* (1886); 5. *Oeuvres èconomiques et philosophiques de François Quesnay* (1888); 6. *Was Sagt die Nationalökonomie als Wissenschaft über die Bedeutung löher und niedriger Getreidepreise?* (1901); 7. *Die Geschichte der Nationalökonomie, Erster Teil: Die Zeit vor Adam Smith* (1902).
Career Agricultural economist and historian of economic ideas who advocated the industrialisation of agriculture and turned to the study of the physiocrats because of their preoccupation with agriculture. He also defended Adam Smith againt German economists of the Historical School and attempted to harmonise the ideas of Smith and Kant.
Secondary Literature S. Bauer, 'Oncken, August', *ESS*, 11.

OPIE, Roger G.

Born 1927, Adelaide, Australia.
Current Post Fellow, Lect. Econ., New Coll. Oxford, 1961–.
Degrees MA Univ. Adelaide, 1950; MPhil, MA Univ. Oxford, 1954, 1961.
Offices and Honours Member, UK Monopolies and Mergers Commission, 1968–81, UK Price Commission, 1977–80; CBE, 1976.
Principal Fields of Interest 113 Economic Planning Theory.
Publications *Articles:* Chapters in 1. *Banking in Western Europe*, ed. R. Sayers (OUP, 1961); 2. *Economic Growth in Britain*, ed. J. M. Henderson, *et al.* (Weidenfeld & Nicolson, 1964); 3. *Unfashionable Economics*, ed. P. Streeten (Weidenfeld & Nicolson, 1969); 4. *The Labour Government's Economic Record*, ed. W. Beckerman (Butterworths, 1971); 5. *Planning and Market Relations*, eds. M. Kaser and R. Portes (Macmillan, 1971); 6. *European Merger Conirol*, ed. K. J. Hopf (de Gruyter, 1982).
Principal Contributions Contributed intensively and extensively to the preparation and writing of the UK National Plan (1965) as Ass. Dir., UK Dept. of Economic Affairs. Later professional work (1967–70) has been to advise the Chairman of the UK National Board for Prices and Incomes and to participate in numerous investigations carried out by the Monopolies and Mergers Commission and the Price Commission.

OPPENHEIMER, Franz*

Dates and Birthplace 1864–1943, Berlin, Germany.
Posts Held Lect., Univ. Berlin, 1909–19; Prof., Univ. Frankfurt, 1919–29.
Degrees MD Univ. Berlin, 1885; PhD Univ. Kiel, 1908.

Publications *Books:* 1. *Die Siedlungs-genossenschaft* (1896, 1922); 2. *Das Grundgesetz der marxschen Gesell-schaftslehre* (1903, 1926); 3. *The State: Its History and Development Viewed Sociologically* (1907, 1926); 4. *Die soziale Frage und der Sozialismus* (1912, 1925); 5. *Kapitalismus- Kommunismus-wissenschaftlicher Sozialismus* (1919); 6. *System der Soziologie*, 4 vols (1922–35); 7. *Erlebtes, Erstrebtes, Erreichtes: Lebenserinnerungen* (1931, 1964).

Career Sociologist who used theoretical models to explain social change. Gossen's marginal utility theory and von der Goltz's theorem — the volume of migration from rural areas is directly related to the proportion of agricultural land in large estates — were major influences on his thinking. His attack on monopoly control of land traced land monopoly through successive social and economic systems. His agrarian socialism led him to oppose dogmatic Marxism whilst accepting aspects of Marx's analysis.

Secondary Literature H. H. Gerth, 'Oppenheimer, Franz', *IESS*, 11.

ORCUTT, Guy Henderson

Born 1917, Wyandotte, MI, USA.
Current Post Prof. Econ. and Stats., Yale Univ., New Haven, CT, USA, 1980–.
Past Posts Instr. Econ., MIT, 1944–6; Sr. Res. Worker, Dept. Appl. Econ., Univ. Camb., 1946–8; Econ., IMF, 1949; Ass. Prof., Assoc. Prof. Econ., Harvard Univ., 1949–58; Brittingham Prof. Econ., Univ. Wisconsin, 1958–69; Vis. Prof., Harvard Univ., 1965–6; Sr. Adviser, IBRD, 1967–8; Dir. Poverty and Inequality Project, Urban Inst., 1968–75; Irving Fisher Vis. Prof., Prof. Econ. and A. Whitney Griswold Prof. Urban Stud., Yale Univ., 1963–70, 1970–80; Chairman, Center Stud. of the City and Its Environment, Dir., ISPS Energy, Environment and Soc. Program, Yale Univ., 1970–3, 1980–1; Mellon Vis. Lect. Econ., School Forestry and Environmental Stud., Yale Univ., 1980–1; Vis. Prof., Inst. Advanced Stud., Vienna, 1980; Fellow, Wissenschaftskolleg zu Berlin, 1983–4.

Degrees BA (Physics), MA, PhD Univ. Michigan, 1939, 1940, 1944.
Offices and Honours Rackham Fellow, 1941–3; Nuffield Fellow, Univ. Oxford, 1947; Carnegie Fellow, 1956; Ford Foundation Faculty Fellow, 1956–7; Fellow, Council Em Soc, 1956, 1961–2, 1968–71; Fellow, Vice-Pres., ASA, 1959, 1959–61; Exec. Comm., AEA, 1972–5; Board Dirs., Treasurer, US SSRC, 1975–8, 1976–8; Humboldt Award, 1983.
Principal Fields of Interest 036 Economic Methodology.
Publications *Books:* 1. *Proposed Equalization and Apportionment, Report Special Commission on Equalization and Apportionment of the Commonwealth of Massachusetts* (Commonwealth Mass., 1956); 2. *Consumer Survey Statistics, Report of the Consultant Committee on Consumer Survey Statistics* (Fed. Reserve System, 1955); 3. *Microanalysis of Socioeconomic Systems: A Simulation Study* (with M. Greenberger, J. Korbel and A. M. Rivlin), (Harper, 1961); 4. *Forecasting on a Scientific Basis* (with H. Wold, et al.), (Inst. Gulbenkian de Ciencia, 1967); 5. *Policy Exploration through Microanalytic Simulation* (with S. Caldwell and R. Wertheimer), (Urban Inst., 1976); 6. *Microsimulation-Models, Methods and Applications*, co-ed. (with R. Bergman and G. Eliasson), (Almqvist & Wiksell, 1980); 7. *Microanalytic Simulation Models to Support Social and Financial Policy*, co-ed. (with J. Merz and H. Quinke), (N-H, 1984).

Articles: 1. 'A study of the autoregressive nature of the time series used for Tinbergen's model of the economic system of the United States, 1919–1932', *JRSS*, Series B, 10(1), 1948; 2. 'Testing the significance of correlation between time series' (with S. F. James), *Biometrika*, 25(3,4), Dec. 1948; 3. 'Application of least square regression to relationships containing autocorrelated error terms' (with D. Cochrane), *JASA*, March 1949; 4. 'Measurement of price elasticities in international trade', *REStat*, 32, May 1950, repr. in *Readings in International Economics*, eds. R. E. Caves and H. G. Johnson (Richard D. Irwin, 1968); 5. 'Actions, consequences and causal relations', *REStat*,

34, Nov. 1952; 6. 'Incentive and disincentive experimentation for income maintenance policy purposes' (with A. Orcutt), *AER*, 58(4), Sept. 1968; 7. 'Data aggregation and information loss' (with H. Watts and J. Edwards), *AER*, 58(4), Sept. 1968; 8. 'Toward a theory of wealth accumulation and distribution: a model of US household wealth accumulation' (with J. D. Smith), *Annales de L'INSEE*, 33–4, Jan.–June 1979; 9. 'An empirical analysis of air pollution dose — response curves' (with R. Mendelsohn), *JEEM*, 6(2), June 1979; 10. 'Unemployment and inflation', *IHS J*, 4, 1980.

Principal Contributions Since coming into economics in 1939 with a background in physics, I have sought to improve the methods, tools and data which are used in trying to determine the consequence of alternative macroeconomic policies. During the 1940s I designed and demonstrated three electromechanical, analogue computing devices. One of these, a multiple regression analyser, was built at MIT and used in Monte-Carlo experiments underlying my early work on testing for significance of relationship between time series having autocorrelation properties similar to real macroeconomic time series. This machine is described in article No 1 above. By the end of the 1940s, my research focus was entirely on the statistical estimation of relationships between macroeconomic time series, such as those being used by Tinbergen and Klein. During the early 1950s I became convinced that evidence remaining in highly aggregated time series was inadequate for the needed development and testing of macroeconometric models of national economies. During subsequent years this led to many, somewhat successful efforts to secure and make available micro-entity cross-sectional and time series panel data. It also led, as I became aware of the impossibility of aggregating nonlinear microlevel relations into macro-level relations between macro variables, to my conception, in 1956, of microanalytic system modelling and simulation, using the large electronic digital computers which were just beginning to emerge. Much of my effort in subsequent years has focussed on the development of microanalytic simulation techinques and concrete models designed for policy application.

ORNSTEIN, Stanley I.

Born 1939, Los Angeles, CA, USA.
Current Post Res. Econ., Grad. School Management, UCLA, USA. 1984.
Past Posts Assoc., Planning Res. Corp., 1968–70; Ass. Res. Econ., Assoc. Res. Econ., Grad. School Management, UCLA, 1970–8, 1978–84.
Degrees BS (Civil Eng.), MS (Bus. Admin.) San Diego Univ., 1960, 1965; PhD UCLA, 1970.
Principal Fields of Interest 611 Market Structure; Industrial Organisation and Corporate Strategy; 612 Public Policy towards Monopoly and Competition; 630 Industry Studies.
Publications *Books:* 1. *The Impact of Large Firms on the US Economy*, co-ed. (with J. F. Weston), (D. C. Heath, 1973); 2. *Advertising Intensity and Industrial Concentration* (AEI, 1977).

Articles: 1. 'Concentration and profits', *J Bus*, 45(4), Oct. 1972; 2. 'Determinants of market structure' (with J. F. Weston, M. Intriligator and R. Shrieves), *SEJ*, 29(4), April 1973; 3. 'Empirical uses of the price-cost margin', *J Ind E*, 24(2), Dec. 1975; 4. 'The advertising-concentration controversy', *SEJ*, 43(1), July 1976; 5. 'Advertising intensity and industrial concentration — an empirical inquiry, 1947 to 1967' (with S. Lustgarten), in *Issues in Advertising: The Economics of Persuasion*, ed. D. Tuerck (AEI, 1978); 6. 'The control of alcohol consumption through price increases', *J. Stud. Alcohol*, 41(9), Sept. 1980; 7. 'Antitrust policy and market forces as determinants of industry structure: case histories in beer and distilled spirits', *Antitrust Bull.*, 26(2), Summer 1981; 8. 'Price and income elasticities of demand in alcoholic beverages' (with D. Levy), in *Recent Development in Alcoholism*, I, eds. M. Galanter and A. Paredes (Plenum, 1983); 9. 'Resale price maintenance and cartels', *Antitrust Bull.*, 30(2), Summer 1985.

Principal Contributions My initial research interests were on the nature of competition and the extent of monopoly power. Early studies examined the relationship between industry concentration, advertising, and profit rates, as well as the determinants of market structure, After an absence, I recently returned to this field of study, examining changes over time in structure-performance relationships since that is the main issue; that is, do changes in concentration lead to changes in advertising or profits and vice versa?

I moved away from this area in the late 1970s, having come to believe that such interindustry studies tell us little about the extent of competition in industries, little of how monopoly is established, and little of how market structures evolve. My focus shifted to individual industry studies, examining first the alcoholic beverage industries. This resulted in studies of the evolution of market structure and performance in beer, wine and distilled spirits; estimates of demand elasticities for distilled spirits and beer and the influence of alcohol control laws on demand; the role of price in controlling the social costs of drinking; and estimates of the monopoly welfare losses due to alcohol control laws.

In recent years my attention has been on individual antitrust issues as a method of studying competition and developing an understanding of monopoly power in real markets. The issues I addressed include resale price maintenance and cartels, advertising as a source of monopoly power, the impact of merger policy on market structure, vertical or collateral restraints, and joint ventures.

ORTES, Giammaria*

Dates and Birthplace 1713–90, Venice, Italy.
Posts Held Clergyman.
Publications *Books:* 1. *Economia Nazionale* (1774); 2. *Reflections on Population* (1790).
Career His idiosyncratic system has something in common with that of Steuart, whom he many have read. His starting point was that consumption was the limiting factor on total output. He attacked the view that money and wealth were identical, arguing that money was merely a symbol of wealth, and expressly excluding if from his list of items that constitute wealth. He drew attention to the disparity between the potential growth of population and the increase of subsistence. He set an absolute limit to population of three billion, suggesting that when the limit was reached parents would eat their children.
Secondary Literature J. J. Spengler, 'Ortes, Giammaria', *ESS*, 11.

OSTER, Sharon

Born 1948, New York City, NY, USA.
Current Post Prof. School Organisation and Management, Yale Univ., New Haven, CT, 1983–.
Past Posts Ass. Prof., Assoc. Prof. Econ., Yale Univ., 1974–8, 1979–83.
Degrees BA Hofstra Univ., NY, 1970; PhD Harvard Univ., 1975.
Principal Fields of Interest 610 Industrial Organisation.
Publications *Articles:* 1. 'Industry differences in the level of discrimination against women', *QJE*, 89(2), May 1975; 2. 'Regulatory barriers to diffusion of innovation' (with J. Quigley), *Bell JE*, 8(2), Autumn 1977; 3. 'Industrial search for new location', *REStat*, 61(2), May 1979; 4. 'Analysis of interstate differences in consumer regulations', *EI*, 18(1), Jan. 1980; 5. 'Optimal order for submitting manuscript', *AER*, 70(3), June 1980; 6. 'Determinants of consumer complaints', *REStat*, 62(4), Nov. 1980; 7. 'Product regulation: a measure of the benefits', *J Ind E*, 30(1), June 1981; 8. 'The diffusion of innovation among steel firms', *Bell JE*, 13(1), Spring 1982; 9. 'Intraindustry structure and the degree of strategic change', *REStat*, 64(3), Aug. 1982; 10. 'The strategic use of regulatory investment by industry sub-groups', *EI*, 20(4), Oct. 1982.

OSTROY, Joseph Martin

Born 1942, Philadelphia, PA, USA.
Current Post Prof. Econ., UCLA, Los Angeles, CA, USA.
Past Posts Lect., Univ. Essex, 1967–8; Acting Ass. Prof., Assoc. Prof., UCLA, 1968–74; Vis. Lect., LSE, 1972–3; Vis. Fellow, Churchill Coll. Camb., 1979; Oskar Morgenstern Vis. Prof., NYU, 1981.
Degrees BS Univ. Penn., 1964; PhD Northwestern Univ., 1970.
Offices and Honours Beta Gamma Sigma Honor Soc.
Principal Fields of Interest 021 General Equilibrium Theory; 022 Microeconomic Theory; 023 Macroeconomic Theory.
Publications *Articles:* 1. 'The informational efficiency of monetary exchange', *AER*, 63(9), Sept. 1973; 2. 'Money and the decentralization of exchange' (with R. M. Starr), *Em*, 42(6), Nov. 1974; 3. 'The no-surplus condition as a characterization of perfectly competitive equilibrium', *JET*, 2, April 1980, repr. in *Non-Cooperative Approaches to the Theory of Perfect Competition*, ed. A. Mas Colell (Academic Press, 1982); 4. 'Flexibility and uncertainty' (with R. Jones), *REStud*, 51(1), Jan. 1984; 5. 'A reformulation of the marginal productivity theory of distribution', *Em*, 52(3), May 1984.
Principal Contributions Research devoted to providing a more decentralised approach to general equilibrium theory, i.e. diminishing the dependence on the auctioneer. One problem is the introduction of money. I have emphasised the sequential, bilateral nature of exchange and the role of money as a monitoring device. Another problem concerns the elimination of the price-making role of the auctioneer. Proposed an alternative, called a no-surplus allocation, to the Walrasian definition of perfectly competitive equilibrium. Have also explored the properties of general equilibrium models with a continuum of agents and an infinite number of commodities.

OTT, Alfred Eugen Maria

Born 1929, Kassel, Germany.
Current Post Ordentlicher Univ. Prof., Univ. Tübingen, Baden-Württemberg, W. Germany, 1963–.
Past Posts Prof., Univ. Sarrlandes Saarbrücken, 1960–3.
Degrees Diplom-Volkswirt, Dr Rer. Pol. Univ. Heidelberg, 1952, 1954; Habilitation, Univ. Munich, 1958.
Offices and Honours Dir., Inst. Angewandte Wirtschaftsforschung, Tübingen; Member, Theoretischen Ausschusses für Unternehmentheorie und -politik, Vereins für Socialpolitik; Cons. Ifo-Inst. für Wirtschaftsforschung, Munich, Bundes der Steuerzahler, Landesverband Baden-Württemberg, Kuratoriums des Inst. Systemtechnik und Innovationforschung, Karlsruhe.
Editorial Duties Ed. Board, *JN*.
Principal Fields of Interest 111 Economic Growth; 227 Prices; 321 Fiscal Theory.
Publications *Books:* 1. *Marktform und Verhaltensweise* (Gustav Fischer, 1959); 2. *Einführung in die dynamische Wirtschaftstheorie* (Vandenhoeck & Ruprecht, 1966); 3. *Grundzüge der Preistheorie* (Vandenhoeck & Ruprecht, 1968, 1984); 4. *Leitlinien für die branchenmassige Lohnfindung* (Stahleisen, 1968); 5. *Die räumliche Disaggregation von Input-Output-Tabellen* (with D. Schwarz and A. Wagner), (J. C. B. Mohr, Paul Siebeck, 1970); 6. *Der EDV-Markt in der Bundesrepublik Deutschland* (with N. Kloten, *et al.*), (J.C.B. Mohr, Paul Siebeck, 1976); 7. *Preistheorie* (Wissenschaftliche Buchgesellschaft, 1978).
Articles: 1. 'Zur dynamischen Theorie der Marktformen', *JNS*, 1955; 2. 'The relation between the accelerator and the capital output ratio', *REStud*, 25, June 1958; 3. 'Technisher Fortschritt', *Handbuch der Sozialwissenschaften*, 10, (Springer, 1959); 4. 'Produktionsfunktion, Technisher Fortschritt und Wirtschaftswachstum', in *Einkommens Vorteilung und technishe Fortschritt*, ed. E. Schneider (Springer, 1959; transl., English in *Internat. Econ. Papers*, 11, Macmillan, 1962); 5. 'Preistheorie', *JSW*, 13, 1962; 6. 'Les systèmes de classification des marchés et l'oligo-

pole', *Econ App*, 15, 1962; 7. 'Wachstumszyklen und der Technische Fortschritt', in *Technische Fortschritte — Ursache und Auswirkung wirtschaftlichen Handels*, ed. H. J. Niedereicholz (Inst. für Wirtschaftsforschung, 1974); 8. 'Zur mathematischen Behandlung von Wachstumszyklen' (with R. Wiegert), *JNS*, 194(2), April 1979.

Principal Contributions Let me first name those two academic teachers that have influenced me most: Erich Preiser and Alexander Rüstow. Both my leaning towards economic theory and towards Keynesianism are due to Preiser's influence. Rüstow, on the other hand, is responsible for my strong sympathy with neoliberal ideas. My early scientific career began in fields that Preiser had not paid much attention to, namely price theory and the theory of economic dynamics. As time went on, new topics arose, such as the theory of technical progress, growth theory and the theory of the trade cycle with various extensions towards the field of stabilisation policy and input-output analysis. In addition, I have paid special interest to the history of economic thought, the emphasis on the economic system of Karl Marx resulting more or less casually. Starting in 1963 I became director of the Institute of Applied Economic Research in Tübingen. The great challenge for me consisted in shouldering the supervision of and responsibility for a great host of highly diversified fields of investigation, extending from the technological gap to the Shop Closing Law. These research activities also gave rise to intriguing questions of regional policy. My research has been paralleled by university teaching. I have always attached great importance to the duty of bringing up new generations of scientists. I have served as a member of the Council of Scientific Advisers of the Prime Minister of Baden-Württemberg.

OVERSTONE, Samuel Jones Lloyd*

Dates and Birthplace 1796–1883, England.
Post Held Banker.

Degrees BA, MA Univ. Camb., 1818, 1822.
Offices and Honours MP for Hythe, 1819–26; Created Baron Overstone, 1860.
Publications *Books:* 1. *Tracts and other Publications on Metallic and Paper Currency* (1858).
Career Influential authority on British banking and finance who favoured convertibility of banknotes. The view of the currency school which he expressed to parliamentary committees in 1833 and 1840 was subsequently embodied in the Bank Act, 1844. Further evidence to committees in 1848 and 1857 was published by him afterwards.
Secondary Literature *The Correspondence of Lord Overstone*, ed. D. P. O'Brien, 3 vols (CUP, 1971).

OWEN, Robert*

Dates and Birthplace 1771–1858, Newtown, Wales.
Posts Held Cotton manufacturer.
Publications *Books:* 1. *A New View of Society* (1816, 1970); 2. *Two Memorials on Behalf of the Working Classes* (1818); 3. *Lectures on an Entire New State of Society* (1830).
Career Successful businessman and critic of industrialism who preached cooperative organisation. His New Lanark Mills in Scotland were organised as a model factory community. He developed this idea further to advocate villages in which collective working would be the basis for social regeneration. In 1824 he set up New Harmony, Indiana as a model community. On his return to Britain in 1829, he was drawn into workers' politics and promoted the Grand National Consolidated Trades Union in 1833 and 1834. This, like his other experiments, failed, but he soon came to be regarded as the father of the co-operative movement.
Secondary Literature A. Briggs, 'Owen, Robert', *IESS*, 11; A. L. Morton, *The Life and Ideas of Robert Owen* (Lawrence & Wishart, 1962); J. F. C. Harrison, *Robert Owen and the Owenites in Britain* (Routledge & Kegan Paul, 1969).

OZAWA, Terutomo

Born 1935, Yokohama, Japan.
Current Post Prof. Econ., Colorado State Univ., Fort Collins, CO, USA, 1974–.
Past Posts Ass. Prof., Assoc. Prof., Colorado State Univ., 1966–8, 1970–4; Vis. Res. Assoc. Center Pol. Alternatives, MIT, 1975–6; Vis. Scholar, Univ. Camb., 1982–3; Cons., World Bank, 1971–2, UNESCAP, 1979–80, 1983, OYCD, 1980–4, UNCTAD, 1983–4.
Degrees BA Tokyo Univ. Foreign Stud., Tokyo, 1958; MBA, PhD Columbia Univ., 1962, 1966.
Principal Fields of Interest 441 International Investment and Capital Markets; 620 Economics of Technological Change.
Publications *Books:* 1. *Japan's Technological Challenge to the West, 1950–74: Motivation and Accomplishment* (MIT Press, 1974); 2. *Multinationalism, Japanese Style: The Political Economy of Outward Dependency* (Princeton Univ. Press, 1979, 1982); 3. *People and Productivity in Japan* (Pergamon, 1982); 4. *Japan's General Trading Companies: Merchants of Economic Development* (with K. Kojima), (OECD, 1984; transl., Japanese, Sanno Press, 1984).
Articles: 1. 'The Rybczynski theorem: a diagrammatic note on a corollary proposition', *Ec*, N.S. 37, Aug. 1970; 2. 'Technology imports and direct foreign investments in Japan', *J. World Trade Law*, 7, Nov.-Dec. 1973; 3. 'The peculiarities of Japanese multinationalism: facts and theories', *BNLQR*, 28, Dec. 1975; 4. 'Commodity trade and factor mobility: comment', *AER*, 66(4), Sept. 1976; 5. 'International investment and industrial structure: new theoretical implications from the Japanese experience', *OEP*, 31(1), March 1979; 6. 'Government control over technology acquisition and firms' entry into new sectors', *Camb JE*, 4, June 1980; 7. 'Technology transfer and Japanese economic growth in the postwar period', in *Technology Transfer and Economic Development*, eds. R. G. Hawkins and A. J. Prasad (JAI Press, 1981); 8. 'A newer type of foreign investment in third world resource development', *RISE*, 29, Dec. 1982; 9. 'The role of transnational corporations in the economic development of the ESCAP region: some available evidence from recent experience', in *Transnational Corporations and Their Impact on Economic Development in Asia and the Pacific* (ESCAP/UNCTC, 1982); 10. 'Technology transfers', in *Encyclopedia of Japan* (Kodansha Internat., 1983).
Principal Contributions Among the first to explore the dynamic factors of Japan's postwar economic growth, such as technological assimilation, research and development activities, and technology exports. Initial work focussed on licensing agreements as the major conduit of technology imports into postwar Japanese industry and their impact on Japan's R&D and export competitiveness in manufactures. Research then extended to Japanese exports of technology and to overseas investments. Have been stressing a new macroeconomic analytical framework to analyse the unique set of economic forces that induce Japanese enterprises, large and small alike, to seek overseas business opportunities through foreign direct investment and nonequity forms of involvement. Have explored the 'new forms of investments' pursued by Japan's distinctive economic institution, the general trading company.

P

PAISH, Frank Walter

Born 1898, London, England.
Current Post Prof. Emeritus, Univ. London, 1965–.
Past Posts Econ., Standard Bank S. Africa, 1921–32; Lect., Reader, Prof. Econ., LSE, 1932–8, 1938–49, 1949–65; Deputy Dir. Programmes, UK Ministry Aircraft Production, 1941–5; Cons., Lloyds Bank, 1965–70.
Degree BA Univ. Camb., 1921.
Offices and Honours Hon. Fellow, LSE, 1970.
Editorial Duties Secretary, Ed., London and Camb. Econ. Service, 1932–41, 1945–9, 1947–9.

Principal Fields of Interest 023 Macroeconomic Theories.

Publications *Books:* 1. *The Post-War Financial Problems and Other Essays* (Macmillan, 1950); 2. *Business Finance* (Pitman, 1953, 1968); 3. *Studies in an Inflationary Economy — The UK 1948–61* (Macmillan, 1962); 4. *Long-Term and Short-Term Interest Rates in the UK* (Manchester Univ. Press, 1966); 5. *Policy for Incomes?* (with J.V. Hennessey), (INEA, 1964, 1968); 6. *The Rise and Fall of Incomes Policy* (INEA, 1969, 1971); 7. *How the Economy Works and Other Essays* (Pitman, 1970); 8. *Benham's Economics*, co-ed. (with A.J. Culyer), (Pitman, 1973).

Principal Contributions In the days when it was unpopular to say so, I was among the few in the 1950s to proclaim the absolute necessity of a margin of spare capacity, in short, 2–3 per cent unemployment, to prevent Keynesian policies from setting off a vicious inflation. This came to be known at the time as the 'Paish doctrine' and is now part of the pre-history of the Phillips curve.

PALGRAVE, Robert Harry Inglis*

Dates and Birthplace 1827–1919, Westminster, London, England.

Post Held Banker.

Offices and Honours Ed., *The Economist*, 1877–83; Fellow, Royal Soc., 1882; Pres., Section F BAAS, 1883; knighted, 1909.

Publications *Books:* 1. *Notes on Banking in Great Britain, Ireland, Sweden, Denmark and Hamburg* (1872); 2. *Analysis of the Transactions of the Bank of England 1844–72* (1873); 3. *Bank Rate and the Money Market* (1903); 4. *Dictionary of Political Economy*, 3 vols, ed. (1894–1908, 1963).

Career Writer on banking from the point of view of a practitioner rather than a theoretician. His interest in the discipline of economics proper is represented by the substantial *Dictionary of Political Economy*, a basic reference work until recent times.

Secondary Literature A.W. Kiddy, 'Obit.: Sir Inglis Palgrave', *EJ*, 29, 1919.

PANTALEONI, Maffeo*

Dates and Birthplace 1857–1924, Frascati, Italy.

Posts Held Prof., various Italian univs; Prof., Univ. Rome, 1901–.

Degree Dr Law Univ. Rome, 1881.

Offices and Honours Member, Italian Chamber Deputies, 1901; Senator, 1923.

Publications *Books:* 1. *Teoria Della Traslazione Dei Tributi* (1882, 1958); 2. *Dall'ammontare probabile Della Ricchezza Privata in Italia* (1884); 3. *Pure Economics* (1889, 1957); 4. *Note in Margine Della Guerra* (1917); 5. *Tra le Incognite* (1917); 6. *Politica* (1918); 7. *Erotemi di Economia*, 2 vols (1925).

Articles: 1. 'Some phenomena of economic dynamics', *Scritti Varii di Economia* (1910), repr. in *Internat. Econ. Papers*, 5, eds. A.T. Peacock, *et al.* (Macmillan, 1955); 2. 'Contribution to the theory of the distribution of public expenditure' (1883, 1904), repr. in *Classics in the Theory of Public Finance*, eds. R.A. Musgrave and A.T. Peacock (Macmillan, 1958).

Career Italian economist who attempted to avoid being identified with any of the contemporary schools. He wrote studies of price fluctuations, discriminatory pricing, industrial cartels and banking, and sought to develop a dynamic theory of economics. In the latter he attempted a synthesis of marginal utility theory with Ricardian value theory. His considerable involvement in quantitative work led him eventually to doubt the usefulness of utility theory in macroeconomic questions; he also rejected the work of the marginalists in public finance.

Secondary Literature P. Sraffa and A. Loria, 'Maffeo Pantaleoni', *EJ*, 34, Dec. 1924; L. Frey, 'Pantaleoni, Maffeo', *IESS*, 11.

PANZAR, John Clifford

Born 1947, Chicago Heights, IL, USA.

Current Post Prof. Econ., Northwestern Univ., Evanston, IL, USA, 1983–.

Past Posts Technical Staff, Head, Econ. Analysis Res. Dept., Bell Lab,

NJ, USA, 1974–83, 1980–3; Vis. Adjunct Assoc. Prof., Univ. Cal. Berkeley, 1977; Vis. Prof. Econ., Univ. Pennsylvania, 1983.

Editorial Duties BA Carleton Coll., 1969; MA, PhD Stanford Univ., 1973, 1975.

Degrees Ed. Board, *JEL*, 1983–., *Info. Econ. and Pol.*, 1982–.

Principal Fields of Interest 610 Industrial Organisation and Public Policy; 022 Microeconomic Theory.

Publications *Books:* 1. *Regulation, Service Quality and Market Performance: A Model of Airline Rivalry* (Garland Press, 1979); 2. *Contestable Markets and the Theory of Industry Structure* (with W.J. Baumol and R.D. Willig), (Harcourt Brace Jovanovich, 1982).

Articles: 1. 'A neoclassical approach to peak load pricing', *Bell JE*, 7(2), Autumn 1976; 2. 'Free entry and the sustainability of natural monopoly' (with R.D. Willig), *Bell JE*, (1), Spring 1977; 3. 'Economics of scale in multi-output production' (with R.D. Willig), *QJE* 91(3), Aug. 1977; 4. 'Public utility pricing under risk: the case of self-rationing' (with D.S. Sibley), *AER*, 68(5), Dec. 1978; 5. 'Equilibrium and welfare in unregulated airline markets', *AER*, 69(2), May 1979; 6. 'Regulation, deregulation and economic efficiency: the case of the CAB', *AER*, 70(2), May 1980; 7. 'The contestability of airline markets during the transition to deregulation' (with E.E. Bailey), *J. Law and Contemporary Problems*, 44(1), Feb. 1981; 8. 'Economies of scope' (with R.D. Willig), *AER*, 71(2), May 1981; 9. 'On the nonlinear pricing of inputs' (with J.A. Ordover), *Int ER*, 23(3), Oct. 1982.

Principal Contributions My work has focussed primarily on the theory of economic regulation. Beginning with my thesis, I have had a continuing interest in the US airline industry. Initially, this research analysed the effects of Civil Aeronautics Board regulation, but more recently it has been an attempt to understand the more complex workings of unregulated airline markets. The other major thrust of my research has been in the theory of the multiproduct firm, particularly the multiproduct natural monopoly. This was a natural by-product of the years I spent as a research economist at Bell Laboratories. In the course of exploring the proper theoretical framework for the analysis of policy issues involved in the regulation of multiproduct natural monopolies, my colleagues and I identified and analysed multiproduct cost concepts such as economies of scope and product-specific economies of scale. These proved to be important concepts in the analysis of monopoly *sustainability*: i.e., the conditions under which a regulator could fix the prices of a natural monopolist and allow free entry into the industry without running the risk of inefficient entry by non-innovative firms. (Thus sustainability requires, *inter alia*, that there be no cross-subsidy among the products of the monopolist.) While the sustainability concept was developed for the case of regulated firms, it occurred to W.J. Baumol, R.D. Willig and myself that it was also an appropriate equilibrium concept for markets in which entry and exit are very easy. (Unregulated airline markets perhaps provide the best real world approximation.) Such *contestable* markets became the focus of our recent book.

PAPANEK, Gustav

Born 1926, Vienna, Austria.
Current Post Prof. Econ., Boston Univ., MA, USA.
Past Posts Dir., Devlp. Advisory Service, Harvard Univ., 1965–70; Dir. Harvard Advisory Group, Planning Commission and Ministry Fin., Govt. Indonesia, 1971–3; Interim Dir. Center Asian Devlp. Stud., Boston Univ., 1977–80.
Degrees BA (Agric. Econ.) Cornell Univ., 1947; MA, PhD Harvard Univ., 1949, 1951.
Offices and Honours Council, Soc. Internat. Devlp., 1970–3; Member, Exec. Comm., Vice-Pres., Pres., Assoc. Comp. Econ. Stud., 1971–3, 1980–1, 1982; Vice-Pres., Pres., Assoc. Asian Stud., New England Conf., 1975–6, 1976–7.
Principal Fields of Interest Economic Studies of Less Industrialised Countries.

Publications *Books:* 1. *Pakistan's Development: Social Goals and Private Incentives* (Harvard Univ. Press, 1967, OUP Karachi, 1968, 1971); 2. *Development Policy — Theory and Practice*, ed. (Harvard Univ. Press, 1968); 3. *Decision Making for Economic Development* (with others), (Houghton-Mifflin, 1971); 4. *Development Policy – – the Pakistan Experience*, co-ed. (Harvard Univ. Press, 1971); 5. *The Indonesian Economy*, ed. and contrib. (Praeger, 1980).

Articles: 1. 'The effect of aid and other resource transfers on savings and growth in less developed countries', *EJ*, 82, Sept. 1972; 2. 'Aid, foreign private investment, savings and growth in less developed countries', *JPE*, 81(1), Jan./Feb. 1973; 3. 'Development theory — the earnest search for a mirage', *EDCC*, 25, Suppl., 1977, repr. in *Essays in Economic Development and Cultural Change*, ed. M. Nash (Univ. Chicago Press, 1977); 4. 'Economic growth, income distribution and the political process in less developed countries', in *Income Distribution and Economic Inequality*, eds. Z. Griliches, et al. (Campus Verlag, 1978); 5. '*Laissez-faire*, growth and equity: Hong Kong', *EJ*, 91, June 1981.

Principal Contributions Work has centred on the use of the market mechanism as a tool to achieve the planned goals of a society, particulary in less developed countries. Specifically, analysis of the possibility of achieving both high rates of growth and greater equality; and the contribution of foreign aid to growth. In teaching: the use of the case method to encourage the application of theory and methodology to the solution of actual problems.

PARETO, Vilfredo*

Dates and Birthplace 1848–1923, Paris, France.

Posts Held Engineer, 1870–92; Prof., Univ. Lausanne, 1893–1900.

Degrees BS Eng., Polytechnic Inst., Turin, 1869.

Offices and Honours Senator.

Publications *Books:* 1. *Cours d'économie politique* (1896–7, 1964); 2. *Systèmes socialistes* (1902–3, 1965); 3. *Manual of Political Economy* (1906, 1909, 1971); 4. *The Mind and Society: A Treatise on General Sociology*, 4 vols (1916, 1963).

Articles: 1. 'Mathematical economics', *Encyclopédie des Sciences Mathématique*, 1911, repr. in *Internat. Econ. Papers*, 5, eds. A.T. Peacock, et al. (Macmillan, 1955); 2. 'Mathematical economics', *Encyclopédie des Sciences Mathématique*, 1(4), repr. in *Precursors in Mathematical Economics: An Anthology*, eds. W.J. Baumol and S.M. Goldfeld (1968).

Career Italian engineer economist, whose mathematical ability led to his appointment as Walras' successor at Lausanne. In the *Manual* ... he worked out an improved version of general equilibrium theory and demonstrated the restricted sense in which perfect competition achieved an optimal solution. He made important contributions to the discussion of the methodology of economics and the place of the discipline in the social sciences as a whole. His distinction between cardinal and ordinal utility and between an individual and a collective optimum were major theoretical contributions.

Secondary Literature J.A. Schumpeter, 'Vilfredo Pareto', in *Ten Great Economists from Marx to Keynes* (OUP, 1951); G.H. Bousquet, *Vilfredo Pareto: Le savant et l'homme* (Payet et Fil, 1960); M. Allais, 'Pareto, Vilfredo: contributions to economics', *IESS*, 11; W.J. Samuels, *Pareto on Policy* (Elsevier, 1974).

PARKIN, Michael

Born 1939, Birdwell, Yorkshire, England.

Current Post Prof. Econ., Univ. Western Ontario, London, Ont., Canada, 1975–.

Past Posts Ass. Lect., Univ. Sheffield, 1963–4; Lect., Univ. Leicester, 1964–6; Lect., Sr. Lect., Univ. Essex, 1967–9, 1969–70; Prof., Univ. Manchester, 1970–5; Vis. Prof., Brown Univ., 1972, Hyderabad Univ., India,

1974; Vis. Sr. Res. Econ., Reserve Bank Australia, 1973, 1974; Vis. Fellow, Hoover Inst., Stanford, 1979–80.

Degrees BA Univ. Leicester, 1963; MA Univ. Manchester, 1970.

Editorial Duties Ed., *MS*, 1974–5; Managing Ed., *CJE*, 1982–; Ed. Boards, *REStud*, *MS*, *JMCB*, *J Mon E*, *AER*.

Principal Fields of Interest 130 Economic Fluctuations; 310 Domestic Monetary Theory; 430 Balance of Payments.

Publications *Books:* 1. *Readings in British Monetary Economics*, co-ed. (with H.G. Johnson, *et al.*), (OUP, 1972); 2. *Incomes Policy and Inflation*, co-ed. (with M.T. Sumner), (Manchester Univ. Press, 1972); 3. *Essays in Modern Economics*, co-ed. (with A.R. Nobay), (Longmans, 1973); 4. *Contemporary Issues in Economics*, co-ed. (with A.R. Nobay), (CUP, 1975); 5. *Current Economic Problems*, co-ed. (with A.R. Nobay), (CUP, 1975); 6. *Inflation in the World Economy*, co-ed. (with G. Zis), (Manchester Univ. Press, Univ. Toronto Press, 1976); 7. *Inflation in Open Economics*, co-ed. (with G. Zis), (Manchester Univ. Press, Univ. Toronto Press, 1976); 8. *Inflation in the United Kingdom*, co-ed. (with M.T. Sumner), (Manchester Univ. Press, Univ. Toronto Press, 1978); 9. *Modern Macroeconomics* (with R. Bade), (Prentice-Hall, 1982, Philip Allan, 1982); 10. *Macroeconomics* (Prentice-Hall, 1984).

Articles: 1. 'Income policy: a re-appraisal' (with R.G. Lipsey), *Ec*, N.S. 37, May 1970; 2. 'Portfolio diversification as optimal precautionary behavior' (with M.R. Gray), in *Theory of Demand, Real and Monetary*, ed. M. Morishima (OUP, 1973); 3. 'Inflation, the balance of payments, domestic credit expansion and exchange rate adjustments', in *National Monetary Policies and the International Financial System*, ed. R.Z. Aliber (Univ. Chicago Press, 1974); 4. 'Inflation expectations' (with J.A. Carlson), *Ec*, N.S. 42, May 1975; 5. 'Inflation: a survey' (with D.E.W. Laidler), *EJ*, 95, Dec. 1975; 6. 'The transition from fixed exchange rates to money supply

targets', *JMCB*, 9(1), Feb. 1977; 7. 'A "monetarist" analysis of the generation and transmission of world inflation: 1958–1971', *AER*, 68(2), May 1977; 8. 'A comparison of alternative techniques of monetary control under rational expectations', *MS*, 46(3), Sept. 1978; 9. 'Some international evidence on output-inflation trade-offs: a reappraisal' (with B. Bentley and C. Fader), in *Development in an Inflationary World*, eds. J.M. Flanders and A. Razin (Academic Press, 1980); 10. 'Unemployment and inflation: facts, theories, puzzles and policies', in *Unemployment in Western Countries*, eds. E. Malinvaud and J-P. Fitoussi (Macmillan, 1980).

Principal Contributions Theoretical and empirical work on portfolio debt and interest-rate selection behaviour of financial institutions, households and firms. A series of papers (written in collaboration with others) derived tight restrictions on portfolio and debt behaviour of a variety of financial institutions. These models were tested on the time series behaviour of UK financial institutions. Further work broadened the scope to deal with dynamic aspects of consumer behaviour and the simultaneous choice of consumption, investment, and financial assets and liabilities.

Inflation and unemployment, and the role of monetary policies and wage and price controls: a series of papers and a major research programme (co-directed with David Laidler) studied wide aspects of these problems. International finance and open economy macroeconomics: the interrelations between foreign shocks, exchange-rate regimes, and domestic economic performance were studied in a series of papers. Empirical work on the aggregate world economy under fixed exchange rates was also undertaken, revealing that closed economy macroeconomic models provide a good guide to the performance of the world economy as a whole when exchange rates are fixed.

The political economy of inflation and the relation between political arrangements and economic policy: a series of papers has sought to explore the relationship between a country's constitutional set-up and its choice of macroeconomic policies.

PARKS, Richard William

Born 1938, Utica, NY, USA.
Current Post Prof. Econ., Univ. Washington, Seattle, WA, USA, 1978–.
Past Posts Ass. Prof. Econ., Univ. Chicago, 1965–70; Cons., Dept. Planning, Govt. Panama, 1966–7; Assoc. Prof., Univ. Washington, 1970–8; Vis. Prof. Econ., Univ. Hawaii, 1972.
Degrees BA Harvard Univ., 1960; MA (Stats.), PhD Univ. Cal. Berkeley, 1965, 1966.
Offices and Honours Phi Beta Kappa, 1960; Cipolla Prize Econ. Hist., 1963; Ford Foundation Dissertation Fellow, 1964–5; Fulbright Lect., Argentina, 1968; Nat. Fellow, Hoover Inst., Stanford Univ., 1976–7.
Principal Fields of Interest 022 Microeconomic Theory; 200 Quantitative Economic Methods and Data; 920 Consumer Economics.
Publications *Articles:* 1. 'Efficient estimation of a system of regression equations when disturbances are both serially and contemporaneously correlated', *JASA*, 62, June 1967; 2. 'Systems of demand relations: an empirical comparison of alternative functional forms', *Em*, 37(4), Oct. 1969; 3. 'Price responsiveness of factor utilization in Swedish manufacturing, 1870–1950', *REStat*, 53(2), May 1971; 4. 'Maximum likelihood estimation of the linear expenditure system', *JASA*, 66, Dec. 1971; 5. 'A cross-country comparison of the effects of prices, income, and population composition on consumption patterns' (with A.P. Barten), *EJ*, 83, Sept. 1973; 6. 'The demand and supply of durable goods and durability', *AER*, 64(1), March 1974; 7. 'Determinants of scrapping rates for post-war vintage automobiles', *Em*, 45(5), July 1977; 8. 'Inflation and relative price variability', *JPE*, 86(1), Feb. 1978; 9. 'Durability, maintenance, and the price of used assets', *EI*, 17(2), April 1979; 10. 'Vertical equity in real estate assessment: a fair appraisal' (with L.A. Kochin), *EI*, 20(4), Oct. 1982.

Principal Contributions In a series of papers I helped to develop the econometric approach to complete systems of consumer and producer demand functions. By standardising the econometric methods, it was possible to get improved comparisons among competing demand models. I developed methods of estimation for equation systems whose errors involve both serial and cross-equation correlation and provided one of the first empirical applications of flexible functional forms. My interest in the intertemporal aspects of consumer demand led to several papers on the economics of consumer durables. I first focussed on the determinants of optimal durability treated as a characteristic determined entirely by the manufacturer. In attempting to apply these ideas to the economic lifetimes of automobiles, I developed a model in which a good's lifetime depends on both built-in characteristics and on the maintenance and care provided by owners. These papers predict a lengthening of the lifetimes of existing cars as a response to attempts to regulate safety and pollution characteristics of new cars, a prediction borne out by US experience in the mid-1970s. Using techniques whose origins lie in my earlier demand system work, I showed a mechanism by which unanticipated inflation could give rise to increased variability in relative price changes and thus to important real effects of inflation. In work with Kochin I showed that a widely-used test for the evaluation of real estate assessments was fatally flawed. A similar error has been made in several contexts involving the evaluation of estimates. A simple modification produces a more reasonable test.

PARNELL, Henry Brooke*

Dates and Birthplace 1776–1842, Ireland.
Posts Held Politician.
Offices and Honours MP, 1797–1803, 1806–41; Member, UK Bullion Comm., 1810; Created 1st Baron Congleton, 1841.
Publications *Books:* 1. *Observations*

upon the State of the Currency of Ireland (1804); 2. *The Principles of Currency and Exchange* (1805); 3. *Treatise on the Corn Trade* (1809); 4. *Observations on Paper Money* (1827); 5. *On Financial Reform* (1830); 6. *A Plain Statement of the Power of the Bank of England* (1832).

Career Whig financial experi whose parliamentary speeches and pamphlets on economic questions were widely respected. He was an enthusiastic defender of the report of the Bullion Committee and attacked the Corn Laws. His treatise, *On Financial Reform*, laid out the basic principles which were adopted with success by Peel and Gladstone.

PARSONS, Donald O.

Born 1944, Pittsburgh, PA, USA.
Current Post Prof. Econ., Ohio State Univ., Columbus, OH, USA, 1977–.
Past Posts Ass. Prof., Assoc. Prof., Ohio State Univ., 1970–3, 1973–7.
Degrees BA Duke Univ., Durham, NC, 1966; PhD Univ. Chicago, 1970.
Offices and Honours Harry Sherman Res. Fellow, NBER, 1975–6.
Editorial Duties Ed. Board, *J. Econ. and Bus.*
Principal Fields of Interest 610 Industrial Organisation and Public Policy; 820 Labour Markets; 850 Human Capital.
Publications *Books:* 1. *Poverty and the Minimum Wage* (AEI, 1980).
Articles: 1. 'Specific human capital: layoffs and quits', *JPE*, 80(6), Nov. 1972; 2. 'Quit rates over time: a search and information approach', *AER*, 63(3), June 1973; 3. 'The United States steel consolidation: the creation of market control' (with E.J. Ray), *J Law E*, 18(1), April 1975; 4. 'Intergenerational wealth transfers and the educational decisions of male youth', *QJE*, 89(4), Nov. 1975; 5. 'The autocorrelation of earnings, human wealth inequality and income contingent loans', *QJE*, 86(6), Nov. 1978; 6. 'The decline in male labor force participation', *JPE*, 88(1), Feb. 1980; 7. 'Unemployment, the allocation of labor, and optimal government intervention', *AER*,

70(4), Sept. 1980; 8. 'Racial trends in male labor force participation', *AER*, 70(5), Dec. 1980; 9. 'The male labor force participation decision: health, reported health and economic incentives', *Ec*, 49, Feb. 1982; 10. 'On the economics of intergenerational control', *Pop. and Devlp. Rev.*, March 1984.

Principal Contributions My first contributions involved the theoretical and empirical analysis of the employment relationship. I developed a theoretical model of firm-specific training, compensation, and job turnover and estimated a job turnover model which indicates that firms and workers share in such investments. An analysis of job search and quit rates revealed that the labour market was responsive to real factors but not to unexpected inflation. More recently I estimated a model of labour transfer between industries which suggests that the transfer rate is largely independent of aggregate effects or industry congestion effects.

I have undertaken several studies of schooling investments. Foregone earnings are shown to be an inappropriate measure of schooling cost in a capital-constrained environment. I estimate that the variance of human capital is not higher for those with more schooling, which explains the lack of demand for income-contingent loans. I have estimated family background effects on schooling attainment, and attempted to unravel the effects of differential productivity, capital costs, and direct consumption value on schooling choice.

In the related area of family economics, I have stressed the interplay of altruism and self-interest in moulding intra-family relationships. I have developed a model of marriage that determines explicit exchange prices for male and female attributes as well as the matching of these attributes. I have also modelled and estimated (with Claudia Goldin) the interplay of parental aspirations for their children's future well-being through schooling and their desire for current child labour income.

I have undertaken several policy analyses, including one of the 1920 US Steel antitrust decision (with Edward

Ray). I have estimated the anti-poverty effects of the minimum wage and found negligible income redistribution effects for low-skilled adult females. Most recently, I have modelled and estimated large labour supply disincentive effects of the social security disability insurance programme.

PASINETTI, Luigi Lodovico

Born 1930, Bergamo, Italy.
Current Post Prof. Econ. Analysis, Universita Cattolica del Sacro Cuore, Milan, Italy.
Past Posts Res. Fellow, Nuffield Coll., Oxford, 1960–1; Fellow, Lect. Econ., King's Coll., Reader, Univ. Camb., 1961–73, 1971–6; Wesley Clair Mitchell Vis. Res. Prof., Columbia Univ., 1971, 1975; Vis. Res. Prof., Indian Stat. Inst., Calcutta, 1975.
Degrees Laurea, Universita Cattolica del Sacro Cuore, Milan, 1953–4; PhD Univ. Camb., 1962.
Offices and Honours Fellow, Em. Soc., 1978; St Vincent Prize Econ., 1979; Council, Exec. Comm., IEA, 1980–.
Editorial Duties Ed. Boards, *REStud*, 1962–4, *Camb. JE*, 1977–, *J Post Keyn E*, 1978–, *Kyk*, 1981–.
Principal Fields of Interest 020 General Economic Theory; 110 Economic Growth, Development and Planning, Theory and Policy; 210 Econometric, Statistical and Mathematical Methods and Models.
Publications *Books:* 1. *A Multisector Model of Economic Growth* (King's Coll., Camb., 1963); 2. *Growth and Income Distribution — Essays in Economic Theory* (CUP, 1974; transls., Italian, Il Mulino, 1977, Spanish, Alianza Editorial, 1978, Portuguese, Zahar Editores, 1979, Japanese, Iwanami Shoten, 1984); 3. *Lectures on the Theory of Production* (Colombia Univ. Press, Macmillan, 1977; transls., Japanese, Orion Press, 1979, Spanish, Fondo Cultura Economica, 1983); 4. *Essays on the Theory of Joint Production*, ed. (Macmillan, 1980); 5. *Structural Change and Economic Growth — A Theoretical Essay on the Dynamics of The Wealth of Nations* (CUP, 1981; transl., Japanese, Nihon Hyoronsha, 1983, Italian, UTET, 1984).
Articles: 1. 'On concepts and measures of changes in productivity', *REStat*, 41, Aug. 1959; 2. 'A new theoretical approach to the problems of economic growth', in *Pontificiae Academiae Scientiarum Scripta Varia*, 28, 1965; 3. 'Changes in the rate of profit and switches of techniques', *QJE*, 80(4), Nov. 1966; 4. 'Switches of techniques and the "rate of return" in capital theory', *EJ*, 79, Sept. 1969; 5. 'The notion of vertical integration in economic analysis', *Metroec.*, 25, 1973; 6. 'On "non-substitution" in production models', *Camb JE*, 1(4), Dec. 1977; 7. 'The rate of interest and the distribution of income in a pure labour economy', *J Post Keyn E*, 3(2), Winter 1980–1.
Principal Contributions I began by giving a mathematical formulation of Ricardo's theoretical system, following the interpretation emerging from Piero Sraffa's edition of Ricardo's works. My name was then associated with two major economic debates of the 1960s: (1) the post-Keynesian claim that the rate of profit and the distribution of income depend on the saving propensities of capitalists and are independent of the saving propensities of workers (known as the 'Pasinetti theorem'); and (2) the capital theory debate originating from Samuelson-Levhari's challenge to Sraffa's analysis of the reswitching of techniques (I was the first to disprove the Samuelson-Levhari's nonswitching theorem). These contributions have placed me among the critics of traditional marginal economics.

On the more positive side, I have pursued a wide investigation into the fundamental dynamics of industrial societies. Along the lines that were adopted after Keynes by Harrod, Domar, Joan Robinson and Kaldor, I went on to enquire into such movements of the economic systems through time that are characterised by nonproportional growth and structural change due to the unevenness from sector to sector of productivity changes and the hierarchical structure of consumers' needs ('Engel's Law'). This work led me to call for the elaboration of new analytical tools (such as vertically integrated sector analysis, as opposed to input-output analysis) and also for changes in the methodology of economics itself, especially with reference to a separation of basic relations typical of industrial societies as such (whether capitalist or socialist) from relations specific to particular institutions. From this analysis many empirical regularities and a number of theoretical contributions, that had earlier been difficult to absorb into marginal theory, seem to find a more natural and satisfactory theoretical explanation.

PATINKIN, Don

Born 1922, Chicago, IL, USA.
Current Post Prof. Econ., Hebrew Univ. Jerusalem, Jerusalem, Israel; Res. Assoc., Maurice Falk Inst. Econ. Res. in Israel, Jerusalem, Israel, 1957–.
Past Posts Res. Ass., Res. Assoc., Cowles Commission Econ. Res., Ass. Prof. Econ., Univ. Chicago, 1946–7, 1947–8, 1947–8; Assoc. Prof. Econ., Univ. Illinois, 1948–9; Lect., Assoc. Prof., Hebrew Univ. Jerusalem, 1949–52; Dir. Res., Maurice Falk Inst. Econ. Res. in Israel, 1956–72; Vis. Prof., Univs., Cal. Berkeley, 1961–2, MIT, 1968, Western Ontario, 1973–9, Chicago, 1972, 1977–9, Columbia, 1980, Northwestern, Johns Hopkins, Europ. Univ. Inst., 1981.
Degrees BA, MA, PhD Univ. Chicago, 1943, 1945, 1947; Hon. DHL Univ. Chicago, 1976, Univ. Western Ontario, 1983.
Offices and Honours Phi Beta Kappa, 1943; Fellow, Pres., Em Soc, 1953, 1974; Rothschild Prize, 1959; Member, Israel Academy Sciences and Humanities, 1963; Foreign Hon. Member, AAAS, 1969; Israel Prize, 1970; Hon. Member, AEA, 1975; Pres., Israel Econ. Assoc., 1976.
Editorial Duties Advisory Board, *JMCB*, Ed. Board, *J Macroecon*.
Principal Fields of Interest 020 General Economic Theory; 031 History of Economic Thought; 311 Domestic Monetary and Financial Theory and Policy.

Publications *Books:* 1. *Money, Interest and Prices: An Integration of Monetary and Value Theory* (Row Peterson, 1956, 1965; transls., Spanish, Aguilar, 1959, Japanese, Keiso Skobo, 1971, French, Presses Univ. de France, 1972, Italian, Cedam, 1978); 2. *Introduction to Economics: Lecture Notes* (Hebrew), (Hebrew Univ. Jerusalem, 1958); 3. *The Israel Economy: The First Decade* (Maurice Falk Inst. Econ. Res. Israel, 1959); 4. *Lectures on Price Theory* (Hebrew) (with Y. Grunfeld and N. Liviatan), (Hebrew Univ. Jerusalem, 1964); 5. *On the Nature of the Monetary Mechanism* (Almqvist & Wiksell, 1967); 6. *Studies in Monetary Economics* (Harper & Row, 1972); 7. *Keynes' Monetary Thought: A Study of Its Development* (Duke Univ. Press, 1976, 1978; transls., German, Vahlen, 1979, Japanese, McGraw-Hill Kogakusha, 1979); 8. *Keynes, Cambridge and 'The General Theory': The Process of Criticism and Discussion Connected with the Development of 'The General Theory'*, co-ed. (with J.C. Leith), (Macmillan, 1977, Toronto Univ. Press, 1978; transl., Japanese, McGraw-Hill Kogakusha, 1979); 9. *Essays On and In the Chicago Tradition* (Duke Univ. Press, 1981); 10. *Anticipations of 'The General Theory'? and Other Essays on Keynes* (Univ. Chicago Press, Blackwell, 1982).
Articles: 1. 'Mercantilism and the readmission of the Jews to England', *Jewish Social Stud.*, 8, 1946; 2. 'Price flexibility and full employment', *AER*, 38(4), Sept. 1948, 39(3), June 1949, repr. in *Readings in Monetary Theory*, eds. F.A. Lutz and L.W. Mints (Blakiston, 1951); 3. 'Financial intermediaries and the logical structure of monetary theory: a review article', *AER*, 51(1), March 1961; 4. 'On the economic theory of price indexes' (with N. Liviatan), *EDCC*, 9, April 1961; 5. 'Some reflections on the brain drain' in *The Brain Drain*, ed. W. Adams (Macmillan, 1968); 6. 'Friedman on the quantity theory and Keynesian economics', *JPE*, 80(5), Sept.–Oct., 1972, repr. in *Milton Friedman's Monetary Framework: A Debate with His Critics*, ed. R.J. Gordon (Univ. Chicago Press, 1974); 7. 'What advanced countries can

learn from the experience with indexation', *Explor. Econ. Res.*, 4(1), Winter 1977; 8. 'Multiple discoveries and the central message: the case of *"The General Theory"'*, *Amer. J. Sociology*, 89, Sept. 1983; 9. 'Keynes and economics today', *AER*, 74(2), May 1984.

Principal Contributions Contributed primarily to monetary and employment theory as well as to the history of this theory from 1870–1940. In early work, developed an integration of value theory and monetary theory by means of a general-equilibrium microeconomic model which introduced a direct effect of real money balances (more generally, net real financial assets) into the demand functions of all markets, including those for commodities. Used model to define proper relationship between the analysis of the real and monetary aspects of the economy respectively (the 'dichotomy issue'). Developed corresponding macroeconomic models, and with these analysed the role of financial intermediaries and the conditions for the neutrality of money in both stationary and growing economics. Extended the model to theory of unemployment and in this context developed first explicit disequilibrium macroeconomic model. Also used the model to show relationship between Keynesian and classical theories of unemployment. Developed an inventory-theoretic analysis of the demand for money based on a stochastic payment process and thus rationalised introduction of real money balances into the utility function. Contributed to the history of monetary theory and published studies of Walras, Wicksell, Fisher, Cambridge School, and others.

In more recent years, have carried out research on the development of macroeconomic theory in interwar period. In this context, studied development of Keynes's monetary and employment theory, as well as of his related policy views. Used Keynes's *General Theory* as test case of Robert Merton's theory of multiple discoveries in science and showed that, contrary to the widely accepted view, neither the Stockholm School nor Kalecki can be credited with the discovery of this theory. Also analysed the interaction between the respective developments of macroeconomic theory and national-income accounting in the 1930s. In earlier years also contributed to price theory: namely, theory of cartels, of consumers' surplus, and of price indexes. From time to time, have studied aspects of the Israeli economy, and have written a history of the first decade of this economy.

PATTANAIK, Prasanta Kumar

Born 1943, Cuttack, Orissa, India.
Current Post Prof. Math. Econ., Univ. Birmingham, Birmingham, England, 1978–.
Past Posts Ass. Lect., Ramjas Coll., Delhi, 1965; Tutor, Lect., Delhi School Econ., 1965–8; Ass. Prof., Harvard Univ., 1968–70; Res. Fellow, Nuffield Coll. Oxford, 1970–1; Vis. Fellow, Reader, Prof., Delhi School Econ., 1971–5; Prof., La Trobe Univ., Melbourne, 1975–7; Vis. Fellow, ANU, 1977; Prof., Southern Methodist Univ., Dallas, 1977–8, 1983; Fellow, Inst. Advanced Stud., Jerusalem, 1983.
Degrees BA Utkal Univ., 1983, MA, PhD Univ. Delhi, 1965, 1968.
Offices and Honours Fellow, Em Soc, 1979–; Member, Soc. Econ. Analysis, 1979.
Editorial Duties Assoc. Ed., *JET*, 1975–; Ed. Board, *REStud*, 1980–3; Ed., *Social Choice and Welfare*, 1984.
Principal Fields of Interest 025 Social Choice; 024 Welfare Theory; 411 International Trade Theory.
Publications *Books:* 1. *Voting and Collective Choice* (CUP, 1971); 2. *Strategy and Group Choice*, (N-H, 1978); 3. *Social Choice and Welfare*, co-ed. (with M. Salles), (N-H, 1983).
Articles: 1. 'Risk impersonality and the social welfare function', *JPE*, 76, Nov.–Dec. 1968; 2. 'Necessary and sufficient conditions for rational choice under majority decision' (with A.K. Sen), *JET*, 1(2), Aug. 1969; 3. 'Factors market imperfections, the terms of trade and welfare' (with R.N. Batra), *AER*, 61(5), Dec. 1971; 4. 'On some suggestions for having non-binary social choice functions' (with R.N.

Batra), *Theory and Decision*, 3, 1972; 5. 'On the stability of sincere voting situations', *JET*, 6(6), Dec. 1973; 6. 'Threats, counter-threats, and strategic voting', *Em*, 44(1), Jan. 1976; 7. 'Counter-threats and strategic manipulation under voting schemes', *REStud*, 43(1), Feb. 1976; 8. 'Strategic voting under minimally binary group decision functions' (with I. MacIntyre), *JET*, 25(3), Dec. 1981; 9. 'The structure of coalitional power under probabilistic group decision rules' (with T. Bandyophyay and R. Deb), *JET*, 27(2), Aug. 1982; 10. 'The structure of general probabilistic group decision rules' (with R. Heiner), in *Social Choice and Welfare, op. cit.*

Principal Contributions My main contribution has been in the area of social choice theory. I have also done some work on trade theory. In social choice theory I have worked on (1) conditions (formulated in terms of restrictions on profiles of individual preferences) for transitivity and quasi-transitivity of different classes of group decision rules; (2) strategic voting (especially for decision rules under which the sets of outcomes may not be singletons); and (3) stochastic social choice. In trade theory, my work concentrated on domestic distributions and welfare.

PATTEN, Simon Nelson*

Dates and Birthplace 1852–1922, Sandwich, IL, USA.
Posts Held Schoolteacher, 1882–8; Prof. Polit Econ., Univ. Pennsylvania, 1888–1917.
Degrees MA, PhD Univ. Halle, Germany, 1878.
Offices and Honours Pres., AEA, 1908.
Publications *Books:* 1. *Premises of Political Economy* (1885); 2. *Theory of Social Forces* (1896); 3. *Development of English Thought* (1899); 4. *Theory of Prosperity* (1902); 5. *Heredity of Social Progress* (1903); 6. *New Basis of Civilisation* (1907).
Career Social philosopher who never limited himself to the traditional field of economic inquiry. Frequently in-volved in intellectual controversy, but his ability to stimulate discussion made him a very successful teacher. He favoured protectionism and national-ism in economic policy.
Secondary Literature H.R. Seager, 'S.N. Patten', in *Essays in Economic Theory*, ed. R.G. Tugwell (Alfred A. Knopf, 1924).

PEACOCK, Alan Turner

Born 1922, Ryton-on-Tyne, England.
Current Post Hon. Prof. Econ., Heriot-Watt Univ. 1978–.
Past Posts Lect., Univ. St Andrews, 1947–8; Lect., Reader Public Fin, LSE, 1948–51, 1951–5; Prof. Econ., Univ. Edinburgh, 1957–62; Prof. Econ., Univ. York, England, 1962–7; Vis. Prof. Econ., Univ. Münster, W. Germany, 1951–, Johns Hopkins Univ., 1958; Vis. Res. Prof., Einaudi Foundation, Turin, 1970; Chief. Econ. Adviser, UK Dept. Trade Industry, 1973–6; Hon. Prof. Econ., Univ. York, 1978–81; Prof. Econ., Vice-Chancellor, Univ. Buckingham, Buckingham, Eng-land, 1978, 1983–4.
Degrees MA Univ. St Andrews 1947; Hon. Dr Univ. Stirling, 1974; Dr (H.C.), Zurich, 1984.
Offices and Honours Member, Advisory Council, INEA, 1961–; Council, RES; Member, Council, Chairman, Econ. Comm., UK SSRC, 1972–3; Member, Royal Comm. Con-stitution, 1971–3; Hon. Pres., Internat. Inst. Public Fin., 1975; Fellow, BA, 1979–; Hon. Fellow, LSE, 1980–; Pres., Atlantic Econ. Soc., 1982; Member, UK Govt., Enquiries Retire-ment Provision, 1984–; Chairman, UK Govt. Commission, BBC Licence Fee, 1985–.
Editorial Duties Assoc. Ed., *Ec*, 1949–56; Co-ed., *SJPE*, 1960–2; *PF*, 1962–; Ed. Boards, *J. Cultural Econ.*, 1982–, *Ec*, 1982–, *Micros*, 1983.
Principal Fields of Interest 320 Fiscal Theory and Policy, Public Finance; 910 Welfare Programmes; 031 History of Economic Thought.
Publications *Books:* 1. *Economics of National Insurance* (Wm. Hodge, 1952; transl., Japanese, Ganshodo, 1954); 2.

Income Redistribution and Social Policy, ed. and contrib. (Cape, 1953; transl., Japanese, 1957); 3. *National Income and Social Accounting* (with H.C. Edey), (Hutchinson, 1954, with R.A. Cooper, 1966; transls., Japanese, DiamondSha, 1956, Portuguese, Zahar Rio de Janeiro); 4. *Classics in the Theory of Public Finance* (with R.A. Musgrave), (Macmillan, 1958, 1967); 5. *The Growth of Public Expenditure in the United Kingdom 1890–1955* (with J. Wiseman), (Princeton Univ. Press, OUP, 1961, A&U, 1967); 6. *Economic Theory of Fiscal Policy* (with G.K. Shaw), (A&U, 1971, 1976; transls., Italian, 1972, Spanish, Fondo de Cultura Economica, 1974); 7. *Welfare Economics: A Liberal Restatement* (with C. Rowley), (Martin Robertson, St Martins Press, 1975; transl., Japanese, 1977); 8. *The Composer in the Market-Place* (with R. Weir), (Faber Music, 1975); 9. *The Economic Analysis of Government* (Martin Robertson, 1979, 1981); 10. *The Political Economy of Taxation*, co-ed. (with F. Forte), (Blackwell, 1981).

Articles: 1. 'The national insurance funds', *Ec*, N.S. 16, Aug. 1949; 2. 'Wage claims and the pace of inflation (1945–51)' (with W.J.L. Ryan), *EJ*, 53, June 1953; 3. 'Built-in flexibility and economic growth', in *Stabile Preise in Wachsender Wirtschaft*, ed. G. Bombach (J.C.B. Mohr, Paul Siebeck, 1960); 4. 'Consumption taxes and compensatory finance' (with J. Williamson), *EJ*, 77, March 1967; 5. 'Welfare economics and public subsidies to the arts', *MS*, 37(4), Dec. 1969, repr. in *The Economics of the Arts*, ed. M. Blaug (Martin Robertson, 1976); 6. 'On the anatomy of collective failure', *PF*, 35(1), 1980; 7. 'Public X-inefficiency: informational and institutional constraints', in *Anatomy of Government Deficiencies*, ed. H. Hanusch (Springer-Verlag, 1983).

Principal Contributions My early approach to economics was entirely derived from a burning interest in policy questions, having been tempted to take an active interest in politics. My first somewhat polemical work was in the then entirely unexplored area of the economics of social security and was an exercise in Keynesian fiscal economics (1952). It was a natural transition to public finance and to the study of the causes and consequences of public-sector growth, and I suppose that my joint work with Jack Wiseman is something of a pioneering effort. Ever-present liberal (in the British sense) views led me to reject Paretian welfare economics as the normative base of public finance, leading to my co-operation with like-minded Charles Rowley (1970s).

As Chief Economic Adviser to the UK Department of Trade and Industry, I was brought face to face with the grubby realities of policy formulation and implementation (1973–6). Rather than lead me to be sceptical of the applications of economic analysis to policy problems, this experience strengthened my conviction that governments need more economics and not less, if only to understand the strict limitations on the effectiveness of State intervention. My recent writing has therefore been concentrated on the economic analysis of government (1977–) and particularly on the 'feedback' effects of government policy on the use by industry and taxpayers/voters of the instruments of political participation, using that term in a wider sense than that employed by public choice theorists. These latter-day preoccupations plus a long-standing interest in the economics of the arts should be enough to allow me to hold a reasonably intelligent conversation with much better trained and more specialised younger economists — at least for a little while longer!

PEARCE, David William

Born 1941, Harrow, Middlesex, England.
Current Post Prof. Polit. Econ., Univ. Coll. London, London, England, 1983–.
Past Posts Ass. Lect., Lect., Lancaster Univ., 1964–5, 1965–7; Lect., Sr. Lect., Southampton Univ., 1969–70, 1970–4; Dir., Public Sector Econ. Res. Centre, Leicester Univ., 1974–6; Prof. Polit. Econ., Aberdeen Univ., Scotland,

1977–82; Vis. Prof., Adelaide Univ., 1983.

Degrees BA, MA Univ. Oxford, 1963, 1967.

Offices and Honours Member, UK Nat. Radiological Protection Board, 1980–; Member, Waste Management Advisory Council, 1975; Member, UK SSRC Energy Panel, 1977–9; Member, US ESRC, Econ. Comm., 1982–; Hon. Vice-Pres., Assoc. Polytechnic Teachers Econ., 1978–81; Fellow, Centre Econ. Pol. Res., London, England, 1983–.

Editorial Duties Ed. Boards, *Internat. J. Social Econ.*, 1975–, *Resources Pol.*, 1975–, *Energy Econ.*, 1978–, *Internat. Environmental Stud.*, 1978, *Futures*, 1982–, *J. Indian Affairs*, 1982–, *Resources and Conservation*, 1982–, *J. Econ. Stud.*, 1983–.

Principal Fields of Interest 721 Natural Resources.

Publications *Books:* 1. *Cost Benefit Analysis* (Macmillan, 1971, 1983); 2. *Cost Benefit Analysis: Theory and Practice* (with A.K. Dasgupta), (Macmillan, 1972); 3. *Natural Resource Depletion*, ed. (Macmillan, 1975); 4. *Environmental Economics* (Longman, 1976); 5. *Price Theory* (with W.J.L. Ryan), (Macmillan, 1977); 6. *Decision Making for Energy Futures* (with L. Edwards and G. Beuret), (Macmillan, 1979); 7. *Social Projects Appraisal* (with C.A. Nash), (Macmillan, 1981); 8. *Macmillan Dictionary of Modern Economics*, ed. (Macmillan, 1981, 1983); 9. *Risk and the Political Economy of Resource Development* (with H. Siebert and I. Walter), (Macmillan, 1984).

Articles: 1. 'The evaluation of urban motorway schemes: a case study — Southampton' (with C.A. Nash), *Urb Stud.*, 10(2), June 1973; 2. 'An incompatibility in planning for a steady state and planning for maximum economic welfare', *Environment and Planning*, 5, 1973; 3. 'An evaluation of cost benefit analysis criteria' (with C.A. Nash and J.K. Stanley), *SJPE*, 22(2), June 1975; 4. 'The limits of cost benefit analysis as a guide to environmental policy', *Kyk*, 29(1), 1976; 5. 'The economics of energy analysis' (with M. Webb), *Energy Pol.*, Dec. 1975; 6. 'The monetary evaluation of noise

nuisance' (with R. Edwards), *Environment Planning and Resource Management*, 1(1), 1979; 7. 'Risk assessment: use and misuse', *Proceedings Royal Soc. London*, 1981; 8. 'World energy demand and crude oil prices to 2000', *J Agric Econ*, 36(3), 1981; 9. 'Ethics, irreversibility, future generations and the social rate of discount', *Internat. J. Environmental Stud.*, 21, 1983; 10. 'Energy consumption in Eastern Europe' (with R. Westoby), *Energy Econ.*, 6(1), 1984.

Principal Contributions Nearly all of my work has its foundations in an early and continuing concern for natural environments and wildlife species. I regarded cost-benefit analysis as the appropriate procedure for assessing the worth of natural environments and continue to believe that it provides a useful way of thinking. From cost-benefit it was a natural progression to environmental economics as a subject in itself. Becoming less enamoured with orthodox economics, I began work on the links between economics and the general science of ecology. At the same time, the implication of energy sources in so much of environmental destruction caused me to divert some attention to energy economics, particulary in developing countries. These themes — the cost-benefit framework, ecology, and energy — continue to define my research and interest in economics.

PEARCE, Ivor Frank

Born 1926, Bristol, Avon, England.

Current Post Prof. Econ., Univ. Southampton, Southampton, Hampshire, England, 1961–.

Past Posts Vis. Prof., Univ. Penn., 1965, 1969, Univ. Cal., 1972, 1980, Inst. Advanced Stud., ANU, 1972, St Hilda's Coll., Melbourne, 1977–8.

Degrees BA Univ. Bristol, 1949; PhD Univ. Nottingham, 1953.

Offices and Honours Fellow, Em Soc; Council Member, INEA, London, 1979–.

Principal Fields of Interest 211 Econometric Models; 400 International Economy.

Publications *Books:* 1. *A Contribu-*

tion to Demand Analysis (OUP, 1964);
2. *International Trade*, 2 vols (Macmillan, Norton, 1970); 3. *A Model of Output, Employment, Wages and Prices in the United Kingdom* (OUP, 1976); 4. *The Incredible Eurodollar* (A&U, 1984).

Articles: 1. 'The place of money capital in the theory of production' (with A. Gabor), *QJE*, 72, Nov. 1958; 2. 'The problem of the balance of payments', *Int ER*, 2, Jan. 1961; 3. 'An exact method of consumer demand analysis', *Em*, 29, Oct. 1961; 4. 'Matrices with dominating diagonal blocks', *JET*, 9(2), Oct. 1974; 5. 'The incredible Eurodollar', *The Banker*, June 1980.

Principal Contributions International balance of payments and money market theory; the theory of value in international trade; the theory of capital and economic growth; general equilibrium and income distribution theory; the theory of consumer behaviour; the theory and practice of large-scale econometric model-building; the theory and measurement of social welfare, and the mathematisation of economics.

PECHMAN, Joseph A.

Born 1918, New York City, NY, USA.

Current Post Sr. Fellow, Brookings Inst., Washington, DC, 1962–.

Past Posts Stat., Nat. Res. Project, Philadelphia, 1937; Res. Ass., Econ., Univ. Wisconsin, 1937–8; Ass. Dir., Wisconsin Income Tax Study, Wisconsin Tax Commission, 1938–9; Res. Assoc., Univ. Wisconsin, 1939–40; Econ., US Office Price Admin., 1941–2; Meteorologist, US Army, 1942–5; Ass. Dir., Tax Advisory Staff, US Treasury, 1946–53; Assoc. Prof. Fin., School Industrial Management, MIT, 1953–4; Econ., US President's Council Econ. Advisers, 1954–6; Econ., Comm. Econ. Devlp., 1956–60; Exec. Dir., Stud. Govt. Fin., Dir., Econ. Stud. Program, Brookings Inst., 1960–70, 1962; Adjunct Prof., Georgetown Univ. Law Center, 1980–.

Degrees BS City Coll. NY, 1937; MA, PhD, Hon. LLD Univ. Wisconsin, 1938, 1942, 1978.

Offices and Honours Phi Beta Kappa, 1937; Pres., AFA, 1971, EEA, 1979; Vice-Pres., AEA, 1978.

Editorial Duties Ed. Board, *AER*.

Principal Fields of Interest 320 Fiscal Theory; 130 Economic Fluctuations; 910 Welfare, Health, and Education.

Publications *Books:* 1. *Federal Tax Policy* (Brookings Inst., 1966, 1977); 2. *Social Security: Perspectives for Reform* (with H.J. Aaron and M.K. Taussig), (Brookings Inst., 1968); 3. *Who Bears the Tax Burden?* (with B.A. Okner), (Brookings Inst., 1974); 4. *Work Incentives and Income Guarantees: The New Jersey Negative Income Tax Experiment*, co-ed. (with P.M. Timpane), (Brookings Inst., 1975); 5. *Tax Reform: The Impossible Dream?* (with G.F. Break), (Brookings Inst., 1975); 6. *Welfare in Rural Areas: The North Carolina-Iowa Income Maintenance Experiment*, co-ed. (with J.L. Palmer), (Brookings Inst., 1978); 7. *Comprehensive Income Taxation*, ed. (Brookings Inst., 1977); 8. *What Should be Taxed: Income or Expenditure?*, ed. (Brookings Inst., 1980); 9. *How Taxes Affect Economic Behaviour*, co-ed. (with H.J. Aaron), (Brookings Inst., 1981); 10. *Setting National Priorities*, ed. (Brookings Inst. Annual, 1976–83).

Articles: 1. 'Is a negative income tax practical?' (with J. Tobin and P. Meiszkowski), *Yale Law J.*, 77(1), Nov. 1967; 2. 'The rich, the poor and the taxes they pay', *Public Interest*, Fall 1969; 3. 'Responsiveness of the Federal individual income tax to changes in income', *Brookings Papers Econ. Activity*, 2, 1973; 4. 'Making economic policy: the role of the economist', in *Handbook of Political Science*, 6, *Policies and Policy-making* (Addison-Wesley, 1975); 5. 'Taxation' (with K. Kaizuka), in *Asia's New Giant: How the Japanese Economy Works*, eds. H. Patrick and H. Rosovsky (Brookings Inst., 1976); 6. 'Taxation', in *Britain's Economic Performance*, eds. R.E. Caves and L.B. Krause (Brookings Inst., 1980); 7. 'Tax Policies for the 1980s', in *Economics in the Public Service: Papers in Honor of Walter W. Heller* (W.W. Norton, 1981); 8. 'Comprehensive income taxation and rate reduction' (with J.K. Scholz), *Tax Notes*, 11, Oct. 1982.

Principal Contributions I have concentrated my attention on the measurement of the incidence taxation, and on budget and tax policy.

PECK, Merton Joseph

Born 1925, Cleveland, OH, USA.

Current Post Thomas DeWitt Guyler Prof. Econ. and Transportation, Yale Univ., New Haven, CT, USA, 1981–.

Past Posts Teaching Fellow, Instr. Econ., Harvard Univ., 1951–5; Ass. Prof. Econ., Univ. Michigan, 1955–6; Ass. Prof., Assoc. Prof. Bus. Admin., Harvard Univ., 1956–61; Dir., Systems Analysis US Office Secretary Defense, 1961–2; Prof. Econ., Yale Univ., 1962–81; Member, US President's Council Econ. Advisers, 1968–9.

Degrees BA Oberlin Coll., 1949; MA, PhD Harvard Univ., 1951, 1954; MA Yale Univ, 1962.

Offices and Honours Ford Faculty Fellow, 1966–7; Nat. Assoc. Educ. Broadcasters, Award for Outstanding Book on TV, 1971.

Principal Fields of Interest 610 Industrial Organisation and Public Policy; 620 Economics of Technological Change; 630 Industry Studies.

Publications *Books:* 1. *Competition in the Transportation Industries* (with J. Meyer, C. Zwick and J. Stenason), (Harvard Univ. Press, 1959); 2. *Competition in the Aluminum Industry* (Harvard Univ. Press, 1962); 3. *Weapon Acquisition: An Economic Analysis* (with F. M. Scherer), (Harvard Bus. School, 1962); 4. *Technology, Economic Growth and Technical Change* (with R. Nelson and E. Kalachek), (Brookings Inst., 1969); 5. *Economic Aspects of Television Regulation* (with R. Noll and J. McGowan), (Brookings Inst., 1973); 6. *Unsettled Questions on Regulatory Reform* (with P. MacAvoy), (AEI, 1978).

Articles: 1. 'The determination of a fair return on investment in regulated industries' (with J. R. Meyer), in *Transportation Economics*, ed. J. R. Mayer (Columbia Univ. Press, 1965); 2. 'Science and technology', in *Britain's Econ-*omic Prospects*, ed. R. Caves (Brookings Inst., 1968); 3. 'The single entity proposal for international telecommunications', in *Essays in Honor of Edward Mason*, ed. J. Markham (Houghton-Mifflin, 1970); 4. 'Television: old theories, current facts and future policies' (with J. McGowan), *AER*, 66(2), May 1976; 5. 'Technology', in *Asia's New Giant: How the Japanese Economy Works*, eds. H. Patrick and H. Rosovsky (Brookings Inst., 1976); 6. 'Technology and economic growth: the case of Japan' (with A. Goto), *Res. Pol.*, 10, 1981; 7. 'Innovation, imitation and comparative advantage: the performance of Japanese color television set manufacturers' (with R. Wilson), in *Merging Technologies: Consequences for Economic Growth, Structural Change and Employment*, ed. H. Giersch (Univ. Kiel, 1981).

Principal Contributions My research has been in the field of industrial organisation broadly defined. My first book, which grew out of my dissertation, was a study of the postwar American aluminum industry. Simultaneously, I worked with my fellow Harvard instructors on a book on the US transportation industries. This volume stressed the competition between industries — particularly that between truck and rail — and it was an early plea for deregulation of the US transportation sector. It was an innovation at the time in its use of econometrics to study cost functions in transportation.

My next research efforts centred on understanding the process of weapons acquisition in the US, a subject that had attracted little attention from economists. This work, with F. M. Scherer, led to an interest in what are now called the high-technology industries and the complexities of technical change. I worked at the Rand Corporation with R. Nelson and E. Kalachek to examine technical change more generally and this research was reported in a Brookings book. My interests then shifted to national science and technology policy, and I wrote two chapters in Brookings volumes comparing science and technology policy in Britain and Japan with the policies and institutions in the US. In the early 1970s, I began work with

Roger Noll and John McGowan on the US television industry, which was changing rapidly with the advent of cable television. The work, reported in still another Brookings volume, relied more than my previous research on econometric estimates of the demand for television programming. Recently I have returned to my first research efforts to examine how the rise in the price of energy has changed the world aluminum industry.

PEJOVICH, Steve

Born 1931, Belgrade, Yugoslavia.
Current Post Prof. Econ., Dir., Center Res. and Educ. in Free Enterprise, Texas A&M Univ., Coll. Station, TX, USA, 1981–.
Past Posts Ass. Prof., St Mary's Coll., TX, 1962–6; Assoc. Prof., Univ. Dallas, 1966–7; Assoc. Prof., Texas A&M Univ., 1967–70; Prof., Ohio Univ., 1970–5; Dean, School Bus., Acting Pres., Univ. Dallas, 1975–80, 1980–1.
Degrees LLB Univ. Belgrade, 1955; PhD Georgetown Univ., Washington, 1963.
Offices and Honours Ford Foundation Fellow, 1962; Vis. Scholar, Hoover Inst., Stanford, 1973; Adjunct Scholar, Heritage Foundation, 1980; Advisory Comm., USIA, 1981–; Earhard Fellow, 1982.
Editorial Duties Ed. Board, *Modern Age*, 1970–, *RSE* 1970–.
Principal Fields of Interest 050 Economic Systems; 610 Industrial Organisation and Public Policy; 025 Social Choice.
Publications *Books:* 1. *Market Planned Economy of Yugoslavia* (Univ. Minn. Press, 1966); 2. *Role of Technical Schools in Improving the Skills and Earning Capacity of Rural Manpower: A Case Study* (US Dept. Labor, 1966); 3. *The Economics of Property Rights: Selected Essays*, co-ed. (with E. Firobotn), (Ballinger, 1974); 4. *Individual Liberty: Selected Works of W. H. Hutt*, co-ed. (with D. Klingaman), (Greenwood Press, 1975); 5. *Governmental Policies and the Free Market: The US Economy in the 1970s*, ed. (Texas A&M Univ. Press, 1977); 6.

The Co-determination Movement in the West, ed. (D. C. Heath, 1976); 7. *Fundamentals of Economics: A Property Rights Approach* (Fisher Inst., 1979); 8. *Life in the Soviet Union: A Report Card on Socialism* (Fisher Inst. 1979); 9. *Social Security System in Yugoslavia* (AEI, 1979); 10. *Economic and Philosophical Foundations of Capitalism*, ed. (D. C. Heath, 1983).
Articles: 1. 'Property rights and economic theory: a survey of recent literature' (with E. Furubotn), *JEL*, 10(4), Dec. 1972; 2. 'The Yugoslav system of contractual self-management and its implications', *RSE*, 38, 1980; 3. 'The economic position of the enterprise in the Yugoslav economy', *Stratsveten skpalig Tidskrift*, 1980; 4. 'Codetermination in the West', *RSE*, 39, 1981; 5. 'Les Derechos de propiedad y la teoria economica' (with E. Furubotn), *Hacienda Publica Española*, 68, 1981; 6. 'Codetermination in the West: the case of Germany', *Heritage Foundation Lecture Series*, 10, 1982; 7. 'Karl Marx, property rights school and the process of social change', *Kyk*, 35(3), 1982; 8. 'Economic objectives of the Reagan administration', *Wirtschafts Polit. Blätter*, 2, 1982; 9. 'Allocative effects of property rights', *J Fin. and Public Choice*, 3, 1983; 10. 'Property rights and incentives', *Proceedings German Econ. Assoc.*, Sept. 1983.
Principal Contributions Research and teaching interests are in the areas of comparative economic systems, economic analysis of law and theory of institutions. In recent years, publications have been primarily in the direction of incorporating the incentive effects of various property rights with standard price theory.

PELTZMAN, Sam

Born 1940, New York City, NY, USA.
Current Post Prof. Bus. Econ., Grad. School Bus., Univ. Chicago, Chicago, IL, USA, 1978–.
Past Posts Ass. Prof., Prof. Econ., UCLA, 1967–73; Vis. Ass. Prof., Ford Foundation Vis. Prof., Grad. School Bus., Univ. Chicago, 1968, 1973; Sr.

Staff Econ., US President's Council Econ. Advisers, 1970–1; Res. Fellow, Inst. Advanced Study, Hebrew Univ., Jerusalem, 1978.

Degrees BBA City Coll. NY, 1960; PhD Univ. Chicago, 1965.

Offices and Honours Adjunct Scholar *AEI*.

Editorial Duties Ed., *JPE*, 1974–84.

Principal Fields of Interest 613 Public Utilities; 610 Industrial Organisation.

Publications *Books:* 1. *Public Policy Toward Mergers*, co-ed. (with F. Weston), (Goodyear, 1968).

Articles: 1. 'Entry in commercial banking', *J Law E*, 8(3), Oct. 1965; 2. 'Capital investment in commercial banking', *JPE*, 78(1), Jan.–Feb. 1970; 3. 'Pricing in public and private enterprise: electric utilities in the United States', *J Law E*, 14(1), April 1971; 4. 'The effect of government subsidies in kind on private expenditures: the case of higher education', *JPE*, 81(1), Jan.–Feb. 1973; 5. 'An evaluation of consumer protection regulation: the 1962 drug amendments', *JPE*, 81(5), Sept.–Oct. 1973; 6. 'The effects of automobile safety regulation', *JPE*, 83(4), Aug. 1975; 7. 'Toward a more general theory of regulation', *JPE*, 19(2), Aug. 1976; 8. 'The gains and losses from industrial concentration', *J Law E*, 20(2), Oct. 1977; 9. 'The growth of government', *J Law E*, 23(2), Oct. 1980.

Principal Contributions My principal interest has been in the relationship between economics and the legal system. In pursuit of this interest, I have done several studies on the effects of government regulation in such fields as banking, drugs, automobile safety, advertising regulation, etc. I have also thought about what common strands run through the diverse gamut of such regulations, so I have done some theoretical work on rational-choice models of regulation. But mainly I regard myself as an empirical researcher, rather than a theorist. In recent years, I have come to realise that regulation and other forms of government activity have much in common, so I have broadened my research to include public spending and politics.

PEN, Jan

Born 1921, Lemmer, The Netherlands.

Current Post Prof. Econ., Faculty Law, Rijksuniv., Groningen, The Netherlands, 1956–.

Past Posts Dir., General Econ. Pol., Dutch Ministry Econ. Affairs, The Hague, 1947–56.

Degrees MA, PhD Univ. Amsterdam, 1946, 1950; Hon. Dr Free Univ., Brussels, 1973.

Offices and Honours Fellow, Royal Netherlands Academy Sciences, 1972.

Editorial Duties Ed. Board, *DE*.

Principal Fields of Interest 023 Macroeconomics; 229 Micro-data; 320 Public Finance.

Publications *Books:* 1. *The Wage Rate under Bargaining* (Harvard Univ. Press, 1958); 2. *Modern Economics* (Penguin, 1965); 3. *Harmony and Conflict in Modern Society* (A&U, 1966); 4. *A Primer on International Trade* (Prentice-Hall, 1969); 5. *Income Distribution* (Macmillan, 1971); 6. *Naar een Brechtvaardiger Inkomengverdeling* (Dutch) (with J. Tinbergen), (Elsevier, 1977); 7. *Macro-economie* (Dutch), (with J. van Gemerden), (Elsevier, 1977); 8. *Kijk, Economie* (Dutch), (Elsevier, 1979); 9. *Among Economists* (N-H, 1985).

Articles: 1. 'A general theory of bargaining', *AER*, 42(1), March 1952; 2. 'The strange adventures of Dutch wage policy', *BJIR*, 1, Nov. 1963; 3. 'Profits as a rich source of puzzlement', *DE*, 128(3), 1980; 4. 'A clear case of levelling: income equalization in the Netherlands', *Social Res*, 46(4), Winter 1979; 5. 'On eclecticism, or we are (almost) all neo-classical neo-Keynesian now', *DE*, 129(1), 1981; 6. 'Stagnation explained?' *DE*, 131(4), 1983.

Principal Contributions American observers see me primarily as a labour economist, British observers as a critic of the Treasury model and a partisan of incomes policies. I like to describe myself as a Keynesian, who is in favour of the welfare state and cultural economics; but also as an environmentalist who believes that nature is becoming painfully scarce. One of my minor contributions is in the field of imagery:

income distribution as a paradigm of dwarfs and giants. The idea was quantified by, *inter alia*, Assar Lindbeck for Sweden. I believe in econometric research (but never did it myself) because the numerical values of parameters define the structure of the economy. This structure should be the backbone of colligation or storytelling and economists should not refrain from telling stories. Basically, I am an economic journalist, who produces a running comment on economic issues in newspapers and magazines. These articles are published in various collections (not mentioned above because they are in Dutch) with titles like *The Surprises of Economics* (1984). My *Look, Economics* (1978) is a picture book stressing the human and everyday aspects of economic life. *Among Economists* (1985) asks the question whether we really are a quarrelsome lot and tries to synthesise Karl Popper and Benjamin Ward.

PENCAVEL, John Harold

Born 1943, London, England.
Current Post Prof. Econ., Stanford Univ., Stanford, CA, USA, 1978–.
Past Posts Ass. Prof., Assoc. Prof., Econ. Stanford Univ., 1969–74, 1974–8.
Degrees BSc, MSc Univ. London, 1965, 1966; PhD Princeton Univ. 1969.
Editorial Duties Assoc. Ed., Ed., *JEL*, 1982–5, 1985–.
Principal Fields of Interest 800 Manpower, Labour, Population; 022 Microeconomic Theory; 211 Econometric and Statistical Methods and Models.
Publications *Books:* 1. *An Analysis of the Quit Rate in American Manufacturing Industry* (Industrial Relations Section, Princeton Univ. 1970).
Articles: 1. 'American trade union growth 1900–1960' (with O. Ashenfelter), *QJE*, 83(3), Aug. 1969; 2. 'Wages, specific training and labor turnover', *Int ER*, 13(1), Feb. 1972; 3. 'Constant-utility index numbers of real wages', *AER*, 67(2), March 1977; 4. 'Wage and employment determination under trade unionism' (with J. Dertouzos), *JPE*, 89(6), Dec. 1981; 5. 'The effects of incomes policies on the frequency

and size of wage changes', *Ec*, N.S. 49, May 1982; 6. 'Dynamic hours of work functions' (with T. R. Johnson), *Em*, 52(2), March 1984; 7. 'The trade-off between wages and employment in trade union objectives', *QJE*, 99(2), May 1984.
Principal Contributions My research has concentrated upon the operation of labour markets. Early work examined the determinants of labour turnover across industries and the determinants of the movement of money wages over time. More recently, my interests have concerned the behaviour of trade unions and aspects of the supply of labour. With respect to trade unions, I have been interested in determining the empirical relevance of different trade union objectives and alternative models describing the way in which wages and employment are set in unionised markets. My research on labour supply has involved the application of the conventional allocation model to a number of different issues, such as the definition of a constant utility index number of real wages and the evaluation of different income maintenance programme including the negative income tax and the wage subsidy scheme.

PENNINGTON, James*

Dates and Birthplace 1777–1862, Kendal, Cumbria, England.
Posts Held Businessman
Offices and Honours Member, Polit. Econ. Club, 1828.
Publications *Books:* 1. *The Currency of the British Colonies* (1848); 2. *A Letter to Kirkman Finlay on the Importation of Foreign Corn* (1840).
Career Expert on currency who was frequently consulted by the British government in the regulation of the currency of the West Indies after 1833. His *Letter to Kirkman Finlay ...* advocated the restriction of Bank of England note issues. Peel consulted him on the framing of the Bank Act 1844 but moved beyond his recommendations by separating the Bank's banking and issue departments.
Secondary Literature R. S. Sayers, ed., *Economic Writings of James Pennington* (LSE, 1963).

PERLMAN, Mark

Born 1923, Madison, WI, USA.
Current Post Prof. Econ., Prof.
Hist., Prof. Econ. Public Health, Univ.
Pittsburgh, Pittsburgh, PA, USA.
1963–.
Past Posts Ass. Prof., Univ. Hawaii,
1951–2; Ass. Prof., Cornell Univ.,
1952–5; Ass. Prof., Assoc. Prof, Vis.
Prof., Johns Hopkins Univ., 1955–8,
1958–63, 1963–4; Vis. Fellow, Clare
Coll. Camb., 1976–7; Fellow, Inst.
Advanced Study, Princeton Univ.,
1981–2; Prof. Oesterreichische Laender-
bank, Schumpeter Univ., Vienna,
1982.
Degrees BA, MA Univ. Wisconsin,
1947, 1947; PhD Columbia Univ.,
1950.
Offices and Honours Res. Training
Fellow, US SSRC, 1949–50; Ford
Foundation Res. Fellow, 1962–3; Fulbright Lect. Econ., Melbourne Univ.,
1968; Res. Scholar, Rockefeller
Center, Bellagio, Italy, 1983; Pres.,
Hist. Econ. Soc., 1984–5.
Editorial Duties Ed. Board, *ILRR*,
1953–55; Ed., *JEL*, 1968–81; Co-ed.,
Surveys Econ. Lit. Series (CUP, 1977–).
Principal Fields of Interest 840
Demographic Economics; 031 History
of Economic Thought; 913 Economics
of Health.
Publications *Books:* 1. *Judges in
Industry: A Study of Labor Arbitration
in Australia* (Melbourne Univ. Press,
1954); 2. *Labor Union Theories in
America: Background and Develop-
ment* (Greenwood, 1958, 1976); 3. *The
Machinists: A New Study in American
Trade Unionism* (Harvard Univ. Press,
1961); 4. *Democracy in the IAM*
(Wiley, 1962); 5. *Health Manpower in a
Developing Economy* (with T. Baker),
(JHUP, 1967); 6. *Spatial, Regional and
Population Economics: Essays in
Honor of Edgar M. Hoover*, co-ed.
(with C. Levin and B. Chinitz),
(Gordon & Breach, 1972); 7. *Eco-
nomics of Health and Medical Care*, ed.
(Halsted Press, 1977); 8. *The Organisa-
tion and Retrieval of Economic Know-
ledge*, ed. (Halsted Press, 1977).
Articles: 1. 'Measuring the effects of
population control on economic
development: Pakistan as a case study'

(with E. M. Hoover), *PDR*, 6(4), 1966;
2. 'Theories of the labor movement',
IESS, 8; 3. 'Some economic growth
problems and the part population
policy plays', *QJE*, 89(2), May 1975; 4.
'Orthodoxy and heterodoxy in economics: a retrospective view of experiences in Britain and the U.S.A.',
ZN, 37(1–2), 1977; 5. 'Reflections on
methodology, persuasion, and Machlup', in *Fritz Machlup: Breadth and
Depth in Economics*, ed. J. S. Dreyer
(D. C. Heath, 1978); 6. 'One man's
Baedeker to productivity growth discussions', in *Contemporary Econ.
Problems, 1979*, ed. W. J. Fellner
(AEI, 1979); 7. 'Schumpeter as a historian of economic thought', 'G. L. S.
Shackle as a historian of economic
thought', in *Research in the History of
Economic Thought and Methodology*,
1, ed. W. J. Samuels (JAI Press, 1983);
8. 'On health, population change and
economic development', in *Spatial,
Regional and Population Economics:
Essays in Honor of Edgar M. Hoover*,
eds. B. Chinitz, C. Levin and M.
Perlman (Gordon & Breach, 1972); 9.
'Collective bargaining and industrial
relations: the past, the present and the
future', in *Contemporary Economic
Problems, 1983–84*, ed. W. J. Fellner
(AEI, 1984); 10. 'National economic
statistics: the case study of American
national accounts', in *The Political
Economy of National Statistics*, eds. W.
Alonso and P. Starr (Russell Sage
Foundation, 1984).
Principal Contributions My initial
interest was in the development of
American industrial government (i.e.
approaches to collective decision-
making in industry). *Judges in Industry*,
a dissertation, was an application of
that initial interest to the operation of
the Australian Arbitration Court and
involved the study of the role of employer and union organisation and the
cost and price structure of particular
industries in getting the losing party to
accept its awards. My study and its
analytical method were used, irrespec-
tive of my original intent, by the
successful counsel in the 1954 Boiler-
makers Case as a basis for finding the
then 50-year-old arbitration system un-
constitutional. A second line of effort

started with a book on the historical study of American labour union theories; it treated them primarily as an area of American economic institutionalism. The next two books dealt further with the practices and theories of American labour unionism.

In 1960, as an offshoot of my work at Johns Hopkins, I became involved in studying the economics of investment in public health; my current interest has a greater emphasis on preventive health care than on the delivery of health care services. In 1963 I started my collaboration with Professor Edgar M. Hoover (of Coale-Hoover model fame) in demographic economics. This work has been particularly concerned with the lag in the profession's consciousness between the demographic empirical changes and the modifications of theoretical models. This interest in theoretical models has led increasingly to work in the history of economic thought.

In 1969 I created the *Journal of Economic Literature* for the AEA; I perceived it as a means of synthesising a discipline which seemed to be intent upon fractionating. I remained its managing editor for over 12 years, during which time I was responsible *inter alia* for commissioning a large number of subfield survey articles and for developing a classification system of articles in economics (the one used in this volume). My work as series co-editor of CUP's *Surveys of Economic Literature* is an outgrowth of my journal editorship.

PERLMAN, Selig*

Dates and Birthplace 1888–1959, Bialystok, Poland.
Posts Held Res. Ass., Prof., Univ. Wisconsin, 1908–59.
Offices and Honours Member, Wisconsin Commission Human Rights, 1947.
Publications *Books:* 1. *History of Trade Unionism in the United States* (1922); 2. *Theory of the Labor Movement* (1928, 1956).
Career Labour historian and theoretician, whose theory of the labour

movement he called the Commons-Perlman theory in tribute to his mentor at Wisconsin. The theory was not abstract but was based on his encyclopedic knowledge of labour history. He believed that job security and not wage bargaining or workers' control was the true explanation of the rise of trade unions.
Secondary Literature E. E. Witte, 'Selig Perlman', *ILRR*, 13, April 1960.

PERRAKIS, Stylianos

Born 1939, Piraeus, Greece.
Current Post Prof. Admin., Univ. Ottawa, Ottawa, Canada, 1980–.
Past Posts Engineer, Greek Powder and Cartridge Co., Athens, 1963–4; Acting Instr., Univ. Cal. Berkeley, 1967–9; Ass. Prof., Assoc. Prof., Univ. Ottawa, 1970–3, 1973–9; Vis. Assoc. Prof. Econ., Univ. Cal. Santa Barbara, 1976–7; Vis. Prof., ESCAE, Reims, France, 1983–4.
Degrees Diploma (Eng.) Nat. Technical Univ., Athens, 1960; MS (Ind. Eng. -OR), PhD (Ind. Eng. -OR) Univ. Cal. Berkeley, 1966, 1970.
Offices and Honours Professional Schools Fellow, Ford Foundation, Univ. Cal. Berkeley, 1967–9; Sr. Staff Award, Univ. Ottawa, 1982–3.
Principal Fields of Interest 026 Economics of Uncertainty and Information; Game Theory and Bargaining Theory; 520 Business Finance and Investment; 610 Industrial Organisation and Public Policy.
Publications *Articles:* 1. 'Resource allocation and scale of operations in monopoly firm: a dynamic analysis' (with I. Sahin), *Int ER*, 13(2), June 1972; 2. 'The evaluation of risky investments with random timing of cash returns' (with C. Henrin), *Management Science*, 21(1), Sept. 1974; 3. 'Certainty equivalents and timing uncertainty', *J. Fin and Quant. Analysis*, 10(1), March 1975; 4. 'Rate-of-return regulation of a monopoly firm with random demand', *Int ER*, 17(1), Feb. 1976; 5. 'On risky investments with random timing of cash returns and fixed planning horizon' (with I Sahin), *Management Science*, 22(7), March 1976; 6. 'On the

regulated price-setting monopoly firm with a randon demand curve', *AER*, 66(3), June 1976; 7. 'On the technological implications of the spanning theorem', *CJE*, 12(3), Aug. 1979; 8. 'Factor-price uncertainty with variable proportions: note', *AER*, 70(5), Dec. 1980; 9. 'Capacity and entry under demand uncertainty' (with G. Warskett), *REStud*, 50(3), July 1983; 10. 'Option pricing bounds in discrete time' (with P. Ryan), *J Fin*, 39(2), June 1984.

Principal Contributions I came to economics through management science and my interest in decision-making techniques. Since the early 1970s I have worked exclusively in the field of uncertainty in its various forms, in so far as they affect economic and financial decisions. As a special domain of application I have chosen industrial organisation, since this happens to be the branch of microeconomics where theory is closest to application. My earliest work was concerned with the way uncertainty in several components of individual decision-making at the level of the investor or the business firm affected well-established rules and results. I have analysed uncertainty arising out of demand, cost or timing factors, and its effects on resource allocation or the acceptance/rejection decision for a particular project. In more recent years I have become interested in the role of financial markets in decision-making under risk and the way they interact with complex long-term decisions of the firm. Some of my work in this area has been empirical, examining the effects of uncertainty in industries such as electricity generation, broadcasting and cable television. Currently I am working in the financial domain on the valuation of contingent claims and other complex financial instruments, as well as on the use of such instruments for policy decisions at the level of the individual firm or industry.

PERROUX, François

Born 1903, Lyons, France.
Current Post Pres., Inst. Sciences Math. Econ. Appl., Paris; Hon. Prof., Coll. de France; Pres., Conseil Scientifique de l'ISMEA, 1975–.
Past Posts Prof., Coll. de France, 1925–75; Prof., Univ. Lyons, 1926–8; Prof., Univ. Paris, Ecole des Hautes Etudes, Sorbonne, 1938–55.
Degrees Licence et Diplôme d'Etudes Supérieures des Lettres, Doctorat de Sciences Econ., Univ. Lyons, 1924, 1932; Agregé des Sciences Econ., Univ. Paris, 1928; Hon. Dr Univs., Sao-Paulo, 1936, Coimbra, Portugal, 1937, Liège, 1955, Frankfurt-am-Main, 1957, Lisbon, 1960, Cordoba, 1963, Montevideo, 1963, Georgetown, Washington, 1963, ICA, Peru, 1964, Lima, 1964–8, Chile, 1967, Barranquilla, Colombia, 1967–8, Bogotá, 1968, Quebec, 1968, Barcelona, 1969, Bucharest, 1969, Ottawa, 1974.
Offices and Honours Grand Croix de l'Order Nat. du Mérite; Commander, Légion d'Honneur; Commander, Palmes Académiques; Conseil Nat. Services Publics, 1945; Conseil Supérieur Comptabilité, 1947; Pres., Congrès Internat. de la Comptabilité, 1948; Pres., Sous-Commission Méthodes, Commission Comptes Budgets Econ.; Conseil Economique et Social; Ministère Fin., 1952; French Co-dir., Europ. Soc. Culture, Venice, 1956; Member, Conseil Internat. Sciences Sociales, 1960; Foreign Member, Accademia Nazionale dei Lincei, 1960; Corresp. Fellow, BA, 1961; Hon. Member, AEA, 1962; CNRS, 1963; Medaille d'Or 'C.C. Söderström', Royal Academy Sciences, Stockholm, 1971; Assoc. Member, Academie de Bruxelles; Member, Royal Academy, Barcelona.
Principal Fields of Interest 020 General Economic Theory; 113 Economic Planning Theory; 941 Regional Economics.
Publications *Books:* 1. *Le problème du profit* (Edns. Marcel Giard, 1926); 2. *La valeur* (Presses Univ. de France, 1943); 3. *Les comptes de la nation* (Presses Univ. de France, 1949); 4. *Théorie générale du progrès économique*(Cahiers de l'ISEA, 1956–7; transl., Greek, 1962); 5. *L'économie du XXème siècle* (Presses Univ. de France, 1961, 1969); 6. *Les techniques quantitative de la planification* (Presses Univ. de France,

1965); 7. *Pouvoir et économie* (Presses Univ. de France, 1975); 8. *Unités activés et mathématiques nouvelles. Révision de la théorie de l'équilibre général* (Dunod, 1975); 9. *A Basic Concept of Development. Basic Trends* (Blackwell, 1983). *Articles:* 1. 'Economic spaces: theory and application', *QJE*, 64(1), Feb. 1950, repr. in *Readings in Regional Development*, ed. J. Friedman (CUP, 1985); 2. 'Prises de vue sur la croissance de l'économie française 1780–1950', *Income and Wealth* 5 (NBER, 1956); 3. 'L'équilibre des unités passives et l'équilibration générale des unités actives', *Econ App*, 3–4, 1978; 4. 'Peregrinations of an economist and the choice of his route', *BNLQR*, 133, June 1980.

Principal Contributions Studies on structure, economic growth, industrialisation, common markets, regional policies, economic spaces, international trade. After thorough study of the static general equilibrium theory, was led to develop a generalised equilibrium theory based on the concept of active units capable of modifying their environment; asymmetrical actions in the irreversible time are combined in a whole whose temporary equilibria engender, under specified conditions, a general 'equilibrium' characterised by the exhaustion of the agent's energy for change. This state provides a framework, in terms of pre-topology, for the active units to hold together and to react on each other through market operations and organisational processes.

Secondary Literature P. Urri, 'On Perroux', in *Contemporary Economists in Perspective*, eds. H. W. Spiegel and W. J. Samuels (JAI Press, 1984).

PESANDO, James Edward

Born 1946, Toronto, Ont., Canada.
Current Post Prof. Econ., Univ. Toronto, Res. Ass., NBER, 1979–.
Past Posts Ass. Prof., Ass. Prof. Econ., Univ. Toronto, 1971–5, 1975–9.
Degrees BA Harvard Univ., 1967; MA Univ. Cal. Berkeley, 1968; PhD Univ. Toronto, 1971.
Editorial Duties Assoc. Ed., *J Fin*, 1977–83.

Principal Fields of Interest 023 Macroeconomic Theory; 313 Capital Markets; 520 Business Finance and Investment.

Publications *Books:* 1. *Public and Private Pensions, in Canada: An Economic Analysis* (with S. A. Rea, Jr.), (Univ. Toronto Press, 1977).
Articles: 1. 'Seasonal variability in distributed lag models', *JASA*, 67, June 1972; 2. 'The money supply and common stock prices: further observations on the econometric evidence', *J Fin*, 29, June 1974; 3. 'A note on the rationality of the Livingston price expectations', *JPE*, 83, Aug. 1975; 4. 'Rational expectations and distributed lag expectations proxies', *JASA*, 71, March 1976; 5. 'Determinants of term premiums in the market for the United States treasury bills', *J Fin*, 30, Dec. 1975; 6. 'On the efficiency of the bond market: some Canadian evidence', *JPE*, 86, Dec. 1978; 7. 'On forecasting interest rates: an efficient markets perspective', *J Mon E*, 8, Nov. 1981; 8. 'Investment risk, bankruptcy risk and pension reform in Canada', *J Fin*, 37, June 1982; 9. 'On expectations, term premiums and the volatility of long-term interest rates', *J Mon E*, 12, Sept. 1983; 10. 'Retirement annuity design in an inflationary climate' (with Z. Bodie), in *Financial Aspects of the U.S. Pension System*, eds. Z. Bodie and J. Shoven (Univ. Chicago Press, 1983).

Principal Contributions Early research interests included distributed lag models and the empirical problem of modelling expectations formation. The term structure of interest rates, with attention to the empirical use of hypothesis of rational expectations formation, became a primary application. Subsequent interests included the question of how short- and long-term interest rates would behave in an efficient capital market. A special concern to me was the question, at both the theoretical and empirical level, of the 'forecastability' of movements in long-term interest rates. For the past three years I have been concerned primarily with issues related to private pension plans and the retirement income system. Specific interests include annuity design, the measurement of pension liabilities, the valuation of benefits by workers, and the problem of accounting for pension costs.

PESCH, Heinrich*

Dates and Birthplace 1854–1926, Germany.

Posts Held Mainz Theological Seminary, 1892–1900.

Degrees Grad. Univ. Bonn, 1875, Univ. Berlin, 1903.

Offices and Honours Member, Soc. of Jesus.

Publications *Books:* 1. *Liberalismus, Sozialismus und christliche Gesellschaftsordnung*, 2 vols (1893–1900); 2. *Lehrbuch der Nationalökonomie*, 5 vols (1905–23).

Career Catholic economist who stressed the moral basis of economics, arguing that economic phenomena should be evaluated in terms of welfare, and called the social system he advocated 'Christian solidarism'. This involved stressing the interdependence of groups within society and the necessity of subordinating private economic interests to the collective welfare of the people.

Secondary Literature G. Briefs, 'Pesch, Heinrich', *ESS*, 12.

PESEK, Boris Peter

Born 1928, Most, Czechoslovakia.

Current Post Prof., Univ. Wisconsin, Milwaukee, WI, USA, 1967–.

Past Posts Prof., Michigan State Univ., 1957–67; Cons., East Europ. Nat. Income Project, Columbia Univ., 1957–63.

Degrees BA Coe Coll., Cedar Rapids, IA, 1951; MA, PhD Univ. Chicago, 1953, 1956.

Offices and Honours Rockefeller Foundation Fellow, Johns Hopkins Univ., 1956–7.

Principal Fields of Interest 023 Macroeconomics; 310 Domestic Monetary Theory.

Publications *Books:* 1. *National Income of Czechoslovakia* (Univ. Chicago Press, 1965); 2. *Money, Wealth and Economic Theory* (with T. R. Saving), (Macmillan, 1967); 3. *The Foundations of Money and Banking* (with T. R. Saving), (Macmillan, 1968).

Articles: 1. 'Monetary reforms and monetary equilibrium', *JPE*, 66(5), Oct. 1958; 2. 'A comparison of the distributional effects of taxation and inflation', *AER*, 50(1), March 1960; 3. 'Economic growth and its measurement', *EDCC*, 9(3), April 1961; 4. 'Kuznet's incremental capital output ratios', *EDCC*, 12(1), Oct. 1963, repr. in *Readings in Economic Development*, ed. D. R. Kammerschen (South-Western, 1965); 5. 'Money versus autonomous expenditures: the quality of evidence', *Bus. Econ.*, 3(2), Spring 1968; 6. 'Monetary theory in Alice's wonderland era', *JEL*, 14(3), Sept. 1976; 7. 'The theory of permanent income', *J Post Keyn E*, 1(4), Summer 1979; 8. 'Modern bank deposits and the theory of optimum undefined money', in *Economic Perspectives*, ed. M. B. Ballabon (Hardwood, 1979); 9. 'There is another bank reform in the wings', *J Post Keyn E*, 4(3), Spring 1982.

Principal Contributions I believe that I have shown that (1) gold, fiat, and bank money earns to its holders an imputed income and thus is not merely an asset offset by a debt; (2) banks not only intermediate (lend what they have borrowed) but also lend what they have not borrowed. (I came to realise that I have merely rediscovered what Chester A. Phillips had known in 1921 and Joseph Schumpeter in 1936); (3) as money starts to earn a higher and higher rate of interest, it will be more and more driven out of circulation. (I came to realise that I have merely rediscovered Gresham's Law); (4) an 'optimum' money earning interest via deflation equal to the rate of return on real capital would cause an economic collapse because then nobody would want to hold real assets. (I came to realise that this had been known to John Maynard Keynes in 1936); and (5) deregulation of the banking industry and the following birth of 'non-banks' which supply checkable deposits makes it impossible for Congress to perform its constitutional duty to 'regulate currency and the price thereof' — failure to regulate money has always caused a financial collapse. While I believe that these contributions merit attention, nobody else thinks so. In this volume I appear only as a result of computer blindness. The citations that put me here usually explain how wrong I am. But it has been said that the next best thing to being loved is being hated; the worst thing is to be ignored. Besides, I know that Emperors hate to be informed about the lack of substance of their clothing.

PESTON, Maurice

Born 1931, London, England.
Current Post Prof. Econ., Queen Mary Coll., London, England, 1979–.
Past Posts Special Adviser, UK Secretary State Educ. and Science, 1974–5; Sr. Special Adviser, UK Secretary of State Prices and Consumer Protection, 1976–9; Chairman, Econ. Board, UK SSRC, 1976–9.
Degrees BSc LSE, 1952.
Offices and Honours Chairman, UK Comm. Nat. Academic Awards, 1967–73.
Editorial Duties Ed., *Appl., Econ.*, 1972–;. Council Member, *RES*, 1978–.
Principal Fields of Interest 023 Macroeconomic Theory.
Publications *Books:* 1. *Public Goods and the Public Sector* (Macmillan, 1972); 2. *Theory of Macroeconomic Policy* (Philip Allan, 1974); 3. *Whatever Happened to Macroeconomics?* (Manchester Univ. Press, 1980).
Articles: 1. 'Random variations risk and returns to scale' (with T. M. Whitin), *QJE*, 68, Nov. 1954; 2. 'Generalising the balanced budget multiplier', *REStat*, 40, Aug. 1958; 3. 'On the sales maximisation hypothesis', *Ec*, N.S. 26, May 1959; 4. 'The correlation between targets and instruments', *Ec*, N.S. 39, Nov. 1972; 5. 'Monetary policy and incomes policy. Complements or substitutes?', *Appl. Econ.*, Dec. 1980.
Principal Contributions Microeconomics: clarification of the analysis of returns to scale, the interpretation of the objectives sought by the firm, the theory of forward markets and the analysis of changes in preferences. Macroeconomics: elaboration of a number of aspects of the balanced budget multi-

plier, the need for interventionist macroeconomic policy, and the nature of macroeconomics itself.

PFOUTS, Ralph William

Born 1920, Atchison, KA, USA.
Current Post Prof. Econ., Univ. N. Carolina Chapel Hill, Chapel Hill, NC, USA, 1968–.
Past Posts Ass. Instr., Univ. Kansas, 1946–7; Part-time Instr., Assoc. Prof. Econ., Univ. N. Carolina, 1947–52, 1952–8, 1962–8; Vis. Prof., Univ. Leeds, 1983; Vis. Res. Scholar, Internat. Inst. Appl. Systems Analysis, Laxenburg, Austria, 1983.
Degrees BA, MA Univ. Kansas, 1942, 1947; PhD Univ. N. Carolina, 1952.
Offices and Honours Pres. N. Carolina Chapter, ASA, 1952–3; US SSRC Fellow, Univ. Camb., 1953–4; Ford Foundation Faculty Res. Fellow, MIT, 1962–3; Vice-Pres., Pres., SEA, 1961–2, 1965–6; Vice-Pres., Pres., Atlantic Econ. Assoc., 1973–6, 1977–8.
Editorial Duties Ed. Boards, *SEJ*, 1955–75, *Metroec.*, 1960–80, *Q.J. Ideology*, 1976–, *Atlantic Econ. J.*, 1973–.
Principal Fields of Interest 022 Microeconomic Theory; 213 Mathematical Methods and Models; 036 Economic Methodology.
Publications *Books:* 1. *The Feasibility of the Shoe and Leather Industries in Kansas* (Univ. Kans. Press, 1947); 2. *Techniques of Urban Economic Analysis*, ed. (Chandler-Davis, 1960); 3. *Essays in Economics and Econometrics: A Volume in Honor of Harold Hotelling*, ed. (Univ. N. Carolina Press, 1960); 4. *Elementary Economics: A Mathematical Approach* (Wiley, 1972).
Articles: 1. 'A theory of the responsiveness of hours of work to changes in wage rates' (with F. Gilbert), *REStat*, 40(2), May 1958; 2. 'Utility, hours of work and savings', in *Essays in Economics and Econometrics, op. cit.*; 3. 'A matrix general solution of linear difference equations with constant coefficients' (with C. E. Ferguson), *Maths. Magazine*, 33, Feb.–March 1960; 4. 'The theory of cost and production in

the multi-product firm', *Em*, 29(4), Oct. 1961; 5. 'Learning and expectations in dynamic duopoly behavior' (with C. E. Ferguson), *Behavioral Science*, 7(2), April 1962; 6. 'A note on systems of simultaneous difference equations with constant coefficients', *Naval Res. Logistics Q.*, 12(3–4), Sept.–Dec. 1965; 7. 'An axiomatic approach to index numbers', *Rev. Internat. Stat. Assoc.*, 34(2), 1966; 8. 'Index number systems', *Em*, 40(5), Sept. 1972; 9. 'Profit maximization in chain retail stores', *J Ind E*, 27(1), Sept. 1978; 10. 'A biextremal principle for a behavioral theory of the firm' (with K. O. Kortanek), *Math. Modelling*, 3(6), 1982.

Principal Contributions Have attempted to act on a sincere belief that economic theory needs to be more realistic. This is taken to mean that the assumptions underlying a theory should describe reality, should be as complete as possible and should not be clearly contrary to fact. Also that the logic applied to the assumptions should be rigorous and clear. This led to an attempt to develop a more realistic prototype of the consumer by including wages, hours of work, savings and non-labour income in the utility function. It also led to a dynamic duopoly model which incorporated learning and expectations. This in turn led to an interest in difference equations as a means of analysing dynamic problems.

The desire for realism also led to research on the multiproduct firm. An inverse belief motivated research on statistical index number formulas which were viewed as realistic but lacking a theoretical basis. Research experience taught me to understand the need for a methodological basis for economics or any empirical science and gave me a continuing interest in methodology as it applies to economics. I have had the good fortune of working with several creative collaborators. I should mention especially the late C. E. Ferguson who was a more than equal partner in our joint efforts.

PHELPS, Edmund S.

Born 1933, Evanston, IL, USA.
Current Post McVickar Prof. Polit. Econ., Columbia Univ., New York City, NY, USA, 1982–.
Past Posts Ass. Instr., Yale Univ., 1958–9; Econ., Rand Corp., CA, 1959–60; Ass. Prof., Assoc. Prof., Yale Univ., 1960–2, 1963–6; Vis. Assoc. Prof., MIT, 1962–3; Prof., Univ. Penn., 1966–71; Prof., Columbia Univ., 1971–8, 1979–82; Prof., NYU, 1978–9.
Degrees BA Amherst Coll., MA, 1955; PhD Yale Univ., 1959.
Offices and Honours US SSRC Fellow, 1965–6; Fellow, Center Advanced Study Behavioral Sciences, Stanford, 1969–70; Wesley C. Mitchell Res. Prof., 1974; Guggenheim Foundation Fellow, 1978; Fellow, Em Soc, 1968, AAAS, 1980, NAS, 1982; Vice-Pres., AEA, 1983–; Pres., Atlantic Econ. Soc., 1984.
Editorial Duties Ed. Board, *AER*, 1971–3.
Principal Fields of Interest 023 Macroeconomic Theory.
Publications *Books:* 1. *Fiscal Neutrality toward Economic Growth* (McGraw-Hill, 1965); 2. *Golden Rules of Economic Growth* (W.W. Norton, 1966, N-H, 1967); 3. *Microeconomic Foundations of Employment and Inflation Theory*, co-ed. and contrib. (W.W. Norton, 1970, Macmillan, 1971); 4. *Inflation Policy and Unemployment Theory* (W. W. Norton, 1972); 5. *Economic Justice: A Reader*, ed. (Penguin, 1974); 6. *Altruism, Morality and Economic Theory*, ed. (Basic Books, Sage Fund, 1975); 7. *Studies in Macroeconomic Theory: Employment and Inflation* (Academic Press, 1979); 8. *Studies in Macroeconomic Theory: Redistribution and Growth* (Academic Press, 1980); 9. *Individual Forecasting and Aggregate Outcomes: 'Rational Expectations Examined'* (CUP, 1983); 10. *Political Economy: An Introductory Text* (W.W. Norton, 1985).
Articles: 1. 'Second essay on the golden rule of accumulation', *AER*, 55(4), Sept. 1965; 2. 'Factor-price-frontier estimation of a "vintage" production model' (with C.D. Phelps),

REStat, 48, Aug. 1966; 3. 'Inflation, expectations and economic theory', in *Inflation and the Canadian Experience*, eds. N. Swan and D. Wilton (Queen's Univ. Industrial Relations Centre, 1971); 4. 'The statistical theory of racism and sexism', *AER*, 62(5), Dec. 1972, repr. in *Human Capital Formation and Economic Development*, ed. R.A. Wykstra (Free Press, 1971), and in *Economics of Women and Work*, ed. A. Amsden (Penguin, 1979); 5. 'Some macroeconomics of population levelling', in *Proceedings of the U.S. Commission on Population Growth and the American Future*, 2 (US Govt. Printing Office, 1972); 6. 'Obstacles to curtailing inflation', in *Essays in Post-Keynesian Inflation*, eds. J. H. Gapinski and C.E. Rockwood (Ballinger, 1979); 7. 'On Okun's micro-macro system', *JEL*, 19(4), Sept. 1981; 8. 'A model of non Walrasian general equilibrium' (with G.A. Calvo), in *Macroeconomics, Prices and Quantities: Essays in Memory of Arthur M. Okun*, ed. J. Tobin (Brookings Inst., 1983); 9. 'Cracks on the demand side: a year of crisis in theoretical macroeconomics', *AER*, 72(2), May 1982; 10. 'Implicit contracts and the social contract', in *Inflation, Debt and Indexation*, eds. R. Dornbusch and M.E. Simonsen (MIT Press, 1983).

Principal Contributions I initiated the expectational formulation of macroeconomic theory, beginning with an algebraic statement of the Natural Rate Hypothesis (1968) and continuing with the earliest constructions of non-Walrasian or imperfect-information, micro-macro models of (expectational) equilibrium and disequilibrium behaviour: a model of firms' competing through their wage scales to retain experienced employees (1968), the 'island parable' of search unemployment (1969), and a model of firms' price competition in customer markets (1970). Subsequent research emphasised the durability of non-synchronicity of price and wage postings or commitments (1968, 1977, and 1978). Later research was directed to the development of a theory of contractual wage arrangements, contingent on only observable variables, arising from mobility costs and consequent moral hazard (1978, partly with G. Calvo).

My previous work, largely in the area of capital theory and growth economics, took several lines. There was the (American) discovery of the Golden Rule result, the analysis of 'vintage'-capital models of the putty-clay and putty-putty type, the study of dynamic inefficiency from excessive capital deepening, and a study of neutral fiscal policy (intertemporally balanced budget). Some of my work in the 1970s turned to other aspects of public finance. I introduced some arguments that a reduction of some tax rates in some tax brackets might actually increase the government's revenue and thus make possible a general increase of economic welfare. These were developed in a series of papers on the economics of maximum tax revenue: a model of efficient wage-income taxation (1973), a model of the best mix of tax rates on capital and labour (1975 and 1979, with J. Ordover), and a new model of the inflation tax (1974). Recent work is on exceptional disequilibrium (1983, partly with R. Frydman), on contracts, and on open-economy, customer-market models of the effects of fiscal stimuli.

PHELPS BROWN, Ernest Henry

Born 1906, Calne, Wiltshire, England.
Current Post Retired.
Past Posts Fellow, New Coll., Oxford, 1930–47; Prof. Econ. Labour, Univ. London, 1947–68.
Degrees MA Univ. Oxford, 1931; Hon. DLitt Heriot-Watt Univ., 1972.
Offices and Honours Pres., RES, 1970–2.
Principal Fields of Interest 820 Labour Markets, Public Policy.
Publications *Books:* 1. *The Framework of the Pricing System* (Chapman & Hall, 1936); 2. *The Growth of British Industrial Relations* (Macmillan, 1959, Papermac, 1965); 3. *The Economics of Labor* (Yale Univ. Press, 1962); 4. *A Century of Pay* (with M.H. Browne), (Macmillan, 1968); 5. *The Inequality of Pay* (OUP, 1977).

Articles: 1. 'The share of wages in national income' (with P.E. Hart), *EJ*, 62, June 1952; 2. 'Seven centuries of the prices of consumables, compared with builders' wage-rates' (with S.V. Hopkins), *Ec*, N.S. 23, Nov. 1956; 3. 'The meaning of the fitted Cobb-Douglas function', *QJE*, 71, Nov. 1957; 4. 'The underdevelopment of economics', *EJ*, 83, March 1972; 5. 'New wine in old bottles: reflections on the changed working of collective bargaining in Great Britain', *BJIR*, 11, Nov. 1973; 6. 'The radical reflections of an applied economist', *BNLQR*, 132, March 1980.

Principal Contributions Study of the movement of money and real wages over time; the relation between real wages and productivity in the course of economic development, and changes in population. Factors in economic development indicated by historical and comparative studies. Pay, profits and productivity in five Western economies, 1860–1960. The pay structure, social and economic influences on differentials. Industrial relations in the light of economic and social history. Contemporary incomes policy.

PHILIPPOVICH VON PHILIPPSBERG, Eugen*

Dates and Birthplace 1858–1917, Vienna, Austro-Hungary.

Posts Held Privatdozent, Univ. Vienna; Prof., Univ. Freiburg, 1885–93, Univ. Vienna, 1893–1917.

Offices and Honours Member, Upper House, Austrian parliament, 1907.

Publications *Books:* 1. *Die Bank von England im Dienste der Finanzverwaltung des Staates* (1885); 2. *Über Aufgabe und Methode der politischen Öonomie* (1886); 3. *Der Badische Staatshaushalt in den Jahren 1868–89* (1889); 4. *Grundriss der politischen Ökonomie*, 2 vols (1893–1907); 5. *Die Entwicklung der wirtschaftspolitischen Ideen im Neunzehnten Jahrhundert* (1910).

Career Early career influenced by the German Historical School, but his later leanings were toward Austrian theory. His *Grundriss . . .* was the lead-

ing German textbook on general economics for 25 years, and reconciled the ideas of the two schools. His political influence, through a group known as the Austrian Fabians, has had a considerable effect on Austrian social legislation.

Secondary Literature F.A. Hayek, 'Phillippovich von Philippsberg, Eugen', *ESS*, 12.

PHILLIPS, Alban William Housego*

Dates and Birthplace 1914–75, Te Rehunga, Dannevirke, New Zealand.

Posts Held Tooke Prof. Econ. Science and Stats., LSE, 1958–67; Prof. Econ., Res. School Social Sciences, ANU, 1967–70.

Degrees BSc, PhD Univ. London, 1949, 1952.

Offices and Honours Member, UK Inst. Electrical Engineers, 1938; Vis. Prof., MIT, 1965–6.

Publications *Articles:* 1. 'Stabilisation policy in a closed economy', *EJ*, 64, June 1954; 2. 'The relation between unemployment and the rate of change of money wage rates in the United Kingdom, 1861–1957', *Ec*, N.S. 25, Nov. 1958; 3. 'The estimation of parameters in systems of stochastic differential equations', *Biometrika*, 461, 1959; 4. 'Employment, inflation and growth', *Ec*, N.S. 29, Feb. 1962; 5. 'Estimation of systems of difference equations with moving average disturbances', Walras–Bowley Lecture, Em Soc, 1966.

Career The originator of the Phillips curve relating the rate of change of money wage rates to the level of unemployment. Pioneered the application of optimal control and control engineering techniques to econometric models. Developed econometric estimation techniques for models with autoregressive, moving average errors.

Secondary Literature L. Lancaster, 'Phillips, A. William', *IESS*, 18; C. A. Blyth, 'A. W. Phillips: 1914–75', *ER*, 51, Sept. 1975.

PIERSON, Nicolaas Gerard*

Dates and Birthplace 1839–1909, The Netherlands.

Posts Held Cotton merchant and Banker; Dir., Pres., Nederlandsche Bank, 1866, 1885–91; Prof., Univ. Amsterdam, 1877.

Offices and Honours Dutch Minister Fin., 1891–4; Prime Minister and Minister Fin., 1897–1901; Member, Dutch Second Chamber, 1905–.

Publications *Books:* 1. *Grondbeginselen der Staathuishoudkunde*, 2 vols (1875–6); 2. *Leerboek der Staathuishoudkunde*, 2 vols (1884–90); 3. *Verspreide economische Geschriften*, 6 vols (1910–11).

Career As a statesman he sought to reform the Dutch tax system according to the principle of the ability to pay — indirect taxes were reduced, and an income tax introduced. His *Leerboek* . . . was his chief publication, and places the emphasis on economics as a means for improving material welfare, rather than on pure theory. His position in Dutch economics was pre-eminent, and substantially influenced the progress of the subject in Holland.

Secondary Literature H.W.C. Bordewijk, 'Pierson, Nicolaas Gerard', *ESS*, 12.

PIGOU, Arthur Cecil*

Dates and Birthplace 1877–1959, Ryde, Isle of Wight, England.

Posts Held Lect., Fellow, Prof. Polit. Econ., King's Coll., Camb., 1901, 1902, 1908–43.

Degrees MA Univ. Camb., 1900.

Offices and Honours Adam Smith Prize, 1903; Fellow, BA, 1927.

Publications *Books:* 1. *Principles and Methods of Industrial Peace* (1905); 2. *Wealth and Welfare* (1912), subsequently *The Economics of Welfare* (1920, 1960); 3. *Unemployment* (1914); 4. *Industrial Fluctuations* (1927, 1929); 5. *A Study in Public Finance* (1928, 1956); 6. *The Theory of Unemployment* (1933); 7. *The Economics of Stationary States* (1935); 8. *Employment and Equilibrium* (1941, 1949); 9. *Keynes' 'General Theory': A Retrospective View* (1950); 10. *Essays in Economics* (1952).

Career Marshall's successor to the Cambridge chair and devoted expositor of Marshall's economics during his tenure of the chair. Pioneered welfare economics in *Wealth and Welfare*, which embodied his own concerns for justice and the protection of the interests of the poor. Singled out by Keynes in *The General Theory* as the leading advocate of the classical views which Keynes rejected, he came to accept much of Keynes's thinking in his later years. The quality of all his books is outstanding but he has only slowly won a place as an economist of first distinction.

Secondary Literature A. Robinson, 'Pigou, Arthur Cecil', *IESS*, 12; D. Collard, 'A.C. Pigou', *Pioneers of Modern Economics in Britain*, eds. D.P. O'Brien and J.R. Presley (Macmillan, 1981).

PINCUS, Jonathan James

Born 1939, Brisbane, Queensland, Australia.

Current Post Fellow, Inst. Advanced Stud., ANU, Canberra, Australia, 1984–.

Past Posts Sr. Tutor, Monash Univ., Melbourne, Australia, 1964–5; Inst., Ass. Prof., Simon Fraser Univ., Canada, 1969–72; Res. Fellow, ANU, 1972–4; Cons., Industries Assistance Comm., Canberra, 1974; Priorities Rev. Staff, Canberra, 1974–5; Vis. Assoc. Prof., Stanford Univ., 1976; Vis. Res. Assoc., Vis. Prof., Public Choice Center, VA, 1980–1, 1982–3; Vis. Fellow, Centre Pol. Stud., Monash Univ., 1980–1, 1983–4.

Degrees BA Univ. Queensland, 1964; MA, PhD Stanford Univ., 1970, 1972.

Offices and Honours Fulbright Travel Award, 1965; Canada Council Dissertation Award, 1970; Nevins Prize, 1972–3; Columbia Univ. Exec. Council, Australian Econ. Hist Assoc., 1977–82.

Editorial Duties Ed. Boards, *Australian Econ. Hist. Rev.*, 1977–82; *Explor. Econ. Hist.*, 1978–84.

Principal Fields of Interest 422 Commercial Policy; 025 Public Choice; 048 Oceanic Economic History.

Publications *Books:* 1. *Pressure Groups and Politics in Antebellum Tariffs* (Columbia Univ. Press, 1977); 2. *Government and Capitalism. Public and Private Choice in Twentieth-Century Australia* (with N.G. Butlin and A. Barnard), (A&U, 1982).

Articles: 1. 'Pressure groups and the pattern of tariffs', *JPE*, 83(4), May–June 1975; 2. 'Public and private sector employment in Australia, 1901–1974' (with A. Barnard and N.G. Butlin), *Australian Econ. Rev.*, 37(1), 1977; 3. 'Tariffs', in *Encyclopedia of American Economic History* (Scribner's Sons, 1980); 4. 'The cyclical effects of incremental export subsidies' (with E. Kleiman), *ER*, 57, June 1981; 5. 'Industry assistance' (with R.G. Gregory), in *Industrial Economics: Australian Studies* (A&U, 1982); 6. 'Regulation' (with G. A. Withers), in *Surveys of Australian Economics*, 3 (A&U, 1983); 7. 'Regulation and public enterprise', in *State Enterprise and Deregulation* (Centre Pol. Stud., 1983); 8. 'Did Australian living standards stagnate between 1890 and 1940?' (with I. W. McLean), *JEH*, 43(1), March 1983; 9. 'Railways and land values', *J. Transport Hist.*, 4(2), Sept. 1983; 10. 'Government expenditure growth and resource allocation: the nebulous connection', *OEP*, 35, Nov. 1983.

Principal Contributions Helped start the rush towards empirical models of public intervention with a study of import tariff-setting that developed the economic analysis of group behaviour within a specific historical, political and institutional setting.

PINDYCK, Robert Stephen

Born 1945, New York City, NY, USA.
Current Post Prof. Appl. Econ., MIT, Cambridge, MA, 1980–.
Past Posts Ass. Prof., Assoc. Prof., Sloan School Management, MIT, 1971–9.
Degrees BS (Electrical Eng.), MS (Electrical Eng.), PhD MIT, 1966, 1967, 1971.

Offices and Honours Pres., Assoc. Environmental and Resource Econ., 1980; Council, Fed. Amer. Scientists.
Editorial Duties Assoc. Ed., *J Ec Dyn.*, *Energy Econ.*, 1978–; Advisory Ed., *J. Energy and Devlp.*, 1980–; Ed. Board, *Energy Systems and Pol.*, 1980–.
Principal Fields of Interest 022 Microeconomic Theory; 610 Industrial Organisation and Public Policy; 720 Natural Resources.

Publications *Books:* 1. *Optimal Planning for Economic Stabilization* (N-H, 1973); 2. *The Economics of the Natural Gas Shortage, 1960–80* (with P.W. MacAvoy), (N-H, 1975); 3. *Price Controls and the Natural Gas Shortage* (with P. W. MacAvoy), (AEI, 1975); 4. *Econometric Models and Economic Forecasts* (with P.W. MacAvoy), (McGraw-Hill, 1976, 1981); 5. *Advances in the Economics of Energy and Resources*, 2 vols, ed. (JAI Press, 1979); 6. *The Structure of World Energy Demand* (MIT Press, 1979).

Articles: 1. 'Optimal policies for economic stabilization', *Em*, 41(3), May 1973; 2. 'Alternative regulatory policies for dealing with the natural gas shortage' (with P.W. MacAvoy), *Bell JE*, 4(2), Autumn, 1973; 3. 'Instruments, intermediate targets, and monetary controllability' (with S.M. Roberts), *Int ER*, 17(3), Oct. 1976; 4. 'Gains to producers from the cartelization of exhaustible resources', *REStat*, 60(2), May 1978; 5. 'Cartel pricing and the structure of the world Bauxite market', *Bell JE*, 8(2), Autumn 1977; 6. 'The optimal exploration and production of non-renewable resources', *JPE*, 86(5), Oct. 1978; 7. 'Interfuel substitution and the industrial demand for energy: an international comparison', *REStat*, 61(2), May 1979; 8. 'Uncertainty and exhaustible resource markets', *JPE*, 88(6), Dec. 1980; 9. 'The pricing of durable exhaustible resources' (with D. Levhari), *QJE*, 96(3), Aug. 1981; 10. 'Dynamic factor demands and the effects of energy price shocke' (with J. Rotemberg), *AER*, 73(5), Dec. 1983.

Principal Contributions Early work focussed on the use of control theoretic methods for the design and analysis of economic policy. This included applications to monetary policy, the design of development planning models, and the analysis of regulatory policies for individual markets. Later my work shifted to the economics of energy and natural resource markets, with a particular interest in the economics of resource exploration and the role of uncertainty. Related to this was an econometric study of sectoral energy demands, an analysis of the world oil market and the behaviour of the OPEC cartel, and studies of cartel pricing and cartel behaviour in general. I have also been interested in the relationship of energy markets to the macroeconomy, and the macroeconomic effects of sudden and drastic changes in energy prices. Finally, my most recent work has dealt with the analysis of capital investment decisions under various kinds of uncertainty, as well as the determinants of secular trends in the stock market.

PIORE, Michael J.

Born 1940, New York City, NY, USA.
Current Post Prof. Econ., Mitsui Prof. Contemporary Technology, MIT, Cambridge, MA, USA, 1975–.
Past Posts Res. Ass., US President's Council Econ. Advisers, Washington, DC, 1960, 1961; Teaching Fellow Econ., Harvard Univ., 1964–6; Res. Co-ordinator, Acting Exec. Dir., Commonwealth Puerto Rico Governors' Advisory Council, 1970–1; Ass. Prof., Labor Econ., Assoc. Prof. Econ., MIT, 1966–70, 1970–5.
Degrees BA, PhD Harvard Univ., 1962, 1966.
Offices and Honours MacArthur Prize Fellow; Hon. Woodrow Wilson Fellow, Phi Beta Kappa; John Harvard Scholar; Detur Prize; Harvard Coll. Scholar.
Principal Fields of Interest 820 Labour Markets.
Publications *Books:* 1. *Internal Labor Markets and Manpower Adjustment* (with P. Doeringer), (D. C. Heath, 1971); 2. *Birds of Passage, Migrant Labor and Industrial Societies* (CUP, 1979); 3. *Unemployment and Inflation: Institutionalist and Structural-*

ist Views, ed. (Sharpe Press, 1979); 4. *Dualism and Discontinuity in Industrial Society* (with S. Berger), (CUP, 1980); 5. *The Second Industrial Divide* (with C. Sabel), (Basic Books, 1984).
Articles: 1. 'On-the-job training and adjustment to technological change', *JHR*, 3(4), Fall 1968; 2. 'The role of immigration in industrial growth: a case study of the origins and character of Puerto Rican migration to Boston', in *The Diverse Society: Implications for Social Policy*, eds. S. J. Pastora, *et al.* (Assoc. Press, 1976); 3. 'Dualism in the labor market: a response to uncertainty and flux, case of France', *RE*, 19(1), Jan. 1978; 4. 'Qualitative research techniques in economics', *Administrative Science Q.*, 24(4), Dec. 1979; 5. 'Union and Politics', in *The Shrinking Perimeter, Unionism and Labor Relations in the Manufacturing Sector*, eds. H. A. Jarvis and M. Roomkin (D. C. Heath, 1980); 6. 'Italian small business development: lessons for US industrial policy' (with C. Sabel), in *American Industry in International Competition: Government Policies and Corporate Strategies*, eds. J. Zeisman and L. Tyson (Cornell Univ. Press, 1982).
Principal Contributions My work has focussed upon the role of institutions, technology and social processes in the structure and evolution of the labour market. It is distinguished from conventional neoclassical labour economics in that it attempts to understand the economy as embedded in the society, and economic structures as the outgrowth of historical processes. I have been influential in the development of several key labour market concepts, notably the notion of the 'internal labour market' (with Peter. B. Doeringer), the dual labour market hypothesis (with Peter B. Doeringer, David Gordon, Michael Reich and Richard Edwards), and flexible specialisation (with Charles Sabel). My most recent work with Charles Sabel attempts to understand the relationship between technology, institutional structure and macroeconomic performance. It draws heavily upon French 'théorie de la regulation'; it attaches to that theory an explicit but nondeterministic theory of

technological development, emphasising the alternatives of mass and craft production, and works out its implications for an understanding of the historical evolution of the American economic structure.

PIROU, Gaëtan*

Dates and Birthplace 1886–1945, France.
Posts Held Prof. Univ. Paris.
Offices and Honours Ed., *REP*, Chef de Cabinet to Pres., French Senate, 1927–30.
Publications *Books:* 1. *Les doctrines économiques* (1925); 2. *Introduction à l'étude de l'économie politique* (1929); 3. *Le corporatisme* (1935); 4. *La monnaie française de 1936 à 1938* (1938); 5. *L'utilité marginale de C. Menger à J. B. Clark* (1938); 6. *Traite d'économie politique* (1942).
Career Teacher of economics who introduced much foreign economic thinking to French universities. His works on general economics makes a very precise distinction between descriptive economics, theoretical economics and economic doctrine. The lack of mathematical content in his work rendered it a little behind the trend of the times but his grasp of the history of economics was broad and firm.
Secondary Literature H. S. Bloch, 'Memorial: Gaëtan Pirou', *AER*, 37(1), March 1947.

PLANT, Arnold*

Dates and Birthplace 1898–1978, London, England.
Posts Held Prof., Univ. Cape Town, S. Africa, 1923–30; Prof. Commerce, LSE, 1930–65.
Degrees BCom, BSc Univ. London, 1922, 1923.
Offices and Honours Adviser UK Comms., Raw Materials Allocation, 1940–6; knighted, 1947; Chairman, UK SSRC, 1955–62.
Publications *Books:* 1. *Selected Economic Essays and Addresses* (1974).
Career Remembered as a teacher, university administrator, official adviser, and expert on the economics of patents.

PLOTT, Charles R.

Born 1938, Frederick, OK, USA.
Current Post Prof. Econ., Dir., Program for Study of Enterprise and Public Pol., Cal. Inst. Technology, Pasadena, CA, USA.
Past Posts Ass. Prof., Assoc. Prof., Purdue Univ., IN, 1965–7, 1968–70; Vis. Prof. Econ., Stanford Univ., 1968–9; Vis. Prof. Law, Univ. S. Cal. Law Center, 1976; Vis. Prof. Econ., Univ. Chicago, 1980; Dir., Lee Pharmaceuticals, Mobile Recreation Systems, Inc.; Cons., General Motors Corp., Analytical Assessments Corp., Polinomics Res. Labs., US Fed. Trade Commission, US Civil Aeronautics Board.
Degrees BS, MS Oklahoma State Univ., 1961, 1964; PhD Univ. Virginia, 1965.
Offices and Honours Ford Foundation Fellow, 1968; Guggenheim Foundation Fellow, 1981–2; Pres., Public Choice Soc., 1976–8; Exec. Comm., SEA, 1977–8.
Editorial Duties Ed. Boards, *Social Science Res.*, 1967–7, *Public Choice*, *J Ec Behav*, 1983–.
Principal Fields of Interest 010 General Economics; 022 Microeconomics; 025 Social Choice.
Publications *Articles:* 1. 'Occupational self regulation: a case study of the Oklahoma dry cleaners', *J Law E*, 8, Oct. 1965; 2. 'A notion of equilibrium and its possibility under majority rule', *AER*, 57(4), Sept. 1967; 3. 'Some organizational influences on urban renewal decisions', *AER*, 58(2), May 1968; 4. 'Path independence, rationality and social choice', *Em*, 41, Nov. 1973; 5. 'A model of agenda influence on committee decisions' (with M. Levine), *AER*, 68(1), March 1978; 6. 'Economic theory of choice and the reference reversal phenomenon', *AER*, 69(4), Sept. 1979; 7. 'Asset valuation in an experimental market' (with R. Forsythe and T. Palfrey), *Em*, 50, May 1978; 8. 'Efficiency of experimental

security markets with insider information: an application of rational expectations models' (with S. Sunder), *JPE*, 90, Aug. 1982; 9. 'The effects of market practices in oligopolistic markets: an experimental examination of the ethyl case' (with D. M. Grether), *EI*, forthcoming, 1985.

Principal Contributions My early work focussed on the relationships between political organisation and economics. The activities of a cartel of Oklahoma dry cleaners first attracted my attention and that paper was followed by a study of political influences on urban renewal spending decisions. This interest in the nonmarket aspects of markets led naturally to the study of the mathematical properties of voting rules and theories of behaviour under alternative voting rules, game theory, etc. Questions of a welfare economic and social philosophy nature could not be avoided so the full generality of the social choice problem attracted my attention. As axiomatic social choice theory became theoretically connected to game theory one could easily generate an overabundance of competing theories about the behaviour of political and economic processes. An insight about how one might study a voting situation in an experimental setting and thereby eliminate some of the competing ideas caused me to turn my attention to experimental methods. The experimental methods used to study voting could be applied with equal force to markets, public goods, and externality situations. The fascination with experimental methods as a basic research tool and as a policy tool has continued to occupy my attention.

PLOURDE, Charles Gordon

Born 1938, Owen Sound, Ont., Canada

Current Post Assoc. Prof. Econ., York Univ., Toronto, Canada, 1977–.

Past Posts Instr. Maths., Queens Univ., Kingston, Ont., 1963–5; Ass. Prof. Econ., Univ. W. Ontario, London, Ont., 1969–76; Vis. Scholar, Concordia Univ., Montreal, 1979; Vis.

Assoc. Prof., Univ. Waterloo, Waterloo, Ont., 1983.

Degrees BA, MA (Maths.) Queens Univ., Kingston, Canada, 1959, 1965; PhD Univ. Minn., 1970.

Offices and Honours Amelia Erhardt Fellow, 1967; Canada SSHRC Fellow, 1966, 1973, 1983.

Principal Fields of Interest 721 Natural Resources; 722 Conservation and Pollution; 022 Microeconomic Theory.

Publications *Books:* 1. *Fisheries Management and Employment in the Newfoundland Economy* (with S. Ferris), (Econ. Council Canada, 1980).

Articles: 1. 'A simple model of replenishable natural resource exploitation', *AER*, 60(3), June 1970, repr. in *Umwelt und wirtschaftliche Entwicklung*, ed. H. Siebert (Wege der Forschung, 1977); 2. 'Exploitation of common-property replenishable natural resources', *WEJ*, 9(3), Sept. 1971, repr. in *Economics of Natural and Environmental Resources*, ed. V. Smith (Gordon & Breach, 1974); 3. 'A model of waste accumulation and disposal', *CJE*, 5(1), Feb. 1972; 4. 'Conservation of extinguishable species', *Natural Resources J.*, Oct. 1975; 5. 'A theory of demand for public characteristics', *Eastern Econ. J.*, April 1976; 6. 'Diagrammatic representation of the exploitation of replenishable natural resources: dynamic iterations', *JEEM*, 6, 1979; 7. 'Seasonal unemployment insurance, crop-sharing contracts and the Newfoundland inshore fisheries' (with S. Ferris), *CJE*, 15(4), Aug. 1982; 8. 'Uncertainty in fisheries management: the role of the discount rate' (with R. Bodell), *J. Marine Econ.*, 1(2), March 1984.

Principal Contributions My early research concentrated on the problems related to the optimal management of dynamic, replenishable natural resources. These include fisheries, forests and common property, unappropriated natural reservoirs, such as air and watersheds which may become polluted or abused. Management policy was directed toward providing quotas or rules for individual agents and optimal taxation. This direction of analysis was applied to a specific cod fishery in Newfoundland where the hypothesis that unemployment benefits were attracting excess employment into the fishery was tested. Although I have maintained an ongoing interest in the practical management of replenishable natural resources, my main interest at present involves the various aspects of uncertainty in the area. Of particular interest is the inability to collect data on sizes of fish stocks and hence problems in estimating production functions. (Most fishery management analysis assumes known cost or production functions.) One interesting manifestation of this stock uncertainty is the inefficiency of wage contracts in fishing and the development of crop-sharing arrangements.

POLACHEK, Solomon William

Born 1945, Washington, DC, USA.
Current Post Prof. Econ., State Univ. NY Binghamton, NY, 1983–.
Past Posts Preceptor, Nat. Planning Assoc., Washington, DC, 1966–70; Preceptor Econ., Columbia Univ., 1971–3; Ass. Prof., Assoc. Prof. Econ., Ford Foundation Vis. Faculty Fellow, Univ. N. Carolina, 1973–83.
Degrees BA George Washington Univ., 1967; PhD Columbia Univ., 1973.
Offices and Honours Earhart Foundation Fellow, 1968–9; Pres. Fellow, Columbia Univ., 1969–72; Post-doctoral Fellow, Univ. Chicago, 1972–3; Scholar, Carolina Pop. Center, 1977–8; Nat. Fellow, Hoover Inst., Stanford Univ., 1979–80.
Principal Fields of Interest 850 Human Capital; 841 Demographic Economics.
Publications *Articles:* 1. 'Family investments in human capital: earnings of women' (with J. Mincer), *JPE*, pt. 2, 82(2), March–April 1974, repr. in *Family Economics: Marriage, Human Capital, and Fertility*, ed. T. W. Schultz (Univ. Chicago Press, 1974), and *The Economics of Women and Work*, ed. A. Amsden (St Martin's Press, 1980); 2. 'Potential biases in measuring male-female discrimination', *JHE*, 10(2), Spring 1975; 3. 'A life cycle approach to

migration: analysis of the perspicacious peregrinator' (with F. Horvath), in *Research in Labor Economics*, ed. R. Ehrenberg (JAI Press, 1977); 4. 'The rate of return to schooling and the business cycle' (with T. J. Kniesner and A. H. Padilla), *JHE*, 13(2), Spring 1978; 5. 'Educational production functions: a microeconomic approach' (with T. Kniesner and H. Harwood), *J. Educ. Stats.*, Autumn 1978, repr. in *Research on Teaching College Economics: Selected Readings*, eds. R. Fels and J. J. Siegfried (Joint Council Econ. Educ., 1982); 6. 'Simultaneous equations models of sex discrimination', in *Income Inequality: Trends and International Comparisons*, ed. J. Morony (D. C. Heath, 1977); 7. 'Economics of discrimination', in *Encyclopedia of Economics*, ed. D. Greenwald (McGraw-Hill, 1983); 8. 'Occupational self-selection: a human capital approach to sex differences in occupational structure', *REStat*, 63(1), Feb. 1981; 9. 'Discrimination: fact or fiction? An examination using an alternative approach' (with R. F. Kamalich), *SEJ*, 49(2), Oct. 1982; 10. 'Occupational segregation: a defense of human capital predictions', *JHR*, forthcoming, 1985.

POLAK, Jacques Jacobus

Born 1914, Rotterdam, The Netherlands.
Current Post Exec. Dir., IMF, Cyprus, Israel, The Netherlands, Romania, Yugoslavia, Washington, DC, 1981–.
Past Posts Econ., League of Nations, Geneva, Switzerland, 1937–40, Princeton, NJ, 1940–3, Netherlands Embassy, Washington, DC, 1944–6; Division Chief, Ass. Dir., Dep. Dir., Dir. Res. Dept., Econ. Counsellor, IMF, 1947–9, 1949–52, 1952–8, 1958–9, 1966–79; Cons., IBRD, 1980; Vis. Prof., Johns Hopkins Univ., 1949–50, George Washington Univ., 1950–5.
Degrees MA, PhD Univ. Amsterdam, 1936, 1937; PhD (Hon.) Erasmus Univ., Rotterdam, 1972.
Offices and Honours Fellow, Em Soc, 1949–50.
Principal Fields of Interest 431 Bal-

ance of Payments: Mechanisms of Adjustment; Exchange Rates; 432 International Monetary Arrangements; 134 Inflation and Deflation.

Publications *Books:* 1. *Publieke Werken als vorm van Conjunctuurpolitiek* (Martinus Nijhoff, 1937); 2. *The National Income of the Netherlands Indies, 1921–1939* (mimeo, 1943), repr. in *Changing Economy in Indonesia*, ed. P. Creutzberg (Martinus Nijhoff, 1979); 3. *The Dynamics of Business Cycles* (with J. Tinbergen), (Univ. Chicago Press, CUP, 1950; 4. *An International Economic System* (Univ. Chicago Press, A&U, 1954); 5. *Some Reflections on the Nature of Special Drawing Rights* (IMF, 1971); 6. *The New International Monetary System*, co-ed. (with R. A. Mundell), (Columbia Univ. Press, 1977); 7. *Thoughts on an International Monetary Fund Based Fully on the SDR* (IMF, 1979).

Articles: 1. 'The international propagation of business cycles', *REStud*, 6, April 1939; 2. 'Balance of payments problems of countries reconstructing with the help of foreign loans', *QJE*, 57, Feb. 1943, repr. in *Readings in the Theory of International Trade*, eds. H. S. Ellis and L. A. Metzler (Blakiston, 1950); 3. 'European exchange depreciation in the early twenties', *Em*, 11, April 1943; 4. 'Monetary analysis of income formation and payments problems', in *The Monetary Approach to the Balance of Payments, IMF Staff Papers*, 6, Nov. 1957; 5. 'Money-national and international', in *Essays in Honour of Thorkis Kristensen* (OECD, 1970); 6. 'The role of the international monetary fund', in *Problems of the International Monetary System, Forty Years after Bretton Woods* (Fed. Reserve Bank Boston, 1984).

Principal Contributions My doctoral dissertation and my initial work dealt with business cycles, including assisting Tinbergen in his 1939 League of Nations model on the US economy. From there I moved toward international business-cycle aspects and other aspects of the international system. My subsequent work in the IMF required a consolidation of monetary analysis with multiplier analysis and the theory of the balance of payments. This had been touched upon

in Article No. 1 above and was given a reasonably satisfactory resolution in my book, *An International Economic System*, which has found widespread application, in the Fund and elsewhere. The design of the Special Drawing Rights began to occupy me in the mid–1960s. Broader issues relating to the role of the fund and international economic policy in general are taken up in more recent work, such as Article No. 6 above and my 1979 IMF pamphlet.

POLENSKE, Karen Rosel

Born 1937, Lewiston, IN, USA.

Current Post Prof. Regional Polit. Econ. and Planning, MIT, Camb., MA, USA, 1981–.

Past Posts Instr., Lect., Res. Assoc., Harvard Univ., 1966–8, 1969–70, 1966–72; Sr. Vis., King's Coll. Camb., 1970–1; Assoc. Prof. Urban Stud. and Planning, MIT, 1972–81; Fellow, Netherlands Inst. Advanced Study, 1980; S. W. Brooks Vis. Lect., Univ. Queensland, 1983.

Degrees BA Oregon State Univ., 1959; MA (Public Admin. and Econ.) Maxwell School, Syracuse Univ., 1961; PhD Harvard Univ., 1966.

Editorial Duties Ed. Boards, *J. Pol. Modeling*, 1979–83, *Rev. Regional Stud.*, 1981–.

Principal Fields of Interest 110 Economic Growth, Development and Planning Theory and Policy; 210 Econometric, Statistical and Mathematical Methods and Models; 940 Regional Economics.

Publications *Books:* 1. *State Estimates of the Gross National Product: 1947, 1958, 1963* (with others), (D. C. Heath, 1972); 2. *Multiregional Input-Output Analysis*, 3 vols, ed. (D. C. Heath, 1972, 1972 and 1973); 3. *State Estimates of Technology, 1963* (with others), (D. C. Heath, 1974); 4. *Advances in Input-Output Analysis*, co-ed. (with J. V. Skolka), (Ballinger, 1976); 5. *The US Multiregional Input-Output Accounts and Model* (D. C. Heath, 1980).

Articles: 1. 'Empirical implementation of a multiregional input-output gravity trade model', in *Contributions to Input-Output Analysis*, eds. A. P. Carter and A. Brody (N-H, 1969); 2. 'An empirical test of interregional input-output models: estimation of 1963 Japanese production', *AER*, 60(2), May 1970; 3. 'An analysis of the US commodity freight shipments', in *Planning Over Time and Space*, eds. G. G. Judge and T. Takaya (N-H, 1973); 4. 'The implementation of a multiregional input-output model for the United States', in *Input- Output Techniques*, eds. A. Brody and A. P. Carter (N-H, 1972); 5. 'Multiregional interactions between energy and transportation', in *Advances in Input-Output Analysis, op. cit.*; 6. 'Energy analyses and the determination of multi-regional prices', *Papers Regional Science Assoc.*, 43, 1979; 7. 'Output, income, and employment input-output multipliers' (with D. Di Pasquale), in *Impact Analysis: Methodology and Applications*, ed. S. Pleeter (Martinus Nijhoff, 1980); 8. 'Regional methods of analysis for stagnating regions', in *Lectures on Regional Stagnation*, eds. W. Buhr and P. Friedrich (NOMOS, 1981); 9. 'Constructing and implementing multiregional models for the study of distributional impacts', in *International Use of Input-Output Analysis*, ed. R. Stäglin (Vandenhoeck & Ruprecht, 1982); 10. 'Growth-pole theory and strategy reconsidered: domination, linkages, and distribution', in *Societies, Boundaries, Regions*, eds. A. Kuklinski and J. G. Lambooy (Moulton/Walter de Gruyter, 1984).

Principal Contributions Twenty years ago my interest in regional economic development became focussed on the analysis of regional economic disparities. I have pioneered in the development for the US of a regional accounting framework comparable to that used at the national level for the analysis of changes in the gross national product. My specific contribution to the field of regional planning has been threefold: (1) the development of a method for constructing a comprehensive set of multi-regional accounts (2) the actual estimation of a set of multi-regional accounts for the US; and (3) the application of the general multi-regional accounting framework to policy issues both in the US and abroad. One of my most valuable contributions to the field has been a description of the conceptual framework and data-estimation procedures required to construct multi-regional accounts. This information was published in a series of six volumes. The sixth volume, *The U.S. Multi-regional Input-Output Accounts and Model*, provides a systematic presentation of the entire theoretical framework of the multi-regional accounts and model as well as a summary of the procedures and data sources used for assembling the accounts. The creative aspect of the work on the basic multi-regional accounts and model is over; they are being used on a day-by-day basis. I am therefore embarking on two new but related areas of research. The first is the development of a technique for quick retrieval of up-to-date information that can be incorporated year by year into a general multi-regional accounting framework. The second is an extension of the initial multi-regional accounting framework to include information on capital, both financial and physical.

POLINSKY, Mitchell A.

Born 1948, St Louis, MO, USA.
Current Post Prof. Law, Assoc. Prof. Econ., Stanford Univ., Res. Assoc., NBER, 1979–.
Past Posts Ass. Prof. Econ., Harvard Univ, 1973–9; Russell Sage Foundation Res. Law and Social Science, Yale Law School, 1975–6, Harvard Law School, 1976–7; Ass. Prof. Law & Econ., Harvard Law School, 1977–9.
Degrees BA Harvard Univ., 1970; PhD MIT, 1973; MSL Yale Law School, 1976.
Offices and Honours Allyn A. Young Prize Econ., Harvard Univ., 1970; Woodrow Wilson Foundation Hon. Fellow, NSF Grad. Fellow, MIT, 1970–1, 1970–3; Hon. Mention, NTA-TIA Outstanding Doctoral Dissertation Awards Program, 1973; Member, Law and Social Sciences Advisory Sub-comm., NSF, 1980–2.
Editorial Duties Ed. Boards, *Supreme Court Econ. Rev.*, *Yale J. Law, Econ. and Organization*.
Principal Fields of Interest 916 Economics of Crime; 610 Industrial

Organisation and Public Policy; 024 Welfare Theory.

Publications *Books:* 1. *An Introduction to Law and Economics* (Little, Brown, 1983).
Articles: 1. 'The optimal tradeoff between the probability and magnitude of fines' (with S. Shavell), *AER*, 69(5), Dec. 1979; 2. 'Private versus public enforcement of fines', *J Legal Stud.*, 9(1), Jan. 1980; 3. 'On the choice between property rules and liability rules', *EI*, 18(2), April 1980; 4. 'Strict liability vs. negligence in a market setting', *AER*, 70(2), May 1980; 5. 'Resolving nuisance disputes: the simple economics of injunctive and damage remedies', *Stanford Law Rev.*, 32(6), July 1980; 6. 'Contribution and claim reduction among antitrust defendants: an economic analysis' (with S. Shavell), *Stanford Law Rev.*, 33(3), Feb. 1981; 7. 'Pigovian taxation with administrative costs' (with S. Shavell), *J Pub E*, 19(3), Dec. 1982; 8. 'Risk sharing through breach of contract remedies', *J. Legal Stud.*, 12(2), June 1983; 9. 'Products liability, consumer misperceptions, and market power' (with W. P. Rogerson), *Bell JE*, 14(2), Autumn 1983.

Principal Contributions My early work was concerned with issues of urban economics, including local public sector economics and housing demand analysis. After attending Yale Law School, 1975–6, my research shifted to the so-called 'new law and economics'. Within this area, my principal interest is the economics of enforcement, broadly defined. For example, I am concerned with whether antitrust laws should be enforced by private individuals using the treble damage remedy or by public regulators using fines and imprisonment as threats. Similar questions arise in the control of pollution, product quality, and tax evasion, other substantive areas of interest to me. Much of my research in this area is summarised in a nontechnical way in my textbook, *An Introduction to Law and Economics*.

POLLAK, Robert A.

Born 1938, New York City, NY, USA.
Current Post Charles and William Day Prof. Econ. and Social Sciences, Univ. Penn., Philadelphia, PA, USA, 1972–.
Past Posts Ass. Prof. Econ., Univ. Penn., 1964–8; Econ., US Bureau Labor Stats., Washington, DC, 1968–9; Assoc. Prof. Econ., Univ. Penn., 1968–79.
Degrees BA Amherst Coll., MA, 1960; PhD MIT, 1964.
Offices and Honours Phi Beta Kappa, 1960; Fellow, Em Soc, 1977.
Editorial Duties Ed., *Int ER*, 1976–.
Principal Fields of Interest 022 Microeconomic Theory; 025 Social Choice; 921 Consumer Economics; Levels and Standards of Living.
Publications *Articles*: 1. 'Estimation of the linear expenditure system' (with J. Wales), *Em*, 37(4), Oct. 1969; 2. 'Generalized separability', *Em*, 40(3), May 1972; 3. 'The relevance of the household production function and its implications for the allocation of time' (with M. L. Wachter), *JPE*, 83(2), April 1975; 4. 'Endogenous tastes in demand and welfare analysis', *AER*, 68(2), May 1978; 5. 'Estimation of complete demand systems from household budget data: the linear and quadratic expenditure system' (with T. J. Wales), *AER*, 68(3), June 1978; 6. 'Towards a more general model of fertility determination: endogenous preferences and natural fertility' (with R. A. Easterlin and M. L. Wachter), in *Population and Economic Change in Less Developed Countries*, ed. R. A. Easterlin (Univ. Chicago Press, 1980); 7. 'The social cost of living index', *J Pub E*, 15(2), June 1981; 8. 'Parental preferences and provision for progeny' (with J. R. Behrman and P. Taubman), *JPE*, 90(1), Feb. 1982; 9. 'Acyclic collective choice rules' (with D. H. Blair), *Em*, 50(4), July 1982; 10. 'Rational collective choice' (with D. H. Blair), *Scientific Amer.*, 249(2), Aug. 1983.

Principal Contributions My research on household behaviour has been shaped by the belief that economic theory can and should provide a framework for empirical analysis. Four threads run through this work, much of it joint with Terence J. Wales. (1) Household budget data: Pollak and Wales (1978) established that, contrary to popular assumption, interesting demand systems such as the LES and QES are identified by as few as two budget studies despite the limited price variability in such data. (2) Demographic effects: I have developed new procedures for incorporating demographic variables such as family size into empirical demand analysis (e.g. demographic translating) and challenged the welfare interpretation of such equivalence scales, arguing that one must distinguish between conditional and unconditional scales. (3) Functional forms: I have developed new forms for empirical demand analysis and new classes of functional forms (generalised separability, additive utility functions and linear Engel curves, and systems quadratic in expenditure). (4) Dynamic specifications: empirical demand analysis must either assume that demand system parameters remain constant or specify how they change with time or past consumption; I have proposed and estimated various dynamic specifications — the statistical superiority of dynamic over static specifications (the common empirical finding) might reflect misspecification or taste change.

I have developed the distinction between 'rational' and 'myopic' habit formation and examined the implications of endogenous preferences for welfare analysis, arguing again that one must distinguish between conditional and unconditional preferences. In collaboration with Jere Behrman and Paul Taubman, I have developed and estimated a 'preference model' of intrafamily resource allocation as an alternative to the standard 'investment model' of human capital theory. I have developed cost-of-living index theory in directions relevant to index number construction (e.g. subindexes, intertemporal indexes, group or social indexes, the treatment of quality). In collaboration with Douglas Blair, I have characterised the class of social choice rules satisfying the Arrow axioms and acyclicity, and argued that acyclicity is the appropriate rationality condition. We show that every such rule must contain a 'vetoer', someone who can veto almost all pairs of alternatives.

POMERY, John Geoffrey

Born 1946, Bournemouth, Hampshire, England.
Current Post Assoc. Prof. Econ., Purdue Univ., W. Lafayette, IN, USA, 1982–.
Past Posts Instr., Ass. Prof., Rice Univ., Houston, TX, 1974–7, 1977–9; Vis. Ass. Prof., Ass. Prof., Northwestern Univ., 1978–9, 1979–82.
Degrees BA (Philo., Polit. & Econ.) Oxford Univ., 1968; MA Univ. Essex, 1970; MA, PhD Univ. Rochester, 1972, 1977.
Principal Fields of Interest 410 International Trade Theory; 020 General Economic Theory.
Publications *Books:* 1. *International Trade and Uncertainty: Simple General Equilibrium Models Involving Randomness* (Garland Publ., 1984).
Articles: 1. 'Uncertainty and international trade', in *International Economic Policy: Theory and Evidence*, eds. R. Dornbusch and J. A. Frenkel (JHUP, 1979); 2. 'Restricted stock markets in simple general equilibrium models with production uncertainty', *J Int E*, 15(3–4), Nov. 1983; 3. 'Uncertainty in trade models', in *Handbook of International Economics, 1*, eds. R. W. Jones and P. B. Kenen (N-H, 1984).
Principal Contributions My initial research involved modelling international exchange in a technologically-uncertain environment using the standard Arrow-Pratt portfolio theory. By emphasising trade in assets with random returns, rather than trade in physical goods, this provided an alternative perspective to the earlier literature (which implicitly treated trade in physical goods as central). My 1983 paper contributes to literature integrating the two perspectives; see also my two survey papers.

My current interests include the implications for international trade theory of implicit uncertainty about behaviour of other economic agents (as well as technological uncertainty). Such an issue cannot arise within a narrow definition of perfectly competitive trade. However, the growth (outside the international trade field) of research focussing on contracts, incentives, property rights, repeated games, etc., plus the greater role (within trade theory) of models of imperfect competition and strategically endogenous government intervention, etc., invite a deeper concern over the potential role of, for example, nation-specific social norms in relation to topics such as comparative advantage, trade dependency, and trade-related intervention.

PONSARD, Claude

Born 1927, Dijon, France.
Current Post Prof., Univ. Dijon, Dijon, France, 1963–.
Past Posts Attaché de recherches, CNRS, 1950–4; Chargé de Mission, INSEE, Paris, 1950–8; Chargé de cours, Faculté de Droit et des Sciences Econ., Univ. Nancy, 1954–8; Prof., Faculté de Droit et des Sciences Econ., Univ. Lyon, 1958–63.
Degrees Dr Univ. Dijon, 1953; Diplôme, Ecole Pratique des Hautes Etudes, Sorbonne, Paris, 1957; Agrégé Paris, 1958.
Offices and Honours Vouters Prize, 1954; Dir., Inst. Econ. Maths., 1969–; Chevalier, Legion d'Honneur, 1980; Ordre National du Mérite, 1971; Officier, Ordre des Palmes Académiques, 1976.
Editorial Duties Ed. Boards, *REP, Internat. J Fuzzy Sets and Systems, Sistemi Urbani.*
Principal Fields of Interest 030 History of Economic Thought; 231 Mathematical Methods and Models; 731 Economic Geography.
Publications *Books:* 1. *Economie et espace* (SEDES, 1955); 2. *Histoire des théories économiques spatiales* (Armand Colin, 1958; transl., English, Springer Verlag, 1983); 3. *Un modèle topologique d'équilibre économique interrégional* (Dunod, 1969); 4. *Une révision de la théorie des aimes de marché* (Sirey, 1974).

Articles: 1. 'Hierarchie des places centrales et graphes phi-flous', *Environment and Planning*, A, 9, 1977; 2. 'Economie urbaine et espaces métriques', *Sistemi Urbani*, 1(1), 1979; 3. 'An application of fuzzy subsets theory to the analysis of the consumer's spatial preferences', *Internat. J. Fuzzy Sets and Systems*, 5(3), 1981; 4. 'L'équilibre spatial du consommateur dans un contexte imprécis', *Sistemi Urbani*, 3(1), 1981; 5. 'Partial spatial equilibria with fuzzy constraints', *J Reg S*, 22(2), 1982; 6. 'Producer's spatial equilibrium with a fuzzy constraint', *Europ. J OR.*, 10(3), 1982; 7. 'A theory of spatial general equilibrium in a fuzzy economy', *Document de Travail I.M.E.*, 65, 1984.
Principal Contributions First works were attempts to integrate space in economic analysis. Subsequently moved away towards formal representations of space and their analytical implications: application of graphs and networks theory and general topology in spatial economic theory. More recently, research has been devoted to the statement of a fuzzy economic spaces theory. Mathematical tools are fuzzy subsets theory and their applications. The results are several contributions on imprecise economic universes and soft economic behaviour under fuzzy constraints (spatial partial equilibria and general equilibrium). Much of my work has been devoted to the history of spatial economic theory.

PORTES, Richard David

Born 1941, Chicago, IL, USA.
Current Post Prof. Econ., Birkbeck Coll., Univ. London, 1972–; Dir., Centre Econ. Pol. Res., London, England, 1983–.
Past Posts Fellow, Tutor Econ., Balliol Coll. Oxford, 1965–9; Ass. Prof. Econ. Internat. Affairs, Princeton Univ., 1969–72; Hon. Res. Fellow, Univ. Coll. London, 1971–2; Vis. Res. Prof., Inst. Internat. Econ. Stud., Univ. Stockholm, 1973, 1974, 1976, 1978; Vis. Prof. Econ., Harvard Univ., 1977–8; Dir. d'Etudes Associés, Ecole

des Hautes Etudes en Sciences Sociales, Paris, 1978–.

Degrees BA (Maths., Philo.), Yale Univ., 1962; MA, DPhil. Univ. Oxford, 1965, 1969.

Offices and Honours Rhodes Scholar, 1962–5; Woodrow Wilson Fellow, 1962; Guggenheim Foundation Fellow, 1977–8; Econ. Affairs Comm., Vice-Chairman, UK SSRC, 1980–; Res. Assoc., NBER, 1980; Fellow, Em Soc, 1983–.

Editorial Duties Ed. Boards, *REStud, 1967–9, 1972–80, Appl. Econ.*, 1973–, *J Comp E*, 1980–, *Econ. Modelling*, 1982–; Foreign Ed., *REStud*, 1969–72.

Principal Fields of Interest 123 Comparative Economic Studies; 052 Socialist and Communist Economic Systems; 023 Macroeconomic Theory.

Publications *Books:* 1. *Planning and Marketing Relations*, co-ed. (with M. Kaser), (Macmillan, 1971); 2. *The Polish Crisis: Western Economic Policy Options* (Royal Inst. Internat. Affairs, 1981); 3. *Deficits and Detente* (Twentieth-Century Fund, 1983).

Articles: 1. 'The enterprise under central planning', *REStud*, 36, April, 1969; 2. 'The strategy and tactics of economic decentralisation', *Soviet Stud.*, 23(4), April 1972; 3. 'The control of inflation: lessons from East European experience', *Ec*, N.S. 44, May 1977, repr. in *Comparative Economic Systems*, ed. M. Bornstein (Richard D. Irwin, 1978); 4. 'Macroeconomic models with quantity rationing' (with J. Muellbauer), *EJ*, 88, Dec. 1978; 5. 'Disequilibrium estimates for consumption goods markets in centrally planned economies' (with D. Winter), *REStud*, 47(1), Jan. 1980; 6. 'Internal and external balance in a centrally planned economy', *J Comp E*, 3, Dec. 1979; 7. 'Effects of the world economic crisis on the East European Economies', *World Economy* 3, June 1980, repr. in *International Economic Policies and Their Theoretical Foundations*, ed. J. M. Letiche (Harcourt Brace, Academic Press, 1982); 8. 'Macroeconomic equilibrium & disequilibrium in centrally planned economies', *EI*, 19(4), Oct. 1981; 9. 'Central planning & monetarism: fellow travellers?', in *Marxism, Planning & the Soviet Economy*, ed. P. Desai (MIT Press, 1983); 10. 'Planning the consumption goods market: preliminary disequilibrium results for Poland 1955–80' (with D. Quandt, D. Winter and S. Yeo), in *Contemporary Macroeconomic Modelling*, eds. P. Malgrange and P. A. Muet (Blackwell, 1984).

Principal Contributions Analysis of enterprise behaviour under central planning; developing macroeconomic theory of closed and open centrally planned economies; macroeconometrics of labour market, consumption goods market and foreign trade under central planning; assessment of economic reforms in CPEs and of East-West economic and financial relations; analysis of macroeconomic models with quantity rationing and inventories; and hypothesis testing with disequilibrium estimation methods.

POSNER, Richard A.

Born 1939, USA.

Current Post Judge, US Court Appeals Seventh Circuit; Sr. Lect., Univ. Chicago Law School, 1983–.

Degrees BA Yale Univ., 1959; LLB Harvard Univ., 1962.

Offices and Honours Member, Amer. Law Inst., Amer. Bar Assoc., AAAS.

Principal Fields of Interest 010 General Economics.

Publications *Books:* 1. *Economic Analysis of Law* (Little, Brown, 1973, 1977); 2. *Antitrust Law: An Economic Perspective* (Univ. Chicago Press, 1976); 3. *The Economics of Justice* (Harvard Univ. Press, 1981).

Articles: 1. 'Taxation by regulation', *Bell JE*, 2(1), Spring 1971; 2. 'A theory of negligence', *J. Legal Stud.*, 1(1), Jan. 1972; 3. 'The social costs of monopoly and regulation', *JPE*, 83(4), Aug. 1975.

Principal Contributions Use of economic theory to explain the common law; economic analysis of antitrust law; and economic analysis of the State.

POSTLETHWAYT, Malachy*

Dates and Birthplace 1707–67, England.
Posts Held Businessman.
Publications *Books:* 1. *The African Trade* (1745); 2. *The National and Private Advantage of the African Trade Considered* (1746); 3. *The Universal Dictionary of Trade and Commerce* (1751); 4. *Great Britain's True System* (1757).
Career Writer on British trade, and the means for improving it, who is chiefly remarkable for the way in which his books conveyed, without acknowledgement, Cantillon's unknown ideas to a British readership. *The Universal Dictionary* . . . , though in large part a translation from the French of Savary des Bruslons, was a successful compendium of practical information for eighteenth-century merchants.
Secondary Literature E. A. J. Johnson, 'Malachy Postlethwayt', in *Predecessors of Adam Smith* (Prentice-Hall, 1937).

POSTLEWAITE, Andrew William

Born 1943, Harvey, IL, USA.
Current Post Prof. Econ., Fin. and Public Management, Univ. Penn., Philadephia, PA, USA, 1982–.
Past Posts Res. Fellow, CORE, Univ. Louvain, 1973–4; Ass. Prof., Assoc. Prof., Univ. Illinois, Urbana, 1974–5; Vis. Prof. Econ., Univ. Cal. San Diego, CA, 1976; Vis. Assoc. Prof., Princeton Univ., 1979–80; Prof. Public Management, Univ. Penn., 1980–2.
Degrees BA Illinois Wesleyan Univ., 1965; PhD Northwestern Univ., 1974.
Offices and Honours Res. Fellow, Univ. Illinois, 1973–4, Inst. Advanced Study, Hebrew Univ., 1983, Inst. Maths and Its Applications, Univ. Minn., 1983.
Editorial Duties Assoc. Ed., *JET*, 1981–.
Principal Fields of Interest 020 Economic Theory; 320 Public Finance; 610 Industrial Organisation and Public Policy.
Publications *Articles*: 1. 'Disadvantageous syndicates' (with R. Rosenthal),

JET, 9(3), Nov. 1974; 2. 'The incentives for price-taking behavior in large exchange economies' (with D. J. Roberts), *Em*, 44(1), Jan. 1976; 3. 'Weak versus strong domination in a market with indivisible goods' (with A. Roth), *J. Math. Econ.*, 4(2), Aug. 1977; 4. 'Disadvantageous monopolies and disadvantageous endowments' (with J. Drèze and J. Gabszewicz), *JET*, 16(1), Oct. 1977; 5. 'A note on the stability of large cartels' (with D. J. Roberts), *Em*, 45(8), Nov. 1977; 6. 'Approximate efficiency of non-Walrasian Nash equilibria' (with D. Schmeidler), *Em*, 46(1), Jan. 1978; 7. 'Barriers to trade and disadvantageous middlemen: nonmonotonicity of the core' (with E. Kalai and J. Roberts), *JET*, 19(1), Oct. 1978; 8. 'A group incentive compatible mechanism yielding core allocations' (with E. Kalai and J. Roberts), *JET*, 20(1), Feb. 1979; 9. 'Manipulation via endowments', *REStud*, 46, April 1979; 10. 'Oligopoly and competition in large markets' (with M. Okuno and J. Roberts), *AER*, 70(1), March 1980.
Principal Contributions My work has concentrated on strategic behaviour in economic models, primarily general equilibrium models. The work has focussed on the theoretical limits of organisational design and performance, where organisations are modelled as games in strategic form and performance is taken to be the game theoretic solution (Nash, Dominant, Bayesian Nash) to these games.

PREBISCH, Raúl

Born 1901, Tucumán, Argentina.
Current Post Dir., CEPAL Rev., UNECLA, Santiago, Chile, 1976–.
Past Posts Exec. Secretary, UNECLA, 1950–63; Secretary-General, UNCTAD, 1963–9.
Degrees BA (Econ.) Univ. Buenos Aires; Hon. degrees; Univs. Colombia Los Andes, Colombia; Penjab, India; Bar Ilan, Israel; Complutense, Spain; Montevideo, Uruguay.
Offices and Honours Jawaharlal Nehru Award Internat. Understanding, 1974; Dag Hammarskjold Hon.

Medal German UN Assoc., 1977; Third World Prize, Third World Foundation, 1981.

Principal Fields of Interest 112 Economic Development Models.

Publications *Books:* 1. *Introducción a Keynes*, ed. (Fondo de Cultura, Económica, 1947); 2. *Una Nueva Política Commercial para el Desarrollo* (Fondo de Cultura Económica, 1964); 3. *Transformación y Desarrollo* (Fondo de Cultura Económica, 1965); 4. *Interpretación del Proceso de Desarrollo Latino-Americano en 1949*, UN Serie conmemorativa del XXV Aniversario de la CEPAL, Santiago (UN, 1973), and in *Estudio Económico de América Latina, 1949* (Fondo de Cultura Económica, 1950); 5. *Capitalismo Periferico. Crisis y Transformación* (Fondo de Cultura Económica, 1981).

Articles: 1. 'Commercial policy in the underdeveloped countries', *AER*, 49(2), May 1959; 2. 'El desarrollo económico della América Latina y algunos de sus principales problemas', *Boletín Econ. Amér. Latina*, 7(1), Feb. 1962.

Principal Contributions The development of the countries of the world economic periphery, particularly those of Latin America, both in the field of theory and in that of the implementation of ideas. In theory, propounded original interpretations respecting relations between the industrial centres and the periphery and the specific internal processes which characterise the development of the latter; proposals for action have had great influence, in particular those relating to the creation of the New International Economic Order.

PREOBRAZHENSKI, Evgeni*

Dates and Birthplace 1886–1937, Russia.

Publications *Books:* 1. *The New Economics* (1926, 1965); 2. *Zakat Kapitalizma* (Russian), (1931); 3. *The Crisis of Soviet Industrialization: Selected Essays*, ed. D. A. Filtzer (1979).

Career Participant in the Soviet economic debate of the late 1920s. He was a leading spokesman of the left-wing opposition, and his writings, though often concerned with particular current issues contain insights of high quality. His starting point was the 'goods famine' of 1925 which he explained in terms of fundamental flaws in the running of the Soviet economy. He favoured a high rate of economic expansion at the expense of the agricultural sector. The defeat of his viewpoint led inevitably to his disappearance in the purges of the 1930s.

Secondary Literature A. Ehrlich, *The Soviet Industrialization Debate, 1924–1928* (Harvard Univ. Press, 1960); N. Spulber, *Soviet Strategy for Economic Growth* (Indiana Univ. Press, 1964).

PRESCOTT, Edward C.

Born 1940, Glen Falls, NY, USA.

Current Post Prof. Econ., Univ. Minnesota-Minneapolis, Econ. Adviser, Fed. Reserve Bank Minneapolis, 1980–.

Past Posts Ass. Prof. Econ., Univ. Penn., 1966–71; Brookings Econ. Pol. Fellow, 1969–70; Ass. Prof., Assoc. Prof., Prof. Econ., Carnegie-Mellon Univ., Pittsburgh, 1971–2, 1972–5, 1975–80; Vis. Prof., Norwegian School Bus. Econ., Bergen, 1974–5; Ford Vis. Res. Prof., Univ. Chicago, 1978–9.

Degrees BA (Maths) Swarthmore Coll., PA, 1962; MS (OR) Case Inst. Technology, 1963; PhD Carnegie-Mellon Univ., 1967.

Offices and Honours Guggenheim Foundation Fellow, 1974–5.

Editorial Duties Assoc. Ed., *J Em*, 1975–82, *Int ER*, 1980–; Ed., *Minnesota Occasional Papers*, 1984–.

Principal Fields of Interest 131 Economic Fluctuations.

Publications *Articles*: 1. 'Investment under uncertainty' (with R. E. Lucas, Jr.), *Em*, 39(5), Sept. 1971; 2. 'Adaptive decision rules for macroeconomic planning', *WEJ*, 9, Dec. 1971; 3. 'A note on price systems in infinite dimensional space' (with R. E. Lucas, Jr.), *Int ER*, 13(2), June 1972; 4. 'Equilibrium search and unemployment' (with R. E. Lucas, Jr.), *JET*, 7(2), Feb. 1974; 5. 'Estimation in the presence of sequential parameter variations' (with T. Cooley), *Em*, 44(1), Jan. 1976; 6. 'Rules rather than discretion: the inconsistency of optimal plans' (with F. E. Kydland), *JPE*, 85(3), June 1977; 7. 'Sequential location among firms with foresight' (with M. Visscher), *Bell JE*, 8(2), Autumn 1977; 8. 'Organization capital' (with M. Visscher), *JPE*, 88(3), June 1980; 9. 'Time-to-build and aggregate fluctuations' (with F. E. Kydland), *Em*, 50(6), Nov. 1982; 10. 'Pareto optimal and competitive equilibria with private information' (with R. Townsend), *Em*, 52(1), Jan. 1984.

Principal Contributions My most important contribution is probably Article No. 9 above, jointly authored by Finn E. Kydland. There we establish that the equilibrium stochastic growth model accounts remarkably well for business-cycle fluctuations. Indeed, given the nature and magnitude of the technological change shocks and given people's willingness and ability to substitute intertemporally, there would be a puzzle if industrial market economies did not display the business-cycle phenomena. A second contribution was the finding that optimal dynamic taxation plans are time inconsistent. This leads one to the conclusion that the role of the economist is to evaluate policy rules with respect to their operating characteristics, rather than evaluating alternative policy actions. This research was also joint with Finn E. Kydland. Methodologically, I have contributed to competitive theory uncertainty. In No. 1 above, the competitive equilibrium is a stationary stochastic process. In No. 4 above the competitive equilibrium is an invariant distribution of market types with each market being subject to a stationary Markov process. Both papers were written jointly with Robert E. Lucas, Jr., who deserves principal credit for formulating the problems and recognising their value in substantive economic analyses. Another contribution was the extension of competitive theory to large private-information contracting economies. Unlike earlier extensions, it was not just a matter of redefining the commodity point. It also required the introduction of lotteries to convexify

the consumption possibility sets. This work was done jointly with Robert M. Townsend. Other research has explored issues in industrial organisation. In No. 8 above, a firm is viewed as an arrangement for producing and using information. In No. 10 above, 'coalitions' are shown to be needed for efficient evaluation and funding of investment projects.

PREST, Alan Richmond*

Dates and Birthplace 1919–85, York, England.

Posts Held Lect. Econ., Univ. Camb., 1949–64; Vis. Prof., Columbia Univ. 1961–2; Prof. Econ., Univ. Manchester, 1964–70; Vis. Prof., Univ. Pittsburgh, 1969; Prof. Econ., LSE, 1970–85; Vis. Fellow, ANU, 1971, 1977, 1978, 1983.

Degrees BA, MA, PhD Univ. Camb., 1940, 1944, 1948; MSc Univ. Manchester, 1967.

Offices and Honours Pres., Section F, BAAS, 1967.

Editorial Duties Ed. Board, *Ec.*

Publications *Books:* 1. *Public Finance in Theory and Practice* (1960, 1974, with N. A. Barr, 1979); 2. *Public Finance in Developing Countries* (1962, 1972); 3. *Self Assessment for Income Tax* (with N. A. Barr and S. R. James), (1977); 4. *Intergovernmental Fiscal Relations in the UK* (1978); 5. *The Taxation of Urban Land* (1981).

Articles: 1. 'National income of the United Kingdom', *EJ*, 58, March 1948; 2. 'The expenditure tax and saving', *EJ*, 69, Sept. 1959; 3. 'Cost benefit analysis: a survey' (with R. Turvey), *EJ*, 75, Dec. 1965, repr. in RES-AEA, *Surveys of Economic Theory*, 3 (Macmillan, St Martin's Press, 1966); 4. 'The budget and interpersonal distribution', *PF*, 32(1–2), 1968; 5. 'The structure and reform of direct taxation', *EJ*, 89, June 1979.

Career His first interest in the immediate postwar period was in problems of developing countries. Work at the department of Applied Economics, Cambridge, soon steered him towards national income accounting and in the early 1950s these two interests coalesced in work on the national income of

Nigeria. Public finance interests then began to develop, partly in relation to the UK and partly in relation to developing countries. This work was the genesis of *Public Finance in Theory and Practice*, which has held its own as the premier public finance text for British students.

PRIBRAM, Karl*

Dates and Birthplace 1877–1973, Prague, Austro-Hungarian Europe.
Posts Held Privatdozent, Ausserordentliche Prof., Univ. Vienna, 1907–14, 1914–19; Econ., Vienna Central Agency Housing Reform, Central Commission for Stats., Austrian Ministry of Trade, Austrian Ministry of Social Admin., 1907–21; Chief, Dept. Res. and Stats., ILO, Geneva, 1921–8; Prof. Econ., Univ. Frankfurt, 1928–33; Econ., Brookings Inst., 1933–5; Econ., US Social Security Board, 1935–42, US Tariff Commission, 1942–51.
Degrees Dr Law Prague Univ., 1900; Habilitation Univ. Vienna, 1907.
Publications *Books:* 1. *Die Entsteliung der individualistischen Sozialphilosophie* (1912); 2. *Cartel Problems* (1935); 3. *Conflicting Patterns of Thought* (1949); 4. *A History of Economic Reasoning* (1983).
Articles: 1. 'World unemployment and its problems', in *Unemployment as a World Problem*, ed., Q. Wright (1931); 2. 'Unemployment', *ESS*, 4.
Career A lifelong interest in prevailing patterns of economic reasoning led him in old age to complete a massive history of economic thought. In earlier years, he was an expert on problems of housing, social security, labour statistics and the problem of interwar unemployment.
Secondary Literature 'Biographical introduction', in K. Pribram, *A History of Economic Reasoning* (JHUP, 1983).

PROUDHON, Pierre-Joseph*

Dates and Birthplace 1809–65, Besançon, France.
Posts Held Printer and political writer.

Publications *Books:* 1. *What is Property?* (1840, 1966); 2. *Du principe federatif* (1863); 3. *De la capacité politique des classes ouvrières* (1865); 4. *Oeuvres complètes*, 20 vols (1923–50).
Career Socialist writer whose doctrine 'property is theft' is self-explanatory. He believed that the current forms of the State had to be replaced by a mutualist organisation of the economy which included free credit and the exchange of services; society would then become a federation of territorial and occupational groups. One of Marx's earliest publications, *The Poverty of Philosophy* (1847), is a polemic against Proudhon.
Secondary Literature M. Prelot, 'Proudhon, Pierre-Joseph', *IESS*, 12; E. Hyams, *Pierre-Joseph Proudhon: His Revolutionary Life, Mind and Works* (Taplinger, 1975).

PRYOR, Frederic LeRoy

Born 1933, Owosso, MI, USA.
Current Post Prof. Econ., Swarthmore Coll., Swarthmore, PA, USA, 1974–.
Past Posts Ass. Prof. Econ., Univ. Michigan, 1955–7; Res. Econ., Yale Univ., 1957–62; Ass. Prof., Assoc. Prof. Econ., Swarthmore Coll., 1962–74; Vis. Prof., Univs., Indiana, 1969, Cal. Berkeley, 1972–3, Inst. Internat. Econ., Geneva, 1977–8, 1982, Paris, 1981.
Degrees BA (Chemistry) Oberlin Coll., 1955; MA, PhD Yale Univ., 1957, 1962.
Editorial Duties Ed. Board, *J Comp E*, 1976–84.
Principal Fields of Interest 050 Economic Systems; 123 Comparative Economic Studies of Development.
Publications *Books:* 1. *The Communist Foreign Trade System* (A&U, 1963; transls., Japanese, 1964, Spanish, 1970); 2. *Public Expenditures in Communist and Capitalist Nations* (A&U, 1968); 3. *Property and Industrial Organization in Communist and Capitalist Nations* (Indiana Univ. Press, 1973); 4. *The Origins of the Economy: A Comparative Study of Distribution in Primitive and Peasant*

Economies (Academic Press, 1977); 5. *A Guidebook to the Comparative Study of Economic Systems* (Prentice-Hall, 1984).

Articles: 1. 'An international comparison of concentration ratios', *REStat*, 54(2), May 1972; 2. 'The rise of manufacturing establishments', *EJ*, 72(2), June 1972; 3. 'The impact of social and economic institutions on the size distribution of income and wealth: a simulation study', *AER*, 63(1), March 1973; 4. 'The Friedman-Savage utility function in cross-cultural perspective', *JPE*, 64(4), Aug. 1976; 5. 'The origins of money', *JMCB*, 9(3), Aug. 1977; 6. 'The classification and analysis of precapitalist economic systems by Marx and Engels', *HOPE*, 14(4), Winter 1982; 7. 'On induced economic change in precapitalist societies' (with S. B. Mauer), *JDE*, 10, June 1982.

Principal Contributions Most of my work has focussed on two questions: What are the causal forces underlying the origins and development of different economic institutions and systems? What is the impact of different economic institutions on the performance of the economy? After carrying out a case study of foreign trade in East Europe, I believed that these two questions could be approached more fruitfully by directly comparing societies with different economic systems. In my next three books I dealt respectively with consumption, production, and distribution and tried to test empirically a variety of hypotheses by means of such inter-societal or international comparisons. In recent years my scholarly interests have broadened: I have tried to analyse a series of questions about economic institutions and systems in both industrial and non-industrial economies and to deal with issues that have not only economic but important social and political aspects as well. Among other things this means that much of my recent work falls in the areas of economic development and economic history.

PSACHAROPOULOS, George

Born 1937, Athens, Greece.
Current Post Manager, Res. Program, Educ. Dept., World Bank, Washington, DC, USA, 1981–.
Past Posts Ass. Prof. Econ., Univ. Hawaii, 1968–9; Lect. Econ., LSE, 1969–81; Cons., OECD, UNESCO, ILO, Greek Govt., World Bank, 1969–81.
Degrees BA Grad. Bus. School, Athens, 1960; MA, PhD Univ. Chicago, 1964, 1968.
Offices and Honours Ford Foundation Fellow, 1964–8; Outstanding Scholar Award, 1969.
Editorial Duties Ed. Boards, *Econ. Educ. Rev.*, 1980–, *Section Educ., Internat. Encyclopedia Educ.* (Pergamon, 1985).
Principal Fields of Interest 022 Microeconomic Theory; 111 Economic Development; 912 Economics of Education.
Publications *Books:* 1. *Returns to Education: An International Comparison* (Elsevier, Jossey-Bass, 1973); 2. *Earnings and Education in OECD Countries* (OECD, 1975; transl., French, 1975); 3. *Post-Secondary Education Development Study Team* (in Greek), (with A. Kazamias), (Greek Center Social Res., Greek Ministry Educ., 1984); 4. *Information: An Essential Factor in Educational Planning and Policy*, ed. (UNESCO, 1980); 5. *Higher Education in Developing Countries: A Cost-Benefit Analysis* (World Bank, 1980); 6. *Hints for Educational Planners: The IIEP Experience in Five Less Developed Countries* (with B. Sanyal), (UNESCO Internat. Inst. Educ. Planning, 1981); 7. *Manpower Issues in Educational Investment: A Consideration of Planning Processes and Techniques* (with K. Hinchliffe, C. Dougherty and R. Hollister), (World Bank, 1983).

Articles: 1. 'Estimating shadow rates of return to investment in education', *JHR*, 5(1), Winter 1970; 2. 'The marginal contribution of education to economic growth', *EDCC*, 21(3), July 1972; 3. 'Substitution assumptions versus empirical evidence in manpower planning', *DE*, 121(6), Nov.–Dec.

1973; 4. 'The screening hypothesis and the returns to education' (with R. Layard), *JPE*, 82(5), Sept.–Oct. 1974; transl., Spanish, *Revista Espanola de Economia*, May–Aug. 1976; 5. 'Schooling and income distribution' (with A. Marin), *REStat*, 58(3), Aug. 1976; 6. 'On the explanation of schooling, occupation and earnings: some alternative path analyses' (with J. Tinbergen), *DE*, 126(4), April–May 1978; 7. 'Human capital and earnings: British evidence and a critique' (with R. Layard), *REStud*, 46(3), July 1979; 8. 'The reward for risk in the labour market: evidence from the United Kingdom and a reconciliation with other studies' (with A. Marin), *JPE*, 90(4), Aug. 1982; 9. 'The contribution of education to economic growth: international comparisons', in *International Productivity Comparisons*, ed. J. Kendrick (Ballinger, 1984).

Principal Contributions Early work was focussed on the returns of education in different country settings, leading to the documentation of certain patterns like the diminishing profitability of investment in education by increasing level of education and *per capita* income. In the mid-1970s, my interest shifted to the role of education as a determinant of earnings and income distribution. I have also studied related topics such as the elasticity of substitution between different types of educated labour, the screening hypothesis, and labour market segmentation. The empirical emphasis of my work has been in LDC labour markets. My recent work concentrates on the development of analytical tools and the derivation of empirical signals that may guide policy-makers in developing countries to make investment decisions in education conducive to economic growth and social equity.

Q

QUANDT, Richard E.

Born 1930, Budapest, Hungary.
Current Post Prof. Econ., Princeton Univ., Princeton, NJ, USA, 1964–.

Past Posts Ass. Prof., Assoc. Prof., Princeton Univ., 1956–9, 1959–64; Vis. Prof., Birkbeck Coll., Univ. London, 1981.
Degrees BA Princeton Univ., 1952; MA, PhD Harvard Univ., 1955, 1957.
Offices and Honours Guggenheim Foundation Fellow, 1958–9; Fellow, Council, Em Soc, 1968, 1975–80; Member, ASA, 1979.
Editorial Duties Assoc. Ed. *REStat*, 1974–80; Ed. Board, *Appl. Econ.*, 1982–.
Principal Fields of Interest 210 Econometric, Statistical and Mathematical Methods and Models; 022 Microeconomic Theory; 027 Economics of Centrally Planned Economies.
Publications *Books:* 1. *Microeconomic Theory: A Mathematical Approach* (with J. M. Henderson), (McGraw-Hill, 1958, 1980); 2. *The New Inflation* (with W. L. Thorp), (McGraw-Hill, 1959); 3. *Strategies and Rational Decisions in the Securities Option Market* (with B. G. Malkiel), (MIT Press, 1969); 4. *The Demand for Travel*, ed. (D. C. Heath, 1970); 5. *Studies in Nonlinear Estimation* (with S. M. Goldfeld), (Ballinger, 1976); 6. *Nonlinear Methods in Econometrics* (with S. M. Goldfeld), (N-H, 1971).

Articles: 1. 'A probabilistic theory of consumer behavior', *QJE*, 70(4), Nov. 1956; 2. 'The estimation of the parameters of a linear regression system obeying two separate regimes', *JASA*, 53, Dec. 1958; 3. 'On the existence of Cournot equilibrium' (with C. H. Frank), *Int ER*, 4(1), Jan. 1963; 4. 'Some tests for homoscedasticity' (with S. M. Goldfeld), *JASA*, 60, June 1965; 5. 'Estimation of model splits', *Transportation Res.*, 2(1), March 1968; 6. 'The supply of money and common stock prices: a comment' (with B. G. Malkiel), *J Fin*, 27(4), Sept. 1972; 7. A comparison of methods for testing nonnested hypotheses', *REStat*, 56(1), Feb. 1974; 8. 'Tests of the equilibrium vs. disequilibrium hypothesis', *Int ER*, 19(2), June 1978; 9. 'A model of rationing and labor supply: theory and estimation' (with J. Eaton), *Ec*, N.S. 50, Aug. 1983; 10. 'Complexity in regulation', *J Pub E*, 22(2), Nov. 1983.
Principal Contributions In the first

few years of professional life I was most interested in micro-theory. This was the period in which the first edition of *Microeconomic Theory: A Mathematical Approach* was published. I soon started, however, to devote most of my energies to econometrics. Sundry problems of estimation and testing occupied me until I encountered substantive transportation oriented problems of estimation (e.g. modal split estimation) which occupied me for some years. Around the same time I developed a strong interest in financial economics, particularly in the use of options as financial strategies. In the last few years I have concentrated most of my efforts on the econometrics of disequilibrium models, with reference to both free market and planned economies.

QUESNAY, François*

Dates and Birthplace 1694–1774, Mèrè, France.
Posts Held Doctor; Consulting physician to Louis XV.
Publications *Books:* 1. *Tableau économique* (1758, 1972); 2. *La physiocratie,* 2 vols (1768); 3. *Oeuvres economiques et philosophiques* (1888). *Articles:* 1. 'Fermiers', *Encyclopédie,* 6, 1756; 2. 'Grains', *Encyclopédie,* 7, 1757.
Career The founder of the physiocratic school, he did not write on economics until he was in his sixties. His two *Encyclopédie* articles introduced the characteristic argument that only agriculture could produce a 'produit-net'. Despite his position close to the seat of power, he wrote articles critical of the régime, some of which were collected in *A Physiocratie*. Arguing from a concept of natural laws, in effect a description of the elements of a free enterprise system, he developed a version of society in which a strong monarch regulates affairs so that the natural order of things can operate freely. Because farmers and landowners were considered the truly productive classes in the physiocratic system, there was a counterbalancing disregard for the contributions of the merchant and industrialist. The criticism of privileged and unproductive groups, which were closely associated with the monarchy as it existed, was what made physiocracy a somewhat subversive doctrine. His *Tableau économique* was first hailed by Marx, and has since come to be regarded as a crude version of input-output analysis, pointing towards general equilibrium theory.
Secondary Literature R. L. Meek, *The Économics of Physiocracy* (A&U, 1962, Harvard Univ. Press, 1963); B. F. Hoselitz, 'Quesnay, François', *IESS,* 13; M. Kuczynski and R. L. Meek, *Quesnay's Tableau Economique* (Augustus M. Kelley, 1972).

QUINN, Joseph Francis

Born 1947, Amherst, MA, USA.
Current Post Prof. Econ., Boston Coll., Chestnut Hill, MA, USA, 1985–.
Past Posts Ass. Prof., Assoc. Prof., Boston Coll., 1975–80, 1980–5; Vis. Ass. Prof., Inst. Res. on Poverty, Madison, WI, 1978, 1979, 1980; Vis. Assoc. Prof., Grad. School Public Pol., Univ. Cal. Berkeley, 1980–4.
Degrees BA Amherst Coll., MA, 1969; PhD MIT, 1975.
Editorial Duties Ed. Boards, *Social Science, J. Gerontology.*
Principal Fields of Interest 820 Labour Markets: Public Policy; 900 Welfare Programmes; 918 Economics of Ageing.
Publications *Articles:* 1. 'The microeconomic determinants of early retirement', *JHR,* 12(3), Summer 1977; 2. 'Wage differentials among older workers in the public and private sectors', *JHR,* 14(1), Winter 1979; 3. 'Labor force participation patterns of older self-employed workers', *Social Security Bull.,* 43(4), April 1980; 4. 'Wage rates and city size' (with K. McCormick), *Industrial Relations,* 20(2), Spring 1981; 5. 'Compensation in the public sector: the importance of pensions', in *Public Finance and Public Employment,* ed. R. Haveman (Wayne State Press, 1982, repr., Italian, in *Problemi di Amministrazione Publica,* 2, 1982); 6. 'Pension wealth of government and private sector workers', *AER,* 72(2), May 1982; 7.

'The effect of pension plans on the pattern of life-cycle compensation' (with R. V. Burkhauser), in *The Measurement of Labor Cost*, ed. J. Triplett (Univ. Chicago Press, 1983); 8. 'Is mandatory retirement overrated? evidence from the 1970s' (with R. V. Burkhauser), *JHR*, 18(3), Summer 1983; 9. 'Influencing retirement behavior: a key issue for social security' (with R. V. Burkhauser), *J. Pol. Analysis & Management*, 3(1), Fall 1983; 10. 'Retirement income rights as a component of wealth', *RIW*, 31(2), June 1985.

Principal Contributions My recent research (much of it with Richard V. Burkhauser of Vanderbilt University) has focussed on the microeconomic determinants of individual retirement decisions — who retires when, and why? I have concentrated on the impact of public policy — mandatory retirement rules and the financial incentives implicit in our social security (SS) and pension systems. Central to this research is the belief that SS and pension rights are best viewed as assets — the present value of future income streams. When receipt of benefits is delayed (e.g., by the decision to continue work), the asset value of future SS or pension rights may rise or fall, depending on whether the benefits foregone today are adequately offset by the increments in benefits in the future. Our research has established that at some age (certainly by 65), the asset value of these rights falls with continued work. This is equivalent to a pay cut, and in many cases a severe one. We find that individuals respond as expected — the higher the loss in SS or pension wealth associated with continued work, the higher the likelihood of retirement. Mandatory retirement, in contrast, is often a redundant constraint — one that is superfluous given the financial inducements in place. Attempts to alter retirement patterns by delaying or eliminating mandatory retirement will have little impact unless the work disincentives facing the elderly are decreased. Fortunately, recent legislation has moved in that direction.

Related work has studied the importance of SS and pension rights in the wealth portfolios of older Americans, total compensation comparisons between those in the public and private sectors, the extent and correlates of partial retirement, the retirement patterns of the self-employed, the impact of unexpected events in retirement plans, mandatory retirement and the university, and the measurement of economic status.

QUIRK, James Patrick

Born 1926, St Paul, MN, USA.
Current Post Prof. Econ., Cal. Inst. Technology, Pasadena, CA, USA, 1971–.
Past Posts Instr., St Mary's Univ., TX, 1949–51; Econ., US Bureau Census, 1951–3; Market Analyst, G. H. Tennan & Co., Minneapolis, 1953–6; Res. Ass., Univ. Minnesota, 1955–9; Instr., Ass. Prof., Assoc. Prof., Purdue Univ., IN, 1959–65; Prof., Univ. Kansas, 1965–71.
Degrees BA, MA, PhD Univ. Minnesota, 1948, 1949, 1959.
Offices and Honours Ford Foundation Fellow, 1963.
Principal Fields of Interest 021 General Equilibrium Theory; 721 Resource Economics; 026 Economics of Uncertainty.
Publications Books: 1. *Introduction to General Equilibrium Theory and Welfare Economics* (with R. Saposnik), (McGraw-Hill, 1968; transls., Japanese, 1972, Spanish, 1972, French, 1980); 2. *Papers in Quantitative Economics*, co-ed. (with A. Zarley), (Univ. Kansas Press, 1969); 3. *Intermediate Microeconomics* (Science Res. Assoc., 1976); 4. *Essays in Contemporary Fields in Economics*, co-ed. (with G. Horwich), (Purdue Univ. Press, 1981); 5. *Economics* (with D. McDougal), (Science Res. Assoc., 1981); 6. *Coal Models and their Use in Government Planning* (with K. Terasawa and D. Whipple), (Praeger, 1982).
Articles: 1. 'Admissibility and measurable utility functions' (with R. Saposnik), *REStud*, 29, Feb. 1962; 2. 'Qualitative economics and the stability of equilibrium' (with R. Rupport), *REStud*, 32, Oct. 1965; 3. 'Qualitative economics and the scope of the correspon-

dence principle' (with L. Bassett and J. Maybee), *Em*, 36, July–Oct. 1968; 4. 'Qualitative problems in matrix theory' (with J. Maybee), *SIAM Rev.*, 11, 1969; 5. 'Complementarity and stability of equilibrium', *AER*, 60(2), June 1970; 6. 'Dynamic models of fishing' (with V. Smith), in *Economics of Fisheries Management: A Symposium* (Univ. British Columbia, 1970); 7. 'The economic theory of a professional sports league' (with M. El Hodiri), in *Government and the Sports Business* (Brookings Inst., 1974); 8. 'Appropriative water rights and the efficient allocation of resources' (with H. Burness), *AER*, 69(1), March 1979; 9. 'Capital contracting and the regulated firm' (with H. Burness and D. Montgomery), *AER*, 70(2), June 1980.

Principal Contributions During the 1960s my main research interests were in general equilibrium theory and qualitative economics of the Samuelson-Lancaster type, exploring the extent to which qualitative information combined with the competitive hypothesis of Walras's Law and homogeneity leads to restrictive comparative status and/or stability results. I also did some work on the economics of uncertainty (the notion of first-degree stochastic dominance and the expected utility hypothesis) and production theory. In the 1970s my interests shifted to several applied areas, including the economics of professional sports, resource economics (and especially water economics), and the economic theory of the regulated firm. My most recent work has been concerned with price patterns on commodity futures markets and in particular research into theoretical explanations for backward action in such markets.

Urbana, 1964–5; Assoc. Prof. Econ., Washington Univ., St Louis, 1965–70; Vis. Prof. Econ., Univ. Rochester, NY, 1971; Vis. Res. Prof. Econ., CORE, Catholic Univ. Louvain, Belgium, 1971.

Degrees BA Univ. Texas, 1959; MA, PhD Yale Univ., 1960, 1963.

Offices and Honours Fellow, Em Soc, 1978.

Principal Fields of Interest 021 General Equilibrium Theory.

Publications *Books:* 1. *Economics of Feudalism* (Gordon & Breach, 1971); 2. *Theory of Microeconomics* (Academic Press, 1972); 3. *Theory of General Economic Equilibrium* (Academic Press, 1972).

Articles: 1. 'Edgeworth exchange and general economic equilibrium', *YES*, 4, Spring 1964, Spring 1965; 2. 'International trade and development in a small country', in *Papers in Quantitative Economics*, eds. J. Quirk and A. Zarley (Univ. Kansas Press, 1968); 3. 'Normally, factor inputs are never gross substitutes', *JPE*, 76, Jan.–Feb. 1968; 4. 'Resource allocation with increasing returns to scale', *AER*, 60(5), Dec. 1970; 5. 'Nice demand functions', *Em*, 41(5), Sept. 1973; 6. 'Pairwise optimality, multilateral optimality and efficiency, with and without externalities', in *Theory and Measurement of Economic Externalities*, ed. S. Y. Lip (Academic Press, 1976); 7. 'Equivalence of consumer surplus, the Divisia index of output and Eisenberg's addilog social utility', *JET*, 13(1), Aug. 1976; 8. 'On factor price equalization', *J Math E* 5(1), March 1978; 9. 'The second theorem of welfare economics when utilities are independent', *JET*, 23(3), Dec. 1980; 10. 'Utility over time: the homothetic case', *JET*, 25(2), Oct. 1981.

R

RADER, John Trout III

Born 1938, TX, USA.
Current Post Prof. Econ., Washington Univ., St Louis, WA, 1970–.
Past Posts Res. Ass., Yale Univ., 1961–2; Ass. Prof. Econ., Univs. Missouri, Columbia, 1962–4, Univ. Illinois,

RADNER, Roy

Born 1927, Chicago, IL, USA.
Current Post Member, Technical Staff, Bell Lab., Murray Hill, NJ, USA, 1980–.
Past Posts Ass. Prof. Cowles Commission, Univ. Chicago, 1954–5; Ass. Prof., Econ. Res. Assoc. Cowles Foundation, Yale Univ., 1955–7; Assoc.

Prof., Prof. Econ. Stats., Univ. Cal Berkeley, 1957–79.

Degrees PhB, BS (Maths), MS (Maths.), PhD (Math. Stats.) Univ. Chicago, 1945, 1950, 1951, 1956.

Offices and Honours Member, Inst. Math. Stats., Amer. Assoc. Advancement Science; Fellow, Center Advanced Study Behavioral Sciences, 1955–6; Guggenheim Foundation Fellow, 1961–2, 1965–6; Overseas Fellow, Churchill Coll., Camb., 1969–70; AAAS, 1970; Vice-Pres., Pres., Em Soc, 1971–3; Member, NAS, 1975, Commission Human Resources, 1976–9; Assembly, Behavioral Social Science, Nat. Res. Council, USA, 1979–82.

Principal Fields of Interest 026 Economies of Uncertainity.

Publications *Books:* 1. *Optimal Replacement Policy* (with D. W. Jorgenson and J. J. McCall), (N-H Rand-McNally, 1967); 2. *Decision and Organization* (with C. B. McGuire), (N-H, 1972); 3. *Economic Theory of Teams* (with J. Marschak), (Yale Univ. Press, 1972); 4. *Demand and Supply in US Higher Education* (with L. S. Miller), (McGraw-Hill, 1975); 5. *Mathematicians in Academia* (with C. V. Kuh), (Conf. Board Math. Sciences, 1980).

Articles: 1. 'Paths of economic growth that are optimal with regard only to final states: a "turnpike theorem"', *REStud*, 28, Feb. 1961; 2. 'Equilibre des marchés a terme et au comptant en cas d'incertitude', *Cahiers d'Econometrie*, 9, 1967; 3. 'Satisficing', *J Math E*, 2, 1975; 4. 'Monitoring cooperative agrreements in a repeated principal-agent relationship', *Em*, 49(5), Sept., 1981; 5. 'Equilibrium under uncertainty', in *Handbook of Mathematical Economics*, eds. K. J. Arrow and M. Intriligator (N-H, 1981).

Principal Contributions Contributions to the theory of decision-making in decentralised organisations; the theory of teams (developed with J. Marschak); game-theoretic analyses of incentives for efficient decision-making in long-lasting organisations; bounded rationality; and existence and optimality of market equilibria under uncertainty including equilibria with private information, equilibrium of plans, prices, and price-expectations, and

rational expectations equilibrium. Characterisation of optimal investment strategies: optimal capital accumulation under certainty (turnpike theory) and uncertainty; and optimal strategies for inspection and maintenance of stochastically failing equipment. Empirical studies of demand and supply in higher education.

RAE, John*

Dates and Birthplace 1796–1872, Scotland.

Posts Held Schoolmaster in Canada, California and Hawaii.

Publications *Books:* 1. *Statement of Some New Principles on the Subject of Political Economy* (1834, 1965).

Career Though working in near complete isolation, he succeeded in creating a theory of capital to which Böhm-Bawerk and others were indebted; in his lifetime some small recognition from J. S. Mill was almost the only notice he obtained. In addition to his capital theory, he discussed the formation of saving, the importance of inventions, and the role of government in redirecting money from luxury expenditure into education, and other forms of public expenditure.

Secondary Literature R. W. James, *John Rae, Political Economist*, 2 vols (Univ. Toronto Press, 1965); J. J. Spengler, 'Rae, John', *IESS*, 13.

RAMSAY, George*

Dates and Birthplace 1800–71, Banff, Scotland.

Posts Held Landowner.

Degrees BA, MA Univ. Camb., 1823, 1826.

Publications *Books:* 1. *Essay on the Distribution of Wealth* (1836).

Career Though an isolated and uninfluential figure, Ramsay's *Essay* ... shows an unusually good grasp of contemporary French economic thought. His grasp of the distinction between capitalist and entrepreneur ('master') is particularly strong.

Secondary Literature J. S. Prybyla, 'The economic writings of George

Ramsay, 1800–1871', *SJPE*, 10, Nov. 1963.

RAMSEY, Frank Plumpton*

Dates and Birthplace 1903–60, Cambridge, England.
Posts Held Fellow, King's Coll. Camb.
Degrees BA Univ. Camb., 1923.
Publications *Books:* 1. *Foundations of Mathematics and Other Essays*, ed. R. B. Braithwaite (1931).
Articles: 1. 'The Douglas proposals', *Univ. Camb. Magazine*, 11(1), Jan. 1922; 2. 'A contribution to the theory of taxation', *EJ*, 37, March 1927; 3. 'A mathematical theory of saving', *EJ*, 38, Dec. 1928; all repr. in *Precursors in Mathematical Economics*, eds. W. J. Baumol and S. M. Goldfeld (1968).
Career In a short but fruitful life he made major contributions to mathematical logic and philosophy. From his undergraduate days, Cambridge economists had tested their theories against his logical abilities and in his two published papers he showed analytical ability to the highest level. Keynes regarded his 1928 article, dealing with the concept of optimal social saving rules, as 'one of the most remarkable contributions to mathematical economics ever made'.
Secondary Literature J. M. Keynes, 'F. P. Ramsey', *Essays in Biography* (Macmillan, 1933, 1972).

RANIS, Gustav

Born 1929, Darmstadt, Germany.
Current Post Frank Altschul Prof. Internat. Econ., Yale Univ., New Haven, CT, USA, 1982–.
Past Posts Econ., Overseas Devlp. Program, Ford Foundation, NY, 1957–8; Joint Dir. Res., Inst. Devlp. Econ., Karachi, Pakistan, 1959–61; Instr., Ass. Prof., Assoc. Dir., Econ. Growth Center, Assoc. Prof., Prof. Econ., Yale Univ., 1956–7, 1960–1, 1961–5, 1961–4, 1964–81; Ass. Admin. Program and Pol., Agency Internat. Devlp., US Dept. State, 1965–7; Ford Foundation Vis. Prof., Univ. Andes, Colombia, 1976–7.

Degrees BA Hon. BA Brandeis Univ., 1952, 1982; MA, PhD Yale Univ., 1953, 1956.
Offices and Honours Jr. Phi Beta Kappa, Brandeis Univ., 1951; Sterling Fellow, Yale Univ., 1954–5; US-SSRC Fellow, Japan, 1955–6; Fellow, Member Board Trustees, Brandeis Univ., 1961–7, 1968–; Ford Foundation Faculty Fellow, Mexico, 1971–2.
Editorial Duties Ed. Board, *Desarrollo y Sociedad*, CEDE, Univ. Andes, Colombia, 1978–, *PDR*, 1978–80, *Econ. Rev.*, Univ. Teheran, 1977.
Principal Fields of Interest 112 Economic Development Models and Theories; 121 Economic Studies of Developing Countries; 440 International Investment and Foreign Aid.
Publications *Books:* 1. *Development of the Labor Surplus Economy: Theory and Policy* (with J. C. H. Fei), (Richard D. Irwin, 1964); 2. *Government and Economic Development*, ed. (Yale Univ. Press, 1971); 3. *The Gap Between Rich and Poor Nations*, ed. (Macmillan, St Martin's Press, 1972); 4. *The U.S. and the Developing Economies*, ed. (W. W. Norton, 1964, 1973); 5. *Sharing in Development: A Programme of Employment, Equity and Growth for the Philippines*, Chief of Mission and ed. (ILO, 1974); 6. *Growth with Equity: The Taiwan Case* (with J. C. H. Fei and S. W. Y. Kuo), (OUP, 1979); 7. *Science, Technology and Economic Development: A Historical and Comparative Study*, co-ed. (with W. Beranek), (Praeger, 1979); 8. *The Theory and Experience of Economic Development: Essays in Honor of Sir W. Arthur Lewis*, co-ed., (with M. Gersovitz, C. Diaz-Alejandro and M. Rosenzweig), (A&U, 1982); 9. *Comparative Development Perspectives: Essays in Honor of Lloyd Reynolds*, co-ed. (with R. West, M. Leiserson and C. Morris), (Westview Press, 1984); 10. *Japan and the Developing Countries: A Comparative Analysis of Development Experience*, co-ed. (with K. Ohkawa), (Blackwell, 1984).
Articles: 1. 'Factor proportions in Japanese economic development', *AER*, 47(4), Sept. 1957; 2. 'Financing economic development', *EHR*, March 1959, repr. in *The Experience of Economic*

Growth: Case Studies in Economic History, ed. B. Supple (Random House, 1963), and *Agriculture and Economic Growth: Japan's Experience* (Univ. Tokyo Press, 1969); 3. 'A theory of economic development' (with J. C. H. Fei), *AER*, 51(4), Sept. 1961; 4. 'Investment criteria, productivity and economic development: an empirical comment', *QJE*, 76, May 1962; 5. 'Innovation, capital accumulation and economic development' (with J. C. H. Fei), *AER*, 53(3), June 1963; 6. 'Innovation intensity and factor bias in the theory of growth' (with J. C. H. Fei), *Int ER*, May 1965; 7. 'A model of growth and employment in the open dualistic economy: the case of Korea and Taiwan' (with J. C. H. Fei), *J Dev Stud*, 11(2), Jan. 1975, repr. in *Employment, Income Distribution and Development*, ed. F. Steward (Frank Cass, 1975); 8. 'Economic development and financial institutions', in *Economic Progress, Private Values and Public Policy: Essays in Honor of William Fellner*, eds. B. Balassa and R. Nelson (N-H, 1977); 9. 'Growth and the family distribution of income by factor components' (with J. C. H. Fei and S. W. Y. Kuo), *QJE*, 42, Feb. 1978, repr. in *El Trimestre Economico*, July–Sept. 1980; 10. 'Typology in development theory: retrospective and prospects', in *Economic Structure and Performance: Essays in Honor of Hollis Chenery*, eds. R. Syrquin, L. Taylor and J. Westphal (Academic Press, 1984).

Principal Contributions Early work was concentrated on analysing Japanese post-Meiji economic development as a case of successful early transition to modern growth. I later moved into comparative Asian development analysis focussing first on Pakistan and later on Korea and Taiwan. My attention was initially concentrated on the analysis of balanced growth in the dual economy, with emphasis on the financing of development and the choice of factor proportions. This work then led me into a long-term collaboration with John Fei, the first product of which, *Development of the Labor Surplus Economy*, presented a two-sector model of development, focusing on both the behavioural and organisational aspects of dualism, as well as on the special role of innovational intensity and bias in non-agricultural production. Later work led me to a further exploration of the importance of technology choices as well as the direction of technology change for LDC employment and growth objectives. At the same time, Fei and I moved into work on the construction of open, i.e. trade-related, dualistic models, including further refinement of the specification of agricultural activities.

In the late 1970s, the emphasis of my work shifted to an analysis of the relationship between patterns of growth and the distribution of income. The tool utilised was a Gini decomposition procedure first empirically applied to the case of Taiwan, leading to a volume entitled *Growth with Equity* (1979). Other country applications have followed since. Most recently I have turned my attention again to the comparative analysis of historical development experiences by contrasting the contemporary Taiwanese and Korean record with that of historical Japan, and moving at the same time to a comparison between the East Asian labour surplus economy and those of other typological representatives, including Mexico and Colombia in Latin America, the Philippines in Asia, and Ghana in Africa. Also in recent years, I have turned my attention increasingly to the role of science and technology in development as well as to the importance of agricultural/industrial linkages in the context of a successful participatory growth path.

RAPPING, Leonard A.

Born 1934, Los Angeles, CA, USA.
Current Post Prof. Econ., Univ. Mass., Amherst, MA, USA, 1985–.
Past Posts Res. Econ., Northwestern Transportation Center, 1959–60; Rand Corp., 1961–2; Lect., UCLA, 1962; Ass. Prof., Prof. Econ., Carnegie-Mellon Univ., 1962–6, 1967–74; Disting. Vis. Prof., Univ. Nevada, 1978; Vis. Prof., Brandeis Univ., MA, 1984.
Degrees BA UCLA, 1956; MA, PhD Univ. Chicago, 1958, 1961.
Offices and Honours Beta Kappa,

1955; Ford Faculty Res. Fellow, 1965; Member, Highway Res. Board, NAS, 1972; Nominating Comm., AEA, 1975–6, EEA, 1977.

Editorial Duties Ed., *Rev. Radical Polit. Econ.*, 1972–4.

Principal Fields of Interest 310 Domestic Monetary and Financial Theory and Institutions; 430 Balance of Payments, International Finance; 820 Labour Markets, Public Policy.

Publications *Books:* 1. *The Economic Value of the United States Merchant Marine* (with A. Ferguson, *et al.*), (Northwestern Transportation Center, 1961); 2. *U.S. Shipping Policy and Military Shipping Requirements* (Rand Corp., 1963); 3. *Racial Discrimination in Organized Baseball* (with A. Pascal), (Rand Corp., 1970).

Articles: 1. 'The impact of Atlantic-Gulf unionism on the relative earnings of unlicensed merchant seamen', *ILRR*, 17(1), Sept.–Oct. 1963; 2. 'Learning and a World War II production function', *REStat*, 46(1), Feb. 1964; 3. 'The role of market variables and key bargains in the maufacturing wage determination process' (with T. W. McGuire), *JPE*, 76(5), Oct. 1968; 4. 'Real wages, employment and inflation' (with R. E. Lucas, Jr.), *JPE*, 77(5), Oct. 1969, repr. in *Microeconomic Foundations of Employment and Inflation Theory*, ed. E. S. Phelps (W. W. Norton, Macmillan, 1970), and *Studies in Business-Cycle Theory*, ed. R. E. Lucas, Jr. (MIT Press, 1981); 5. 'Price expectations and the Phillips curve' (with R. E. Lucas, Jr.), *AER*, 59(3), June 1969; 6. 'The supply of labor and manufacturing wage determination in the United States: an empirical examination' (with T. W. McGuire), *Int ER*, 11(2), June 1970; 7. 'The 1975 report of the President's Council of Economic Advisers: a radical critique' (with J. Crotty), *AER*, 65(5), Dec. 1975; 8. 'The great recession of the 1970s: domestic and international considerations', in *Alternative Directions in Economic Policy*, eds. F. J. Bonello and T. R. Swartz (Notre Dame Press, 1978); 9. 'The domestic and international aspects of structural inflation', in *Post-Keynesian Theories of Inflation*, eds. J. Gipinsky and C. Rockwood (Ballinger, 1979); 10. 'Bureaucracy, the corporation and economic policy', *J. Post Keyn E*, 9(3), Spring 1984.

Principal Contributions Initially, I empirically investigated collective bargaining and technological processes in merchant shipping and shipbuilding. This industry-specific research was followed by a more general econometric analysis of labour markets. Union wage effectiveness, monopoly wage effects and racial discrimination were investigated in the context of competitive, equilibrium, labour market models. This micro-foundation facilitated later macro research into the theoretical and empirical basis of aggregate labour supply and business cycles. Again assuming continuously clearing, competitive labour markets, the determination of aggregate real wages, employment and inflation were studied.

The drift of my interests from narrower to broader issues continued. Abandoning the closed economy assumption, my attention turned to global forces and their impact on domestic inflation, employment and associated public and private institutions. Having abandoned the idea that variations in economic activity can be explained in traditional business-cycle terms I turned to a structural approach to this problem. Global economic, political and military events constrain domestic economic policy and force the restructuring of domestic economic institutions. The associated research agenda is to identity these global forces as well as the process whereby domestic institutions adapt.

RAU, Karl Heinrich*

Dates and Birthplace 1792–1870, Germany.

Posts Held Prof., Univ. Erlangen, 1816–22, Univ. Heidelberg, 1822.

Publications *Books:* 1. *Ansichten der Volkswirtschaft* (1821); 2. *Über die Kameralwissenschaft* (1825); 3. *Lehrbuch der politischen Ökonomie*, 3 vols (1826–37); 4. *Über Beschränkungen der Freiheit in der Volkswirtschaftspflege* (1847).

Articles: 1. 'Report to the Bulletin of the Royal Academy of Sciences of

Brussels', 8(2), 1841, repr. in *Precursors in Mathematical Economics: An Anthology*, eds. W. J. Baumol and S. M. Goldfeld (1968).

Career The author of the most successful mid-nineteenth-century textbook of economics in Germany. The 3-volume treatment (economic laws, economic policy and public finance) exercised a lasting influence on the structure of German economics teaching. Following the success of the Historical School, his emphasis on classical economic principles caused his reputation to decline.

RAYMOND, Daniel*

Dates and Birthplace 1786–1849, CT, USA.

Posts Held Lawyer.

Publications *Books:* 1. *The Missouri Question* (1819); 2. *Thoughts on Political Economy* (1820), 2nd edn. *The Elements of Political Economy*, 2 vols (1823).

Career First American author of formal treatise on political economy. He favoured an element of government intervention, particularly in the case of protective tariffs. On currency, he supported a gold-backed government issue, and strongly opposed the issue of bank notes by private banks. He denounced slavery on both economic and moral grounds and, like many American writers, did not accept Malthus on population.

Secondary Literature A. D. H. Kaplan, 'Raymond, Daniel', *ESS*, 13.

READ, Samuel*

Dates and Birthplace ?

Publications *Books:* 1. *On Money and the Bank Restriction Laws* (1816); 2. *The Problem Solved in the Explication of a Plan of a Safe Steady and Secure Government Paper Currency* (1818); 3. *Exposure of Certain Plagiarisms of J. R. McCulloch* (1819); 4. *General Statement of an Argument on the Subject of Population* (1821); 5. *Political Economy* (1829).

Career *Political Economy*, his chief

work, led the anti-Ricardian spirit of the times, and bears affinities to the work of Samuel Bailey. The analysis of profit and interest exercised some influence on his contemporaries.

Secondary Literature E. R. A. Seligman, 'On some neglected British economists, Pts I–II', *EJ*, 13, Sept., Dec. 1903.

REAGAN, Barbara Ruth Benton

Born 1920, San Antonio, TX, USA.

Current Post Prof. Econ., Southern Methodist Univ., Dallas, TX, 1967–.

Past Posts Econ., Sr. Project Leader, Agric, Res. Service, US Dept. Agric., Washington, DC, 1942–7, 1949–55; Prof., Texas Woman's Univ., 1959–67; Assoc. Dean, Univ. Coll., Ass. Pres., Southern Methodist Univ., 1975–6; Disting. Vis. Prof. Econ., Kenyon Coll., OH, 1979.

Degrees BS Univ. Texas, Austin, 1941; MA (Stats.) Amer. Univ., Washington, DC, 1947; MA, PhD Harvard Univ., 1949, 1952.

Offices and Honours Ferguson Fellow, Harvard Univ., 1947–9; Econ. Res. Advisory Comm., US Dept. Agric., 1965–70; Advisory Comm. Agric. Pol. Inst., N. Carolina State Univ., Kellogg Foundation, 1965–70; Nat. Advisory Food and Drug Council, 1968–71; Outstanding Teacher Award, Willis M. Tate Award Outstanding Faculty Member, Southern Methodist Univ., 1972, 1982; Manpower Council, N. Texas Council of Govts., 1972–4; Comm. Status of Women in the Econ. Profession, AEA, 1972–8; Board of Trustees and Instructional TV Comm., Public Communication Foundation N. Texas, 1973–6; Dallas Economists Club, 1975–; Dallas Chamber Commerce Comm. Urban Affairs, 1975; Pres., Phi Beta Kappa, Pres., Faculty Senate Board, Governors Board Trustees, Southern Methodist Univ., 1975–6, 1981–2, 1981–4, 1981–3; Board Dirs., Dallas Urban League, 1975–9; Univ. Advisory Council, Amer. Council Life Insurance, Washington, DC, 1977–81; Advisers Comm., White House Conf. Balanced Nat. Growth and Econ. Devlp., 1977–8; Cons., Ford Foundation, 1980; Dallas

Outstanding Women, Women's Centre Dallas, 1980; Dallas *Morning News* Board Econ., 1982–; AAUW Laurel Award, 1983; Advisory Board Econ., Wharton Econometric Forecasting Assoc., 1983–; Dir., Fed. Home Loan Bank, Region IX, 1981–5.

Editorial Duties Ed. Boards, *JEL*, 1977–9, *J. Econ. Educ.*, 1984–.

Principal Fields of Interest 820 Labour Markets; 910 Economics of Education, Poverty, and Discrimination; 921 Consumer Economics and Levels of Living.

Publications *Books:* 1. *Wage and Wage Rates of Hired Farm Labor* (US Dept. Agric., 1946–7); 2. *Mexican-American Industrial Migrants* (Southern Methodist Univ. Press, 1971); 3. *Women in the Workplace: Implications of Occupational Segregation*, co-ed. and contrib. (Univ. Chicago Press, 1976); 4. *Issues in Federal Statistical Needs Relating to Women*, ed. and contrib. (US Bureau Census, 1979); 5. *Economic Foundations of Women in the Labor Force* (Southern Methodist Univ. Press, 1981).

Articles: 1. 'Economic consequence of free or administered price in agriculture', *Southwestern Social Science Q.*, March 1959, repr. in *Capitalism, Socialism and Central Planning, Readings in Comparative Economic Systems*, ed. W. A. Leeman (Houghton Mifflin, 1963); 2. 'Consumer economics research and the definition of poverty', *J. Home Econ.*, April 1967; 3. 'Condensed versus detailed schedule in expenditure surveys', *Agric. Econ. Res.*, 6(2), 1954; 4. 'Guidelines to obviate role prejudice and sex discrimination', *AER*, 63(5), Dec. 1973; 5. 'Sex discrimination in universities: an approach through internal labor market analysis', *AAUP Bull.*, March 1974; 6. 'Two supply curves for economists? Implications of mobility and career attachment of women', *AER*, 67(1), Feb. 1977, 68(2), May 1978; 7. 'De facto job segregation', in *American Women Workers in a Full Employment Economy: A Compendium* (US Govt. Printing Office, 1977, repr. in *Readings in Labor Economics and Labor Relations*, ed. R. L. Rowan (Richard D. Irwin, 1980); 8. 'Stocks and flows of academic economists', *AER*, 69(2), May 1979; 9. 'Causes and effects of inflation', in *Outlook Proceedings* (US Dept. Agric., Fall 1978).

Principal Contributions Survey analysis and methodology were the focus of my early work on national surveys of income and expenditure, levels of living, small farmers' credit and ability to repay, and agricultural wages. My most quoted article on methods was the comparative study of short and long enumerative schedules for collecting expenditure data. I have had a career-long respect for quality economic data and econometric methods. From full-time research, I made a change in career direction by moving to full-time graduate and undergraduate teaching in a university that stressed teaching and professional service. After nepotism rules collapsed, I moved to a university that stressed research and teaching. I was first asked to develop core curriculum in cross-disciplinary approaches to the social sciences, and then returned to straight economics.

My research interests centred on labour migration of Blacks and Mexican Americans emphasising effects of re-training programmes. After national attention turned to discrimination against women, I was asked to help SMU clarify its own situation. This led to the article in the *AAUP Bulletin* explaining the methods used by the AEA to help the economics profession overcome discrimination against women. I quantified revolving-door effects on hiring and replacing faculty, analysed occupational segregation by sex, extended the human capital model into male-female wage differences, criticised misuse of residual methods of measuring discrimination, and examined federal statistical needs related to women. My recent research has centred on factors affecting women's labour supply.

RECKTENWALD, Horst Claus

Born 1920, Spiesen, Germany.

Current Post Prof. Econ., Dir. Inst. für Volkswirtschaftslehre, Friedrich-Alexander Univ., Erlangen-Nürnberg, W. Germany, 1983–.

Past Posts Privatdozent., Univ.

Mainz, 1957–8; Prof., Tech. Hochschule, Darmstadt, 1958–9; Vis. Prof., Univ. Erlangen, 1959; Prof., Univ. Freiburg, 1959–63; Dean Faculty, Rector, Friedrich-Alexander Univ., Erlangen-Nürnberg, 1965, 1968, 1973.

Degrees Dr Rer. Pol., Univ. Mainz, 1954, 1957.

Offices and Honours Foundation Councils, New Univ. Regensburg, Augsburg, München (Hochschule der Bundeswehr) and Passau, 1967–9; Advisory Councils, Bundesministerien, 1968–81; Board Dirs., Internat. Inst. Management, Verwaltung (Wissenschaftszentrum), Berlin, W. Germany, 1970–9; Award for *Tax Incidence and Income Redistribution*, Outstanding Academic Book, USA, 1972; Deutsche Forschungsgemeinschaft, Bonn, 1978; Order Fed. Republic Germany (Bundesverdientstkreuz) First Class, 1976, Grobes BV-Kreuz, 1981; Pres., Inst. Internat. Fin. Publiques, Paris, 1978–81; Hon. Pres., IIPF, Paris, 1981–.

Editorial Duties Ed., *Abhandlung zum Wirtschaftlichen Staatswissenschaften*, 1968–; Ass. Ed., *J Pub E*, 1972–; Ed. Board, *Public Fin. Q.*, 1973–.

Principal Fields of Interest 300 Domestic Monetary and Fiscal Theory and Institutions; 031 History of Economic Thought; 036 Economic Methodology.

Publications *Books:* 1. *Steuerinzidenztheorie* (Duncker & Humbolt, 1958, 1967; transl., Spanish, Editorial, 1970); 2. *Finanztheorie und Finanzpolitik*, ed. (Kiepenheuer & Witsch, 1968, 1970); 3. *Finanz- und Geldpolitik im Umbruch* (with H. Haller), (Kohler & Hause, 1969); 4. *Nutzen-Kosten-Analyse und Programmbudget* (Mohr-Siebeck, 1970); 5. *Tax Incidence and Income Redistribution* (Wayne State Univ. Press, 1971); 6. *Political Economy* (Macmillan, 1973; transl., Spanish, Universitaria, 1977); 7. *Adam Smith — Sein Leben und sein Werk* (C. H. Beck, 1976); 8. *Tendances à long terme du secteur public*, ed. (Edns. Cujas, 1978); 9. *Markt und Staat* (Vandenhoeck & Ruprecht, 1980); 10. *Staatswirtschaft und Geldwirtschaft* (C. H. Beck, 1983). *Articles:* 1. 'Zur Lehr von den Marktformen', *WA*, 67(2), 1951, repr. in *Preistheorie*, ed. A. E. Ott (Kiepenheuer & Witsch, 1968); 2. 'Effizienz

und innere Sicherheit', *Kyk*, 20(2), 1967; 3. 'Grundlagen einer intergrierten Wirtschafts — und finanz — politik', *ZN*, 29, 1969, repr. Spanish, *Hacienda Publica Espanola*, 21, 1973; 4. 'German income tax reform — a simulation model', *J Pub E*, 1, 1972; 5. 'Falsification of Wagner's law', in *Secular Trends of the Public Sector*, ed. (Edns. Cujas, 1978); 6. 'An Adam Smith renaissance anno 1976? a reappraisal of his scholarship', *JEL*, 16(1), March 1978, repr. in *Tokyo Smith-Seminar*, ed. H. Mizuta (Maruzen, Pergamon, 1982), and in *Adam Smith — Critical Assessments*, ed. J. C. Wood (Croom Helm, 1984), and in *Ethik, Markt und Staat* (Wissenschaftliche Buches, 1984); 7. 'Justitia distributiva durch Unverteilung? Eine Analyse der personalen Inzidenz' (with K. D. Gruske), *Kyk*, 33(1), 1980; 8. 'Karl Marx anno 1983', *JNS*, 199(6), 1983; 9. 'The public waste syndrome — contours of a theory', in *The Search for Efficiency in the Public Sector*, eds. H. Hanusch and W. Stolper (Wayne State Univ. Press, 1984); 10. 'Federalisme fiscale — analyse empirique à long terme', in *Melanges Gaudemet*, ed. J. Molinier (Edns. Univ., 1984), repr. as 'Falsifizierung des Popitz-Gesetz', in *Staat, Steuern und Finanzausgleich*, eds. W. A. S. Koch, *et al.* (Duncker & Humblot, 1984).

Principal Contributions Earlier interests included failures of static market structure theory, stressing the changing pattern of evolutionary competition, and the inefficient behaviour of an absolute public monopolist. Empirical research concentrated on public sector economics (badly labelled public finance) and tested and falsified Wagner's Law (growing State's share), Popitz's Law (alleged centralisation in federalism), and the 'displacement effect', applying secular trend analysis. Tried to develop contours of a theory of the public waste syndrome by way of revealing and combining the causes for O- and R-inefficiency and emphasising the negative correlation (at least conflict) between self- and group-interest and *bonum commune*. Initiated research on the poor integration of State and technology in fifty-to-fifty mixed economies, revealing the dubious validity of empirical work using cost-benefit analysis.

More recently returned to analysing tax burden additional to tax payments by way of criticising both the partial Jevons-Marshall excess burden theorem (which ignores excess benefits) and (Ramsey's) optimal taxation 'movement' with its naive policy suggestions. Research directed to the process of personal budget incidence, medium-run redistribution effects, and allocative misintegration of the State in GNP. Continued to trace and analyse Adam Smith's opus as an Aristotelean entity of ethics, economics, and politics, proving (1) its catholicity, consistency, originality and failures, (2) Smith's eminent power to reasonably sythesise, and (3) refuting Viner's dictum of Smith's eclecticism and alleged contradictions. Translated *Wealth of Nations* into German and contributed to bringing economics alive by modern historical techniques and intellectual biographies, emphasising (Wicksellian-like) the renaissance of political economy. Wrote a novel (systematic plus lexicographic) textbook on public and monetary economics.

REDDAWAY, William Brian

Born 1913, Cambridge, England.
Current Post Retired Cons.
Past Posts Ass., Bank England, 1934–5; Res. Fellow, Univ. Melbourne, 1936–7; Fellow, Clare Coll. Camb., 1938–; Stat., UK Board Trade, 1940–7; Econ. Dir., OEEC, Paris, 1951–2; Lect. Econ., Dir., Dept. Appl. Econ., Prof. Polit. Econ., Univ. Camb., 1939–55, 1955–70, 1969–80; Vis. Econ., MIT Centre Internat. Studies, Delhi, 1959–60; Vis. Lect., World Bank, Washington, 1960–5; Econ., Harvard Devlp. Advisory Service, Ghana, 1967; Econ. Adviser part-time, Conf. British Industry, 1971–83; Econ., Bangladesh Inst. Devlp. Stud., 1974–5. Cons., Prices Justification Tribunal, Australia, 1974.
Degrees BA (Maths. & Econ.), MA Univ. Camb., 1934, 1938.
Offices and Honours Adam Smith Prize, Univ. Camb., 1934–5; Fellow, BA, 1967; Member, UK Nat. Board

Prices and Incomes, 1967–71; CBE, 1971.
Editorial Duties Ed. *London and Camb. Econ. Service*, 1947–74, *EJ*, 1971–6.
Principal Fields of Interest 100 Economic Growth and Development; Planning; Fluctuations; 300 Domestic Monetary and Fiscal Theory and Institutions; 400 International Economics.
Publications *Books:* 1. *Russian Financial System* (Macmillan, 1935); 2. *Economics of a Declining Population* (A&U, 1939); 3. *Measurement of Production Movements* (CUP, 1946, with F. Carter and P. Stone, 1965); 4. *Development of the Indian Economy* (A&U, 1962); 5. *Effects of UK Direct Investment Overseas*, 2 vols (CUP, 1967, 1968); 6. *Effects of the Selective Employment Tax*, 2 vols (CUP, HMSO 1970, 1973).

Articles: 1. 'General Theory of employment, interest and money', *ER*, 12, June 1936, repr. in *Keynes' 'General Theory': Reports of Three Decades*, ed. R. Lekachman (St Martin's Press, 1964); 2. 'Rationing', in *Lessons of the British War Economy*, ed. D. N. Chester (CUP, 1951); 3. 'Wage flexibility and the distribution of labour', *LBR*, 54, Oct. 1959, repr. in *The Labour Market*, eds. B. J. McCormick and E. O. Smith (Penguin, 1968); 4. 'The economics of under-developed countries', *EJ*, 73, March 1963; 5. 'The economics of newspapers', *EJ*, 73, June 1963; 6. 'Rising prices for ever?', *LBR*, 81, July 1966; 7. 'OPEC surpluses, the world recession and the UK economy' (with G. H. Feinstein), *MBR*, 60, Spring 1978, repr. in *Contemporary Problems of Economic Policy*, eds. R. C. O. Mathews and J. P. Sargent (Methuen, 1983); 8. 'Portfolio selection in practice', in *Macroeconomic Analysis*, ed. J. Currie, A. R. Nobay and P. Peel (Croom Helm, 1981); 9. 'An alternative economic strategy' (with B. Hopkin, M. Miller), *Camb JE*, 6, March 1982; 10. 'Problems and prospects for the UK economy', *ER*, 59, Sept. 1983.
Principal Contributions I have attempted to tackle *practical* problems, whether on full employment, growth, underdeveloped economics, inflation, the effects of direct investment over-

seas, the selective employment tax, or the investment of portfolios. To do so, I have sought to combine theory with realistic data and to look for the factors which are quantitatively important, rather than those which are intellectually stimulating. I have tried to be pragmatic in my choice of methods for tackling problems and to be clear about the alternative position with which comparisons are effectively being made (and to be sure that it is a meaningful and consistent one). Favourite slogan for pupils and research colleagues: 'It is better to be roughly right than to be precisely wrong (or irrelevant).'

REDER, Melvin Warren

Born 1919, San Francisco, CA, USA.
Current Post Prof. Urban and Labor Econ., Grad. School Bus., Univ. Chicago, 1974–.
Past Posts Instr., Bryn Mawr Coll., 1942–3, Brooklyn Coll., 1943–5; Ass. Prof., Carnegie Inst. Technology, 1946–8; Assoc. Prof., Univ. Penn., 1948–9; Assoc. Prof., Prof., Stanford Univ., 1949–53, 1953–71; Vis. Prof., LSE, 1967; Res. Assoc., NBER, 1971–4; Disting. Prof. Econ., Grad. Center, City Univ. NY, 1971–4.
Degrees BA Univ. Cal. Berkeley, 1939; MA Univ. Chicago, 1941; PhD Columbia Univ., 1946.
Offices and Honours Guggenheim Foundation Fellow, 1955–6; Fellow, Center Advanced Study Behavioral Science, Stanford, 1957–8; Ford Faculty Fellow, 1961–2.
Editorial Duties Ed., *J Bus*; Ed. Board, *J. Labor Res.*
Principal Fields of Interest 020 General Economic Theory; 030 History of Economic Thought; Methodology; 800 Manpower; Labour Population.
Publications *Books:* 1. *Studies in the Theory of Welfare Economics* (Columbia Univ. Press, 1947); 2. *Labor in a Growing Economy* (Wiley, 1957).
Articles: 1. 'Theoretical problems of a national wage-price policy', *CJE*, 14, Feb. 1948; 2. 'The theory of occupational wage differentials', *AER*, 45(5), Dec. 1955; 3. 'Alternative theories of labor's share', in *The Allocation of Econ-

omic Resources*, ed. M. Abromovitz (Stanford Univ. Press, 1959); 4. 'Wage structure theory and measurement', in *Aspects of Labor Economics*, ed. A. Rees (NBER, 1963); 5. 'Economic consequence of increased immigration', *REStat*, 45, Aug. 1963; 6. 'Some aspects of the size distribution of earnings', in *The Distribution of National Income*, eds. J. Marshal and B. Ducros (Macmillan, 1968); 7. 'An Economic analysis of medical malpractice', *J. Legal Stud.*, 5, June 1976; 8. 'Chicago economics: permanence and change', *JEL*, 20, March 1982; 9. 'Output and strike activity in US manufacturing: how large are the losses?' (with G. R. Neumann), *ILRR*, Jan. 1984.

Principal Contributions In graduate school and the first few years thereafter I concentrated upon economic theory, writing about welfare economics and macro and micro topics. In the late 1940s, my primary focus shifted to labour economics where it since has remained, despite occasional and continuing flirtations with other research areas. I have always interpreted labour economics broadly to include the interface of trade union wage behaviour with monetary-fiscal policy (Article No. 1 above), the theory of income distribution among factor shares (Article No. 3 above) and among individuals (Article No. 6), the theory of wage structure (Article No. 2), the effects of immigration (Article No. 5) and the analysis of strikes (Article No. 9). So interpreted, labour economics continues to be the centre of my professional interest. However, I have also worked in a number of other branches of the subject: medical economics (Article No. 7); and the methodology and history of economic thought (Article No. 8).

REES, Albert Everett

Born 1921, New York City, NY, USA.
Current Post Pres., Alfred P. Sloan Foundation, New York City, NY, USA, 1979–.
Past Posts Instr., Roosevelt Coll., Chicago, IL, 1947–8; Res. Assoc.,

NBER, 1953–4, 1978–9; Staff Member, US President's Council Econ. Advisers, 1954–5; Fellow, Center Advanced Study Behavioral Sciences, Stanford, CA, 1959–60; Ass. Prof., Assoc. Prof., Prof. Econ., Univ Chicago, 1948–54, 1954–61, 1961–6; Prof. Econ., Provost, Princeton Univ., 1966–79, 1975–7; Dir., US Council Wage and Price Stability, 1974–5.

Degrees BA Oberlin Coll., 1943; MA, PhD Univ. Chicago, 1947, 1950.

Editorial Duties Ed., *JPE*, 1954–9; Assoc. Ed., *Internat. Encyclopedia Social Sciences*, ed. D. L. Sills (Free Press, 1968), 1962–7.

Principal Fields of Interest 820 Labour Markets; 830 Trade Unions; 220 Economic and Social Statistics.

Publications *Books:* 1. *Real Wages in Manufacturing, 1890–1914* (Princeton Univ. Press, 1961); 2. *The Economics of Trade Unions* (Univ. Chicago Press, 1962); 3. *Workers and Wages in an Urban Labor Market* (with G. P. Shultz), (Univ. Chicago Press, 1970); 4. *Discrimination in Labor Markets*, co-ed. (with O. Ashenfelter), (Princeton Univ. Press, 1973); 5. *Economics of Work and Pay* (with D. S. Hamermesh), (Harper & Row, 1973, 1984); 6. *Striking a Balance: Making National Economic Policy* (Univ. Chicago Press, 1984).

Articles: 1. 'Wage determination and involuntary unemployment', *JPE*, 59, April 1951; 2. 'Postwar wage determination in the basic steel industry', *AER*, 60(4), Sept. 1952; 3. 'Industrial conflict and business fluctuations', *JPE*, 60, Oct. 1952; 4. 'Union wage policies', in *Interpreting the Labor Movement* (IRRA, 1952); 5. 'Alternative retail price indexes for selected nondurable goods, 1947–59', in *The Price Statistics of the Federal Government* (NBER, 1961); 6. 'The effects of unions on resource allocation', *J Law E*, 6, Oct. 1963; 7. 'The Phillip's curve as a menu for policy choice', *Ec*, N.S. 37, Aug. 1970; 8. 'Compensating Wage Differentials', in *Essays on Adam Smith*, eds. A. Skinner and T. Wilson (Clarendon Press, 1975).

Principal Contributions Contributed to the understanding of the influence of trade unions on wages, the sources of wage differences within occupations and the historical measurement of changes in real wages. Also participated in one of the first uses of experimental methods to measure economic behaviour.

REIFFERS, Jean-Louis

Born 1941, Paris, France.

Current Post Prof. Econ. Science; Dir. Internat. Econ. and Fin. Center (CEFI), Univ. d'Aix-Marseille II, France, 1974–.

Past Posts Ass. Econ., Aix-en-Provence, 1964–9; Maître de Conf. Agrégé, Univ. Toulon, 1970–3; Cons., ILO, Morocco, Ivory Coast, Mali, UNESCO, 1978–84, Internat. Inst. Higher Educ., 1983–4.

Degrees Licence Sciences Econ., Dr d'Etat Univ. Aix-Marseille, 1964, 1969; Agrégé Sciences Econ., Paris, 1970.

Offices and Honours Vice-Pres., Univ. d'Aix-Marseille, 1974–7.

Editorial Duties Ed. Boards, *Dunod*, 1979–84, *Mondes en Devlp. Rev.*, 1979–84, *Cahiers de l'ISMEA*, 1984–.

Principal Fields of Interest 400 International Economics; 800 Manpower; Labour; Population.

Publications *Books:* 1. *L'union douanière Européenne et l'avantage collectif mondial. Diffusée avec le concours de la CEE* (Univ. d'Aix-Marseille, 1969); 2. *Le role de l'immigration des travailleurs étrangers dans la croissance de la République Federale Allemande* (ILO, 1970); 3. *L'occident en desarroi, ruptures d'un système économique*, co-ed. (with X. Greffe), (Dunod, 1978; transl., Spanish, Blume Editorial, 1981); 4. *Sociétés transnationales et developpement endogène* (with A. Cartapanis, W. Experton, J. L. Fuguet), (UNESCO, 1981; transls., English, Spanish, 1982); 5. *Economie et finances internationales*, ed. (Dunod, 1982); 6. *La montée des protectionnismes dans les années 80*, co-ed. (with B. Lassudrie-Duchène), (Economica, 1984).

Articles: 1. 'Reflexions sur le paradoxe de Leontief', *Econ App*, 25(1), 1972; 2. 'La transformation organisée', in *L'Occident en Desarroi, op cit.*; 3. 'Insertion dans la DIT et espace social du travail', *Rev. Econ. Industrielle*, 4, 1980; 4. 'Differenciation nationales et système mondial: élements de méthode', *RISE*, 28(12), Dec. 1981; 5. 'The new world order and its implications for higher education in France', in *Higher Education and the New International Order*, ed. B. Sanyal (Frances Pinter, UNESCO, 1982); 6. 'La production national de l'avantage comparatif', in *Internationalisation et Autonomie*, ed. H. Bourguinat (Economica, 1982).

Principal Contributions Writing and teaching in the areas of international economics. Early work was concentrated on customs union issues and especially world welfare incidences. More recently my concern has been to establish the links between the international specialisation and the 'labour social space', which is supposed to characterise each country. The hypothesis is that a country modifies its technology and market laws by its own social organisation. Numerous tests have been done on industrialised countries to explain that the dominant functionalist viewpoint is irrelevant. Normative work conducted by myself has led me to think that a nation has a capacity to develop an unique path to take advantage of the international division of labour. I have applied this methodology to conduct studies for UNESCO on the effects of transnational corporations on national cultures.

REYNOLDS, Lloyd G.

Born 1910, Alberta, Canada.
Current Post Sterling Prof. Econ. Emeritus, Yale Univ., 1980–.
Past Posts Instr. Econ., Harvard Univ., 1936–9; Ass. Prof. Econ., Johns Hopkins Univ., 1939–45; Assoc. Prof., Prof. Econ., Yale Univ., 1945–80.
Degrees BA, Hon. LLD Univ. Alberta, 1931, 1957; MA McGill Univ. 1933; PhD Harvard Univ., 1936; Hon. MA Yale Univ., 1948.
Offices and Honours Exec. Comm., Vice-Pres., AEA, 1952–5, 1959; Pres., IRRA, 1955.
Principal Fields of Interest 110 Economic Growth.
Publications *Books:* 1. *The Structure of Labor Markets* (Harper, 1951); 2.

The Evolution of Wage Structure (with C. T. Morris), (Yale Univ. Press, 1956); 3. *The Three Worlds of Economics* (Yale Univ. Press, 1972); 4. *Agriculture in Development Theory* (Yale Univ. Press, 1975); 5. *Image and Reality in Economic Development* (Yale Univ. Press, 1977); 6. *Economic Growth in the Third World, 1850–1980* (Yale Univ. Press, 1984).
Articles: 1. 'The spread of economic growth to the Third World 1850–1980' *JEL*, 21(3), Sept. 1983.
Principal Contributions Price theory; the theory of labour markets and wage determination; the applicability of Western economic theory to centrally planned economies and developing economies; and development theory and development experience.

RICARDO, David*

Dates and Birthplace 1772–1823, London, England.
Posts Held Stockjobber and loan contractor, 1793–1814; Country landowner, 1814–23.
Offices and Honours Founder Member, Geological Soc.; MP Portarlington, Ireland, 1819–23; Founder, Polit. Econ. Club, 1821.
Publications *Books:* 1. *The High Price of Bullion* (1810); 2. *Essay on the Influence of a Low Price of Corn on the Profits of Stock* (1814); 3. *On the Principles of Political Economy and Taxation* (1817); 4. *On Protection to Agriculture* (1822); 5. *Plan for the Establishment of a National Bank* (1824); 6. *David Ricardo: Works and Correspondence*, 11 vols, eds. P. Sraffa and M. H. Dobb (CUP, 1951–73).
Career Successor to Adam Smith's pre-eminent position in British economics, his influence continued to dominate the aims and methods of the discipline throughout the nineteenth century. Despite his own considerable practical experience, his writings are severely abstract and frequently difficult. His chief emphasis was on the principle of diminishing returns in connection with the rent of land, which he believed also regulated the profits of capital. He attempted to deduce a theory of value from the application of labour, but found

it difficult to separate the effects of changes in distribution from changes in technology. The questions thus raised about the labour theory of value were taken up by Marx and the so-called 'Ricardian socialists' as a theoretical basis for criticism of established institutions.

Ricardo's law of rent was probably his most notable and influential discovery. It was based on the observation that the differing fertility of land yielded unequal profits to the capital and labour applied to it. Differential rent is the result of this variation in the fertility of land. This principle was also noted at much the same time by Malthus, West, Anderson, and others. His other great contribution, the law of comparative cost, or comparative advantage, demonstrated the benefits of international specialisation, while furnishing an explanation of the commodity composition of international trade. This was at the root of the free trade argument which set Britain firmly on the course of exporting manufactures and importing foodstuffs. His success in attaching other economists, particularly James Mill and McCulloch, to his views largely accounted for the remarkable dominance of his ideas long after his own lifetime. Though much of this was eventually rejected, his abstract method and much of the theoretical content of his work became the framework for economic science at least until the 1870s.

Secondary Literature M. Blaug, 'Ricardo, David', *IESS*, 13; M. Blaug, *Ricardian Economics. A Historical Study* (Greenwood Press, 1973); B. Gordon, *Political Economy in Parliament, 1819–23* (Barnes & Noble, 1977); S. Hollander, *The Economics of David Ricardo* (Univ. Toronto Press, 1979).

RICCI, Umberto*

Dates and Birthplace 1879–1946, Chieti, Italy.

Posts Held Statistician, Internat. Inst. Agric., 1910; Prof., Univs. Macerta, Parma, Pisa, Bologna, Rome, 1924–8, Cairo, 1929–40, Istanbul, 1942–6.

Publications *Books:* 1. *Reddito e Imposta* (1914); 2. *Les bases théore-*

tiques de la statistique agricole internationale (1914); 3. *Politica e Economia* (1920); 4. *Dal Protezionismo al Sindacalismo* (1926); 5. *La Politica Annonaria dell'Italia durante la Grande Guerra* (1939); 6. *Eléments d'économie politique pure: théorie de la valeur* (1951).

Career Beginning his career as an administrator he rose, via his work on agricultural economics, to become a major theoretician. He wrote on capital, supply and demand curves, theory of wants, savings and taxation, and dealt with applied economics in various journals. One of these articles was the immediate cause of the Fascist government depriving him of his Rome chair.

Secondary Literature L. Einaudi, 'Obit. Umberto Ricci', *AER*, 36(4), Sept. 1946.

RICHARDSON, George Barclay

Born 1924, London, England.

Current Post Secretary to Chief Exec., OUP, Oxford, England, 1974–.

Past Posts Third Secretary, UK Foreign Service, London, 1949; Univ. Reader Econ., Univ. Oxford, 1969–73; Econ. Adviser, UK Atomic Energy Authority, 1968–74; Member, Econ. Devlp. Comm., UK Electrical Eng. Industry, 1964–73; UK Monopolies Commission, 1969–74; UK Royal Commission Environmental Pollution, 1973–4; Delegate, OUP, 1971–4.

Degrees BSc (Physics and Maths.) Aberdeen Univ., 1944; MA (Philo., Polit. and Econ.) Univ. Oxford, 1949.

Offices and Honours CBE.

Principal Fields of Interest 020 General Economic Theory; 610 Industrial Organisation.

Publications *Books:* 1. *Information and Investment* (OUP, 1960); 2. *Economic Theory* (OUP, 1964); 3. *The Future of the Heavy Electrical Plant Industry* (OUP, 1969).

Articles: 1. 'Imperfect knowledge and economic efficiency', *OEP*, 5, June 1953; 2. 'Equilibrium, expectations and information', *EJ*, 69, June 1959; 3. 'The growth of firms' (with N. H. Leyland), *OEP*, 16, March 1964; 4. 'The limits to a firm's rate of growth', *OEP*, 16, March 1964; 5. 'The theory of restrictive trade practices', *OEP*, 17, March 1965; 6. 'Ideal and reality in the choice of techniques', *OEP*, 17, July 1965; 7. 'Price notification schemes', *OEP*, 19, Nov. 1967; 8. 'Planning versus competition', *Soviet Stud.*, 22(3), Jan. 1971; 9. 'Adam Smith on competition and increasing returns', in *Essays on Adam Smith*, eds. T. Wilson and A. S. Skinner (OUP, 1975).

Principal Contributions My central theoretical interest developed from the appreciation that the market structure identified with perfect competition would not permit the attainment of the associated equilibrium configuration, whatever definition were given to the perfect knowledge, usually assumed to be requisite to this end. This led me to consider the market conditions under which this equilibrium could be reached and I found, paradoxically, that these involved so-called 'imperfections' such as small numbers, understandings on price, goodwill, and so on. These ideas were advanced in my book *Information and Investment*. Given these theoretical preoccupations, it was natural for me to become interested in industrial economics and the problems of monopoly and competition. My pamphlet on the heavy electrical industry in the UK is an example reflecting this interest. My theoretical interests also led me to write an introductory textbook (*Economic Theory*) that started with normative rather than positive economics, i.e. by identifying the conditions for optimal allocation and then discussing the market arrangements favourable to the attainment of this allocation in practice.

RIDKER, Ronald Gene

Born 1931, Chicago, IL, USA.
Current Post Sr. Econ. Pol. Planning Div., World Bank, Washington, DC, 1980–.
Past Posts Fulbright Scholar, 1955–6; Instr., Ass. Prof., Washington Univ., St Louis, 1956–8, 1958–64; Dir. Econ., Air Pollution Project, US Public Health Service, 1963–5; Assoc. Prof. Econ., Maxwell School, Syracuse Univ., 1964–7; Vis. Res. Prof. Internat. Econ., Brookings Inst., 1965–6; Ass. Chief,

Chief Pol. Planning Div., US Agency Internat. Devlp., 1966–7, 1969–70; Econ. Adviser, USAID Mission India, New Delhi, 1967–9; Dir., Program, Pop. Resources and the Environment, Resources for Future, 1970–80; Cons., UNESCO, Thailand, 1963, Hudson Inst., 1964–7, US Commission Pop. Growth, 1970–2, ILO, Pop. and Labor Pol. Branch, 1975, Ford Foundation, Manila, 1979, Argonne Nat. Lab., 1979.
Degrees BA Univ. Cal. Berkeley, 1952; MA (Internat. Relations) Fletcher School Law and Diplomacy, 1953; PhD Univ. Wisconsin, 1958.
Offices and Honours Adviser, Pop. Resource Center, Public Interest Econ. Center, Technology and World Pop. Study, US Office Technology Assessment, 1979–80.
Principal Fields of Interest 840 Demographic Economics; 112 Economic Development Models and Theories.
Publications *Books:* 1. *Educational Investment Programming in Thailand. Report to the Government of Thailand*, ed. (UNESCO, 1963); 2. *Economic Costs of Air Pollution, Studies in Measurement* (Praeger, 1967); 3. *Employment and Unemployment Problems of the Near East and South Asia*, co-ed. (with H. Lubell), (Vikas Publ., 1971); 4. *Population, Resources and the Environment, Research Reports of the Commission on Population Growth and the American Future*, III, ed. and contrib. (US Govt. Printing Office, 1972); 5. *Changing Resource Problems of the Fourth World*, ed. and contrib. (JHUP, 1976); 6. *Population and Development: The Search for Selective Interventions*, ed. and contrib. (JHUP, 1976); 7. *Labour Policy and Fertility in Developing Countries* (with O. S. Nordberg), (ILO, 1976); 8. *To Choose a Future: Resource and Environmental Consequences of Alternative Growth Paths* (with W. D. Watson), (JHUP, 1980).
Articles: 1. 'Discontent and economic growth', *EDCC*, 11(1), Oct. 1962, repr. in *Ekistics*, 16(93), Aug. 1963; 2. 'An evaluation of the forecasting ability of the Norwegian national budgeting system', *REStat*, 45(1), Feb. 1963; 3. 'On the economics of post world war III', *JPE*, 71(4), Aug. 1963;

4. 'Burial costs and premature death' (with A. G. Holtmann), *JPE*, 73(3), June 1965; 5. 'The determinants of residential property values, with special reference to air pollution' (with J. A. Henning), *REStat*, 49(2), May 1967; 6. 'The economic determinants of discontent, an empirical investigation', *J Dev Stud*, 4, Jan 1968; 7. 'Population and pollution in the United States', *Science*, 176, June 9, 1972; 8. 'Incentives for family welfare and fertility reduction: an illustration for Malaysia' (with R. Muscat), *Stud. Family Planning*, 4(1), Jan. 1973; 9. '"To grow or not to grow": that is not the relevant question', *Science*, 182, Dec. 28, 1973; 10. 'The no-birth bonus scheme — an evaluation of the use of savings accounts for family planning in South India', *Pop. and Devlp. Rev.*, 6(1), March 1980.

Principal Contributions While I have worked in a variety of fields, one characteristic of most of my work has been the attempt to integrate disparate elements of a picture to answer specific, concrete questions. This was true in attempting to explain the linkage between discontent and economic growth, and between population, resources and environmental pressures, and in trying to understand the determinants (mostly economic) of population growth that would be amenable to policy influence and then apply what was learned to the design of specific population control programmes. It was even true in attempting to develop an integrated picture of the economic costs of air pollution. Most recently I have turned on a full-time basis to economic development problems, which of course also require an integrative approach.

RIPLEY, William Zebina*

Dates and Birthplace 1867–1941, Medford, MA, USA.
Posts Held Lect. Sociology, Columbia Univ., 1893–1901; Prof. Econ., MIT, 1895–1901; Prof. Polit. Econ., Harvard Univ., 1901–33.
Degrees BA MIT, 1890; MA, PhD, LittD Columbia Univ., 1892, 1893, 1929; LLD Univ. Wisconsin, 1930, Univ. Rochester, NY, 1931.

Offices and Honours Dir., C.R. I&P Railways, 1917–33; Admin. Labor Standards, US War Dept., 1918; Chairman, Nat. Adjustment Comm., US Shipping Board, 1919–20.
Publications *Books:* 1. *Trusts, Pools and Corporations* (1905); 2. *Railway Problems* (1907); 3. *Railroads — Rates and Regulation* (1912); 4. *Railroads — Finance and Organization* (1942); 5. *Main Street and Wall Street* (1927).
Career Leading American transport and industrial economist in the pre-World War I and interwar period.

RIST, Charles*

Dates and Birthplace 1874–1955, Lausanne, Switzerland.
Posts Held Prof. Polit. Econ., Univs. Montepellier, Paris, 1913–33; Dep. Governor, Bank of France, 1926; Pres., Banque Ottomaine.
Degrees Lic. és Lettre, Dr en droit, Univ. Paris.
Offices and Honours Officer, Légion d'Honneur; Pres., Assoc. Française des Sciences Econ.; Member, Inst. de France.
Publications *Books:* 1. *A History of Economic Doctrines* (with C. Gide), (1915, 1948); 2. *La deflation en pratique* (1923); 3. *Historie des doctrines relatives au crédit et la monnaie* (1938); 4. *Précis des mécanisme économique élémentaires* (1946).
Career Invited by Charles Gide to co-operate in his history of economics when he succeeded Gide to the Montepellier chair. In addition to this work, he was also a successful adviser to foreign governments, undertaking financial missions in Romania, Turkey, Spain and Austria.
Secondary Literature 'Charles Rist: l'homme — la pensée — l'action', *REP*, Nov./Dec. 1955.

RIVLIN, Alice Mitchell

Born 1931, Philadelphia, PA, USA.
Current Post Dir., Econ. Stud. Program, Brookings Inst., Washington, DC, 1983–.
Past Posts Brookings Inst., 1957–66;

Dep. Ass. Secretary, Ass. Secretary, US Dept. Health, Educ. and Welfare, 1966–9; Sr. Fellow, Brookings Inst., 1969–75; Dir., Congressional Budget Office, US Congress, 1975–83.

Degrees BA Bryn Mawr Coll., 1952; PhD Ratcliffe Coll., Harvard Univ., 1958.

Offices and Honours W. S. Woytinsky Lect. Award, Univ. Michigan, 1972; Gladys M. Kammerer Award, 1972; Charles E. Merriam Award, 1977; Member, Amer. Polit. Science Assoc.; Exec. Comm., Vice-Pres., Pres., AEA, 1979, 1981, 1986; MacArthur Foundation Fellow, 1983; Godkin Lect., Harvard Univ., 1984.

Principal Fields of Interest 513 Business and Public Administration.

Publications *Books:* 1. *Setting National Priorities*, co-author (Brookings Inst., 1971, 1972, 1973); 2. *Systematic Thinking for Social Action* (Brookings Inst., 1971); 3. *Ethical and Legal Issues of Social Experiments*, co-author (Brookings Inst., 1975); 4. *Income Distribution — Can Economists Help?* (Brookings Inst., 1975); 5. *How Can Experiments be more Useful?* (Brookings Inst., 1976); 6. *Economic Choices 1983*, ed. (Brookings Inst., 1984).

Principal Contributions Academic career devoted to policy analysis of federal budgetary problems in US and two tours of duty in the government, managing analytical staffs devoted to improving the budgetary decision process — principal contributions, the organisation of the Congressional Budget Office to improve the analysis and information available to Congress for budget decisions.

ROBBINS, Lionel Charles*

Dates and Birthplace 1898–1984, Harmondsworth, Middlesex, England.

Posts Held Fellow, Lect., New Coll., Oxford, 1924, 1927–9; Lect., Prof. Econ., LSE, 1925–7, 1929–61; Dir., Econ. Section UK Cabinet, 1941–5; Chairman, *Financial Times*, 1961–70; Chairman, UK Comm. Higher Educ., 1961–4; Chairman, Court of Governors, LSE, 1968–74; Pres., BA, 1962–7; Member, UK House of Lords, 1959–84;

Dir., Econ. Intelligence Unit, London, 1971–84.

Degrees BSc LSE, 1923; MA Univ. Oxford, 1924; Hon. Degrees Univs., Dunelm, Exeter, Strathclyde, Sheffield, Heriot-Watt, Columbia, Cambridge, Leicester, Strasbourg, Cal., London, Lisbon, York, Stirling, Royal Coll. Art, PA.

Offices and Honours Member, UK Econ. Advisory Council, 1930–7; Companion of the Bath, 1944; Hon. Fellow, Univ. Coll. London, Manchester Coll. Science and Technology, LSE, London Grad. School Bus. Stud., Courtauld Inst.; Fellow, Pres., BA, 1942, 1962–7; Trustee, Nat. Gallery London, 1952–74, Tate Gallery, London, 1953–9, 1962–7; Pres., RES, 1954–5; Life Peer, 1959; Companion of Honour, 1968; Dir., Royal Opera House, London, 1955–80; Chancellor, Stirling Univ., Scotland, 1968–78; Disting. Fellow, Hist. Econ. Soc., USA, 1984.

Editorial Duties Adviser, *LBR*.

Principal Fields of Interest 030 History of Economic Thought; Methodology; 134 Inflation and Deflation; 430 Balance of Payments; International Finance.

Publications *Books:* 1. *An Essay on Nature and Significance of Economic Science* (1934, 1984); 2. *The Great Depression* (1934, 1938); 3. *The Economic Basis of Class Conflict* (1939); 4. *The Economic Causes of War* (1947); 5. *The Theory of Economic Policy in English Classical Political Economy* (1952, 1978); 6. *Robert Torrens and the Evolution of Classical Economics* (1963); 7. *Politics and Economics* (1963); 8. *Autobiography of an Economist* (1971); 9. *Against Inflation* (1979); 10. *Higher Education Revisited* (1980).

Articles: 1. 'The dynamics of capitalism', *Ec*, 6, March 1926; 2. 'The representative firm', *EJ*, 38, Sept. 1928; 3. 'The economic effects of variations of hours of labour', *EJ*, 39, March 1929; 4. 'The present position of economic science', *Ec*, 10, March 1930; 5. 'The concepts of stationary equilibrium', *EJ*, 40, June 1930; 6. 'On the elasticity of demand for income in terms of effort', *Ec*, 10, June, 1930; 7. 'Consumption and the trade cycle', *Ec*, 12, Nov. 1932; 8. 'Live and dead issues in the methodology of economics', *Ec*, N.S. 5, Aug.

1938; 9. 'The teachings of economics in schools and universities', *EJ*, 65, Dec. 1955; 10. 'Economics and political economy', *AER*, 71(2), May 1981.

Career (Statement submitted Feb. 1984.) My earliest intellectual allegiance was to Guild Socialism. After graduating at the LSE in 1923, I shed any remnants of my one-time socialism, at any rate so far as the organisation of production was concerned. I was and am an economic liberal but without belonging to any political party; my time in the House of Lords has been spent on the cross-benches. At the LSE in the 1930s, the main focus of intellectual activity was the seminar, usually chaired by myself, which was held by myself and Fritz von Hayek.

I have been involved at various times in the formation of UK economic policy. As a member of the Economic Advisory Council committee chaired by Keynes, in 1930, I was in a minority of one: I was an anti-expansionist where public expenditure was concerned, at a time when, as I now think, I should have been on the other side. My feelings are quite otherwise in regard to my opposition to the abandonment of the policy of free imports. Later, in World War II, I became Director of the Economic Section of the War Cabinet. I was a UK delegate at the Hot Springs and the Bretton Woods Conferences in the latter years of the war, dealing with external problems which involved some of the most difficult matters of general economic analysis.

After the war, I should like to think that I had played some part in the scholarly revival of interest in the English classical political economists which has taken place in recent years. My interest in the history of economic thought, always something of a passion, involved me in the piquant intellectual exercise of writing up Robert Torrens, a figure high up in the second class. It is this work by which I would most wish to be judged as a scholar.

The chairmanship of the Robbins Committee on Higher Education is one of the most rewarding experiences I have had. The supplementary material published with the committee's report, for which I can claim no credit, seems to me to be one of the most notable achievements of social studies in our time. On balance, when surveying the way in which all the recommendations of other such enquiries were quietly shelved, I had little cause for dissatisfaction, either with the notice attracted by the report or with the degree to which its suggestions were accepted.

ROBERTSON, Dennis Holme*

Dates and Birthplace 1890–1963, Lowestoft, Suffolk, England.

Posts Held Fellow, Reader Econ., Prof., Trinity Coll. Camb., 1914–38, 1930–8, 1944–57; Prof. Econ., Univ. London, 1939–44.

Degrees MA Univ. Camb., 1912.

Offices and Honours Fellow, BA, 1932, Pres., RES, 1948–50; Knighted, 1953.

Publications *Books:* 1. *A Study of Industrial Fluctuation* (1915); 2. *Money* (1922, 1928); 3. *The Control of Industry* (1923); 4. *Banking Policy and the Price Level* (1926); 5. *Essays in Monetary Theory* (1940); 6. *Britain in the World Economy* (1954); 7. *Growth, Wages, Money* (1961).

Career Monetary economist; his work on industrial fluctuations was also very significant. Keynes's pupil and then collaborator, he later became a prominent critic of Keynes's *General Theory*. This did not prevent his return to Cambridge and to the chair of economics, after which he devoted much of his attention to teaching. His major contribution is to the study of business cycles, but his contribution to the development of Keynesian economics, despite his well-known reservations, is also important.

Secondary Literature S. R. Dennison, 'Robertson, Dennis Holme', *IESS*, 13; J. R. Presley, *Robertsonian Economics* (Macmillan, 1979).

ROBERTSON, Hector Menteith*

Dates and Birthplace 1905–84, Leeds, Yorkshire, England.

Posts Held Ass. Lect., Univ. Leeds, 1928–9; Sr. Lect., Univ. Cape Town,

1930–49; Jagger Prof., Emeritus Prof. Econ., Univ. Cape Town, 1950–70, 1970–84; Vis. Prof., Univ. Melbourne, 1956, 1971.

Degrees BA, MA Univ. Leeds, 1925, 1926; PhD Univ., Camb., 1929.

Offices and Honours Gladstone Memorial Prize, English Univ., 1925; Ellen McArthur Prize, Univ. Camb., 1932; Joint Ed., *SAJE*, 1947–75, Ass. Ed. (Civil), *Union War Histories, South Africa*, 1947–58; Fellow, Univ. Cape Town, 1958–68; Corresp. for S. Africa *RES*, 1953–84; Pres., Econ. Soc. S. Africa, 1950–2; Carnegie Corp. Vis., USA, 1956.

Publications *Books:* 1. *Aspects of the Rise of Economic Individualism: A Criticism of Max Weber and his School* (1933, 1959), repr. in part in *Protestantism and Capitalism: The Weber Thesis and its Critics*, ed. R. W. Green (1959); 2. *The Adam Smith Tradition* (1950); 3. *South Africa, Economic and Political Aspects* (1957).

Articles: 1. 'Sir Bevis Bulmer: a large-scale speculator of Elizabethan and Jacobean times', *J Econ. and Bus. Hist.*, 4, Nov. 1931; 2. '150 years of economic contact between black and white', *SAJE*, 2, Dec. 1934, 3, March 1935; 3. 'Economic development of the Cape under van Riebeek', *SAJE*, 13, March, June, Sept., Dec., 1945; 4. 'European economic developments in the 16th century', *SAJE*, 18, March 1950, repr. in *Aspects of the Rise of Economic Individualism* (1959); 5. 'Adam Smith's approach to the theory of value' (with W. L. Taylor), *EJ*, 67, June 1957, repr. in *Essays in Economic Thought: Aristotle to Marshall*, eds. J. J. Spengler and W. R. Allen (1960); 6. 'Marx, Menger, Mercantilism and Max Weber', in *Studi in Onore di Amintore Fanfani*, ed. D. A. Giuffre (1962); 7. 'Immigration in the South African economy', in *Economics of International Migration*, ed. B. Thomas (1958); 8. 'Alfred Marshall's aims and methods illustrated from his treatment of distribution', *HOPE*, 2(1), Spring 1970, repr. in *Alfred Marshall: Critical Assessments*, ed. J. C. Wood (1982); 9. 'Euge! Belle! Dear Mr Smith: The Wealth of Nations, 1776–1976', *SAJE*, 44, Dec. 1976; 10. 'Fifty years of the South African Journal of Economics', *SAJE*, 51, March 1983.

Principal Contributions (Written by H. M. Robertson shortly before his death.) I believe that elucidation of changes in Western European economies during 'early modern times' suffered from injudicious adoption of general explanations, based on ingeniously conceived, attractively developed psycho-sociological constructs such as a 'spirit of capitalism' emanating from a protestant work-ethic. Written reluctantly to help emancipate historical research from such constraints, my first book was long received with little understanding or open-mindedness. I avoided controversy; but once restated my views at a seminar (see No. 4 above). In 1956 Gerschenkron induced me to talk to his graduate students at short notice. I retained the notes; and expanded them later for an appropriate tribute to Fanfani (see No. 6 above). South Africa has provided opportunities for varied economic and historical research.

An early contribution was '150 years of economic contact between black and white' (Article No. 2). Various articles and much unpublished research have followed intensive study of Dutch East India Co. records. Control over company outstations, distant both in space and time, involved detailed written communications between local officials and the central administration by slow, irregularly-calling ships. These provide well-documented information on economic 'events' and about economic thinking, within the company, on reasons for their occurrence, their expected results and control — *viz*. about links between economic thinking and action. My chief interests have always lain in the border areas between economic history and the history of economic thought. Teaching duties helped me to make my own assessments of past economists. Most detailed is a review of a major element in Marshall's work (Article No. 8). I derived most pleasure from those which brought me into the congenial company of Adam Smith (Article No. 9).

Secondary Literature V. de V. Graaff, 'H. M. Robertson, 1905–84', *SAJE*, 52, Sept. 1984.

ROBINSON, Edward Austin Gossage

Born 1897.

Current Post Emeritus Prof. Econ., Univ. Camb., 1966–.

Past Posts Fellow, Corpus Christi Coll. Camb., 1923–6; Tutor to HH The Maharaja of Gwalior, 1926–8; Univ. Lect., Fellow, Sidney Sussex Coll. Camb., Prof. Econ., Univ. Camb., 1929–49, 1931–, 1950–65; Member, Econ. Section, UK War Cabinet, Office 1939–42; Econ. Adviser, UK Ministry Production, 1942–5, UK Board Trade, 1946; Dir. Econ., UK Ministry Power, 1967–8.

Degrees BA, MA Univ. Camb., 1921, 1923.

Offices and Honours Secretary, RES, 1945–70; Treasurer, Pres., IEA, 1950–9, 1959–62; Member, Council, DSIR, 1954–9; Chairman, Council, NIESR, 1949–62; Europ. Advisory Comm., OEEC, 1957–62; Exec. Comm., Overseas Develp. Inst.; Knighted, 1957.

Editorial Duties Joint Ed., *EJ*, 1944–70.

Principal Fields of Interest 121 Economic Studies of Less Industrialised Countries.

Publications *Books:* 1. *The Structure of Competitive Industry* (Macmillan, 1931); 2. *Monopoly* (Macmillan, 1941); 3. *Economic Consequences of the Size of Nations*, ed. (Macmillan, 1960); 4. *Economic Development of Africa South of the Sahara*, ed. (Macmillan, 1964); 5. *Problems in Economic Development* (Macmillan, 1965); 6. *The Economics of Education*, co-ed. (with J. Vaizey), (Macmillan, 1966); 7. *Backward Areas in Advanced Countries*, ed. (Macmillan, 1969); 8. *Economic Development of South Asia*, ed. (Macmillan, 1970); 9. *The Economic Development of Bangladesh Within a Socialist Framework*, co-ed. (with others), (Macmillan, 1974).

ROBINSON, Joan*

Dates and Birthplace 1903–83, Camberley, Surrey, England.

Posts Held Lect., Reader, Prof. Econ., Univ. Camb., 1932–49, 1949–65, 1965–71.

Degrees MA Univ. Camb., 1927; Hon. LLD Univs. London, Liège.

Publications *Books:* 1. *Economics of Imperfect Competition* (1933); 2. *Accummulation of Capital* (1956, 1969); 3. *Aspects of Development and Underdevelopment* (1979); 4. *Collected Economic Papers*, 5 vols (1979).

Career Her early work on imperfect competition, which she later repudiated, taught an entire generation of economists the geometrics of price theory that now figures so heavily in elementary textbooks. A leading propagator of Keynesian economics before the war, she moved after the war towards a dynamisation of Keynesian economics, gradually converting it into a theory of growth along what is nowadays called 'post-Keynesian' lines. Becoming increasingly scornful of orthodox economics, she led the battle against Samuelson and Solow in the 1960s and 1970s, denying in particular the neoclassical theory of distribution based on the principle of marginal productivity.

Secondary Literature G. C. Harcourt, 'Robinson, Joan', *IESS*, 18; T. Skouras, 'The economics of Joan Robinson', in *Twelve Contemporary Economists*, eds. J. R. Shackleton and G. Locksley (Macmillan, 1981); 'Robinson Memorial Issue', *Camb JE*, 7, Jan. 1983.

RODBERTUS, Johann Karl*

Dates and Birthplace 1805–75, Greifswald, Sweden.

Posts Held Barrister, Prussian Civil Service, 1826–32.

Publications *Books:* 1. *Die Forderungen der arbeitenden Klassen* (1839); 2. *Zur Erkenntnis unserer staatswirtschaftlichen Zustände* (1842); 3. *Overproduction and Crises* (1850–1, 1898); 4. *Zur Erklärung und Abhälfe der heutigen Creditnoth des Grundbesitzes* (1868–9); 5. *Briefe und socialpolitische Aufsätze*, 2 vols (1882); 6. *Schriften*, 4 vols, ed. A. Wagner (1899).

Career German State socialist, particularly associated with Lassalle and Wagner. His programme for relieving the distress of the working classes attendant on industrialisation, was economic rather than political. The private ownership of land and of the means of production was to be eliminated not by revolution or political organisation, but by a gradual evolutionary process. While enjoying a considerable reputation in his own lifetime, he is nowadays little read.

Secondary Literature B. Fritsch, 'Rodbertus, Johann Karl', *IESS*, 13.

ROEMER, John E.

Born 1945, Washington, DC, USA.
Current Post Prof. Econ., Univ. Cal. Davis, USA, 1981–.
Past Posts Ass. Prof., Assoc. Prof., Univ. Cal. Davis, 1974–80; Vis. Prof., Yale Univ., 1980.
Degrees BA (Maths.) Harvard Univ., 1966; PhD Univ. Cal. Berkeley, 1974.
Offices and Honours US SSRC Fellow, 1977; NSF Post-doctoral Fellow, 1979; Guggenheim Foundation Fellow, 1980.
Editorial Duties Ed. Marxian Economics, *Encyclopedia of Economics* (McGraw-Hill); Co-ed., Book Series 'Marxism and Modern Social Theory' (CUP); Ed. Board, *Econ. and Philo.*
Principal Fields of Interest 020 General Economic Theory; 036 Economic Methodology.
Publications *Books:* 1. *US–Japanese Competition in International Markets* (Inst. Internat. Stud., 1975); 2. *Analytical Foundations of Marxian Economic Theory* (CUP, 1981); 3. *A General Theory of Exploitation and Class* (Harvard Univ. Press, 1982).
Articles: 1. 'Continuing controversies on the falling rate of profit: fixed capital and other issues', *Cam JE*, 3(4), Dec. 1979; 2. 'A general equilibrium approach to Marxian economics', *Em*, 48(2), March 1980; 3. 'Innovation, rates of profit, and uniqueness of von Neumann prices', *JET*, 24(3), June 1980; 4. 'Rawlsian justice as the core of a game' (with R.E. Howe), *AER*, 71(5), Dec. 1981; 5. 'Origins of exploitation and class: value theory of pre-capitalist economy', *Em*, 50(1), Jan. 1982; 6. 'Exploitation alternatives and social-ism', *EJ*, 92, March 1982; 7. 'New directions in the Marxian theory of exploitation and class', *Polit. and Soc.*, 11(3), Summer 1982; 8. 'Property relations vs. surplus value in Marxian exploitation', *Philo. and Public Affairs*, 11(4), Fall 1982; 9. 'Are socialist ethics consistent with efficiency?', *Philo. Forum*, 14, Spring–Summer 1983; 10. 'Unequal exchange, labor migration and international capital flows: a theoretical synthesis', in *Marxism, Central Planning and the Soviet Economy: Economic Essays in Honor of Alexander Erlich*, ed. P. Desai (MIT Press, 1984).
Principal Contributions PhD dissertation studied competition in international markets among five major capitalist countries, describing a cycle of four stages with respect to trade and foreign investment concentration. Published a monograph and four articles on the subject. Other work during this period was on systematic biases in comparative growth statistics of socialist and capitalist economies (a theoretical paper), and empirical work on post-fiscal distribution of income in the US.

In 1980, began applying general equilibrium methods to formulating ideas of Marxian economics. Displayed main ideas of Marxian economics in a general equilibrium setting, summarised in 1981 book. This work led to investigating foundations of exploitation theory. Could one propose a general theory of exploitation in which Marxian exploitation is a special case, but which would allow a comparative discussion of exploitation under feudalism, capitalism, and socialism? In the 1982 book, such a theory is proposed, using general equilibrium and game-theoretic techniques, and it is seen that the labour theory of value is irrelevant for Marxism, both as a theory of price and as a theory of exploitation. That book also develops a precise theory of class in a general equilibrium model, in which classes emerge endogenously from agent behaviour subject to constraints. The methodological presumption underlying this work is rational choice and micro-foundation: Marxism must abandon its teleological method and seek to explain phenomena as the consequence of rational choice.

Most generally, I adhere to an 'analytical Marxism' which applies the tools of contemporary economics to analysing the foundations of Marxian ideas which are intuitively and historically compelling, thus putting that theory on a sounder basis. In the process, some parts of the received theory are vitiated, and some parts remain, and are thereby strengthened.

ROGERS, James Edwin Thorold*

Dates and Birthplace 1823–90, W. Meon, Hampshire, England.
Posts Held Clergyman, Private Tutor, Univ. Oxford, 1846–59; Prof. Econ. Stats., King's Coll., London, 1859–90; Drummond Prof., Univ. Oxford, 1862–8, 1888–90.
Offices and Honours MP, 1880–6.
Publications *Books:* 1. *A History of Agriculture and Prices in England*, 7 vols (1866–1902); 2. *A Manual of Political Economy for Schools* (1868, 1876); 3. *Six Centuries of Work and Wages* (1884, 1949); 4. *The Economic Interpretation of History* (1888); 5. *The Relations of Economic Science to Social and Political Action* (1888); 6. *The Industrial and Commercial History of England*, ed. A.G.L. Rogers (1892).
Career On leaving the Church to pursue economic studies, he developed an idiosyncratic system based on the use of empirical evidence, but retaining much of the *laissez faire* liberalism of the classical economists he so despised. His opinionated, anti-establishment views interrupted his Oxford career, but his monumental publications of price data secured his scholarly reputation.
Secondary Literature A.W. Coats, 'Rogers, James E. Thorold', *IESS*, 13; N.B. De Marchi, 'On the early dangers of being too political an economist: Thorold Rogers and the 1868 election to the Drummond Professorship', *OEP*, 28(3), Nov. 1976.

ROMER, Thomas

Born 1947, Nyiregyhaza, Hungary.
Current Post Prof. Econ. and Polit. Econ., Grad. School Industrial Admin., Carnegie-Mellon Univ., Pittsburgh, PA, USA, 1981–.
Past Posts Lect., Ass. Prof., Univ. Western Ont., 1972–5; Ass. Prof., Assoc. Prof., Prof., Carnegie-Mellon Univ., 1975–80; Vis. Econ., US Fed. Trade Commission, Washington, 1979–80.
Degrees BSc MIT, 1968; MPhil, PhD Yale Univ., 1971, 1974.
Offices and Honours Joint Council Econ. Educ. Award, 1975; Duncan Black Award, Public Choice Soc., 1980.
Editorial Duties Co-ed., *Carnegie Papers on Polit. Economy* (1980–).
Principal Fields of Interest 025 Social Choice; Bureaucratic Performance; 320 Fiscal Theory and Policy; Public Finance; 931 Urban Economics and Public Policy.
Publications *Articles:* 1. 'Individual welfare, majority voting, and the properties of a linear income tax', *J Pub E*, 4, May 1975; 2. 'Majority voting on tax parameters: some further results', *J Pub E*, 7, Feb. 1977; 3. 'Political resource allocation, controlled agendas, and the status quo' (with H. Rosenthal), *Public Choice*, 33, Winter 1978; 4. 'Bureaucrats vs. voters: on the political economy of resource allocation by direct democracy' (with H. Rosenthal), *QJE*, 93, Nov. 1979; 5. 'The elusive median voter' (with H. Rosenthal), *J Pub E*, 12, Oct. 1979; 6. 'Asymmetric information and agenda control: the bases of monopoly power in public spending' (with R. Filimon and H. Rosenthal), *J Pub E*, 17, Feb. 1982; 7. 'Median voters or budget maximizers: evidence from school expenditure referenda' (with H. Rosenthal), *ZN*, Suppl. 2, 1982; 8. 'Housing, voting, and moving: equilibrium in a model of local public goods with multiple jurisdictions' (with D. Epple and R. Filimon), in *Research in Urban Economics*, 3, ed. J.V. Henderson (JAI Press, 1983); 9. 'Warranties, performance, and the resolution of buyer-seller disputes' (with T. Palfrey), *Bell JE*, 14, Spring 1983.
Principal Contributions The focus of my research has been the interaction of market and nonmarket forces in re-

source allocation, particularly in the political economy of the public sector. This has involved both theoretical work and empirical (econometric, experimental) investigation. Early work dealt with determinants of income tax rates, using a highly streamlined representation of the political process. The structure of political decision-making is modelled in greater detail in my work on local public spending (in collaboration with H. Rosenthal), where considerations of agenda control and asymmetric and incomplete information play important roles. Most recently, I have begun detailed analysis of the connections between political campaign finance and political/economic outcomes. Another developing interest is the relationship between legal processes (dispute resolution) and product markets (particularly warranties).

ROPER, Don

Born 1940, Lubbock, TX, USA.
Current Post Prof. Econ., Univ. Utah, Salt Lake City, UT, USA, 1982–.
Past Posts Econ., Fed. Reserve Board, Washington, DC, 1969–75; Vis. Scholar, Univ. Stockholm, 1974, ANU, 1978, Julame Univ., 1980; Bailey Prof. Money and Banking, Univ. Illinois, 1981–2.
Degrees BS (Industrial Eng.) Texas Technological Univ., 1963; MA Northwestern Univ., 1965; PhD Univ. Chicago, 1969.
Principal Fields of Interest 430 International Monetary Economics; 210 Mathematics and Econometrics; 040 Economic History.
Publications *Articles:* 1. 'Macroeconomic policies and the distribution of the world money supply', *QJE*, 85, Feb. 1971; 2. 'Role of expected value analysis for speculation', *QJE*, 89, Feb. 1975; 3. 'A monetary model of exchange market pressure', *AER*, 67(4), Sept. 1977; 4. 'J. Laurence Laughlin and the quantity theory of money' (with L. Girton), *JPE*, 86, Aug. 1978; 5. 'Optimal exchange market intervention' (with S. Turnovsky), *CJE*, 42, May 1980; 6. 'Theory of currency sub-stitution and monetary integration' (with L. Girton), *Econ App*, 33(1), 1980; 7. 'Optimum monetary aggregate for stabilization policy' (with S. Turnovsky), *QJE*, 94, Sept. 1980; 8. 'Theory and implications of currency substitution' (with L. Girton), *JMCB*, 13, Feb. 1981; 9. 'Capitalization formulas with time varying yields', *PF*, 37(1), 1982.

Principal Contributions Early work focussed on asset substitution in general versus substitution between monies *per se*. The latter, referred to as 'currency substitution', has implications that can be explained only by reference to the essential property of money, which, I have argued, is the independence of money's own rate from the value of money (measured in any *numéraire*). In more recent work I have used this property of money to explain Keynes's view that the rate on money 'ruled the roost' in the Great Depression and to show that it is the source of neutrality theorems in monetary economics. In work on monetary reform, I have considered new forms of contract on deposit monies which eliminate neutrality and the possibility of secular overissue (inflation). In other work, with Stephen Turnovsky, the definition of 'money' was viewed as the weighted average of financial instruments with weights chosen for stabilisation objectives. Lance Girton and I have separated the behaviour of private participants in exchange markets from central bank intervention through the use of a concept called 'exchange market pressure'. This, we think, addresses the simultaneity problem found in empirical work on the monetary approach to the balance of payments and exchange-rate determination. In work on monetary history, L. Girton and I have developed the argument that the driving force underlying the evolution of monetary institutions arises from the conflict between efforts to maintain confidence in the value of monetary liabilities and efforts to replace commodity with fiat money. As a major example of this viewpoint we have argued that the Great Depression can be seen, in part, as the collapse of an international system made vulnerable to a gold scramble by efforts to restore confidence with prewar parities while introducing gold-economising measures.

RÖPKE, Wilhelm*

Dates and Birthplace 1899–1966, Schwarmstedt, Germany.
Posts Held Privatdozent, Univs. Jena and Graz; Prof., Univs. Marburg, 1928–33, Istanbul, 1933–7, Grad. Inst., Geneva, 1937–66.
Degrees PhD Univ. Marburg, 1921.
Publications *Books:* 1. *Die Lehre von der Wirtschaft* (1937); 2. *Die Gesellschaftskrisis der Gegenwart* (1942); 3. *Civitas Humana* (1944); 4. *Internationale Ordnung* (1945); 5. *Jenseits von Angebot und Nachfrage* (1958).
Career Extremely prolific and wide-ranging writer whose chief aim was the rehabilitation of the market economy. As an opponent of the Nazis he was an exile after 1933; he was equally a critic of socialist economics. Through his close friendship with Ludwig Erhard, he was a major architect of the German 'economic miracle'.
Secondary Literature P. Boarman, 'Wilhelm Röpke', *German Econ. Rev.*, 4(2), 1966.

ROSCHER, Wilhelm Georg Griedrich*

Dates and Birthplace 1817–94, Germany.
Posts Held Lect., Prof., Univ. Göttingen, 1840–8; Prof., Univ. Leipzig, 1848–94.
Publications *Books:* 1. *Grundriss zu Vorlesungen über die Staatswirtschaft nach geschichtlicher Methode* (1843); 2. *Principles of Political Economy*, 2 vols, 1854–94, 1882); 3. *Geschichte der National Ökonomie in Deutschland* (1874, 1924).
Career One of the founders of the German Historical School who explicitly excluded normative in favour of positive economics. The value of historical study, he argued, was that it showed that all nations proceed through stages of development and decay. He also wrote on purely historical and philosophical topics, as well as venturing comprehensively into the history of economic thought.
Secondary Literature E. Salin, 'Roscher, Wilhelm', *IESS*, 13.

ROSE, Klaus

Born 1928, Bochm, Germany.
Current Post Inst. für Allgemeine und Aussenwirtschaftstheorie, Univ. Mainz, W. Germany, 1962–.
Degrees Diplom-Volkswirt, Dr Rer. Pol., Privatdozent Univ. Cologne 1950, 1952, 1957; Ordentlicher Prof., Univ. Mainz, 1961.
Offices and Honours Instr. Econ., Foreign Office, Bonn, W. Germany.
Editorial Duties Ed. Boards, *Jahrbuch für Sozialwissenschaften*, *Handwörterbuch der Wirtschaftswissenschaften* (Vandenhoek & Ruprecht, Mohr, Fisher).
Principal Fields of Interest 420 Trade Relations; 111 Economic Growth Theory.
Publications *Books:* 1. *Theorie der Aussenwirtschaft* (Vahlen-Verlag, 1964, 1981); 2. *Theorie der internationalen Wirtschaftsbeziehungen*, ed. (Kiepenheuer & Witsch, 1965, 1971); 3. *Gleichgewichtswachstum and Stabilitat* (J.C.B. Mohr, 1970); 4. *Grundlagen der Wachstumstheorie* (Vandenhoeck & Reprecht, 1971, 1977); 5. *Theorie der Einkommensverteilung* (Gabler, 1965).
Articles: 1. 'Die Bedeutung des Akzelerationsprinzips für die Dynamisierung des Keynesschen Systems', *Jahrbücher für Nationalökonomie und Statistik*, 165, 1953; 2. 'Der Erkenntniswert der Wachstumsmodelle', *Jahrbücher für Nationalökonomie und Statistik*, 168, 1956; 3. 'Wachstums- und Konjunkturtheorie', *Jahrbuch für Sozialwissenschaften*, 13, 1962; 4. 'Friehandle, Optimalzoll und wirtschaftlicher Wohlstand', *WA*, 96, 1966; 5. 'Einkommens- und Beschäftigungstheorie', in *Kompendium der Volkswirtschaftslehre*, 1, ed. H. Ehrlicher, *et al.* (Vandenhoeck & Ruprecht, 1967, 1975); 6. 'Heckscherohlinsches Theorem und technischer Fortschritt', in *Beiträge zur Theorie der Aussenwirtschaft, Schriften des Vereins für Sozialpolitik*,

56 (Duncker & Humblot, 1970); 7. 'Flexible Wechselkurse und Inflationsimport' (with D. Bender), *Jahrbücher für Nationalökonomie und Statistik*, 187(6), Aug. 1973; 8. 'Der monetäre Ansatz in der Zahlungsbilanztheorie', *Jahrbuch für Sozialwissenschaften*, 28, 1977; 9. 'Wechselkurs', in *Handwörterbuch der Wirtschaftswissenschaften* (Vandenhoeck & Ruprecht, Mohr, Fischer, 1980); 10. 'Freie Wechselkurse, Finanzmarkttheorie und Kaufkraftparität', in *Politik und Markt* (Fischer, 1980).

Principal Contributions During my studies of economics at the University of Cologne, I was especially interested in business-cycle theory and wrote my master's thesis (Dipl. Volkswirt) on neo-Austrian business-cycle theory. The thesis for the doctorate also treated problems of business-cycle theory, particularly Hick's model of cycle and growth. The renaissance of interest in growth theory — initiated by Domar and Harrod — caused me to write an inaugural dissertation (*Habilitationsschrift*) about questions of stability during phases of economic growth. The results of this work were published in several articles.

At the beginning of the 1960s, my interest shifted to international economic relations. The fast expansion of world trade connected with the increasing convertibility of currencies gave new interest to questions of international economic relations. This was the incentive to write *Theorie der Aussenwirtschaft* (Theory of International Trade), now in its eighth edition. First I was interested in the pure theory of international trade but later on I concentrated on the monetary aspects of international relations. This is illustrated by several articles concerned with balance-of-payments and exchange-rate problems. My preferences for didactics led me to write books and articles in the theory of income and employment which is standard fare at most German universities. Moreover, I wrote *Wachstumstheorie* (Growth Theory), because I had the impression that the complicated and technical literature on this subject was too difficult for many students. In the

following years I worked mainly on questions in applied economic science. This is exemplified by an article about the German experience of flexible exchange rates since 1973, which I have just finished (see Article No. 10 above).

ROSEN, Howard

Born 1917, Newark, NJ, USA.
Current Post Private Cons., 1980–.
Past Posts Price and Industrial Econ., Bureau Labor Stats., US Dept. Labor, 1945–7; Ass. Prof., Hampton Inst., VA, 1947–51; Labor Econ., Bureau Labor Stats., US Dept. Labor, Washington, DC, 1951–62; Professorial Lect., George Washington Univ., 1962–80; Dir., Office Res. & Devlp., Employment & Training Admin., US Dept. Labor, 1980–5; Cons., Nat. Centre Res. Vocational Educ., Ohio State Univ., 1980–1; Vis. Prof., Brandeis Univ., Waltham, MA, 1980–1; Sr. Scientist, Abt Assoc. Inc., Cambridge, MA, 1984–.
Degrees BA Rutgers Univ., 1939; MA NJ State Teachers Coll., 1942; PhD Amer. Univ., Washington, DC, 1956; Hon. Dr (Humane Letters) Ohio State Univ., 1980.
Offices and Honours Disting. Career Service Award, US Dept. Labor.
Editorial Duties Ed. Board, *JHR*, 1975–80.
Principal Fields of Interest 810 Manpower Training and Allocation; Labour Force and Supply; 811 Manpower Training and Development; 820 Labour Markets; Public Policy.
Publications *Books:* 1. *Responsiveness of Training Institutions to Changing Labor Market Demands* (with R.E. Taylor and F.C. Pratzner), (Ohio State Univ. Press, 1983); 2. *Displaced Workers: Implications for Educational and Training Institutions — 1984* (with K. Hollenbecke and F.C. Pratzner), (Ohio State Univ. Press, 1984); 3. *Servants of the People: The Uncertain Future of the Federal Civil Service* (Olympus, 1985).
Articles: 1. 'Social research: a challenge to the new generation', in *Growth and Change* (Univ. Kentucky, 1970); 2. 'An administrator's reflections', in

Employment and Training R&D: Lessons Learned and Future Directions (Upjohn Inst. Employment Res., 1984).

Principal Contributions I began my career in the Bureau of Labor Statistics in the US Dept. of Labor where I worked as a price economist and industrial economist in the price and productivity divisions. Upon moving to the manpower division in BLS I administered the preparation of industry and blue-collar occupation studies for the Occupational Outlook Handbook. In 1961 I was asked to contribute to the development of the country's legislation on manpower and employment — known as the Manpower Development and Training Act (MDTA). From 1962 to 1980 I administered the US Dept. of Labor's R&D programme concerned with problems of unemployment, underdevelopment and the special labour market difficulties of minorities, women, the handicapped and disadvantaged workers. While administering this programme I also taught at George Washington University and The American University in Washington, DC. In addition to sponsoring social science research my office funded some 500 PhD candidates to write their dissertations in the employment and training field. My governmental assignments involved me in many of the important policy issues affecting the training of disadvantaged workers in our society. Since 1980 I have been a consultant to both public and private organisations. I have also finished a book about the 2.4 million career employees of the US government.

ROSEN, Sherwin

Born 1938, Chicago, IL, USA.
Current Post Edwin A. and Betty L. Bergman Prof. Econ., Univ. Chicago, Chicago, IL, USA, 1977–.
Past Posts Ass. Prof., Assoc. Prof., Prof., Kenan Prof. Econ., Univ. Rochester, NY, 1967–70, 1970–5, 1975–7; Vis. Prof., Univ. Buffalo, 1970; Harvard Univ., 1972–3, Columbia Univ., 1974, Stanford Univ., 1976; Adjunct Scholar, AEI; Cons., US Dept. Labor,

Fed. Communications Commission, US Social Security Admin.
Degrees BS Purdue Univ., IN, 1960; MA, PhD Univ. Chicago, 1962, 1966.
Offices and Honours Ford Foundation Dissertation Fellow, 1963–4; NBER, 1967; Sr. Res. Fellow, Fellow, Em Soc, 1976; Vis. Scholar, Hoover Inst., Palo Alto, 1983–; Res. Assoc. Nat. Opinion Res. Center, 1977; Member, Conf. Income and Wealth, 1978.
Editorial Duties Ed. Boards, *AER*, 1970–4, 1982–; Assoc. Ed., *J Em*, 1970–4; *REStat*, 1973–; *Em*, 1975–84; *Econ. Letters*, 1978–; *Bell JE*, 1981–3; *Rand J. Econ.*, 1984–; *J Labor Econ*, 1983–.
Principal Fields of Interest 022 Microeconomic Theory; 800 Manpower, Labour, Population; 611 Market Structure.
Publications Books: 1. *A Disequilibrium Model of Demand for Factors of Production* (with M.I. Nadiri), (NBER, 1974); 2. *Studies in Labour Markets*, ed. (Univ. Chicago Press, 1981).
Articles: 1. '1. Short-run employment variation on class-I railroads in the U.S., 1947–64', *Em*, 36, Oct. 1968; 2. 'Trade union power, threat effects and extent of organization', *REStud*, 36, April 1969; 3. 'Learning and experience in the labor market', *JHR*, 7(3), Summer 1972; 4. 'Hedonic prices and implicit markets: product differentiation in pure competition', *JPE*, 82(4), Jan.–Feb. 1974; 5. 'The value of saving a life: evidence from the labor market' (with R. Thaler), in *Household Production and Consumption*, ed. N. Terleckyj (Columbia Univ. Press, 1976); 6. 'Substitution and division of labor', *Ec*, N.S. 45, Aug. 1978; 7. 'Education and self-selection' (with R. Willis), *JPE*, 87(5), pt. 2, Oct. 1979; 8. 'Rank-order tournaments as optimal labor contracts' (with E. Lazear), *JPE*, 89(5), Oct. 1981; 9. 'The economics of superstars', *AER*, 71(5), Dec. 1981; non-technical version in *The Amer. Scholar*, 52(4), Autumn 1983; 10. 'Authority, control and the distribution of earnings', *Bell JE*, 13(2), Autumn 1982.
Principal Contributions Early work elaborated the role of production complementarities and adjustment costs for understanding demands for inputs in

time-series data, and demonstrated a buffer-inventory function for input utilisation rates in intertemporal resource allocation. From there I studied human capital accumulation, spelling out its behavioural implications for life-cycle earning dynamics, learning by experience, sequential job assignments, job mobility and educational selection. Theoretical and empirical work supports the idea that educational choices go along comparative advantage lines, requiring multifaceted concepts of ability rather than single-factor concepts such as IQ.

An overriding theme of almost all my work has been the analysis of spatial equilibrium in markets with heterogeneous goods and agents, showing how buyers and sellers are matched together and what inferences can be drawn from price and location data about the underlying structure of preferences and technology. This work clarifies the nature of equilibrium in markets characterised by product differentiation, and its relationship to market structure. It also has many applications for labour economics and the theory of equalising differences. My own applications include estimation of the value of human life for risk-benefit assessments, the value of urban amenities and disamenities for quality of life indexes, and the nature of teacher preferences over racial and other characteristics of students. I have recently turned to the microeconomics of incentive and other labour market contracts and their relation to the size distribution of income and output. I have also contributed to the measurement of trade union differentials, the analysis of social security and empirical connections between health and wealth. My current research concerns empirical problems in economic dynamics.

ROSENBLUTH, Gideon

Born 1921, Berlin, Germany.
Current Post Prof. Econ., Univ. British Columbia, Vancouver, British Columbia, Canada, 1962–.
Past Posts Ass. Econ., Res. Div., Wartime Prices and Trade Board, Ottawa, 1943–6; Stat., Canadian Labour and Prices Div., Ottawa, 1946–8; Econ., Econ. Res. and Devlp. Branch, Canadian Dept. Trade and Commerce, Ottawa, 1949; Instr., Princeton Univ., 1949–50; Res. Assoc., NBER, NY, 1951–2; Ass. Prof. Econ., Stanford Univ., 1952–4; Assoc. Prof. Econ., Queen's Univ., 1954–62; Vis. Assoc. Prof., Univ. Washington, 1961.
Degrees BA Univ. Toronto, 1943; PhD Columbia Univ., 1953.
Offices and Honours US SSRC Training Fellow, NBER, NY, 1950–1; Pres., CEA, 1978–9, Canadian Assoc. Univ. Teachers, 1966–7; Fellow, Royal Soc. Canada.
Editorial Duties Ed. Board, Managing Ed., *CJE*, 1976–8, 1972–6; Ed. Board, *Western Econ. Rev.*, 1984–.
Principal Fields of Interest 131 Economic Fluctuatons; 611 Market Structure; 612 Public Policy towards Monopoly.
Publications *Books:* 1. *Wages, Salaries and Supplementary Labour Income in Canada by Months, January 1946 to April 1947* (Dominion Bureau Stats., 1947); 2. *Concentration in Canadian Manufacturing Industries* (Princeton Univ. Press, 1957); 3. *Canadian Anti-Combines Administration, 1952 to 1960* (with H.D. Thorburn), (Univ. Toronto Press, 1963); 4. *The Canadian Economy and Disarmament* (Macmillan, 1967).
Articles: 1. 'Measures of concentration', in *Business Concentration and Price Policy*, ed. G.J. Stigler (Princeton Univ. Press, 1955); 2. 'Changes in Canadian sensitivity to United States business fluctuations', *CJE*, 23, Nov. 1957; 3. 'Wage rates and the allocation of labour', *CJE*, 3, Aug. 1968; 4. 'Input-output analysis: a critique', *Stat. Hefte*, 9(4), 1968; 5. 'The relation between foreign control and concentration in Canadian industry', *CJE*, 3(1), Feb. 1970; 6. 'A contribution to the new theory of demand: a rehabilitation of the Giffen good' (with R.G. Lipsey), *CJE*, 3(2), May 1971; 7. 'The new theory of consumer demand and monopolistic competition' (with G. C. Archibald), *QJE*, 89, Nov. 1975; 8. 'Economists and the growth controversy', *Canadian Public Pol.*, 2(2), Spring 1976; 9. 'Publishing economics', *CJE*,

12(4), Nov. 1979; 10. 'The challenge of the eighties: economics', *Transactions Royal Soc. Canada*, 18, Series 4, 1980.

Principal Contributions My main interest has been in empirical research that would improve our understanding of how the Canadian economy works and contribute to the appraisal of government policies. I have pursued this interest in the field of industrial organisation where I have contributed to the quantitative study of concentration, its causes and effects, and have applied the economist's tools to the positive analysis of the government's competition policy. In the same general area I have worked on the peculiarly Canadian problem of foreign ownership and control of Canadian industry, both as a phenomenon to be explained and as a problem of public policy.

A second focus of interest has been the relation between business fluctuations in the US and Canada. The study that I consider my most important contribution in this field, using spectral techniques, is unpublished but served as foundation for the work of others. From my early days as a statistician in the Federal government, I have retained an interest in the construction and use of macroeconomic statistics. This has led to some contributions to the theory of input-output models. I have also applied input-output analysis to the study of the economic impact in Canada of Canadian and US military expenditures as part of a study of the economics of disarmament.

Academic self-interest, I guess, has caused me to study the economics of universities and the related problems of government policy. This has led, by natural stages, to an interest in the economics of scholarly publishing, the economics of publishing in general, and government financial support of cultural activities. Recent political developments in British Columbia have aroused my interest, along with that of some of my colleagues, in the economics of regional development, and the development of this particular region in particular. The resulting research programme is now producing a number of significant papers.

ROSENZWEIG, Mark Richard

Born 1947, New York, NY, USA.
Current Post Prof. Econ., Univ. Minnesota, Minneapolis, MN, USA, 1982–.
Past Posts Ass. Prof., Assoc. Prof., Yale Univ., 1973–8, 1978–9; Dir. Res., Select Commission Immigration and Refugee Pol., Washington, DC, 1979–80; Assoc. Prof., Univ. Minn., 1979–82; Vis. Assoc. Prof., Princeton Univ., 1982.
Degrees BA Columbia Coll., NYC, 1969; MA, PhD Columbia Univ., 1971, 1973.
Offices and Honours Woodrow Wilson Dissertation Fellow, 1972–3; Nat. Inst. Health Res. Service Fellow, 1976–7; US SSRC Training Fellow, 1976–7; Member, Social Sciences and Pop. Study Section, NIH, 1980–4; Panel on Immigration Stats., Nat. Res. Council, NAS, 1983–4.
Principal Fields of Interest 100 Economic Growth; Development; 840 Demographic Economics; 850 Human Capital.
Publications *Books:* 1. *Contractual Arrangements, Employment and Wages in Rural Labor Markets: A Critical Review* (with H. Binswanger), (Agric. Devlp. Council, 1981); 2. *The Theory and Experience of Economic Development: Essays in Honour of Sir W. Arthur Lewis*, co-ed. (with M. Gersovitz, C. Diaz-Alejandro and G. Ranis), (A&U, 1982); 3. *Contractual Arrangements, Employment and Wages in Rural Labor Markets in Asia*, co-ed. (with H. Binswanger), (Yale Univ. Press, 1984).
Articles: 1. 'Fertility, schooling and the economic contribution of children' (with R. Evenson), *Em*, 45(5), June 1977; 2. 'Rural wages, labor supply and land reform: a theoretical and empirical analysis', *AER*, 68(5), Dec. 1978; 3. 'Neoclassical theory and the optimizing peasant', *QJE*, 94(1), Feb. 1980; 4. 'Testing the quantity-quality model of fertility: the use of twins as a natural experiment' (with K. Wolpin), *Em*, 48(1), Jan. 1980; 5. 'Life cycle labor supply and fertility: causal inferences from household models' (with K. Wolpin), *JPE*, 88(2), Feb. 1980; 6.

'Educational subsidy, agricultural development and fertility change', *QJE*, 97(1), Feb. 1982; 7. 'Education and contraceptive choice: a conditional demand framework' (with D. Seiver), *Int ER*, 23(1), Feb. 1982; 8. 'Market opportunities, genetic endowments and intrafamily resource distribution: child survival in rural India' (with T.P. Schultz), *AER*, 72(4), Sept. 1982; 9. 'Estimating a household production function: heterogeneity, the demand for health inputs and their effect on birthweight' (with T.P. Schultz), *JPE*, 91(5), Oct. 1983; 10. 'Schooling, search and spouse selection: testing economic theories of marriage and household behaviour' (with B. Boulier), *JPE*, 92(4), Aug. 1984.

Principal Contributions My work has principally been concerned with obtaining a better understanding of household decision-making in a variety of economic settings, with particular attention to the allocation of time and the formation of human capital. My initial work examined the empirical and theoretical foundations of rural employment and wage determination, which forms the underpinnings of most macro development models. Data on labour supply behaviour and rural wages in developing countries, evidently not used by development theorists, were exploited to test various pervasive assumptions in the development literature. The 'trade-offs' between fertility and the supply of time by women to the market and the investment of resources in children were the foci of another set of papers. These were concerned with illuminating the meaning of such trade-offs when all three variables are decision variables and with testing propositions about their interrelationship and their relevance to various development and educational policies. This led to work on estimating the technology of household production, on the identification of the technical or biological parameters describing the relationships between household resource use (household services, health habits) and outcomes (health) when households are optimising and heterogeneous. Differentiation between technical and behavioural

relations presumably provides better estimates of the effects of behaviour on such produced goods as health outcomes and an improved understanding of the roles of education in the non-market sector. Recent work has been concerned with the interplay between the economic environment, the intrafamily allocation of consumption and investment resources across household members with differing characteristics (age, gender, ability), and the formation and structure of households. Understanding the behaviour of individuals making collective household decisions when the membership of the household is itself endogenously determined is a formidable task which occupies my current research resources.

ROSENSTEIN-RODAN, Paul N.*

Dates and Birthplace 1902–85, Austro-Hungary.

Posts Held Prof. Polit. Econ., Univ. Coll. London, 1934–47; Econ. Adviser, IBRD, 1947–52; Prof., MIT, 1952–68, Univ. Texas, 1968–72, Univ. Boston, 1972–85.

Degrees Dr Univ. Vienna.

Principal Fields of Interest 110 Economic Growth; Development.

Publications *Books:* 1. *Disguised Unemployment and Under-Employment in Agriculture* (MIT Centre for Internat. Stud., 1956).

Articles: 1. 'Marginal utility', in *Handwörterbuch der Staatswissenschaften*, 4 (1927), and *Internat. Econ. Papers*, 10 (Macmillan, 1960); 2. 'The role of time in economic theory', *Ec*, N.S. 1, Feb. 1934; 3. 'Problems of industrialisation of eastern and south-eastern Europe', *EJ*, 53, June–Sept. 1943; 4. 'International aid for under-developed countries', *REStat*, 43, May 1961; 5. 'Criteria for evaluation of national development effort', *J Developmental Planning*, 1, Jan. 1969.

Principal Contributions Development economics, particularly as an adviser to governments. Writings shifted from purely theoretical approach to development problems towards an applied economics approach. The concepts of complementarity in consumption and production, the time sequence of economic adjustments, and the importance of economies of scale in production, all of which are to be found in my early theoretical work, recur in later contributions to the practice of development.

Secondary Literature R.S. Eckaus, 'Rosenstein-Rodan, Paul N.', *IESS*, 18.

ROSOVSKY, Henry

Born 1927, Free City of Danzig (now Gdansk), Poland.

Current Post Lewis P. and Linda L. Geyser Univ. Prof., Harvard Univ., USA.

Past Posts Ass. Prof., Prof. Econ. and Hist., Univ. Cal. Berkeley, 1958–65; Prof. Econ., Harvard Univ., 1965–; Vis. Prof., Univs., Hitotsubashi, Tokyo, Stanford, Hebrew, Jerusalem; Dean, Faculty of Arts and Sciences, Harvard Univ., 1973–84.

Degrees BA, Hon. LLD Coll. William and Mary, 1949, 1976; MA, PhD Harvard Univ., 1953, 1959; Hon. LHD Univs. Yeshiva, 1977, Hebrew Union Coll., 1978, Colgate Univ., 1979; PhD (h.c.) Hebrew Univ., 1982; LHD Univ. Hartford, CT, 1984, Brandeis Univ., MA, 1984; LLD Queen's Univ., 1984.

Offices and Honours Schumpeter Prize, Harvard Univ., 1963; Board Dirs., Assoc. Asian Stud., 1963–6; Chairman, Pol. Advisory Board, Econ. Inst., Boulder, CO, 1967–74; Assoc. Dir., East Asia Res. Center, Harvard Univ., 1967–9; Chairman, Council Res. Econ. Hist., 1968–71; Fellow, AAAS, 1969.

Editorial Duties Ed., *Explor. Entrepreneurial Hist.*, 1954–6; Assoc. Ed., *JEH*, 1958–61.

Principal Fields of Interest 045 Asian Economic History.

Publications *Books:* 1. *Capital Formation in Japan, 1868–1940* (Free Press, 1961); 2. *Quantitative Japanese Economic History: An Annotated Bibliography and a Survey of US Holdings* (Univ. Cal. Press, 1961); 3. *Japanese Economic Growth: Trend Acceleration in the Twentieth Century* (with K. Ohkawa), (Stanford Univ. Press, 1973);

4. *Asia's New Giant: How the Japanese Economy Works*, co-ed. (with H. Patrick), (Brookings Inst., 1975); 5. *The Modernization of Japan and Russia* (with others), (Free Press, 1975).

Articles: 1. 'The indigenous components in the modern Japanese economy' (with K. Okahawa), *EDCC*, 9, April 1961; 2. 'Japan's transition to modern economic growth, 1868–1885', in *Industrialization in Two Systems*, ed. H. Rosovsky (Wiley, 1966); 3. 'What are the lessons of Japanese economic history?', in *Economic Development in the Long Run*, ed. A.J. Youngson (A&U, 1972).

Principal Contributions As an economic historian, specialised in the study of modern economic growth in nineteenth-century Japan. Also attempted to consider Japanese economic growth in comparative perspective.

ROSSI, Pellegrino Luigi Edoardo*

Dates and Birthplace 1787–1848, Carrara, Italy.

Posts Held Prof. Law, Univ. Bologna, 1813; Prof., Univ. Geneva, 1819; Prof. Econ., then Constitutional Law, Collège de France, 1833; French Ambassador to Rome, 1845; Papal Prime Minister, 1848.

Offices and Honours Involved in drafting Swiss constitution, 1832; Member, French Academy, 1836; Peer of France, 1839.

Publications *Books:* 1. *Traité de droit pénal*, 3 vols (1829); 2. *Cours d'économie politique*, 4 vols (1840–54); 3. *Mélanges d'économie politique, d'histoire et de philosophie*, 2 vols (1857).

Career Say's successor in the chair at the Collège de France and a member of the school which dominated the chief journals and institutions of economic life in France throughout the nineteenth century. His economics was the conventional Ricardianism of his day but the *Cours* ... achieved considerable success. His varied academic and political career ended in assassination in Rome.

Secondary Literature L. Ledermann, 'Rossi, Pellegrino Luigi Edoardo', *ESS*, 13.

ROSTOW, Walt Whitman

Born 1916, New York City, NY, USA.

Current Post Rex G. Baker Jr. Prof. Polit. Econ., Univ. Texas, Austin, TX, USA.

Past Posts Instr. Econ., Columbia Univ., 1940–1; Major, US Army, 1942–5; Ass. Chief, German-Austrian Econ. Div., US Dept. State, Washington, DC, 1945–6; Harmsworth Prof. Amer. Hist., Oxford Univ., 1946–7; Ass., Exec. Secretary, EEC, Geneva, 1947–9; Pitt Prof. Amer. Hist.; Lect., Camb. Univ., 1949–50, 1958; Prof. Econ. Hist., MIT, Staff Member, Center Internat. Stud., MIT, 1951–61; Dep. Special Ass., Special Ass., US President for Nat. Security Affairs, 1961, 1966–9; Chairman, Pol. Planning Council, Counselor, US Dept. State, 1961–6; US Member, Inter-Amer. Comm. Alliance for Progress (Ambassador), 1964–6.

Degrees BA, PhD Yale Univ., 1936, 1940; MA Oxford Univ., 1946; MA Camb. Univ., 1949, Hon. LLD Carnegie Inst. Technology, Pittsburgh, 1962, Univ. Miami, 1965, Univ. Notre Dame, 1966, Middelbury Coll., VT, 1967; Hon. Dr Humane Letters, Jacksonville Univ., FL, 1974.

Offices and Honours US SSRC Fellow, 1939–40; Hon. OBE (military), 1945; Legion of Merit, 1945; AAAS, 1957; Presidential Medal Freedom with Distinction, 1969; Member, Board Foreign Scholarships, 1969–71; Omicron Delta Kappa Soc., Amer. Philo. Soc., 1983; Disting. Fulbright Vis. Lect., India, 1983–4; Res. Scholar, Rockefeller Foundation Center, Bellagio, Italy, 1983.

Principal Fields of Interest 040 Economic History; 020 Economic Theory; 112 Economic Development.

Publications *Books:* 1. *Essays on the British Economy of the Nineteenth Century* (Clarendon Press, 1948, Greenwood Press, 1981); 2. *The Process of Economic Growth* (W.W. Norton, 1952, 1960, Clarendon Press, 1953); 3. *A Proposal: Key to an Effective Foreign Policy* (with M.F. Millikan), (Harper, 1957); 4. *The Stages of Economic Growth: A Non-Communist Manifesto* (CUP, 1960, 1971); 5. *How it All Began: Origins of the Modern Economy* (McGraw-Hill, 1975); 6. *The World Economy: History and Prospect* (Univ. Texas Press, Macmillan, 1978); 7. *Getting from Here to There* (McGraw-Hill, Macmillan, 1978); 8. *Why the Poor get Richer and the Rich Slow Down: Essays in the Marshallian Long Period* (Univ. Texas Press, Macmillan, 1980); 9. *British Trade Fluctuations, 1868–1896: A Chronicle and a Commentary* (Arno Press, 1981); 10. *The Barbaric Counter-Revolution: Cause and Cure* (Univ. Texas Press, 1983).

Articles: 1. 'Marx was a city boy, or why communism may fail', *Harper's Magazine*, Feb. 1955; 2. 'Some general reflections on capital formation and economic growth', in *Capital Formation and Economic Growth* (Princeton Univ. Press, 1955); 3. 'The interrelation of theory and economic history', *JEH*, 17, Dec. 1957; 4. 'Some lessons of history for Africa', in *Pan-Africanism Reconsidered*, ed. Amer. Soc. African Culture (Univ. Cal. Press, 1962); 5. 'The past quarter-century as economic history and the tasks of international economic organization', *JEH*, 30(1), March 1970; 6. 'The bankruptcy of neo-Keynesian economics', *Intermountain Econ. Rev.*, 7(1), Spring 1976; 7. 'A national policy towards regional change', *New England Econ. Indicators*, May 1977; 8. 'How close is a planned economy?', *The Wharton Magazine*, 2, 1977; 9. 'Comment from a not quite empty box', *EJ*, 92, March 1982; 10. 'Foreign aid: justice for whom?', in *The Search for Justice* (Univ. Texas, 1983).

Principal Contributions I have tried to do three things in the field of economics. First, to bring to bear modern economic theory and statistical analysis on economic history. Second, to generate from historical and contemporary experience systematic views about the process of economic development, including the role of noneconomic variables. Third, to contribute to the emergence of a general, dynamic theory of prices and production which would differ from conventional macro- and micro-theory in that it (1) embraces as endogenous demographic change, the generation and diffusion of new technologies, and trend movements in the prices of basic commodities relative to industrial products; and (2) systematically links sectoral and aggregate analysis.

On the whole, my colleagues have generously acknowledged, not without criticism, my efforts in economic history and development, while ignoring or resisting actively my theoretical propositions. But the special character of whatever contribution I may have made to historical and development analysis stems directly from the distinctive, dynamic, disaggregated theoretical framework I have devised and used. Incomplete at present, that framework nevertheless seeks to meet head-on the formidable challenges posed in any effort to deal systematically with the Marshallian long period. Much of the weakness, irrelevance, and even bankruptcy of contemporary mainstream economics flows from its evasion of those challenges because, contrary to Keynes's famous dictum, long-period forces are actively at work every day of our lives.

ROTHBARTH, Erwin*

Dates and Birthplace 1913–44, Frankfurt-am-Main, Germany.
Past Posts Stat. Ass., Camb. Univ., 1938–42.
Degrees BSc LSE, 1936.
Offices and Honours Gladstone Memorial Prize, LSE; Gerstenberg Student; Leverhulme Res. Scholar.
Editorial Duties Ed. Board, *REStud*, 1937–44.
Publications *Articles:* 1. 'The measurement of changes in real income under conditions of rationing', *REStud*, 8, Feb. 1941; 2. 'A note on the index number problem', *REStud*, 11(2), 1944; 3. 'Causes of the superior efficiency of USA industry as compared to British industry', *EJ*, 56, Sept. 1946.
Career Inventor of the concept of the 'virtual' price system in the theory of rationing, who worked closely with Keynes in preparing the national income estimates that appeared as an appendix to Keynes's *How to Pay for the Wars* (1940).
Secondary Literature L. Cuyvers, 'Erwin Rothbarth's Life and Work', *J Post Keyn E*, 6(2), 1983–4.

ROTHENBERG, Jerome

Born 1924, New York City, NY, USA.
Current Post Prof. Econ., MIT, Cambridge, MA, USA, 1966–; Vis. Prof., Univ. Cal. Berkeley, USA, 1983–4.
Past Posts Fellow, Nat. Inst. Public Affairs, 1945; Fiscal Analyst, US Bureau Budget, 1946; Instr. Econ., Rutgers Univ., 1948–9; Econ., NY State Hospital Study, 1948–9; Instr. Econ., Amherst Coll., MA, 1949–54; Instr. Econ., Univ. Mass., Amherst, 1953; Ass. Prof. Econ., Univ. Cal., 1954–7; Fellow, Center Advanced Study Behavioral Sciences, 1956–7; Ass. Prof. Econ., Univ. Chicago, 1957–60; Task Force, Governor Illinois Study State Tax System, 1961; Assoc. Prof., Prof. Econ., Northwestern Univ., 1960–3, 1963–6; Vis. Fellow, Nuffield Coll. Oxford, 1965–6; Faculty Assoc., Joint Center Urban Stud., MIT, Harvard Univ., 1966–; Vis. Prof., NSF Summer Inst. Urban Econ., Stanford Univ., 1970, 1971, 1972; Academic Vis., LSE, 1973–4.
Degrees BA, MA, PhD Columbia Univ., 1945, 1947, 1954.
Offices and Honours NY State Undergrad. Scholar, Grad. Scholar; Phi Beta Kappa, 1945; Fellow, Nat. Inst. Public Affairs, 1945–6; Ford Foundation Faculty Res. Fellow; Co-Chairman, Comm. Urban Pub. Econ., 1976–.
Editorial Duties Ed. Board, *JUE*.
Principal Fields of Interest 930 Urban Economics; 320 Fiscal Theory and Policy; Public Finance; 020 General Economic Theory.
Publications *Books:* 1. *The Measurement of Social Welfare* (Prentice-Hall, 1961); 2. *Economic Evaluation of Urban Renewal* (Brookings Inst., 1967); 3. *Approach to the Welfare Analysis of Intertemporal Resource Allocation* (Athens Center Planning Econ. Res., 1967); 4. *Readings in Urban Econ-*

omics, co-ed. (with M. Edel), (Macmillan, 1972); 5. *Intra-metropolitan Location and the Public Sector* (US Dept. Commerce, 1971); 6. *Transport and the Urban Environment*, co-ed. (with I.G. Heggie), (Macmillan, 1974); 7. *The Management of Water Quality and the Environment*, co-ed. (with I.G. Heggie), (Macmillan, 1974); 8. *Regulation of the U.S. Copper Industry* (with N. Sheldon, R. Sheldon and A. Dorenfeld), (NSF, 1981).

Articles: 1. 'Non-convexity, aggregation and Pareto optimality', *JPE*, 68(5), Oct. 1960; 2. 'Consumer sovereignty and the economics of television programming', *Stud. in Public Communication*, 4, Autumn 1962; 3. 'A model of economic and political decision-making', in *The Public Economy of Urban Communities*, ed. J. Margolis (Resources for the Future, 1965); 4. 'The economics of congestion and pollution: an integrated view', *AER*, 60(2), May 1970; 5. 'On the microeconomics of internal migration', in *Comparative Analysis of Internal Migration*, eds. A. Brown and E. Neuberger (Academic Press, 1976); 6. 'Endogenous city-suburb governmental rivalry through household location', in *The Political Economy of Multi-Level Government*, ed. W. Oates (D.C. Heath, 1976); 7. 'Urban housing markets & housing policy', in *Selected Readings in Quantitative Urban Analysis*, eds. S.J. Bernstein and W.G. Mellon (Pergamon, 1978); 8. 'Neighborhood deterioration and the urban housing market complex', in *Urban Housing* (Fed. Home Loan Bank San Francisco, 1979); 9. 'Simultaneous estimation of the supply and demand for housing location in a multizoned metropolitan area' (with K. Bradbury, R. Engle, and O. Irvine), in *Residential Location and Urban Housing Markets*, ed. G.K. Ingram (Ballinger, 1980); 10. 'Housing investment, housing consumption and tenure choice', in *Urban Housing and Land Use*, ed. R. Grieson (D.C. Heath, 1982).

Principal Contributions My earliest research was in the field of health-care economics. I gradually shifted to pure welfare theory and through this to utility theory, to individual and group decision-making, to public choice and to an elaborate modelling of representative government as an abstract decision-making system, including in this a novel theory of coalitions. This led to more and more applications of welfare theory in several large branches. One of these involved substantial research commitments to the economics of environment and urban economics. My later work developed into a full specialisation in urban economics, with attention to location and spatial economics, urban transportation, housing, slums, urban renewal and other policies, and local government.

Another research branch stemmed from utility and decision theory. It led to research in the microeconomics of migration, to a new systematisation of the economics of criminal behaviour (including so-called 'irrational crime'), and to individual and group risk behaviour. This latter has coalesced with my work in pollution theory and policy.

A third branch derived from my public choice interests, along with my urban concentration. It involved theoretical research on the functioning of a federal governmental structure, and on sources of inefficiency in that functioning. This has combined in the urban context with theoretical and institutional problems in the governance of metropolitan areas, and interacts strongly with problems of State and local government, and of specific sectoral urban policy problems.

Other derived and *ad hoc* areas of interest have been (in the 1960s) a considerable commitment to strategy and defence economics, a more sporadic but durable interest in market structure and performance, production theory in extractive industry, government regulation, and most recently, the study of the post-Cultural Revolution structural changes in the economy of the People's Republic of China.

ROTHSCHILD, Kurt Wilhelm

Born 1914, Vienna, Austro-Hungary.
Current Post Prof. Econ., Johannes Kepler Univ., Linz, Austria, 1982–.
Past Posts Ass. Lect., Glasgow Univ.,

1940–7; Sr. Res. Worker, Austrian Inst. Econ. Res., Vienna, 1947–66; Prof., Univ. Linz, Austria, 1966–82; Vis. Prof., Univs. Dundee, 1959–60, Strathclyde, 1966, Saarbrücken, 1968–9, Salford, 1975, Monash, 1981.

Degrees Dr Jur. (Law) Univ. Vienna, 1938; MA Glasgow Univ., 1940.

Offices and Honours Social Science Award, City Vienna, 1980; Science Award, City Linz, 1983.

Editorial Duties Ed. Board, *Kyk*, *Empirica*, *Empirical Econ.*, *WD*, *Ökonomie und Gesellschaft*.

Principal Fields of Interest 020 General Economic Theory; 824 Labour Market Studies, Wages, Employment; 411 International Trade Theory.

Publications *Books:* 1. *Austria's Economic Development between the Two Wars* (F. Muller, 1947); 2. *The Austrian Economy since 1945* (Royal Inst. Internat. Affairs, 1950); 3. *The Theory of Wages* (Blackwell, 1954, 1965; transls., Japanese Tokyo Sogen-Sha, 1956, Spanish, Aguilar, 1957, German, Vahlen, 1963, Portuguese, and Hindustani); 4. *Market Forms and International Trade* (Europa-Verlag, 1966); 5. *Economic Forecasting* (Springer-Verlag, 1969); 6. *Power in Economics*, ed. (Penguin, 1971; transls., Italian, Franco Angeli, 1976, Spanish, 1976); 7. *Determinants of Wage Movements* (with E. Nowotny and G. Schwodianer), (Springer-Verlag, 1972); 8. *Accelerating Inflation* (with H.J. Schmahl), (Weltardir, 1973); 9. *Unemployment in Austria 1955–75* (Inst. Labour Market Pol., 1977); 10. *Introduction to Disequilibrium Theory* (Springer-Verlag, 1981).

Articles: 1. 'The degree of monopoly', *Ec*, N.S. 9, April 1942; 2. 'Price theory and oligopoly', *EJ*, 37, Sept. 1947, repr. in *Readings in Price Theory*, eds. G.J. Stigler and K.E. Boulding (Richard D. Irwin, 1953), and *Industrial Organization and Public Policy: Selected Readings*, ed. W. Sichel (Houghton Mifflin, 1967), and *Readings in Modern Economics: Monopoly and Competition*, ed. A. Hunter (Penguin, 1969), and (German) in *Preistheorie*, ed. A.E. Ott (Kieponhener & Witsch, 1965), (Italian) in *Economisti Moderni*, ed. F. Caffe (Milano, 1962),

and *Valore, prezzi e equilibrio generale*, ed. G. Lunghini (Mulino, 1971); 3. 'The Phillips curve and all that', *SJPE*, 18(3), Nov. 1971, repr. (German) in *Lohne, Preise, Beschäftigung*, ed. E. Nowong (Fischer, 1974); 4. 'Export structure, export flexibility and competitiveness', *WA*, 111(2), 1975; 5. 'Arbeitslose: Gibt's die?', *Kyk*, 31(1), 1978; 6. 'Aussenhandelstheorie, aussenhandelspolitik und aunpassungsdruk', *Kyk*, 32(1–2), 1979; 7. 'Stagflation: was Bleibt von der Phillips-kurve?', *Wirtschaft und Gesellschaft*, 8(2), 1982; 8. 'Observations on the economics, politics and ethics of the welfare State', *ZGS*, 138(3), Sept. 1982; 9. 'Geldmenge, Wahrumgoreserven und wechselkursanderungen', *JNS*, 198(4), July 1983; 10. 'Schumpeter and socialism', in *Schumpeterian Economics*, ed. H. Frisch (Praeger, 1982), repr. in Spanish in *Revista de Occidente*, 21(2), 1983.

Principal Contributions Starting off mainly with work on microeconomic problems of price and wage theory, my interests then turned increasingly to macroeconomic Keynesian-type themes with labour-market and working-class questions in the foreground: full employment (theory and policy), wage formation, income distribution and economic systems. Parallel with this (and in connection with my work at the Austrian Res. Inst.) I also worked in the field of international trade with special stress on the problem of small open economies. My methodological 'credo' is to try to deal in an undogmatic way with real-world economic and social problems. This has led to some polemics against the rigidities of neoclassical orthodoxy.

ROTHSCHILD, Michael

Born 1942, Chicago, IL, USA.

Current Post Prof. Econ., Univ. Cal. San Diego, CA, USA, 1982–.

Past Posts Instr., Boston Coll., 1968–9; Ass. Prof., Harvard Univ., 1969–73; Lect., Assoc. Prof., Prof., Princeton Univ., 1972–6; Prof. Econ., Univ. Wisconsin, Madison, 1976–82; Vis. Prof., Hebrew Univ., Jerusalem, 1972.

Degrees BA (Anthrop.) Reed Coll.,

1963; MA (Internat. Relations) Yale Univ., 1965; PhD MIT, 1969.

Offices and Honours Fellow, Council Member, Em Soc, 1972, 1979–84; Oskar Morgenstern Disting. Fellowship, Mathematica Inc., Princeton, NJ, 1981–2; Rommnes Faculty Fellow, Univ. Wisconsin, 1977; Guggenheim Foundation Fellow, 1978–9.

Editorial Duties Assoc. Ed., *JET*, 1973–, *Em*, 1970–3, 1979–; Ed. Board, *JEL*, 1981–3.

Principal Fields of Interest 022 Microeconomic Theory; 026 Economics of Uncertainty; 610 Industrial Organisation.

Publications *Books:* 1. *Uncertainty in Economics: Readings and Exercises*, co-ed. (with P.A. Diamond), (Academic Press, 1978).

Articles: 1. 'Increasing risk: 1. A Definition' (with J.E. Stiglitz), *JET*, 2(3), Sept. 1970; 2. 'Towards an economic theory of replacement investment' (with M.S. Feldstein), *Em*, 42, May 1974; 3. 'Models of market organisation with imperfect information: a survey', *JPE*, 81(6), Nov.–Dec. 1972; 4. 'Searching for the lowest price when the distribution of prices is unknown', *JPE*, 82(4), July–Aug., 1974; 5. 'On the allocation of effort' (with R. Radner), *JET*, 10(3), June 1975; 6. 'Equilibrium in competitive insurance markets: an essay on the economics of imperfect information' (with J.E. Stiglitz), *QJE*, 90, Nov. 1976.

Principal Contributions I was seduced into economics by James Tobin who showed me that economics, in sharp contrast to political science which I was studying at the time, was a field which welcomed rigorous formal models that were analytically interesting and relevant to practical problems. It's hard to imagine a more pleasant intellectual occupation than doing economic theory. The world keeps creating practical puzzles of interest and importance; to understand them it is often necessary (or at least legitimate) to learn new and beautiful mathematics.

ROWLEY, Charles Kershaw

Born 1939, Southampton, Hampshire, England.

Current Post Prof. Econ., Center Res. Assoc., Center Study Public Choice, George Mason Univ., VA, USA, 1983–.

Past Posts Lect. Econ., Univ. Nottingham, 1962–5; Lect., Sr. Lect. Econ., Univ. Kent, England, 1965–70; Vis. SSRC Fellow, Sr. Lect., Reader Econ. and Social Stats., Univ. York, 1968–9, 1970–2; David Dale Prof. Econ., Univ. Newcastle-upon-Tyne, 1972–83; Res. Assoc., Center Study Public Choice, Virginia Polytechnic and State Univ., 1974, 1979.

Degrees BA, PhD Univ. Nottingham, 1960, 1964.

Offices and Honours Member, Mont Pelerin Soc., 1967–; Member, UK Radioactive Waste Management Advisory Comm., 1977–83; Pres., Europ. Public Choice Soc., 1980–2.

Editorial Duties Ed. Boards, *Appl. Econ.*, 1969–82, *Econ. Affairs*, 1979–, *Industrial Econ.*, 1978–80; Ed., *Internat. Rev. Law and Econ.*, 1980–.

Principal Fields of Interest 020 General Economic Theory; 600 Industrial Organisation; 900 Welfare Programmes.

Publications *Books:* 1. *The British Monopolies Commission* (A&U, 1966); 2. *Steel and Public Choice* (McGraw-Hill, 1971); 3. *Anti-trust and Economic Efficiency* (Macmillan, 1973); 4. *Readings in Industrial Economics*, ed. 2 vols (Macmillan, 1973); 5. *Welfare Economics: A Liberal Restatement* (with A.T. Peacock), (Martin Robertson, 1975); 6. *A Study of Effluent Discharges to the River Tees* (HMSO, 1979); 7. *Frihet, Rattvisa, Effectivitet* (Timbro, 1979); 8. *Prepayments and Insolvency* (UK Office Fair Trading, 1984); 9. *The Economics of Politics* (Blackwell, 1984).

Articles: 1. 'Mergers and public policy', *J Law E*, 11, April 1968; 2. 'The monopolies commission and rate of return on capital', *EJ*, 79, March 1969; 3. 'On allocative efficiency, X-efficiency and the measurement of welfare loss' (with M.A. Crew), *Ec*, N.S. 38, May 1971; 4. 'X-theory versus management discretion theory' (with M.A. Crew and M.W. Jones-Lee), *SEJ*, 38(2), Oct. 1971; 5. 'Pareto optimality and the political economy of liberalism' (with A.T. Peacock), *JPE*, 80(3), May–June 1972; 6. 'Welfare economics and the public regulation of natural monopoly' (with A.T. Peacock), *J Pub E*, 1(3), June 1972; 7. 'The economics of accidental oil pollution by tankers in coastal waters' (with P. Burrows), *J Pub E*, 3(3), Aug. 1974; 8. 'Pareto optimality and the gains from trade: a public choice interpretation', *Public Choice*, 29, Spring, 1977; 9. 'Property rights and the performance of regulation and public enterprise', *Internat. Rev. Law and Econ.*, June 1981; 10. 'Social sciences and law: the relevance of economic theories', *Oxford J. Legal Stud.*, 1981.

Principal Contributions My early work was in the field of industrial organisation, commencing with an institutional study of the British Monopolies Commission, but moving on to the application of structure-conduct-performance theory to industrial analysis. An interest in the concept of X-efficiency shifted my interest to welfare economics. A major research collaboration with Alan Peacock led to a range of contributions to a liberal political economy and this is an abiding interest. Following a period of writing in the field of environmental economics, emphasising the relevance of market studies, my interests shifted significantly towards public choice and law and economics and most of my recent and current research is in these important fields. The influence of the Virginia school upon my work is obvious and I have now moved location to my true home. Still, my love for the 'old' Chicago remains, influences my work, and creates a constructive tension with Virginian-blend economics. Of the new Chicago, the least said the better.

RUBIN, Paul Harold

Born 1942, Boston, MA, USA.
Current Post Ass. Dir., Bureau Econ., US Fed. Trade Commission, Washington, DC, USA, 1983–.

Past Posts Ass. Prof., Assoc. Prof., Prof., Univ. Georgia, 1968–82; Sr. Staff Econ., US President's Council Econ. Advisers, 1981–2; Prof., Baruch Coll., City Univ. NY, 1982–3.
Degrees BA Univ. Cincinnati, 1963; MA, MS, PhD Purdue Univ., IN, 1964, 1968, 1970.
Offices and Honours Liberty Fund-Center Libertarian Stud. Fellow, 1979; City Univ. NY Faculty Fellow, 1983.
Principal Fields of Interest 025 Public Choice; 613 Economics of Regulation.
Publications *Books:* 1. *Congressmen, Constituents and Contributors; Determinants of Roll Call Voting in the House of Representatives* (with J. B. Kau), (Martinus Nijhoff, 1982); 2. *Business Firms and the Common Law: the Evolution of Efficient Rules* (Praeger, 1983).

Articles: 1. 'The expansion of firms', *JPE*, 81(4), July–Aug. 1973; 2. 'Why is the common law efficient?', *J. Legal Stud.*, 6(1), Jan. 1977; 3. 'The theory of the firm and the structure of the franchise contract', *J Law E*, 21(1), April 1978; 4. 'Voting on minimum wages: a time series analysis' (with J. B. Kau), *JPE*, 86(2), pt. 1, April 1978; 5. 'Self interest, ideology, and logrolling in congressional voting' (with J. B. Kau), *J Law E*, 22(2), Oct. 1979; 6. 'An economic analysis of the law of false advertising' (with E. Jordan), *J. Legal Stud.*, 8(3), June 1979; 7. 'An evolutionary model of taste for risk' (with C. Paul), *EI*, 16(4), Oct. 1979; 8. 'A general equilibrium model of congressional voting' (with J. B. Kau and D. Keenan), *QJE*, 97(2), May 1982; 9. 'Common law and statute law', *J Legal Stud.*, 11(2), June 1982; 10. 'Evolved ethics and efficient ethics', *J Ec Behav*, 3(2), June 1982.

Principal Contributions My initial research interests were in the theory of the firm. This led to an interest in industrial organisation. However, the questions which I found most interesting in this area dealt with issues of government intervention and regulation: more specifically, I became interested in the determinants of government intervention in markets. This has in turn led to my two main research interests: public choice and law and economics.

In the area of public choice, my major research has been empirical studies of congressional voting, co-authored with James Kau. It was our belief that the voting behaviour of Congress provided a set of data which could be used to test various theories of legislation. In particular, we wanted to determine the extent to which Stigler's theory (that legislation could be explained as a result of economic self-interest) was valid. Our results, published in several articles and summarised in *Congressmen, Constituents, and Contributors*, indicate that, while economic interest is important, ideological factors are also significant in explaining legislation.

In the area of law and economics, I developed the theory that legislation evolves towards efficiency if the parties to disputes are chosen 'correctly'. In particular, this means that if business firms are litigants, efficiency will tend to result; if government agencies are litigants, efficiency is less likely. This research was published in several papers and in *Business Firms and the Common Law*. Finally, I have read in the area of sociobiology and have published some papers attempting to provide evolutionary arguments for the forms of human tastes. I have applied these arguments to tastes for risk and ethical beliefs.

RUEFF, Jacques Leon*

Dates and Birthplace 1897–1978, Paris, France.

Posts Held Finance Section, League of Nations, 1927–30; Prof., L'Ecole Libre des Sciences Polit., 1930–40; Inspector General of Finances, 1945–50.

Degrees L'Ecole Polytechnique, 1921; l'Ecole des Sciences Polit., 1923.

Offices and Honours Commander, Légion d'Honneur; Pres., Polit. Econ. Stat. Socs., Paris; Vice-Pres., Internat. Inst. Stats.; Croix de Guerre, 1914–8; Member, Inst. de France, 1964.

Publications *Books:* 1. *Des sciences physiques aux sciences morales* (1922); 2. *Théorie des phénomènes monétaries* (1927); 3. *Epître aux dirigistes* (1949); 4. *The Age of Inflation* (1963); 5. *Balance of Payments* (1965); 6. *La réforme*

du système monétaire international (1973).

Articles: 1. 'L'assurance-chômage cause du chômage permanente', *REP*, April 1931; 2. 'Nouvelle discussion sur la chômage, les salaires det les prix', *REP*, Sept.–Oct. 1951.

Career A premature 'monetarist' and thorough-going anti-Keynesian, who emerged in postwar France under de Gaulle as an extremely influential proponent of orthodox monetary policies, including the return to the gold standard.

RUGGLES, Richard

Born 1916, Columbus, OH, USA.
Current Post Stanley Rezor Prof. Econ., Yale Univ., USA, 1962–.
Degrees BA, PhD Harvard Univ., 1939, 1942.
Offices and Honours Fellow, ASA, Em Soc.
Editorial Duties Managing Ed., *RIW*, 1975–.
Principal Fields of Interest 221 National Income Accounting.
Publications *Books:* 1. *National Income Accounts and Income Analysis* (with N. D. Ruggles), (McGraw-Hill, 1956); 2. *Design of Economic Accounts* (with N. D. Ruggles), (NBER, 1971).

Articles: 1. 'Integrated economic accounts for the United States, 1947–80' (with N. D. Ruggles), *Survey Current Bus.*, 1982.

Principal Contributions The development of national economic accounts and their integration with microdata bases for enterprises, households and governments.

RUTTAN, Vernon W.

Born 1924, Alden, MA, USA.
Current Post Prof. Agric. and Appl. Econ., Univ. Minnesota, MN, USA, 1965–.
Past Posts Econ., Div. Regional Stud., 1951–3; Gen. Manager, US Tennessee Valley Authority, 1954; Ass. Prof., Assoc. Prof., Prof. Agric. Econ., Purdue Univ., IN, 1955–7, 1957–60, 1960–3; Exec. Office Pres.,

Staff Econ., US President's Council Econ. Advisers, 1961–3; Agric. Econ., Rockefeller Foundation, Internat. Rice Res. Inst., Philippines, 1963–5; Trustee, Pres., Agric. Devlp. Council Inc., 1967–73, 1973–7.

Degrees BA Yale Univ., 1948; MA, PhD Univ. Chicago, 1950, 1952; Hon. LLD Rutgers Univ., 1978.

Offices and Honours Publication Award, AAEA, 1956, 1957, 1962, 1966, 1967, 1971, 1979; Fellow, AAEA, 1974, AAAS, 1976.

Principal Fields of Interest 620 Economics of Technical Change; 710 Agricultural Economics; 110 Economic Growth and Development.

Publications *Books:* 1. *The Economic Demand for Irrigated Acreage: New Methodology and Some Preliminary Projections, 1954–80* (JHUP, 1965); 2. *Plant Science: An Introduction to World Crops* (with J. Janick, *et al.*), (W. H. Freeman, 1969); 3. *Agricultural Development: An International Perspective* (with Y. Hayami), (JHUP, 1971); 4. *Induced Innovation: Technology, Institutions and Development* (with H. P. Binswanger), (JHUP, 1978); 5. *Agricultural Research Policy* (Univ. Minn. Press, 1982).

Articles: 1. 'The contribution of technological progress to farm output: 1970–75', *REStat*, 38, Feb. 1956; 2. 'Agricultural policy in an affluent society', *JFE*, 48(5), Dec. 1966; 3. 'Factor prices and technical change in agricultural development: the United States and Japan, 1880–1960' (with Y. Hayami), *JPE*, 78(5), Sept.–Oct. 1970; 4. 'Technology and the environment', *AJAE*, 53(5), Dec. 1971; 5. 'Economic benefits from research: an example from agriculture' (with R. Evenson and P. Waggoner), *Science*, 205, Sept. 14, 1979; 6. 'Bureaucratic productivity: the case of agricultural research', *Public Choice*, 35(5), 1980; 7. 'Toward a theory of induced institutional innovation', *J Dev Stud*, 20(4), July 1984.

Principal Contributions Theory and measurement of productivity growth; extension and testing of the theory of induced technical change; development of the theory of induced institutional change; and empirical analyses of the rate of technical and institutional change on agricultural development, and research policy.

RYBCZYNSKI, Tadeusz Mieczyslaw

Born 1923, Lwow, Poland.

Current Post Econ. Adviser (Dir., Lazard Securities Ltd., 1969–), Lazard Bros. & Co., London, England, 1954–.

Past Posts Lloyds Bank, London, 1949–53; Part-time Lect., LSE, 1958–9; Vis. Prof., Univ. Surrey, 1968–74, City Univ. London, 1974–.

Degrees BCom, MSc Univ. London, 1949, 1952.

Offices and Honours Chairman, Society of Bus. Econ., 1962–75; Governor, Member, Council Management & Exec. Comm., NIESR, 1966; Member, Scientific Comm., Internat. Centre Banking and Monetary Stud., Univ. Geneva, 1967; Member, Governing Body, Trade and Pol. Res. Centre, London, 1968–; Council Member, Treasurer, RES, 1969–76, 1976–; Member, Econ. Council, UK SSRC, 1973–8; Member, Advisory Board Banking and Fin., Univ. Aston Management Centre, Birmingham, 1973–81; Member, Financial Comm. Confed. British Industry, 1974–8; Member Board Governors, Brunel Univ., England, 1976–9; Member, UK Monopolies and Mergers Commission, 1978–81; Member, Parliamentary and Whitehall Comm., City Communications Centre, London, 1978–; Member, Monetary Commission, Internat. Chamber Commerce, 1978–; Comm. Member, Foreign Affairs Club, Vice-Pres., Section F, 1980–; Member, Econ. and Social Affairs Comm., British Inst. Management, London, 1980–; Member, Research Comm., Royal Inst. Internat. Affairs, London, 1980–; Bernard Harms Medal Outstanding Contribut. to Econ. Profession, Inst. World Economy, Univ. Kiel.

Editorial Duties Ed. *Bus. Econ.*, 1969–75; Ed. Board, *World Economy*, 1977–; Ed. Comm., *Round Table*, 1982–.

Principal Fields of Interest 400 International Economics; 100 Economic Growth, Development and Fluctuations; 310 Domestic Monetary and Financial Theory and Institutions.

Publications *Books:* 1. *The Economist in Business*, ed. and contrib. (Blackwell, 1967); 2. *Value Added Tax — the UK Position and the European Experience*, ed. and contrib. (Blackwell, 1969); 3. *Towards an Open World Economy — A Report by an Advisory Group* (with others), (Macmillan, 1972); 4. *A New Era in Competition*, ed. and contrib. (Blackwell, 1973); 5. *The Economics of the Oil Crisis*, ed. and contrib. (Macmillan, 1976); 6. *Structural Changes in the World Economy* (Univ. Kiel, 1983).

Articles: 1. 'Factor endowment and relative community prices', *Ec*, N.S. 84, Nov. 1955, repr. in *Readings in International Economics*, eds. R. E. Caves and H. G. Johnson (A&U, 1968); 2. 'Banking in the USSR', in *Comparative Banking*, ed. H. W. Auburn (Waterlow, 1960); 3. 'Long range planning and capital requirements', in *Long Range Planning*, ed. H. Dunoud, *et al.* (Prentice-Hall, 1967); 4. 'U.K. financial sector since Radcliffe — non-clearing banks', in *Money in Britain 1959–69*, eds. R. Croome and H. G. Johnson (OUP, 1970); 5. 'The cost and sources of capital', in *Problems of Investment*, ed. R. Shone (Blackwell, 1971); 6. 'Economics, economists and industry', in *Users of Economics*, ed. G. D. N. Worswick (Blackwell, 1972); 7. 'Memorandum on "international monetary arrangements"', in *Fourth Report from the House of Commons Treasury and Civil Service Commission*, III (HMSO, 1983); 8. 'Internationalisation of financial markets', in *The International Monetary System 1971–80*, eds. T. Thompson and L. Tsoukalis (Blackwell, 1983); 9. 'The role of banks in international capital markets', in *International Lending in a Fragile World Economy* (Martinus Nijhoff, 1984).

Principal Contributions My main contribution has been the attempt to see when the factor-price equalisation theorem, developed by Samuelson and Stolper and forming part of Heckscher-Ohlin international trade theory, holds good.

S

SACHS, Jeffrey David

Born 1954.
Current Post Prof. Econ., Harvard Univ., Res. Assoc., NBER, Cambridge, MA, USA; Member, Brookings Panel Econ., Brookings Inst., Washington, DC, USA, 1983–.
Past Posts Staff. Ass., Subcomm. Antitrust and Monopolies, Judiciary Comm. US Senate, 1973; Staff Ass., US Senator Phillip A. Hart, 1974; Student Intern, Fed. Reserve Board, Washington, DC, 1977; Vis. Scholar, Inst. Internat. Econ. Stud., Stockholm, 1978; Jr. Fellow, Harvard Soc. Fellows, 1978–80; Res. Assoc., Falk Inst. Econ. Res., Jerusalem, 1979, 1980; Vis. Res. Assoc., LSE, 1981; Cons., IMF, Washington, DC, 1982; Vis. Prof., Ecole des Hautes Etudes, Paris, 1983; Cons., OECD, Paris, 1983.
Degrees BA, MA PhD Harvard Univ., 1976, 1978, 1980.
Offices and Honours Merit Scholar, 1972; John Harvard Scholar Highest Academic Achievement, 1973–6; Detur Book Prize, 1976; Whitaker Prize, Harvard Univ., 1976; John Williams Prize, Harvard Univ., 1976; Leontief Award Outstanding Dissertations, EEA, 1981; Wells Prize Econ. Dissertations, Harvard Univ., 1981; Irving Fisher Award Outstanding Dissertations, Omicron Delta Epsilon Soc., 1982; Member, Council Foreign Relations, NYC, 1981–.
Principal Fields of Interest 023 Macroeconomic Theory; 130 Economic Fluctuations; 430 Balance of Payments; International Finance.
Publications *Books:* 1. *Economics of Worldwide Stagflation* (with M. Bruno), (Harvard Univ. Press, 1985).
Articles: 1. 'Wages, profits, and macroeconomic adjustment; a comparative study', *Brookings Papers Econ. Activity*, 2, 1979; 2. 'Wages, flexible exchange rates, and macroeconomic policy', *QJE*, 94(4), June 1980; 3. 'Supply vs. demand approaches to the problem of stagflation' (with M. Bruno), in *Macroeconomic Policies for*

Growth and Stability, ed. H. Giersch (Inst. für Weltwirtschaft, 1981); 4. 'Energy and growth under flexible exchange rates', in *The International Transmission of Economic Disturbance*, eds. J. Bhandari and R. Putnam (MIT Press, 1983); 5. 'The current account and macro adjustment in the 1970s', *Brookings Papers Econ. Activity*, 1, 1981; 6. 'Input price shocks and the slowdown in economic growth' (with M. Bruno), *REStud*, Suppl., 1982; 7. 'LDC debt: problems and prospects', in *Crises in the Economic and Financial Structure*, ed. P. Wachtel (D. C. Heath, 1982); 8. 'Anticipation, recessions, and policy: an intertemporal disequilibrium model' (with O. Blanchard), *Annales de l'Insée*, 47–48, July–Dec. 1982; 9. 'Theoretical issues in international borrowing', in *Essays in International Finance* (Internat. Fin. Section, Princeton Univ., 1984); 10. 'Macroeconomic policy coordination among the industrial economies' (with G. Oudiz), *Brookings Papers Econ. Activity*, 1, 1984.

Principal Contributions My work has focussed on three areas of international economics: comparative macroeconomic performance of the OECD economies, the scope of macroeconomic policy among these economies, and the nature of international lending to developing countries. On the first topic, I collaborated with Michael Bruno for several years in the study of the supply shocks of the 1970s and early 1980s and the ensuing stagflation in the industrialised economies. That work led to an investigation of the role of external disturbances (such as higher energy prices) in macroeconomic adjustment, and more importantly, to the role of labour market institutions in the adjustment process. We were among the first researchers to point out that European wage indexation was a major factor in the prolonged high unemployment since 1973. The work is pulled together in our book, *Economics of Worldwide Stagflation*. On the topic of international policy co-ordination, I have undertaken theoretical and empirical work to investigate the potential macroeconomic gains of closer co-ordination of macroeconomic policies among the industrial economies. Starting from the theoretical result that nonco-operative policy-making is likely to be Pareto-inefficient, I have used large-scale econometric models to investigate the magnitude of the inefficiency. On the issue of international lending, I have been investigating the origins of the international debt crisis in the 1980s, as well as trying to identify the structural features of international lending that make the loan markets susceptible to such crises. The work stresses the non-enforceability of international loans, and the types of market failures that can result therefrom. Also, I am designing large-scale econometric models of global macroeconomic balance that can help to assess the prospects for continued debt servicing.

SAINT-SIMON, Claude Henri de Rouvroy*

Dates and Birthplace 1760–1825, Paris, France.

Posts Held Army officer, 1777–81; Businessman and speculator, 1781–1804; Writer and journalist, 1804–25.

Publications *Books:* 1. *Introduction aux travaux scientifiques du dix-neuvième siècle* (1807); 2. *Mémoire sur la science de l'homme* (1813); 3. *New Christianity* (1825); 4. *Selected Writings*, ed. F. M. H. Markham (1925).

Career His influence on Comte and social reformers, rather than his publications, is the source of his fame. His indentification of the phenomenon of 'industrialisation', advocacy of a science of society, and 'evolutionary organicist' theory of society are his major contributions. He advocated planned industrialisation and peaceful social change led by engineers, manufacturers and scientists. His last work, *New Christianity*, inspired a movement involving many intellectuals, which eventually split, with Enfantin leading one wing towards mystical religion.

Secondary Literature M. V. Martel, 'Saint-Simon', *IESS*, 13; K. Taylor, *Henri Saint-Simon* (Croom Helm, 1975).

SALIN, Edgar*

Dates and Birthplace 1892–1974, Frankfurt-am-Main, Germany.

Posts Held Prof. Univ. Heidelberg, 1924–7; Prof., Rector, Univ. Basle, 1927–74, 1971.

Offices and Honours Founder, Friedrich List Gesellschaft.

Publications *Books:* 1. *Platon und die griechische Utopie* (1921); 2. *Geschichte der Volkswirtschaftslehre* (1923, 1951); 3. *Wirtschaft und Staat* (1932); 4. *Jakob Burkhardt und Nietzsche* (1938); 5. *Ökonomik der Atomkraft* (1955); 6. *Die Entwicklung des internationalen Verkehrs* (1964).

Articles: 1. 'Economics: romantic and universalist economics', *ESS*, 5.

Career A follower of Otto Spann's 'universalist economics', which enjoyed a brief spell of fame in Germany in the first quarter of this century, being a typical German holistic reaction to the atomism of mainstream anglophone economics. In his *Geschichte* . . . , the entire history of economic thought is depicted as a struggle between collectivist and individualist ideas. During this early period, he made a major contribution to the historical understanding of Greek economics. In later years he turned his attention to modern topics, including atomic energy and international monetary fluctuations.

SALOP, Steven C.

Born 1946, Reading, PA, USA.

Current Post Prof. Econ., Georgetown Univ. Law Center, Washington, DC, USA, 1981–.

Past Posts Econ., Fed. Reserve Board, Washington, DC, 1972–7; Econ., US Civil Aeronautics Board, 1971–8; Econ., Deputy Ass., Dir., US Consumer Protection, Ass. Dir., Industry Analysis, Assoc. Dir., Special Projects, US Fed. Trade Commission, 1978–9, 1979–80, 1980–1; Adjunct Prof., George Washington Univ., 1975–8, Univ. Penn., 1978–9.

Degrees BA Univ. Penn., 1968; MPhil, PhD Yale Univ., 1971, 1972.

Offices and Honours Phi Beta Kappa, 1962; Shoenboun Prize Econ., 1968; NSF Fellow, 1968–72; Nomination Comm., AEA, 1982; Secr. Antitrust Section, Amer. Assoc. Law Schools.

Editorial Duties Assoc. Ed., *Internat. J. Industrial Organization*; Econ. Ed. Adviser, *J. Consumer Res.*, 1982.

Principal Fields of Interest 022 Microeconomic Theory; 600 Industrial Organisation; 026 Economics of Uncertainty and Information.

Publications *Books:* 1. *Consumer Information Remedies*, ed. (Fed. Trade Commission, 1979); 2. *Consumer Post-Purchase Remedies*, ed. (Fed. Trade Commission, 1980); 3. *Strategy, Predation and Antitrust Analysis*, ed. (Fed. Trade Commission, 1981).

Articles: 1. 'Strategic entry deterrence', *AER*, 73(2), May 1979; 2. 'The noisy monopolist: information, price dispersion and price discrimination', *REStud*, 44(3), Oct. 1977; 3. 'Bargains and ripoffs: a model of monopolistically competitive price dispersion' (with J. Stiglitz), *REStud*, 44(3), Oct. 1977; 4. 'Parables of information transmission in markets', in *The Effect of Information on Consumer and Market Behavior*, ed. A. Mitchell (Amer. Marketing Assoc., 1978); 5. 'A model of the natural rate of unemployment', *AER*, 69(1), March 1979; 6. 'Monopolistic competition with outside goods', *Bell JE*, 10(1), Spring 1979; 7. 'Efficient regulation of consumer information' (with H. Beales and R. Craswell), *J Law E*, 24(3), Dec. 1981; 8. 'Raising rivals' cost' (with D. Scheffman), *AER*, 73(2), May 1983; 9. 'Judo economics: capacity limitations and coupon competition' (with J. Gelman), *Bell JE*, 14(2), Autumn 1983; 10. 'Practices that (credibly) facilitate oligopoly coordination', in *New Developments in Market Structure*, ed. J. E. Stiglitz (MIT Press, 1984).

Principal Contributions My thesis showed how imperfect information in the labour market leads to monopsony and an inefficiently large 'natural rate' of unemployment. Turning to the product market, 'Noisy monopolist' and 'Bargains and ripoffs' explored the interaction of market power, imperfect information and self-selection in consistent equilibrium models. The resulting need to better understand imperfectly competitive equilibria led into monopolistic competition theory and then to industrial organisation, deregulation and antitrust.

Work on a number of Federal Trade Commission rule-makings, interdisciplinary task forces and staff reports resulted in a number of summary articles on consumer information policy. That work represents a merger of the economic theory of imperfect information and legal conceptions of deception and unfairness. My managerial functions at FTC then turned from consumer protection and towards antitrust and strategic competition. My recent research attempts to formulate rigorous economic theories of antitrust liability. This work concerns both pricing co-ordination and exclusionary practices. It applies recently developed ideas from economic theory to traditional issues of competition policy.

I have tried throughout my work to create rigorous yet simple economic models, presented in an aesthetically appealing manner. In this regard, I have combined the lessons of my primary teachers: Edmund Phelps, David Cass and Joseph Stiglitz. The art form of economic theory has always interested me. I prefer to capture my ideas by constructing self-contained examples rather than by formulating fully generalised, highly abstract models. And I enjoy the connections between economic theory and everyday experience — whether by interpreting the signal inherent in a red sports car or in choosing judo economics as a way of life.

SAMUELS, Warren Joseph

Born 1933, New York City, NY, USA.

Current Post Prof. Econ., Mich. State Univ., East Lansing, MI, USA, 1968–.

Past Posts Ass. Prof. Econ., Univ. Missouri, Columbia, 1957–8, Georgia State Univ., Atlanta, 1958–9; Ass. Prof., Assoc. Prof. Econ., Univ. Miami, FL, 1959–68.

Degrees BBA Univ. Miami, 1954; PhD Univ. Wisconsin, 1955, 1957.

Offices and Honours Pres., History of Econ. Soc., 1981–2.

Editorial Duties Ed., *JEI*, 1971–81; Ed. Board, *HOPE*, 1969–, *SEJ*, 1967–8, *J Post Keyn E*, 1977–, *Pol. Stud. J*, 1979–; Ed., *Res. in the History of Econ. Thought and Methodology* (JAI Press), 1983–.

Principal Fields of Interest 031 History of Economic Thought; 036 Methodology; 320 Domestic Fiscal Policy and Public Finance.

Publications *Books:* 1. *The Classical Theory of Economic Policy* (World, 1966); 2. *A Critique of Administrative Regulation*, co-ed. (with H. M. Trebing), (Inst. Public Utilities, 1972); 3. *Pareto on Policy* (Elsevier, 1974); 4. *The Chicago School of Political Economy*, ed. (Div. Res. Mich. State Univ., 1976); 5. *The Economy as a System of Power*, 2 vols, ed. (Transaction Books, 1979); 6. *The Methodology of Economic Thought*, ed. (Transaction Books, 1980); 7. *Taxing and Spending Policy*, co-ed. (with L. L. Wade), (Lexington, 1980); 8. *Law and Economics* (with A. A. Schmid), (Martinus Nijhoff, 1981); 9. *Contemporary Economists in Perspective*, 2 vols, co-ed. (with H. W. Spiegel), (JAI Press, 1984).

Articles: 1. 'The physiocratic theory of economic policy', *QJE*, 76, Feb. 1962; 2. 'The economy as a system of power and its legal bases: the legal economics of Robert Lee Hale', *Univ. Miami Law Rev.*, 27, Spring–Summer 1973; 3. 'The history of economic thought as intellectual history', *HOPE*, 6(3), Fall 1974; 4. 'The political economy of Adam Smith', *Nebraska J. Econ.*, 15, Summer 1976, repr. in *Ethics*, 87, April 1977; 5. 'Ideology in Economics', in *Modern Economic Thought*, ed. S. Weintraub (Univ. Penn. Press, 1977); 6. 'Normative premises in regulatory theory', *J Post Keyn E*, 1(1), Fall 1978; 7. 'The state, law, and economic organization', *Res. Law and Sociology*, 2, 1979; 8. 'Economics as a science and its relation to policy: the example of free trade', *JEI*, 14, March, 1980; 9. 'A critique of the discursive systems and foundation concepts of distribution analysis', *Analyse & Kritik*, 4, Oct. 1982.

Principal Contributions From the

very beginning of my career I have been interested in generating greater clarity as to the economic role of government both in the history of economic thought and in contemporary economics. This often has taken the form of identifying fundamentals otherwise obscured by abstract and misleading or incomplete ideological and theoretical formulations. This quest has channelled most, although not all, of my work in the history of economic thought and in the legal-economic fundamentals of welfare economics, regulation, property rights and law and economics.

For the last decade or so I also have been involved in researching the conceptual and sociological origins of modern economics in the period 1870–1914. This has involved work in identifying the nature and consequences of different modes of doing intellectual history; the dynamics of theoretical and school development; the identification of the considerations which seem to have governed economists during that period in making their choices as to what constituted economics and how economics was to be done; and the consequences for the practice of economics of those choices; in short, a sociological or social history of economics which is neither internalist nor externalist (as those concepts generally have been used) but which focusses on status-oriented considerations operating within the increasingly self-conscious and professionalising discipline. As in my work on the economic role of government, I am less interested in the ideological self-perceptions of economists than in what those self-perceptions have generated in terms of disciplinary practice.

SAMUELSON, Paul Anthony

Born 1915, Gary, IN, USA.
Current Post Inst. Prof., MIT, Camb., MA, USA, 1960–.
Past Posts MIT, 1940–.
Degrees BA Univ. Chicago, 1935; MA, PhD Harvard Univ., 1936, 1941; Hon. DLL, DSci., DLit., DLetters, DEcon., various univs.
Offices and Honours David Wells Prize, Univ. Harvard, 1941; John Bates Clark Medal, Pres., AEA, 1947, 1961; Pres., Em Soc, 1953; Pres., Hon. Pres., IEA, 1965–8, 1968–; Albert Einstein Medal, 1970; Nobel Prize in Econ., 1970.
Editorial Duties Contrib. Ed., *Newsweek*.
Principal Fields of Interest 020 General Economic Theory.
Publications *Books:* 1. *Foundations of Economic Analysis* (Harvard Univ. Press, 1947, 1983, 1985); 2. *Economics* (McGraw-Hill, 1948, 1981); 3. *Linear Programming and Economic Analysis* (with R. Dorfman and R. Solow), (McGraw-Hill, 1958); 4. *Collected Scientific Papers of Paul A. Samuelson*, 1, 2, ed. J.E. Stiglitz, 3, ed. R.C. Merton, 4, eds. H. Nagatani and K. Crowley (MIT Press, 1966, 1972, 1977).
Principal Contributions The theory of consumers' behaviour and capital theory; growth theory; various topics in mathematical economics; welfare economics; international trade theory; fiscal policy and income determination; the pure theory of public expenditure; the methodology of economics; the history of economic thought; portfolio selection and the theory of speculative markets; and the economics of population.
Secondary Literature A. Lindbeck, 'Paul Anthony Samuelson's contributions to economics', *Swed JE*, 72(1), Jan. 1970, repr. in *Contemporary Economists in Perspective*, eds. H.W. Spiegel and W.J. Samuels (JAI Press, 1984); A. Kendry, 'Paul Samuelson and the scientific awakening of economics', *Twelve Contemporary Economists*, eds. J.R. Shackleton and G. Locksley (Macmillan, 1981); *Paul Samuelson and Modern Economic Theory*, eds. E.C. Brown and R.M. Solow (McGraw-Hill, 1983).

SAMUELSON, William Frank

Born 1952, Boston, MA, USA.
Current Post Assoc. Prof. Econ., Boston Univ., Boston, MA, USA, 1984–.
Past Posts Ass. Prof. Econ., Boston Univ., 1978–84.

Degrees BA, PhD Harvard Univ., 1974, 1978.

Principal Fields of Interest 022 Microeconomics; 026 Economics of Uncertainty and Information; 511 Organisation and Decision Theory.

Publications *Articles:* 1. 'The object-distribution problem revisited', *QJE*, 95(1), Feb. 1980; 2. 'First-offer bargains', *Management Science*, 26(2), Feb. 1980; 3. 'Optimal auctions', *AER*, 71(3), June 1981; 4. 'Competitive bidding in defense contracting', in *Auctions, Bidding and Contracting: Uses and Theory* (NYU Press, 1983); 5. 'Bargaining under incomplete information', *Operations Res*, 31(5), Sept. 1983; 6. 'I won the auction but don't want the prize', *J. Conflict Resolution*, 27(4), Dec. 1983; 7. 'Bargaining under asymmetric information', *Em*, 52(4), July 1984; 8. 'Dividing coastal waters', *J. Conflict Resolution*, 29(1), March 1985; 9. 'The winner's curse in bilateral negotiations', in *Research in Experimental Econ.*, 3 (JAI Press, 1985); 10. 'A comment on the Coase theorem', in *Game-Theoretic Models of Bargaining* (CUP, 1985).

Principal Contributions According to the conventional description, microeconomics is about the functioning of markets and the behaviour of economic agents in the presence (and occasionally in the absence) of markets. My research has focussed on the latter area, individual decisions and behaviour, principally, in nonmarket contexts. This focus has come about partly by chance, partly by inertia but primarily by the belief that increasing our understanding of nonmarket allocation methods — auctions and competitive bidding, negotiation and bargaining, arbitration and fair division, voting and group decision-making — is at least as important as painting an additional wrinkle on the well-known 'face' of market behaviour.

My research has aimed at developing and experimentally testing models of normative behaviour in bidding and bargaining settings under incomplete information. In the former area, my work has analysed optimal bidding behaviour of competing buyers at auction and has characterised revenue-maximising auction methods available to the seller. In the latter area, my work has examined optimal bargaining strategies under both incomplete and asymmetric information and the implications of these strategies for bargaining efficiency. In a comparison of bidding and bargaining methods, my research has re-examined the Coase theorem by demonstrating the inherent limitations of bargaining solutions to externality problems under incomplete information and showing that forgoing an initial rights assignment and allocating the right by competitive bid leads to Pareto-superior outcomes. Finally, my research in arbitration and fair division has examined equitable ways to divide a collection of goods among recipients and methods for determining maritime boundaries for mineral and fishing rights in ocean waters under dispute.

SANDMO, Agnar

Born 1938, Tøsberg, Norway.

Current Post Prof. Econ., Norwegian School Econ. and Bus. Admin., Bergen, Norway, 1971–.

Past Posts Ass. Prof., Assoc. Prof., Acting Prof., Norwegian School Econ. and Bus. Admin., 1966–71; Vis. Researcher, CORE, Univ. Louvain, Belgium, 1969–70; Vis. Prof., Univ. Essex, 1975–6.

Degrees Siviløkonom, Licentiat, Dr oecon. Norwegian School Econ. and Bus. Admin., 1961, 1966, 1970.

Offices and Honours Fellow, Em Soc, 1976; Council Member, Member, Norwegian Academy Sciences, 1984–.

Editorial Duties Ed. *Statsøkonomisk Tidsskrift*, 1974–; Ed. Board, *Scand JE*, 1976–; Assoc. Ed., Co-ed., *J Pub E*, 1973.

Principal Fields of Interest 020 General Economic Theory; 320 Fiscal Theory and Policy; Public Finance.

Publications *Books:* 1. *Essays on Public Economics: The Kiryat Anavim Papers*, ed. (D.C. Heath, 1978); 2. *Kalkulasjonsrente og prosjektvurdering* (The Social Discount Rate and Project Evaluation) (with K.P. Hagen), (Universitetsforlaget, 1983).

Articles: 1. 'Capital risk, consumption

and portfolio choice', *Em*, 37(4), Oct. 1969; 2. 'On the theory of the competitive firm under price uncertainty', *AER*, 61(1), March 1971; 3. 'Discount rates for public investment in closed and open economies' (with J.H. Drèze), *Ec*, N.S. 38, Nov. 1971; 4. 'Discount rates for public investment under uncertainty', *Int ER*, 13(2), June 1972, repr. in *Allocation under Uncertainty: Equilibrium and Optimality*, ed. J.H. Drèze (Macmillan, 1974); 5. 'Income tax evasion: a theoretical analysis' (with M.G. Allingham), *J Pub E*, 1(3–4), Nov. 1972; 6. 'Public goods and the technology of consumption', *REStud*, 40(4), Oct. 1973; 7. 'Optimal taxation: an introduction to the literature', *J Pub E*, 6(1,2), July–Aug. 1976; transls., Spanish, *Hacienda Publica Espanola*, 1976, German, *Optimale Finanzpolitik*, eds. M. Rose, H.D. Wenzel and W. Wiegard (Gustav Fischer, 1981); 8. 'Portfolio theory asset demand and taxation', *REStud*, 44(2), June 1977; 9. 'Welfare implications of the taxation of savings' (with A.B. Atkinson), *EJ*, 90, Sept. 1980; 10. 'Tax evasion, labour supply and the equity-efficiency trade-off', *J Pub E*, 16(3), Dec. 1981.

Principal Contributions First published work was in the economics of uncertainty, where my main aim was to explore the implications of the expected utility theorem and hypotheses about risk aversion for saving, portfolio and production decisions of consumers and firms. Later turned my attention to public economics, particularly as it related to welare economics and the theory of the second best. Topics within that area include the following: the derivation of the social rate of discount when there are imperfections in the form of tax distortions or incomplete markets; the theory of public goods and externalities with emphasis on the 'household production' approach; optimum tax theory, both in general and with special application to labour supply and saving, tax evasion, etc., and taxation and risk-taking.

SARGAN, John Denis

Born 1924, Doncaster, Yorkshire, England.

Current Post Prof. Emeritus, LSE, 1984–.

Past Posts Lect., Univ. Leeds, 1948–63; Vis. Prof., Univ. Minnesota, 1958–9, 1959–60; Ass. Prof., Univ. Chicago, 1959–60; Reader, Prof. Em, LSE, 1963–4, 1964–84; Vis. Prof., Yale Univ., 1974, Florida, 1982.

Degrees BA (Maths.), MA (Maths.), BA Univ. Camb., 1944, 1946, 1948.

Offices and Honours Pres., Em. Soc., 1980.

Editorial Duties Ex-Assoc. Ed., *Em*; Ex-Ed., *REStud*.

Principal Fields of Interest 211 Econometric Methods; 212 Construction of Econometric Models; 213 Mathematical Methods.

Publications *Articles:* 1. 'The estimation of relationships with autocorrelated residuals by use of instrumental variables', *RSS*, Series B, 21, 1959; 2. 'The maximum likelihood estimation of economic relationships with autoregressive residuals', *Em*, 29, July 1961; 3. 'Wages and prices in the U.K.: a study in econometric methodology', in *The Calston Papers* (Butterworths, 1964); 4. 'Econometric estimations and the Edgeworth approximation', *Em*, 44(3), July 1976; 5. 'The consumer price equation in the post-war British economy: an exercise in equation specification testing', *REStud*, 47(1), Jan. 1980; 6. 'A model of wage price inflation', *REStud*, 47(1), Jan. 1980; 7. 'Some tests of dynamic specification for a single equation', *Em*, 48(4), May 1980.

Principal Contributions I had an early interest in economic theory and econometrics, but after my first visit to the USA I decided to concentrate on econometric theory and applied econometric work on inflation. My first two articles listed above contain the econometric theory relevant to the empirical work of the third article. I came back to wage inflation in No. 6 above. I still regard the idea that workers strive for a target value of real wages as an important explanation of current inflationary behaviour. The use of instrumental variables to give a general technique for estimating economic relationships is now widely adopted.

A second development was based upon the fear that asymptotic (large sample) theory gives poor approximations in estimating some econometric models where sample sizes are less than one hundred. It is very difficult to discuss the exact distributions of estimations and test statistics from econometric models, but my 1976 article (No. 4 above) does contain some theoretical results, which however lead to difficult numerical computations. A much simpler alternative is to use approximation distributions, which consist of series of approximation terms in which each term is relatively small compared with the next earlier term, and the error in the approximation is of order equal to some initial power of the sample size. For sufficiently large sample size, these approximations may be sufficiently good to give a much better approximation to the exact distribution than the standard asymptotic distribution. For estimations it is almost always possible to make use of the Edgeworth expansion, and for test statistics to make use of the chi-squared expansions. The practical problem is to develop computer programs to compute these approximations in sufficiently realistic models. Such programs have been written and implemented successfully by me and my students.

SARGENT, Thomas J.

Born 1943, Pasadena, CA, USA.
Current Post Prof. Econ., Univ. Minnesota, USA, 1982–.
Past Posts Vis. Prof., Univ. Chicago, 1976–7, Harvard Univ., 1981–2.
Degrees BA Univ. Cal. Berkeley, 1964; PhD Harvard Univ., 1968.
Offices and Honours Phi Beta Kappa, 1963; Fellow, Em Soc, 1976; Mary Elizabeth Morgan Prize, Univ. Chicago, 1979–80.
Principal Fields of Interest 023 Macroeconomic Theory.
Publications *Books:* 1. *Macroeconomic Theory* (Academic Press, 1979); 2. *Rational Expectations and Econo-*

metric Practice, co-ed. (with R.E. Lucas, Jr.), (Univ. Minn. Press, 1981).
Articles: 1. 'Rational expectations and the dynamics of hyperinflation' (with N. Wallace), *Int ER*, 14(2), June 1973; 2. 'Interpreting economic time series', *JPE*, 89(1), Feb. 1981.
Principal Contributions Studies of the role of expectations in macroeconomic models, and the relationship between dynamic economic theory and time series analysis.

SATO, Kazuo

Born 1927, Sapporo, Hokkaido, Japan.
Current Post Prof. Econ., Rutgers Univ., New Brunswick, NJ, USA, 1983–.
Past Posts Ass. Prof., Assoc. Prof., Inst. Social and Econ. Res., Osaka Univ., 1959–64; Econ. Affairs Officer, UN, 1962–70; Vis. Prof., MIT, 1969–70; Prof., State Univ. NY, Buffalo, 1970–83; Vis. Prof., Univs. Pittsburgh, 1976, Tsukuba, 1977, Albany, 1978, Columbia, 1981–3.
Degrees BA Hokkaido Univ., 1953; MA, PhD Yale Univ., 1956, 1960.
Offices and Honours Member, Comm. Japanese Econ. Stud., 1978–; Assoc. Dir., Comm. Asian Econ. Stud., 1983–5.
Editorial Duties Ed., *Japanese Econ. Stud.*, 1972–.
Principal Fields of Interest 023 Macroeconomic Theory; 111 Economic Growth Theory and Models; 123 Comparative Economic Studies.
Publications *Books:* 1. *Production Functions and Aggregation* (N-H, 1975); 2. *Essays in Modern Capital Theory*, co-ed. (with M. Brown and P. Zarembka), (N-H, 1976); 3. *Industry and Business in Japan*, co-ed. (M.E. Sharpe), (Croom Helm, 1980); 4. *The Anatomy of Japanese Business*, co-ed. (M.E. Sharpe), (Croom Helm, 1984); 5. *Production Functions* (Japanese), (Sobunsha, 1975); 6. *Contemporary Economic Theory* (Japanese), co-ed. (Shinhyoron Sha, 1979).
Articles: 1. 'Price-cost structure and behavior of profit margins', *YEE*, 1, Fall 1961; 2. 'A model of investment

behavior: fixed investment and capacity in Japanese manufacturing, 1952–1963', *Econ. Stud. Q.*, 16, June 1964, repr. in *Econometric Studies of Japan*, eds. R. Kosobud and R. Minami (Univ. Illinois Press, 1977); 3. 'The neoclassical theorem and distribution of income and wealth', *REStud*, 33, Oct. 1966, repr. in *Readings in the Theory of Growth*, ed. F.H. Hahn (Macmillan, 1971); 4. 'A two-level constant-elasticity-of-substitution production function', *REStud*, 34, April, 1967; 5. 'Taxation and neo-classical growth, *PF*, 33, 1967; 6. 'The neo-classical postulate and the technology frontier in capital theory', *QJE*, 88(3), Aug. 1974; 7. 'A simultaneous equation model of savings in developing countries' (with N.H. Leff), *JPE*, 83(6), Dec. 1975; 8. 'The meaning and measurement of the real value added index', *REStat*, 58(4), Nov. 1976; 9. 'The demand function for industrial exports: a cross-country analysis', *REStat*, 59(4), Nov. 1977; 10. 'Macroeconomic adjustment in developing countries: instability, short-run growth, and external dependency' (with N.H. Leff), *REStat*, 62(1), May 1980.

Principal Contributions Early work has been concerned with theory of economic growth (the role of technical progress, income and wealth distribution, the role of taxes), theory of production functions (aggregation of microunits into a macro-production function), theory of capital (theoretical basis), index number theory (based on economic theory), economic development (macroeconomic adjustments in developing countries), and quantitative studies of economic behaviour (consumer demand functions, investment function, export function, constructions of macroeconomic models). More recently, have moved on to study the macroeconomic equilibrium process under quantity constraints on the one hand and developments in the contemporary Japanese economy as well as quantitative economic history of the interwar Japan on the other.

SATO, Ryuzo

Born 1931, Yuzawa-shi, Akita-Ken, Japan.

Current Post Prof. Econ., Brown Univ., Providence, RI, USA, 1967–; Adjunct Prof. Public Theory, J.F. Kennedy School Govt., Harvard Univ., Cambridge, MA, USA, 1982–.

Past Posts Vis. Assoc. Prof. Econ., Brown Univ., 1965–6; Vis. Scholar, Univ. Camb., 1970–1; Vis. Prof. Econ., Univ. Bonn, 1974–5, Dept. Eng., Kyoto Univ., Japan, 1982–3; Assoc., Center Internat. Affairs (US–Japan), Harvard Univ., 1982–3; Vis. Prof., Internat. Univ. Japan, 1983–; Res. Assoc., NBER, 1982–; Lect., Matsushita School Govt. and Bus., 1983–.

Degrees BEc, Dr Econ. Hitotsubashi Univ., Tokyo, 1954, 1969; PhD Johns Hopkins Univ., 1962.

Offices and Honours Nikkei Econ. Prize, Japan, 1968; Ford Foundation Fellow, 1970–1; Guggenheim Foundation Fellow, 1974–5.

Editorial Duties Ed. Boards, *JEL*, 1975–8, *Lecture Notes on Econ. and Math. Systems*, 1972–.

Principal Fields of Interest 020 General Economic Theory; 111 Economic Growth Theory and Models; 620 Economics of Technological Change.

Publications *Books:* 1. *Theory of Economic Growth* (Japanese), (Keiso-Shobo, 1968); 2. *Mathematical Economic Theory* (German), co-ed. (with M.J. Beckmann), (Kiepenheuer & Witsch, 1975); 3. *Resource Allocation and Division of Space*, co-ed. (with T. Fujii), (Springer-Verlag, 1977); 4. *Double Up-Bringing Experiences — USA and Japan* (Japanese), (with K. Sato), (Diamond Publ., 1981); 5. *Theory of Technical Change and Economic Invariance: Application of Lie Groups* (Academic Press, 1981); 6. *New Macroeconomics* (Japanese), (McGraw-Hill Kogakusha, 1982); 7. *Invariance Principle and Structure of Technology* (with T.Nono), (Springer-Verlag, 1983); 8. *Technology, Organization and Economic Structure, Essays in Honor of Isamu Yamada*, co-ed. (with R. Sato and M.J. Beckmann), (Springer-Verlag, 1983), 9. *Research and Productivity: Endogenous Technical*

Change (with G. Suzawa), (Auburn Publ., 1983); 10. *'Me' Society vs. 'We' Society: USA vs. Japan* (Japanese), (Nihon Keizi Shimbum, 1983).

Articles: 1. 'Fiscal policy in a neoclassical growth model: an analysis of time required for equilibrating adjustment', *REStud*, 30(1), Feb. 1963; 2. 'Productivity, factor prices, and economic growth' (with J.W. Kendrick), *AER*, 53(5), Dec. 1963; 3. 'The estimation of biased technical progress and the production function', *Int ER*, 11(2), June 1970; 4. 'Optimal savings policy when labor grows endogenously' (with E. Davis), *Em*, 39(4), Nov. 1971; 5. 'The stability of the competitive system which contains gross complementary goods', *REStud*, 39(4), Oct. 1972; 6. 'On the most general class of CES functions', *Em*, 43(5–6), Sept.–Nov. 1975; 7. 'Self-dual preferences', *Em*, 44(5), Sept. 1976; 8. 'The impact of technological change on the holotheticity of production functions', *REStud*, 47(4), July 1980; 9. 'A theory of endogenous technical progress: dynamic Böhm-Bawerk effect and optimal R&D policy' (with T. Nono), *ZN*, Feb. 1982; 10. 'Unattainability of integrability and definiteness conditions in the general case of demand for money and goods' (with P.A. Samuelson), *AER*, 74(4), Sept. 1984.

Principal Contributions My early work in economics concentrated on the theory of economic growth. My 1968 book, *Theory of Economic Growth*, presented a comprehensive analysis of modern growth theories, including classical, Schumpeterian, Harrod-Domar, neoclassical theories, and contemporary optimal growth theory. Production function analysis and the estimation of technical progress followed as a result of work with John Kendrick in the 1960s. A model of biassed technical progress was first formulated and applied to US data in the late 1960s. In the early 1970s, my interest shifted to the formulation of modern production theory incorporating technical progress functions. This research endeavour led to the study of invariance problems in economics and culminated in the 1981 book, *Theory of Technical Change*. Subjects covered in the book include (1) analysis of technical change and returns to scale, (2) self-duality of preference and technologies, (3) general recoverability problem of optimal dynamic behaviour, (4) economic conservation laws and (5) invariant index number problems.

Some recent contributions include the application of Noether's invariance principle to uncover some hidden dynamic symmetries and conservation laws, the study (with P. Samuelson) of the integrability conditions in the general case of demand for money and goods, and the development of an endogenous theory of technical progress presented in *Research and Productivity* (with G. Suzawa). Current research interest is in the application of differential games to areas like the Schumpeterian hypothesis, market structure, and international rivalry in R&D and international trade.

SAUVY, Alfred

Born 1898, Villeneuve de la Raho, France.

Current Post Retired, 1972–.

Past Posts UN Commission Pop., 1947–; Conseil Econ. et Social, 1947–74; Prof., Collège de France, 1959–70.

Degrees Ancien élève l'Ecole Polytechnique; Dr h.c., Univs., Geneva, Brussels, Liège, Utrecht, Montreal, Palermo.

Offices and Honours Grad. Officier, Legion d'Honneur; Commandeur, la Sante Publique; Commondeur d'Academie; Ancien Pres. De la Conjoncture et du Plan au Conseil Econ. et Social.

Principal Fields of Interest 131 Economic Fluctuations; 841 Demographic Economics.

Publications *Books:* 1. *Le pouvoir et l'opinion* (Payot, 1949); 2. *General Theory of Population*, 2 vols (Presses Univ. de France, 1954, 1966; transls., Spanish, Russian, Chinese); 3. *La montée des jeunes* (Calmann-Levy, 1958); 4. *Histoire économique de la France entre les deux guerres*, 4 vols (Fayard, 1965, 1975, 3 vols, Economica, 1984); 5. *De Paul Reynaud a Charles de Gaulle* (Casterman, 1972); 6. *Le* *cout et la valeur de la vie humaine* (Hermann, 1977); 7. *Humour et politique* (Calmann-Levy, 1979); 8. *La machine et le chômage* (Dunod, 1980); 9. *La vie en plus* (Calmann-Levy, 1981); 10. *Mondes en marche* (Calmann-Levy, 1982).

Principal Contributions Short-term economic fluctuations and demographic changes in the world; the effects of technical change on total employment; the struggle for clarity in statistical information bearing on matters of economic policy.

Secondary Literature J. Bourgeois-Pichat, 'Sauvy, Alfred', *IESS*, 18.

SAVING, Thomas Robert

Born 1933, Chicago, IL, USA.

Current Post Prof. Econ., Texas A&M Univ., Coll. Station, TX, USA, 1968–.

Past Posts Ass. Prof., Univ. Washington, Seattle, 1960–1; Ass. Prof., Assoc. Prof., Prof., Michigan State Univ., 1961–3, 1963–6, 1966–8.

Degrees BA Michigan State Univ., 1957; MA, PhD Univ. Chicago, 1958, 1960.

Offices and Honours Ford Foundation Fellow, 1971–2; Pres., WEA, 1971–2; Pres., Southern Econ. Assoc., 1980–1.

Editorial Duties Ed. Boards, *AER*, 1970, *SEJ*, 1973–4, *WEJ*, 1970, *JMCB*, 1980–4.

Principal Fields of Interest 310 Monetary Economics; 610 Industrial Organisation; 020 General Economic Theory.

Publications *Books:* 1. *Money, Wealth and Economic Theory* (with B. P. Pesek), (Macmillan, 1967; transls., Spanish, Chinese); 2. *The Foundations of Money and Banking* (with B. P. Pesek), (Macmillan, 1968).

Articles: 1. 'Monetary policy, taxes, and the rate of interest' (with B. P. Pesek), *JPE*, 71, Aug. 1963; 2. 'Long-run adjustments in a perfectly competitive firm and industry' (with C. E. Ferguson), *AER*, 59(5), Dec. 1969; 3. 'Outside money, inside money and the real balance effect', *JMCB*, 2(1), Feb. 1970; 4. 'Inside money, competitive

rents, and the real balance effect', *JMCB*, 3(2), May 1971; 5. 'Transactions costs and the demand for money', *AER*, 61(3), June 1971; 6. 'On the neutrality of money', *JPE*, 81, Jan.–Feb. 1973; 7. 'Product quality, uncertainty and regulations: the trucking industry' (with A. De Vany), *AER*, 67(4), Sept. 1977; 8. 'Money supply theory with competitively determined deposit rates and activity charges', *JMCB*, 11(1), Feb. 1979; 9. 'Life-cycle job choice and the demand and supply of entry level jobs: some evidence from the air force' (with A. S. De Vany), *REStat*, 64(4), Aug. 1982; 10. 'The economics of quality' (with A. S. De Vany), *JPE*, 20(3), Dec. 1983.

Principal Contributions Early work concentrated in industrial organization estimated the optimal scale of enterprise using the survivor technique and firm size distributions. I worked with Carl Brehm on an early negative income tax paper published in *AER*. My interest turned to the microeconomic foundations of monetary theory where my work with Boris Pesek changed the way money and money substitutes were viewed as contributors to net monetary wealth. The approach developed by Pesek and myself, first reported in our book *Money, Wealth and Economic Theory*, forms the foundation for user cost-weighted measures of the money supply.

Research interest shifted to the theory of the firm and its implications for money supply determination, concentrating on banks as firms and the banking industry as a competitive industry. The special feature of the banking industry is the externality that arises because of the relationship of banks to their customers. Banks and their customers compete for a necessary scarce factor of production, base money.

My interest in microeconomics and the importance that market constraints place on outcomes led me in two additional directions: the theory of factor demand and extensions of the theory of the firm. The latter led to the development of quantity restrictions as a basis for short-run rationing in competitive markets. A series of ten papers, most in collaboration with Arthur D. Vany and culminating in *JPE*, 1983, laid the foundations for extending the theory of the firm to the case where quality and quantity supplied are not independent. An inverse relation between quality and quantity arises most obviously in service industries where queues develop, but in other industries increased output affects quality. This approach improves understanding of monopolistic competition as well as capacity allocation.

SAX, Emil*

Dates and Birthplace 1845–1927, Jauernig, Austro-Hungary.
Posts Held Prof., Univ. Prague, 1879–93.
Publications *Books:* 1. *Die Verkehrsmittel in Volks-und Staatswirtschaft*, 2 vols (1878–9); 2. *Grundlegung der theoretischen Staatswirtschaft* (1887); 3. *Der Kapitalzins* (1916).
Articles: 1. 'The valuation theory of taxation' (1924, 1956), repr. in *Classics in the Theory of Public Finance*, eds. R. A. Musgrave and A. T. Peacock (1958).
Career Extended the marginal theory of value to public finance and transportation. His *Grundlegung* ... was a major influence on the development of the theory of taxation and *Die Verkehrsmittel* ... was a standard work on transportation economics.
Secondary Literature E. Lindahl, 'Sax, Emil', *ESS*, 13.

SAY, Horace Emile*

Dates and Birthplace 1794–1860, France.
Posts Held Businessman.
Offices and Honours Founder of Soc. d'Econ. Polit. and *J. des Economistes*; Member, Tribunal de Commerce; Councillor, State, 1849–51; Member, l'Académie des sciences morales et politiques, 1857.
Publications *Books:* 1. *Histoire des relations commerciales entre la France et le Brésil* (1830); 2. *Etudes sur l'administration de la ville de Paris* (1846); 3. *Statistique de l'industrie à Paris* (1858).

Career Son of J.-B. Say and his father's devoted follower, his work on commercial relations with Brazil arose from his own business experience there. His work on industrial statistics was based on a massive survey conducted under his supervision by the Paris Chamber of Commerce.

SAY, Jean-Baptiste*

Dates and Birthplace 1767–1832, Lyon, France.
Posts Held Journalist and Ed., *La Décade*, 1793–99; Cotton manufacturer, 1806–13; Prof. Industrial Econ., Conservatorie des Arts et Métiers, Paris, 1817; Prof. Polit. Econ., Collège de France, Paris, 1830–2.
Offices and Honours Member, French Tribunate, 1799–1806.
Publications *Books:* 1. *A Treatise on Political Economy* (1803, 1880, 1971); 2. *Catechism of Political Economy* (1815); 3. *Letters to Malthus* (1821, 1965); 4. *Cours complet d'économie politique pratique*, 6 vols (1828–9, 1852).
Career Inspired by Smith's *Wealth of Nations*, he wrote his *Treatise* ... which introduced Smithian ideas to France and other European countries. His analysis developed beyond Smith's, including an emphasis on the role of the entrepreneur. The famous law of markets (Say's law) became widely accepted as a statement of the eternal ability of market forces to produce equilibrium of production and demand. His influence dominated officially-taught economics in France for most of the nineteenth century: unorthodox views and different approaches tended to be kept outside the conventional academic world and were confined to such institutions as the écoles which trained engineers.
Secondary Literature G. Leduc, 'Say, Jean-Baptiste', *IESS*, 14.

SAY, Leon*

Dates and Birthplace 1826–96, France.
Posts Held Politician, financier and journalist.

Offices and Honours Member, French Senate and Chamber of Deputies; Member, French Academy; Pres., Senate; Prefect of the Seine; French Ambassador to London; French Minister of Fin., 1872–9, 1882.

Publications *Books:* 1. *Critical Enquiry into the Financial Situation of Paris* (1866); 2. *Ten Days in Upper Italy* (1883); 3. *State Socialism* (1886); 4. *Democratic Solutions of the Problems of Taxation* (1886).

Career An economist of the *laissez faire* liberal tradition, and a follower of his grandfather, J.-B. Say, on most issues. Responsible for many major financial transactions, notably the liquidation of the war debt to Germany, and the establishment of redeemable government stock. Despite an association in the 1860s with the co-operative movement, he was a determined opponent of socialism and an anti-protectionist.

Secondary Literature C. Gide, 'Say, Leon', *EJ*, 6, June 1896.

SAYERS, Richard Sidney

Born 1908, Bury St Edmunds, Suffolk, England.

Current Post Emeritus Prof. Econ., Univ. London, 1968–.

Past Posts Ass. Lect. Econ., LSE, 1931–5; Lect. Econ., Exeter, Corpus Christi and Pembroke Coll. Oxford, 1935–45; Fellow, Pembroke Coll. Oxford, 1939–45; Econ., UK Ministry of Supply, 1940–5; Econ. Adviser, UK Cabinet Office, 1945–7; Cassel Prof. Econ., LSE, 1947–68; Member, UK Radcliffe Comm. Monetary System, 1957–9; OECD Comm. Fiscal Measures, 1966–8; Member, UK Monopolies Commission, 1968.

Degrees MA Univ. Camb., 1933; MA Univ. Oxford, 1936; Hon. DLitt Univ. Warwick, 1967; Hon. DCL Univ. Kent, 1967.

Offices and Honours Pres., Section F BA, 1960; Vice-Pres., BA, 1966–7; Pres., Econ. Hist. Soc., 1972–4; Vice-Pres., RES, 1973–6; Hon. Fellow, St Catherine's Coll. Camb., LSE, Inst. Bankers.

Principal Fields of Interest 312 Commercial Banking.

Publications *Books:* 1. *Bank of England Operations, 1890–1914* (OUP, 1936); 2. *Modern Banking* (OUP, 1938, 1967); 3. *American Banking System* (OUP, 1948); 4. *Banking in the British Commonwealth*, ed. (OUP, 1952); 5. *Papers in English Monetary History*, co-ed. (with T. S. Ashton), (Macmillan, 1953); 6. *Financial Policy, 1939–45* (HMSO, Longman, 1956); 7. *Central Banking After Bagehot* (OUP, 1957); 8. *Lloyds Bank in the History of English Banking* (OUP, 1957); 9. *Economic Writings of James Pennington*, ed. (LSE, 1963); 10. *The Bank of England 1891–1944* (OUP, 1976).

Principal Contributions English monetary history; relationship between monetary policy and theory and institutions, as exemplified in report of the committee on the working of the monetary system (Radcliffe Report) 1959.

SCARF, Herbert Eli

Born 1930, Philadelphia, PA, USA.

Current Post Sterling Prof. Econ., Yale Univ., New Haven, CT, USA, 1979–.

Past Posts Rand Corp., Santa Monica, CA, 1954–7; Ass. Prof., Assoc. Prof. Stats., Stanford Univ., 1957–63; Prof. Econ., Yale Univ., 1963–79.

Degrees BA (Maths.) Temple Univ., 1951; PhD (Maths.) Princeton Univ., 1954; LHD h.c. Univ. Chicago, 1978.

Offices and Honours Fellow, Center Advanced Study, Stanford, CA, 1963; Fellow, Pres., Em Soc, 1963, 1983; Fellow, AAAS, 1971; Member, NAS, 1976; Lanchester Prize Von Neumann Medal, OR Soc. Amer., 1974, 1983.

Principal Fields of Interest 021 General Equilibrium Theory; 026 Game Theory; 213 Mathematical Methods.

Publications *Books:* 1. *Studies in the Mathematical Theory of Inventory and Production* (with K. J. Arrow and S. Karlin), (Stanford Univ. Press, 1958); 2. *Contributions to the Theory of Inventory and Replacement* (with K. J. Arrow and S. Karlin), (Stanford Univ. Press, 1961); 3. *Multistage Inventory Models and Techniques*, co-ed. (with

D. M. Guilford and M. W. Shelley), (Stanford Univ. Press, 1963); 4. *The Computation of Economic Equilibria* (with T. Hansen), (Yale Univ. Press, 1973).

Articles: 1. 'The optimality of (S,s) policies in the dynamic inventory problem', in *First Stanford Symposium on Mathematics in the Social Sciences* (Stanford Univ. Press, 1961); 2. 'Some examples of global instability of the competitive equilbrium', *Int ER*, 1(3), Sept. 1960; 3. 'A limit theorem on the core of an economy' (with G. Debreu), *Int ER*, 4(3), Sept. 1963; 4. 'The core an n-person game', *Em*, 35(1), Jan. 1967; 5. 'The approximation of fixed points of a continuous mapping', *Siam J. Appl. Maths.*, 15(5), Sept. 1967; 6. 'The solution of systems of piecewise linear equations' (with B. C. Eaves), *Maths. of Operations Res.*, 1(1), Feb. 1976; 7. 'Production sets with indivisibilities', *Em*, 49(1), Jan. 1981, 49(2), March 1981.

Principal Contributions After receiving a PhD in mathematics from Princeton, I left academic life to work for the Rand Corporation for several years. I became interested in the mathematical theory of inventory management and several years later produced a proof of the optimality of (S,s) policies for the dynamic inventory problem under fairly general conditions. While teaching in the department of statistics at Stanford I learned about recent work on the stability of the competitive equilibrium, and constructed several examples of models of exchange for which the Walrasian adjustment mechanism was globally unstable. It was this work which led to my subsequent interest in developing algorithms for the computation of economic equilibria. In 1963 I published a paper with Gerard Debreu demonstrating that the core of an economy converged to the set of competitive equilibria as the number of agents tended to infinity in a particular way. My recent work has concentrated on the study of indivisibilities in production, in particular the replacement of price-guided tests for optimality in non-convex programs by searches in quantity space.

SCHAFFLE, Albert Eberhard Friedrich*

Dates and Birthplace 1831–1904, Nürtingen, Germany.
Posts Held Journalist with *Schwäbischer Merkur*; Prof. Polit Econ., Univ. Tübingen, 1860, Univ. Vienna, 1868–71.
Offices and Honours Member, Wurttemberg parliament, 1861–5; Austrian Minister of Commerce, 1871.
Publications *Books:* 1. *Hand-und Lehrbuch der Nationalökonomie* (1861); 2. *Uber die Theorie der ausschliessenden Absatzverhältnisse* (1867); 3. *Capitalism and Socialism* (1869); 4. *Quintessenz des Sozialismus* (1874); 5. *Bau und Leben des sozialen Körpers*, 4 vols (1875–8); 6. *Aussichtslosigkeit der Sozialdemokratie* (1884); 7. *Steuren*, 2 vols (1895–7).
Career German academic socialist whose *Quintessenz* . . . was widely read and translated. The early theoretical works, and his brief period of ministerial office in Austria, were succeeded by a long period as a writer in Stuttgart, when he produced a large number of works on a wide range of economic and financial topics. His influence, both as an opponent of *laissez faire* liberalism and a reconciler of German philosophy and the inductive method of economic investigation, was considerable.
Secondary Literature F. K. Mann, 'Schaffle, Albert Eberhard Friedrich', *ESS*, 13.

SCHALL, Lawrence Delano

Born 1940, Los Angeles, CA, USA.
Current Post Prof. Fin. and Bus. Econ., Grad. School Bus., Univ. Washington, Seattle, WA, USA.
Degrees BA UCLA, 1962; MA, PhD Univ. Chicago, 1967, 1969.
Offices and Honours Phi Beta Kappa, 1962; MIMH Fellow, Bowman Lingle Fellow, Univ. Chicago, 1964–7, 1967–8; Bank Amer. Excellence Award, 1983.
Principal Fields of Interest 520 Business Finance and Investment; 024 Welfare Theory; 540 Accounting.

Publications *Books:* 1. *The Theory of Financial Decisions* (with C.W. Haley), (McGraw-Hill, 1973, 1979); 2. *Introduction to Financial Management* (with C.W. Haley), (McGraw-Hill, 1977, 1983); 3. *Evaluating Business Ventures* (with K. Henderson and R.G. May), (US Nat. Bank Oregon, 1982); 4. *Evaluating Business Ventures, Cases and Problems* (with K. Henderson and R.G.May), (US Nat. Bank Oregon, 1982); 5. *Administracion Financiera* (with C.W. Haley), (Editorial McGraw-Hill, 1983).

Articles: 1. 'Firm financial structure and investment', *J. Fin. and Quant. Analysis*, 6, June 1971; 2. 'Technological externalities and resource allocation', *JPE*, 79, Sept.–Oct. 1971; 3. 'Asset valuation, firm investment and firm diversification', *J Bus.*, 45, Jan. 1972; 4. 'Interdependent utilities and Pareto optimality', *QJE*, 86, Feb. 1972; 5. 'To lease or buy and asset acquisition decisions', *J Fin*, 29, Sept. 1974; 6. 'Corporate bankruptcy and conglomerate merger' (with R.C. Higgins), *J Fin*, 30, March 1975; 7. 'Urban renewal policy and economic efficiency', *AER*, 66(4), Sept. 1976; 8. 'Problems with the concept of the cost of capital' (with C.W. Haley), *J. Fin. and Quant. Analysis*, 13, Dec. 1978; 9. 'Commodity chain systems and the housing market', *JUE*, 10, Sept. 1981; 10. 'Taxes, inflation and corporate financial policy', *J Fin*, 39, March 1984.

Principal Contributions Early work focussed on financial economics, welfare theory, and urban economics. My first book, *The Theory of Financial Decisions* (with C.W. Haley), appeared in the early 1970s and was an advanced text on financial theory. It was intended as a comprehensive presentation of the major concepts in the area. Since the mid-70s, my research and publications have, with few exceptions, centred on financial economics topics, including valuation, corporate financial planning (mergers, leasing, investment and financing analysis, etc.), and taxes. In recent years, I have also pursued an interest in the uses of computers in financial analysis.

SCHELLING, Thomas Crombie

Born , 1921, Oakland, CA, USA.
Current Post Lucius N. Littauer Prof. Polit Econ., Harvard Univ., Cambridge, MA, USA, 1969–.
Past Posts Econ., US Govt., Copenhagen, Paris, Washington, 1948–53; Assoc. Prof., Prof. Econ., Yale Univ., 1953–8; Prof. Econ., Center Internat. Affairs, Harvard Univ., 1958–69; Sr. Staff Member, Rand Corp., 1958–9; Res. Fellow, Inst. Strategic Stud., London, 1965; Acting Dir., Center Internat. Affairs, Harvard Univ., 1967–8; Lady Davis Vis. Prof., Hebrew Univ., Jerusalem, 1976.
Degrees BA Univ. Cal. Berkeley, 1943; PhD Harvard Univ. 1951.
Offices and Honours Jr. Fellow, Harvard Univ., 1948; Frank E. Seidman Disting. Award Polit. Econ., 1977; Member, Inst. Medicine, NAS; Fellow, AAAS; Member, Amer. Assoc. Advancement Science.
Editorial Duties Board Syndics, Harvard Univ. Press; Ed. Boards, *Public Pol. and Management*, *J. Strategic Stud*, *Internat. Security*, *Econ. and Philos.*, *QJE*, *REStat*.
Principal Fields of Interest 911 General Welfare Programmes; 920 Consumer Economics.
Publications *Books:* 1. *National Income Behavior* (McGraw-Hill, 1951; transl., Spanish, Inst. Interamer. Estradistica, 1956); 2. *International Economics* (Allyn & Bacon, 1958); 3. *The Stategy of Conflict* (Harvard Univ. Press, 1960, 1980, OUP, 1963; transls. Spanish, Editorial Tecnos S.A., 1964, French, Presses Univ., 1984); 4. *Strategy and Arms Control* (with M.H. Halperin), (Twentieth Century Fund, 1961; transl., Italian, Il Mulino, 1962); 5. *Arms and Influence* (Yale Univ. Press, 1966; transls., Italian, Il Mulino, 1968, Hebrew, Armed Services Pub., 1982); 6. *Micromotives and Macrobehaviour* (W.W. Norton, 1978; transl., French, Presses Univ., 1980); 7. *Thinking Through the Energy Problem* (Comm. Econ. Develp., 1979); 8. *Incentives for Environmental Protection*, ed. (MIT Press, 1983); 9. *Choice and Consequence* (Harvard Univ. Press, 1984).

Articles: 1. 'Reciprocal measures for arms stabilization', *Daedalus*, Fall 1960; 2. 'Arms control: proposal for a special surveillance force', *World Politics*, 13(1), Oct. 1960; 3. 'Experimental games and bargaining theory', *World Politics*, 14(1), Oct. 1961; 4. 'The role of deterrence in total disarmament', *Foreign Affairs*, April 1962; 5. 'Dynamic models of segregation', *J. Math. Sociology*, 1, 1971; 6. 'On the ecology of micro-motives', *Public Interest*, 25, Fall 1971; 7. 'A process of residential segregation: neighborhood tipping', in *Racial Discrimination in Economic Life*, ed. A.H. Pascal (D.C. Heath, 1972); 8. 'Prices as regulatory instruments', in *Incentives for Environmental Protection*, ed. T.C. Schelling (MIT Press, 1983); 9. 'Climatic changes: implications for welfare and policy', in *Changing Climate Report of the Carbon Dioxide Assessment Committee* (Nat. Academy Press, 1983); 10. 'Self-command in practice, in policy, and in a theory of rational choice', *AER*, 74(2), May 1984.

Principal Contributions Bargaining caught my interest in graduate school, and I spent 1948–53 in foreign aid negotiations in Europe and Washington, then went to Yale as an international economist interested in bargaining. Within a few years I switched to military strategy and arms control as the most inviting field of application, spent some time with the Rand Corporation, became a member of various advisory boards on military technology and arms control, moved to Harvard in 1959 divided between the economics department and the Center for International Affairs, and concentrated on national security strategy and defence economics through the 1960s.

The same interest in bargaining led into the study of crime, protest and terrorism. Government connections were severed in 1970 but I pursued the subject of nuclear proliferation, which took me into energy policy for several years. Meanwhile an interest in race and other social divisions led to some modelling of segregation and integration and ultimately *Micromotives and Macrobehavior*. That same interest in bargaining drew me into fields as apparently distant as the social arrangements for dying and global prospects for climate change from the concentration of greenhouse gasses in the atmosphere. Finally, having always been intrigued by the problems people have in managing their own behaviour, I began working on addictive behaviours in the 1970s and by the early 1980s had settled on 'self-command' as my theoretical preoccupation, and smoking as a subject of applied research.

SCHERER, Frederic Michael

Born 1932, Ottawa, IL, USA.
Current Post Prof. Econ., Swarthmore Coll., Swarthmore, PA, USA, 1982–.
Past Posts Res. Assoc., Harvard Bus. School, 1958–63; Ass. Prof., Princeton Univ., 1963–6; Prof. Econ., Univ. Michigan, 1966–72; Sr. Res. Fellow, Internat. Inst. Management, Berlin, 1972–4; Dir., Bureau Econ., US Fed. Trade Commission, 1974–6; Prof. Econ., Northwestern Univ. 1976–82.
Degrees BA Univ. Michigan, 1954; MBA, PhD Harvard Univ., 1958, 1963.
Offices and Honours Baker Scholar, Copeland Award, Harvard Bus. School, 1957; Ford Foundation Fellow, 1961–2; Lanchester Prize, ORSA, 1964; Advisory Panels, NSF, 1978–84.
Editorial Duties Ed. Board, *AER*, 1977–80, *REStat*, 1977–, *J Ind E*, 1982–: Field Ed., *Encyclopaedia of Econ.* (McGraw-Hill).
Principal Fields of Interest 600 Industrial Organisation; 620 Economics of Technical Change; 022 Micro-theory.
Publications *Books:* 1. *The Weapons Acquisition Process: An Economic Analysis* (with M. J. Peck), (Harvard Bus. School, 1962); 2. *The Weapons Acquisition Process: Economic Incentives* (Harvard Bus. School, 1964); 3. *Industrial Market Structure and Economic Performance* (Rand McNally, Houghton Mifflin, 1970, 1980); 4. *The Economics of Multi-Plant Operation: An International Comparisons Study* (with others), (Harvard Univ. Press, 1975); 5. *Innovation and Growth: Schumpeterian Perspectives* (MIT Press, 1984).

Articles: 1. 'The theory of contractual incentives for cost reduction', *QJE*, 78, May 1964; 2. 'Market structure and the stability of investment', *AER*, 59(2), May 1969; 3. 'The determinants of industrial plant size in six nations', *REStat*, 55(2), May 1973; 4. 'Economies of scale and industrial concentration', in *Industrial Concentration: The New Learning* (Little, Brown, 1974); 5. 'Regulatory dynamics and economic growth', in *Toward a New U.S. Industrial Policy?* (Univ. Penn. Press, 1981); 6. 'Demand-pull and technological innovation: Schmookler revisited', *J Ind E*, 28, March 1982; 7. 'The lag structure of returns to R&D' (with D. Ravenscraft), *Appl. Econ.*, 14, Dec. 1982.

Principal Contributions Much of my professional career has been shaped by the early recognition, following Schumpeter, that technological change is by far the most potent contributor to improvements in economic well-being. My research has explored many facets of technological change, e.g. in rough chronological order, the impact of the patent system in large corporations, the economics of advanced weapons development, the links between market structure and innovative vigour, the nature and magnitude of scale economies, the structure of interindustry technology flows, and the productivity growth consequences of industrial research and development investments. Occasional digressions from this preoccupation have carried me to a broader array of industrial structure and behaviour questions, notably, in my treatise-textbook, *Industrial Market Structure and Economic Performance*, and in my most recent work on the behavioural consequences of mergers and spin-offs. In this work, I have continued to place more than the conventional amount of emphasis on dynamic, and on a methodological approach combining close observation of real-world behaviour (e.g. through interviews and case studies) with theory-building and statistical analysis.

SCHMALENSEE, Richard Lee

Born 1944, Belleville, IL, USA.
Current Post Prof. Appl. Econ. Sloan School Management, MIT, Cambridge, MA, USA, 1979–.
Past Posts Ass. Prof., Assoc. Prof., Univ. Cal. San Diego, 1970–7; Res. Fellow, Univ. Louvain, 1973–4; Assoc. Prof., Sloan School, MIT, 1977–9; Cons., US Fed. Trade Commission, 1972–7; Special Cons., Nat. Econ. Res. Assoc., 1981–.
Degrees BS, PhD MIT, 1965, 1970.
Offices and Honours Res. Fellow, Univ. Louvain, 1973–4; NSF Fellow, 1975–7, 1981–4; Res. Advisory Comm., Center Study Govt. Regulation, AEI, 1980–; Fellow, Em Soc, 1982–.
Editorial Duties Ed. Boards, *J Ind E*, 1977, *Res. Econ. de Louvain*, 1979, *AER*, 1982, *Internat. J. Industrial Organization*, 1982.
Principal Fields of Interest 610 Industrial Organisation and Public Policy; 022 Microeconomic Theory; 500 Administration; Business Finance; Marketing; Accounting.
Publications *Books:* 1. *The Economics of Advertising* (N-H, 1972); 2. *The Control of Natural Monopolies* (D. C. Heath, 1979); 3. *Markets for Power: An Analysis of Electric Utility Deregulation* (with P. L. Joskow), (MIT Press, 1983).

Articles: 1. 'A note on the theory of vertical integration, *JPE*, 81, March–April 1973; 2. 'Brand loyalty and barriers to entry, *SEJ*, 40, April, 1974; 3. 'A model of promotional competition in oligopoly, *REStud*, 43, Oct. 1976; 4. 'A model of advertising and product quality, *JPE*, 87, June 1978; 5. 'Entry deterrence in the ready-to-eat breakfast cereal industry', *Bell JE*, 9, Autumn 1978; 6. 'Output and welfare implications of monopolistic third-degree price discrimination', *AER*, 71(1), March 1981; 7. 'Monopolistic two-part pricing arrangements, *Bell JE*, 11, Autumn 1981; 8. 'Economies of scale and barriers to entry', *JPE*, 89, Dec. 1981; 9. 'Product differentiation advantages of pioneering brands', *AER*, 72(3), June 1982; 10. 'Advertising and entry deterrence: an exploratory model', *JPE*, 91, Aug. 1983.

Principal Contributions I began my career thinking of myself as a micro-economist interested in lots of things. And I worked on lots of things, from macroeconomic modelling to cost/benefit analysis. Over time, my interests have focussed more sharply on industrial economics, though I still shop around to some extent. In industrial economics, two principal themes of my work have been, in retrospect, the power of theory to illuminate market reality, and the importance of nonprice competition in modern markets. I continue to enjoy using a variety of techniques to explore a variety of problems, and I remain committed to the proposition that economics is concerned with understanding the world as it is.

SCHMIDT, Kurt

Born 1924, Sobernheim, Germany.
Current Post Prof. Econ., Univ. Mainz, 1968–.
Past Posts Wissenschaftlicher Ass., Privatdozent, Univ. Bonn, 1951–7, 1957–63; Prof., Technische Hochschule Berlin, 1963–8.
Degrees Diplom-Volkswirt, Dr Rer. Pol., Habilitation (Privatdozent) Univ. Bonn, 1965, 1952, 1957.
Offices and Honours Rockefeller Fellow USA, 1960–1; Vis. Prof., Res. Assoc., Bologna, 1962–3, Univ. Cal. Berkeley, 1966, Univ. York, England, 1969; Member, Wissenschaftlicher Beirat, German Ministry of Fin.; Member, Sachverständigenrat zur Begutachtung der gesamtwirtschaftlichen Entwicklung.
Editorial Duties Co-ed., *Handwörterbuch der Wirtschaftswissenschaft* (Mohr-Siebeck).
Principal Fields of Interest 010 General Economics; 020 General Economic Theory; 300 Domestic Monetary and Fiscal Theory and Institutions.
Publications *Books:* 1. *Die Steuerprogression* (Mohr-Siebeck, 1960); 2. *Die mehrjahrige Finanzplanung, Wunsch und Wirklichkeit* (with E. Wille), (Mohr-Siebeck, 1970).
Articles: 1. 'Zur Reform der Unternehmensbesteuerung', *Finanzarchiv*, 22, 1962–3; 2. 'Entwicklungstendenzen

der offentlichen Ausgaben im demokratischen Gruppenstaat', *Finanzarchiv*, 25, 1966; 3. 'Das Leistungsfähigkeitsprinzip und die Theorie vom proportionalen Opfer', *Finanzarchiv*, 26, 1967; 4. 'Kollektivbedurfnisse und Staatstatigkeit', in *Theorie und Praxis des finanzpolitischen Interventionismus (Fritz Neumark zum 70 Geburtstag)*, (Mohr-Siebeck, 1970); 5. 'Zur politischen Reaktion auf Nachfragewogen in der Staatswirtschaft', *Finanzarchiv*, N.F. 33, 1974; 6. 'Korruption' (with C. Garschagen), in *Handwörterbuch der Wirtschaftswissenschaft*, 4 (Mohr-Siebeck, 1978); 7. 'Grundprobleme der Besteuerung', in *Handbuch der Finanzwissenschaft*, 2 (Mohr-Siebeck, 1978); 8. 'Finanzpolitik fur mehr wirtschaftliches Wachstum', in *Wirtschaftswissenschaft als Grundlage staatlichen Mandelns (Festschrift fur Heinz Haller zum 65 Geburtstag)* (Mohr-Siebeck, 1979); 9. 'Verlockungen und Gefahren der Schattenwirtschaft', *Rheinisch-westfälische Akademie der Wissenschaft*, 1982.

Principal Contributions My Habilitationsschrift (*Progressive Taxation*, 1960) was a critical review of the arguments in favour of progressive taxation. My articles on public expenditures (Nos. 2, 4 and 5 above) treat the problems in a political-sociological way. The book on medium-term fiscal planning (1970) covers the experiences in Germany during the first three years of the *Finanzplanung* and discusses measures to improve it. The article 'Corruption' (No. 6) is an economic treatment of a problem seldom discussed in economic theory. In No. 8 a more growth-oriented fiscal policy is demanded, and an overview of possible measures is given. No. 7 summarises the main problems connected with the allocation, stabilisation, distribution and growth-functions of taxation.

SCHMOLLER, Gustav*

Dates and Birthplace 1838–1917, Württemberg, Germany.
Posts Held Prof. Staatswissenschaften, Univ. Halle, 1864–72, Univ. Strasbourg, 1872–82, Univ. Berlin, 1882–1913.

Degrees Grad. Univ. Tübingen, 1860.

Offices and Honours Founder, *Verein für Sozialpolitik*; Member, Prussian State Council, 1884; Upper House of Parliament, 1889.

Publications *Books:* 1. *Zur Geschichte der deutschen Kleingewerke im 19 Jahrhundert* (1870); 2. *Über einige Grundfragen der Sozialpolitik und der Volkswirtschaftslehre* (1874–97, 1904); 3. *The Mercantile System and its Historical Significance* (1897); 4. *Grundriss der allgemeinen Volkswirtschaftslehre* (1900–4, 1923).

Career Founder of the 'younger historical school' ('academic socialists') and promoter of research in the social sciences in Germany. Menger's attack on his ideas inaugurated the famous *Methodenstreit*. Schmoller's major work, the *Grundriss*, is wide in scope but lacks coherence. His political stance — between conservatism and revolutionary socialism — was boldly maintained, and achieved a good deal of public support.

Secondary Literature W. Fischer, 'Schmoller, Gustav', *IESS*, 14.

SCHMOOKLER, Jacob*

Dates and Birthplace 1918–67, NJ, USA.

Posts Held Instr., Univ. Penn., 1946–51; Ass. Prof., Michigan State Univ., 1951–7; Prof. Econ., Univ. Minnesota, 1957–67.

Degrees BA Temple Univ., 1940; PhD Univ. Penn., 1951.

Publications *Books:* 1. *Invention and Economic Growth* (1966); 2. *Patents, Invention and Economic Change*, eds. Z. Griliches and L. Hurwicz (1972).

Career He began the quantitative study of technical progress in the late 1940s, well before the subject was fashionable. In his major work, *Invention and Economic Growth*, he argued for the endogenous nature of technical progress, again years before that point of view commanded the attention of others.

SCHNEIDER, Erich*

Dates and Birthplace 1900–70, Germany.

Posts Held Schoolteacher, 1925–36; Prof., Univs. Aarhus, 1936–46, Kiel, 1946–68; Dir., Inst. World Econ., Univ. Kiel, 1961–9.

Degrees Dr Rer. Pol. Univ. Frankfurt, 1922.

Offices and Honours Pres., Verein für Sozialpolitik, 1963–6; List Gold Medal, 1965.

Publications *Books:* 1. *Reine Theorie monopolistischer Wirtschaftsformen* (1932); 2. *Theorie der Produktion* (1934); 3. *Einführung in die Wirtschaftstheorie*, 4 vols (1947–62); 4. *Pricing and Equilibrium* (1952); 5. *Volkswirtschaft und Betriebswirtschaft: ausgewählte Aufsätze* (1964); 6. *Zahlungsbilanz und Wechselkurs* (1968); 7. *Die Wirtschaft im Schulunterricht* (1968); 8. *Joseph A. Schumpeter: Leben und Werk eines grossen Sozialökonomen* (1970).

Career His contribution to price theory and particularly the theory of monopoly made his name, but his *Einführung ...* was his chief achievement. It gave German students a grounding in modern analysis based on his very wide knowledge of the international literature of economic. Part 4 is a masterly history of price theory from Smith to Marshall.

Secondary Literature W. Vogt, 'Erich Schneider and economic theory', *German Econ. Rev.*, 9(4), 1971.

SCHOFIELD, Norman James

Born 1944, Rothesay, Bute, Scotland.

Current Post Reader Econ., Univ. Essex, England, 1979–.

Past Posts Lect., Univ. Essex, 1970–6; Vis. Lect., Yale Univ., 1973; Assoc. Prof., Univ. Texas, Austin, 1976–9.

Degrees BSc (Physics and Maths.) Liverpool Univ., 1965; BSc (Maths.), PhD Univ. Essex, 1966, 1976.

Offices and Honours BA Wolfson Fellow, 1976; Leverhulme Faculty Fellow, 1977; NSF Fellow, 1979; Hallsworth Fellow, Univ. Manchester, 1982–3; Sherman Fairchild Disting. Scholar, Cal. Inst. Technology, 1983–4.

Editorial Duties Ed. Board, *Social Choice and Welfare*, 1983–.

Principal Fields of Interest 021 General Equilibrium Theory; 025 Social Choice; 026 Game Theory and Bargaining Theory.

Publications *Books:* 1. *Data Analysis and the Social Sciences*, co-ed. (with D. McKay and P. Whiteley), (Frances Pinter, St Martins Press, 1983); 2. *Crisis in Economic Relations between North and South*, ed. (Gower Publ., 1984); 3. *Mathematical Methods in Economics* (Croom Helm, 1984).

Articles: 1. 'Transitivity of preferences on a smooth manifold', *JET*, 14, Feb. 1977; 2. 'Generalized bargaining sets for cooperative games', *Internat. J Game Theory*, 7, Dec. 1978; 3. 'Instability of simple dynamic games', *REStud*, 45, Oct. 1978; 4. 'Generic properties of simple Bergson-Samuelson welfare functions', *J. Math. Econ.*, 7, Oct. 1980; 5. 'Bargaining set theory and stability in coalition governments', *Math. Social Sciences*, 3, Oct. 1982; 6. 'Equilibria in simple dynamic games', in *Social Choice and Welfare*, eds. P. Pattanaik and M. Salles (N-H, 1983); 7. 'Generic instability of majority rule', *REStud*, 50, Oct. 1983; 8. 'General relevance of the impossibility theorem in smooth social choice', *Theory and Decision*, 16, Jan. 1984; 9. 'Social equilibrium and cycles on compact sets', *JET*, 32, June 1984.

Principal Contributions My original training was in physics and mathematics, and as a graduate student at Liverpool I studied differential topology and dynamical systems. I was particularly impressed by the work of René Thom in catastrophe theory, and by the applications of this theory to the social sciences made by Chris Zeeman. While in the mathematics department at Essex I did some work in game theory and social choice, and was happy to move over to the department of government. In the early 1970s I came across the work of Steven Smale on applying singularity theory to general equilibrium theory, and eventually wrote up a doctoral thesis on the applications of singularity theory to social choice. Some of this work was published in the *REStud*, and *JET*. Over the next few years at the University of Texas, Austin, I developed these methods to show that general social choice processes involving coalitions are fundamentally chaotic. More precisely I showed that such processes are *classified* by two integers, the stability and instability dimensions. Below the stability dimension, equilibria exist, while above the instability integers, chaos occurs almost always. Although the theorem has obvious relevance in political theory, there is no reason to suppose that economic systems are not similarly classifiable. My other interests are in game theory, with application, for example, in international economics, and I am becoming increasingly interested in the theory of knowledge. It seems to me that games (of chess, of life, of economic behaviour, etc.) are only partly describable in terms of utility maximisation but instead have as a key feature the generation of knowledge (about nature, other players, etc.). It is not clear as yet how to represent such games and the more fundamental question is how to represent knowledge itself.

SCHULTZ, Henry*

Dates and Birthplace 1893–1938, Poland.

Posts Held Prof. Econ., Univ. Chicago, 1926–38.

Degrees BA City Coll. NY; PhD Columbia Univ., 1926.

Publications *Books:* 1. *Statistical Laws of Demand and Supply* (1928); 2. *The Theory and Measurement of Demand* (1938).

Articles: 1. 'Theoretical considerations relating to supply', *JPE*, 35, Aug. 1927; 2. 'Marginal productivity and the general pricing process', *JPE*, 37, Oct. 1929; 3. 'Interrelations of demand', *JPE*, 41, Aug. 1933; 4. 'Interrelations of demand, price and income', *JPE*, 43, Aug. 1935.

Career Econometrician whose early years were spent conducting statistical investigations for various government departments. Inspired by his teacher H. L. Moore, and having a detailed grasp of Cournot, Walras and Pareto, he was able to make a synthesis of theory and empirical work on demand. His work on statistical demand analysis involved several contributions to statistical theory.

Secondary Literature H. Hotelling, 'The work of Henry Schultz', *Em*, 7, April 1939; K. A. Fox, 'Schultz, Henry', *IESS*, 14.

SCHULTZ, T. Paul

Born 1940, Ames, IA, USA.
Current Post Malcolm K. Bradman Prof. Econ. and Pop., Dir., Yale Econ. Growth Center, Yale Univ., New Haven, CT, USA, 1977–, 1983–.
Past Posts Res. Econ., Dir. Pop. Res., Rand Corp., 1965–8, 1968–72; Prof. Econ., Univ. Minn., 1972–5; Prof. Econ., Yale Univ., 1974–7; Hooker Vis. Prof., McMasters Univ., Canada, 1983.
Degrees BA Swarthmore Coll., PA, 1961; PhD MIT, 1966.
Offices and Honours Member, Internat. Union Scientific Study Pop., 1972–; Fellow, AAAS, 1980–; Res. Advisory Panels, NIH, 1968–78; Steering Group, Pop. and Employment Project, ILO, 1971–8; Member, UN Study Group on Pop., 1969–71, UN World Food and Nutrition, 1976–7; Advisory Comm., US Census Bureau on Pop. Stat., 1980–5, Pop. Growth and Devlp., 1984–5.
Editorial Duties Co-ed., *Res. in Pop. Econ.*, 1981–; *Demographic Econ. Rev.*, 1985–.
Principal Fields of Interest 840 Demographic Economics; 820 Labour Markets, Public Policy; 122 Economic Studies of Developing Countries.
Publications *Books:* 1. *The Distribution of Personal Income* (US Govt. Printing Office, 1964); 2. *Love and Life Between the Censuses: A Model of Family Decision-Making in Puerto Rico* (with M. Nerlove), (Rand Corp., 1970); 3. *Structural Change in a Developing Economy* (with R. R. Nelson and R. L. Slighton), (Princeton Univ. Press, 1971); 4. *Evaluation of Population Policies: A Framework for Analysis and its Application to Taiwan's Family Planning Program* (Rand Corp., 1971); 5. *Fertility Determinants: A*

Theory, Evidence and an Application to Policy Evaluation (Rand Corp., 1974); 6. *Economics of Population* (Addison-Wesley, 1981).
Articles: 1. 'An economic model of family planning and fertility', *JPE*, 77(2), March–April 1969; 2. 'An economic perspective on population growth', in *Rapid Population Growth* (JHUP, 1971); 3. 'Explanations of birth rate change over space and time: a study of Taiwan', *JPE*, 81(2), pt. 2, March–April 1974, repr. in *Economics of the Family*, ed. T. W. Schultz (Univ. Chicago Press, 1974); 4. 'Interrelationships between mortality and fertility', in *Population and Development: The Search for Selective Interventions*, ed. R. G. Ridker (JHUP, 1976); 5. 'Estimating labor supply functions for married women', in *Female Labor Supply: Theory and Estimation*, ed. J. P. Smith (Princeton Univ. Press, 1980); 6. 'Effective protection and the distribution of personal income by sector in Colombia', in *Trade and Employment in Developing Countries*, ed. A. Krueger (Univ. Chicago Press, 1982); 7. 'Market opportunities, genetic endowments and the intrafamily distribution of resources: child survival in rural India' (with M. R. Rosenzweig), *AER*, 72(4), Sept. 1982; 8. 'Estimating a household production function: heterogeneity and the demand for health inputs' (with M. R. Rosenzweig), *JPE*, 91(5), Oct. 1983.
Principal Contributions I first sought to understand the determinants of fertility in terms of microeconomic theory of household demand behaviour. This perspective was used to assess the contribution of policy to slow population growth in Taiwan, and the analysis was extended to encompass the determinants of interrelated family behaviour in various countries, such as child health and schooling, family labour supply, mobility, and marriage patterns. Some conditions that initially were regarded as exogeneously affecting fertility and investments in children were subsequently re-examined as simultaneously determined with fertility over the family's life-cycle, such as child mortality. Intra-household resource allocations among children and between

genders were shown to have economic origins; heterogeneity in individual unobserved endowments, for example, healthiness and fecundity, was shown to bias direct inferences of the effect on child health and fertility of self-selected input behaviour. Migration was approached as a process that matches the heterogeneous preferences of people to local prices and opportunities, modifying behaviour of migrants across regions. In several studies of the personal distribution of income, I have tried to assess which aspects of development, changes in age and household compositions associated with demographic trends, and educational investments in people, help to account for empirical regularities in inequality associated with modern economic growth.

SCHULTZ, Theodore W.

Born 1902, SDak, USA.
Current Post Charles L. Hutchinson Disting. Service Prof. Emeritus, Univ. Chicago, Chicago, IL, USA, 1972–.
Past Posts Faculty Econ., Iowa State Coll., 1930–43; Prof. Econ., Univ. Chicago, 1943–52; Charles L. Hutchinson Disting. Service Prof., 1952–72.
Degrees BS, S. Dakota State Coll., 1928; MS, PhD Univ. Wisconsin, Madison, 1928, 1930; Hon. LLD, Grinnell Coll. 1949; Hon. Dr, S. Dakota State Coll., 1959; Hon. LLD, Univs. Michigan State, 1962, Illinois, 1968, Wisconsin, 1968, Catholic Univ. Chile, 1979, Dijon, 1981.
Offices and Honours Fellow, Center Advanded Study Behavioral Sciences, Stanford, CA, 1956–67; Amer. Farm. Econ. Assoc., 1957–; AAAS, 1958–; Amer. Philo. Soc., 1962–; Pres., Disting. Fellow, Francis A. Walker Medal, AEA, 1960, 1965–, 1972; Founding Member, Nat. Academy Educ., 1965; Disting. Service Award, AAEA, 1973; Member, NAS, 1974–; Leonard Elmhirst Medal, Internat. Agric. Econ. Assoc., 1976; Joint Nobel Prize in Econ., 1979; Hon. Life Member, Phi Kappa Phi, 1981, Sociedade Rural Brasileira, 1981, Gdanski Medal Univ. Poland, 1981.

Editorial Duties Ed., *JFE*, 1939–42, *JPE*, Suppls., 1962, 1972, 1973, 1974.
Principal Fields of Interest 710 Agriculture; Natural Resources; 850 Human Capital; 912 Economics of Education.
Publications *Books:* 1. *Food for the World*, ed. (Univ. Chicago Press, 1945); 2. *Agriculture in an Unstable Economy* (McGraw-Hill, 1945); 3. *The Economic Organization of Agriculture* (McGraw-Hill, 1953); 4. *The Economic Value of Education* (Columbia Univ. Press, 1963); 5. *Transforming Traditional Agriculture* (Yale Univ. Press, 1964, Univ. Chicago Press, 1983); 6. *Investment in Human Beings*, ed. (Univ. Chicago Press, 1962); 7. *Investment in Human Capital: The Role of Education and of Research* (Free Press, 1971); 8. *Economics of the Family: Marriage, Children and Human Capital*, ed. (Univ. Chicago Press, 1975); 9. *Distortions of Agricultural Incentives*, ed. (Indiana Univ. Press, 1978); 10. *Investing in People: The Economics of Population Quality* (Univ. Cal. Press, 1981; transls., Thai, Arabic, Indian, French, German, and Japanese).

Articles: 1. 'Capital rationing, uncertainty and farm-tenancy reform', *JPE*, 48, June 1940; 2. 'Reflections and poverty within agriculture', *JPE*, 58, Feb. 1950; 3. 'Declining economic importance of agricultural land', *EJ*, 59, Dec. 1951; 4. 'Reflections on agricultural production, output and supply', *JFE*, 3, Aug. 1956; 5. 'Investment in human capital', *AER*, 51(1), March 1961, repr. in *Penguin Economics Readings: Economics of Education, 1*, ed. M. Blaug (Penguin, 1969); 6. 'Institutions and the rising economic value of man', *AJAE*, 50, Dec. 1968; 7. 'The value of the ability to deal with disequilibria', *JEL*, 13(3), Sept. 1975; 8. 'Nobel lecture: the economics of being poor', *JPE*, 88, Aug. 1980; 9. 'On the economics of the increases in the value of human time over time', in *Economic Growth Revisited, 2*, ed. R. C. O. Matthews (Macmillan, 1980); 10. 'Distortions by the international donor community', in *Promoting Increased Food Production in the 1980s* (World Bank, 1981).

Principal Contributions Reared in the protest culture of the Dakotas nurtured by the Non-Partisan League, for me to have become an agnostic came naturally, except for a strong belief in uncertainty. I sought intellectual comfort at the University of Wisconsin.

The economy was in serious disarray. Banks closed. Corn was used as fuel. Irving Fisher came at Ames to see how script money was helping employment and trade. A lifetime subscription to the *Economic Journal* cost me a pittance. Hard times are good for economists. I persistently overrated the utility of economics, underinvested in history, and paid too little attention to my doubts. Yet, taking the long view, I perceived the decline in the economic importance of land and saw the increasing role of human capital.

In 1932, I presented some evidence for doubting the validity of Marshall's use of diminishing returns to land in forecasting 'future developments'. Owners of farm land were becoming less and less important as an economic class, contrary to Ricardo who still held sway over Marshall on this point.

We hanker for the prestige that is accorded to scientists. But hard as economists must try, they will not succeed in obtaining a divorce from the social attributes of society and humanism.

Well-reasoned doubts are good for economics. Neither theory, nor data, nor mathematics can fully resolve them. Paraphrasing Bridgman, the physicist, economic behaviour is more complex than our thoughts about it; our thoughts, however, are more comprehensive than standard theory; and, standard theory is more comprehensive than mathematical economics. Each of these has its advantages. What is known from all of them is nevertheless subject to doubts. Economics would be better if we would subsitiue reasoned doubts for our parochial economic doctrines.

SCHUMPETER, Joseph Alois*

Dates and Birthplace 1883–1950, Triesch, Austro-Hungary.
Posts Held Teacher, Univs. Czernovitz and Graz, 1909–18; Pres., Biederman Bank, 1920–4; Prof., Univ. Bonn, 1925–32; Prof., Harvard Univ., 1932–50.

Degrees Grad. Univ. Vienna.
Offices and Honours Minister of Fin., Austria, 1919–20; Pres., AEA, 1949; Founding member, Pres., Em Soc, 1933.
Publications *Books:* 1. *Das Wesen und der Hauptinhalt der theoretischen Nationalökonomie* (1908); 2. *The Theory of Economic Development* (1912, 1934, 1949); 3. *Economic Doctrines and Method* (1914, 1954); 4. *The Crisis of the Tax State* (1918), repr. in *Internat. Econ. Papers*, 4 (1954); 5. *Business Cycles*, 2 vols (1939); 6. *Imperialism and Social Classes* (1927, 1951); 7. *Capitalism, Socialism and Democracy* (1942, 1950); 8. *Ten Great Economists* (1951); 9. *Essays of J. A. Schumpeter*, ed. R. V. Clemence (1951); 10. *History of Economic Analysis* (1954).
Career Great teacher and historian of economics, his own economic theory was complex and wide-ranging. The distinction between statics and dynamics was essential to his account of capitalism — certain periods approximating to equilibrium, and other exhibiting considerable change. His analysis of business cycles started from this point and distinguished the types and behaviour of cycles. The posthumous *History . . .* shows a prodigious grasp of the literature of economics. In this, as in his major book *Capitalism, Socialism and Democracy*, he relates economic phenomena and ideas to a wider context of social analysis. The latter, whilst rejecting the Marxian analysis, still envisages capitalism as moving by its own internal forces towards Schumpeter's vision of a socialist society.
Secondary Literature S. E. Harris, *Schumpeter: Social Scientist* (Harvard Univ. Press, 1951); W. F. Stolper, 'Schumpeter, Joseph A,', *IESS*, 14; A. Heertje, ed. *Schumpeter's Vision: Capitalism, Socialism and Democracy After 40 Years* (Praeger, 1981); H. Frisch, ed. *Schumpeterian Economics* (Praeger, 1981).

SCHWARTZ, Anna Jacobson

Born 1915, New York City, NY, USA.
Current Post Res. Assoc., NBER, NY, 1941–.

Past Posts Res. Assoc., Columbia Univ., US SSRC, 1936–41; Instr., Brooklyn Coll., 1952; Instr., Baruch Coll., NY, 1959–60; Adjunct Prof., Grad. Division, Hunter Coll., NY, 1967–9; Adjunct Prof., NYU Grad. School Arts and Science, 1969–70; Staff Dir., US Gold Commission, 1981–2.

Degrees BA Barnard Coll., NY, 1934; MA, PhD Columbia Univ., 1935, 1964.

Offices and Honours Phi Beta Kappa; Murray Fellow, Barnard Coll., 1934–5; Member, Shadow Open Market Comm., 1973–; Hon. Vis. Prof., City Univ. Bus. School, London, 1984–; Pres., WEA, 1987–.

Editorial Duties Ed. Boards, *AER*, 1972–8, *JMCB*, 1974–5, 1984–; *J Mon E*, 1975–.

Principal Fields of Interest 130 Economic Fluctuations; Stabilisation and Inflation; 310 Domestic Monetary and Financial Theory and Institutions; 430 Balance of Payments; International Finance.

Publications *Books:* 1. *The Growth and Fluctuation of the British Economy, 1790–1850* (with A. D. Gayer and W. W. Rostow), (Clarendon Press, 1953, Harvester Press, 1975); 2. *A Monetary History of the United States, 1867–1960* (with M. Friedman), (Princeton Univ. Press, 1963); 3. *Monetary Statistics of the United States* (with M. Friedman), (Columbia Univ. Press, 1970); 4. *A Century of British Market Interest Rates, 1874–1975* (City Univ. Centre Banking and Internat. Fin., 1981); 5. *Monetary Trends in the United States and the United Kingdom: Their Relation to Income, Prices and Interest Rates, 1867–1975* (with M. Friedman), (Univ. Chicago Press, 1982); 6. *Report to the Congress of the Role of Gold in the Domestic and International Monetary Systems*, 1 (US Govt. Printing Office, 1982); 7. *The International Transmission of Inflation* (with M. R. Darby, *et al.*), (Univ. Chicago Press, 1983); 8. *A Retrospective on the Classical Gold Standard, 1821–1931*, co-ed. (with M. D. Bordo), (Univ. Chicago Press, 1984).

Articles: 1. 'The beginning of competitive banking in Philadelphia, 1782–1809', *JPE*, 55, Oct. 1947; 2. 'An attempt at synthesis in American banking history', *JEH*, 7, Nov. 1947; 3. 'Gross dividend and interest payments by corporations at selected rates in the 19th century', in *Trends in the American Economy in the Nineteenth Century*, Stud. Income and Wealth, 24 (NBER, 1960); 4. 'Money and business cycles' (with M. Friedman), *REStat*, pt. 2, 45, Feb. 1963; 5. 'Why money matters', *LBR*, 94, Oct. 1969; 6. 'Secular price change in historical perspective', *JMCB*, pt. 2, 5, Feb. 1973; 7. 'Has growth of money substitutes hindered monetary policy?' (with P. Cagan), *JMCB*, 7, May 1975; 8. 'Understanding 1929–1933', in *The Great Depression Revisited*, ed. K. Brunner (Martinus Nijhoff, 1981); 9. 'Reflections on the gold commission report', *JMCB*, pt. 1, 14, Nov. 1981; 10. 'Real and pseudo-financial crises', in *Financial Crises and the World Banking System*, ed. G. E. Wood (Macmillan, 1985).

Principal Contributions The research project I was first associated with, the growth and fluctuation of the British economy, 1790–1850, was a wide-ranging historical study that provided experience in careful data collection and anlysis of cyclical developments based on NBER statistical measures, but deficient in what I later came to regard as significant: the role assigned to monetary policy, the interpretation of the behaviour of interest rates, and price *level* rather than *relative* price changes. Emphasis on these economic factors I owe to the influence of Milton Friedman on my intellectual development. He was the central figure, I hardly need say, in inspiring the post-World War II revival of professional interest in money demand and supply and their interaction with nominal and real variables. The findings of our research supported the conclusion that changes in the quantity of money have important and broadly predictable economic effects among which the following may be noted: (1) changes in the growth rate of money affect the growth rate of nominal income; (2) instability in the growth rate of money is associated with instability in the growth of nominal income; (3) long-run changes in the growth rate of money relative to growth in output determine the long-run behaviour of prices, while short-run changes in the growth rate of money are an important element in the ordinary business cycle; (4) a sustained change in the growth rate of money tends to be followed by a change in the inflation rate in the same direction after a lag of several years; (5) short-run changes in the growth rate of money tend to be followed by changes in the same direction of real output after a lag of several quarters; and (6) substantial contractions in the growth rate of money over short periods have been a major factor in producing severe economic contractions.

SCITOVSKY, Tibor

Born 1910, Budapest, Hungary.
Current Post Retired, 1983–.
Past Posts Clerk, Hungarian Gen. Creditbank, Budapest, 1934–5; Res. Econ., London & Camb. Econ. Service, 1938–9; Econ., US Dept. Commerce, Washington, DC, 1946; Assoc. Prof., Prof. Econ., Stanford Univ., 1946–58; Prof., Univ. Cal. Berkeley, 1958–68; Vis. Prof., Harvard Univ., 1965–6; Fellow, Devlp. Centre, OECD, Paris, 1966–8; Heinz Prof. Econ., Yale Univ. 1968–70; Eberle Prof. Devlp. Econ., Stanford Univ., 1970–6; Prof., LSE, 1976–8; Vis. Prof., Univ. Cal. Santa Cruz, 1978–82; Prof. recalled to duty, Stanford Univ., 1978–81; Vis. Fellow, All Souls Coll., Oxford, 1983.
Degrees Dr Juris, Univ. Budapest, 1932; MSc LSE, 1938.
Offices and Honours Guggenheim Foundation Fellow, 1949; Vice Pres., Disting. Fellow, AEA, 1970, 1973; Member, AAAS, 1966–; Corresp. Fellow, BA, 1981; Hon. Fellow, LSE, 1982.
Editorial Duties Ed. Board, *AER*.
Principal Fields of Interest 020 General Economic Theory; 110 Economic Development; 400 Internal Economics.
Publications Books: 1. *Welfare and Competition* (Richard D. Irwin, 1951, 1971; transl., Spanish, Amorrortu, 1967); 2. *Mobilizing Resources for War*, (with E. S. Shaw and L. Tarshis), (McGraw-Hill, 1951); 3. *Economic Theory & Western European Integra-*

tion (A&U, 1958; transls., Italian, Feltrinelli, 1961, Spanish, Aguilar, 1964); 4. *Papers on Welfare and Growth* (Stanford Univ. Press, 1964; transl., Spanish, Tecnos, 1970); 5. *Money & the Balance of Payments* (Rand McNally 1969; transl., Japanese); 6. *Industry & Trade in Some Developing Countries* (with I. M. D. Little and M. F. Scott), (OUP, 1970; transls., Spanish, Fondo de cultura economica, 1975, French, Presse de l'Univ. de Quebec, 1975); 7. *The Joyless Economy* (OUP, 1976; transls., German, Campus, 1977, French, Calmann-Levy, 1976, Japanese).

Articles: 1. 'What's wrong with the arts is what's wrong with society', *AER*, 62(2), May 1972; 2. 'Notes on the producer society', *DE*, 121(3), 1973; 3. 'The place of economic welfare in human welfare', *QREB*, 13(3), Autumn 1973; 4. 'Are men rational or economists wrong?', in *Nations & Households in Economic Growth*, eds. P. A. David and M. W. Reder, (Academic Press, 1974); 5. 'Market power and inflation', *Ec*, 45, Aug. 1978; 6. 'Asymmetries in economics', *SJPE*, 25(3), Nov. 1978; 7. 'The desire for excitement in modern society', *Kyk*, 34(1), 1981; 8. 'Excess demand for job importance and its implications', in *Wert und Praeferenzprobleme in den Sozialwissenschaften*, ed. R. Tietz, (Duncker & Humblot, 1981).

Principal Contributions I find it easier and more meaningful to list my concerns rather than my contributions — perhaps because the latter have been too simple-minded, fragmented and scattered to mention. My main concern has been to guard against the economist's predilection for an oversimplified and overmechanical approach by explaining the behaviour of economic variables in terms of the underlying human actions, reactions, their motivation and often by the asymmetries between buyers and sellers, price makers and price takers, and between the same person's upward and downward adjustment of prices or quantities. The nature and forms of competition, saving behaviour, balance-of-payments adjustment, inflation, stagflation are among the many and varied subjects on which that approach throws new light. My other main concern has been to point out some of the anomalies of the traditional theory of rational consumer behaviour and to facilitate and encourage the introduction of physiological psychology into the field.

SCOTT, Anthony Dalton

Born 1923, Vancouver, British Columbia, Canada.

Current Post Prof. Econ., Univ. British Columbia, Vancouver, Canada, 1965–.

Past Posts Res. Ass., Dept. Appl. Econ., Camb. Univ., 1949; Ass. Lect., LSE, 1949–53; Instr., Lect., Ass. Prof., Univ. British Columbia, 1949–65; Res. Staff, Royal Commission Canada's Econ. Prospects, Ottawa, 1955–6; Vis. Fellow, York Univ., Canada, 1963; Lily Fellow, Univ. Chicago, 1965; Reserve Bank Fellow, ANU, 1978; Mackenzie King Vis. Prof., Harvard Univ., 1983–4; Cons., OECD, Paris, 1971–5; Commissioner, Internat. Joint Commission, 1968.

Degrees BCom, BA Univ. British Columbia, 1946, 1947; MA Harvard Univ., 1949; PhD Univ. London, 1953; Hon. LLD, Guelph Univ., Canada, 1980.

Offices and Honours Member, Canada SSRC, 1963–7; Nominating Comm., Exec. Council, Exec. Comm., AEA, 1956–7, 1966–70; Pres., Amer. Assoc. Environmental Econ., 1975–8; Vice-Pres., Corresp., CEA, 1978–80, 1980; Fellow, Royal Soc. Canada, 1969–; Pres., Academy II, 1979–80; Officer, Order Canada, 1982.

Editorial Duties Ed. Board, *JEEM*, 1973–, *Land Econ.*, 1969–75, *WEJ*, 1968–71.

Principal Fields of Interest 325 Intergovernmental Finance; 720 Natural Resources.

Publications *Books:* 1. *Output, Labour and Capital in the Canadian Economy* (with W. C. Hood), (Queen's Printers, 1958); 2. *Guide to Benefit–Cost Analysis*, co-ed. (with W. R. D. Sewell, J. Davis, and D. W. Ross), (Queen's Printers, 1962); 3. *The Common Wealth in Ocean Fisheries* (with F.

T. Christy, Jr.), (JHUP, 1965, 1973); 4. *Economics of Fisheries Management: A Symposium*, ed. (Inst. Animal Resource Ecology, Univ. British Columbia, 1970); 5. *Natural Resources: The Economics of Conservation* (McClelland & Stewart, 1971); 6. *The Brain Drain: Determinants, Measurement and Welfare Effects* (with H. G. Grubel), (Wilfred Laurier Univ. Press, 1977); 7. *Natural Resource Revenues: A Test of Federalism*, ed. (Univ. British Columbia Press, 1976); 8. *The Economic Constitution of Federal States* (with A. Breton), (Univ. Toronto Press, 1978); 9. *The Design of Federations* (with A. Breton), (Inst. Res. Public Pol., 1980); 10. *Canada in Fiscal Conflict: Resources and the West* (with J. Helliwell), (Pemberton Securities Ltd., 1981).

Articles: 1. 'A note on grants in federal countries', *Ec*, N.S. 17, Nov. 1950; 2. 'The evaluation of federal grants', *Ec*, N.S. 19, Nov. 1952; 3. 'Notes on user cost', *EJ*, 63, June 1953; 4. 'The fishery: the objectives of sole ownership', *JPE*, 63(2), April 1955; 5. 'Development of the extractive industries', *CJE*, 28, Feb. 1962; 6. 'Theory of the mine under conditions of certainty', in *Extractive Resources and Taxation*, ed. M. Gaffney (Univ. Wisconsin Press, 1967); 7. 'Investing and protesting', *JPE*, 77(6), Nov.–Dec. 1969; 8. 'Transfrontier pollution: are new institutions necessary?', in *Economics of Transfrontier Pollution*, ed. H. Smets (OECD, 1976); 9. 'Costs of learning about the environmental damage of mining projects' (with H. Campbell), *ER*, 56, March 1980; 10. 'Property rights and property wrongs', *CJE*, 16, Nov. 1983.

Principal Contributions Since 1953 I have been concerned with the economics of natural resources. My 1953 thrice-republished thesis on *Conservation* led to numerous articles and a few books in the economics of fisheries (with Christy, Nehan and others); mining, water resources (with Sewell and others); and environmental economics. Also in 1953 I began a series on the economics of government grants, culminating in two joint books with Albert Breton on the economics of federal constitutions. In 1956 I did some intensive statistical work on capital stocks and their measurement (with W. C. Hood). In the mid-1960s with Harry Johnson and Herbert Grubel I turned to the economics of the 'Brain Drain'; a book was published collecting our papers in 1977. In the 1970s at OECD and in Canada, I wrote extensively on international environmental relationships, linked in part tc my position on the Canadian–American Boundary Waters Treaty Commission. After the books with Breton I turned to the economics of property rights, with emphasis on both their public choice aspects and on the precise characteristics of proprietory rights in resources.

SCOTT, William Robert*

Dates and Birthplace 1868–1940, Lisnamallard, Northern Ireland.
Posts Held Lect., St Andrews Univ., 1896–1915; Adam Smith Prof., Univ. Glasgow, 1915–40.
Degrees BA, MA, DLitt Trinity Coll., Dublin, 1889, 1891, 1902; DPhil St Andrews Univ., 1900.
Offices and Honours Fellow, BA; Pres., Section F BAAS, 1915; Pres., EHS, 1928, RES, 1935–7
Publications *Books:* 1. *Francis Hutcheson* (1900); 2. *Constitution and Finance of English, Scottish and Irish Joint-stock Companies to 1720*, 3 vols (1910–12); 3. *Report to the Board of Agriculture for Scotland* (1914); 4. *Economic Problems of Peace after War*, 2 vols (1917–18); 5. *Adam Smith as Student and Professor* (1937, 1968).
Career Economic historian whose account of joint-stock companies is based on massive scholarship and a sound grasp of business procedures. He did valuable work on contemporary economic problems, some of it for official commissions and much of it published in article form. His work on Smith involved the patient assembly of new factual material.
Secondary Literature J. H. Clapham, 'Obit.: William Robert Scott', *EJ*, 50, June–Sept. 1940.

SCROPE, George Julius Poulett*

Dates and Birthplac 1797–1876, England.
Posts Held Private income.
Degree BA Univ. Camb., 1821.
Offices and Honours Fellow, Royal Soc., 1826; MP for Stroud, 1833–68.
Publications *Books:* 1. *Principles of Political Economy* (1833, 1969); 2. *Friendly Societies* (1872).
Articles: 1. 'The political economists', *Quarterly Rev., 1831.*
Career He adopted the name Scrope on marrying the heiress of that family, and his interest in the state of the workers on the Scrope family estate turned his attention partially away from geology, in which he had already made a name, to political economy. He wrote many pamphlets on economic questions, opposing the Malthusian theory of population, defending the Poor Laws, advocating unemployment insurance, criticising the gold standard and commenting on other issues. He was, however, more than just a current commentator, attributing business cycles to psychological causes aggravated by monetary phenomena, and using the concept of equilibrium to analyse supply and demand. Despite the high quality of his work and his publication of a systematic treatise, his contribution was largely ignored.
Secondary Literature R. Opie, 'A neglected English economist: George Poulett Scrope', *QJE*, 44, Nov. 1929.

SEAGER, Henry Rogers*

Dates and Birthplace 1870–1930, USA.
Posts Held Prof., Univs. Penn., Columbia.
Offices and Honours Pres., AEA, 1922.
Publications *Books:* 1. *Introduction to Economics* (1904); 2. *Social Insurance* (1910); 3. *Principles of Economics* (1913); 4. *Trust and Corporation Problems* (1929); 5. *Labor and Other Economic Essays* (1931).
Career Labour economist and expert on trusts whose arguments for social insurance were considered highly effective.

Through his writings and public activities he achieved some success in changing government attitudes towards corporations and trusts.

Secondary Literature C. A. Gulick, 'Seager, Henry Rogers', *ESS*, 14.

SEERS, Dudley*

Dates and Birthplace 1920–82, London, England.

Posts Held Chief, Survey Section, UNECLA, 1957–61; Vis. Prof., Yale Univ., 1961–3; Dir., Econ. Devlp. Div., UNECA, 1963–4; Dir. General, Econ. Planning Staff, UK Ministry Overseas Devlp., 1964–7; Dir., Professorial Fellow, Inst. Devlp. Stud., Univ. Sussex, 1967–73, 1973–82.

Degrees BA Univ. Camb., 1941.

Offices and Honours Ed. Board, *J. Dev. Stud.*; Pres., Soc. Internat. Devlp., 1968–70; Council, RES, 1975–8; Pres., Europ. Assoc. Devlp. Res. and Training Insts., 1975–8; Companion, Order St Michael and St George, 1975.

Publications *Books:* 1. *Towards Full Employment. A Programme for Colombia, Prepared by an Inter-agency Team Organised by the ILO* (with others), (ILO, 1970); 2. *Matching Employment Opportunities and Expectations. A Programme of Action for Ceylon,* 2 vols (with others), (ILO, 1971); 3. *Under-developed Europe: Studies in Core-periphery Relations*, co-ed. (with B. Schaffer and M. Kiljunen), (Harvester Press, 1979); 4. *Integration and Unequal Development: The Experience of the EEC*, co-ed. (with C. Vaitsos), (Macmillan, 1980); 5. *The Second Enlargement of the EEC: Integration of Unequal Partners*, co-ed. (with C. Vaitsos), (Macmillan, 1981).

Articles: 1. 'The limitations of the special case', in *The Teaching of Development Economics*, eds. K. Martin and J. Knapp (Frank Cass, 1967); 2. 'What are we trying to measure?', *J Dev. Stud.*, 8(3), April 1972; 3. 'The political economy of national accounting', in *Employment, Income Distribution and Development Strategy: Problems of the Developing Countries — Essays in Honour of H. W. Singer*, eds. A. K.

Cairncross and M. Puri (Macmillan 1975); 4. 'Life expectancy as an integrating concept in social and demographic analysis and planning', *RIW*, 23(3), Sept. 1977; 5. 'The congruence of Marxism and other neo-classical doctrines', in *Towards a New Strategy of Development* (Pergamon, 1980).

Career Originally stressed the relativism of economics — the danger in particular of transferring economic propositions uncritically from industrial countries to the Third World. Later he placed more emphasis on the extent to which European countries, and the European economic system as a whole, show problems familiar to those in the development field, suggesting that theory and practical experience in that field may throw light on the problems of industrialised countries. Other main interests were in criticising the massive transfer of statistical categories and frameworks to the Third World, and suggesting what might be more appropriate.

SEKINE, Thomas Tomohiko

Born 1933, Tokyo, Japan.

Current Post Prof. Econ. and Social and Polit. Thought, York Univ., Downsview, Ont., Canada, 1984–.

Past Posts Stat., UN Stats. Office, NY, 1960–2; Lect., Sir George Williams Coll., 1963–4; Res. Assoc., Univ. Birmingham, 1965–6; Ass. Prof., Simon Fraser Univ., 1966–8; Vis. Res. Assoc., Northwestern Univ.; Ass. prof., Assoc. Prof., York Univ., Canada, 1968–72, 1972–83; Vis. Prof., Internat. Christian Univ., Tokyo, 1982–4.

Degrees BA (Social Science) Hitotsubashi Univ., Tokyo, 1957; MA McGill Univ., Montreal, 1964; PhD Univ. London, 1967.

Offices and Honours Canada Council Non-Resident Fellow, 1958–60.

Principal Fields of Interest 020 Economic Theory; 036 Economic Methodology; 050 Economic Systems.

Publications *Books:* 1. K. Uno, *Principles of Political Economy, Theory of a Purely Capitalist Society*, ed. (Harvester Press, 1980); 2. *The Dialectic of Capital, A Study of the Inner Logic of*

Capitalism, A Preliminary Edition (Yushindo Press, 1984).

Articles: 1. 'Commodity reserve currency and international equilibrium', *Metroec.*, 22, 1970; 2. 'Stability of monetary equilibrium in a classical exchange economy', *Metroec.*, 24, 1972; 3. 'Investment dynamics of a two-sector production model', *ZN*, 32(2–3), Sept. 1972; 4. 'Classical monetary theory and the non-optimality theorem', *ZN*, 33(1–2), 1973; 5. 'Uno-Riron: a Japanese contribution to Marxian political economy', *JEL*, 13(3), Sept. 1975; 6. 'The necessity of the law of value', *Science and Society*, 44(3), Fall 1980; 7. 'The circular motion of capital', *Science and Society*, 45(3), Fall 1981; 8. 'Economic theory and capitalism', *York Stud. in Polit. Economy*, 1, 1982; 9. 'Productive and unproductive labor', *York Stud. in Polit. Economy*, 2, 1983; 10. 'The law of market value', *Science and Society*, 46(4), Winters 1982–3.

Principal Contributions After abandoning my earlier interest in the neoclassical theory of money and its application to international economics, I concentrated on a reformulation of Marx's economic theory (as propounded in *Capital*) according to the method of the late Professor Kozo Uno. The reformulation (see my *Dialectic of Capital*) involves, in addition to some expository modernisation, a reassertion of the structural correspondence between the economic theory of capitalism and Hegelian dialectical logic. More recently I have taken increasing interest in 'political economy' in the broader sense in which I include designs of a new society (presumably socialist) free from the alienation of labour and environmental crises. I believe this to be the right direction in which to seek a paradigmic change in economic science.

SELDEN, Richard Thomas

Born 1922, Pontiac, MI, USA.
Current Post Carter Glass Prof. Econ., Univ. Virginia, Charlottesville, VA, USA, 1969–.
Past Posts Instr. Bus. Admin., Univ. Mass., 1949–50; Ass. Prof, Assoc. Prof. Econ. and Bus. Admin, Vanderbilt Univ., TN, 1952–9; Res. Assoc., NBER, 1958–9; Assoc. Prof. Banking, Columbia Univ., 1959–63; Member, Res. Staff, NBER, 1959–63; Prof. Econ., Cornell Univ., 1963–9; Vis. Prof. Econ., Stanford Univ., 1967; Vis. Scholar, Univ. Stockholm, 1978; Vis. Prof. Econ., Bombay Univ., 1981; Assoc. Prof. Univ. Strasbourg, 1982, 1983.
Degrees BA Univ. Chicago, 1948; MA Columbia Univ., 1949; PhD Univ. Chicago, 1954.
Offices and Honours Guggenheim Foundation Fellow, 1964–5; Fulbright Advanced Res. Scholar, Belgium, 1965; Ford Foundation Faculty Fellow, Cornell Univ., 1968–9.
Editorial Duties Ed. Board, *JMCB*, 1969–72.
Principal Fields of Interest 310 Domestic Monetary and Financial Theory and Institutions; 134 Inflation and Deflation; 123 Comparative Economic Studies involving both Developed and Developing Countries.
Publications *Books:* 1. *Trends and Cycles in the Commercial Paper Market* (NBER, 1963); 2. *Time Deposit Growth and the Employment of Bank Funds* (with G. R. Morrison), (Assoc. Reserve City Banker, 1965); 3. *Capitalism and Freedom: Problems and Prospects,* ed. (Univ. Press Virginia, 1975).

Articles: 1. 'Accelerated amortization and industrial concentration', *REStat*, 37(3), Aug. 1955; 2. 'Monetary velocity in the United States', in *Studies in the Quantity Theory of Money*, ed. M. Friedman (Univ. Chicago Press, 1956); 3. 'Cost–push versus demand–pull inflation, 1955–57', *JPE* 67(1), Feb. 1959; 4. 'The postwar rise in the velocity of money: a sectoral analysis', *J Fin*, 16(4), Dec. 1961; 5. 'Stable monetary growth', in *In Search of a Monetary Constitution*, ed. L. B. Yeager (Harvard Univ. Press, 1962); 6. 'Business pricing policies and inflation' (with H. J. De Podwin), *JPE*, 71(2), April 1963; 7. 'A critique of Dutch monetarism', *J Mon E*, 1(2), April 1975; 8. 'Monetary growth and the long-run rate of inflation', *AER*, 65(2), May 1975; 9. 'Monetarism', in *Modern*

Economic Thought, ed. S. Weintraub (Univ. Penn. Press, 1976); 10. 'Inflation and monetary growth: experience in fourteen countries of Europe and North America since 1958', *Fed. Reserve Bank Richmond, Econ. Rev.*, Nov.–Dec. 1981.

Principal Contributions The focus of my research has been the demand for money. Two early studies examined trends in monetary velocity in the US. More recent work has dealt with the role of monetary growth as a cause of inflation, not only in the US but in other industrialised countries as well. Most of this work has involved extensive empirical analysis. Some of it — for example, on the markets for commercial paper and consumer instalment credit — has consisted of fairly detailed examinations of financial institutions. The basic aim of all my research (apart from the 1955 paper on accelerated amortisation) has been to improve our understanding of the way in which monetary policy does its work. I expect to pursue this aim in the future through further comparative (cross-country) studies of monetary policy.

SELIGMAN, Edwin Robert Anderson*

Dates and Birthplace 1861–1939, New York City, NY, USA.

Posts Held Lect., Prof., Columbia Univ., 1885–1931.

Degrees BA, MA, LLB, PhD Columbia Univ., 1879, 1884, 1885.

Offices and Honours Founder, Pres., AEA, 1902–4; Founder, Pres., AAUP, 1919–20; Chief Ed., *ESS*, 1927–35.

Publications *Books:* 1. *The Shifting and Incidence of Taxation* (1892, 1927); 2. *Progressive Taxation in Theory and Practice* (1894, 1908); 3. *Essays in Taxation* (1895, 1928); 4. *The Economic Interpretation of History* (1902, 1934, 1961); 5. *Principles of Economics* (1905, 1929); 6. *The Income Tax: A Study of the History, Theory and Practice of Income Taxation at Home and Abroad* (1911, 1914); 7. *Studies in Public Finance* (1925); 8. *Essays in Economics (1925)*.

Career Expert on public finance,

member of innumerable tax commissions, and a key figure in the professionalisation of American economics. His work on income tax concentrated on the equity case for a progressive income tax in terms of ability to pay, but he also explored the incidence of taxation and the effects of taxes on production. Also wrote on general economics, where the influence of his earlier German studies is revealed by his high estimation of the value of historical studies. His interest in the history of economic thought was reflected in his remarkable personal library which he bequeathed to Columbia University.

Secondary Literature C.S. Shoup, 'Seligman, Edwin R.A.', *IESS*, 14.

SEN, Amartya Kumar

Born 1933, Santiniketan, Bengal, India.

Current Post Drummond Prof. Polit. Econ., Fellow, All Souls Coll. Oxford, 1981–.

Past Posts Prof. Econ., Delhi Univ., 1963–71; Prof. Econ., LSE, 1971–7; Prof. Econ., Univ. Oxford, 1977–80.

Degrees BA Calcutta Univ., 1953; BA, PhD Univ. Camb., 1955, 1959; Hon. DLitt Visva-Bharati Univ., India, 1982; Hon. DSc Univ. Bath, 1963; Hon. DU Univ. Essex, 1983.

Offices and Honours Fellow, BA; Fellow, Em Soc; Foreign Hon. Member, AAAS; Andrew D. White Prof., Cornell Univ.; Chairman, UN Expert Group Role Advanced Skill and Technology, 1968; Mahalanobis Prize, 1976; Pres., Em Soc, 1984.

Principal Fields of Interest 110 Economic Growth; Development.

Publications *Books:* 1. *Choice of Techniques* (Blackwell, 1960, 1968, Indian edn., CUP, 1960); 2. *Collective Choice and Social Welfare* (Holden-Day, 1970, Oliver & Boyd, 1971, N-H, 1980); 3. *On Economic Inequality* (OUP, W. W. Norton, 1973; Indian edn., OUP, 1973; transls., German, 1975, Japanese, 1975, Spanish, 1979); 4. *Employment, Technology and Development* (OUP, 1975, Indian edn., OUP, 1975); 5. *Poverty and Famines:*

An Essay on Entitlement and Deprivation (OUP, 1981); 6. *Choice, Welfare and Measurement* (Blackwell, MIT Press, 1982, Indian edn., OUP, 1983); 7. *Resources, Values and Development* (Blackwell, 1984).

Principal Contributions Works in welfare economics and social choice theory, particularly in expanding their informational bases, incorporating considerations of liberty and rights, and exploring problems of collective rationality. Contributions to methods and techniques of economic measurement, particularly of real national income, poverty, inequality and unemployment. Exploration of the analytic foundations of rational choice and of the behavioural bases of economic theory. Contributions to the choice of technology in developing countries, and to methods of shadow pricing and cost–benefit analysis. Developing a theory of the causation of famines, focussing on entitlement relations and general economic interdependence rather than just on food supply, and application to particular famines in Asia and Africa.

SENIOR, Nassau William*

Dates and Birthplace 1790–1864, Compton Beauchamp, England.
Posts Held Lawyer; Drummond Prof., Univ. Oxford, 1825–30, 1847–52.
Degrees BA, MA Univ. Oxford, 1812, 1815.
Offices and Honours Barrister, 1819; Member, Polit. Econ. Club, 1823; Member, numerous govt. comms, including Poor Laws, 1833, Factory conditions, 1837, Popular education, 1857.
Publications *Books:* 1. *Two Lectures on Population* (1829); 2. *Three Lectures on the Transmission of the Precious Metals* (1828, 1931); 3. *Three Lectures on the Costs of Obtaining Money* (1830, 1931); 4. *An Outline of the Science of Political Economy* (1836, 1951); 5. *Letters on the Factory Act* (1837); 6. *Lecture on the Production of Wealth* (1847); 7. *Four Introductory Lectures on Political Economy* (1852); 8. *Historical and Philosophical Essays*, 2 vols (1865).

Career As an adviser to the Whig party, he exercised a marked influence on social and economic policy during the 1830s. He also made considerable theoretical contributions in the lectures given during his terms as Drummond Professor. His rigorous restatement of the theory of value, his abstinence theory of capital, his treatment of population, money and international trade, and his distinction between the science and art of political economy, all received favourable notice.

Secondary Literature M. Bowley, *Nassau Senior and Classical Economics* (Kelly, 1949); M. Bowley, 'Senior, Nassau William', *IESS*, 14.

SETON, Francis

Born 1920, Vienna, Austria.
Current Post Sr. Fellow, Nuffield Coll., Oxford, 1978–.
Past Posts Res. Fellow, Official Fellow, Nuffield Coll., Oxford; Res. Assoc., Russian Res. Center, Harvard Univ.; Special Lect., Univ. Oxford; Cons., UK Nat. Exec. Devlp. Office, Dept. Econ. Affairs, UK Board Trade, 1960–70, UNECE, 1961–2, UN Human Rights Comm., 1972; Adviser, Govt. Iran, 1966–70, Govt. Chile, 1969, 1970, Govt. Indonesia, 1972–3; Vis. Prof., Columbia Univ., 1958, Osaka Univ., 1958, Wharton School, Penn. Univ., 1963, Univ. of the South, TN, USA, 1982.
Degrees BA, MA, DPhil Univ. Oxford, 1948, 1949, 1954.
Editorial Duties Ed., *OEP*, 1960–75, *J Post Keyn E*, *J Comp E*.
Principal Fields of Interest 021 General Equilibrium Theory; 123 Comparative Economic Studies; 222 Input–output.
Publications *Books:* 1. *The Tempo of Soviet Industrial Expansion* (Manchester Stat. Soc., 1957); 2. *The Effect of Fiscal Codes on the Yield of Capital Projects* (UK Board Trade, 1969); 3. *Shadow Wages in the Chilean Economy* (OECD Devlp. Centre, 1972); 4. *Industrial Management — East and West*, co-ed. (with A. Silberston), (Praeger, 1973); 5. *Cost, Use and Value* (OUP, 1985).

Articles: 1. 'The social accounts of the Soviet Union in 1934', *REStat*, 36, Aug. 1954; 2. 'Productivity, trade balance, and international structure', *EJ*, 66, Dec. 1956; 3. 'The transformation problem', *REStud*, 24, June 1957, repr. in *The Economics of Marx*, eds. M. C. Howard and J. E. King (Penguin, 1976); 4. 'Ideological obstacles to rational price setting in communist countries', in *The Socialist Price Mechanism*, ed. A. Abouchar (Duke Univ. Press, 1977); 5. 'A quasi-competitive price basis for intersystem comparisons of economic structure and performance', *J Comp E*, 5(4), Dec. 1981.

Principal Contributions Price and value concepts in the theory and practice of centrally planned economies, e.g. the Marxian 'transformation problem'; economic development and policy in the Soviet Union; problems of planning, trade, and aid for developing countries; and shadow pricing for project appraisal.

SHACKLE, George Lennox Sharman

Born 1903, Cambridge, England.
Current Post Emeritus Prof., Univ. Liverpool, 1969–.
Past Posts Brunner Prof. Econ. Science, Univ. Liverpool, 1951–69.
Degrees BA, PhD Univ. London, 1931, 1937; DPhil Univ. Oxford, 1940; Hon. DSc New Univ. Ulster, 1974; Hon. DSoc. Sc. Univ. Birmingham, 1978.
Offices and Honours Council, RES, 1955–69; Prof. F. de Vries Lect., Rotterdam School Econ., 1957; Vis. Prof., Columbia Univ., 1957, Pittsburgh Univ., 1967; Pres. Section F. BAAS, 1966; Fellow, BA, 1967–; Keynes Lecturer, BA, 1976.
Principal Fields of Interest 031 History of Economic Thought.
Publications *Books:* 1. *Expectations, Investment and Income* (CUP, 1938, 1968); 2. *Expectation in Economics* (CUP, 1949, 1952); 3. *Decision, Order and Time in Human Affairs* (CUP, 1961, 1969); 4. *The Years of High Theory* (CUP, 1967); 5. *Epistemics &*

Economics (CUP, 1972); 6. *Imagination and the Nature of Choice* (Edinburgh Univ. Press, 1979).
Articles: 1. 'Some notes on monetary theories of the trade cycle', *REStud*, 1(1), Oct. 1933; 2. 'A theory of investment decisions', *OEP*, 6, April 1942; 3. 'Recent theories concerning the nature and role of interest', *EJ*, 71, June 1961; 4. 'Time and choice', The Keynes Lecture (BA, 1976); 5. 'Imagination, formalism and choice', in *Time, Uncertainty and Disequilibrium*, ed. M. J. Rizzo (D. C. Heath, 1979); 6. 'A student's pilgrimage', *BNLQR*, 145, June 1983.

Secondary Literature M. Perlman, 'On Shackle', in *Contemporary Economists in Perspective*, eds. H. W. Spiegel and W. J. Samuels (JAI Press, 1984); B. J. Loasby, M. Perlman, A. Heertje, 'G. L. S. Shackle as a historian of economic thought', in *Research in the History of Economic Thought and Methodology, The Craft of the Historian of Economic Thought*, ed. W. V. Samuels (JAI Press, 1983); F. Stephen, 'Expectation possibility and interest: an appraisal of the economics of G. L. S. Shackle', *J Econ. Stud.*, 12(1/2), 1985.

SHARPE, William F.

Born 1934, Cambridge, MA, USA.
Current Post Timken Prof. Fin., Grad. School Bus., Stanford Univ., CA, USA, 1973–.
Past Posts Econ., Rand Corp., 1959–61; Ass. Prof., Assoc. Prof., Prof., Univ. Washington, 1961–3, 1963–7, 1967–8; Prof., Univ. Cal. Irvine, 1968–70; Prof., Stanford Univ., 1970–3.
Degrees BA, MA, PhD UCLA, 1955, 1956, 1961.
Offices and Honours Phi Beta Kappa, 1955.
Editorial Duties Assoc. Ed., *J. Fin. and Quant. Analysis*, 1966–72, *Management Science*, 1970–2, *Bell JE*, 1970–3, *J Fin*, 1983–; Ed. Adviser, Fin. and Computer Science (Praeger).
Principal Fields of Interest 313 Capital Markets; 022 Microeconomic Theory; 521 Business Finance.
Publications *Books:* 1. *The Econ-*

omics of Computers (Columbia Univ. Press, 1969); 2. *Portfolio Theory and Capital Markets* (McGraw-Hill, 1970); 3. *Introduction to Managerial Economics* (Columbia Univ. Press, 1973); 4. *BASIC: An Introduction to Computer Programming Using the BASIC Language* (with N. L. Jacob), (Free Press, 1979); 5. *Investments* (Prentice-Hall, 1981).

Articles: 1. 'A simplified model for portfolio analysis', *Management Science*, 9(2), Jan. 1963; 2. 'Capital asset prices — a theory of market equilibrium under conditions of risk', *J Fin*, 19(3), Sept. 1964; 3. 'Mutual fund performance', *J Bus*, 39(1), pt. 2, Jan. 1966; 4. 'Risk-return classes of New York stock exchange common stocks, 1931–1967' (with G. M. Cooper), *Fin. Analysts J.*, March–April 1972; 5. 'Closed-end investment companies in the United States' (with H. B. Sosin), in *European Finance Association, 1974 Proceedings*, ed. B. Jacquillat (N-H., 1975); 6. 'Corporate pension funding policy', *J Fin Econ*, June 1976; 7. 'The capital asset pricing model: a 'multi-beta' interpretation', in *Financial Decision Making Under Uncertainty*, eds. H. Levy and M. Sarnt (Academic Press, 1977); 8. 'Bank capital adequacy, deposit insurance, and security values', *J. Fin. and Quant. Analysis*, Nov. 1978; 9. 'Decentralized investment management', *J Fin*, 36(2), May 1981; 10. 'Some factors in New York stock exchange security returns, 1931–1979', *J. Portfolio Management*, Summer 1982.

Principal Contributions Work has combined an interest in normative approaches to financial decision-making under uncertainty and positive theories of equilibrium in financial markets characterised by uncertainty. The former is subsumed under the title portfolio theory, the latter under the title capital market theory.

SHAW, Graham Keith

Born 1938, Rochdale, Lancashire, England.

Current Post Rank Foundation Prof. Econ., Dean, School of Accounting, Bus. and Econ., Univ. Buckingham, Buckingham, England, 1980–.

Past Posts Ass. Prof. Econ., NYU, 1966–7; Lect. Econ., Univ. York, England, 1967–70; Reader Econ., Univ. St Andrews, 1971–9, Univ. E. Anglia, 1979–80; Vis. Prof. Econ., Univ. Puerto Rico, 1971, Vassar Coll., NY, 1972, Univ. Toledo, OH, 1983; Tax and Fiscal Pol. Cons., OECD Devlp. Centre, Paris, 1969–71, Harvard Univ. Devlp. Advisory Service, 1972–3, Nederlands Econ. Inst., 1979.

Degrees BSc London Univ., 1960; PhD Columbia Univ., 1966.

Principal Fields of Interest 320 Fiscal Theory and Policy, Public Finance; 023 Macroeconomic Theory; 112 Economic Development Models and Theories.

Publications *Books:* 1. *The Economic Theory of Fiscal Policy* (with A. Peacock), (A&U, 1971, 1976; transls., Italian, 1972, Japanese, 1973, Spanish, 1974); 2. *An Introduction to the Theory of Macroeconomic Policy* (Martin Robertson, 1971, 1977; transl., Spanish, 1974); 3. *Macroeconomic Theory and Policy in the UK* (with D. Greenaway), (Martin Robertson, 1983); 4. *Rational Expectations: An Elementary Exposition* (Wheatsheaf, 1984).

Articles: 1. 'Monetary-fiscal policy for growth and the balance of payments constraint', *Ec*, N.S. 34, May 1967, repr. in *Readings in Macro-economics*, ed. N. J. Keiser (Prentice-Hall, 1976), and in *Letture di Politica Fiscale*, ed. A. Pedone (Societa Editrice il Multino, 1972); 2. 'Fiscal measures to improve employment in developing countries: a technical note' (with A. T. Peacock), *PF*, 26(3), 1971; 3. 'The tax mix and aggregate demand: a respecification' (with B. A. Forster), *PF*, 31(2), 1976; 4. 'The measurement of fiscal influence', in *Current Issues in Fiscal Policy* (Martin Robertson, 1979); 5. 'On the economics of tax aversion' (with R. B. Crose), *PF*, 37(1), 1982; 6. 'Tax evasion and tax revenue loss' (with A. T. Peacock), *PF*, 37(2), 1982.

Principal Contributions Macroeconomic theory and policy particularly with reference to fiscal policy and the economics of the budget constraint, with occasional forays into specific aspects of taxation generally, as for example, tax evasion and taxation aspects peculiar to less advanced economies.

SHELL, Karl

Born 1938, Paterson, NJ, USA.
Current Post Prof. Econ., Co-Dir., Center Analytic Res. Econ. and Social Sciences, Univ. Penn., USA, 1970–.
Past Posts Systems Analyst, Proctor & Gamble, 1959; Econ., US President's Council Econ. Advisers, 1962; Act. Instr. Econ., Stanford Univ., 1962–3; Ass. Prof., Assoc. Prof. Econ., MIT, 1964–7, 1967–8; Assoc. Prof. Econ., Univ. Penn., 1968–70; Vis. Prof. Econ., Stanford Univ., 1972–3; Adjunct Res., CEPREMAP, Paris, 1977–8; Adjunct Prof. Econ., Univ. Paris XII, 1979; Adjunct Prof. Econ., Univ. Paris I, 1981.
Degrees BA (Maths.), Princeton Univ., 1960; PhD Stanford Univ., 1965; Hon. MA Univ. Penn., 1971.
Offices and Honours ITT Prize Scholar, 1959–60; Sigma Xi Res. Prize, 1960; Soc. Sigma Xi, 1960; Woodrow Wilson Nat. Fellow, 1960–1; Woodrow Wilson Disting. Fellow, 1963–4; Ford Faculty Res. Fellow, 1967–8; Fellow, Em. Soc., 1973; Guggenheim Foundation Fellow, 1977–8; Fellow, Center Advanced Study Behav. Sciences, Stanford, CA, 1984–5.
Editorial Duties Ed. *JET*, 1968–; Ed., Monographs Econ. Theory, Math. Econ., and Econometrics (Academic Press, 1968–.).
Principal Fields of Interest 020 General Economic Theory; 111, Economic Growth Theory; 321 Fiscal Theory.
Publications *Books:* 1. *Essays on the Theory of Optimal Economic Growth*, ed. (MIT Press, 1967); 2. *Economic Theory of Price Indices* (with F. M. Fisher), (Academic Press, 1972); 3. *Mathematical Methods in Investment and Finance*, co-ed. (with G. P. Szego), (N-H, 1972); 4. *The Hamiltonian Approach to Dynamic Economics*, co-ed. (with D. Cass), (Academic Press, 1976).
Articles: 1. 'Toward a theory of inventive activity and capital accumulation', *AER*, 51(2), May 1965; 2. 'The

allocation of investment in a dynamic economy' (with J. E. Stiglitz), *QJE*, 81(4), Nov. 1967; 3. 'Capital gains, income and saving' (with M. Sidrauski and J. E. Stiglitz), *REStud*, 36(1), Jan. 1969; 4. 'Applications of Pontryagin's maximum principle to economics', in *Mathematical Systems Theory and Economics, 1*, ed. H. W. Kuhn and G. P. Szego (Springer, 1969); 5. 'Public debt, taxation and capital intensiveness' (with E. S. Phelps), *JET*, 1(3), Oct. 1969; 6. 'An exercise in the theory of heterogeneous capital accumulation' (with C. Caton), *REStud*, 38(1), Jan. 1971; 7. 'Notes on the economics of infinity', *JPE*, 79(5), Sept.–Oct. 1971; 8. 'The structure and stability of competitive dynamical systems' (with D. Cass), *JET* 12(2), Feb. 1976; 9. 'The overlapping-generations model' (with Y. Balasko), *JET*, 23(3), Dec. 1980; 24(1), Feb. 1981; 10. 'Do sunspots matter?' (with D. Cass), *JPE*, 91(2), April, 1983.

Principal Contributions The theory of intertemporal resource allocation: pioneered in inventive activity and capital accumulation. Showed (with Stiglitz) how long-run perfect-foresight excludes errant trajectories in saddle-point dynamical systems of heterogeneous capital accumulation. Analysed indeterminacy of equilibrium in economies with government debt. Established (with Phelps) that the debt is not necessarily burdensome: a larger debt can be associated with a higher long-run capital intensity. Established that restrictions on market participation are not essential in the perfect-foresight overlapping-generations economy; the double infinity of consumers and dated commodities is the source of intertemporal inefficiency. Showed (with Cass) how dynamic stability of the optimal growth model is dependent on the geometry of the Hamiltonian function. Provided (with Balasko) a detailed analysis of equilibrium and welfare in overlapping-generations economies. Inventor (with Cass) of the 'sunspots model'; showed that incomplete market participation plays an essential role in economies facing extrinsic uncertainty.

Other research: extensive work

(with Fisher) on the theory of economic price indices; the theory of taxes denominated in money units; applied work on financing higher education in the US.

SHEPHERD, William Geoffrey

Born 1936, Ames, IA, USA.
Current Post Prof. Econ., Univ. Michigan, Ann Arbor, MI, USA, 1971–.
Past Posts Instr., Yale Univ., 1961–3; Ass. Prof., Assoc. Prof., Univ. Michigan, 1963–6, 1966–71; Special Econ. Ass., Ass. Attorney General for Antitrust, US Dept. Justice, Washington, DC, 1967–8; Vis. Prof., Williams Coll., MA, 1982, Nankai Univ., Tianjin, China, 1983, Univ. Mass., 1984–5.
Degrees BA Amherst Coll., MA, 1957; MA, PhD Yale Univ., 1958, 1963.
Offices and Honours Fulbright Fellow, 1959–60; Chairman, Transportation and Public Utilities Group, AEA, 1976–7.
Editorial Duties Ed. Boards, *Antitrust Bull.*, *Industrial Organization Rev.*, *REStat*.
Principal Fields of Interest 610 Industrial Organisation and Public Policy; 614 Public Enterprises; 620 Economics of Technological Change.
Publications *Books:* 1. *Economic Performance under Public Ownership: British Fuel and Power* (Yale Univ. Press, 1965; transl., Italian, CIRIEC, 1968); 2. *Utility Regulation: New Directions in Theory and Policy*, co-ed. (with T. G. Gies), (Random House, 1966); 3. *Market Power and Economic Welfare* (Random House, 1970; transl., Chinese, 1980); 4. *The Treatment of Market Power* (Columbia Univ. Press, 1975); 5. *Public Policies toward Business* (with C. Wilcox), (Richard D. Irwin, 1975, 1985); 6. *Public Policies Toward Business: Readings and Cases*, ed. (Richard D. Irwin, 1975, 1979); 7. *Public Enterprise: Economic Analysis of Theory and Practice*, ed. (D. C. Heath, 1976); 8. *The Economics of Industrial Organization* (Prentice-Hall, 1979, 1985); 9. *Economic Regulation: Essays in Honor of James R. Nelson*, co-ed. (with K. D.

Boyer), (Michigan State Univ. Press, 1981); 10. *Economics* (with L. Anderson and A. Putallaz), (Prentice-Hall, 1983).
Articles: 1. 'Cross-subsidising and allocation in public firms', *OEP*, N.S. 16, March 1964; 2. 'Trends of concentration in American manufacturing industry, 1947–58', *REStat*, 46, May 1964; 3. 'What does the survivor technique show about economies of scale?', *SEJ*, 35, July 1967; 4. 'Alternatives for public expenditure', in *Britain's Economic Prospects*, ed. R. E. Caves, *et al.* (Brookings Inst., 1968); 5. 'Market power and racial discrimination in white-collar employment', *Antitrust Bull.*, 16, Spring 1969; 6. 'The elements of market structure', *REStat*, 54, Feb. 1972; 7. 'Entry as a substitute for regulation', *AER*, 63(2), May 1973; 8. 'Monopoly profits and economies of scale', in *Industrial Organization, Antitrust, and Public Policy*, ed. J. Craven (Kluwer Nijhoff, 1982); 9. 'Causes of increased competition in the US economy, 1939–80', *REStat*, 64, Nov. 1982; 10. '"Contestability" versus "competition"', *AER*, 74(4), Sept. 1984.
Principal Contributions The nature and effects of markets structure, in concept and fact. Developed early econometric analysis of market structures in the US and UK. Established market share as the central element of market structure relations of employment discrimination to market structure. Also, prepared early econometric tests of the performance of British public enterprises. Helped develop the analysis of marginal-cost pricing, the rate-base effect of regulation, and entry into regulated markets. Recent work measures the rise of competition in the US economy, shows problems of 'sustainability' and 'contestability', and explores the nature of competition. Monographs deal with market power and alternative policies toward monopoly. Textbooks cover industrial organisation, public policies toward business, and elementary economics.

SHESHINSKI, Eytan

Born 1939, Haifa, Israel.
Current Post Sir Isaac Wolfson Prof. Public Fin., Hebrew Univ., Jerusalem, Israel, 1979–.
Past Posts Vis. Prof. Econ., Stanford Univ., 1976; Oskar Morgenstern Disting. Fellow, Princeton Univ., 1980; Fellow, Center Advanced Study Behavioral Sciences, Stanford, 1981.
Degrees BA, MA Hebrew Univ., Jerusalem, 1961, 1963; PhD MIT, 1966.
Editorial Duties Co-ed., *Em*, 1977–81.
Offices and Honours Fellow, Em Soc; Council, Em Soc, 1979–81; Wicksell Lectures, 1980; Walras-Bowley Lecture, Em Soc, 1981.
Principal Fields of Interest 022 Microeconomic Theory.
Publications *Articles:* 1. 'The optimal linear income-tax', *REStud*, 39, July 1972, repr. in *Economic Justice*, ed. E. S. Phelps (Penguin, 1973); 2. 'Direct versus indirect remedies for externalities' (with J. Green), *JPE*, pt. 4, 84(4), Aug. 1976; 3. 'Inflation and costs of price adjustment' (with Y. Weiss), *REStud*, 44(2), June 1977; 4. 'Efficiency in the optimum supply of public goods' (with L. Lau and J. Stiglitz), *Em*, 46(2), March 1978.
Principal Contributions Switching of techniques in linear open input–output models; the theory of optimum income taxation; externalities and corrective taxation; firm's optimum behaviour under inflation; and social security and theory of intergenerational transfers.

SHIBATA, Hirofumi

Born 1929, Fujisawa, Japan.
Current Post Prof. Econ., Osaka Univ., Toyonaka, Japan, 1979–.
Past Posts Assoc. Prof. Econ., Queen's Univ., Canada, 1965–8; Reader Econ., Univ. York, 1968–71; Vis. Assoc. Prof. Econ., Univ. Maryland, 1970–1; Prof. Econ., Univ. Kentucky, 1971–9; Sr. Econ. Affairs Officer, UN, 1971; Cons., Canadian Dept. Fin., 1965, Urban Inst., Washington, DC, 1972.

Degrees BA Kobe Univ., Japan, 1953; MA McGill Univ., 1962; PhD Columbia Univ., 1965.
Offices and Honours Res. Fellow, Private Planning Assoc. Canada (Montreal), 1965–8; Canada Council Fellow; Fulbright Fellow; Bronfman Fellow; Internat. Econ. Integration Program Fellow.
Editorial Duties Ed. Board, *PF*, 1983–; Ed., *Growth and Change: J Regional Devlp.*, 1977–83.
Principal Fields of Interest 421 Trade Relations; 722 Conservation and Pollution.
Publications *Books:* 1. *Harmonization of National Economic Policies under Free Trade* (with H. J. Johnson and P. Wonnacott), (Univ. Toronto Press, 1968); 2. *Fiscal Harmonization under Freer Trade: Principles and their Applications to a Canada–US Free Trade Area* (Univ. Toronto Press, 1969); 3. *Public Economics* (Japanese), (Toyo Keizai Shinpo Sha, 1985); 4. *Australia's Federal System, Resource Developments and Resource Trade* (with P. Drysdale), (A&U, 1985).
Articles: 1. 'On the equivalence of tariffs and quotas', *AER*, 58(1), March, 1968; 2. 'A bargaining model of the pure theory of public expenditure', *JPE*, 79(1), Jan.–Feb. 1971; 3. 'Pareto optimality, trade and the Pigovian corrective tax', *Ec*, N.S. 39, May 1972; 4. 'Pareto optimality and gains from trade: a further elucidation', *Ec*, N.S. 41, Feb. 1974; 5. 'A theory of group consumption and group formation', *PF*, 34(3), 1979; 6. 'Control of pollution when the offended defend themselves' (with J. S. Winrick), *Ec*, N.S. 50, Nov. 1983; 7. 'Economics of representative democracy: a model of skewed representations', in *Public Finance and the Quest for Efficiency*, ed. H. Hanush (Wayne State Univ. Press, 1984).
Principal Contributions The first analysis of 'voluntary export control', explaining voluntarism in terms of non-equivalence of tariffs and quotas: introduction of an analytical method of free-trade areas as distinct from customs unions in their economic effects; introduction of a new concept 'the restricted origin principle of taxation' and use of it in analyses of international tax

harmonisation; analysis of pure public goods, geometrically showing possibilities of overproduction of public goods; clarification of externalities under which a unilaterally imposed Pigovian tax can be successful; analysis of group consumption goods and group formation processes; stability analysis of internationalisation of an externality under a corrective tax; analysis of interactions between control policies of polluters and the victims' defensive activities; and economic analysis of representative democracies.

SHILLER, Robert James

Born 1946, Detroit, MI, USA.
Current Post Prof. Econ., Cowles Foundation and School Organization and Management, Yale Univ., New Haven, CT, USA, 1982–.
Past Posts Ass. Prof., Univ. Minnesota, 1972–4; Res. Fellow, NBER, Camb., MA, 1974–5; Assoc. Prof., Prof. Econ., and Fin., Wharton School, Univ. Penn., 1974–81, 1981–2; Vis. Prof., MIT, 1981–2.
Degrees BA Univ. Michigan, 1967; MSc, PhD MIT, 1968, 1972.
Offices and Honours Vis. Scholar, Fed. Reserve Bank, Philadelphia, 1977–8; Res. Assoc., NBER, 1979–; Fellow, Em Soc, 1980; Econ. Panel, NSF, 1983–5; Brookings Panel Econ. Activity, 1984–5.
Editorial Duties Assoc. Ed., J Em, 1980–3, J. Portfolio Management, 1983–; Foreign Ed., REStud, 1981–.
Principal Fields of Interest 023 Macroeconomic Theory.
Publications Articles: 1. 'A distributed lag estimator derived from smoothness priors', Em, 41(4), July 1973; 2. 'Inflation, rational expectations and the term structure of interest rates' (with F. Modigliani), Ec, N.S. 40, Feb. 1973; 3. 'The Gibson paradox and historical movements in real long term interest rates' (with J. J. Siegel), JPE, 85(5), Oct. 1977; 4. 'Rational expectations and the dynamic structure of macroeconomic models: a critical review', J Mon E, 4, Jan. 1978; 5. 'The volatility of long term interest rates and expectations models of the term struc-ture', JPE, 87, Dec. 1979; 6. 'Can the federal reserve control real interest rates?', in Rational Expectations and Economic Policy, ed. S. Fischer (Univ. Chicago Press, 1980); 7. 'Do stock prices move too much to be justified by subsequent changes in dividends?', AER, 71(3), June 1981; 8. 'The determinants of the variability of stock market prices' (with S. Grossman), AER, 71(7), May 1981; 9. 'Forward rates and future policy: interpreting the term structure of interest rates' (with J. Y. Campbell and K. L. Schoenholtz), Brookings Papers Econ. Activity, 1, 1983; 10. 'Smoothness priors and non-linear regression', JASA, forthcoming, 1985.
Principal Contributions Contributed to empirical macroeconomics and finance with techniques that make better use of information and lead to more robust models. Showed how the high volatility of prices of speculative assets may call into question some fundamental ideas in finance theory. Studied the behaviour of financial asset prices over the business cycle in connection with theoretical models that use a minimum of restrictive assumptions. Described the time series behaviour of the term structure of interest rates and its implications for monetary policy. Developed distributed lags and nonlinear regression estimation methods based on smoothness priors.

SHONE, Robert Minshull

Born 1906, Birkenhead, England.
Current Post Retired, 1983–.
Past Posts Lect., LSE, 1935–6; Head, Dir. Econ. and Stats. Dept., British Iron and Steel Fed., 1936–9, 1946–53; Gen. Dir., Iron and Steel Control, 1940–5; Exec. Member, Iron and Steel Board, 1953–62; Dir. General, NEDC, 1962–6; Vis. Prof., City Univ., London, England, 1967–83; Special Prof., Nottingham Univ., 1971–3; Dir., various public companies, 1968–82.
Degrees BEng, MEng Liverpool Univ., 1927, 1929; MA Univ. Chicago, 1934.
Offices and Honours CBE 1949;

Knighted 1955; Pres., Soc. of Bus. Econ., 1963–8; Hon. Fellow, LSE.

Principal Fields of Interest 110 Economic Growth; 522 Business Investment; 620 Economics of Technical Change.

Publications *Books:* 1. *Modern Business Problems* (with others), (Longmans Green, 1937); 2. *Industrial Future of Great Britain* (with others), (Europa Publ., 1948); 3. *Models for Decision* (with others), (English Univ. Press, 1965); 4. *Britain and the Common Market* (with others), (BBC Publ., 1967); 5. *Problems of Investment*, ed. and contrib. (Blackwell, 1971); 6. *Price and Investment Relationships* (Paul Elek, 1975; transl., Japanese, Kern Assoc., 1978).

Articles: 1. 'Industrial production and steel consumption' (with H. R. Fisher), *JRSS*, 121, pt. 3, 1958; 2. 'Economic ends and means', *J. Inst. Actuaries*, 94, Dec. 1958; 3. 'Planning for economic growth in a mixed economy', *EJ*, 75, March 1965.

Principal Contributions My first job was building up the statistical and economic work at the central organisation in the UK steel industry. This later led to developing the wartime steel allocation plan and helping at the birth of the Controlled Material Plan in the USA. From early Chicago and LSE days I was concerned with the impact of technical progress on investment and prices. This led, as executive member of the Iron and Steel Board, in 1957 to the supervision of steel prices on a long-term marginal cost basis. Prices were related to costs at a new plant embodying the latest technology. This enabled the supervision of both price and development policy to be integrated. It also influenced the adoption in 1967 of a similar policy as the key factor in the government's policy for nationalised industries. As the first Director-General of the National Economic Development Council (NEDC), I established its organisation and that of the industrial EDCs (1962). This structure has remained essentially unchanged for over 20 years and through six successive governments. Our first task was preparing the plan for *Growth of the UK Economy to 1966* and *Conditions Favourable to Faster Growth* on the policy changes needed; and then we reported on progress a year later. On returning to academic and company life in 1966 my main concern was with the significance of technical change for growth and for price and investment decisions, and with a model for such decision-making. The need to measure the real return and cost of capital for both company and public purposes was emphasised. These issues were covered in my book *Price and Investment Relationships* and in other publications.

SHONFIELD, Andrew Akiba*

Dates and Birthplace 1917–81, England.

Posts Held Journalist, *Financial Times*, 1947–57, *Observer*, 1958–61; Dir. Stud., Res. Fellow, Dir., Royal Inst. Internat. Affairs, 1961–8, 1969–71, 1972–7; Prof. Econ., Europ. Univ. Inst., Florence, 1978–81.

Degree BA Univ. Oxford, 1939.

Offices and Honours Chairman, UK SSRC, 1969–71; Knighted, 1978.

Publications *Books:* 1. *British Economic Policy since the War* (1958); 2. *Attack on World Poverty* (1960); 3. *Modern Capitalism* (1965); 4. *Europe: Journey to an Unknown Destination* (1973); 5. *In Defence of the Mixed Economy*, ed. Z. Shonfield (1984).

Career As a journalist, he put forward a view of British economic and political affairs which was sympathetic to the Left in a non-doctrinaire fashion, and was concerned with helping Britain rid herself of delusions about her economic strength and political importance. His books carefully related economic problems to his understanding of social problems, and were directed at educating the public rather than solving technical problems. His appointment to a chair at the European University Institute was a reflection of his own commitment to the idea of European union.

Secondary Literature (Obit.) 'Sir Andrew Shonfield: distinguished journalist and economist', *The Times*, 24 January 1981.

SHOUP, Carl Sumner

Born 1902, San Jose, CA, USA.
Current Post McVickar Prof. Emeritus Polit. Econ., Columbia Univ.; Cons., Public Fin. Res. and Pol. Projects, 1971–.
Past Posts Ass. Prof., Assoc. Prof., Prof., Columbia Univ., 1928–71; Dir., Tax Study, Ass., Res. Cons., US Treasury, 1934, 1937–8, 1938–46, 1962–8; Chief Tax Mission, Japan, 1949–50, Fin. Study (with R. M. Haig), 1950–2; Fulbright Prof., Univs. Paris and Strasbourg, 1953–4; Member, Fiscal and Fin. Comm., EEC, 1960–2, US President's Comm. Budget Concepts, 1967; Vis. Prof., ANU, 1968; Interregional Adviser, Tax Reform, UN, 1971–4; Killam Fellow, Dalhousie Univ., Canada, 1974–5; Vis. Prof., Monash Univ., 1980; Res. Cons., Fiscal Survey, Venezuela, 1958, Fiscal Harmonization Common Markets, 1962–4, Fed. Estate and Gift Taxation, 1964–6, Tax Mission, Liberia, 1969, Carnegie Center Transportation Stud., 1976, Tax Stud., Venezuela, 1981–3.
Degrees BA (Law) Stanford Univ., 1924; PhD Columbia Univ., 1930; Hon. Dr Univ. Strasbourg, 1967.
Offices and Honours Pres., Nat. Tax Assoc., 1949–50; Pres., IIPF, 1950–3; Disting. Fellow, AEA; Order of Sacred Treasure, Japan.
Editorial Duties Ed., *Bull. Nat. Tax Assoc.*, 1931–55.
Principal Fields of Interest 031 History of Economic Thought; 221 National Income Accounting; 320 Public Finance; Fiscal Theory and Policy.
Publications *Books:* 1. *The Sales Tax in France* (Columbia Univ. Press, 1930); 2. *The Sales Tax in the United States* (with others), (Columbia Univ. Press, 1934); 3. *Facing the Tax Problem* (with R. Blough and M. Newcomer), (Twentieth Century Fund, 1937); 4. *The Prospects for a Study of the Economic Effects of Payroll Taxes* (SSRS, 1941); 5. *Principles of National Income Analysis* (Houghton Mifflin, 1947); 6. *Report on Japanese Taxation* (with others), (SCAP, 1949; transl., Japanese, SCAP, 1949); 7. *Ricardo on Taxation* (Columbia Univ. Press, 1960); 8. *Federal Estate and Gift Taxes* (Brook-

ings Inst., 1966); 9. *Public Finance* (Aldine, 1969; transls., Japanese, Yuhikaku, 1974, Spanish, Inst. de Estudios Fiscales, 1980); 10. *Quantitative Research on Taxation and Government Expenditures* (NBER, 1972).
Articles: 1. 'The taxation of excess profits', *Polit. Science Q.*, 55(4), 56(1, 2), Dec. 1940, March–June 1941; 2. 'Taxation aspects of international economic integration', in *Aspects Financiers et Fiscaux de l'Integration* (Inst. Internat. de fin. Publiques, 1954), repr. in *Penguin Modern Economic Readings: International Economic Integration*, ed. P. Robson (Penguin, 1971); 3. 'Theory and background of the value added tax', *Proceedings, 48th Conference* (NTA, 1955), repr. in *Bobbs-Merrill Economics Rep. Series* (Bobbs-Merrill, 1964); 4. 'Debt financing and future generations', *EJ*, 72, Dec. 1962, repr. in *Public Debt and Future Generations*, ed. C. E. Ferguson (Univ. Carolina Press, 1964), and in *Readings in Modern Economics: Public Finance*, ed. H. W. Houghton (Penguin, 1970); transl., Spanish, *Hacienda Publica Espanola*, 71, 1972; 5. 'Linear programming in public finance', *Finanzarchiv*, 22(3), Aug. 1963; 6. 'Standards for distributing a free governmental service: crime prevention', *PF*, 19(4), 1964; 7. 'Public goods and joint production', in *Essays in Honor of Marco Fanno*, ed. T. Bagiotti (Cedam, 1966); 8. 'Production from consumption', *PF*, 20(1–2), 1965; 9. 'Risk as a dimension in measuring level of service', in *Uncertainty and Expectations in Economics: Essays in Honour of G. L. S. Shackle*, eds. C. F. Carter and J. L. Ford (Blackwell, 1982); 10. 'Economic limits to taxation', *Atlantic Econ.*, 9(1), March 1981; transl., Spanish, *Hacienda Publica Espanola*, 82, 1983.
Principal Contributions My early interest in tax policy problems and taxation techniques developed as I assisted, while a graduate student and later as a member of the Columbia University faculty — initially in the Graduate School of Business, then in the Department of Economics — in a number of research and policy studies by R. M. Haig, E. R. A. Seligman and Roswell Magill with respect to the tax systems of

the US (Federal), New York State, Cuba and France. Here I absorbed attitudes, values and goals that proved helpful in the years 1949–69 in directing tax missions to Japan, Venezuela, and Liberia. In the earlier years my teaching schedule included, from time to time, courses in tax technique, economic theory, and national income analysis. In later years I explored the neglected field of measurement and distribution of public services. All this I tried to bring together in my treatise, *Public Finance*, in 1969.

Throughout my career, fate or disposition has led me to spend much time and effort in other countries, which in turn aided me in my post-Columbia assignment with the UN for three years as adviser to developing countries on their tax policy problems. I have found that one of the more difficult tasks of the tax economist is to divide the time optimally between gaining and keeping familiarity with the intricacies of tax techniques, while also remaining proficient in the economic theory applicable to those techniques. Moreover, the field of public finance has expanded so far beyond its earlier emphasis on taxation that here too one's allocation of time among branches of the discipline becomes an increasingly more complex decision.

SHOVE, Gerald Frank*

Dates and Birthplace 1887–1947, England.

Posts Held Fellow, King's Coll., Reader Econ., Univ. Camb., 1929–47.

Degree MA Univ. Camb., 1910.

Publications *Articles:* 1. 'Varying costs and marginal net profits', *EJ*, 38, 1928; 2. 'The representative firm and increasing returns', *EJ*, 40, March 1930; 3. 'The place of Marshall's *Principles* in the development of economic theory', *EJ*, 52, Dec. 1942; 4. 'Mrs Robinson on Marxian economics', *EJ*, 54, April 1944.

Career A colleague of Keynes who was not, however, a member of the famous 'circus' that criticised Keynes's work. His teaching, and his small number of articles, were inspired by a desire to make a useful contribution to thinking in a wider political and ethical sphere. His chief contribution was towards the restatement of the theories of value and distribution.

Secondary Literature F. Shove, *Fredegond and Gerald Shove* (CUP, 1952).

SHUBIK, Martin

Born 1926, New York City, NY, USA.

Current Post Seymour H. Knox Prof. Math. Institutional Econ., Yale Univ., New Haven, CT, USA, 1975–.

Past Posts Demonstrator Physics, Univ. Toronto, 1948–9; Res. Ass., Res. Assoc., Princeton Univ., 1951–3, 1953–5; Fellow, Center Advanced Stud., Palo Alto, CA, 1955–6; Cons., General Electric Co., 1956–60; Adjunct Res. Prof., Penn. State Univ., 1957–9; Vis. Prof. Econ., Prof. Econ. Organization, Yale Univ., 1960–1, 1963–75; Staff Member, T. J. Watson Res. Labs., IBM, 1961–3; Vis. Prof., Univ. de Chile, Santiago, 1965, Inst. Advanced Stud., Vienna, 1968, 1970; Cons., Rand Corp., Santa Monica, CA, 1970–1; Vis. Prof., Univ. Melbourne, 1973; Dir., Cowles Foundation Res. Econ., Yale Univ., 1973–6.

Degrees BA (Maths.), MA Univ. Toronto, 1947, 1949; MA, PhD Princeton Univ., 1951, 1953.

Offices and Honours Fellow, Center Advanced Study Behavioral Sciences, 1955; Fellow, Em Soc, 1971; Fellow, World Academy Arts and Sciences, 1975; Hon. Prof. Vienna, 1978; Medal, Collège de France, 1978.

Editorial Duties Assoc. Ed., *Management Science* (Basic Books); Ed. Boards, *RIW*, *Simulation and Games*, *J. Conflict Resolution*, *Eastern Econ. J.*; Advisory Boards, *Internat. J. Game Theory*, *Internat. Stud. Series*.

Principal Fields of Interest 022 Microeconomics; 213 Mathematical Methods.

Publications *Books:* 1. *Strategy and Market Structure* (Wiley, 1959; transls., Spanish Omega, 1962, French, Dunod, 1964); 2. *Games for Society, Business and War* (Elsevier, 1975); 3. *The Aggressive Conservative Investor* (with M.

J. Whitman), (Random House, 1979); 4. *The War Game* (with G. Brewer), (Harvard Univ. Press, 1979); 5. *Market Structure and Behavior* (with R. E. Levitan), (Harvard Univ. Press, 1980); 6. *Game Theory in the Social Sciences*, 2 vols. (MIT Press, 1982, 1984); 7. *The Mathematics of Conflict* (N-H, 1983).

Articles: 1. 'A method for evaluating the distribution of power in a committee system' (with L. S. Shapley), *Amer. Polit. Science Rev.*, 48(3), Sept. 1954; 2. 'Games of economic survival' (with G. Thompson), *Naval Res. Logistics Q.*, 6(2), June 1959; 3. 'Edgeworth market games', in *Contributions to the Theory of Games*, eds. A. W. Tucker and R. D. Luce (Princeton Univ. Press, 1950–9), repr. in *Mathematische Wirtshafts-Theorie* (Verlag Kiepenheuer, 1960); 4. 'Incentives, decentralized control, the assignment of joint costs and internal pricing', *Management Science*, 8(2), April 1962, repr. in *Management Controls: New Directions in Basic Research*, ed. S. Eilon (McGraw-Hill, 1964), and *Readings in Management Decision*, ed. L. R. Amey (Longmans, 1966); 5. 'Pure competition, coalition power and fair division' (with L. S. Shapley), *Int ER*, 10(3), Oct. 1969; 6. 'On market games' (with L. S. Shapley), *JET*, 1(1), June 1969; 7. 'Commodity money, oligopoly, credit and bankruptcy in a general equilibrium model', *WEJ*, 11(1), March 1973; 8. 'Bankruptcy and optimality in a closed trading economy modelled as a noncooperative game' (with P. Dubey), *J Math E*, 6(2), July 1979; 9. 'Efficiency properties of strategic market games: an axiomatic approach' (with P. Dubey and A. Mas-Colell), *JET*, 22(2), April 1980.

Principal Contributions My goal has been to reconcile the development in modern mathematical economics with the classical scope of political economy. My first steps were to reconcile three diverse sets of economic models. They are the Walrasian general equilibrium system, the Cournot-Nash noncooperative equilibrium, primarily applied to models of oligopolistic markets in strategic or extensive form, and the Edgeworth contract curve, core value and other co-operative solutions primarily applied to bargaining. In collaboration with Lloyd Shapley, the models of a Market Game and Strategic Market Game were developed and related to general equilibrium. This work provides the answer to how to embed oligopolistic structures in a closed economic model.

But this is a preliminary to the analysis of two broader sets of problems: (1) money and financial institutions as the neutral network or control system, linking individual economic agents into a macroeconomic system and (2) 'the games within the game' or the political and bureaucratic control structure, which provides the controllers of the control system. If individuals are regarded as finite machines, then as a first approximation the culture-free, institution-free individual maximising models which characterise much of microeconomic theory provide only working models of 'local rationality', which apply to short periods of time and local problems. These are embedded in broader environments encompassing larger scope and lengthier time periods. The reconciliation of local maximising behaviour with the broader sweeps of the economy, polity and society comes through the conventions, traditions, law and other codings provided by institutions, historical, cultural and biological process. The future direction of mathematical institutional political economy lies in the development of a theory of money and financial institutions, stressing the concept of minimal institution as the simplest description of the rules of the game required to guide the process. The next step is to further develop models of limited rationality in a societal context.

SIDGWICK, Henry*

Dates and Birthplace 1838–1900, Skipton, Yorkshire, England.

Posts Held Fellow, Lect., Trinity Coll., Praelector Moral Polit. Philo., Knightsbridge Prof., Univ. Camb., 1859–69, 1859–75, 1875–83, 1883–1900.

Publications *Books:* 1. *The Methods of Ethics* (1874, 1901); 2. *Principles of Political Economy* (1883, 1901); 3. *The*

Scope and Method of Economic Science (1885); 4. *The Elements of Politics* (1891, 1908).

Career Philosopher who taught moral sciences and who was deeply involved in university reform. He is regarded as one of the founder figures of the Cambridge School, despite having written little on economics. His *Principles* . . . is largely based on Mill, but includes several innovations such as a clear recognition of market failure due to externalities in production.

Secondary Literature A. and E. Sidgwick, *Henry Sidgwick: A Memoir* (Macmillan, 1906); B. Corry, 'Sidgwick, Henry', *IESS*, 14.

SIEGEL, Jeremy James

Born 1945, Chicago, IL, USA.
Current Post Assoc. Prof. Fin., Wharton School, Univ. Penn., Philadelphia, PA, USA, 1976–.
Past Post Ass. Prof. Bus. Econ., Grad. School Bus., Univ. Chicago, 1972–6.
Degrees BA (Maths. Econ.) Columbia Univ. 1967; PhD MIT, 1971.
Offices and Honours Phi Beta Kappa, Columbia Coll., 1967; Woodrow Wilson Nat. Fellow, 1967–8; NSF Grad. Fellow, 1967–71; NSF Post-doctoral Fellow, 1971–2.
Editorial Duties Assoc. Ed., *JMCB*, 1984.
Principal Fields of Interest 023 Macroeconomic Theory; 310 Domestic Monetary and Financial Theory and Institutions; 311 Domestic Monetary and Financial Theory and Policy.
Publications *Articles:* 1. 'Risk, interest rates and the forward exchange', *QJE*, 86(2), May 1972; 2. 'Stability of Keynesian and classical macroeconomic systems', *J Mon E*, 2(2), April 1976; 3. 'Indexation, the risk-free asset, and capital market equilibrium' (with J. Warner), *J Fin*, 32(4), Sept. 1977; 4. 'The Gibson paradox, and historical movements in real interest rates' (with R. Shiller), *JPE*, 85(5), Oct. 1977; 5. 'Inflation-induced distortions in government and private saving statistics', *REStat*, 61(2), April 1979; 6. 'Bank regulation and macroeconomic

stability' (with A. Santomero), *AER*, 71(1), March 1981; 7. 'Bank reserves and financial stability', *J Fin*, 36(5), Dec. 1981; 8. 'Monetary stabilization and the informational value of monetary aggregates', *JPE*, 90(1), Feb. 1982; 9 'A general equilibrium money and banking paradigm' (with A. Santomero), *J Fin*, 37(2), May 1982; 10. 'Operational interest rate rules', *AER*, 73(5), Dec. 1983.

Principal Contributions My early work concentrated on the effect of inflation on the macroeconomy, particularly such issues as the stability of an inflationary equilibrium (the subject of my PhD thesis), the efficiency of the inflation tax, and the distortions caused by inflation in national income statistics. During this period I analysed, with Robert Shiller, the Gibson paradox, or the long-term historical correlation of the price level and the nominal rate of interest. Our econometric techniques rejected the Irving Fisher hypothesis, which maintained that movements in long-term interest rates are primarily due to inflationary expectations. My interest in monetary policy led to the development, with Anthony Santomero, of a general equilibrium model in which to analyse banking regulation. This model enabled us to analyse the effects of deposit rate and reserve regulation on the stability of prices and interest rates. In a later paper, I determined that the reserve ratio on transactions deposits which minimises the variability of the price level is below the level set by the Monetary Control Act of 1980.

Presently my research concentrates on the nature of optimal monetary policy and the informational value of nominal monetary aggregates. In response to the prevailing beliefs that an optimal stabilising policy requires too much knowledge about the structure of the economy, I developed a simple criterion by which the monetary authority can control money so as to minimise the variance of unanticipated price level and output changes. I also show that the nominal money supply may reveal sufficient information so that monetary policy has no influence on the dispersion of economic agents' estimates of the price level. My most recent research demonstrates that the correlation between interest-rate movements and money-supply announcements may not be caused by monetary policy but instead reflects the correlation of both variables with real output.

SIEGFRIED, John J.

Born 1945, Allentown, PA, USA.

Current Post Prof. Econ., Vanderbilt Univ., Nashville, TN, USA, 1981–.

Past Posts Instr., Penn. State Univ., 1968–9; Lect., Univ. Wisconsin Extension, 1970–2; Ass. Prof., Assoc. Prof., Vanderbilt Univ., 1972–5, 1975–81; Econ., Fed. Trade Commission, Washington, DC, 1976–6; Sr. Staff Econ., US President's Council Econ. Advisers, Washington, DC, 1976–7.

Degrees BS Rensselaer Polytechnic Inst., NY, 1967; MA Penn. State Univ., 1968; PhD Univ. Wisconsin, 1972.

Offices and Honours Phi Kappa Phi; Member, Exec. Comm, SEA, 1983–5.

Editorial Duties Ed. Board, *Industrial Organization Rev.*, 1976–80.

Principal Fields of Interest 600 Industrial Organisation; 012 Teaching of Economics.

Publications *Books:* 1. *Recent Advances in Economics*, co-ed. (with R. Fels), (Richard D. Irwin, 1974); 2. *Economic Analysis and Antitrust Law*, co-ed. (with T. Calvani), (Little, Brown 1979); 3. *The Economics of Crime: An Anthology of Recent Work*, co-ed. (with L. Andreano), (Schenkman Publ., 1980); 4. *The Economics of Firm Size, Market Structure and Social Performance*, ed. (Fed. Trade Commission, 1980); 5. *Research on Teaching College Economics: Selected Readings*, co-ed. (with R. Fels), (Joint Council Econ. Educ., 192).

Articles: 1. 'The welfare cost of monopoly: and interindustry analysis' (with T. K. Tiemann), *EI*, 12(2), June 1974; 2. 'The determinants of antitrust activity', *J Law E*, 18(2), Oct. 1975; 3. 'In defense of the average concentration ratio', *JPE*, 83(6), Dec. 1975; 4. 'Is teaching a good way to learn?: an evaluation of the benefits and costs to

undergraduate student proctors in a PSI Course', *SEJ*, 43(3), Jan. 1977; 5. 'Economic power and political influence: the impact of industry structure on public policy' (with L. M. Salamon), *Amer. Polit. Science Rev.* 71(3), Sept. 1977; 6. 'Research on teaching college economics: a survey' (with R. Fels), *JEL*, 16(3), Sept. 1979; 7. 'The incidence of price changes in the U.S. economy' (with K. Maddox McElroy and G. H. Sweeney), *REStat*, 64(2), May 1982; 8. 'The economics curriculum in the U.S.: 1980' (with J. T. Wilkinson), *AER*, 72(2), May 1982; 9. 'The economic cost of suboptimal manufacturing capacity in the U.S.' (with K. D. Evans and G. H. Sweeney), *J Bus*, 56(1), Jan. 1983; 10 'A profile of students majoring in economics' (with J. Raymond), *AER*, 74(2), May 1984.

Principal Contributions Early research was on the rate of return to the PhD in economics, publishing of economics papers, and its influence on academic salaries. I then developed a methodology for evaluating hypotheses relating corporate political power to firm and market characteristics, using the effectiveness of corporations in lowering tax rates to measure political power. Subsequent research related firm size and market structure to the income redistribution effects of monopoly and corporate contributions to charity, culminating in an edited volume on several non-efficiency effects of firm size and market structure. Using the US input–output matrix and the BLS Consumer Expenditure Survey, I developed estimates of the effect of price changes on different income groups, considering their indirect purchases as well as their direct purchases of various commodities. I have applied microeconomic principles and empirical measurement to the welfare cost due to monopoly, the determinants of antitrust activity, the market for lawyers, professional teams sports, suboptimal manufacturing capacity, and estimating the demand for minor-league baseball and coffee.

Throughout my career I worked in a second major line of research: economics education. This research includes studies of self-paced instruction learning by teaching, differences between men and women in learning economics, the methodology for empirical studies of the effectiveness of experimental teaching methods, the economics curriculum in the US, the structure of the introductory economics course, and a profile of senior economics majors and what influences their understanding of economics. The economics education work led to a survey of the literature on research on teaching college economics, and an edited collection of the better research on this subject.

SILBERBERG, Eugene

Born 1940, New York City, NY, USA.
Current Post Prof. Econ., Univ. Washington, Seattle, WA, USA, 1979–.
Past Posts Ass. Prof. Bus., State Univ. NY, Binghamton, 1964–7; Ass. Prof., Assoc. Prof. Econ., Univ. Washington, 1967–73, 1973–9.
Degrees BS (Maths. and Physics) City Coll. NY, 1960; PhD Purdue Univ., IN, 1964.
Principal Fields of Interest 022 Microeconomic Theory; 213 Mathematical Methods and Models; 025 Social Choice; Political Economy.
Publications *Books:* 1. *The Structure of Economics* (McGraw-Hill, 1978).
Articles: 1.'Duality and the many consumer's surpluses', *AER*, 62(5), Dec. 1972; 2. 'Is the act of voting rational?' (with Y. Barzel), *Public Choice*, 13, Autumn 1973; 3. 'A revision of comparative statics methodology in economics, or how to do comparative statics on the back of an envelope', *JET*, 7(2), Feb. 1974; 4. 'The theory of the firm in "long-run" equilibrium', *AER*, 64(4), Sept. 1974; 5. 'Shipping the good apples out: the Alchian and Allen substitution theorem reconsidered' (with T. Borcherding), *JPE*, 86(1), Feb. 1978.
Principal Contributions My early work concentrated in two areas. I developed the analysis of consumer's surplus as a line integral and showed that consumer's surplus was a meaningful, i.e. operational, concept only if

the associated line integral was path-independent. Functions identifying monetary evaluations of changes in utility are non-existent except under special conditions. Meaningful consumer's surplus measures exist only in terms of a consumer's willingness to pay (or be paid) to change the constraints in specified ways. These measures are all changes in the expenditure function.

My other work concentrated on comparative statics methodology. My article in *JET*, expanded in my text, *The Structure of Economics*, generalised the methods first presented by Samuelson. I showed that the envelope theorems and all comparative statics theorems (including the LeChatelier effects) could easily be derived by maximising the difference between the direct and indirect objective functions with respect to both the choice variables and the parameters. My current research deals with incorporating the rationality postulate into the characteristics approach to consumer theory to develop new implications of changes in incomes, and propositions concerning the formation of rules of behaviour.

SILBERTSON, Zangwill Aubrey

Born 1922, London, England.
Current Post Prof. Econ., Imperial Coll. Science and Technology, Univ. London, London, England, 1978–.
Past Posts Econ., Courtaulds Ltd., 1946–50; Lect. Econ., Univ. Camb., 1951–71; Res. Fellow, St Catharine's Coll., St John's Coll. Camb., 1950–3, 1958–71; Fellow, Nuffield Coll. Oxford, 1971–8; Vis. Prof., Univ. Queensland, 1977, Univ. South Sewanee, TN, USA, 1984.
Degrees BA, MA Univ. Camb., 1942, 1950; MA Univ. Oxford, 1971.
Offices and Honours Rockefeller Foundation Fellow, 1959–60; Member, UK Monopolies Commission, 1965–8; Board Member, British Steel Corp., 1967–76; Member, Dept. Comm. Patent System UK Banks Comm., 1967–70; Econ. Comm. UK SSRC, 1969–73; Econ. Adviser, Confed. British Industry, 1972–4; Member, UK

Royal Comm. Press, 1974–77; Adviser, Bank England, 1979–81; Secretary-Gen., RES, 1979–.

Editorial Duties Ed. Board, *J Ind E*, 1980–.

Principal Fields of Interest 610 Industrial Organisation and Public Policy; 620 Economics of Technological Change; 440 International Investment and Foreign Aid.

Publications *Books:* 1. *Education and Training for Industrial Management* (Management Publ., 1955); 2. *The Motor Industry* (with G. Maxcy), (A&U, 1959); 3. *Economies of Large-Scale Production in British Industry* (with C. Pratten and R. M. Dean), (CUP, 1965); 4. *The Patent System-Administration* (with K. H. Boehm), (CUP, 1967); 5. *Economic Impact of the Patent System* (with C. T. Taylor), (CUP, 1973); 6. *The Steel Industry* (with A. Cockerill), (CUP, 1974); 7. *Microeconomic Efficiency and Macroeconomic Performance* (with D. Shepherd and J. Turk), (Philip Allan, 1983); 8. *British Overseas Investment* (with D. Shepherd and R. Strange), (British Overseas Investment, 1984); 9. *Industrial Policy and International Trade*, ed. with A. M. Schaefer (British Overseas Investment, 1984).

Articles: 1. 'Monopoly investigation and the rate of return on capital employed' (with D. Solomons), *EJ*, 62, Dec. 1952; 2. 'Hire purchase controls and the demand for cars', *EJ*, 73, March 1963; 3. 'Size of plant, size of enterprise and concentration in British manufacturing industry 1935–58', (with A. Armstrong), *JRSS*, 128, pt.3, 1965; 4. 'International comparisons of labour productivity in the automobile industry 1950–65' (with C. Pratten), *BOIS*, 29, Nov. 1967; 5. 'Price behaviour of firms', *EJ*, 80, Sept. 1970; 6. 'Economies of scale in theory and practice', *EJ*, 83, March 1972; 7. 'Alternative managerial objectives' (with G. M. Heal), *OEP*, 24(2), July 1972; 8. 'The ownership and control of industry' (with S. Nyman), *OEP*, 30(1), March 1978; 9. 'Factors affecting the growth of firms-theory and practice,' in *Microeconomic Analysis*, eds. D. Currie, D. Peel and W. Peters (Croom Helm, 1981); 10. 'Some aspects of the techno-

logical balance of payments' (with M. Ledic), *Manchester Stat. Soc.*, April 1983.

Principal Contributions My work in Courtaulds as an economist at the start of my career aroused my interest in industrial economics. When I was appointed a lecturer at Cambridge, I was asked to lecture on specific industries, and my book on the motor industry with George Maxcy grew out of this. Other work on specific industries followed, especially on the steel industry, once I had been appointed a part-time Board member of the British Steel Corporation. At the same time I was interested in more general questions of industrial analysis and policy and was much involved in the work at Cambridge on measuring economies of scale. My next major field of interest was innovation and the patent system, culminating in my 1973 book with Christopher Taylor.

When I moved to Oxford in 1971 I became interested in the growth of firms and published a number of articles in that field. At Imperial College I have worked on British overseas investment, among other areas, and a book on this subject has been completed. I have also returned to my earlier interest in innovation, including now its international aspects. I would say that my major work has been on the motor industry, on economies of scale, and on innovation. I have worked a good deal in collaboration, usually with younger scholars, with the division of work between us varying from case to case.

SIMON, Herbert Alexander

Born 1916, Milwaukee, WI, USA.

Current Post Richard King Mellon Univ. Prof. Computer Science and Psychology, Carnegie-Mellon Univ., Pittsburgh, PA, USA, 1955–.

Past Posts Staff Member, Internat. City Managers' Assoc., Chicago, 1938–9; Dir., Admin. Measurement Stud., Bureau Public Admin., Univ. Cal. Berkeley, 1939–42; Ass. Prof. Polit. and Social Science, Illinois Inst. Technology, 1942–7; Cons., Rand Corp.,

1960–1; Prof., Carnegie Inst. Technology, 1949–55.

Degrees BA, PhD Univ. Chicago, 1936, 1943; Hon. DSc Case Inst. Technology, 1963, Univs., Yale, 1963, Marquette, Canada, 1981, Columbia, 1983, Gustavus Adolphus, Sweden, 1984; LLD Univs. Chicago, 1964, McGill, 1970, Michigan, 1978, Pittsburgh, 1979; Fil. Dr Univ. Lund, Sweden, 1968; Dr Econ. Science Univ. Erasmus, Rotterdam, 1973; DPhil Univ. Paul Valery, Montpellier, 1984.

Offices and Honours Disting. Fellow, AEA, 1976; Disting. Scientific Contrib. Award, Amer. Psychol. Assoc., 1969; Turing Award, Assoc. Computing Machinery; James Madison Award, Amer. Polit. Science Assoc.; Procter Prize, Sigma Xi; Nobel Prize in Econ., 1978.

Editorial Duties Assoc. Ed., *Econ. Behav. & Organisation*; Advisory Board, *Managerial and Decision Econ.*; sometime Assoc. Ed., *Em.*

Principal Fields of Interest 020 General Economic Theory; 210 Econometric Methods and Models; 510 Administration.

Publications *Books:* 1. *Administrative Behavior* (Macmillan, 1947, 1976); 2. *Models of Man* (Wiley, 1956; 3. *Organizations* (with J. G. March), (Wiley, 1958); 4. *New Science of Management Decision* (Prentice-Hall, 1960, 1977); 5. *The Sciences of the Artificial* (MIT Press, 1968, 1981); 6. *Human Problem Solving* (with A. Newell), (Prentice-Hall, 1972); 7. *Skew Distributions and Business Firm Sizes* (with Y. Ijiri), (N-H, 1976); 8. *Models of Discovery* (Reidel, 1977); 9. *Models of Thought* (Yale Univ. Press, 1979); 10. *Models of Bounded Rationality* (MIT Press, 2 vols, 1982).

Principal Contributions My principal aim has been to understand human rationality. Troubled by the inapplicability of classical optimisation theory to the realities of public decision-making, I was early led to a theory of choice based on the thesis that human rationality is bounded: that because of limitations of knowledge and processing capacity, people satisfice. Set forth in *Administrative Behavior* and in papers on rational choice, organisational equil-

ibrium, and the employment contract (Books 9 and 10 above), the theory led me into empirical studies of governmental and business decision-making that supported it. About 1955, Allen Newell and I, using the then novel computer and the list-processing programming languages we invented with J. C. Shaw, discovered how to program computers to simulate human problem solving, using heuristic search based on bounded rationality. This research provided the foundation for artificial intelligence and for the 'information processing revolution' in cognitive psychology, and enabled me subsequently to make a number of contributions to human cognition, artificial intelligence and management science. During the past ten years I have sought to explore the implications of this research for economics. My enjoyment of applied mathematics has led me into other problems in economics and philosophy of science. The products include an analysis of the incidence of the property tax, a theorem on the existence of solutions of input-output matrices, a theorem on the dynamics of nearly-decomposable systems, a theorem on certainty equivalence, linear decision rules for production planning, a theory of business firm size distributions, and explorations of causality and its relations with identifiability and structural equations. In philosophy, I have clarified the notions of definability of terms and falsifiability of theories. My chief current preoccupation, bridging many interests, is with a computer-modelled theory of scientific discovery — possibly autobiographical.

Secondary Literature A. K. Ando and W. J. Baumol, 'Herbert Simon's contributions to economics', *Scand JE*, 80(1), Jan. 1979, repr. in *Contemporary Economists in Perspective*, eds. H. W. Spiegel and W. J. Samuels (JAI Press, 1984).

SIMONS, Henry Calvert*

Dates and Birthplace 1899–1946, Virden, ILL, USA.

Posts Held Prof., Univ. Iowa, 1920–7, Univ. Chicago, 1927–46.

Degree BA Univ. Michigan, 1920.

Publications *Books:* 1. *Personal Income Taxation* (1938); 2. *Economic Policy for a Free Society* (1948); 3. *Federal Tax Reform* (1950).

Articles: 1. 'Some reflections on syndicalism', *JPE*, 52, March 1944.

Career One of the founders of the Chicago School, he set out to redefine the relations between government and a *laissez faire* economy in the context of the considerable government intervention practised during the 1930s depression. He argued that government should provide a framework for the operation of the economy by creating appropriate monetary and competitive conditions; government was not to support monopolies and was to limit the growth of trade union power. His ideas on taxation were most fully worked out and have had a long-term influence on the federal income tax system.

Secondary Literature H. Stein, 'Simons, Henry C.', *IESS*, 14; J. R. Davies, *The New Economics and the Old Economists* (Iowa State Univ. Press, 1971).

SIMS, Christopher Albert

Born 1942, Washington, DC, USA.

Current Post Prof. Econ., Univ. Minnesota, Minneapolis, MN, USA, 1975–.

Past Posts Ass. Prof. Econ., Harvard Univ., 1967–70; Res. Fellow, NBER, 1970–1; Ass. Prof. Econ., Univ. Minnesota, 1970–4; Vis. Prof. Econ., Yale Univ., 1974; MIT, 1979–80.

Degrees BA (Maths.), PhD Harvard Univ., 1963, 1968.

Offices and Honours Fellow, Council Em Soc., 1975, 1979–80.

Editorial Duties Co-ed., *Em*, 1977–81; Amer. Em Ed., *REStud*, 1973–5.

Principal Fields of Interest 023 Macroeconomic Thoery; 130 Economic Fluctuations; 210 Econometrics.

Publications *Books:* 1. *New Methods in Business Cycle Research*, ed. (Fed. Reserve Bank Minneapolis, 1977).

Articles: 1. 'Discrete approximations in continuous time distributed lags in econometrics', *Em*, 39(3), May 1971; 2. 'Distributed lag estimation when the parameter space is explicitly infinite dimensional', *Annals Math. Stats.*, 42(5), 1971; 3. 'Money, income and causality', *AER*, 62(4), Sept. 1972; 4. 'Seasonality in regression', *JASA*, 69(3), Sept. 1974; 5. 'Exogeneity and causal orderings in macroeconomic models', in *New Methods in Business Cycle Research*, *op. cit.*; 6. 'Business cycle modelling without pretending to have too much a priori economic theory', in *New Methods in Business Cycle Research*, *op. cit.*; 7. 'Macroeconomics and reality', *Em*, 48(1), Jan. 1980; 8. 'Policy analysis with econometric models', *Brookings Papers Econ. Acitivity*, 1, 1982; 9. 'Is there a monetary business cycle?', *AER*, 72(2), May 1983.

Principal Contributions I have aimed since the start of my research career at making econometric analysis of data more practically useful by freeing it from conventional assumptions, known to be untrue, whose effects must be allowed for by judgemental adjustment of results. My aim has not been iconoclastic, however, and usually I have proceeded in the spirit of clarifying, modifying, and formalising the methods used by the best people actually analysing data. In early papers I wrote on the roles of the assumptions that time is discrete and that an exact finite-dimensional 'time' model exists in distributed lag models. My work on the relation of exogeneity to Granger-caused priority was motivated by the observation that regression models with right-hand-side variables taken as exogenous were pervasive in economics, and that economists regularly justified the choice of right-hand-side variable by vague appeals to notions of causal priority. It turned out that the notion of causal priority required was Granger's.

In recent years I have been aiming at building a multiple time series methodology as useful as conventional simultaneous equations modelling for macroeconomics, yet with a formal probability model which can be taken seriously. While the components of the methodology I have been using are not in themselves new, the style — elaborate modelling of the predicitive structure of the data preceding a cautious and sometimes informal application of *a priori* knowledge to interpret the results — is different from much previous econometric work. The methodology is increasingly being applied for forecasting and policy analysis, has provided 'stylised facts' as grist for the mill of 'pure theory' and is undergoing rapid development by other economists as well as myself. It does make heavy demands on its user's tolerance for ambiguity, however, and this may preclude its becoming standard.

SINGER, Hans Wolfgang

Born 1910, Elberfeld (now Wuppertal), Rhineland, Germany.

Current Post Retired, 1985–.

Past Posts Member, Pilgrim Trust, 1936–8; Ass. Lect. Econ., Manchester Univ., 1938–45; Econ. Res. Officer, UK Ministry Town and Country Planning, 1945–6; Lect. Polit. Econ., Glasgow Univ., 1946–7; Dir., UN Secretariat, 1947–69; Vis. Prof., New School Social Res., NY, 1947–69; Vis. Prof., William Coll., USA, 1963–4; Prof. Univ. Sussex, 1969–75; Emeritus Prof., Professorial Fellow, Inst. Devlp. Stud., Univ. Sussex, Brighton, England, 1969, 1975–85.

Degrees Econ. Dipolma Univ. Bonn, 1931; PhD Univ. Camb., 1936.

Offices and Honours Francis Wood Memorial Prize, 1940; Fellow, Inst. Social Stud., The Hague; Pres., NY Chapter, Soc. Internat. Devlp., 1966–9; Pres., UK Chapter, Soc. Internat. Devlp., 1980–3.

Editorial Duties Ed. Board, *Canadian J. Devlp. Stud.*, *J. Devlp. Areas*, *Pakistan J. Appl. Econ.*; Ed. *Industry and Development* (UNIDO).

Principal Fields of Interest 110 Economic Growth; Development and Planning Theory and Policy; 420 Trade Relations; Commerical Policy; International Economic Integration; 440 International Investment and Foreign Aid.

Publications *Books:* 1. *Men without Work: A Report to the Pilgrim Trust* (with A. D. K. Owen and W. Oakeshott), (CUP, 1937); 2. *Unemployment and the Unemployed* (King & Son, 1940); 3. *Can We Afford Beveridge?* (Fabian Soc., 1943); 4. *The Role of the*

Economist as Official Adviser (with W. A. Johr), (A&U, 1955; transl., German, 1956); 5. *Perspectives in Economic Development* (with S. Schiavo-Campo), (Houghton Mifflin, 1970); 6. *Employment, Incomes and Equality: A Strategy for Increasing Productive Employment in Kenya* (with R. Jolly), (ILO, 1972); 7. *Technologies for Basic Needs* (ILO, 1977, 1983); 8. *Rich and Poor Countries* (with J. Ansari), (A&U, 1977, 1981; transls., Portuguese, Ed Piramide, 1982, Japanese, 1976); 9. *The International Economy and Industrial Development: Trade and Investment in the Third World* (with J. Ansari and R. H. Ballance), (Wheatsheaf Books, 1982).

Articles: 1. 'Some notes on duopoly and spatial competition' (with A. P. Lerner), *JPE*, 45, April 1937; 2. 'An index of urban land rents and house rents in England and Wales, 1845–1913', *Em*, 9, July–Oct. 1942; 3. 'Gains and losses from trade and investment in under-developed countries', *AER*, 40(2), May 1950; 4. 'Mechanics of economic development', *Indian Econ. Rev.*, Aug. 1952, Feb. 1953; 5. 'Dualism revisited: a new approach to the problems of the dual society in developing countries, *J Devlp. Stud.*, 7(1), Oct. 1969; 6. 'Unemployment in an African setting: lessons of the employment mission to Kenya' (with R. Jolly), *Int Lab Rev*, 25(2), Feb. 1973; 7. 'The distribution of gains from trade and investment — revisited', *J Devlp. Stud.*, 11(4), July 1975; 8. 'Food aid: its potential disincentives to agriculture' (with P. J. Isenman), *Devlp. Digest*, 15(2), April 1977; 9. 'Introduction', 'Policy implications of the Lima target', *Industry and Development*, 3 (Third Gen. Conf. UNIDO, 1979); 10. 'The role of human capital in development', *Pakistan J. Appl. Econ.*, 2(1), 1983.

Principal Contributions Before the war my chief interests and contributions centred upon unemployment problems and living conditions among the unemployed in prewar Britain. During the war, I studied war economics including the German war economy (a series of 13 articles in the *Economic Journal* throughout the war) and problems of wartime planning in the UK.

On joining the UN in 1947 my interest turned to the problems and developing countries, where it has remained since. I started off with studies on terms of trade of developing countries (at that time almost exclusively exporters of primary commodities) and as a result of historical studies and economic analysis developed a hypothesis that there is a general tendency for terms of trade to move against developing countries (the Prebisch-Singer thesis). This I subsequently extended to analysis of the more generally inferior position or handicaps of developing countries in the global economic system, moving beyond terms of trade and primary commodities to questions of technology, negotiating power and international finance.

I also developed an early interest in te role of human resources in development and specifically in the problems of children. This has been maintained to the present day, recently culminating a study (jointly with some others) on the impact of the world recession on the condition of children (special issue of *World Development*, March 1984). Another major long-term interest has been in relation to aid — directly derived from trade pessimism due to deteriorating terms of trade — and specifically in food aid. This dates back to my role as Chairman of the group of experts setting up the UN World Food Programme. This interest has continued and led to a number of books, articles, reports and studies. Based on my post as Director of the Economic Division of UNIDO, I also studied problems of industrialisation and industrialisation policies, as evidence by my 1982 book (jointly with Ansari and Ballance).

SISMONDI, Jean Charles Leonard Simonde De*

Dates and Birthplace 1773–1842, Geneva, Switzerland.

Posts Held Bank clerk, farmer and professional writer.

Publications *Books:* 1. *Tableau de l'agriculture toscane* (1801); 2. *De la richesse commerciale*, 2 vols (1803); 3. *Historie des républiques italiennes du moyen age*, 16 vols (1809–18); 4. *Nouveaux principes d'économie politique*, 2 vols (1819, 1827, 1953); 5. *Histoire des français*, 31 vols (1821–44); 6. *Political Economy*, ed. M. Mignot (1847).

Articles: 1. 'Two papers on demand', *Revue Encyclopédique*, 1824, repr. in *Internat. Econ. Papers*, 7, eds. A. T. Peacock, *et al.* (Macmillan, 1957).

Career Historian whose economic ideas passed through different phases. The acceptance of free-trade principles in *De la richesse commerciale* was abandoned in favour of a critical posture towards free trade and industrialisation. *Nouveaux principes ...* attacked wealth accumulation both as an end in itself, and for its detrimental effect on the poor. His critique was noticed by Malthus, Ricardo and J. S. Mill, but despite his favourable attitude towards the poor, he was attacked by Marx, Lenin and other socialists.

Secondary Literature G. Sotiroff, 'Simonde de Sismondi, J. C. L.', *IESS*, 14; T. Sowell, 'Sismondi: A Neglected Pioneer', *HOPE*, 4(1), Spring 1972.

SLICHTER, Sumner Huber*

Dates and Birthplace 1892–1959, Madison, WI, USA.

Posts Held Instr., Ass. Prof., Prof., Cornell Univ., 1920–30; Prof., Harvard Univ., 1930–59.

Degrees BA, MA Univ. Wisconsin, 1913, 1914; PhD Univ. Chicago, 1918.

Offices Pres., AEA, 1941; Pres., IRRA, 1949.

Publications *Books:* 1. *The Turnover of Factory Labor* (1919); 2. *Modern Economic Society* (1931); 3. *Union Policies and Industrial Management* (1941); 4. *The Challenge of Industrial Relations* (1947); 5. *The American Economy: Its Problems and Prospects* (1948); 6. *The Impact of Collective Bargaining on Management* (1960); 7. *Potentials of the American Economy: Selected Essays*, ed. J. T. Dunlop (1961).

Career Economic commentator, whose chief concern was with labour relations on which he did extensive field research. His faith in the potential for expansion of the American economy was considerable. He was deeply suspicious of trade unions, and argued that that ability of unions to influence the state of the economy should be restricted by legislation. He wrote extensively for newspapers and magazines, spoke on innumerable public platforms, and did much to popularise economic thinking on labour problems.

Secondary Literature J. T. Dunlop, 'Sumner Huber Slichter', in S. H. Slichter, *Potentials of the American Economy* (Harvard Univ. Press, 1961).

SLUTSKY, Eugen*

Dates and Birthplace 1880–1948, Yaroslavl, Russia.

Posts Held Teacher Law, Technical Coll., 1911–18; Prof. Polit. Econ., Kiev Inst. Commerce, 1918–26; Inst. Bus. Cycles, Moscow, 1926–31; Central Inst. Meteorology, 1931–4; Math. Inst., Academy of Sciences, 1934–48.

Degrees Grad. Law, Polit. Econ. Univ. Kiev, 1911, 1918.

Publications *Books:* 1. *Izbrannye Trudy: Teoriia Veroiatnostei, Matematicheskaia Statistika* (1960).

Articles: 1. 'On the criterion of goodness of fit of the regression lines and on the best method of fitting them to the data', *JRSS*, 77, 1913; 2. 'On the theory of the budget of the consumer', *Giornale degli Economisti*, 1915, repr. in *Readings in Price Theory*, eds. K. E. Boulding and G. J. Stigler (1953); 3. 'The summation of random causes as the source of cyclic processes', *Em*, 5, April 1937.

Career Mathematician and economist whose main achievement was in consumer behaviour. 'Slutsky's relation' deals with the relationship of the substitution effect and the income effect due to changes in the price of a commodity. Later work was on mathematical statistics and probability theory. His contribution to the theory of stochastic processes reflects on the question of the causation of fluctuations or cycles in economic and other phenomena.

Secondary Literature R. D. G. Allen, 'The work of Eugen Slutsky', *Em*, 18, July 1950; A. A. Koniis, 'Slutsky, Eugen', *IESS*, 14.

SMART, William*

Dates and Birthplace 1853–1915, Renfrewshire, Scotland.

Posts Held Businessman, Lect., Univ. Dundee, 1866–7, Univ. Glasgow, 1886–96; Prof., Univ. Glasgow, 1896–1915.

Degrees MA Univ. Glasgow.

Offices and Honours Pres., Section F BAAS, 1904; Member, UK Poor Laws Commission, 1905–9.

Publications *Books:* 1. *An Introduction to the Theory of Value* (1891, 1926); 2. *Studies in Economics* (1895); 3. *The Distribution of Income* (1899); 4. *Taxation of Land Values and the Single Tax* (1900); 5. *The Return to Protection* (1904); 6. *Economic Annals of the Nineteenth Century*, 2 vols (1910–17).

Career Translator of the Austrian economists and largely responsible for making their works known in Britain. His own books exhibit a balance between his practical experience of the business world and his enthusiasm for marginal utility theory.

Secondary Literature T. Jones, 'Smart, William', *ESS*, 14.

SMITH, Adam*

Dates and Birthplace 1723–90, Kirkcaldy, Scotland.

Posts Held Prof. Logic, Prof. Moral Philo., Univ. Glasgow, 1751–2, 1752–63; Tutor to Duke of Buccleuch, 1764–6; Adviser to Charles Townshend, 1766–7; Commissioner of Customs for Scotland, 1778–90.

Degrees MA Univ. Glasgow, 1740.

Publications *Books:* 1. *The Theory of Moral Sentiments* (1759); 2. *An Inquiry into the Nature and Causes of the Wealth of Nations* (1776); 3. *Works and Correspondence of Adam Smith*, various eds, 6 vols (OUP, 1976–81).

Career Moral philosopher, often regarded as the founder of modern political economy. Though he wrote and lectured on a wide range of subjects, *Moral Sentiments* and the *Wealth of Nations* were his only full-length treatises, whose underlying philosophy and methodology seems to have been established early in his life, and both, though superficially inconsistent, reflect a single view of the world. In *Moral Sentiments* he explored the ethical conduct of men under the influence of social pressures; the *Wealth of Nations* was concerned with economic processes resulting from the operation of self-interest, and was used to illustrate the nature of economic relations in a market society, including the economic policies appropriate to such an order. Its remarkable success meant that it effectively defined the scope and content of political economy for later generations and was widely cited as an authority in favour of free market, *laissez faire* economics, but is much more than the unsubtle apologia for private enterprise that it has been made to seem, allowing as it does an important regulating function to government.

Secondary Literature J. Viner, 'Smith, Adam', *IESS*, 14; S. Hollander, *The Economics of Adam Smith* (Univ. Toronto Press, 1973); J. R. Lundgren, *The Social Philosophy of Adam Smith* (Martinus Nijhoff, 1974); *Essays on Adam Smith*, eds., A. S. Skinner and T. Wilson (OUP, 1976); D. Winch, *Adam Smith's Politics* (CUP, 1978); A. S. Skinner, *A System of Social Science* (OUP, 1979); J. C. Wood, ed., *Adam Smith: Critical Assessments*, 4 vols (Croom Helm, 1984).

SMITH, James P.

Born 1943, New York City, NY, USA.
Current Post Sr. Econ., Rand Corp., Santa Monica, CA, USA, 1974–.
Past Posts Ass. Prof., Grad. Center, City Univ. NY, 1971–4; Res. Assoc., NBER, 1972–4; Vis. Scholar, LSE, 1980.
Degrees BA Fordham Univ., MA, 1965; PhD Univ. Chicago, 1972.
Offices and Honours Phi Beta Kappa.
Editorial Duties Ed. Board, *AER*, 1982–3; Assoc. Ed., *EI*, 1978–80.
Principal Fields of Interest 824 Labour Market Studies, Wages and Employment; 850 Human Capital; 121 Economic Studies of Developing Countries.
Publications *Books:* 1. *Female Labor Supply: Theory and Estimation* (Princeton Univ. Press, 1980).

Articles: 1. 'On the labor supply effects of age-related income maintenance programs', *JHR*, 18(1), Winter 1975; 2. 'Family labor supply over the life cycle', *Explor. Econ. Res.*, 4(2), Spring 1977; 3. 'Black-white male wage rations: 1960–1970', *AER*, 67(3), June 1977; 4. 'Assets, savings and labor supply', *EI*, 6(4), Oct. 1977; 5. 'The improving economic status of black Americans', *AER*, 68(2), May 1978; 6. 'Race differences in earnings: a survey and new evidence', in *Issues in Urban Economics*, 2, eds. P. Mieszkowski and M. Strasszheim (JAI Press, 1979); 7. 'Inequality: race differences in the distribution of earnings', *Int ER*, 29(2), June 1979; 8. 'The distribution of family earnings', *JPE*, 87(5), Oct. 1979; 9. 'Asset accumulation and family size', *Demography*, 17(3), Aug. 1980; 10. 'Race and human capital', *AER*, 74(4), Sept. 1984.

Principal Contributions Early work concentrated on life-cycle models of decision-making, including decisions of families to work, invest and consume. From this research, I developed an interest in estimation issues concerning female labour supply, which would eventually culminate in a book of essays dealing with the changing economic position of blacks and women in America. While the early research concentrated on 1960 trends, more recently my interest has moved to a more historical approach spanning periods of over 100 years. My most recent research interest has centred on labour markets in developing countries, and in particular the transformation of these markets as the development process proceeds.

SMITH, V. Kerry

Born 1945, Jersey City, NJ, USA.
Current Post Centennial Prof. Econ., Vanderbilt Univ., Nashville, TN, USA, 1983–.
Past Posts Ass. Prof. Assoc. Prof. Stats., Bowling Green State Univ., OH, 1969–71, 1971–2; Res. Assoc., Fellow, Sr. Fellow, Resources for the Future, Washington, DC, 1971–3, 1976–7, 1977–9; Assoc. Prof., Prof. Econ., State Univ. NY Binghamton,

1973–5, 1975–8; Prof. Econ., Univ. N. Carolina, 1979–83.

Degrees BA, PhD Rutgers Univ., 1966, 1970.

Offices and Honours Phi Beta Kappa; Guggenheim Foundation Fellow, 1976–7; Exec Comm., SEA, 1981–3; Vice-Pres., Pres., Assoc. Environmental and Resource Econ., 1979–80, 1984–.

Editorial Duties Ed. Board, *Land Econ.*, 1977–, *QREB*, 1981–; Ed., *Advances Appl. Micro-Econ.*, 1981–.

Principal Fields of Interest 721 Natural Resources; 211 Econometric and Statistical Methods and Models; 613 Public Utilities and Costs of Government Regulation.

Publications *Books:* 1. *Monte Carlo Methods: Their Role for Econometrics* (D. C. Heath, 1973); 2. *Technical Change, Relative Prices and Environmental Resource Evaluation* (JHUP, 1974); 3. *The Costs of Congestion: An Econometric Analysis of Wilderness Recreation* (with C. J. Cicchetti), (Ballinger, 1976); 4. *Structure and Properties of a Wilderness Travel Simulator: An Application to the Spanish Peaks Area* (with J. V. Krutilla), (JHUP, 1976); 5. *The Economic Consequences of Air Pollution* (Ballinger, 1976); 6. *Scarcity and Growth Reconsidered* (JHUP, 1979); 7. *Explorations in Natural Resource Economics*, co-ed. (with J. V. Krutilla), (JHUP, 1982); 8. *Environmental Policy Under Reagan's Executive Order: The Role of Benefit-Cost Analysis*, ed. (Univ. N. Carolina Press, 1984).

Articles: 1. 'A comparison of maximum likelihood versus blue estimators' (with T. W. Hall), *REStat*, 54(2), May 1972; 2. 'The small-sample properties of selected econometric estimators in the context of alternative macromodels', *Internat. Stat. Rev.*, 40, 1972; 3. 'Inter-temporal production externalities, technical change and public expenditure analysis', *JEEM*, 1, Aug. 1974; 4. 'The economic value of statute reform: the case of liberalized abortion' (with T. A. Deyak), *JPE*, 84(1), Feb. 1976; 5. 'An econometric evaluation of a generalized consumer surplus measure: the mineral king controversy' (with C. J. Cicchetti and A. C. Fisher), *Em*, 44(6), Nov. 1976; 6. 'Resource and

environmental constraints to growth' (with J. V. Krutilla), *Amer. J. Agric. Econ.*, 61(3), Aug. 1979; 7. 'The evaluation of natural resource adequacy: elusive quest or frontier of economic analysis?', *Land Econ.*, 56, Aug. 1980; 8. 'Measuring factor substitution with neoclassical models: an experimental evaluation (with R. J. Kopp), *Bell JE*, 11(2), Autumn 1980; 9. 'Option value: a conceptual overview', *SEJ*, 49(3), Jan. 1983; 10. 'The measurement of nonneutral technological change' (with R. J. Kopp), *Int ER*, 25(3), Oct. 1984.

Principal Contributions Early work investigated the small sample properties of simultaneous equation estimators using economically relevant models for Monte Carlo experiments. Initial research in resource and environmental economic develops three areas: (1) treatment of changes in relative prices in benefit-cost analyses involving unique natural environments; (2) modelling the demand for and supply of wilderness recreation with alternative levels of congestion; and (3) estimating the role of substitute facilities in modelling the demand for and valuation of outdoor recreational facilities. Continued research associated with modelling the demand for outdoor recreation, including cases where skill was important to recreation, the spatial limits to the Hotelling-Clawson-Knetsch travel cost demand model, and, most recently, the role of site attributes including water quality for the demand for recreation.

Following this research, research efforts directed toward the evaluation of the adequacy of natural resources, including the measurement of natural resource scarcity and evaluation, in general, and the treatment of natural resources in economic models. In process of evaluating the role of natural resources in economic models, conducted with R. J. Kopp, an evaluation of the authenticity of neoclassical models descriptions of factor input substitution and nonneutral technical change. Most recent work has been directed in two areas: the modelling and estimation of individuals' willingness to pay for risk reductions and the evaluation of the performance of partial equilibrium measures of welfare changes.

SMITH, Vernon Lomax

Born 1927, Wichita, KA, USA.
Current Post Prof. Econ., Univ. Arizona, Tucson, AZ, USA, 1975–.
Past Posts Instr. Econ., Univ. Kansas, 1951–2; Econ., Harvard Econ. Res. Project, 1954–5; Management Sciences Res. Group, Ass. Prof., Assoc. Prof., Prof., Purdue Univ., IN, 1955–6, 1957–9, 1961–7; Vis. Prof., Stanford Univ., 1961–2; Prof., Brown Univ., 1967–8; Prof., Univ. Mass., 1968–75; Vis., Cowles Foundation, Yale Univ., 1971; Vis. Prof., Univ. Southern Cal. Tech., 1974–5; Advisory Council, Inst. Marine Resources, Univ. Cal., 1974–5.
Degrees BSEE Cal. Inst. Technology, 1949; MA Univ. Kansas, 1952; PhD Harvard Univ., 1955.
Offices and Honours Faculty Res. Fellow, Ford Foundation, 1958–9; Fellow, Center Advanced Study Behavioral Sciences, 1972–3; Sherman Fairchild Disting. Scholar, Cal. Tech., 1973–4; Best *EI* Article, WEA, 1980, 1982; Adjunct Scholar, Cato Inst., 1983.
Editorial Duties Contributing Ed., *Bus. Scope*, 1957–62; Ed. Board, *AER*, 1969–72, *Cato J.*, 1983–.
Principal Fields of Interest 022 Microeconomic Theory; 029 Experimental Economics; 721 Natural Resources.
Publications *Books:* 1. *Economics: An Analytical Approach* (with K. Davidson and J. Wiley), (Richard D. Irwin, 1958, 1962); 2. *Investment and Production* (Harvard Univ. Press, 1961); 3. *Economics of Natural and Environmental Economics* (Gordon & Breach, 1971); 4. *Research in Experimental Economics*, 1, 2, 3 (JAI Press, 1979, 1982, 1984).
Articles: 1. 'The theory of investment and production', *QJE*, 73, Feb. 1959; 2. 'An experimental study of competitive market behavior', *JPE*, 70, April 1962; 3. 'Economics of production from natural resources', *AER*, 58(3), June 1968; 4. 'Corporate financial theory under uncertainty', *QJE*, 84(3), Aug. 1970; 5. 'Economics of the primitive hunter culture with applications to pleistocene extinction and the rise of agriculture', *JPE*, 83(4), July-Aug. 1975; 6. 'Incentives and behavior in English, Dutch and sealed-bid auctions' (with V. Coppinger and J. Titus), *EI*, 18(1), Jan. 1980; 7. 'Microeconomic systems as an experimental science', *AER*, 72(5), Dec. 1982; 8. 'Auction market theory of heterogeneous bidders' (with J. Cox and J. Walker), *Econ. Letters*, 9, 1982; 9. 'On divestiture and the creation of property rights in public lands', *Cato J.*, Winter 1982; 10. 'Market contestability in the presence of sunk costs' (with D. Coursey, M. Issac and M. Luke), *Rand JE*, 1, Spring 1984.

Principal Contributions My research, 1955–65, centred on the integration of investment, capital and production theory. This work was extended to deal with problems of production, investment and pricing decisions over time, and with tax and depreciation policies. The economics of uncertainty, particularly corporate financial theory, occupied the period 1966–72, leading to the unpopular result that the M-M theorem fails when corporate bonds are subject to default risk. My research in natural resource economics (1966–77) emphasised the bionomic and geonomic stockflow and property right failure, characteristics of production from natural resources. This work provides an explanation of the agricultural revolution which coincides suspiciously with the late Pleistocene extinction of the favorite animals hunted by man. This was the critical period in the creation of modern man in the sense that agriculture appears to have forced the development of much more sophisticated property right systems, and their derived exchange systems, than had characterised man as a nomadic hunter.

My first experimental market was conducted in the spring of 1956, leading to the *JPE* article in 1962. The experimental study of market performance under alternative institutions of contract has continued to excite my research interest down to the present time. The importance of this work is in providing a methodology which makes it possible for us, as economists, to demonstrate what is that we think we know about market allocation. Unfortunately, a great deal of what we what we think we know, and what we teach, is either not true or not demonstrated. This should be disturbing only to the insufferably arrogant since man as a species distinct from other animals has been around for about one million years; exchange and property rights systems of the kind made possible by the agricultural revolution date from 10–15,000 years ago; and we began the serious study of economics only in the last 200 years.

SMITHIES, Arthur*

Dates and Birthplace 1907–81, Hobart, Tasmania, Australia.
Posts Held Instr. Econ., Univ. Michigan, 1934–5; Econ, Australian Treasury Dept., 1935–8; Ass. Prof., Assoc. Prof., Univ. Michigan, 1938–43; Econ., Chief, Econ. Bureau, US Bureau Budget, 1943–8; Dir., Fiscal and Trade Pol. Div., UNECA, 1948–9; Prof. Econ., Harvard Univ., 1949–74; Econ. Adviser, US Office Defense Mobilization, 1951–2; Cons., Hoover Comm., 1954; Fulbright Vis. Prof., Univ. Oxford, 1955–6; Vis. Prof., ANU, 1962–3.
Degrees LLB Univ. Tasmania, 1929; BA Univ. Oxford, 1932; PhD Harvard Univ., 1934.
Offices and Honours Rhodes Scholar, Univ. Oxford, 1931–2; Commonwealth Fund Fellow, Harvard Univ., 1932–4; Guggenheim Foundation Fellow, 1955–6; Fellow, Em Soc.
Editorial Duties Ed., *QJE*, *J. Econ. Abstracts*.
Publications *Books:* 1. *The Budgetary Process in the United States* (1954).
Articles: 1. 'Optimum location in spatial competition', *JPE*, 49, June, 1941; 2. 'Process analysis and equilibrium analysis', *Em*, 10, Jan. 1942; 3. 'Joseph A. Schumpeter, 1883–1950', *AER*, 40, Sept. 1950; 4. 'Economic fluctuations and growth', *Em*, 25, Jan. 1957.
Career Macroeconomist and expert on the US budgetary process who also wrote authoritatively on a wide range of topics from location theory to Schumpeterian economics.

SMOLENSKY, Eugene

Born 1932, New York City, NY, USA.
Current Post Prof. Econ., Univ. Wisconsin, 1961–.

Past Posts Dir., Inst. Res. Poverty, Univ. Wisconsin, 1978–82.
Degrees BA Brooklyn Coll., 1952; MA Amer. Univ., Washington, DC, 1956; PhD Univ. Penn., 1961.
Principal Fields of Interest 122 Economic Studies of More Industrialised Countries.
Publications *Books:* 1. *Aggregate Supply and Demand Analyses* (with P. Davidson), (Harper & Row, 1964); 2. *Public Expenditures, Taxes and the Distribution of Income* (with M. Reynolds), (Academic Press, 1977).
Principal Contributions The finding that income inequality in the US has been unchanged throughout the 20th century, except for a one-time decline during World War II. Expanding the accounting framework to contain regional and sectoral shifts, the growth transfer payments, changing household living arrangements, permanent as opposed to nominal income, has all been in vain.

SOHMEN, Egon*

Dates and Birthplace 1930–77, Linz, Austria.
Degrees MBA Univ. Vienna, 1952; Dr Rer. Pol. Univ. Tübingen, 1954; PhD MIT, 1958.
Offices and Honours Fulbright Scholar, Univ. Kansas, 1952–3; Woodrow Wilson Fellow, Smithsonian Inst., Washington, DC, 1975.
Posts Held Ass. Prof. Econ., Yale Univ., 1958–61, Prof. Econ., Univ. Saarbrücken, 1961–9; Prof. Econ., Univ. Heidelberg, 1969–77.
Publications *Books:* 1. *Flexible Exchange Rates* (1961, 1969; transls., German, 1973, Italian, 1974, Japanese, 1975); 2. *International Monetary Problems and the Foreign Exchanges* (1963; transls., German, 1964, Japanese, 1964); 3. *The Theory of Forward Exchange* (1966; transl., Japanese, 1968); 4. *Marktwirtschaft, Presse und Werbung* (1971); 5. *Allokationstheorie und Wirtschaftspolitik* (1976).
Career His path-breaking book on *Flexible Exchange Rates* did much to swing the weight of economic opinion in the USA towards the regime of float-

ing exchange rates that came into being in the mid-1970s. During his brief academic career of 19 years, he was a vigorous advocate of flexible exchange rates, competiton and the market mechanism.

SOLOMON, Ezra

Born 1920, Rangoon, Burma.
Current Post Dean Witter Prof. Fin., Stanford Univ., USA, 1976–.
Past Posts Faculty, Univ. Chicago, 1948–61, Grad. School Bus., Stanford Univ., 1961–76; Member, US President's Council Econ. Advisers, 1971–3.
Degrees BA Univ. Rangoon, 1940; PhD Univ. Chicago, 1950.
Offices and Honours Member, US Presidential Commission Fin. Structure Regulation, 1970–1.
Editorial Duties Ed. Boards, *J Fin*, 1963–5, *J Quant. Fin. Analysis*, 1965–6, *J Bus Fin*, 1968–70.
Principal Fields of Interest 521 Business Finance.
Publications *Books:* 1. *The Management of Corporate Capital*, ed. (Free Press, 1959); 2. *Metropolitan Chicago — An Economic Analysis* (with A. Bilbija), (Free Press, 1960); 3. *The Theory of Financial Management* (Columbia Univ. Press, 1963; transls., Spanish, 1965, Portuguese, 1969, Turkish, 1970, French, 1971, Japanese, 1971, Italian, 1972); 4. *The Anxious Economy* (Stanford Univ. Press, 1975, San Francisco Books, 1976); 5. *Introduction to Financial Management* (with J. Pringle), (Goodyear Publ., 1977, 1980; transl., Portuguese, 1981).
Articles: 1. 'Measuring a company's cost of capital', *J Bus*, 28, Oct. 1955; 2. 'The arithmetic of capital-budgeting decisions', *J Bus*, 29, April 1956; 3. 'Leverage and the cost of capital', *J Fin*, 18, May 1963; 4. 'Return on investment: the relation of book-yield to true yield', in *Basic Research in Accounting Measurement* (AAA, 1965); 5. 'Alternative rate of return concepts and their implication for utility regulation', *Bell JE*, 1(1), Spring 1970, repr. in *Bell Yearbook 1*, ed. P. W. MacAvoy (Praeger, 1970).
Principal Contributions Early work,

with others, unified the then descriptive field of corporation finance with the abstractions of capital theory into a modern theory of financial management dealing with the pricing of corporate capital assets and securities under conditions of uncertainty. Later work pioneered exploring systematic differences between conventional accounting rates of return and underlying true rates of return.

SOLOW, Robert M.

Born 1924, New York City, NY, USA.
Current Post Inst. Prof., MIT, Camb., MA, USA, 1973–.
Past Posts Ass. Prof. Stats., Ass. Prof. Econ., Prof. Econ., MIT, 1949–54, 1954–8, 1958–73; Sr. Staff Econ., US President's Council Econ. Advisers, 1961–2; Eastman Vis. Prof., Fellow, Balliol Coll. Oxford, 1968–9; Overseas Fellow, Churchill Coll. Camb., 1984.
Degrees BA, MA, PhD Harvard Univ., 1947, 1948, 1951; Hon. Dr Univs. Chicago, Brown, Paris I, Warwick, Geneva, Williams, Wesleyan Lehigh, Tulane.
Offices and Honours David A. Wells Prize, Harvard Univ., 1951; John Bates Clark Medal, AEA, 1961; Pres., Em Soc, 1964, AEA, 1978; Fellow, AAAS, Amer. Philo. Soc., Corresp. Fellow, BA; Member, NAS; Frank Killian Lect., MIT, 1979; Seidman Award Polit. Econ., 1983.
Principal Fields of Interest 020 General Economic Theory; 023 Macroeconomics Pure and Applied.
Publications *Books:* 1. *Linear Programming and Economic Analysis* (with R. Dorfman, P. Samuelson), (McGraw-Hill, 1958); 2. *Capital Theory and the Rate of Return* (N-H, 1965; transls., French, Polish); 3. *Price Expectations and the Behaviour of the Price Level* (Manchester Univ. Press, 1968); 4. *The Nature and Sources of Unemployment in the US* (Almqvist & Wiksell, 1964); 5. *Growth Theory: An Exposition* (OUP, 1969; transls., French, German, Italian, Spanish, Japanese).
Articles: 1. 'A contribution of the theory of economic growth', *QJE*, 70,

Feb. 1956, repr. in *Readings in Mathematical Economics*, ed. P. Newman (JHUP, 1968); 2. 'Technical change and the aggregate production function', *REStat*, 39, Aug. 1957, repr. in *Readings in Economic Statistics and Econometrics*, ed. A. Zellner (Nettle, Brown, 1968); 3. 'Analytical aspects of anti-inflation policy' (with P. Samuelson), *AER*, 50(2), May 1960; 4. 'Output, employment and wages in the short run' (with J. Stiglitz), *QJE*, 82, Nov. 1968; 5. 'Does fiscal policy matter?' (with A. J. Blinder), *J Pub E*, 2(4), Nov. 1973; 6. 'Intergenerational equity and exhaustible resources', *REStud*, Symposium, 1974; 7. 'The economics of resources or the resources of economics', *AER*, 64(2), May 1974; 8. 'On theories of unemployment', *AER*, 70(1), March 1980; 9. 'Wage bargaining and employment' (with I McDonald), *AER*, 71(3), June 1981.

Principal Contributions My most persistent research interest has been aggregative economics. (Even my work on the economics of non-renewable resources originated from curiosity about the extent to which gradual resource scarcity becomes a drag on economic growth). The obvious bias toward small transparent models reflects a desire to use theory as a guide for interpreting concrete events and policies. My early work on growth theory was an attempt to define an equilibrium path around which pathological economic fluctuations occur as a result of market failure. Short-run macroeconomics is mainly an attempt to isolate those features of modern industrial capitalist economies that account for those pathologies, especially unemployment and inflation. Most recently, I have concentrated on the ways and reasons why labour markets do not function like a classical spot market.

SOMBART, Werner*

Dates and Birthplace 1863–1941, Ermsleben, Germany.
Posts Held Syndic with Bremen Chamber of Commerce, 1888–90; Assoc. Prof. Polit. Econ., Univ. Breslau, 1890–1906; Prof., Handelshoch-

schule, Berlin, 1906–18, Univ. Berlin, 1918–.
Degree PhD Univ. Berlin, 1888.
Publications *Books:* 1. *Socialism and the Social Movement* (1896, 1909); 2. *Der moderne Kapitalismus*, 3 vols (1902, 1924–7); 3. *Die Deutsche Volkswirtschaft im 19 Jahrhundert* (1903, 1927); 4. *The Jews and Modern Capitalism* (1911, 1962); 5. *The Quintessence of Capitalism* (1913, 1915); 6. *Studien zur Entwicklungsgeschicte des modernen Kapitalismus*, 2 vols (1913); 7. *A New Social Philosophy*, ed. K. F. Geises (1934, 1937).
Articles: 1. 'Economic theory and economic history', *EHR*, 2, Jan. 1929.

Career Writer on capitalism, whose viewpoint swung so sharply from Marxism to ultra-conservatism to national socialism that he is virtually impossible to categorise. His chief work *Der Moderne Kapitalismus* is eclectic and sometimes unreliable, but presents a historical analysis of capitalism which differs from the Marxian version in regarding modern capitalism as an improvement on early competitive capitalism.
Secondary Literature J. Kuczynski, 'Sombart, Werner', *IESS*, 15.

SONNENFELS, Joseph von*

Dates and Birthplace 1732–1817, Nikolsburg, Austro-Hungary.
Post Held Prof. Cameral Science, Univ. Vienna, 1763.
Offices and Honours Served as adviser to Austrian govt on various occasions; Ennobled, 1797; Freiherr, 1804.
Publications *Books:* 1. *Grundsätze der Polizi, Handlung und Finanzwissenschaft*, 2 vols (1763–7); 2. *Betrachtungen über die neuen politischen Handlungsgrundsätze der Engländer* (1764); 3. *Leitfaden in den Handlungswissenschaften* (1776); 4. *Gesammelte Schriften*, 10 vols (1783–7).
Career Neo-cameralist, who advised successive Austrian emperors and advocated enlightened absolutism —e.g. the State had the positive role of ensuring basic standards of life, including hospitals and reformed prisons. He believed in the virtues of a growing popula-

tion and consequently favoured labour-intensive industries and small land proprietorship. He saw money not merely as a medium of exchange, but as a productive factor. Though many of his views were not particularly original, his ideas were influential, chiefly through the use of his *Grundsätze . . .* as a textbook.

Secondary Literature K. Zielenziger, 'Sonnenfels, Freiherr Joseph von', *ESS*, 14.

SONNENSCHEIN, Hugo Freund

Born 1940, New York City, NY, USA.
Current Post Prof. Econ., Princeton Univ., Princeton, NJ, USA, 1976–.
Past Posts Ass. Prof., Assoc. Prof., Prof. Econ., Univ. Minnesota, 1964–70; Vis. Prof., Univ. Andes, Colombia, 1965, Penn. State Univ., 1968–9; Prof. Econ., Univ. Mass., 1970–3; Vis. Prof., Univs. Tel Aviv and Hebrew, Jerusalem, 1972; Prof. Econ., Northwestern Univ., 1973–6; Vis. Prof., Univs. Parix XII, 1978, Aix-en-Provence, France, 1978, McMaster, Canada, 1981, Strasbourg, 1983.
Degrees BA Univ. Rochester, 1961; MS PhD Purdue Univ. IN, 1964.
Offices and Honours US-SSRC Fellow, Dept. Maths., Univ. Michigan, 1967–8; Ford Foundation Faculty Res. Fellow, 1970–1; Fellow, Em Soc., 1973; Guggenheim Foundation Fellow, 1976–7.
Editorial Duties Assoc. Ed., *JET*, 1972–5; Ed. Board, *J Math E*, 1974–; Irving Fisher & Frank Taussig Competitions, 1973–6, *SIAM J.*, 1976–80; Co-ed., Ed., *Em*, 1975–7, 1977–84; Advisory Ed., *Em Soc.* Monograph Series, 1980–; Ed., *Fund. Econ.*, 1981–.
Principal Fields of Interest 021 General Equilibrium Theory; 213 Mathematical Methods and Models; 022 Microeconomic Theory.
Articles: 1. 'Price distortion and economic welfare' (with E. M. Foster), *Em*, 39(2), March 1970; 2. 'Do Walras' law and continuity characterize the class of community excess demand functions?', *JET*, 10(4), Aug. 1973; 3. 'An axiomatic characterization of the competitive mechanism' (with W. Shafer), *Em*, 42(3), May 1974; 4. 'Equilibrium in abstract economies without ordered preferences', *J Math E*, Dec. 1975; 5. 'On the foundations of the theory of monopolistic competition' (with D. J. Roberts), *Em*, 45(1), Jan. 1977; 6. 'Cournot and Walras equilibrium' (with W. Novshek), *JET*, 15(6), Dec. 1978; 7. 'On the existence of rational expectations equilibrium (with R. Anderson), *JET*, 19(2), April 1982; 8. 'Price dynamics based on the adjustment of firms', *AER*, 72(5), Dec. 1982.

Principal Contributions From the start I was attracted by the axiomatic method: Debreu's *Theory of Value* and Arrow's *Social Choice and Individual Values* were most influential. My first paper to receive attention demonstrated that general equilibrium existence theory could be carried out without transitive preferences. Subsequently, I applied the formal general equilibrium model to situations with trade and taxation. I next investigated the extent to which the utility hypothesis restricts the form of market excess demand functions. This was motivated by my concern that structure might be lost via aggregation; this has been my most influential work. My approach to general equilibrium changed radically when I read Debreu's lemma on 'abstract economies' and its application by Arrow and Debreu. Working with Wayne Shafer, I extended Debreu's lemma. This led to my interest in equilibrium with monopolistic elements, and D. John Roberts and I worked on the foundations of that theory.

I have had a continuing interest in the demand theory of the individual consumer, and in social choice theory, and continue to publish in these areas. Some recent contributions: with William Novshek, I have constructed noncooperative Cournot-type foundations for the Walrasian model. These foundations apply when average cost functions are U-shaped, entry is free and firms are small relative to the market. With Bob Anderson, I have established existence theorems for economies in which agents condition on the information communicated by prices. Also, I have studied the dynamics of the adjustment of myopic firms to differential profits; I am interested in the adequacy of profits as signals for driving the distribution of firms to an optimum. A major long-term research goal is to present a unified treatment of general equilibrium theory that incorporates, along with classical perspectives, recent lessons learned from game theory, the economics of incentives, and the economics of uncertainty.

SOWELL, Thomas

Born 1936, Gastonia, NC, USA.
Current Post Sr. Fellow, Hoover Inst., Stanford Univ., Stanford, CA, USA, 1980–.
Past Posts Labor Econ., US Dept. Labor, 1961–2; Instr., Douglass Coll., Rutgers Univ., 1962–3; Lect., Howard Univ., 1963–4; Econ. Analyst, AT&T, 1964–5; Ass. Prof., Cornell Univ., 1965–9; Assoc. Prof., Brandeis Univ., MA, 1969–70; Assoc. Prof., Prof., UCLA, 1970–2, 1979–80; Proj. Dir., Urban Inst., Washington, DC, 1972–4; Fellow, Center Advanced Study Behavioral Sciences, Stanford, CA, 1976–7; Fellow, Hoover Inst., 1977; Vis. Prof., Amherst Coll., MA, 1977.
Degrees BA Harvard Univ., 1958; MA Columbia Univ., 1959; PhD Univ. Chicago, 1968.
Principal Fields of Interest 030 History of Economic Thought; 040 Economic History; 810 Manpower Training.
Publications *Books:* 1. *Economics: Analysis and Issues* (Scott, Foresman, 1971); 2. *Say's Law: An Historical Analysis* (Princeton Univ. Press, 1972); 3. *Classical Economics Reconsidered* (Princeton Univ. Press, 1974); 4. *Race and Economics* (David McKay, 1975); 5. *Knowledge and Decisions* (Basic Books, 1980); 6. *Ethnic America* (Basic Books, 1981); 7. *Markets and Minorities* (Basic Books, 1981); 8. *The Economics and Politics of Race: An International Perspective* (William Morrow, 1983).
Articles: 1. 'Marx's "increasing misery" doctrine', *AER*, 50(1), March 1960; 2. 'Marxian value reconsidered', *Ec*, N.S. 30, Aug. 1963; 3. 'The general glut controversy reconsidered', *OEP*, 15(3), Nov. 1963; 4. 'The shorter work week controversy', *ILRR*, 18(2), Jan. 1965; 5. 'Marx's capital after one hundred years', *CJE*, 33(1), Feb. 1967; 6. 'The "evolutionary" economics of Thorstein Veblen', *OEP*, 19(2), July 1967; 7. 'Sismondi: a neglected pioneer', *HOPE*, 4(1), Spring 1972; 8. 'Adam Smith in theory and practice', in *Adam Smith and Modern Political Economy*, ed. G. P. O'Driscoll, Jr. (Iowa State Univ. Press, 1979).
Principal Contributions My early work (1960–75) was primarily in the history of economic theory. If there was any recurring theme in this work, it was that too often current issues and ideas are read back into economists of the past, creating gross distortions. When my interests shifted to other areas, I discovered that this was part of a more general recklessness with facts in the interest of preconceived visions. Since the mid-1970s, my work has been concerned with (1) racial and ethnic groups and (2) social theory. My principal book in the first area is *The Economics and Politics of Race*. My principal book applying the economic approach to social theory in general is *Knowledge and Decisions*. I am currently at work on another book in social theory, *A Conflict of Visions*. It seeks to explain why a few different underlying assumptions about the nature of man, knowledge, and social causation translate into repeated and drastic differences on a vast spectrum of social and political issues.

SPANN, Othmar*

Dates and Birthplace 1878–1950, Vienna, Austro-Hungary.
Posts Held Studied in Zürich, Berne and Tübingen; Prof., Technical High School, Berlin, 1909, Univ. Vienna, 1919–38.
Degrees Dr Polt. Science, Univ. Tübingen, 1903.
Publications *Books:* 1. *The History of Economics* (1910, 1930).
Career German Romantic economist and social theorist who developed a philosophical standpoint known as 'universalism', the antithesis of the atomism and individualism which was said to characterise Anglo-Saxon econ-

omics. His *History of Economics* went through 19 editions and until the 1930s was the most widely read history of economic thought in the German-speaking countries.

Secondary Literature E. Salin, 'Economics: romantic and universalist economics', *ESS*, 5; W. Heinrich, 'Spann, Othmar', *Handwörterbuch der Sozialwissenschaft*, 9 (Fischer Verlag, 1958).

SPENCE, Andrew Michael

Born 1943, Montclair, NJ, USA.
Current Post George Gund Prof. Econ. and Bus. Admin., Harvard Univ., Camb., MA, USA, 1977–.
Past Posts Ass. Prof., Harvard Univ., 1971–3; Assoc. Prof., Stanford Univ., 1973–5; Hon. Res. Fellow, Harvard Univ., 1975–6; Vis. Prof., Harvard Univ., 1976–7.
Degrees BA (Philo.) Princeton Univ., 1966; BA, MA (Maths.) Oxford Univ., 1968; PhD Harvard Univ., 1972.
Offices and Honours Hons Thesis Prize Philo., Princeton Univ., 1966; Rhodes Scholar, 1966–8; Danforth Fellow, 1966–70; David A Wells Prize, Harvard Univ., 1972; J. K. Galbraith Prize Excellence in Teaching, Harvard Univ., 1978; John Bates Clark Medal, AEA, 1981; Fellow, AAAS, 1983.
Editorial Duties Ed. Board, *AER*, *Bell JE*, *JET*, and *Public Pol.*
Principal Fields of Interest 010 General Economics; 520 Business Finance and Investment; 600 Industrial Organisation.
Publications *Books:* 1. *Market Signaling: Informational Transfer in Hiring and Related Processes* (Harvard Univ. Press, 1974); 2. *Industrial Organization in an Open Economy* (with R. E. Caves and M. E. Porter), (Harvard Univ. Press, 1980); 3. *Competitive Structure in Investment Banking* (with S. Hayes and D. Marks), (Harvard Univ. Press, 1983).
Articles: 1. 'Blue whales and applied control theory', in *Systems Approaches to Environmental Problems* (Bavarian Academy Sciences, 1973); 2. 'Job market signaling', *QJE*, 87(3), Aug. 1973; 3. 'Competitive and optimal responses to signals: an analysis of efficiency and

distribution', *JET*, 7(3), March 1974; 4. 'Product selection, fixed costs, and monopolistic competition', *REStud*, 43(2), June 1976; 5. 'Consumer misperceptions, product failure and producer liability', *REStud*, 64(3), Oct. 1977; 6. 'Entry, capacity, investment and oligopolistic pricing', *Bell JE*, 8(2), Autumn, 1977; 7. 'Investment, strategy and growth in a new market', *Bell JE*, 10(1), Spring 1979; 8. 'Multi-product quantity-dependent prices and profitability constraints', *REStud*, 47(5), Oct. 1980; 9. 'The learning curve and competition, *Bell JE*, 12(1), Spring 1981; 10. 'Cost reduction, competition and industry performance', *Em*, 52(1), Feb. 1984.

Principal Contributions My first interest developed during a faculty seminar on the economics of discrimination. A subject which seemed tangentially related at the time was the informational structure of markets, and after thinking about the subject for a while, I decided I didn't know what in principle would constitute a signal that could, in an equilibrium appropriately defined, persistently carry information. The result was a class of models called 'signalling models'. They turned out to have rather interesting properties. Without ever really moving on, I added product differentiation and monopolistic competition, the theory (not new) of how (and with what welfare results) markets select products. I then turned to a broad group of subjects that fall under the heading of dynamic aspects of competition. That interest really developed as a result of dissatisfaction with models (including my own) of entry and entry deterrence. The dynamics of the competitive process with special emphasis on the underlying structure that influences the process has occupied me for the past four or five years.

SPENGLER, Joseph J.

Born 1902, Piqua, OH, USA.
Current Post James B. Duke Prof. Emeritus Econ., Duke Univ., NC, USA, 1972–.
Past Posts Regional Price Exec. US

Office Price Admin., 1942–3; Ass. Prof., Assoc. Prof., Prof. Econ., Duke Univ., 1934–72, Univ. N. Carolina, 1972–3.

Degrees BA, MA, PhD, Dr Humane Letters (Hon.) Ohio State Univ., 1926, 1929, 1930, 1965; Hon. Dr Science Alma Coll., 1968; Hon. Dr Law Tulane Univ., 1978.

Offices and Honours Phi Beta Kappa, 1927; US SSRC, 1945–60; Pres., SEA, 1947, PAA, 1957, AEA, 1965, Hist. Econ. Soc., 1975–6, Atlantic Econ. Soc., 1976–7; Fellow, ASA, 1950, Amer. Assoc. Advancement Science, 1950, Amer. Philo. Soc., 1954, AAAS, 1962, Mont Pelerin Soc., 1963, World Academy Arts and Sciences, 1966.

Principal Fields of Interest 840 Demographic Economics.

Publications *Books:* 1. *France Faces Depopulation* (Duke Univ. Press, 1938, 1979); 2. *Indian Economic Thought* (Duke Univ. Press, 1971); 3. *Population Economics, Selected Essays* (Duke Univ. Press, 1972); 4. *Facing Zero Population Growth: Reactions and Interpretations, Past and Present* (Duke Univ. Press, 1978); 5. *Origins of Economic Thought and Justice* (Southern Illinois Univ. Press, 1980).

Articles: 1. 'Population doctrines in the United States, pts I–II', *JPE*, 41, Aug., Oct. 1933; 2. 'French population theory since 1800, pts I–II', *JPE*, 44, Oct., Dec. 1936; 3. 'Monopolistic competition and the use and price of urban land service', *JPE*, 54, Oct. 1946; 4. 'Aspects of the economics of population growth, pts I–II', *SEJ*, 14, Oct. 1947, Jan. 1948; 5. 'Smith v Hobbes: economy vs. polity', in *Adam Smith and the Wealth of Nations*, ed. F. R. Glahe (Univ. Colorado Press, 1978).

Principal Contributions Study of decline in fertility, and of history of economics; identification and analysis of the interrelations between various population movements and phenomena, and economic phenomena, together with the nature of interrelations between population phenomena and aspects of macro- and microeconomics; ageing effects and changes in the composition of 'economic thought' over time.

SPIETHOFF, Arthur*

Dates and Birthplace 1873–1957, Germany.

Posts Held Taught at Berlin, Prague and Bonn Univs.

Editorial Duties Ass. Ed., Ed., *Schmoller's Jahrbuch*, 1899, 1908.

Publications *Books:* 1. *Die wirtschaftlichen Wechsellagen*, 2 vols (1955).

Articles: 1. 'Vorbemerkungen zu einer Theorie der Überproducktion', *Schmoller's Jahrbuch*, 26, 1902; 2. 'The "historical" character of economic theories', *JEH*, 12(2), 1952; 3. 'Business cycles', (1923), repr. in *Internat. Econ. Papers*, 3 (1953); 4. 'Pure theory and economic gestalt theory', in *Enterprise and Secular Change*, eds. F. C. Lane and J. C. Riemersma (1953).

Career Beginning his work on business cycles, he discovered the need for a new general theory of economics to replace the Historical School orthodoxy in which he had been trained. Within the framework of his historical-realistic theory he was then able to pursue his empirical work on cycles. He considered cycles, including the long waves, which he identified independently, as part of the essential pattern of capitalist economics. He also did valuable work on the capital and money market, and on land utilisation and housing, using the same conceptual framework.

Secondary Literature G. Clausing, 'Spiethoff, Arthur', *IESS*, 15.

SPULBER, Nicolas

Born 1915, Brasov, Romania.

Current Post Disting. Prof. Emeritus Econ., Indiana Univ., Bloomington IND, USA, 1980–.

Past Posts Res. Assoc., MIT, 1952–4; Lect., Assoc. Prof., Prof. Econ., Indiana Univ., 1954–80; Vis. Prof. Econ., City Coll. NY, 1963–4; Scholar, Internat. Res. Center, Indiana Univ., 1967–72.

Degrees MA, PhD Grad. Faculty, New School Social Res., NY, 1950, 1952.

Offices and Honours Halle Fellow, New School Social Res., 1951–2; Ford Faculty Res. Fellow, 1961.

Principal Fields of Interest 113 Economic Planning Theory and Policy; 213 Mathematical Methods and Models.

Publications *Books:* 1. *The Economics of Eastern Europe* (MIT, Wiley, 1957, Greenwood Press, 1976); 2. *Soviet Strategy for Economy Growth* (Indiana Univ. Press, 1964; transl., Italian, Einaudi, 1970); 3. *The State and Economic Development in Eastern Europe* (Random House, 1966); 4. *The Soviet Economy: Structure, Principles, Problems* (W. W. Norton, 1962, 1969); 5. *Socialist Managment and Planning* (Indiana Univ. Press, 1971); 6. *Quantitative Economic Policy and Planning: Theory and Models* (with I. Horowitz), (W. W. Norton, 1976); 7. *Organizational Alternatives in Soviet-Type Economies* (CUP, 1979); 8. *Resources & Planning in Eastern Europe*, co-ed. (Indiana Univ. Press, 1957); 9. *Study of the Soviet Economy*, ed. (Indiana Univ. Press, 1961); 10. *Foundations of Soviet Strategy for Economic Growth*, ed. (Indiana Univ. Press, 1963, 1965).

Articles: 1. 'Effects of the embargo on Soviet trade', *Harvard Bus. Rev*, 3(6), Dec. 1952; 2. 'The operation of trade within the Soviet bloc' (with F. Gehrels), *REStat*, 15(2), May 1958, repr. in *Readings on the Soviet Economy*, ed. F. Holzman (Rand McNally, 1962); 3. 'Taux de profit et croissance dans les economies planifiées', *Econ App*, 10(4), Oct.–Dec. 1957; 4. 'Contrasting economic patterns: Chinese and Soviet strategies of development', *Soviet Stud.*, 15(3), July 1963, repr. in *Communist Political Systems*, ed. A. Z. Rubinstein, (Prentice-Hall, 1966); 5. 'Socialism, industrialization and convergence', *Yearbook of E. Europen Econ.*, 2, 1971; 6. 'On some issues in the theory of the socialist economy', *Kyk*, 25(4), 1972; 7. 'Is there an economic system based on the sovereignty of each consumer' (with G. M. von Furstenberg), *ZN*, 33(3–4), 1973; 8. 'Welfare criteria for comparing changes within and between systems' (with G. M. von Furstenberg), *WA*, 110(4), Fall, 1974; 9. On the pioneering stage in input-output economics: the Soviet national economic balance 1923–24 after fifty years' (with K. Moayed-Dadkah), *REStat*, 57(1), Feb. 1975; 10. 'Percep-

tions Americaines du pouvoir economique Sovietique', *Cadmos*, 4(13), Spring 1981.

Principal Contributions My earliest work focussed on the study of the economic relations between the Soviet Union and Eastern Europe after World War II (this was the subject of my PhD dissertation). Subsequently I turned my attention to the changes undergone by the East European economies through the adoption and implementation of the Soviet economic model. Viewed through the prismatic refractions of six different countries with dissimilar traditions and different levels of development and resources, certain accepted assumptions concerning the role, scope and pace of nationalisation and collectivisation, and the Soviet strategy of growth, could be retested and examined under new angles (Book 1 above).

I then examined in three interrelated analytical works (1) the formulation and the rationale of the Soviet approaches to growth and development (Book 2 above); (2) the Soviet planning system and the *modus operandi* of the Soviet economy (Book 4 above); and (3) the most decisive attempts of modify the Soviet-type system without fully challenging all its premises and its rationale (Book 7 above). In the meantime I also focussed on the relations between the Soviet planning concepts and methods (Book 5 above) and the models and methods developed in the West (Book 6 above). This latter volume provided a *single* quantitative framework for the formulation of policy decisions, the use of instruments for carrying them out, and the choosing of the methods for integrating policies and instruments into consistent national, regional, or sectoral plans. My current research concerns the evolution of economic polices in certain mixed economies.

SRAFFA, Piero*

Dates and Birthplace 1898–1983, Turin, Italy.

Posts Held Prof. Polit. Econ., Univ. Perugia, 1924–6; Prof. Polit. Econ., Univ. Cagliari, Sardinia, Italy, 1926–7;

Lect., Univ. Camb., 1927; Fellow, Trinity Coll., Camb., 1927–83.

Degree Grad. Univ. Turin.

Publications *Books:* 1. *Works and Correspondence of David Ricardo*, 11 vols, co-ed. (with M. H. Dobb), (1951–73); 2. *Production of Commodities by Means of Commodities: Prelude to a Critique of Economic Theory* (1960, 1975).

Articles: 1. 'The bank crisis in Italy', *EJ*, 32, 1922; 2. 'Sulle relazioni fra costs e quantita prodotta', *Annali di Economia*, 2, 1925; 3. 'The laws of returns under competitive conditions', *EJ*, 36, Dec. 1926, repr. in *Readings in Price Theory*, eds. G. J. Stigler and K. E. Boulding (1953); 4. 'Increasing returns and the representative firm: a symposium', *EJ*, 40, March 1930; 5. 'Dr Hayek on money and capital', *EJ*, 42, March 1932, 42, June 1932.

Career Criticism of Marshall's theory of the firm, and the perfect competition model current in the 1920s. Editing of the works and correspondence of Ricardo. Re-examination of classical theories of value and income distribution which has led others to reexamine and abandon marginalist economic theory.

Secondary Literature L. L. Pasinetti, 'Sraffa, Piero', *IESS*, 18; A. Roncaglia, *Sraffa and the Theory of Prices* (Wiley, 1978).

SRINIVASAN, Thirukodikaval N.

Born 1933, Tirupati, India.

Current Post Samuel C. Park Jr. Prof. Econ., Yale Univ., New Haven, CT, USA, 1980–.

Past Posts Stat. Quality Control Officer, Indian Stat. Inst., Bombay, 1955–7; Instr., Ass. Prof., Member, Cowles Commission Res. Econ., Yale Univ., 1960–1, 1961–4; Vis., Inst. Econ. Growth, New Delhi, 1962–3; Vis. Prof., Ford Faculty Res. Fellow, Stanford Univ., 1967–8; Prof., Indian Stat. Inst., New Delhi, 1964–79; Vis. Prof., MIT, 1972–3, 1977–8; Vis. Lect., Johns Hopkins Univ., 1980; Special Adviser, Devlp. Res. Center, Cons., World Bank, 1977–80, 1980–.

Degrees BA (Maths.), MA (Maths.),

Madras Univ., India, 1953, 1954; PhD Yale Univ., (Maths.) 1958, 1962.

Offices and Honours Merit Scholarship, Indian Stat. Inst., 1954–5; Ford Management Fellow, 1958–9; Ford Doctoral Dissertation Fellow, 1959–60; Ford Faculty Res. Fellow, 1967; Fellow, Em Soc, 1970; Hon. Member, AEA, 1976; Mahalanobis Memorial Medal (Internat. Award), Indian Em Soc, 1975; Fellow, AAAS, 1982.

Editorial Duties Co-ed., *Em*, 1974–8, *JDE*, 1972–6; Assoc. Ed., *J Int E*, 1972–6, *Int ER*, 1972; Ed. Secretary, *Sankhya, Quant. Econ. Issues*, 1974–6; Ed. Board, *PDR*, 1980.

Principal Fields of Interest 022 Microeconomic Theory; 112 Economic Development Models and Theories; 411 International Trade Theory.

Publications *Books:* 1. *Scheduling the Operations of the Bhakra System* (with B. S. Minhas, *et al.*), (Stat. Publ. Soc., 1972); 2. *Poverty and Income Distribution in India*, co-ed. (with P. K. Bardhan), (Stat. Publ. Soc., 1974); 3. *Optimal Requirements of Fertilizers for the Fifth Plan Period* (with K. S. Parikh), (Fertilizer Assoc. India, 1974); 4. *Foreign Trade Regimes and Economic Development: India* (with J. N. Bhagwati), (NBER, 1975); 5. *Lectures on International Trade* (with J. Bhagwati), (MIT Press, 1983).

Articles: 1. 'Optimum savings in a two sector model of growth', *Em*, 32, July 1964, 33, April 1965; 2. 'Optimum savings under uncertainty' (with D. Levhari), *REStud*, 36, April 1969; 3. 'Approximations to finite sample moments of estimators whose exact sampling distributions are unknown', *Em*, 38(3), May 1970; 4. 'The theory of wage differentials: production response and factor price equalisation' (with J. Bhagwati), *J Int E*, 1(1), Feb. 1971; 5. 'Tax evasion — a model', *J Pub E*, 2(4), Nov. 1973; 6. 'Development, poverty and basic human needs: some issues', *Food Res. Inst. Stud.*, 11(2), 1977; 7. 'Credit and sharecropping in agrarian societies: economies of developing countries' (with A. Braverman), *JDE*, 9(3), Nov. 1981; 8. 'General equilibrium theory, project evaluation and economic development', in *The Theory and Experience of Economic Development:*

Essays in Honor of Sir W. Arthur Lewis, eds. M. Gersovitz, *et al.* (A&U, 1982); 9. 'International factor movements, commodity trade and commercial policy in a specific factor model', *J Int E*, 14 (3/4), May 1983; 10. 'Hunger: defining it, estimating its global incidence and alleviating it', in *Role of Markets in the World Food Economy*, eds. D. G. Johnson and E. Schuh (Westview Press, 1983).

Principal Contributions Starting from my doctoral dissertation, I have continued to work on dynamic models of economic growth and development. My dissertation (and my later article in *Em*) included a demonstration of what Edmund Phelps christened as the Golden Rule of Accumulation at about the same time he published it. In my work with Levhari, I extended optimal savings (and accumulation) rules to situations involving uncertainty. Bhagwati and I analysed optimal growth in an open economy. I have also built empirical planning models for India.

Singly and in collaboration with Bhagwati, I have been contributing since the mid-1960s to the pure theory of international trade. The basic thrust of these contributions is to analyse the welfare consequences and implications for factor prices of commercial and other policies in what may be loosely described as 'distorted' economies. The policies included tariffs and quotas, factor accumulation, intra- and international factor movements, foreign aid and other capital inflows, etc.

A third area of my continuing interest is economics of uncertainty — in a number of articles I have explored the effect of various forms of uncertainty on savings, on the relationship between farm size and productivity in agriculture, on tax evasion in a context of uncertain discovery of evasion, on commercial policy, etc. I have also contributed to the study of poverty and income distribution as well as trade and development policy issues in India. I have analysed the relationship between poverty, undernutrition and malnutrition. Problems of agricultural development, including analysis of institutions such as tenancy and share-cropping, inter-linkages of credit, land, labour

and product markets in situations in which a complete set of Arrow-Debreu contingent commodity markets do not exist, optimal use of inputs such as irrigation water and fertilizers, continue to attract my analytical interest. More recently I have been collaborating with Kirit Parikh and N. S. S. Narayana on a dynamic computable general equilibrium model of Indian agricultural development.

STACKELBERG, Heinrich von*

Dates and Birthplace 1905–46, Kudinowo, Russia.
Posts Held Privatdozent, Univs. Cologne and Berlin; Prof. Univ. Bonn, 1941–3, Univ. Madrid, 1943–6.
Degree PhD Univ. Cologne, 1932.
Publications *Books:* 1. *Grundlagen einer reiner Kostentheorie* (1932); 2. *Marktform und Gleichgewicht* (1934); 3. *Grundzüge der theoretischen Volkswirtschaftslehre* (1943).
Career Mathematical economist whose early economic interest was in pricing under conditions of oligopoly. Later work was on capital theory, and at the time of his death he was attempting a theory of the whole economic process. A stalwart opponent of central planning, he worked out his criticism in a mathematical form.
Secondary Literature W. Eucken, 'Obit.: Heinrich von Stackelberg', *EJ*, 58, March 1948.

STAMP, Josiah Charles*

Dates and Birthplace 1880–1941, Bexley, London, England.
Posts Held UK, civil servant, 1896–1919; Dir., Nobel Industries, 1919–26; ICI, 1926–8 and other cos.; Cons., British Govt., 1935–; Member of many official commissions and comms.
Degrees BSc, DSc Univ. London, 1911, 1916.
Offices and Honours Dir., Bank of England; Pres., Section F BAAS, 1926, RSS, 1930–2; created Baron, 1938.
Publications *Books:* 1. *The Fundamental Principles of Taxation* (1921, 1936); 2. *Wealth and Taxable Capacity*

(1922); 3. *Some Economic Factors in Modern Life* (1929); 4. *The Calculus of Plenty* (1935); 5. *The Science of Social Adjustment* (1937); 6. *The National Capital and other Statistical Studies* (1937).

Career Statistician and expert on taxation who did much to restructure the British tax system. His work was analytical and statistical rather than theoretical. The concept of excess profits, which could be taxed at a higher than normal rate, and the index of profits he developed in 1932, were two of his contributions in this field. His public lectures and articles included expositions of the problems of the national income and capital, as well as taxation questions.

Secondary Literature J. H. Jones, *Josiah Stamp: Public Servant* (Pitman, 1964); J. Mogey, 'Stamp, Josiah Charles', *IESS*, 15.

STEEDMAN, Ian Williamson

Born 1941, London, England.
Current Post Prof. Econ., Univ. Manchester, England, 1976–.
Past Posts Lect., Sr. Lect. Econ., Univ. Manchester, 1967–73, 1973–6; Nuffield Foundation Fellow, Florence, 1970–1.
Degrees BA Univ. Camb., 1964; PhD Univ. Manchester, 1967.
Editorial Duties Assoc. Ed., *Camb JE*, *Metroec.*; Book Rev. Ed., *MS*.
Principal Fields of Interest 022 Microeconomic Theory; 031 History of Economic Thought; 411 International Trade Theory.
Publications *Books:* 1. *Saggi sulla teoria del commercio internazionale*, ed. (Biblioteca Marsilio, 1977); 2. *Marx After Sraffa* (New Left Books, 1977; transls., Italian, Japanese, and Spanish); 3. *Fundamental Issues in Trade Theory*, ed. (Macmillan, 1979); 4. *Trade Amongst Growing Economies* (CUP, 1979).
Articles: 1. 'Reswitching and primary input use' (with J. S. Metcalfe), *EJ*, 82, March 1972, repr. in *Fundamental Issues in Trade Theory*, ed. I. Steedman (Macmillan, 1978); 2. 'Jevons's theory of capital and interest', *MS*, 40(1),

March 1972; 3. 'On foreign trade' (with J. S. Metcalfe), *Econ Int*, 26(3–4), Aug.–Nov. 1973; 4. 'Positive profits with negative surplus value', *EJ*, 85, March 1975, repr. in *Marx After Sraffa* (New Left Books, 1977); 5. 'Reswitching, primary inputs and the Heckscher-Ohlin-Samuelson theory of trade' (with J. S. Metcalfe), *J Int E*, 7(2), May 1977, repr. in *Fundametal Issues in Trade Theory*, *op cit.*; 6. 'Basics, non-basics and joint production, *EJ*, 87, June 1977, repr. in *Essays on the Theory of Joint Production*, ed. L. L. Pasinetti (Macmillan, 1980); 7. 'Heterogeneous labour and "classical" theory', *Metroec.*, 1980; 8. 'Marx on Ricardo', in *Marxian and Classical Political Economy. Essays in Honour of Ronald Meek*, eds. I. Bradley and M. Howard (Macmillan, 1981); 9. 'Time preference, the rate of interest and abstinence from accumulation', *AEP*, 20(37), Dec. 1981; 10. 'Joint production and the wage-rent frontier', *EJ*, 92, March 1982.

Principal Contributions My first response to any theory is 'What precisely is it saying and assuming?', and my second, not far behind, is 'What is wrong with it?'. I find economic theory fascinating but share J. S. Mill's respect for 'negative logic' — 'that which points out weaknesses in theory ... without establishing positive truths'. I find it implausible that any economic theory should be more than partially true and am always surprised by the apparent confidence of many economists who firmly advocate the adoption or the abandonment of particular economic policies. A respectful but sceptical view of economic theory is perhaps strengthened both by a concern with the history of thought. (I have studied Ricardo, Marx, Jevons and Wicksteed) and by the influence of Sraffa's writings. Italian economists have been and are important to the development of my own work in various fields, including the history of thought, capital theory, pure trade theory and the theory of joint production.

STEIN, Herbert

Born 1916, Detroit, MI, USA.
Current Post Sr. Fellow, AEI, Washington, DC, USA, 1984–.
Past Posts Econ., US Govt., Washington, DC, 1938–45; US Navy, 1944–5; Econ., Res. Dir., Comm. Econ. Devlp., Washington, DC., 1945–67; Fellow, Center Study Behavioral Sciences, Stanford, CA, 1965–6; Sr. Fellow, Brookings Inst., Washington, DC, 1967–8; Member, Chairman, US President's Council Econ. Advisers, 1969–71, 1972–4; Prof. Univ. Virginia, 1974–84.
Degrees BA Williams Coll., MA, 1935; PhD Univ. Chicago, 1958; Hon. LLD Rider Coll., 1971, Univ. Hartford, CT, 1978, Roanoke Coll., 1984, Williams Coll., 1980.
Offices and Honours First Prize, Pabst Postwar Employment Awards, 1944; Chairman, Pres., Nat. Econ. Club, 1966–8; Pres., SEA, 1983–4.
Editorial Duties Ed., *AEI Econ.*, 1977–.
Principal Fields of Interest 320 Fiscal Theory and Policy; Public Finance; 130 Economic Fluctuations; Forecasting; Stabilisation and Inflation; 042 North American Economic History.
Publications *Books:* 1. *Government Price Policy in the United States during the World War* (Williams Coll. Press, 1938); 2. *Jobs and Markets* (with T. O. Yntema, *et al.*), (Comm. Econ. Devlp., 1947); 3. *Policies to Combat Depression* (Arno Press, 1956); 4. *Fiscal Revolution in America* (Univ. Chicago Press, 1969); 5. *The Economic System in an Age of Discontinuity, Long Range Planning or Market Reliance?* (with W. Leontief), (NYU Press, 1976); 6. *On the Brink* (with B. Stein), (Simon & Schuster, 1977); 7. *Moneypower: How to Make Inflation Make you Rich* (with B. Stien), (Harper & Row, 1979); 8. *Presidential Economics: The Making of Economic Policy from Roosevelt to Reagan and Beyond* (Simon & Schuster, 1984).
Articles: 1. 'Managing the federal debt'. *J Law E*, 1, Oct. 1958; 2. 'High employment and economic growth' (with E. Denison), in *Goals for Americans* (Prentice-Hall, 1960); 3. 'Unem-

ployment, inflation and economic stability'. in *Agenda for the Nation*, ed. K. Gordon (Brookings Inst., 1968); 4. 'Don't fall for industrial policy', *Fortune*, Nov. 1983; 5. 'Fiscal policy: reflections on the past decade', in *Contemporary Economic Problems*, ed. W. Fellner (AEI, 1976); 6. 'Spending and getting', in *Contemporary Economic Problems*, ed. W. Fellner (AEI, 1977); 7. 'Price fixing as seen by a price fixer: Part II' in *Contemporary Economic Problems*, ed. W. Fellner (AEI, 1979); 9. 'The chief executive as chief economist', in *Contemporary Economic Problems*, ed. W. Fellner (AEI, 1981); 10. 'Fiscal policy: overview', in *International Encyclopedia of the Social Sciences*', ed. D. L. Sills (Macmillan, Free Press, 1968).
Principal Contributions In the period after World War II, participation in the development and dissemination of a strategy of economic policy that synthesised a positive marcroeconomic role for government with a free market. As a key part of that strategy, elaborated the implications of a policy of balancing the budget at high employment. In two books (1969 and 1984) told the history of the interaction of economic conditions, economic science and political forces in the evolution of economic policy in the US from 1929 to 1984. As member and chairman of the President's Council of Economic Advisers brought to Presidential decision-making the information and advice that contemporary economics had to offer. Continuing effort to supply objective analysis of economic policy issued to lay public through writing in newspapers and magazines and through lectures.

STERN, Nicholas Herbert

Born 1946, London, England.
Current Post Prof. Econ., Univ. Warwick, Coventry; Dir., Devlp. Econ. Res. Centre, Univ. Warwick, Coventry, England, 1978–.
Past Posts Univ. Lect. Industrial Maths., Fellow Tutor Econ., St Catharine's Coll. Oxford, 1970–7; Res. Assoc. Econ., MIT, 1972; Overseas Vis. Fellow, Ford Foundation Vis.

Prof., Indian Stat. Inst., 1974–5, 1981–2; CNRS Vis., Lab. d'Econ., Ecole Polytechnique, Paris, 1977; Vis. Scholar, Fiscal Affairs Dept., IMF, 1983.

Degrees BA (Maths.) Univ. Camb., 1967; DPhil Univ. Oxford, 1972.

Offices and Honours Scholar, William Heron Res. Student Econ., Peterhouse Coll. Camb., 1967, 1967–8; Nuffield Student, Nuffield Coll. Oxford, 1968–9; Jr. Res. Fellow Econ., Queen's Coll. Oxford, 1969–70; Fellow, Em Soc, 1978.

Editorial Duties Ed. Board, *REStud*, 1969–79; Joint Managing Ed., (with A. B. Atkinson), *OEP*, 1976–7; Advisory Ed., *Econ. Letters*.

Principal Fields of Interest 020 General Economic Theory; 110 Economics of Development; 320 Public Economic.

Publications *Books:* 1. *An Appraisal of Tea Production on Smallholdings in Kenya* (OECD, 1972); 2. *Theories of Economic Growth*, co-ed. (with J. A. Mirrlees), (Macmillan, 1973); 3. *Crime, the Police and Criminal Statistics* (with R. A. Carr-Hill), (Academic Press, 1979); 4. *Palanpur: The Economy of an Indian Village* (with C. J. Bliss), (OUP, 1982).

Articles: 1. 'Fairly good plans' (with J. A. Mirrlees), *JET*, 4(2), April 1972; 2. 'Optimum development in a dual economy', *REStud*, 39(2), April 1972; 3. 'The optimal structure of market areas' (with B. Boilobas), *JET*, 4(2), April 1972; 4. 'An econometric model of the supply and control of recorded offences in England and Wales' (with R. A. Carr-Hill), *J Pub E*, 2(4), Nov. 1973; 5. 'Pigou, taxation and public goods' (with A. B. Atkinson), *REStud*, 4(1), Jan. 1974; 6. 'Optimum saving with economies of scale' (with A. K. Dixit and J. A. Mirrlees), *REStud*, 42(3), July 1975; 7. 'Productivity, wages and nutrition: Part I: the theory' (with C. J. Bliss), *JDE*, 5(4), Dec. 1978; 8. 'Optimum taxation with errors in administration', *J Pub E*, 17(2), March 1982; 9. 'On the switch from direct to indirect taxation' (with A. B. Atkinson and J. Gomulka), *J Pub E*, 14(2), March 1980; 10. 'Oligopoly and welfare' (with A. K. Dixit), *Europ ER*, 19(1), 1982.

Principal Contributions From the beginning of my research, I have studied public economics and the economics of developing countries. The approach has sometimes been purely theoretical but a substantial element has always been applied. A major theme has been the use of the tools of quantitative analysis to study the consequences of government policy, and the systematic application of criteria to evaluate those policies. Examples range from the social cost-benefit analysis of a small-holder tea scheme in Kenya to the pure theory of optimum investment and growth policies and the theory of optimum income taxation. Careful policy formation involves the understanding of the way individuals behave and how they interact with markets. Thus development economics requires the study of village economies and in 1974–5 Christopher Bliss and I studied the economy of the village Palanpur in West Uttar Pradesh in India and our results were published in our book entitled *Palanpur*. Similary, use of the criminal statistics in discussion of crime and policy should be based on an understanding of how individuals, society and institutions interact to generate the figures, and my book on the British crime statistics with Roy Carr-Hill was directed to this end. More recently my research has concentrated on empirical work on public finance in both developing countries (particularly India, Pakistan and Mexico) at the Development Economics Research Centre of the University of Warwick, and the UK at the Taxation, Incentives and Distribution of Income Programme directed together with Professors Atkinson and King at LSE.

STEUART, James Denham*

Dates and Birthplace 1712–80, Edinburgh, Scotland.

Post Held Landowner.

Publications *Books:* 1. *An Inquiry into the Principles of Political Economy*, 2 vols (1767, 1976); 2. *Works, Political, Metaphysical and Chronological*, 6 vols (1805).

Career Jacobite exile, whose continental travels provided abundant material for his *Inquiry* . . . The Book is an expression of the Scottish philosophical school of the eighteenth century, couched in sophisticated mercantilist terms. His view of society was dynamic: free nations succeeding slave societies, and states passing through various phases of development; government should intervene when necessary in the operations of the market and little advantage is to be gained from free trade. His ideas were little noticed in Britain but received some attention from the German Historical School.

Secondary Literature W. Stark, 'Steuart, James Denham', *IESS*15; A. S. Skinner, 'Introduction', J. Steuart, *Inquiry*, vol. 1 (Oliver & Boyd, 1976).

STEUER, Max David

Born 1930, New York City, NY, USA.

Current Post Reader Econ., LSE, London, England, 1972–.

Past Posts Lect., Sr. Lect., LSE, 1960–7, 1967–72; Econ., UK Nat. Econ. Devlp. Office, 1962–4; Econ., Econ. Res. Group, UK Board Trade, 1964–6; Project Dir., UK Dept. Trade and Industry, 1967–70; Vis. Prof., Univ. Penn., 1969; Prof. Econ., Univ. Ghana, 1971–4.

Degrees BA, MA Columbia Univ., 1954, 1955.

Principal Fields of Interest 010 General Economics; 121 Economic Studies of Developing Countries; 411 International Trade Theory.

Publications *Books:* 1. *Mathematical Sociology, a Selective Annotated Bibliography* (with J. Holland), (Weidenfeld & Nicolson, 1969); 2. *The Impact of Foreign Direct Investment on the United Kingdom* (with P. Abell, *et al.*), (HMSO, 1973); 3. *After the Crisis — Longer Term Prospects for the Economy of Ghana* (Ghana Univ. Press, 1973).

Articles: 1. 'The relation between profits and wage rates' (with R. G. Lipsey), *Ec*, N.S. 28, May 1961; 2. 'A note on Kleiman on comparative advantage', *Ec*, N.S. 28, Aug. 1961; 3. 'Skill categories and the allocation of labour' (with M. D. Godfrey), *BJIR*, 1, June 1963; 4. 'An elementary exposition of the policy problem of maintaining internal and external balance' (with P. Saunders), *SJPE*, 11, June 1964; 5.

'Import substitution and Chenery's patterns of industrial growth: a further study' (with C. Voivodas), *EI*, 18, Feb. 1965; 6. 'An empirical test of the Gatt hypothesis' (with G. F. Erb), *JPE*, 74, June 1966; 7. 'The relationship between United Kingdom export performance in manufactures and the internal pressure of demand' (with R. J. Ball and J. R. Eaton), *EJ*, 76, Sept. 1966; 8. 'The effect of waiting times on foreign orders for machine tools' (with R. J. Ball and J. R. Eaton), *Ec*, N.S. 33, Nov. 1966; 9. 'Price and output decisions of firms — a critique of E. S. Mills' theory' (with A. P. Budd), *MS*, 36, March 1968; 10. 'The industrial relations of foreign owned subsidiaries in the United Kingdom' (with J. Gennard), *BJIR*, 9, July, 1971.

Principal Contributions Almost every area of economics is of interest to me and to compound the problem, I am particularly interested in interactions between economics and other social sciences. I am often struck by the analytical similarity between areas and also by the extent of interdependence. It is both a strength and a weakness of economics that it offers explanations largely without reference to the history or the culture of the people whose economic life is being explained. It manages to do this by relying too much on traditional maximising theory. I am interested in bringing something else to bear in addition to conventional rationality. The trick is to make that 'something' analytically tractable. At the moment, evolutionary economic theory seems to me to offer some hope. Without knowing exactly how to achieve it, I like the idea of economics having empirical content. I also think it should be of potential policy use. In very small and indirect ways my work has reflected this stance.

STEWART, Dugald*

Dates and Birthplace 1753–1828, Edinburgh, Scotland.

Posts Held Prof. Moral Philo., Univ. Glasgow, 1785–1810.

Publications *Books:* 1. *Outlines of Moral Philosophy* (1793); 2. *Account* *of the Life and Writings of Adam Smith* (1795), repr. in A. Smith, *Essays on Philosophical Subjects*, eds. W. P. D. Wightman and J. C. Bryce (1980); 3. *Philosophical Essays* (1810); 4. *Collected Works*, 11 vols (1854–60).

Career His lectures on political economy were extremely well attended and influential, many future statesmen, including Lord Palmerston, being amongst his students. The content of the lectures was derived very closely from Adam Smith, though differed slightly on some matters – e.g. he was rather more sympathetic towards the physiocrats than Smith. He was the author of the first biography of Smith.

Secondary Literature M. Stewart, *Memoir of the Late Dugald Stewart* (1838).

STEWART, Frances Julia

Born 1940, Kendal, Westmoreland, England.

Current Post Fellow, Somerville Coll. Sr. Res. Officer, Inst. Commonwealth Stud., Oxford Univ., 1972–.

Past Posts Econ. Ass., Treasury, London, 1961–2; Econ. Ass., Nat. Econ. Develp. Office, London, 1962–4; Econ. Ass., Econ. Adviser, UK Dept. Econ. Affairs, London, 1964–7; Lect., Univ. E. Africa, Nairobi, 1967–; Res. Officer, Queen Elizabeth House, Oxford, 1970–2; Full time Cons., Pol. Planning Div. World Bank, 1978–9.

Degrees BA (Philo., Polit. and Econ.), MA, DPhil Univ. Oxford, 1961, 1967, 1976.

Offices and Honours Jr., Sr., Webb Medley Prize Econ., Univ. Oxford, 1960, 1961; Council, Intermediate Technology Devlp. Group, 1981–; Council, RES, 1984–.

Editorial Duties Ed. Board, *WD*.

Principal Fields of Interest 112 Economic Development Models and Theories:; 121 Economic Studies of Developing Countries; 621 Technological Change; Innovation; Research and Development.

Publications *Books:* 1. *Employment, Income Distribution and Development*, ed. (Frank Cass, 1975); 2. *Technology and Underdevelopment* (Macmillan,

1977, 1978; transl., Spanish, Fondo de Cultura Economica, 1983); 3. *International Cooperation, A Framework for Change* (with A. Sengupta), (Frances Pinter, 1982); 4. *The Economics of New Technology in Developing Countries*, co-ed. (with J. James), (Frances Pinter, 1982); 5. *Work, Income and Inequality: Payments Systems in the Third World*, ed. (Macmillan, 1983); 6. *Planning to Meet Basic Needs* (Macmillan, 1985).

Articles: 1. 'Conflicts between output and employment objectives in developing countries' (with P. Streeten), *OEP*, 23(2), July 1971, repr. in *The Struggle for Economic Development*, ed. M. P. Todaro (Longman, 1983); 2. 'Choice of technique in developing countries', *JDS*, 9(1), Oct. 1972; 3. 'A note on social cost benefit analysis and class conflict in LDCs', *WD*, 3(1), repr. in *The Political Economy of Development and Underdevelopment*, ed. C. Wilber (Random House, 1979); 4. 'Kenya, strategies for development', in *Development Paths in India and China*, eds. G. Routh, *et al.* (Macmillan, 1975); repr. in *Papers on the Kenyan Economy*, ed. T. Killick (Heinemann, 1982); 5. 'Capital goods in developing countries', in *Employment, Income Distribution and Development Strategy*, eds. A. Cairncross and M. Puri (Macmillan, 1976), and *Development Economics and Policy Readings*, ed. I. Livingstone (A&U, 1981); 6. 'New strategies for development: poverty, income distribution and growth' (with P. Streeten), *OEP*, 28(3), Nov. 1976, repr. in *Distribution del Ingreso en America Latina*, ed. O. Munoz; 7. 'A new currency for trade among developing countries' (with M. Stewart), *Trade and Devlp.*, 2, Autumn 1980; 8. 'New products: a discussion of the welfare effects of new products in developing countries' (with J. James), *OEP*, 33(1), March 1981; 9. 'Work and welfare', in *Human Resources, Employment and Development*, eds. P. Streeten and H. Maier (Macmillan, 1983); 10. 'New theories of international trade: some implications for the south', in *Monopolistic Competition and International Trade*, ed. H. Kierzkowski (OUP, 1984).

Principal Contributions A predominant interest has been in technology and Third World Countries. This led to analysis of strategies of development, especially the Basic Needs approach. A parallel, and related, concern has been with the international system as it affects the Third World. From a theoretical perspective, my work has led to recognition of the limitations of pure neoclassical models — the need to allow for a wider range of influences and motives, and for substantial discontinuities, especially with respect to technology. I have worked within a structuralist framework (loosely defined), recognising, and attempting to analyse rigorously, the influence of interest groups on policies. Significant contributions have been: (1) extension of the neoclassical view of technology choice to include a wider range of influences. One consequence was to emphasise the importance of the composition of units (i.e. the proportion of investible resources controlled by different types of decision-maker) as a determinant of choice of technique; (2) development of the concept of *appropriate products* as part of appropriate technology, adopting a Lancaster approach to consumption; (3) recognition of the role of the capital goods sector in Thirld World countries, as a way of realising a different direction of technology change; (4) early (1973) recognition of the potential for South-South trade. With Michael Stewart, I developed the idea of a Third World currency to promote such trade; (5) the development of a macro-planning framework for 'Basic Needs' (with John Fei and Gustav Ranis). One important element is the recognition that ultimate welfare does not occur at the point of the consumption of goods, but depends on the impact of these goods on health and well-being. The metaproduction function relates to human well-being; and (6) attempts to analyse operational interest groups rigorously to understand policy formulation domestically and internationally.

STIGLER, George Joseph

Born 1911, Renton, WA, USA.
Current Post Charles R. Walgreen

Disting. Service Prof. Emeritus, Dir. Center for Study of the Economy and the State, Univ. Chicago, 1981–.

Past Posts Ass. Prof., Iowa State Univ., 1936–8; Ass. Prof., Assoc. Prof., Prof., Univ. Minnesota, 1938–46; Res. Staff, NBER, 1941–76; Prof., Brown Univ., 1946–7; Lect., LSE, 1948; Prof., Columbia Univ., 1947–58; Prof., Univ. Chicago, 1958–81.

Degrees BBA, Univ. Washington, 1931, MBA Northwestern Univ., 1932; PhD Univ. Chicago, 1938; Hon. DSc Carnegie-Mellon Univ., 1973, Univ. Rochester, NY, 1974, Helsinki School Econ., 1976, Northwestern Univ., 1979; Hon. LLD Brown Univ., 1980, DePaul Univ., MN, 1983.

Offices and Honours Member, Attorney General's Comm. Study Antitrust Laws, 1954–5; Guggenheim Foundation Fellow, 1955; Fellow, Center Advanced Study Behavioral Sciences, Stanford, CA, 1957–8; Pres., AEA, 1964; Member, Blue Ribbon Defense Panel, 1969–70; Vice-Chair., Dir., Securities Investor Protection Corp., 1971–4; Pres., Hist. Econ. Soc., 1977; Pres., Mont Pelerin Soc., 1977–8; Dir., Chicago Board Trade, 1980–3; Nobel Prize in Econ., 1982; Member, NAS; Fellow, ASA, Em Soc.

Editorial Duties Ed., *JPE*, 1974–.

Principal Fields of Interest 020 General Economic Theory; 030 History of Thought; 600 Industrial Organisation.

Publications Books: 1. *Production and Distribution Theories* (Macmillan, 1941); 2. *The Theory of Price* (Macmillan, 1942, 1966); 3. *Five Lectures on Economic Problems* (LSE, Longmans, Green, 1949); 4. *Supply and Demand for Scientific Personnel* (with D. Blank), (Princeton Univ. Press, 1957); 5. *The Economist as Preacher and Other Essays* (Univ. Chicago Press, 1962); 6. *Capital and Rates of Return in Manufacturing Industries* (Princeton Univ. Press, 1963); 7. *Essays in the History of Economics* (Univ. Chicago Press, 1965); 8. *The Organization of Industry* (Richard D. Irwin, 1968); 9. *The Behavior of Industrial Prices* (with J. K. Kindahl), (Columbia Univ. Press, 1970); 10. *The Citizen and the State: Essays on Regulation* (Univ. Chicago Press, 1975).

Articles: 1. 'Production and distribution in the short run', *JPE*, 47, June 1939; 2. 'The cost of subsistence', *JFE*, 27, May 1945; 3. 'The kinky oligopoly demand curve and rigid prices', *JPE*, 55, Oct. 1947; 4. 'The division of labor is limited by the extent of the market', *JPE*, 59, June 1951; 5. 'The economics of information', *JPE*, 69, June 1961; 6. 'A theory of oligopoly', *JPE*, 72, Feb. 1964; 7. 'Law enforcement, malfeasance and compensation of enforcers', *J Law E*, 3, Jan. 1974.

Principal Contributions Subject to the usual rule that everything has been anticipated, I have done early work in (1) the economics of information, which was treated as a standard economic quantity with demand and supply conditions, specialisation in production, etc. (Article No. 5 above); (2) the economic theory of regulation, which viewed the political market-place for regulation as also displaying the usual rational behaviour of all participants; this was preceded by a decade of studies of the effects of regulation; (3) linear programming, on the diet problem (Article No. 2); (4) a theory of collusive oligopoly and the limitations it encounters (Article No. 6); (5) the measurement of productivity when output is related to the sum of all inputs; (6) the measurement of economies of scale by the temporal pattern of the outputs of firms of different sizes, the so-called 'survivor' method (in Book 8); and (7) a variety of empirical tests of theories of industrial organisation (Article No. 3).

STIGLITZ, Joseph Eugene

Born 1943, Gary, IN, USA.
Current Post Prof. Econ., Princeton Univ., Princeton, NJ, USA, 1979–.
Past Posts Vis. Fellow, St Catherine's Coll. Oxford, 1973–4; Prof. Econ., Yale Univ., 1970–4; Prof. Econ., Stanford Univ., CA, 1974–6; Drummond Prof. Polit. Econ., Oxford Univ., 1976–9; Oskar Morgenstern Disting. Fellow, Vis. Prof., Inst. Advanced Stud. and Maths., Princeton, NJ, 1978–9; Vis. Scholar, Hoover Inst., Stanford, 1984.
Degrees BA Amherst Coll., MA, 1964; PhD MIT, 1966; Hon. MA Camb. Univ., 1970, Yale Univ., 1970, Oxford Univ., 1976; Hon. DHL Amherst Coll., 1974.
Offices and Honours Fulbright Fellow, 1965–6; Guggenheim Foundation Fellow, 1969–70; Fellow, Secretary, Em Soc, 1972–, 1972–5; John Bates Clark Medal, Exec. Comm. AEA, 1979, 1982; Elected Fellow, AAAS, 1983.
Editorial Duties General Ed., *Em Soc Repr. Series*, 1972–5; Co-ed., *JPE*; Assoc. Ed., *Managerial and Decision Econ.*
Principal Fields of Interest 020 General Economic Theory; 026 Economics of Uncertainty and Information; 320 Public Finance.
Publications *Books:* 1. *Collected Scientific Papers of Paul A. Samuelson*, 1, 2, ed. (MIT Press, 1965); 2. *Readings in Modern Theory of Economic Growth*, co-ed. (MIT Press, 1960); 3. *Lectures in Public Economics* (with A. B. Atkinson), (McGraw-Hill, 1980); 4. *Theory of Commodity Price Stabilization* (with D. Newbery), (OUP, 1981).
Articles: 1. 'Output, employment and wages in the short run' (with R. Solow), *QJE*, 82, Nov. 1968; 2. 'Distribution of income and wealth among individuals', *Em*, 37(3), July 1969; 3. 'Increasing risk: 1. A definition' (with M. Rothschild), *JET*, 2(3), Sept. 1970; 4. 'Taxation, corporate financial policy and the cost of capital', *JPE*, 2(1), Feb. 1973; 5. 'Incentives and risk sharing in share-cropping', *REStud*, 41(2), April 1974; 6. 'The design of tax structure: direct versus indirect taxation' (with A. B. Atkinson), *JPE*, 6(4), July–Aug. 1976; 7. 'Equilibrium in competitive insurance markets: an essay on the economics of imperfect information' (with M. Rothschild), *QJE*, 80(4), Nov. 1976; 8. 'On the impossibility of informationally efficient markets' (with S. Grossman), *AER*, 70(3), June 1980; 9. 'Credit rationing in markets with imperfect information' (with A. Weiss), *AER*, 71(3), June 1981; 10. 'Equilibrium unemployment as a worker discipline device' (with C. Shapiro), *AER*, 74(3), June 1984.
Principal Contributions The focus of my research during the past decade has been to extend our understanding of how imperfect and costly information

affects economic behaviour and market equilibrium. This work has shown that the basic existence, characterisation and welfare theorems of perfect competition are not robust (under weak conditions, market equilibrium does not exist; when it does, it is characterised by nonlinear price schedules; it is, in general, not constrained Pareto-efficient and, in equilibrium, demand may not equal supply). It has also laid the foundations of a more general theory which explicitly incorporates imperfect information. This work has explored detailed applications of this theory to the behaviour of monopolists and the government in labour, capital and product markets. This work has included detailed investigations of both moral hazard and adverse selection problems in both competitive and noncompetitive environments. Among the important applications are the microfoundations for macroeconomics (a theory of credit rationing and a theory of unemployment), the development of Pareto-efficient taxation (which takes into account the fact that lump-sum redistributive taxes are not feasible), a more general theory of competition (taking into account the information conveyed by relative performance), the theory of partial discriminating monopolists (which explains nonlinear pricing, commodity bundling, the theory of share-cropping, and the interlinkage of markets in LDCs) and the new theory of the firm, in which the manager is viewed as having considerable discretion.

STOCKING, George W.*

Dates and Birthplace 1892–1975, Clarendon, TX, USA.

Posts Held Ass. Prof., Prof. Econ., Univ. Texas, 1925–6, 1926–47; Prof. Econ., Vanderbilt Univ., TN, 1947–63; Fellow, Fund Res. Social Science, 1928–9; Guggenheim Foundation Fellow, 1932; Technical Adviser, US Labor Advisory Board, 1933–5; Member, Chairman, Petroleum Labor Pol. Board, NRA, 1933–4, 1934–5; Chairman, Nat. Longshoremen's Mediation Board, 1935–6; Member, Advisory Council Security Board, 1937–8; Ass. Dir.,

Bureau Res. and Stats., 1940; Econ. Cons., US Dept. Justice, 1941–4; Member, Nat. Defense Mediation Board, 1941; Dir., Fuels Div. Office Price Admin., 1942; Member, War Labor Board, 1943, Nat. Railway Labor Panel, 1943–6; Dir., Fed. Reserve Bank, San Antonio, TX, 1943–6.

Degrees BA, MA Univ. Texas, 1918, 1921; PhD Columbia Univ., 1925.

Offices and Honours Pres., SEA, 1952, AEA, 1958.

Publications *Books:* 1. *The Oil Industry and the Competitive System* (1925, 1973); 2. *The Potash Industry: A Study in State Control* (1933); 3. *Cartels in Action* (with M. W. Watkins), (1946); 4. *Cartels or Competition* (with M. W. Watkins), (1948); 5. *Monopoly and Free Enterprise* (with M. W. Watkins), (1951); 6. *Basing Point Pricing and Regional Development* (1954); 7. *Workable Competition and Antitrust Policy* (1961); 8. *Middle East Oil: A Study in Political and Economic Controversy* (1970).

Articles: 1. 'Labour problems in the American bituminous coal industry', *EJ*, 37(2), June 1927; 2. 'Stabilization of the oil industry: its economic and legal aspects', *AER*, 23(1), Suppl., March 1938; 3. 'The progress of concentration in industry', *AER*, 38(2), May 1948; 4. 'The antitrust laws: a symposium', *AER*, 39(4), June 1949; 5. 'The economics of basing point pricing', *Law and Contemporary Problems*, 15(2), Spring 1950; 6. 'Saving free enterprise from its friends', *SEJ*, 19(4), April 1953; 7. 'The rule of reason, workable competition, and the legality of trade association activities', *Univ. Chicago Law Rev.*, 21, Summer 1954; 8. 'The rule of reason, workable competition, and monopoly', *Yale Law J.*, 64(8), July 1955; 9. 'The duPont-General Motors case and the Sherman Act', *Virginia Law Rev.*, 44(1), Jan. 1958; 10. 'Institutional factors in economic thinking', *AER*, 49(1), March 1959.

Career George Stocking's main contributions were in the area where economics, law and policy overlap: industrial organisation, market behaviour, and antitrust policy. He was widely known for his strong belief in the virtues of open competition and the diffusion of power; he held 'Populist' attitudes toward large corporations and market concentration. His work dealt with the international aspects of monopoly and cartels as well as with the origins of monopoly and oligopoly. His advocacy of structural reorganisation of monopoly markets was also developed in a number of articles and in testimony before government agencies, while other publications analysed several important antitrust cases. Stocking also contributed to the economics of international oil in his last important work, which examined the role of major oil companies in the Middle East during the critical periods before an after World War II.

Secondary Literature J. W. McKie, 'George W. Stocking (obit.)', *AER*, 62(3), June 1976.

STOLL, Hans R.

Born 1939, Regensburg, Germany.
Current Post Walker Prof. Fin., Owen Grad. School Management, Vanderbilt Univ., Nashville, TN, USA, 1977–.
Past Posts Instr. Bus. Econ., Grad. School Bus., Univ. Chicago, 1965–6; Ass. Prof., Assoc. Prof. Fin., Wharton School, Univ. Penn., 1966–80; Vis. Prof., Board Governors Fed. Reserve System, 1968–9; Sr. Econ., Inst. Investors Study, Securities and Exchange Commission, Washington, DC, 1969–70; Vis. Assoc. Prof. Fin., Grad. School Bus., Univ. Chicago, 1975–6; Sr. Fulbright-Hays Acting Vis. Lect., Ecole Supérieure des Sciences Econ. et Commerciales, Paris, 1976–7.
Degrees BA Swarthmore Coll., PA, 1961; MBA, PhD Univ. Chicago, 1963, 1966.
Editorial Duties Ed. Boards, *Fin. Management*, *J. Fin. Res.*
Principal Fields of Interest 310 Domestic Monetary and Financial Theory and Institutions; 520 Business Finance and Investment.
Publications *Books:* 1. 'Taxes, Financial Policy and Small Business (with T. Day and R. Whaley), (D. C. Heath, 1985).
Articles: 1. 'An empirical study of the forward exchange market under fixed and flexible exchange rate systems', *CJE*, 1, Feb. 1968; 2. 'The relationship between put and call optional prices', *J Fin*, 24, Dec. 1969; 3. 'Price impacts of block trading on the NYSE' (with A. Kraus), *J Fin*, 27, June 1972; 4. 'The supply of dealer services in securities markets', *J Fin*, 33, Sept. 1978; 5. 'The pricing of security dealer services: an empirical study of NASDAQ stocks', *J Fin*, 33, Sept. 1978; 6. 'Commodity futures and spot price determination and hedging in capital market equilibrium', *J. Fin. and Quant. Analysis*, 14, Nov. 1979; 7. 'Optimal dealer pricing under transactions and return uncertainty' (with T. Ho), *J Fin. Econ.*, 9, March 1981; 8. 'Transaction costs and the small firm effect' (with R. E. Whaley), *J Fin. Econ.*, 12, June 1983; 9. 'The dynamics of dealer markets under competition' (with T. Ho), *J Fin*, 38, Sept. 1983; 10. 'Spot and futures prices and the law of one price' (with A. Protopapadakis), *J Fin*, 38, Dec. 1983.

Principal Contributions After completing a dissertation on the forward foreign exchange market at the Graduate School of Business of the University of Chicago, I began teaching corporate finance and speculative markets at the Wharton School. Among other things, this teaching responsibility led to an interest in speculative markets and led to research on options markets and the derivation of the put-call parity relationship for options on common stocks and empirical tests of that relationship. A stint at the Securities and Exchange Commission on its Institutional Investors Study generated research on the impact of institutional investors on securities prices. Also in part as a result of this experience at the SEC, I worked on the impact of the deregulation of New York Stock Exchange commission rates and wrote a number of papers on the provision of dealer services in securitites markets. These papers provide a theory of the dealer in securities markets and carry out some empirical tests using over-the-counter bid-ask spread data. I also developed an interest in commodity futures, published a paper on the determination of spot and futures prices in capital market equilbrum as well as a more recent paper examining international purchasing power parity using commodity futures prices. Finally, I have had an interest in small business financing issues, having completed several papers on this subject and most recently co-authored a book that examines taxes and financial policies of small firms.

STOLPER, Wolfgang Friedrich

Born 1912, Vienna, Austro-Hungary.
Current Post Prof. Emeritus, Univ. Michigan, Ann Arbor, MI, USA, 1982–.
Past Posts Instr., Tutor, Harvard Univ., 1936–41; Ass. Prof., Assoc. Prof., Swarthmore Coll., 1941–9; Assoc. Prof., Prof., Dir., Center Res. Econ. Devlp., Univ. Michigan, 1949–82, 1963–70; Vis. Prof., Univ., Zurich, 1952, 1969, 1971, 1973–9, Heidelberg, 1966, Munster, 1966, Bern 1971, Ibadan (Nigeria), 1974, Hawaii at Manoa, 1982; Head, Econ. Planning Unit, Fed. Ministry Econ. Devlp., Lagos, 1960–2; Member, Econ. Section, IBRD, 1967; Cons., IBRD, USAID, Ford Foundation.
Degrees MA, PhD Harvard Univ., 1935, 1938; Hon. Dr Rer. Pol. Univ. Saarbrücken, W. Germany.
Offices and Honours Charles W. Holtzer Fellow, Univ. Fellow, Harvard Univ., 1934–5, 1935–6; Guggenheim Foundation Fellow, 1947–8; August Lösch Memorial Ring, City of Heidenheim and Internat. Regional Sciences Assoc., 1982; Grosses Verdientkreuz Fed. Republic Germany, 1982.
Principal Fields of Interest 031 History of Economic Thought; 113 Economic Planning Theory and Policy; 411 International Trade Theory.
Publications *Books:* 1. *Germany Between East and West* (Nat. Planning Assoc., 1960); 2. *The Structure of the East German Economy* (Harvard Univ. Press, 1960); 3. *Planning Without Facts* (Harvard Univ. Press, 1966); 4. *Budget, Economic Policy and Economic Performance in Underdeveloped Countries* (J. C. B. Mohr, P. Siebeck, 1971).
Articles: 1. 'British monetary policy and the housing boom', *QJE*, pt. 2, 16(1), Nov. 1941; 2. 'Protection and real wages' (with P. A. Samuelson), *REStud*, 9, Nov. 1941, repr. in *Read-*ings in the Theory of International Trade*, eds. H. S. Ellis and L. A. Metzler (Blakiston, 1949), and *International Trade*, ed. J. Bhagwati (Penguin, 1969), and *Collected Scientific Papers of P. A. Samuelson* (MIT Press, 1966); transl., German, *Theorie der Internationalen Wirtschaftsbezieung*, ed. K. Ruse (Fischer Verlag, 1965); 3. 'Notes on the dollar shortage', *AER*, 40(3), June 1950; 4. 'A method of constructing community indifference curves', *Schweizzeitschaft für Volkswirts*, 86(2), 1950; 5. 'Spatial order and the economic growth of cities', *EDCC*, 3(2), 1955; 6. 'An input-output table of East Germany with application to foreign trade' (with K. W. Roskamp), *BOIS*, 23, Nov. 1961; 7. 'Social factors in economic planning', *E. African Econ. Rev.*, 1964; 8. 'Aspects of Schumpeter's theory of evolution', in *Schumpeterian Economics*, ed. H. Frisch (Praeger, 1982); 9. 'Fiscal and monetary policy in the context of development', in *Public Finance and Economic Growth*, eds. D. Biehl, K. Roskamp and W. Stolper (Praeger, 1983).

Principal Contributions The joint article with Samuelson analyses for the first time the precise relationship between the prices of goods and relative shares of factors. The other trade articles establish an 'import multiplier'. The East German input-output study, measures the gains from trade as defined by Samuelson, i.e. as an improvement in the input-output relationship as the consequence of factor reallocations due to trade. *The Structure of the East German Economy* measures the GNP of a communist country from the production side; it is also a product by product comparison with West German developments, the only instance in which the differences between two economies is due solely to the difference in types of economic system. The work on underdeveloped countries deals with problems and ways of translating theoretical insights into economic policies under actual (Nigerian and other African) circumstances. It is argued that the recurrent budget rather than the plan or development budget is the central concern of economic policy-making where all decisions come together and all distortions and mistakes become apparent. The work on Schumpeter tries to show his relationship to later theoretical developments. It also deals with his economic policy writings and activities.

STONE, John Richard Nicholas

Born 1913, London, England.
Current Post Emeritus Prof., Univ. Camb., 1980–.
Past Posts UK Office War Cabinet, Central Stat. Office, 1940–5; Dir., Dept. Appl. Econ., Univ. Camb., 1945–55; P.D. Leake Prof. Fin. Accounting, Univ. Camb., 1955–80; Vis. Scholar, Inst. Advanced Study, Princeton, 1945; Cons., Chairman, League of Nations Subcomm. Nat. Income Stats., 1945; Dir., OEEC, Nat. Accounts Res. Unit, Camb., 1949–51; Cons., Chairman, UN Expert Group Nat. Accounts, 1972; Vis. Prof., Johns Hopkins Univ., 1953; Vis. Prof., School Stats. and Planning, Warsaw, 1960; Cons., Chairman, UN Expert Group Revision Nat. Accounts, 1963–8; Cons., OECD Comm. Scientific and Technical Personnel, 1966–71; Vis. Prof., Univ. Havana, 1971; Cons. Member, UN Expert Group System of Social and Demographic Stats., 1969–75; Vis. Prof., Univ. Geneva, 1979.
Degrees BA, MA, DSc Univ. Camb., 1953, 1938, 1957; Hon. Dr, Univs. Oslo, Free Univ. Brussels, 1965, Geneva, 1971, Warwick, 1975, Pantheon-Sorbonne, Paris I, 1977, Bristol, 1978.
Offices and Honours Fellow, King's Coll. Camb., 1945–; CBE, 1946; Member, Internat. Stat. Inst., 1946; Fellow, Pres., Em Soc., 1946, 1955; Hon. Member, Soc. Incorporated Accountants Auditors, 1954; Fellow, BA, 1956; Foreign Hon. Member, AAAS, 1968; Hon. Member, AEA, 1976; Hon. Fellow, Gonville and Caius Coll. Camb., 1976; Knighted, 1978; Pres., RES, 1978–80, Nobel Prize in Econ., 1985.
Editorial Duties Ed. Board, *JRSS Series B*, 1949–56, *Metroec.*, 1949–; *Em*, 1951–66, *Econ. Modelling*, 1984–; Ed. *Nat. Accounts Stud.* (OEEC), 1951–3, *Stud. Nat. Income and Expenditure of UK, 1920–38* (*CUP*, 1953–72),

A Programme for Growth (Chapman & Hall, 1962–74).
Principal Fields of Interest 100 Economic Growth; Development; Planning; Fluctuations. 200 Quantitative Economic Methods and Data; 900 Welfare Programmes; Consumer Economics; Urban and Regional Economics.
Publications *Books:* 1. *National Income and Expenditure* (with J. E. Meade), (OUP, 1944, Bowes & Bowes, 1948, 1957), (with G. Stone), (Bowes & Bowes, 1961, 1977; transls., Spanish, 1965, Japanese 1969); 2. *The Role of Measurement in Economics* (CUP 1951); 3. *The Measurement of Consumers' Expenditure and Behaviour in the United Kingdom, 1920–1938*, 2 vols. (with D. A. Rowe, *et al.*), (CUP, 1954, 1966); 4. *Quantity and Price Indexes in National Accounts* (OEEC, 1956); 5. *Input-Output and National Accounts* (OEEC, 1961, transl, Russian, 1964); 6. *A Computable Model of Economic Growth* (with J. A. C. Brown), (Chapman & Hall 1962; transl., Czech, 1965); 7. *Mathematics in the Social Sciences and Other Essays* (Chapman & Hall, 1966; transl., Polish, 1970); 8. *Mathematical Models of the Economy and Other Essays* (Chapman & Hall, 1970); 9. *Demographic Accounting and Model-Building* (OECD, 1971); 10. *Towards a System of Social and Demographic Statistics* (with A. Aidenoff), (UN, 1975).
Articles: 1. 'Definition and measurement of the national income and related totals', in *Measurement of National Income and the Construction of National Accounts* (UN, 1947); 2. 'On the interdependence of blocks of transactions', *JRSS Suppl*, 9(1–2), 1947; 3. 'Prediction from autoregressive schemes and linear stochastic difference systems', in *Proceedings Internat. Stat. Conf.*, 5, 1951; 4. 'Linear expenditure systems and demand analysis', *EJ*, 64, Sept. 1954, repr. in *The Structural Interdependence of the Economy* (Wiley, Giuffrè, 1955); 5. 'Transition and admission models in social demography', *Social Science Res.*, 2(2), 1973, repr. in *Social Indicator Models* (Russell Sage, 1975); 6. 'Direct and indirect constraints in the adjustment of observations', in *Nasjonalrgnskap, Modeller og Analyse* (Statistisk Sentralbyra, 1975); 7. 'Sig-

moids', *Bull. Appl Stats.*, 7(1), 1980; 8. 'The relationship of demographic accounts to national income and product accounts', in *Social Accounting Systems*, eds. F. T. Juster and K. C. Land (Academic Press, 1982); 9. 'Model design and simulation', *Econ. Modelling*, 1(1), 1984; 10. 'Balancing the national accounts', in *Demand, Trade and Equilibrium* (Macmillan, 1984).

Principal Contributions Econometric application of mathematical and statistical techniques to economic and social processes: demand analysis with single equations and systems of equations (linear expenditure system); aggregate consumption and saving functions; input-output; systems of index-numbers; adjustment of observations; seasonal variation; projection errors; economic control; sigmoid growth; and simulation. National accounting systems: first official estimates of British national income and expenditure (Book 1 above); standardised systems of national accounts (Article 1 and Books 4 and 5 above) an integrated system of social and demographic statistics and its links with the economy (Books 9 and 10 above); and The 'Cambridge Growth Project', a disaggregated model of the British economy (Book 6 above).

STORCH, Heinrich Friedrich Von*

Dates and Birthplace 1766–1835, Riga, Russia.

Post Held Russian Govt. Employee, 1789.

Offices and Honours Member, Russian Academy Sciences.

Publications *Books:* 1. *Statistische Uebersicht der Staatshalterschaften des Russischen Reiches* (1795); 2. *Historisch-statistisches Gemälde des Russischen Reiches*, 9 vols (1797–1803); 3. *Cours d'économie politique*, 6 vols (1815); 4. *Considérations sur la nature du revenu national* (1824).

Career His historical-statistical work on Russia and published lectures on political economy were his two sources of fame. Though basically a Smithian, he developed a theory of stages in economic development, with different economic principles needed to explain the workings of each stage. His later work was largely concerned with questions of national income.

Secondary Literature V. Gelesnoff, 'Storch, Heinrich Friedrich von', *ESS*, 14.

STREETEN, Paul Patrick

Born 1917, Vienna, Austro-Hungary.

Current Post Dir., World Devlp Inst., Prof., Boston Univ., Boston, MA, USA, 1983–.

Past Posts Fellow, Balliol Coll. Oxford, 1948–66, 1968–78; Vis. Fellow, Johns Hopkins Univ., 1955–6; Fellow, Advanced Stud., Wesleyan Univ., 1962–3; Dep. Dir. Econ. Planning, UK Ministry Overseas Devlp., 1964–6; Fellow, Acting Dir., Prof. Econ., Inst. Devlp. Stud., Univ. Sussex, 1966–8; Warden, Queen Elizabeth House, DIR., Inst. Commonwealth Stud., Univ. Oxford, 1968–79; Special Adviser, World Bank, 1976–80; Dir. Stud., Overseas Devlp. Inst., Washington, 1979–80; Dir., Asian Devlp. Stud., Boston Univ., 1980–3; Leader, ILO Basic Needs Mission, Tanzania, 1981.

Degrees MA Aberdeen Univ., 1944; BA, MA, DLitt Univ. Oxford, 1947, 1952, 1976; Hon. LLD Aberdeen Univ., 1980.

Offices and Honours Rockefeller Fellow, 1950–1; Member Board, Commonwealth Devlp. Corp., 1967–72; Member, UK Nat. Commission, UNESCO, 1966–70; Vice-Chairman, UK Social Sciences Advisory Comm; Member, Royal Commission Environmental Pollution, 1974–6; Provisional Council, Univ. Mauritius, 1966–72; Statutory Commission, Univ. Malta, 1972–; Advisory Panel, Canadian Univ. Service Overseas; Governing Body, Queen Elizabeth House, Univ. Oxford, 1966–8, Inst. Devlp. Stud, Univ. Sussex, 1968–80, Dominion Students' Hall Trust, London House, Overseas Devlp. Inst., London, 1972–7, Trade Pol. Res. Center, London, 1972–83.

Editorial Duties Ed., *BOIS*, 1961–6; Ed. Board, *J Dev Stud*, 1966–70.

Principal Fields of Interest 133 Economic Planning Theory and Policy; 400

International Investment and Aid; 036 Economic Methodology.

Publications *Books:* 1. *The Political Element in the Development of Economic Theory*, G. Myrdal, ed. (Routledge & Kegan Paul, 1953; transls., German, 1963, French, Italian, Portuguese.); 2. *Economic Integration: Aspects and Problems* (Sythoff, 1961, 1964); 3. *The Crisis of Indian Planning*, co-ed. (with M. Lipton), (OUP, 1968); 4. *Unfashionable Economics*, ed. (Weidenfeld & Nicolson, 1970); 5. *Diversification and Development: The Case of Coffee* (with D. Elson), (Praeger, 1971); 6. *Aid to Africa* (Praeger, 1972); 7. *The Frontiers of Development Studies* (Macmillan, 1972; transl., Spanish, 1982); 8. *Foreign Investment, Transnationals and Developing Countries* (with S. Lall), (Macmillan, 1977); 9. *Development Perspectives* (Macmillan, 1981); 10. *First Things First: Meeting Basic Human Needs in Developing Countries* (with S. J. Burki, *et al.*), (OUP, 1981).

Articles: 1. 'Economics and value judgements' *QJE*, 64, Nov. 1950; 2. 'The inappropriateness of simple "elasticity" concepts in the theory of international trade' (with T. Balogh), *BNLQR*, 3, Oct.–Dec. 1950, and *BOIS*, 13, March 1951; 3. 'The effect of taxation on risktaking' *OEP*, 5(3), Sept. 1953; 4. 'Programs and prognoses' *QJE*, 68(3), Aug. 1954; 5. 'A note on Kaldor's speculation and economic stability', *REStud*, 26(1), Oct. 1958; 6. 'Unbalanced growth', *OEP*, 11, June 1959; 7. 'Domestic vs. foreign investment' (with T. Balogh), *BOIS*, 22, Aug. 1960; 8. 'Wages, prices and productivity', *Kyk*, 15(3), Oct. 1962, repr. in *Penguin Modern Economics Readings: Inflation*, eds. R. J. Ball and P. Doyle (Penguin, 1969); 9. 'The coefficient of ignorance' (with T. Balogh), *BOIS*, 25(2), 1963, repr. in *Penguin Modern Economics Readings: Economics of Education, 1*, ed. M. Blaug (Penguin, 1969); 10. 'The limits of development research', *WD*, 2, 10–12, Oct.–Dec. 1974.

Principal Contributions Having had to cover a very wide area as tutorial fellow with a heavy teaching load and without opportunity for graduate studies, I never acquired the taste for specialisation in a 'field' (or patch). Work on methodology, welfare economics, public finance and international trade emphasised the importance of changing institutions. Early critique of welfare economics, international trade theory, and flexible exchange rates made for scepticism of models that pour out the baby instead of the bathwater, and for emphasis on discontinuities, asymmetries, irreversibilities, and indivisibilities. In my first book, *Economic Integration*, I criticised the European Community and balanced growth. Work with Myrdal on *Asian Drama* and in the UK Development Ministry changed my interest from theory to policy, especially development, and how to bridge the gap between thinkers and doers. Experience in planning for a very small country (Malta) and a very large one (India) led to work on different kinds of interaction between domestic and international factors.

As something of an expert in imperial decay (Austria and Britain), I stressed the gap between technological advances and institutional inertia and the need for exercise of intitutional imagination, interdisciplinary approaches and explicit introduction of value premises. In this light, contributions to public finance, welfare economics, theory of inflation, international trade and development can be seen as attempts to loosen intellectual muscles to avoid intellectual cramps induced by 'Rigour' that is irrelevant to the world we live in. As an early critic of the advocacy of 'maximising' growth, I was put in charge of World Bank's work on Basic Needs, but never felt happy as propagandist or apologist. Return to academia led to the return to a more critical stance.

STROTZ, Robert Henry

Born 1922, Aurora, IL, USA.

Current Post Pres., Northwestern Univ., Evanston, IL, USA, 1970–.

Past Posts Instr., Ass. Prof., Assoc. Prof., Prof. Econ., Dean, College of Arts and Sciences, Northwestern Univ., 1947–51, 1951–2, 1952–8, 1958–70, 1966–70; Vis. Prof., MIT, 1958–9.

Degrees BA, PhD Univ. Chicago, 1942, 1951; Hon LLD Illinois Wesleyan Univ., 1976, Millikin Univ., 1979.

Offices and Honours Rockefeller Foundation Grant, 1955–6; Member, Chairman, Social Science Advisory Comm., NSF, 1968–71, 1969–70; Fellow, Em Soc, 1959; Member, Nat. Board Grad. Educ., 1971–5.

Editorial Duties Managing Ed., *Em*, 1953–68; Assoc. Ed., *Int ER*, 1960–4; Special Ed. Econometrics, *Internat. Encyclopedia Social Sciences*, ed. D.L. Sills (Free Press, 1968), 1962–8.

Principal Fields of Interest 024 Welfare Theory; 036 Economic Methodology; 021 General Equilibrium Theory.

Publications *Books:* 1. *Problems for Economic Analysis* (with C. L. Allen and A. Morgner), (Prentice-Hall, 1948); 2. *Problems in the Theory of Price* (with C.L. Allen and A. Morgner), (Prentice-Hall, 1954).

Articles: 1. 'Long-run marginal cost and fluctuating output' (with H. M. Oliver), *SEJ*, 18, Oct. 1951, repr. in *Readings in Microeconomics*, ed. S. M. Blummer (Internat. Textbook, 1969); 2. 'Cardinal utility', *AER*, 43(2), May 1953, repr. in *Readings in Microeconomics*, ed. D. R. Kemerschen (World Publ., 1970); 3. 'Myopia and inconsistency in dynamic utility maximization', *RES*, 23(3), 1956; 4. 'The empirical implications of a utility tree', *Em*, 25, April 1957; 5. 'How income ought to be distributed: a paradox in distributive ethics', *JPE*, 66, June 1958; 6. 'Recursive vs. nonrecursive systems', (with H. O. A. Wold), *Em*, 28, April 1960; 7. 'How income ought to be distributed: paradox regained', *JPE*, 69, June 1961; 8. 'Flight insurance and the theory of choice' (with R. Eisner), *JPE*, 69, Aug. 1961; 9. 'The Keynesian model with a generalized money illusion', *RISE*, 10, Oct. 1965, repr. in *Essays in Honor of Marco Fanno*, *Studi in Onore di Marco Fanno*, 11 (Cedam 1966); 10. 'Econometrics', in *Internat. Encyclopedia Social Sciences*, ed. D. L. Sills, (Macmillan, Free Press, 1968).

STRUMILIN, Stanislav Gustavovich*

Dates and Birthplace 1877–1974, Dashkovtsy, Russia.

Posts Held Employee, Soviet State Planning Comm., 1921–37, 1943–51; Taught, Moscow State Univ., 1921–3, Inst. Nat. Econ., 1929–30, Moscow State Inst. Econ., 1931–50, Academy Social Sciences, 1948–74.

Offices and Honours Member, Soviet Academy, 1931; Lenin Prize, 1958; Hero of Socialist Labour, 1967.

Publications *Books:* 1. *Wealth and Labour* (1905); 2. *Problems of the Economics of Labour* (1925); 3. *Essays on the Soviet Economy* (1928); 4. *The Industrial Revolution in Russia* (1944).

Articles: 1. 'The economic significance of national education', *Planovoe Khoziaistvo*, 9–10, 1924, repr. in *Readings in the Economics of Education*, eds. M.J. Bowman, *et al.* (UNESCO, 1968); 2. 'The economics of education in the USSR', *Internat. Social Science J.*, 14(4), 1962.

Career His career spanned the entire Stalinist era and covered a wide range of activities; his more than 700 publications range through statistics, social sciences and economic history. He devised an index of labour productivity (the 'Strumilin index') and until his death he presided over all Soviet debates on economic questions.

STUBBLEBINE, William Craig

Born 1936, West Point, NY, USA.

Current Post Von Tobel Prof. Polit. Econ., Res. Prof., Center Study Law Structures, Claremont McKenna Coll., CA, 1977–.

Past Posts Ass. Prof., Univ. Virginia, 1961–3; Ass. Prof., Univ. Delaware, 1963–6; Nat. Science Fellow, MIT, 1965–6; Assoc. Prof., Prof., Claremont Men's Coll. and Claremont Grad. School, 1966–76, 1976–9; Fulbright Scholar, Univ. Turin, 1967–8; Vis. Prof., Southern Methodist Univ., TX, 1971; Virginia Polytechnic Inst., 1972; Dir., Center Study Law Structures, Claremont McKenna Coll., 1977–84.

Degrees BS Univ. Delaware, 1958; PhD Univ. Virginia, 1963.

Offices and Honours Amer. Polit. Science Assoc.; Mont Pelerin Soc.; Public Choice Soc; WEA; Snavely Prize, Univ. Virginia, 1965; Vice-Pres., Western Tax Assoc., 1979–81.

Principal Fields of Interest 822 Public Policy.

Publications *Books:* 1. *Balanced Budget — Tax Limitation Amendment* (with S. J. Markman), (US Senate Comm. on Judiciary, 1981); 2. *Reaganomics: A Mid-Term Report*, co-ed. (with T. D. Willett), (ICS, 1983).

Articles: 1. 'Externality' (with J. M. Buchanan), *Ec*, N.S. 29, Nov. 1962; 2. 'Institutional elements in the finance of education', *SEJ*, 32, Nov. 1965; 3. 'On property rights and institutions', in *Explorations in the Theory of Anarchy* (Virginia Polytechnic Inst., 1972); 4. 'California and the finance of education' (with R. K. Teeples), in *Property Taxation and the Finance of Education* (Univ. Wisconsin Press, 1974); 5. 'Price of electricity under different alternatives' and 'On changing the law', in *Electric Power Reform* (Univ. Michigan, 1976); 6. 'California and property tax limitation' (with E. F. Toma), *Nevada Rev. Bus. and Econ.*, 2, Winter 1978–9; 7. 'SJR 56; the Federal limit', Proposed Constitutional amendment to balance the Federal budget, *Hearings*, US Senate, Series No. 96–41 (US Govt. Printing Office, 1980); 8. 'Balancing the budget versus limiting spending', in *The Constitution and the Budget* (AEI, 1980); 9. 'Practical problems of constitutional reform', in *Constitutional Economics* (D. C. Heath, 1982); 10. 'The balanced budget/tax limitation amendment', *Hastings Constitutional Law Q.*, 10, Summer 1983.

Principal Contributions Participated in the rethinking of externality theory, public good theory, and property rights theory, as well as theoretical and practical applications of public choice theory. Contributions to the development of constitutional limits on government taxing and spending has had a major impact, including adoption of constitutional amendments in several American states.

SUITS, Daniel Burbidge

Born 1918, St Louis, MO, USA.

Current Post Prof. Econ., Michigan State Univ., E. Lansing, MI, USA, 1974–.

Past Posts Ass. Prof., Assoc. Prof., Prof. Econ., Instr., Univ. Michigan, 1946–50, 1950–55, 1955–9, 1959–69; Res. Assoc., NBER, 1953; Dir. Amer. Stud. Seminar; Lect., Kyoto Univ., Doshisha Univ., Kyoto, Japan, 1958; Res. Assoc., Center Econ. Res., Athens, 1963; Vis. Prof., Univ. Hawaii, 1966, 1973–4, 1976; Prof. Econ., Univ. Cal. Santa Cruz, 1969–74.

Degrees BA(Philo.), MA, PhD Univ. Michigan, 1940, 1941, 1948.

Offices and Honours Fellow, Em Soc, ASA, East-West Pop. Inst.; Disting. Faculty Award, Michigan State Univ., 1980.

Principal Fields of Interest 111 Economic Growth Theory and Models; 210 Econometric, Statistical and Mathematical Methods and Models; 840 Demographic Economics.

Publications *Books:* 1. *Statistics: An Introduction to Quantitative Economic Research* (Rand McNally, 1963; transl., Japanese, 1980); 2. *Theory and Application of Econometric Models* (Center Econ. Res., 1963); 3. *An Econometric Model of the Greek Economy* (Center Econ. Res., 1964; transl., Greek, 1964); 4. *Principles of Economics* (Harper & Row, 1970, 1973; transl., Japanese, 1978).

Articles: 1. 'An econometric model of the watermelon market', *JFE*, 37(2), May 1955; 2. 'The demand for automobiles in the United States, 1929–1956', *REStat*, 40(3), Aug. 1958; transl., Japanese, Machine Industry Council, 1960, repr. in *Readings in Managerial Economics*, eds. T. J. Coyne, *et al.* (Bus. Publ., 1977); 3. 'Forecasting and analysis with an econometric model', *AER*, 52(1), March 1962, repr. in *Readings in Business Cycles*, eds. R. A. Gordon and L. R. Klein (Richard D. Irwin, 1965), and *Readings in Economics and Statistics*, ed. A. Zellner (Little, Brown, 1968); 4. 'Determinants of consumer expenditure', in *Impacts of Monetary Policy*, eds. D. B. Suits, *et al.* (Prentice-Hall, 1963); 5. 'Birth control in an econometric simulation' (with W. Mardfin, *et al.*), *Int ER*, 16(1), Feb. 1975; 6. 'Gambling taxes: regressivity and revenue potential', *Nat. Tax J.*, 16(1), Feb. 1977; 7. 'Measurement of tax progressivity', *AER*, 67(4), Sept. 1977; 8. 'Spline functions fitted by standard least squares methods' (with A. Mason and L. Chan), *REStat*, 60(1), Feb. 1978; 9. 'Measuring the gains from population control: results of an econometric simulation' (with A. Mason), in *Research in Population Economics*, ed. L. Simon (JAI Press, 1982).

Principal Contributions I suppose it was the experience of the Great Depression that led me into economics. From the beginning, I found the greatest appeal in quantitative economics: the testing of economic theory and the measurement of theoretically meaningful economic relationships. This has continued to be the centre of my research activity. Aside from sporadic *ad hoc* attacks on individual problems (most recently on the economics of gambling), my research has been organised around econometric models: models of individual markets for products ranging from automobiles to watermelons; models of the short-run behaviour of the US economy; and most recently (in close collaboration with A. Mason at the East-West Population Institute), models of long-run economic development and demographic change. Experience with these models has taught me several important principles of econometric research. First, models are best evaluated by their performance, preferably by regular public forecasts. Secondly, there is no perfect model. At best, models are crude approximations to a continuously shifting reality. For this reason, a model should always be treated as a continuing research project. Econometric models are immense fun, and they have probably contributed something to economic stability, but increasingly I believe that the single most important thing an academic economist can do is to teach principles. Chipping away at frontiers makes occasional marginal contributions to understanding, but the general level of economic performance depends, at bottom, on how well the elect-orate and the millions of economic actors understand the elementary principles that govern the day to day behaviour of our economic system.

SWAN, Peter Lawrence

Born 1944, Melbourne, Victoria, Australia.
Current Post Prof. Management, Australian Grad. School Management, Univ. New South Wales, Sydney, NSW, Australia, 1983–.
Past Posts Sr. Teaching Fellow, Monash Univ., Melbourne, 1970–2; Sr. Projects Officer, Australian Tariff Board, 1972; Vis. Ass. Prof., Grad. School Bus., Univ. Chicago, 1973; Lect., Sr. Lect., Reader Econ., ANU, Canberra, 1974–83; Vis. Prof., Univ. Hawaii, 1979.
Degrees BEc ANU, 1966; PhD Monash Univ., 1972.
Offices and Honours Member, New South Wales Council, Australia.
Principal Fields of Interest 022 Microeconomic Theory; 611 Market Structure: Industrial Organisation and Corporate Strategy; 613 Public Utilities and Costs of Government Regulation.
Publications *Articles:* 1. 'Market structure and technological progress: the influence of monopoly on product innovation', *QJE*, 84, Nov. 1971; 2. 'Durability of consumption goods', *AER*, 60(5), Dec. 1970; 3. 'Monopoly and competition in the market for durable goods' (with E. Sieper), *REStud*, 40, July, 1973; 4. 'Optimum replacement of capital goods with labor-saving technical progress: a comparison of the early New England and British textile firm', *JPE*, 84, Dec. 1976; 5. 'Income taxes, profit taxes and neutrality of optimizing decisions', *ER*, 52, June 1976; 6. 'The Mathews report on business taxation', *ER*, 54, April 1978; 7. 'On buying a job: the regulation of taxi cabs in Canberra', *Centre Independent Stud.*, Pol. Monograph 1, 1979; 8. 'Alcoa: the influence of recycling on monopoly power', *JPE*, 88, Feb. 1980; 9. 'An optimum business tax structure for Australia', in *Australian Fin. System Inquiry, Commissioned Stud. and*

Selected Papers, (Australian Govt. Printing Service, 1981); 10. 'Participation rules for Pareto-optimum clubs' (with A. L. Hillman), *J Pub E*, 20(1), Feb. 1983.

Principal Contributions Although my PhD thesis on the automobile industry and much of my work has an applied bent to it, my first love is theory in the form of thinking through the implications of simple postulates, such as profit maximisation, no matter how unpopular the conclusions. Much of my early work on monopoly and durability has been involved in trying to break down the prejudice that many economists feel against profit-maximising monopolies despite their acceptance of the proposition that self-seeking behaviour may have socially beneficial effects. State-run monopolies in electricity generation etc., that adopt other goals, may do far more harm. My work on the intertemporal allocation of resources has broadened out to include issues in tax reform relating to inflation adjustment and to the nature of income and cash-flow (consumption) taxes. My interest in the economics of regulation stems from a recognition that most monopolies rely heavily on State patronage to implement and police barriers to entry. The taxicab industry worldwide (with a few notable exceptions) is an example of this. I also have a growing interest in law and economics as well as in extreme forms of regulation, such as State ownership, and the reasons for it.

SWEEZY, Allan R.

Born 1907.
Current Post Prof. Emeritus, Cal. Inst. Technology, CA, 1977–.
Past Posts Instr. Econ., Harvard Univ., 1934–8; Cons., US Treasury, 1934–5; Econ., Fed. Reserve Board, 1938–9; Econ., Fed. Works Agency, 1939–40; Assoc. Prof., Prof. Econ., Williams Coll., 1940–6, 1946–7; Vis. Prof. Econ., Prof. Econ., Cal. Inst. Technology, 1949–50, 1950–77; Assoc. Dir., Caltech Pop. Program, 1970–5.
Degrees BA, PhD Harvard Univ., 1929, 1934.

Offices and Honours Lionel de Jersey Harvard Student, Univ. Camb., 1929–30; Sheldon Fellow, Univ. Vienna and LSE, 1932–3.
Principal Fields of Interest 840 Demographic Economics.
Publications *Articles:*1. 'The interpretation of subjective value theory, in the writings of the Austrian economists', *REStud*, 1, June 1934; 2. 'Collected works of Carl Menger', *QJE*, 50, Aug. 1936; 3. 'Population growth and investment opportunity', *QJE*, 55, Nov. 1940; 4. 'The economic explanation of fertility changes in the United States', *Pop. Stud.*, 14, July 1971; 5. 'Attitudes toward limitation', in *Population: Perspective, 1971*, eds. H. Brown and A. R. Sweezy (Freeman & Cooper, 1972); 6. 'The Keynesians and government policy, 1933–1939', *AER*, 62(2), May 1972; 7. 'Socioeconomic development and fertility', in *Population: Perspective, 1973*, ed. H. Brown, *et al.* (Freeman & Cooper, 1973); 8. 'The impact of population growth on employment' (with A. Owens), *AER*, 64(2), May 1974; 9. 'The natural history of the stagnation thesis', in *Zero Population Growth Implications*, ed. J. Spengler (Carolina Pop. Center, Univ. N. Carolina, 1975); 10. 'Multiplier', in *Encyclopedia of Economics*, ed. D. Greenwald (MacGraw-Hill, 1982).

SWEEZY, Paul Marlor

Born 1910, New York City, NY, USA.
Current Post Co-ed., *Monthly Rev.*, New York, NY, USA, 1949–.
Past Posts Instr., Ass., Prof. Econ., Harvard Univ., 1934–46; Vis. Prof., Univs., Cornell, Stanford, New School Social Res., NY, Yale, Cal. Davis, Manchester.
Degrees BA, PhD Harvard Univ., 1931, 1937; Hon. LLD Jawaharlal Univ., India, 1983.
Offices and Honours David A. Wells Prize, Harvard Univ., 1938; Exec. Comm., AEA, 1973–5.
Editorial Duties Co-ed., *Monthly Rev.*, 1949–.
Principal Fields of Interest 020

General Economic Theory; 040 Economic History; 050 Economic Systems.
Publications *Books:* 1. *Monopoly and Competition in the English Coal Trade, 1550–1850* (Harvard Univ Press, 1938); 2. *The Theory of Capitalist Development* (OUP, 1942); 3. *Socialism* (McGraw-Hill, 1949); 4. *The Present as History* (Monthly Rev. Press, 1953); 5. *Cuba: Anatomy of a Revolution* (with L. Huberman), (Monthly Rev. Press, 1960); 6. *Monopoly Capital: An Essay on the American Economic and Social Order* (with P. A. Baran), (Monthly Rev. Press, 1966); 7. *Modern Capitalism and Other Essays* (Monthly Rev. Press, 1975); 8. *The End of Prosperity* (with H. Magdoff), (Monthly Rev. Press, 1981); 9. *Post-Revolutionary Society* (Monthly Rev. Press, 1982); 10. *Four Lectures on Marxism* (Monthly Rev. Press, 1982).
Principal Contributions I became a Marxist during a year of study at LSE in 1932–3 when I became convinced that mainstream economics of the kind I had been taught at Harvard had little to contribute toward understanding the major events and trends of the twentieth century. On returning to the US, I discovered that North-American Marxism was practically nonexistent. In these circumstances, I acquired what I later described as 'a mission in life', i.e., to do whatever I could to make Marxism an integral and respected part of the intellectual life of the country — or, in other terms, to contribute to establishing a serious and authentic North-American brand of Marxism. I pursued this mission by means of teaching, writing and publishing — since 1949 through the medium of *Monthly Review* magazine and Monthly Review Press publishing house. During this period I have been closely associated with a distinguished group of colleagues, all of us together being sometimes referred to as a 'Monthly Review School', (Leo Huberman, Paul A. Baran, Harry Braverman and Harry Magdoff). We have, I think, played an important part in establishing Marxism on a firm foundation in the US. We have also of course sought to advance Marxist social science through theoretical and empirical studies. My own dis-

tinctive contributions have tended to be mainly in two areas: the functioning of capitalism in its latest (monopoly, imperialist, global) stage, and the transition between social systems (feudalism to capitalism, and capitalism to socialism).

SYLOS-LABINI, Paolo

Born 1920, Rome, Italy.
Current Post Prof. Écon., Univ. Rome, Italy, 1962–.
Past Posts Ass. Lect. Econ., Univ. Rome, 1944–56; Ass. Prof. Econ., Univ. Sassari, Sardinia, 1955–7; Prof. Econ., Univ. Catania, 1957–60; Prof. Econ., Univ. Bologna, 1960–2; Vis. Prof., Univs. Oxford and Camb., 1960, 1966, MIT, Harvard, 1965, UNAM Mexico, 1976, Yamaguchi, Japan, 1978, Rio De Janeiro, 1979, Sydney, 1980.
Degree Dr Jurisprudence Univ. Rome, 1942.
Offices and Honours Adviser Oil Law, Italian Prime Minister, 1955; Member, Italian Commission for Problems of Energy, 1958; Member, Technical-Scientific Comm., Italian Minister Budget, 1964–74; Member, Comité d'Econ. Industriale, CNR, France; Premio Nitti, Accademia dei Lincei, 1978; Premio Napoli, Premio Napoli Foundation, 1983.
Editorial Duties Ed. Board, *Internat. J. Industrial Organization*, 1983–, *Moneta e credito*, BNLQR, 1983–.
Principal Fields of Interest 110 Economic Growth; Development; and Planning Theory and Policy; 610 Industrial Organisation and Public Policy; 620 Economics of Technological Change.
Publications *Books:* 1. *Oligopolio e progresso tecnico* (Giuffre, 1956, 1957, Eidaudi, 1961, 1975; transls., English, Harvard Univ. Press, 1962, 1969, Polish, Panstwowe Wydawnictwo Nankowe, 1963, Japanese, Tokyo Keizai, 1964, 1970, Spanish, Oilos-tau, 1966, Czech, Nakladalelstvi Svoboda, 1967, Portuguese, Editoria Forense Univ., 1980); 2. *Problemi dell'economia siciliana*, ed. and contrib. (Feltrinelli, 1966); 3. *Problemi dello sviluppo economico* (Laterza, 1970, 1974; transl., Japanese,

Nihon Hyoron, 1973); 4. *Sindacati, inflazione e produttivita* (Laterza, 1972, 1977; transl., English, Saxon House, 1974); 5. *Saggio sulle classi sociali* (Laterza, 1974, 1982; transls., Japanese, Nihon Hyoron, 1976, Catalan, Edicions, 1962, 1979, Spanish, Ediciones Peninsula, 1981, Portuguese, Zahae Editores, 1983); 6. *Prezzi relativi e distribuzione del reddito*, ed. (Bringhieri, 1973); 7. *Il sottosviluppo e l'economia contemporanea* (Laterza, 1983; transl., Spanish, Editorial Critica, 1984); 8. *Le forze dello sviluppo e del declino* (Laterza, 1984; transl., English, MIT Press, 1984).

Articles: 1. 'Saggio dell'interesse e reddito nazionale', *Atti dell'Academia Nazionale dei Lincei*, 1948; transl., French, Sept. 1951; 2. 'Le problème des cycles de longue durée', *Econ App*, 3–4, 1950; 3. 'Precarious employment in Sicily', *ILRR*, May 1964; 4. 'Prices and wages: a theoretical and statistical interpretation of Italian experience', *J Ind E*, 15, April, 1967; 5. 'Prices, costs and profits in the manufacturing industry: Italy and Japan', *RISE*, 2, 1980; 6. 'On the instability of raw materials prices and the problem of gold', in *The Gold Problem — Economic Perspectives*, ed. A. Curzio (Macmillan, 1982); 7. 'La "teoria generale": riflessioni critiche suggerite da alcuni grandi problemi del nostro tempo', in *Attualita di Keynes* (Laterza, 1983; transl., English, Macmillan, 1984); 8. 'Nuovi aspetti dello sviluppo ciclico dell' economia', *Moneta e Credito*, Dec. 1983, *BNLQR*, March 1984.

Principal Contributions As a young student at the University of Rome in 1940, I chose to prepare a dissertation on the economic consequences of inventions: I was fascinated by the great technical inventions of our time. To my surprise, I discovered that Joseph Schumpeter was one of the few modern economists who had devoted systematic attention to technical innovations and economic growth; otherwise it was necessary to go back to the great classical economists and to Karl Marx. Growth and technical progress then have always been my main intellectual interests. Gradually I became convinced that to understand the process of economic growth it was necessary to study, at the same time, innovations, changes in market forms and changes in income distribution — these being the three specific processes that constitute the general process of economic growth. My interests in growth did not remain on the purely theoretical plane but soon moved to empirical and econometric analyses, as well as to practical questions of economic policy (for a period I was one of the advisers to the Minister of the Budget). Also my recent book on underdeveloped countries combines theoretical analysis and empirical research. The guideline of all my work can be summarised as follows. The ideal future development of economic analysis would be a combination of Ricardian rigour with Smithian wisdom in which history is not a field left to specialists but the necessary background of theoretical economics.

T

TAGGART, Robert Alexander, Jr.

Born 1946, Detroit, MI, USA.

Current Post Prof. Fin., Boston Univ., Boston, MA, USA, 1978–.

Past Posts Ass. Prof., Assoc. Prof. Fin., Northwestern Univ., 1974–83; Econ., Fed. Reserve Bank Boston, 1976–7; Vis. Assoc. Prof., Harvard Bus. School, 1982–4.

Degrees BA(Maths.) Amherst Coll., MA, 1974; SM, PhD MIT, 1969, 1974.

Offices and Honours Phi Beta Kappa, Res. Assoc., NBER.

Editorial Duties Ed., *Fin. Management*; Assoc. Ed., *J Fin and Quant. Analysis*.

Principal Fields of Interest 520 Business Finance and Investment; 312 Commercial Banking; 613 Public Utilities and Costs of Government Regulation.

Publications *Articles:* 1. 'Bond refunding: a clarifying analysis' (with A. R. Ofer), *J Fin*, 32(1), March 1977; 2. 'A model of regulation under uncertainty and a test of regulatory bias' (with D. Baron), *Bell JE*, 8(1), Spring 1977; 3. 'A model of corporate financing decisions', *J Fin*, 32(5), Dec. 1977;

4. 'Effects of deposit rate ceilings: the evidence from Massachusetts savings banks', *JMCB*, 10(2), May 1978; 5. 'Bank capital and public regulation' (with S. Greenbaum), *JMCB*, 10(2), May 1978; 6. 'Future investment opportunities and the value of the call provision on a bond' (with Z. Bodie), *J Fin*, 33(4), Sept. 1978; 7. 'Taxes and corporate capital structure in an incomplete market', *J Fin*, 35(3), June 1980; 8. 'Capital budgeting and the financing decision: an exposition', in *Readings in Financial Management*, ed. D. F. Scott, *et al.* (Academic Press, 1982), repr. in *Financial Management: Cases and Readings*, eds. V. L. Andrews, C. W. Young and P. Hunt (Richard D. Irwin, 1982); 9. 'Implications of corporate capital structure theory for banking institutions' (with Y. Orgler), *JMCB*, 15(3), May 1983; 10. 'Capital structure equilibrium under market imperfections and incompleteness' (with L. Senbet), *J Fin*, 39(1), March 1984.

Principal Contributions As a student, I was primarily interested in the linkage between the financial and real sectors of the economy. I wanted to understand how the structure of the financial system affects capital formation and how the financial sector interacts with the corporate sector in allocating capital. I took up the study of finance initially in the hope of finding some clues to this linkage. In one sense, I found the answer that finance theory offers to be disappointing. Over and over, the theory's fundamental results stress that purely financial transactions are a veil; only the real side of the economy matters. However, this theme does serve to emphasise the fluidity and adaptability of the financial system. Financial transactions can typically be performed by many agents and in many substitute ways. Any profit opportunities afforded by such transactions can be expected to erode rather quickly under the force of competition. What has come to fascinate me is the continual adaptation of this competitive process. Much of my work has centred around the ways in which nonfinancial corporations adapt their financing to such forces as taxation, government regulation, inflation and incentive problems. I have also studied financial intermediaries' adaptation to these forces, particularly government regulation and taxation. This work has not, of course, provided a complete understanding of the linkage between financial and real sectors. It has, however, convinced me that any solid explanation of this linkage should account for the process by which corporations, financial institutions, governments and households all compete with one another to provide financial services.

TAKAYAMA, Akira

Born 1932, Yokohama, Japan.
Current Post Vandeveer Prof. Econ., Southern Illinois Univ., Carbondale, IL, USA, 1983–.
Past Posts Instr., Ass. Prof., Internat. Christian Univ., Tokyo, Japan, 1962–4; Fellow Econ. Stats., Univ. Manchester, 1964–5; Vis. Assoc. Prof., Univ. Minnesota, 1965–6; Vis. Assoc. Prof., Prof., Purdue Univ., IN, 1966–80; Vis. Prof., Prof., Texas A&M Univ., 1978–82; Prof., Kyoto Univ., Japan, 1982–; Vis. Fellow, ANU, 1968, 1977; Vis. Prof., Univ. Rochester, NY, 1969–70; Univ. Hawaii, 1971–2, Univ. Tokyo, 1974, 1975.
Degrees BA Internat. Christian Univ., 1957; MA, PhD Univ. Rochester, 1960, 1962; Dr Econ. Hitotsubashi Univ., Tokyo, 1964.
Editorial Duties Advisory Ed., *Econ Letters*; Assoc. Ed., *J Macroecon*.
Principal Fields of Interest 020 General Economic Theory; 112 Economic Development Models and Theories; 400 International Economics.
Publications *Books:* 1. *International Economics* (Japanese), (Toyo Keizai Shimposha, 1963); 2. *International Trade: An Approach to Theory* (Holt, Rinehart & Winston, 1972); 3. *Mathematical Economics* (Dryden Press, 1974, CUP, 1985).
Articles: 1. 'Economic growth and international trade', *REStud*, 31(3), July 1964; 2. 'On the biased technological progress', *AER*, 75(4), Sept. 1974; 3. 'Devaluation, the specie flow mechanism, and the steady state' (with R. K. Anderson), *REStud*, 44(2), June 1977; 4. 'The wealth effect, the capital

account, and alternative policies under fixed exchange rates', *QJE*, 92(1), Feb. 1978; 5. 'An antinomy in the theory of comparative advantage' (with J.Z. Drabicki); *J Int E*, 9(2), May 1979; 6. 'Does monetary policy matter?', *ZCS*, 136(4), Dec. 1980; 7. 'Dynamic-behaviour of the firm with adjustment costs, under regulatory constraint' (with M. A. El-Hodiri), *J Ec Dyn*, 3(1), Feb. 1981; 8. 'An optimal monetary policy in a neoclassical model of economic growth' (with J. Z. Drabicki), *J Macroecon*, 5(1), Winter, 1983; 9. 'Money, national debt, and economic growth' (with J.Z. Drabicki), *JET*, 33(2), Aug. 1984; 10. 'Consumer's surplus, path independence, compensating and equivalent variations', *ZGS*, 140(4), Dec. 1984.

Principal Contributions Synthesised diversified topics in mathematical economics into a coherent whole in *Mathematical Economics*; likewise with international economics in *International Trade*. Major contributions in papers: *International trade* — in showing that the usual procedure of comparing two commodities in determining comparative advantage is false in a multi-commodity world; *Growth theory* — in proving that the Nurkse balanced growth hypothesis is in general false and that the usual instability result of neoclassical monetary growth models can be reversed if securities are introduced in the model; *Macroeconomics* — in proposing a money supply formula in which the money supply is endogeneous depending on the rate of interest, and in putting into proper perspective the long-debated problem of stocks and flows; *Monetary approach to the balance of payments* — in finding the proper understanding of the classical mechanism of international adjustment and proving the equivalence of the devaluation condition and the stability condition of the long-run equilibrium; *Open macro models* — in expressing into a clear and consistent analytical framework the issue of fiscal and monetary policies under fixed and flexible exchange rates. *Industrial organisation* — in presenting the first correct analysis of the behaviour of the firm under a regulatory constraint, and

then later in recapitulating the argument in a dynamic framework; *Microtheory* — in clarifying (hopefully once and for all) the concept of consumer's surplus; *American economic history* — in empirically establishing that US economic growth is neither Hicks-neutral nor Harrod-neutral but rather Solow labour-saving, and that the elasticity of substitution between labour and capital is fairly constant and is approximately equal to 0.64.

TAUBMAN, Paul

Born 1939, Fall River, MA, USA.

Current Post Prof. Econ., Univ. Penn., Philadelphia, PA, USA, 1972–.

Past Posts Ass. Prof. Econ., Harvard Univ., 1964–6; Staff Member, US President's Council Econ. Advisers, Washington, DC, 1965–6; Assoc. Prof. Econ., Univ. Penn., 1966–72; Vis. Scholar, Univ. Cal. Berkeley, 1972–3; Member, Board Human Resources, NAS, 1971–4; Res. Assoc., NBER, NYC, 1970–3, Palo Alto, CA, 1977–.

Degrees BS, PhD Univ. Penn., 1961, 1964.

Offices and Honours Fellow, Em Soc; Member, Internat. Soc. Twin Stud. (NBER).

Editorial Duties Assoc. Ed., *JASA*, 1970–2, *REStat*, 1974–.

Principal Fields of Interest 200 Quantitative Economic Methods; 824 Labour Market Studies; 850 Human Capital.

Publications *Books:* 1. *Policy Simulations of the Brookings Model* (with G. Fromm), (Brookings Inst., 1968); 2. *Mental Ability and Higher Educational Attainment in the Twentieth Century* (with T. J. Wales), (NBER, Carnegie Commission Higher Educ., 1972); 3. *Public Economic Theory and Policy* (with G. Fromm), (Macmillan, 1973); 4. *Education as an Investment and as a Screening Device* (with T. J. Wales), (NBER, Carnegie Commission Higher Educ., 1974); 5. *Sources of Inequality of Earnings* (N-H, 1975); 6. *Kinometrics: The Determinants of Socioeconomic Success within and between Families*, ed. (N-H, 1977); 7. *Income Distribution and Redistribution* (Addison-Wesley, 1978); 8. *Inter- and*

Intragenerational Determinants of Socioeconomic Success with Special Reference to Genetic, Family and Other Environments (with J. Behrman, T. J. Wales, and Z. Hrubec), (N-H, 1980).

Articles: 1. 'A forecasting model of federal government purchases of goods and services' (with M. Brown). *JASA*, 57, Sept. 1962; 2. 'Impact of investment subsidies in a neoclassical growth model' (with T. J. Wales), *REStat*, 51(3), Aug. 1969; 3. 'User cost, capital utilization, and investment theory' (with M. Wilkinson), *Int ER*, 11(2), June 1970; 4. 'Subsidies, taxes and real estate investment', in *Economics of Federal Subsidy Programs*, Joint Econ. Comm. (US Govt. Printing Office, 1972); 5. 'Higher education, mental ability and screening' (with T. J. Wales), *JPE*, 81(1), Jan.–Feb. 1973; 6. 'Earnings, education, genetics and environment', *JHR*, 11(4), Fall 1976; 7. 'The determinants of earnings: genetics, family and other environments: a study of white male twins', *AER*, 66(5), Dec. 1976; 8. 'Parental preferences and provision for progeny' (with J. R. Behrman and R. A. Pollak), *JPE*, 90(1), Feb. 1982; 9. 'On heritability', *Ec*, N.S. 48, Nov. 1982; 10. 'Changes in life cycle earnings: what do social security data show?' (with S. Rosen), *JHR*, 17(3), Summer 1982.

Principal Contributions Initially I estimated and used saving functions and macro models. To evaluate investment tax incentives, I used a general equilibrium model and demonstrated that if savings' interest elasticity is small, investment incentives will primarily drive up real interest rates.

Next I turned to estimating the monetary returns to education net of the effect of ability using several major bodies of data generated by T. J. Wales and myself. The sample contains measures of four abilities, numerous aspects of family background, and direct reports on earnings in 1955 and 1969. We found big biasses in returns if ability and background were not controlled. Mathematical ability was important; verbal ability, finger dexterity, and spatial perception were not.

Using a Twin Sample, we found that within pair differences in schooling, identical twins (at age 50) have coefficients about half the coefficient for individuals even after making an appropriate allowance for measurement error. Using data on both identical and fraternal twins, the variance in any variable is decomposable into genetic, common and specific environment components. We translate the environment into investment in human capital which depends on genetic endowments, family income and prices. Include this genetic impact with any direct genetic impact; assume prices are constant across families; then the variation in common environment occurs because of differences in family income. We treat family income as a latent variable in a system of equations, which are identified. For earnings, the decomposition of the variance is 45% genetic endowments, 12% common environment, and the rest specific environment. The 12% indicates the maximum gain from eliminating inequality of opportunity, that part of inequality which may be reduced without incurring inefficiency losses. We also find parents slightly reinforce initial endowment differences in allocating resources among siblings.

TAUSSIG, Frank William*

Dates and Birthplace 1859–1940, St Louis, MO, USA.

Posts Held Instr., 1885–92, Prof. Econ., 1892–1935, Harvard Univ.

Degrees BA, PhD, LLB Harvard Univ., 1879, 1883, 1886.

Offices and Honours Member, govt commissions; Adviser, President Wilson; Ed., *QJE*, 1896–1936.

Publications *Books:* 1. *The Tariff History of the United States* (1888, 1931); 2. *Wages and Capital* (1896, 1932); 3. *Principles of Economics*, 2 vols (1911, 1939); 4. *Some Aspects of the Tariff Question* (1915, 1931); 5. *International Trade* (1927).

Career Neoclassical economist who, through his teaching, the *Principles . . .*, and his editorship of the *QJE*, exercised a considerable influence on successive generations of American economists. International trade was his principal theoretical interest and he devoted much of his attention to the question of tariffs. In his writings on general economic theory he stressed the continuity between classical and neoclassical theory, arguing that there was only one continuous body of ideas which had subsequently been elaborated and refined.

Secondary Literature J. A. Schumpeter, *Ten Great Economists from Marx to Keynes* (OUP, 1951); G. Haberler, 'Taussig, Frank W.', *IESS*, 15.

TAWNEY, Richard Henry*

Dates and Birthplace 1880–1962, Calcutta, India.

Posts Held Ass., Univ. Glasgow, 1906–8; Teacher, 1908–14, Fellow Balliol Coll., Oxford, 1918–21; Prof. Econ. Hist., LSE, 1931–49.

Degree BA Univ. Oxford, 1903.

Offices and Honours Member, official comms. and commissions, Pres., Workers' Educational Ass., 1928–44; Fellow, BA, 1935.

Publications *Books:* 1. *The Agrarian Problem in the Sixteenth Century* (1912, 1963); 2. *Studies in the Minimum Wage*, 2 vols (1914); 3. *The Acquisitive Society* (1920, 1948); 4. *Religion and the Rise of Capitalism* (1926, 1963), 5. *Equality* (1931, 1952, 1961); 6. *Land and Labour in China* (1932, 1964); 7. *Business and Politics under James I: Lionel Cranfield as Merchant and Minister* (1958).

Career Economic historian whose *Religion and the Rise of Capitalism*, elaborating the Weber thesis on the Protestant ethic, is a major work of scholarship which has had an inspiring effect on generations of readers. A pioneer member of the Fabian society, his *Acquisitive Society* and *Equality* are fundamental statements of opposition to the moral values of capitalism and class privelege.

Secondary Literature L. Stone, 'Tawney, R. H.', *IESS*, 15.

TAYLOR, Fred Manville*

Dates and Birthplace 1855–1932, Northville, MI, USA.

Posts Held Prof., Albion Coll., 1879–92; Ass. Prof., Prof., Univ. Michigan, 1894–1929.

Degrees BA Northwestern Univ.; PhD Univ. Michigan, 1888.

Offices and Honours Pres., AEA, 1928.

Publications *Books:* 1. *Some Chapters on Money* (1906), 2. *Principles of Economics* (1911).
Articles: 1. 'The guidance of production in a socialist state', *AER*, 19(1), March 1929, repr. in *On the Economic Theory of Socialism*, ed. B. E. Lippincott (1938).

Career Originally a political scientist, his early economic interests were in applied and, particularly, monetary questions, however, he developed an increasing interest in theory, and his *Principles of Economics* reflects the development of his ideas through teaching general economics, in which he placed a strong emphasis on theoretical rigour. Many of his pupils became distinguished economists. His theoretical position was a modified version of the doctrines of the Austrian School. His 1929 article was an answer to von Mises' argument that socialism was impractical.

TAYLOR, John Brian

Born 1946, Yonkers, NY, USA.

Current Post Prof. Econ. and Public Affairs, Princeton Univ., Princeton, NJ, USA, 1980–.

Past Posts Ass. Prof., Assoc. Prof., Prof. Econ., Columbia Univ., 1973–7, 1977–9, 1979–80; Sr. Staff Econ., US President's Council Econ. Advisers, 1976–7; Vis. Prof., Yale Univ., 1980; Vis. Scholar, Fed. Reserve Bank Philadelphia, 1978–9.

Degrees BA Princeton Univ., 1968; PhD Stanford Univ., 1973.

Offices and Honours Guggenheim Foundation Fellow, 1983–4.

Editorial Duties Assoc. Ed., *Em*, 1981–, *J Mon E*, 1978–83, *J Ec Dyn*, 1978.

Principal Fields of Interest 130 Economic Fluctuations, Forecasting; 210 Econometric, Statistical and Mathematical Methods; 300 Monetary and Fiscal Theory and Institutions.

Publications *Books:* 1. *Macroeconomics* (with R. E. Hall), (W. W. Norton, 1984).

Articles: 1. 'Asymptotic properties of multiperiod control rules in the linear regression model', *Int ER*, 15(2), June 1974; 2. 'Monetary policy during a transition to rational expectations', *JPE*, 83(5), Oct. 1975; 3. 'Strong consistency of least squares estimates in normal regression' (with T. W. Anderson), *Annals Stats.*, 4(4), July 1976; 4. 'Stabilizing powers of monetary policy under rational expectations' (with E. S. Phelps), *JPE*, 85(1), Feb. 1977; 5. 'Conditions for unique solutions in stochastic macroeconomic models with rational expectations', *Em*, 45(5), Sept. 1977; 6. 'Estimation and control of a rational expectations model with rational expectations', *Em*, 47(5), Sept. 1979; 7. 'Aggregate dynamics and staggered contracts', *JPE*, 88(1), Feb. 1980; 8. 'The Swedish investment fund system as a stabilization policy rule', *Brookings Papers Econ. Activity*, 1, 1982; 9. 'Solution and maximum likelihood estimation of dynamic nonlinear rational expectations models', *Em*, 51(4), July 1983; 10. 'Union wage settlement during a disinflation', *AER*, 73(5), Dec. 1983.

Principal Contributions Research interest in macroeconomic questions began with an investigation of the impact of countercyclical policies on long-term growth, in an undergraduate thesis at Princeton. I then turned to theoretical econometric and optimal control issues relating to macro-policy. The effect of different policy rules on the information about how policy works was studied in my Stanford PhD thesis and in several papers, some joint with T. W. Anderson. I began to study the role of expectations in macro-policy soon after moving to Columbia where I benefitted greatly from collaborations with E. S. Phelps. My first concern was with how people would come to learn enough during transition periods to form expectations ration-

ally. I also investigated the problem of non-uniqueness due to the self-fulfilling properties of rational expectations. Previous research in macroeconomics with rational expectations had assumed perfectly flexible prices, which I viewed as unrealistic, and therefore Phelps and I developed a sticky price model with rational expectations. Monetary policy has a role in this framework, but one which is different quantitatively than earlier sticky price models. I became interested in developing empirical models that could be used for policy when expectations are consistent, and estimated a small model that satisfied the rational expectations requirements. A policy was characterised as a choice of a rule that trades off output fluctuations against inflation fluctuations. In developing the aggregate supply side, I found that staggered overlapping contracts for wages played an important role, and therefore began a systematic investigation of staggered wage setting, using data for the US. More recently I have been working on the international aspects of macro-policy using the framework developed in my earlier studies.

TAYLOR, Lester Dean

Born 1938, IA, USA.

Current Post Prof. Econ., Univ. Arizona, Tucson, AZ, USA, 1974–.

Past Posts Instr., Harvard Univ., 1963–4; Ass. Prof., Harvard Univ., 1964–8; Staff Econ., US President's Council Econ. Advisers, 1964–5; Adviser, Harvard Devlp. Advisory Service, Bogotá, Colombia, 1967–8; Assoc. Prof., Univ. Michigan, 1969–74; Vis. Prof., Univ. Arizona, 1972–3.

Degrees BA Univ. Iowa, 1960; PhD Harvard Univ., 1963.

Offices and Honours Phi Beta Kappa; Woodrow Wilson Fellow.

Editorial Duties Assoc. Ed., *REStat*, *J Consumer Res*.

Principal Fields of Interest 010 General Economics; 210 Econometrics; 610 Industrial Organisation and Public Policy.

Publications *Books:* 1. *Consumer Demand in the United States* (with H. S.

Houthakker), (Harvard Univ. Press, 1966, 1970); 2. *Telecommunications Demand* (Ballinger, 1980); 3. *Probability and Mathematical Statistics* (with T. A. Wilson and S. J. Turnovsky), (Harper & Row, 1974); 4. *Inflation in North American Manufacturing* (Info. Canada, 1973).

Articles: 1. 'On the estimation of dynamic demand functions' (with D. Weiserbs), *REStat*, 54(4), Nov. 1972; 2. 'Estimation by minimizing the sum & absolute errors', in *Frontiers in Econometrics*, ed. P. Zarembka (Academic Press, 1974); 3. 'The demand for electricity: a survey', *Bell JE*, 6(1), Spring 1975; 4. 'Experiments in seasonal-time-of-day-pricing of electricity to residential users' (with J. T. Wenders), *Bell JE* 7(2), Fall 1976; 5. 'Some problems and issues in building econometric models of energy demand', in *Perspectives on Resource Modeling: Energy and Minerals*, eds. M. Auriel and R. Arnit (Ballinger, 1982).

Principal Contributions Research interests have focussed on the theory and measurement of consumer demand, aggregate consumption and saving, pricing policies in the regulated industries, and econometric and statistical techniques. Current interests include the reformulation of money and capital theory fusing Keynes and Schumpeter (I believe post-Keynesians are correct in their interpretation of Keynes, but wrong in their policy prescriptions; no one has attempted to show the basic similarities of the interest and capital theories of Keynes and Schumpeter) and the development of a dynamic theory of consumer choice in association with a believable psychology of human motivation. The opponent-process models of the psychologist Richard Solomon and his followers provide my present point of departure for the latter research.

TEIGEN, Ronard Leslie*

Dates and Birthplace 1931–84, Kenyon, MN, USA.
Posts Held Market Res. Analyst, General Electric Co., IN, 1956–8; Ass. Prof., Assoc. Prof., Prof. Econ., Univ.

Michigan, 1962–72, 1972–84; Vis. Prof., Norwegian School Econ. and Bus. Admin., Bergen, 1969–84; Cons., Comm. Nobel Prize in Econ., Stockholm, 1970; Res. Fellow, Inst. Internat. Econ. Stud., Univ. Stockholm, 1970–84; Dept. Ass. Dir., Fiscal Analysis, US Congressional Budget Office, 1975–6.
Degrees BBA, MA Univ. Minnesota, 1952, 1955; PhD MIT, 1962.
Offices and Honours Ford Foundation Faculty Res. Fellow, Univ. Michigan, 1965–6; Fellow, Em Soc.
Editorial Duties Assoc. Ed., *J Fin*, 1968–72.
Publications *Books:* 1. *Financial Development and Stabilization Policy: A Study of the Scandinavian Economies* (1976); 2. *Readings in Money, National Income and Stabilization Policy*, co-ed. (with W. L. Smith), (1965, 1978).
Career Wrote on monetary and macroeconomic theory.

TELSER, Lester C.

Born 1931, Chicago, IL, USA.
Current Post Prof. Econ., Univ. Chicago, Chicago, IL, USA, 1965–.
Past Posts Res. Ass., Cowles Commission Res. Econ., 1952–4; Co-op Agent, US Dept. Agric., Econ. Dept., Univ. Chicago, 1954–5; Ass. Prof. Econ., Iowa State Coll., 1955–6; US Army, 1956–8; Faculty, Grad. School Bus., Univ. Chicago, 1958–65; Vis. Res. Fellow, Cowles Foundation Res. Econ., Yale Univ., 1964–5; Ford Faculty Res. Fellow, CORE, Univ. Louvain, Belgium, 1969–70.
Degrees BA Roosevelt Univ., IL, 1951; MA, PhD Univ. Chicago, 1953, 1956.
Offices and Honours Fellow, Em Soc. ASA; Member, Econ. Advisory Panel, NSF, 1971–3.
Editorial Duties Assoc. Ed., *JASA*, 1966–9, *REStat*, 1972–, *J. Futures Markets*, 1980–.
Principal Fields of Interest 026 Economics of Uncertainty and Information; 600 Industrial Organisation; 213 Mathematical Methods and Models.
Publications *Books:* 1. *Functional Analysis in Mathematical Economics* (with R. L. Graves), (Univ. Chicago

Press, 1972); 2. *Competition, Collusion and Game Theory* (Aldine-Atherton, 1972); 3. *Economic Theory and the Core* (Univ. Chicago Press, 1978).

Articles: 1. 'Safety first and hedging', *REStud*, 23(1), Jan. 1955; 2. 'Futures trading and the storage of cotton and wheat', *JPE*, 66, June 1958; 3. 'A theory of speculation relating profitability and stability', *REStat*, 41, Aug. 1959; 4. 'Why should manufacturers want fair trade?', *J Law E*, 3, Oct. 1960; 5. 'The demand for branded goods as estimated from consumer panel data', *REStat*, 44, Aug. 1962; 6. 'Advertising and competition', *JPE*, 72(6) Dec. 1964; 7. 'Organized futures markets: costs and benefits' (with H. N. Higinbotham), *JPE*, 85(5), Oct. 1977; 8. 'A theory of self-enforcing agreements', *J Bus*, 53(1), Jan. 1980; 9. 'Why there are organized futures markets', *J Law E*, 24(1), April 1981; 10. 'A theory of innovation and its effects', *Bell JE*, 13(1), Spring 1982.

Principal Contributions Starting with my doctoral dissertation completed in 1956, I have continued to work on various aspects of organised futures markets. This research began with an investigation of monetary theory. My current research still draws close analogies between monetary theory and the theory of these markets.

My interest in trade and exchange led me to the theory of the core. This theory has furnished me with a powerful tool to study various problems of industrial organisation, including departure from marginal cost pricing, the balance between co-operation and competition, and a deeper understanding of the competitive process. The focus of this work is on the many ways that are used to advance the mutual gain of buyer and seller by devising methods of sharing the costs and benefits from long-term investments of all sorts. These raise free-rider problems for which business firms have found ingenious solutions such as resale price maintenance. Though many economists regarded such practices as anti-competitive, I explain them and similar ones as solutions of free-rider problems that enhance consumer welfare. Many departures from marginal cost pricing that seem at first blush anti-competitive

have a similar explanation as a solution of a free-rider problem in disguise; the theory of self-enforcing agreements grows from this work. This theory poses the problem of what penalties the parties to a co-operative venture can invoke in order to secure compliance to it if they have no recourse to a third-party as an enforcer. The Prisoners' Dilemma is the best-known example where the problem arises. In real situations, people find ways of solving these dilemmas by an appropriate design of self-enforcing agreements. I view the nonco-operative equilibrium, which is usually inefficient, as the punishment or as the alternative to an efficient co-operative agreement. Either by forming coalitions or by devising suitable strategies, people invent incentives to advance their mutual gains from co-operation.

TEMIN, Peter

Born 1937, Philadelphia, PA, USA.
Current Post Prof. Econ., MIT, Cambridge, MA, USA, 1970–.
Past Posts Teaching Ass., MIT, 1961–2; Ass. Prof., Assoc. Prof., MIT, 1965–7, 1967–70; Res. Assoc., NBER, 1982–.
Degrees BA Swarthmore Coll., PA, 1959; PhD MIT, 1964.
Offices and Honours Woodrow Wilson Fellow, MIT, 1959–60; NSF Co-op. Fellow, MIT, 1960–1; Res. Fellow, Harvard Univ., 1961–2; Jr. Fellow, Soc. Fellows, Harvard Univ., 1962–5; Vis. Fellow, Charles Warren Center Stud. Amer. Hist., Harvard Univ., 1976–7.
Principal Fields of Interest 040 Economic History; 913 Health Economics.
Publications *Books:* 1. *Iron and Steel in Nineteenth Century America: An Economic Inquiry* (MIT Press, 1964); 2. *The Jacksonian Economy* (W. W. Norton, 1969); 3. *The New Economic History*, ed. (Penguin, 1972); 4. *Causal Factors in American Economic Growth in the Nineteenth Century* (Macmillan, 1975); 5. *Did Monetary Forces Cause the Great Depression?* (W. W. Norton, 1976); 6. *Reckoning with Slavery* (with P. David, *et al.*), (OUP, 1976); 7. *Taking Your Medicine: Drug Regulation in the*

United States (Harvard Univ. Press, 1980).

Articles: 1. 'Physician prescribing behavior: is there learning by doing?', in Drug and Health: Economic Issues and Policy Objectives, ed. R. E. Helms, (AEI, 1981); 2. 'Discussion', in The Second Pharmaceutical Revolution, ed. N. Wells (Office of Health Econ., 1983); 3. 'Patterns of cotton agriculture in postbellum Georgia', JEH, 43(3), Sept. 1983; 4. 'Monetary trends and other phenomena', JEH, 43(3), Sept. 1983; 5. 'Cost and benefits in switching drugs from Rx to OTC', JHE, 1, Dec. 1983.

Principal Contributions A contributor to the 'new economic history'. This analysis typically starts with a formal model of some aspects of economic behaviour, assembles historical data for use in the model, and draws conclusions by joining the data and the model. Work has centred on questions of monetary history, technical change, and industrial organisation in nineteenth- and twentieth-century America.

THEIL, Henri

Born 1924, Amsterdam, The Netherlands.

Current Post McKethan-Matherly Prof. Econometrics and Decision Sciences, Univ. Florida, USA, 1981–.

Past Posts Prof. Econometrics, Dir., Econometric Inst., Netherlands School Econ., Rotterdam, 1953–66, 1956–66; Univ. Prof., Dir. Center Math. Stud. Bus. Econ., Univ. Chicago, 1965–81.

Degrees PhD Univ. Amsterdam, 1951; LLD Univ. Chicago, 1964; Dr h.c. Free Univ., Brussels, 1974, Erasmus Univ., Rotterdam, 1983.

Offices and Honours Pres., Em Soc, 1961.

Principal Fields of Interest 212 Econometric Models.

Publications Books: 1. Linear Aggregation of Economic Relations (N-H., 1954); 2. Economic Forecasts and Policy (N-H., 1958, 1961); 3. Principles of Econometrics (Wiley, 1971); 4. Theory and Measurement of Consumer Demand, 2 (N-H., 1975); 5. The System-

Wide Approach to Microeconomics (Univ. Chicago Press, 1980).

Principal Contributions Econometric methodology; the application of informational measures in economics; and consumption and production theory.

THIRLWALL, Anthony Philip

Born 1941, Workington, Cumbria, England.

Current Post Prof. Appl. Econ., Univ. Kent, Canterbury, England, 1976–.

Past Posts Ass. Lect., Univ. Leeds, 1964–6; Vis. Prof., W. Virginia Univ., 1967; Lect. Sr. Lect., Reader, Univ. Kent, Canterbury, 1966–76; Econ. Adviser, UK Dept. Employment, 1968–70; Res. Assoc., Industrial Relations Section, Princeton Univ., 1971–2; Vis. Econ., Univ. Papua, New Guinea, 1974, Gezira, Sudan, 1978, Univ. Camb., 1979, Messina, 1983; Vis. Prof., Melbourne Univ., 1981.

Degrees BA Leeds Univ., 1962; MA Clark Univ., 1963; PhD Leeds Univ., 1967.

Offices and Honours Council, Exec. Comm., RES, 1979–; Governor, NIESR, 1979–.

Editorial Duties Ed. Board, J Dev Stud, 1979–.

Principal Fields of Interest 112 Economic Development Models and Theories; 431 Balance of Payments; 824 Labour Market Studies.

Publications Books: 1. 'Growth and Development; with Special Reference to Developing Economies (Macmillan 1972, 1983); 2. Inflation, Saving and Growth in Developing Economies (Macmillan 1974, St Martins Press, 1975; transl., Spanish, El Manuel Moderno, 1976); 3. Regional Growth and Unemployment in the UK (with R. Dixon), (Macmillan, Holmes & Meier, 1975); 4. 'Financing Economic Development (Macmillan, 1976; transls., Greek, Spanish, Turkish); 5. Keynes and International Monetary Relations, ed. (Macmillan, 1976); 6. Keynes and Laissez Faire, ed. (Macmillan, 1978); 7. Balance of Payments Theory and U.K. Experience (Macmillan, 1980); 8. Keynes and the Bloomsbury Group, co-ed. (with D. Crabtree), (Macmillan 1980); 9. *Keynes as a Policy Adviser*, ed. (Macmillan, 1982).

Articles: 1. 'Technical progress: a survey' (with C. Kennedy), *EJ*, 82, March 1972; 2. 'Population growth and the growth of output and living standards in a production function framework', *MS*, 40(4), Dec. 1972; 3. 'An empirical estimate for Britain of the impact of the real balance effect on income and interest', *SEJ*, 30(2), Oct. 1972; 4. 'The Keynesian multiplier with interest rate, redistribution and real balance effects', *OBES*, 36(4), Nov. 1974; 5. 'Types of unemployment in the regions of Great Britain', *MS*, 42(4), Dec. 1974; 6. 'A model of regional growth rate differences on Kaldorian lines' (with R. Dixon), *OEP*, 27(2), July 1975; 7. 'The balance of payments constraint as an explanation of international growth rate differences', *BNLQR*, 128, March 1979; 8. 'The input-output formulation of the foreign trade multiplier' (with C. Kennedy), *AEP*, 18(32), June 1979; 9. 'Import penetration, export promotion and Harrod's trade multiplier' (with C. Kennedy), *OEP*, 31(2), July 1979; 10. 'The balance of payments constraint, capital flows and growth rate differences between developing countries' (with M. N. Hussain), *OEP*, 34(3), Oct. 1982.

Principal Contributions The understanding of 'regional' economic differences, the theory of cumulative causation, and the concept of balance-of-payments constrained growth; the measurement of types of unemployment; the development of models of inflation and growth, and of population and growth.

THOMPSON, Thomas Perronet*

Dates and Birthplace 1783–1869, Hull, Yorkshire, England.

Posts Held Naval officer, 1803–6; Army officer, 1806–8, 1810–68, appointed General, 1868; Governor, Sierra Leone, 1808–10.

Degree BA Univ. Camb., 1802.

Offices and Honours Fellow, Royal Soc., 1828; MP for Hull, 1836–7, Bradford, 1847–52, 1857–9.

Publications *Books:* 1. *The True Theory of Rent in Opposition to Mr. Ricardo and Others* (1826, 1827); 2. *Catechism on the Corn Laws* (1827, 1940); 3. *The Instruments of Exchange* (1830, 1842); 4. *Catechism on the Currency* (1848).

Career Active service in the army terminated in 1822, when he turned to writing, founding the *Westminster Review*, the organ of the 'philosophical radicals'. He was the proprietor of the paper and chief contributor to it from 1829–36. His anti-Corn Law writings were his most successful publications and he played a major role in the Anti-Corn Law League.

THOMPSON, William*

Dates and Birthplace 1775–1833, Cork, Ireland.

Post Held Private income.

Publications *Books:* 1. *An Inquiry into the Principles of the Distribution of Wealth* (1824, 1963); 2. *Appeal of One Half of the Human Race, Women, Against the Pretensions of the Other Half, Men* (1825, 1831); 3. *Labour Rewarded* (1827); 4. *Practical Directions for the Establishment of Communities* (1830).

Career British 'utilitarian' socialist and feminist. His earliest theoretical concerns were with problems of distribution, which led him to advocate co-operation rather than competition. He rapidly became recognised as the chief theorist of the co-operative movement and concentrated on the attempt to mobilise opinion amongst the labouring classes in favour of consumers' and producers' co-operatives.

Secondary Literature R. K. P. Pankhurst, *William Thompson: Britain's Pioneer Socialist, Feminist and Co-operator* (Watts, 1954); A. Briggs, 'Thompson, William', *IESS*, 16.

THORNTON, Henry*

Dates and Birthplace 1760–1815, Clapham, London, England.

Posts Held Banker.

Offices and Honours MP Southwark, 1782–1815; Member of commissions and comms. on Suspension of Cash Payments, 1797, Irish Currency, 1804, Bullion, 1810, Corn Trade, 1813.

Publications *Books:* 1. *An Enquiry into the Nature and Effects of the Paper Credit of Great Britain* (1802, 1939).

Career Monetary theorist who systematised ideas on money, the velocity of circulation, interest, prices and employment, and international economic relations in his *Enquiry*. . . . These ideas are embedded in a defence of the Bank of England's policy regarding the suspension of cash payments. He later became more critical of the Bank, and favoured a reduced circulation of notes. Though very successful in his own day, the *Enquiry* was gradually forgotten until Hollander, Viner, and others rediscovered it and drew attention to its anticipations of modern monetary theory.

Secondary Literature S. Meacham, *Henry Thornton of Clapham* (Harvard Univ. Press, 1964); T. W. Hutchinson, 'Thornton, Henry', *IESS*, 16; P. Beaugrand, *Henry Thornton. Un precurseur de J. M. Keynes* (Presses Univ. de France, 1984).

THORNTON, William Thomas*

Dates and Birthplace 1813–80, Burnham, Somerset, England.

Posts Held Employee, East India Co., 1836–58; Secretary, public works, India Office, 1858–80.

Offices and Honours CBE, 1873.

Publications *Books:* 1. *Overpopulation and its Remedy* (1845); 2. *A Plea for Peasant Proprietors* (1848); 3. *On Labour, its Wrongful Claims and Rightful Dues* (1869); 4. *Indian Public Works and Cognate Topics* (1875).

Career Colleague and friend of J. S. Mill, he advocated land reforms as a remedy for rural distress, particularly that of Ireland. It was Thornton's criticism of the wages fund theory that induced Mill's retraction on the subject.

THÜNEN, Johann Heinrich von*

Dates and Birthplace 1783–1850, Oldenburg, Germany.

Posts Held Landowner and farmer.

Publications *Books:* 1. *Der Isolierte Staat in Beziehung auf Landwirtschaft und Nationalökonomie*, 3 vols (1826–63), (English transl. pt. 1, 1826, selections from pt. 2, 1850, ed. P. Hall, 1966, and pt. 2, 1850, in B. W. Dempsey *The Frontier Wage*, 1960).

Career Founder of location theory, mathematical economist and econometrician whose work, though little appreciated in his own time, has since been re-evaluated as one of the outstanding early contributions to economics. The 'isolated state' refers to an abstract spatial model which he used to develop theories of rent, location, wages and interest. His ideas were built on the meticulous accumulation of data from farming experiments on his estate. He expressed his ideas verbally, arithmetically and in algebraic terms, also making some use of calculus. He developed an exact theory of marginal productivity and applied the theory to questions of production and distribution. The *Isolated State* . . . was not a systematic treatise, and his very great number of achievements have to be disinterred from amongst much other material, such as practical discussions of agricultural economics. Despite this it is one of the great economic classics.

Secondary Literature A. H. Leigh, 'Thünen, Johann Heinrich von', *IESS*, 16; P. A. Samuelson, 'Thünen at two hundred', *JEL*, 21(4), Dec. 1983; M. Blaug, 'The economics of Johann von Thünen' in *Research in the History of Economic Thought and Methodology*, 3, ed. W. J. Samuels (JAI Press, 1986).

THUROW, Lester Carl

Born 1938, Livingston, MT, USA.

Current Post Gordon Y. Billard Prof. Management and Econ., Sloan School Management, MIT, Cambridge, MA, 1983–.

Past Posts Econ., US President's Council Econ. Advisers, 1964–5; Ass. Prof. Econ., Harvard Univ., 1965–8;

Prof. Econ. and Management, MIT, 1968–83; Prof., Univ. Arizona, 1975, 1980; Econ. Commentator, Radio WGBH–2, Boston, 1968–75; Pres. Appointee, US Nat. Comm. Manpower Pol., 1978–9.

Degrees BA Williams Coll., MA, 1960; MA (Philo., Polit. and Econ.) Oxford Univ., 1962; PhD Harvard Univ., 1964; Hon Dr Williams Coll., 1980, Montana State Univ., 1982, Muhlenberg Coll., 1982.

Offices and Honours Tying Scholar, Jr. Phi Beta Kappa, Williams Coll.; Rhodes Scholar, Univ. Oxford, 1962; Wells Prize, Grad. Nat. Fellow, Harvard Univ; '200 Rising Leaders', *Time*, July 15, 1974; Gerald Loeb Award Econ. Writing, 1982; Champion Media Awards, 1983; Fellow, AAAS, 1984.

Editorial Duties Ed. Board, *NY Times*, 1979; Board Econ., *Time*, 1980–1, 1984–; Contrib. Ed., *Newsweek*, 1981–3.

Principal Fields of Interest 320 Fiscal Theory and Policy; 400 International Economics; 820 Labour Markets.

Publications *Books:* 1. *Poverty and Discrimination* (Brookings Inst., 1969); 2. *Investment in Human Capital* (Wadsworth, 1970); 3. *The Impact of Taxes on the American Economy* (Praeger, 1971); 4. *The Economic Problem* (Prentice-Hall, 1974); 5. *Generating Inequality* (Basic Books, 1975); 6. *The Zero-Sum Society* (Basic Books, 1980); 7. *Five Economic Challenges* (with R. Heilbroner), (Prentice-Hall, 1981); 8. *Economics Explained* (with R. Heilbroner), (Prentice-Hall, 1982); 9. *Dangerous Currents: The State of Economics* (Random House, 1983); 10. *World Class — A Strategy for American Success* (Simon & Schuster 1985).

Articles: 1. 'Stagflation and the distribution of real economic resources', *Data Resources Rev.*, Dec. 1978, repr. in *Readings in Macro-Economics* (McGraw-Hill, 1981); 2. 'Indirect incidence of government expenditures', *AER*, 70(2), May 1980; 3. 'The productivity problem', *Technology Rev.*, Oct. 1980; 4. 'The moral equivalent of defeat', *Foreign Pol.*, Spring 1981; 5. 'Why economists disagree', *Dissent*, Spring 1982; 6. 'America's banks in

crises', *NY Times Magazine*, Sept. 24, 1984; 7. 'A strategy for revitalizing American industry', *Cal. Managment Rev.*, 1, Fall 1984; 8. 'Building a world-class economy', *Social Science and Modern Soc.*, Nov.–Dec. 1984; 9. 'Learning to say 'no'', *New England J. Medicine*, Dec. 13, 1984.

Principal Contributions My professional publications began with an interest in income distribution economics and this remains a central concern. The nature of the interest however has changed. Initially the articles were written from the perspective of what one can learn about how one might alter the distribution of income and wealth to produce more equality. Tax policies, expenditure policies, and labour market mechanisms to increase education and training were of central concern. Over the years I have come to the conclusion that income distribution economics is in some sense the back side of economics from whence springs most of the problems of central concern on the front side of economics. Wages, for example, simply don't adjust as they should adjust given the simple supply and demand market clearing mechanisms that we all teach. I would argue that this 'non-clearance' is not a market imperfection but evidence that an efficient labour market works in a very different manner from that usually specified. Figuring out how this and related efficient but not price-auction market-clearing, mechanisms work is of central concern, starting with the book *Generating Inequality*.

TIDEMAN, Thorwald Nicolaus

Born 1943, Chicago, IL, USA.
Current Post Assoc. Prof. Econ., Virginia Polytech. Inst. & State Univ., Blacksburg, VA, USA, 1974.
Past Posts Ass. Prof., Harvard Univ., 1969–74; Sr. Staff Econ., US President's Council Econ. Advisers, 1970–1; Res. Assoc., Kennedy School Govt., Harvard Univ., 1979–80; Vis. Prof., Univ. Buckingham, England, 1983, 1985.
Degrees BA Reed Coll., 1965; PhD Univ. Chicago, 1969.

Offices and Honours Dissertation Fellow, Comm. Urban Econ., Resources for the Future, 1967–8; Postdoctoral Fellow, Travelers Insurance Co., 1970; Post-doctoral Fellow, Center Study of Public Choice, Virginia Polytech. Inst. & State Univ., 1973–5; Certificate Disting. Res. in Educ., VA Educ. Res. Assoc., 1976.

Principal Fields of Interest Ed. Board, *Public Fin. Q*

Principal Fields of Interest 025 Social Choice; Bureaucratic Performance; 822 Public Policy; Role of Government; 324 State and Local Government Finance.

Publications *Books:* 1. *Tax and Expenditure Limitations*, co-ed. (with H. Ladd), (Urban Inst., 1981).

Articles: 1. 'Measures of concentration' (with M. Hall), *JASA*, 62, March 1967; 2. 'Efficient provision of a local non-private good' (with E. Smolensky and R. Burton), *Geographic Analysing*, 2, July 1970; 3. 'Discrimination by waiting time in merit goods' (with D. Nichols and E. Smolensky), *AER*, 61(3), June 1971; 4. 'From individual to collective ordering through multidimensional attribute space' (with I. J. Good), *Proc. Royal Soc. London*, A347, Jan. 1976; 5. 'The capabilities of voting rules in the absence of coalitions', *Pol. and Politics*, 4, June 1976; 6. 'A new and superior process for making social choices' (with G. Tullock), *JPE*, 84, Dec. 1976, repr. in Spanish, *Hacienda Publico Espanola*, 60, 1979; 7. 'Liability rules, compulsory exchange, and compensated incentive compatibility', in *Essays in the Law and Economics of Local Governments* (Urban Inst., 1979); 8. 'Deciding what to kill', in *Ethics and Animals* (Humana Press, 1983); 9. 'A collective conception of collective value', *Perspectives on Local Public and Fin. and Public Pol.*, 1, 1983; 10. 'An experiment in the demand revealing process', *Public Choice*, 41(3), Summer 1983.

Principal Contributions My first publication resulted from collaboration with a teacher (Marshall Hall) to characterise measures of concentration. The principal theme of my work, however, has been how appropriate action is identified and implemented. When first introduced to welfare economics an an undergraduate, I was awed, fascinated and puzzled by the idea that economic analysis could specify what collective action was appropriate when individuals disagreed. My doctoral dissertation dealt with ways of achieving efficiency in land use in the face of interdependencies. Part of the dissertation was a collaboration with Gene Smolensky and Dick Burton on the efficient size and spacing of public goods. A separate collaboration with Smolensky and Don Nichols dealt with waiting time as an imperfect device for rationing public services to just the most needy. But my chief interest has been decision rules. One branch of this work has dealt with new one-person-one-vote voting rules, some of this work in collaboration with I. J. Good. Another branch has dealt with identifying suitable weights for combining the preferences of different persons. This led to a variety of explorations of the demand-revealing process, some in collaboration with Gordon Tullock. Seeing how the demand-revealing process, works made it clear that it is not just efficiency that is needed in collective decision rules but adherence to appropriate treatment of individuals. This has led me, in current work, to suggest that traditional approaches to normative economics should be replaced by a Lockean approach, and that a restructured society could finance efficient local public goods without coercive taxes.

TINBERGEN, Jan

Born 1903, The Hague, The Netherlands.

Current Post Retired, 1972–.

Past Posts Stat., Netherlands Central Bureau Stat., 1929–45; Econ., League of Nations, Geneva, 1936–8; Dir., Central Planning Bureau, The Hague, 1945–55; Ass. Prof., Netherlands School Econ., Rotterdam, 1933–55; Cleveringa Prof., Univ. Leiden 1956–72; Adviser World Bank, Various govts., 1956–7; Vis. Prof., Harvard Univ., 1956–7.

Degrees Dr (Physics) Univ. Leiden,

1929; Hon. Degrees, Econ. and Social Sciences, 20 univs.

Offices and Honours Erasmus Prize, 1967; Joint Nobel Prize in Econ. Science 1969.

Editorial Duties Ed. Boards, *DE, Econ. Stat. Berichten.*

Principal Fields of Interest 112 Economic Development; 211 Econometric and Statistical Methods.

Publications *Books:* 1. *Business Cycles in the USA, 1921–33* (League of Nations, 1939); 2. *Business Cycles in the UK, 1870–1914* (N-H, 1956); 3. *Methematical Models of Economic Growth* (with H. C. Bos), (McGraw-Hill, 1962); 4. *Economic Policy: Principles and Design* (N-H, 1967); 5. *Income Distribution: Analysis and Policies* (N-H, 1975).

Articles: 1. 'The appraisal of road construction: two calculation schemes', *REStat*, 39, Aug. 1957; 2. 'Testing and applying a theory of utility' (with N. Bouma and B. M. S. van Praag), *Europ ER*, 8(2), Aug. 1976; 3. 'How to reduce the incomes of the two labour elites', *Europ ER*, 10(2), Nov. 1977; 4. 'Two approaches to quantify the concept of equitable income distribution?', *Kyk*, 33(1), 1980; 5. 'Market-determined and residual incomes — some dilemmas' (with J. Kol), *Econ App*, July 1980.

Principal Contributions Perhaps: construction of first econometric model (Netherlands 1923–35); similar model for USA 1919–32, for UK 1870–1914; semi-input-output model (taking into account non-tradables); improvement of estimation of production functions as invented by Peter T. Gottschalk; and allocation of workers over jobs, as characterised by level of schooling.

Secondary Literature B. Hansen, 'Jan Tinbergen's contributions to economics', *Scand JE*, 71(1), Jan. 1969, repr. in *Contemporary Economists in Perspective*, eds. H. W. Spiegel and W. J. Samuels (JAI Press, 1984).

TOBIN, James

Born 1918, Champaign, IL, USA.
Current Post Sterling Prof. Econ.,

Yale Univ., New Haven, CT, USA, 1957–.

Past Posts Jr. Econ., US Office Price Admin., Washington, DC, 1941–2; US Naval Reserve, 1942–6; Jr. Fellow, Soc. Fellows, Harvard Univ., 1947–50; Assoc. Prof., Prof. Econ., Yale Univ., 1950–5, 1955–7; Dir., Acting Dir., Cowles Foundation Res. Econ., Yale Univ., 1955–61, 1964–5; Member, US President's Council Econ. Advisers, Washington, DC, 1961–2; Rockefeller Foundation, Vis. Prof., Univ. Nairobi, Inst. Devlp. Stud., Kenya, 1972–3, Vis. Prof., Univ. Minnesota, Minneapolis, 1978; Ford Vis. Res. Prof., Univ. Cal. Berkeley, 1983.

Degrees BA, MA, PhD Harvard Univ., 1930, 1940, 1947; LLD (h.c.) Syracuse Univ., 1967, Univ. Illinois, 1969, Dartmouth Coll., MA, 1970, Swarthmore Coll., PA, 1980, New School Social Res., NY, 1982, NYU, 1982, Hofstra Univ., NY, 1983, Univ. Hartford, CT, 1984, Colgate Univ., 1984; Dr. Econ. (h.c.) New Univ., Lisbon, 1980; Hon. Dr. Humane Letters, Bates Coll., 1982.

Offices and Honours Fellow, Vice-Pres., Pres., Em Soc, 1957, 1958; US SSRC Faculty Res. Fellow, 1952–5; John Bates Clark Medal, Vice-Pres., Pres., AEA, 1955, 1964, 1971; Member, Secretary Class V, Behavioral and Social Sciences, NAS, 1972, 1979–82; Pres., EEA, 1977; Nobel Member, Amer. Philo. Soc.; Fellow, Amer. Academy Sciences; Corresp. Fellow, BA; Nobel Prize in Economics, 1981.

Editorial Duties Amer. Ed., *REStud*, 1952–4; Ed. Boards, *JMCB*, 1968–, *J Mon E*, 1980.

Principal Fields of Interest 020 General Economics; 111 Economic Growth; 310 Domestic Monetary and Financial Theory.

Publications *Books:* 1. *The American Business Creed* (with S. E. Harris, *et al.*), (Harvard Univ. Press, 1956); 2. *National Economic Policy* (Yale Univ. Press, 1966); 3. *Essays in Economics: Vol 1, Macroeconomics* (Markham, 1971, N-H, 1974); 4. *The New Economics One Decade Older* (Princeton Univ. Press, 1974); 5. *Essays in Economics Vol II: Consumption and Econometrics* (N-H, 1975); 6. *Asset*

Accumulation and Economic Activity
(Blackwell, 1980); 7. *Essays in Econo-
mics Vol III: Theory and Policy* (MIT
Press, 1982); 8. *Risk Aversion and
Portfolio Choice*, co-ed. (with D.
Hester), (Wiley, 1967); 9. *Studies of
Portfolio Behavior*, co-ed. (with D.
Hester), (Wiley, 1967); 10. *Financial
Markets and Economic Activity*, co-ed.
(with D. Hester), (Wiley, 1967).

Principal Contributions Clarification
and extension of Keynesian macroeconomic models with respect to money
wages, inflation, money demand, consumption and saving, and fiscal and
monetary policies. Development of
theory of portfolio choice under uncertainty, including the separation
theorem basic to capital asset pricing
model; and application of the theory to
macroeconomics. Incorporation of
money and inflation in growth theory.
Empirical studies of consumption, saving, asset demand. Origination of
method (TOBIT) for estimating relationships involving limited to truncated
dependent variables. Theory of capital
investment emphasising importance of
ratio of market value to replacement
cost, 'q'.

Secondary Literature D. D. Purvis,
'James Tobin's contributions to economics', *Scand JE* 84(1), Jan. 1982, repr.
in *Contemporary Economists in Perspective*, eds. H. W. Spiegel and W. J.
Samuels (JAI Press, 1984).

TODARO, Michael P.

Born 1942, New York City, NY,
USA.
Current Post Prof. Econ., NYU; Sr.
Assoc., Center Pol. Stud., Pop. Coun-
cil, New York City, NY, USA, 1978–.
Past Posts Vis. Rockefeller Lect
Econ., Makerere Coll., Uganda, 1964–
5; Instr. Econ., Yale Univ., 1967–8;
Res. Fellow, Inst. Devlp. Stud., Vis.
Sr. Lect. Econ., Nairobi, 1968–70,
1974–6; Assoc. Dir., Social Sciences,
Rockefeller Foundation, 1970–6; Vis.
Prof. Econ., Univ. Cal. Santa Barbara,
1976; Dep. Dir., Sr. Assoc., Center
Pol. Stud., Pop. Council, 1976–8.
Degrees BA Haverford Coll., 1964;
MPhil, PhD Yale Univ., 1966, 1967.

Offices and Honours Phi Beta
Kappa, 1964; Woodrow Wilson Fel-
low, 1965; NDEA Fellow, 1966–7;
Member, Internat. Advisory Comm.,
Pop. Inst., East-West Center, Hawaii,
1972–4; William Pyle Philips Disting.
Vis., Haverford Coll., 1977; Member,
Council Foreign Relations, 1973.
Editorial Duties Ed. Board, *Pop. and
Devlp. Rev.*, 1977–, *PDR*, 1983.
Principal Fields of Interest 112 Eco-
nomic Development Models and
Theories; 121 Economic Studies of
Less Industrialised Countries; 840
Demographic Economics.
Publications *Books:* 1. *Economic
Theory* (with P.W. Bell), (OUP, 1969,
1973); 2. *Development Planning: Mod-
els and Methods* (OUP, 1972); 3. *Inter-
nal Migration in Developing Countries*
(ILO, 1976); 4. *Economics for a Developing World* (Longman, 1977, 1983;
transls., Spanish, Portuguese, Indonesian); 5. *Economic Development in the
Third World* (Longman 1977, 1981,
transl., Japanese); 6. *City Bias and Rural Neglect* (Pop. Council, 1981); 7. *The
Struggle for Economic Development*,
ed. (Longman, 1983).
Articles: 1. 'A model of labor migration and urban unemployment in less
developed countries', *AER*, 59(1),
March 1969; 2. 'Technological transfer,
labour absorption, and economic development' (with H. Pack), *OEP*,
21(3), Nov. 1969; 3. 'Migration, unemployment, and development: a two-
sector analysis' (with J.R. Harris),
AER, 60(1), March 1970; 4. 'Income
expectations, rural-urban migration
and employment in Africa', *Int Lab
Rev*, 101(5), Nov. 1971; 5. 'Industrialization, unemployment and the urban
environment', in *Employment Creation
in Developing Societies*, ed. K. Wohl-
muth (Praeger, 1973); 6. 'Educational
demand and supply in the context of
growing unemployment in less developed nations' (with E.O. Edwards),
WD, 1(3–4), March 1973; 7. 'Urban job
expansion, induced migration and rising unemployment: a formulation and
simplified empirical test for LDCs',
JDE 3(3), Sept. 1976; 8. 'Development
policy and population growth: framework for planners', *Pop. and Devlp.
Rev.*, 3(1–2), March–June 1977; 9.

'Internal migration in developing countries: a survey', in *Population and Economic Change in Developing Countries*, ed. R.A. Easterlin (Univ. Chicago Press, 1980); 10. 'Intergenerational income-fertility linkages in developing countries: a conceptual framework', in *Comparative Development Perspectives: Essays in Honor of Lloyd Reynolds*, eds. G. Ranis and R.L. West (Westview Press, 1984).

Principal Contributions Known most widely for seminal theoretical writings on the relationship between rural-urban migration and urban unemployment in less developed countries, I have also made significant contributions to research on urbanisation, population and development interactions, issues in the economics of education and the technology/employment fields. I am also internationally known for my leading textbooks on economic development, which have been used in over 40 countries and translated into five languages. My theory of migration first demonstrated the economic rationality of continued migration in the face of rising urban unemployment and inflexible urban wages. An important policy implication of this model is that the creation of more urban jobs would probably worsen rather than relieve the urban unemployment problem (the so-called 'Todaro paradox'). This helped to reorient development theory and practice away from exclusive emphasis on industrialisation and towards putting greater emphasis on raising agricultural incomes and promoting rural development. It also underlined the powerful economic forces at work in causing the continued extraordinary growth rates of Third World cities.

TOOKE, Thomas*

Dates and Birthplace 1774–1858, Kronstadt, Russia.

Posts Held Merchant in the Russian trade; Governor, Royal Exchange Insurance Co.

Offices and Honours Fellow, Royal Soc., 1821; Founder Member, Polit. Econ. Club, 1821–58; Witness before govt. comms; Member, Commission on Child Employment, 1833, 1840.

Publications *Books:* 1. *Thoughts and Details on the High and Low Prices of the Thirty Years from 1793 to 1822* (1823, 1829); 2. *Considerations on the State of the Currency* (1826); 3. *On the Currency in Connexion with the Corn Trade* (1829); 4. *A History of Prices and the State of Circulation from 1792 to 1856*, 6 vols (with W. Newmarch), (1838–57); 5. *An Inquiry into the Currency Principle* (1844, 1959); 6. *On the Bank Charter Act of 1844* (1856).

Career Major Spokesman for free trade, and author of the Merchants' Petition, 1820. Defended the gold standard on many occasions before espousing the Banking Principle that note issues need no rigid controls. Although he rejected the quantity theory of money, he never developed a complete monetary theory. His interest in the effect of monetary policy on prices led him into his lifelong work on price data. Though he and his collaborator, William Newmarch, constructed no indices on the basis of the data, the raw material was used by others, including Jevons.

Secondary Literature T.E. Gregory, *An Introduction to Tooke and Newmarch's 'A History of Prices'* (LSE, 1928, 1962); F.W. Fetter, 'Tooke, Thomas', *IESS*, 16.

TORRENS, Robert*

Dates and Birthplace 1780–1864, Ireland.

Posts Held Army officer, 1797–1835; Proprietor, *Globe* newspaper.

Offices and Honours Fellow, Royal Soc., 1818; Founder, Member, Polit. Econ. Club, 1821; MP for Ashburton, 1831–2, Bolton, 1832–5.

Publications *Books:* 1. *The Economist Refuted* (1808, 1858); 2. *An Essay on Money and Paper Currency* (1812); 3. *An Essay on the External Corn Trade* (1815, 1829); 4. *An Essay on the Production of Wealth* (1821, 1970); 5. *Letters on Commercial Policy* (1833, 1958); 6. *The Budget* (1841–2, 1965); 7. *The Principles and Practical Operation of Sir Robert Peel's Bill of 1844* (1848, 1858).

Career Critic of the labour theory of value, and an independent discoverer of the principle of comparative advantage. He wrote extensively on economic questions for over 50 years. As an advocate of the principle of colonisation as a remedy for over-population, he promoted schemes for the colonisation of Australia. His views on international trade were unusual for the day in rejecting unilateral free trade, arguing instead that tariffs might be optimal under certain circumstances. Although his early writings had put the case for paper currency, he soon became a major spokesman of the Currency School. Though influential in his day, he had little effect posthumously and was rediscovered only recently.

Secondary Literature L. Robbins, *Robert Torrens and the Evolution of Classical Economics* (Macmillan, 1958); B. Corry, 'Torrens, Robert', *IESS*, 16.

TOWNSEND, Harry

Born 1925, Blackburn, Lancashire, England.

Current Post Prof. Econ., Univ. Lancaster, 1972–.

Past Posts Lect. Econ., Univ. Sheffield, 1950–5; Lect., Reader Econ., LSE, 1955–72.

Degrees BSc Univ. London, 1949.

Offices and Honours Leverhulme Scholar, LSE, 1946–9; Knoop Res. Fellow, Univ. Sheffield, 1950–1; Nursey Premium, Soc. Engineers, 1968.

Publications *Books:* 1. *Business Enterprise* (with R.S. Edwards), (Macmillan, 1958; transl., Spanish, 1966); 2. *Studies in Business Organisation* (with R.S. Edwards), (Macmillan, 1961); 3. *Business Growth* (with R.S. Edwards), (Macmillan, 1966); 4. *Scale, Innovation, Merger and Monopoly* (Pergamon, 1968; Italian transl., 1970); 5. *Price Theory*, ed. (Penguin, 1971, 1980).

Articles: 1. 'Economic theory and the cutlery trades', *Ec*, N.S. 21, Aug. 1954; 2. 'The cutlery trade', in *The Structure of British Industry*, vol. 2, ed. D.L. Burn (Macmillan, 1958); 3. 'Price theory and petrol prices', in *Essays in*

Honour of Lord Robbins, eds. M.H. Preston and B.A. Corry (Weidenfeld & Nicolson, 1972); 4. 'Big business and big science', *Science Public Pol.*, Dec. 1974; 5. 'Economics of consumerism', Univ. Lancaster, 1974.

Principal Contributions Application of price theory to industry: analysis of industrial organisation in terms of market, administrative and co-operative integration.

TOYNBEE, Arnold*

Dates and Birthplace 1852–83, London, England.

Posts Held Lect., Tuturial Fellow, Balliol Coll. Oxford, 1878–83.

Degrees BA Univ. Oxford, 1878.

Publications *Books:* 1. *Lectures on the Industrial Revolution* (1884, 1956).

Career Coined the phrase 'industrial revolution' and introduced the concept of a single, decisive transformation of the British economy in the third quarter the eighteenth century. He turned to economics because of its relevance to social reform, and rejected the deductive in favour of the historical method. He argued that economic policies were appropriate or not, according to historical circumstances, and therefore rejected *laissez faire* in favour of a kind of municipal socialism for his own time. He is remembered for his inspiring teaching which influenced many Oxford contemporaries to accept a socially-committed version of economics.

Secondary Literature A. Milner, *Arnold Toynbee* (1901); R. Lekachman, 'Toynbee, Arnold', *IESS*, 16.

TRIFFIN, Robert

Born 1911, Flobecq, Belgium.

Current Post Invited Prof., Univ. de Louvain la Neuve, Belgium; Part-time Cons., EEC, Brussels, Belgium, 1977–.

Past Posts Lect., Univ. Louvain, Belgium, 1938–9; Instr., Harvard Univ., 1939–42; Chief, Latin Amer. Section, Fed. Reserve Board, 1942–6; Dir., Exchange Control Div., Head, Technical Representative in Europe, Observer,

OECC Payments Comm., IMF, 1946–8, 1948–9; Special Adviser, Alternate US Representative, Europ. Payments Union, Europ. Recovery Admin., Paris, 1949–51; Pelatiah Perit Prof. Polit. and Social Science, Frederick William Beinnecke Prof. Econ., Yale Univ., 1958–67, 1967–80; Master, Berkeley Coll., Yale Univ., 1969–77; Adviser, Monetary and Banking Reforms Honduras, Paraguay, Guatemala, Dominican Republic, Ecuador; Cons., UN, OEEC, Jean Monnet Action Comm. for United States of Europe; US President's Council Econ. Advisers.

Degrees BA (Philo.), Dr en Droit, Licencie Econ., Louvain Univ., 1933, 1934, 1935; PhD Harvard Univ., 1939; Hon. Dr Univs. Louvain, 1970, Yale, 1976, Amer. Coll. Switzerland, 1982.

Offices and Honours Commander, Orden del Merito, Paraguay, 1944; Commander, Orden del Quetzal, Guatemala, 1971; Commander, Ordre de la Couronne, Belgium, 1973; Member, World AAAS, AAAS, Académie Royale de Belgique, Council Foreign Relations; Vice-Pres., AEA, 1967–8.

Editorial Duties Ed. Boards, *Asuntos Europeus, PDR.*

Principal Fields of Interest 423 Economic Integration; 431 Balance of Payments; 432 International Monetary Arrangements.

Publications *Books:* 1. *Monopolistic Competition and General Equilibrium Theory* (Harvard Univ. Press, 1942); 2. *Europe and the Money Muddle: From Bilateralism to Near Convertibility 1947–1956* (Yale Univ. Press, 1957, Greenwood Press, 1976; transl., Spanish *El Caos Monetario*, Fondo de Cultura Economica, 1961); 3. *Gold and the Dollar Crisis: The Future of Convertibility* (Yale Univ. Press, 1960, 1961; transls., Japanese, 1961, French, Presses Univ. de France, 1962, Spanish, Fondo de Cultura Economica, 1962); 4. *The World Money Maze: National Currencies in International Payments* (Yale Univ. Press, 1966); 5. *Gull og Penger* (Studieselskapet Samfunn og Noeringsliv, 1966); 6. *Maintaining and Restoring Balance in International Payments* (with W. Fellner, F. Machlup, *et al.*), (Princeton Univ. Press, 1966; transl., Spanish, Editorial Gustavo Gili, 1969); 7. *Wegweiser vom Währungswirrarr* (Berlin Verlag, 1967); 8. *Our International Monetary System: Today and Tomorrow* (Random House, 1968; transls., Japanese, Diamond Publ., 1968, French, Firmin Didot Etude et Edns Clé, 1969, Spanish, Amorrortu Editores, 1970, Italian, Einaudi, 1973, Portuguese, Editora Expresao e Cultura, 1972); 9. *Gold and the Dollar Crisis: Yesterday and Tomorrow* (Princeton Univ. Press, 1978); 10. *Europe's Money: Problems of European Monetary Coordination and Integration* (with R. S. Masera, *et al.*), (OUP, 1984).

Articles: 1. 'La théorie de la surévaluation monétaire et la dévaluation belge', *Bull. de l'Inst. des Sciences Econ.*, Nov. 1937; transl., Spanish, *El Trimestre Economico*, 1948; 2. 'National central banking and the international economy', in *Postwar Economic Studies* (Board of Governors, Fed. Reserve System, 1947); transl., Spanish, *El Trimestre Economico*, 1948; 3. 'Institutional developments in the intra-European monetary system', in *Money, Trade, and Economic Growth, Essays in Honor of John H. Williams* (Macmillan, 1951); 4. 'The size of the nation and its vulnerability to economic nationalism', in *The Economic Consequences of the Size of Nations*, ed. E. A. G. Robinson (St Martins Press, 1960); 5. 'Integration économique européenne et politique monétaire', *La Restauration des Monnaies Européennes, REP*, 1960; 6. 'Payments arrangements within the ECAFE region', in *Report and Recommendations of the Seminar on Financial Aspects of Trade Expansion* (ECAFE, 1967); 7. 'On the creation of a European reserve fund', *BNLQR*, 91, Dec. 1969; transls., French, *Moneta e Credito*, 1970, Spanish, CEMLA, 1970; 8. 'A common currency for the common market', *Morgan Guaranty Survey*, 1970; 9. 'The use of SDR finance for collectively agreed purposes', *BNLQR*, 96, March 1971; transls., Italian, *Moneta e Credito*, 1971, Spanish, *Revista Bancaria*, 1971; 10. 'An economist's career: what? why? how?', *BNLQR*, 138,

Sept. 1981; transl., Italian, *Moneta e Credito*, 1981.

Principal Contributions My early interest in general equilibrium theory was inspired by Professors Schumpeter and Leontief. Most of my career, however, has been devoted to the twin problems of world monetary reform and regional monetary integration, in which I saw the best opportunity for an economist to serve deeply entrenched pacifist convictions, inspired by Einstein and my revulsion for Hitlerism on the eve of World War II.

I saw, from the very beginning, these two goals as complementary, as demonstrated by the contribution of the European Payments Union (which I designed in 1947 and helped to negotiate in 1949–50) to the return to worldwide convertibility. Regional groups can carry international co-operation further than is yet feasible on a world scale, and improve the ability of participating countries to progress, even though more slowly, toward worldwide co-operation commitments. I was (alas!) a good forecaster of the 'gold and dollar crisis' of 1960 and later years, but failed (also alas!) to persuade the officials to negotiate in time the fundametal reforms needed to avoid it.

I was somewhat more successful in my advocacy of regional monetary integration particularly in Europe and in Central America. The ECU-anchored European Monetary system is an obvious successor of the European Payments Union and implements — even though imperfectly still — the mechanisms suggested in my reports (to the Monnet Committee for the United States of Europe and to the Commission of the European Communities) for a European Reserve Fund, and defended by Chancellor Brandt, at the first Summit Meeting of the Hague in 1969.

The following suggestions might enhance the chances of success of incipient international economists: (1) Long-term historical trends, derived from comprehensive 'Tableaux à la Quesnay', are more important than short-term analysis and econometric models based on unrealistic assumptions, chosen for their better amenability to mathematical treatment. (2) 'Compatibility' is a more fruitful concept than 'equilibrium'. (3) Institutions must be designed primarily to erect a 'defence in depth' — rather than a 'Maginot line' — against possible disturbances. (4) 'Communicability' is as essential as good economics: you will not influence policy if you don't speak a language understandable and convincing to policy-makers.

Any reader interested in these suggestions should glance at Article No. 10 above.

TSIANG, Sho-chieh

Born 1918, Shanghai, China.
Current Post Pres., Dhung-Hua Institution Econ. Res., Taipei, Taiwan, Republic China, Prof. Emeritus, Cornell Univ., 1985–.
Past Posts Econ., Central Bank China, 1945–6; Prof. Econ., Nat. Univ. Peking, 1946–8; Prof. Econ., Nat. Taiwan Univ., 1948–9; Econ., IMF, 1949–60; Prof. Econ., Univ. Rochester, NY, 1960–9; Cons., UN Secretariat, 1963–4; Vis. Fellow, Jesus Coll. Oxford, 1966–7; Prof. Econ., Cornell Univ., 1969–85; Rockefeller Prof., Univ. Philippines, 1972–3; Vis. Fellow, Nuffield Coll. Oxford, 1976–7; Vis. Lect., Inst. Advanced Stud., Vienna, 1982, Keio Univ., Tokyo, 1984.
Degrees BSc, PhD LSE, 1941, 1945; DSc London Univ., 1975.
Offices and Honours British Council Fellow, 1942–4; Hutchinson Silver Medal, LSE, 1945–6; Member, Academia Sinica, ROC, 1958–; Guggenheim Foundation Fellow, 1966–7.
Editorial Duties Ed. Board, *AER*, 1974–6.
Principal Fields of Interest 110 Economic Growth, Development and Planning Theory and Policy; 310 Domestic Monetary and Financial Theory and Institutions; 430 Balance of Payments; International Finance.
Publications Books: 1. *Variations of Real Wages and Profit Margins in Relation to Trade Cycles* (Pitman, 1947); 2. *Quantitative Economics and Development*, co-ed. (with L. Klein and M. Nerlove), (Academic Press, 1980); 3.

Inflation in East Asian Countries, co-ed. (with J. C. H. Fei), (Chung-Hua Inst. Econ. Res., 1984).

Articles: 1. 'Liquidity preference and loanable funds theories, multiplier and velocity analysis: a synthesis', *AER*, 46(4), Sept. 1956; 2. 'The theory of forward exchange and effects of government intervention of the foreign exchange market', *IMF Staff Papers*, April 1959; 3. 'The role of money in trade balance stability: synthesis of the elasticity and absorption approaches', *AER*, 51(5), Dec. 1961; 4. 'A model of growth in Rostovian stages', *Em*, 32(4), Oct. 1964; 5. 'Walras' law, Say's law and liquidity preference in general equilibrium analysis', *Int ER*, 1(3), Sept. 1966; 6. 'The rationale of the mean standard deviation analysis, skewness preference and the demand for money', *AER*, 52(3), June 1972; 7. 'The dynamics of international capital flows and internal and external balance', *QJE*, 89(2), May 1975; 8. 'The monetary theoretic foundation of the modern monetary approach to the balance of payments', *OEP*, 29(3), Nov. 1977; 9. 'The diffusion of reserves and the money supply multiplier', *EJ*, 88, June 1978; 10. 'Keynes's "finance" demand for liquidity, Robertson's loanable funds theory, and Friedman's monetarism', *QJE*, 94(2), May 1980.

Principal Contributions Demonstrated in 1943 that Keynes's theory of speculative demand for money is really a theory of speculative arbitrage between short-term financial assets and long-term bonds, and that such speculation does not render the entire interest structure inflexible, but merely makes the long-term rate less flexible that the short-term rate, thus shifting the whole burden of adjustment to the latter. Later (1956 and 1980) exposed the logical defect of the Keynesian liquidity preference theory due to Keynes's self-admitted neglect of the 'demand for finance', and demonstrated that the liquidity preference and loanable funds theories are reconcilable when the former's neglect of the demand for finance is mended. Other contributions include the formulation of a theory of precautionary money demand on the basis of inventory theory; critical examination of mean-variance analysis of asset demand for money; the first comprehensive theory on the forward exchange rate that takes into account all three categories of operations; hedging, covered interest arbitrage, and speculation; the construction of a theory on foreign exchange speculation as well as a theory on international capital flows including transient portfolio reallocations in addition to sustainable flows; criticisms of modern monetary theory of the balance of payments, and of the indiscriminate application of Walras' law to monetary analysis: and application of modified Markov chain analysis to money supply determination. On the practical policy side, formulated a theoretical model of economic take-off for a poor developing country, and helped to apply this model successfully through advisory work to the government of Taiwan, which has developed the nation into a remarkable paradigm of rapid and self-sustained economic growth.

TSURU, Shigeto

Born 1912, Tokyo, Japan.

Current Post Ed. Adviser, Asahi Shimbum, Tokyo, Japan, 1975–.

Past Posts Vice-Minister, Econ. Stabilization Board, Japan Govt., 1947–8; Prof. Econ., Pres., Hitotsubashi Univ., Tokyo, 1948–72, 1972–5; Cons., ECAFE, 1954, 1955; Vis. Prof., Harvard Univ., 1956–7, Yale Univ., 1960, Univ. Minnesota, 1960, Johns Hopkins Univ., 1960–1, Univ. Rochester, NY, 1961, Delhi Univ., 1952–3.

Degrees BA, MA, PhD Harvard Univ., 1935, 1936, 1940; Hon. LLD Lawrence Univ., Canada, 1972.

Offices and Honours Vice-Pres., Internat. Social Science Council, 1967–73; Exec. Comm., Vice-Pres., Pres., IEA, 1971–4, 1974–7, 1977–80; Hon. Member, AEA.

Editorial Duties Ed. Boards, *Majingira, JEEM*.

Principal Fields of Interest 113 Economic Planning Theory and Policy; 620 Economics of Technological Change; 720 Conservation and Pollution.

Publications *Books:* (All in Japanese except 6) 1. *Essays on Marxian Economics* (Science Council Japan, 1956); 2. *Essays on Japanese Economy* (Kinokuniya, 1958); 3. *Has Capitalism Changed?*, ed. (Iwanami, 1959); 4. *Essays on Economic Development* (Kinokuniya, 1968); 5. *Towards a New Political Economy* (Kodansha, 1976); 6. *The Mainsprings of Japanese Growth: A Turning Point?* (Atlantic Inst., 1976); 7. *Collected Works*, 13 vols (Kondasha, 1975–6).

Articles: 1. 'On reproduction schemes', in P. M. Sweezy, *The Theory of Capitalist Development* (OUP, 1942); 2. 'Business cycles in post-war Japan', in *The Business Cycles in the Post-war World*, ed. E. Lundberg (Macmillan, 1955); 3. 'Growth and stability of the post-war Japanese economy', *AER*, 51(2), May 1961; 4. 'Merits and demerits of the mixed economy in economic development: lessons from India's experience', in *Studies on Developing Countries* (Polish Scientific Publ., 1964); 5. 'Survey of economic research in post-war Japan: major issues of theory and public policy arising out of post-war economic problems', *AER*, 65(4), Sept. 1964; 6. 'A peripatetic economist', *BNLQR*, 142, Sept. 1982.

Principal Contributions The resuscitation of political economy, as contrasted to economics, in an attempt to reappraise the viability of the capitalist system. Have questioned the welfare significance of the national income (or GNP) concept years before it become fashionable and wrote on development planning and other welfare-related fields of applied economics, such as medical economics, environment and urban problems. A self-assessment is given in Article No. 6 above.

TUCKER, George*

Dates and Birthplace 1775–1861, Bermuda.

Posts Held Prof. Moral Philo., Univ. Virginia, 1825–45.

Offices and Honours Congressman, 1819–25.

Publications *Books:* 1. *Laws of Wages, Profits and Rent Investigated* (1837); 2. *The Theory of Money and Banks Investigated* (1839); 3. *Progress of the United States in Population and Wealth in Fifty Years* (1843); 4. *Banks or No Banks* (1857); 5. *Political Economy for the People* (1859); 6. *Essays Moral and Metaphysical* (1860).

Career Writer on various subjects whose economic work was probably his most significant. He was a critic of Ricardo, and questioned Malthusian population theory. Though a Southerner, he was critical of slavery on both economic and moral grounds.

Secondary Literature H. U. Faulkner, 'Tucker, George', *ESS*, 15; T. R. Snaveley, *George Tucker* (Univ. Virginia Press, 1964).

TUCKER, Josiah*

Dates and Birthplace 1712–99, Laugharne, Wales.

Posts Held Clergyman, 1737–99.

Degrees BA, MA, DD Univ. Oxford, 1836, 1839, 1755.

Publications *Books:* 1. *A Brief Essay on the Advantages and Disadvantages Which Respectively Attend France and Great Britain with Regard to Trade* (1749); 2. *The Elements of Commerce and Theory of Taxes* (1755); 3. *The Case of Going to War, for the Sake of Procuring, Enlarging or Securing of Trade, Considered in a New Light* (1763); 4. *A Letter from a Merchant in London to his Nephew in North America* (1766); 5. *The True Interest of Great Britain Set Forth in Regard to the Colonies* (1774).

Career Pamphleteer, who wrote frequently on economic topics and on the question of the American colonies, whose independence he favoured. His attacks on monopolies and his belief that trade was not benefitted by the conflict with the colonies were favourably noticed by subsequent writers, including McCulloch.

Secondary Literature W. E. Clark, *Josiah Tucker: Economist* (1903); J. F. Rees, 'Tucker, Josiah', *ESS*, 15.

TUGAN-BARANOVSKY, Mikhail Ivanovich*

Dates and Birthplace 1865–1919, Kharkov, Russia.
Posts Held Privatdozent, Univ. St Petersburg, 1894–9, 1905–15; Dean Faculty Law, Univ. Kiev, 1917–19.
Degrees Grad., MA Univ. Kharkov, 1888, 1890.
Offices and Honours Member, Ukrainian Academy Sciences; Fin. Minister, Ukrainian Republic, 1918.
Publications *Books:* 1. *Crises industrielle en Angleterre* (1894, 1913); 2. *The Russian Factory* (1898); 3. *Modern Socialism in its Historical Development* (1906, 1910); 4. *Osnovy Politicheskoi Ekonomii* (1909, 1918); 5. *Sotsial'nyia Osnovy Kooperatsiia* (1916, 1921).
Career Opponent of the Populists, who argued that Russia could bypass capitalism and become a peasant socialist country. His study of crises in England was designed to refute this by showing the way capitalism had evolved in England. His critique of Marxism in other works led him to be regarded as a revisionist. His disproportionality theory of crises — in which crises occur because some sectors of industry expand out of proportion to others — was widely admired by contemporaries. In later years he abandoned Marxism, becoming interested in co-operative movements.
Secondary Literature O. Crisp, 'Tugan-Baranovskii', *IESS*, 16; A. Nove, 'M. I. Tugan-Baranovsky (1865–1919)', *HOPE*, 2(2), Fall 1970.

TUGWELL, Rexford Guy*

Dates and Birthplace 1891–1979, Sinclairville, NY, USA.
Posts Held Instr. Econ., Univ. Penn., 1915–7; Ass. Prof. Econ., Univ. Washington, 1917–8; Instr., Ass. Prof., Assoc. Prof., Prof. Econ., Univ. Columbia, 1920–2, 1922–6, 1926–31, 1931–7; Ass. Secretary, Under-Secretary, US Dept. Agric., 1933, 1934–6; Administrator, US Resettlement Admin., 1936–8; Head, Planning Dept., NYC Planning Comm., 1938; Governor, Puerto Rico, 1941; Member, Carib-

bean Comm., 1942–7; Dir., Polit. Science, Univ. Chicago Inst. Planning, 1946–52, 1946–57; Vis. Prof., LSE, 1949–50, Harvard Univ., 1959; Res. Prof. Polit. Science, Univ. S. Illinois, Carbondale, 1965–6.
Degrees BS, MA, PhD Wharton School, Univ. Penn., 1915, 1916, 1922; DLitt Univ. New Mexico, 1933, Univ. Puerto Rico, 1953, Univ. Penn., 1971.
Offices and Honours Woodrow Wilson Foundation Award, 1958; Silver Medal, Amer. Assoc. Planning Office, 1967; Bancroft Prize, 1969.
Publications *Books:* 1. *The Economic Basis of Public Interest* (1922); 2. *The Trend of Economics* (with others), (1924); 3. *American Economic Life* (with T. Munro and R. E. Stryker); 4. *Soviet Russia in the Second Decade* (with others), (1928); 5. *The Place of Planning in Society* (1954); 6. *The Democratic Roosevelt* (1957); 7. *The Act of Politics* (1958); 8. *Tugwell's Thoughts on Planning* (1975).
Career A prominent institutionalist in the 1920s, he joined Roosevelt's brain trust in 1933 and soon emerged as a vigorous spokesman for the New Deal. In the course of his long career, he increasingly turned towards political science and wrote no economics after 1945.
Secondary Literature A. G. Gruchy, *Modern Economic Thought. The American Contribution* (Prentice-Hall, 1947), chap. 6.

TULLOCK, Gordon

Born 1922, Rockford, IL, USA.
Current Post Disting. Prof. Econ. and Public Choice, George Mason Univ., Fairfax, VA, 1983–.
Past Posts Foreign Service Officer, China, 1947–56; Ass. Prof., Assoc. Prof., Univ. S. Carolina, 1959–60, 1960–2; Assoc. Prof., Univ. Virginia, 1962–7; Prof. Econ. and Polit. Science, Rice Univ., TX, 1967–8; Prof. Econ. and Public Choice, Virginia Polytechnic Inst. and State Univ., 1968–72.
Offices and Honours Post-doctoral Fellow, Univ. Virginia, 1958–9; Ed., Dir., Center for Study of Public Choice, 1968–; Dir., Dodger Products,

Eldorado, IA; Pres., SEA; Secretary, Public Choice Soc., 1965–.

Principal Fields of Interest 025 Social Choice.

Publications *Books:* 1. *The Calculus of Consent* (with J. M. Buchanan), (Univ. Michigan Press, 1962); 2. *The Politics of Bureaucracy* (Public Affairs Press, 1965); 3. *The Logic of the Law* (Basic Books, 1971); 4. *The Social Dilemma: Economics of War and Revolution* (Center Study Public Choice, 1974); 5. *The New World of Economics* (with R. B. McKenzie), (Basic Books, 1975); 6. *Trials on Trial* (1979); 7. *Toward a Theory of the Rent-Seeking Society* (with J. M. Buchanan and R. D. Tollison), (Texas A&M Univ. Press, 1981).

TURGOT, Anne Robert Jacques*

Dates and Birthplace 1727–81, Paris, France.

Posts Held Intendant, Limoges, 1761–74; Contrôleur général of France, 1774–6.

Publications *Books:* 1. *Reflections on the Formation and the Distribution of Wealth* (1769–70, 1973); 2. *Oeuvres de Turgot et documents le concernant*, ed. G. Schelle, 5 vols (1913–23).

Career Reforming administrator and minister whose efforts were cut short by the resistance of the privileged classes. His attempts to rationalise the tax burdens and obligations of French society were justified in theoretical terms of physiocratic variety. His *Reflections . . .* is frequently described as one of the most important general treatises on political economy written before Smith's *Wealth of Nations* and there is little doubt that it was a major influence on Adam Smith. His other economic writings have only recently become available in English.

Secondary Literature W. Stark, 'Turgot, Anne Robert Jacques', *IESS*, 16; R. L. Meek, *Turgot on Progress, Sociology and Economics* (CUP, 1973); P. D. Groenewegen, *The Economics of A. R. J. Turgot* (Martinus Nijhoff, 1977).

TURNOVSKY, Stephen John

Born 1941, Wellington, New Zealand.

Current Post Prof. Econ., Univ. Illinois, Urbana-Champaign, IL; Res. Assoc., NBER, Cambridge, MA, USA, 1982.

Past Posts Jr. Lect., Victoria Univ., Wellington, 1963; Ass. Prof., Univ. Penn., 1968–71; Assoc. Prof., Univ. Toronto, 1971–2; Prof. Econ., ANU, 1972–82; Vis. Prof., School Bus. Admin., Univ. Cal. Berkeley, 1975, Univ. Paris-Dauphine, 1979, Univ. Minnesota, 1979; Vis. Res. Assoc., CEPREMAP, Paris, 1979; Vis. Fellow, Nuffield Coll. Oxford, 1979.

Degrees BA, MA (Maths.) Victoria Univ., Wellington, 1962, 1963; PhD Harvard Univ., 1968.

Offices and Honours Fellow, Academy Social Sciences, Australia, 1976–; Fellow, Em Soc, 1981–; Pres., Soc. Econ. Dynamics and Control, 1982–4.

Editorial Duties Joint Ed., *ER*, 1973–7; Ed., *J Ec Dyn*, 1981–; Ed. Board, *Australian Econ. Rev.*, 1973–4, *Int ER*, 1972–, *J Ec Dyn*, 1979–81, *JMCB*, 1977–, *J Pub. Econ*, 1982–.

Principal Fields of Interest 023 Macroeconomic Theory; 131 Economic Fluctuations; 430 Balance of Payments; International Finance.

Publications *Books:* 1. *The Inflationary Process in North American Manufacturing* (with L.D. Taylor and T.A. Wilson), (Prices and Incomes Commission, 1973); 2. *Applications of Control Theory to Economic Analysis*, co-ed. (with J.D. Pitchford), (N-H, 1977); 3. *Macroeconomic Analysis and Stabilization Policy* (CUP, 1977; transl., Japanese, 1980).

Articles: 1. 'Empirical evidence on the formation of price expectations,', *JASA*, 65(4), Dec. 1970; 2. 'The stability properties of optimal economic policies', *AER*, 64(1), March 1974; 3. 'The dynamics of fiscal policy in an open economy', *J Int E*, 6(2), May 1976; 4. 'Expectations and the dynamics of devaluation', *REStud*, 47(3), July 1980; 5. 'Consumer's surplus, price instability and price stabilization' (with H. Shalit and A. Schmitz', *Em*, 48(1), Jan. 1980; 6. 'The analysis of macroeconomic policies in perfect foresight equilibrium' (with W.A. Brock), *Int ER*, 22(1), Feb. 1981; 7. 'Monetary policy and foreign price disturbances under flexible exchange rates', *JMCB*, 13(2), May 1981; 8. 'Incidence of taxes; a dynamic macroeconomic analysis', *J Pub E*, 18(2), July 1982; 9. 'The determination of spot and futures prices with storable commodities', *Em*, 51(5), Sept. 1983; 10. 'Covered interest parity, uncovered interest parity and exchange rate dynamics' (with J. Eaton), *EJ*, 93, Sept. 1983.

Principal Contributions I have worked extensively in macroeconomic theory, particularly in the modelling and analysis of consistently specified dynamic systems. Much of the emphasis of this work has been on inflation, inflationary expectations, and their interaction with other macroeconomic variables. I am also interested in rational expectations, both the methodological issues and the policy questions. More recently my interests have moved in the direction of international macroeconomic theory. This work has centred around the dynamic behaviour of exchange rates, as well as the analysis of economies subject to stochastic disturbances of various kinds. I have a continuing interest in issues pertaining to macroeconomic stabilisation policy. This extends from traditional dynamic optimal feedback policy to more current interests in optimal exchange market intervention, and more generally, optimal stabilisation of stochastic economies. I have also worked on problems of price stabilisation. This has concerned the analysis of various schemes directed at the stabilisation of prices and the allocation of the benefits and losses resulting from them. My recent work in this area has focussed on the effectiveness of futures markets as a means of stabilising the spot price.

TURVEY, Ralph

Born 1927, Birmingham, England.
Current Post Chief, Dept. Labour Info. and Stats., ILO, Geneva, Switzerland, 1975–.

Past Posts Lect., Reader, Vis. Prof., LSE, 1948–64, 1973–5; Vis. Lect., Johns Hopkins Univ., 1953; Ford Foundation Vis. Prof., Univ. Chicago, 1958; Econ. Adviser, UK Treasury, 1960–2; Centre Econ. Res., Athens, 1963; Chief Econ., UK Electricity Council, 1964–7; Member, Joint Dep. Chairman, UK Nat. Board Prices and Incomes, 1967–71; Econ. Cons., Scientific Control Systems, 1971–5.
Degrees BSc, DSc Univ. London, 1947, 1971.
Offices and Honours Council Member, RES, 1971–6; Member, UK Nat. Water Council, 1974–5, UK Inflation Accounting Comm, 1974–5; Governor, Kingston Polytechnic, London, 1972–5.
Editorial Duties Ed. Boards, *REStud*, *Internat. Econ. Papers*, *J Pub E*, *Benefit Cost Analysis Annual*.
Principal Fields of Interest 220 Economic and Social Statistical Data and Analysis; 613 Public Utilities; 614 Public Enterprises.
Publications Books: 1. *The Economics of Real Property* (A&U, 1957); 2. *Interest Rates and Asset Prices* (A&U, 1960); 3. *Studies in Greek Taxation* (with G. Break), (Athens Centre Econ. Res., 1964); 4. *Optimal Pricing and Investment in Electricity Supply* (A&U, 1968); 5. *Economic Analysis and Public Enterprises* (A&U, 1971); 6. *Demand and Supply* (A&U, 1971); 7. *Report to the Government of Pakistan on the Prices of Essential Commodities* (Govt. of Pakistan, 1974); 8. *Electricity Economics* (with D. Anderson), (JHUP, 1977; transls., French, Spanish).
Articles: 1. 'Some aspects of the theory of inflation in a closed economy', *EJ*, 61, Sept. 1951; 2. 'Some notes on multiplier theory', *AER*, 43(3), 1953; 3. 'On divergences between social cost and private cost', *Ec*, N.S. 30, Aug. 1963; 4. 'Optimisation and sub-optimisation in fishery regulation', *AER*, 54(1), March 1964; 5. 'Cost-benefit analysis: a survey' (with A. Prest), *EJ*, 75, Dec. 1965, repr. in AES-RES, *Surveys of Economic Theory*, 3 (Macmillan, 1966); 6. 'Analysing the marginal cost of water supply', *Land Econ.*, 52, May 1976; 7.

'Structural change and structural unemployment', *Int Lab Rev*, 116, Sept.–Oct. 1977; 8. 'The treatment of seasonal items in consumer price indices', *ILO Bull. Lab. Stat.*, 4, 1979; 9. 'Durable goods, dwellings and credit in consumer price indices', *ILO Bull. Lab. Stat.*, 1, 1981.

Principal Contributions Started as economic theorist in the days when it was possible to keep up with everything in economics, then gradually concentrated on the applied aspects of efficient resource allocation. Since 1964 I have in particular specialised in electricity economics, having estimated the marginal cost structure in some dozen electricity enterprises scattered round the world. In this work, and in prices and incomes work, I endeavoured to combine economic analysis with industry-specific knowledge. More recently I have turned to labour statistics and some practical problems of consumer price indices.

U

ULMAN, Lloyd

Born 1920, New York City, NY, USA.
Current Post Prof. Econ. and Industrial Relations, Univ. Cal. Berkeley, CA, USA, 1968–.
Past Posts Ass. Prof., Assoc. Prof., Prof. Econ., Univ. Minnesota, 1950–8; Sr. Labor Econ., US President's Council Econ. Advisers, 1961–2; Cons., Fed. Reserve Board, 1966–7, US President's Council Econ. Advisers, 1963–8; Vis. Fellow, All Souls Coll. Oxford 1973–4; Dir., Inst. Industrial Relations, Univ. Cal. Berkeley, 1963–81.
Degrees BA Columbia Univ., 1940; MA Univ. Wisconsin, 1941; PhD Harvard Univ., 1950.
Offices and Honours Guggenheim Foundation Fellow, 1966–7; Order Northern Star, Sweden, 1979; Pres., IRRA, 1986.
Editorial Duties Ed. Boards, *Industrial Relations*, 1961–, *AER*, 1969–.
Principal Fields of Interest 820 Labour Markets; Public Policy; 830

Trade Unions; Collective Bargaining; Labour–Management Relations.

Publications *Books:* 1. *The Government of the Steel Workers' Union* (Wiley, 1962); 2. *The Rise of the National Trade Union* (Harvard Univ. Press, 1955); 3. *Wages and Labor Mobility* (with P. de Wolff, *et al.*), (OECD 1965); 4. *Manpower Programs in the Policy Mix*, ed. (Wiley, 1971); 5. *Challenges to Collective Bargaining*, ed. (Wiley, 1967); 6. *Wage Restraint: A Study of Incomes Policies in Western Europe* (with R.J. Flanagan), (Univ. Cal. Press, 1971); 7. *Unionism, Economic Stabilization and Incomes Policies: The European Experience* (with R.J. Flanagan and D. Soskice), (Wiley, 1983).

Articles: 1. 'Marshall and Friedman on union strength', *REStat*, 37, Nov. 1955; 2. 'Influence of the economic environment on the structure of the steel workers' union', in *Proceedings of the 14th Annual Meeting of the IRRA*, 1961; 3. 'The development of trade and labor unions', and 'Unionism and collective bargaining in the modern period', in *American Economic History*, ed. S.E. Harris (McGraw-Hill, 1961); 4. 'Collective bargaining and industrial efficiency', in *Britain's Economic Prospects*, ed. R.E. Caves (Brookings Inst., 1968); 5. 'The uses and limits of manpower policy', *Public Interest*, Winter 1974; 6. 'Connective bargaining and competitive bargaining', *SJPE*, 21(2), June 1974; 7. 'Multinational unionism: incentives, barriers, and alternatives', *Industrial Relations*, 14(1), Feb. 1975.

Principal Contributions My work has primarily been concerned with the historical determinants, distinctive characteristics, and economic effects of trade unionism and collective bargaining. I began studying the historic determinants and structural properties of American systems and have continued to work in that area. Subsequently, I paid considerable attention to the wider significance of policies of direct wage restraint for the light which such policies shed on the workings of the institutions themselves and on the interaction among collective bargaining, the political process, and economic stabilisation policies. This interest has led me farther afield and into work on unionism and macroeconomic developments in postwar European countries.

ULMER, Melville Jack

Born 1911, New York City, NY, USA.
Current Post Prof. Emeritus, Univ. Maryland, College Park, MD, 1982–.
Past Posts Chief, General Price Res. Section, US Bureau Labor Stats., 1940–5; Ass. Chief, Reports Division, Smaller War Plants Corp., 1945–6; Section Chief, Office Bus. Econ., US Dept. Commerce, 1946–8; Res. Assoc., NBER, 1950–60; Assoc. Prof., Prof. Econ., American Univ., Washington, DC, 1950–2, 1952–60; Vis. Prof. Econ., Netherlands School Econ., Rotterdam, 1958–9, 1965–6; Prof. Econ., Univ. Maryland, 1961–82.
Degrees BS, MA NYU, 1937, 1938; PhD Columbia Univ., 1948.
Offices and Honours Disting. Assoc. Award, Atlantic Econ. Soc., 1982; Foreign Lect. Awards, US State Dept., 1976, 1977, 1978; Sr. Fellow, Nat. Endowment Humanities, 1974–5; Sr. Fulbright Lect. Awards, 1958–9, 1965–6; AAAS Fellow, 1956–; Wilton Park Fellow, UK, 1966; Disting. Lect., Univ. Nebraska, Lincoln, 1976, St Lawrence Univ., 1975; American Lect. Fellow., Internat. People's College, Denmark, 1966.
Editorial Duties Ed., *Survey Current Bus.*, 1948–50; Contrib. Ed., *New Republic*, 1970–9; Ed. Board, *JEI*, 1971–3.
Principal Fields of Interest 023 Macroeconomic Theory; 133 General Outlook and Stabilisation Theories and Policies; 321 Fiscal Theory and Policy.
Publications *Books:* 1. *The Theory and Measurement of International Price Competitiveness* (US Bureau Budget, 1969); 2. *The Welfare State: U.S.A.* (Houghton Mifflin, 1969); 3. *Economics: Theory and Practice* (Houghton Mifflin, 1958, 1965); 4. *Capital in Transportation, Communication, and Public Utilities* (Princeton Univ. Press, 1960); 5. *Trends and Cycles in Capital Formation by U.S. Railroads,* *1870–1950* (NBER, 1954); 6. *The Economic Theory of Cost of Living Index Numbers* (Columbia Univ. Press, 1949); 7. *Wartime Prices, I* (with J.M. Blair), (US Dept. Labor, 1944); 8. *Small Business and Civic Welfare* (with C. Wright Mills), (Senate Document No. 136, 79th Congress, 2nd Session, 1946).
Articles: 1. 'Autonomous and induced investment', *AER*, 62(4), Sept. 1952; 2. 'Long term trends in the financing of regulated industries', *J Fin.*, Spring 1955; 3. 'Some reflections on the economic theory of power', *DE*, May 1959, repr. in *Revue de Sociologie*, 2, 1960; 4. 'The limitations of revenue sharing', *Annals American Academy Political and Social Science*, Sept. 1971, repr. in *Current Issues of Economic Policy*, eds. L.G. Reynolds, D. Lewis and C.D. Green (Richard D. Irwin, 1973); 5. 'Toward public employment and economic stability', *JEI*, 6(4), Dec. 1972; 6. 'Human values and economic science', *JEI*, 8(2), June 1974; 7. 'A comment on Lerner's Keynesianism', in *Fiscal Responsibility in Constitutional Democracy*, ed. J.M. Buchanan and R.E. Wagner (Martinus Nijhoff, 1978); 8. 'Old and new fashions in employment and inflation theory', *JEI*, 7(1), March 1979; 9. 'Multinational corporations and third world capitalism', *JEI*, 14(2), June 1980; 10. 'Ideologies and economic science', *Atlantic Econ. J.*, 12(3), March 1983.
Principal Contributions My interest in economic fluctuations and in stabilization policies began as a student of Wesley C. Mitchell. As a side issue, when still at Columbia, I explored the theory of consumer choice and its application to the economic theory of cost of living index numbers. Here, in my doctor's dissertation, I developed a model that has remained the starting point for most studies of this subject since that date. Later, at the National Bureau of Economic Research, I came closer to the main theme of my interest in a study of long-term trends and cycles in the regulated industries, which required the development of entirely new data on capital formation for the years from 1870 to 1950. From that point onward I concentrated more

directly on the central problem of economic stabilization. In *The Welfare State: U.S.A.*, I developed what I believe was the first analysis and explanation for the phenomenon that was later on generally termed 'stagflation'. There and in subsequent articles I also developed, through application of the balanced budget multiplier, a scheme for achieving full employment without inflation by means of a nationally co-ordinated public employment programme, accompanied by appropriate fiscal and monetary policies.

For proper execution, the plan just referred to would require a level of public administration and rigorous supervision which in subsequent years, through the 1970s, seemed to grow even more distant from possible realisation. In more recent studies I explored the alternative possibility of strengthening and expanding the range of automatic stabilisers. Coordinate studies led me to the analysis of revenue-sharing, in which I exposed as early as 1970 the difficulties that more than a decade later led to general disenchantment with this fiscal device. My most recent studies have been in the broader problems of public finance, including fiscal policy, and in perhaps the broadest of all topics, economic methodology. Also, in 1980 I formulated a statistical analysis demonstrating a close relationship between the per capita volume of multinational corporation investment in Third World countries and the rates of economic growth prevailing in these countries, a finding that I also related to the progress of capitalism in the Third World.

UNWIN, George*

Dates and Birthplace 1870–1925, Stockport, Lancashire, England.

Posts Held Private Secretary to Leonard Courtney; Lect., Prof. Econ., Univ. Edinburgh, 1908–10, 1910–25.

Publications *Books:* 1. *Industrial Organisation in the Sixteenth and Seventeenth Centuries* (1904, 1957); 2. *The Guilds and Companies of London* (1908, 1964); 3. *Finance and Trade under Edward III* (1918, 1962); 4. *Samuel*

Oldknow and the Arkwrights (1924); 5. *Studies in Economic History*, ed. R.H. Tawney (1927).

Career Economic historian, who attributed the success of the industrial revolution to the decline of State intervention in the late eighteenth century. His interpretations were much more in line with those of economists and sociologists than was usual in historical writing and he influenced subsequent generations in this approach, both through his teaching and his writings.

Secondary Literature T.S. Ashton, 'Unwin, George', *IESS*, 16.

USHER, Abbot Payson*

Dates and Birthplace 1883–1965, Lynn, MA, USA.

Posts Held Prof., Cornell Univ., 1910–20, Univ. Boston, 1920–2; Prof. Econ., Harvard Univ., 1922–49.

Degrees BA, MA, PhD Harvard Univ., 1904, 1905, 1910.

Publications *Books:* 1. *The History of the Grain Trade in France 1400–1710* (1913); 2. *Introduction to the Industrial History of England* (1920); 3. *A History of Mechanical Inventions* (1929, 1954); 4. *The Early History of Deposit Banking in Mediterranean Europe* (1943).

Articles: 1. 'The industrialization of modern Britain', *Technology and Culture*, 1, 1960.

Career Economic historian whose work drew on his knowledge of a range of disciplines, and emphasised the theoretical and statistical elements. His studies of inventions, markets and banking, all drew striking modern parallels.

Secondary Literature J.H. Dales, 'Usher, Abbott P.', *IESS*, 16.

USHER, Dan

Born 1934, Montreal, Quebec, Canada.

Current Post Prof. Econ., Queen's Univ., Kingston, Ont., Canada.

Past Posts Econ., UNECAFE, Bangkok, Thailand, 1960–1; Halsworth Fellow Econ., Univ. Manchester, 1961–3; Res. Fellow Econ., Nuffield Coll.

Oxford, 1963–6; Ass. Prof., Grad. School Bus., Columbia Univ., 1966–7; Killam Fellow Canada Council, Queen's Univ., 1971–3; Cons., Canadian Econ. Devlp. Agency, 1969; Cons., Nat. Accounts Div., Canada Dominion Bureau Stat., 1970, Econ. Planning Unit, Govt. Malaysia, Harvard Devlp. Advisory Service, 1974; Nat. Fellow, Hoover Inst. War Revolution and Peace, Stanford, CA, 1978–9.

Degrees BA McGill Univ., 1955; MA, PhD Univ. Chicago, 1958, 1960.

Offices and Honours Fellow, Royal Soc. Canada.

Principal Fields of Interest 220 Economic and Social Statistical Data and Analysis; 320 Fiscal Theory; 020 General Economic Theory.

Publications *Books:* 1. *The Price Mechanism and the Meaning of National Income Statistics* (OUP, 1969, Greenwood Press, 1979); 2. *The Measurement of Economic Growth* (Blackwell, Mott, 1980); 3. *The Measurement of Capital*, ed. (Univ. Chicago Press, 1980); 4. *The Economic Prerequisite to Democracy* (Blackwell, Mott 1981; transls., Japanese, German).

Articles: 1. 'The transport bias in comparisons of national income', *Ec*, N. S. 30, May 1963; 2. 'The Thai national income at United Kingdom prices', *BOIS*, 25, Aug. 1963; 3. 'The welfare economics of invention', *Ec*, N.S. 31, Aug. 1964; 4. 'Traditional capital theory', *REStud*, 32, April 1965; 5. 'The derivation of demand curves from indifference curves', *OEP*, 17, March 1965; 6. 'Equalizing differences in income and the interpretation of national income statistics', *Ec*, N. S. 32, Aug. 1965; 7. 'An imputation to the national accounts for changes in life-expectancy', in *The Measurement of Economic and Social Performance*, ed. M. Moss (*NBER*, 1973); 8. 'The suitability of the Divisia index for the measurement of economic aggregates', *RIW*, 20(3), Sept. 1974; 9. 'Public property and the effects of migration upon other residents of the migrant's countries of origin and destination', *JPE*, 85(3), Oct. 1977; 10. 'Welfare economics of the socialization of commodities', *J Pub, E*, 8(2), Oct. 1977.

Principal Contributions The greater part of my research has been devoted to aspects of two quite different subjects: the measurement of real national income across countries or over time and the connection, if any, between the form of economic organisation and the maintenance of democratic government. My studies of national accounting began when I was working for the UN in Bangkok. One could not help but notice the discrepancy between the exceedingly low numbers commonly used to characterise the national incomes of poor countries and the simple biological fact that people in many of these countries did manage to remain alive and to prosper. This observation gave rise to the statistical problem of constructing better numbers and to the theoretical problem of why the available numbers appeared to be so far off the mark. These matters are examined in *The Price Mechanism and the Meaning of National Income Statistics*. I then went on to write *The Measurement of Economic Growth* about the comparison of incomes over time with special reference to the construction of alternative measures for Canada over the period 1926 to 1974.

The Economic Prerequisite to Democracy is a development of the observation that certain well-known weaknesses in majority rule as a means of allocating income among citizens carry strong implications about how the economy must be organised if government by majority rule is to be preserved. The book is in part an attempt to explain why democratic government has usually been associated with some forms of economic organisation but not others, and it is in part an attempt to use the maintenance of democratic government as a criterion, to be set along with efficiency and equality, in the evaluation of economic policy.

Over the years I have dabbled in a variety of topics: capital theory, the theory of demand, invention, international trade, migration, industrial policy and public finance.

UZAWA, Hirofumi

Born 1928, Tottori, Japan.
Current Post Prof. Econ., Univ. Tokyo, Tokyo, Japan, 1969–.
Past Posts Res. Assoc., Appl. Maths. and Stats. Labs., Stanford Univ., 1956–62; Lect. Econ., Act. Ass. Prof. Econ., Stanford Univ., 1958–9; 1959–60; Ass. Prof. Econ. and Maths., Univ. Cal. Berkeley, 1960–1; Assoc. Prof. Econ. and Stats., Stanford Univ., 1961–4; Prof. Econ., Univ. Chicago, 1964–9.
Degrees BS (Maths.) Univ. Tokyo, 1951; PhD Tohoku Univ., Japan, 1963.
Offices and Honours Fellow, Vice-Pres., Pres., Em Soc, 1961, 1974–5, 1976; Fellow, AAAS, 1966–; Foreign Hon. Fellow, AEA; Matsunaga Prize, 1969; Yoshino Prize, 1970; Mainichi Prize, 1974; Person of Cultural Merit, Govt. Japan, 1983.
Editorial Duties Ed. Board *AER*, 1962–7; Foreign Ed., *REStud*, 1961–7.
Principal Fields of Interest 023 Macroeconomics; 213 Mathematical Economics.
Publications *Books:* 1. *Studies in Linear and Non-linear Programming* (with K. J. Arrow and L. Hurwicz), (Stanford Univ. Press, 1958); 2. *Price Theory* (Japanese) (with K. Imai, *et al.*), 3 vols, (Iwanami Shoten, 1972); 4. *Social Costs of the Automobile* (Japanese), (Iwanami Shoten, 1974); 5. *Re-examination of Modern Economics* (Japanese), (Iwanami Shoten, 1974).
Articles: 1. 'Preference and rational choice in the theory of consumption', *Proceedings of the First Stanford Symposium on Math. Methods in the Social Sciences* (Stanford Univ. Press, 1960); 2. 'Neutral inventions and the stability of growth equilibrium', *REStud*, 28, Feb. 1961; 3. 'The stability of dynamic processes', *Em*, 29, Oct. 1961; 4. 'On a two-sector model of economic growth I–II', *REStud*, 29, Oct. 1961, 30, June 1963; 5. 'Production functions with constant elasticities of subistitution', *REStud*, 29, Oct. 1962; 6. 'Optimal growth in a two-sector model of capital accumulation', *REStud*, 31, Jan. 1964; 7. 'Time preference and the Penrose effect in a two-class model of economic growth', *JPE*, 77(4), pt. 2, July-Aug. 1969; 8. 'On the dynamic stability of economic growth: the neoclassical versus Keynesian approaches', in *Trade, Stability, and Macroeconomics*, eds. G. Horwich and P. A. Samuelson (Academic Press, 1974); 9. 'Sur la théorie économique du capital collectif social', *Cahiers du Seminaire d'Econométrie*, 1974.

Principal Contributions Earlier work covered various topics in economic theory, such as the construction of the logical framework for the analysis of consumer's behaviour, the duality of production functions and cost functions, the stability problem of price mechanism in a market economy, and the analysis of non-tâtonnement processes. Then my interest shifted to the problems of economic growth in a capitalist economy with particular emphasis upon the role played by the interaction of the consumption good industry and the investment good industry. This was accomplished by the construction of a two-sector model of economic growth, which was later utilised to examine the pattern of optimum economic growth. Further research on the process of price and quantity adjustment in a decentralised market economy has shown the instability of such processes, and my research interest has been concentrated upon the dynamic analysis of disequilibrium processes. Later, research has been extended to cover the problems of environmental disruption, economics of medicare, and social costs of automobiles.

UZTÁRIZ, Gerónimo*

Dates and Birthplace 1670–1732, Spain.
Posts Held Member, Spanish Council of Trade and Council of the Indies.
Publications *Books:* 1. *Teórica y Práctica de Comercio y de Marina* (1724).
Career Possibly the best-known Spanish mercantilist whose *Teórica ...* was translated and widely admired. It is an assemblage of facts and criticism rather than theoretical analysis — even his recognition that economic conditions govern population levels, rather than vice versa, was hardly new. His advocacy of industrialisation and arma-

ment for Spain is interesting, since this is presumably the policy he had recommended to Cardinal Alberoni when he was one of the latter's advisers.

Secondary Literature E. J. Hamilton, 'The mercantilism of Gerónimo de Uztáriz', in *Economics, Sociology and the Modern World*, ed. N. E. Himes (Univ. Chicago Press, 1935).

V

VANDERKAMP, John

Born 1934, Aalten, The Netherlands.
Current Post Dean, Prof. Social Science, Univ. Guelph, Guelph, Canada, 1981–.
Past Posts Econ., Res. Dept. Bank Canada, Ottawa, 1959–62; Assoc. Prof., Univ. British Columbia, 1964–71; Vis., Univ. Essex, 1969–70; Prof., Univ. Guelph, 1971–80; Vis. Fellow, Inst. Social and Econ. Res., York Univ., Canada, 1976–7; Vis. Prof., Hebrew Univ., Jerusalem, 1980; Disting. Vis., Univ. Alberta, 1984.
Degrees BEcSc (Candidaats) Free Univ., Amsterdam, 1957; MBA Univ. Toronto, 1959; PhD LSE, 1964.
Offices and Honours Studentship, LSE, 1962–4; Canada Council Leave Fellow, 1969–70; Exec. Council, CEA, 1972–82.
Editorial Duties Ed. Board, *CJE*, 1968–9; Ed., *Canadian Public Pol. — Analyse de Politiques*, 1974–82.
Principal Fields of Interest 820 Labour Markets; Public Policy; 831 Trade Unions; 851 Human Capital.
Publications *Books:* 1. *Labour Markets Adjustment* (with T. Montague), (Inst. Industrial Relations, Univ. British Columbia, 1966); 2. *Mobility Patterns in the Canadian Labour Force* (Econ. Council Canada, 1973); 3. *The Economic Causes and Effects of Migration: Canada 1964–71* (with E. K. Grant), (Econ. Council Canada, 1976).
Articles: 1. 'Wage and price level determination: an empirical model for Canada', *Ec*, N.S. 33, May 1966; 2. 'An application of Lipsey's concept of structural unemployment', *REStud*, 33(3), Nov. 1966; 3. 'Interregional

mobility in Canada: a study of the time pattern of migration', *CJE*, 1(3), Aug. 1968; 4. 'The effect of out-migration on regional employment', *CJE*, 3(4), Nov. 1970; 5. 'Migration flows and their determinants and the effects of return migration', *JPE*, 79, Sept.–Oct. 1971; 6. 'Wage adjustment, productivity and price change expectations', *REStud*, 39, Jan. 1972; 7. 'Inflation: a simple Friedman theory with a Phillips twist', *J Mon E*, 1(1), Jan. 1975; 8. 'The role of population size in migration studies', *CJE*, 9(3), Aug. 1976; 9. 'The effects of migration on income: a micro study with Canadian data, 1965–71' (with E. K. Grant), *CJE*, 12(3), Aug. 1980; 10. 'A micro-econometric analysis of strike activity in Canada' (with R. Swidinsky), *J Labour Res.*, 3(4), Fall 1982.

Principal Contributions Two principal themes are characteristic of most of my research and publications. The first relates to substance: labour market adjustment in its various forms. And the second concerns approach, since most of my work is empirical in nature. The term empirical connotes both hypothesis testing and attempts to explain observed patterns of behaviour or 'real-world' phenomena. Observed patterns are analysed in the light of pertinent economic theory and institution arrangements using appropriate econometric techniques. All of the empirical work relates to adjustment aspects of the Canadian labour market. Initial work concentrated on wage adjustment and its relation to unemployment with macroeconomic overtones. The notion of structural unemployment, the link between unemployment and vacancies, and the phenomenon of labour hoarding were analysed in this context. My work on strike behaviour can also be related to this area of interest. Gradually another area of adjustment, viz. on the supply side, became the dominant interest, with particular emphasis on migration. Human capital hypotheses were tested also in terms of outcomes after migration and the results provided only weak support. This had led to some rethinking about the whole of the interregional adjustment process. More recent work has been concerned with regional disparities in incomes and unemployment, and with the role of regional employment growth.

VANDERLINT, Jacob*

Dates and Birthplace ?–1740.
Publications *Books:* 1. *Money Answers All Things* (1734).
Career English pamphleteer whose one important work was often mentioned favourably during the nineteenth century because it argued for free trade. He called for the cultivation of more land to increase the amounts of food available and to reduce its price, which in turn would give the country a competitive advantage in foreign trade.
Secondary Literature J. F. Rees, 'Vanderlint, Jacob', *ESS*, 15.

VANEK, Jaroslav

Born 1930, Prague, Czechoslovakia.
Current Post Carl Marks Prof. Internat. Stud., Cornell Univ., Ithaca, NY, USA, 1969–.
Past Posts Res. Ass., EEC, UN, Geneva, 1952–4; Teaching Econ., MIT, 1956–7; Instr., Ass. Prof., Harvard Univ., 1957–64; Vis. Prof., Univ. Geneva, 1961–2; Cons., Res. Project, Dir., Agency Internat. Devlp., Washington, DC, 1964; Assoc. Prof., Prof. Econ., Cornell Univ., 1964–7, 1966–9; Cons., Govt. Peru, 1971; Vis. Prof., Inst. Econ. Science, Belgrade, 1972, Univ. Catholique de Louvain, Belgium, 1974, Inst. Social Stud., The Hague, 1978–9; Econ. Adviser, Turkish Prime Minister Ecevit, 1978–9; Dir. STEVEN (Solar Technology and Energy for Vital Econ. Needs Foundation), 1983.
Degrees Certificate (Stat.) Sorbonne, Paris, 1952; Licence Econ., Univ. Geneva, 1954; PhD, MIT, 1957.
Offices and Honours Guggengeim Foundation Fellow, 1961–2; Ford Foundation Faculty Res. Fellow, 1967–8; Scholar, Netherlands Inst. Advanced Study Humanities and Social Sciences, 1975–6; Co-founder, *People for Self-Management* (Assoc. for Enterprise Democracy), *Federation for Economic Democracy* (now Industrial Cooperative Assoc).

Editorial Duties Selection Comm., NSF, 1966.
Principal Fields of Interest 400 International Economics; 833 Labour-management Relations.
Publications *Books:* 1. *International Trade: Theory and Economic Policy* (Richard D. Irwin, 1962); 2. *The Natural Resource Content of United States Foreign Trade, 1870–1955* (MIT Press, 1963); 3. *General Equilibrium of International Discrimination: The Case of Customs Unions* (Harvard Univ. Press, 1965); 4. *Maximal Economic Growth* (Cornell Univ. Press, 1968); 5. *The General Theory of Labor-Managed Market Economies* (Cornell Univ. Press, 1970); 6. *The Participatory Economy: An Evolutionary Hypothesis and a Development Strategy* (Cornell Univ. Press, 1971; transls., Spanish, German, Swedish); 7. *Self-Management: Economic Liberation of Man*, ed. (Penguin, 1975); 8. *The Labor-Managed Economy: Essays by Jaroslav Vanek* (Cornell Univ. Press, 1977); 9. *The Praxis of Popular Participation in the Development Process* (UNESCO, 1980); 10. *The Manual of STEVEN* (Solar Technology and Energy for Vital Econ. Needs, 1983).
Articles: 1. 'Growth with technological change, variable returns to scale and a general savings function' (with J. B. Trent), *RISE* 16(8), Aug. 1969; 2. 'The subsistence income, effort and development potential of labor management and other economic systems', *EJ*, 82, Sept. 1972; repr. in *Self-Management: Economic Liberation of Man, op. cit.*, transl., Spanish, *El Trimestre Economico*, April–June, 1972); 3. 'Some fundamental considerations on financing and the right of property under labor management', in *Economic Structure and Development: Essays in Honour of Jan Tinbergen* (N-H, 1973); 4. 'The macroeconomic theory and policy of an open worker-managed economy', *Ekonomska-Analiza*, Summer, 1972.
Principal Contributions In my life to date, I have engaged in a series of transformations, or what I call praxis progressions, going from critical reflection to action: from Stalin's serfdom to freedom of the Western white upper class; from capitalism to economic

democracy and self-management; from neoclassical economics to a critical, history-based and human-oriented study going beyond the confines of economics; from comfortable agnosticism to deep and all-pervasive Christian faith; from believing in economic development Western-style to assisting a sustainable human betterment of the poorest in the world through co-operation, solar energy and human technology; from the AEA to association as much as possible with the poor of Calcutta, Lima, Nairobi or Manila, who indirectly are victims of the former.

The $10,000 income and $2,000 worth of energy *per capita*, and $100,000 of capital per job enjoyed (or suffered) by the rich of the world cannot for many reasons ever become the way of life of the 80% poor. The sane level at which all humanity can survive indefinitely is somewhere near the order of ten times less than today's rich, and ten times more than today's poorest. For the latter, who also are wealthy in permanent solar energy, this promises a significant improvement in the long haul. That and the process going with it, I would call the economics of hope. By, contrast, the potentially cataclysmic road down from the 'non-renewable' and 'cancerous' standards implicit in the present self-centred mainstream economics and 'atom defence' of our ill-gotten riches is an adjustment process which is mind-boggling: it is what I call the economics of damnation. The road up appears bright for the poor (if the rich do not destroy it), and assisting and learning from it appears to me to be the only way of redemption for the rich.

VAN PRAAG, Bernard M. S.

Born 1939, Amsterdam, The Netherlands.

Current Post Prof. Maths. Econ., Em Inst., Erasmus Univ., Rotterdam, The Netherlands, 1984–.

Past Posts Ass. Prof., Econometric Inst., Rotterdam, 1964–70; Assoc. Prof. Econ., Free Univ. Brussels, 1969–70; Assoc. Prof. Econ., Grad. School Management, Delft 1970–2; Prof. Econ., Leiden Univ. 1972–84;

Co-Dir. Center Prof. Public Econ., Leiden, 1975–84.

Degrees Candidatt (Actuarial Sciences), Candidaat, Dr Univ. Amsterdam, 1960, 1964, 1968.

Offices and Honours Member, Internat. Stat. Inst.; Res. Scholar, Netherlands Inst. Advanced Study in Humanities and Social Sciences, 1983–4.

Editorial Duties Assoc. Ed., *JHE*, *Econ. Letters*.

Principal Fields of Interest 022 Microeconomic Theory; 210 Economic, Statistical and Mathematical Methods and Models; 841 Demographic Economics.

Publications *Books:* 1. *The Theory of Individual Welfare Functions and Consumer Behavior* (N-H, 1968).
Articles: 1. 'The welfare function of income in Belgium: an empirical investigation', *Europ ER*, 2, 1971; 2. 'The introduction of an old-age pension in a growing economy' (with G. Poeth), *J Pub E*, 4(1), Feb. 1975; 3. 'A new approach to the construction of family equivalence scales' (with A. Kapteyn), *Europ ER*, 7(4), May 1976; 4. 'The poverty line: concept and measurement' (with T. Goedhart, *et al.*), *JHR*, 12(4), Fall 1977; 5. 'Model-free regression', *Econ. Letters*, 7, 1981; 6. 'A dynamic model of the interaction between the state and the private sector' (with F. van Winden), *J Pub E*, 16(1), Aug. 1981; 7. 'Poverty in Europe' (with A. Hagenaars and J van Weeren), *RIW*, 28, 1982; 8. 'The influence of classification and observation errors on the measurement of income inequality' (with A. Hagenaars and W. van Eck), *Em*, 51(4), Aug. 1983; 9. 'The social security trap' (with A. Kapteyn), *Challenge*, 26(3), July–Aug. 1983; 10. 'Least-squares theory based on general distributional assumptions with an application to the incomplete observations problem' (with T. Dylistra and J. van Velzen), *Psychometrica*, 1984.

Principal Contributions In my monograph (1968), I tried to draw an analogy between probability distribution functions for random variables and cardinal utility functions for commodities. On the basis of the central limit theorem of probability theory, I showed that under fairly general assumptions, individual welfare functions (i.e. cardinal utility functions) tend to become lognormal (multivariate) distribution functions. In subsequent empirical research, I and my colleagues succeeded in estimating such welfare functions, at least for the one-dimensional concept of an individual welfare function of income. This was done on the basis of attitude questions in surveys. The results, corroborated in about twenty large-scale surveys carried out from 1970 up to 1984 in European countries and the USA, may be used for the estimation of family equivalence scales, the assessment of the monetary value of household work and for poverty and income inequality analysis. They also provide information on the formation of norms on the basis of past experience and anticipated future and on the influence on an individual of his social reference group. Secondary subjects of interest are the introduction of social security in an economic system with its effects for retirement and employment and statistical-econometric estimation of linear models. In the last field, the population-sample decomposition approach was developed, which is quite helpful in understanding and solving problems with respect to missing data, sample selectivity and panel analysis.

VARIAN, Hal R.

Born 1947, Wooster, OH, USA.
Current Post Prof. Econ. and Fin., Univ. Michigan, Ann Arbor, MI, USA, 1983–.
Past Posts Ass. Prof., Prof. Econ., Univ. Mich., 1973–7, 1977–83; Academic Vis., Nuffield Coll. Oxford, 1980–1.
Degrees BS MIT, 1969; MA (Maths.), PhD Univ. Cal. Berkeley, 1973, 1973.
Offices and Honours NSF Fellow, 1970–3; Guggenheim Foundation Fellow, 1979–80; Fellow, Em Soc, 1983.
Principal Fields of Interest 020 General Economic Theory; 600 Industrial Organisation; 320 Public Finance.
Publications *Books:* 1. *Microeconomic Analysis* (W. W. Norton, 1978, 1984; transls., Spanish, Bosch, 1981, German, Oldenbourg, 1981, Japanese forthcoming).

Articles: 1. 'Equity, envy and efficiency', *JET*, 9(1), Sept. 1974; 2. 'Distributive justice, welfare economics and the theory of fairness', *Philo. and Public Affairs*, 4(3), 1975, repr. in *Philosophy and Economic Theory*, eds. F. Hahn and M. J. Hollis (OUP, 1979); 3. 'On non-Walrasian equilibria', *Em*, 45(3), April 1977; 4. 'Redistributive taxation as social insurance', *J Pub E*, 14(1), Aug. 1980; 5. 'A model of sales', *AER*, 70(4), Sept. 1980; 6. 'The non-parametric approach to demand analysis', *Em*, 50(4), July 1982; 7. 'Nonparametric tests of consumer behaviour', *REStud*, 50(1), Jan. 1983.
Principal Contributions My early work in economics was concerned with axiomatic notions of 'fair distribution' which were based on concepts of symmetric treatment. The main concern here is the relationship between the philosophical concepts and their economic consequences. That work was followed by a brief excursion into the disequilibrium foundations of macroeconomics. More recently I investigated the theory of optimal taxation and social insurance and models of price discrimination by means of randomisation. Finally, my current interests involve the 'nonparametric' approach to econometric analysis. This approach allows an econometrician to test and use microeconomic theory on observed choice behaviour without postulating any restrictive functional forms. At the moment I am also engaged in several other projects involving public goods, price discrimination, demand estimation and financial markets.

When I look back at my research interests I am struck by their eclectic nature. I have always worked on the basis of ideas, not fields, and have found it very rewarding to do so. I should also mention my contribution to economics through my textbook *Microeconomic Analysis*. This started as class notes based on journal articles and classes I had taken; it has evolved into one of the major graduate texts. This has been very gratifying to me and, I hope, useful to the profession.

VEBLEN, Thorstein Bunde*

Dates and Birthplace 1857–1929, Cato, WI, USA.

Posts Held Teacher, Univ. Chicago, 1892–1906. Stanford Univ., 1906–9, Univ. Missouri, 1911–18, New School for Social Res., NY, 1918–26.

Degrees BA Carleton Coll., 1880; PhD Yale Univ., 1884.

Publications *Books:* 1. *The Theory of the Leisure Class* (1899, 1953, 1959); 2. *The Theory of Business Enterprise* (1904, 1965); 3. *The Instinct of Workmanship* (1914, 1964); 4. *Imperial Germany and the Industrial Revolution* (1915, 1964); 5. *The Higher Learning in America* (1918, 1957); 6. *Absentee Ownership and Business Enterprise in Recent Times* (1923, 1967); 7. *Essays in our Changing Order* (1934, 1964); 8. *The Place of Science in Modern Civilisation* (1918, 1961).

Career Economist and sociologist who criticised American society from an evolutionary and cosmopolitan viewpoint. His scathing indictment of capitalism did not, however, lead him to involvement with programmes for reform. He viewed society as a conflict between an acquisitive and a technocratic instinct. The terms 'conspicuous consumption' and 'pecuniary emulation' have entered the language from Veblen's works. He enjoyed a wide readership in his own day and was highly regarded by some of his pupils, who sustained him through the difficulties of his academic career. He soon came to be regarded as the founder of an American institutionalist school, which survives to this day. American institutionalism, however, owes perhaps more to Mitchell and Commons than to Veblen, who was too idiosyncratic to be capable of imitation and development.

Secondary Literature J. Dorfman, *Thorstein Veblen and his America* (Kelly, 1961); A. K. Davis, 'Veblen, Thorstein', *IESS*, 16; J. Dorfman, ed., *Thorstein Veblen: Essays, Reviews and Reports — Previously Uncollected Writings* (Augustus M. Kelley, 1973); J. P. Diggin, *The Bard of Savagery: Thorstein Veblen and Modern Social Theory* (Harvester Press, 1978).

VERNON, Raymond

Born 1913, New York City, NY, USA.

Current Post Prof. Internat. Affairs, Harvard Univ., USA, 1978–.

Past Posts US Securities and Exchange Commission, 1935–46; US State Dept., 1946–54; Planning and Control Dir., Hawley and Hovis, 1954–6; Dir., NY Metropolitan Region Study, Harvard Univ., 1956–9; Prof., Harvard Bus. School, 1959–78; Adjunct Prof., Fletcher School, Tufts Univ., 1981–3.

Degrees BA City Coll. NY, 1933; PhD Columbia Univ., 1941; Hon. MA Harvard Univ., 1959.

Offices and Honours Board Overseers, Heller School, Brandeis Univ. MA; Dir., World Peace Foundation; Dir., US/UN Assoc. Meritorious Service Award, US Dept. State; Member, AAAS, US Council Foreign Relations.

Editorial Duties Ed., *J Pol. Analysis and Management*, 1981–.

Principal Fields of Interest 123 Comparative Economic Studies; 442 International Business; 614 Public Enterprise.

Publications *Books:* 1. *The Regulation of Stock Exchange Members* (Columbia Univ. Press, 1941); 2. *Anatomy of a Metropolis* (with E. M. Hoover), (Harvard Univ. Press, 1960); 3. *Metropolis, 1985* (Harvard Univ. Press, 1960); 4. *The Dilemma of Mexico's Development* (Harvard Univ. Press, 1966; transl., French, Eds Economie et Humanisme, Eds Ouvrières, 1966); 5. *The Myth and Reality of our Urban Problems* (Harvard Univ. Press, 1966); 6. *Sovereignty at Bay: The Multinational Spread of U.S. Enterprises* (Basic Books, 1971; transls., Swedish, Alb. Bonniers Boktryckeri, 1972, Spanish, Fondo de Cultura Economica, 1973, Japanese, Tokyo, 1973); 7. *The Economic Environment of International Business* (with L. T. Wells, Jr.), (Prentice-Hall, 1972, 1980); 8. *Storm Over the Multinationals: The Real Issues* (Harvard Univ. Press, 1977); transls., Korean, Hyon-am Publ., 1979, Russian, Mockba 'Ilporpecc', 1982, Spanish, Fondo de Cultura Economica, 1980, Portuguese, Zadhar Editores, 1980); 9. *Two Hungry Giants: The United States and Japan in* *the Quest for Oil and Ores* (Harvard Univ. Press, 1983).

Articles: 1. 'State-owned enterprises in Latin American exports', *QREB*, 21(2), Summer 1981, repr. in *Export Diversification and the New Protectionism: The Experiences of Latin America*, eds. W. Baer and M. Gillis (Univ. Illinois Press, 1981); 2. 'International trade policy in the 1980s: prospects and problems', *Internat. Stud. Q.*, 26, Dec. 1982; 3. 'Technology's effects on international trade: a look ahead', in *Emerging Technologies: Consequences for Economic Growth, Structural Change and Employment*, eds. H. Giersch (Inst. Weltwirtschaft, 1982); 4. 'State-owned enterprises in the world economy: the case of iron ore' (with Brian Levy), in *Public Enterprise in Less-Developed Countries*, ed. L. P. Jones, (CUP, 1982); 5. 'The politics of comparative national statistics', in *Conference on the Politics of National Statistics* (US–SSRC, 1983); 6. 'Linking managers with ministers: dilemmas of the state-owned enterprise', *J. Pol. Analysis and Management*, 3(4), Summer 1984; 7. 'The analytical challenge', in *Reversing America's Industrial Decline: Lessons from our Competitors*, eds. W. H. Davidson and M. S. Hochmuth (Ballinger, 1984); 8. 'Uncertainty in the resource industries: the special role of state-owned enterprises', in *Risk and the Political Economy of Resource Development*, eds. D. W. Pearce, H. Siebert and I. Walter (Macmillan, 1984); 9. 'Organizational and institutional responses to international risk', in *Managing International Risk*, ed. R. J. Herring (CUP, 1984).

Principal Contributions For fifty years I have pursued the by-ways of economics, the subjects that ordinarily appear in the footnotes rather than the main texts. My interest in the by-ways began with my thesis, written in the 1930s, on the regulation of stock exchange members. As a government official concerned with the regulation of securities exchanges, I had come to know their operations quite intimately at a time when our profession had not yet become fascinated with the properties of efficient markets. At that time I could not have imagined, even in moments of the sheerest fantasy, that the stock market would come to be viewed as the case par excellence of such a market.

The tasks that followed kept me concentrated on the footnotes of the profession. There was nearly a decade in the State Department; there were several challenging years as an executive in the candy business; there were four exciting years as the director of an ambitious study of the New York Metropolitan Region; and there were more than two decades at the Harvard Business School, trying to understand and explain the behaviour of international business.

With a background of that sort, it is hardly surprising that I look indifferently on much of what occupies the economic mainstream. From my special viewpoint, the most interesting economic puzzles lie mainly in phenomena that our profession has largely passed by. I am interested in observing and understanding the regularities that are to be found in a world in which information is lacking, oligopoly is the rule, and increasing returns to scale prevail; and I am indifferent to the fact that those regularities, once discovered and understood, cannot easily be attached to the general equilibrium paradigm.

VERRI, Pietro*

Dates and Birthplace 1728–97, Milan, Italy.

Posts Held Official, Austrian administration of Milan.

Offices and Honours Founder, Societa dei Pugni, Milan; Ed., *Il Caffe*, 1764–6.

Publications *Books:* 1. *Elementi del Commercio* (1760); 2. *Bilancio del Commercio Dello Stato di Milano* (1764); 3. *Riflessioni Sulle Leggi Vincolanti* (1769); 4. *Meditazioni Sull'economia Politica* (1771).

Career His economic work, though chiefly the underpinning of policy recommendations, was scientifically of the highest standard. His concept of economic equilibrium was based ultimately on the calculus of pleasure and pain, for like his contemporary Beccaria he was a utilitarian. As an administrator he had access to copious supplies of facts and wove them into his argument in the most apposite fashion. His work on the calculation of balance of payments figures is just one of his achievements in the quantitative field, and his other original contributions include a constant-outlay demand curve.

Secondary Literature C. Pagui, 'Verri, Pietro', *ESS*, 15.

VICKERS, Douglas William

Born 1924, Rockhampton, Queensland, Australia.

Current Post Prof. Econ., Univ. Massachusetts, Amherst, MA, USA, 1977–.

Past Posts Prof. Fin., Univ. Penn., 1957–72; Prof. Econ., Univ. Western Australia, 1972–7; Vis. Prof. Fin., Univ. Penn., 1976.

Degrees BCom Univ. Queensland, 1949; BSc, PhD Univ. London, 1952, 1956; MA Univ. Penn., 1971.

Offices and Honours Fellow, Academy Social Sciences Australia, 1976.

Principal Fields of Interest 031 History of Economic Thought; 311 Domestic Monetary and Financial Theory and Policy; 521 Business Finance.

Publications *Books:* 1. *Studies in the Theory of Money 1690–1776* (Chilton, 1959); 2. *The Theory of the Firm: Production, Capital and Finance* (McGraw-Hill, 1968); 3. *Man in the Maelstrom of Modern Thought* (Presbyterian & Reformed, 1975); 4. *Financial Markets in the Capitalist Process* (Univ. Penn. Press, 1978); 5. *A Christian Approach to Economics and the Cultural Condition* (Exposition Press, 1982); 6. *Money, Banking and the Macroeconomy* (Prentice-Hall, 1985).

Articles: 1. 'Disequilibrium structures and financing decisions in the firm' *J. Bus. Fin. and Accounting*, 1(3), Autumn, 1974; 2. 'Finance and false trading in non-*tâtonnement* markets', *AEP*, 14, Dec. 1975; 3. 'Adam Smith and the status of the theory of money', in *Essays on Adam Smith*, eds. A. T. Wilson and A. Skinner (Clarendon Press, 1976); 4. 'Financial theory of the firm', in *Modern Economic Thought*, ed. S. Weintraub (Univ. Penn. Press, 1977); 5. 'Uncertainty, choice and the

marginal efficiencies', *J Post Keyn E*, 2(2), Winter 1979; 6. 'Uncertainty and the uses of money', *J. Bus. Fin. and Accounting*, 5(3), October 1979; 7. 'Real time and the choice-decision point', *J Post Keyn E*, 3(4), Summer 1981; 8. 'The money capital "factor"', *J Post Keyn E*, 4(2), Winter 1981; 9. 'The marginal efficiency of (money) capital', *J Bus. Fin. and Accounting*, 8(2), Summer 1981; 10. 'Formalism, finance and decisions in real economic time', in *Methodological Controversy in Economics*, ed. A. W. Coats (JAI Press, 1983).

Principal Contributions A re-examination of the development of the theory of money and cognate intellectual history in the eighteenth century, published in *Studies in the Theory of Money* and further elaborated in *Essays on Adam Smith*; an integration of the theory of money and the problems of money capital into the theory of the firm, published in *The Theory of the Firm*; and a subsequent series of papers; a reconsideration of the relevance of uncertainty, disequilibrium, and time for the theory of finance and the displacement of timeless Walrasian statics, published in *Financial Markets in the Capitalist Process* and subsequent papers; and an examination of the relation between philosophico-theological, Christian and orthodox economic thought, notably in *Man in the Maelstrom of Modern Thought* and *A Christian Approach to Economics*.

VICKREY, William

Born 1914, Victoria, British Columbia, Canada.

Current Post Prof. Econ. Emeritus, Columbia Univ., NY, USA, 1979–.

Past Posts Fellow, Center Advanced Study Behavioral Sciences, Stanford, CA, 1967–8; Vis. Lect., Monash Univ., Australia, 1971; Public Fin. Cons., UN Center Devlp. Programs, Planning and Pol., 1974–5; McVickar Prof. Polit. Econ., Columbia Univ., NY, 1950–9.

Degrees BS Yale Univ., 1935; MA, PhD Columbia Univ., 1937, 1947; Dr. Humane Letters, Univ. Chicago, 1979.

Offices and Honours Chairman,

Metropolitan Econ. Assoc., NY, 1964–5; Fellow, Em Soc, 1967; Dir., NBER, 1973–7; Fellow, AAAS, 1974; Disting. Fellow, AEA, 1978.

Principal Fields of Interest 323 National Taxation; 613 Public Utilities.

Publications *Books:* 1. *Agenda for Progressive Taxation* (Ronald Press, 1949, 1971); 2. *The Revision of the Rapid Transit Fare Structure of the City of New York* (Fin. Project, Mayor's Comm. Management Survey, 1952); 3. *Microstatics* (Harcourt Brace & World, 1964); 4. *Metastatics and Macroeconomics* (Harcourt Brace & World, 1964).

Articles: 1. 'Utility, strategy, and social decision rules', *QJE*, 74, Nov. 1960, repr. in *Readings in Welfare Economics*, eds. K. J. Arrow and T. Scitovsky (Richard D. Irwin, 1969); 2. 'Counter-speculation, auctions, and competitive sealed tenders', *J. Fin*, 16, 1961; 3. 'Responsive pricing of utility services', *Bell JE*, 2, 1971; 4. 'The city as a firm', in *The Economics of Public Services*, eds. M. S. Feldstein and R. P. Inman (Macmillan, 1977); 5. 'Optimal transit subsidy policy', *Transportation*, 9, 1980.

Principal Contributions Progressive taxation reform proposals: cumulative averaging assessment, bequeathing power succession tax, age difference graduation of succession taxes, taxable tax credit for government interest, rationalisation of undistributed profits tax, of earned income credit. Theory and application of marginal cost pricing: responsive pricing, urban congestion charges, simulated futures markets in airline reservation, impacts of inflation on utility regulation, pricing and fare collection methods. Public choice theory: demand revealing procedures, auctions and bidding theory, self-policing imputation sets in game theory, social welfare functions. Land value taxation: short- versus long-term impacts and relationships with marginal cost pricing.

VIETORISZ, Thomas

Born 1926, Budapest, Hungary.
Current Post Prof. Econ., New School Social Res., NYC, 1970–.
Past Posts Assoc. Dir., Econ. Development Training Program, UNECLA, 1957–60; Res. Staff Member, T. J. Watson Res. Center, IBM Corp., 1961–3; Vis. Prof., Univ. Cornell, MIT, 1970–81.

Degrees Absolutorium (Chem. Eng.), Technical Univ., Budapest, 1946; MS (Chem. Eng.) PhD MIT, 1948, 1956.

Offices and Honours Cons., UN, World Bank, OECD, Inter-Amer. Bank, US Govt., US State Govts., Govts. of Mexico and Puerto Rico, and numerous private firms and organisations, 1964–81.

Principal Fields of Interest 113 Economic Planning Theory and Policy.

Publications *Books:* 1. *Industrial Complex Analysis and Regional Development* (with W. Isard and E. W. Schooler), (MIT Press, Wiley, 1959); 2. *Techniques of Sectoral Economic Planning: The Chemical Industries* (UN, 1966); 3. *Engineering Industry, Chemical Industry* (UNIDO, 1969); 4. *The Economic Development of Harlem* (with B. Harrison), (Praeger, 1970); 5. *Planning and Programming of Metalworking Industries with Special View to Exports* (with R. Lissak), (UN, 1972).

Articles: 1. 'Locational choices in planning', in *National Economic Planning*, ed. M. Milligan (Columbia Univ. Press, 1967); 2. 'Decentralization and project evaluation under economies of scale and indivisibilites', *UN Industrialization and Productivity Bull.*, 11, 1968; 3. 'Quantized preferences and planning by priorities', *AER*, 60(2), May 1970; 4. 'Indicators of labor market functioning and urban social distress' (with R. Mier and J. Giblin), in *Urban Affairs Annual Rev.*, 1975; 5. 'The use of input-output computer information in programming for chemical processes', in *Advances in Input-output Analysis* (Ballinger, 1976).

Principal Contributions Methods of strategic planning: industrial planning (chemical industries, engineering industries); regional planning (Third World countries, metropolitan areas); mathematical planning models (linear and integer programming, simulation); political economy of development and planning in industrially advanced countries, Third World areas, and socialist economies.

of the impact of government risk regulation failed to reveal any significant safety impact of the regulations. A potential problem of these policy interventions is the uncertainty they create for business decisions. Such uncertainty will depress productivity even in situations in which firms are risk-neutral and have accurate perceptions of the likelihood of future regulations. An alternative policy approach would be to remedy the informational inadequacies of the market directly. My recent research has focussed on the effect of chemical labels on individual behaviour. In terms of risk perceptions and other labour market impacts, I have shown that chemical labels have the expected impact. The most important result in this area is that it is not simply the risk conveyed by the information, but the informational content of the label that is also of consequence. As predicted by the two-armed bandit model, workers prefer to face risks known with less precision.

VON WEIZSAECKER, Carl Christian

Born 1938, Berlin, Germany.
Current Post Prof. Econ., Univ. Berne, Switzerland, 1982–.
Past Posts Prof. Econ., Univ. Heidelberg, 1965–72; Vis. Prof., MIT, 1968–70; Prof. Econ., Univ. Bielefeld, 1972–4, Univ. Bonn, 1974–82.
Degrees DPhil, Habilitation Univ. Basel, Switzerland, 1961, 1965.
Offices and Honours Fellow, Em Soc, 1969; Member, Advisory Board, W. German Ministry Econ. Affairs, 1977–; Foreign Hon. Member, AAAS, 1979.
Degrees Co-Ed., *Em*, 1969–74, *Internat. J. Industrial Organisation*, 1982–, *Kyk*, 1980–.
Principal Fields of Interest 022 Microeconomic Theory; 620 Economics of Technological Change; 613 Public Utilities and Government Regulation.
Publications *Books:* 1. *Wachstum, Zins und Optimale Investitionsquote* (Mohr-Siebeck, 1962); 2. *Zur ökonomischen Theorie des technischen Fortschritts* (Vandenhoeck & Ruprecht,

1966); 3. *Steady State Capital Theory* (Springer, 1971); 4. *Barriers to Entry, A Theoretical Treatment* (Springer, 1980); 5. *Die Rolle des Wettbewerbs im Fernmedebereich* (with G. Knieps and J. Müller), (Baden-Baden, 1981).
Articles: 1. 'Existence of optimal programs of accumulation for an infinite time horizon', *REStud*, 32, April 1965; 2. 'Notes on endogenous change of tastes', *JET*, 3(4), Dec. 1971; 3. 'Substitution along the time axis', *Kyk*, 27(4), 1974, repr. in *Essays in Modern Capital Theory*, eds. M. Brown, K. Sato and P. Zarembka (N-H, 1975); 4. 'A welfare analysis of barriers to entry', *Bell JE*, 11(2), Autumn 1980; 5. 'Rechte und Verhältnisse in der modernen Wirtschaftslehre', *Kyk*, 34(3), 1981; 6. 'The costs of substitution', *Em*, 52(5), Sept. 1984.
Principal Contributions Theory of optimal growth: 'golden rule' and 'overtaking criterion'. Theory of technical progress: theory of induced technical change. Capital theory: duality relations in capital theory; steady state capital theory; coefficient of intertemporal substitution. Welfare economics of endogenous tastes. Concept of barriers to entry. Proposals for reform of the telecommunications sector.

W

WACHTER, Michael L.

Born 1943, New York City, NY, USA.
Current Post Prof. Econ. and Management, Dir., Inst. Law and Econ., Univ. Penn., Philadelphia, PA, USA, 1976–.
Past Posts Ass. Prof., Assoc. Prof., Univ. Penn., 1969–73, 1973–6; Vis. Res. Assoc., Econ., Princeton Univ., 1974; Sr. Adviser, Brookings Panel Econ. Activity, 1976–; Commisioner, Minimum Wage Study Commission, US Congressional Commission, 1978–81; Res. Assoc., NBER, 1978–.
Degrees BS Cornell Univ., 1964; MA, PhD Harvard Univ., 1967, 1970.
Offices and Honours Woodrow Wil-

son Fellow, 1964–5; Bers Prof. Social Sciences, Univ. Penn., 1972–3.

Principal Fields of Interest 824 Labour Market Studies.

Publications *Books:* 1. *Toward a New U.S. Industrial Policy?*, co-ed. (with S. M. Wachter), (Univ. Penn. Press, 1982); 2. *Removing Obstacles to Economic Growth*, co-ed. (with S. M. Wachter), (Univ. Penn. Press, 1984).

Articles: 1. 'Cyclical variation in the interindustry wage structure', *AER*, 60(1), March 1970; 2. 'Wage determination, inflation and the industrial structure' (with S. A. Ross), *AER*, 63(4), Sept. 1973; 3. 'The primary and secondary labor market mechanism: a critique of the dual approach', *Brookings Papers Econ. Activity*, 3, 1974; 4. 'The relevance of the household production function and its implications for the allocation of time' (with R. A. Pollak), *JPE*, 83(2), April 1975; 5. 'Understanding the employment relation: the analysis of idiosyncratic exchange' (with O. E. Williamson and J. E. Harris), *Bell JE*, 6(1), Spring 1975; 6. 'Intermediate swings in labor-force participation', *Brookings Papers Econ. Activity*, 2, 1977; 7. 'A production function-nonaccelerating inflation approach to potential output: is measured potential output too high?' (with J. M. Perloff), *Carnegie-Rochester Conf. Series*, 10, 1979; 8. 'The labor market mechanism and illegal immigration: the outlook for the 1980s', *ILRR*, 33(3), April, 1980; 9. 'Time series changes in youth joblessness' (with C. Kim), in *The Youth Labor Market Problem: Its Nature, Causes and Consequences*, ed. R. B. Freeman and D. A. Wise (Univ. Chicago Press, 1982); 10. 'Levelling the peaks and troughs of the demographic cycle: an application to school enrolment rates' (with W. L. Wascher), *REStat*, 66(2), May 1984.

Principal Contributions Work has focussed on functioning of labour markets with particular reference to interindustry wage determination, differential unemployment, labour force behaviour of different age-sex groups, and the impact of immigration on secondary labour markets. Related research has focussed on the estimation of equilibrium unemployment rates and potential output. Projects have focussed on short- and long-run fluctuations in productivity growth and new law and economics approaches to collective bargaining.

WAGNER, Adolph Heinrich Gotthelf*

Dates and Birthplace 1835–1917, Erlangen, Germany.

Posts Held Teacher, Vienna, Hamburg, Dorpat, Freiburg im Breisgau, 1858–70; Prof. Polit. Econ., Univ. Berlin, 1870–1917.

Degree Dr Univ. Göttingen, 1857.

Offices and Honours Founder, *Verein für Sozialpolitik*, 1872; Member, Lower House, Prussian Diet, 1882–5; Member Upper House, 1910–17.

Publications *Books:* 1. *Beiträge zur Lehre von den Banken* (1857); 2. *Die Geld- und Credittheorie der Peel'schen Bankacte* (1862); 3. *Finanzwissenschaft*, 4 vols (1871–2); 4. *Theoretische Sozialökonomik*, 2 vols (1907–9); 5. *Adolph Wagner, Briefe, Dokumente, Augenzeugenberichte 1851–1971*, ed. H. Rubner (1978).

Career Conservative critic of *laissez faire* economics who sought by the intervention of the State to secure social justice for the working classes. His economics was based on theoretical principles and he was largely on the Austrian side in the 'Methodenstreit'. His greatest contribution was in public finance where he integrated the subject with general economics and gave it strong theoretical principles. He stressed the redistributive potential of taxation and accepted the growth of public expenditure by the modern State. He also made important contributions to monetary and banking policy.

Secondary Literature G. Meyer, 'Wagner, Adolf', *IESS*, 16; *Classics in the Theory of Public Finance*, eds. R. A. Musgrave and A. T. Peacock (Macmillan, 1958).

WAKEFIELD, Edward Gibbon*

Dates and Birthplace 1796–1862, London, England.

Publications *Books:* 1. *Letter from Sydney* (1829, 1929); 2. *Facts Relating to the Punishment of Death in the Metropolis* (1831); 3. *View of the Art of Colonisation* (1849); 4. *Collected Works*, ed. M. F. Lloyd-Prichard (1969).

Career Colonisation theorist, whose scheme was based on the sale not grant of land to colonists, both to ensure that the purchasers cultivated it properly and also to provide funds for the development of the colonisation process; he also argued for self-government once the colony was sufficiently large. The colony of S. Australia was organised according to his principles, and proved very successful. He also advised Lord Durham on his *Report on the Affairs of British North America* which set Canada on the course towards self-government, and gave similar advice on the colonisation of New Zealand. His defence of colonisation, based on the notion that Britain was suffering from an excess of both capital and labour, influenced the later classical economists, such as J. S. Mill, in taking a more sceptical attitude towards Say's law and the so-called impossibility of general gluts.

Secondary Literature R. Lekachman, 'Wakefield, Edward Gibbon', *IESS*, 16.

WALD, Abraham*

Dates and Birthplace 1902–50, Cluj, Romania.

Posts Held Austrian Inst. Bus. Cycle Res., Vienna, 1932–8; Res. Fellow, Columbia Univ., 1938–50.

Publications *Books:* 1. *Sequential Analysis* (1947); 2. *Statistical Decision Functions* (1950).

Articles: 1. 'On the unique non-negative solvability of the new production equations' (pts. 1, 2), *Ergebnisse eines mathematische Kolloquiums*, Heft 6, 1933–4, Heft 7, 1934–5, ed. K. Menger (1935, 1936), repr. in *Precursors in Mathematical Economics: An Anthology*, eds. W. J. Baumol and S. M. Goldfeld (1968); 2. 'On some systems of equations of mathematical economics', *ZN*, 7, 1936; *Em*, 19, Oct. 1951; 3. 'On the statistical treatment of linear stochastic difference equations (with H. B. Mann), *Em*, 11, July–Oct. 1943.

Career Mathematical statistician whose work on decision theory and sequential analysis is of outstanding importance. He also did original work in econometrics and mathematical economics, including existence proofs for general equilibrium, seasonal corrections of time series, formulae for index numbers, the Cournot duopoly problem, and stochastic difference equations.

Secondary Literature H. Freeman, 'Wald, Abraham', *IESS*, 16.

WALKER, Amasa*

Dates and Birthplace 1799–1875, Woodstock, CT, USA.

Posts Held Businessman; Teacher Polit. Econ., Oberlin Coll, MA, 1842–8, Amherst Coll., MA.

Offices and Honours Massachussetts Secretary State, Member Legislature; Congressman, 1862.

Publications *Books:* 1. *The Nature and Uses of Money and Mixed Currency* (1857); 2. *Science of Wealth* (with F. A. Walker), (1866).

Career In addition to his public and political life, he taught and wrote on political economy. He was the chief American advocate of the currency school. He illustrated his argument that prices are determined by the quantity of money by the use of charts. His economics was in general orthodox and he was a supporter of free trade. His son Francis, who co-operated on the *Science of Wealth*, attained a similar position of eminence in the discipline.

Secondary Literature H.E. Miller, 'Walker, Amasa', *ESS*, 15.

WALKER, Francis Amasa*

Dates and Birthplace 1840–97, Boston, MA, USA.

Posts Held Chief Treasury Bureau Stats, 1869–70; Superintendent US Censuses, 1870, 1880; Prof., Yale Univ., 1872–81; Pres., MIT, 1881–97.

Degree BA Amherst Coll., MA, 1860.

Offices and Honours Pres., ASA, 1883–96, AEA, 1886–92.

Publications *Books:* 1. *The Wages Question* (1876); 2. *Money* (1878); 3. *Money in its Relations to Trade and Industry* (1879); 4. *Land and its Rent* (1883); 5. *Political Economy* (1883); 6. *International Bimetallism* (1896); 7. *Discussions in Economics and Statistics*, 2 vols (1899).

Career After his experience of statistical work, and under the tutelage of his father, he took up economics and became a chief figure in the discipline. He was concerned to establish economics as a science rather than a branch of practical politics. He developed his own distribution theory, vigorously repudiating the wages fund doctrine, argued for bimetallism and pioneered the use of graphic presentation of data. He also encouraged the creation of permanent census staff and fostered the use of statistics by economists.

Secondary Literature H. W. Spiegel, 'Walker, Francis A.', *IESS*, 16.

WALLACE, Neil

Born 1939, New York City, NY, USA.

Current Post Prof. Econ., Univ. Minnesota, Minneapolis, MN, USA, 1974–.

Past Posts Res. Ass., Res. Dept., Fed. Reserve Bank St Louis, 1962; Instr., Ass. Prof.,Assoc. Prof., Univ. Minnesota, 1963–4, 1964–9, 1969–74; Resident Cons., Logistics Dept., Rand Corp., 1965–6; Res. Fellow, NBER, 1968–9; Cons., Fed. Reserve Bank Minneapolis, 1970–.

Degrees BA Columbia Univ., 1960; PhD Univ. Chicago, 1964.

Offices and Honours Fellow, Em Soc.

Editorial Duties Assoc. Ed., *JET*; *Monetary Theory*, *Fundamentals of Pure and Appl. Econ.*

Principal Fields of Interest 023 Macroeconomic Theory; 310 Domestic Monetary and Financial Theory and Institutions; 430 Balance of Payments; International Finance.

Publications *Books:* 1. *Models of Monetary Economies*, co-ed. (with J. Kareken), (Fed. Reserve Bank Minneapolis, 1980).

Articles: 1. 'The stability of models of money and growth with perfect foresight' (with T. Sargent), *Em*, 41(6), Nov. 1973; 2. 'Deposit insurance and bank regulation: a partial equilibrium exposition' (with J. Kareken), *J Bus*, 51(3), July 1978; 3. 'The overlapping generations model of fiat money', in *Models of Monetary Economies, op. cit.*; 4. 'On the indeterminacy of equilibrium exchange rates' (with J. Kareken), *QJE*, 96(2), May 1981; 5. 'A Modigliani-Miller theorem for open market operations', *AER*, 71(3), June 1981; 6. 'A hybrid fiat-commodity monetary system', *JET*, 25(3), Dec. 1981; 7. 'The real bills doctrine vs. the quantity theory: a reconsideration' (with T. Sargent), *JPE*, 90(6), Dec. 1982; 8. 'A legal restrictions theory of the demand for 'money' and the role of monetary policy', *Fed. Reserve Bank Minneapolis Q.Rev.*, 7, Winter 1983; 9. 'A model of commodity money' (with T. Sargent), *J Mon E*, 12(2), July 1983; 10. 'A price discrimination analysis of monetary policy' (with J. Bryant), *REStud*, 51(2), April 1984.

Principal Contributions My research during the past few years has been directed toward analysing alternative monetary standards and alternative regulatory schemes of private financial intermediation, including the accompanying central bank lending or open-market operation scheme. For these questions, it matters how one explains two observations: the first is the relatively low rate of return on the assets typically labelled 'money' the second is the fiat component in the value of some of these assets. My current view is that an explanation of the first of these must include an appeal to legal restrictions that inhibit arbitrage between interest-bearing securities and non-interest-bearing currency — for example, arbitrage carried out by financial intermediaries that buy default-free interest-bearing securities and sell small denomination notes, which promise the bearer some amount of the payoff on the securities. If permitted, such arbitrage would limit nominal interest rates on default-free securities to magnitudes commensurate with spreads charged by mutual funds and, barring significant scale economies, would make central bank lending irrelevant. Given that the relatively low return on some assets is explained by legal restrictions, the fiat component in the value of some assets can be analysed using versions of overlapping generations models. I have used such models to study a variety of monetary standards.

WALLACE, Robert*

Dates and Birthplace 1697–1771, Kincardine, Scotland.
Posts Held Clergyman.
Offices and Honours Moderator, General Assembly, Church of Scotland, 1743; Royal Chaplain for Scotland, 1744.
Publications *Books:* 1. *Dissertation on the Numbers of Mankind* (1753); 2. *Characteristics of the Present State of Great Britain* (1758); 3. *Various Prospects of Mankind, Nature and Providence* (1761).
Career Pre-Malthusian writer on population who disputed Hume's contention that population had increased since ancient times. However, on returning to the question in *Various Prospects . . .* , he argued that the capacity for mankind to reproduce itself would frustrate the prospects for more perfect forms of society. Godwin attempted to refute this; Malthus found it congenial towards his own views. Wallace's writings in general are in the traditions of the Scottish Enlightenment.
Secondary Literature J. F. Rees, 'Wallace, Robert', *ESS*, 15.

WALLICH, Henry Chirstopher

Born 1914, Berlin, Germany.
Current Post Board Governors, Fed. Reserve System, Washington, DC, USA, 1974–.
Past Posts Export Bus., Argentina, Chile, 1933–5; Foreign Dept., Security Analysis Dept., Chemical Bank Trust Co, 1935; Hackney, Hopkinson & Sutphen, Security Analyst, 1936–40; Foreign Res. Div., Fed. Reserve Bank

NY, 1946–51; Prof. Econ., Yale Univ., 1951–74; Ass. Sr. Cons., US Secretary Treasury, 1958–9, 1969–74; Member, President's Council Econ. Advisers, 1959–61; Ed. writer part-time, *Washington Post*, 1961–4; Guggenheim Foundation Fellow, 1962–3; Columnist, *Newsweek*, 1965–74.
Degrees MA, PhD Harvard Univ., 1941, 1944.
Principal Fields of Interest 311 Domestic Monetary and Financial Theory and Policy.
Publications *Books:* 1. *Monetary Problems of an Export Economy* (Harvard Univ. Press, 1950); 2. *Public Finance in a Developing Country, El Salvador, A Case Study* (with J. H. Adler), (Harvard Univ. Press, 1951); 3. *Monetary and Banking Legislation of the Dominican Republic, 1947* (with T. Triffin), (Fed. Reserve Bank, 1953); 4. *Mainsprings of the German Revival* (Yale Univ. Press, 1955); 5. *The Cost of Freedom* (Harper, 1960); 6. *Monetary Policy and Practice — A View from the Federal Reserve Board* (D. C. Heath, 1981).
Articles: 1. 'From multiplier to quantity theory', in *Economic Progress Private Values and Public Policy. Essays in Honor of William Fellner*, ed. B. Balassa and R. R. Nelson (N-H, 1977); 2. 'Stabilization policy and vicious and virtuous circles', in *Flexible Exchange Rates and the Balance of Payments, Essays in Memory of Egon Sohmen*, eds. J. S. Chipman and C. P. Kindleberger (N-H, 1980); 3. 'Samuelson and trends in monetary policy', in *Samuelson and Neoclassical Economics*, ed. G. R. Feiwel (Kluwer-Nijhoff, 1981); 4. 'Federal reserve policy' (with T. F. Brady), *Encyclopedia of Economics*, ed. D. Greenwald (McGraw-Hill, 1982); 5. 'Federal reserve system' (with T. F. Brady), *Encyclopedia of Economics, op. cit.*; 6. 'Incomes policy' (with R. Rainey), *Encyclopedia of Economics, op. cit.*
Principal Contributions See my 'Some Uses of Economics', *BNLQR*, 141, June 1982, which says it all.

WALLIS, Kenneth Frank

Born 1938, Mexborough, Yorkshire, England.
Current Post Prof. Econ., Dir., US ESRC Macroecon. Modelling Bureau, Univ. Warwick, Coventry, England, 1977–.
Past Posts Res. Staff Econ., Lect., Cowles Foundation, Yale Univ., 1965–6; Lect., Reader Stats., LSE, 1966–7.
Degrees BSc (Maths.), MScTech (Industrial Admin.) Univ. Manchester, 1959, 1961; PhD Stanford Univ., 1966.
Offices and Honours Fellow, Em Soc, 1975; Council, Royal Stat. Soc., 1972–6; Governor, NIESR, 1978–; Member, UK Treasury Academic Panel, 1980–.
Editorial Duties Co-ed., *Em*, 1977–83; Joint Ed., *Ec*, 1973–6; Ed. Board, *REStud*, 1971–6.
Principal Fields of Interest 211 Econometric and Statistical Methods and Models; 132 Economic Forecasting and Econometric Models; 212 Construction, Analysis and Use of Econometric Models.
Publications *Books:* 1. *Topics in Applied Econometrics* (Blackwell, Univ. Minnesota Press, 1973, 1979); 2. *Introductory Econometrics* (Blackwell, Halsted Press, 1972, with M. B. Stewart, 1981); 3. *Econometrics and Quantitative Economics*, co-ed. (with D. F. Hendry), (Blackwell, 1984).
Articles: 1. 'Lagged dependent variables and serially correlated errors: a reappraisal of three-pass least squares', *REStat*, 49, Nov. 1967; 2. 'Some recent developments in applied econometrics: dynamic models and simultaneous equation systems', *JEL*, 7(4), Sept. 1969; 3. 'Wages, prices and incomes policies: some comments', *Ec*, N.S. 39, Aug. 1971, repr. in *Incomes Policy and Inflation*, eds. M. Parkin and M. T. Sumner (Manchester Univ. Press, 1972); 4. 'Testing for fourth order autocorrelation in quarterly regression equations', *Em*, 40, July 1972; 5. 'Seasonal adjustment and relations between variables', *JASA*, 69, March 1974; 6. 'Modelling macroeconomic time series' (with D. L. Prothero), *JRSS*, A, 139, 1976; 7. 'Multiple time series analysis and the final form of econometric models', *Em*, 45, Sept. 1977; 8. 'Econometric implications of the rational expectations hypothesis', *Em*, 48, Jan. 1980, repr. in *Rational Expectations and Econometric Practice*, eds. R. E. Lucas and T. J. Sargent (Univ. Minnesota Press, A&U, 1981); 9. 'Model validation and forecast comparisons: theoretical and practical considerations' (with M. H. Salmon), in *Evaluating the Reliability of Macroeconomic Models*, eds. G. C. Chow and P. Corsi (Wiley, 1982); 10. 'Seasonal adjustment and revision of current data: linear filters for the x–11 method', *JRSS*, A, 145, 1982.
Principal Contributions Contributions to the development of statistical methods for the econometric analysis of economic time series.

WALRAS, Antoine Auguste*

Dates and Birthplace 1801–66, Montpellier, France.
Posts Held Educational administrator.
Publications *Books:* 1. *De la nature de la richesses, et de l'orgine de la valeur* (1831, 1938); 2. *Théorie de la richesse sociale* (1849); 3. *Esquisse d'une théorie de la richesse* (1863).
Career Rejecting utility and labour, he suggested 'rareté' as the true source of value. This placed the emphasis on the quantity of commodity available, and led him to argue that political economy should be a mathematical science. In the *Théorie* ... he developed a doctrine of property which involved public ownership of land. Not least of his achievements was the formative influence he exercised on the ideas of his son, Léon.
Secondary Literature E. Antonelli, 'Walras, Antoine Auguste', *ESS*, 15.

WALRAS, Marie-Esprit Leon*

Dates and Birthplace 1834–1910, Evreux, France.
Posts Held Journalist, railway official, bank employee; Prof., Univ. Lausanne, 1870–92.

Degrees Bacc. (lettres), (science), Univ. Paris, 1851, 1853.

Publications *Books:* 1. *L'économie politique et la justice* (1860); 2. *Recherche de l'idéal social* (1868); 3. *Elements of Pure Economics* (1874–7, 1926, 1954); 4. *Théorie mathématique du bimétallisme* (1881); 5. *Etudes d'économie sociale* (1896, eds. F. Rouge, R. Picher and R. Durand Anzies, 1936, 1983); 6. *Etudes d'économie politique appliquée* (1898, 1936); 7. *Correspondence of Leon Walras and Related Papers*, 3 vols, ed. W. Jaffé (1965).

Career Co-discoverer with Jevons and Menger of marginal utility theory, he was also the first economist to produce a multi-equational model of general equilibrium. He divided his economic work into three parts; pure, applied and social, the latter being normative and concerned with questions of justice. His first economic publication (1860) was in this area and very much in the tradition of the work of his father, Auguste. On obtaining the Lausanne chair, he concentrated on pure economics and taught himself mathematics. The results appear in the *Elements* ... which, through successive editions, became an increasingly sophisticated version of his general equilibrium model. He also did significant work on monetary reform, concentrating on bimetallism and the question of bank note issue. However, he was never able to produce the systematic treatises on applied and social economics which he had envisaged. Though well known to economists of his time through his voluminous correspondance, true appreciation of his monumental achievements only came posthumously in the 1930s.

Secondary Literature W. Jaffé, 'Walras, Leon', *IESS*, 16; *William Jaffé's Essays on Walras*, ed. D. A. Walker (CUP, 1983).

WALTERS, Alan Arthur

Born 1926, Leicester, England.

Current Post Prof. Econ., Johns Hopkins Univ., Baltimore, MD, USA, 1975–, Res. Scholar, AEI, 1983–.

Past Posts Lect., Prof. Econometrics and Stats., Univ. Birmingham, 1952–68; Prof. Econ., LSE, 1968–75; Vis. Prof., Northwestern Univ., Univ. Virginia, Monash Univ.; Member, UK Commission London's Third Airport (Roskill), 1968–70; Econ. Adviser, World Bank, 1976–80; Personal Adviser, UK Prime Minister, 1981–3.

Degrees BSc Univ. London 1951; MA Univ. Oxford, 1981; Hon. DLitt Univ. Leicester, 1981; Hon. DSocSc Univ. Birmingham, 1984.

Offices and Honours Fellow, Em Soc, 1969; Francis Boyer Lecture Award, AEI; Knighted, 1983.

Editorial Duties Managing Ed., *REStud*, 1967–9; Ed. Boards, *J. Transport Econ. and Pol.*, 1969, *Econ. Modelling*, 1983–.

Principal Fields of Interest 120 Country Studies; 310 & 320 Domestic Monetary and Fiscal Policy.

Publications *Books:* 1. *Growth without Development* (with R. W. Clower, G. Dalton and M. Harwitz), (Northwestern Univ. Press, 1966); 2. *Integration in Freight Transport* (INEA, 1968); 3. *The Economics of Road User Charges* (JHUP, 1968); 4. *An Introduction of Econometrics* (Macmillan, 1968, 1970); 5. *Money in Boom and Slump* (INEA, 1968, 1971); 6. *Economics of Ocean Freight Rates* (with E. Bennathan), (Praeger, 1969); 7. *Penguin Modern Economics Readings: Money and Banking*, ed. (Penguin, 1970); 8. *Noise and Prices* (OUP, 1975); 9. *Microeconomic Theory* (with P. R. G. Layard), (McGraw-Hill, 1978); 10. *Port Pricing and Investment* (with E. Bennathan), (OUP, 1979).

Articles: 1. 'Track costs and motor taxation', *J Ind E*, 2, April 1954; 2. 'Expectations and the regression fallacy in estimating cost functions', *REStat*, 12(2), pt. 1, May 1960; 3. 'The theory and measurement of marginal private and social cost of highway congestion', *Em*, 29, Oct. 1961; 4. 'Production and cost functions: a survey', *Em*, 31, April 1963; 5. 'Professor Friedman on the demand for money', *JPE*, 73, Oct. 1965; 6. 'Demand for money in the U.K.' (with N. J. Kavanagh), *BOIS*, 28(2), July 1966; 7. 'The stability of Keynesian and monetary multiplier' (with C. R. Barrett), *REStat*, 48(4),

Nov. 1966; 8. 'Incremental capital-output ratios', *EJ*, 76, Dec. 1966; 9. 'Consistent expectations, distributed lags and the quantity theory', *EJ*, 81, June 1971; 10. 'Airports — an economic survey', *J. Transport Econ. and Pol.*, 12(2), May 1978.

Principal Contributions Early work was in economic statistics, particularly the distribution of income, but became more interested in applied economics and econometric testing, particularly in the transport industries. My main contribution here was in the development of pricing principles and practice in industrial and developing countries and in the problem of dealing with urban traffic congestion and public sector pricing generally. I believe that as a result there was a change in professional and official views on pricing. This led to an interest in the econometrics of production and cost functioning generally. But this was quickly overtaken (in 1959) by my curiosity about monetary policy in the UK and monetary economics and theory.

The problem was first to establish lines for the quantity of money, then to examine the evidence of money demand and monetary multipliers for the UK. I became more involved in general discussions about British economic policy and performance but also I continued my work on pricing and cost-benefit studies — the latter with my membership of the Commission on London's Third Airport (1968–70). Policy dominated my interests and I was able to bring the experience to the job of advising the Prime Minister on all matters of economic policy. Finally, I have recently been concerned with the state of economics — and particularly macroeconomics — and the advice which economists can, with good conscience, give. A review of the policies and performance of the British economy is under way.

WARBURTON, Clark*

Dates and Birthplace 1896–1979, Shady Grove, NY, USA.
Posts Held Instr., Ewing Christian Coll., 1921–5, Rice Inst., 1925–9; Assoc. Prof., Emory Univ., Atlanta, GA, 1929–31; Member, Board, Res. Staff, Fed, Reserve, 1932, Brookings Inst., 1932–4; Econ., Fed. Deposit Insurance Corp., 1934–65; Vis. Prof., Univ. Cal. Davis, 1966–7.
Degrees BA, MA Cornell Univ., 1921, 1928; PhD Columbia Univ., 1932.
Offices and Honours Pres., SEA, 1963–4.
Publications *Books:* 1. *Depression, Inflation and Monetary Policy: Selected Papers 1945–1953* (1966).
Articles: 1. 'Plateaux of prosperity and plains of depression', in *Economic Essays in Honor of Wesley Clair Mitchell* (1935); 2. 'Monetary disturbances and business fluctuations in two centuries of American history', in *In Search of a Monetary Constitution*, ed. L. B. Yeager (1962); 3. 'Monetary disequilibrium in the first half of the twentieth century', *HOPE*, 13(2), Summer, 1981.
Career Pioneer monetarist whose contribution to the modern restatement of the quantity theory of money was long unrecognised. His published papers in the 1940s were unusual in their opposition to the current Keynesian tide. His writings have a strong empirical bias, originally related to his research for the Federal Deposit Insurance Corporation.
Secondary Literature M. D. Bordo and A. J. Schwartz, 'Clark Warburton: pioneer monetarist', *J Mon E*, 5, 1979; L. B. Yeager, 'Clark Warburton, 1896–1979', *HOPE*, 13(2), Spring 1981.

WARD, Barbara Mary*

Dates and Birthplace 1914–81, York, Yorkshire, England.
Posts Held Univ. Extension Lect., 1936–9; Ass. Ed., Foreign Ed., Contrib. Ed., *The Econ.*, 1939–40, 1940–50, 1950–8; UK Ministry Info., Washington, Stockholm, 1942; Adviser, Govts. India, Pakistan, 1942; Vis. Scholar, Harvard Univ., 1957–68; Albert Schweitzer Prof. Internat. Econ. Devlp., Columbia Univ., 1968–73.
Offices and Honours Pres., Internat.

Inst. Environment and Devlp., 1973–80; Council, Royal Inst. Internat. Affairs, London, England, 1943–4; Member, Pontifical Comm. Justice and Peace, 1967–81; Trustee, Governor, Sadler's Wells-Old Vic, 1943–81, 1944–53; Governor, BBC, 1946–50; Pres., Conservation Soc., 1973, Catholic Women's League; Christophos Literary Award, 1954, 1959; Campion Award, 1964; Audubon Medal, Nat. Audubon Soc., 1973; Jawaharlal Nehru Prize, India, 1974; Hon. Fellow, LSE, 1976; Created Baroness, 1976; Hon. Fellow, Somerville Coll. Oxford, 1978.

Degrees BA (Philo., Polit and Econ.) Somerville Coll. Oxford; Hon Dr, Fordham Univ., MA, 1949, Smith Coll., MA, 1949, Columbia Univ., 1954, Kenyon Coll., OH, 1957, Harvard Univ., 1957, Brandeis Univ., MA, 1961.

Publications *Books:* 1. *The West at Bay* (1948); 2. *The Rich Nations and the Poor Nations* (1962); 3. *Women in New Asia* (1963); 4. *Plan Under Pressure: An Observer's View* (1963); 5. *Why Help India?* (with M. Zinkin), (1963); 6. *Two Views on Aid to Underdeveloped Countries* (with P. T. Bauer), (1967); 7. *The Widening Gap* (1971); 8. *Only One Earth: The Care and Maintenance of a Small Planet* (with R. Dubos), (1972); 9. *Progress for a Small Planet* (1979).

Career Her meteoric career took her from journalism to development planning to environmental protection. Although she wrote almost twenty books, an equal number of pamphlets, and literally thousands of magazine atricles, her true power was only revealed by hearing her speak. (In a wartime newspaper poll she was voted the second most popular speaker in Britain).

WATTS, Harold Wesley

Born 1932, Salem, OR, USA.
Current Post Prof. Econ., Columbia Univ., NY, 1976–; Sr. Fellow, Mathematica Pol. Res., Princeton, NJ, 1978–.
Past Posts Ass. Dir., Cowles Foundation Res. Econ., Yale Univ., 1957–61;
Dir., Inst. Res. Poverty, Prof. Econ., Univ. Wisconsin, 1966–71, 1966–76; Dir., Center Social Sciences, Columbia Univ., 1976–9.
Degrees BA Univ. Oregon, 1954; MA, PhD Yale Univ., 1955, 1957.
Offices and Honours Irving Fisher Res. Prof., Yale Univ., 1971–2; Carnegie Council Children, 1972–7; Guggenheim Foundation Fellow, 1975–6; Fellow, Em Soc, 1979–; Paul F. Lazarsfeld Award, 1980; Fellow, APPAM, 1983–; ASA/Census Fellow, 1984–5.
Principal Fields of Interest 850 Human Capital; 914 Economics of Poverty.
Publications *Books:* 1. *Income Maintenance and Labor Supply: Econometric Studies* (with G. C. Cain), (Univ. Wisconsin, Inst. Res. Poverty Monograph Series, 1973); 2. *The New Jersey Income Maintenance Experiment*, vols 2–3 (with A. Rees), (Academic Press, 1977).

Articles: 1. 'An economic definition of poverty', in *On Understanding Poverty: Perspectives from the Social Sciences*, ed. D. P. Moynihan (Basic Books, 1969); 2. 'Problems in making policy inferences from the Coleman report' (with G. Cain), *Amer. Sociological Rev.*, 35(2), April 1970; 3. 'The labor-supply response of husbands', *JHR*, 9(2), Spring 1974; 4. 'A model of the endowment of human wealth or let's look at social policy through the eyes of the 21st century's adults', in *Economic Progress, Private Values and Public Policy, Essays in Honor of William Fellner*, eds. B. Belassa and R. Nelson (N-H, 1977); 5. 'Why, and how well, do we analyse inequality?', in *Major Social Issues, A Multidisciplinary View*, eds. J. M. Yinger and S. J. Cutler (Free Press, 1978).
Principal Contributions Clarification of conceptual basis of economic poverty, and implementation of alternative concepts in analysing income distributions; analysis of negative income tax and other linear tax and transfer schemes; development and implementation of first major social experiment — the New Jersey negative tax experiment; development of method for optimising experimental designs to estimate functions of linear regression parameters. Analysis of the child development

process as a human capital accumulation programme.

WAUD, Roger Neil

Born 1938, Detroit, MI, USA.
Current Post Prof. Econ., Univ. N. Carolina, USA, 1972–.
Past Posts Ass. Prof., Grad. School Bus., Univ. Chicago, 1964–9; Assoc. Prof. Econ., Univ. N. Carolina, 1969–72; Sr. Econ., Board Governors, Fed. Reserve System, 1973–5; Res. Assoc., NBER, 1982–; Vis. Scholar, Univ. Camb., 1983.
Degrees BA Harvard Univ., 1960; MA (Appl. Stats.), PhD Univ. Cal. Berkeley, 1962, 1965.
Offices and Honours Exec. Comm., SEA, 1977–9.
Editorial Duties Ed. Board, *SEA*, 1970–3.
Principal Fields of Interest 300 Domestic Monetary and Fiscal Theory and Institutions; 210 Econometric, Statistical and Mathematical Methods and Models.
Publications *Books:* 1. *Economics* (Harper & Row, 1980, 1983); 2. *Macroeconomics* (Harper & Row, 1980, 1983); 3. *Microeconomics* (Harper & Row, 1980, 1983).
Articles: 1. 'Misspecification in the "partial adjustment" and "adaptive expectations" models', *Int ER*, 9, June 1968; 2. 'Public interpretation of Federal Reserve discount rate changes', *Em*, 38(2), March 1970; 3. 'The Almon lag technique and the monetary versus fiscal policy debate' (with P. Schmidt), *JASA*, 68, March 1973; 4. 'Net outlay, uncertainty and liquidity preference as behavior towards risk', *JMCB*, 7(4), Nov. 1975; 5. 'Further international evidence on output-inflation trade-offs' (with R. Froyen), *AER*, 70(3), June 1980; 6. 'The state of the Federal budget and the state of the economy' (with R. Abrams and R. Froyen), *EI*, 21, Oct. 1983.
Principal Contributions Early work focussed on problems of estimating and identifying distributed lag models commonly used in consumption and investment studies. Subsequently became interested in problems of estimating and testing for effects of monetary and fiscal policy. Later research along these lines examined the role of supply-side versus demand-side effects in explaining the output-inflation trade-off. Have tried to develop and emphasise concept of money's role as a contrivance for dealing with the lack of synchronisation both in time and magnitude between income and outlay, and to integrate this concept into portfolio theory.

WAUGH, F. V.*

Dates and Birthplace 1898–1974, Burlington, VA, USA.
Posts Held Econ., NJ Dept. Agric., 1923–4, Ct. Agric. Extension Service, 1925–6, MA Division Markets, 1926–7, New England Res. Council, 1928–32; US Dept. Agric., 1932–45; Advisor, US Office War Mobilization and Reconversion, 1945–6; Sr. Staff, US President's Council Econ. Advisors, 1946–51; Econ. US Dept. Agric., 1951–65.
Degrees BA Mass. Agric. Coll., 1922; MS (Agric. Econ.) Rutgers Univ., 1924; PhD (Agric. Econ.) Columbia Univ., 1929.
Offices and Honours Croix de Guerre, France, 1918; Cons., FAO 1965–72, US Dept. Commerce, 1965–74; Vice Pres., Amer. Farm Econ. Assoc., 1939, 1946; Vice-Pres., ASA, 1941; Hon. Fellow, Amer. Farm Econ. Assoc., ASA, Em Soc.
Publications *Articles*: 1. *Selected Writings on Agricultural Policy and Economic Analysis*, eds. J. P. Houck and M. E. Abel (1984).
Career Pioneer in agricultural economics and the practical blending of economic theory, mathematics, statistics and econometrics. Broke new ground on such topics as the opitmal allocation of product sales among separate markets, subsidized food stamps for low-income people, the merits of price stability for agricultural products, the size and composition of grain reserve stocks, linear programming as a tool for agricultural economics and the causes of cyclical behaviour in farm output and prices.

WEBB, Beatrice*

Dates and Birthplace 1858–1943, Gloucester, England.

Posts Held Social investigator and writer.

Offices and Honours Member, Royal Commission on the Poor Laws, 1905–9; Member, various other commissions and comms., including Comm. on Equal Pay, 1919.

Publications *Books:* 1. *The Co-operative Movement in Great Britain* (1891, 1899); 2. *The Wages of Men and Women: Should They Be Equal?* (1919); 3. *My Apprenticeship* (1926, 1950); 4. *Our Partnership* (1948). See also Webb, Sydney.

Career Co-operative work with her husband, Sidney, on a multitude of social and political issues. She came from a prosperous but radical background and began her career as a social investigator on Charles Booth's study of London life and labour. Though less in the public eye than her husband, she was fully involved in all his activities, was co-author of all their major publications and a strong influence on innumerable politicians, social scientists and writers.

Secondary Literature M. Cole, 'Webb, Sidney and Beatrice', *IESS*, 16.

WEBB, Sidney James*

Dates and Birthplace 1859–1947, London, England.

Posts Held Clerk, 1875–8; Civil Servant, 1878–91; Journalist, writer and politician.

Offices and Honours Member, Exec. Comm., Fabian Soc.; Founder LSE; Member, London County Council, 1892–1910; MP, 1922–9; Member, Labour govts., 1924, 1929–31; created Lord Passfield, 1929.

Publications *Books:* 1. *Facts for Socialists* (1887); The following all jointly with Beatrice Webb; 2. *The History of Trade Unionism* (1894, 1950); 3. *Industrial Democracy*, 2 vols (1897, 1920); 4. *English Local Government*, 10 vols (1906–29); 5. *The Break-up of the Poor Law* (1909); 6. *The Consumers' Co-operative Movement* (1921); 7. *The*

Decay of Capitalist Civilisation (1923); 8. *English Poor Law History*, 3 vols (1927–30); 9. *Methods of Social Study* (1932); 10. *Soviet Communism*, 2 vols (1935, 1947).

Career Already established as a theorist of the Fabian Society, and a collector of social and economic information, his marriage in 1892 to Beatrice Potter began the extraordinary partnership which achieved so much in research and socialist politics. Their position was basically utilitarian, and they sought to achieve a socialist society by the replacement of private ownership with a range of public and co-operative forms of ownership. Gradual change was to be the means for this and the trades unions, co-operative movement and Labor Party were amongst the agencies they employed to spread their views. The pamphlets of the Fabian Society best expressed their programme. Much of their research was in economic history, but their efforts on government commissions, including the *Minority Report of the Commission on the Poor Laws* (1909), were extremely influential. They later came to see Soviet communism as a vision of the society they wished for Britain, but violent revolution was never part of their programme.

Secondary Literature M. Cole, 'Webb, Sidney and Beatrice', *IESS*, 16; G. J. Stigler, *Essays in the History of Economics* (Univ. Chicago Press, 1965), chap. 9.

WEBER, Alfred*

Dates and Birthplace 1868–1958, Erfurt, Germany.

Posts Held Prof., Univ. Berlin, 1899–1904, Univ. Prague, 1904–7, Univ. Heidelberg, 1907–33.

Degrees Dr Univ. Berlin, 1895.

Publications *Books:* 1. *Theory of the Location of Industries* (1909, 1929, 1957); 2. *Die Krise des modernen Staatsgedankens in Europa* (1925); 3. *Kulturgeschichte als Kultursoziologie* (1935, 1950); 4. *Abschied von der bisherigen Geschichte* (1946); 5. *Der dritter oder der vierte Mensch* (1953).

Articles: 1. 'Location theory and trade policy', *Archiv für Sozialwissen-*

schaft, 1911, repr. in *Internat. Econ. Papers*, 8, eds. A. T. Peacock, *et al.* (Macmillan, 1958).

Career Although better known in Germany for his sociological writings, his first book is a landmark in the history of location theory. He developed von Thünen's analysis by his examination of the factors governing the location of industry. His writings were suppressed by the Nazis, but he re-emerged after World War II as a political and intellectual influence on the new German State.

Secondary Literature E. Salin, 'Weber, Alfred', *IESS*, 16.

WEBER, Max*

Dates and Birthplace 1864–1920, Erfurt, Germany.

Posts Held Prof. Econ., Univ. Freiburg, 1894–6, Univ. Heidelberg, 1896–1904.

Publications *Books:* 1. *The Protestant Ethic and the Spirit of Capitalism* (1904–5, 1930); 2. *The Theory of Social and Economic Organisation*, eds. A. M. Henderson and T. Parsons (1922, 1947); 3. *On the Methodology of the Social Sciences*, eds. E. A. Shils and H. A. Finch (1949); 4. *General Economic History* (1923, 1961).

Career One of the major figures in sociology whose system was based on the meaning individuals attached to their actions. This led him to reject various other systems, including the utilitarianism of the marginalists. His famous thesis on Protestantism and capitalism was intended to resolve the paradox of the condemnation of the acquisitive spirit in Protestant theology and the evident economic success of members of Protestant sects. Much of his other work was on the sociology of religion and the methodology of the social sciences. In *Wirtschaft und Gesellschaft* he examined economic activity for what it revealed about the social behaviour of groups. Owing to ill-health, much of his written work is in unfinished fragments which have been edited and published posthumously. Even his finished writings, however, are tortuously written and have created endless controversies.

Secondary Literature M. Weber, *Max Weber: A Biography* (1926, 1957); R. Bendix, 'Weber, Max', *IESS*, 16.

WEBER, Warren E.

Born 1945, Evanston, IL, USA.

Current Post Sr. Econ. and Manager, Monetary Stud., Fed. Reserve Bank, Minneapolis, MN, USA, 1984–.

Past Posts Ass. Prof., Assoc. Prof. Prof., Virginia Polytechnic Inst. State Univ., 1968–72, 1972–6, 1978–84; Vis. Assoc. Prof., Duke Univ., Durham, NC, 1976–7; Assoc. Prof., Tulane Univ., LO, 1977–8.

Degrees BA (English) Wesleyan Univ., CT, 1965; MS, PhD Carnegie-Mellon Univ., 1968, 1969.

Offices and Honours Phi Beta Kappa, 1965.

Editorial Duties Ed. Board, *SEJ*, 1975–7.

Principal Fields of Interest 311 Domestic Monetary and Financial Theory and Policy; 211 Econometric and Statistical Methods and Models; 431 Balance of Payments; Mechanisms of Adjustment; Exchange Rates.

Publications *Articles*: 1. 'The effect of interest rates on aggregate consumption', *AER*, 60(4), Sept. 1970; 2. 'Monetary assets, net wealth and banking structure', *JMCB*, 7(3), Aug. 1975; 3. 'Competition, monopoly and the organization of government in metropolitan areas' (with R. E. Wagner), *J Law E*, 18(3), Dec. 1975; 4. 'Interest rates, inflation and consumer expenditures', *AER*, 65(5), Dec. 1975; 5. 'Consumer behavior and quantity constraints: some implications for monetary theory' (with R. J. Mackay), *JMCB*, 9(1), Feb. 1977; 6. 'The effect of real and monetary disturbances on the price level under alternative commodity reserve standards', *Int ER*, 21(3), Oct. 1980; 7. 'Ouput variability under monetary policy and exchange rate rules', *JPE*, 89(4), Aug. 1981; 8. 'New evidence on the free banking era' (with A. J. Polnick), *AER*, 73(5), Dec. 1983; 9. 'A method for estimating distributed lags when observations are randomly missed' (with M. J. Hinich), *JASA*, 79, June 1984.

Principal Contributions Early work empirically examined the effects of interest-rate changes on aggregate consumer expenditures. The nonlinear models estimated were based upon intertemporal utility maximisation on the part of consumers. The studies found that interest-rate changes significantly affected consumption. Recent work explores the implications of the experience of the Free Banking Era in the US (1839–63) for regulation of current financial institutions. This work calls into question the notion that wildcat banking was prevalent during this period. Frequency domain methods for estimation of distributed lag models with missing observations or errors-in-variables are also currently being researched. The variability of ouput under alternative exchange-rate regimes has been and continues to be a research area.

WEILLER, Jean Sylvian

Born 1905, Saint-Die, Vosges, France.

Current Post Hon. Prof., Univ. Paris, 1; Dir. d'études écon. internat., Ecole des Hautes Etudes en Sciences Sociales, Paris, 1978–.

Past Posts Ass., Faculté de Droit, Sorbonne, Paris, 1930; Conseiller technique, Ministère du Commerce (Accords commerciaux), 1930–5; Prof. Doyen, Faculté de Droit, Univ. Poitiers, 1936–45, 1954–5; Prof., Faculté de Droit et des Sciences Econ., Univ. de Paris, 1955; Dir. d'études, l'Ecole Pratique des Hautes Etudes, 1949; Prof., Univ. Paris, 1, Pantheon-Sorbonne, 1970–7.

Degrees Dr Faculté de Droit de Paris, 1929.

Offices and Honours Rockefeller Foundation Fellow, 1939; Member, League of Nations Econ. Dept., 1939–41; Member, Inst. Advanced Study, Princeton, NJ, 1942–3; Cons., FAO, Rome, Abidjan, Accra, 1961.

Degrees Ed. Boards, *Rev. d'Histoire Econ. et Sociale*, 1945–; *RE*, 1950–; *Cahiers Economies et Sociétés*, 1975–.

Principal Fields of Interest 031 History of Economic Thought; 400 International Economics.

Publications *Books:* 1. *L'influence du change sur le commerce exterieur* (M. Rivière, 1936), 2. *Problemes d'économie internationale: Les ecranges du capitalisme liberal* (Presses Univ. de France, 1946); 3. *Une nouvelle experience, l'organisation internationale des échanges* (Presses Univ. de France, 1950); 4. *Histoire de la pensée économique au XX siecle* (with E. James), (Presses Univ. de France, 1955); 5. *La balance des paiements* (Presses Univ. de France, 1968, 1979; transl., Spanish, Fondo de Cultura Economica, 1979); 6. *Induction, Growth and Trade, Essays in Honour of Sir Roy Harrod*, co-ed. (Clarendon Press, 1970); 7. *Les cadres sociaux de la pensée économique* (with G. D. Desroussiles), (Presses Univ. de France, 1974); 8. *Economie internationale, faits théorie et politiques, 1, automatismes et structures* (with J. Coussy, et al.), (Mouton, 1975); 9. *Internationalisation et integration — ou cooperation* (with B. Ducros, et al.), (Mouton, 1979).

Articles: 1. 'Structure économique et commerce exterieur', *REP*, Nov.–Dec. 1935; 2. 'Le bloc sterling et all réprise britannique', *Annales du droit et des sciences sociales*, 1935; 3. 'The size of the economy and its relation to stability and steady progress' (with L. Tarshis, G. Leduc, et al.), in *The Consequences of the Size of Nations*, ed. A. G. Robinson (Macmillan, 1960); 4. 'Capital et revenu dans les relations économiques internationales', *Kyk*, 2, 1948; 5. 'Les preferences nationales de structure et le deséquilibre structurel', *REP*, 1949; 6. 'Existing international payments and exchange systems', in *International Trade Theory in a Developing World*, eds. R. F. Harrod and D.C. Hague (Macmillan, 1963); 7. 'Anti-cyclical policies in relation to foreign trade patterns and tariffs: an historical approach', *EI*, 2, 1969; 8. 'La politique commerciale des Etats-Unis, le jeu institutionnel et l'inégalite des nations', *Economies et Sociétés*, 19, 20, 21, June 1971, June–July 1972, July–Aug. 1973; 9. 'Preferences pour un mode d'expansion en économie ouverte', *Economies et Sociétés*, 26, 27, 1978; 10. 'Dèsequilibres et preferences de politique économique; secondes lectures de Keynes, d'Albert Aftalion et de quelques autres', *RE*, Jan. 1982.

Principal Contributions The main contributions relate to international economics but very often efforts have been made to clarify the connections between economics and other disciplines at different levels of analysis (historical and sociological, more or less abstract or concrete, etc.). In international economics I have been concerned to challenge leading orthodox opinion with regard to 'equilibrium' and the price mechanism or policies of adjustment under fixed or flexible exchange rates. It is not sufficient to ask how effectively the price mechanism or the rate of interest will work and the reflections on the difficulties encountered are quite different for countries more or less developed and integrated in an international trade and payments system. The starting point of a series of considerations with regards to freer trade, protectionism and international economic co-operation is to be traced to the interventions deemed necessary during long waves (Kondratieff cycles) in prices. Long-run tendencies in foreign patterns appear especially in the light of the French experiment from 1880 until World War II. In these circumstances, the persistence of a similar trade pattern from year to year proves the persistence of the same national preferences for certain structures as far as the main categories of imports or exports are concerned. The eventuality of conflicting national structural preferences makes international co-operation even more vital. Several of my papers are concerned with different aspects of the need for economic co-operation rather than international or transnational integration. Nowadays, the search for co-operation and intergovernmental negotiation is the antidote to many evils and threats of a long-run recession.

WEINTRAUB, Eliot Roy

Born 1943, New York City, NY, USA.

Current Post Prof. Econ., Duke Univ., Durham, NC, USA, 1980–.

Past Posts Ass. Prof., Rutgers Coll.,

1968–70; Ass. Prof., Assoc. Prof., Duke Univ., 1970–80; Vis. Lect., Univ. Bristol, England, 1971–2; Vis. Prof., Univ. Hawaii, 1978, UCLA, 1982.

Degrees BA Swarthmore Coll., PA (Maths), 1964; MS, PhD (Appl. Maths.) Univ. Penn., 1967, 1969.

Editorial Duties Ed. Board *JEL*, 1978–, *AER*, 1981–.

Principal Fields of Interest 021 General Equilibrium Theory; 031 History of Economic Thought; 036 Economic Methodology.

Publications *Books:* 1. *General Equilibrium Theory* (Macmillan, 1974; transls., Spanish, 1978, Italian, 1978); 2. *Conflict and Cooperation in Economics* (Macmillan, 1975); 3. *Microfoundations* (CUP, 1979; transl., French, 1980); 4. *Mathematics for Economists* (CUP, 1982); 5. *General Equilibrium Analysis: Studies in Appraisal* (CUP, 1985).

Articles: 1. 'Stochastic stability of short run market equilibrium', *QJE*, 84(1), Feb. 1970; 2. 'Stochastic stability of a general equilibrium system under adaptive expectations' (with S. Turnovsky), *Int ER*, 12(1), Feb. 1971; 3. 'Transactions costs and convergence of a "trade-out-of-equilibrium" model' (with D. Graham and E. Jacobson), *Int ER*, 13(2), June 1972; 4. 'Uncertainty and the Keynesian revolution', *HOPE*, 7(4), Dec. 1975; 5. 'On convergence to Pareto allocations' (with D. Graham), *REStud*, 42(3), July 1975; 6. 'Trades-commodity parity theorems' (with D. Graham, *et al.*), *JET*, 12(3), June 1976; 7. 'Real transactions costs are inessential' (with H. Baligh, *et al.*), *Kyk*, 29(3), Sept. 1976; 8. 'Microfoundations of macroeconomics: a critical survey', *JEL*, 15(1), March 1977; 9. 'Catastrophe theory and intertemporal equilibria', *Econ App*, 33(2), 1980; 10. 'The existence of a competitive equilibrium: 1930–54', *JEL*, 21(1), March 1983.

Principal Contributions Early work, based on my doctoral dissertation, concerned the effects of imposing random shocks on *tâtonnement* processes for general equilibrium models. Most result were negative in the sense that stochastic shocks destabilised *tâtonnement* adjustments. This led to my concern with non-*tâtonnement* processes based on actual trading behaviour, in which transactions costs, information costs, and trading strategies intrude. These ideas linked up with my work in monetary theory and, in an attempt to sort out the issues, I was led to survey the area of 'micro-foundations of macroeconomics'. This survey also resulted from concerns with Keynes-versus-Keynesian problems which I had addressed in several articles. These ideas led me to a more self-conscious analysis of just what general equilibrium analysis could, or could not, do in economics. The result was a shift of interest to the 'modern' history of economic thought and method, which reached fruition with a history of competitive equilibrium theory from Wald to Debreu, and a book on appraising general equilibrium analysis. I have had a continuing secondary interest in mathematical ideas in economics, and this has led to books on game theory and mathematics for economists and, more recently, on the usefulness of catastrophe theory for economics.

WEINTRAUB, Sidney*

Dates and Birthplace 1914–83, New York City, NY, USA.

Posts Held Grad. Faculty, New School Social Res., NY, 1951–7, Univ. Minnesota, 1959, Univ. Hawaii, 1967, Univ. Waterloo, Canada, 1969–71, Univ. Western Australia, 1974; Prof. Econ., Univ. Penn., 1975–81; Disting. Prof., Univ. South, 1981–3.

Degrees Student, LSE, 1938–9; PhD NYU, 1941.

Offices and Honours Cons., US Treasury, US State Dept., US Forest Service, US Federal Communications Comm., US Federal Power Comm., Prices and Incomes Comm. (Canada), Econ. Council Canada, Univ. Puerto Rico, Council Appl. Econ. Res. (India); Co-ed. and co-founder, *J Post Keyn E*; Ed., *Puerto Rico Econ. Q.*

Publications *Books:* 1. *Price Theory* (1949, 1979); 2. *An Approach to the Theory of Income Distribution* (1958, 1979); 3. *Employment Growth and Income Distribution* (1966); 4. *Capitalism's Inflation and Unemployment Crisis*

(1978); 5. *Keynes, Keynesians and Monetarists* (1978).

Articles: 1. 'A Jevonian seditionist: a munity to enhance the economic bounty?', *BNLQR* 36(146), Sept. 1983.

Career Development and integration of aggregate demand, aggregate supply, and macro-distribution; conceptualisation and formalisation of theory of general price level, consumer price level, and the price level in the open economy; theory of growth and distribution in underemployed and unsteady states; generalising Kalecki and simplifying macroeconomics; interpreting Keynes; TIP, a tax-based incomes policy as a contribution to economic policy of inflation; a theory of profits; and economic dissent from popular orthodoxy for two decades.

Secondary Literature A. Bloomfield and P. Davidson, 'On Weintraub', in *Contemporary Economists in Perspective*, eds. H.W. Spiegel and W.J. Samuels (JAI Press, 1984); 'Symposium: a tribute to Sidney Weintraub', *J Post Keyn E*, 7(4), Summer 1985.

WEISBROD, Burton A.

Born 1931, Chicago, IL, USA.

Current Post Prof. Econ., Dir., Center Health Econ. and Law, NIMH Training Program Health and Mental Health Econ., Univ. Wisconsin, Madison, WI, USA, 1966–, 1983–.

Past Posts Lect., Northwestern Univ., 1954–5; Instr., Carleton Coll., 1955–7; Instr., Ass. Prof., Assoc. Prof., Washington Univ., 1957–8, 1958–62, 1962–4; Vis. Prof., Princeton Univ., 1962–3; Sr. Staff member, US President's Council Econ. Advisers, 1963–4; Assoc. Prof., Univ. Wisconsin, 1964–6; Vis. Prof., State Univ. Binghamton, 1972; Sr. Fulbright Lect., Univ. Autonoma de Madrid, 1970; Vis. Scholar, Brotman Fellow, Kennedy School Govt., Harvard Univ., 1982–3; Vis. Prof., Brandeis Univ., MA, 1982–3.

Degrees BA (Management) Univ. Illinois, 1951; MA, PhD Northwestern Univ., 1952, 1958.

Offices and Honours Guggenheim Foundation Fellow, 1969–70; Ford Foundation Faculty Fellow, 1971–2;

Member, Exec. Comm., NBER, Conf. RIW, 1975–7; Exec. Comm., AEA, 1975–7; Member, Govt. Council, NAS Inst. Medicine, 1976–83; Nat. Fellow, Educ. Fin. and Productivity Center, Univ. Chicago, 1978–; Sr. Res. Fellow, Brookdale Inst., Jerusalem, 1978–.

Editorial Duties Ed. Boards, *Public Fin. Q.*, 1972, *J Pub E*, 1971–, *Managerial & Decision Econ.*, 1980–3, *JHR*, 1966–81, *Internat. J. Social Econ.*, 1972–, *QREB*, 1980–.

Principal Fields of Interest 024 Welfare Theory; 322 National Government Expenditures and Budgeting; 913 Economics of Health.

Publications *Books:* 1. *The Economics of Poverty* (Prentice-Hall, 1965); 2. *Benefits, Cost and Finance of Public Higher Education* (with W. Lee Hansen), (Markham Publ., 1969); 3. *The Daily Economist*, co-ed. (with H.G. Johnson), (Prentice-Hall, 1974); 4. *American Health Policy: Perspectives and Choices* (with R. Andreano), (Markham Publ., 1974); 5. *Disease and Economic Development: The Case of Parasitic Diseases in St. Lucia, West Indies* (with R. Andreano, *et al.*), (Univ. Wisconsin Press, 1974); 6. *The Voluntary Nonprofit Sector: An Economic Analysis* (D.C. Heath, 1978); 7. *Public Interest Law: An Economic and Institutional Analysis* (with J.F. Handler and N.K. Komesar), (Univ. Cal. Press, 1978); 8. *Economics and Mental Health*, co-ed. (with T. McGuire), (NIMH, 1981); 9. *Human Resources, Employment and Development, Vol 3: The Problems of Developed Countries and the International Economy*, co-ed. (with H. Hughes), (Macmillan, 1983); 10. *Economics and Medical Research* (AEI for Public Pol. Res., 1983).

Articles: 1. 'Medical research: the key to health care cost containment?' (with J. Goddeeris), *Colloquium*, 2, May 1982; 2. 'Clinical evaluation vs. economic evaluation: the case of a new drug' (with J. Geweke), *Medical Care*, 20(8), Aug. 1982; 3. 'Scholarships, citations and salaries: economic rewards in economics' (with D. Hamermesh and H.G. Johnson), *SEJ*, 49, Oct. 1982; 4. 'Why can't workers, retirees share economic ups, downs?', *Los Angeles Times*, Dec. 1982; 5. 'Economic ap-

proaches to evaluating a new medical technology: the drug cimetidine', in *Economic and Medical Evaluation of Health Care*, eds. A.J. Culyer and B. Horisberger (Springer Verlag, 1982); 6. 'Competition in the health care market: a cautionary view', in *Market Reforms in Health Care*, ed. J. Meyer (AEI, 1983); 7. 'A guide to benefit-cost analysis as seen through a controlled experiment in treating the mentally ill', *JHR*, 16(4), Fall 1983, repr. in *Social Policy Evaluation: An Economic Perspective*, eds. A. Razin, E. Helpman and E. Sadka (Academic Press, 1983); 8. 'Nonprofit and proprietary sector behavior: wage differentials among lawyers', *J Law E*, 1(3), July 1983; 9. 'Charities can't patch government safety net' (with J. Schiff), *St Louis Post-Dispatch*, July 1983, *Milwaukee Journal*, Aug. 1983, *Des Moines Register*, 1983; 10. 'Expenditure effects of technological change: the case of a new drug', *Evaluation Rev.*, Spring 1984.

Principal Contributions Welfare economics — theoretic and applied — attracted me to economics. From this base it was natural to direct my research to areas such as education and medical care which, involving both investments in human capital and powerful distributional equity considerations, have become central focusses of governmental policy. Research included studies on external effects of education, and various works within a benefit-cost analytic framework — sometimes theoretic, focussing on the role of distributional weights, and sometimes applied, as on the evaluation of polio research. In the last decade my research on the economics of health has increased, much of it continuing to focus on programme evaluation and the economics of medical research. At the same time I have broadened my public sector focus to encompass other 'nonmarket' institutions, particularly the private 'nonprofit' sector. The actual and the efficient roles of various types of institution — private market, governmental, and private nonprofit — have become a major interest. Questions on which I have been focussing include: the rationale for public subsidies to nonprofits, the nature of systematic differences in economic behaviour across institutional types, and the forces leading to the existence of 'mixed' industries such as hospitals, day care centres, and schools — in which two or more ownership-types of institution coexist.

WEITZMAN, Martin L.

Born 1942, New York City, NY, USA.
Current Post Prof. Econ., MIT, Cambridge, MA, USA, 1974–.
Past Posts Res. Staff, Cowles Foundation, Yale Univ., 1967–72; Ass. Prof., Assoc. Prof. Econ., Yale Univ., 1967–70, 1970–2; Assoc. Prof. Econ., MIT, 1972–4.
Degrees BA Swarthmore Coll. PA (Maths. and Physics), 1963; MS (Stats. and OR) Stanford Univ., 1964; PhD MIT, 1967.
Offices and Honours Phi Beta Kappa; Sigma Xi; NSF Fellow, 1963–5; Woodrow Wilson Fellow, 1963–4; Ford Foundation Dissertation Fellow, 1966; Guggenheim Foundation Fellow, 1970–1; Fellow, Em Soc, 1976.
Editorial Duties Assoc. Ed.: *J Comp E*, *Econ. Letters*.
Principal Fields of Interest 020 General Economic Theory; 050 Economic Systems.
Publications *Books:* 1. *The Share Economy* (Harvard Univ. Press, 1984). *Articles:* 1. 'Soviet postwar economic growth and capital labor substitution', *AER*, 60(4), Sept. 1970; 2. 'Optimal growth with economies of scale in the creation of overhead capital', *REStud*, 37(4), Oct. 1970; 3. 'Prices vs. quantities', *REStud*, 41(4), Oct. 1974; 4. 'A Marxian model of enclosures' (with J.S. Cohen), *JDE*, 1(4), Feb. 1975; 5. 'On the welfare significance of national product in a dynamic economy', *QJE*, 90, Feb. 1976; 6. 'Optimal search for the best alternative', *Em*, 47(3), May 1979; 7. 'Funding criteria for research, development and exploration projects' (with K. Roberts), *Em*, 48(4), Sept. 1981; 8. 'Increasing returns and the foundations of unemployment theory', *EJ*, 92, Dec. 1982; 9. 'Some macroeconomic implications of alternative compensation systems', *EJ*, 97, Dec. 1983.

Principal Contributions My abiding interest is in the field of comparative economic systems, broadly defined. I have worked intensively in the theory of economic planning and in optimal growth theory. Specific contributions were made in analysing the choice between price and quantity instruments, and optimal resource allocation under economies of scale. I have followed developments in the Soviet economy and applied to it production-function analysis. Another area of interest is the economics of project selection in research and development. Work on the economics of common property resources led to an investigation of the English enclosure movement. Currently I have been applying the comparative systems approach to macroeconomic issues, arguing that stagflation is essentially a problem of a wage system that is largely absent from profit-sharing versions of capitalist economies.

WELCH, Finis R

Born 1938, Olney, TX, USA.
Current Post Prof. Econ., UCLA, CA, USA, 1978–; Pres., Welch Assoc., Santa Monica, CA, USA, 1984–.
Past Posts Ass. Prof. Econ., Univ. Chicago, 1964–6; Assoc. Prof. Econ., Southern Methodist Univ., Dallas, 1966–9; Res. Assoc., NBER, NY, 1969–73; Exec. Officer, PhD Program Econ., City Univ. NY, 1971–3; Dir., Labour and Pop. Stud. Program, Rand Corp., Santa Monica, CA, 1973–8; Pres., Unicon Res. Corp., Santa Monica, CA, 1978–84.
Degrees BS Univ. Houston, 1961; PhD Univ. Chicago, 1965.
Offices and Honours Fellow, Em Soc, 1980; Member, Nat. Academy Educ., 1980, Member, Conf. Income and Wealth, NBER, 1984.
Editorial Duties Ed. Boards, *AER*, 1974–7, *AJAE*, 1974–7, *Econ. Educ. Rev.*, 1979–, *J. Labor Res.*, 1980–, *JEL*, 1980–, *J. Labor Econ.*, 1982–.
Principal Fields of Interest 800 Labour Market Studies, Wages, Employment.
Publications *Articles*: 1. 'Education in production', *JPE*, 78(1), Jan. 1970; 2. 'Education and racial discrimination',

in *Discrimination in Labor Markets*, eds. O. Ashenfelter and A. Rees (Princeton Univ. Press, 1974); 3. 'Employment quotas for minorities', *JPE*, 84(4), pt. 2, Aug. 1976; 4. 'Do sex preferences really matter?' (with Y. Ben-Porath), *QJE*, 90(2), May 1976; 5. 'Black-white male wage ratios, 1960–1970' (with J. Smith), *AER*, 67(3), June 1977; 6. 'Effects of minimum wages on the level and age composition of youth employment' (with J. Cunningham), *REStat*, 60(1), Feb. 1978; 7. 'Local labor markets and cyclic components in demand for college trained manpower' (with J. Smith), *Annales de L'INSEE*, March 1978; 8. 'Effects of cohort size on earnings', *JPE*, 87(5), pt. 2, Oct. 1979; 9. 'Earnings of Hispanic men: the role of English language proficiency' (with W. McManus and W. Gould), *J. Labor Econ.*, 1, April 1983; 10. 'Affirmative action in labor markets' (with J. Smith), *J. Labor Econ.*, 2, April 1984.

Principal Contributions My work concentrates on determinants of labour earnings and is intensely empirical. Early work on returns to schooling was followed by a prolonged series on group differences in earnings. Several compare blacks and whites and one contrasts Hispanics and Anglos. Much of the work is descriptive, characterising patterns and the evolution of group differences through time. The behavioural work, in the context of competitive markets, concentrates on determinants of major swings in earnings patterns. Income differences by age, schooling level, and race are examined for responses to changes in labour force composition and protective legislation. Analysis of effects of cohort size on age-learning profiles traces early results and future implications for the baby boom cohorts. Effects of rising education levels are contrasted with growth in labour productivity and cyclical swings in tracing changes in patterns of income differences by schooling. Currently involved with implications of modern and discriminatory legislation, together with its enforcement apparatus, and the comparison of evolving patterns of income and employment differences between those protected and those not protected by the legislation.

WELLISZ, Stanislaw Henryk

Born 1925, Warsaw, Poland.
Current Post Prof. Econ., Columbia Univ., New York City, NY, USA, 1964–.
Past Posts Instr., Williams Coll., MA, 1955–7; Ass. Prof., Assoc. Prof., Grad. School Bus., Univ. Chicago, 1957–60, 1961–4; Ford Foundation Vis. Prof., Warsaw Univ., Central School Planning and Stats., Warsaw, 1950–60; Chief Econ. Adviser, Calcutta Metropolitan Planning Organisation, Calcutta, 1961–3; Dir., Harlem Devlp., Project, 1967–8; Sr. Econ. Cons., Greater Istanbul Master Plan Bureau, 1975–6; Cons. Nat. Econ. Budgeting, Venezuelan Parliamentary Commission Fiscal Reform, 1982; Cons. Trade and Industrialisation, Govt. Mauritius, 1983–4; Vis. Prof., Catholic Univ., Lublin, Poland, 1983–4.
Degrees BA, MA, PhD Harvard Univ., 1947, 1949, 1954.
Offices and Honours Phi Beta Kappa; Fulbright Fellow; Camb. Pres., Middle East Econ. Assoc.
Principal Fields of Interest 110 Economic Growth; Development, Planning and Policy; 411 International Trade Theory; 927 Economics of Centrally Planned Economies.
Publications *Books:* 1. *The Economies of the Soviet Bloc* (McGraw-Hill, 1964; transls., Japanese, 1965, Spanish, 1966, French, 1968).
Articles: 1. 'Economic planning in The Netherlands, France and Italy', *JPE*, 68(3), June 1960; 2. 'Regulation of natural gas pipeline companies: an economic analysis', *JPE*, 71(1), Feb. 1963; 3. 'On external diseconomies and the government assisted invisible hand', *Ec*, N.S. 31, Nov. 1964, repr. in *Theories of International Politics*, ed. B. M. Russet (Markham, 1968); 4. 'Dual economies, disguised unemployment and the unlimited supply of labor', *Ec*, N.S. 35, Feb. 1968; 5. 'Lessons of twenty years' experience in developing countries', *Ec*, N.S. 38, May 1971; 6. 'Project evaluation, shadow prices and trade policy' (with R. Findlay), *JPE*, 84(3), June 1976; 7. 'Hierarchy, ability and income distribution' (with G. Calvo), *JPE*, 87(5), pt. 2, Oct. 1979; 8.

'Rent-seeking, welfare and the political economy of trade restrictions' (with R. Findlay), in *Import Competition and Responses*, ed. J. Bhagwati (NBER, 1982).

Principal Contributions My interest in the interaction between institutions and market forces pervades my research, which ranges from welfare economics, through studies of economic development and planning, to my recent work on neoclassical political economy, and which includes such 'out-riders' as my papers (with G. Calvo) on the economics of hierarchies. Among my significant contribution I would rank my early paper on the regulation of natural gas companies in which I advanced a hypothesis, simultaneously with Avrech and Johnson, that rate return regulation encourages overcapitalisation on the part of regulated companies.

In the middle and late 1960s I explored the then popular notions of 'disguised unemployment', upholding the thesis that the phenomenon was the product of market-distorting institutions. I even undertook a lengthy study of Indian agriculture which showed, at least to my satisfaction, that in the absence of such distortions Lewis-type unemployment did not exist. I also showed the relation (later associated with the names of Harris and Todaro) between urban minimum wage and urban unemployment in developing countries.

Most recently I have been collaborating with R. Findlay on problems of trade barriers and factor-price distortions in open economies. In this field, our contributions include the rigorous derivation of the relation between protection policies and shadow prices of factors. We have also modelled general equilibrium systems in which protection is generated through the interaction between the economy and the policy, and we have explored the effects of diverse poltical configurations on trade regimes. We are currently extending our work to encompass problems of international factor mobility and of coalitions among international interest groups.

WELLS, David Ames*

Dates and Birthplace 1828–98, Springfield, MA, USA.
Posts Held Chairman, US Nat. Revenue Commission, 1865–6; Special Commission Revenue, 1866–70; Chairman, NY State Tax Commission, 1870–6.
Degrees Grad. Williams Univ., 1847, Lawrence Scientific School, 1851.
Publications *Books:* 1. *Our Burden and Strength* (1864); 2. *Reports of the Special Commissioner of the Revenue* (1866–9); 3. *Recent Economic Changes* (1889); 4. *The Theory and Practice of Taxation* (1900).
Career Originally a geologist and chemist, he turned to economics in middle life. He was an able collector of statistics and his ability to draw worthwhile conclusions from imperfect material was considerable. Tariffs, currency, theory of money and taxation were his chief economic interest. He became a determined free-trader.
Secondary Literature E. R. A. Seligman, 'Wells, David Ames', *ESS*, 15.

WEST, Edward*

Dates and Birthplace 1782–1828, London, England.
Posts Held Fellow, Univ. Coll., Univ. Oxford, 1807; Lawyer, 1814; Chief Justice, Bombay, 1823–8.
Degrees BA, MA Univ. Oxford, 1804, 1807.
Offices and Honours Knighted, 1822.
Publications *Books:* 1. *Essay on the Application of Capital to Land* (1815); 2. *Treatise of the Law and Practice of Extents in Chief and in Aid* (1817); 3. *The Price of Corn and Wages of Labour* (1826).
Career One of the independent discoverers of the theory of differential rent, more usually associated with Ricardo. His *Essay* . . . contains a clear statement of the principle of diminishing returns. His writings contain various anticipations of later doctrine, e.g. the idea that international trade tends to equalise factor prices between countries.
Secondary Literature W. D. Grampp, 'West, Edward', *IESS*, 16; W. D.

Grampp, 'Edward West Reconsidered', *HOPE*, 2(2), Fall 1970.

WEST, Edwin George

Born 1922, Yorkshire, England.
Current Post Prof. Econ., Carleton Univ., Ottawa, Ont., Canada, 1970–.
Past Posts Lect., Guildford Coll. Technology, England, 1951–6; Sr. Lect, Oxford Coll. Technology, 1956–62; Lect., Univ. Newcastle-upon-Tyne, 1962–5; Post-doctoral Fellow, Univ. Chicago, 1965–6; Reader, Univ. Kent, 1966–70; Vis. Res. Scholar, Univ. Cal. Berkeley, 1974, Virginia Polytechnic Inst., 1975–7; Vis. Prof., Emory Univ., GA, USA, 1983–4.
Degrees BSc, PhD Univ. London, 1948, 1964.
Offices and Honours Adjunct Scholar, Heritage Foundation, Washington, 1978–; Member, Mont Pelerin Soc., 1964–; Board Advisers, Pacific Inst. Public Pol. Res., San Francisco, 1981–.
Editorial Duties Ed. Boards, *INEA*, 1981, *Econ. Educ. Rev.*, 1980–3, *Reason Papers*, 1975–, *Pol. Report* (CATO Inst., 1978–), *Carleton Econ. Papers*, 1980–.
Principal Fields of Interest 031 History of Economic Thought; 322 National Government Expenditures and Budgeting; 822 Public Policy; Role of Government.
Publications *Books:* 1. *Education and the State: A Study in Political Economy* (INEA, 1965, 1970); 2. *Economics, Education and the Politician* (INEA, 1968); 3. *Education and the Industrial Revolution* (Batsford, 1975); 4. *Adam Smith: The Man and His Works* (Arlington, 1969, Liberty Fund, 1976); 5. *The Political Economy of American Public School Legislation* (Center Independent Educ., 1977); 6. *Economics Today — The Macro View* (with R. L. Miller), (Harper & Row, 1978); 7. *Economics Today — The Micro View* (with R. L. Miller), (Harper & Row, 1978); 8. *Minimum Wages in Canada: New Issues in Theory, Evidence, Policy and Politics* (with M. McKee), (Econ. Council Canada, 1980); 9. *Tax Credits for Education* (Heritage Foundation, 1981); 10. *Non-Public School Aid:* *The Law, Economics, and Politics of American Education* (D. C. Heath, 1986).
Articles: 1. 'The public versus the private sector in education: a classical economic dispute', *JPE*, 72, Oct. 1964, repr. in *The Classical Economists and Economic Policy*, ed. A. W. Coats (Methuen, 1971); 2. 'The political economy of public school legislation', *J Law E*, 10, Oct. 1967; 3. 'Resource allocation and growth in early nineteenth century education', *EHR*, 33, April 1970; 4. 'Adam Smith's public economics', *CEJ*, 10, Feb. 1977; 5. 'John Stuart Mill's redistribution policy: new political economy or old?', *EI*, 16(4), Oct. 1978; 6. 'Literacy and the industrial revolution', *EHR*, 31(3), Aug. 1978, repr. in *Industry, Education and the Economy*, ed. G. Roderick (Falmer Press, 1980); 7. 'John Stuart Mill, unions and the wages fund' (with R. Hafer), *QJE*, 92(4), Nov. 1978; 8. 'The theory of second best: a solution in search of a problem' (with M. McKee), *EI*, 19(3), July 1981; 9. 'Marx's hypotheses on the length of the working day', *JPE*, 91(2), April 1983; 10. 'De Gustibus Non Est Disputandum: the phenomenon of "merit wants"' (with M. McKee), *AER*, 73(5), Dec. 1983.
Principal Contributions I began writing from the discipline of public finance and especially from the government expenditure side. My first application, in *Education and the State* (1965), was an investigation into the rationale of government-provided schooling in Britain. This led me to a similar investigation into the public finance of American education in the later 1960s and in the 1970s into the history of intervention in British education from 1760. Simultaneously I have worked in the history of economic thought with predominant attention to Adam Smith, John Stuart Mill and Karl Marx. I have frequently researched on government intervention in labour matters.

My interest in public choice is reflected in recent work on minimum wages as well as current writing on the choice between alternative methods of financing education (voucher, loans and full-cost fees). In welfare economic theory, my chief interest has been in the economics of second best and the concept of merit goods. Consistent also with my welfare economics and public finance background, I am currently studying public subsidies to the performing arts in Canada. My latest work in education is engaging me in the law and economics of the subject in the US and especially with respect to the most recent Supreme Court decisions on aid to private schools.

WESTON, J. Fred

Born 1916, Fort Wayne, IN, USA.
Current Post Prof., Grad. School Management, UCLA, CA, USA, 1956–.
Past Posts Teaching Fellow, Univ. Chicago, 1941–3; Fin. Dept., US Army, 1943–5; Econ. Cons., President Amer. Bankers Assoc., 1945–6; Instr., Ass. Prof., Univ. Chicago, 1947–9; Assoc. Prof., UCLA, 1949–55.
Degrees BA (Polit. Science), MBA, PhD Univ. Chicago, 1937, 1943, 1948.
Offices and Honours Pres., WEA, 1962, AFA, 1966, WFA, 1979–80; Ford Foundation Faculty Res. Fellow, 1962–7; Disting. Teaching Award, UCLA, 1978; J. Fred Weston Doctoral Fellow, 1979–.
Editorial Duties Assoc. Ed., *J Fin*, 1948–55, *Bus. Econ.*, 1975–, *J. Fin. Res.*, 1978–; Cons. Ed., *J. Bus. Res.*, 1973–; Ed. Boards, *J Fin*, 1957–9, *Fin. Analysis J.*, 1965–70, *Bus. Econ.*, 1965–, *WEJ*, 1963–5, *J. Fin. and Quant. Analysis*, 1969–76, *J. Accounting, Auditing and Fin.*, 1977–, *Chase Fin. Q.*, 1981–.
Principal Fields of Interest 420 Trade Relations; Commercial Policy; International Economic Integration; 520 Business Finance and Investment; 610 Industrial Organisation and Public Policy.
Publications *Books:* 1. *Public Policy Toward Mergers* (with S. Peltzman), (Goodyear, 1969); 2. *The Impact of Large Firms on the US Economy* (with S. I. Ornstein), (D. C. Heath, 1973); 3. *Industrial Concentration: The New Learning*, co-ed. and contrib. (with J. J. Goldschmid and H. M. Mann), (Little, Brown, 1974); 4. *Large Corporations in a Changing Society* (NYU Press, 1975);

5. *Treasurer's Handbook*, co-ed. (with M. G. Goudzwaard), (Dow-Jones-Irwin, 1976); 6. *Concentration and Efficiency: The Other Side of the Monopoly Issue* (Hudson Inst., 1978); 7. *Domestic Concentration and International Competition* (Macmillan, 1980); 8. *Mergers and Economic Efficiency*, 1 (US Govt. Printing Office, 1980); 9. *Industrial Concentration, Mergers and Growth*, 2 (US Dept. Commerce, 1981); 10. *Corporate Enterpise in a New Environment*, co-ed. (with M. E. Granfield), (KCG Productions, 1982).
Articles: 1. 'A note on capital budgeting and the three Rs' (with N. Chen), *Fin. Management*, 9, Spring 1980; 2. 'Comment on analysis of credit policy changes' (with P. D. Tuan), *Fin. Management*, 9, Winter 1980; 3. 'From practice to theory', *Fin. Management*, 10, Spring 1981; 4. 'Developments in finance theory', *Fin. Management*, 10, June 1981, repr. in *Financial Analysis and Planning: Theory and Application* (Addison-Wesley, 1983); 5. 'Price behavior of deep discount bonds' (with C. Hsia), *J Bank Fin.*, June 1981; 6. 'Section 7 enforcement: implementation of outmoded theories', *Antitrust Law J.*, 1982; 7. 'Trends in anti-trust policy', *Chase Fin. Q.*, 1, Spring 1982; 8. 'A note on the evaluation of cancellable operating leases' (with T. E. Copeland), *Fin. Management*, 11, Summer 1982; 9. 'Some aspects of merger theory' (with K. S. Chung), *J. Midwest Fin. Assoc.*, 12, 1983.
Principal Contributions Early work was on the economic concept of profit and its implications for tax policy, antitrust and other regulatory policies. Articles and books on mergers from the standpoint of strategic diversification planning and public policy effects. Other research in the area of financial analysis and policy such as corporate tax incidents, investment decisions using asset pricing models, and capital structure theory. Co-author of leading texts on managerial finance and on financial theory and corporate policy. Current research is on mergers, joint ventures, antitrust policy and industrial policy.

WHATELY, Richard*

Dates and Birthplace 1787–1863, London, England.

Posts Held Fellow, Oriel Coll., Drummond Prof., Univ. Oxford, 1811, 1829–31; Archbishop of Dublin, 1831–63.

Degrees BA, BD, DD Univ. Oxford, 1808, 1812, 1825.

Offices and Honours Chairman, Royal Commission Irish Poor, 1833–6; Vice-Pres., Royal Irish Academy, 1848.

Publications *Books:* 1. *Elements of Logic* (1826); 2. *Introductory Lectures on Political Economy* (1831); 3. *Easy Lessons on Money Matters* (1837); 4. *Miscellaneous Lectures and Reviews* (1861).

Career A prolific writer (chiefly on religious topics) his writings on political economy derive essentially from the view expressed in his *Elements of Logic*. Here he rejected induction as extra-logical. His economics is abstract and deductive and contributed little that was new. However, by instituting the Whately Chair at Trinity College, Dublin, he made possible a distinguished tradition. His involvement in Irish education led him to write various textbooks, including one on economic topics.

Secondary Literature L. M. Fraser, 'Whately, Richard', *ESS*, 15.

WHEATLEY, John*

Dates and Birthplace 1722–1830, Erith, London, England.

Posts Held Lawyer, 1797; Businessman in the West India trade; Clerk, Supreme Court, Calcutta, 1825–30.

Degrees BA Univ. Oxford, 1793.

Publications *Books:* 1. *Remarks on Currency and Commerce* (1803); 2. *Thoughts on the Object of the Foreign Subsidy* (1805); 3. *Essay on the Theory of Money and Principles of Commerce*, 2 vols (1807–22); 4. *Letter to Lord Grenville on the Distress of the Country* (1816); 5. *Report on the Reports of the Bank Committees* (1819); 6. *Letter to the Duke of Devonshire on the State of Ireland* (1824).

Career Writer on money who stated much of the theory which later came to be associated with Ricardo and the Bullion Report, 1810. He argued that there is an optimum quantity of money in a country which keeps prices in equilibrium with other countries; hence, an issue of paper money in excess of this amount depreciates a currency.

Secondary Literature F.W. Fetter, 'Life and writings of John Wheatley', *JPE*, 50, June 1942.

WHEWELL, William*

Dates and Birthplace 1794–1866, Lancaster, Lancashire, England.

Posts Held Fellow, Tutor, Master, Trinity Coll., Camb., 1817–66; Prof. Mineralogy, Prof. Moral Philo., Univ. Camb., 1828–32, 1838–55.

Offices and Honours Founder, Camb. Philo. Soc., 1818; Vice-Chancellor, Univ. Camb., 1842–3.

Publications *Articles:* 1. 'Mathematical exposition of some doctrines of political economy', *Camb. Philo. Soc. Transactions*, 3, 1830; 2. 'Mathematical exposition of some of the leading doctrines in Mr. Ricardo's *Principles*', *Camb. Philo. Soc. Transactions*, 4, 1831; 3. 'Mathematical exposition of some doctrines of political economy', *Camb. Philo. Soc. Transactions*, 9, 1850.

Career Mathematician, philosopher of science and university administrator, who published early papers on economics using mathematical language. There is some dispute as to whether this was genuine mathematical economics or merely economics set out algebraically. In pursuit of the encouragement of the inductive method in economics, he cajoled his friend Richard Jones into completing and publishing at least a part of his projected major work on economics.

Secondary Literature R.D. Theocharis, 'Whewell, William', *IESS*, 16; J.L. Cochrane, 'The first mathematical Ricardian model', *HOPE*, 2(2), Fall 1970.

WHITAKER, John King

Born 1933, Burnley, Lancashire, England.

Current Post Prof. Econ., Univ. Virginia, Charlottesville, VA, USA, 1969–.

Past Posts Res. Fellow, Johns Hopkins Univ., 1959–60; Lect., Prof. Econ. Theory, Univ. Bristol, 1960–6, 1966–9, Vis. Prof. Econ., Univ. Virginia, 1967–8.

Degrees BA Univ. Manchester, 1956; MA Johns Hopkins Univ., 1957; PhD, Camb. Univ., 1962.

Offices and Honours Stevenson Prize, Univ. Camb., 1958; Vice-Pres., Pres., Hist. Econ. Soc., 1981–2, 1982–3.

Editorial Duties Ass. Ed., *REStud*, 1965–9; Ed. Boards, *HOPE*, 1983–, *Res. in the Hist. Econ. and Econ. Methodology* (JAI Press, 1983–).

Principal Fields of Interest 030 History of Economic Thought: Methodology; 020 General Economic Theory.

Publications *Books:* 1. *Econometric Analysis for National Economic Planning* (with P.E. Hart and G. Mills), (Butterworths, 1964); 2. *The Early Economic Writings of Alfred Marshall, 1867–1890*, ed. (Macmillan, Free Press, 1975).

Articles: 1. 'Cycles, accumulation and the growth of capacity', *MS*, 27, Sept. 1959; 2. 'Vintage capital models and econometric production functions', *REStud*, 33, Jan. 1966; 3. 'Capital aggregation and optimality conditions', *REStud*, 35, Oct. 1968; 4. 'Alfred Marshall; the years 1877–1885', *HOPE*, 4, Spring 1972, repr. in *Alfred Marshall Critical Assessments*, ed. J.C. Woods (Croom Helm, 1982); 5. 'Private wealth as an obstacle to Pareto optimality?', *REStud*, 39, July 1972; 6. 'John Stuart Mill's methodology: a review article', *JPE*, 83, Oct. 1975; 7. 'Some neglected aspects of Alfred Marshall's economic and social thought', *HOPE*, 9, Summer 1977, repr. in *Alfred Marshall Critical Assessments*, ed. J.C. Wood (Croom Helm, 1982); 8. 'The effectiveness of fiscal feedback rules and automatic stabilisers under rational expectations' (with B.T. McCallum), *J Mon E*, 5, April 1979; 9. 'An essay on the pure theory of commodity money', *OEP*, 31, Nov. 1979; 10. 'A neglected classic in the theory of distribution', *JPE*, 90, April 1982.

Principal Contributions I began my professional career by thinking of myself as an economic theorist and still retain a 'middlebrow' interest in modern economic theory. But I have found my interests focussing increasingly on the history of economics, especially the history of economic theory. In part this is doubtless a natural consequence of changing comparative advantage over the professional life-cycle — I hope, indeed, that the history of economics is the exceptional area in which *absolute* advantage increases with age: there are certainly some suggestive examples! I feel, though, that it is also a matter of a natural bent reasserting itself, after perhaps being suppressed for some years. As a 'high-school dropout', I came to undergraduate economics partly because at that time my lack of Latin ruled out a history degree. Not that I regret the choice. Economics still retains a great intellectual appeal. But, unlike most of my colleagues, I find that I am happiest when rummaging among dusty old books, hoping to uncover forgotten pearls, rather than when crunching numbers at a keyboard. Without ever intending it, I realise, looking back, that I have drifted into setting myself up as a kind of intellectual conscience of the profession — setting straight historical priorities and rescuing neglected or forgotten contributors. My work in this regard has focussed on the last third of the nineteenth century and especially on Alfred Marshall, whose early manuscripts I brought to light and edited and whose correspondence I am currently editing, I believe this kind of work has social value — perhaps on the ground that those who forget history are doomed to repeat it — although it is by its nature something of a minority avocation.

WICKSELL, Knut*

Dates and Birthplace 1851–1926, Stockholm, Sweden.

Posts Held Lect., journalist and pamphleteer; Ass. Prof., Univ. Uppsala, 1899; Assoc. Prof., Prof., Univ. Lund, 1900, 1903–17.

Degrees Licentiate (Maths.), Dr Univ. Uppsala, 1876, 1895.

Offices and Honours Pres., Economists Club, Stockholm, 1917.

Publications *Books:* 1. *Value, Capital and Rent* (1893, 1954); 2. *Finanztheoretische Untersuchungen nebst Darstellung und Kritik des Steuerwesens Schwedens* (1896); 3. *Interest and Prices* (1898, 1936); 4. *Lectures on Political Economy*, 2 vols (1901–6, 1935–51); 5. *Selected Papers on Economic Theory* (1958).

Career Theorist and political activist whose rigorous work on the marginalist theory of price and distribution and on monetary theory are models of their kind. The *Lectures on Political Economy* has been aptly called a 'textbook for professors'. In an unusually chequered career (including a brief spell of imprisonment) he wrote and lectured tirelessly on radical issues. He was an advocate of social and economic reforms of various kinds, most notably neo-Malthusian population controls. In his later years he was revered by the new generation of economists who became known as the Stockholm School. They developed his ideas on 'the cumulative process' into a dynamic theory of monetary macroeconomics simultaneously with but independently of the Keynesian revolution.

Secondary Literature T. Gårdlund, *The Life of Knut Wicksell* (Almqvist & Wiksell, 1958); C.G. Uhr, *Economic Doctrines of Knut Wicksell* (Univ. Cal. Press, 1960); T. Gårdlund, 'Wicksell, Knut', *IESS*, 16; S. Stern and B. Thalberg, eds., *The Theoretical Contributions of Knut Wicksell* (Macmillan, 1979).

WICKSTEED, Philip Henry*

Dates and Birthplace 1844–1927, Leeds, Yorkshire, England.

Posts Held Clergyman, 1867–97; Univ. Extension Lect., 1887–1918.

Degrees MA Univ. London, 1866.

Publications *Books:* 1. *The Alphabet of Economic Science* (1888, 1955); 2. *An Essay on the Co-ordination of the Laws of Distribution* (1894, 1932); 3. *The Common Sense of Political Economy*, 2 vols (1910, 1950).

Career Writer on theology, literature and philosophy, who turned to economics in middle life, influenced by socialist sentiments and his membership of the Fabian Society. He was Jevons's first major follower and wrote on opportunity costs, the reversability of the supply curve and distribution theory. His principle of maximisation, though chiefly valuable in his economic writings, was intended to provide a guide to choices and behaviour in all aspects of life.

Secondary Literature C.H. Herford, *Philip Henry Wicksteed: His Life and Work* (Dent, 1931); W.D. Grampp, 'Wicksteed, Philip Henry', *IESS*, 16.

WIESER, Friedrich von*

Dates and Birthplace 1851–1926, Vienna, Austro-Hungary.

Posts Held Civil servant, 1872–84; Lect., Univ. Vienna, 1883; Prof., Univ. Prague, 1884, Univ. Vienna, 1903.

Offices and Honours Austrian Minister of Commerce, 1917.

Publications *Books:* 1. *Überden Ursprung und die Hauptgesetze des wirtschaftlichen Werthes* (1884); 2. *Natural Value* (1889, 1956); 3. *Social Economics* (1914, 1967); 4. *Das Gesetz der Macht* (1926); 5. *Gesammelte Abhandlungen*, ed. F. A. von Hayek (1929).

Career Member of the Austrian School of economists, whose early interest in sociology was diverted towards economics by the publication of Menger's *Grundsätze*. His early work was on the theory of cost; he later wrote on currency, taxation and social and economic policy. In *Social Economics* he produced the only systematic treatise by any of the older Austrian School. After World War I he returned to sociology, and developed his 'law of small numbers' which described the action of élites.

Secondary Literature F. A. von Hayek, 'Wieser, Friedrich von', *IESS*, 16; R. B. Ekelund, Jr., 'Power and utility: the normative economics of Friedrich von Wieser', *RSE*, 28(2), Sept. 1970.

WILES, Peter John De La Fosse

Born 1919, Rugby, Warwickshire, England.
Current Post Prof. Russian Social and Econ. Stud., LSE, London, England, 1965–.
Past Posts Fellow, New Coll. Oxford, 1948–60; Prof. Econ., Brandeis Univ., MA, 1960–3; Res. Assoc., Inst. Internat. Ekonomi, Stockholm, 1963–4; Vis. Prof., City Coll. NY, 1964–5.
Degrees BA Univ. Oxford, 1941.
Principal Fields of Interest 053 Comparative Economic Systems.
Publications *Books:* 1. *Price, Cost and Output* (Blackwell, 1962); 2. *Political Economy of Communism* (Blackwell, 1962); 3. *Communist International Economics* (Praeger, Blackwell, 1969); 4. *Distribution of Income East and West* (N-H, 1974); 5. *Economic Institutions Compared* (Blackwell, 1978); 6. *The New Communist Third World*, ed. (Croom Helm, 1982).
Articles: 1. 'Agenda for the age of inflation', *Econom*, Aug.–Sept. 1951; 2. 'The Soviet economy outpaces the West', *Foreign Affairs*, July 1953; 3. 'The nation's intellectual investment', *BOIS*, 18, Aug. 1956; 4. 'On the Co-Com-embargo', in *Probleme des Industrialismus Ost und West*, eds. W. Gumpel and D. Keese (Springer, 1973); 5. 'Cost inflation and the state of economic theory', *EJ*, 83, June 1973.
Principal Contributions Sovietology: demonstration that allocative inefficiency is compatible with rapid economic growth in Soviet-type systems and that economic convergence between East and West is highly improbable. Theory of the capitalist firm: administered prices, cost inflation, extreme insufficiency of orthodoxy. Practical central planning: institutions and motivations, especially military, behind international technology transfer. Human capital: seminal general article and later critique of the rationality assumptions.

WILLETT, Thomas D.

Born 1942, Staunton, VA, USA.
Current Post Horton Prof. Econ.,

Claremont Grad. School, Claremont McKenna Coll., Claremont, CA, USA, 1978–.
Past Posts Ass. Prof. Econ., Harvard Univ., 1967–70; Assoc. Prof. Econ., Cornell Univ., 1970–2; Dep. Ass. Secretary, Dir. Internat. Monetary Res., US Treasury, 1972–7.
Degrees BA William and March Coll., MA, 1964; PhD Univ. Virginia, 1967.
Editorial Duties Ed. Boards, *QJE*, 1968–76, *REStat*, 1968–76, *J Econ Bus*, 1970–8, *Pol. Analysis*, 1974–80; *SEJ*, 1976–9, *Internat. Stud. Q.*, 1980–; *Internat. Organisation*, 1981–; Co-ed., *Public Pol.*, 1969–72.
Principal Fields of Interest 310 Domestic Monetary and Financial Theory; 320 Public Economics; 400 International Economics.
Publications *Books:* 1. *A Strategy for US Balance of Payments Policy* (with G. Haberler), (AEI, 1968); 2. *The Oil Transfer Problem and International Economic Stability* (Internat. Fin. Section, Princeton Univ., 1975); 3. *The Economic Approach to Public Policy* (with R. Amacher and R. Tollison), (Cornell Univ. Press, 1976); 4. *The Theory of Optimum Currency Areas* (with E. Tower), (Internat. Fin. Section, Princeton Univ., 1976); 5. *Floating Exchange Rates and International Monetary Reform* (AEI, 1977); 6. *Challenges to a Liberal International Economic Order* (with R. Amacher and G. Haberler), (AEI, 1979); 7. *International Liquidity Issues* (AEI, 1980); 8. *The International Monetary System* (with J. Dreyer and G. Haberler), (AEI, 1982); 9. *Reaganomics* (with C. Stubblebine), (Inst. for Contemporary Stud., 1983).
Articles: 1. 'International specie flows and American monetary stability, 1834–1860', *JEH*, 28(1), March 1968; 2. 'Interest rate policy and external balance' (with F. Forte), *QJE*, 83(2), May 1969; 3. 'Reserve asset preference and the confidence problem in the crisis zone' (with L. H. Officer), *QJE*, 83(4), Nov. 1969; 4. 'On equalizing the distribution of political income' (with D. Mueller and R. Tollison), *JPE*, 82, March–April 1974; 5. 'Market failure, the common pool problem, and ocean

resource exploitation' (with R. Sweeney and R. Tollison), *J Law E*, 17(1), April 1974; 6. 'A note on the relation between the rate and variability of inflation' (with D. E. Logue), *Ec*, N.S. 43, May 1976; 7. 'An economic theory of mutually advantageous issue linkages' (with R. Tollison), *Internat. Organization*, 33, Autumn 1979; 8. 'Presidential politics, budget deficits and monetary policy in the United States, 1960–76' (with L. Laney), *Public Choice*, 40(1), 1983; 9. 'The vicious circle debate' (with M. Wolf), *Kyk*, 36(2), 1983; 10. 'US monetary policy and world liquidity', *AER*, 73(2), May 1983.

Principal Contributions International monetary problems: especially the stability and reform of the international monetary system and analysis of flexible exchange rates; applied public choice analysis of various political institutions; analysis of the causes and effects of inflation; and application of public choice theory to the analysis of macroeconomic policy and international economic relations.

WILLGERODT, Hans

Born 1924, Hildesheim, Germany.
Current Post Dir., Wirschaftspolitisches Seminar, Univ. Cologne, W. Germany, 1963–.
Past Posts Prof., Dir., Inst. Wirtschaftspolitik, Univ. Cologne, 1963, 1970.
Degrees Diplom-Volkswirt, Doctorate, Habilitation, Privatdozent Univ. Bonn, 1950, 1954, 1959.
Offices and Honours Member, Mont Pelerin Soc., Deutsche Gesellschaft für auswärtige Politik, List-Gesellschaft, Gesellschaft für Wirtschafts- und Sozialwissenschaften (Verein für Sozialpolitik); Ludwig Erhard-Stiftung, Arbeitsgemeinschaft deutscher wirtschaftswissenschäftlischer Forschungs Inst.
Editorial Duties Ed. Boards, *ORDO-Yearbook*, *Zeitschrift für Wirtschaftspolitik*.
Principal Fields of Interest 420 Trade Relations; 430 Balance of Payments; 713 Agricultural Policy.
Publications *Books*: 1. *Handelsschranken im Dienste der Währungs-*

politik (Helmut Küpper, 1962); 2. *Vermögen für Alle* (with A. Bomsch, *et al.*), (Econ. Verlag, 1971); 3. *Wege und Irrwege zur europäischen Währungsunion* (Rombach, 1972); 4. *Der 'gemeinsame Agrarmarkt der EWG'* (J. C. B. Mohr, Paul Siebeck, 1974); 5. *Die Krisenempfindlichkeit des internationalen Währungssystems* (with K. Bartel and U. Schillert), (Duncker & Humbolt, 1981).
Articles: 1. 'Sectoral integration: agriculture, transport, energy and selected industries', in *Economic Integration Worldwide, Regional Sectoral*, ed. F. Machlup (Macmillan, 1976); 2. 'Planning in West Germany: the social market economy', in *The Politics of Planning, A Review and Critique of Centralized Economic Planning* (Inst. Contemporary Stud., 1976); 3. 'Von der Macht des Kapitals — Mythen und Wirklichkeit', *Sozioökonomische Forschungen*, 8, 1976; 4. 'Die motivierte Zahlungsbilanztheorie — vom "schicksalhaften Zahlungsbilanzdefizit" und der unsterblichkeit falscher Inflationslehren', in *Internationale Wirtschaftsordnung*, eds. H. Gröner and A. Schüller (G. Fischer, 1978); 5. 'Stabilitätsförderung durch marktwirtschaftliche Ordnungspolitik — Notwendigkeit und Grenzen', in *Probleme der Wirtschaftspolitik*, ed. E. Teichmann (G. Fischer, 1978); 6. 'Wirtschaftsordnung und Staatsverwaltung', *ORDO*, 3, 1979; 7. 'Economic order and public administration', in *Standard Texts on the Social Market Economy*, eds. W. Stützel, *et al.* (Stuttgart, New York, 1982); 8. 'Die Agrarpolitik der europäischen Gemeinschaft in der Krise', *ORDO*, 34, 1983.

Principal Contributions Problems created when using trade barriers as a means of balance-of-payments policy. International monetary order: early analysis and prediction of the economic and politial difficulties of a monetary union of the EEC; proof that convertibility and flexible exchange rates reduce the alleged danger of petro-dollars and political fund transfers. New international economic order: criticism of the Corea-Plan and the report of the North-South Commission; in contrast a liberal economic order is advocated. Proposition of a supply-side policy to fight stag-flation and rejection of Keynesian instruments; recommendation to foster private property as a basic element of a sound economic and political order. Critical analysis of the European agriculture policy.

WILLIAMS, Alan

Born 1927, Birmingham,England.
Current Post Prof. Econ., Univ. York, 1972–.
Past Posts Lect. Econ., Univ. Exeter, 1954–63; Vis. Lect., Woodrow Wilson School, Princeton Univ., 1963–4; Dir. Econ. Stud., UK Treasury Centre Admin. Stud., London, 1966–8.
Degrees BCom Univ. Birmingham, 1951; Hon. DPhil Univ. Lund, 1977.
Offices and Honours Member, UK Nat. Water Council; Member, UK SSRC Health and Health Services Panel; Founder-member, UK SSRC Health Economists Study Group; Member, UK Royal Comm. NHS, UK Dept. Health Social Security Chief Scientist's Res. Comm., UK SSRC Social Science Law Comm., Yorkshire Water Authority, Council Chartered Inst. Public Fin. Accountancy.
Principal Fields of Interest 913 Economics of Health.
Publications *Books:* 1. *Public Finance and Budgeting Policy* (A&U, 1962); 2. *Output Budgeting and the Contribution of Microeconomics to Efficiency in Government* (HMSO, 1967); 3. *Current Issues in Cost-Benefit Analysis* (with H.G. Walsh), (HMSO, 1969); 4. *Efficiency in the Social Services* (with R. Anderson), (Blackwell, Martin Robertson, 1975); 5. *The Principles of Practical Cost Benefit Analysis* (with R. Sugden), (OUP, 1978).
Articles: 1. 'The optimal provision of public goods in a system of local government', *JPE*, 74, Feb. 1966; 2. 'Cost-benefit analysis: bastard science? and/or insidious poison in the body politic', *J Pub E*, 1(2), Aug. 1972; 3. 'Measuring the effectiveness of health care systems', *British J. Preventive Social Medicine*, 28, Aug. 1974; 4. 'Health service planning', in *Studies in Modern Economic Analysis*, eds. M.J. Artis

and A.R. Nobay (Blackwell, 1977); 5. 'Welfare economics and health status measurement', in *Health, Economics and Health Economics*, eds. M. Perlman and J. van der Graag (N-H, 1981).
Principal Contributions Early work concentrated on the welfare economies of multi-level government but later emphasis shifted to the expenditure side of the budget, and specifically to the problem of economic appraisal of public expenditure, especially in the broad area of social services. Recent work directed at finding theoretically correct, yet operationally feasible ways of valuing the benefits of public services, which do not rely on willingness or ability to pay but on some explicit egalitarian principle other than similar preferences; concentrating on the problems facing the NHS.

WILLIAMS, Anne Douglas

Born 1943, Montreal, Quebec, Canada.
Current Post Assoc. Prof. Econ., Bates Coll., Lewiston, ME, USA, 1981–.
Past Posts Ass. Prof. Econ., Univ. Penn., 1975–81; Res. Dir., US House Representatives, Select Comm. Pop., 1977–8.
Degrees BA Smith Coll., MA, 1965; MA, PhD Univ. Chicago, 1972, 1976.
Offices and Honours Chair, Dorothy S. Thomas Award Comm. Pop. Assoc. Amer., 1980–1; Member, Nat. Res. Council Comm. Pop., 1983–.
Principal Fields of Interest 840 Demographic Economics.
Publications *Books:* 1. *Effects of Economic Development on Fertility* (G.E. Tempo, 1974); 2. *Domestic Consequences of United States Population Change* (with L.G. Martin, L.F. Bouvier and M.C. Parks), (US Govt. Printing Office, 1978); 3. *Consequences of Changing US Population*, 3 vols, co-ed. (with L.G. Martin, L.F. Bouvier and M.C. Parks), (US Govt. Printing Office, 1978).
Articles: 1. 'Bayesian analysis of the Federal Reserve-MIT-Penn model's Almon lag consumption function' (with A. Zellner), *Em*, 1(3), Oct. 1973, repr.

in *Bayesian Analysis in Econometrics and Statistics*, ed. A. Zellner (N-H, 1980); 2. 'Determinants of fertility in developing countries: review and evaluation of the literature', in *Population Public Policy and Economic Development*, ed. M.C. Keeley (Praeger, 1976); 3. 'Measuring the impact of child mortality on fertility', *Demography*, 14(4), Nov. 1977; 4. 'Comments on Ben Porath "Child mortality and fertility"', in *Population and Economic Change in Developing Countries*, ed. R.A. Easterlin (Univ. Chicago Press, 1980).

Principal Contributions Measurement of the determinants of fertility in the US. Emphasis on the effects of child mortality on fertility, and statistical biasses of these measures, with the finding of nonlinear responses. Analysis of the relative income hypothesis using cross-sectional data of twins, confirming the importance of female labour force participation.

WILLIAMSON, Jeffrey Gale

Born 1935, New Haven, CT, USA.
Current Post Laird Bell Prof., Harvard Univ., Cambridge, MA, 1984–.
Past Posts Ass. Prof., Vanderbilt Univ., TN, 1961–3; Ass. Prof., Assoc. Prof., Prof., Univ. Wisconsin, 1963–4; 1964–8, 1968–83; Vis. Prof., Prof., Univ. Harvard, 1972, 1983; Vis. Prof., Univ. Philippines, 1967–8, Stanford Univ., 1976–7, Camb. Univ., 1978; Res. Cons., World Bank, 1981–2.
Degrees BA (Maths.) Wesleyan Univ., CT, 1957; MA, PhD Stanford Univ., 1959, 1961; Hon. MA Harvard Univ., 1983.
Offices and Honours Vice Pres., EHA, 1982–3; Guggenheim Foundation Fellow, 1976–7; Cole Prize, 1971.
Editorial Duties Ed. Boards, *Explor. Econ. Hist.*, 1965–9, 1973–4, 1977–85, *EDCC*, 1969–, *REStat*, 1972–, *JEH*, 1983–; Co-ed., Assoc. Ed., *Explor. Econ. Hist.*, 1969–73, 1974–7.
Principal Fields of Interest 040 Economic History; 100 Economic Development.
Publications *Books:* 1. *American Growth and the Balance of Payments, 1920–31* (Univ. N. Carolina Press,

1964); 2. *Dualistic Economic Development: Theory and History* (with A.C. Kelley and R.J. Cheetham), (Chicago Univ. Press, 1972); 3. *Lessons from Japanese Development: An Analytical Economic History* (with A.C. Kelley), (Chicago Univ. Press, 1974); 4. *Late Nineteenth-Century American Development: A General Equilibrium History* (CUP, 1974); 5. *American Inequality: A Macroeconomic History* (with P.H. Lindert), (Academic Press, 1980); 6. *What Drives Third World City Growth?* (with A.C. Kelley), (Princeton Univ. Press, 1984); 7. *Did British Capitalism Breed Inequality?* (A&U, 1984).

Articles: 1. 'Regional inequality and the process of national development: a description of the patterns', *EDCC*, 13(4), pt. 2, Suppl., July 1965, repr. in *Regional Analysis*, ed. L. Needleman (Penguin, 1968); 2. 'Capital accumulation, labor saving and labor absorption once more', *QJE*, 85(1), Feb. 1971; 3. 'Writing history backwards: Meiji Japan revisited' (with A.C. Kelley), *JEH*, 31(4), Dec. 1971; 4. 'Watersheds and turning points: conjectures on the long term impact of civil war financing', *JEH*, 34(3), Sept. 1974; 5. 'The sources of American inequality, 1896–1948', *REStat*, 58(4), Nov. 1976; 6. 'Savings, accumulation and modern economic growth: the contemporary relevance of Japanese history' (with L. DeBever), *J. Japanese Stud.*, 4, Fall 1977; 7. 'Inequality, accumulation and technological imbalance: a growth-equity conflict in American history?', *EDCC*, 27(2), Jan. 1979; 8. 'The limits to urban growth: suggestions for macromodelling third world economies' (with A.C. Kelley), *EDCC*, 30(3), April 1982; 9. 'Was the industrial revolution worth it? Disamenities and deaths in 19th-century British towns', *Explor. Econ. Hist.*, 19(3), July 1982; 10. 'English workers' living standards during the industrial revolution: a new look' (with P.H. Lindert), *EHR*, Second Series, 36(1), Feb. 1983.

Principal Contributions My contributions to economic development in the Third World have been mainly in the general equilibrium analysis of multi-sectoral dualistic models, the operation of labour markets, the determinants of inequality, and the accumulation process. These interests have recently culminated in my collaborative work with Allen Kelley on Third-World city growth problems. My contributions to economic history departed from conventional empirical analysis in about 1971. Since that time I have devoted almost all of my efforts to the application of applied general equilibrium models to industrial revolution experience in Japan, America and Britain. It is in this area that my cliometric contributions have been most significant. Almost all of my work has dealt with the quantitative documentation and understanding of economic growth from low income levels. Recently, however, my interests have shifted to problems of inequality and demographic change, especially those which centre on urban growth.

WILLIAMSON, John Harold

Born 1937, Hereford, England.
Current Post Sr. Fellow, Inst. Internat. Econ., Washington, DC, 1981–.
Past Posts Lect., Univ. York, England, 1963–8; Vis. Ass. Prof., MIT, 1967; Adviser, HM Treasury, 1968–70; Prof., Univ. Warwick, 1970–7; Adviser, IMF, 1972–4; Prof., Public Univ., Rio de Janeiro, 1977–81; Vis. Prof., MIT, 1980.
Degrees BSc LSE, 1958; PhD Univ. Princeton, 1963.
Offices and Honours Council, RES, 1976–7.
Editorial Duties Ed. Board, *REStud*, 1965–72; Ass. Ed., *EJ*, 1976; Book Rev. Ed., *J Int E*, 1977–83.
Principal Fields of Interest 432 International Monetary Arrangements; 431 Balance of Payments; 441 International Investment.
Publications *Books:* 1. *The Crawling Peg* (Princeton Univ. Press, 1965); 2. *The Failure of World Monetary Reform, 1971–74* (Nelson, 1977); 3. *The Financing Procedures of British Foreign Trade* (with S. Carse and G.E. Wood), (CUP, 1980); 4. *Exchange Rate Rules*, ed. (Macmillan, 1981); 5. *The Lending Policies of the IMF* (Inst. Internat. Econ., 1982); 6. *IMF Conditionally*, ed. (Inst. Internat. Econ.,

1982); 7. *The Open Economy and the World Economy* (Basic Books, Harper & Row, 1983); 8. *The Exchange Rate System* (Inst. Internat. Econ., 1983); 9. *A New SDR Allocation?* (Inst. Internat. Econ., 1984).
Articles: 1. 'Liquidity and the multiple key currency proposal', *AER*, 53(3), June 1983; 2. 'Profit, growth and sales maximinization', *Ec*, N.S. 33, Feb. 1966; 3. 'On the normative theory of balance of payments adjustment', in *Monetary Theory and Monetary Policy in the 1970s*, eds. G. Clayton, J.C. Gilbert and R. Sedgwick (OUP, 1971); 4. 'The impact of customs unions on trade in manufactures' (with A.T. Bottrill), *OEP*, 23(3), Nov. 1971; 5. 'Another case of profitable destabilizing speculation', *J Int E*, 3(1), Feb. 1973; 6. 'International liquidity — a survey', *EJ*, 83, Sept. 1973; 7. 'Payments objectives and economic welfare', *IMF Staff Papers*, 20(3), Nov. 1973; 8. 'The international financial system', in *Higher Oil Prices and the World Economy* (Brookings Inst., 1975).
Principal Contributions Initial work concerned the theory of the firm and macroeconomic theory as well as international monetary economics, and is doubtless best remembered for having coined the term 'crawling peg'. My spell in government concentrated my mind on applied issues, primarily in international economics, notably reform of the international monetary system. Appraisal of the post-Bretton Woods nonsystem, and how to improve it, has remained a central preoccupation. Living in Latin America sparked an interest in the design of stabilisation/ adjustment programmes, and in monitoring the role of the IMF as guardian of the adjustment process.

WILLIAMSON, Oliver Eaton

Born 1932, Superior, WI, USA.
Current Post Gordon B. Tweedy Prof. Econ., Law and Organisation, Univ. Penn., Philadelphia, PA, 1976–.
Past Posts Ass. Prof. Econ., Univ. Cal. Berkeley, 1963–5; Assoc. Prof. Econ., Univ. Penn., 1965–76; Special Econ. Ass., Antitrust Div., US Dept.

Justice, 1966–7; Vis. Prof., Univ. Warwick, 1973; Disting. Vis. Prof., Univ. Kyoto, Japan, 1983.

Degrees BS MIT, 1955; MBA Stanford Univ., 1960; PhD Carnegie-Mellon Univ., 1963.

Offices and Honours Fellow, Em Soc, 1977; Fellow AAAS, 1983.

Editorial Duties Co-ed., *J. Law, Econ. and Organization.*

Principal Fields of Interest 010 General Economics; 510 Administration; 610 Industrial Organisation.

Publications *Books:* 1. *The Economics of Discretionary Behavior* (Prentice-Hall, 1964); 2. *Corporate Control and Business Behavior* (Prentice-Hall, 1970); 3. *Markets and Hierarchies* (Free Press, 1975); 4. *The Economic Institutions of Capitalism* (Free Press, 1985); 5. *Economic Organization* (Wheatsheaf Books, 1986).

Articles: 1. 'Managerial discretion and business behavior', *AER*, 53(5), Dec. 1983; 2. 'Hierarchical control and optimum firm size', *JPE*, 76, April 1967; 3. 'Economies as an antitrust defense', *AER*, 58(1), March 1968; 4. 'The vertical integration of production', *AER*, 61(1), May 1971; 5. 'Understanding the employment relation' (with M. Wachter and J. Harris), *Bell JE*, 6, Spring 1975; 6. 'Franchise bidding for natural monpolies', *Bell JE*, 7, Spring 1976; 7. 'Transaction cost economics', *J Law E*, 22, Oct. 1979; 8. 'The modern corporation', *JEL*, 19(4), Dec. 1981; 9. 'Credible commitments: using hostages to support exchange', *AER*, 73(4), Sept. 1983.

Principal Contributions I became an economist with interdisciplinary interests because, in the convoluted course of events, that was the natural thing to do. Being a PhD student at Carnegie-Mellon in the early 1960s was an exciting experience. The study of economic organisation — within and between markets and hierarchies, to include both standard and nonstandard forms of contracting — became an obsession thereafter. The four key academic figures in my research on problems of economic organisation were Kenneth Arrow, Alfred D. Chandler, Jr., Ronald Coase, and Herbert Simon. Although I had only two (Arrow and Simon) in

the classroom, I regard Chandler and Coase as my teachers nonetheless. From Arrow I learned about the importance of information and not to shoe-horn difficult problems into orthodox boxes. Chandler taught me that organisational innovation was an important and neglected phenomenon that had pervasive ramifications for understanding American industry. Coase taught me that transaction costs were central to the study of economic organisation and that such studies should be performed in a comparative institutional manner. And Simon taught me that behavioural assumptions were important and not to be intimidated by disciplinary boundaries. It has given me statisfaction to have been a participant in helping to shape the 'new institutional economics' during the past 20 years and to see research contributions reflected in public policy reforms — especially in the area of antitrust. Not only do the revised 'merger guidelines' reflect the importance of economies as an antitrust defence, but the concept of the firm as a governance structure (rather than as a production function) has taken a secure hold.

WILLIG, Robert D.

Born 1947, New York City, NY, USA.

Current Post Prof. Econ. and Public Affairs, Princeton Univ., Princeton, NY, USA, 1978–.

Past Posts Lect., Stanford Univ., 1971–3; Technical Staff, Supervisor, Econ. Res. Dept., Bell Labs., 1973–7, 1977–8; Inst. Math. Stud. Social Sciences, Stanford Univ., 1975; Vis. Fellow, Univ. Warwick, 1977; Lect., Princeton Univ., 1977–8.

Degrees BA (Maths.) Harvard Univ., 1967; MS (Operations Res.), PhD Stanford Univ., 1968, 1973.

Offices and Honours Fellow, Em Soc, 1981–; Member, Organizing Comm. Telecommunications Pol Res. Conf., 1977–8; Aspen Task Force Future of Postal Service, 1978–80; AEI Res. Advisory Comm., 1980–; AEA Nominating Comm., 1980–1.

Editorial Duties Ed. Board, *Series on*

Govt. Regulation Econ. Activity (MIT Press, 1979–), *AER*, 1980–3.

Principal Fields of Interest 022 Microeconomic Theory; 024 Welfare Theory; 610 Industrial Organisation and Public Policy.

Publications *Books:* 1. *Contestable Markets and the Theory of Industry Structure* (with W. J. Baumol and J. C. Panzar), (Harcourt Brace Jovanovich, 1982); 2. *Welfare Analysis of Policies Affecting Prices and Products* (Garland Press, 1980).

Articles: 1. 'Consumer's surplus without apology', *AER*, 66(4), Sept. 1976; 2. 'Free entry and the sustainability of natural monopoly' (with J. Panzar), *Bell JE*, 8(1), Spring 1977; 3. 'Pareto superior nonlinear outlay schedules', *Bell JE*, 9(1), Spring 1978; 4. 'Incremental consumer's surplus and hedonic price adjustment', *JET*, 17(2), April 1978; 5. 'Multiproduct technology and market structure', *AER*, 69(2), May 1979; 6. 'Industry performance gradient indexes' (with R. Dansby), *AER*, 69(3), June 1979; 7. 'What can markets control?', in *Perspective on Postal Service Issues*, ed. R. Sherman (AEI, 1980); 8. 'Social welfare dominance', *AER*, 71(2), May 1981; 9. 'An economic definition of predation: pricing and product innovation' (with J. Ordover), *Yale Law J.*, 90, Dec. 1981; 10. 'Sector differentiated capital taxation with imperfect competition and inter-industry flows', *J Pub E*, 21(2), July 1983.

Principal Contributions From the outset, my work has focussed on welfare theory, on industrial organisation, and on their combination. As first inspired by the example of my PhD mentor, James Rosse, my interest in industrial organisation has been motivated by the rich set of policy issues concerning the relationship between government and business, and the public interest performance of the private and quasi-private sectors. One necessity for the analysis of such issues is a welfare economics that is at once rigorously based on understandable values and amenable to practical application. My work on welfare theory has been motivated by this need, and I have been pleased to obtain useful results on consumer's surplus, the welfare evaluation of changes in product variety and quality, social welfare dominance methods, and techniques for assessing the welfare impact of changes in prices of intermediate goods in complex economies.

My work on public utilities was motivated by the question of whether optimal pricing is consistent with open entry in natural monopoly markets, and whether potential entry can enforce socially desirable behaviour. Contestability theory was the natural generalisation of this line of research to other market structures. Contestability has turned out to be an extremely rich area for research, as well as an extremely controversial one. Fortunately, the steam now seems to be abating, and careful empirical and theoretical evaluations as well as valuable extensions, are replacing heated rhetoric. It has been gratifying to participate in applications of state-of-the-art work to reforms in the practice of regulatory and antitrust policy. Pressing policy issues have been a powerful stimulus to research, while industrial organisation theory is proving, in some significant areas, to be an effective guide to policy formulation.

WILLIS, Robert J.

Born 1940, Great Falls, MT, USA.

Current Post Prof. Econ., State Univ. NY Stony Brook, Res. Assoc., Econ. Res. Center, Assoc. Dir., Pop. Res., Nat. Opinion Res. Center, Chicago, IL, USA, 1978–.

Past Posts Lect., Ass. Prof., Wesleyan Univ., CT, 1966–71; Ass. Prof., Assoc. Prof., Grad. Center, City Univ. NY, 1971–4; Res. Fellow, NBER, 1971; Vis. Assoc. Prof., Assoc. Prof., Vis. Prof., Stanford Univ., 1974–5, 1975–8, 1982–3; Vis. Prof., UCLA, 1977–8; Nat. Fellow, Hoover Inst., 1982–3.

Degrees BA Dartmouth Coll., MA, 1962; MA, PhD Univ. Washington, Seattle, 1965, 1971.

Offices and Honours Ford Foundation Dissertation Fellow; Res. Fellow, NBER, 1970–1; Member, Internat. Union Scientific Study Pop., 1980–;

Member, Pop. and Social Sciences Study Section, Nat. Inst. Child Health and Human Devlp., Nat. Inst. Health, 1978–82; Member, Panel Determinants Fertility Behavior Developing Countries, NAS, 1978–82.

Editorial Duties Ed. Board, *J Labor Econ.*, 1982–.

Principal Fields of Interest 840 Demographic Economics; 823 Labour Mobility.

Publications *Articles:* 1. 'A new approach to the economic theory of fertility behavior', *JPE*, Suppl., March–April 1973, repr. in *Economics of the Family: Marriage, Children and Human Capital*, ed. T.W. Schultz (Univ. Chicago Press, 1974); 2. 'Contraception and fertility: household production under uncertainty' (with R.T. Michael), in *Household Production and Consumption*, ed. N.E. Terleckyj (Columbia Univ. Press, 1975); 3. 'Estimation of a stochastic model of reproduction' (with J.J. Heckman), in *Household Production and Consumption, op. cit.*; 4. 'A beta-logistic model for the analysis of sequential labor force participation by married women' (with J.J. Heckman), *JPE*, 85(1), Feb. 1977; 5. 'Dynamic aspects of earnings mobility' (with L.A. Lillard), *Em*, 46(5), Sept. 1978; 6. 'Education and self-selection' (with S. Rosen), *JPE*, Suppl., 87(5), Oct. 1979, repr. in *Evaluation Studies Review Annual*, eds. E.W. Stromsdorfer and G. Farkas (Sage Publ., 1980); 7. 'On managerial rewards and self-selection; risk-taking in public enterprises' (with E. James and E. Neuberger), *J Comp E*, 3(4), Dec. 1979; 8. 'The old age security hypothesis and population growth', in *Demographic Behavior: Interdisciplinary Perspectives*, ed. T.K. Burch (Westview Press, 1980); 9. 'The direction of intergenerational transfers and demographic transition: the Caldwell hypothesis reexamined', *Pop. and Devlp. Rev.*, 8, Suppl., 1982.

Principal Contributions Beginning with my PhD thesis, the focus of much of my research has been on the determinants and consequences of population growth. Initially, the emphasis was on microeconomic models of family behaviour, including determinants of the number and quality of children and the use and efficacy of fertility control. In the last five years, I have been attempting to build a theory of demographic transition which links micro- and macro-level economic demographic interactions within the framework of the overlapping generations model. This emphasises the role of intergenerational transfers within families and the effects of population growth on the equilibrium interest rate and rates of accumulation of human and physical capital. Lately I have also been doing theoretical research on a 'contractual view' of the family and its implications for divorce settlements and child support. I am just now beginning a major data collection effort which will allow empirical investigation of issues concerning marriage and divorce and also issues concerning intergenerational transfers within families in the US. Another line of research involves the application of econometric methods to problems of labour supply and human capital using longitudinal data. This work includes studies of sequential labour force participation by married women, the dynamics of earnings and transitions into and out of poverty, and the role of unmeasured ability factors in determining schooling choice and subsequent life-cycle earnings.

WILSON, James*

Dates and Birthplace 1805–60, Hawick, Scotland.

Posts Held Businessman, 1821–44; Proprietor, Chief writer, *The Economist*, 1843–60.

Offices and Honours MP, 1847–59; Fin. Secretary, UK Treasury, 1853–8; Fin. member, Council of India, 1859–60.

Publications *Books:* 1. *Influences of the Corn Laws* (1839); 2. *Fluctuations of Currency, Commerce and Manufactures* (1840); 3. *The Revenue, or What Shall the Chancellor Do?* (1841); 4. *Capital, Currency and Banking* (1847).

Career Businessman whose acute comments on current issues were first made public in pamphlet form and then through *The Economist*. In parliament he spoke effectively on economic issues and was a highly regarded financial minister. In India he began a reform of the taxation system and introduced a paper currency. His economic ideas were the conventional orthodoxy of the day — anti-Corn Law, pro-free trade, and in favour of a sound, convertible currency. His 1840 work, *Fluctuations* ..., is regarded as one of the first systematic accounts of the phenomenon of business cycles.

WILSON, Robert Butler

Born 1937, Geneva, NB, USA.
Current Post McBean Prof. Decision Sciences, Grad. School Bus., Stanford Univ., Stanford, CA, USA, 1971–.
Past Posts Ass. Prof., Univ. Cal. Berkeley, 1963–4; Ass. Prof., Assoc., Prof., Stanford Univ., 1964–71.
Degrees BA (Maths.), MBA, DBA Harvard Univ., 1959, 1961, 1963.
Offices and Honours Fellow, Em Soc, 1976, AAAS, 1981; Ford Foundation Fellow, 1967–8; Fellow, Centre Advanced Study Behavioral Sciences, Stanford, 1977–8; Guggenheim Foundation Fellow, 1982–3.
Editorial Duties Assoc. Ed., *Em*, 1979–; Member, *Econ. Panel NSF*, 1980–2.
Principal Fields of Interest 020 General Economic Theory; 213 Mathematical Methods and Models; 510 Administration.
Publications *Articles:* 1. 'Theory of syndicates', *Em*, 36(1), Jan. 1968; 2. 'Computing equilibria of n-person games', *SIAM J. Appl. Maths.*, 21(1), July 1971; 3. 'On the theory of aggregation', *JET*, 10(1), Feb. 1975; 4. 'A bidding model of "perfect" competition', *REStud*, 4(3), Oct. 1977; 5. 'The bilinear complementarity problem and competitive equilibria of piecewiselinear economic models', *Em*, 46(2), Jan. 1978; 6. 'Competitive exchange', *Em*, 46(3), May 1978; 7. 'Information, efficiency, and the core of an economy', *Em*, 46(4), July 1978; 8. 'Sequential equilibria' (with D. Kreps), *Em*, 50(4), July 1982; 9. 'Reputation and imperfect information' (with D. Kreps), *JET*, 27(2), Aug. 1982; 10. 'Capacity

pricing' (with S. Oren and S. Smith), *Em*, 53, forthcoming, 1985.
Principal Contributions I think it is possible to reconstruct economic theory from a foundation in game theory, and indeed many contributors are advancing the task. The methodology has improved (though much remains) and it enables inclusion of realistic features: strategic behaviour, informational disparities, timing and dynamics. Capturing the effects of incentives on efficiency is primary, both in trading processes (bargaining, auctions, bid-ask markets, etc.) and in contracting and the organisation of firms. Pricing strategy is also a candidate, especially discriminatory practices and public-utility pricing where selfselection is important, but also competitive battles (price wars, entry and exit). The fine structure of markets is poorly modelled, in my view, and the theory barely conveys the richness of practice; this would be fine if theory captured the main features but actually it misses essentials. The challenge is more often the right formulation than the analysis. A genuine welfare economics awaits a better understanding of product and factor (especially labour) markets. The reliance of game theory on assumed common knowledge and perfect 'rationality' is an analytical strength and a practical deficiency. The robustness of this approach depends mainly on showing that simple strategies suffice for the important economic institutions.

Practical studies of management, and especially investment and pricing, are my best source of theoretical topics; I continue to be amazed at the estrangement of so much economic theory, and many economists, from current practice in the field they study. I intend to return to social choice theory and political science with the tools of game theory. I see social science as modern philosophy with a realistic bent, and think it can make a difference by explicating classical conundrums; e.g., an analysis of a bargaining game sheds more light than any axiomisation. I retain an interest in risk-sharing, public enterprises, and even markets, that achieve co-operatively efficient outcomes with economies of numbers, scale, or information; public utility investments and pricing need considerable work. My early interest in computational topics waned as micro-seconds became cheaper. Working with doctoral students is a great pleasure.

WILSON, Thomas

Born 1916, Belfast, Northern Ireland.
Current Post Emeritus Prof. Polit. Econ., Univ. Glasgow, 1982–.
Past Posts UK Ministry Econ. Warfare, 1940–1; UK Ministry Aircraft Production, 1941–2; UK Prime Minister's Stat. Branch, UK War Cabinet Office, Econ. Section, 1942–5, 1945–6; Fellow, Univ. Coll. Oxford, 1946–58; Adam Smith Prof. Polit. Econ., Univ. Glasgow, 1958–82; Vis. Fellow, All Souls Coll. Oxford, 1974–5; Vis. Fellow, ANU Centre Res. Fed. Fin. Relations, Canberra, 1982.
Degrees BA Queen's Univ., Belfast, 1938; PhD London Univ., 1940; MA Oxford Univ., 1946; Hon. Dr Univ. Stirling, 1982.
Offices and Honours OBE; Fellow, BA, Royal Soc. Edinburgh; Hon. Fellow, LSE; Hon. Res. Fellow, Univ. Glasgow; Council, Pres., Scottish Econ. Soc., 1958–78, 1977–8; UK SSRC Econ. Comm., 1969–73; Exec. Comm., NIESR, 1971–9.
Editorial Duties General Ed., *OEP*, 1948–58; Ed. Board, *J Ind E*, 1960–80.
Principal Fields of Interest 023 Macroeconomics; 131 Economic Fluctuations.
Publications *Books:* 1. *Fluctuations in Income and Employment* (Pitman, 1947); 2. *Modern Capitalism and Economic Progress* (Macmillan, 1950); 3. *Oxford Studies in the Price Mechanism*, co-ed. (with P. W. S. Andrews), (OUP, 1951); 4. *Inflation* (Blackwell, Harvard Univ. Press, 1961); 5. *Planning and Growth* (Macmillan, 1964); 6. *Pensions, Inflation and Growth*, ed. (Heinemann, 1974); 7. *Essays on Adam Smith*, co-ed. (with A. S. Skinner), (OUP, 1975); 8. *The Market and the State*, co-ed. (with A. S. Skinner), (OUP, 1976); 9. *The Political Economy of the Welfare State* (with D. J. Wilson), (A&U,

1982); 10. *Monetarism, Keynesianism and the Market* (OUP, 1985).
Articles: 1. 'The economic outlook: some basic issues', *SJPE*, 26(1), Feb. 1979; 2. 'The price of oil: a case of negative marginal revenue', *J Ind E*, 27(4), June 1979; 3. 'Proverty and selectivity', in *Discussing the Welfare State* (Pol. Stud. Inst., 1980); 4. '1929–1933: could it happen again?', *Three Banks Rev.*, Dec. 1980; 5. 'Robertson, money and monetarism', *JEL*, 18(4), Dec. 1980; 6. 'Welfare economics and the welfare state', *Scand JE*, 83(1), 1981; 7. 'Issues of regional finance: fiscal transfers between regions and between members of the EC', *Proceedings of the Internat. Inst. of Public Fin.*, 1979 (Elsevier, 1981).
Principal Contributions Fluctuations in output and employment with particular reference to the USA and the UK (this was extended in an early study of inflation); exploration of the ground between Keynesianism and monetarism, leading to the revival of interest in Robertson's non-Walrasian monetarism; the relationship between difference branches of economics with an extension of work into price theory, regional economics, including fiscal federalism, and international monetary adjustments; the respective roles of the market and the State; the basis in welfare economies of policy recommendations, with welfare programmes in Britain and other countries as one field of application.

WINCH, Donald Norman

Born 1935, London, England.
Current Post Prof. Hist. Econ., Univ. Sussex, Brighton, England, 1969–.
Past Posts Vis. Lect., Univ. Cal. Berkeley, 1959–60; Lect., Univ. Edinburgh, 1960–3; Lect., Reader, Univ. Sussex, 1963–6, 1966–9; Vis. Prof., Rice Univ., TX, 1965; Vis. Fellow, Inst. Advanced Study, Princeton Univ., 1974–5, ANU, 1983; Vis. Prof., Tulane Univ., LO, 1984.
Degrees BSc Univ. London, 1956; PhD Princeton Univ., 1960.
Offices and Honours Publications

Secretary, RES, 1971–; Dean, School Social Sciences, Univ. Sussex, 1974.

Editorial Duties Book Rev. Ed., *EJ*, 1976–83; Ed. Board, *HOPE*, 1969–84.

Principal Fields of Interest 031 History of Economic Thought.

Publications *Books:* 1. *Classical Political Economy and Colonies* (LSE, Harvard Univ. Press, 1965; transl., Japanese, 1972); 2. *James Mill: Selective Economic Writings* (Oliver & Boyd, 1966); 3. *Economics and Policy: A Historical Study* (Hodder & Stoughton, 1969, 1972); 4. *The Economic Advisory Council, 1930–39: A Study in Economic Advice during Depression and Recovery* (with S. K. Howson), (CUP, 1976); 5. *Adam Smith's Politics: An Essay in Historiographic Revision* (CUP, 1978); 6. *That Nobel Science of Politics: A Study in Nineteenth-century Intellectual History* (with S. Collini and J. Burrow), (CUP, 1983).

Articles: 1. 'What price the history of economic thought?', *SJPE*, 9, Nov. 1962; 2. 'Classical economics and the case for colonization', *Ec*, N.S. 30, Nov. 1963; 3. 'The Keynesian revolution in Sweden', *JPE*, 74, April 1966; 4. 'Introduction', to J. S. Mill, *Principles of Political Economy*, ed. (Penguin, 1970); 5. 'The emergence of economics as a science', *Fontana Econ. Hist. of Europe*, 3 (Fontana, 1979); 6. 'Marginalism and the boundaries of economic science', in *The Marginal Revolution in Economics*, eds. R. D. C. Black, *et al.* (Duke Univ. Press, 1979); 7. 'Jacob Viner as intellectual historian', in *The Craft of the Historian of Economic Thought*, ed. W. J. Samuels (JAI Press, 1983); 8. 'Adam Smith's enduring particular result: a political and cosmopolitan perspective', in *Wealth and Virtue: The Shaping of Political Economy in the Scottish Englightenment* (CUP, 1983); 9. 'Science and the legislator: Adam Smith and after', *EJ*, 93, Sept. 1983.

Principal Contributions My main interest has always been concentrated on the history of economic thought, usually with particular reference to the relationship between theory and policy. Early work on the classical period was followed by studies of Keynesian ideas in twentieth-century Britain, the US,

and Sweden. In recent years my interests have returned to the classical period, beginning with work on Adam Smith's politics considered within its eighteenth-century context and followed by related work on the connections between political economy and the science of politics in Britain during the nineteenth century. My historiographic preferences favour non-teleological history, and I would now describe myself more as an intellectual historian concerned with economic, social and political ideas, than as a historian of economic thought, *tout court*.

WINSTON, Gordon Chester

Born 1929, San Francisco, CA, USA.

Current Post Prof. Econ., Williams Coll., MA, USA.

Past Posts Sr. Res. Adviser, Head of Project, Yale Univ. Pakistan Project, 1966–8, 1970–1; Member, Inst. Advanced Study, Princeton Univ., 1978–9; Vis. Scholar, Inst. Internat. Econ. Stud., Stockholm, 1979–80.

Degrees BA Swarthmore Coll., PA, 1956; MA, PhD Yale Univ., 1957, 1964.

Principal Fields of Interest 121 Economic Studies of Less Industrialised Countries; 820 Labour Markets.

Publications *Books:* 1. *Industrial Capacity and Employment Promotion: Case Studies of Sri Lanka, Nigeria, Morocco and Overall Survey of other Developing Countries* (with N. Phan Thuy, *et al.*), (Gower Publ., 1981); 2. *The Timing of Economic Activities: Firms, Households and Markets in Time-specific Analysis* (Gower, 1981).

Articles: 1. 'An international comparison of income and hours of work', *REStat*, 48, Feb. 1966; 2. 'Capital utilization in economic development', *EJ*, 81, March 1971; 3. 'Shift working, employment and economic development: a study of industrial workers in Pakistan' (with G. Farooq), *EDCC*, 26(2), Jan. 1978; 4. 'On measuring factor proportions in industries with different seasonal and shift patterns or, did the Leontief paradox ever exist?', *EJ*, 89, Dec. 1979; 5. 'Addiction and backsliding: a theory of compulsive consumption', *J Ec Behav*, 1(1), Dec. 1980.

Principal Contributions Development of a theory of optimal capital utilisation with its implications for capital productivity, growth, productive capacity, and the meaning and measurement of factor proportions; the analysis of efficient time-shaped production of perishable products; time-specific analysis of household work and consumption activities; a theory of time-shaped markets and peak loads; the theoretical and empirical (international cross-section) analysis of long-run aggregate labour supply based on household work-leisure choices; the integration of these into a time-specific theory that reveals the economic importance of the timing of processes within the analytical 'unit time' of orthodox analysis.

WINTER, Sidney Graham

Born 1935, Iowa City, IA, USA.
Current Post Prof. Econ. and Management, Yale Univ., New Haven, CT, USA, 1977–.
Past Posts Res. Econ., Rand Corp., 1959–61, 1966–8; Staff Member, US President's Council Econ. Advisers, Washington, DC, 1961–2; Acting Ass. Prof., Ass. Prof., Acting Assoc. Prof., Univ. Cal. Berkeley, 1963–6; Prof. Econ. Res. Assoc., Inst. Public Pol. Stud., Univ. Michigan, 1968–76; Vis. Prof. Econ., Yale Univ., 1976, Univ. Cal. Davis, 1983.
Degrees BA Swarthmore Coll., PA, 1956; MA, PhD Yale Univ., 1957, 1964.
Offices and Honours Fellow, Em Soc, 1968–.
Editorial Duties Assoc. Ed., *JET*, 1969–71, *Admin. Science Q.*, 1969–72, *Behavioral Science*, 1968–79; Founding Co-ed., *J Ec Behav*, 1980–.
Principal Fields of Interest 022 Microeconomic Theory; 611 Market Structure: Industrial Organisation and Corporate Strategy; 621 Technological Change; Innovation; Research and Development.
Publications *Books:* 1. *An Evolutionary Theory of Economic Change*

(with R. R. Nelson), (Harvard Univ. Press, 1982).

Articles: 1. 'Economic "natural selection" and the theory of the firm', *YEE*, 4, Spring 1964; 2. 'The norm at a closed technology and the straight-down-the-turnpike theorem', *REStud*, 34, Jan. 1967; 3. 'A single remark on the second optimality theorem of welfare economics', *JET*, 1, June 1969; 4. 'Optimal price policy under atomistic competition' (with E. S. Phelps), in *Microeconomic Foundations of Employment and Inflation Theory*, eds. E. S. Phelps, *et al.* (W. W. Norton, 1970); 5. 'Satisficing, selection and the innovating remnant', *QJE*, 85, May 1971; 6. 'Neoclassical vs. evolutionary theories of economic growth' (with R. R. Nelson), *EJ*, 84, Dec. 1974; 7. 'Optimization and evolution in the theory of the firm', in *Adaptive Economic Models*, eds. R. Day and T. Groves (Academic Press, 1975); 8. 'Forces generating and limiting concentration under Schumpeterian competition' (with R. R. Nelson), *Bell JE*, 9, Autumn 1978; 9. 'Attention allocation and input proportions', *J Ec Behav*, 2, March 1981; 10. 'An essay on the theory of production', in *Economics and the World Around It*, ed. S. Hymons (Univ. Michigan Press, 1982).

Principal Contributions As a graduate student, I set out to do a dissertation on the determinants of corporate spending on research and development. The quest for an appropriate theoretical framework for this sort of empirical inquiry led me to abandon that specific dissertation topic, but has contributed the dominant themes for much of my work. At an early stage I became convinced that the methodological doctrine of 'as if' profit maximisation, allegedly supported by the 'natural selection' argument, did not provide compelling reasons for rejecting direct behavioural evidence at the level of the individual firm. My work since then — much of it reported in *An Evolutionary Theory of Economic Change* (with R. R. Nelson) — has focussed on the development of an evolutionary economics of the firm and industry, a theoretical framework capable of accommodating behavioural evidence at the firm level, but also explicit about the long-run constraints that market systems impose on behaviour. The economics of technological change remains the primary arena of application of this framework. Recently, the problem of productive knowledge, particularly the question of what it means for a firm to 'know' something, has become an important subsidiary focus, along with the problem of understanding the 'life-cycle' dynamics of firm and industry evolution.

WISEMAN, Jack

Born 1919, Burnley, Lancashire, UK.

Current Post Prof. Econ., Univ. York, York, UK, 1982–.

Past Posts Ass. Lect., Lect., Sr. Lect., LSE, 1949–63; Dir. (part-time), London Office Inst. Science Econ. Appliquée, Paris, 1959–62; Vis. Prof. Econ., Univ. Cal. Berkeley, 1962–3; Prof. Econ., Dir., Inst. Social and Econ. Res., Univ. York, UK, 1964–82; Staff Cons., Canadian Royal Commission Taxation, 1964; Vis. Prof., George Mason Univ., Fairfax, VA, 1984; Vis. Scholar, Center Study Public Choice, George Mason Univ., 1985.

Degrees BSc, Univ. London, 1947.

Offices and Honours Silver Medal, Royal Society Arts, 1939; Vice-Pres., Pres., Hon. Pres., Internat. Inst. Public Fin, 1966–75; Adjunct Scholar, Adam Smith Inst.; Advisory Cons., Committee Fiscal Affairs, OECD, 1966–.

Editorial Duties Joint General Ed., *Univ. York Studies Econ.*, 1964–78; Ed. Boards, *Public Fin. Q., J Econ. Stud.*

Principal Fields of Interest 320 Domestic Fiscal Theory and Policy: Public Finance; 910 Welfare, Health and Education; 010 General Economics.

Publications *Books:* 1. *The Economics of Fisheries*, co-ed. (with R. Turvey), (Internat. Econ. Assoc., FAO, 1957); 2. *The Growth of Public Expenditure in the United Kingdom* (with A. T. Peacock), (Princeton Univ. Press, OUP, 1961, 1967); 3. *A Course in Applied Economics* (with G. H. Phelps Brown), (Pitman, 1964; transl., Spanish, Compania Bibliografica Espanola, 1966); 4. *Education for Democrats* (with A. T. Peacock), (INEA, 1963); 5. *Comparative Aspects of the Taxation of Business in the United Kingdom and Germany* (Anglo-German Foundation, 1979); 6. *Beyond Positive Economics*, ed. (Macmillan, 1983); 7. *Public Production*, co-ed. (with D. Bos and T. A. Musgrave), (Springer-Verlag, 1982); 8. *Public Sector and Political Economy Today*, co-ed. (with H. Hanusch and K. Roskamp), (Fischer-Verlag, 1985); 9. *A Comprehensive Classified Annotated Bibliography of Health Economics* (with C. A. Blades, A. J. Culyer and A. Walker), (Wheatsheaf, 1986).

Articles: 1. 'The raw cotton commission, 1948–1952' (with B. S. Yamey), *OEP*, Feb. 1956, repr. in *Markets, Market Control and Marketing Reform*, eds. P. T. Bauer and B. S. Yamey (Weidenfeld & Nicolson, 1968); 2. 'The theory of public utility price — an empty box', *OEP*, Feb. 1957, repr. in *LSE Essays on Cost*, eds. J. M. Buchanan and G. F. Thirlby (Weidenfeld & Nicolson, 1973), and in *Readings in Industrial Economics: Vol. 2, Private Enterprise and State Intervention*, ed. C. K. Rowley (Macmillan, 1972); 3. 'The economics of education' and 'The economics of education: a rejoinder', *SJPE*, 6, Feb. 1959, repr. in *Economics of Education, 2*, ed. M. Blaug (Penguin, 1969); 4. 'The logic of national debt policy', *Westminster Bank Review*, Aug. 1961, repr. in *Public Debt and Future Generations*, ed. J. M. Ferguson (Richard D. Irwin, 1964), and *Monetary Theory and Policy*, ed. R. A. Ward (Wiley, 1966); 5. 'Cost-benefit analysis in education', *SEJ*, July 1965, repr. in *Educational Investment in an Urban Society: Costs, Benefits and Public Policy*, eds. M. R. Levin and A. Shank (Teachers College Press, 1969) and in *Human Capital Formation and Manpower Development*, ed. R. A. Wykstra (Collier Macmillan, 1971); 6. 'The economics of disability policy' (with J. G. Cullis), in *Economic Policies and Social Goals: Aspects of Public Choice*, ed. A. J. Culyer (Martin Robertson, 1974); 7. 'The political economy of nationalised industry', in *The Economics of Politics* (INEA, 1978); 8. 'Costs and decisions', in *Contemporary Economic Analysis*, eds. D. A. Currie and W. Peters (Croom Helm, 1979); 9. 'Uncertainty, costs and collective economic planning', *Ec.*, May 1983, repr. in *LSE Essays on Cost*, eds. J. M. Buchanan and G. F. Thirlby (Weidenfeld & Nicolson, 1973); 10. 'Principles of public policy relevant to smoking' (with S. C. Littlechild), *Policy Studies*, Jan. 1984.

Principal Contributions Distrusts undue specialisation. Major interest has shifted from industrial economics to public finance/public sector studies/public choice with a continuing interest in social policy and economics of human resources. A permanent preoccupation has been with the inadequacy of economic theory in respect particularly of its assumptions about human behaviour and knowledge and the related treatment of uncertainty. This interest and contribution is reflected in the selection of publications. It has evolved from an early interest in cost theory, leading to rejection of objective-cost pricing rules, to a concern with the inadequacies of a positivist economics. While retaining a research and teaching interest in the listed special areas, the ongoing intellectual preoccupation is with the development and propagation of subjectivist ideas, and with the 'marriage' of subjectivism, mainstream positivism, and public choice. Major specific contributions have been to the study of public expenditures, public utility pricing and cost theory generally, economics of health and education. At the policy level, the propagation of understanding of the role and value of free markets and libertarian principles.

WITTE, Ann Dryden

Born 1942, Oceanside, NY, USA.
Current Post Prof. Econ., Univ. N. Carolina, Chapel Hill, NC, USA, 1983–.
Past Posts Econ. Analyst, Systems Analyst, US Govt., Washington, DC, 1963–6, 1966–7; Instr. Econ., Tougaloo Coll., MS, 1967–8; Instr. Econ., N. Carolina State Univ., 1970–2; Vis. Ass. Prof. Econ., Vis. Ass. Prof. Public Law and Govt., Univ. N. Carolina, 1972–3, 1973–4; Ass. Prof. Econ., Assoc. Prof. Econ., Univ. N. Carolina, 1974–9, 1979–83; Vis. Prof. Econ., Wellesley Coll., MA, 1984–5.

Degrees BA (Polit. Science and Hist.) Univ. Florida, 1963; MA Columbia Univ., 1965; PhD N. Carolina State Univ., 1971.

Offices and Honours Phi Beta Kappa; Woodrow Wilson Grad. Fellow; Adviser, N. Carolina Governor's Office, Criminal Justice Planning, 1977; Member, Special Comm., Correctional Programs NC Employment and Training Council, 1982; Chair, AEA Census Advisory Comm., 1981; Res. Scholar, Rockefeller Center, Bellagio, Italy, 1983.

Editorial Duties Ed. Board, *Rev. Regional Stud.*, 1976–9; Advisory Ed., *Evaluation Rev.*, 1982–3; Advisory Board, *Criminological Res. Advances in Quant. Method and Application*, 1983–.

Principal Fields of Interest 212 Construction, Analysis and Use of Econometric Models; 022 Microeconomic Theory; 900 Welfare Programmes, Consumer Economics, Urban and Regional Economics.

Publications *Books:* 1. *Work Release in North Carolina: The Program and the Process* (Inst. Govt., 1973); 2. *Work Release in North Carolina: An Evaluation of its Post Release Effects* (Inst. Res. Social Sciences, 1975); 3. *Basic Issues in Correction Performance* (with G. A. Grizzle, *et al.*), (US Dept. Justice, 1982); 4. *Beating the System: The Underground Economy* (with C. Simon), (Auburn House, 1982); 5. *An Economic Analysis of Crime and Justice: Theory, Methods and Applications* (with P. Schmidt), (Academic Press, 1984); 6. *Advances in Applied Macroeconomics, 3*, co-ed. (with V. K. Smith), (JAI Press, 1984).

Articles: 1. 'Alternative estimates of capital-labor substitution in Peru', *Em*, 39(6), Nov. 1971; 2. 'Employment in the manufacturing sector of developing economies', *J Dev Stud*, 10(1), Oct. 1973; 3. 'An analysis of recidivism, using the truncated lognormal distribution' (with P. Schmidt), *JRSS*, Series C, 26(3), 1977; 4. 'Vacant and urban land holdings: portfolio considerations and owner characteristics' (with J. E. Bachman), *SEJ*, 45(2), Oct. 1978; 5. 'An estimate of a structural hedonic price model of the housing market: an application of Rosen's theory of implicit markets' (with H. Sumka and H. Erekson), *Em*, 47(5), Sept. 1979; 6. 'Estimating the economic model of crime with individual data', *QJE*, 94(1), Feb. 1980; 7. 'Determinants of the costs of operating large scale prisons with implications for correctional standards' (with W. Trumbull), *Law and Soc. Rev.*, 16(1), 1981–2; 8. 'Increased costs of office building operation and construction: effects on the costs of office space and the equilibrium distribution of offices' (with H. Tauchen), *Land Econ.*, 59(3), Aug. 1983; 9. 'Socially optimal and equilibrium distributions of office activities: models with exogenous and endogenous contacts' (with H. Tauchen), *JUE*, 15(1), Jan. 1984; 10. 'The new law and economics: a critical review' (with H. Barreto and T. A. Husted), *Amer. Bar Foundation Res. J.*, Oct. 1984.

Principal Contributions Mine has been a highly diverse career. I began analysing the agricultural and labour situation in the USSR largely because I had learned Russian as an undergraduate and I was too broke to go on to graduate school. My employer decided that I would make a good economist and sent me to get a masters degree in economics. I returned from graduate school to become part of the newly established Planning, Programming and Budgeting System of the US Government. From the federal government, I went to teach at a small black college in Mississippi, Tougaloo College, during the height of the civil rights movement. After Martin Luther King was shot, the position of white faculty on black campuses became very difficult and I returned to graduate school to obtain the PhD. My dissertation work was devoted to a study of employment in Latin American countries. Latin America has been a continual interest of mine and somewhere along the way I have managed to learn both Portuguese and Spanish.

After the birth of a child, travel became difficult and I began to develop an interest in applying microeconomics and econometrics to a wide range of issues. One of the first domestic issues that I studied was the way in which jobs affected the behaviour of criminal offenders. I have continued and broadened my interest in law and economics and also studied real-estate markets and the location of businesses and households. At the present time I am studying domestic violence, tax compliance and office location. I feel that my principal contributions have been to stimulate students, creatively address important economic issues, and to work to improve policy at the State, local and national level.

WOLD, Herman

Born 1908, Skien, Norway.
Current Post Prof. Emeritus, Univ. Uppsala, Uppsala, Sweden, 1975–.
Past Posts Prof. Stats., Univ. Uppsala, 1942–70; Prof. Stats., Univ. Göteborg, 1970–5; Prof. Invité, Univ. Geneva, 1975–80.
Degrees Studentexamen Skara Coll., 1927; Fil. Kandidate, Fil. Licentiate, Fil. Dr Univ. Stockholm, 1930, 1933, 1938.
Offices and Honours Vice-Pres., Internat. Stat. Inst., 1957–61; Member, Royal Swedish Academy Science, 1961–; Pres., Em Soc, 1966; Hon. Dr Technical Univ. Liston, 1966; Member, Royal Swedish Academy Science Comm. Nobel Prize Econ., 1968–80; Hon. Member, AEA, 1979; Hon. Foreign Member, AAAS, 1979.
Principal Fields of Interest 211 Econometric and Statistical Methods.
Publications *Books:* 1. *A Study in the Analysis of Stationary Time Series* (Almqvist & Wiksell, 1938, 1954); 2. *Demand Analysis: A Study in Econometrics* (with L. Jureen), (Almqvist & Wiksell, 1952, Wiley, 1953); 3. *Fix-Point Estimation in Theory and Practice* (with R. Gergström), (Vandenhoeck & Ruprecht, 1983); 4. *Systems under Indirect Observation*, 1–2, co-ed. (with K. G. Jöreskog), (N-H, 1981); 5. *Evaluating School Systems using Partial Least*

Squares (with R. Noonan), (Pergamon, 1984).

Articles: 1. 'A synthesis of pure demand analysis, I–III', *Skandinavisk Aktuarietidskrift*, 26, 1943, 27, 1944; 2. 'Causal inference from observational data. A review of ends and means', *JRSS*, A, 119, 1956; 3. 'On the consistency of least squares regression', *Sankhyā*, A, 25(2), 1963; 4. 'Cycles', *Internat. Encyclopedia Stats.*, 2 (Free Press, 1978); 5. 'Models for knowledge', in *The Making of Statisticians*, ed. J. Gani (Springer, 1982).

Principal Contributions Stationary time series and stochastic processes: decomposition theorem; applications of autoregressive and moving average processes; analysis of consumer demand: synthesis of utility theory, statistical method, and empirical applications; path models with directly observed variables: causal chain systems vs. interdependent (ID) systems; the fix-point method for estimation of ID systems: strengthening the philosophical foundations by general definitions of the notions of model and cause-effect relations: systems analysis by path models with indirectly observed variables: soft modelling using PLS (Partial Least Squares) estimation: prediction accuracy vs. parameter accuracy.

WONNACOTT, G. Paul

Born 1933, London, Ont., Canada.
Current Post Prof. Econ., Univ. Maryland, College Park, MD, USA, 1962–.
Past Posts Fellow, Brookings Inst., Washington, 1957–8; Ass. Prof., Columbia Univ., 1958–62; Staff, Canadian Royal Commission Banking and Fin. 1962; Staff, US President's Council Economic Advisers, 1968–70; Assoc. Dir., Div. Internat. Fin., Board Governors, Fed. Reserve System, Washington, DC, 1974–5; Res. Staff, US Treasury, 1980.
Degrees BA (Hist.) Univ. Western Ontario, 1955; MA, PhD Princeton Univ., 1957, 1959.
Offices and Honours Brookings Inst.

Fellow, 1957–8; Ford Foundation Fellow, 1963–4.

Principal Fields of Interest 430 International Finance; 423 Economic Integration; 311 Domestic Monetary Theory and Policy.

Publications *Books:* 1. *The Canadian Dollar* (Univ. Toronto Press, 1960, 1965); 2. *Free Trade between the United States and Canada: The Potential Economic Effects* (with R. J. Wonnacott), (Harvard Univ. Press, 1967); 3. *Harmonization of National Economic Policies under Free Trade* (with H. G. Johnson and H. Shibata), (Univ. Toronto Press, 1968); 4. *Macroeconomics* (Richard D. Irwin, 1974, 1984); 5. *Economics* (with R. J. Wonnacott), (McGraw-Hill, 1979, 1982; transls., Spanish, 1981, Portuguese, with Y. R. Crusius and C. R. Crusius, 1982, Canadian ed., with A. Blomqvist, 1983); 6. *U.S. Intervention in the Market for DM* (Princeton Stud. in Internat. Fin., 1982).

Articles: 1. 'Disguised and overt unemployment in less developed economies', *QJE*, 76(2), May 1962; 2. 'A suggestion for the revaluation of gold', *J Fin*, 18(1), March 1963; 3. 'Canadian automotive protection: content provisions, the Bladen plan, and recent changes', *CJE*, 31(1), Feb. 1965; 4. 'The automotive agreement of 1965' (with R. J. Wonnacott), *CJE*, 33(2), May 1967; 5. 'The similarity of quantity theory and Keynesian policy prescriptions in recent years', in *Monetary Process and Policy*, ed. G. Horwich, (Richard D. Irwin, 1967); 6. 'U.S. investment in the Canadian economy', *Int J Econ.*, 27(2), Spring 1972; 7. 'The marginal utility of income does not increase: borrowing, lending and Friedman-Savage gambles' (with M. J. Bailey and M. Olson), *AER*, 70(2), June 1980; 8. 'Is unilateral tariff reduction preferable to a customs union?' (with R. J. Wonnacott), *AER*, 71(4), Sept. 1981; 9. 'Free trade between the United States and Canada: fifteen years later' (with R. J. Wonnacott), *Canadian Public Pol.*, Oct. 1982; 10. 'How general is the case for unilateral tariff reduction?' (with R. J. Wonnacott), *AER*, 74(2), June 1984.

Principal Contributions Early work

concentrated on economic relations between Canada and the US. My doctoral dissertation, *The Canadian Dollar*, concluded that flexible exchange rates had worked quite well for Canada in the 1950s. The study on the potential effects of free trade between the US and Canada (with R. J. Wonnacott) concluded that the gains to Canada would be very large, primarily because of economies of scale and the possibility of reorganising the 'branch plant' industry of Canada. Interest in international trade and financial policies led to service on the senior staffs of the Council of Economic Advisers and the Federal Reserve Board.

My intermediate text, *Macroeconomics*, was an attempt to move away from the Keynesian approach of most texts of the day, and to present some of the problems in Keynesian theory, particularly as an equilibrium system. I attempted to present a balanced evaluation of the Keynesian and classical approaches in a way which was readable and understandable by undergraduates.

Recent research has concentrated in two areas: exchange-market intervention and customs union theory. In my Princeton study, I found that US intervention in the market for the DM in the late 1970s had been stabilising, in the sense that purchases (sales) had been made when the rate was below (above) the 12-month moving average. I rejected profitability of intervention as the principal criterion for intervention; it is not clear why it should be the sole basis for judging exchange-market intervention, when practically nobody would use it for judging domestic open-market operations. My work on customs union theory (with R. J. Wonnacott) has shown the narrowness of the common argument that customs unions are dominated by unilateral tariff reduction.

WONNACOTT, Ronald Johnston

Born 1930, London, Ont., Canada.
Current Post Prof. Econ., Univ. Western Ont., London, Ont., Canada, 1965–.

Past Posts Lect., Harvard Law School, 1956–7; Ass. Prof., Assoc. Prof., Univ. Western Ontario, 1958–61, 1962–5; Vis. Assoc. Prof., Univ. Minnesota, 1961–2.
Degrees BA Univ. Western Ontario, 1955; MA, PhD Harvard Univ., 1957, 1959.
Offices and Honours Woodrow Wilson Fellow, 1955–6; Ford Foundation Faculty Fellow, 1957; Pres, CEA, 1981–2; Board Dirs., Social Science Fed. Canada, 1982–3; Fellow, Royal Soc. Canada, 1983–.
Principal Fields of Interest 420 Trade Relations and Commercial Policy; 210 Econometrics.
Publications *Books:* 1. *Canadian American Dependence: An Interindustry Analysis of Production and Prices* (N-H, 1961); 2. *Cost of Capital in Canada* (with G. L. Reuber), (Resources for the Future, 1961); 3. *Free Trade Between the US and Canada* (with P. Wonnacott), (Harvard Univ. Press, 1967); 4. *Introductory Statistics* (with T. H. Wonnacott), (Wiley, 1972, 1984; transls., Japanese, Baifukan, 1978, Italian, Editore Franco Angeli, 1972, 1974, Spanish, Editorial Limusa, 1979, Portuguese, Editora Livros Tecnicos e Cientificos, 1980). 5. *Econometrics* (with T. H. Wonnacott), (Wiley 1970, 1979; transls., Portuguese, Editora Livros Tecnicos e Cientificos, 1976, Italian, ISEDI, 1974, Japanese, Baifukan, 1975, Spanish, Biblioteca de Ciencias Sociales, 1982); 6. *Introductory Statistics for Business and Economics* (with T. H. Wonnacott), (Wiley 1973, 1984; transls., Spanish, Editorial Limusa, 1979, Portuguese, Editora Livros Tecnicos e Cientificos, 1981); 7. *Canada's Trade Options* (Econ. Council Canada, 1975; transl., French, Econ. Council Canada, 1975); 8. *Economics* (with P. Wonnacott), (McGraw-Hill, 1979, 1982; transls., Portuguese, McGraw-Hill do Brasil, 1982, Spanish, Editorial McGraw-Hill Latinoamericana, 1981); 9. *Regression* (with T. H. Wonnacott), (Wiley 1981); 10. *Statistics: Discovering Its Power* (with T. H. Wonnacott), (Wiley, 1982).
Articles: 1. 'Wage level and employment structure in the United States Regions: a free trade precedent', *JPE*,

72(4), Aug. 1964; 2. 'Possible economic effects of Canadian-U.S. tariff elimination', *Atlantic Community Q.*, Spring 1965; 3. 'Automotive agreement of 1965' (with P. Wonnacott), *CJE*, 33(2), May 1967; 4. 'The political economy of a Canada-U.S. free trade area', *Internat. J.*, 20(4), Fall 1974; 5. 'Canada's future in a world of trade blocs: a proposal', *Canadian Public Pol.*, 1(1), Winter 1975; 6. 'Industrial strategy: a Canadian substitute for trade liberalization?', *CJE*, 8(4), Nov. 1975; 7. 'Least distance estimators' (with T. H. Wonnacott), *Internat. J. Math. Science and Technology*, 8(3), 1977; 8. 'Is unilateral tariff liberalization preferable to a customs union? The curious case of the missing foreign tariffs' (with P. Wonnacott), *AER*, 71(4), Sept. 1981; 9. 'Controlling trade and foreign investment in the Canadian economy: some proposals', *CJE*, 15(4), Nov. 1982; 10. 'The Canadian content proposals of the task force on the automobile industry', *Canadian Public Pol*, 10(1), March 1984.

Principal Contributions Developed a two-country input-output model and its dual to describe the output and price linkages between the Canadian and US economies; a regional analysis of the location of industry in the US which was later extended to North America, and became the point of departure for a five-year study of the effects of Canada-US free trade. This study was undertaken with Paul Wonnacott, with whom I have also co-authored several articles on customs union theory, and the Canada-US Auto Pact, and a textbook in economics. Contributed to trade policy debate in Canada by an analysis of topics such as industrial strategy, tariffs, various imaginative new forms of nontariff protection, and the economics of foreign investment. Co-authored with Tom Wonnacott several books on statistics, econometrics and regression (and a new least-distance econometric estimator). Obviously, my most important single decision: my choice of brothers/co-authors.

WOOD, Stuart*

Dates and Birthplace 1853–1914, Philadelphia, PA, USA.
Posts Held Iron founder, cotton merchant, banker and property speculator.
Degree PhD Harvard Univ., 1875.
Offices Vice-Pres., AEA, 1901.
Publications *Articles:* 1. 'A new view of the theory of wages Pts. I–II', *QJE*, 3, Oct. 1888, July 1889; 2. 'The theory of wages', *AEA Publ.*, 4, 1889; 3. 'A critique of wages theories', *Annals Amer. Academy of Pol. and Social Sciences*, 1, 1890.
Career Probably the first American PhD in economics, and an independent discoverer of marginal productivity theory. He also published a review article on the history of the wage-fund doctrine.
Secondary Literature G. J. Stigler, *Essays in the History of Economics* (Univ. Chicago Press, 1965), chap. 10.

WORSWICK, George David Norman

Born 1916, London, England.
Current Post Emeritus Fellow, Magdalen Coll. Oxford, 1982–.
Past Posts Res. Officer, Univ. Oxford Inst. Stats., 1940–60; Fellow, Tutor Econ., Magdalen Coll. Oxford, 1945–65; Dir., NIESR, London, 1965–82; Vis. Prof., MIT, 1962–3.
Degrees BA (Maths.), MA Univ. Oxford 1937, 1941; Hon. DSc City Univ. London, 1975.
Offices and Honours Fellow, BA, 1979; Pres., Section F, BAAS, 1971; RES., 1982–4; CBE
Editorial Duties Ass. Ed., Ed., *BOIS*, 1940–60.
Principal Fields of Interest 010 General Economics; 130 Economic Fluctuations; Forecasting and Inflation.
Publications *Books:* 1. *The British Economy 1945–50*, co-ed. (OUP, 1952); 2. *The British Economy in the 1950s*, co-ed. (OUP, 1962); 3. *Profits in the British Economy* (with D. G. Tipping), (Blackwell, 1967); 4. *Uses of Economics*, ed. (OUP, 1972); 5. *The Concept and Measurement of Involuntary Unemployment*, ed. (OUP, 1976);

6. *Keynes and the Modern World*, co-ed. (OUP, 1983).

Articles: 1. 'Points, prices and consumer choice, *BOIS*, 6(3), Feb. 1944; 2. 'Stability and flexibility of full employment', in *Economics of Full Employment* (Blackwell 1944); 3. 'A note on the adding-up criterion', *REStud*, 22(1), 1954; 4. 'Mrs. Robinson on simple accumulation', *OEP*, 12(2), June 1959; 5. 'Fiscal policy and stabilization in Britain', *JMCB*, 1(3), Aug. 1969; 6. 'Is progress in economic science possible?', *EJ*, 82, March 1972.

Principal Contributions An Oxford college tutor must be a generalist, trying to keep up with principal developments in economic theory, while continuing to keep in touch with the real world. Interest in theory led to rationing, the adding-up criterion and economic growth. Particular interests in applied economics have included profits and the service industries, and I was involved in editing and contributing to books on the British economy. At NIESR, I became involved in economic modelling and forecasting. Throughout my professional life I have advocated an incomes policy as a means to achieve full employment without inflation.

WRIGLEY, Edward Anthony

Born 1931, Manchester, England.
Current Post Prof. Pop. Stud., LSE, London, England, 1979–.
Past Posts Fellow, Peterhouse Coll., Univ. Lect., Univ. Camb., 1958–, 1958–74; Member, Inst. Advanced Study, Princeton Univ., 1970–1; Dir., SSRC Camb. Group Hist. Pop. and Social Structure, 1974–; Hinkley Vis. Prof., Johns Hopkins Univ., 1975; Tinbergen Vis. Prof., Erasmus Univ., Rotterdam, 1979.
Degrees BA, PhD Univ. Camb., 1952, 1957.
Offices and Honours William Volker Res. Fellow, Univ. Chicago, 1953–4; Ellen Macarthur Prize, 1958; Pres., British Soc. for Pop. Stud., 1978–9; Fellow, BA, 1980–; Pop. Investigation Comm., 1980–; Council, EHS, 1982–.
Editorial Duties Ed. Boards, *Camb. Geographical Stud.*, 1969–81, *J. Inter-*disciplinary Hist.*, 1970–, *Camb. Stud. in Pop., Econ. and Society in Past Time*, 1983–.
Principal Fields of Interest 040 Economic History; 841 Demographic Economics.
Publications *Books:* 1. *Industrial Growth and Population Change* (CUP, 1961); 2. *An Introduction to English Historical Demography* (Weidenfeld & Nicholson, 1966); 3. *Population and History*, ed. (Weidenfeld & Nicholson, 1969); 4. *Nineteenth Century Society*, ed. (CUP, 1972); 5. *Identifying People in the Past*, ed. (Edward Arnold, 1973); 6. *Towns and Societies*, co-ed. (with P. Abrams), (CUP, 1978); 7. *The Population History of England* (with R. S. Schofield), (Edward Arnold, 1981).

Articles: 1. 'The supply of raw materials in the industrial revolution', *EHR*, 2(15), Aug. 1961; 2. 'Family limitation in pre-industrial England', *EHR*, 19, April 1966; 3. 'A simple model of London's importance in changing English society and economy', *Past and Present*, 37, 1967; 4. 'The process of modernization and the industrial revolution in England', *J. Interdisciplinary Hist.*, 3, 1972; 5. 'Parasite or stimulus: the town in a pre-industrial economy', in *Towns and Societies*, eds. R. Abrams and E. A. Wrigley (CUP, 1978); 6. 'Fertility strategy for the individual and the group', in *Historical Studies of Changing Fertility*, ed. C. Tilly (Princeton Univ. Press, 1978); 7. 'Marriage, fertility and population growth in eighteenth century England', in *Marriage and Society*, ed. R. B. Outhwaite (Europa, 1981); 8. 'The growth of population in eighteenth-century England: a conundrum resolved', *Past and Present*, 98, 1983.

Principal Contributions My work has always centred round the phenomenon of the industrial revolution, the phase of fundamental change in economic affairs which for the first time in human history made poverty, so to speak, optional. It was a change which may be defined in economic terms but must be understood by considering matters which extend well beyond economic affairs, and which include investigating the ways in which West European society evolved into something substantially different from other advanced civilisations. I have been especially interested in the strikingly different demographic history of the West, and especially in the West European marriage pattern, so constituted as to make reproduction and so population growth responsive to fluctuating economic circumstances in a manner not found elsewhere. This work culminated in the publication of *The Population History of England* in 1981. I have, however, also maintained an abiding interest in more 'conventional' topics, including urban growth, the triggers and concomitants of technological change, the circumstances in which agricultural productivity increased in the past (beating the Ricardian trap of declining marginal returns), and modernisation theory.

Y

YAARI, Menahem E.

Born 1935, Jerusalem, Israel.
Current Post S. A. Schonbrunn Prof. Math. Econ., Hebrew Univ., Jerusalem, 1971–.
Past Post Vis. Prof., Univ. Penn., 1979–80.
Degrees BA Hebrew Univ., 1958; PhD Stanford Univ., 1962.
Offices and Honours Member, Israel Econ. Assoc.; Fellow, Em Soc, Walras-Bowley Lecture, 1970, 1977.
Editorial Duties Co-ed., *Em*, 1968–75.
Principal Fields of Interest 022 Microeconomic Theory.
Publications *Books:* 1. *Linear Algebra for Social Sciences* (Prentice-Hall, 1971).
Articles: 1. 'Repeated insurance contracts and moral hazard' (with A. Rubinstein), *JET*, 30(1), June 1983; 2. 'On dividing justly' (with M. Bar-Hillel), *Social Choice and Welfare*, 1(1), 1984.
Principal Contributions Studies in consumer theory, economics of uncertainty and moral hazard, changes of tastes, and distributive justice.

YAWITZ, Jess Barry

Born 1946, St Louis, MO, USA.
Current Post John E. Simon Prof. Fin., Washington Univ., St Louis, MO, USA, 1981–.
Past Posts Ass. Prof., Assoc. Prof., Prof. Bus. Econ. and Fin., School Bus., Washington Univ., 1971–6, 1976–9, 1979–81; Vis. Scholar, Stanford Univ., School Bus., 1978; Dir., Inst. Banking and Fin Markets, School Bus., Washington Univ., 1980; Res. Assoc., NBER, 1983.
Degrees BA, MA, PhD Washington Univ., 1968, 1969, 1972.
Offices and Honours Univ. Disting. Faculty Award, 1983.
Editorial Duties Assoc. Ed., *J. Fin. Res.*, 1979, *J. Midwest Fin Assoc.*, 1979, *Fin. Management*, 1978–82.
Principal Fields of Interest 312 Commerical Banking; 313 Capital Markets; 521 Business Finance.
Publications *Books:* 1. *Financial Management of Financial Institutions* (with G. Hempel), (Prentice-Hall, 1976); 2. *Macroeconomics* (with M. Eaker), (Prentice-Hall, 1984).
Articles: 1. 'The relative importance of duration and yield volatility on bond price volatility', *JMCB*, 9(1), pt. 1, 1977; 2. 'An analytical model of interest rate differentials and different default recoveries', *J. Fin. and Quant. Analysis*, 12(3), Sept. 1977; 3. 'Externalities and risky investments', *J Fin*, 32(4), Sept. 1977; 4. 'The effect of bond refunding on shareholder wealth' (with J. A. Anderson), *J Fin*, 32(5), Dec. 1977; 5. 'The technology of risk and return' (with E. Greenberg and W. J. Marshall), *AER*, 68(3), June 1978; 6. 'Risk premia on municipal bonds', *J Fin. and Quant. Analysis*, 13(3), Sept. 1978; 7. 'Measuring the effect of callability on bond yields' (with W. J. Marshall), *JMCB*, 13(1), Feb. 1981; 8. 'Firm behavior under uncertainty and the theory of finance' (with W. J. Marshall and E. Greenberg), *QREB*, 23(2), Summer 1983; 9. 'The effect of risk on the firm's optimal capital stock: a note' (with W. J. Marshall and K. Maloney), *J Fin*, 38(4), Sept. 1983; 10. 'Incentives for diversification and the structure of the conglomerate firm' (with E. Green-

berg and W. J. Marshall), *SEJ*, 50(7), July 1984.

YEAGER, Leland Bennett

Born 1924, Oak Park, IL, USA.
Current Post Ludwig von Mises Disting. Prof. Econ., Auburn Univ., Auburn, Al, 1983–.
Past Posts Instr., Texas A&M Coll., 1949–50; Instr., Ass. Prof., Univ. Maryland, 1952–7; Ass. Prof., Assoc. Prof., Prof., Paul Goodloe McIntire Prof. Econ., Univ. Virginia, 1957–; Vis. Prof., Southern Methodist Univ., TX, 1962, UCLA, 1975, NYU, 1979, Auburn Univ., 1983, George Mason Univ., VA, 1983.
Degrees BA Oberlin Coll., 1948; MA, PhD Columbia Univ., 1949, 1952.
Offices and Honours Pres., SEA, 1974–5; Vice-Pres., Atlantic Econ. Soc., 1976–7; Adjunct Scholar, AEI and Cato Inst.
Editorial Duties Ed. Boards, *SEJ*, 1960–3, *Atlantic Econ. J.*, 1973–.
Principal Fields of Interest 311 Monetary Theory; 411 International Trade and Theory; 970 Economics of Politics.
Publications *Books:* 1. *Free Trade: America's Opportunity* (Schalkenbach, 1954); 2. *In Search of a Monetary Constitution*, ed. (Harvard Univ. Press, 1962); 3. *International Monetary Relations: Theory, History and Policy* (Harper & Row, 1966, 1976; transl., Spanish, Alianza Editorial, 1984); 4. *Trade Policy and the Price System* (with D. Tuerck), (Intext, 1966); 5. *The International Monetary Mechanism* (Holt, Rinehart & Winston, 1968; transl., Japanese, Minerva, 1971); 6. *Monetary Policy and Economic Performance* (AEI, 1972); 7. *Experiences with Stopping Inflation* (with others), (AEI, 1983; transl., Spanish, Ed Tres Tempos, 1983); 8. *Ludwig von Mises, Nation, State and Economy*, ed. (NYU Press, 1983).
Articles: 1. 'Some questions about growth economics', *AER*, 44(1), March 1954; 2. 'A cash-balance interpretation of depression', *SEJ*, 22, April 1956; 3. 'A rehabilitation of purchasing-power parity', *JPE*, 66, Dec. 1958; transl., Spanish, *Fundacion de Investigaciones Economicas Latinoamericanas*, 1966; 4. 'Methodenstreit over demand curves', *JPE*, 68, Feb. 1960; 5. 'Essential properties of the medium of exchange', *Kyk*, 21(1), 1968, repr. in *Monetary Theory*, ed. R. Clover (Penguin, 1969); 6. 'Absorption and elasticity: a fuller reconciliation', *Ec, N.S.* 37, Feb. 1970; 7. 'Toward understanding some paradoxes in capital theory', *EI*, 14, Sept. 1976; 8. 'Pareto optimality in policy espousal', *J. Libertarian Stud.*, 2, Fall 1978; 9. 'Inflation, output and employment: some clarifications' (with D. Birch and A. Rabin), *EI*, 20, April 1982; 10. 'A laissez faire approach to monetary stability' (with R. Greenfield), *JMCB*, 15, Aug. 1983.
Principal Contributions I like to think that I have made contributions toward understanding the role of money in balance-of-payments disequilibrium and adjustment and reconciling the elasticities, absorption, and monetary approaches to the topic (especially in Book No. 3. above, and in Article No. 6); grasping the implications for macroeconomic performance of the fact that money serves as the medium of exchange and lacks a market and price of its own (in Article No.5, the co-authored Article, No. 9, and elsewhere); more fully understanding our existing monetary system by comparing it with a radically deregulated system in which money as we now know it, especially government money, no longer existed and in which media of exchange and payments services were provided entirely by private enterprise; understanding, further, how such a system would eliminate major macroeconomic troubles (Article No. 10, with Greenfield, and more recent work); and clarifying the nature of capital and interest and showing how their proper conceptualisation dissolves the 'Cambridge' paradoxes (eg. Article No. 7). I have long had an interest in the overlap between economics and philosophy — for example, in how egalitarian ideas underlie much policy discussion, and the bases of those ideas, and in what economics can contribute to ethics. In recent years these interests have been occupying a large share of my time.

YOTOPOULOS, Pan A.

Born 1933, Athens, Greece.
Current Post Prof. Econ., Food Res. Inst., Stanford Univ., Stanford, CA, USA. 1972–.
Past Posts Instr., Ass. Prof., Assoc. Prof., Prof. Econ., Univ. Wisconsin, Milwaukee, 1960–7; Sr. Assoc., Dir. Res., Acting Dir. General, Center Planning and Econ. Res., Athens, 1961, 1963–5; Assoc. Prof. Econ., Dir., Econ. Res. Center, Univ. Hawaii, 1967–8; Assoc. Prof. Econ., Food Res. Inst., Stanford Univ., 1968–72; Member, World Bank Basic Econ. Missions, Syria, 1977, United Arab Emirates, 1978; Internat. Fund for Agric. Devlp. Mission, Zambia, 1981.
Degrees Diploma (Law), Diploma (Polit. Science and Econ.) Univ. Athens, 1954, 1956; MA Univ. Kansas, 1957; PhD UCLA, 1958.
Offices and Honours Fulbright Fellow, 1956; AAEA Award Professional Excellence Published Res., 1969; Sr. Fellow Award, East-West Center, Honolulu, 1974; Vis. Fellow, Res. School Pacific Stud., ANU, 1975; Adviser to Pres., Faculty Devlp. Nat. Agrarian Univ., Lima, 1982–; Nuffield and NSF Fellow, Univ. Warwick, 1983.
Editorial Duties Ed. Boards, *JDE*, 1977–, *Greek Econ. Rev.*, 1977–; *PDR*, 1979–; Managing Ed., *J. Econ. Devlp.* 1983–.
Principal Fields of Interest 112 Economic Development Models and Theories; 711 Agicultural Supply and Demand Analysis; 841 Demographic Economics.
Publications *Books:* 1. *Surplus Labor in Greek Agriculture* (with A. A. Pepelasis), (Center of Planning and Econ. Res., 1962; transl., Greek, Center Planning and Econ. Res., 1963); 2. *The Elasticity of the Labor Supply Curve: A Theory and an Evaluation of Greek Agriculture* (Centre Planning and Econ. Res., 1964); 3. *Economic Analysis and Economic Policy*, ed. (Center of Planning and Econ. Res., 1966); 4. *Allocative Efficiency in Economic Development* (Center of Planning and Econ. Res., 1973); 5. *Economics of Development: Empirical Investigations* (with J. B. Nugent), (Harper & Row,

1976; transls., Spanish, Fondo de Cultura Economica, 1981, Japanese, Keio Univ. Press, 1984); 6. *The Population Problem and the Development Solution* (Stanford Univ., Food Res. Inst. Stud., 1977); 7. *Resource Use in Agriculture: Application of the Profit Function to Selected Countries* (with L. J. Lau), (Stanford Univ., Food Res. Inst. Stud., 1979).
Articles: 1. 'From stock to flow capital inputs for agricultural production functions: a micro-analytic approach', *JFE*, 49, May 1967; 2. 'The empirical content of economic rationality: a test for a less developed economy' (with J. Wise), *JPE*, 77(6), Nov.–Dec. 1969; 3. 'A test for relative efficiency and an application to Indian agriculture' (with L. J. Lau), *AER*, 61(1), March 1971; 4. 'A test for relative efficiency: some further results' (with L. J. Lau), *AER*, 63(1), March 1973; 5. 'The balanced-growth version of the linkage hypothesis: a test' (with J. B. Nugent), *QJE*, 87(2), May 1973; 6. 'The linear logarithmic expenditure system: an application to consumption-leisure choice' (with L. J. Lau and W. L. Lin), *Em*, 46(4), July 1978; 7. 'What has orthodox economics learned from recent experience?' (with J. B. Nugent), *WD*, 7, June 1979; 8. 'The microeconomics of distribution: a simulation of the farm economy' (with L. J. Lau, S. E. Chou and W. L. Lin), *J. Pol. Modeling*, 3(2), 1981; 9. 'A micro economic-demographic model of the agricultural household in the Philippines', *Food Res. Inst. Stud.* 19(1), 1983; 10. 'Middle-income classes and food crises: the "new" food-feed competition', *EDCC*, 34(3), April 1985.
Principal Contributions The attempt to bring theories of economic development to bear upon facts, and vice versa, lies at the core of my research. It is exemplified by my advanced text (book 5 above). In this quest I happened to make a few original contributions by forging some new tools, modifying some theories and filling in certain gaps in our understanding of economic development. In my research on agriculture in economic development, I started from conventional tests of economic efficiency. These led to raising ques-

tions about the meaning of rationality and the context of efficiency in a world of imperfect markets, imperfect foresight and differences in initial endowments. New tools based on the production and profit function were created to handle these questions by distinguishing the components of technical, price and economic efficiency. Next, extending the concept of production efficiency in the context of welfare maximisation led to employing expenditure systems to make operational the concept of equilibrium in the new economics of the household. The integration of the demographic decision with the production and consumption behaviour of the household is the most recent aspect of this reasearch.

In my research on the importance of the economic and social structure for economic development, I started from the concepts of balanced-unbalanced growth and linkages. This has led to my more recent interest on the role of socio-economic classes in the development process and to linking class-specific consumption behaviour to the process of economic and social (dis)articulation of the developing economy through social accounting matrices.

YOUNG, Allyn Abbott*

Dates and Birthplace 1876–1929, Kenton, OH, USA.
Posts Held Prof., Univs. Leland, Stanford, Washington, Cornell, Harvard and London, 1902–29.
Degree PhD Univ. Wisconsin, 1902.
Offices Various advisory posts, US govt, the League of Nations; Member, Polit. Econ. Club; Pres., Section F, BAAS.
Publications *Books:* 1. *Economic Problems New and Old* (1927); 2. *Analysis of Banking Statistics for the United States* (1928).
Articles: 1. 'Increasing returns and economic progress', *EJ*, 38, Dec. 1928.
Career His extremely wide qualifications, his practical work for government and his busy academic career left him no time for a major treatise. However, his published articles and his teaching ensured a great reputation for

him among his contemporaries. Banking and currency were among the many specific areas on which he had worked, but before his early death he had begun a systematic treatise on economic theory.
Secondary Literature C. P. Blitch, 'Allyn A. Young: a curious case of professional neglect', *HOPE*, 15(1), Spring 1983.

Z

ZABEL, Edward

Born 1927, Orange, NJ, USA.
Current Post Matherly Prof. Econ. and Decision Sciences, Univ. Florida, Gainesville, FL, 1983–.
Past Posts Econ., Rand Corp., 1956–8; Ass. Prof., Assoc. Prof., Prof., Univ. Rochester, NY, 1958–62, 1962–7, 1967–81; Vis. Fellow, Yale Univ., 1964–5, LSE, 1968–9, Univ. Florida, 1980; Prof., Univ. Florida, 1981–3.
Degrees BA (Polit. Science) Syracuse Univ., NY, 1950; MA PhD Princeton Univ., 1953, 1956.
Offices and Honours Phi Beta Kappa, 1950; Sanxay Fellow, Proctor Fellow, Princeton Univ., 1952–3, 1953–4; Ford Foundation Faculty Res. Fellow, 1964–5.
Editorial Duties Assoc. Ed., *Management Science*, 1969–73; Ed. Board, *Appl. Econ.*, 1973–.
Principal Fields of Interest 022 Microeconomic Theory; 026 Economics of Uncertainty; 213 Mathematical Methods and Models.
Publications *Articles:* 1. 'A note on the optimality of (S,s) policies in inventory theory', *Management Science*, 9(1), Oct. 1962; 2. 'Efficient accumulation of capital for the firm', *Em*, 31(1–2), Jan.–April 1963; 3. 'A dynamic model of the competitive firm', *Int ER*, 8(2), June 1967; 4. 'Monopoly and uncertainty', *REStud*, 37(2), April 1970; 5. 'Risk and the competitive firm', *JET*, 3(2), June 1971; 6. 'Multi-period monopoly under uncertainty', *Jet*, 5(3), Dec. 1972; 7. 'Consumer choice, portfolio decisions and transaction costs', *Em*, 41(2), March 1973; 8. 'Consumer behavior under risk in disequilibrium

trading', *Int ER*, 18(2), June 1977; 9. 'Price adjustment in a competitive market and the securities exchange specialist' (with J. Bradfield), in *General Equilibrium, Growth and Trade* (Academic Press, 1979); 10. 'Competitive price adjustment without market clearing', *Em*, 49(5), Sept. 1981.

Principal Contributions My earlier papers analyse firm and consumer behaviour under uncertainty in multi-period models. These papers consider the competitive firm's search for high prices over time, the monopolistic firm's responses to random deviations in demand, and the consumer's commodity and portfolio decisions when portfolio changes incur transaction costs. Later papers attempt to use insights obtained in earlier work to analyse multi-period trading processes when markets need not be cleared each period. For example, two papers analyse trading in organised securities exchanges which use the specialist system and derive explicit characteristics of stationary market price distributions from properties of the specialist's price-making decisions. Recent work focusses on the role of explicit, optimising price-makers in purely competitive markets, emphasising the resulting implications for equilibria, adjustments and stability of competitive systems.

ZAGHINI, Enrico

Born 1938, Rome, Italy.
Current Post Prof. Em, Univ. 'La Sapienza', Rome, Italy, 1976–.
Past Posts Stat., Italian Stat. Central Office, Rome, 1961–5; Lect., Univ. Rome, 1965–72; Prof. Econ. and Banking, Siena, Italy, 1972–6.
Degrees BS (Stats.), PhD Univ. Rome, 1962, 1969.
Editorial Duties Ed. Board, *Economia Politica Rivista*, 1983.
Principal Fields of Interest 021 General Equilibrium Theory; 211 Econometric and Statistical Methods and Models; 213 Mathematical Methods and Models.
Publications *Books:* 1. *Matematica applicata all'economia* (Facolta di Scienze Stat., 1965); 2. *Saggi sull'-accumulazione di capitale nei modelli di equilibrio generale* (Edizioni dell'-Ateneo, 1967; one essay transl., English, as 'One-period equilibrium in the von Neumann Model', *Keio Econ. Stud.*, 8(2), 1971); 3. *Prezzi naturali e prezzi di mercato* (Edizioni dell'Ateneo, 1970); 4. *Lezioni di Econometria* (Edizioni dell' Ateneo, 1970).

Articles: 1. 'On non-basic commodities', *Schweizerische Zeitschrift für Volkswirtschaft und Statistik*, 103(2), 1967; 2. 'Sur la condition de resolubilité du modèle ferme de Leontief', *Econ App*, 4, 1967; 3. 'Solow prices and the dual stability paradox in the Leontief dynamic system', *Em*, 39(3), May 1971; 4. 'A lecture on price theory: flexible *tâtonnements* and existence of solutions for Walras model of capital formation, *Econ. Notes*, 2(2), 1973; 5. 'Sull 'esistenza di equilibri con disoccupazione involontaria', *Rassegna Economica*, 38(5), 1974; 6. 'A note on capital goods durability in the Walrasian theory of capital formation and credit', *ZN*, 35(1–2), 1975; 7. 'Price systems with a non-uniform profit rate', *Econ. Notes*, 4(1), 1975; 8. 'On the existence of involuntary unemployment equilibria', *ZN*, 37(1–2), 1977; 9. 'Un modello di equilibrio generale non concorrenziale', *Rassegna Economica*, 43(3), 1979; 10. 'Modelli econometrici e previsione di lungo periodo', *Note economiche*, 1, 1979.

Principal Contributions My first field of research was the interconnection between the models of Leontief, von Neumann and Walras. While it was common to say that the three models were radically different, I proved that the mechanism of capital goods accumulation and of price formation was basically the same in all three. In doing this, I considered various problems concerning the existence of meaningful solutions for Walras' model of capital formation. This analysis led me to consider the connection between classical natural prices and Walrasian prices in the context of the capital accumulation model. My contention was that Walrasian prices are the rigorous formulation of classical market prices constituting the basis for natural prices. In proving the above, I introduced non-static expectations into the Walrasian model. The study of this problem led me to a critique of the perfect foresight prices usually associated with the Leontief dynamic model and to a solution of the so-called 'dual stability paradox'. Afterwards I studied a group of models in which non-competitive conditions are prevailing and in which involuntary unemployment may emerge. In the last years I have been interested in the econometric forecasting of public revenues and expenditures.

ZAJAC, Edward Eugene

Born 1926, Cleveland, OH, USA.
Current Post Prof. Econ., Univ. Arizona, Tucson, AZ, USA, 1983–.
Past Posts Member, Technical Staff, Maths. and Stats. Res. Center, Bell Lab., 1954–66; Member, Task Force on FCC Investigation, AT&T, 1965–6; Vis. Prof., Electrical Eng., Polytechnic Inst. NY, 1966–7; Head, Math. Physics Dept., Econ. and Graphics Res. Dept., Dir., Econ. Res., Bell Labs., 1967–8, 1968–78, 1978–83.
Degrees BME (Mech. Eng.) Cornell Univ., 1950; MSE (Mech. Eng.) Princeton Univ., 1952; PhD (Eng. Mechanics) Stanford Univ., 1954.
Offices and Honours Henry Crathorne Phillips Fellow, Princeton Univ., 1950–1; NSF Fellow, 1953–4.
Editorial Duties Ed. Board, *J Appl. Mechanics*, 1965.
Principal Fields of Interest 020 General Economic Theory; 610 Industrial Organisation and Public Policy; 620 Economics of Technological Change.
Publications *Books:* 1. *Fairness or Efficiency. An Introduction to Public Utility Pricing* (Ballinger, 1978).
Articles: 1. 'Bounds on the decay rate of damped linear systems', *Q. Appl. Maths.*, 20, Jan. 1963; 2. 'Computer-made perspective movies as a scientific and communication tool', *Communications of the ACM*, 7, March 1964; 3. 'Note on overly-stable difference approximations', *J. Maths. and Physics*, 1, March 1964; 4. 'A geometric treatment of Averch-Johnson's behavior of the firm model', *AER*, 60(1), March

1970, excerpts repr. in *Public Policies Toward Business*, ed. W. G. Shepherd (Irvin, 1979); 5. 'Lagrange multiplier values at constrained optima', *JET*, 4, April 1972; 6. 'Note on "gold plating" or "rate base padding"', *Bell JE*, 3, Spring 1972; 7. 'Dupuit-Marshall consumer's surplus, utility, and revealed preference', *JET*, 20, April 1979.
Principal Contributions For the first ten years following my PhD in engineering mechanics, my research and publications were principally in the fields of my training. Starting in 1962, I made some of the earliest computer-animated films, including *A Pair of Paradoxes*, and worked on the application of computer animation to science education films. Subsequently my research interests turned to economics. Starting in 1968, with the help of Elizabeth Bailey, Gerald Faulhaber and others, I gradually built a group of about 25 outstanding researchers, concentrating on regulation and industrial organisation, finance, theoretical and applied econometrics, labour economics and the economics of information. My own research has focussed on regulation, public utility pricing and economic justice.

ZAREMBKA, Paul

Born 1942, St Louis, MO, USA.
Current Post Prof. Econ., State Univ. NY Buffalo, Buffalo, NY, USA, 1976–.
Past Posts Ass. Prof. Econ., Univ. Cal. Berkeley, 1967–72; Lect., Pacific Univ., Omori Res. Inst. Internat Relations, Tokyo, 1968; Vis. Prof., Alfred-Weber Inst., Heidelberg Univ., 1970–1, Ibero-Amer. Inst., Univ. Göttingen, 1971, 1972; Assoc. Prof. Econ., State Univ. NY Buffalo, 1973–6; Sr. Res. Officer, World Employment Programme, Geneva, 1974–7; Researcher, Group for Study and Res. on Science, Louis Pasteur Univ., Strasbourg, 1978, 1979.
Degrees BA (Maths.) Purdue Univ., IN, 1964; MS, PhD Univ. Wisconsin, 1967, 1967.
Offices and Honours Fulbright-Hayes Lect., Academy Econ. Stud., Poznan, Poland, 1979.

Editorial Duties Ed., *Res. Polit. Economy* (JAI Press, 1977–).

Principal Fields of Interest 051 Capitalist Economic Systems; 052 Socialist and Communist Economic Systems; 112 Economic Development Models and Theories.

Publications *Books:* 1. *Toward a Theory of Economic Development* (Holden-Day, 1972); 2. *Frontiers in Econometrics*, ed. (Academic Press, 1974); 3. *Essays in Modern Capital Theory*, co-ed. (with M. Brown and K. Sato), (N-H, 1976).

Articles: 1. 'Manufacturing and agricultural production functions and international trade: United States and northern Europe', *JFE*, 48(4), pt. 1, Nov. 1966; 2. 'On the empirical relevance of the CES production function', *REStat*, 52(1), Feb. 1970; 3. 'Marketable surplus and growth in the dual economy', *JET*, 2(2), June 1970; 4. 'Notes on testing symmetry conditions between factor demand equations', *Ec*, N.S. 38, Feb. 1971; 5. 'Transformation of variables in econometrics', in *Frontiers in Econometrics*, *op cit.*; 6. 'Capital heterogeneity, aggregation and the two-sector model', *QJE*, 89(1), Feb. 1975; 7. 'Investment and saving in capitalist society: an interpretation of the Cambridge position', in *On the Stability of Contemporary Economic Systems*, eds. O. Kynx and W. Schrettl (Vandenhoeck & Ruprecht, 1979); 8. 'Accumulation of capital in the periphery', in *Res. in Polit. Economy*, 2 (JAI Press, 1979); 9. 'Accumulation and the state in Venezuelan industrialization' (with J. P. P. Sainz), *Latin Amer. Perspectives*, 6(3), Issue 22, Summer 1979; 10. 'Lenin on the economics of socialist transformation and Polish solidarity, *Res. in Polit. Economy*, 5 (JAI Press, 1982).

Principal Contributions My initial research interests were in the application of neoclassical economic theory and econometric methods to the description of Third World economies, and in the development of transformation-of-variable methods in econometrics. These interests were complemented by research activity in the econometrics of production economics, under an implicit premise that production econ-

omics is the base of all economics. This latter interest was particularly stimulated by the Cambridge controversy in capital theory in which I became exposed to the possibility of standing up against the whole neoclassical tradition that is so deeply embedded in US academic economics. Thus, regardless of some disagreements with the Cambridge School in capital theory, I remain indebted to their challenge. After a reading outside of economics into political theory, economic anthropology, and philosophy, I became exposed in Geneva to a deeper intellectual interest in Marx and Marxism than I had experienced in the US (even at Berkeley in the Vietnam era). All of this culminated in a break in conceptual thinking, centred upon Marx's *Capital* in its a-Hegelian, a-economistic interpretation (associated with the French philosopher Louis Althusser). Within Marxist intellectuals, Althusser is highly controversial, but I support the basic correctness of that approach to understanding human society. My own work within Marxism has then been centred on a reinterpretation of accumulation of capital to include a process of the penetration of non-capitalist forms of production and I have applied this reinterpretation to twentieth-century social developments.

ZARNOWITZ, Victor

Born 1919, Lancut, Poland.

Current Post Prof. Econ. and Fin., Grad. School Bus., Univ. Chicago, Chicago, IL, USA, 1965–.

Past Posts Tutor, Instr., Univ. Heidelberg, and Grad. School Bus., Mannheim, 1949–51, Res. Ass., Lect., Vis. Ass. Prof., Columbia Univ. NY, 1956–9; Res. Ass., Staff Member, Res. Assoc., NBER, 1956–62, 1963–; Assoc. Prof. Fin., Grad, School Bus., Univ. Chicago, 1959–64; Cons., Bureau Econ. Analysis, US Dept. Commerce, 1972–.

Degrees MA, PhD Univ. Heidelberg, 1949, 1951.

Offices and Honours Post-doctoral Res. Fellow, US-SSRC, 1953–4; Ford Foundation Faculty Res. Fellow, 1963–

4; Fellow, ASA, 1976; Member, Co-ordinating Comm. US Center, Internat. Res. Econ. Tendency Surveys (CIRET), Paris, France.

Editorial Duties Co-ed., *Econ. Outlook*, *J. Forecasting*.

Principal Fields of Interest 131 Economic Fluctuations; 132 Economic Forecasting; 200 Quantitative Economic Methods and Data.

Publications *Books:* 1. *Die Theorie der Einkammensverteilung* (J. C. B. Mohr, Paul Siebeck 1951); 2. *Unfilled Orders, Price Changes and Business Fluctuations* (NBER, 1962); 3. *An Appraisal of Short-Term Economic Forecasts* (Columbia Univ. Press, 1967); 4. *The Business Cycle Today*, ed. and contrib. (Columbia Univ. Press, 1972); 5. *Orders, Production and Investment: A Cyclical and Structural Analysis* (Columbia Univ. Press, 1973).

Articles: 1. 'Technology and price structure in general equilibrium systems', *REStud*, 23(2), June 1956; 2. 'Cause and consequence of changes in retailers' buying' (with R. P. Mack), *AER*, 48(1), March 1958; 3. 'Index numbers and the seasonality of quantities and prices', in *The Price Statistics of the Federal Government* (NBER, 1961); 4. 'Cyclical aspects of incorporations and the formation of new business enterprises', in *Business Cycle Indicators*, I, ed. G. H. Moore (NBER, 1961); 5. 'Business cycle analysis of econometric model simulations' (with G. H. Moore and C. Boschan), in *Econometric Models of Cyclical Behavior*, I, ed. B. G. Hickman (NBER, 1972); 6. 'Cyclical indicators: an evaluation and new leading indexes' (with C. Boschan), *Bus. Conditions Digest*, May 1975; 7. 'An analysis of annual and multiperiod quarterly forecasts of aggregate income, output and the price level', *J Bus*, 52(1), Jan. 1979; 8. 'On functions, quality and timeliness of economic information', *J Bus*, 55(1), Jan. 1982.

Principal Contributions Contributed to the study of the nature and sources of business cycles and their various aspects and manifestations. Worked on the cyclical behaviour of prices; orders and production; inventories; business failures; new business formation; and fixed capital investment. Studied the interrelations of business cycles, growth and inflation; problems of identifying and dating historical expansions and contractions; and implications for cyclical analysis of macroeconometric model simulations. Analysed the properties and accuracy of different types of economic forecasts: judgemental, econometric, based on survey data and time-series models. Sought to provide a systematic basis for comparative studies in this area by directing and evaluating quarterly surveys of multiperiod forecasts of the US economy. Conducted research resulting in the revision of the system of leading, coincident, and lagging business-cycle indicators for the US.

ZECKHAUSER, Richard Jay

Born 1940, Philadelphia, PA, USA.

Current Post Prof. Polit. Econ., J. F. Kennedy School Govt., Harvard Univ., Cambridge, MA, USA, 1972–.

Past Posts Ass. Prof., Assoc. Prof., Harvard Univ., 1968–70, 1970–2.

Degrees BA, PhD Harvard Univ., 1962, 1969.

Offices and Honours Jr. Fellow, Soc. Fellow, John Williams Award, Harvard Univ., H. B. Earhart Fellow, NSF; Res. Assoc., Center Bus. and Govt., Harvard Univ., NBER, 1981–; Dir., Niederhoffer, Cross and Zeckhauser Inc., NY, 1967–83.

Principal Fields of Interest 022 Microeconomic Theory; 026 Economics of Uncertainty and Information; Game Theory and Bargaining Theory; 822 Public Policy; Role of Government.

Publications *Books:* 1. *Benefit Cost and Policy Analysis Annual*, co-ed. (with others), (Aldine, 1971, 1972, 1973, 1974); 2. *A Primer for Policy Analysis* (with E. Stokey), (W. W. Norton, 1978); 3. *Demographic Dimensions of the New Reupublic* (with P. McClelland), (CUP, 1982); 4. *What Role for Government?*, ed. (Duke Univ. Press, 1983).

Articles: 1. 'Insurance, information, and individual action' (with M. Spence), *AER*, 61(2), May 1971; 2. 'Optimal mechanisms for income transfer',

AER, 61(3), June 1971; 3. 'Voting systems, honest preferences and Pareto optimality', *Amer. Polit. Science Rev.*, Sept. 1973; 4. 'Risk spreading and distribution', in *Redistribution Through Public Choice*, eds. H. M. Hochman and G. E. Peterson (Columbia Univ. Press, 1974, repr. in *Benefit Cost and Policy Analysis Annual 1974, op. cit.*; 5. 'The optimal consumption of depletable natural resoures' (with M. C. Weinstein), *QJE*, 89(3), Aug. 1975; 6. 'Procedures for valuing lives', *Public Pol.*, Fall 1975; 7. 'Impossibility of Bayesian group decision making with separate aggregation of beliefs and values' (with W. Hylland), *Em*, 47(6), Nov. 1979; 8. 'Long term effects of interventions to improve survival in mixed populations' (with D. Shepard), *J. Chronic Diseases*, 1980; 9. 'Market index futures contracts' (with V. Niederhoffer), *Fin. Analysts J.*, Jan.–Feb. 1980, repr. in *Handbook of Financial Markets: Securities, Options, Futures*, eds. F. J. Fabozzi and F. G. Zarb (Dow Jones-Irwin, 1982), and *Interest Rate Futures: Concepts and Issues*, eds. G. D. Gay and R. W. Kolb (Robert F. Dame, 1982); 10. 'Survival versus consumption' (with D. Shepard), *Management Science*, April 1984.

Principal Contributions The primary challenge facing our society is how to allocate resources in accordance with the preferences of the citizenry. Unfortunately, centralised decision-making is hopelessly distorted by a political process that encourages individuals to misrepresent their preferences and inevitably favours certain groups over others. Thus my conceptual work has tried to discover possibilities for decentralised allocation procedures, particularly when uncertainty and asymmetric information are problems. This work has naturally focussed on incentives for honest revelation.

Welcome results are (1) that paying the expected externality effectively decentralises multi-stage externality and group decision problems under uncertainty, and (2) that a point-voting-type mechanism for public goods can elicit honest preferences and lead to an efficient bundle. Similarly I have shown that involuntary unemployment is

a consequence of worker and firm heterogeneity; that groups employing Bayesian decision methods cannot preserve Pareto optimality; that a fundamental nonconvexity arises if externality leads to shutdown; and that voting mechanisms must be inefficient if intensities of preference matter. Other work has dealt with agency theory, insurance, and populations with heterogeneous risk.

I have also been involved in a variety of policy investigations, exploring ways to promote the health of human beings, to help labour markets and financial markets operate more efficiently, and to foster informed and appropriate choices by individuals and government agencies. Cross-fertilisation between these policy investigations and my conceptual work has been of great value. In considering such topics as risk analysis (life valuation, calibration of probabilities) and the redesign of regulatory processes, I have found uncertainty and decentralisation to be important issues, and a major theme of my current work on human resources and health is the importance of heterogeneity (possibly unobservable) in the population.

ZELLNER, Arnold

Born 1927, New York City, NY, USA.

Current Post H. G. B. Alexander Prof. Econ. and Stats., Grad School Bus., Univ. Chicago, Chicago, IL, USA, 1966–.

Past Posts Ass. Prof., Assoc. Prof. Econ., Univ. Washington, 1955–9; Vis. NSF Post-doctoral Fellow, Cowles Foundation, Yale Univ., 1957; Vis. Fulbright Prof., Netherlands School Econ., 1960–1; Assoc. Prof;, Prof. Econ., Univ. Wisconsin, Madison, 1960–6; Vis. Ford Foundation Prof. Econ., Univ. Chicago, 1964–5, Univ. Cal. Berkeley, 1971; Vis. Scholar, Stanford Univ., 1980–1; Vis. Prof. Em., Monash Univ., Australia, 1983, Univ. Southern Cal., 1984.

Degrees BA (Physics) Harvard Univ., 1949; PhD Univ. Cal. Berkeley, 1957.

Offices and Honours Dir., H. G. B.

Alexander Res. Foundation, Univ. Chicago; Fellow, Council, Em Soc., ASA, AAAS; Chair, AEA Census Advisory Comm.; Member, Board Dirs., NBER; John R. Commons Award; McKinsey & Co. Outstanding Teaching Award; ASA Chicago Chapter Outstanding Stat. of Year Award; Pres., Leonard J. Savage Memorial Trust Fund.

Editorial Duties Ed., *ASA, J. Bus and Econ. Stats.*; Co-ed., *J Em*; Assoc. Ed., *Em, JEL*.

Principal Fields of Interest 010 General Economics; Theory; History Systems; 130 Economic Fluctuations; Forecasting; Stabilisation; and Inflation; 210 Econometric, Statistical, and Mathematical Methods and Models.

Publications *Books:* 1. *Economic Aspects of the Pacific Halibut Fishery* (with J. A. Crutchfield), (US Govt. Printing Office, 1963); 2. *Readings in Economic Statistics and Econometrics*, ed. (Little, Brown, 1968); 3. *Systems Simulation for Regional Analysis: An Application to River-Basin Planning* (with H. R. Hamilton, *et al.* (MIT Press, 1969); 4. *An Introduction to Bayesian Inference in Econometrics* (Wiley, 1971; transl., Russian, 1980); 5. *Estimating the Parameters of the Markov Probability Model from Aggregate Time Series Data* (with T. C. Lee and G. G. Judge), (N-H, 1970, 1977; transl., Russian, 1977); 6. *Studies in Bayesian Econometrics and Statistics in Honor of Leonard J. Savage*, co-ed. (with S. E. Feinberg), 2 vols (N-H, 1975, 1977); 7. *Seasonal Analysis of Economic Time Series*, ed. (US Govt. Printing Office, 1978); 8. *Bayesian Analysis in Econometrics and Statistics: Essays in Honor of Harold Jeffreys*, ed. (N-H, 1980); 9. *Applied Time Series Analysis of Economic Data*, ed. (US Govt. Printing Office, 1983); 10. *Basic Issues in Econometrics* (Univ. Chicago Press, 1985).

Articles: 1. 'An efficient method of estimating seemingly unrelated regressions and tests for aggregation bias', *JASA*, 57, June 1962; 2. 'Estimators for seemingly unrelated regression equations: some exact finite sample results', *JASA*, 58, Dec. 1963; 3. 'Specification and estimation of Cobb-Douglas production function models' (with J. Kmenta and J. Drèze), *Em*, 34, Oct. 1966; 4. 'Estimation of regression relationships containing unobservable independent variables', *Int ER*, 11, Oct. 1970; 5. 'Bayesian and alternative approaches in econometrics', in *Frontiers in Quantitative Economics*, ed. M. D. Intriligator (N-H, 1971); 6. 'Time series analysis and simultaneous equation models' (with F. Palm), *J Em*, 2, May 1974; 7. 'Bayesian and non-Bayesian analysis of the regression model with multivariate student-t error terms', *JASA*, 71, June 1976; 8. 'Estimation of functions of population means and regression coefficients including structural coefficients: a minimum expected loss (MELO) approach', *J Em*, 8, Oct. 1978; 9. 'Causality and econometrics', in *Three Aspects of Policy and Policymaking*, eds. K. Brunner and A. H. Meltzer (N-H, 1979); 10. 'Statistical analysis of econometric models', *JASA*, 74, Sept. 1979.

Principal Contributions For many years I have devoted my research efforts toward improving methods and applications of econometrics. This has involved me in both theoretical and applied studies since I believe that a strong interaction between theory and application promotes progress, a point that I have emphasised in my writings and teaching. A good deal of my work has involved a comparative analysis of Bayesian and non-Bayesian econometrics under grants since the 1960s. Also, this work has involved development of computer programs for Bayesian analysis and work with a number of colleagues and students. My 1983 Fisher-Schultz Econometric Society Lecture, entitled 'Bayesian Econometrics', to be published in *Econometrica*, summarises some major points regarding the need for use of prior information in econometrics and Bayesian methods for effective use of it. In addition, my 1985 book treats philosophical issues, time series modelling problems, and Bayes/non-Bayes issues.

Secondary Literature J. B. Ramsey, 'On Zellner', in *Contemporary Economists in Perspective*, eds. H. W. Spiegel and W. V. Samuels (JAI Press, 1984).

ZEUTHEN, Frederik*

Dates and Birthplace 1888–1959, Copenhagen, Denmark.
Posts Held Civil Servant, 1912–30; Prof., Univ. Copenhagen, 1928–58.
Degrees Grad., PhD Univ. Copenhagen, 1912, 1928.
Offices Fellow, Em Soc.
Publications *Books:* 1. *Den Ökonomiske Fordeling* (1928); 2. *Problems of Monopoly and Economic Warfare* (1930); 3. *Arbejdslön og Arbejdslöshed* (1939); 4. *Economic Theory and Method* (1955).
Career Economist who made early contributions to the theory of bargaining, the use of inequalities in the Walras system and the theory of monopolistic competition.
Secondary Literature H. Brems, 'From the years of high theory: Frederik Zeuthen (1888–1959)', *HOPE*, 8(3), Fall 1976.

Appendix 1

INDEX OF PRINCIPAL FIELDS OF INTEREST

Every respondent was asked to select three principal fields of interest from the American Economic Association's classification scheme of fields in economics, included in every issue of the *Journal of Economic Literature* and in all 22 volumes of the A.E.A. Index of Economic Articles.* This index refers to living economists only and to the first of these three principal fields of interest.

000 General Economics; Theory; History; Systems
    010 General Economics

Albach, H.
Allingham, M.
Archibald, G.C.
Budd, E.C.
Caravale, G.A.
Clower, R.W.
Coase, R.H.
Collard, D.
Cotta, A.
Culbertson. J.M.
Daly, G.
Harcourt, G.C.
Heilbroner, R.L.
Heller, W.W.
Helmstadter, E.
Hicks, J.
Hirschman, A.O.
Kosters, M.H.
Kuska, E.A.
Little, I.M.D.

MacDougall, G.D.A.
Mincer, J.
Mirrlees, J.A.
Modigliani, F.
Mohring, A.
Möller, H.O.
Mortensen, D.T.
Muth, J.F.
Nelson, R.R.
Nuti, D.M.
Olson, M.L.
Plott, C.R.
Posner, R.A.
Schmidt, K.
Spence, A.M.
Steuer, M.D.
Taylor, L.D.
Williamson, O.E.
Zellner, A.

    011 General Economics
    012 Teaching of Economics

Bach, G.L.
Cairncross, A.K.
Fels, R.

Johnston, B.F.
Lumsden, K.G.

    020 General Economic Theory

Benassy, J-P.E.
Baron, D.P.
Boulding, K.E.
Brems, H.J.
Bruto, D.L.
Bronfenbrenner, M.
Burmeister, E.
Carlson, J.A.
Champernowne, D.G.
Cheung, S.N.S.
Cyert, R.M.
Desai, M.J.
Diamond, P.A.
Diewert, W.E.
Dolbear, F.T. Jr.
Ericson, R.E.
Foldes, L.P.

Foley, D.K.
Ford, J.L.
Friedman, J.W.
Friedman, M.
Gäfgen, G.F.M.
Georgescu-Roegen, N.
Gintis, H.M.
Gorman, W.
Greenhut, M.L.
Groves, T.F.Jr.
Guitton, H.
Hayek, F.A.V.
Heertje, A.
Intriligator, M.D.
Iwai, K.
Kahn, R.F.
Kornai, J.

---

* Respondents whose principal field of interest is the economics of the family, the economics of law, the economics of politics, game theory, Marxian economics and policy modelling had difficulty in using the scheme. Nevertheless, despite some deficiencies the A.E.A. scheme is the only one widely known and used by economists.

Kregel, J.
Kurz, M.
Laffont, J-J.
Lancaster, K.J.
Leftwich, R.H.
Leijonhufvud, A.S.B.
Liebhafsky, H.H.
Lind, R.C.
Lindsay, C.M.
Lydall, H.F.
Malinvaud, E.C.
Meade, J.E.
Newberry, D.M.G.
Newman, P.K.
Oi, W.Y.
Pasinetti, L.L.
Patinkin, D.
Perroux, F.
Postlewaite, A.W.
Reder, M.W.
Richardson, G.B.

Roemer, J.E.
Rothschild, K.W.
Rowley, C.K.
Samuelson, P.A.
Sandmo, A.
Sato, R.
Scitovsky, T.
Sekine, T.T.
Shell, K.
Simon, H.A.
Solow, R.M.
Stern, N.H.
Stigler, G.J.
Stiglitz, J.E.
Sweezy, P.M.
Takayama, A.
Tobin, J.
Varian, H.R.
Weitzman, M.L.
Wilson, R.B.
Zajac, E.E.

021 General equilibrium theory

Bergstrom, T.C.
Bewley, T.F.
Bliss, C.J.E.
Borch, K.H.
Cass, D.
Chetty, V.K.
Debreu, G.
Dehez, P.J.E.
Dixon, P.B.
Drèze, J.
Ellickson, B.
Fisher, F.M.
Gale, D.M.
Grandmont, J-M.
Hahn, F.H.

Hudson, E.A.
Kuenne, R.E.
Laroque, G.R.
Mas-Colell, A.
McKenzie, L.W.
Morishima, M.
Negishi, T.
Ostroy, J.M.
Quirk, J.P.
Rader, J.T.
Scarf, H.E.
Schofield, N.J.
Seton, F.
Sonnenschein, H.F.
Weintraub, E.R.

022 Micro-economic theory

Akerlof, G.A.
Alchian, A.A.
Asimakopulos, A.
Barten, A.P.
Barzel, Y.
Baumol, W.J.
Bishop, R.L.
Blackorby, C.
Bohm, P.J.G.
Borcherding, T.E.
Bowman, M.J.
Bradford, D.F.
Chiswick, B.R.
Comanor, W.S.
Crocker, T.T.
Dewey, D.J.
Dorfman, R.
Eaton, B.C.
Feldman, A.M.
Fishburn, P.C.
Frech, H.E.
Gabor, A.
Gaertner, W.
Garegnani, P.
Gordon, D.F.

Gould, J.P.
Gould, J.R.
Graham, D.A.
Green, J.R.
Harsanyi, J.C.
Hart, O.S.
Hausman, J.A.
Helpman, E.
Hirschleifer, J.
Holt, C.A.
Houthakker, H.
Hurter, A.P.
Jaskold-Grabszewicz, J.
Kamien, M.I.
Katzner, D.W.
Koutsoyiannis, A.
Lesourne, J.F.
Lim, C.
Lovell, M.
Markham, J.W.
McCall, J.J.
McFadden, D.L.
Miyazaki, H.
Moore, J.C.
Muellbauer, J.N.

Ng, Y-K.
Parks, R.W.
Pfouts, R.W.
Pindyck, R.S.
Pollak, R.A.
Psacharapoulos, G.
Rosen, S.
Rothschild, M.
Salop, S.C.
Samuelson, W.F.
Sheskinski, E.
Shubik, M.

Silberberg, E.
Smith, V.L.
Srinivasan, T.N.
Steedman, I.
Swan, P.L.
Van Praag, B.M.S.
Von Weizsaecker, C.C.
Willig, R.D.
Winters, S.G.
Yaari, M.E.
Zabel, E.
Zeckhauser, R.J.

023 Macro-economic theory

Abel, A.B.
Ackley, H.G.
Ando, A.K.
Avernheimer, L.
Azariados, C.
Barro, R.J.
Bator, F.M.
Brechling, F.P.R.
Brown, M.
Bruno, M.
Burstein, M.L.
Carr, J.L.
Casarosa, C.
Chiang, A.C.
Chow, G.
Clark, P.K.
Cooley, T.F.
Courbis, R.
Davidson, P.
Domar, E.D.
Eisner, R.
Fair, R.C.
Fan, L-S.
Feldstein, M.
Fitoussi, J-P.
Friedman, B.M.
Gallaway, L.E.
Grossman, H.
Hines, A.G.

Howitt, P.W.
Jorgenson, D.W.
Kaldor, N.
Komiya, R.
Leroy, S.F.
Levi, M.D.
Lowe, A.
Lucas, R.E.Jr.
Maccini, L.J.
McCallum, B.T.
Meltzer, A.H.
Mishkin, F.S.
Paish, F.W.
Pen, J.
Pesando, J.E.
Pesek, B.P.
Phelps, E.S.
Peston, M.
Sachs, J.D.
Sargent, T.J.
Sato, K.
Shiller, R.J.
Siegel, J.J.
Sims, C.A.
Turnovsky, S.J.
Ulmer, M.J.
Uzawa, H.
Wallace, N.
Wilson, T.

024 Welfare theory

Barnett, A.H.
Bergson, A.
Blau, J.H.
Buchanan, J.M.
Deaton, A.S.

Hammond, P.J.
Hennipman, P.
Mishan, E.J.
Strotz, R.H.
Weisbrod, B.A.

025 Social choice; bureaucratic performance

Bish, R.L.
Black, D.
Friedman, D.D.
Furubotn, E.G.
Margolis, J.
Mueller, D.C.

Pattanaik, P.K.
Romer, T.
Rubin, P.H.
Tideman, T.N.
Tullock, G.

026 Economics of uncertainty and information

Aumann, R.J.
Casson, M.C.
Cheng, P.L.
Ehrlich, I.
Hakansson, N.H.
Hart, A.G.
Hellwig, M.F.

Henderson, J.V.
Lippman, S.A.
Markowitz, H.M.
Merton, R.C.
Perrakis, S.
Radner, R.
Telser, L.C.

030 History of Economic Thought; Methodology

Hutchison, T.W.	Loasby, B.J.
Laidler, D.E.W.	Sowell, T.
Lazonick, W.H.	Whitaker, J.K.

031 History of economic thought

Bartoli, H.	Lekachman, R.
Black, R.D.C.	Moggridge, D.E.
Campbell, R.	O'Brien, D.P.
Coats, A.W.	Samuels, W.J.
Corry, B.A.	Shackle, G.L.S.
De Marchi, N.B.	Shoup, C.S.
Elelund, R.B.Jr.	Stolper, W.F.
Eltis, W.A.	Vickers, D.W.
Fetter, F.W.	Weiller, J.S.
Glahe, F.R.	West, E.G.
Hollander, S.	Winch, D.N.
Kloten, N.W.	

036 Economic methodology

Blaug, M.	Orcutt, G.H.
Boland, L.A.	

040 Economic History

Adelman, I.	Morris, C.T.
Feinstein, C.H.	North, D.C.
Genovese, E.D.	Rostow, W.W.
Habakkuk, H.J.	Temin, P.
Hannah, L.	Williamson, J.G.
Lindert, P.H.	

041 Economic history; general

Deane, P.M.	Maddison, A.
Engerman, S.L.	McCloskey, D.N.

042 North American (excluding Mexico) economic history

David, P.A.	Fogel, R.W.
DeCanio, S.J.	Meyer, J.R.

043 Ancient and medieval economic history until 1453

044 European economic history

Cameron, R.E.	Landes, D.S.
Ford, A.G.	

045 Asian economic history

Rosovsky, H.

046 African economic history

047 Latin American and Caribbean economic history

Diaz-Alejandro, C.F.	Furtado, C.

048 Oceanic economic history

050 Economic Systems

Bos, H.C.	Pejovich, S.
Brittan, S.	Pryor, F.L.
Hurwicz, L.	

051 Capitalist economic systems

Galbraith, J.K.	Monsen, R.J.
Gordon, D.M.	Zarembka, P.
Melman, S.	

052 Socialist and communist economic systems

Bettelheim, C.O.	Lavigne, M.
Grossman, G.	Nove, A.
Kantorovich, L.V.	

053 Comparative economic systems

Ellman, M.J.	Neuberger, E.
Lindblom, C.E.	Wiles, P.J.F.

100 Economic Growth; Development; Planning; Fluctuations

Cline, W.R.
Mundlak, Y.
Reddaway, W.B.

Rosenzweig, M.R.
Stone, J.R.N.

110 Economic Growth; Development; and Planning Theory and Policy

Abramovitz, M.
Aldcroft, D.H.
Bailey, M.N.
Balassa, B.
Hansen, B.
Harrison, B.
Hickman, B.G.
Lewis, W.A.

Nichols, D.A.
Polenske, K.R.
Reynolds, L.G.
Rosenstein-Rodan, P.N.
Sen, A.K.
Shone, R.S.
Sylos-Labini, P.
Tsiang, S.
Wellisz, S.H.

111 Economic growth theory and models

Ben-Porath, Y.
Brock, W.A.
Clague, C.K.
Clark, C.G.
Fabricant, S.
Harris, D.J.

Hulten, C.R.
Kennedy, C.M.
Levhari, D.
Ott, A.E.M.
Suits, D.B.

112 Economic development models and theories

Butz, W.F.
Chenery, H.B.
Eckaus, R.S.
Frank, C.R.Jr.
Hagen, E.E.
Higgins, B.H.
Hoselitz, B.F.
Ilchman, W.F.
Lal, D.K.
Leff, N.H.

Meier, G.M.
Myint, H.
Myrdal, G.
Prebisch, R.
Ranis, G.
Thirlwall, A.P.
Tinbergen, J.
Todaro, M.P.
Yotopoulos, P.A.

113 Economic planning theory and policy

Berg, E.J.
Chamberlain, N.W.
Opie, R.G.
Spulber, N.

Streeten, P.P.
Tsuru, S.
Vietorisz, T.

114 Economic war, defence, and disarmament

120 Country Studies

Walters, A.A.

121 Economic studies of less industrialised countries

Alexander, S.S.
Barlow, R.
Bauer, P.T.
Behrman, J.R.
Berry, R.A.
Dasgupta, P.S.

Fishlow, A.
Griffin, K.B.
Hutcheson, T.L.
Lall, S.
Papanek, G.
Robinson, E.A.G.
Winston, G.C.

122 Economic studies of more industrialised countries

Denison, E.F.
Hart, P.E.

Matthews, R.C.O.
Smolensky, E.

123 Comparative economic studies

Gordon, R.J.
Krueger, A.O.

Portes, R.D.
Vernon, R.

130 Economic Fluctuations; Forecasting; Stabilisation; and Inflation

Adams, F.G.
Aoki, M.
Artis, M.J.
Ball, R.J.

Blinder, A.S.
Buiter, W.H.
Flemming, J.S.
Friend, I.

Gordon, M.J.   Parkin, M.
Gutowski, A.F.   Schwartz, A.J.
Keyserling, L.H.   Taylor, J.B.
Mizon, G.E.
131 Economic fluctuations
Burns, A.F.   Prescott, E.C.
Hall, R.E.   Rosenbluth, G.
Kydland, F.E.   Sauvy, A.
Lundberg, E.F.   Zarnowitz, V.
132 Economic forecasting and econometric models
Latane, H.A.   Minford, A.P.
133 General outlook and stabilisation theories and policies
134 Inflation and deflation
Brown, A.J.   Lipsey, R.G.
Hazledine, T.   Marquez, J.R.
200 Quantitative Economic Methods and Data
Christensen, L.R.   Jaffee, D.M.
Faulhaber, G.R.   Lee, T.H.
Gastwirth, J.L.   Liu, B-C.

210 Econometric, Statistical, and Mathematical Methods and Models
Christ, C.F.   Johnston, J.
Dhrymes, P.J.   Kuh, E.
Goldfeld, S.M.   Leamer, E.E.
Huffman, W.E.   Quandt, R.E.
Johnson, T.
211 Econometric and statistical methods and models
Aigner, D.J.   Heckman, J.J.
Amemiya, T.   Hendry, D.F.
Ashenfelter, O.C.   Klein, L.R.
Basmann, R.L.   Kmenta, J.
Bergmann, B.R.   Koot, R.S.
Berndt, E.R.   Maddala, G.S.
Byron, R.P.   Nelson, C.R.
Cragg, J.G.   Nerlove, M.L.
Durand, D.   Pearce, I.F.
Granger, C.W.J.   Sargan, J.E.
Griliches, Z.   Wallis, K.F.
Haitovsky, Y.   Wold, H.
212 Construction, analysis, and use of econometric models
Bodkin, R.G.   Theil, H.
Boskin, M.J.   Witte, A.D.
Goldberger, A.S.
213 Mathematical methods and models
Beckmann, M.J.   Maital, S.
Coen, R.M.   Makarov, V.L.
214 Computer programs
Ijiri, Y.

220 Economic and Social Statistical Data and Analysis
Miller, H.P.   Usher, D.
Turvey, R.
221 National income accounting
Beckerman, W.   Marchal, J.
Frankel, S.H.   Marczewski, J.W.
Jaszi, G.   Ruggles, R.
222 Input–output analysis
Carter, A.P.   Leontief, W.
223 Financial accounts
224 National wealth and balance sheets
Copeland, M.A.   Goldsmith, R.W.

514 Goals and objectives

520 Business Finance and Investment
    Ekern, S.   Schall, L.D.
    Hamada, R.S.   Taggart, R.A.Jr.
    Landskroner, Y.
   521 Business finance
      Bierwag, G.O.   Johnson, R.W.
      Black, F.   Leland, H.E.
      Elton, E.J.   Miller, M.H.
      Fama, E.F.   Solomon, E.
   522 Business investment

530 Marketing
   531 Marketing and advertising

540 Accounting
   541 Accounting

600 Industrial Organization; Technological Change; Industry Studies
    Adams, W.   Mason, E.S.
    Jacquemin, A.P.   Masson, R.T.
    Kamerschen, D.R.   Scherer, F.M.
    Landes, W.M.   Siegfried, J.J.

610 Industrial organization and public policy
    Bailey, E.E.   Landes, E.
    Bain, J.S.   Levin, R.C.
    Benham, L.K.   Littlechild, S.C.
    Braeutigam, R.R.   Mead, W.J.
    Chiplin, B.   Oster, S.
    Cowling, K.G.   Panzar, J.C.
    Demsetz, H.   Parsons, D.O.
    Gort, M.   Peck, M.J.
    Grabowski, H.G.   Schmalensee, R.L.
    Joskow, P.L.   Shepherd, W.G.
    Kaysen, C.   Silberston, Z.A.
   611 Market structure
      Means, G.C.   Ornstein, S.I.
   612 Public policy towards monopoly and competition
      Allen, B.T.
   613 Public utilities and government regulation of other industries
      Cicchetti, C.J.   Peltzman, S.
   614 Public enterprises
      Bos, D.J.
   615 Economics of transportation

620 Economics of Technological Change
    Binswanger, H.   Ruttan V.W.
    Mansfield, E.
   621 Technological change; motivation; research and development

630 Industry Studies

640 Economic Capacity

700 Agriculture; Natural Resources
   710 Agriculture
      Gardner, B.   Just, R.E.
      Hayami, Y.   Kislev, Y.
      Hazell, P.B.R.   Mellor, J.W.
      Hoch, I.   Schultz, T.W.

720 Natural Resources
    721 Natural resources
        Canes, M.E.   Mikesell, R.F.
        Clawson, M.   Mills, E.S.
        D'Arge, R.C.   Pearce, D.W.
        Freeman, A.M.   Plourde, C.G.
        Kneese, A.V.   Smith, V.K.
        Krutilla, J.V.
    722 Conservation and pollution
        Knetsch, J.L.
    723 Energy
        Adelman, M.A.   Manne, A.S.
        Danielsen, A.L.   Nordhaus, W.D.
        Heal, G.M.

730 Economic Geography

800 Manpower; Labor; Population
        Fleisher, B.M.   Pencavel, J.H.
        Johnson, G.E.   Welch, F.R.
        Keeley, M.C.

810 Manpower Training and Allocation, Labor Force and Supply
        Doeringer, P.B.   Main, B.G.M.
        Levin, H.M.   Rosen, H.
    811 Manpower training and development
        Vincens, J-M.
    812 Occupation
    813 Labor force
        Finnegan, T.A.   Lloyd, C.B.
        Gilroy, C.L.

820 Labor Markets; Public Policy
        Bluestone, B.A.   Leslie, D.G.
        Cain, G.G.   Lester, R.A.
        Dunlop, J.T.   Phelps-Brown, E.H.
        Edwards, R.C.   Piore, M.J.
        Ehrenberg, R.G.   Quinn, J.F.
        Freeman, R.B.   Reagan, B.R.B.
        Hamermesh, D.   Rees, A.E.
        Hanoch, G.   Ulman, L.
        Hansen, W. Lee   Vanderkamp, J.
        Layard, P.R.G.   Viscusi, W.K.
        Lazear, E.P.
    821 Theory of labor markets and leisure
        Gronau, R.
    822 Public Policy; role of government
        Macavoy, P.W.   Stubblebine, W.C.
    823 Labor mobility
        Greenwood, M.J.   Harris, J.R.
    824 Labor market studies, wages, employment
        DeTray, D.N.   Lillard, L.A.
        Galenson, W.   Smith, J.P.
        Greenhalgh, C.A.   Wachter, M.L.
        Hendricks, W.
    825 Labor productivity
    826 Labor markets; demographic characteristics
        Leibowitz, A.

830 Trade Unions; Collective Bargaining

840 Demographic Economics

Alonso, W.	Ridker, R.G.
Arthur, W.B.	Schultz, T.P.
Easterlin, R.A.	Spengler, J.J.
Kelley, A.C.	Sweezy, A.R.
Leibenstein, H.	Williams, A.D.
Perlman, M.	Willis, R.J.

850 Human Capital

Becker, G.S.	Polachek, S.W.
Bell, C.S.	Taubman, P.
Bowles, S.	Watts, H.W.

900 Welfare Programmes; Consumer Economics; Urban and Regional Economics

  911 General Welfare programmes

Babeau, A.Y.G.	Schelling, T.C.
Haveman, R.H.	

  912 Economics of education

Bowen, H.R.	Carnoy, M.

  913 Economics of health

Culyer, A.J.	Newhouse, J.P.
Enthoven, A.	Williams, A.

  914 Economics of poverty

  Levitan, S.A.

  915 Social security

  Kotlikoff, L.J.

  916 Economics of Crime

Block, M.K.	Polinsky, M.A.

  917 Economics of minorities

920 Consumer Economics

930 Urban Economics

Moses, L.N.	Rothenberg, J.
Muth, R.F.	

  931 Urban economics and public policy

Aarron, H.J.	Downs, A.
Blomquist, G.C.	

  932 Housing economics

  933 Urban transportation economics

Beesley, M.E.	Kain, J.F.

940 Regional Economics

  941 Regional economics

Isard, W.	Mackay, R.R.
Lasnen, J-R.	

Appendix 2

INDEX OF COUNTRY OF RESIDENCE
IF NOT USA

(dead economists are starred)

AUSTRALIA
Arndt, H.W.
Bryon, R.P.
Clark, C.G.
Corden, W.M.
Dixon, P.B.
Gregory, R.G.
*Hearn, W.E.
Kemp, M.C.
Ng, Y.K.
Pincus, J.J.
Swan, P.L.

AUSTRIA
*Auspitz, R.
*Bauer, O.
*Böhm-Bawerk, E.
*Lieben, R.
*Menger, A.
*Menger, C.
*Mises, L.v.
*Philippovich, E.
Rothschild, K.W.
*Sonnenfels, J.
*Spann, O.
*Wieser, F.v.

BELGIUM
Barten, A.P.
*Denis, H.
Drèze, J.
Jacquemin, A.P.
Jaskold-Grabszewicz, J.
*Lavelaye, E.L.
*Molinari, G. de
Triffin, R.

CANADA
Ahmad, S.
Archibald, G.C.
Asimakopulos, A.
Berry, R.A.
Boadway, R.W.
Boland, L.A.
Breton, A.
Burstein, M.L.
Carr, J.L.
Cheng, P.L.
Cragg, J.G.
Diewert, W.E.

Easton, B.C.
Gordon, M.J.
Grubel, H.G.
Helleiner, G.K.
Hazledine, T.
Hollander, S.
Howitt, P.W.
*Innis, H.A.
Koutsoyiannis, A.
Laidler, D.E.W.
Levi, M.D.
Lim, C.
Lipsey, R.G.
Moggridge, D.E.
Parkin, M.
Perrakis, S.
Pesando, J.E.
Plourde, C.G.
Scott, A.D.
Sekine, T.T.
Usher, D.
Vanderkamp, J.
Wonnacott, R.J.

CHILE
Prebisch, R.

CHINA
Cheung, S.N.S.

DENMARK
*Zeuthen, F.

FRANCE
*Aftalion, A.
Allais, M.F.C.
*Aupetit, A.
Babeau, A.Y.G.
Bartoli, H.
Bastiat, F.
Benassy, J-P.E.
*Bertrand, J.L.F.
Betelheim, C.O.
Bienaymé, A.N.A.P.
*Blanc, J.J.L.
*Blangui, J.A.
*Boisguilbert, P.L.
Boiteux, M.P.
*Canard, N.F.
*Cantillon, E.

*Chevalier, M.
*Cheysson, J-J.E.
*Colson, C-L.
*Condillac, E.B. de
*Condorcet, M.J.A.
Cotta, A.
Courbis, R.
*Courcelle-Seneuil, J.G.
*Cournot, A.A.
*Destutt de Tracy, A.
*Dunoyer, C.
*Dupont de Nemours, P.S.
*Dupuit, A.J.
Fitoussi, J-P.
*Fourier, C.
Furtado, C.
*Garnier, J.G.
*Garnier, G.
*Gide, C.
*Gonnard, R.
Grandmont, J-F.
Guitton, H.
*Halévy, E.
*Isnard, A-N.
*Juglar, C.
Laffont, J-J.
*Landry, M.A.
Laroque, G.R.
Lavigne, M.
*Law, J.
*Leroy-Beaulieu, P.
*Lescure, J.
Lesourne, J-F.
*Levasseur, E.
*Mantoux, P.J.
Marchal, J.
Marczewski, J.W.
*Mercier de la Rivière, P.P.
*Mirabeau, V.R.
*Morellet, A.
Perroux, F.
*Pirou, G.
Ponsard, C.
*Proudhon, P-J.
*Quesnay, F.
Reiffers, J-L.
*Rist, C.
*Rueff, J.L.
*Saint-Simon, C.H.
Sauvy, A.
*Say, H.S.

Kuska, E.A.
Lal, D.K.
Lall, S.
*Lardner, D.
*Landerdale, J.M.
*Lavington, F.
Layard, P.R.G.
Leslie, D.G.
Little, I.M.D.
Littlechild, S.C.
*Lloyd, W.F.
Loasby, B.J.
*Locke, J.
*Longe, F.D.
*Lowe, J.
Lumsden, K.G.
Lydall, H.F.
MacDougall, G.D.A.
MacKay, R.R.
*MacLeod, H.D.
Main, B.G.M.
Malcomson, J.M.
*Malthus, T.R.
*Mandeville, B.
*Marcet, J.
*Marshall, A.
*Marshall, M.P.
*Martin, H.
*Martineau, H.
Matthews, R.C.O.
*McCulloch, J.R.
Meade, J.E.
*Meek, R.L.
*Mill, J.
*Mill, J.S.
Miller, M.M.
Minford, A.P.
Mirrlees, J.A.
Mishan, E.J.
Mizon, G.E.
Muellbauer, J.N.
Nevin, A.T.
Newberry, D.M.G.
Newman, P.K.
*Newmarch, W.
*Nicholson, J.S.

*Norman, G.W.
Nove, A.
O'Brien, D.P.
Opie, R.G.
*Overstone, S.J.L.
*Owen, R.
Paish, F.W.
*Palgrave, R.H.I.
Pattanaik, P.K.
Peacock, A.T.
Pearce, D.W.
Pearce, I.F.
*Pennington, J.
Peston, M.
Phelps-Brown, E.H.
*Phillips, A.W.H.
*Pigou, A.C.
*Plant, A.
Portes, R.D.
*Postlethwayt, M.
*Prest, A.R.
*Rae, J.
*Ramsay, G.
*Ramsey, F.P.
*Read, S.
Reddaway, W.B.
*Ricardo, D.
Richardson, G.B.
*Robbins, L.C.
*Robertson, D.H.
Robinson, E.A.G.
*Robinson, J.
*Rogers, J.E.T.
*Rothbart, E.
Roy, A.D.
Rybczynski, T.M.
Sargan, J.D.
Schofield, N.J.
*Scott, W.R.
*Scrope, G.J.P.
*Seers, D.
Sen, A.K.
*Senior, N.W.
Seton, F.
Shackle, G.L.S.
Shaw, G.K.

Shone, R.S.
*Shove, G.F.
*Sidgwick, H.
Silberston, Z.A.
Singer, H.W.
*Smart, W.
*Smith, A.
*Sraffa, P.
*Stamp, J.C.
Steedman, I.
Stern, N.H.
*Steuart, J.D.
Steuer, M.D.
*Stewart, D.
Stewart, F.J.
Stone, J.R.N.
*Tawney, R.H.
Thirlwall, A.P.
*Thompson, T.P.
*Thompson, W.
*Thornton, H.
*Thornton, W.T.
*Tooke, T.
*Torrens, R.
Townsend, H.
*Toynbee, A.
*Tucker, J.
*Unwin, G.
*Vanderbilt, J.
*Wakefield, E.G.
*Wallace, R.
Wallis, K.F.
*Webb, B.
*Webb, S.J.
*West, E.
*Whateley, R.
*Wheatley, J.
*Whewell, W.
*Wicksteed, P.H.
Wiles, P.J.F.
*Wilson, J.
Wilson, T.
Winch, D.N.
Wiseman, J.
Worswick, G.D.N.
Wrigley, E.A.

Appendix 3

INDEX OF COUNTRY OF BIRTH IF NOT USA

(dead economists are starred)

*Mahalanobis, P.C.
Miller, M.M.
Pattanaik, P.K.
Sen, A.K.
Srinivasan, T.N.
*Tawney, R.H.

IRELAND
Black, R.D.C.
*Butt, I.
*Cairnes, J.E.
*Cantillon, E.
*Edgeworth, F.Y.
*Hancock, W.N.
*Hearn, W.E.
*Hutcheson, F.
*Ingram, J.K.
*Lardner, D.
*Leslie, T.E.C.
*Longfield, S.M.
Neary, J.P.
*O'Brien, G.A.
*Parnell, H.B.
*Torrens, R.

ISRAEL
Barzel, Y.
Ben-Porath, Y.
Berglas, E.
Canes, M.E.
Ehrlich, I.
Frenkel, J.A.
Gronau, R.
*Grunfeld, Y.
Kislev, Y.
Kreinin, M.E.
Kurz, M.
Levhari, D.
Sheshinski, E.
Yaari, M.E.

ITALY
*Amoroso, L.
*Barone, E.
Basevi, G.
*Beccaria, C.B.
*Bresciani-Turroni, C.
Caravale, G.A.
Casarosa, C.
*Cossa, L.
*Del Vecchio, G.
*De Viti de Marco
*Divisia, F.
*Einaudi, L.
*Ferrara, F.
*Galiani, F.
Garegnani, P.
*Genovesi, A.
*Loria, A.
*Mazzola, U.
Modigliani, F.
Nuti, D.M.
*Ortes, G.

*Pantaleoni, M.
Pasinetti, L.L.
*Ricci, U.
*Rossi, P.L.E.
*Sraffa, P.
Sylos-Labini, P.
*Verri, P.
Zaghini, E.

JAMAICA
Girvan, N.P.
Harris, D.J.
Hines, A.G.

JAPAN
Amemiya, T.
Ando, A.K.
Aoki, M.
Hamada, K.
Hayami, Y.
Ijiri, Y.
Iwai, K.
Komiya, R.
Miyazaki, H.
Morishima, M.
Negishi, T.
Ozawa, T.
Sato, K.
Sato, R.
Sekine, T.T.
Shibata, H.
Takayama, A.
Tsuru, S.
Uzawa, H.

KOREA
Lee, T.H.

LITHUANIA
Griliches, Z.
Haitovsky, Y.
Levitan, S.A.

LUXEMBOURG
Gäfgen, G.F.M.

MALAYSIA
Lin, C.
Ng, Y-K.

MEXICO
Brito, D.L.
Eicson, R.E.

NETHERLANDS
Barten, A.P.
Blaug, M.
Bos, H.C.
Buiter, W.H.
*Cohen Stuart, A.J.
Heertje, A.
Hennipman, P.

Houthakker, H.
*Koopmans, T.
Leeuw, F. de.
*Mandeville, B.
Pen J.
*Pierson, N.G.
Polak, J.J.
Theil, H.
Tinbergen, J.
Vanderkamp, J.
Van Praag, B.S.

NEW ZEALAND
Falvey, R.E.
Hazledine, T.
Hudson, E.A.
*Meek, R.L.
*Phillips, A.W.H.
Turnovsky, S.V.

NORWAY
Borch, K.H.
Eikern, S.
*Frisch, R.A.K.
*Johansen, L.
Kydland, F.E.
Sandmo, A.
Wold, H.

PAKISTAN
Khan, M.S.

PANAMA
Griffin, K.B.

POLAND
Carnoy, M.
Kamien, M.I.
*Lange, O.
Marczewski, J.W.
Mieszkowski, P.M.
Mincer, J.
Mundlak, Y.
Rosovsky, H.
Rybczynski, T.M.
*Schultz, H.
Wellisz, S.H.
Zarnowitz, V.

ROMANIA
Georgescu-Roegen, N.
Spulber, N.
*Wald, A.

RUSSIA
*Baran, P.A.
*Bortkiewicz, L.V.
*Bukharin, N.I.
*Dmitriev, V.K.
Domar, E.D.
*Gerschenkron, A.
Gort, M.

Grossman, G.
Helpman, E.
Hurwicz, L.
*Kalecki, M.
Kantorovich, L.V.
*Kondratieff, N.D.
*Kuznets, S.
Landskroner, Y.
*Lenin, V.I.
Leontief, W.
*Lerner, A.R.
Letiche, J.M.
*Luxemburg, R.
Makarov, V.L.
Marshak, J.
*Novozhilov, V.V.
Nove, A.
*Preobrazhenski, E.
*Slutsky, E.
*Stackelberg, H.v.
*Storch, H.F.v.
*Strumilin, S.G.
*Tooke, T.
*Tugan-Baranovsky, M.I.
Weiller, J.S.

SOUTH AFRICA
Feinstein, C.H.
Frankel, S.H.
Lydall, H.F.

SPAIN
*Antonelli, E.J.
*Blanc, J.J.L.
*Cannan, E.
Donges, J.B.
*Florez Estrada, A.
Lasuen, J-R.
Mas-Colell, A.
*Uztariz, G.

ST LUCIA
Lewis, W.A.

SWEDEN
*Akerman, J.H.
Bohm, P.J.G.
*Cassel, G.K.
Hakansson, N.H.
*Heckscher, E.P.
Leijonhufvud, A.
*Lindahl, E.R.
Lindbeck, A.
Murdal, G.
*Ohlin, B.G.
*Rodbertus, J.K.
*Wicksell, K.

SWITZERLAND
*Bernoulli, D.
Binswanger, H.
Brunner, K.
*Cherbuliez, A.E.

Frey, B.S.
*Sismondi, J.S. de

TUNISIA
Fitoussi, J-P.

UNITED KINGDOM
Aldcroft, D.H.
*Allen, R.G.D.
Allingham, M.
*Anderson, J.
*Andrews, P.W.S.
Archibald, G.C.
*Armstrong, W.E.
Arthur, W.B.
Artis, M.J.
*Ashley, W.J.
Atkinson, A.B.
*Attwood, T.
*Babbage, C.
*Bagehot, W.
Bailey, M.N.
*Bailey, S.
Ball, R.J.
Barlow, R.
*Barton, J.
*Bastable, C.F.
Beckerman, W.
Beesley, M.E.
*Benham, F.C.C.
*Bentham, J.
*Berkeley, G.
*Berry, A.
*Beveridge, W.H.
*Bickerdike, C.F.
Black, D.
Bliss, C.J.E.
*Bonar, J.
Boulding, K.E.
*Bowley, A.L.
*Bray, J.F.
Brittan, S.
Brown, A.J.
*Buchanan, D.
*Burns, A.R.
Cairncross, A.K.
Casson, M.C.
*Chadwick, E.
*Chalmers, T.
Champernowne, D.G.
*Chapman, S.J.
Chiplin, B.
*Clapham, J.H.
Clark, C.G.
*Clay, H.
Coase, R.H.
Coats, A.W.
*Cobden, R.
*Coddington, A.
*Cole, G.D.H.
Collard, D.A.
*Colguhoun, P.
Corry, B.A.

Cowling, K.G.
*Crossland, C.A.
Culyer, A.J.
*Cunningham, W.
*Dalton, E.H.
*Davenant, C.
Deaton, A.S.
*De Quincey, T.
*Dickinson, H.D.
Dicks-Mireaux, L.
*Dobb, M.
Dougherty, C.R.S.
Dunning, J.H.
*Durbin, E.F.M.
*Eden, F.M.
*Edgeworth, F.Y.
Ellman, M.J.
*Farrell, M.J.
*Fawcett, H.
*Ferguson, A.
Flemming, J.S.
*Flux, A.W.
Ford, A.G.
Ford, J.L.
*Foxwell, H.S.
*Fullarton, J.
*Gaitskell, H.T.N.
*Giffen, R.
*Godwin, W.
*Gonner, E.C.K.
Goodhart, C.A.E.
Gorman, W.
*Goschen, G.J.
Gould, J.R.
Granger, C.W.J.
*Gray, J.
*Gray, S.
*Green, H.A.J.
Greenhalgh, C.A.
*Gregory, T.E.G.
Habakkuk, H.J.
*Hall, C.
Hammond, P.J.
Hannah, L.
*Harris, J.
*Harrod, R.F.
Hart, O.S.
Hart, P.E.
*Hawtrey, R.G.
Hazell, P.B.R.
Heal, G.M.
*Heaton, H.
*Henderson, H.D.
Hendry, D.F.
*Hewins, W.A.S.
Hicks, J.
*Higgs, H.
*Hobson, J.A.
*Hodgskin, T.
Hollander, S.
*Horner, F.
*Hume, D.
Hutt, W.H.

*Hyndman, H.M.
Ingham, A.
*Jenkin, H.C.F.
*Jevons, W.S.
*Johnson, W.E.
Johnston, J.
*Jones, R.
*Joplin, T.
Kahn, R.F.
Keesing, D.
Kennedy, C.M.
*Keynes, J.M.
*Keynes, J.N.
King, M.A.
Laidler, D.E.W.
*Lauderdale, J.M.
*Lavington, F.
*Law, J.
Layard, P.R.G.
*Lehfeldt, R.A.
Leslie, D.G.
Levi, M.D.
Little, I.M.D.
Littlechild, S.C.
*Lloyd, W.F.
Loasby, B.J.
*Locke, J.
*Longe, F.D.
Lumsden, K.G.
MacDougall, G.D.A.
*MacLeod, H.D.
Maddison, A.
Main, B.G.M.
Malcomson, J.M.
*Malthus, T.R.
*Marcet, J.
*Marshall, A.
*Marshall, M.P.
*Martin, H.
*Martineau, H.
Matthews, R.C.O.
*McCulloch, J.R.
Meade, J.E.
*Mill, J.
*Mill, J.S.
Minford, A.P.
Mirrlees, J.A.
Mishan, E.J.
Mizon, G.E.
Nevin, E.T.
Newberry, D.M.G.
Newman, P.K.
*Newmarch, W.

*Nicholson, J.S.
*Norman, G.W.
O'Brien, D.P.
*Overstone, S.V.L.
*Owen, R.
Paish, F.W.
*Palgrave, R.H.I.
Parkin, M.
Peacock, A.T.
Pearce, D.W.
Pearce, I.F.
*Pennington, J.
Pencavel, J.H.
Peston, M.
Phelps-Brown, E.H.
*Pigou, A.C.
*Plant, A.
Pomery, J.G.
*Postlethwayt, M.
*Prest, A.R.
*Rae, J.
*Ramsay, G.
*Ramsey, F.P.
*Read, S.
Reddaway, W.B.
*Ricardo, D.
Richardson, G.B.
*Robbins, L.C.
*Robertson, D.H.
*Robertson, H.M.
*Robinson, E.A.G.
*Robinson, J.
*Rogers, J.E.T.
Roy, A.D.
Rowley, C.K.
Sargan, J.D.
Schofield, N.J.
*Scott, W.R.
*Scrope, G.J.P.
*Seers, D.
Senior, N.W.
Shackle, G.L.S.
Shaw, G.K.
Shone, R.S.
*Shonfield, A.A.
*Shove, G.F.
*Sidgwick, H.
Silberston, Z.A.
*Smart, W.
*Smith, A.
*Stamp, J.C.
Steedman, I.
Stern, N.H.

*Steuart, J.D.
Steuer, M.D.
*Stewart, D.
Stewart, F.J.
Stone, J.R.N.
Thirlwall, A.P.
*Thompson, T.P.
*Thompson, W.
*Thornton, H.
*Thornton, W.T.
Townsend, H.
*Toynbee, A.
*Tucker, J.
Turvey, R.
*Unwin, G.
*Vanderlint, J.
*Wakefield, E.G.
*Wallace, R.
Wallis, K.F.
Walters, A.A.
*Ward, B.M.
*Webb, B.
*Webb, S.J.
*West, E.
West, E.G.
*Whateley, R.
*Wheatley, J.
*Whewell, W.
Whitaker, J.K.
*Wicksteed, P.H.
Wiles, P.J.F.
Williamson, J.H.
*Wilson, J.
Wilson, T.
Winch, D.N.
Wiseman, J.
Worswick, G.D.N.
Wrigley, E.A.

VENEZUELA
Marquez, J.R.

YUGOSLAVIA
Neuberger, E.
Pejovich, S.

ZAIRE
Jaskold-Grabszewicz, J.

ZAMBIA
Fisher, S.

Appendix 4

NAMES WITHOUT AN ENTRY

Our computer program of the 1,000 most frequently cited economists in the years 1972–83 turned up some 123 names of economists who failed to return their form even after a second and third mailing. It is impossible to tell how many of these received a form but refused to fill it in because of some studious opposition to any *Who's Who*, whatever its purpose, and how many never received the form because they were on leave or had recently changed their place of employment. In any case, here is a list of those names:

R.S. Ahlbrandt	R.S. Hartman	G. Norman
R.J. Allard	M. Hartwell	G.P. O'Driscoll
C. Almon	J.G. Head	M.V. Pauly
S. Almon	D.B. Hertz	J.A. Peckman
E. Ames	B.V. Hindley	A. Piatier
J.E. Anderson	W.G. Hoffmann	A. Piettre
R.W. Anderson	P. Howitt	H. Raiffa
H. Averch	M.D. Hurd	K.N. Raj
R.W. Bacon	J. Jewkes	R.H. Rasohe
P. Balestra	W.R. Johnson	S. Reiter
B.J.Z. Berry	R.W. Jones	J. Richardson
H.G. Bowen	E. Kauder	M.K. Richter
W.H. Branson	J.W. Kendrick	R.W. Roll
M.J. Brennan	R.E. Kihlstrom	R.V. Roosa
R. Brenner	C.C. Killingsworth	J. Ropke
P.G. Burrows	B.F. King	S. Rose-Ackerman
A. Charmes	I.M. Kirzner	N. Rosenberg
J. Ciccolo	A.K. Klevorick	T.J. Rothenberg
R.A. Cohn	M.B. Krauss	J.W. Salmon
R. Craine	J.J. Lambin	A. Sapir
J.A. Crutchfield	J.S. Lane	L.V. Savage
B.L. Currie	D.R. Lee	H. Schneider
D.A. Currie	T. Levitt	G. Schultz
C.J. Dahlman	H.G. Lewis	L.S. Shapley
G. Dalton	N. Liviatan	R.W. Shephard
R.H. Day	D.T. Llewellyn	N.V. Simler
A.S. DeVany	H.R. Lorie	L.A. Sjaastad
W. Dolde	S.H. Lustgaten	H.M. Somers
M.K. Evans	S.A. Marglin	D.A. Starrett
E.L. Feige	F.B. Massell	J.A. Trevithick
C.D. Foster	S. McManus	B.D. Udis
D. Gale	D.L. Meadows	A. Ulph
J.S. Gallagher	H. Mendershausen	P.K. Verlegesit
D. Gately	E.J. Mitchell	K.F. Wacks
J. Geiveke	D.J. Mullineaux	T.D. Wallace
V.P. Goldberg	R.A. Mundell	B. Ward
W.H. Gruber	M. Mussa	L. Waverman
M. Hadjimichalakis	M.I. Nadiri	W.C. Wheaton
J.A. Hanson	C. Napoleoni	P. Wolfe
J.P. Harkness	S.J. Nickell	E. Zaleski
J.E. Harris	A.R. Nobay